LONGMAN

Active Study
Dictionary

5ᵀᴴ EDITION

KT-415-941

Pearson Education Limited
Edinburgh Gate
Harlow
Essex CM20 2JE
England
and Associated Companies throughout the world

www.pearsonelt.com/dictionaries

First edition published 1983
Second edition 1991
Third edition 1998
Fourth edition 2004
Fifth edition 2010

ISBN Paperback   978 1 4082 1832 7
      20 19
      IMP 15 14 13 12 11 10

      Paperback + CD   978 1 4082 3236 1
      20 19
      IMP 16 15 14 13

Set in Whitney by Letterpart, UK
Printed in China
SWTC/13

Contents

Pronunciation table   inside front cover
Guide to the Dictionary   iv
Acknowledgements   vi
Labels   vii
Photo acknowledgements   viii

The Dictionary A-Z   1-1037

Picture dictionary   A2
Language notes   A14
Grammar reference   A44

Irregular verbs   1038

Guide to the Dictionary

Active words are printed in red letters. This shows which are the most important words to know.

alphabet /ˈælfəbet/ n [C] a set of letters that are used when writing a language: *the Greek alphabet*

Pronunciation is shown using the International Phonetic Alphabet.

alpine /ˈælpaɪn/ adj relating to the Alps or other high mountains: *alpine flowers*

Part of speech is shown first, then information about whether a word is countable, uncountable, transitive, intransitive etc.

altar /ˈɔːltə $ ˈɔːltər/ n [C] a kind of holy table, especially used in a church for religious ceremonies

Labels before the definition show if a word is used in informal, formal, literary, legal, or technical English.

altercation /ˌɔːltəˈkeɪʃən $ ˌɔːltər-/ n [C] *formal* a noisy argument

Definitions explain the meaning of the word in clear simple language, using the 2000-word Longman Defining Vocabulary.

The meanings of each word are listed in order of frequency. The most common meaning is shown first.

although /ɔːlˈðəʊ $ ɔːlˈðoʊ/ linking word
1 in spite of the fact that something is true: *Although the car's old, it still runs well.* | *He lent his friend £20, although he didn't have much money himself.*
2 but: *You can copy my answers, although I'm not sure they're right.*

Common grammar patterns are shown before the examples, so that you can see clearly how the word operates in a sentence.

amazement /əˈmeɪzmənt/ n [U] when you feel very surprised: **in amazement** *I stared at him in amazement.* | **sb's amazement** *To my amazement, Neal got up and left without a word.*

arm¹ /ɑːm $ ɑːrm/ n [C]
1 BODY PART one of the two long parts of your body between your shoulders and your hands: **left/right arm** *He had a tattoo on his left arm.* | *I put my arms around him.* | *They walked along arm in arm* (=with their arms bent around each other's). | **cross/fold your arms** (=bend your arms so that they are resting on top of each other against your body) | **under your arm** *I was carrying a pile of books under my arm.* → see picture on page A2
2 CLOTHES the part of a piece of clothing that covers your arm SYN sleeve

Useful natural examples show you how to use the word.

Idioms, fixed phrases, and phrasal verbs are listed in alphabetical order after the main senses of the word.

PHRASES
be up in arms about sth to be very angry about something: *The whole town is up in arms about the closure of the hospital.*
welcome sb/sth with open arms to show that you are very happy and eager to see someone or to accept an idea or plan: *We welcomed the offer with open arms.*

Synonyms, opposites, and related words are shown after the definition.

arm² v [I,T] to provide weapons for someone OPP disarm

Derived forms are shown at the end of the entry.

artful /ˈɑːtfəl $ ˈɑːrt-/ adj good at deceiving people —**artfully** adv

Grammar boxes give you extra grammatical information about a word, and help you avoid making mistakes.

Collocations boxes show you the other words that are commonly used with that word.

advice /əd'vaɪs/ *n* [U] the things you say to someone when you tell them what you think they should do: **[+on/about]** *a book that's full of advice on baby care* | *Can you give me some advice about buying a house?*

Grammar
Advice is an uncountable noun. Do not say 'advices'.
Do not say 'He gave me a good advice.' Say *He gave me some good advice.* or *He gave me a good piece of advice.*

COLLOCATIONS

verbs
to give sb advice *Can I give you some advice?*
to offer advice *The tourist office can offer advice on places to visit.*
to get advice *I got some good advice from my teacher about applying to college.*
to ask sb's advice (*also* **to ask for advice**) *My friends often ask my advice.*
to take/follow sb's advice (=to do what someone advises you to do) *She followed his advice and took up yoga.*

adjectives
good/useful advice *The book is full of good advice.*
bad advice *I now realise that this was bad advice.*
sound advice (=sensible advice) *My mother always gave me sound advice.*
practical advice *The website has practical advice on starting your own business.*
legal/medical/financial etc advice *I think you should get some legal advice.*

phrases
a piece/bit of advice *Let me give you a piece of advice*

aim¹ /eɪm/ *n*
1 [C] something that you want to achieve: **[+of]** *The aim of the research is to discover what causes the illness.* | *Our **main aim** is to provide a good service.* | **with the aim of doing sth** *I flew to the US with the aim of finding a job.*
2 [singular, U] someone's ability to hit the thing they are trying to hit: *Mark's aim wasn't very good.*
PHRASES
take aim to point a weapon at someone or something: **[+at]** *He took aim at the target.*

THESAURUS

aim something you want to achieve: *His aim is to make as much money as possible.*
goal something important that you hope to achieve in the future, even though it may take a long time: *Their long-term goal is to set up a base on the Moon.*
ambition something that you very much want to achieve in your life: *Her ambition was to be a doctor.*
target a particular amount or total that you want to achieve: *Our target is to reduce greenhouse gases by 50% by 2020.*
objective a particular thing that someone is trying to achieve, especially in business or politics: *We met to set the business objectives for the coming year.*

Thesaurus boxes help you expand your vocabulary, by showing you other similar words and explaining clearly the difference between them.

author Ac /'ɔːθə $ 'ɒːθər/ *n* [C] someone who has written a book SYN **writer**: *a well-known American author* | **[+of]** *Robert Louis Stevenson was the author of 'Treasure Island'.*

Word Choice: author or writer?
Author is more formal than **writer** and is used especially about someone who writes books that are of a high standard, which are considered to be literature: *He is influenced by American authors such as Hemingway and Faulkner.*
Writer is a more general word. You use it about anyone who writes books, articles for magazines etc: *I've always wanted to be a writer.*

Word Choice boxes explain clearly the difference between pairs of very similar words.

Acknowledgements

Director
Michael Mayor

Publishing Manager
Laurence Delacroix

Managing Editor
Chris Fox

Senior Editor
Rosalind Combley

Editors
Evadne Adrian-Vallance
Karen Cleveland Marwick
Lucy Hollingworth
Elizabeth Manning
Michael Murphy
Dr Martin Stark
Laura Wedgeworth

Pronunciation Editor
Dinah Jackson

Proofreaders
Lynda Carey
Pat Dunn
Ruth Hillmore
Alison Sadler

Project Manager
Alan Savill

**Computational Linguist and
CD-ROM Project Management**
Allan Ørsnes

Language Notes
Diane Schmitt
Chris Fox

Editorial Manager
Paola Rocchetti

Production Editor
Željka Letica Finnerty

Technical Support Manager
Trevor Satchell

Production Manager
Keeley Everitt

Design
Matthew Dickin

**Project and Database
Administrator**
Denise McKeough

Network Administrator
Robert Stringer

Keyboarder
Denise McKeough

Administrative Assistance
Angela Wright

Picture Research
Sandra Hilsdon
Jack Holgarth

Illustrations
Chris Pavely
Christen Stewart (Debora Wolf
Illustration)
Fiammetta Dogi
John Carrozza
John Schriener (Debora Wolf
Illustration)
Mark Turner (Beehive Illustration)
Tony Wilkins

The Publishers and editorial team would like to thank the lexicographic team who worked on the *Longman Active Study Dictionary* (fourth edition) and the many people who have contributed advice to the making of this latest edition, in particular the Linglex Dictionary and Corpus Advisory Committee:

Lord Quirk (Chair), Professor David Crystal, Professor Geoffrey Leech, Professor John Wells, Della Summers

The Publishers and editors of the *Longman Active Study Dictionary* would like to thank all of the teachers who took part in the research for the current edition:

Simon Adams, Tina Alexander, Melinda Allan, Clementine Annabell, Matt Armstrong, James Barnett, Daragh Behrman, James Bury, Ben Butler, Nick Canning, Graham Cartmell, John Cater, Jill Elliott, E Augusta Fisher, Will Frost, John Gallagher, Josephine Hagard, Richard Mark Hamer, Ryan Hannan, Kathleen Hargreaves, Henriette Heise, Jake Hogg, Chris Horsey, Grant Ibbs, John Johannesen, Andy Johnson, Rob Julian, Iffaf Khan, Mary Lawrence, Simon Manners, Sara L. Marlow, William G Martin, Eve McEllirrey, Louise Miller, Steven Miller, Harry Newman, Gary Nixon, Joanna Novcic, Jolanta Nyczke, Julian Oakley, Andrea Regina Paschoal, Vanessa Pasini, Frank Pinner, Michael Robinson, Dave Ruchpaul, Mick Sheahan, Jane Sherlock, Miles Smith, Nadege Sokolowski, Phillipa Stallard, Joanna Stansfield, Gary Thompson, Caroline Tillotson, Duncan Watson, Michael Whyte, Sarah Zamora-Smith

Every effort has been made to include the names of all the teachers who took part in the research. If your name has been inadvertently omitted please contact us and we will be happy to insert it in a future reprint.

Labels

The following labels are used in this dictionary:

BrE British English
AmE American English
formal – used in formal speech or writing
informal – used when speaking or writing to people you know well, but not in essays, business letters etc
spoken – used in spoken English
written – used in written English
approving – used when you approve of someone or something
disapproving – used when you do not approve of someone or something
humorous – used in a joking way
literary – used mainly in literature
old-fashioned – this word was much more common in the past. These days it sounds old-fashioned
technical – used by doctors, scientists and other people who have special knowledge about a subject
law – used by lawyers
trademark – used as the official name of a product

Parts of speech

adj = adjective
adv = adverb
auxiliary verb (the verbs 'be', 'do', and 'have')
determiner (words such as 'a', 'the', 'that', and 'this')
linking word (a word that joins words, phrases, and clauses together, for example 'and')
modal verb (verbs such as 'could', 'might', and 'shall')
n = noun
number ('five', 'sixty' etc)
prefix ('un-', 're-', 'anti-' etc)
prep = preposition
pron = pronoun
suffix ('-ness', '-ly' etc)
v = verb

Grammar codes

nouns:
[C] = countable
[U] = uncountable
[C,U] = countable or uncountable
[singular] = only used in the singular
[plural] = only used in the plural
[C usually singular] = the singular form is much more common
[C usually plural] = the plural form is much more common

verbs:
[T] = transitive
[I] = intransitive
[I,T] = intransitive or transitive
[I + adv/prep] = a verb that is always followed by an adverb or preposition
[linking verb] = a verb used in descriptions, such as 'be' or 'seem'

adjectives:
[not before noun] = an adjective that never comes before a noun
[only before noun] = an adjective that always comes before a noun
[only after noun] = an adjective that always comes after a noun

Abbreviations

sb = somebody
sth = something

Photo acknowledgements

The publisher would like to thank the following for their kind permission to reproduce their photographs:

(Key: b-bottom; c-centre; l-left; r-right; t-top) **www.dreamstime.com:** 3 (Goose), 3 (Horse), 8, 8 (Electric), 59 (Backpack), 71 (Single), 81 (Wastepaper), 85, 130tr, 159tc, 237br, 237tl, 281tr, 337, 338, 343 (Chrysanthemum), 343 (Geranium), 343 (Iris), 343 (Poppy), 381c, 381tr, 412bl, 412cl, 412tl, 437b, 437cl, 437cr, 437tr, 482br, 482tc, 508, 517bl, 517tr, 548tr, 594bl, 596tr, 609, 610tr, 640br, 640tr, 641br, 651 (Floral), 651 (Zigzag), 655l, 820, 874 (Folder), 888l, 907, 910bl, 910tr; **Action Plus Sports Images:** 9 (Hockey); **Alamy Images:** 3 (Swordfish); Andrew Darrington 343 (Bluebell); D Hurst 684; Judith Collins 123tl; Martin Lee 190 (Crisps), 190 (Tuna); Mike Booth 910; Steve Skjold 190 (Cheese); V&A Images 910br; **Corbis:** Denis Scott 3 (Whale); **DK Images:** 3 (Mackerel), 3 (Shark), 12 (Console), 190 (Honey), 237tr, 399, 412tr, 482tr, 522t, 615, 640tl, 866, 938bl, 938br, 938tl, 952 (Taxi); Dave King 36 (Chimp), 36 (Orangutan), 69 (Brown); Jerry Young 69 (Polar); Steve Gorton 71 (Futon), 111tl; **Hemera Photo Objects:** 6, 102, 110, 113l, 139, 229, 318tl, 318tr, 325, 338tr, 361, 369 (Can), 369 (Mower), 369 (Rake), 369 (Shears), 369 (Spade), 369 (Trowel), 369 (Wheelbarrow), 405, 419, 491, 499, 517tc, 517tl, 522br, 550, 583l, 600, 623b, 629, 727br, 755, 818, 845b, 845t, 926, 944, 957, 964, 1004; **iStockphoto:** 12 (DVD player), 12 (Laptop), 12 (Memory Stick), 12 (Mobile), 12 (MP3), 12 (Palmtop), 12 (Phone), 12 (TV), 29, 40, 47 (Asleep), 47 (Awake), 59 (Handbag), 59 (Holdall), 61 (Balloon), 61 (Hot air balloon), 71 (Bunk), 71 (Cot), 71 (Double), 75, 81 (Dustbin), 81 (Rubbish), 85t, 91br, 91tr, 99bl, 99tl, 99tr, 106b, 106t, 111bl, 111r, 118tl, 118tr, 120, 123b, 123r, 130bl, 130br, 130tl, 137tl, 148b, 159b, 162 (Boxer shorts), 162 (Bra), 162 (Dress), 162 (Jacket), 162 (Jeans), 162 (Jumper), 162 (Knickers), 162 (Pants), 162 (Scarf), 162 (Shorts), 162 (Skirt), 162 (Socks), 162 (Sweatshirt), 169, 176r, 183l, 190 (Margarine), 190 (Milk), 190 (Pickles), 190 (Toothpaste), 208, 273, 281, 281bl, 283, 287, 295, 314, 333, 343 (Carnation), 343 (Daffodil), 343 (Daisy), 343 (Sunflower), 343 (Thistle), 343 (Tulip), 343 (Violet), 356, 361 (Tadpoles), 369 (Fork), 376, 379tl, 381bl, 381br, 381tl, 390, 409l, 415, 429b, 433, 461, 466bl, 466br, 466tc, 466tl, 466tr, 482 (Bracelet), 482bl, 482tl, 489, 526bl, 526tl, 530l, 561, 583r, 610bl, 610br, 610cl, 610cr, 610tc, 610tl, 623r, 623t, 641bl, 641t, 651 (Checked), 651 (Spotted), 655cl, 655cr, 655r, 661tl, 661tr (Dog), 669t, 678t, 688bl, 688br, 689, 705, 721, 725, 727, 744, 744tr, 766b, 771t, 777, 792l, 800, 805, 810, 820 (Boots), 820 (Slippers), 820 (Stilettos), 820 (Trainers), 829l, 834 (Skates), 844r, 865, 874 (Clips), 874 (Eraser), 874 (Highlighter), 874 (Hole punch), 874 (Scissors), 874 (Sharpener), 874 (Stapler), 885, 891, 902t, 915, 930, 938tr, 952 (Bike), 952 (Bus), 952 (Coach), 952 (Ferry), 952 (Helicopter), 952 (Motorboat), 952 (Train), 952 (Tram), 952 (Yacht), 952 (Car), 980, 997, 1015, 1020b, 1020tr; Andy Gehrig 3 (Robin); Brigitte Magnus 9 (Climbing); David T Gomez 3 (Giraffe); Eliza Snow 9 (Rowing); Eva Serrabassa 486tl; Gerrit David de Vries 3 (Hippo); Hubert Gruner 9 (Biking); Ian McDonnell 404 (Dreadlocks); Jason Lugo 162 (T-shirt); Jeanne Hatch 404 (Bob); Joe Belanger 195tl; Jon Helgason 651 (Pinstripe); Maxim Kulko 3 (Wolf); Michael Olson 9 (Kayaking); Nico Smit 596b; Oleksandr Dibrova 3 (Impala); Serghei Starus 9 (Tennis); **Jupiter Unlimited:** 3 (Koala), 3 (Penguin), 9 (Basketball), 31, 36 (Gorilla), 59 (Shopping), 69 (Panda), 71 (Camp), 81b, 91bl, 91tl, 99br, 113r, 131, 137tr, 146bc, 146bl, 146br, 148t, 150, 159r, 159tl, 162 (Belt), 162 (Coat), 162 (Shirt), 162 (Tie), 162 (Waterproof), 176l, 183br, 183tr, 190 (Chocolates), 190 (Cola), 195bl, 195br, 195tr, 211, 214, 222, 237bl, 241, 255b, 259, 281br, 333tr, 343 (Lily), 343 (Orchid), 343 (Rose), 345bl, 345br, 369 (Gloves), 369 (Pot), 379bx, 379tr, 389, 393, 404 (Bald), 404 (Bun), 404 (Curly), 404 (Plait), 404 (Ponytail), 404 (Receding), 404 (Straight), 404 (Wavy), 409r, 412br, 412cr, 425, 429, 437tl, 442, 444, 446b, 473b, 486bl, 486br, 486tr, 495tl, 495tr, 499 (Lamb), 499 (Sheep), 507, 518bl, 518tr, 522bl, 526r, 548bl, 548br, 548tl, 572, 576l, 576r, 580, 588b, 588tl, 588tr, 593, 593b, 593tr, 594, 594tl, 618, 638br, 638l, 638tr, 640bl, 642, 651 (Plain), 651 (Striped), 651 (Tartan), 661bl, 661br, 667 (Bread), 667 (Cake), 667 (Cheese), 667 (Coal), 667 (Concrete), 667 (Ice cubes), 667 (Meat), 667 (Soap), 669b, 678b, 688, 688tl, 700, 729c, 729l, 729r, 766t, 771bl, 771br, 779, 786, 789, 792r, 794, 799, 815, 820 (Shoes), 826, 829r, 834 (Blades), 834 (Ice), 844, 847, 860, 878c, 878l, 888b, 888r, 902b, 902r, 944 (Axe), 952 (Cruiser), 952 (Scooter), 952 (Van), 987, 1020tl, 1030, 1033, 1036; Photos.com 3 (Rhino); Stockxpert 3 (Cows), 3 (Donkey), 3 (Duck), 3 (Fox), 3 (Owl), 9 (Baseball); ThinkStock Images 9 (Skiing); **Pearson Education Ltd:** 4 (Fruit), 5 (Vegetables), 12 (CD), 12 (Scanner), 770; Getty/Photodisc 12 (Computer); Photodisc.com/Musical Instruments 6 (Musical); **Photolibrary.com:** 473t; Photodisc/Ryan McVay 139br; Sven Olof 820 (Clogs); **PunchStock:** Portraits 404 (Pigtails), 404 (Spiky); Westend61 654; **shutterstock:** 118; Dimitry Yashkin 9 (Speed skating); Eoghan McNally 9 (Rugby); Jonathan Larsen 9 (Table tennis); Kondrashov Mikhail Evgenevich 9 (Karate); nikkytok 162 (Trousers); Olga Besnard 9 (Ice skating); photobank.ch 530r; Terekhov Igor 162 (Tracksuit); Vaclav Voirab 9 (Cycling); WizData,Inc 9 (Boxing)

All other images © Pearson Education

Every effort has been made to trace the copyright holders and we apologise in advance for any unintentional omissions. We would be pleased to insert the appropriate acknowledgement in any subsequent edition of this publication.

Aa

A, a /eɪ/ n [C,U] (*plural* **A's, a's**) **1** the first letter of the English alphabet **2** the sixth note in the musical SCALE of C MAJOR, or the musical KEY based on this note **3** the highest mark that a student can get in an examination or for a piece of work: *I got an A in French.*

a /ə; *strong* eɪ/ (*also* **an** *before a vowel sound*) determiner
1 used to show that you are talking about something or someone that has not been mentioned before, or that the listener does not know about → **the:** *There was a problem with the car.* | *I saw a really good film last week.*
2 used to show that you are talking about a general type of thing, not a specific thing → **the:** *Do you have a car?* | *Her boyfriend is an artist.* | *Have a look at this* (=Look at this).
3 one: *a thousand pounds* | *a dozen eggs*
4 used in some phrases that say how much of something there is: *a few weeks from now* | *a lot of people*
5 every or each: *A square has four sides.* | **once a week/$100 a day etc** (=one time each week, $100 each day etc) *He gets paid $100,000 a year.*
6 used before two nouns that are often mentioned together: *a knife and fork*

> **Word Choice: a or an?**
> You usually use **a** when the next word begins with a consonant (**b**, **c**, **d**, **f** etc): *a big cat* | *a small dog* | *a hotel*
> You use **an** when the next word begins with **h**, when the **h** is not pronounced: *an hour* | *an honest man*
> You usually use **an** when the next word begins with a vowel (**a**, **e**, **i**, **o**, or **u**): *an old man* | *an umbrella*
> You use **a** when the next word begins with **u**, when this is pronounced like 'you': *a university* | *a union*

A & E /ˌeɪ ənd ˈiː/ n [U] *BrE* (**accident and emergency**) the department in a hospital where people go if they are injured or suddenly become ill

aback /əˈbæk/ adv **be taken aback** to be very surprised or shocked: *I was taken aback by Linda's rudeness.* **THESAURUS** SURPRISED

abacus /ˈæbəkəs/ n [C] a wooden frame with small balls which are moved along wires, used for counting and calculating

abandon Ac /əˈbændən/ v [T] **1** to leave a person or thing, especially one that you are responsible for, and not go back for them: *The baby had been abandoned outside a hospital.* | *The thieves abandoned the car nearby.* **2** to stop doing or using something

because of problems: *The new policy had to be abandoned.* —**abandonment** n [U]

abandoned Ac /əˈbændənd/ adj not being used or looked after any more: *an abandoned building*

abashed /əˈbæʃt/ adj embarrassed or ashamed: *They both looked slightly abashed.*

abate /əˈbeɪt/ v [I] *formal* to become less strong: *The storm showed no signs of abating.*

abattoir /ˈæbətwɑː $ -ɑːr/ n [C] *BrE* a place where animals are killed for their meat **SYN** **slaughterhouse**

abbey /ˈæbi/ n [C] a large church, especially one used by a group of MONKS or NUNS

abbot /ˈæbət/ n [C] a man who is in charge of a MONASTERY

abbreviate /əˈbriːvieɪt/ v [T] *formal* to make a word, story etc shorter

abbreviation /əˌbriːviˈeɪʃən/ n [C] a shorter form of a word: **[+for/of]** *'Dr' is the written abbreviation for 'Doctor'.*

abdicate /ˈæbdɪkeɪt/ v **1** [I] to officially give up the position of being king or queen **2** **abdicate (your) responsibility** *formal* to refuse to continue being responsible for something —**abdication** /ˌæbdɪˈkeɪʃən/ n [C,U]

abdomen /ˈæbdəmən, æbˈdəʊ- $ -ˈdoʊ-/ n [C] *technical* the part of your body between your chest and the top of your legs, including your stomach —**abdominal** /æbˈdɒmənəl $ -ˈdɑː-/ adj

abduct /əbˈdʌkt, æb-/ v [T] to take someone away by force: *Police believe that the woman has been abducted.* —**abduction** /əbˈdʌkʃən, æb-/ n [C,U]

aberration /ˌæbəˈreɪʃən/ n [C,U] *formal* something that is completely different from what usually happens or from what someone usually does: *a temporary psychological aberration*

abet /əˈbet/ v (**abetted, abetting**) → **aid and abet** at AID[2]

abhor /əbˈhɔː $ əbˈhɔːr, æb-/ v [T] (**abhorred, abhorring**) *formal* to hate something because you think it is morally wrong: *He abhorred violence in any form.* —**abhorrence** /əbˈhɒrəns $ -ˈhɔː-/ n [U]

abhorrent /əbˈhɒrənt $ -ˈhɔːr-/ adj *formal* behaviour or beliefs that are abhorrent seem very bad and morally wrong

abide /əˈbaɪd/ v
PHRASES
can't abide sb/sth to hate someone or something very much: *I can't abide his stupid jokes.*

PHRASAL VERBS
abide by sth to obey a law, agreement etc: *You have to abide by the rules of the game.*

abiding /əˈbaɪdɪŋ/ adj [only before noun] *literary* an abiding feeling or belief continues for a long time: *her abiding love of the English countryside* → **LAW-ABIDING**

ability /əˈbɪləti/ n [C,U] (*plural* **abilities**) the state of being able to do something, or your level of skill at doing something: **ability to do sth** *A manager must have the ability to communicate well.* |

athletic/academic/linguistic etc ability *a young girl with great musical ability | We just have to play to the best of our ability* (=as well as we can).

abject /ˈæbdʒekt/ *adj* **1 abject poverty/misery/failure** when someone is extremely poor, unhappy, or unsuccessful **2 abject apology** an abject apology shows that you are ashamed of what you have done

ablaze /əˈbleɪz/ *adj* [not before noun] **1** burning with a lot of flames: *The ship was set ablaze by the explosion.* **2** very bright with colour or light: *a garden ablaze with summer flowers*

able /ˈeɪbəl/ *adj*
1 be able to do sth a) to have the power, skill, knowledge etc you need to do something OPP **unable**: *I'd love to be able to play the piano.* **b)** to be in a situation where it is possible for you to do something OPP **unable**: *Will you be able to come tonight?*
THESAURUS ▶ CAN
2 clever or good at doing something: *a very able student*

-able /əbəl/ *suffix* used to say that something can have something done to it: *a washable fabric | a noticeable change*

able-'bodied *adj* physically strong and healthy, especially when compared with someone who is DISABLED: *a team of both disabled and able-bodied athletes*

ably /ˈeɪbli/ *adv* skilfully or well: *The director was ably assisted by his team of experts.*

abnormal Ac /æbˈnɔːməl $ -ˈnɔːr-/ *adj* different from what is normal, especially in a way that is strange, worrying, or dangerous OPP **normal**: *abnormal behaviour | abnormal levels of chlorine in the water* —**abnormally** *adv* —**abnormality** /ˌæbnɔːˈmæləti $ -nər-/ *n* [C,U]: *a serious genetic abnormality*

aboard /əˈbɔːd $ əˈbɔːrd/ *adv, prep* on or onto a ship, plane, or train: *The boat swayed as he climbed aboard. | Everyone aboard the plane was killed.*

abode /əˈbəʊd $ əˈboʊd/ *n* [C] *formal* the place where you live: **right of abode** (=the right to live in a country)

abolish /əˈbɒlɪʃ $ əˈbɑː-/ *v* [T] to officially end a law, system etc: *plans to abolish the death penalty* —**abolition** /ˌæbəˈlɪʃən/ *n* [U]: *the abolition of slavery*

abominable /əˈbɒmɪnəbəl, -mənə- $ əˈbɑː-/ *adj* extremely unpleasant or bad —**abominably** *adv*

aborigine /ˌæbəˈrɪdʒɪni/ (also **aboriginal** /ˌæbəˈrɪdʒɪnəl◂/) *n* [C] a member of the race of people who have lived in Australia from the earliest times —**aboriginal** *adj*

abort /əˈbɔːt $ -ɔːrt/ *v* [T] **1** to stop an activity because it would be too difficult or dangerous to continue: *The flight had to be aborted because of computer problems.* **2** to deliberately end a PREGNANCY when the baby is still too small to live

abortion /əˈbɔːʃən $ əˈbɔːr-/ *n* [C,U] when a PREGNANCY is deliberately ended while the baby is still too small to live: *She considered having an abortion.*

abortive /əˈbɔːtɪv $ əˈbɔːr-/ *adj* an abortive action or attempt to do something is not successful

abound /əˈbaʊnd/ *v* [I] *literary* to exist in large

numbers: *a river where fish abound*
PHRASAL VERBS
abound in/with sth to contain a lot of something: *The park abounds with wildlife.*

about¹ /əˈbaʊt/ *prep*
1 relating to a subject or person: *a book about astrology | What was he talking about? | We're all very upset about it. | Tell me all about* (=everything about) *it.*
2 *BrE* in many different directions or in different parts of a place SYN **around**: *Clothes were scattered about the room.*
3 in the character or nature of a person or thing: *There's something odd about him.*
PHRASES
| **do something about sth** to do something to solve a problem: *We must do something about the shower – it's still dripping.*
| **what/how about sb/sth** *spoken* **1** used to make a suggestion: *'What shall I get her?' 'What about some chocolates?' |* **what/how about doing sth** *How about coming round for a barbecue?* **2** used to ask someone to consider and talk about someone or something else involved in a situation: *What about Jack? We can't just leave him here.*

THESAURUS

about relating to a subject or person: *We talked about a lot of things. | What's the film about?*
on you use **on** when saying that a book, programme, report etc deals with a particular subject: *a book on French cooking | a programme on Islamic art*
concerning/regarding *formal* about something: *If you have any further questions concerning your course, contact your tutor.*
with regard to sth *formal* about something – used especially when you start talking or writing about something: *Dear Sir, I'm writing with regard to your advertisement in 'The Times'.*

---

about² *adv*
1 a little more or less than a number or amount SYN **approximately, roughly**: *I live about 10 miles from here. | We left the restaurant at round about 10.30.* THESAURUS ▶ APPROXIMATELY
2 be about to do sth to be ready to start doing something: *We were about to leave when Jerry arrived.*
3 just about almost: *Dinner's just about ready.* THESAURUS ▶ ALMOST
4 *BrE* in many different directions or in different parts of a place SYN **around**: *People were lying about on the floor.*
5 *BrE* near to where you are now SYN **around**: *Is Patrick about? There's a phone call for him.*

a,bout-'face (also **a,bout-'turn** *BrE*) *n* [singular] a complete change in the way someone thinks or behaves

above /əˈbʌv/ *adv, prep*
1 in or to a higher position than something else OPP **below**: *Raise your arm above your head. | There's a light above the entrance. | The noise came from the room above.* → see picture on page A8

2 more than a number, amount, or level OPP **below**: *Temperatures rose above zero today.* | *and/or above suitable for children aged 7 and above*
3 louder than other sounds: *He couldn't hear her voice above the noise.*
4 *formal* before, in the same piece of writing OPP **below**: *Write to the address above for further information.*
5 higher in rank, more powerful, or more important: *officers above the rank of lieutenant*
6 be above suspicion/criticism etc to be so good that no one can doubt or criticize you
PHRASES
| **above all** *formal* most importantly: *Above all, I would like to thank my parents.*

a,bove 'board / $.'../ *adj* [not before noun] something such as a business deal that is above board is honest and legal **THESAURUS** HONEST

abrasive /ə'breɪsɪv/ *adj* **1** rude and not gentle: *his abrasive manner* **2** having a rough surface that can be used to rub off the surface of other things

abreast /ə'brest/ *adv* **two/three/four abreast** with two, three, or four people moving along next to each other: *The cyclists were riding three abreast, so no one could pass them.*
PHRASES
| **keep abreast of sth** to make sure that you know the most recent facts about a subject: *I listen to the radio to keep abreast of the news.*

abridged /ə'brɪdʒd/ *adj* an abridged form of a book, play etc has been made shorter: *the **abridged version** of the novel* —**abridge** *v* [T]

abroad /ə'brɔːd $ ə'brɒːd/ *adv* in or to a foreign country: *He often has to **go abroad** on business.* | *Did you enjoy **living abroad**?* | *the President's image both **at home and abroad** (=in this country and in other countries)* | *from abroad workers hired from abroad*

abrupt /ə'brʌpt/ *adj* **1** sudden and unexpected: *an abrupt change in the attitudes of voters* **2** not polite or friendly, especially because you do not want to waste time: *She was rather abrupt on the phone.* —**abruptly** *adv* —**abruptness** *n* [U]

abs /æbz/ *n* [plural] *informal* the muscles on your ABDOMEN (=stomach): *exercises that improve your abs*

abscess /'æbses/ *n* [C] a swollen place on your body that is infected and contains a yellow liquid

abscond /əb'skɒnd, æb- $ æb'skɑːnd/ *v* [I] *formal* to leave a place without permission, or to leave somewhere after stealing something: *She had absconded from a children's home.*

abseil /'æbseɪl/ *v* [I] *BrE* to go down a cliff etc by sliding down a rope and pushing against the cliff with your feet

absence /'æbsəns/ *n* **1** [C,U] when you are not in the place where people expect you to be, or the time that you are away: [+from] *frequent absences from work* | *in/during sb's absence The vice president will handle things in my absence.* **2** [U] the lack of something: *In the absence of any firm evidence (=because there wasn't any), the police had to let him go.*

absent /'æbsənt/ *adj* **1** not in the place where you are normally expected to be OPP **present**: [+from] *Why was she absent from school yesterday?* | *I had to do the work of an absent colleague.* **2** *formal* not in a place, thing, or situation: *Controversy was rarely absent.*

absentee /ˌæbsən'tiː◂/ *n* [C] **1** *formal* someone who is supposed to be in a place but is not there **2 absentee landlord/owner** the owner of a building or piece of land who lives far away

absenteeism /ˌæbsən'tiːɪzəm/ *n* [U] regular absence from work or school without a good reason

absently /'æbsəntli/ *adv* in a way that shows you are not interested or not thinking about what is happening: *Rachel smiled absently and went on with her work.*

absent-'minded *adj* someone who is absent-minded often forgets or does not notice things because they are thinking of something else —**absent-mindedness** *n* [U] —**absent-mindedly** *adv*

absolute /'æbsəluːt/ *adj* **1** complete and total: *There was absolute silence.* | *a ruler with absolute power* **2** used to emphasize your opinion: *You're an absolute genius!* **3** definite and not likely to change: *I can't give you any absolute promises.*

absolutely[1] /'æbsəluːtli, ˌæbsə'luːtli/ *adv* completely or totally: *Are you absolutely sure?* | *This is absolutely delicious!* | **absolutely no/nothing** (=none or nothing at all) *He knows absolutely nothing about politics.*

absolutely[2] *spoken* used to say 'yes' or show that you agree in a strong way: *'Do you think I should go?' 'Absolutely.'* | *'Don't you believe me?' '**Absolutely not** (=no).'*

absolve /əb'zɒlv $ -ɑːlv/ *v* [T] *formal* to say publicly that someone should not be blamed for something, or to forgive them

absorb /əb'sɔːb, əb'zɔːb $ -ɔːrb/ *v* [T] **1** if something absorbs liquid, heat etc, it takes it in through its surface: *The towel absorbed most of the water.* **2** to learn, understand, and remember new information: *She's a good student who absorbs information quickly.* **3 be absorbed in sth** to be very interested in something that you are doing, watching etc: *I was completely absorbed in the book.* **4** if something is absorbed, it becomes part of something larger: **be absorbed into sth** *countries that had become absorbed into the Soviet Union* —**absorption** /-'sɔːpʃən $ -ɔːr-/ *n* [U]

absorbent /əb'sɔːbənt, -'zɔː- $ -ɔːr-/ *adj* something that is absorbent can take in liquids through its surface: *absorbent paper*

absorbing /əb'sɔːbɪŋ, -'zɔː- $ -ɔːr-/ *adj* very interesting and keeping your attention: *an absorbing article about space travel* **THESAURUS** INTERESTING

abstain /əb'steɪn/ *v* [I] **1** *formal* to not do something that you would normally enjoy doing: [+from] *Patients were advised to abstain from alcohol.* **2** to deliberately not vote —**abstention** /əb'stenʃən/ *n* [C,U]

abstinence /'æbstənəns/ n [U] when someone stops doing something that they would normally enjoy, especially for religious reasons

abstract $\boxed{Ac}$ /'æbstrækt/ adj **1** based on ideas rather than specific examples or real events: *Beauty is an **abstract idea**.* | *abstract arguments about justice* **2** abstract art consists of shapes and patterns that do not look like real things or people → see picture at **PAINTING**

absurd /əb'sɜːd, -'zɜːd $ -ɜːrd/ adj completely unreasonable or silly: *an absurd situation* | ***It seems absurd** to go all that way just for the day.* **THESAURUS** **STUPID** —**absurdly** adv —**absurdity** n [C,U]

abundance /ə'bʌndəns/ n [singular, U] formal a very large quantity of something: **[+of]** *There is an abundance of creative talent.* | **in abundance** *Wild flowers grow here in abundance.*

abundant /ə'bʌndənt/ adj existing in large quantities: *an abundant supply of fresh fruit*

abundantly /ə'bʌndəntli/ adv **1 abundantly clear/plain** very easy to understand: *He made it **abundantly clear** that he was dissatisfied.* **2** in large quantities

abuse¹ /ə'bjuːs/ n **1** [C,U] when someone uses something in a way it should not be used: **[+of]** *government officials' abuse of power* | **drug/alcohol abuse** (=when people take illegal drugs or drink too much) **2** [U] cruel or violent treatment of someone: *a police investigation into **child abuse*** | *victims of **sexual abuse*** **3** [U] rude and insulting things that someone says when they are angry: *The family suffered constant **verbal abuse**.*

abuse² /ə'bjuːz/ v [T] **1** to do cruel or violent things to someone: **sexually/physically abused** *He was sexually abused as a child.* **2** to use something too much or in the wrong way: *He had **abused** his **position** as mayor by offering jobs to his friends.* **3** to say rude and insulting things to someone

abusive /ə'bjuːsɪv/ adj using words that are rude and insulting: *an abusive letter*

abysmal /ə'bɪzməl/ adj very bad: *the country's abysmal record on human rights* —**abysmally** adv

abyss /ə'bɪs/ n [C] **1** a very dangerous or frightening situation: *the abyss of nuclear war* **2** literary a very deep hole or space that seems to have no bottom

academic¹ $\boxed{Ac}$ /ˌækə'demɪk◄/ adj **1** relating to education, especially in a college or university: *students' **academic achievements*** | **academic work/study/research** | **the academic year** (=the period of the year when there are school or university classes) **2** if a subject in a discussion is academic, it is not important to discuss it because you cannot change the situation: *We don't have any money, so the question of where to go on holiday is purely academic.* **3** good at studying: *She was never a very academic child.*

academic² $\boxed{Ac}$ n [C] a teacher in a college or university

academy /ə'kædəmi/ n [C] (plural **academies**) **1** a school or college that trains students in a special subject or skill: *a military academy* **2** an organization whose purpose is to encourage the development of art, science, or literature

accede /ək'siːd, æk-/ v

PHRASAL VERBS

accede to sth formal to agree to a request or demand

accelerate /ək'seləreɪt/ v **1** [I] if a car driver accelerates, they start to go faster: *Melissa accelerated as she drove onto the highway.* **2** [I,T] if a process accelerates or if you accelerate it, it starts to happen more quickly: *a plan to accelerate economic growth* —**acceleration** /ək,selə'reɪʃən/ n [U]

accelerator /ək'seləreɪtə $ -ər/ n [C] the part of a car that you press with your foot to make it go faster

accent /'æksənt $ 'æksent/ n [C] **1** a way of pronouncing words that someone has because of where they were born or live: *He's got a strong northern accent.* **THESAURUS** **LANGUAGE 2 the accent on sth** the importance given to something: *a training programme with the accent on safety* **3** a mark written above some letters, for example é or â: *The 'é' in fiancée has an acute accent.*

COLLOCATIONS

verbs

to have an accent *She had a strong French accent.*

to speak with an accent *The man spoke with a New York accent.*

to lose your accent *His English was good, but he never lost his German accent.*

adjectives

a French/American etc accent *I noticed that she had a Spanish accent.*

a strong/broad/thick accent (=very noticeable) *His accent was so strong I found it hard to understand what he was saying.*

a slight/faint accent *She has a very slight Irish accent.*

a foreign accent *I got a call from a man with a foreign accent.*

---

accentuate /ək'sentʃueɪt/ v [T] to make something easier to notice

accept /ək'sept/ v

1 OFFER/ADVICE/INVITATION [I,T] to take or agree to something that someone offers you or suggests: *They offered me the job and I accepted.* | **accept an offer/invitation** *We would be happy to accept your invitation.* | **accept advice/suggestions** *Jackie won't accept any advice.* | **accept sth from sb** *officials accused of accepting bribes from criminals* **2 SITUATION** [T] to admit that an unpleasant fact or difficult situation is true: **[+that]** *I accept that we've made mistakes.* | *Arthur soon **accepted the fact that** he wasn't going to get the job.* | *Everyone **accepts the need** for change.* **THESAURUS** **BELIEVE** **3 LET SB JOIN** [T] to let someone join an organization, university course etc $\boxed{OPP}$ **reject**: *She applied to Columbia College and was accepted.* **4 WELCOME SB** [T] to let someone new become part of a group and to treat them in the same way as other members: *It was a long time before the other kids at school accepted him.* **5 CREDIT CARDS/CHEQUES** [T] to let customers pay for something in a particular way → **take**: *We don't accept credit cards.*

6 RESPONSIBILITY/BLAME **accept responsibility/blame for sth** to admit that you are responsible for something bad that has happened: *The company have accepted responsibility for the accident.*

acceptable /ək'septəbəl/ *adj*
1 good enough, especially for a particular purpose: **[+to]** *an agreement which is acceptable to everyone* | **acceptable level/standard/quality** *Do staff provide an acceptable level of service?*
2 if behaviour is acceptable, people approve of it and think that it is appropriate OPP **unacceptable**: *It is socially acceptable for men to marry younger women.* | *It's simply not an acceptable way to do business.* | *Her suggestion seems perfectly acceptable.* —**acceptability** /ək,septə'bɪləti/ *n* [U]

acceptance /ək'septəns/ *n* [U] **1** when you agree to accept something that is offered to you: **[+of]** *The board has recommended acceptance of the offer.* | *She gave a brief **acceptance speech** (=a speech to accept an award, position etc).* **2** when people agree that something is right or true: **[+of]** *There is widespread acceptance of the need for economic reform.* | **[+that]** *the general acceptance that global temperatures have risen* | **gain/find acceptance** (=become popular) *His ideas soon gained acceptance from scientists.* **3** when you decide that there is nothing you can do to change an unpleasant situation **4** when someone is allowed to become part of a group or society: **[+into]** *the immigrants' gradual acceptance into the community*

accepted /ək'septɪd/ *adj* an accepted idea or way of doing something is one that most people think is right or reasonable: **generally/widely/universally etc accepted** *a generally accepted principle of international law*

access¹ Ac /'ækses/ *n* [U] **1** the right to enter a place, use something, see someone etc: **[+to]** *In some areas there is no access to clean water.* | *Students need to **have access to** the computer system.* **2** the way you enter a building or get to a place, or how easy this is: **[+to]** *The only access to the farm is along a narrow track.* | **[+for]** *improved access for disabled customers* | **get/gain access (to sth)** formal (=enter) *The thieves gained access through the upstairs window.*

access² Ac *v* [T] to find and use information, especially on a computer: *software for accessing the Internet*

accessible Ac /ək'sesəbəl/ *adj* **1** easy to reach, find, or use OPP **inaccessible**: *The park is not accessible by road.* | *a wide range of information that is **easily accessible*** **2** easy to understand and enjoy OPP **inaccessible**: **[+to]** *He makes a difficult subject accessible to the ordinary reader.* —**accessibility** /ək,sesə'bɪləti/ *n* [U]

accessory /ək'sesəri/ *n* [C] (*plural* **accessories**) **1** something such as a bag, belt, or jewellery that you wear or carry because it is attractive: *fashion accessories* **2** something that you can add to a machine, tool, car etc which is not necessary but is useful or attractive **3** *law* someone who helps a criminal

accident /'æksɪdənt/ *n* [C] a situation in which someone is hurt or something is damaged without anyone intending it to happen: *He died in a car accident.* | *Sam had an accident at work and had to go to hospital.* | *The accident happened in the early hours of Sunday morning.* | *I didn't do it on purpose – **it was an accident**.*

PHRASES

by accident in a way that is not intended or planned OPP **on purpose**: *The cure was discovered almost by accident.* | *I met her **quite by accident**.*

COLLOCATIONS

adjectives

a bad/serious/major accident *There was a bad accident right outside our house.*

a terrible/nasty/horrific accident *It looked like a very nasty accident.*

a fatal accident (=in which someone is killed) *The number of fatal accidents has gone down.*

a minor accident (=not serious) *His car was involved in a minor accident.* ⚠ Do not say 'a small accident'. Say **a minor accident**.

verbs

to have an accident *I've never had an accident before in my life.*

to be involved in an accident formal: *Her parents were involved in a car accident when she was 6 years old.*

to prevent an accident *Speed cameras can help prevent accidents.*

noun + accident

a car/road/traffic accident *The actor was killed in a tragic car accident.*

a rail/train accident *Most rail accidents are caused by human error.*

THESAURUS

accident an event in which something is damaged or someone is hurt, without anyone intending it to happen: *Drive carefully – you don't want to have an accident.*

crash a bad accident in which a car, train, plane etc hits something else: *a car crash* | *Buddy Holly died in a plane crash just when he was becoming famous.*

collision an accident in which two or more cars, trains, planes etc hit each other: *a mid-air collision between two planes*

pile-up an accident in which several cars, trucks etc hit each other while travelling in the same direction: *a motorway pile-up*

disaster a very bad accident involving a train, plane, or boat, in which a lot of people are killed or injured: *It was the country's worst ever air disaster.*

---

accidental /,æksə'dentl◄/ *adj* if something that happens is accidental, it was not planned or intended OPP **deliberate**: *insurance against accidental damage* | *Was the explosion accidental or deliberate?* —**accidentally** *adv*: *I accidentally set off the alarm.*

'accident-prone *adj* someone who is accident-prone often has accidents

acclaim /ə'kleɪm/ *n* [U] a lot of public praise for someone or something: **international/great/widespread etc acclaim** *His first novel received widespread acclaim.* | *The show won critical acclaim.*

acclaimed /ə'kleɪmd/ *adj* praised by a lot of people: **highly/widely acclaimed** *the band's highly acclaimed debut album* —**acclaim** *v* [T]

acclimatize (*also* **-ise** *BrE*) /ə'klaɪmətaɪz/ (*also* **acclimate** *AmE* /ə'klaɪmət $ 'ækləmeɪt, ə'klaɪmət/) *v* [I,T] to become used to the weather, way of living etc in a new place, or to make someone do this: **[+to]** *It takes the astronauts a few days to get acclimatized to conditions in space.* —**acclimatization** /ə,klaɪmətaɪ'zeɪʃən $ -tə-/ *n* [U]

accolade /'ækəleɪd/ *n* [C] praise given to someone because people think they are very good, or a prize given to them for their work

accommodate Ac /ə'kɒmədeɪt $ ə'kɑː-/ *v* [T] **1** to have enough space for a particular number of people or things: *The hall can accommodate 300 people.* **2** to give someone a place to live, stay, or work: *A new hostel was built to accommodate the students.* **3** *formal* to provide someone with what they need, or do what they want: *The centre is designed to accommodate the needs of all visitors.*

accommodating /ə'kɒmədeɪtɪŋ $ ə'kɑː-/ *adj* helpful and willing to do what someone else wants

accommodation Ac /ə,kɒmə'deɪʃən $ ə,kɑː-/ *BrE*, **accommodations** *AmE n* a place to live, stay, or work: *The college provides accommodation for all new students.* | *Rented accommodation is getting very expensive.*

> **Grammar**
> In British English, **accommodation** is uncountable and is not used in the plural with 's'. You say: *They gave me a list of accommodation.*
> In American English, people usually use the plural form **accommodations**. The singular form is rare. You say: *They gave me a list of accommodations.*

accompaniment Ac /ə'kʌmpənɪmənt/ *n* [C] **1** *formal* something that is good to eat or drink with another food: **[+to]** *White wine is an excellent accompaniment to fish.* **2** music played while someone sings or plays another instrument: *a piano accompaniment*

accompany Ac /ə'kʌmpəni/ *v* [T] (**accompanied**, **accompanying**, **accompanies**) **1** *formal* to go somewhere with someone: **[+to]** *I accompanied her to the station.* | **be accompanied by sb** (=have sb with you) *Children under 12 must be accompanied by an adult.* **2** to play a musical instrument while someone is playing or singing the main tune **3** to happen, exist etc with something else: *Depression may be accompanied by fear in some cases.*

accomplice /ə'kʌmplɪs $ ə'kɑːm-, ə'kʌm-/ *n* [C] someone who helps a criminal to do something wrong

accomplish /ə'kʌmplɪʃ $ ə'kɑːm-, ə'kʌm-/ *v* [T] to succeed in doing something: *The new government has accomplished a great deal.*

accomplished /ə'kʌmplɪʃt $ ə'kɑːm-, ə'kʌm-/ *adj* very skilful, especially in art, writing, music etc: *a highly accomplished poet*

accomplishment /ə'kʌmplɪʃmənt $ ə'kɑːm-, ə'kʌm-/ *n* **1** [C] *formal* a skill, especially in art, writing, music etc **2** [U] when you succeed in doing something: **[+of]** *the accomplishment of his ambition*

accord[1] /ə'kɔːd $ -ɔːrd/ *n* [C] an official agreement

PHRASES

in accord (with sb/sth) *formal* in agreement with someone or something, or the same as something: *These results are in accord with earlier research.*

of your own accord willingly, and not because someone has asked you or forced you to do something: *He left of his own accord.*

accord[2] *v* [T] *formal* to treat someone or something in a special way, or give them special attention: *On his return he was accorded a hero's welcome.*

accordance /ə'kɔːdəns $ ə'kɔːr-/ *n* **in accordance with sth** *formal* according to a system or rule: *Safety checks were made in accordance with the rules.*

accordingly /ə'kɔːdɪŋli $ ə'kɔːr-/ *adv* **1** in a way that is suitable for a particular situation: *If you work extra hours, you will be paid accordingly.* **2** *formal* as a result of something SYN **therefore**

ac'cording to *prep* **1** as shown by something or said by someone: *According to our records, she hasn't paid her bill.* | *According to Angela, he's married.* **2** in the way that has been planned or that is based on a system: *Everything went according to plan and we arrived on time.* | *The game must be played according to the rules.*

accordion /ə'kɔːdiən $ ə'kɔːr-/ *n* [C] a musical instrument like a box that you hold in both hands. You play it by pulling the sides in and out and pushing buttons to produce different notes.

ACCORDION

accost /ə'kɒst $ ə'kɒːst, ə'kɑːst/ *v* [T] if someone you do not know accosts you, they come and speak to you in an unpleasant or threatening way

account[1] /ə'kaʊnt/ *n* [C] **1** REPORT a written or spoken description of something that has happened: **[+of]** *She was able to give an account of the accident.* | *Holroyd has written a detailed account of the war.* | **eye-witness/first-hand account** (=description of events by someone who saw them) *his eye-witness account of the shootings*

2 AT A BANK (*also* **bank account**) an arrangement with a bank that allows you to keep your money there and take money out when you need it: *Would* you like to **open an account** (=make this arrangement)? | *Your salary will be **paid into** your bank **account**. | I've **withdrawn** £250 **from** my account. | What's your **account number**?*

3 FINANCIAL RECORDS **accounts** [plural] a record of the money that a business has received and spent: *Their **annual accounts** showed a loss of £4 million.*

4 WAY OF PAYING an arrangement with a shop or company that allows you to buy things or use a service now and pay later: **on account** *Can I buy this on account?* | *I'd like to **charge** this **to** my **account** (=pay using this arrangement). | an Internet account | **pay/settle your account** (=pay what you owe) You must settle your account within thirty days.*

PHRASES

by/from all accounts according to what people say: *He was, by all accounts, a shy man.*

not on my account spoken not for me or because of me: *Don't stay up late on my account.*

on account of sth because of something: *Some trains were cancelled on account of the storm.*

on no account/not on any account formal used to emphasize that someone must not do something: *On no account open the door to a stranger.*

take account of sth/take sth into account to consider particular facts when judging or deciding something: *These statistics do not take account of age.*

account² v

PHRASAL VERBS

account for sth **1** to be a particular part of an amount: *Oil and gas account for 60% of our exports.* **2** to be the reason for something, or to explain the reason for something: *If he's taking drugs, that would account for his behaviour.* | *Can you account for what you did?*

accountable /əˈkaʊntəbəl/ adj [not before noun] responsible for what you do and willing to explain it or accept criticism: **[+to]** *The government is accountable to the people.* | **[+for]** *Managers must be accountable for their decisions.* | *If students fail exams, can their teachers be **held accountable** (=considered responsible)?* —**accountability** /əˌkaʊntəˈbɪləti/ n [U]

accountancy /əˈkaʊntənsi/ BrE, **accounting** /əˈkaʊntɪŋ/ AmE n [U] the job of being an accountant

accountant /əˈkaʊntənt/ n [C] someone whose job is to write or check financial records

accredited /əˈkredɪtɪd/ adj having official approval

accumulate Ac /əˌkjuːmjəleɪt/ v [I,T] to gradually increase in amount, or to make the amount of something gradually increase: *Dirt and dust had accumulated in the corners of the room.* | **accumulate money/knowledge/wealth etc** *He had accumulated over £300,000.* —**accumulation** /əˌkjuːmjəˈleɪʃən/ n [C,U]

accuracy Ac /ˈækjərəsi/ n [U] the quality of being exact or correct OPP **inaccuracy**: *He passes the ball with amazing accuracy.*

accurate Ac /ˈækjərət/ adj exact and correct OPP **inaccurate**: *Patients should be given accurate information about their treatment.* | *These figures are*

not completely accurate. | *an accurate shot* THESAURUS ▶ RIGHT —**accurately** adv

accusation /ˌækjəˈzeɪʃən/ n [C] a statement saying that someone has done something wrong or illegal: **[+against]** *Both boys **made** serious **accusations** against each other.*

accuse /əˈkjuːz/ v [T] to say that someone has done something wrong or illegal: **accuse sb of (doing) sth** *Are you accusing me of lying?* | *He was accused of theft.* —**accuser** n [C]

accused /əˈkjuːzd/ n **the accused** [singular or plural] the person or people accused of a crime in a court of law

accusing /əˈkjuːzɪŋ/ adj showing that you think someone has done something wrong: *She gave him an accusing look.* —**accusingly** adv

accustom /əˈkʌstəm/ v **accustom yourself to (doing) sth** to make yourself get used to something and accept it: *He had accustomed himself to living alone.*

accustomed /əˈkʌstəmd/ adj formal **be accustomed to (doing) sth** to be used to something and accept it as normal: *She was accustomed to a life of luxury.* | **become/get/grow accustomed to sth** *Ed's eyes quickly grew accustomed to the dark.*

ace¹ /eɪs/ n [C] **1** a PLAYING CARD with one symbol on it, that has the highest or lowest value in a game: **[+of]** *the ace of hearts* → see picture at **PLAYING CARD 2** a first hit in tennis or VOLLEYBALL that is so good that your opponent cannot reach it **3** someone who is very skilful at doing something: *a soccer ace*

ace² adj informal very good or skilful

ache¹ /eɪk/ v [I] **1** if part of your body aches, you feel a continuous pain there: **ache from (doing) sth** *My legs were aching from walking so far.* **2** to want to do or have something very much: **[+to]** *Jenny was aching to go home.* | **[+for]** *I was aching for sleep.*

ache² n [C] a continuous pain: **have a headache/backache/toothache etc** *(=have a continuous pain in your head etc) Tommy has an earache.* | *a bad stomach ache* THESAURUS ▶ PAIN —**achy** adj

achieve Ac /əˈtʃiːv/ v [T] to succeed in getting a good result or in doing something you want: *Most of our students **achieve** excellent exam **results**.* | **achieve an aim/ambition/goal** *She had finally **achieved** her **ambition** to sail around the world.* THESAURUS ▶ SUCCEED —**achiever** n [C]: *a high achiever* (=someone who is very successful) —**achievable** adj

achievement Ac /əˈtʃiːvmənt/ n

1 [C] something good and impressive that you succeed in doing: **great/major/remarkable etc achievement** *Putting a man on the moon was one of our greatest achievements.* | *an impressive achievement of 144 points*

2 [U] when you succeed in doing or getting something you want: **[+of]** *the achievement of a lifetime's ambition* | *educational achievement* | *the sense of achievement you get from doing a job well*

Achilles' heel /əˌkɪliːz ˈhiːl/ n [C] a fault in someone's character, which could cause them to fail or be defeated: *I think his vanity is his Achilles' heel.*

acid¹ /'æsɪd/ n [C,U] a liquid chemical substance that has a pH of less than 7. Some types of acid can damage things. → **alkali**: *Vinegar contains a kind of acid.* —**acidic** /ə'sɪdɪk/ adj —**acidity** /ə'sɪdəti/ n [U]

acid² adj **1** having a very sour taste **2 acid remark/ comment** something you say that uses humour in an unkind way to criticize someone **3** containing acid: *an acid solution*

,acid 'rain n [U] rain that contains acid chemicals, for example from factory smoke and cars, and that is harmful to the environment

acknowledge Ac /ək'nɒlɪdʒ $ -'nɑː-/ v [T] **1** to accept or admit that something is true or official: **[+(that)]** *Angie acknowledged that she'd made a mistake.* | *They are refusing to acknowledge the court's decision.* **2** [usually passive] to recognize how good or important someone or something is: **acknowledge sth as sth** *These beaches are acknowledged as the cleanest in Europe.* | **acknowledge sth to be sth** *He's widely acknowledged to be the best in his field.* **3** to write to someone telling them that you have received something they sent you: *They still haven't acknowledged my letter.* **4** to show someone that you have seen them or heard what they said: *Tom acknowledged her presence with a quick smile.*

acknowledgement Ac , **acknowledgment** /ək'nɒlɪdʒmənt $ -'nɑː-/ n **1** [C,U] when you show that you accept something is true: **[+of]** *He bowed his head in acknowledgement of defeat.* **2** [C] a letter that tells someone has received something sent them: *Have you received an acknowledgement yet?* **3** [singular, U] when you make a movement to show you have noticed someone or heard what they said: **a nod/smile/wave etc of acknowledgement 4 acknowledgements** [plural] a short piece of writing in a book in which the writer thanks the people who have helped with it

acne /'ækni/ n [U] a skin problem that causes spots to appear on the face and is common among young people

acorn /'eɪkɔːn $ -ɔːrn, -ərn/ n [C] the nut of an OAK tree

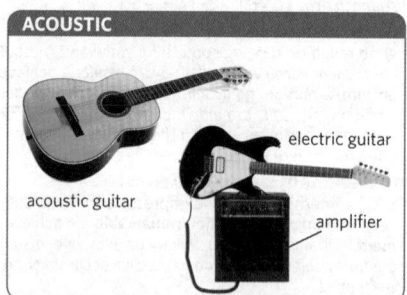

ACOUSTIC

electric guitar

acoustic guitar

amplifier

acoustic /ə'kuːstɪk/ adj **1** relating to sound and the way people hear things **2** an acoustic musical instrument is not electric: *an acoustic guitar*

acoustics /ə'kuːstɪks/ n [plural] the way in which the shape and size of a room affect how well or badly you can hear music, speech etc

acquaintance /ə'kweɪntəns/ n [C] someone you know, but do not know well
PHRASES
make sb's acquaintance formal to meet someone for the first time: *I would be delighted to make Mrs McGough's acquaintance.*

acquainted /ə'kweɪntɪd/ adj formal **1** if you are acquainted with someone, you have met them a few times but do not know them very well: *Doug and I are already acquainted.* **2 be acquainted with sth** to know about something, because you have seen it, read it, used it etc: *My lawyer's already acquainted with the facts.*

acquiesce /ˌækwi'es/ v [I] formal to agree to do what someone wants, or to allow something to happen, although you do not like it —**acquiescence** n [U]

acquire Ac /ə'kwaɪə $ ə'kwaɪr/ v [T] formal **1** to get something, especially by buying it: *The museum acquired the painting for £6.8 million.* THESAURUS ► BUY **2** to learn something: **acquire knowledge/skills** *He's acquired some knowledge of Arabic.*

acquisition Ac /ˌækwə'zɪʃən/ n **1** [U] the process of getting or learning something: **[+of]** *the acquisition of wealth* **2** [C] something that you have obtained, especially by buying it: *This sofa's a new acquisition.*

acquit /ə'kwɪt/ v [T usually passive] (**acquitted, acquitting**) to decide in a court of law that someone is not guilty of a crime: **acquit sb of sth** *Simons was acquitted of murder.*

acquittal /ə'kwɪtl/ n [C,U] an official statement in a court of law that someone is not guilty

acre /'eɪkə $ -ər/ n [C] a unit for measuring an area of land, equal to 4,840 square yards or about 4,047 square metres

acrid /'ækrɪd/ adj having a very strong and unpleasant smell that hurts your nose or throat: *a cloud of acrid smoke*

acrimonious /ˌækrə'məuniəs◄ $ -'mou-/ adj an acrimonious meeting, argument etc involves a lot of anger and disagreement: *an acrimonious divorce* —**acrimoniously** adv

acrobat /'ækrəbæt/ n [C] someone who does skilful physical actions to entertain people, for example balancing on a high rope —**acrobatic** /ˌækrə'bætɪk◄/ adj

acrobatics /ˌækrə'bætɪks/ n [plural] skilful actions like those of an acrobat

acronym /'ækrənɪm/ n [C] a word made from the first letters of the name of something. For example, NATO is an acronym for the North Atlantic Treaty Organization.

across /ə'krɒs $ ə'krɒːs/ adv, prep
1 from one side of something to the other side: *the first flight across the Atlantic* | *There wasn't a bridge so we swam across.* | **go/run/come etc straight across** (=go across in a direct line or without stopping) *The road runs straight across the desert.* | **10 feet/5 metres etc across** (=used to show how wide something is) *In places, the river is 2 km across.* → see picture on page A8

2 on the opposite side of something: *Andy lives across the road.* | **across (sth) from sb/sth** *France is just across the Channel from here.*

PHRASES

across the board affecting everyone or everything: *a pay increase of 8% across the board*

acrylic /əˈkrɪlɪk/ *adj* acrylic paints or cloth are made from chemical substances, not natural ones

act¹ /ækt/ *v*

1 DO STH [I] to do something: *Unless the UN acts soon, more people will die.* | **act on advice/orders/instructions** (=do what someone says) *We're acting on the advice of our lawyer.*

2 BEHAVE [I] to behave in a particular way: *Nick's been acting strangely recently.* | *Do you think the company acted reasonably?* | **[+like]** *Stop acting like a baby!* | **act cool/crazy/tough etc** *a gang of boys trying to act tough* | *He's not really upset – he's just acting* (=pretending to be upset)!

3 IN A PLAY/FILM [I,T] to perform in a play or film: *She started acting when she was 12.* | *Which character are you acting?*

4 HAVE A USE/EFFECT [I] to have a particular use or effect: **[+as]** *Salt acts as a preservative.* | **[+on]** *the way that drugs act on the brain* | **act as agent/chairman/consultant etc** (=do a particular job, especially for a short time) *Mr Compton has kindly agreed to act as Secretary for this event.*

PHRASAL VERBS

act sth ↔ **out** to show how something happened by performing it like a play: *The children read the story and then acted it out.*

act up if a child acts up, he or she behaves badly

act² *n*

1 SOMETHING YOU DO [C] something that you do: **[+of]** *an act of kindness* | **in the act of doing sth** (=at the moment that you are doing something) *The man was caught in the act of leaving the building.* | *a criminal act*

2 LAW (*also* **Act**) [C] a law that has been officially accepted by the government: *The Criminal Justice Act* | *Act of Congress/Parliament*

3 PART OF PLAY (*also* **Act**) [C] one of the main parts of a play, OPERA etc: *Hamlet kills the king in Act 5.*

4 PERFORMANCE [C] a short piece of entertainment on television or stage: *a comedy act*

5 PRETENDING [singular] behaviour that is not sincere: *He never loved me – it was just an act.*

PHRASES

get in on the act *informal* to become involved in a successful activity that someone else has started: *Geoff had the idea of setting up the club, but Brian soon wanted to get in on the act.*

get your act together *informal* to start to do things in a more organized way: *You'll have to get your act together before the exams.*

acting¹ /ˈæktɪŋ/ *adj* **acting manager/director etc** someone who does an important job until the usual person comes back, or until a new person is chosen

acting² *n* [U] the job or skill of performing in plays or films

action /ˈækʃən/ *n*

1 [U] when you do something, especially to achieve a particular thing: *The government must take action to stop the rise in crime.* | **course/plan of action** (=way of dealing with a situation) *The best course of action is to tell her the whole story.* | **firm/tough/direct etc action** *He realized the need for immediate action.* | *Most people are against military action.*

2 [C] something that you do: *You cannot be responsible for other people's actions.* | **quick/swift/prompt action** *Tanya's prompt action saved his life.*

3 [U] *informal* exciting things that are happening: *New York's where the action is.* | **an action movie** (=one with a lot of fast exciting scenes) | **action-packed** *holidays for teenagers*

4 [U] fighting in a war: *Ann's husband was killed in action.* | *buildings destroyed by enemy action*

5 the action the events in a story, film, play etc: *The action takes place in southern Italy.*

6 [C,U] the process of deciding something in a court of law: *They threatened to take legal action against him.*

7 [singular] the way something moves or works, or the effect it has on something: **[+of]** *the action of the heart* | *the action of bacteria on the skin*

PHRASES

in action doing a particular job, activity, or sport: *photos of ski jumpers in action* | *a chance to see the new technology in action*

out of action broken and not working, or injured and not able to do things such as sport: *The photocopier's out of action again.* | *His injury put him out of action for a month.*

ˌaction ˈreplay *n* [C] *BrE* an exciting moment in a sports game that is shown again on television immediately after it happens SYN **instant replay** *AmE*

activate /ˈæktɪveɪt/ *v* [T] *formal* to make something start working: *This switch activates the alarm.*

active¹ /ˈæktɪv/ *adj*

1 always doing things, or moving around a lot OPP **inactive**: *games for active youngsters* | *She's 80, but still very active.*

2 involved in an organization or activity by doing things for it: **active member/supporter** *an active member of the local football club* | *Students should take an active part in discussions.*

3 *technical* something that is active is ready or able to work as expected: *The virus is active even at low temperatures.* | **an active volcano** (=able to explode at any time)

4 *technical* an active verb or sentence has the person or thing doing the action as its SUBJECT. In 'The boy kicked the ball', the verb 'kick' is active. → PASSIVE → PROACTIVE

active² *n* **the active (voice)** the active form of a verb → PASSIVE

actively /ˈæktɪvli/ *adv* in a way that involves doing things or taking part in something: *Parents must be actively involved in their children's education.*

activist /ˈæktɪvɪst/ *n* [C] someone who works to achieve social or political change

activity /ækˈtɪvəti/ *n* (*plural* **activities**)
1 [C usually plural] something that you do for enjoyment in a regular organized way: **leisure/ recreational/social etc activities** *outdoor activities such as hiking and climbing*
2 [C,U] things that people do to achieve a particular aim: **political/business/economic etc activity** *the department's research activities* | *terrorist activity*
3 [U] when a lot of things are happening, or when people are moving around OPP **inactivity**: *The house is full of activity once the kids get home.*

actor /ˈæktə $ -ər/ *n* [C] someone who performs in a play or film

---

THESAURUS

actor someone who performs in a play or film: *The actors came back onto the stage.* | *He won the award for best actor.*
actress a woman who performs in a play or film. Women usually prefer to be called **actors** rather than **actresses**: *She's one of my favourite actresses.*
star a famous actor: *a Hollywood star* | *She looked like a movie star.*
the star the person who has the most important part in a play or film: *Daniel Craig is the latest star of the 'Bond' films.*
co-star one of two or more famous actors who have important parts in a play or film: *His co-star is Angelina Jolie.*
the lead the main part in a play or film: *Tom Cruise will play the lead.*
the cast all the actors in a play or film: *The film features an all-star cast* (=all the actors are stars).

---

actress /ˈæktrɪs/ *n* [C] a woman who performs in a play or film THESAURUS **ACTOR**

actual /ˈæktʃuəl/ *adj* real or exact: *Were those his actual words?* | *Germany won, but I don't know the actual score.* | **In actual fact** (=actually), *she's older than me.*

actually /ˈæktʃuəli, -tʃəli/ *adv especially spoken*
1 used to emphasize that something is true, especially when it is a little surprising or unexpected: *Prices have actually fallen.* | *'Disappointed?' 'No, actually I feel rather glad.'* | *Actually he's 45.*
2 used to politely give more information, give your opinion etc: *I've known him all my life, actually.* | *Actually, I think I prefer this one.*

acumen /ˈækjəmən, əˈkjuːmən/ *n* [U] the ability to think quickly and make good decisions: **business acumen**

acupuncture /ˈækjəˌpʌŋktʃə $ -ər/ *n* [U] a way of treating pain or illness by putting thin needles into parts of the body

acute /əˈkjuːt/ *adj* **1** very serious or severe: *an **acute shortage** of teachers* | *acute pain* | *an acute infection of the throat* THESAURUS **SERIOUS 2** good at understanding things quickly and clearly: *an acute mind* **3** an acute sense or feeling is very strong: *an acute sense of smell* | *acute feelings of anxiety* **4** *technical* an acute angle is less than 90 degrees → see picture at **ANGLE**[1]

acutely /əˈkjuːtli/ *adv* feeling or noticing something very strongly: *We are **acutely aware** of the problem.* | *acutely embarrassed*

ad /æd/ *n* [C] *informal* an advertisement THESAURUS **ADVERTISEMENT**

AD /ˌeɪ ˈdiː/ (*Anno Domini*) used to show that a date is a particular number of years after the birth of Christ → **BC**: *453 AD*

adage /ˈædɪdʒ/ *n* [C] a well-known phrase that says something wise about life

adamant /ˈædəmənt/ *adj formal* determined not to change your opinion, decision etc —**adamantly** *adv*

Adam's apple /ˌ... ˈ.../ *n* [C] the lump at the front of your neck that moves when you talk or swallow

adapt /əˈdæpt/ *v* **1** [I,T] to change your behaviour or ideas because it is necessary in a new situation: **[+to]** *Children may find it hard to adapt to a new school.* | **adapt yourself/itself etc (to sth)** *Insects adapt themselves to many environments.* THESAURUS **CHANGE 2** [T] to change something so that it is suitable for a different purpose: **[+to]** *Our car has been adapted to take unleaded fuel.* | **adapt sth for sb/sth** *Her first novel was **adapted for television** (=changed and made into a film or television programme).* **3 be well adapted to sth** to be especially suitable for something: *flowers that are well adapted to the cold winters*

adaptable Ac /əˈdæptəbəl/ *adj* able to change and be successful in new and different situations —**adaptability** /əˌdæptəˈbɪləti/ *n* [U]

adaptation Ac /ˌædæpˈteɪʃən/ *n* **1** [C] a play, film, or television programme that is based on a book **2** [U] when someone or something changes in order to be suitable for a new situation: **[+to]** *successful adaptation to retirement*

adapter, adaptor /əˈdæptə $ -ər/ *n* [C] an object you use to connect two pieces of electrical equipment, or to connect more than one piece of equipment to the same power supply

add /æd/ *v*
1 PUT WITH STH ELSE [T] to put something with something else, or with a group of other things: *Just add a little water.* | **add sth to sth** *Do you want to add your name to the mailing list?*
2 MATHS [T] to put numbers or amounts together to calculate the total OPP **subtract**: **add sth and sth** *Add 5 and 3 to make 8.* | **add sth to sth** *The interest will be added to your savings every six months.*
3 INCREASE [I,T] to increase the amount or cost of something: **add (sth) to sth** *Sales tax adds 15% to the bill.* | *Let's try not to add to the problem.*
4 SAY MORE [T] to say something extra about what you have just said: *'It's too late anyway,' he added.* | **[+that]** *The judge added that this case was the worst she had ever seen.* THESAURUS **SAY**
PHRASES
add insult to injury to make a bad situation even worse for someone who has already been treated badly: *Not only did she lie to him, but to add insult to injury, she also stole his wallet.*

PHRASAL VERBS

add sth ↔ **on** to put another part or amount on something, so that it is bigger: *They're going to add on another bedroom.* | **[+to]** *A service charge will be added on to your bill.*

add up

1 to calculate the total of several numbers or amounts: **add sth ↔ up** *Add your scores up and see who's won.*

2 not add up to not seem true or reasonable: *His story* (=explanation) *doesn't add up*.

added /'ædɪd/ *adj* more than what is usual or natural SYN **extra**: *This method has an **added advantage**.* | *fruit juice with no added sugar*

adder /'ædə $ -ər/ *n* [C] a small poisonous snake

addict /'ædɪkt/ *n* [C] **1** someone who is unable to stop taking drugs: *a heroin addict* **2** someone who likes something very much and does it a lot: *television addicts*

addicted /ə'dɪktɪd/ *adj* **1** unable to stop taking a drug: **[+to]** *Marvin soon became addicted to sleeping pills.* **2** liking something so much that you do not want to stop doing it or having it: **[+to]** *My kids are addicted to surfing the Net.* THESAURUS LIKE —**addiction** /ə'dɪkʃən/ *n* [C,U]: *addiction to nicotine*

addictive /ə'dɪktɪv/ *adj* **1** if a drug is addictive, it is difficult to stop taking it: *Tobacco is **highly addictive**.* **2** an activity that is addictive is so enjoyable that you do not want to stop

addition /ə'dɪʃən/ *n* **1** [U] the act of adding something to something else: **the addition of sth** *The addition of herbs and spices improves the flavour.* **2** [U] the process of adding together several numbers or amounts to get a total → **subtraction 3** [C] something that is added: *The tower is a later addition to the cathedral.*

PHRASES

in addition used to add another piece of information to what you have just said: *The group meets four times a week; in addition, we have individual counselling sessions.* | **[+to]** *In addition to her teaching job, she plays in a band.*

additional /ə'dɪʃənəl/ *adj* more than you already have, or more than was agreed or expected → **extra**: *Additional information can be obtained from the centre.* THESAURUS MORE —**additionally** *adv*

additive /'ædətɪv/ *n* [C usually plural] a substance that is added to food to make it taste or look better or to keep it fresh

address¹ /ə'dres $ ə'dres, 'ædres/ *n* [C]

1 the details of where someone lives or works, including the number of the building, name of the street and town etc: *What's your new address?*

2 a series of letters or numbers used to send an email to someone, or to reach a page of information on the Internet: *Give me your **email address**.*

3 a formal speech: *the Gettysburg Address*

COLLOCATIONS

adjectives

sb's full address *Please write your full address, including your postcode.*

the same address/a different address *Do you know if they are still at the same address?*

a false address *At the police station, she gave the police a false address.*

a forwarding address (=a new address for sending letters to after you have moved) *He did not leave a forwarding address.*

noun + address

sb's home address *His home address is 5, Orton Road, London N31 8HW.*

sb's work/business address *My business address is on my card.*

sb's email address *Can you let me have your email address?*

verbs

to give sb your address *You should always be careful when giving people your address.*

to have/know sb's address *I think I have his address somewhere.*

sb's address has changed *The company's address had changed.*

address² /ə'dres/ *v* [T]

1 to write a name and address on an envelope, package etc: **address sth to sb** *There's a letter here addressed to you.*

2 *formal* to speak directly to a person or group: *A guest speaker then addressed the audience.* | **address sth to sb** *You should address your question to the chairman.*

3 *formal* if you address a problem, you start trying to solve it: **address a problem/issue/question** *We are now starting to address the problem of oil on the beaches.*

4 to use a particular name or title when speaking or writing to someone: **address sb as sth** *The President should be addressed as 'Mr. President'.*

adept /'ædept, ə'dept $ ə'dept/ *adj* good at doing something that needs care or skill OPP **inept**: *He became adept at cooking his favourite dishes.* —**adeptly** *adv*

adequate Ac /'ædɪkwət/ *adj* **1** enough in quantity or of a good enough quality for a particular purpose OPP **inadequate**: *Her income is hardly adequate to pay the bills.* THESAURUS ENOUGH **2** fairly good, but not excellent: *Her performance was adequate but lacked originality.* —**adequately** *adv* —**adequacy** *n* [U]

adhere /əd'hɪə $ -'hɪr/ *v* [I] to stick firmly to something: **[+to]** *The eggs of these fish adhere to plant leaves.*

PHRASAL VERBS

adhere to sth to continue to behave according to a particular rule, agreement, or belief: *I have adhered strictly to the rules.*

adherent /əd'hɪərənt $ -'hɪr-/ *n* [C] someone who supports a particular belief, plan, political party etc —**adherence** *n* [U]: *adherence to democratic principles*

adhesion /əd'hiːʒən/ *n* [U] when one thing sticks to another thing

adhesive /əd'hiːsɪv/ n [C,U] a substance such as glue that can stick things together —**adhesive** adj: adhesive tape

ad hoc /ˌæd 'hɒk◂ , -'hɑːk◂ , -'hoʊk◂/ adj done when necessary, rather than planned or regular: I work for them **on an ad hoc basis**. —**ad hoc** adv

adj. (also **adj** BrE) the written abbreviation of **adjective**

adjacent Ac /ə'dʒeɪsənt/ adj formal next to something: a door leading to the adjacent room | **[+to]** buildings adjacent to the palace

adjective /'ædʒɪktɪv/ n [C] a word that tells you more about a noun. 'Big', 'funny', and 'hot' are all adjectives. —**adjectival** /ˌædʒək'taɪvəl◂/ adj: an adjectival phrase

adjoining /ə'dʒɔɪnɪŋ/ adj next to something, and connected to it: adjoining rooms —**adjoin** v [T]

adjourn /ə'dʒɜːn $ -ɜːrn/ v [I,T] to stop a meeting or a legal process for a short time or until a later date: The committee adjourned for an hour. —**adjournment** n [C,U]

adjudicate /ə'dʒuːdɪkeɪt/ v [I,T] formal to be the judge in a competition or make an official decision about a problem or argument: The European Court was asked to adjudicate in the dispute. —**adjudicator** n [C] —**adjudication** /əˌdʒuːdɪ'keɪʃən/ n [U]

adjust Ac /ə'dʒʌst/ v **1** [I,T] to make small changes to the way you do things in order to get used to a new situation or condition: **[+to]** We're gradually adjusting to the new way of working. **2** [T] to change or move something slightly to improve it or make it more suitable for a particular purpose: Check and adjust the brakes regularly. —**adjustable** adj: an adjustable lamp

adjustment Ac /ə'dʒʌstmənt/ n [C,U] **1** a small change made to a machine, system, or calculation: I've **made a few adjustments to** our original calculations. **2** a change in the way you behave or think: a **period of adjustment**

ad-lib /ˌæd 'lɪb/ v [I,T] (**ad-libbed, ad-libbing**) to say things that you have not prepared or planned to say when you are performing or giving a speech: She forgot her lines and had to ad-lib. —**ad-lib** n [C]

administer /əd'mɪnɪstə $ -ər/ v [T] **1** to manage the work or money of a company or organization: officials who administer the transport system **2** to provide or organize something officially as part of your job: **administer sth to sb** The test was administered to all 11-year-olds. **3** formal to give someone a drug or medical treatment: The medicine was administered in regular doses.

administration Ac /ədˌmɪnə'streɪʃən/ n [U] **1** (also **admin**) the activities that are involved in managing the work of a company or organization: Have you any experience in administration? **THESAURUS** GOVERNMENT **2** the government of a country at a particular time: the Kennedy Administration

administrative Ac /əd'mɪnəstrətɪv $ -streɪtɪv/ adj relating to the work of managing a company or organization: The job is mainly administrative. —**administratively** adv

administrator /əd'mɪnəstreɪtə $ -ər/ n [C] someone whose job involves managing the work of a company or organization

admirable /'ædmərəbəl/ adj having many good qualities that you respect and admire: an admirable achievement —**admirably** adv

admiral /'ædmərəl/ n [C] an officer who has a very high rank in the navy

admiration /ˌædmə'reɪʃən/ n [U] a feeling of great respect and liking for something or someone: **in admiration** He gazed at her in admiration. | **[+for]** I'm **full of admiration** for the people who built this.

admire /əd'maɪə $ -'maɪr/ v [T]
1 to like someone because they have done something that you think is good, or to like the skills or qualities that someone has: **admire sb for (doing) sth** I always admired my mother for her courage and patience. | I really **admire the way** she brings up those kids.
2 to look at something and think how beautiful or impressive it is: We stopped halfway to admire the view. —**admirer** n [C]: I'm a great admirer of yours. —**admiring** adj: an admiring look —**admiringly** adv

---

THESAURUS

admire to like someone because they have done something that you think is good, or to like the skills or qualities that someone has: You know how much I admire you. | I admire his honesty.
look up to sb to admire someone who is older than you, or who has more experience: He had always looked up to his father when he was young.
idolize/worship to admire someone so much that you think they are perfect: Monroe was idolized by millions of fans around the world.

---

admissible /əd'mɪsəbəl/ adj formal admissible reasons, facts etc are acceptable or allowed, especially in a court of law OPP **inadmissible**: admissible evidence

admission /əd'mɪʃən/ n **1** [C] when you admit that something is true or that you have done something wrong: **[+of]** If he resigns, it will be an admission of guilt. **2** [C,U] permission given to someone to enter a building or place, or to become a member of a school, club etc: **[+to]** Tom has applied for admission to Oxford next year. **3** [C,U] the process of taking someone into a hospital for treatment, tests, or care: There are 13,000 hospital admissions annually due to playground accidents. **4** [U] the price charged when you go to a film, sports event, concert etc: Admission $6.50.

admit /əd'mɪt/ v (**admitted, admitting**)
1 [I,T] to say that you have done something wrong or illegal OPP **deny**: **[+(that)]** The chairman of the company admitted that mistakes had been made. | **[+to]** He'll never admit to the murder.
2 [I,T] to agree unwillingly that something is true OPP **deny**: 'OK, I was scared,' she admitted. | **[+(that)]** You may not like her, but you have to admit that she is good at her job.
3 [T] to allow someone to enter a public place to watch a game, performance etc: Only ticket holders will be admitted into the stadium.

4 be admitted to be taken into hospital because you are ill

THESAURUS

admit to say that you have done something wrong or illegal: *I admit that it was a silly mistake.* | *She admitted that she had lied to the police.*

confess to tell someone that you have done something very bad, especially when people have been asking you questions and trying to persuade you to do this: *He later confessed in court that he had killed his wife.*

own up to sth to tell someone that you did something, especially something not very serious: *One of the boys owned up to drawing the picture on the wall.*

admittance /əd'mɪtəns/ n [U] permission to enter a place: *Journalists were refused admittance to the meeting.*

admittedly /əd'mɪtɪdli/ adv used when you are admitting that something is true: *This has led to financial losses, though admittedly on a fairly small scale.*

admonish /əd'mɒnɪʃ $ -'mɑː-/ v [T] literary to tell someone that they have done something wrong —**admonishment** n [C,U]

ado /ə'duː/ n **without more/further ado** without any more delay

adolescence /ˌædə'lesəns/ n [U] the period when a young person is developing into an adult, usually between the ages of 12 and 18

adolescent /ˌædə'lesənt◂/ n [C] a young person who is developing into an adult **THESAURUS** YOUNG —**adolescent** adj

adopt /ə'dɒpt $ ə'dɑːpt/ v **1** [I,T] to take someone else's child into your home and legally become its parent: *Sally was adopted when she was four.* **2** [T] to begin to use a particular plan or way of doing something: *The police are adopting more forceful methods.* **3** [T] to formally approve a suggestion: *The committee voted to adopt our proposals.* —**adoption** /ə'dɒpʃən $ ə'dɑːp-/ n [C,U]: *children put up for adoption* | *the adoption of new technology* —**adopted** adj: *their adopted daughter*

adoptive /ə'dɒptɪv $ ə'dɑːp-/ adj [only before noun] an adoptive parent is one who has adopted a child

adorable /ə'dɔːrəbəl/ adj very attractive: *an adorable little puppy*

adore /ə'dɔː $ ə'dɔːr/ v [T] **1** to love and admire someone very much: *Tim absolutely adores his older brother.* **THESAURUS** LOVE **2** to like something very much: *I simply adore chocolate.* **THESAURUS** LIKE —**adoration** /ˌædə'reɪʃən/ n [U] —**adoring** adj: *Kylie's adoring fans*

adorn /ə'dɔːn $ -ɔːrn/ v [T] formal **be adorned with sth** to be decorated with something: *church walls adorned with religious paintings* —**adornment** /ə'dɔːnmənt $ -ɔːr-/ n [C,U]

adrenalin /ə'drenəlɪn/ n [U] a chemical produced

by your body that gives you more energy when you are frightened, excited, or angry

adrift /ə'drɪft/ adv a boat that is adrift is not tied to anything, and is moved around by the ocean or wind

PHRASES

come adrift if something comes adrift, it becomes separated from the thing it should be fastened to: *The exhaust had come adrift from the underside of the car.*

adroit /ə'drɔɪt/ adj clever and skilful, especially at thinking and speaking —**adroitly** adv

adulation /ˌædʒə'leɪʃən/ n [U] formal praise and admiration for someone that is more than they really deserve

adult¹ Ac /'ædʌlt, ə'dʌlt/ n [C] a fully grown person or animal

adult² adj

1 [only before noun] fully grown or developed: *an adult lion* | *the adult population* | *He lived most of his* **adult life** *in Scotland.*

2 typical of an adult: *an adult view of the world*

3 [only before noun] adult films, magazines etc are about sex or related to sex

adultery /ə'dʌltəri/ n [U] sex between someone who is married and someone who is not their wife or husband: *She had* **committed adultery** *on several occasions.* —**adulterous** adj

adulthood /'ædʌlthʊd, ə'dʌlt-/ n [U] the time when you are an adult → **childhood**

adv. (also **adv** BrE) the written abbreviation of **adverb**

advance¹ /əd'vɑːns $ əd'væns/ n **1** [C,U] a change, discovery, or invention that brings progress: *medical advances* **2** [C] a movement forward to a new position, especially by an army OPP **retreat**: *Napoleon's advance towards Moscow* **3** [C usually singular] money paid to someone before the usual time: **[+on]** *Could I have a small advance on my salary?* **4 advances** [plural] an attempt to start a sexual relationship with someone: *She accused her boss of* **making advances to** *her.*

PHRASES

in advance (of sth) before something happens or is expected to happen: *The airline suggests booking tickets 21 days in advance.* **THESAURUS** BEFORE

advance² v **1** [I,T] to develop or progress, or to make something develop or progress: *Their analysis does not really advance our understanding of the problem.* | *He agreed to take the job because he hoped it would* **advance** *his* **career**. **2** [I] to move forward to a new position OPP **retreat**: **[+on]** *Troops advanced on the rebel stronghold.* —**advancement** n [C,U]: *the advancement of science*

advance³ adj [only before noun] done or given before an event: **advance planning/warning/ booking etc** *advance warning of a hurricane* | *You can make an advance booking with your credit card.*

advanced /əd'vɑːnst $ əd'vænst/ adj

1 very modern: *advanced technology* | *advanced weapon systems*

2 studying or dealing with a school subject at a difficult level: *advanced learners of English* | *advanced physics*

3 having reached a late point in time or development: *By this time, the disease was too far advanced to be treated.*

advantage /əd'vɑːntɪdʒ $ əd'væn-/ *n* [C,U]
1 something that helps you to be better or more successful than other people OPP **disadvantage**: [+of] *He has the advantage of a good education.* | [+over] *Her previous experience gave her an advantage over the other students.*
2 a good feature which something has, which makes it better or more useful than other things OPP **disadvantage**: [+of] *Good public transport is just one of the advantages of living in a big city.* | [+over] *The new system has a number of advantages over the old one.* | *They discussed the plan and decided that the advantages outweighed the disadvantages* (=the advantages were more important).

PHRASES

take advantage of sth/sb 1 to use a situation to help you do or get something you want: *I took advantage of the good weather to paint the shed.* **2** to treat someone unfairly in order to get something for yourself: *I don't mind helping, but I resent being taken advantage of.*

use/turn sth to your advantage to use something that you have or that happens in order to achieve something: *How could he turn the situation to his advantage?*

work/be to sb's advantage to help someone to be better or more successful than other people: *Sometimes a lack of experience can work to your advantage.*

COLLOCATIONS

verbs

to have an advantage *He has an advantage because he's much bigger than me.*
to get/gain an advantage *In business, everyone is always trying to get an advantage for themselves.*
to give sb an advantage *Her knowledge of Russian gave her an advantage.*

adjectives

a big/great/major advantage *The team started the competition with a big advantage.*
a slight advantage *Being taller gives you a slight advantage.*
an unfair advantage *Children with rich parents have an unfair advantage.*

---

advantageous /ˌædvən'teɪdʒəs, ˌædvæn-/ *adj* helpful and likely to make you more successful

advent /'ædvent/ *n* **the advent of sth** the time when something first begins to be used a lot or by a lot of people: *the advent of the computer*

adventure /əd'ventʃə $ -ər/ *n* [C,U] an exciting experience in which dangerous or unusual things happen: *a great adventure* | *an adventure story* —**adventurer** *n* [C]

adventurous /əd'ventʃərəs/ *adj* **1** (also **adventuresome** /əd'ventʃəsəm $ -tʃər-/ *AmE*) wanting to do new, exciting, or dangerous things: *Andy is a very adventurous rock-climber.* THESAURUS BRAVE
2 exciting and involving danger —**adventurously** *adv*

adverb /'ædvɜːb $ -vɜːrb/ *n* [C] a word that adds to the meaning of a verb, an adjective, another adverb, or a whole sentence, such as 'slowly' in 'He ran slowly', 'very' in 'It's very hot', or 'naturally' in 'Naturally, we want you to come' —**adverbial** *adj*

adversary /'ædvəsəri $ 'ædvərseri/ *n* [C] (*plural* **adversaries**) *formal* a country or person you are fighting or competing against

adverse /'ædvɜːs $ -ɜːrs/ *adj formal* not good or favourable: *the recession's adverse effect on the building industry* | *adverse weather conditions* —**adversely** *adv*

adversity /əd'vɜːsəti $ -ɜːr-/ *n* [C,U] difficulties or problems in your life: *his courage in the face of adversity*

advert /'ædvɜːt $ -ɜːrt/ *n* [C] *BrE* an advertisement THESAURUS ADVERTISEMENT

advertise /'ædvətaɪz $ -ər-/ *v* [I,T]
1 to tell the public about a product or service in order to persuade them to buy it or use it: *a poster advertising sportswear* | *I saw your car advertised in the evening paper.* | *We can't afford to advertise all year round.*
2 to make an announcement, for example in a newspaper, that a job is available, an event is going to happen etc: [+for] *RCA is advertising for an accountant.* —**advertiser** *n* [C]

advertisement /əd'vɜːtəsmənt $ ˌædvər'taɪz-/ (*also* **ad** *informal*, **advert** *BrE*) *n* [C] a picture, set of words, or short film that is intended to persuade people to buy something, or that gives information about a concert, film, job etc: [+for] *The Sunday papers are full of advertisements for cars.*

THESAURUS

advertisement a picture, set of words, or short film that is intended to persuade people to buy something, or that gives information about a concert, film, job etc: *advertisements for beauty products* | *a job advertisement*
ad (*also* **advert** *BrE*) *informal* an advertisement: *an ad for a new Toshiba computer*
commercial an advertisement for a product or shop on television or radio: *a television commercial for Levi jeans*
poster a picture or sign used to advertise something in a public place: *I saw a poster for the film outside the cinema.*
billboard a big sign next to a road, with an advertisement on it: *the huge billboards on the freeway*
junk mail letters advertising things that are sent to a lot of people, especially ones that people do not want: *We get so much junk mail through our letter box.*
spam emails advertising things that are sent to a lot of people and that they do not want: *There are various ways to prevent spam reaching your inbox.*

advertising /ˈædvətaɪzɪŋ $ -ər-/ n [U] the business of advertising things on television, in newspapers etc: *a career in advertising | advertising executive*

advice /ədˈvaɪs/ n [U] the things you say to someone when you tell them what you think they should do: **[+on/about]** *a book that's full of advice on baby care | Can you give me some advice about buying a house?*

Grammar
Advice is an uncountable noun. Do not say 'advices'.
Do not say 'He gave me a good advice.' Say *He gave me some good advice.* or *He gave me a good piece of advice.*

COLLOCATIONS

verbs

to give sb advice *Can I give you some advice?*
to offer advice *The tourist office can offer advice on places to visit.*
to get advice *I got some good advice from my teacher about applying to college.*
to ask sb's advice (*also* **to ask for advice**) *My friends often ask my advice.*
to take/follow sb's advice (=to do what someone advises you to do) *She followed his advice and took up yoga.*

adjectives

good/useful advice *The book is full of good advice.*
bad advice *I now realise that this was bad advice.*
sound advice (=sensible advice) *My mother always gave me sound advice.*
practical advice *The website has practical advice on starting your own business.*
legal/medical/financial etc advice *I think you should get some legal advice.*

phrases

a piece/bit of advice *Let me give you a piece of advice.*
a word of advice *spoken* (=used when advising someone) *A word of advice: read the contract very carefully.*

advisable /ədˈvaɪzəbəl/ adj something that is advisable should be done in order to avoid problems or risks OPP **inadvisable**: *It is advisable to wear a safety belt at all times.* —**advisability** /ədˌvaɪzəˈbɪləti/ n [U]

advise /ədˈvaɪz/ v
1 [I,T] to tell someone what you think they should do: **advise sb to do sth** *The doctor advised me to take more exercise.* | **advise (sb) against (doing) sth** *I'd advise you against saying anything to the press.* | **advise (sb) on sth** *Franklin advises us on financial matters.* | **advise (sb) that** *The doctor advised him that a period of complete rest was the only remedy.*
2 [T] *formal* to officially tell someone something: *You will be advised when the work is completed.*
PHRASES
you would be well advised to do sth used to strongly advise someone to do something: *You would be well advised to see a lawyer.*

THESAURUS

advise to tell someone what you think they should do, especially when you know more about the situation than they do: *He advises people about how to invest their money.*
tell sb to do sth/say sb should do sth to tell someone what you think they should do. These phrases are often used instead of **advise** in everyday conversation: *I told her not to worry.* | *My friends said that I should wait.*
recommend to advise someone to do something, especially after studying the subject carefully: *Doctors recommend eating plenty of fruit and vegetables.*
urge to strongly advise someone to do something, because you think it is important: *Police are urging people not to travel unless their journey is absolutely necessary.*

adviser, advisor /ədˈvaɪzə $ -ər/ n [C] someone whose job is to give advice about a subject: *a financial adviser*

advisory /ədˈvaɪzəri/ adj having the purpose of giving advice: *an advisory committee*

advocate[1] Ac /ˈædvəkeɪt/ v [T] *formal* to publicly say that something should be done: *Extremists were openly advocating violence.* —**advocacy** /-kəsi/ n [U]

advocate[2] Ac /ˈædvəkət, -keɪt/ n [C] **1** someone who publicly supports someone or something: **[+of]** *an advocate of prison reform* **2** *law* a lawyer who defends someone in a court of law

aerial[1] /ˈeəriəl $ ˈer-/ adj [only before noun] from a plane or happening in the air: *aerial photos | aerial attacks*

aerial[2] n [C] *BrE* a piece of metal or wire used for receiving or sending radio or television signals SYN **antenna** *AmE* → see picture at **CAR**

aerobic /eəˈrəʊbɪk $ eˈroʊ-/ adj aerobic exercise makes your heart and lungs stronger

aerobics /eəˈrəʊbɪks $ eˈroʊ-/ n [U] active physical exercise done to music, usually in a class: *Are you going to aerobics tonight?*

aerodynamics /ˌeərəʊdaɪˈnæmɪks $ ˌeroʊ-/ n [U] the scientific study of how objects move through the air —**aerodynamic** adj

aeroplane /ˈeərəpleɪn $ ˈerə-/ *BrE*, **airplane** *AmE* n [C] a flying vehicle with wings and at least one engine SYN **plane** → see picture on p. 16

aerosol /ˈeərəsɒl $ ˈerəsɑːl/ n [C] a small metal container in which a liquid substance is kept under pressure. You press a button on the container to make the liquid come out in very small drops.

aerospace /ˈeərəʊspeɪs $ ˈeroʊ-/ n [U] the industry that designs and builds aircraft and space vehicles: *the aerospace industry*

aesthetic (*also* **esthetic** *AmE*) /iːsˈθetɪk, es- $ es-/ adj relating to beauty and the study of beauty: *the aesthetic qualities of literature* —**aesthetically** /-kli/ adv: *aesthetically pleasing*

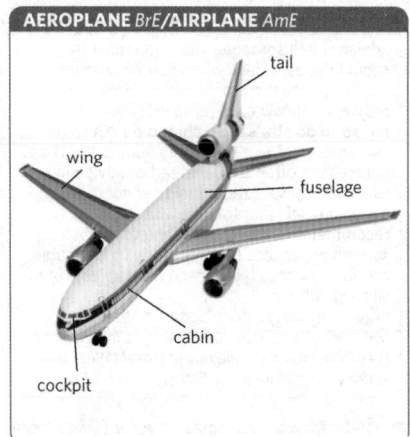

AEROPLANE *BrE/***AIRPLANE** *AmE*

tail

wing

fuselage

cabin

cockpit

aesthetics (*also* **esthetics** *AmE*) /iːsˈθetɪks, es-$ es-/ *n* [U] the study of beauty, especially beauty in art

afar /əˈfɑː $ əˈfɑːr/ *adv* **from afar** *literary* from a long distance away

affable /ˈæfəbəl/ *adj* friendly and easy to talk to SYN **pleasant**: *an affable guy* —**affably** *adv*

affair /əˈfeə $ əˈfer/ *n* [C]
1 POLITICS **affairs** [plural] public or political events and activities: *a foreign affairs correspondent for CNN*
2 PERSONAL/FINANCIAL SITUATION **affairs** [plural] things connected with your personal life, your financial situation etc: *I don't want to discuss my financial affairs.*
3 EVENT an event or set of related events, especially unpleasant ones: *the Watergate affair* | *The whole affair was a disaster.*
4 SEXUAL RELATIONSHIP a secret sexual relationship between two people, when at least one of them is married to someone else: **[+with]** *Ed's having an affair with his boss's wife.* → **CURRENT AFFAIRS**, **LOVE AFFAIR**, **STATE OF AFFAIRS**
PHRASES
be sb's affair if something is your affair, you do not want other people to know about it or become involved in it: *What I do in my free time is my affair.*

affect Ac /əˈfekt/ *v* [T]
1 to cause a change in someone or something, or to change the situation they are in: *Help is being sent to areas affected by the floods.* | *decisions which affect our lives*
2 [usually passive] to make someone feel strong emotions: *We were all deeply affected by her death.*

Word Choice: affect or effect?
Affect is a verb: *Smoking affects your health.*
Effect is usually a noun: *Too much sun can have a bad effect on your skin.*
Effect can also be used as a verb in very formal English, meaning 'to make something happen'. Do not confuse it with **affect**: *It is difficult to effect changes in society.*

affectation /ˌæfekˈteɪʃən/ *n* [C,U] *disapproving* when someone behaves or speaks in a way that is not natural or sincere

affected /əˈfektɪd/ *adj* not sincere or natural OPP **unaffected**: *an affected laugh*

affection /əˈfekʃən/ *n* [C,U] a feeling of liking or loving someone: **[+for]** *Barry felt a great affection for her.*

affectionate /əˈfekʃənət/ *adj* showing that you like or love someone: *an affectionate child* —**affectionately** *adv*

affidavit /ˌæfɪˈdeɪvɪt/ *n* [C] *law* a written statement that you swear is true, used in a court of law

affiliate /əˈfɪlieɪt/ *v* [I,T usually passive] if a group or organization affiliates to or with another larger one, it forms a close connection with it —**affiliated** *adj*: *The Society is not affiliated with any political party.* —**affiliation** /əˌfɪliˈeɪʃən/ *n* [C,U]: *What are the group's political affiliations?*

affinity /əˈfɪnəti/ *n* (*plural* **affinities**) **1** [singular] the feeling you have when you like and understand someone or something: **[+for/with/between]** *She felt a natural affinity for these people.* **2** [C,U] a close relationship between two things because of qualities or features that they share

affirm /əˈfɜːm $ -ɜːrm/ *v* [T] *formal* to say definitely that something is true: *The President affirmed his intention to reduce taxes.* —**affirmation** /ˌæfəˈmeɪʃən $ ˌæfər-/ *n* [C,U]

affirmative /əˈfɜːmətɪv $ -ɜːr-/ *adj* *formal* an affirmative answer or action means 'yes' or shows agreement OPP **negative**: *an affirmative nod* —**affirmative** *n* [C]: *She answered in the affirmative.* —**affirmatively** *adv*

affix /ˈæfɪks/ *n* [C] *technical* a group of letters added to the beginning or end of a word to change its meaning or use, for example 'un' or 'ness' → **prefix**, **suffix**

afflict /əˈflɪkt/ *v* [T] *formal* to affect someone or something in an unpleasant way, and make them suffer: **afflict sb/sth with/by sth** *Towards the end of his life he was afflicted with blindness.* | *a country afflicted by famine* —**affliction** /əˈflɪkʃən/ *n* [C,U]

affluent /ˈæfluənt/ *adj* having a lot of money, nice houses, expensive things etc → **wealthy**: *an affluent suburb of Paris* | *affluent families* THESAURUS **RICH** —**affluence** *n* [U]

afford /əˈfɔːd $ -ɔːrd/ *v* [T]
1 can/could afford a) to have enough money to pay for something: *I wish we could afford a new computer.* | **afford to do sth** *I can't afford to buy a new car.* THESAURUS **EXPENSIVE b)** if you can afford to do something, you can do it, because it will not cause any problems for you: **afford to do sth** *We can't afford to offend our regular customers.*
2 *formal* to provide something: *The walls afforded some protection from the wind.* —**affordable** *adj*: *affordable housing*

affront /əˈfrʌnt/ *n* [singular] a remark or action that offends or insults someone: *The accusation was an affront to his pride.*

afield /əˈfiːld/ *adv* **far/further afield** far or further away: *As he grew more confident, he started to wander further afield.*

afloat /əˈfləʊt $ əˈfloʊt/ *adj, adv* floating on water

PHRASES

keep (sb/sth) afloat/stay afloat to have enough money to pay your debts and continue in business: *She had to borrow more money just to keep the company afloat.*

afoot /əˈfʊt/ *adj* [not before noun] being planned or happening: *There were plans afoot for a second attack.*

afraid /əˈfreɪd/ *adj* [not before noun]

1 frightened because you think that you may get hurt or that something bad may happen **SYN** **frightened**, **scared**: *There's no need to be afraid.* | **[+of]** *kids who are afraid of the dark* | **afraid to do sth** *She was afraid to go back into the house.* **THESAURUS**

FRIGHTENED

2 worried about something: **afraid of doing sth** *A lot of people are afraid of losing their jobs.* | **afraid to do sth** *Don't be afraid to ask for help.* | **[+(that)]** *He was afraid that the others would laugh at him.* | **afraid for sb/sth** (=worried that something bad may happen to a particular person or thing) *I thought you were in danger and I was afraid for you.*

PHRASES

I'm afraid *spoken* used to politely tell someone something that may annoy, upset, or disappoint them: *I won't be able to come with you, I'm afraid.* | **[+(that)]** *I'm afraid this is a no smoking area.* | *'Are we late?' 'I'm afraid so* (=yes).*' | *'Are there any tickets left?' 'I'm afraid not* (=no).'*

afresh /əˈfreʃ/ *adv* **start afresh** to start again from the beginning: *We decided to move to Sydney and start afresh.*

African American /ˌæfrɪkən əˈmerɪkən/ *n* [C] an American with dark skin, whose family originally came from the part of Africa south of the Sahara Desert

Afro-Caribbean /ˌæfrəʊ kærəˈbiːən $ ˌæfroʊ-/ *adj* relating to a person whose family originally came from Africa, and who was born or whose parents were born in the Caribbean

after /ˈɑːftə $ ˈæftər/ *prep, linking word, adv*

1 when something has happened, or when someone has done something **OPP** **before**: *What are you doing after class?* | *After you called the police, what did you do?* | **after doing sth** *After leaving school, he worked in a restaurant.* | **the day/week/year etc after (sth)** *I'll see you again tomorrow or the day after.* | **an hour/two weeks etc after (sth)** *We left an hour after daybreak.* | *He discovered the jewel was a fake a month after he bought it.* | **soon/not long/shortly after (sth)** *We arrived soon after they did.*

2 when a particular amount of time has passed **OPP** **before**: *After 10 minutes remove the cake from the oven.* | *After a while, the woman returned.*

3 following someone or something else in a list or piece of writing, or in order of importance: *Whose name is after mine on the list?* | *After football, tennis is my favourite sport.*

4 following someone in order to stop or speak to them: *Go after him and apologize.*

5 *AmE* used to say how many minutes past the hour it is when saying the time **SYN** **past** *BrE*: *It's ten after five.*

6 because of something that has happened: *I'm surprised he came, after the way you treated him.*

7 when someone has left a place or has finished doing something: *I spend all day cleaning up after the kids.*

8 in spite of something: *After all the trouble I had, Reese didn't even say thank you.*

9 **be after sb/sth a)** to be looking for someone or something: *He's always in trouble – the police are after him again.* **b)** to want to have something that belongs to someone else: *You're just after my money!*

10 **be called/named after sb** to be given the same name as someone else: *She was named Sarah, after my grandmother.*

PHRASES

after all 1 used to say that what you expected did not happen: *Rita didn't have my pictures after all. Jake did.* | *It didn't rain after all.* **2** used when saying something that shows why you are right: *Don't shout at him – he's only a baby, after all.*

day after day/year after year etc continuously for a very long time: *Day after day we waited, hoping she'd call.*

one after the other/one after another if a series of events or actions happen one after another, each one happens soon after the previous one: *Ever since we moved here it's been one problem after another.*

THESAURUS

after when something has happened, or a period of time has passed. You use **after** especially when talking about the past: *After the concert, we went out for a meal.* | *She felt a lot better after a few days in bed.*

in five minutes/a month etc five minutes, a month etc after now, or after a particular time: *I'll be ready in ten minutes.* | *In a couple of days the exams would be over.*

within a month/two weeks etc after less than a month, two weeks etc – used especially when the time seems short: *He was able to solve the problem within seconds.*

two days/six weeks etc from now two days etc after now: *Ten days from now I'll be back in France.*

later some time after now, or after the time you are talking about: *Let's talk about it later.* | *She came back five minutes later.*

'after-ef,fect *n* [C usually plural] a bad effect that remains after something has ended: **[+of]** *the after-effects of an illness*

afterlife /ˈɑːftəlaɪf $ ˈæftər-/ *n* [singular] the life that some people believe you have after you die

aftermath /ˈɑːftəmæθ $ ˈæftər-/ *n* [singular] the time after an important or bad event: **in the aftermath of** *the refugee crisis in the aftermath of the civil war*

afternoon /ˌɑːftəˈnuːn◂ $ ˌæftər-/ n [C,U] the period of time after the morning and before the evening → **morning, evening**: It was very hot in the afternoon. | **on Monday/Friday etc afternoon** I'll see you on Tuesday afternoon. | Do you want to go swimming **this afternoon** (=today in the afternoon)? | **yesterday/tomorrow afternoon** We met yesterday afternoon. | an afternoon sleep → **GOOD AFTERNOON**

aftershave /ˈɑːftəʃeɪv $ ˈæftər-/ n [C,U] a liquid with a nice smell that a man puts on his face

aftertaste /ˈɑːftəteɪst $ ˈæftər-/ n [C usually singular] a taste that stays in your mouth after you eat or drink something: a drink with a strong aftertaste

afterthought /ˈɑːftəθɔːt $ ˈæftərθɔːt/ n [C usually singular] something that you mention or add later because you did not think of it before: 'Bring Clare too,' he added as an afterthought.

afterwards /ˈɑːftəwədz $ ˈæftərwərdz/ (also **afterward** AmE) adv after an event or time that has been mentioned: Charles arrived **shortly afterwards**. | For years afterwards, I felt guilty about what happened. | Two days afterwards, I received a call. | Afterwards, he told me they were getting married.

again /əˈgen, əˈgeɪn $ əˈgen/ adv
1 one more time: Could you say that again? I didn't hear. | I'll never go there again. | **yet/once again** (=used to emphasize that something has happened before) He had to apologize yet again. | The cake burned so we had to start **all over again** (=from beginning).
2 back to the same condition, situation, or place as before: I'll come and see you when I'm well again. | It's great to have you home again.

PHRASES
again and again many times: He read the letter again and again. **THESAURUS** OFTEN
then/there again spoken used to add a fact that is different from what you have just said or makes it seem less true: I prefer showers **but then again** I do like having a bath occasionally.

against /əˈgenst, əˈgeɪnst $ əˈgenst/ prep
1 not agreeing with something: John was against the idea of selling the house. | We are against testing cosmetics on animals.
2 used to say who is affected by something in a bad way: violence against elderly people | discrimination against women
3 used to say who someone is competing or fighting with: The team will play against Hungary on Saturday.
4 trying to stop something from happening: the battle against crime | We must take action against homelessness.
5 **against the law/the rules** not allowed by the law or the rules: It is against the law to sell alcohol to children.
6 **against sb's wishes/advice/orders etc** if you do something against someone's wishes etc, you do it even though they tell you not to do it: She got married against her parents' wishes.
7 touching a surface: The cat's fur felt soft against her face. | Chris leaned back against the wall. → see picture on page A8

8 in the opposite direction to the movement or flow of something: sailing against the wind
9 protecting you from something: insurance against injury

PHRASES
have sth against sb/sth to dislike or disapprove of someone or something: I have nothing against dogs but I don't want one myself.

age¹ /eɪdʒ/ n
1 [C,U] the number of years someone has lived or something has existed: games for children of all ages | Patrick is the same age as me. | **be 10/25 etc years of age** You must be 18 years of age to enter. | **at the age of 12/50 etc** She married at the age of 19. | **over/under the age of 16/30 etc** people over the age of 65 | **for your age** (=compared with other people of the same age) Judy's very tall for her age. | **(of) your own age** (=the same age as you) He doesn't have many friends his own age.
2 [U] the age when you are legally old enough to do something: **under age** You can't buy alcohol, you're under age. | I went back to work when the children reached **school age**. → **UNDER-AGE**
3 [C,U] a period in someone's life: women of child-bearing age | The teens are often a difficult age.
4 [C] a period of history: the modern age | **[+of]** the age of new technology **THESAURUS** PERIOD
5 [U] the state of being old: The building was already showing signs of age. | **with age** Wine often improves with age (=as it gets older).
6 **ages** [plural] informal a long time: It's ages since I saw him. | **for ages** I haven't been there for ages.

PHRASES
come of age 1 to reach the age when you are legally an adult: When he comes of age, we'll have a special celebration. **2** if something comes of age, people start to accept and respect it: The festival has finally come of age.

COLLOCATIONS

adjectives
an early/a young age He loved music from an early age.
old age (=the time when you are old) People don't want to think about the problems of old age.
middle age (=between about 40 and 60) I'd say she was in late middle age.
the same age You're the same age as me.

noun + age
working age Less than half the people of working age have jobs.
retirement age Can you continue working after you reach retirement age?
the voting age The voting age is 18.

age + noun
an age group/range The books are aimed at the 12–16 age group.
an age limit The upper age limit for the competition was 25.

verbs
to reach the age of 5/50 etc Most girls here are married before they reach the age of 21.

age² v [I,T] (*present participle* **ageing** *or* **aging**) to become or look older, or to make someone look older: *He has aged a lot since his wife died.* —**ageing** *BrE*, **aging** *AmE adj*: *an aging rock star*

aged¹ /eɪdʒd/ *adj* **aged 5/15 etc** 5, 15 etc years old: **[+between]** *Police are searching for a man aged between 25 and 30.*

aged² /'eɪdʒɪd/ *adj* **1** very old: *his aged parents* **2 the aged** old people: *the cost of caring for the sick and aged*

age group *n* [C] the people between two ages, considered as a group: *people in the 18-44 age group*

ageist /'eɪdʒɪst/ *adj* treating older people unfairly because of a belief that they are less important than younger people —**ageism** *n* [U]

ageless /'eɪdʒləs/ *adj* never seeming old or old-fashioned: *furniture with an ageless quality*

agency /'eɪdʒənsi/ *n* [C] (*plural* **agencies**) **1** a business that provides a particular service for people or organizations: *an advertising agency* **2** an organization or government department that does a particular job: *the UN agency responsible for helping refugees* → **TRAVEL AGENCY**

agenda /ə'dʒendə/ *n* [C] **1** a list of things that an organization is planning to do: **on the agenda** *This has put environmental issues on the political agenda.* | **be high on/top of the agenda** (=be one of the most important things that should be done first) *Health care reforms are high on the President's agenda.* | *The government set an agenda for constitutional reform.* **2** a list of the subjects that will be discussed at a meeting: **on the agenda** *The next item on the agenda is finance.* **THESAURUS** **LIST 3 hidden agenda** *disapproving* the secret purpose behind something that you do: *Was there a hidden agenda behind their decision?*

agent /'eɪdʒənt/ *n* [C] **1** a person or company that arranges services or does work for other people: *Our agent in Rome handles all our Italian contracts.* **2** someone who tries to get secret information about another government or organization → **ESTATE AGENT, TRAVEL AGENT**

age-'old *adj* having existed for a very long time: *age-old traditions*

aggravate /'ægrəveɪt/ *v* [T] **1** to make a bad situation, illness, or injury worse: *Exercise may aggravate the injury.* **2** to annoy someone —**aggravating** *adj* —**aggravation** /ˌægrə'veɪʃən/ *n* [C,U]

aggregate Ac /'ægrɪgət/ *n* [C,U] *formal* a total —**aggregate** *adj*

aggression /ə'greʃən/ *n* [U] angry or violent behaviour or feelings: *an act of aggression* | **[+towards]** *Our dogs have never shown any aggression towards other dogs.*

aggressive /ə'gresɪv/ *adj* **1** behaving in an angry or violent way towards someone: *an aggressive attitude* **2** very determined to succeed: *aggressive marketing* —**aggressively** *adv* —**aggressiveness** *n* [U]

aggressor /ə'gresə $ -ər/ *n* [C] a person or country that starts a fight or war

aggrieved /ə'griːvd/ *adj* angry or unhappy because you think you have been treated unfairly

aghast /ə'gɑːst $ ə'gæst/ *adj* [not before noun] *written* shocked: **[+at]** *They were aghast at the verdict.* | *She stared at him aghast.*

agile /'ædʒaɪl $ 'ædʒəl/ *adj* **1** able to move quickly and easily: *She was strong and agile.* **2** someone who has an agile mind is able to think quickly and intelligently —**agility** /ə'dʒɪləti/ *n* [U]

agitate /'ædʒɪteɪt/ *v* [I] *formal* to protest in order to achieve social or political changes: **[+for/against]** *workers agitating for higher pay* —**agitator** *n* [C]

agitated /'ædʒɪteɪtɪd/ *adj* very worried or upset: *He was in an agitated state.* —**agitation** /ˌædʒɪ'teɪʃən/ *n* [U]

AGM /ˌeɪ dʒiː 'em/ *n* [C] *BrE* (**annual general meeting**) a meeting that a business or organization has every year

agnostic /æg'nɒstɪk, əg- $ -'nɑː-/ *n* [C] someone who believes that it is not possible to know whether God exists → **atheist** —**agnostic** *adj* —**agnosticism** /-tɪsɪzəm/ *n* [U]

ago /ə'gəʊ $ ə'goʊ/ *adv* used to say how far back in the past something happened: **ten years/a moment/a long time etc ago** *Jeff left an hour ago.* | *We went there a long time ago.*

agonize (*also* **-ise** *BrE*) /'ægənaɪz/ *v* [I] to think and worry for a long time about a decision: **[+about/over]** *For a long time she had agonized about what she should do.*

agonizing (*also* **-ising** *BrE*) /'ægənaɪzɪŋ/ *adj* extremely painful or difficult: *an agonizing decision* —**agonizingly** *adv*

agony /'ægəni/ *n* [C,U] (*plural* **agonies**) very severe pain, sadness, or worry: **in agony** *He was lying on the floor in agony.* | **[+of]** *the agony of loneliness*

'agony ˌaunt *n* [C] *BrE* someone who answers people's letters in a magazine or newspaper, giving them advice about their personal problems

agoraphobic /ˌægərə'fəʊbɪk $ -'foʊ-/ *adj* afraid of open spaces and public places → **claustrophobic** —**agoraphobia** *n* [U]

agree /ə'griː/ *v*
1 [I,T] to have the same opinion as someone else **OPP disagree**: **[+with]** *I agree with Karen. It's much too expensive.* | **[+that]** *Most doctors agree that the condition is caused by stress.* | **[+about/on]** *My first husband and I never agreed about anything.* **THESAURUS** **DISAGREE**

> **Grammar**
> Do not say 'I agree you.' or 'I agree your opinion.'
> Say *I agree with you.* or *I agree with your opinion.*

2 [I,T] to say yes to a suggestion, plan etc **OPP refuse**: **agree to do sth** *She agreed to stay at home with Charles.* | **[+to]** *He would never agree to such a plan.*
3 [I,T] to make a decision with someone after discussing something: **agree to do sth** *We agreed to*

meet next week. | **[+on]** *We're still trying to agree on a date for the wedding.* | **[+that]** *It was agreed that the elections would be held in May.*
4 [I] if two pieces of information agree, they say the same thing: **[+with]** *The names you've given me don't agree with those on my list.*

PHRASAL VERBS

agree with sb/sth

1 to think that something is the right thing to do: *I don't agree with killing animals for food.*
2 sth **does not agree with** sb if something that you ate or drank does not agree with you, it makes you feel ill

---

THESAURUS

agree to have the same opinion as someone, or to think that a statement is correct: *I completely agree.* | *Most people would agree with that statement.*

(I think) sb is right used in conversation when agreeing with someone: *I think you're right. It's better to wait and see what happens.*

be in agreement if two or more people are in agreement about something, they have the same opinion: *Not all scientists are in agreement about this issue.*

be of the same opinion formal to have the same opinion as someone: *Dr Clegg was of the same opinion as Professor Collins.*

share sb's views/concerns formal to have the same opinions or concerns as another person: *They shared his views about the war.* | *I share your concerns about the cost.*

unanimous if a group of people are unanimous about a decision, they all agree: *The jury were unanimous and found him not guilty.* | *a unanimous decision*

---

agreeable /əˈɡriːəbəl/ *adj* **1** *old-fashioned* pleasant: *an agreeable man* **2** acceptable: **[+to]** *a solution that's agreeable to both parties* **3** **be agreeable to sth** *formal* to be willing to do or allow something —**agreeably** *adv*: *I was agreeably surprised.*

agreed /əˈɡriːd/ *adj* **1** an agreed price, method, arrangement etc is one that people have discussed and accepted **2** **be agreed** if people are agreed, they all agree about something: **[+on]** *Are we all agreed on the date for the meeting?*

agreement /əˈɡriːmənt/ *n*
1 [C] an arrangement or promise to do something, made by two or more people, organizations etc: **[+between]** *an agreement between Britain and Germany* | **[+on]** *an international agreement on environmental standards*
2 [U] when people have the same opinion **OPP** **disagreement**: **[+on]** *There is general agreement on the need for prison reform.* | **[+that]** *There was unanimous agreement that the meeting should be cancelled.* | **in agreement** *All parties were in agreement.* **THESAURUS** **AGREE**

COLLOCATIONS

verbs

to make an agreement *The president has made new trade agreements.*

to come to/reach an agreement *We took hours to reach an agreement about what to do.*
to sign an agreement *The two countries signed a peace agreement.*
to have an agreement (=to have already agreed something) *I thought we had an agreement.*

types of agreement

a written agreement *The members of any business partnership should make a written agreement.*
a verbal agreement (=one that is not written down) *It was only a verbal agreement, but I trusted him.*
a formal agreement *They have not yet signed a formal agreement.*
a peace/trade agreement

nouns

the terms of an agreement *Under the terms of the agreement, governments must cut carbon emissions by 30%.*

---

agriculture /ˈæɡrɪˌkʌltʃə $ -ər/ *n* [U] the work or study of growing crops and keeping animals on farms —**agricultural** /ˌæɡrɪˈkʌltʃərəl◂/ *adj*

aground /əˈɡraʊnd/ *adv* **run/go aground** if a ship runs aground, it becomes stuck because the water is not deep enough

ah /ɑː/ *spoken* used to show surprise, happiness etc or that you have just understood something: *Ah, yes, I see what you mean.*

aha /ɑːˈhɑː/ *spoken* used when you suddenly understand or realize something: *Aha! So that's where you've been hiding!*

ahead /əˈhed/ *adv*
1 in front of someone or something: *She was staring straight ahead.* | **[+of]** *Jane was walking ahead of him.* | **up ahead** *We could see the lights of the city up ahead.*
2 in or into the future: **[+of]** *We* **have** *a busy day ahead of us.* | **the months/years/weeks ahead** *The months ahead are going to be difficult for him.* | *You need to* **plan ahead** (=plan for the future).
3 before someone or something else: **[+of]** *There were two people ahead of me at the doctor's.* | *He's giving a series of concerts ahead of his international tour.*
4 making more progress or more developed than other people or things: **[+of]** *She is well ahead of the rest of her class.* | *a design that's way ahead of others* | **get/stay ahead** *You need to work hard if you want to get ahead.* | **ahead of your/its time** (=very advanced or new and not understood or accepted)
5 winning in a game, competition etc: *Two shots from Gardner* **put** *the Giants 80–75* **ahead**. **THESAURUS** **WIN**

PHRASES

ahead of schedule/time earlier than planned: *The building was completed ahead of schedule* **THESAURUS** **EARLY**

aid¹ Ac /eɪd/ *n* **1** [U] money, food, or services that an organization or government gives to help people *The UN is sending aid to the earthquake victims.* | *a £15*

A

billion aid package | **military/financial/medical etc aid** 2 [C] a thing that helps you do something: *study aids*

PHRASES

come/go to sb's aid to help someone: *The school is hoping that businesses will come to its aid and finance the project.*

in aid of sth in order to collect money for a CHARITY: *She's been raising money in aid of a children's charity.*

with/without the aid of sth using or not using something to help you do something: *We finally got there with the aid of a map.*

aid² Ac *v* [T] *formal* to help someone, or help something to happen: *Exercise can aid relaxation.*
THESAURUS HELP

PHRASES

aid and abet *law* to help someone do something illegal: *He was found guilty of aiding and abetting the murder of Frank Taylor.*

aide (*also* **aid** *AmE*) /eɪd/ *n* [C] someone whose job is to help a person who has an important job: *a presidential aide*

AIDS /eɪdz/ *n* [U] (**Acquired Immune Deficiency Syndrome**) a very serious disease that stops your body from defending itself against infection: *the AIDS virus* | *AIDS sufferers*

ailing /'eɪlɪŋ/ *adj* weak or ill: *an ailing economy* | *his ailing mother*

ailment /'eɪlmənt/ *n* [C] an illness that is not very serious: ***minor ailments***

aim¹ /eɪm/ *n*

1 [C] something that you want to achieve: **[+of]** *The aim of the research is to discover what causes the illness.* | *Our **main aim** is to provide a good service.* | **with the aim of doing sth** *I flew to the US with the aim of finding a job.*

2 [singular, U] someone's ability to hit the thing they are trying to hit: *Mark's aim wasn't very good.*

PHRASES

take aim to point a weapon at someone or something: **[+at]** *He took aim at the target.*

THESAURUS

aim something you want to achieve: *His aim is to make as much money as possible.*

goal something important that you hope to achieve in the future, even though it may take a long time: *Their long-term goal is to set up a base on the Moon.*

ambition something that you very much want to achieve in your life: *Her ambition was to be a doctor.*

target a particular amount or total that you want to achieve: *Our target is to reduce greenhouse gases by 50% by 2020.*

objective a particular thing that someone is trying to achieve, especially in business or politics: *We met to set the business objectives for the coming year.*

aim² *v*

1 [I] to try or intend to achieve something: **aim to do sth** *We aim to finish by Friday.* | **[+for]** *We're aiming for a reduction in pollution levels.*

2 [I,T] to point a weapon at someone or something that you want to hit: **[+at]** *The gun was aimed at his head.*

3 aim sth at sb to do or say something that is intended for a particular person or group: *advertising aimed at children* | *criticism aimed at the government*

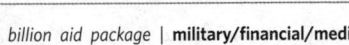
AIM

aimless /'eɪmləs/ *adj* without a clear purpose or reason —**aimlessly** *adv*

ain't /eɪnt/ a way of saying or writing 'am not', 'is not', 'are not', 'has not', or 'have not', which many people think is incorrect

air¹ /eə $ er/ *n*

1 GAS WE BREATHE [U] the gases around the Earth, which we breathe: *Let's go outside and get some fresh air.* | **in the air** *There was a smell of burning in the air.*

2 ABOVE THE GROUND if something is in the air, it is in the space above the ground: **in/into the air** *David threw the ball up into the air.* | *The plane was already in the air.*

3 PLANES **air travel/safety etc** travel, safety etc involving or relating to planes: *the world's worst air disaster*

4 QUALITY [singular] a quality that someone or something seems to have: **[+of]** *There was an air of mystery about her.*

5 FEELING IMPORTANT **airs** [plural] a way of behaving that shows someone thinks they are more important than they really are: *You shouldn't have to **put on airs** with your own friends.* → **HOT AIR, MIDAIR, in the open air** at **OPEN¹, thin air** at **THIN¹**

PHRASES

by air travelling by or using a plane: *Most people travel to the islands by air.*

be in the air 1 to be likely to happen very soon: *Romance is in the air.* **2** if a feeling is in the air, a lot of people have it: *There was a tension in the air.*

be on/off (the) air to be broadcasting or not broadcasting on television or radio: *The radio station is temporarily off air.*

be up in the air if something is up in the air, no one has made a decision about it yet: *The decision about expanding the airport is still up in the air.*

COLLOCATIONS

adjectives

fresh air *I felt better when I was outside in the fresh air.*

clean air *These plants only grow where the air is clean.*

polluted air *In the rush hour, the air is very polluted.*

warm/hot air *Warm air rises.*

cool/cold air *It was October, and the air was turning colder.*

noun + air

sea/mountain/country air *I breathed in the cool mountain air.*

the morning/evening/night air *We could smell flowers on the evening air.*

air + noun

air pollution *Forests are badly affected by air pollution.*

air quality *Air quality in the city has seriously declined.*

an air current (*also* **a current of air**) *The kite rose up on a current of air.*

air² *v*

1 OPINION [T] to express your opinions publicly: **air your views/grievances/complaints** *Everyone will get a chance to air their views.*

2 PROGRAMME [I,T] to broadcast a programme on television or radio: *'Star Trek' first aired in 1966.*

3 CLOTHES (*also* **air out** *AmE*) [I,T] to put clothes outdoors or in a warm place so that they smell clean

4 ROOM (*also* **air out** *AmE*) [I,T] to let fresh air into a room —**airing** *n* [singular]

airbag /'eəbæg $ 'er-/ *n* [C] a bag in a car that fills with air to protect the driver or passenger in an accident

airbase /'eəbeɪs $ 'er-/ *n* [C] a place where members of an air force live and military aircraft fly from

airborne /'eəbɔːn $ 'erbɔːrn/ *adj* flying or carried through the air

'air con,ditioning *n* [U] a system that makes the air in a room, building, or vehicle stay cool —**air conditioned** *adj*

aircraft /'eəkrɑːft $ 'erkræft/ *n* [C] (*plural* **aircraft**) a plane or other vehicle that can fly

'aircraft ,carrier *n* [C] a ship that planes can fly from and land on

airfare /'eəfeə $ 'erfer/ *n* [C] the price of a ticket to fly somewhere

airfield /'eəfiːld $ 'er-/ *n* [C] a place where military or small planes fly from → **airport**

'air force *n* [C] the part of a country's military organization that uses planes to fight

airhead /'eəhed $ 'er-/ *n* [C] *informal* someone who behaves in a stupid way

'air ,hostess *n* [C] *BrE old-fashioned* a woman who serves food and drink to passengers on a plane → **flight attendant**

airily /'eərəli $ 'er-/ *adv* in a way that shows you do not think something is important: *'I know all that,' she said airily.*

'airing ,cupboard *n* [C] *BrE* a warm cupboard where you keep sheets and clothes that have just been washed and dried

airless /'eələs $ 'er-/ *adj* without fresh air

airlift /'eə,lɪft $ 'er-/ *n* [C] an occasion when people or things are taken to a place by plane, because it is

too difficult or dangerous to get there by road —**airlift** *v* [T]

airline /'eəlaɪn $ 'er-/ *n* [C] a company that carries passengers by plane

airliner /'eə,laɪnə $ 'e,laɪnər/ *n* [C] a large plane for passengers

airmail /'eəmeɪl $ 'er-/ *n* [U] the system of sending letters and packages by plane: *Do you want to send this by airmail?*

airman /'eəmən $ 'er-/ *n* [C] (*plural* **airmen** /-mən/) someone who is a member of a country's air force

airplane /'eəpleɪn $ 'er-/ *n* [C] *AmE* a vehicle with wings and an engine that flies in the air SYN **aeroplane** *BrE*, **plane**

airplay /'eəpleɪ $ 'er-/ *n* [U] the number of times that a particular song is played on the radio: *The new single is getting lots of airplay.*

airport /'eəpɔːt $ 'erpɔːrt/ *n* [C] a place where planes take off and land, with buildings for passengers to wait in

'air raid (*also* **'air strike**) *n* [C] an attack by military planes

airship /'eə,ʃɪp $ 'er-/ *n* [C] a large aircraft with an engine but no wings, which is filled with gas

airsick /'eə,sɪk $ 'er-/ *adj* feeling sick because of the movement of a plane

airspace /'eəspeɪs $ 'er-/ *n* [U] the sky above a particular country, which is controlled by that country

'air strike *n* [C] an air raid

airstrip /'eə,strɪp $ 'er-/ *n* [C] a long narrow piece of land that planes can fly from and land on

airtight /'eətaɪt $ 'er-/ *adj* not allowing air to get in or out: *airtight containers*

airtime /'eətaɪm $ 'er-/ *n* [U] the amount of time that a radio or television station gives to a particular subject, advertisement etc

,air 'traffic con,troller *n* [C] someone at an airport whose job is to give instructions to pilots by radio

airwaves /'eəweɪvz $ 'er-/ *n* **the airwaves** *informal* radio and television broadcasts: *a subject that's been debated on the airwaves*

airy /'eəri $ 'eri/ *adj* an airy room or building has a lot of space and fresh air

aisle /aɪl/ *n* [C] a passage between rows of seats in a church, theatre, or plane, or between rows of shelves in a shop

ajar /ə'dʒɑː $ ə'dʒɑːr/ *adj* [not before noun] a door that is ajar is slightly open

a.k.a. /,eɪ keɪ 'eɪ, ,ækə/ *adv* (**also known as**) used when giving someone's real name together with the name they are known by: *John Phillips, a.k.a. The Mississippi Mauler*

akin /ə'kɪn/ *adj* **akin to sth** *formal* similar to something: *He looked at her with something akin to pity.*

à la carte /ˌæ lə ˈkɑːt, ˌɑː lɑː- $ -ˈkɑːrt/ adj, adv if food in a restaurant is à la carte, each dish has a separate price

alarm¹ /əˈlɑːm $ əˈlɑːrm/ n
1 WARNING SOUND [C] a piece of equipment that makes a noise to warn people of danger: **burglar/ fire/smoke alarm** Did you remember to set the burglar alarm? | He **set off the alarm** (=made it start ringing) by accident. | Someone's car **alarm** was **going off** (=making a noise).
2 FEELING OF FEAR [U] a feeling of fear because something bad might happen: **[+at]** Many people expressed alarm at the plans. | **in alarm** They both jumped back in alarm.
3 CLOCK [C] an alarm clock: I've **set the alarm** for six o'clock. → **false alarm** at FALSE
PHRASES
> **alarm bells ring** if alarm bells ring, you worry that something bad is about to happen: When she didn't arrive by 9, alarm bells started to ring.
> **raise/sound the alarm** to warn people that something bad is happening: A neighbour heard shouting and raised the alarm.

alarm² v [T] to make someone feel worried or frightened —**alarmed** adj: He was rather alarmed to find her there.

a'larm clock n [C] a clock that makes a noise to wake you up → see picture at **CLOCK¹**

alarming /əˈlɑːmɪŋ $ -ɑːr-/ adj making you feel worried or frightened: an alarming increase in crime

alarmist /əˈlɑːmɪst $ -ɑːr-/ adj making people feel worried about dangers that do not exist: alarmist reports of health risks

alas /əˈlæs/ formal used when mentioning a fact that you wish was not true

albatross /ˈælbətrɒs $ -trɔːs, -trɑːs/ n [C] a very large sea bird

albeit Ac /ɔːlˈbiːɪt $ ɒːl-/ linking word formal although

albino /ælˈbiːnəʊ $ ælˈbaɪnoʊ/ n [C] (plural **albinos**) a person or animal who has pink eyes and white skin and hair

album /ˈælbəm/ n [C] **1** a CD, record, or TAPE with several songs on it: Their latest album will be released next week. **2** a book that you put photographs, stamps etc in: a photograph album

alcohol /ˈælkəhɒl $ -hɒːl/ n [U]
1 drinks such as beer or wine that can make you drunk: Avoid drinking alcohol if you're driving. | **alcohol abuse/problems** (=when someone regularly drinks too much) the effects of alcohol abuse
2 the substance in beer, wine etc that makes you drunk

alcoholic¹ /ˌælkəˈhɒlɪk◀ $ -ˈhɒː-/ adj containing alcohol OPP **non-alcoholic**: an alcoholic drink

alcoholic² n [C] someone who regularly drinks too much alcohol and cannot stop: His father was an alcoholic.

alcoholism /ˈælkəhɒlɪzəm $ -hɒː-/ n [U] the medical condition of being an alcoholic

alcove /ˈælkəʊv $ -koʊv/ n [C] a place in the wall of a room that is built further back than the rest of the wall

ale /eɪl/ n [U] a type of beer

alert¹ /əˈlɜːt $ -ɜːrt/ adj always watching and ready to notice anything strange, unusual, or dangerous: I knew that I had to remain wide awake and alert. | **[+to]** Cyclists must always be alert to the dangers on a busy road.

alert² v [T] to warn someone of a problem or of possible danger: As soon as we suspected it was a bomb, we alerted the police.

alert³ n [C] a warning to be ready for possible danger: a flood alert
PHRASES
> **on the alert** ready to notice and deal with a problem: **[+for]** Police are on the alert for trouble. | All our troops are on **full alert** (=ready to deal with a serious problem).

A level /ˈeɪ ˌlevəl/ n [C] an examination in a particular subject taken in England and Wales, usually at the age of 18

algae /ˈældʒiː, -giː/ n [U] a very simple plant without stems or leaves that grows in or near water

algebra /ˈældʒəbrə/ n [U] a type of mathematics that uses letters and signs to show numbers and amounts —**algebraic** /ˌældʒəˈbreɪ-ɪk◀/ adj: algebraic formulae

alias¹ /ˈeɪliəs/ prep used when you are giving a name that someone uses instead of their real name: the spy Margaret Zelle, alias Mata Hari

alias² n [C] a false name used by a criminal

alibi /ˈæləbaɪ/ n [C] something that proves that someone was not where a crime happened and therefore could not have done it: **[+for]** He **had an alibi** for the night of the murder.

alien¹ /ˈeɪliən/ adj **1** very different and strange: **[+to]** Her way of life is totally alien to me. **2** relating to creatures from other worlds: alien life-forms

alien² n [C] **1** formal someone who lives and works in a country but is not a citizen: The clinic provides health care for **illegal aliens**. **2** a creature that comes from another world

alienate /ˈeɪliəneɪt/ v [T] **1** to do something that makes someone stop supporting you: The latest tax increases will alienate many voters. **2** to make someone feel they no longer belong to your group: We don't want to alienate kids who already have problems at school. —**alienated** adj —**alienation** /ˌeɪliəˈneɪʃən/ n [U]: a feeling of alienation from society

alight¹ /əˈlaɪt/ adj [not before noun] **1** burning: Several cars were **set alight** by rioters. **2** if your face or eyes are alight, they look happy and excited

alight² v [I] formal **1** if a bird or insect alights on something, it stops flying and comes down onto it **2** to step out of a vehicle at the end of a journey: **[+from]** She alighted from the train.

align /əˈlaɪn/ v [I,T] **1** be aligned with sb/align yourself with sb to say that you support a political group, country, or person: Some Democrats have *aligned themselves with the Republicans on this issue.* | *a country **closely aligned with** the West* **2** to arrange something so that it is in the same line as something else: *It looks like your wheels need aligning.* —**alignment** *n* [C,U]

alike¹ /əˈlaɪk/ *adj* [not before noun] very similar: *All small cars look alike to me.*

alike² *adv* **1** in a similar way: *When we were younger we dressed alike.* **2** equally: *The new rule was criticized by teachers and students alike.*

alimony /ˈæləməni $ -moʊni/ *n* [U] money that someone has to pay regularly to their former wife or husband after a DIVORCE

A-list /ˈeɪ lɪst/ *n* **the A-list** film stars, musicians etc who are very famous and popular → **B-list, Z-list**: *A-list celebrities* —**A-lister** *n* [C]

alive /əˈlaɪv/ *adj* [not before noun]
1 living and not dead: *They didn't expect to find anyone alive after the explosion.* | *My grandparents are **still alive**.* | *I'm amazed my plants have **stayed alive** in this weather.* | *He was **kept alive** on a life-support machine.*
2 continuing to exist: *Ancient traditions are very much alive in rural areas.*
3 full of energy or activity: [+with] *The stadium was alive with excitement.* | *The streets **come alive** after ten o'clock.*

Word Choice: alive or living?
You use **alive** when saying that someone is not dead: *Jack and his friends were lucky to be alive.*
You use **living** when saying that someone is living now: *an exhibition of works by living artists*
You also use **living** when talking about all plants and animals that live and die: *The chemical is harmful to all living creatures.*

---

alkali /ˈælkəlaɪ/ *n* [C,U] a chemical substance that has a pH of more than 7 → **acid** —**alkaline** *adj*

all¹ /ɔːl $ ɒːl/ *determiner, pron*
1 the whole of an amount or period of time: *Have we spent all the money?* | *I've been waiting all day for him to call.* | [+of] *All of this land belongs to me.* | *Bill talks about work **all the time** (=very often).*
2 every one of a group of people or things: *Did you answer all the questions?* | *We all wanted to go home.* | [+of] *Listen, all of you, I have an important announcement.*
3 the only thing: *Is that all you're going to eat?* | *He had dark hair. That's all I can remember.* → **after all** at AFTER, **all the same** at SAME²
PHRASES
all sorts/kinds/types of sth very many different types of things, people, or places: *You can buy all kinds of things in the bazaar.*
(not) at all used to say that something is not even slightly true, or to ask if something is even slightly true: *The place hasn't changed at all.* | *Was anyone at all interested in my idea?*
for all ... in spite of something: *For all his faults, he was a good father.*

Grammar
You use **all** with a singular verb if the noun is uncountable: *All the wine **is** finished.*
You use **all** with a plural verb if the noun is plural: *All my friends **are** coming to the party.*

---

all² *adv*
1 completely: *Ruth was sitting all alone.* | *She got all upset when he had to leave.* | *The judges were dressed all in black.*
2 5 all/20 all etc used to say that the two players or teams in a game both have the same number of points: *The score was 2 all at half-time.* → **ALL RIGHT¹**
PHRASES
all along during all of a period of time: *I knew all along that I couldn't trust him.*
be all for sth *informal* to support something strongly: *I'm all for the idea of women priests.*
all the better/easier etc used to emphasize that something was better or easier etc because of the situation: *The job was made all the easier by having the right tools.*
all but almost completely: *It was all but impossible to find anywhere to park.*
all in all considering everything: *All in all, the evening went well.*
all over 1 in every part of a place: *We've been looking all over for you.* | *There were papers all over the floor.* **2** finished: *I'm just glad it's all over.*
all through sth through the whole time that something continues: *He sat there quietly all through the film.*

Allah /ˈælə/ *n* the Muslim name for God

all-aˈround *adj* [only before noun] *AmE* good at doing a lot of different things, especially in sports SYN **all-round** *BrE*: *a good all-around player*

allay /əˈleɪ/ *v* [T] *formal* **allay sb's worries/fears/ suspicions etc** to make someone feel less worried, frightened etc: *I did my best to allay her fears.*

all ˈclear *n* **the all clear** a message saying that it is safe to do something: *We have to wait for the all clear from the safety committee before we can start.*

allegation /ˌælɪˈgeɪʃən/ *n* [C] a statement saying that someone has done something wrong or illegal, which is not supported by proof: [+that] *There are allegations that the police tortured prisoners.* | [+against] *The teacher **made** serious **allegations** against a colleague.* | [+of] *He faces allegations of fraud.*

allege /əˈledʒ/ *v* [T] *formal* to say that someone has done something wrong or illegal, without showing proof: *Baldwin is alleged to have killed two people.*

alleged /əˈledʒd/ *adj* [only before noun] *formal* supposed to be true, but not proved: *the group's alleged connections with organized crime* —**allegedly** /əˈledʒɪdli/ *adv*

allegiance /əˈliːdʒəns/ *n* [C] loyalty or support that you give to a leader, country, or idea: [+to] *pledge allegiance to the flag of the United States of America.*

allegory /ˈæləgəri $ -gɔːri/ *n* [C,U] (*plural* **allegories**) a story, poem, or painting in which the events and characters represent good and bad qualities

allergic /əˈlɜːdʒɪk $ -ɜːr-/ *adj* **1** if you are allergic to something, you become ill if you eat, touch, or breathe it: **[+to]** *He's allergic to cats.* **2** caused by an allergy: *an **allergic reaction** to the bee sting*

allergy /ˈælədʒi $ -ər-/ *n* [C] (*plural* **allergies**) a condition that makes you ill when you eat, touch, or breathe something: **[+to]** *He **has** an **allergy** to peanuts.*

alleviate /əˈliːvieɪt/ *v* [T] *formal* to make something less bad or severe: *These tablets will alleviate the pain.*

alley /ˈæli/ (*also* **alleyway** /ˈæliweɪ/) *n* [C] a narrow street between buildings

alliance /əˈlaɪəns/ *n* [C] an agreement between countries or groups of people to work together or support each other: **[+between]** *an alliance between an American and a Japanese company* | **[+with]** *The Liberals **formed** an **alliance** with the new Social Democratic Party.*

allied /ˈælaɪd, əˈlaɪd/ *adj* joined by a political or military agreement: *allied soldiers* | *The two leaders were closely allied during the Gulf War.*

alligator /ˈæləɡeɪtə $ -ər/ *n* [C] a large animal like a CROCODILE that lives in the US and China → see picture at REPTILE

alliteration /əˌlɪtəˈreɪʃən/ *n* [U] the use of a series of words that begin with the same sound in order to make a special effect, for example in 'Round the rocks runs the river'

allocate Ac /ˈæləkeɪt/ *v* [T] to decide to use an amount of money, time etc for a particular purpose: **allocate sth for sth** *The hospital has allocated $500,000 for AIDS research.*

allocation Ac /ˌæləˈkeɪʃən/ *n* **1** [C] an amount of something that you have decided to use for a particular purpose **2** [U] the decision to allocate something: **[+of]** *the allocation of state funds to the university*

allot /əˈlɒt $ əˈlɑːt/ *v* [T] (**allotted, allotting**) to use an amount of something for a particular purpose, or give an amount of something to a particular person: **allot sth to sth/sb** *He allotted 20 minutes a day to exercise.* | **allot sb sth** *Each person was allotted two tickets.*

allotment /əˈlɒtmənt $ əˈlɑːt-/ *n* **1** [C,U] when an amount of something is given to someone as their share: **[+of]** *the allotment of funds* **2** [C] *BrE* a small area of land that people can rent for growing vegetables

all 'out *adv* **go all out to do sth** to try to do something with a lot of effort and determination: *We'll be going all out to win.* —**all-out** *adj*: *an all-out effort*

allow /əˈlaʊ/ *v* [T]
1 to say that someone can do or have something: *Smoking is not allowed in the library.* | **allow sb to do sth** *My parents would never allow me to stay out late.* | **allow sb sth** *We're allowed four weeks holiday a year.* | **allow sb in/out/up etc** *You're not allowed in here.*
2 to make it possible for something to happen or for someone to do something: **allow sb/sth to do sth** *The new headlights allow drivers to see even in very*

foggy weather. | *We mustn't allow the situation to get any worse.*
3 to plan that a particular amount of time, money etc will be needed for a particular purpose: *Allow 14 days for delivery.* | **allow yourself sth** *Allow yourself two hours to get to the airport.* —**allowable** *adj*

PHRASAL VERBS
allow for sth to include the possible effects of something in your plans so that you can deal with them: *Even allowing for delays, we should finish early.*

> **THESAURUS**
> **allow** to say that someone can do or have something: *You're not allowed to use your mobile phone in class.* | *They allowed him to stay in the country.*
> **let** to allow someone to do something. **Let** is much more common in spoken English than **allow**. It is not used in the passive: *My Dad won't let me go to the concert.*
> **permit** *formal* if something is permitted, it is allowed according to the rules – used especially on signs and in announcements: *Ball games are not permitted outside this building.*
> **give sb permission** used when someone in an important position allows someone to do something: *He was given permission to take some time off work.*
> **give your consent** *formal* to say that you will allow someone to do something, when you have a legal right to say 'no': *Her parents refused to give their consent to the marriage.*

allowance /əˈlaʊəns/ *n* [C usually singular] **1** an amount of money that you are given: *His father gives him a small monthly allowance.* | *a travel allowance* **2** an amount of something that you are allowed to have: *Passengers' baggage allowance is 75 pounds per person.*

PHRASES
make allowances for sb to be kind to someone and not criticize them because you know that they have a problem or disadvantage: *Dad's under pressure – we have to make allowances for him.*

alloy /ˈælɔɪ $ ˈælɔɪ, əˈlɔɪ/ *n* [C] a metal made by mixing two or more different metals

all-'purpose *adj* [only before noun] able to be used in any situation: *an all-purpose cleaner*

all 'right¹ *adj* [not before noun], *adv* spoken
1 satisfactory, but not very good: *'How's the food?' 'It's all right, but I've had better.'* | *Did everything go all right* (=happen in a satisfactory way)? **THESAURUS** SATISFACTORY
2 well and happy: *Kate was looking very pale – I hope she's all right.* | *Are you feeling all right?*
3 suitable or convenient SYN OK: *We need to fix a time for our meeting. Would Thursday afternoon be all right?*

PHRASES
is it all right if ...?/would it be all right if ...? used to ask for someone's permission to do something: *Is it all right if I close the window?*
that's all right 1 used to reply when someone thanks you: *'Thanks for your help!' 'That's all right.'*

2 used to tell someone you are not angry when they say they are sorry: *'Sorry I'm late!' 'That's all right!'*

all 'right² *spoken* used to say that you agree with a plan or suggestion: *'Let's go now.' 'All right.'*

,all-'round *adj* [only before noun] *BrE* good at doing a lot of different things, especially in sports [SYN] **all-around** *AmE: an all-round athlete* —**all-rounder** *n* [C]

'all-time *adj* used when you compare things to say that one of them is the best, worst etc that there has ever been: **an all-time high/low** *The price has reached an all-time low.* | *my all-time favorite film*

allude /əˈluːd/ *v*
PHRASAL VERBS
allude to sb/sth *formal* to mention something or someone in an indirect way

allure /əˈljʊə $ əˈlʊr/ *n* [U] an exciting quality that attracts people: **[+of]** *the allure of travel*

alluring /əˈljʊərɪŋ $ əˈlʊr-/ *adj* very attractive: *an alluring smile*

allusion /əˈluːʒən/ *n* [C,U] *formal* when you mention something or someone in an indirect way: *His poetry is full of historical allusions.*

ally¹ /ˈælaɪ $ ˈælaɪ, əˈlaɪ/ *n* [C] (*plural* **allies**) **1** a country that helps another country during a war: *the US and its European allies* **2** a person who supports you in a difficult situation

ally² /əˈlaɪ $ əˈlaɪ, æˈlaɪ/ *v* [I,T] (**allied, allying, allies**) **ally yourself to/with sb** to join with another person, organization, or country and support them

almighty /ɔːlˈmaɪti $ ɒːl-/ *adj* **1** having the power to do anything: *Almighty God* | **the Almighty** (=God) **2** [only before noun] very big or loud: *We heard an almighty crash.*

almond /ˈɑːmənd $ ˈɑː-, -æ-, ˈæl-/ *n* [C] a flat white nut with a slightly sweet taste → see picture at NUT

almost /ˈɔːlməʊst $ ˈɒːlmoʊst, ɒːlˈmoʊst/ *adv* nearly but not completely: *Are we almost there?* | *It was almost midnight.* | *Almost all children like to read.* | *I'm sorry, I almost forgot to call you.*

THESAURUS

almost nearly but not completely: *I've almost finished my essay.* | *She's almost 12.*
nearly *especially BrE* almost. You can use 'very' before **nearly** but not before **almost**: *It's nearly 10 o'clock.* | *It's very nearly time to go home.*
practically/virtually almost completely – used before adjectives and before **all**, **every**, **everyone**. Not used before numbers: *The room was practically empty.* | *Virtually everyone had left.*
more or less (*also* **just about/pretty much** *spoken*) very nearly – used especially when saying that things are nearly the same: *All the rooms are more or less the same size.* | *That's pretty much what I expected.*
not quite almost, but not yet: *I'm not quite ready yet.*
getting on for sth *BrE*, **getting on toward sth** *especially AmE informal* almost a particular time or age – used especially when you are not sure

---

of the exact time or age: *It's getting on for 10 years since we saw each other.*

alms /ɑːmz $ ɑːmz, ɑːlmz/ *n* [plural] *old-fashioned* money and food given to poor people

aloft /əˈlɒft $ əˈlɒːft/ *adv literary* high up in the air: *They held the banner aloft for everyone to see.*

alone /əˈləʊn $ əˈloʊn/ *adj, adv*
1 [not before noun] without any other people, or without help from anyone else: *She lives alone.* | *I was all alone* (=completely alone) *in a strange city.* | *You shouldn't leave a child alone in the house.* | *My wife and I like to spend time alone together* (=away from everyone else).
2 sb/sth alone only one person or thing: *You alone must make this decision.* | *This disease cannot be cured by drugs alone.*
PHRASES
leave/let sb alone to stop annoying someone: *'Leave me alone!' she screamed.*
leave/let sth alone to stop touching something: *Leave that clock alone or you'll break it.*

Word Choice: alone, on your own, or by yourself?
Alone is used especially in more formal written English: *He lived alone.* | *The killer acted alone.* In everyday spoken English, you usually say that someone does something **on his/her own** or **by himself/herself**: *My sister lived by herself in a small apartment.* | *He built the house on his own.*

---

along¹ /əˈlɒŋ $ əˈlɒːŋ/ *prep*
1 from one place on a line, road, river etc to another place on it: *We took a walk along the river.* | *She looked anxiously along the line of faces.* | *They've put up a fence along the road.*
2 at a particular place on a line, road, river etc: *The house is somewhere along this road.*

along² *adv*
1 going forward: *I was driving along, listening to the radio.*
2 with you: **take/bring sb/sth along** *Do you mind if I bring a friend along?* | **go along/come along** *We're going to a party – you're welcome to come along!* → **all along** at ALL²
PHRASES
along with in addition to someone or something else: *Diane was chosen for the job along with three other people.*
be along/come along to arrive: *The next bus should be along in a minute.*
get along/come along to develop or make progress: *How are you getting along in your new job?* | *Your English is coming along very well.*

alongside /əˌlɒŋˈsaɪd $ əˌlɒːŋ-/ *adv, prep* **1** next to the side of something: *We parked alongside a white van.* [THESAURUS] **NEXT 2** working or doing something with someone else: *Charles spent a week working alongside the miners.*

aloof /əˈluːf/ *adj* **1** deliberately staying away from other people or not talking to them, especially because you think you are better than they are: *She* seemed cold and aloof. **2** if you stay aloof from something, you do not become involved in it

aloud /ə'laʊd/ adv in a voice that people can hear: Will you please read the poem aloud? | He cried aloud with pain.

alphabet /'ælfəbet/ n [C] a set of letters that are used when writing a language: the Greek alphabet

alphabetical /ˌælfə'betɪkəl◀/ adj arranged according to the letters of the alphabet: The names are listed **in alphabetical order**. —**alphabetically** /-kli/ adv

alpha 'male n [C] **1** the male with the highest rank in a group of animals such as CHIMPANZEES **2** humorous the man who has the most power and influence and the highest social position in a particular group

alpine /'ælpaɪn/ adj relating to the Alps or other high mountains: alpine flowers

already /ɔːl'redi $ ɒːl-/ adv **1** before now, or before a particular time: I've seen that film already. | By the time he arrived, the room was already crowded. **2** sooner than expected: Are you leaving already? | I've forgotten the number already.

alright /ɔːl'raɪt $ ˌɒːl-/ adv another spelling of ALL RIGHT that some people consider to be incorrect

also /'ɔːlsəʊ $ 'ɒːlsoʊ/ adv in addition to something you have mentioned: We specialize in shoes, but we also sell handbags. | She sings beautifully and also plays the piano.

> **Usage**
> **Also**, **too** and **as well** all mean the same thing.
> **As well** and **too** are used especially in spoken English. They usually come at the end of a sentence: He's a nice guy and he's really good-looking as well. | Will your mother be there too?
> **Also** is usually used before a verb, or after the verb **to be**: The DVD also includes a number of extra features.| Timing is also an important factor. If there are two or more verbs together, **also** comes after the first one: She can also speak Italian.

altar /'ɔːltə $ 'ɒːltər/ n [C] a kind of holy table, especially used in a church for religious ceremonies

alter Ac /'ɔːltə $ 'ɒːltər/ v [I,T] to change, or to make something or someone change: Her face hadn't altered much over the years. | They had to alter their plans. **THESAURUS** CHANGE

alteration Ac /ˌɔːltə'reɪʃən $ ˌɒːl-/ n [C,U] a change in something, or the process of changing it: **[+to]** I have just **made** a couple of minor **alterations** to the drawings.

altercation /ˌɔːltə'keɪʃən $ ˌɒːltər-/ n [C] formal a noisy argument

alternate¹ Ac /'ɔːltɜːnət $ 'ɒːltər-, 'æl-/ adj [only before noun] **1** happening in a regular way, first one thing and then the other thing: Arrange the meat and rice in alternate layers. **2 alternate days/weeks etc** one of every two days, weeks etc: We visit my parents on alternate Sundays. **3** used to replace another thing of the same type SYN alternative —**alternately** adv

alternate² Ac /'ɔːltəneɪt $ 'ɒːltər-, 'æl-/ v [I,T] if two things alternate, or if you alternate them, first you do one thing or one thing happens, then the other, then the first one again: **[+between]** Her moods alternated between joy and sadness. —**alternating** adj: alternating layers of sand and stone

alternative¹ Ac /ɔːl'tɜːnətɪv $ ɒːl'tɜːr-, æl-/ adj [only before noun] **1** used instead of something else: The main road is blocked, so drivers should choose an alternative route. **2** different from what is usual or accepted: an alternative lifestyle | alternative medicine

alternative² Ac n [C] something you can choose instead of something else: There are a number of alternatives. | **[+to]** Milk is a healthier alternative to cream. | I **had no alternative** but to report him to the police.

alternatively /ɔːl'tɜːnətɪvli $ ɒːl'tɜːr-, æl-/ adv used to suggest an alternative to your first suggestion: I could come to your house, or alternatively we could meet in town.

although /ɔːl'ðəʊ $ ɒːl'ðoʊ/ linking word **1** in spite of the fact that something is true: Although the car's old, it still runs well. | He lent his friend £20, although he didn't have much money himself. **2** but: You can copy my answers, although I'm not sure they're right.

altitude /'æltɪtjuːd $ -tuːd/ n [C,U] the height of something above sea level: **high/low altitude** Breathing becomes more difficult at high altitudes.

alto /'æltəʊ $ -toʊ/ n [C,U] (plural altos) a female singer with a low voice, or a male singer with a high voice

altogether /ˌɔːltə'geðə◀ $ ˌɒːltə'geðər◀/ adv **1** completely: Bradley seems to have disappeared altogether. | I'm not altogether sure what this word means. **2** including everything or everyone: There were five of us altogether. **3** in general, considering everything: It did rain a lot, but altogether I'd say it was a good trip.

> **Word Choice: altogether or all together?**
> You use **altogether** to talk about the total amount of people or things: You owe me £5 altogether.
> You use **all together** to say that people or things are together in a group: When we're all together, we have a great time.

altruistic /ˌæltru'ɪstɪk◀/ adj caring more about other people's needs and happiness than about your own —**altruism** /'æltruɪzəm/ n [U]

aluminium /ˌælə'mɪniəm/ BrE, **aluminum** /ə'luːmənəm/ AmE n [U] a silver-white metal that is light and easy to bend

alumni /ə'lʌmnaɪ/ n [plural] the former students of a school, college etc

always /ˈɔːlwəz, -weɪz $ ˈɒːl-/ *adv*
1 every time, or at all times: *Always lock your car.* | *We're always ready to help you.*
2 forever, or for all your life: *I will always love you.*
3 for a very long time: *I've always loved his music.* | *I've always wanted to go to China.*
4 very often: *The stupid car is always breaking down!*
PHRASES

| **you could always …** *spoken* used to make a polite suggestion: *You could always try calling her.*

Grammar
You normally use **always** before a verb: *We always go on holiday in August.*
You use **always** after the verb **be**: *Jeff is always late for school.*
If there are two or more verbs together, **always** comes after the first one: *I have always lived in this town.*

THESAURUS – sense 2
always forever, or for all your life: *Don't worry – things won't always be this bad!* | *We will always have each other.*
forever if something lasts or continues forever, it continues for all future time: *Our planet will not last forever.* | *She wanted the holidays to go on forever.*
permanently for a very long time, often for the rest of your life – used about a change that happens: *They decided to move to Portugal permanently.* | *Her hearing was permanently damaged by the explosion.*
for life for the rest of your life: *They should put that man in prison for life.* | *Marriage should be for life.*
for good *especially spoken* for a very long time and possibly forever – used especially when saying that someone or something goes away or comes back permanently: *This time he says he's coming back for good.* | *Those days have gone for good.*

Alzheimer's disease /ˈæltshaɪməz dɪˌziːz $ -mərz-/ *n* [U] a disease that affects someone's brain, and makes it difficult for them to remember things

am /m, əm; *strong* æm/ the first person singular present tense of the verb BE

a.m. (*also* **am** *BrE*) /ˌeɪ ˈem/ used in times from 12 o'clock at night until 12 o'clock in the day → **p.m.**: *I start work at 9:00 a.m.*

amalgamate /əˈmælgəmeɪt/ *v* [I,T] to join two organizations together to become a bigger organization, or to join together in this way: *The two companies are amalgamating to form a huge multinational corporation.* —**amalgamation** /əˌmælgəˈmeɪʃən/ *n* [C,U]

amass /əˈmæs/ *v* [T] *formal* if you amass money, knowledge, information etc, you gradually collect a large amount of it: *He **amassed a fortune** in the years before the war.*

amateur¹ /ˈæmətə, -tʃʊə, -tʃə, ˌæmətɜː $ ˈæmətʃʊr, -tər/ *adj* doing something because you enjoy it, not because it is your job: *an amateur boxer* | *amateur football*

amateur² *n* [C] **1** someone who does something because they enjoy it, not because it is their job **OPP** **professional 2** someone who is not very good at doing something: *It looked as if the building had been decorated by a bunch of amateurs.*

amateurish /ˈæmətərɪʃ, -tʃʊə-, -tʃə- ˌæməˈtɜːrɪʃ $ ˈæmətʃʊr-, -tɜːr-/ *adj* done in a way that is not very skilful: *his amateurish attempts at painting*

amaze /əˈmeɪz/ *v* [T] to make someone feel very surprised: *Kay amazed her friends by saying she was getting married.* | *It amazes me how much she has improved.*

amazed /əˈmeɪzd/ *adj* [not before noun] very surprised: **[+at/by]** *We were amazed at how quickly the kids learned the song.* | **[+(that)]** *I'm amazed that you remember him.* **THESAURUS** SURPRISED

amazement /əˈmeɪzmənt/ *n* [U] when you feel very surprised: *in amazement I stared at him in amazement.* | **to sb's amazement** *To my amazement, Neal got up and left without a word.*

amazing /əˈmeɪzɪŋ/ *adj* very surprising: *What an amazing story!* **THESAURUS** SURPRISING —**amazingly** *adv*: *an amazingly generous offer*

ambassador /æmˈbæsədə $ -ər/ *n* [C] an important official who represents his or her government in a foreign country: **[+to]** *the Mexican ambassador to Canada* —**ambassadorial** /æmˌbæsəˈdɔːriəl/ *adj*

amber /ˈæmbə $ -ər/ *n* [U] **1** a hard yellowish-brown clear substance that is used for making jewellery: *an amber necklace* **2** a yellowish-brown colour: *The traffic lights turned to amber.* —**amber** *adj*

ambidextrous /ˌæmbɪˈdekstrəs◂/ *adj* able to use both your hands equally well

ambience (*also* **ambiance** *AmE*) /ˈæmbiəns/ *n* [U] the character of a place and the way this makes you feel: *a restaurant with a lovely friendly ambience*

ambiguity Ac /ˌæmbɪˈɡjuːəti/ *n* [C,U] (*plural* **ambiguities**) when something can have more than one possible meaning: **[+in]** *There were several ambiguities in the letter.*

ambiguous Ac /æmˈbɪɡjuəs/ *adj* something that is ambiguous has more than one possible meaning: *His answer was ambiguous.*

ambition /æmˈbɪʃən/ *n*
1 [C] a strong desire to do or achieve something: *Her ambition is to climb Mount Everest.* | **ambition to do sth/of doing sth** *Miles had finally achieved his ambition of being an author.* **THESAURUS** AIM
2 [U] a strong determination to become successful or powerful: *a young politician with a lot of ambition*

COLLOCATIONS
verbs
to have an ambition *Have you always had an ambition to act?*
to achieve/fulfil an ambition (=to do what you wanted to do) *We never thought she would achieve this ambition.*

adjectives

sb's main ambition *My main ambition has always been to have a family.*
sb's greatest/ultimate ambition *Her ultimate ambition is to win an Olympic gold medal.*
a lifelong ambition (=one that you have had all your life) *He fulfilled a lifelong ambition by meeting his hero.*
a burning ambition (=a very strong desire to do something) *He had no burning ambitions to succeed at work.*

ambitious /æm'bɪʃəs/ *adj* **1** determined to be successful or powerful: *He is young and very ambitious.* **THESAURUS** DETERMINED **2** an ambitious plan aims to achieve something very great but very difficult: *the most ambitious engineering project of modern times*

ambivalent /æm'bɪvələnt/ *adj* not sure whether you like something or whether you want it: **[+about]** *I think Carla's ambivalent about getting married.* —**ambivalence** *n* [U]

amble /'æmbəl/ *v* [I] to walk slowly in a relaxed way

ambulance /'æmbjələns/ *n* [C] a special vehicle for taking ill or injured people to hospital: *the ambulance service* | **by ambulance** *Mike had to be taken by ambulance to hospital.*

ambush /'æmbʊʃ/ *n* [C] a sudden attack by people who have been waiting and hiding: *Two soldiers were killed in an ambush near the border.* **THESAURUS** ATTACK —**ambush** *v* [T]

ameliorate /ə'miːliəreɪt/ *v* [T] *formal* to make something better

amen /ɑː'men, eɪ-/ *spoken* said at the end of a Christian or Jewish prayer

amenable /ə'miːnəbəl $ ə'miːn- ə'men-/ *adj* willing to listen or do something: **[+to]** *I'm sure they'll be amenable to your suggestions.*

amend Ac /ə'mend/ *v* [T] to make small changes or improvements, especially to something that has been written: *The law has been amended several times.*

amendment Ac /ə'mendmənt/ *n* [C,U] a change made in the words of a law or document: *constitutional amendments* | **[+to]** *an amendment to the new Finance Bill*

amends /ə'mendz/ *n* **make amends** to do something to show that you are sorry for something bad or wrong that you did: *I tried to make amends by inviting him to lunch.*

amenity /ə'miːnəti $ ə'me-/ *n* [C usually plural] (*plural* **amenities**) something that makes a place comfortable and easy to live in: *The hotel's amenities include a pool and two bars.*

American[1] /ə'merɪkən/ *adj* from or connected with the United States: *Her mother is American.* | *American cars*

American[2] *n* [C] someone from the United States → NATIVE AMERICAN

AMERICAN FOOTBALL

A,merican 'football *n* [U] *BrE* a game played in the US in which two teams wearing HELMETS and special protective clothes carry, kick, or throw an OVAL ball **SYN** **football** *AmE*

A,merican 'Indian *n* [C] NATIVE AMERICAN

Americanism /ə'merɪkənɪzəm/ *n* [C] a word or phrase that is typically used in American English

Americanize (*also* **-ise** *BrE*) /ə'merɪkənaɪz/ *v* [T] to change a society, language, system etc so that it becomes more like America —**Americanization** /ə,merɪkənaɪ'zeɪʃən $ -nə-/ *n* [U]

amethyst /'æmɪθɪst/ *n* [C,U] a purple stone used in jewellery

amiable /'eɪmiəbəl/ *adj* friendly and pleasant: *an amiable young man* —**amiably** *adv* —**amiability** /,eɪmiə'bɪləti/ *n* [U]

amicable /'æmɪkəbəl/ *adj* friendly and without arguments: *an amicable divorce* —**amicably** *adv*

amid /ə'mɪd/ (*also* **amidst** /ə'mɪdst/) *prep formal* among something, or while something is happening: *surviving amid the horrors of war*

amiss[1] /ə'mɪs/ *adj* if something is amiss, there is a problem: *She sensed something was amiss.*

amiss[2] *adv* **1** **take sth amiss** to feel offended or upset about something someone has said or done **2** **sth would not go/come amiss** to be useful or suitable in a particular situation: *Two hundred pounds wouldn't go amiss right now.*

ammonia /ə'məʊniə $ -'moʊ-/ *n* [U] a clear liquid with a strong bad smell that is used for cleaning things or in cleaning products

ammunition /,æmjə'nɪʃən/ *n* [U] things such as bullets, bombs etc that are fired from guns

amnesia /æm'niːziə $ -ʒə/ *n* [U] the medical condition of not being able to remember anything

amnesty /'æmnəsti/ *n* [C,U] (*plural* **amnesties**) **1** an official order by a government that allows prisoners to be free: **[+for]** *an amnesty for political prisoners* **2** a period of time when you can admit to doing something illegal without being punished

amoeba /ə'miːbə/ *n* [C] a very small creature that has only one cell

amok /ə'mɒk $ ə'mɑːk/ *adv* **run amok** to behave in an uncontrolled way

among /ə'mʌŋ/ (also **amongst** /ə'mʌŋst/) prep
1 in a particular group of people or things: *The decision has caused a lot of anger among women.* | *Relax, you're among friends here.* | *When they were children they were always fighting among themselves.*
2 in the middle of, through, or between: *We found him hiding among the bushes.* | *Rescue teams searched among the wreckage for survivors.*
3 if something is divided or shared among a group of people, each person is given a part of it: *His money will be divided among his three children.*
4 used when you are mentioning one or two people or things from a larger group: *Swimming and diving are among the most popular Olympic events.* | *We discussed, among other things, ways to raise money.*

amoral /eɪ'mɒrəl, æ- $ eɪ'mɔː-, -'mɑː-/ adj behaving in a way that shows you do not care if what you are doing is wrong

amorous /'æmərəs/ adj full of sexual desire or feelings of love

amorphous /ə'mɔːfəs $ -ɔːr-/ adj without a definite shape

amount¹ /ə'maʊnt/ n [C] how much of something there is: **[+of]** *I was surprised at the amount of work I had to do.* | *They spent a **considerable amount** (=a lot) of time on the project.* | *Please pay **the full amount** (=all the money you owe) by the end of the month.* | *There's a **certain amount** of risk (=some risk) with any investment.*

amount² v
PHRASAL VERBS
amount to sth **1** to have the same meaning or effect as something, without being exactly that thing: *What he said amounted to an apology.* **2** to add up to a particular total: *Jenny's debts amount to $1,000.*

amp /æmp/ (also **ampere** /'æmpeə $ -pɪr/) n [C]
1 a unit for measuring electric current **2** *informal* an AMPLIFIER

amphetamine /æm'fetəmiːn, -mɪn/ n [C,U] a drug that gives people more energy and makes them feel excited

amphibian /æm'fɪbiən/ n [C] an animal such as a FROG that can live on land and in water

amphibious /æm'fɪbiəs/ adj able to live both on land and in water: *amphibious creatures*

amphitheatre BrE, **amphitheater** AmE /'æmfəˌθɪətə $ -ər/ n [C] a large circular building without a roof and with many rows of seats, where people can sit and watch public performances

ample /'æmpəl/ adj more than enough: *You'll have ample time for questions later.* | *There's ample room in here for everyone.* —**amply** adv

amplifier /'æmpləfaɪə $ -faɪər/ n [C] a piece of electronic equipment used to make music and other sounds louder → see picture at ACOUSTIC

amplify /'æmplɪfaɪ/ v [T] (**amplified, amplifying, amplifies**) **1** to make sounds louder using electronic equipment **2** *formal* to make something such as a feeling stronger: *These stories only amplified her fears.* —**amplification** /ˌæmplɪfɪ'keɪʃən/ n [U]

amputate /'æmpjəteɪt/ v [I,T] to cut off someone's arm, leg, finger etc during a medical operation: *After the accident, the doctors had to amputate her leg.* —**amputation** /ˌæmpjə'teɪʃən/ n [C,U]

amuse /ə'mjuːz/ v [T] **1** to make someone laugh or smile: *Harry's jokes always amused me.* **2** to make time pass in an enjoyable way, so that you don't get bored: *She brought along some games to amuse the children on the flight.* | *The kids **amused themselves** playing hide-and-seek.*

amused /ə'mjuːzd/ adj smiling or laughing because something is funny: *The man looked a little amused.* | **[+at/by]** *Ellen seemed amused by the whole situation.* | *I could see she was **highly amused** (=very amused).*
PHRASES
> **keep sb amused** to entertain or interest someone for a long time so that they do not get bored: *It's hard work trying to keep the kids amused on rainy days.*

amusement /ə'mjuːzmənt/ n **1** [U] the feeling you have when something makes you laugh or smile: **in/with amusement** *She looked at him in amusement.* **2** [C,U] something that entertains you and makes time pass in an enjoyable way: *childhood amusements* | *What do you do for amusement (=in order to enjoy yourself) in this town?*

a'musement arˌcade n [C] BrE a place where people can play games on machines by putting coins in them

a'musement ˌpark n [C] a large park where people can ride on big machines, for example ROLLER COASTERS

amusing /ə'mjuːzɪŋ/ adj funny and entertaining: *a **highly amusing** (=very amusing) story* | *I didn't **find** your comment amusing.* THESAURUS FUNNY

an /ən; *strong* æn/ determiner used instead of 'a' when the following word begins with a vowel sound → **a**: *an orange* | *an X-ray* | *an hour*

anachronism /ə'nækrənɪzəm/ n [C] someone or something that seems to be in the wrong historical time: *The royal family seems something of an anachronism nowadays.* —**anachronistic** /əˌnækrə'nɪstɪk◂/ adj

anaemia BrE, **anemia** AmE /ə'niːmiə/ n [U] a medical condition in which you do not have enough red cells in your blood —**anaemic** adj

anaesthetic BrE, **anesthetic** AmE /ˌænəs'θetɪk◂/ n [C,U] a drug that stops you feeling pain, used during a medical operation: **under anaesthetic** *The operation will be done under anaesthetic (=using anaesthetic).* | *The doctor gave him a **local anaesthetic** (=one that only affects a particular part of your body).* | *You will need to have a **general anaesthetic** (=one that makes you completely unconscious).*

anaesthetist BrE, **anesthetist** AmE /ə'niːsθətɪst $ ə'nes-/ n [C] someone whose job is to give anaesthetics to people in hospitals

anaesthetize (also **-ise** BrE, **anesthetize** AmE) /ə'niːsθətaɪz $ ə'nes-/ v [T] to make someone unable to feel pain by giving them an anaesthetic

anagram /'ænəgræm/ n [C] a word or phrase made by changing the order of the letters in another word or phrase: *'Silent' is an anagram of 'listen'.*

anal /'eɪnl/ adj relating to the ANUS

analogous Ac /ə'næləgəs/ adj formal similar to another situation or thing: [+to/with] *Operating the system is analogous to driving a car.*

analogy Ac /ə'nælədʒi/ n [C,U] (plural **analogies**) a way of explaining something by saying it is similar to something else: [+between] *We can draw an analogy* (=make a comparison) *between the brain and a computer.*

analyse Ac BrE, **analyze** AmE /'ænəl-aɪz/ v [T] to examine or think about something carefully in order to understand it: *We're trying to analyse what went wrong.* | *The patient's blood is tested and analyzed.*

analysis Ac /ə'næləsɪs/ n [C,U] (plural **analyses** /-siːz/) careful examination of something in order to understand it better or find out what it consists of: [+of] *The team are carrying out a **detailed analysis** of the test results.* | *statistical analysis* | **for analysis** *Blood samples were sent to the laboratory for analysis.*

analyst Ac /'ænəlɪst/ n [C] **1** someone whose job is to analyse a subject and advise other people about it: *a computer analyst* **2** a PSYCHOANALYST

analytical Ac /ænəl'ɪtɪkəl/, **analytic** /-'ɪtɪk/ adj using methods that help you examine things carefully: *an analytical mind*

analyze /'ænəlaɪz/ v the American spelling of ANA-LYSE

anarchist /'ænəkɪst $ -ər-/ n [C] someone who believes that governments, laws etc are not neces-sary —**anarchism** n [U]

anarchy /'ænəki $ -ər-/ n [U] a situation in which no one obeys rules or laws and there is no control or government: *The nation is in danger of falling into anarchy.* —**anarchic** /æ'nɑːkɪk $ -ɑːr-/ adj

anathema /ə'næθəmə/ n [singular, U] formal something you hate because it is the opposite of what you believe in: [+to] *His political views were anathema to me.*

anatomy /ə'nætəmi/ n **1** [U] the scientific study of the structure of the body: *human anatomy* **2** [singular] the structure of a living thing, organiza-tion, or social group, and how it works: [+of] *the anatomy of modern society* —**anatomical** /ænə'tɒmɪkəl $ -'tɑː-/ adj —**anatomically** /-kli/ adv

ancestor /'ænsəstə, -sɛs- $ -sestər/ n [C] a member of your family who lived a long time ago, before your grandparents → **descendant**: *His ancestors came from Italy.* **THESAURUS** RELATIVE —**ancestral** /æn'sestrəl/ adj

ancestry /'ænsəstri, -ses- $ -ses-/ n [C,U] (plural **ancestries**) the members of your family who lived in past times: *people of Scottish ancestry*

anchor¹ /'æŋkə $ -ər/ n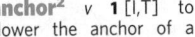
[C] **1** a heavy metal object that is lowered into the water to prevent a ship or boat from moving **2** AmE someone who reads the news on television or radio and is in charge of the programme **SYN** news-reader BrE

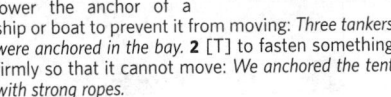

anchor² v **1** [I,T] to lower the anchor of a ship or boat to prevent it from moving: *Three tankers were anchored in the bay.* **2** [T] to fasten something firmly so that it cannot move: *We anchored the tent with strong ropes.*

anchovy /'æntʃəvi $ æntʃouvi/ n [C,U] (plural **anchovies**) a small fish that tastes of salt

ancient /'eɪnʃənt/ adj
1 belonging to a time in history that was thousands of years ago: *ancient Rome* **THESAURUS** OLD
2 humorous very old: *I look absolutely ancient in that photograph!*

and /ənd, ən; strong ænd/ linking word
1 used to join two words or parts of sentences: *a knife and fork* | *They started shouting and screaming.* | *Martha was going to the store, and Tom said he'd go with her.*
2 used to say that one thing happens after another: *Grant knocked and went in.*
3 spoken used instead of 'to' after certain verbs such as 'come', 'go', 'try': *Try and finish your homework before dinner.*
4 used in numbers and when adding numbers: *Six and four make ten.* | *three and a half*
5 used to say that one thing is caused by something else: *I missed lunch and I'm starving!*

android /'ændrɔɪd/ n [C] a ROBOT that looks com-pletely human

anecdotal /ænɪk'dəʊtl◂ $ -'doʊ-/ adj consisting of stories based on someone's personal experience: *The report is based on **anecdotal evidence** rather than serious research.*

anecdote /'ænɪkdəʊt $ -doʊt/ n [C] a short inter-esting story about a particular person or event

anemia /ə'niːmiə/ n the American spelling of ANAE-MIA —**anemic** adj

anesthetic /ænəs'θetɪk◂/ n the American spelling of ANAESTHETIC

anesthetist /ə'niːsθɜːtɪst $ ə'nes-/ n the American spelling of ANAESTHETIST

anesthetize /ə'niːsθətaɪz $ ə'nes-/ v the American spelling of ANAESTHETIZE

anew /ə'njuː $ ə'nuː/ adv literary in a new or differ-ent way: *She started life anew in New York.*

angel /'eɪndʒəl/ n [C] **1** a SPIRIT who is God's serv-ant in heaven, and who is often shown as a person dressed in white with wings **2** spoken a very kind person: *Oh, thanks! You're an angel!* —**angelic** /æn'dʒelɪk/ adj

anger¹ /'æŋgə $ -ər/ n [U] a strong feeling of

wanting to hurt or criticize someone because they have done something bad to you or been unkind to you: **[+at]** *Emily was filled with anger at the way she had been treated.* | **in anger** (=when you are angry) *You should never hit a child in anger.*

anger² v [T] to make someone feel angry: *The court's decision angered environmentalists.*

ANGLES

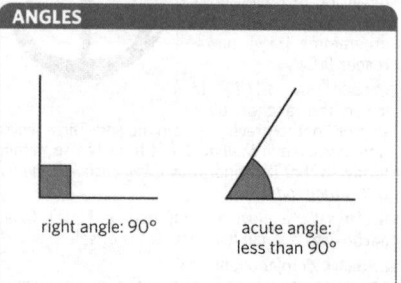

right angle: 90°

acute angle:
less than 90°

angle¹ /ˈæŋɡəl/ n [C]

1 the space between two lines or surfaces that meet or cross each other, measured in degrees: *an angle of 45°*

2 a way of considering a problem or situation: *Let's try to look at the problem from a different angle.*

3 the direction from which you look at something: *From that angle, he could just see the corner of the roof.*
→ **RIGHT ANGLE**

PHRASES

at an angle sloping, not upright or level: *The tree was growing at an angle.*

angle² v [T] **1** to turn or move something so that it is not straight or upright: *You could angle the table away from the wall.* **2** to present information from a particular point of view for a specific group of people: *The book is angled towards a business audience.*

PHRASAL VERBS

angle for sth to try to get something you want without asking directly for it: *I think she's angling for an invitation to the party.*

Anglican /ˈæŋɡlɪkən/ adj relating to the Church of England —**Anglican** n [C] —**Anglicanism** n [U]

angling /ˈæŋɡlɪŋ/ n [U] the activity of fishing with a hook and a line —**angler** n [C]

Anglo- /ˈæŋɡləʊ $ -ɡloʊ/ prefix relating to England or Britain and another country: *Anglo-American relations*

angry /ˈæŋɡri/ adj feeling or showing anger: *He was beginning to get angry.* | **[+with/at]** *She was angry with him because he had lied to her.* | *Jess laughed, which made me even angrier.* | **[+about]** *Don't you feel angry about the way you've been treated?* | **[+that]** *The workers are angry that they haven't been paid for the week.* —**angrily** adv

THESAURUS

angry feeling or showing anger: *He gets really angry if people are late.* | *angry voices*
mad [not before noun] *informal* angry: *Dad was mad at me for damaging the car.*

cross [not before noun] *spoken* a little angry – used when speaking to people you know well: *Don't be cross with me.*
annoyed [not before noun] a little angry, but not very angry: *I was annoyed that the class was cancelled again.*
irritated a little angry about something silly or unpleasant that keeps happening: *He was clearly irritated by their stupid questions.*
furious/livid very angry: *He was furious when he found out what they'd done to his car.*
outraged very shocked and angry: *There were hundreds of complaints from outraged viewers.*
bad-tempered a bad-tempered person becomes angry easily and often: *a bad-tempered old man*
in a bad mood if someone is in a bad mood, they seem angry and behave in an unfriendly way, often for no particular reason: *I woke up in a bad mood.*

angst /æŋst/ n [U] strong feelings of anxiety that you have over a long period of time when you are worried about your life

anguish /ˈæŋɡwɪʃ/ n [U] *written* very great pain or worry: *the anguish of not knowing the truth* —**anguished** adj: *anguished cries for help*

angular /ˈæŋɡjələ $ -ər/ adj having sharp corners

animal¹ /ˈænəməl/ n [C]

1 any living creature, like a cow or dog, that is not a bird, insect, fish, or person: *farm animals* | *wild animals* | *the enormous diversity of the animal kingdom*

2 any living creature that can move around: *Humans are highly intelligent animals.*

animal² adj connected with or made from animals: *animal fats*

animate /ˈænəmət/ adj *formal* living OPP **inanimate**

animated /ˈænɪmeɪtɪd/ adj **1** showing a lot of interest and energy: *an animated debate* **2** **animated cartoon/film etc** a film in which pictures and MODELS seem to move and talk —**animatedly** adv

animation /ˌænəˈmeɪʃən/ n **1** [U] the process of making animated films **2** [U] energy and excitement: **with animation** *They were talking with animation.*

animosity /ˌænəˈmɒsəti $ -ˈmɑː-/ n [C,U] (*plural* **animosities**) *formal* strong dislike or hatred: *There was a lot of animosity between the two leaders.*

ankle /ˈæŋkəl/ n [C] the part of your body where your foot joins your leg → see picture on page A2

annals /ˈænlz/ n **in the annals of** sth in the whole history of a particular subject: *one of the most unusual cases in the annals of crime*

annex /əˈneks $ əˈneks, ˈæneks/ v [T] to take control of a country or area next to your own, especially by using force —**annexation** /ˌænekˈseɪʃən/ n [C,U]

annexe *BrE*, **annex** *AmE* /ˈæneks/ n [C] a separate building that has been added to a larger one: *a hospital annexe*

annihilate /əˈnaɪəleɪt/ v [T] to destroy something or defeat someone completely: *Their army was annihilated in just three days.* —**annihilation** /əˌnaɪəˈleɪʃən/ n [U]

anniversary /ˌænəˈvɜːsəri $ -ɜːr-/ n [C] (plural **anniversaries**) a date on which something special or important happened in a previous year: *Our **wedding anniversary** is May 3.* | **[+of]** *the 50th anniversary of India's independence*

Anno Domini /ˌænəʊ ˈdɒmənaɪ $ ˌænoʊ ˈdɑː-/ formal → **AD**

announce /əˈnaʊns/ v [T]
1 to officially tell people about something so that everyone knows: *The winner of the competition will be announced shortly.* | **[+(that)]** *A police spokesman announced that a man had been arrested.* **THESAURUS** TELL
2 to say something in a loud and confident way: **[+(that)]** *Liam suddenly announced that he was leaving the band.*

announcement /əˈnaʊnsmənt/ n
1 [C] an important official statement about something that has happened or will happen: *We all waited for the captain to **make an announcement**.* | **[+(that)]** *We were shocked by the announcement that the mayor was resigning.*
2 [singular] when someone tells a lot of people about something: **[+of]** *the announcement of the election results*

announcer /əˈnaʊnsə $ -ər/ n [C] someone who gives information or introduces people on television or radio

annoy /əˈnɔɪ/ v [T] to make someone feel a little angry: *Jane wouldn't stop complaining and it was beginning to annoy me.*

annoyance /əˈnɔɪəns/ n **1** [U] the feeling of being annoyed: *Mia's annoyance never showed.* **2** [C] something that annoys you: *The dog next door is a constant annoyance.*

annoyed /əˈnɔɪd/ adj a little angry: **[+with]** *Are you annoyed with me just because I'm a bit late?* | **[+at/about]** *She was really annoyed at the way he just ignored her.* | **[+(that)]** *My sister's annoyed that we didn't call.* **THESAURUS** ANGRY

annoying /əˈnɔɪ-ɪŋ/ adj making you feel annoyed: *an annoying habit of interrupting* | *It's annoying that we didn't know about this before.* —**annoyingly** adv

annual¹ Ac /ˈænjuəl/ adj **1** happening once every year: *the annual conference* **2** calculated over a period of one year: *He has an annual income of around $500,000.* —**annually** adv

annual² n [C] **1** a plant that lives for one year or season **2** a book, especially for children, that is produced once a year with the same title but different stories, pictures etc

annuity /əˈnjuːəti $ əˈnuː-/ n [C] (plural **annuities**) a fixed amount of money that is paid each year to someone, usually until they die

annul /əˈnʌl/ v [T] (**annulled, annulling**) formal to officially state that a marriage or legal agreement no longer exists —**annulment** n [C,U]

anomalous /əˈnɒmələs $ əˈnɑː-/ adj formal different from what you expected to find: *a highly anomalous situation*

anomaly /əˈnɒməli $ əˈnɑː-/ n [C,U] (plural **anomalies**) formal something that is noticeable because it is different from what is usual: *In those days, a woman professor was still an anomaly.*

anon /əˈnɒn $ əˈnɑːn/ the written abbreviation of **anonymous**, used especially to show that the writer of a poem or song is not known

anonymity /ˌænəˈnɪməti/ n [U] when other people do not know who you are or what your name is: *The author prefers anonymity.*

anonymous /əˈnɒnɪməs $ əˈnɑː-/ adj **1** not known by name: *the anonymous author of a collection of poems* | *The person concerned wishes to **remain anonymous**.* **2** done, sent, or given by someone who does not want their name to be known: *an anonymous letter* —**anonymously** adv

anorak /ˈænəræk/ n [C] BrE a short coat with a HOOD that keeps out the wind and rain

anorexia /ˌænəˈreksiə/ (also **anorexia nervosa** /ˌænəˌreksiə nɜːˈvəʊsə $ -nərˈvoʊ-/) n [U] a mental illness that makes people, especially young women, stop eating so that they become dangerously thin

anorexic /ˌænəˈreksɪk◂/ adj suffering from or relating to anorexia

another /əˈnʌðə $ -ər/ determiner, pron
1 one more person or thing of the same kind: *Do you want another beer?* | *Buy one CD and we'll give you another, completely free.* **THESAURUS** MORE
2 a different person or thing: *You'll just have to find another job.* | *She lives in another part of the country.* | *He left his wife for another woman.* → **ONE ANOTHER**

> **Grammar**
> **Another** is written as one word. Do not write it as 'an other'.

answer¹ /ˈɑːnsə $ ˈænsər/ v
1 QUESTION [I,T] to say something to someone when they have asked you a question or spoken to you: *'I don't know,' she answered.* | *I had to **answer** a lot of **questions** about my previous job.* | *Why don't you answer me?* | **[+(that)]** *Clare answered that she was not interested in their offer.*
2 IN A TEST [T] to reply to a question in a test, competition etc: *Please answer as many questions as you can.*
3 TELEPHONE/DOOR [I,T] to pick up the telephone when it rings or go to the door when someone knocks or rings the bell: *The phone rang and rang, but no one answered.*
4 LETTER [I,T] to send a letter as a reply to an advertisement or to a letter that someone has sent to you: *They never answered my letter.*
PHRASAL VERBS
answer back to reply in a rude way to someone you are supposed to obey: **answer sb back** *Don't answer me back, young man!*
answer for sth to explain to people in authority why you did something wrong or why something happened, and be punished if necessary: *One day you'll have to answer for this.*

> **THESAURUS**
> **answer** to say something to someone after they have asked you a question or spoken to you: *He*

didn't answer my question. | *I said 'hello' to her but she didn't answer.*

reply to answer someone – used especially in written English to report what someone said: *He replied that he was busy until 12 o'clock.*

get back to sb to answer someone's question later, when you are less busy or have more information to give – used especially in spoken English: *Can I get back to you later today?*

write back to write a letter or email to someone who has written to you: *She never wrote back to me.*

respond to say or do something when someone says or does something to you – a rather formal use: *He responded by raising his hands up in the air.*

answer² *n*

1 **TO A QUESTION** [C,U] something you say when you reply to a question that someone has asked you: *Give me an answer as soon as possible.* | **[+to]** *Mark never got an answer to his letter.* | **In answer to** *your question, I think Paul's right.* | *I told you before,* **the answer is no!**

2 **TO A PROBLEM** [C] something that solves a problem: *There is no easy answer.* | **[+to]** *A bit more money would be the answer to all our problems.*

3 **IN A TEST** [C] something that you write or say in reply to a question in a test or competition: *What was the answer to question 7?* | **the right/wrong/correct/incorrect answer** *Score two points for each correct answer.*

answerable /ˈɑːnsərəbəl $ ˈæn-/ *adj* **be answerable to sb (for sth)** to have to explain your actions to someone in authority: *These officials are answerable to Parliament.*

ˈanswering maˌchine (also **answerphone** *BrE* /ˈɑːnsəfəʊn $ ˈænsərfoʊn/) *n* [C] a machine that records messages from people who telephone you when you are not there

ant /ænt/ *n* [C] a small black or red insect that lives in large groups

antagonism /ænˈtæɡənɪzəm/ *n* [U] when people strongly dislike or oppose someone or something: **[+between]** *the long-standing antagonism between the two countries* | **[+towards]** *their antagonism towards tourists*

antagonistic /ænˌtæɡəˈnɪstɪk◂/ *adj* opposing an idea or plan, or showing that you dislike someone: **[+to/towards]** *groups which are antagonistic to one another*

antagonize (also **-ise** *BrE*) /ænˈtæɡənaɪz/ *v* [T] to make someone feel angry or unfriendly towards you: *He was deliberately trying to antagonise her.*

Antarctic /ænˈtɑːktɪk $ -ɑːr-/ *n* **the Antarctic** the very cold area around the South Pole → **the Arctic** —**Antarctic** *adj*

antelope /ˈæntələʊp $ ˈæntəl-oʊp/ *n* [C] an animal with long horns that can run very fast → see picture on page A3

antenatal /ˌæntɪˈneɪtl◂/ *adj BrE* relating to the medical care given to women who are going to have a baby **SYN** **prenatal** → **postnatal**: *an antenatal clinic*

antenna /ænˈtenə/ *n* [C] **1** (*plural* **antennae** /-niː/) one of two long thin parts on an insect's head that it uses to feel things **2** (*plural* **antennas**) *especially AmE* a wire or piece of metal that receives or sends television or radio signals **SYN** **aerial** *BrE* → see picture at **CAR**

anthem /ˈænθəm/ *n* [C] a special song that is sung at religious, sports, or political ceremonies → **NATIONAL ANTHEM**

anthology /ænˈθɒlədʒi $ ænˈθɑː-/ *n* [C] (*plural* **anthologies**) a set of stories, poems etc by different people collected together in one book

anthrax /ˈænθræks/ *n* [U] a serious disease affecting cattle and sheep, which can affect humans

anthropology /ˌænθrəˈpɒlədʒi $ -ˈpɑː-/ *n* [U] the scientific study of people, societies, customs, and beliefs —**anthropologist** *n* [C] —**anthropological** /ˌænθrəpəˈlɒdʒɪkəl $ -ˈlɑː-/ *adj*

anti- /ˈænti $ ænti, æntaɪ/ *prefix* **1** strongly opposed to something or someone, or strongly disliking something or someone **OPP** **pro-**: *anti-American feeling* **2** having the effect of preventing something: *antifreeze (=liquid added to a car's engine to prevent freezing)*

antibiotic /ˌæntibaɪˈɒtɪk◂ $ -ˈɑː-/ *n* [C usually plural] a drug that is used to kill BACTERIA and cure infections —**antibiotic** *adj*

antibody /ˈæntiˌbɒdi $ -ˌbɑː-/ *n* [C] (*plural* **antibodies**) a substance produced by your body to fight disease

anticipate Ac /ænˈtɪsəpeɪt/ *v* [T] to expect something to happen and to prepare for it: *We don't anticipate any problems.* | **[+(that)]** *It is anticipated that prices will rise.*

anticipation Ac /ænˌtɪsəˈpeɪʃən/ *n* [U] **1** happy feelings when you think something good is going to happen: *Her eyes sparkled with anticipation.* **2** **in anticipation of sth** because you expect something to happen: *He raised his fists in anticipation of a fight.*

anticlimax /ˌæntiˈklaɪmæks/ *n* [C,U] an event that seems disappointing because it happens after something that was much better: *The rest of the journey was an anticlimax.*

anticlockwise /ˌæntiˈklɒkwaɪz◂ $ -ˈklɑː-/ *adj, adv BrE* in the opposite direction to the way the hands of a clock move **SYN** **counterclockwise** *AmE* **OPP** **clockwise**: *Turn the handle anticlockwise.*

antics /ˈæntɪks/ *n* [plural] funny, silly, or strange behaviour

antidepressant /ˌæntidɪˈpresənt/ *n* [C] a drug used to treat DEPRESSION (=a medical condition in which you are very unhappy)

antidote /ˈæntidəʊt $ -doʊt/ *n* [C] **1** something that makes an unpleasant situation better: **[+to]** *Laughter is a good antidote to stress.* **2** a substance that stops the effects of a poison

antifreeze /ˈæntifriːz/ *n* [U] a liquid that is put in the water of a car's engine to stop it from freezing

antipathy /ænˈtɪpəθi/ *n* [U] *formal* a feeling of strong dislike towards someone or something: **[+to/towards]** *his antipathy to women*

,anti-'perspirant n [U] a substance that you put under your arms to prevent yourself from SWEATing → **deodorant**

antiquated /'æntɪkweɪtɪd/ adj old-fashioned and not suitable for modern needs or conditions: *anti-quated laws*

antique /æn'tiːk◂/ n [C] a piece of furniture, jewellery etc that is old and valuable: *priceless antiques | an **antique shop** (=one that sells antiques)* **THESAURUS** OLD —**antique** adj: *beautiful antique furniture*

antiquity /æn'tɪkwəti/ n (plural **antiquities**) **1** [U] ancient times: **in antiquity** *In antiquity a variety of methods were used.* **2** [U] the state of being very old: *a building of great antiquity* **3** [C usually plural] a building or object made in ancient times: *Roman antiquities*

anti-semitism /ˌænti'semətɪzəm/ n [U] hatred of Jewish people —**anti-semitic** /ˌæntisə'mɪtɪk◂/ adj

antiseptic /ˌæntə'septɪk◂/ n [C,U] a medicine that you put onto a wound to stop it becoming infected —**antiseptic** adj: *antiseptic cream*

antisocial /ˌænti'səʊʃəl $ -'soʊ-/ adj **1** antisocial behaviour upsets, harms, or annoys other people **2** unwilling to meet other people and talk to them: *I'm feeling a bit antisocial at the moment.*

antithesis /æn'tɪθɪsɪs/ n [C] (plural **antitheses** /-siːz/) formal the exact opposite of something: **[+of]** *Love is the antithesis of selfishness.*

antler /'æntlə $ -ər/ n [C] one of the two horns on the head of male DEER → see picture at **DEER**

antonym /'æntənɪm/ n [C] technical a word that means the opposite of another word → **synonym**

anus /'eɪnəs/ n [C] the hole in your bottom through which solid waste leaves your body

anvil /'ænvəl/ n [C] an iron block on which pieces of hot metal are shaped using a hammer

anxiety /æŋ'zaɪəti/ n (plural **anxieties**) **1** [C,U] the feeling of being very worried about something: **[+about/over]** *his anxiety about the future | My mother's ill health was a constant **source of anxiety***. **2** [U] a feeling of wanting to do something very much: **anxiety to do sth** *I nearly fell in my anxiety to get downstairs.*

anxious /'æŋkʃəs/ adj **1** worried about something: **[+about]** *I'm quite anxious about my exams. | an anxious look | an **anxious moment/time** etc* (=one in which you feel worried) **THESAURUS** WORRIED **2** feeling strongly that you want to do something or want something to happen: **anxious to do sth** *I was anxious to get home. | **[+(that)]** We're very anxious that no one else hears about this.* —**anxiously** adv: *Mom waited anxiously by the phone.*

any¹ /'eni/ determiner, pron **1** some or even the smallest amount or number – usually used in questions and negative statements: *Have you got any money? | It won't make any difference. | **[+of]** They didn't invite any of us. | Are there **any other** questions? | 'Don't you want butter?' 'I couldn't find any.'* **2** used to refer to a person or thing of a particular type when what you are saying is true of all people or things of that type: *a question that any child could answer | Any help would be welcome.* → **in any case** at CASE, **at any rate** at RATE¹

PHRASES

any moment/minute/day etc (now) very soon: *He'll be here any minute.*

> **Usage**
> Do not say 'Any parents love their children.' Say *All parents love their children.*
> Do not say 'Any country has these problems.' Say *Every country has these problems.*

any² adv even a small amount – used before a COMPARATIVE form, usually in questions and negative statements: *Are you feeling any better? | Is she any happier now? | I can't run any faster.*

anybody /'eniˌbɒdi, 'enibədi $ -ˌbɑːdi/ pron ANYONE

anyhow /'enihaʊ/ adv informal ANYWAY

any more, **anymore** /ˌeni'mɔː $ -'mɔːr/ adv **not any more** if something does not happen any more, it used to happen in the past but it does not happen now: *Nick doesn't live here any more.*

anyone /'eniwʌn/ (also **anybody**) pron **1** a person – used in questions and negative statements: *Is anyone at home? | I haven't seen anyone all day. | Do you know **anyone else** who wants a ticket?* **2** any person or any people, when it does not matter who: *Anyone can learn to cook. | We offer advice to anyone who is unemployed.*

anyplace /'enipleɪs/ adv AmE ANYWHERE

anything /'eniθɪŋ/ pron **1** any thing, event, situation etc, when it is not important which one: *Take anything you want. | Anything would be better than feeling like this. | Can I do anything to help?* **2** something – used in questions and negative statements: *Do you need anything? | Her father didn't know anything about it. | Would you like **anything else** to eat? | **or anything** spoken (=or anything similar) It's not dangerous or anything.*

PHRASES

anything but not at all: *Maria is anything but stupid.*
anything like sb/sth similar in any way to something or someone: *Belinda doesn't look anything like her sister. | If you're anything like me, you hate ironing.*
as important/clear/big etc as anything informal extremely important, clear etc: *He's as excited as anything.*

anyway /'eniweɪ/ (also **anyhow** informal) adv **1** in spite of the fact that you have just mentioned: *Tom was ill, but I went to the party anyway. | This idea probably won't work, but let's try it anyway.* **2** used when you are adding something to support or explain what you have just said: *I haven't got time to do it now. **And anyway**, I don't have the right tools. | He decided to sell his bike – he never used it anyway.* **3** used when you are changing the subject of a conversation or returning to a previous subject: *Anyway, how are things with you? | I think she's around my age, **but anyway**, she's pregnant.*

4 used when adding something that corrects or slightly changes what you have just said: *I'm not thinking of changing my job. Not this year, anyway.*

anywhere /'eniweə $ -wer/ (*also* **anyplace** *AmE*) *adv*

1 in or to any place, when it is not important where: *Sit anywhere you like.* | *I could study anywhere.* | *I wouldn't want to live **anywhere else**.*

2 used in questions and negative statements to mean 'somewhere' or 'nowhere': *Did you go anywhere last night?* | *Have you looked **anywhere else**?* | *I don't have anywhere to live.*

PHRASES

anywhere between one and ten/20 and 30 etc used to mean any age, number, amount etc between the ones that you say: *She could have been anywhere between 45 and 60 years of age.*

not anywhere near not at all: *She doesn't practise **anywhere near as much as** Sam.*

apart /ə'pɑːt $ -ɑːrt/ *adv*

1 if people or things are apart, they are not close to each other or touching each other: *Plant the seeds 8 inches apart.* | *They have offices **as far apart as** India and Peru.* | *He and his wife are now **living apart**.* | **[+from]** *Tim and Kate sat together, slightly apart from the others.*

2 if something comes apart, or if you take it apart, it separates into different pieces: *He took the camera **apart** to clean it.*

3 if two events are a particular time apart, that is the length of time between them: *Our birthdays are only two days apart.*

PHRASAL VERBS

fall apart if something falls apart, it fails completely: *His marriage fell apart.*

a'part from *prep*

1 except for: *Apart from the ending, it's a really good film.* | *I don't see any of my family, apart from my sister.* **THESAURUS** EXCEPT

2 in addition to: *Apart from Rory, Claire has two other children.*

apartheid /ə'pɑːtaɪt, -teɪt, -taɪd $ -ɑːr-/ *n* [U] the system that used to exist in South Africa, in which only white people had full political and legal rights

apartment /ə'pɑːtmənt $ -ɑːr-/ *n* [C] *especially AmE* a set of rooms on one floor of a large building, where someone lives **SYN** flat *BrE* **THESAURUS** HOUSE

a'partment ˌbuilding (*also* **a'partment ˌhouse**) *n* [C] *AmE* a building that is divided into separate apartments

apathetic /ˌæpə'θetɪk◂/ *adj* not interested in something, and not willing to make any effort to change things: **[+about]** *He's totally apathetic about politics.*

apathy /'æpəθi/ *n* [U] the feeling of not being interested in something, and not willing to make any effort to change things: *public apathy about the coming election*

APES

gorilla

chimpanzee

orangutang

ape /eɪp/ *n* [C] an animal that is similar to a monkey but has no tail or only a very short tail

aperitif /ə,perə'tiːf/ *n* [C] an alcoholic drink that you have before a meal

aperture /'æpətʃə $ 'æpərtʃʊr/ *n* [C] *formal* a small hole, especially one that lets light into a camera

apex /'eɪpeks/ *n* [C] *formal* **1** the top or highest part of something pointed or curved: *the apex of the roof* **2** the most important position in an organization or society

aphrodisiac /ˌæfrə'dɪziæk◂/ *n* [C] a food, drink, or drug that makes someone want to have sex

apiece /ə'piːs/ *adv* each: *Roses cost £2 apiece.*

Apocalypse /ə'pɒkəlɪps $ ə'pɑː-/ *n* **the Apocalypse** the destruction and end of the world

apocalyptic /ə,pɒkə'lɪptɪk◂ $ ə,pɑː-/ *adj* warning people about terrible events that will happen in the future

apolitical /ˌeɪpə'lɪtɪkəl◂/ *adj* not interested in politics, or not connected with any political party

apologetic /ə,pɒlə'dʒetɪk◂ $ ə,pɑː-/ *adj* showing or saying that you are sorry that you did something bad or were responsible for it: *The manager was very apologetic.* | *an **apologetic** smile* —**apologetically** /-kli/ *adv*

apologize (*also* **-ise** *BrE*) /ə'pɒlədʒaɪz $ ə'pɑː-/ *v* [I] to tell someone that you are sorry that you have upset them or caused them problems: **apologize for (doing) sth** *He apologized for being late.* | **[+to]** *Apologize to your sister now!* | *I apologise. I was selfish.*

apology /ə'pɒlədʒi $ ə'pɑː-/ *n* [C] (*plural* **apologies**) something that you say or write to someone to show them that you are sorry for upsetting them or causing them problems

COLLOCATIONS

verbs

to make an apology *He made no apology for what had happened.*

to issue an apology (=to make an official public

apology) *The company issued an apology for the delay.*

to get/receive an apology *We got no apology or explanation from the school.*

to accept sb's apology *Please accept our apologies for the mistake.*

to demand an apology *He wrote a letter to the BBC demanding an apology.*

to owe sb an apology (=because you have been bad or unfair to them) *I was wrong. I owe you an apology.*

adjectives

a public apology *She won a public apology from her former boss.*

a full apology *He advised the newspaper to publish a full apology.*

a written apology *The family want a written apology.*

a formal apology *The government refused to make a formal apology for the war.*

apostle /əˈpɒsəl $ əˈpɑː-/ n [C] one of the 12 men chosen by Christ to teach people about the Christian religion

apostrophe /əˈpɒstrəfi $ əˈpɑː-/ n [C] **1** the sign (') that is used in writing to show that numbers or letters have been left out, for example 'don't' (=do not) and '86 (=1986) **2** the sign (') used before or after the letter 's' to show that something belongs or relates to someone or something, for example 'Laura's coat' or 'the boys' father' **3** the sign (') used before 's' to show the plural of letters and numbers: *Your r's look like v's.*

app /æp/ n [C] *informal* a piece of computer software which does a particular job SYN **application**

appal *BrE*, **appall** *AmE* /əˈpɔːl $ əˈpɒːl/ v [T] (**appalled**, **appalling**) if something appals you, it shocks and upsets you: *I was appalled by their racism.* —**appalled** adj

appalling /əˈpɔːlɪŋ $ əˈpɒː-/ adj **1** terrible and shocking: *children living in appalling conditions* **2** *informal* very bad: *The weather was appalling.* —**appallingly** adv

apparatus /ˌæpəˈreɪtəs $ -ˈræ-/ n [C,U] (*plural* **apparatus** or **apparatuses**) a set of equipment that is used for a particular purpose: *firemen wearing breathing apparatus*

apparel /əˈpærəl/ n [U] *formal* clothes

apparent Ac /əˈpærənt/ adj **1** easy to notice: *It soon became apparent that he hadn't read the report.* | *Suddenly, for no apparent reason, she started to cry.* **2** seeming to be real or true, although it may not be: *He was frustrated by his apparent lack of progress.*

apparently /əˈpærəntli/ adv **1** used to say that you have heard that something is true, but you are not completely sure about it: *Apparently, it's not the first time she's left him.* | *The conference was apparently a great success.* **2** according to the way someone looks or a situation appears, although you cannot be sure: *the unexplained death of an apparently healthy baby*

apparition /ˌæpəˈrɪʃən/ n [C] **1** a GHOST **2** someone who looks strange or frightening

appeal¹ /əˈpiːl/ n **1** [C] an urgent public request for help, money, information etc: [+for] *Police have issued an appeal for information.* | *The girl's parents have made a public appeal for her safe return.* | *The hospital has launched an appeal to raise £150,000.* **2** [C,U] a formal request to a court or to someone in authority asking for a decision to be changed: [+to] *an appeal to the European Court of Human Rights* | [+against] *He lost his appeal against a 6-month jail sentence.* **3** [U] if something has appeal, people think it is attractive or interesting: [+of] *the popular appeal of football* → SEX APPEAL

appeal² v **1** [I] to make a serious public request for help, money, information etc: [+for] *The President has appealed for calm.* | *Police are appealing for witnesses.* | **appeal to sb (to do sth)** *Hungary has appealed to foreign zoos to find the animals a home.* **2** [I,T] to make a formal request to a court or someone in authority asking for a decision to be changed: [+against] *He plans to appeal against his conviction.* **3** [I] if something appeals to you, you think it is attractive or interesting: [+to] *That idea doesn't appeal to me at all.*

appealing /əˈpiːlɪŋ/ adj attractive or interesting

appear /əˈpɪə $ əˈpɪr/ v **1** SEEM [linking verb] to seem: **appear to be/do sth** *The noise appeared to come from the bedroom.* | **appear worried/annoyed etc** *Mrs Poole appeared calm.* | **it appears that** *It appears that she's changed her mind.* THESAURUS ▶ SEEM **2** BE SEEN/ARRIVE [I] if someone or something appears, they can suddenly be seen or they suddenly arrive OPP **disappear**: *A man suddenly appeared from behind a tree.* | *Ruth appeared in the doorway.* **3** IN A FILM/PLAY [I] to take part in a film, play, concert, television programme etc: [+in/on] *He is currently appearing in 'Blood Brothers' at the Lyric Theatre.* **4** IN A BOOK/NEWSPAPER [I] to be written or shown in a newspaper, book, magazine etc: [+in] *The article appeared in the 'Independent' on 31st August.* **5** BE AVAILABLE [I] to become available or known about for the first time: *The calendars will appear in the shops in September.*

appearance /əˈpɪərəns $ əˈpɪr-/ n **1** WAY SB/STH LOOKS [C,U] the way that someone or something looks or seems: *Annette was always very concerned about her appearance.* | *The government wanted to give the appearance of doing something.* **2** IN A PUBLIC EVENT/FILM ETC [C] when someone takes part in a public event, play, concert, television programme etc: *I made my first TV appearance in 1957.* | *a series of public appearances* **3** FIRST USE [singular] when something new begins to exist or starts being used: [+of] *the appearance of the mini-skirt in 1965* **4** ARRIVAL [C usually singular] the unexpected or sudden arrival of someone or something: **[+of]** *The sudden appearance of her daughter startled her.*

appease /ə'pi:z/ v [T] *formal* to make someone less angry by giving them something that they want: *an attempt to appease critics of his regime* —**appeasement** n [C,U]

append Ac /ə'pend/ v [T] *formal* to add something to a piece of writing

appendage /ə'pendɪdʒ/ n [C] *formal* something that is attached to something bigger or more important

appendicitis /ə,pendɪ'saɪtɪs/ n [U] an illness in which your appendix swells and causes pain

appendix Ac /ə'pendɪks/ n [C] **1** (*plural* **appendixes**) a small organ near your BOWEL, which has little or no use **2** (*plural* **appendixes** or **appendices** /-dəsi:z/) a part at the end of a book that has additional information

appetite /'æpətaɪt/ n [C,U] **1** a desire for food: *I seem to have lost my appetite lately.* **2** a desire or liking for a particular activity: **[+for]** *her amazing appetite for work*

COLLOCATIONS

verbs

to have an appetite *She had no appetite, but she tried to eat.*

to lose your appetite *I was so excited I completely lost my appetite.*

to give sb an appetite *The walk has given us an appetite.*

to spoil/ruin your appetite (=to make you not feel like eating a meal) *Don't eat that now – it will spoil your appetite for dinner.*

adjectives

a big/huge appetite *All our family have huge appetites.*

a good/healthy appetite *He seems fine – he certainly has a good appetite.*

a small appetite *The reason she stays so slim is that she only has a small appetite.*

---

appetizer (*also* **-iser** *BrE*) /'æpətaɪzə $ -ər/ n [C] a small amount of food that you eat at the beginning of a meal SYN **starter** *BrE*

appetizing (*also* **-ising** *BrE*) /'æpətaɪzɪŋ/ adj food that is appetizing looks or smells very good

applaud /ə'plɔ:d $ ə'plɒ:d/ v **1** [I,T] to hit your hands together to show that you have enjoyed a play, concert, speaker etc SYN **clap**: *The audience applauded.* **2** [T] *formal* to praise something that someone does: *She should be applauded for her honesty.*

applause /ə'plɔ:z $ ə'plɒ:z/ n [U] the sound of people hitting their hands together to show that they have enjoyed a play, concert, speaker etc: *He was given a big round of applause* (=period of applause).

apple /'æpəl/ n [C,U] a hard round fruit that has a green, red, or yellow skin and is white inside: *apple pie* → see picture on page A4

appliance /ə'plaɪəns/ n [C] a piece of electrical equipment, such as a REFRIGERATOR or a WASHING MACHINE, that is used in people's homes

applicable /ə'plɪkəbəl, 'æplɪkəbəl/ adj affecting or concerning a particular person, group, or situation: **[+to]** *The legislation will be applicable to the whole country.*

applicant /'æplɪkənt/ n [C] someone who has formally asked, usually in writing, for a job, university place etc

application /,æplɪ'keɪʃən/ n

1 REQUEST [C] a formal request, usually in writing, for something such as a job, a university place, or permission to do something: **[+for]** *an application for a grant* | *job applications* | *You'll need to **fill in** an **application form***.

2 USE [C,U] a practical purpose for which a machine, idea etc can be used: *The research has many **practical applications***.

3 ON A COMPUTER [C] a piece of computer software which does a particular job

4 OF PAINT/CREAM ETC [C,U] when you put something such as paint or cream onto a surface

applied /ə'plaɪd/ adj **applied science/physics/ linguistics etc** a subject that is studied for a practical purpose → **pure**

apply /ə'plaɪ/ v (**applied**, **applying**, **applies**)

1 ASK FOR [I] to make a formal request, usually in writing, for something such as a job, a university place, or permission to do something: **[+for]** *Rob's **applied for** a job in Canada.* | *The company is **applying for** permission to demolish the building.* | **apply to do sth** *I've **applied to** join the army.* THESAURUS ▶ ASK

2 CONCERN [I] to concern or affect a particular person, group, or situation: **[+to]** *Do the same rules apply to part-time workers?*

3 USE [T] to use something such as a method, idea, or law: **apply sth to sth** *the value of applying these techniques to archaeology* THESAURUS ▶ USE

4 WORK HARD **apply yourself (to sth)** to work very hard and carefully on something, especially for a long time: *If only he had applied himself to his studies!*

5 PAINT/CREAM [T] to put something such as paint or cream onto a surface: *Apply the paint using a sponge.* | *a brush for applying make-up*

appoint /ə'pɔɪnt/ v [T] to formally give someone a job or position: *The school's just appointed a new head teacher.* | **appoint sb to sth** *She's been appointed to the Board of Directors.* | **appoint sb (as) sth** *He was appointed Chief Engineer.*

appointed /ə'pɔɪntɪd/ adj **the appointed day/ time/place etc** the time, date etc that has or had been decided: *I reported to H.Q. at the appointed time.*

appointment /ə'pɔɪntmənt/ n

1 [C] an arrangement for a meeting at an agreed time and place, for a particular purpose: *I don't want to be late for my appointment.* | **[+with]** *She has an appointment with a client at 10.30.* THESAURUS ▶ **MEETING**

2 [C,U] an occasion when someone is formally given a job or position: **[+of]** *the appointment of a new Archbishop*

COLLOCATIONS

verbs

to have an appointment *I have an appointment with Dr Simons.*

to make/arrange an appointment *She made an appointment to see her lawyer.*

to cancel an appointment *I had to cancel my appointment at the hairdresser's.*

to miss an appointment (=to not go to a meeting you have arranged) *She got stuck in traffic and missed the appointment.*

types of appointment

a doctor's appointment *He may be a little late – he has a doctor's appointment.*

a dentist's/dental appointment *I called to make a dental appointment.*

a business appointment *She has business appointments all morning.*

---

apportion /əˈpɔːʃən $ -ɔːr-/ v [T] formal to decide how something should be shared between various people: *We are not here to **apportion blame** (=say who deserves to be blamed).*

appraisal /əˈpreɪzəl/ n [C,U] an official description of how valuable, effective, or successful someone or something is: *an annual appraisal of employees' work*

appraise /əˈpreɪz/ v [T] formal to carefully decide how valuable, important etc something is: *She appraised her handiwork.*

appreciable Ac /əˈpriːʃəbəl/ adj formal noticeable or important: *Three years in China had had an appreciable effect on him.* —**appreciably** adv

appreciate Ac /əˈpriːʃieɪt/ v [T] 1 to understand how serious or important a situation or problem is or what someone's feelings are: *He did not **fully** appreciate the significance of signing the contract.* | *[+that/how etc] I don't think you appreciate how busy I am.* 2 to be grateful for something: *Aunt Kate really appreciated the card you sent.* | *I'd appreciate it if you came along tonight* (=please come). 3 to understand how good or useful someone or something is: *The Americans, however, appreciated his talents.*

appreciation Ac /əˌpriːʃiˈeɪʃən/ n 1 [U] pleasure you feel when you realize something is good, useful, or well done: *[+of] She has a fine appreciation of music.* 2 [U] a feeling of being grateful to someone: *Let's **show** our **appreciation** by buying her a small gift.* 3 [C,U] an understanding of the importance or meaning of something: *[+of] The course helped me gain a better appreciation of children's needs.*

appreciative /əˈpriːʃətɪv/ adj showing that you have enjoyed something or feel grateful for it —**appreciatively** adv

apprehend /ˌæprɪˈhend/ v [T] formal if the police apprehend a criminal, they catch them and take them to a police station SYN **arrest**

apprehension /ˌæprɪˈhenʃən/ n [U] anxiety or fear about something in the future: *She felt sick with apprehension.*

apprehensive /ˌæprɪˈhensɪv◂/ adj anxious or afraid about something in the future —**apprehensively** adv

apprentice /əˈprentɪs/ n [C] someone who works for an employer for a fixed amount of time in order to learn a skill

apprenticeship /əˈprentəʃɪp/ n [C,U] the job of being an apprentice, or the period of time in which you are an apprentice

approach¹ Ac /əˈprəʊtʃ $ əˈprəʊtʃ/ v
1 [I,T] to move nearer to someone or something: *Slowly, he approached the bed.* | *A car approached and stopped.*
2 [T] to ask someone to do something, especially when you are not sure if they will want to do it: *She's been approached by two schools about a teaching job.*
3 [I,T] if an event or particular time is approaching, or if you are approaching it, it will happen soon: *It was approaching 4.15 p.m.*
4 [T] to begin to deal with a situation or problem in a particular way: *It all depends on how you approach the problem.*

approach² Ac n
1 WAY OF DOING STH [C] a general way of doing something or dealing with a problem: *[+to] a new approach to teaching languages* THESAURUS ▶ WAY
2 REQUEST [C] a request: *[+to] An approach to the landlord may be necessary.*
3 OF A FUTURE EVENT the fact that a future time or event is getting closer: *the approach of winter*
4 MOVEMENT CLOSER [U] movement closer to something: *Our approach frightened the birds.*
5 ROAD/PATH [C] a road or path leading to a place: *an approach road*

approachable /əˈprəʊtʃəbəl $ əˈprəʊtʃ-/ adj friendly and easy to talk to OPP **unapproachable**

approbation /ˌæprəˈbeɪʃən/ n [U] formal praise or approval

appropriate¹ Ac /əˈprəʊpri-ət $ əˈprəʊ-/ adj suitable for a particular time, situation, or purpose OPP **inappropriate**: *[+for] clothes that are appropriate for a job interview* | *[+to] an education system which is more appropriate to the needs of the students* | *It would not **be appropriate** for me to discuss that now.* THESAURUS SUITABLE —**appropriately** adv —**appropriateness** n [U]

appropriate² /əˈprəʊprieɪt $ əˈprəʊ-/ v [T] formal to steal or take something

approval /əˈpruːvəl/ n [U]
1 when a plan, decision, or person is officially accepted: *[+for] We have obtained approval for the funding.* | *The president has already **given** his **approval** to the plan.*
2 the opinion that someone or something is good OPP **disapproval**: *I was always trying to **win** my father's **approval**.* | *Does the design **meet** with your **approval** (=do you like it)?*

approve /əˈpruːv/ v
1 [T] to officially accept a plan or idea: *We are waiting for our proposals to be approved.*
2 [I] to think that someone or something is good, right, or suitable OPP **disapprove**: *[+of] My parents didn't approve of my friends.* | *I don't approve of taking drugs.*

approving /ə'pruːvɪŋ/ *adj* showing support or agreement for something OPP **disapproving**: *an approving nod* —**approvingly** *adv*

approx /ə'prɒks $ ə'prɑːks/ the written abbreviation of **approximately**

approximate[1] Ac /ə'prɒksəmət $ ə'prɑːk-/ *adj* not exact, but nearly right: *These figures are only approximate.*

approximate[2] Ac /ə'prɒksɪmeɪt $ ə'prɑːk-/ *v* [I, linking verb] *formal* to be similar to but not exactly the same as something else —**approximation** /ə,prɒksə'meɪʃən $ ə,prɑːk-/ *n* [C,U]

approximately /ə'prɒksəmətli $ ə'prɑːks-/ *adv* a little more or a little less than an exact number, amount etc: *The plane will be landing in approximately 20 minutes.*

THESAURUS

approximately a little more or less than an exact number, amount etc: *Birmingham is approximately 100 miles from London.*

about/around approximately. **About** and **around** are much more common than **approximately** in everyday spoken English: *I'll be back at about 5:30.*

roughly approximately – used especially when the exact number or amount is not very important: *We're expecting roughly 100 people to come.*

or so *informal* used after a number or amount to show that it may be a little more or less: *I'm going on holiday in a month or so.*

---

apricot /'eɪprəkɒt $ 'æprəkɑːt/ *n* [C] a small soft yellow fruit with one large seed → see picture on page A4

April /'eɪprəl/ *n* [C,U] (*written abbreviation* **Apr.**) the fourth month of the year, between March and May: **next/last April** *I'm going to Cuba next April.* | **in April** *Our new office opened in April.* | **on April 6th** *The meeting was on April 6th.*

April 'Fool's Day *n* [singular] April 1, a day when people play tricks on each other

apron /'eɪprən/ *n* [C] a piece of clothing that you wear to protect your clothes, especially when you are cooking

apt /æpt/ *adj* **1** exactly suitable: *an apt remark* **2** **be apt to do sth** to be likely to do something: *They're good kids but apt to get into trouble.* —**aptly** *adv*

aptitude /'æptɪtjuːd $ -tuːd/ *n* [C,U] a natural ability to do something well

aquarium /ə'kweəriəm $ ə'kwer-/ *n* [C] **1** a clear glass or plastic container for fish and other water animals **2** a building where people go to look at fish and other water animals

Aquarius /ə'kweəriəs $ ə'kwer-/ *n* **1** [U] the sign of the Zodiac of people born between January 21 and February 19 **2** [C] someone who has this sign

aquatic /ə'kwætɪk, ə'kwɒ- $ ə'kwæ-, ə'kwɑː-/ *adj* living or happening in water: *aquatic plants* | *aquatic sports*

aqueduct /'ækwədʌkt/ *n* [C] a structure like a bridge that takes water across a valley

Arab /'ærəb/ *n* [C] someone whose language is Arabic and whose family come from the Middle East or North Africa —**Arab** *adj*: *Arab countries*

Arabic /'ærəbɪk/ *n* [U] the language of Arab people and the religious language of Islam

arable /'ærəbəl/ *adj* relating to growing crops: *arable land*

arbiter /'ɑːbɪtə $ 'ɑːrbɪtər/ *n* [C] **1** someone who settles an argument between two opposing sides **2** **arbiter of fashion/taste etc** someone who judges what is fashionable, attractive etc

arbitrary Ac /'ɑːbɪtrəri, -tri $ 'ɑːrbətreri/ *adj* decided or arranged without any reason or plan, often unfairly: *an arbitrary decision* —**arbitrarily** /'ɑːbɪtrərəli $,ɑːrbə'trerəli/ *adv*

arbitrate /'ɑːbɪtreɪt $ 'ɑːr-/ *v* [I,T] to officially judge how an argument between two opposing sides should be solved —**arbitrator** *n* [C] —**arbitration** /,ɑːbɪ'treɪʃən $,ɑːr-/ *n* [U]

arc /ɑːk $ ɑːrk/ *n* [C] part of a circle or any curved line

arcade /ɑː'keɪd $ ɑːr-/ *n* [C] **1** a place where people go to play games on machines: *an amusement arcade* **2** (*also* **shopping arcade** BrE) a large building where there are a lot of shops

ARCH

arch[1] /ɑːtʃ $ ɑːrtʃ/ *n* [C] **1** a structure with a curved top that supports the weight of a bridge or building: *We walked under an arch into a small courtyard.* **2** the curved middle part of the bottom of your foot —**arched** *adj*: *an arched doorway*

arch[2] *v* [I,T] to form a curved shape, or to make something form a curved shape: *The cat arched her back and hissed.*

archaeology (*also* **archeology** AmE) /,ɑːki'ɒlədʒi $,ɑːrki'ɑː-/ *n* [U] the study of ancient societies by examining what remains of their buildings, tools, places they were buried etc —**archaeologist** *n* [C]: *The site is being studied by archaeologists.* —**archaeological** /,ɑːkiə'lɒdʒɪkəl◂ $,ɑːrkiə'lɑː-/ *adj*: *an archaeological site*

archaic /ɑː'keɪ-ɪk $ ɑːr-/ *adj* very old-fashioned or no longer used: *archaic words*

archbishop /,ɑːtʃ'bɪʃəp◂ $,ɑːrtʃ-/ *n* [C] a Christian priest of the highest rank, who is in charge of all the churches in a particular area

archeology /ˌɑːkiˈɒlədʒi $ ˌɑːrkiˈɑː-/ n an American spelling of ARCHAEOLOGY

archery /ˈɑːtʃəri $ ˈɑːr-/ n [U] the sport of shooting ARROWS from a BOW —**archer** n [C]

archetype /ˈɑːkɪtaɪp $ ˈɑːr-/ n [C usually singular] a perfect example of something, because it has all the most important features, qualities etc of that thing —**archetypal** /ˌɑːkɪˈtaɪpəl◂ $ ˌɑːr-/ adj: Byron was the archetypal Romantic hero.

architect /ˈɑːkətekt $ ˈɑːr-/ n [C] someone who designs buildings

architecture /ˈɑːkətektʃə $ ˈɑːrkətektʃər/ n [U] **1** the style and design of buildings: medieval architecture **2** the job or skill of designing buildings —**architectural** /ˌɑːkəˈtektʃərəl◂ $ ˌɑːr-/ adj

archive /ˈɑːkaɪv $ ˈɑːr-/ n [C usually plural] a place where a lot of historical records are stored, or the records that are stored

archway /ˈɑːtʃweɪ $ ˈɑːrtʃ-/ n [C] a passage or entrance under an ARCH

Arctic¹ /ˈɑːktɪk $ ˈɑːrk-/ adj **1** relating to the most northern part of the world near the North Pole **2** (also **arctic**) extremely cold: arctic conditions

Arctic² n **the Arctic** the very cold area around the North Pole → **Antarctic**

ardent /ˈɑːdənt $ ˈɑːr-/ adj supporting or wanting something very strongly: an ardent football supporter | an ardent desire to win

ardour BrE, **ardor** AmE /ˈɑːdə $ ˈɑːrdər/ n [U] formal very strong admiration or love

arduous /ˈɑːdjuəs $ ˈɑːrdʒuəs/ adj involving a lot of strength and hard work: an **arduous task** | an **arduous journey**

are /ə; strong ɑː $ ər; strong ɑːr/ v the present tense plural and second person singular of BE

area Ac /ˈeəriə $ ˈeriə/ n [C]
1 a part of a country, town etc: Dad grew up in the Portland area. | [+of] a working-class area of Birmingham
2 a part of a house, office, garden etc that is used for a particular purpose: Their apartment has a large kitchen area.
3 a particular subject or type of activity: The course covers three main **subject areas**.
4 the size of a flat surface: an area of 200 square miles → **CATCHMENT AREA, NO-GO AREA**

COLLOCATIONS

adjectives

a big/wide/large area The snow fell over a wide area.

your local area We don't have a supermarket in our local area.

a rural area (=in the countryside) There is a need for better public transport in rural areas.

a remote area (=a long way from towns and cities) They visited a remote area of northeast Afghanistan.

an urban area (=in a town or city) Most people live in urban areas.

a built-up area (=with a lot of buildings and people) Speed limits are lower in built-up areas.

a residential/industrial area (=mostly containing people's homes/industry) This is a quiet residential area of Bristol.

'area ˌcode n [C] the part of a telephone number that you have to add for a different town or country

arena /əˈriːnə/ n **1** [C] a building with a large flat central area surrounded by raised seats, used for sports or entertainment: a sports arena **2** **the political/public/international etc arena** all the people and activities connected with politics, the government etc: Women are entering the political arena in larger numbers.

aren't /ɑːnt $ ˈɑːrənt/ **1** the short form of 'are not': They aren't here. **2** the short form of 'am not', used in questions: I'm in big trouble, aren't I?

arguable /ˈɑːgjuəbəl $ ˈɑːr-/ adj **1** it is arguable that used to say that something might be true: It's arguable that the new law will make things better. **2** not certain, or not definitely true, and therefore easy to doubt: Whether he's the right person for the job is arguable.

arguably /ˈɑːgjuəbli $ ˈɑːr-/ adv used to say that there are good reasons for saying that something is true: Senna was arguably the greatest racing driver of all time.

argue /ˈɑːgjuː $ ˈɑːr-/ v
1 [I] to shout and say angry things to someone because you disagree with them: We could hear the neighbours arguing. | [+about/over] They always seem to be arguing about money. | [+with] Stop arguing with me!
2 [I,T] to clearly explain why you think something is true or should be done: [+that] She argued that most teachers are underpaid. | [+for/against] Baker argued against cutting the military budget. | She **argued the case** for changing the law.

argument /ˈɑːgjəmənt $ ˈɑːr-/ n [C]
1 a situation in which people speak angrily to each other because they disagree about something: [+about/over] an argument about who was responsible for the accident | [+with] I had an argument with my mother.
2 a set of reasons that show that something is true or untrue, right or wrong etc: [+for/against] a **powerful argument** against smoking | [+that] the familiar argument that the costs outweigh the benefits

COLLOCATIONS

verbs

to have an argument My boyfriend and I had a big argument.

to get into an argument They were always getting into arguments with their neighbours.

to start an argument She seemed to want to start an argument.

to win/lose an argument Are you the sort of person who can't bear to lose an argument?

an argument breaks out (=it starts) An argument broke out between two women waiting in line.

adjectives

a big/huge/massive argument There was a massive argument about who was right.

a heated/furious argument (=involving very strong feelings) *I could hear people having a heated argument.*

argument a situation in which people speak angrily to each other because they disagree about something: *The woman was having an argument with the waiter.*

row *BrE*, **fight** *especially AmE* an argument between people who know each other well, in which they shout at each other: *The couple were always having rows with each other.*

quarrel *especially BrE* an argument in which people who know each other well get very angry and upset, and which often lasts a long time: *a family quarrel* | *He had a violent quarrel with his father and they didn't speak to each other for years.*

disagreement a situation in which people disagree, but without shouting or getting angry: *There was a slight disagreement over the rules of the game.*

squabble a short argument about something that is not important: *The children were having a squabble about who should sit in the front of the car.*

dispute an argument when two people, groups, or countries publicly disagree about something: *The workers were involved in a bitter dispute over pay.* | *a border dispute*

argumentative /ˌɑːgjəˈmentətɪv◂ $ ˌɑːr-/ *adj* someone who is argumentative often argues or likes arguing

aria /ˈɑːriə/ *n* [C] a song that is sung by only one person in an OPERA

arid /ˈærɪd/ *adj formal* very dry and with very little rain: *arid land* | *an arid climate*

Aries /ˈeəriːz, ˈeəriiːz $ ˈeriːz/ *n* **1** [U] the sign of the Zodiac of people born between March 21 and April 20 **2** [C] someone who has this sign

arise /əˈraɪz/ *v* [I] (*past tense* **arose** /əˈrəʊz $ əˈroʊz/*, past participle* **arisen** /əˈrɪzən/) **1** if a problem or difficult situation arises, it begins to happen: *A crisis has arisen in the Foreign Office.* **2** *literary* to get out of bed, or to stand up

aristocracy /ˌærəˈstɒkrəsi $ -ˈstɑː-/ *n* [C] (*plural* **aristocracies**) the people in the highest social class, who traditionally have a lot of land, money, and power: *a member of the aristocracy* —**aristocrat** /ˈærɪstəkræt, əˈrɪs- $ əˈrɪs-/ *n* [C]: *a wealthy aristocrat* —**aristocratic** /ˌærɪstəˈkrætɪk/ *adj*

arithmetic /əˈrɪθmətɪk/ *n* [U] the science of numbers involving adding, multiplying etc → **mathematics** —**arithmetic** /ˌærɪθˈmetɪk◂/ *adj* —**arithmetically** /-kli/ *adv*

arm¹ /ɑːm $ ɑːrm/ *n* [C]
1 BODY PART one of the two long parts of your body between your shoulders and your hands: **left/right arm** *He had a tattoo on his left arm.* | *I put my arms around him.* | *They walked along arm in arm* (=with their arms bent around each other's). | **cross/fold**

your arms (=bend your arms so that they are resting on top of each other against your body) | **under your arm** *I was carrying a pile of books under my arm.* → see picture on page A2
2 CLOTHES the part of a piece of clothing that covers your arm SYN **sleeve**
3 CHAIR the part of a chair that you rest your arm on
4 WEAPONS **arms** [plural] weapons: *the sale of arms to other countries* | *the arms trade* | *an arms dealer* (=a company that sells weapons) | *a new international agreement on arms control* (=limiting the number of weapons that countries are allowed to have)
5 LONG OBJECT a long part of an object or piece of equipment: *The cutting wheel is on the end of a steel arm.* → **twist sb's arm** at TWIST¹

PHRASES
be up in arms about sth to be very angry about something: *The whole town is up in arms about the closure of the hospital.*
welcome sb/sth with open arms to show that you are very happy and eager to see someone or to accept an idea or plan: *We welcomed the offer with open arms.*

arm² *v* [I,T] to provide weapons for someone OPP **disarm**

armaments /ˈɑːməmənts $ ˈɑːr-/ *n* [plural] weapons and military equipment: *nuclear armaments*

armband /ˈɑːmbænd $ ˈɑːrm-/ *n* [C] a band of material that you wear around the top part of your arm

armchair /ˈɑːmtʃeə, ˌɑːmˈtʃeə $ ˈɑːrmtʃer, ˌɑːrmˈtʃer/ *n* [C] a comfortable chair with sides that you can rest your arms on → see picture at CHAIR¹

armed /ɑːmd $ ɑːrmd/ *adj*
1 carrying weapons: *an armed guard* | **[+with]** *The suspect is armed with a shotgun.* | *He got ten years in prison for armed robbery* (=stealing using a gun).
2 **armed with sth** having something useful that you need: *I went into the meeting armed with a copy of the report.*

armed 'forces *n* **the armed forces** a country's military organizations such as the army

armful /ˈɑːmfʊl $ ˈɑːrm-/ *n* [C] the amount of something that you can hold in one or both arms: **[+of]** *an armful of books*

armistice /ˈɑːmɪstɪs $ ˈɑːrm-/ *n* [C] an agreement to stop fighting

armour *BrE*, **armor** *AmE* /ˈɑːmə $ ˈɑːrmər/ *n* [U]
1 metal or leather clothing worn in past times by men in battle: *a suit of armour* **2** a layer of strong material that protects something

armoured *BrE*, **armored** *AmE* /ˈɑːməd $ ˈɑːrmərd/ *adj* protected against bullets or other weapons by a strong layer of metal: *an armoured car*

armoury *BrE*, **armory** *AmE* /ˈɑːməri $ ˈɑːr-/ *n* (*plural* **armouries**) a place where weapons are stored

armpit /ˈɑːmpɪt $ ˈɑːrm-/ *n* [C] the hollow place under your arm where it joins your body

'arms race n [C usually singular] the competition between different countries to have a larger number of powerful weapons

army /ˈɑːmi $ ˈɑːr-/ n [C] (plural **armies**)
1 a military force that fights wars on land: *He joined the army when he was 17.* | **in the army** *Her son is in the army.* | *the US army*
2 a large group of people or animals involved in the same activity: **[+of]** *an army of ants*

A-road /ˈeɪ rəʊd $ -roʊd/ n [C] a main road in Britain that is smaller than a MOTORWAY

aroma /əˈrəʊmə $ əˈroʊ-/ n [C] a strong pleasant smell: **[+of]** *the aroma of fresh coffee* **THESAURUS** SMELL **—aromatic** /ˌærəˈmætɪk◂/ adj: *aromatic oils*

aromatherapy /əˌrəʊməˈθerəpi $ əˌroʊ-/ n [U] the use of pleasant smelling plant oils to make you feel healthy and relaxed **—aromatherapist** n [C]

arose /əˈrəʊz $ əˈroʊz/ v the past tense of ARISE

around /əˈraʊnd/ (also **round** BrE) adv, prep
1 surrounding something or someone: *We put a fence around the yard.* | *Mario put his arms around her.*
2 in a circular movement: *Water pushes the wheel around.* | *They danced around the bonfire.*
3 to or in many parts of a place: *Stan showed me around the office.* | *an international company with offices all around the world*
4 in or near a particular place: *Is there a bank around here?* | *Is your dad around?*
5 on or to the other side of something: *There's a door around the back.*
6 existing: *That joke's been around for years.*
7 used to say that someone or something turns so that they face in the opposite direction: *I'll turn the car around and pick you up at the door.*
8 (also **about** especially BrE) used when guessing a number, amount, time etc, without being exact **SYN approximately**: *The stadium seats around 50,000 people.* **THESAURUS** APPROXIMATELY

arouse /əˈraʊz/ v [T] **1** to make someone have a particular feeling: *Her behaviour aroused the suspicions of the police.* **2** to make someone feel sexually excited **—arousal** n [U]

arrange /əˈreɪndʒ/ v
1 [I,T] to make plans and preparations for something to happen: *I've arranged a meeting with Jim.* | **arrange to do sth** *Have you arranged to play football on Sunday?* | **arrange for sb to do sth** *Dave arranged for someone to drive us home.* | **[+that]** *We arranged that I would go and stay with them for the weekend.*
2 [T] to put a group of things or people in a particular order or position: *The list is arranged alphabetically.* | *She arranged the flowers in a vase.*

ar,ranged 'marriage n [C,U] a marriage in which your parents choose a husband or wife for you

arrangement /əˈreɪndʒmənt/ n
1 [C usually plural] plans and preparations that you must make so that something can happen in the future: **[+for]** *Lee's still making arrangements for the wedding.* | *We haven't finalized our travel arrangements yet.*

2 [C,U] something that has been organized or agreed on **SYN agreement**: **[+with]** *We have a special arrangement with the bank.* | **arrangement to do sth** *Max cancelled our arrangement to meet.*
3 [C] a group of things in a particular position or order: *a flower arrangement*

array /əˈreɪ/ n [C usually singular] a group of people or things, especially one that is large or impressive: **[+of]** *a dazzling array of young dancers*

arrears /əˈrɪəz $ əˈrɪrz/ n [plural] money that is owed and should already have been paid: *You'll have to pay off the arrears later.*
PHRASES
  be in arrears to owe someone money because your regular payment to them is late: *We're six weeks in arrears with the rent.*

arrest¹ /əˈrest/ v [T]
1 if the police arrest someone, the person is taken away because the police think they have done something illegal: **arrest sb for sth** *The police arrested Eric for shoplifting.*
2 formal to stop something happening: *drugs that are used to arrest the spread of the disease*

arrest² n [C,U] when the police take someone away and guard them because they may have done something illegal: *The police expect to make an arrest soon.* | **under arrest** *A man is under arrest following the murder of two teenage girls.*

arrival /əˈraɪvəl/ n
1 [U] when you arrive somewhere **OPP departure**: *Shortly after our arrival in Florida, Lottie got robbed.*
2 **the arrival of sth** the time when a new idea, method, product etc is first used or discovered: *The arrival of the personal computer changed the way we work.*
3 [C] a person or thing that has arrived recently: *a new arrival at the school*

arrive /əˈraɪv/ v [I]
1 **REACH A PLACE** to get to a place: *Your letter arrived yesterday.* | **[+in/at]** *The train finally arrived in New York at 8.30 p.m.* | *He arrived late as usual.* | *We arrived home at ten o'clock.*
2 to happen: *At last the big day arrived!*
3 **REACH A DECISION/SOLUTION** to reach a decision, solution etc: *The committee finally arrived at a decision.*
4 **START EXISTING** to begin to exist or to start being used: *Our sales have doubled since computer games arrived.*
5 **BABY** to be born: *It was just past midnight when the baby arrived.*

> **Grammar**
> You **arrive in** a country, city, or town: *He arrived in Australia on 24th July.* | *We arrived in Paris in August.*
> You **arrive at** a building or place: *We arrived at our hotel.* | *They finally arrived at Los Angeles Airport.* | *I arrived back at my house at 8.30.*
> You do not use a preposition with **here**, **there**, and **home**: *What time do you think he will arrive here?* | *We arrived there at one o'clock.* | *I arrived home after midnight.*

A

arrive to get to the place you are going to: *It was late when we arrived in Madrid.* | *I phoned to say that I'd arrived safely.*

get (to) to arrive somewhere. **Get to** is much more common in everyday spoken English than **arrive**: *What time did you get home?* | *By the time I got to the bank it was closed.*

reach to arrive somewhere, especially after a long or difficult journey: *It took them three days to reach the top of the mountain.*

turn up *informal* to arrive somewhere – used when you are waiting for someone, especially when they are late or do not come: *Steve turned up late as usual.*

get in to arrive – used about the time a plane, train etc arrives. Also used about the time you arrive home from work: *When does the next boat get in?* | *She normally gets in at about 6.30.*

arrogant /ˈærəgənt/ *adj* behaving in an unpleasant or rude way because you think you are more important than other people: *an arrogant, selfish man* **THESAURUS** PROUD —**arrogantly** *adv* —**arrogance** *n* [U]

arrow /ˈærəʊ $ ˈæroʊ/ *n* [C] **1** a thin straight weapon with a point at one end that you shoot from a BOW **2** a sign in the shape of an arrow, used to show direction

arsenal /ˈɑːsənəl $ ˈɑːr-/ *n* [C] a large number of weapons, or the building where they are stored

arsenic /ˈɑːsənɪk $ ˈɑːr-/ *n* [U] a very strong poison

arson /ˈɑːsən $ ˈɑːr-/ *n* [U] the crime of deliberately making a building burn **THESAURUS** CRIME —**arsonist** *n* [C]

art /ɑːt $ ɑːrt/ *n*
1 [U] the activity or skill of producing paintings, photographs etc, or paintings etc that are produced using this skill: *He's very good at art.* | **modern/contemporary art** | *lovers of* **fine art** (=paintings etc that are considered to be very high quality) | *important* **works of art**
2 the arts [plural] art, music, theatre, film, literature etc all considered together: *Government funding for the arts has been reduced.*
3 arts (*also* **the arts**) [plural] subjects you can study that are not scientific, for example history, languages etc
4 [C,U] the skill involved in making or doing something: **[+of]** *the art of writing* → CLIP ART, MARTIAL ART, PERFORMING ARTS

artefact *especially BrE*, **artifact** *especially AmE* /ˈɑːtəfækt $ ˈɑːr-/ *n* [C] an object such as a tool or weapon that was made in the past and is historically important: *Egyptian artefacts*

artery /ˈɑːtəri $ ˈɑːr-/ *n* [C] (*plural* **arteries**) **1** one of the tubes that takes blood from your heart to the rest of your body → see Word Choice at VEIN
2 *formal* a main road, railway line, or river

artful /ˈɑːtfəl $ ˈɑːrt-/ *adj* good at deceiving people —**artfully** *adv*

'art ,gallery *n* [C] a building where paintings are shown to the public

arthritis /ɑːˈθraɪtɪs $ ɑːr-/ *n* [U] a disease that causes the joints of your body to become swollen and very painful —**arthritic** /-ˈθrɪtɪk/ *adj*: *arthritic fingers*

artichoke /ˈɑːtɪtʃəʊk $ ˈɑːrtətʃoʊk/ *n* [C] a round green vegetable with thick pointed leaves and a firm base

article /ˈɑːtɪkəl $ ˈɑːr-/ *n* [C]
1 IN A NEWSPAPER a piece of writing in a newspaper or magazine: **[+on/about]** *an article on fishing* | *I read a very interesting article about the problem of teenage pregnancy.*
2 OBJECT a thing: *The museum has some very valuable articles.* | *an* **article of clothing** (=a shirt, sock etc)
3 IN GRAMMAR *technical* in grammar, the word 'the' (=the definite article), or the words 'a' or 'an' (=the indefinite article)

articulate¹ /ɑːˈtɪkjələt $ ɑːr-/ *adj* able to express your thoughts and feelings clearly OPP **inarticulate**: *a bright and articulate child* —**articulately** *adv*

articulate² /ɑːˈtɪkjəleɪt $ ɑːr-/ *v* [T] to put your thoughts or feelings into words: *She found it difficult to articulate her fears.*

articulated /ɑːˈtɪkjəleɪtɪd $ ɑːr-/ *adj especially BrE* an articulated vehicle has two parts joined together to make it easier to turn: *an articulated lorry*

artifact /ˈɑːtəfækt $ ˈɑːr-/ *n* [C] *especially AmE* another spelling of ARTEFACT

artificial /ˌɑːtɪˈfɪʃəl◂ $ ˌɑːr-/ *adj*
1 not real or natural but made to be like something that is real or natural OPP **natural**: *a vase of artificial flowers* | *foods that contain artificial flavourings and sweeteners*
2 *disapproving* not natural or sincere OPP **genuine**: *an artificial smile* —**artificially** *adv*

artificial not real or natural, but made to be like something real or natural: *artificial snow* | *artificial light* | *She has an artificial leg.*

synthetic synthetic materials or substances are made by chemical processes, not natural processes: *synthetic materials like polyester* | *synthetic rubber*

man-made man-made materials, lakes, hills etc are made by people and are not made naturally: *man-made fibres* | *a man-made lake*

imitation not real, but made to look exactly like something real – used especially about guns, jewellery, and leather: *The man was carrying an imitation gun.* | *The diamonds aren't real – they're imitation.*

false false teeth, EYELASHes etc are made to look like real ones: *He was wearing a false moustache.* | *a false beard*

virtual used about something that you experience by watching a computer screen, rather than in the real world: *You can take a virtual tour of the house online.* | *a virtual world*

artificial in'telligence n [U] (written abbreviation **AI**) the science of how to make computers do things that people can do, such as make decisions and understand language

artificial respi'ration n [U] a way of making someone breathe again when they have stopped, by blowing air into their mouth

artillery /ɑːˈtɪləri $ ɑːr-/ n [U] big heavy guns, usually on wheels

artisan /ˌɑːtɪˈzæn $ ˈɑːrtɪzən/ n [C] formal someone who does skilled work, making things by hand

artist /ˈɑːtɪst $ ˈɑːr-/ n [C]
1 someone who produces art, especially paintings
2 a professional performer such as a singer or dancer

artiste /ɑːˈtiːst $ ɑːr-/ n [C] formal a professional performer such as a singer or dancer

artistic /ɑːˈtɪstɪk $ ɑːr-/ adj **1** [only before noun] relating to art or culture: the artistic director of the Metropolitan Opera **2** good at painting, drawing etc: She was so artistic and creative. —**artistically** /-kli/ adv

artistry /ˈɑːtəstri $ ˈɑːr-/ n [U] great skill in a particular activity

artwork /ˈɑːtwɜːk $ ˈɑːrtwɜːrk/ n **1** [U] pictures, photographs etc that are prepared for a book, magazine etc **2** [C,U] paintings and other pieces of art: an exhibition of contemporary artworks

arty /ˈɑːti $ ˈɑːrti/ BrE, **artsy** /ˈɑːtsi $ ˈɑːrt-/ AmE adj disapproving showing an interest in art in a way that seems pretended: an arty film

as /əz; strong æz/ adv, prep, linking word
1 used to compare people or things: **as ... as** Her hands were as cold as ice. | We must decide **as soon as possible** (=very soon). | You're **the same** age **as** me. | Tom works **just as** hard as the others.
2 used to say what job someone has or what purpose something has: Mum worked as a teacher before she married. | What can we use as a bandage?
3 in a particular way or state: Please leave my desk as it is.
4 used when what you are saying is already known about: **As you know**, I'm leaving at the end of this month. | **As I said before**, money is our biggest problem.
5 while something is happening: As I was walking home, I realized I had left my bag behind. | The phone rang **just as** I was leaving.
6 because: As you've apologised, I won't tell anyone. → **as long as** at LONG², **as a matter of fact** at MATTER¹, **so as to do sth** at SO², **such as** at SUCH, **as well (as sb/sth)** at WELL¹, **as yet** at YET¹

PHRASES
as for sb used when you are starting to talk about a different person: John's ill and as for me, I'm too busy to help.
as if/as though used when you are saying how someone or something seems: She looked as if she had been crying. | It looks as though it might rain.
as of/as from today/next week etc formal starting from a particular time: The change comes into effect as of January 1.

asap /ˌeɪ es eɪ ˈpiː, ˈeɪsæp/ adv the abbreviation of **as soon as possible**

asbestos /æsˈbestəs/ n [U] a grey material that does not burn and was used in buildings in the past

ascend /əˈsend/ v [I,T] formal to move to a higher position **OPP** **descend**: The plane ascended rapidly.
PHRASES
ascend the throne to become king or queen: A new emperor, Dinh Bo Linh, ascended the throne in 967.
in ascending order arranged so that each thing in a group is bigger, more important etc than the one before: Their ages, in ascending order, are 4, 7, 10, and 14.

ascendancy, **ascendency** /əˈsendənsi/ n [U] formal a position of increasing power, influence, or control: Conservative ideals are **in the ascendancy**.

ascent /əˈsent/ n formal **1** [C usually singular] when someone or something moves to a higher position **OPP** **descent**: the ascent of Mount Everest **2** [U] when someone becomes more important or successful **3** [C] a path or hill that goes upwards: a **steep ascent**

ascertain /ˌæsəˈteɪn $ ˌæsər-/ v [T] formal to discover the truth about something: **ascertain who/whether/what etc** The investigation failed to ascertain how she died.

ascetic /əˈsetɪk/ adj living a simple life with no physical comforts

ascribe /əˈskraɪb/ v
PHRASAL VERBS
ascribe sth **to** sb/sth formal to say that something is caused by a particular person or thing: Can we ascribe the rise in asthma to an increase in pollution?

asexual /eɪˈsekʃuəl/ adj technical not having or using sexual organs: asexual reproduction

ash /æʃ/ n **1** [U] the grey powder that is left after something has burned: cigarette ash → see picture at **VOLCANO** **2** **ashes** [plural] the powder that remains after a dead body has been CREMATEd (=burned) **3** [C,U] a type of tree that grows in forests in Britain and North America

ashamed /əˈʃeɪmd/ adj [not before noun] feeling very sorry or guilty about something bad you have done, or someone in your family has done: **[+of]** Mike **felt ashamed** of his own behaviour. | Some children are ashamed of their parents. | Crying is **nothing to be ashamed of** (=you shouldn't feel ashamed). | **be ashamed to do sth** I'm ashamed to admit I only scored 20. | **[+that]** They were ashamed that they had not offered to help.

THESAURUS

ashamed feeling very sorry and guilty about something bad you have done, or someone in your family has done: I felt ashamed that I had lied to her.
embarrassed feeling uncomfortable and worried that you look silly, for example because you have made a mistake: He was embarrassed that he couldn't remember her name.
humiliated very embarrassed and upset because someone has made you seem weak or

stupid: *She humiliated him in front of all his friends.*
feel bad/guilty to feel bad or guilty because of something that you did or should have done: *I feel bad about forgetting your birthday.*

ashen /'æʃən/ *adj* very pale because of shock or fear: *Her face was ashen.*

ashore /ə'ʃɔː $ ə'ʃɔːr/ *adv* towards the side of a lake or sea: *His body was **washed ashore**.*

ashtray /'æʃtreɪ/ *n* [C] a small dish used to collect cigarette ASH (=the powder that is produced when it burns)

Asian /'eɪʃən, 'eɪʒən $ 'eɪʒən, 'eɪʃən/ *n* [C] someone who comes from Asia, or whose family came from Asia —**Asian** *adj*

aside¹ /ə'saɪd/ *adv* **1** if you keep something aside, you keep it so that you can use it or think about it later: **set/put sth aside** *Set aside an hour a week for practice.* **2** if you move something aside, you move it away from you, to the side: **move/step/push etc aside** *Bob pushed her aside in disgust.*

PHRASES

aside from sb/sth except for someone or something: *Aside from Stephen, everyone arrived on time.*

aside² *n* [C] something funny you say quietly so that only a few people hear

ask /ɑːsk $ æsk/ *v* [I,T]

1 QUESTION to speak or write to someone in order to get an answer: *'What time is it?' she asked.* | *Can I **ask a question**?* | *Let's **ask the way**.* | **ask sb sth** *I don't like it when people ask me my age.* | **ask (sb) who/what/if etc** *The officer asked who we were.* | *Ask Tom if he's got a spare pen.* | **ask (sb) about sth** *Did they ask about your experience?* | *She asked me about my job.*

Grammar
Do not say 'I will ask to him.' Say *I will ask him.*

2 FOR HELP/ADVICE/PERMISSION to make a request for help, advice, or permission: *If you need anything, just ask.* | **ask (sb) for sb/sth** *I had to ask my parents for money.* | *She rang the hospital and asked for Dr Harvey* (=asked whether she could speak to him). | **ask sb to do sth** *I asked Paula to email me the file.* | **ask (sb) if/whether** *Ask your mom if you can stay over.* | *I asked if I could use the phone.* | **ask to do sth** *Karen has asked to leave early on Friday.*
3 INVITE to invite someone to go somewhere: **ask sb out** (=invite someone to a film, restaurant etc because you like them) *Mark's too shy to ask girls out.* | **ask sb in/into sth** (=invite someone into your house, room etc) *Don't ask strangers into your house.* | **ask sb over/round** *informal* (=invite someone to your house) *They asked us over for a meal.*
4 PRICE to want a particular amount of money for something you are selling: *How much are you asking for the house?* | **ask £20/$2,000 etc for sth** *They're asking £5,000 for their old car.*
5 THINK CAREFULLY **ask yourself sth** to think very carefully and honestly about something: *Have you asked yourself whether you're doing the right thing?*

PHRASES

be asking for trouble/be asking for it *informal* used to say that doing something will cause problems: *Driving a motorbike without a helmet is just asking for trouble.*
don't ask me! *spoken informal* used to say that you do not know the answer to a question: *'When will you be finished?' 'Don't ask me!'*
if you ask me *spoken* used to emphasize your opinion: *If you ask me, you're all wrong.*

PHRASAL VERBS

ask after sb to ask someone about another person's health: *Jill was asking after you.*

THESAURUS

to ask a question

ask to speak or write to someone in order to get an answer: *Can I ask you a question?*
inquire/enquire *formal* to ask for information about something: *I'm writing to inquire about the job that was advertised in yesterday's 'Times'.*
consult *formal* to ask a doctor, lawyer, expert etc for information or advice: *If the problem continues, you may need to consult a doctor about it.*
question to ask someone a lot of questions, in order to get information about something, or to find out what they think: *Police are questioning a man about the attack.* | *Most of the people we questioned thought that the government was doing a good job.*
interrogate to ask someone a lot of questions for a long time, especially in an aggressive way: *The prisoners were interrogated and not allowed to sleep.*

to ask for something

ask for sth to tell someone that you want them to give you something: *I went to the bank and asked for a loan.*
order to ask for food or drink in a restaurant, or to ask a company to send you goods: *Daniel ordered another bottle of wine.* | *You can order direct from their website.*
apply to ask formally for a job, a place at a university etc by writing to someone or completing a form: *Which universities have you applied to?*
request *formal* to ask for something, especially official permission to do something: *The pilot requested permission to land.*
demand to ask for something in a firm or angry way: *Angry parents are demanding an explanation.*
beg to ask for something that you want or need very much, in an urgent way: *He begged me to stay.*
nag to keep asking someone for something, in an annoying way: *My parents are always nagging me to clean my room.*

askew /ə'skjuː/ *adv, adj* [not before noun] not straight or level: *His tie was askew and he smelt of brandy.*

asleep /ə'sliːp/ *adj* [not before noun] sleeping OPP **awake**: *Quiet! The baby's asleep.* | **fast/sound**

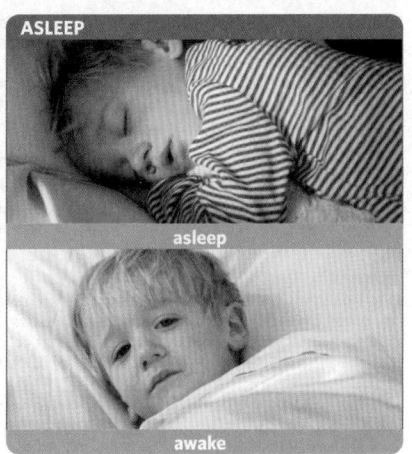

ASLEEP

asleep

awake

asleep (=sleeping very deeply) | *I **fell asleep*** (=started sleeping) *in front of the fire.* | *I was **half asleep*** (=very tired) *by the time we got home.* THESAURUS SLEEP

asparagus /əˈspærəgəs/ n [U] a long thin green vegetable → see picture on page A5

aspect `Ac` /ˈæspekt/ n [C] one part of a situation, plan, or subject: **[+of]** *What's the most interesting aspect of your work?*

aspersion /əˈspɜːʃən, -ʒən ʃ əˈspɜːrʒən/ n [C] *formal* an unkind remark or an unfair judgment: *No one is **casting aspersions on** you or your work.*

asphalt /ˈæsfælt ʃ ˈæsfɔːlt/ n [U] a hard black substance used on the surface of roads

asphyxiate /æsˈfɪksieɪt, əs-/ v [T] *formal* to stop someone breathing SYN **suffocate**: *Three children were asphyxiated by smoke.* —**asphyxiation** /æsˌfɪksiˈeɪʃən, əs-/ n [U]

aspiration /ˌæspəˈreɪʃən/ n [C usually plural, U] a strong desire to have or achieve something: **[+of]** *the **political aspirations** of their leaders*

aspire /əˈspaɪə ʃ əˈspaɪr/ v [I] to have a strong desire to achieve something: **[+to]** *students who aspire to a career in law* —**aspiring** adj [only before noun]: *an aspiring politician*

aspirin /ˈæsprɪn/ n [C,U] (*plural* **aspirin** or **aspirins**) a drug sold as small TABLETS that reduces pain and fever: *I **took an aspirin** and went to bed.*

ass /æs/ n [C] old-fashioned a DONKEY

assailant /əˈseɪlənt/ n [C] *formal* someone who attacks another person SYN **attacker**

assassin /əˈsæsɪn/ n [C] someone who murders an important person: *Who was Kennedy's assassin?*

assassinate /əˈsæsəneɪt ʃ -səneɪt/ v [T] to murder an important person: *a plot to assassinate the President* THESAURUS KILL —**assassination** /əˌsæsəˈneɪʃən ʃ -sənˈeɪ-/ n [C,U]: *an assassination attempt*

assault¹ /əˈsɔːlt ʃ əˈsɒːlt/ n **1** [C,U] *formal* the crime of attacking a person: **[+on/against]** *sexual assaults on women* | *He was **charged with assault**.* **2** [C] an attack by an army to take control of a place: **[+on]** *an assault on enemy lines*

assault² v [T] to attack someone violently: *He claims the teacher assaulted him.*

assemble `Ac` /əˈsembəl/ v **1** [I,T] if you assemble people or things, or if people assemble, they are brought together in the same place: *A crowd had assembled in front of the White House.* **2** [T] to put the different parts of something together: *The book-case was quite easy to assemble.* → see picture at BUILD¹ THESAURUS BUILD

assembly `Ac` /əˈsembli/ n (*plural* **assemblies**) **1** [C] a group of people who are elected to make decisions for a country or organization: *the United Nations General Assembly* **2** [C,U] a regular meeting of all the students and teachers in a school: *I'll see you after assembly.* **3** [U] the process of making something by joining its different parts together

as'sembly ˌline n [C] a system for making large quantities of things in a factory. The products move past a line of workers who each check or make one part.

assent /əˈsent/ n [U] *formal* official agreement: *They will be asked to **give** their **assent** to the proposal.* —**assent** v [I]

assert /əˈsɜːt ʃ -ɜːrt/ v [T] **1** to say firmly that something is true: **[+that]** *The company has vigorously asserted that it is not breaking the law.* **2** to behave in a determined and confident way to make people respect you: **assert your rights/ independence etc** *A teacher must assert his authority.* | **assert yourself** *In the 1960s, women began to assert themselves politically.* —**assertion** /əˈsɜːʃən ʃ -ɜːr-/ n [C,U]: *a confident assertion*

assertive /əˈsɜːtɪv ʃ -ɜːr-/ adj behaving confidently to make people listen to you —**assertiveness** n [U] —**assertively** adv

assess `Ac` /əˈses/ v [T] **1** to make a judgment about a person, situation etc after considering it: *a study to **assess the impact** of crime on people's lives* **2** to calculate the value, cost, or level something has: **assess sth at £100/31 per cent etc** *The cost of the earthquake was assessed at $2.2 billion.* —**assessment** n [C,U]: *reading assessment tests*

asset /ˈæset/ n **1** [C usually singular] something or someone that helps you to succeed: **[+to]** *You're an asset to the company, George.* **2 assets** [plural] a company's assets are the things it owns: *a firm with $1.3 billion in assets*

assiduous /əˈsɪdjuəs ʃ -dʒuəs/ adj *formal* working with great care —**assiduously** adv

assign `Ac` /əˈsaɪn/ v [T] *formal* to give something to someone: **assign sth to sb** *We assigned a different task to each student.* | *Victoria has been assigned a personal bodyguard.*

assignment `Ac` /əˈsaɪnmənt/ n [C,U] a job or piece of work that is given to someone: *Students have to do three written assignments.* | **on assignment** (=doing a job) *He's on assignment in Russia at the moment.*

Word Choice: assignment or essay?
You use **assignment** about a piece of work that you are asked to do for your studies or your work. This can involve writing, reading, or trying to find information about something: *As part of our assignment, we had to look at different companies' websites on the Internet.*
You use **essay** about a piece of writing on a particular subject, which you write as part of your school or college work: *She's writing an essay about the causes of the Russian Revolution.*

assimilate /əˈsɪməleɪt/ v **1** [T] to learn and understand information: *The children were quick to **assimilate** new ideas.* **2** [I,T] if people assimilate, or if they are assimilated, they gradually become part of a new group or country they have joined: [**+into**] *The immigrants soon assimilated into Canadian society.* —**assimilation** /əˌsɪməˈleɪʃən/ n [U]

assist Ac /əˈsɪst/ v [I,T] *formal* to help someone do something: **assist (sb) in/with sth** *She returned to the kitchen to assist in the preparations.* | *Shall I assist you with carrying your bags?* **THESAURUS ▶ HELP**

assistance Ac /əˈsɪstəns/ n [U] *formal* help: *Shall I give you some **assistance**?* | *Can I be of any assistance* (=help you)? | *A passer-by came to her assistance* (=helped her). | **financial/legal/military etc assistance** | *with the assistance of sb/sth We put the shed up with the assistance of a few friends.*

assistant /əˈsɪstənt/ n [C]
1 someone whose job is to help someone more important: *Meet Jane, my new assistant.*
2 *BrE* someone whose job is to help customers in a shop **SYN clerk** *AmE*: *a sales assistant*
3 the assistant manager/director etc someone whose job is just below the position of manager, director etc

as,sisted 'suicide n [C,U] when a doctor or other person helps a person who is seriously ill to kill themselves in order to end their suffering

associate¹ /əˈsəʊʃieɪt, əˈsəʊsi- $ əˈsoʊ-/ v [T] if you associate two people or things, or if they are associated, you see that they are connected in some way: **associate sb/sth with sth** *You don't normally associate sunshine with England.* | *Cancer is definitely associated with smoking.*

PHRASAL VERBS
associate with 1 associate with sb *formal* to spend time with someone: *I don't like the people she associates with.* **2 associate yourself with sb/sth** to show support for someone or something

associate² /əˈsəʊʃiət, əˈsəʊsi- $ əˈsoʊ-/ n [C] someone that you work or do business with: *business associates*

associate³ /adj [only before noun] an associate position or job is at a lower level and has fewer rights than similar positions or jobs

association /əˌsəʊsiˈeɪʃən, əˌsəʊʃi- $ əˌsoʊ-/ n **1** [C] an organization for people who do the same kind of work or have the same interests: *the Association of University Teachers* **THESAURUS ▶ ORGANIZATION**
2 [C,U] a connection or relationship with another

person or group: **in association with sb** *The award was presented by Hydro UK in association with the Fellowship of Engineering.* | *his close associations with the Green Party* **3** [C usually plural] a memory or feeling that is related to a particular place, event etc: *a building with romantic associations*

assorted /əˈsɔːtɪd $ -ɔːr-/ adj of various different types: *a box of assorted cookies*

assortment /əˈsɔːtmənt $ -ɔːr-/ n [C] a mixture of different types of the same thing: [**+of**] *an assortment of cakes and biscuits*

assume Ac /əˈsjuːm $ əˈsuːm/ v [T]
1 to think that something is true, although you have no proof: [**+(that)**] *Your light wasn't on, so I assumed you were out.* | **let's assume that/assuming that** *Let's assume for a moment that you are the father of that child.*
2 *formal* to take control, power, or a particular position: **assume power/responsibility/authority etc** *Mark will **assume the role of** Managing Director.*
3 to pretend to feel something or be something you are not: *Gail assumed an air of indifference.*

assumed /əˈsjuːmd $ əˈsuːmd/ adj if you have an assumed name or IDENTITY you use a false name or pretend to be someone else

assumption Ac /əˈsʌmpʃən/ n **1** [C] something that you think is true although you have no proof: [**+that**] *We're **working on the assumption** that prices will rise.* | [**+about**] *Don't **make assumptions** about people you don't know.* **2** [singular] when someone starts to have power, control, or a new position

assurance Ac /əˈʃʊərəns $ əˈʃʊr-/ n **1** [C] a promise that something is true or will happen: [**+that**] *He gave me an **assurance** that the work would be complete by now.* **2** [U] confidence in your abilities or the truth of what you are saying: *Cindy spoke with quiet assurance.*

assure Ac /əˈʃʊə $ əˈʃʊr/ v [T] **1** to tell someone that something is definitely true or will happen, to try to stop them worrying: **assure sb (that)** *She kept assuring me that she felt quite well.* | **I can assure you,** *the painting is quite genuine.* **2** to make something certain to happen or be successful: *enough money to assure the success of the project*

assured /əˈʃʊəd $ əˈʃʊrd/ adj **1** showing confidence in your abilities **SYN self-assured**: *a mature assured manner* **2** certain to be achieved: *A Republican victory seemed assured.* **3 be/feel assured of sth** if you are assured of something, you are sure that it will happen: *The Queen can be assured of a warm welcome in Australia.*

asterisk /ˈæstərɪsk/ n [C] a mark like a star (*), used in writing to point out that something is interesting, important, or missing

asteroid /ˈæstərɔɪd/ n [C] a large object made of rock that moves around in space

asthma /ˈæsmə $ ˈæzmə/ n [U] an illness that makes it difficult to breathe: *people who suffer from asthma* | *an asthma attack* —**asthmatic** /æsˈmætɪk $ æz-/ adj

astonished /əˈstɒnɪʃt $ əˈstɑː-/ adj very surprised: **[+at/by]** We were astonished at her ignorance. | **[+that]** He was quite astonished that she actually agreed. | **astonished to see/learn/discover etc** I was astonished to discover she was younger than me. **THESAURUS** SURPRISED —**astonish** v [T]: The result astonished everyone.

astonishing /əˈstɒnɪʃɪŋ $ əˈstɑː-/ adj very surprising: an astonishing decision | **It's astonishing that** you didn't know about this. —**astonishingly** adv

astonishment /əˈstɒnɪʃmənt $ əˈstɑː-/ n [U] complete surprise: **in astonishment** We all stared in astonishment. | **to sb's astonishment** To her astonishment, she won.

astound /əˈstaʊnd/ v [T] to make someone feel very surprised: The result astounded us. —**astounding** adj: an astounding success —**astounded** adj: I was absolutely astounded when he told me. —**astoundingly** adv

astray /əˈstreɪ/ adv **1 go astray** to be lost: The letter went astray in the post. **2 lead sb astray** to encourage someone to do bad or immoral things

astride /əˈstraɪd/ adv, prep with one leg on each side of something: a girl **sitting astride** a motorbike

astrology /əˈstrɒlədʒi $ əˈstrɑː-/ n [U] the study of the position and movements of PLANETS and stars and how they might affect people's lives → **astronomy** —**astrologer** n [C] —**astrological** /ˌæstrəˈlɒdʒɪkəl◂ $ -ˈlɑː-/ adj: astrological predictions

astronaut /ˈæstrənɔːt $ -nɒːt, -nɑːt/ n [C] someone who travels in a spacecraft

astronomical /ˌæstrəˈnɒmɪkəl◂ $ -ˈnɑː-/ adj **1** informal astronomical prices are very high **THESAURUS** EXPENSIVE **2** [only before noun] connected with the scientific study of the stars and PLANETS —**astronomically** /-kli/ adv

astronomy /əˈstrɒnəmi $ əˈstrɑː-/ n [U] the scientific study of the stars and PLANETS —**astronomer** n [C]

astute /əˈstjuːt $ əˈstuːt/ adj quick to understand a situation and how to get an advantage from it: an astute businessman

asylum /əˈsaɪləm/ n **1** [U] protection that a government gives to people who have left their country because they are in danger for political reasons: He arrived in Britain and **applied for asylum**. | He was granted **political asylum**. **2** [C] old-fashioned a hospital for people with mental illness

a'sylum-ˌseeker n [C] someone who escapes to another country because they are in danger for political reasons **SYN** refugee

asymmetrical /ˌeɪsəˈmetrɪkəl/ adj having two sides of different shapes or lengths

at /ət; strong æt/ prep
1 used to say where someone or something is or where something happens: I met my husband at university. | Does this train stop at Preston? | **at the top/bottom/end etc (of sth)** We live at the end of the street. | We're meeting at Mike's (=Mike's house). | John's at work (=in the place where he works).
2 used to say when something happens: The movie starts at 8:00. | at night | What are you doing at the weekend?
3 used to show the price, speed, level etc of something: gas selling at $2.75 a gallon | a car traveling at 50 mph
4 used to show who or what a particular action or feeling is directed towards: That guy's staring at me. | None of the kids laughed at his joke. | I'm really surprised at you.
5 used to say which activity you are talking about when you say how well someone can do it: **good/bad etc at (doing) sth** I'm pretty good at maths.
6 in a particular state: children at risk | The two countries were at war.
7 the symbol @, used in EMAIL addresses → **(not) at all** at ALL[1], **at first** at FIRST[1], **at least** at LEAST[1]

ate /et, eɪt $ eɪt/ v the past tense of EAT

atheist /ˈeɪθiɪst/ n [C] someone who does not believe in God → **agnostic** —**atheism** n [U]

athlete /ˈæθliːt/ n [C] someone who competes in sports such as running or jumping

athletic /æθˈletɪk, əθ-/ adj **1** physically strong and good at sport: a tall man with an athletic build **2** [only before noun] connected with athletes or athletics

athletics /æθˈletɪks, əθ-/ n [U] **1** BrE sports such as running and jumping **2** AmE sports in general: high school athletics

atlas /ˈætləs/ n [C] a book of maps: a road atlas

ATM /ˌeɪ tiː ˈem/ n [C] AmE (**Automated Teller Machine**) a machine that you use with a card to get money from your bank account **SYN** cash machine BrE

atmosphere /ˈætməsfɪə $ -fɪr/ n
1 [C usually singular, U] the feeling that a place, situation, or event gives you: The atmosphere at home was tense. | a hotel with a relaxed atmosphere | **[+of]** an atmosphere of excited expectation
2 [singular] the mixture of gases that surrounds the Earth or another PLANET
3 [singular] the air in a room: a small pub with a smoky atmosphere

> **Word Choice**: atmosphere or mood?
> You use **atmosphere** to describe the general feeling a place, situation, or event gives you: The hotel has a friendly relaxed atmosphere. You use **mood** to describe the way that a person or group of people feel at a particular time, especially when this can change quickly: Alan wasn't in a very good mood this morning. | Their mood of optimism quickly vanished.

atmospheric /ˌætməsˈferɪk◂/ adj **1** relating to the Earth's atmosphere: atmospheric pressure **2** if a place or sound is atmospheric, it seems beautiful and mysterious: atmospheric music

atom /'ætəm/ n [C] the smallest part of an ELE-MENT that can exist alone: *carbon atoms*

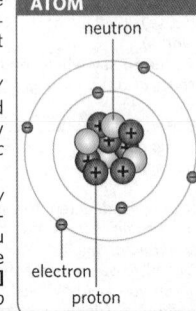

ATOM
neutron
electron
proton

atomic /ə'tɒmɪk $ ə'tɑː-/ adj relating to atoms and the energy produced by splitting them: *the atomic bomb*

atone /ə'təʊn $ ə'toʊn/ v [I] formal to do something to show that you are sorry for having done something wrong: **[+for]** *Richard was anxious to atone for his crimes.*

atop /ə'tɒp $ ə'tɑːp/ prep written on top of something

atrium /'eɪtriəm/ n [C] a large open space with a glass roof in the centre of a building

atrocious /ə'trəʊʃəs $ ə'troʊ-/ adj very bad or severe: *Your spelling's atrocious.* | *atrocious weather* —**atrociously** adv

atrocity /ə'trɒsəti $ ə'trɑː-/ n [C,U] (plural **atrocities**) a very cruel or violent action: *the atrocities of war*

attach Ac /ə'tætʃ/ v [T]

1 FASTEN/JOIN to fasten or join one thing to another: **attach sth to sth** *Please attach a photograph to your application.* | **the attached cheque/form etc** *Please sign and return the attached slip.* **THESAURUS** ▶ JOIN

2 EMAIL to connect a document or FILE to an email so that you can send them together: *Please see attached document.*

3 LIKE SB/STH **be attached to sb/sth** to like someone or something very much because you have known them for a long time: *Tom was very attached to his old teddy bear.*

4 IMPORTANCE/VALUE **attach importance/value etc to sth** to believe that something is important, valuable etc: *Don't attach much importance to what Nick says.*

5 BE PART OF STH to belong to or be part of a bigger organization: *The Medical School is attached to the University of Sussex.*

attachment Ac /ə'tætʃmənt/ n **1** [C,U] formal a strong feeling of loyalty, love, or friendship: **[+to/for]** *his strong attachment to his sister* **2** [C] a part that you fasten to a machine to make it do a particular job: *Use the brush attachment to clean wooden floors.* **3** [C] a FILE that you send with an email message: *I can't open the attachment.*

attack¹ /ə'tæk/ v

1 [I,T] to use violence to try to hurt or kill someone, or to cause damage to a place: *She was attacked as she walked home from school.* | **attack sb with sth** *The man attacked him with a knife.* | *The rebels attacked the town with tanks.*

2 [T] to criticize someone strongly: **attack sb for (doing) sth** *The government has been attacked for failing to tackle street crime.*

3 [T] if a disease, insect, or substance attacks something, it damages it: *The virus attacks the body's immune system.*

4 [I,T] in sport, to move forward in order to score points

attack to use violence against a person or place: *A gang of boys attacked him and started punching him.* | *The town was attacked by US forces.*
invade to enter a country and try to get control of it using force: *Germany invaded Russia in 1941.*
ambush if a group of people ambush someone, they hide and wait for them and then attack them: *He was ambushed by gunmen as he drove to work.*
retaliate to attack someone who has attacked you: *The demonstrators threw stones at the police, who retaliated by firing rubber bullets.*
mug to attack someone in a public place in order to steal from them: *I don't like walking home after dark – I'm worried I'll get mugged.*
stab to attack someone with a knife: *She tried to stab him with a kitchen knife.*

attack² n

1 [C,U] a violent action that is intended to hurt or kill someone: **[+on]** *the terrorist attack on the World Trade Center* | **bomb/knife/arson etc attack** *fears of a nuclear attack* | *The army launched an attack.* | **be/come under attack** *We were under attack from enemy forces.*

2 [C,U] strong criticism: **[+on]** *He launched a personal attack on the President.* | **be/come under attack** *He came under fierce attack for his ideas.*

3 [C] a short period of time when you are ill, worried, afraid etc: **[+of]** *an attack of flu* | *She suffers from panic attacks.*

4 [C,U] in sport, an attempt by the players in a team to get points: **in attack** (=when a team is attacking) *Brazil look very impressive in attack.* → HEART ATTACK

attacker /ə'tækə $ -ər/ n [C] someone who attacks someone else: *Her attacker dragged her into the bushes.*

attain Ac /ə'teɪn/ v [T] to achieve something after trying for a long time: *More women are now attaining high positions in business.* —**attainment** n [C,U] —**attainable** adj

attempt¹ /ə'tempt/ n [C] when you try to do something: **attempt to do sth** *All attempts to resolve the problem have failed.* | **[+at]** *his first attempt at this exam* | **in an attempt to do sth** *In an attempt to save money, I offered to do the work myself.*

verbs
to make an attempt *She made no attempt to help him.*
to give up/abandon an attempt *They tried to reach him one more time before abandoning their attempt.*
to fail/succeed in your attempt *They completely failed in their attempt to convince the public.*
an attempt fails/succeeds *Her attempt to break the world record failed.*

adjectives
a successful/unsuccessful attempt *She made an unsuccessful attempt to get him to change his mind.*

a deliberate attempt *This was a deliberate attempt to disrupt the elections.*
the first/second etc attempt *That was amazingly good for a first attempt.*
a vain/futile attempt (=one that does not succeed) *He started singing in a vain attempt to cheer her up.*
a desperate attempt (=one that you very much want to succeed, but that is likely to fail) *She made a desperate attempt to catch the glass before it fell.*

attempt² *v* [T] to try to do something, especially something difficult: *The second question was so difficult I didn't even attempt it.* | **attempt to do sth** *Now I will attempt to explain why the revolution started.*
THESAURUS TRY

attempted /ə'temptɪd/ *adj* [only before noun] tried, but not successfully achieved: *He was charged with attempted murder.*

attend /ə'tend/ *v* [I,T] *formal* to go to an event such as a meeting or class: *More than 2,000 people are expected to attend the conference.* | *Please let us know if you are unable to attend.*
PHRASAL VERBS
attend to sb/sth *formal* to give attention to someone or something: *I may be late – I've got some things to attend to.*

attendance /ə'tendəns/ *n* [C,U] **1** the number of people who attend an event, such as a meeting, concert etc: *Church attendances have fallen in recent years.* **2** when someone goes to a meeting, class etc: **[+at]** *The course involves 8 hours' attendance at college each week.*

attendant /ə'tendənt/ *n* [C] someone whose job is to look after customers in a public place: *a car parking attendant*

attention /ə'tenʃən/ *n* [U]
1 when you watch, listen, or think carefully because you are interested in something: *You should pay more attention in class.* | *We need to give more attention to the needs of older people.* | *My attention wasn't really on the game.* | *The game is fun and will keep the attention of any child.* | *Attention to detail is essential in this job.* | *Most children have a short attention span* (=period of time that they are interested in watching, listening etc to something).
→ **undivided attention** at UNDIVIDED
2 when people notice something or are interested in it: *We waved to attract the attention of the waiter.* | *We wanted to draw attention to this problem* (=make people notice it). | **public/media/press attention** *Her story attracted a lot of media attention.* | *Johnny enjoyed being the centre of attention* (=the person that everyone is interested in).
3 special care or treatment: *Some of the children required urgent medical attention.*
PHRASES
stand at/to attention if soldiers stand to attention, they stand very straight, with their feet together: *The major stood to attention and saluted.*

attentive /ə'tentɪv/ *adj* **1** listening or watching carefully: *an attentive audience* **2** making sure that

someone has everything they need: *an attentive host*
—**attentively** *adv*

attic /'ætɪk/ *n* [C] a room at the top of a house, just below the roof

attire /ə'taɪə $ ə'taɪr/ *n* [U] *formal* clothes

attitude Ac /'ætɪtjuːd $ -tuːd/ *n* [C,U] what you think and feel about something: **[+to/towards]** *Many people have negative attitudes towards old age.* | *He has a very positive attitude towards his work.* | *These people have a different attitude of mind* (=way of thinking).

attorney /ə'tɜːni $ -ɜːr-/ *n* [C] *AmE* a lawyer

attract /ə'trækt/ *v* [T]
1 to make someone like something or feel interested in it: **attract sb to sth** *What attracted me to the job was the chance to travel.* | **attract attention/interest etc** *The story has attracted a lot of attention from the media.*
2 to make someone come to a place: *The exhibition has attracted a lot of visitors.*
3 to like someone in a sexual way: *I've always been attracted to blondes.*
4 if something attracts things, it makes them move towards it: *Left-over food attracts flies.*

attraction /ə'trækʃən/ *n* **1** [C,U] a feeling of liking someone, especially in a sexual way: *The attraction between them was immediate.* **2** [C] something that is interesting or enjoyable to see or do: *The beautiful beaches are the island's main attraction.* | *The castle is a major tourist attraction* (=place that many tourists visit).

attractive /ə'træktɪv/ *adj*
1 pretty or pleasant to look at: *an attractive young woman* | *Women seem to find him attractive.*
THESAURUS BEAUTIFUL
2 having qualities that make you want to accept something or be involved in it: **[+to]** *a political movement that is attractive to young people* | *The club have made him a very attractive offer.* **THESAURUS** GOOD —**attractively** *adv*

attribute¹ Ac /ə'trɪbjuːt $ -bjət/ *v*
PHRASAL VERBS
attribute sth **to** sb/sth **1** to believe or say that a situation or event was caused by something: *The increase in crime can be attributed to social changes.* **2** to believe that something was written, said, or made by a particular person: *a painting attributed to Rembrandt*

attribute² Ac /'ætrəbjuːt/ *n* [C] a good or useful quality: *What attributes should a good manager have?*

attributive /ə'trɪbjətɪv/ *adj* an attributive adjective comes before a noun and describes the noun. For example, in the phrase 'big city', 'big' is an attributive adjective, and in the phrase 'school bus', 'school' is a noun in an attributive position. → **predicative**

atypical /eɪ'tɪpɪkəl/ *adj formal* not typical or usual

aubergine /'əʊbəʒiːn $ 'oʊbər-/ *n* [C] *BrE* a large dark purple vegetable **SYN** eggplant *AmE* → see picture on page A5

auburn /'ɔːbən $ 'ɒːbərn/ *adj* auburn hair is a reddish brown colour

auction /'ɔːkʃən $ 'ɒːk-/ n [C] an event at which things are sold to the person who offers the most money —**auction** v [T]

auctioneer /ˌɔːkʃə'nɪə $ ˌɒːkʃə'nɪr/ n [C] someone who is in charge of an auction

audacity /ɔː'dæsəti $ ɒː-/ n [U] when someone is brave enough to do something that seems shocking or rude: *I can't believe he had the audacity to ask for more money.* —**audacious** /ɔː'deɪʃəs $ ɒː-/ adj

audible /'ɔːdəbəl $ 'ɒː-/ adj loud enough to be heard [OPP] **inaudible**: *Her voice was barely audible.* —**audibly** adv

audience /'ɔːdiəns $ 'ɒː-, 'ɑː-/ n [C also + plural verb BrE]
1 the people who watch or listen to a performance: *One member of the audience described the opera as boring.* | *The audience were* (=each member was) *clapping and cheering.*
2 BrE the people who watch a particular television programme, read a particular book or magazine etc: *The show attracts a regular audience of 20 million viewers.* | *a new magazine aimed at a teenage audience*
3 a formal meeting with someone who is very important: [+with] *an audience with the Pope*

audio /'ɔːdiəʊ $ 'ɒːdioʊ/ adj [only before noun] for recording and broadcasting sound: *audio tapes* | *audio equipment*

audiovisual /ˌɔːdiəʊ'vɪʒuəl◂ $ ˌɒːdioʊ-/ adj [only before noun] using recorded pictures and sound: *audiovisual equipment*

audit /'ɔːdɪt $ 'ɒː-/ n [C] when someone officially examines a company's financial records to check that they are correct —**audit** v [T] —**auditor** n [C]

audition /ɔː'dɪʃən $ ɒː-/ n [C] a short performance by an actor, singer etc to test whether he or she is good enough to perform in a play, concert etc —**audition** v [I,T]

auditorium /ˌɔːdə'tɔːriəm $ ˌɒː-/ n [C] the part of a theatre where people sit to watch a performance

augment /ɔːg'ment $ ɒːg-/ v [T] formal to increase the size or value of something

augur /'ɔːgə $ 'ɒːgər/ v **augur well/ill** formal to be a sign that something good or bad will happen in the future

August /'ɔːgəst $ 'ɒː-/ n [C,U] (*written abbreviation* **Aug.**) the eighth month of the year, between July and September: **next/last August** *I was there last August.* | **in August** *His birthday's in August.* | **on August 6th** *The new store opened on August 6th.*

aunt /ɑːnt $ ænt/ (*also* **auntie** /'ɑːnti $ 'æn-/ *informal*) n [C] the sister of your father or mother, or the wife of your UNCLE → **AGONY AUNT**

au pair /əʊ 'peə $ oʊ 'per/ n [C] a young person who stays with a family in a foreign country and looks after their children

aura /'ɔːrə/ n [C] a quality or feeling that seems to come from a person or place: *Inside the church there was an aura of complete tranquillity.*

aural /'ɔːrəl/ adj relating to the sense of hearing → **oral**: *aural skills*

auspices /'ɔːspɪsɪz $ 'ɒː-/ n **under the auspices of sth** formal with the help and support of an organization: *The research was done under the auspices of Harvard Medical School.*

auspicious /ɔː'spɪʃəs $ ɒː-/ adj formal an auspicious time or event makes you expect success in the future [OPP] **inauspicious**

austere /ɔː'stɪə, ɒ- $ ɒː'stɪr/ adj **1** very plain and simple: *Life in the monastery was very austere.* | *an austere style of painting* **2** very strict and serious: *a cold, austere woman*

austerity /ɔː'sterəti, ɒ- $ ɒː-/ n [U] bad economic conditions in which people do not have enough money to live: *the austerity of the post-war years*

authentic /ɔː'θentɪk $ ɒː-/ adj something that is authentic really is what it seems to be: *authentic Indian food* | *an authentic Picasso painting*
[THESAURUS] GENUINE —**authentically** /-kli/ adv —**authenticity** /ˌɔːθen'tɪsəti $ ˌɒː-/ n [U]

author Ac /'ɔːθə $ 'ɒːθər/ n [C] someone who has written a book [SYN] **writer**: *a well-known American author* | [+of] *Robert Louis Stevenson was the author of 'Treasure Island'.*

> **Word Choice**: author or writer?
> **Author** is more formal than **writer** and is used especially about someone who writes books that are of a high standard, which are considered to be literature: *He is influenced by American authors such as Hemingway and Faulkner.*
> **Writer** is a more general word. You use it about anyone who writes books, articles for magazines etc: *I've always wanted to be a writer.*

authoritarian /ɔːˌθɒrə'teəriən◂ $ ɒːˌθɑːrə'ter-, əˌθɒː-/ adj forcing people to obey strict rules or laws and not allowing any freedom: *an authoritarian regime*

authoritative Ac /ɔː'θɒrətətɪv, ə- $ ɒː'θɑːrəteɪtɪv, ə'θɒː-/ adj **1** an authoritative book, statement etc can be trusted because it was written by someone who knows a lot about a subject: *an authoritative textbook on European history* **2** behaving or speaking in a confident determined way that makes people respect and obey you: *The captain spoke in a calm and authoritative voice.* —**authoritatively** adv

authority Ac /ɔː'θɒrəti, ə- $ ə'θɑː-, ə'θɒː-/ n (*plural* **authorities**)
1 [U] the power that a leader, government etc has: [+over] *Which country has authority over these islands?* | **in authority** *Could I speak to someone in authority* (=who has a position of power), *please?* | *He is now in a position of authority.* | **authority to do sth** *She doesn't have the authority to dismiss staff.*
[THESAURUS] EXPERT
2 [C] an organization or government department that makes official decisions and controls public services: *Write a letter of complaint to the local authority.* | *the San Diego Water Authority* | *an agreement between the US and Colombian authorities*
[THESAURUS] GOVERNMENT
3 [C] someone who is respected because of their

knowledge about a subject: **[+on]** *Dr Ballard is a leading authority on tropical diseases.*

authorize (also **-ise** *BrE*) /ˈɔːθəraɪz $ ˈɒː-/ v [T] to give official permission for something: *an authorized biography* | **authorize sb to do sth** *No one authorized you to spend this money.* —**authorization** /ˌɔːθəraɪˈzeɪʃən $ ˌɒːθərə-/ n [C,U]

autistic /ɔːˈtɪstɪk $ ɒː-/ adj having a mental condition that makes it hard for someone to understand other people and form relationships —**autism** /ˈɔːtɪzəm $ ˈɒː-/ n [U]

auto /ˈɔːtəʊ $ ˈɒːtoʊ/ adj especially AmE relating to cars SYN **motor** BrE: *the auto industry* | *auto insurance*

autobiography /ˌɔːtəbaɪˈɒɡrəfi $ ˌɒːtəbaɪˈɑː-/ n [C] (plural **autobiographies**) a book that someone writes about their own life THESAURUS BOOK —**autobiographical** /ˌɔːtəbaɪəˈɡræfɪkəl $ ˌɒː-/ adj

autograph /ˈɔːtəɡrɑːf $ ˈɒːtəɡræf/ n [C] if a famous person gives you their autograph, they sign their name on something for you → see Word Choice at SIGNATURE —**autograph** v [T]: *an autographed picture*

automated Ac /ˈɔːtəmeɪtɪd $ ˈɒː-/ adj using computers and machines to do a job rather than people: *The production process is now **fully automated**.* —**automation** /ˌɔːtəˈmeɪʃən $ ˌɒː-/ n [U]

automatic¹ Ac /ˌɔːtəˈmætɪk◄ $ ˌɒː-/ adj
1 an automatic machine is designed to work by itself without much human control: *an automatic gearbox*
2 certain to happen because of a rule or system: *We get an automatic pay increase every year.*
3 done without thinking: *an automatic reaction* —**automatically** /-kli/ adv: *You shouldn't automatically assume that your teacher is right.*

automatic² n [C] **1** a weapon that can shoot bullets continuously **2** a car with a system of GEARS that operate themselves

automobile /ˈɔːtəməbiːl $ ˈɒːtəmoʊ-/ n [C] AmE a car

automotive /ˌɔːtəˈməʊtɪv◄ $ ˌɒːtəˈmoʊ-/ adj [only before noun] relating to cars: *automotive technology*

autonomous /ɔːˈtɒnəməs $ ɒːˈtɑː-/ adj having the power to make independent decisions or rules: *an autonomous state* —**autonomy** n [U]: *The region wants political autonomy.*

autopsy /ˈɔːtɒpsi $ ˈɒːtɑːp-/ n [C] (plural **autopsies**) AmE an official examination of a dead body to discover why the person has died SYN **post-mortem** BrE

autumn /ˈɔːtəm $ ˈɒː-/ n [C,U] the season between summer and winter, when the leaves fall off the trees SYN **fall** AmE —**autumnal** /ɔːˈtʌmnəl $ ɒː-/ adj

auxiliary /ɔːɡˈzɪljəri, ɔːk- $ ɒːɡˈzɪljəri, -ˈzɪləri/ adj giving extra help or support: *auxiliary nurses* —**auxiliary** n [C]

aux,iliary 'verb n [C] a verb that is used with another verb to form questions, negative sentences, and tenses. In English the auxiliary verbs are 'be', 'do', and 'have'.

avail¹ /əˈveɪl/ n **to no avail** without success: *They had searched everywhere, but to no avail.*

avail² v **avail yourself of sth** formal to accept an offer or use an opportunity: *Students should avail themselves of every opportunity to improve their English.*

available Ac /əˈveɪləbəl/ adj
1 if something is available, you can have it, buy it, or use it: **[+at/in/from]** *Tickets are available from the box office.* | **[+to]** *Not enough data is available to scientists.* | **[+for]** *land that is available for development* | **readily/widely available** *Illegal drugs are readily available in our cities.*
2 [not before noun] someone who is available is not busy and has enough time to talk to you: *Dr Wright is not available at the moment.* —**availability** /əˌveɪləˈbɪləti/ n [U]

avalanche /ˈævəlɑːntʃ $ -læntʃ/ n [C] **1** a large amount of snow that falls down the side of a mountain **2 an avalanche of sth** a very large number of things that happen or arrive at the same time: *The school received an avalanche of letters.*

avant-garde /ˌævɒŋ ˈɡɑːd◄ $ ˌævɑːŋ ˈɡɑːrd◄/ adj avant-garde literature, music, or art is very modern and different from existing styles: *an avant-garde film*

avarice /ˈævərɪs/ n [U] formal an extreme desire for wealth SYN **greed**

Ave. (also **Ave** BrE) the written abbreviation of **Avenue**: *36, Rokesly Ave*

avenge /əˈvendʒ/ v [T] literary to punish someone because they have harmed you or your family: *He wanted to avenge his brother's death.*

avenue /ˈævənjuː $ -nuː/ n [C] **1** a road in a town: *Fifth Avenue* THESAURUS ROAD **2** a possible way of achieving something: *We must explore every avenue in order to achieve peace.*

average¹ /ˈævərɪdʒ/ adj
1 [only before noun] the average amount is the amount you get when you add together several figures and divide this by the total number of figures: *The **average cost** of making a movie has risen by 15%.* | *Last winter was colder than average.*
2 [only before noun] an average person or thing is the usual or most typical size or type: *They have an average size garden.* | *In an average week I drive about 250 miles.* THESAURUS NORMAL
3 not very good but not very bad: *I didn't think it was a great movie – just average really.*

average² n
1 [C] the amount that you get by adding several figures together and then dividing the result by the number of figures: **[+of]** *The average of 3, 8 and 10 is 7.* | *Each person raised an average of £60.*
2 [C,U] the usual level or amount for most people or things: **above/below average** *students of above average ability*
PHRASES
on average based on a calculation of what usually happens: *On average, men still earn more than women.*

average³ v [T] to be a particular amount as an average: *The train travelled at speeds averaging 125 mph.*
PHRASAL VERBS
average out to result in a particular average amount: **[+at]** *Our weekly profits average out at about $750.*

averse /əˈvɜːs $ əˈvɜːrs/ *adj* **not be averse to sth** *formal* to quite enjoy something: *Charles was not averse to the occasional cigar.*

aversion /əˈvɜːʃən $ əˈvɜːrʒən/ *n* [singular] *formal* a strong dislike of something: **[+to]** *She has a strong aversion to cats.*

avert /əˈvɜːt $ -ɜːrt/ *v* [T] *formal* **1** to prevent something unpleasant from happening: *negotiations aimed at averting a crisis* **2 avert your eyes/gaze** to look away from something: *Henry averted his eyes as she undressed.*

aviary /ˈeɪviəri $ ˈeɪvieri/ *n* [C] (*plural* **aviaries**) a large CAGE in which birds are kept

aviation /ˌeɪviˈeɪʃən $ ˌeɪ-, ˌæ-/ *n* [U] the activity of flying or making aircraft

avid /ˈævɪd/ *adj* [only before noun] eager: *an avid reader of romantic novels* —**avidly** *adv*

avocado /ˌævəˈkɑːdəʊ◄ $ -doʊ◄/ *n* [C,U] (*plural* **avocados**) a fruit with a thick dark green skin that is green inside and has a large seed in the middle → see picture on page A4

avoid /əˈvɔɪd/ *v* [T]
1 to prevent something bad from happening: **avoid doing sth** *The refugees left to avoid getting bombed.* | *Alan narrowly avoided an accident.*
2 to deliberately not go near a person or place: *I have the impression John's trying to avoid us.*
3 to deliberately not do something: **avoid doing sth** *Try to avoid spending too much.* —**avoidance** *n* [U] —**avoidable** *adj*

> **Grammar**
> **Avoid** is not followed by an infinitive.
> Do not say 'He avoided to serve in the army.'
> Say *He avoided serving in the army.*

THESAURUS

avoid a person/place

avoid to deliberately not go near a place, or deliberately try not to meet someone and talk to them: *It's best to avoid the town centre – it gets very busy.* | *Every time I see her, she avoids me.*
keep away/stay away to not go near a person or place, especially because they are dangerous: *Keep away from the fire!* | *I'd stay away from that dog if I were you.*
make a detour to not go to a place by the most direct way, especially because there is a problem on the road that you would usually take: *I made a detour to avoid the traffic.*

not do sth

avoid to not do something that you are expected to do: *He always tries to avoid doing the housework.* | *Some people will do anything to avoid paying taxes.*

---

get out of sth to avoid having to do something. **Get out of** is often used instead of **avoid** in everyday spoken English: *I said I'd take him to see the film. I can't get out of it now.*
get around sth to avoid a problem, difficult situation, law, or rule: *I can't see any other way of getting around the problem.* | *Companies are always trying to get around the regulations.*
evade *formal* to avoid dealing with a question or subject, or having responsibility for doing something: *The Minister tried to evade the question.* | *He somehow managed to evade responsibility for his actions.*

await /əˈweɪt/ *v* [T] *formal* **1** to wait for something: *Briggs is awaiting trial for murder.* **2** if a situation or event awaits someone, it is going to happen to them: *A warm welcome awaits you.*

awake¹ /əˈweɪk/ *adj* [not before noun] not sleeping: *How do you stay awake during boring lectures?* | *Emma lay awake half the night, worrying.* | *The noise brought him wide awake (=completely awake).* | *The storm kept us awake all night.* → see picture at ASLEEP

awake² *v* [I,T] (*past tense* **awoke** /əˈwəʊk $ əˈwoʊk/, *past participle* **awoken** /əˈwəʊkən $ əˈwoʊkən/) *formal* to wake up, or to wake someone up: *I awoke early the next morning.*

awaken /əˈweɪkən/ *v* [I,T] *formal* **1** to wake up, or to make someone wake up: *The noise awakened me.* **2** [T] to make someone have a sudden feeling: *Several strange events had already occurred to awaken our suspicions.*
PHRASAL VERBS
awaken sb to sth *formal* to make someone begin to realize something: *We must awaken people to the dangers of pollution.*

awakening /əˈweɪkənɪŋ/ *n* [singular, U] when you suddenly start to realize a fact or experience a feeling: *His political awakening took place in 1943.*

award¹ /əˈwɔːd $ -ɔːrd/ *n* [C]
1 a prize that someone gets for something that they have achieved: **[+for]** *She won an award for her book.* → see Word Choice at REWARD
2 an amount of money that is given to someone because of a judge's decision: **[+for]** *an award for unfair dismissal*

COLLOCATIONS

verbs

to win an award *The advertisement won several awards.*
to get/receive an award *He was the first Briton to receive the award.*
to give sb an award *She was given an award for her charity work.*
to present an award (=to give it to someone) *The company director will present the award.*
an award goes to sb/sth (=they win it) *The award for best film went to 'Schindler's List'.*

types of award

a top/major award *The restaurant has won several top awards.*

a prestigious award (=one that people think is very important) *This is one of the most prestigious poetry awards.*
a film/music/poetry etc award

award + noun

an award winner *Last year's award winner will present the prize.*
an awards ceremony *We were all invited to the awards ceremony.*

award² v [T] to officially give someone a prize or money: **award sth to sb** *A prize will be awarded to the winner.* | **award sb sth** *The judge awarded me first prize.* **THESAURUS** GIVE

aware Ac /əˈweə $ əˈwer/ adj
1 [not before noun] if you are aware of something, you know about it or realize that it is there **OPP** unaware: **[+of]** *The children are aware of the danger.* | *He was aware of the wind in his face.* | **[+that]** *Were you aware that Joe had a problem with his knee?* **THESAURUS** KNOW
2 interested in something and knowing a lot about it: **politically/environmentally etc aware** *Young people are becoming more politically aware.* **—awareness** n [U]

awash /əˈwɒʃ $ əˈwɔːʃ, əˈwɑːʃ/ adj [not before noun] **1** covered with water: *The streets were awash with flood water.* **2** having too much of something: **[+with]** *Hollywood is awash with rumours.*

away¹ /əˈweɪ/ adv
1 moving further from a place, or staying far from a place: *Go away!* | *Diane drove away quickly.* | **[+from]** *Keep away from the fire!* **THESAURUS** AVOID
2 in a different direction: *Tim turned away and looked out of the window.* | *She blushed and looked away.*
3 not at home, at work, or in school: *Kate is away on holiday.* | **[+from]** *Simon's away from school.*
4 used to say how far it is to a place, thing, or time in the future: **five miles/ten feet etc away** *Geneva is only 20 miles away.* | *Christmas is only a month away.*
5 used to say how close someone is to achieving something or experiencing something: **[+from]** *At one point they were only two points away from victory.*
6 into a safe place: *Put your money away, I'm paying.*
7 used to say that something disappears or is removed: *The music died away.* | *Cut away all the dead wood.* | *He gave his money away to charity.*
8 without stopping: *They've been hammering away all day.*
9 if a team plays away, they play at their opponent's field or sports hall → **right away** at RIGHT²

away² adj **away game/match** a sports game that is played at your opponent's field or sports hall **OPP** home

awe /ɔː $ ɒː/ n [U] a feeling of great respect for someone or something: **in awe of sb** *We were all in awe of the headmaster* (=we respected him a lot).

'awe-in,spiring adj very impressive: *an awe-inspiring achievement*

awesome /ˈɔːsəm $ ˈɒː-/ adj **1** very impressive, often in a way that is slightly frightening: *an awesome responsibility* **2** *especially AmE informal* very good

awful /ˈɔːfəl $ ˈɒː-/ adj
1 very bad or unpleasant: *The weather was awful.* | *He's a pretty awful driver.* **THESAURUS** BAD
2 [only before noun] *spoken* used to emphasize how much, how good, how bad etc something is: *It's going to cost an awful lot of* (=a large amount of) *money.* | *She made me feel an awful fool.*
3 look/feel awful to look or feel ill

awfully /ˈɔːfəli $ ˈɒː-/ adv spoken very: *I'm awfully sorry – I didn't mean to disturb you.*

awkward /ˈɔːkwəd $ ˈɒːkwərd/ adj
1 embarrassing: *I hope he won't ask any awkward questions.* | *an awkward silence* **THESAURUS** DIFFICULT
2 not relaxed: *Geoff looked uneasy and awkward.* | *I had been sitting in an awkward position.*
3 difficult to deal with or use: *The cupboard was an awkward shape and wouldn't fit into the room.*
4 not suitable: *They came at an awkward time.* **—awkwardly** adv **—awkwardness** n [U]

awning /ˈɔːnɪŋ $ ˈɒː-/ n [C] a sheet of material outside a shop, tent etc to keep off the sun or the rain

awoke /əˈwəʊk $ əˈwoʊk/ v the past tense of AWAKE
awoken /əˈwəʊkən $ əˈwoʊ-/ v the past participle of AWAKE

awry /əˈraɪ/ adj **go awry** to not happen in the way that was planned: *All their plans had gone awry.*

axe¹ (also **ax** *AmE*) /æks/ n [C] a tool used for cutting wood, with a wooden handle and a metal blade → see picture at TOOL

axe² (also **ax** *AmE*) v [T] *informal* to get rid of a plan, service, or someone's job: *a decision to axe 2,000 staff*

axis /ˈæksɪs/ n [C] (plural **axes** /-siːz/) **1** the imaginary line around which a large round object, such as the Earth, turns → see picture at GLOBE **2** a line at the side or bottom of a GRAPH, used for marking measurements

axle /ˈæksəl/ n [C] the bar that connects two wheels on a vehicle

aye /aɪ/ adv *spoken informal* a word meaning 'yes', used especially in Scotland and the North of England

Bb

B, b /biː/ n [C,U] (plural **B's**, **b's**) **1** the second letter of the English alphabet **2** the seventh note in the musical SCALE of C MAJOR, or the musical KEY based on this note **3** a mark given to a student's work to show that it is good but not excellent: *I got a B in history.*

BA, B.A. /ˌbiː 'eɪ/ n [C] (**Bachelor of Arts**) a university degree in a subject such as history or literature → **BSc**

babble /'bæbəl/ v [I] to talk quickly in a way that is silly or difficult to understand: *What are you babbling on about?* —**babble** n [U]

babe /beɪb/ n [C] **1** literary a baby **2** spoken informal an attractive young woman

baboon /bə'buːn $ bæ-/ n [C] a large monkey

baby /'beɪbi/ n [C] (plural **babies**)
1 a very young child: *She had a baby in her arms.*
2 baby bird/rabbit/elephant etc a very young animal

COLLOCATIONS

verbs
a baby is born *Our baby was born in June.*
to have a baby (also **to give birth to a baby** formal) *Most UK women have their babies in hospital.*
to be expecting a baby (also **be having a baby**) (=to be pregnant) *His wife is expecting another baby.* ⚠ Do not say 'be waiting a baby'. Say **be expecting a baby** or **be having a baby**.

adjectives
a baby is due (=is expected to be born) *When is her baby due?*
an unborn baby (=not yet born) *You can sing or talk to your unborn baby.*
a newborn baby *They had a newborn baby, and weren't getting much sleep.*

baby + noun
a baby boy/girl (also **a baby son/daughter**) *We had a beautiful baby boy.*
a baby brother/sister *Joe now has a baby brother.*

'baby ,boomer n [C] someone born during a period when a lot of babies were born, especially between 1946 and 1964

'baby ,carriage (also **'baby ,buggy**) n [C] AmE a thing like a bed on wheels that you put a baby in and push along **SYN** **pram** BrE

babysitter /'beɪbi,sɪtə $ -ər/ n [C] someone who looks after children while their parents go out for a short time —**babysitting** n [U]: *I earn some extra money from babysitting.* —**babysit** v [I,T]

bachelor /'bætʃələ $ -ər/ n **1** [C] a man who has never been married **2 Bachelor of Arts/Science/Education etc** a university degree

back¹ /bæk/ n [C]
1 BODY PART the part of your body from your neck and shoulders down to your bottom: *Always sit with your back straight.* | *He fell and injured his back.* | *He lay on his back listening to music.* | *people who suffer from back pain*
2 NOT FRONT [usually singular] the part of something that is furthest from the front **OPP** **front**: **on the back (of sth)** *a T-shirt with a picture of a snake on the back* | *Write your name on the back of the cheque.* | **in the back (of sth)** (=in the part of a vehicle behind the driver) *Do you want to sit in the back of the car?* | **at the back (of sth)** (=in the part of a room or building that is behind the front) *We sat at the back of the hall.* | *My bedroom's at the back of the house.* | **out back** AmE (=behind a building)
3 OF A CHAIR the part of a seat that you lean against when you are sitting: **[+of]** *He rested his arm on the back of the sofa.* → **turn your back on sb/sth** at **TURN¹**

PHRASES
at/in the back of your mind if a thought is at the back of your mind, it is there even when you are thinking about other things: *There was a slight worry at the back of his mind.*
back to back 1 with the backs of two people or things towards each other: *Stand back to back and see who's tallest.* **2** happening one after the other: *The team had a couple of wins back to back.*
back to front BrE with the back of something where the front should be: *You've got your sweater on back to front.*
behind sb's back without someone knowing, especially in an unkind way: *They're always talking about her behind her back.*
get off sb's back informal to stop annoying someone or asking them to do something: *I told him to get off my back and leave me alone.*
be glad/pleased etc to see the back of sb/sth informal to be happy that someone is leaving or that something is ending: *I was glad to see the back of that awful woman.*
be on sb's back informal to tell someone to do something again and again, or to criticize them a lot: *The boss has been on her back again, complaining that she's always late for work.*

back² adv
1 where someone or something was before: **[+in/ to/into etc]** *Put the milk back in the refrigerator.* | *When do you go back to school?* | *The jumper didn't fit so I took it back to the shop.* | *I'll be back* (=return) *in an hour.* | *He ran all the way back home.*
2 into the state that someone or something was in before: **[+to]** *Would you go back to being married?* | *I couldn't get back to sleep.*
3 in the direction that is behind you: *Dan walked away and didn't look back.*
4 doing the same thing to someone that they have done to you: *I'll call you back later.* | *Gina smiled, and the boy smiled back.*
5 at or to a time in the past: **[+to]** *I often think back to my childhood.* | **three years/two months etc back** *This all happened about two years back.*

6 away from someone or something: *'Keep back (=stay away)!'* shouted one of the firefighters. | **[+from]** *The house was set back from the road.*

PHRASES

back and forth in one direction and then in the opposite direction several times: *The two boys were kicking a football back and forth between them.*

back³ v

1 SUPPORT **[T]** to support someone or something, especially by using your money or power: *The Bank gave £45,000 to back the programme.* | *Several witnesses came forward to back him.*

2 GO BACKWARDS **[I,T]** to move in the direction that is behind you, or to make a vehicle move in this way: **back (sth) into/out of/away etc** *He slowly backed away from the dog.* | *Teresa backed the car into the garage.*

3 GAMBLE **[T]** to risk money by guessing that a particular horse, team etc will win something: *I backed Goliath at 10–1.*

> **Usage**
> Do not use **back** as a verb when you mean 'go back'. For example, do not say 'I back to my home.' Say *I went back to my home.* or *I went back home.*

PHRASAL VERBS

back down to agree not to do something, or to admit that you are wrong: **[+on]** *The government has backed down on its proposal.* | *Neither side was prepared to back down.*

back off

1 to move away from something: *She backed off, turned, and ran.*

2 especially *AmE spoken* to stop telling someone what to do, or to stop criticizing someone: *Back off! I don't need your advice.*

back onto sth if a building backs onto a place, the back of the building faces it: *The house backs onto the river.*

back out to decide not to do something that you had promised to do: **[+of]** *They backed out of the deal at the last minute.*

back up

1 back sb/sth ↔ up to support what someone is saying, or show that it is true: *Will you back me up?*

2 back sth ↔ up to make a copy of information stored on a computer: *Don't forget to back up your files.*

3 back sth ↔ up to move backwards, or to make a vehicle go backwards: *He backed the car up a few feet.*

back⁴ adj [only before noun]

1 at the back of something: *the back door | in the back garden | Mum sat in the back seat of the car.*

2 back street/road a street that is away from the main streets

3 back rent/taxes/pay money that someone owes from an earlier date

PHRASES

take a back seat to be less involved in something than you used to be: *Our boss is nearing retirement and takes more of a back seat at meetings these days.*

backache /ˈbækeɪk/ *n* **[C,U]** a pain in your back
THESAURUS **PAIN**

backbench /ˌbækˈbentʃ◂/ *adj* [only before noun] *BrE* a backbench Member of Parliament is one who does not have an important official position
—**backbencher** *n* **[C]**

backbenches /ˌbækˈbentʃɪz/ *n* **the backbenches** [plural] *BrE* the seats in Parliament where backbench politicians sit

backbone /ˈbækbəʊn $ -boʊn/ *n* **1** **[C]** the bone down the middle of your back SYN **spine** → see picture on page A2 **2 the backbone of sth** the most important part of something: *A good manager is the backbone of the team.*

backbreaking /ˈbækbreɪkɪŋ/ *adj* backbreaking work is very hard physical work THESAURUS **TIRING**

backdate /ˌbækˈdeɪt $ ˈbækdeɪt/ *v* **[T]** to make something have its effect from an earlier date: **backdate sth to/from sth** *The pay increase will be backdated to January.*

backdrop /ˈbækdrɒp $ -drɑːp/ *n* **[C]** **1** the situation in which something happens: *a love story set against the backdrop of war* **2** (also **backcloth** /-klɒθ $ -klɔːθ/) the painted cloth at the back of a stage

backer /ˈbækə $ -ər/ *n* **[C]** someone who supports a plan, especially by providing money

backfire /ˌbækˈfaɪə $ ˈbækfaɪr/ *v* **[I]** if something you do backfires, it has the opposite effect to the one you wanted

backgammon /ˈbækɡæmən/ *n* **[U]** a game for two players, using flat round pieces and DICE on a board

background /ˈbækɡraʊnd/ *n*

1 **[C]** someone's education, family, and experience: *All the kids here come from very different backgrounds.* | *He has a background in Computer Science.* | **social/cultural/family etc background** *What's her educational background?*

2 [singular, U] the general situation in which something happens: **[+to]** *Let me explain the background to this case.* | **against a background** *The deal came against a background of rising political tension.* | *He gave us some background information.*

3 [C usually singular] the area that is behind the main things that you look at in a picture: **in the background** *You can see some houses in the background.* | **on/against a background** *a pattern of roses on a blue background*

4 [singular] sounds that are in the background are not the main ones that you can hear: *There was a lot of background noise.* | **in the background** *I could hear music playing in the background.*

PHRASES

in the background if someone stays in the background, they work or do things quietly, so that other people do not notice them: *A waiter stood quietly in the background.*

backhand /ˈbækhænd/ *n* [C usually singular] a way of hitting the ball in tennis etc, with the back of your hand turned towards the ball

backing /ˈbækɪŋ/ *n* **[U]** support or help, especially with money: *We managed to get **financial backing** for the project.*

backlash /'bæklæʃ/ n [C] a strong reaction from people against an idea or person: **[+against]** *a public backlash against the President*

backlog /'bæklɒg $ -lɔːg, -lɑːg/ n [C usually singular] a lot of work that needs doing and that you should have done earlier

backpack[1] /'bækpæk/ n [C] a bag used to carry things on your back, especially when you go walking → see picture at **BAG**[1]

backpack[2] v [I] to go walking or travelling carrying a backpack —**backpacker** n [C] —**backpacking** n [U]

backpedal /ˌbæk'pedl $ 'bæk,pedl/ v [I] (**backpedalled, backpedalling** BrE, **backpedaled, backpedaling** AmE) to change your opinion or not do something that you had said you would do $\boxed{\text{SYN}}$ **backtrack**: *They are backpedalling on the commitment to cut taxes.*

backside /'bæksaɪd/ n [C] *informal* the part of your body that you sit on $\boxed{\text{SYN}}$ **bottom**

backslash /'bækslæʃ/ n [C] a line (\) used in writing to separate words, numbers, or letters

backstage /ˌbæk'steɪdʒ◂/ adv, adj behind the stage in a theatre

backstroke /'bækstrəʊk $ -stroʊk/ n [singular] a style of swimming on your back → see picture at **SWIM**[1]

back-to-'back adj [only before noun] happening one after another: *The team has had five back-to-back wins.*

backtrack /'bæktræk/ v [I] to change your opinion or not do something that you had said you would do $\boxed{\text{SYN}}$ **backpedal**: *The minister denied that he was backtracking.*

backup /'bækʌp/ n **1** [C,U] extra help or support that can be used if it is needed: *Four more police cars provided backup.* **2** [C] a copy of a computer document or program that you can use if the original one is lost or damaged: **[+of]** *Have you made a backup of the file?*

backward /'bækwəd $ -wərd/ adj **1** [only before noun] in the direction that is behind you: *She gave a backward glance.* **2** developing or learning more slowly than normal: *a backward child*

backwards /'bækwədz $ -wərdz/ (also **backward** especially AmE) adv
1 in the direction that is behind you $\boxed{\text{OPP}}$ **forwards**: *She stepped backwards in surprise.*
2 towards the past or the beginning of something $\boxed{\text{OPP}}$ **forwards**: *Count backwards from 100.*
3 with the back part in front: *You've got your T-shirt on backwards.*
PHRASES
backwards and forwards first in one direction, then in the opposite direction several times: *The hotel sign was swinging backwards and forwards in the wind.*

backwater /'bækwɔːtə $ -wɒːtər, -wɑː-/ n [C] a quiet uninteresting town

backyard /ˌbæk'jɑːd◂ $ -'jɑːrd◂/ n [C] **1** BrE a small enclosed area behind a house covered with a hard surface **2** AmE an area of land behind a house $\boxed{\text{SYN}}$ **garden** BrE

bacon /'beɪkən/ n [U] meat from a pig that has been put in salt and cut into thin pieces: *bacon and eggs*

bacteria /bæk'tɪəriə $ -'tɪr-/ n [plural] very small living things that sometimes cause disease —**bacterial** adj

bad /bæd/ adj (comparative **worse** /wɜːs $ wɜːrs/, superlative **worst** /wɜːst $ wɜːrst/)
1 $\boxed{\text{NOT GOOD}}$ not good or pleasant: *I'm afraid there's some bad news.* | *a bad smell* | *That's bad luck.* | *Dad's in a bad mood today.*
2 $\boxed{\text{LOW QUALITY}}$ of a low quality or standard: *That was the worst meal I've ever had.*
3 $\boxed{\text{NOT SKILFUL}}$ if you are bad at something, you cannot do it very well: *a bad skier* | **[+at]** *I was bad at tennis.* | **bad at doing sth** *I'm really bad at remembering people's names.*
4 $\boxed{\text{SERIOUS}}$ serious or severe: *a bad cold* | *The situation's getting worse.*
5 $\boxed{\text{NOT MORALLY GOOD}}$ not morally good: *He was a bad man.*
6 $\boxed{\text{NOT WELL-BEHAVED}}$ not behaving well: *Put it down, you bad boy!*
7 $\boxed{\text{HARMFUL}}$ **be bad for sb/sth** to be harmful: *Smoking is bad for you.* | *It's bad for your teeth to eat sweets.*
8 $\boxed{\text{TIME}}$ **a bad time/moment** a time that is difficult, unsuitable, or inconvenient: *Is this a bad time to call?*
9 $\boxed{\text{REGRET}}$ **feel bad** to feel ashamed or sorry about something: **[+about]** *I felt really bad about missing your birthday.* $\boxed{\text{THESAURUS}}$ ▶ ASHAMED
10 $\boxed{\text{HEART/LEG/BACK ETC}}$ a bad heart, leg etc is injured or does not work properly: *He had to take some time off work because he had a bad back.*
11 $\boxed{\text{NOT SAFE TO EAT}}$ food that is bad is not safe to eat because it is not fresh: *The milk has gone bad.* → be in sb's bad books at **BOOK**[1]
PHRASES
not bad *spoken* quite good: *The movie wasn't bad.*
too bad *spoken* **1** BrE used to say that you do not care about something: *'We need the report by tomorrow.' 'Too bad, I can't finish it until next week.'* **2** especially AmE used to say that you are sorry about something that has happened: *It's too bad she missed all the fun.*

THESAURUS

bad not good or pleasant: *a bad idea* | *The film was really bad.*

not very good not good – used as a more gentle way of saying that something was bad or disappointing: *Jo's exam results weren't very good.*

awful/terrible very bad: *Those colours look awful together.* | *It was a terrible mistake.*

horrible very bad, especially in a way that shocks or upsets you: *a horrible accident* | *What a horrible thing to say!*

disgusting smelling or tasting very bad: *The soup tasted disgusting.*

poor not as good as it could be or should be. *Poor* sounds rather formal: *The animals were in very poor condition.* | *His performance at school has been poor.*

disappointing not as good as you hoped or expected: *The team has had a very disappointing season.*

lousy *informal* very bad – used especially when you feel annoyed about something. Also used when saying that you feel unwell: *I've had a really lousy day.* | *He got up the next morning feeling lousy.*

baddie, **baddy** /'bædi/ n [C] *BrE informal* a bad person in a film or book **OPP** **goodie**

bade /bæd, beɪd/ v the past tense and past participle of BID

badge /bædʒ/ n [C] *BrE* a piece of metal, plastic, or cloth with writing or a picture on it that you wear to show which school you go to, which job you do etc **SYN** **button**, **pin** *AmE*: *the school badge* | *Her badge said '4 today!'* | *a sheriff's badge*

badger¹ /'bædʒə $ -ər/ n [C] an animal with black and white fur that lives under the ground

badger² v [T] to keep trying to persuade someone to do or allow something: *My friends keep badgering me to get a cell phone.* | *Tom badgered me into going.*

bad 'language n [U] words that are rude or used for swearing: *The film was full of bad language.*

badly /'bædli/ adv (comparative **worse** /wɜːs $ wɜːrs/, superlative **worst** /wɜːst $ wɜːrst/)
1 in a way that is not good **OPP** **well**: *The book was badly written.* | *Rob did badly in the test.*
2 very much or very seriously: *The refugees badly need clean water.* | *Our roof was leaking badly.* | *I could see that he was badly injured.*

badly 'off adj [not before noun] *especially BrE* poor or in a bad situation **OPP** **well-off**

badminton /'bædmɪntən/ n [U] a game in which you hit a small object with feathers on it over a net

badmouth /'bædmaʊθ/ v [T] *especially AmE informal* to criticize someone

bad-'tempered adj someone who is bad-tempered is easily annoyed **THESAURUS** **ANGRY**

baffle /'bæfəl/ v [T] if something baffles you, you cannot understand it: *Her behaviour baffled me.*
—**baffling** adj

bag¹ /bæg/ n [C]
1 a container that you can carry things in: *a shopping bag* | *a brown paper bag*
2 *BrE* a container that women use for carrying money and personal things **SYN** **handbag**: *a black leather bag*
3 a large container used to carry clothes when you are travelling: *John packed his bags and left.*
4 the amount a bag can contain: **[+of]** *He ate a whole bag of sweets.* → **CARRIER BAG**, **let the cat out of the bag** at **CAT**, **SHOULDER BAG**, **SLEEPING BAG**, **TOILET BAG**

PHRASES

bags of sth *especially BrE informal* a lot of something: *They've got bags of money!*

bags under your eyes dark circles or loose skin under your eyes

BAGS

backpack/rucksack *BrE*

shopping bag

handbag *BrE*/purse *AmE*   holdall *BrE*/carryall *AmE*

bag² v [T] (**bagged**, **bagging**) **1** (*also* **bag up**) to put things in a bag **2** *informal* to get something before other people get it: *I'll get there early and bag some seats.*

bagel /'beɪgəl/ n [C] a type of bread, shaped like a ring → see picture at **BREAD**

baggage /'bægɪdʒ/ n [U] **1** the bags that you carry when you are travelling **SYN** **luggage**: *Check your baggage in at the desk.* **2** problems and emotional difficulties that you continue to have from a situation in the past: *She's carrying a lot of emotional baggage.*

Grammar

Baggage is not used in the plural. Do not say 'You can leave baggages here.' Say *You can leave your baggage here.*

baggy /'bægi/ adj baggy clothes are big and loose **OPP** **tight**

'bag lady n [C] *informal* an offensive word for a homeless woman who carries all her possessions with her

bagpipes /'bægpaɪps/ n [plural] a musical instrument played especially in Scotland, by blowing air into a bag and forcing it out through pipes

baguette /bæ'get/ n [C] a long thin LOAF of bread

bail¹ /beɪl/ n [U] when someone pays money to a court so that they can stay out of prison until they appear before the court, or the amount of money that they pay: **grant/refuse sb bail** *The defendant was granted bail until April 27.* | **release/free sb on bail** (=let someone go free when bail is paid)

bail² v [T usually passive] *BrE* if someone is bailed, they pay an amount of money and are allowed to stay out of prison until they appear in a court of law

PHRASAL VERBS

bail sb ↔ **out 1** to help someone get out of trouble, especially by giving them money: *Young people often expect their parents to bail them out.* **2** to money with a court of law so that someone can stay out of prison until they appear in court

bailiff /ˈbeɪlɪf/ *n* [C] **1** *BrE* someone whose job is to take people's property when they owe money **2** *AmE* someone whose job is to guard prisoners in a court of law

bait¹ /beɪt/ *n* [singular, U] **1** food that you use to attract fish or animals so that you can catch them **2** something that is offered to someone to persuade them to do something

bait² *v* [T] **1** to put food on a hook or in a trap to catch fish or animals **2** to deliberately try to annoy someone by laughing at them or making jokes about them

bake /beɪk/ *v* [I,T] to cook something such as bread or cakes in an OVEN: *I'm baking a cake.* | *baked potatoes* | **bake (sth) at 180/200 etc degrees** *Bake at 250 degrees for 20 minutes.* → see picture at **COOK¹**
THESAURUS COOK

baked 'beans *n* [plural] beans that are cooked in a tomato sauce and sold in cans

baker /ˈbeɪkə $ -ər/ *n* [C] **1** someone whose job is making bread, cakes etc **2 baker's** *BrE* a shop that sells bread, cakes etc

bakery /ˈbeɪkəri/ *n* [C] (*plural* **bakeries**) a place where bread, cakes etc are made or sold

baking /ˈbeɪkɪŋ/ *adj* very hot: *a baking hot day*

balance¹ /ˈbæləns/ *n*
1 [U] when you are able to stand and walk steadily, without falling: *I put my arms out to help me keep my balance.* | *Jim lost his balance on the ice.* | *The blow knocked his opponent off balance.* **THESAURUS** FALL
2 [singular, U] when you give the right amount of importance to different things in a sensible way: *Try to keep a balance between work and play.* | *It's not always easy to strike the right balance.*
3 [singular, U] when the correct relationship exists between different things OPP imbalance: [+between] *the need to maintain the balance between cost and profit* | [+of] *pesticides that upset the balance of nature*
4 [C] **a)** the amount of money that you have left to use: *Can I check my bank balance please?* **b)** the amount of money that you owe for something: *You can pay a deposit now and the balance later.*
PHRASES
be/hang in the balance if something hangs in the balance, you do not know yet whether the result will be bad or good: *The president's future hung in the balance.*
on balance used to tell someone your opinion after considering all the facts: *On balance, I prefer the new system.*

balance² *v*
1 [I,T] to be in a steady position, without falling, or to put something in this position: [+on] *Can you balance on one leg?* | **balance sth on sth** *The woman was balancing a large vase on her head.*
2 [T] to consider one thing in relation to something else, especially so that you give the right amount of importance to both: **balance sth against sth** *Our rights have to be balanced against our responsibilities.* | **balance sth and sth** *It can be hard to balance family life and a career.*

3 (*also* **balance out**) [I,T] if two or more things balance, or if one balances the other, the effect of one equals the effect of the other: *Job losses in some departments were balanced by increases in others.*
PHRASES
balance the books/budget to make sure that you do not spend more money than you have: *The company is finding it difficult to balance the books.*

balanced /ˈbælənst/ *adj* **1** fair and sensible: *a balanced approach to the problem* **2** including a good mixture of things: *a balanced diet* → WELL-BALANCED

balance of 'payments (*also* balance of 'trade) *n* [singular] *especially BrE* the difference between the amount of money that a country earns from selling goods and services abroad and the amount it spends

balance of 'power *n* **the balance of power** the way in which power is divided between people, countries, or organizations

balance sheet *n* [C] a written statement of how much a business has earned and how much it has spent

balancing act *n* [singular] when you are trying to please two different people or groups, or achieve two different things: *The Prime Minister is attempting a difficult balancing act.*

balcony /ˈbælkəni/ *n* [C] (*plural* **balconies**) **1** a structure built onto an outside wall of a building, that you reach through an upstairs door **2** the seats upstairs in a theatre

bald /bɔːld $ bɒːld/ *adj* **1** someone who is bald has no hair or very little hair on their head → see picture at **HAIR 2** [only before noun] bald facts or statements are very direct —**baldness** *n* [U]

balding /ˈbɔːldɪŋ $ ˈbɒːl-/ *adj* losing hair on your head

baldly /ˈbɔːldli $ ˈbɒːld-/ *adv* in a clear direct way, without trying to be polite: *'I want you to leave,' she said baldly.*

bale¹ /beɪl/ *n* [C] a large amount of something such as paper or HAY, tied tightly together

bale² *v*
PHRASAL VERBS
bale out *BrE*, **bail out** *AmE* to escape from a plane, using a PARACHUTE

baleful /ˈbeɪlfəl/ *adj formal* angry or evil

balk /bɔːk, bɔːlk $ bɒːk, bɒːlk/ *v* the American spelling of BAULK

ball /bɔːl $ bɒːl/ *n* [C]
1 a round object that you throw, hit, or kick in a game or sport: *tennis balls* | *Do you want to come and play ball* (=play a game with a ball)?
2 something rolled into a round shape: [+of] *a ball of wool* | *Form the pastry into a ball.*
3 a large formal occasion where people dance
THESAURUS PARTY
4 the rounded part at the base of the toes or at the base of the thumb → **play ball** at **PLAY¹**

something: *We will ballot our members to find out how much support there is for a strike.*

PHRASES

have a ball *informal* to enjoy something very much: *We had a ball last night!*

be on the ball *informal* to be able to think or react very quickly: *You need to be on the ball in a job interview.*

set/start the ball rolling *informal* to start something happening: *Just a small donation will start the ball rolling.*

ballad /'bæləd/ *n* [C] a long song or poem that tells a story

ballerina /ˌbælə'riːnə/ *n* [C] a woman who dances in ballets

ballet /'bæleɪ $ bæ'leɪ, 'bæleɪ/ *n* **1** [C,U] a type of dancing that tells a story with music but no words, or a performance of this type of dancing: *We went to see a ballet in London.* | *I'm **going to the ballet** (=going to watch a ballet) this evening.* | *a **ballet dancer*** **2** [C] a group of ballet dancers who work together: *the Royal Ballet*

'ball game *n* [C] *AmE* a game of baseball, football, or BASKETBALL

PHRASES

sth is a whole new ball game/a different ball game used when saying that a situation is very different from the one you are used to: *Now that the country is in recession, it's a whole new ball game.*

ballistic /bə'lɪstɪk/ *adj* **go ballistic** *informal* to suddenly become very angry

bal,listic 'missile *n* [C] a powerful weapon that can travel very long distances through the air

BALLOONS

balloon

hot air balloon

balloon¹ /bə'luːn/ *n* [C] a small coloured rubber bag that you blow air into and use as a toy or decoration: *Can you **blow up** these **balloons**?* | *Suddenly the **balloon burst**.* → HOT AIR BALLOON

balloon² *v* [I] to suddenly become much larger: *The company's debt ballooned to $350 million.*

ballot¹ /'bælət/ *n* [C,U] a system of voting in secret, or an occasion when people vote in this way: *Workers **held a ballot** and rejected strike action.* | *a **ballot paper** (=piece of paper that you use to vote)* | *He won 54% of **the ballot** (=the number of votes in an election).*

ballot² *v* [T] *especially BrE* to ask people to vote for

something: *We will ballot our members to find out how much support there is for a strike.*

'ballot box *n* [C] **1 the ballot box** the system of voting in an election: *Voters will make their views known through the ballot box.* **2** the box where people put the papers they have used for voting

ballpark /'bɔːlpɑːk $ 'bɔːlpɑːrk/ *n* [C] **1** *AmE* a field for playing baseball, with seats for people to watch the game **2 a ballpark figure/estimate** a number or amount that is almost but not exactly correct

PHRASES

in the right/same etc ballpark *informal* used to say that numbers or amounts are almost correct, almost the same etc: *All the bids are expected to be in the same ballpark.*

ballpoint pen /ˌbɔːlpɔɪnt 'pen $ ˌbɔːl-/ (*also **ballpoint***) *n* [C] a pen with a small ball at the end, which rolls ink onto the paper

ballroom /'bɔːlrʊm, -ruːm $ 'bɔːl-/ *n* [C] a large room for formal dances

ˌballroom 'dancing *n* [U] a formal type of dancing that is done with a partner and has different steps for different types of music

balmy /'bɑːmi $ 'bɑːmi, 'bɑːlmi/ *adj* balmy air or weather is warm and pleasant: *a balmy evening*

baloney /bə'ləʊni $ -'loʊ-/ *n* [U] *informal* something that is silly or not true: *Don't give me that baloney!*

balustrade /ˌbælə'streɪd $ 'bæləstreɪd/ *n* [C] a row of posts along the edge of a BALCONY or bridge

bamboo /ˌbæm'buː◂/ *n* [U] a tall tropical plant with hollow stems, often used for making furniture

bamboozle /bæm'buːzəl/ *v* [T] *informal* to trick or confuse someone

ban¹ /bæn/ *n* [C] an official order saying that people must not do something: **[+on]** *The government **imposed** (=started) a ban on tobacco advertising.* | *The committee agreed to **lift** (=end) the ban on meat imports.*

ban² *v* [T] (**banned, banning**) to officially say that people must not do something: *Smoking is banned inside the building.* | **ban sb from doing sth** *He was banned from driving for a year.* **THESAURUS** ▶ FORBID

banal /bə'nɑːl, bə'næl/ *adj* ordinary and not interesting: *a banal conversation* —**banality** /bə'næləti/ *n* [C,U]

banana /bə'nɑːnə $ -'næ-/ *n* [C] a long curved yellow fruit → see picture on page A4

band¹ /bænd/ *n* [C]

1 MUSICIANS [also + plural verb *BrE*] a group of musicians who play popular music together: *Her boyfriend was in a band.* | *The band was playing old Beatles' songs.*

2 GROUP OF PEOPLE a group of people who have the same beliefs or aims: **[+of]** *a loyal band of supporters*

3 ROUND OBJECT a narrow piece of something, with one end joined to the other to form a circle: *papers held together with a **rubber band***

4 NUMBERS/AMOUNTS a range of numbers or amounts in a system: *tax/age/income band taxpayers in higher tax bands*

5 OF COLOUR/LIGHT a narrow area of colour or light that is different from the areas around it: *a fish with a black band along its back* → **BOY BAND, ELASTIC BAND**

COLLOCATIONS

verbs

to be/play/sing in a band *She had always wanted to be in a band.*

to form a band *They formed the band while they were at school.* ⚠ Do not say 'make a band'. Say **form a band.**

a band plays/performs *His band played at the Glastonbury festival.*

a band splits (up) *The band split after making only one album.*

types of band

a live band (=playing music that is not recorded) *Do you ever go to see live bands?*

a rock/jazz etc band *He plays sax in a jazz band.*

a brass band (=with brass instruments such as trumpets)

band + noun

a band member (*also* **a member of a band**) *He was one of the original band members.*

band² *v*

PHRASAL VERBS

band together if people band together, they work with each other to achieve something: *Local people have banded together to fight the company's plans.*

bandage¹ /ˈbændɪdʒ/ *n* [C] a long piece of cloth that you tie around a wound or injury

bandage² (*also* **bandage up**) *v* [T] to tie a bandage around a wound or injury

Band-Aid *n* [C] *trademark AmE* a small piece of material that you stick over a small wound on your skin SYN **plaster** *BrE*

bandanna, bandana /bænˈdænə/ *n* [C] a piece of coloured cloth that you wear around your head or neck

B and B, B & B /ˌbiː ənd ˈbiː/ *n* [C] the abbreviation of **bed and breakfast** THESAURUS **HOTEL**

bandit /ˈbændɪt/ *n* [C] someone who robs people who are travelling through hills or mountains

bandstand /ˈbændstænd/ *n* [C] a structure in a park, used by a band playing music

bandwagon /ˈbændˌwægən/ *n* [C] an activity or idea that suddenly becomes popular or fashionable: *the keep-fit bandwagon of the 1980s* | *All the political parties are trying to **jump on the** environmental **bandwagon** (=start supporting it because it is fashionable).*

bandwidth /ˈbændwɪdθ/ *n* [U] *technical* the amount of information that can be carried through a telephone wire or computer connection at one time

bandy /ˈbændi/ *v* (**bandied, bandying, bandies**) **be bandied about/around** to be mentioned by a lot of people: *Rumours of an affair had been bandied about in the media.*

bane /beɪn/ *n* **be the bane of sb/sth** to be the person or thing that annoys someone or causes problems for them: *Commuting is the bane of my life.*

bang¹ /bæŋ/ *n* [C] **1** a sudden loud noise such as an explosion or something hitting a hard surface: *There was a loud bang, followed by the sound of breaking glass.* | *The door closed with a bang.* → see picture on page A7 **2** an occasion when part of your body hits something: **[+on]** *He got a nasty bang on the head.* **3** **bangs** [plural] *AmE* hair that is cut straight across the front of your head, above your eyes SYN **fringe** *BrE* → see picture at **HAIR**

PHRASES

go with a bang *informal* if an event goes with a bang, it is very successful: *ideas to make sure your party goes with a bang*

bang² *v* [I,T] **1** to make a loud noise, especially by hitting something against something hard: **[+on]** *Someone was banging on the door.* | *She banged her fists on the table.* | *A door banged downstairs.* THESAURUS **HIT 2** to hit part of your body against something by accident: **bang sth on sth** *I banged my knee on the corner of the bed.* | **[+into]** *He banged into the doorpost.*

bang³ *adv informal* directly or exactly: *The train arrived **bang on time**.* | *The technology is **bang up to date**.*

PHRASES

bang goes sth *BrE spoken* used to show that you are unhappy because something you had planned will not happen: *Oh well, bang goes our night out.*

banger /ˈbæŋə $ -ər/ *n* [C] *BrE informal* **1** a SAUSAGE **2** an old car in bad condition **3** a FIREWORK that makes a loud noise

bangle /ˈbæŋɡəl/ *n* [C] a band of metal, wood etc that you wear around your wrist

banish /ˈbænɪʃ/ *v* [T] **1** to get rid of something: *facial massage that can help banish wrinkles* | **banish sth from sth** *a show that's been banished from our TV screens* | **banish the thought/feeling etc** *She tried to banish the memory from her mind.* **2** to make someone leave a place as a punishment: **banish sb from/to sth** *He was banished from the country.* —**banishment** *n* [U]

banister /ˈbænɪstə $ -ər/ *n* [C] the piece of wood that you hold onto at the side of stairs → see picture at **STAIRCASE**

banjo /ˈbændʒəʊ $ -dʒoʊ/ *n* [C] (*plural* **banjos**) a musical instrument with a round body and strings that you pull with your fingers → see picture on page A6

bank¹ /bæŋk/ *n* [C]

1 PLACE FOR MONEY the company or place where you can keep your money or borrow money: **in the bank** *I think I'll put the money in the bank.*

2 OF RIVER land along the side of a river or lake: **[+of]** *the banks of the River Thames* | *the river bank*

3 OF BLOOD/INFORMATION ETC a store of something that is kept until people need it: *a blood bank* | *a data bank* | **[+of]** *a bank of information*

4 OF EARTH/SNOW ETC a large sloping mass of earth, sand, snow etc: *a grassy bank* | [+of] *a huge bank of earth*
5 OF CLOUD/FOG a mass of cloud or FOG → BOTTLE BANK, FOOD BANK, PIGGY BANK

COLLOCATIONS

verbs

to go to the bank *I'm going to the bank to get some money.*
to borrow (sth) from a bank *They were forced to borrow from the bank.*
to put sth in the bank *She went to put some cheques in the bank.*

bank + noun

a bank account *We had almost nothing in our bank account.*
your bank balance (=the amount in your bank account at a particular time) *You can check your bank balance online.*
a bank loan *He tried to get a bank loan to start a business.*
a bank statement (=a record of all the money taken out of and put into a bank account) *I read my bank statement every month.*

---

bank² *v* **1** [T] to put money in a bank: *Have you banked the cheque yet?* **2** [I] to use a particular bank: [+with/at] *I bank with the National Bank now.* **3** [I] if a plane banks, it slopes to one side when it is turning
PHRASAL VERBS
bank on sb/sth to depend on something happening: *I was banking on him being here.*

'bank ac,count *n* [C] an arrangement that allows you to keep your money in a bank and take it out when you want to

'bank ,balance *n* [C] the amount of money someone has in their bank account

banker /'bæŋkə $ -ər/ *n* [C] someone who has an important job in a bank

,bank 'holiday *n* [C] *BrE* an official holiday when banks and most companies are closed

banking /'bæŋkɪŋ/ *n* [U] the business of a bank

'bank note, banknote *n* [C] a piece of paper money SYN note *BrE*, bill *AmE*

bankroll /'bæŋkrəʊl $ -roʊl/ *v* [T] to provide the money that someone needs for a business, plan etc SYN finance: *Who is bankrolling the campaign?*

bankrupt¹ /'bæŋkrʌpt/ *adj* without enough money to pay your debts: *Many small businesses went bankrupt last year.*

bankrupt² *v* [T] to make someone become bankrupt: *The deal nearly bankrupted us.*

bankruptcy /'bæŋkrʌptsi/ *n* [C,U] (*plural* bankruptcies) when a person or company cannot pay their debts: *a company on the verge of bankruptcy*

banner /'bænə $ -ər/ *n* [C] a long piece of cloth with writing on it: *The crowds were cheering and waving banners.*

PHRASES
under the banner of sth 1 doing something because of a principle or belief: *an election fought under the banner of social justice* **2** doing something as part of a particular organization: *a force operating under the NATO banner*

banquet /'bæŋkwɪt/ *n* [C] a very formal meal for a lot of people THESAURUS MEAL

banter /'bæntə $ -ər/ *n* [U] friendly conversation with a lot of jokes in it: *He always enjoyed a bit of banter with his customers.*

bap /bæp/ *n* [C] *BrE* a round soft bread ROLL

baptism /'bæptɪzəm/ *n* [C,U] a religious ceremony in which a priest puts water on someone to make them a member of the Christian church → **christening** —baptismal /bæp'tɪzməl/ *adj*

Baptist /'bæptɪst/ *n* [C] a member of a Christian group that believes baptism should only be for those old enough to understand its meaning

baptize (*also* -ise *BrE*) /bæp'taɪz $ 'bæptaɪz/ *v* [T] to make someone a member of the Christian church by a baptism

bar¹ /bɑː $ bɑːr/ *n* [C]
1 WHERE PEOPLE DRINK ALCOHOL **a)** a place where alcoholic drinks are sold and can be drunk: *We met in the hotel bar.* **b)** *BrE* one of the rooms inside a PUB
2 COUNTER where alcoholic drinks are served: **at the bar** *They stood at the bar.* | **behind the bar** *The woman behind the bar was very friendly.*
3 SELLING FOOD/COFFEE coffee/snack/burger etc bar a place where a particular type of food or drink is served
4 BLOCK a small block of something: [+of] *a bar of soap* | *a bar of chocolate* | *a candy bar* → see picture at PIECE¹ THESAURUS PIECE
5 OF METAL/WOOD a long narrow piece of metal or wood: *iron bars*
6 IN MUSIC a group of notes in printed music, separated from others by a vertical line: *the opening bars of the song*
7 ON A COMPUTER a row of pictures on a computer screen that you can choose and CLICK on: *the menu bar*
8 OBSTACLE something that prevents something else from happening: *His lack of a formal education was not a bar to his success.*
9 LAWYERS the bar the profession of being a lawyer, or lawyers considered as a group
PHRASES
behind bars *informal* in prison: *He was back behind bars last night.*
raise the bar/set the bar high to do something very well, so that other people feel they have to try harder: *He has raised the bar for other film-makers.*

bar² *v* [T] (**barred, barring**) **1** to officially prevent someone from doing something: **bar sb from (doing) sth** *He was barred from playing in the tournament.* **2** to prevent someone from going somewhere by putting something in front of them: *A tall gate **barred** their way.* **3** to close and lock a door or window

bar³ *prep* except: *It was a great performance, bar one mistake.*

PHRASES

bar none used to emphasize that someone or something is the best: *It's the best restaurant in town, bar none.*

barbarian /bɑːˈbeəriən $ bɑːrˈber-/ *n* [C] someone who is rough, violent, and uneducated and does not respect art, education etc

barbaric /bɑːˈbærɪk $ bɑːr-/ (also **barbarous** /ˈbɑːbərəs $ ˈbɑːr-/) *adj* violent and cruel: *a barbaric act of terrorism* **THESAURUS** CRUEL —**barbarism** *n* [U]

barbarous /ˈbɑːbərəs $ ˈbɑːr-/ *adj literary* cruel and shocking: *barbarous crimes* —**barbarously** *adv*

barbecue /ˈbɑːbɪkjuː $ ˈbɑːr-/ *n* [C] **1** an occasion when you cook and eat food outdoors **SYN** BBQ: *We had a barbecue on the beach.* **2** a piece of equipment for cooking food outdoors —**barbecue** *v* [T]: *barbecued sausages*

barbed /bɑːbd $ bɑːrbd/ *adj* a barbed remark is unkind

barbed 'wire *n* [U] wire with sharp points on it, used to stop people getting into a place

barber /ˈbɑːbə $ ˈbɑːrbər/ *n* [C] a man whose job is to cut men's hair

'bar chart (also **'bar graph**) *n* [C] a picture of boxes of different heights, in which each box represents a different amount or quantity

'bar code *n* [C] a row of black lines on a product that a computer can read to get information such as the price

bard /bɑːd $ bɑːrd/ *n* [C] *literary* a poet

bare¹ /beə $ ber/ *adj* **1** not covered by clothes: *children running around in bare feet* | **bare-chested/bare-legged etc 2** empty, or not covered by anything: *The room was very bare.* | *a bare hillside* **THESAURUS** EMPTY **3** basic and with nothing extra: *a report giving just the bare facts* | *a room with the bare minimum of furniture* | **the bare necessities/essentials** (=the basic things you need) —**bareness** *n* [U]

PHRASES

with your bare hands without using a weapon or tool: *Firefighters dug with their bare hands to rescue survivors.*

bare² *v* [T] to let people see part of your body by removing something that is covering it: *I don't usually bare my skin to the sun.* | *The dog bared its teeth and growled.*

barefoot /ˈbeəfʊt $ ˈber-/ *adj, adv* not wearing any shoes or socks: *walking barefoot in the sand*

barely /ˈbeəli $ ˈberli/ *adv* **1** only just: *They had barely enough money to live on.* | *I could barely stay awake.* | *The cabin was barely visible in the rain.* **2** used to emphasize that something happens immediately after something else: *He'd barely sat down when the phone rang.*

barf /bɑːf $ bɑːrf/ *v* [I] *AmE informal* to VOMIT —**barf** *n* [U]

bargain¹ /ˈbɑːgɪn $ ˈbɑːr-/ *n* [C] **1** something you buy cheaply or for less than its usual price: *The table was a real bargain.* | *books at bargain prices* | **bargain hunters** (=people looking for things that are cheap) **THESAURUS** CHEAP **2** an agreement between two or more people, in which each person agrees to do something in return for something else: **make/strike a bargain** *I'll make a bargain with you. You cook and I'll wash up.* | *I've kept my side of the bargain and I expect you to keep yours.*

PHRASES

into the bargain *especially BrE* in addition to everything else: *She found a new job and a new husband into the bargain.*

bargain² *v* [I] to discuss the conditions of a sale, agreement etc in order to get a fair deal: **[+with]** *people bargaining with traders* | **[+for]** *They're trying to bargain for better pay.* | **[+over]** *union leaders bargaining over wages*

PHRASAL VERBS

bargain for/on sth to expect that something will happen: *I hadn't bargained on getting stuck in traffic.* | *The thief got more than he bargained for when his victim fought back.*

barge¹ /bɑːdʒ $ bɑːrdʒ/ *n* [C] a boat for carrying goods on a CANAL or river

barge² *v* [I,T] to walk somewhere so quickly or carelessly that you push people or hit things: **[+through/past]** *He barged past the guards at the door.* | *She barged her way through the crowds.*

PHRASAL VERBS

barge in (also **barge into** sth) to enter somewhere rudely, or to rudely interrupt someone: *Sorry to barge in while you're having a meal.*

baritone /ˈbærɪtəʊn $ -toʊn/ *n* [C] a male singing voice that is fairly low, but not the lowest

bark¹ /bɑːk $ bɑːrk/ *v* **1** [I] when a dog barks, it makes a short loud sound: **[+at]** *The dog always barks at strangers.* **2** (also **bark out**) [I,T] to say something in a loud angry voice: *The teacher barked instructions at us.* | **[+at]** *'What are you doing?' he barked at her.*

PHRASES

be barking up the wrong tree *spoken* to be doing something that will not get the result you want: *You're barking up the wrong tree – I had nothing to do with any of this.*

bark² *n* **1** [C] the rough loud sound that a dog makes **2** [U] the outer covering of a tree → see picture at PLANT¹

barley /ˈbɑːli $ ˈbɑːrli/ *n* [U] a grain used for making food and alcohol

barmaid /ˈbɑːmeɪd $ ˈbɑːr-/ *n* [C] *BrE* a woman who serves drinks in a bar **SYN** **bartender** *especially AmE*

barman /ˈbɑːmən $ ˈbɑːr-/ *n* [C] (plural **barmen** /-mən/) *BrE* a man who serves drinks in a bar **SYN** **bartender** *AmE*

bar mitzvah /ˌbɑː ˈmɪtsvə $ ˌbɑːr-/ *n* [C] the religious ceremony held when a Jewish boy reaches the age of 13

barmy /'bɑːmi $ 'bɑːrmi/ adj BrE informal slightly crazy

barn /bɑːn $ bɑːrn/ n [C] a large farm building for keeping crops or animals in

barometer /bə'rɒmɪtə $ -'rɑːmɪtər/ n [C]
1 something that shows any changes in a situation: **[+of]** an industry that's a good barometer of the state of the economy **2** an instrument for measuring changes in air pressure and weather

baron /'bærən/ n [C] **1** a man in Britain or Europe of a high social rank **2** someone who has a lot of power in a particular business: **press/drug barons**

baroness /'bærənəs/ n [C] a woman in Britain or Europe of a high social rank

baroque /bə'rɒk, bə'rəʊk $ bə'rouk, -'rɑːk/ adj relating to the style of art, music, building etc popular in Europe in the 17th century

barrack /'bærək/ v [I,T] BrE to shout criticism at a speaker, performer, or sports player: He was barracked by a section of the crowd.

barracks /'bærəks/ n [plural] a group of buildings where soldiers live

barrage /'bærɑːʒ $ bə'rɑːʒ/ n **1** [singular] a lot of complaints, questions etc: **[+of]** We've received a barrage of complaints from viewers. **2** [C usually singular] the continuous shooting of guns

barred /bɑːd $ bɑːrd/ adj a barred window has bars across it

barrel /'bærəl/ n [C] **1** a large container for liquids such as beer: a beer barrel | **[+of]** a barrel of oil **2** the part of a gun that bullets are fired through

barren /'bærən/ adj barren land or soil is not good enough for plants to grow

barricade¹ /'bærəkeɪd, ˌbærə'keɪd/ n [C] something that is put across a road or door to stop people going through: Demonstrators erected barricades across the streets.

barricade² v [T] to use a barricade to prevent someone or something from going somewhere: **barricade sb in/into sth** Students barricaded themselves in and refused to leave.

barrier /'bæriə $ -ər/ n [C] **1** something that prevents people from doing something: a new deal to abolish trade barriers | The **language barrier** prevents many people from working abroad. | **[+to]** Disability need not be a barrier to success. **2** an object that keeps people or things separate or prevents people from entering a place: barriers to hold back the crowds

barring /'bɑːrɪŋ/ prep unless something happens: Barring accidents, she should win.

barrister /'bærɪstə $ -ər/ n [C] a lawyer in Britain who can work in the higher law courts

barrow /'bærəʊ $ -roʊ/ n [C] a small vehicle that is pushed or pulled along

bartender /'bɑːˌtendə $ 'bɑːrˌtendər/ n [C] especially AmE someone whose job is to serve drinks in a bar

barter /'bɑːtə $ 'bɑːrtər/ v [I,T] to exchange goods or services without using money: **barter sth for sth**

BARRIER

barrier

obstruction   obstacle

Farmers bartered grain for machinery. —**barter** n [U]

base¹ /beɪs/ v [T] to use somewhere as your main place of business: **be based somewhere** The company is based in Denver. | **London-based/Tokyo-based etc** a London-based publisher

PHRASAL VERBS
base sth **on/upon** sth to use something as the thing you develop something else from: The movie is based on the author's childhood experiences.

base² n [C]
1 BOTTOM OF OBJECT the lowest part of something: **[+of]** the base of the skull THESAURUS ▶ BOTTOM
2 FOR DEVELOPING STH a situation or idea that something else can develop from: **[+for]** The research has been used as a base for many other studies.
3 ARMY/NAVY a place where people in the army, navy etc live and work: an army base
4 PLACE TO WORK/STAY the main place where someone works or stays, or from which work is done: The firm has its main base in London. | **[+for]** The hotel is an ideal base for sightseeing.
5 SUPPORTERS the group of people who support a person or organization: Mandela had a broad base of political support. | a company with a large client base
6 MAIN SUBSTANCE the main part of a substance, to which other things can be added: paint with an oil base
7 IN BASEBALL one of the four places that a player must touch in order to get a point in baseball
PHRASES
| **be off base** AmE informal to be completely wrong: His estimate was way off base.

base³ adj formal morally bad: base instincts

baseball /'beɪsbɔːl $ -bɒːl/ n
1 [U] a game in which two teams try to get points by hitting a ball and running around four bases → see picture on page A9
2 [C] the ball used in baseball

baseless /'beɪsləs/ adj not true: baseless rumours

baseline /'beɪslaɪn/ n [C usually singular]
1 technical a measurement or fact against which

other measurements or facts are compared: *a baseline against which to judge waste reduction* **2** the line at the back of the court in games such as tennis

basement /'beɪsmənt/ *n* [C] the rooms in a building that are below the level of the ground

bases /'beɪsiːz/ *n* the plural of BASIS

bash¹ /bæʃ/ *v* **1** [I,T] to hit something or someone hard: **bash sth on/against sth** *He bashed his head on the back of the seat.* **2** [T] *informal* to criticize someone publicly

bash² *n* [C] **1** *informal* a party: *a birthday bash* **2** a hard hit

PHRASES

> **have a bash at (doing) sth** *BrE spoken* to try to do something: *I'm going to have a bash at putting these shelves up.*

bashful /'bæʃfəl/ *adj* shy —**bashfully** *adv*

basic /'beɪsɪk/ *adj*
1 basic things are the most simple or most important things → **basics**: *the basic principles of chemistry* | *The basic idea is simple.*
2 something that is basic is simple, with nothing extra: *The rooms are fairly basic.* | *food and basic necessities*

basically /'beɪsɪkli/ *adv*
1 *spoken* used to give a simple explanation of something: *Basically, I'm just lazy.*
2 in the most important ways, without considering small details: *All cheeses are made in basically the same way.*

basics /'beɪsɪks/ *n* [plural] the most important facts or things that you need: **[+of]** *I know **the basics** of first aid.* | *people without basics like food and education*

basil /'bæzəl $ 'beɪ-/ *n* [U] a HERB with a strong smell and taste

basin /'beɪsən/ *n* [C] **1** *BrE* a round container attached to a wall, in which you wash your hands and face SYN **sink** *AmE* → see picture at **BATHROOM** **2** *BrE* a bowl for liquids or food: *Pour the hot water into a basin.* **3** *technical* a large area of land that is lower at the centre: *the Amazon basin*

basis /'beɪsɪs/ *n* [C] (*plural* **bases** /-siːz/)
1 the information, facts, or thing on which something is based: **form/provide a basis for sth** *The video will provide a basis for class discussion.* | **the basis for/of sth** *Bread forms the basis of their daily diet.* | **on the basis of sth** (=using particular facts or reasons) *On the basis of the present evidence, he is not guilty.*
2 on a ... basis used to say how something is organized or done: *They work on a **voluntary basis**.* | *We offer this service on a **commercial basis**.* | **on the basis that** *He was employed on the basis that he would work 37 hours per week.* | **on a regular/daily/weekly etc basis** *Meetings are held on a regular basis.*

bask /bɑːsk $ bæsk/ *v* [I] **1** to enjoy sitting or lying in the warmth of the sun: **[+in]** *A lizard was basking in the sun.* **2** to enjoy the approval that you are getting from other people: **[+in]** *Nigel was still basking in the glory of his first book.*

basket /'bɑːskɪt $ 'bæ-/ *n* [C]
1 a container made from thin pieces of wood, plastic, wire etc, used to carry things or put things in: *a **shopping basket** | a wicker **laundry basket** (=for dirty clothes) | **[+of]** a basket of fruit*
2 the net in basketball → **WASTEPAPER BASKET**

basketball /'bɑːskɪtbɔːl $ 'bæskətbɒːl/ *n* **1** [U] a game between two teams, in which each team tries to throw a ball through a net → see picture on page A9 **2** [C] the ball used in this game

bass /beɪs/ *n* **1** [C] a very low male singing voice, or a man with a voice like this **2** [U] the lower half of the whole range of musical notes **3** (*also* ˌbass gui'tar*) [C,U] an electric GUITAR that plays low notes **4** [C] a DOUBLE BASS

bassoon /bə'suːn/ *n* [C] a very long wooden musical instrument with a low sound that you play by blowing into it → see picture on page A6

baste /beɪst/ *v* [I,T] to pour liquid or melted fat over food that is cooking

bastion /'bæstiən $ -tʃən/ *n* [C] a place, organization etc that protects old beliefs or ways of doing things

bat¹ /bæt/ *n* [C] **1** a piece of wood used to hit the ball in games such as baseball and CRICKET: *a cricket bat* → see picture on page A9 **2** a small animal that flies at night, like a mouse with wings

bat² *v* [I] (**batted**, **batting**) to be the person or team that is trying to hit the ball in CRICKET or baseball

PHRASES

> **not bat an eyelid/eye** to not be upset or surprised by something: *He didn't bat an eyelid when he was threatened.*

batch /bætʃ/ *n* [C] a group of things or people that arrive or are dealt with at the same time: **[+of]** *She had just baked another batch of cookies.*

bated /'beɪtɪd/ *adj* **with bated breath** feeling very anxious or excited

bath¹ /bɑːθ $ bæθ/ *n* [C]
1 *BrE* a long container in which you sit to wash yourself SYN **bathtub** *AmE* → see picture at **BATHROOM**
2 [usually singular] when you wash your body in the water that you put in a bath: **have/take a bath** *Suzy had a bath and went to bed.* | *All I wanted was a nice **hot bath** (=wash with hot water).* | *Shall I **run a bath** (=put water in a bath) for you?*
3 a bathroom, used especially in advertising: *All our bedrooms have a **private bath**.*

bath² *v* [I,T] *BrE* to wash yourself or someone else in a bath SYN **bathe** *AmE*: *Mum's upstairs bathing the baby.*

bathe /beɪð/ *v* **1** [I,T] *especially AmE* to wash yourself or someone else in a bath **2** [T] to put water or another liquid on part of your body as a medical treatment **3** [I] *BrE old-fashioned* to swim **4 be bathed in light** if something is bathed in light, a lot of light is shining on it

bathing suit /'beɪðɪŋ suːt, -sjuːt $ -suːt/ *n* [C] *especially AmE old-fashioned* a SWIMSUIT

bathrobe /'bɑːθrəʊb $ 'bæθroʊb/ *n* [C] a loose

piece of clothing like a coat that you wear before or after a bath

bathroom /ˈbɑːθrʊm, -ruːm $ ˈbæθ-/ n [C]
1 a room where there is a bath and often a toilet: *a house with two bathrooms* **THESAURUS** ▸ TOILET
2 *AmE* a room where there is a toilet: *I need to go to the bathroom* (=use a toilet).

bathtub /ˈbɑːθtʌb $ ˈbæθ-/ n [C] *especially AmE* a long container in which you wash yourself **SYN** bath *BrE* → see picture at **BATHROOM**

baton /ˈbætɒn, -tn $ bæˈtɑːn, bə-/ n [C] **1** a stick that a police officer uses as a weapon **2** a stick used to control the way music is played by a group of musicians **3** a stick passed from one runner to another in a race

batsman /ˈbætsmən/ n [C] (*plural* **batsmen** /-mən/) the person who is trying to hit the ball in cricket

battalion /bəˈtæljən/ n [C] a large group of soldiers

batter¹ /ˈbætə $ -ər/ v [I,T] to hit someone or something very hard many times: *He was battered to death.* | [+at/on/against etc] *People were battering at the door.*

batter² n **1** [C,U] a mixture of flour, eggs, and milk, used in cooking **2** [C] the person who is trying to hit the ball in baseball

battered /ˈbætəd $ -ərd/ *adj* **1** old and in bad condition: *a battered suitcase* **2 battered woman/**

wife/baby etc someone who has been attacked by their husband, a parent etc

battery /ˈbætəri/ n (*plural* **batteries**)
1 [C] an object that provides electricity for something such as a radio, car, or toy: *It needs a **new battery**.* | **flat battery** *BrE*, **dead battery** *AmE* (=one with no power) | **rechargeable batteries**
2 [U] *law* the crime of hitting someone: *He was charged with **assault and battery**.*
3 battery chickens/hens chickens that are kept in very small cages, so the farm can produce a lot of eggs → **recharge your batteries** at RECHARGE

battle¹ /ˈbætl/ n
1 **IN A WAR** [C,U] a fight between two armies or groups, especially in a war: [+of] *the Battle of Trafalgar* | **in battle** *Her son was killed in battle.*
2 **ARGUMENT** [C] a situation in which people or groups compete or argue with each other: [+with/ between] *a long battle with my parents about clothes* | [+for] *the battle for power* | *a **legal battle***
3 **ATTEMPT TO DO STH** [C] an attempt to stop something happening or to achieve something difficult: [+against] *the battle against disease* | **the battle to do sth** *the battle to protect the English countryside* | *We're **fighting a losing battle** (=trying to do something but not succeeding).* | **win/lose a battle** (=succeed or not succeed in doing something)
PHRASES
be half the battle to be an important part of achieving something: *Having enough confidence is half the battle.*

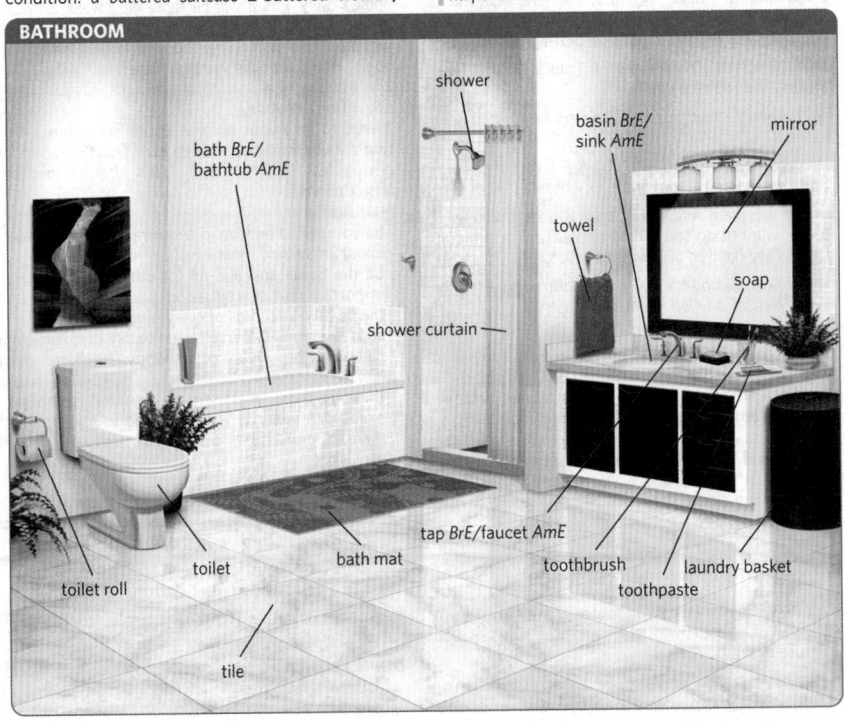

BATHROOM

shower

bath *BrE/* bathtub *AmE*

basin *BrE/* sink *AmE*

mirror

towel

soap

shower curtain

tap *BrE/*faucet *AmE*

toothbrush

laundry basket

toothpaste

toilet roll

toilet

bath mat

tile

B

COLLOCATIONS

verbs

to fight (in) a battle *A famous battle was fought there in 1916.*

to win/lose a battle *Who won the Battle of Waterloo?*

to die/be killed in a battle *Hundreds died in the battle.*

a battle takes place *During the Civil War a battle took place near here.*

adjectives

a great battle *There was a great battle, in which the English were defeated.*

a famous/historic battle *This was the site of the famous Battle of Hastings.*

a bloody battle (=in which a lot of people are killed or wounded) *the bloodiest battle of the American Civil War*

battle² *v* [I,T] to try very hard to achieve something difficult: **[+against/with]** *She battled bravely against cancer.* | **[+to]** *Doctors battled to save his life.*
PHRASES
  battle it out to continue to try and win or get what you want for as long as possible: *The two politicians are battling it out to see who will become the party's candidate in the election.*

battlefield /ˈbætlfiːld/ (*also* **battleground** /ˈbætlɡraʊnd/) *n* [C] **1** a place where a battle is fought **2** a subject that people do not agree about: *Education has become a **political battleground**.*

battlements /ˈbætlmənts/ *n* [plural] a low wall around the top of a castle

battleship /ˈbætlʃɪp/ *n* [C] a very large ship used in wars

bauble /ˈbɔːbəl $ ˈbɒː-/ *n* [C] *BrE* a round decoration that is used to decorate a CHRISTMAS TREE

baulk *BrE*, **balk** *AmE* /bɔːk, bɔːlk $ bɔːk, bɒːlk/ *v* [I] to not want to do something unpleasant or difficult: **[+at]** *They baulked at paying so much.*

bawl /bɔːl $ bɒːl/ *v* [I,T] to shout or cry loudly: *'Fares please!' bawled the bus conductor.*

bay /beɪ/ *n* [C]
1 a place where the coast curves around the sea: *a view **across the bay*** | *San Francisco Bay*
2 a small area that is used for a particular purpose: *a **loading bay** (=for goods)*
PHRASES
  keep/hold sth at bay to prevent something dangerous or unpleasant from happening or from coming too close: *The police were struggling to hold the rioters at bay.*

bayonet /ˈbeɪənət, -net/ *n* [C] a long knife fixed to the end of a long gun

bay ˈwindow *n* [C] a window that sticks out from the wall of a house, with glass on three sides → see picture at **WINDOW**

bazaar /bəˈzɑː $ -ˈzɑːr/ *n* [C] **1** a market in Asian or Middle Eastern countries **2** an event when people

sell a lot of different things to collect money for an organization: *a church bazaar*

BBC /ˌbiː biː ˈsiː◂/ *n* **the BBC** (**the British Broadcasting Corporation**) the British radio and television company that is paid for by the state

BBQ *n* [C] the written abbreviation of **barbecue**

BC /ˌbiː ˈsiː/ *adv* (**before Christ**) used after a date → **AD**: *2600 BC*

be¹ /bɪ; *strong* biː/ *auxiliary verb* (*past tense* **was**/**were**, *past participle* **been**, *present participle* **being**)
1 used with a present participle to form the CONTINUOUS tenses of verbs: *Jane was reading by the fire.* | *He isn't leaving, is he?*
2 used with a past participle to form the PASSIVE: *Smoking is not permitted on this flight.* | *The house is being painted.*
3 used to talk about imagined situations, in CONDITIONAL sentences: **if sb was/were (to do) sth** *If I were rich, I'd buy a Rolls Royce.* | *If he was to offer me the job, I'd accept.*
4 sb is to do sth *formal* **a)** used to say what must happen: *You are not to go out.* **b)** used to say what will happen: *They are to be married in June.*
5 sb/sth is to be seen/found/heard etc *formal* used to say that someone or something can be seen etc: *The only sound to be heard was the birds' singing.*

be² *v* [linking verb]
1 used to give or ask for information about someone or something, or to describe them: *I'm hungry.* | *Her name's Sally.* | *Tom will be three next week.* | *Where are my keys?* | *The party's on Saturday.* | *Mr Cardew was a tall thin man.* | *Their house is huge.* | *Is this your bag?* | *How long have you been here?*
2 to behave in a particular way: *He was just being silly.* | *Don't be rude.*
3 used to give your opinion about something: **it's/that's nice/possible/strange etc** | *'John's passed his driving test.' 'That's great!'* | *It's strange that she hasn't phoned.*
PHRASES
  be yourself to behave in a natural way: *Don't worry about impressing others – just be yourself.*
  be the be-all and end-all (of sth) to be the most important part of a situation: *Losing the match isn't the be-all and end-all of everything.*
  sb is not himself/herself used to say that someone seems to be unwell or unhappy: *He hasn't been himself for days.*
  there is/there are used to say that something exists or happens: *There's a hole in my shoe.* | *Is there a problem?* | *Suddenly there was a loud explosion.*

beach /biːtʃ/ *n* [C] an area of sand or small stones at the edge of the sea: *a **sandy beach*** | **on/at the beach** *We spent the day on the beach.* | *a beach resort*

beachfront /ˈbiːtʃfrʌnt/ *adj* [only before noun] next to a beach: *beachfront apartments*

beacon /ˈbiːkən/ *n* [C] a light or electronic signal, used to guide boats, planes etc

bead /biːd/ *n* [C] **1** a small round ball of wood, plastic, or glass, used in jewellery **2** a small drop of liquid such as water or blood

beady /'biːdi/ *adj* beady eyes are small, dark, and shiny

beak /biːk/ *n* [C] the hard pointed mouth of a bird → see picture on page A3

beaker /'biːkə $ -ər/ *n* [C] *BrE* a cup with straight sides and no handle

beam¹ /biːm/ *n* [C] **1** a line of light or energy: **[+of]** *the beam of the flashlight* | *a laser beam* **2** a long piece of wood or metal used in building houses, bridges etc **3** a big happy smile

beam² *v* [I] to smile very happily: **[+at]** *Grandad beamed at us proudly.* **THESAURUS** SMILE **2** [T] to send a radio or television signal: **beam sth across/ up/to etc sth** *News from any part of the world can be beamed to us by satellite.*

bean /biːn/ *n* [C]
1 a seed or case that seeds grow in, cooked as food: *kidney beans* | *green beans*
2 coffee/cocoa beans the seeds used in making coffee or chocolate

bear¹ /beə $ ber/ *v* (*past tense* **bore** /bɔː $ bɔːr/, *past participle* **borne** /bɔːn $ bɔːrn/)
1 ACCEPT [T] to bravely accept or deal with something that is unpleasant **SYN** **stand, tolerate**: *For Etty, the loss was very hard to bear.* | *The pain was almost more than she could bear.* | *They just had to grin and bear it* (=not complain).
2 BE RESPONSIBLE [T] to be responsible for something: **bear the responsibility/blame** *He must bear some of the blame.* | **bear the burden/costs** *Why should the taxpayer have to bear the burden of paying for the games?*
3 BE SIMILAR **bear a resemblance/relation to sb/sth** to be similar to or related to someone or something: *The child bore a striking resemblance to his father.*
4 NAME/APPEARANCE [T] *formal* to have a particular name or appearance **SYN** **have**: *the company that bore her father's name* | *The town still bore the scars of war.*
5 WEIGHT [T] to support the weight of something **SYN** **hold**: *Her ankle was sore, but it was bearing her weight.*
6 BAD FEELINGS [T] *formal* to have bad feelings towards someone **SYN** **hold**: *I don't bear a grudge* (=still feel angry about something).
7 CARRY/BRING [T] *formal* to bring or carry something: *They came bearing gifts.*
8 TURN **bear right/left** to turn towards the right or left: *Bear left at the lights.*
9 BABY [T] *formal* to give birth to a baby → **bear the brunt of sth** at **BRUNT**

PHRASES
bear fruit if a plan or decision bears fruit, it is successful
bear in mind sth to not forget a fact or idea: **[+that]** *Bear in mind that this method may not work.*
bear with me *spoken* used to politely ask someone to wait while you do something: *Bear with me for a moment and I'll check.*
bear witness to sth *formal* to show that something is true or exists: *The film bears witness to her skill as a director.*
can't bear sb/sth to dislike someone or something

very much, or to feel unable to do something because it is so unpleasant **SYN** **can't stand**: *She really can't bear him.* | **can't bear (sb) doing sth** *I can't bear people shouting at me.* | *He can't bear the thought of starting again.* | **can't bear to do sth** *It was so horrible I couldn't bear to watch.* **THESAURUS** HATE

sth doesn't bear thinking about used to say that something is very upsetting or shocking: *The long-term effects don't bear thinking about.*

PHRASAL VERBS
bear down on sb/sth to move quickly towards someone or something in a threatening way: *The truck bore down on them.*
bear sth ↔ **out** to show that something is true: *Our fears were borne out by the research.*
bear up to succeed in being brave and determined during a difficult or upsetting time: *How's she bearing up?*

BEARS

bear

panda

polar bear

bear² *n* [C] a large strong animal with thick fur → **POLAR BEAR, TEDDY BEAR**

bearable /'beərəbəl $ 'ber-/ *adj* something that is bearable is possible to accept or deal with, although it is very unpleasant

beard /bɪəd $ bɪrd/ *n* [C] the hair that grows on a man's chin → see picture at **MOUSTACHE** —**bearded** *adj*

bearer /'beərə $ 'berər/ *n* [C] someone who brings or carries something: **[+of]** *the bearer of bad news*

bearing /'beərɪŋ $ 'ber-/ *n* **1 have a bearing on sth** to have an influence or effect on something: *His age had no bearing on our decision.* **2 lose your bearings** to become confused about where you are **3 get your bearings** to find out where you are or what you should do

beast /biːst/ *n* [C] *literary* a wild animal

beat¹ /biːt/ *v* (*past tense* **beat**, *past participle* **beaten** /'biːtn/)
1 DEFEAT [T] to get more points, votes etc than other people in a game or competition: *Spain beat Italy 3–1.* | *It was clear that the Democrats could not*

beat the Republicans. | **beat the record/score etc** (=do something better, faster etc than it has been done before) *He beat the world record by 11 seconds.*

THESAURUS WIN

2 HIT [T] to hit someone or something violently many times: *He had been badly beaten.* | *The girl was beaten to death.* | **beat the door down/in** (=hit it until it opens or breaks) **THESAURUS** HIT

3 KNOCK AGAINST [I,T] to hit against the surface of something continuously, or to make something do this: **[+on/against]** *The rain beat loudly on the roof.* | **beat sth on/against sth** *A bird was beating its wings against the wire netting.*

4 MIX [T] to mix food together quickly using a fork or a kitchen tool: *Beat the eggs.*

5 HEART/DRUM [I] to make a regular movement or sound: *My heart was beating.* | *We could hear drums beating.*

6 DEAL WITH [T] to deal successfully with a problem, illness etc: *The government has promised to beat inflation.* | *advice on how to beat depression*

7 BE BETTER [T] *spoken* to be better or more enjoyable than something: **beat doing sth** *It beats going to work.* | *You can't beat a good book* (=nothing is better). → **off the beaten track/path** at BEATEN

PHRASES

beat about/around the bush to avoid talking about something unpleasant or embarrassing: *Don't beat about the bush – what is it?*

beat a (hasty) retreat to leave very quickly, in order to avoid trouble: *We had to beat a hasty retreat from the restaurant after Bill upset one of the waiters.*

(it) beats me *spoken* used to say that you do not understand or know something: *'What's his problem?' 'Beats me!'*

PHRASAL VERBS

beat down

1 if the sun beats down, it shines brightly and is hot

2 if the rain beats down, it rains very hard

beat sb/sth ↔ **off** to succeed in defeating someone who is attacking you

beat sb **to** sth to get or do something before someone else: *I applied for the job but someone beat me to it.*

beat sb ↔ **up** to hit someone until they are badly hurt

beat² *n* **1** [C] one of a series of regular movements or sounds: **[+of]** *the steady beat of his heart* **2** [singular] the pattern of sounds in a piece of music **3** [singular] the area that a police officer walks around regularly: *We need more police on the beat* (=walking around the streets).

beat³ *adj especially AmE informal* very tired

beaten /'biːtn/ *adj* **off the beaten track/path** far away from places that people usually visit

beating /'biːtɪŋ/ *n* [C] when someone is hit many times, for example in a fight: *a brutal beating*

PHRASES

take a beating to lose very badly in a game or competition: *Arsenal took a 5–1 beating from Tottenham Hotspur.*

beat-up *adj informal* a beat-up car, bicycle etc is old and in bad condition

beautician /bjuː'tɪʃən/ *n* [C] someone whose job is to give beauty treatment to your skin, hair etc

beautiful /'bjuːtəfəl/ *adj*

1 extremely nice to look at: *She was **the most beautiful woman in the world.*** | *a **stunningly beautiful** area*

2 very good or giving you great pleasure SYN **lovely**: *The weather was beautiful.* | *a beautiful piece of music* —**beautifully** *adv*

THESAURUS

beautiful extremely nice to look at – used especially about a girl, woman, or child: *She was still a very beautiful woman.* | *a beautiful baby girl*

good-looking nice to look at. **Good-looking** is very common in spoken English: *He's a good-looking guy.*

attractive nice to look at, especially in a way that makes you feel sexually interested: *All the boys found her attractive.*

pretty used about a girl or young woman who looks nice, especially one who has a nice face: *She was very pretty and had short blonde hair.*

handsome *especially written* used especially about a man with a nice face who is tall and strong: *He was tall, dark, and handsome.*

lovely *especially BrE* very nice – used especially when telling a woman that she looks nice: *You look lovely tonight.* | *You have lovely eyes.*

cute *spoken* nice to look at – used especially about animals, babies, children, and young adults: *a cute little puppy* | *She thinks you're cute!*

beauty /'bjuːti/ *n* (*plural* **beauties**)

1 [U] the quality of being beautiful: *a woman of **great beauty*** | **[+of]** *the beauty of the Swiss Alps* | *beauty treatments/products* (=to make you more attractive)

2 [C] *informal* something that is very good or impressive: *That motorcycle's **a real beauty.***

3 used to explain why something is especially good: *The beauty of email is that it's so quick.*

4 [C] *old-fashioned* a woman who is very beautiful

beauty salon / $ '...,./ (*also* **beauty parlor** *AmE*) *n* [C] a place where you can have beauty treatments for your skin, hair etc

beauty spot *n* [C] a beautiful place in the countryside

beaver¹ /'biːvə $ -ər/ *n* [C] a North American animal with thick fur and a wide flat tail

beaver² *v*

PHRASAL VERBS

beaver away to work hard in a very busy way

became /bɪ'keɪm/ *v* the past tense of BECOME

because /bɪ'kɒz, bɪkəz $ bɪ'kɔːz, bɪkəz/ *linking word* used when you are giving the reason for something: *You can't go because you're too young.* | *partly/largely/mainly because I'd never leave, partly because I'd get homesick.* | *Students lose marks **simply because** they haven't read the question properly.* | **because of sth/sb** *We didn't have a picnic because of the rain.*

PHRASES

just because ... *spoken* used to say that although one thing is true, it does not mean that something else is true: *Just because you're older, it doesn't mean you can tell me what to do.*

beck /bek/ n **be at sb's beck and call** to always be ready to do what someone wants

beckon /'bekən/ v [I,T] to move your hand to show that you want someone to move towards you: **beckon (to) sb to do sth** *He beckoned to them to follow him.*

become /bɪ'kʌm/ v [linking verb] (*past tense* **became** /-'keɪm/, *past participle* **become**) to begin to be something, or begin to have a feeling: *Kennedy became the first Catholic president.* | *It is becoming harder to find good staff.* | *Helen was becoming increasingly anxious.*

PHRASES

become of sb/sth to happen to someone or something: *Whatever became of those old photos?* | *I don't know what will become of him when she dies.*

THESAURUS

become to begin to be something, or begin to have a feeling – used before nouns and adjectives: *Car crime has become a major problem.* | *He suddenly became angry.*
get to become – used before adjectives, but not before nouns. **Get** is less formal than **become** and is used especially in spoken English: *It was getting dark.* | *They were getting tired.*
grow old/tired/louder etc to become old, tired, louder etc gradually. **Grow** sounds rather formal and is used especially in written English: *People were growing anxious.* | *The wind grew quieter.*
go blue/deaf/blind/mad etc to become a different colour. Also used about people becoming unable to see or hear well, or becoming crazy: *Her hair was going grey.* | *He went blind.* | *I think I'm going mad.*
turn brown/cold/nasty to become a different colour. Also used about the weather or people's behaviour changing: *The leaves were turning brown.* | *He suddenly turned nasty.*
change/turn into sth to become something completely different, often in a surprising way: *The town has changed into a modern city.*

---

bed /bed/ n
1 FOR SLEEPING [C,U] a piece of furniture for sleeping on: *a comfortable bed* | **in bed** *It was half past ten, but Richard was still in bed.* | **time for bed** (=time to go to bed) *Come on kids, it's time for bed.*
2 OF OCEAN/RIVER/LAKE [C] the ground at the bottom of the ocean, a river, or a lake: *the sea bed* THESAURUS▶ BOTTOM
3 FOR PLANTS [C] an area of ground that has been prepared for plants to grow in: *flower beds*
4 FOR PUTTING STH ON [singular] a layer of something that is a base for something else: *on a bed* prawns on a bed of lettuce

---

BEDS

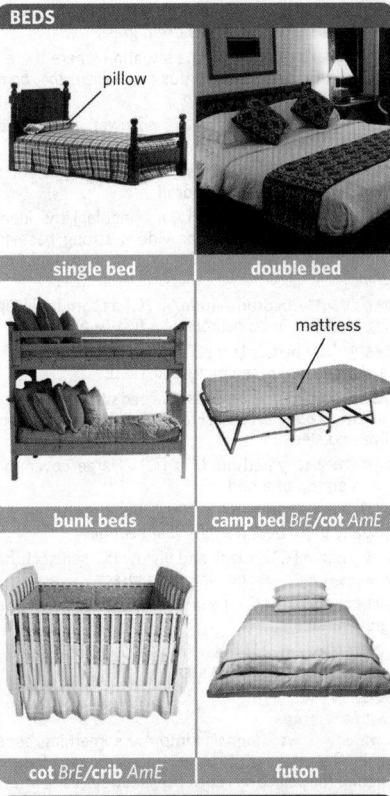

pillow

single bed

double bed

mattress

bunk beds

camp bed *BrE*/cot *AmE*

cot *BrE*/crib *AmE*

futon

COLLOCATIONS

verbs

to go to bed *I usually go to bed about 11.*
to get into/out of bed *It's time to get out of bed.*
to lie in bed *Sam lay in bed thinking.*
to stay in bed *I felt awful, so I decided to stay in bed.*
to put sb to bed (=to put a child in their bed) *I'll put the baby to bed.*
to make the bed (=to arrange the sheets and covers on the bed) *Can you make the bed?*

types of bed

a single bed (=for one person) *The only things in the room were a chair and a single bed.*
a double bed (=for two people) *Would you like a double bed or twin beds?*
twin beds (=two single beds in a room)

---

bed and 'breakfast (*also* **B & B**) n [C] a house or a small hotel where you pay to sleep and have breakfast THESAURUS▶ HOTEL

bedclothes /'bedkləʊðz, -kləʊz $ -kloʊðz, -kloʊz/ [plural] BEDDING

bedding /'bedɪŋ/ n [U] **1** the sheets, BLANKETs etc

that you put on a bed **2** something soft that an animal sleeps on, such as dried grass

bedlam /'bedləm/ *n* [U] a situation where there is a lot of noise and confusion: *When the bomb exploded, there was bedlam.*

bedraggled /brˈdrægəld/ *adj* wet and untidy **THESAURUS** UNTIDY

bedridden /'bed,rɪdn/ *adj* not able to get out of bed because you are old or ill

bedrock /'bedrɒk $ -rɑːk/ *n* [singular] the ideas, people, or facts which provide a strong base for something: *Honesty is the bedrock of a good relationship.*

bedroom /'bedrʊm, -ruːm/ *n* [C] a room for sleeping in: *John's in his bedroom.* | *a two-bedroom flat*

bedside /'bedsaɪd/ *n* [C] the area around a bed: *a bedside table* → see picture at **TABLE**[1]

bedsit /ˌbedˈsɪt/, **bedsitter** /ˌbedˈsɪtə $ -ər/, **bed-'sitting room** *n* [C] BrE a rented room which you live and sleep in

bedspread /'bedspred/ *n* [C] a large cover that goes on top of a bed

bedtime /'bedtaɪm/ *n* [C,U] the time when you usually go to bed: *It's past your bedtime!*

bee /biː/ *n* [C] a black and yellow flying insect that makes HONEY → see picture at **INSECT**

beech /biːtʃ/ *n* [C,U] a large tree that has a smooth grey surface

beef[1] /biːf/ *n* [U] meat from a cow: *roast beef* | *a joint of beef* → **GROUND BEEF**

beef[2] *v*

PHRASAL VERBS

beef sth ↔ **up** *informal* to improve something, especially by making it bigger or stronger: *Security around the palace has been beefed up since the attack.*

beefburger /'biːfbɜːɡə $ -bɜːrɡər/ *n* [C] BrE very small pieces of beef made into a flat round shape and cooked **SYN** burger, hamburger

beefy /'biːfi/ *adj informal* a beefy man is big and strong

beehive /'biːhaɪv/ *n* [C] a place where BEES are kept to produce HONEY **SYN** hive

beeline /'biːlaɪn/ *n* **make a beeline for sb/sth** *informal* to go quickly and directly towards someone or something: *The children made a beeline for the food.*

been /biːn, bɪn $ bɪn/ *v* **1** the past participle of BE **2 have been to (do) sth** used to say that someone has gone to a place and come back: *Kate has just been to Japan.* | *Have you been to see the new James Bond film yet?*

beep /biːp/ *v* **1** [I] if a machine beeps, it makes a short high sound: *The heart monitor started beeping.* **2** [I,T] if a horn beeps, or you beep it, it makes a loud noise —**beep** *n* [C]

beeper /'biːpə $ -ər/ *n* [C] a small machine that you carry with you, which makes a sound to tell you to telephone someone **SYN** pager

beer /bɪə $ bɪr/ *n* [C,U] an alcoholic drink made from grain, or a glass of this drink: *a pint of beer* | *Would you like a beer?*

beet /biːt/ *n* [C,U] **1** (*also* sugar beet) a vegetable that sugar is made from **2** AmE a dark red vegetable that is the root of a plant **SYN** beetroot BrE → see picture on page A5

beetle /'biːtl/ *n* [C] an insect with a hard round back → see picture at **INSECT**

beetroot /'biːtruːt/ *n* [C] BrE a dark red vegetable that is the root of a plant **SYN** beet AmE → see picture on page A5

befall /brˈfɔːl $ -ˈfɒːl/ *v* [I,T] (*past tense* befell /-ˈfel/, *past participle* befallen /-ˈfɔːlən $ -ˈfɒːlən/) *formal* if something unpleasant or dangerous befalls you, it happens to you: *the terrible things that had befallen him*

befit /brˈfɪt/ *v* [T] (befitted, befitting) *formal* to seem suitable or good enough for someone: *a funeral befitting a national hero*

before[1] /brˈfɔː $ -ˈfɔːr/ *prep* **1** earlier than something or someone **OPP** after: *I usually shower before breakfast.* | *We got home before the others.* | *You need to check in an hour before your flight.* | *We got back the day before yesterday* (=two days ago). **2** in front of someone or something else in a list or order **OPP** after: *S comes before T in the alphabet.* **3** used to say that one thing or person is considered more important than another: *She always puts her family before her career.* **4** if one place is before another as you go towards it, you will reach it first **OPP** after: *Turn right just before the station.* **5** *formal* in front of: *The priest knelt before the altar.*

THESAURUS

before earlier than something happens, or someone else: *I was very nervous before the interview.* | *Stella got married before me.*
by not later than a particular time or date: *I'll be home by 6 o'clock.* | *Hand your essays in by Friday.*
previously before now, or before a time in the past: *He's been married twice previously.*
in advance/beforehand if you do something in advance, you do it before something happens, so that you are ready for it: *You should book your tickets well in advance.* | *Let me know beforehand when you will be arriving.*
formerly *formal* in the past: *The country was formerly known as Rhodesia.*

before[2] *adv* at an earlier time: *They'd met before, at one of Sally's parties.* | **the day/week/month etc before** *We were in Paris last week and Rome the week before.*

before[3] *linking word* **1** earlier than the time when something happens: *John wants to talk to you before you go.* **2** so that something does not happen: *You'd better lock your bike before it gets stolen.* | *I sat down before she could change her mind.*

beforehand /brˈfɔːhænd $ -ˈfɔːr-/ *adv* before something happens: *When you give a speech, it's natural to feel nervous beforehand.* **THESAURUS** BEFORE

B

befriend /brˈfrend/ v [T] to become someone's friend, especially someone who needs your help

befuddled /brˈfʌdld/ adj completely confused

beg /beg/ v (**begged, begging**) **1** [I,T] to ask for something in a way which shows you want it very much: **beg (sb) to do sth** I begged her to stay, but she wouldn't. | a prisoner begging to be released | **beg (sb) for sth** They begged for mercy. | He rang a friend to beg for his help. **THESAURUS** ASK **2** [I] to ask someone for food, money etc because you are very poor: children begging in the streets

PHRASES

I beg your pardon spoken **1** used to ask someone politely to repeat something: 'It's 7 o'clock.' 'I beg your pardon?' 'I said it's 7 o'clock.' **2** formal used to say sorry for something you have said or done: Oh, I beg your pardon, did I step on your toe? **3** formal used to show that you strongly disagree: 'New York's a terrible place.' 'I beg your pardon, that's my home town!'

beggar /ˈbegə $ -ər/ n [C] someone who lives by asking people for food and money

begin /brˈgɪn/ v (past tense **began** /-ˈgæn/, past participle **begun** /-ˈgʌn/, present participle **beginning**) **1** [I,T] to start doing something, or to start to happen or exist: The meeting will begin at 10:00. | Tomorrow the President will begin talks with several European heads of state. | **begin to do sth** It's beginning to rain. | He began to cry. | **begin doing sth** I began teaching in 1992. **THESAURUS** START **2** [I] if you begin with something or begin by doing something, you do it first: **[+with]** Let's begin with exercise 5. | **begin by doing sth** May I begin by thanking you all for coming. **3** [I] if a book, film, word etc begins with something, that is how it starts: It begins with a description of the author's home.

PHRASES

to begin with 1 used to introduce the first or most important point: To begin with, you mustn't take the car without asking. **2** used to say what something was already like before something else happened: I didn't break it! It was like that to begin with. **3** in the first part of an activity or process: The children helped me to begin with, but they soon got bored.

beginner /brˈgɪnə $ -ər/ n [C] someone who has just started to do or learn something: a class for beginners

beginning /brˈgɪnɪŋ/ n [C usually singular] the start or first part of something: **[+of]** the beginning of the war | We've been here since the beginning of the year. | **at the beginning** At the beginning of the film, she's in London. | **from the beginning** Read it again, from the beginning. | **in the beginning** You should have told me in the beginning if there was a problem.

Grammar
Do not say 'on the beginning'. Say **at the beginning** or **in the beginning**.

THESAURUS

beginning the first part of an event, story, period of time etc: I've only read the beginning of

the story. | the beginning of the 20th century

start the time when something begins, or the way something begins: March is usually the start of spring. | I was late on my first day, which was a bad start.

origin the place where something first came from, or how it started to exist: a new theory about the origin of life on our planet

dawn literary the beginning of an important period of time in history: the dawn of civilization

begrudge /brˈgrʌdʒ/ v [T] to feel upset and angry about something: Honestly, I don't begrudge him his success. | I begrudge spending so much money on train fares.

beguiling /brˈgaɪlɪŋ/ adj literary attractive and interesting

begun /brˈgʌn/ v the past participle of BEGIN

behalf **Ac** /brˈhɑːf $ brˈhæf/ n **on behalf of sb/on sb's behalf** instead of someone: He agreed to speak on my behalf.

behave /brˈheɪv/ v [I]
1 to do things of a particular kind: He's been behaving very oddly recently. | He began behaving differently towards me. | She behaved in a very responsible **way**. | **[+like]** Stop behaving like a child!
2 to be polite and not cause trouble **OPP** misbehave: Will you boys please behave! | **behave yourself** If you behave yourself you can have an ice cream. | **well-behaved/badly behaved** a badly behaved class

behaviour BrE, **behavior** AmE /brˈheɪvjə $ -ər/ n [U]
1 the things that a person or animal does: I'm not very pleased with your behaviour. | **good/bad behaviour** Reward your children for good behaviour. | **[+towards]** violent behaviour towards police officers | **human/social/sexual etc behaviour** normal patterns of human behaviour
2 technical the things that something in science normally does: the behaviour of cancer cells —**behavioural** adj

Grammar
Behaviour is not usually used in the plural. Do not say 'good behaviours'. Say good behaviour.

behead /brˈhed/ v [T] to cut someone's head off as a punishment

beheld /brˈheld/ v the past tense and past participle of BEHOLD

behind¹ /brˈhaɪnd/ prep
1 at the back of something: the person standing behind me | He stepped out from behind the counter. | The car park is **right behind** (=just behind) the supermarket. → see picture on page A8
2 not as successful or making as much progress as someone or something else: We're three points behind the other team. | The building work is three months **behind schedule** (=later than it should be). **THESAURUS** LATE
3 responsible for something or causing it to happen: The same gang is believed to be behind all the robberies.

4 supporting a person, idea etc: *We're all behind the plan.*

PHRASES

behind the times old-fashioned: *He's rather behind the times as regards his taste in music.*

behind² *adv*

1 at the back of something: *George was following close behind.* | **from behind** *He grabbed me from behind.*

2 in the place where someone or something was before: *I decided to stay behind and work.* | *When I got there I realized I'd left the tickets behind.*

3 be/get behind to be late or slow in doing something: *We are three months behind with the rent.*

behind³ *n* [C] *informal* the part of your body that you sit on SYN bottom

behold /bɪˈhəʊld $ -ˈhoʊld/ *v* [T] (*past tense and past participle* **beheld** /-ˈheld/) *literary* to see something —**beholder** *n* [C]

beige /beɪʒ/ *n* [U] a pale brown colour —**beige** *adj*

being¹ /ˈbiːɪŋ/ *v* the present participle of BE

being² *n* [C] a living person or imaginary creature: *strange beings from outer space*

PHRASES

come into being to begin to exist: *a law that came into being in 1912*

belated /bɪˈleɪtɪd/ *adj* happening or arriving late: *a belated birthday card* —**belatedly** *adv*

belch /beltʃ/ *v* **1** [I] to let air come out noisily through your mouth from your stomach SYN **burp 2** [T] to produce a lot of smoke or fire: *factories belching black smoke* —**belch** *n* [C]

beleaguered /bɪˈliːɡəd $ -ərd/ *adj formal* having a lot of problems: *the country's beleaguered motor industry*

belie /bɪˈlaɪ/ *v* [T] (**belied, belying, belies**) *formal* to give you a wrong idea about something: *He has an energy that belies his 85 years.*

belief /bɪˈliːf/ *n*

1 [singular, U] the feeling that something is definitely true or definitely exists: **[+that]** *the belief that children learn best through playing* | **[+in]** *a strong belief in magic* | **Contrary to popular belief** (=despite what most people believe), *exercise is not always good for you.*

2 [singular] the feeling that someone or something is good, important, or right: **[+in]** *He has a strong belief in the importance of education.*

3 [C usually plural] an idea or set of ideas that you think are true: *different communities with different religious beliefs*

PHRASES

beyond belief used to emphasize that something is very bad, good, strange etc: *It seemed cruel beyond belief.*

believe /bɪˈliːv/ *v*

1 [T] to think that something is true or that someone is telling the truth: *Do you believe his story?* | *I don't believe you!* | **[+(that)]** *I can't believe he's only 25!* | *I found his explanation hard to believe.*

THESAURUS ▶ THINK

2 [T] to have a particular opinion about something, without being completely sure: **[+(that)]** *I believe she'll be back on Monday.* | **It is believed that** *three people were killed in the accident.*

3 [T] used in some phrases to show that you are surprised or shocked: **can't/don't believe sth** *I can't believe you lied to me!* | **Would you believe it,** *he even remembered my birthday!* | *He could hardly believe his eyes* (=was very surprised) *when he looked out of the window.*

4 [I] to have religious faith —**believable** *adj*

PHRASES

believe it or not *spoken* used when something is true but surprising: *Believe it or not, I don't actually dislike him.*

PHRASAL VERBS

believe in sth

1 to be sure that something or someone definitely exists: *Do you believe in ghosts?*

2 to think that someone or something is good, important, or right: *We believe in democracy.* | *I believe in being honest and telling the truth.*

> **Grammar**
> Do not say 'You must believe on yourself.' Say *You must believe in yourself.*

THESAURUS

to believe something

believe to think that something is true or that someone is telling the truth: *Don't believe everything you read in the newspapers.* | *I believe you. Thousands wouldn't!*

accept to believe that something is true, especially because someone has persuaded you to believe it: *His wife accepted his explanation for why he was late.*

take sb's word for it *especially spoken* to believe what someone says is true, even though you have no proof or experience of it yourself: *I wasn't there when the accident happened, so I'll just have to take your word for it.*

be taken in by sth/fall for sth to be tricked into believing something that is not true: *A lot of people were taken in by these claims.*

---

believer /bɪˈliːvə $ -ər/ *n* [C] **1** someone who believes that a particular idea or thing is very good: **firm/great believer in sth** *I'm a great believer in healthy eating.* **2** someone who believes in a particular religion

belittle /bɪˈlɪtl/ *v* [T] *formal* to say that something is less important than it really is: *Why do they always try to belittle our efforts!*

bell /bel/ *n* [C]

1 a piece of electrical equipment that makes a ringing sound: *I rang the front door bell but no one answered.*

2 a metal object that makes a ringing sound when you hit it or shake it → **ring a bell** at RING²

belligerent /bɪˈlɪdʒərənt/ *adj formal* wanting to fight or argue

bellow /ˈbeləʊ $ -loʊ/ *v* [I,T] to shout something in a very loud voice

belly /'beli/ n [C] (plural **bellies**) informal your stomach, or the part of your body between your chest and the top of your legs

'belly ,button n [C] informal the small hole just below your waist on the front of your body SYN navel

belong /bɪ'lɒŋ $ bɪ'lɔːŋ/ v [I]
1 if something belongs in a place, that is the place where it should go: [+in/on/by etc] Books like that don't belong in the classroom. | Please put the chair back where it belongs.
2 if you belong somewhere, you feel happy there: She felt she didn't belong in the city.
PHRASAL VERBS
belong to sb/sth
1 if something belongs to you, you own it: Does this umbrella belong to you? THESAURUS OWN
2 if you belong to an organization, you are a member of it: I don't belong to the tennis club.

belongings /bɪ'lɒŋɪŋz $ bɪ'lɔːŋ-/ n [plural] the things that you own, especially things that you carry with you: Please take all your **personal belongings** with you. THESAURUS PROPERTY

beloved /bɪ'lʌvɪd/ adj literary loved very much: my beloved wife, Fiona

below /bɪ'ləʊ $ -'loʊ/ adv, prep
1 in a lower place or position than someone or something else OPP above: Jake lives in the apartment below. | fish that feed just below the surface of the water THESAURUS UNDER → see picture on page A8
2 less than a particular number or amount OPP over: Anything below £500 would be a good price. | The temperature was well **below zero**.
3 on a later page or lower on the same page OPP above: For more information, **see below**.
4 lower in rank: Is a captain below a general?

belt¹ /belt/ n [C]
1 FOR TROUSERS a band of leather or cloth that you wear around your waist → see picture at CLOTHES
2 ON A MACHINE a circular band of material such as rubber that moves parts of a machine: the car's fan belt
3 AREA a large area of land: America's farming belt → CONVEYOR BELT, GREEN BELT, SAFETY BELT, SEAT BELT
PHRASES
have sth under your belt to have already done something useful or important: I want to get this qualification under my belt.

belt² v [T] informal to hit someone or something hard
PHRASAL VERBS
belt sth ↔ **out** to sing a song very loudly

belying /bɪ'laɪ-ɪŋ/ v the present participle of BELIE

bemoan /bɪ'məʊn $ -'moʊn/ v [T] formal to say that you are unhappy about something: He was **bemoaning the fact that** lawyers charge so much.

bemused /bɪ'mjuːzd/ adj slightly confused: a bemused expression

bench /bentʃ/ n **1** [C] a long wooden seat for two or more people: We sat on a **park bench** to eat our sandwiches. **2 the bench** law the judges who work in a court

BENCH

benchmark /'bentʃmɑːk $ -mɑːrk/ n [C] something that is used for comparing and measuring other things: [+for] The test results provide a benchmark for measuring student achievement.

bend¹ /bend/ v (past tense and past participle **bent** /bent/)
1 [I,T] to move a part of your body so that it is not straight or so that you are not standing upright: Bend your knees slightly. | [+down/over] He bent down to tie his shoelace. → see picture on page A11
2 [T] to push or press something so that it is no longer flat or straight: You've bent the handle. → **bend the rules** at RULE¹
PHRASES
bend over backwards to try very hard to help someone: Our new neighbours bent over backwards to help us when we moved house.

bend² n [C] a curve in something, especially a road or river: a sharp bend in the road → HAIRPIN BEND

beneath /bɪ'niːθ/ adv, prep
1 under or below something: the warm sand beneath her feet | He stood on the bridge, looking at the water beneath. THESAURUS UNDER
2 if someone or something is beneath you, you think that they are not good enough for you: She seemed to think that talking to us was beneath her.

benefactor /'benəˌfæktə $ -ər/ n [C] formal someone who gives money or help to someone else

beneficial Ac /ˌbenɪ'fɪʃəl◂/ adj helpful or useful: [+to] The agreement will be beneficial to both groups.

beneficiary Ac /ˌbenə'fɪʃəri $ -'fɪʃieri/ n [C] (plural **beneficiaries**) formal someone who gets an advantage from something which happens: Businesses were the main beneficiaries of the tax cuts.

benefit¹ Ac /'benəfɪt/ n
1 [C,U] an advantage or improvement that you get from something: [+of] What are the benefits of contact lenses? | The new credit cards will **be of** great **benefit to** our customers. | **for sb's benefit** (=in order to help them) Liu Han translated what the minister said for my benefit.
2 [C,U] BrE money that you get from the government when you are ill or when you do not have a job SYN welfare AmE: You may be entitled to unemployment benefit. | **on benefit(s)** (=receiving benefits) All his family are on benefits.
3 [C] a performance, concert etc that makes money for a CHARITY → CHILD BENEFIT, FRINGE BENEFIT

PHRASES

give sb the benefit of the doubt to believe or trust someone even though it is possible that they are lying or are wrong: *I gave him the benefit of the doubt although I wasn't sure that he was telling the truth.*

benefit² Ac v [I,T] (*past tense and past participle* **benefited** *or* **benefitted**, *present participle* **benefiting** *or* **benefitting**) if you benefit from something or if it benefits you, it helps you: *The new policy changes mainly benefit small companies.* | **[+from/by]** *Most of these children would benefit from an extra year at school.*

benevolent /bə'nevələnt/ *adj formal* kind and generous —**benevolence** *n* [U]

benign /bɪ'naɪn/ *adj* **1** *technical* a benign TUMOUR is not caused by CANCER **OPP malignant** **2** *formal* kind and gentle

bent¹ /bent/ *v* the past tense and past participle of BEND

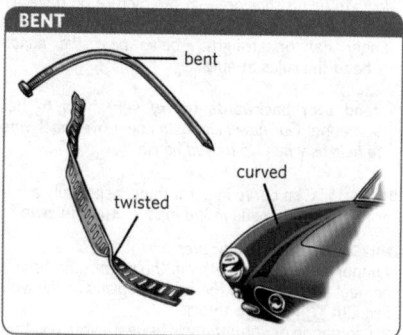

BENT

bent

curved

twisted

bent² *adj* **1** no longer straight or flat: *a bent nail* | *She was* ***bent double*** (=with the top part of her body leaning forward) *in pain.* **2** *BrE informal* someone who is bent is not honest
PHRASES

be bent on (doing) sth to be determined to do something or have something: *Mendoza was bent on getting a better job.*

bent³ *n* [singular] *formal* a skill or interest that someone has: *readers of a more literary bent*

bequeath /bɪ'kwiːð, bɪ'kwiːθ/ *v* [T] *formal* to arrange that someone will get something you own after you die

bequest /bɪ'kwest/ *n* [C] *formal* something that you arrange to give to someone after you have died

berate /bɪ'reɪt/ *v* [T] *formal* to speak angrily to someone because they have done something wrong

bereaved /bə'riːvd/ *adj formal* if someone is bereaved, someone they love has died —**bereavement** *n* [C,U]

bereft /bə'reft/ *adj formal* **1** feeling sad and alone **2 bereft of sth** completely without something: *bereft of all hope*

beret /'bereɪ $ bə'reɪ/ *n* [C] a soft round flat hat → see picture at HAT

berry /'beri/ *n* [C] (*plural* **berries**) a small soft fruit with small seeds

berserk /bɜː'sɜːk, bə- $ bɜːr'sɜːrk, 'bɜːrsɜːrk/ *adj* **go berserk** *informal* to become very angry and violent in a crazy way: *The guy went berserk and started hitting Paul.*

berth /bɜːθ $ bɜːrθ/ *n* [C] **1** a place to sleep on a train or boat **2** the place where a ship comes to land

beseech /bɪ'siːtʃ/ *v* [T] (*past tense and past participle* **besought** /-'sɔːt $ -'sɔːt/ *or* **beseeched**) *literary* to eagerly and anxiously ask someone for something **SYN beg**

beset /bɪ'set/ *v* [T] (*past tense and past participle* **beset**, *present participle* **besetting**) *formal* to cause trouble for someone: *The family was beset by financial difficulties.*

beside /bɪ'saɪd/ *prep*
1 next to or very close to someone or something: *Gary sat down beside me.* | *a cabin* ***right beside*** *the lake* **THESAURUS** NEXT → see picture on page A8
2 used to compare two people or things: *This year's sales figures don't look very good beside last year's.*
PHRASES

be beside yourself (with anger/fear/grief/joy etc) to feel a particular emotion very strongly: *The boy was beside himself with fury.*

be beside the point to not be important: *'I'm not hungry.' 'That's beside the point, you need to eat!'*

besides /bɪ'saɪdz/ *adv, prep* **1** *spoken* used when adding another reason: *I wanted to help her out. Besides, I needed the money.* **2** in addition to something or someone else: *Was there anyone else you knew besides Steve?* | **besides doing sth** *Besides going to college, she works 15 hours a week.*

besiege /bɪ'siːdʒ/ *v* **1 be besieged by people/worries/thoughts etc** to be surrounded by a lot of people or to be very worried etc: *a rock star besieged by fans* **2 be besieged with letters/questions/demands etc** to receive a lot of letters, be asked a lot of questions etc: *The radio station was besieged with letters of complaint.* **3** [T] if an army besieges a place, soldiers surround it

besotted /bɪ'sɒtɪd $ bɪ'sɑː-/ *adj* loving someone or something so much that you seem silly: **[+with]** *He's completely besotted with her.*

besought /bɪ'sɔːt $ -'sɔːt/ *v* the past tense and past participle of BESEECH

bespectacled /bɪ'spektəkəld/ *adj formal* wearing glasses

best¹ /best/ *adj* better than anyone or anything else: *the best player on the team* | *What's the* ***best way*** *to get to El Paso?* | *The* ***best thing*** *to do is to ask Mum first.* | *Who is your* ***best friend***? → SECOND BEST

best² *adv*
1 more than anyone else or anything else: *Helen knows him best.* | *Which song do you like best?* | *She's* ***best known*** *for her role in 'Friends'.*
2 in a way that is better than any other: *It works best if you warm it up first.*

B

PHRASES

as best you can as well as you can: *She would have to manage as best she could.*

best³ *n* **the best a)** someone or something that is better than any others: *Which stereo is the best?* **b)** the most successful situation or results you can achieve: *All parents want the best for their children.*

PHRASES

at best used to emphasize that something is not very good, even when you consider it in the best possible way: *At best, only a few trains will be running over the holiday period.*

at your best doing something as well as you are able to: *The movie shows Hollywood at its best.*

do/try your best to try as hard as you can to achieve something: *I did my best, but I still didn't pass.* **THESAURUS** **TRY**

it's (all) for the best used to say that something seems bad now, but might have a good result later: *I'll be sad to see her leave, but maybe it's for the best.*

make the best of sth to accept a bad situation and do what you can to make it better: *It's not going to be easy, but we'll just have to make the best of it.*

best 'man *n* [singular] a friend of a BRIDEGROOM (=man who is getting married), who helps him to get ready and stands next to him during the wedding

bestow /bɪˈstəʊ $ -ˈstoʊ/ *v* [T] *formal* to give someone something of great value or importance

bestseller /ˌbestˈselə $ -ər/ *n* [C] a popular product, especially a book, which a lot of people buy —**best-selling** *adj* [only before noun]: *a best-selling novel*

bet¹ /bet/ *v* [I,T] (*past tense and past participle* **bet**, *present participle* **betting**) to try to win money by saying what the result of a race, game, or competition will be: **bet (sb) that** *I bet him £5 that he wouldn't win.* | **bet (sth) on sth** *She bet all her money on a horse that came last.* —**betting** *n* [U]

PHRASES

I bet *spoken* **1** used to say that you are sure that something is true or happened: *I bet they'll be late.* | *I bet she was surprised when she saw you at the party.* **2** used to show that you agree with someone or understand how they feel: *'I was furious.' 'I bet you were!'* **3** used to show that you do not believe someone: *'I'm definitely going to give up smoking.' 'Yeah, I bet.'*

you bet! *spoken* used to say 'yes' in a very definite way: *'Would you like to come?' 'You bet!'*

bet² *n* [C]

1 if you have a bet on something, you try to win money by saying what the result of a game, race, or competition will be: **[+on]** *I had a bet on the match.* | **win/lose a bet** *If he scores now, I'll win my bet.*

2 the money that you risk in order to try to win more money: *a $10 bet* → **hedge your bets** at HEDGE²

PHRASES

a good/safe bet something that is likely to be useful or successful: *This shop is always a good bet for presents.*

your best bet *spoken* used when advising someone what to do: *Your best bet would be to avoid the motorway.*

betray /bɪˈtreɪ/ *v* [T]

1 **PERSON** to behave dishonestly towards someone who loves you or trusts you: *Her husband had betrayed her by lying to her.*

2 **COUNTRY** to be disloyal to your country, company etc, for example by giving secret information to its enemies

3 **FEELINGS** to show feelings that you are trying to hide: *His voice betrayed his nervousness.*

betrayal /bɪˈtreɪəl/ *n* [C,U] when someone betrays another person

better¹ /ˈbetə $ -ər/ *adj*

1 of higher quality, or more useful, interesting, skilful etc **OPP** **worse**: *We need a better computer.* | **[+than]** *Your stereo is better than mine.* | *My sister's better at maths than I am.* | **much/a lot/far better** *We now have a much better understanding of the disease.* | **better still/even better** *It was even better than last year.* | *Your English is getting better* (=improving).

2 less ill than you were, or no longer ill **OPP** **worse**: *She's a little better today.* | *Are you feeling better?* | *I hope your sore throat gets better soon.* **THESAURUS** **HEALTHY**

PHRASES

have seen better days *informal* to be in a bad condition: *The sofa had seen better days.*

it is better/it would be better used to give advice about what someone should do: **it is better to do sth** *It's much better to get a proper written agreement.* | **it would be better if** *It would be better if you stayed here.*

the sooner the better/the bigger the better etc used to say that something should happen as soon as possible, be as big as possible etc: *Fetch a large vase, the bigger the better.*

better² *adv*

1 to a higher standard or quality: **[+than]** *He speaks English better than I do.*

2 more: *This jacket suits me better.* | **[+than]** *I knew her better than anyone else.*

PHRASES

do better to perform better or reach a higher standard: **[+than]** *We did better than all the other schools.*

had better *spoken* **1** used to say what someone should do: *You'd better go and get ready.* | *I think I'd better leave now.* **2** used to threaten someone: *You'd better keep your mouth shut about this.*

better³ *n* **the better** the one that is the higher in quality, more suitable etc when you are comparing two similar people or things: *It's hard to decide which one's better.*

PHRASES

for the better in a way that improves the situation: *a definite change for the better*

get the better of sb 1 if a feeling gets the better of you, you do not control it when you should: *His curiosity got the better of him and he opened the letter.* **2** to defeat someone

better⁴ v [T] *formal* to achieve something that is better than something else: *Jim's total of five gold medals is unlikely to be bettered.*

better 'off *adj* **1** if you are better off, you have more money than you had before: *We plan to reduce taxes and make all families better off.* **2** happier, improved, more successful etc: **[+with/without]** *She's better off without him.* **3 you/he/she etc would be better off doing sth** *spoken* used to say what someone should do: *You'd be better off doing the exam next year, when you're ready for it.*

'betting ,shop n [C] *BrE* a place where people go to BET on the results of races, games etc
SYN **bookmaker**

between /bɪˈtwiːn/ *adv, prep*
1 (*also* **in between**) with one thing or person on each side: *He sat between the two women on the sofa.* | *two houses with a narrow path in between →* see picture on page A8
2 used to say that a place is in the middle with other places at a distance from it: *Oxford is between London and Birmingham.*
3 used to say which two places are connected by something: *They're building a new road between Manchester and Sheffield.*
4 (*also* **in between**) after one event or time and before another: *I didn't see my parents at all between Christmas and Easter.* | *He had a year off between leaving school and going to university.* | *I have a lesson at nine o'clock and another at three o'clock, but nothing in between.*
5 used to show a range of amounts, by giving the largest and smallest: *My journey to school takes between 30 and 40 minutes.* | *children aged between 7 and 11*
6 used to show who is involved in a relationship, agreement, fight etc: *The relationship between them has always been friendly.* | *an agreement between the company and the trade unions* | *the war between England and France*
7 used to say that something is shared by each person in a group: *Tom divided his money between his children.*
8 used to say which two things or people you are comparing: *the contrast between town and country life*
9 if people have an amount of money between them, that is the total amount they have: *We had ten dollars between us. →* **GO-BETWEEN**

> **Word Choice: between or among?**
> You use **between** when there is one person or thing on each side of someone or something: *I sat between Alex and Sarah.*
> You use **among** when there are several people or things around someone or something: *The hut was hidden among the trees.*

beverage /ˈbevərɪdʒ/ n [C] *formal* a drink: *We don't sell alcoholic beverages.*

beware /bɪˈweə $ -ˈwer/ v [I,T] used to warn someone to be careful: **[+of]** *Beware of the dog!* | **beware of doing sth** *They should beware of making hasty decisions.*

bewildered /bɪˈwɪldəd $ -ərd/ *adj* confused and not sure what to do or think: *The children looked bewildered and scared.* —**bewilderment** n [U]

bewildering /bɪˈwɪldərɪŋ/ *adj* confusing: *a bewildering variety of choices*

bewitch /bɪˈwɪtʃ/ v [T] if something bewitches you, you are so interested in it that you cannot think about anything else: *He was bewitched by her smile.*

beyond /bɪˈjɒnd $ -ˈjɑːnd/ *prep, adv*
1 if something is beyond a place, it is on the side of it that is farthest away from you: *There was a forest beyond the river.* | *We got a lovely view of the river, and the mountains beyond.*
2 past a particular time or date: *The project will continue beyond 2010.* | *our plans for the year 2011 and beyond*
3 more than a particular amount, level, or limit: *Inflation has risen beyond the 5% level.*
4 outside the limits of what someone or something can do: *Such tasks are far beyond the abilities of the average student.*
5 used to say that something cannot be done: *The TV is beyond repair.* | *The concert was cancelled due to circumstances beyond our control.*
6 used to mean 'except' in negative sentences: *The island doesn't have much industry beyond tourism.*
PHRASES
> **it's beyond me** *spoken* used to say that you do not understand something: *It's beyond me why she's so popular.*

bi- /baɪ/ *prefix* two: *He's bilingual (=able to speak two languages well).*

bias Ac /ˈbaɪəs/ n [singular, U] an opinion about a person, group, or idea which makes you treat them unfairly or differently: **political/gender/racial etc bias** *He has accused his employers of racial bias.* | **[+against/towards/in favour of]** *Some employers have a bias against women.*

biased Ac /ˈbaɪəst/ *adj* supporting one person or group in an unfair way, when you should treat everyone fairly: *The referee was definitely biased!* | **[+against/towards/in favour of]** *Some newspapers are biased in favour of the government.* THESAURUS UNFAIR

bib /bɪb/ n [C] a piece of cloth or plastic that you tie under a baby's chin to protect its clothes when it is eating

bible /ˈbaɪbəl/ n **1 the Bible** the holy book of the Christian religion **2** [C] a copy of the Bible —**biblical** /ˈbɪblɪkəl/ *adj*

bibliography /ˌbɪbliˈɒɡrəfi $ -ˈɑːɡ-/ n [C] (*plural* **bibliographies**) a list of books on a particular subject

bicentenary /ˌbaɪsenˈtiːnəri $ -ˈtenəri, -ˈsentəneri/ *especially BrE*, **bicentennial** /-ˈteniəl/ *AmE* n [C] (*plural* **bicentenaries**) the day or year exactly 200 years after an important event: **[+of]** *the bicentenary of Mozart's death*

biceps /ˈbaɪseps/ n [C usually plural] (*plural* **biceps**) the large muscle on the front of your upper arm

bicker /'bɪkə $ -ər/ v [I] to argue about something unimportant: **[+about/over]** *The kids were bickering about who was the fastest runner.*

bicycle /'baɪsɪkəl/ n [C] a vehicle with two wheels that you ride by pushing the PEDALS with your feet: *Can he ride a bicycle?* | **by bicycle** *She came by bicycle.*

bid¹ /bɪd/ n [C] **1** an offer to pay a particular price for something: **[+for]** *We made a bid of £400 million for the company.* | *a takeover bid for the company* **2** an offer to do work for someone at a particular price: **[+for]** *The company accepted the lowest bid for the cleaning contract.* **3** an attempt to achieve or get something: **[+for]** *a bid for power* | **bid to do sth** *a desperate bid to save the child's life*

bid² v [I,T] (past tense and past participle **bid**, present participle **bidding**) to offer to pay a particular price that several people want to buy: **bid (sb) sth for sth** *She bid $50,000 for the painting.* —**bidder** n [C]

bid³ v [T] (past tense **bade** /bæd, beɪd/ or **bid**, past participle **bid** or **bidden** /'bɪdn/, present participle **bidding**) literary **bid sb good morning/goodbye etc** to greet someone

bidding /'bɪdɪŋ/ n [U] when people bid for goods in an AUCTION
PHRASES
do sb's bidding *formal* to do what someone tells you to do: *The servants always had to be ready to do their master's bidding.*

bide /baɪd/ v **bide your time** to wait until the right time to do something

bidet /'biːdeɪ $ bɪ'deɪ/ n [C] a large bowl that you sit on to wash your bottom

biennial /baɪ'eniəl/ adj a biennial event happens once every two years

bifocals /baɪ'fəʊkəlz $ 'baɪfoʊ-/ n [plural] glasses with an upper part made for seeing things that are far away, and a lower part made for reading

big /bɪg/ adj
1 large, or larger than the average size **OPP small**: *a big red balloon* | *the biggest city in the world* | *How big is their new house?* **THESAURUS FAT**
2 important or serious **OPP small**: *a big decision* | *This is a very big match for our team.* | *We have some big problems.* | *It was the biggest mistake of my life.* **THESAURUS IMPORTANT**
3 successful or popular: *His last film was a big hit.* | *He'll never make it big* (=become successful) *as a professional golfer.*
4 **big sister/brother** *informal* your big sister or brother is older than you are
PHRASES
big deal *spoken* used when you do not think something is as important as someone else thinks it is: *It's just a game. If you lose, big deal.* | *It's no big deal* (=it's not important).
big money (*also* **big bucks** *AmE*) *informal* a lot of money: *He was offered big money for his life story.*

BICYCLE

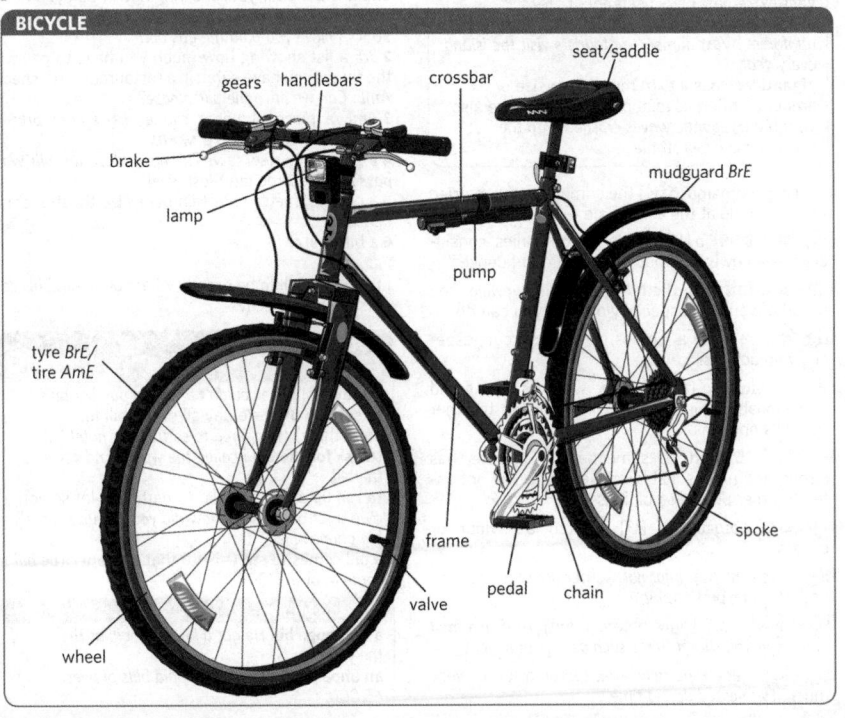

seat/saddle
gears | handlebars | crossbar
brake
mudguard *BrE*
lamp
pump
tyre *BrE*/
tire *AmE*
frame
spoke
valve | pedal | chain
wheel

THESAURUS

big you use **big** when talking about the size of something. You also use it when talking about things that are very serious or important: *a big country* | *a big man* | *a big mistake* | *a big decision*
large you use **large** when talking about the size of something. You also use it when talking about numbers or amounts. **Large** sounds more formal than **big** and is the usual word to use in written English: *a large painting* | *The museum attracts a large number of visitors.*
major big and important or serious, especially when compared to others of the same kind: *Pollution is a major problem.* | *the major political parties* | *a major earthquake*
substantial rather big. **Substantial** sounds more formal than **big** and is used especially when writing about amounts and numbers, increases and decreases: *A new roof will cost a substantial amount of money.* | *a substantial increase in the number of homeless people*

very big

great very big – used especially when something has a big effect or seems very impressive: *The show was a great success.* | *There have been great changes in society.* | *Luckily the damage wasn't very great.*
huge/massive/enormous extremely big: *Their house is huge.* | *There is an enormous amount of work to do.* | *a massive increase in oil prices*
vast extremely big – used about areas, distances, numbers, or amounts: *a vast area of rainforest* | *Vast numbers of tourists visit the island every year.*
gigantic/colossal extremely big in size or amount – often used about things that are also very high: *Gigantic waves crashed onto the beach.* | *a colossal statue*

bigamy /ˈbɪɡəmi/ n [U] the crime of being married to two people at the same time —**bigamist** n [C]

big 'business n [U] very large companies, considered as a powerful group with a lot of influence

big-headed /ˌbɪɡˈhedɪd◂/ adj disapproving too proud of yourself, especially of what you can do

big 'name n [C] a famous person or group, especially an actor, singer etc

bigot /ˈbɪɡət/ n [C] someone who has strong and unreasonable opinions and will not listen to other people's opinions

bigoted /ˈbɪɡətɪd/ adj someone who is bigoted has strong and unreasonable opinions and will not listen to other people's opinions

bigotry /ˈbɪɡətri/ n [U] bigoted behaviour or beliefs

'big shot n [C] informal someone who has an important or powerful job

big-'ticket adj [only before noun] AmE informal expensive: *big-ticket items such as cars or jewelry*

'big time[1] adv especially AmE spoken a lot, or very much: *He messed up big time.*

big time[2] n **the big time** informal when someone is very successful or important, for example in politics or sports: *The 46-year-old author has finally hit the big time.* —**big-time** adj [only before noun]: *big-time drug dealers*

bigwig /ˈbɪɡwɪɡ/ n [C] informal an important person

bike[1] /baɪk/ n [C] informal
1 a bicycle: *He likes riding his bike.* | **by bike** *I came here by bike.*
2 a MOTORCYCLE → **MOUNTAIN BIKE**

bike[2] v [I + adv/prep] informal to ride a bicycle

biker /ˈbaɪkə $ -ər/ n [C] someone who rides a MOTORCYCLE

bikini /bəˈkiːni/ n [C] a piece of clothing in two parts that women wear on the beach when it is hot

bilateral /baɪˈlætərəl/ adj involving two groups or countries: *a bilateral trade agreement* | *bilateral negotiations between Israel and Syria* —**bilaterally** adv

bile /baɪl/ n [U] a bitter green-brown liquid produced by your LIVER, which helps you to DIGEST fat

bilingual /baɪˈlɪŋɡwəl/ adj **1** able to speak two languages very well **2** written or spoken in two languages: *a bilingual dictionary*

bill[1] /bɪl/ n [C]
1 a list of things that you have bought or that someone has done for you, showing how much you have to pay for them: **[+for]** *The bill for the repairs came to $650.* | *Have you paid the gas bill?*
2 BrE a list showing how much you have to pay for the things you have eaten in a restaurant SYN **check** AmE: *Can we have the bill, please?*
3 AmE a piece of paper money SYN **note** BrE: *a ten-dollar bill* THESAURUS **MONEY**
4 a plan for a new law: *The new education bill was passed* (=became law) *last week.*
5 a programme of entertainment at a theatre, concert etc
6 a bird's BEAK
PHRASES
fit/fill the bill to be exactly what you need: *This car fits the bill perfectly.*

COLLOCATIONS

verbs

to pay a bill *She couldn't afford to pay her bills.*
to settle a bill (=to pay all of the bill for something) *He offered to settle their hotel bill.*
to ask for the bill *I called the waiter and asked for the bill.*
to run up a bill (=to use something a lot so you owe a lot of money) *How did you run up such a big phone bill?*
a bill comes to sth (=is for that amount) *The bill came to over $100.*

types of bill

a big/huge bill *He got a huge tax bill at the end of the year.*
an unpaid bill *They had unpaid bills of over £5,000.*

an electricity/gas/phone bill *The gas bill has gone up again.*
a hotel bill *He paid the hotel bill by credit card.*

bill² v [T] to send a bill to someone: **bill sb for sth** *They've billed me for things I didn't order.*
PHRASAL VERBS
bill sth **as** sth to advertise or describe something in a particular way: *The boxing match was billed as 'the fight of the century'.*

billboard /'bɪlbɔːd $ -bɔːrd/ n [C] a big sign next to a road, that is used to advertise something
SYN **hoarding** *BrE* **THESAURUS** ADVERTISEMENT

billet /'bɪlɪt/ v [T] to put soldiers in people's houses to live for a short time —**billet** n [C]

billfold /'bɪlfəʊld $ -foʊld/ n [C] *AmE* a small flat case that you use for carrying paper money
SYN **wallet** *BrE*

billiards /'bɪljədz $ -ərdz/ n [U] a game played on a table that is covered in cloth, in which you hit balls with a CUE (=long stick) and try to knock them into pockets at the edge of the table

billing /'bɪlɪŋ/ n [U] the importance of the position of a performer's name, for example at the beginning of a film: *He promised me I'd get **top billing**.*

billion /'bɪljən/ number (plural **billion** or **billions**)
1 the number 1,000,000,000: **two/three/four etc billion** *3.5 billion years ago* | **billions of pounds/dollars etc**
2 an extremely large number of things or people: **a billion** *A billion stars shine in the sky.* | **billions of sth** *There are billions of things I want to say.* —**billionth** adj —**billionth** n [C]

billow /'bɪləʊ $ -loʊ/ v [I] **1** (also **billow out**) if something made of cloth billows, it moves in the wind and fills with air: *The boat's sails billowed in the wind.* **2** if smoke billows, a lot of it rises into the air: **[+out of/up etc]** *Smoke billowed out of the chimney.* —**billow** n [C]

bimbo /'bɪmbəʊ $ -boʊ/ n [C] (plural **bimbos**) *informal* an offensive word meaning an attractive but stupid woman

bimonthly /baɪ'mʌnθli/ adj appearing or happening once every two months or twice each month: *a bimonthly trade magazine* —**bimonthly** adv

bin /bɪn/ n [C]
1 a large container where you put small things that you no longer want: *She threw the letter in the bin.* | *wastepaper bin*
2 a container that you use to store things: *a flour bin*

binary /'baɪnəri/ adj **the binary system** *technical* a system of counting that only includes the numbers 0 and 1, used especially in computers: *The binary system was discovered by a Hungarian.*

bind¹ /baɪnd/ v (past tense and past participle **bound** /baʊnd/) **1** [T] to tie something together firmly, with string or rope: *They bound his legs with a rope.* **2** (also **bind together**) [T] *formal* to form a strong connection between two people, groups, or countries: *Their shared experiences helped to bind the two men together.* **3** [T usually passive] if you are bound by an agreement or promise, you must do what you

BINS

wastepaper basket *BrE*/wastebasket *AmE*

dustbin *BrE*/garbage can *AmE*   rubbish bin

agreed or promised to do: *Each country is bound by the treaty.* **4** [I,T] *technical* to stick together in a mass, or to make small pieces of something stick together **5** [T] to fasten the pages of a book together and put them in a cover: *The book was printed and bound in India.*

bind² n **a bind** *informal* an annoying or difficult situation: *It's a real bind having to look after the children.*

binding¹ /'baɪndɪŋ/ adj a contract or agreement that is binding must be obeyed: *The contract isn't binding until you sign it.*

binding² n [C] the cover of a book

binge /bɪndʒ/ n [C] *informal* an occasion when you eat or drink a lot in a very short time: *He **goes on** alcohol **binges** that last all weekend.* —**binge** v [I]: *I sometimes binge on chocolate.*

binge ,drinking n [U] the activity of drinking a large amount of alcohol in a short period of time —**binge drinker** n [C]

bingo /'bɪŋgəʊ $ -goʊ/ n [U] a game played for money or prizes in which numbers are chosen and called out. If you have the right numbers on your card, you win.

binoculars /bɪ'nɒkjələz, baɪ- $ -'nɑːkjələrz/ n [plural] an object like a large pair of glasses that you hold up and look through to see things that are far away

BINOCULARS
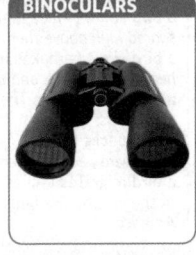

bio- /baɪəʊ, baɪə $ baɪoʊ, baɪə/ prefix relating to or using living things: *biochemistry* | *biofuels*

biochemistry
/ˌbaɪəʊ'keməstri $ ˌbaɪoʊ-/ n [U] the scientific study of the chemistry of living things —**biochemist** n [C] —**biochemical** adj

biodegradable /ˌbaɪəʊdɪˈgreɪdəbəl◀ $ ˌbaɪoʊ-/ *adj* a material that is biodegradable can be destroyed by natural processes, in a way that does not harm the environment: *biodegradable plastic*

biodiesel /ˈbaɪəʊˌdiːzəl $ ˈbaɪoʊ-/ *n* [U] a liquid made from vegetable oil or animal fat, which can be used instead of DIESEL in engines

biodiversity /ˌbaɪəʊdaɪˈvɜːsəti, -də- $ ˌbaɪoʊdaɪˈvɜːr-, -də-/ *n* [U] *technical* the number of different plants and animals in a place

biographer /baɪˈɒgrəfə $ -ˈɑːgrəfər/ *n* [C] someone who writes a biography of someone else

biography /baɪˈɒgrəfi $ -ˈɑːg-/ *n* [C] (*plural* **biographies**) a book about a person's life THESAURUS▶ BOOK —**biographical** /ˌbaɪəˈgræfɪkəl◀/ *adj*

biological /ˌbaɪəˈlɒdʒɪkəl◀ $ -ˈlɑː-/ *adj* 1 relating to the natural processes performed by living things: *a biological process* 2 relating to biology 3 **biological weapons/warfare/attack etc** weapons, attacks etc that involve the use of living things, including BACTERIA, to harm people —**biologically** /-kli/ *adv*

biology /baɪˈɒlədʒi $ -ˈɑːl-/ *n* [U] the scientific study of living things —**biologist** *n* [C]

biopsy /ˈbaɪɒpsi $ -ɑːp-/ *n* [C] (*plural* **biopsies**) the removal of cells from someone's body to find out more about a disease they may have

biosecurity /ˌbaɪəʊsɪˈkjʊərəti $ ˌbaɪoʊsɪˈkjʊr-/ *n* [U] things that are done to prevent diseases from spreading between people, animals, or crops: *biosecurity measures on poultry farms*

biotechnology /ˌbaɪəʊtekˈnɒlədʒi $ ˌbaɪoʊtekˈnɑː-/ *n* [U] the use of living things such as cells and BACTERIA to make drugs, destroy waste matter etc

bipartisan /ˌbaɪpɑːtɪˈzæn $ baɪˈpɑːrtɪzən/ *adj* involving two political parties: *a bipartisan committee*

birch /bɜːtʃ $ bɜːrtʃ/ *n* [C,U] a tree with smooth BARK and thin branches, or the wood from this tree

bird /bɜːd $ bɜːrd/ *n* [C] an animal with wings and feathers that can usually fly → **kill two birds with one stone** at KILL¹ → see picture on page A3

COLLOCATIONS

verbs

a bird flies *A bird flew out of the tree.*

a bird soars (=flies high in the sky) *The birds soared high above them.*

a bird sings (=makes musical sounds) *It was a beautiful morning, and the birds were singing.*

a bird lays its eggs *The birds lay their eggs in the rocky cliffs.*

a bird pecks (at) sth (=bites it with its beak) *Birds were pecking at crumbs on the path.*

a bird migrates (=flies each year to another part of the world) *The birds migrate from South America.*

noun + bird

a flock of birds (=a large number of birds together) *A flock of birds flew across the evening sky.*

---

bird + noun

bird song (=musical sounds that birds make) *She was woken by bird song.*

bird-watching (=the activity of watching wild birds) *One of his hobbies is bird-watching.*

a bird's nest *The boys found a bird's nest.*

types of bird

a wild bird *The future of our wild birds is under threat.*

a common/rare bird *The forest is home to a number of rare birds and animals.*

a bird of prey (=that hunts and eats small animals) *The mice are hunted by birds of prey.*

---

birdie /ˈbɜːdi $ ˈbɜːrdi/ *n* [C] *AmE* a small object with feathers that you hit across a net in the game of BADMINTON SYN **shuttlecock** *BrE*

bird of ˈprey *n* [C] (*plural* **birds of prey**) a bird that kills and eats other birds and small animals

ˈbird-ˌwatcher *n* [C] someone who watches wild birds and tries to recognize different types —**bird-watching** *n* [U]

Biro /ˈbaɪərəʊ $ ˈbaɪroʊ/ *n* (*plural* **Biros**) trademark *BrE* a type of pen

birth /bɜːθ $ bɜːrθ/ *n*
1 [C,U] the time when a baby comes out of its mother's body: **at birth** (=when someone is born) *She weighed 3 kg at birth.* | **from/since birth** *He has been blind from birth.* | **date of birth** *especially BrE*/ **birth date** *especially AmE*: *What's your date of birth?*
2 [U] someone's family origin: **by birth** *Her father was French by birth.*
3 birth parent/mother/father someone's birth parent is their real mother or father, rather than someone who looked after them or ADOPTED them
4 [singular] the time when something new starts to exist: **[+of]** *the birth of a nation*
PHRASES
give birth if a woman gives birth, she produces a baby from her body: **[+to]** *She's just given birth to twins.*

ˈbirth cerˌtificate *n* [C] an official document that shows when and where you were born

ˈbirth conˌtrol *n* [U] methods of stopping a woman becoming PREGNANT

birthday /ˈbɜːθdeɪ $ ˈbɜːr-/ *n* [C] the date in each year on which you were born → **anniversary**: *When's your birthday?*
PHRASES
Happy birthday! *spoken* used for greeting someone on their birthday: *Happy birthday, darling!*

COLLOCATIONS

adjectives

sb's 18th/40th etc birthday *It's my sister's 16th birthday next week.*

a happy birthday *I just wanted to wish you a happy birthday.*

verbs

to have a good/nice birthday *I had a really nice birthday.*

to get sth for your birthday *Did you get anything special for your birthday?*

to remember/forget sb's birthday *People always remember my birthday because it's on January 1st.*

birthday + noun

a birthday card/present/gift *Don't forget to send Grandma a birthday card.*

a birthday party *She invited me to her birthday party.*

a birthday cake *I'm making Joe a birthday cake.*

a birthday treat (=something special you do on your birthday) *What would you like to do for a birthday treat?*

birthmark /ˈbɜːθmɑːk $ ˈbɜːrθmɑːrk/ n [C] an unusual mark on someone's skin that is there when they are born

birthplace /ˈbɜːθpleɪs $ ˈbɜːrθ-/ n [C usually singular] the place where someone was born **THESAURUS** ORIGIN

birthrate /ˈbɜːθreɪt $ ˈbɜːrθ-/ n [C] the average number of babies born during a particular period of time in a country or area

biscuit /ˈbɪskɪt/ n [C]
1 *BrE* a thin sweet cake **SYN** **cookie** *AmE*: *a chocolate biscuit*
2 *AmE* a kind of bread that you bake in small round shapes

bisexual /baɪˈsekʃuəl/ adj sexually attracted to both men and women —**bisexual** n [C] —**bisexuality** /ˌbaɪsekʃuˈæləti/ n [U]

bishop /ˈbɪʃəp/ n [C] a Christian priest with a high rank who is in charge of the churches and priests in a large area

bison /ˈbaɪsən/ n [C] (*plural* **bison** or **bisons**) an animal that looks like a large cow with long hair on its head and shoulders, and lives in the United States **SYN** **buffalo**

bistro /ˈbiːstrəʊ $ -troʊ/ n [C] (*plural* **bistros**) a small restaurant

bit¹ /bɪt/ n [C]
1 **PIECE** a small piece of something: **[+of]** *a few bits of broken glass* | *The car was **blown to bits** (=broken into small pieces) in the explosion.* **THESAURUS** PIECE
2 **PART** *BrE informal* a part of something: **[+of]** *the best bit of the film*
3 **A LITTLE** **a bit of sth** especially *BrE informal* a small amount of something: **[+of]** *He may need a bit of help.*
4 **SLIGHTLY** **a bit** especially *BrE* slightly: *Could you turn the TV up a bit?* | *Aren't you being a little bit unfair?* | *Carol looks a bit like my sister.* | **a bit better/older/easier etc** *I feel a bit better now.* | **not a bit/not one bit** (=not at all) *You're not a bit like your brother.*
5 **SLIGHT** **a bit of a ...** especially *BrE* used especially in spoken English when you are describing something: *The news came as a bit of a shock* (=it was rather shocking). | *There has been a bit of a change of plan* (=the plan has changed slightly).
6 **SHORT TIME/DISTANCE** especially *BrE* a short period of time or a short distance: *You'll have to wait a bit.* | **in a bit** *I'll see you in a bit.* | **for a bit** *We sat around for*

a bit chatting. | **after a bit** *After a bit, he got used to the idea.* | *I walked on a bit and then turned back.*
7 **COMPUTER** the smallest unit of information that a computer uses
8 **ON A DRILL** the sharp part of a tool for cutting or making holes: *a drill bit*
9 **ON A HORSE** a metal bar that is put in the mouth of a horse and used to control its movements
PHRASES
bit by bit especially *BrE* gradually: *Bit by bit, I was starting to change my mind.* **THESAURUS** SLOWLY
bits and pieces *informal* any small things of various kinds: *Let me get all my bits and pieces together.*
do your bit *informal* to do a fair share of the work or effort that is needed to achieve something: *We wanted to do our bit for the local community.*
every bit as important/bad/good etc especially *BrE* equally important, bad etc as something else: *Peter was every bit as good-looking as his brother.*
love sb to bits *BrE informal* to like someone very much: *I love him to bits.*
quite a bit a fairly large amount: *She's quite a bit older than him.* | **[+of]** *He does quite a bit of travelling.*

bit² v the past tense of BITE

bitch¹ /bɪtʃ/ n **1** [C] a female dog **2** [C] an offensive word for a woman that you dislike: *She's such a bitch!* **3** **be a bitch** *informal* to cause problems or be difficult: *I love this sweater but it's a bitch to wash.*

bitch² v [I] **1** *informal* to make unpleasant remarks about someone: **[+about]** *He never bitches about other members of the team.* **2** *AmE* to complain continuously

bitchy /ˈbɪtʃi/ adj *informal* unkind and unpleasant about other people —**bitchily** adv —**bitchiness** n [U]

bite¹ /baɪt/ v (*past tense* **bit** /bɪt/, *past participle* **bitten** /ˈbɪtn/, *present participle* **biting**)
1 [I,T] to use your teeth to eat something or attack someone: *Be careful of the dog. Jerry said he bites.* | **[+into/through/at/down]** *She bit into an apple.* | *A shark can easily bite through a man's leg.* | **bite sth off** *a man whose arm was bitten off by an alligator* | *I wish I could stop **biting** my **nails** (=biting the nails on my fingers).*
2 [I,T] if an insect or snake bites, it injures someone by making a hole in their skin → **sting**: *I think I've been bitten by a mosquito.*
3 [I] to start to have an unpleasant effect: *The new tobacco taxes have begun to bite.*
PHRASES
bite the bullet to start dealing with an unpleasant situation because you can no longer avoid it: *I finally bit the bullet and paid.*
bite the dust *informal* to die, fail, or be defeated: *Their hopes of winning the championship have finally bitten the dust.*

THESAURUS

bite to use your teeth to eat something or attack someone: *He bit into the apple.* | *That cat bites people!*
chew to keep biting something that is in your

mouth: *Helen was chewing a piece of gum.* | *Always chew your food thoroughly before you swallow it.*

nibble to bite a lot of small pieces off something: *She was nibbling a biscuit.* | *The rabbit was nibbling a carrot.*

gnaw if an animal gnaws something, it bites it repeatedly with a lot of force, in order to eat it or make a hole in it: *The dog was in the yard gnawing on a bone.* | *Mice had gnawed a hole in the box.*

sting if an insect stings you, it makes a very small hole in your skin and hurts you. You use **sting** about BEES, WASPS, and SCORPIONS, and **bite** about other insects, SPIDERS, and snakes: *Ouch! I think I've just been stung by a wasp.*

bite² *n*
1 [C] when you cut or chew something with your teeth: **take/have a bite (of sth/out of sth)** *He took a bite of the cheese.* | *Can I have a bite of your apple?* | **give sb a bite** *The dog gave her a nasty bite.* | *Antonio ate half his burger in one bite.*
2 [C] a wound made when an animal or insect bites you → **sting**: *snake/mosquito/ant etc bites* *I'm covered in mosquito bites!*
3 a bite (to eat) *informal* a small meal: *Let's have a bite to eat before we go.*

biting /ˈbaɪtɪŋ/ *adj* **1** a biting wind is extremely cold **2** a biting criticism or remark is cruel or unkind

bitten /ˈbɪtn/ *v* the past participle of BITE

bitter¹ /ˈbɪtə $ -ər/ *adj*
1 ANGRY angry and upset because you feel you have been treated unfairly: **[+about]** *I feel very bitter about what happened.* | *a bitter old man* | *She gave a bitter laugh.*
2 DISAPPOINTMENT/BLOW [only before noun] making you feel very unhappy and upset: **a bitter disappointment/blow** *His exam results were a bitter disappointment to his parents.* | *She knew from bitter experience that they wouldn't agree.*
3 ARGUMENT a bitter argument is one in which people feel very strong anger or hatred towards each other: *The couple are locked in a bitter legal dispute over the children.* | *They are bitter enemies.*
4 TASTE something that is bitter has a strong taste that is not sweet OPP **sweet** → **sour**: *a fruit with a horrible bitter taste* THESAURUS **TASTE**
5 WEATHER bitter weather is extremely cold: *a bitter wind* —**bitterness** *n* [U]
PHRASES
to/until the bitter end continuing until the end, even though this is difficult: *They say they will fight the closure to the bitter end.*

bitter² *n* [C,U] *BrE* beer with a bitter taste, or a glass of this: *A pint of bitter, please.* | *Two bitters, please.*

bitterly /ˈbɪtəli $ -ər-/ *adv* with a lot of anger or sadness: *I was bitterly disappointed.* | *He complained bitterly.*
PHRASES
bitterly cold very cold: *It was a bitterly cold December morning.*

bitter-'sweet *adj* making you feel both happy and sad: *bitter-sweet memories*

bitty /ˈbɪti/ *adj BrE informal* having too many small parts that do not seem to be related to each other: *I thought the film was rather bitty.*

bizarre /bəˈzɑː $ -ˈzɑːr/ *adj* very unusual and strange: *a bizarre coincidence* THESAURUS **STRANGE** —**bizarrely** *adv*

black¹ /blæk/ *adj*
1 COLOUR having the darkest colour, like coal or night: *a black dress* | *her jet black* (=very black) *hair* | *Outside, it was pitch black* (=completely black).
2 PEOPLE belonging to a race of people who have dark brown skin → **white**: *Over half the students here are black.*
3 TEA/COFFEE black coffee or tea does not have milk in it OPP **white**
4 VERY SAD sad and without hope for the future: *a mood of black despair*
5 HUMOUR/COMEDY humour that makes jokes about serious subjects
6 ANGRY angry or disapproving: *He gave me a black look.* —**blackness** *n* [U]
PHRASES
black and blue *informal* having a lot of BRUISES on your body: *The victim's body had been battered black and blue.*
black and white showing pictures or images only in black, white, and grey: *an old black and white film*
black mark if there is a black mark against you, someone has a bad opinion of you because of something you have done: *It is almost impossible to borrow money if you have any black marks against you.*

black² *n*
1 [C,U] the dark colour of coal or night: *She was wearing black.*
2 (*also* **Black**) [C] someone belonging to a race of people with dark skin: *discrimination against blacks*
PHRASES
in black and white written or printed: *The rules are there in black and white.*
be in the black to have money in your bank account

black³ *v*
PHRASAL VERBS
black out to suddenly become unconscious → **blackout**: *Sharon blacked out and fell to the floor.*

'black belt *n* [C] a high rank in JUDO and KARATE, or someone who has this rank

blackberry /ˈblækbəri $ -beri/ *n* [C] (*plural* **blackberries**) a small sweet black fruit → see picture on page A4

blackbird /ˈblækbɜːd $ -bɜːrd/ *n* [C] a common bird, the male of which is completely black

blackboard /ˈblækbɔːd $ -bɔːrd/ *n* [C] a dark smooth board that you write on with CHALK in schools → see picture at CLASSROOM

blackcurrant /ˌblækˈkʌrənt◂ $ -ˈkɜːr-/ *n* [C] a small blue-black fruit → see picture on page A4

blacken /ˈblækən/ *v* [I,T] to become black, or make

something black: *Smoke had blackened the kitchen walls.*

PHRASES

blacken sb's name to say unpleasant things about someone so that other people have a bad opinion of them: *The senator was accused of setting up a campaign to blacken the other candidate's name.*

black 'eye *n* [C] an area of dark skin around someone's eye that is the result of them being hit

blackhead /'blækhed/ *n* [C] a small dark spot on the skin, with a black centre

black 'hole *n* [C] an area in outer space into which everything near it, including light, is pulled

blacklist /'blæklɪst/ *v* [T] to put someone or something on a list of people or things that are considered bad or dangerous: *Members of the Communist Party have been blacklisted and are unable to find work.* —**blacklist** *n* [C]

black 'magic *n* [U] evil magic connected with the Devil

blackmail /'blækmeɪl/ *n* [U] when someone makes you pay them money or do what they want by threatening to tell your secrets **THESAURUS** **THREATEN** —**blackmail** *v* [T]: *He had tried to blackmail me.* —**blackmailer** *n* [C]

black 'market *n* [C] when things are bought or sold illegally: **on the black market** *drugs that were only available on the black market*

blackout /'blækaʊt/ *n* [C] **1** a period of darkness caused by failure of the electricity supply **2** a situation in which people are not allowed to report any news about something **3** a period during a war when lights must be turned off or covered at night **4** when you suddenly become unconscious: *He's suffered from blackouts since the accident.*

black 'sheep *n* [C] someone who is considered to be bad or embarrassing by the rest of their family

blacksmith /'blæk,smɪθ/ *n* [C] someone who makes and repairs things made of iron

blackspot /'blækspɒt $ -spɑːt/ *n* [C] *BrE* a place where the situation is very bad: *an **accident blackspot** (=where there are a lot of road accidents)*

black 'tie *adj* a black tie event is one at which people wear special formal clothes

blacktop /'blæktɒp $ -tɑːp/ *n* [U] *AmE* the thick black substance used to cover roads **SYN** **Tarmac** *BrE*

bladder /'blædə $ -ər/ *n* [C] the part of your body where URINE is stored before it leaves your body → see picture on page A2

blade /bleɪd/ *n* [C]
1 the flat sharp cutting part of a knife, tool, or weapon: *the blade of a knife | a **razor blade***
2 the flat wide part of an OAR or PROPELLER
3 **blade of grass** a single thin flat leaf of grass

blah /blɑː/ *n* **blah, blah, blah** *spoken* used instead of completing what you are saying, because it is boring or easy to guess: *She was saying, 'He's great, he's so cool, blah, blah, blah.'*

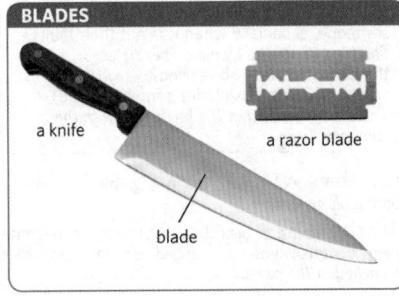

BLADES

a knife

a razor blade

blade

blame¹ /bleɪm/ *v* [T] to say or think that someone or something is responsible for something bad: *Don't blame me – it's not my fault.* | **blame sb/sth for sth** *Marie still blames herself for Patrick's death.* | *Poor weather conditions were blamed for the accident.* | **blame sth on sb** *She blamed the broken computer on me.* | *I'm sure he was **to blame for** the fire.* | *The increase in interest rates was **widely blamed** for the crisis.* **THESAURUS** **GUILTY**

PHRASES

I don't blame you/you can hardly blame them etc *spoken* used to say that you can understand why someone did something: *'She's left her husband.' 'I don't blame her, after the way he treated her.'*

THESAURUS

blame to say or think that someone or something is responsible for something bad that happens: *You shouldn't blame yourself for what happened.* | *The pilot was blamed for the crash.*

say it's sb's fault to say that someone is responsible for something bad that has happened. This phrase is often used instead of **blame** in everyday spoken English: *He said it was my fault that we lost the game.*

put/place/lay the blame on sb/sth to say that someone or something is responsible for something bad that happens. **Place** and **lay** sound rather formal and are used especially in written English: *She always tries to put the blame on me! | The report placed the blame firmly on the city authorities.*

---

blame² *n* [U] responsibility for a mistake or something bad: **[+for]** *I always get the blame for his mistakes.*

PHRASES

to point the finger of blame at sb to say that someone is responsible for something bad: *It's easy to point the finger of blame at someone else.*

COLLOCATIONS

verbs

to get the blame (=to be blamed) *A window was broken, and James got the blame.*

to take the blame (=to say that something is your fault) *I'm not going to take the blame for something I didn't do.*

to put/pin/lay the blame on sb (=to blame someone, especially when it is not their fault) *She tried to put the blame on her sister.*
the blame lies with sb (=used to say that someone is responsible for something bad) *There is no doubt that the blame lies with the company.*

blameless /ˈbleɪmləs/ *adj* not guilty of anything bad: *a blameless life*

blanch /blɑːntʃ $ blæntʃ/ *v* [I] *literary* to become pale because you are afraid or shocked: *Nick blanched at the news.*

bland /blænd/ *adj* **1** without any excitement, strong opinions, or special qualities: *a bland TV quiz show* **2** bland food has very little taste: *a very bland white sauce* **THESAURUS** TASTE

blank¹ /blæŋk/
1 something that is blank has nothing written or recorded on it: *a blank cassette* | *Leave the last page blank.* **THESAURUS** EMPTY
2 a blank expression or look shows no emotion, understanding, or interest → **blankly** → POINT-BLANK
PHRASES
go blank if your mind goes blank, you are suddenly unable to remember something: *When she saw the exam questions, her mind went blank.* **THESAURUS** FORGET

blank² *n* [C] an empty space on a piece of paper, for you to write a word or letter in: *Fill in the blanks on the form.* → **draw a blank** at DRAW¹

blank 'cheque *BrE*, **blank 'check** *AmE n* [C] a cheque that has been signed, but has not had the amount written on it

blanket¹ /ˈblæŋkɪt/ *n*
1 [C] a cover for a bed, usually made of wool
2 [singular] a thick layer of something that covers something: **[+of]** *The hills were covered with a blanket of snow.*

blanket² *v* [T] to cover something completely: **be blanketed in/with sth** *The coast was blanketed in fog.*

blanket³ *adj* **blanket statement/rule/ban** a statement, rule etc that affects everyone or includes all possible kinds of something: *a blanket ban on all types of hunting*

blankly /ˈblæŋkli/ *adv* without showing any emotion or understanding: *Anna stared blankly at the wall.*

blare /bleə $ bler/ (*also* **blare out**) *v* [I,T] to make a very loud unpleasant noise: *Horns blared in the street outside.* | *music blaring out from her car* —**blare** *n* [singular]

blasphemy /ˈblæsfəmi/ *n* [C,U] (*plural* **blasphemies**) something you say or do that insults God or insults people's religious beliefs —**blasphemous** *adj*: *blasphemous talk* —**blaspheme** /blæsˈfiːm/ *v* [I]

blast¹ /blɑːst $ blæst/ *n* **1** [C] a sudden strong movement of wind or air: **[+of]** *a blast of icy air* **2** [C] an explosion: *a bomb blast* | *Thirty-six people died in the blast.* **3** [C] a sudden very loud noise: *a*

long trumpet blast **4 a blast** *AmE spoken* an enjoyable and exciting experience: *We had a blast at Mitch's party.*
PHRASES
(at) full blast as strongly or loudly as possible: *The TV was on full blast.*

blast² *v* **1** [I,T] to break something into pieces using explosives: *They blasted a tunnel through the side of the mountain.* **2** (*also* **blast out**) [I,T] to produce a lot of loud noise, especially music: **[+from]** *Dance music blasted from the stereo.* | *a loudspeaker blasting rock music* **3** [T] to attack a place or person with bombs or guns: *Two gunmen blasted their way into the building.*

blast³ *spoken* used when you are annoyed about something: *Blast! I've lost my keys!*

blatant /ˈbleɪtənt/ *adj* done openly, with no effort to hide bad or dishonest behaviour: *a blatant lie* —**blatantly** *adv*

blaze¹ /bleɪz/ *n* **1** [C] a large fire: *Helicopters were used to fight the blaze.* **2 a blaze of light/colour** a lot of very bright light or colour: *The garden was a blaze of colour.*
PHRASES
(in a) blaze of glory/publicity receiving a lot of praise or public attention: *He launched the new paper in a blaze of publicity.*

blaze² *v* [I] to burn or shine very brightly and strongly: *a huge log fire blazing in the hearth*

blazer /ˈbleɪzə $ -ər/ *n* [C] a jacket, sometimes with the special sign of a school or club on it: *a school blazer*

blazing /ˈbleɪzɪŋ/ *adj* **1** extremely hot: *a blazing summer day* **2** very angry: *a blazing row*

bleach¹ /bliːtʃ/ *n* [U] a chemical used to clean things or make them whiter

bleach² *v* [T] to make something white or lighter in colour by using chemicals or the light from the sun: *Her hair had been bleached by the sun.*

bleachers /ˈbliːtʃəz $ -ərz/ *n* [plural] *AmE* rows of seats where people sit to watch sports games

bleak /bliːk/ *adj* **1** without anything to make you feel happy or hopeful: *Without a job, the future seemed bleak.* **2** cold and unattractive: *a bleak November day* | *the bleak landscape of the northern hills* —**bleakness** *n* [U]

bleary /ˈblɪəri $ ˈblɪri/ *adj* unable to see clearly because you are tired or have been crying: *Sam came down to breakfast looking bleary-eyed.* —**blearily** *adv*

bleat /bliːt/ *v* [I] **1** to make the sound that a sheep or goat makes **2** *informal* to complain in a silly or annoying way: *He's always bleating about wanting more money.* —**bleat** *n* [C]

bleed /bliːd/ v [I] (*past tense and past participle* **bled** /bled/) to lose blood because of an injury: *His head was bleeding badly.* | *Tragically, she* **bled to death.** —**bleeding** n [U]: *Tom kept pressure on the vein to try and stop the bleeding.*

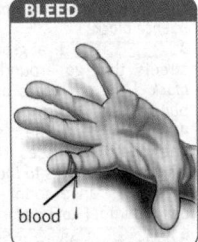
BLEED
blood

bleep /bliːp/ n [C] a high electronic sound: *the shrill bleep of the alarm clock* —**bleep** v [I]

bleeper /ˈbliːpə $ -ər/ n [C] *BrE* a small electronic machine you carry with you that makes a high sound when it receives a message for you **SYN** **pager**

blemish /ˈblemɪʃ/ n [C] a mark that spoils something: *a blemish on her cheek* **THESAURUS** **MARK** —**blemished** adj

blend¹ /blend/ v **1** [I,T] to combine two different features: *a story that blends fact and fiction* **2** [T] to mix two or more things together thoroughly: *Blend the butter and sugar together.*

PHRASAL VERBS
blend in if something blends in, it looks suitably similar to everything around it: [+with] *curtains that blend in with the wallpaper*

blend² n [C] a mixture of two or more things: [+of] *a unique blend of Brazilian and Colombian coffee* | *the right blend of sunshine and soil for growing grapes*

blender /ˈblendə $ -ər/ n [C] a small electric machine that you use to mix food

bless /bles/ v [T] (*past tense and past participle* **blessed** or **blest** /blest/) **1** **be blessed with sth** to be lucky and have a special ability or good quality: *George was blessed with good health.* **2** to ask God to protect someone or something, or to make something holy: *Their mission had been blessed by the Pope.*

PHRASES
bless him/her etc *spoken* used to show you really like someone or are pleased by them: *He's always willing to help. Bless him!*
bless you *spoken* words you say when someone SNEEZES

blessed /ˈblesɪd/ adj **1** [only before noun] *spoken* used to show that you are annoyed: *Now where have I put that blessed book?* **2** [only before noun] enjoyable or desirable: *a moment of blessed silence* **3** *formal* holy and loved by God: *the Blessed Virgin Mary*

blessing /ˈblesɪŋ/ n **1** [C] something good that improves your life or makes you happy: *The rain was a real blessing after all that heat.* **2** [U] someone's approval or encouragement: **with/without sb's blessing** *They were determined to marry, with or without their parents' blessing.* **3** [singular, U] protection and help from God, or the prayer in which you ask for this

PHRASES
a blessing in disguise something that seems to be bad but that you later realize is good: *The lack of tourism on the island could be a blessing in disguise.*
a mixed blessing something that is both good and bad: *Living close to the office was a mixed blessing.*
count your blessings to be glad because of the good things that you have: *We should count our blessings that we're all in reasonable health.*

blew /bluː/ v the past tense of BLOW

blight¹ /blaɪt/ n [singular, U] something which damages or spoils things: [+on] *the poverty that is a blight on our nation*

blight² v [T] to damage or spoil something: *an area blighted by unemployment*

blimey /ˈblaɪmi/ *BrE spoken informal* used to express surprise: *Blimey, look at that!*

blind¹ /blaɪnd/ adj
1 **UNABLE TO SEE** **a)** unable to see: *She's almost blind in her right eye.* | **totally/completely/almost/partially blind** | *He was slowly going blind* (=becoming unable to see). | *Beverley was born blind.* **b)** the blind people who cannot see: *special facilities for the blind*
2 **UNABLE TO NOTICE** **be blind to sth** to completely fail to notice or realize something → **blindly**: *He was blind to the faults of his own children.*
3 **DONE WITHOUT THINKING** **blind faith/loyalty/panic** strong feelings that make you do things without thinking – used to show disapproval: *a story about blind loyalty*
4 **CORNER/BEND** a blind corner or bend in a road is one that you cannot see round when you are driving —**blindness** n [U] → **COLOUR-BLIND**

PHRASES
turn a blind eye (to sth) to ignore something that you know should not be happening: *Teachers were turning a blind eye to smoking in the school.*

blind² v [T] **1** to make someone unable to see, either permanently or for a short time: *The deer was blinded by our headlights.* **2** to make someone unable to notice or realize the truth about something: **blind sb to sth** *Being in love blinded me to his faults.*

blind³ n [C] a piece of cloth or other material that you pull down to cover a window

blind ˈdate n [C] a romantic meeting arranged between a man and a woman who have not met each other before: *They met on a blind date.*

blindfold¹ /ˈblaɪndfəʊld $ -foʊld/ n [C] a piece of cloth that is put over someone's eyes so that they cannot see

blindfold² v [T] to cover someone's eyes with a piece of cloth so that they cannot see: *The hostages were blindfolded and led to the cellar.*

blinding /ˈblaɪndɪŋ/ adj **1** a blinding light is very bright: *Suddenly there was a blinding flash of light.* **THESAURUS** **BRIGHT 2** **blinding headache** a very painful headache: *I had a blinding headache and decided to lie down for a while.*

blindly /ˈblaɪndli/ adv **1** without thinking or understanding: *Don't blindly accept what they tell you.* **2** not seeing or not noticing what is around you: *She sat staring blindly out of the window.*

blind spot n [C] **1** something that you are unable or unwilling to understand: *He has a blind spot for computers.* **2** a part of the road that you cannot see when you are driving

bling /blɪŋ/ n [U] *informal* expensive objects, for example JEWELLERY, that are worn in a way that is very easy to notice

blink¹ /blɪŋk/ v **1** [I,T] to close and open your eyes quickly: *He blinked as he stepped out into the sunlight.* **2** [I] if a light blinks, it goes on and off

blink² n [C] the action of blinking

PHRASES
| **on the blink** *informal* not working properly: *The phone's on the blink.*

blinkered /ˈblɪŋkəd $ -ərd/ adj refusing to accept new or different ideas: *a blinkered attitude to life*

blip /blɪp/ n [C] **1** a flashing light on the screen of a piece of electronic equipment **2** *informal* a small temporary change from what usually happens: *This month's rise in prices could be just a blip.*

bliss /blɪs/ n [U] complete happiness: *I didn't have to get up till 11 – sheer bliss!*

blissful /ˈblɪsfəl/ adj very happy: *the first blissful weeks after we married* —**blissfully** adv: *She seemed blissfully unaware of the problems ahead.*

B-list /ˈbiː lɪst/ adj [only before noun] fairly famous or popular, but not the most famous or popular → **A-list**: *B-list celebrities*

blister /ˈblɪstə $ -ər/ n [C] a small area of skin that is swollen and full of liquid because it has been rubbed or burned —**blister** v [I,T]

blistering /ˈblɪstərɪŋ/ adj **1** extremely hot: *blistering heat* **2** *blistering attack/criticism etc* remarks expressing angry criticism: *a blistering attack on the government*

blithely /ˈblaɪðli/ adv without thinking about dangers or problems: *They blithely ignored the danger.* —**blithe** adj

blitz /blɪts/ n **1 the Blitz** the attack on British cities from the air during the Second World War **2** [C] when you use a lot of effort to achieve something in a short time: *The campaign starts next month with a TV advertising blitz.* —**blitz** v [T]

blizzard /ˈblɪzəd $ -ərd/ n [C] a storm with a lot of wind and snow THESAURUS STORM

bloated /ˈbləʊtɪd $ ˈbloʊ-/ adj full of liquid, gas, food etc, so that you look or feel much larger than normal: *I feel bloated after that meal.*

blob /blɒb $ blɑːb/ n [C] a small drop of a thick liquid: **[+of]** *a few blobs of paint*

bloc /blɒk $ blɑːk/ n [C] a group of countries with the same political aims, working together: *the former Soviet bloc*

block¹ /blɒk $ blɑːk/ n [C]
1 LARGE PIECE a large solid piece of wood, stone, ice etc: **[+of]** *a block of concrete* | *a model made of wooden blocks* → see picture at PIECE¹
2 BUILDING *BrE* a large building divided into a lot of homes, offices, or CLASSROOMS: **[+of]** *a block of flats* |

an office block | *an apartment block* | *the school science block*
3 PART OF A TOWN a group of buildings with four streets that go around it: *Let's walk around the block.* | *the other kids on the block* (=living in the buildings)
4 DISTANCE *AmE* the distance along a street from one road that crosses it to the next that crosses it: *It's just three blocks to the store from here.*
5 AMOUNT an amount that something has been divided into: **[+of]** *a block of text*
6 PREVENTING PROGRESS something that makes it difficult to move or progress: **[+to]** *This incident could be a block to the peace process.*
7 PREVENTING THINKING *have a block (about sth)* to be unable to think clearly or remember something for a short time: *I had a mental block about his name.*
→ BUILDING BLOCK, *be a chip off the old block* at CHIP¹, SUN BLOCK, TOWER BLOCK

block² v [T]
1 (*also* **block up**) to prevent people or things from moving through something: *A fallen tree was blocking the road.* | *block sb's way/path/exit etc A ten foot wall blocked my escape.* | *be blocked (up)* (=contain something that is preventing movement) *The drain's blocked up.*
2 to stop something from happening or developing: *Why did the council block the plan?*
3 to stop someone from seeing something by being in a particular position: *A tall man in front of me was blocking my view.*

PHRASAL VERBS
block sth ↔ **off** to close a road or path so that people cannot use it: *The freeway exit's been blocked off by police.*

block sth ↔ **out**
1 to stop light from reaching a place: *Thick smoke blocked out the light.*
2 to stop yourself thinking about something unpleasant: *She waited, trying to block out her anxiety.*

blockade /blɒˈkeɪd $ blɑː-/ n [C] when an army or navy surrounds a place to stop people or supplies from leaving or entering: *a blockade of the city* | *a naval blockade* —**blockade** v [T]

blockage /ˈblɒkɪdʒ $ ˈblɑː-/ n [C] something that is blocking a tube or pipe: *There seems to be a blockage in the pipe.*

blockbuster /ˈblɒkˌbʌstə $ ˈblɑːkˌbʌstər/ n [C] *informal* a film or book that is very exciting and successful: *the latest Hollywood blockbuster*

block 'capitals (*also* **block 'letters**) n [plural] letters in their large form, for example A, B, C, instead of a, b, c

blog /blɒg $ blɑːg/ n [C] a web page containing information or opinions from a particular person or about a particular subject, to which new information is added regularly —**blog** v [I] —**blogger** n [C]

bloke /bləʊk $ bloʊk/ n [C] *BrE informal* a man

blonde¹, **blond** /blɒnd $ blɑːnd/ adj
1 blonde hair is pale or yellow
2 someone who is blonde has pale or yellow hair

blonde² n [C] *informal* a woman who has pale or yellow hair: *a good-looking blonde*

blood /blʌd/ n
1 [U] the red liquid that flows around your body: *Blood was flowing from the wound.* → see picture at **BLEED**
2 [U] the family that you belong to: *a woman of **royal blood*** → **in cold blood** at **COLD¹**, **your own flesh and blood** at **FLESH¹**
PHRASES
| **bad blood** feelings of anger and hate between people: *There's a lot of bad blood between the father and the son in that family.*
| **be/run in sb's blood** to be a strong and natural part of someone's character: *A love of politics was in his blood.*
| **new blood** new people in an organization who bring new ideas and energy: *We need some new blood in the department.*

COLLOCATIONS

verbs
blood flows *Blood flows around the body.*
blood comes from/out of sth *There was blood coming from his nose.*
to lose blood (=to bleed) *She lost a lot of blood during the operation.*
to be covered in/with blood *His face was covered in blood.*
to give/donate blood (=to provide blood from your body for the medical treatment of other people) *She gives blood regularly.*

noun + blood
a drop of blood *There were drops of blood on his shirt.*
a pool of blood *Police found him lying in a pool of blood.*

blood + noun
a blood test (=a test done on your blood to check your health) *The doctors did some blood tests.*
a blood cell *Red blood cells carry oxygen.*

bloodbath /'blʌdbɑːθ $ -bæθ/ n [singular] when a lot of people are violently killed

bloodcurdling /'blʌdˌkɜːdlɪŋ $ -ɜːr-/ adj a blood-curdling sound is very frightening: *We heard a **blood-curdling scream**.*

'blood ˌdonor n [C] someone who gives their blood to be used in medical treatment

'blood group n [C] BrE one of the types of blood that human blood is divided into SYN **blood type** AmE

bloodhound /'blʌdhaʊnd/ n [C] a large dog which can find things using its sense of smell

bloodless /'blʌdləs/ adj without killing or violence: *a bloodless revolution*

'blood ˌpressure n [U] the force with which your blood moves around your body: *Older people often **have high blood pressure**.*

bloodshed /'blʌdʃed/ n [U] when people are killed in fighting or war: *talks aimed at **avoiding** further bloodshed*

bloodshot /'blʌdʃɒt $ -ʃɑːt/ adj bloodshot eyes are slightly red

'blood sport n [C] a sport that involves killing animals

bloodstain /'blʌdsteɪn/ n [C] a mark or spot of blood: *bloodstains on the carpet* —**bloodstained** adj: *his bloodstained clothes*

bloodstream /'blʌdstriːm/ n [singular] the blood flowing in your body: *The drug is injected straight into the bloodstream.*

bloodthirsty /'blʌdˌθɜːsti $ -ɜːr-/ adj enjoying killing and violence

'blood transˌfusion n [C,U] a medical treatment that involves putting more blood into someone's body

'blood type n [C] AmE one of the types of blood that human blood is divided into SYN **blood group** BrE

'blood ˌvessel n [C] one of the tubes in your body that blood flows through → **artery**, **vein**

bloody¹ /'blʌdi/ adj **1** covered in blood: *a bloody nose* **2** with a lot of killing and injuries: *a bloody battle*

bloody² adj, adv BrE spoken used to emphasize what you are saying in a slightly rude or angry way: *It's bloody cold out there.* | *Where's my bloody hat?* | *That was a bloody stupid thing to do.*

bloody-'minded adj deliberately making things difficult for other people —**bloody-mindedness** n [U]

bloom¹ /bluːm/ n [C] a flower: *beautiful yellow blooms*
PHRASES
| **in (full) bloom** with the flowers fully open: *The roses were in bloom.*

bloom² v [I] **1** if a plant blooms, its flowers open **2** to be happy, healthy, and successful: *Jo seemed to be blooming.*

blossom¹ /'blɒsəm $ 'blɑː-/ n [C,U] a flower or the flowers on a tree or bush: *huge white blossoms* | **blossom** (=with the flowers open) → see picture at **PLANT¹**

blossom² v [I] **1** if trees blossom, they produce flowers **2** (also **blossom out**) to become happier, more beautiful, or more successful: **[+into]** *She blossomed into a beautiful young woman.*

blot¹ /blɒt $ blɑːt/ v [T] (**blotted, blotting**) to dry wet spots on something using soft paper or a cloth
PHRASAL VERBS
blot sth ↔ **out 1** to cover or hide something completely: *Black clouds blotted out the sun.* **2** to stop yourself thinking about something unpleasant: *He tried to blot out the memory of that night.*

blot² n [C] a drop of liquid such as ink that has fallen onto a piece of paper

blotch /blɒtʃ $ blɑːtʃ/ n [C] a pink or red mark on your skin or a coloured mark on something —**blotchy** adj: *blotchy leaves*

'blotting ˌpaper n [U] soft paper used for drying ink on a page

blouse /blaʊz $ blaʊs/ n [C] a shirt for a woman or girl: *She was wearing a silk blouse.*

blow¹ /bləʊ $ bloʊ/ v (*past tense* **blew** /bluː/, *past participle* **blown** /bləʊn $ bloʊn/)
1 WIND a) [I] if wind or a current of air blows, it moves: *A cold wind was blowing hard.* | *A sudden draught of air blew in.* **b)** [I,T] to move in the wind, or to make something move somewhere in the wind: **[+in]** *Her hair was blowing in the breeze.* | **blow sth across/into etc sth** *The wind blew leaves across the path.* | **blow (sth) in/out/down etc** *My ticket blew away.* | *Trees had been blown down.* | **blow (sth) open/shut** *The door blew shut behind me.*
2 AIR/SMOKE [I,T] to push air out through your mouth: **blow (sth) into/onto/through etc sth** *Renee blew on her soup to cool it down.* | *He blew the smoke right into my face.*
3 WHISTLE/TRUMPET [I,T] to make a sound by pushing air into a whistle, horn, or musical instrument: *The referee's whistle blew.* | *A truck went by and blew its horn at her.*
4 EXPLOSION blow sth off/away/out etc to damage or destroy something violently with an explosion or shooting: *Part of his leg had been blown off.*
5 CHANCE blow your chances/blow it *informal* to lose a good opportunity by making a mistake: *By failing this exam I've blown my chances of getting into university.*
6 MONEY [T] *informal* to spend a lot of money in a careless way: *He blew all his savings on a trip to Hawaii.*
7 FUSE [I,T] if a FUSE blows, or something blows a FUSE, it suddenly stops working because too much electricity has passed through it: *My hairdryer's blown a fuse.*
PHRASES
blow your nose to clear your nose by forcing air through it into a cloth or piece of paper: *He blew his nose on a paper tissue.*
PHRASAL VERBS
blow sb **away** *spoken* to make someone feel very surprised and pleased: *Their kindness just blew me away.*
blow sth ↔ **out** to blow air on a flame and make it stop burning: *Blow out all the candles.*
blow over if an argument or storm blows over, it ends
blow up
1 to destroy something, or to be destroyed, with an explosion: *Their plane blew up in mid-air.* | **blow sth** ↔ **up** *The bridge was blown up by terrorists.* **THESAURUS** EXPLODE
2 blow sth ↔ **up** to fill something with air or gas: *Come and help me blow up the balloons.*

blow² n [C]
1 something very sad and disappointing that happens to you: *Her mother's death was a terrible blow.*
2 a hard hit with a hand, tool, or weapon: **[+to/on]** *The victim suffered several blows to the head.*
3 when you blow air out of your mouth or nose: *One blow and the candles were out.* → **BODY BLOW**

PHRASES
come to blows if two people come to blows, they start fighting: *The two men came to blows in an argument over money.*

blow-by-'blow adj **a blow-by-blow account/ description etc** a description of an event that gives all the details exactly as they happened

'blow-dry v [T] (**blow-dried**, **blow-drying**, **blow-dries**) to dry your hair using an electric HAIRDRYER —**blow-dry** n [singular]: *a cut and blow-dry*

blown /bləʊn $ bloʊn/ v the past participle of BLOW

blowout /'bləʊaʊt $ 'bloʊ-/ n [C] *informal* **1** a tyre that bursts suddenly **2** a big expensive meal or a large party

blubber¹ /'blʌbə $ -ər/ (*also* **blub** /blʌb/) v [I] *BrE informal* to cry noisily

blubber² n [U] the fat of sea animals, especially WHALES

bludgeon /'blʌdʒən/ v [T] to hit someone several times with something heavy: *He was bludgeoned to death.*

blue¹ /bluː/ adj
1 having the colour of the sky on a fine day: *the blue lake* | **dark/light/pale/bright blue** *a dark blue dress*
2 [not before noun] *informal* sad: *I've been feeling kind of blue lately.*
3 blue joke/movie a joke or film about sex → **black and blue** at BLACK¹, **NAVY BLUE**, **once in a blue moon** at ONCE¹, **ROYAL BLUE**

blue² n [C,U] **1** the colour of the sky on a fine day: *I like greens and blues best.* | *She was dressed in blue.*
2 blues (*also* **the blues** [plural]) a slow sad style of music that came from the southern US: *He sings the blues.*
PHRASES
have/get the blues *informal* to feel sad and alone
out of the blue *informal* if something happens out of the blue, it is unexpected: *The letter came completely out of the blue.* **THESAURUS** SUDDENLY

bluebell /'bluːbel/ n [C] a small plant with blue flowers that often grows in forests → see picture at FLOWER¹

blueberry /'bluːbəri $ -beri/ n [C] (*plural* **blueberries**) a small round dark blue fruit → see picture on page A4

blue-'blooded adj a blue-blooded person belongs to a royal or NOBLE family

'blue-chip adj **blue-chip companies/shares etc** companies or SHARES that are very unlikely to lose money

blue-'collar adj blue-collar workers do physical work, rather than working in offices → **white-collar**

blueprint /'bluːprɪnt/ n [C] a plan for achieving something, or showing how to build something: **[+for]** *a blueprint for health care reform* | *the blueprint for a new shopping mall*

blue 'ribbon n [C] the first prize in a competition, sometimes a small piece of blue material

bluff¹ /blʌf/ v [I,T] to pretend that you are going to do something or that you know about something, in order to get what you want: *I don't believe you – I think you're bluffing!*

bluff² *n* [C,U] an attempt to make someone believe that you are going to do something when you do not really intend to: *He threatened to resign, but I'm sure it's a bluff.*

PHRASES

call sb's bluff to tell someone to do what they are threatening to do because you do not believe they will really do it: *She was tempted to call his bluff, hardly able to believe he would carry out his threat.*

blunder¹ /'blʌndə $ -ər/ *n* [C] a careless or stupid mistake: *a political blunder*

blunder² *v* [I] **1** to move in an unsteady way as if you cannot see properly: [+into/past/through etc] *Jo came blundering down the stairs.* **2** to make a careless or stupid mistake

blunt¹ /blʌnt/ *adj* **1** not sharp or pointed: *a blunt knife* **2** saying exactly what you think, even if it upsets people: *Julian's blunt words hurt her.* —**bluntness** *n* [U]

blunt² *v* [T] to make someone's feelings less strong: *Too much alcohol blunted my reactions.*

bluntly /'blʌntli/ *adv* speaking in a direct honest way that sometimes upsets people: ***To put it bluntly***, *you're not going to pass the exam.*

blur¹ /blɜː $ blɜːr/ *n* [singular] something that you cannot see clearly or cannot remember clearly: *Below me, the island was already a blur. | The crash is just a blur in my mind.*

blur² *v* [I,T] (**blurred**, **blurring**) to become less clear, or to make something less clear: *His writing blurred beneath her tired eyes. | Electronic resources have **blurred the distinction between** learning and play.*

Blu-ray /'bluː reɪ/ *n* [U] *trademark* a way of storing very clear video images on a DISC

blurb /blɜːb $ blɜːrb/ *n* [singular] a short description giving information about a book or new product

blurred /blɜːd $ blɜːrd/ (*also* **blurry** /'blɜːri/) *adj* not clear: *blurry photos | a blurred memory*

blurt /blɜːt $ blɜːrt/ (*also* **blurt out**) *v* [T] to say something suddenly and without thinking, especially something that you should keep secret: *Pete blurted out the news at a party.*

blush /blʌʃ/ *v* [I] to become red in the face, especially because you are embarrassed: *The way he looked at her made her blush. |* [+with] *Toby blushed with pride.* —**blush** *n* [C]

blusher /'blʌʃə $ -ər/ (*also* **blush** *AmE*) *n* [C,U] cream or powder that you put on your face to make it look pink and attractive

bluster /'blʌstə $ -ər/ *v* [I] to speak in a loud angry way —**bluster** *n* [U]

blustery /'blʌstəri/ *adj* blustery weather is very windy: *a blustery winter day*

BO /ˌbiː 'əʊ $ -'oʊ/ *n* [U] (**body odour**) an unpleasant smell from someone's body caused by SWEAT

boa constrictor /'bəʊə kənˌstrɪktə $ 'boʊə kənˌstrɪktər/ *n* [C] a large snake that is not poisonous, but kills animals by crushing them

boar /bɔː $ bɔːr/ *n* [C] **1** a male pig **2** a wild pig

BOARDS

cheese board

ironing board

chessboard

skateboard

board¹ /bɔːd $ bɔːrd/ *n*

1 FOR WRITING/PUTTING INFORMATION [C] a piece of wood or plastic on a wall where you can write or put information: **on the board** *The teacher wrote a few words on the board. | Can I put this notice on the board? | Remember to check the board for dates and times.*

2 FOR CUTTING/PLAYING GAMES ETC [C] a flat piece of wood or plastic that you use for a particular purpose: *a **chopping board** (=for chopping food) | a **chessboard/dartboard etc** (=for playing these games)*

3 IMPORTANT GROUP (*also* **Board**) [C also + plural verb] *BrE* the group of people in a company or organization who make important decisions: [+of] *The Board of Directors met yesterday. | a board meeting | one of the **board members***

4 ORGANIZATION **Board** used in the names of some organizations: *the Electricity Board | the Board of Trade*

5 ON FLOOR/FENCE [C] a long thin flat piece of wood used for making floors, fences etc

6 MEALS [U] the meals that are provided for you when you pay to stay somewhere: **full board/half board** (=all meals or only breakfast and dinner) *How much is a single room with full board? |* **board and lodging** *BrE,* **room and board** *AmE* (=meals and a room) *The cost covers the student's board and lodging.* → BULLETIN BOARD, DIVING BOARD, DRAINING BOARD, DRAWING BOARD, IRONING BOARD

BLUNT

sharp

blunt

board

PHRASES

across the board affecting everyone or everything: *Prices have been reduced right across the board.*

on board on a ship, plane, or spacecraft: *There were over 1,000 passengers on board.*

board² v **1 a)** [I,T] to get on a plane, ship, or train: *Passengers in rows 15 to 25 may now board.* | **boarding card/pass** (=a card you must show in order to get on a plane) **b) be boarding** if a plane or ship is boarding, passengers are getting on it: *Flight 503 for Lisbon is now boarding.* **2** [I] to pay to stay in a room in someone's house: *Most students board with local families.* **3** [I] *especially BrE* to live at school rather than going home at night

PHRASAL VERBS

board sth ↔ **up** to cover windows or doors with wooden boards: *The house next door has been boarded up for months.*

boarder /ˈbɔːdə $ ˈbɔːrdər/ n [C] **1** *especially BrE* a child who lives at school **2** *AmE* someone who pays to live in someone else's house and have meals there SYN **lodger** *BrE*

board game n [C] an indoor game that you play by moving small pieces around on a special board

boarding house n [C] a private house where you pay to sleep and eat

boarding school n [C] a school where students live rather than going home at night

boardroom /ˈbɔːdruːm, -rʊm $ ˈbɔːrd-/ n [C] a room where the important people in a company have meetings

boardwalk /ˈbɔːdwɔːk $ ˈbɔːrdwɒːk/ n [C] *AmE* a raised path made of wood, usually built next to the sea

boast¹ /bəʊst $ boʊst/ v **1** [I] to talk too much about your own abilities and achievements in a way that annoys other people: **[+about]** *He's always boasting about how much money he has.* **2** [T] if a place boasts something good, the place has it: *The health club boasts an Olympic-sized swimming pool.*

boast² n [C] something that you like telling people because you are proud of it: *Her proud boast was that she had never had a day's illness.*

boastful /ˈbəʊstfəl $ ˈboʊst-/ adj talking too much about your own abilities and achievements —**boastfully** adv

boat /bəʊt $ boʊt/ n [C] a vehicle that travels across water → **ship**: **by boat** *You can only get to the island by boat.* → **HOUSEBOAT**, **miss the boat/bus** at **MISS¹**, **MOTORBOAT**, **rock the boat** at **ROCK²**

PHRASES

be in the same boat (as sb) to be in the same unpleasant situation as someone else: *We're all in the same boat, so stop complaining.*

COLLOCATIONS

verbs

to sail a boat *I've never sailed a boat before.*

to row a boat (=using oars) *They rowed a little boat across the lake.*

to take a boat (=to go in a boat as a passenger) *He took a boat to France.*

to tie up/moor a boat (=to tie it to something so that it stays in one place) *We tied up the boat in the harbour.*

a boat sinks *His boat hit a rock and sank.*

a boat capsizes (=turns over in the water) *The boat capsized in a storm.*

types of boat

a fishing boat *The harbour was full of fishing boats.*

a sailing boat *BrE*, **a sailboat** *AmE* *They have a small sailing boat.*

a rowing boat *BrE*, **a rowboat** *AmE* *A rowing boat passed us on the river.*

a pleasure boat (=a small boat that people use on a lake or river)

boat + noun

a boat trip *You can take a boat trip to the islands.*

boating /ˈbəʊtɪŋ $ ˈboʊt-/ n [U] the activity of travelling in a small boat for pleasure: *a boating holiday in Norfolk*

bob¹ /bɒb $ bɑːb/ v [I] (**bobbed, bobbing**) to move up and down on water: *a small boat bobbing up and down*

bob² n [C] a way of cutting your hair so that it hangs straight down to the level of your chin → see picture at **HAIR**

bobbin /ˈbɒbɪn $ ˈbɑː-/ n [C] a small round object that you wind thread onto, especially on a SEWING MACHINE

bobby /ˈbɒbi $ ˈbɑːbi/ n [C] (*plural* **bobbies**) *BrE informal old-fashioned* a policeman

bobby pin n [C] *AmE* a thin piece of metal that women use to hold their hair in place SYN **hairgrip** *BrE*

bode /bəʊd $ boʊd/ v **bode well/ill** *literary* to be a good or bad sign for the future: *The recent survey bodes ill for the Democrats.*

bodice /ˈbɒdɪs $ ˈbɑː-/ n [C] the part of a woman's dress above her waist

bodily¹ /ˈbɒdəli $ ˈbɑː-/ adj relating to the human body: *He did not suffer any bodily harm.*

bodily² adv if you move someone bodily, you lift them or carry them: *I had to lift him bodily onto the bed.*

body /ˈbɒdi $ ˈbɑːdi/ n (*plural* **bodies**)

1 OF PERSON/ANIMAL [C] the physical structure of a person or animal: *He had mud and dirt all over his body.* | *the **human body*** | *exercise that's good for the body and mind* → see picture on page A2

2 NOT LEGS OR HEAD [C] the central part of a person or animal's body, not including the arms, legs, or head: *Keep your arms close to your body.*

3 DEAD PERSON [C] the dead body of a person: **[+of]** *The body of a girl has been found in the river.*

4 OFFICIAL GROUP [C] an official group of people who work together: *the official body responsible for safety at work*

5 OF INFORMATION a large amount of information, knowledge etc: *There's a **body of evidence** in favour of this idea.*

6 the main part of something, especially a piece of writing: *The first paragraph should prepare the way for the body of your essay.*

7 OF A PLANE/CAR [C] the main structure of a vehicle, not the engine, wheels etc: *The body of the plane was not damaged.*

8 OF HAIR [U] hair that has body is thick and healthy

'body blow *n* [C] a serious disappointment or shock

'body ,building *n* [U] doing physical exercises to make your muscles bigger and stronger —**body builder** *n* [C]

bodyguard /'bɒdigɑːd $ 'bɑːdigɑːrd/ *n* [C] someone whose job is to protect an important person

THESAURUS ▶ GUARD

'body ,language *n* [U] movements you make without thinking, that show what you are feeling or thinking: *I could tell from his body language that he was nervous.*

bodywork /'bɒdiwɜːk $ 'bɑːdiwɜːrk/ *n* [U] the metal structure of a vehicle, not the engine, wheels etc

bog¹ /bɒg $ bɑːg, bɔːg/ *n* [C,U] an area of soft muddy ground

bog² *v* **get/be bogged down (in sth)** to be unable to make any progress because you have become so involved with a problem: *Let's not get bogged down in minor details.*

bogeyman /'bəʊgimæn $ 'boʊ-/ *n* [C] (*plural* **bogeymen** /-men/) an evil SPIRIT, especially in children's imagination or stories

boggle /'bɒgəl $ 'bɑː-/ *v* **the/your mind boggles** *spoken* used to say that something is difficult to imagine or believe: *The amount of money involved makes your mind boggle.*

boggy /'bɒgi $ 'bɑː-, 'bɔːgi/ *adj* boggy ground is wet and muddy

,bog-'standard *adj* BrE *informal disapproving* not special in any way

bogus /'bəʊgəs $ 'boʊ-/ *adj* not true or real, although someone is pretending that it is: *bogus insurance claims*

bohemian /bəʊ'hiːmiən, bə- $ boʊ-, bə-/ *adj* living in a very relaxed way and not accepting society's rules of normal behaviour —**bohemian** *n* [C]

boil¹ /bɔɪl/ *v* [I,T]

1 if a liquid boils, or if you boil it, it becomes hot enough to change into steam: *Drop the noodles into boiling salted water.* | **[+at]** *Water boils at 100°C.*

THESAURUS ▶ COOK

2 a) to cook something in boiling water: *Boil the rice for ten minutes.* | *a boiled egg* **b)** to heat a container so the liquid in it boils: *Will you boil the kettle and make some tea?* | *The kettle's boiling.* → see picture at **COOK¹**

PHRASAL VERBS

boil down to sth if a situation or statement boils down to something, that is the most important fact or the basic meaning: *It all boils down to how much money you have.*

boil over

1 to boil and flow over the sides of a pan

2 if a situation or emotion boils over, people begin to get angry

boil² *n* **1 the boil** *BrE*, **a boil** *AmE* a state of boiling: **Bring** the soup **to the boil.** | *Wait until the water* **comes to the boil.** **2** [C] a painful infected swelling under your skin

boiler /'bɔɪlə $ -ər/ *n* [C] a container for heating water, that provides hot water in a house or steam for an engine

'boiler suit *n* [C] *BrE* a piece of loose clothing like trousers and a shirt joined together, that you can wear over your clothes to protect them when you are working

boiling /'bɔɪlɪŋ/ *adj* extremely hot: *It's* **boiling hot** *in here.* THESAURUS ▶ HOT

'boiling point *n* [singular] the temperature at which a liquid boils

boisterous /'bɔɪstərəs/ *adj* noisy and full of energy: *boisterous children*

bold¹ /bəʊld $ boʊld/ *adj* **1** confident and willing to take risks: *a bold and imaginative plan* | *She was bold enough to ask for more money.* THESAURUS ▶ BRAVE **2** very clear and strong or bright: *a bold, bright red* | *The graphics are bold and colourful.* —**boldly** *adv* —**boldness** *n* [U]

bold² *n* [U] a style of printed letters that are darker and thicker than ordinary letters: *The chapter headings are in bold.*

bollard /'bɒləd, -ɑːd $ 'bɑːlərd/ *n* [C] *BrE* a short thick post in the street, used to control traffic

bolster /'bəʊlstə $ 'boʊlstər/ (*also* **bolster up**) *v* [T] to improve something by giving support and encouragement: *She tried to bolster his confidence.*

bolt¹ /bəʊlt $ boʊlt/ *n* [C] **1** a metal bar that slides across to fasten a door or window **2** a screw with no point, used with a NUT to fasten things together

PHRASES

a bolt from the blue something that is completely unexpected: *Her promotion was a bolt from the blue.*

bolt² *v* **1** [I] to run away suddenly: *A gun fired, and the horse bolted.* **2** [T] to fasten two things together, using a bolt: *The chairs are bolted to the floor.* **3** [T] to lock a door or window with a bolt **4** (*also* **bolt down**) [T] to eat something very quickly: *He bolted down his lunch.*

bolt³ *adv* **sit/stand bolt upright** to sit or stand with your back very straight: *He suddenly sat bolt upright in bed.*

bomb¹ /bɒm $ bɑːm/ *n* [C] a weapon made of material that will explode: *The bomb went off in a crowded street.* → **TIME BOMB**

PHRASES

cost a bomb *informal* to cost a lot of money: *The party must have cost a bomb.*

COLLOCATIONS

verbs

a bomb goes off/explodes *A bomb exploded at the station.*

to set off a bomb (*also* **to detonate a bomb** *formal*) (=to make a bomb explode) *The police safely detonated the bomb.*
to plant a bomb (=to put a bomb somewhere) *Terrorists planted a bomb in a crowded shopping centre.*
to drop a bomb (=from a plane) *Hundreds of bombs were dropped on the city.*
a bomb falls *Bombs fell all around them.*

types of bomb
a nuclear/atomic bomb *They had the technology to make a nuclear bomb.*
a car bomb (=put inside a car) *The judge was killed by a car bomb.*

bomb + noun
a bomb attack *No one claimed responsibility for the bomb attack.*
a bomb threat (=a message saying there is a bomb) *The building was evacuated after a bomb threat.*
a bomb scare (=when people think there might be a bomb) *Flights were delayed because of a bomb scare.*

bomb² *v* [T] **1** to attack a place with bombs: *Terrorists bombed the railway station.* **2** [I] *informal* to be unsuccessful: *Her latest movie bombed.* **3** [I always + adv/prep] *BrE informal* to move very quickly

bombard /bɒmˈbɑːd $ bɑːmˈbɑːrd/ *v* [T] **1** to attack a place for a long time with guns and bombs: *They bombarded the enemy camp.* **2** to ask a lot of questions or give a lot of information or criticism, so that it is difficult for someone to deal with: *Viewers bombarded the TV station with complaints.* —**bombardment** *n* [C,U]

ˈbomb disˌposal *n* [U] the job of making bombs safe when they have not yet exploded

bomber /ˈbɒmə $ ˈbɑːmər/ *n* [C] **1** a plane that drops bombs **2** someone who puts a bomb somewhere

bombshell /ˈbɒmʃel $ ˈbɑːm-/ *n* [C] a shocking piece of news: *Then she **dropped** the **bombshell**: she was pregnant.*

bona fide /ˌbəʊnə ˈfaɪdi $ ˈbəʊnə faɪd/ *adj* real and not intending to deceive anyone: *The pool is for bona fide members only.*

bonanza /bəˈnænzə, bəʊ- $ bə-, bəʊ-/ *n* [C] a situation in which people make a lot of money: *The discovery could represent an amazing cash bonanza.*

bond¹ Ac /bɒnd $ bɑːnd/ *n* [C] **1** a shared feeling or interest that unites people: **[+between]** *the bond between a mother and child* | **[+with]** *Britain has a special bond with the US.* **2** an official document promising that a government or company will pay back money that it has borrowed, often with INTEREST: *government bonds*

bond² Ac *v* [I] **1** if two things bond, they become firmly fixed or glued together **2** to develop a special relationship with someone: *You all have to bond as a team.* —**bonding** *n* [U]

bondage /ˈbɒndɪdʒ $ ˈbɑːn-/ *n* [U] a situation in which people have no freedom → **slavery**

bone /bəʊn $ boʊn/ *n* [C,U] one of the hard parts that form the frame of the body: *Sam **broke** a **bone** in his foot.* | **hip/thigh/cheek etc bone** *She was so thin her hip bones stuck out.* | *fragments of bone*
PHRASES
a bone of contention something that causes arguments
make no bones about (doing) sth to say or do something in an open way, because you are not ashamed about it: *She makes no bones about her ambitions.*
the bare bones (of sth) the most basic and important details of something: *He began his talk by describing the bare bones of the situation.*

ˌbone ˈdry *adj* completely dry

ˈbone ˌmarrow *n* [U] the substance in the middle of bones SYN **marrow**

bonfire /ˈbɒnfaɪə $ ˈbɑːnfaɪr/ *n* [C] a large outdoor fire

ˈBonfire ˌNight *n* [U] November 5th, when people in Britain light FIREWORKS and have large outdoor fires

bonkers /ˈbɒŋkəz $ ˈbɑːŋkərz/ *adj informal* crazy
THESAURUS ▸ CRAZY

bonnet /ˈbɒnɪt $ ˈbɑː-/ *n* [C] **1** *BrE* the front part of a car that covers the engine SYN **hood** *AmE* → see picture at CAR **2** a hat that ties under the chin, worn by babies or by women in the past

bonny /ˈbɒni $ ˈbɑːni/ *adj BrE* pretty and healthy – used mainly in northern Britain: *a bonny baby*

bonus /ˈbəʊnəs $ ˈboʊ-/ *n* [C] **1** money added to someone's usual pay, especially as a reward for good work: *a Christmas bonus* **2** something good that you do not expect in a situation: *We work well together – the fact that we're friends is a bonus.*

bony /ˈbəʊni $ ˈboʊ-/ *adj* **1** very thin: *bony fingers* **2** containing a lot of bones: *bony fish*

boo¹ /buː/ *v* [I,T] to shout 'boo' to show that you do not like a person, performance etc —**boo** *n* [C]

boo² *spoken* said loudly and suddenly to someone in order to frighten them, as a joke

boob /buːb/ *n* [C] *informal* **1** [usually plural] a woman's breast **2** *BrE* a silly mistake

ˈboo-boo *n* [C] *informal* a silly mistake: *I **made** a bit of a **boo-boo** asking her about David!*

ˈbooby prize /ˈbuːbi praɪz/ *n* [C] a prize given as a joke to the person who is last in a competition

ˈbooby trap *n* [C] a hidden bomb that will explode when anyone or anything touches something connected to it —**booby-trapped** *adj*

book¹ /bʊk/ *n* [C]
1 a set of printed pages held together in a cover so that you can read them: **[+by]** *I'm reading a book by Zadie Smith.* | **[+about/on]** *a book on Ethiopia*
2 sheets of paper that you can write on held together in a cover: *a red **address book** | a **sketch book***
3 a set of things such as stamps or tickets held together inside a paper cover: **[+of]** *a book of raffle tickets* | *a **cheque book***
4 books [plural] written records of a company's financial accounts: *a company that is having problems **balancing the books*** → PHONE BOOK, PHRASE BOOK

PHRASES

by the book exactly according to the rules: *They **do** everything **strictly by the book**.*

a closed book a subject that you do not understand anything about: *Philosophy is a closed book to me.*

be in sb's good/bad books *informal* used to say that someone is pleased or annoyed with you: *She'll be in the manager's bad books if she arrives late again.*

COLLOCATIONS

verbs

to read a book *Have you read any of her books?*
to write a book *The book was written by Graham Greene.*
to open/close a book *She opened the book and began to read.*
to publish a book *The book is published by Penguin.*
a book comes out (=it is published) *The book came out about a year ago.*

noun + book

the cover of a book (*also* **the book cover**) *His name is on the cover of the book.*
the title/name of a book *I've forgotten the title of the book.*
a chapter of a book *For homework, read the next chapter of the book.*

THESAURUS

novel a book about imaginary people and events: *a historical novel* | *Jane Eyre is the main character in the novel.*
fiction books about imaginary people and events: *She reads a lot of romantic fiction.*
non-fiction books about things that really exist or really happen: *I like non-fiction, especially travel books.*
literature novels, plays, and poems that are important works of art: *He's studying American literature at university.*
science fiction books about imaginary events in the future, or space travel
reference book a book which you look at to find information such as a DICTIONARY or an ENCYCLOPEDIA
textbook a book about a particular subject that you use in a classroom
coursebook *BrE* a book that you have to study as part of your course
guidebook a book telling visitors about a city or country
hardback *BrE* (*also* **hardcover** *especially AmE*) a book that has a hard stiff cover
paperback a book that has a paper cover
biography a book about a real person's life, written by another person
autobiography a book that someone has written about their own life

book² *v*

1 RESTAURANT/TICKET/PLANE ETC [I,T] to arrange to have or do something at a particular time in the future: **book a ticket/flight/seat/room etc** *Have you booked a holiday this year?* | **book ahead/in advance** *The restaurant is very popular so it's best to book ahead.* | *The flight is **fully booked** (=there are no seats left).* | **book sb sth** *I've booked you a room at the Plaza.* | **book sb into/onto sth** *I was booked onto the early flight.*
2 MUSICIAN/PERFORMER [T] to arrange for someone to perform at a particular place and time: *We've booked a jazz band for the wedding.*
3 POLICE [T] to ARREST someone
4 REFEREE [T] *BrE* if a REFEREE in a sports game books a player, they write their name in an official book because they have broken the rules

PHRASAL VERBS

book in (*also* **book into** sth) *BrE* to arrive at a hotel and say who you are SYN **check in**

bookcase /'bʊk-keɪs/ *n* [C] a piece of furniture with shelves to hold books → see picture at **CLASSROOM**

bookie /'bʊki/ *n* [C] *informal* a BOOKMAKER

booking /'bʊkɪŋ/ *n* [C] an arrangement to use a hotel room, travel by train etc, at a particular time in the future: *Can I **make a booking** for next Saturday?*

'booking ˌoffice *n* [C] *BrE* a place where you buy train or bus tickets

bookkeeping /'bʊkˌkiːpɪŋ/ *n* [U] the job or activity of recording the financial accounts of an organization —**bookkeeper** *n* [C]

booklet /'bʊklɪt/ *n* [C] a small book that gives information SYN **leaflet**: *a booklet on immunization*

bookmaker /'bʊkˌmeɪkə $ -ər/ *n* [C] *formal* someone whose job is to collect money that people BET (=risk) on the result of games, races etc and to pay them if they win

bookmark /'bʊkmɑːk $ -mɑːrk/ *n* [C] **1** a piece of paper that you put in a book so that you can find the page you want **2** a way of saving the address of a page on the Internet so that you can find it easily —**bookmark** *v* [T]

bookshelf /'bʊkʃelf/ *n* [C] (*plural* **bookshelves** /-ʃelvz/) a shelf that you keep books on → see picture at **CLASSROOM**

bookshop /'bʊkʃɒp $ -ʃɑːp/ *especially BrE*, **bookstore** /'bʊkstɔː $ -stɔːr/ *AmE n* [C] a shop that sells books

bookstall /'bʊkstɔːl $ -stɒːl/ *n* [C] *BrE* a small shop with an open front that sells books and magazines, especially at a railway station

bookworm /'bʊkwɜːm $ -wɜːrm/ *n* [C] *disapproving* someone who likes reading very much

boom¹ /buːm/ *n* **1** [singular] a sudden increase in business activity or in the popularity of something OPP **slump**: **[+in]** *a boom in sales* | *the postwar* **property boom** | *The* **economic boom** *is over.* **2** [C] a deep loud sound, like the sound of an explosion

boom² *v* **1** [I] if business or the ECONOMY is booming, it is very successful and growing quickly **2** [I,T] to make a loud deep sound —**booming** *adj*: *a booming economy*

boomerang /'buːməræŋ/ n [C] a curved stick that comes back to you when you throw it

boon /buːn/ n [C] something that is useful and makes your life easier or better: *My new car is a boon.*

boorish /'buərɪʃ $ 'bʊr-/ adj literary rude

boost /buːst/ v [T] to increase or improve something: *The publicity **boosts** your **confidence**. | Winning really **boosts** your **confidence**.* —**boost** n [singular]: *The news gave a boost to the economy.*

booster /'buːstə $ -ər/ n [C] **1** something that increases or improves something, especially a person's confidence: *His speech was a real **morale booster**.* **2** a small quantity of a drug that increases the effect of one that was given before **3** a ROCKET that provides extra power for a SPACECRAFT

boot¹ /buːt/ n [C]
1 a type of shoe that covers your whole foot and the lower part of your leg: *She wore high-heeled boots.* | **walking/hiking/football boots** → see picture at SHOE¹
2 *BrE* an enclosed space at the back of a car, used for carrying bags etc [SYN] **trunk** *AmE* → CAR BOOT SALE → see picture at CAR

PHRASES

> **get/be given the boot** *informal* to be forced to leave your job: *She got the boot after being caught stealing.*

boot² v **1** (*also* **boot up**) [I,T] to start the program that makes a computer ready to be used: *My PC won't boot.* **2** [T] *informal* to kick someone or something hard

booth /buːð $ buːθ/ n [C] a small enclosed area, often used for doing something privately: *a **voting booth** | a telephone booth*

bootleg¹ /'buːtleg/ adj [only before noun] bootleg products are made and sold illegally

bootleg² n [C] a musical recording that has been made illegally

booty /'buːti/ n [U] valuable things taken by a group of people, especially an army that has won a battle

booze¹ /buːz/ n [U] informal alcoholic drink

booze² v [I] informal to drink a lot of alcohol

border¹ /'bɔːdə $ 'bɔːrdər/ n [C]
1 the official line that separates two countries or states: **[+between]** *the border between England and Wales* | **[+with]** *an area of Brazil **on the border** with Bolivia* | **across/over the border** *He escaped over the border.* | *This is where we **cross the border** into Canada.*
2 a band around the edge of something: *paper with a black border*

border² v [T] **1** to share a border with another country: *Arab states that border Israel* **2** to form a line along the edge of something: *trees bordering the river*

PHRASAL VERBS

border on sth to be very close to being something extreme or bad: *a relaxed attitude bordering on negligence*

borderline¹ /'bɔːdəlaɪn $ 'bɔːrdər-/ adj very nearly not good enough or close to not reaching a particular standard: *In **borderline cases** a second examiner will review your work.*

borderline² n [singular] the point at which one quality, condition etc ends and another begins: *the borderline between sleep and being awake*

bore¹ /bɔː $ bɔːr/ v **1** [T] to make someone feel bored: *Am I boring you?* | **bore sb with sth** *I won't bore you with the details.* **2** [I,T] to make a deep round hole in a hard surface: *They bored a tunnel into the rock.*

bore² n **1** [singular] something that is not interesting or annoys you: *School is such a bore.* **2** [C] someone who talks too much about uninteresting things

bore³ v the past tense of BEAR

bored /bɔːd $ bɔːrd/ adj tired and impatient because something is uninteresting or you have nothing to do: *I'm bored – let's go!* | *After an hour people started to **get bored**.* | **[+with]** *She's bored with doing the same thing every day.* | *I'm so bored with my job.* | **bored stiff/bored to tears** (=extremely bored)

boredom /'bɔːdəm $ 'bɔːr-/ n [U] the feeling you have when you are bored: *They sang songs to **relieve the boredom**.*

boring /'bɔːrɪŋ/ adj not interesting in any way: *His job sounds so boring.* | *I got stuck talking to a really boring man.*

THESAURUS

boring not interesting in any way: *a boring film | Her husband is so boring!*

not very interesting rather boring. This phrase is often used in everyday English, instead of saying directly that something is boring: *The programme wasn't very interesting and I decided to go to bed.*

dull rather boring, because nothing interesting or exciting happens. **Dull** sounds less strong than **boring** and is more common in written descriptions: *He came home after another dull day at the office. | History seemed rather a dull subject when I was at school.*

tedious very boring – used when something that you do is slow or difficult and takes a long time: *a tedious task | The process of getting a visa was tedious and slow.*

monotonous boring – used when something continues in the same way and never changes: *Factory work can be very monotonous. | He had a slow monotonous voice.*

---

born¹ /bɔːn $ bɔːrn/ v
1 be born when a person or animal is born, they come out of their mother's body or out of an egg: *Where were you born?* | *lambs that have only just been born* | **[+in]** *His wife was born in India.* | *Shakespeare was born in 1564.* | **[+on]** *Her baby was born on May 5th.* | **be born into sth** (=be in a particular situation when you are born) *children born into poor families*
2 be born when something such as an idea is born, it starts to exist
3 be born to do sth to have a natural ability to do a particular job or activity: *She was born to perform.*

born² adj **born leader/teacher etc** someone who has a natural ability to lead, teach etc

born-again 'Christian n [C] someone who has started to have very strong religious beliefs

borne /bɔːn $ bɔːrn/ v the past participle of BEAR → **AIRBORNE**

borough /ˈbʌrə $ -roʊ/ n [C] a town or part of a large city that is responsible for managing its own schools, hospitals, roads etc

borrow /ˈbɒrəʊ $ ˈbɑːroʊ, ˈbɔː-/ v
1 [I,T] to use something that belongs to someone else and give it back to them later → **lend, loan**: Can I borrow the car tonight, dad? | **borrow sth from sb** She borrowed money from her friends. | **[+from]** The company had to borrow from the bank.
2 [I,T] to take or copy ideas or words: **borrow sth from sth/sb** English has borrowed many words from French. | **[+from]** His act **borrows heavily** (=a lot) from other comedians. —**borrowing** n [C,U] —**borrower** n [C]

bosom /ˈbʊzəm/ n **1** [singular] the front part of a woman's chest **2** [C usually plural] one of a woman's breasts
PHRASES
| **bosom friend/buddy** a very close friend: Tim was his bosom buddy.

boss¹ /bɒs $ bɔːs/ n [C]
1 the person who employs you or who is in charge of you at work: She asked her boss for the day off. | We've got a new boss at work. | I like being **my own boss** (=working for myself, not an employer).
2 the person who controls a relationship or situation: You have to show a dog that you're the boss.

THESAURUS

boss the person who employs you, or the person who is in charge of you at work. **Boss** sounds rather informal. In more formal situations you use **manager**: I didn't want to get into trouble with my boss.
manager the person in charge of a business such as a shop, bank, or hotel, or of part of a business: I'd like to speak to the hotel manager. | the sales manager
head the person who is in charge of an organization, or a department in an organization: He's the head of the CIA. | the head of the French department at school
president especially AmE the person who is in charge of a large company, or a department in a company: the president of Warner Bros
managing director BrE the person who is in charge of the way a company or organization is managed: He's the managing director of PC World.
line manager the person above you in your company, who is in charge of your work: If you have any problems, talk to your line manager.

boss² (also **boss around**) v [T] to tell people to do things, especially when you have no authority to do it: Stop bossing me around!

bossy /ˈbɒsi $ ˈbɔːsi/ adj always telling other people what to do, in a way that is annoying: a bossy little

girl —**bossily** adv —**bossiness** n [U]

botany /ˈbɒtəni $ ˈbɑː-/ n [U] the scientific study of plants —**botanist** n [C] —**botanical** /bəˈtænɪkəl/ adj

botch /bɒtʃ $ bɑːtʃ/ (also **botch up**) v [T] informal to do something badly and carelessly: The surgeon really botched the operation.

both /bəʊθ $ boʊθ/ determiner, pron
1 used to talk about two people or things together → **either, neither**: Anne and John are both scientists. | They can both speak Spanish. | Hold it in both hands. | She loved both her parents. | **[+of]** Both of his sisters are blonde. | We could go bowling, or dancing, or both.
2 both ... and ... used to emphasize that something is true not only of one thing or person but also of another: a game enjoyed by both adults and children

Usage
Do not say 'the both'. For example, do not say 'The both men were killed'. Say Both men were killed. or Both the men were killed. or Both of the men were killed.
Do not say 'his/her both'. For example, do not say 'his both sisters'. Say both of his sisters or both his sisters.

bother¹ /ˈbɒðə $ ˈbɑːðər/ v
1 [I,T] to make the effort to do something: **bother to do sth** He didn't bother to lock the door. | **bother doing sth** Did anyone bother filling in the form? | **[+with/about]** I'm not going to bother with changing my clothes. | 'Shall I get you a ticket?' 'No, **don't bother.**'
2 [I,T] to make someone feel slightly worried or upset: Being in a crowd really bothers me. | Does **it bother** you **that** he forgets your name?
3 [T] to annoy someone, especially by interrupting what they are doing: Stop bothering me – I'm trying to work.
PHRASES
| **can't be bothered (to do sth)** BrE used to say that you do not have enough interest or energy to do something: I can't be bothered to cook tonight.

bother² n [U] especially BrE trouble or difficulty caused by small problems: **[+with]** He's had some bother with his back. | 'Thanks.' 'That's okay – **it's no bother** (=I am happy to help).'

bother³ BrE spoken used when you are annoyed about something

bothered /ˈbɒðəd $ ˈbɑːðərd/ adj [not before noun] spoken **1** worried or upset: He doesn't seem at all **bothered about** what she said. **THESAURUS** WORRIED **2 not bothered** especially BrE used to say that something is not important to you: 'What shall we have to eat?' 'I'm not bothered.'

Botox /ˈbəʊtɒks $ ˈboʊtɑːks/ n [U] trademark a substance that is put into areas of your face so that they do not move and get lines

bottle¹ /ˈbɒtl $ ˈbɑːtl/ n [C]
1 a) a glass or plastic container with a narrow top, used for keeping liquids in: **[+of]** a bottle of beer | a **wine/beer/water etc bottle b)** the amount that a

bottle contains: **[+of]** *She drank a whole bottle of milk.*

2 a container for a baby to drink from with a rubber part on the top: *Will you give Joe his bottle?*
→ **HOT-WATER BOTTLE**

bottle² v [T] to put a liquid into a bottle: *This wine is bottled in Burgundy.* —**bottled** *adj: bottled water*

PHRASAL VERBS

bottle sth ↔ **up** to not allow yourself to show strong feelings: *It's not good to bottle up anger.*

'bottle bank n [C] a container in the street that you put empty bottles in, so that the glass can be used again

bottleneck /'bɒtlnek $ 'bɑː-/ n [C] **1** a place where traffic cannot pass easily, so that there are delays **2** a part of a process that causes delays

bottom¹ /'bɒtəm $ 'bɑː-/ n
1 LOWEST PART the lowest part or side of something OPP **top**: **[+of]** *Hold the bottom of the ladder.* | **at the bottom (of sth)** *a picture with his name at the bottom* | *She stood at the bottom of the stairs.* | **on the bottom (of sth)** *What's that on the bottom of your shoe?* | **in the bottom (of sth)** *I found my keys in the bottom of my bag.*
2 LOWEST RANK the lowest position in an organization, company, or group OPP **top**: **at the bottom (of sth)** *United are at the bottom of the league.* | *He started at the bottom and worked his way up to become managing director.*
3 OF THE SEA ETC the ground under an ocean, river, pool etc: *I can't touch the bottom of the pool.* | **at the bottom (of sth)** *creatures that live at the bottom of the sea*
4 BODY PART [C] the part of your body that you sit on
5 CLOTHES [C usually plural] the part of a set of clothes that you wear on the lower part of your body: **pyjama/bikini bottoms** → **ROCK BOTTOM, from top to bottom** at **TOP¹**

PHRASES

be at the bottom of sth to be the basic cause of a problem or situation: *Jealousy is probably at the bottom of her behaviour.*

get to the bottom of sth to find out the cause of a problem or situation: *The police are trying to get to the bottom of the mystery.*

THESAURUS

the bottom the lowest part of something: *the bottom of the page | the bottom of the ocean | The village is at the bottom of a big hill.*

the underside (*also* **the underneath** *BrE*) the outside surface which is under something: *the underside of the boat | The mechanic took a look at the underneath of the car.*

base the lowest part of something – especially the part that supports the rest of an object or building: *The lamp has a square base. | the base of the tower*

the sea/river bed the ground at the bottom of a river or the sea: *The fish lay their eggs on the sea bed.*

---

bottom² adj
1 [only before noun] in the lowest place or position: **the bottom drawer/shelf/corner etc** *Dictionaries are on the bottom shelf.*
2 the least successful or important: **be/come bottom** *I was bottom in the spelling test.*

bottomless /'bɒtəmləs $ 'bɑː-/ adj extremely deep, or seeming to have no limit: *a bottomless hole | The government does not have a bottomless pit* (=a supply with no limits) *of money to spend on public services.*

,bottom 'line n **the bottom line** the most basic and important fact about a situation: *The bottom line is that we have to finish the project on time.*

bough /baʊ/ n [C] literary a large tree branch

bought /bɔːt $ bɒːt/ v the past tense and past participle of **BUY**

boulder /'bəʊldə $ 'boʊldər/ n [C] a very large rock

boulevard /'buːlvɑːd $ 'bʊːləvɑːrd, 'bʊ-/ n [C] a wide road in a town or city

bounce¹ /baʊns/ v
1 BALL [I,T] if something such as a ball bounces, or if you bounce it, it hits a surface and then immediately moves away from it: **[+off]** *The ball bounced off the post and into the goal.* | **bounce sth on/against etc sth** *Two boys were bouncing a basketball against the wall.*
2 JUMP [I] to jump up and down on a soft surface: **[+on]** *Don't bounce on the bed.* → see picture at **JUMP¹**
3 CHEQUE [I,T] if you write a cheque and it bounces, or your bank bounces it, the bank will not pay the amount written on the cheque because there is not enough money in your bank account
4 WALK [I] to walk quickly and with a lot of energy: **[+into/along etc]** *The children came bouncing into the room.*
5 EMAIL (*also* **bounce back**) [I,T] if an email that you send bounces or is bounced, it is returned to you and the other person does not receive it because of a technical problem or error: *I sent you three emails, but they all bounced back.*

PHRASAL VERBS

bounce back to feel better after being ill, or to become successful again after failing or being defeated: *The team bounced back after a series of defeats.*

bounce² n [C] when something bounces

bouncer /'baʊnsə $ -ər/ n [C] someone whose job is to keep people who behave badly out of a club or bar THESAURUS **GUARD**

bouncy /'baʊnsi/ adj **1** something that is bouncy bounces easily: *a bouncy ball* **2** someone who is bouncy is happy and full of energy

bound¹ /baʊnd/ v the past tense and past participle of **BIND**

bound² adj [not before noun]
1 be bound to do sth to be very likely to do something or to happen: *Madeleine's bound to make friends.* | *Interest rates are bound to go up.*
2 be bound (by sth) to be forced to do what a law or agreement says you must do: *The company is bound*

by law to provide us with safety equipment.
3 *written* a ship, plane etc that is bound for a particular place is going there: **[+for]** *a ship bound for Peru | a Tokyo-bound flight*
4 be bound up with sth to be closely related to something: *Jake's self-image is very much bound up with his job.*

bound³ *v* [I] to move quickly with long steps and a lot of energy: **[+up/towards/across etc]** *Grace came bounding down the stairs.*

bound⁴ *n* **1 bounds** [plural] the limits of what is possible or acceptable: *That behaviour is **beyond the bounds** of decency.* **2** [C] *written* a long or high jump
PHRASES
| **out of bounds** if a place is out of bounds, you are not allowed to go there: *This room is out of bounds for children.*

boundary /'baundəri/ *n* [C] (*plural* **boundaries**)
1 the line that marks the edge of an area of land → **border**: **[+between]** *The Ohio River forms a **natural boundary** between Ohio and Kentucky.* **2** the limit of what is acceptable or thought to be possible: **[+of]** *the boundaries of human knowledge*

boundless /'baundləs/ *adj* having no limit or end: *boundless energy*

bountiful /'bauntɪfəl/ *adj literary* if something is bountiful, there is more than enough of it: *a bountiful supply of fresh food*

bounty /'baunti/ *n* [C] (*plural* **bounties**) money that is given to someone as a reward for helping to catch a criminal

bouquet /bəʊ'keɪ, buː-/ $ bou-, buː-/ *n* [C] a number of flowers fastened together, that you give to someone

bourbon /'buəbən $ 'bɜːr-/ *n* [U] a type of American WHISKY

bourgeois /'buəʒwɑː $ bur'ʒwɑː/ *adj disapproving* too concerned with having a lot of money, possessions, and a high position in society

bourgeoisie /ˌbuəʒwɑː'ziː $ ˌbur-/ *n* **the bourgeoisie** the people in a society who are rich, educated, own land etc → **middle class**

bout /baut/ *n* [C] **1** a short period of illness: **[+of]** *a bout of flu* **2** a BOXING or WRESTLING match

boutique /buː'tiːk/ *n* [C] a small shop that sells fashionable clothes

bovine /'bəʊvaɪn $ 'bou-/ *adj technical* relating to cows

bow¹ /baʊ/ *v* [I,T] to bend the top part of your body forward in order to show respect for someone: *The actors bowed and left the stage.* | **[+before/to]** *He bowed respectfully to the king.*
PHRASAL VERBS
bow out to decide to stop doing something that you have been doing for a long time: **[+of]** *It's time for him to bow out of politics.*
bow to sb/sth to finally agree to do something that people want you to do, even though you do not want to do it: *The government will have to bow to the wishes of the people.*

bow² /baʊ/ *n* [C] **1** when someone bows **2** the front part of a ship → **stern**

bow³ /bəʊ $ boʊ/ *n* [C] **1** a band of cloth or string with a knot in the middle and a circle on each side, used as decoration in your hair or to tie shoes: *hair tied back in a bow* **2** a weapon that you use for shooting ARROWS **3** a long piece of wood with material fastened to it, used for playing instruments with strings, such as a VIOLIN → see picture on page A6

bowel /'baʊəl/ *n* [C usually plural] the part inside your body that carries solid waste food away from your stomach and out of your body

bowl¹ /bəʊl $ boʊl/ *n* [C]
1 a round container that is open at the top, in which you put food or liquid → **dish**: *a soup bowl*
2 (*also* **bowlful** /'bəʊlfʊl $ 'boʊl-/) the amount that a bowl will hold: **[+of]** *a bowl of rice*
3 bowls an outdoor game in which you roll large wooden balls towards a smaller ball

bowl² *v* [I,T] **1** to roll a ball along a surface when you are playing the games of BOWLS or BOWLING **2** to throw a ball towards the BATSMAN in cricket
PHRASAL VERBS
bowl sb ↔ **over** to make someone very pleased, excited, or surprised: *When Ian met Sue, he was completely bowled over.*

bow-legged /ˌbəʊ'legd◂, -'legɪd◂ $ ˌboʊ-/ *adj* a bow-legged person has legs that curve out at their knees

bowler /'bəʊlə $ 'boʊlər/ *n* [C] **1** a player who throws the ball towards the BATSMAN in CRICKET **2** *BrE* (*also* **bowler hat**) a hard round black hat that businessmen sometimes wear

bowling /'bəʊlɪŋ $ 'boʊ-/ *n* [U] an indoor game in which you roll a heavy ball along a wooden track in order to knock over pieces of wood called PINS

bow tie /ˌbəʊ 'taɪ $ ˌbou taɪ/ *n* [C] a man's tie fastened in the shape of a BOW

BOXES

trunk
tool box
tin
cardboard box

box¹ /bɒks $ bɑːks/ *n* [C]
1 CONTAINER a container for putting things in, especially one with four straight sides, or the amount that this container can hold: *a cardboard box* | **[+of]** *a box of chocolates* → see picture at **CONTAINER**
2 IN A THEATRE/COURT a small area of a theatre or

box

court that is separate from where other people are sitting: *the jury box*

3 SMALL SQUARE a small square on a page where you write a figure or other information: *Tick the box if you would like to join our mailing list.*

4 FOR POST **box (number) 25/232 etc** a number used instead of an address, especially in newspaper advertisements → **PO Box**

5 TELEVISION **the box** *especially BrE informal* the television → **BALLOT BOX, CALL BOX, TELEPHONE BOX**

box² v **1** (*also* **box up**) [T] to put things in boxes: *It took us a day to box up everything in the study.* **2** [I] to take part in the sport of BOXING

PHRASAL VERBS

box sb/sth ↔ **in** to surround someone or something so that they cannot get out or get away

boxer /ˈbɒksə $ ˈbɑːksər/ n [C] someone who does boxing as a sport

'boxer ,shorts n [plural] loose cotton underwear for men → see picture at **CLOTHES**

boxing /ˈbɒksɪŋ $ ˈbɑːk-/ n [U] a sport in which two people wearing big leather GLOVES hit each other → see picture on page A9

'Boxing Day n [C,U] *BrE* December 26th, the day after Christmas Day, which is a national holiday in the UK

'box ,office n [C] a place in a theatre, concert HALL etc where you buy tickets

boy¹ /bɔɪ/ n [C]

1 a male child or a young man → **girl**: *a school for boys* | *a group of* **teenage boys**

2 a son: *How old is your* **little boy** *now?* → **PAPER BOY**

boy² *AmE spoken informal* used to emphasize what you are saying: *Boy, that chicken smells good!*

'boy band n [C] a group of attractive young men who make POP records

boycott /ˈbɔɪkɒt $ -kɑːt/ v [T] to refuse to buy or use something as a protest: *Catholic groups plan to boycott the movie.* —**boycott** n [C]

boyfriend /ˈbɔɪfrend/ n [C] a man that you are having a romantic relationship with → **girlfriend**

boyhood /ˈbɔɪhʊd/ n [U] the time during a man's life when he is a boy

boyish /ˈbɔɪ-ɪʃ/ adj like a young man: *his slim, boyish figure*

bra /brɑː/ n [C] a piece of underwear that a woman wears to support her breasts → see picture at **CLOTHES**

brace¹ /breɪs/ v [T] to prepare yourself for something unpleasant: *Boris braced himself for a fight.*

brace² n **1** [C] something that is used to strengthen or support something: **neck/back/knee etc brace** *Jill had to wear a neck brace for six weeks.* **2 braces** [plural] *BrE* two narrow bands that you wear over your shoulders and fasten to your trousers to stop them from falling down SYN **suspenders** *AmE* **3** [C] (*also* **braces** *AmE* [plural]) a wire frame that some people wear to make their teeth straight

bracelet /ˈbreɪslɪt/ n [C] a piece of jewellery that you wear around your wrist → see picture at **JEWELLERY**

bracing /ˈbreɪsɪŋ/ adj bracing air or weather is cold and makes you feel healthy: *a bracing sea breeze*

bracken /ˈbrækən/ n [U] a plant that often grows in forests and becomes reddish brown in the autumn

bracket¹ /ˈbrækɪt/ n [C] **1** one of the pairs of signs ( ) put around words to show additional information SYN **parenthesis** *AmE*: **in brackets** *Last year's sales figures are given in brackets.* **2 income/tax/age etc bracket** a particular level of income, tax etc: *Price's new job puts him in the highest tax bracket.* **3** a piece of metal or wood fixed to a wall to support a shelf

bracket² v [T] **1** to consider a group of people or things as similar: *Don't bracket us with those idiots.* **2** to put brackets around a word

brag /bræg/ v [I] (**bragged**, **bragging**) to talk too proudly about yourself SYN **boast**: **brag about sth** *Ray likes to brag about his success with women.*

braid¹ /breɪd/ n **1** [U] a narrow band made of threads that are twisted together, used to decorate the edges of clothes: *gold braid* **2** [C] *AmE* a length of something, especially hair, made by twisting three pieces together SYN **plait** *BrE* → see picture at **HAIR** —**braided** adj

braid² v [T] *AmE* to twist three long pieces of hair, rope etc together to make one long piece SYN **plait** *BrE*

braille /breɪl/ n [U] a type of printing that blind people can read by touching the page

brain /breɪn/ n

1 [C] the part of your body inside your head which you use to think, feel, and move: *Jorge suffered* **brain damage** *in the accident.* | *a brain tumour* → see picture on page A2

2 [C usually plural, U] the ability to think well: *If you had any brains, you'd know what I mean.* | *Come on,* **use** *your* **brain**, *John.*

3 [C usually plural] *informal* someone who is very intelligent: *Some of the best brains in the country are here tonight.* → **pick sb's brain(s)** at PICK¹, **rack your brain(s)** at RACK²

PHRASES

be the brains behind sth to be the person who thought of and developed a plan, system, organization etc, especially a successful one: *He's the brains behind the company's success.*

brainchild /ˈbreɪntʃaɪld/ n [singular] *informal* an idea, plan, organization etc that one person has thought of: **[+of]** *The personal computer was the brainchild of Steve Jobs.*

'brain dead adj in a state where your brain is so damaged that you cannot breathe without help, even though your heart is still beating

brainless /ˈbreɪnləs/ adj completely stupid

brainstorm /ˈbreɪnstɔːm $ -stɔːrm/ n [singular] **1** *informal* an American word for BRAINWAVE THESAURUS IDEA **2** *BrE* when you are suddenly unable to think clearly

brainstorming /ˈbreɪnstɔːmɪŋ $ -ɔːr-/ n [U] when a group of people meet in order to try to develop ideas or solve problems

brainwash /'breɪnwɒʃ $ -wɒːʃ, -wɑːʃ/ v [T] to force someone to believe something that is not true by telling them many times that it is true: *People are brainwashed into believing that being fat is some kind of crime.* —**brainwashing** n [U]

brainwave /'breɪnweɪv/ n [C] BrE a very good idea that you have suddenly SYN **brainstorm** AmE
THESAURUS IDEA

brainy /'breɪni/ adj informal intelligent

brake¹ /breɪk/ n [C] the part of a vehicle that makes it go more slowly or stop: *You need good brakes on a motorbike.* | *cars fitted with **anti-lock brakes*** → see picture at BICYCLE
PHRASES
put the brakes on sth to make something develop more slowly or happen less: *The government is trying to put the brakes on rising prices.*

brake² v [I] to make a vehicle go more slowly or stop, using its brake: *Brake gently as you approach the bend.*

bramble /'bræmbəl/ n [C] a wild BLACKBERRY bush

bran /bræn/ n [U] the crushed skin of wheat and other grain, often used in bread

branch¹ /brɑːntʃ $ bræntʃ/ n [C]
1 OF A TREE a part of a tree that grows out from the TRUNK (=the main part) → see picture at PLANT¹
2 OF A SHOP/COMPANY a local business, shop etc that is part of a larger business etc: *The shop has **opened branches** all over the country.*
3 OF A SUBJECT one part of a large subject of study or knowledge: **a branch of medicine/physics/philosophy etc**

branch² (*also* **branch off**) v [I] to divide into two or more smaller, narrower, or less important parts: *When you reach Bread Street, the road branches into two.*
PHRASAL VERBS
branch out to start doing something different from the work or activities that you normally do: **[+into]** *The bank has begun to branch out into selling insurance.*

brand¹ /brænd/ n [C] **1** a product that a particular company makes: **[+of]** *a new brand of soap* **2** a particular quality or way of doing something: **[+of]** *Nat's special brand of humour*

brand² v [T] **1** to describe someone as a very bad type of person: **brand sb (as) sth** *Ryan was branded a liar by the media.* **2** to make or burn a mark on an animal in order to show who it belongs to

branded /'brændɪd/ adj a branded product is made by a well-known company and has the company's name on it

brandish /'brændɪʃ/ v [T] to wave a weapon around in a threatening way: *Chisholm burst into the office brandishing a knife.*

'brand ,name n [C] the name a company gives to a product it makes

,brand-'new adj completely new: *a brand-new car*

brandy /'brændi/ n [C,U] (*plural* **brandies**) a strong alcoholic drink made from wine, or a glass of this drink

brash /bræʃ/ adj disapproving behaving too confidently and speaking too loudly: *a brash young senator*

brass /brɑːs $ bræs/ n [U] **1** a shiny yellow metal that is a mixture of COPPER and ZINC **2 a)** musical instruments that are made of metal, such as the TRUMPET: *a **brass band*** **b) the brass (section)** the people in an ORCHESTRA or band who play musical instruments that are made of metal

brat /bræt/ n [C] informal a badly behaved child: *a **spoiled brat***

bravado /brə'vɑːdəʊ $ -doʊ/ n [U] behaviour that is intended to show that you are brave and confident, even when you are not

brave¹ /breɪv/ adj showing that you are not afraid to do something that is dangerous, frightening, or difficult: *brave firefighters* | *It was very brave of you to tell her the truth.* —**bravely** adv: *The troops fought bravely until the end.* —**bravery** n [U]: *medals awarded for bravery*

THESAURUS

brave not afraid to do something that is dangerous, frightening, or difficult: *the brave men who fought in the war* | *It was a brave thing to do.*
courageous very brave – used especially about someone fighting for what they believe in, or fighting against a disease: *She is an extraordinary and courageous woman, who has struggled to bring democracy to her country.* | *his courageous fight against cancer*
daring willing to try doing something that involves a lot of danger or risk: *a daring escape from a prison camp* | *a daring artist*
bold behaving in a confident way that shows you are not afraid to take difficult decisions, or do things that other people may disagree with: *Starting her own company was a bold decision.* | *No one felt bold enough to ask that question.*
adventurous used about someone who enjoys going to new places, or doing exciting and dangerous things: *If you are feeling adventurous, you can go diving in the Red Sea.*

---

brave² v [T] to be brave enough to do something difficult, dangerous, or unpleasant: *The crowd braved icy wind and rain to see the procession.*

bravo /brɑː'vəʊ, brɑː'vəʊ $ -voʊ/ spoken something that you shout to show that you like something

brawl /brɔːl $ brɒːl/ n [C] a noisy fight among a group of people: *a drunken brawl* **THESAURUS** FIGHT —**brawl** v [I]

brawn /brɔːn $ brɒːn/ n [U] physical strength —**brawny** adj: *brawny arms*

brazen¹ /'breɪzən/ adj used to describe a person or the actions of a person who is not embarrassed about behaving in a wrong or immoral way: *a brazen lie* —**brazenly** adv

brazen² v
PHRASAL VERBS
brazen sth out to deal with a situation in which you have done something bad by continuing to say that you acted correctly

brazier /ˈbreɪziə $ -ər/ *n* [C] a metal container that holds a fire and is used to keep people warm outside

breach /briːtʃ/ *n* [C,U] when you break a law, rule, or agreement: **[+of]** *You are in breach of your contract.* —**breach** *v* [T]

BREAD

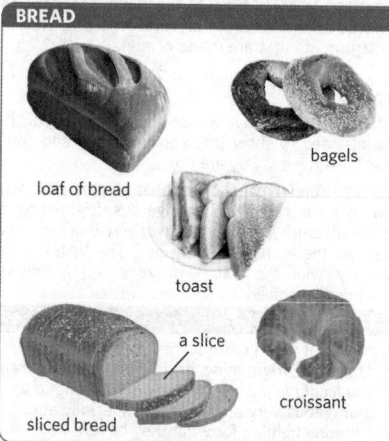

bagels

loaf of bread

toast

a slice

croissant

sliced bread

bread /bred/ *n* [U] a common food made by baking a mixture of FLOUR and water

COLLOCATIONS

nouns + bread

a slice/piece of bread *Serve the soup with pieces of crusty bread.*

a loaf of bread *She put a loaf of bread on the table.*

verbs

to make/bake bread *He makes his own wholewheat bread.*

to cut/slice bread *I'll cut some bread for the sandwiches.*

types of bread

fresh bread *There's nothing nicer than fresh bread.*

stale bread (=hard and no longer fresh) *The bread is a bit stale.*

white/brown bread *Would you like white bread or brown bread?*

wholewheat bread (*also* **wholemeal bread** *BrE*) (=made with flour that contains all of the grain)

bread + noun

a bread roll (=bread in a round shape, for one person) *For lunch I had a bread roll with some cheese.*

breadcrumbs /ˈbredkrʌmz/ *n* [plural] very small pieces of bread, often used in cooking

breadline /ˈbredlaɪn/ *n* **the breadline** a very low level of income which allows people to eat but not have any extra things: *a family living on the breadline*

breadth /bredθ, bretθ/ *n* **1** [C,U] the distance from one side of something to the other **SYN** width

2 [U] the quality of including a lot of different people, things, or ideas: **[+of]** *No one could equal Dr Brenninger's breadth of knowledge.*

PHRASES

a hair's breadth a very small distance or amount: *The bullet missed his heart by a hair's breadth.*

breadwinner /ˈbredˌwɪnə $ -ər/ *n* [C] the person in a family who earns most of the money that the family needs

break¹ /breɪk/ *v* (*past tense* **broke** /brəʊk $ broʊk/, *past participle* **broken** /ˈbrəʊkən $ ˈbroʊ-/)

1 SEPARATE INTO PIECES [I,T] if something breaks, or if you break it, it separates into pieces, usually because it has been dropped, hit etc: *I had to break a window to get into the house.* | *Be careful – those glasses break easily.* | **break sth in half/two** *He broke the biscuit in half.*

2 BONE [T] to damage a bone in your body by making it crack or split: **break your leg/arm etc** *She fell down and broke her hip.* THESAURUS HURT

3 DAMAGE [I,T] if you break a tool or a machine, or if it breaks, it no longer works properly: *He was playing with the camera and broke it!* THESAURUS DAMAGE

4 LAW/RULE [T] to disobey a law or rule: *Williams denied breaking the law.* | *Students who break the rules will be punished.*

5 PROMISE/AGREEMENT [T] to not do what you promised to do: *The mayor broke a promise to improve schools.* | *You broke your word.*

6 STOP/REST [I,T] to stop for a short time in order to have a rest or eat something: **[+for]** *We broke for lunch at 12:30.* | *We can break our journey in Oxford.*

7 MAKE STH END [T] to stop something from continuing: *The sound of gunfire broke the silence.*

8 NEWS [I] if news about an important event breaks, it becomes known: *News of his resignation broke yesterday afternoon.*

9 DAY/DAWN [I] if day or DAWN breaks, light begins to show in the sky as the sun rises

10 BOY'S VOICE [I] when a boy's voice breaks, it becomes lower and starts to sound like a man's voice

11 WEATHER [I] if the weather breaks, it suddenly changes: *We went to the coast for a few days until the weather broke.*

12 STORM [I] if a storm breaks, it begins

PHRASES

break sb's concentration to stop someone from being able to think about what they are doing: *A shout from the crowd broke the golfer's concentration.*

break even to neither make a profit nor lose money: *We broke even in our first year of business.*

break a habit to stop doing something that you do regularly, especially something that you should not do: *The program is designed to help drug addicts break their habit.*

break sb's heart to make someone very unhappy, especially by ending a relationship with them

break the ice *informal* to make people who have just met feel less nervous and more willing to talk to each other: *I suggested a game to break the ice.*

break loose/free to escape: *The cattle broke loose during the night.*

break the news (to sb) to tell someone about

something bad that has happened: *Ellie called him into her office to break the news.*

break a record to do something faster, better etc than anyone has ever done it before: *an attempt to break the 10,000 metres* **world record**

THESAURUS

to break something

break to damage something and make it separate into pieces: *Careful you don't break those glasses.* | *I think I've broken my arm.*

smash to break something with a lot of force: *The ball smashed one of the windows.*

snap to deliberately break something hard into two pieces, making a sharp noise: *He snapped the sticks in two.*

fracture to damage a bone, especially so that a line appears on the surface: *I fell over and fractured my wrist.*

to become broken

break to become damaged and separate into pieces: *I dropped the plate and it broke.*

shatter to break into a lot of small pieces: *The glass shattered when it hit the floor.*

crack if something cracks, a line appears on its surface, which means that it may break into separate pieces later: *The ice on the river was starting to crack.*

burst if a tyre, balloon, pipe etc bursts, it gets a hole in it and air or liquid suddenly comes out: *A water pipe in the roof had burst.*

split to tear or break in a straight line: *My jeans were so tight that they split.*

crumble to break into a powder or a lot of small pieces: *The bricks were starting to crumble.*

PHRASAL VERBS

break away

1 to move away from someone who is holding you: *She started crying and tried to break away.*

2 to leave a group or organization and form another group, usually because of a disagreement: **[+from]** *They broke away from the national union and set up their own local organization.*

break down

1 if a car or a machine breaks down, it stops working: *My car broke down on the way to work.*

2 to fail: *Negotiations broke down after only two days.* | *She moved back to America when her* **marriage broke down**.

3 if someone breaks down, they start crying: *Imelda* **broke down in tears** *at the funeral.* **THESAURUS** ▶ CRY

4 break sth ↔ down if you break down a door, you hit it so hard that it breaks and falls to the ground

5 if a substance breaks down, or if something breaks it down, it changes or separates into smaller parts as a result of a chemical process: **break sth ↔ down** *Food is broken down in the stomach.*

break in to use force to enter a building, especially in order to steal something: *Burglars broke in during the night and took the stereo.* **THESAURUS** ▶ ENTER

break into sth

1 to use force to enter a building or car, especially in order to steal something: *They broke into the room through the back window.* **THESAURUS** ▶ ENTER

2 to suddenly start doing something: *He* **broke into a run** *as he came round the corner.* | *Her face suddenly* **broke into a smile.**

3 to become involved in a new job or business activity: *American companies are trying to break into Eastern European markets.*

break off

1 if something breaks off, or if you break it off, it is separated from the main part of something: **break sth ↔ off** *She broke off a piece of cheese.* | *One of the car's wing mirrors had broken off.*

2 break sth ↔ off to end a relationship: *The US has broken off diplomatic relations with Iran.* | *She* **broke off** *their* **engagement** *a week before they were due to be married.*

3 to suddenly stop doing something or talking to someone: **break sth ↔ off** *Without explanation, management broke off contract negotiations.*

break out

1 if a disease, fire, or war breaks out, it starts: *Nine months later, war broke out in Korea.* **THESAURUS** ▶ START

2 to escape from prison: **[+of]** *Two inmates broke out of prison and murdered a police officer.*

3 break out in spots/a rash/sweat etc if you break out in spots etc, they appear on your skin

break through (sth) to use force to get through something that is stopping you from moving forward: *Demonstrators tried to break through police lines.*

break up

1 break sth ↔ up to separate something into smaller parts: *They plan to break the company up into several smaller companies.*

2 if something breaks up, or if you break it up, it breaks into small pieces: *The ship broke up on the rocks.* | **break sth ↔ up** *We used shovels to break up the soil.*

3 to end a relationship with a husband, wife, BOY-FRIEND etc: *Troy and I broke up last month.* | **[+with]** *She's broken up with Glen.*

4 break sth ↔ up to stop a fight or argument: *Three policemen were needed to break up the fight.*

5 if a meeting or party breaks up, people start to leave

6 *BrE* when a school breaks up, it closes for a holiday: **[+for]** *When do you break up for Easter?*

break with sb/sth to leave a group of people or an organization, after a disagreement with them: *Yugoslavia under Tito soon broke with Stalin's Russia.*

**break² ** n [C]

1 REST a period of time when you stop what you are doing in order to rest, eat etc: *Let's take a ten-minute break.* | **lunch/coffee/tea break**

2 HOLIDAY a short holiday: *We flew off for a week's break in Spain.* | **(the) Christmas/Easter/summer etc break** *Are you going anywhere over the Easter break?* | *luxury* **weekend breaks**

3 ON A BONE the place where something, such as a bone in your body, has been broken: *The break has not healed correctly.*

4 PAUSE a period of time when something stops happening before it starts again: **[+in]** *a break in the conversation*

5 GAP a space or hole in something: **[+in]** *a break in the clouds*

6 OPPORTUNITY a chance to become successful: *The band's **big break** came when they sang on a local TV show.*

7 CHANGE **a break with tradition/the past** a time when people stop following old customs and do something in a completely different way: *Clark made a complete break with the past and moved to Chile.*

PHRASES

the break of day *literary* the morning, when it starts getting light

breakable /ˈbreɪkəbəl/ *adj* made of a material that breaks easily: *Make sure you pack breakable ornaments carefully.*

breakage /ˈbreɪkɪdʒ/ *n* [C usually plural] something that someone breaks: *All breakages must be paid for.*

breakaway /ˈbreɪkəweɪ/ *adj* a breakaway group of people has separated from a larger group because of a disagreement: *a **breakaway group** of journalists*

breakdown /ˈbreɪkdaʊn/ *n* **1** [C,U] the failure of a relationship or system: **[+of]** *He moved away after the breakdown of his marriage.* | **[+in]** *a breakdown in the peace talks* **2** [C] a mental condition in which someone becomes unable to continue with their normal life: *Two years ago he **had a nervous breakdown**.* **3** [C] an occasion when a car or a piece of machinery stops working: *We **had a breakdown** on the motorway.* **4** [C] a statement explaining the details of something: **[+of]** *I'd like a breakdown of these figures, please.*

breaker /ˈbreɪkə $ -ər/ *n* [C] a large wave with a white top that rolls onto the shore

breakfast /ˈbrekfəst/ *n* [C,U] the meal you have in the morning: *I usually **have breakfast** at 7.30.* | **for breakfast** *Would you like tea or coffee for breakfast?* | **English breakfast** (=a cooked breakfast of BACON, eggs, TOAST etc) | **continental breakfast** (=a breakfast of coffee and bread with butter and JAM) → BED AND BREAKFAST

break-in *n* [C] a situation in which someone enters a building by force, especially to steal things: *There was a break-in at the college last night.*

breaking point *n* [U] when a person or system can no longer work well because there are so many problems: *The relationship has **reached breaking point**.*

breakneck /ˈbreɪknek/ *adj* **at breakneck speed/pace** extremely fast: *She was driving at breakneck speed.*

breakout /ˈbreɪkaʊt/ *n* [C] an escape from a prison, especially one involving a lot of prisoners

breakthrough /ˈbreɪkθruː/ *n* [C] an important new discovery or development: **[+in]** *Police have **made a breakthrough** in their hunt for the killers.*

breakup /ˈbreɪkʌp/ *n* [C] **1** the ending of a marriage or relationship **2** the separation of an organization or country into smaller parts: **[+of]** *the breakup of the Soviet Union*

breast /brest/ *n*
1 [C] one of the two round parts on a woman's chest that produce milk when she has a baby
2 [C,U] the front of a bird's body, or the meat from this: *turkey breast* → see picture on page A3
3 [C] *literary* the top of your body at the front → DOUBLE-BREASTED

breast-feed *v* [I,T] (*past tense and past participle* **breast-fed**) if a woman breast-feeds, she feeds a baby with milk from her breasts

breaststroke /ˈbrest-strəʊk $ -stroʊk/ *n* [U] a way of swimming in which you push your arms forward and then pull them back in a circle towards you → see picture at SWIM¹

breath /breθ/ *n*
1 [U] air that you send out of your lungs when you breathe: *He has **bad breath** (=his breath smells unpleasant).* | *I could **smell** alcohol **on his breath**.*
2 [C,U] air that you take into your lungs: *She talked without **pausing for breath**.* | **take a (deep/big/long) breath** *He took a deep breath and dived into the water.*

Usage

Do not confuse **breath** (noun) and **breathe** (verb). Do not say 'I found it hard to breath.' Say *I found it hard to breathe.*

PHRASES

a breath of fresh air 1 something that is new, different, and enjoyable: *This exciting young designer has **brought a breath of fresh air to** the fashion world.* **2** clean air outside: *I'm just going out for a breath of fresh air.*

catch your breath/get your breath back to rest after running, climbing etc until you can breathe normally again: *I stopped at the top of the hill to catch my breath.*

don't hold your breath *spoken* used to say that something is not going to happen soon: *He promised to pay back the money he owes you, but don't hold your breath.*

hold your breath to deliberately stop breathing in and out for a short while: *Can you hold your breath under water?*

out of breath/short of breath having difficulty breathing, especially after exercise: *He was leaning against the wall, completely out of breath.*

take your breath away if something takes your breath away, it is very beautiful or exciting: *a view that will take your breath away*

under your breath in a quiet voice, so that other people cannot hear: *'I hate you,' he muttered under his breath.*

Breathalyzer (*also* **-lyser** *BrE*) /ˈbreθəl-aɪzə $ -ər/ *n* [C] *trademark* a piece of equipment used by the police to test whether a driver has drunk too much alcohol —**breathalyze** *v* [T]

breathe /briːð/ *v* [I,T] to take air into your lungs and send it out again: *Grandad got up, **breathing heavily** (=with long slow breaths).* | *Relax and **breathe deeply** (=take in a lot of air).* | *Try not to breathe the fumes.* —**breathing** *n* [U]

PHRASES

be breathing down sb's neck *informal* to watch someone carefully and make them feel nervous or annoyed: *I can't work with you breathing down my neck.*

not breathe a word to not say anything about something that is secret: *Promise not to breathe a word to anyone.*

PHRASAL VERBS
breathe in to take air into your lungs: *The doctor told her to breathe in.* | **breathe sth ↔ in** *They breathed in the fresh sea air.*
breathe out to let air out of your lungs: *Jim breathed out deeply.*

THESAURUS

breathe to take air into your lungs and send it out again: *The patient was breathing normally.*
snore to breathe noisily while you are sleeping: *I couldn't sleep because my husband was snoring.*
sigh to send air out slowly through your mouth, making a noise that shows you are disappointed, tired, RELIEVED etc: *We all sighed with relief when we finally got home.*
gasp to breathe with difficulty through your mouth because you are ill, have been running etc: *He collapsed on the floor, gasping for breath.*
pant to breathe quickly and noisily through your mouth when you are running or hurrying, or because you feel hot: *Steve came panting up the hill towards us.*
wheeze to breathe with difficulty, making a noise in your throat and chest, because you are ill: *If he is wheezing, he may have a chest infection.*

---

breather /'briːðə $ -ər/ *n* [singular] *informal* a short rest from what you are doing: *Let's take a breather.*

breathing space *n* [singular, U] a short period when you have a rest from doing something before starting again

breathless /'breθləs/ *adj* having difficulty breathing because you are tired, excited, frightened etc: **[+with]** *They waited, breathless with anticipation.* —**breathlessly** *adv* —**breathlessness** *n* [U]

breathtaking /'breθˌteɪkɪŋ/ *adj* very impressive, beautiful, or surprising: *a breathtaking view* —**breathtakingly** *adv*

breed¹ /briːd/ *v* (*past tense and past participle* **bred** /bred/) **1** [I] if animals breed, they have babies: *Rats can breed every six weeks.* **2** [T] to keep animals or plants in order to produce young animals or develop new plants: *He breeds cattle.* **3** [T] to cause a particular feeling, situation etc to develop: *Arguments can breed insecurity in a child.*

breed² *n* [C] **1** a particular type of an animal: **[+of]** *a rare breed of sheep* **2** a particular type of person or thing: **[+of]** *The island is catering for a new breed of tourist.*

breeder /'briːdə $ -ər/ *n* [C] someone who breeds animals or plants: *a dog breeder*

breeding /'briːdɪŋ/ *n* [U] **1** when animals produce babies: *the breeding season* **2** the activity of keeping animals or plants in order to produce others with particular qualities: *animal breeding programmes*

breeding ground *n* [C] **1** a place or situation where something bad develops: **[+for]** *Stale milk is a*

breeding ground for germs. **2** a place where animals or birds go to breed

breeze¹ /briːz/ *n* [C] a gentle wind: *a **light** breeze* **THESAURUS** WIND

breeze² *v* [I] to walk somewhere in a relaxed confident way: **[+in/out/along etc]** *She breezed into my office and asked for a job.*

breezy /'briːzi/ *adj* **1** a breezy person is confident and relaxed **2** if the weather is breezy, there is quite a lot of wind —**breezily** *adv*

brethren /'breðrən/ *n* [plural] *old-fashioned* the members of an organization, especially a religious group

brevity **Ac** /'brevəti/ *n* [U] *formal* the quality of being short and quick → **brief**: **[+of]** *the brevity of human life* | *Michelle answered with brevity.*

brew¹ /bruː/ *v* **1** [T] to make beer **2** [T] to make a drink of tea or coffee: *freshly brewed coffee* **3** [I] if tea or coffee brews, it is left in hot water for a few minutes so that the taste gets stronger **4** **be brewing** if trouble or a storm is brewing, it will happen soon

brew² *n* [C] *informal* **1** a type of beer **2** a pot of hot tea

brewer /'bruːə $ -ər/ *n* [C] a person or company that makes beer

brewery /'bruːəri/ *n* [C] (*plural* **breweries**) a place where beer is made, or a company that makes beer

bribe¹ /braɪb/ *v* [T] to give someone money or a gift to persuade them to do something, especially something dishonest: **bribe sb to do sth** *He bribed one of the guards to smuggle out a note.*

bribe² *n* [C] money or a gift that is given to someone to persuade them to do something, especially something dishonest: **accept/take a bribe** *The judge admitted that he had accepted bribes.*

bribery /'braɪbəri/ *n* [U] when someone offers or accepts bribes

bric-a-brac /'brɪk ə ˌbræk/ *n* [U] small objects from people's houses that are not worth very much money

brick /brɪk/ *n* [C,U] a hard block of baked clay used for building walls, houses etc: *a brick wall* | *The houses are made of brick.*

bricklayer /'brɪkˌleɪə $ -ər/ *n* [C] someone whose job is to build walls with bricks —**bricklaying** *n* [U]

bridal /'braɪdl/ *adj* relating to a bride or a wedding: *a bridal gown*

bride /braɪd/ *n* [C] a woman who is getting married or has just got married → **groom**

bridegroom /'braɪdɡruːm, -ɡrʊm/ *n* [C] a man who is getting married or has just got married

bridesmaid /'braɪdzmeɪd/ *n* [C] a girl or woman who helps the bride on the day of her wedding

BRIDGES

footbridge

suspension bridge

bridge¹ /brɪdʒ/ n

1 OVER A RIVER/ROAD [C] a structure built over a river, road etc so that people or vehicles can cross it: **[+over/across]** *a bridge over the Mississippi* | *They* **crossed** *the* **bridge** *over the railway line.*

2 CONNECTION [C] something that makes a connection between people, situations, ideas etc: **[+between]** *The training programme is seen as a bridge between school and work.* | *The police must* **build bridges** (=develop a better relationship) *with the community.*

3 ON A SHIP [C usually singular] the high part of a ship from which it is controlled

4 GAME [U] a card game for four players

5 ON YOUR NOSE **the bridge of your nose** the upper part of your nose between your eyes → **SUSPENSION BRIDGE**

bridge² v [T] **1** to reduce the difference between two things or people: **[+between]** *Are we doing enough to* **bridge the gap** *between rich and poor?* **2** to build or form a bridge over something: *A fallen tree bridged the stream.*

bridle¹ /'braɪdl/ n [C] a set of leather bands that is put over a horse's head to control its movements

bridle² v [I,T] *written* to become angry or offended about something: **[+at]** *She bridled at the question.*

brief¹ Ac /briːf/ adj

1 continuing for only a short time: *a brief visit* **THESAURUS ▸ SHORT**

2 using only a few words: *The letter was very brief.* | *a brief statement*

3 **be brief** to say or write something using only a few words: *Ladies and gentlemen, I'll try to be brief.* —**briefly** adv

brief² Ac n [C] **1** instructions that explain someone's duties or jobs: *My brief is to increase our sales.* **2** **briefs** [plural] men's or women's underwear worn on the lower part of the body

PHRASES

in brief using only a few words: *Here is the sports news in brief.*

brief³ Ac v [T] to give someone the information or instructions they need: **brief sb on sth** *The president has been* **fully briefed** *on the current situation.*

briefcase /'briːfkeɪs/ n [C] a flat case used to carry papers or books for work → see picture at **CASE**

briefing Ac /'briːfɪŋ/ n [C,U] an occasion when people are given information or instructions: *a* **press briefing** (=when people who report the news are given information)

brigade /brɪ'ɡeɪd/ n [C] a large group of soldiers forming part of an army → **FIRE BRIGADE**

brigadier /ˌbrɪɡə'dɪə◂ $ -'dɪr◂/ n [C] an important officer in the British army

bright /braɪt/ adj

1 LIGHT shining strongly: *The torch was very bright.* | *the bright lights of the city*

2 PLACE/DAY full of light: *a large bright room* | *a bright summer's day* (=with the sun shining)

3 CLEVER intelligent: *Vicky is a very bright child.* | *He is always full of bright ideas.* **THESAURUS ▸ INTELLIGENT**

4 COLOURS bright colours are strong and easy to see: *Her dress was bright red.*

5 HAPPY happy or cheerful: *a bright smile* | *She sounded bright on the phone.*

6 FUTURE a bright future is one that is likely to be successful: *Looking ahead,* **the future looks bright**. —**brightly** adv: *brightly coloured balloons* —**brightness** n [U]

THESAURUS

bright a bright light shines strongly: *The plant needs plenty of bright light.*

strong strong light is very bright and often hot: *Strong sunshine can be dangerous.*

brilliant extremely bright, especially in a way that is beautiful: *The garden was full of brilliant autumn sunshine.*

dazzling a dazzling light is so bright that you cannot look at it: *the dazzling reflection of the sun on the ice*

blinding a blinding light is so bright that it makes you unable to see after you have looked at it: *There was a blinding flash and then a huge explosion.*

---

brighten /'braɪtn/ (*also* **brighten up**) v **1** [I,T] to become brighter or more pleasant, or to make something brighter or more pleasant: *The weather should brighten up in the afternoon.* | *She bought flowers to brighten the room.* **2** [I,T] to become happier, or to make someone happier: *She brightened up when she saw us coming.*

brilliant /'brɪljənt/ adj

1 LIGHT/COLOUR brilliant light or colour is very bright and strong: *brilliant sunshine* | *brilliant blue eyes* **THESAURUS ▸ BRIGHT**

2 INTELLIGENT very clever, skilful, or successful: *a brilliant scientist* | *That's a brilliant idea!* | *He's had a brilliant career.* **THESAURUS ▸ INTELLIGENT**

3 VERY GOOD *BrE informal* extremely nice or enjoyable: *'How was your holiday?' 'It was brilliant!'* **THESAURUS ▸ NICE** —**brilliance** n [U] —**brilliantly** adv

brim[1] /brɪm/ n [C] **1** the bottom part of a hat that sticks out **2** the top edge of a container: *The glass was full to the brim* (=completely full).

brim[2] v [I] (**brimmed**, **brimming**) **1** if your eyes brim with tears, you start to cry **2 be brimming (over) with sth** to have a lot of something: *Rob was brimming with confidence*.

brine /braɪn/ n [U] salty water, often used for preserving food

bring /brɪŋ/ v [T] (past tense and past participle **brought** /brɔːt $ brɒːt/)
1 a) to take something or someone with you to a place: *I brought these pictures to show you.* | **bring sb/sth with you** *Bring the children with you.* | **bring sb/sth to sth** *Our teacher brought a real owl to class.* **b)** to get something for someone and take it to them: **bring sb sth** *Rob brought her a glass of water.*
THESAURUS TAKE
2 to move something somewhere: **bring sth out/up/down etc** *Bring your arms up level with your shoulders.* | *She reached into her bag and brought out a pen.*
3 to make something happen: *The strikes brought chaos.* | *His words brought a smile to her face* (=made her smile). | **bring sth to an end/close etc** (=make something stop) *The trial was brought to a sudden halt.* | *Bring the sauce to the boil* (=make it boil by heating it).
4 if something brings people to a place, it makes them go there: *The fair brings a lot of people to the town.*
5 to make something available for people to have or enjoy: **bring sth to sb/sth** *Investment has brought jobs to the region.* | **bring sb sth** *Football brought him wealth and fame.*
PHRASES
can't bring yourself to do sth to not be able to do something, especially because it is unpleasant: *I couldn't bring myself to look.*

> **THESAURUS**
> **bring** to take something or someone to the place where you are now, or the place where you are going: *I've brought a book you might like to read.* | *Remember to bring your passport!*
> **take** to take something or someone to another place: *What clothes should I take?* | *He was taken to hospital.*
> **get** (*also* **fetch** *especially BrE*) to go to another place and bring something or someone back with you: *I went upstairs to get my jacket.*

PHRASAL VERBS
bring sth ↔ **about** to make something happen: *The war brought about huge social and political changes.*
THESAURUS CAUSE
bring sb/sth **around/round**
1 bring the conversation around/round to sth to deliberately and gradually change the subject of a conversation: *Helen tried to bring the conversation around to the subject of marriage.*
2 to make someone become conscious again
bring sth/sb ↔ **back**
1 to return from somewhere with something or

someone: **[+for]** *I'll bring back some sweets for the kids.*
2 to start using something again that was used in the past: *Some people want to bring back the death penalty.*
3 to make you remember something: *Seeing him brought back a lot of memories.*
bring sb/sth **down**
1 to reduce something to a lower level: *Better farming methods have brought down the price of food.*
THESAURUS REDUCE
2 bring down a government/president etc to force a government etc to stop ruling a country
3 to make something or someone fall: *An enemy plane was brought down by rocket launchers.*
bring sth ↔ **forward**
1 to change the date or time of something so that it happens sooner: **[+to]** *The meeting was brought forward to Wednesday.*
2 *formal* to introduce new plans or ideas for people to discuss
bring sb/sth ↔ **in**
1 to introduce a new law: *The council will bring in new regulations to restrict parking.*
2 to ask someone with special knowledge, skills etc to do a particular job: **bring sb in to do sth** *The FBI were brought in to help with the search.*
3 to earn or produce an amount of money: *The sale should bring in more than £2 million.*
bring sth ↔ **off** to succeed in doing something difficult **SYN** **pull off**: *They brought off the most daring robbery in history.*
bring sth ↔ **on** to cause a pain or an unpleasant situation: *Stress can bring on a headache.*
bring sth ↔ **out**
1 to make something easier to notice: *The spices bring out the flavour of the meat.*
2 to produce something that will be sold to the public: *They're bringing out a new album next month.*
3 bring out the best/worst in sb to make someone show the best or worst part of their character: *Becoming a dad has brought out the best in Dan.*
bring sb ↔ **together** to make people do things together or feel more friendly to each other: *War brings a community together.*
bring sb/sth ↔ **up**
1 to start to talk about something **SYN** **raise**: *She wished she'd never brought up the subject of money.*
2 *especially BrE* to look after children until they are adults **SYN** **raise** *AmE*: *Rachel had been brought up by her grandmother.* | **bring sb up to do sth** (=teach a child at home to behave in a particular way) *We were brought up to be polite.* | **well/badly brought up** (=behaving well or badly because of the way you were taught at home)
3 *BrE* if you bring food up, it comes back up from your stomach and out of your mouth **SYN** **vomit**

brink /brɪŋk/ n **be on the brink (of sth)** to be almost in a new situation, especially a bad one: *The world seemed on the brink of war.*

brisk /brɪsk/ adj **1** quick or full of energy: *a brisk walk* | *Her voice sounded brisk.* **2** trade or business that is brisk is very busy and a lot of things are sold —**briskly** adv —**briskness** n [U]

bristle[1] /ˈbrɪsəl/ n **1** [C,U] short stiff hair that feels rough: *His chin was covered with bristles.* **2** [C] a short stiff hair, wire etc on a brush —**bristly** *adj*

bristle² *v* [I] **1** to show that you are very annoyed: [+with] *She bristled with indignation.* **2** if an animal's fur bristles, it stands up stiffly because of fear or anger

PHRASAL VERBS

bristle with sth to be full of something: *streets bristling with tourists*

Brit /brɪt/ *n* [C] *informal* someone from Britain

British¹ /'brɪtɪʃ/ *adj* from or relating to Britain

British² *n* the British [plural] the people of Britain

Briton /'brɪtn/ *n* [C] *formal* someone from Britain

brittle /'brɪtl/ *adj* hard but easily broken: *The branches were dry and brittle.*

broach /brəʊtʃ $ broʊtʃ/ *v* **broach the subject/ matter/question etc** to mention a subject that may be embarrassing or unpleasant: *At last he broached the subject of her divorce.*

broad /brɔːd $ brɒːd/ *adj*

1 wide OPP **narrow** → **breadth**: *broad shoulders* | *He gave her a broad smile.*

2 including many different kinds of things or people OPP **narrow**: *a broad range of interests*

3 general, and without a lot of details: *a broad outline of the plan*

4 a broad ACCENT (=way of speaking) clearly shows where you come from SYN **strong**: *a broad Scottish accent*

PHRASES

| **in broad daylight** during the day, when it is light: *He was attacked in broad daylight.*

> **Word Choice: broad or wide?**
> **Wide** is the usual word to use when talking about roads, rivers, lakes, rooms etc.
> You use **broad** when talking about someone's shoulders or their chest, or when saying that someone has a broad smile or a broad grin.
> **Broad** is also used especially in literature to describe rivers, lakes etc.

B-road /'biː rəʊd $ -roʊd/ *n* [C] a type of road in Britain that is smaller than an A-ROAD

broadband /'brɔːdbænd $ 'brɒːd-/ *n* [U] a system of connecting computers to the Internet and moving information at a very high speed —**broadband** *adj*

broadcast¹ /'brɔːdkɑːst $ 'brɒːdkæst/ *n* [C] a programme on radio or television: *a news broadcast*

broadcast² *v* [I,T] (*past tense and past participle* **broadcast**) to send out a radio or television programme: *The match will be broadcast live* (=while it is happening) *on Channel 5.* —**broadcasting** *n* [U]

broadcaster /'brɔːdkɑːstə $ 'brɒːdkæstər/ *n* [C] someone who speaks on radio and television programmes

broaden /'brɔːdn $ 'brɒːdn/ *v* [I,T] **1** to include more people, ideas, activities etc, or to make something do this SYN **widen**: *The social world of the child slowly broadens.* | *The party must broaden its appeal to younger voters.* | *Travel broadens the mind* (=helps

you to understand more about people and the world). **2** (*also* **broaden out**) to become wider, or to make something wider: *The river broadens out here.*

broadly /'brɔːdli $ 'brɒːd-/ *adv* in a general way: *We reached broadly similar conclusions.* | *Broadly speaking, there are two interpretations.*

PHRASES

| **smile/grin broadly** to have a big smile on your face: *Rob came into the room grinning broadly.*

broad-minded /,brɔːd'maɪndɪd◂ $,brɒːd-/ *adj* willing to accept behaviour or ideas that are very different from your own OPP **narrow-minded**

broadsheet /'brɔːdʃiːt $ 'brɒːd-/ *n* [C] a serious newspaper printed on large sheets of paper → **tabloid** THESAURUS **NEWSPAPER**

broadside /'brɔːdsaɪd $ 'brɒːd-/ *n* [C] a strong criticism of someone or something

brocade /brə'keɪd $ broʊ-/ *n* [U] thick cloth that has a pattern of gold and silver threads

broccoli /'brɒkəli $ 'brɑː-/ *n* [U] a vegetable with green stems and green or purple flowers → see picture on page A5

brochure /'brəʊʃə, -ʃʊə $ broʊ'ʃʊr/ *n* [C] a thin book that gives information or advertises something: *a holiday brochure*

broil /brɔɪl/ *v* [T] *AmE* to cook something under or over direct heat SYN **grill** *BrE*: *broiled chicken*

broiler /'brɔɪlə $ -ər/ *n* [C] *AmE* a special area of a STOVE used for cooking food under direct heat SYN **grill** *BrE*

broke¹ /brəʊk $ broʊk/ *adj* [not before noun] *informal* having no money at all: *I can't pay you now – I'm broke.* THESAURUS **POOR**

PHRASES

| **go broke** if a business goes broke, it has to close because it has no money: *A lot of businesses went broke during the recession.*

broke² *v* the past tense of BREAK

broken¹ /'brəʊkən $ 'broʊ-/ *adj*

1 DAMAGED damaged or in small pieces because of being hit, dropped etc: *Be careful of the broken glass.* | **a broken arm/leg etc** (=one in which the bone is badly damaged) | *Wrap the plates up so they won't get broken.*

2 NOT WORKING a machine or piece of equipment that is broken does not work: *The CD player's broken.*

3 NOT CONTINUOUS not continuous: *a broken white line* | *Expect broken sleep in your baby's early months.*

4 HOME/MARRIAGE **broken home/family/marriage** a family in which the husband and wife have ended their relationship and do not live together any more: *a broken marriage* | *kids from broken homes*

5 LANGUAGE **broken English/French etc** if you speak in broken English, French etc, you speak the language slowly and not very well

6 SAD **a broken heart** a feeling of great sadness, especially because someone you love has died or left you: *She died of a broken heart.*

THESAURUS

not working

broken a machine or piece of equipment that is broken does not work: *The heater's broken.*

there's something wrong with sth used when saying that a car, machine etc is not working properly and you do not know why: *There's something wrong with my car – it's making a funny noise.*

out of order if a machine used by the public is out of order, it is not working for a temporary period: *The toilet is out of order.*

down if a computer system is down, it is not working: *I'm afraid we can't help you – our computer system is down at the moment.*

broken² *v* the past participle of BREAK

broken-'down *adj* not working or in bad condition: *a broken-down truck*

broken-'hearted *adj* very sad, especially because someone you love has died or left you

broker¹ /'brəukə $ 'brəukər/ *n* [C] someone whose job is to buy and sell property, insurance etc for someone else: *a real estate broker* → **STOCKBROKER**

broker² *v* **broker a deal/settlement/treaty etc** to arrange the details of a plan, plan etc so that everyone can agree to it: *an agreement brokered by the UN*

brolly /'brɒli $ 'brɑːli/ *n* [C] (*plural* **brollies**) *BrE informal* an UMBRELLA

bronchitis /brɒŋ'kaɪtɪs $ brɑːŋ-/ *n* [U] an illness that affects your breathing and makes you cough

bronze /brɒnz $ brɑːnz/ *n* [U] **1** a dark red-brown metal **2** a dark reddish brown colour —**bronze** *adj*: *a bronze statue*

bronzed /brɒnzd $ brɑːnzd/ *adj* having skin that is attractively brown because you have been in the sun

bronze 'medal *n* [C] a prize, especially a round piece of bronze, that is given to someone who comes third in a race or competition

brooch /brəutʃ $ brəutʃ/ *n* [C] a piece of jewellery that you fasten to your clothes with a pin

brood¹ /bruːd/ *v* [I] to keep thinking about something that you are worried, angry, or upset about: [+over/about/on] *You can't just sit there brooding over your problems.*

brood² *n* [C] a family of young birds

brook¹ /brʊk/ *n* [C] a small stream

brook² *v* **not brook sth/brook no sth** *formal* to not allow or accept something

broom /bruːm, brʊm/ *n* [C] a brush with a long handle, used for sweeping floors → see picture at MOP²

broomstick /'bruːmstɪk, 'brʊm-/ *n* [C] the type of broom that a WITCH is supposed to fly on, in stories

broth /brɒθ $ brɔːθ/ *n* [U] soup made with meat or vegetables: *chicken broth*

brothel /'brɒθəl $ 'brɑː-, 'brɔː-/ *n* [C] a house where men pay to have sex with PROSTITUTES

brother /'brʌðə $ -ər/ *n* [C]
1 a man or boy who has the same parents as you → **sister**: *Sam was playing with his little brother.*
2 a man who belongs to the same race, religion, organization etc as you
3 a man who is a member of a religious group, especially a MONK

COLLOCATIONS

older/elder brother *This is Will, my older brother.*
younger brother *I have a younger brother and an older sister.*
big brother (=an older brother – used especially by children) *My big brother always looks after me.*
little brother (=a younger brother – used especially by children) *Why is your little brother crying?*
baby brother *Lucy has a new baby brother.*
twin brother *Tom is Brendan's twin brother.*

brotherhood /'brʌðəhʊd $ -ər-/ *n* **1** [U] a feeling of friendship between people: *the spirit of brotherhood* **2** [C] an organization of people who share the same political or religious ideas

'brother-in-law *n* [C] (*plural* **brothers-in-law**) **1** the brother of your husband or wife **2** the husband of your sister

brotherly /'brʌðəli $ -ər-/ *adj* **brotherly love/ feeling** the kind of love or feeling you expect a brother to show

brought /brɔːt $ brɔːt/ *v* the past tense and past participle of BRING

brow /braʊ/ *n* [C] **1** *literary* the part of your face above your eyes and below your hair SYN **forehead 2** an EYEBROW **3 the brow of a hill** *BrE* the top part of a hill

browbeat /'braʊbiːt/ *v* [T] (*past tense* **browbeat**, *past participle* **browbeaten** /-biːtn/) to try to force someone to do something, especially in a threatening way

brown¹ /braʊn/ *adj*
1 having the colour of earth, wood, or coffee: *brown shoes* | *Jenny has light brown hair.*
2 having skin that has become darker in the sun: *You look brown. Have you been on holiday?* —**brown** *n* [C,U]: *Is the jacket available in brown?*

brown² *v* [I,T] if food browns, or if you brown it, you cook the food until it is brown

brownfield site /'braʊnfiːld ˌsaɪt/ *n* [C] *BrE* land in a city that used to have factories etc on it, but is now used for building new houses → **greenfield site**

brownie /'braʊni/ *n* [C] **1** a thick flat chocolate cake **2 Brownie** a young member of the Guides

browse /braʊz/ *v*
1 IN A SHOP [I] to look at the goods in a shop without looking for a particular thing to buy: *'Can I help you?' 'No thanks. I'm just browsing.'*
2 BOOK/MAGAZINE [I] to look through a book or magazine without a particular purpose: [+through] *I was browsing through the catalogue.*
3 INTERNET [I,T] to search for information on a computer or on the Internet

browser /'braʊzə $ -ər/ n [C] a computer program that finds information on the Internet and shows it on your computer screen: *a Web browser*

bruise /bruːz/ n [C] a dark mark on your skin where you have fallen, been hit etc **THESAURUS** HURT —**bruise** v [T]: *He fell and bruised his knee.* —**bruising** n [U]

brunch /brʌntʃ/ n [C,U] a meal eaten in the late morning, instead of breakfast and LUNCH

brunette /bruːˈnet/ n [C] a woman with dark brown hair

brunt /brʌnt/ n **bear/take the brunt of sth** to suffer the worst part of something unpleasant: *I had to bear the brunt of his anger.*

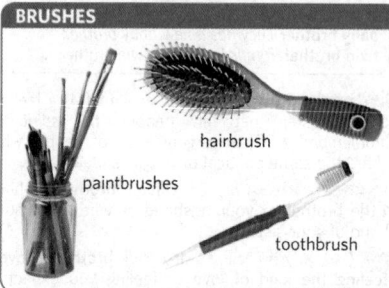

BRUSHES

hairbrush

paintbrushes

toothbrush

brush¹ /brʌʃ/ n
1 [C] a thing that you use for cleaning, painting, tidying your hair etc → **broom**: *a scrubbing brush | a brush and comb*
2 [singular] a movement of brushing something: *I'll just give my hair a quick brush.*
3 [U] small bushes and trees that cover an area
4 brush with sth a time when something unpleasant almost happens to you: *a brush with death | His first brush with the law occurred when he was a teenager.*
→ **HAIRBRUSH, NAILBRUSH, PAINTBRUSH, TOOTHBRUSH**

brush² v
1 [T] to clean something or make something smooth and tidy, using a brush → **sweep**: *Go brush your teeth. | Ella brushed her hair slowly.*
2 [T] to remove something with a brush or your hand: **brush sth off/from sth** *She brushed the crumbs off her lap. |* **brush sth away** *He brushed his tears away.*
3 [I,T] to touch someone or something lightly as you go past them: *Something brushed his shoulders. |* **[+against/past]** *Her hair brushed against my arm.*
PHRASAL VERBS
brush sb/sth ↔ **aside/off** to refuse to listen to someone or what they say, especially by ignoring them: *He brushed aside her accusations.*
brush up (on) sth to practise your skill or knowledge of something so that you are as good at it as you were in the past: *I have to brush up on my French before I go to Paris.*

'brush-off n [singular] *informal* rude or unfriendly behaviour that shows you are not interested in someone: *She gave me the brush-off.*

brusque /bruːsk, brʊsk $ brʌsk/ adj using very few

words when you speak, in a way that seems rude: *a brusque manner* —**brusquely** adv

Brussels sprout /ˌbrʌsəlz ˈspraʊt/ n [C] a small round green vegetable → see picture on page A5

brutal /'bruːtl/ adj **1** very cruel and violent: *a brutal attack* **THESAURUS** VIOLENT **2** not pleasant and not sensitive to people's feelings: *He replied with brutal honesty.* —**brutally** adv: *He was brutally murdered.* —**brutality** /bruːˈtæləti/ n [C,U]

brutalize (*also* **-ise** *BrE*) /'bruːtəl-aɪz/ v [T] to make someone violent, cruel, and unable to feel sympathy: *the brutalizing effects of war*

brute¹ /bruːt/ n [C] a cruel violent man

brute² adj **brute force/strength** physical strength rather than intelligence and careful thinking

BSc /ˌbiː es ˈsiː/ *BrE*, **B.S.** /ˌbiː ˈes/ *AmE* n [C] Bachelor of Science; a university degree in a science subject

BSE /ˌbiː es ˈiː/ n [U] (**bovine spongiform encepha-lopathy**) a disease of the brain that affects cows and usually kills them

BTW the written abbreviation of **by the way**, used in email or TEXT MESSAGES

bubble¹ /'bʌbəl/ n [C] a ball of air or gas in a liquid: **[+of]** *A few bubbles of air rose to the surface of the water. | champagne bubbles*

bubble² v [I] **1** to produce bubbles: *Heat the sauce until it starts to bubble.* **2** (*also* **bubble over**) to be excited: **[+with]** *Mary was bubbling over with excitement.*

'bubble bath n [U] a liquid soap that smells nice and makes bubbles in your bath water

'bubble gum n [U] a type of CHEWING GUM that you can blow into a bubble

bubbly /'bʌbli/ adj **1** cheerful and full of energy: *a bubbly personality* **2** full of bubbles

buck¹ /bʌk/ n [C] **1** *informal* a US, Canadian, or Australian dollar: *Could you lend me 20 bucks? | He was just trying to* **make a buck** (=earn some money). **2** the male of some animals, for example DEER and rabbits
PHRASES
| **pass the buck** to make someone else responsible for something that you should deal with

buck² v [I] if a horse bucks, it kicks its back feet into the air, or jumps with all four feet off the ground

bucket /'bʌkɪt/ n [C]
1 a round open container with a handle over the top, used for carrying things, especially liquids → see picture at MOP²
2 (*also* **bucketful** /-fʊl/) the amount that a bucket holds: **[+of]** *a bucket of water*

buckle¹ /'bʌkəl/ v **1** [I,T] to bend because of heat or pressure, or to make something bend in this way: *The front wheel on my bike had buckled.* **2** [I] if your knees or legs buckle, they become weak and bend **3** (*also* **buckle up**) [I,T] to fasten a buckle or be fastened with a buckle: **buckle sth on** *He buckled on his sword.*

B

PHRASAL VERBS

buckle down *informal* to start working seriously: *You'd better buckle down or you'll never pass your exams.*

buckle² *n* [C] a thing made of metal, used for fastening a belt, shoe, bag etc → see picture at WATCH²

bud /bʌd/ *n* [C] a young flower or leaf before it opens → see picture at PLANT¹

Buddhism /'bʊdɪzəm $ 'buː-, 'bʊ-/ *n* [U] a religion of east and central Asia, based on the teaching of Buddha —**Buddhist** *n* [C] —**Buddhist** *adj*

budding /'bʌdɪŋ/ *adj* beginning to develop or be successful: *a budding relationship | a budding artist*

buddy /'bʌdi/ *n* [C] (*plural* **buddies**) *informal* a friend: *We're good buddies.*

budge /bʌdʒ/ *v* [I,T] *informal* **1** if someone or something does not budge, they do not move, or you cannot make them move: *The car won't budge.* | [+from] *Mark hasn't budged from his room all day.* **THESAURUS** MOVE 2 if someone will not budge or be budged, they refuse to change their opinion: *Once Dad's made up his mind, he won't budge.*

budgerigar /'bʌdʒərɪgɑː $ -gɑːr/ *n* [C] *BrE* a small brightly coloured bird that people keep as a pet

budget¹ /'bʌdʒɪt/ *n* [C] **1** the money that is available to an organization or person, or a plan of how it will be spent: [+of] *We have a budget of £100 a week for food.* | **defence/education/training etc budget** *an increase in the public health budget* | **over/under budget** (=spending more or less than what was planned) *The project's gone over budget again.* | *The mayor is raising taxes in order to **balance the budget** * (=not spend more than is available). | *families **on a tight budget*** (=with only a small amount of money to spend) **2** (*also* **Budget**) *BrE* an official statement that a government makes about how much it intends to spend and what taxes will be necessary

budget² *v* [I] to carefully plan and control how you will spend your money: [+for] *We've budgeted for a new car next year.*

budget³ *adj* very low in price – used in advertisements: *a budget flight* **THESAURUS** CHEAP

budgetary /'bʌdʒətəri $ -teri/ *adj* relating to a budget: *budgetary control*

budgie /'bʌdʒi/ *n* [C] a BUDGERIGAR

buff¹ /bʌf/ *n* [C] **wine/computer/opera etc buff** someone who is interested in wine, computers etc and knows a lot about them

buff² (*also* **buff up**) *v* [T] to polish something with a cloth

buffalo /'bʌfələʊ $ -loʊ/ *n* [C] (*plural* **buffaloes** *or* **buffalo**) an animal that looks like a cow with very long horns

buffer /'bʌfə $ -ər/ *n* [C] someone or something that helps to protect a person or thing from being harmed or damaged: [+against] *Support from friends provides a buffer against stress.* —**buffer** *v* [T]

buffet¹ /'bʊfeɪ $ bə'feɪ/ *n* [C] a meal in which people get their own food from a table and then move away to eat

buffet² /'bʌfɪt/ *v* [T usually passive] if wind, rain, or the sea buffets something, it hits it with a lot of force: *Chicago was buffeted by storms last night.*

buffet car /'bʊfeɪ kɑː $ bə'feɪ kɑːr/ *n* [C] *BrE* the part of a train where you can buy food and drink

buffoon /bə'fuːn/ *n* [C] *old-fashioned* someone who does silly things that make you laugh

bug¹ /bʌg/ *n* [C]
1 ILLNESS *informal* an illness that people get very easily from each other but is not very serious: *There's **a nasty bug going round*** (=which a lot of people have caught). | *a **stomach bug*** (=illness affecting your stomach) **THESAURUS** ILLNESS
2 INSECT a small insect
3 COMPUTERS a small mistake in a computer program that stops it from working correctly: *There's a bug in the system.* **THESAURUS** FAULT
4 SECRET DEVICE a small piece of electronic equipment for listening secretly to other people's conversations
5 INTEREST *informal* a strong interest in doing something: **the travel/acting etc bug** *She's got the sailing bug.*

bug² *v* [T] (**bugged**, **bugging**) **1** *spoken* to annoy someone: *Stop bugging me!* **2** to use electronic equipment to listen secretly to other people's conversations

buggy /'bʌgi/ *n* [C] (*plural* **buggies**) *BrE* a light folding chair on wheels that you push small children in **SYN** **stroller** *AmE*

bugle /'bjuːgəl/ *n* [C] a musical instrument like a TRUMPET —**bugler** *n* [C]

BUILD

build

assemble   construct

build¹ /bɪld/ *v* (*past tense and past participle* **built** /bɪlt/)
1 [I,T] to make a building, road, bridge etc: *They're building new houses for local people.* | *The Brooklyn Bridge was built in the 1870s.* | **be built of sth** *Most churches were built of stone.* | [+on] *Are there any plans to build on that land?* **THESAURUS** MAKE
2 (*also* **build up**) [T] to develop something slowly: *She had **built a reputation** as a criminal lawyer.* | *My father **built up the business** himself.*

build

PHRASAL VERBS

build sth **into** sth

1 to make something a permanent part of a wall, room etc: *There are three cash machines built into the wall.*

2 to make something a permanent part of a system, agreement etc

build on sth

1 to use something you have done as a base for achieving more: *We hope to build on what we learned last year.*

2 build sth on sth to base something on an idea or feeling: *Our relationship is built on trust.*

build up

1 if something builds up, it gradually increases: *Excitement was building up inside her.*

2 build sb's hopes up to make someone think they will get what they want, when in fact it is unlikely: *Don't build her hopes up.*

THESAURUS

build to make a building, bridge, road etc: *When was your house built?*

construct to build a large building, bridge, road etc. **Construct** is more formal than **build**: *The company plans to construct a new factory on the site.*

put up/erect to build a wall, fence, building, or STATUE. **Erect** is more formal than **put up**: *The neighbours have put up a new wooden fence. | A monument was erected in his honour.*

assemble to put all the parts of something together: *The furniture is easy to assemble.*

---

build² *n* [singular, U] the shape and size of someone's body: *Maggie's tall with a slim build.*

builder /ˈbɪldə $ -ər/ *n* [C] especially BrE a person or a company that builds or repairs buildings

building /ˈbɪldɪŋ/ *n*

1 [C] a structure such as a house, church, or factory that has a roof and walls

2 [U] the process or business of building things: *land used for building* → BODY BUILDING

COLLOCATIONS

types of building

a tall building *We walked through a narrow alley between tall buildings.*

a brick/stone/wooden building *The town hall is a large brick building.*

an office/apartment/school etc building *They live in an apartment building near the park.*

a high-rise building (=very tall with many floors) *His office is on the top floor of a high-rise building.*

a single-storey/two-storey etc building (=with one/two etc floors) *Her house is a modern, single-storey building.*

a historic building *The city is full of historic buildings.*

verbs

to put up a building (*also* **to erect a building** formal) *They are not allowed to put up any new buildings here.*

to knock down/demolish a building *Many of the old buildings were knocked down after the war.*

ˈbuilding ˌblock *n* [C] a block of wood or plastic for young children to build things with

PHRASES

building blocks [plural] the pieces or parts which together make it possible for something big or important to exist: *Reading and writing are the building blocks of our education.*

ˈbuilding ˌsite *n* [C] a place where a house, factory etc is being built

ˈbuilding soˌciety *n* [C] BrE a type of bank where you can save money or borrow money to buy a house

ˈbuild-up *n* [C usually singular] **1** a gradual increase: [+of] *The build-up of traffic is causing major problems in cities.* **2** the length of time spent preparing for an event: [+to] *the long build-up to the opening of the new mall*

built /bɪlt/ *v* the past tense and past participle of BUILD

ˌbuilt-ˈin *adj* fixed permanently somewhere and not possible to remove: *built-in cupboards*

ˌbuilt-ˈup *adj* a built-up area has a lot of buildings and not many open spaces

bulb /bʌlb/ *n* [C] **1** the glass part of an electric light, where the light shines from: *a 60 watt bulb* **2** a round root that grows into a plant: *tulip bulbs* → see picture at PLANT¹

bulbous /ˈbʌlbəs/ *adj* fat and unattractive: *a bulbous nose*

bulge¹ /bʌldʒ/ *n* [C] a curved place on the surface of something, caused by something under or inside it: *The gun made a bulge under his jacket.*

bulge² (*also* **bulge out**) *v* [I] to stick out in a rounded shape: *Jeffrey's stomach bulged over his trousers. | [+with] Her eyes were bulging with fear.*

bulimia /bjuːˈlɪmiə, bʊ-, -ˈliː-/ *n* [U] an illness in which someone eats too much and then deliberately VOMITs as a way of controlling their weight —**bulimic** *adj*

bulk Ac /bʌlk/ *n* **1 the bulk (of sth)** the main or largest part of something: *The bulk of the work has already been done.* **2** [U] the size of something or someone, especially a large size: *His bulk made it difficult for him to move quickly enough.*

PHRASES

in bulk in large quantities: *It's cheaper to buy things in bulk.*

bulky Ac /ˈbʌlki/ *adj* big and difficult to move: *a bulky package*

bull /bʊl/ *n* [C] a male cow, or the male of some other large animal such as an ELEPHANT

bulldog /ˈbʊldɒg $ -dɔːg/ *n* [C] a powerful dog with a short neck and short thick legs

bulldoze /ˈbʊldəʊz $ -doʊz/ *v* [T] to destroy buildings or move earth and rocks with a bulldozer

bulldozer /ˈbʊldəʊzə $ -doʊzər/ *n* [C] a large

powerful vehicle used for destroying buildings or moving earth and rocks

bullet /'bʊlɪt/ n [C] a small piece of metal that is fired from a gun: *He was killed by a single bullet.* | *a bullet wound in the shoulder*

bulletin /'bʊlətɪn/ n [C] **1** a short news report on television or radio: *Our next news bulletin is at six o'clock.* **2** a regular letter or report that an organization produces to tell people its news

'bulletin ,board n [C] **1** AmE a board on a wall where you can put information for people to see SYN **noticeboard** BrE → see picture at **CLASSROOM** **2** a place in a computer system where you can leave or read messages

'bullet point n [C] a thing in a list, with a symbol in front of it

'bullet-,proof adj made of a material that stops bullets from going through it: *bullet-proof glass*

bullfight /'bʊlfaɪt/ n [C] a type of entertainment popular in Spain, in which a man fights and often kills a BULL —**bullfighter** n [C] —**bullfighting** n [U]

bullhorn /'bʊlhɔːn $ -hɔːrn/ n [C] AmE old-fashioned a piece of equipment that you hold up to your mouth to make your voice louder SYN **megaphone**

bullion /'bʊljən/ n [U] bars of gold or silver

bullish /'bʊlɪʃ/ adj feeling confident about the future: *He's bullish about the company's prospects.*

bullock /'bʊlək/ n [C] a young male cow

bully¹ /'bʊli/ v [T] (**bullied, bullying, bullies**) to deliberately frighten or upset someone who is smaller or weaker than you, especially to make them do something you want: **bully sb into (doing) sth** *He had bullied his wife into giving up her career.* —**bullying** n [U]

bully² n [C] (plural **bullies**) someone who deliberately frightens or upsets a person who is smaller or weaker than they are

'bull's-eye n [C] the point in the exact centre of an object that you try to hit when shooting or in a game like DARTS

bum¹ /bʌm/ n [C] informal **1** BrE the part of your body that you sit on SYN **bottom 2** AmE someone who has no home or job

bum² v [T] (**bummed, bumming**) informal to ask someone if you can borrow or have something: *Can I bum a cigarette?*

PHRASAL VERBS

bum around (sth) informal to travel around, living very cheaply, without having any plans: *I spent the summer bumming around Europe.*

bumblebee /'bʌmbəlbiː/ n [C] a large BEE

bumbling /'bʌmblɪŋ/ adj [only before noun] not clever or skilful, and making a lot of mistakes

bumf /bʌmf/ n [U] BrE informal boring written information that you have to read

bummer /'bʌmə $ -ər/ n **a bummer** informal a situation that is disappointing or annoying

bump¹ /bʌmp/ v **1** [I,T] to hit or knock against something, especially by accident: *Mind you don't*

bump your head! | **[+into/against]** *It was so dark I bumped into a tree.* **2** [I] to move in an uneven way because the ground is not smooth: **[+along]** *The truck bumped along the rough track.*

PHRASAL VERBS

bump into sb informal to meet someone when you were not expecting to: *Guess who I bumped into this morning?*

bump sb ↔ off informal to kill someone

bump sth ↔ up informal to increase something: *In the summer they bump up the prices by 10 per cent.*

bump² n [C] **1** a hard lump on your skin where you have hit it on something: **[+on]** *Derek's got a nasty bump on his head.* **2** a small raised area on a surface: **[+in]** *a bump in the road* **3** a movement in which one thing hits against another thing, or the sound that this makes: *Danny sat down with a bump.*

bumper¹ /'bʌmpə $ -ər/ n [C] the bar across the front and back of a car that protects it if it hits anything

bumper² adj [only before noun] larger than usual: *a bumper crop*

'bumper ,sticker n [C] a small sign with a message on it on the bumper of a car

bumpy /'bʌmpi/ adj not smooth: *a bumpy road* THESAURUS ▶ ROUGH

bun /bʌn/ n [C] **1** BrE a small sweet cake: *We had iced buns for tea.* **2** bread that is made in a small round shape: *a hamburger bun* **3** a way of arranging long hair by fastening it in a round shape on the top of your head → see picture at **HAIR**

BUNCH

a bunch of flowers   a bunch of grapes

bunch¹ /bʌntʃ/ n

1 THINGS [C] a group of things that are held or joined together: **[+of]** *a bunch of grapes* | *a beautiful bunch of violets* THESAURUS ▶ GROUP

2 PEOPLE [singular] informal a group of people: *My class are a really nice bunch.* | **[+of]** *a bunch of idiots*

3 LOTS [singular] AmE informal a large amount: **[+of]** *The doctor asked me a bunch of questions.*

4 HAIR **bunches** [plural] BrE if a girl wears her hair in bunches, she ties it together at each side of her head

bunch² (also **bunch up, bunch together**) v [I,T] **1** to stay close together in a group, or to make a group: *The children were bunched together by the door.* **2** to pull material together tightly in folds: *My skirt got all bunched up in the car.*

bundle¹ /'bʌndl/ n [C] a group of things that are

fastened or tied together: **[+of]** *a bundle of newspapers* **THESAURUS** GROUP

PHRASES

be a bundle of nerves/fun etc *informal* to be very nervous, a lot of fun etc: *She was a bundle of nerves before the race.*

bundle² *v* [T] to make someone move by pushing them roughly: **bundle sb into/through/out of etc** *The police bundled Jason into the back of the van.*

PHRASAL VERBS

bundle sth ↔ **up** to make a bundle by tying things together: *Bundle up the newspapers and we'll take them to be recycled.*

bung¹ /bʌŋ/ *n* [C] *BrE* a round piece of rubber, wood etc used to close the top of a container

bung² *v* [T] *BrE informal* to put something somewhere quickly and carelessly: **bung sth in/on etc** *Bung the butter in the fridge, will you?*

PHRASAL VERBS

bung sth ↔ **up** *informal* **1** to block a hole by putting something in it **2 be bunged up** to be unable to breathe through your nose because you have a cold

bungalow /'bʌŋɡələʊ $ -loʊ/ *n* [C] a house that is built on one level → see picture at **HOUSE¹**
THESAURUS HOUSE

bungee jumping /'bʌndʒi ˌdʒʌmpɪŋ/ *n* [U] a sport in which you jump off something very high with a long length of ELASTIC (=rope that stretches) tied to your legs, so that you do not hit the ground —**bungee jump** *n* [C] —**bungee jumper** *n* [C]

bungle /'bʌŋɡəl/ *v* [T] to do something badly: *The builders bungled the job completely.* —**bungling** *n* [U]

bunk /bʌŋk/ *n* [C] a narrow bed on a train or ship, which is joined to the wall → see picture at **BED**

PHRASES

bunk beds two beds that are one on top of the other

do a bunk *BrE informal* to suddenly leave a place without telling anyone: *Ivor was planning to do a bunk.*

bunker /'bʌŋkə $ -ər/ *n* [C] **1** a strongly built room under the ground, built to protect people from bombs **2** *BrE* a wide hole on a GOLF COURSE filled with sand **SYN** **sandtrap** *AmE*

bunny /'bʌni/ (*also* **bunny ˌrabbit**) *n* [C] (*plural* **bunnies**) a rabbit – used especially by children or when you are talking to children

buoy¹ /bɔɪ $ 'buːi, bɔɪ/ *n* [C] an object that floats on the sea to show which parts are safe or dangerous

buoy² (*also* **buoy up**) *v* [T] to make someone feel happier or more confident: *Jill was buoyed up by success.*

buoyant /'bɔɪənt $ 'bɔɪənt, 'buːjənt/ *adj* **1** happy and confident: *Bob was in a buoyant mood.* **2** buoyant prices or profits are at a high level **3** able to float —**buoyancy** *n* [U]

burble /'bɜːbəl $ 'bɜːr-/ *v* [I,T] to make a sound like a stream flowing over stones

burden¹ /'bɜːdn $ 'bɜːrdn/ *n* [C] **1** something difficult or worrying that you have to deal with: **[+on]** *I don't want to be a burden on my children when I'm old.* **2** *formal* something heavy that you have to carry

burden² *v* [T] **1** to cause a lot of problems for someone: **burden sb with sth** *We won't burden her with any more responsibility.* **2 be burdened (down) with sth** to be carrying something very heavy: *She struggled up the hill, burdened down with shopping.*

bureau /'bjʊərəʊ $ 'bjʊroʊ/ *n* [C] (*plural* **bureaus** or **bureaux** /-rəʊz $ -roʊz/) **1** an office or organization that collects or provides information: *an employment bureau* **2** *especially AmE* a government department: *the Federal Bureau of Investigation* **3** *BrE* a piece of furniture with drawers and a sloping lid that you can open and use as a desk

bureaucracy /bjʊəˈrɒkrəsi $ bjʊˈrɑː-/ *n* (*plural* **bureaucracies**) **1** [U] an official system that is annoying or confusing because it has too many rules and takes too long to make decisions **2** [C,U] the officials in a government or business who are employed and not elected

bureaucrat /'bjʊərəkræt $ 'bjʊr-/ *n* [C] someone who works in a government organization and uses official rules very strictly

bureaucratic /ˌbjʊərəˈkrætɪk◂ $ ˌbjʊr-/ *adj* involving a lot of official rules and processes

burgeoning /'bɜːdʒənɪŋ $ 'bɜːr-/ *adj formal* growing quickly: *the burgeoning market for digital cameras*

burger /'bɜːɡə $ 'bɜːrɡər/ *n* [C] a mixture of meat or vegetables that is made into a round flat shape and cooked

burglar /'bɜːɡlə $ 'bɜːrɡlər/ *n* [C] someone who goes into buildings in order to steal things
THESAURUS THIEF

'burglar aˌlarm *n* [C] a piece of equipment that makes a loud noise when a burglar gets into a building

burglarize /'bɜːɡləraɪz $ 'bɜːr-/ *v* [T] *AmE* to go into a building and steal things **THESAURUS** STEAL

burglary /'bɜːɡləri $ 'bɜːr-/ *n* [C,U] (*plural* **burglaries**) the crime of going into a building in order to steal things **THESAURUS** CRIME

burgle /'bɜːɡəl $ 'bɜːr-/ *v* [T] *BrE* to go into a building and steal things: *Their house was burgled while they were away.* **THESAURUS** STEAL

burgundy /'bɜːɡəndi $ 'bɜːr-/ *adj* dark red

burial /'beriəl/ *n* [C,U] when a dead body is put into the ground

burly /'bɜːli $ 'bɜːrli/ *adj* a burly man is big and strong

burn¹ /bɜːn $ bɜːrn/ *v* (*past tense and past participle* **burnt** /bɜːnt $ bɜːrnt/ *or* **burned**)

1 DAMAGE WITH FIRE/HEAT [T] to damage or destroy something with fire or heat: *We can burn all this rubbish.* | *The iron had **burnt a hole in** my shirt.*

2 INJURE WITH FIRE/HEAT [T] to hurt yourself or someone else with fire or something hot: **burn sb/sth on sth** *I burnt my hand on the iron.* | *She was **badly burned** in a road accident.*

3 PRODUCE FLAMES [I] to produce heat and flames: *Is*

the fire still burning? | My toast is burning!

4 SUN [I,T] if the sun burns your skin, or if your skin burns, it becomes red and painful from the heat of the sun: Don't forget, you can still **get burned** when it's cloudy.

5 FUEL [T] if something burns a FUEL, it uses it to produce power, heat or light: The car burns a lot of fuel.

6 FEEL HOT [I,T] if a part of your body is burning, or if something burns it, it feels unpleasantly hot: My eyes were burning from the smoke.

7 LIGHT [I] literary if a light or lamp is burning, it is shining

8 CD [T] to put music, images, or other information onto a CD or DVD

9 UPSET **be/get burned** to have your feelings hurt: It's not the first time he's been burned.

10 LOSE MONEY **be/get burned** informal to lose a lot of money, especially in a business deal: She got burned when the company went out of business. —**burned** adj

PHRASAL VERBS

burn down if a building burns down or is burned down, it is destroyed by fire: **burn sth ↔ down** The old church was burned down.

burn sth ↔ **off**

1 to use energy that is stored in your body by doing physical exercise: I decided to go for a run to try and burn off a few calories.

2 to remove something by burning it

burn (itself) **out** if a fire burns out, it stops burning because there is no coal, wood etc left

burn up if something burns up or is burned up, it is completely destroyed by fire: **burn sth ↔ up** Most of the woodland has now been burnt up.

THESAURUS

burn to produce heat and flames: A warm fire was burning in the sitting room.

be on fire if a building, car, piece of clothing etc is on fire, it is burning and the fire is damaging it: The car's engine was on fire.

catch fire to start burning accidentally: A shop caught fire after a customer dropped a cigarette.

burst into flames to start producing a lot of flames very suddenly, in a way that causes a lot of damage: The plane crashed and burst into flames.

smoulder BrE, **smolder** AmE to burn slowly and continuously, producing smoke but no flames: In the garden, the fire was still smouldering.

---

burn² n [C] an injury or mark caused by fire or heat → **sunburn**: Many of the victims suffered severe burns.

burned 'out (also **burnt 'out**) adj **1** tired or ill because you have been working too hard: I was completely burned out after my exams. **2** a burned out building or car has had the inside of it destroyed by fire

burner /'bɜːnə $ 'bɜːrnər/ n [C] the top part of a COOKER that produces heat or a flame

PHRASES

put sth on the back burner informal to delay dealing with something until a later time: The government quietly put the scheme on the back burner.

burning /'bɜːnɪŋ $ 'bɜːr-/ adj **1** on fire: a burning house **2** feeling very hot: burning cheeks **3 burning ambition/need etc** a very strong wish, need etc **4 burning question/issue** a very important question that must be dealt with

burnished /'bɜːnɪʃt $ 'bɜːr-/ adj burnished metal has been rubbed until it shines —**burnish** v [T]

burnt¹ /bɜːnt $ bɜːrnt/ v a past tense and past participle of BURN

burnt² adj damaged or hurt by burning: Sorry the toast is a little burnt.

burnt 'out adj BURNED OUT

burp /bɜːp $ bɜːrp/ v [I] informal if you burp, gas comes up from your stomach and makes a noise —**burp** n [C]

burrow¹ /'bʌrəʊ $ 'bɜːroʊ/ v [I,T] to make a hole or small TUNNEL in the ground: **[+under]** Rabbits had burrowed under the wall.

burrow² n [C] a hole in the ground made by an animal such as a rabbit

bursar /'bɜːsə $ 'bɜːrsər/ n [C] someone at a college or school who is responsible for money that is paid or received

bursary /'bɜːsəri $ 'bɜːr-/ n [C] (plural **bursaries**) BrE money that is given to a student to help them pay for their university studies SYN **scholarship**

burst¹ /bɜːst $ bɜːrst/ v (past tense and past participle **burst**)

1 [I,T] to break open suddenly and violently, or to make something do this: The kids burst all the balloons with pins. | One of the tyres had burst. THESAURUS BREAK

2 be bursting with sth to be very full of something: Rome is always bursting with tourists. | Your mum's **bursting with pride** for you. | Classrooms are **bursting at the seams** (=too full). THESAURUS FULL

3 [I] to move quickly and suddenly: **[+into/through etc]** Jenna burst into the room. | The door **burst open** and 20 or 30 policemen rushed in.

4 be bursting to do sth informal to want to do something very much: Becky's just bursting to tell you her news.

PHRASAL VERBS

burst in on sb/sth to interrupt something by entering a room when people do not expect it: I'm sorry to burst in on you like this. THESAURUS ENTER

burst into sth to suddenly begin doing something: The car hit a tree and **burst into flames** (=began burning). | Ellen **burst into tears** (=began crying).

burst out

1 burst out laughing/crying to suddenly start to laugh or cry

2 to suddenly say something quite loudly: 'I don't believe it!' Duncan burst out.

burst² n [C] **1** a short sudden period of activity or noise: **[+of]** a burst of applause | In a sudden **burst of energy** Denise cleaned the whole house. **2** when something breaks suddenly, or the place where it has broken: a burst in the water pipe

burst³ adj broken, so that liquid or air can get out: a burst pipe | burst blood vessels

bury /'beri/ v [T] (**buried, burying, buries**)
1 to put a dead body into the ground: *She was buried in Woodlawn Cemetery.*
2 to cover something with something else so that it cannot be seen: *The dog was burying a bone.* | **bury sth under sth** *Dad's glasses were buried under a pile of newspapers.*
3 to hide your face by pressing it into something, usually because you are upset: *She **buried her face in** her hands and began to cry.*

bus¹ /bʌs/ n [C] (*plural* **buses**) a large vehicle that people pay to travel on: **on a bus** *All the people on the bus stared at me.* | **by bus** *I usually go to school by bus.*
→ see picture at **TRANSPORT¹**

COLLOCATIONS

verbs

to get/catch a bus *You can get a bus to the airport from here.*

to ride a bus *AmE It was the first time Craig had ridden a bus downtown by himself.*

to go on/take the bus (=to travel by bus) *I usually go on the bus to work.*

to get on/off a bus *A woman with a baby got on the bus.* ⚠ Do not say 'get in a bus'. Say **get on a bus.**

to wait for a bus *I was standing at the bus stop waiting for a bus.*

to miss a bus *If we don't leave now, we'll miss the bus.*

bus + noun

a bus ride/journey *He has a 30-minute bus ride to school.*

a bus stop (=a place where a bus stops for passengers) *Get off at the next bus stop for the museum.*

a bus station (=a place where buses start and finish their journeys) *Dad met me at the bus station.*

bus fare (=the money you pay for a bus journey) *She gave me 50p for my bus fare.*

bus² v [T] (**bussed, bussing** *BrE*, **bused, busing** *AmE*) to take a group of people somewhere in a bus: **bus sb to/into etc** *Many children are being bussed to schools in other areas.*

bush /bʊʃ/ n **1** [C] a plant like a small tree with a lot of branches → **shrub, tree**: *a rose bush* | *The child was hiding in the bushes.* **2 the bush** an area of Australia or Africa that is still wild

bushy /'bʊʃi/ adj bushy hair or fur grows thickly: *a bushy tail*

busily /'bɪzəli/ adv in a busy way: *The class were all busily writing.*

business /'bɪznəs/ n
1 SELLING THINGS [U] the activity of producing or selling goods or services, in order to make money: *You need a lot of money to succeed in business.*
2 HOW MUCH YOU SELL [U] the amount of work a company's doing, or the amount of money a company is making: **business is good/bad/slow etc** *Business is always slow during the winter.*
3 COMPANY [C] an organization that produces or

sells things: *Graham **runs** a printing **business**.* | *a small family business* **THESAURUS** COMPANY
4 FOR YOUR JOB [U] the work that you do as your job to earn money: *Al's gone to Japan **on business** (=as part of his job).* | *a **business trip***
5 STH CONCERNS YOU [U] if something is your business, it concerns you and other people do not have a right to know about it: *'Are you going out with Ben tonight?' **'That's my business.'*** | *It's **none of your business** how much I earn.* | *'Who's that girl you were with?' **'Mind your own business** (=don't ask questions about something that does not concern you).'*
6 THINGS TO DO/DISCUSS [U] things that need to be done or discussed: *Okay, let's **get down to business** (=start doing or discussing something).*
7 SITUATION [singular] a situation or event: *Her divorce was a very upsetting business.* | *Tanya found **the whole business** ridiculous.* → **BIG BUSINESS, SHOW BUSINESS**

PHRASES

go out of business if a company goes out of business, it closes because it is not making enough money: *Many small companies have recently gone out of business.*

have no business doing sth/have no business to do sth to do something you should not be doing: *He was drunk and had no business driving.*

stay in business if a company stays in business, it makes enough money and continues: *Some stores are finding it hard to stay in business.*

COLLOCATIONS

verbs

to do business (=to be involved in buying or selling goods or services) *We do a lot of business with Russia.* ⚠ Do not say 'make business'. Say **do business.**

to go into business (=to start producing or selling something) *She went into business with a friend selling flowers.*

to set up/start up in business *He set up in business as an antiques dealer.*

noun + business

the music/entertainment/computer etc business *It can be very hard to get into the music business.*

business + noun

a business deal *They were discussing a business deal.*

business activities *You have to pay tax on any money you make from your business activities.*

the business world *The business world is changing.*

'business ,class n [U] travelling conditions on an aircraft that are more expensive than the ordinary conditions, but not as expensive as FIRST CLASS

businesslike /'bɪznəslaɪk/ adj sensible and practical in the way you do things: *a businesslike manner*

businessman /'bɪznəsmən/ n [C] (*plural* **businessmen** /-mən/) a man who works in business

businesswoman /'bɪznəs,wʊmən/ n [C] (*plural* **businesswomen** /-,wɪmɪn/) a woman who works in business

busk /bʌsk/ v [I] BrE to play music in a public place to earn money —**busker** n [C]

'bus pass n [C] a special ticket that gives you cheap or free bus travel

'bus stop n [C] a place at the side of a road, marked with a sign, where buses stop for passengers

bust¹ /bʌst/ v [T] (past tense and past participle **bust** or **busted**) informal **1** to break something: Someone's bust my skateboard! **2** if the police bust someone, they find them doing something illegal: He got busted for possession of drugs.

bust² n [C] **1** a woman's breasts, or the measurement around a woman's breasts and back: a 34 inch bust **2** informal a situation in which the police go into a place in order to catch people doing something illegal: a major **drug bust 3** a MODEL of someone's head and shoulders, usually made of stone or metal: [+of] a bust of Shakespeare

bust³ adj informal broken: The TV's bust again.
PHRASES
> **go bust** if a business goes bust, it has to close because it does not have enough money: More and more small businesses are going bust each year.

bustle¹ /'bʌsəl/ n [singular] busy and noisy activity: [+of] the bustle of the big city —**bustling** adj

bustle² v [I] to move around and do things in a busy quick way: [+about/around] Linda was bustling around in the kitchen.

'bust-up n [C] informal a fight or argument

busy¹ /'bɪzi/ adj
1 if you are busy, you have a lot of things to do: Alex is busy studying for his exams. | [+with] I'm busy with a customer at the moment. Can I call you back? | There were lots of activities to **keep** the kids **busy**.
2 a busy time is a time when you have a lot of things that you must do: I've had a really **busy day**. | December is the busiest time of year for shops.
3 a busy place is full of people or vehicles: a busy airport | The roads were very busy this morning.
4 especially AmE a telephone line that is busy is being used [SYN] **engaged** BrE —**busily** adv

THESAURUS

busy if you are busy, you have a lot of things to do. Also used about a time when you have a lot to do: We're busy getting ready for the wedding. | It's been a busy week.
have a lot to do to have a lot of things you need to do: Hurry up, we have a lot to do today.
be rushed off your feet especially BrE to be very busy in a way that is very tiring, because you have too many things to do: Before Christmas, everyone is rushed off their feet.
be snowed under especially BrE to have too many things that you have to deal with, so that you feel that you cannot deal with them all: I can't stop for lunch – I'm completely snowed under.
hectic a hectic time or situation is extremely busy, so that you are always hurrying: The president has a hectic schedule today. | She had a hectic social life.

busy² v (**busied, busying, busies**) **busy yourself with sth** to make yourself busy by doing a particular job or activity: Josh busied himself with cleaning the house.

busybody /'bɪzi,bɒdi $ -,bɑːdi/ n [C] (plural **busybodies**) someone who is too interested in other people's private lives

but¹ /bət; strong bʌt/ linking word
1 used before you say something that is different or surprising: Grandma didn't like the song, but we loved it. | Learning Chinese was difficult, but it meant that I got this job. [THESAURUS] **EXCEPT**
2 used before you give the reason why something did not happen or was not possible: Carla was supposed to come tonight, but her husband took the car.
3 spoken used to show surprise at what someone has just said: 'I have to go tomorrow.' 'But you only just arrived!'
4 spoken used after phrases such as 'excuse me' and 'I'm sorry': Excuse me, but haven't we met before?
PHRASES
> **but then (again) ...** used to add some information that makes what you have just said less surprising: I didn't understand the film. But then I was really tired.

but² prep except: Joe can come any day but Monday. | Nobody but Liz knows the truth.

butch /bʊtʃ/ adj an offensive word used to describe a woman who looks, dresses, or behaves like a man

butcher¹ /'bʊtʃə $ -ər/ n [C] **1** someone who owns or works in a shop that sells meat **2 butcher's** a shop that sells meat

butcher² v [T] **1** to kill animals and prepare their meat as food **2** to kill people in a cruel way: Thousands of innocent people were butchered. —**butchery** n [U]

butler /'bʌtlə $ -ər/ n [C] the most important male servant in a big house

butt¹ /bʌt/ n [C] **1** AmE informal the part of your body that you sit on **2** the end of a cigarette after it has been smoked **3 be the butt of sth** to be the person that other people often make jokes about: John is always the butt of the class's jokes. **4** the end of the handle of a gun

butt² v [I,T] to hit or push against someone or something with your head
PHRASAL VERBS
butt in informal to join a conversation or activity without being asked: Sorry, I didn't mean to butt in.

butter¹ /'bʌtə $ -ər/ n [U] a solid yellow food made from cream that you spread on bread or use in cooking: a slice of bread and butter

butter² v [T] to spread butter on something: hot buttered toast
PHRASAL VERBS
butter sb ↔ **up** informal to say nice things to someone so that they will do what you want

buttercup /'bʌtəkʌp $ -ər-/ n [C] a small yellow wild flower

butterfly

butterfly /'bʌtəflaɪ $ -ər-/ n [C] (plural **butterflies**) an insect with large coloured wings → see picture at **INSECT**

PHRASES

have butterflies (in your stomach) informal to feel very nervous: It's natural to have butterflies in your stomach before a first date. **THESAURUS** NERVOUS

buttock /'bʌtək/ n [C usually plural] one of the two parts of your body that you sit on

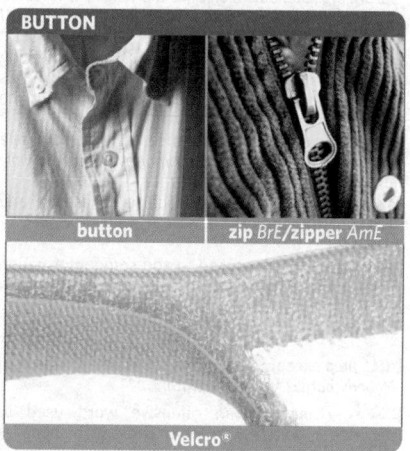

BUTTON

button | zip BrE/zipper AmE

Velcro®

button¹ /'bʌtn/ n [C]
1 ON CLOTHES a small round thing on a shirt, coat etc that you put through a hole to fasten the shirt etc: a jacket with gold buttons | Sam undid (=unfastened) his buttons. | **do up a button** BrE (=fasten a button)
2 ON A MACHINE a small part on a machine that you press to make it start, stop etc: **push/press a button** Just press the 'on' button. | You can close the roof **at the touch of a button**.
3 FOR DECORATION AmE a small piece of metal or plastic with a message or picture on it that you fasten to your clothes SYN **badge** BrE

button² (also **button up**) v [I,T] to fasten something with buttons, or to be fastened with buttons

buttonhole /'bʌtnhəʊl $ -hoʊl/ n [C] a hole which you put a button through

buttress /'bʌtrəs/ v [T] formal to do something to support a system, argument etc

buxom /'bʌksəm/ adj a buxom woman has large breasts

buy¹ /baɪ/ v (past tense and past participle **bought** /bɔːt $ bɒːt/)
1 [I,T] to get something by paying money for it OPP sell: Sam's just bought a new computer. | **buy sb sth** Let me buy you a drink. | **buy sth for sb/sth** He bought a diamond ring for his wife. | **buy sth from sb** I'm buying a car from a friend. | **buy sth for $10/£20 etc** She bought those shoes for £15.
2 [T] informal to believe something that someone tells you: I just don't buy that story.

PHRASES

buy (sb) time informal to make more time for yourself to do something, especially by delaying something: Keep him talking to buy us more time.

PHRASAL VERBS
buy into sth
1 to buy part of a business
2 informal to believe an idea: I don't buy into this idea that women must have perfect bodies.
buy sb ↔ **off** to pay someone to stop causing you trouble
buy sb/sth ↔ **out** to get control of a business by buying all the SHARES in it
buy sth ↔ **up** to quickly buy as much as you can of something: Property developers are buying up all the land in the area.

THESAURUS

buy to get something by paying money for it: I need to buy a new computer.
get to buy something – used especially in spoken English about ordinary things you buy: Can you get me some milk? | Where did you get that tie?
purchase formal to buy something: They purchased the house in 2006. | Tickets may be purchased from the box office.
acquire formal to buy something, especially in order to make money, or as part of a business: The land was acquired by a group of investors.
snap sth up informal to buy something quickly, before other people can buy it: Shoppers are snapping up bargains.
pick sth up informal to buy something, especially without thinking carefully about what you are buying: 'Where did you get the vase?' 'Oh, it's just something I picked up in Venice.'

buy² n **be a good/excellent etc buy** to be something that is good to buy because it is cheap, good quality etc: The Brazilian wine is a good buy.

buyer /'baɪə $ -ər/ n [C] someone who buys something: **[+for]** We've found a buyer for our house.

buyout /'baɪaʊt/ n [C] a situation in which someone gets control of a company by buying all or most of its SHARES

buzz¹ /bʌz/ v [I] **1** to make a continuous noise like the sound of a BEE: a loud buzzing noise **2** to be full of activity, excitement, ideas etc: The office was **buzzing with activity**. | My mind was **buzzing** with new **ideas**.

buzz² n **1** [C] a continuous noise like the sound of a BEE: **[+of]** the buzz of mosquitoes → see picture on page A7 **2** [singular] informal a feeling of excitement or success: I **get a real buzz** from living in New York.

buzzer /'bʌzə $ -ər/ n [C] a small electronic thing that makes a buzzing sound when you press it: **Press your buzzer** if you know the answer.

buzzword /'bʌzwɜːd $ -wɜːrd/ n [C] a word or phrase from a particular area of activity which is fashionable because people think it refers to something important: the latest management buzzwords

B

by /baɪ/ *adv, prep*
1 used to show who did something or what caused something, especially after a PASSIVE verb: *a film made by Steven Spielberg* | *Sylvie was hit by a car.* | **a book/song/painting etc by sb** *a play by Shakespeare*
2 used to say what means or method you use to do something: *Send it by airmail.* | *Hold it by the handle.* | **by doing sth** *Carol earns extra money by babysitting.* | **by car/plane/train/bus etc** *We travelled across India by train.* **THESAURUS** TRAVEL
3 beside or near something: *We sat by the river.*
4 not later than a particular time: *Your report has to be done by 5:00.* **THESAURUS** BEFORE
5 **by mistake/accident/chance** without intending to do something: *Hugh locked the door by mistake.*
6 according to something: **By law**, *you must be over 16 to marry.* | *It's 9.30 by my watch.*
7 past: *Sophie ran by me on her way to the bus.* | *Two cars went by, but nobody stopped.*
8 used to give the measurements of something, or to multiply and divide numbers: *The room is 14 feet by 12 feet.* | *What's 7 multiplied by 8?* | **by the day/metre/hundred etc** (=used to show how the amount of something is measured) *Anne gets paid by the hour.* → **by the way** at WAY¹

PHRASES
(all) by yourself completely alone: *They left the boy by himself for two days!*
by and large used when you are talking generally about something: *By and large, I agree with what he said.*
by day/by night during the day or night: *animals that hunt by night*
day by day/bit by bit/one by one etc used to mean gradually: *Day by day, he grew weaker.*

bye /baɪ/ (*also* ˌbye-ˈbye*) *spoken* goodbye: *Bye Sandy! See you later.*

ˈby-eˌlection *n* [C] *BrE* an election to replace a politician who has left Parliament or died

bygone /ˈbaɪɡɒn $ -ɡɔːn/ *adj* **bygone days/age/era etc** a period of time in the past

bygones /ˈbaɪɡɒnz $ -ɡɔːnz/ *n* **let bygones be bygones** to decide to forget something bad that someone did in the past and to forgive them

bypass¹ /ˈbaɪpɑːs $ -pæs/ *n* [C] **1** a road that takes traffic around the outside of a town: *the Winchester bypass* **THESAURUS** ROAD **2** **(heart) bypass surgery** an operation on someone's heart to make the blood avoid the part that is not working properly

bypass² *v* [T] to go around or avoid something: *The road bypasses the town.* | *Why don't you bypass the agent and contact the seller directly?*

ˈby-ˌproduct *n* [C] **1** something that is made during the process of making something else: **[+of]** *Plutonium is a by-product of nuclear processing.* **2** an unplanned or unexpected result of something: **[+of]** *an unfortunate by-product of the war*

bystander /ˈbaɪˌstændə $ -ər/ *n* [C] someone who is standing, walking etc near something that happens, for example an accident: *Several **innocent bystanders** were killed by the explosion.*

byte /baɪt/ *n* [C] a unit for measuring computer information, equal to eight BITS (=the smallest unit of information)

byword /ˈbaɪwɜːd $ -wɜːrd/ *n* **be/become a byword for sth** to be the name of someone or something that is well-known for having a particular quality: *Hollywood is a byword for glamour.*

B

Cc

C, c /siː/ n [C,U] (plural **C's, c's**) **1** the third letter of the English alphabet **2** the first note in the musical SCALE of C MAJOR, or the musical KEY based on this note **3** a mark given to a student's work to show that it is of average quality: *I got a C in geography.*

C 1 the written abbreviation of **Celsius** or **Centigrade** **2** the written abbreviation of **cent 3** the written abbreviation of **century**

cab /kæb/ n [C] **1** a TAXI: *I took a cab to the airport.* **2** the part of a truck or train where the driver sits

cabaret /'kæbəreɪ $ ˌkæbə'reɪ/ n [C,U] entertainment such as music and dancing performed in a restaurant or club

cabbage /'kæbɪdʒ/ n [C,U] a large round vegetable with thick green or purple leaves → see picture on page A5

cabbie /'kæbi/ n [C] *informal* a taxi driver

cabin /'kæbɪn/ n [C] **1** a small house made of wood: *a log cabin* **2** a small room on a ship where you sleep **3** the area inside a plane where the passengers sit → see picture at **AEROPLANE**

'cabin crew n [plural] the people whose job is to take care of the passengers on a plane → **flight attendant**

cabinet /'kæbɪnɪt/ n [C] **1** a piece of furniture with doors and shelves, used for storing things: *a drinks cabinet* | *a bedside cabinet* **2** (*also* **the Cabinet**) an important group of politicians who make decisions or advise the leader of a government: *a member of the Cabinet* | *cabinet meetings*

cable /'keɪbəl/ n **1** [C,U] a plastic or rubber tube containing wires that carry electronic signals, telephone messages etc: *an underground telephone cable* **2** [U] a system of broadcasting television by using cables under the ground: **on cable** *I'll wait for the movie to come out on cable.* | **cable network/channel/programme 3** [C,U] a thick strong metal rope

'cable car n [C] a vehicle that hangs from a metal rope and carries people up mountains

ˌcable 'television (*also* **cable ˌTV**) n [U] a system of broadcasting television by using cables under the ground

cache /kæʃ/ n [C] a number of things that are hidden, or the place where they are hidden: **[+of]** *a cache of weapons*

CABLE CAR

cackle /'kækəl/ v [I] to laugh in an unpleasant loud way —**cackle** n [C]

cacophony /kə'kɒfəni $ kə'kɑː-/ n [singular] a loud unpleasant mixture of sounds

cactus /'kæktəs/ n [C] (*plural* **cacti** /-taɪ/ *or* **cactuses**) a desert plant covered with small sharp points

caddie, **caddy** /'kædi/ n [C] someone who carries the equipment for someone who is playing golf

cadence /'keɪdəns/ n [C] a regular pattern of sound, especially the sound of someone's voice rising or falling

cadet /kə'det/ n [C] someone who is training to be an officer in the army, navy, AIR FORCE, or police

cadge /kædʒ/ v [T] *BrE informal* to ask someone you know for money, food, cigarettes etc because you do not have any: **cadge sth from/off sb** *I managed to cadge ten quid off Dad.*

caesarean, **cesarean** /sə'zeəriən $ -'zer-/ (*also* **ˌcaeˌsarean 'section**) n [C] an operation in which a woman's body is cut open to take a baby out

cafe, café /'kæfeɪ $ kæ'feɪ, kə-/ n [C] a small restaurant which sells drinks and simple food: *a little Italian cafe* | **in/at a cafe** *We had coffee in a pavement cafe.* | **a transport/motorway/station etc cafe** **THESAURUS** RESTAURANT

cafeteria /ˌkæfə'tɪəriə $ -'tɪr-/ n [C] a restaurant where people get their own food and take it to a table to eat it: *the college cafeteria* **THESAURUS** RESTAURANT

cafetière /ˌkæfə'tjeə $ -'tjer/ n [C] a special pot for making fresh coffee

caffeine /'kæfiːn $ kæ'fiːn/ n [U] a substance in coffee, tea, and some other drinks that makes you feel more active

cage /keɪdʒ/ n [C] a structure made of wires or bars, used for keeping birds or animals in: *a hamster cage* —**caged** adj: *a caged animal*

cagey /'keɪdʒi/ adj *informal* not willing to talk about your plans, intentions etc: *He was very cagey about the deal.*

cagoule /kə'guːl/ n [C] *BrE* a thin coat with a HOOD that stops you from getting wet

cahoots /kə'huːts/ n **be in cahoots (with sb)** *informal* to be working secretly with others, especially to do something dishonest

cajole /kə'dʒəʊl $ -'dʒoʊl/ v [T] to persuade someone to do something by being nice to them or making promises

cake /keɪk/ n
1 [C,U] a sweet food made by baking a mixture of flour, butter, sugar, and eggs: *Would you like some chocolate cake?*
2 fish/rice/potato etc cake fish etc that is made into a flat round shape and then cooked
PHRASES
have your cake and eat it to have all the advantages of something without its disadvantages: *You can't have your cake and eat it too.*

COLLOCATIONS

verbs

to make/bake a cake He made a cake for my birthday. ⚠ Do not say 'cook a cake'. Say **make a cake** or **bake a cake**.
to cut a cake Shall I cut the cake?

nouns + cake

a piece/slice of cake Would you like another piece of fruit cake?

types of cake

a birthday/Christmas/wedding cake She blew out the candles on her birthday cake.
a fruit cake (=one with dried fruit in it) | **a sponge cake** (=one made from flour, butter, sugar, and eggs) | **a chocolate/coffee/lemon cake** (=a sponge cake with a chocolate etc flavour)

caked /keɪkt/ adj **be caked in/with sth** to be covered with a thick layer of something: boots caked with mud

calamity /kəˈlæməti/ n [C,U] (plural **calamities**) an unexpected event that causes a lot of damage or suffering SYN **disaster**

calcium /ˈkælsiəm/ n [U] a silver-white metal that helps to form teeth, bones, and CHALK

calculate /ˈkælkjəleɪt/ v [T]
1 to find out how much something will cost, how long something will take etc, by using numbers: **calculate how much/how many etc** I'm trying to calculate how much paint we need. | **[+(that)]** Sally calculated that the trip would cost about £2,000.
2 to guess something using the information you have: **[+what/whether/how etc]** It's difficult to calculate what effect these changes will have. | **[+(that)]** He'd calculated that she would be home by now.
3 be calculated to do sth to be intended to have a particular effect: It seemed his letter was calculated to upset her.

calculated /ˈkælkjəleɪtɪd/ adj **1 calculated risk/gamble** something you do after thinking carefully, although you know it may have bad results **2** done after thinking carefully, in a clever or dishonest way: It was a calculated attempt to deceive the public.

calculating /ˈkælkjəleɪtɪŋ/ adj someone who is calculating makes careful plans to get what they want, without caring about how this affects other people: a cold and calculating man

calculation /ˌkælkjəˈleɪʃən/ n [C,U]
1 when you use numbers to find out an amount, price etc: a simple **mathematical calculation** | **[+of]** an approximate calculation of the cost | **by/according to some/sb's calculations** According to some calculations, nearly 80% of teenagers have tried drugs. | **do/make a calculation** Dyson did some **rough calculations** (=involving numbers that are not very exact). **2** careful planning to get what you want, especially without caring about how it affects other people

calculator /ˈkælkjəleɪtə $ -ər/ n [C] a small electronic machine that can add, multiply etc → see picture at CLASSROOM

calendar /ˈkæləndə $ -ər/ n [C]
1 a set of pages showing the days and months of a year, that you usually hang on a wall
2 the Roman/Muslim/Jewish etc calendar a system that divides and measures time in a particular way
3 the golfing/sporting/racing etc calendar all the events in a year that are important for a particular activity: Wimbledon, the high point of the tennis calendar
4 a calendar year/month a period of time from the first day of the year or month to the last day of the year or month: Salaries are paid at the end of each calendar month.

calf /kɑːf $ kæf/ n [C] (plural **calves** /kɑːvz $ kævz/)
1 the back of your leg between your knee and foot
2 a baby cow → see picture on page A3

calibre BrE, **caliber** AmE /ˈkælɪbə $ -ər/ n **1** [U] someone's level of ability or quality: players of the highest calibre **2** [C] the width of a bullet or the inside of a gun

call¹ /kɔːl $ kɒːl/ v
1 NAME [T] to use a particular name or word for someone or something, or to give someone a name: **call sb sth** His friends call him Andy. | They finally decided to call the baby Joel. | What do you call this thing? | **be called sth** (=have a particular name) They have a dog called Toby. | We're meeting at a restaurant called Al Paso.
2 PHONE [I,T] to telephone someone: I called about six o'clock but no one was home. | I'll call you tomorrow. | **call a doctor/the police/a taxi etc** (=telephone someone and ask them to come) Has anyone called an ambulance? | **call in sick** (=telephone your work place to say that you are too ill to come to work) | **call collect** AmE (=make a telephone call that is paid for by the person who receives it) THESAURUS **PHONE**

> **Grammar**
> Do not say 'He called to me yesterday.' Say He called me yesterday.

3 DESCRIBE [T] to describe someone or something in a particular way: **call sb/sth sth** Critics are already calling the film a hit. | Are you calling me a liar? | **call sb names** (=use insulting names for someone) The other kids used to call me names.
4 ASK SB TO COME [T] to ask or order someone to come to you: I can hear Mom calling me. | **call sb in/over/across etc** The headmaster called me into his office.
5 SAY/SHOUT (also **call out**) [I,T] to say something loudly or to shout: 'I'm coming!' Paula called down the stairs. | Someone called out my name.
6 STOP AT [I] if a train, ship, bus etc calls at a place, it stops there for a short time: **[+at]** This train calls at all stations to Broxbourne.
7 ARRANGE [T] to arrange for something to happen: **call a meeting/strike/election etc** A meeting was called for 3 pm Wednesday.
8 VISIT SB (also **call by/round/in**) [I] BrE to visit someone or their home for a short time: Your friend Alex called earlier.

PHRASES

call it a day *informal* to stop working, especially because you are tired: *Come on, guys, let's call it a day.*

call the shots/tune if someone calls the shots, they make the important decisions about what should be done: *She likes situations in which she can call the shots.*

PHRASAL VERBS

call back

1 to telephone someone again: *Okay, I'll call back around three.* | **call sb back** *Sorry, she's busy. Can she call you back later?*

2 *BrE* to return to a place that you went to earlier: *I'll call back tonight to pick it up.*

call for sth/sb

1 to demand something publicly: *Congressmen are calling for an investigation into the scandal.*

2 to need something: *It's a project that calls for careful planning.*

3 *BrE* to go to someone's home to collect them: *I'll call for you at about eight.*

call sth ↔ **off** to decide that a planned event will not happen: *The game was called off due to bad weather.* **THESAURUS** CANCEL

call on/upon sb to formally ask someone to do something: **call on sb to do sth** *The UN has called on both sides to start peace talks.*

call sb ↔ **out** to ask someone to come and deal with something difficult or dangerous: *The doctor's been called out to an emergency.* **THESAURUS** SHOUT

call sb/sth ↔ **up**

1 *especially AmE* to telephone someone: *Why don't you call Suzie up?*

2 be called up *BrE* to be ordered to join the army, navy, or AIR FORCE **SYN** draft *AmE*

call² n [C]

1 PHONE when you speak to someone on the telephone: **[+for]** *There's a phone call for you.* | **[+from]** *I got a call from Teresa yesterday.* | *Just give me a call from the airport.* | *Can I make a quick call?* | *Why didn't you return my calls* (=telephone me after I tried to telephone you)? **THESAURUS** PHONE

2 SHOUT a shout or cry, or the sound that an animal makes: *a call for help* | **[+of]** *the call of an owl*

3 VISIT a short visit: *Should we pay a call on Nadia while we're in Paris?*

4 DEMAND when people say publicly that they want something to happen: **[+for]** *a call for tougher controls* | **call for sb to do sth** *There have been calls for the minister to resign.* → **be at sb's beck and call** at BECK, CONFERENCE CALL, ROLL CALL

PHRASES

be on call to be ready to go to work if you are needed: *Heart surgeons are on call 24 hours a day.*

there is no call for sth used to say that something is not needed or wanted: *There's no call for typewriters nowadays – everybody has got a computer on their desk.*

'call box n [C] **1** *BrE* a small structure containing a public telephone **2** *AmE* a public telephone beside a road or FREEWAY used to telephone for help

'call ‚centre *BrE*, **call center** *AmE* n [C] an office where people answer customers' questions, make sales etc by using the telephone

caller /ˈkɔːlə $ ˈkɒːlər/ n [C] someone who makes a telephone call

'call-in n [C] *AmE* a radio or television programme in which people telephone to give their opinions **SYN** phone-in *BrE*

calling /ˈkɔːlɪŋ $ ˈkɒː-/ n [C] a strong feeling that you should do a particular kind of work, especially work that helps other people: *a calling to the priesthood*

callous /ˈkæləs/ adj not caring that other people are suffering —**callously** adv —**callousness** n [U]

'call-up n [C] *BrE* **1** an order to join the army, navy etc **SYN** draft *AmE* **2** an opportunity or invitation to play for a professional sports team, especially a national one

calm¹ /kɑːm $ kɑːm, kɑːlm/ adj

1 PERSON relaxed and not angry or upset: **keep/stay/remain calm** *Please, everyone, try to keep calm!* | *a calm voice*

2 PLACE/SITUATION if a place or situation is calm, there is not much activity or trouble: *The streets are calm again after last night's riots.*

3 SEA/LAKE a sea or lake that is calm does not have many waves: *The water was much calmer in the bay.*

4 WEATHER calm weather is not windy or stormy: *Calmer weather is expected later in the week.* —**calmly** adv —**calmness** n [U]

calm² (*also* **calm down**) v [T] to make someone quiet after they have been angry, excited, or upset: *Matt was trying to calm the baby.*

PHRASAL VERBS

calm down to become quiet after you have been angry, excited, or upset: *Calm down and tell me what happened.*

calm³ n [singular, U] a time when it is peaceful and quiet: **[+of]** *the calm of the evening* | *The police appealed for calm* (=asked people to stay calm) *following the shooting.*

calorie /ˈkæləri/ n [C] a unit for measuring the amount of energy food produces: *An average potato has about 90 calories.* | **low calorie/high calorie** *a low-calorie diet*

calorific /ˌkæləˈrɪfɪk◂/ adj food that is calorific tends to make you fat

calves /kɑːvz $ kævz/ n the plural of CALF

camaraderie /ˌkæməˈrɑːdəri $ -ˈræ-, -ˈrɑː-/ n [U] the feeling that a group of people have when they enjoy being together, especially when they work together: **[+of]** *the camaraderie of office life*

camcorder /ˈkæmˌkɔːdə $ -ˌkɔːrdər/ n [C] a small video camera that you can carry around with you

came /keɪm/ v the past tense of COME

camel /ˈkæməl/ n [C] a large desert animal with a long neck and one or two HUMPS

cameo /ˈkæmiəʊ $ -oʊ/ n [C] (*plural* **cameos**) a small part in a film or play acted by a famous actor: *Whoopi Goldberg makes a cameo appearance in the movie.*

CAMERAS

camera

video camera

webcam

camera /ˈkæmərə/ n [C] a piece of equipment used to take photographs, or make films or programmes: **television/video etc camera** *They posed for the TV cameras.* | **on/off camera** (=while a camera is recording or not recording) *The thieves were caught on camera.*

cameraman /ˈkæmərəmæn/ n [C] (*plural* **cameramen** /-mən/) someone who operates a camera for a television or film company

> **Word Choice**: cameraman or photographer?
> A **cameraman** makes films or television programmes: *a television cameraman*
> A **photographer** takes photographs: *a fashion photographer*

cameraphone /ˈkæmərəˌfəʊn $ -ˌfoʊn/ n [C] a MOBILE PHONE that you can use to take photographs

camouflage /ˈkæməflɑːʒ/ n [C,U] clothes or colours that hide you by making you look the same as the things around you: **in camouflage** *a soldier in camouflage* —**camouflage** v [T]: *Hunters camouflage the traps with leaves.*

camp¹ /kæmp/ n [C,U]
1 a place where people stay in tents for a short time: *After hiking all morning, we returned to camp.* | *We* **set up camp** (=made the camping place ready) *at the lake.*
2 a place where children go to stay for a short time and do special activities: *summer camp*
3 **prison/army/refugee etc camp** a place where prisoners, soldiers etc have to stay in tents or temporary buildings → **CONCENTRATION CAMP**

camp² v [I] **1** (*also* **camp out**) to put up a tent and stay there for a short time: *Where should we camp tonight?* **2 go camping** to have a holiday in which you sleep in tents —**camping** n [U]: *camping equipment*

camp³ adj **1** a man who is camp moves or speaks in a way that people used to think was typical of HOMOSEXUALS **2** (*also* **campy** /ˈkæmpi/ *AmE*) clothes, decorations etc that are camp are very strange, bright, or unusual

campaign¹ /kæmˈpeɪn/ n [C]
1 a series of actions intended to get a particular social or political result: **an election campaign** | an **advertising campaign** | **[+for/against]** *a campaign for equal rights*
2 a series of military attacks

campaign² v [I] to do a series of things intended to get a particular social or political result: **[+for/against]** *The group were campaigning against the destruction of the rainforests.* —**campaigner** n [C]

camp 'bed /ˌ ˈ $ ˈ ˌ/ n [C] *BrE* a narrow bed that folds flat and is easy to carry [SYN] **cot** *AmE* → see picture at **BED**

camper /ˈkæmpə $ -ər/ n [C] **1** someone who is staying in a tent for a short time **2** (*also* '**camper van** *BrE*) a vehicle that has cooking equipment and beds in it

campsite /ˈkæmpsaɪt/ *BrE*, **campground** /ˈkæmpɡraʊnd/ *AmE* n [C] an area where people can stay in tents, often with a water supply and toilets

campus /ˈkæmpəs/ n [C,U] the land and buildings of a college or university: **on campus** *Most first-year students live on campus.*

can¹ /kən; *strong* kæn/ *modal verb* (*negative short form* **can't**)
1 to be able to do something or to know how to do something: *You can swim, can't you?* | *Jess can speak French fluently.* | *I can't meet you now – I'm busy.* | **sb can see/hear/feel/taste/smell/understand sth** (=used with these verbs to mean that someone is able to see etc something now): *I can see the sea!* | *He can't understand why you're so upset.*
2 *spoken* used to ask someone to give you something or to do something: *Can I have a chocolate biscuit?* | *Can you help me lift this box?*
3 used to ask for permission to do something, or to give permission: *Can we go home now?* | *You can go out when you've finished your homework.* | *You can't park there!*
4 *spoken* used to offer to do something: *Can I help you?*
5 used to say that something is possible: *I'm sure it can be done.* | *Can he be alive after all this time?* | *We can't go on like this.*
6 *spoken* used in negatives and questions to say that you do not believe that something is true, or to express surprise or anger: *This can't be the right road.* | *You can't be serious!* | *How can you be so stupid?*
7 used to say what sometimes happens or how someone sometimes behaves: *It can be cold here at night.* | *He can be very charming.*

> **THESAURUS**
>
> **can do sth** to be able to do something, or to know how to do something: *He can run really fast.* | *Can you drive?*
> **be able to do sth** to have the skill, knowledge, strength etc you need to do something – used especially instead of **can** in more formal English: *We are looking for someone who is able to speak French and Spanish.* | *The young birds are now able to fly.*
> **have the ability to do sth** to be able to do something that needs skill, or that most people cannot do: *He had the ability to influence people.*
> **be in a position to do sth** *formal* to be able to do something because you have the knowledge,

power, money, or equipment to do it: *Without that information, we are not in a position to decide.*

> **Word Choice**: can or may?
> **Can** and **may** are both used when asking for or giving permission. **Can** is the usual word to use in everyday English: *Can I stay at your place tonight?*
> **May** is used in polite or formal situations: *If you wish to do so, you may leave early.*

can² /kæn/ *n* [C] a metal container in which food or liquid is kept without air SYN **tin** *BrE*: *a Coke can* | [+of] *a can of tuna fish* | *a can of paint* → see picture at CONTAINER → GARBAGE CAN, WATERING CAN

PHRASES

can of worms a complicated situation that causes a lot of problems when you start to deal with it: *The investigations opened up a whole can of worms.*

can³ *v* [T] (**canned, canning**) to preserve food by putting it in a closed metal container with no air SYN **tin** *BrE*

canal /kəˈnæl/ *n* [C] a long narrow area of water made for ships or boats to travel along → see picture at RIVER

canary /kəˈneəri $ -ˈneri/ *n* [C] (*plural* **canaries**) a small yellow bird that people often keep as a pet

cancel /ˈkænsəl/ *v* [I,T] (**cancelled, cancelling** *BrE*, **canceled, canceling** *AmE*)
1 to say that something that was planned will not happen: *I had to cancel my trip to Rome.* | *You'll have to ring them and cancel.*
2 to end an agreement or arrangement that you do not want any more: *I phoned the hotel to cancel my reservation.* —**cancellation** /ˌkænsəˈleɪʃən/ *n* [C,U]: *Passengers are fed up with cancellations and delays.*

PHRASAL VERBS

cancel sth ↔ **out** if two things cancel each other out, each stops the other from having any effect: *The gains and losses will cancel each other out.*

> ### THESAURUS
> **cancel** to say that something that was planned will not happen: *I was feeling better so I cancelled my doctor's appointment.*
> **call sth off** to cancel an event that you have organized. **Call off** is less formal than **cancel** and is very common in everyday English: *The game was called off.* | *We had to call off the party at the last minute.*
> **postpone** to arrange to do something at a later date, instead of the date that was planned: *The meeting has been postponed until Tuesday.*

cancer /ˈkænsə $ -ər/ *n* [C,U] a serious disease in which cells in someone's body start to grow in a way that is not normal: *lung cancer* | *He died of cancer.* —**cancerous** *adj*

Cancer *n* **1** [U] the sign of the Zodiac of people born between June 22 and July 23 **2** [C] someone who has this sign

candid /ˈkændɪd/ *adj* honest, even about things that are unpleasant or embarrassing SYN **frank**: *a candid article about his drug addiction* —**candidly** *adv*

candidacy /ˈkændədəsi/ *n* [C,U] (*plural* **candidacies**) the position of being a candidate: *She announced her candidacy at the convention.*

candidate /ˈkændədət $ -deɪt, -dət/ *n* [C]
1 someone who is being considered for a job or is competing in an election: [+for] *She's a likely candidate* (=likely to be chosen) *for the job.* | *a presidential candidate* **2** *BrE* someone who is taking an examination

candle /ˈkændl/ *n* [C] a stick of WAX that you burn to produce light: **light/blow out a candle** → see picture at LIGHT¹

candlelight /ˈkændl-laɪt/ *n* [U] the light that a candle produces —**ˈcandle-ˌlit** *adj*

candlestick /ˈkændl-stɪk/ *n* [C] an object used to hold a candle

candour *BrE*, **candor** *AmE* /ˈkændə $ -ər/ *n* [U] the quality of being honest, even about things that are unpleasant or embarrassing

candy /ˈkændi/ *n* [C,U] (*plural* **candies**) *especially AmE* a sweet food made of sugar or chocolate SYN **sweet** *BrE*: *a piece of candy*

cane¹ /keɪn/ *n* **1** [C,U] the hard stem of some plants, used to make furniture or to support plants in the garden: *cane furniture* **2** [C] a long thin stick used to help you walk **3** [C] a stick used by teachers in the past to hit children as a punishment

cane² *v* [T] to punish someone by hitting them with a cane

canine /ˈkeɪnaɪn, ˈkæ- $ ˈkeɪ-/ *adj* relating to dogs

canister /ˈkænɪstə $ -ər/ *n* [C] a metal container: *a gas canister*

cannabis /ˈkænəbɪs/ *n* [U] *especially BrE* an illegal drug that some people smoke SYN **marijuana**

canned /kænd/ *adj AmE* canned food is preserved in a round metal container SYN **tinned** *BrE*: *canned tomatoes* | *canned fruit*

cannibal /ˈkænəbəl/ *n* [C] someone who eats human flesh —**cannibalism** *n* [U]

cannon /ˈkænən/ *n* [C] a large powerful gun used in the past to fire heavy iron balls

ˈcannon ball, **cannonball** *n* [C] a heavy iron ball fired from a cannon

cannot /ˈkænət, -nɒt $ -nɑːt/ a negative form of 'can' SYN **can't**: *I cannot accept your offer.*

canny /ˈkæni/ *adj* clever and not easy to deceive

canoe /kəˈnuː/ *n* [C] a long narrow boat that is pointed at both ends, which you move using a PADDLE → see picture at TRANSPORT¹ —**canoe** *v* [I] —**canoeing** *n* [U]

canon /ˈkænən/ *n* [C] a Christian priest who works in a CATHEDRAL

ˈcan ˌopener *n* [C] a tool for opening cans of food SYN **tin opener** *BrE* → see picture at OPENER

canopy /ˈkænəpi/ n [C] (plural **canopies**) a cover above a bed or seat, used as a decoration or for shelter

can't /kɑːnt $ kænt/ the short form of 'cannot': I can't come today.

cantankerous /kænˈtæŋkərəs/ adj getting annoyed easily and complaining a lot

canteen /kænˈtiːn/ n [C] BrE a place in a factory, school etc where people can get meals, usually cheaply **THESAURUS** RESTAURANT

canter /ˈkæntə $ -ər/ v [I,T] if a horse canters, it runs fairly fast but not as fast as it can → **gallop** —**canter** n [singular]

canvas /ˈkænvəs/ n 1 [U] a type of strong cloth used to make bags, tents, shoes etc: a canvas bag 2 [C] a painting done on canvas, or the cloth it is painted on

canvass /ˈkænvəs/ v 1 [I,T] to try to persuade people to vote for your political party in an election: [+for] Someone was here canvassing for the Green Party. 2 [T] to ask people what their opinion is about something: The company canvassed 600 people who used their product.

canyon /ˈkænjən/ n [C] a deep valley with steep sides: the Grand Canyon

cap¹ /kæp/ n [C]
1 a) a soft hat with a curved part sticking out at the front: a baseball cap → see picture at **HAT** b) a covering that fits closely to your head: a swimming cap
2 something that covers and protects the end or top of something **SYN** top: Put the cap back on the bottle. → **ICE CAP**

cap² v [T] (**capped, capping**) 1 **be capped with sth** to have a particular substance on top: mountains capped with snow 2 to do or say something that is even better or worse than has already been done: Lewis capped a brilliant season by beating the world record. 3 to limit the amount of money that can be used or demanded: Our council has had its spending capped.

capability Ac /ˌkeɪpəˈbɪləti/ n [C,U] (plural **capabilities**) the ability to do something, especially something difficult: [+to] The country **has the capability** to produce nuclear weapons.

capable Ac /ˈkeɪpəbəl/ adj 1 **capable of (doing) sth** having the qualities or ability needed to do something **OPP** incapable: [+of] Do you think he's capable of murder?

> **Grammar**
> Do not say 'He is capable to look after himself.'
> Say He is **capable of** looking after himself.

2 able to do things well: Sue's an extremely capable lawyer.

capacity Ac /kəˈpæsəti/ n (plural **capacities**)
1 [singular] the amount that can fit inside a container, space, building etc: The fuel tank has a **capacity** of 50 litres. | The theatre was **filled to capacity** (=completely full). 2 [C,U] someone's ability to do something: [+for] a child's capacity for learning 3 [singular] someone's job, position, or duty: (**do sth) in your capacity as sth** She travelled a lot in her capacity as a journalist. 4 [singular, U] the amount that a factory or machine can produce: The factory is working **at full capacity** (=producing as much as it can).

cape /keɪp/ n [C] 1 a long loose coat without sleeves that fastens around your neck and hangs from your shoulders 2 a large piece of land surrounded on three sides by water: Cape Cod

caper /ˈkeɪpə $ -ər/ n [C] informal something you do for fun, especially something that is not sensible: I'm too old for this sort of caper.

capillary /kəˈpɪləri $ ˈkæpəleri/ n [C] (plural **capillaries**) a very small narrow tube that carries blood around your body → **artery, vein**

capital¹ /ˈkæpətl/ n
1 [C] an important city where the main government of a country, state etc is: [+of] What's **the capital** of Poland? | a **capital city THESAURUS** CITY
2 **MONEY** [singular, U] money or property, especially when it is used to start a business or to make more money: The government is eager to attract foreign capital. | **capital gains** (=money made from businesses, property etc)
3 **LETTER** (also ˌcapital ˈletter) [C] a letter of the alphabet that is written in its large form, for example at the beginning of a name or sentence: **Write your name in capitals.** | a capital 'T'

capital² adj **capital offence/crime** a crime that can be punished by death

capitalism /ˈkæpətl-ɪzəm/ n [U] an economic and political system in which businesses belong mostly to private owners, not to the government → **communism, socialism** —**capitalist** n [C]

capitalize (also **-ise** BrE) /ˈkæpətl-aɪz/ v
PHRASAL VERBS
capitalize on sth to use something good that you have to get an advantage for yourself: Ecuador has capitalized on its natural beauty to attract tourism.

ˌcapital ˈpunishment n [U] the punishment of killing someone who has committed a serious crime → **death penalty THESAURUS** PUNISHMENT

capitulate /kəˈpɪtʃəleɪt/ v [I] formal to accept or agree to something that you have been opposing —**capitulation** /kəˌpɪtʃəˈleɪʃən/ n [C,U]

cappuccino /ˌkæpəˈtʃiːnəʊ $ -noʊ/ n [C,U] (plural **cappuccinos**) Italian coffee made with hot milk

capricious /kəˈprɪʃəs/ adj likely to change very suddenly: capricious spring weather

Capricorn /ˈkæprɪkɔːn $ -kɔːrn/ n 1 [U] the sign of the Zodiac of people born between December 22 and January 20 2 [C] someone who has this sign

capsize /kæpˈsaɪz $ ˈkæpsaɪz/ v [I,T] if a boat capsizes or you capsize it, it turns over in the water

capsule /ˈkæpsjuːl $ -səl/ n [C] 1 a very small tube of medicine that you swallow 2 the part of a spacecraft in which people live and work

captain¹ /ˈkæptɪn/ n [C]
1 the leader of a team or group of people: [+of] Rod's captain of the football team. | the US **team captain**

captain

2 (*also* **Captain**) someone who is in charge of a ship or plane

3 (*also* **Captain**) a military officer with a fairly high rank

captain[2] *v* [T] to be the captain of a team, ship, or plane

captaincy /ˈkæptənsi/ *n* [C,U] (*plural* **captaincies**) the position of being captain of a team

caption /ˈkæpʃən/ *n* [C] words written above or below a picture in a book, newspaper etc to explain what it is about

captivate /ˈkæptɪveɪt/ *v* [T] to attract and interest you very much: *Alex was captivated by her beauty.* —**captivating** *adj*

captive[1] /ˈkæptɪv/ *adj* kept somewhere and not allowed to leave: *captive animals* | *His son had been **taken captive** (=made a prisoner) during the raid.*
PHRASES
| **captive audience** people who listen to or watch something because they have to, not because they want to: *His family were a captive audience, especially at meal times.*

captive[2] *n* [C] someone who is kept as a prisoner, especially in a war

captivity /kæpˈtɪvəti/ *n* [U] when a person or animal is kept in a prison, cage etc and not allowed to leave: **in captivity** *Many animals won't breed in captivity.*

captor /ˈkæptə $ -ər/ *n* [C] *formal* someone who is keeping another person as a prisoner

capture[1] /ˈkæptʃə $ -ər/ *v* [T]
1 CATCH to catch a person or animal and keep them as a prisoner: *He was captured at the airport.*
2 GET CONTROL to get control of something: *The town was captured by enemy troops after ten days' fighting.* | *Sega and Nintendo soon **captured half the market** (=the business available).*
3 DESCRIBE to succeed in showing or describing something, using pictures or words: *His new book captures what the 1920s were like.*
4 MAKE SB INTERESTED **capture sb's imagination/attention etc** to make someone feel very interested in something: *Her stories have captured children's imagination for years.*

capture[2] *n* [U] **1** when someone captures a person or animal **2** when someone gets control of something: *the capture of the village*

car /kɑː $ kɑːr/ *n* [C]
1 a vehicle with four wheels and an engine, that can carry a small number of passengers: *He wasn't old enough to drive a car.* | **by car** *Did you come by car?* → see picture at TRANSPORT[1]
2 dining/buffet/sleeping car *BrE* a part of a train used for eating or sleeping
3 *AmE* one of the connected parts of a train SYN **carriage** *BrE* → CABLE CAR

CAR

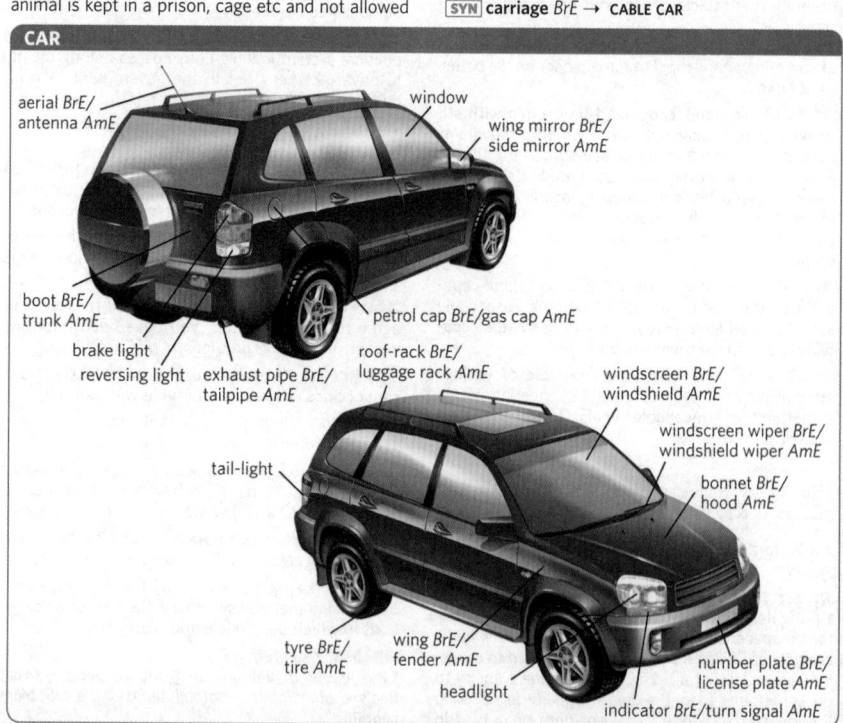

aerial *BrE*/antenna *AmE*

window

wing mirror *BrE*/side mirror *AmE*

boot *BrE*/trunk *AmE*

brake light
reversing light

exhaust pipe *BrE*/tailpipe *AmE*

petrol cap *BrE*/gas cap *AmE*

roof-rack *BrE*/luggage rack *AmE*

windscreen *BrE*/windshield *AmE*

tail-light

windscreen wiper *BrE*/windshield wiper *AmE*

bonnet *BrE*/hood *AmE*

tyre *BrE*/tire *AmE*

wing *BrE*/fender *AmE*

headlight

number plate *BrE*/license plate *AmE*

indicator *BrE*/turn signal *AmE*

verbs

to get in/into a car *She got into her car and drove off.* ⚠ Do not say 'get on a car' or 'go into a car'. Say **get in a car** or **get into a car**.

to get out of a car *Two men got out of the car.*
to drive a car *He never learned to drive a car.*
to park a car *I can't remember where I parked the car.*
a car breaks down (=stops working) *I'm so sorry I'm late – the car broke down.*

car + noun

a car crash/accident (*also* **a car wreck** *AmE*) *There was a car crash on the motorway.*
a car park *There's a car park at the back of the hotel.*
a car door/engine/key *She left the car engine running.*

carafe /kəˈræf, kəˈrɑːf/ *n* [C] a glass container used for serving wine and water at meals

caramel /ˈkærəməl, -mel/ *n* [C,U] boiled sugar, butter, and milk used in food or made into a brown sweet

carat (*also* **karat** *AmE*) /ˈkærət/ *n* [C] a unit for measuring how pure gold is, or how heavy jewels are

caravan /ˈkærəvæn/ *n* [C] **1** *BrE* a vehicle that can be pulled by a car, and that people can live and sleep in SYN **trailer** *AmE* **2** *BrE* a vehicle that is pulled by a horse, and that people can live in SYN **wagon** *AmE*: *a gypsy caravan* **3** a group of people who travel together with animals or vehicles

carbohydrate /ˌkɑːbəʊˈhaɪdreɪt, -drət $ ˌkɑːrbou-/ *n* [C,U] a substance in foods such as sugar, bread, and potatoes that provides your body with heat and energy

carbon /ˈkɑːbən $ ˈkɑːr-/ *n* [U] a chemical substance that is found in all living things, and in coal, DIAMONDS, petrol etc

carbonated /ˈkɑːbəneɪtɪd $ ˈkɑːr-/ *adj* carbonated drinks contain small bubbles → **fizzy**

carbon ˈcopy *n* [C] something or someone that is very similar to another thing or person: *The robbery is a carbon copy of the one last year.*

carbon diˈoxide *n* [U] the gas produced when people or animals breathe out

carbon ˈfootprint *n* [C] the amount of carbon dioxide that a person or organization produces by the things they do, used as a way of measuring how much they harm the environment: *There are lots of ways you can reduce your carbon footprint.*

carbon moˈnoxide *n* [U] a poisonous gas produced when engines burn petrol

carbon ˈneutral *adj* if an organization or activity is carbon neutral, it takes as much carbon dioxide out of the air as it produces

car ˈboot ˌsale *n* [C] *BrE* an event when people sell things they do not want from the back of their cars

carburettor *BrE*, **carburetor** *AmE* /ˌkɑːbjəˈretə, -bə- $ ˈkɑːrbəreɪtər/ *n* [C] the part of a car engine where air and petrol mix

carcass /ˈkɑːkəs $ ˈkɑːr-/ *n* [C] the body of a dead animal

carcinogen /kɑːˈsɪnədʒən $ ˌkɑːr-/ *n* [C] *technical* a substance that can cause CANCER —**carcinogenic** /ˌkɑːsənəˈdʒenɪk $ ˌkɑːr-/ *adj*

card /kɑːd $ kɑːrd/ *n*

1 WITH INFORMATION [C] a small piece of plastic or stiff paper that gives information about someone or something: *an identity card* | *Here's my business card.* | *a set of recipe cards* | *Please bring your medical card.*

2 FOR PAYING [C] a small piece of plastic which you use to pay for goods or to get money: *my credit card* | *a phone card*

3 FOR CHRISTMAS/BIRTHDAYS ETC [C] a folded piece of stiff paper with a picture on the front that you send to people on special occasions: **birthday/greetings/ Christmas etc card**

4 FOR GAMES [C] one of a set of 52 small pieces of stiff paper with pictures or numbers on them that are used to play games SYN **playing card**: *Let's play cards* (=a game using cards). | **pack** (=complete set) **of cards** *BrE*, **deck of cards** *AmE*

5 POSTCARD [C] a POSTCARD: *Don't forget to send me a card.*

6 STIFF PAPER [U] *BrE* thick stiff paper → **cardboard**

7 IN FOOTBALL **red/yellow card** a card that the REFEREE holds up in football to show that a player has done something wrong

8 IN COMPUTER [C] the thing inside a computer that the CHIPS are attached to, that allows the computer to do specific things: *a graphics card* → **CASH CARD, CHARGE CARD, CREDIT CARD, DEBIT CARD, SWIPE CARD**

PHRASES

be on the cards *BrE*, **be in the cards** *AmE* to seem likely to happen: *I've left Brenda. It's been on the cards for a long time.*

put/lay your cards on the table to be completely honest about your plans and intentions: *Let's put our cards on the table and discuss this calmly.*

cardboard /ˈkɑːdbɔːd $ ˈkɑːrdbɔːrd/ *n* [U] very stiff thick paper, used especially for making boxes → see picture at BOX¹

cardiac /ˈkɑːdi-æk $ ˈkɑːr-/ *adj* [only before noun] *technical* relating to the heart: *cardiac arrest* (=when the heart stops working)

cardigan /ˈkɑːdɪɡən $ ˈkɑːr-/ *n* [C] a piece of clothing like a SWEATER but with buttons that you fasten down the front

cardinal¹ /ˈkɑːdənəl $ ˈkɑːr-/ *n* [C] a priest of high rank in the Roman Catholic church

cardinal² *adj* [only before noun] very important or basic: *a cardinal rule*

cardinal ˈnumber *n* [C] a number such as 1, 2, or 3 that shows how many of something there are → **ordinal number**

cardiovascular /ˌkɑːdiəʊˈvæskjələ $ ˌkɑːrdiouˈvæskjələr/ *adj* *technical* relating to the heart and the tubes through which blood flows in your body

care¹ /keə $ ker/ v

1 [I,T] to be concerned about or interested in someone or something: **[+about]** *He doesn't seem to care about other people.* | *A lot of people just don't care about politics.* | **[+what/who/how etc]** *I don't care what you do.*

2 [I] to like or love someone → **caring**: *Buy her flowers to show that you care.* | **[+about/for]** *She obviously cares about you a lot.*

PHRASES

sb couldn't care less *spoken* used to say that someone is not at all concerned about or interested in something: *I really couldn't care less what you think!*

who cares? *spoken* used to say that you do not think something is important or interesting: *It's rather an old car but who cares?*

would you care for sth?/would you care to do sth? *formal* used to ask someone if they want something or want to do something: *Would you care for a drink?*

PHRASAL VERBS

care for sb/sth

1 to look after someone or something **SYN** **take care of**: *Angie gave up her job to care for her mother.*

2 **not care for sb/sth** *formal* to not like someone or something: *I don't care for his brother.*

> **Word Choice: I don't care or I don't mind?**
> You use **I don't care** when saying that you are not interested, especially because you are annoyed or upset: *'Do you want to go out, or stay home and watch a DVD?' 'I really don't care. I've had such a bad day today.'*
> You use **I don't mind** when saying that you are happy to accept either thing: *'Would you prefer tea or coffee?' 'I don't mind.'*

care² n

1 [U] the process of looking after someone or something: *Your father will need constant **medical care**.* | **[+of]** *They shared the care of their children.* | **skin/hair/health etc care** *advice on dental care* | **in sb's care** (=being looked after by someone) *The children had been left in the care of a babysitter.*

2 [U] when you do something carefully in order not to make a mistake or damage something: *You need to **put** more **care into** your work.* | **with care** *Fragile! Handle with care.*

3 [C,U] a worry or problem: *Forget all your cares.* | *Alex looked as though he **didn't have a care in the world** (=did not have any problems or worries).* → **DAY CARE, HEALTH CARE, INTENSIVE CARE**

PHRASES

in care *BrE* a child who is in care is being looked after by government organizations, not by their parents: *When their father was sent to prison, the kids were **taken into care**.*

take care 1 *informal* used to say goodbye to family or friends: *See you tomorrow – take care!* **2** to be careful: **[+to]** *Take care to follow the instructions.*

take care of sb/sth 1 to look after someone or something: *Who's taking care of the baby?* | *Karl took care of the house while we were on holiday.* **2** to deal with something that needs doing: **take care of (doing) sth** *I'll take care of making the reservations.* **THESAURUS** DEAL

career¹ /kə'rɪə $ -'rɪr/ n [C]

1 a job or profession that you have been trained for, and which you usually do for a long time: *a teaching career* | **[+in]** *a career in law* | ***Career prospects*** (=job opportunities) *within the company are excellent.* **THESAURUS** JOB

2 the time in your life that you spend working or doing a particular type of work: *Ted spent most of his career as a teacher.* | **[+as]** *My career as a writer didn't last long.*

career² v [I] *BrE* to move quickly forwards without control: **[+down/through/off etc]** *A couple of boys on bikes careered down the hill.*

carefree /'keəfri: $ 'ker-/ adj without any problems or worries: *a carefree childhood*

careful /'keəfəl $ 'ker-/ adj

1 someone who is careful tries hard not to make mistakes, damage things etc **OPP** **careless**: *a careful driver* | **[+to]** *Anna was careful not to upset Steven.* | **[+(that)]** *We were very careful that he didn't find out.* | **(be) careful!** *spoken* (=used to tell someone to do this) *Be careful with that ladder!*

2 giving a lot of thought and attention to something: *Any school trip requires careful planning.* | **[+about]** *I'm always careful about what I buy.* —**carefully** *adv:* *Please listen carefully.*

> **THESAURUS**
> **careful** someone who is careful tries hard not to make mistakes or damage things. Also used about something that you do with a lot of thought and attention: *Be careful not to drop those glasses.* | *A successful meeting requires careful preparation.*
> **cautious** careful to avoid problems or danger and not wanting to take risks: *a cautious driver* | *Investors are becoming much more cautious.*
> **thorough** careful to check and deal with everything, so that you do not miss something important: *The doctors were very thorough and they did a lot of tests.* | *a thorough investigation*
> **conscientious** careful to do everything that you are told to do, or that it is your duty to do: *She's very conscientious about her work.*
> **meticulous** extremely careful about every small detail: *He kept meticulous records of his experiments.* | *Wendy was always meticulous about her appearance.*
> **painstaking** painstaking work, preparation etc takes a long time and is done in a very careful way: *The book took years of painstaking research.*

careless /'keələs $ 'ker-/ adj not giving enough thought and attention to something, so that you make mistakes, damage things etc **OPP** **careful**: *a careless mistake* | **be careless of sb** *It was careless of you to leave your keys in the car.* —**carelessly** *adv* —**carelessness** *n* [U]

> **THESAURUS**
> **careless** not giving enough thought and attention to what you are doing, so that you make mistakes, damage things etc: *a careless worker* | *The essay was full of careless mistakes.*
> **thoughtless** not thinking about other people or how your actions or words will affect them: *I'm sorry I didn't phone – it was thoughtless of me.*

clumsy someone who is clumsy often drops or breaks things because they move in a careless or awkward way: *As a child he was tall and clumsy.*

tactless speaking in a careless way and saying things that are likely to upset or embarrass someone: *It was a bit tactless to ask about her divorce.* | *a tactless remark*

reckless behaving in a dangerous and stupid way, without thinking about other people's safety: *He was arrested for reckless driving.*

rash deciding to do something without thinking carefully, so that you later regret what you have done: *a rash decision* | *Don't do anything rash.*

carer /ˈkeərə $ ˈkerər/ *n* [C] someone who looks after a child, or a person who is old or ill

caress /kəˈres/ *v* [T] *literary* to touch someone gently in a way that shows you love them **THESAURUS** TOUCH —**caress** *n* [C]

caretaker /ˈkeəˌteɪkə $ ˈkerˌteɪkər/ *n* [C] *BrE* someone whose job is to look after a building, especially a school **SYN** **janitor** *AmE*

cargo /ˈkɑːgəʊ $ ˈkɑːrgoʊ/ *n* [C,U] (*plural* **cargos** or **cargoes**) goods that are carried in a ship or plane: **[+of]** *a cargo of oil* | *a cargo ship*

Caribbean /ˌkærəˈbiːən◂/ *adj* from or relating to the islands in the Caribbean sea, such as Jamaica and Barbados —**Caribbean** *n* [C]

caricature /ˈkærɪkətʃʊə $ -tʃʊr/ *n* [C,U] a funny drawing or description of someone that makes them seem silly **THESAURUS** PICTURE —**caricature** *v* [T]

caring /ˈkeərɪŋ $ ˈker-/ *adj* someone who is caring is kind to other people and tries to help them: *a warm and caring person*

carjacking /ˈkɑːˌdʒækɪŋ $ ˈkɑːr-/ *n* [U] the crime of forcing the driver of a car to give you the car or drive you somewhere, using a weapon —**carjacker** *n* [C]

carnage /ˈkɑːnɪdʒ $ ˈkɑːr-/ *n* [U] *formal* when a lot of people are killed or injured

carnal /ˈkɑːnl $ ˈkɑːrnl/ *adj formal* relating to sex: *carnal desire*

carnation /kɑːˈneɪʃən $ kɑːr-/ *n* [C] a white, pink, or red flower that smells nice → see picture at **FLOWER**[1]

carnival /ˈkɑːnəvəl $ ˈkɑːr-/ *n* [C,U] a public event when people play music, wear special clothes, and dance in the streets: *carnival time in Rio*

carnivore /ˈkɑːnəvɔː $ ˈkɑːrnəvɔːr/ *n* [C] an animal that eats meat —**carnivorous** /kɑːˈnɪvərəs $ kɑːr-/ *adj*

carol /ˈkærəl/ *n* [C] a song that people sing at Christmas: ***Christmas carols***

carousel /ˌkærəˈsel/ *n* [C] **1** the moving thing at an airport from which passengers collect their bags **2** *AmE* a large machine with has toy animals, cars etc for people to ride on as it turns around **SYN** **merry-go-round**

carp[1] /kɑːp $ kɑːrp/ *n* [C,U] (*plural* **carp**) a large fish that lives in lakes or rivers and can be eaten

carp[2] *v* [I] *disapproving* to complain a lot about something: **[+about]** *people who constantly carp about the price of petrol*

ˈcar park *n* [C] *BrE* an area or building where people can park their cars **SYN** **parking lot** *AmE*

carpenter /ˈkɑːpəntə $ ˈkɑːrpəntər/ *n* [C] someone whose job is making and repairing wooden objects

carpentry /ˈkɑːpəntri $ ˈkɑːr-/ *n* [U] the skill or work of a carpenter

carpet /ˈkɑːpɪt $ ˈkɑːr-/ *n*
1 [C,U] material for covering floors, often made of wool, or a piece of this material → **rug**: *All the rooms had **fitted carpets*** (=carpets cut to exactly fit a room). | *I'd like red carpet in the hall.*
2 a carpet of leaves/flowers etc *literary* a thick layer of leaves etc on the ground —**carpet** *v* [T] → **RED CARPET**

carriage /ˈkærɪdʒ/ *n* [C] **1** *BrE* one of the separate parts of a train where passengers sit **SYN** **car** *AmE* **2** a vehicle pulled by a horse and used for passengers

carriageway /ˈkærɪdʒweɪ/ *n* [C] *BrE* one of the sides of a MOTORWAY or main road, used by vehicles travelling in the same direction: *the northbound carriageway* → **DUAL CARRIAGEWAY**

carrier /ˈkæriə $ -ər/ *n* [C] **1** a company that moves goods or passengers from one place to another: *an international carrier* **2** someone who passes a disease to other people without having it themselves → **AIRCRAFT CARRIER**

ˈcarrier ˌbag *n* [C] *BrE* a bag that you are given in a shop to carry the things you have bought

carrot /ˈkærət/ *n*
1 [C,U] a long orange vegetable that grows under the ground → see picture on page A5
2 [C] something that is offered to someone to persuade them to do something: **[+of]** *The government **held out the carrot** of lower interest rates.* | *a **carrot and stick** approach* (=both offering something good and threatening something bad)

carry /ˈkæri/ *v* (**carried, carrying, carries**)
1 **HOLD** [T] to hold something in your hands or arms, or on your back, as you go somewhere: *Let me carry that bag for you.* | **carry sth in/on sth** *Angie was carrying the baby in her arms.* | **carry sth to sth/sb** *The waiter carried our drinks to the table.* → see picture on page A11
2 **TAKE** [T] to take people or things from one place to another: *The bus was carrying 25 passengers.* | **carry sth into/across/through etc sth** *A network of pipes carry oil across the desert.*
3 **IN YOUR POCKET/BAG** [T] to have something with you in your pocket, bag etc as you go somewhere: *I never carry much money.* | *It's illegal to carry a gun.*
4 **DISEASE** [T] to have a disease which can be given to others → **carrier**: *Many diseases are carried by insects.*
5 **INFORMATION/ARTICLE ETC** [T] to contain a particular piece of information or news: *Tobacco products must carry a health warning.* | *The magazine **carries articles** on scientific developments.*
6 **HAVE A RESULT/EFFECT** [T] to have a particular

result or effect: *sports that* **carry a risk** *of injury* | **carry weight/authority** (=have influence over people) *He's someone whose opinion carries weight.* | *Murder carries a life sentence.*

7 **WEIGHT** [T] to support the weight of something: *Two columns carry the whole roof.*

8 **SOUND** [I] if a sound carries, it can be heard for a long way

9 **PROPOSAL** **be carried** if something that is suggested at a meeting is carried, most of the people there agree with it and vote for it: *The* **motion was carried** *by 20 votes to 12.*

PHRASES

carry sth too far/to extremes to do or say something too much or for too long: *It was funny at first, but you've* **carried the joke too far**. **be/get carried away** to be so excited, interested etc that you are not completely in control of what you do or say

PHRASAL VERBS

carry sth ↔ **off** to do something difficult successfully: *No one believed he could carry the plan off.*

carry on

1 to continue doing something: **carry on doing sth** *You'll get ill if you carry on working like that.* | **[+with]** *I decided to carry on with the course.* **THESAURUS** CONTINUE

2 to continue moving in the same direction: *Carry* **straight on** *to the traffic lights.*

carry sth ↔ **out** to do something that has been planned or discussed, or that someone has told you to do: *The students carried out a survey on attitudes to drugs.* | *Have you* **carried out** *her* **instructions**? **THESAURUS** DO

carry sth ↔ **through** to complete or finish something successfully

carryall /ˈkæri-ɔːl $ -ɒːl/ *n* [C] *AmE* a large soft bag **SYN** holdall *BrE* → see picture at **BAG¹**

carrycot /ˈkærikɒt $ -kɑːt/ *n* [C] *BrE* a small bed used to carry a baby

'carry-on *adj* [only before noun] carry-on bags are ones that you take onto a plane with you → **hand luggage**

'carry-out *n* [C] *AmE* food that you can take away from a restaurant to eat, or a restaurant that sells food like this **SYN** takeaway *BrE*

carsick /ˈkɑːˌsɪk $ ˈkɑːr-/ *adj* feeling sick when you are travelling in a car —**carsickness** *n* [U]

cart¹ /kɑːt $ kɑːrt/ *n* [C] **1** a vehicle pulled by a horse and used to carry things **2** *AmE* a large wire basket on wheels that you use in a SUPERMARKET **SYN** trolley *BrE* → see picture at **TROLLEY**

cart² *v* [T] *informal* to carry or take something or someone somewhere, especially with difficulty: **cart sth around** *I'm sick of carting this suitcase around.*

carte blanche /ˌkɑːt ˈblɑːnʃ $ ˌkɑːrt-/ *n* [U] the freedom to do something in exactly the way you want: *Her parents* **gave** *her* **carte blanche** *to organize a party.*

cartel /kɑːˈtel $ kɑːr-/ *n* [C,U] a group of companies that work together to control prices and increase their profits

cartilage /ˈkɑːtəlɪdʒ $ ˈkɑːrtəlɪdʒ/ *n* [C,U] a strong substance that can bend, which is around the joints in your body

cartography /kɑːˈtɒɡrəfi $ kɑːrˈtɑː-/ *n* [U] the skill or work of making maps —**cartographer** *n* [C]

carton /ˈkɑːtn $ ˈkɑːrtn/ *n* [C] a box that contains food or drink, made from stiff paper or plastic: **[+of]** *a carton of juice* | *a milk carton* → see picture at **CONTAINER**

cartoon /kɑːˈtuːn $ kɑːr-/ *n* [C]

1 a film that uses characters that are drawn and not real **THESAURUS** PROGRAMME

2 a funny drawing or set of drawings in a newspaper or magazine

cartoonist /kɑːˈtuːnɪst $ kɑːr-/ *n* [C] someone whose job is to draw cartoons

cartridge /ˈkɑːtrɪdʒ $ ˈkɑːr-/ *n* [C] **1** a small container that you put inside something to make it work: *The printer needs a new* **ink cartridge**. **2** a tube containing explosive powder and a bullet, used in a gun

cartwheel /ˈkɑːt-wiːl $ ˈkɑːrt-/ *n* [C] a movement in which you throw your body sideways onto your hands and bring your legs over your head —**cartwheel** *v* [I]

carve /kɑːv $ kɑːrv/ *v* **1** [T] to cut a piece of wood or stone in order to make an object or make a pattern on the surface: **carve sth from/out of sth** *All the figures are carved from a single tree.* | **carve sth on/onto sth** *Kids had carved their names on the desks.* **2** [I,T] to cut a large piece of cooked meat into thin pieces with a knife → see picture at **CUT¹** **THESAURUS** CUT

PHRASAL VERBS

carve out sth **carve out a career/niche/role etc** to succeed in getting a job, position etc that suits you

carve sth ↔ **up** *disapproving* to divide land, a company etc into smaller parts: *The country was carved up after the war.*

carving /ˈkɑːvɪŋ $ ˈkɑːr-/ *n* **1** [C,U] an object or pattern made by cutting wood, stone etc **2** [U] the activity of cutting wood, stone etc into objects or patterns

cascade /kæˈskeɪd/ *n* [C] *literary* something that flows or hangs down in large amounts: **[+of]** *Her hair was a cascade of soft curls.* —**cascade** *v* [I]: *Waterfalls cascaded down the mountainside.*

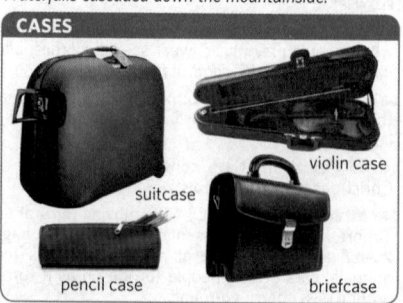

CASES

violin case

suitcase

pencil case

briefcase

case /keɪs/ *n* [C]

1 **SITUATION** a particular situation, or an example of that situation: *In this case there are several possible solutions.* | **in some/many/most etc cases** *In most cases, excessive speed was the cause of the accident.* | **in sb's case** *They say men don't age and in his case it was true.* | *In the case of special education, the issues are different.* | [+of] *a case of wrongful imprisonment*

2 POLICE/COURT CASE something that is being dealt with by lawyers or the police: [+of] *a case of armed robbery* | *a murder case*

3 OF A DISEASE an occasion when someone has an illness, or someone who has an illness: [+of] *The first cases of the disease were reported in 1978.*

4 REASONS FOR DOING STH [usually singular] a number of reasons why something should be done or believed: [+for/against] *There's a strong case for changing the law.* | *Student representatives met to put forward their case.*

5 SUITCASE *BrE* a SUITCASE: *Our cases are all packed.*

6 CONTAINER a container for storing or protecting something: *a packing case* | *a pencil case* | *Always keep your guitar in its case.* → **LOWER CASE, UPPER CASE**

PHRASES

in any case *spoken* used to give a reason for doing something, or to express determination to do it SYN **anyway**: *We'll take you home – we're going that way in any case.* | *I think I could win. In any case, I'm going to try.*

in case of sth *formal* if or when something happens: *In case of fire, break the glass.*

(just) in case 1 as a way of being prepared for something that might happen: *Take your umbrella in case it rains.* **2** *AmE* if: *In case I'm late, start without me.*

in that case if that is the situation: *'It will only take five minutes.' 'In that case, I'll wait.'*

it's a case of (doing) sth *spoken* used to say what is needed to do something: *Anyone can get fit. It's just a case of taking enough exercise.*

be on sb's case *informal* to criticize someone a lot in a way that seems unfair: *Dad's always on my case about something.*

be on the case *BrE* to be dealing with something: *The email isn't working at the moment, but I'm on the case.*

be the case to be true: *It may be the case that science is badly taught in schools.*

'case ,study *n* [C] a detailed report about a person, group, or situation studied over a period of time

cash¹ /kæʃ/ *n* [U]

1 money in the form of coins and notes: *There's a small discount if you pay cash.* | **in cash** *I usually have about £50 in cash with me.* THESAURUS **MONEY**

2 *informal* money in any form: *I'm short of cash just now.* | *The company had problems raising cash for the deal.* → **hard cash** at **HARD¹**

cash² *v* [T] to exchange a cheque for money

PHRASAL VERBS

cash in on sth *disapproving* to get money or other advantage from a situation in a way that other people think is wrong

cashback /'kæʃbæk/ *n* [U] **1** a way of getting money from a shop when you pay for the things you are buying with a DEBIT CARD. The total amount is taken from your bank account. **2** an amount of

money that is offered to customers who are buying a car, piece of furniture etc as a way of reducing what they have to pay for it

'cash card *n* [C] a plastic card used for getting money from a CASH MACHINE

'cash crop *n* [C] a crop that is grown to be sold, not used by the people growing it

'cash desk *n* [C] *BrE* the desk in a shop where you pay

cashew /'kæʃuː, kə'ʃuː/ *n* [C] a small curved nut → see picture at **NUT**

'cash flow *n* [U] the movement of money into and out of a business or someone's bank account: *I've had a few cash flow problems.*

cashier /kæ'ʃɪə $ -'ʃɪr/ *n* [C] someone whose job is to receive and pay out money in a bank, shop etc

CASH MACHINE

'cash ma,chine (also **'cash di,spenser** *BrE*) *n* [C] a machine that you get money from using a plastic card, especially in a wall outside a bank or SUPERMARKET SYN **ATM**

cashmere /'kæʃmɪə $ 'kæʒmɪr, 'kæʃ-/ *n* [U] a type of fine soft wool

Cashpoint /'kæʃpɔɪnt/ *n* [C] *trademark BrE* a CASH MACHINE

'cash ,register *n* [C] a machine used in shops to keep money in and record the amount of money received SYN **till**

casing /'keɪsɪŋ/ *n* [C] a layer of rubber, metal etc that covers and protects something, for example a wire

casino /kə'siːnəʊ $ -noʊ/ *n* [C] (*plural* **casinos**) a place where people try to win money by playing card games or ROULETTE

cask /kɑːsk $ kæsk/ *n* [C] a round wooden container used to store alcohol

casket /'kɑːskɪt $ 'kæs-/ *n* [C] *AmE* the box a dead person is buried in SYN **coffin** *BrE*

casserole /'kæsərəʊl $ -roʊl/ *n* **1** [C,U] meat and vegetables in liquid cooked together slowly in an OVEN: *chicken casserole* **2** [C] a large covered dish used for cooking casseroles

cassette /kə'set/ *n* [C] a small flat plastic case with tape inside on which music, speech, a film etc has been recorded or can be recorded: **an audio/ video cassette** | *a blank cassette* (=with nothing recorded on it yet) | **on cassette** *Is the album still* *available on cassette?* → **VIDEO CASSETTE RECORDER**

cas'sette ,player n [C] a machine used for listening to cassettes

cast¹ /kɑːst $ kæst/ v [T] (*past tense and past participle* **cast**)

1 FOR A FILM/PLAY to choose a particular actor for a part in a film, play etc: **cast sb as sb** *Who was cast as Harry Potter?*

2 THROW/SEND *literary* to throw something somewhere, or send something in a particular direction: **cast sth across/on/into etc sth** *The fishermen cast their nets into the sea.* | *The fire cast a soft light on her face.* | **cast a look/glance at sb/sth** *She cast an anxious glance at Guy.*

3 MAKE [usually passive] to make an object by pouring hot metal into a hollow container: **cast sth in/from sth** *a statue cast in bronze*

4 VOTE **cast a vote** to vote in an election

PHRASES

cast doubt/suspicion on sth to make people feel less certain about something: *Recent information has cast doubt on the evidence.*

cast an eye over sth to read or look at something quickly: *He cast an eye over the letter.*

cast light on/onto sth to explain something or provide new information about it: *Can you cast any light on these figures?*

cast your mind back to try to remember something that happened in the past: [+to] *Try to cast your mind back to that first day at school.*

cast a shadow/cloud over sth to make people enjoy something less or feel less happy: *The bad news cast a shadow over his visit.*

cast a spell on/over sb/sth 1 to use magic to make something happen: *witches casting spells* **2** to interest or attract people very much, as if by magic: *Hong Kong casts a spell over its visitors as soon as they land.*

PHRASAL VERBS

cast around/about for sth to try to find or get something: *On leaving school he cast around for a job.*

cast sb/sth ↔ **aside** to get rid of something or someone: *Never cast aside your old friends.*

cast off to untie the rope that fastens a boat to something

cast² n [C] **1** all the actors in a film, play etc: *an all-star cast* (=all the actors are famous)
THESAURUS ACTOR **2** a PLASTER CAST

castaway /'kɑːstəweɪ $ 'kæst-/ n [C] someone who is alone on an island after their ship has sunk

caste /kɑːst $ kæst/ n [C,U] one of the social classes that people belong to in India: *the **caste system***

caster /'kɑːstə $ 'kæstər/ n another spelling of CASTOR

castigate /'kæstɪgeɪt/ v [T] *formal* to criticize someone severely

'casting ,vote n [singular] the vote of the person in charge of a meeting, used to decide something when there are an equal number of votes supporting and opposing it

,cast 'iron n [U] **1** a type of iron that is very hard: *a cast-iron frying pan* **2 cast-iron excuse/alibi/**

guarantee etc an excuse etc that is very definite and that people will believe

castle /'kɑːsəl $ 'kæ-/ n [C] a very large strong building with high walls, built in the past to protect the people inside from attack: *a 12th-century castle* | *Windsor Castle*

'cast-offs n [plural] clothes that you do not want any more and give to someone else —**cast-off** adj

castor, caster /'kɑːstə $ 'kæstər/ n [C] one of a set of small wheels fixed to the bottom of a piece of furniture so that it can be moved about easily

castrate /kæ'streɪt $ 'kæstreɪt/ v [T] to remove the sexual organs of a male animal or man —**castration** /kæ'streɪʃən/ n [C,U]

casual /'kæʒuəl/ adj

1 RELAXED relaxed and not worried, or seeming not to care about something: [+about] *She's always been pretty casual about her appearance.* | *His **casual attitude** towards work annoyed me.*

2 NOT SERIOUS OR CAREFUL [only before noun] not done in a serious, careful, or planned way: *a **casual glance** at the newspapers* | *She wanted something more than a **casual relationship**.* | *the dangers of **casual sex***

3 CLOTHES casual clothes are comfortable and not worn in formal situations OPP **formal**: *He changed into a **casual jacket** and jeans.*

4 WORK casual work is temporary, or not regular: *casual employment* | *people who work **on a casual basis*** —**casually** adv: *He was dressed casually in faded jeans.*

casualty /'kæʒuəlti/ n (*plural* **casualties**) **1** [C usually plural] someone who is hurt or killed in an accident or war: *road casualties* | *a battle with **heavy casualties*** (=a lot of people hurt or killed) *on both sides* **2 be a casualty of sth** to suffer because of a difficult economic situation or other event: *The city library is the latest casualty of the financial cuts.* **3** [U] *BrE* the part of a hospital that people are taken to when they need urgent treatment SYN **emergency room** *AmE*

cat /kæt/ n [C]

1 a small animal that people keep as a pet, and that often kills birds, mice etc → **feline** → see picture at PET¹

2 a large wild animal that is related to cats, such as a lion

PHRASES

let the cat out of the bag *informal* to tell someone a secret without intending to: *She accidentally let the cat out of the bag.*

cataclysm /'kætəklɪzəm/ n [C] *literary* a serious event that causes great changes or damage: *the cataclysm of the First World War* —**cataclysmic** /ˌkætə'klɪzmɪk◂/ adj

catalogue¹ (*also* **catalog** *AmE*) /'kætəlɒg $ -lɔːg, -lɑːg/ n **1** [C] a complete list of things that you can buy or look at: *our new Spring catalogue* | *an online catalog* **2 a catalogue of injuries/complaints/ disasters etc** a series of injuries etc that happen one after another

catalogue² (*also* **catalog** *AmE*) v [T] to make a complete list of something

catalyst /'kætl-ɪst/ n [C] someone or something

that causes important changes: **[+for]** *His election may **act as a catalyst** for reform.*

catalytic converter /ˌkætl-ɪtɪk kən'vɜːtə $ -'vɜːrtər/ *n* [C] a piece of equipment fitted to a car's EXHAUST system that reduces the amount of poisonous gases the engine sends out

catamaran /ˌkætəmə'ræn/ *n* [C] a sailing boat with two separate HULLS (=the part that goes in the water)

catapult¹ /'kætəpʌlt/ *v* [T] **1** to make someone or something move through the air very quickly: **catapult sb/sth across/through/into etc sth** *The explosion catapulted him into the air.* **2 catapult sb to fame/stardom** to make someone suddenly become famous

catapult² *n* [C] *BrE* a small stick in the shape of a Y with a band of rubber between the ends, used by children to throw stones

cataract /'kætərækt/ *n* [C] a medical condition that affects the eye and makes you slowly lose your sight

catarrh /kə'tɑː $ -'tɑːr/ *n* [U] *BrE* thick liquid that blocks your nose and throat when you have a cold

catastrophe /kə'tæstrəfi/ *n* [C] a terrible event that causes a lot of destruction or suffering —**catastrophic** /ˌkætə'strɒfɪk◄ $ -'strɑː-/ *adj*: *the catastrophic effects of the floods*

catch¹ /kætʃ/ *v* (past tense and past participle **caught** /kɔːt $ kɒːt/)

1 BALL ETC [T] to stop and hold something that is moving through the air: *Tom leapt up and **caught the ball**.* | **catch sb/sth in sth** *She jumped and he caught her in his arms.* → see picture on page A11

2 STOP SB ESCAPING [T] **a)** to stop a person or an animal that is running away: *'You can't catch me,' she yelled over her shoulder.* **b)** to find a criminal and put them somewhere so that they cannot escape → **capture**: *The police have caught the man suspected of the murder.*

3 FISH/ANIMAL [T] to get a fish or animal by using a trap, net, or hook: *I haven't caught anything all day.*

4 SEE SB DOING STH [T] to see someone doing something wrong or secret: **catch sb doing sth** *I caught him looking through my letters.* | *The thieves were **caught in the act**.* | *She was **caught red-handed** taking the money.*

5 ILLNESS [T] to get an illness: *Put your coat on or you'll **catch a cold**.*

6 TRAIN/PLANE/BUS [T] to get on a bus, train etc: *I caught the 7.30 train to London.*

7 NOT BE TOO LATE [T] to not be too late to see something, talk to someone etc OPP **miss**: *We only caught the end of the movie.* | *If you hurry, you'll catch her before she leaves.*

8 GET STUCK (*also* **be/get caught**) [I] to become stuck on or in something by mistake: *His shirt caught on the fence and tore.*

9 MAKE SB NOTICE [T] if something catches your attention, you notice it and feel interested in it: **catch sb's attention/interest etc** *One article on the front page caught my attention.*

10 HIT SB [T] to hit a particular part of someone: **catch sb in/on sth** *The punch caught him in the face.*

11 CANNOT AVOID STH **be caught in/without etc sth** to be unable to avoid an unpleasant situation: *We were caught in the rain.*

12 NOT HEAR **not catch sth** *spoken* to not hear clearly what someone says: *I'm sorry, I didn't catch your name.* THESAURUS ► HEAR

13 NOT EXPECT **catch sb by surprise/unawares/off guard** if something catches you by surprise, it happens when you are not expecting it

PHRASES

catch fire to start burning, especially accidentally: *One of the plane's engines caught fire.*

catch the light if something catches the light, it is bright because of light shining on it: *Her ring caught the light.*

catch sight of/catch a glimpse of to suddenly see someone or something for a moment: *Tony caught sight of Louisa in the crowd.* THESAURUS ► SEE

catch sb's eye if an object catches your eye, you notice it because it is interesting or attractive: *There was one red dress that really caught my eye.* THESAURUS ► NOTICE

catch you later *spoken* used to say goodbye: *'I'm off now.' 'OK. Catch you later.'*

PHRASAL VERBS

catch on

1 to become popular or fashionable: *The idea never caught on in this country.*

2 to begin to understand something: *With careful training, a puppy will soon catch on.*

catch sb ↔ out *BrE* to make someone make a mistake, especially by asking them a difficult question: *Some interviewers may try to catch you out.*

catch up

1 to reach someone in front of you by going faster than them: **[+with]** *I had to run to catch up with her.* | **catch sb up** *You go ahead, and we'll catch you up.*

2 to reach the same standard as other people: *If you miss classes, it's difficult to catch up.*

3 **be/get caught up in sth** to become involved in something, especially without wanting to: *young people who get caught up in crime*

catch up on sth to do something that you have not had time to do yet: **[+on]** *I need to catch up on some work this weekend.*

catch² *n* [C] **1** an act of catching a ball: *Hey! Nice catch!* **2** [usually singular] *informal* a hidden problem involved in something that seems good or cheap: *It's a very good deal – is there a catch?* THESAURUS ► DISADVANTAGE **3** a quantity of fish caught at one time **4** a hook for fastening something and keeping it shut

'catch-all *adj* intended to include all possibilities: *a vague catch-all clause in the contract*

catching /'kætʃɪŋ/ *adj* [not before noun] an illness or feeling that is catching spreads easily from one person to another

catchment area /'kætʃmənt ˌeəriə $ -ˌeriə/ *n* [C] *BrE* the area that a school, hospital, or business gets its students, PATIENTS, or customers from

catchphrase /'kætʃfreɪz/ *n* [C] a short phrase that is well known because a famous person often uses it

Catch-22 /ˌkætʃ twenti'tuː/ *n* [singular] a situation in which, whatever you do, you are prevented from achieving what you want: *It's a Catch-22 situation because you can't get a job without experience and you can't get experience without a job.*

catchy /'kætʃi/ *adj* a catchy tune or phrase is easy to remember

catechism /'kætə,kɪzəm/ *n* [singular] a set of questions and answers about the Christian religion that people learn to become members of a church

categorical /,kætɪ'gɒrɪkəl◄ $ -'gɔː-, -'gɑː-/ *adj* stating that something is completely certain: *a categorical assurance* —**categorically** /-kli/ *adv*: *He categorically denied the rumours.*

categorize (*also* **-ise** *BrE*) /'kætəgəraɪz/ *v* [T] to put people or things into groups according to what type, level etc they are: *The students were categorized according to ability.* | *categorize sb/sth as sth books categorized as 'modern classics'*

category Ac /'kætəgəri $ -gɔːri/ *n* [C] (*plural* **categories**) a group of people or things that are all of the same type: **[+of]** *There are several categories of patients.* | *Voters fell into (=belonged in) three main categories.*

cater /'keɪtə $ -ər/ *v* [I,T] to provide and serve food and drinks at a party, meeting etc, especially as a business: **[+for]** *a company that caters for weddings* —**caterer** *n* [C]

PHRASAL VERBS

cater for/to sb to provide a particular group of people with what they need or want: *a hotel that caters for young children*

catering /'keɪtərɪŋ/ *n* [U] the job of providing and serving food and drinks at parties, meetings etc: *the catering industry*

caterpillar /'kætə,pɪlə $ -tər,pɪlər/ *n* [C] a small creature with a lot of legs that eats leaves. It becomes a BUTTERFLY or MOTH.

cathartic /kə'θɑːtɪk $ -ɑːr-/ *adj* helping you to get rid of unpleasant emotions: *a cathartic experience* —**catharsis** *n* [C,U]

cathedral /kə'θiːdrəl/ *n* [C] the most important church in an area

catholic /'kæθəlɪk/ *adj formal* including a great variety of things: *He had very catholic tastes in music.*

Catholic *adj* relating to the Roman Catholic church —**Catholic** *n* [C] —**Catholicism** /kə'θɒləsɪzəm $ kə'θɑː-/ *n* [U]

Catseye /'kætsaɪ/ *n* [C] *trademark BrE* one of the small objects in the middle of a road that shine when lit by a car's lights, and help the driver to see the road at night

catsup /'kætsəp/ *n* an American spelling of KETCHUP

cattle /'kætl/ *n* [plural] cows and BULLS kept on a farm: *a herd of (=large group of) cattle*

catwalk /'kætwɔːk $ -wɒːk/ *n* [C] the structure that models walk along in a fashion show SYN **runway** *AmE*

Caucasian /kɔː'keɪziən $ kɔː'keɪʒən/ *adj* belonging to the race of people with white skin —**Caucasian** *n* [C]

caught /kɔːt $ kɒːt/ *v* the past tense and past participle of CATCH

cauldron, **caldron** /'kɔːldrən $ 'kɒːl-/ *n* [C] a large round metal pot for boiling liquids over a fire

cauliflower /'kɒlɪ,flaʊə $ 'kɒːli,flaʊər, 'kɑː-/ *n* [C,U] a vegetable with green leaves around a large firm white centre → see picture on page A5

cause¹ /kɔːz $ kɒːz/ *n*

1 [C] a person, event, or thing that makes something happen → **effect**: **[+of]** *Heart disease is a common cause of death.* | **main/major cause** *Sewage is a major cause of water pollution.* | *researchers investigating the causes of depression*

2 [C,U] a reason for doing something or having a particular feeling: **[+for]** *The birth of a baby is a cause for celebration.* | **cause for concern/alarm** *There is no cause for alarm.* | **have (good) cause to do sth** *I think you've good cause to complain.*

3 [C] an organization or aim that a group of people support or fight for: **[+of]** *the cause of freedom* | **good/worthy cause** (=an organization that helps people who need it) *I don't mind giving money if it's for a good cause.*

cause² *v* [T] to make something happen, especially something bad: *Heavy traffic is causing long delays.* | **cause sb sth** *The injury was causing him a lot of pain.* | **cause sb/sth to do sth** *Their divorce had caused her to feel very bitter.* | **cause problems/trouble/damage etc**

THESAURUS

cause to make something happen, especially something bad: *The problem was caused by an electrical fault.* | *Smoking causes lung cancer.*

make sb/sth do sth to cause someone or something to do something: *What made you give up your career?* | *Plants need sun to make them grow.*

be responsible for sth if someone or something is responsible for something bad, they cause it to happen: *The group claimed that it was responsible for the attack.*

bring about sth to make something happen, especially changes or improvements: *The Internet has brought about enormous changes in society.*

lead to sth/result in sth to cause something to happen later – used when talking about the effects of something: *The disease can lead to blindness if it is not treated quickly.* | *Problems in the US led to a downturn in the world economy.*

---

causeway /'kɔːzweɪ $ 'kɒːz-/ *n* [C] a raised road or path across wet ground or through water

caustic /'kɔːstɪk $ 'kɒːs-/ *adj* **1** a caustic remark criticizes someone in a way that is clever but unkind **2** a caustic substance contains chemicals that can burn through things

caution¹ /'kɔːʃən $ 'kɒː-/ *n* **1** [U] when you are very careful to avoid danger or taking risks: **with caution** *The animals should be handled with caution.* | **treat/view sth with caution** (=think about something carefully because it might not be true) *These statistics must be treated with caution.* **2** [C,U] a warning telling you to be careful: **word/note of caution** *A word of caution – be sure to make copies of all files.* **3** [C] *BrE* an official warning that a police officer or judge gives to someone who has done something wrong

caution² v **1** [I,T] to warn someone that something might be dangerous, difficult etc: **caution (sb) against sth** Advisers have cautioned against tax increases. **2** [T] BrE to warn someone officially that the next time they do something wrong they will be punished

cautionary /'kɔːʃənəri $ 'kɒʃəneri/ adj giving a warning: a **cautionary tale** (=story used to warn people)

cautious /'kɔːʃəs $ 'kɒː-/ adj careful to avoid problems or danger: a cautious driver | **cautious about (doing) sth** He was cautious about making any predictions. —**cautiously** adv

cavalcade /ˌkævəl'keɪd, 'kævəlkeɪd/ n [C] a line of people on horses or in vehicles, moving along as part of a ceremony

cavalier /ˌkævə'lɪə◀ $ -'lɪr◀/ adj not caring enough about things that are important: a **cavalier attitude** to human life

cavalry /'kævəlri/ n [U] soldiers who fought on horses in the past

cave¹ /keɪv/ n [C] a large natural hole in the side of a cliff or hill, or under the ground

cave² v

PHRASAL VERBS

cave in 1 if the top or sides of something cave in, they fall down or inwards: The roof caved in. **2** to stop opposing something

caveat /'kæviæt, 'keɪv-/ n [C] formal warning that something may not be completely true, effective etc

caveman /'keɪvmæn/ n [C] (plural **cavemen** /-men/) someone who lived in a cave a long time ago

cavern /'kævən $ -ərn/ n [C] a large deep cave

caviar, **caviare** /'kæviɑː $ -ɑːr/ n [U] fish eggs, eaten as a very special expensive food

cavity /'kævəti/ n [C] (plural **cavities**) **1** a hole or space inside something **2** a hole in a tooth, that a DENTIST fills

cavort /kə'vɔːt $ -ɔːrt/ v [I + adv/prep] to jump or dance around in an excited or sexual way

cc /ˌsiː 'siː/ **1** the abbreviation of **cubic centimetre**: a 2,000 cc engine **2** used in a business letter or email to show that you are sending a copy to someone else

CCTV /ˌsiː siː tiː 'viː/ n [U] BrE (**closed circuit television**) a system of cameras and television, used in public places to protect people from crime

CD /ˌsiː 'diː◀/ n [C,U] (**compact disc**) a small circular piece of plastic on which music or computer information is recorded → see picture on page A12

CD player n [C] a piece of equipment used to listen to music recorded on a CD

CD-R /ˌsiː diː 'ɑː $ -'ɑːr/ n [C,U] (**compact disc recordable**) a CD that you can use only once to record music or computer information

CD-ROM /ˌsiː diː 'rɒm $ -'rɑːm/ n (**compact disc read-only memory**) a CD on which a lot of computer information is stored

CD-RW /ˌsiː diː ɑː 'dʌbəljuː $ -ɑːr-/ n [C,U] (**compact disc rewritable**) a CD that you can use several times to record music or computer information

cease Ac /siːs/ v [I,T] formal to stop doing something, or stop happening: **cease to do sth** The old hotel had **ceased to exist**. | **cease doing sth** After his son's death, Hugo ceased writing.

ceasefire /'siːsfaɪə $ -faɪr/ n [C] an agreement between two countries or groups to stop fighting: a **ceasefire agreement**

ceaseless /'siːsləs/ adj formal continuing for a long time: ceaseless rain —**ceaselessly** adv

cedar /'siːdə $ -ər/ n [C,U] a tall EVERGREEN tree with leaves shaped like needles, or the wood of this tree

cede /siːd/ v [T] formal to give land, power etc to another country or person

ceiling /'siːlɪŋ/ n [C]
1 the inside surface at the top of a room → **roof**: the bathroom ceiling | rooms with **high ceilings**
2 the largest amount of something which is officially allowed: [+of] a ceiling of 5.5% on wage increases

celeb /sə'leb/ n [C] informal a CELEBRITY

celebrate /'seləbreɪt/ v [I,T] to do something enjoyable because it is a special occasion or because something good has happened: John passed his exams so we're having a party to celebrate. | How do you want to celebrate your birthday?

celebrated /'seləbreɪtɪd/ adj famous: a celebrated actor

celebration /ˌselə'breɪʃən/ n [C,U] the activity of celebrating something special, or an occasion or party when you celebrate something: a time of joy and celebration | the New Year's celebrations | We're having a little celebration. | **in celebration of sth** a party in celebration of her 80th birthday THESAURUS
PARTY

celebrity /sə'lebrəti/ n [C] (plural **celebrities**) a famous living person: TV celebrities

---

Word Choice: celebrity or star?
A **celebrity** is a well-known person who often appears on television or in newspapers and magazines: The magazine is full of gossip about minor celebrities. | a celebrity chef
A **star** is a very famous actor, musician, or sports player who many people admire: a Hollywood star

---

celery /'seləri/ n [U] a vegetable with long hard pale green stems, eaten raw or cooked: a **stick of celery** → see picture on page A5

celestial /sə'lestiəl $ -tʃəl/ adj relating to the sky or heaven

celibate /'seləbət/ adj someone who is celibate does not have sex —**celibacy** /-bəsi/ n [U]

cell /sel/ n [C]
1 the smallest part of a living thing: red blood cells
2 a small room where prisoners are kept: a prison cell

cellar /ˈselə $ -ər/ n [C] a room under a house, used for storing things

cellist /ˈtʃelɪst/ n [C] someone who plays the cello

cello /ˈtʃeləʊ $ -loʊ/ n [C] (plural **cellos**) a large wooden musical instrument that you hold between your knees and play by pulling a BOW (=special stick) across the strings → **cellist** → see picture on page A6

Cellophane /ˈseləfeɪn/ n [U] trademark a thin transparent material used for wrapping things

'cell phone (also ˌcellular 'phone) n [C] especially AmE a telephone that you carry with you $\boxed{\text{SYN}}$ **mobile phone** BrE → see picture on page A12

cellular /ˈseljələ $ -ər/ adj **1** relating to the cells in a plant or animal **2** relating to cellular phones: cellular networks

cellulite /ˈseljəlaɪt/ n [U] fat just below someone's skin that makes it look uneven and unattractive

celluloid /ˈseljəlɔɪd/ n [U] a substance like plastic, used in the past to make film

cellulose /ˈseljələʊs $ -loʊs/ n [U] a substance that forms the walls of plant cells

Celsius /ˈselsiəs/ n [U] a scale of temperature in which water freezes at 0° and boils at 100° $\boxed{\text{SYN}}$ **Centigrade**

Celtic /ˈkeltɪk, ˈseltɪk/ adj relating to the Celts (=the people of Ireland, Scotland, or Wales) or their languages

cement¹ /sɪˈment/ n [U] a grey powder used in building, that is mixed with sand and water and allowed to dry and become hard

cement² v [T] **1** to make a relationship, position etc stronger: a deal that will cement their relationship **2** to cover or fix something with cement

cemetery /ˈsemətri $ -teri/ n [C] (plural **cemeteries**) a place where dead people are buried

censor¹ /ˈsensə $ -ər/ v [T] to examine books, films etc and remove anything that is offensive, politically dangerous etc —**censorship** n [U]

censor² n [C] someone whose job is to censor books, films etc

censure /ˈsenʃə $ -ər/ v [T] formal to officially criticize someone —**censure** n [U]

census /ˈsensəs/ n [C] (plural **censuses**) an occasion when a government collects information about the number of people in a country, their ages, jobs etc

cent /sent/ n [C] 1/100th of the standard unit of money in some countries, for example the US

centenary /senˈtiːnəri $ -ˈten-, ˈsentəneri/ especially BrE, **centennial** /senˈteniəl/ especially AmE n [C] (plural **centenaries**) the day or year exactly one hundred years after an important event: [+of] the centenary of the composer's birth

center /ˈsentə $ -ər/ n, v the American spelling of CENTRE

Centigrade /ˈsentəgreɪd/ n [U] a scale of temperature in which water freezes at 0° and boils at 100° $\boxed{\text{SYN}}$ **Celsius**

centilitre BrE, **centiliter** AmE /ˈsentiˌliːtə $ -ər/ n [C] (written abbreviation **cl**) a unit for measuring an amount of liquid. There are 100 centilitres in one litre.

centimetre BrE, **centimeter** AmE /ˈsentəˌmiːtə $ -ər/ n [C] (written abbreviation **cm**) a unit for measuring length. There are 100 centimetres in one metre.

central /ˈsentrəl/ adj **1** [only before noun] in the middle of an object or area: central London | a central courtyard | Central Asia **2** [only before noun] having control over the rest of a system, organization etc: central and local government | the system's central control unit **3** more important than anything else: She had a **central role** in the negotiations. | [+to] the loving relationships that are central to family life **4** a place that is central is near the centre of a town: The hotel is very central. —**centrally** adv

ˌcentral 'heating n [U] a system of heating buildings in which heat is produced in one place and taken to the rest of the building by pipes

centralize (also **-ise** BrE) /ˈsentrəlaɪz/ v [T] to control a country, organization, or system from one place: plans to centralize the company's European operations —**centralized** adj —**centralization** /ˌsentrəlaɪˈzeɪʃən $ -lə-/ n [U]

ˌcentral reser'vation n [C] BrE a narrow piece of ground that divides the two parts of a MOTORWAY or other main road

centre¹ BrE, **center** AmE /ˈsentə $ -ər/ n [C] **1** $\boxed{\text{MIDDLE}}$ the middle part or point of something: [+of] the center of a circle | **in the centre (of sth)** There was a table in the centre of the room.

> **Grammar**
> Do not say 'My house is on the centre of town.' Say My house is **in the centre of** town.

2 $\boxed{\text{BUILDING}}$ a building used for a particular purpose: a **sports centre** | [+for] the Centre for Modern Art **3** $\boxed{\text{IMPORTANT PLACE FOR STH}}$ a place where there is a lot of a particular type of business or activity: **business/commercial/banking etc centre** London is a major financial centre. **4** $\boxed{\text{OF A CITY/TOWN}}$ BrE the part in the middle of a city or town where most of the shops, restaurants etc are $\boxed{\text{SYN}}$ **downtown** AmE: **town/city centre** shops in the city centre | [+of] the centre of York **5** $\boxed{\text{IN POLITICS}}$ a political position which does not support extreme views: a politician who is popular with **the centre** | **left/right of centre** left of centre policies → COMMUNITY CENTRE, GARDEN CENTRE, HEALTH CENTRE, LEISURE CENTRE, SHOPPING CENTRE

PHRASES

be (at) the centre of sth to be very involved in something, or to have a very important part in something: He's **at the centre of a row** over school fees. | Lizzy loves to be **the centre of attention** (=the person everyone is talking to, looking at etc).

be/take centre stage if something or someone is centre stage, they have an important position and get a lot of attention: After his father's death, he rose to power and took centre stage.

centre² BrE, **center** AmE v [T] to move something to a position at the centre of something else
PHRASAL VERBS
centre on/around sth if something centres on a particular thing, that is the most important thing in it or what it mainly concerns: *The film centres on his early life.*

centre of 'gravity n [singular] the point in an object around which its weight balances

centrepiece BrE, **centerpiece** AmE /'sentəpiːs $ -ər-/ n [singular] the most important, attractive, or noticeable part of something: **[+of]** *The painting will be the centrepiece of the exhibition.*

-centric /sentrɪk/ suffix giving most attention to a particular thing, person, or group: *malecentric* (=giving males most attention)

centrifugal force /ˌsentrɪfjuːgəl 'fɔːs, senˌtrɪfjəgəl- $ senˌtrɪfjəgəl 'fɔːrs/ n [U] a force that makes things move away from the centre of something when they are moving or turning quickly around it

centurion /sen'tjʊəriən $ -'tʊr-/ n [C] an officer who was in charge of a group of 100 soldiers in the Roman army

century /'sentʃəri/ n [C] (plural **centuries**) a period of 100 years – used especially in dates

---

COLLOCATIONS

adjectives

the 14th/20th etc century (=in the 1300s/1900s etc) *The church was built in the 13th century.*

this century *This has been the hottest summer this century.*

the last/next century *He was writing at the beginning of the last century.*

nouns + century

the beginning/end of the century *She was born at the end of the 19th century.*

the turn of the century (=the time when a new century begins) *The book was written at the turn of the century.*

CEO /ˌsiː iː 'əʊ $ -'oʊ/ n [C] (**Chief Executive Officer**) the person with the most authority in a large company

ceramics /sə'ræmɪks/ n [plural, U] pots, plates etc made from clay, or the art of making them —**ceramic** adj: *ceramic tiles*

Word Choice: ceramics or pottery?
Ceramics and **pottery** both mean the activity of making things from clay, or objects that are made from clay.
You use **ceramics** when talking about this as an art. You use **pottery** when talking about this as an everyday thing. Compare these sentences: *a collection of ceramics by Picasso* | *She found a piece of old pottery in the garden.*

cereal /'sɪəriəl $ 'sɪr-/ n
1 [C,U] breakfast food made from grain and usually eaten with milk: *a bowl of cereal*
2 [C] a plant grown to produce grain for food, for

CEREAL
a bowl of cereal   cereal crops

example wheat or rice: *cereal crops*

cerebral /'serəbrəl $ sə'riː-, 'serə-/ adj [only before noun] technical relating to your brain

cerebral 'palsy n [U] a medical condition that affects someone's ability to move or speak, caused by damage to the brain at birth

ceremonial /ˌserə'məʊniəl $ -'moʊ-/ adj used in a ceremony, or done as part of a ceremony: *a ceremonial procession*

ceremony /'serəməni $ -moʊni/ n (plural **ceremonies**)
1 [C] a formal event that happens in public on a special occasion: *the opening ceremony of the Olympic Games*
2 [U] the formal actions and words always used on particular occasions: **with ceremony** *The statue was erected with great ceremony in 1905.*

COLLOCATIONS

verbs

to hold a ceremony *Where will the wedding ceremony be held?*

to perform a ceremony *The ceremony was performed by a priest.*

to attend a ceremony *Her parents attended her graduation ceremony.*

a ceremony takes place *The funeral ceremony took place in the local church.*

types of ceremony

a wedding/marriage ceremony *They had a traditional wedding ceremony.*

a religious ceremony *The event begins with a short religious ceremony.*

an awards ceremony (=where prizes are given) *Many stars attended the BAFTA awards ceremony.*

the opening ceremony (=when an event begins or a new place opens) *Our guest of honour will perform the opening ceremony.*

---

certain /'sɜːtn $ 'sɜːr-/ adj
1 SURE ABOUT STH [not before noun] completely sure: **[+(that)]** *I'm absolutely certain I left the keys here.* | **[+about/of]** *Are you certain about that?* | **[+what/how etc]** *I'm not certain when it will happen.*
THESAURUS SURE
2 SURE TO HAPPEN/BE TRUE sure to happen or be true: **[+that]** *It seems certain that she will win.* | **certain to**

do sth *Many people **look certain** to lose their jobs.* | *Prisoners faced **certain death**.*

3 PARTICULAR [only before noun] used to talk about a particular person, thing etc without naming or describing them exactly: *The work must be done by a certain date.* | *You are not allowed to park in certain areas.* | *This only applies to certain people.*

4 SOME some but not a lot: *a certain amount of confusion* | **to a certain extent/degree** (=partly but not completely) *I agree with you to a certain extent.*

5 DIFFICULT TO DESCRIBE difficult to describe exactly: *She had a **certain** elegance.*

PHRASES

for certain without any doubt SYN **for sure**: *know/say (sth) for certain Exactly what happened is not known for certain.*

make certain 1 to check that something is correct or true: [+(that)] *He made certain no one could see him.* **2** to do something in order to be sure something will happen: [+(that)] *I'll make certain he knows about it.*

certainly¹ /'sɜːtnli $ 'sɜːr-/ *adv* without any doubt SYN **definitely**: *His lawyers will **almost certainly** appeal.* | *She's **certainly** not shy.*

certainly² *spoken* used to agree or to give your permission SYN **of course**, **go ahead**: *'Can I use your phone?' 'Certainly!'*

certainty /'sɜːtnti $ 'sɜːr-/ *n* (*plural* **certainties**) **1** [U] when you are completely sure about something: **with certainty** *She knew with certainty that he was lying.* **2** [C] something that is definitely true or will definitely happen: *The job losses aren't a certainty.*

certificate /sə'tɪfɪkət $ sər-/ *n* [C] an official document that shows something is true or correct: *Keep all your **exam certificates** (=showing the exams you have passed and their marks).* | **birth/marriage/death certificate** (=giving details of someone's birth etc)

certify /'sɜːtɪfaɪ $ 'sɜːr-/ *v* [T] (**certified**, **certifying**, **certifies**) **1** to officially state that something is correct or true: [+(that)] *Engineers certified that the aircraft was safe.* **2** [usually passive] to give someone an official document to show that they have trained to work in a particular profession: *certified accountants*

cervix /'sɜːvɪks $ 'sɜːr-/ *n* [C] (*plural* **cervices**) the entrance to a woman's UTERUS —**cervical** /'sɜːvɪkəl, sə'vaɪkəl $ 'sɜːrvɪkəl/ *adj*

cesarean /sə'zeəriən $ -'zer-/ *n* another spelling of CAESAREAN

cessation /se'seɪʃən/ *n* [C,U] *formal* when something stops: [+of] *a cessation of violence*

cesspit /'ses,pɪt/ (*also* **cesspool** /'ses,puːl/) *n* [C] a large hole or container under the ground for collecting waste water from a building

cf used in writing to introduce something else that should be compared

CFC /ˌsiː ef 'siː/ *n* [C] (**chlorofluorocarbon**) a gas used in AEROSOLS and FRIDGES, which causes damage to the OZONE LAYER

CGI /ˌsiː dʒiː 'aɪ/ *n* [U] (**computer-generated**

imagery) the use of computers to produce artificial images in films: *a new CGI movie from Disney*

chafe /tʃeɪf/ *v* [I,T] if part of your body chafes, or if something chafes it, your skin becomes sore because something is rubbing against it: *The shoes were chafing her heels.*

chagrin /'ʃægrɪn $ ʃə'grɪn/ *n* [U] *formal* when you feel disappointed and annoyed: **to sb's chagrin** *To her chagrin he got the job.*

chain¹ /tʃeɪn/ *n*

1 METAL RINGS [C,U] a line of metal rings connected together: *He wore a gold chain around his neck.* | *My bicycle chain* (=that makes the wheels turn) *has come off.* | **in chains** (=having chains around your legs to stop you escaping) *The prisoners were in chains.* → see picture at BICYCLE

2 OF SHOPS/HOTELS [C] a group of shops, hotels etc that are owned by the same person or company: [+of] *a chain of restaurants* | *a supermarket chain*

3 OF MOUNTAINS/ISLANDS [C] a series of similar things in a line: *a mountain chain* | [+of] *a chain of islands*

4 OF EVENTS/ACTIONS [C] a series of related events or actions: *the **chain of events** leading up to the war* → FOOD CHAIN

chain² *v* [T] to fasten one thing or person to another, using a chain: **chain sb/sth to sth** *John chained his bicycle to the fence.*

chain re'action *n* [C] a series of related events or chemical changes, with each one causing the next

chainsaw /'tʃeɪnsɔː $ -sɒː/ *n* [C] a tool for cutting wood, which has a circular chain with sharp edges, and is powered by a motor

'chain-smoke *v* [I,T] to smoke cigarettes one after another —**chain-smoker** *n* [C]

'chain store *n* [C] one of a group of shops owned by the same company

chair¹ /tʃeə $ tʃer/ *n*

1 FOR SITTING ON [C] a piece of furniture for one person to sit on: **in/on a chair** *He was sitting in an old leather chair.*

2 OF A MEETING [singular] someone who is in charge of a meeting or committee: **in the chair** *The president, Al Shaw, was in the chair.*

3 PROFESSOR [singular] the position of being a university PROFESSOR: [+of] *She was **appointed** the **chair** of Medicine.*

COLLOCATIONS

verbs

to sit in/on a chair *She sat in her favourite chair.*

to get up from your chair *My father got up from his chair and walked to the window.*

to lean back in your chair *He leant back in his chair and took out his pipe.*

to take a chair (=to sit down on a chair) *Brian took a chair beside his wife.*

---

chair² *v* [T] to be in charge of a meeting or committee

chairman /'tʃeəmən $ 'tʃer-/, **chairwoman** /'tʃeə,wʊmən $ 'tʃer-/, **chairperson** /'tʃeə,pɜːsən $ 'tʃer,pɜːrsən/ *n* [C] **1** someone who is in charge of a

CHAIRS

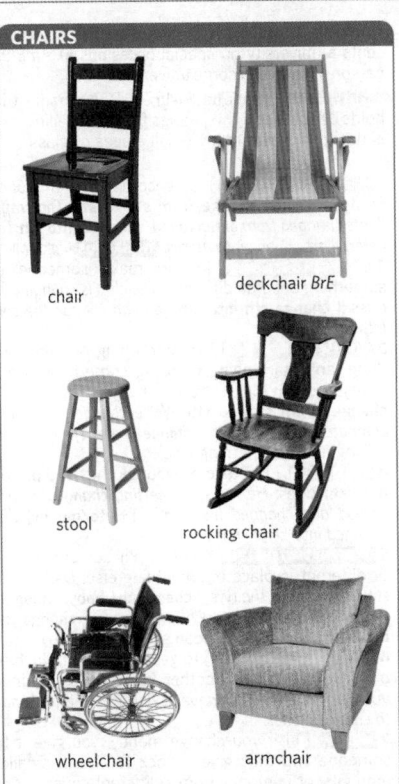

chair

deckchair *BrE*

stool

rocking chair

wheelchair

armchair

meeting or committee **2** someone who is in charge of a large company or organization: **[+of]** *the chairman of British Airways* —**chairmanship** *n* [C,U]

chalet /'ʃæleɪ $ ʃæ'leɪ/ *n* [C] a wooden house, especially one in a mountain area

chalk¹ /tʃɔːk $ tʃɔːk/ *n* **1** [U] soft white rock **2** [C,U] a small stick of soft white or coloured rock, used for writing or drawing → see picture at **CLASSROOM**
PHRASES
be like chalk and cheese *BrE* to be completely different from each other: *The two brothers are like chalk and cheese.*

chalk² *v* [T] to write or draw something with chalk
PHRASAL VERBS
chalk sth ↔ up *informal* to succeed in doing something, especially winning a game, competition etc: *They've chalked up their third win of the season.*

chalkboard /'tʃɔːkbɔːd $ 'tʃɔːkbɔːrd/ *n* [C] *AmE* a BLACKBOARD

chalky /'tʃɔːki $ 'tʃɔː-/ *adj* similar to chalk, or containing chalk

challenge¹ Ac /'tʃæləndʒ/ *n*
1 [C,U] something that tests your skill or ability, especially in a way that is interesting: *The race is a*

tough challenge for any athlete. | **[+of]** *I enjoy the challenge of a new job.*
2 [C] a situation in which other people want to take the power or the top position away from someone else: **[+to]** *The crisis resulted in a challenge to his leadership.* | **[+for]** *the challenge for the Championship*
3 [C] an invitation from someone to try to beat them in a fight, game, argument etc: **[+to]** *The club* **accepted the challenge** *to compete.* | *He looked at her as if* **throwing down a challenge**.

challenge² Ac *v* [T] **1** to refuse to accept that something is right, fair, or legal: *She is* **challenging** *the court's* **decision**. **2** to invite someone to compete or fight against you: **challenge sb to sth** *I've challenged Mike to a game of tennis.*

challenger /'tʃæləndʒə $ -ər/ *n* [C] someone who is trying to win a competition, position of power etc: *the main challenger for the world title*

challenging Ac /'tʃæləndʒɪŋ/ *adj* difficult in an interesting or enjoyable way: *a challenging year*
THESAURUS **DIFFICULT**

chamber /'tʃeɪmbə $ -ər/ *n* [C]
1 LARGE ROOM a large room in a public building used for important meetings: *the Council chamber*
2 OF PARLIAMENT one of the two parts of a parliament: **upper/lower chamber** (=the House of Lords and the House of Commons, in Britain)
3 BELOW GROUND a room, especially one that is below the ground or used for something unpleasant: *a burial chamber*
4 IN YOUR BODY/A MACHINE an enclosed space in your body or inside a machine: *the chambers of the heart*

chambermaid /'tʃeɪmbəmeɪd $ -ər-/ *n* [C] a woman whose job is to clean and tidy hotel BEDROOMS

'chamber ,music *n* [U] CLASSICAL music for a small group of instruments

chameleon /kə'miːliən/ *n* [C] a LIZARD that can make its skin the colour of the things around it → see picture at **REPTILE**

champ /tʃæmp/ *n* [C] *informal* a champion

champagne /ʃæm'peɪn/ *n* [U] a French white wine with a lot of BUBBLES, drunk on special occasions

champion¹ /'tʃæmpiən/ *n* [C]
1 someone who has won a competition, especially in sport: *the world snooker champion* | *a champion cyclist*
2 someone who fights for and defends an aim or idea: *a champion of women's rights*

champion² *v* [T] to publicly fight for and defend an aim or idea: *He* **championed the cause of** *the poor for many years.*

championship /'tʃæmpiənʃɪp/ *n* **1** [C] (*also* **championships** [plural]) a competition to find the best player or team in a particular sport: *the US basketball championships* **2** [singular] the position of being a champion

chance¹ /tʃɑːns $ tʃæns/ *n*
1 POSSIBILITY [C,U] a possibility that something will happen: **[+(that)]** *Is there any chance that he'll recover?* | **[+of]** *Sue had no chance of winning.* | **sb's chances of doing sth** (=how likely someone is to succeed) *What are his chances of getting the job?*

Grammar
Do not say 'His chances to win the game are very small.' Say His **chances of** winning the game are very small.

2 OPPORTUNITY [C] an opportunity to do something that you want to do: **[+to]** She **had the chance** to meet the leading actors. | I never **get a chance** to relax. | Will you **give** me **a chance** to explain? | Friday is our **last chance** to see the show.
3 LUCK [U] when things happen without being planned or caused by people: **by chance** By chance, I met her in town on Saturday. | It was **pure chance** (=not planned at all) that we ended up in the same office. → OFF-CHANCE

PHRASES

any chance of ...? spoken used to ask if you can have something or if something is possible: Any chance of a coffee?
by any chance spoken used to ask politely if something is true or possible: Are you Loren, by any chance?
(the) chances are (that) informal used to say that something is likely: The chances are she'll say no.
no chance/not a chance! spoken used to emphasize that you do not think something will happen
take a chance to do something that involves a risk: I'm **not taking any chances**. | **[+on/with]** The Director took a chance on her and gave her the part.

COLLOCATIONS

verbs

to have/stand a chance He doesn't have much chance of persuading her.
to increase/improve the chance of sth These tips will increase your chance of survival in an emergency.

adjectives

little/no/not much chance He had little chance of escape.
some chance They say there's some chance of sunshine tomorrow.
a good chance (=something that is quite likely) There's a good chance that she'll win.
a small/slight/slim chance The operation has only a small chance of success.
a remote chance (=a very small chance) The chance of being struck by lightning is remote.
a fifty-fifty chance (=an equal chance of happening or not happening) I think I have a fifty-fifty chance of getting an interview.

chance² v **1** [T] informal to do something that involves a risk: The bus might get me there on time but I don't want to **chance** it. **2** [I] literary to do something in a way that was not planned: **[+to]** I chanced to hear their conversation.

chance³ adj [only before noun] not planned or expected: a **chance meeting**

chancellor /'tʃɑːnsələ $ 'tʃænsələr/ n [C] **1** (also **Chancellor of the Ex'chequer**) the British government minister in charge of taxes and government spending **2** the leader of the government in some

countries **3 a)** BrE the person who officially represents a university on special occasions **b)** AmE the person in charge of some universities

chandelier /ˌʃændə'lɪə $ -'lɪr/ n [C] a frame that holds CANDLES or lights, hangs from the ceiling, and is decorated with many small pieces of glass

change¹ /tʃeɪndʒ/ v
1 BECOME DIFFERENT [I] to become different: She's changed a lot. | **change from sth to sth** The traffic lights changed from green to red. | **change into sth** The caterpillars change into moths. THESAURUS ▸ BECOME
2 MAKE STH DIFFERENT [T] to make someone or something become different: The club is changing its rules. | **change sth into sth** You can change the sofa into a bed.
3 DO/USE STH NEW [I,T] to stop doing or using one thing, and start doing or using something else: changed jobs in May. | Are you changing your name? **change (from sth) to sth** We've changed to a new computer system. | Let's **change the subject** (=start talking about something else).
4 CLOTHES [I,T] to take off your clothes and put on different ones: He's upstairs **getting changed**. | Tony shaved and changed his shirt. | **[+into/out of]** She changed into her swimsuit.
5 TYRE/NAPPY/SHEET ETC [T] to put something new or different in place of something else: Dad had to stop and change the tyre. | **change the baby/change a nappy** (=put a clean NAPPY on a baby) | **change the bed/the sheets** (=put clean sheets on a bed)
6 TRAIN/PLANE/BUS [I,T] to get out of one train, bus or aircraft and into another in order to continue your journey: **[+at]** Change at Baker Street. | We had to change planes.
7 MONEY [T] if you change money, you give it to someone and they give it back to you in smaller amounts, or in money from a different country: **Can you change a £20 note?** | **change sth into/for sth** I'd like to change these pounds into euros.
8 STH YOU BOUGHT [T] BrE to take something you bought back to the shop and get something else instead, or to allow a customer to do this SYN **exchange** AmE: I'd like to change this sweater – it's too small.

PHRASES

change hands to become someone else's property: The hotel's changed hands.
change your mind to change your decision or opinion about something: **[+about]** I've changed my mind about leaving school.
change your tune informal to start expressing a different opinion about something: You've changed your tune all of a sudden!

PHRASAL VERBS

change over to stop doing or using one thing and start doing or using something different SYN **switch: change over (from sth) to sth** We're changing over to the new software next month.

THESAURUS

change to make something different: You've changed your hairstyle.
alter to change something so that it is better or more suitable: You can alter the colour using the menu at the top of the screen. | The law has since

been altered to prevent people from using this excuse.

modify to make small changes to something: *We will need to modify the design.*

adapt to change something so that it can be used in a different way: *The building has been adapted so that disabled people can use it.*

turn sth into sth to change something into a completely different thing with a different purpose: *There are plans to turn the theatre into a casino.* | *They want to turn the book into a film.*

reform to change a law or system in order to make it fairer or more effective: *The government wants to reform the tax system.*

transform/revolutionize to change something completely, especially so that it is much better: *Picasso transformed the way we think about art.*

twist/distort to deliberately change facts, ideas, or words, especially in order to deceive people: *They twisted the facts to support their argument.*

change² n

1 **STH BECOMES DIFFERENT** [C,U] something that has become different, or a situation in which something becomes different: **[+in]** *recent changes in the law* | *the need for political change* | **[+of]** *his sudden changes of mood*

2 **STH NEW AND INTERESTING** [singular] something that is interesting or enjoyable because it is different from what is usual: *I need a change.* | *Let's eat out for a change.* | *'Ron was on time.' 'That makes a change.'*

3 **STH IS REPLACED** [C] an action or event that involves replacing one thing with another: *The car needs an oil change.* | **[+of]** *a change of government* | **change from sth to sth** *the change from pounds to kilograms*

4 **MONEY** [U] **a)** the money you get back when you pay more than something costs: *Here's your change, sir.* **b)** coins, not paper money: **in change** *I have about a dollar in change.* **c)** coins or paper money that add up to the same value as a larger unit of money: **[+for]** *Do you have change for $1?* **THESAURUS** ▶ MONEY

5 **CLOTHES** a change of clothes/underwear etc another set of clothes that you can use if necessary → SMALL CHANGE

PHRASES

have a change of heart to change your attitude about something: *She was thinking of leaving, but then she had a sudden change of heart.*

COLLOCATIONS

adjectives

a big/major/great change *There have been some big changes in my life recently.*

a slight/small/minor change *There has to be a slight change of plan.*

a gradual change *The change in his attitude was very gradual.*

a fundamental/radical change *There will have to be fundamental changes in the way we use energy.*

verbs

to make a change *We've made some changes to the design.*

---

to bring about a change (=to cause it) *The war brought about many changes.*

to introduce a change *The government introduced a number of changes to education.*

changeable /ˈtʃeɪndʒəbəl/ adj likely to change or changing often **SYN** **variable**: *changeable weather*

changeover /ˈtʃeɪndʒˌəʊvə $ -ˌoʊvər/ n [C] a change from one activity or system to another **SYN** **switch**: *the changeover from military to civilian rule*

'changing room n [C] a room where you change your clothes when you play sport, try on clothes in a shop etc

channel¹ Ac /ˈtʃænl/ n [C]

1 **TELEVISION** a television station: *What's on Channel 4?* | *Do you mind if I change channels?* | **channel hopping/surfing** (=when you change quickly from one channel to another many times)

2 **METHOD OF COMMUNICATION** [usually plural] a way that you use to communicate information, ideas etc: *Apply through the usual channels.* | **[+of]** *channels of communication*

3 **AREA OF WATER** **the (English) Channel** the narrow area of water between England and France

4 **PASSAGE FOR LIQUID** a passage that water or other liquids flow along: *an **irrigation channel***

5 **FOR SHIPS** the deepest part of a river, sea etc, especially where it is deep enough for ships to sail

channel² Ac v [T] (**channelled, channelling** BrE, **channeled, channeling** AmE) to direct something towards a particular purpose, place, or situation: **channel sth into sth** *He began to **channel** his **energies** into sport.*

chant¹ /tʃɑːnt $ tʃænt/ v [I,T] **1** to repeat a word or phrase many times: *Protestors **chanted** anti-government **slogans**.* **2** to sing a religious song or prayer using only one or two notes

chant² n [C] **1** words or phrases repeated many times: **[+of]** *chants of 'Long live the King!'* **2** a religious song or prayer that is sung using only one or two notes

chaos /ˈkeɪɒs $ -ɑːs/ n [U] a situation in which everything is confused and nothing is happening in an organized way: *The floods **caused chaos**.* | **in chaos** *The game ended in **absolute chaos**.*

chaotic /keɪˈɒtɪk $ -ˈɑːtɪk/ adj confused and without any order: *The city was crowded and chaotic.*

chap /tʃæp/ n [C] especially BrE informal a man

chapel /ˈtʃæpəl/ n [C] a small church or room in which Christians pray and have religious services

chaperone /ˈʃæpərəʊn $ -roʊn/ n [singular] an older woman who goes somewhere with a young woman, to make sure that she behaves well

chaplain /ˈtʃæplɪn/ n [C] a priest who works for the army, a hospital, a university etc

chapped /tʃæpt/ adj chapped lips or hands are sore, dry, and cracked

chapter Ac /ˈtʃæptə $ -ər/ n [C]

1 one of the parts into which a book is divided: *See Chapter 3.* **THESAURUS** ▶ PART

2 a particular period in someone's life or in history: **[+of/in]** *a terrible chapter of history*

character /ˈkærəktə $ -ər/ *n*

1 [C,U] the qualities that make a person, place, or thing different from any other: *The two brothers were totally **different** in character.* | *The character of the school has changed.* | **in character/out of character** (=typical or untypical of someone's character) *He swore, which was completely out of character.*

2 [C] a person in a book, play, film etc: *Julia Roberts played the main character.*

3 [C] a particular kind of person: *Dan's a strange character.* | **a (real) character** (=someone who is interesting and amusing)

4 [U] good qualities such as courage, loyalty, and honesty that people admire: *She had great **strength of character**.*

5 [U] qualities that make someone or something special and interesting: *a house with a lot of character*

6 [C] a letter, mark, or sign used in writing, printing, or on a computer

> **Usage**
> When describing someone's character, you can say, for example: *She's very nice.* | *She's a kind person.* | *She always seems so friendly.*
> Do not say 'Her character is nice.' or 'She has a kind character.'

> **COLLOCATIONS – sense 2**
> **adjectives**
> **the main/central character** *The main character in the book is a lawyer.*
> **a minor character** *I play a minor character in the film.*
> **a fictional character** (=someone who does not exist in real life) *Why do people care so much about fictional characters?*
> **noun + character**
> **a television/film/movie character** *He played many well-known television characters.*
> **a cartoon character** *Minnie Mouse is a famous cartoon character.*
> **verbs**
> **to play a character** *The character of Harry Potter was played by Daniel Radcliffe.*

characteristic¹ /ˌkærəktəˈrɪstɪk◂/ *n* [C usually plural] a quality or feature that is typical of someone or something and makes them different from others: **[+of]** *the characteristics of different schools* | *We inherit **physical characteristics** from our parents.*

characteristic² *adj* typical of a particular person or thing: **[+of]** *These problems are characteristic of modern life.* | *one of the **characteristic features** of his books* —**characteristically** /-kli/ *adv*

characterization (*also* **-isation** *BrE*) /ˌkærəktəraɪˈzeɪʃən $ -tərə-/ *n* [U] the way that the people in a book, play etc are described

characterize (*also* **-ise** *BrE*) /ˈkærəktəraɪz/ *v* [T]
1 to be typical of someone or something: *the bright colours that characterize her paintings* **2** to describe

the qualities of someone or something in a particular way: **characterize sb/sth as (being) sth** *He is often characterised as a Catholic writer.*

charade /ʃəˈrɑːd $ ʃəˈreɪd/ *n* [C] a situation in which people pretend to think, feel etc something, although they clearly do not: *All their talk of unity was only a charade.*

charcoal /ˈtʃɑːkəʊl $ ˈtʃɑːrkoʊl/ *n* [U] a black substance made of burned wood, used as FUEL or for drawing

charge¹ /tʃɑːdʒ $ tʃɑːrdʒ/ *n*

1 FEE [C,U] the amount of money you have to pay for something: **[+of]** *an **admission charge** of £2.50* | **[+for]** *charges for eye tests* | *We deliver **free of charge** (=you do not have to pay for it).* THESAURUS COST

2 ACCUSATION [C] a statement that says that someone has done something illegal or bad: **charge of assault/murder/robbery etc** (=an official statement that the police make) *He appeared in court on a charge of criminal damage.* | **bring/press charges** (=officially say that you think someone is guilty of a crime) | **charge that** *She rejected the charge that she had acted irresponsibly.*

3 SUDDEN MOVE FORWARD [C] an attack in which people or animals move forward quickly

4 ELECTRICITY [U] electricity that is put into an item of electrical equipment such as a BATTERY → **SERVICE CHARGE**

PHRASES

> **be in charge** to have control over or responsibility for something or someone: *Who's in charge?* | **[+of]** *He's in charge of the finances.*
> **take charge** to start to have control of something or someone: *I'm taking charge while she's away.* | **[+of]** *Cathy's taken charge of the department.*

charge² *v*

1 COST [I,T] to ask someone to pay a particular amount of money for goods, a service etc: **charge (sb) £10/$30 etc (for sth)** *We were charged £80.* | **[+for]** *Do you charge for delivery?* | *Many gyms **charge** a joining fee.*

2 WITH CRIME [T] to state officially that someone might be guilty of a crime: **charge sb with sth** *Soames was charged with murder.*

3 MOVE FORWARDS [I,T] to move quickly forwards, especially in a threatening way: **[+into/past/ towards etc]** *Police charged into the house, guns ready.* THESAURUS RUN

4 BATTERY (*also* **charge up**) [I,T] if a BATTERY charges, or if you charge it, it takes in and stores electricity

charge card *n* [C] a plastic card from a particular shop that you can use to buy goods there and pay for them later → **credit card**

charged /tʃɑːdʒd $ tʃɑːrdʒd/ *adj* a charged situation is full of strong emotions: *the **highly charged** atmosphere of the trial*

chariot /ˈtʃæriət/ *n* [C] a vehicle with two wheels pulled by a horse, used in ancient times in battles and races

charisma /kəˈrɪzmə/ *n* [U] the natural ability to attract and influence other people —**charismatic** /ˌkærəzˈmætɪk◂/ *adj*

charitable /ˈtʃærətəbəl/ adj **1** relating to charities and their work: *charitable donations* **2** kind and sympathetic —**charitably** adv

charity /ˈtʃærəti/ n (plural **charities**)
1 [C,U] an organization that gives money, goods, or help to people who are poor, sick etc: **[+for]** *a charity for the homeless* | *The money raised will go to charity* (=be given to a charity). | **charity concert/dinner etc** (=an event etc organized to collect money for a charity) **THESAURUS** ORGANIZATION
2 [U] money or gifts given to help people who are poor, sick etc: *people who live on charity*
3 [U] formal kindness or sympathy towards other people

ˈ**charity shop** n [C] BrE a shop that sells used clothes, books etc to collect money for a charity **SYN** **thrift shop** AmE

charlatan /ˈʃɑːlətən $ ˈʃɑːr-/ n [C] literary disapproving someone who pretends to have special skills or knowledge

charm¹ /tʃɑːm $ tʃɑːrm/ n **1** [C,U] a quality someone or something has that makes people like them: *Lee's boyish charm* | **[+of]** *the charm of Italy* **2** [C] something you wear, have etc because you believe it brings you good luck: *a lucky charm*

charm² v [T] to attract or please someone: *a story that has always charmed children* —**charmer** n [C]

charmed /tʃɑːmd $ tʃɑːrmd/ adj **have/lead a charmed life** to be very lucky, especially by succeeding in avoiding danger, injury etc

charming /ˈtʃɑːmɪŋ $ ˈtʃɑːr-/ adj very pleasing or attractive: *her charming brother* **THESAURUS** NICE —**charmingly** adv

charred /tʃɑːd $ tʃɑːrd/ adj black from having been burned: *charred wood* —**char** v [I,T]

chart¹ Ac /tʃɑːt $ tʃɑːrt/ n [C] **1** a drawing, set of numbers, GRAPH etc that shows information: *The chart shows last year's sales.* **2** a map, especially of the sea or stars **3** **the charts** [plural] the official list of the most popular songs, produced each week

chart² Ac v [T] **1** to record information about something over a period of time: *Teachers chart each student's progress through the year.* **2** to make a map of an area of land, sea, or sky

charter¹ /ˈtʃɑːtə $ ˈtʃɑːrtər/ n **1** [C] a written statement of the principles, duties, and purposes of an organization: *the UN charter* **2** [U] when someone rents a boat, aircraft etc from a company, usually for a short time: **for charter** *yachts available for charter* | *a charter boat* | **charter flight/service** (=using aircraft that travel companies rent but do not own, so that the flight is usually cheaper than usual)

charter² v [T] to rent a boat, aircraft etc from a company

chartered /ˈtʃɑːtəd $ ˈtʃɑːrtərd/ adj [only before noun] BrE **chartered accountant/surveyor etc** a trained ACCOUNTANT etc who has passed all the necessary examinations

ˌ**charter ˈmember** n [C] AmE someone who helps to establish a new organization or club **SYN** **founder member** BrE

CHASE

chase

follow

chase¹ /tʃeɪs/ v
1 [I,T] to quickly follow someone or something, especially to catch them **SYN** **pursue**: *The car was chased by police.* | **[+after]** *'My glove!' he shouted, chasing after the dog.* | **chase sb away/off** (=make someone leave a place, by chasing them) *He managed to chase away his attacker.* **THESAURUS** FOLLOW
2 [I,T] to try very hard to get something: *Too many people are chasing too few jobs.* | **[+after]** *reporters chasing after a story*

chase² n [C] an act of following someone or something quickly to catch them: *a car chase* | *A policeman saw him and gave chase* (=chased him).

chasm /ˈkæzəm/ n literary **1** [C] a very deep space between two areas of rock or ice **2** [singular] a big difference between two people, groups, or things **SYN** **gulf**

chassis /ˈʃæsi:/ n [C] (plural **chassis** /-si:z/) the frame on which the body of a vehicle is built

chaste /tʃeɪst/ adj old-fashioned not having sex, or not showing sexual feelings

chasten /ˈtʃeɪsən/ v [T] formal to make someone realize that their behaviour was wrong

chastise /tʃæˈstaɪz/ v [T] formal to criticize or punish someone

chastity /ˈtʃæstəti/ n [U] when someone lives without having sex: *a vow of chastity*

chat¹ /tʃæt/ v [I] (**chatted**, **chatting**) to talk in a friendly informal way, especially about unimportant things: **[+to/with]** *Jo was chatting to Sam.* | **[+about]** *We chatted about sailing.* **THESAURUS** TALK
PHRASAL VERBS
chat sb ↔ **up** BrE informal to talk to someone in a way that shows you are sexually attracted to them

chat² n [C,U] a friendly informal conversation: **[+with]** *I've had a chat with Sue about it.* **THESAURUS** TALK

chateau /ˈʃætəʊ $ ʃæˈtoʊ/ n [C] (plural **chateaux** /-təʊz $ -ˈtoʊz/) a castle or large country house in France

chatroom /'tʃætru:m, -rʊm/ n [C] a place on the Internet where you can have a conversation with people by writing messages to them and immediately receiving their reply

'chat show n [C] BrE a television or radio show on which people are asked questions about themselves SYN **talk show** AmE

chatter /'tʃætə $ -ər/ v [I] **1** to talk quickly in a friendly way about unimportant things, especially for a long time **2** if your teeth are chattering, they are knocking together because you are cold or afraid —**chatter** n [U]

chatty /'tʃæti/ adj informal **1** liking to talk a lot in a friendly way **2** having a friendly informal style: a **chatty letter**

chauffeur /'ʃəʊfə, ʃəʊ'fɜ: $ 'ʃoʊfər, ʃoʊ'fɜ:r/ n [C] someone whose job is to drive a car for someone else —**chauffeur** v [T]

chauvinist /'ʃəʊvɪnɪst $ 'ʃoʊ-/ n [C] disapproving **1** a man who thinks that men are better than women **2** someone who believes that their country or race is better than any other —**chauvinism** n [U]

cheap¹ /tʃi:p/ adj
1 costing little money, or less money than you expect OPP **expensive**: The jacket was quite cheap. | Property's cheaper in Spain. | cheap flights | **dirt cheap** informal (=extremely cheap)
2 disapproving low in price and quality: cheap jewellery
3 AmE disapproving not liking to spend money SYN **mean** BrE —**cheaply** adv: How did he buy the land so cheaply? —**cheapness** n [U]

THESAURUS

cheap costing very little money, or less than you expected: cheap flights | The jacket was really cheap. It was only $20.
low low prices, rents, or fees do not cost a lot of money: The rent is very low. | They sell good food at surprisingly low prices.
budget budget flights, airlines, hotels etc have specially low prices: You can get a budget flight to Amsterdam for only £19.
be a bargain especially spoken to be extremely cheap: The coat was a real bargain.
be good/great value to be worth the money that you pay: At £12.50, the book is good value.
inexpensive formal not expensive compared to other things of the same kind: Hotels are relatively inexpensive compared to London.
reasonable a reasonable price seems fair and is not too high: The restaurant serves good food at reasonable prices.
economical cheap because it uses less money or fuel: It is more economical to buy in large quantities. | an economical car

---

cheap² adv informal for a low price: I got it cheap. | The house was **going cheap** (=being sold for a lower price than normal).

cheapen /'tʃi:pən/ v **1** [I,T] to become lower in value or price, or to make something do this **2** [T] to make something or someone seem to deserve

less respect: Don't cheapen yourself by answering his insults.

cheapo /'tʃi:pəʊ $ -oʊ/ adj [only before noun] informal low in price and low in quality → **cheap**: a cheapo camera

cheapskate /'tʃi:pskeɪt/ n [C] informal disapproving someone who does not like spending money

cheat¹ /tʃi:t/ v
1 [I] to behave in a dishonest way in order to win or get an advantage: **[+at]** He always cheats at cards. | **cheat in an exam** BrE, **cheat on an exam** AmE: She was caught cheating in a maths test.
2 [T] to deceive or trick someone: **cheat sb out of sth** He cheated the old woman out of all her money. | I **felt cheated** (=felt I had been treated unfairly).
PHRASAL VERBS
cheat on sb if someone cheats on their husband, girlfriend etc, they have a secret sexual relationship with another person

cheat² n [C] someone who cheats

check¹ /tʃek/ v
1 [I,T] to look at or test something carefully in order to be sure that it is correct, in good condition, safe etc: You'd better check our tickets. | Check the eggs before you buy them. | **[+(that)]** Did you check that the door's locked? | **[+whether/how/who etc]** He checked whether he was being followed. | **double-check** (=check something twice)
2 [I,T] to ask someone about something: **[+(that)]** I called to check that they'd received my letter. | **[+with]** Check with your doctor before going on a diet.
3 [T] to stop something bad from getting worse SYN **halt**: measures to check the growth in crime
4 [T] to suddenly stop yourself from saying or doing something: **check yourself** Ruby wanted to laugh, but checked herself.
5 [T] AmE to take your bags to a desk at an airport, so that they can be put on the plane SYN **check in** BrE
6 [T] AmE to put a mark by an answer to show that it is correct, or on a list to show that you have dealt with something SYN **tick** BrE → **DOUBLE-CHECK**
PHRASAL VERBS
check in (also **check into** sth) to go to the desk at an airport or hotel to say that you have arrived: Check in two hours before your flight.
check sth ↔ **off** to put a mark next to something on a list to show that you have dealt with it
check (up) on sb/sth to find out if something or someone is all right, doing what they should be doing etc: I'll just go check on dinner. | Mom's always checking up on me.
check out
1 check sth ↔ **out** to get more information about something, especially to find out if it is true or correct: Did you check out his story?
2 check sb/sth ↔ **out** informal to visit a place or look at something or someone to see if you like them: Check out our new website.
3 to pay the bill and leave a hotel

THESAURUS

check to look at something to make sure that it is correct, in good condition, safe etc: The inspector checked my ticket.

make sure (that) to check that the situation is how it should be, or how you expect it to be: *Can you make sure that the gas is turned off? | I wanted to make sure that you had got back safely.*
double-check to check something again so that you are completely sure: *I double-checked that I had my ticket and my passport with me.*
verify *formal* to officially check something and show that it is correct: *The bank will need to verify your personal details.*

check² n

1 [C] a careful look at or test of something, to see if it is safe, correct, in good condition etc: **[+on]** *a safety check on gas appliances* | **carry out/run/make a check** *A medical check was carried out.*
2 [C usually singular] something that controls something else and stops it from increasing: **[+on]** *Higher interest rates are a check on public spending.* | **keep/hold sth in check** (=keep something under control) *He managed to keep his temper in check.*
3 [C,U] a pattern of squares, especially on cloth: *blue and white check trousers*
4 the American spelling of CHEQUE
5 [C] *AmE* a list that you are given in a restaurant showing what you have eaten and how much you must pay SYN **bill** *BrE*
6 [C] *AmE* a mark (✔) that you put next to an answer to show that it is correct or next to something on a list to show that you have dealt with it SYN **tick** *BrE* → **RAIN CHECK**

checkbook /ˈtʃekbʊk/ *n* the American spelling of CHEQUEBOOK

checked /tʃekt/ *adj* having a regular pattern of different coloured squares: *a checked shirt* → see picture at PATTERN

checkered (*also* **chequered** *BrE*) /ˈtʃekəd $ -ərd/ *adj* **1** marked with squares of two different colours: *a checkered flag* **2 checkered history/past etc** periods of failure as well as success in someone's or something's past: *The car has had a chequered history.*

checkers /ˈtʃekəz $ -ərz/ *n* [U] *AmE* a game for two players, using 12 flat round pieces each and a special board with 64 squares SYN **draughts** *BrE*

'check-in *n* [singular] a place where you report your arrival at an airport, hotel etc: *The check-in desks seem to be crowded.*

'checking ac,count *n* [C] *AmE* a bank account that you can take money out of at any time SYN **current account** *BrE*

checklist /ˈtʃeklɪst/ *n* [C] a list that helps to remind you of all the things you have to do for a particular job or activity THESAURUS LIST

checkmate /ˈtʃekmeɪt/ *n* [U] the position in a game of CHESS when the KING cannot escape and the game has ended

checkout /ˈtʃek-aʊt/ *n* [C] the place in a SUPERMARKET where you pay for goods

checkpoint /ˈtʃekpɔɪnt/ *n* [C] a place where an official person stops people and vehicles to examine them

checkup, **check-up** /ˈtʃek-ʌp/ *n* [C] an occasion when a doctor or DENTIST examines you to see if you are healthy: *It's important to have regular checkups.*

cheddar /ˈtʃedə $ -ər/ *n* [U] a firm smooth yellow cheese

cheek /tʃiːk/ *n*
1 [C] the soft round part of your face below each of your eyes: *Billy had rosy cheeks and blue eyes.* | *her tear-stained cheeks* → see picture on page A2
2 [singular, U] *BrE* behaviour that is rude or not respectful: **have the cheek to do sth** *He had the cheek to ask me for more money.*

cheekbone /ˈtʃiːkbəʊn $ -boʊn/ *n* [C] the bone just below your eye → see picture on page A2

cheeky /ˈtʃiːki/ *adj BrE* rude or showing no respect, sometimes in an amusing way: *a little boy with a cheeky grin* | *Don't be so cheeky!* THESAURUS RUDE

cheer¹ /tʃɪə $ tʃɪr/ *n* [C] a shout of approval, happiness, or encouragement

cheer² *v* [I,T] to shout approval, encouragement etc: *The spectators cheered him wildly.* THESAURUS SHOUT

PHRASAL VERBS
cheer sb ↔ **on** to encourage a person or a team by cheering for them: *Her family and friends were cheering her on.*
cheer up to become happier, or to make someone feel happier: *Cheer up! The worst is over.* | **cheer** sb ↔ **up** *Here's a bit of news that will cheer you up.*

cheerful /ˈtʃɪəfəl $ ˈtʃɪr-/ *adj* **1** happy, or behaving in a way that shows you are happy: *He is feeling more cheerful than before.* | **cheerful voice/smile/manner etc** *'I'm Robyn,' she said with a cheerful smile.* THESAURUS HAPPY **2** bright, pleasant, and making you feel happy: *a cheerful kitchen* —**cheerfully** *adv* —**cheerfulness** *n* [U]

cheerleader /ˈtʃɪəˌliːdə $ ˈtʃɪrˌliːdər/ *n* [C] a member of a team of young women that encourages a crowd to cheer at a US sports event

cheerless /ˈtʃɪələs $ ˈtʃɪr-/ *adj* cheerless weather, places, or times make you feel sad and bored: *a cheerless winter day*

cheers /tʃɪəz $ tʃɪrz/ *spoken* **1** what you say just before you drink a glass of alcohol with someone, to show friendly feelings towards them **2** *BrE informal* thank you **3** *BrE informal* goodbye

cheery /ˈtʃɪəri $ ˈtʃɪri/ *adj* happy or making you feel happy: *a cheery smile* —**cheerily** *adv*

cheese /tʃiːz/ *n* [C,U] a solid food made from milk, that is usually white or yellow: **a cheese sandwich** | **a piece/bit/slice/lump etc of cheese** | *Sprinkle the pasta with grated cheese.* → see picture at BOARD¹

cheeseburger /ˈtʃiːzbɜːgə $ -bɜːrgər/ *n* [C] a HAMBURGER cooked with a piece of cheese on top of the meat

cheesecake /ˈtʃiːzkeɪk/ *n* [C,U] a sweet cake made with soft white cheese: *a slice of strawberry cheesecake*

cheesy /ˈtʃiːzi/ *adj informal* cheap and not of good quality: *a cheesy soap opera*

cheetah /'tʃi:tə/ n [C] an African wild cat that has black spots and is able to run very fast → see picture at TIGER

chef /ʃef/ n [C] a skilled cook, especially the most important cook in a restaurant

chemical¹ Ac /'kemɪkəl/ n [C] a substance used in or produced by a chemical process: **toxic/ hazardous/dangerous chemicals** the disposal of toxic chemicals

chemical² Ac adj relating to substances, the study of substances, or processes involving changes in substances: a chemical reaction | K is the chemical symbol for potassium. | chemical weapons —**chemically** /-kli/ adv

chemist /'kemɪst/ n [C] **1** a scientist who does work related to chemistry: a research chemist **2** BrE someone who is trained to prepare drugs and medicines for sale in a shop SYN **pharmacist 3** (also **chemist's**) BrE a shop where you can buy medicines, beauty products etc SYN **drugstore** AmE

chemistry /'kemɪstri/ n [U]
1 the science that studies the structure of substances and the way they change or combine with each other → **biochemistry**
2 the way substances combine in a process, thing, person etc: a person's body chemistry
3 if there is chemistry between two people, they like each other or work well together

chemotherapy /ˌki:məʊ'θerəpi, ˌkem- $ -moʊ-/, **chemo** informal n [U] the use of drugs to control and try to cure CANCER

cheque BrE, **check** AmE /tʃek/ n [C] a printed piece of paper that you sign and use to pay for things: **[+for]** a cheque for £100 | Can I **pay by cheque**? | **cash a cheque** (=get cash in exchange for a cheque) → **BLANK CHEQUE**

chequebook BrE, **checkbook** AmE /'tʃekbʊk/ n [C] a small book of cheques

'cheque card (also **cheque guaran'tee card**) n [C] BrE a card given to you by your bank that you must show when you write a cheque, which promises that the bank will pay out the amount written on the cheque

chequered /'tʃekəd $ -ərd/ adj a British spelling of CHECKERED

cherish /'tʃerɪʃ/ v [T] **1** if you cherish something, it is very important to you: **cherish a hope/idea/ dream etc** Mary cherished the dream of being a pop star. **2** to take care of someone or something you love very much

cherry /'tʃeri/ n (plural **cherries**) **1** [C] a small round red or black fruit with a stone in the middle: a bunch of cherries → see picture on page A4 **2** [C,U] a tree that produces cherries, or the wood from this tree

cherub /'tʃerəb/ n [C] an ANGEL shown in paintings as a small child with wings

chess /tʃes/ n [U] a board game for two players in which you must trap your opponent's KING in order to win → see picture at BOARD¹

chest /tʃest/ n
1 [C] the front part of your body between your neck and stomach: a hairy chest | chest pains → see picture on page A2
2 [C] a large strong box with a lid, that you use to keep things in: a large wooden chest
PHRASES
get sth off your chest informal to tell someone about something that has worried or annoyed you for a long time: There's something I need to get off my chest.

chestnut /'tʃesnʌt/ n **1** [C] a smooth red-brown nut you can eat → see picture at NUT **2** [C] the tree on which these nuts grow **3** [U] a reddish brown colour —**chestnut** adj

,chest of 'drawers n [C] (plural **chests of drawers**) a piece of furniture with drawers, used for keeping clothes in SYN **dresser** AmE

chew /tʃu:/ v [I,T] **1** to bite food several times before swallowing it: The meat's so tough I can hardly chew it. **THESAURUS** ▶ BITE **2** to bite something several times without eating it: **chew your lip/nails** She chewed her lip and said nothing.
PHRASAL VERBS
chew sb ↔ **out** AmE informal to speak angrily to someone who has done something wrong: My boss chewed me out for being late.
chew sth ↔ **over** to think carefully about a problem, idea etc SYN **consider, mull over**

'chewing gum (also **gum**) n [U] a type of sweet that you chew for a long time, but do not swallow

chewy /'tʃu:i/ adj needing to be chewed a lot before it can be swallowed: chewy toffee

chic /ʃi:k/ adj fashionable and showing good style SYN **stylish**

chick /tʃɪk/ n [C] **1** a baby bird, especially a baby chicken → see picture at CHICKEN¹ **2** especially AmE informal a young woman

CHICKEN

hen

chick

cock BrE/
rooster AmE

chicken¹ /'tʃɪkɪn/ n
1 [C] a farm bird that is kept for its meat and eggs → **chick, cock, hen, rooster**
2 [U] the meat from a chicken: roast chicken | chicken soup

chicken² v
PHRASAL VERBS
chicken out informal to decide at the last moment not to do something because you are not brave enough: You're not chickening out, are you?

chicken³ /tʃɪf/ *adj informal* not brave enough to do something SYN **cowardly**: *Dave's too chicken to ask her out.*

chicken pox, chickenpox /'tʃɪkən pɒks $ -pɑːks/ *n* [U] a common illness that children get, that causes a fever and red spots on the skin

chief¹ /tʃiːf/ *adj* [only before noun]
1 highest in rank: *the government's chief medical officer*
2 most important SYN **main, principal**: *One of the chief causes of crime is drugs.* | *Safety is our chief concern.* THESAURUS **IMPORTANT**

chief² *n* [C] **1** the leader of a group or organization: [+of] *the chief of police* **2** the ruler of a tribe

Chief Ex'ecutive *n* the **Chief Executive** the President of the US

chiefly /'tʃiːfli/ *adv* mostly SYN **mainly, principally**: *a book that is intended chiefly for students of art*

chieftain /'tʃiːftɪn/ *n* [C] the leader of a tribe

chiffon /'ʃɪfɒn $ ʃɪ'fɑːn/ *n* [U] very thin soft cloth used for making women's clothing

child /tʃaɪld/ *n* [C] (*plural* **children** /'tʃɪldrən/)
1 a young person who is not yet an adult: *The film is not suitable for children under 12.* | *I was very happy as a child* (=when I was a child).
2 a son or daughter of any age: *Both our children are married now.* | *She has three grown-up children.* | *Alex is an only child* (=he has no brothers or sisters).
PHRASES
be child's play to be very easy to do: *Cooking for a family is child's play after running a restaurant.*

THESAURUS

child someone who is not yet an adult. You do not usually use **child** to talk about babies or teenagers: *Many children are scared of the dark.* | *He's just a child.*
kid *informal* a child. **Kid** is the usual word to use in everyday spoken English: *He's a smart kid.* | *Kids all know how to use computers.*
little boy/little girl a young male or female child: *I lived there when I was a little girl.* | *Little boys love dinosaurs.*
teenager someone between the ages of 13 and 19 years old: *The cafe was a popular meeting place for teenagers.*
adolescent a young person who is developing into an adult – used especially when talking about the problems these people have: *Adolescents are often very self-conscious about the way they look.*
minor *law* a young person who is not yet legally an adult: *It is illegal to sell alcohol to minors.*

---

childbearing /'tʃaɪldˌbeərɪŋ $ -ˌber-/ *n* [U] **1** the process of giving birth to children **2 childbearing age** the period of a woman's life during which she can have babies

child 'benefit *n* [U] money that the British government gives every week to families with children

childbirth /'tʃaɪldbɜːθ $ -bɜːrθ/ *n* [U] the act of having a baby

childcare /'tʃaɪldkeə $ -ker/ *n* [U] an arrangement in which someone looks after children whose parents are at work

childhood /'tʃaɪldhʊd/ *n* [C,U] the time when you are a child: *Sara had a very happy childhood.*

childish /'tʃaɪldɪʃ/ *adj* **1** relating to or typical of a child: *a childish voice* **2** *disapproving* behaving in a silly way that makes you seem much younger than you are: *Stop being so childish.* —**childishly** *adv* —**childishness** *n* [U]

childless /'tʃaɪldləs/ *adj* having no children: *childless couples*

childlike /'tʃaɪldlaɪk/ *adj* having the good qualities of a child, such as natural or trusting behaviour: *childlike innocence*

childminder /'tʃaɪldˌmaɪndə $ -ər/ *n* [C] *BrE* someone who is paid to look after young children while their parents are at work —**childminding** *n* [U]

childproof /'tʃaɪldpruːf/ *adj* designed to prevent a child from being hurt: *a childproof lock*

children /'tʃɪldrən/ *n* the plural of CHILD

'child sup,port *n* [U] money that someone pays regularly to their former wife or husband in order to help look after their children SYN **maintenance**

chill¹ /tʃɪl/ *n* **1** [singular] a feeling of coldness: *There was a slight chill in the air.* **2** [C] a sudden feeling of fear: *The sound of his laugh sent a chill through her.* **3** [C] a slight illness like a cold: *Take off those wet clothes before you catch a chill.*

chill² *v* **1** [T] to make something or someone cold: *Champagne should be chilled before serving.* **2** (*also* **chill out**) [I] *informal* to relax instead of feeling angry or nervous: *Chill out, Dave, it doesn't matter.*

chilli *BrE*, **chili** *AmE* /'tʃɪli/ *n* (*plural* **chillies** *BrE*, **chilies** *AmE*) **1** [C,U] a small thin red or green vegetable with a very hot taste: *chilli sauce* **2** (*also* **chilli con carne** *BrE*, **chili con carne** *AmE* /-kɒn 'kɑːni $ -kɑːn 'kɑːrni/) [U] a dish made with beans, meat, and chillies

chilling /'tʃɪlɪŋ/ *adj* making you feel frightened: *the chilling sound of wolves howling*

chillout music /'tʃɪlaʊt ˌmjuːzɪk/ (*also* **chillout**) *n* [U] music that you listen to when you want to relax

chilly /'tʃɪli/ *adj* **1** cold enough to make you feel uncomfortable: *a chilly morning* | *It's a bit chilly in here.* THESAURUS **COLD 2** behaving in an unfriendly way: *The results received a chilly reception on the stock markets.*

Word Choice: chilly or cool?
You use **chilly** when the temperature of the air feels a little cold and uncomfortable: *The weather was rather chilly and I wished I'd brought my coat.*
You use **cool** when the temperature of the air or a liquid is a little cold in a way that feels or tastes good: *There was a nice cool breeze.* | *I'd like a cool drink.* | *a cool mountain stream*

chime /tʃaɪm/ *v* [I,T] if a clock or bell chimes, it makes a ringing sound: *The clock chimed six.* —**chime** *n* [C]

PHRASAL VERBS

chime in to say something in order to add your opinion to a conversation: *'The kids could go too,'* Maria chimed in.

chimney /ˈtʃɪmni/ n [C] a vertical pipe that takes smoke up from a fire and out through the roof, or the part of this pipe that is above the roof

'chimney sweep n [C] someone whose job is to SWEEP (=clean) the inside of chimneys

chimpanzee /ˌtʃɪmpænˈziː, -pən-/ (also **chimp** /tʃɪmp/ informal) n [C] an African animal like a monkey without a tail → see picture at **APE**

chin /tʃɪn/ n [C] the front part of your face below your mouth: *He rubbed his chin thoughtfully.* → see picture on page A2

china /ˈtʃaɪnə/ n [U] **1** a hard white substance used for making plates, cups etc **2** plates, cups, and dishes made from china: *I'll get my best china out.*

chink /tʃɪŋk/ n [C] **1** a narrow crack or hole in something: *I could see light through a chink in the wall.* **2** BrE a high ringing sound made by metal or glass objects touching each other: *the chink of coins*

chinos /ˈtʃiːnəʊz $ -noʊz/ n [plural] loose trousers made from cotton

chintz /tʃɪnts/ n [U] smooth cotton cloth with flower patterns on it: *chintz covers on the chairs*

CHIPS

crisps BrE/chips AmE

chips BrE/fries AmE

chip¹ /tʃɪp/ n [C]

1 FOOD [usually plural] **a)** BrE a long thin piece of potato cooked in oil SYN **fries, French fries** AmE: *fish and chips* | *a portion of chips* **b)** AmE a thin flat round piece of food such as potato cooked in very hot oil and eaten cold SYN **crisp** BrE: *a bag of potato chips*
2 COMPUTER a small piece of SILICON with electronic parts on it, that is used in computers: *a silicon chip*
3 WOOD/STONE a small piece of wood, stone etc that has broken off something: *wood chips*
4 DAMAGED PART a small hole or mark on a plate, cup etc where a piece has broken off: *a bowl with a chip in it*
5 GAMBLING a small flat coloured piece of plastic used in GAMBLING games instead of money → **BLUE-CHIP**

PHRASES

be a chip off the old block informal to be very similar to your mother or father in appearance or character: *His son is a chip off the old block.*
have a chip on your shoulder to have an angry attitude to life because you think you have been treated unfairly in the past: *He's always had a chip on his shoulder about not going to college.*
when the chips are down spoken in a serious or difficult situation: *When the chips are down, it's time to show how strong you are.*

chip² v (**chipped, chipping**) **1** [I,T] if you chip something, or if it chips, a small piece accidentally breaks off: *She fell and chipped a tooth.* **2** [T] to break small pieces off something: **chip sth away/off** *Sandy chipped away the plaster covering the tiles.* —**chipped** adj: *a chipped cup*

PHRASAL VERBS

chip away at sth to gradually make something less effective or destroy it: *The government is chipping away at our democratic rights.*
chip in 1 to interrupt a conversation by saying something: *'It won't be easy,' Jeff chipped in.* **2** if each person in a group chips in, they each give a small amount of money so that they can buy something together SYN **contribute**: *We all chipped in to buy Amy a present.*

chipmunk /ˈtʃɪpmʌŋk/ n [C] a small North American animal that looks like a SQUIRREL and has black and white lines on its fur

chiropodist /kəˈrɒpədɪst, ʃə- $ -ˈrɑː-/ n [C] BrE someone whose job is to treat and care for people's feet SYN **podiatrist** AmE —**chiropody** n [U]

chirp /tʃɜːp $ tʃɜːrp/ v [I] if a bird or insect chirps, it makes short high sounds: *sparrows chirping in the trees* —**chirp** n [C]

chirpy /ˈtʃɜːpi $ ˈtʃɜːrpi/ adj BrE informal happy and active: *You seem very chirpy this morning.*

chisel /ˈtʃɪzəl/ n [C] a metal tool with a sharp end, used to cut wood or stone

chit /tʃɪt/ n [C] an official note that shows that you are allowed to have something

'chit-chat n [C,U] informal informal conversation about unimportant things

chivalrous /ˈʃɪvəlrəs/ adj formal a man who is chivalrous behaves in a polite and honourable way to women —**chivalry** n [U]

chives /tʃaɪvz/ n [plural] the long thin leaves of a plant with purple flowers. Chives taste of onion and are used in cooking.

chlorine /ˈklɔːriːn/ n [U] a yellow-green gas that is used to keep swimming pools clean

chlorophyll /ˈklɒrəfɪl, ˈklɔː- $ ˈklɔː-/ n [U] the green substance in plants, which they use to make food using energy from sunlight

chock-a-block /ˌtʃɒk ə ˈblɒk◂ $ ˈtʃɑːk ə ˌblɑːk/ adj **be chock-a-block (with sth)** BrE to be completely full of people or things

ˌchock-ˈfull adj [not before noun] informal completely full or containing a very large amount of something: **[+of]** *The pond was chock-full of weeds.*

chocoholic, chocaholic /ˌtʃɒkəˈhɒlɪk $ ˌtʃɑːkəˈhɒː-, ˌtʃɔː-/ n [C] informal someone who likes chocolate very much and eats a lot of it

chocolate /ˈtʃɒklət $ ˈtʃɑːkələt, ˈtʃɔː-/ n
1 [U] a sweet brown food eaten as a sweet or used in cooking: **milk chocolate** | **plain/dark chocolate**

(=chocolate with no milk and very little sugar) | **a bar of chocolate** (=a large piece with straight sides)

2 [C] a small sweet covered with chocolate: *Would you like a chocolate?* | *a box of chocolates*

3 [U] a drink made from hot milk and chocolate: *a mug of hot chocolate*

choice¹ /tʃɔɪs/ n

1 [C,U] if you have a choice, you can choose between several things → **choose**: **[+between]** *Voters have a choice between three political parties.* | **[+of]** *You have a choice of hotel or self-catering accommodation.* | *He has to make some important choices.*

2 [singular] the range of people or things that you can choose from: **[+of]** *There is a choice of four colours.* | *We offer a **wide choice** of wines and beers.* | *Consumers these days are **spoilt for choice** (=have a lot of things to choose from).*

3 [C usually singular] the person or thing that someone has chosen: **[+of]** *I don't like her choice of shoes.* | *London was a **good choice** to go to.* | *The law was my **first choice** as a career (=the career I wanted to do most).* → **MULTIPLE CHOICE**

PHRASES

by choice if you do something by choice, you do it because you want to: *She lives alone by choice.*

freedom of choice the freedom to choose what you want: *Patients should have more freedom of choice.*

have no choice but to do sth used when you have to do something because there is nothing else that you can do: *We had no choice but to wait.*

sth of your choice the one that you would most like to choose: *Many children are not able to go to the school of their choice.*

COLLOCATIONS

verbs

to have a choice *We had a choice between soup and salad.*

to make a choice (=to choose something) *She now has to make a choice of university.*

to give sb a choice *She gave me a choice: give up smoking or move out.*

to be faced with a choice (=to have to make a choice) *The government is faced with a difficult choice.*

adjectives

the right/wrong choice *Here's some information to help you make the right choice.*

a difficult/hard choice *It was a hard choice, but in the end I decided to stay.*

---

choice² *adj* of high quality: *choice plums*

choir /kwaɪə $ kwaɪr/ n [C] a group of people who sing together, especially in a church or school: *Susan sings in the school choir.*

choke¹ /tʃəʊk $ tʃoʊk/ v

1 CANNOT BREATHE [I,T] to prevent someone from breathing or be prevented from breathing, because the throat is blocked or because there is not enough air: *The smoke was choking me.* | **[+on]** *He choked on a piece of bread.*

2 CANNOT TALK [I,T] to be unable to talk properly because of strong emotion: *He was choking with rage.*

3 CANNOT MOVE THROUGH (*also* **choke up**) [T] to fill a place so that things cannot move through it: **be choked (up) with sth** *The gutters were choked up with leaves.* | *roads choked with traffic*

PHRASAL VERBS

choke sth ↔ **back** to control yourself so that you do not show how angry, sad etc you are: *Anna **choked back tears** as she tried to speak.*

choke² n [C] **1** a part of a car that controls the amount of air going into the engine **2** the sound someone makes when they are choking

choker /ˈtʃəʊkə $ ˈtʃoʊkər/ n [C] a piece of jewellery or narrow cloth that fits closely around your neck

cholera /ˈkɒlərə $ ˈkɑː-/ n [U] a serious disease that affects the stomach and BOWELS

cholesterol /kəˈlestərɒl $ -roʊl/ n [U] a substance in your body which doctors think may cause heart disease

choose /tʃuːz/ v [I,T] (*past tense* **chose** /tʃəʊz $ tʃoʊz/, *past participle* **chosen** /ˈtʃəʊzən $ ˈtʃoʊ-/)

1 to decide which one of several things or possibilities you want: **[+between/from]** *You can choose between ice cream and apple tart.* | **choose to do sth** *I chose to learn Italian rather than Spanish.* | **choose sb/sth to do sth** *They chose Donald to be their leader.* | **choose sb/sth for sth** *Why did you choose me for the job?*

2 to decide to do something: **choose to do sth** *I chose to ignore his advice.*

PHRASES

there is little/nothing to choose between sth used to say that two or more things are equally good: *There is little to choose between the two candidates for the job.*

THESAURUS

choose to decide to have or use a particular person or thing: *Why did you choose that colour?*

pick to choose someone or something, especially quickly. **Pick** is more informal than **choose**: *Pick any number from one to ten.*

select to choose something or someone, especially thinking carefully. **Select** is more formal than **choose**: *The committee will meet to select a new chairman.*

decide on sth to make a final decision when you are choosing something: *Have you decided on a name for the baby?*

opt for to choose one thing instead of another: *Many drivers opt for foreign cars.*

go for *especially spoken* to choose one thing instead of another – used especially when telling someone which thing you have chosen: *I think I'll go for the salad.*

---

choosy /ˈtʃuːzi/ adj difficult to please: *Jean's very choosy about what she eats.*

chop¹ /tʃɒp $ tʃɑːp/ (*also* **chop up**) v [T] (**chopped, chopping**) to cut something into smaller pieces: *He is outside chopping wood for the fire.* | *Can you chop up some carrots for me?* | **chop sth into pieces/chunks**

etc *Chop the meat into small cubes.* → see picture at
CUT¹ **THESAURUS** CUT

PHRASES

chop and change *BrE informal* to keep changing
your opinion: *I wish he would make his mind up
instead of chopping and changing all the time.*

PHRASAL VERBS

chop sth ↔ **down** to make a tree fall down by
cutting it with a sharp tool
chop sth ↔ **off** to remove something by cutting it
with a sharp tool: *Be careful you don't chop your
fingers off.*

chop² n [C] **1** a small flat piece of meat on a bone: *a
pork chop* **2** a quick hard hit with the side of your
hand or with a heavy sharp tool: *a karate chop* **3 the
chop** *BrE* if you get or are given the chop, you lose
your job

chopper /ˈtʃɒpə $ ˈtʃɑːpər/ n [C] *informal* a HELICOP-
TER

choppy /ˈtʃɒpi $ ˈtʃɑːpi/ adj choppy water has a lot
of waves and is not smooth to sail on

chopsticks /ˈtʃɒpstɪks
$ ˈtʃɑːp-/ n [plural] a pair
of thin sticks used for
eating food in China,
Japan etc

CHOPSTICKS

chopsticks

choral /ˈkɔːrəl/ adj relating to music that is sung
by a large group of
people → **chorus**: *an
evening of choral music*

chord /kɔːd $ kɔːrd/ n
[C] two or more musical
notes played at the same
time

chore /tʃɔː $ tʃɔːr/ n [C] a job that you have to do,
especially a boring one: *household chores*

choreography /ˌkɒriˈɒgrəfi, ˌkɔː- $ ˌkɔːriˈɑːg-/ n [U]
the art of arranging how dancers should move during a performance —**choreographer** n [C]
—**choreograph** /ˈkɒriəgrɑːf, ˈkɔː- $ ˈkɔːriəgræf/ v [T]

chortle /ˈtʃɔːtl $ ˈtʃɔːrtl/ v [I] *written* to laugh, espe-
cially because you are pleased about something
—**chortle** n [C]

chorus /ˈkɔːrəs/ n [C] **1** the part of a song that is
repeated after each VERSE **2** a large group of people
who sing together **3 the chorus** a group of singers,
dancers, or actors who perform together in a show
but do not have the main parts **4 a chorus of
thanks/disapproval/criticism etc** something that a
lot of people say at the same time: *The minister was
greeted with a chorus of boos.*

chose /tʃəʊz $ tʃoʊz/ v the past tense of CHOOSE

chosen /ˈtʃəʊzən $ ˈtʃoʊ-/ v the past participle of
CHOOSE

Christ /kraɪst/ (also **Jesus Christ**) n the man who
Christians believe is the son of God. Christianity is
based on Christ's life, death, and teaching.

christen /ˈkrɪsən/ v [T] **1** to officially give a child

its name at a Christian religious ceremony → **baptize**: *She was christened Mary Ann.* **2** to give something or someone a name

christening /ˈkrɪsənɪŋ/ n [C] a Christian ceremony in which a baby is officially given a name
and becomes a member of a Christian church
→ **baptism**

Christian¹ /ˈkrɪstʃən, -tiən/ adj related to Christian-
ity: *Christian beliefs | the Christian Church*

Christian² n [C] someone whose religion is Christianity

Christianity /ˌkrɪstiˈænəti/ n [U] the religion that
is based on the life and teachings of Jesus Christ

Christian name n [C] someone's first name: *I
can't remember his Christian name.* **THESAURUS** NAME

Christmas /ˈkrɪsməs/ n [C,U] the period around
December 25th when Christians celebrate the birth
of Christ and give each other presents: *Are you
going home for Christmas? | Merry Christmas! | a
Christmas card from her sister | an unwanted Christ-
mas present* → **FATHER CHRISTMAS**

Christmas ˈcarol n [C] a Christian song that
people sing at Christmas

Christmas ˈDay n [C,U] December 25th, the day
when most Christians celebrate the birth of Christ

Christmas ˈEve n [C,U] December 24th, the day
before Christmas Day

ˈChristmas tree n [C] a tree that people put
inside their house and decorate for Christmas

chrome /krəʊm $ kroʊm/ (also **chromium**
/ˈkrəʊmiəm $ ˈkroʊ-/) n [U] a hard shiny silver
metal that is used for covering objects: *doors with
chrome handles*

chromosome /ˈkrəʊməsəʊm $ ˈkroʊməsoʊm/ n
[C] *technical* a part of every living cell, which contains the GENEs that control the size, shape etc that
a plant or animal has

chronic /ˈkrɒnɪk $ ˈkrɑː-/ adj if a problem or illness
is chronic, it is serious and likely to continue for a
long time: *a chronic back problem | a chronic shortage
of teachers* —**chronically** /-kli/ adv: *patients who are
chronically ill*

chronicle /ˈkrɒnɪkəl $ ˈkrɑː-/ n [C] a written record
of events which mentions them in the order in
which they happened —**chronicle** v [T]: *The book
chronicles Flanagan's brave battle with cancer.*

chronological /ˌkrɒnəˈlɒdʒɪkəl $ ˌkrɑːnəˈlɑː-/ adj
arranged in the same order as events happened: *a
list of World Cup winners in chronological order*
—**chronologically** /-kli/ adv

chrysalis /ˈkrɪsəlɪs/ n [C] a MOTH or BUTTERFLY at
the stage of development when it has a hard outer
shell and is changing into its adult form → **cocoon**

chrysanthemum /krɪˈsænθəməm/ n [C] a garden
plant that has large brightly coloured flowers → see
picture at **FLOWER¹**

chubby /ˈtʃʌbi/ adj slightly fat: *chubby cheeks*
THESAURUS FAT

chuck /tʃʌk/ v [T] *informal* to throw something:
Chuck that magazine over here. **THESAURUS** THROW

chuck sth ↔ **away** *informal* to throw something away

chuck sth ↔ **in** *BrE informal* to leave your job: *If you hate the job so much, why don't you chuck it in?*

chuck sb/sth ↔ **out** *informal* **1** to throw something away: *We chucked out a lot of stuff when we moved.* **2** to make someone leave a place: **[+of]** *We were chucked out of the restaurant for smoking.*

chuckle /'tʃʌkəl/ v [I] to laugh quietly: *What are you chuckling about?* **THESAURUS** LAUGH —**chuckle** n [C]

chuffed /tʃʌft/ adj [not before noun] *BrE informal* very pleased or happy

chug /tʃʌg/ v [I] (**chugged, chugging**) if a car, train etc chugs somewhere, it moves there slowly, with the engine making a repeated low sound: **[+along/up/around etc]** *The little boat chugged slowly along the canal.*

chum /tʃʌm/ n [C] *old-fashioned* a good friend —**chummy** adj

chunk /tʃʌŋk/ n [C] **1** a large piece of something: **[+of]** *a chunk of cheese* → see picture at PIECE[1] **THESAURUS** PIECE **2** a large part or amount of something: *Hospital bills took a big chunk out of her savings.*

chunky /'tʃʌŋki/ adj **1** thick, solid, and heavy: *chunky jewellery* **2** someone who is chunky has a broad heavy body: *a short, chunky man*

church /tʃɜːtʃ $ tʃɜːrtʃ/ n
1 [C] a building where Christians go to pray → **cathedral**
2 [U] the religious ceremonies in a church: *How often do you* **go to church**?
3 (*also* **Church**) [C] one of the separate groups within the Christian religion: *the Catholic Church* **THESAURUS** RELIGION

> **Grammar**
> When you are talking about ceremonies in churches, you do not use **a** or **the**: *He goes to church every Sunday.*
> When you are talking about a church as a building, you often use **a** or **the**: *We visited a famous church.* | *the famous church of Saint Peter's in Rome*

churchgoer /'tʃɜːtʃˌgəʊə $ 'tʃɜːrtʃˌgoʊər/ n [C] someone who goes to church regularly

Church of 'England n **the Church of England** the state Christian organization in England → **Anglican**

churchyard /'tʃɜːtʃjɑːd $ 'tʃɜːrtʃjɑːrd/ n [C] a piece of land around a church where dead people are buried

churlish /'tʃɜːlɪʃ $ 'tʃɜːr-/ adj *formal* not polite or friendly: *It seemed churlish to refuse her invitation.*

churn[1] /tʃɜːn $ tʃɜːrn/ v
1 STOMACH [I] if your stomach churns, you feel sick because you are nervous or frightened: *Thinking about the exam made my stomach churn.*
2 WATER/MUD (*also* **churn up**) [I,T] if water, mud etc churns, or if something churns it, it moves about violently: *The storm churned up the sea bed.* | *a brown, churning river*
3 BUTTER [T] to make butter by using a churn

churn sth ↔ **out** *informal* to produce large quantities of something quickly, especially without caring about quality: *The nation's film industry churns out more than 50 movies a year.*

churn[2] n [C] **1** a container that is filled with milk and shaken to make butter **2** (*also* **milk churn**) *BrE* a large metal container used to carry milk

chute /ʃuːt/ n [C] **1** a long narrow structure that slopes down, so that things or people can slide down it: *a laundry chute* **2** *informal* a PARACHUTE

chutney /'tʃʌtni/ n [U] a cold mixture of fruit, sugar, and spices that is eaten especially with cheese or meat

CIA /ˌsiː aɪ 'eɪ/ n (**Central Intelligence Agency**) **the CIA** the department of the US government that collects information about other countries, especially secretly

CID /ˌsiː aɪ 'diː/ n [U] (**Criminal Investigation Department**) the department of the British police that deals with serious crimes

cider /'saɪdə $ -ər/ n [C,U] **1** *BrE* a drink made from apples that contains alcohol **2** *AmE* a drink made from apples that does not contain alcohol

cigar /sɪ'gɑː $ -'gɑːr/ n [C] a tube-shaped object made of tobacco leaves that people smoke

cigarette /ˌsɪgəˈret $ ˈsɪgəˌret, ˌsɪgəˈret/ n [C] a paper tube filled with tobacco that people smoke → **cigar**: *a packet of cigarettes*

cilantro /sɪˈlæntrəʊ $ -ˈlɑːtroʊ/ n [U] *AmE* a herb, used especially in Asian cooking **SYN** **coriander** *BrE*

cinch /sɪntʃ/ n **be a cinch** *informal* to be very easy: *The test was a cinch.*

cinder /'sɪndə $ -ər/ n [C] a very small piece of burnt wood, coal etc

cinema /'sɪnəmə/ n
1 [C] *BrE* a building where you go to see films **SYN** **movie theater** *AmE*: *Shall we* **go to the cinema** (=go to see a film) *tonight?*
2 [U] the art or industry of making films: *the influence of Hollywood on Indian cinema*

cinnamon /'sɪnəmən/ n [U] a sweet-smelling spice

circa /'sɜːkə $ 'sɜːr-/ prep *formal* used before a date to show that something happened close to that time, but you do not know exactly when: *He was born circa 1100.*

circle[1] /'sɜːkəl $ 'sɜːr-/ n [C]
1 SHAPE a round shape like the letter O, or a group of people or things arranged in this shape: **[+of]** *a circle of stones* | *The children were dancing in a circle.* → see picture at SHAPE[1]
2 GROUP a group of people who know each other and meet regularly, or who have the same interests or type of job: **[+of]** *She has a wide* **circle of friends**. | **in political/legal/academic etc circles** *Myers' new book has been praised in literary circles.*
3 THEATRE *BrE* the upper floor of a theatre, where the seats are in curved rows **SYN** **balcony** *AmE*: *We have seats in* **the circle**. → **TRAFFIC CIRCLE, VICIOUS CIRCLE**

PHRASES

go around/round in circles to think or argue about something without achieving anything: *This conversation's going around in circles.*

circle² v **1** [I,T] to move in a circle around something: *Our plane circled the airport several times.* **2** [T] to draw a circle around something: *Circle the correct answer.*

circuit /'sɜːkɪt $ 'sɜːr-/ n [C] **1** a set of wires etc that an electrical current flows around: *an electrical circuit* **2** a path that forms a circle around an area, or a journey along this path: *We **did a circuit** of the old city walls.* **3** *BrE* a track where people race cars, bicycles etc **4 the tennis/lecture/club etc circuit** all the places that are usually visited by someone who plays tennis etc: *a well-known speaker on the international lecture circuit*

circuitry /'sɜːkətri $ 'sɜːr-/ n [U] a system of electric circuits

circular¹ /'sɜːkjələ $ 'sɜːrkjələr/ adj **1** shaped like a circle: *a circular table* **2** moving around in a circle: *a circular walk*

circular² n [C] a printed advertisement or notice that is sent to lots of people at the same time

circulate /'sɜːkjəleɪt $ 'sɜːr-/ v **1** [I,T] to move around within a system, or to make something do this: *Blood circulates around the body.* **2** [I] if information or ideas circulate, they become known by many people: ***Rumours** are **circulating** that the mayor's health is getting worse.* **3** [T] to give written information to a number of people: *I'll circulate the report at the meeting.*

circulation /ˌsɜːkjə'leɪʃən $ ˌsɜːr-/ n **1** [singular, U] the movement of blood around your body: *Exercise can improve the circulation.* **2** [singular] the number of copies of a newspaper or magazine that are usually sold each day, week, month etc: **[+of]** *a magazine with a circulation of 400,000*

PHRASES

in/out of circulation if something is in circulation, it is being used by people in a society and passing from one person to another: *Police believe there are thousands of illegal guns in circulation.*

circumcise /'sɜːkəmsaɪz $ 'sɜːr-/ v [T] **1** to cut off the skin at the end of the PENIS (=male sex organ) **2** to cut off the CLITORIS (=part of the female sex organs) —**circumcision** /ˌsɜːkəm'sɪʒən $ ˌsɜːr-/ n [C,U]

circumference /səˈkʌmfərəns $ sər-/ n [C,U] the distance around the outside of something round: *The earth's circumference is nearly 25,000 miles.*

circumspect /'sɜːkəmspekt $ 'sɜːr-/ adj formal thinking carefully about things before doing them **SYN** cautious: *I advise you to be more circumspect about what you say in public.*

circumstance Ac /'sɜːkəmstæns, -stəns $ 'sɜːr-/ n **1** [C usually plural] the conditions that affect a situation, action, event etc: **under/in ... circumstances** *Under normal circumstances she would never have left her child with a stranger.* | *Non-members will*

be admitted only **in special circumstances**. **2** sb's cir cumstances *formal* the conditions in which you live especially how much money you have: *Everyone wi be taxed according to their circumstances.*

PHRASES

under/in/given the circumstances used to say tha a particular situation makes something necessar or acceptable when it would not normally be: *think we did the best we could in the circumstances.*
under/in no circumstances used to emphasize tha something must not happen: *Under no circum stances should you leave this house.*

circumstantial /ˌsɜːkəm'stænʃəl◂ $ ˌsɜːr-/ adj cir cumstantial evidence *law* facts or signs that mak something seem like it is true but do not definitel prove it: *The case against McCarthy is based largely o circumstantial evidence.*

circumvent /ˌsɜːkəm'vent $ ˌsɜːr-/ v [T] formal dis approving to avoid having to obey a rule or law especially in a dishonest way: *The senator is accuse of circumventing the tax laws.*

circus /'sɜːkəs $ 'sɜːr-/ n [C] a group of performer and animals that travel to different places doin tricks and other kinds of entertainment: *circus per formers*

cistern /'sɪstən $ -ərn/ n [C] a large container tha water is stored in

citadel /'sɪtədəl, -del/ n [C] a strong castle wher people in the past could go to be safe if their cit was attacked

citation Ac /saɪˈteɪʃən/ n [C] **1** an official state ment publicly praising someone's actions o achievements: **[+for]** *a citation for bravery* **2** phrase or sentence taken from a book, speech etc: citation from the Bible

cite Ac /saɪt/ v [T] **1** to mention something as a example or proof of something else: *The mayor cite the latest crime figures as proof of the need for mor police.* **2** *AmE law* to order someone to appea before a court of law: *He was cited for speeding.*

citizen /'sɪtɪzən/ n [C]
1 someone who lives in a particular town, state, o country → **national**: *The mayor urged citizens to begi preparing for a major storm.*
2 someone who has the legal right to live and wor in a particular country: *a Brazilian citizen* → **SENIO CITIZEN**

citizenship /'sɪtɪzənʃɪp/ n [U] the legal right t belong to a particular country: *She's applied fo French citizenship.*

citrus /'sɪtrəs/ (also **'citrus fruit**) n [C] (*plura citrus*) a fruit such as an orange or LEMON

city /'sɪti/ n [C] (*plural cities*)
1 a large important town: *Leeds is the third largest cit in England.* | *New York City*
2 the people who live in a city: *The city has bee living in fear since last week's earthquake.* → **INNE CITY**

THESAURUS

city a large important town: *She wasn't used to life in the big city.*

town a large area with houses, shops, offices etc that is smaller than a city: *Southwold is a pretty seaside town.*
capital (*also* **capital city**) the city where a country or state has its government: *Kyoto was the ancient capital of Japan.*
suburb an area around the edge of a city, where many people live: *Ipanema is a fashionable suburb of Rio de Janeiro.*
urban relating to towns and cities: *Pollution is particularly bad in urban areas.*

civic /ˈsɪvɪk/ *adj* relating to a town or city, or the people who live in it: *John Golden was an important civic and business leader.* | *It is your **civic duty** to vote in the local elections.*

civics /ˈsɪvɪks/ *n* [U] *AmE* a school subject dealing with the rights and duties of citizens and the way government works

civil Ac /ˈsɪvəl/ *adj* **1** not related to military or religious organizations: *the civil aircraft industry* | *We were married in a civil ceremony, not in church.* **2 civil unrest/disorder etc** violence involving different groups within a country **3** relating to laws that deal with people's rights, not laws that are related to crimes: *a civil trial* | *civil law* **4** polite but not very friendly: *Please try to be civil.*

civil engiˈneering *n* [U] the planning, building, and repair of roads, bridges, large buildings etc

civilian /səˈvɪljən/ *n* [C] anyone who is not a member of a military organization or the police: *Many innocent civilians were killed.* —**civilian** *adj*: *civilian clothes*

civilization (*also* **-isation** *BrE*) /ˌsɪvəl-aɪˈzeɪʃən $ -vələ-/ *n* **1** [C,U] a society that is well organized and developed: *ancient civilizations* **2** [U] when people live in a well-organized society and have a comfortable way of life: *all the benefits of **modern civilization***

civilize (*also* **-ise** *BrE*) /ˈsɪvəl-aɪz/ *v* [T] to improve a society so that it is more organized and developed: *The Romans hoped to civilize all the tribes of Europe.*

civilized (*also* **-ised** *BrE*) /ˈsɪvəl-aɪzd/ *adj* **1** a civilized society is well organized and has laws and customs: *Care for the elderly is essential in a civilized society.* **2** behaving politely and sensibly: *Let's discuss this in a civilized way.*

civil ˈliberties *n* [plural] (*also* **civil liberty** [U]) the right of all citizens to be free to do whatever they want while respecting the rights of other people

civil ˈrights *n* [plural] the legal rights that every person has

civil ˈservant *n* [C] someone who works in the civil service

civil ˈservice *n* **the civil service** all the government departments and the people who work in them

civil ˈwar *n* [C,U] a war between groups of people from the same country

CJD /ˌsiː dʒeɪ ˈdiː/ *n* [U] a brain disease that kills people, which may be caused by eating meat infected with BSE

cl the written abbreviation of **centilitre**

clad /klæd/ *adj literary* **1** wearing a particular kind of clothing: **[+in]** *a young man clad in shorts and a bike helmet* **2 snow-clad/ivy-clad etc** covered in a particular thing

claim¹ /kleɪm/ *v*
1 SAY STH IS TRUE [T] to say that something is true, even though it might not be: **[+(that)]** *Evans claimed that someone tried to murder him.* | **claim to do/be sth** *There's a man at the door claiming to be your son.* | *George claims to remember exactly what the gunman looked like.*
2 ASK FOR STH [I,T] to ask for something because you have a right to have it or because it belongs to you: *Elderly people can claim £10 a week heating allowance.* | *No one's claimed this wallet that was left behind.*
3 WAR/ACCIDENT/VIOLENCE [T] *written* if a war, accident etc claims lives, people die because of it: *Officials say the violence has **claimed** 21 **lives**.*

claim² *n* [C]
1 a statement that something is true, even though it might not be: **[+that]** *Garcia denied claims that he was involved in drug smuggling.*
2 an official request for money that you think you have a right to: *insurance claims* | **[+for]** *She **put in** a claim for travel expenses.*
3 a right to have or do something: **[+to/on]** *Surely they **have a claim** to their father's land?*
PHRASES
claim to fame a place's or person's claim to fame is the most important or interesting fact about them: *His claim to fame is once having played basketball with Michael Jordan.*

claimant /ˈkleɪmənt/ *n* [C] someone who claims something, especially money, from the government, a court etc because they think they have a right to it: *benefit claimants*

clairvoyant /kleəˈvɔɪənt $ kler-/ *n* [C] someone who says they can see what will happen in the future

clam¹ /klæm/ *n* [C,U] a small sea animal with a shell, that people eat → see picture at SHELLFISH

clam² *v* (**clammed**, **clamming**)
PHRASAL VERBS
clam up *informal* to suddenly stop talking: *Tom always clams up if you ask him about his girlfriend.*

clamber /ˈklæmbə $ -ər/ *v* [I] to climb over something with difficulty, using your hands and feet: **[+over/out/up etc]** *He clambered over the rocks.*

clammy /ˈklæmi/ *adj* slightly wet in an unpleasant way: *clammy hands* THESAURUS DAMP

clamour¹ *BrE*, **clamor** *AmE* /ˈklæmə $ -ər/ *n* [singular, U] **1** a loud noise made by a large group of people or animals: **[+of]** *a clamour of voices in the next room* **2** a complaint or a demand for something made by a lot of people: **[+for]** *the clamour for lower taxes*

clamour² BrE, **clamor** AmE v [I] to demand something loudly: **[+for]** *All the kids were clamouring for attention.*

clamp¹ /klæmp/ v [T] **1** to hold something tightly in a particular position so that it does not move: **clamp sth over/between etc sth** *He clamped his hand over her mouth.* **2** BrE to fasten a piece of equipment onto the wheel of a car that has been parked illegally, so that it cannot be moved SYN **boot** AmE

PHRASAL VERBS

clamp down to become very strict in order to stop people from doing something: **[+on]** *The police are clamping down on drunk drivers.*

clamp² n [C] **1** a piece of equipment for holding things together **2** BrE a piece of equipment that can be fastened onto the wheel of a car that is illegally parked, so that it cannot be moved SYN **boot** AmE

clampdown /ˈklæmpdaʊn/ n [singular] sudden firm action to stop or reduce crime: **[+on]** *a clampdown on illegal immigration*

clan /klæn/ n [C] **1** informal a large family: *The whole clan will be here for Christmas.* **2** a large group of families that often share the same name: *the Campbell clan*

clandestine /klænˈdestɪn/ adj secret: *a clandestine affair*

clang /klæŋ/ v [I,T] to make a loud sound like metal being hit: *The gate clanged shut behind him.* —**clang** n [C]

clank /klæŋk/ v [I] if a metal object clanks, it makes a loud heavy sound: *clanking chains* —**clank** n [C]: *the clank of machinery*

clap¹ /klæp/ v [I,T] (**clapped, clapping**) to hit your hands together several times to show that you approve of something, or want to attract someone's attention → **applause**: *The audience was clapping and cheering.* | *The coach* **clapped** *his* **hands** *and yelled, 'OK, listen!'* —**clapping** n [U] → see picture on page A10

PHRASES

clap your hand on/over/to sth to put your hand somewhere quickly and suddenly: *She clapped her hand over her mouth, realizing she had said too much.*
clap sb on the back/shoulder to hit someone lightly on the back or shoulder with your hand in a friendly way: *He gave Joe a friendly clap on the shoulder.*

clap² n [C usually singular] **1** a sudden loud noise: *a* **clap of thunder** **2** the loud sound that you make when you clap

clarify Ac /ˈklærɪfaɪ/ v [T] (**clarified, clarifying, clarifies**) to make something easier to understand: *I need you to clarify a few points.* —**clarification** /ˌklærɪfɪˈkeɪʃən/ n [C,U]

clarinet /ˌklærəˈnet/ n [C] a wooden musical instrument like a long black tube that you play by blowing into it → see picture on page A6

clarity Ac /ˈklærəti/ n [U] the quality of being clear: *the clarity of Irving's writing style*

clash¹ /klæʃ/ v **1** [I] to fight, argue, or disagree: **[+with]** *Demonstrators clashed with police.* **2** [I] if

colours or clothes clash, they do not look nice together: **[+with]** *That tie clashes with your jacket.* **3** [I] if two events clash, they happen at the same time, so you cannot go to one of them: **[+with]** *Unfortunately, the concert clashes with my class.* **4** [I,T] if two pieces of metal clash, they hit each other and make a loud sound: *the clashing of cymbals*

clash² n [C] **1** an argument or fight between two people, groups, or armies: **[+between/with]** *Ten soldiers were wounded in a clash with the rebels.* | *a clash between the President and Republicans in the Senate* **2** a loud sound made by two metal objects hitting together: *the clash of the cymbals*

clasp¹ /klɑːsp $ klæsp/ n **1** [C] a small metal object used to fasten a bag, jewellery etc **2** [singular] when you hold something tightly SYN **grip**: *the firm clasp of her father's hand*

clasp² v [T] to hold someone or something tightly: **clasp sb/sth in your hands/arms** *She clasped the baby in her arms.*

class¹ /klɑːs $ klæs/ n

1 LESSON [C,U] a period of time when someone teaches a group of students SYN **lesson** BrE: *What time is your computer class?* | **in class** (=during the class) *No talking in class.*

2 COURSE [C] a set of lessons in a particular subject SYN **course** BrE: *I'm doing an evening class next year.* | **[+in]** *a class in photography*

3 GROUP OF STUDENTS [C also + plural verb BrE] a group of students who are taught together → **classmate**: **in a class** *Is Jodie in your class?* | *Gary was* **top of the class.** | **class of 1999/2002 etc** AmE (=all the students who finished school in 1999, 2002 etc) | *My class are going to the Lake District.*

4 SOCIAL GROUP [C,U] the social group that you belong to, based on your job, income, and education, or the system of dividing people in this way: **upper/middle/working class** *a* **working-class background** | *a member of the* **ruling classes** | *success based on class, not ability*

5 TYPE [C] the group that people or things belong to when they are arranged according to their quality, abilities, or type: *What class of vehicle are you qualified to drive?* | **first/business/tourist etc class** (=on a train, aircraft etc) *We traveled* **economy class.** | **first/second class post/mail** | **nice/better etc class (of sth)** *You get a nicer class of people in this area.* | *The car is* **in a class of its own** (=very good quality). | *a* **second class** *university degree*

6 STYLE/SKILL [U] informal a high level of style or skill → **classy**: **have/show class** *The team showed real class today.* | *furniture that is guaranteed to add a* **touch of class** *to your home* → **HIGH-CLASS, WORLD-CLASS**

COLLOCATIONS

verbs

to go to a class (also **to attend a class** formal) *I go to a yoga class on Mondays.*
to take/do a class (=to go to classes as a student) *I was thinking about taking acting classes.*
to teach a class *She teaches evening classes in computing.*

---

types of class

a French/art etc class *I have a science class this afternoon.*
an elementary/intermediate/advanced class *My sister is taking advanced classes in Spanish.*
a beginners' class *There's a beginners' class for people who can't swim at all.*
an evening class/a night class (=when you study a subject in the evenings)

---

class² *v* [T] to put someone or something in a particular group: **class sth as sth** *Cocaine is classed as a hard drug.*

classic¹ Ac /'klæsɪk/ *adj* [only before noun]
1 recognized as having good qualities that last and that people admire: *classic designs of the last century | a classic dark suit* **2** typical of a particular thing or situation: **classic example/mistake/case** *Many students make the classic mistake of revising too much.*

classic² Ac *n* **1** [C] a book, film, or play that is recognized as being important, serious, and with qualities that last for a long time: *'Moby Dick' is a classic of American literature.* **2** classics [plural] the language, literature, and history of ancient Rome and Greece

classical Ac /'klæsɪkəl/ *adj* [only before noun]
1 using traditional styles and ideas and considered to be serious and important: **classical music/composer/dance etc** *classical ballet*

2 connected with the language, literature, and history of ancient Rome and Greece: *classical architecture* —**classically** /-kli/ *adv*: *a classically trained violinist*

classification /ˌklæsɪfɪ'keɪʃən/ *n* [C,U] the process of putting things in groups according to their age, type etc: **[+of]** *the classification of wines*

classified /'klæsɪfaɪd/ *adj* classified information, documents etc are officially secret **THESAURUS** → **SECRET**

classified 'ad *n* [C] a small advertisement that you put in a newspaper to buy or sell something **SYN** small ad *BrE*, want ad *AmE*

classify /'klæsɪfaɪ/ *v* [T] (**classified, classifying, classifies**) to put things into groups according to their age, type etc: **classify sth as/under sth** *Whales are classified as mammals.*

classmate /'klɑːsmeɪt $ 'klæs-/ *n* [C] someone who is in the same class as you at school or college

classroom /'klɑːs-ruːm, -rʊm $ 'klæs-/ *n* [C] a room where students are taught

classwork /'klɑːswɜːk $ 'klæswɜːrk/ *n* [U] work that students do in class, not at home → **homework**

classy /'klɑːsi $ 'klæsi/ *adj informal* expensive and fashionable: *a classy restaurant*

clatter /'klætə $ -ər/ *v* [I,T] if something clatters, it makes a loud noise when it hits something: *The dishes clattered to the floor.* —**clatter** *n* [singular, U]

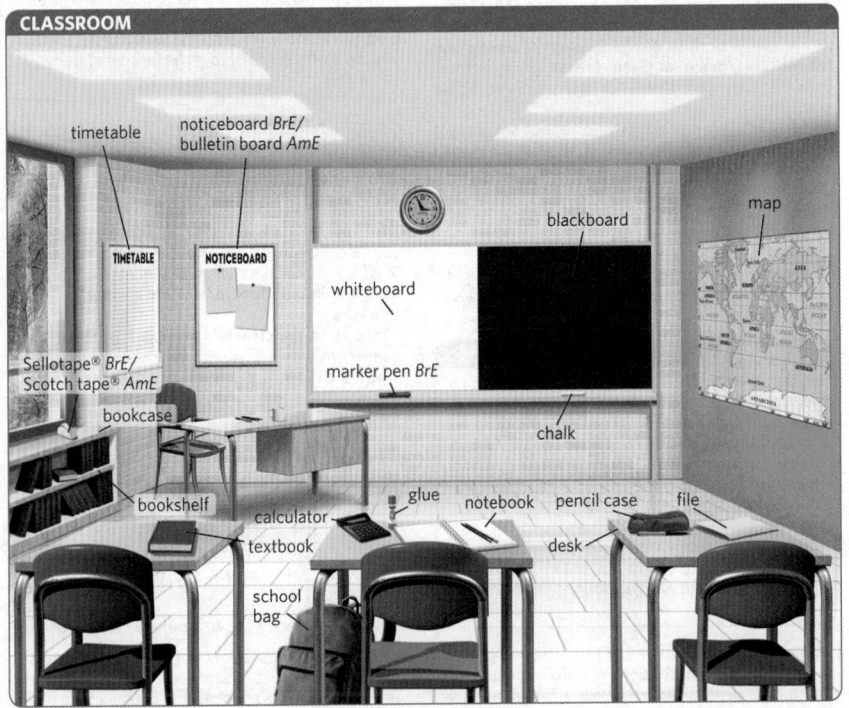

CLASSROOM

clause

clause Ac /klɔːz $ klɒːz/ n [C] **1** part of a legal document covering a particular subject: *clause 14(a) of the Disability Act* **2** in grammar, a group of words that is part of a sentence → MAIN CLAUSE, RELATIVE CLAUSE, SUBORDINATE CLAUSE

claustrophobic /ˌklɔːstrəˈfəʊbɪk $ ˌklɒːstrəˈfoʊ-/ *adj* afraid of being in a small space or a crowd: *Elevators make me claustrophobic.* —**claustrophobia** n [U]

claw¹ /klɔː $ klɒː/ n [C] a sharp curved nail on an animal or bird → see picture on page A3

claw² v [I,T] **1** to tear or pull at something, using your fingers or nails: **[+at]** *The kitten clawed at my trousers.* **2** if you claw your way somewhere, you use a lot of effort and determination to reach a place or position: **claw your way up/back etc** *Hanson has clawed his way to the top.*

clay /kleɪ/ n [U] a type of heavy sticky earth that is used to make pots and bricks

clean¹ /kliːn/ *adj*
1 NOT DIRTY without any dirt, marks etc → **cleanliness**: *Do you have any clean towels?* | *clean air* | *Her room is always* **nice and clean.** | **keep sth clean** *Work surfaces must be kept* **spotlessly clean** (=completely clean). | **wipe/sweep/scrub etc sth clean** *Wipe the sink clean when you're done.* | **clean energy/fuel** (=not causing pollution) *The government wants us to use more clean energy.*
2 HONEST honest or legal and showing that you have not broken any rules or made any mistakes: *a clean fight* | *a clean driving licence* | **clean sheet/slate** (=a record showing that someone has not made any mistakes or done anything wrong) | **come clean (about sth)/make a clean breast of it** *informal* (=admit that you have not been honest about something)
3 NOT OFFENSIVE not offensive or about sex, or not doing anything immoral: *Most of his jokes are clean.* | *a movie that is just* **good clean fun** | *The band has a* **clean image.**
4 NOT ROUGH having a smooth neat edge or surface: *a clean cut*
PHRASES
a clean sweep victory in every part of a competition: *He made a clean sweep of swimming medals at the Olympics.*

> **THESAURUS**
> **clean** not dirty: *The rooms were clean and tidy.* | *a clean shirt* | *clean drinking water*
> **pure** pure water or air is very clean and does not contain any dirt or POLLUTION: *I breathed in the pure mountain air.*
> **hygienic** clean, so that diseases cannot spread: *You eat food that's been on the floor. It's not very hygienic.* | *hygienic conditions*
> **spotless** completely clean – used especially about rooms, houses, clothes, sheets etc: *My mother's house was always spotless.* | *a spotless white blouse*

clean² (*also* **clean up**) v [I,T] to remove dirt from something → **clean-up: clean sth off/from sth** *Use a soft cloth to clean dirt from the lens.* | *The carpets* **need**

cleaning. | *Does your husband help to clean the house?* | *plans to clean up our beaches* | *Have you* **cleaned** *your teeth? BrE* —**cleaning** n [U]: *Who does your office cleaning?* —**clean** n [singular] *BrE*: *It's time you gave the car a good clean.* → SPRING-CLEAN
PHRASAL VERBS
clean sb/sth **out**
1 clean sth ↔ out to make the inside of a room, house etc clean or tidy: *We spent Sunday cleaning out the attic.*
2 *informal* if buying something cleans you out, it is so expensive you have no money left
clean sth ↔ **up** to remove crime, bad behaviour etc from a place or organization: *More police are needed to clean up our city centres.*

> **THESAURUS**
> **clean** to remove dirt from something: *I cleaned the floor.* | *The sheets need cleaning.*
> **wash** to clean something with water and usually soap: *She's washing her hair.* | *You have to wash this sweater by hand.*
> **wipe** to clean a surface with a cloth, often a wet cloth: *Wipe the cooker when you finish.*
> **scrub** to wash something by rubbing it hard, especially with a brush: *I scrubbed the pans until they were clean and shiny.*
> **vacuum** to clean floors, carpets etc with a special machine that sucks up all the dust: *We usually vacuum the carpet about once a week.*
> **do the dishes** (*also* **do the washing-up** *BrE*) to wash plates and pans after a meal: *It's your turn to do the dishes.*
> **do the laundry** (*also* **do the washing** *BrE*) to wash clothes: *I need to go home and do the laundry.*

clean³ *adv informal* completely: *The thieves got* **clean** *away.* | *I* **clean forgot** *you were coming.*

clean-'cut *adj approving* someone who is clean-cut is clean and neat in their appearance

cleaner /ˈkliːnə $ -ər/ n **1** [C] *BrE* someone whose job is to clean offices, houses etc: *office cleaners* **2** [C,U] a machine or substance used to clean things: **toilet/bathroom/sink etc cleaner**
PHRASES
take sb to the cleaner's *informal* **1** to defeat someone completely: *Chelsea took Arsenal to the cleaners with a 3-0 victory.* **2** to cheat someone, taking all their money etc: *He was taken to the cleaners by a conman.*

cleanliness /ˈklenlinəs/ n [U] when you keep yourself or your things clean: *a high standard of cleanliness*

cleanly /ˈkliːnli/ *adv* **1** done quickly, smoothly, and neatly: *It snapped (=broke)* **cleanly** *in two.* **2** without producing dirt, harmful substances etc: *fuel that burns cleanly*

cleanse /klenz/ v [T] to carefully clean your skin

cleanser /ˈklenzə $ -ər/ n [C,U] **1** a creamy substance you use to clean your face **2** a substance used for cleaning surfaces in a house, office etc

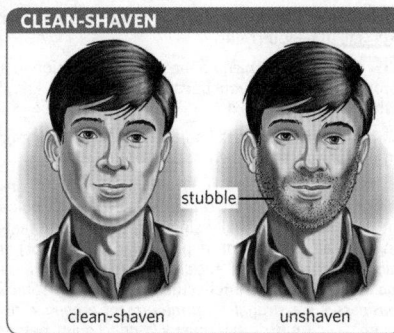

CLEAN-SHAVEN

stubble

clean-shaven   unshaven

,clean-'shaven *adj* a man who is clean-shaven does not have a BEARD or MOUSTACHE (=hair on his face)

'clean-up (*also* cleanup) /'kliːnʌp/ *n* [C usually singular] the process of removing dirt, waste, or harmful substances from a place: *the cleanup of the oil spill*

clear¹ /klɪə $ klɪr/ *adj*
1 EASY TO UNDERSTAND easy to understand, see, read, or hear → **clarity**: **clear idea/description/ explanation etc** *clear instructions* | [+about/on] *The law isn't completely clear on this matter.* | [+to] *It's clear to me that you don't care.* | **make sth clear/make it clear (that)** *Hugh had made it perfectly clear he wasn't interested.* | **make yourself clear** (=express your ideas so that people understand)
2 NO DOUBT impossible to doubt → **clearly**: *clear evidence* | *a clear victory* | **it is clear whether/how/ what etc** *It's not clear how it happened.* | **it is clear (that)** *It became clear that she had lied.* | *a clear case of racism*
3 NOT CONFUSED [not before noun] feeling sure that you understand something: [+about/on] *I'm not clear about what you want me to do.* | [+to] *He nodded as if things were now clear to him.*
4 NO CLOUDS weather that is clear is bright with no rain or clouds: *a clear sky*
5 TRANSPARENT a substance or liquid that is clear is easy to see through: *clear glass bottles* | *a crystal clear lake*
6 NOT BLOCKED/COVERED not blocked, hidden, or covered by anything: *The roads were clear last night.* | *clear skin* | **keep sth clear (of sth)** *Keep paths clear of weeds.* | **clear view/look** *a clear view over the bay*
7 NO GUILT a clear conscience when you know that you did the right thing and do not feel guilty → **the coast is clear** at COAST¹, CRYSTAL CLEAR

clear² *v*
1 TIDY UP (*also* **clear up**) [T] to tidy or empty a place by removing things → **clear-out**: **clear sth off/from sth** *Please clear all books from the library desks.* | **clear sth of sth** *The roads had been cleared of snow.* | **clear sth away** (=put things where they belong) *John, clear your toys away, please.* | **clear sth out** (=remove things you do not want) *I spent the afternoon clearing out my desk.* | *After meals, I clear the table* (=remove the plates, glasses etc) *and start again.* | *Can you clear a space for my books?*

2 NOT GUILTY [T] to prove that someone is not guilty of something: **clear sb of (doing) sth** *Johnson was cleared of murdering his wife.*
3 PERMISSION [T] to give or get official permission to do something: *The plane has now been cleared for take-off.* | **clear sth with sb** *Has the order been cleared with Mr Herrick?*
4 WEATHER (*also* **clear up**) [I] if the weather or sky clears, it gets brighter
5 FENCE/WALL [T] to go over a fence, wall etc without touching it
6 CHEQUE [I] if a cheque that is made out to you clears, the bank puts the money into your account
PHRASES
    clear the air to talk about a problem in order to solve a disagreement with someone: *It's about time you called her to clear the air.*
    clear your throat to cough a little so that you can speak clearly: *He cleared his throat nervously.*

PHRASAL VERBS
clear off *BrE informal* to leave a place quickly: *Clear off and leave me alone!*
clear up
1 clear sth ↔ up to explain or solve something, or make it clearer: *I need to clear up some details with you.*
2 if an infection clears up, it gets better

clear³ *adv* away from someone or something: [+of] *Firefighters pulled the driver clear of the wreckage.* | **stand/stay/steer/keep clear (of sth/sb)** (=not see someone or do something that may cause you problems) *Steer clear of Neil – he's trouble.*

clear⁴ *n* **in the clear** not guilty of something

clearance /'klɪərəns $ 'klɪr-/ *n* [C,U] **1** official permission to do something: *We're waiting for security clearance to enter the port.* | [+for] *clearance for landing* **2** the removal of unwanted things from a place: **snow/land/forest clearance** | **clearance sale** (=when things that are not wanted are sold very cheaply) **3** the distance between two objects that is needed to stop them touching: *Allow two inches of clearance between the lights.*

'clear-cut *adj* certain or definite: *no clear-cut solutions*

,clear-'headed *adj* able to think clearly and sensibly

clearing /'klɪərɪŋ $ 'klɪr-/ *n* [C] a small area in a forest where there are no trees

clearly /'klɪəli $ 'klɪrli/ *adv*
1 without any doubt: *Clearly, the situation was very serious.* | *She was clearly drunk.*
2 in a way that is easy to see, hear etc: *Speak slowly and clearly.*
3 if you cannot think clearly, you are confused

'clear-out *n* [C] *BrE* a process of removing things you do not want

cleavage /'kliːvɪdʒ/ *n* [C,U] the space between a woman's breasts

cleaver /'kliːvə $ -ər/ *n* [C] a knife with a large square blade: *a meat cleaver*

clef /klef/ *n* [C] a sign used in written music to show the PITCH of the notes

clemency /'klemənsi/ n [U] *formal* when someone is forgiven or punished less severely for a serious crime

clementine /'klemənti:n, -taɪn/ n [C] *BrE* a kind of small orange

clench /klentʃ/ v [T] to close your hands, mouth etc tightly: *Hal clenched his fists in anger.*

clergy /'klɜ:dʒi $ 'klɜ:r-/ n **the clergy** [plural] the official leaders of organized religions

clergyman /'klɜ:dʒimən $ 'klɜ:r-/, **clergywoman** /'klɜ:dʒi,wʊmən $ -ɜ:r-/ n [C] a man or woman who is a member of the clergy

cleric /'klerɪk/ n [C] a member of the clergy

clerical /'klerɪkəl/ adj **1** relating to office work: *clerical workers* **2** relating to the clergy

clerk /klɑ:k $ klɜ:rk/ n [C] **1** someone whose job is to do the written work or accounts in an office **2** *AmE* someone whose job is to help people in a shop [SYN] **assistant** *BrE* **3** *AmE* someone whose job is to help hotel guests when they arrive or leave: *Leave the keys with the **desk clerk**.*

clever /'klevə $ -ər/ adj
1 *especially BrE* someone who is clever is intelligent and understands things quickly [SYN] **smart** *AmE*: *a clever student* | *My brothers are all very clever.* | *It was very clever of you to work it out.* [THESAURUS] INTELLIGENT
2 things, ideas etc that are clever are skilfully designed: *clever advertising* | *a clever little gadget*
3 [not before noun] skilled in a particular activity [SYN] **good**: **clever at doing sth** *Heidi's quite clever at spotting a bargain.* | *He's always been **clever with** his hands* (=good at making things). —**cleverly** adv —**cleverness** n [U]

cliché /'kli:ʃeɪ $ kli:'ʃeɪ/ n [C] a phrase that has been repeated so often that it is no longer effective or interesting: *tired old clichés* [THESAURUS] PHRASE —**clichéd** adj

click¹ /klɪk/ v
1 [SHORT SOUND] [I,T] to make a short hard sound, or to make something produce this sound: *The door **clicked shut**.* | *Ed **clicked** his **fingers*** (=made a sound by moving his thumb and fingers together quickly).
2 [COMPUTER] [I,T] to press a button on a computer MOUSE to make the computer do something: **[+on]** *Double-click* (=click twice) *on the icon.* → see picture on page A7
3 [UNDERSTAND] [I] *informal* if something clicks, you suddenly understand the truth about it: *It all **clicked into place** – she was Jim's wife.*
4 [GET ON WELL] [I] *informal* if two people click, they like each other straight away: *We just **clicked** the moment we met.*

click² n [C,U] a short hard sound: *the **click** of her heels*

client /'klaɪənt/ n [C] someone who pays a person or organization for a service: *an important client* [THESAURUS] CUSTOMER

clientele /,kli:ən'tel $,klaɪən'tel, ,kli:-/ n [singular] the people who regularly use a shop, hotel etc: *Our clientele consists mainly of young people.*

cliff /klɪf/ n [C] a large area of rock with steep sides, often beside the sea: *the white cliffs of Dover* [THESAURUS] MOUNTAIN

cliffhanger /'klɪf,hæŋə $ -ər/ n [C] a situation in a story that excites you because you do not know what will happen next

climactic /klaɪ'mæktɪk/ adj forming the exciting or important part at the end of a story or event

climate /'klaɪmət/ n **1** [C] the typical weather conditions in an area: *a dry climate* → see Word Choice at WEATHER **2** [C usually singular] the general feelings in a situation at a particular time: **[+of]** *a climate of racial tolerance* | **political/economic/intellectual etc climate** *Small businesses are struggling in the present economic climate.* —**climatic** /klaɪ'mætɪk/ adj [only before noun]

'climate change n [U] important changes in the weather of the whole world: *the effects of climate change on agriculture*

climax /'klaɪmæks/ n [C] the most important or exciting things that come at the end of a story or experience: **[+of]** *the climax of his career* | *The festival **reaches** a **climax** with a firework display.* —**climax** v [I]

climb /klaɪm/ v
1 (also **climb up**) [I,T] to move towards the top of something: *a cat climbing a tree* | *The aircraft was still climbing steadily.* | *the first man to climb Mount Everest*
2 [I] to move somewhere with difficulty, using your hands and feet: **[+down/along/over etc]** *We all climbed into the back of the truck.*
3 [I] if a number or amount climbs, it increases: *The temperature was climbing steadily.* —**climb** n [C]: *a steep climb*
PHRASAL VERBS
climb down *BrE* to admit that you were wrong about something: **[+over]** *The management had to climb down over the pay claim.*

climbdown /'klaɪmdaʊn/ n [C usually singular] when someone is forced to admit that they are wrong: *a humiliating climbdown for the government*

climber /'klaɪmə $ -ər/ n [C] someone who climbs rocks or mountains as a sport

climbing /'klaɪmɪŋ/ n [U] the sport of climbing mountains or rocks: *The boys love to **go climbing**.* → see picture on page A9

clinch /klɪntʃ/ v [T] *informal* to succeed in getting something after trying hard: **clinch a match/race etc** *They clinched the cup with a last-minute goal.*

cling /klɪŋ/ v [I] (past tense and past participle **clung** /klʌŋ/) **1** to hold someone or something tightly because you do not feel safe: **[+to/on/together]** *a little girl clinging to her mother* **2** to stick to something: **[+to]** *Sand clung to her arms and legs.*
PHRASAL VERBS
cling on to try to keep something, even though it is difficult: **[+to]** *He is **clinging on** to power.*
cling to sth to continue to believe something, even though it may no longer be true: *She clung to the hope of rescue.*

clingfilm /ˈklɪŋfɪlm/ n [U] BrE thin transparent plastic used to wrap food SYN **Saran Wrap** AmE

clingy /ˈklɪŋi/ adj **1** disapproving someone who is clingy is too dependent on another person and will often hold onto them: a clingy child **2** clingy clothing or material sticks tightly to your body and shows its shape: a clingy dress

clinic /ˈklɪnɪk/ n [C] **1** a place where people get medical treatment: **dental/outpatient etc clinic 2** AmE a group of doctors who share the same offices SYN **practice** BrE

clinical Ac /ˈklɪnɪkəl/ adj **1** [only before noun] relating to medical tests or the treatment of people who are sick: **clinical trials/research 2** disapproving not influenced by personal feelings: His attitude was cold and clinical. —**clinically** /-kli/ adv

clinician /klɪˈnɪʃən/ n [C] technical a doctor who examines and treats people who are sick rather than studying disease

clink /klɪŋk/ v [I,T] if glass or metal objects clink, or if you clink them, they make a short high sound when they touch: Dad clinked his glass with a spoon. —**clink** n [C,U]

clip¹ /klɪp/ n [C] **1** a small metal or plastic object used to hold things together **2** a short part of a film or television programme that is shown separately: **[+from]** clips from the new Bond movie

clip² v (**clipped, clipping**) **1** [I,T] to fasten things together, using a clip: **clip (sth) to/onto sth** He clipped the dog's lead to its collar. **2** [T] to cut small amounts from something to make it neater: clipped hedges **3** [T] to hit something at an angle: The truck clipped a parked car.

'clip art n [U] pictures that you can copy from CD-ROMS or WEBSITES to use on your computer

clipboard /ˈklɪpbɔːd $ -bɔːrd/ n [C] **1** a small flat board with a clip that holds paper onto it **2** part of a computer MEMORY that stores information when you cut, copy, or move it

clipped /klɪpt/ adj a clipped voice is quick and clear but not very friendly: a clipped military accent

clippers /ˈklɪpəz $ -ərz/ n [plural] a tool used for cutting small pieces off something: nail clippers → see picture at **NAIL¹**

clipping /ˈklɪpɪŋ/ n **1** [C] an article, picture etc that has been cut out of a newspaper or magazine **2** **clippings** [plural] small pieces that have been cut from something: grass clippings

clique /kliːk/ n [C] disapproving a small group of people who know each other well but who are not friendly towards other people —**cliquey** adj

clitoris /ˈklɪtərɪs/ n [C] a part of a woman's outer sex organs where she can feel sexual pleasure

cloak¹ /kləʊk $ kloʊk/ n **1** [C] a warm piece of clothing like a coat without sleeves **2** [singular] disapproving an organization or activity that deliberately keeps something secret: a cloak for terrorist activities

cloak² v [T usually passive] **1** to deliberately hide facts, feelings etc so that people do not see or understand them – used especially in news reports:

The talks have been **cloaked in secrecy**. **2** literary to cover something, for example with darkness or snow

cloakroom /ˈkləʊkrʊm, -ruːm $ ˈkloʊk-/ n [C] a small room where you can leave your coat, bag etc

clobber /ˈklɒbə $ ˈklɑːbər/ v [T] informal **1** to hit someone hard **2** to defeat someone easily **3** to affect someone badly: The steel industry was clobbered in the recession.

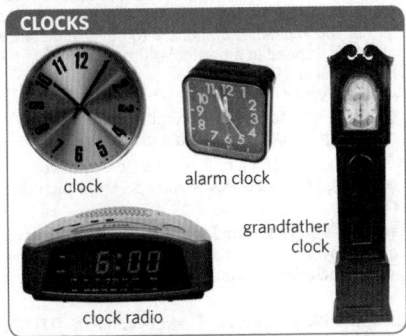

CLOCKS

clock

alarm clock

grandfather clock

clock radio

clock¹ /klɒk $ klɑːk/ n
1 [C] an instrument that shows the time. Clocks are fixed on a wall or kept in a room: What time does that clock say? | **by the church/kitchen etc clock** (=according to a particular clock) It was 5.30 am by the kitchen clock.
2 [C] an instrument in a vehicle that tells you how far it has travelled or how fast it is going → **O'CLOCK**
PHRASES
against the clock if you do something against the clock, you do it as fast as possible, because you do not have much time: We were racing against the clock to get everything ready in time.
around the clock (also **round the clock** BrE) all day and all night without stopping: Rescue teams **worked around the clock**.
the clocks go back the time is changed in the autumn, so that it is one hour earlier: The clocks go back this weekend.
the clocks go forward the time is changed in the spring, so that it is one hour later
turn/put the clock back to make a situation the same as it was in the past: They want to turn the clock back to the Middle Ages.

COLLOCATIONS

verbs
to look at the clock I was bored and kept looking at the clock.
to set a clock Mary set her alarm clock for 7 a.m.
the clock says eight/nine etc (=shows a particular time) The clock by my bed said nine thirty. ⚠ Do not say 'the clock shows two o'clock'. Say **the clock says two o'clock**.
a clock strikes eight/nine etc (=makes eight, nine etc sounds according to the hour) Downstairs, the clock struck midnight.
a clock ticks (=makes regular quiet sounds) The clock ticked on the mantelpiece.

types of clock

an alarm clock (=that makes a noise to wake you up) *My alarm clock goes off at quarter past six.*
a grandfather clock (=an old-fashioned tall clock that stands on the floor) | **a wall clock** (=that hangs on a wall)

clock² v [T] **1** to measure the speed at which someone or something is moving: *The police clocked him at 160 kilometres an hour.* **2** to cover a distance or reach a speed in a particular time: *Karen won the race, clocking 49.2 seconds.*

PHRASAL VERBS
clock up sth to reach a number or amount: *We clocked up 125,000 miles on our old car.*

clock 'radio n [C] a radio with a clock that you can set so that the radio wakes you up → see picture at CLOCK¹

clockwise /'klɒk-waɪz $ 'klɑːk-/ adj, adv in the same direction as the hands of a clock move OPP **anticlockwise, counterclockwise**: *Turn the dial clockwise.*

clockwork /'klɒk-wɜːk $ 'klɑːk-wɜːrk/ n [U] BrE clockwork toys have parts inside that move when you turn a key
PHRASES
go/run like clockwork to happen in exactly the way you planned: *The fire drill went like clockwork.*
(as) regular as clockwork always happening in the same way at the same time: *Matt comes round every Friday morning as regular as clockwork.*

clog¹ /klɒg $ klɑːg/ (also **clog up**) v [I,T] (**clogged, clogging**) to block something completely: **clog sth up** *Leaves had clogged up the drain.*

clog² n [C] a shoe made of wood → see picture at SHOE¹

cloister /'klɔɪstə $ -ər/ n [C] a covered path between a church building and a garden

clone /kləʊn $ kloʊn/ n [C] technical an exact copy of an animal or plant that scientists produce from one of its cells —**clone** v [T]: *Scientists have managed to clone a sheep.*

close¹ /kləʊz $ kloʊz/ v
1 WINDOW/DOOR/EYES ETC [I,T] to shut something, or to become shut SYN **shut** OPP **open**: *Do you mind if I close the window? | He closed the lid of the box. | The door closed quietly behind her. | Close your eyes and go to sleep.*
2 SHOP/BUILDING [I,T] if a shop or building closes, or if someone closes it, it shuts for some time: *What time does the library close tonight?*
3 BUSINESS/FACTORY [I,T] if a business or factory closes, or someone closes it, it stops existing or operating: *The factory closed last month.*
4 PERFORMANCE/SPEECH ETC [I,T] if a show, discussion, speech etc closes, or someone closes it, it ends: *The show closed after only a few weeks. | close (sth) with sth He closed his speech with a quotation from Shakespeare.*
5 BANK ACCOUNT [T] to stop having an account at a bank: *I've closed my bank account.*

6 DEAL **close a deal/sale/contract** to successfully agree a business deal
7 GAP **close the gap** to make the distance or difference between two things smaller: *an attempt to close the gap between rich and poor*
PHRASAL VERBS
close down if a shop or business closes down, it stops existing: *The cinema will close down next year. |* **close sth ↔ down** *They closed down their London offices last year.*
close in
1 to move closer to someone or something, especially in order to attack them: **[+on]** *Rebel soldiers are closing in on the town.*
2 if night closes in, it starts to get dark
close sth ↔ **off** if a road or area is closed off, people cannot go into it

THESAURUS

close to stop being open, or to make something stop being open: *Do you mind if I close the window? | Her eyes slowly closed.*
shut to close something. **Shut** sometimes has the feeling of closing something quickly and firmly: *The windows had all been shut. | The door suddenly shut with a loud bang.*
slam to close a door or lid quickly and noisily, especially because you are angry: *'I'm not coming back!' she said, slamming the door behind her.*
draw the curtains to close curtains by pulling them across a window: *The curtains were all drawn, so I assumed they had gone to bed.*
put the top/lid on sth to close a container by putting a top or lid onto it: *He never puts the top back on the toothpaste.*

close² /kləʊs $ kloʊs/ adj, adv
1 DISTANCE not far from someone or something → **closely**: **[+to]** *The house was close to the beach. | The closest shops are a mile away. |* **[+together]** *They sat close together. |* **[+behind]** *I followed close behind. | Her parents lived close by (=near). | Close up (=from a short distance), he was less attractive. | at close range/quarters (=from a short distance)*
THESAURUS ▸ NEAR
2 TIME near to something in time: **[+to]** *It was close to midnight. |* **[+together]** *Our birthdays are quite close together.*
3 NUMBER/AMOUNT near to a number: **[+to]** *Inflation is now close to 6%. | They've been married for close on 20 years (=nearly 20 years).*
4 ALMOST DOING STH if you are close to something, you are likely to experience it soon: **close to (doing) sth** *They are close to agreeing a deal. | She was close to tears. | He came close to death (=he almost died).*
5 CAREFUL [only before noun] giving careful attention to something: *Pay close attention to this. | Take a closer look. | Keep a close eye on him.*
6 LIKE SB A LOT if people are close, they like or love each other very much: *We were very close friends. |* **[+to]** *Are you close to your sister?*
7 GOOD RELATIONSHIP if you have a close relationship with another person, organization, or country, you often discuss things with each other and you get on well: **close ties/links/cooperation/relationship** *The*

government would seek closer ties with Europe. | *She has* **kept in close contact** *with him over the years.*

8 FAMILY MEMBERS **close relations/relatives/family** family members such as your parents, brother, or sister

9 GAME/COMPETITION a close competition or game is won or lost by only a few points

10 WEATHER *BrE* if the weather is close, it is warm and uncomfortable —**closeness** *n* [U]

PHRASES
| **(you're) close** *spoken* used to tell someone that they almost have the correct answer: *'He looks about 40.' 'You're close – he's 39.'*
| **a close shave/thing/call** a lucky escape from a bad situation

close³ /kləʊz $ kloʊz/ *n* [singular] the end of an activity or period of time: *The summer was* **drawing to a close.** | *It's time to* **bring** *the meeting* **to a close.** | **at the close of sth** *I was sent to Spain at the close of the war.*

closed /kləʊzd $ kloʊzd/ *adj*
1 not open SYN **shut**: *She kept her eyes* **tightly closed.** | *The door was* **firmly closed.**
2 if a shop or public building is closed, it is not open and people cannot go into it or use it SYN **shut**
3 restricted to a particular group of people or things OPP **open**: *a closed meeting*
4 not willing to accept new ideas or influences OPP **open**: *Don't go with a closed mind.*

PHRASES
| **behind closed doors** privately, without involving other people: *The deal was made behind closed doors.*

closed circuit 'television *n* [C,U] (*abbreviation* **CCTV**) cameras which are used in public places to help prevent crime

close-knit /ˌkləʊs 'nɪt◂ $ ˌkloʊs-/ (*also* **closely-'knit**) *adj* a close-knit family or group of people know each other well and help each other a lot

closely /'kləʊsli/ *adv* **1** very carefully: *I was* **watching** *him* **closely.** | *a closely guarded secret* **2** if you work closely with someone, you work with them and help them **3** **closely related/connected etc** having a strong connection: *The two problems are closely related.* **4** **follow closely** to happen soon after something else: *a flash of lightning followed closely by thunder*

close-set /ˌkləʊs 'set◂ $ ˌkloʊs-/ *adj* close-set eyes are very near to each other

closet¹ /'klɒzɪt $ 'klɑː-, 'klɔː-/ *n* [C] *especially AmE* a cupboard for keeping clothes in SYN **wardrobe** *BrE*

closet² *adj* [only before noun] used to describe someone who keeps their true opinions or way of life a secret: *a closet fascist*

close-up /'kləʊs ʌp $ 'kloʊs-/ *n* [C,U] a photograph that is taken from very near to someone or something

closing /'kləʊzɪŋ $ 'kloʊ-/ *adj* happening or done at the end of something: *the closing stages of the race* | *his closing speech to the conference* | *The closing date* (=last possible date) *for applications is today.*

THESAURUS LAST

closure /'kləʊʒə $ 'kloʊʒər/ *n* **1** [C,U] when an institution, building, or road is closed: **[+of]** *the closure of the hospital* **2** [U] when a bad situation has ended and you can stop thinking about it

clot /klɒt $ klɑːt/ *n* [C] a mass of blood which has become almost solid —**clot** *v* [I,T]

cloth /klɒθ $ klɔːθ/ *n*
1 [U] material used for making clothes and other things: **cotton/woollen/silk cloth** *a coat made of thick woollen cloth*
2 [C] a piece of cloth that you use for cleaning things: *Wipe the surface with a damp cloth.*

clothe /kləʊð $ kloʊð/ *v* [T] to provide clothes for someone: *He needed money to feed and clothe his children.*

clothed /kləʊðd $ kloʊðd/ *adj formal* dressed: *He was* **fully clothed.**

clothes /kləʊðz, kləʊz $ kloʊðz, kloʊz/ *n* [plural] things that people wear such as shirts, skirts, or trousers → PLAIN-CLOTHES → see picture on p. 162

Grammar
Clothes are always plural. There is no singular form. When talking about one shirt, one sock etc, you say **a piece of clothing** or **an article of clothing**: *She picked up each piece of clothing and folded it carefully.*

COLLOCATIONS

verbs
to wear clothes *He likes to wear fashionable clothes.*
to put your clothes on *Just let me put some clothes on.*
to take off your clothes *She took off her clothes and got into bed.* ⚠ Do not say 'I put off my clothes.' Say **I took off my clothes.**
to change your clothes (=to put on different clothes) *Don't you want to change your clothes for the party?*

types of clothes
warm clothes *Make sure you wear warm clothes.*
clean/dirty clothes *Mum, I don't have any clean clothes!*
sb's best clothes *She dressed the children in their best clothes.*
casual clothes *Casual clothes are not suitable for an interview.*
formal clothes *It's best to wear formal clothes for an interview.*
smart clothes *BrE Do you have to wear smart clothes to work?*
work/school clothes *He changed into his work clothes.*
fashionable/trendy clothes *The club was full of people wearing trendy clothes.*
designer clothes (=made by a well-known designer) *She spends hundreds of pounds on designer clothes.*

THESAURUS

clothes things that people wear such as shirts, skirts, or trousers: *I need to buy some new clothes.* | *a clothes shop*

clothing clothes – used especially when talking about a type of clothes, or about companies that make clothes. Also used in the phrase **a piece of clothing** (=a shirt, a sock etc): *Students should bring warm clothing on the trip.* | *You should wear protective clothing.* | *Workers in the clothing industry are often badly paid.* | *They found a piece of clothing in the bushes.*

garment *formal* one thing that you wear. Also used when talking about companies that make and sell clothes: *a long velvet garment* | *the garment industry in India* | *garment workers*

costume a set of clothes that you wear for acting in a play or performance. Also used about the traditional clothes of a country: *The actors were all in 16th century costumes.* | *the national costume of Austria*

clothesline, **clothes line** /'kləʊðzlaɪn, 'kləʊz- $ 'kloʊðz-, 'kloʊz-/ *n* [C] a rope that you hang clothes on so that they will dry

'clothes peg *BrE*, **clothes pin** /'kləʊðzpɪn/ *AmE n* [C] a small object that you use to fasten clothes to a clothesline

clothing /'kləʊðɪŋ $ 'kloʊ-/ *n* [U] *formal* clothes: *It's cold, so wear warm clothing.* **THESAURUS ▶ CLOTHES**

COLLOCATIONS

adjectives

warm clothing *They had no blankets or warm clothing.*

light clothing (=made from thin materials) *You should be able to swim 50 metres in light clothing.*

tight/loose clothing *Remove any tight clothing or jewellery.*

outdoor clothing *The shop sells ski-wear and other outdoor clothing.*

protective clothing *Hospital cleaners have to wear protective clothing.*

phrases

a piece of clothing *He threw away every piece of clothing he owned.*

an item/article of clothing *formal* (=a piece of clothing) *You may bring a few items of clothing.*

cloud¹ /klaʊd/ *n*

1 [C,U] a white or grey mass in the sky, from which rain sometimes falls: *There were no clouds in the sky.* | **Black clouds** were gathering overhead. | **Storm clouds** hung low over the island.

2 [C] a mass of smoke, dust, or gas: **[+of]** *a huge cloud of dust*

3 [C] something that makes you feel worried or upset: **[+of]** *the cloud of economic recession* | *The only* **cloud on the horizon** *was her mother's illness.* | **every cloud has a silver lining** (=every bad thing has a good side)

CLOTHES

shirt | T-shirt | jacket | waterproof jacket | jumper *BrE*/sweater | sweatshirt | coat | scarf | dress | jeans | tie | belt | knickers *BrE*/panties *AmE* | skirt | bra | socks | shorts | tracksuit *BrE* | boxer shorts | underpants | trousers/pants *AmE*

PHRASES

be/live in cloud-cuckoo land to believe that a situation is much better than it really is: *If she thinks he will come back to her, she's living in cloud-cuckoo land.*

on cloud nine *informal* very happy because something good has happened: *When she first got the job she was on cloud nine.*

under a cloud affected by a bad or unpleasant situation: *He returned under a cloud of gloom and despair.*

cloud² v **1** [T] to make it more difficult to form an opinion or to deal with a problem: *Don't allow personal feelings to **cloud** your **judgment**.* | *He should not be **clouding** the **issue** with irrelevant remarks.* **2** (*also* **cloud up**) [I,T] to become difficult to see through, or to make this happen: *The windows had clouded up.* | *Tears clouded his eyes.*

PHRASAL VERBS

cloud over if the sky clouds over, clouds appear or cover the sun

cloudless /ˈklaʊdləs/ *adj* a cloudless sky has no clouds

cloudy /ˈklaʊdi/ *adj*
1 if it is cloudy, there are a lot of clouds in the sky
2 a cloudy liquid is not clear: *The water looked cloudy.*

clout /klaʊt/ *n informal* **1** [U] the ability to influence important people: *He's still got some **political clout**.* **2** [singular] *BrE* when someone hits you

clove /kləʊv $ kloʊv/ *n* [C] **1** a piece of GARLIC **2** a strong sweet spice with a pointed stem

clover /ˈkləʊvə $ ˈkloʊvər/ *n* [C] a small plant with three round leaves on each stem

clown¹ /klaʊn/ *n* [C] a person with a red nose, painted face, and funny clothes, whose job is to make people laugh

clown² (*also* **clown around/about**) *v* [I] to behave in a silly or funny way: *Stop clowning around!*

club¹ /klʌb/ *n* [C]
1 ORGANIZATION [also + plural verb *BrE*] an organization for people who share an interest or who enjoy similar activities: **football/rugby/golf etc club** | *I'm a **member** of the local drama club.* | *He's **joined** a health club.* | *She **belongs to** the tennis club.* | **[+for]** *a club for unemployed youngsters* | *The group has a huge **fan club**.* THESAURUS ORGANIZATION
2 BUILDING the building used by the members of a club: *We had lunch at the golf club.*
3 FOR MUSIC/DANCING a place where people go to dance, listen to music, and meet socially: *Shall we **go to** a club?* | *a jazz club*
4 FOR PLAYING GOLF a stick used in golf to hit the ball SYN **golf club**
5 WEAPON a heavy stick used as a weapon
6 IN CARD GAMES **clubs** [plural] in card games, the cards with black symbols with three round parts: *the king of clubs* → see picture at PLAYING CARD

club² *v* [T] (**clubbed**, **clubbing**) to hit someone with a large heavy object: *The seals were **clubbed to death**.*

PHRASAL VERBS

club together if people club together, they all give money in order to pay for something together

clubbing /ˈklʌbɪŋ/ *n* [U] when people go to clubs to dance and be with friends: *She **goes clubbing** most weekends.*

clubhouse /ˈklʌbhaʊs/ *n* [C] the main building of a sports club where people can meet and talk

cluck /klʌk/ *v* [I] if a chicken clucks, it makes a short low sound —**cluck** *n* [C]

clue /kluː/ *n* [C] a piece of information or an object that helps to solve a crime or mystery: *The police are still **searching for clues**.* | **[+(as) to]** *He uncovered a clue as to her whereabouts.* | *The shoes could **provide a clue** to his identity.* | *I don't know – **give** me a **clue**!*

PHRASES

not have a clue *informal* to definitely not know or understand something: *'Where's Karen?' 'I haven't got a clue.'* | **[+what/where/how etc]** *I didn't have a clue what to do.*

clued-'up *BrE*, **clued-'in** *AmE adj* knowing a lot about something

clueless /ˈkluːləs/ *adj disapproving* having no understanding or knowledge of something

clump¹ /klʌmp/ *n* [C] a group of trees or plants growing together

clump² *v* [I + adv/prep] to walk with slow noisy steps

clumsy /ˈklʌmzi/ *adj* **1** moving in an awkward way, often knocking things and making them fall over: *The girl was really clumsy and dropped the bag on the floor.* THESAURUS CARELESS **2** large, heavy, and difficult to use: *big clumsy shoes* **3** if you say or do something in a clumsy way, you do it in a careless way, without considering other people's feelings: *Dave made a **clumsy attempt** to comfort us.* —**clumsily** *adv* —**clumsiness** *n* [U]

> **Word Choice: clumsy or awkward?**
> If someone is **clumsy**, they drop things or knock against things, especially in a way that other people find annoying: *The clumsy idiot spilled paint on the bedroom carpet!*
> If someone is **awkward**, they move or behave in a way that does not seem relaxed and natural: *I was a shy awkward teenager.*

clung /klʌŋ/ *v* the past tense and past participle of CLING

cluster¹ /ˈklʌstə $ -ər/ *n* [C] a group of things that are close together: **[+of]** *a small cluster of buildings*

cluster² *v* [I,T] to form a group of people or things: **[+around/round/together]** *Everyone clustered around her.*

clutch¹ /klʌtʃ/ *v* [I,T] to hold something tightly: *She clutched her case.* | **[+at]** *She clutched at his arm* (=tried to hold it). THESAURUS HOLD

clutch² *n* [C] **1** the part of a car that you press with your foot to change GEAR **2** sb's **clutches** if you are in someone's clutches, they control you: *He was trying to **escape** his mother's **clutches**.* **3** a clutch of sth a group of people or things

clutter¹ /ˈklʌtə $ -ər/ (*also* **clutter up**) *v* [T] to fill a space in an untidy way: *Piles of books cluttered up his desk.*

clutter² n [U] things that fill a space in an untidy way

cm the written abbreviation of **centimetre**

co- /kəʊ $ koʊ/ prefix with someone else, or together: We co-wrote the book.

c/o the written abbreviation of **care of**, used in addresses, for example when you are sending a letter to someone who is living in another person's house: John Simms c/o Mrs R. Pearce

Co. /kəʊ $ koʊ/ **1** the abbreviation of **Company**: Hilton, Brooks & Co. **2** the written abbreviation of **County**: Co. Durham

coach¹ /kəʊtʃ $ koʊtʃ/ n [C]
1 someone who trains a person or team in a sport: **basketball/football/tennis etc coach** THESAURUS TEACHER
2 BrE a bus with comfortable seats used for long journeys SYN **bus** AmE: **by coach** We went to Paris by coach. | **on a coach** They came on a coach. | **coach trip/tour** → see picture at TRANSPORT¹
3 BrE one of the parts of a train in which passengers sit SYN **car** AmE
4 a vehicle pulled by horses

coach² v [I,T] **1** to train a person or team in a sport: He coaches the local football team. **2** to give someone extra private lessons —**coaching** n [U]

coal /kəʊl $ koʊl/ n
1 [U] a hard black substance that you can burn to provide heat: Put some coal on the fire. | a lump of coal | a coal fire
2 coals [plural] burning pieces of coal

PHRASES
| **haul/rake sb over the coals** to speak angrily to someone who has done something wrong

coalition /ˌkəʊəˈlɪʃən $ ˌkoʊə-/ n [C,U] when two or more groups work together, usually in politics: The two parties have decided to **form a coalition**. | a **coalition government**

coarse /kɔːs $ kɔːrs/ adj **1** rough and thick, not smooth or fine: a coarse woollen blanket THESAURUS ROUGH **2** rude and offensive —**coarsely** adv —**coarseness** n [U]

coast¹ /kəʊst $ koʊst/ n [C] the land next to the sea: **[+of]** the west coast of Africa | **on the coast** They've rented a cottage on the coast. | **off the coast** (=in the water near the land) a small island off the coast

PHRASES
| **the coast is clear** if the coast is clear, there is no one around in a place, so no one will see you or catch you: I looked down the corridor and checked that the coast was clear.

coast² v [I] **1** to achieve something without effort: **[+to]** He coasted to an easy victory. **2** to move forward without using the engine of a car

coastal /ˈkəʊstl $ ˈkoʊstl/ adj [only before noun] near the coast: **coastal waters** | a **coastal town**

ˈcoast guard, coastguard n [C] a person or organization that helps people in danger on the sea

coastline /ˈkəʊstlaɪn $ ˈkoʊst-/ n [C,U] the land along the edge of the sea

coat¹ /kəʊt $ koʊt/ n [C]
1 a piece of clothing that you wear over other clothes to keep you warm when you go outside: Put your coat **on** if you're going out. → see picture at CLOTHES
2 a piece of clothing that a doctor wears over other clothes
3 an animal's fur
4 a layer of a substance such as paint: **[+of]** a coat of varnish

coat² v [T] to cover a surface with a layer of something: **coat sth with/in sth** The books were coated with dust.

coating /ˈkəʊtɪŋ $ ˈkoʊ-/ n [C] a layer of something that covers a surface: **[+of]** a light coating of snow

ˌcoat of ˈarms n [C] (plural **coats of arms**) a design that is the symbol of a family, town, or institution

coax /kəʊks $ koʊks/ v [T] to gently persuade someone to do something: **coax sb into doing sth** We managed to coax him into eating something. | **coax sb down/out/back etc** Firefighters coaxed the man down.

cobble¹ /ˈkɒbəl $ ˈkɑː-/ v
PHRASAL VERBS
cobble sth ↔ **together** to quickly produce or make something that is useful but not perfect: The script had been cobbled together by several writers.

cobble² /ˈkɒbəl $ ˈkɑː-/ (also **cobblestone** /ˈkɒbəlstəʊn $ ˈkɑːbəlstoʊn/) n [C usually plural] a round stone that was used in the past for making road surfaces —**cobbled** adj: cobbled streets

cobbler /ˈkɒblə $ ˈkɑːblər/ n [C,U] old-fashioned someone whose job is to make or repair shoes

cobra /ˈkəʊbrə $ ˈkoʊ-/ n [C] a poisonous snake that can make its neck look wider when it is going to attack something

cobweb /ˈkɒbweb $ ˈkɑːb-/ n [C] a structure of fine threads made by a SPIDER

cocaine /kəʊˈkeɪn, kə- $ koʊ-/ n [U] an illegal drug

cock¹ /kɒk $ kɑːk/ n [C] **1** BrE a male chicken SYN **rooster** AmE **2** a rude word for a PENIS

cock² v [T] to raise or move part of your head or face: John **cocked** his **head** to one side.
PHRASES
| **cock a snook at sb/sth** BrE to show clearly that you do not respect someone or something: He always tried to cock a snook at authority.

cockerel /ˈkɒkərəl $ ˈkɑː-/ n [C] a male chicken

ˌcock-ˈeyed adj informal **1** not sensible or practical: a cock-eyed idea **2** not straight or level: His hat was all cock-eyed.

cockney /ˈkɒkni $ ˈkɑːk-/ n **1** [C] a person from East London **2** [U] the form of English used by people from East London

cockpit /ˈkɒkpɪt $ ˈkɑːk-/ n [C] the part of a plane where the pilot sits → see picture at AEROPLANE

cockroach /ˈkɒkrəʊtʃ $ ˈkɑːkroʊtʃ/ n [C] a large insect that sometimes lives in places where there is food

cocktail /ˈkɒkteɪl $ ˈkɑːk-/ n **1** [C] an alcoholic drink which is a mixture of different drinks: *a cocktail party* **THESAURUS** ▶ **PARTY 2 fruit/seafood/prawn cocktail** a mixture of fruit, SEAFOOD etc **3** [C] a powerful or dangerous combination: **[+of]** *a poisonous cocktail of gases*

'cock-up *n* [C] *BrE spoken informal* a rude word for a mistake

cocky /'kɒki $ 'kɑːki/ *adj informal* too confident, in a way which people do not like —**cockiness** *n* [U]

cocoa /'kəʊkəʊ $ 'koʊkoʊ/ *n* [U] **1** brown powder that tastes of chocolate **2** a hot chocolate drink

coconut /'kəʊkənʌt $ 'koʊ-/ *n* [C,U] a very large brown nut which is white inside and has liquid in the middle → see picture at **NUT**

cocoon[1] /kə'kuːn/ *n* [C] **1** a silk cover around an insect **2** a situation in which you feel safe: *the cocoon of a loving family*

cocoon[2] *v* [T] to protect or surround someone: *She lay cocooned in her warm bed.*

cod /kɒd $ kɑːd/ *n* [C,U] (*plural* **cod**) a large sea fish that you can eat

code[1] /kəʊd $ koʊd/ *n*
1 [C] a set of rules or principles: *She followed a strict moral code.* | **code of conduct/behaviour** | **code of practice/ethics** (=rules that people in a particular business agree to obey)
2 [C] a set of numbers, letters, or symbols that gives information about something: *Please write the product code number on your order form.*
3 [C,U] a system of words, letters, or symbols, used instead of ordinary writing to keep something secret: **in code** *The messages were written in code.* | *a secret code* | *It took several months to crack the enemy's code* (=to understand it).
4 (*also* **dialling code**) [C] *BrE* the part of a telephone number that you use for a particular area or country **SYN** **area code** *AmE*: **[+for]** *The code for Manchester is 0161.* → **AREA CODE, BAR CODE, ZIP CODE**

code[2] Ac *v* [T] to use a code to show something: *All the information was coded and entered into the computer.*

coded Ac /'kəʊdɪd $ 'koʊ-/ *adj* using a system for giving information, for example with letters, symbols, or colours: *a coded message*

co-ed /ˌkəʊ 'ed◂ $ 'koʊ ed/ *adj* a co-ed school is one in which boys and girls study together

coerce /kəʊ'ɜːs $ 'koʊɜːrs/ *v* [T] *formal* to force someone to do something by threatening them: *He was coerced into signing.* —**coercion** /kəʊ'ɜːʃən $ koʊ'ɜːrʒən/ *n* [U]

coexist /ˌkəʊɪɡ'zɪst $ ˌkoʊ-/ *v* [I] to exist together: **[+with]** *People can coexist with animals.* —**coexistence** *n* [U]

coffee /'kɒfi $ 'kɔːfi, 'kɑːfi/ *n*
1 [U] a hot dark brown drink that has a slightly bitter taste: *I don't like coffee.* | *Would you like a cup of coffee?* | **black/white coffee** (=without/with milk)
2 [C] a cup of coffee: *Who wants a coffee?*
3 [U] whole coffee beans, crushed coffee beans, or a powder from which you make coffee: *a jar of coffee* | **instant coffee** (=coffee powder) | **real coffee** (=(crushed) coffee beans)

4 [U] a light brown colour: *a coffee-coloured blouse*

'coffee ˌtable *n* [C] a low table in a LIVING ROOM → see picture at **TABLE**[1]

coffers /'kɒfəz $ 'kɒːfərz, 'kɑː-/ *n* [plural] the money that an organization has: *The firm's coffers are empty.*

coffin /'kɒfɪn $ 'kɒː-, 'kɑː-/ *n* [C] a box in which a dead person is put **SYN** **casket** *AmE*

cog /kɒg $ kɑːg/ *n* [C] a wheel that turns in a machine and makes another wheel turn

COG

PHRASES
a cog in the wheel/ machine one of many people in an organization or situation: *I want to be more than just a cog in the wheel.*

cogent /'kəʊdʒənt $ 'koʊ-/ *adj formal* a cogent explanation or opinion is clear and reasonable, and people will believe it

cognac /'kɒnjæk $ 'koʊ-, 'kɑː-/ *n* [C,U] a strong alcoholic drink from France **SYN** **brandy**

cognitive /'kɒgnətɪv $ 'kɑːg-/ *adj formal* relating to the process of knowing, understanding, and learning something —**cognitively** *adv*

cohabit /kəʊ'hæbɪt $ koʊ-/ *v* [I] *formal* to live as husband and wife, without being married —**cohabitation** /kəʊˌhæbɪ'teɪʃən $ koʊ-/ *n* [U]

coherent Ac /kəʊ'hɪərənt $ koʊ'hɪr-/ *adj* **1** clear and easy to understand: *He put forward a coherent argument in favour of stricter laws.* **2** if someone is coherent, they are talking in a way that is easy to understand: *He was slightly drunk, and not very coherent.* **3** something that is coherent has parts that go together well: *They are not a coherent group.* —**coherently** *adv*

cohesion /kəʊ'hiːʒən $ koʊ-/ *n* [U] when all the people in a group are united and work together well

coil[1] /kɔɪl/ (*also* **coil up**) *v* [I,T] to wind or twist into a round shape, or to make something do this: *The snake coiled around the branch.* | *I coiled the rope around a post.*

coil[2] *n* [C] a piece of wire or rope that has been wound into a circular shape

coin[1] /kɔɪn/ *n* [C] a round piece of money made of metal → **note**, **bill**: *a pound coin*
PHRASES
the other side of the coin a different fact or way of thinking about something: *Making the rules is only part of it. How the rules are carried out is the other side of the coin.*
toss/flip a coin to decide something by throwing a coin into the air and guessing which side will show when it falls: *Let's flip a coin to see who goes first.*
two sides of the same coin two ideas which are closely related: *Love and hate are two sides of the same coin.*

coin[2] *v* [T] to invent a new word or phrase that

coincide

many people start to use: *Who first coined the term 'acid rain'?*

coincide Ac /ˌkəʊənˈsaɪd $ ˌkoʊ-/ v [I] to happen at the same time as something else: **[+with]** *The show was timed to coincide with the launch of the book.*

coincidence /kəʊˈɪnsɪdəns $ koʊ-/ n [C,U] when two things happen together, in a surprising way: *It was **pure coincidence** that we were on the same train.* | **by coincidence** *By coincidence, he was in London at the same time as I was.* | **It's no coincidence that** *most of the protesters are women.* —**coincidental** /kəʊˌɪnsəˈdentl $ koʊ-/ adj —**coincidentally** adv

cola /ˈkəʊlə $ ˈkoʊ-/ n [C,U] a sweet brown drink containing bubbles, or a bottle, can, or glass of this drink

colander /ˈkʌləndə, ˈkɒ- $ ˈkʌləndər, ˈkɑː-/ n [C] a bowl with a lot of small holes in it, used for washing food or separating liquid from food

cold¹ /kəʊld $ koʊld/ adj
1 something that is cold has a low temperature OPP **hot**, **warm**: *The house was cold and empty.* | *We slept on the cold ground.* | *a blast of cold air* | **ice/stone/freezing cold** (=very cold) *freezing cold water* | *My coffee's **gone cold**.* | **be/feel/look/get cold** *I feel so cold!* | *It's **cold** outside.* | *The day was **bitterly cold**.*
2 cold food is cooked, but is not eaten hot: *a cold buffet* | *Serve the potatoes cold.*
3 without friendly feelings OPP **warm**: *a polite but cold greeting* THESAURUS **UNFRIENDLY** —**coldness** n [U]

PHRASES
  get/have cold feet *informal* to start to feel that you are not brave enough to do something: *She was getting cold feet about getting married.*
  give sb the cold shoulder *informal* to deliberately ignore someone or be unfriendly to them, especially because they have upset or offended you: *I tried to talk to her, but she gave me the cold shoulder.*
  in cold blood in a cruel and deliberate way: *innocent civilians murdered in cold blood*
  leave sb cold if something leaves you cold, you are not at all interested in it: *Most poetry leaves me cold.*

THESAURUS

cold having a low temperature: *a cold winter day* | *This room gets very cold at night.* | *It's cold outside!* | *I'm cold!* | *a cold drink*
cool a little cold, especially in a pleasant way: *a nice cool breeze* | *It's cooler in the shade.*
chilly a little cold in a way that feels rather uncomfortable: *a chilly night* | *It's getting chilly – you may need a coat.*
freezing very cold and very uncomfortable: *It's freezing outside.* | *The freezing weather continued.* | *I'm freezing!*
icy very cold – used especially when the temperature is near or below zero: *an icy wind* | *the icy waters of the lake*
draughty *BrE*, **drafty** *AmE* a draughty room or building has cold air blowing in from outside,

especially because the doors and windows do not fit well: *Old houses can be very draughty.*

cold² n **1** [C] a common illness that makes you cough, and makes it difficult to breathe through your nose: *I've got a bad cold.* **2** [U] when you feel cold: *I was shivering with cold.* **3** the cold cold weather: *Come in out of the cold.*

PHRASES
  be left out in the cold to not be included in an activity: *Anyone who didn't join the gang was left out in the cold.*

COLLOCATIONS

verbs
to have a cold (*also* **to have got a cold** *spoken*) *I'm not going to come because I've got a cold.*
to be getting a cold (=to be starting to have a cold) *Don't exercise if you think you're getting a cold.*
to catch a cold *Everyone in the family caught his cold.*
to come down with a cold (*also* **to go down with a cold** *BrE*) *informal* (=to start to have a cold) *A lot of people come down with colds at this time of year.*

adjectives
a bad cold *He was off school today with a bad cold.*
a nasty cold (*also* **a heavy cold** *BrE*) (=a very bad cold) *She had a nasty cold and couldn't play.*
a slight cold/a bit of a cold *It's only a slight cold – I'll be fine tomorrow.* ⚠ Do not say 'a little cold'. Say **a slight cold** or **a bit of a cold**.

---

cold³ adv *AmE* suddenly and completely: *In the middle of his speech, he stopped cold.*

PHRASES
  out cold *informal* unconscious: *The boxer was knocked out cold.*

cold-blooded /ˌkəʊld ˈblʌdɪd◄ $ ˌkoʊld-/ adj
1 cruel and showing no feelings: *a cold-blooded killer*
2 a cold-blooded animal, such as a snake, has a body temperature that changes with the temperature around it → **warm-blooded** —**cold-bloodedly** adv

cold-hearted /ˌkəʊld ˈhɑːtɪd◄ $ ˌkoʊld ˈhɑːr-/ adj showing no kindness or sympathy: *a cold-hearted man*

coldly /ˈkəʊldli $ ˈkoʊld-/ adv in a very unfriendly way: *Jan looked at her coldly.*

ˌcold ˈturkey n **go cold turkey** to feel ill because you have stopped taking a drug that you are ADDICTED to

coleslaw /ˈkəʊlslɔː $ ˈkoʊlslɑː/ n [U] a SALAD made with thinly cut raw vegetables

colic /ˈkɒlɪk $ ˈkɑː-/ n [U] pain in the stomach that babies often get

collaborate /kəˈlæbəreɪt/ v [I] **1** to work together to produce or achieve something: **[+with]** *She often collaborates with other writers.* | **[+on]** *Two companies collaborated on this project.* **2** to help an enemy army or government that controls your country: [+with] *It seems that he collaborated with the secret police.* —**collaborator** *n* [C] —**collaboration** /kəˌlæbəˈreɪʃən/ *n* [U] —**collaborative** /kəˈlæbərətɪv $ -reɪ-/ *adj*

collage /ˈkɒlɑːʒ $ kəˈlɑːʒ/ *n* [C,U] a picture made by sticking pieces of paper, cloth etc onto a surface, or the art of making pictures in this way

collapse¹ Ac /kəˈlæps/ *v* [I]
1 to fall down suddenly: *Many buildings collapsed during the earthquake.*
2 to suddenly fall down or become unconscious because you are ill or very weak: *He collapsed with a dangerously high fever.* THESAURUS ▶ FALL
3 to fail suddenly and completely: *The luxury car market has collapsed.*

collapse² Ac *n* [C,U] **1** the sudden failure of a business, system, or plan: [+of] *the collapse of the Soviet Union* | *economic collapse* **2** when something suddenly falls down: *Floods caused the collapse of the bridge.* **3** when someone suddenly falls down or becomes unconscious because of an illness or injury: *The prisoner was in a state of collapse.*

collapsible /kəˈlæpsəbəl/ *adj* something collapsible can be folded so that it can be stored or carried: *a collapsible table*

collar¹ /ˈkɒlə $ ˈkɑːlər/ *n* [C]
1 the part of a shirt, coat, dress etc that fits around your neck: *a dress with a white collar*
2 a narrow band of leather or plastic that is fastened around an animal's neck → BLUE-COLLAR, WHITE-COLLAR

collar² *v* [T] *informal* to catch and hold someone: *Two policemen collared him before he could get away.*

collarbone /ˈkɒləbəʊn $ ˈkɑːlərboʊn/ *n* [C] one of the bones that go from the base of your neck to your shoulders → see picture on page A2

collateral /kəˈlætərəl/ *n* [U] *technical* property or money that you promise to give to someone if you cannot pay back a debt: *He offered his house as collateral for the loan.*

colleague Ac /ˈkɒliːɡ $ ˈkɑː-/ *n* [C] someone you work with: *my colleagues at the bank*

collect¹ /kəˈlekt/ *v*
1 GET THINGS TOGETHER [T] to get things and bring them together: *I'll collect everyone's papers at the end of the test.*
2 INTERESTING OBJECTS [T] to keep objects of the same type because they interest you: *Ann collects teddy bears.*
3 MONEY [I,T] to ask people to give money for a particular purpose: [+for] *I'm collecting for Children in Need.*
4 CROWD [I] to come together in a place: *A crowd had collected at the scene of the accident.*
5 FETCH SB [T] *especially BrE* to go to a particular place and bring someone or something away SYN **pick up**: **collect sb from sth** *Can you collect the kids from school?*
PHRASES
collect yourself/your thoughts to make yourself calmer and able to think more clearly: *I want to collect my thoughts before the meeting begins.*

collect² *adj, adv AmE* **1 call/phone sb collect** if you call someone collect, the person who gets the telephone call pays for it SYN **reverse the charges** *BrE* **2 collect call** a telephone call that is paid for by the person who gets it

collected /kəˈlektɪd/ *adj* **1** [only before noun] **collected poems/stories etc** all the poems, stories etc of a particular writer included together in one book: *the collected works of Shakespeare* **2** calm and in control of yourself and your thoughts and feelings

collection /kəˈlekʃən/ *n*
1 [C] a set of objects of the same type that you keep because they interest you: *my CD collection* | [+of] *a fine collection of paintings*
2 [U] when you bring together things of the same type from different places: [+of] *the collection of reliable information*
3 [C,U] when you ask people for money for a particular purpose: [+for] *a collection for cancer research*
4 [C,U] when something is taken away from a place: *Garbage collections are made every Tuesday.*
5 [singular] *informal* a group of people that are together in the same place: [+of] *There was an odd collection of people at the party.*

collective¹ /kəˈlektɪv/ *adj* [only before noun] shared by every member of a group or society: *a collective decision* | *our collective responsibility for the environment* —**collectively** *adv*

collective² *n* [C] a business or organization owned and controlled by the people who work in it

collector /kəˈlektə $ -ər/ *n* [C] **1 ticket/tax/debt etc collector** someone whose job is to collect tickets or money from people **2** someone who collects things that are interesting to them: *a stamp collector*

college /ˈkɒlɪdʒ $ ˈkɑː-/ *n*
1 [C,U] a school for advanced education, especially in a particular profession or skill: *an art college* | **at college** *We were great friends at college.*
2 [C,U] *AmE* a university: *college students*
3 [C] a part of a university, especially in Britain: *King's College, Cambridge* → COMMUNITY COLLEGE, JUNIOR COLLEGE

Grammar
When you are talking about the time when someone is studying at a college, do not use 'a' or 'the' before **college**: *They met while they were at college together.*

COLLOCATIONS
verbs
to go to college (*also* **to attend college** *formal*) *She'd like to go to teacher training college.*
to finish college *When I finish college, I plan to travel.*
to leave college *He started his own business after he left college.*

types of college
an art/music/drama college *The Music College was founded in 1869.*
an agricultural/secretarial/technical college *I wanted a job in farm management so I went to agricultural college.*

a teacher training college (=where you learn to be a teacher) | a sixth form college BrE (=where students in Britain can go at 16, instead of going to a school)

collide /kəˈlaɪd/ v [I] to crash violently into something or someone → **collision**: The two trains collided in a tunnel. | [+with] Her car collided with a lorry.

colliery /ˈkɒljəri $ ˈkɑːl-/ n [C] (plural **collieries**) BrE a coal mine and the buildings and machinery connected with it

collision /kəˈlɪʒən/ n [C,U] a violent crash in which one vehicle hits another: Two people were killed in a **head-on collision** (=between two vehicles that are moving directly towards each other). **THESAURUS** ACCIDENT

colloquial /kəˈləʊkwiəl $ -ˈloʊ-/ adj colloquial language is the kind of language used in informal conversations: a colloquial expression —**colloquially** adv —colloquialism n [C]

collusion /kəˈluːʒən/ n [U] formal a secret agreement between people to do something dishonest —collude /kəˈluːd/ v [I]: She colluded in the plot.

cologne /kəˈləʊn $ -ˈloʊn/ n [U] a liquid that smells slightly of flowers or plants, that you put on your neck or wrists

colon /ˈkəʊlən $ ˈkoʊ-/ n [C] the mark (:) used in writing to introduce a list or an example

colonel /ˈkɜːnl $ ˈkɜːr-/ n [C] an officer with a high rank in the army, marines, or the US air force

colonial /kəˈləʊniəl $ -ˈloʊ-/ adj relating to colonialism or a colony: the struggle against colonial rule

colonialism /kəˈləʊniəlɪzəm $ -ˈloʊ-/ n [U] the system by which a powerful country rules another less powerful country → **imperialism** —colonialist adj, n [C]

colonize (also -ise BrE) /ˈkɒlənaɪz $ ˈkɑː-/ v [T] to get control of another country or area and make it a colony: Australia was colonized in the 18th century. —colonist n [C] —colonization /ˌkɒlənaɪˈzeɪʃən $ ˌkɑːlənə-/ n [U]

colony /ˈkɒləni $ ˈkɑː-/ n [C] (plural **colonies**) **1** a country or area that is controlled by a more powerful country: Algeria was formerly a French colony. **2** a group of people with the same interests who live together: an artists' colony **3** a group of the same kind of animals living together: an ant colony

color /ˈkʌlə $ -ər/ n, v the American spelling of COLOUR

colossal /kəˈlɒsəl $ kəˈlɑː-/ adj extremely large: They've run up colossal debts. **THESAURUS** BIG

colour¹ BrE, color AmE /ˈkʌlə $ -ər/ n
1 [C,U] red, blue, yellow etc: What colour is your new car? | the colours of the rainbow | **in colour** The meat should be pale pink in colour. | The sky slowly changed colour.
2 [U] if something has colour, it has bright colours and looks nice: flowers that will **add colour** to your garden
3 [U] a colour photograph, film etc shows all the

different colours, not just black and white **OPP** black and white: a large colour TV | **in colour** The magazine was printed in colour.
4 [C,U] how dark or light someone's skin is: people of all colours
5 [U] the appearance of someone's skin on their face, which shows how healthy they are: The fresh air has brought some colour to her cheeks.
6 [U] interesting or exciting qualities: a story full of life, colour, and adventure
7 colours [plural] the colours that are used to represent a team, school, club, country etc: Australia's national colours are gold and green. → **OFF-COLOUR**

COLLOCATIONS

adjectives

a **red/green/blue etc colour** The leaves were a lovely red colour.

a **bright colour** (=strong and noticeable) She likes to wear bright colours.

a **dark colour** (=more like black than white) Dark colours make a house seem smaller.

a **light/pale colour** (=not dark or strong) All the bedrooms are painted in light colours.

a **primary colour** (=red, yellow, or blue) Why are children's toys always in primary colours?

---

colour² BrE, color AmE v [T] **1** to make something a particular colour: Do you colour your hair or is it natural? **2** (also colour in) to use paint, pencils etc to put colours inside the lines of a picture: Draw a picture and colour it in. **3** colour sb's judgment/opinion etc to influence someone's opinion about something: Personal feelings coloured his judgment.

'colour-blind BrE, color-blind AmE adj not able to see the difference between some colours —colour-blindness n [U]

coloured BrE, colored AmE /ˈkʌləd $ -ərd/ adj having a colour or colours other than black or white: coloured glass | a brightly coloured shirt

colourful BrE, colorful AmE /ˈkʌləfəl $ -lər-/ adj **1** having a lot of bright colours: a garden full of colourful flowers | colourful costumes **2** interesting, exciting, and full of variety: He's led a very colourful life.

colouring BrE, coloring AmE /ˈkʌlərɪŋ/ n **1** [U] the colour of someone's hair, skin, and eyes: Mandy had her mother's dark colouring. **2** [C,U] a substance used to give a particular colour to food: green **food colouring**

colourless BrE, colorless AmE /ˈkʌlələs $ ˈkʌlər-/ adj **1** having no colour: a colourless liquid **2** not interesting or exciting: His books always seemed rather dull and colourless.

'colour scheme BrE, color scheme AmE n [C] the combination of colours that someone chooses for a room

colt /kəʊlt $ koʊlt/ n [C] a young male horse

column /ˈkɒləm $ ˈkɑː-/ n [C]
1 a tall solid upright stone post used to support a building: the marble columns of a Greek temple
2 numbers or words written under each other down a page → **row**: Add up the numbers in each column. | [+of] a column of figures

3 lines of print that go down the page of a newspaper or book
4 an article on a particular subject that appears regularly in a newspaper or magazine: *He writes a weekly column for 'The Times'.* | *a gardening column*
5 something with a long narrow shape: **[+of]** *a column of smoke*
6 a long moving line of people or vehicles: **[+of]** *a column of soldiers on the march* → **GOSSIP COLUMN**

columnist /'kɒləmɪst, -ləmnɪst $ 'kɑ:-/ n [C] someone who regularly writes articles for a newspaper or magazine

coma /'kəʊmə $ 'koʊ-/ n [C,U] someone who is in a coma has been unconscious for a long time, usually because of a serious illness or injury: **in a coma** *Ben was in a coma for six days.*

comatose /'kəʊmətəʊs $ 'koʊmətoʊs/ adj
1 *technical* in a coma **2** deeply asleep

comb[1] /kəʊm $ koʊm/ n **1** [C] a piece of plastic or metal with a row of thin teeth, that you use to make your hair tidy → **brush 2** [singular] when you use a comb: *Your hair needs a good comb.*

comb[2] v [T] **1** to make your hair tidy with a comb: *Have you combed your hair?* **2** to search a place thoroughly: **comb sth for sth** *Police are combing the area for more bombs.*

combat[1] /'kɒmbæt $ 'kɑːm-/ n [C,U] fighting during a war: **in combat** *Her husband was killed in combat.* | **unarmed combat** (=without weapons)

combat[2] /'kɒmbæt, kəm'bæt $ 'kɑːmbæt/ v [T] (**combated** or **combatted**, **combating** or **combatting**) to try to stop something bad from happening or getting worse: *new technology to combat crime* | *measures to combat inflation*

combatant /'kɒmbətənt $ kəm'bætnt/ n [C] someone who fights in a war

combative /'kɒmbətɪv $ kəm'bætɪv/ adj ready to fight or argue: *Paul was in a combative mood.*

combination /ˌkɒmbə'neɪʃən $ ˌkɑːm-/ n
1 [C,U] two or more different things that are used, put, or mixed together: **[+of]** *Doctors now treat this disease with a combination of drugs.* | *a combination of bad management and inexperience*
2 [C] a set of numbers or letters you need to open a combination lock

combi'nation lock n [C] a lock that is opened by using a special set of numbers or letters → see picture at **LOCK**[2]

combine /kəm'baɪn/ v
1 [I,T] to join or mix two or more things together: **combine sth with sth** *Combine the flour with the milk and eggs.* | **combined with sb/sth** *Diets are most effective when combined with exercise.* | *The combined*

a comb

COMB

effects of the war and the drought resulted in famine.
THESAURUS MIX
2 [T] to do two different activities at the same time: **combine sth with/and sth** *She manages to combine family life with a career.*

combine harvester /ˌkɒmbaɪn 'hɑːvɪstə $ ˌkɑːmbaɪn 'hɑːrvɪstər/ (*also* **combine**) n [C] a large machine used by farmers to cut grain and separate the seeds from it

combustible /kəm'bʌstəbəl/ adj technical able to burn easily: *Gasoline is highly combustible.*

combustion /kəm'bʌstʃən/ n [U] the process of burning

come /kʌm/ v [I] (*past tense* **came** /keɪm/, *past participle* **come**)
1 to move towards you or arrive at the place where you are **OPP** go: **[+in/into/out of etc]** *A young woman came into the room.* | *Someone was coming towards me.* | *Can you come here for a minute?* | *What time are you coming home?* | **come and do sth** *Come and have dinner with us.* | **come to do sth** *I've come to see Phil.* | **here comes sb/sth** *spoken* (=used to say that someone or something is coming towards you) *Here comes Karen now.*
2 to travel to a place: *Which way did you come?* | **[+to/from/through etc]** *They came over the mountains in the north.* | **come by car/train/bus etc** *Did you come by car?*
3 if someone comes with you, they go to a place with you: **[+with]** *I asked her if she'd like to come with us.*
4 if a letter or package comes, it is delivered to you by post: *The phone bill came yesterday.*
5 if a time or event comes, it arrives or starts to happen: *Spring came early that year.* | *The time has come to make some changes.*
6 to be in a particular position in an order, a series, or a list: **[+before/after]** *What letter comes after 'u'?* | **come first/second/last etc** *I came last in the cycle race.* **THESAURUS** WIN
7 to reach a particular level or place: **[+up/down]** *The water only came up to my knees.*
8 to be produced or sold with particular features: **[+in]** *The sweaters come in four sizes.* → **how come?** at **HOW**[1]

PHRASES
come and go 1 to be allowed to go into and leave a place whenever you want: *Students come and go as they please.* **2** to keep starting and stopping: *The pain comes and goes.*
come as a surprise/shock etc to make someone feel surprised etc: *Her death came as a shock to everyone.*
come naturally/easily (to sb) to be easy for someone to do, say etc: *Acting came naturally to Rae.*
come of age to reach the age when you are legally considered to be an adult: *He'll receive the money when he comes of age.*
come open/undone/loose etc to become open etc: *Your shoelace has come undone.*
come to do sth to begin to have a feeling or opinion: *I came to believe that he was innocent after all.*
come to think of it *spoken* used to add something

that you have just realized or remembered: *Come to think of it, Cooper did mention the accident to me.*
in (the) years/days etc to come in the future: *I think we shall regret this decision in the years to come.*

PHRASAL VERBS

come about to happen or develop: *How did this extraordinary situation come about?*

come across

1 come across sb/sth to meet or find someone or something by chance: *I came across an old diary in her desk.* **THESAURUS** FIND

2 if someone comes across in a particular way, they seem to have particular qualities: **[+as]** *He comes across as a nice guy.*

come along

1 to develop or improve: *Terry's work has really come along this year.*

2 to appear or arrive: *I'm ready to take any job that comes along.*

3 to follow someone or go with them: *Can I come along too?*

come apart *especially BrE* to break into pieces: *The book just came apart in my hands.*

come at sb to move towards someone in a threatening way: *She came at him with a knife.*

come away *BrE*

1 to become separated from the main part of something: *I pulled, and the handle came away.*

2 to leave a place with a particular feeling or idea: *We came away thinking we had done quite well.*

come back

1 to return: *When is your sister coming back from Europe?*

2 if something comes back to you, you suddenly remember it: **[+to]** *Then, everything William had said came back to me.*

3 to become fashionable or popular again → **comeback**: *Long skirts are coming back.*

come between sb to cause trouble between people: *I didn't want the question of money to come between us.*

come by

1 come by sth to get something that is rare or difficult to find: *How did you come by these pictures?* | *Jobs are very hard to come by in the winter months.*

2 to visit someone for a short time: *Veronica came by to see me today.* **THESAURUS** VISIT

come down

1 if a price or level comes down, it gets lower: *Wait until prices come down before you buy.*

2 to fall to the ground: *A lot of trees came down in the storm.*

come down on sb/sth

1 to punish someone or criticize them severely: *We need to come down hard on young offenders.*

2 come down on the side of sb/sth to decide to support something or someone: *The court came down on the side of the boy's father.*

come down to sth if a complicated situation or problem comes down to something, that is the single most important thing: *It all comes down to money in the end.*

come down with sth *informal* to get an illness: *I think I'm coming down with flu.*

come forward to offer help to someone, or offer to do something: *Witnesses are asked to come forward with information about the robbery.*

come from sth

1 to be born, obtained from, or made somewhere: *His mother came from Texas.* | *A lot of drugs come from quite common plants.* | *The idea came from America.*

2 to be the result of something: **come from doing sth** *Most of her problems come from expecting too much of people.*

come in

1 to enter a place: *Come in and sit down.* **THESAURUS** ENTER

2 to arrive: *What time does your train come in?*

3 to be received: *Reports are coming in of an earthquake in Japan.*

4 to become fashionable or popular: *I remember when miniskirts first came in.*

5 to finish a race: **come in first/second etc** *His horse came in second to last.*

6 come in useful/handy to be useful: *Bring some rope – it might come in handy.*

7 when the TIDE comes in, the sea moves towards the land and covers the edge of it

come in for sth to receive something, especially something unpleasant: *After the riots the police **came in for** a lot of **criticism**.*

come into sth

1 to be involved in something: *Where do I come into all this?*

2 to receive money or property from someone who has died: *I came into some money when my grandfather died.*

come of sth to result from something: *We wanted to start a pop group, but nothing ever came of it.*

come off

1 come off sth to become removed from something: *A button had come off his coat.*

2 to happen as planned: *In the end the trip never came off.*

3 to succeed: *It was a good idea, but it didn't quite come off.*

4 come off well/badly etc to get into a good or bad situation as a result of something: *If we have an argument, I always come off worst.*

5 come off it! *spoken* used to tell someone that you do not believe what they are saying: *Oh, come off it! Don't pretend you didn't know.*

come on

1 to start working: *The lights suddenly came on in the cinema.*

2 come on! *spoken* **a)** used to tell someone to hurry, or to encourage them to do something: *Come on! We'll be late.* | *Come on, it's not that hard.* **b)** used to tell someone that you do not believe them: *Oh come on, don't lie to me!*

3 if an illness comes on, you start to be ill with it: *I can feel a headache coming on.*

come out

1 to become known: *The truth will come out one day.*

2 if a book, record etc comes out, it becomes available for people to buy: *When does his new book come out?*

3 to state your opinions clearly and directly: *Why*

don't you just come out and say what you really think?
4 if something you say comes out in a particular way, that is how it sounds or how it is understood: *I tried to explain, but it came out all wrong.*
5 if dirt or a mark comes out, it is removed by washing or cleaning it
6 if a photograph comes out, it shows a clear picture: *The wedding photos came out really well.*
7 if the sun, moon, or stars come out, they appear in the sky

come out in sth **come out in spots/a rash** *BrE* to become covered in spots because you are ill

come out with sth to say something, especially something that is not expected: *Tanya comes out with some stupid remarks.*

come over
1 to visit you at your house: *Can I come over to your place tonight?* **THESAURUS** VISIT
2 come over sb if a feeling comes over you, it affects you strongly: *A wave of sleepiness came over her.* | *I'm sorry I was so rude – I don't know what came over me!*
3 if someone or something comes over in a particular way, that is how they seem to people: **[+as]** *She comes over as a very cold woman.*

come round *BrE* (also **come around** *AmE*)
1 to visit someone: *Paul is coming round to my house for tea.* **THESAURUS** VISIT
2 to change your opinion so that you now agree with someone: **[+to]** *I'm sure he'll come round to our way of thinking.*
3 to become conscious again: *When she came round her mother was sitting by the bed.*
4 to happen as a regular event: *Christmas will soon be coming round again.*

come through
1 come through sth to continue to exist or succeed after a difficult or dangerous time: *We've come through all kinds of trouble together.*
2 if a piece of news or a result comes through, it becomes known or arrives: *His divorce should come through next month.*

come to
1 come to a conclusion/decision/agreement etc to reach a particular result: *After a long discussion, we finally came to a decision.*
2 come to sth a) to develop so that something bad happens: *We need to be prepared to fight, but hopefully it won't come to that.* **b)** to add up to a total amount: *That comes to $24.50.*
3 come to sb if a thought or idea comes to you, you realize or remember it: *I can't remember her name just now, but it'll come to me.*
4 to become conscious again: *When I came to, I was lying on the grass.*

come under sth
1 come under attack/fire/pressure etc to be attacked, shot at etc: *The students have come under pressure to report their friends.*
2 to be controlled by something: *These schools come under the control of the Department of Education.*
3 to be in a particular part of a book or information system: *Skiing? That'll come under 'Sport'.*

come up
1 if someone comes up to you, they come close to you, especially in order to speak to you: *One of the*

teachers came up and spoke to me.
2 to be mentioned or suggested: *The subject didn't come up at the meeting.*
3 be coming up to be happening soon: *Is your birthday coming up soon?*
4 if a problem comes up, it suddenly happens: *Something's come up, so I won't be able to go with you.*
THESAURUS HAPPEN
5 when the sun or moon comes up, it appears in the sky

come up against sb/sth to have to deal with problems or difficulties: *Black politicians often come up against racist attitudes.*

come up to sb/sth to be as good as something: *This work doesn't come up to your usual standard.*

come up with sth to think of an idea, plan, or reply: *They still haven't come up with a name for the baby.*
THESAURUS INVENT

comeback /'kʌmbæk/ *n* [C usually singular] when someone or something becomes popular or successful again: *Miniskirts are **making a comeback**.*

comedian /kə'miːdiən/ *n* [C] someone whose job is to tell jokes and make people laugh

comedown /'kʌmdaʊn/ *n* [singular] *informal* a situation that is not as good as something you had before: *It was a comedown compared with his old job.*

comedy /'kɒmədi $ 'kɑː-/ *n* (plural **comedies**)
1 [U] entertainment intended to make people laugh: **comedy series/show/writer/actor etc** | **stand-up comedy** (=telling jokes in front of people)
2 [C] a funny film or play: *All my favourite films are comedies.* | *a TV comedy*

comet /'kɒmɪt $ 'kɑː-/ *n* [C] a very bright object in the sky like a star with a tail

comfort¹ /'kʌmfət $ -ərt/ *n*
1 [U] when you feel physically relaxed, happy, and without pain **OPP** **discomfort**: *I dress for comfort, not fashion.* | **built/made/designed for comfort** *Our shoes are designed for comfort.* | **in comfort** *I prefer to travel in comfort.* | *Use the Internet to do your shopping from **the comfort of your own home**.*
2 [U] if someone or something gives you comfort, they make you feel happier when you are upset or worried: *Whenever Bob was upset, he turned to Meg for comfort.* | **give/provide/offer comfort** *a book which offers comfort to people with cancer* | **great/much/little comfort** *My faith is a **source of great comfort**.*
3 [singular] someone or something that helps you feel happier or less worried: **be a comfort (to sb)** *Ann's been a **great comfort** to me since Ian died.*
4 [U] when you have enough money to buy all the things you need: *They had enough money to **live in comfort**.*
5 comforts [plural] all the things that make your life easier and more comfortable: *home comforts*

comfort² *v* [T] to make someone feel happier when they are upset or worried: *The boy's mother tried to comfort him.* —**comforting** *adj*: *a comforting thought* —**comfortingly** *adv*

comfortable /'kʌmftəbəl, 'kʌmfət- $ 'kʌmfərt-, 'kʌmft-/ *adj*
1 something that is comfortable makes you feel

physically relaxed: **comfortable chair/bed/sofa etc**
The bed wasn't very comfortable. | **comfortable room/
lounge/hotel etc** *a comfortable flat* | **comfortable
clothes/shoes/boots etc** *loose, comfortable clothing*
2 if you are comfortable, you feel physically relaxed:
Are you comfortable sitting on the floor? | *Sit down and
make yourself comfortable.* **THESAURUS** ▶ RELAXED
3 emotionally relaxed and not worried: **[+with]** *I feel
comfortable with him whenever we're together.*
4 having enough money to buy all the things you
need or want: *a comfortable retirement*
—**comfortably** *adv*: *The hotel is comfortably furnished.*

> **THESAURUS**
>
> **comfortable** making you feel physically relaxed,
> or feeling physically relaxed: *The hotel was very
> comfortable.* | *Are you comfortable in that chair?*
> **comfy** *informal* comfortable – used especially
> about furniture and clothes: *a big comfy sofa* | *a
> nice comfy sweater*
> **cosy** *BrE*, **cozy** *AmE* comfortable and warm –
> used especially about small rooms, houses etc:
> *a cosy little room with a real fire*
> **smooth** a smooth journey is comfortable,
> especially because there are no delays, your
> plane does not shake, or the sea is not rough:
> *The flight was very smooth and we actually got
> there early.* | *a smooth crossing*
> **luxurious** a luxurious hotel, ship etc is
> extremely comfortable because it has large
> rooms, expensive furniture etc: *a luxurious 5-star
> hotel*

comforter /ˈkʌmfətə $ -fərtər/ *n* [C] *AmE* a cover
for a bed that is filled with soft warm material
SYN duvet *BrE*

comfy /ˈkʌmfi/ *adj informal* comfortable
THESAURUS ▶ COMFORTABLE

comic¹ /ˈkɒmɪk $ ˈkɑː-/ *adj* funny or amusing: *a
comic novel*

comic² *n* [C] **1** (*also* **'comic book**) a magazine that
tells stories using sets of pictures **2** someone
whose job is to tell jokes and make people laugh

comical /ˈkɒmɪkəl $ ˈkɑː-/ *adj* funny: *She looked so
comical I burst out laughing.* —**comically** /-kli/ *adv*

'comic strip *n* [C] a set of pictures in a newspaper
or magazine that tell a short funny story

coming¹ /ˈkʌmɪŋ/ *n* **1 the coming of sth** when
something new comes or begins: *The coming of the
railways changed the town considerably.* **2 comings
and goings** the movements of people as they arrive
at and leave places: **[+of]** *the comings and goings of
the visitors*

coming² *adj* [only before noun] *formal* happening
soon: *the coming months*

comma /ˈkɒmə $ ˈkɑːmə/ *n* [C] the mark (,) used in
writing to show a short pause

command¹ /kəˈmɑːnd $ kəˈmænd/ *n*
1 ORDER [C] an order that must be obeyed: *Shoot
when I give the command.*
2 IN CHARGE [U] if someone is in command, they
are responsible for deciding what people, especially

soldiers, should do: **in command (of sth)** *Lieutenant
Peters is in command.* | **under sb's command** *troops
under the command of General Fox* | **take command
(of sth)** (=begin controlling a group or situation and
making decisions) *When the fire was discovered, Carl
took command.* | **at sb's command** *He has a large staff
at his command.*
3 ON A COMPUTER [C] an instruction to a computer
to do something
4 KNOWLEDGE knowledge of something, especially a
language: **good/excellent/poor etc command of sth**
He has a good command of English.

command² *v* [T] **1** to order someone to do something: **command sb to do sth** *The King commanded
him to stay.* **THESAURUS** ▶ ORDER **2** to control an army
or group of soldiers: *Major Grey commanded the
troops.* **3** to get something such as respect or attention because you do something well or are important or popular: *a teacher who commands respect*

commandant /ˌkɒmənˈdænt $ ˈkɑːməndænt/ *n* [C]
the army officer in charge of a place or group of
people

commandeer /ˌkɒmənˈdɪə $ ˌkɑːmənˈdɪr/ *v* [T] to
take someone's property for military use: *The hotel
was commandeered for use as a hospital.*

commander /kəˈmɑːndə $ kəˈmændər/ *n* [C] **1** an
officer in charge of a military organization or group
2 an officer with a middle rank in the navy

commanding /kəˈmɑːndɪŋ $ kəˈmæn-/ *adj* [only
before noun] **1** *approving* having great confidence
which makes people respect and obey you: *his commanding presence* **2** a commanding position is one
from which you are likely to win: *He now has a
commanding lead in the championship.*

com,manding 'officer *n* [C] the officer in charge
of a group of soldiers

commandment /kəˈmɑːndmənt $ kəˈmænd-/ *n*
[C] one of ten rules given by God in the Bible that
tell people how they must behave

commando /kəˈmɑːndəʊ $ kəˈmændoʊ/ *n* [C]
(*plural* **commandos**) a soldier who is trained to
make quick attacks into enemy areas

commemorate /kəˈmeməreɪt/ *v* [T] if something
commemorates an event or group of people, it
exists so that people will remember that event or
group with respect: *The monument commemorates
the war of independence.* —**commemorative**
/kəˈmemərətɪv/ *adj* —**commemoration**
/kəˌmeməˈreɪʃən/ *n* [U]

commence Ac /kəˈmens/ *v* [I,T] *formal* to begin:
Work on the building will commence soon.
THESAURUS ▶ START —**commencement** *n* [C,U]

commend /kəˈmend/ *v* [T] *formal* to praise someone or something publicly or formally: *She was
commended for her years of service to the community.*
—**commendation** /ˌkɒmənˈdeɪʃən $ ˌkɑː-/ *n* [C,U]

commendable /kəˈmendəbəl/ *adj formal* deserving praise: *Your enthusiasm is highly commendable.*
—**commendably** *adv*

commensurate /kəˈmenʃərət/ *adj formal* matching something in size, quality, or length of time:
[+with] *The salary is commensurate with experience.*

comment¹ Ac /'kɒment $ 'kɑː-/ *n* [C,U] an opinion that you give about someone or something: **[+on/about]** *He made rude comments about her.*
PHRASES
no comment *spoken* used when you do not want to answer a question: *'Are you going to resign because of this scandal, Prime Minister?' 'No comment.'*

COLLOCATIONS
verbs

to make a comment *People made some interesting comments.*
to have a comment (=to want to make a comment) *If you have any comments, please let me know.*
to welcome comments *We would welcome your comments and suggestions.*

adjectives

a positive/negative comment (=expressing a good/bad opinion of something) *I've had some very positive comments about the idea.*
a helpful/constructive comment (=one that helps you make progress) *Thank you for your helpful comments.*
a quick/brief comment *He finished his speech with a few brief comments on equal opportunities.*

---

comment² Ac *v* [I,T] to give your opinion about someone or something: **[+on]** *He refused to comment on the rumour.* | **[+that]** *She commented that the food was poor.* **THESAURUS** SAY

commentary Ac /'kɒməntəri $ 'kɑːmənteri/ *n* [C,U] (*plural* **commentaries**) **1** a spoken description on the television or radio of an event while it is happening: **[+on]** *the commentary on the race* **2** a book or article that explains or discusses a book, poem, idea etc: *political commentary*

commentator Ac /'kɒmənteɪtə $ 'kɑːmənteɪtər/ *n* [C] **1** someone on television or radio who describes an event as it is happening: *a **sports commentator*** **2** someone who knows a lot about a subject, and who writes about it or discusses it on the television or radio: *political commentators* —**commentate** *v* [I]

commerce /'kɒmɜːs $ 'kɑːmɜːrs/ *n* [U] the activity of buying and selling things in business

commercial¹ /kə'mɜːʃəl $ -ɜːr-/ *adj* relating to the buying and selling of things and with making money: *The film was a commercial success.* —**commercially** *adv*

commercial² *n* [C] an advertisement on television or radio: *TV commercials* **THESAURUS** ADVERTISEMENT

commercialized (*also* **-ised** *BrE*) /kə'mɜːʃəlaɪzd $ -ɜːr-/ *adj disapproving* too concerned with making money: *The resort is too commercialized.* —**commercialism** *n* [U]

commiserate /kə'mɪzəreɪt/ *v* [I] *formal* to express your sympathy for someone who is unhappy —**commiseration** /kə,mɪzə'reɪʃən/ *n* [U] (*also* **commiserations** [plural])

commission¹ /kə'mɪʃən/ *n* **1** [C] an official group whose job is to find out about or control an activity: *the International Whaling Commission* **2** [C,U] extra money that you are paid every time you sell something: *20% commission* **3** [C,U] a request for an artist, designer, or musician to do a piece of work

commission² Ac *v* [T] to ask someone to do a particular piece of work for you: *The government commissioned the report last year.* | **commission sb to do sth** *He was commissioned to design a bridge.*

commissioner /kə'mɪʃənə $ -ər/ *n* [C] someone with an important position in an official organization: *a police commissioner*

commit /kə'mɪt/ *v* (**committed, committing**)
1 [T] to do something wrong or illegal: *the gang that **committed** the **crime*** | **commit murder/rape/arson etc** *Most murders are committed by men.* | **commit suicide** (=kill yourself deliberately) **THESAURUS** DO
2 [I,T] to say that you will definitely do something: **commit sb to (doing) sth** *He **committed** his government to solving the crisis.* | *Meeting them doesn't **commit** us to anything.* | **commit yourself** *I'd committed myself and there was no turning back.*
3 [T] to decide to use money, time, people etc for a particular purpose: **commit sth to sth** *A lot of money has been committed to the project.*
4 [T] to order someone to be put in a hospital or prison: *The judge committed him to prison.*

commitment /kə'mɪtmənt/ *n* **1** [C] a promise or arrangement to do something: *a long-term commitment* | **commitment to do sth** *They made a commitment to work together.* | **[+to]** *a commitment to electoral reform* | *family **commitments*** **2** [U] determination to work hard and continue with something: *The team showed commitment.* | **[+to]** *her commitment to her job*

committed /kə'mɪtɪd/ *adj* wanting to work hard at something: *a committed teacher*

committee /kə'mɪti/ *n* [C also + plural verb *BrE*] an official group of people who meet to decide what needs to be done about something: **[+of]** *the International Committee of the Red Cross* | **[+on]** *a committee on safety* | **be on a committee** (=be a member of it) *He's on the finance committee.* | *a committee meeting* | *The committee have elected John as chairman.*

commodity /kə'mɒdəti $ kə'mɑː-/ *n* [C] (*plural* **commodities**) a product that is bought and sold: *agricultural commodities*

common¹ /'kɒmən $ 'kɑː-/ *adj*
1 something that is common is often seen or often happens OPP **rare**: *Rabbits are a common wild animal in this area.* | *a common mistake* | **[+among]** *The illness is common among children.* | *It's **common** for new fathers to feel jealous of their babies.* | **common practice** (=a usual way of doing something) *Working from home is common practice.*
2 shared by two or more people or things: *We have a common interest in films.* | *a common goal* | **[+to]** *These problems are common to all schools.* | **common ground** (=things that people or groups agree about or are interested in) *There was little common ground between the two sides.* | **the common good** (=what is best for everyone) *We need to work together for the common good.* | **common knowledge** (=something

everyone knows) *It's common knowledge* that he's an alcoholic.
3 [only before noun] ordinary and not special in any way: *common salt* | **the common man** (=ordinary people)
4 *BrE old-fashioned* behaving in a way that is typical of someone who belongs to a low social class: *She's so common!*

PHRASES

have sth in common (with sb/sth) to be similar in some way: *The two towns have many things in common.* | *We may have grown up together, but we* **have nothing in common** (=are not similar in any way).* | *I have a lot in common with him.* THESAURUS

DIFFERENT

in common with sb/sth in the same way as someone or something else: *In common with other schools, we suffer from overcrowded classrooms.*

common² *n* [C] a large area of grass in a town or village that people walk or play sport on

'common-law *adj* **common-law husband/wife** someone you have lived with for a long time as if they were your husband or wife

commonly /'kɒmənli $ 'kɑː-/ *adv* often or usually: *People with this illness commonly complain of headaches.*

commonplace /'kɒmənpleɪs $ 'kɑː-/ *adj* very common and not unusual: *Divorce is commonplace.*

'common room *n* [C] *BrE* a room in a school or college that a group of teachers or students use when they are not teaching or studying

Commons /'kɒmənz $ 'kɑː-/ *n* **the Commons** the larger and more powerful of the two parts of the British Parliament, whose members are elected by citizens → **the Lords**

,common 'sense *n* [U] the ability to do sensible things: *Use your common sense.*

Commonwealth /'kɒmənwelθ $ 'kɑː-/ *n* **the Commonwealth** an organization of about 50 countries that were once part of the British EMPIRE

commotion /kə'məʊʃən $ -'moʊ-/ *n* [singular, U] sudden noise or activity: *They heard a commotion.*

communal /'kɒmjʊnəl, kə'mjuːnl $ 'kɑː-/ *adj* shared by a group of people: *a communal bathroom*

commune¹ /'kɒmjuːn $ 'kɑː-, kə'mjuːn/ *n* [C] a group of people who live together and share work and possessions

commune² /kə'mjuːn/ *v*

PHRASAL VERBS

commune with sb/sth *formal* **1** to communicate with a person, god, or animal, especially in a mysterious SPIRITUAL way **2 commune with nature** to spend time in the countryside, enjoying it in a quiet peaceful way

communicate Ac /kə'mjuːnɪkeɪt/ *v* [I,T] if people communicate with each other, they give each other information by speaking, writing letters etc: *We communicate by email.* | **[+with]** *It's difficult to communicate with people if you don't speak their language.* | **communicate sth to sb** *the way a conductor communicates his or her ideas to the orchestra* | *A*

baby communicates its needs by crying.

communication /kə,mjuːnɪ'keɪʃən/ *n*
1 [U] when people talk to each other or give each other information: **[+between]** *communication between teachers and parents* | **be in communication with sb/sth** *The pilot stayed in communication with the control tower.* | *The Internet is an important* **means of communication**.
2 communications [plural] ways of sending and receiving information using computers, telephones, radios etc: *Modern communications enable people to work from home.*
3 communications [plural] roads, railways etc that are used for travelling and sending goods: **[+with]** *Paris has good communications with many European cities.*
4 [C] *formal* a letter, message, or telephone call

communicative Ac /kə'mjuːnəkətɪv $ -keɪtɪv/ *adj* someone who is communicative tells people things: *My son isn't very communicative.*

Communion /kə'mjuːnjən/ (*also* Holy Communion) *n* [U] a Christian ceremony in which people eat bread and drink wine

communiqué /kə'mjuːnəkeɪ $ kə,mjuːnə'keɪ/ *n* [C] an official report or announcement

communism, Communism /'kɒmjənɪzəm $ 'kɑː-/ *n* [U] a political system based on the idea that people are equal and that the state should own companies

communist, Communist /'kɒmjənɪst $ 'kɑː-/ [C] someone who believes in communism —**communist, Communist** *adj: the Communist Party*

community /kə'mjuːnəti/ *n* [C also + plural verb *BrE*] (*plural* **communities**)
1 a group of people who live in the same town or area: *The library serves the whole community.* | *a* **rural community** (=people who live in the country) | *the* **local community**
2 a group of people who are similar in some way, for example because they have the same religion or do the same job: **ethnic communities** | **the gay/black/Asian etc community** *protests from the gay community* | **the business/academic/scientific etc community**

com'munity ,centre *BrE*, **community center** *AmE n* [C] a place where people from the same area can go for social events, classes etc

com'munity ,college *n* [C] **1** a SECONDARY SCHOOL in the UK that students from the local area can go to, which also has classes for adults **2** a college in the US that students can go to for two years in order to learn a skill or prepare for university

com,munity 'service *n* [U] work that someone does to help other people without being paid, especially as a punishment for a crime

commute /kə'mjuːt/ *v* [I] to regularly travel a long distance to work: **[+to/from/between]** *He commutes to York.* THESAURUS TRAVEL —**commute** *n* [C]: *My morning commute takes 45 minutes.* —**commuter** *n* [C]: *The train was packed with commuters.*

compact¹ /kəm'pækt, 'kɒmpækt $ kəm'pækt/ *adj* small and neat: *a compact design*

compact² /kəmˈpækt/ v [T] to press something soft together so that it becomes smaller or more solid

compact 'disc n [C] a CD

companion /kəmˈpænjən/ n [C] someone you spend a lot of time with, or who travels somewhere with you: his **constant companion** | a **travelling companion**

companionship /kəmˈpænjənʃɪp/ n [U] the good feeling that you have when you are not alone but have a friend with you: She joined the club for companionship.

company /ˈkʌmpəni/ n (plural **companies**)
1 [C also + plural verb BrE] an organization that makes or sells something or provides a service: The company makes washing machines. | He set up his own company.
2 [U] a situation in which someone is with you and you are not alone: I **enjoy** his **company** (=like being with him). | I'll stay here to **keep** you **company** (=be with you so you are not alone). | She had the dog as company. | Tim is **good company** (=someone you enjoy being with). | **in sb's company** (=with someone) He felt relaxed in the company of women.
3 [C] a group of actors, dancers, or singers who work together: a ballet company → **LIMITED COMPANY, PARENT COMPANY**

COLLOCATIONS

verbs

to work for a company She works for an insurance company.
to join a company Some new trainees are joining the company.
to run/manage/be in charge of a company Lisa runs a catering company.
to set up/start/form a company We decided to set up our own company.
a company goes bankrupt (also **a company goes bust** informal) (=stops doing business after losing money) Unfortunately, the holiday company went bust.

adjectives

a large/big/major company We are a large manufacturing company.
a small company His father is the director of a small company.
an international/multinational company She works for a major international company.

THESAURUS

company an organization that makes or sells something, or provides a service: I work for a big American company. | an insurance company
firm a company, especially one that provides a service rather than producing goods: a law firm | a firm of accountants
business a company - often one that employs only a small number of people: She started her own jewellery business. | a family business
corporation a large company or group of companies - used especially in the names of

large companies: the president of the Volvo Car Corporation | the British Broadcasting Corporation
multinational/multinational company a very large company with offices in many different countries: The big multinational oil companies have made enormous profits.
subsidiary a company that is owned by a larger company: The firm is a subsidiary of Hewlett-Packard.

comparable /ˈkɒmpərəbəl $ ˈkɑːm-/ adj formal similar to something else in size, number, quality etc, so that you can make a comparison: a car of **comparable size**

comparative¹ /kəmˈpærətɪv/ adj **1 comparative comfort/freedom/safety etc** comfort etc that is quite good when compared to how comfortable etc something or someone else is: the comparative safety of the hut **2 comparative study/analysis etc** a study etc that involves comparing something with something else: She's working on a comparative study of the two writers.

comparative² n **the comparative** the form of an adjective or adverb that you use when saying that something is bigger, better etc than another thing or than before. For example 'taller' is the comparative of 'tall', and 'more expensive' is the comparative of 'expensive'.

comparatively /kəmˈpærətɪvli/ adv compared with something else: Videos are still comparatively expensive.

compare /kəmˈpeə $ -ˈper/ v
1 [T] if you compare things, you examine them in order to find out how they are similar or different: We went to different shops to compare prices. | **compare sth with/to sth** Compare this list with yours. | **Compared to** me, Al is very tall. | a 5% increase **compared with** last year
2 [I,T] if you compare two things, you say that they are similar in some way: **compare sth to/with sth** Critics have compared him to De Niro.
3 sth doesn't/can't compare (with sth) if something does not compare with something else, it is not as good, large etc: This CD doesn't compare with his last one.

PHRASES

compare notes (with sb) informal to talk to someone to find out if their experience of something is the same as yours: The meetings give salesmen a chance to compare notes.

comparison /kəmˈpærəsən/ n
1 [C,U] when you compare things: **[+of]** a comparison of prices | **in comparison (with/to sth)** In comparison to other video games, this one isn't very exciting. | **by comparison (with sth)** His brother's crime was minor by comparison. | **for comparison (with sth)** These figures are provided for comparison with previous studies.
2 [C] a statement that something is like something else: **[+between]** The article **makes** a **comparison** between the two poems. | The writer **draws comparisons** between the two men.

PHRASES

there's no comparison *spoken* used when you think that one thing is much better than another: *There's no comparison between canned and fresh vegetables.*

compartment /kəm'pɑːtmənt $ -ɑːr-/ *n* [C] **1** a separate space or area inside something: *a purse with many compartments* **2** a separate area inside a railway carriage: *a first-class compartment*

COMPASS

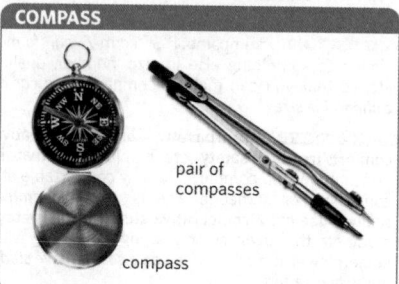

pair of compasses

compass

compass /'kʌmpəs/ *n* [C] **1** an instrument that shows the direction you are travelling in, with a needle that always points north **2** (*also* **compasses**) an instrument for drawing circles

compassion /kəm'pæʃən/ *n* [U] sympathy for someone who is suffering: **[+for]** *compassion for the sick*

compassionate /kəm'pæʃənət/ *adj* feeling sympathy for people who are suffering: *a compassionate man*

compatible Ac /kəm'pætəbəl/ *adj* **1** two people who are compatible have similar ideas or interests, and are able to have a good relationship **2** two things that are compatible are able to exist or be used together without problems: **[+with]** *Is the software compatible with your PC?* —**compatibility** /kəm,pætə'bɪləti/ *n* [U]

compatriot /kəm'pætriət $ -'peɪt-/ *n* [C] someone who is from the same country

compel /kəm'pel/ *v* [T] (**compelled**, **compelling**) to force someone to do something: **compel sb to do sth** *The bad weather compelled me to turn back.* | *She **felt compelled to** resign because of the scandal.* **THESAURUS** FORCE

compelling /kəm'pelɪŋ/ *adj* **1** very interesting or exciting: *a compelling film* **2** a compelling argument, reason etc seems very strong or good: *a **compelling reason** for resigning*

compensate Ac /'kɒmpənseɪt $ 'kɑːm-/ *v* **1** [I] to do something so that something bad has a smaller effect: **[+for]** *He bought her flowers to compensate for being late.* **2** [I,T] to pay someone money because they have suffered injury, loss, or damage: **compensate sb for sth** *The firm compensated workers for loss of earnings.*

compensation Ac /,kɒmpən'seɪʃən $,kɑːm-/ *n* **1** [U] money that someone is given because they have been injured or badly treated: **in compensation** *The holiday company paid the Taylors £150 in*

compensation. | **[+for]** *Farmers are **demanding compensation** for their losses.* **2** [C,U] something that makes a bad situation better: *Being unemployed has its compensations, like not having to get up early.*

compère /'kɒmpeə $ 'kɑːmper/ *n* [C] *BrE* someone who introduces the performers on a television programme, in a theatre show etc

compete /kəm'piːt/ *v* [I] to try to win something or to be more successful than someone else: **[+in]** *Ten runners are competing in the race.* | **[+with/against]** *We compete with teams from other villages.* | *Small firms cannot compete against large companies.* | **[+for]** *The stores are competing for customers.*

competent /'kɒmpɪtənt $ 'kɑːm-/ *adj* good at your work or able to do something well: *a **highly competent** doctor* —**competence** *n* [U] —**competently** *adv*

competing /kəm'piːtɪŋ/ *adj* [only before noun] **1** competing stories, ideas etc cannot all be right or accepted: *Several people gave **competing accounts** of the accident.* **2** competing companies or products are trying to be more successful than each other

competition /,kɒmpə'tɪʃən $,kɑːm-/ *n*
1 [C] an organized event in which people or teams compete against each other: *Who won the competition?*
2 [U] a situation in which people or organizations compete with each other: **[+for]** *Competition for the job was intense.* | **[+between/among]** *fierce competition among supermarkets* | **be in competition with sb** *She is in competition with four other people.*
3 [singular, U] the people or groups that compete against you, especially in business or sport: *Our aim is to be better than **the competition**.* | *You'll have no competition.*

COLLOCATIONS

verbs

to enter a competition *I entered a poetry competition.*

to take part in a competition *Anyone under 16 can take part in the competition.*

to win a competition *She won an international dance competition.*

to come first/second etc in a competition *We came second in a school science competition.*

to hold/run/have a competition *The village is holding a competition for the best garden.*

types of competition

a music/painting/cookery etc competition *He won first prize in a photography competition.*
a national/international competition

competitive /kəm'petətɪv/ *adj* **1** determined to be more successful than other people: *Boys are more competitive than girls.* **2** a competitive situation is one in which people or organizations try to be more successful than others: *a **highly competitive** industry* | *competitive sports* **3** competitive prices or products are fairly cheap: *Our rates are very competitive.* —**competitiveness** *n* [U]

competitor /kəm'petɪtə $ -ər/ *n* [C] a person, team, or company that competes with another: *We* *sell more than our main competitors.*

compilation Ac /ˌkɒmpəˈleɪʃən $ ˌkɑːm-/ n [C] a CD, record, or book which contains songs or stories from different CDs, records, or books: **[+of]** *a compilation of love songs*

compile Ac /kəmˈpaɪl/ v [T] to make a book, list etc using different pieces of information

complacent /kəmˈpleɪsənt/ adj *disapproving* too pleased with what you have achieved so that you no longer try to improve: *We mustn't get too complacent.* —**complacency** n [U] —**complacently** adv

complain /kəmˈpleɪn/ v [I,T]
1 to say that you are not satisfied with something or not happy about something: *They're complaining because the price has increased.* | *'No one ever tells me anything!' Ian complained.* | **[+(that)]** *Teachers complain that they do not get enough support from parents.* | **[+about]** *The kids complained about the food.* | **[+to]** *She complained to the manager.*
2 to say that you feel ill or have a pain: **[+of]** *He complained of stomach pains.*

THESAURUS

complain to say that you are not satisfied with something, or not happy about something: *Dear Sir, I am writing to complain about the service I received at your hotel.*
make a complaint to formally complain about something to someone in authority: *I'm going to make an official complaint to your manager.*
protest to complain about something that you think is wrong, especially publicly: *The demonstrators are protesting against the war.*
object to say that you disagree with a plan or suggestion, or that you do not approve of someone's behaviour: *Would anyone object if we have a quick break?* | *I object to some of his comments about women.*
grumble to keep complaining in a bad-tempered way: *He's always grumbling about his knee.*
moan/whine (*also* **whinge** *BrE*) *informal* to keep complaining in an annoying and unreasonable way: *We all have to work, so stop moaning about it.*

complaint /kəmˈpleɪnt/ n
1 [C,U] something that you say or write when you are not happy about something: **[+about]** *We've received complaints about the noise.* | **[+against]** *complaints against the police* | **[+from]** *complaints from residents* | **[+to]** *I made a complaint to the boss.*
THESAURUS ▶ COMPLAIN
2 [C] something that you complain about: *My only complaint is that the restaurant is far too expensive.*
3 [C] an illness that affects part of your body: *a chest complaint*

COLLOCATIONS

verbs

to make a complaint *She made a complaint to the manager.*
to have a complaint (=to want to complain) *I didn't have any complaints about the service.*
to receive/get/have a complaint *The BBC received a huge number of complaints about the programme.*

to deal with/handle a complaint *The hospital employs someone to deal with complaints.*

types of complaint

a formal/official complaint *Ms Smith has made a formal complaint against her boss.*
customer complaints *We take all customer complaints seriously.*

nouns + complaint

a letter of complaint *I wrote a letter of complaint to the hotel manager.*
cause/grounds for complaint (=a good reason to complain) *I hope you will not have any cause for complaint.*

complement¹ Ac /ˈkɒmpləmənt $ ˈkɑːm-/ n [C] *formal* **1** something that makes a good combination with another thing: **[+to]** *The wine was the perfect complement to the meal.* **2** the number of people or things that is needed or usual: **[+of]** *The school has its **full complement** of teachers.* **3** in grammar, a word or phrase that follows a verb and describes its subject

complement² Ac /ˈkɒmpləment $ ˈkɑːm-/ v [T] to make a good combination with something else: *The curtains complement the carpet.*

complementary Ac /ˌkɒmpləˈmentəri◂ $ ˌkɑːm-/ adj complementary things go well together, although they are usually different: *Their skills are complementary – she is artistic and he is very good with money.*

complementary 'medicine n [U] *especially BrE* complementary medicine uses treatments that are not part of traditional Western medicine

complete¹ /kəmˈpliːt/ adj
1 [only before noun] used when emphasizing what you are saying: *The news came as a **complete surprise** (=I was very surprised).* | *The police are in **complete control** of the situation (=they control everything that happens).* | *It was a **complete waste of time**.* | **complete fool/idiot etc** *I've been a complete fool (=I have been very stupid).*
2 something that is complete has all the parts it should have OPP **incomplete**: *a complete set of china* | *the **complete works** of Shakespeare* | *The collection is complete.*
3 finished: *Work on the bridge is complete.*
4 complete with sth having particular equipment or features OPP **incomplete**: *The house comes complete with a sauna.* —**completeness** n [U]

complete² v [T] **1** to finish doing or making something: *We hope to complete the work soon.* | *The building took a year to complete.* THESAURUS ▶ FINISH
2 to make something whole or perfect by adding what is missing: *I need one more stamp to complete the set.* **3** to write information on a form: *Sixty-five people completed the questionnaire.*

completely /kəmˈpliːtli/ adv in every way: *I completely forgot about your birthday.* | *Geoff's a completely different person since he retired.*

completion /kəmˈpliːʃən/ n [U] when something is finished: *When's the **completion date** for the building work?* | **[+of]** *the completion of an $80 million project*

complex¹ Ac /ˈkɒmpleks $ ˌkɑːmˈpleks◂/ *adj* something that is complex has a lot of different parts and is difficult to understand or deal with: *a **complex system** of highways* | *a **highly complex** issue* —**complexity** /kəmˈpleksəti/ *n* [C,U]: *They don't realise the complexity of the problem.*

complex² Ac /ˈkɒmpleks $ ˈkɑːm-/ *n* [C] **1** a group of buildings or one large building used for a particular purpose: *a new shopping complex* **2** an emotional problem in which someone feels very anxious about something: *I think she's got an inferiority complex.*

complexion /kəmˈplekʃən/ *n* **1** [C,U] the natural colour and appearance of the skin on your face: *a young woman with a pale complexion* **2** [singular] the way something appears to be: *This **puts** an entirely **new complexion** on things* (=makes them seem completely different).

compliance /kəmˈplaɪəns/ *n* [U] *formal* when people obey a rule or law: [+with] *compliance with company regulations*

compliant /kəmˈplaɪənt/ *adj* willing to obey other people's wishes and demands

complicate /ˈkɒmplɪkeɪt $ ˈkɑːm-/ *v* [T] to make a problem or situation more difficult: *Don't tell Michael about this. It'll only **complicate matters**.*

complicated /ˈkɒmplɪkeɪtɪd $ ˈkɑːm-/ *adj* something that is complicated has a lot of different parts and is difficult to understand or deal with OPP **simple**: *The instructions are much too complicated.* | *an extremely complicated process* THESAURUS DIFFICULT

> **Word Choice: complicated or complex?**
> **Complicated** is the usual word to use in everyday English when something is difficult because it has a lot of parts: *Some of the questions were really complicated.*
> **Complex** is used especially in technical or more formal English. Things that are **complex** often have a lot of parts that are connected with each other in different ways: *The vitamin has a complex chemical structure.*

complication /ˌkɒmplɪˈkeɪʃən $ ˌkɑːm-/ *n* **1** [C,U] a problem that makes a situation more difficult to understand or deal with: *The journey is difficult enough without further complications.* **2** [C usually plural] another medical problem or illness that happens when someone is already ill: *There were complications following surgery.*

complicity /kəmˈplɪsəti/ *n* [U] when someone allows another person to do something bad or illegal

compliment¹ /ˈkɒmpləmənt $ ˈkɑːm-/ *n* [C] something nice that you say about someone or something, in order to praise them: *I was trying to **pay her a compliment**.* | *I wasn't sure exactly what they meant, but I **took** it **as a compliment**.*
PHRASES
with the compliments of sb/with sb's compliments *formal* used by an organization when they send or give something to you: *Please accept these tickets with our compliments.*

compliment² /ˈkɒmpləmənt $ ˈkɑːm-/ *v* [T] to say something nice to someone in order to praise them: **compliment sb on sth** *They complimented Kentaro on his excellent English.* THESAURUS PRAISE

complimentary /ˌkɒmpləˈmentəri◂ $ ˌkɑːm-/ *adj* **1** given free to someone: *complimentary tickets* **2** saying that you like something and think it is good: [+about] *He was very complimentary about the food.*

comply /kəmˈplaɪ/ *v* [I] (**complied, complying, complies**) *formal* to obey an order or request: [+with] *Anyone who fails to comply with the regulations will be fined.*

component Ac /kəmˈpəʊnənt $ -ˈpoʊ-/ *n* [C] one of the different parts of a machine or system: *car components* | [+of] *Exercise is one of the key components of a healthy lifestyle.*

compose /kəmˈpəʊz $ -ˈpoʊz/ *v* **1** **be composed of sth** to be formed from a number of different things, parts, or people: *The workforce is composed largely of women.* **2** [T] to write a piece of music: *Nyman composed the music for the film 'The Piano'.* **3** **compose yourself** to become calm after feeling angry, upset, or excited → **composed 4** [T] to write a letter or speech, thinking very carefully about it as you write it

composed /kəmˈpəʊzd $ -ˈpoʊzd/ *adj* calm and not upset or angry → **composure**: *She remained composed throughout the interview.*

composer /kəmˈpəʊzə $ -ˈpoʊzər/ *n* [C] someone who writes music

composite /ˈkɒmpəzət $ kɑːmˈpɑː-/ *adj* made up of different parts: *a composite image* —**composite** *n* [C]

composition /ˌkɒmpəˈzɪʃən $ ˌkɑːm-/ *n* **1** [U] the way that something is made up of different parts, things, or people: [+of] *the chemical composition of soil* | *the composition of the jury* **2** [C] a piece of music that someone has written: *one of Beethoven's early compositions* **3** [U] the art or process of writing music or poetry **4** [U] the way in which the different parts of a painting or photograph are arranged **5** [C,U] a short piece of writing about a subject by a student SYN **essay**

compost /ˈkɒmpɒst $ ˈkɑːmpoʊst/ *n* [U] a mixture of decayed leaves and plants that you add to the soil to help plants grow

composure /kəmˈpəʊʒə $ -ˈpoʊʒər/ *n* [singular, U] when someone appears or feels calm and confident: **regain/recover/keep your composure** *She stopped crying and regained her composure.*

compound¹ Ac /ˈkɒmpaʊnd $ ˈkɑːm-/ *n* [C] **1** a chemical compound is a substance that consists of two or more different substances **2** an area that contains a group of buildings and is surrounded by a wall or fence: *a prison compound* **3** (*also* **compound noun/adjective/verb**) two or more words that are used together as a noun, adjective, or verb

compound² Ac /kəmˈpaʊnd/ *v* [T] to make a difficult situation worse: *Our problems were compounded by appalling weather conditions.*

comprehend /ˌkɒmprɪˈhend $ ˌkɑːm-/ v [I,T] formal to understand something: **comprehend what/ how/why etc** They don't seem to comprehend how serious this is. **THESAURUS** UNDERSTAND

comprehensible /ˌkɒmprɪˈhensəbəl $ ˌkɑːm-/ adj easy to understand OPP **incomprehensible**: [+to] language that is comprehensible to the average reader

comprehension /ˌkɒmprɪˈhenʃən $ ˌkɑːm-/ n **1** [U] the ability to understand something: The whole situation is completely **beyond** my **comprehension** (=impossible for me to understand). **2** [C,U] an exercise to test how well students understand written or spoken language: a listening comprehension test

comprehensive Ac /ˌkɒmprɪˈhensɪv $ ˌkɑːm-/ adj including everything: a comprehensive account of the war —**comprehensively** adv

compre'hensive ˌschool (also **comprehensive**) n [C] a school in Britain for students aged between 11 and 18, who are of all levels of ability

compress /kəmˈpres/ v [I,T] formal to press something or make something smaller so that it takes up less space or takes less time **THESAURUS** PRESS —**compression** /-ˈpreʃən/ n [U]

comprise Ac /kəmˈpraɪz/ v formal **1 be comprised of sb/sth** to consist of particular parts, groups, or people: The committee is comprised of eight members. **2** [T] to form part of a larger group: Women comprise over 75% of our staff.

compromise¹ /ˈkɒmprəmaɪz $ ˈkɑːm-/ n [C,U] when people or groups accept less than they really want, especially in order to make an agreement: **make/reach a compromise** Talks will continue until a compromise is reached. | [+between] a compromise between the government and trade unions

compromise² v **1** [I] to accept something that is not exactly what you want: President Obama has said that he would be ready to compromise. **2** [T] to do something that is against your principles, beliefs etc and so seems dishonest or embarrassing: **compromise your beliefs/principles/integrity etc** artists who refuse to compromise their principles | **compromise yourself** The UN is afraid of compromising itself.

compromising /ˈkɒmprəmaɪzɪŋ $ ˈkɑːm-/ adj making it seem that someone has done something dishonest or wrong: some compromising photographs of the President

compulsion /kəmˈpʌlʃən/ n **1** [C usually singular] a strong desire to do something that is wrong: I had a sudden compulsion to hit her. **2** [U] when someone is forced to do something that they do not want to do → **compel**

compulsive /kəmˈpʌlsɪv/ adj **1** compulsive behaviour is very difficult to stop or control: compulsive eating **2 compulsive liar/gambler etc** someone who has a strong desire to lie, GAMBLE etc, which they cannot control —**compulsively** adv

compulsory /kəmˈpʌlsəri/ adj if something is compulsory, you must do it OPP **voluntary**: compulsory military service **THESAURUS** NECESSARY

compunction /kəmˈpʌŋkʃən/ n **have no compunction about (doing) sth** to not feel guilty about doing something, even though other people may think it is wrong

computer Ac /kəmˈpjuːtə $ -ər/ n [C] an electronic machine that can store and arrange large amounts of information, which can be used to do many different things: Always switch off your computer at the end of the day. | **on computer** All our data is kept on computer. → see picture on page A12

COLLOCATIONS

verbs

to use a computer He mostly uses his computer for gaming.

to log onto a computer (=to start using it by typing a password) When I tried to log onto my computer, I got an error message.

to start up/boot a computer (=to make it start working) It takes a long time to start up the computer.

to shut down a computer (=to close the programs and stop it working) Do you shut down your computer completely every night?

a computer crashes (=suddenly stops working) The computer crashed when I tried to save.

a computer is down (=is not working) All the office computers are down this morning.

computer + noun

a computer system The hospital is bringing in a new computer system.

a computer network A virus had infected the entire computer network.

a computer screen/keyboard Make sure your computer screen is at the right height.

a computer program/game We're learning how to write simple computer programs.

computerize (also **-ise** BrE) /kəmˈpjuːtəraɪz/ v [T] to use a computer to store information or to control the way something is done: plans to computerize all our financial records —**computerization** /kəmˌpjuːtəraɪˈzeɪʃən $ -rə-/ n [U]

com,puter-'literate adj able to use a computer —**computer literacy** n [U]

computing Ac /kəmˈpjuːtɪŋ/ n [U] the use or study of computers

comrade /ˈkɒmreɪd, -rɪd $ ˈkɑːmræd/ n [C] a friend, especially someone who fights together with you in a war —**comradeship** n [U]

con¹ /kɒn $ kɑːn/ v [T] (**conned, conning**) informal to trick someone in order to get something that you want: **con sb into (doing) sth** You conned me into thinking I could trust you. | **con sb out of sth** She was conned out of £300.

con² n [C usually singular] informal a trick to get someone's money or to make someone do something: The website says they're offering free holidays, but it's all a big con. → **the pros and cons (of sth)** at PRO

concave /ˌkɒnˈkeɪv, kən- $ ˌkɑːnˈkeɪv, kən-/ adj having a surface that curves inwards OPP **convex**: a concave mirror

conceal /kənˈsiːl/ v [T] to hide something carefully: *Cannabis was found concealed in the suitcase.* | **conceal sth from sb** *Sue tried hard to conceal her disappointment from the others.* **THESAURUS** HIDE —**concealment** n [U]

concede /kənˈsiːd/ v **1** [T] to admit that something is true, although you do not want to: **[+(that)]** *She reluctantly conceded that I was right.* **2** [I,T] to let someone have something although you do not want to: **concede sth to sb** *Japan was forced to concede the islands to Russia.* | *In the end the government conceded to the terrorists' demands* (=agreed to do what they asked). **3** [I,T] to admit that you are not going to win a game, argument etc: *Perot conceded defeat* (=accepted he had lost) *in the election.*

conceit /kənˈsiːt/ n [U] an attitude that shows that you are too proud of what you can do, how you look etc

conceited /kənˈsiːtɪd/ adj disapproving too proud of yourself, especially of what you can do: *I don't want to seem conceited, but I know I'll win.* **THESAURUS** PROUD —**conceitedly** adv

conceivable Ac /kənˈsiːvəbəl/ adj something that is conceivable could possibly happen or be true OPP **inconceivable**: **[+that]** *It is conceivable that the experts are wrong.* —**conceivably** adv

conceive Ac /kənˈsiːv/ v **1** [I,T] to be able to imagine something: **[+of]** *It is impossible to conceive of the size of the universe.* **2** [T] to think of a new idea or plan: *How was the idea first conceived?* | **conceive sth as sth** *The exhibition was originally conceived as a temporary tourist attraction.* **3** [I,T] to become PREGNANT → **conception**

concentrate Ac /ˈkɒnsəntreɪt $ ˈkɑːn-/ v **1** [I] to think very carefully about something you are doing: *With all this noise, it's hard to concentrate.* | *Will you please concentrate!* | **[+on]** *I'm trying to concentrate on reading this article.* **2 be concentrated on/in/around etc sth** to exist in large numbers or amounts in a particular place: *Most of New Zealand's population is concentrated in the North Island.*

PHRASAL VERBS

concentrate (sth) **on** sth to give most of your attention to one thing: *I want to concentrate on my career for a while before I have kids.* | **concentrate your efforts/attention/energy etc on sth** *They are concentrating their efforts on raising public awareness.*

concentrated /ˈkɒnsəntreɪtɪd $ ˈkɑːn-/ adj **1** a concentrated liquid has been made stronger by removing most of the water from it: *concentrated orange juice* **2** [only before noun] showing a lot of effort or determination: *He made a concentrated effort to improve his French.*

concentration Ac /ˌkɒnsənˈtreɪʃən $ ˌkɑːn-/ n **1** [U] when you think very carefully about something you are doing: *They soon get tired and lose their concentration.* | *She needed all her powers of concentration to stop herself slipping.* **2** [U] when you put a lot of attention, time, or energy into one thing: **[+on]** *There was too much concentration on one type of industry.* **3** [C,U] a large amount of something in

the same place: **[+of]** *high concentrations of minerals in the water*

concenˈtration ˌcamp n [C] a prison where large numbers of people are kept in very bad conditions, usually during a war

concentric /kənˈsentrɪk/ adj concentric circles are of different sizes and have the same centre

concept Ac /ˈkɒnsept $ ˈkɑːn-/ n [C] a general idea or principle: **[+of]** *the concept of freedom for all* **THESAURUS** IDEA —**conceptual** /kənˈseptʃuəl/ adj

conception Ac /kənˈsepʃən/ n **1** [C] a general idea about what something is like, or a way of understanding what something is like: **[+of]** *changing conceptions of the world* **2** [U] when a woman or female animal becomes PREGNANT → **conceive**

concern¹ /kənˈsɜːn $ -ɜːrn/ n

1 [C,U] a feeling of worry about something important: **[+about/over]** *There is growing concern about pollution in our cities.* | **[+for]** *concern for her children's welfare* | **[+that]** *renewed concern that the virus could spread* | *The research findings gave serious cause for concern* (=reason to worry). | *the concerns expressed by parents*

2 [C,U] something that is important to you or that involves you: *Our main concern is for passengers' safety.* | **of concern (to sb)** *The destruction of the rain forests is of concern to us all.*

3 [C] a company or business: *The restaurant is a family concern.*

concern² v [T]

1 to affect or involve someone: *What we're planning doesn't concern you.*

2 to make someone feel worried or upset: *The teenage drug problem concerns most parents.*

3 if a book, report etc concerns something, it is about it: *The film concerns a group of school friends.*

4 concern yourself (with sth) to become involved in something that interests or worries you: *You don't need to concern yourself with this, Jan.*

concerned /kənˈsɜːnd $ -ɜːrnd/ adj

1 involved in something or affected by it: *Divorce is always painful, especially when children are concerned.* | **[+with]** *organizations concerned with animal welfare* | *It was a difficult time for all concerned* (=everyone involved or affected).

2 worried about something important: **[+about]** *I'm concerned about his eyesight.* | **[+for]** *We are all concerned for their safety.* | **[+that]** *Many people are concerned that the system is not safe.* **THESAURUS** WORRIED

PHRASES

| **as far as sb is concerned** used to show someone's opinion: *As far as I'm concerned, the whole idea is crazy.*

| **as far as sth is concerned** used to show which subject or thing you are talking about: *As far as money is concerned, the club is doing fairly well.*

concerning /kənˈsɜːnɪŋ $ -ɜːr-/ prep about or relating to something: *Police are asking for information concerning the incident.* **THESAURUS** ABOUT

concert /ˈkɒnsət $ ˈkɑːnsərt/ n [C] a performance given by musicians or singers

concerted /kən'sɜːtɪd $ -ɜːr-/ adj **concerted effort/ attempt/action etc** a very determined effort, attempt etc: We should all **make a concerted effort** to raise this money.

concertina /ˌkɒnsə'tiːnə $ ˌkɑːnsər-/ n [C] a musical instrument that you hold with both hands and play by pushing the sides together and pulling them apart

concerto /kən'tʃɜːtəʊ $ -'tʃertoʊ/ n [C] (plural **concertos**) a piece of CLASSICAL music, usually for one instrument and an ORCHESTRA

concession /kən'seʃən/ n [C] **1** something that you agree to in order to end an argument: The government will never **make concessions** to terrorists. **2** a special right given to someone by the government, an employer etc: tax concessions for married people **3** BrE a reduction in the price of tickets for certain groups of people, for example students

concessionary /kən'seʃənəri $ -neri/ adj **1** given as a concession **2** BrE specially reduced in price, for example for old people or children

conciliation /kənˌsɪli'eɪʃən/ n [U] formal the process of trying to end an argument between people

conciliatory /kən'sɪliətəri $ -tɔːri/ adj formal intended to stop arguments, and lead to agreement or friendship: Both sides in the dispute have now adopted a more conciliatory approach.

concise /kən'saɪs/ adj short and clear, without using too many words: a concise answer —**concisely** adv

conclude Ac /kən'kluːd/ v **1** [T] to decide something after considering all the information you have: **[+that]** The report concluded that the accident was preventable. **2** [T] formal to complete something that you have been doing: The study was concluded last month. | **conclude an agreement/treaty/deal etc** (=to complete a political or business agreement successfully) **3** [I,T] to end a meeting, speech, book, or event by doing or saying one final thing: **[+with]** The seminar concluded with a question and answer session. —**concluding** adj: concluding remarks

conclusion Ac /kən'kluːʒən/ n

1 [C] something you decide after considering all the information you have: **[+that]** I've **come to** the **conclusion** that she's lying. | The appeal court **reached** the same **conclusion**. | It's important not to **jump to conclusions** (=to decide something too quickly without all the facts). | We can **draw** two main **conclusions** from the data.

2 [C] the end or final part of something: the conclusion of his essay

3 [U] when a political or business agreement is completed: **[+of]** the conclusion of a peace agreement → **FOREGONE CONCLUSION**

conclusive Ac /kən'kluːsɪv/ adj proving that something is true: There is no **conclusive evidence** connecting him with the crime. —**conclusively** adv

concoct /kən'kɒkt $ -'kɑːkt/ v [T] **1** to invent a story, plan, or excuse, especially to deceive someone: She concocted a story about her mother being sick. **2** to make something unusual by mixing different things together —**concoction** /kən'kɒkʃən $ -'kɑːk-/ n [C,U]

concourse /'kɒŋkɔːs $ 'kɑːŋkɔːrs/ n [C] a large HALL or open place in a public building such as an airport

concrete¹ /'kɒŋkriːt $ 'kɑːŋ-/ n [U] a substance used for building that is made by mixing sand, water, small stones, and CEMENT —**concrete** v [T]

concrete² /'kɒŋkriːt $ kɑːn'kriːt/ adj **1** made of concrete: a concrete floor → see picture at **MATERIAL¹**
2 clearly based on facts, not on beliefs or guesses: **concrete information/evidence/facts etc** We need concrete information about the man's identity.

concur /kən'kɜː $ -'kɜːr/ v [I] (**concurred, concurring**) formal to agree with someone: **[+with]** Dr. Hastings concurs with our decision.

concurrent Ac /kən'kʌrənt $ -'kɜːr-/ adj existing or happening at the same time: He is serving two concurrent prison sentences. —**concurrently** adv

concussion /kən'kʌʃən/ n [C,U] slight damage to your brain that makes you become unconscious or feel sick: He was taken to hospital with concussion. —**concussed** /kən'kʌst/ adj: He was slightly concussed.

condemn /kən'dem/ v [T] **1** to say very strongly that you do not approve of someone or something: Politicians were quick to condemn the bombing. **2** to give a severe punishment to someone who is guilty of a crime: The murderer was **condemned to death**. **3** to force someone to live in an unpleasant way or to suffer: **condemn sb to sth** families who are condemned to a life of poverty **4** to say officially that a building is not safe enough to be used

condemnation /ˌkɒndəm'neɪʃən, -dem- $ ˌkɑːn-/ n [C,U] an expression of very strong disapproval: **[+of]** international condemnation of the plans

condensation /ˌkɒnden'seɪʃən, -dən- $ ˌkɑːn-/ n [U] small drops of water that appear when steam or hot air touches a cold surface

condense /kən'dens/ v **1** [I,T] if gas or hot air condenses, it becomes a liquid as it becomes colder **2** [T] to make a speech or piece of writing shorter by using fewer words to say the same thing **3** [T] to make a liquid thicker by removing some of the water from it: *condensed milk*

condescend /ˌkɒndɪˈsend $ ˌkɑːn-/ v [I] to agree to do something even though you think you are too important to do it: **condescend to do sth** *He might condescend to see us later.* —**condescension** /-ˈsenʃən/ n [U]

PHRASES

condescend to sb to behave as if you are better or more important than someone else

condescending /ˌkɒndɪˈsendɪŋ◂ $ ˌkɑːn-/ adj showing that you think you are better or more important than other people: *He gave us a condescending smile.*

condition¹ /kənˈdɪʃən/ n

1 [C,U] the state that something or someone is in: **[+of]** *the condition of the local roads* | **in (a) good/bad/terrible etc condition** *The bike is still in pretty good condition.* | **in (a) stable/critical/comfortable etc condition** *The driver is in a critical condition in hospital.* | **in no condition to do sth** (=too ill, drunk, upset etc to do something) *Molly is in no condition to return to work.* THESAURUS ILLNESS

2 conditions [plural] the situation in which something happens: **under these/certain/normal etc conditions** *Under such conditions, the plants will grow rapidly.* | *The trip was cancelled because of adverse* **weather conditions**. | *They managed to make a profit, despite difficult* **economic conditions**.

3 conditions [plural] the environment in which people live or work, that affects their life: **living/working conditions** *protests against poor working conditions* | *Nurses are demanding better* **pay and conditions**.

4 [C] something that you must agree to or that must happen before something else can happen: **[+for]** *the conditions for getting into college* | *your* **terms and conditions** *of employment* | *The application was approved,* **subject to** *certain* **conditions**. | *We'll agree to your proposal* **on condition that** *we receive some of the money immediately.* | *You can go out* **on one condition**: *you must be home by eleven o'clock.*

5 [C] an illness: *a heart condition* | *a child with a serious* **medical condition**

THESAURUS

in good condition

in good condition if something is in good condition, it looks good or works well: *They have kept the house in very good condition.* | *The car is in good condition, considering its age.*
in perfect/mint condition in very good condition, with no marks or faults: *The book is 100 years old, but it's still in perfect condition.*
as good as new looking or working like a new one – used especially about something that has just been cleaned or repaired: *If I polish the table, it will look as good as new.*

in bad condition

in bad condition used about something that is damaged, dirty, or not working properly: *Parts of the road were in very bad condition.*
in a terrible state very dirty and untidy, or badly damaged: *Her flat was in a terrible state.*

shabby shabby clothes, furniture, rooms etc are in bad condition because they have been used a lot: *An old man in a shabby suit answered the door.* | *The curtains and carpets looked shabby.*
tattered tattered clothes and books are old and torn: *a tattered brown jacket* | *His textbooks were all tattered.*
dilapidated a dilapidated building is in bad condition because it has not been looked after: *Inside, the hotel was slightly dilapidated.*

condition² v [T] **1** to make a person or animal behave in a particular way by training or influencing them over a period of time: **condition sb/sth to do sth** *The horses are conditioned to expect food from people.* **2** to add a special liquid to your skin or hair to keep it healthy —**conditioning** n [U]

conditional /kənˈdɪʃənəl/ adj **1** if an offer, agreement etc is conditional, it will only happen if something else happens: **[+on]** *His college place is conditional on his exam results.* **2** a conditional sentence is one that begins with 'if' or 'unless', and expresses something that must happen before something else can happen

conditioner /kənˈdɪʃənə $ -ər/ n [C,U] a liquid that you put on your hair after washing it to keep it in good condition

condo /ˈkɒndəʊ $ ˈkɑːndoʊ/ n [C] (plural **condos**) *AmE informal* a condominium THESAURUS HOUSE

condolence /kənˈdəʊləns $ -ˈdoʊ-/ n [C usually plural, U] sympathy for someone when someone they love has died: *Please offer my condolences to your mother.*

condom /ˈkɒndəm $ ˈkɑːn-, ˈkʌn-/ n [C] a thin piece of rubber that a man wears over his PENIS during sex to stop a woman becoming PREGNANT, or to protect against disease

condominium /ˌkɒndəˈmɪniəm $ ˌkɑːn-/ (also **condo** *informal*) n [C] *AmE* a building with several apartments, each of which is owned by the people living in it, or one of these apartments THESAURUS HOUSE

condone /kənˈdəʊn $ -ˈdoʊn/ v [T] to accept or allow behaviour that most people think is wrong: *cannot condone the use of violence.*

conducive /kənˈdjuːsɪv $ -ˈduː-/ adj formal **be conducive to sth** if a situation is conducive to something, it makes that thing possible or likely to happen: *The sunny climate is conducive to outdoor activities.*

conduct¹ Ac /kənˈdʌkt/ v
1 DO [T] to do or organize something: **conduct an experiment/test** *The pupils are conducting an experiment with two magnets.* | **conduct an interview/survey/investigation etc** *We're conducting a survey into children's eating habits.* | *The group* **conducted** *a terrorist* **campaign** *in the 1970s.*
2 MUSIC [I,T] to stand in front of musicians or singers and direct their playing or singing
3 ELECTRICITY/HEAT [T] if something conducts electricity or heat, it allows the electricity or heat to travel along or through it

4 BEHAVE **conduct yourself** the way that you conduct yourself is the way that you behave: *Public figures have a duty to conduct themselves correctly.*

conduct² Ac /ˈkɒndʌkt $ ˈkɑːn-/ *n* [U] **1** the way someone behaves, especially in public or in their job SYN **behaviour**: *standards of professional conduct* **2** the way an activity is organized and done: [+of] *complaints about the conduct of the election*

conductor /kənˈdʌktə $ -ər/ *n* [C]
1 MUSIC someone who conducts a group of musicians or singers
2 ELECTRICITY/HEAT something that allows heat or electricity to travel along or through it
3 TRAIN *AmE* someone who is in charge of a train or the workers on it
4 BUS *BrE* someone whose job is to collect payments from passengers on a bus

CONES

ice cream cone/
cornet *BrE*

traffic cone   pine cone

cone /kəʊn $ koʊn/ *n* [C] **1** a hollow or solid object with a round base, sloping sides, and a point at the top: *a traffic cone* **2 ice cream cone** a container for ICE CREAM that is shaped like a cone and that you can eat SYN **cornet** *BrE* **3** a thing that grows on PINE and FIR trees, which contains the seeds of the tree SYN **pine cone**

confectionery /kənˈfekʃənəri $ -neri/ *n* [U] sweets and cakes

confederation /kənˌfedəˈreɪʃən/ (*also* **confederacy** /kənˈfedərəsi/) *n* [C] a group of people, political parties, or organizations that have joined together to achieve an aim —**confederate** /kənˈfedərət/ *adj*

confer Ac /kənˈfɜː $ -ˈfɜːr/ *v* (**conferred, conferring**) **1** [I] to discuss something with other people so that everyone can express their opinion: [+with] *You may confer with the other team members.* **2 confer a degree/honour etc on sb** to officially give someone a degree etc

conference Ac /ˈkɒnfərəns $ ˈkɑːn-/ *n* [C] a large meeting, often lasting for several days, at which members of an organization, profession etc discuss things related to their work: [+on] *an international*

conference on the Environment | **conference centre/hall/facilities etc** THESAURUS MEETING → PRESS CONFERENCE

conference call *n* [C] a telephone call in which several people can all talk to each other

confess /kənˈfes/ *v* [I,T] **1** to admit that you have done something bad, illegal, or embarrassing: **confess to (doing) sth** *He has confessed to the crime.* | [+(that)] *Max confessed that he'd forgotten my birthday.* | **I have to/must confess** *spoken* (=used to admit something embarrassing) *I have to confess, I don't know much about it.* THESAURUS ADMIT **2** to tell a priest or God about bad things you have done —**confessed** *adj*

confession /kənˈfeʃən/ *n* **1** [C] a statement admitting that you have done something bad, illegal, or embarrassing: *He made a full confession to the police.* | *I have a confession to make* – *I've lost your keys.* **2** [C,U] when you tell a priest or God about bad things you have done: *She decided to go to confession.*

confetti /kənˈfeti/ *n* [U] small pieces of paper that you throw over a man and woman who have just got married

confidant /ˈkɒnfədænt, ˌkɒnfəˈdænt, -ˈdɑːnt $ ˈkɑːnfədænt/ *n* [C] someone you tell your secrets to or who you talk to about personal things

confidante /ˈkɒnfədænt, ˌkɒnfəˈdænt, -ˈdɑːnt $ ˈkɑːnfədænt/ *n* [C] a female confidant

confide /kənˈfaɪd/ *v* [I,T] to tell someone about personal things that you do not want other people to know: *'I quite like him,' she confided.* | **confide to sb that** *He had confided to friends that he was unhappy.*
PHRASAL VERBS
confide in sb to tell someone about something personal and secret, because you feel you can trust them: *I've never been able to confide in my sister.*

confidence /ˈkɒnfɪdəns $ ˈkɑːn-/ *n*
1 [U] belief in your ability to do things well or be liked by people: [+in] *I didn't have any confidence in myself.* | **confidence to do sth** *I wouldn't have the confidence to wear that.* | **with confidence** *It's important that children learn to read with confidence.*
2 [U] the feeling that you can trust someone or something to be good or successful: [+in] *The survey reveals a lack of confidence in the police.* | *Most parents have total confidence in the school.* | *a bid to restore confidence in the government* | **public/business/consumer confidence**
3 gain/win/earn sb's confidence if you gain someone's confidence, they start to trust you
4 [C] a secret or some personal and secret information: *We spent the evening talking and sharing confidences.*
PHRASES
in confidence if you say something in confidence, you tell someone something and trust them not to tell anyone else: *I'll tell you something about Marie – in confidence of course.*

COLLOCATIONS

verbs

to have confidence *You should have the confidence to say what you think.*

to gain confidence *Each day she gained a little more confidence.*
to give sb confidence *Doing the course has given me a lot of confidence.*
to be full of confidence *She's doing well and she's full of confidence.*
to lack confidence *He's good at his job, but he lacks confidence.*
to lose confidence *After three defeats, the team were losing confidence.*
to boost sb's confidence (=to make someone feel more confident) *One of my stories was published, which really boosted my confidence.*

confident /ˈkɒnfɪdənt $ ˈkɑːn-/ *adj*
1 sure that something is true or that something will happen in the way you want or expect: **[+(that)]** *She was confident that the problem would be sorted out.* | **confident of (doing) sth** *Owens is confident of success.* | **[+about]** *I feel very confident about the future.* **THESAURUS** SURE
2 sure that you are able to do things well or deal with situations successfully: **[+about]** *I'm much more confident about my ability.* | **confident smile/manner/voice etc** —**confidently** *adv* → SELF-CONFIDENT

THESAURUS – sense 2

confident sure that you can do things well or deal with situations successfully: *The players were in a confident and relaxed mood before the game.* | *a confident leader*
self-confident confident when you are dealing with other people, and not shy or nervous: *Jess was only 12, but she was very self-confident.* | *I soon became more self-confident as a public speaker.*
sure of yourself sure about your opinions and abilities, even when other people do not agree with you: *He was so sure of himself that I didn't try to argue with him.*
extrovert someone who likes talking and being with other people: *Most actors are natural extroverts.*
shy nervous and embarrassed about talking to people, especially people you do not know: *As a teenager, she was very shy.*

confidential /ˌkɒnfɪˈdenʃəl◂ $ ˌkɑːn-/ *adj* secret and not intended to be shown or told to other people: *confidential information* | **highly/strictly confidential** *The report is highly confidential.* **THESAURUS** SECRET —**confidentially** *adv* —**confidentiality** /ˌkɒnfədenʃiˈæləti $ ˌkɑːn-/ *n* [U]

configuration /kənˌfɪɡəˈreɪʃən, -ɡjə- $ -ɡjə-/ *n* [C,U] *formal or technical* the shape or arrangement of the parts of something

confine Ac /kənˈfaɪn/ *v* [T] **1** if you confine yourself or your activities to one thing, you do only that thing, or you do something, using only that thing **SYN** limit, restrict: **confine sth to sth** *We confined our research to young people.* | **confine yourself to (doing) sth** *He confined himself to writing plays.* **2** to stop something bad from spreading **SYN** limit, restrict: **confine sth to sth** *Firefighters managed to*

confine the fire to the ground floor. **3** to make someone stay in a place: **confine sb to sth** *An accident had confined him to a wheelchair.*

confined Ac /kənˈfaɪnd/ *adj* **1** **be confined to sb/sth** to exist in or affect only a particular place or group: *Demand for the book seems to be confined to women.* **2** a confined space or area is very small

confinement /kənˈfaɪnmənt/ *n* [U] when someone is forced to stay in a place: *They were held in confinement.* → SOLITARY CONFINEMENT

confines /ˈkɒnfaɪnz $ ˈkɑːn-/ *n* [plural] the limits or edge of something: *You must stay **within the confines of** the hotel.*

confirm Ac /kənˈfɜːm $ -ɜːrm/ *v* [T]
1 to show or prove that something is true or right: *Blood tests confirmed the diagnosis.* | **[+that]** *Can you confirm that the money has been paid?* | **[+what]** *Today's events confirm what we already know.* | **confirm sb's suspicions/belief/fears** *A telephone call confirmed my suspicions.*
2 to tell someone that an arrangement is now definite: *Please confirm your booking.*
3 **be confirmed** to be made a full member of the Christian church in a special ceremony

confirmation Ac /ˌkɒnfəˈmeɪʃən $ ˌkɑːnfər-/ *n* [C,U] **1** a statement, document etc saying that something is true or definite: **[+of]** *There is still no official confirmation of the report.* **2** a ceremony in which someone is made a full member of the Christian church

confirmed /kənˈfɜːmd $ -ɜːr-/ *adj* **confirmed bachelor/atheist etc** someone who has been something for a long time and is unlikely to change

confiscate /ˈkɒnfəskeɪt $ ˈkɑːn-/ *v* [T] to officially take something away from someone: *Customs officers confiscated his passport.* —**confiscation** /ˌkɒnfəˈskeɪʃən $ ˌkɑːn-/ *n* [C,U]

conflict¹ Ac /ˈkɒnflɪkt $ ˈkɑːn-/ *n* [C,U] **1** fighting: *the conflict in Afghanistan* | **[+between]** *a conflict between rival gangs* **2** a strong disagreement or argument: *He was always careful to avoid conflict.* | **[+over]** *conflicts over land* | **in conflict (with sb)** *She was always in conflict with her parents.* | **3** a big difference between two ideas, influences, needs etc: **[+between]** *the conflict between religion and science* | **in conflict (with sth)** *Individual aims may be in conflict with company aims.*
PHRASES

conflict of interest(s) a situation in which you cannot do your job fairly because you are personally affected by the decisions that you make: *There is a clear conflict of interests between her job as a politician and her business activities.*

conflict² Ac /kənˈflɪkt/ *v* [I] if two ideas, statements, needs etc conflict, they cannot both be true or exist together: **[+with]** *evidence that conflicts with previous findings* | **conflicting advice**

conform Ac /kənˈfɔːm $ -ɔːrm/ *v* [I] **1** to behave in the way that people expect or in the same way as other people: *There's always pressure on children to conform.* | **[+to]** *He was determined not to conform to the stereotype of a police officer.* **2** to obey a law, rule etc: **[+to]** *Products must conform to safety standards.* —**conformity** *n* [U]

conformist Ac /kən'fɔːmɪst $ -ɔːr-/ *adj* thinking and behaving in the same way as most other people OPP **nonconformist** —**conformist** *n* [C]

confound /kən'faʊnd/ *v* [T] to surprise people by showing that what they expected was wrong: *Her amazing recovery has confounded doctors.* | *He confounded his critics by winning the election.*

confront /kən'frʌnt/ *v* [T] **1** if a problem, difficulty etc confronts you, you have to do something about it: *the problems confronting the government* | **be confronted with sth** *Children are often shy when confronted with new situations.* **2** to do something to deal with a difficult or unpleasant problem, situation etc: *We need to confront the issue.* **3** to stand in front of someone in a threatening way: *She was confronted by two men.* **4** to try to make someone admit something, especially by showing them proof: *Eventually she confronted him about the affair.*

confrontation /ˌkɒnfrən'teɪʃən $ ˌkɑːn-/ *n* [C,U] an argument or fight: **[+with/between]** *confrontations between countries*

confrontational /ˌkɒnfrən'teɪʃənəl◄ $ ˌkɑːn-/ *adj* likely to cause arguments or make people angry: *a confrontational style of management*

confuse /kən'fjuːz/ *v* [T] **1** to make someone feel that they cannot think clearly or understand something: *His directions really confused me.* **2** to think wrongly that a person or thing is someone or something else: **confuse sb/sth with sb/sth** *It's easy to confuse Sue with her sister.* **3** to make something more complicated or difficult to understand: *The media were accused of **confusing** the **issue**.*

confused /kən'fjuːzd/ *adj*
1 unable to understand something, especially because it does not seem to make sense: *He was totally confused by the tax form.* | **[+about]** *I'm still confused about what happened.*
2 unable to think clearly, so that you do not know what is happening around you: *Old people sometimes get confused.*
3 complicated and difficult to understand: *a confused situation*

confusing /kən'fjuːzɪŋ/ *adj* unclear and difficult to understand: *It's all very confusing.* | *The results of the survey are confusing and contradictory.*

confusion /kən'fjuːʒən/ *n* [C,U]
1 a feeling that you do not understand something or do not know what to do: **[+over/as to/about]** *There's a lot of confusion about the new rules.* | **in confusion** *Marcus frowned in confusion.*
2 when you wrongly think that a person or thing is someone or something else: *To avoid confusion, the teams wore different colours.* | **[+between]** *confusion between flu and the common cold*
3 a confusing situation in which a lot of things are happening: **[+of]** *a confusion of noise and lights*

congeal /kən'dʒiːl/ *v* [I] if a liquid such as blood congeals, it becomes thick or solid

congenial /kən'dʒiːniəl/ *adj formal* pleasant in a way that makes you feel comfortable and relaxed: *a congenial atmosphere*

congenital /kən'dʒenətl/ *adj* affecting someone from the time they are born: *a congenital heart problem*

congested /kən'dʒestɪd/ *adj* full or blocked: *The roads were **heavily congested** (=full of traffic).* | *His nose was congested (=blocked, especially because he had a cold).* —**congestion** /-'dʒestʃən/ *n* [U]

con'gestion ˌcharging *n* [U] *BrE* a way of reducing traffic in city centres by charging drivers money to enter

conglomerate /kən'ɡlɒmərət $ -'ɡlɑː-/ *n* [C] a large company consisting of several companies that have joined together

conglomeration /kənˌɡlɒmə'reɪʃən $ -ˌɡlɑː-/ *n* [C] *formal* a group of many different things or people gathered together

congratulate /kən'ɡrætʃəleɪt/ *v* [T] to tell someone that you are happy because they have achieved something, or because something good has happened to them: **congratulate sb on (doing) sth** | *congratulated him on his success.* THESAURUS ▶ PRAISE

congratulations /kənˌɡrætʃə'leɪʃənz/ *n* [plural] used to congratulate someone: *You won? Congratulations!* | **[+on]** *Congratulations on your engagement!* | **[+to]** *Congratulations to all the winners!*

congregate /'kɒŋɡrɪɡeɪt $ 'kɑːŋ-/ *v* [I] to come together in a group: *A group of protesters had congregated outside.*

congregation /ˌkɒŋɡrə'ɡeɪʃən $ ˌkɑːŋ-/ *n* [C] the people who are in a church for a religious service

congress /'kɒŋɡres $ 'kɑːŋɡrɪs/ *n* [C] a large formal meeting of members of different organizations, countries etc

Congress *n* [C,U] the group of people elected to make laws for the US, consisting of the Senate and the House of Representatives —**congressional** /kən'ɡreʃənəl/ *adj*

congressman /'kɒŋɡrəsmən $ 'kɑːŋ-/ *n* [C] (*plural* **congressmen** /-mən/) a man who is elected to be in Congress THESAURUS ▶ POLITICIAN

congresswoman /'kɒŋɡrəsˌwʊmən $ 'kɑːŋ-/ *n* [C] (*plural* **congresswomen** /-ˌwɪmɪn/) a woman who is elected to be in Congress THESAURUS ▶ POLITICIAN

conical /'kɒnɪkəl $ 'kɑː-/ *adj* shaped like a CONE

conifer /'kəʊnəfə, 'kɒ- $ 'kɑːnəfər/ *n* [C] a tree that keeps its leaves in winter and has CONES containing its seeds —**coniferous** /kə'nɪfərəs $ koʊ-, kə-/ *adj*

conjecture /kən'dʒektʃə $ -ər/ *n* [C,U] *formal* when you form ideas or opinions about something without having much information to base them on SYN **guesswork**: *The statement is pure conjecture.* —**conjecture** *v* [I,T]

conjugal /'kɒndʒəɡəl $ 'kɑːn-/ *adj* [only before noun] *formal* relating to marriage

conjugate /'kɒndʒəɡeɪt $ 'kɑːn-/ *v* [T] to give the different forms that a verb can have —**conjugation** /ˌkɒndʒə'ɡeɪʃən $ ˌkɑːn-/ *n* [C,U]

conjunction /kən'dʒʌŋkʃən/ *n* [C] **1 in conjunction with sb/sth** working, happening, or being used with someone or something else: *The worksheets should be used in conjunction with the video.* **2** a word such as 'but', 'and', or 'because', which joins parts of a sentence

conjure /ˈkʌndʒə $ ˈkɑːndʒər, ˈkʌn-/ v
PHRASAL VERBS
conjure sth ↔ **up 1** to bring a thought, memory, or picture to someone's mind: *Smells can often conjure up memories.* **2** to make, get, or achieve something, as if by magic: *Dean conjured up a last-minute goal.*

conjurer, conjuror /ˈkʌndʒərə $ ˈkɑːndʒərər, ˈkʌn-/ n [C] someone who does magic tricks

conjuring /ˈkʌndʒərɪŋ $ ˈkɑː-, ˈkʌn-/ n [U] when someone does magic tricks and makes things appear and disappear

conman /ˈkɒnmæn $ ˈkɑːn-/ n [C] (*plural* **conmen** /-men/) a man who tries to get money by tricking people

connect /kəˈnekt/ v
1 [T] to join two or more things together SYN **link**: *The M11 connects London and Cambridge.* | *Connect the speakers to the stereo.* THESAURUS **JOIN**
2 [T] to realize or show that a fact, event, person etc is related to or involved in something SYN **link**: **connect sb/sth with sth** *There is little evidence to connect him with the crime.*
3 [T] to join something to a supply of electricity, gas, or water, or to a computer or telephone network OPP **disconnect**: *Has the phone been connected yet?* | [+to] *Click here to connect to the Internet.*
4 [I] if a plane, train etc connects with another one, it arrives just before the other one leaves so you can change from one to the other: *a connecting flight to Rio*

connected /kəˈnektɪd/ adj
1 if two things are connected with each other, they are related in some way: [+with] *problems connected with homelessness* | *Bad diet is closely connected with many illnesses.* THESAURUS **RELATED**
2 joined to something else: [+to] *The computer is connected to a printer.* → **WELL-CONNECTED**

connection /kəˈnekʃən/ n
1 RELATIONSHIP [C,U] a relationship between things: [+between] *the connection between smoking and cancer* | [+with/to] *Does this have any connection with the project?* | *the close connection between opera and poetry*
2 ELECTRIC WIRE [C] a piece of wire or metal joining two parts of a machine together or to an electrical system
3 TO INTERNET/TELEPHONE ETC [C,U] when two or more machines or telephones are joined together or joined to a larger system, using an electrical connection: *free Internet connection* | [+to] *The socket allows connection to a PC.*
4 PLANE/TRAIN ETC [C] a plane, train etc that is arranged so that people from an earlier plane, train etc can use it: *I missed my connection.*
5 PEOPLE **connections** [plural] people you know who can help you, especially because they are in positions of power: *He has connections in high places.*
PHRASES
in connection with sth concerning something: *Police are questioning a man in connection with the crime.*

connector /kəˈnektə $ -ər/ n [C] an object which is used to join two pieces of equipment together

connive /kəˈnaɪv/ v [I] to work secretly to do something bad or allow something bad to happen: **connive (with sb) to do sth** *Together, they connived to deceive her.* —**connivance** n [C,U]

connoisseur /ˌkɒnəˈsɜː $ ˌkɑːnəˈsɜːr/ n [C] someone who knows a lot about something such as art, food, or music: [+of] *a connoisseur of fine wines* THESAURUS **EXPERT**

connotation /ˌkɒnəˈteɪʃən $ ˌkɑː-/ n [C] an idea or quality that a word makes you think of, in addition to its basic meaning: [+of] *the word 'discipline' and its connotations of punishment*

conquer /ˈkɒŋkə $ ˈkɑːŋkər/ v **1** [I,T] to get control of a country or area by fighting: *The Normans conquered England in 1066.* **2** [T] to succeed in controlling something, especially a problem or strong feeling: *efforts to conquer inflation* | *I didn't think I'd ever conquer my fear of flying.* —**conqueror** n [C]

conquest /ˈkɒŋkwest $ ˈkɑːŋ-/ n [C,U] when someone gets control of a group of people, area, or situation: [+of] *the Spanish conquest of Central America* | *the conquest of space*

conscience /ˈkɒnʃəns $ ˈkɑːn-/ n [C,U] the part of your mind that tells you whether what you are doing is morally right or wrong: *He had a guilty conscience* (=feeling of guilt). | *I knew I could face them with a clear conscience* (=when you know you have done nothing wrong). | **pang/twinge of conscience** (=a slight feeling of guilt)
PHRASES
on sb's conscience making you feel guilty: *I lied and it's been on my conscience ever since.*

conscientious /ˌkɒnʃiˈenʃəs◂ $ ˌkɑːn-/ adj approving careful to do everything that it is your job or duty to do: *a conscientious teacher* THESAURUS **CAREFUL** —**conscientiously** adv

conscientious ob'jector n [C] someone who refuses to fight in a war because of their moral beliefs

conscious /ˈkɒnʃəs $ ˈkɑːn-/ adj **1** [not before noun] noticing something or being aware that it exists: **conscious of (doing) sth** *People are increasingly conscious of the need to exercise.* | [+that] *John was conscious that she was watching him.* **2** awake and able to understand what is happening OPP **unconscious**: *Owen was still conscious when they got to the hospital.* **3** **conscious effort/decision/attempt etc** a deliberate effort, decision etc: *Lyn had made a conscious decision to have a baby.* **4** thinking that something is very important: **health-conscious/fashion-conscious etc** *fashion-conscious teenagers* | [+of] *She's very conscious of safety.* —**consciously** adv → **SELF-CONSCIOUS**

consciousness /ˈkɒnʃəsnəs $ ˈkɑːn-/ n **1** [U] the condition of being awake and understanding what is happening: *She lost consciousness in the accident.* | *It was two weeks before he regained consciousness.* **2** [U] someone's mind, thoughts, and ideas: *research into human consciousness* **3** [singular, U] when you know that something exists or is important: **[+of]** *We need to increase public consciousness of the problem.*

conscript[1] /ˈkɒnskrɪpt $ ˈkɑːn-/ *n* [C] someone who has been made to join the army, navy etc

conscript[2] /kənˈskrɪpt/ *v* [T] to make someone join the army, navy etc —**conscription** /-ˈskrɪpʃən/ *n* [U]

consecrate /ˈkɒnsəkreɪt $ ˌkɑːn-/ *v* [T] to make something holy by performing a religious ceremony —**consecration** /ˌkɒnsəˈkreɪʃən $ ˌkɑːn-/ *n* [U]

consecutive /kənˈsekjətɪv/ *adj* happening one after the other: *It rained for three consecutive days.* —**consecutively** *adv*

consensual /kənˈsenʃuəl/ *adj formal* **1** involving the agreement of all or most people in a group: *a consensual style of management* **2** consensual sexual activity is wanted and agreed to by the people involved

consensus Ac /kənˈsensəs/ *n* [singular, U] agreement between everyone in a group: **[+on/about]** *Ministers failed to reach a consensus on the issue.* | **[+that]** *a general consensus among teachers that the policy should be changed* | *The consensus of opinion is that Smith should resign.*

consent[1] Ac /kənˈsent/ *n* [U] permission: **without sb's consent** *He took the car without the owner's consent.* | *Her parents gave their consent to the marriage.* THESAURUS ALLOW

consent[2] Ac *v* [I] to give your permission for something, or agree to something: **[+to]** *He had not consented to medical treatment.*

consequence Ac /ˈkɒnsəkwəns $ ˈkɑːnsəkwens/ *n* [C] something that happens as a result of something else: **[+of]** *the environmental consequences of road building* | **[+for]** *The policy will have serious consequences for Britain.* | *The accident happened as a consequence of poor safety procedures.* THESAURUS THEREFORE

PHRASES

of little/no consequence *formal* not important: *matters of little consequence*

consequent Ac /ˈkɒnsəkwənt $ ˈkɑːn-/ *adj* [only before noun] *formal* happening as a result of something else: *terrorism and the consequent decline in tourism*

consequently Ac /ˈkɒnsəkwəntli $ ˈkɑːnsəkwentli/ *adv* as a result: *He did no work and consequently failed the exam.*

conservation /ˌkɒnsəˈveɪʃən $ ˌkɑːnsər-/ *n* [U] **1** the protection of natural things such as animals, plants, forests etc: **[+of]** *conservation of the countryside* | *conservation groups* **2** when you prevent something from being wasted: **[+of]** *the conservation of resources* —**conservationist** *n* [C]

conservatism /kənˈsɜːvətɪzəm $ -ɜːr-/ *n* [U] dislike of change and new ideas

conservative[1] /kənˈsɜːvətɪv $ -ɜːr-/ *adj* **1** not willing to accept changes or new ideas: *a conservative attitude to education* **2 Conservative** belonging or

relating to the Conservative Party in Britain: *a Conservative MP* **3 a conservative estimate/guess** a guess that is deliberately lower than the real amount probably is

conservative[2] *n* [C] someone who does not like changes

Conservative *n* [C] a member or supporter of the Conservative Party in Britain

Conˈservative ˌParty *n* **the Conservative Party** a political party in Britain that supports RIGHT-WING ideas

conservatory /kənˈsɜːvətəri $ -ˈsɜːrvətɔːri/ *n* [C] (*plural* **conservatories**) a room with glass walls and a glass roof, that is joined to the side of a house

conserve /kənˈsɜːv $ -ˈsɜːrv/ *v* [T] to prevent something from being wasted, damaged, or destroyed: *the need to conserve the countryside*

consider /kənˈsɪdə $ -ər/ *v*

1 [I,T] to think about something carefully, especially before making a decision: **consider doing sth** *I considered resigning.* | **[+whether/what etc]** *He was considering whether to apply for the job.* | *You should consider the possibility of hiring a lawyer.* THESAURUS THINK

2 [T] to think of someone or something in a particular way: **[+that]** *They considered that the film was not suitable for children.* | **consider sb/sth (to be) sth** *Mrs. Gillan was considered to be an excellent teacher.*

3 [T] to think about someone and their feelings so you do not upset them: *He doesn't consider my feelings at all.*

considerable Ac /kənˈsɪdərəbəl/ *adj* large enough to be important or have an effect: *a considerable amount of money* —**considerably** *adv*

considerate /kənˈsɪdərət/ *adj* thinking about other people's feelings and needs OPP **inconsiderate**: *He was always kind and considerate.* THESAURUS KIND —**considerately** *adv*

consideration /kənˌsɪdəˈreɪʃən/ *n* **1** [U] *formal* careful thought and attention: **under consideration** *Several plans are under consideration.* **2** [C] a fact that you think about when deciding something: *financial considerations* **3** [U] when you think about other people's feelings and needs: **[+for]** *He shows no consideration for others.*

PHRASES

take sth into consideration to think about something when making a decision: *We'll take into consideration the fact that you were ill.*

considered /kənˈsɪdəd $ -ərd/ *adj* a considered opinion, judgment etc is one that you have thought about carefully

PHRASES

all things considered when you think about all parts of a situation: *All things considered, I think the day went well.*

considering /kənˈsɪdərɪŋ/ *prep, linking word* used to say that you are thinking about a particular fact when giving your opinion: **[+(that)]** *She did very well considering it was her first attempt.*

consign /kən'saɪn/ v

PHRASAL VERBS

consign sb/sth **to** sth **1** to cause someone or something to be in a bad situation: *a decision that consigned him to political obscurity* **2** to put something somewhere, especially in order to get rid of it

consignment /kən'saɪnmənt/ n [C] a quantity of goods that is sent somewhere: **[+of]** *a consignment of toys*

consist [Ac] /kən'sɪst/ v

PHRASAL VERBS

consist of sth to be formed from two or more things or people: **consist mainly/entirely/largely of sth** *The audience consists largely of teenagers.*

consistency [Ac] /kən'sɪstənsi/ n [C,U] (*plural* **consistencies**) **1** *approving* the quality of always happening or being done in the same way [OPP] **inconsistency**: **[+in]** *Consistency in approach is important.* **2** how thick, smooth etc a substance is: *a dessert with a creamy consistency*

consistent [Ac] /kən'sɪstənt/ adj **1** *approving* always happening or doing something in the same way [OPP] **inconsistent**: *the team's most consistent player* | **[+in]** *He is consistent in his opposition to the plan.* **2** containing facts, ideas etc that agree with other facts etc: **[+with]** *His story is not consistent with the facts.* —**consistently** adv: *consistently good marks*

consolation /ˌkɒnsə'leɪʃən $ ˌkɑːn-/ n [C,U] something that makes you feel better when you are sad or disappointed: **[+for/to]** *The news will be little consolation for those who have lost their jobs.*

console¹ /kən'səʊl $ -'soʊl/ v [T] to make someone feel better when they are sad or disappointed: *No one could console her when her dog died.* | **console yourself with sth** *I consoled myself with the thought that I had done my best.*

console² /'kɒnsəʊl $ 'kɑːnsoʊl/ n [C] a flat board that contains the controls for a machine, piece of electrical equipment, computer etc

consolidate /kən'sɒlədeɪt $ -'sɑː-/ v [I,T] **1** to make your power or success stronger so that you continue to be successful: *The company has consolidated its position in the Japanese market.* **2** to combine things so that they are more effective or easier to manage: *a loan to consolidate debts* —**consolidation** /kənˌsɒlə'deɪʃən $ -ˌsɑː-/ n [C,U]

consonant /'kɒnsənənt $ 'kɑːn-/ n [C] any letter of the English alphabet except a, e, i, o, and u → **vowel**

consort /kən'sɔːt $ -ɔːrt/ v

PHRASAL VERBS

consort with sb *formal* to spend time with someone who other people do not approve of

consortium /kən'sɔːtiəm $ -ɔːr-/ n [C] (*plural* **consortia** /-tiə/ or **consortiums**) a group of companies or organizations who are working together: **[+of]** *a consortium of banks*

conspicuous /kən'spɪkjuəs/ adj easy to notice [OPP] **inconspicuous**: *The notice must be displayed in a conspicuous place.* —**conspicuously** adv

conspiracy /kən'spɪrəsi/ n [C,U] (*plural* **conspiracies**) a secret plan made by two or more people to do something bad or illegal: **conspiracy to do sth** *a*

conspiracy to evade taxes | **[+against]** *a conspiracy against the police* **THESAURUS** ▶ **PLAN**

conspirator /kən'spɪrətə $ -ər/ n [C] someone who is part of a group planning a conspiracy —**conspiratorial** /kənˌspɪrə'tɔːriəl/ adj

conspire /kən'spaɪə $ -'spaɪr/ v [I] **1** to secretly plan with other people to do something bad or illegal: **conspire to do sth** *The men admitted conspiring to steal cars.* **2** *formal* if events conspire to do something, they happen at the same time and have a bad result: **conspire to do sth** *Pollution and neglect have conspired to ruin the city.*

constable /'kʌnstəbəl $ 'kɑːn-/ n [C] a British police officer of the lowest rank

constabulary /kən'stæbjələri $ -leri/ n [C] (*plural* **constabularies**) the police force of a particular area or country

constant [Ac] /'kɒnstənt $ 'kɑːn-/ adj **1** happening regularly or all the time: *a constant stream of vehicles* | *the constant threat of violence* **2** staying the same: *a constant speed* —**constancy** n [U]

constantly [Ac] /'kɒnstəntli $ 'kɑːn-/ adv all the time or regularly: *The English language is constantly changing.* **THESAURUS** ▶ **OFTEN**

constellation /ˌkɒnstə'leɪʃən $ ˌkɑːn-/ n [C] a group of stars that has a name **THESAURUS** ▶ **STAR**

consternation /ˌkɒnstə'neɪʃən $ ˌkɑːnstər-/ n [U] a feeling of shock or worry: **in consternation** *She stared at him in consternation.*

constipation /ˌkɒnstə'peɪʃən $ ˌkɑːn-/ n [U] when someone is unable to get rid of solid waste easily out of their body —**constipated** /'kɒnstɪpeɪtɪd $ 'kɑːn-/ adj

constituency [Ac] /kən'stɪtʃuənsi/ n [C] (*plural* **constituencies**) *BrE* an area of a country that elects someone to a parliament, or the people who live and vote there

constituent [Ac] /kən'stɪtʃuənt/ n [C] **1** someone who votes in a particular area **2** one of the parts that form something: **[+of]** *the constituents of blood* —**constituent** adj

constitute [Ac] /'kɒnstɪtjuːt $ 'kɑːnstɪtuːt/ v linking verb **1** to be considered to be something: *The rise in crime constitutes a threat to society.* **2** if several parts constitute something, they form it: *the 50 states that constitute the USA*

constitution [Ac] /ˌkɒnstɪ'tjuːʃən $ ˌkɑːnstɪ'tuː-/ n [C] **1** (*also* **Constitution**) a set of laws and principles that a country or organization is governed by: *the Constitution of the United States* **2** someone's health and ability to fight illness: **(have) a strong/weak constitution**

constitutional [Ac] /ˌkɒnstɪ'tjuːʃənəl◄ $ ˌkɑːnstɪ'tuː-/ adj relating to the constitution of a country: *constitutional reform* —**constitutionally** adv

constrain [Ac] /kən'streɪn/ v [T] *formal* to limit something, or to stop someone from doing what they want to do: *The project was constrained by lack of money.*

constrained Ac /kən'streɪnd/ adj **feel constrained to do sth** formal to feel that you must do something

constraint Ac /kən'streɪnt/ n [C,U] something that limits your freedom to do what you want: **[+on]** The government has **placed constraints** on further research.

constrict /kən'strɪkt/ v **1** [I,T] to become narrower or tighter, or to make something do this: Her throat constricted. **2** [T] to limit someone's freedom to do what they want —**constriction** /-'strɪkʃən/ n [C,U]

construct Ac /kən'strʌkt/ v [T] to build something such as a house, bridge, road etc: The Empire State Building was constructed in 1931. → see picture at BUILD¹ **THESAURUS** BUILD

construction Ac /kən'strʌkʃən/ n **1** [U] the process of building something such as a house, bridge, or road: the construction of a new airport | **under construction** (=being built) The hotel is under construction. | a road construction project **2** [C] formal something that has been built: a wooden construction **3** [C] the way in which words are put together in a sentence: difficult **grammatical constructions**

constructive Ac /kən'strʌktɪv/ adj useful and helpful: constructive criticism —**constructively** adv

construe /kən'struː/ v [T] formal to understand a remark or action in a particular way: **construe sth as sth** Comments like that may be construed as sexist.

consul /'kɒnsəl $ 'kɑːn-/ n [C] a government official in a foreign city whose job is to help citizens of his or her own country who are there —**consular** /'kɒnsjələ $ 'kɑːnsələr/ adj

consulate /'kɒnsjələt $ 'kɑːnsələt/ n [C] the building in which a consul lives and works → **embassy**

consult Ac /kən'sʌlt/ v **1** [T] to ask someone for advice or information, or to look for it in a book, on a map etc: Consult your doctor if the headaches continue. | **consult sb about sth** I consulted an accountant about tax. **THESAURUS** ASK **2** [I,T] to discuss something with someone so that you can make a decision together: He sold the car without consulting me! | **[+with]** The President consulted with European leaders.

consultancy Ac /kən'sʌltənsi/ n [C,U] (plural **consultancies**) a company that gives advice on a particular subject, or the advice that they give: a management consultancy | consultancy fees

consultant Ac /kən'sʌltənt/ n [C] **1** someone whose job is to give advice about a particular subject: a marketing consultant **2** BrE a hospital doctor of the highest rank who knows a lot about a particular area of medicine **THESAURUS** DOCTOR

consultation Ac /ˌkɒnsəl'teɪʃən $ ˌkɑːn-/ n **1** [C] a discussion or meeting that you have in order to get information or advice: **[+between]** consultations between teachers and parents | a medical consultation **2** [U] when you discuss something with someone in order to get information or advice: **for consultation** A counsellor is always available for consultation. | **in consultation with sb** The plans were drawn up in consultation with engineers. **3** [U] when you look for information in a book: **for consultation** Old exam papers are available for consultation.

consumables /kən'sjuːməbəlz $ -'suːm-/ n [plural] goods that people use and then buy again

consume Ac /kən'sjuːm $ -'suːm/ v [T] **1** to use energy, goods, time etc: Only 27% of the paper we consume is recycled. **2** formal to eat or drink something **3** **be consumed with guilt/rage/passion etc** literary to feel extremely guilty, angry etc **4** if fire consumes something, it destroys it completely

consumer Ac /kən'sjuːmə $ -'suːmər/ n [C] someone who buys or uses goods and services → **consumption**: Consumers are enjoying lower airfares. | a wider choice of goods for **the consumer** (=consumers in general) **THESAURUS** CUSTOMER

consumerism /kən'sjuːmərɪzəm $ -'suːr-/ n [U] the buying and selling of goods and services: the power of consumerism today

consuming /kən'sjuːmɪŋ $ -'suːr-/ adj [only before noun] a consuming feeling or interest is very strong and important in your life: a consuming ambition

consummate¹ /kənˈsʌmət, ˈkɒnsəmət $ ˈkɑːnsəmət/ adj formal showing great skill: He performed **with consummate skill**.

consummate² /'kɒnsəmeɪt $ 'kɑːn-/ v [T] to make a marriage or relationship complete by having sex —**consummation** /ˌkɒnsə'meɪʃən $ ˌkɑːn-/ n [U]

consumption Ac /kən'sʌmpʃən/ n [U] **1** the amount of electricity, gas, oil etc that is used: **energy/fuel etc consumption** the need to reduce petrol consumption **2** formal when people eat or drink something: **[+of]** the consumption of alcohol

contact¹ Ac /'kɒntækt $ 'kɑːn-/ n
1 [U] communication with a person, organization, or country: **[+with/between]** There is little contact between the two tribes. | **be/get/keep/stay in contact (with sb)** We stay in contact by email. | She moved away and they **lost contact**. | It'd be good to **make contact with** other local schools.
2 [U] when two people or things touch against each other: **[+with/between]** Babies need **physical contact** with a loving adult. | Don't let raw meat **come into contact with** other food.
3 [C] someone you know who may be able to help you or give you advice: Do you have any contacts in the area?

contact² Ac v [T] to telephone or write to someone: Who can we contact in an emergency? | She contacted the police.

'contact ˌlens n [C] a small round piece of plastic you put on your eye to help you see clearly

contagious /kən'teɪdʒəs/ adj **1** a contagious disease can be passed from one person to another by touch **2** a feeling, attitude etc that is contagious spreads quickly among people: Her laughter was contagious.

contain /kən'teɪn/ v [T]
1 to have something inside: His wallet contained $45. | This product may contain nuts.
2 to include something: Her letter contained information about his business activities. | Does the film contain violence?
3 to control the emotions you feel: Jane couldn't

contain her amusement. | **contain yourself** *He was so excited he could hardly contain himself.*

4 to stop something from spreading or escaping: *Doctors are struggling to contain the epidemic.* —**containment** *n* [U] *formal: containment of public expenditure*

container /kən'teɪnə $ -ər/ *n* [C] something such as a box or bowl that you keep things in: *Ice cream is sold in plastic containers.*

contaminate /kən'tæmɘneɪt/ *v* [T] if a dirty or poisonous substance contaminates something, it gets into it and makes it dangerous: *Chemical waste had contaminated the water supply.* —**contamination** /kən,tæmɘ'neɪʃən/ *n* [U]

contemplate /'kɒntɘmpleɪt $ 'kɑːn-/ *v* [T] to think about something in a serious way: **contemplate doing sth** *Have you contemplated resigning?* —**contemplation** /,kɒntɘm'pleɪʃən $,kɑːn-/ *n* [U]

contemporary¹ Ac /kən'tempərəri, -pəri $ -pəreri/ *adj*
1 belonging to the present time SYN **modern**: **contemporary music/art/dance etc** *an exhibition of contemporary art*
2 done or existing at the same time: *contemporary accounts of the war* | **[+with]** *letters contemporary with his earliest compositions*

contemporary² Ac *n* [C] (*plural* **contemporaries**) someone who lives or works at the same time as someone else: *Mozart was admired by his contemporaries.*

contempt /kən'tempt/ *n* [U] the feeling that someone or something does not deserve respect: *Stuart treated his wife with* **utter contempt.**
PHRASES
  contempt of court *law* when someone does not obey a court of law: *He was jailed for seven days for contempt of court.*

contemptible /kən'temptɘbəl/ *adj* not deserving any respect: *contemptible behaviour* —**contemptibly** *adv*

contemptuous /kən'temptʃuəs/ *adj* showing that you think someone or something deserves no respect: *a contemptuous glance* —**contemptuously** *adv*

contend /kən'tend/ *v* **1** [I] to compete against someone to get something: **[+for]** *Twelve teams contended for the title.* **2** [T] to say or argue that something is true: **[+that]** *Democrats contend that the tax is unfair.*
PHRASAL VERBS
contend with sth to have to deal with something difficult or unpleasant: *The builders* **had to contend with** *bad weather.*

contender /kən'tendə $ -ər/ *n* [C] someone who is competing to get or win something

content¹ /'kɒntent $ 'kɑːn-/ *n*
1 contents [plural] **a)** the things that are inside a box, bag, room etc: **[+of]** *Suzy looked through the contents of her handbag.* | *The gallery's contents were*

CONTAINERS

can of cola

tin/can of tuna

pot of honey

bag of crisps *BrE*/chips *AmE*

tube of toothpaste

packet of cheese

jar of pickles

carton of milk

tub of margarine

box of chocolates

damaged in the fire. **b)** the things that are written in a letter, book etc: **[+of]** *He kept the contents of the letter a secret.*
2 [singular] the amount of a substance that something contains: **fat/protein/alcohol etc content** *the* **high fat content** *of cheese*
3 [singular] the ideas or information contained in a speech, book, programme etc: **[+of]** *Is the content of the magazine suitable for children?*

content² /kənˈtent/ *adj* [not before noun] satisfied and happy: **[+with]** *She seems content with her life.* | **content to do sth** *I was* **quite content** *to let Steve do the talking.* —**contentment** *n* [U] → **do sth to your heart's content** at HEART

content³ *v* **content yourself with (doing) sth** to accept something even though it is not what you really want: *We'll have to content ourselves with a cheaper holiday this year.*

contented /kənˈtentɪd/ *adj* satisfied and happy **OPP discontented**: *a contented smile* **THESAURUS** HAPPY —**contentedly** *adv*

contention /kənˈtenʃən/ *n formal* **1** [C] a strong opinion that someone expresses **2** [U] arguments and disagreements between people
PHRASES
| **be in contention (for sth)** to be competing for something: *France remains in contention for the World Cup.*

contentious /kənˈtenʃəs/ *adj formal* likely to cause an argument

contest¹ /ˈkɒntest $ ˈkɑːn-/ *n* [C] a competition: **[+for]** *the contest for the world title* | *I only* **entered the contest** *for fun.* | *The election will be a* **close contest** (=one which either party, team etc could win, because they are equally popular, good etc).

contest² /kənˈtest/ *v* [T] **1** to say formally that you do not think something is correct or fair: *His brothers contested the will.* **2** to try to win something, especially an election

contestant /kənˈtestənt/ *n* [C] someone who competes in a competition

context **Ac** /ˈkɒntekst $ ˈkɑːn-/ *n* [C,U] **1** the situation, events etc that are related to something and help you understand it: **in context/out of context** (=in relation to this situation etc, or not) *You need to consider these events in their historical context.* **2** the words that come before and after a word or phrase and help you understand its meaning

continent /ˈkɒntɪnənt $ ˈkɑːn-/ *n* [C] **1** one of the seven main areas of land on the Earth: *the continent of Africa* **2 the Continent** *BrE* Western Europe, not including Britain

continental /ˌkɒntɪˈnentl◂ $ ˌkɑːn-/ *adj* **1** relating to a continent but not its islands: *flights across the continental US* **2** *BrE old-fashioned* relating to the continent of Europe, not including Britain

contingency /kənˈtɪndʒənsi/ *n* [C] (*plural* **contingencies**) an event or situation that might happen in the future and could cause problems: *a* **contingency plan**

contingent¹ /kənˈtɪndʒənt/ *adj formal* depending

on something else in order to happen: **[+on/upon]** *Further investment is contingent on the company's performance.*

contingent² *n* [C] **1** a group of people at an event who all come from the same area, organization etc: *Has the Scottish contingent arrived?* **2** a group of soldiers sent to help a larger group

continual /kənˈtɪnjuəl/ *adj* [only before noun] happening all the time without stopping, or happening many times: *five weeks of continual rain* | *the continual threat of terrorism* —**continually** *adv*: *The phone rang continually.*

continuation /kənˌtɪnjuˈeɪʃən/ *n* **1** [C] something that follows something else and seems a part of it: **[+of]** *The book is a continuation of his autobiography.* **2** [singular, U] when something continues to exist or happen: *measures to ensure the continuation of food supply*

continue /kənˈtɪnjuː/ *v*
1 [I,T] to not stop happening, existing, or doing something → **discontinue**: **[+for]** *The strike continued for four weeks.* | **[+with]** *Will the team continue with their research?* | **continue to do sth** *The city's population has continued to grow.* | **continue doing sth** *Most elderly people want to continue living at home.*
2 [I,T] to start again after a pause: *After a brief ceasefire, fighting continued.* | *Rescue teams will continue the search tomorrow.* | **continue doing sth** *He picked up his book and continued reading.*
3 [I] to go further in the same direction: **[+down/along/into etc]** *We continued along the road.* —**continued** *adj*: *Thank you for your continued support.*

THESAURUS
continue to not stop happening, existing, or doing something: *The good weather seems likely to continue.* | *The business may not be able to continue.* | *He continued talking.*
last to continue – used especially when saying how long something continues for: *The trial lasted for six days.*
go on (*also* **carry on** *especially BrE*) to continue. **Go on** is less formal than **continue**, and is very common in everyday English: *The meeting went on till five o'clock.* | *She's going to carry on working till the baby's born.*
keep on doing sth to continue doing something: *Keep on going in this direction until you see the church.* | *I kept on telling him, but he wouldn't listen.*
drag on if something drags on, it seems boring and continues for much longer than necessary: *The film dragged on for another hour.*

continuity /ˌkɒntəˈnjuːəti $ ˌkɑːntəˈnuː-/ *n* [U] when something continues over a long period of time without stopping or changing: *There should be continuity of care between hospital and home.*

continuous /kənˈtɪnjuəs/ *adj*
1 happening or existing without stopping: *a* **continuous flow** *of information* | *The problems have been continuous.*
2 *technical* the continuous form of a verb shows that an action is continuing. In English, this is formed by

contort

the verb 'be' followed by a PRESENT PARTICIPLE as in 'I was watching TV'. —**continuously** adv

> **Word Choice: continuous or continual?**
> These words both mean that something continues to happen or exist. You say *a continuous/continual supply of water* | *a continuous/continual process*
> You often use **continual** when something bad or annoying keeps happening: *continual problems* | *continual interruptions*

contort /kən'tɔːt $ -ɔːrt/ v [I,T] if your face or body contorts, or is contorted, it is twisted into an unnatural shape: **[+with/in]** *His body contorted in agony*. —**contortion** /-'tɔːʃən $ -ɔːr-/ n [C,U]

contour /'kɒntʊə $ 'kɑːntʊr/ n [C] **1** the shape of the outer edges of something: *the contours of the hills* **2** (also **'contour line**) a line on a map joining points of equal height

contraband /'kɒntrəbænd $ 'kɑːn-/ n [U] goods that are brought into a country illegally

contraception /ˌkɒntrə'sepʃən $ ˌkɑːn-/ n [U] the methods that stop a woman becoming PREGNANT **SYN** birth control

contraceptive /ˌkɒntrə'septɪv◂ $ ˌkɑːn-/ n [C] something that is used to stop a woman becoming PREGNANT —**contraceptive** adj: *the contraceptive pill*

contract¹ Ac /'kɒntrækt $ 'kɑːn-/ n [C] an official agreement between two or more people: *Read the contract carefully before you sign it.* —**contractual** /kən'træktʃuəl/ adj: *a contractual arrangement*

COLLOCATIONS

verbs

to sign a contract *She has just signed a contract with the BBC.*

to have a contract *We have a contract to install a new computer system at the company.*

to agree to a contract (also **to agree a contract** BrE) *He has agreed a new one-year contract with Arsenal.*

to break a contract (=to do something that your contract does not allow) *She left, breaking her contract of employment.*

types of contract

a recording/building etc contract *The band was soon offered a recording contract.*

a one-year/two-year etc contract | **a contract of employment** (also **an employment contract**)

---

contract² Ac /kən'trækt/ v **1** [I] to become smaller **OPP** expand: *Metal contracts as it cools.* **2** [T] formal to get a serious illness: *Sharon contracted AIDS from a dirty needle.* **3** [I,T] to sign a contract with someone agreeing what you or they will do

contraction /kən'trækʃən/ n **1** [C] technical a very strong painful movement of a woman's muscles during the birth of her baby **2** [U] the process of becoming smaller **OPP** expansion: *the contraction of the coal industry* **3** [C] technical a shorter form of a word or words: *'Don't' is a contraction of 'do not'.*

contractor Ac /kən'træktə $ 'kɑːntræktər/ n [C] a person or company that does work or supplies goods for another company: *a building contractor*

contradict Ac /ˌkɒntrə'dɪkt $ ˌkɑːn-/ v **1** [I,T] to disagree with something, especially by saying that the opposite is true: *The article **flatly contradicts** their claims.* **2** [T] if one statement, story etc contradicts another, they are different, and both cannot be true: *The witnesses' accounts **contradict each other**.*

contradiction Ac /ˌkɒntrə'dɪkʃən $ ˌkɑːn-/ n **1** [C] a difference between two statements, facts etc which means they cannot both be true: **[+between]** *the contradiction between our figures and the official ones* **2** [U] when you say that someone else's opinion, statement etc is wrong

contradictory Ac /ˌkɒntrə'dɪktəri◂ $ ˌkɑːn-/ adj if two statements are contradictory, they are different and cannot both be true

contralto /kən'træltəʊ $ -toʊ/ n [C,U] (plural **contraltos**) a female singer with a low voice → **alto**

contraption /kən'træpʃən/ n [C] a machine or piece of equipment that looks strange or unlikely to work **THESAURUS** MACHINE

contrary¹ Ac /'kɒntrəri $ 'kɑːntreri/ n formal **1 on/quite the contrary** used to emphasize that the opposite of what someone has just said is actually true: *It wasn't a good thing; on the contrary it was a mistake.* **2 to the contrary** saying or showing the opposite of something: *Despite rumours to the contrary, their relationship is very good.*

contrary² Ac adj **1** completely different from each other, or opposed to something: *They expressed contrary opinions.* | **[+to]** *The government's actions are contrary to the public interest.* **2 contrary to popular belief/opinion** opposite to what people think: *Contrary to popular belief, a desert can be very cold.*

contrast¹ Ac /'kɒntrɑːst $ 'kɑːntræst/ n **1** [C,U] a very noticeable difference between people, things etc: **[+between]** *the contrast between the rich and the poor* | **[+with]** *The marble makes **a strong contrast** with the wooden floor.* **2 in/by contrast (to/with sth)** used when comparing two people, things etc that are very different from each other: *There was brilliant sunshine outside, in contrast to the interior.* **3** [C] something that is very different to something else: **[+to]** *The theatre was **quite a contrast** to the ones we'd performed in before.*

contrast² Ac /kən'trɑːst $ -'træst/ v **1** [I] if two things contrast, the difference between them is very noticeable: **[+with]** *These results **contrast sharply** with other medical tests.* **2** [T] to compare two people, ideas, objects etc and show how they are different from each other: **contrast sth with sth** *The speaker contrasted this approach with earlier methods.* —**contrasting** adj: *contrasting colours*

contravene /ˌkɒntrə'viːn $ ˌkɑːn-/ v [T] formal to do something that is not allowed by a law or rule —**contravention** /-'venʃən/ n [C,U]

contribute Ac /kən'trɪbjuːt/ v [I,T] **1** to give money, help, ideas etc to something that other people are also involved in: *Everyone was expected to contribute £2.* | **contribute (sth) to/towards sth** *I hope you'll all contribute towards the discussion.* | *The* volunteers *contribute their own time to the project.* **THESAURUS** **GIVE 2** to help to make something happen: **[+to]** *Alcohol contributes to 100,000 deaths a year in the US.* **3** to write for a newspaper or magazine —**contributor** *n* [C]

contribution Ac /ˌkɒntrəˈbjuːʃən $ ˌkɑːn-/ *n* [C] **1** something that you give or do to help make something successful: **[+to]** *Einstein's enormous contribution to science* | *I'd like to think I'd* **made a contribution** *to society.* **2** an amount of money that you give to help pay for something: **[+of]** *A contribution of £25 will buy 15 books.*

contributory /kənˈtrɪbjətəri $ -tɔːri/ *adj* [only before noun] helping to cause something: *Smoking is a* **contributory factor** *in lung cancer.*

contrite /ˈkɒntraɪt $ ˈkɑːn-/ *adj formal* feeling guilty and sorry for something bad that you have done —**contritely** *adv* —**contrition** /kənˈtrɪʃən/ *n* [U]

contrive /kənˈtraɪv/ *v* [T] **1** *formal* to succeed in doing something difficult: **contrive to do sth** *Somehow she contrived to escape.* **2** to deliberately make something happen in a clever or dishonest way: *The companies are accused of contriving the oil shortage.*

contrived /kənˈtraɪvd/ *adj* seeming false and not natural: *The novel's characters seem contrived.*

control¹ /kənˈtrəʊl $ -ˈtroʊl/ *n*
1 [U] the power or ability to make someone or something do what you want: **[+of/over]** *Babies have very little control over their movements.* | **under control** (=happening or behaving in the way you want) *'Do you need any help?' 'No, it's all under control, thanks.'* | **out of control** (=not happening or behaving in the way you want) *The car spun out of control and hit a tree.*
2 [U] the power to decide how a country, place, company etc is organized, and what it does: **[+of]** *The family* **has control** *of the company.* | **in control of sth** *Rebel forces are still in control of the area.* | *China* **took control** *of the island in 1683.*
3 [C,U] when you limit something, or a rule, law etc that limits it: **[+of]** *the control of inflation* | **[+on]** *There are* **strict controls** *on international trade.* | **under control** (=being prevented from increasing) *Firefighters had the fire under control by midnight.*
4 [U] the ability to remain calm, even when you are angry, upset, or excited: *David* **lost control of himself** *and started yelling.*
5 [C] a thing that you press or turn to make a machine, television etc work: *the TV* **remote control**
6 [C,U] the place where something is officially checked: *passport control* → **BIRTH CONTROL**

control² *v* [T] (**controlled, controlling**)
1 to have power over a country, place, organization etc, and decide what happens there: *The Republicans now control the Senate.* | **Labour-/Republican-/Democrat- etc controlled** *a Conservative-controlled council*
2 to make someone or something do what you want, or to make something work in a particular way: *a teacher who can't control the kids* | *The temperature inside is carefully controlled.*
3 to limit the amount or growth of something: *a chemical used to control weeds*
4 to make yourself behave calmly, even if you feel angry, excited, or upset: *Sarah tried to control her anger.* —**controller** *n* [C]

con'trol ˌfreak *n* [C] *informal* someone who wants to control all the details of every situation they are in

controversial Ac /ˌkɒntrəˈvɜːʃəl◂ $ ˌkɑːntrəˈvɜːr-/ *adj* causing a lot of disagreement among people: *The site of the new road has been a* **controversial issue**. —**controversially** *adv*

controversy Ac /ˈkɒntrəvɜːsi, kənˈtrɒvəsi $ ˌkɑːntrəˈvɜːrsi/ *n* [C,U] (*plural* **controversies**) a lot of disagreement about an idea or plan, involving many people: **[+over/about]** *There's been some controversy over increasing students' fees.*

conurbation /ˌkɒnɜːˈbeɪʃən $ ˌkɑːnɜːr-/ *n* [C] a group of towns that have spread and become joined together

convalesce /ˌkɒnvəˈles $ ˌkɑːn-/ *v* [I] to spend time getting well after an illness —**convalescence** *n* [U]: *a long period of convalescence*

convection /kənˈvekʃən/ *n* [U] *technical* the movement caused by warm gas or liquid rising, and cold gas or liquid sinking

convene Ac /kənˈviːn/ *v* [I,T] *formal* to come together or bring people together for a meeting

convenience /kənˈviːniəns/ *n* [U] the quality of being suitable or useful for a particular purpose **OPP** **inconvenience**: **the convenience of doing sth** *Most people like the convenience of using credit cards.* |

for convenience *I bought a house near the station for convenience.*

con'venience ˌfood n [C,U] food that is prepared already and that is sold frozen or in cans, packages etc, so that it can be prepared quickly and easily

con'venience ˌstore n [C] a shop where you can buy food, alcohol, magazines etc, that is often open 24 hours each day

convenient /kənˈviːniənt/ adj
1 a convenient time is good for you because you are not doing anything else then OPP **inconvenient**: *Would 10:30 be a convenient time to meet?* | [+for] *Eleven o'clock is convenient for me.*
2 a convenient way of doing something is useful and easy OPP **inconvenient**: **convenient to do sth** *Mail order catalogues are a convenient way to shop.*
3 a convenient place is near and easy to get to OPP **inconvenient**: *The shops are very convenient.* —**conveniently** adv

convent /ˈkɒnvənt $ ˈkɑːnvent/ n [C] a place where NUNS live

convention Ac /kənˈvenʃən/ n **1** [C] a formal meeting of people who belong to the same profession, organization etc: *a teachers' convention* **2** [C] a formal agreement between countries: [+on] *the European Convention on Human Rights* **3** [C,U] the normal and traditional way of behaving and thinking in a society: *social conventions*

conventional Ac /kənˈvenʃənəl/ adj **1** [only before noun] of the usual type that has been used for a long time: *a conventional oven* **2** thinking and behaving in the normal and traditional way OPP **unconventional**: [+in] *Tom is conventional in his approach to life.* **3** [only before noun] conventional weapons and wars do not use NUCLEAR power: *conventional forces* —**conventionally** adv

converge /kənˈvɜːdʒ $ -ˈvɜːrdʒ/ v [I] to come from different directions and meet at the same place: [+on] *Reporters converged on the scene.*

conversant /kənˈvɜːsənt $ -ɜːr-/ adj [not before noun] formal having knowledge or experience of something: [+with] *Staff members are conversant with the issues.*

conversation /ˌkɒnvəˈseɪʃən $ ˌkɑːnvər-/ n [C,U] an informal talk between two or more people: [+with] *I had a short conversation with the teacher.* | [+about] *an interesting conversation about Italian opera* THESAURUS ➤ TALK —**conversational** adj

COLLOCATIONS
verbs
to have a conversation *We had a really interesting conversation.*
to carry on/hold a conversation *It's impossible to carry on a conversation with all this noise.*
to make conversation (=to talk in order to be polite) *We sat there and tried to make conversation.*
to get into conversation with sb (=to start talking with someone) *She got into conversation with one of the women in the queue.*

adjectives
a long/short conversation *A customer was having a long conversation with the waitress.*
a private conversation *Go away! This is a private conversation.*

converse¹ /kənˈvɜːs $ -ˈvɜːrs/ v [I] formal to have a conversation with someone

converse² Ac /ˈkɒnvɜːs $ ˈkɑːnvɜːrs/ n **the converse** formal the converse of a fact, word, statement etc is the opposite of it

conversely Ac /kənˈvɜːsli, ˈkɒnvɜːsli $ kənˈvɜːrsli, ˈkɑːnvɜːrsli/ adv used when one situation is the opposite of another: *American consumers prefer white eggs; conversely, British buyers like brown eggs.*

conversion Ac /kənˈvɜːʃən $ -ˈvɜːrʒən/ n [C,U] **1** when you change something from one system or purpose to another: [+into/of/to] *the conversion of waste into energy* **2** when someone changes to a different religion or belief: [+to/from] *her conversion to Catholicism*

convert¹ Ac /kənˈvɜːt $ -ˈvɜːrt/ v [I,T] **1** to change from one system or purpose to another, or to change something in this way: [+to/into] *a sofa that converts into a bed* | *The old houses have been converted into flats.* **2** to accept a different religion, opinion etc, or to make someone do this: **convert (sb) to sth** *Steve has converted to Islam.*

convert² /ˈkɒnvɜːt $ ˈkɑːnvɜːrt/ n [C] someone who has been persuaded to change their religion or beliefs

convertible Ac /kənˈvɜːtəbəl $ -ɜːr-/ n [C] a car with a roof that you can fold back or remove

convex /ˌkɒnˈveks◂, kən-, ˈkɒnveks $ ˌkɑːnˈveks◂, kən-, ˈkɑːnveks/ adj having a surface that curves OUTWARDS, like part of the outside of a ball or tube OPP **concave**

convey /kənˈveɪ/ v [T] **1** to express ideas, feelings etc: *What does this poem convey?* **2** formal to take something from one place to another, especially in a vehicle

con'veyor belt n [C] a long moving band of rubber or metal, used to move things from one place to another

convict¹ /kənˈvɪkt/ v [T] to officially decide in a court of law that someone is guilty of a crime OPP **acquit**: **convict sb of sth** *She was convicted of shoplifting.*

convict² /ˈkɒnvɪkt $ ˈkɑːn-/ n [C] someone who has been proved guilty of a crime and sent to prison

conviction /kənˈvɪkʃən/ n **1** [C,U] a very strong belief or opinion: **with/without conviction** *She spoke with great conviction* (=showing strong belief in what she said). **2** [C] a decision in a court of law that someone is guilty of a crime: [+for] *He had a conviction for theft.*

convince Ac /kənˈvɪns/ v [T]
1 to make someone feel certain that something is true: *Her arguments didn't convince me.* | **convince sb (that)** *She convinced us she could do it.* | **convince sb**

of sth *He tried to convince them of his innocence.*
THESAURUS PERSUADE
2 to persuade someone to do something **SYN** **persuade**: **convince sb to do sth** *I couldn't convince Liz to come.*

convinced Ac /kənˈvɪnst/ *adj* [not before noun] completely certain that something is true: *You don't* **sound convinced.** | **[+(that)]** *I am convinced the treatment is safe.* | **[+of]** *Is she convinced of his guilt?*
THESAURUS SURE

convincing Ac /kənˈvɪnsɪŋ/ *adj* **1** making you believe that something is true or right: **convincing evidence/proof/arguments etc** *It was a convincing excuse.* | *He was* **utterly convincing** *in the role* (=he acted the part very well). **2** **convincing victory/win** a victory that someone wins very easily: *This was the convincing win the team needed.* —**convincingly** *adv*

convivial /kənˈvɪviəl/ *adj formal* friendly and cheerful

convoluted /ˈkɒnvəluːtɪd $ ˈkɑːn-/ *adj formal* complicated and difficult to understand

convoy /ˈkɒnvɔɪ $ ˈkɑːn-/ *n* [C] a group of vehicles or ships travelling together: **[+of]** *a convoy of trucks*

convulsion /kənˈvʌlʃən/ *n* [C] a sudden shaking movement of your body, caused by illness

coo /kuː/ *v* [I] **1** when DOVES or PIGEONS coo, they make a low soft sound **2** to speak in a soft loving way

COOK

boil   fry

bake   roast

cook¹ /kʊk/ *v*
1 [I,T] to prepare food for eating, using heat: *Where did you learn to cook?* | **cook lunch/dinner/supper etc** *It's your turn to cook dinner.* | **cook sb sth** *I've cooked you a delicious curry.* | **cook (sth) for sb** *Jamie's cooking for us tonight.* | *slices of cooked ham*
2 [I] if food cooks, it is being prepared to eat, using heat: *While the pasta's cooking, grate some cheese.*
PHRASAL VERBS
cook sth ↔ **up** *informal* to invent an excuse, plan etc, especially in order to deceive someone

---

THESAURUS

cook to prepare food or a meal for eating, using heat: *I'm cooking pasta for supper.* | *He's offered to cook supper for me.*
make to make a meal or a particular dish, by cooking or putting food together: *Are you making lunch?* | *I think I'll make a salad.*

different ways of cooking

bake to cook bread, cakes etc in an oven: *Tom baked a cake for my birthday.*
roast to cook vegetables or meat in an oven: *Roast the potatoes for an hour.*
fry to cook food in hot oil: *She was frying some mushrooms.*
stir-fry to quickly fry small pieces of food in a small amount of oil and keep moving them in the pan: *I'm going to stir-fry the vegetables.*
grill to cook food over or under strong heat: *grilled fish*
boil to cook something in very hot water: *a boiled egg*
steam to cook vegetables over hot water: *Steaming vegetables is healthier than boiling them.*
poach to cook fish or eggs slowly in hot liquid: *Poach the fish in a little milk.*
microwave to cook food in a microwave oven: *I microwave vegetables if I'm short of time.*

cook² *n* [C] **1** someone whose job is to prepare and cook food **SYN** **chef 2** **good/bad/terrible etc cook** someone who is good, bad etc at cooking

cookbook /ˈkʊkbʊk/ *especially AmE* (also ˈcookery book *BrE*) *n* [C] a book that tells you how to prepare and cook food

cooker /ˈkʊkə $ -ər/ *n* [C] *BrE* a large piece of kitchen equipment used for cooking food **SYN** **stove** *AmE*: *a gas cooker* → see picture at **KITCHEN**

cookery /ˈkʊkəri/ *n* [U] *BrE* the art or skill of preparing and cooking food **SYN** **cooking**

cookie /ˈkʊki/ *n* [C] *especially AmE* a small flat sweet cake **SYN** **biscuit** *BrE*
PHRASES
  tough/smart cookie *informal* someone who is clever and knows how to get what they want: *She's a smart cookie and will probably do well.*

cooking /ˈkʊkɪŋ/ *n* [U] **1** the activity of preparing food so that it is ready to eat, usually by heating it: *Who* **does the cooking** *in your house?* | *cooking implements* **2** food made in a particular way or by a particular person: *Indian cooking*

cool¹ /kuːl/ *adj*
1 COLD fairly cold: *a lovely cool drink* | *a cool breeze* | *It* **gets** *quite cool in the evenings.* **THESAURUS** COLD
2 CALM calm and not nervous or excited: **keep/stay cool** *He's good at staying cool in a crisis.*
3 GOOD *informal* attractive, fashionable, or interesting in a way that people admire: *You* **look cool** *in that hat.* | *'He's in a band.' 'Cool!'*
4 AGREEING *spoken* used to say that you agree with something or are not annoyed about it: *If you want to go now,* **it's cool** *with me.*
5 UNFRIENDLY not as friendly as you expect: *They received a cool reception.* —**coolness** *n* [U]

cool² v 1 [I,T] to become a little colder, or to make something a little colder: *Leave the cakes to cool.* | *We stopped to cool our faces in the stream.* 2 [I] if a feeling or relationship cools, it becomes less strong
PHRASAL VERBS
cool (sb) **down/off 1** to return to a normal temperature after being hot: *Let's go for a swim to cool off.* 2 to become calm after being angry, or to make someone become calm: *She'll cool down in a day or two.*

cool³ n 1 **keep your cool** to stay calm in a difficult situation: *Rick was yelling, but she kept her cool.* 2 **lose your cool** to stop being calm in a difficult situation 3 **the cool (of sth)** a temperature that is pleasantly cool: *the cool of the evening*

cooler /'ku:lə $ -ər/ n [C] a container for keeping food and drinks cold

coolly /'ku:l-li/ adv 1 in a way that seems unfriendly: *'Fine,' she said coolly.* 2 calmly: *He coolly walked over and kissed her.*

coop¹ /ku:p/ n [C] a building for chickens

coop² v **be cooped up** to be kept in a very small place, or to be made to stay indoors: *I hate being cooped up in an office all day.*

cooperate Ac (also **co-operate** BrE) /kəʊˈɒpəreɪt $ koʊˈɑːp-/ v [I] 1 to work with someone else to achieve something you both want: **[+with]** *Many species cooperate with each other when hunting.* | **[+on/in]** *Several countries cooperated on the project.* | **[+to]** *Parents and teachers can cooperate to solve the problem.* 2 to be helpful by doing what someone wants you to do: **[+with]** *When questioned, he refused to co-operate with the police.*

cooperation Ac (also **co-operation** BrE) /kəʊˌɒpəˈreɪʃən $ koʊˌɑːp-/ n [U] 1 when you work with someone else to achieve something that you both want: **[+between]** *the need for* **close co-operation** *between East and West* | **in cooperation with sb** *The study was done in cooperation with local businesses.* 2 when you are helpful and do what someone wants: *No smoking. Thank you for your cooperation.*

cooperative¹ Ac (also **co-operative** BrE) /kəʊˈɒpərətɪv $ koʊˈɑːp-/ adj 1 willing to help SYN **helpful**: *She was very cooperative.* 2 done by people working together: *a cooperative effort* —**cooperatively** adv

cooperative² (also **co-operative** BrE) n [C] a business or organization owned equally by all the people working there

coordinate¹ Ac (also **co-ordinate** BrE) /kəʊˈɔːdəneɪt $ koʊˈɔːr-/ v 1 [T] to organize an activity so that people work together effectively: *We need to coordinate our efforts.* 2 [T] to make the parts of your body move well together: *Some children find it hard to coordinate their movements.* 3 [I,T] if clothes or colours coordinate, or if you coordinate them, they look nice together

coordinate² Ac (also **co-ordinate** BrE) /kəʊˈɔːdənət $ koʊˈɔːr-/ n [C] technical one of a set of numbers that give the exact position of a point on a map

coordination Ac (also **co-ordination** BrE) /kəʊˌɔːdəˈneɪʃən $ koʊˌɔːr-/ n [U] 1 the ability to make the different parts of your body do what you want: *Most sports will help to improve your coordination.* 2 the organization of people and things so that they work together well: **[+of]** *the coordination of military exercises*

coordinator Ac (also **co-ordinator** BrE) /kəʊˈɔːdəneɪtə $ koʊˈɔːrdəneɪtər/ n [C] someone who organizes the way people work together

cop /kɒp $ kɑːp/ n [C] informal a police officer

cope /kəʊp $ koʊp/ v [I] to succeed in dealing with everything you have to do, especially when it is very difficult: *Sometimes I just can't cope.* | **[+with]** *How does she cope with six kids?*

copier /'kɒpiə $ 'kɑːpiər/ n [C] a PHOTOCOPIER

copious /'kəʊpiəs $ 'koʊ-/ adj [only before noun] large in quantity: *She took* **copious notes.** —**copiously** adv

'cop-out n [C] informal something you do or say in order to avoid doing or accepting something: *He said he couldn't come because he was ill, but I think that was just a cop-out.*

copper /'kɒpə $ 'kɑːpər/ n 1 [U] a soft orange-brown metal 2 [C] BrE informal a police officer

copse /kɒps $ kɑːps/ n [C] a small group of trees or bushes

copy¹ /'kɒpi $ 'kɑːpi/ n [C] (plural **copies**) 1 a document, object etc that has been made to look exactly like the original one: **[+of]** *We'll need to see a copy of your birth certificate.* | *Always* **make copies** *of your files.* | *The chair is a copy of an original design.* 2 one of many books, magazines, CDs etc which have been produced: **[+of]** *Have you got a copy of today's paper?* | *Their album sold millions of copies.* → **CARBON COPY**

copy² v (**copied, copying, copies**) 1 [I,T] to make a document, object etc that is exactly the same as an earlier or original one: *Copy the letter and send it out.* | **copy (sth) from sth** *The design was copied from an 18th century wallpaper.* | **copy sth into/onto sth** *You can copy the file onto a floppy disk.* 2 [T] to do something that someone else has done, or behave like someone else: *Kids often copy what they see on TV.* 3 [I,T] to cheat by looking at someone's work and writing what they have written: *Stop copying me!* 4 (also **copy down/out**) [T] to write something exactly as it is written somewhere else: *I'd like you to copy down this poem.* | **copy sth into sth** *Here are some questions to copy into your books.*
PHRASAL VERBS
copy sb ↔ **in** to send someone a copy of an email message that you have written to someone else

copyright /'kɒpiraɪt $ 'kɑː-/ n [C,U] the legal right to be the only person or company that produces or sells a book, play, film etc —**copyright** adj

coral /'kɒrəl $ 'kɔː-, 'kɑː-/ n [U] a hard pink, white, or red substance formed from the bones of very small sea animals

cord /kɔːd $ kɔːrd/ n 1 [C,U] a piece of thick string

or thin rope **2** [C,U] wire covered with plastic for connecting equipment to a supply of electricity SYN **cable 3 cords** [plural] trousers made from COR-DUROY

cordial /'kɔːdiəl $ 'kɔːrdʒəl/ adj formal friendly and polite —**cordially** adv

cordless /'kɔːdləs $ 'kɔːrd-/ adj a cordless piece of equipment is not connected to its power supply by wires: a cordless phone

cordon¹ /'kɔːdn $ 'kɔːrdn/ n [C] a line of police or soldiers around an area to stop people going there: a police cordon

cordon² v
PHRASAL VERBS
cordon sth ↔ **off** to surround and protect an area with police or soldiers: Police cordoned off the street where the body was found.

corduroy /'kɔːdʒərɔɪ, -dʒə- $ 'kɔːrdə-/ n [U] thick strong cotton cloth with raised lines on it

core Ac /kɔː $ kɔːr/ n [C]
1 FRUIT the hard central part of an apple or PEAR → see picture on page A4
2 MAIN PART the most important or central part of something: **[+of]** Money is **at the core of** the problem. | **core beliefs/subjects/skills etc** Students have to study five core subjects.
3 PLANET the central part of the Earth or another PLANET → **HARDCORE**
PHRASES
to the core completely or extremely: The news shook me to the core.

coriander /ˌkɒri'ændə $ ˌkɔːri'ændər/ n [U] BrE a herb, used especially in Asian cooking SYN **cilantro** AmE

cork /kɔːk $ kɔːrk/ n **1** [U] material that comes from the BARK (=outer part) of a Mediterranean tree: cork floor tiles **2** [C] a small round piece of cork that is put into the top of a bottle to close it

corkscrew /'kɔːkskruː $ 'kɔːrk-/ n [C] the tool you use to pull a cork out of a bottle → see picture at OPENER

corn /kɔːn $ kɔːrn/ n
1 [U] BrE plants such as wheat, from which we get grain and seeds: fields of corn | an **ear of corn** (=the top part of the plant where seeds grow)
2 [U] AmE **a)** a tall plant with large yellow seeds SYN **maize** BrE **b)** the seeds of this plant eaten as food SYN **sweetcorn** BrE → see picture on page A5

corner¹ /'kɔːnə $ 'kɔːrnər/ n [C]
1 OF A PAGE/BED/SQUARE ETC the point at which two lines, edges, or walls meet: **[+of]** Fold the corner of the page. | **in the corner** a room with a piano in the corner | Click the icon in the top left-hand corner of the screen. | **on the corner** She sat on the corner of the bed.
2 OF A ROAD the place where two roads or streets meet: **[+of]** We walked to the corner of the street. | **on/at the corner** a hotel on the corner of 5th and Maine | Wait for me at the corner. | **around the corner** There's a bar just around the corner.
3 OF YOUR MOUTH/EYE the side of your mouth or eye: I saw him **out of the corner of my eye** (=without turning my head).

4 DIFFICULT SITUATION a difficult situation that you cannot easily escape from: **in/into a corner** She found herself in a **tight corner**. | He forced me **into a corner** and I had to accept.
5 FAR PLACE a place that is far away and not well known: **[+of]** She's gone to work in a **remote corner** of Africa.
6 IN SPORT (also **corner kick**) a kick that one team is allowed to take from a corner at their opponent's end of the field in soccer → **cut corners** at CUT¹

corner² v **1** [T] to force someone into a position from which they cannot easily escape: He cornered me and demanded an answer. **2** [I] if a car corners, it goes around a corner
PHRASES
corner the market to get total control of the supply of a particular type of goods: The company has cornered 98% of the fried chicken market.

'corner shop n [C] BrE a small shop near houses, that sells food, cigarettes, and other things needed every day

cornerstone /'kɔːnəstəʊn $ 'kɔːrnərstoʊn/ n [C] something that is very important because everything else depends on it: **[+of]** Trust is the cornerstone of any relationship.

cornet /'kɔːnɪt $ kɔːr'net/ n [C] **1** a musical instrument like a small TRUMPET **2** a sweet food that you put ICE CREAM in, and hold in your hand to eat SYN **cone** → see picture at CONE

cornflakes /'kɔːnfleɪks $ 'kɔːrn-/ n [plural] small flat pieces of corn, usually eaten at breakfast with milk

cornflour /'kɔːnflaʊə $ 'kɔːrnflaʊr/ BrE, **cornstarch** /'kɔːnstɑːtʃ $ 'kɔːrnstɑːrtʃ/ AmE n [U] a fine white flour made from corn, used in cooking

corny /'kɔːni $ 'kɔːrni/ adj informal very silly or repeated too often to be funny or interesting: corny jokes

coronary¹ /'kɒrənəri $ 'kɔːrəneri, 'kɑː-/ adj relating to the heart: coronary disease

coronary² n [C] (plural **coronaries**) a HEART ATTACK

coronation /ˌkɒrə'neɪʃən◂ $ ˌkɔːr-, ˌkɑː-/ n [C] an official ceremony in which someone is made a king or queen

coroner /'kɒrənə $ 'kɔːrənər, 'kɑː-/ n [C] an official whose job is to discover the cause of someone's death, especially when it is sudden or unusual

corporal /'kɔːpərəl $ 'kɔːr-/ n [C] a low rank in the army or AIR FORCE

corporal 'punishment n [U] punishment that involves hitting someone THESAURUS PUNISHMENT

corporate Ac /'kɔːpərət $ 'kɔːr-/ adj [only before noun] relating to a corporation or the people in it: Our corporate headquarters are in Houston. | corporate responsibilities

corporation Ac /ˌkɔːpə'reɪʃən $ ˌkɔːr-/ n [C] a large company or organization THESAURUS COMPANY

corps /kɔː $ kɔːr/ n [C] (plural **corps** /kɔːz $ kɔːrz/) **1** a group in an army, especially one with special duties: *the medical corps* **2** a group of people who do a particular job: *the press corps*

corpse /kɔːps $ kɔːrps/ *n* [C] a dead body

corpus /'kɔːpəs $ 'kɔːr-/ *n* [C] (*plural* **corpuses** or **corpora** /-pərə/) *technical* a large collection of written or spoken language, used for studying the language

corral /kəˈrɑːl $ kəˈræl/ *n* [C] an enclosed area for cattle or horses, especially in the US

correct¹ /kəˈrekt/ *adj*
1 right or without any mistakes [SYN] **right** [OPP] **incorrect**: *He gave the **correct answer**.* | *'Is your name Ives?' 'Yes, that's correct.'* [THESAURUS] RIGHT
2 suitable for a particular situation: *Hold the wheel in the correct position.* → **POLITICALLY CORRECT**
—**correctly** *adv*: *Have you spelled it correctly?* —**correctness** *n* [U]

correct² *v* [T]
1 to make something right or make it work the way it should: *Please correct the mistakes in your homework.* | *Most eyesight problems are easy to correct.*
2 to tell or show someone what mistakes they have made: *He always corrects my pronunciation.*

correction /kəˈrekʃən/ *n* [C,U] a change that makes something right or better, or when you change something in this way: *She **made** a few **corrections** to the text.*

corrective /kəˈrektɪv/ *adj* formal intended to make something right or better: *corrective lenses*

correlate /'kɒrəleɪt $ 'kɔː-, 'kɑː-/ *v* [I,T] if two or more facts, ideas etc correlate or if you correlate them, they are closely connected to each other or one causes the other: [+with] *Poverty and poor housing correlate with a shorter life expectancy.*

correlation /ˌkɒrəˈleɪʃən $ ˌkɔː-, ˌkɑː-/ *n* [C,U] a connection between two things, especially when one causes the other: [+between] *There is a correlation between poverty and ill health.*

correspond [Ac] /ˌkɒrəˈspɒnd $ ˌkɔːrəˈspɑːnd, ˌkɑː-/ *v* [I] **1** if two things correspond, they are the same or very similar: *The text and the pictures don't seem to correspond.* | [+with/to] *The French 'baccalauréat' exam corresponds to British 'A levels'.* **2** if two people correspond, they write letters to each other

correspondence [Ac] /ˌkɒrəˈspɒndəns $ ˌkɔːrəˈspɑːn-, ˌkɑː-/ *n* **1** [U] letters that people write, or the activity of writing and getting letters: *She keeps all her correspondence.* | *Their correspondence continued for years.* **2** [C] a relationship or connection between two things: *There's a **close correspondence** between their accounts.*

corre'spondence ˌcourse *n* [C] a course of lessons in which the student works at home and sends completed work to their teacher by post

correspondent /ˌkɒrəˈspɒndənt $ ˌkɔːrəˈspɑːn-, ˌkɑː-/ *n* [C] someone whose job is to report news from a particular area or on a particular subject: *Here's our sports correspondent.*

corresponding [Ac] /ˌkɒrəˈspɒndɪŋ◂ $ ˌkɔːrəˈspɑːn-, ˌkɑː-/ *adj* [only before noun] relating or similar to

something else: *Sales are up 10% on the corresponding period last year.* —**correspondingly** *adv*

corridor /'kɒrɪdɔː $ 'kɔːrədər, 'kɑː-/ *n* [C] a long narrow area between two rows of rooms: **in the corridor** *Please wait in the corridor.* | **along/down the corridor** *Her office is just down the corridor.*

corroborate /kəˈrɒbəreɪt $ kəˈrɑː-/ *v* [T] *formal* to provide information that supports or proves someone's statement: *We have new evidence to corroborate her story.* —**corroboration** /kəˌrɒbəˈreɪʃən $ -ˌrɑː-/ *n* [U]

corrode /kəˈrəʊd $ -ˈroʊd/ *v* [I,T] if metal corrodes, or if water, chemicals etc corrode it, it is slowly destroyed: *Many of the pipes have corroded.*

corrosion /kəˈrəʊʒən $ -ˈroʊ-/ *n* [U] the gradual destruction of metal by water, chemicals etc —**corrosive** /-sɪv/ *adj*: *highly corrosive chemicals*

corrugated /'kɒrəgeɪtɪd $ 'kɔː-, 'kɑː-/ *adj* **corrugated iron/cardboard** iron etc that is made in the shape of waves or folds

corrupt¹ /kəˈrʌpt/ *adj* **1** dishonest or immoral: *corrupt judges* | *a corrupt political system* [THESAURUS] **DISHONEST 2** computer information that is corrupt has been damaged and spoiled

corrupt² *v* **1** [I,T] to make someone dishonest or immoral: *Power can corrupt.* | *films that corrupt people's minds* **2** [T] to damage the information on a computer so that it does not work properly: *Somehow the file got corrupted.*

corruption /kəˈrʌpʃən/ *n* [U] dishonest or immoral behaviour, especially by people with power: *Two officials were charged with corruption.*

corset /'kɔːsɪt $ 'kɔːr-/ *n* [C] a piece of tight underwear worn by women to make them look thinner, especially in the past

cos /kəz/ *linking word BrE spoken informal* because

cosmetic /kɒzˈmetɪk $ kɑːz-/ *adj* **1** intended to make your skin or body more beautiful: *cosmetic products* | **cosmetic surgery** (=medical operations to improve the way you look) **2** involving only small unimportant changes, instead of more important ones: **cosmetic changes** *to the law*

cosmetics /kɒzˈmetɪks $ kɑːz-/ *n* [plural] creams, powders etc that you use to make your face and body more attractive

cosmic /'kɒzmɪk $ 'kɑːz-/ *adj* relating to space or the universe

cosmonaut /'kɒzmənɔːt $ 'kɑːzmənɒːt/ *n* [C] an ASTRONAUT from the former Soviet Union

cosmopolitan /ˌkɒzməˈpɒlətən◂ $ ˌkɑːzməˈpɑː-/ *adj* **1** a cosmopolitan place has people from many different parts of the world: *a vibrant, cosmopolitan city* **2** a cosmopolitan person, attitude etc shows a lot of experience of different people and places

cosmos /'kɒzmɒs $ 'kɑːzməs/ *n* **the cosmos** the whole universe

cost¹ /kɒst $ kɒːst/ *n*
1 [C,U] the amount of money that you have to pay in order to buy or do something: [+of] *the high cost of accommodation in London* | **at a cost (of sth)** *We repaired the roof at a cost of £15,000.* | *Baby seats are*

available **at no extra cost**. | **running/living/travel etc costs** *The car has very low running costs.* | **the cost of living** (=the amount of money you need to spend on things like food and clothes)

2 [singular] what you have to lose, give away etc in order to achieve something else: **[+to]** *The cost to the environment was high.* | *He saved his career, but at what cost to his marriage?* | **at all costs/at any cost** (=whatever you have to do to achieve something) *We must avoid a scandal at all costs.*

3 (*also* **cost price**) [singular, U] *especially AmE* the price that someone paid for something they are going to sell: *Her uncle let her have the car at cost.*

PHRASES

find/know/learn etc sth to your cost to know or find out about something because of an unpleasant experience: *Motor racing is a dangerous sport, as many drivers have discovered to their cost.*

THESAURUS

cost the amount of money that you have to pay in order to buy or do something: *The cost of fuel keeps going up.* | *Companies are always looking at ways of cutting costs.*

price the amount of money that someone wants you to pay for something: *Their prices are much lower than other supermarkets.* | *Can you ask him to lower the price?* | *How much is the price of a plane ticket to New York?*

value the amount of money that something is worth: *The value of your shares can go down as well as up.*

charge the amount that you have to pay for a service or to use something: *There is a small charge for using the Internet in your hotel room.* | *bank charges*

fee the amount you have to pay to enter a place or join a group, or for the services of a professional person such as a lawyer or doctor: *The entrance fee is £5.* | *Lawyers' fees can be very expensive.*

fare the amount you have to pay to travel somewhere by bus, plane, train etc: *How much is the train fare from London to Paris?*

cost² *v* (*past tense and past participle* **cost**)
1 [linking verb] to have a particular price: *This dress cost $75.* | *How much did your computer cost?* | **cost sb sth** *A first class ticket will cost you a lot.* | **it costs sth to do sth** *It costs £6 to get into the museum.* | **cost (sb) a fortune/a bomb** *The meal cost a fortune.* | **not cost (sb) a penny/a thing** *A kind word doesn't cost you a thing.*
2 [T] to make someone lose something important: **cost sb sth** *That one mistake cost him his life.*
3 [T] (*past tense and past participle* **costed**) to calculate how much money is needed to pay for something: *Have you costed your proposals?*

co-star¹ /ˈkəʊ stɑː $ ˈkoʊ stɑːr/ *n* [C] one of two or more famous actors who appear together in a film or play **THESAURUS** ACTOR

co-star² *v* [I] (**co-starred**, **co-starring**) to be working in a film or play with other famous actors: **[+with/in]** *Penelope Cruz co-starred with Tom Cruise.*

cost-ˌcutting *n* [U] the things which a company or organization does in order to reduce its costs: *As part of a cost-cutting exercise, the company is reducing its workforce by 60 jobs.*

ˌcost efˈfective, cost-effective *adj* producing the best profits or advantages at the lowest cost: *a cost-effective solution*

costly /ˈkɒstli $ ˈkɒːstli/ *adj* **1** costing a lot of money **SYN** **expensive**: *a costly procedure* **2** causing a lot of problems: *The mistake proved costly.*

costume /ˈkɒstjʊm $ ˈkɑːstuːm/ *n* [C,U] **1** a set of clothes worn by an actor, or to make someone look like a particular type of person, animal etc → **outfit**: *the costumes for 'Hamlet'* | *She wore a rabbit costume.* **THESAURUS** CLOTHES **2** clothes that are typical of a particular country or time in the past: **in costume** | *dancers in national costume* → SWIMMING COSTUME

cosy *BrE*, **cozy** *AmE* /ˈkəʊzi $ ˈkoʊzi/ *adj* warm and comfortable: *a cosy bed* **THESAURUS** COMFORTABLE

cot /kɒt $ kɑːt/ *n* [C] **1** *BrE* a small bed with high sides for a young child **SYN** **crib** *AmE* → see picture at BED **2** *AmE* a CAMP BED → see picture at BED

ˈcot ˌdeath *n* [C] *BrE* the sudden, unexpected, and unexplained death of a baby while it is sleeping **SYN** **crib death** *AmE*

cottage /ˈkɒtɪdʒ $ ˈkɑː-/ *n* [C] a small house in the country, especially an old one: *a country cottage* | *holiday cottages* → see picture at HOUSE¹ **THESAURUS** HOUSE

ˌcottage ˈcheese / $ ˈ.../ *n* [U] soft white cheese

ˌcottage ˈindustry *n* [C] an industry that consists of people working at home

cotton¹ /ˈkɒtn $ ˈkɑːtn/ *n* [U]
1 cloth or thread made from the cotton plant: *a cotton shirt* | *a reel of black cotton* (=thread used for sewing)
2 a plant with white hairs used for making cotton cloth and thread
3 *AmE* a soft mass of cotton, used especially for cleaning your skin **SYN** **cotton wool** *BrE* → see picture at PAD¹

cotton² *v*
PHRASAL VERBS
cotton on *informal* to begin to understand something **SYN** **realize**: **[+to]** *I soon cottoned on to what he was doing.*

ˌcotton ˈwool *n* [U] *BrE* a soft mass of cotton, used for cleaning the skin, wounds etc **SYN** **cotton** *AmE* → see picture at PAD¹

couch¹ /kaʊtʃ/ *n* [C] a long comfortable piece of furniture on which you can sit or lie

couch² *v* **be couched in sth** to be expressed in a particular way: *His refusal was couched in polite terms.*

ˈcouch poˌtato *n* [C] *humorous* someone who spends a lot of time sitting and watching television

cough¹ /kɒf $ kɔːf/ v [I]
if you cough, air suddenly comes out of your throat with a short loud sound, for example because you are ill: *He was awake coughing all night.*

COUGH

PHRASAL VERBS

cough up

1 *informal* to give someone money, information etc when you do not really want to: *Come on, cough up!* | **cough sth ↔ up** *I had to cough up £200 for a new printer.*

2 cough sth ↔ up if you cough up a substance such as blood, it comes from your lungs or throat into your mouth when you cough

cough² n [C]

1 when someone coughs, or the sound of someone coughing: *I heard a loud cough behind me.*

2 an illness that makes you cough: *Amy has a bad cough.*

> **COLLOCATIONS - sense 2**
>
> **verbs**
>
> **to have (got) a cough** *I felt ill and I had a cough.*
>
> **to get/catch a cough** *She often gets colds and coughs.*
>
> **adjectives**
>
> **a bad/nasty cough** *He was absent from school with a bad cough.*
>
> **a slight cough** (also **a bit of a cough** *spoken*) *He has a slight cough but I don't think he's really ill.*

could /kəd; *strong* kʊd/ *modal verb* (*negative short form* **couldn't**)

1 used as the past tense of 'can' to say what someone was able to do or was allowed to do in the past: *She said she couldn't find it.* | *The teacher said we could all go home.* | **sb could see/hear etc sth** (=saw, heard etc sth on a particular occasion) *I could hear laughter.*

2 a) used to say that something is possible or might happen: *Most accidents in the home could be prevented.* | *You could be right, I suppose.* | *It could be weeks before we get a reply.* **THESAURUS** **MAYBE** **b)** used to say that something was possible in the past, but did not actually happen: *She could have been killed.*

3 *spoken* used to make a polite request: *Could I ask you a couple of questions?* | *Could you open the window?*

4 used to suggest doing something: *You could try calling his office.* | *We could always stop and ask directions.*

5 *spoken* used to emphasize how happy, angry etc you are by saying how you want to express your feelings: *I was so angry I could have killed her.*

couldn't /ˈkʊdnt/ the short form of 'could not'

could've /ˈkʊdəv/ the short form of 'could have'

council /ˈkaʊnsəl/ n [C]

1 the organization that is responsible for local government in a particular area: *Northampton Borough Council* | **local council** *elections*

2 a group of people who make rules, laws, or decisions, or give advice: *the UN Security Council*

3 council house/flat a house or flat in Britain that is provided by the local council for a very low rent: *There's a shortage of council houses in the area.*

ˈcouncil esˌtate n [C] *BrE* an area in a town or city with streets of council houses

councillor *BrE*, **councilor** *AmE* /ˈkaʊnsələ $ -ər/ n [C] a member of a council

counsel¹ /ˈkaʊnsəl/ v [T] (**counselled, counselling** *BrE*, **counseled, counseling** *AmE*) to advise or support someone who has problems: *a new unit to counsel alcoholics* —**counselling** n [U]: *a counselling service for drug users* —**counsellor** n [C]: *a marriage counsellor*

counsel² n [U] **1** a lawyer who speaks for someone in court: *counsel for the prosecution* **2** *literary* advice

count¹ /kaʊnt/ v

1 CALCULATE (*also* **count up**) [T] to try to find out how many people or things there are in a group: *It took hours to count all the votes.*

2 SAY NUMBERS [I] to say numbers in the correct order: *Can you count in Japanese?*

3 CONSIDER AS [T] to think of someone or something in a particular way: **count sb/sth as sth** *I've always counted Rob as one of my best friends.* | *You should* **count** *yourself* **lucky** *that you weren't hurt.*

4 BE IMPORTANT [I] to be important or valuable: **[+for]** *First impressions count for a lot.*

5 BE ALLOWED [I] to be allowed or accepted: *You cheated, so your score doesn't count.*

6 INCLUDE [T] to include someone or something in a total: *There are five in our family, counting me.*

PHRASES

> **count me in/out** *spoken* used to say that you want to be involved in something or do not want to be involved: *I don't want to go anywhere this evening - so count me out.*
>
> **don't count your chickens (before they're hatched)** *spoken* used to say that you should not make plans that depend on something good happening, because it might not: *You'll probably get the job, but don't count your chickens just yet.*

PHRASAL VERBS

count on sb/sth

1 to depend on someone or something: *You can always count on Doug in a crisis.*

2 to expect something: *We hadn't counted on so many people coming.*

count sth ↔ **out** to put things down one by one as you count them: *He counted out ten $50 bills.*

count² n [C] **1** the process of counting, or the total that you get when you count things: *Hold your breath for a count of ten.* **2** one of the crimes that the police say someone is guilty of: *Davis was found not guilty on all counts.* **3** a European man with a high social rank → HEAD COUNT, POLLEN COUNT

PHRASES

> **lose count (of sth)** to forget how many there are of something: *There have been so many accidents here, the police have lost count.*

on all/several/both etc counts in every way, in several ways etc: *We were proved wrong on both counts.*

countable /ˈkaʊntəbəl/ *adj* a countable noun has both a singular and a plural form OPP **uncountable**

countdown /ˈkaʊntdaʊn/ *n* [C usually singular] **1** when numbers are counted backwards to zero before something happens: **[+to]** *the countdown to lift-off* **2** the period before an important event happens, when it gets closer and closer: **[+to]** *the countdown to the World Cup*

countenance¹ /ˈkaʊntənəns/ *n* [C] *literary* your face

countenance² *v* [T] *formal* to accept, support, or approve of something SYN **tolerate**

counter¹ /ˈkaʊntə $ -ər/ *n* [C]
1 the place where you pay or are served in a shop, bank etc: *He wondered if the girl **behind the counter** recognised him.*
2 *AmE* a flat surface in the kitchen where you prepare food SYN **worktop** *BrE* → see picture at KITCHEN
3 a small round object used in some games that are played on a board → OVER-THE-COUNTER

counter² *v* [T] **1** to do something in order to prevent something bad from happening or to reduce its bad effects: *efforts to counter inflation* **2** to say something to show that what someone has just said is not true: *'That's not what the statistics show,' she countered.*

counter³ *adv* **run/be counter to sth** *formal* to be the opposite of something: *ideas that run counter to the Church's traditional view of marriage*

counter- /ˈkaʊntə $ -tər/ *prefix* **1** the opposite of something: *counter-productive* **2** done as a reaction to something or to oppose something: *The men made a counter-claim against the police.*

counteract /ˌkaʊntərˈækt/ *v* [T] to reduce or prevent the bad effect of something, by doing something that has the opposite effect: *Try relaxation exercises to counteract the effects of stress.*

counterattack /ˈkaʊntərəˌtæk/ *n* [C] an attack that you make against someone who has attacked you, in a sport, war, or argument —**counterattack** *v* [I]

counterbalance /ˌkaʊntəˈbæləns $ -tər-/ *v* [T] to have an equal and opposite effect to something else: *Riskier investments tend to be counterbalanced by high rewards.* —**counterbalance** /ˈkaʊntəˌbæləns $ -tər-/ *n* [C]

counterclockwise /ˌkaʊntəˈklɒkwaɪz $ -tərˈklɑːk-/ *adj, adv AmE* ANTICLOCKWISE OPP **clockwise**

counterfeit /ˈkaʊntəfɪt $ -tər-/ *adj* made to look exactly like the real thing in order to deceive people: *counterfeit money* THESAURUS FALSE —**counterfeit** *v* [T]

counterpart /ˈkaʊntəpɑːt $ -tərpɑːrt/ *n* [C] a person or thing that has the same job or purpose as someone or something else in a different place: *Belgian officials are discussing the matter with their French counterparts.*

counterproductive, **counter-productive** /ˌkaʊntəprəˈdʌktɪv $ -tər-/ *adj* causing the opposite result to the one you want: *Punishing children can be counterproductive.*

countersign /ˈkaʊntəsaɪn $ -ər-/ *v* [T] to sign a paper that has already been signed by someone else: *Your doctor should countersign the form.*

countess /ˈkaʊntɪs/ *n* [C] a European woman with a high social rank

countless /ˈkaʊntləs/ *adj* [only before noun] very many: *a drug that has saved countless lives*

country¹ /ˈkʌntri/ *n* (*plural* **countries**)
1 [C] an area of land that is controlled by its own government, president, king etc → **nation**: *Russia is the largest country in the world.*
2 **the country** land that is away from towns and cities SYN **countryside**: *I've always lived in the country.*
3 **the country** all the people who live in a country: *a government that has the support of the country*
4 [U] a type of land: *mountainous country*

COLLOCATIONS

adjectives

a foreign country *He was in a foreign country, and he was lost.*
a European/African/Asian etc country *In many African countries, the radio is the most popular source of news.*
a rich/poor country *We live in one of the richest countries in the world.*
a developing country (=poor and trying to increase its industry and trade) *Bangladesh is a developing country in South East Asia.*
a developed/industrialized country (=rich and with a lot of industry) *This disease is now rare in developed countries.*

noun + country

your home country (=where you were born or live permanently) *These people have been forced to leave their home country.*

verbs

to visit a country *She had always wanted to visit other countries.*
to run/govern a country *Is he the right person to run the country?*
to represent your country *Her ambition was to represent her country at swimming.*

THESAURUS

country an area of land controlled by its own government, president, king etc: *Brazil is one of the biggest countries in the world.*
nation a country, its people, and its political or economic system: *The events shocked the whole nation.* | *leaders of the world's most powerful nations*
superpower one of the most powerful countries in the world: *China is now an economic superpower.*
land written a country – used in stories: *The princess lived in a faraway land.*

country² *adj* [only before noun] in or relating to the countryside SYN **rural** OPP **urban**: *country people | country roads*

'country ,club *n* [C] a sports and social club, especially one for rich people

,country 'house *n* [C] *BrE* a large house in the countryside, especially one that is old and interesting

countryman /'kʌntrimən/ *n* [C] (*plural* **countrymen** /-mən/) someone from your own country

'country ,music (*also* ,**country and 'western**) *n* [U] a type of music from the southern and western US

countryside /'kʌntrisaɪd/ *n* [U] the area that is not near big towns and cities: *the beauty of the English countryside | open countryside*

county /'kaʊnti/ *n* [C] (*plural* **counties**) an area of a state or country that has its own local government

coup /kuː/ *n* [C] **1** (*also* **coup d'état** /ˌkuː deɪˈtɑː $ -deˈtɑː/) when a group of people suddenly take control of a country, especially by using force: *a military coup* **2** [usually singular] an impressive achievement: *Winning that contract was a real coup.*

couple¹ Ac /'kʌpəl/ *n*
1 [C] two people who are married or have a romantic relationship: *the couple next door | married couples*
2 a couple two or a few: [+of] *There were a couple of kids in the back of the car. | I'll be ready in a couple of minutes.*

couple² Ac *v* **coupled with sth** together with something: *Low rainfall coupled with high temperatures destroyed the crops.*

coupon /'kuːpɒn $ -pɑːn/ *n* [C] **1** a small piece of printed paper that gives you the right to pay less for something or get something free: *a coupon for 30 pence off a jar of coffee* **2** a printed form, used when you order something, enter a competition etc

courage /'kʌrɪdʒ $ 'kɜːr-/ *n* [U] the quality you have when you do not let fear affect you in a frightening situation SYN **bravery** OPP **cowardice**: *She showed great courage throughout her illness. | Driving again after his accident must have taken a lot of courage. |* **the courage to do sth** *He did not have the courage to tell Nicola that he was leaving her.* —**courageous** /kəˈreɪdʒəs/ *adj: a courageous decision* —**courageously** *adv* → **pluck up (the) courage (to do sth)** at PLUCK¹

courgette /kʊəˈʒet $ kʊr-/ *n* [C] *BrE* a long vegetable with a dark green skin SYN **zucchini** *AmE* → see picture on page A5

courier /'kʊriə $ -ər/ *n* [C] someone whose job is to deliver documents and packages

course¹ /kɔːs $ kɔːrs/ *n*
1 LESSONS [C] a series of lessons or a period of study in a particular subject SYN **class** *AmE*: *Andy's doing a computer course. |* [+in/on] *a degree course in engineering*
2 PART OF MEAL [C] one of the parts of a meal: *a three-course meal | the main course*
3 WAY STH DEVELOPS [singular] the way that something develops or happens: [+of] *events that changed the course of history | run/take its course*

(=develop in the usual way) *You'll just have to let things take their course.*
4 THING TO DO [C] something that you can do to deal with a situation: *The best course of action would be to speak to her privately.*
5 MEDICINE course of treatment/antibiotics etc *especially BrE* medicine or medical treatment that someone has regularly for a period of time
6 DIRECTION [C,U] the planned direction taken by a boat or plane to reach a place: *The plane changed course to avoid the storm. |* **on/off course** (=going in the right or wrong direction) *The ship was blown off course.*
7 FOR SPORTS [C] an area of land or water where races are held, or an area of land designed for playing golf: *a race course | an 18-hole course* → CRASH COURSE, **in due course** at DUE¹, **as a matter of course** at MATTER¹

PHRASES

in/during/over the course of sth during a period of time or a process: *During the course of our conversation, I found out that he had worked in France.*
in the course of time after some time passes: *The situation will improve in the course of time.*
of course *spoken* **1** used to show that what you are saying is expected or already known and so not surprising: *Of course there are exceptions to every rule. | The insurance has to be renewed every year, of course.* **2** used to say yes very strongly or to give permission politely: *'Can I borrow your notes?' 'Of course you can.'*
of course not *spoken* used to say no very strongly: *'Do you mind if I'm a bit late?' 'Of course not.'*
be on course (for sth/to do sth) to be likely to achieve something because you have already had some success: *Hodson is on course to break the world record.*

COLLOCATIONS

verbs

to take a course (*also* **to do a course** *BrE*) *I'm doing a Spanish course.* ⚠ Do not say 'make a course'. Say **take a course** or **do a course**.
to go on a course *BrE You should go on a first aid course.*
to pass/fail a course *You need to attend 60% of classes to pass the course.*
to teach a course (*also* **to give a course**) *She is teaching a course in Art and Design.*

types of course

a language/art/computer etc course *His company sent him on a computer course.*
a training course *She decided to do a management training course.*
a college/university course *He dropped out of his college course.*
a full-time/part-time course *You can do the diploma as a part-time course.*

---

course² *v* [I] *literary* to flow quickly: [+down/through] *Tears coursed down her cheeks.*

coursebook /'kɔːsbʊk $ 'kɔːrs-/ *n* [C] *BrE* a book that students use regularly during a set of lessons on a particular subject THESAURUS ▸ BOOK

coursework /'kɔːswɜːk $ 'kɔːrswɜːrk/ n [U] work that students do during a course of study, rather than in examinations, and that forms part of their final mark

court¹ /kɔːt $ kɔːrt/ n

1 LAW [C,U] the people who make a legal judgment, for example about whether someone is guilty of a crime, or the place where these judgments are made: *the European Court of Justice* | *The court decided that West was guilty.* | *a court of law* | *The court case lasted six weeks.* | *If they don't pay, we'll take them to court* (=bring a legal case against them). | *He will appear in court today, charged with murder.*

2 SPORTS [C] an area made for playing games such as tennis: *a squash court* | *on court The players are due on court in an hour.* → see picture on page A9

3 KING/QUEEN [C] **a)** the place where a king or queen lives and works: *the royal courts of Europe* **b)** the king or queen, their family, and their friends, advisers etc: *Court officials denied the rumours.*

COLLOCATIONS

verbs

to go to court (=to take legal action) *The costs of going to court are very high.*

to take sb to court (=to take legal action against someone) *She took the company to court for sex discrimination.*

to appear in court *A man has appeared in court charged with cruelty to animals.*

a court hears a case (=a case is presented to the court for a decision) *The court will hear the case next month.*

court + noun

a court case (=a problem or crime that is dealt with in a court of law) *a recent court case involving the death of a baby*

a court of law *You may be asked to give evidence before a court of law.*

types of court

a High Court (=an important court, with more power than an ordinary court) *Their convictions were upheld in the High Court.*

the Supreme Court (=the most important court in some countries or US states) *The Supreme Court ruled in his favor.*

a magistrates' court (=a local court which deals with less serious crimes) *His case will be heard in the magistrates' court.*

---

court² v **1** [T] to try to please someone so that they will support you: *Both parties are courting young voters.* **2** be courting if a man and woman are courting, they are having a romantic relationship and may get married **3** court disaster/danger to do something that is likely to have very unpleasant results

courteous /'kɜːtiəs $ 'kɜːr-/ adj formal very polite OPP **discourteous** THESAURUS ► POLITE —**courteously** adv

courtesy /'kɜːtəsi $ 'kɜːr-/ n (plural **courtesies**) **1** [U] polite behaviour: *She didn't even have the*

courtesy to apologize. **2 courtesies** [plural] things that you say or do to be polite in formal situations: *The President was exchanging courtesies with his guests.*

PHRASES

| **courtesy of sb** used to say in a grateful way who provided or did something for you: *The winner will receive three CDs, courtesy of Hyperion Records.*

courthouse /'kɔːthaʊs $ 'kɔːrt-/ n [C] a building containing courts of law and government offices

courtier /'kɔːtɪə $ 'kɔːrtɪr/ n [C] someone in the past with an important position at a royal court

court 'martial /$ '. ,../ n [C] a military court or an occasion when a soldier is judged by a military court —**court-martial** v [T]

courtroom /'kɔːtruːm, -rʊm $ 'kɔːrt-/ n [C] a room in a law court where cases are judged

courtship /'kɔːt-ʃɪp $ 'kɔːrt-/ n [C,U] old-fashioned when a man and woman are having a romantic relationship before marrying

courtyard /'kɔːtjɑːd $ 'kɔːrtjɑːrd/ n [C] an open space surrounded by walls or buildings

cousin /'kʌzən/ n [C] a child of your AUNT or UNCLE: *Jane and I are cousins.* | **first cousin** (=a cousin)

cove /kəʊv $ koʊv/ n [C] part of the coast where a small area of sea is partly surrounded by land → **bay**

cover¹ /'kʌvə $ -ər/ v [T]

1 PUT STH OVER STH (also **cover up**) to put something over the top of something else to protect, close, or hide it OPP **uncover**: *Cover the pan and let the sauce simmer.* | *Cover the furniture up before you start painting.* | **cover sth with sth** *Dan covered his face with his hands.* | *tables covered with clean white cloths*

2 FORM A LAYER if something covers a surface, it forms a layer over it: *Snow covered the ground.* | **be covered in/with sth** *Your boots are covered in mud!*

3 INCLUDE to include or deal with something: *The course covers all aspects of business.*

4 PAY FOR to be enough money to pay for something: *The award should be enough to cover her college fees.* | *Will $200 cover the cost of textbooks?*

5 TRAVEL to travel a particular distance: *We had covered 20 kilometres by lunchtime.* | *A leopard can cover a lot of ground very quickly.*

6 AREA used to say how big a town, forest etc is: *The city covers an area of 20 square kilometres.*

7 INSURANCE if your insurance covers you or your possessions, it promises to pay you money if you have an accident, something is stolen etc: **cover sb against/for sth** *This policy covers you against accident or injury.*

8 REPORT to report the details of an event for a newspaper, television, or radio: *I'd just returned from covering the Cambodian war.*

9 WITH A GUN to aim a gun somewhere to protect someone from being attacked or to prevent someone from escaping: *Police officers covered the back entrance.*

PHRASAL VERBS

cover for sb

1 to do someone else's work because they are ill or

are somewhere else: *I'll be covering for Sandra next week.*
2 to prevent someone from getting into trouble by lying for them, especially about where they are or what they are doing

cover sth ↔ **up** to prevent people from discovering a mistake or an unpleasant fact: *The whole thing was covered up and never reached the papers.* **THESAURUS** HIDE

cover² n

1 FOR PUTTING OVER STH [C] something that is put on top of or around something else to protect it: *a cushion cover*

2 OF A BOOK/MAGAZINE [C] the outer front or back part of a book, magazine etc: **front/back cover** *His picture was on the front cover of 'Newsweek'.* | *I read the book from cover to cover.*

3 INSURANCE [U] *BrE* the protection your insurance gives you, so that it pays you money if you are injured, something is stolen etc **SYN** coverage *AmE*: *temporary medical cover* | **[+for/against]** *cover against fire and theft*

4 SHELTER [U] protection from bad weather or attack: *We took cover under a tree.* | *Everyone ran for cover when the shooting started.*

5 DECEIVING [singular] something that is used to hide what someone is really doing, especially because it is illegal: **[+for]** *The company is just a cover for the Mafia.* | *I wasn't sure they would believe my cover story.*

6 ON A BED **the covers** [plural] the sheets etc that are over you when you are in bed → UNDERCOVER

coverage /ˈkʌvərɪdʒ/ *n* [U] **1** when a subject or event is reported on television or radio, or in newspapers: **media/press coverage** *Her death attracted widespread media coverage.* **2** the range of subjects and facts included in a book, website, class etc: **[+of]** *Dunn's website provides good coverage of the subject.* **3** *AmE* the protection your insurance gives you **SYN** cover *BrE*

coveralls /ˈkʌvərɔːlz $ -ɔːrlz/ *n* [plural] *AmE* OVERALLS

covering /ˈkʌvərɪŋ/ *n* [singular] something that covers or hides something: **[+of]** *a light covering of snow*

covering ˈletter *BrE*, **ˈcover ˌletter** *AmE n* [C] a letter that you send with a document or package, which gives more information about it

covert /ˈkʌvət, ˈkəʊvɜːt $ ˈkoʊvərt/ *adj* secret or hidden: *covert operations* —**covertly** *adv*

ˈcover-up *n* [C] an attempt to prevent the public from discovering the truth about something: *CIA officials denied there had been a cover-up.*

ˈcover ˌversion *n* [C] a new recording of a song that was originally recorded by a different person or group

covet /ˈkʌvɪt/ *v* [T] *literary* to want something very much, especially something that someone else has —**coveted** *adj*: *The FA Cup is the most coveted prize in English football.*

cow¹ /kaʊ/ *n* [C] a large animal that is kept on farms and used to produce milk or meat → **bull**: *dairy cows* | *a herd of cows* → see picture on page A3

PHRASES
till the cows come home forever – used when saying that something takes too long: *We can talk about this till the cows come home, but we're never going to agree.*

cow² *v* [T] to frighten someone in order to make them do something: *The children were cowed into obedience.*

coward /ˈkaʊəd $ -ərd/ *n* [C] someone who is not at all brave: *They called me a coward because I wouldn't fight.* —**cowardly** *adj*: *a cowardly thing to do*

cowardice /ˈkaʊədɪs $ -ər-/ *n* [U] a lack of courage **OPP** bravery

cowboy /ˈkaʊbɔɪ/ *n* [C] **1** in the US, a man who rides a horse and whose job is to look after cattle **2** *BrE informal* someone whose work is bad or who is dishonest in business: *cowboy builders*

cower /ˈkaʊə $ -ər/ *v* [I] to bend low and move back because you are frightened: *The hostages were cowering in a corner.*

co-worker /ˌkəʊ ˈwɜːkə $ ˌkoʊ ˌwɜːrkər/ *n* [C] someone who you work with → **colleague**

coy /kɔɪ/ *adj* **1** shy or pretending to be shy in order to attract people's interest: *a coy smile* **2** not wanting to tell people about something: *Tania was always coy about her age.* —**coyly** *adv*

coyote /ˈkɔɪ.əʊt, kɔɪˈəʊti $ ˈkaɪ.oʊt, kaɪˈoʊti/ *n* [C] a small wild dog that lives in Northwest America and Mexico

cozy /ˈkəʊzi $ ˈkoʊ-/ *adj* the American spelling of COSY **THESAURUS** COMFORTABLE

crab /kræb/ *n* [C,U] a sea animal with a round flat shell and ten legs, the front two of which have PINCERS on them, or the meat from this animal

crack¹ /kræk/ v

1 BREAK [I,T] if something cracks or is cracked, it breaks so that it gets a line on its surface, and may then break into pieces: *The ice was starting to crack.* | *cracked plates* | *He cracked a couple of eggs into a pan.* **THESAURUS** BREAK

2 HIT [T] to hit someone or something hard: **crack sth on/against sth** *She fell and cracked her head on the step.*

3 SOLVE [T] *informal* to find the answer to a difficult problem **SYN** solve: *Yes! I've finally cracked it!* | *This new evidence could help detectives to crack the case.*

4 TOO MUCH PRESSURE [I] to become unable to deal with a situation because there is too much pressure on you: *She was beginning to crack under the strain of trying to do two jobs.*

5 SUDDEN SOUND [I,T] to make a sudden sharp sound, or to make something do this: *He cracked his knuckles.* | *Thunder cracked overhead.*

PHRASES
crack a joke *informal* to tell a joke: *He kept cracking jokes about my new haircut.*

get cracking *BrE spoken* to start doing something or going somewhere quickly: *It's late, so we'd better get cracking.*

not all it's cracked up to be not as good as people think: *Life as a model isn't all it's cracked up to be.*

PHRASAL VERBS

crack down to become more strict in dealing with a problem and punishing the people involved: **[+on]** *The police are **cracking down hard** on violent crime.*
crack up *informal*
1 to become mentally ill because you have a lot of problems
2 to start laughing

crack² *n*

1 PLACE WHERE STH IS BROKEN [C] a thin line on the surface of something when it is broken but has not actually come apart: *A huge crack had appeared in the ceiling.*
2 WEAKNESS [C] a weakness or fault in a system, relationship etc, which will cause problems later: **[+in]** *The cracks in their relationship were starting to show.*
3 SPACE [C] a very narrow space between two things or two parts of something: **[+in]** *a crack in the curtains*
4 SUDDEN SOUND [C] a sudden loud sharp sound: *The firework exploded with a loud crack.*
5 JOKE [C] a clever joke or rude remark: **[+about]** *Stop **making cracks about** my sister!*
6 ATTEMPT [C] *informal* an attempt to do something: **[+at]** *Okay, let's **have a crack** at fixing this bike.*
7 DRUG [U] a very dangerous illegal drug
PHRASES

| **at the crack of dawn** very early in the morning: *We were woken at the crack of dawn by the birds singing.*

crack³ *adj* [only before noun] having a lot of experience and skill: *crack troops* | *He's a **crack shot** (=very good at shooting).*

crackdown /'krækdaʊn/ *n* [C usually singular] action that is taken to deal more strictly with bad or illegal behaviour: **[+on]** *a crackdown on drunk driving*

cracked /krækt/ *adj* something that is cracked has lines on the surface because it is damaged but not completely broken: *a cracked mirror* | *He escaped with a cracked rib.*

cracker /'krækə $ -ər/ *n* **1** [C] a thin BISCUIT often eaten with cheese **2** [C] a brightly coloured paper tube containing a small present, which people pull open at Christmas **3** [singular] *BrE informal* something that is very good: *Thompson's goal was a real cracker!*

crackers /'krækəz $ -ərz/ *adj* [not before noun] *BrE informal* crazy: *You're crackers!* THESAURUS CRAZY

crackle /'krækəl/ *v* [I] to make a lot of short sharp noises: *the sound of logs crackling on the fire* → see picture on page A7

crackpot /'krækpɒt $ -pɑːt/ *adj* [only before noun] slightly crazy: *Whose crackpot idea was this?*

cradle¹ /'kreɪdl/ *n* **1** [C] a baby's bed with bars around the sides **2 the cradle of sth** the place where something important began: *Athens was the cradle of western democracy.*

cradle² *v* [T] to hold someone or something gently in your arms: *Tony cradled the baby in his arms.*

craft¹ /krɑːft $ kræft/ *n* [C] **1** (*plural* **crafts**) a skilled activity in which you make something using your hands: *traditional country crafts such as pottery and weaving* **2** (*plural* **craft**) a boat

craft² *v* [T] to make something with your hands, using a special skill: *Each doll is crafted individually by specialists.*

craftsman /'krɑːftsmən $ 'kræfts-/ *n* [C] (*plural* **craftsmen** /-mən/) someone who is very skilled at making things with their hands: *furniture made by the finest craftsmen*

craftsmanship /'krɑːftsmənʃɪp $ 'kræfts-/ *n* [U] the skill of making something beautiful with your hands

crafty /'krɑːfti $ 'kræf-/ *adj* good at getting what you want by cleverly deceiving people: *He's a crafty old devil.* —**craftily** *adv*

crag /kræg/ *n* [C] a steep rough rock on a hill or mountain

craggy /'krægi/ *adj* **1** craggy ground is very steep and covered with large rocks **2** a craggy face has a lot of lines

cram /kræm/ *v* (**crammed**, **cramming**) **1** [T] to force a lot of people or things into a small space: **cram sth into sth** *She managed to cram all her clothes into one suitcase.* **2 be crammed with sth** to be full of people or things: *The streets were crammed with tourists.* **3** [I] to prepare yourself for an examination by learning a lot of information very quickly: *Julia stayed up all night cramming for her final.* —**crammed** *adj*: *a crammed train*

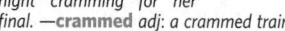
CRAM

cramp /kræmp/ *n* [C,U] a bad pain in your muscles that makes it difficult to move: *I've got cramp in my foot.*

cramped /kræmpt/ *adj* a cramped room or building does not have enough space for the people or things in it

cranberry /'krænbəri $ -beri/ *n* [C] (*plural* **cranberries**) a small red sour fruit: *cranberry sauce*

crane¹ /kreɪn/ *n* [C] **1** a tall machine with a long metal arm for lifting heavy things **2** a water bird with very long legs

crane² *v* [I,T] to stretch your neck forward in order to see or hear something: *He craned his neck to get a better view of the stage.*

crank¹ /kræŋk/ *n* [C] **1** *informal* someone who has unusual ideas and behaves strangely: *a religious crank* **2** a handle that you turn to make a machine work

crank² *v*
PHRASAL VERBS
crank sth↔ **up** *informal* to make the sound of something, especially music, louder: *Crank up the volume!*

cranny /'kræni/ *n* [C] (*plural* **crannies**) a small

crash

narrow hole in a wall or rock → **every nook and cranny** at NOOK

crash¹ /kræʃ/ v

1 HAVE AN ACCIDENT [I,T] to have an accident in a car, plane etc, especially by hitting something else → **collide**: *The jet crashed shortly after takeoff.* | [+into/through etc] *We crashed straight into the car in front.* | **crash a car/bus/plane etc** *He was drunk when he crashed the car.*

> **Grammar**
> Do not say 'The car crashed with a wall.' Say *The car **crashed into** a wall.*

2 HIT [I] to hit something hard, causing a lot of damage or making a loud noise: [+into/through/against etc] *A brick crashed through the window.* | *the sound of waves crashing against the rocks*
3 LOUD NOISE [I] to make a loud noise: *Thunder crashed and boomed outside.*
4 COMPUTER [I] if a computer crashes, it suddenly stops working: *The system keeps crashing.*
5 STOCK MARKET [I] if a STOCK MARKET crashes, prices suddenly fall by a large amount

crash² n [C]
1 ACCIDENT an accident in which a vehicle hits something else → **collision**: *Six vehicles were involved in the crash.* | **car/plane/train etc crash** *All 265 passengers were killed in the plane crash.* | *a **head-on crash** between two trains* THESAURUS ACCIDENT
2 LOUD NOISE a loud noise made by something falling or breaking: *We were woken by the sound of a loud crash downstairs.* | **with a crash** *The tray fell to the floor with a crash.* → see picture on page A7
3 COMPUTER when a computer suddenly stops working
4 STOCK MARKET when prices on a STOCK MARKET suddenly fall by a large amount: *a stock market crash*

'**crash ,barrier** n [C] BrE a fence that divides the two sides of a road or that prevents a crowd from moving forward

'**crash course** n [C] a short course in which you study a subject very quickly

'**crash ,helmet** n [C] a hard hat worn by MOTORCYCLISTS, racing drivers etc to protect their heads

,**crash-'land** / $ '../ v [I,T] to bring a plane down to the ground in a more dangerous way than usual because the plane has a problem —**crash landing** n [C]

crass /kræs/ adj stupid and rude: *a crass remark*

crate /kreɪt/ n [C] a large box used for carrying fruit, bottles etc: *a crate of beer*

crater /'kreɪtə $ -ər/ n [C] **1** the round open top of a VOLCANO → see picture at **VOLCANO 2** a round hole in the ground made by something that has fallen on it or by an explosion

cravat /krə'væt/ n [C] a piece of loosely folded material that a man ties around his neck → **tie**

crave /kreɪv/ v [T] to want something very much: *He craved affection.*

craving /'kreɪvɪŋ/ n [C] a very strong desire for something: *a craving for chocolate*

crawl¹ /krɔːl $ krɒːl/ v [I]
1 BABY/PERSON to move on your hands and knees: *The baby is just learning to crawl.* | [+into/out of/through etc] *We crawled through a hole in the fence.* → see picture on page A11
2 INSECT if an insect crawls, it moves along the ground: [+over/up etc] *Flies were crawling all over the food.*
3 VEHICLE if a vehicle crawls, it moves very slowly: *We crawled all the way into town.*
4 TO AN IMPORTANT PERSON disapproving to be very pleasant to someone because they are important or can help you: [+to] *He's always crawling to the boss.*
5 COVERED WITH STH **be crawling with sth** to be completely covered with insects or people: *The tent was crawling with ants!*

crawl² n **1** [singular] a very slow speed: *cars moving along at a crawl* **2 the crawl** a way of swimming in which you lie on your stomach and move one arm, and then the other, over your head → **backstroke, breaststroke, butterfly** → see picture at **SWIM¹**

crayon /'kreɪən, -ɒn $ -aːn, -ən/ n [C] a stick of coloured WAX or a coloured pencil that children use to draw pictures

craze /kreɪz/ n [C] a fashion, game, type of music etc that is very popular for a short time: *the latest craze to hit New York*

crazed /kreɪzd/ adj behaving in a wild and uncontrolled way like someone who is mentally ill

crazy /'kreɪzi/ adj (comparative **crazier**, superlative **craziest**)
1 very strange or not sensible SYN **mad**: *Our friends all think we're crazy.* | *It's an absolutely **crazy idea**.* THESAURUS STUPID
2 angry or annoyed: *Stop it, you're **driving** me **crazy** (=making me very annoyed)!* | *Dad will **go crazy** when he hears about this.*
3 mentally ill SYN **mad**: *a crazy old woman* —**crazily** adv —**craziness** n [U]
PHRASES
be crazy about sb/sth to like someone or something very much: *Lee's crazy about cats.* THESAURUS LIKE
go crazy if a group of people go crazy, they become very excited: *England scored and the fans went crazy.*
like crazy very much or very quickly: *We're going to have to work like crazy to get this finished on time.*

> **THESAURUS**
>
> **crazy** very strange or not sensible: *Don't listen to him – he's crazy.* | *It was a crazy thing to do.*
> **mad** BrE crazy: *Are you completely mad?* | *Whose mad idea was that?*
> **nuts** (also **crackers/bonkers** BrE) informal crazy: *That guy is nuts.* | *The whole thing sounds bonkers.*
> **insane** informal completely crazy and stupid: *She should never have lent him the money – she must be insane.*

creak /kriːk/ v [I] if something such as a door or wooden floor creaks, it makes a long high noise when it moves: *The door creaked shut behind him.*

—**creak** n [C] —**creaky** adj → see picture on page A7

cream¹ /kriːm/ n
1 [U] a thick white liquid that comes from milk: *strawberries and cream* | *fresh cream*
2 [C,U] a thick smooth substance that you put on your skin to make it softer or less painful: *face cream* | *sun cream*
3 the best people or things in a group: **the cream of** *Europe's footballers* → ICE CREAM, SUN CREAM

cream² adj pale yellow-white in colour: *a cream-coloured carpet*

‚cream **'cheese** / $ '../ n [U] a type of soft white cheese

creamy /'kriːmi/ adj containing cream or thick and smooth like cream: *The sauce was smooth and creamy.*

crease¹ /kriːs/ n [C] a line on cloth or paper where it has been folded or crushed: *She smoothed the creases from her skirt.* THESAURUS LINE

crease² v [I,T] if a piece of cloth or paper creases, or you crease it, it becomes marked with a line after it has been folded or crushed → **crumple**: *Try not to crease your jacket.* —**creased** adj

create Ac /kriˈeɪt/ v [T]
1 to make something new exist or happen: *The new factory should create 450 jobs.* | *The increase in traffic has created a lot of problems.* THESAURUS MAKE
2 to invent or design something: *This dish was created by our chef Jean Richard.* THESAURUS INVENT
—**creator** n [C]: *Walt Disney, the creator of Mickey Mouse*

creation Ac /kriˈeɪʃən/ n **1** [U] when something new is created: **[+of]** *the creation of a United Europe* | *a* **job** *creation scheme* **2** [C] something that has been created: *the artist's latest creation* **3 Creation** according to many religions, the time when the universe and everything in it was made by God

creationism /kriˈeɪʃənɪzəm/ n [U] the belief that God created the world in the way described in the Bible —**creationist** adj, n [C]

creative /kriˈeɪtɪv/ adj **1** a creative person is good at thinking of new ideas: *one of Japan's most talented and creative film directors* **2** involving the use of imagination to produce new ideas or things: *a creative solution to the problem* —**creatively** adv —**creativity** /ˌkriːeɪˈtɪvəti/ n [U]: *artistic creativity*

creature /'kriːtʃə $ -ər/ n [C]
1 an animal, fish, or insect: *We should respect all living creatures.*
2 an imaginary animal or person, or one that is very strange and frightening: *creatures from outer space*
3 beautiful/gorgeous/stupid etc creature someone who is beautiful, gorgeous etc

‚creature **'comforts** n [plural] all the things that make life comfortable and enjoyable: *The hotel had all the creature comforts of his home in London.*

crèche /kreʃ $ kreʃ, kreɪʃ/ n [C] BrE a place where babies are looked after while their parents are at work SYN **day care center** AmE

credence /'kriːdəns/ n [U] when something is accepted as true: *This new evidence* **lends credence to** *the theory.*

credentials /krɪˈdenʃəlz/ n [plural] **1** someone's education, achievements, and experience that prove they have the ability to do something: *She has excellent academic credentials.* **2** a document which proves who you are

credibility /ˌkredəˈbɪləti/ n [U] when someone or something can be trusted and believed by people: *The scandal has damaged the government's credibility.*

credible /'kredəbəl/ adj if someone or something is credible, people can trust them or believe them: *a credible witness*

credit¹ Ac /'kredɪt/ n
1 [U] a way of buying goods in which you arrange to pay for them later: **on credit** *The TV and the washing machine were bought on credit.*
2 [U] praise given to someone for doing something: *It's not fair – I do all the work and he* **gets** *all the* **credit**. | **[+for]** *You've got to* **give** *him* **credit** *for trying.*
3 [C] a successfully completed part of a course at a university or college
4 [C] a payment made into a bank account
5 the credits [plural] the list of the people who helped to make a television programme or film

PHRASES
be a credit to sb/sth to behave so well or be so successful that the people around you are proud of you: *You're a credit to the school!*
be in credit to have money in your bank account: *There are no bank charges if you are in credit.*
have sth to your credit to have achieved something: *She already has two novels to her credit.*

credit² Ac v [T] **1** to add money to a bank account OPP **debit**: **credit sth to sth** *The cheque will be credited to your account.* **2 credit sb with (doing) sth** to believe that someone has a good quality or has done something good: *Credit me with some intelligence, please!* **3 be credited to sb/sth** if something is credited to someone or something, they are said to have achieved it or be the reason for it: *Much of Manchester United's success can be credited to their manager.* **4** to believe that something surprising is true: *Would you credit it! He's won!*

creditable /'kredətəbəl/ adj deserving praise or approval: *The French team finished a creditable second.*

'**credit card** n [C] a small plastic card that you use to buy goods or services and pay for them later: **by credit card** *Can I pay by credit card?*

'**credit crunch** n [singular] a time when borrowing money becomes difficult because banks are less willing to lend money

creditor Ac /'kredɪtə $ -ər/ n [C] a person or organization that you owe money to

'**credit ‚rating** n [C] a judgment made by a bank or other company about how likely a person or business is to pay their debts

credo /'kriːdəʊ, 'kreɪ- $ -doʊ/ n [C] (*plural* **credos**) a short statement that expresses a belief or rule

creed /kriːd/ n [C] a set of beliefs or principles: *People of all creeds were there.* | *a* **religious creed**

creek /kriːk/ n [C] **1** BrE a narrow area of water where the sea flows into the land **2** AmE a small narrow stream or river

PHRASES

be up the creek (without a paddle) spoken to be in a difficult situation: I'll really be up the creek if I don't get my passport by Friday.

creep¹ /kriːp/ v [I] (past tense and past participle **crept** /krept/) **1** to move very quietly so that no one will notice you: [+down/in/out etc] She crept down the stairs in the dark. THESAURUS WALK **2** to move somewhere very slowly → **crawl**: The car was creeping along in heavy traffic. **3** to gradually start to happen: [+into/in/over etc] A note of panic had crept into his voice. **4** to gradually increase: [+up] The total number of people out of work crept up to five million.

PHRASAL VERBS

creep up on sb **1** to surprise someone by walking up behind them quickly: I wish you wouldn't creep up on me like that! **2** if a feeling, problem, or bad situation creeps up on you, it gradually affects you without you realizing it: Tiredness can creep up on you when you're stressed at work. **3** if an event creeps up on you, it seems to happen sooner than you expect: Somehow, the end of term had crept up on us.

creep² n [C usually singular] someone who you dislike a lot: Go away, you little creep!

PHRASES

give you the creeps to make you feel nervous or frightened: That guy gives me the creeps!

creeper /ˈkriːpə $ -ər/ n [C] a plant that grows up walls or along the ground

creepy /ˈkriːpi/ adj informal making you feel nervous and slightly frightened: a creepy movie

cremate /krɪˈmeɪt $ ˈkriːmeɪt/ v [T] to burn the body of a dead person at a funeral ceremony —**cremation** /krɪˈmeɪʃən/ n [C,U]

crematorium /ˌkreməˈtɔːriəm $ ˌkriː-/ n [C] (plural **crematoriums** or **crematoria** /-riə/) a building in which the bodies of dead people are burned at a funeral ceremony

crept /krept/ v the past tense and past participle of CREEP

crescendo /krəˈʃendəʊ $ -doʊ/ n [C] (plural **crescendos**) when a piece of music becomes gradually louder

crescent /ˈkresənt, ˈkrez-/ n [C] **1** a curved shape that is wider in the middle and pointed at the ends: a **crescent moon** → see picture at SHAPE¹ **2 Crescent** used in the names of streets that have a curved shape: Turn left into Woodford Crescent.

cress /kres/ n [U] a small plant with round green leaves that are eaten raw

crest /krest/ n [C] **1** the top of a hill or wave **2** a group of upright feathers on a bird's head **3** a special picture used as the sign of a school, town, important family etc

crestfallen /ˈkrestˌfɔːlən $ -ˌfɔːl-/ adj formal sad or disappointed

crevasse /krɪˈvæs/ n [C] a deep open crack in the thick ice on a mountain

crevice /ˈkrevɪs/ n [C] a narrow crack, especially in rock

crew /kruː/ n [C]
1 all the people that work together on a ship, plane etc THESAURUS GROUP
2 a group of people who work together on something: an ambulance crew

crewman /ˈkruːmən/ n [C] (plural **crewmen** /-mən/) a member of the crew on a boat or ship

crib¹ /krɪb/ n [C] AmE a baby's bed with bars around the sides SYN **cot** BrE → see picture at BED

crib² v [T] (**cribbed**, **cribbing**) old-fashioned to dishonestly copy someone else's work: **crib sth off/from sb** He didn't want anyone to crib the answers off him.

'crib death n [C] AmE the sudden, unexpected, and unexplained death of a baby while it is sleeping SYN **cot death** BrE

crick /krɪk/ n **a crick in sb's neck** a pain in someone's neck that is caused by the muscles becoming stiff: I woke with a crick in my neck.

CRICKET

cricket /ˈkrɪkɪt/ n **1** [U] a game in which two teams try to get points by hitting a ball and running between two sets of sticks **2** [C] a small brown insect that can jump and makes a rough sound by rubbing its wings together

cricketer /ˈkrɪkɪtə $ -ər/ n [C] BrE someone who plays cricket

crime /kraɪm/ n
1 [U] illegal activities in general: There was very little crime when we moved here.
2 [C] an illegal action that can be punished by law: He committed a number of crimes in the area.

PHRASES

it's a crime spoken used to say that something is morally wrong: It's a crime to waste food.
the scene of the crime the place where a crime has happened: Detectives were already at the scene of the crime.

COLLOCATIONS

verbs

to commit (a) crime I have not committed any crime. ⚠ Do not say 'do a crime'. Say **commit a crime** or **carry out a crime**.
to carry out a crime They both planned and carried out the crime.

to turn to crime (=to start committing crimes) *He turned to crime to pay off his debts.*
to solve a crime *The crime was never solved.*
to fight crime *How can we help the police to fight crime?*

adjectives

serious crime (=bad crime) *Have you ever been the victim of a serious crime?*
petty crime (=crime that is not very serious) *As a teenager, he became involved in petty crime.*
violent crime *The level of violent crime has gone down.*

crime + noun

the crime rate *Japan has a very low crime rate.*
a crime wave (=a sudden increase in crime in an area) *The city has been hit by a crime wave.*

THESAURUS
different types of crime

robbery the crime of stealing from a bank, shop etc, especially using violence: *They stole £100,000 in the robbery.* | *a daring bank robbery*
burglary the crime of breaking into someone's home in order to steal things: *There was a burglary in the house across the street.*
theft *formal* the crime of stealing something: *Car theft is a big problem.* | *thefts of mobile phones*
shoplifting the crime of taking small things from shops without paying for them: *She was arrested in the supermarket for shoplifting.*
mugging the crime of attacking and robbing someone in a public place: *There have been several muggings on the High Street.*
murder the crime of deliberately killing someone: *He was charged with his wife's murder.*
fraud the crime of deceiving people in order to get money: *credit card fraud*
arson the crime of deliberately setting fire to a building: *The school was destroyed in an arson attack.*
vandalism the crime of deliberately damaging public property: *Vandalism has been a serious problem on the railways.*

criminal¹ /ˈkrɪmɪnəl/ *adj*
1 [only before noun] relating to crime: ***criminal behaviour*** | *He has a long **criminal record** (=an official record of the crimes he has committed).* | *The case will be tried in a **criminal court**.*
2 wrong, dishonest, and unacceptable: *It's criminal that teachers are paid so little money.* —**criminally** *adv*

criminal² *n* [C] someone who has done something wrong or illegal: *Police have described the man as a violent and dangerous criminal.*

crimson /ˈkrɪmzən/ *adj* having a deep red colour —**crimson** *n* [U]

cringe /krɪndʒ/ *v* [I] **1** to feel embarrassed by something: *It **makes** me **cringe** when I think how stupid I was.* **2** to move away from someone or

something because you are afraid: *She cringed away from him in horror.*

crinkle /ˈkrɪŋkəl/ (*also* **crinkle up**) *v* [I,T] to become covered with small folds, or make something do this: *Mandy crinkled her nose in disgust.* —**crinkled** *adj* —**crinkly** *adj*

cripple¹ /ˈkrɪpəl/ *n* [C] a word for someone who cannot walk properly, which is now considered to be offensive

cripple² *v* [T] **1** to hurt someone so they can no longer walk: *He was crippled in a car accident.* **2** to seriously damage something or make it much weaker: *The country's economy has been crippled by drought.* —**crippled** *adj* —**crippling** *adj*: *a crippling illness* | *crippling debts*

crisis /ˈkraɪsɪs/ *n* [C,U] (*plural* **crises** /-siːz/) a time when a situation is very bad or dangerous → **emergency**: *The country now faces an **economic crisis**.* | *a **major political crisis*** | *an emotional crisis* | **in crisis** *The car industry is now in crisis.* → MIDLIFE CRISIS

crisp¹ /krɪsp/ *adj* **1** something that is crisp is hard, and makes a pleasant sound when you break it: *She kicked at the crisp leaves at her feet.* **THESAURUS** HARD **2** fresh, firm, and pleasant to eat: *a nice crisp salad* **THESAURUS** HARD **3** weather that is crisp is cold and dry: *a crisp winter morning* **4** cloth that is crisp looks clean and new: *crisp clean sheets* **5** a picture that is crisp is clear —**crisply** *adv*

crisp² *n* [C] *BrE* a thin flat round piece of potato cooked in very hot oil and eaten cold as a SNACK **SYN** **chip** *AmE*: *a packet of crisps* → see picture at CHIP¹

crispy /ˈkrɪspi/ *adj* crispy food is pleasantly hard: *crispy bacon* **THESAURUS** HARD

crisscross /ˈkrɪskrɒs $ -krɔːs/ *v* [I,T] to make a pattern of straight lines that cross each other: *Motorways crisscross the countryside.*

criterion Ac /kraɪˈtɪəriən $ -ˈtɪr-/ *n* [C usually plural] (*plural* **criteria** /-riə/) a standard that you use to judge something or make a decision about something: **[+for]** *What are the criteria for selecting the winner?*

critic /ˈkrɪtɪk/ *n* [C] **1** someone whose job is to give their opinion of a film, book etc: *a literary critic for 'The Times'* **2** someone who says that a person or idea is bad or wrong: **[+of]** *an outspoken critic of the government*

critical /ˈkrɪtɪkəl/ *adj* **1** if you are critical of someone or something, you say that you think they are bad or wrong: **[+of]** *Economists are critical of the plans.* | *She made some **highly critical** remarks.* **2** very important: **[+to]** *The talks are critical to the future of the peace process.* | *The effects of climate change are **of critical importance**.* **3** serious or dangerous: *The driver is still **in a critical condition** (=seriously ill or injured) in hospital.* **4** [only before noun] judging how good a play, film, book etc is: *a **critical analysis** of Shakespeare* —**critically** /-kli/ *adv*: *She's critically ill.*

criticism /ˈkrɪtɪsɪzəm/ *n*
1 [C,U] when you say that a person or thing is bad or wrong **OPP** praise: **[+of]** *I don't think his criticisms*

of the project are justified. | **strong/harsh/severe criticism** She **faced harsh criticism** when she resigned. | **provoke/attract/draw criticism** His speech attracted widespread criticism. | **take/accept criticism** (=be willing to accept that it may be true) Kate doesn't **take criticism well**. | **constructive criticism** (=meant to help someone improve)
2 [U] when someone gives their judgment of a film, play, book etc: literary criticism

criticize (also **-ise** BrE) /ˈkrɪtɪsaɪz/ v [I,T] to say what faults you think someone or something has OPP **praise**: You do nothing but criticize. | **criticize sb for (doing) sth** The regime has been criticized for its record on human rights. | **criticize sth strongly/sharply/heavily etc** The government's policies have been strongly criticized. | The new law has been **widely criticized** (=criticized by a lot of people).

critique /krɪˈtiːk/ n [C] a piece of writing describing the good and bad qualities of a play, film, book etc

croak /krəʊk $ kroʊk/ v **1** [I] to speak in a low rough voice: 'Hello,' he croaked. **2** [I,T] if a FROG croaks, it makes a low deep sound —**croak** n [C]

crochet /ˈkrəʊʃeɪ $ kroʊˈʃeɪ/ v [I,T] to make clothes by twisting wool together using a needle with a hook at one end —**crochet** n [U]

crock /krɒk $ krɑːk/ n [C] old-fashioned a clay pot

crockery /ˈkrɒkəri $ ˈkrɑː-/ n [U] BrE cups, plates, and dishes

crocodile /ˈkrɒkədaɪl $ ˈkrɑː-/ n [C] a large REPTILE with a long mouth and sharp teeth, that lives in lakes and rivers in hot countries

crocus /ˈkrəʊkəs $ ˈkroʊ-/ n [C] a small purple, yellow, or white flower that appears in spring → see picture at **FLOWER¹**

croissant /ˈkwɑːsɒŋ $ krɔːˈsɑːnt/ n [C] a curved piece of soft bread, eaten for breakfast, especially in France → see picture at **BREAD**

crony /ˈkrəʊni $ ˈkroʊni/ n [C] (plural **cronies**) informal disapproving one of a group of friends who use their power or influence to help each other: one of his **political cronies**

crook¹ /krʊk/ n **1** [C] informal a criminal or dishonest person: a bunch of crooks **2 the crook of sb's arm** the inside of someone's arm, where it bends

crook² v [T] if you crook your finger or arm, you bend it

crooked /ˈkrʊkɪd/ adj **1** not straight: crooked streets THESAURUS **DISHONEST 2** informal dishonest

croon /kruːn/ v [I,T] to sing or speak softly about love

crop¹ /krɒp $ krɑːp/ n
1 [C] plants such as wheat, fruit, vegetables etc that farmers grow and sell: Our main crops are rice and oats. → see picture at **CEREAL**
2 [C] the amount of wheat, fruit etc that a farmer produces in a season: **[+of]** a **bumper crop** (=a very large amount) of broad beans
3 [singular] a group of people or things that arrive at the same time: **[+of]** this year's crop of novels

4 [C] a short whip used in horse riding → **CASH CROP**

crop² v [T] (**cropped, cropping**) to make something shorter by cutting it: His hair was cropped short. | We use sheep to keep the grass cropped.
PHRASAL VERBS
crop up to suddenly appear or happen: A problem's cropped up.

cropper /ˈkrɒpə $ ˈkrɑːpər/ **come a cropper** BrE informal **a)** to fail unexpectedly **b)** to fall over

croquet /ˈkrəʊkeɪ, -ki $ kroʊˈkeɪ/ n [U] a game played on grass in which you hit balls under bent wires using a wooden hammer

cross¹ /krɒs $ krɔːs/ v
1 TO THE OTHER SIDE (also **cross over**) [I,T] to go from one side of a road, river, room etc to the other: Take care when you **cross the road**. | We **crossed the border** into Italy. | **[+to]** The boat had crossed safely to the other side. | the first ship to cross the Pacific | A cheering crowd greeted the first runner to cross the finish line. THESAURUS **TRAVEL**
2 LINES/PATHS/ARMS ETC [I,T] if two straight things cross, or if you cross them, they are arranged so that one goes over the other: The road crosses the railway here. | **cross your arms/legs/ankles** She sat down and crossed her legs.
3 MIX ANIMALS/PLANTS [T] to mix two different types of animal or plant to produce young animals or plants: **cross sth with sth** Wolves can be crossed with domestic dogs.
4 IN SPORT [I,T] to pass the ball across the playing area in a game such as football: Norbury crossed the ball into the penalty area.
5 MAKE SB ANGRY [T] to oppose someone or disagree with them, so that they become very angry: Those who crossed him soon had cause for regret.
6 IN RELIGION **cross yourself** to touch your head, chest, and shoulders in turn to show respect for God → **DOUBLE-CROSS**
PHRASES
cross your fingers/fingers crossed used to say that you hope something will happen: All we can do is cross our fingers and hope for the best.
cross your mind if a thought crosses your mind, it suddenly comes into your mind: It crossed my mind that he might think we were lovers.
PHRASAL VERBS
cross sth ↔ **off** to draw a line through something on a list to show that you have dealt with it: Cross off their names as they arrive.
cross sth ↔ **out** to draw a line through something you have written because it is not correct

cross² n [C]
1 a mixture of two things: **[+between]** It looks like a cross between a dog and a rat.
2 a) an upright wooden post with another post fixed across it. In the past, people were punished by being fastened to the post and left to die: **the cross** (=the cross that Christ died on) **b)** an object, sign etc in the shape of a cross, used to represent the Christian faith: a tiny gold cross | He made **the sign of the cross** (=moved his hand in the shape of a cross).
3 BrE a mark (x) put on paper to show where

something is or that something is not correct: **put/ mark a cross** I've put a cross to show where the pub is. **4** when a player kicks the ball across the playing area in a game such as football

cross³ adj BrE annoyed: **[+with]** Are you cross with me? | **[+about]** She's still cross about losing all that money. **THESAURUS** ANGRY

cross- /krɒs $ krɔːs/ prefix **1** going from one side of something to the other: a cross-Channel ferry | cross-border fighting **2** mixing two different things: cross-cultural influences

crossbar /'krɒsbɑː $ 'krɔːsbɑːr/ n [C] **1** the bar that joins two GOALPOSTS → see picture at **FOOTBALL** **2** the bar on a bicycle that joins the seat and the HANDLEBARS → see picture at **BICYCLE**

crossbow /'krɒsbəʊ $ 'krɔːsbou/ n [C] a weapon used to shoot ARROWS

cross-'country adj [only before noun] a cross-country race is one that goes across fields and not along roads —**cross-country** n [C,U]

cross-ex'amine v [I,T] to officially ask someone questions to discover whether they have been telling the truth: In court, the two women were cross-examined. —**cross-exami'nation** n [C,U]

cross-'eyed / $ '../ adj having eyes that look inwards

crossfire /'krɒsfaɪə $ 'krɔːsfaɪr/ n [U] **1** bullets travelling towards each other from different directions: Red Cross workers were **caught in the crossfire**. **2** a situation in which you are badly affected by a disagreement, even though it does not involve you: I don't want to get **caught in the** political **crossfire**.

crossing /'krɒsɪŋ $ 'krɔː-/ n [C] **1** a place where you can safely cross a road, river etc **2** a place where two roads, lines etc cross **3** a journey across water

cross-legged /ˌkrɒs 'legəd◂, -'legd◂ $ 'krɔːs ˌlegəd, -ˌlegd/ adv, adj in a sitting position with your knees apart and one foot over the opposite leg: Children **sat cross-legged** on the floor.

CROSS-LEGGED

crossover /'krɒsəʊvə $ 'krɔːsouvər/ n [C,U] when something or someone is popular or successful in different areas or is liked by different types of people, for example when a popular song is liked by people who usually only like serious music: The song has enjoyed crossover success on the country and pop charts.

cross-'purposes n [plural] **at cross-purposes** if two people are at cross-purposes, they become confused because they think they are talking about the same thing, although they are not

cross-'reference / $ '. ,.../ n [C] a note in a book telling you to look on a different page for more information

crossroads /'krɒsrəʊdz $ 'krɔːsroudz/ n [C] (plural **crossroads**) **1** a place where two roads cross each

other → **junction, T-junction: at the crossroads** Turn left at the crossroads. **2** a time when you have to make an important decision about your future: **at a crossroads** Neil is at a crossroads in his career.

'cross ˌsection, cross-section n [C] **1** a picture of something that shows what it would look like if you cut it in half, or an object cut in this way **2** a group of people or things that is typical of a larger group: **[+of]** a cross-section of the American public

crosswalk /'krɒswɔːk $ 'krɔːswɒːk/ n [C] AmE a marked place where people can cross a road safely **SYN** pedestrian crossing BrE

crossword /'krɒswɜːd $ 'krɔːswɜːrd/ (also **'crossword ˌpuzzle**) n [C] a game in which you write the answers to CLUES (=questions) in boxes arranged in a black and white pattern: I usually **do the crossword** in the newspaper. → see picture at **PUZZLE¹**

crotch /krɒtʃ $ krɑːtʃ/ (also **crutch** BrE) n [C] the place where your legs join at the top, or the part of a pair of trousers etc that covers this

crouch /krautʃ/ (also **crouch down**) v [I] to bend your knees and back so you are close to the ground → see picture on page A11

crow¹ /krəʊ $ krou/ n [C] a large black bird that makes a loud sound

PHRASES

as the crow flies used to describe the distance between two places when measured in a straight line: My house is ten miles from here as the crow flies.

crow² v [I] **1** if a COCK (=male chicken) crows, it makes a loud sound **2** to talk very proudly about yourself or your achievements: **[+about/over]** She keeps crowing about her exam results.

crowbar /'krəʊbɑː $ 'kroubɑːr/ n [C] a strong iron bar used to open things

crowd¹ /kraud/ n
1 [C] a large group of people in one place: **[+of]** a large crowd of football supporters | A **crowd gathered** outside the building. | Police used tear gas to **disperse the crowd**. | Shop online and **avoid the crowds**. **THESAURUS** GROUP
2 [singular] ordinary people: He likes to **stand out from the crowd** (=be different from ordinary people).
3 [singular] informal a group of people who know each other well

crowd² v [I,T] if people crowd somewhere, they are there in large numbers: **[+around/into/in etc]** The students crowded round my desk for a better look. | **be crowded together** The prisoners were all crowded together in a small cell. | Holiday-makers crowd the beaches in high season.
PHRASAL VERBS
crowd sb/sth ↔ **out** to force someone or something to leave a place: Supermarkets have crowded out the small grocery stores.

crowded /'kraudɪd/ adj very full of people or things: a crowded room | The train was **over-crowded** (=carrying too many people).

crown¹ /kraun/ n [C]
1 a circle made of gold and jewels, which a king or queen wears on their head

2 the Crown the power and position of a king or queen, or their government

3 a cover that is fixed over a damaged tooth

4 the top of a hill, your head, or a hat: **[+of]** *the crown of the hill*

crown² v [I,T] **1** to put a crown on someone's head, as part of a ceremony that officially makes them the ruler of a country: **crown sb king/queen/tsar etc** *She was crowned queen 50 years ago.* **2** to make something complete or perfect by adding to it: *His career was crowned by a Nobel Prize.*

crowning /ˈkraʊnɪŋ/ adj [only before noun] better, more important etc than anything else: *Winning this award was the **crowning achievement** of his career.*

crucial [Ac] /ˈkruːʃəl/ adj very important: **[+to]** *Money is crucial to the aid program.* **THESAURUS** ▶ IMPORTANT —**crucially** adv: *a crucially important meeting*

crucifix /ˈkruːsəfɪks/ n [C] a cross with a figure of Christ on it

crucify /ˈkruːsɪfaɪ/ v [T] (**crucified, crucifying, crucifies**) **1** to kill someone by fastening them to a cross **2** *informal* to criticize someone very strongly —**crucifixion** /ˌkruːsəˈfɪkʃən/ n [C,U]

crude /kruːd/ adj **1** [only before noun] crude oil, rubber etc is in a natural condition **2** offensive or rude: *His jokes are crude.* **3** not made to a high standard: *a crude shelter* **4** not exact or detailed: *a crude estimate* —**crudely** adv

crude 'oil (*also* **crude**) n [U] oil that is in its natural condition, as it comes out of an OIL WELL, before it is made more pure or separated into different products

cruel /ˈkruːəl/ adj hurting people or animals or making them suffer [OPP] **kind: [+to]** *People who are cruel to animals make me mad.* | *His death was **a cruel blow** (=it affected someone very badly).* —**cruelly** adv: *She was treated very cruelly.*

THESAURUS

cruel deliberately hurting people or animals or making them suffer: *Children can be very cruel to each other.* | *The prisoners were treated in a cruel way.*

heartless not feeling any pity and not caring about other people: *a cold heartless killer* | *How can you be so heartless?*

vicious very violent and cruel, especially by suddenly attacking someone: *a vicious attack on an old man* | *Some dogs can be vicious.*

brutal very cruel and violent, and without normal human feelings: *a brutal dictator* | *a brutal murder*

barbaric extremely cruel, in a way that shocks people: *The bombing was a barbaric act.* | *Hunting is a barbaric sport.*

---

cruelty /ˈkruːəlti/ n [C,U] (*plural* **cruelties**) behaviour or actions that are unkind or cause suffering [OPP] **kindness: [+to]** *cruelty to animals* | *cruelties committed in the name of religion*

cruise¹ /kruːz/ v [I] **1** if a plane, boat, car etc

cruises, it moves at a steady speed **2** to win something easily: **cruise to victory/success etc**

cruise² n [C] a holiday on a large ship

cruise 'missile n [C] a powerful weapon that can be aimed from a very long distance away

cruiser /ˈkruːzə $ -ər/ n [C] a type of ship → see picture at TRANSPORT¹

crumb /krʌm/ n [C] **1** a very small piece of bread, cake etc **THESAURUS** ▶ PIECE **2** a very small amount: **[+of]** *She offered us a few crumbs of comfort.*

crumble /ˈkrʌmbəl/ v **1** [I,T] to break into small pieces, or to make something do this: *She crumbled the bread onto the ground.* | *The walls had crumbled away.* **THESAURUS** ▶ BREAK **2** [I] if a system or relationship crumbles, it fails: *His marriage had crumbled.*

crummy /ˈkrʌmi/ adj informal of poor quality: *a crummy hotel room*

crumple /ˈkrʌmpəl/ (*also* **crumple up**) v [I,T] to crush paper or cloth —**crumpled** adj: *crumpled sheets*

crunch¹ /krʌntʃ/ v [I,T] to make a noise like something being crushed: **[+on/over]** *I heard boots crunching on the gravel.* | *Rob crunched an apple.*

crunch² n **1** [singular] a noise like the sound of something being crushed: **[+of]** *the crunch of footsteps in the snow* → see picture on page A7 **2** [singular] *informal* the moment in a situation when you must make an important decision: **When it came to the crunch,** *I couldn't bring myself to do it.* **3** [C] an exercise in which you lie on the floor and move your head and shoulders up and down

crunchy /ˈkrʌntʃi/ adj food that is crunchy is pleasantly firm and makes a sound when you bite it

crusade /kruːˈseɪd/ n [C] a determined attempt to change something you feel is morally wrong: **[+against/for]** *a crusade against violence* —**crusade** v [I] —**crusader** n [C]

crush¹ /krʌʃ/ v [T]

1 to press something so hard that it breaks or is damaged: *The car was crushed by a falling tree.* | **crush sb/sth under/ beneath/against etc sth** *She was crushed under the wheels of a car.* | *People were **crushed to death** by the crowd.* **THESAURUS** ▶ PRESS

2 to use severe methods to defeat someone: **crush a rebellion/uprising/revolt etc** *The revolt was crushed by the government.* **3** to make someone lose all hope, confidence etc: **crush sb's hopes/enthusiasm etc** *Her hopes were cruelly crushed.*

crush² n **1** [C] a strong feeling of love for someone that continues only for a short time: *I had a huge **crush** on my tutor.* **THESAURUS** ▶ LOVE **2** [singular] a crowd of people in a very small space: *At last we managed to get through the crush.*

crushing /ˈkrʌʃɪŋ/ adj **1** very hard to deal with, and making you lose hope and confidence: *The army* suffered a **crushing defeat**. **2** a crushing remark, reply etc contains a very strong criticism

crust /krʌst/ n [C,U] **1** the baked outside part of bread, a PIE etc **2** a hard layer on the surface of something: *the Earth's crust*

crusty /ˈkrʌsti/ adj food that is crusty has a hard crust: *nice crusty bread*

crutch /krʌtʃ/ n [C]
1 FOR HELP WALKING [usually plural] one of a pair of sticks that you lean on to help you walk: **on crutches** *I was on crutches for weeks.*
2 FOR EMOTIONAL HELP something that someone uses to help them, especially when this is not good for them: *Tom uses drugs as a crutch.*
3 PLACE ON BODY BrE the place where your legs join at the top, or the part of a pair of trousers etc that covers this SYN **crotch**

crux /krʌks/ n [singular] the most important part of a problem or question: **[+of]** *The crux of the matter is whether he intended murder.*

cry¹ /kraɪ/ v (cried, crying, cries)
1 [I] to produce tears from your eyes: **[+over/about]** *What are you crying about?* | **[+for]** *the sound of a baby crying for its mother* | **[+with]** *She could have cried with joy.*
2 (also **cry out**) [I,T] written to say something loudly: *'Stop!' she cried.* | *He cried her name out in anguish.* | **[+for]** *voices crying for help* THESAURUS SHOUT
3 [I] if animals or birds cry, they make a loud high sound → **a shoulder to cry on** at SHOULDER¹
PHRASES
be crying out for sth to need something urgently: *We're crying out for math teachers.*
cry over spilt milk informal to worry about a mistake that cannot be changed: *There's no point crying over spilt milk.*
cry wolf to keep asking for help when you do not need it, so that when you really need help, no one believes you: *Is he just crying wolf again?*

THESAURUS

cry to produce tears from your eyes, especially because you are unhappy or in pain: *Don't cry – everything will be all right.*
be in tears to be crying: *She was in tears by the end of the film.*
burst into tears to suddenly start crying: *Sara read the letter and burst into tears.*
break down to start crying after trying hard not to cry: *After the funeral, he just broke down.*
sob to cry in a noisy way: *I could hear someone sobbing in the next room.*
weep written to cry – used in stories and written descriptions: *The woman was weeping over the body of her son.*
your eyes water to have tears in your eyes, for example because of smoke, or when you are cutting onions: *The onions are making my eyes water.*

---

cry² n (plural **cries**)
1 [C] the sound someone makes when they feel a strong emotion, for example when they are very sad

or are in pain: **[+of]** *He gave a cry of pain.* | *She let out a cry of delight.* | **cry of pain/joy/fear** etc *Letting out a cry of delight, he grasped her hands.* | **[+for]** *cries for help*
2 [singular] BrE when someone cries: **have a cry** | *You'll feel better after **a good cry*** (=crying for a long time).
3 [C] a sound made by an animal or bird: *the cries of gulls*
PHRASES
a cry for help something someone does that shows they are unhappy and need help: *A suicide attempt is a cry for help.*
be a far cry from sth to be very different from something else: *The Olympics were a far cry from the spectacle we see now.*

crying /ˈkraɪ-ɪŋ/ adj **1 it's a crying shame** spoken used to say that something is very sad **2 a crying need for sth** an urgent need for something: *There's a crying need for better public transport.*

crypt /krɪpt/ n [C] a room under a church

cryptic /ˈkrɪptɪk/ adj having a meaning that is hard to understand: *a cryptic comment*

crystal /ˈkrɪstl/ n **1** [U] high quality glass: *crystal wine glasses* **2** [C] a small evenly shaped object that forms naturally when a liquid becomes solid: *ice crystals* **3** [C,U] a type of clear pale rock

crystal 'ball n [C] a glass ball that some people think can show future events

crystal 'clear adj **1** clearly stated and easy to understand: *I made my orders crystal clear.* **2** completely clear and clean

crystallize (also **-ise** BrE) /ˈkrɪstəlaɪz/ v [I,T] **1** if liquid crystallizes, it forms crystals **2** if an idea or plan crystallizes, it becomes clear or certain

cub /kʌb/ n [C] **1** a young bear, lion etc → see picture at LION **2 Cub** a young member of the Scouts

cube /kjuːb/ n [C] **1** a solid square object with six equal sides: *an ice cube* → see picture at SHAPE¹ **2** the cube of a number is the number produced when you multiply it by itself twice —**cube** v [T]

cubic /ˈkjuːbɪk/ adj relating to a measurement of space which is calculated by multiplying the length of something by its width and height: **cubic centimetre/inch** etc

cubicle /ˈkjuːbɪkəl/ n [C] a small separate area in a room: *a shower cubicle*

cuckoo /ˈkʊkuː $ ˈkuːkuː, ˈkʊ-/ n [C] a bird that lays its eggs in the NESTS of other birds and makes a sound like the sound of its name

cucumber /ˈkjuːkʌmbə $ -ər/ n [C] a long thin green vegetable that you eat raw → see picture on page A5

cuddle

cuddle /ˈkʌdl/ v [I,T] to put your arms around someone or something as a sign of love: *Dan cuddled the puppy.* —**cuddle** n [C]

CUDDLE

PHRASAL VERBS
cuddle up to lie or sit very close to someone: **[+to]** *Come and cuddle up to me.*

cuddly /ˈkʌdli/ adj soft, warm, and nice to hold: *cuddly toys*

cue /kjuː/ n [C] **1** an action or event that is a signal for something else to happen: **[+for]** *That was a cue for us to leave.* **2** a word or action in a play that tells an actor to do something: *Tony waited nervously for his cue.* **3** a long straight wooden stick used to hit the ball in games such as SNOOKER

PHRASES
(right/as if) on cue happening at exactly the right moment: *As if on cue, Sam came in.*
take your cue from sb to copy what someone else does because they do it correctly: *With interest rates, the smaller banks will take their cue from the Federal Bank.*

cuff¹ /kʌf/ n [C] the end part of a sleeve, where it fastens

cuff² v [T] to hit someone lightly

'cuff link, cufflink n [C] a small piece of jewellery that a man can use to fasten his shirt sleeves → see picture at **JEWELLERY**

cuisine /kwɪˈziːn/ n [U] a particular style of cooking: *French cuisine*

cul-de-sac /ˈkʌl də ˌsæk, ˈkʊl- $ ˌkʌl də ˈsæk, ˌkʊl-/ n [C] a street with no way out at the end

culinary /ˈkʌlənəri $ ˈkʌləneri, ˈkjuːl-/ adj [only before noun] formal relating to cooking: *culinary skills*

cull /kʌl/ v [T] **1** to kill some of the animals in a group **2** formal to collect information from different places: **cull sth from sth** *The data was culled from many sources.* —**cull** n [C]

culminate /ˈkʌlməneɪt/ v

PHRASAL VERBS
culminate in/with sth to end with a particular event, especially a big or important one: *The meeting culminated in a vote.*

culmination /ˌkʌlməˈneɪʃən/ n **the culmination of sth** something important that happens after a period of development: *The book is the culmination of ten years' work.*

culpable /ˈkʌlpəbəl/ adj formal deserving blame —**culpability** /ˌkʌlpəˈbɪləti/ n [U]

culprit /ˈkʌlprɪt/ n [C] **1** someone who has done something wrong: *The police caught the culprit.* **2** informal the reason for a problem or difficulty: *Tax is the main culprit.*

cult¹ /kʌlt/ n [C] a small religious group whose members often have unusual beliefs: *a religious cult* **THESAURUS** RELIGION

cult² adj a cult film, TV show etc is very popular among a small group of people, but is not known about or liked by most people: *'Donnie Darko' is something of a cult movie.*

cultivate /ˈkʌltɪveɪt/ v [T] **1** to prepare land for growing crops, or to grow a particular crop **2** to try to develop a friendship with someone who can help you: *You need to cultivate useful contacts.* **3** to work hard to develop a particular skill, attitude, or quality —**cultivation** /ˌkʌltɪˈveɪʃən/ n [U]

cultivated /ˈkʌltɪveɪtɪd/ adj **1** someone who is cultivated is intelligent and knows a lot about music, art, literature etc: *a **highly cultivated** man* **2** cultivated land is used for growing crops or plants

cultural Ac /ˈkʌltʃərəl/ adj **1** relating to a particular society and its way of life: *cultural differences | cultural traditions* **2** relating to art, literature, music etc: *the city's cultural life* —**culturally** adv

culture Ac /ˈkʌltʃə $ -ər/ n **1** [C,U] the ideas, way of life, traditions etc of a particular society: *You have to spend time in a country to understand its culture. | the differences between the two cultures | **Western/American/Japanese etc culture*** **2** [U] art, music, literature etc: *If it's culture you're looking for, the city has several museums. | **popular culture** (=the music, films etc that are liked by a lot of people)* **3** [C,U] technical BACTERIA or cells grown for scientific use, or the process of growing them

cultured /ˈkʌltʃəd $ -ərd/ adj intelligent, polite, and interested in art, literature, music etc

'culture ˌshock n [singular, U] the feeling of being confused or anxious when you visit a country that is very different from your own

cumbersome /ˈkʌmbəsəm $ -bər-/ adj **1** heavy and difficult to move or use: *a cumbersome machine* **2** a process or system that is cumbersome is slow and difficult: *Getting a passport is a cumbersome process.*

cumulative /ˈkjuːmjələtɪv $ -leɪtɪv/ adj increasing gradually: *the **cumulative effects** of stress and overwork* —**cumulatively** adv

cunning /ˈkʌnɪŋ/ adj clever, especially in a dishonest or unfair way: *a cunning plan | a cunning opponent* **THESAURUS** INTELLIGENT —**cunning** n [U] —**cunningly** adv

cup¹ /kʌp/ n [C] **1** a small container with a handle that you drink from, or the drink that it contains → **saucer**: *a cup and saucer | **[+of]** a cup of coffee* → see picture at **CUP¹** **2** a metal container that is given as a prize in a competition, or the competition itself: *They **won the** European **Cup**.* **3** a unit used in the US for measuring food when cooking: *Stir in a cup of flour.*

cup² v [T] (**cupped, cupping**) to form your hands

into the shape of a cup: **[+around]** *She **cupped her hands** around the mug.*

cupboard /'kʌbəd $ -ərd/ n [C] a piece of furniture with doors and sometimes shelves, used for storing clothes, plates, food etc → **closet**, **wardrobe**: *kitchen/food/medicine etc cupboard Your coat's in the bedroom cupboard.* | **fitted cupboards** (=ones that are fixed in position and not possible to remove) → see picture at **KITCHEN** → **AIRING CUPBOARD**

curable /'kjʊərəbəl $ 'kjʊr-/ adj an illness that is curable can be cured

curate /'kjʊərət $ 'kjʊr-/ n [C] a priest of low rank whose job is to help the priest who is in charge of an area

curator /kjʊ'reɪtə $ -ər/ n [C] someone who is in charge of a MUSEUM

curb¹ /kɜːb $ kɜːrb/ n [C] **1** something that controls or limits something: **[+on]** *The new tax should act as a curb on spending.* **2** AmE the edge of the PAVEMENT, where it joins the road SYN **kerb** BrE

curb² v [T] to control or limit something: *new measures to curb crime*

curdle /'kɜːdl $ 'kɜːrdl/ v [I,T] if a liquid curdles, it becomes unpleasantly thick: *Milk curdles in warm weather.*

cure¹ /kjʊə $ kjʊr/ v [T]
1 to make an illness or injury better → **heal**: *This type of cancer can be cured.* | **cure sb of sth** *Ninety per cent of patients can be cured of the disease.*
2 to solve a problem, or improve a bad situation: *an attempt to cure unemployment*
3 to preserve food by drying it, hanging it in smoke, or covering it with salt: *cured ham*

cure² n [C] **1** a medicine or treatment that makes an illness go away: **[+for]** *a cure for AIDS* **2** something that solves a problem: **[+for]** *There's no easy cure for poverty.*

curfew /'kɜːfjuː $ 'kɜːr-/ n [C] a law that forces people to stay indoors after a particular time at night: *The army imposed a curfew.*

curiosity /ˌkjʊəri'ɒsəti $ ˌkjʊri'ɑːs-/ n [singular, U] the desire to know about something: *I opened the box to **satisfy** my **curiosity**.* | **out of curiosity** (=because of curiosity) *She followed him out of curiosity.* | **[+about]** *Children have a **natural curiosity** about the world around them.*

curious /'kjʊəriəs $ 'kjʊr-/ adj
1 wanting to know or learn about something: *Puppies are naturally curious.* | **[+about]** *I'm curious about how the system works.* | **curious to know/see/hear etc** *Sue was curious to know what happened.*
THESAURUS STRANGE
2 strange or unusual: *a curious noise* | **[+that]** *It's curious that she left without saying goodbye.*
—**curiously** adv

curl¹ /kɜːl $ kɜːrl/ v [I,T] to form a curve or curves, or to make something do this: *Her long hair curled down her back.* | **curl (sth) around/round sth** *He curled his arm around her waist.*
PHRASAL VERBS
curl up 1 to lie or sit comfortably with your legs bent close to your body: *She curled up on the sofa.*

2 if paper, leaves etc curl up, the edges bend upwards

curl² n [C] something in the shape of a curve, especially a piece of hair: *a girl with blonde curls* | **[+of]** *a curl of smoke*

curler /'kɜːlə $ 'kɜːrlər/ n [C] a small metal or plastic tube for making hair curl

curly /'kɜːli $ 'kɜːrli/ adj curly hair has a lot of curls → see picture at **HAIR**

currant /'kʌrənt $ 'kɜːr-/ n [C] a small dried GRAPE used in cakes

currency Ac /'kʌrənsi $ 'kɜːr-/ n (plural **currencies**)
1 [C,U] the type of money that a country uses: **foreign currency** | the **local currency** THESAURUS MONEY **2** [U] when something is accepted or used by a lot of people: *The idea soon **gained currency**.*

current¹ /'kʌrənt $ 'kɜːr-/ adj happening, existing, or being used now: *her current boyfriend* | *The word is still current in some circles.* —**currently** adv

current² n [C]
1 a flow of water or air in a particular direction: ***Strong currents** are dangerous for swimmers.*
2 a flow of electricity through a wire

current ac·count n [C] BrE a bank account that you can take money out of at any time SYN **checking account** AmE

current af·fairs n [U] important political or social events that are happening now

curriculum /kə'rɪkjələm/ n [C] (plural **curricula** /-lə/ or **curriculums**) the subjects that students learn at a school, college etc

curriculum vitae /kəˌrɪkjələm 'viːtaɪ/ n [C] BrE formal a CV

curry /'kʌri $ 'kɜːri/ n [C,U] (plural **curries**) meat or vegetables cooked in a spicy sauce

curse¹ /kɜːs $ kɜːrs/ v **1** [I] to use rude language because you are angry SYN **swear**: *He cursed loudly.* **2** [T] to say or think bad things about someone or something because they have made you angry: **curse sb/sth for (doing) sth** *He cursed himself for believing her lies.*

curse² n [C] **1** a rude word or words that you use when you are angry **2** magic words that bring someone bad luck: *a witch's curse* **3** something that causes trouble or harm: **[+of]** *Noise is a curse of modern life.*

cursor /'kɜːsə $ 'kɜːrsər/ n [C] a shape on a computer screen that moves to show where you are writing

cursory /'kɜːsəri $ 'kɜːr-/ adj done very quickly and without much attention: *a cursory glance*

curt /kɜːt $ kɜːrt/ adj using very few words in a way that seems rude: *a curt reply* —**curtly** adv —**curtness** n [U]

curtail /kɜː'teɪl $ kɜːr-/ v [T] formal to reduce or limit something: *The new law curtailed police powers.* —**curtailment** n [C,U]

curtain /'kɜːtn $ 'kɜːrtn/ n [C] a piece of cloth that you pull across a window at night, use to divide a room etc: *a new **pair of curtains*** | *Lisa **drew the curtains*** (=opened or closed them). **THESAURUS** CLOSE → see picture at **BATHROOM**

curtsy, curtsey /ˈkɜːtsi $ ˈkɜːr-/ *v* [I] (**curtsied, curtsying, curtsies**) if a woman curtsies, she bends her knees with one foot in front of the other, as a sign of respect for an important person —**curtsy** *n* [C]

curve[1] /kɜːv $ kɜːrv/ *n* [C] a line or shape which bends round like part of a circle: *a **sharp curve** in the road* | *Look at the curve on this graph.* → **LEARNING CURVE**

curve[2] *v* [I,T] to bend or move in the shape of a curve, or to make something do this: *The ball curved through the air.* → see picture at **BENT**[2] —**curved** *adj*

cushion[1] /ˈkʊʃən/ *n* [C]
1 a bag filled with soft material that you put on a chair or the floor to make it more comfortable → **pillow**
2 something that stops one thing from hitting another: *Good sports shoes **provide a cushion** when running.*

cushion[2] *v* [T] **1** if something soft cushions a fall or a hit, it makes it less painful: *His landing was cushioned by the snow.* **2** to reduce the effects of something unpleasant

cushy /ˈkʊʃi/ *adj informal* a cushy job or situation is very easy or pleasant

cuss /kʌs/ *v* [I] *AmE spoken* to say rude words because you are angry [SYN] **swear**

custard /ˈkʌstəd $ -ərd/ *n* [U] *BrE* a thick sauce that you pour over sweet food

custodial /kʌˈstəʊdiəl $ -ˈstoʊ-/ *adj* custodial sentence *BrE* the punishment of being sent to prison

custodian /kʌˈstəʊdiən $ -ˈstoʊ-/ *n* [C] *formal* someone who takes care of a public building or something valuable

custody /ˈkʌstədi/ *n* [U] **1** the legal right to look after a child: **[+of]** *His ex-wife **has custody** of the kids.* **2** when someone is kept in prison until they go to court: **hold/keep sb in custody**

custom /ˈkʌstəm/ *n*
1 [C,U] something that people in a particular society do because it is traditional: **local/ancient/ French etc custom** *She follows Islamic custom by covering her hair.* | **it is the custom (for sb) to do sth** *It's the custom for the bride's father to pay for the wedding.*
2 customs [plural] the place where your bags are checked for illegal goods when you enter a country → **immigration**: *All baggage must **go through customs**.*
3 [U] *formal* when people regularly use a particular shop or business: *The shop **lost custom** when a supermarket opened nearby.*

custom- /ˈkʌstəm/ *prefix* **custom-made/custombuilt/custom-designed etc** made, built etc for a particular person: *He always wore custom-made suits.*

customary /ˈkʌstəməri $ -meri/ *adj* usual or normal: **it is customary (for sb) to do sth** *It is customary*

for the bride to wear white. —**customarily** /ˈkʌstəmərəli $ ˌkʌstəˈmerəli/ *adv*

customer /ˈkʌstəmə $ -ər/ *n* [C] someone who buys things from a shop or company: *a **regular customer*** | *the importance of good **customer service***

THESAURUS

customer someone who buys goods or services from a shop or company: *The shop assistant was serving a customer.* | *The firm is one of our biggest customers.*
client someone who pays for a service from a professional person or company: *I have a meeting with an important business client.*
guest someone who pays to stay in a hotel: *The swimming pool is for hotel guests only.*
consumer any person who buys goods or uses services – used when talking about these people as a group: *More competition means lower prices for consumers.* | *the rights of the consumer*
market the number of people who want to buy a product, or the type of people who want to buy it: *There's a big market for organic vegetables.* | *His clothes are mainly aimed at the youth market.*

customize (also **-ise** *BrE*) /ˈkʌstəmaɪz/ *v* [T] to change something to make it more suitable for a particular person or purpose

cut[1] /kʌt/ *v* (*past tense and past participle* **cut**, *present participle* **cutting**)
1 [INTO PIECES] [I,T] to divide something into two or more pieces using a knife or scissors: *Shall I cut the cake?* | *She **cut** the string **in half** (=into two pieces).* | **cut sth into slices/pieces** *Cut the apple into slices.* | **cut sb a slice/piece (of sth)** (=separate a piece of something from the main part) *Can you cut me a piece of bread, please?* | **[+along/across/round etc]** *Cut along the dotted line.*
2 [MAKE SHORTER] [I,T] to make something shorter with a knife, scissors etc: **cut the lawn/grass/hedge etc** *The grass **needs cutting**.* | **have/get your hair cut** *It's time you got your hair cut.*
3 [REDUCE] [T] to reduce the amount of something: *Try to cut the amount of sugar in your diet.* | *Seventy jobs were lost in order to **cut costs**.* **THESAURUS** REDUCE
4 [INJURE YOURSELF] [T] to hurt yourself with a knife or something else that is sharp: *I cut my finger chopping carrots.* | **cut yourself (on sth)** *Be careful you don't cut yourself.* **THESAURUS** HURT
5 [FILMS/BOOKS/SPEECHES] [T] to remove parts of a film, book, speech etc: *A sex scene was cut from the film.* **THESAURUS** REMOVE
6 [MAKE A HOLE/MARK] [T] to make a mark in the surface of something, open something etc using a sharp tool: **cut sth into sth** *Strange letters were cut into the stone.* | **Cut open** *the chillies and remove the seeds.*
7 [GO A SHORTER WAY] [I] to go somewhere by a quicker and more direct way than usual: **[+through/ across etc]** *I cut across the field.*
8 [ON COMPUTER] [T] to remove writing, a picture etc from a computer document: **Cut and paste** *the picture into a new file* (=remove it and move it to another place).

CUT

slice

dice

shred

chop

grate

carve

PHRASES

cut class/school *AmE informal* to deliberately not go to school: *We cut class and went to hang out at the mall.*

cut corners to do something less well than you should in order to save time, effort, or money: *The airline was accused of cutting corners on safety.*

cut your losses to stop doing something that is failing so that you do not waste any more money, time, or effort: *We decided to cut our losses and close the business.*

cut sth short to stop doing something earlier than you had planned: *The band had to cut short its concert tour.*

PHRASAL VERBS

cut across sth if a problem or feeling cuts across different groups of people, they are all affected by it: *The drug problem cuts across all social classes.*

cut back to make an amount, number, cost etc smaller: **[+on]** *Hospitals are cutting back on staff.* | **cut** sth ↔ **back** *Funding will be cut back.*

cut down

1 to eat, drink, or use less of something, especially in order to improve your health: **[+on]** *I'm trying to cut down on cigarettes.*

2 cut sth ↔ **down** to cut a tree so that the whole of

it falls to the ground: *Large areas of forest have been cut down.*

cut in to interrupt someone who is speaking by saying something: *Do you mind if I cut in?*

cut sb/sth ↔ **off**

1 (*also* **cut** sth **off** sth) to separate something from the main part with a knife etc: *His finger was cut off in the accident.* | *Cut the fat off the meat.*

2 to stop the supply of something to someone: *They'll cut off the electricity if you don't pay the bill.* | *The US has cut off aid to the country.*

3 be/get cut off if you are cut off while you are talking on the telephone, the telephone suddenly stops working

4 be cut off if a place is cut off, it is difficult or impossible to get to: *The city was cut off by floods.*

cut out

1 cut sth ↔ **out** to remove something by cutting it with a knife or scissors: **[+from]** *He was cutting out pictures from the magazine.*

2 cut it/that out! *spoken* used when you want someone to stop doing something that is annoying you: *Hey, Kate, cut it out! That hurts!*

3 be cut out for sth/to be sth to have the qualities that you need for a particular job or activity: *I wasn't cut out to be a teacher.*

4 if an engine cuts out, it suddenly stops working

cut sth ↔ **up** to cut something into small pieces: *Cut up the fruit into pieces.*

THESAURUS

cut to divide something into two or more pieces, using a knife, SCISSORS etc: *He cut the apple into quarters.*

chop to cut wood, vegetables, or meat into pieces: *Chop the onion into small pieces.* | *Bill was chopping wood for the fire.*

slice to cut bread, meat, or vegetables into thin pieces: *Can you slice the bread for the sandwiches?*

carve to cut thin pieces from a large piece of cooked meat: *He began carving the chicken.*

peel to cut the thin outside part off a potato, apple etc: *Peel the potatoes and boil them for about ten minutes.*

saw to cut wood using a SAW (=a tool that you push backwards and forwards on the surface of wood): *I sawed the wood in half.*

snip to quickly cut something using SCISSORS: *Lisa snipped the label off her new sweater.*

mow to cut the grass in a garden, park etc: *Dad was mowing the lawn.*

cut² *n* [C]

1 REDUCTION a reduction in the size, number, or amount of something: **[+in]** *The company announced* **big cuts** *in prices.* | *We need to* **make some cuts** *in spending.* | *tax/pay/job etc cuts*

2 INJURY an injury that you get when something sharp cuts your skin: **[+on]** *He had bruises and cuts on his hands.* **THESAURUS** INJURY

3 HOLE/MARK a hole or mark in a surface made by something sharp: **[+in]** *Make a cut in the paper.*

4 HAIRCUT [usually singular] a HAIRCUT

5 SHARE [usually singular] a share of something,

C

especially money: **[+of]** *Do we all get a cut of the winnings?*

6 OF MEAT a piece of meat that comes from a particular part of an animal: *Use cuts of meat with less fat.* → **SHORT CUT**

PHRASES

be a cut above sb/sth to be better than someone or something else: *This movie is a cut above the rest.*

cut and 'dried *adj* a situation, decision, or result that is cut and dried cannot be changed

cutback /'kʌtbæk/ *n* [C usually plural] a reduction in something, especially to save money: **[+in]** *The government has made cutbacks in the armed forces.*

cute /kjuːt/ *adj* attractive: *a cute little puppy*
THESAURUS ► BEAUTIFUL

cutlery /'kʌtləri/ *n* [U] knives, forks, and spoons **SYN** silverware *AmE*

cutlet /'kʌtlɪt/ *n* [C] a small flat piece of meat on a bone: *a lamb cutlet*

'cut-off (*also* **cutoff**) /'kʌtɒf $ -ɒːf/ *n* [C] a time or level at which something stops: *April's the cut-off date.*

cut-'price (*also* cut-'rate *especially AmE*) *adj* cheaper than normal: *cut-price petrol*

cutter /'kʌtə $ -ər/ *n* [C] a tool used for cutting something: *wire cutters*

'cut-throat *adj* a cut-throat activity or business involves people competing with each other in an unpleasant way: *cut-throat competition*

cutting¹ /'kʌtɪŋ/ *n* [C] **1** a piece that you cut from a plant and use to grow a new plant **2** *BrE* a piece of writing that you cut from a newspaper or magazine **SYN** clipping *AmE*

cutting² *adj* a cutting remark is unkind and intended to upset someone

cutting 'edge *n* **the cutting edge (of sth)** the newest design or way of doing something —**cutting-edge** *adj*: *cutting-edge technology*

CV /ˌsiː 'viː/ *n* [C] *BrE* (**curriculum vitae**) a list of

your education and previous jobs, which you send to employers when you are looking for a job **SYN** résumé *AmE*

cwt the written abbreviation of **hundredweight**

cyanide /'saɪənaɪd/ *n* [U] a very strong poison

cybercafe /'saɪbəkæfeɪ $ -bərkæˌfeɪ/ *n* [C] a CAFE where you can use computers connected to the Internet

cyberspace /'saɪbəspeɪs $ -bər-/ *n* [U] the imaginary place where electronic messages go when they travel from one computer to another

cycle¹ Ac /'saɪkəl/ *n* [C] **1** a number of events that happen many times in the same order: **[+of]** *the cycle of the seasons* **2** *especially BrE* a bicycle or MOTORCYCLE

cycle² Ac *v* [I] *especially BrE* to ride a bicycle **SYN** bike *AmE*: **[+to/down/home etc]** *She cycled to my house.* —**cyclist** *n* [C] —**cycling** *n* [U] → see picture on page A9

cyclic Ac /'saɪklɪk/ (*also* **cyclical** /'sɪklɪkəl, 'saɪ-/) *adj* happening again and again in a regular pattern

cyclone /'saɪkləun $ -kloun/ *n* [C] a very strong wind that moves in a circle

cygnet /'sɪgnɪt/ *n* [C] a young SWAN

cylinder /'sɪləndə $ -ər/ *n* [C] **1** an object in the shape of a tube → see picture at **SHAPE¹** **2** the part of an engine that is shaped like a tube, where another part moves backwards and forwards —**cylindrical** /sə'lɪndrɪkəl/ *adj*

cymbal /'sɪmbəl/ *n* [C] one of a pair of round metal plates that you hit to make a musical sound

cynic /'sɪnɪk/ *n* [C] a cynical person —**cynicism** /-sɪzəm/ *n* [U]

cynical /'sɪnɪkəl/ *adj* unwilling to believe that people have good, honest, or sincere reasons for doing something: **[+about]** *The public is cynical about election promises.* —**cynically** /-kli/ *adv*

cyst /sɪst/ *n* [C] a LUMP containing liquid that grows in your body or under your skin

czar /zɑː $ zɑːr/ *n* [C] another spelling of TSAR

Dd

D, d /diː/ *n* [C,U] (*plural* **D's, d's**) **1** the fourth letter of the English alphabet **2** the second note in the musical SCALE of C MAJOR, or the musical KEY based on this note **3** a mark given to a student's work to show that it is not very good: *I got a D in chemistry.*

-'d /d/ the short form of 'would' or 'had': *She'd like to come.* | *Nobody knew where he'd gone.*

D.A. /ˌdiː 'eɪ/ *n* [C] the abbreviation of **district attorney**

dab¹ /dæb/ *v* [I,T] (**dabbed, dabbing**) to touch something lightly several times, usually with a cloth: *She dabbed her eyes with a handkerchief.* | **dab sth on/onto sth** *Joe was dabbing sun lotion on his face.*

dab² *n* [C] **1** a small amount of something: **[+of]** *a dab of butter* **2** a light touch

dabble /'dæbəl/ *v* [I] to be something in a way that is not very serious: **[+in]** *He dabbled in drugs.*

dad /dæd/ (*also* **daddy** /'dædi/) *n* [C] *informal* father: *Dad took me to the zoo.* | *Dad, can I borrow the car?*

daffodil /'dæfədɪl/ *n* [C] a tall yellow flower that grows in spring → see picture at **FLOWER¹**

daft /dɑːft $ dæft/ *adj BrE spoken informal* silly: *Me, jealous? **Don't be daft!***

dagger /'dægə $ -ər/ *n* [C] a short pointed knife used as a weapon

daily¹ /'deɪli/ *adj*
1 happening, done, or produced every day: *a daily newspaper*
2 relating to a single day: *a daily rate of pay* —**daily** *adv*: *The park is open daily.*
PHRASES
| **daily life** the ordinary things that you do: *Computers are part of daily life in North America.*

daily² *n* [C] (*plural* **dailies**) a newspaper that is printed and sold every day, or every day except Sunday

dainty /'deɪnti/ *adj* small, pretty, and delicate: *dainty white flowers* —**daintily** *adv*

dairy¹ /'deəri $ 'deri/ *n* [C] (*plural* **dairies**) **1** a place on a farm where milk is kept, and butter and cheese are made **2** a company that sells milk and makes cheese, butter etc

dairy² *adj* [only before noun] **1** made from milk: **dairy products/produce 2** connected with the production of milk: **dairy farmer/farm/cattle**

daisy /'deɪzi/ *n* [C] (*plural* **daisies**) a small white flower with a bright yellow centre → see picture at **FLOWER¹**

dam /dæm/ *n* [C] a wall built across a river to stop the water and make a lake —**dam** *v* [T]

damage¹ /'dæmɪdʒ/ *n*
1 [U] physical harm that is done to something, so that it is broken or spoiled: *I hope the storm doesn't do too much damage.* | **[+to]** *Was there any damage to your car?*

> **Grammar**
> Do not say 'Pollution causes damage of the environment.' Say *Pollution causes damage to the environment.*

2 [U] a bad effect on someone or something: **[+to]** *The damage to his reputation was considerable.*
3 damages [plural] *law* money that a court orders someone to pay to someone else for harming that person or their property → **compensation**: *The court awarded her £5,000 in damages.*

COLLOCATIONS

verbs
to do damage *The storm did a lot of damage.*
⚠ Do not say 'make damage'. Say **do damage**.
to cause damage *Did the leak cause any damage?*
to repair the damage *How much will it cost to repair the damage?*
to suffer damage *formal* (=to be damaged by something) *You could suffer damage to your liver.*

adjectives
serious/severe damage *Smoking causes serious damage to your health.*
extensive damage *formal* (=covering a large area) *The bomb did extensive damage.* ⚠ Do not say 'big damage'. Say **a lot of damage** or **extensive damage**.
permanent damage (=that cannot be repaired) *He suffered permanent brain damage.*
minor damage *The water did only minor damage.*

noun + damage
fire/storm/flood etc damage (=caused by fire, storm, flood etc) *Their house suffered serious flood damage.*
brain/liver/nerve etc damage

damage² *v* [T]
1 to cause physical harm to something: *The house has been badly damaged by fire.*
2 to have a bad effect on someone or something: *He claimed that the article had damaged his reputation.* —**damaging** *adj*: *the damaging effects of sunlight*

THESAURUS

damage to cause physical harm to something, or to have a bad effect on something: *The other car wasn't damaged.* | *Smoking can damage your health.*
break to damage a machine or piece of equipment so that it does not work: *I hope I haven't broken your camera.*
smash to damage something by hitting it hard: *Someone had smashed the windows of my car.*
harm to have a bad effect on something: *We need to develop new fuels that won't harm the environment.*

spoil to make something less good or enjoyable: *The view was spoiled by an ugly modern building. | We didn't let the rain spoil our holiday.*
vandalize to deliberately and illegally damage buildings, public property etc: *The classroom had been vandalized and paint sprayed all over the walls.*
sabotage to secretly damage machines or equipment in order to harm an enemy: *The power lines supplying the town's electricity had been sabotaged.*

dame /deɪm/ *n* [C] **1** a British title that is given to a woman because of her achievements: *Dame Judi Dench* **2** *AmE old-fashioned* a woman

damn¹ /dæm/ *spoken* used when you are annoyed or disappointed: *Damn! I forgot to bring my wallet!*

damn² (*also* **damned**) *adv, adj spoken* used to emphasize something: *Everything was so damn expensive. | Turn off that damn TV. | I'll do what I damn well want.*

damn³ *n* **not give a damn** *spoken* to not care at all about something: *I don't give a damn what he thinks.*

damn⁴ *v* [T] *spoken* **1** **damn it/you etc** used when you are very angry: *Damn those kids!* **2** **I'll be damned** used when you are surprised

damned /dæmd/ *adj, adv* another form of 'damn', used especially in writing

damning /ˈdæmɪŋ/ *adj* showing that someone has done something very bad or wrong: **damning indictment/evidence/report/criticism** *a damning report on the state of school discipline*

damp /dæmp/ *adj* slightly wet: *The house was cold and damp. | a damp cloth* —**damp, dampness** *n* [U]

THESAURUS

things

damp slightly wet: *a damp sponge | My clothes were still damp.*
moist slightly wet – used when this is a good thing because it is how something should be: *The cake was lovely and moist. | Make sure that the soil is moist.*
clammy clammy skin is covered in cold sweat, in a way that feels unpleasant: *My hands were all clammy.*

weather/air

damp if the weather is damp, or a place is damp, the air feels wet, especially in a cold unpleasant way: *a damp day in February | a cold damp basement*
humid if the weather is humid, it is very hot and the air feels very wet: *Bangkok gets very humid in the summer.*
muggy if the weather is muggy, it is warm and the air feels wet and uncomfortable: *It was a very muggy evening and I wished it would rain.*

dampen /ˈdæmpən/ *v* [T] **1** (*also* **dampen down** *BrE*) to make something such as a feeling or activity less strong: *Nothing could dampen their enthusiasm.* **2** to make something slightly wet: *The fine rain dampened her hair.*

damper /ˈdæmpə $ -ər/ *n* **put a damper on sth** to stop something from being enjoyable: *Heavy rain put a damper on the event.*

damsel /ˈdæmzəl/ *n* [C] **damsel in distress** *humorous* a young woman who needs help

dance¹ /dɑːns $ dæns/ *n*
1 [C] a special set of movements performed to a particular type of music: *Let's have one more dance. | The only dance I know is the waltz.*
2 [U] the art or activity of dancing: *modern dance | dance lessons*
3 [C] a social event or party where you dance: *a school dance*

dance² *v* [I]
1 to move your body in a way that matches the style and speed of music: **[+with]** *Who's that dancing with Tom? | Do you want to dance?*
2 to move around quickly, because you are excited or full of energy: *She danced round him, trying to grab the letter.* —**dancer** *n* [C] —**dancing** *n* [U]

dandelion /ˈdændəlaɪən/ *n* [C] a small bright yellow wild flower

dandruff /ˈdændrəf, -drʌf/ *n* [U] small white pieces of dead skin from your head

danger /ˈdeɪndʒə $ -ər/ *n*
1 [singular, U] the possibility that someone or something will be harmed, or that something bad will happen: **[+of]** *Is there any danger of infection?* | **in danger** (=in a dangerous situation) *They believe their lives are in danger.* | **out of danger** (=no longer in a dangerous situation) | **be in danger of (doing) sth** *The bridge was in danger of collapsing.* | **[+that]** *There is a danger that these opportunities may be missed.*
2 [C] something or someone that may harm you: **[+to]** *He's a danger to others.* | **[+of]** *the dangers of smoking*

COLLOCATIONS

verbs

to be in danger *Don't worry, you're not in any danger.*
to put sb/sth in danger *He put his own life in danger.*
danger passes (=there is no longer any danger) *They hid until the danger had passed.*

adjectives

great danger *He warned me that I was in great danger.*
serious danger (=very great) *There's a serious danger of flooding.*
constant danger (=continuing all the time) *They are in constant danger of attack.*

danger + noun

a danger area/zone (=an area that could be dangerous) *Houses in the danger zone were evacuated.*

dangerous /ˈdeɪndʒərəs/ *adj* likely to cause physical harm or death, or something bad to happen: **be dangerous (for sb) to do sth** *It's dangerous to walk alone at night around here.* | **[+to/for]** *The virus is not dangerous to humans. | This man is highly dangerous.*

—**dangerously** adv: They were standing dangerously close to the edge.

dangle /'dæŋgəl/ v [I,T] to hang or swing loosely, or to make something do this: **[+from]** The keys were dangling from his belt. | **dangle sth in/over etc sth** I dangled my feet in the water.

dank /dæŋk/ adj unpleasantly wet and cold: a dank cellar

dapper /'dæpə $ -ər/ adj a dapper man is small and neatly dressed

dappled /'dæpəld/ adj marked with spots of colour, light, or shade: **dappled shade/sunlight**

dare¹ /deə $ der/ v **1** [I] to be brave enough to do something – used especially in negative sentences: He wanted to ask her, but he didn't dare. | **dare (to) do sth** I daren't tell mum. **2 dare sb to do sth** to try to persuade someone to do something dangerous: I dare you to jump!
PHRASES
don't you dare spoken used to tell someone that they must not do something: Don't you dare talk to me like that!
how dare you/he etc spoken used when you are very angry about what someone has said or done: How dare you call me a liar!
I dare say (also **I daresay**) especially BrE spoken used when saying that something may be true: I dare say things will improve.

dare² n [C] something dangerous that you have dared someone to do

daredevil /'deədevəl $ 'der-/ n [C] someone who likes doing dangerous things —**daredevil** adj

daren't /deənt $ dernt/ the short form of 'dare not': I daren't tell him. He'd be furious!

daresay /ˌdeə'seɪ $ 'derseɪ/ → DARE¹

daring /'deərɪŋ $ 'der-/ adj **1** willing to do dangerous things: a daring rescue attempt **THESAURUS** BRAVE **2** new or unusual in a way that may shock people: a daring new play —**daring** n [U] —**daringly** adv

dark¹ /dɑːk $ dɑːrk/ adj
1 NO LIGHT if it is dark, there is little or no light **OPP light**: Turn on the light; it's dark in here. | **It gets dark** (=night begins) early in winter. | Suddenly the room **went dark** (=became dark).
2 COLOUR closer to black than to white in colour **OPP light, pale**: dark hair | **dark blue/green/red etc** | a dark suit
3 PERSON a dark person has black hair, brown skin etc **OPP fair**: a small, dark man
4 SECRET mysterious or frightening: a dark secret
5 TIMES/DAYS a dark time is unhappy or without hope: the dark days of the war
PHRASES
dark horse someone who is not well known, and who surprises people by winning a competition or doing something that you do not expect: The champion was defeated by a dark horse, Jack Fleck.

dark² n **1 the dark** when there is no light: My son is afraid of the dark. **2 after/before dark** at night or before night begins: I don't like walking home after dark.
PHRASES
in the dark informal not knowing about something important because no one has told you about it: We had been **kept in the dark** about the sale.

darken /'dɑːkən $ 'dɑːr-/ v [I,T] to become darker, or to make something darker: The sky darkened and rain began to fall. | a darkened room

dark 'glasses n [plural] glasses that you wear to protect your eyes from the sun **SYN** sunglasses

darkly /'dɑːkli $ 'dɑːrk-/ adv in a sad, angry, or threatening way

darkness /'dɑːknəs $ 'dɑːrk-/ n [U] when there is no light: **Darkness fell** (=it got dark) around 5 pm. | **in darkness** (=without any light) The room was in darkness.

darkroom /'dɑːkruːm, -rʊm $ 'dɑːrk-/ n [C] a room with a red light or no light, where film from a camera is made into photographs

darling¹ /'dɑːlɪŋ $ 'dɑːr-/ n [C] used when speaking to someone you love: Come here, darling.

darling² adj [only before noun] much loved: my darling daughter

darn¹ /dɑːn $ dɑːrn/ v [T] to repair a hole in clothes by stitching wool across it

darn² (*also* **darned** /dɑːnd $ dɑːrnd/) *adv, adj AmE spoken* used to emphasize what you are saying: *a darn good idea*

DARTS

dart¹ /dɑːt $ dɑːrt/ *n* **1** [C] a small pointed object that is thrown in a game of darts or used as a weapon **2 darts** [U] a game in which you throw darts at a circular board: *a game of darts* **3** [C] a small fold stitched into a piece of clothing to make it fit

dart² *v* [I] to move suddenly and quickly in a particular direction: **[+back/out/forward etc]** *A child had darted out into the road.*

dash¹ /dæʃ/ *v* **1** [I] to go somewhere very quickly: **[+into/across/out etc]** *She dashed into the room.* | *Tim had to dash off after class.* **THESAURUS** HURRY **2** [T] to make something hit violently against something else: **dash sth against/on sth** *The ship was dashed against the rocks.*

PHRASES

dash sb's hopes to destroy someone's hopes: *Hopes of peace have been dashed.*

I must dash/I have to dash *spoken* used to say you have to leave quickly: *Must dash, I've got a meeting.*

dash² *n* **1** [singular] a small amount of a liquid: *a dash of lemon* **2** [C] a mark (–) used in writing or printing to separate parts of a sentence

PHRASES

make a dash for sth to run very quickly towards something: *He made a dash for the door.*

dashboard /ˈdæʃbɔːd $ -bɔːrd/ *n* [C] the part in front of the driver in a car that has the controls on it

dashing /ˈdæʃɪŋ/ *adj* a dashing man is attractive and confident: *a dashing young doctor*

data Ac /ˈdeɪtə, ˈdɑːtə/ *n* [U, plural] information or facts: *He's* **collecting data** *for his report.* | **data storage/retrieval**

database /ˈdeɪtəbeɪs/ *n* [C] a large amount of information stored in a computer system

data processing *n* [U] the use of computers to store and organize information

date¹ /deɪt/ *n* [C]

1 DAY a particular day of the month or of the year, shown by a number: *'What's today's date?' 'It's August the eleventh.'* | *Please write down your* **date of birth** (=the day you were born). | **set/fix a date** (=choose a day when something will happen) *Have you set a date for the wedding?*

2 MEETING **a)** an arrangement to meet someone, especially someone you like in a romantic way: *Mike's* **got a date** *tonight.* | *Let's* **make a date** (=arrange a time) *to meet up.* **THESAURUS** MEETING **b)** *AmE* someone you go on a date with: *My date's taking me out to dinner.*

3 FRUIT a sweet sticky brown fruit with a long seed → OUT-OF-DATE, SELL-BY DATE, UP-TO-DATE

PHRASES

to date until now: *This is the best research on the subject to date.*

date² *v*

1 [T] to write the date on something: *a letter dated May 1st, 1923*

2 [T] to find out the age of something that is very old: *Geologists can date the rocks by examining fossils in the same layer.*

3 [I,T] to seem old-fashioned, or to make something seem old-fashioned: *His designs have hardly dated at all.*

4 [I,T] *AmE* to have a romantic relationship with someone: *How long have you been dating Monica?*

PHRASAL VERBS

date from sth (*also* **date back to** sth) to have existed since a particular time: *The cathedral dates from the 13th century.*

dated /ˈdeɪtɪd/ *adj* not fashionable any more: *That dress looks a bit dated now.* **THESAURUS** OLD-FASHIONED

daub /dɔːb $ dɒːb/ *v* [T] to put paint or a soft substance on a surface in a careless way: *The walls are daubed with graffiti.*

daughter /ˈdɔːtə $ ˈdɒːtər/ *n* [C] someone's female child: *They have two daughters.*

daughter-in-law *n* [C] (*plural* **daughters-in-law**) the wife of someone's son

daunted /ˈdɔːntɪd $ ˈdɒːn-/ *adj* feeling afraid or worried: **[+by]** *Don't be daunted by the technology.*

daunting /ˈdɔːntɪŋ $ ˈdɒːn-/ *adj* frightening or worrying: **daunting task/prospect/challenge**

dawdle /ˈdɔːdl $ ˈdɒː-/ *v* [I] to take a long time to go somewhere: *Stop dawdling – we'll be late.*

dawn¹ /dɔːn $ dɒːn/ *n* [U] **1** the time of day when light first appears: **at dawn** *We were up at dawn.* | *As* **dawn broke** (=it started to get light) *the rain stopped.* **2 the dawn of civilization/time etc** the time when something began or first appeared **THESAURUS** BEGINNING

dawn² *v* [I] if day or morning dawns, it begins: *The morning dawned fresh and clear.*

PHRASAL VERBS

dawn on sb if a fact dawns on you, you realize it for the first time: *It dawned on me that Jo had been right all along.*

day /deɪ/ *n*

1 [C] a period of time equal to 24 hours → **daily**: *We went to Paris for ten days.* | *They arrived two days ago.* | *I'll call you in a couple of days.* | *'What day is it today?' 'It's Friday.'*

2 [C,U] the period of time between when it becomes light in the morning and when it becomes dark in the evening **OPP** **night**: *The days begin to get* *longer in the spring.* | *It's rained **all day**.*

3 [C usually singular] the time during the day when you are usually awake: *My day usually begins at six o'clock.* | *It's been **a long day** (=used when you had to get up early and were busy all day).*

4 [C] the hours you work in a day: *Jean works an eight-hour day.*

5 [C] (*also* **days** [plural]) a particular time in the past: ***In my day** (=when I was young) very few people had cars.* | *Life was hard **in those days** (=then).*

6 sb's days the time when someone is alive: *She ended her days in Kent.* → DAY-TO-DAY, MODERN-DAY, OPEN DAY, PRESENT-DAY, TODAY, TOMORROW, YESTERDAY

PHRASES

day after day/day in day out used to emphasize that something bad or boring continues to happen: *I'm sick of sitting at the same desk day after day.*

day by day slowly and gradually: *She was getting stronger day by day.*

have had its day to not be popular or successful any more: *I think the band has had its day.*

make sb's day *informal* to make someone very happy: *That card really made my day.*

one day on a day in the past: *She just walked in here one day.*

one day/some day at some time in the future: *I'd like to visit the States some day.*

the other day *spoken* a few days ago: *I saw Roy the other day.* THESAURUS RECENTLY

these days used to talk about the situation that exists now: *Children have lots more opportunities these days.*

to this day until and including now: *To this day we don't know what really happened.*

COLLOCATIONS

adjectives

every day *She washes her hair every day.*

the next/the following day (=the day after something happened) *The following day, a letter arrived.*

the previous day (=the day before something happened) *It had rained the previous day.*

a big day (=a day when something important is planned) *The big day finally arrived.*

a historic day (=a day when something very important happens) *This is a historic day for our country.*

noun + day

sb's wedding day *I was so happy on my wedding day.*

election/market etc day *It's less than a week until election day.*

Christmas/Easter/Independence etc Day *We spent Christmas Day at home.*

Usage

You use **on** to talk about a particular day of the week: *I'm going to a party on Saturday.*

You use **next** to talk about a day in the week after the present one: *I'll meet you next Tuesday.* Do not say 'on next Tuesday'.

You use **this** to talk about a day during the present week: *Her birthday is this Friday.* Do not say 'on this Friday'.

You use **last** to talk about a day in the week before the present one: *He died last Friday.*

---

daybreak /'deɪbreɪk/ *n* [U] the time of day when light first appears SYN **dawn**: **at daybreak** *We set off at daybreak.*

'day care /'deɪkeə $ -ker/ *n* [U] care of young children, or of sick or old people, during the day

'day care ,center *AmE*, **day care centre** *BrE n* [C] a place where babies are cared for while their parents are at work SYN **nursery** *BrE*

'day ,centre (*also* **'day care ,centre**) *n* [C] *BrE* a place where people who are old or ill can be cared for during the day

daydream /'deɪdriːm/ *v* [I] to think about pleasant things so that you forget what you should be doing: **[+about]** *Jessica sat at her desk, daydreaming about Tom.* THESAURUS DREAM —**daydream** *n* [C] —**daydreamer** *n* [C]

daylight /'deɪlaɪt/ *n* [U] the light produced by the sun during the day: *The park is open during **daylight hours**.* | *A young girl has been attacked **in broad daylight** (=during the day when it is light).*

PHRASES

beat/knock the (living) daylights out of sb to hit someone many times and hurt them badly: *If you're lying, I'll knock the living daylights out of you!*

sth is daylight robbery *BrE informal* used to say that something costs a lot more than is reasonable: *Five pounds for a cup of tea? It's daylight robbery.*

scare/frighten the (living) daylights out of sb *informal* to frighten someone a lot: *'You frightened the daylights out of me!' she gasped.*

,day re'turn *n* [C] *BrE* a train or bus ticket that lets you go somewhere at a cheaper price than usual, if you go there and back on the same day: *a day return to Oxford*

daytime /'deɪtaɪm/ *n* [U] the period between the time when it gets light and the time when it gets dark OPP **night-time**: **in/during the daytime** *Owls sleep in the daytime.* | *daytime television*

,day-to-'day *adj* [only before noun] happening every day as a normal part of your life: **day-to-day work/business/life etc** *the day-to-day running of the company*

daze /deɪz/ *n* **in a daze** confused and unable to think clearly: *He wandered around in a daze.*

dazed /deɪzd/ *adj* unable to think clearly, usually because you are shocked or have been in an accident: **dazed look/expression**

dazzle /'dæzəl/ *v* [T] **1** if a strong light dazzles you, it is so strong that you cannot see for a short time **2** if someone or something dazzles you, you think they are very impressive: *They were clearly dazzled by her talent and charm.*

dazzling /'dæzəlɪŋ/ *adj* **1** a dazzling light is so bright that you cannot see for a short time after you look at it THESAURUS BRIGHT **2** very impressive, exciting, or interesting: *a dazzling performance*

de- /diː, dɪ/ *prefix* used to talk about removing something or making it less: *decaffeinated coffee* (=coffee which has had the caffeine removed) | *The government have devalued the currency* (=reduced its value).

deacon /'diːkən/ *n* [C] a religious official in some Christian churches

deactivate /diː'æktɪveɪt/ *v* [T] *formal* to make something stop working OPP **activate**: *Type in the code number to deactivate the alarm.*

dead¹ /ded/ *adj*

1 NOT ALIVE no longer alive: *Her mother's been dead for two years.* | *I think that plant's dead.* | *the dead body of a young boy* | *Two men were shot dead by the terrorists.*

2 NOT WORKING an engine, telephone etc that is dead is not working because there is no power: *Is the battery dead?* | *Suddenly the phone went dead.*

3 NOT ACTIVE/SUCCESSFUL no longer active or being used: *He says the peace plan is dead.*

4 BORING a place that is dead is boring because nothing interesting happens there: *This place is dead during the week.*

5 NO FEELING a part of your body that is dead has no feeling in it for a short time: *My feet have gone dead.*

6 COMPLETE [only before noun] complete: *We all stood waiting in dead silence.* | *The train came to a dead stop.*

7 EXACT [only before noun] exact: *The arrow hit the dead centre of the target.*

8 NO LONGER USED a dead language is no longer used by people OPP **living**

PHRASES

over my dead body *spoken* used when you are determined not to allow something to happen: *You'll marry him over my dead body!*

Word Choice: dead or died?

Dead is an adjective used to describe someone or something that is no longer alive: *a dead fish*

Died is the past tense and past participle of the verb **to die**: *He died of a heart attack in 2002.* Do not say 'They thought he was died.' Say *They thought he was dead.* or *They thought he had died.*

dead² *adv informal* **1** completely or exactly: *dead right/wrong* *'It's a crazy idea.' 'You're dead right!'* | *She stopped dead when she saw us.* | *You can't miss it – it's dead ahead at the lights.* | *The plane landed dead on time.* **2** *BrE spoken* very: *dead easy/simple/boring etc* *The film was dead good.*

dead³ *n* **1 the dead** people who are dead OPP **the living 2 in the dead of night/winter** in the middle of the night or in the middle of winter

deaden /'dedn/ *v* [T] to make a feeling or sound less strong: *drugs to deaden the pain*

dead 'end *n* [C] **1** a street with no way out at one end **2** a situation from which no progress is possible

dead 'heat *n* [C] the result of a race in which two people finish at exactly the same time

deadline /'dedlaɪn/ *n* [C] a date or time by which you must finish something: *He failed to meet the deadline.*

deadlock /'dedlɒk $ -lɑːk/ *n* [singular, U] when people, organizations etc cannot agree: *an attempt to break the deadlock*

deadly¹ /'dedli/ *adj* very dangerous and likely to cause death: *a deadly poison*

deadly² *adv* **deadly serious/boring etc** very serious, boring etc

deadpan /'dedpæn/ *adj* sounding and looking completely serious when you are not

deaf /def/ *adj*

1 physically unable to hear, or unable to hear well → **hearing impaired**: *deaf children* | *Pa's going* (=becoming) *deaf.*

2 the deaf [plural] people who are deaf: *a school for the deaf*

3 be deaf to sth unwilling to listen to something: *She was deaf to all his appeals.* —**deafness** *n* [U]

deafen /'defən/ *v* [T] to make it difficult for you to hear anything —**deafening** *adj*: *The noise was deafening.*

deal¹ /diːl/ *n*

1 [C] an agreement or arrangement, especially in business or politics: *The union did a deal with the government.*

2 a great/good deal a large quantity of something SYN **a lot**: [+of] *I spend a great deal of time abroad.* | **a great deal more/longer/cheaper etc** *Ian is a great deal older than Sue.*

3 [C usually singular] the way someone is treated in a situation: **a good/fair etc deal** *Children deserve a better deal.* | **a rough/raw deal** (=unfair treatment) *He has had a raw deal.* → **big deal** at BIG

PHRASES

be a done deal *informal* to have been agreed or settled: *The sale of the building is practically a done deal.*

it's a deal *spoken* used when you make an agreement with someone: *'I'll go if you go.' 'OK, it's a deal.'*

COLLOCATIONS

verbs

to do/make a deal *I did a deal with him to buy his car.*

to reach/strike a deal *The two sides have finally reached a deal.*

to clinch a deal (=to finally get a deal that you want) *The salesman was eager to clinch the deal.*

a deal falls through (=things do not happen as arranged) *They were going to make a film together, but the deal fell through.*

noun + deal

a business deal *I'd like your advice on a business deal.*

a pay deal *The staff are negotiating a new pay deal.*

a record deal (=one between a singer or band and a recording company) *The band doesn't have a record deal yet.*

adjectives
a good deal (=a good price, offer, or arrangement) *I think I got a good deal.*

deal² v [I,T] (past tense and past participle **dealt** /delt/)
1 (also **deal out**) to give playing cards to all of the players in a card game: *It's your turn to deal.*
2 to buy and sell illegal drugs: *He deals to finance his own habit.* —**dealing** n [U]
PHRASES
| **deal a blow (to sb/sth)** to harm someone or something: *The ban dealt a severe blow to local tourism.*

PHRASAL VERBS
deal in sth to buy and sell a particular product: *She deals in antiques.*
deal with sb/sth
1 to do what is necessary, especially in order to solve a problem: *Who deals with complaints?*
2 to be about a particular subject: *Chapter 6 deals with taxation.*
3 to do business with someone: *We deal with companies all over Europe.*

THESAURUS
to deal with something

deal with sth to do what is necessary, especially in order to solve a problem: *The new president has so many problems to deal with. | We asked the police to deal with the matter.*
handle to deal with a problem or situation - used especially when talking about how well or badly someone does this: *I thought you handled the situation really well.*
tackle to start to deal with a problem in a determined way: *The government needs to do something to tackle unemployment.*
solve if you solve a problem, you deal with it successfully: *I finally solved the problem by getting a new keyboard for my computer.*
take care of sth to do the work or make the arrangements that are necessary, especially in order to help someone else: *Don't worry about locking the doors - I'll take care of that. | Can you take care of the travel arrangements for me?*

dealer /'diːlə $ -ər/ n [C] **1** someone who buys and sells a particular product: *a car dealer* **2** the person who gives out the cards in a card game

dealership /'diːləʃɪp $ -ər-/ n [C] a business that sells a particular company's product, especially cars

dealings /'diːlɪŋz/ n [plural] business or personal relations with someone: **[+with]** *I've had dealings with Baylis before.*

dean /diːn/ n [C] **1** a priest with a high rank in the Christian church **2** a university official with a high rank: *the Dean of Arts*

dear¹ /dɪə $ dɪr/ **oh dear** spoken used when you are surprised, upset, or annoyed: *Oh dear, I've broken it.*

dear² n [C] spoken used when speaking to someone you like or love: *You look nice, dear.*

dear³ adj
1 used before a name at the beginning of a letter: *Dear Mr. Todd, ... | Dear Meg, ...*
2 [not before noun] BrE expensive: *Petrol is a lot dearer in the UK.*
3 used to show that you like someone or something very much: *Mark's a very dear friend. | dear old Aunt Rose*

dearly /'dɪəli $ 'dɪrli/ adv very much: *Sam loved her dearly. | I would dearly like to see him.*

dearth /dɜːθ $ dɜːrθ/ n [singular] formal a lack of something: **[+of]** *the dearth of information*

death /deθ/ n
1 [C,U] the end of someone's life **OPP** birth: *her father's death | the cause of death | [+from] deaths from cancer | bleed/starve etc to death* (=die in this way) *He froze to death. | put/sentence/condemn sb to death* (=kill someone, or decide that they should be killed, as a legal punishment) *He was found guilty and sentenced to death.*
2 the death of sth the permanent end of something: *the death of Communism*
PHRASES
| **be scared/bored etc to death** informal be very frightened, bored etc: *He's scared to death of dogs.*

deathbed /'deθbed/ n **on his/her etc deathbed** when someone is dying

deathly /'deθli/ adj, adv reminding you of death or of a dead body: **deathly cold/white/pale** *She turned deathly pale. | A deathly hush* (=complete silence) *fell over the room.*

'death ˌpenalty n [singular] when someone is killed as a legal punishment → **capital punishment**
THESAURUS PUNISHMENT

death row /ˌdeθ 'rəʊ $ -'roʊ/ n [U] the part of a prison where prisoners are kept before they are killed as a punishment: *Troy is on death row.*

'death squad n [C] a group of people who have been ordered to kill someone's political opponents

'death toll n [singular] the number of people who have died in an accident, war etc: *As the unrest continues, the death toll has risen to 15.*

'death trap n [C] informal a vehicle, building etc that is in such bad condition that it might injure or kill someone

debacle /deɪˈbɑːkəl, dɪ-/ n [C] an event or situation that is a complete failure: *The media blamed the Chancellor for the current economic debacle.*

debar /dɪˈbɑː $ -ˈbɑːr/ v [T] (**debarred, debarring**) formal to officially prevent someone from doing something: *groups which are debarred from voting*

debase /dɪˈbeɪs/ v [T] formal to make someone or something lose their value or people's respect —**debasement** n [C,U]

debatable Ac /dɪˈbeɪtəbəl/ adj an idea, fact, or decision that is debatable may be right but it could easily be wrong: **It's debatable whether** *this book is as good as her last.*

debate¹ Ac /dɪˈbeɪt/ n
1 [C,U] discussion of a subject that often continues

for a long time and in which people express different opinions: *The school's future became the **subject of** much **debate**.*

2 [C] a formal discussion of a subject, for example in parliament, in which people express different opinions, and sometimes vote: **[+on]** *Friday's debate on immigration*

debate² Ac *v* **1** [I,T] to discuss a subject formally so that you can make a decision or solve a problem: *The issue was debated on Monday.* **2** [T] to think about something carefully before making a decision: **debate who/what etc** *I debated whether to phone Kim.*

debauchery /dɪˈbɔːtʃəri $ dɪˈbɒ:-, dɪˈbɑ:-/ *n* [U] immoral behaviour involving drugs, alcohol, sex etc

debilitating /dɪˈbɪlɪteɪtɪŋ/ *adj formal* a debilitating illness or problem makes you very ill or weak

debit¹ /ˈdebɪt/ *n* [C] an amount of money that has been taken out of your bank account OPP **credit**

debit² *v* [T] when a bank debits your account, it takes money away from it because you have spent it OPP **credit**: *Twenty-five pounds has been debited from your account.*

'debit card *n* [C] a plastic card that you can use to pay for things. The money is taken directly from your bank account.

debonair /ˌdebəˈneə◂ $ -ˈner◂/ *adj old-fashioned* fashionable and confident

debrief /ˌdiːˈbriːf/ *v* [T] to get information from someone such as a soldier by officially asking them questions about a job they have just done or an experience they have had → **brief** —**debriefing** *n* [C,U]

debris /ˈdebriː, ˈdeɪ- $ dəˈbriː, deɪ-/ *n* [U] the pieces remaining from something that has been destroyed: *debris from the explosion*

debt /det/ *n*

1 [C,U] if you have debts, or if you are in debt, you owe money to someone: **[+of]** *debts of £50 million* | **in debt (to sb)** *I was heavily in debt.* **THESAURUS** **OWE**

2 [C usually singular] the degree to which you have been influenced by, or helped by, someone or something: *Years later, she acknowledged the **debt** she **owed** him for his help in London.* | **be in sb's debt** *formal* (=be thankful for something someone has done for you)

COLLOCATIONS

verbs

to have debts *He has debts of almost £30,000.*

to run up debts (=borrow more and more money) *She ran up big debts while she was at college.*

to get/fall into debt *I was terrified of getting into debt.*

to pay off a debt (=to pay the money back) *He sold the house to pay off his debts.*

to write off/cancel a debt (=to say officially that it does not have to be paid) *The bank finally agreed to write off the debt.*

adjectives

a big/large/huge debt *The company has huge debts.*

a bad debt (=one that is unlikely to be paid) *How can banks protect themselves against bad debts?*

debtor /ˈdetə $ -ər/ *n* [C] someone who owes money

debunk /ˌdiːˈbʌŋk/ *v* [T] to show that an idea or belief is false

debut /ˈdeɪbjuː, ˈdeb- $ deɪˈbjuː, dɪ-/ *n* [C] the first time that a performer or sports player performs in public: *He made his **debut** for Wales in 98.* | **debut match/appearance etc** *He scored a brilliant goal in his debut match.* —**debut** *v* [I]

Dec. the written abbreviation of **December**

decade Ac /ˈdekeɪd, deˈkeɪd/ *n* [C] a period of ten years

decadent /ˈdekədənt/ *adj* having low moral standards and interested only in pleasure —**decadence** *n* [U]

decaf /ˈdiːkæf/ *n* [C,U] *informal* decaffeinated coffee

decaffeinated /diːˈkæfɪneɪtɪd/ *adj* decaffeinated drinks have had the CAFFEINE removed

decapitate /dɪˈkæpɪteɪt/ *v* [T] to cut off someone's head

decay¹ /dɪˈkeɪ/ *v* [I] **1** to be slowly destroyed by a natural chemical process: *dead or decaying plants* **2** if buildings decay, they are slowly destroyed because no one takes care of them: *Many prisons are old and decaying.* —**decayed** *adj*

decay² *n* [U] when something decays: *tooth decay* | *The house **fell into decay**.*

deceased /dɪˈsiːst/ *n* **the deceased** someone who has recently died —**deceased** *adj*

deceit /dɪˈsiːt/ *n* [C,U] behaviour that tries to make people believe something that is not true: *lies and deceit* —**deceitful** *adj*

deceive /dɪˈsiːv/ *v* [T] to make someone believe something that is not true SYN **trick** → **deception**: *I was completely deceived.* | **deceive sb into doing sth** *He deceived his victim into giving him £500.* | **deceive yourself** *I thought she loved me, but I was deceiving myself.* **THESAURUS** **TRICK**

December /dɪˈsembə $ -ər/ *n* [C,U] (*written abbreviation* **Dec.**) the 12th month of the year, between November and January: **next/last December** *Last December they visited Prague.* | **in December** *We got married in December.* | **on December 6th** *The meeting was on December 6th.*

decency /ˈdiːsənsi/ *n* [U] morally correct behaviour: *At least he **had the decency to** apologize.*

decent /ˈdiːsənt/ *adj* **1** good enough or fairly good: *a decent salary* | *decent food* **2** honest and good: *ordinary decent people* **3** wearing enough clothes, so that you are not showing too much of your body: *Don't come in, I'm not decent!* —**decently** *adv*

decentralize (*also* **-ise** *BrE*) /ˌdiːˈsentrəlaɪz/ *v* [T] to change a government or organization so that decisions are made in a lot of different places, instead of only one place —**decentralization** /ˌdiːˌsentrəlaɪˈzeɪʃən $ -lə-/ *n* [U]

deception /dɪˈsepʃən/ *n* [C,U] the act of deliberately making someone believe something that is not true: *The money was obtained by deception.*

deceptive /dɪˈseptɪv/ *adj* something that is deceptive seems very different from how it really is: *She seems OK, but appearances can be deceptive.* —**deceptively** *adv*

decibel /ˈdesəbel, -bəl/ *n* [C] a unit for measuring the loudness of sound

decide /dɪˈsaɪd/ *v*
1 [I,T] to make a choice to do something, or a judgment about something: *'Where will you live?' 'We haven't decided yet.'* | **decide to do sth** *She decided to accept.* | *Ali decided that the house was too small.* | *I decided I would call her.* | **[+whether/what/when etc]** *Have you decided what to wear?* | **decide against (doing) sth** (=decide not to do something) *They decided against taking the dog.*
2 [T] to be the reason why something has a particular result: *the goal that decided the match*
3 [T] to be the reason for someone making a particular choice: **decide sb to do sth** *What decided you to come all the way out here?*
PHRASAL VERBS
decide on sth to choose one thing from among many: *Have you decided on a name for the baby?*
THESAURUS ▶ CHOOSE

THESAURUS

decide to make a choice to do something: *We decided to celebrate by having a party.*
make up your mind *especially spoken* to decide something, especially after thinking about it for a long time: *I can't make up my mind what to wear.*
choose to do sth to decide to do something – especially when this is different from what people expect or tell you to do: *She chose to ignore my advice.*
make a decision to decide after thinking carefully, especially about something very important: *Have you made a decision about where you want to go to university?*
come to/reach a decision to decide about something important after discussing or considering it – used especially about groups of people: *The jury took several hours to reach a decision.*

decided /dɪˈsaɪdɪd/ *adj* [only before noun] definite and easily noticed: *The new house was a decided improvement on the old one.*

decidedly /dɪˈsaɪdɪdli/ *adv* very much, in a way that is easy to notice: *Chris looked decidedly uncomfortable.*

deciduous /dɪˈsɪdʒuəs/ *adj* deciduous trees lose their leaves in winter → **evergreen**

decimal¹ /ˈdesəməl/ *n* [C] a number, for example 0.8 or 0.263, which is less than one and is shown as

a FULL STOP followed by the number of TENTHS, HUNDREDTHS etc

decimal² *adj* a decimal system is based on the number ten

decimal 'point *n* [C] the mark (.) in a decimal

decimate /ˈdesɪmeɪt/ *v* [T] to destroy a large part of something: *The village had been decimated by war.*

decipher /dɪˈsaɪfə $ -ər/ *v* [T] to find the meaning of something that is difficult to read or understand

decision /dɪˈsɪʒən/ *n* [C] a choice or judgment that you make: **decision to do sth** *Scott's decision to join the navy* THESAURUS ▶ DECIDE

COLLOCATIONS

verbs

to make a decision *I've made my decision: I'm leaving.*
to take a decision *BrE* (=to make an important or formal decision) *The company took the decision to close the factory.*
to come to/reach a decision (=to make a decision after a lot of thought) *The jury took three days to reach a decision.*

adjectives

an important/major decision *Don't make any important decisions without talking to me.*
a big decision (=an important decision) *It was a big decision and I needed some time to think about it.*
a difficult/hard/tough decision *She was facing a difficult decision.*
a good/bad decision *I admit I've made some bad decisions in the past.*
the right/wrong decision *I'm sure you've made the right decision.*

decisive /dɪˈsaɪsɪv/ *adj* **1** having an important effect on the result of something: *a decisive moment in his career* **2** good at making decisions quickly and firmly: *a decisive leader* **3** a decisive victory, result etc is very definite and clear —**decisively** *adv*: *A manager must be able to act decisively.* —**decisiveness** *n* [U]

deck¹ /dek/ *n* [C] **1 a)** the flat top part of a ship, that you can walk on: **on deck** *Let's go up on deck.* **b)** one of the levels on a ship, plane, or bus: *the lower deck* **2** *AmE* a wooden floor built out from the back of a house, where you can sit outdoors **3** *AmE* a set of playing cards SYN **pack** *BrE*

deck² (*also* **deck out**) *v* [T] to decorate something with flowers, flags etc: *The church was decked with flowers.*

deckchair /ˈdektʃeə $ -tʃer/ *n* [C] *BrE* a folding chair with a long seat made of cloth → see picture at **CHAIR¹**

decking /ˈdekɪŋ/ *n* [U] a wooden floor next to a house or in a garden

declaration /ˌdekləˈreɪʃən/ *n* [C,U] an official statement about something: *a declaration of war*

declare /dɪˈkleə $ -ˈkler/ *v* [T]
1 to state officially and publicly that a particular situation exists or that something is true: *She*

declared her **intention** to stand for president. | In 1853, Turkey **declared war** on Russia. | **declare sb/sth (to be) sth** The strike was **declared** illegal. | **[+(that)]** The company declared there was no risk.
2 to say something in a clear firm way: 'It's not fair,' Jane declared.
3 to state the value of things that you have bought or own, because you may have to pay tax on them

decline¹ Ac /dɪˈklaɪn/ n [C,U] a decrease in the quality, quantity, or importance of something: **[+in]** a decline in profits | **in decline** The city was in decline.

decline² Ac v **1** [I] to decrease in quantity, quality, or importance: Coffee production declined. | His health continued to decline. **THESAURUS** DECREASE **2** [I,T] formal to say no to an invitation, offer, or request, usually politely: Mary **declined** Jay's **invitation** to dinner. | **decline to do sth** Murray declined to comment. **THESAURUS** REFUSE

declutter /diːˈklʌtə $ -ər/ v [I,T] to make a place tidy by removing things you do not want or need: I decided it was time to declutter my bedroom.

decode /ˌdiːˈkəʊd $ -ˈkoʊd/ v [T] to discover the meaning of a secret or complicated message

decommission /ˌdiːkəˈmɪʃən/ v [T] to stop using a ship, weapon, or NUCLEAR REACTOR and to take it to pieces

decompose /ˌdiːkəmˈpəʊz $ -ˈpoʊz/ v [I,T] to be slowly destroyed by a natural process: a partially decomposed body

decor /ˈdeɪkɔː $ -kɔːr/ n [C,U] the way that the inside of a building is decorated: The decor was very modern.

decorate /ˈdekəreɪt/ v
1 [T] to make something look more attractive by putting something pretty on it: Paintings decorated the walls. | **decorate sth with sth** Decorate the cake with cherries.
2 [I,T] BrE to paint or put paper onto the walls of a room or building: We need to decorate the bathroom. | I spent Saturday decorating.

decoration /ˌdekəˈreɪʃən/ n
1 [C,U] something pretty that you put onto something else in order to make it more attractive: Christmas decorations | Save some of the nuts for decoration.
2 [U] the style in which something is decorated, or the activity of decorating something: changes in the decoration of churches

decorative /ˈdekərətɪv $ ˈdekərə-, ˈdekəreɪ-/ adj pretty and used as a decoration: decorative features
—**decoratively** adv

decorator /ˈdekəreɪtə $ -ər/ n [C] especially BrE someone who paints houses and puts paper on the walls as their job

decorum /dɪˈkɔːrəm/ n [U] formal behaviour that is polite and suitable for a particular occasion

decoy /ˈdiːkɔɪ/ n [C] a person or object that is used to trick a person or animal into going somewhere or doing something

decrease /dɪˈkriːs/ v [I,T] to become less, or to make something do this **OPP** increase: Crime decreased by 30%. | **[+to]** By 1881, the population had decreased to 5.2 million. | the need to decrease costs

—**decrease** /ˈdiːkriːs/ n [C,U]: a decrease in sales

THESAURUS

decrease to become less: In the UK, the size of families has decreased.
go down to decrease. **Go down** is less formal than **decrease** and is the usual word to use in everyday English: Prices usually go down in January.
fall/drop to decrease, especially by a large amount: Prices have fallen by 50%. | The number of accidents has dropped dramatically.
decline formal to decrease, especially gradually – used especially about the standard or level of something: Standards of health care have declined in recent years.

decree /dɪˈkriː/ n [C] an official order or decision
—**decree** v [T]

decrepit /dɪˈkrepɪt/ adj old and in bad condition: his decrepit car

decriminalize (also **-ise** BrE) /diːˈkrɪmənəlaɪz/ v [T] to state officially that something is not illegal any more —**decriminalization** /diːˌkrɪmənəlaɪˈzeɪʃən $ -lə-/ n [U]

dedicate /ˈdedɪkeɪt/ v [T] **1** to give all your attention and effort to one thing: **dedicate yourself/your life to (doing) sth** She dedicated her life to helping the poor. **2** to say that a book, film, song etc has been written, made, or performed for someone, to show that you respect or love them: The book is dedicated to his wife.

dedicated /ˈdedɪkeɪtɪd/ adj working very hard at something because you think it is important: a dedicated musician

dedication /ˌdedɪˈkeɪʃən/ n **1** [U] when you work very hard because you believe that what you are doing is important: the skill and dedication of our staff | **[+to]** his dedication to the sport **2** [C] an act of dedicating something to someone, or a ceremony where this is done **3** [C] the words used when dedicating a book, film, song etc to someone

deduce Ac /dɪˈdjuːs $ dɪˈduːs/ v [T] formal to decide that something is true using the information that you have

deduct /dɪˈdʌkt/ v [T] to take away an amount from a total: Taxes are deducted from your pay.
—**deductible** adj

deduction Ac /dɪˈdʌkʃən/ n **1** [C] an amount that is taken away from a total: I earn about $2,000 a month, after deductions. **2** [C,U] when you decide that something is likely to be true, using the information that you have: his formidable **powers of deduction**

deed /diːd/ n [C] **1** formal something that someone does: **good deeds 2** law an official paper that is a record of an agreement, especially an agreement concerning who owns property

deem /diːm/ v [T] formal to decide that something is true: The material was deemed faulty.

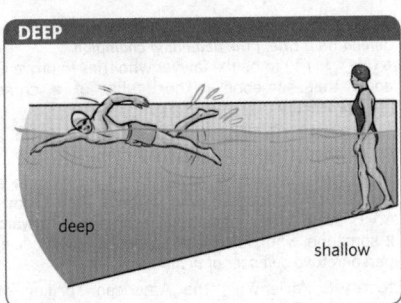

DEEP

deep

shallow

deep¹ /diːp/ adj

1 **FROM TOP TO BOTTOM** if something is deep, there is a long distance from the surface to the bottom OPP **shallow** → **depth**: *The water's not very deep.* | *a deep cut*

2 **FROM FRONT TO BACK** if something is deep, there is a long distance from the front to the back: *a deep shelf*

3 **IN MEASUREMENTS** 3 centimetres/7 feet etc deep measuring 3 centimetres, 7 feet etc from the surface to the bottom or from the front to the back: *The pool was 5 metres deep.*

4 **SERIOUS/SEVERE** serious or severe: *the **deep divisions** within the party* | *She's **in deep trouble**.*

5 **BREATH/SIGH** a deep breath/sigh if you take a deep breath or give a deep SIGH, you take a lot of air into your lungs before letting it out again

6 **FEELING/BELIEF** a deep feeling or belief is felt very strongly: *Colin felt a **deep sense** of despair.*

7 **SOUND/VOICE** a deep sound or voice is very low

8 **COLOUR** a deep colour is dark and strong OPP **light**, **pale**: *a deep blue carpet*

9 **SLEEP** a deep sleep if someone is in a deep sleep, it is difficult to wake them

10 **DIFFICULT TO UNDERSTAND** serious and often difficult to understand: *Some of his books are a bit deep for me.* → **KNEE-DEEP**

PHRASES

deep in thought/conversation thinking or talking so much that you do not notice anything else: *He was too deep in thought to notice me.*

deep² adv

1 a long way into or below the surface of something: *He thrust his hands deep in his pockets.* | *deep beneath the ground*

2 **two/three etc deep** if things or people are two deep, three deep etc, there are two, three etc rows or layers of them: *People were standing four deep at the bar.*

PHRASES

deep down 1 if you feel or know something deep down, you are sure about it: *Deep down, I knew she was right.* **2** if someone is kind, cruel etc deep down, that is what they are really like, even though they seem not to be: *Deep down, she is a very caring person.*

run/go deep if a feeling runs deep or goes deep, people feel it very strongly: *Resentment against the police ran deep.*

deepen /ˈdiːpən/ v [I,T] to become worse, or make something become worse: *The crisis deepened.*

deep 'freeze n [C] a large metal box in which food can be stored at very low temperatures for a long time SYN **freezer**

deep 'fried adj cooked in a lot of hot oil

deeply /ˈdiːpli/ adv extremely or very much: *She was deeply upset.*

deep-'seated (*also* **deep-'rooted**) adj a deep-seated feeling or idea is strong and very difficult to change

deep-'set adj deep-set eyes are deep in the surface of the face

deer /dɪə $ dɪr/ n [C] (*plural* **deer**) a large wild animal that can run very fast, eats grass, and has horns on its head

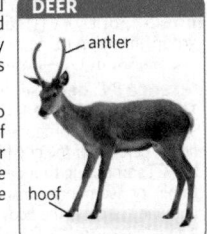

DEER

antler

hoof

deface /dɪˈfeɪs/ v [T] to spoil the appearance of something by writing or making marks on it: *the vandals who defaced the statue*

defamation /ˌdefəˈmeɪʃən/ n [U] *law* when someone says or writes bad and untrue things about someone else —**defamatory** /dɪˈfæmətəri $ -tɔːri/ adj

default¹ /dɪˈfɔːlt $ -ˈfɑːlt/ n [C] the way in which things are arranged on a computer screen unless you decide to change them: *The default page length is 58 lines.*

PHRASES

by default if something happens by default, it happens only because something else does not happen: *The other team never arrived, so we won by default.*

default² v [I] to not do something that you have legally agreed to do: **[+on]** *He defaulted on his loan payments.*

defeat¹ /dɪˈfiːt/ n [C,U]

1 failure to win or succeed: *their 2-0 defeat against Manchester United* | *On 2 March, they **suffered** their worst **defeat** of the war.*

2 victory over someone or something: **[+of]** *her defeat of Democrat Abe Robbins*

defeat² v [T]

1 to win a victory over someone in a war, competition, game etc SYN **beat**: *In the last match, Venus Williams defeated her sister 6-3, 6-4.* THESAURUS **WIN**

2 if a problem or piece of work defeats you, it is so difficult that you cannot solve it or do it: *It was the last question on the paper that defeated me.*

3 to make something fail: *The plan was defeated by a lack of money.*

Word Choice: defeat or beat?
Defeat is used especially in written English: *The National Party narrowly defeated the ruling Labour government.*

D

Beat sounds less formal and is used especially in spoken English. You use it especially about defeating someone in a game, race, or competition: *Do you think Murray will beat Nadal in the final?*

defeatist /dɪˈfiːtɪst/ *adj* behaving in a way that shows you expect to fail: *a defeatist attitude* —**defeatism** *n* [U] —**defeatist** *n* [C]

defecate /ˈdefɪkeɪt/ *v* [I] *formal* to get rid of solid waste from your body

defect¹ /ˈdiːfekt, ˈdiːˌfekt/ *n* [C] a fault in the way something is made or the way it works: **[+in]** *defects in the product* **THESAURUS** FAULT —**defective** /dɪˈfektɪv/ *adj*: *defective machinery*

defect² /dɪˈfekt/ *v* [I] to leave your own country or group in order to go to or join an opposing one —**defector** *n* [C] —**defection** /dɪˈfekʃən/ *n* [C,U]

defence *BrE*, **defense** *AmE* /dɪˈfens $ ˈdiːfens/ *n*
1 AGAINST ATTACK **a)** [U] the act of protecting something or someone from attack: **[+of]** *their heroic defence of the city* | *the defense of human rights* **b)** [C] something that can be used to protect something or someone from attack: **[+against]** *The immune system is the body's defence against infection.*
2 AGAINST CRITICISM [C,U] something that you say or do in order to support someone or something who is being criticized: **in sb's/sth's defence** *Jill wrote a letter to their boss in Mike's defense.*
3 WEAPONS/ARMIES [U] the weapons, soldiers etc that a country uses to protect itself from attack: *spending on defence* | *the Defense Department*
4 IN LAW **a)** [C] the things that are said in a court of law to prove that someone is not guilty of a crime: *His defence was that he intended only to wound the thief.* **b)** **the defence** the lawyers in a court who try to prove that someone is not guilty of a crime: *The defense called only one witness.*
5 IN SPORTS [C,U] the players in a game such as football whose main job is to stop the other team from getting points → **SELF-DEFENCE**

defenceless *BrE*, **defenseless** *AmE* /dɪˈfensləs/ *adj* weak and unable to protect yourself: *a defence-less child*

defend /dɪˈfend/ *v*
1 AGAINST ATTACK [T] to protect someone or something from attack: **defend sb/sth against/from sth** *a castle built to defend the island against invaders* | **defend yourself** *The course teaches women to defend themselves.*
2 AGAINST CRITICISM [T] to say something to support someone or something that has been criticized: *The school has defended its decision.* | **defend yourself (against sth)** *He defended himself against the allegations.* | *She vigorously defended her husband.*
3 MAKE STH CONTINUE [T] to make sure that something can continue to exist, and is not taken away: *It is important to defend democracy.* | *The workers are fighting to defend their jobs.*
4 IN SPORTS [I,T] to try to prevent your opponents from getting points in a game such as football: *Liverpool defended well.*
5 IN A COMPETITION [T] to try to win a competition

that you won last time: *The team are preparing to* **defend** *their* **title.** | **the defending champion**
6 IN LAW [I,T] to be the lawyer who tries to prove in court that someone is not guilty of a crime **OPP** prosecute

defendant /dɪˈfendənt/ *n* [C] the person in a court who has been ACCUSED of a crime

defender /dɪˈfendə $ -ər/ *n* [C] **1** a player in a game such as football who defends their team's GOAL from the opposing team → **forward** **2** someone who defends a particular idea, belief, person etc: *a defender of democracy*

defense /dɪˈfens/ *n* the American spelling of DEFENCE

defenseless /dɪˈfensləs/ *adj* the American spelling of DEFENCELESS

defensive¹ /dɪˈfensɪv/ *adj* **1** intended to protect people from attack: *defensive weapons* **2** behaving in a way that shows you think someone is criticizing you: *He was very defensive about his work.* —**defensively** *adv*

defensive² *n* **on the defensive** ready to defend yourself: *Jane was angry and on the defensive.*

defer /dɪˈfɜː $ -ˈfɜːr/ *v* [T] (**deferred**, **deferring**) *formal* to delay something until a later date: *Further discussions will be deferred until April.*

deference /ˈdefərəns/ *n* [U] *formal* behaviour that shows that you respect someone or something: **in deference to sb/sth** *They wore black in deference to tradition.* —**deferential** /ˌdefəˈrenʃəl◂/ *adj*

defiance /dɪˈfaɪəns/ *n* [U] when you refuse to obey a person or rule → **defy**: **act/gesture of defiance** *an act of defiance against his parents* | **in defiance (of sb/sth)** *Some stores opened in defiance of the law.*

defiant /dɪˈfaɪənt/ *adj* refusing to obey a person or rule: *a defiant gesture* —**defiantly** *adv*

deficiency /dɪˈfɪʃənsi/ *n* [C,U] (*plural* **deficiencies**) **1** a lack of something that you need: *a vitamin deficiency* **2** a fault that makes something or someone not good enough: **[+in/of]** *the deficiencies of the system*

deficient /dɪˈfɪʃənt/ *adj* **1** not containing enough of something: **[+in]** *a diet that is deficient in iron* **2** not good enough: *a deficient immune system*

deficit /ˈdefɪsɪt/ *n* [C] the difference between the amount of something you have and the higher amount you need: **[+of]** *a trade deficit of $3 billion*

defile /dɪˈfaɪl/ *v* [T] *formal* to spoil something that is beautiful, good, or pure

define Ac /dɪˈfaɪn/ *v* [T]
1 to describe something correctly and thoroughly: *We need to define our clients' needs.* | **clearly/well defined** *The aims need to be clearly defined.*
2 to explain the meaning of a word → **definition**: *It's difficult to define the word exactly.* | **define sth as sth** *A budget is defined as 'a plan of action expressed in money terms'.*

definite Ac /ˈdefɪnət, ˈdefənət/ *adj*
1 without any doubt: *I can't give you a definite answer.* | *The study shows a definite link between sun exposure and skin cancer.*

2 a definite arrangement or promise is certain to happen: *We haven't made any definite arrangements.* **3** [not before noun] saying something firmly so that people are certain what you mean: [+about] *She's very definite about what she wants.*

definite 'article *n* [singular] the word 'the' in English → **indefinite article**

definitely Ac /'defɪnətli, 'defənətli/ *adv* without any doubt SYN **certainly**: *That's definitely true.* | *The museum is definitely worth visiting.*

definition Ac /ˌdefəˈnɪʃən/ *n* [C] a phrase or sentence that says what a word means: [+of] *There are many definitions of the word 'feminism'.*

PHRASES

by definition having a particular quality because all things or people of the same type have it: *Children are, by definition, immature.*

definitive Ac /dɪˈfɪnətɪv/ *adj* **1** a definitive book is better than any other book on the same subject: *the definitive guide to wine* **2** a definitive agreement, statement etc is certain and unlikely to change: *I can't give a definitive answer yet.* —**definitively** *adv*

deflate /ˌdiːˈfleɪt, dɪ-/ *v* **1** [T] to make someone feel less important or confident: *I felt deflated by his criticism.* **2** [I,T] if a tyre, BALLOON etc deflates, or if you deflate it, it gets smaller because the air comes out

deflect /dɪˈflekt/ *v* **1** [T] to do something to stop people paying attention to you and criticizing you: **deflect sth (away) from sth** *attempts to deflect attention away from his private life* **2** [T] to take someone's attention away from what they are trying to do: **deflect sb from sth** *She refused to be deflected from her aims.* **3** [I,T] to make something move in a different direction, especially after hitting something: *He deflected the ball away from the goal.* —**deflection** /-ˈflekʃən/ *n* [C,U]

deforestation /diːˌfɒrəˈsteɪʃən $ -ˌfɔː-, -ˌfɑː-/ *n* [singular, U] when all the trees in an area are cut down or destroyed

deformed /dɪˈfɔːmd $ -ɔːrmd/ *adj* something that is deformed has the wrong shape, especially because it has grown or developed wrongly: *deformed hands*

deformity /dɪˈfɔːməti $ -ɔːr-/ *n* [C,U] (plural **deformities**) a part of someone's body that is not the normal shape: *children with physical deformities*

defraud /dɪˈfrɔːd $ -ˈfrɒːd/ *v* [T] to get money from an organization by deceiving them: **defraud sb of sth** *attempts to defraud the bank of almost $30,000*

defrost /ˌdiːˈfrɒst $ -ˈfrɒːst/ *v* [I,T] **1** if frozen food defrosts, or if you defrost it, it becomes warmer and stops being frozen **2** to turn off a FREEZER or REFRIGERATOR so that the ice inside it melts

deft /deft/ *adj* quick and skilful: *deft movements* —**deftly** *adv*

defunct /dɪˈfʌŋkt/ *adj* not existing or useful any more

defuse /ˌdiːˈfjuːz/ *v* [T] **1** to improve a difficult or violent situation by making people less angry: **defuse a situation/crisis/row** *an attempt to defuse*

the crisis **2** to stop a bomb from exploding by removing the FUSE

defy /dɪˈfaɪ/ *v* [T] (**defied, defying, defies**) **1** to refuse to obey someone or something → **defiance**: *people who openly defy the law* **2 defy description/ analysis/belief etc** to be impossible to describe or understand: *Its size defies description.* **3 defy sb to do sth** to ask someone to try to do something that you think is not possible

degenerate¹ /dɪˈdʒenəreɪt/ *v* [I] to become worse: [+into] *The discussion soon degenerated into an argument.*

degenerate² /dɪˈdʒenərət/ *adj* morally unacceptable: *his degenerate lifestyle* —**degenerate** *n* [C]

degrade /dɪˈɡreɪd/ *v* [T] to treat someone in a way that makes people have less respect for them: *an advert which degrades women* —**degrading** *adj* —**degradation** /ˌdeɡrəˈdeɪʃən/ *n* [U]

degree /dɪˈɡriː/ *n*

1 TEMPERATURE [C] a unit for measuring temperature: **30 degrees Celsius/80 degrees Fahrenheit etc** (=30°C/80°F etc)

2 ANGLE [C] a unit for measuring angles: *a 90 degree angle* (=90°)

3 AMOUNT OF STH [C,U] the amount or level of something: [+of] *an operation with a high degree of risk* | *The treatment has been used with* **varying degrees** *of success.* | **to a degree/to some degree/to a certain degree** (=partly) *Your weight depends to some degree on your genes.*

4 QUALIFICATION [C] a QUALIFICATION that you get when you finish a course at university: [+in] *She* **has a degree** *in physics.* | **do/take a degree** *He did a degree in French.* → **MASTER'S DEGREE**

dehydrated /ˌdiːhaɪˈdreɪtɪd $ diːˈhaɪdreɪ-/ *adj* not having enough water in your body —**dehydration** /ˌdiːhaɪˈdreɪʃən/ *n* [U]

deity /'deɪəti, 'diː-/ *n* [C] (plural **deities**) a god or GODDESS

déjà vu /ˌdeɪʒɑː ˈvuː/ *n* [U] the feeling that you are having exactly the same experience as you have had before: *I had a sudden feeling of déjà vu.*

dejected /dɪˈdʒektɪd/ *adj* sad and disappointed: *He looked slightly dejected.*

delay¹ /dɪˈleɪ/ *n* [C,U] when you have to wait for something to happen, or the time you have to wait: *There are* **long delays** *on the motorway.* | *There may be a* **slight delay.** | **without delay** (=immediately) *He replied to the letter without delay.*

delay² *v*

1 [I,T] to wait until a later time to do something: *He agreed to delay the decision.* | **delay sth until sth** *The elections will be delayed until June.* | **delay doing sth** *Don't delay seeking help if your child is unwell.*

2 [T] to make someone or something late, or make something happen more slowly: *Our flight was delayed by bad weather.* | *A good diet can delay the onset of the disease.*

THESAURUS

delay to wait until a later time to do something: *They decided to delay the announcement about the wedding.* | *Don't delay – buy now!*

postpone to change an event to a later time or date: *The match has been postponed.*

put sth off to delay doing something. **Put off** is less formal than **delay** or **postpone** and is very common in everyday English: *I've been putting off painting the house, but it really needs doing.* | *I can't put it off any longer.*

procrastinate *formal* to delay doing something that you should do: *The government cannot procrastinate any longer on the issue.*

delectable /dɪˈlektəbəl/ *adj formal* very pleasant, especially to taste or smell

delegate¹ /ˈdelɪɡət/ *n* [C] someone who has been chosen to represent a group at a meeting

delegate² /ˈdelɪɡeɪt/ *v* [I,T] to give part of your work or responsibilities to someone else: *Some of the tasks can be delegated to assistants.*

delegation /ˌdeləˈɡeɪʃən/ *n* **1** [C] a group of people who represent a country or organization: **[+of]** *a delegation of French officials* **2** [U] when you give someone else part of your work or responsibilities: **[+of]** *the delegation of responsibility*

delete /dɪˈliːt/ *v* [T] to remove something from a piece of writing or from the information on a computer: **delete sth from sth** *The data has been deleted from the file.* **THESAURUS** REMOVE —**deletion** /-ˈliːʃən/ *n* [C,U]

deli /ˈdeli/ *n* [C] a DELICATESSEN

deliberate¹ /dɪˈlɪbərət/ *adj* **1** intended or planned: *a **deliberate** attempt to embarrass her* | *a deliberate mistake* **2** slow and careful: *His steps were slow and deliberate.*

deliberate² /dɪˈlɪbəreɪt/ *v* [I,T] to think about something carefully

deliberately /dɪˈlɪbərətli/ *adv*
1 done in a way that is intended or planned [OPP] **accidentally**: *The fire was started deliberately.*
2 in a slow and careful way: *He spoke very slowly and deliberately.*

> ### THESAURUS
>
> **deliberately** if you do something deliberately, you choose to do it, and it does not happen by chance: *She deliberately waited until after they had left the room.*
> **on purpose** *especially spoken* deliberately, especially in order to annoy someone or get an advantage for yourself: *I didn't push her on purpose – it was an accident.*
> **intentionally** deliberately. **Intentionally** sounds a little more formal than **deliberately** and is used especially when saying that someone has thought carefully before doing something: *The advertisement was intentionally misleading.* | *The police couldn't prove that she did it intentionally.*

deliberation /dɪˌlɪbəˈreɪʃən/ *n* [C,U] careful thought or discussion: *After much deliberation the prize was awarded to Murray.*

delicacy /ˈdelɪkəsi/ *n* (*plural* **delicacies**) **1** [U] when something is soft, light, or easily damaged: *the delicacy of the petals* **2** [U] when you behave in a careful

way so that you do not upset people: *a situation that needs to be handled with delicacy* **3** [C] a rare or expensive food that is good to eat: *local delicacies*

delicate /ˈdelɪkət/ *adj*
1 easily damaged or broken: *delicate china*
2 small and attractive: *delicate flowers* | *her delicate hands*
3 needing to be dealt with very carefully so that you do not upset people: *This is a very delicate matter.*
4 a delicate colour, taste, or smell is not very bright or strong: *a delicate shade of pink*
5 *old-fashioned* often ill: *a delicate child* **THESAURUS** WEAK —**delicately** *adv*

delicatessen /ˌdelɪkəˈtesən/ *n* [C] a shop that sells good quality cheeses, cooked meats, SALADS etc

delicious /dɪˈlɪʃəs/ *adj* very pleasant to taste or smell: *a delicious meal* **THESAURUS** TASTE

> ### THESAURUS
>
> **delicious** food or drink that is delicious tastes very good: *This bread's delicious! Did you make it yourself?* | *a delicious fruit drink*
> **tasty** *especially spoken* if something is tasty, you like the taste: *a tasty sauce* | *tasty snacks*
> **yummy/scrumptious** *informal* delicious: *This chocolate cake is yummy!*
> **mouth-watering** mouth-watering food looks or smells delicious and makes you want to eat it: *There was a cafe serving mouth-watering Italian ice cream.*

delight¹ /dɪˈlaɪt/ *n* **1** [U] a feeling of great pleasure: **with/in delight** *The children screamed with delight.* | **to sb's delight** *The plans were rejected to the delight of local people.* | *He **took** great **delight in** (=enjoyed) telling me I was wrong.* **2** [C] something that gives you pleasure: *The game was a delight to watch.* | **the delights of sth** *a chance to enjoy the delights of Tuscany*

delight² *v* [T] to give someone great pleasure and enjoyment: **delight sb with sth** *She delighted fans with her performance.*
PHRASAL VERBS
delight in sth to enjoy something very much, especially something unpleasant: *She delights in shocking people.*

delighted /dɪˈlaɪtɪd/ *adj* very pleased: **delighted to do sth** *Yoko will be delighted to see you.* | **[+(that)]** *I'm delighted you can come.* | **[+with/by/at]** *Helen absolutely delighted with the results.* **THESAURUS** HAPPY

> **Grammar**
> Do not say 'I was very delighted with the present.' Say *I was absolutely delighted with the present.*

delightful /dɪˈlaɪtfəl/ *adj formal* very pleasant: *a delightful garden* —**delightfully** *adv*

delinquency /dɪˈlɪŋkwənsi/ *n* [U] *formal* bad or illegal behaviour by young people —**delinquent** *n* [C]: *a young delinquent* —**delinquent** *adj*: *delinquent behaviour* → **JUVENILE DELINQUENT**

delirious /dɪˈlɪriəs/ adj **1** talking in a confused way because you are ill **2** literary extremely happy —**deliriously** adv

delirium /dɪˈlɪriəm/ n [U] when someone is very confused because they are ill

deliver /dɪˈlɪvə $ -ər/ v
1 [I,T] to take something to a place: **deliver sth to sth** The letter was delivered to his home. | I'm having some flowers **delivered** for her birthday. THESAURUS TAKE
2 [T] to say something formally: **deliver a speech/lecture etc** He delivered a televised speech. | **deliver a judgment/verdict** The jury delivered a verdict of unlawful killing.
3 [I,T] to do the things that you have promised: **[+on]** It's time the government started delivering on its promises. | the failure of some services to **deliver the goods** (=do what they have promised)
4 [T] to help a woman give birth to her baby

delivery /dɪˈlɪvəri/ n (plural **deliveries**) **1** [C,U] when something is taken to a place, or the things that are taken: There's free delivery on orders over £25. | a delivery service **2** [U] when people provide a service or do something that they have promised to do: **[+of]** the delivery of care for the elderly **3** [C,U] the process of giving birth to a baby

delta /ˈdeltə/ n [C] an area of low land near the sea where a river separates into many smaller rivers

delude /dɪˈluːd/ v [T] to make someone believe something that is not true: She deluded herself that she was in love.

deluge /ˈdeljuːdʒ/ n [singular] **1** a lot of things that happen or arrive at the same time: **[+of]** a deluge of complaints **2** formal a large flood —**deluge** v [T]: We were deluged with mail.

delusion /dɪˈluːʒən/ n [C,U] something you believe that is not true: the delusion that things were better in the past

deluxe /dəˈlʌks $ -ˈlʊks/ adj very good and expensive: a deluxe hotel

delve /delv/ v [I] **1** to try to find out more about something: **[+into]** attempts to delve further into the subject **2** to put your hand deep inside a bag or box in order to find something: **[+into]** He delved into his pocket and brought out a pen.

demand¹ /dɪˈmɑːnd $ dɪˈmænd/ n
1 [singular, U] the need or desire that people have for goods and services: **[+for]** There's a great demand for new housing. | the **growing demand** for organic produce | skills that are **much in demand**
2 [C] a very determined request for something: **[+for]** demands for political reform
3 demands [plural] the difficult or tiring things you have to do, or the skills you need: **[+of]** the demands of modern life | **[+on]** The play **makes** considerable **demands** on the actors' talents.

PHRASES
on demand whenever someone wants something: Do you feed your baby on demand?

demand² v [T]
1 to ask for something in a determined way: The President demanded the release of all the hostages. |

[+that] They demanded that he should resign. | **demand to know/see etc sth** They demanded to see my passport. | 'Where are you going?' she demanded angrily. THESAURUS ASK

Grammar
Do not say 'He demanded for a pay rise.' Say He demanded a pay rise.

2 if one thing demands another thing, it needs that thing in order to be successful: Learning a language demands a great deal of time and effort.

demanding /dɪˈmɑːndɪŋ $ dɪˈmæn-/ adj **1** needing a lot of time, ability, and effort: a demanding job THESAURUS DIFFICULT **2** always wanting attention in a way that is annoying: a demanding child

demeaning /dɪˈmiːnɪŋ/ adj making you feel that you are not important or respected: a demeaning job

demeanour BrE, **demeanor** AmE /dɪˈmiːnə $ -ər/ n [singular, U] formal the way someone behaves, dresses, speaks etc: her cheerful demeanour

demented /dɪˈmentɪd/ adj behaving in a crazy way

dementia /dɪˈmenʃə, -ʃiə $ -tʃə/ n [U] an illness that gradually affects someone's brain and memory

demise /dɪˈmaɪz/ n [singular] formal **1** the end of something that used to exist: **[+of]** the demise of the steel industry **2** someone's death

demo /ˈdeməʊ $ -moʊ/ n [C] (plural **demos**) **1** BrE a DEMONSTRATION: an anti-war demo **2** an example of something that is produced to show what it is like or how it works: demo software

democracy /dɪˈmɒkrəsi $ dɪˈmɑː-/ n [C,U] (plural **democracies**) the political system in which everyone can vote to choose the government, or a country that has this system: the struggle for democracy | Western democracies

democrat /ˈdeməkræt/ n [C] someone who supports the idea of democracy

Democrat n [C] someone who supports the Democratic Party in the US

democratic /ˌdeməˈkrætɪk◂/ adj **1** a democratic government or leader has been elected by the people of a country **2** organized according to the idea that everyone should be involved in making decisions: a democratic style of management —**democratically** /-kli/ adv: He was democratically elected.

Democratic Party n the Democratic Party one of the two main political parties in the US → **the Republican Party**

demolish /dɪˈmɒlɪʃ $ dɪˈmɑː-/ v [T] **1** to destroy a building: The house was demolished in 1968. THESAURUS DESTROY **2** to prove that an idea or opinion is completely wrong: The theory has been demolished by recent research. —**demolition** /ˌdeməˈlɪʃən/ n [C,U]

demon /ˈdiːmən/ n [C] an evil SPIRIT —**demonic** /dɪˈmɒnɪk $ -ˈmɑː-/ adj

demonstrate Ac /ˈdemənstreɪt/ v
1 [T] to show that something is true: The accident demonstrated the importance of wearing seat belts. |

[+that] *The study demonstrates that fewer graduates are finding jobs.*
2 [T] to show someone how to do something or how something works: **[+how]** *Instructors should demonstrate how to use equipment.* **THESAURUS** EXPLAIN
3 [I] to protest with other people in a public place: **[+against]** *Huge crowds demonstrated against war.*
4 [T] to show that you have a particular skill, quality, or feeling: *Students must demonstrate an ability to work under pressure.*

demonstration Ac /ˌdemənˈstreɪʃən/ n
1 [C] an occasion when a large group of people meet to show that they disagree with or support something: **[+against]** *a demonstration against the government* | *Thousands of students* **took part in** the **demonstration**.
2 [C,U] when you show someone how to do something or how something works: **[+of]** *She* **gave** *us a* **demonstration** *of how to use the software.* | *a cookery demonstration*
3 [C] something that shows someone or something has a particular quality or feeling: **[+of]** *This is a clear demonstration of the country's commitment to peace.*

> **Word Choice: demonstration or protest?**
> A **demonstration** is a large public event in which people gather together or walk together to show that they disagree with or support something: *an anti-war demonstration*
> A **protest** is any action taken by a person or group to show their disapproval of something they think is wrong or unfair: *He left the party as a protest against the war.* | *The people took control of the airport* **in protest** *against the government.*

demonstrative Ac /dɪˈmɒnstrətɪv $ dɪˈmɑːn-/ adj willing to show that you care about someone
demonstrator Ac /ˈdemənstreɪtə $ -ər/ n [C] someone who takes part in a demonstration
demoralized (also **-ised** BrE) /dɪˈmɒrəlaɪzd $ -ˈmɔː-, -ˈmɑː-/ adj no longer feeling confident or hopeful: *I came out of the interview feeling totally demoralized.*
demoralizing (also **-ising** BrE) /dɪˈmɒrəlaɪzɪŋ $ -ˈmɔː-, -ˈmɑː-/ adj making you feel less confident and hopeful: *They suffered a demoralizing defeat.* —**demoralize** v [T]
demote /dɪˈməʊt $ -ˈmoʊt/ v [T] to give someone a less important job OPP **promote** —**demotion** /-ˈməʊʃən $ -ˈmoʊ-/ n [C,U]
demure /dɪˈmjʊə $ -ˈmjʊr/ adj shy, quiet, and polite
den /den/ n [C] **1** the home of some wild animals **2** informal a room in a house where people can relax **3** a place where secret or illegal activities happen
denial Ac /dɪˈnaɪəl/ n **1** [C,U] a statement saying that something is not true → **deny**: *The government* **issued** *an official* **denial** *of the reports.* **2** [U] when someone is not allowed to have or do something: **[+of]** *the denial of basic human rights*
denigrate /ˈdenɪɡreɪt/ v [T] to criticize someone or something unfairly

denim /ˈdenɪm/ n [U] strong cotton cloth used for making JEANS
denomination /dɪˌnɒməˈneɪʃən $ dɪˌnɑː-/ n [C] a religious group with slightly different beliefs from other groups in the same religion
denote Ac /dɪˈnəʊt $ -ˈnoʊt/ v [T] to mean or represent something: *Each H on the map denotes a hospital.*
denounce /dɪˈnaʊns/ v [T] to criticize someone or something publicly: **denounce sb/sth as sth** *The election was denounced as a farce.*
dense /dens/ adj **1** containing a lot of things or people close together: *dense pine forests* **2** dense smoke or cloud is difficult to see through —**densely** adv
density /ˈdensəti/ n [C,U] (plural **densities**) **1** the number of people or things there are in an area, in relation to the size of the area: *Taiwan has a high* **population density**. | **[+of]** *the density of housing* **2** technical the relationship between an object's weight and the amount of space it fills

dent¹ /dent/ n [C] a hollow area in the surface of something, where it has been hit: *a dent in the car door*
dent² v [T] **1** to have a bad effect on something: *The affair severely dented his reputation.* **2** to make a hollow area on the surface of something by hitting it

DENT
a dent in the car door

dental /ˈdentl/ adj relating to teeth: *dental care*
dental 'floss n [U] special string that you use for cleaning between your teeth
dentist /ˈdentɪst/ n [C] someone whose job is to treat people's teeth: *I'm* **going to the dentist's** *this afternoon.* —**dentistry** n [U]
dentures /ˈdentʃəz $ -ərz/ n [plural] a set of artificial teeth
denunciation /dɪˌnʌnsiˈeɪʃən/ n [C,U] a public statement in which you criticize someone or something
deny Ac /dɪˈnaɪ/ v [T] (**denied, denying, denies**) **1** to say that something is not true OPP **admit** → **denial**: *In court they denied all the charges.* | **[+(that)]** *He strongly denied that he had taken the money.* | **deny doing sth** *Wilks denies murdering his wife.*
2 to not let someone have something: **deny sb sth** *Many people are being denied basic human rights.*
deodorant /diːˈəʊdərənt $ -ˈoʊ-/ n [C,U] a substance that you put under your arms to stop your body smelling unpleasant
depart /dɪˈpɑːt $ -ɑːrt/ v [I] formal to leave: **[+from]** *The train will depart from Platform 4.* | **[+for]** *He departed for Rome immediately.* **THESAURUS** LEAVE
department /dɪˈpɑːtmənt $ -ɑːr-/ n [C] one of the parts of a large organization such as a college,

government, or company: *the marketing department* —**departmental** /ˌdiːpɑːˈtmentl◂ $ -ɑːr-/ *adj*

de'**partment ˌstore** *n* [C] a large shop that sells many different types of things

departure /dɪˈpɑːtʃə $ -ˈpɑːrtʃər/ *n* **1** [C,U] when a person, plane, train etc leaves a place: *Check in at the airport an hour before departure.* | **[+for]** *her departure for Japan* **2** [C] a change from what is usual or expected: **[+from]** *a significant departure from previous methods*

depend /dɪˈpend/ *v* **it/that depends** *spoken* used to say that you are not sure about something, because other things might affect what happens: *'Are you coming to my house later?' 'It depends. I might have to work.'*

PHRASAL VERBS

depend on/upon sb/sth

1 if something depends on something else, it is directly affected by that thing: *Your grade will depend on your performance in the final exam.*

2 to need help from someone or something: *We depend entirely on donations from the public.*

3 to trust someone or something: *I know I can always depend on Jon.*

dependable /dɪˈpendəbəl/ *adj* someone or something that is dependable will always do what you need them to do: *a dependable employee* | *a dependable car*

dependant *BrE*, **dependent** *AmE* /dɪˈpendənt/ *n* [C] a person, especially a child, who needs someone else to pay for their food, clothes etc

dependent /dɪˈpendənt/ *adj* **1** needing someone or something in order to exist, be successful, healthy etc OPP **independent**: **[+on/upon]** *The local economy is dependent on tourism.* THESAURUS **NEED** **2 be dependent on/upon sth** *formal* to be directly affected by something else: *Starting salary is dependent on experience.* —**dependence** (also **dependency**) *n* [U]

depict /dɪˈpɪkt/ *v* [T] to show someone in a picture or to describe them in a story: *The god is depicted as a bird with a human head.* —**depiction** /dɪˈpɪkʃən/ *n* [C,U]

deplete /dɪˈpliːt/ *v* [T] to reduce the amount of something: *Many forests have been depleted by acid rain.* —**depletion** /dɪˈpliːʃən/ *n* [U]: *the depletion of the ozone layer*

deplorable /dɪˈplɔːrəbəl/ *adj formal* very bad: *The prisoners were held in deplorable conditions.*

deplore /dɪˈplɔː $ -ˈplɔːr/ *v* [T] *formal* to say that you think something is very bad and that you strongly disapprove of it: *a statement deploring the use of chemical weapons*

deploy /dɪˈplɔɪ/ *v* [T] to move soldiers and military equipment to a place so that they can be used if necessary —**deployment** *n* [C,U]: *the deployment of UN troops*

deport /dɪˈpɔːt $ -ɔːrt/ *v* [T] to force someone to leave a country and return to the country they came from —**deportation** /ˌdiːpɔːˈteɪʃən $ -pɔːr-/ *n* [C,U]

depose /dɪˈpəʊz $ -ˈpoʊz/ *v* [T] to remove a leader

from their position: *The king was recently deposed by the military.*

deposit¹ /dɪˈpɒzɪt $ dɪˈpɑː-/ *n* [C] **1** a part of the cost of something that you pay before paying the total amount later: *We* **put down a deposit** *on the house.* | **[+of]** *We require a deposit of 10%.* **2** an amount of money that you pay into a bank account OPP **withdrawal**: *I'd like to* **make a deposit** *please.* **3** money that you pay when you rent something such as an apartment or car, which will be given back if you do not damage it: *We paid one month's rent in advance, plus a deposit of $500.* **4** a layer of a mineral, metal etc that is left in soil or rocks through a natural process: *oil and mineral deposits*

deposit² *v* [T] **1** to put money into a bank account or valuable things into a safe place: *We deposited the money in a Swiss bank account.* **2** *formal* to put something down in a particular place: *She deposited her bag by the front door.* **3** to gradually leave a layer of a substance on a surface: *The river deposits silt along its bed.*

de'**posit ac,count** *n* [C] *BrE* a bank account that pays INTEREST on the money that you leave in it

depot /ˈdepəʊ $ ˈdiːpoʊ/ *n* [C] a place where buses, trains etc are kept when they are not being needed

depraved /dɪˈpreɪvd/ *adj* morally bad or evil: *Michael thought we were all depraved gamblers.*

depreciate /dɪˈpriːʃieɪt/ *v* [I] to decrease in value or price: *A new car depreciates as soon as it is driven.* —**depreciation** /dɪˌpriːʃiˈeɪʃən/ *n* [U]

depress Ac /dɪˈpres/ *v* [T] **1** to make someone feel very unhappy: *His films depress me.* **2** to reduce the value of something, or make something less successful: *The bad weather has depressed sales.* | *A war will depress the global economy.*

depressed /dɪˈprest/ *adj* **1** very unhappy: *She felt lonely and depressed.* THESAURUS **SAD 2** not having enough jobs or business activity: *depressed inner-city neighbourhoods*

depressing /dɪˈpresɪŋ/ *adj* making you feel sad: *a depressing book*

depression Ac /dɪˈpreʃən/ *n* [C,U] **1** a feeling of great sadness, or a medical condition that makes you have this feeling: *The patient is* **suffering from depression**. **2** a long period during which there is very little business activity and many people do not have jobs: *a severe* **economic depression** → see Word Choice at **RECESSION**

deprive /dɪˈpraɪv/ *v*

PHRASAL VERBS

deprive sb **of** sth to prevent someone from having something that they need or should have: *Prisoners were deprived of sleep for three days.*

deprived /dɪˈpraɪvd/ *adj* not having the things that are necessary for a comfortable or happy life: *a deprived childhood* THESAURUS **POOR** —**deprivation** /ˌdeprɪˈveɪʃən/ *n* [U]

depth /depθ/ *n* **1** [C,U] **a)** the distance from the top of something to the bottom of it → **deep**: **[+of]** *The lake has an average depth of six to eight metres.* **b)** the distance from the front of an object to the

back of it: **[+of]** *The depth of the shelves is about 35 cm.* → see picture at **DIMENSION 2** [U] (*also* **depths**) how strong an emotion is or how serious a situation is: **[+of]** *People need to realize the depth of the problem.* | *I was in* **the depths of depression** (=very unhappy). **3 the depths of the ocean/forest** etc the part of an ocean etc that is furthest away from people, and most difficult to reach → **IN-DEPTH**
PHRASES

in depth including all the details: *The book examines the issue* **in great depth**.

be out of your depth to be in a situation that is too difficult for you to understand or deal with: *For the first week at her new job she felt hopelessly out of her depth.*

the depths of winter the middle of winter, when it is coldest: *Stews are great, especially in the depths of winter.*

deputize (*also* **-ise**) /ˈdepjʊtaɪz/ v [I] *BrE* to do the work of someone of a higher rank than you for a short time because they are unable to do it: **[+for]** *Jed could deputize for Stewart, if necessary.*

deputy /ˈdepjʊti/ n [C] (*plural* **deputies**) someone in an organization who is directly below another person in rank, and who is officially in charge when that person is not there

derail /ˌdiːˈreɪl, dɪ-/ v [I,T] if a train derails or is derailed, it goes off the tracks —**derailment** n [C,U]

deranged /dɪˈreɪndʒd/ adj behaving in a crazy or dangerous way: *a deranged criminal*

deregulation /diːˌregjəˈleɪʃən/ n [U] when rules and controls are removed in an area of business

derelict /ˈderəlɪkt/ adj a derelict building or piece of land is in very bad condition because it has not been used for a long time

deride /dɪˈraɪd/ v [T] *formal* to say or show that you think that someone or something is silly or unimportant —**derision** /dɪˈrɪʒən/ n [U] —**derisive** /dɪˈraɪsɪv/ adj: *derisive laughter*

derisory /dɪˈraɪsəri/ adj an amount of money that is derisory is so small that it is not worth considering seriously: *a derisory pay increase*

derivation Ac /ˌderəˈveɪʃən/ n [C,U] what something developed from, especially a word

derive Ac /dɪˈraɪv/ v **1** [T] to get something, especially an advantage or a pleasant feeling, from something: *It's important that I* **derive** *some* **pleasure** *from my work.* **2** [I,T] to develop or come from something: **[+from]** *The word is derived from Latin.*

dermatologist /ˌdɜːməˈtɒlədʒɪst $ ˌdɜːrməˈtɑː-/ n [C] a doctor who treats skin diseases

derogatory /dɪˈrɒgətəri $ dɪˈrɑːgətɔːri/ adj insulting and disapproving: *derogatory remarks about his family*

descend /dɪˈsend/ v [I,T] *formal* to go down **OPP** **ascend**: *He slowly descended the steps.*
PHRASES

be descended from sb to be related to someone who lived a long time ago: *She is descended from a family of French aristocrats.*

descendant /dɪˈsendənt/ n [C] someone who is

related to a person who lived a long time ago → **ancestor**: *a descendant of slaves* **THESAURUS** **RELATIVE**

descent /dɪˈsent/ n **1** [C,U] when a plane, person etc goes down to a lower place **OPP** **ascent**: *The plane began its descent.* **2** [U] your family origins, especially the country they lived in in the past: **of Italian/Russian etc descent** *a young man of Asian descent*

describe /dɪˈskraɪb/ v [T] to say what someone or something is like or to explain something that has happened: *Police asked the woman to describe her attacker.* | **describe sb/sth as sth** *The victim's neighbors described him as a gentle man who loved children.* | **describe sb/sth to sb** *Ava was just describing to me her trip to Egypt.* | **[+how/what/why etc]** *It's hard to describe how I felt.*

Grammar
Do not say 'She described me the house.' Say *She described the house to me.*

description /dɪˈskrɪpʃən/ n [C,U]
1 something you say or write that tells people what someone or something is like: **[+of]** *The police issued a* **detailed description** *of the missing woman.* | **brief/short/full/complete description** *The catalog gives a description of each product.* | **fit/match/answer a description** (=be like the person described)
2 a type of something: *I think it's a weapon* **of some description**. | *People* **of all descriptions** *came to see the show.* → **JOB DESCRIPTION**

descriptive /dɪˈskrɪptɪv/ adj a descriptive word or piece of writing describes something

desecrate /ˈdesɪkreɪt/ v [T] to damage something holy or respected —**desecration** /ˌdesɪˈkreɪʃən/ n [singular, U]

desert[1] /ˈdezət $ -ərt/ n [C,U] a large area of very hot dry land where few plants grow: *the Sahara desert*

desert[2] /dɪˈzɜːt $ -ˈzɜːrt/ v **1** [T] if you desert a person or place, you leave them and never go back: *Her boyfriend deserted her when she got pregnant.* | *People have* **deserted** *the villages and moved to the cities.* **2** [I] to leave the army without permission —**desertion** /-ˈzɜːʃən $ -ˈzɜːr-/ n [C,U]

deserted /dɪˈzɜːtɪd $ -ɜːr-/ adj a deserted place is empty and quiet: *At night the streets are deserted.* **THESAURUS** **EMPTY**

deserter /dɪˈzɜːtə $ -ˈzɜːrtər/ n [C] a soldier who leaves the army without permission

desert 'island n [C] a tropical island where nobody lives

deserve /dɪˈzɜːv $ -ɜːrv/ v [T] if you deserve something, you should get it because of something you have done: *After all that work you deserve a break.* | **deserve to do sth** *We didn't really deserve to win.* | *What had he done to* **deserve** *this* **punishment**? | *People who are sent to prison for drunk-driving* **get what** *they* **deserve**. —**deserved** adj: *a well-deserved rest* —**deservedly** /dɪˈzɜːvɪdli $ -ɜːr-/ adv

deserving /dɪˈzɜːvɪŋ $ -ɜːr-/ adj [only before noun] needing help and support: *The money is intended to help deserving students.*

design¹ Ac /dɪˈzaɪn/ n
1 [C,U] the way that something is planned or made: *We've made some changes to the computer's original design.*
2 [C] a pattern used to decorate something: *curtains with a floral design*
3 [C,U] a drawing that shows how something will be made or what it will look like, or the process of making one of these drawings: *The new plane is in its final design stage.* | [+for] *the design for the new office building* → **GRAPHIC DESIGN, INTERIOR DESIGN**

design² Ac v [T]
1 to draw or plan something that you will make or build: *The palace was designed by an Italian architect.*
2 to make something for a particular purpose or person: **design sth to do sth** *These exercises are designed to strengthen muscles.* | **be designed for sb/sth** *a computer specifically designed for children*

designate /ˈdezɪɡneɪt/ v [T] to choose someone or something for a particular job or purpose: *The building was designated as a temporary hospital.*
—**designation** /ˌdezɪɡˈneɪʃən/ n [C,U]

designer¹ /dɪˈzaɪnə $ -ər/ n [C] someone whose job is to design new styles of clothes, cars etc: *a fashion designer* | *an interior designer* (=someone who designs the inside of a building)

designer² adj [only before noun] designer clothes are made by a famous fashion designer: *designer suits*

desirable /dɪˈzaɪərəbəl $ -ˈzaɪr-/ adj something that is desirable is something you want because it is good or useful: *a desirable neighborhood*
—**desirability** /dɪˌzaɪərəˈbɪləti $ -ˌzaɪr-/ n [U]

desire¹ /dɪˈzaɪə $ -ˈzaɪr/ n
1 [C,U] a strong feeling that you want something very much: [+for] *a desire for peace* | **desire to do sth** *a desire to win at all costs* | *She had no desire to marry him.*
2 [U] when you feel strongly that you want to have sex with someone

desire² v [T] **1** *formal* to want something very much: *The hotel has **everything** you **could** possibly desire.* **2** to find someone sexually attractive
PHRASES
have the desired effect/result to have the effect or result you wanted: *Her remarks had the desired effect.*

desk /desk/ n [C] a table where you sit and write or work → see picture at **CLASSROOM** → **CASH DESK**

desktop /ˈdesktɒp $ -tɑːp/ n [C] **1** the main area on a computer where you can find the ICONS that represent PROGRAMS, and where you can do things to manage the information on the computer **2** the top surface of a desk

desktop publishing n [U] (abbreviation **DTP**) when you arrange the writing and pictures for a magazine, book etc using a computer

desolate /ˈdesələt/ adj **1** a place that is desolate has no people or activity and is not attractive: *a*

desolate highway **2** someone who is desolate is very sad and lonely —**desolation** /ˌdesəˈleɪʃən/ n [U]

despair¹ /dɪˈspeə $ -ˈsper/ n [U] a feeling that you have no hope at all: *She killed herself **in despair**.*

despair² v [I] *formal* to feel that there is no hope at all: *Despite his illness, Ron never despaired.*
—**despairing** adj

despatch /dɪˈspætʃ/ n, v a British spelling of DISPATCH

desperate /ˈdespərət/ adj
1 willing to do anything to change a bad situation, even if it is dangerous or unpleasant: *Joe had been unemployed for over a year and was **getting desperate**.* | *a desperate attempt to escape*
2 needing or wanting something very much: [+for] *The team is desperate for a win.* | **desperate to do sth** *After a week in the hospital he was desperate to go home.* **THESAURUS** ▶ NEED
3 a desperate situation is very bad or serious: *a **desperate shortage** of food* —**desperately** adv: *The doctors tried desperately to save her life.*
—**desperation** /ˌdespəˈreɪʃən/ n [U]

despicable /dɪˈspɪkəbəl, ˈdespɪ-/ adj extremely bad or cruel: *a despicable crime* —**despicably** adv

despise /dɪˈspaɪz/ v [T] to hate someone very much: *He was a nasty man who despised children.*
THESAURUS ▶ HATE

despite Ac /dɪˈspaɪt/ prep used to say that something happened or is true, even though this is not what you expected: *She loved him despite the way he treated her.*

despondent /dɪˈspɒndənt $ dɪˈspɑːn-/ adj very unhappy and without hope: *Taylor was broke and increasingly despondent about finding work.*
—**despondently** adv

despot /ˈdespɒt, -ət $ ˈdespət, -ɑːt/ n [C] someone, especially a ruler, who uses power in a cruel and unfair way —**despotic** /deˈspɒtɪk $ -ˈspɑː-/ adj
—**despotism** /ˈdespətɪzəm/ n

DESSERTS

gateau *BrE*

apple pie

sponge cake

sundae

dessert /dɪˈzɜːt $ -ɜːrt/ n [C,U] sweet food that you eat after the main part of a meal: *What's for dessert?*

destabilize (also **-ise** BrE) /diːˈsteɪbəlaɪz/ v [T] to make something such as a government or ECONOMY become less successful or more likely to get worse

destination /ˌdestəˈneɪʃən/ n [C] the place that you are travelling to: *We have just enough fuel to reach our destination.*

destined /ˈdestɪnd/ adj certain to do or become something: **destined to do sth** *She was destined to become her country's first woman Prime Minister.* | **[+for]** *He's destined for greatness.*

destiny /ˈdestɪni/ n [C,U] (plural **destinies**) the things that will happen to someone in the future **SYN fate**: *a nation fighting to control its own destiny*

destitute /ˈdestɪtjuːt $ -tuːt/ adj having no money, no home, no food etc: *The floods left thousands of people destitute.* —**destitution** /ˌdestɪˈtjuːʃən $ -ˈtuː-/ n [U]

destroy /dɪˈstrɔɪ/ v [T] to damage something very badly, so that it no longer exists, or cannot be repaired: *The building was completely destroyed by fire.* | *Condon destroyed any evidence that linked him to the crime.*

THESAURUS

destroy to damage something very badly, so that it no longer exists, or cannot be repaired: *Their house was destroyed by a bomb.* | *We are destroying our planet.*
devastate to damage a large area very badly and destroy the buildings, trees etc in it: *Large areas of the city were devastated by an earthquake.*
wreck to damage a building, room, car etc very badly, especially so that it is in pieces: *The fans wrecked the train.* | *Hundreds of homes were wrecked by the storm.*
ruin to spoil something completely, especially so that it looks very bad: *My new carpet was ruined.* | *The new houses will ruin the view.*
demolish to completely destroy a building, either deliberately or by accident: *The cinema had to be demolished because it was unsafe.* | *The explosion demolished the school.*
knock down to get rid of a building, wall etc, especially in order to build something new: *We decided to knock down the old wooden garage.*

---

destroyer /dɪˈstrɔɪə $ -ər/ n [C] a small fast military ship with guns

destruction /dɪˈstrʌkʃən/ n [U] when something is destroyed: **[+of]** *the destruction of the rainforest*

destructive /dɪˈstrʌktɪv/ adj causing a lot of damage to people or things: *the destructive power of a hurricane*

detach /dɪˈtætʃ/ v [T] to remove part of something that has been made so that you can remove it —**detachable** adj

detached /dɪˈtætʃt/ adj **1** not reacting to or involved in something in an emotional way: *Smith remained cold and detached throughout his trial.* **2** BrE a detached house is not joined to another house → see picture at **HOUSE¹**

detachment /dɪˈtætʃmənt/ n **1** [U] when someone does not react in an emotional way or feel involved

in something **2** [C] a group of soldiers who are sent to do something

detail¹ /ˈdiːteɪl $ dɪˈteɪl/ n
1 [C,U] a fact or piece of information about something: *The documentary included a lot of historical detail.* | **in detail** (=using a lot of details) *He describes the events in great detail.*
2 details [plural] information that helps to complete what you know about something: *She refused to give any details about what had happened.*

detail² v [T] to give all the facts or information about something: *The list detailed everything we would need for our trip.*

detailed /ˈdiːteɪld $ dɪˈteɪld/ adj including a lot of information: *a detailed account of their conversation*

detain /dɪˈteɪn/ v [T] if the police detain someone, they keep them in a POLICE STATION and do not allow them to leave

detainee /ˌdiːteɪˈniː/ n [C] formal someone who is kept in a prison, usually because of their political views

detect Ac /dɪˈtekt/ v [T] to notice something that is not easy to see, hear etc: *Paul detected a note of disappointment in his mother's voice.* **THESAURUS** NOTICE —**detectable** adj —**detection** /-ˈtekʃən/ n [U]

detective Ac /dɪˈtektɪv/ n [C] a police officer whose job is to discover who is responsible for crimes

detector Ac /dɪˈtektə $ -ər/ n [C] a piece of equipment that tells you if there is a particular substance somewhere: *a metal detector*

detention /dɪˈtenʃən/ n **1** [U] when someone is kept in prison **2** [C,U] a school punishment in which you have to stay at school after the other students have left

deter /dɪˈtɜː $ -ˈtɜːr/ v [T] (**deterred**, **deterring**) if something deters you from doing something, it makes you not want to do it: *The security camera was installed to deter people from stealing.*

detergent /dɪˈtɜːdʒənt $ -ɜːr-/ n [C,U] a liquid or powder that you use for washing clothes, dishes etc

deteriorate /dɪˈtɪəriəreɪt $ -ˈtɪr-/ v [I] to become worse: *David's health deteriorated rapidly.* —**deterioration** /dɪˌtɪəriˈreɪʃən $ -ˌtɪr-/ n [U]

determination /dɪˌtɜːməˈneɪʃən $ -ɜːr-/ n [U] the desire to continue trying to do something even when it is difficult: **determination to do sth** *I admire his determination to work his way through law school.*

determine /dɪˈtɜːmɪn $ -ɜːr-/ v [T] **1** to find out the facts about something: *Experts have been unable to determine the cause of the explosion.* **2** to directly influence or affect something: *Training will determine how well you perform in a race.* **3** to officially decide something: *The date of the court case has not yet been determined.*

determined /dɪˈtɜːmɪnd $ -ɜːr-/ adj wanting to do something very much, so that you will not let anything stop you: **determined to do sth** *She was determined to start her own business.* | **[+(that)]** *I'm* determined that my children will have the best education possible. | a **determined effort** to stop smoking

---

THESAURUS

determined if you are determined to do something, you have decided you will definitely do it and you will not let anything stop you: *He's determined to win the championship.* | *a very determined woman*

stubborn refusing to change your mind about something, especially when other people think you are wrong: *I wish you would stop being so stubborn.*

firm showing by your behaviour that you are strong and in control: *You have to be firm with young children.*

single-minded working very hard to achieve one thing, and thinking that everything else is much less important: *A professional tennis player must be completely single-minded.*

ambitious determined to be successful, rich, powerful, or famous: *He was very ambitious and wanted to be a millionaire by the time he was 20.*

ruthless determined to get what you want in a very unpleasant way, and not caring if you harm other people: *a ruthless dictator*

---

determiner /dɪˈtɜːmənə $ -ˈtɜːrmənər/ n [C] in grammar, a word you use before a noun to show which thing you mean. In the phrases 'the car' and 'some new cars', 'the' and 'some' are determiners.

deterrent /dɪˈterənt $ -ˈtɜːr-/ n [C] something that makes people less likely to do something: *an effective deterrent to car thieves*

detest /dɪˈtest/ v [T] formal to hate someone or something very much: *I was going out with a boy my mother detested.* **THESAURUS** HATE

detonate /ˈdetəneɪt/ v [I,T] if you detonate a bomb, or if it detonates, it explodes —**detonation** /ˌdetəˈneɪʃən/ n [C,U]

detonator /ˈdetəneɪtə $ -ər/ n [C] a piece of equipment used to make a bomb explode

detour /ˈdiːtʊə $ -tʊr/ n [C] a way of going somewhere that takes longer than the usual way: *We made a detour to avoid the street repairs.* **THESAURUS** AVOID —**detour** v [I,T]

detox /ˈdiːtɒks $ -tɑːks/ n [C,U] informal **1** treatment to help people stop drinking alcohol or taking drugs SYN **rehab**: *She spent a month in detox.* **2** a period of time when you only eat and drink particular things, to try and remove harmful substances from your body —**detox** v [I]

detract /dɪˈtrækt/ v

PHRASAL VERBS

detract from sth to make something seem less good: *One small mistake isn't going to detract from your achievements.*

detractor /dɪˈtræktə $ -ər/ n [C] someone who says bad things about someone or something, in order to make them seem less good than they really are: *Even the President's detractors admit that his decision was right.*

detriment /ˈdetrəmənt/ n **to the detriment of sth** having a harmful effect on something: *He started working longer hours, to the detriment of his health.* —**detrimental** /ˌdetrəˈmentl◂/ adj

devalue /diːˈvæljuː/ v [I,T] to reduce the value of a country's money **2** [T] to make someone or something seem less important or valuable: *History has tended to devalue the contributions of women.* —**devaluation** /diːˌvæljuˈeɪʃən/ n [C,U]

devastate /ˈdevəsteɪt/ v [T] **1** to damage something very badly: *Bombing raids devastated the city of Dresden.* **THESAURUS** DESTROY **2** to make someone feel extremely shocked and sad —**devastation** /ˌdevəˈsteɪʃən/ n [U]

devastating /ˈdevəsteɪtɪŋ/ adj **1** causing a lot of damage: *Chemical pollution has had a **devastating effect** on the environment.* **2** making someone feel very sad and shocked: *Losing my job was a devastating experience.*

develop /dɪˈveləp/ v

1 GROW/IMPROVE [I,T] if something develops, or if you develop it, it gets bigger or becomes more important: *plans to develop the local economy* | [+into] *Wright is fast developing into one of this country's most talented players.* | [+from] *The book developed from a magazine article he had written earlier.*

2 NEW PRODUCT/IDEA [T] to make a new product or idea over a period of time: *Scientists are developing new drugs to fight AIDS.*

3 ILLNESS/FEELING [T] to begin to have an illness or feeling: *Her baby developed a fever during the night.* | *She soon developed a dislike for him.*

4 PROBLEM/SITUATION [I,T] if a problem or difficult situation develops, it begins to happen or exist, or it gets worse: *A crisis seems to be developing within the Conservative Party.* | *The plane developed engine problems and crashed.*

5 PHOTOGRAPHS [T] to make pictures from photographic film, using special chemicals

6 BUILD ON LAND [T] to build houses, offices etc on a piece of land —**developed** adj: *a highly developed sense of smell*

developer /dɪˈveləpə $ -ər/ n [C] a person or company that makes money by buying land and building houses, factories etc on it

development /dɪˈveləpmənt/ n

1 [U] the process of growing, changing, or becoming better: *Vitamins are necessary for a child's growth and development.* | [+of] *the development of computer technology*

2 [C] a new event that changes a situation: *Our reporter has news of the latest developments in Moscow.*

3 [C] a change that makes something better: *We've seen significant developments in the treatment of breast cancer.*

4 [C,U] a group of new buildings, or the process of building them: *a new **housing development*** | *The land was sold for development.*

deviant /ˈdiːviənt/ (also **deviate** /-viət/ AmE) adj formal different, in a bad way, from what is considered normal: *deviant behaviour* —**deviant** n [C]

deviate Ac /ˈdiːvieɪt/ v [I] to change and become different from what is normal or expected: [+from]

The results of the survey deviate from what we expected. —**deviation** /ˌdiːviˈeɪʃən/ *n* [C,U]

device Ac /dɪˈvaɪs/ *n* [C] **1** a machine or tool used for a particular purpose: *a small electronic device* **THESAURUS** MACHINE **2** a special way of doing something that makes it easier to do: *a memory device*

devil /ˈdevəl/ *n* **1 the Devil** the most powerful evil SPIRIT in some religions, especially in Christianity **2** [C] an evil SPIRIT
PHRASES
better the devil you know *spoken* used when saying that it is better to have someone or something that you are familiar with, rather than a new thing or person
speak of the devil (*also* **talk of the devil** *BrE*) *spoken* used when you suddenly see someone that you have just been talking about: *Speak of the devil. Here comes John now.*
who/what/where the devil *spoken* used when asking a question, when you are very annoyed or surprised: *Where the devil have you been?*

devilish /ˈdevəlɪʃ/ *adj* **1** very evil: *devilish schemes* **2** morally bad, but in a way that is attractive: *He looked at her with a devilish grin.* —**devilishly** *adv*

devil's 'advocate *n* **play/be devil's advocate** to pretend to disagree with someone in order to have a good discussion with them

devious /ˈdiːviəs/ *adj* using tricks or lies to get what you want: *a devious scheme for making money* **THESAURUS** DISHONEST —**deviously** *adv* —**deviousness** *n* [U]

devise /dɪˈvaɪz/ *v* [T] to think of a new way of doing something: *He's devised a game to help kids learn English.*

devoid /dɪˈvɔɪd/ *adj* **devoid of sth** to have no particular quality at all: *The area is completely devoid of charm.*

devote Ac /dɪˈvəʊt $ -ˈvoʊt/ *v* [T] to use most of your time, effort etc doing something: **devote your time/effort/energy etc (to sth)** *She devoted most of her spare time to tennis.*

devoted Ac /dɪˈvəʊtɪd $ -ˈvoʊ-/ *adj* giving someone or something a lot of love and attention: *a devoted father* | [+to] *She's devoted to her cats.* —**devotedly** *adv*

devotee /ˌdevəˈtiː/ *n* [C] someone who likes or admires someone or something very much: [+of] *a devotee of 1930s films*

devotion Ac /dɪˈvəʊʃən $ -ˈvoʊ-/ *n* [U] **1** when you love someone a lot and show this by giving them a lot of attention: [+to] *Their devotion to each other grew stronger over the years.* **2** when you give a lot of effort or loyalty to something: [+to] *a musician's devotion to his art* | *a soldier's devotion to duty* **3** strong religious feeling

devour /dɪˈvaʊə $ -ˈvaʊr/ *v* [T] **1** to eat something quickly: *She devoured three burgers and a pile of fries.* **2** to read something quickly and eagerly, or watch something with great interest

devout /dɪˈvaʊt/ *adj* very religious: *a devout Catholic* —**devoutly** *adv*

dew /djuː $ duː/ *n* [U] small drops of water that form on the surfaces of things that are outside during the night

dexterity /dekˈsterəti/ *n* [U] skill in using your hands to make or do things

diabetes /ˌdaɪəˈbiːtiːz, -tɪs/ *n* [U] a disease in which your body cannot control the amount of sugar in your blood —**diabetic** /-ˈbetɪk◂/ *adj* —**diabetic** *n* [C]

diabolical /ˌdaɪəˈbɒlɪkəl◂ $ -ˈbɑː-/ *adj* **1** evil or cruel: *a diabolical killer* **2** *BrE informal* very bad: *That hotel was diabolical.*

diagnose /ˈdaɪəgnəʊz $ -noʊs/ *v* [T] to find out what illness a person has: **diagnose sb with sth** *She was diagnosed with breast cancer.*

diagnosis /ˌdaɪəgˈnəʊsɪs $ -ˈnoʊ-/ *n* [C,U] (*plural* **diagnoses** /-siːz/) when a doctor says what illness someone has

diagnostic /ˌdaɪəgˈnɒstɪk◂ $ -ˈnɑː-/ *adj* **diagnostic methods/tests etc** methods, tests etc that are used to help make a diagnosis

diagonal /daɪˈægənəl/ *adj* **1** a diagonal line joins two opposite corners of a square shape **2** straight and sloping: *a dress with diagonal stripes* —**diagonal** *n* [C] —**diagonally** *adv*: *Tony was sitting diagonally opposite me.*

diagram /ˈdaɪəgræm/ *n* [C] a drawing that uses simple lines to show what something looks like, where something is, or how something works: [+of] *a diagram of a car engine*

dial[1] /ˈdaɪəl/ *n* [C] **1** the round part of a clock, watch, or machine that has numbers showing you the time or a measurement **2** the part of a radio, THERMOSTAT etc that you turn to change something, such as the radio station or temperature **3** part of an older telephone that you turn to dial a number

dial[2] *v* [I,T] (**dialled, dialling** *BrE*, **dialed, dialing** *AmE*) to press the buttons or turn the dial on a telephone: *I must have dialled the wrong number.*

dialect /ˈdaɪəlekt/ *n* [C,U] a form of a language that is spoken in one part of a country: *We couldn't understand the local dialect.* **THESAURUS** LANGUAGE

dialogue (*also* **dialog** *AmE*) /ˈdaɪəlɒg $ -lɒːg, -lɑːg/ *n* [C,U] **1** a conversation in a book, play, or film: *a boring film with bad dialogue* **2** a discussion between two groups or countries: [+between/with] *an opportunity for dialogue between the opposing sides*

diameter /daɪˈæmɪtə $ -ər/ *n* [C,U] a line from one side of a circle to the other, passing through the circle's centre: **three inches/one meter etc in diameter** *The wheel was about two feet in diameter.*

diametrically /ˌdaɪəˈmetrɪkli/ *adv* **diametrically opposed** completely different and opposite

diamond /ˈdaɪəmənd/ *n* **1** JEWEL [C,U] a very hard clear valuable stone, used in jewellery: *a diamond ring* **2** SHAPE [C] a shape with four straight but sloping sides of equal length that stands on one of its points

3 IN CARD GAMES **diamonds** [plural] in card games, the cards with red diamond shapes on them: *the ace of diamonds* → see picture at **PLAYING CARD**

4 IN BASEBALL [C] the field where people play BASE-BALL

diaper /'daɪəpə $ 'daɪpər/ n [C] AmE a piece of soft cloth or paper you put on a baby's bottom to hold liquid and solid waste SYN **nappy** BrE

diaphragm /'daɪəfræm/ n [C] **1** the muscle between your lungs and your stomach that controls your breathing **2** a round rubber object that a woman uses as a CONTRACEPTIVE

diarrhoea BrE, **diarrhea** AmE /ˌdaɪə'rɪə/ n [U] an illness in which waste from your BOWELs is very watery

diary /'daɪəri $ 'daɪri/ n [C] (plural **diaries**)
1 a book in which you write down things that have happened to you: *Tony kept a daily diary* (=wrote in a diary every day).
2 especially BrE a book with spaces for each day where you can write down meetings, events etc that are planned for the day SYN **calendar** AmE: *I'll put that meeting in my diary.* | *I think I'm free that day, but I'll just check my diary.*

diatribe /'daɪətraɪb/ n [C] formal a piece of writing or speech full of criticism

dice¹ /daɪs/ n [C] (plural **dice**) a small block with six sides and a different number of spots on each side, used in games: *Throw the dice to start the game.*

dice² v [T] to cut food into small square pieces: *Dice the carrots.* → see picture at **CUT¹** —**diced** adj

dicey /'daɪsi/ adj informal slightly dangerous: *The future looks dicey for small businesses.*

dichotomy /daɪ'kɒtəmi $ -'kɑː-/ n [C] (plural **dichotomies**) formal the difference between two opposite things or ideas

dictate /dɪk'teɪt $ 'dɪkteɪt/ v **1** [I,T] to say words for someone else to write down: **dictate sth to sb** *She dictated the letter to her secretary.* **2** [I,T] to tell someone what they must do or how they must behave: **dictate who/what/how etc** *We can't dictate how the money will be spent.* **3** [T] to influence or control something: **dictate what/how etc** *Funds dictate what we can do.*

dictation /dɪk'teɪʃən/ n **1** [U] when you say words for someone else to write down **2** [C,U] sentences that a teacher reads out to test a student's ability to hear and write the words correctly: *French dictation*

dictator /dɪk'teɪtə $ 'dɪkteɪtər/ n [C] a leader who has complete power —**dictatorial** /ˌdɪktə'tɔːriəl◂/ adj

dictatorship /dɪk'teɪtəʃɪp $ -'teɪtər-/ n [C,U] a system in which a dictator controls a country
THESAURUS ► **GOVERNMENT**

diction /'dɪkʃən/ n [U] formal how clearly someone pronounces words

dictionary /'dɪkʃənəri $ -neri/ n [C] (plural **dictionaries**) a book that gives a list of words in alphabetical order, with their meanings in the same or another language: *a German–English dictionary*

did /dɪd/ v the past tense of DO

didn't /'dɪdnt/ the short form of 'did not'

die /daɪ/ v [I] (**died**, **dying**, **dies**)
1 to stop living: *He died at the age of 78.* | [+of] *patients who are dying of cancer* | [+from] *She eventually died from her injuries.* | *Mary died peacefully in her sleep.* | *The bullet entered his brain and he died instantly.*
2 to disappear or stop existing: *Poetry will never die.*
PHRASES
be dying for sth/to do sth informal to want something very much: *I'm dying for a beer.* | *We're dying to see what it is.* THESAURUS ► WANT
be dying of hunger/thirst/boredom etc to be very hungry, thirsty, bored etc: *I was dying of boredom and couldn't wait to leave.*
sth is to die for informal used when saying that something is very good: *The views are to die for.*

PHRASAL VERBS
die away if something, especially a sound, dies away, it becomes weaker and stops: *The footsteps died away.* | *Her voice died away into a mumble.*
die down to become less strong, active, or violent: *The excitement finally died down.*
die out to disappear or stop existing completely: *All but three of the lake's fish species have died out.*

THESAURUS

die to stop living because of old age, illness, or injury: *Her father died last week.*
be killed if someone is killed, they die in an accident, attack etc: *Three people were killed when their car hit a tree.*
pass away formal a polite expression used to avoid saying 'die', in order to show respect or to not upset someone: *The doctor told us that she'd passed away in the night.*
lose your life to be killed in a terrible event: *Hundreds of people lost their lives when the ship sank.*

diehard /'daɪhɑːd $ -hɑːrd/ n [C] informal someone who is against change and refuses to accept new ideas

diesel /'diːzəl/ n [U] a type of oil used in the engines of some vehicles

diet¹ /'daɪət/ n
1 [C] if you are on a diet, you only eat certain foods, in order to become thinner or to improve your health: *a salt-free diet* | **on a diet** (=eating little in order to lose weight) *Lynn is always on a diet.*
2 [C,U] the kind of food that you eat each day: **balanced/healthy/poor etc diet** *It is important to eat a healthy diet.* | [+of] *The animals live on a diet of fruit and insects.*

DICE

COLLOCATIONS

verbs

to be on a diet *You're not eating much – are you on a diet?*
to go on a diet (=to start being on a diet) *I went on a diet and lost ten pounds.*
to follow a diet (=to eat only certain types of food) *How long have you been following the diet?*
to stick to a diet (=to continue to follow a diet) *It's hard to stick to a diet when you're on holiday.*
⚠ Do not say 'keep a diet'. Say **stick to a diet**.

adjectives

a strict diet (=in which your food is very limited) *The doctor said I had to follow a very strict diet.*
a crash diet (=an attempt to lose weight very quickly over a short time) *Crash diets are not usually a good idea.*

diet² v [I] to eat less in order to become thinner: *Try to exercise when dieting.*

diet³ adj [only before noun] diet drinks or foods contain less sugar or fat than ordinary ones

dietary /ˈdaɪətəri $ -teri/ adj related to the food someone eats

differ /ˈdɪfə $ -ər/ v [I] **1** to be different: [+from] *The new system differs from the old in important ways.* **THESAURUS** DISAGREE **2** to have different opinions: *We differ on this matter.*

difference /ˈdɪfərəns/ n
1 [C] the way in which one person or thing is different from another [OPP] similarity: [+between] *What's the difference between a song and a poem?* | [+in] *Researchers found important differences in the way boys and girls learn.*
2 [singular] an amount by which one thing is different from another: **difference in age/size etc** *There's not much difference in price.* | *There's a five-hour **time difference** between London and New York.*
3 our/your/their differences disagreements: *We're friends now but we've **had our differences** in the past.*
PHRASES
a difference of opinion a slight disagreement: *Guy and Virginia had a difference of opinion.*
it makes no difference to sb used to say that it does not matter to someone which thing happens, is chosen etc: *Morning or afternoon. It makes no difference to me.*
make a/the difference to have an important effect or influence on someone or something: [+to] *The programme made a big difference to my life.* | *Having a good teacher **made all the difference** to Alex.*

COLLOCATIONS

adjectives

a big/major difference *There's a big difference between forgetting something and telling a deliberate lie.*
an important/significant difference *They found significant differences in quality.*
a slight/small difference *There is just one small difference.*

a subtle difference (=not obvious) *You have to be aware of subtle differences in meaning.*

verbs

to know the difference (=to know how two things are different) *They don't know the difference between right and wrong.*
sb can tell/see the difference (=can recognize how two things are different) *I can't see the difference between them.*
to notice a difference *He has noticed a difference in the way people treat him.*

different /ˈdɪfərənt/ adj
1 not like something or someone else [OPP] similar: [+from] *Our sons are **very different** from each other.* | [+to] *Her jacket is **completely different** to mine.* | [+than] *AmE: He seemed different than he did in New York.* | *a **slightly different** way of doing things*
2 [only before noun] used to talk about two or more separate things: *I went to three different shops.* | *We can approach this problem in several different ways.* | **different types/kinds etc** *There are many different types of fabric.* —**differently** adv

> **Grammar**
> Do not say 'different of'. Say **different from** or **different than**.
> **Different from** is used in both British and American English: *I felt I was **different from** the other kids at school.*
> American speakers also say **different than**: *I felt I was **different than** the other kids at school.*
> You will also hear some British speakers say **different to**, but many teachers think that this use is wrong.

THESAURUS

different not like something or someone else, or not like you were before: *My new job is very different from my old one.* | *You look different. Have you had your hair cut?*
unlike sb/sth used when describing in what way people or things are different from each other: *Our company is doing well, unlike most of our competitors.* | *Unlike me, my brother went to university.*
unique something that is unique is the only one of its kind: *He has his own unique style of painting.* | *the island's unique wildlife*
distinctive a distinctive style, sound, colour etc makes something very different or unusual, in a way that is easy to recognize: *Male birds have distinctive blue and yellow markings.*
have nothing in common to be completely different – used especially when saying that people are interested in very different things, and therefore cannot have a friendly relationship: *My father and I had nothing in common.* | *The two stories have nothing in common.*

differential /ˌdɪfəˈrenʃəl◂/ n [C] formal a difference between things: **wage/pay differentials**

differentiate Ac /ˌdɪfəˈrenʃieɪt/ v [I,T] to recognize or express the difference between things or people: **[+between]** *It's important to differentiate between fact and opinion.*

difficult /'dɪfɪkəlt/ *adj*

1 not easy to do, understand, or deal with OPP **easy**: *a difficult question* | **it is difficult to do sth** *It is difficult to see how we can save money.* | **it is difficult for sb to do sth** *It is difficult for me to travel now.* | *He's finding it difficult to get a job.*

2 involving problems or causing trouble or worry: *The strike is making things difficult for commuters.*

3 someone who is difficult never seems pleased or satisfied: *a difficult customer*

THESAURUS

difficult not easy to do, understand, or deal with: *a difficult task* | *a difficult problem* | *It's difficult to talk about these things.*

hard difficult. **Hard** is less formal than **difficult** and is very common in everyday English: *The test was really hard.* | *It's hard to say sorry.*

tough very difficult, because you have to use a lot of effort, or be very determined: *It was a tough race.* | *Managers sometimes have to make some tough decisions.*

complicated something that is complicated is difficult to understand because it has many parts: *The rules of the game are very complicated.* | *a complicated system*

tricky difficult, especially because there are many possible problems and you could easily make a mistake: *Finding your way out of the forest can be tricky, especially at night.* | *a tricky situation*

awkward an awkward situation, question etc is difficult or embarrassing to deal with: *You've put me in a very awkward position.*

challenging difficult in an interesting and enjoyable way: *I wanted a job that was more challenging.*

demanding a demanding job or task is difficult and tiring, because it takes a lot of time and hard work: *It can be demanding bringing up young children.*

---

difficulty /'dɪfɪkəlti/ *n* (*plural* **difficulties**)

1 [U] when something is not easy to do: **have difficulty (in) doing sth** *Did you have difficulty finding the house?* | **with/without difficulty** *She stood up with difficulty.* **THESAURUS** ▶ PROBLEM

Grammar
Do not say 'He had difficulty to sleep.' Say *He had difficulty sleeping.*

2 [C] a problem: *the country's severe economic difficulties* | *We've had a few difficulties recently.* | **get/run into difficulties** *The boat ran into difficulties in rough seas.*

3 [U] a situation in which you have problems: **in difficulty** *Many families are in financial difficulty.*

diffident /'dɪfɪdənt/ *adj* not behaving in a confident way

diffuse /dɪ'fjuːz/ *v* [I,T] to spread over a large area, or to make something spread over a large area: *These ideas diffused quickly across Europe.*

---

dig¹ /dɪg/ *v* [I,T] (*past tense and past participle* **dug** /dʌg/, *present participle* **digging**) to move earth, snow etc so that you make a hole in the ground, especially using a tool such as a SPADE: *We'll have to dig a large hole.* | **dig sb/sth out of sth** *Two survivors were dug out of the rubble.* | **[+down]** *Dig down about six inches.* | **[+for]** *digging for treasure*

PHRASES

dig your heels in to refuse to do something that other people are trying to make you do: *Monica dug her heels in and turned down the invitation.*

PHRASAL VERBS

dig in (*also* **dig** sth **into** sth) to push a hard or pointed object into something, or to press into something, often causing pain: **dig sth ↔ in** *The cat dug its claws in.*

dig sth ↔ **up**

1 to take something out of the ground, using a tool: *Make sure that you dig up all the roots.*

2 to make holes in an area of ground or road: *It costs millions to dig up the streets and install cables.*

3 to find hidden or forgotten information by searching carefully: *Newspapers began to **dig up the dirt** (=find embarrassing information) on the President.*

dig² *n* [C] **1** *informal* an unkind thing that you say about someone in order to criticize them: *He's always **having a dig at** me about my weight.* **2** a quick hard push, using your finger or a sharp object: *a dig in the ribs* **3** the process or a place where people dig into the ground to find ancient objects to study: *an archaeological dig*

digest /daɪ'dʒest, də-/ *v* [T] **1** when you digest food, your stomach changes it into a form that your body can use: *Babies can't digest the food that adults eat.* **2** to understand new or difficult information after thinking about it: *It took us a while to digest the news.* —**digestible** *adj*

digestion /daɪ'dʒestʃən, də-/ *n* [C,U] the process of digesting food —**digestive** /-tɪv/ *adj*: *your digestive system*

digicam /'dɪdʒɪkæm/ *n* [C] a type of camera that takes pictures that can be stored on a computer rather than on film

digit /'dɪdʒɪt/ *n* [C] a single number from 0 to 9: **three-digit/four-digit etc number** *Choose a four-digit number such as 3,709.*

digital /'dɪdʒətl/ *adj* **1** digital equipment, such as cameras or televisions, uses a system in which pictures and sound are recorded, stored, or sent out in the form of numbers: **digital TV/television/radio** **2** showing information in a series of numbers: *a digital clock*

dignified /'dɪgnɪfaɪd/ *adj* behaving in a calm and serious way that makes other people respect you: *a dignified leader*

dignitary /'dɪgnətəri $ -teri/ *n* [C] (*plural* **dignitaries**) someone with an important official position

dignity /'dɪgnəti/ *n* [U] **1** the ability to behave in a calm serious way, even in difficult situations: **with dignity** *She spoke with courage and dignity.* | *He struggled to **maintain** his **dignity**.* **2** the quality of being serious and formal: *the dignity of the presidency*

digress /daɪˈgres/ v [I] *formal* to begin to talk or write about something that is not related to what you were saying before —**digression** /daɪˈgreʃən/ n [C,U]

dike /daɪk/ n [C] another spelling of DYKE

dilapidated /dɪˈlæpɪdeɪtɪd/ adj a dilapidated building, vehicle, or piece of furniture is old and in bad condition THESAURUS CONDITION

dilate /daɪˈleɪt/ v [I,T] if the PUPILS of your eyes dilate, they open and become wider: *dilated pupils*

dilemma /dəˈlemə, daɪ-/ n [C] a situation in which you must make a difficult choice between two things: **in a dilemma** *He now finds himself in a terrible dilemma.* | *The president faces a dilemma about accepting these gifts.* | *a moral dilemma*

diligent /ˈdɪlɪdʒənt/ adj *formal* someone who is diligent works very hard and carefully: *a diligent student* —**diligently** adv —**diligence** n [U]

dilute /daɪˈluːt $ dɪˈluːt, daɪ-/ v [T] to make a liquid weaker by adding another liquid to it: *diluted fruit juice* THESAURUS MIX —**dilute** /ˌdaɪˈluːt◂/ adj

dim¹ /dɪm/ adj **1** not bright, clear, or easy to see: *the dim light of a winter evening* **2** a dim memory is not very clear in your mind: *I had only a dim memory of my grandparents.* **3** *informal* stupid: *She can be a bit dim.* —**dimly** adv
PHRASES
take a dim view of sth to strongly disapprove of something: *He took a dim view of the way the war was being fought.*

dim² v [I,T] (**dimmed, dimming**) if a light dims, or if you dim it, it becomes less bright

dime /daɪm/ n [C] a coin worth ten CENTS

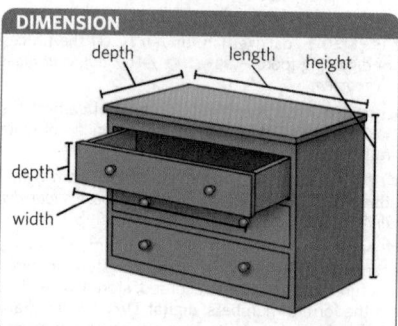

DIMENSION: depth, length, height, depth, width

dimension [Ac] /daɪˈmenʃən, də-/ n **1** [C] a particular part of a situation that affects the way you think about it: **[+of]** *the spiritual dimension of life* | **new/different/another dimension** *The baby has added a new dimension to their life.* **2 dimensions** [plural] the size of something measured by its length, width, and height: **[+of]** *What are the dimensions of the room?*

diminish [Ac] /dəˈmɪnɪʃ/ v [I,T] to become smaller or less important: *The country's political influence has diminished recently.*

diminutive /dəˈmɪnjətɪv/ adj *formal* very small: *a diminutive old lady*

dimple /ˈdɪmpəl/ n [C] a small hollow place on your cheek or chin that appears when you smile —**dimpled** adj

din /dɪn/ n [singular] a loud unpleasant noise that continues for a long time: *Her kids were making such a din upstairs!* THESAURUS NOISE

dine /daɪn/ v [I] *formal* to eat a meal, especially in the evening: *He's dining with friends at the Ritz.*
PHRASAL VERBS
dine out *formal* to eat in a restaurant

diner /ˈdaɪnə $ -ər/ n [C] **1** *especially AmE* a restaurant that serves cheap food THESAURUS RESTAURANT **2** someone who is eating in a restaurant

dinghy /ˈdɪŋi, ˈdɪŋɪ/ n [C] (*plural* **dinghies**) a small open boat: *a rubber dinghy* | *sailing dinghies*

dingy /ˈdɪndʒi/ adj a dingy place is dirty, dark, and unpleasant: *a dark, dingy office*

'dining room n [C] a room where you eat your meals in a house or hotel

dinner /ˈdɪnə $ -ər/ n
1 [C,U] the main meal of the day, which most people eat in the evening: *What's for dinner?* → see Word Choice at LUNCH
2 [C] a formal occasion in the evening when a large group of people eat a meal to celebrate something THESAURUS PARTY → TV DINNER

COLLOCATIONS
verbs
to have/eat dinner *What time do you usually have dinner?*
to make/cook dinner *It's time to start cooking dinner.*
to have sth for dinner *We're having pizza for dinner.*
to come for/to dinner *Mike and Linda are coming for dinner tonight.*
to go out for/to dinner (=to go and eat in a restaurant) *Let's go out for dinner.*
take sb out for/to dinner *He's taking me out for dinner.*
types of dinner
Sunday/Christmas/Thanksgiving dinner *After Christmas dinner, they opened their presents.*
a three-course/four-course etc dinner *The cost of the hotel includes a three-course dinner.*
dinner + noun
a dinner party *She's having a dinner party for eight people.*
dinner time *Wash your hands, it's dinner time!*

'dinner jacket n [C] *BrE* a black or white jacket that men wear for formal occasions SYN **tuxedo** *AmE*

dinosaur /ˈdaɪnəsɔː $ -sɔːr/ n [C] a large animal that lived about 200 million years ago and is now EXTINCT (=no longer exists)

diocese /ˈdaɪəsɪs/ n [C] the area that a BISHOP is in charge of

dip¹ /dɪp/ v (**dipped, dipping**) **1** [T] to put something into a liquid for a short time and lift it out again: **dip sth in/into sth** *Janet dipped her feet into the water.* | *strawberries dipped in chocolate* **2** [I] to go down to a lower level: *The sun dipped below the horizon.* | *Share prices have **dipped sharply** (=quickly).*

PHRASAL VERBS

dip into sth to use part of an amount of money: *Medical bills forced her to dip into her savings.*

dip² n

1 DECREASE [C] a drop in the level or amount of something: [+in] *a dip in temperature*

2 SWIM [C] *informal* a quick swim: *She **went for a dip** in the pool.*

3 IN STH'S SURFACE [C] a place where the surface of something goes down suddenly: [+in] *a dip in the road*

4 FOR FOOD [C,U] a thick SAUCE that you dip food into before you eat it: *a sour cream dip*

diploma /dəˈpləʊmə $ -ˈploʊ-/ n [C] an official document that you are given when you have successfully finished a course of study: *a teaching diploma* | [+in] *a diploma in nursing*

diplomacy /dəˈpləʊməsi $ -ˈploʊ-/ n [U] **1** the job or skill of keeping the relationships between countries friendly: *international diplomacy* **2** the skill of dealing with people without upsetting them: *The situation demands **tact and diplomacy**.*

diplomat /ˈdɪpləmæt/ n [C] someone who officially represents their government in a foreign country

diplomatic /ˌdɪpləˈmætɪk◂/ adj **1** relating to the relationships between countries: *The U.S. wants to establish **diplomatic relations** with China.* **2** good at dealing with people without upsetting them: *She's usually very diplomatic.* —**diplomatically** /-kli/ adv

dire /daɪə $ daɪr/ adj very serious or bad: *It will have **dire consequences** for the stock market.* | *The farming industry is **in dire straits** (=in a very difficult situation).*

direct¹ /dəˈrekt, daɪˈrekt◂/ adj

1 without other places, people, or processes coming between OPP **indirect**: *a direct flight to Egypt* | *staff who work in **direct contact** with the public* | *Keep medicines out of **direct sunlight**.* | *The building took a **direct hit** (=was hit by a bomb).* | **direct result/consequence** *Ten people die every day as a direct result of smoking.* | *There's a **direct link** between poverty and crime.*

2 exact, without any changes: *a direct quote from the President*

3 saying exactly what you mean OPP **indirect**: *Can I ask you a direct question?* —**directness** n [U]

direct² v

1 AIM [T] to aim something at a particular person: **direct sth at/towards sb/sth** *His anger is mainly directed at his father.*

2 PLAY/FILM [I,T] to control the way a play, film, or television programme is made by telling the actors what they should do

3 GIVE DIRECTIONS [T] to tell someone how to get to a place: **direct sb to sth** *Can you direct me to the airport?*

4 CONTROL [T] to control and organize something: *a police officer directing traffic*

direct³ adv **1** without stopping or changing direction: *You can fly direct from London to Nashville.* **2** without dealing with anyone else first: *Contact the bank direct.*

di,rect 'debit n [C] an instruction that you give to your bank to pay money regularly from your bank account to a particular person or organization: **by direct debit** *You can pay your bill by direct debit.*

direction /dəˈrekʃən, daɪ-/ n

1 WHERE SB/STH IS FACING OR MOVING [C] the place or point that you are moving, facing, or pointing towards: *We met Jim coming in the opposite direction.* | **in a direction** *Jill pointed in my direction.* | *We walked in the direction of the hotel.* | **from a direction** *We heard a scream from the direction of the pool.* | *People were running in all directions.* | **right/wrong direction** *Are we going in the right direction?* | *Maurice **changed direction** and went back towards town.*

2 HOW TO GET TO A PLACE **directions** [plural] instructions about how to reach a place or do something: *Could you **give** me **directions** to the bus station?* | *Always **read the directions** before using weedkiller.*

3 DEVELOPMENT [C] the general way that something develops: *Our lives have gone in very different directions.* | *This is a **new direction** for the company.* | *The law is **a step in the right direction** (=a good development).*

4 CONTROL [U] the act of managing an organization and telling people what to do: **under sb's direction** *The company has expanded under his direction.*

5 PURPOSE [U] a purpose or aim: *I feel that there is a **lack of direction** in my life.*

PHRASES

sense of direction the ability to know which way to go: *Bill's always getting lost – he has no sense of direction.*

directive /dəˈrektɪv, daɪ-/ n [C] an official order to do something: [+on] *the EU directive on maternity leave*

directly /dəˈrektli, daɪ-/ adv **1** with no other person, process etc between: *You can order the book directly from the publisher.* | *Are you **directly involved** in planning the event?* **2** **directly opposite/in front/behind** etc exactly in a particular position: *Lucas sat directly behind us.* **3** done in a clear way that shows what you honestly feel: *He didn't **answer** my question directly.*

direct 'object n [C] in grammar, the person or thing that is affected by the action of a TRANSITIVE verb, for example 'Mary' in the sentence 'I saw Mary' → **indirect object**

director /dəˈrektə, daɪ- $ -ər/ n [C]

1 someone who controls or manages an organization or company: *the new marketing director* | [+of] *a director of the company* | *The company is run by a **board of directors** (=a group of directors).*

2 someone who is in charge of making a film, play, or television programme and who tells the actors etc what to do: *a famous **movie director*** | [+of] *the director of the 'Star Wars' films*

D

directory /daɪˈrektəri, də-/ n [C] (plural **directories**) **1** a book or list of names, facts etc, arranged in alphabetical order: *the telephone directory* **2** a place on a computer where FILES or programs are kept

di,rect 'speech n [U] a way of reporting what someone says in which you say or write their actual words, as in 'I don't want to go,' said Julie → **indirect speech**

dirt /dɜːt $ dɜːrt/ n [U]
1 DUST/MUD a substance such as dust or mud that makes things dirty: *His hands were covered in dirt.*
2 SOIL earth or soil: *He left them lying in the dirt.* | **dirt track/road** (=one with a surface of soil and small stones)
3 HARMFUL SECRETS *informal* secret information about someone's life, that would harm them if other people knew about it: **[+on]** *The papers were trying to dig up the dirt* (=find harmful information) *on the President.*

dirty¹ /ˈdɜːti $ ˈdɜːr-/ adj
1 not clean: *dirty dishes* | *How did you get so dirty?*
2 relating to sex in a way that might offend people: *dirty jokes* | *He's got a dirty mind* (=thinks about sex a lot).
3 unfair or dishonest: *That was a dirty trick.*
PHRASES
| **do sb's dirty work** to do an unpleasant or dishonest job for someone: *I told them to do their own dirty work.*

THESAURUS

dirty not clean: *a dirty cloth*
filthy very dirty: *The whole place was absolutely filthy.*
muddy covered with mud: *It had been raining hard and the path was muddy.*
greasy covered with oil or GREASE: *Greasy food is bad for your health.*
grimy covered in thick black dirt: *My hands were all grimy.* | *the grimy walls of the prison*
polluted polluted air or water contains harmful chemicals from cars, factories etc: *In the centre of the city, the air is very polluted.*
contaminated contaminated food, water, or land is not safe to use because dangerous chemicals or bacteria have got into it: *The disease is spread through contaminated drinking water.*
unhygienic not clean and likely to cause disease: *The food had been prepared under unhygienic conditions.*

dirty² v [T] (**dirtied, dirtying, dirties**) to make something dirty

dis- /dɪs/ prefix **1** not: *a disrespectful remark* | *He acted dishonestly.* **2** used to talk about removing or stopping something: *Disconnect the plug.* | *Disinfect the wound.*

disability /ˌdɪsəˈbɪləti/ n [C,U] (plural **disabilities**) a permanent illness or injury that makes it difficult for someone to do ordinary things such as seeing, walking etc: *wheelchair access for people with **physical disabilities*** | *Her child has a **learning disability**.*

disabled /dɪsˈeɪbəld/ adj
1 someone who is disabled cannot use a part of their body properly: *a **severely disabled** patient* | **mentally disabled** *people*
2 the disabled [plural] people who are disabled

disadvantage /ˌdɪsədˈvɑːntɪdʒ $ -ˈvæn-/ n [C,U] a bad feature of something, which causes problems or makes it worse than other things: **[+of]** *the disadvantages of living in a city* | **be at a disadvantage** *Disabled people are at a disadvantage in the job market.*

THESAURUS

disadvantage a bad feature of something, which causes problems or makes it worse than other things: *The car uses a lot of fuel, which is a big disadvantage.*
drawback a disadvantage – used when something has good features which are usually more important: *It's a great camera. The only drawback is the price.*
catch *especially spoken* a disadvantage or problem which you do not realise at first: *There is a catch – you can only make cheap calls after 10 pm.*
bad point a disadvantage – used when comparing the advantages and disadvantages of something: *Both designs have their good points and bad points.*
the downside the disadvantage of a situation that seems good in most ways: *I love my job. The downside is that I don't get much free time.*

disadvantaged /ˌdɪsədˈvɑːntɪdʒd◂ $ -ˈvæn-/ adj someone who is disadvantaged is poor and does not have a good education, good health etc: *disadvantaged kids from the inner cities*

disaffected /ˌdɪsəˈfektɪd◂/ adj people who are disaffected are no longer happy with their lives or their government: *disaffected voters*

disagree /ˌdɪsəˈɡriː/ v [I]
1 to have a different opinion from someone else OPP **agree**: **[+with]** *My boss doesn't like people disagreeing with her.* | **[+about/on/over]** *We disagree about most things.*
2 to be different: *The statements of the two witnesses disagree.*

> **Grammar**
> Do not say 'I disagree him.' or 'I disagree that idea.' Say *I disagree with him.* or *I disagree with that idea.*

THESAURUS

disagree/not agree to have a different opinion from someone else about something: *'I think it looks nice.' 'I don't agree – I think it looks horrible.'* | *She was the only one who disagreed with me.*
be divided/split if a group of people is divided or split on something, some have one opinion and others have a different opinion: *The jury was divided on the verdict.*
differ *formal* if two or more people differ, they have different opinions about something: *The two leaders differed on how to handle the situation.* |

Opinions differ (=people have different opinions) on the best way to tackle the problem of climate change.

not see eye to eye to have different opinions and ideas, so that it is difficult for you to be friends or work together: *We didn't always see eye to eye about what kind of music the band should play.*

disagreeable /ˌdɪsəˈɡriːəbəl◂/ adj formal
1 unpleasant: *a disagreeable smell* **2** unfriendly and bad-tempered: *a rude, disagreeable woman* —**disagreeably** adv

disagreement /ˌdɪsəˈɡriːmənt/ n [C,U] when people express different opinions about something and sometimes argue: **[+over/about/on]** *There is some disagreement over the price.* | *He and his brother **had a disagreement** over money.* | **[+between/among]** *a disagreement between the two countries* **THESAURUS ARGUMENT**

disallow /ˌdɪsəˈlaʊ/ v [T] to officially refuse to allow something, because a rule has been broken: *Their first goal was disallowed.*

disappear /ˌdɪsəˈpɪə $ -ˈpɪr/ v [I]
1 if something disappears, you can no longer see it: *My keys have disappeared.* | *The sun briefly disappeared behind a cloud.* | **[+from]** *Some books have disappeared from the library.*
2 to stop existing: *The rainforests may disappear forever.* —**disappearance** n [C,U]: *Police are investigating the woman's disappearance.*

THESAURUS

disappear if something disappears, you can no longer see it, or it stops existing: *The cat disappeared over the wall.* | *Large parts of the forest have already disappeared.*
vanish to completely disappear, especially suddenly or in a mysterious way: *When she came back, her bag had vanished.*
go away to stop existing – used about something that you hope will stop, such as a pain or problem: *I wish this headache would go away.*
fade away to gradually become less clear, strong, or bright, and finally disappear: *The sound of her steps faded away and there was silence.*
become extinct if a type of animal or plant becomes extinct, it stops existing: *The polar bear could become extinct if the ice keeps melting.*

disappoint /ˌdɪsəˈpɔɪnt/ v [T] to make someone unhappy because something they hoped for did not happen: *I'm sorry to disappoint you, but we can't go.* —**disappointing** adj: *His exam results were very disappointing.*

disappointed /ˌdɪsəˈpɔɪntɪd◂/ adj unhappy because something you hoped for did not happen, or was not as good as you expected: *disappointed customers* | **[+at/with/about]** *Jake seems **bitterly disappointed** (=very disappointed) with the result.* | **[+in]** *I'm very disappointed in you, Mark.* | **[+that]** *He was disappointed that Kerry couldn't come.* | **disappointed to hear/find/see etc sth** *I was very*

disappointed to hear you'd failed your test.

THESAURUS

disappointed unhappy because something you hoped for did not happen, or was not as good as you expected: *I was disappointed that I hadn't won.*
feel let down to feel disappointed, especially because something is not as good as you hoped, or someone did not do what they promised: *Fans felt let down after the singer cancelled her concert at the last minute.*
be/feel sorry used when saying that you are disappointed or sad and wish the situation was different: *I'm sorry he can't be with us today.*
disillusioned disappointed because you realize that a person, belief, system etc is not as good as you thought: *The economic situation is getting worse and people are becoming disillusioned with the government.*
heartbroken very sad and upset because of something that has happened: *She was heartbroken when their relationship ended.*

disappointment /ˌdɪsəˈpɔɪntmənt/ n **1** [U] a feeling of unhappiness because something is not as good as you expected, or has not happened in the way you hoped: **[+at/about/over]** *The family **expressed** their **disappointment** at the court's decision.* | *She tried to **hide** her **disappointment**.* **2** [C] someone or something that is not as good as you hoped or expected: *The party was **a bit of a disappointment**.*

disapprove /ˌdɪsəˈpruːv/ v [I] to think that someone or something is bad or wrong: **[+of]** *Her parents **strongly disapprove** of her lifestyle.* —**disapproving** adj: *She gave me a disapproving look.* —**disapproval** n [U]

disarm /dɪsˈɑːm $ -ˈɑːrm/ v **1** [I] if a country disarms, it reduces the number of weapons and soldiers it has: *Both sides must disarm before the peace talks can begin.* **2** [T] to take away someone's weapons: *Police managed to disarm the gunman.* **3** [T] to make someone feel less angry and more friendly: *His tact and political skills disarmed his critics.* —**disarming** adj: *a disarming smile*

disarmament /dɪsˈɑːməmənt $ -ˈɑːr-/ n [U] when a country reduces the number of soldiers and weapons it has: *nuclear disarmament*

disarray /ˌdɪsəˈreɪ/ n [U] **be in disarray** to be very untidy, disorganized, or confused: *Her hair was in disarray.*

disassociate /ˌdɪsəˈsəʊʃieɪt, -sieɪt $ -ˈsoʊ-/ v another form of DISSOCIATE

disaster /dɪˈzɑːstə $ dɪˈzæstər/ n [C,U]
1 an event such as an accident, flood, or storm that causes a lot of harm or suffering: *an air disaster in which 329 people died* | **ecological/environmental/natural etc disaster** *The drought was the worst natural disaster this century.* | *the Chernobyl **nuclear disaster*** | *The country is on the edge of **economic disaster**.* | **[+for]** *The flood could **spell disaster** for wildlife* (=cause a lot of harm in the future). **THESAURUS ACCIDENT**

2 something that is a complete failure: *Our Christmas party was a **complete disaster**.*

disastrous /dɪˈzɑːstrəs $ dɪˈzæ-/ *adj* very bad, or ending in failure: **disastrous consequences/results/effects** *Climate change could have disastrous effects on Earth.*

disband /dɪsˈbænd/ *v* [I,T] *formal* to stop existing as an organization, or to make something do this

disbelief /ˌdɪsbəˈliːf/ *n* [U] a feeling that you do not believe something: **in disbelief** *I looked at him in disbelief.* —**disbelieve** *v* [T]: *I see no reason to disbelieve him.*

disc (*also* **disk** *especially AmE*) /dɪsk/ *n* [C] **1** a round flat shape or object: *a revolving metal disc* **2** a record or CD **3** a computer DISK **4** a flat piece of soft bone between the bones in your back

discard /dɪsˈkɑːd $ -ɑːrd/ *v* [T] *formal* to throw something away: *Discard any old cleaning materials.* | *discarded paper*

discern /dɪˈsɜːn $ -ɜːrn/ *v* [T] *formal* to see, notice, or understand something: *I could just discern the outline of the bridge in the fog.* —**discernible** *adj*

discerning /dɪˈsɜːnɪŋ $ -ɜːr-/ *adj* able to make good judgments, especially about art, style etc: *a superb hotel for the discerning traveller* —**discernment** *n* [U]

discharge /dɪsˈtʃɑːdʒ $ -ɑːr-/ *v* [T] **1** to officially allow someone to leave a place: **discharge sb from sth** *Blanton was discharged from hospital last night.* **2** to send out gas, liquid, smoke etc: *Sewage is discharged directly into the sea.* **3** *formal* to perform a duty or promise: *The trustees failed to **discharge** their **duties** properly.* —**discharge** /ˈdɪstʃɑːdʒ $ -tʃɑːrdʒ/ *n* [U]: *his discharge from the army*

disciple /dɪˈsaɪpəl/ *n* [C] someone who believes in the ideas of a great teacher or leader, especially a religious one

disciplinarian /ˌdɪsəpləˈneəriən $ -ˈner-/ *n* [C] someone who makes people obey strict rules: *Dad was always the disciplinarian in the family.*

discipline¹ /ˈdɪsɪplɪn/ *n*
1 OF CHILDREN/EMPLOYEES [U] a way of training someone so that they learn to control their behaviour and obey rules: *The school has very high standards of discipline.* | *serious **discipline** problems in the police force*
2 OF YOURSELF [U] a way of training your mind or body, or of learning to control your behaviour: *It took him a lot of hard work and discipline to make the Olympic team.*
3 SUBJECT [C] a particular subject of study → SELF-DISCIPLINE

discipline² *v* [T] **1** to teach someone to obey rules and control their own behaviour: *Some parents are not very good at disciplining their children.* **2** to punish someone who has disobeyed an organization's rules —**disciplinary** /ˈdɪsəplɪnərə, ˌdɪsəˈpli- $ ˈdɪsəplɪneri/ *adj* [only before noun]

disciplined /ˈdɪsɪplɪnd/ *adj* a disciplined person obeys rules and controls their behaviour: *a disciplined, well-trained army*

'disc jockey *n* [C] a DJ

disclaim /dɪsˈkleɪm/ *v* [T] *formal* to say that you are not responsible for something or do not know anything about it

disclaimer /dɪsˈkleɪmə $ -ər/ *n* [C] a statement saying that you are not responsible for something, or that you do not know about it

disclose /dɪsˈkləʊz $ -ˈkloʊz/ *v* [T] to make something publicly known, especially after it has been kept secret: *The newspaper refused to disclose where their information came from.* —**disclosure** *n* [C,U]: *the disclosure of private medical information*

disco /ˈdɪskəʊ $ -koʊ/ *n* [C] (*plural* **discos**) a place or event where people dance to popular music

discolour *BrE*, **discolor** *AmE* /dɪsˈkʌlə $ -ər/ *v* [I,T] to change colour, or to make something change colour, so that it looks unattractive

discomfort /dɪsˈkʌmfət $ -ərt/ *n* **1** [U] slight pain, or a feeling of being physically uncomfortable: *Your injury isn't serious, but it may cause some discomfort.* **2** [C] something that makes you uncomfortable: *the discomforts of long-distance travel*

disconcerting /ˌdɪskənˈsɜːtɪŋ◄ $ -ɜːr-/ *adj* making you feel slightly confused, embarrassed, or worried: *a disconcerting question* —**disconcerted** *adj*

disconnect /ˌdɪskəˈnekt/ *v* [T] **1** to remove the supply of power, gas, water etc from a machine or piece of equipment: *Always disconnect the machine from the mains first.* **2** to separate two things that are connected

discontented /ˌdɪskənˈtentɪd◄/ *adj* unhappy or not satisfied: **[+with]** *After two years, I became discontented with my job.* —**discontent** *n* [U]

discontinue /ˌdɪskənˈtɪnjuː/ *v* [T] to stop doing something

discord /ˈdɪskɔːd $ -ɔːrd/ *n* [U] *formal* disagreement between people: *marital discord*

discount¹ /ˈdɪskaʊnt/ *n* [C] a reduction in the usual price of something: *Members **get** a 10% **discount**.* | **at a discount** *Employees can buy books at a discount.* —**discount** /dɪsˈkaʊnt $ ˈdɪskaʊnt/ *v* [T]

discount² /dɪsˈkaʊnt $ ˈdɪskaʊnt/ *v* [T] to consider something unlikely to be true or important: *Larry tends to discount any suggestion I ever make.*

discourage /dɪsˈkʌrɪdʒ $ -ˈkɜːr-/ *v* [T] **1** to persuade someone not to do something OPP **encourage**: *attempts to discourage illegal immigration* | **discourage sb from doing sth** *They're trying to discourage staff from smoking at work.* **2** to make someone less confident or less willing to do something OPP **encourage**: *Don't let one failure discourage you.* —**discouragement** *n* [C,U]

discouraged /dɪsˈkʌrɪdʒd $ -ˈkɜːr-/ *adj* no longer having the confidence you need to continue doing something: *Some players **get discouraged** and quit.* —**discouraging** *adj*

discourse /ˈdɪskɔːs $ -ɔːrs/ *n* [C,U] *formal* a serious talk, piece of writing, or discussion

discourteous /dɪsˈkɜːtiəs $ -ɜːr-/ *adj* *formal* not polite

discover /dɪsˈkʌvə $ -ər/ *v* [T]
1 FIND SB/STH to find someone or something, either

by accident or because you were looking for them: *The body was discovered in a field.*
2 **FIND OUT STH** to learn something that you did not know about before: **[+who/what/how etc]** *Did you ever discover who sent you the flowers?* | **[+(that)]** *She discovered that she was pregnant.*
3 **FIND STH NEW** if someone discovers a new place, fact, substance etc, they are the first person to find it or know that it exists: *The Curies are best known for discovering radium.* **THESAURUS** FIND —**discoverer** *n* [C]

discovery /dɪsˈkʌvəri/ *n* (*plural* **discoveries**)
1 [C] a fact or piece of knowledge that someone learns about, when it was not known before: *Astronomers have made significant discoveries about our galaxy.* | **[+that]** *the discovery that bees can communicate with each other*
2 [U] when someone discovers something: **[+of]** *the discovery of oil in Alaska*

discredit /dɪsˈkredɪt/ *v* [T] to make people stop trusting or respecting someone or something: *The defense lawyer will try to discredit our witnesses.*

discreet /dɪˈskriːt/ *adj* careful about what you say or do so that you do not upset or embarrass people: *Can you please be discreet about this?* —**discreetly** *adv*

discrepancy /dɪˈskrepənsi/ *n* [C,U] (*plural* **discrepancies**) a difference between two things that should be the same: **[+between]** *Police found discrepancies between the two men's statements.*

discretion Ac /dɪˈskreʃən/ *n* [U] **1** if someone uses their discretion, they make a decision about exactly what should be done in a particular situation: *Promotions are left to the discretion of the manager.* | **at sb's discretion** *Tipping is entirely at the customer's discretion.* **2** when you are careful about what you say or do, so that you do not upset or embarrass people: *This situation must be handled with discretion.*

discretionary Ac /dɪˈskreʃənəri $ -neri/ *adj* relating to or based on a decision by someone in a position of authority: **discretionary award/grant etc**

discriminate Ac /dɪˈskrɪməneɪt/ *v* [I] **1** to treat one person or group differently from another in an unfair way: **[+against]** *Under federal law, it is illegal to discriminate against women.* **2** to recognize a difference between two things

discriminating /dɪˈskrɪməneɪtɪŋ/ *adj* able to judge what is of good quality and what is not: *a book that will appeal to discriminating readers*

discrimination /dɪˌskrɪməˈneɪʃən/ *n* [U] **1** when one group of people is treated unfairly: **[+against]** *widespread discrimination against older people in the job market* | **racial/sex/religious etc discrimination** *a victim of racial discrimination* **THESAURUS** PREJUDICE
2 the ability to recognize the difference between two or more things: *children's shape discrimination*

Word Choice: discrimination or prejudice?
Discrimination is the unfair treatment of a particular group, for example by not giving them good jobs: *Discrimination against disabled people in the workplace is illegal.*
Prejudice is an unfair attitude, which makes

you treat a group of people badly because they are different from you: *There is still a lot of prejudice against black people.*

discriminatory /dɪˈskrɪmənətəri $ -tɔːri/ *adj* formal treating one person or group differently from another in an unfair way

discus /ˈdɪskəs/ *n* [C] a heavy flat circular object which people throw as far as possible as a sport: *He came first in the discus* (=the sport of throwing a discus).

discuss /dɪˈskʌs/ *v* [T] to talk about something with someone in order to exchange ideas or decide something: *We're meeting today to discuss our science project.* | *If you would like to discuss the matter further, please call me.* | **discuss sth with sb** *I'd like to discuss this with my father first.* | **[+what/who/where etc]** *We are discussing how to deal with the situation.* **THESAURUS** TALK

Grammar
Do not say 'We discussed about our plans.' Say *We discussed our plans.* or *We talked about our plans.*

discussion /dɪˈskʌʃən/ *n* [C,U] when people discuss something: **[+about/on]** *In class we had a discussion about global warming.* | **[+of]** *the discussion of important issues* | **under discussion** (=being discussed) *The project is under discussion.*

disdain /dɪsˈdeɪn/ *n* [U] formal a lack of respect for someone or something, because you think they are not important or good enough: **[+for]** *his disdain for manual labour* —**disdainful** *adj*: *He gave me a disdainful look.*

disease /dɪˈziːz/ *n* [C,U] an illness which affects a person, animal, or plant: *She suffers from a rare disease of the blood.* **THESAURUS** ILLNESS —**diseased** *adj*

COLLOCATIONS

verbs
to have a disease (*also* **to suffer from a disease**) *He has had the disease since childhood.*
to catch/get a disease *You can catch the disease from drinking dirty water.*
to cause a disease *Smoking causes heart disease.*
to cure a disease *The disease can be cured easily.*
a disease spreads *Within a year the disease had spread across Europe.*

types of disease
a common/rare disease *He has a rare kidney disease.*
a serious disease *Many serious diseases are preventable.*
a fatal disease (=that causes death) *The disease is rarely fatal.*
an incurable disease (=that cannot be cured) *She is dying of an incurable disease.*
an infectious/contagious disease (=that spreads from one person to another) *Children should be vaccinated against infectious diseases.*
heart/liver/kidney etc disease *He is being treated for kidney disease.*

disembark

Ac = words from the Academic Word List

nouns + disease

a cure for a disease *There is no known cure for this disease.*
an outbreak of a disease (=when a disease appears in a number of people or animals) *There has been an outbreak of the disease in Wales.*

Word Choice: disease or illness?
A **disease** is an illness that is passed from one person to another, or that affects a particular part of the body: *The disease is spread by mosquitoes.* | *He has heart disease.*
An **illness** is a serious health problem which causes someone to be ill: *It took him a long time to recover from his illness.* | *a hospital for people who suffer from mental illness*
Do not use **illness** about mild problems such as a headache or a cold. Do not use **disease** about mental health problems.

disembark /ˌdɪsəmˈbɑːk $ -ˈɑːrk/ v [I] to get off a ship or plane —**disembarkation** /ˌdɪsembɑːˈkeɪʃən $ -bɑːr-/ n [U]

disembodied /ˌdɪsəmˈbɒdid◀ $ -ˈbɑː-/ adj a disembodied sound or voice comes from someone who cannot be seen

disenchanted /ˌdɪsɪnˈtʃɑːntɪd $ -ˈtʃænt-/ adj disappointed with someone or something, and no longer believing that they are good: **[+with]** *Anne was becoming disenchanted with her marriage.* —**disenchantment** n [U]

disengage /ˌdɪsənˈɡeɪdʒ/ v [I,T] to separate two things that were connected: *Disengage the gears when you park the car.*

disentangle /ˌdɪsənˈtæŋɡəl/ v [T] **1 disentangle yourself (from sb/sth)** to escape from a difficult situation that you are involved in **2** to untie ropes, strings etc that have become twisted or tied together

disfigure /dɪsˈfɪɡə $ -ˈfɪɡjər/ v [T] to spoil someone's appearance: *His face was badly disfigured in the accident.* —**disfigurement** n [C,U]

disgrace¹ /dɪsˈɡreɪs/ n **1 be a disgrace** to be very bad and unacceptable: *The UK rail system is a national disgrace.* | **[+to]** *Doctors like you are a disgrace to the medical profession.* **2** [U] when someone loses other people's respect because they have done something that other people strongly disapprove of: **in disgrace** *Harry left the school in disgrace.* —**disgrace** v [T]: *How could you disgrace us all like that?*

disgraceful /dɪsˈɡreɪsfəl/ adj very bad: *Your behaviour has been disgraceful!* —**disgracefully** adv

disgruntled /dɪsˈɡrʌntld/ adj annoyed, disappointed, and not satisfied: *disgruntled employees*

disguise¹ /dɪsˈɡaɪz/ v [T] **1** to change your appearance or voice so that people will not recognize you: **disguise yourself as sb/sth** *She disguised herself as a man.* **THESAURUS** ▶ HIDE **2** to hide a fact or feeling so that people will not notice it: *Dan couldn't disguise his feelings for Katie.*

disguise² n [C,U] things that you wear to change your appearance and hide who you really are: *The glasses were part of his disguise.* | **in disguise** *The woman turned out to be a police officer in disguise.*

disgust¹ /dɪsˈɡʌst, dɪz-/ n [U] a strong feeling of dislike, annoyance, or disapproval: **with disgust** *Everybody looked at me with disgust.* | **in disgust** *We left in disgust.*

disgust² v [T] to make someone feel very annoyed or upset about something that is not acceptable: *Pornography shocks and disgusts decent people.* —**disgusted** adj: *We felt disgusted by the way we'd been treated.*

disgusting /dɪsˈɡʌstɪŋ, dɪz-/ adj
1 shocking and unacceptable: *The way he treats her is disgusting.*
2 extremely unpleasant and making you feel sick: *a disgusting smell* | *Smoking is a disgusting habit.*
THESAURUS ▶ TASTE —**disgustingly** adv: *They're disgustingly rich.*

Usage
Do not say 'very disgusting'. Just say **disgusting**.

dish¹ /dɪʃ/ n [C]
1 FOR SERVING FOOD a round container with low sides, used for holding food → **bowl**: *a serving dish* | **[+of]** *a large dish of spaghetti*
2 FOOD food cooked or prepared in a particular way: *a wonderful pasta dish* | *You can serve this soup as a main dish* (=the biggest part of a meal).
3 ALL PLATES/CUPS ETC dishes [plural] all the plates, cups, bowls etc that are used during a meal: **do/wash the dishes** *Who's going to do the dishes?*
THESAURUS ▶ WASH → SATELLITE DISH

dish² v
PHRASAL VERBS
dish sth ↔ **out** *informal* to give something to people: *He's always dishing out unwanted advice.*

disheartened /dɪsˈhɑːtnd $ -ɑːr-/ adj disappointed because you do not think you will be able to achieve something

disheartening /dɪsˈhɑːtnɪŋ $ -ɑːr-/ adj making you lose hope and confidence: *It was disheartening to see how little had been done.*

dishevelled *BrE*, **disheveled** *AmE* /dɪˈʃevəld/ adj having very untidy clothes and hair: *She looked tired and dishevelled.*

dishonest /dɪsˈɒnɪst $ -ˈɑː-/ adj someone who is dishonest deceives people, for example by lying, stealing, or cheating **OPP honest**: *a dishonest politician* | *a dishonest thing to do* —**dishonesty** n [U] —**dishonestly** adv

THESAURUS

dishonest someone who is dishonest deceives people, for example by lying, stealing, or cheating: *I wouldn't keep the money – that would be dishonest.* | *The goods had been obtained by dishonest means.*
corrupt using power in a dishonest way to get advantages for yourself – used about people in official positions: *Most of the city's politicians are corrupt.*

crooked *informal* dishonest and involved in illegal activities: *a crooked businessman*

devious good at thinking of clever plans to trick people and get what you want: *Some companies are very devious and charge you for things you haven't asked for.*

sly hiding what you are really thinking or doing in order to get what you want: *She had a sly expression on her face, as if she knew something that I didn't.*

sneaky *informal* doing things secretly and tricking people in order to get what you want: *It was sneaky of him not to tell us till the very last minute.*

suspicious making you think that someone is doing something dishonest or illegal: *Did you notice anything suspicious about him?*

dishonour BrE, **dishonor** AmE /dɪsˈɒnə $ -ˈɑːnər/ n [U] *formal* when people no longer respect you or approve of you because you have done something dishonest or immoral: *His behaviour* **brought dishonour on** *the family.* —**dishonour** v [T] —**dishonourable** adj —**dishonourably** adv

dishtowel /ˈdɪʃˌtaʊəl/ n [C] AmE a cloth used for drying dishes SYN **tea towel** BrE

dishwasher /ˈdɪʃˌwɒʃə $ -ˌwɔːʃər, -ˌwɑː-/ n [C] a machine that washes dishes → see picture at **KITCHEN**

disillusion /ˌdɪsəˈluːʒən/ v [T] to make someone realize that something they thought was true or good is not: *I hate to disillusion you, but she's never coming back.*

disillusioned /ˌdɪsəˈluːʒənd◂/ adj unhappy because you have lost your belief that someone or something is true or good THESAURUS **DISAPPOINTED** —**disillusionment** (also **disillusion**) n [U]

disincentive /ˌdɪsənˈsentɪv/ n [C] something that makes people less willing to do something: *High interest rates can be a disincentive to expanding a business.*

disinfect /ˌdɪsənˈfekt/ v [T] to clean something with a chemical that destroys BACTERIA —**disinfection** /-ˈfekʃən/ n [U]

disinfectant /ˌdɪsənˈfektənt/ n [C,U] a chemical that destroys BACTERIA

disinherit /ˌdɪsɪnˈherɪt/ v [T] to prevent someone from receiving any of your money or property after your death

disintegrate /dɪsˈɪntɪgreɪt/ v [I] **1** to break up into small pieces: *The whole plane just disintegrated in mid-air.* **2** to become weaker and be gradually destroyed: *Pam kept the kids when the marriage disintegrated.* —**disintegration** /dɪsˌɪntɪˈgreɪʃən/ n [U]

disinterested /dɪsˈɪntrɪstɪd/ adj able to judge a situation fairly because you will not get any advantages for yourself from it: *disinterested advice* —**disinterest** n [U]

disjointed /dɪsˈdʒɔɪntɪd/ adj a disjointed speech or piece of writing is not easy to understand because the words or ideas are not arranged in a clear order

disk /dɪsk/ n [C]
1 a small flat piece of plastic or metal used for storing information in a computer
2 an American spelling of DISC → **FLOPPY DISK, HARD DISK**

disk drive n [C] the part of a computer where you put a disk when you want to copy information onto it or from it

disk jockey n [C] an American spelling of DISC JOCKEY → **DJ**

dislike¹ /dɪsˈlaɪk/ v [T] to not like someone or something OPP **like**: *Why do you dislike her so much?* | **dislike doing sth** *I dislike being the centre of attention.*

THESAURUS

dislike/not like to not like someone or something. **Dislike** sounds stronger than **not like**: *I don't like getting up in the morning.* | *She disliked him from the moment they met.*

not be very keen on sth *informal* (also **not be very fond of sth**) *especially* BrE used to say that you do not like something, but in a polite and gentle way: *I'm not very keen on golf.*

go off sb/sth BrE *informal* to stop liking someone or something: *I used to like his music but I've gone off it now.*

put sb off sb/sth BrE to make you stop liking someone or something: *He got terribly drunk and it really put me off him.*

dislike² /dɪsˈlaɪk, ˈdɪslaɪk/ n [C,U]
1 a feeling of not liking someone or something OPP **like**: [+of/for] *She shared her mother's dislike of housework.* | *They* **took an instant dislike** *to each other.*
2 **dislikes** [plural] the things that you do not like: *I know all her* **likes and dislikes.**

dislocate /ˈdɪsləkeɪt $ -loʊ-/ v [T] to make a bone come out of its normal place: *I dislocated my shoulder playing football.* —**dislocation** /ˌdɪsləˈkeɪʃən $ -loʊ-/ n [C,U]

dislodge /dɪsˈlɒdʒ $ -ˈlɑːdʒ/ v [T] to force something to move when it is stuck somewhere: *Lee dislodged a few stones as he climbed over the wall.*

disloyal /dɪsˈlɔɪəl/ adj doing or saying things that do not support your friends, your country, or the group you belong to: *He felt he had been disloyal to his friends.* —**disloyalty** n [U]

dismal /ˈdɪzməl/ adj making you feel unhappy and without hope: *dismal weather* | *We faced a dismal future.*

dismantle /dɪsˈmæntl/ v [T] **1** to take something apart so that it is in separate pieces: *Chris dismantled the bike in five minutes.* **2** to gradually get rid of a system or organization: *an election promise to dismantle the existing tax laws*

dismay¹ /dɪsˈmeɪ/ n [U] a strong feeling of disappointment and worry: **to sb's dismay** *I found to my dismay that I had left my money behind.*

dismay² v [T] to make someone feel very disappointed and worried: *The poor election turn-out dismayed politicians.*

dismember /dɪsˈmembə $ -ər/ v [T] *formal* to cut a body into pieces

dismiss /dɪsˈmɪs/ v [T]
1 NOT CONSIDER STH to refuse to consider someone's idea or opinion because you think it is not serious, true, or important: **dismiss sb/sth as sth** *He dismissed the idea as impossible.*
2 SACK *formal* to make someone leave their job: *If you're late again you'll be dismissed!*
3 ALLOW SB TO LEAVE to send someone away or allow them to go: *Classes will be dismissed early tomorrow.* —**dismissal** n [C,U]

dismissive /dɪsˈmɪsɪv/ adj if you are dismissive of someone or something, you refuse to consider them seriously: **[+of]** *She tends to be dismissive of anyone who complains.* —**dismissively** adv

dismount /dɪsˈmaʊnt/ v [I] to get off a horse, bicycle, or MOTORCYCLE

disobedient /ˌdɪsəˈbiːdiənt◂, ˌdɪsəʊ- $ ˌdɪsə-, ˌdɪsoʊ-/ adj refusing to do what someone in authority tells you to do: *a disobedient child* —**disobedience** n [U] —**disobediently** adv

disobey /ˌdɪsəˈbeɪ, ˌdɪsəʊ- $ ˌdɪsə-, ˌdɪsoʊ-/ v [I,T] to refuse to do what someone in authority tells you to do: *She would never disobey her parents.*

disorder /dɪsˈɔːdə $ -ˈɔːrdər/ n **1** [U] when things or people are very untidy or disorganized: *The house was in a state of complete disorder.* **2** [U] a situation in which a lot of people behave in an uncontrolled, noisy, or violent way in public: **public/civil disorder** **3** [C] an illness that prevents part of your body from working properly: *a rare liver disorder*

disordered /dɪsˈɔːdəd $ -ˈɔːrdərd/ adj *formal* **1** not tidy **2** mentally confused

disorderly /dɪsˈɔːdəli $ -ˈɔːrdər-/ adj **1** untidy: *clothes left in a disorderly heap* **2** disorderly behaviour is noisy or violent: *Jerry was charged with being* **drunk and disorderly.**

disorganized (*also* -**ised** *BrE*) /dɪsˈɔːɡənaɪzd $ -ˈɔːr-/ adj not arranged or planned very well: *The meeting was completely disorganized.* —**disorganization** /dɪsˌɔːɡənəˈzeɪʃən $ -ˌɔːrɡənə-/ n [U]

disoriented /dɪsˈɔːrientɪd/ (*also* **disorientated** /dɪsˈɔːriəntertɪd/ *BrE*) adj confused and not able to understand what is happening or where you are: *After the long flight, I was tired and disoriented for a week.* —**disorienting, disorientating** adj —**disorientation** /dɪsˌɔːriənˈteɪʃən/ n [U]

disown /dɪsˈəʊn $ -ˈoʊn/ v [T] to say that you no longer have any connection with someone or something: *Frankly, I'm not surprised her family disowned her.*

disparaging /dɪˈspærədʒɪŋ/ adj a disparaging remark or look shows that you do not think someone or something is very good or important: *She made some* **disparaging remarks** *about the royal family.*

disparate /ˈdɪspərət/ adj *formal* disparate things are very different and not related to each other: *a meeting covering many disparate subjects* —**disparity**

/dɪˈspærəti/ n [C,U]: *the disparities between rich and poor*

dispassionate /dɪsˈpæʃənət/ adj not influenced by personal feelings: *a dispassionate opinion* —**dispassionately** adv: *We must look at the situation dispassionately.*

dispatch¹ (*also* **despatch** *BrE*) /dɪˈspætʃ/ v [T] to send someone or something somewhere: *The packages were dispatched yesterday.*

dispatch² (*also* **despatch** *BrE*) n [C] **1** a message sent between military or government officials: *a dispatch from headquarters* **2** a report sent to a newspaper from one of its writers who is in another town or country

dispel /dɪˈspel/ v [T] (**dispelled, dispelling**) *formal* to make something go away, especially a belief, idea, or feeling: *Mark's calm words dispelled our fears.*

dispensary /dɪˈspensəri/ n [C] (*plural* **dispensaries**) a place where medicines are prepared and given out

dispensation /ˌdɪspənˈseɪʃən, -pen-/ n [C,U] special permission to do something that is not usually allowed

dispense /dɪˈspens/ v [T] **1** to give something to people: *The machines in the hall dispense drinks.* **2** to prepare and give medicines to people
PHRASAL VERBS
dispense with sth *formal* to not use something that you usually use, because it is not necessary: *Ann suggested that they dispense with speeches altogether at the wedding.*

dispenser /dɪˈspensə $ -ər/ n [C] a machine from which you can get things such as drinks or money: *a cash dispenser*

disperse /dɪˈspɜːs $ -ɜːrs/ v [I,T] to scatter in different directions, or to make something do this: *Police used tear gas to disperse the crowd.* —**dispersal** n [U]

dispirited /dɪˈspɪrɪtɪd/ adj sad and no longer hopeful: *She looked tired and dispirited.*

displace Ac /dɪsˈpleɪs/ v [T] **1** to take the place of someone or something SYN **replace**: *The yen displaced the dollar as the world's most important currency.* **2** to make a group of people leave the place where they normally live: *Millions of people were displaced by war.* —**displacement** n [U] —**displaced** adj

display¹ Ac /dɪˈspleɪ/ n [C]
1 FOR PEOPLE TO SEE an arrangement of objects for people to look at: **[+of]** *a display of African masks* | **on display** (=being displayed) *The pictures are on display in the cafeteria.*
2 PERFORMANCE a public performance or entertainment: *a firework display* | **[+of]** *a display of dancing*
3 FOR SHOWING INFORMATION the part of a piece of equipment that shows information, for example a computer screen: *A light flashed on the display.*
4 FOR SHOWING EMOTION display of affection/temper etc an occasion when someone clearly shows a particular attitude or quality: *a shocking display of aggression*

display² Ac /v [T] **1** to put things in a place where people can see them easily: *a row of tables displaying pottery* | *Results will be displayed on the noticeboard.* **2** to clearly show a feeling or quality: *He displayed no emotion at the funeral.* **3** if a computer displays information, it shows it: *An error message was displayed.*

displeased /dɪs'pliːzd/ *adj formal* annoyed: *She looked displeased.* —**displeasure** /-'pleʒə $ -ər/ *n* [U]

disposable Ac /dɪ'spəʊzəbəl $ -'spoʊ-/ *adj* intended to be used once or for a short time and then thrown away: *disposable nappies*

dis,posable 'income *n* [U] the amount of money that you have available to spend each month after you have paid for rent, food etc

disposal Ac /dɪ'spəʊzəl $ -'spoʊ-/ *n* [U] when you get rid of something: **[+of]** *the disposal of radioactive waste*
PHRASES
at sb's disposal available for someone to use: *He had a lot of cash at his disposal.*

dispose Ac /dɪ'spəʊz $ -'spoʊz/ *v*
PHRASAL VERBS
dispose of sth to get rid of something: *safer ways of disposing of waste*

disposed /dɪ'spəʊzd $ -'spoʊzd/ *adj formal* **1 well/favourably/kindly disposed to sb/sth** liking someone or something: *countries that are well disposed to the West* **2 be/feel disposed to do sth** to be willing to do something: *He did not feel disposed to argue.*

disposition /ˌdɪspə'zɪʃən/ *n* [C] *formal* someone's usual character: *a cheerful disposition*

disproportionate Ac /ˌdɪsprə'pɔːʃənət◂ $ -ɔːr-/ *adj* too much or too little in relation to something: *She gets a disproportionate amount of publicity.* —**disproportionately** *adv*

disprove /dɪs'pruːv/ *v* [T] to show that something is definitely wrong or not true: *The facts disprove his argument.*

dispute¹ /dɪ'spjuːt, 'dɪspjuːt/ *n* [C,U] a serious argument or disagreement: **[+with]** *He was involved in a legal dispute with his neighbour.* | **[+over]** *The two men got into a dispute over money.* | **be in dispute (with sb)** *They are in dispute with a local building firm.* | **pay/industrial dispute** (=between employers and workers) *Flights have been disrupted by a pilots' pay dispute.* THESAURUS ARGUMENT
PHRASES
beyond dispute if something is beyond dispute, everyone agrees that it is true: *His loyalty is beyond dispute.*

dispute² /dɪ'spjuːt/ *v* [T] to say that you think something is not correct or true: *He claims he won, but I dispute that.*

disqualify /dɪs'kwɒlɪfaɪ $ -'kwɑː-/ *v* [T usually passive] (**disqualified, disqualifying, disqualifies**) to stop someone from taking part in an activity because they have broken a rule: **disqualify sb from sth** *He was disqualified from the race.* —**disqualification** /dɪsˌkwɒlɪfɪ'keɪʃən $ -kwɑː-/ *n* [C,U]

disquiet /dɪs'kwaɪət/ *n* [U] *formal* anxiety or unhappiness about something: **[+about]** *public disquiet about animal testing*

disregard /ˌdɪsrɪ'ɡɑːd $ -ɑːrd/ *v* [T] to ignore something: *The judge told the jury to disregard that statement.* —**disregard** *n* [U]: *He showed total disregard for my feelings.*

disrepair /ˌdɪsrɪ'peə $ -'per/ *n* [U] buildings that are in disrepair are in bad condition because they have not been cared for: *The old house had **fallen into disrepair.***

disreputable /dɪs'repjətəbəl/ *adj* dishonest, illegal, or bad OPP **reputable**: *a disreputable businessman*

disrepute /ˌdɪsrɪ'pjuːt/ *n* **bring sth into disrepute** *formal* to make people no longer admire or respect something: *behaviour which has brought the medical profession into disrepute*

disrespect /ˌdɪsrɪ'spekt/ *n* [U] lack of respect for something or someone: **[+for]** *his disrespect for the law* —**disrespectful** *adj*

disrupt /dɪs'rʌpt/ *v* [T] to prevent something from continuing normally by causing problems: *Road works are seriously disrupting traffic.* —**disruptive** *adj*: *disruptive students* —**disruption** /-'rʌpʃən/ *n* [C,U]

dissatisfied /dɪˌsætəsfaɪd, dɪs'sæ-/ *adj* not happy because something is not as good as you had expected OPP **satisfied**: *dissatisfied customers* | **[+with]** *If you are dissatisfied with our service, please let us know.* —**dissatisfaction** /dɪˌsætəs'fækʃən, dɪsˌsæ-/ *n* [U]

dissect /dɪ'sekt, daɪ-/ *v* [T] to cut up the body of a plant or animal in order to study it

disseminate /dɪ'semɪneɪt/ *v* [T] *formal* to spread information or ideas to as many people as possible: *a network to disseminate medical information*

dissent /dɪ'sent/ *n* [U] refusal to agree with an accepted opinion or decision: *political dissent* —**dissent** *v* [I]: *Few historians dissent from this view.* —**dissenter** *n* [C]

dissertation /ˌdɪsə'teɪʃən $ ˌdɪsər-/ *n* [C] a long piece of writing that you do for a university degree

disservice /dɪ'sɜːvəs, dɪs'sɜː- $ -ɜːr-/ *n* **do sb/sth a disservice** to make people have a bad opinion of someone or something, especially when this is unfair: *The critics have done this play a great disservice.*

dissident /'dɪsɪdənt/ *n* [C] someone who publicly criticizes the government in a country where this is a crime —**dissident** *adj*: *dissident writers*

dissimilar Ac /dɪ'sɪmələ, dɪs'sɪ- $ -ər/ *adj* not the same: *The Breton language is **not dissimilar to** (=is quite like) Welsh.* —**dissimilarity** /dɪˌsɪmə'lærəti, dɪsˌsɪ-/ *n* [C,U]

dissipate /'dɪsəpeɪt/ *v* [I,T] *formal* to gradually disappear, or to make something do this

dissociate /dɪ'səʊʃieɪt, -sieɪt $ -'soʊ-/ *v* [T] to say that you do not agree with someone or something: **dissociate yourself from sth** *He tried to dissociate himself from the chairman's remarks.*

D

dissolution /ˌdɪsəˈluːʃən/ n [U] when a parliament, marriage, or business arrangement is formally ended → **dissolve**

dissolve /dɪˈzɒlv $ dɪˈzɑːlv/ v

1 MIX INTO LIQUID [I,T] if a solid dissolves, or if you dissolve it, it mixes with a liquid and becomes liquid itself: *Stir the mixture until the sugar dissolves.* | **dissolve sth in sth** *Dissolve the tablets in water.*

2 END STH [T] to formally end a parliament, marriage, or business arrangement

3 DISAPPEAR [I] to gradually disappear: *My shyness soon dissolved.*

PHRASES

dissolve into tears/laughter etc to start crying or laughing a lot: *She threw herself into a chair and dissolved into tears.*

dissuade /dɪˈsweɪd/ v [T] *formal* to persuade someone not to do something: **dissuade sb from (doing) sth** *a campaign to dissuade young people from smoking*

distance[1] /ˈdɪstəns/ n

1 [C,U] the amount of space between two places or things: **[+from/between]** *What's the distance from London to Harlow?* | *the distance between two cars* | **at a distance of 20 feet/30 metres etc** *I followed at a distance of about 10 metres.* | **within walking/ travelling/commuting distance** (=near enough to walk or travel to) *The school is within easy walking distance.* **THESAURUS** NEAR

2 [singular] a place that is far away: **in the distance** *I heard bells ringing in the distance.* | **at/from a distance** *We watched from a safe distance.* → **LONG-DISTANCE**

PHRASES

keep your distance 1 to stay far enough away to be safe: *The dogs looked fierce, so I kept my distance.* **2** to avoid becoming too friendly with someone: *He tends to keep his distance from employees.*

COLLOCATIONS

adjectives

a long/great distance *People now drive longer distances each day.*

a short distance *My house is just a short distance from here.*

some distance (=quite a long distance) *His parents live some distance away.*

a safe distance (=enough space to be safe) *Keep a safe distance from the edge of the cliff.*

verbs

to travel a great/long etc distance *They travel long distances to find work.*

to measure the distance *Measure the distance between the two walls.*

---

distance[2] v **distance yourself** to say that you are not involved with someone or something: *The party is distancing itself from its violent past.*

distant /ˈdɪstənt/ adj

1 far away in space or time: *the sound of distant laughter* | *The building is a relic of **the distant past**.* **THESAURUS** FAR

2 not friendly or not interested: *She seemed cold and distant.*

3 [only before noun] not closely related to you **OPP** **close**: *a distant relative* —**distantly** adv

distaste /dɪsˈteɪst/ n [singular, U] a feeling that something or someone is unpleasant or offensive: **[+for]** *her distaste for gossip*

distasteful /dɪsˈteɪstfəl/ adj unpleasant or offensive

distill, **distil** /dɪˈstɪl/ v [T] (**distilled**, **distilling**) **1** to make a liquid more pure by heating it until it becomes gas and then letting it cool: *distilled water* **2** to get the main ideas or facts from a large amount of information: *The wisdom in this book has been distilled from years of experience.* —**distillation** /ˌdɪstəˈleɪʃən/ n [C,U]

distillery /dɪˈstɪləri/ n [C] (*plural* **distilleries**) a factory where strong alcoholic drink such as WHISKY is produced

distinct Ac /dɪˈstɪŋkt/ adj **1** clearly different or separate: *Spanish and Catalan are two entirely distinct languages.* **2** if something is distinct, you can see, hear, or notice it easily: *There was a distinct smell of burning.*

PHRASES

as distinct from used to emphasize that you are talking about one thing and not another: *I am talking about childhood as distinct from adolescence.* —**distinctly** adv: *I distinctly remember his words.*

distinction Ac /dɪˈstɪŋkʃən/ n

1 DIFFERENCE [C] a clear difference between things: **[+between]** *The law **makes** a **distinction** between children and adults.*

2 GOOD QUALITY [U] when someone or something is special and very good: *an artist of great distinction*

3 GOOD WORK [C,U] a special mark given to a student whose work is excellent: *She passed the exam with distinction.*

distinctive Ac /dɪˈstɪŋktɪv/ adj different from other things and very easy to recognize: *The band have a distinctive sound.* **THESAURUS** DIFFERENT —**distinctively** adv

distinguish /dɪˈstɪŋɡwɪʃ/ v

1 SEE THE DIFFERENCE [I,T] to recognize or understand the difference between things or people: **[+between]** *He is old enough to distinguish between fiction and reality.*

2 BE THE DIFFERENT THING [T] to be the thing that makes someone or something different from other people or things: *What distinguishes us is the quality of our research.*

3 SEE/HEAR STH [T] to be able to see or hear something, even if it is difficult: *It was too dark for me to distinguish anything clearly.* —**distinguishable** adj

distinguished /dɪˈstɪŋɡwɪʃt/ adj successful and respected: *a distinguished scientist*

distort Ac /dɪˈstɔːt $ -ɔːrt/ v [T] **1** to change the shape or sound of something so it is strange or unclear: *Tall buildings can distort radio signals.* **2** to report something in a way that changes its meaning: *The press distorted what I said.* **THESAURUS** CHANGE —**distorted** adj —**distortion**

/dɪˈstɔːʃən $ -ɔːr-/ n [C,U]: *a distortion of the facts*

distract /dɪˈstrækt/ v [T] to take someone's attention away from what they are doing: *Don't distract me while I'm driving! | The government is trying to distract attention from its failures.*

distracted /dɪˈstræktɪd/ adj unable to think clearly because you are worried about something

distraction /dɪˈstrækʃən/ n [C,U] something that takes your attention away from what you are doing: *I can't study at home – there are too many distractions.*
PHRASES
| **drive sb to distraction** to annoy someone very much: *He drove his teachers to distraction.*

distraught /dɪˈstrɔːt $ -ˈstrɑːt/ adj extremely upset: *Friends comforted his distraught parents.*

distress¹ /dɪˈstres/ n [U] **1** a feeling of extreme unhappiness: *Their divorce caused him great distress.* **2** a very difficult situation where someone needs help: *charities who help families in distress*

distress² v [T] to make someone feel very upset: *The news distressed her.*

distressing /dɪˈstresɪŋ/ adj making you feel very upset: *a distressing dream* —**distressingly** adv

distribute Ac /dɪˈstrɪbjuːt/ v [T] **1** to share things among a group of people: *I'll distribute copies of the report.* | **distribute sth to/among sb** *Food and blankets were distributed among the refugees.* **2** to supply goods to shops and companies in a particular area: *The tape is distributed by American Video.* —**distribution** /ˌdɪstrəˈbjuːʃən/ n [U]

distributor /dɪˈstrɪbjʊtə $ -ər/ n [C] a company or person that supplies goods to shops or companies

district /ˈdɪstrɪkt/ n [C] an area of a city or country: **shopping/residential/business etc district** *Edinburgh's main shopping district | the Ludhiana district of East Punjab*

district at'torney n [C] *AmE* a lawyer who works for the government in one particular area

distrust¹ /dɪsˈtrʌst/ n [U] a feeling that you cannot trust someone SYN **mistrust**: **[+of]** *He had a deep distrust of the police.* —**distrustful** adj

distrust² v [T] to not trust someone or something SYN **mistrust** OPP **trust**: *Meg had always distrusted banks.*

disturb /dɪˈstɜːb $ -ɜːrb/ v [T]
1 INTERRUPT to interrupt someone so that they cannot continue what they are doing: *Sorry to disturb you, but it's urgent. | Noise from the street disturbed her sleep.*
2 WORRY SB to make someone feel worried or upset: *Something about the situation disturbed him.*
3 MOVE STH to move something: *If you go into my office, please don't disturb anything.*

disturbance /dɪˈstɜːbəns $ -ɜːr-/ n **1** [C] a situation in which people behave violently in public: *a disturbance outside a bar* **2** [C,U] something that interrupts what you are doing: *The builders will cause as little disturbance as possible.*

disturbed /dɪˈstɜːbd $ -ɜːrbd/ adj not behaving in a normal way because of mental or emotional problems: *a disturbed child*

disturbing /dɪˈstɜːbɪŋ $ -ɜːr-/ adj worrying or upsetting: *a disturbing increase in crime*

disuse /dɪsˈjuːs/ n [U] when something is no longer used: *The building eventually fell into disuse.*

disused /ˌdɪsˈjuːzd◂/ adj [only before noun] no longer used: *a disused railway*

ditch¹ /dɪtʃ/ n [C] a long narrow hole dug at the side of a field or road to hold or carry away water

ditch² v [T] *informal* to get rid of something or someone: *The government quickly ditched the plan.*

dither /ˈdɪðə $ -ər/ v [I] to be unable to make a decision: **[+over/about]** *I was still dithering over what to wear.*

ditto¹ /ˈdɪtəʊ $ -toʊ/ adv used instead of repeating something, to say that what has been said is also true in another case: *Friday nobody showed up. Ditto Monday and Tuesday.*

ditto² n [C] (plural **dittos**) a mark (") that you write under a word in a list so that you do not have to write the same word again

diva /ˈdiːvə/ n [C] a very successful female singer

divan /dɪˈvæn $ ˈdaɪvæn/ n [C] **1** a bed with a thick base **2** a long low soft seat with no arms or back

DIVE

dive

scuba diving

dive¹ /daɪv/ v [I] (past tense **dived** also **dove** /dəʊv $ doʊv/ *AmE*, past participle **dived**)
1 INTO WATER to jump into the water with your head and arms first: **[+into/off etc]** *Harry dived into the pool. | It is dangerous to dive off the cliffs.* THESAURUS JUMP
2 UNDER WATER/SEA to swim under water using breathing equipment: *You can swim and dive in the crystal clear waters.*
3 MOVE DOWNWARDS to travel down through air or water: *The plane began to dive.* | **[+down/onto etc]** *Seabirds were diving down to catch fish.*
4 MOVE QUICKLY to move or jump quickly: **[+into/after etc]** *He dived into a doorway to get out of the rain.* | *Shots were heard and everyone dived for cover.*

dive² n [C]
1 QUICK MOVEMENT a sudden movement in one

direction: *She made a dive for the ball.*
2 DECREASE a sudden fall in the amount, value, or success of something: *Share prices took a dive.*
3 MOVEMENT DOWNWARDS a movement down through air or water: *The plane suddenly went into a dive.*
4 INTO WATER a jump into water with your head and arms first

diver /ˈdaɪvə $ -ər/ *n* [C] someone who swims under water with breathing equipment

diverge /daɪˈvɜːdʒ, də- $ -ɜːrdʒ/ *v* [I] to be different or to develop in a different way: **[+from]** *At this point his version of events diverges from hers.* —**divergence** *n* [C,U] —**divergent** *adj*: *divergent views*

diverse Ac /daɪˈvɜːs $ dəˈvɜːrs, daɪ-/ *adj formal* different from each other: *London is home to people of many diverse cultures.* —**diversity** *n* [U]

diversify Ac /daɪˈvɜːsɪfaɪ $ dəˈvɜːr-, daɪ-/ *v* [I,T] (**diversified**, **diversifying**, **diversifies**) to begin to make different products or get involved in new areas of business: **[+into]** *a cosmetics company that is diversifying into clothing* —**diversification** /daɪˌvɜːsɪfɪˈkeɪʃən $ dəˌvɜːr-, daɪ-/ *n* [U]

diversion /daɪˈvɜːʃən, də- $ -ɜːrʒən/ *n*
1 CHANGE IN STH'S DIRECTION [C,U] a change in the direction something is going in, or its purpose: **[+of]** *the diversion of a section of the river*
2 STH FUN [C,U] an enjoyable activity that stops you from being bored: *Computer games can be a great diversion for kids.*
3 CHANGE YOUR ATTENTION [C] something that takes your attention away from something else: *One man creates a diversion while the other steals your purse.*
4 ON ROADS [C] *BrE* a different way that traffic is sent when the usual way is blocked

divert /daɪˈvɜːt, də- $ -ɜːrt/ *v* [T] **1** to change the direction or purpose of something: *We should divert more resources into research.* | *Traffic is being diverted to avoid the accident.* **2 divert (sb's) attention from sth** to take someone's attention away from something: *The war will divert attention from the government's problems.*

divest /daɪˈvest, də-/ *v*
PHRASAL VERBS
divest sb/sth of sth *formal* to remove something or get rid of something: *He divested himself of his coat.*

divide¹ /dəˈvaɪd/ *v*
1 SEPARATE INTO PARTS [I,T] if something divides, or if you divide it, it separates into two or more parts: **divide sth into sth** *The teacher divided the class into groups.* | **[+into]** *The story divides into three sections.*
2 KEEP APART (*also* **divide off**) [T] to keep two areas separate from each other: *The river divides the North and South sides of the city.* | **divide sth from sth** *A curtain divided his sleeping area from ours.*
3 SHARE (*also* **divide up**) [T] to separate something into parts and give parts to different people, activities etc: **divide sth between/among sth/sb** *He divided the money equally among his children.* | *She divides her time between New York and London.*
4 MATHS [T] to calculate how many times one number contains another number → **multiply**: **divide sth by sth** *15 divided by 5 is 3.*

5 DISAGREE [T] to make people disagree with each other: *The issue has divided voters.* THESAURUS▸
DISAGREE

divide² *n* [C usually singular] a strong difference between the beliefs of two groups: *They're on opposite sides of the political divide.*

dividend /ˈdɪvədənd, -dend/ *n* [C] a part of a company's profit that is paid to people who have SHARES in the company
PHRASES
| **pay dividends** to bring a lot of advantages: *Exercise now will pay dividends when you're older.*

di'viding ˌline *n* [singular] the difference between two similar things: **[+between]** *the dividing line between popular fiction and serious literature*

divine /dəˈvaɪn/ *adj* relating to God or a god: *divine power*

diving /ˈdaɪvɪŋ/ *n* [U] **1** the sport of swimming under water using breathing equipment **2** the activity of jumping into water with your head and arms first

'diving board *n* [C] a board above a SWIMMING POOL that people can jump from

divinity /dəˈvɪnəti/ *n* [U] **1** *AmE* the study of God and religious beliefs SYN **theology** *BrE* **2** being God or like a god

divisible /dəˈvɪzəbəl/ *adj* able to be divided by a number: **[+by]** *27 is divisible by 9 and 3.*

division /dəˈvɪʒən/ *n*
1 SEPARATION [C,U] when you separate something into parts, or the way these parts are separated: **the division of sth into/between/among sth** *the division of words into syllables*
2 DISAGREEMENT [C,U] disagreement among the members of a group: **[+within/among/between]** *There are deep divisions within the party.*
3 MATHS [U] when you calculate how many times one number contains another → **multiplication**
4 PART OF A GROUP [C] a group within a large company, army, or organization: *He heads our IT division.* | *They sent a division of tanks.*
5 SPORT [C] one of the groups of teams that a sports competition is divided into: **First/Second etc Division** *Manchester City were in the First Division.*

divisional /dəˈvɪʒənəl/ *adj* [only before noun] relating to a group within a large company, army, or organization: *a divisional manager*

divisive /dəˈvaɪsɪv/ *adj* causing a lot of disagreement among people: *a very divisive issue*

divorce¹ /dəˈvɔːs $ -ɔːrs/ *n* [C,U] the legal ending of a marriage → **separation**: *She wants to get a divorce.* | *Many marriages end in divorce.*

divorce² *v* **1** [I,T] to legally end a marriage → **separate**: *His parents divorced when he was six.* | *Why did she divorce him?* | *They decided to get divorced.* **2** [T] *formal* to separate two things completely: **divorce sth from sth** *It is difficult to divorce religion from politics.* —**divorced** *adj*: *a divorced woman*

divorcee /dəˌvɔːˈsiː/ *n* [C] *BrE* someone who is divorced

divulge /daɪˈvʌldʒ, də-/ *v* [T] to give someone

secret information: *Doctors cannot divulge information about their patients.*

Diwali, **Divali** /dɪˈwɑːli/ n a Hindu FESTIVAL, celebrated in the autumn

DIY /ˌdiː aɪ ˈwaɪ/ n [U] *BrE* (**do-it-yourself**) when you make or repair things in your house yourself rather than paying other people to do the work

dizzy /ˈdɪzi/ adj feeling that you are losing your balance, for example because you have been spinning around or you are ill: *She felt dizzy when she stood up.* | *He suffers from dizzy spells.* —**dizziness** n [U]

DJ /ˌdiː ˈdʒeɪ◂/ n [C] (**disc jockey**) someone who plays records on the radio or in a club where you can dance

DNA /ˌdiː en ˈeɪ◂/ n [U] (**deoxyribonucleic acid**) a substance that carries GENETIC information in a cell

DNA ˈfingerprinting n [U] the process of examining the pattern of someone's GENES, for example to find out whether blood, hair etc found where a crime was committed belongs to them [SYN] **genetic fingerprinting**

do¹ /duː/ auxiliary verb (past tense **did** /dɪd/, past participle **done** /dʌn/, third person singular **does** /dəz; strong dʌz/)
1 used with another verb to form questions or negatives: *Do you like pasta?* | *What did he say?* | *I don't know her name.* | *Don't push me!*
2 used to form QUESTION TAGS: *You know Tom, don't you?* | *She didn't understand, did she?*
3 used to avoid repeating another verb: *She eats a lot more than I do.* | *so/neither do I* '*I have to go.*' '*So do I.*' | *Paul didn't like it and neither did I.*
4 used to emphasize the main verb in a sentence: *He did tell me, but I forgot.* | *Do be careful.*

do² v (past tense **did**, past participle **done**, third person singular **does**)
1 [ACTION/ACTIVITY] [T] to perform an action or activity: *What are you doing?* | *I have to do my homework.* | *All he does is watch TV.* | **do something/anything** *Why isn't anybody doing anything to help?*
2 [DO STH WELL/BADLY] [I] used to talk or ask about how successful someone is: *How is she doing at university?* | **do well/badly** *She did well at school.*
3 [HAVE AN EFFECT] [T] to have a particular effect on someone or something: *It will do you good to have a break.* | **do nothing/a lot/something etc for sb/sth** *The scandal has done nothing for his reputation.* | *The new job did a lot for her confidence.*
4 [JOB] [T] to have a particular job: *What do you do?* | *She doesn't know what she wants to do.*
5 [BE GOOD ENOUGH] [I] used to say that something is acceptable or enough: *Butter is best, but oil would do.* | *My old black shoes will have to do.* | *All these excuses just won't do.* [THESAURUS] SATISFACTORY
6 [HAIR/NAILS ETC] **do your hair/nails/make-up etc** to make your hair etc look nice
7 [STUDY] [T] *BrE* to study a subject at school or college: *We didn't do Latin at school.*
8 [COOK] [T] to cook a type of food: *I'm doing steak tonight.*
9 [TRAVEL] [T] to achieve a particular speed or distance: *He was doing over 90 miles an hour.*

10 [PROVIDE] [T] to provide a service or sell a product: *They do home deliveries.*
PHRASES
what is sb/sth doing? used when you are surprised or annoyed that someone or something is in a particular place or doing a particular thing: *What is my jacket doing on the floor?* | *What are you doing with my purse?*

PHRASAL VERBS
do away with sb/sth *informal*
1 to get rid of something: *We should do away with those old customs.*
2 to kill someone
do sth **over** *AmE* to do something again, especially because you did it wrong the first time
do up
1 to fasten something, or to be fastened: *The dress does up at the back.* | **do sth** ↔ **up** *Do up your shoelaces.*
2 **do sth** ↔ **up** to repair a building or car, and improve its appearance: *They bought an old house and did it up.*
do with sb/sth
1 **could do with sth** to need or want something: *I could do with some help.*
2 **be/have to do with sb/sth** to be related to or involved with something or someone: *The conversation mostly had to do with work.* | *I'm sorry, but it's* **nothing to do with me** (=I am not responsible or involved).
3 **do sth with sth** to deal with something, usually by putting it somewhere: *I don't know what to do with these boxes.* | *What have you done with my bag* (=where have you put it)?
do without
1 **do without (sth)** to live or manage without having something: *I couldn't do without a car.*
2 **could do without sth** used to say that something is annoying you or causing problems: *I could do without this noise.*

THESAURUS

do to do something – used especially in the following phrases: **do a job/task** *There are one or two jobs that need doing in the garden.* | **do your homework/the housework** *Have you done your homework yet?* | **do the shopping/cooking/cleaning etc** *Who usually does the cooking in your house?* | **do a test/experiment/some research** *Scientists did some tests on mice.* | **do a course** *Do you know which course you want to do at university?*

make to do something – used in the following phrases: **make a speech** *The Prince made a short speech.* | **make a comment/suggestion/joke** *Can I make a suggestion?* | **make a decision** *She still hasn't made a final decision.* | **make a mistake** *Don't worry if you make a mistake.*

give to do a talk, speech, or performance: *He gave a wonderful talk on birds.* | *The band gave a brilliant performance.*

carry out sth to do something, or to do what someone tells you to do – used especially in the following phrases: **carry out work/a task** *They carried out the work very efficiently.* | **carry out**

research/an experiment/an operation *The hospital carries out research into cancer.* | **carry out sb's orders** *You will be punished if you fail to carry out orders.*

perform *formal* to do a task, duty, or operation: *A team of surgeons performed the operation.* | *The machine can perform several tasks at once.*

commit to do something that is a crime: *Women commit fewer crimes than men.*

do³ *n* [C] (*plural* **dos**) *informal* a party or other social event: *We're going to a do on Saturday.*

PHRASES

dos and don'ts things that you should and should not do: *the dos and don'ts of having a pet*

doable /'du:əbəl/ *adj* [not before noun] *spoken informal* able to be done or completed: *Is the task really doable?*

docile /'dəʊsaɪl $ 'dɑːsəl/ *adj* quiet and easy to control: *a docile animal*

dock¹ /dɒk $ dɑːk/ *n* **1** [C] the place in a port where goods are taken on and off ships **2 the docks** [plural] the area around and including a port **3 the dock** the part of a law court where the person who is charged with a crime stands

dock² *v* [I,T] if a ship docks, it sails into a dock

PHRASES

dock sb's pay to reduce the amount of money that you pay someone as a punishment: *The company has threatened to dock the officers' pay.*

'dock ,worker (*also* **docker** /'dɒkə $ 'dɑːkər/ *BrE*) *n* [C] a person whose job is to move goods on and off ships **SYN** **longshoreman** *AmE*

doctor¹ /'dɒktə $ 'dɑːktər/ *n* [C]

1 (*written abbreviation* **Dr**) someone who is trained to treat people who are ill: *You should go to the doctor with that cough.* | *Dr. Brown is busy at the moment.*

2 someone who has the highest level of degree given by a university: *a Doctor of Philosophy* → **SPIN DOCTOR, WITCH DOCTOR**

COLLOCATIONS

verbs

to go to the doctor *If I don't feel better tomorrow, I'll go to the doctor.*

to see a doctor *He needs to see a doctor immediately.*

to ask a doctor (*also* **to consult a doctor** *formal*) *For further advice, consult your family doctor.*

to call/get a doctor (=to ask one to come to you) *I think we should call a doctor.*

a doctor examines sb *The doctor who examined him said he was perfectly healthy.*

a doctor prescribes sth (=writes an order for medicine for someone) *The doctor prescribed painkillers.*

THESAURUS

doctor someone who is trained to treat people who are ill: *If you have a chest pain, you should see a doctor.*

GP *BrE* a doctor who treats the people who live in a local area: *My GP gave me some antibiotics.*

physician *especially AmE formal* a doctor: *the American physician, Dr James Tyler Kent*

surgeon a doctor who does operations in a hospital: *a heart surgeon*

consultant *BrE* a very senior doctor in a hospital, with knowledge about a particular area of medicine: *a consultant in disease control*

psychiatrist a doctor who is trained to treat people with mental illnesses: *a child psychiatrist*

vet (*also* **veterinarian** *especially AmE*) a doctor who treats animals: *We took the cat to the vet.*

doctor² *v* [T] to change something in a dishonest way in order to gain an advantage: *Do you think the police doctored the evidence?*

doctorate /'dɒktərət $ 'dɑːk-/ *n* [C] a university degree at the highest level

doctrine /'dɒktrɪn $ 'dɑːk-/ *n* [C,U] a set of religious or political beliefs

docudrama /'dɒkjʊˌdrɑːmə $ 'dɑːkjʊˌdrɑːmə, -ˌdræmə/ *n* [C] a television programme which shows real events in the form of a story

document¹ Ac /'dɒkjəmənt $ ˌdɑːk-/ *n* [C] **1** a piece of paper that has official information written on it: *a legal document* | *historical documents* **2** a piece of work that you write and keep on a computer: *Click on the document you want to open.* —**documentary** /ˌdɒkjə'mentəri $ ˌdɑːk-/ *adj*: *documentary evidence*

document² Ac /'dɒkjəment $ 'dɑːk-/ *v* [T] to record information about something by writing about it, photographing it etc: *The programme documents the life of a teenager.*

documentary /ˌdɒkjə'mentəri◂ $ ˌdɑːk-/ *n* [C] (*plural* **documentaries**) a film or television programme that gives information about a subject: **[+on/about]** *They are **making** a **documentary** about volcanoes.* **THESAURUS** ▶ **PROGRAMME**

documentation Ac /ˌdɒkjəmən'teɪʃən, -men- $ ˌdɑːk-/ *n* [U] documents that show that something is true or correct

doddle /'dɒdl $ 'dɑːdl/ *n* **be a doddle** *BrE informal* to be very easy: *The exam was a doddle.*

dodge¹ /dɒdʒ $ dɑːdʒ/ *v* **1** [I,T] to move quickly to avoid someone or something: **[+between/through/into etc]** *They **dodged** through the **traffic**.* | *We had to dodge the bullets.* **2** [T] to deliberately avoid discussing something or doing something: *The Senator dodged the crucial question.*

dodge² *n* [C] *informal* a way of avoiding something that you should do: *a **tax dodge*** (=a way of avoiding paying tax)

dodgy /'dɒdʒi $ 'dɑː-/ *adj BrE informal* **1** not working properly or not in good condition: *a dodgy hard disk* **2** dishonest, or not to be trusted: *dodgy business dealings*

doe /dəʊ $ doʊ/ *n* [C] a female rabbit or **DEER**

does /dəz; *strong* dʌz/ *v* the third person singular of the present tense of **DO**

doesn't /'dʌzənt/ the short form of 'does not'

dog¹ /dɒg $ dɒːg/ n [C]
1 a very common animal with four legs, fur, and a tail. Dogs are often kept as pets or as working animals. → **puppy**, **bitch**: *I could hear a dog barking.* → see picture at **PET¹**
2 a male dog, FOX, or WOLF → **HOT DOG**

COLLOCATIONS

verbs

to have a dog (=to keep one as a pet) *We have one dog and two cats.*
to walk a dog (also **to take a dog for a walk**) *Alison is out walking the dog.*
a dog barks (=makes short loud sounds) *I wish that dog would stop barking!*
a dog growls (=makes a long deep angry sound) *The dog growled at him, showing its teeth.*
a dog wags its tail (=moves its tail to show pleasure) *The dog was jumping around and wagging its tail.*

types of dog

a pet dog *Some owners give their pet dogs too much food.*
a stray dog (=a pet dog that is lost) *A stray dog followed them down the street.*
a guide dog (=trained to guide a blind person) |
a guard dog (=trained to guard a building)

noun + dog

a breed of dog (=a type of dog) *What breed of dog is it?*

dog² v [T] (**dogged**, **dogging**) if a problem dogs you, it causes trouble for a long time

'dog ,collar n [C] *informal* a white collar worn by priests

dog-eared /ˈdɒg ɪəd $ ˈdɔːg ɪrd/ adj dog-eared books have been used so much that the corners of their pages are folded or torn

dogged /ˈdɒgɪd $ ˈdɔː-/ adj [only before noun] determined to do something even though it is difficult: *a dogged determination to succeed* —**doggedly** adv

doghouse /ˈdɒghaʊs $ ˈdɔːg-/ n [C] *AmE* a small building outdoors for a dog to sleep in **SYN kennel** *BrE*

PHRASES

be in the doghouse *informal* to have annoyed someone or made them angry with you: *I'm in the doghouse for forgetting my girlfriend's birthday.*

dogma /ˈdɒgmə $ ˈdɔːgmə, ˈdɑːgmə/ n [C,U] beliefs that people are expected to accept as true without asking for any explanation: *religious dogma*

dogmatic /dɒgˈmætɪk $ dɔːg-, dɑːg-/ adj someone who is dogmatic is completely certain of their beliefs and expects other people to accept them without arguing —**dogmatically** /-kli/ adv

do-gooder /ˌduː ˈgʊdə $ -ər/ n [C] *informal* someone who thinks they are helping others, but who often gets involved when they are not wanted

dogsbody /ˈdɒgz,bɒdi $ ˈdɔːgz,bɑːdi/ n [C] (*plural* **dogsbodies**) *BrE* someone who has to do all the small boring jobs in a place: *I'm just the office dogsbody.*

doing¹ /ˈduːɪŋ/ n **1 be sb's (own) doing** to be someone's own fault: *His bad luck was all his own doing.*
2 take some doing *informal* to be hard work: *Getting the place clean is going to take some doing.*

doing² v the present participle of DO

,do-it-your'self n [U] DIY

doldrums /ˈdɒldrəmz $ ˈdoʊl-, ˈdɑːl-, ˈdɔːl-/ n **in the doldrums a)** if something is in the doldrums, it is not doing well or developing: *Sales have been in the doldrums for months.* **b)** if you are in the doldrums, you are feeling sad

dole¹ /dəʊl $ doʊl/ n [U] *BrE* money that the British government gives to people who are unemployed: **be/go on the dole** (=be receiving government money) *He's been on the dole for two years.*

dole² v

PHRASAL VERBS

dole sth ↔ **out** *informal* to give money, food, advice etc to more than one person: [+to] *Vera was doling out candy to the kids.*

doleful /ˈdəʊlfəl $ ˈdoʊl-/ adj *formal* very sad: *a doleful song*

doll /dɒl $ dɑːl, dɔːl/ n [C] a toy that looks like a small person or baby: *a small wooden doll*

dollar /ˈdɒlə $ ˈdɑːlər/ n [C]
1 written sign $; the standard unit of money in the US, Australia, Canada, and some other countries: *That will be three dollars, please.* | *a ten-dollar bill*
2 the dollar the value of US money in relation to the money of other countries: *The pound has* **risen** **against the dollar** (=increased in value in relation to the dollar).

dollop /ˈdɒləp $ ˈdɑː-/ n [C] a small amount of soft food, usually dropped from a spoon: *a dollop of thick cream* → see picture at **PIECE¹**

dolphin /ˈdɒlfɪn $ ˈdɑːl-, ˈdɔːl-/ n [C] a very intelligent sea animal with a long grey pointed nose

DOLPHIN

domain Ac /dəˈmeɪn, dəʊ- $ də-, doʊ-/ n [C] *formal* **1** an area of activity, interest, or knowledge, especially one that a particular person or organization deals with: **outside/within the domain of sth/sb** *This problem is outside the domain of medical science.*
2 an area that was controlled by someone in past times

dome /dəʊm $ doʊm/ n [C] a round roof on a building —**domed** adj

domestic Ac /dəˈmestɪk/ adj
1 WITHIN A COUNTRY happening within one country and not involving any others: *US foreign and domestic policy*
2 WITHIN A FAMILY [only before noun] relating to

family relationships and life at home: *We share the* **domestic chores**. | *women who suffer from* **domestic violence** | **domestic appliances** (=machines used in the home) *such as washing machines*

3 PERSON someone who is domestic enjoys doing jobs in the home, such as cooking

4 ANIMALS [only before noun] a domestic animal lives on a farm or in someone's home

domesticated Ac /də'mestɪkeɪtɪd/ *adj* domesticated animals work for people or live with them as pets

domesticity /ˌdəʊme'stɪsəti $ ˌdoʊ-/ *n* [U] life at home with your family

dominant Ac /'dɒmɪnənt $ 'dɑː-/ *adj* **1** strongest, most important, or most noticeable: *a company that is quite dominant in this market* **2** wanting to control people or events: *a dominant personality* —**dominance** *n* [U]

dominate Ac /'dɒmɪneɪt $ 'dɑː-/ *v* **1** [I,T] to control someone or something: *Five large companies dominate the car industry.* **2** [I,T] to be the strongest, most important, or most noticeable feature of something: *Education issues dominated the election campaign.* —**domination** /ˌdɒmə'neɪʃən $ ˌdɑː-/ *n* [U]

domineering /ˌdɒmə'nɪərɪŋ◂ $ ˌdɑːmə'nɪr-/ *adj* trying to control other people too much: *a domineering father*

dominion /də'mɪnjən/ *n* **1** [U] *literary* the power or right to rule people **2** [C] *formal* the land owned or controlled by a ruler or government: *the king's dominions*

domino /'dɒmənəʊ $ 'dɑːmənoʊ/ *n* (*plural* **dominoes**) **1** [C] one of a set of small pieces of wood or plastic with spots on, used for playing a game **2 dominoes** [U] the game that you play using dominoes

don¹ /dɒn $ dɑːn/ *n* [C] *BrE* a university teacher

don² *v* [T] (**donned, donning**) *formal* to put on a piece of clothing

donate /dəʊ'neɪt $ 'doʊneɪt/ *v* [T] to give something, especially money, to a person or organization that needs help: **donate sth to sb/sth** *Our school donated £500 to the Red Cross.* THESAURUS ▶ GIVE

donation /dəʊ'neɪʃən $ doʊ-/ *n* [C,U] something, especially money, that you give to help a person or organization: [+to/from] *Please* **make** *a* **donation** *to the hospital fund.*

done¹ /dʌn/ *v* the past participle of DO

done² *adj* **1** finished or completed: *The job's nearly done.* | *I'll be glad when the exams are* **over and done with** (=completely finished). **2** cooked enough to eat: *Is the pasta done yet?*

PHRASES
be done for *informal* to be in serious trouble or likely to fail: *If we get caught, we're done for.*

done³ *spoken* used to agree to and accept a deal: *'I'll give you $50 for it.' 'Done!'*

donkey /'dɒŋki $ 'dɑːŋki/ *n* [C] a grey or brown animal like a small horse with long ears → see picture on page A3

PHRASES
for donkey's years *BrE spoken* for a very long time: *I've known Kevin for donkey's years.*

'donkey ˌwork *n* **do the donkey work** *BrE* to do the hard or boring part of a job

donor /'dəʊnə $ 'doʊnər/ *n* [C] **1** someone who gives something, especially money, to an organization in order to help people: *The Museum received $10,000 from an* **anonymous donor**. **2** someone who gives some of their blood or part of their body to help a person who is ill: *a blood donor*

donut /'dəʊnʌt $ 'doʊ-/ *n* [C] *especially AmE* another spelling of DOUGHNUT

don't /dəʊnt $ doʊnt/ the short form of 'do not': *I don't know.*

doodle /'duːdl/ *v* [I,T] to draw shapes or patterns while you are thinking about something else: *I spent most of the class doodling in my notebook.* THESAURUS ▶ DRAW —**doodle** *n* [C]

DOODLE

doom¹ /duːm/ *v* [T] **be doomed to sth** if you are doomed to something unpleasant, it is certain to happen to you: *We are all doomed to die.* —**doomed** *adj*: *passengers on the doomed flight*

doom² *n* [U] when something very bad is certain to happen soon: *a sense of* **impending doom** (=coming very soon) | **doom and gloom/gloom and doom** (=when there seems to be no hope for the future) *Despite the bad figures,* **it's not all doom and gloom**.

door /dɔː $ dɔːr/ *n* [C]
1 the thing that you open and close to get into or out of a house, room, or car → **gate**: *Could you open the door for me?* | *Is the back door shut?*

2 the space made by an open door: **in/out of the door** *Rick ran out of the door.* | **in/out through the door** *She walked in through the door.* → NEXT DOOR

PHRASES
at the door if someone is at the door, they are waiting for you to open it so that they can come inside: *I think there's somebody at the door.*
(from) door to door 1 *especially BrE* from one building to another: *How long is the journey, door to door?* **2** going to each house on a street to sell something or talk to people: *The police went from door to door, asking if anyone had seen anything.* | *a door-to-door salesman*
out of doors outside: *I prefer working out of doors.* THESAURUS ▶ OUTSIDE

COLLOCATIONS

verbs

to open the door *Mum opened the door with a big smile on her face.*
to close/shut the door *Please close the door behind you.*

a door opens/closes/shuts *The car door opened and a woman got out.*
to slam the door (=to shut it loudly, usually because you are angry) *He went out, slamming the door behind him.*
to answer the door (=to open it for someone who has knocked or pressed the bell) *Will someone please answer the door?*
to lock/unlock a door *He never locks the bathroom door.*

types of door
the front/back/side door (=of a house) *Reporters were waiting outside the front door.*
the kitchen/bedroom/bathroom etc door | **a car door**

door + noun
a door handle (=that you move up or down to open a door) *Ella reached for the door handle.*
a door knob (=that you turn to open a door)

doorbell /'dɔːbel $ 'dɔːr-/ *n* [C] a button outside a house that makes a sound when you push it so that people inside know you are there: *I rang the doorbell but no one answered.*

doorknob /'dɔːnɒb $ 'dɔːrnɑːb/ *n* [C] a round handle used to open a door

doorman /'dɔːmæn, -mən $ 'dɔːr-/ *n* [C] (plural **doormen** /-men, -mən/) a man who works at the door of a hotel or theatre, helping people who are coming in and out

doormat /'dɔːmæt $ 'dɔːr-/ *n* [C] **1** a piece of material by a door for you to clean your shoes on **2** informal someone who lets other people treat them badly

doorstep /'dɔːstep $ 'dɔːr-/ *n* [C] a step just outside a door to a building
PHRASES
on sb's/the doorstep very near to where you live: *Wow! The beach is right on your doorstep!*

doorway /'dɔːweɪ $ 'dɔːr-/ *n* [C] the space where the door opens into a room or building

dope /dəʊp $ doʊp/ *n* [U] informal an illegal drug, especially MARIJUANA

dork /dɔːk $ dɔːrk/ *n* [C] informal a stupid person

dormant /'dɔːmənt $ 'dɔːr-/ *adj* not active now, but able to be active at a later time: *a dormant volcano*

dormitory /'dɔːmətəri $ 'dɔːrmətɔːri/ (plural **dormitories**) (also **dorm** /dɔːm $ dɔːrm/) *n* [C] **1** especially BrE a large room where a lot of people sleep **2** AmE a large building at a school or college where students live SYN **hall of residence** BrE

dosage /'dəʊsɪdʒ $ 'doʊ-/ *n* [C] the amount of a medicine that you should take: [+of] *a high dosage of morphine*

dose /dəʊs $ doʊs/ *n* [C] **1** a measured amount of medicine: **high/low dose** *Start with a low dose.* | [+of] *an extra dose of painkillers* **2** the amount of something that you experience at one time: *I quite like Jamie in small doses* (=in limited amounts but not often).

dosh /dɒʃ $ dɑːʃ/ *n* [U] BrE informal money

doss /dɒs $ dɑːs/ (also **doss down**) *v* [I] BrE informal to sleep somewhere that is not your usual place or not your usual bed: *I dossed down on the couch.*

dossier /'dɒsieɪ $ 'dɔːsjeɪ, 'dɑː-/ *n* [C] a set of papers that include detailed information about someone or something: [+on] *a dossier on the organization's political activities*

dot¹ /dɒt $ dɑːt/ *n* [C] a small round mark or spot: *a pattern of dots on the screen* | *The plane shrank to a black dot in the sky.*
PHRASES
on the dot informal exactly at a particular time: **at three o'clock/seven thirty etc on the dot** *He arrived at six on the dot.*

dot² *v* [T] (**dotted, dotting**) **1** to mark something by putting a dot on it **2** to spread things out within an area: **be dotted with sth** *The lake was dotted with sailboats.*

dot-com, dot.com /ˌdɒt ˈkɒm $ ˌdɑːt ˈkɑːm/ *adj* [only before noun] informal a dot-com company is one whose business is done using the Internet

dote /dəʊt $ doʊt/ *v*
PHRASAL VERBS
dote on/upon sb to love someone very much, so that you cannot see their faults: *Steve dotes on his son.*

doting /'dəʊtɪŋ $ 'doʊ-/ *adj* [only before noun] doting parents love their children very much and cannot see their faults

dotted 'line *n* [C] a line of small printed spots or lines: *Cut along the dotted lines.*
PHRASES
sign on the dotted line informal to officially agree to something by signing a contract: *Before you sign on the dotted line, think about alternative investments.*

dotty /'dɒti $ 'dɑːti/ *adj* old-fashioned informal slightly crazy

double¹ /'dʌbəl/ *adj*
1 having two parts that are similar or exactly the same: *the double doors of the cathedral* | *Don't park on double yellow lines.*
2 combining or involving two things of the same type: *a double murder case*
3 twice the usual amount, size, or number: *a double whiskey* | *walls of double thickness*
4 made to be used by two people or things → **single**: *a double bed* | *a double garage* → see picture at **BED**
PHRASES
double figures BrE, **double digits** especially AmE the numbers from 10 to 99 → **single figures**: *Inflation reached double figures.*

double² *n* **1** [C,U] something that is twice as big or twice as much as usual or as something else: *Scotch and water please – make it a double.* | *'They offered me £10,000.' 'I'll give you double.'* **2 doubles** [plural] a game played between two pairs of people, especially in tennis → **singles 3** [C] a room for two people in a hotel → **single 4 sb's double** someone who looks very similar to someone else

double³ v [I,T] to become twice as large or twice as much, or to make something do this: *The church has doubled its membership.* | **double in size/number/value etc** *The company has doubled in size.* | **double the size/number/amount etc (of sth)** *We will double the number of police.* **THESAURUS** INCREASE

PHRASAL VERBS

double as sb/sth to have a second use, job, or purpose: *The sofa doubles as a bed.*

double back to turn around and go back the way you have just come: *He doubled back and headed for Howard Bay.*

double up/over to bend at the waist because you are in pain or laughing a lot: **double up with pain/laughter** *They all doubled up with laughter.*

double⁴ determiner twice as big, twice as much, or twice as many: **double the amount/number/size etc** *We'll need double this amount for eight people.*

double-barrelled BrE, **double-barreled** AmE /ˌdʌbəl ˈbærəld/ adj **1** a double-barrelled gun has two parts that bullets are fired through **2** BrE a double-barrelled family name has two parts

double bass /ˌdʌbəl ˈbeɪs/ n [C] a very large wooden musical instrument like a VIOLIN that you play standing up → see picture on page A6

double-breasted /ˌdʌbəl ˈbrestɪd/ adj a double-breasted jacket or coat has two sets of buttons

double-'check v [I,T] to check something again so that you are completely sure: *I think I turned off the oven, but I'll double-check.* **THESAURUS** CHECK

double-'click v [I] to press a button on a computer MOUSE twice

double-'cross v [T] to cheat someone when you are involved in something dishonest together —**double cross** n [C]

double-decker /ˌdʌbəl ˈdekə $ -ər/ n [C] a bus with two levels → see picture at TRANSPORT¹

double 'glazing n [U] BrE two layers of glass in windows or doors, that help keep a room warmer and quieter —**double glaze** v [T]

double 'life n [C] if someone leads a double life, they have another secret family, job, or activity

double 'standard n [C] a rule or principle that is unfair because it treats one person or group differently from another: *They accuse the government of double standards.*

double 'take n **do a double take** to look at someone or something again because you are surprised by what you saw or heard

doubly /ˈdʌbli/ adv **1 doubly difficult/important/interesting etc** much more difficult, important etc than usual: *The journey will be doubly difficult in winter.* **2** in two ways or for two reasons: *You are doubly mistaken.*

doubt¹ /daʊt/ n [C,U] a feeling that you have when you are not certain whether something is true or possible: **[+about]** *I have doubts about his ability to do the job.* | **[+(that)]** *There's no doubt that their marriage was a mistake.*

PHRASES

beyond doubt/without doubt used to say that something is definitely true: *The state must prove beyond reasonable doubt that he is guilty.* | *I knew without a shadow of doubt* (=without any doubt at all) *that I would lose.*

be in doubt 1 if something is in doubt, it may not succeed or be able to continue: *The future of the peace talks is in doubt.* **2** if something is in doubt, you think that it may not be true: *Her honesty was never in doubt.*

be in no doubt (also **not be in any doubt**) to have no doubt or any doubt about something: *I was in no doubt that I had done the right thing.* **THESAURUS** SURE

no doubt used to say that you think something is true: *No doubt they'll win.* | *She was a top student, no doubt about it* (=used to emphasize that something is definitely true).

COLLOCATIONS

verbs

to have doubts *He had always had doubts about the project.*

to have no doubt *I have no doubt that we will succeed.*

to cast doubt on sth (=to make people unsure about something) *New evidence has cast doubt on her story.*

to raise doubts about sth (=to make people unsure about something) *The disaster raised doubts about the safety of nuclear power.*

adjectives

serious/considerable doubts *I was beginning to have serious doubts about moving to California.*

grave doubts formal (=very serious doubts) *There are grave doubts about the future of the company.*

a lingering/nagging doubt (=one that does not go away) *There were still some lingering doubts in my mind.*

doubt² v [T]

1 to think that something may not be true or that it is unlikely: *Do you doubt her story?* | **[+(that)]** *I doubt we will ever see her again.* | **[+if]** *I doubt if she can see us.* | *He might come, but I doubt it.*

2 to not trust or believe someone or something: *Nobody doubts his ability to stay calm in a crisis.* | *Do you doubt my word* (=think I am lying)?

THESAURUS

doubt to think that something may not be true or that it is unlikely: *Some people doubt these claims.* | *I doubt that they'll agree.*

I don't think so/I shouldn't think so spoken used when saying that you do not think something is true: *'Do you think she's married?' 'I don't think so.'*

be doubtful/dubious to think that something is unlikely to be a good idea, or is unlikely to happen or be true: *Mum was doubtful when I suggested having a party for all my friends.*

be sceptical BrE, **be skeptical** AmE to not be sure that something is true, or that something will work: *Scientists are skeptical about the benefits of the treatment.*

have mixed feelings to be unsure exactly how you feel about something because there are both good and bad things about it: *I had very mixed feelings about leaving home.*

have second thoughts to start feeling unsure about whether a decision you have just made is the right one: *She was beginning to have second thoughts about going skiing. It sounded rather dangerous.*

doubtful /ˈdaʊtfəl/ *adj* **1** probably not true, or unlikely to happen: **it is doubtful if/whether** *It is doubtful whether she will survive.* **THESAURUS** DOUBT **2** not certain about something: **[+if/whether]** *I'm still doubtful if I should take the job.* —**doubtfully** *adv*

doubtless /ˈdaʊtləs/ *adv* used when saying that something is very likely to happen or be true: *There will doubtless be someone at the party that you know.*

dough /dəʊ $ doʊ/ *n* [U] a mixture containing flour that you use to make bread or PASTRY

doughnut, **donut** /ˈdəʊnʌt $ ˈdoʊ-/ *n* [C] a small cake that is usually shaped like a ring

dour /dʊə, ˈdaʊə $ daʊr, dʊr/ *adj* looking unfriendly and serious: *a dour expression*

douse, dowse /daʊs/ *v* [T] to pour water or another liquid over something: *Firefighters quickly doused the blaze.* | *They doused the wood with petrol and set it alight.*

dove¹ /dʌv/ *n* [C] a type of small white bird often used as a sign of peace

dove² /dəʊv $ doʊv/ *v AmE* a past tense of DIVE

dowdy /ˈdaʊdi/ *adj* unattractive or unfashionable

down¹ /daʊn/ *adv, prep*
1 towards or in a lower place OPP **up**: *Dave bent down to tie his shoelace.* | *Get down off the table.* | *They came running down the stairs.* | *She looked down into the courtyard.* | *The bathroom is down those stairs.* → see picture on page A8
2 into a sitting or lying position: *Please sit down.* | *I think I'll go and lie down.*
3 at or to a place which is further along a path, road etc: *She's just gone down to the shops.* | *There's a cafe a hundred yards down the road.* | *A boy was running down the street.*
4 in or towards the south OPP **up**: *They drove all the way down from Boston to Miami.* | *He's bought a villa down south.*
5 to or at a lower rate or amount OPP **up**: *Keep your speed down.* | *Can you turn the radio down?* | **[+to]** *He cut his report down to three pages.*
6 **write/note/take etc sth down** to write something on paper: *I'll write down the address for you.* | *Start by jotting down a few ideas.*
7 if you are down for something, you are on a list of people who will do something: **[+for]** *Purvis is down for the 200 metres race.*
8 from an earlier time to a later time: *The story was handed down in the family from father to son.* | **[+to]** *traditions that have come down to us from medieval times*

down² *adj* [not before noun] **1** unhappy: *I've never seen Brett looking so down.* **THESAURUS** SAD **2** behind in a game by a particular number of points: *We were down by 6 points at half-time.* **3** a computer that is down is not working **THESAURUS** BROKEN

down³ *v* [T] to drink something quickly: *Matt downed his coffee and left.*

down⁴ *n* [U] thin soft feathers or hair

down-and-ˈout *n* [C] someone who has no home, job, or money —**down-and-out** *adj*

downcast /ˈdaʊnkɑːst $ -kæst/ *adj* **1** sad or upset **2** downcast eyes are looking down

downer /ˈdaʊnə $ -ər/ *n informal* **1** [singular] an experience that makes you feel unhappy: *a movie that ends on a real downer* **2** [C] a drug that makes you feel relaxed

downfall /ˈdaʊnfɔːl $ -fɔːl/ *n* [singular] when someone stops being successful: *the scandal that led to his downfall*

downgrade /ˈdaʊngreɪd/ *v* [T] to make someone or something seem less important

downhearted /ˌdaʊnˈhɑːtɪd◂ $ -ɑːr-/ *adj* sad, especially because of not achieving what you want

downhill /ˌdaʊnˈhɪl◂/ *adj, adv* towards the bottom of a hill, or on a slope that goes down OPP **uphill**: *The truck rolled downhill.* | *downhill skiing*
PHRASES
be all downhill/be downhill all the way to become easier: *The worst is over. It's all downhill from here.*
go downhill to become worse: *After Bob lost his job, things went downhill rapidly.*

Downing Street /ˈdaʊnɪŋ striːt/ *n* the place where the British Prime Minister lives and works – also used to refer to the British Prime Minister or government

download /ˌdaʊnˈləʊd $ ˈdaʊnloʊd/ *v* [T] to receive information or programs on a computer, especially using the INTERNET

downmarket /ˌdaʊnˈmɑːkɪt◂ $ -ɑːr-/ *adj BrE* cheap and not of good quality SYN **downscale** *AmE*: *They wanted to change their downmarket image.*

down ˈpayment *n* [C] the first payment that you make when you are going to pay for something in regular payments: *We've made a down payment on a new car.*

downplay /ˌdaʊnˈpleɪ $ ˈdaʊnpleɪ/ *v* [T] to make something seem less important than it really is SYN **play down**: *The police downplayed the seriousness of the situation.*

downpour /ˈdaʊnpɔː $ -pɔːr/ *n* [C usually singular] a lot of rain that falls in a short time **THESAURUS** RAIN

downright /ˈdaʊnraɪt/ *adv, adj* used to emphasize what you are saying, especially when you are saying that something is bad: *It's downright dangerous!* | *It's a downright disgrace.*

downscale /ˈdaʊnskeɪl/ *adj AmE* downscale goods or services are cheap and not of very good quality SYN **downmarket** *BrE*

downshifting /ˈdaʊnʃɪftɪŋ/ *n* [U] when you

change your job so that you earn less but have a nicer life —**downshift** v [I]

downside /'daʊnsaɪd/ n [singular] the bad part of something: [+of] The downside of the plan is the cost. **THESAURUS** DISADVANTAGE

downsize /'daʊnsaɪz/ v [I,T] to reduce the number of workers in a company —**downsizing** n [U]

'Down's ,Syndrome (also **Downs**) n [U] a condition that someone is born with, that stops them from developing normally both mentally and physically

downstairs /ˌdaʊn'steəz◂ $ -'sterz◂/ adj, adv on or towards a lower level of a building, especially a house OPP **upstairs**: Go downstairs and answer the door. | There was a sound **from downstairs**. | He was downstairs. | A light was on in one of the **downstairs rooms**.

downstream /ˌdaʊn'striːm◂/ adv in the same direction that a river or stream is flowing OPP **upstream**

down-to-'earth adj practical and direct in a sensible honest way: She's very friendly and down-to-earth.

downtown /ˌdaʊn'taʊn◂/ adj, adv especially AmE to or in the centre or main business area of a city OPP **uptown**: Do you want to go downtown? | an office in **downtown** New York | **downtown** offices/hotels

downtrodden /'daʊnˌtrɒdn $ -ˌtrɑː-/ adj treated badly by people who have power

downturn /'daʊntɜːn $ -tɜːrn/ n [C usually singular] a time when there is less business activity and conditions become worse: [+in] a downturn in the economy

downwards /'daʊnwədz $ -wərdz/ especially BrE, **downward** especially AmE adv **1** moving or pointing towards a lower position OPP **upwards**: The balloon drifted slowly downwards. **2** decreasing to a lower level OPP **upwards**: The dollar moved downwards against the pound. —**downward** adj

downwind /ˌdaʊn'wɪnd/ adj, adv in the same direction that the wind is moving

dowry /'daʊəri $ 'daʊri/ n [C] (plural **dowries**) money or property which, in some societies, is given to a man by his wife's family when they marry

dowse /daʊs/ v another spelling of DOUSE

doze /dəʊz $ doʊz/ v [I] to sleep lightly, usually for a short time: Graham dozed for an hour. **THESAURUS** SLEEP

PHRASAL VERBS

doze off to fall asleep: I was just dozing off when they arrived.

dozen /'dʌzən/ number (plural **dozen** or **dozens**)
1 twelve: a dozen eggs | **two/three/four etc dozen** (=24, 36, 48 etc) The number of deaths has risen to more than two dozen. | Chris, Helen, and **half a dozen** others went on holiday together. | **A dozen or so** (=about 12) cars were parked near the entrance.
2 a lot of: **a dozen** I've heard this story a dozen times before. | **dozens of sth** We asked dozens of people.

Dr BrE, **Dr.** especially AmE the written abbreviation of **Doctor**

drab /dræb/ adj not interesting or bright: Everything looked so drab and colourless. —**drabness** n [U]

draconian /drə'kəʊniən $ -'koʊ-/ adj extremely strict, in an unpleasant way: **draconian measures**

draft¹ Ac /drɑːft $ dræft/ n [C] **1** a piece of writing or a drawing that is not yet in its finished form: [+of] the first draft of his novel | **a rough draft** | The **final draft** (=final form) had been completed. | **a draft report** **2** a written order for money to be paid by a bank **3** the American spelling of DRAUGHT¹ **4** **the draft** AmE a system in which people must join the armed forces

draft² Ac v [T] **1** to write a plan, letter, report etc that will change before it is finished: The House plans to **draft a bill** on education. **2** AmE to order someone to join the armed forces SYN **conscript**: **draft sb into sth** Brad's been drafted into the army.

draft³ Ac adj the American spelling of DRAUGHT²

draftsman /'drɑːftsmən $ 'dræfts-/ n the American spelling of DRAUGHTSMAN

drafty /'drɑːfti $ 'dræfti/ adj the American spelling of DRAUGHTY **THESAURUS** COLD

drag¹ /dræg/ v (**dragged, dragging**)
1 PULL [T] to pull someone or something somewhere: **drag sth away/along/through etc** Ben dragged his sledge through the snow. → see picture at PULL¹ **THESAURUS** PULL
2 ON COMPUTER [T] to move words, pictures etc on a computer screen by pulling them with the mouse: You can **drag and drop** text like this.
3 MAKE SB GO [T] to make someone go somewhere, although they do not want to: **drag sb to/into/out of etc sth** My mother used to drag me to church every week. | **drag yourself away from the TV** (=stop watching TV)
4 PASS SLOWLY [I] if time or an event drags, it seems to pass slowly and you feel bored: History lessons always seemed to drag.
5 TOUCH THE GROUND [I] if something is dragging along the ground, part of it is touching the ground as you move: Your coat's dragging in the mud.

PHRASES

drag your feet/heels to delay doing something: The government were dragging their feet over reforms.

PHRASAL VERBS

drag sb/sth into sth to involve someone or something in an unpleasant situation: I'm sorry to drag you into this mess.

drag on to continue for too long: The meeting dragged on all afternoon. **THESAURUS** CONTINUE

drag sth ↔ out to make a situation or event last longer than necessary: How much longer are you going to drag this argument out?

drag sth out of sb to force someone to tell you something

drag² n **1 a drag** informal something or someone that is annoying or boring: 'I have to stay in tonight.' 'What a drag.' **2** [C] when someone breathes in smoke from their cigarette: *He took a drag on his cigarette.*

PHRASES

in drag a man in drag is wearing women's clothes: *The whole performance is done in drag.*

the main drag *especially AmE informal* the main road through a town

dragon /ˈdrægən/ *n* [C] an imaginary animal that breathes fire and has wings and a tail

dragonfly /ˈdrægənflaɪ/ *n* [C] (*plural* **dragonflies**) a flying insect with a long brightly-coloured body → see picture at INSECT

drain¹ /dreɪn/ *v* **1 a)** [T] to make the water or liquid in something flow away: *Can you drain the pasta, please?* | **drain sth from sth** *Drain the water from the peas.* **b)** [I] if a liquid drains away, it flows away: **[+away/off/from]** *The bath water slowly drained away.* **c)** [I] if something drains, the liquid from it flows away: *Leave the dishes to drain.* **2 drain your glass/cup** to drink all the liquid in your glass or cup: *Hurriedly draining her cup, she reached for her purse.* **3** [T] to make you very tired: *The experience drained her completely.* **4** [T] to use too much of something, especially money

drain² *n* [C] **1** a pipe or hole through which waste liquids are carried away: *a blocked drain* **2 a drain on sb/sth** something that uses too much time, money, or strength: *The war was an enormous drain on economic resources.*

PHRASES

down the drain *informal* being wasted: *He doesn't want to see all his work going down the drain.*

drainage /ˈdreɪnɪdʒ/ *n* [U] the system or process by which water or waste liquid flows away from a place

drained /dreɪnd/ *adj* very tired: *Afterwards I felt completely drained.*

draining board (also **drain board** *AmE*) *n* [C] an area next to a kitchen SINK where you put wet dishes to dry

drainpipe /ˈdreɪnpaɪp/ *n* [C] *BrE* a pipe that carries rainwater down from the roof of a building

drama Ac /ˈdrɑːmə $ ˈdrɑːmə, ˈdræmə/ *n* **1** [C,U] a play for the theatre, television, or radio, or plays in general: *a new TV drama* | *performances of dance, music, and drama* **2** [U] the study of performing in plays: *drama classes* | *the new drama teacher* **3** [C,U] exciting or unusual things that happen: *a night of high drama*

dramatic Ac /drəˈmætɪk/ *adj* **1** sudden and surprising: *a dramatic change in temperature* **2** exciting and impressive: *a dramatic speech* **3** related to the theatre or plays: *Miller's dramatic works* THESAURUS EXCITING **4** showing your feelings in a way that makes other people notice you: *Tony threw up his hands in a dramatic gesture.* —**dramatically** /-kli/ *adv*

dramatist Ac /ˈdræmətɪst/ *n* [C] someone who writes plays

dramatize Ac (also **-ise** *BrE*) /ˈdræmətaɪz/ [T] **1** to make a book or event into a play: *a novel*

dramatized for TV **2** to make something seem more serious than it really is: *Do you always have to dramatize everything?* —**dramatization** /ˌdræmətaɪˈzeɪʃən $ -tə-/ *n* [C,U]

drank /dræŋk/ *v* the past tense of DRINK

drape /dreɪp/ *v* [T] to put cloth or clothing over or around something: **drape sth over/across/around sth** *He draped his coat over a chair.* | **be draped in sth** *The coffin was draped in black.*

drapes /dreɪps/ *n* [plural] *AmE* long heavy curtains

drastic /ˈdræstɪk/ *adj* drastic action is extreme, and has an effect immediately: *The President promised drastic changes in health care.* —**drastically** /-kli/ *adv*: *Prices have been drastically reduced.*

draught¹ *BrE*, **draft** *AmE* /drɑːft $ dræft/ *n* **1** [C] a current of air blowing through a room **2 draughts** [U] *BrE* a game played by two people, each with 12 round pieces, on a board of 64 squares SYN **checkers** *AmE*

PHRASES

on draught beer that is on draught is served from a large container rather than a bottle: *The pub has a wide variety of beers on draught.*

draught² *BrE*, **draft** *AmE adj* [only before noun] draught beer is served from a large container rather than a bottle

draughtsman *BrE*, **draftsman** *AmE* /ˈdrɑːftsmən $ ˈdræfts-/ *n* [C] (*plural* **draughtsmen**) someone who draws the parts of a new building or machine

draughty *BrE*, **drafty** *AmE* /ˈdrɑːfti $ ˈdræfti/ *adj* a draughty room has cold air blowing through it THESAURUS COLD

draw¹ /drɔː $ drɒː/ *v* (*past tense* **drew** /druː/, *past participle* **drawn** /drɔːn $ drɒːn/)

1 PICTURE [I,T] to make a picture of something with a pencil or pen: *She was drawing a picture of a tree.* | **draw sb sth** *Can you draw me a map?* | *I can't draw very well.*

2 COMPARISON **draw a comparison/distinction** to say that two things are similar or different: *The report drew a distinction between 'helping' and 'caring'.*

3 REACTION [T] to get a reaction or support from someone or something: *His comments drew an angry response.* | **draw sth from sth** *I drew comfort from her kind words.*

4 WEAPON **draw a gun/knife/sword** to take a weapon from its container or from your pocket

5 MONEY FROM BANK [T] to take money from your bank account: *I'd just drawn £50 out of the bank.*

6 RECEIVE MONEY [T] to receive official payments, for example because you are ill or old: *I'll be drawing my pension soon.*

7 MAKE SB INTERESTED [T] to attract or interest someone: **draw sb to sth** *What first drew you to acting?* | *Her eye was drawn to a painting on the wall.*

8 PULL [T] to pull something or someone in a particular direction: **draw sb/sth aside/up/into etc** *He drew her into his arms.* | **draw sth out/from sth** *He reached into his pocket and drew out a piece of paper.*

9 MOVE [I] to move in a particular direction: **[+away/out of/past]** *The car drew away.*

10 SAME SCORE [I,T] *especially BrE* if two teams or

players draw, they have the same number of points: **[+with]** *Ireland drew with France.* | *They* **drew 3–3**.

11 PICK WINNER [T] to pick tickets or cards in order to decide who will win a prize

12 NOT TALK **refuse to be drawn (on sth)** if you refuse to be drawn on a subject, you refuse to talk about it: *She refused to be drawn on the subject of her divorce.*

PHRASES

draw (sb's) attention to sb/sth to make someone notice something: *I'd like to draw your attention to the last paragraph.* | *She didn't want to* **draw attention to herself**.

draw a blank to be unable to find something or think of something: *I just drew a blank on the last test question.*

draw blood to make blood come out of someone's skin: *The dog bit her hand so hard he drew blood.*

draw breath 1 to take air into your lungs **2** to rest when you are busy: *I needed a moment to draw breath.*

draw conclusions to decide something, based on information that you have: *They have not drawn any conclusions from the data.*

draw near *literary* to move closer in time or space: *The summer holidays are drawing near.*

draw the curtains to open or close curtains: *Can you draw the curtains – it's getting dark.*

draw the line (at sth) to refuse to do something because you do not approve of it, although you will do other things: *I don't mind helping you, but I draw the line at telling lies.*

draw to an end/a close/a halt to end or stop: *Another year was drawing to an end.*

PHRASAL VERBS

draw in if the days or nights are drawing in, it is getting dark earlier in the evening

draw sb into sth to involve someone in something that they do not want to do: *Keith refused to be drawn into our argument.*

draw on sth to use something, for example information or experience, for a particular purpose: *His books* **draw heavily on** *his experience as a therapist.*

draw up

1 draw sth ↔ up to prepare a document: *We* **drew up** *a* **list** *of the options.*

2 if a vehicle draws up, it stops: *Another car drew up beside ours.*

THESAURUS

draw to make a picture with a pencil or pen: *We had to draw a picture of a horse.*

sketch/do a sketch to draw a picture quickly and without a lot of detail: *He did a quick sketch of how the house would look.*

illustrate to draw the pictures in a book: *She illustrates children's stories.*

doodle to draw shapes or patterns without really thinking about what you are doing: *'What's that supposed to be?' 'Oh, nothing. I was just doodling.'*

trace to copy a picture by putting a piece of thin paper over it and drawing the lines that you can see through the paper: *I traced the original design onto another sheet of paper.*

---

draw² *n* [C] **1** *especially BrE* a game that ends with both teams or players having the same number of points: *The match* **ended in a draw**. | *a* **goalless** *draw* **2** when someone or something is chosen by chance, for example the winning ticket in a competition, or the teams who will play against each other in a competition: *a* **prize draw** | **[+for]** *the draw for the World Cup* **3** something that attracts visitors: *The museum will be a* **big draw**.

drawback /ˈdrɔːbæk $ ˈdrɒː-/ *n* [C] a disadvantage: **[+of/to]** *The only drawback to a holiday in Scotland is the weather.* THESAURUS DISADVANTAGE

drawer /drɔː $ drɒːr/ *n* [C] part of a piece of furniture, which can be pulled out and is used for keeping things in: *Put it in the* **desk drawer**. | *the* **bottom/top/left-hand drawer**

drawing /ˈdrɔːɪŋ $ ˈdrɒː-/ *n*
1 [C] a picture you make with a pen or pencil: **[+of]** *She showed us a drawing of the house.*
2 [U] the art or skill of making pictures with a pen or pencil: *I've never been good at drawing.*

ˈdrawing board *n* **go back to the drawing board** to start working on a new plan or idea, because the one you tried before failed

ˈdrawing pin *n* [C] *BrE* a short pin with a wide flat top, used for fastening paper to a board SYN **thumbtack** *AmE*

ˈdrawing room *n* [C] *old-fashioned* a large room in a house where people can sit and talk and meet visitors

drawl /drɔːl $ drɒːl/ *v* [I,T] to speak slowly with long vowel sounds —**drawl** *n* [singular]: *a slow Texas drawl*

drawn¹ /drɔːn $ drɒːn/ *v* the past participle of DRAW

drawn² *adj* looking tired, worried, or ill

ˌdrawn-ˈout *adj* continuing for a very long time: *a* **long drawn-out** *process*

dread¹ /dred/ *v* [T] to feel very worried about something that is going to happen: *Phil's really dreading his interview tomorrow.* | **dread doing sth** *I always dread going to the dentist's.* | *I* **dread to think** *what effect it will have* (=it will be very bad).

dread² *n* [U] a feeling of worry or fear: *She* **lives in dread** *of the disease returning.*

dreadful /ˈdredfəl/ *adj* very bad or unpleasant: *What dreadful weather!* —**dreadfully** *adv*

dreadlocks /ˈdredlɒks $ -lɑːks/ *n* [plural] a style of arranging your hair so that it hangs in thick pieces like rope → see picture at HAIR

dream¹ /driːm/ *n* [C]
1 the thoughts, images, and experiences that come into your mind when you are asleep → **daydream**: **[+about]** *I had a dream about you last night.*
2 something that you hope will happen: *It was his dream to play football for his country.* | **[+of]** *He* **fulfilled** *his* **dream** *of becoming a police officer.* | **beyond your wildest dreams** (=better than anything you imagined or hoped) *The whole experience has been a* **dream come true** (=as good as I hoped). | *the* **man/home/holiday etc of your dreams** (=the perfect man, home etc)

a dream **world** a good situation which exists only in your imagination: *If you believe that, you're living in a dream world*.
in a **dream** not noticing or paying attention to what is happening: *Ruth went about her tasks in a dream*.
like a **dream** 1 if something is like a dream, it does not seem real: *The last few days have seemed like a dream*. 2 extremely well: *The plan worked like a dream*.
Sweet dreams! *spoken* said to someone who is going to bed

COLLOCATIONS
verbs
to have a dream *Were you having a bad dream?*
adjectives
a bad dream (=unpleasant or frightening) *The movie gave the kids bad dreams.*
a strange dream (also a weird dream *informal*) *I had such a strange dream last night!*
a vivid dream (=very clear) *The dream was so vivid it seemed completely real.*
a recurring dream (=one that you have many times) *I used to have a recurring dream in which I was late for work.*

THESAURUS
dream the thoughts, images, and experiences that come into your mind when you are asleep: *I had a strange dream last night – you and I were in some sort of forest.*
nightmare a very unpleasant and frightening dream: *She still has terrible nightmares about the accident.*
daydream a series of pleasant thoughts that you have when you are awake, which make you not notice what is happening around you: *Neil was in a daydream, and didn't hear the teacher call his name.*
fantasy something exciting that you imagine happening to you, which is extremely unlikely to happen: *I used to have fantasies about becoming the next Sherlock Holmes.*

dream² v (past tense and past participle **dreamed** or **dreamt** /dremt/)
1 [I,T] to have a dream while you are asleep → **day-dream**: [+(that)] *I often dream that I'm falling.* | [+about] *I dreamt about you last night.*
2 [I,T] to think about something that you would like to happen: [+of/about] *We dream of having our own home.* | [+(that)] *Cath never dreamt she'd be offered the job* (=she did not expect it to happen).

Grammar
Do not say 'We dreamt to open our own restaurant.' Say *We dreamt of opening our own restaurant.*

PHRASES
wouldn't dream of (doing) sth *spoken* used to say that you would never do something, because you think it is wrong: *I wouldn't dream of letting her go on her own.*

PHRASAL VERBS
dream sth ↔ **up** to think of a plan or idea, especially an unusual one: *Who dreams up these TV commercials?*

dream³ adj [only before noun] perfect, or exactly what you wanted: *They had built their dream home.*

dreamer /'driːmə $ -ər/ n [C] someone who has plans or ideas that are not practical

dreamy /'driːmi/ adj 1 imagining pleasant things and not paying attention: *a dreamy look* 2 pleasant, peaceful, and relaxing: *dreamy music* —**dreamily** adv

dreary /'drɪəri $ 'drɪri/ adj dull and uninteresting: *the same old dreary jobs* —**drearily** adv

dredge /dredʒ/ v [T] to move mud or sand from the bottom of a river or lake, or to search for something by doing this
PHRASAL VERBS
dredge sth ↔ **up** to start talking about something bad or unpleasant that happened a long time ago: *Why do the papers have to dredge up that old story?*

dregs /dregz/ n [plural] a small amount of a drink, sometimes with bits in, left at the bottom of a cup, glass, or bottle

drench /drentʃ/ v [T] to make something completely wet —**drenched** adj: *I was drenched in sweat.*

dress¹ /dres/ n
1 [C] a piece of clothing worn by a woman or girl, which covers the top of her body and part or all of her legs → **skirt**: *She was wearing a white dress.* | *a beautiful wedding dress* → see picture at **CLOTHES**
2 [U] clothing of a particular type: *The audience wore evening dress* (=formal clothes worn to important social events). | *He has no dress sense* (=ability to choose nice clothes). | *The club has a strict dress code* (=rules about what you can wear). THESAURUS ▸ CLOTHES → FANCY DRESS

dress² v
1 [I,T] to put clothes on someone or on yourself: *Hurry up and get dressed!* | *Can you dress the kids?*

Grammar
In everyday English, you usually say 'She **got dressed**.' 'She dressed' sounds more formal and is mainly used in written descriptions.

2 be dressed to be wearing clothes: *Are you dressed yet?* | be dressed in sth *He was dressed in a suit.* | smartly/elegantly/casually etc dressed *a smartly dressed young officer* | well/badly dressed (=wearing tidy clothes or untidy clothes) | *She lay down on the bed fully dressed* (=wearing all her clothes).
3 [I] to wear particular clothes: *Dress warmly – it's cold outside.* | [+for] *a splendid hotel where everyone dresses for dinner* (=wears formal clothes for an evening meal)
4 dress a wound/cut to clean and cover a wound to protect it: *Clean the wound and dress it carefully.*
PHRASAL VERBS
dress down to wear clothes that are less formal

than the ones you usually wear: *She dressed down in old jeans and a T-shirt.*

dress up
1 to wear special clothes for fun: **[+as]** *I went to the party dressed up as a gorilla.* | **[+in]** *At Halloween, the kids dress up in costumes and collect candy.*
2 to wear clothes that are more formal than the ones you usually wear: *It's only a small party. You don't need to dress up.*

dresser /ˈdresə $ -ər/ n [C] **1** *BrE* a large piece of furniture with shelves for holding dishes and plates **2** *AmE* a piece of furniture with drawers for holding clothes SYN **chest of drawers** *BrE*

dressing /ˈdresɪŋ/ n **1** (*also* **salad dressing**) [C,U] a mixture of oil and VINEGAR that you pour over SALAD **2** [C] a piece of material used for covering a wound: *The nurse changed his dressing.*

'dressing gown n [C] *BrE* a long piece of clothing worn before going to bed or after getting out of bed SYN **robe** *AmE*

'dressing room n [C] a room where performers get ready for a show

'dressing ˌtable n [C] *BrE* a piece of furniture with a mirror in a bedroom, where you do your hair or MAKE-UP → see picture at **TABLE**[1]

'dress reˌhearsal n [C] the final practice for a show, using all the clothes and objects which will be used in the show

drew /druː/ v the past tense of DRAW

dribble /ˈdrɪbəl/ v [I,T] **1** *BrE* if you dribble, liquid comes out of your mouth onto your face SYN **drool** *AmE*: *The baby's dribbling on your jacket.* **2** to flow slowly in irregular drops: **[+from/down/out]** *Blood dribbled down the side of his face.* **3** to move a ball using repeated movements of your arm or leg: *Dribble the ball up to the net.* —**dribble** n [C,U]

dribs and drabs /ˌdrɪbz ən ˈdræbz/ n **in dribs and drabs** in small amounts, not all at once: *The guests arrived in dribs and drabs.*

dried /draɪd/ v the past tense and past participle of DRY

drier /ˈdraɪə $ -ər/ n [C] another spelling of DRYER

drift¹ /drɪft/ v [I] **1** to move slowly on water or in air: **[+out/towards/along etc]** *The boat slowly drifted out to sea.* | *Smoke was drifting across the road.* **2** to move or do something gradually, without any plan or purpose: **[+towards/across/away etc]** *People were drifting out of the stadium.* | **your mind/thoughts drift** *His thoughts drifted back to their earlier conversation.* **3** if snow or sand drifts, the wind moves it into large piles

PHRASAL VERBS
drift apart if people drift apart, they gradually stop being friends
drift off to gradually go to sleep: *I drifted off to sleep in front of the telly.*

drift² n [C] **1** a large pile of snow or sand that has been blown by the wind: *massive snow drifts* **2** **the drift/sb's drift** the general meaning of what someone is saying: **catch/get the drift** (=understand the general meaning) *I think I caught the drift of his argument.* **3** a gradual movement from one place to

another: *the drift away from the countryside to the big cities in the North*

drill¹ /drɪl/ n **1** [C] a machine used for making holes in something hard: *an electric drill* | *a dentist's drill* → see picture at **TOOL 2** [C,U] a method of teaching something by making people repeat the same thing many times: *a pronunciation drill* **3** when you practise what you should do in a dangerous situation, such as a fire or emergency **4** [U] when soldiers practise marching

drill² v **1** [I,T] to make a hole with a drill: *Drill a hole in each corner.* | **drill for oil/gas etc** (=look for oil, gas etc under the ground) **2** [T] to teach someone by making them repeat the same thing many times

drily /ˈdraɪli/ adv another spelling of DRYLY

drink¹ /drɪŋk/ v (*past tense* **drank** /dræŋk/, *past participle* **drunk** /drʌŋk/)
1 [I,T] to take liquid into your mouth and swallow it: *Would you like something to drink?* | *I drink too much coffee.* | *Is this water safe to drink?*
2 [I] to drink alcohol, especially regularly: *Ahmet doesn't drink, does he?* | *Don't drink and drive.* —**drinking** n [U]

PHRASAL VERBS
drink to sb/sth to wish someone success, good health etc when you have an alcoholic drink: *Let's drink to Patrick's success in his new job.*

THESAURUS

drink to take liquid into your mouth and swallow it: *Drink plenty of water.*
have to have a drink of something: *Do you want to have a cup of tea?* | *He's had three beers already.*
sip to drink something slowly, in small amounts: *Mark was sipping his coffee and reading the newspaper.*
slurp *informal* to drink something in a noisy way: *Try not to slurp your soup.*
gulp sth down to drink all of something very quickly: *I gulped down the tea and ran out of the house.*

---

drink² n [C,U]
1 liquid that you drink: **[+of]** *Can I have a drink of water please?* | *Bring your own food and drink.*
2 an alcoholic drink: *Do you want to go for a drink after work?*

COLLOCATIONS

verbs

to have a drink (=especially an alcoholic drink) *We had a drink after work.*
to go for a drink (=in a pub or bar) *I'm going for a drink with my friends tonight.*
to buy/get sb a drink (=in a pub or bar) *He offered to buy me a drink.*
to pour sb a drink *Sylvia poured herself another drink.*
to make sb a drink (=usually tea or coffee) *Come in and I'll make us a drink.*

adjectives

a hot/cold etc drink *I usually have a hot drink before bed.*

a **soft drink** (=which does not contain alcohol) *They love snacks and soft drinks.*
an **alcoholic drink** (=containing alcohol) *Beer, wine, and other alcoholic drinks will be available.*
a **fizzy drink** *BrE*, a **carbonated drink** *AmE* (=with bubbles of gas)

drink-'driving n [U] *BrE* the crime of driving a car after drinking too much alcohol SYN **drunk driving** *AmE* —**drink-driver** n [C]

drinker /'drɪŋkə $ -ər/ n [C] someone who often drinks alcohol: *He's quite a **heavy drinker** (=he drinks a lot).*

'drinking ,water n [U] water which is clean enough to drink

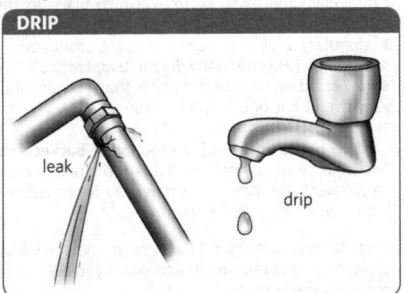

DRIP

leak

drip

drip¹ /drɪp/ v [I,T] (**dripped**, **dripping**) to let liquid fall in small drops: *That tap's still dripping.* | *Don't drip blood on the carpet!* | [+from/off/through etc] *Water was dripping through the ceiling.* | **be dripping with water/sweat etc** *They were both dripping with sweat.*

drip² n **1** [C] a small drop of liquid that falls from something: *She put a bucket on the floor to catch the drips.* **2** [singular] the sound of a liquid falling in small drops: *the steady drip of rain from the roof* **3** [C] *BrE* a piece of hospital equipment used for putting liquids directly into a person's blood SYN **IV** *AmE*: **on a drip** *She was put on a drip after the operation.* **4** [C] *informal* someone who is boring and weak

drive¹ /draɪv/ v (*past tense* **drove** /drəʊv $ droʊv/, *past participle* **driven** /'drɪvən/)
1 VEHICLE **a)** [I,T] to make a car, bus, or truck move forward: *Can you drive?* | *Fiona drives a BMW.* **b)** to take someone somewhere in a car: **drive sb to sth** *Can I drive you to the station?* | *After the party, he drove her home.* **c)** [I] to travel somewhere in a car: [+to/down/off etc] *I drive to work every day.* | *Do you want to take a bus or drive?* → see Word Choice at RIDE
2 MAKE SB MOVE [T] to force people or animals to move to a different place: *Crime drives business away from an area.*
3 MAKE SB DO STH [T] to strongly influence someone to do something: **drive sb to sth** *Marriage problems eventually drove her to drink.*
4 MAKE SB ANGRY/ANNOYED [T] to make someone very angry or excited: **drive sb crazy/mad/nuts/insane** (=make sb very angry) *This cough is driving me mad.*
5 HIT NAILS ETC [T] to hit something such as a stick or nail very hard into a surface: **drive sth into sth** *a tool for driving nails into floorboards*
6 WORK HARD [T] to make a person or animal work very hard: *Dad's driving himself too hard.*
7 PROVIDE POWER [T] to provide the power for a machine: *a petrol-driven lawnmower*

PHRASES
what sb is driving at what someone is really trying to say: *Look, just what are you driving at?*

PHRASAL VERBS
drive sb ↔ **away** to behave in a bad way that makes someone leave: *Her husband's violence finally drove her away.*
drive sb ↔ **off** to force someone to go away

drive² n
1 JOURNEY [C] a journey in a car: *Let's **go for a drive** along the coast.* | *Chris **took** the kids **for a drive**.* | **long/short drive** *It's a long drive home.* THESAURUS JOURNEY
2 FOR PARKING [C] a wide path that joins someone's house to the street, which you can park on or drive down SYN **driveway**: *There was a big Mercedes in the drive.*
3 STREET [singular] used in the names of small streets: *They live at 28, Springfield Drive.*
4 NATURAL NEED [C] a strong natural need: *the male sex drive*
5 PLANNED EFFORT [C] a planned effort to achieve a particular result: *Five hundred jobs have gone as part of an economy drive* (=effort to save money). | **drive to do sth** *a nationwide drive to crack down on crime*
6 DETERMINATION [U] determination and energy to succeed: *Mel's got tremendous drive.*
7 ON A COMPUTER [C] a piece of equipment in a computer that can read and store information: *a CD-ROM drive*
8 ON A CAR/TRUCK [U] the power from an engine that makes the wheels of a vehicle go round: *a truck with four-wheel drive* → DISK DRIVE, ZIP DRIVE

'drive-by adj **drive-by shooting/killing etc** when someone is shot from a moving car

'drive-in adj **drive-in restaurant/cinema/movie** a restaurant, cinema etc where you can buy food or watch a film without leaving your car —**drive-in** n [C]

drivel /'drɪvəl/ n [U] nonsense: *He **talks** such **drivel** sometimes!*

driven /'drɪvən/ v the past participle of DRIVE

driver /'draɪvə $ -ər/ n [C] someone who drives a car, truck, bus etc: *a taxi driver*
PHRASES
back seat driver a passenger in the back of a car who gives unwanted advice to the driver about how to drive: *The last thing I needed was a back seat driver.*

'driver's ,license n [C] *AmE* a DRIVING LICENCE

'drive-through adj **drive-through restaurant/bank etc** a restaurant, bank etc that you can use without getting out of your car

driveway /'draɪvweɪ/ (*also* **drive**) n [C] a small road that leads up to a person's house

driving¹ /ˈdraɪvɪŋ/ n [U] when someone drives a car, or the way someone drives: I'm having **driving lessons**. | He was convicted of **dangerous driving**. → DRINK-DRIVING

driving² adj **1** driving rain/snow rain or snow that is falling very heavily and fast **2** the driving force (behind sth) the person or organization who is mainly responsible for making something happen: Her father is the driving force behind her tennis career.

'driving ,licence BrE, **'driver's ,license** AmE n [C] an official card that says that you are legally allowed to drive a car

drizzle /ˈdrɪzəl/ v [I] to rain very lightly: It had been drizzling off and on for days. THESAURUS RAIN —drizzle n [U]: The rain slowed to a fine drizzle.

drone /drəʊn $ droʊn/ v [I] to make a low continuous noise: A plane droned overhead. —drone n [singular]

PHRASAL VERBS

drone on to talk in a boring way for a long time: [+about] Joe kept droning on about work.

drool /druːl/ v [I] **1** if you drool, the liquid in your mouth runs out onto your chin: The dog was drooling at the sight of the food. **2** to show in a silly way that you like someone or something a lot: [+over] teenagers drooling over the lead singer

droop /druːp/ v [I] if something droops, it hangs down, for example because it is weak or heavy: The plants need watering. They're starting to droop.

drop¹ /drɒp $ drɑːp/ v (dropped, dropping)
1 LET STH FALL [T] to let something you are holding fall to the ground: Tom dropped his bag by the door. | Enemy aircraft dropped bombs on the city. → see picture on page A11
2 FALL [I] to fall to or towards the ground: [+from/off/onto etc] She dropped onto the sofa as soon as she came in from work. | The sword dropped from his hand.
3 VISIT [I] to visit someone you know, usually without telling them that you are coming: [+by/round/in] I dropped by to see if you're feeling better. | Why don't you drop in for a drink one evening? THESAURUS VISIT
4 DECREASE [I,T] to fall to a lower level or amount, or to reduce the level or amount of something: The number of deaths on this road has dropped sharply. | The temperature can drop to -15° overnight. | Have you asked them to **drop the price**? THESAURUS DECREASE
5 STOP DOING STH [T] to stop doing something or continuing with something: Students are allowed to drop history in year nine. | I couldn't ask him to **drop everything** (=stop what he was doing) just to drive me to London.
6 TAKE SB SOMEWHERE [T] to take someone to a place in a car, before continuing to somewhere else: Just drop me here - I can walk the rest of the way. | **drop sb off** She drops the kids off at school on her way to work.
7 NOT INCLUDE [T] to decide not to include someone in a team: **drop sb from sth** He's been dropped from the England squad for the second test.
8 STOP TALKING [I,T] to stop talking about something: If you think I'm going to **let it drop**, you're wrong. | Just **drop it**, will you? I don't want to argue.

PHRASES
drop dead informal to die suddenly and unexpectedly: He just dropped dead in the street one day.
drop sb a line informal to write a letter to someone: Drop me a line when you get there.

PHRASAL VERBS
drop off informal to go to sleep
drop out to stop going to university or school before you have completed your studies, or to stop doing an activity before you finish it: [+of] He had dropped out of college. THESAURUS LEAVE

drop² n
1 [C] a very small amount of liquid: [+of] drops of rain | coffee with a little drop of brandy THESAURUS PIECE
2 [singular] the distance from a high place to the ground: There is a **sheer drop** to the valley below.
3 [singular] a fall in the amount, level, or number of something: [+in] a sudden **drop in temperature**
4 eye/ear drops liquid medicine that you put into your eye or ear one drop at a time

PHRASES
a drop in the ocean BrE, **a drop in the bucket** AmE an amount of something that is too small to have any effect: Ten new teachers will be appointed, but this is just a drop in the ocean.

'drop-down ,menu n [C] a list of choices which appears on a computer screen when you CLICK on a place on the screen

droplet /ˈdrɒplɪt $ ˈdrɑːp-/ n [C] a very small drop of liquid: [+of] tiny **droplets of water**

dropout /ˈdrɒpaʊt $ ˈdrɑːp-/ n [C] **1** someone who leaves school or college without completing their course: a high school dropout **2** someone who does not want to be part of normal society

droppings /ˈdrɒpɪŋz $ ˈdrɑː-/ n [plural] solid waste from animals or birds

drought /draʊt/ n [C,U] a long period of dry weather when there is not enough water: a region hit by severe drought

drove /drəʊv $ droʊv/ v the past tense of DRIVE

droves /drəʊvz $ droʊvz/ n [plural] crowds of people: **in droves** Tourists come in droves to see the White House.

drown /draʊn/ v **1** [I,T] to die by being under water for too long, or to kill someone in this way: The boys almost drowned in the river. | Hundreds of people were drowned when the ferry sank. | He saved his brother from drowning. **2** (also **drown out**) [T] to prevent a sound from being heard by making a louder noise: We put on some music to drown out their yelling.

drowsy /ˈdraʊzi/ adj tired and almost asleep SYN sleepy: The tablets might make you feel drowsy. THESAURUS TIRED —drowsiness n [U]

drudgery /ˈdrʌdʒəri/ n [U] boring work: the drudgery of housework

drug¹ /drʌɡ/ n [C]
1 [usually plural] an illegal substance that people take to make them feel happy, relaxed, excited etc: **take/use drugs** Many teenagers admitted taking

drugs at some time. | *No thanks, I don't* **do drugs.** | **on drugs** (=taking drugs) *She looks as though she's on drugs.* | **soft drugs** (=less strong drugs such as MARIJUANA) | **hard drugs** (=strong drugs such as COCAINE and HEROIN) | *Reports say he died of a* **drug overdose** (=he took too much of a drug).
2 a medicine or a substance for making medicines: *a new drug to treat depression* | *the cost of* **prescription drugs** (=medicines from your doctor)

drug² v [T] (**drugged, drugging**) **1** to give someone drugs, usually to stop them feeling pain or to make them sleep **2** to put a drug into someone's food or drink: *His wine had been drugged.*

'**drug ,addict** n [C] someone who cannot stop taking illegal drugs

drugstore /'drʌgstɔː $ -stɔːr/ n [C] *AmE* a shop where you can buy medicines, beauty products etc SYN **chemist's** *BrE*

drum¹ /drʌm/ n [C]
1 a round musical instrument played by hitting it with your hand or a stick → **drummer**: *Jason* **plays the drums.** | **bang/beat a drum** *A thousand people marched, beating drums.* → see picture on page A6
2 a large round container for storing liquids such as oil or chemicals

drum² v [I,T] (**drummed, drumming**) to hit something many times in a way that sounds like drums: *I could hear the rain drumming on the roof.*
PHRASAL VERBS
drum sth **into** sb to say something to someone so often that they cannot forget it: *The risks of smoking were drummed into us at school.*
drum sth ↔ **up** to try to get help, money etc by asking a lot of people: *We need to* **drum up** *more* **support.**

drummer /'drʌmə $ -ər/ n [C] someone who plays the drums

drumstick /'drʌmˌstɪk/ n [C] **1** the leg of a chicken, TURKEY etc, which has been cooked as food **2** a stick that you use to play a drum

drunk¹ /drʌŋk/ v the past participle of DRINK

drunk² adj unable to control your behaviour because you have drunk too much alcohol OPP **sober**: *Bill* **got** *really* **drunk** *at Sue's party.* | *He was too drunk to walk home.*

Word Choice: drunk or drunken?
The usual word to use is **drunk**. You say *My father was always drunk.* (Not 'My father was always drunken.') **Drunk** is not usually used before a noun, except in the American expression **drunk driver/driving.**
Drunken is only used before a noun. It is used especially in certain fixed phrases: *a drunken rage* | *He fell into a drunken stupor* (=he became unconscious from drinking too much). You also use **drunken** about people who have drunk too much and are behaving badly: *drunken football fans*
---

drunk³ (also **drunkard** /'drʌŋkəd $ -ərd/) n [C] someone who is drunk or who often gets drunk

,**drunk 'driving** (also **drunken driving**) n [U] *AmE* the crime of driving a car after drinking too much alcohol SYN **drink-driving** *BrE* —**drunk driver** n [C]

drunken /'drʌŋkən/ adj [only before noun] behaving in a way that shows that you are drunk: *a drunken crowd* —**drunkenness** n [U]

dry¹ /draɪ/ adj
1 NOT WET if something is dry, it has no water or other liquid inside it or on its surface OPP **wet**: *Is the washing dry yet?* | *Store in a cool, dry place.*
2 WEATHER/DAY with very little rain OPP **wet**: *hot and dry weather* | *plants which grow in* **dry conditions**
3 SKIN/MOUTH/HAIR if your mouth, skin, or hair is dry, it does not have enough natural liquid or oil in it: *She licked her dry lips.* | *shampoo for dry hair*
4 HUMOUR someone who has a dry sense of humour seems serious when they are making a joke
5 BORING not interesting or exciting to read or listen to: *dry political debates*
6 WINE dry wine does not have a sweet taste OPP **sweet** —**dryness** n [U] → BONE DRY

dry² v [I,T] (**dried, drying, dries**) to become dry, or to make something dry: *Hang on, I've just got to dry my hair.* | *I hung my towel up to dry.* | *Here,* **dry** *your* **eyes** (=wipe away your tears). —**dried** adj: *dried fruit* → BLOW DRY
PHRASAL VERBS
dry off to become dry, or to make something dry: *We dried off in the sun.* | **dry** sth ↔ **off** *Clean the cut and dry it off carefully.*
dry out to dry completely, or to dry something completely: *Put your coat on the radiator to dry out.*
dry up
1 if a supply of something dries up, there is no more of it: *Our research project was cancelled when the money dried up.*
2 if a river or lake dries up, the water in it disappears
3 *BrE* to dry plates, dishes etc that have been washed: **dry** sth ↔ **up** *Could you just dry those glasses up?*

,**dry-'clean** / $ '../ v [T] to clean clothes with chemicals instead of water

,**dry 'cleaner's** n [C] (plural **dry cleaner's**) a shop where you take clothes to be dry-cleaned

dryer, drier /'draɪə $ -ər/ n [C] a machine that dries things, especially clothes or hair: *a hand dryer*

dryly, drily /'draɪli/ adv said in a way that sounds serious although you are really joking

dual /'djuːəl $ 'duːəl/ adj [only before noun] having two of something, or two parts: *a* **dual purpose** *vehicle* | *My wife has* **dual nationality.** *She has Swiss and British passports.*

,**dual 'carriageway** n [C] *BrE* a main road that has two lines of traffic travelling in each direction

dub /dʌb/ v [T] (**dubbed, dubbing**) **1** to change the original spoken language in a film or television programme into another language: **dub** sth **into** sth *an Italian film dubbed into English* **2** to give someone or something a name that describes them in some way: **dub** sb sth *They immediately dubbed him 'Fatty'.*

dubious /'djuːbiəs $ 'duː-/ *adj* **1** [not before noun] not sure whether something is good or true: **[+about]** *I'm very dubious about this idea.* **2** not seeming honest, safe, or valuable: *Some of his business activities seem a bit dubious.*

duchess /'dʌtʃɪs/ *n* [C] a woman with the highest social rank below a PRINCESS, or the wife of a DUKE: *the Duchess of York*

duck¹ /dʌk/ *n* [C,U] a common water bird with short legs and a wide beak, or the meat from this bird: *roast duck* → **LAME DUCK** → see picture on page A3

duck² *v* **1** [I,T] to lower your body or head very quickly to avoid being hit or seen: *She ducked her head to go through the doorway.* | **[+behind/under etc]** *He ducked behind a hedge.* **2** [T] *informal* to avoid something that is difficult or unpleasant: *The minister has been accused of* **ducking** *the real* **issue**. **3** [T] *BrE* to push someone under water for a short time as a joke `SYN` **dunk** *AmE*

DUCK

duckling /'dʌklɪŋ/ *n* [C] a young duck

duct /dʌkt/ *n* [C] **1** a tube in a building for carrying air or electric wires **2** a thin narrow tube inside your body that liquid or air goes through: *a tear duct*

dud /dʌd/ *adj informal* useless or not working: *a dud light bulb* —**dud** *n* [C]

dude /djuːd $ duːd/ *n* [C] *especially AmE informal* a man: *Are you okay, dude?*

due¹ /djuː $ duː/ *adj*
1 [not before noun] expected to happen or arrive at a particular time: **be due to do sth** *The film is due to start at 10.30.* | **[+in/on/at]** *The flight from Munich was due at 7:48 pm.* | **[+back]** *My library books are due back tomorrow.* | **[+for]** *The car's due for a service soon.*
2 if an amount of money is due, it must be paid: *The first payment of £25 is now due.*
3 if you are due something, you deserve it, or someone owes it to you: *He never got the recognition he was due.*
PHRASES
| **due to sth** because of something: *Our bus was late due to heavy traffic.*
| **in due course/time** at a more suitable time in the future: *Your complaints will be answered in due course.*

due² *adv* **due north/south/east/west** exactly north, south etc

due³ *n* **dues** [plural] money that you pay regularly to be a member of an organization: *union dues*
PHRASES
| **give sb his/her etc due** to admit that someone deserves something: *But to give him his due, he is good at his job.*

duel /'djuːəl $ 'duːəl/ *n* [C] a fight between two people with guns or swords —**duel** *v* [I]

duet /djuˈet $ duˈet/ *n* [C] a piece of music for two performers

dug /dʌɡ/ *v* the past tense and past participle of DIG

duke /djuːk $ duːk/ *n* [C] a man with the highest social rank below a PRINCE

dull¹ /dʌl/ *adj*
1 `BORING` not interesting or exciting: *a pretty dull party* | *The meetings are usually* **deadly dull** (=very dull). `THESAURUS` ▶ **BORING**
2 `NOT BRIGHT` not bright or shiny: *a dull green colour* | *a dull, cloudy day*
3 `NOT LOUD` a dull sound is not clear or loud: *I heard a* **dull thud**.
4 `PAIN` a dull pain is not strong: *a* **dull ache** *in my shoulder* —**dully** *adv* —**dullness** *n* [U]

dull² *v* [T] to make something become less severe or less clear: *a drug to dull the pain*

duly /'djuːli $ 'duːli/ *adv formal* at the correct time or in the correct way: *His objection was duly noted.*

dumb¹ /dʌm/ *adj* **1** *informal* stupid: *What a dumb question!* **2 a)** not able to speak because you are so surprised, angry etc: *We were all* **struck dumb** *for a moment.* **b)** *old-fashioned* someone who is dumb is not able to speak. This use is now usually considered to be offensive. —**dumbly** *adv*

dumb²
PHRASAL VERBS
dumb sth ↔ **down** *disapproving* to present something in a way which is easy to understand, but which is too simple and not interesting: *the dumbing down of TV news*

dumbfounded /dʌmˈfaʊndɪd/ *adj* extremely surprised: *He stared at me, absolutely dumbfounded.*

dummy /'dʌmi/ *n* [C] (*plural* **dummies**) **1** a figure of a person: *a dressmaker's dummy* **2** a copy of a weapon, tool, vehicle etc that you cannot use: *It wasn't a real gun, just a dummy.* **3** *BrE* a rubber object that you put into a baby's mouth for it to suck `SYN` **pacifier** *AmE*

dump¹ /dʌmp/ *v* [T] **1** to put something somewhere in a careless way: **dump sth in/on/down etc** *They dumped their bags on the floor and left.* `THESAURUS` ▶ **PUT 2** to get rid of something that you do not want: *Waste chemicals are simply dumped in the river.*

dump² *n* [C] **1** a place where unwanted waste is taken and left: *a rubbish dump* **2** *informal* a place that is very dirty and ugly: *This town's a real dump.*
PHRASES
| **be down in the dumps** *informal* to feel very unhappy: *She was feeling a bit down in the dumps after losing the game.*

dumpling /'dʌmplɪŋ/ *n* [C] a round mixture of flour and fat cooked in boiling liquid: *chicken and dumplings*

Dumpster /'dʌmpstə $ -ər/ *n* [C] *trademark AmE* a large metal container for holding waste `SYN` **skip** *BrE*

dumpy /'dʌmpi/ adj informal short and fat: a dumpy woman

dune /djuːn $ duːn/ n [C] a hill of sand

dung /dʌŋ/ n [U] solid waste from animals

dungarees /ˌdʌŋɡəˈriːz/ n [plural] BrE trousers with thin pieces that go over your shoulders and a square piece of cloth that covers your chest **SYN** overalls AmE

dungeon /'dʌndʒən/ n [C] a dark underground prison used in the past

dunk /dʌŋk/ v **1** [T] to put something into a liquid for a short time and take it out again, especially something you are eating: I like to dunk biscuits in my tea. **2** [T] AmE to push someone under water for a short time as a joke **SYN** duck BrE

DUNK

dunno /'dʌnəʊ $ -noʊ/ spoken informal a way of writing or saying 'I do not know', which many people think is incorrect

duo /'djuːəʊ $ 'duːoʊ/ n [C] (plural **duos**) two people who sing, dance etc together

dupe¹ /djuːp $ duːp/ v [T] to tell lies in order to make someone believe or do something: **dupe sb into doing sth** She was duped into giving him the money.

dupe² n [C] someone who is deceived by someone else

duplex /'djuːpleks $ 'duː-/ n [C] AmE a house that is divided into two parts, so that it has two separate homes in it

duplicate¹ /'djuːplɪkeɪt $ 'duː-/ v [T] **1** to copy something: Could you duplicate this letter for me? **2** to repeat something in exactly the same way: Staff were duplicating each other's work. —**duplication** /ˌdjuːplɪˈkeɪʃən $ ˌduː-/ n [U]

duplicate² /'djuːplɪkət $ 'duː-/ adj [only before noun] a duplicate copy of something is made so that it is exactly the same: a **duplicate copy** of the letter

duplicate³ n [C] an exact copy of something: **[+of]** He made a **duplicate** of the key.

durable /'djʊərəbəl $ 'dʊr-/ adj staying in good condition for a long time: Plastic is a durable material. —**durability** /ˌdjʊərəˈbɪləti $ ˌdʊr-/ n [U]

duration Ac /djʊˈreɪʃən $ dʊ-/ n [U] formal the length of time that something continues: He slept **for the duration of** the journey.

duress /djʊˈres $ dʊ-/ n [U] if you do something under duress, you do it because you are threatened by someone, not because you want to: The confession was obtained under duress.

during /'djʊərɪŋ $ 'dʊr-/ prep **1** through all of a period of time: During the summer she worked as a waitress. | Foxes sleep during the day. **2** at one point in a period of time: The car was stolen during the night.

Word Choice: during or for?
You use **during** when saying that something happens at some point in a period of time: The baby was sick during the night.
You use **for** when saying how long something continues: I watched TV for a couple of hours. Do not say 'I studied French during five years.' Say I studied French for five years.

THESAURUS

during through all of a period of time, or at one point in a period of time: During the war people had very little to eat. | Something woke me up during the night.
all through (also **throughout**) during all of a period of time – used when something is continuous: They were together all through the summer.
over at some point or at various points during a period of days, weeks, months etc: It will be interesting to see what happens over the next few years.
within before a period of time has ended: Within a week she was starting to feel better.

---

dusk /dʌsk/ n [U] when it starts to get dark at the end of the day → **dawn**: **at dusk** They arrived at dusk.

dusky /'dʌski/ adj literary rather dark

dust¹ /dʌst/ n [U] very small bits of dirt or soil that look like a powder: The furniture was **covered in dust**. | a thick **layer of dust** on the table | a **speck of dust** | The car drove off in a **cloud of dust**.

dust² v [I,T] to clean the dust from something with a cloth: He dusted the shelves.
PHRASAL VERBS
dust sth ↔ **off** to remove dust, dirt etc from something by brushing it with your hands: He dusted off the crumbs. | **dust yourself off** He got to his feet and dusted himself off.

dustbin /'dʌstbɪn/ n [C] BrE a large container outside your home where you put waste so that it can be taken away **SYN** garbage can AmE → see picture at BIN

duster /'dʌstə $ -ər/ n [C] a cloth for removing dust from furniture

dustman /'dʌstmən/ n [C] (plural **dustmen** /-mən/) BrE someone whose job is to take away waste that people leave in dustbins **SYN** garbage collector AmE

dustpan /'dʌstpæn/ n [C] a flat container with a handle that you use with a brush to remove dust and waste from the floor

dusty /'dʌsti/ adj covered with dust: dusty old bottles

dutiful /'djuːtɪfəl $ 'duː-/ adj a dutiful person does what they are expected to do: a dutiful son —**dutifully** adv

duty /'djuːti $ 'duː-/ n (plural **duties**)
1 RESPONSIBILITY [C,U] something that you should do because it is right: I promise I will **do my duty**. | **duty to do sth** It is our duty to help her. | Parents **have a duty** to protect their children.

2 JOB [C usually plural, U] something you have to do as part of your job: *Her duties included typing.* | *He was carrying out his duties as ambassador.*

3 TAX [C,U] a tax you pay on something you buy: [+on] *the duty on cigarettes* → **HEAVY-DUTY, NIGHT DUTY**

PHRASES

on/off duty if a doctor, nurse, police officer etc is on or off duty, they are working or not working at a particular time: *Ann goes on duty* (=starts working) *at half past ten.* | *What time do you go off duty* (=finish work)?

duty-'free *adj* duty-free goods can be brought into a country without paying tax on them: *duty-free cigarettes* —**duty-free** *adv*

duvet /'duːveɪ, 'djuː- $ duː'veɪ/ *n* [C] *especially BrE* a thick warm cover that you put on top of you when you are in bed SYN **comforter** *AmE*

DVD /ˌdiː viː 'diː/ *n* [C] (**digital video disc**) a flat round object like a CD that you use on a computer or a piece of equipment called a DVD player to play films, pictures, and sound → see picture on page A12

DVD-'ROM *n* [C,U] (**digital video disc read-only memory**) a type of computer DISC that can store more information than a CD-ROM

dwarf¹ /dwɔːf $ dwɔːrf/ *n* [C] (*plural* **dwarfs** or **dwarves** /dwɔːvz $ dwɔːrvz/) **1** an imaginary creature that looks like a small man: *Snow White and the Seven Dwarfs* **2** a person who is much shorter than usual. Many people think this use is offensive.

dwarf² *v* [T] something that dwarfs other things is so big that it makes them seem very small: *The church is dwarfed by skyscrapers.*

dwarf³ *adj* [only before noun] a dwarf plant or animal is much smaller than the usual size

dwell /dwel/ *v* [I] (*past tense and past participle* **dwelt** /dwelt/ or **dwelled**) *literary* to live in a particular place

PHRASAL VERBS

dwell on/upon sth to think or talk for too long

about something unpleasant: *That is not a subject I want to dwell on.*

dweller /'dwelə $ -ər/ *n* [C] **city/town/cave etc dweller** someone who lives in a particular place

dwelling /'dwelɪŋ/ *n* [C] *formal* a house, apartment etc where people live

dwindle /'dwɪndl/ (*also* **dwindle away**) *v* [I] to gradually become less or smaller: *The town's population is dwindling.* —**dwindling** *adj*

dye¹ /daɪ/ *n* [C,U] a substance that you use to change the colour of hair, cloth etc

dye² *v* [T] (**dyed, dyeing, dyes**) to change the colour of something, using a dye: *Her hair was dyed blonde.*

dying /'daɪ-ɪŋ/ *v* the present participle of DIE

dyke, dike /daɪk/ *n* [C] **1** a wall or bank built to keep back water and prevent flooding **2** *especially BrE* a long narrow hole cut in the ground to take water away

dynamic Ac /daɪ'næmɪk/ *adj* **1** full of energy and ideas: *a dynamic businessman* **2** continuously changing: *a dynamic economy* **3** *technical* a dynamic force causes movement: *dynamic energy* —**dynamically** /-kli/ *adv* —**dynamism** /'daɪnəmɪzəm/ *n* [U]

dynamics /daɪ'næmɪks/ *n* [plural] the way in which things or people behave and affect each other: *group dynamics*

dynamite /'daɪnəmaɪt/ *n* [U] **1** a powerful explosive **2** something or someone that is exciting or likely to cause trouble

dynasty /'dɪnəsti $ 'daɪ-/ *n* [C] (*plural* **dynasties**) a family of rulers who have controlled a country for a long time: *the Ming dynasty* —**dynastic** /dɪ'næstɪk $ daɪ-/ *adj*

dysentery /'dɪsəntəri $ -teri/ *n* [U] a serious disease that causes severe DIARRHOEA

dysfunctional /dɪs'fʌŋkʃənəl/ *adj* not behaving or working normally

dyslexia /dɪs'leksiə/ *n* [U] a condition that makes it difficult for someone to read and spell —**dyslexic** *adj*

Ee

E, e /iː/ n [C,U] (*plural* **E's, e's**) **1** the fifth letter of the English alphabet **2** the third note in the musical SCALE of C MAJOR, or the musical KEY based on this note **3** a mark given to a student's work to show that it is of very low quality: *I got an E in physics.* **4 Ecstasy** (=an illegal drug)

E the written abbreviation of **east** or **eastern**

e-, E- /iː/ *prefix* using or involving the Internet: *e-commerce* | *e-shopping*

each /iːtʃ/ *determiner, pron, adv* every person or thing: *She had a bottle in each hand.* | *Tickets cost £5 each* (=each ticket costs £5). | **[+of]** *Each of the children sang a song.* | *We were given ten minutes each* (=each of us was given ten minutes). | **each day/week/month etc** (=on each day, in each week etc) *I get one day off each week.*

> **Word Choice**: each, every, or all?
> You use **each** when you are considering people or things separately. **Each** is followed by a singular noun: *Each student has a desk.* | *Each car is carefully checked before it leaves the factory.* You use **every** or **all** when you are considering all the people or things together as a group. **Every** is followed by a singular noun, and **all** is followed by a plural noun: *Every child in the class passed the test.* | *All the children enjoyed the trip.*

each 'other *pron* used to show that each of two or more people does something to the other or others → **one another**: *We all hugged and kissed each other.* | *Claire and Kay looked at each other.*

eager /ˈiːgə $ -ər/ *adj* wanting to do something very much, or waiting with excitement for something to happen: **eager to do sth** *Rosie was eager to leave.* | **[+for]** *We were always eager for news from home.* —**eagerly** *adv* —**eagerness** *n* [U]

eagle /ˈiːgəl/ *n* [C] a very large strong bird, with a beak like a hook, that kills and eats small animals

ear /ɪə $ ɪr/ *n*
1 [C] one of the two parts of your body that you hear with: *He whispered something in her ear.* → see picture on page A2
2 [C] the top part of a plant such as wheat that produces grain: **[+of]** *an ear of corn*
3 [singular] the ability to learn music or copy sounds that you hear: **[+for]** *I've always had an ear for accents.*
PHRASES
 be all ears *informal* be very interested to hear what someone is going to say: *Go ahead, I'm all ears.*
 be smiling/grinning from ear to ear to be smiling a lot: *When she came out of her office she was grinning from ear to ear.*

earache /ˈɪəreɪk $ ˈɪr-/ *n* [singular, U] a pain inside your ear: *I've got terrible earache.* **THESAURUS** PAIN

eardrum /ˈɪədrʌm $ ˈɪr-/ *n* [C] a thin piece of skin inside your ear that allows you to hear sound

earl /ɜːl $ ɜːrl/ *n* [C] a man with a high social rank

earlobe /ˈɪələʊb $ ˈɪr-/ *n* [C] the soft piece of flesh at the bottom of your ear

early /ˈɜːli $ ˈɜːrli/ *adj, adv* (*comparative* **earlier**, *superlative* **earliest**)
1 before the usual or expected time OPP **late**: *You're early! It's only five o'clock!* | **[+for]** *I was a few minutes early for my appointment.* | *They came home early.*
2 in the first part of a period of time or an event OPP **late**: *in the early 1960s* | *the early part of her career* | *the early morning sun* | **[+in]** *Harry was killed early in the war.* | *The store will open early next year.* | **early on** (=at an early stage) *I realized early on that I couldn't trust him.*
PHRASES
 at the (very) earliest not before the time or date mentioned: *The tunnel won't open until July at the earliest.*
 it's early days *BrE* used to say that it is too soon to know what the result of something will be: *Things are looking good, but it's early days yet.*
 the early hours the time between MIDNIGHT and morning: *The attack happened in the early hours of Sunday morning.*
 an early night if you have an early night, you go to bed earlier than usual: *I was feeling a bit tired so I decided to have an early night.*

> **THESAURUS**
>
> **early** before the usual or expected time: *The bus arrived a few minutes early.* | *We left the party early.*
> **on time** arriving or happening at the right time: *The train was on time.* | *I managed to finish my essay on time.*
> **in good time/in plenty of time** *especially BrE* long enough before something happens, so that you are ready in case something goes wrong: *Make sure that you are at the airport in good time.*
> **ahead of schedule** before the official time that was agreed: *The work was finished ahead of schedule.*
> **first thing** *especially spoken* immediately after you get up, or as soon as you start work: *I'll speak to him first thing in the morning.*

earmark /ˈɪəmaːk $ ˈɪrmaːrk/ *v* [T] to decide that someone will do a particular job or something will be used for a particular purpose: **earmark sb/sth for sth** *The land was earmarked for a golf course.*

earn /ɜːn $ ɜːrn/ *v*
1 [I,T] to be paid money for your work: *She earns £27,000 a year.* | *You don't **earn** much **money** being a nurse.* | *Dad did all sorts of jobs to **earn a living*** (=earn enough money for the things you need to live).
2 [T] to make a profit from business or from putting money in a bank: *You could **earn** a higher rate of **interest** elsewhere.*
3 [T] to deserve something, for example because

you have worked hard: *I think we've **earned a rest** after all that work!*
4 [T] if your actions or qualities earn you something, you get it because of them: **earn sb sth** *That performance earned her an Oscar.* —**earner** *n* [C]: *He is the only wage earner in the family.*

THESAURUS

earn to be paid money for your work, especially your regular job: *Doctors can earn over £100,000 a year.*

get to earn money. **Get** is less formal than **earn** and is very common in everyday English: *She gets $12 an hour.*

make to earn money – used about people and businesses: *He made $9 million last year.* | *The shop wasn't making enough money.*

be on sth *BrE especially spoken* to earn a particular amount of money each year: *'How much are you on?' 'About £25,000 a year'.*

be/get paid to earn money from someone who pays you, rather than from your own business: *The workers are paid very low wages.* | *He gets paid more than I do.* → **SALARY**

earnest /ˈɜːnɪst $ ˈɜːr-/ *adj* very serious and sincere: *an earnest young man* —**earnestly** *adv*
PHRASES
be in earnest to really mean what you are saying: *She wasn't sure whether he was in earnest or not.*
start/begin in earnest if something starts happening in earnest, it starts happening properly or seriously: *On Monday your training **begins in earnest!***

earnings /ˈɜːnɪŋz $ ˈɜːr-/ *n* [plural] your earnings are the money that you earn by working: *Average earnings have risen by 3%.* **THESAURUS** **SALARY**

earphones /ˈɪəfəʊnz $ ˈɪrfoʊnz/ *n* [plural] a small piece of equipment that you put in or over your ears to listen to music so that only you can hear it

earplug /ˈɪəplʌg $ ˈɪr-/ *n* [C usually plural] a small piece of rubber that you put into your ear to keep out noise

earring /ˈɪərɪŋ $ ˈɪr-/ *n* [C] a piece of jewellery that you wear on your ear → see picture at **JEWELLERY**

earshot /ˈɪəʃɒt $ ˈɪrʃɑːt/ *n* **within earshot/out of earshot** near enough or not near enough to hear what someone is saying: *She waited until he was out of earshot before continuing.*

'ear-ˌsplitting *adj* very loud: *an ear-splitting explosion*

earth /ɜːθ $ ɜːrθ/ *n*
1 **PLANET** (*also* **the earth**, **the Earth**) the PLANET that we live on → **world**: *The earth revolves around the sun.* | *The space shuttle returned to earth.* | **on earth** *one of the hottest places on earth* | *the future of planet Earth* → see Word Choice at **WORLD**
2 **SOIL** [U] the substance that plants grow in **SYN** soil: *the smell of wet earth* **THESAURUS** **GROUND**
3 **THE GROUND** [U] the hard surface of the world, as opposed to the sea or air: *We watched in horror as the plane **fell to earth**.* | *The earth began to shake beneath our feet.*

4 **ON ELECTRICAL EQUIPMENT** [C usually singular] *BrE* a wire that makes a piece of electrical equipment safe by connecting it with the ground **SYN** **ground** *AmE* → **DOWN-TO-EARTH**
PHRASES
come down to earth/bring sb down to earth to get back to your normal life again after a period of great excitement, or to make someone do this: *After he won the Olympic gold medal, it took him a few weeks to come back down to earth.*
cost/pay/charge the earth *informal* to cost, pay etc a very large amount of money: *That dress must have cost the earth!*
what/why/how etc on earth ...? *spoken* used to ask a question when you are very surprised or angry: *What on earth did you do that for?*

earthenware /ˈɜːθənweə, -ðən- $ ˈɜːrθənwer, -ðən-/ *adj* an earthenware pot, bowl etc is made of very hard baked clay —**earthenware** *n* [U]

earthly /ˈɜːθli $ ˈɜːrθli/ *adj* **no earthly reason/use etc** no reason, use etc at all: *There was no earthly reason to stay.*

earthquake /ˈɜːθkweɪk $ ˈɜːrθ-/ *n* [C] a sudden shaking of the earth's surface that often causes a lot of damage

'earth ˌscience *n* [C usually plural] a science such as GEOLOGY which involves the study of the physical world

earthworm /ˈɜːθwɜːm $ ˈɜːrθwɜːrm/ *n* [C] a thin brown WORM that lives in soil

earthy /ˈɜːθi $ ˈɜːrθi/ *adj* **1** tasting, smelling, or looking like earth or soil: *earthy colours* **2** talking about sex and the human body in a relaxed direct way: *earthy language*

ease¹ /iːz/ *n* [U]
PHRASES
at ease feeling relaxed: **[+with]** *She felt completely **at ease** with Barry.* | *The nurse soon **put** me **at my ease** (=made me feel relaxed).* | *He looked shy and **ill at ease** (=not relaxed).* **THESAURUS** **RELAXED**
with ease if you do something with ease, it is very easy for you to do it: *They won with ease.*

ease² *v* [I,T] **1** if something unpleasant eases, or if you ease it, it gradually improves: *The doctor gave me something to ease the pain.* **THESAURUS** **REDUCE**
2 to move someone or something slowly and carefully into a place: *Phil eased himself into an armchair.*
PHRASAL VERBS
ease off if something eases off, it becomes less: *The rain had eased off a bit.*
ease up to work less hard or do something with less energy than before: *Just relax and ease up a little.*

easel /ˈiːzəl/ *n* [C] a frame that you put a painting on while you paint it

easily /ˈiːzəli/ *adv*
1 without difficulty: *She found the house easily.*
2 **could/can/might easily** used to say that something is possible or is very likely to happen: *Teenage parties can easily get out of control.*
3 **easily the best/biggest/most stupid etc** definitely the best, biggest etc: *She is easily the most intelligent girl in the class.*

east¹, East /iːst/ n [singular, U] (written abbreviation **E**)

1 the direction from which the sun rises: *Which way is east?* | **from/towards the east** *The army is approaching from the east.* | **to the east (of sth)** *the region to the east of Munich*
2 the east the eastern part of a country or area: *Rain will spread to the east later.* | **[+of]** *the east of Scotland*
3 the East a) the countries in Asia, especially China and Japan: *The Oriental is one of the most famous hotels in the East.* **b)** the countries in the eastern part of Europe and central Asia **c)** AmE the part of the US east of the Mississippi River, especially the states north of Washington DC

east², East adj [only before noun] (written abbreviation **E**) **1** in the east or facing the east: *the east coast of Africa* | *We live in East London.* **2** an east wind comes from the east

east³ adv (written abbreviation **E**) towards the east: *We drove east along Brooklyn Avenue.* | **[+of]** *a small village 18 miles east of Paris*

eastbound /ˈiːstbaʊnd/ adj travelling or leading towards the east: *an eastbound train*

Easter /ˈiːstə $ -ər/ n [C,U] a holiday in March or April when Christians remember the death of Christ and his return to life: **at Easter** *We always go away at Easter.* | *the Easter holidays*

ˈEaster egg n [C] **1** BrE a chocolate egg that people eat at Easter **2** AmE an egg that has been coloured and decorated to celebrate Easter

easterly /ˈiːstəli $ -ərli/ adj **1** towards or in the east: *We drove off in an easterly direction.* **2** an easterly wind comes from the east

eastern, Eastern /ˈiːstən $ -ərn/ adj (written abbreviation **E**)

1 in or from the east of a country or area: *the eastern shore of the island* | *Eastern Europe*
2 in or from the countries in Asia, especially China and Japan: *Eastern religions*

easternmost /ˈiːstənməʊst $ -ərnmoʊst/ adj furthest east: *the easternmost part of the country*

eastwards /ˈiːstwədz $ -wərdz/ (also **eastward**) adv towards the east: *We sailed eastwards.* —**eastward** adj: *We followed an eastward course up the river.*

easy¹ /ˈiːzi/ adj

1 not difficult OPP **difficult, hard**: *The test was really easy.* | *an easy job* | **easy to do sth** *It's a lovely car and very easy to drive.* | *Having a computer will make things a lot easier.*
2 comfortable, relaxed, and not worried: *I felt easy and at home.* | *He'll do anything for an easy life.*
PHRASES
| **I'm easy** informal used to say that you are happy to do what other people want to do: *You choose – I'm easy.*

THESAURUS

easy not difficult and not needing a lot of effort or skill: *The test was easy.* | *It's easy to see why she's unhappy.*

---

simple not complicated and not having a lot of parts or things that you need to understand: *a simple way of dealing with the problem* | *The idea seems so simple.*
straightforward easy to do or understand, and not likely to cause problems: *Installing the software should be a fairly straightforward job.*
user-friendly easy to use: *The camera is very user-friendly.*
be a piece of cake informal to be very easy to do: *Driving in Tokyo was a piece of cake compared to driving in London.*

easy² adv
PHRASES
sth comes easy to sb used when saying that it is easy for someone to do something, because they are used to doing it: *Admitting that he was wrong didn't come easy to him.*
(that's) easier said than done used to say that something would be very difficult to do: *'Find him and bring him back.' 'That's easier said than done.'*
go easy on sb informal to be more gentle and less strict or angry with someone: *Go easy on Peter – he's having a hard time at school.*
go easy on sth informal used to tell someone not to use, eat, or drink too much of something: *Go easy on salty foods.*
take it easy 1 (also **take things easy**) to relax and not do very much: *You should take it easy for a few days.* **2** informal used to tell someone to become less upset or angry: *Just take it easy and tell us what happened.*

ˈeasy chair n [C] a large comfortable chair

easygoing /ˌiːziˈɡəʊɪŋ◂ $ -ˈɡoʊ-/ adj not easily upset, annoyed, or worried

ˌeasy ˈlistening n [U] music with pleasant tunes that is relaxing to listen to

eat /iːt/ v [I,T] (past tense **ate** /et, eɪt $ eɪt/, past participle **eaten** /ˈiːtn/)

1 to put food in your mouth and swallow it: *We sat eating our sandwiches.* | *He began to eat.* | *Would you like something to eat?* THESAURUS **MEAL**
2 to have a meal: *We usually eat at six.* | *Have you eaten lunch yet?*
3 I could eat a horse spoken informal used to say you are very hungry THESAURUS **HUNGRY**
PHRASAL VERBS
eat away to gradually remove or reduce something: **eat sth ↔ away** *Rust had eaten the metal away.* | **[+at]** *Pollution was eating away at the stone.*
eat into sth
1 to gradually use time, money etc so that less is available: *My job often eats into the weekend.*
2 to damage something: *Acid eats into the metal, damaging the surface.*
eat out to eat in a restaurant: *Let's eat out for a change.*
eat up spoken to eat all of something: *Eat up, there's a good girl.* | **eat sth ↔ up** *He ate it all up.*

THESAURUS

eat to put food in your mouth and swallow it: *You've eaten all the chocolates!* | *I didn't feel like eating.*

have to eat a particular kind of food, or to eat a particular meal: *I usually have toast for breakfast.* | *What time do you have lunch?*

feed on sth to eat a particular kind of food – used about animals: *Owls feed on mice and small birds.*

munch to eat something with big movements of your mouth, especially when you are enjoying your food: *He was munching an apple.*

nibble to eat something by biting off very small pieces: *The rabbit was nibbling on a carrot.*

pick at sth to eat only a small amount of your food because you are not hungry or do not like the food: *She looked miserable and picked at the food on her plate.*

stuff yourself to eat too much food, until you cannot eat anything else: *We stuffed ourselves with donuts and pancakes.*

eater /ˈiːtə $ -ər/ n [C] **big/light/fussy etc eater** someone who eats a lot, not much, only particular things etc: *I've never been a big eater.*

'eating dis,order n [C] a medical condition in which someone does not eat normal amounts of food, especially because they are frightened of getting fat → **anorexia, bulimia**

eaves /iːvz/ n [plural] the edges of a roof that stick out beyond the walls: *Birds had nested under the eaves.*

eavesdrop /ˈiːvzdrɒp $ -drɑːp/ v [I] (**eavesdropped, eavesdropping**) to secretly listen to other people's conversations → **overhear** THESAURUS HEAR —**eavesdropper** n [C]

EAVESDROP

ebb¹ /eb/ (*also* **ebb tide**) n [singular] the flow of the sea away from the land, when the TIDE goes out

PHRASES

be at a low ebb to be weak and not strong: *His confidence is at a low ebb.*

ebb and flow when something keeps increasing and decreasing: *the ebb and flow of the conversation*

ebb² v [I] **1** if the TIDE ebbs, it flows away from the land **2** (*also* **ebb away**) to gradually decrease: *Lucy's strength ebbed away.*

ebony /ˈebəni/ n [U] a hard black wood —**ebony** adj

ebullient /ɪˈbʌliənt, ɪˈbʊ-/ adj formal very happy and excited: *his ebullient personality*

eccentric¹ /ɪkˈsentrɪk/ adj strange or unusual: *Aunt Nessy was always a bit eccentric.* | *eccentric habits* THESAURUS STRANGE —**eccentricity** /ˌeksenˈtrɪsəti, -sən-/ n [C,U]: *Kate's mother had a reputation for eccentricity.*

eccentric² n [C] someone who behaves in a way that is strange or unusual

ecclesiastical /ɪˌkliːziˈæstɪkəl/ (*also* **ecclesiastic** /-ˈæstɪk◂/) adj relating to the Christian church or its priests: *ecclesiastical history*

echelon /ˈeʃəlɒn $ -lɑːn/ n [C usually plural] a level or rank in an organization, business etc, or the people at that level: **upper/higher/lower etc echelons (of sth)** *the upper echelons of government*

echo¹ /ˈekəʊ $ ˈekoʊ/ n [C] (*plural* **echoes**) **1** a sound that you hear again when it comes back off a wall or rock **2** something that is very similar to what has happened or been said before: **[+of]** *The article contains echoes of an earlier report.*

echo² v (**echoed, echoing, echoes**) **1** [I] if a sound or place echoes, you hear sounds repeated when they come back off walls or rock: *Children's voices echoed through the big old house.* **2** [T] to repeat and agree with what someone else has said: *Kaletsky, writing in 'The Times', echoed this view.*

eclectic /ɪˈklektɪk/ adj including a mixture of many different things or people: *a wonderfully eclectic mix of furniture* | *His taste in music was eclectic.*

eclipse¹ /ɪˈklɪps/ n [C] when the Sun or the Moon seems to disappear, because one of them is passing between the other one and the Earth

eclipse² v [T] **1** to become more important, powerful, or famous than someone or something else, so that they are no longer noticed: *British cinema had been largely eclipsed by that of Hollywood.* **2** to make the Sun or Moon disappear in an eclipse

eco- /iːkəʊ $ iːkoʊ/ prefix relating to the environment: *ecofriendly products* | *an ecosystem*

ecofriendly /ˈiːkəʊˌfrendli $ ˈiːkoʊ-/ adj not harmful to the environment: *ecofriendly products*

ecological /ˌiːkəˈlɒdʒɪkəl $ -ˈlɑː-◂/ adj relating to the relationship of living things to each other and to their environment: *The ecological balance in the area could be destroyed.* | *an ecological disaster* —**ecologically** /-kli/ adv

ecology /ɪˈkɒlədʒi $ ɪˈkɑː-/ n [singular, U] the relationship of living things to each other and to their environment, or the scientific study of this —**ecologist** n [C]

e-commerce /ˈiː ˌkɒmɜːs, $ -kɑːmɜːrs/ n [U] (**electronic commerce**) when people buy and sell goods and services using a computer and the Internet: *the growth of e-commerce*

economic Ac /ˌiːkəˈnɒmɪk◂, ˌi:- $ -ˈnɑː-/ adj **1** [only before noun] relating to trade, industry, and the management of money → **economy**: *the government's economic policy* | *Economic growth in Britain has been slow.* | *an economic crisis* **2** a business activity that is economic produces enough profit to continue: *It is no longer economic for us to run the service.* —**economically** /-kli/ adv: *economically developed countries*

> **Word Choice: economic or economical?**
> **Economic** means relating to trade, industry etc.
> **Economical** means using less fuel or money.
> Do not say 'This car is very economic.' Say *This car is very economical.*

economical Ac /ˌekəˈnɒmɪkəl, ˌiː- $ -ˈnɑː-/ adj if something is economical, it does not use a lot of fuel or cost a lot of money: a smaller and more economical car | It's more economical to use coal. **THESAURUS** CHEAP —**economically** /-kli/ adv: Food is produced as efficiently and economically as possible.

economics Ac /ˌekəˈnɒmɪks, ˌiː- $ -ˈnɑː-/ n **1** [U] the study of the way in which money, goods, and services are produced and used: a professor of economics **2** [plural] the amount of money that something will cost and earn: I think we need to look at the economics of the project again.

Word Choice: economics or economy?
Economics is the study of how money and goods are made and used. A country's **economy** is its system for producing money or goods: The Japanese economy grew by 2%.
Do not say 'He is studying economy.' Say He is studying economics.

economist Ac /ɪˈkɒnəmɪst $ ɪˈkɑː-/ n [C] someone who studies economics

economize (also **-ise** BrE) /ɪˈkɒnəmaɪz $ ɪˈkɑː-/ v [I] to reduce the amount of money or goods that you use: [+on] We're trying to economize on heating.

economy¹ Ac /ɪˈkɒnəmi $ ɪˈkɑː-/ n (plural economies)
1 [C] the system by which a country's money and goods are produced and used, or a country considered in this way: a capitalist economy | the slowdown in the Japanese economy | the economies of Eastern Europe
2 [C,U] the careful use of things so that nothing is wasted and less money is spent: We will have to **make** some **economies**. | **For reasons of economy**, we are not having a Christmas party this year. → MARKET ECONOMY

economy² adj [only before noun] cheap or intended to save money: an economy class air ticket | a large economy pack

ecosystem /ˈiːkəʊˌsɪstəm $ ˈiːkoʊ-/ n [C] all the animals and plants in an area, and their relationship to each other and their environment

ecotourism /ˈiːkəʊˌtʊərɪzəm $ ˈiːkoʊˌtʊr-/ n [U] the business of organizing holidays to natural areas where people can visit and learn about the area in a way that will not hurt the environment —**ecotourist** n [C]

ecstasy /ˈekstəsi/ n (plural **ecstasies**) **1** [C,U] a feeling of extreme happiness: an expression of pure ecstasy **2** (also **Ecstasy**) [U] an illegal drug that gives people a feeling of happiness and energy

ecstatic /ɪkˈstætɪk, ek-/ adj feeling extremely happy: Peter was ecstatic when he heard the news.

eczema /ˈeksəmə $ ˈeksəmə, ˈegz-, ɪgˈziːmə/ n [U] a medical condition in which someone's skin is dry, red, and sore

eddy /ˈedi/ n [C] (plural **eddies**) a circular movement of water or air

edge¹ /edʒ/ n
1 [C] the part of something that is furthest from the centre: **the edge of sth** Billy sat on the edge of the bed. | He stood at the water's edge, staring across the lake.
2 [C] the thin sharp part of a tool used for cutting: the edge of the knife
3 [C] an area beside a very steep slope: Don't stand so close to the edge.
4 [singular] something that gives you an advantage over others: [+over/on] That's where the Europeans **have an edge** over the Americans. → CUTTING EDGE
PHRASES
on edge nervous: I'm a little on edge after what happened last night. **THESAURUS** NERVOUS

edge² v **1** [I,T] to move slowly and gradually, or to make something do this: The car edged forwards. | **edge your way along/towards etc** She edged her way along the path. **2** [T] to put something along the edge of something to decorate it: The city square was edged by trees.

edgeways /ˈedʒweɪz/ (also **edgewise** AmE /-waɪz/) adv with the part that is usually the edge facing forwards SYN **sideways**: We carried it up the stairs edgeways. → **get a word in (edgeways)** at WORD¹

edgy /ˈedʒi/ adj nervous and worried: Are you OK? You seem a little edgy.

edible /ˈedəbəl/ adj if something is edible, you can eat it OPP **inedible**

edict /ˈiːdɪkt/ n [C] formal an official order that is given by someone in a position of power

edifice /ˈedɪfɪs/ n [C] formal a large building

edit /ˈedɪt/ v [T] to correct mistakes in a piece of writing or a film, and decide which parts to keep —**edit** n [C]

edition Ac /ɪˈdɪʃən/ n [C] **1** one copy or form of a book, newspaper, magazine etc: **first/second/third etc edition** The first edition of the book was published in 1836, and the second edition a year later. | The paperback edition costs £7.95. | The article is in today's edition of 'The Times'. **2** one of a series of television or radio programmes that is broadcast regularly: last week's edition of 'Friends'

editor Ac /ˈedɪtə $ -ər/ n [C] the person who decides what should be included in a book, newspaper, magazine etc, and checks for mistakes —**editorial** /ˌedəˈtɔːriəl/ adj: They made a few editorial changes.

editorial Ac /ˌedəˈtɔːriəl◄/ n [C] a piece of writing in a newspaper that gives the editor's opinion about something

educate /ˈedjʊkeɪt $ ˈedʒə-/ v [T] **1** to teach someone in a school or college: He was educated at Westminster School. **2** to give someone information about something so that they understand it: **educate sb about sth** a campaign to educate teenagers about HIV —**educator** n [C] especially AmE

educated /ˈedjʊkeɪtɪd $ ˈedʒə-/ adj an educated person has a high standard of knowledge and education: a well-educated young woman
PHRASES
educated guess a guess that is likely to be correct because you have enough information: I don't

know exactly how much the ring is worth, but I could make an educated guess.

education /ˌedjuˈkeɪʃən $ ˌedʒə-/ n [singular, U] the process of teaching and learning, usually at school, college, or university: *The government has promised to spend more on education.* | *the education system* | *the importance of **getting a** good **education*** → FURTHER EDUCATION, HIGHER EDUCATION, PHYSICAL EDUCATION

educational /ˌedjuˈkeɪʃənəl◂ $ ˌedʒə-/ adj **1** relating to education: *universities and other educational institutions* **2** teaching you something: *Working in Tanzania was a very **educational experience**.* | *educational toys* —**educationally** adv

Edwardian /edˈwɔːdiən $ -ˈwɔːr-/ adj relating to the time of King Edward VII of Britain (1901-1910): *an Edwardian house*

eel /iːl/ n [C] a long thin fish that looks like a snake

eerie /ˈɪəri $ ˈɪri/ adj strange and frightening: *an eerie sound* —**eerily** adv

effect[1] /ɪˈfekt/ n

1 [C,U] a change or result that happens because of an event or action: **[+of]** *We can already see the effects of climate change.* | **[+on]** *My parents' divorce had a big effect on me.* → see Word Choice at AFFECT
2 [C] a feeling that an artist, speaker, book etc tries to give you: **[+of]** *The play's clever lighting **created** the **effect** of oil lamps.*
3 effects [plural] *formal* someone's effects are the things that they own SYN **belongings**: *I went to collect his effects from the hospital.* → AFTER-EFFECT, GREENHOUSE EFFECT, SIDE EFFECT

PHRASES

for effect if someone does something for effect, they do it in order to make people notice: *She **paused for effect**, then carried on speaking.*
in effect used when you are describing what you think are the real facts of a situation: *In effect, I'll be earning less than I was last year.*
put/bring sth into effect to make a plan or idea happen: *It won't be easy to put the changes into effect.*
take effect 1 (*also* **come into effect**) if a law, rule, or system takes effect or comes into effect, it officially starts: *The new rules come into effect in June.* **2** to start to produce results: *The tablets soon began to take effect.*
to this/that effect used to say that you are giving the general meaning of what someone said, not their exact words: *The report says he's no good at his job, or words to that effect.*

COLLOCATIONS

verbs

to have an effect *The Internet has had a big effect on our lives.*
to feel an effect (=to notice it) *He is still feeling the effects of his injury.*
to reduce the effect of sth *Exercise can reduce the effects of stress.*
the effect lasts *How long do the effects of the drug last for?*

the effect wears off (=gradually stops) *The effect of the anaesthetic was beginning to wear off.*

adjectives

a big/great/huge effect *Her experience in Africa had a huge effect on her.*
a small effect *For most people, the effect of the changes will be quite small.*
little effect (=not much effect) *Changing his diet had little effect on his weight.*
a good effect *Going to college seems to have had a good effect on him.*
a bad/harmful effect *The harmful effects of alcohol are well known.*
the long-term/short-term effect *No one knows what the long-term effects of the changes will be.*

THESAURUS

effect a change or result that is caused by an event or action: *the harmful effects of smoking* | *The treatment didn't seem to have any effect.*
impact a big effect, especially one that is important and permanent: *New technology has had a huge impact on the way we work.*
influence an effect that changes people's opinions, behaviour, or the way something develops: *His father had a big influence on him.* | *the influence of advertisements on consumers*
side effect an unwanted effect that something, especially a drug or treatment, has: *Side effects of the drug may include headaches and sickness.*

effect[2] v [T] *formal* to make something happen: *an attempt to **effect** major **change***

effective /ɪˈfektɪv/ adj
1 having the result that you want OPP **ineffective**: *an effective way to teach reading* | *a **highly effective** method* THESAURUS **SUCCESSFUL**
2 [not before noun] if a law, agreement, or system becomes effective, it officially starts: **[+from]** *The new regulations are effective from April 5th.* —**effectiveness** n [U] → COST EFFECTIVE

effectively /ɪˈfektɪvli/ adv **1** in a way that gets the result you want: *She controlled the class very effectively.* **2** used to describe what you think is really true or really happens: *The poor are effectively excluded from politics.*

effeminate /ɪˈfemənət/ adj a man who is effeminate looks or behaves like a woman

effervescent /ˌefəˈvesənt◂ $ -fər-/ adj **1** a liquid that is effervescent produces small bubbles of gas SYN **fizzy** **2** someone who is effervescent seems to be full of energy and happiness —**effervescence** n [U]

efficient /ɪˈfɪʃənt/ adj working well, without wasting time or energy: *an efficient way of organizing your work* | *an efficient secretary* —**efficiently** adv —**efficiency** n [U]

effigy /ˈefɪdʒi/ n [C] (*plural* **effigies**) a model of a real person, which people sometimes burn as a protest

effluent /ˈefluənt/ n [C,U] *formal* liquid waste, especially chemicals or SEWAGE

EGGS

scrambled eggs | boiled eggs

fried egg | poached egg

effort /'efət $ 'efərt/ n
1 [U] hard work: *She puts a lot of effort into her work.* | **it takes effort (to do sth)** *It took a lot of effort to find him.* | *He lifted the box easily, without using much effort.*
2 [C,U] an attempt to do something: *Kim is making an effort to lose weight.* | **sb's efforts to do sth** *I was impressed with his efforts to stop smoking.* | **in an effort to do sth** *In an effort to reduce crime, more police are being hired.* THESAURUS ▶ TRY
PHRASES
| **be an effort** to be difficult or painful to do: *I was so weak that even standing up was an effort.*

effortless /'efətləs $ 'efərt-/ adj if something is effortless, you can do it very easily: *His running looks effortless.* —**effortlessly** adv

effusive /ɪ'fjuːsɪv/ adj showing your happiness, friendship etc in a very excited way: *an effusive greeting* —**effusively** adv

EFL /ˌiː ef 'el/ n [U] (**English as a Foreign Language**) the teaching of English to people who speak a different language

e.g. (also **eg** BrE) /ˌiː 'dʒiː/ the written abbreviation of **for example**: *science subjects e.g. chemistry and physics*

egalitarian /ɪˌɡælə'teəriən $ -'ter-/ adj based on the belief that everyone should have equal rights: *egalitarian principles* —**egalitarian** n [C]

egg¹ /eg/ n
1 [C] a round object that contains a baby bird, insect, snake etc: *Blackbirds lay their eggs in March.*
2 [C,U] an egg from a chicken that you can cook and eat: **fried/boiled/poached etc eggs** | *He had bacon and eggs for breakfast.*
3 [C] a cell produced inside a woman or female animal that can develop into a baby → **EASTER EGG, NEST EGG**
PHRASES
| **put all your eggs in one basket** to depend completely on one thing in order to get success so that

you have no other plans if this fails: *You shouldn't put all your eggs in one basket.*

egg² v
PHRASAL VERBS
egg sb ↔ **on** to encourage someone to do something that they should not do: *He didn't want to jump, but his friends kept egging him on.*

eggcup /'eg-kʌp/ n [C] a container that holds a boiled egg while you eat it

eggplant /'egplɑːnt $ -plænt/ n [C,U] AmE a large vegetable with a smooth shiny purple skin SYN **aubergine** BrE → see picture on page A5

eggshell /'egʃel/ n [C,U] the hard outside part of an egg

'egg white n [C,U] the part of an egg that becomes white when cooked → **yolk**

ego /'iːgəʊ, 'egəʊ $ -goʊ/ n [C] (plural **egos**) the good opinion that you have about yourself: **big/enormous ego** *He has an enormous ego* (=thinks he is very clever and important). | *The promotion boosted her ego* (=made her feel better about herself).
PHRASES
| **ego trip** disapproving if someone is on an ego trip, they think that they are better or more important than other people: *Power is the ultimate ego trip for many people.*

egocentric /ˌiːgəʊ'sentrɪk◂, ˌeg- $ -goʊ-/ adj thinking only about yourself and not about other people

egotism /'iːgətɪzəm, 'eg-/ (also **egoism** /'iːgəʊɪzəm, 'eg- $ -goʊ-/) n [U] the belief that you are much better or more important than other people —**egotist, egoist** n [C] —**egotistic** /ˌiːgə'tɪstɪk◂, ˌeg-/, **egoistic** /ˌiːgəʊ'ɪstɪk◂, ˌeg- $ -goʊ-/, **egotistical** adj

eh /eɪ/ spoken **1** BrE used to ask someone to say something again: *'You need a modem.' 'Eh?'* **2** used when you want someone to reply to you or agree with you: *Maybe he isn't as stupid as we thought, eh?*

eiderdown /'aɪdədaʊn $ -dər-/ n [C] a thick warm cover for a bed, filled with duck feathers

eight /eɪt/ number the number 8: *eight dollars* | *Dinner is at eight* (=eight o'clock). | *She is eight* (=eight years old).

eighteen /ˌeɪ'tiːn◂/ number the number 18: *Eighteen people were hurt.* | *Jim is eighteen* (=18 years old). —**eighteenth** adj, pron: *his eighteenth birthday* | *I'm leaving on the eighteenth* (=the 18th day of the month).

eighth¹ /eɪtθ/ adj coming after seven other things in a series: *in the eighth century* | *her eighth birthday* —**eighth** pron: *He's arriving on the eighth* (=the eighth day of the month).

eighth² n [C] one of eight equal parts of something

eighty /'eɪti/ number
1 the number 80
2 **the eighties** (also **the '80s, the 1980s**) [plural] the years from 1980 to 1989: **the early/mid/late eighties** *The band was very successful in the mid-eighties.* —**eightieth** adj: *his eightieth birthday*

PHRASES

be in your eighties to be aged between 80 and 89: **early/mid/late eighties** *Hilda Simpson was a woman in her early eighties.*

in the eighties if the temperature is in the eighties, it is between 80 degrees and 89 degrees F: *The temperature at the height of summer was often in the eighties.*

either¹ /ˈaɪðə $ ˈiːðər/ *linking word* **either … or** used when showing a choice: *We can either have lunch here or go out. | She's the kind of person you either love or hate. | Either she leaves or I will!*

either² *determiner, pron*
1 one of two things or people → **any**: *There's tea or coffee – you can have either. | She has a British and a Canadian passport so that she can live in either country. | [+of] Can either of you lend me £5?*
2 either side/end/hand etc both sides, ends, hands etc SYN **each**: *He sat in the back of the car with a policeman on either side.*

> **Grammar**
> You use **either** with a singular noun and a singular verb: *I can meet you on Wednesday or Thursday – either day is good for me.*
> You use **either of** with a plural noun and a singular verb: *Either of the films is worth seeing. | Has either of them telephoned yet?*

either³ *adv* used in negative sentences to mean 'also' → **neither**: *I haven't seen the movie and my brother hasn't either. | 'I don't like him.' 'I don't either.'*

ejaculate /ɪˈdʒækjəleɪt/ *v* [I,T] when a male ejaculates, SEMEN comes out of his PENIS —**ejaculation** /ɪˌdʒækjəˈleɪʃən/ *n* [C,U]

eject /ɪˈdʒekt/ *v* **1** [T] *formal* to make someone leave a place by using force: **eject sb from sth** *He was ejected from the club for fighting.* **2** [I,T] to make something come out of a machine by pressing a button: *How do I eject the CD?* **3** [I] if a pilot ejects from a plane, he or she escapes from it by using a special seat that throws the pilot out

eke /iːk/ *v*
PHRASAL VERBS
eke sth ↔ **out 1 eke out a living/existence** to live with very little money or food **2** to make a small supply of something last longer by only using small amounts of it

elaborate¹ /ɪˈlæbərət/ *adj* having a lot of small details or complicated parts: *an elaborate pattern | an elaborate plan* —**elaborately** *adv*

elaborate² /ɪˈlæbəreɪt/ *v* [I,T] *formal* to give more details about something: **[+on]** *He refused to elaborate on his reasons for resigning.*

elapse /ɪˈlæps/ *v* [I] *formal* if a period of time elapses, it passes

elastic /ɪˈlæstɪk/ *n* [U] a rubber material that can stretch and then go back to its usual shape and size: *socks with elastic around the top* —**elastic** *adj*

e,lastic 'band *n* [C] *BrE* a thin circle of rubber for holding things together SYN **rubber band** → see picture at STATIONERY

elated /ɪˈleɪtɪd/ *adj* extremely happy: *He felt elated.* —**elation** /ɪˈleɪʃən/ *n* [U]

elbow¹ /ˈelbəʊ $ -boʊ/ *n* [C]
1 the joint in the middle of your arm, where your arm bends: *I've hurt my elbow.* → see picture on page A2
2 the part of a shirt etc that covers your elbow
PHRASES
elbow room enough space in which to move easily: *Give me some elbow room.*

elbow² *v* [T] to push someone with your elbow: **elbow your way through/past/into etc sth** *He elbowed his way through the crowd.*

elder¹ /ˈeldə $ -ər/ *adj especially BrE* the elder child in a family is the older one of two: *Their elder son is now at university.* THESAURUS → OLD

> **Word Choice: elder or older?**
> **Elder** sounds rather formal. In everyday English, people usually say **older**: *She looks just like her older sister.*
> You say *He is **older** than me.* (Not 'He is elder than me.')

elder² *n* [C usually plural] **1 be sb's elder** *formal* to be older than someone else: **be two/ten etc years sb's elder** *Janet's sister is eight years her elder.* **2 sb's elders (and betters)** people who are older than you and who you should respect: *You should listen to your elders and betters.* **3** a member of a social group who is important and respected because they are old: *the village elders*

elderly /ˈeldəli $ ˈeldərli/ *adj* **1** an elderly person is old: *an elderly woman* THESAURUS → OLD **2 the elderly** people who are old: *a home for the elderly*

eldest /ˈeldɪst/ *adj especially BrE* the eldest child in a family is the oldest one: *He is **the eldest** of six children.*

elect¹ /ɪˈlekt/ *v* [T]
1 to choose someone for a job by voting: **elect sb (as) president/leader/mayor etc** *She was elected President.* THESAURUS → VOTE
2 elect to do sth *formal* to choose to do something: *He elected to stay at home.*

elect² *adj* **president-elect/governor-elect/prime minister-elect etc** the person who has been elected as president etc, but who has not yet officially started their job

election /ɪˈlekʃən/ *n*
1 [C] an occasion when people vote to choose a leader or government: *He won the presidential election. | the right to vote in elections*
2 [U] a situation in which someone is chosen as leader, or a party is chosen: *the election of a new leader | stand for election (=to try to be elected) There are very few women standing for election.* → BY-ELECTION —**electoral** /ɪˈlektərəl/ *adj*

COLLOCATIONS
verbs

to have/hold an election *An election will be held on March 22nd.*
to call an election (=to arrange for an election

to happen) *The Prime Minister decided to call an election.*

to win/lose an election *Who do you think will win the election?*

types of election

a general/national election (=one to elect a national government) *He may resign before the next general election.*

a local/regional/state election *They have had success in local elections.*

a presidential election (=one to elect a new president) *She was a candidate in last year's presidential election.*

a democratic election *These were the country's first ever democratic elections.*

election + noun

the election results *The election results will not be announced until tomorrow morning.*

an election campaign *He fought a very good election campaign.*

an election victory/defeat *It was his fourth election victory.*

elective /ɪ'lektɪv/ *adj formal* **1** an elective position is one that you must be elected for: *the House of Assembly's elective seats* **2** elective medical treatment is treatment that you choose to have, although you do not have to: **elective surgery** *such as hip replacements*

elector /ɪ'lektə $ -tər, -tɔːr/ *n* [C] someone who has the right to vote in an election **SYN voter**

electorate /ɪ'lektərət/ *n* [singular] all the people in a country who have the right to vote: *the British electorate*

electric /ɪ'lektrɪk/ *adj*
1 something that is electric works using electricity: **electric light/kettle/cooker etc** | *an electric guitar* | **electric current/power/charge** (=a flow of electricity)
2 very exciting: *The* **atmosphere** *in the room was* **electric.**

electrical /ɪ'lektrɪkəl/ *adj* using or relating to electricity: **electrical equipment/goods/appliances etc** | *an electrical fault* | *an electrical engineer*

e,lectric 'chair *n* **the electric chair** a chair in which criminals are killed using electricity

electrician /ɪ,lek'trɪʃən, ,elɪk-/ *n* [C] someone whose job is to fit electrical wires and repair electrical equipment

electricity /ɪ,lek'trɪsəti, ,elɪk-/ *n* [U] the power that is carried by wires and used to make lights and machines work: *The cooker works by electricity.* | *the* **electricity supply** | *the* **electricity bill**

electrics /ɪ'lektrɪks/ *n* [plural] *BrE* the parts of a machine that use electrical power

e,lectric 'shock *n* [C] a sudden painful feeling you get if you accidentally touch electricity

electrify /ɪ'lektrɪfaɪ/ *v* [T] (**electrified, electrifying, electrifies**) **1** if a performance or speech electrifies people, they think it is very interesting and exciting **2** to change a railway so that it uses electrical

power, or to supply a place with electricity —**electrified** *adj* —**electrifying** *adj*: *Her words had an electrifying effect.*

electrocute /ɪ'lektrəkjuːt/ *v* [T] to kill someone by passing electricity through their body —**electrocution** /ɪ,lektrə'kjuːʃən/ *n* [U]

electrode /ɪ'lektrəʊd $ -troʊd/ *n* [C] a small piece of metal or a wire that sends electricity through something

electron /ɪ'lektrɒn $ -trɑːn/ *n* [C] a part of an atom that has a NEGATIVE electric CHARGE → see picture at **ATOM**

electronic /ɪlɪk'trɒnɪk◂, ɪ,lek- $ -'trɑː-/ *adj* electronic equipment uses electricity and MICROCHIPS —**electronically** /-kli/ *adv*

electronics /ɪ,lek'trɒnɪks, ,elɪk- $ -'trɑː-/ *n* [U] the science of making electronic equipment, such as computers or televisions: **electronics company/industry/firm etc** | *He's got a degree in electronics.*

elegant /'eləgənt/ *adj* graceful and attractive: *an elegant woman* —**elegance** *n* [U] —**elegantly** *adv*

elegy /'elɪdʒi/ *n* [C] (*plural* **elegies**) a sad poem or song, especially about someone who has died

element Ac /'eləmənt/ *n* [C]
1 CHEMICAL a simple chemical substance that consists of only one kind of atom → **compound**
2 SMALL AMOUNT element of surprise/truth/risk/doubt etc a small amount of surprise etc: *There's an element of risk in every sport.*
3 FEATURE one part or feature of something: *Speed is an important element of the game.*
4 PART OF A GROUP a group of people who are part of a larger group: *communist elements in the party*
5 WEATHER the elements [plural] the weather, especially bad weather: *A cave provided shelter from the elements.*
6 ON A HEATER the part of a piece of electrical equipment that produces heat

elementary /,elə'mentəri◂/ *adj* **1** simple or basic: *an elementary mistake* **2** [only before noun] relating to the first and easiest part of a subject: *elementary science* **3** [only before noun] *AmE* elementary education is the first six years of children's education **SYN primary** *BrE*: *Fairbrook* **Elementary School**

elephant /'eləfənt/ *n* [C] a large grey animal with big ears and a long TRUNK

ELEPHANT

tusk

trunk

PHRASES

the elephant in the room an important subject or problem that everyone knows about but no one mentions: *Her illness was the elephant in the room.*

elevate /'elɪveɪt/ *v* [T]
formal to move someone or something to a higher position: **elevate sb/sth to sth** *He was elevated to Secretary of State.*

elevated /'elɪveɪtɪd/ *adj formal* in a high position or at a high level

elevation /ˌeləˈveɪʃən/ n **1** [singular] a height above the level of the sea: **[+of]** The village is situated at an elevation of 300 metres. **2** [U] formal when someone moves to a more important position or rank: **[+to]** her elevation to international stardom

elevator /ˈeləveɪtə $ -ər/ n [C] AmE a machine that takes you up and down in a building [SYN] lift BrE

eleven /ɪˈlevən/ number the number 11: She was sent to jail for eleven months. | I went to bed at eleven (=11 o'clock). | He is eleven (=11 years old).

eleventh¹ /ɪˈlevənθ/ adj coming after ten other things in a series: her eleventh birthday —**eleventh** pron: I'm planning to leave on **the eleventh** (=the 11th day of the month).

eleventh² n [C] one of 11 equal parts of something

elf /elf/ n [C] (plural **elves** /elvz/) a small imaginary person with pointed ears and magical powers

elicit /ɪˈlɪsɪt/ v [T] formal to get information or a reaction from someone: Her letter didn't **elicit** a **response**.

eligible /ˈelɪdʒəbəl/ adj **1** if you are eligible for something, you have the right to have it or do it: **[+for]** Are you eligible for a loan? | **eligible to do sth** If you are 18, you are eligible to vote. **2** [only before noun] an eligible man or woman is good to marry because they are rich, attractive, and not married: an **eligible bachelor** —**eligibility** /ˌelɪdʒəˈbɪləti/ n [U]

eliminate [Ac] /ɪˈlɪməneɪt/ v [T] **1** to completely get rid of something that is unnecessary or unwanted: Credit cards **eliminate** the **need** to carry cash. | **eliminate sth from sth** You should eliminate animal fats from your diet. **2 be eliminated** if you are eliminated in a sports competition, you can no longer be in it, for example because you lost a game: Pete was eliminated in the first game.

elimination [Ac] /ɪˌlɪməˈneɪʃən/ n [U] **1** the removal or destruction of something: **[+of]** the elimination of nuclear weapons **2** the defeat of a team or player in a competition, so that they no longer take part in it

PHRASES

process of elimination a way of finding the right answer by proving that all the other answers are wrong: We chose the right person for the job by a process of elimination.

elite /eɪˈliːt, ɪ-/ n [C] a group of people who have a lot of power because they have money, knowledge, or special skills

elitist /eɪˈliːtəst, ɪ-/ adj an elitist system is one in which a small group of people have much more power than others —**elitism** n [U]

Elizabethan /ɪˌlɪzəˈbiːθən◂/ adj relating to the time of Queen Elizabeth I of England (1558–1603): Elizabethan drama

elliptical /ɪˈlɪptɪkəl/ (also **elliptic** /-tɪk/) adj shaped like a long circle but with slightly flat sides [SYN] oval

elm /elm/ n [C,U] a tall tree with broad leaves

elocution /ˌeləˈkjuːʃən/ n [U] the skill of speaking clearly and correctly

elongated /ˈiːlɒŋgeɪtɪd $ ɪˈlɔːŋ-/ adj longer than normal

elope /ɪˈləʊp $ ɪˈloʊp/ v [I] if two people elope, they leave home secretly to get married

eloquent /ˈeləkwənt/ adj able to express your ideas and opinions well: an eloquent speaker —**eloquently** adv —**eloquence** n [U]

else /els/ adv used when talking about someone or something that is different from the one already mentioned: Can I get you anything else? | He was sitting in someone else's seat. | Where else could she be?

PHRASES

or else 1 used to say that there will be a bad result if someone does not do something: Hurry up or else we'll miss the train. **2** used to say what another possibility might be: The salesman will reduce the price or else include free insurance. **3** used to threaten someone: You'd better give it back or else!

elsewhere /elsˈweə, ˈelsweə $ ˈelswer/ adv in or to another place: goods imported from the US and elsewhere

ELT /ˌiː el ˈtiː/ n [U] especially BrE (**English Language Teaching**) the teaching of English to people whose first language is not English

elucidate /ɪˈluːsədeɪt/ v [I,T] formal to explain something by providing more information

elude /ɪˈluːd/ v [T] formal **1** to avoid being caught by someone, especially by tricking them: He eluded the police for six weeks. **2** if something you want eludes you, you do not find or achieve it: Success eluded her. **3** if a fact eludes you, you cannot remember it: Her name eludes me at the moment.

elusive /ɪˈluːsɪv/ adj difficult to find: a shy and elusive animal

elves /elvz/ n the plural of ELF

'em /əm/ pron informal sometimes used as a short form of 'them': Go on, Bill, you tell 'em!

emaciated /ɪˈmeɪʃieɪtəd, -si-/ adj very thin because you are ill or do not have enough food

email, e-mail /ˈiː meɪl/ n
1 [C] an electronic message sent from one computer to another: I got an email from Joe.
2 [U] (**electronic mail**) a system for sending electronic messages by computer: Email is a very quick form of communication. —**email** v [T]: I emailed the hotel to say when we would be arriving.

COLLOCATIONS
verbs

to send an email Someone sent me an email about the meeting.
to get/receive an email Did you get my email?
to read an email When I read your email, I thought it was a joke.
to write an email I spent the morning writing emails.
to reply to an email/answer an email Why haven't you replied to my email?
to check your email (=to see if new messages have arrived) How often do you check your email?

email + noun

an **email address** *I'll give you my email address.*
an **email message** *I can send email messages on my phone.*

emanate /'eməneɪt/ v
PHRASAL VERBS
emanate from sth *formal* if a smell, light etc emanates from somewhere, it comes from that place: *Wonderful smells emanated from the kitchen.*

emancipate /ɪ'mænsəpeɪt/ v [T] *formal* to give people the political or legal rights that they did not have before —**emancipated** *adj* —**emancipation** /ɪˌmænsə'peɪʃən/ n [U]

embalm /ɪm'bɑːm $ -'bɑːm, -'bɑːlm/ v [T] to preserve a dead body by using chemicals and oils

embankment /ɪm'bæŋkmənt/ n [C] a wall of earth or stones to stop water from flooding an area, or to support a road or railway

embargo /ɪm'bɑːɡəʊ $ -'bɑːrɡoʊ/ n [C] (*plural* **embargoes**) an official order to stop trade with another country: **impose/lift an embargo** (=start or end one) *The UN lifted the oil embargo.*

embark /ɪm'bɑːk $ -ɑːrk/ v [I] to get on a ship or plane —**embarkation** /ˌembɑː'keɪʃən $ -bɑːr-/ n [C,U]
PHRASAL VERBS
embark on/upon sth to start something new: *She left school to embark on a career as a model.*

embarrass /ɪm'bærəs/ v [T] to make someone feel ashamed, stupid, or uncomfortable: *My parents always embarrass me.*

embarrassed /ɪm'bærəst/ *adj* if you feel embarrassed, you feel nervous or uncomfortable about what other people think of you: **[+about/at]** *I felt embarrassed about how untidy the house was.* | **embarrassed to do sth** *He was too embarrassed to admit his mistake.* THESAURUS ASHAMED

embarrassing /ɪm'bærəsɪŋ/ *adj* if something is embarrassing, it makes you feel embarrassed: *It was very embarrassing being called up onto the stage.* | *an embarrassing question*

embarrassment /ɪm'bærəsmənt/ n 1 [U] the feeling of being embarrassed: *Eric went red in the face with embarrassment.* | **to sb's embarrassment** *To her embarrassment, she couldn't remember his name.* THESAURUS SHAME 2 [C] something or someone that makes you feel embarrassed: **[+to/for]** *The scandal is an embarrassment to the government.*

embassy /'embəsi/ n [C] (*plural* **embassies**) a group of OFFICIALS who live and work in a foreign country, and whose job is to help people from their own country who are also living or working there. The building these people work in is also called an embassy.

embattled /ɪm'bætld/ *adj formal* 1 [only before noun] an embattled person, organization etc has a lot of problems or difficulties: *The embattled president had to resign.* 2 surrounded by enemies, especially in war or fighting: *the embattled capital, Sarajevo*

embed /ɪm'bed/ v [I,T] (**embedded, embedding**) to put something firmly and deeply into something else: **be embedded in sth** *A piece of glass was embedded in her hand.*

embellish /ɪm'belɪʃ/ v [T] 1 to make something more beautiful by adding decorations 2 to make a story more interesting by adding details that are not true —**embellishment** n [C,U]

ember /'embə $ -ər/ n [C usually plural] a piece of wood or coal that stays red and very hot after a fire has stopped burning

embezzle /ɪm'bezəl/ v [I,T] to steal money from the place where you work —**embezzlement** n [U]

embittered /ɪm'bɪtəd $ -ərd/ *adj* angry or full of hate because bad or unfair things have happened to you

emblazoned /ɪm'bleɪzənd/ *adj* [not before noun] if something is emblazoned with a name or design, it has that design on it where it can be seen clearly

emblem /'embləm/ n [C] a picture, shape, or object that is used to represent a country, organization etc

embodiment /ɪm'bɒdɪmənt $ ɪm'bɑː-/ n the **embodiment of sth** someone or something that represents an idea or quality, or is a typical example of that idea or quality: *He is the embodiment of evil.*

embody /ɪm'bɒdi $ ɪm'bɑːdi/ v [T] (**embodied, embodying, embodies**) to be a very good example of an idea or quality: *She embodies everything I admire in a teacher.*

embrace /ɪm'breɪs/ v [T] *formal* 1 to put your arms around someone and hold them in a loving way: *She warmly embraced her son.* 2 *formal* to eagerly accept a new idea, opinion, religion etc: *We hope these regions will embrace democratic reforms.* 3 *formal* to include something: *This course embraces different aspects of psychology.* —**embrace** n [C]: *He held her in a loving embrace.*

embroider /ɪm'brɔɪdə $ -ər/ v 1 [I,T] to decorate cloth by sewing a picture or pattern on it 2 [T] to make a story more interesting by adding details that are not true

embroidery /ɪm'brɔɪdəri/ n (*plural* **embroideries**) 1 [C,U] a pattern sewn onto cloth, or cloth with patterns sewn onto it 2 [U] the act of sewing patterns onto cloth

embroil /ɪm'brɔɪl/ v [T] **be embroiled in sth** to be involved in a difficult situation: *I didn't want to become embroiled in their argument.*

embryo /'embriəʊ $ -brioʊ/ n [C] (*plural* **embryos**) an animal or human that has just begun to develop inside its mother's body

embryonic /ˌembri'ɒnɪk◄ $ -'ɑːn-/ *adj* 1 at a very early stage of development: *The plans are only in embryonic form.* 2 relating to an embryo: *embryonic cells*

emerald /'emərəld/ n [C] a bright green jewel

emerge Ac /ɪ'mɜːdʒ $ -ɜːrdʒ/ v [I] 1 to appear or come out from somewhere: **[+from]** *He emerged from his hiding place.* 2 to become known: *Eventually the truth emerged.* | *Later it emerged that she had been having an affair.* 3 to come out of a difficult experience: **[+from]** *She emerged from the divorce a stronger person.* —**emergence** *n* [U]

emergency /ɪˈmɜːdʒənsi $ -ɜːr-/ *n* [C] (*plural* **emergencies**) a dangerous situation that happens suddenly, and in which people might be hurt or killed: *Come quickly – it's an emergency!* | **in an emergency** *Make sure your children know what to do in an emergency.* | **In case of emergency**, *press the alarm button.* | **emergency exit/supplies etc** (=used in an emergency) → **STATE OF EMERGENCY**

eˈmergency ˌbrake *n* [C] *AmE* a handle in a car that you pull up with your hand to stop the car from moving SYN **handbrake** *BrE*

eˈmergency ˌroom *n* [C] *AmE* the part of a hospital where people are taken when they need urgent treatment SYN **casualty** *BrE*

eˈmergency ˌservices *n* [plural] official organizations such as the police that deal with crimes, fires, or helping people who are badly hurt

emerging Ac /ɪˈmɜːdʒɪŋ $ -ɜːr-/ (*also* **emergent** /-dʒənt/) *adj* [only before noun] in an early state of development: *the country's emerging oil industry*

emigrant /ˈemɪɡrənt/ *n* [C] someone who leaves their country to live in a different one → **immigrant**

emigrate /ˈemɪɡreɪt/ *v* [I] to leave your country to go and live in a different one: **[+to/from]** *They emigrated to France.* THESAURUS **LEAVE** —**emigration** /ˌemɪˈɡreɪʃən/ *n* [U]

eminent /ˈemɪnənt/ *adj* famous and respected: *an eminent scientist*

eminently /ˈemɪnəntli/ *adv* formal approving completely and certainly: *He's **eminently suitable** for the role.*

emission /ɪˈmɪʃən/ *n* [C usually plural, U] a substance that is sent out into the air, or the act of sending it out: *gas emissions*

eˈmissions ˌtrading *n* [U] the practice of buying or selling permission to produce a particular amount of a substance that can harm the environment

emit /ɪˈmɪt/ *v* [T] (**emitted**, **emitting**) to send out gas, heat, a sound etc

emotion /ɪˈməʊʃən $ ɪˈmoʊ-/ *n* [C,U] a strong feeling such as love, hate, anger etc: **with emotion** *She trembled with emotion.* | **hide/show/control emotion** *He could not hide his emotions.* | *Her face showed no **sign of emotion**.* THESAURUS **FEELING**

emotional /ɪˈməʊʃənəl/ *adj* connected with feelings such as anger, pity, sadness etc: *children with **emotional problems*** | *She needs **emotional support**.* | **become/get emotional** (=get upset, cry etc) *He becomes emotional easily.* —**emotionally** *adv*: *an emotionally cold man*

emotive /ɪˈməʊtɪv $ ɪˈmoʊ-/ *adj* causing strong feelings of anger, sadness etc: *Abortion is an **emotive issue**.*

empathize (*also* **-ise** *BrE*) /ˈempəθaɪz/ *v* [I] to be able to understand someone else's problems, especially because you have had similar problems → **sympathize: [+with]** *I found it hard to empathize with her.*

empathy /ˈempəθi/ *n* [U] the ability to understand someone's feelings and problems → **sympathy**

emperor /ˈempərə $ -ər/ *n* [C] a man who rules an EMPIRE

emphasis Ac /ˈemfəsɪs/ *n* (*plural* **emphases** /-siːz/) **1** [C,U] special importance or attention that you give something: **(place/put) emphasis on (doing) sth** *The Japanese put a lot of emphasis on manners.* **2** [C usually singular] *technical* special importance given to a word or phrase, for example by saying it louder → **stress**

emphasize Ac (*also* **-ise** *BrE*) /ˈemfəsaɪz/ *v* [T] if you emphasize something you say or write, you give it special importance so that people will notice it: **emphasize that/how** *I emphasized that I was not criticizing her.* | *The report **emphasizes the importance of** education.*

emphatic Ac /ɪmˈfætɪk/ *adj* expressing your meaning strongly: *an emphatic 'no'* —**emphatically** /-kli/ *adv*

empire /ˈempaɪə $ -paɪr/ *n* [C] a group of countries or organizations that are all controlled by one person, government etc: *the Roman Empire*

empirical Ac /ɪmˈpɪrɪkəl/ *adj* [only before noun] based on practical tests and experience, not ideas OPP **theoretical**: *empirical evidence*

employ /ɪmˈplɔɪ/ *v* [T]
1 to pay someone to do a job: *The factory employs 2,000 people.* | **employ sb as sth** *He was employed as a teacher.* THESAURUS **USE**
2 *formal* to use something: *The network employs the latest technology.*

employee /ɪmˈplɔɪiː, ˌemplɔɪˈiː/ *n* [C] someone who receives a SALARY (=payment) to work for an organization, person, or company SYN **worker**: *government employees* | *employee rights*

employer /ɪmˈplɔɪə $ -ər/ *n* [C] an organization, person, or company that pays people to do a job: *Please give the name of your previous employer.*

employment /ɪmˈplɔɪmənt/ *n* [U]
1 when an organization, person, or company pays someone to do a job OPP **unemployment**: **in employment** *Are you in **full-time employment**?* | **[+of]** *We are opposed to the employment of children.* | **employment rights** for part-time workers | **find/seek/offer employment** *What are her chances of finding employment?*
2 the number of people who have jobs: *Farm jobs represent 12% of the region's total employment.* | *You're never going to get **full employment** (=when everyone has a job).*
3 *formal* the use of a particular object or method to achieve something SYN **use**: **[+of]** *the employment of military force*

empower /ɪmˈpaʊə $ -ˈpaʊr/ *v* [T] **1** to give someone confidence or skills so that they have more control over their life: *Education can empower you.* **2** *formal* to give someone the official power to do something —**empowerment** *n* [U]

empress /ˈemprɪs/ *n* [C] a woman who rules an EMPIRE, or the wife of an EMPEROR

EMPTY

empty   half-full   full

empty¹ /'empti/ adj (comparative **emptier**, superlative **emptiest**)
1 an empty container or place has nothing or no one in it: Noticing her empty wine glass, he refilled it. | By midnight, the streets were empty. | I've left an **empty space** for your signature. | The train was **half-empty** (=there were not many people on it).
2 without meaning, value, or importance: **empty words/promises/threats etc** a government's empty promises | Without him, my life would be empty. —**emptiness** n [U]: a feeling of emptiness

THESAURUS

empty an empty container has nothing in it. An empty place has no one in it: an empty bottle | The house looked empty.
bare a bare room or cupboard has very little in it. Bare walls have no pictures on them: The room was bare except for a small table.
blank a blank screen or piece of paper has no writing or pictures on it. A blank tape, CD etc has nothing recorded on it: I kept staring at the blank sheet of paper.
hollow a hollow tree, wall etc has an empty space inside: The insects live in hollow trees.
free a free seat, space, or room is available because no one else is using it: Is this seat free?
vacant a vacant room or building is available for people to pay to use: a vacant apartment
deserted a deserted place is quiet because all the people have gone away: The streets were deserted.
uninhabited an uninhabited place has no one living there: an uninhabited island

empty² v (**emptied**, **emptying**, **empties**) **1** (also **empty out**) [T] if you empty a container, you remove everything from it: The thieves had emptied out the desks. | **empty sth into/onto sth** Rachel emptied the soup into a pan. **2** [I] if a place empties, people leave it: The stores were already emptying.

empty-'handed adj without getting what you wanted: The thieves **fled empty-handed**.

emulate /'emjəleɪt/ v [T] formal if you emulate someone, you try to be like them because you admire them: Children emulate their heroes.

emulsion /ɪ'mʌlʃən/ (also e'**mulsion paint**) n [C,U] BrE a type of paint used on inside walls or ceilings that is not shiny when it dries

enable Ac /ɪ'neɪbəl/ v [T] to make it possible for

someone to do something or for something to happen: **enable sb/sth to do sth** The money enabled me to buy a house.

enact /ɪ'nækt/ v [T] **1** law to make a proposal become law: Congress will not enact the Bill. **2** formal to perform a story, event etc by acting it

enamel /ɪ'næməl/ n [U] **1** a hard substance used to decorate or protect things made of metal, clay etc **2** the hard surface on your teeth

enamoured BrE, **enamored** AmE /ɪ'næməd $ -ərd/ adj [not before noun] formal liking or loving someone or something very much: [+with] You don't seem too enamoured with your job.

encampment /ɪn'kæmpmənt/ n [C] a large temporary camp, especially of soldiers: a military encampment

encapsulate /ɪn'kæpsjəleɪt $ -sə-/ v [T] formal to express or show something complicated in a short way SYN **sum up**: **encapsulate sth in sth** Encapsulate your ideas in a few words.

encase /ɪn'keɪs/ v [T] to cover something completely: **be encased in sth** The reactor is encased in concrete.

enchant /ɪn'tʃɑːnt $ ɪn'tʃænt/ v [T] **1** if something enchants you, it makes you feel happy, interested, and excited: Her beauty enchanted us all. **2** literary to use magic on someone or something —**enchanted** adj: an enchanted castle

enchanting /ɪn'tʃɑːntɪŋ $ ɪn'tʃæn-/ adj very pleasant or attractive: She has an enchanting smile.

encircle /ɪn'sɜːkəl $ -ɜːr-/ v [T] to surround someone or something: a baby encircled by wolves

enclave /'enkleɪv, 'eŋ-/ n [C] a small place that is different from the area around it because the people living there belong to a different nationality: a Spanish enclave in Africa

enclose /ɪn'kləʊz $ -'kloʊz/ v [T] **1** to put something in an envelope with a letter: Please enclose your payment. | **Please find enclosed** the agenda for our meeting. **2** to surround something with a fence or wall —**enclosed** adj

enclosure /ɪn'kləʊʒə $ -'kloʊʒər/ n [C] **1** an area that is separated by a wall or fence **2** something that you put in an envelope with a letter

encompass /ɪn'kʌmpəs/ v [T] formal **1** to include many ideas, subjects etc **2** to cover or surround an area

encore /'ɒŋkɔː $ 'ɑːŋkɔːr/ n [C] an extra piece of music a performer plays because the AUDIENCE wants it

encounter¹ Ac /ɪn'kaʊntə $ -ər/ v [T] **1** to experience something that causes difficulty: **encounter problems/opposition etc** The government **encountered resistance** to its plans. **2** formal to meet someone when you did not plan to SYN **come across**: I first encountered him at Oxford.

encounter² Ac n [C] an occasion when you meet someone or experience something when you did not plan to: [+with/between] a **chance encounter** with a famous actor

E

encourage /ɪnˈkʌrɪdʒ $ ɪnˈkɜːr-/ v [T]
1 to try to help someone succeed, for example by giving them confidence or determination OPP **discourage**: **encourage sb to do sth** You are **actively encouraged** to contribute to school life. | **encourage sb in sth** My dad encouraged me in my ambitions. THESAURUS▸ PERSUADE
2 to make something more likely to happen: Violent movies encourage anti-social behaviour. —**encouraged** adj [not before noun]: I felt encouraged to continue. —**encouragement** n [C,U]: words of encouragement | Henry needed no encouragement to work hard. —**encouraging** adj: encouraging news on jobs

encroach /ɪnˈkrəʊtʃ $ -ˈkroʊtʃ/ v
PHRASAL VERBS
encroach on/upon sth to gradually take more of someone's time, power, space etc: Don't let work encroach on your private life.

encrusted /ɪnˈkrʌstɪd/ adj covered with a hard layer of something: [+with] boots encrusted with mud

encyclopedia (also **encyclopaedia** BrE) /ɪnˌsaɪkləˈpiːdiə/ n [C] a book or CD containing facts about many subjects, or detailed facts about one subject

end¹ /end/ n
1 [singular] the last part of a period of time, activity, book etc OPP **beginning**, **start**: [+of] I get paid **at the end of** the week. | **By the end of** the test she was sure she'd failed. | **In the end** (=after a period of time) we decided to go. | I watched the film **from beginning to end**.
2 [singular] when something is finished or no longer exists: **put/bring an end to sth** We must put an end to the war. | **come to an end** His life came to an abrupt end. | **be at an end** 'This conversation is at an end,' she snapped. | **the end of the road/line** Our marriage had **reached the end of the line**. THESAURUS▸ STOP
3 [C] the part of a place or thing that is furthest from its beginning or centre: [+of] Walk to the end of the road with me. | We sat at **opposite ends** of the table. | desks arranged **end to end** (=with their ends touching)
4 [C usually plural] a purpose, aim, or result: political/military/personal etc ends She'd do anything to **achieve** her own **ends**. → DEAD END, ODDS AND ENDS, get (hold of) the wrong end of the stick at WRONG
PHRASES
| **days/hours etc on end** many days, hours etc without stopping: It rained **for days on end**.
| **it's not the end of the world** spoken informal used to say that a problem is not as bad as it seems: If you don't get the job, it's not the end of the world.
| **make ends meet** to get just enough money to buy what you need: We could barely make ends meet after Ray lost his job.
| **no end of trouble/problems etc** informal lots of trouble etc: This will cause no end of trouble.
| **reach the end of your rope/tether** to get to the stage when you cannot deal with a bad situation:

She reached the end of her tether when she lost her job.

THESAURUS
end the last part of a period of time, or of an activity, book, film etc: Her birthday is at the end of July. | I missed the end of the programme.
ending the way that a story, film etc ends: The story has a happy ending.
finish the end of a race or competition: The race had a thrilling finish.
finale the impressive last part of a performance, event etc: The show will be a dramatic finale to the Olympic Games.

end² v [I,T] to finish or stop, or to make something finish OPP **begin**, **start**: What time does the film end? | talks aimed at ending the conflict | [+with/in] Their marriage ended in divorce. → NEVER-ENDING
PHRASES
| **the year/week etc ending sth** used to refer to a year that ends on a particular date: accounts for the year ending 31 July 2004
PHRASAL VERBS
end up to finally be in a particular place, situation, or state without intending to: **end up doing sth** When I diet, I always end up putting weight back on. | [+like/as] I don't want to end up like my parents.

THESAURUS
end to finish – used especially about a situation, story, or event: No one knows when the war will end. | How does the story end?
finish to stop happening – used especially to say what time an event or activity stops: School finishes at 3:30. | The party didn't finish till 4 in the morning!
be over if an event or activity is over, it has ended – used especially when you are glad that something has finished, or when someone is too late for something: At last all the exams were over. | By the time I arrived, the meeting was already over.
come to an end to end – used about a situation or activity that has continued for a long time: It was August and the holiday was coming to an end.

endanger /ɪnˈdeɪndʒə $ -ər/ v [T] to put someone or something in a dangerous or harmful situation: Smoking **endangers your life**. | The whale is an **endangered species** (=one that may soon no longer exist).

endear /ɪnˈdɪə $ ɪnˈdɪr/ v
PHRASAL VERBS
endear sb **to** sb to make someone popular: His remarks did not endear him to the audience. —**endearing** adj: an endearing smile

endearment /ɪnˈdɪəmənt $ ɪnˈdɪr-/ n [C,U] words that express your love for someone

endeavour BrE, **endeavor** AmE /ɪnˈdevə $ -ər/ v [I] formal to try to do something new or difficult: **endeavour to do sth** I endeavoured to reassure him. —**endeavour** n [C,U]: Darwin's scientific endeavours

endemic /enˈdemɪk, ɪn-/ adj an endemic disease

or problem is always there → **epidemic**: *Crime is endemic in cities.*

ending /'endɪŋ/ n [C] **1** the way that a story, film, activity etc ends: **[+to]** *cheese – the perfect ending to a meal* | **happy/surprise etc ending** *I like stories with a happy ending.* **THESAURUS** **END 2** the last part of a word: *Past participles have an 'ed' ending.*

endless /'endləs/ adj in large quantities or for long periods of time: **endless amounts of** *paperwork* —**endlessly** adv

endorse /ɪn'dɔːs $ -ɔːrs/ v [T] to express support or approval of someone or something: *The president did not endorse the views of his deputy.* —**endorsement** n [C,U]

endow /ɪn'daʊ/ v [T] to give a college, hospital etc a large sum of money —**endowment** n [C,U]

PHRASAL VERBS

endow sb/sth **with** sth formal to make someone or something have a particular quality: *He was endowed with supernatural strength.*

'end-product n [C] something that is produced at the end of a process or activity

end re'sult n [C usually singular] the final result of a process or activity: *The end result is likely to be fewer farms and farmers.*

endurance /ɪn'djʊərəns $ ɪn'dʊr-/ n [U] the ability to continue doing something difficult or painful: *a test of physical and mental endurance*

endure /ɪn'djʊə $ ɪn'dʊr/ v [T] to be in a difficult or painful situation for a long time without complaining

enduring /ɪn'djʊərɪŋ $ ɪn'dʊr-/ adj continuing for a long time: *music's **enduring** appeal*

'end user n [C] the person who uses a product, rather than the people who made it

enemy /'enəmi/ n (plural **enemies**)
1 [C] someone who hates you and wants you to fail: *He **made** many **enemies**.* | *He's a dangerous enemy to have.* | **bitter/sworn enemy** *Jo and Jay are sworn enemies.*
2 [singular] the country that your country is fighting in a war: *territory controlled by **the enemy*** | **enemy aircraft/territory/fire etc**

energetic Ac /ˌenə'dʒetɪk◄ $ -ər-/ adj strong, active, and working hard: *a young energetic leader* | **energetic in doing sth** *The government could be more energetic in helping the poor.* —**energetically** /-kli/ adv

energy Ac /'enədʒi $ -ər-/ n [C,U] (plural **energies**)
1 power from oil, coal etc that produces heat, movement etc: *Switch off lights and save energy.*
2 the physical and mental strength that makes you able to do things without getting tired: *Kids are always **full of energy**.* | **(have) the energy to do sth** *I didn't have the energy to walk.* | *Managers put **time and energy** into their artists' careers.*

COLLOCATIONS

types of energy

solar energy (=from sunlight) *They use solar energy for heating water.*

nuclear/atomic energy *Some countries rely heavily on nuclear energy.*

wind energy *Wind energy is used to generate electricity.*

renewable energy (=from things that will always exist or can be replaced) *The government wants to encourage the use of renewable energy.*

clean energy (=which does not cause pollution) *Could this be a source of cheap, clean energy?*

verbs

to use energy *We should try to use energy efficiently.*

to save energy *The website gives information on how to save energy in your home.*

to generate/produce energy *The wind farm can produce enough energy to supply 2,000 homes.*

energy + noun

energy use (also **energy consumption** formal) *How can we cut energy use?*

energy efficiency *There is an urgent need to improve energy efficiency.*

energy resources *The world's energy resources will not last forever.*

noun + energy

a source/form of energy *We must explore other sources of energy.*

enforce Ac /ɪn'fɔːs $ -ɔːrs/ v [T] to make people obey a rule or law: **enforce a law/ban etc** *We will enforce the speed limit.* —**enforcement** n [U] —**enforceable** adj

engage /ɪn'geɪdʒ/ v [T] formal **1** if something engages your interest or attention, it makes you stay interested: *The toy didn't **engage** her **attention** for long.* | **engage sb in sth** *I tried to **engage** him **in** conversation.* **2** formal to employ someone: **engage sb as sth/to do sth** *She was engaged as a nanny for their two children.*

PHRASAL VERBS

engage in sth (also **be engaged in** sth) formal to do an activity: *Ken was engaged in prayer.*

engaged /ɪn'geɪdʒd/ adj **1** if two people are engaged, they have agreed to marry: **[+to]** *Isn't she engaged to Phil?* | *Viv and Tony **got engaged** last year.* **THESAURUS** **MARRIED 2** BrE if a telephone line is engaged, it is already being used **SYN** **busy** AmE: **engaged tone/signal** (=the sound you hear when this happens)

engagement /ɪn'geɪdʒmənt/ n [C] **1** an agreement between two people to marry, or the period of time before they marry: *Their **engagement** was **announced** last week.* **2** an official arrangement for someone important to do something: *The Minister **has** a **speaking engagement**.*

engaging /ɪn'geɪdʒɪŋ/ adj pleasant and attractive: *an engaging smile*

engender /ɪn'dʒendə $ -ər/ v [T] formal to cause a particular situation or feeling: *a poster engendering racial hatred*

engine /'endʒɪn/ n [C]
1 the part of a vehicle that produces the power that makes it move → **motor**: **start/turn/switch an**

engine on/off *He pulled in and turned off the engine.* | **car/jet etc engine** | *an engine that runs on gas*
2 a vehicle that pulls a railway train → **FIRE ENGINE, JET ENGINE, SEARCH ENGINE**

engineer¹ /,endʒə'nɪə $ -'nɪr/ *n* [C]
1 someone whose job is to design, build, or repair roads, bridges, machines etc: **mechanical/ electrical/software etc engineer**
2 *AmE* someone whose job is driving a train

engineer² *v* [T] **1** to arrange something secretly: *the enemies who engineered his downfall* **2** to change the GENETIC structure of a plant or animal: *genetically engineered wheat*

engineering /,endʒə'nɪərɪŋ $ -'nɪr-/ *n* [U] the work of designing, building, or repairing roads, bridges, machines etc → **GENETIC ENGINEERING**

English /'ɪŋglɪʃ/ *n*
1 [U] the language used in Britain, the US, Australia, and some other countries: *Do you speak English?* | *He's Chinese, but his English is excellent.*
2 the English [plural] people from England: *The English do not always behave well abroad.* —**English** *adj*: *English literature*

engrave /ɪn'greɪv/ *v* [T] to cut words or pictures into metal, wood, glass etc: *a watch engraved with his initials*

engraving /ɪn'greɪvɪŋ/ *n* [C] a picture printed from a piece of engraved metal

engrossed /ɪn'grəʊst $ -'groʊst/ *adj* so interested in something that you do not think of anything else: **[+in]** *Dad was engrossed in the paper.*

engulf /ɪn'gʌlf/ *v* [T] **1** to have a very strong effect on a person, place, or thing: *Despair engulfed him.* **2** to completely surround something: *The house was engulfed in flames.*

enhance Ac /ɪn'hɑːns $ ɪn'hæns/ *v* [T] to improve something: *Salt enhances flavour.* —**enhanced** *adj* —**enhancement** *n* [C,U]

enigma /ɪ'nɪgmə/ *n* [C] someone or something that is mysterious or difficult to understand: *Russia will always be an enigma.* —**enigmatic** /,enɪg'mætɪk◂/ *adj*: *an enigmatic smile*

enjoy /ɪn'dʒɔɪ/ *v* [T] to get pleasure from something: **enjoy doing sth** *My wife enjoys riding.* | **enjoy yourself** *Did you enjoy yourself at the party?*

> **Grammar**
> Do not say 'Pete enjoys to play tennis.' Say *Pete enjoys playing tennis.*

enjoyable /ɪn'dʒɔɪəbəl/ *adj* giving you pleasure: *an enjoyable movie* **THESAURUS** ▶ **NICE**

enjoyment /ɪn'dʒɔɪmənt/ *n* [U] pleasure that something gives you: **give/bring sb enjoyment** *Music gives me great enjoyment.* | **[+from]** *He gets great enjoyment from driving.*

enlarge /ɪn'lɑːdʒ $ -ɑːrdʒ/ *v* [T] if you enlarge something, or if it enlarges, it gets bigger: *Can I have these photos enlarged?* —**enlargement** *n* [C,U]

PHRASAL VERBS
enlarge on/upon sth *formal* to provide more information about something you have already mentioned

enlighten /ɪn'laɪtn/ *v* [T] *formal* to explain something to someone: **enlighten sb as to/about sth** *Would you enlighten me as to your whereabouts?* —**enlightening** *adj*

enlightened /ɪn'laɪtnd/ *adj approving* having a sensible and modern attitude: *an **enlightened approach** to women's rights*

enlightenment /ɪn'laɪtnmənt/ *n* [U] *formal* when you understand something clearly, or when you help someone do this: *Isabel looked to Ron for enlightenment.*

enlist /ɪn'lɪst/ *v* **1** [I] to persuade someone to help you: *She **enlisted help** from friends.* **2** [I,T] to join the army, navy etc —**enlistment** *n* [C,U]

enliven /ɪn'laɪvən/ *v* [T] to make something more interesting: *Use games to enliven seminars.*

en masse /,ɒn 'mæs $,ɑːn-/ *adv* together as a group: *They resigned en masse.*

enmity /'enmɪti/ *n* [C,U] (*plural* **enmities**) *formal* a strong feeling of hatred towards someone: **[+between/towards]** *enmity between nations*

enormity Ac /ɪ'nɔːməti $ -ɔːr-/ *n* [singular] how big, serious, or difficult something is: **[+of]** *the **enormity of** his crimes*

enormous Ac /ɪ'nɔːməs $ -ɔːr-/ *adj* very big in size, amount, or degree: *It cost **an enormous amount** of money.* | *The team made **an enormous effort.***
THESAURUS ▶ **BIG** —**enormously** *adv*: *an enormously popular writer*

enough¹ /ɪ'nʌf/ *adv*
1 to the amount or degree that you need or want: **[+for]** *The water wasn't hot enough for a bath.* | **enough to do sth** *The room is just big enough to take a bed.* | *Do you think this meat is cooked enough?*
2 if something is nice, good etc enough, it is fairly nice, good etc, but not very nice, good etc: **happy/ nice/pleasant etc enough** *He seems a nice enough young man.*
3 sth is bad/difficult/hard etc enough (without sth) *spoken* used to say a situation is already bad, and you do not want it to get worse: *Life's hard enough if you were born here.* → **sure enough** at **SURE**

PHRASES
> **strangely/oddly/funnily enough** used when saying that something is connected with what you have just been talking about, in a surprising way: *Funnily enough, you're the third person who has asked me that question.*

> **Grammar**
> **Enough** is used after adjectives and adverbs: *These jeans aren't big enough.* | *He's not working quickly enough.*
> **Enough** is used before nouns: *There isn't enough space in this office.*

enough² *determiner, pron* as much or as many as you need or want: **(have) enough (sth) to do sth** *The police don't have enough evidence to convict him.* | *Have you had enough to eat?* | **[+for]** *Is there enough wine for everyone?* | *You've had **more than enough** time to prepare.*

PHRASES
| **have had enough (of sth)** spoken used to say you are tired of a situation and you want it to end: By 10.00 pm, I'd just about had enough.

THESAURUS

enough as much or as many as you need or want: I don't have enough money. | Do we have enough chairs?

plenty more than enough – used especially when saying that you do not need to worry about having more: There's no need to hurry – we have plenty of time.

sufficient formal enough for a particular purpose: The court did not have sufficient evidence to find him guilty.

adequate formal enough – used especially when saying if something is a good enough standard: They weren't given adequate training. | The equipment should be adequate for most purposes.

enquire /ɪnˈkwaɪə $ -ˈkwaɪr/ v [I,T] especially BrE another spelling of INQUIRE **THESAURUS** ASK

enquiry /ɪnˈkwaɪəri $ ɪnˈkwaɪri, ˈɪŋkwəri/ n [C] (plural **enquiries**) especially BrE another spelling of INQUIRY

enrage /ɪnˈreɪdʒ/ v [T] to make someone very angry: a programme that has enraged parents

enrich /ɪnˈrɪtʃ/ v [T] to improve the quality of something by adding to it —**enrichment** n [U]

enrol BrE, **enroll** AmE /ɪnˈrəʊl $ -ˈroʊl/ v [I,T] (**enrolled, enrolling**) if you enrol at a college, university etc, or the college etc enrols you, you officially arrange to join a course there: [+on/for] BrE: I enrolled on the wine course. [+in] AmE: He plans to enroll in medical school. —**enrolment** n [C,U]

en route /ɒn ˈruːt $ ˌɑːn-/ adv on the way: [+to/from] a flight en route to Moscow

ensconce /ɪnˈskɒns $ ɪnˈskɑːns/ v [T] to settle yourself in a place where you feel safe or comfortable: [+at/in/on etc] Martha was **firmly ensconced** at the bar.

ensemble /ɒnˈsɒmbəl $ ɑːnˈsɑːm-/ n [C] **1** BrE a small group of musicians, actors etc who perform together **2** a set of things that belong together

enshrine /ɪnˈʃraɪn/ v [T] formal if a right, power etc is enshrined, it is protected by law: [+in] These rights are enshrined in the Constitution.

enslave /ɪnˈsleɪv/ v [T] formal **1** to trap someone in a situation from which they cannot escape **2** to make someone a slave

ensue /ɪnˈsjuː $ ɪnˈsuː/ v [I] formal to happen after or as a result of something: A long silence ensued. —**ensuing** adj [only before noun]

en suite /ɒn ˈswiːt $ ɑːn-/ adj BrE an en suite bathroom is joined onto a bedroom —**en suite** n [C]: The main bedroom has an en suite.

ensure Ac especially BrE, **insure** AmE /ɪnˈʃʊə $ -ˈʃʊr/ v [T] to make certain that something happens or is done: [+(that)] Ensure that the fire doors are kept clear.

entail /ɪnˈteɪl/ v [T] formal to involve something or

make it necessary: Does your job entail much travelling?

entangle /ɪnˈtæŋgəl/ v [T] **1** to make something become caught or twisted in a net, rope etc: [+in/with] a fish **got entangled** with the line **2** to involve someone in a situation that is difficult to get away from: [+in/with] Jay became romantically entangled with her boss. —**entanglement** n [C,U]

enter /ˈentə $ -ər/ v
1 **PLACE** [I,T] to go or come into a place → **entrance**, **entry**: Everyone stopped talking when he entered. | No one is allowed to enter the building. | We entered the city late at night.
2 **PROFESSION** [T] to start working in a particular job: He entered politics in 1990.
3 **SITUATION/WAR** [T] to start to become involved in something: America entered the war in 1917.
4 **COMPETITION/EXAMINATION** [I,T] to arrange to take part in a competition or examination, or to arrange for someone to do this: She entered the competition and won. | **enter (sb) for sth** He was entered for a talent contest.
5 **INFORMATION** [T] to put information onto a document or into a computer: **enter sth in/on etc sth** Enter your name on the form. | Enter your password. **THESAURUS** WRITE
6 **PERIOD OF TIME** [T] to begin a period of time: The talks are now entering their third week.
PHRASAL VERBS
enter into sth
1 **enter into an agreement/contract etc** formal to make an official agreement to do something
2 to become involved in something: Both sides must enter into negotiations.
3 to affect a situation: It was pure skill – luck didn't enter into it at all.

THESAURUS

enter to go or come into a place: The burglars entered the house through a back window.

go in/into sth to enter a place. Go in/into is less formal than enter and is more common in everyday English: I went in and looked around. | The two men went into the hotel.

come in/into sth to enter a place – used when you are already in that place: Come in and sit down. | When you come into the village, the church is on your right.

get in/into sth to enter a place, especially when it is difficult. You also use **get in/into** about going into a car: I can't get in! The door's locked. | Julian got into the car beside her.

break in/into sth to enter a building using force, especially in order to steal something: If anyone tries to break in, the alarm will go off.

burst in/into sth to enter a room or building very suddenly and noisily: The men burst in and started shouting.

Word Choice: enter or join?

You say that someone **enters** a particular type of work, for example politics, teaching, or the legal profession.

You usually say that someone **joins** a company or organization: She joined the company last year.

Enter is less common and more formal in this meaning.

enterprise /'entəpraız $ -tər-/ n **1** [C] a company or business: *a small family-run enterprise* **2** [C] a large and complicated project: *The film festival is a huge enterprise.* **3** [U] the ability to think of new ideas and make them work, especially in business: *a spirit of enterprise and adventure* → FREE ENTERPRISE

enterprising /'entəpraızıŋ $ -tər-/ adj able to think of new ideas and make them work: *an enterprising young student*

entertain /,entə'teın $ -tər-/ v **1** [T] to amuse people by doing something they enjoy watching or listening to: **entertain sb with sth** *A magician entertained the children with tricks.* **2** [I,T] to invite people to have food and drink with you: *I often have to entertain clients.* **3** [T] *formal* to consider an idea: *He would never entertain the thought of divorce.*

entertainer /,entə'teınə $ -tər'teınər/ n [C] someone whose job is to tell jokes, sing etc in order to entertain people

entertaining /,entə'teınıŋ◄ $ -tər-/ adj interesting and enjoyable: *an entertaining evening* | *an entertaining game*

entertainment /,entə'teınmənt $ -tər-/ n [C,U] things such as television, films, and shows that are intended to amuse or interest people: *The hotel offers* **live entertainment.** | *Many resorts have entertainments for children.* | **the entertainment industry/business/world**

enthral *BrE*, **enthrall** *AmE* /ın'θrɔːl $ -'θrɔːl/ v [T] (**enthralled**, **enthralling**) if something enthrals you, it makes you feel very interested or excited: *The audience was enthralled by his performance.* —**enthralling** *adj*

enthuse /ın'θjuːz $ ın'θuːz/ v [I] to talk about something in a very excited way: **[+about/over]** *She enthused about the beauty of Lake Garda.*

enthusiasm /ın'θjuːziæzəm $ ın'θuː-/ n [U] a strong feeling of interest and enjoyment: **[+for]** *She* **shares** *your* **enthusiasm** *for jazz.* | *He welcomed us* **with great enthusiasm.** —**enthusiast** *n* [C]

enthusiastic /ın,θjuːzi'æstık◄ $ ın,θuː-/ adj interested and excited: **enthusiastic about (doing) sth** *Everyone was very enthusiastic about the project.* | *She wasn't very enthusiastic about going to London.* | *an enthusiastic crowd* —**enthusiastically** /-klı/ adv

entice /ın'taıs/ v [T] to persuade someone to do something by offering them something nice: **entice sb into/away from etc** *Good window displays entice customers into the store.* —**enticing** adj: *an enticing menu*

entire /ın'taıə $ -'taır/ adj [only before noun] used to emphasize that you mean all of something: *It was the best day of my entire life.* | *The hurricane destroyed entire villages.*

entirely /ın'taıəli $ -'taır-/ adv completely: *an entirely different way of life* | *I'm not entirely convinced about it.* | *The charity depends entirely on donations.*

entirety /ın'taıərəti $ -'taır-/ n **in its/their entirety** *formal* including every part: *The film will be shown in its entirety.*

entitle /ın'taıtl/ v [T] **1** to give someone the right to have or do something: **be entitled to (do) sth** *Employees are entitled to free health insurance.* | *You are not entitled to be here.* | **entitle sb to sth** *a voucher which entitles you to free membership of the club* **2 be entitled sth** if a book, play etc is entitled something, that is its name: *a poem entitled 'Pride of Youth'* —**entitlement** *n* [C,U]

entity Ac /'entəti/ n [C] (*plural* **entities**) *formal* something that exists as a single and complete unit: *The two stores are run as* **separate entities.**

entourage /'ɒntʊrɑːʒ $ 'ɑːn-/ n [C] a group of people who travel with an important person: *the president and his entourage*

entrance /'entrəns/ n
1 [C] a door or gate that you go through to enter a place OPP **exit** → **entry**: **[+to/of]** *the entrance to the tower* | *the school's* **main entrance** | *the hotel entrance* | **front/back/side entrance** *We got in through the back entrance.*
2 [U] the right to go into a place or join an organization, college etc: **[+to]** *Entrance to the museum is free.* | *There's a $30* **entrance fee** (=money you pay to get in somewhere). | *the qualifications required for university entrance*
3 [C usually singular] when someone enters a place: *Jane* **made** *a dramatic* **entrance.**

entranced /ın'trɑːnst $ -'trænst/ adj giving all your attention to something or someone because they are so beautiful or interesting: *She listened, entranced.*

entrant /'entrənt/ n [C] *formal* someone who enters a competition, organization, profession, or examination: **[+to]** *new entrants to teaching*

entreat /ın'triːt/ v [T] *formal* to ask someone for something in an emotional way SYN **beg**

entrée /'ɒntreı $ 'ɑːn-/ n [C] *AmE* the main part of a formal meal SYN **main course** *BrE*

entrenched /ın'trentʃt/ adj entrenched ideas have existed for a long time and are not likely to change

entrepreneur /,ɒntrəprə'nɜː $,ɑːntrəprə'nɜːr/ n [C] someone who starts a new business —**entrepreneurial** adj

entrust /ın'trʌst/ v [T] to make someone responsible for something: **entrust sb with sth** *I was entrusted with the task of looking after the money.* | **entrust sth to sb** *The design of the new building was entrusted to a young architect.*

entry /'entri/ n (*plural* **entries**)
1 INTO A PLACE [C,U] when someone goes into a place OPP **exit**: **[+to/into]** *Entry to the gardens is free.* | *How did the thieves* **gain entry** (=get in)? | *Refugees were* **refused entry** (=they were not allowed in) *to the country.* | *They were charged with illegal entry.*
2 INTO AN ORGANIZATION [U] when someone joins an organization, college etc: **[+into/to]** *Britain's entry into the European Union* | *the entry requirements for a university course*
3 FOR A COMPETITION [C] something you make or

write in order to try to win a competition: *The closing date for entries is January 6.* | *the **winning entry*** **4 IN A BOOK** [C] a short piece of writing in a book containing information: *an entry in his diary* | *a dictionary entry*

5 ON A COMPUTER [U] the process of putting information into a computer: *data entry*

6 DOOR [C] a door or gate that you go through to enter a place → **RE-ENTRY**

entwine /ɪn'twaɪn/ v [I,T] **1** to twist one thing around another thing **2 be entwined** to be closely related in a complicated way: *Physical and mental health are closely entwined.*

enumerate /ɪ'njuːməreɪt $ ɪ'nuː-/ v [T] *formal* to name all the things on a list

envelop /ɪn'veləp/ v [T] to cover or surround something completely: **be enveloped in sth** *The room was soon enveloped in flames.*

envelope /'envələʊp $ -loʊp/ n [C] a paper cover that you put a letter in before you send it

enviable /'enviəbəl/ *adj* an enviable situation or quality is one that other people would like to have: *The hotel has an enviable position.*

envious /'enviəs/ *adj* wanting something that someone else has: **[+of]** *Tom became increasingly envious of his brother.* → see Word Choice at **JEALOUS**
—**enviously** *adv*

environment Ac /ɪn'vaɪrənmənt/ n [C,U]
1 the environment the land, water, and air that people, animals, and plants live in: *chemicals that are damaging to the environment*
2 the people and things around you that affect your life: *Schools should provide a **safe environment** for children.* | **working/learning environment** *a pleasant working environment*

COLLOCATIONS

verbs
to protect the environment *We have a duty to protect the environment.*
to harm/damage the environment *We use techniques that don't harm the environment.*
⚠ Do not say 'hurt the environment'. Say **harm the environment** or **damage the environment**.
to pollute the environment (=to make it dirty) *They produce chemicals which pollute the environment.*

adjectives
good for the environment *Cycling is better for the environment than driving.*
bad for/harmful to the environment *These activities are harmful to the environment.*

noun + environment
effect/impact on the environment *Some types of farming can have a very bad effect on the environment.*
the destruction of the environment *the destruction of the environment caused by oil exploration*

environmental Ac /ɪnˌvaɪrən'mentl◂/ *adj* relating

to the land, water, and air on Earth: *serious environmental damage* | **environmental issues** | **environmental groups** (=groups who want to protect the environment) —**environmentally** *adv*: *chemicals that are environmentally safe*

environmentalist Ac /ɪnˌvaɪrən'mentəlɪst/ n [C] someone who tries to protect the environment

en,viron,mentally 'friendly *adj* not harmful to the environment: *environmentally friendly products*

envisage /ɪn'vɪzɪdʒ/ (*also* **envision** /-'vɪʒən/) v [T] to think that something will be possible in the future: *I can't envisage moving from here.*

envoy /'envɔɪ/ n [C] someone who is sent to another country as an official representative

envy[1] /'envi/ v [T] (**envied, envying, envies**) to wish you had something that someone else has: *She has a lifestyle most people would envy.* | **envy sb (for) sth** *I envied her her good looks.* | *I **don't envy** you your job.*

envy[2] n [U] **1** the feeling of wanting something that someone else has → **jealousy**: **with envy** *He gazed with envy at the car.* **2 be the envy of** sb to be something that other people admire and want: *Our facilities are the envy of most other schools.*

enzyme /'enzaɪm/ n [C] a chemical that is produced in plants and animals and causes a chemical process to start

ephemeral /ɪ'femərəl/ *adj formal* existing only for a short time

epic[1] /'epɪk/ n [C] a long book, poem, or film with many exciting adventures

epic[2] *adj* long and exciting: *an epic journey*

epidemic /ˌepə'demɪk◂/ n **1** [C] a situation in which a lot of people have a disease: *a flu epidemic* | **[+of]** *an epidemic of cholera* **2** [singular] a sudden increase in something bad: *an epidemic of car crime* —**epidemic** *adj* [only before noun]

epilepsy /'epələpsi/ n [U] a medical condition affecting someone's brain that can make them suddenly unconscious and unable to control their movements —**epileptic** /ˌepə'leptɪk◂/ *adj*: *an epileptic fit* —**epileptic** n [C]

epilogue /'epəlɒg $ -lɔːg, -lɑːg/ n [C] a speech or piece of writing added to the end of a book, film, or play → **prologue**

episode /'epəsəʊd $ -soʊd/ n [C] **1** one of the parts of a television or radio story that is broadcast separately: **[+of]** *He watches every episode of 'Friends'.* **THESAURUS** PART **2** an important event or period of time: *an exciting episode in her career*

epitaph /'epətɑːf $ -tæf/ n [C] a piece of writing on the stone over someone's GRAVE (=place where they are buried)

epitome /ɪ'pɪtəmi/ n **the epitome of sth** a very typical example of something: *She was the epitome of elegance.*

epitomize (*also* **-ise** *BrE*) /ɪ'pɪtəmaɪz/ v [T] to be a typical example of something: *a situation which epitomizes the problems in this industry*

epoch /'iːpɒk $ 'epək/ n [C] a period of history

equal¹ /ˈiːkwəl/ adj
1 the same in size, value, or amount: **equal number/amount (of sth)** *There was an equal number of men and women.* | **of equal importance/value/size etc** *jobs of equal importance* | **[+in]** *two squares equal in size* | **[+to]** *One inch is equal to 2.54 centimetres.*
2 having the same rights and opportunities as everyone else: *Democracy is based on the idea that all people are equal.* | **equal rights/opportunities** *Women do not yet have equal rights at work.*
3 be equal to sth to have the ability to do something successfully: *I'm not sure he's equal to the task.*
4 be equal to sth to be as good as something else: *The architecture here is equal to any in the world.*

equal² v [T] (**equalled, equalling** BrE, **equaled, equaling** AmE) **1** to be the same size, number, or amount as something else: *4 plus 4 equals 8.* **2** to be as good as something or someone else: *Johnson has equalled the Olympic record.*

equal³ n [C] someone or something that is as good as another person or thing and has the same importance or value: *Men and women should be treated as equals.* | **be the equal of sb/sth** (=be as good as someone or something) *a company that's the equal of its US competitors* | **without equal** (=better than anyone or anything else) *Good champagne is without equal.*

equality /ɪˈkwɒləti $ ɪˈkwɑː-/ n [U] when people have the same rights and opportunities **[OPP] inequality**: *the struggle for racial equality* | *They are demanding equality for men and women.* | **[+of]** *equality of opportunity* | **[+between]** *equality between the sexes*

equalize (also **-ise** BrE) /ˈiːkwəlaɪz/ v **1** [T] to make two things the same in size, value etc: *a vote to equalize wages* **2** [I] BrE to get a point in a game so that you have the same number of points as your opponent: *Spain equalized in the 75th minute.*

equally /ˈiːkwəli/ adv
1 to the same level or amount: *Diet and exercise are equally important in maintaining good health.*
2 in equal parts or amounts: *We divided the money equally.*
3 spoken used when you are saying something that is just as important as what you have just said: *There was no enthusiasm for the idea, but equally there was no opposition.*
4 in a way that is fair because it is the same for everyone: *We tried to treat everyone equally.*

'equals sign BrE, **'equal sign** AmE n [C] the sign (=) that you use in mathematics to show that two numbers, amounts etc are the same

equanimity /ˌiːkwəˈnɪməti, ˌekwə-/ n [U] formal calmness in the way you react to things

equate [Ac] /ɪˈkweɪt/ v [T] formal to consider that two things are similar or related: **equate sth with sth** *Most people equate wealth with success.*

equation [Ac] /ɪˈkweɪʒən/ n [C] a statement in mathematics showing that two amounts are equal: *In the equation 2y + 4 = 10, what is y?*

equator /ɪˈkweɪtə $ -ər/ n **the equator** the imaginary line around the Earth that is exactly the same distance from the North Pole and the South Pole → see picture at **GLOBE**

equestrian /ɪˈkwestriən/ adj relating to horse-riding

equilateral triangle /ˌiːkwɪˈlætərəl ˈtraɪæŋɡəl/ n [C] technical a TRIANGLE whose three sides are all the same length

equilibrium /ˌiːkwəˈlɪbriəm/ n [singular, U] a balance between different things: *The government is anxious not to upset the economic equilibrium.*

equip [Ac] /ɪˈkwɪp/ v [T] (**equipped, equipping**) **1** to provide someone with the tools or equipment they need: **equip sb/sth with sth** *The researchers equipped themselves with cameras.* | **be equipped with sth** *The hotel's rooms are equipped with a TV and telephone.* | **well/fully/poorly etc equipped** *a well equipped hospital* **2** to give someone the information and skills they need: **equip sb with sth** *We equip students with the skills they will need to succeed in life.* | **equip sb for sth** *training that will equip you for the job*

equipment [Ac] /ɪˈkwɪpmənt/ n [U] the things that you need to do a job or sport: *new computer equipment* | *an expensive piece of equipment*

> **Grammar**
> **Equipment** is an uncountable noun. It is not used in the plural. You say *Their equipment is very modern.* (Not 'Their equipments are very modern.')
> When talking about a single thing, you say **a piece of equipment**: *I need to buy a new piece of equipment for my camera.*

equitable /ˈekwətəbəl/ adj formal fair and equal: *equitable treatment of all staff*

equity /ˈekwəti/ n [U] formal when everyone is treated fairly and equally

equivalent¹ [Ac] /ɪˈkwɪvələnt/ adj having the same value or meaning as something else: **[+to]** *a qualification that is equivalent to a degree*

equivalent² [Ac] n [C] something that has the same value or meaning as something else: **[+of]** *He was fined £600 – the equivalent of two weeks' wages.* | *a French word with no English equivalent*

er /ɜː, ə $ ɜːr, ər/ spoken a sound you make when you are not sure what to say next: *Well, er, I don't really know.*

-er /ə $ ər/ suffix someone who does something: *a footballer* | *bad drivers*

ER /ˌiː ˈɑː $ -ˈɑːr/ n [C] AmE the abbreviation of **emergency room**

era /ˈɪərə $ ˈɪrə/ n [C] a period of time in history: *the post-war era* | **[+of]** *a new era of peace* **THESAURUS** ▶ **PERIOD**

eradicate /ɪˈrædɪkeɪt/ v [T] to get rid of something such as a disease or social problem: *attempts to eradicate poverty* —**eradication** /ɪˌrædɪˈkeɪʃən/ n [U]

erase /ɪˈreɪz $ ɪˈreɪs/ v [T] **1** to remove written or recorded information: *Some of the names had been erased.* **THESAURUS** ▶ **REMOVE 2** to get rid of a memory or feeling: *He wanted to erase the memory of their last meeting.*

E

eraser /ɪ'reɪzə $ -sər/ n [C] a piece of rubber used for removing pencil marks from paper SYN **rubber** BrE → see picture at STATIONERY

erect¹ /ɪ'rekt/ v [T] formal to build something, or put it in an upright position: The church was erected in 1121. | The police erected barriers. THESAURUS BUILD

erect² adj in a straight upright position: He stood erect.

erection /ɪ'rekʃən/ n **1** [C] if a man has an erection, his PENIS becomes stiff and upright because he is sexually excited **2** [U] when something is built or put in an upright position: **[+of]** the erection of a fence

ergonomics /ˌɜːɡə'nɒmɪks $ ˌɜːrɡə'nɑː-/ n [U] the way in which the careful design of equipment helps people to work better and more quickly —**ergonomic** adj: a new ergonomic design —**ergonomically** /-kli/ adv

erode Ac /ɪ'rəʊd $ ɪ'roʊd/ v [I,T] **1** if the weather or sea erodes land or rocks, it gradually destroys them: The coastline is being eroded. **2** to gradually reduce someone's power or confidence: Their political rights have been eroded. —**erosion** /ɪ'rəʊʒən $ ɪ'roʊ-/ n [U]

erotic /ɪ'rɒtɪk $ ɪ'rɑː-/ adj involving sexual excitement: erotic dreams

err /ɜː $ ɜːr/ v [I] **err on the side of caution/ generosity etc** to be more careful, generous etc than is necessary, in order to make sure nothing bad happens

errand /'erənd/ n [C] a short trip to do something for someone: She's **running an errand** for me.

errant /'erənt/ adj [only before noun] formal behaving badly: his errant father

erratic /ɪ'rætɪk/ adj changing often, or not following a regular pattern: erratic behavior —**erratically** /-kli/ adv

erroneous Ac /ɪ'rəʊniəs $ ɪ'roʊ-/ adj formal not correct: erroneous beliefs

error Ac /'erə $ 'erər/ n [C,U] a mistake: **[+in]** an error in our calculations | Police admitted they had **made** several **errors**. | a serious **error of judgment** | **in error** (=because of a mistake) The letter was opened in error. | an accident caused by **human error** (=a mistake by a person) | a computer **error message** (=message telling you the program cannot do what you want) THESAURUS MISTAKE

erstwhile /'ɜːstwaɪl $ 'ɜːrst-/ adj [only before noun] formal former: his erstwhile friend

erupt /ɪ'rʌpt/ v [I] **1** if a fight or argument erupts, it starts suddenly: A political row has erupted. **2** if a VOLCANO erupts, smoke, fire, and rock come out of it **3** if a place erupts, the people there suddenly become very angry or excited: The stadium erupted when England scored. —**eruption** /ɪ'rʌpʃən/ n [C,U]: a volcanic eruption

escalate /'eskəleɪt/ v [I,T] **1** if an argument or fight escalates, or if someone escalates it, it quickly becomes worse: Fighting has escalated in the area. | **[+into]** a dispute which has escalated into violence **2** to increase, or make something increase: Costs

have escalated. —**escalation** /ˌeskə'leɪʃən/ n [C,U]

escalator /'eskəleɪtə $ -ər/ n [C] moving stairs that take people from one level of a building to another

ESCALATOR

escapade /'eskəpeɪd/ n [C] an exciting adventure

escape¹ /ɪ'skeɪp/ v
1 [I,T] to leave a place or dangerous situation when someone is trying to catch you or stop you: **[+from/through etc]** He escaped from prison. | **[+with]** She escaped with minor injuries. | **escape unhurt/unharmed**
2 [I,T] to avoid something bad: **escape death/injury** The driver narrowly escaped death. | Schools have not escaped criticism.
3 [T] if something escapes you, you cannot remember it or do not notice it: Her name escapes me. | **escape sb's notice/attention** His behaviour did not escape the notice of police.
4 [I] if gas or liquid escapes from somewhere, it comes out —**escaped** adj: escaped prisoners

THESAURUS

escape to leave a place or dangerous situation when someone is trying to catch you or stop you: The prisoners escaped while the guards were sleeping. | He escaped from his attackers.
get away to escape from someone who is chasing you. **Get away** is more informal than **escape**: A police officer ran after him but he got away.
get out to leave a building or room which is locked, or when the way out is blocked: Make sure you know how to get out of the building if there is a fire.
flee written to leave a dangerous place very quickly, especially a country: Many Jewish people fled to America.

escape² n
1 [C,U] when someone gets away from a place or situation: **[+from]** Passengers talked about their escape from the wreckage. | She tried to **make** her **escape**. | The couple **had a lucky escape** (=were lucky not to be hurt or killed) when their car hit a tree. | the firm's **narrow escape** from bankruptcy
2 [singular, U] a way to forget about your life and problems for a short time: **[+from]** a welcome escape from the pressures of work → FIRE ESCAPE

escapee /ˌeskeɪ'piː, ɪˌskeɪ'piː/ n [C] someone who has escaped

escapism /ɪ'skeɪpɪzəm/ n [U] activities or entertainment that help you forget about your life and problems for a short time: Books were a form of escapism for him. —**escapist** adj

escort¹ /ɪ'skɔːt $ -ɔːrt/ v [T] to take someone somewhere, especially in order to protect or guard them: **escort sb back/into etc sth** Armed guards

escorted the prisoners into the courthouse.
THESAURUS TAKE

escort² /'eskɔːt $ -ɔːrt/ n **1** [C,U] a person or group of people who go with someone in order to protect or guard them: *He was given a **police escort**.* | **under escort** *He was taken to prison under armed escort.* **2** [C] someone who goes with another person to a formal social event

Eskimo /'eskəməʊ $ -moʊ/ n [C] (plural **Eskimo** or **Eskimos**) old-fashioned an INUIT. Many people now consider this word offensive.

ESL /ˌiː es 'el/ n [U] (**English as a Second Language**) teaching English to students who are living in an English-speaking country, but whose first language is not English

esoteric /ˌesə'terɪk◂, ˌiːsə-/ adj known or understood by only a few people who have special knowledge

ESP /ˌiː es 'piː/ n [U] (**English for Specific/Special Purposes**) the teaching of English to business people, scientists etc whose first language is not English

esp. the written abbreviation of **especially**

especially /ɪ'speʃəli/ adv
1 used when something concerns one situation, person, thing etc more than others: *The town is very busy, especially in summer.* | *I like all the boys but especially Jake.*
2 for one particular person or reason: **[+for]** *He played that song especially for me.* | *She bought new clothes especially for the trip.*
PHRASES
not especially not very: *The hotel isn't especially nice.*

espionage /'espiənɑːʒ/ n [U] the activity of finding out secret information and giving it to a country's enemies or a company's competitors **SYN** spying

espouse /ɪ'spaʊz/ v [T] formal to support an idea or belief

espresso /e'spresəʊ, ɪ'spre- $ -soʊ/ n [C,U] (plural **espressos**) strong black Italian coffee

essay /'eseɪ/ n [C] a piece of writing that discusses a subject: **[+on/about]** *He wrote an essay on French politics.* → see Word Choice at **ASSIGNMENT**

COLLOCATIONS

verbs

to write/do an essay *The students were asked to write an essay on their favourite poet.*
to give in/hand in an essay *I want you to hand in your essays on Friday.*
to mark an essay BrE, **to grade an essay** AmE *She had a pile of essays to mark.*

types of essay

an English/history/politics etc essay *He got a good grade for his English essay.*
a school essay *I used to make lots of spelling mistakes in my school essays.*

essence /'esəns/ n **1** [singular, U] the most basic and important part of something: **[+of]** *The essence of his argument is simple.* | **in essence** (=basically) *In essence, we have three choices.* **2** [C,U] a liquid obtained from a flower or plant, that is used in cooking to give a particular flavour to food: *vanilla essence*

essential /ɪ'senʃəl/ adj
1 important and necessary: **[+for/to]** *A balanced diet is essential for good health.* | **It is essential that** *we make a decision soon.* | **it is essential to do sth** *It is essential to book tickets early.* **THESAURUS** NECESSARY
2 most important or basic: *The essential difference between them is their size.*

essentially /ɪ'senʃəli/ adv used when giving the most basic fact about something: *It is essentially an old-fashioned romance story.*

es,sential 'oil n [C] an oil from a plant

essentials /ɪ'senʃəlz/ n [plural] things that are important and necessary: *They almost ran out of food and other essentials.*

establish Ac /ɪ'stæblɪʃ/ v [T]
1 to start a company, organization, or system: *Our goal is to establish a new research center.* | *The company was established in 1974.*
2 establish relations/contacts/links etc to start a relationship with another organization, country etc: *Many businesses have established links with local schools.*
3 to discover facts which prove something: *We have been unable to establish the cause of the fire.* | **[+whether/what etc]** *Detectives are trying to establish whether the crimes are related.* | **[+that]** *We have established that the disease is caused by a virus.*
4 to make people accept that you are good at doing something: *She has **established** a **reputation** in the fashion industry.* | **establish sb/sth as sth** *He has already established himself as a top chef.*
—**established** adj

establishment Ac /ɪ'stæblɪʃmənt/ n **1** [C] formal an institution, organization, or business: *a research establishment* **2 the Establishment** the people in a society or profession who have a lot of power and do not like new ideas: *a scandal that shocked the Establishment* | **the medical/military/religious etc establishment 3** [U] when someone starts an organization, relationship, or system: **[+of]** *the establishment of NATO*

estate Ac /ɪ'steɪt/ n [C] **1** a large area of land in the countryside that is owned by one person **2** BrE an area where a lot of houses or other buildings have been built: *a housing estate* | *an industrial estate* **3** all the property and money that someone leaves when they die **4** an estate car

es'tate ,agent n [C] BrE someone whose job is to buy and sell houses and land for people **SYN** real estate agent, Realtor AmE

es'tate car n [C] BrE a large car with a door at the back and a lot of space behind the back seats for bags etc **SYN** station wagon AmE

esteem¹ /ɪ'stiːm/ n [U] formal respect and admiration for someone: *She was **held in high esteem**.*

esteem² v [T] formal to respect and admire someone: *He was **highly esteemed** as a philosopher.*

esthetic /i:s'θetɪk $ es-/ adj an American spelling of AESTHETIC

estimate¹ Ac /'estɪmeɪt/ v [T] to decide what you think the value, size etc of something is, partly by guessing and partly by calculating: **[+that]** We estimate that 75% of our customers are teenagers. | **estimate sth at sth** The cost has been estimated at $1,500. —**estimated** adj: An estimated 10,000 people took part in the demonstration.

estimate² Ac /'estəmət/ n [C]
1 what you think the value, size etc of something is, after calculating it quickly: According to some estimates, two-thirds of the city was destroyed. | At **a rough estimate**, I'd say it's 300 years old.
2 a statement of how much it will probably cost to build or repair something: I got three estimates.

estimation Ac /,estə'meɪʃən/ n [U] someone's judgment or opinion: Philip has really **gone down in my estimation** (=I respect him less).

estranged /ɪ'streɪndʒd/ adj formal **1** no longer living with your husband or wife **2** no longer communicating with your family or friends because of an argument: **[+from]** He was estranged from his family. —**estrangement** n [C,U]

estrogen /'i:strədʒən $ 'es-/ n the American spelling of OESTROGEN

estuary /'estʃuəri, -tʃəri $ -tʃueri/ n [C] (plural **estuaries**) where a river joins the sea

etc. /et 'setərə/ adv (**et cetera**) used after a list to show that there are other similar things or people that you could add: information in the form of books, leaflets, videos etc.

etch /etʃ/ v [I,T] to make lines or patterns on metal, glass, or stone, using tools or chemicals
PHRASES
  be etched in/on sb's memory/mind to be impossible to forget: Every detail is etched in my memory.

eternal /ɪ'tɜ:nəl $ -ɜ:r-/ adj continuing for always: the hope of **eternal** life —**eternally** adv

eternity /ɪ'tɜ:nəti $ -ɜ:r-/ n **1** [U] time that continues for always **2** an eternity informal a very long time: We waited for **what seemed like an eternity**.

ethereal /ɪ'θɪəriəl $ ɪ'θɪr-/ adj delicate, and not seeming real: ethereal beauty —**ethereally** adv

ethic Ac /'eθɪk/ n [C] **1** a belief that influences people's behaviour: He had a strong **work ethic** (=belief that work is important). **2** ethics [plural] ideas or rules about what is morally right and wrong: the **medical ethics** committee **3** the ethics of (doing) sth whether or not something is morally right: a discussion on the ethics of capital punishment

ethical Ac /'eθɪkəl/ adj **1** connected with principles of what is right and wrong: **ethical issues/questions/problems 2** morally good and correct: It would not be ethical to lie to them. —**ethically** /-kli/ adv

ethnic Ac /'eθnɪk/ adj relating to a particular race of people: an **ethnic minority**

ethnic 'cleansing n [U] when people from a particular ethnic group are forced to leave an area

ethnicity /eθ'nɪsəti/ n [U] the fact that someone belongs to a particular race of people

ethos /'i:θɒs $ 'i:θɑ:s/ n [singular] the moral attitudes within a group or institution: The **whole ethos** of our society has changed.

etiquette /'etɪket $ -kət/ n [U] the rules of polite behaviour

etymology /,etə'mɒlədʒi $ -'mɑ:-/ n [U] the study of the origins and changing meanings of words —**etymological** /,etəmə'lɒdʒɪkəl◀ $ -'lɑ:-/ adj —**etymologically** /-kli/ adv

EU /,i: 'ju:/ n the EU (**the European Union**) the political and economic organization that most European countries belong to

eulogy /'ju:lədʒi/ n [C,U] (plural **eulogies**) a speech or piece of writing in which you praise someone or something very much

euphemism /'ju:fəmɪzəm/ n [C,U] a word or phrase that is used to avoid saying something shocking or embarrassing —**euphemistic** /ju:fə'mɪstɪk◀/ adj —**euphemistically** /-kli/ adv

euphoria /ju:'fɔ:riə $ ju-/ n [U] extreme happiness and excitement —**euphoric** /-'fɒrɪk $ -'fɔ:-, -'fɑ:-/ adj

euro /'juərəu $ 'jurou/ n [C] (plural **euros**) the unit of money used by most countries in the European Union

Euro- /juərəu $ jurou/ prefix relating to Europe or the EU: the Euro-elections (=elections for the European Parliament)

European¹ /,juərə'pi:ən◀ $,jurə-/ adj relating to Europe or the EU: the European Parliament

European² n [C] someone from Europe

European 'Union n the EU

euthanasia /,ju:θə'neɪziə $ -'neɪʒə/ n [U] when someone is helped to die because they are suffering

evacuate /ɪ'vækjueɪt/ v [T] to move people to a safer place —**evacuation** /ɪ,vækju'eɪʃən/ n [C,U]

evacuee /ɪ,vækju'i:/ n [C] someone who was evacuated during a war

evade /ɪ'veɪd/ v [T] **1** to avoid doing something you should do, or avoid talking about something: She evaded my question. **THESAURUS** ▶ AVOID **2** to escape from someone who is trying to catch you: He evaded capture.

evaluate Ac /ɪ'væljueɪt/ v [T] formal to judge how good, useful, or successful something is **SYN** assess: Teachers meet regularly to evaluate students' progress. —**evaluation** /ɪ,vælju'eɪʃən/ n [C,U]

evangelical /,i:væn'dʒelɪkəl◀/ adj **1** evangelical Christians believe that they must tell people about Christ **2** very keen to share your beliefs or ideas —**evangelical** n [C]

evaporate /ɪ'væpəreɪt/ v **1** [I,T] if a liquid evaporates, it changes into a gas: The **water** had **evaporated**. **2** [I] if a feeling evaporates, it disappears: His fears evaporated. —**evaporation** /ɪ,væpə'reɪʃən/ n [U]

evasion /ɪ'veɪʒən/ n [C,U] when you avoid doing something: **tax evasion**

evasive /ɪˈveɪsɪv/ *adj* trying to avoid doing something or saying something: *an evasive answer* —**evasively** *adv* —**evasiveness** *n* [U]

eve /iːv/ *n* **on the eve of sth** just before the day when something important happens: *Speaking on the eve of the match, he sounded confident.*

even¹ /ˈiːvən/ *adv*
1 used to emphasize something that is surprising or unexpected: *Even the youngest children enjoyed the concert.* | **not/never** *I don't even know what he looks like.* | *He never even sent me a card.* | **may/might even** *He might even agree.*
2 even bigger/better/more etc used to emphasize that something is bigger, better etc: *If you could finish it today, that would be even better.* | *She knows even less about it than I do.*
3 used to add a word which is stronger or more exact: *He was surprised, even a little disappointed.*
PHRASES
even if/when/after used to emphasize that something will not or did not change a situation: *I'll never speak to her again, even if she apologizes.* | *Even when he found her, he couldn't stop crying.*
even now/then in spite of what happened: *Even now I find it hard to believe he lied.*
even so in spite of this: *They made more money that year, but even so the business failed.*
even though although: *She wouldn't go, even though Tom offered to take her.*

even² *adj* **1** flat, level, or smooth OPP **uneven**: *You need an even surface to work on.* | *He has lovely even teeth.* THESAURUS ▶ FLAT **2** an even rate or temperature does not change much: *an even body temperature* **3** involving equal amounts or numbers: *an even distribution of wealth* | *They have an even chance of winning.* **4** even numbers can be divided exactly by two OPP **odd** → **break even** at BREAK¹, **on an even keel** at KEEL¹
PHRASES
get even (with sb) *informal* to harm someone as much as they have harmed you: *I'll get even with you one day!*

even³ *v*
PHRASAL VERBS
even out if differences even out, or if you even them out, they become less: **even sth ↔ out** *Things seem to have evened themselves out a bit.*

evening /ˈiːvnɪŋ/ *n* [C,U] the end of the day and the early part of the night: *We visited them one evening.* | *I'll see you this evening.* | **on Monday etc evening(s)** *especially BrE*: *I have a class on Thursday evenings.* | **Monday etc evening(s)** *especially AmE*: *He was interviewed Friday evening.* | **in the evening(s)** *In the evenings it was very cold.* | *We spent a very pleasant evening with them.* | **evening class/paper/meal** *We had just finished our evening meal.*
PHRASES
(good) evening *spoken* used to greet someone when you meet them in the evening: *Evening, Rick.*

Grammar
Do not say 'On the evening, I watched TV.' Say *In the evening, I watched TV.*

You use **on** when talking about a particular evening: *She'll be back on Thursday evening.* | *He was out on the evening when the robbery happened.*

ˈevening dress *n* **1** [U] formal clothes that people wear for formal social events in the evening **2** (*also* **evening gown**) [C] a formal dress that a woman wears to a formal social event in the evening

evenly /ˈiːvnli/ *adv* **1** in an equal way: *a more evenly distributed workload* | *The Senate is split evenly between the two parties.* **2** in a regular or steady way: *He was breathing more evenly.* **3 evenly matched** having an equal chance of winning: *The two teams are very evenly matched.*

event /ɪˈvent/ *n* [C]
1 something that happens, especially something important, interesting, or unusual: *The opening of the factory was a **major event** locally.* | *Police are trying to work out the **sequence of events**.* | *They were not happy about the **course of events** (=the way things happened).* | *Her **version of events** (=what she said happened) was completely different.*
2 a performance, competition, party etc that has been arranged for a particular date or time: *The next event will be the 100 metres.* | **social/sporting event** *The biggest social event of the year.* → NON-EVENT
PHRASES
in any/either event (*also* **at all events**) whatever happens: *In any event, it's likely prices will rise.*
in the event used when saying what actually happened, especially when you expected something else: *In the event we didn't have to wait long for the results.*
in the event of sth *formal* if a particular thing happens: *Britain agreed to support the US in the event of war.*
in the normal course of events used to say what would usually happen: *In the normal course of events, she would not agree.*

eventful /ɪˈventfəl/ *adj* full of interesting or important events: *an eventful life*

eventual Ac /ɪˈventʃuəl/ *adj* [only before noun] happening after a long time: *the eventual outcome* | *the eventual winner*

eventuality Ac /ɪˌventʃuˈæləti/ *n* [C] (*plural* **eventualities**) *formal* something that might happen, especially something bad: *We must **prepare for** any eventuality.*

eventually Ac /ɪˈventʃuəli, -tʃəli/ *adv* after a long time: *Eventually he got a job.* THESAURUS ▶ FINALLY

ever /ˈevə $ ˈevər/ *adv*
1 at any time – used mainly in questions and negative sentences: *Have you ever eaten snails?* | *Nothing ever makes Paula angry.* | *If you're ever in London, give us a call.* | **the best/biggest etc ever** *That was the best meal I've ever had.* | *They **hardly ever** (=almost never) watch TV.* | *She **never ever** forgot him.*
THESAURUS ▶ RARELY

Grammar
Do not say 'I have ever been to London.' Say *I have been to London before.*

2 hotter/thinner/better etc than ever even hotter

etc than before: *I woke up the following morning feeling worse than ever.*

3 always or continuously: *Ever optimistic, I kept trying.* | *He joined the firm in 1980, and has been here* **ever since** (=continuously since then). | **ever-growing/ever-increasing etc** (=continuing to grow, increase etc) *the ever-growing population* | *Joe was late,* **as ever** (=like always). | **as popular/bad/happy etc as ever** *She was looking as cheerful as ever.* | *His name will live* **forever** (=always in the future).

PHRASES

ever so/ever such a *BrE spoken* used to emphasize what you are saying: *It's ever so cold in here.* | *He's ever such a nice man.*

evergreen /'evəgriːn $ -ər-/ *adj* an evergreen tree has leaves that do not fall off in winter → **deciduous** —**evergreen** *n* [C]

everlasting /ˌevəˈlɑːstɪŋ◄ $ ˌevərˈlæ-/ *adj* continuing for ever: *everlasting peace*

evermore /ˌevəˈmɔː $ ˌevərˈmɔːr/ *adv literary* always in the future

every /'evri/ *determiner*

1 each one of a group of people or things: *Every student will take the test.* | **every single/last** (=with nothing or no one missing) *He told Jan every single thing.*

2 used to say how often something happens: **every day/month/year etc** (=on each day, in each month etc) *He goes running every day.* | **Every time** *the phone rang, she jumped.* | **every few feet/ten yards etc** *Every few yards she stopped.*

3 the greatest possible: *I'll make* **every effort** *to be there.* | *There is* **every chance** *that he will succeed.* → **ALL¹**

PHRASES

every bit as good/important etc used to emphasize that something is as good, important etc as something else: *I dislike him* **every bit as much as** *you do.*

every now and then/every so often sometimes, but not often: *I still see her every now and then.*

THESAURUS SOMETIMES

every other the first, third, fifth etc or the second, fourth, sixth etc: *Water the plants* **every other day**.

every which way *informal* in every direction: *People were running every which way.*

one in every hundred/two in every thousand etc used to show how common something is: *a disease that will kill one in every thousand babies*

Grammar
Every is followed by a singular verb. You say *Almost every house has a computer nowadays.* (Not 'Every house have a computer.')

everybody /'evribɒdi, -bədi $ -bɑːdi/ *pron* EVERYONE

everyday /'evrideɪ/ *adj* [only before noun] ordinary, usual, or happening every day: *It's just part of everyday life.* **THESAURUS** NORMAL

everyone /'evriwʌn/ (also **everybody**) *pron* every person: *Is everyone ready to go?* | **Everyone else** *had gone.*

Word Choice: everyone or every one?
Everyone means all of the people in a group: *The new law affects everyone.*
You use **every one** when you want to emphasize that you mean each person or thing in a group: *I've seen every one of his films.*
Everyone and **every one** are both followed by a singular verb.

everyplace /'evripleɪs/ *adv AmE spoken* EVERYWHERE

everything /'evriθɪŋ/ *pron* each thing or all things: *She criticizes everything I do.* | *Is everything all right?* | *Jim does the dishes, but I do* **everything else**.

PHRASES

and everything *spoken* used instead of mentioning other things: *He's a nice guy and everything, but not very bright.*

be/mean everything (to sb) to be more important than anything else: *Money isn't everything.*

everywhere /'evriweə $ -wer/ *adv*

1 in or to every place: *I've looked* **everywhere else**.

2 be everywhere to be very common: *Internet cafes are everywhere.*

evict /ɪ'vɪkt/ *v* [T] to force someone to leave their home, for example because they have not paid rent —**eviction** /ɪ'vɪkʃən/ *n* [C,U]

evidence¹ Ac /'evɪdəns/ *n* [U]

1 facts or signs that show that something is true or that something exists: [**+of**] *You must be able to provide evidence of your ability.* | [**+that**] *Do you have any evidence that this treatment works?* | [**+for**] *There is no evidence for these claims.*

2 facts given or objects shown in a court of law in order to prove that someone is guilty or not guilty: [**+against**] *There was very little evidence against him.*

PHRASES

be in evidence *formal* to be easily seen or noticed: *Armed police were much in evidence at the airport.*

give evidence to tell a court what you know about a case: *He refused to give evidence at the trial.*

Grammar
Evidence is an uncountable noun. It is not used in the plural. You say *There was a lot of evidence against him.* (Not 'There were a lot of evidences.')
When talking about a single thing, you say **a piece of evidence**: *The knife was an important piece of evidence in the trial.*

COLLOCATIONS

verbs

to have evidence *The police did not have enough evidence to charge him.*

to look for/search for evidence *Scientists have been searching for evidence about the origins of the universe.*

to find/get evidence *They found evidence of a plot to kill the president.*

to consider/examine/study the evidence *Having considered all the evidence, the court found him not guilty.*

adjectives

scientific/medical/historical evidence *There is no scientific evidence that the vitamin prevents cancer.*

good/clear/strong evidence *There is no clear evidence that they ever met.*

hard/solid evidence (=very clear and reliable evidence) *They think that he is guilty, but they don't have any hard evidence.*

new/fresh evidence *His lawyers say that they have found fresh evidence that he is innocent.*

noun + evidence

a piece of evidence *A vital piece of evidence was missing.*

evidence² v formal **be evidenced by/in sth** to be shown or proven by something

evident Ac /ˈevɪdənt/ adj formal easily noticed SYN **clear, obvious**: *It was evident that they were not satisfied.* | *Her deafness became evident when she was 12.*

evidently Ac /ˈevədəntli $ -dənt-, -dent-/ adv **1** used to say that something is true and can easily be noticed SYN **clearly, obviously**: *The President was evidently unwell.* **2** used to talk about something that you have heard about SYN **apparently**: *He evidently studied hard and was popular.*

evil¹ /ˈiːvəl/ adj
1 very bad or harmful, or morally wrong: *his evil deeds* | *an evil dictator*
2 connected with the devil: *evil spirits*
3 very unpleasant: *an evil smell*

evil² n [C,U] something that is very bad or harmful, or that is morally wrong: **[+of]** *the evils of racism* | *They chose the lesser of two evils* (=the thing which seemed less bad). | *They see the process as a necessary evil.* | *the choice between good and evil*

evocative /ɪˈvɒkətɪv $ ɪˈvɑː-/ adj making you remember or imagine something: **[+of]** *Her novel is wonderfully evocative of village life.*

evoke /ɪˈvəʊk $ ɪˈvoʊk/ v [T] to make someone feel or remember something: *The film evoked memories of my childhood.* —**evocation** /ˌevəˈkeɪʃən, ˌiːvəʊ- $ ˌevə-, ˌiːvoʊ-/ n [C,U]

evolution Ac /ˌiːvəˈluːʃən, ˌevə- $ ˌevə-, ˌiːvoʊ-/ n [U] **1** the gradual development of plants and animals over millions of years: *Darwin's theory of evolution* **2** the gradual development of an idea, situation, or object: **[+of]** *the evolution of computer technology* —**evolutionary** adj

evolve Ac /ɪˈvɒlv $ ɪˈvɑːlv/ v **1** [I,T] to develop, or to make something develop: **[+into]** *Our relationship evolved into a warm friendship.* **2** [I] if animals or plants evolve, they gradually develop over a very long period

ewe /juː/ n [C] a female sheep

ex /eks/ n [C] informal someone who used to be your husband, wife, boyfriend, or girlfriend

ex- /eks/ prefix former: **ex-wife/husband/girlfriend etc** THESAURUS **PREVIOUS**

exacerbate /ɪɡˈzæsəbeɪt $ -sər-/ v [T] to make something worse: *This will only exacerbate the problem.*

exact¹ /ɪɡˈzækt/ adj
1 correct in every detail: *I can remember his exact words.* | *the exact nature of the problem* | *I met her years ago – seven years ago, to be exact.* | **exact date/time/number/amount** *I can't remember the exact date.* | **exact location/position/spot** THESAURUS **RIGHT**
2 used to emphasize that something is the same or precise SYN **very**: *He said the exact same thing.* | *He's the exact opposite of his brother.* | *He arrived at the exact moment I mentioned his name.*
PHRASES

sth is not an exact science used to say that something involves opinions and guessing, rather than definite facts: *Predicting the weather is not an exact science.*

exact² v [T] formal to take something from someone: *The war exacted a heavy price.*

exacting /ɪɡˈzæktɪŋ/ adj needing or demanding a lot of effort or care: *She set herself exacting standards.*

exactly /ɪɡˈzæktli/ adv
1 used to emphasize that something is no more and no less than a number or amount, or is completely correct in every detail: *We got home at exactly six o'clock.* | **exactly what/how/where etc** *I know exactly where she lives.* | **what/how/where etc exactly?** *What exactly is going on?* | *That's exactly right.*
2 used to emphasize that something is the same or different: *They were wearing exactly the same dress.* | *He was exactly the opposite of his brother.* THESAURUS **SAME**
3 spoken used to show that you agree completely with someone: *'We should sell the car.' 'Exactly!'*
PHRASES

not exactly spoken **1** used to reply that something is not completely true: *'Sheila's ill, is she?' 'Not exactly, she's just tired.'* **2** used to say that something is definitely not true SYN **hardly**: *Why's Tim on a diet? He's not exactly fat.*

THESAURUS

exactly used to emphasize that something is no more or no less than a particular number or amount, or is completely correct in every detail: *She weighed exactly 50 kilos.* | *I'm going to tell you exactly what happened.*
precisely exactly – used especially in more formal or technical contexts: *The space rocket was launched at precisely 18:00 hours.*
just used especially when saying that something is exactly right, the same, or the opposite: *This is just the right colour for the room.* | *Everything was just the same as before.*
right especially spoken exactly in a particular position: *The hotel is right in the middle of the town.*
on the dot informal at exactly a particular time, and no earlier or later: *He usually arrives home at 5.30 p.m. on the dot.*

exaggerate /ɪgˈzædʒəreɪt/ v [I,T] to make something seem better, larger, worse etc than it really is: *He says everyone hates him, but he's exaggerating.* | **grossly/wildly exaggerated** *The problems have been grossly/wildly exaggerated.* —**exaggerated** adj: *He gave an exaggerated sigh.* —**exaggeration** /ɪgˌzædʒəˈreɪʃən/ n [C,U]: *It is no exaggeration to say that he saved my life.*

exalted /ɪgˈzɔːltɪd $ -ɔːl-/ adj formal of a very high rank or highly respected: *an exalted position*

exam /ɪgˈzæm/ n [C]
1 an official test of knowledge or ability in a particular subject: *He's taking his exams at the moment.*
THESAURUS ▶ TEST
2 AmE a set of medical tests: *an eye exam*

COLLOCATIONS

verbs

to take/do an exam (*also* **to sit an exam** BrE) *When does she take her exam?* ⚠ Do not say 'make an exam'. Say **take an exam** or **do an exam**.
to pass/fail an exam *He worked hard and passed all his exams.*
to do well/badly in an exam BrE, **to do well/badly on an exam** AmE *She always does well in exams.*
to study for an exam (*also* **revise for an exam** BrE) *I was up late revising for my exams.*

types of exam

a chemistry/French etc exam *I failed my physics exam.*
a written exam *She still has to take a written exam.*
an oral exam (=a spoken exam) *We had our French oral exam yesterday.*
a final exam (=at the end of a course) *We take our final exams at the end of this year.*
an entrance exam (=to enter a school or university) *He passed the school entrance exam.*

exam + noun

exam results *When do you get your exam results?*
an exam paper *You can turn over your exam papers now.*
an exam question *Read the exam questions carefully.*

---

examination /ɪgˌzæməˈneɪʃən/ n
1 [C] formal an official test of knowledge or ability in a particular subject: *The examination results will be announced in September.* | **pass/fail an examination** *He passed all his examinations.* **THESAURUS** ▶ TEST
2 [C] a set of medical tests: *He was given a thorough medical examination.*
3 [C,U] when someone looks at or considers something carefully: **[+of]** *a detailed examination of the data* | *On closer examination, the painting was found to be a forgery.*

examine /ɪgˈzæmɪn/ v [T]
1 to look at something carefully in order to find out more about it: *The doctor examined her ankle.*
2 to consider an idea or plan carefully: *The proposals will be examined in detail.* | **[+how/whether/what]**

This chapter examines how the law actually operates.
3 formal to test someone's knowledge of a subject

examiner /ɪgˈzæmənə $ -ər/ n [C] the person who officially judges how well students perform in an examination

example /ɪgˈzɑːmpəl $ ɪgˈzæm-/ n [C]
1 something that you mention because it is typical of the kind of thing you are talking about: *Let me give you an example.* | **[+of]** *There are plenty of examples of countries that have done this.*
2 someone whose behaviour is good and should be copied, or their behaviour: **[+to]** *She's an example to us all.* | *Parents should* **set** *an* **example** *for their children* (=show them how to behave). | *I suggest you* **follow** *her* **example** (=do what she did).
PHRASES
for example used when you are giving an example to show what you mean: *Food prices have increased greatly. For example, the price of meat has doubled.* | *Many countries, for example Mexico and Japan, have a lot of earthquakes.*
make an example of sb to punish someone so that other people will not do what they did: *I think the judge just wanted to make an example of him.*

exasperated /ɪgˈzɑːspəreɪtɪd $ -ˈzæs-/ adj very annoyed: *I was so exasperated with him.* —**exasperate** v [T] —**exasperation** /ɪgˌzɑːspəˈreɪʃən $ -ˌzæs-/ n [U]

exasperating /ɪgˈzɑːspəreɪtɪŋ $ -ˈzæs-/ adj very annoying

EXCAVATE

excavate

dig

excavate /ˈekskəveɪt/ v [I,T] to dig in the ground, especially in order to find ancient objects —**excavation** /ˌekskəˈveɪʃən/ n [C,U]

exceed Ac /ɪkˈsiːd/ v [T] formal to go beyond a particular amount or level: *The* **cost** *must not* **exceed** *$150.* | *His performance* **exceeded** *our* **expectations.** | *She was fined for* **exceeding** *the speed* **limit.**

exceedingly /ɪkˈsiːdɪŋli/ adv formal extremely: *an exceedingly difficult task*

excel /ɪkˈsel/ v [I] (**excelled, excelling**) formal to do something very well: [**+at/in**] I never excelled at sport.
PHRASES

excel yourself BrE to do something better than you have done it before: The meal was wonderful - you've excelled yourself.

excellent /ˈeksələnt/ adj

1 extremely good or of very high quality: What an excellent idea! **THESAURUS** GOOD

> **Grammar**
> Do not say 'very excellent'. Just say **excellent**.

2 spoken used to show that you approve of something: 'I'll bring them over tonight.' 'Excellent.' —**excellently** adv —**excellence** n [U]: a reputation for excellence in research

except /ɪkˈsept/ linking word, prep

1 not including someone or something: We're open every day except Monday. | [**+for**] Everyone went to the show, except for Scott. | [**+when/where/what etc**] I don't know anything about it, except what I've read. | [**+(that)**] I have earrings just like those, except they're silver.

2 used to give the reason why something did not happen: I would have gone, except we had visitors.

THESAURUS

except not including someone or something: I got all the answers right except the last one.
apart from sth used when mentioning one or two things that are different, especially when they do not change the main part of what you are saying: Apart from the ending, it was a good film. | The weather was good, apart from a couple of cloudy days.
excluding/not including used when the total number or amount does not include something: The bill came to $56, not including service.
but except - used especially after **nothing, no one, everything,** or **everyone**: There was nothing but desert, as far as the eye could see.

---

excepted /ɪkˈseptɪd/ adj formal not included: He doesn't have any interests, politics excepted.

excepting /ɪkˈseptɪŋ/ prep not including **SYN** except: All the students, excepting three or four, spoke fluent English.

exception /ɪkˈsepʃən/ n [C,U] someone or something that is not included in a general statement: [**+to**] There's an **exception** to every **rule**. | **notable/important exception** There was one notable exception. | He was generally rude, and today **was no exception**. | **with the exception of sb/sth** Everyone came to the party, with the exception of Mary. | **without exception** All of his films, without exception, have been a huge success. | We'll **make an exception** in your case (=not include you in a rule).
PHRASES

take exception to sth to be offended by something: He took exception to one of the interviewer's remarks.
the exception that proves the rule the only person

or thing that makes a general statement not completely true: Books seldom make great movies, but this one is the exception that proves the rule.

exceptional /ɪkˈsepʃənəl/ adj **1** unusually good **SYN** **outstanding**: an exceptional student **2** unusual and not likely to happen often: We would do this only **in exceptional circumstances**. **THESAURUS** UNUSUAL —**exceptionally** adv

excerpt /ˈeksɜːpt $ -ɜːrpt/ n [C] a short piece taken from a book, poem, piece of music etc: [**+from**] an excerpt from his poem

excess¹ /ɪkˈses, ˈekses/ n **1** [singular, U] a larger amount of something than is suitable: [**+of**] The problem was caused by an excess of enthusiasm. **2 excesses** [plural] harmful or bad things which people do too much: [**+of**] the **worst excesses** of the rock star's lifestyle
PHRASES

do sth to excess to do something too much: He smoked and drank to excess.
in excess of sth more than an amount or level: Our profits were in excess of $5 million.

excess² /ˈekses/ adj [only before noun] more than is wanted or allowed: He wanted to lose some **excess weight**.

excessive /ɪkˈsesɪv/ adj too much or too great: Avoid **excessive amounts** of coffee. —**excessively** adv

exchange¹ /ɪksˈtʃeɪndʒ/ n

1 [C,U] when you give, send, or say something to someone, and they give, send, or say something to you: [**+of**] Our main aim is to encourage the **exchange of information**. | **exchange of ideas/views** A very frank exchange of views took place. | There was **an exchange of fire** (=both sides were shooting). | **in exchange for sth** The Europeans traded weapons in exchange for gold.

2 [C] a conversation, especially between people who are angry: They had a **heated exchange**.

3 [C] **a)** when you visit another student, usually in another country, and afterwards they visit you **b)** a temporary arrangement in which you have someone else's job or house, while they have your job or house

4 [U] technical money that is changed into money from another country: **foreign exchange**

5 [C] a STOCK EXCHANGE

exchange² v [T] to give, send, or say something to someone who gives, sends, or says something to you: The two armies exchanged prisoners. | **exchange sth for sth** I'd like to exchange this shirt for a smaller one. | **exchange information/ideas/views** a place where people can chat and exchange ideas | **exchange glances/greetings/words etc** The two women exchanged glances and laughed.

exˈchange rate n [C] the value of money from one country compared with money from another country: What's the exchange rate?

excise /ˈeksaɪz/ n [C,U] tax on goods produced and used inside a country

excitable /ɪkˈsaɪtəbəl/ adj becoming excited very easily

excite /ɪkˈsaɪt/ v [T] **1** to make someone feel excited **2** formal to cause a particular feeling or reaction SYN **arouse**: The photographs **excited** great **interest**.

excited /ɪkˈsaɪtɪd/ adj happy, interested, or hopeful because something good has happened or is expected: **[+about]** The kids are **getting** really **excited** about the trip. | **excited to do sth** She was so excited to be home. —**excitedly** adv

excitement /ɪkˈsaɪtmənt/ n [C,U] the feeling of being excited, or a situation in which you are excited: **[+of]** the excitement of her new job | She was flushed with excitement. | **in sb's/the excitement** In his excitement, he had forgotten to switch his camcorder on.

exciting /ɪkˈsaɪtɪŋ/ adj making you feel excited: an exciting discovery | Their trip sounded really exciting.

> **THESAURUS**
>
> **exciting** making you feel excited: New York is one of the world's most exciting cities.
> **thrilling** very exciting and enjoyable: England won a thrilling game against Argentina. | a thrilling adventure
> **gripping** a gripping film, story, game etc is so exciting that you cannot stop watching or reading it: a gripping film about the war in Afghanistan
> **exhilarating** an exhilarating experience makes you feel very excited and full of energy: Skiing down the mountains is an exhilarating experience.
> **dramatic** dramatic events or parts of a story, film etc are very exciting to watch or hear about: the dramatic events on the stock market

exclaim /ɪkˈskleɪm/ v [T] written to suddenly say something loudly, because you are surprised, excited, or angry: 'No!' she exclaimed angrily.

exclamation /ˌekskləˈmeɪʃən/ n [C] something you say suddenly and loudly because you are surprised or angry

excla'mation mark especially BrE (also **excla'mation point** AmE) n [C] the mark (!) that is written after an exclamation

exclude Ac /ɪkˈskluːd/ v [T] **1** to not allow someone to go into a place or take part in something: **exclude sb from (doing) sth** Until 1994 the black population was excluded from voting. **2** to not include something OPP **include**: **exclude sth from sth** We have excluded this data from the report. **3** to decide that something is not possible: Police have **excluded the possibility** that she killed herself.

excluding Ac /ɪkˈskluːdɪŋ/ prep not including: The cost of hiring a car is £180 a week, excluding insurance. THESAURUS EXCEPT

exclusion Ac /ɪkˈskluːʒən/ n [U] when someone is not allowed to go into a place or take part in something OPP **inclusion**: the exclusion of professional athletes from the Olympics

> PHRASES
> **do sth to the exclusion of sth** to do one thing so much that you do not do or think about something

else: She's been studying hard to the exclusion of everything else.

exclusive¹ Ac /ɪkˈskluːsɪv/ adj **1** available to only one person or group, and not shared: an **exclusive interview** with Nelson Mandela | The club has **exclusive use** of the pool during the day. **2** very expensive: an exclusive hotel

> PHRASES
> **exclusive of sth** not including something OPP **inclusive**: The price of the trip is $450, exclusive of meals.

exclusive² n [C] a news story that is only in one newspaper or magazine

exclusively Ac /ɪkˈskluːsɪvli/ adv only: This offer is available exclusively to club members.

excrement /ˈekskrəmənt/ n [U] formal solid waste from a person's or animal's body

excrete /ɪkˈskriːt/ v [I,T] technical to get rid of waste from the body —**excretion** /ɪkˈskriːʃən/ n [C,U]

excruciating /ɪkˈskruːʃieɪtɪŋ/ adj extremely painful: The pain in my knee was excruciating. —**excruciatingly** adv

excursion /ɪkˈskɜːʃən $ ɪkˈskɜːrʒən/ n [C] a short trip for pleasure: an excursion to the island of Burano

excusable /ɪkˈskjuːzəbəl/ adj behaviour that is excusable can be forgiven OPP **inexcusable**

excuse¹ /ɪkˈskjuːz/ v [T]

1 to forgive someone, usually for something that is not very serious: Please excuse my bad handwriting. | **excuse sb for (doing) sth** Please excuse me for being so late.

2 to allow someone not to do something: **excuse sb from (doing) sth** You are excused classes for the rest of the week.

3 if something excuses bad behaviour, it is the reason why it happened, which makes it possible to understand or forgive: Nothing can excuse lying to your parents.

> PHRASES
> **excuse me** spoken **1** used to politely get someone's attention: Excuse me, is this the right bus for the airport? **2** used to politely say you are sorry for doing something: Oh, excuse me, I didn't see you there. **3** used to politely tell someone that you are leaving a place: Excuse me a moment, there's someone at the door.

excuse² /ɪkˈskjuːs/ n [C]

1 a reason that you give to explain why you did something wrong: **[+for]** What's your excuse for being late? | I'm sure he has a good excuse for not calling. THESAURUS REASON

2 a reason that you invent to explain why you do something: **excuse to do sth** Karl was glad of an excuse to leave. | He **made** some **excuse** about a dentist's appointment and left. | At least it **gave** me an **excuse** to get out of the house.

> PHRASES
> **make excuses for sb/sth** to give reasons why someone has made a mistake or behaved badly: You shouldn't make excuses for her behaviour.

there is no excuse for sth used for saying that something is not acceptable: *There is no excuse for what he did.*

execute /'eksəkju:t/ v [T] **1** to kill someone as a punishment for a crime THESAURUS KILL **2** *formal* to do something that has been planned or ordered: *a carefully executed plan* —**execution** /ˌeksə'kju:ʃən/ n [U]

executioner /ˌeksə'kju:ʃənə $ -ər/ n [C] someone whose job is to kill criminals as a punishment

executive¹ /ɪg'zekjətɪv/ n [C] **1** an important manager in a company: *a sales executive* **2 the executive** the people in an organization who have the power to make decisions: *the union's national executive*

executive² *adj* **1** relating to making decisions in a company or organization: *an executive committee* **2** expensive and suitable for people who have important jobs: *executive homes*

exemplary /ɪg'zempləri/ *adj formal* exemplary behaviour is excellent and can be used as an example for other people to copy

exemplify /ɪg'zemplɪfaɪ/ v [T] (**exemplified, exemplifying, exemplifies**) *formal* to be a typical example of something: *Stuart exemplifies the kind of student we like at our school.*

exempt¹ /ɪg'zempt/ *adj* not having to do something or pay for something: [**+from**] *He was exempt from military service.* | *Medical products are exempt from tax.*

exempt² v [T] to give someone permission not to do something: **exempt sb from sth** *Anyone who is mentally ill is exempted from military service.* —**exemption** /ɪg'zempʃən/ n [C,U]

exercise¹ /'eksəsaɪz $ -ər-/ n
1 [C,U] physical activity that you do to stay strong and healthy: *I really need to take more exercise.* | *You can do special exercises to strengthen your back.*
2 [C] something you do to help you practise a skill: *relaxation exercises*
3 [C] a set of written questions to test a student's knowledge: *For homework, do exercises 1 and 2.*
4 [C] a set of activities for training soldiers: *a military exercise*

COLLOCATIONS

verbs
to do exercise (*also* **to take exercise** BrE) *I feel like doing some exercise.*
to get exercise *Do you get much exercise?*

adjectives
good exercise *Walking is good exercise.*
regular exercise *Regular exercise will help keep your weight down.*
physical exercise *Most adults don't do enough physical exercise.*
hard/vigorous exercise (=involving a lot of physical effort) *You must not do any hard exercise.*
gentle/light/moderate exercise (=not involving too much physical effort) *The patients are encouraged to do gentle exercise.*

exercise² v
1 [I,T] to do physical activities so that you stay strong and healthy: *It is important to exercise regularly.* | *You need to exercise the muscles in your back.*
2 [T] *formal* to use a power or right that you have: *She exercised her influence to get him the job.* THESAURUS USE

exert /ɪg'zɜ:t $ -ɜ:rt/ v [T] **1 exert authority/ influence/pressure etc** to use your authority or influence to make something happen: [**+on**] *The UN is exerting pressure on the two countries to stop the war.* **2 exert yourself** to make a great effort

exertion /ɪg'zɜ:ʃən $ -ɜ:r-/ n [C,U] when you make a great effort: *He was worn out by his exertions.*

exhale /eks'heɪl/ v [I,T] to breathe out OPP **inhale**: *Take a deep breath, then exhale slowly.*

exhaust¹ /ɪg'zɔ:st $ -'zɒ:st/ v [T] **1** to make someone very tired: *The trip totally exhausted us.* **2** to use all of something: *Eventually, the world's oil supply will be exhausted.*

exhaust² n **1** (*also* **ex'haust pipe**) [C] a pipe on a car that waste gas comes out of → see picture at **CAR 2** [U] the waste gas that is produced when an engine is working: *exhaust fumes*

exhausted /ɪg'zɔ:stɪd $ -'zɒ:s-/ *adj* extremely tired: [**+by/from**] *I was still exhausted from the race.* THESAURUS TIRED —**exhaustion** /ɪg'zɔ:stʃən $ -'zɒ:s-/ n [U]: *He collapsed with exhaustion.*

exhausting /ɪg'zɔ:stɪŋ $ -'zɒ:s-/ *adj* making you feel extremely tired: *a long and exhausting journey* THESAURUS TIRING

exhaustive /ɪg'zɔ:stɪv $ -'zɒ:s-/ *adj* thorough and complete: *an exhaustive search of the area*

exhibit¹ Ac /ɪg'zɪbɪt/ v **1** [I,T] to show something in a public place so that people can see it: *His paintings will be exhibited in the National Gallery.* **2** [T] *formal* to show a quality or feeling: *The prisoner exhibited no signs of remorse.* —**exhibitor** n [C]

exhibit² Ac n [C] an object that is shown in a public place for people to look at

exhibition Ac /ˌeksɪ'bɪʃən/ n
1 a) [C] a public show where people can go and see paintings, photographs etc: [**+of**] *an exhibition of historical photographs* **b)** [U] when something, such as a painting, is shown in public: **on exhibition** *The paintings are currently on exhibition in Paris.*
2 exhibition of sth when someone shows a skill, feeling, or kind of behaviour: *an impressive exhibition of athletic skill*

exhibitionist /ˌeksɪ'bɪʃənɪst/ n [C] *disapproving* someone who likes to behave or dress in a way that makes other people notice them —**exhibitionist** *adj*

exhilarated /ɪg'zɪləreɪtɪd/ *adj* extremely happy and excited: *He was exhilarated by the speed and the risk.* —**exhilaration** /ɪgˌzɪlə'reɪʃən/ n [U]

exhilarating /ɪg'zɪləreɪtɪŋ/ *adj* making you feel extremely happy and excited: *an exhilarating experience* THESAURUS EXCITING

exhort /ɪgˈzɔːt $ -ɔːrt/ v [T] formal to try to persuade someone to do something —**exhortation** /ˌeksɔːˈteɪʃən $ -ɔːr-/ n [C,U]

exile /ˈeksaɪl, ˈegzaɪl/ n **1** [U] when someone is forced to leave their country and live somewhere else, usually for political reasons: **in/into exile** a writer who lives in exile | She went into exile. **2** [C] someone who has had to leave their country and live somewhere else: Cuban exiles living in the US —**exile** v [T]: He was exiled from Russia in the 1930s. —**exiled** adj

exist /ɪgˈzɪst/ v [I] to happen or to be real or alive: Do ghosts really exist? | a custom that still exists in some areas | Border controls will **cease to exist** after June.

existence /ɪgˈzɪstəns/ n **1** [U] when something exists: **[+of]** Do you believe in the existence of God? | **in existence** Mammals have been in existence for many millions of years. **2** [C usually singular] the type of life that someone has: He **led a** miserable **existence**.

existing /ɪgˈzɪstɪŋ/ adj [only before noun] happening or being used now: We need new computers to replace the existing ones.

exit¹ /ˈegzɪt, ˈeksɪt/ n [C]
1 a door that you go through to leave a place: There are two exits at the back of the plane. | **emergency/fire exit**
2 when you leave a place: The President **made a** quick **exit** after his speech.
3 a place where you can leave a MOTORWAY: Take exit 23 for the city.

exit² v **1** [I] formal to leave a place: The band exited through a side door. **2** [I,T] to finish using a computer PROGRAM: Press F3 to exit.

exodus /ˈeksədəs/ n [singular] when a lot of people leave a place at the same time: the exodus of Russian scientists to America

exonerate /ɪgˈzɒnəreɪt $ ɪgˈzɑː-/ v [T] formal to officially say that someone who has been blamed for something is not guilty: Ross was exonerated from all blame.

exorbitant /ɪgˈzɔːbətənt $ -ɔːr-/ adj an exorbitant price is much higher than it should be —**exorbitantly** adv

exorcize (also -ise BrE) /ˈeksɔːsaɪz $ -ɔːr-/ v [T] to force an evil SPIRIT to leave a place by using special prayers and ceremonies —**exorcism** /-sɪzəm/ n [C,U] —**exorcist** n [C]

exotic /ɪgˈzɒtɪk $ ɪgˈzɑː-/ adj something that is exotic seems unusual and exciting because it is from a foreign country: an exotic flower | exotic food

expand Ac /ɪkˈspænd/ v [I,T] to become larger, or to make something larger: The population **expanded rapidly** in the '60s. | Water expands as it freezes.
THESAURUS ▶ INCREASE —**expandable** adj
PHRASAL VERBS
expand on/upon sth formal to add more details or information to something that you have already said: Could you expand on your last comment, please?

expanse /ɪkˈspæns/ n [C] a very large area of land, sea, or sky: the vast expanse of the Pacific Ocean

expansion Ac /ɪkˈspænʃən/ n [U] when something increases in size, number, or amount: a period of economic expansion

expansionism Ac /ɪkˈspænʃənɪzəm/ n [U] disapproving when a country or group tries to increase the amount of land or power it has —**expansionist** adj: the country's expansionist policy

expansive Ac /ɪkˈspænsɪv/ adj very friendly and willing to talk a lot: Alan was in an expansive mood.

expatriate /eksˈpætriət, -trieɪt $ -ˈpeɪ-/ (also **ex-pat** /ˌeksˈpæt/) n [C] someone who lives in a foreign country

expect /ɪkˈspekt/ v [T]
1 to think that something will probably happen: **expect (sb) to do sth** Do you expect to travel a lot this year? | He expected me to drive him home! | **[+(that)]** We expect the meeting will finish about 5 o'clock. | **As expected**, Rebecca passed easily.
2 to believe that someone must do something because it is their duty: The officer expects absolute obedience from his men. | **expect sb to do sth** We're expected to work late sometimes.
3 to believe that someone or something is going to arrive: I'm expecting a letter from Japan. | What time do you expect him home? —**expected** adj: the expected rise in interest rates
PHRASES
be expecting (a baby) informal if a woman is expecting, she is going to have a baby: Sarah's expecting a baby in September.
I expect especially BrE spoken used to say that you think something is probably true: **[+(that)]** It's late and I expect you're tired. | 'Do you think he'll get the job?' 'Yes, **I expect so**.'

expectancy /ɪkˈspektənsi/ n [U] the feeling that something exciting or interesting is going to happen: There was a look of expectancy on the children's faces. → LIFE EXPECTANCY

expectant /ɪkˈspektənt/ adj **1** hopeful that something good or exciting will happen: an expectant crowd **2** **expectant mother/father** a mother or father whose baby will be born soon: The Pregnancy Book is given free to all first-time expectant mothers. —**expectantly** adv: They looked at Jos expectantly.

expectation /ˌekspekˈteɪʃən/ n **1** [C,U] what you hope or believe will happen: **[+that]** the expectation that prices will rise | **[+of]** We have a reasonable expectation of success. **2** [C usually plural] something good that you think will happen: The trip didn't **live up to** our **expectations** (=it wasn't as good as we hoped). | Many refugees arrive in the country with **high expectations**.

expedient¹ /ɪkˈspiːdiənt/ adj if something you do is expedient, it helps you but it is not morally right: She thought it would be expedient to use a false name. —**expediency** (also **expedience**) n [U]

expedient² n [C] a clever way of dealing with a situation

expedite /ˈekspədaɪt/ v [T] to make a process or action happen more quickly **SYN** speed up

E

expedition /ˌekspəˈdɪʃən/ n [C] **1** a long and carefully organized journey: *an expedition to the North Pole* **THESAURUS** ▶ JOURNEY **2** a short trip that you make for a particular purpose: *a shopping expedition*

expel /ɪkˈspel/ v [T] (**expelled, expelling**) **1** to officially order someone to leave a school, organization, or country: **expel sb from sth** *Jake was expelled from school for smoking.* **2** *formal* to force air, water, or gas out of something

expend /ɪkˈspend/ v [T] *formal* to use money, time, or energy: *A lot of effort has been expended on creating the right image for the company.*

expendable /ɪkˈspendəbəl/ adj if something or someone is expendable, they are not needed and you can get rid of them: *workers who are regarded as expendable*

expenditure /ɪkˈspendɪtʃə $ -ər/ n [U] *formal* **1** the total amount of money that a government, organization, or person spends: **[+on]** *Expenditure on medical care has doubled.* **2** when someone spends money or uses time or effort: *the wasteful expenditure of time*

expense /ɪkˈspens/ n
1 [C,U] the amount of money you spend on something: **household/medical/living expenses** (=money that you spend for a particular purpose) *All his money went on medical expenses.* | *All rooms were fully equipped **at great expense** (=costing a lot of money).*
2 expenses [plural] money that you spend on travel, hotels etc when you are working, and then get back from your employer: *They pay £300 a week plus expenses.* | **on expenses** *Don't worry, I'll put the taxi on expenses.*
PHRASES
at sb's expense 1 if you do something at someone's expense, they pay for you to do it: *a trip to Japan at the tax-payer's expense* **2** in a way that makes someone seem stupid: *Louis kept making jokes at his wife's expense.*
at the expense of sb/sth if something is done at the expense of something or someone else, it is achieved by harming the other person or thing: *A medical career requires commitment at the expense of family life.*

expensive /ɪkˈspensɪv/ adj something that is expensive costs a lot of money **OPP** cheap: *an expensive restaurant*

THESAURUS

expensive something that is expensive costs a lot of money: *an expensive present* | *Land is very expensive.*
high high prices, rents, taxes, or fees cost a lot of money. Do not use **expensive** with these words: *People are worried about the high price of fuel.* | *The rent is too high.*
pricey *informal* expensive: *£550 for a plane ticket does sound rather pricey.*
fancy *informal* something that is fancy looks expensive: *We stayed in a fancy hotel.* | *fancy clothes*
overpriced things that are overpriced cost more than they should: *overpriced restaurants* | *The food was overpriced.*

astronomical astronomical prices, costs, rents, or fees cost a very large amount of money, especially too much money: *Some people paid astronomical prices for tickets to the game.*
cost a fortune *informal* to be very expensive: *The meal cost a fortune!*
sb can't afford sth someone does not have enough money to buy or do something: *A lot of young people can't afford to buy a house.*

experience¹ /ɪkˈspɪəriəns $ -ˈspɪr-/ n
1 [U] knowledge or skill that you learn when you do something yourself, or when something happens to you: *He's a very good teacher with a lot of experience.* | **[+of/in/with]** *Do you **have** any **experience** in marketing?* | *He has no **previous experience** of working with animals.* | **In my experience**, *a credit card is always useful.* | **know/learn/speak from experience** *I speak from personal experience.*
2 [C] something that happens to you: *I **had** a very strange **experience** last week.* | *Going to China was a wonderful experience.*

experience² v [T] if you experience something, it happens to you: **experience problems/difficulties etc** *We're experiencing a few problems with our website.* | *You may **experience** some **pain**.*

experienced /ɪkˈspɪəriənst $ -ˈspɪr-/ adj someone who is experienced has a lot of skill or knowledge because they have done something before **OPP** inexperienced: *a very experienced pilot* | **[+in]** *doctors who are experienced in these techniques*

experiment¹ /ɪkˈsperəmənt/ n [C]
1 a scientific test to find out or prove something: **[+on/with]** *experiments on rats*
2 an occasion when you try something new to see if it will be successful: **[+in/with]** *an experiment in bilingual education* —**experimental** /ɪkˌsperəˈmentl◂/ adj: *experimental farming techniques*

COLLOCATIONS

verbs
to do/carry out an experiment *The scientists did a series of experiments on rats.* ⚠ Do not say 'make an experiment'. Say **do an experiment** or **carry out an experiment**.
to perform/conduct an experiment *formal* (=to do an experiment) *The experiment was performed in a laboratory.*
an experiment shows/proves sth *His experiments showed that his theory worked.*

types of experiment
a scientific experiment *They did a scientific experiment to find out how different people react to stress.*
a laboratory experiment (=one that takes place in a laboratory) *In laboratory experiments, volunteers were given small quantities of the drug.*
animal experiments (=experiments using animals) *Are animal experiments necessary in medical research?*

experiment² /ɪkˈsperəmənt/ v [I] **1** to try using different things or doing something in different ways: **[+with]** *Many teenagers experiment with drugs.* **2** to do a scientific test in order to find out or prove something: **[+on/with]** *Do you think it's right to experiment on animals?* —**experimentation** /ɪkˌsperəmenˈteɪʃən/ n [U]

expert Ac /ˈekspɜːt $ -ɜːrt/ n [C] someone who has a lot of knowledge about a subject or is very skilful at doing something: **[+on/in]** *an expert on ancient Egyptian art* | **medical/technical/financial etc expert** —**expert** adj: *expert advice* —**expertly** adv

THESAURUS

expert someone who has a lot of knowledge about a subject or is very skilful at doing something: *a bird expert* | *I'm not really an expert on cars.*
authority an expert whose opinions are greatly respected by many people: *He is one of the world's leading authorities on green technology.*
specialist an expert on a particular technical or medical subject: *She went to see a cancer specialist at the Royal Marsden Hospital.*
connoisseur an expert on art, food, or music, who knows when something is of good quality: *a connoisseur of fine wines*

expertise Ac /ˌekspɜːˈtiːz $ -ɜːr-/ n [U] special skills or knowledge that you learn by experience or training: *medical expertise*

expire /ɪkˈspaɪə $ -ˈspaɪr/ v [I] if a document or legal agreement expires, the period of time in which you can use it ends —**expiration** /ˌekspəˈreɪʃən/ n [U]

expiry /ɪkˈspaɪəri $ -ˈspaɪri/ n [U] BrE the end of a period of time in which something can be used, or the end of a period of authority: *What's the **expiry date** on your passport?* | *the expiry of the President's term of office*

explain /ɪkˈspleɪn/ v [I,T] **1** to give someone the information they need to understand something: **explain sth to sb** *I explained the rules to Sara.* | **[+how/what/why etc]** *Can someone explain how this thing works?* | **[+that]** *He explained that it had been a difficult film to make.*

> **Grammar**
> Do not say 'He explained me the idea.' Say *He explained the idea to me.*

2 to give the reason for something: **[+why/how etc]** *Brad never explained why he was late.* | **[+that]** *I explained that I'd missed the bus.*
PHRASAL VERBS
explain sth ↔ **away** to make something seem less important or less serious, by giving reasons for it: *Claire tried to explain away the bruises on her arm.*

THESAURUS

explain to give someone the information they need to understand something: *The teacher explained what the word meant.*
tell to explain something to someone. **Tell** is often used instead of **explain** in everyday English: *Can you tell me the way to the station?*

show to explain to someone how to do something, by doing it while they watch you: *Do you want me to show you how to use the cooker?*
demonstrate to show people the right way to do something by doing it while they watch you, especially when this is part of your job: *The instructor demonstrated how to reverse the car around a corner.*
go through sth to explain something carefully, often more than once, to make sure that people understand it: *Could you go through the instructions again?*

explanation /ˌekspləˈneɪʃən/ n **1** [C,U] the reasons why something happened or why you did something: **[+for]** *Is there any explanation for his behaviour?* | *She was given no explanation.* **THESAURUS** REASON **2** [C] something you say or write to describe how something works or to make something easier to understand: **[+of]** *a detailed explanation of how to use the program* | *She **gave** a good, clear **explanation**.*

COLLOCATIONS

verbs
to think of an explanation *I can't think of any other explanation.*
to give an explanation *He gave no explanation for what happened.*
to believe/accept an explanation *She accepted his explanation without question.*
to have an explanation *Scientists still do not have an explanation for this phenomenon.*
to demand an explanation *She went to see the manager and demanded an explanation.*

adjectives
a possible explanation *It seemed the only possible explanation.*
the most likely explanation *The most likely explanation is that she simply forgot.*
a simple explanation *There must be a perfectly simple explanation for all this.*
a satisfactory/good enough explanation *No one has been able to come up with a satisfactory explanation.*
a logical explanation *I can't think of any logical explanation.*

explanatory /ɪkˈsplænətəri $ -tɔːri/ adj giving information about something or explaining how something works: *an explanatory booklet* → **SELF-EXPLANATORY**

expletive /ɪkˈspliːtɪv $ ˈeksplətɪv/ n [C] formal a swear word

explicable /ekˈsplɪkəbəl/ adj something that is explicable can be easily understood or explained **OPP** **inexplicable**

explicit Ac /ɪkˈsplɪsɪt/ adj **1** explaining something in a way that is very clear and easy to understand: *Could you be more explicit?* **2** showing or describing sex or violence in a detailed way: *explicit love scenes* —**explicitly** adv

explode /ɪkˈspləʊd $ -ˈsploʊd/ v
1 [I,T] to burst loudly and violently, or to make something do this → **explosion**: *The car bomb exploded at 6:16.*
2 [I] to suddenly increase a lot in size or amount: *The population of the area exploded after the war.*
3 [I] to suddenly become very angry: *Susie exploded when I told her about the car.*

THESAURUS

explode if a bomb explodes, it bursts suddenly and violently with a loud noise, often causing a lot of damage: *A bomb exploded on a crowded subway train.*
go off if a bomb goes off, it explodes. **Go off** is less formal than **explode** and is very common in everyday English: *A series of bombs went off in the middle of London.*
blow up if a building, car, plane etc blows up, or someone blows it up, it bursts suddenly and violently into pieces: *The plane blew up in midair.* | *The men were planning to blow up the parliament building.*
set off to make a bomb explode, either deliberately or by mistake: *They set off a bomb in a crowded café.* | *The slightest movement could set off the bomb.*

---

exploit¹ **Ac** /ɪkˈsplɔɪt/ v [T] **1** to treat someone in an unfair way, by not paying as much as they deserve: *Many foreign workers are abused and exploited.* **2** to use something effectively so that you get as much advantage as possible from it: *We must exploit the country's mineral resources.* —**exploitation** /ˌeksplɔɪˈteɪʃən/ n [U]

exploit² /ˈeksplɔɪt/ n [C usually plural] something brave or interesting that someone has done: *a book about his exploits in Latin America*

exploratory /ɪkˈsplɒrətəri $ ɪkˈsplɔːrətɔːri/ adj done in order to find out more about something: *exploratory surgery*

explore /ɪkˈsplɔː $ -ˈsplɔːr/ v
1 [I,T] to travel around an area to find out what it is like: *We spent a week exploring the Oregon coastline.*
2 [T] to discuss or think about something carefully: *Explore all the possibilities before you make a decision.* —**exploration** /ˌekspləˈreɪʃən/ n [C,U]: *a voyage of exploration*

explorer /ɪkˈsplɔːrə $ -ər/ n [C] someone who travels to places that people have not visited before

explosion /ɪkˈspləʊʒən $ -ˈsploʊ-/ n [C]
1 when something such as a bomb explodes, or the noise it makes → **explode**: *We heard a huge explosion.* | *The force of the explosion shook the building.* | **bomb/nuclear etc explosion**
2 [usually singular] a sudden large increase: *the population explosion* | [+of] *the recent explosion of interest in African music*

explosive¹ /ɪkˈspləʊsɪv $ -ˈsploʊ-/ adj **1** something that is explosive can cause an explosion: *an explosive mixture of gases* **2** likely to make people become violent or angry: *an explosive situation* | *Abortion is an explosive issue.*

explosive² n [C] a substance that can cause an explosion

exponent /ɪkˈspəʊnənt $ -ˈspoʊ-/ n [C] an exponent of an idea or belief tries to persuade other people that it is good: *an exponent of socialism*

export¹ **Ac** /ˈekspɔːt $ -ɔːrt/ n
1 [U] the business of selling goods to another country **OPP** **import**: [+of] *the export of live animals*
2 [C] a product that is sold to another country **OPP** **import**: *Oil is now one of Malaysia's main exports.*

export² **Ac** /ɪkˈspɔːt $ -ɔːrt/ v [I,T] to sell goods to another country **OPP** **import**: **export (sth) to sb** *Japan exports electronic equipment to dozens of countries.* —**exporter** n [C]

expose **Ac** /ɪkˈspəʊz $ -ˈspoʊz/ v [T]
1 **UNCOVER** to show something that is usually covered or hidden: **expose sth to sth** *When a wound is exposed to the air, it heals more quickly.* **THESAURUS** **SHOW**
2 **PUT SB IN DANGER** to put someone in a situation or place that may be harmful or dangerous: **be exposed to sth** *workers who were exposed to high levels of radiation*
3 **TELL TRUTH** to tell people the truth about something bad or dishonest: *The report exposed corruption among officials.*
4 **EXPERIENCE STH** to let someone experience new ideas, ways of life etc: **be exposed to sth** *Children who have been exposed to different cultures are less likely to be prejudiced.*
5 **FILM** to allow light onto a piece of film in a camera in order to produce a photograph

exposé /ekˈspəʊzeɪ $ ˌekspoʊˈzeɪ/ n [C] a story in a newspaper or on television that shows the truth about something, especially something dishonest or shocking

exposed **Ac** /ɪkˈspəʊzd $ -ˈspoʊzd/ adj not protected from the weather: *an exposed hillside*

exposure **Ac** /ɪkˈspəʊʒə $ -ˈspoʊʒər/ n **1** [C,U] when someone is put in a situation where they are not protected from something harmful: [+to] *Too much exposure to the sun can cause skin cancer.* **2** [C,U] when newspapers or television show the true facts about something bad or dishonest: *the exposure of his business dealings* **3** [U] the harmful effects of being outside for a long time when the weather is extremely cold: *Three climbers died of exposure.* **4** [C] the amount of film that is used each time you take a photograph: *a film with 36 exposures*

expound /ɪkˈspaʊnd/ v [I,T] formal to explain or talk about something in detail: [+on] *Evans continued to expound on his theory.*

express¹ /ɪkˈspres/ v [T]
1 to tell people what you are thinking or feeling: **express your views/opinions/concerns** *A number of people expressed their concern.* | *She expressed an interest in becoming a member.* | **express sth in/through/by sth** *The idea is difficult to express in words.* | **express yourself** (=clearly say what you think or feel)
2 to show your thoughts or feelings by the way you

look or your actions: *The look on Paul's face expressed utter despair.*

express² *adj* [only before noun] **1** an express wish or purpose is clear and definite: *It was her express wish that you should inherit her house.* **2** an express train or bus is very fast

express³ *n* [C] a fast train or bus which stops at only a few stations

expression /ɪkˈspreʃən/ *n*
1 [C,U] when you say, write, or do something to show what you are thinking or feeling: *I'm sending these flowers as an expression of my gratitude.*
2 [C] a look on someone's face: [+of] *an expression of shock* | *He came back with a cheerful expression on his face.*
3 [C] a word or phrase that has a particular meaning: *What does the expression 'head over heels' mean?*
THESAURUS PHRASE

expressionless /ɪkˈspreʃənləs/ *adj* an expressionless face or voice does not show what someone is feeling or thinking

expressive /ɪkˈspresɪv/ *adj* showing what someone is thinking or feeling: *expressive eyes*

expressly /ɪkˈspresli/ *adv formal* **1** clearly and firmly: *Students are expressly forbidden to enter.* **2** for a particular purpose: *a building expressly designed for the disabled*

expressway /ɪkˈspresweɪ/ *n* [C] a wide road in a city on which cars can travel fast → **freeway**, **highway**, **motorway** **THESAURUS** ROAD

expulsion /ɪkˈspʌlʃən/ *n* [C,U] when someone is officially ordered to leave a place → **expel**: [+of/from] *his expulsion from the Soviet Union*

exquisite /ɪkˈskwɪzət, ˈekskwɪ-/ *adj* beautiful and delicate: *an exquisite diamond ring* —**exquisitely** *adv*

ext. the written abbreviation of **extension** when you mean a particular telephone line

extend /ɪkˈstend/ *v* **1** [T] to make something continue for longer than previously arranged or planned: *Could you extend your visa for six months?* **2** [T] to make something include or affect more things or people: **extend sth to sth** *The UK wants to extend the ban to EU countries.* **3** [I] to cover a particular distance or area: [+across/over/through etc] *The river extends 2,000 km to the south.* **4** [T] to make a building, road etc bigger: *plans to extend the road network* **5** [T] *formal* to officially offer help, thanks, sympathy etc: **extend sth to sb** *I'd like to extend a warm welcome to our visitors.* **6** [T] to stretch out your hand, arm, or leg: *Perry extended a hand in greeting.*

extended /ɪkˈstendɪd/ *adj* [only before noun] long: *an extended period of neglect*

ex,tended 'family *n* [C] a family group that consists of parents, children, and also of grandparents, AUNTS, UNCLES etc → **nuclear family**

extension /ɪkˈstenʃən/ *n* **1** [U] the process of making a building, road etc bigger: [+of] *the extension of the southern vineyards* **2** [C usually singular] a new part that is added to something such as a house: [+to] *BrE: We built an extension to the kitchen.* **3** [C usually singular] an extra period of time allowed for

something: *I need an extension to finish my essay.* **4** [singular, U] the development of something so that it affects more things or people: [+of] *the extension of voting rights to women* **5** [C] one of several telephones that are connected to the same line: *What's your extension number?*

extensive /ɪkˈstensɪv/ *adj* large in amount or area: *The exhibition received extensive media coverage.*

extent /ɪkˈstent/ *n* [U] how big, important, or serious something is: [+of] *What is the full extent of his injuries?* | **to some/a certain extent** (=partly) *To a certain extent, it was my fault.* | **to a large/greater/lesser extent** | *Crime increased to the extent that people were afraid to go out.*

exterior /ɪkˈstɪəriə $ -ˈtɪriər/ *n* [C usually singular] **1** the outside of something **OPP interior**: [+of] *the exterior of the building* **2** **calm/confident etc exterior** someone's behaviour, which does not show their real feelings or nature: *Beneath that calm exterior, she's angry.* —**exterior** *adj*

exterminate /ɪkˈstɜːməneɪt $ -ɜːr-/ *v* [T] to kill all of a particular group or type of animals or people —**extermination** /ɪkˌstɜːməˈneɪʃən $ -ɜːr-/ *n* [C,U]

external Ac /ɪkˈstɜːnl $ -ɜːr-/ *adj*
1 relating to the outside of a thing or person's body **OPP internal**: *repairs to the external walls* | *For external use only* (=used on medicines that you must put on your skin, not eat).
2 from outside your organization, country, university etc **OPP internal**: *external examiners*

extinct /ɪkˈstɪŋkt/ *adj* **1** a type of animal or plant that is extinct no longer exists: *Activists fear that the tiger may become extinct.* **THESAURUS** DISAPPEAR **2** an extinct VOLCANO does not ERUPT (=send out hot rock, smoke etc)

extinction /ɪkˈstɪŋkʃən/ *n* [U] when a type of animal or plant stops existing: *The whales are in danger of extinction.*

extinguish /ɪkˈstɪŋgwɪʃ/ *v* [T] *formal* to make a fire or light stop burning or shining **SYN** put out: *Please extinguish all cigarettes.*

extinguisher /ɪkˈstɪŋgwɪʃə $ -ər/ *n* [C] a FIRE EXTINGUISHER

extol /ɪkˈstəʊl $ -ˈstoʊl/ *v* [T] (**extolled**, **extolling**) *formal* to praise something very highly: **extol the virtues/benefits etc of sth**

extort /ɪkˈstɔːt $ -ɔːrt/ *v* [T] if someone extorts money from you, they threaten you to make you give them money —**extortion** /ɪkˈstɔːʃən $ -ɔːr-/ *n* [U]

extortionate /ɪkˈstɔːʃənət $ -ɔːr-/ *adj disapproving* extortionate prices, demands etc are too big

extra¹ /ˈekstrə/ *adj, adv* in addition to the usual things or amount: *pizza with extra cheese* | *Drivers should take extra care in icy conditions.* | *Dinner prices are fixed at $15, but wine is extra.* | *Do you get paid extra at weekends?* | *Henry's been working extra hard.* | *an extra hour in bed* | **one/a few/some extra** *I bought a few extra just in case.* **THESAURUS** MORE

extra² *n* [C] **1** something that can be added to a product or service and that makes it cost more: *The*

extract

DVD and scanner are **optional extras**. **2** an actor in a film who has a small unimportant part

extract¹ Ac /ɪkˈstrækt/ v [T] **1** formal to remove something from a place or thing: **extract sth from sth** Precious gems are extracted from the mine. | I had **a tooth extracted**. **2** if someone extracts information or money from you, they get it from you, even though you did not want to give it to them: **extract sth from sth** The police failed to extract **a confession** from him. —**extraction** /ɪkˈstrækʃən/ n [U]

extract² Ac /ˈekstrækt/ n **1** [C] a small part taken from a story, poem etc: **[+from]** an extract from the film **2** [C,U] a substance that is removed from a plant: **vanilla/plant etc extract**

extracurricular /ˌekstrəkəˈrɪkjələ◂ $ -ər◂/ adj [only before noun] extracurricular activities are those that are not part of the course that a student is studying

extradite /ˈekstrədaɪt/ v [T] to send someone who may have committed a crime back to the country where it happened so that they can be dealt with there —**extradition** /ˌekstrəˈdɪʃən/ n [C,U]

extramarital /ˌekstrəˈmærətl◂/ adj [only before noun] an extramarital sexual relationship is one that a married person has with a person who is not their husband or wife

extraneous /ɪkˈstreɪniəs/ adj formal not directly related to a particular subject: extraneous details

extraordinary /ɪkˈstrɔːdənəri $ ɪkˈstrɔːrdn-eri, ˌekstrəˈɔːr-/ adj very unusual, surprising, or special: **It's extraordinary that** he didn't tell you. | an extraordinary talent **THESAURUS** SURPRISING —**extraordinarily** /ɪkˈstrɔːdənərəli $ ɪkˌstrɔːrdnˈerəli, ˌekstrəˈɔːrdn-erəli/ adv

extrapolate /ɪkˈstræpəleɪt/ v [I,T] formal to use facts about a current situation in order to say what might happen in another: **extrapolate (sth) from sth** Extrapolating from these results, we predict future trends.

extraterrestrial /ˌekstrətəˈrestriəl◂/ adj in or from a place that is not the Earth: the search for extraterrestrial life

extravagant /ɪkˈstrævəgənt/ adj **1** spending or costing too much money: an extravagant lifestyle **2** extravagant claims, promises etc are not likely to be true —**extravagantly** adv —**extravagance** n [C,U]

extravaganza /ɪkˌstrævəˈgænzə/ n [C] a large expensive event or entertainment

extravert /ˈekstrəvɜːt $ -ɜːrt/ n another spelling of EXTROVERT

extreme¹ /ɪkˈstriːm/ adj
1 [only before noun] very great in amount or severity: extreme poverty | extreme weather conditions | **extreme cases/circumstances** In extreme cases, the child may die.
2 [only before noun] the furthest part of a place in a particular direction: the extreme north
3 extreme opinions are very strong and most people think they are unreasonable: His views were extreme, and led to political isolation.
4 [only before noun] extreme sports are done in a way that is more dangerous than the usual form of that sport: **extreme surfing/boxing etc**

extreme² n [C] something that is much greater, more severe etc than usual: **[+of]** Bacteria can withstand extremes of heat and cold. | **at the other/opposite extreme** (=used when two things are as different as possible) At the other extreme, Austria has almost zero unemployment. | **take/carry sth to extremes/go to extremes** disapproving (=do something to the greatest possible extent) Caution is sensible, but not if parents go to extremes.

PHRASES

in the extreme extremely: These experiments are cruel in the extreme.

extremely /ɪkˈstriːmli/ adv more than very: I'm extremely sorry. | He finds it extremely difficult to talk about what happened.

extremist /ɪkˈstriːmɪst/ n [C] disapproving someone with very strong political or religious opinions → **fundamentalist**: left-wing extremists —**extremist** adj: an extremist group —**extremism** n [U]

extremity /ɪkˈstreməti/ n [C] (plural extremities) formal the part that is furthest from the centre of something

extricate /ˈekstrɪkeɪt/ v [T] to get yourself or someone else out of a bad situation: **extricate yourself/sb from sth** How could he extricate himself from the debt?

extrovert, extravert /ˈekstrəvɜːt $ -ɜːrt/ n [C] someone who is confident and likes being with people **OPP introvert** **THESAURUS** CONFIDENT —**extrovert, extroverted** /-vɜːtɪd $ -vɜːr-/ adj

exuberant /ɪgˈzjuːbərənt $ ɪgˈzuː-/ adj very happy, excited, and full of energy: an exuberant personality —**exuberance** n [U]

exude /ɪgˈzjuːd $ ɪgˈzuːd/ v formal **1** [T] someone who exudes love, confidence, power etc shows a lot of love etc **2** [I,T] to flow out slowly, or to make something do this

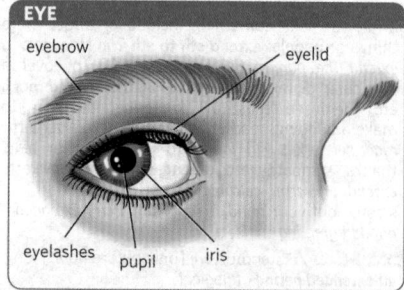

EYE

eyebrow — eyelid

eyelashes — pupil — iris

eye¹ /aɪ/ n [C]
1 one of the two things in your face that you see with: Close your eyes and go to sleep. | There were tears in her eyes. | His eyes were full of fear.
2 a particular way of judging or understanding something: He surveyed her with **a critical eye**. | **in the eyes of sb** Joe can do no wrong in the eyes of his partner. | **through the eyes of sb** (=from a particular person's point of view) a story **seen through the eyes**

of a child | **a (good) eye for sth** (=the ability to recognize or judge something) *To be a proofreader you need* ***a good eye for detail****.*
3 the hole in a needle that you put the thread through → **not bat an eye** at BAT², **could not believe your eyes** at BELIEVE, **BLACK EYE**, **turn a blind eye (to sth)** at BLIND¹, **catch sb's eye** at CATCH¹, **with/to the naked eye** at NAKED, **see eye to eye** at SEE

PHRASES

sb cannot take their eyes off sb/sth used to say that someone cannot stop looking at someone or something because they are attractive or interesting: *I couldn't take my eyes off her all evening.*

close/shut your eyes to sth to ignore something bad that is happening: *We could not shut our eyes to what was going on here.*

do sth with your eyes open to do something when you know what problems you might have: *I went into the job with my eyes open, so I've only myself to blame.*

drop/lower your eyes to look down at the ground: *He lowered his eyes in embarrassment.*

have your eye on sth to want something that you think might become available: *He's got his eye on the store next door.*

keep an eye on sb/sth to watch someone or something to make sure nothing bad happens: *Police have* ***kept a close eye on*** *Taylor since she came out of prison.* | *Louise was* ***keeping half an eye on*** *the baby* (=watching without her full attention).
THESAURUS ▶ WATCH

keep an eye open/out (for sb/sth) to be ready to notice something when it appears: *Keep an eye out for traffic.*

keep your eyes peeled/skinned (for sth) *spoken* to watch carefully for something: *Keep your eyes peeled for bargains at the market.*

look sb in the eye to look at someone's eyes when speaking to them: *Look me in the eye and tell me the truth.*

run/cast your eye over sth to read something quickly: *She cast her eye over the letter.*

set/lay/clap eyes on sb/sth *informal* to see someone or something, especially for the first time: *It was the most beautiful building I had ever laid eyes on.*

be up to your eyes in sth *BrE informal* to be very busy doing something: *I'm up to my eyes in paperwork.*

COLLOCATIONS

adjectives

brown/blue/grey/green eyes *She has blonde hair and blue eyes.*
hazel eyes (=pale brown and slightly green or golden) *He was fair, with hazel eyes.*
dark eyes *She looked into his dark eyes.* ⚠ Do not say 'black eyes' when you mean **dark eyes**. 'To have a black eye' means to have a bruise around your eye.

red eyes (=because you are upset, tired, ill etc) *Her eyes were red from crying.*
big/small eyes *She looked at me with her big brown eyes.*
sb's eyes are open/closed/shut *His eyes were still shut.*

verbs

to open your eyes *He opened his eyes and looked around.*
to close/shut your eyes *Close your eyes and go back to sleep.*
to rub your eyes *'I'm so sleepy,' he said, rubbing his eyes.*
sb's eyes sparkle/shine (=show happiness or excitement) *Jenny's eyes sparkled with excitement.*

---

eye² v [T] (*present participle* **eyeing** *or* **eying**) to look at someone or something with great interest

eyeball /'aɪbɔːl $ -bɔːl/ n [C] the whole of your eye, including the part inside your head

eyebrow /'aɪbraʊ/ n [C] the line of short hairs above your eye: *He* ***raised*** *his* ***eyebrows*** *in surprise.* → see picture at EYE¹

'**eye-,catching** adj unusual, attractive, or noticeable

'**eye contact** n [U] when two people look at each other's eyes: *The boy avoided making eye contact with me and I knew he was lying.*

-eyed /aɪd/ suffix used to say that someone has eyes of a particular colour or type: *a brown-eyed girl*

eyelash /'aɪlæʃ/ n [C] one of the small hairs growing on the edge of your eyelids → see picture at EYE¹

eyelid /'aɪlɪd/ n [C] one of the pieces of skin that cover your eyes when you close them → see picture at EYE¹

eyeliner /'aɪ,laɪnə $ -ər/ n [C,U] a type of MAKE-UP that you put along the edges of your eyelids

'**eye-,opener** n [singular] an experience from which you learn something new or surprising

'**eye-,shadow** n [U] coloured MAKE-UP that you put on your eyelids

eyesight /'aɪsaɪt/ n [U] the ability to see: **poor/good/perfect etc eyesight**

eyesore /'aɪsɔː $ -sɔːr/ n [C] a building or area that is very ugly: *Those old tower blocks are an eyesore.*
THESAURUS ▶ UGLY

eyewitness /'aɪ,wɪtnəs/ n [C] someone who sees a crime or accident: *According to eyewitnesses, four men were in the bank.* | *an* ***eyewitness account*** *of the incident*

Ff

F, f /ef/ *n* [C,U] (*plural* **F's, f's**) **1** the sixth letter of the English alphabet **2** the fourth note in the musical SCALE of C MAJOR, or the musical KEY based on this note

F the written abbreviation of **Fahrenheit**

fable /ˈfeɪbəl/ *n* [C] a traditional story that teaches a moral lesson

fabled /ˈfeɪbəld/ *adj* famous and often mentioned in traditional stories SYN **legendary**: *the fabled Fountain of Youth*

fabric /ˈfæbrɪk/ *n* **1** [C,U] cloth: **woollen/silk/synthetic etc fabric 2** [singular] the structure and customs of a society: *a change in the fabric of society* **3** [singular] the walls, floor, and roof of a building

fabricate /ˈfæbrɪkeɪt/ *v* [T] to invent a story or information in order to deceive someone: *The police were accused of **fabricating evidence**.* —**fabrication** /ˌfæbrɪˈkeɪʃən/ *n* [C,U]

fabulous /ˈfæbjələs/ *adj* very good: *You look fabulous!*

facade, façade /fəˈsɑːd, fæ-/ *n* [C] **1** [usually singular] a way of behaving that hides your real feelings or character: *Behind the cheerful facade, she's lonely.* **2** the front of a building

face¹ /feɪs/ *n* [C]
1 the front of your head, where your eyes, nose, and mouth are: *her beautiful face* | *He was lying face down* (=with his face towards the ground). | *There was a big smile on his face.* → see picture on page A2
2 the expression on someone's face that shows how they feel: *Why does she always have such a sad face?* | *I saw the disappointment in his face.*
3 a person: **new/famous/familiar etc face** *She's a familiar face to British audiences.*
4 the front or surface of something such as a clock or mountain: *a clock face* | *a cliff face* → see picture at WATCH² → IN-YOUR-FACE
PHRASES
sb's face falls used to say that someone suddenly looks sad: *'I have to go now,' he said. Her face fell.*
sb's face lights up used to say that someone suddenly looks happy: *His face lit up when he saw her.*
face to face while physically close to someone: **meet/talk etc face to face** *I'd rather explain face to face, not on the phone.*
in the face of sth in a difficult situation: *courage in the face of danger*
keep a straight face to stop yourself from smiling or laughing: *When I heard this, I could hardly keep a straight face.*
lose face/save face to lose the respect of other people, or to avoid losing their respect: *Is there any way that the government can save face?*
make/pull a face to change your expression to make people laugh or to show that you do not like something: *Roy took one bite and pulled a face.*
on the face of it when you first consider something, before you know the details: *On the face of it, it seemed reasonable.*
to sb's face if you say something to someone's face, you say it directly to them when you are with them: *I told him to his face just what I thought of him.*

COLLOCATIONS
adjectives
a pretty/beautiful/handsome etc face *Her face was very pretty.*
a round/oval/square face *He had curly hair and a round face.*
a thin/fat face *The teacher was tall, with a long, thin face.*
a pale/red face *Her eyes looked enormous in her pale face.*
a sad/happy/worried/puzzled face *I remember his sad face at the window.*
a smiling face *Your reward will be the kids' smiling faces.*
a long face (=an unhappy expression) *People were going round with long faces.*

verbs
sb's face goes/turns red (=with embarrassment or anger) *Anna's face went bright red as she realized her mistake.*
sb's face goes pale/white (=with shock or fear) *I saw her face go pale when he walked in.*

---

face² *v* [T]
1 (*also* **be faced with**) to have to deal with a difficult situation: **face problems/difficulty/a challenge etc** *The team **faces** the impossible **task** of beating Brazil.* | *Alan is faced with an uncertain future.*
2 (*also* **face up to sth**) to accept that an unpleasant situation exists: **face facts/the truth/the fact that** *Many couples can't face the fact that their marriage is over.* | *Let's face it – you'll never be a star player.*
3 sb can't face (doing) sth used to say that someone does not feel able to do something, especially because it upsets them: *He couldn't face driving all the way to Los Angeles.*
4 to be opposite or pointing towards someone or something: *Dean **turned to face** me.* | *Her apartment faces the sea.* | **north-facing/south-facing etc** *a south-facing garden*
PHRASES
face the music to experience the results of something bad you have done: *I went home to face the music.*

faceless /ˈfeɪsləs/ *adj disapproving* a faceless person, organization etc is not clearly known and seems unfriendly or not worth caring about: *faceless bureaucrats*

facelift /ˈfeɪslɪft/ *n* [C] **1** a medical operation to make your face look younger **2** work to improve the appearance of a building, city etc: *The offices were given a facelift.*

facet /'fæsɪt/ n [C] one of several parts of someone's character, a situation etc SYN **aspect**

facetious /fə'si:ʃəs/ adj disapproving saying things in order to be funny or clever, in a way that is silly and annoying: *facetious comments* —**facetiously** adv —**facetiousness** n [U]

,**face-to-'face** adj [only before noun] a face-to-face meeting, conversation etc is one where you are with another person: *Do you prefer telephone or face-to-face interviews?*

,**face 'value** n [singular, U] the value or cost shown on a coin, ticket etc

PHRASES

take sth at face value to accept what you are told without thinking carefully first: *Don't take what adverts tell you at face value.*

facial¹ /'feɪʃəl/ adj on or relating to your face: *facial hair*

facial² n [C] a beauty treatment to clean the skin on your face and make it softer

facile /'fæsaɪl $ 'fæsəl/ adj a facile remark, argument etc is too simple and shows a lack of careful thought or understanding: *a facile answer to a complex problem*

facilitate Ac /fə'sɪlɪteɪt/ v [T] formal to make it easier for something to happen: *The Web could facilitate learning.* —**facilitator** n [C]

facility Ac /fə'sɪləti/ n (plural **facilities**) 1 **facilities** [plural] rooms, equipment, or services that are provided for a particular purpose: **library/conference/ leisure etc facilities** *All rooms have **private facilities*** (=a private bathroom and toilet). 2 [C usually singular] a helpful service or feature that a machine or system has: *Does your bank offer an overdraft facility?* 3 [C] formal a building used for a particular activity: *a top-secret research facility*

facsimile /fæk'sɪməli/ n [C] an exact copy of a picture, piece of writing etc

fact /fækt/ n
1 [C] something that is true: **[+about]** ***facts and figures*** *about the Philippines* | **interesting/well-known fact** *It's a well-known fact that new cars lose their value quickly.* | **the fact that** *They lost, **despite the fact that** their opponents were reduced to 10 men.* | **in fact/as a matter of fact** (=used to add something surprising or unusual that is true) *It looks difficult, but **in actual fact** it's quite easy.* | **the fact (of the matter) is (that)** (=used to emphasize a fact) *The fact of the matter is we need more time.* | *I **know for a fact that** she's married.* | *Just **stick to the facts** (=only say what you know is true).* THESAURUS ▶ TRUE
2 [U] things that really happen or exist OPP **fiction**: *A journalist must separate fact from fiction.* → **MATTER-OF-FACT**

PHRASES

a fact of life something bad that people must accept: *Violent crime is a fact of life in our cities.*
the facts of life if you tell a child the facts of life, you explain how people have sex to produce a baby: *Most parents have difficulty talking to their children about the facts of life.*

faction /'fækʃən/ n [C] a small group of people who are part of a larger group and who have different ideas that they want the other members to accept: *The President hopes to unite his party's **warring factions**.*

factor Ac /'fæktə $ -ər/ n [C] 1 one of several things that influence or cause a situation: **[+in]** *Vaccination is an **important factor** in improving the nation's health.* | **social/economic factor** *Crime is due to economic factors.* 2 a particular position on a scale that measures the strength or effect something has: *factor 15 sun cream* 3 **by a factor of five/ten etc** if something increases or decreases by a factor of five, ten etc, it increases or decreases by five times, ten times etc: *The number of cars with airbags has increased by a factor of 10 since 1993.*

factory /'fæktəri/ n [C] (plural **factories**) a building where goods are produced in large quantities: *a car factory*

factual /'fæktʃuəl/ adj based on or relating to facts: **factual information/knowledge etc** | *factual errors* —**factually** adv

faculty /'fækəlti/ n (plural **faculties**) 1 [C] a group of departments in a university: **[+of]** *the Faculty of Law* 2 [C,U] AmE all the teachers in a school or college 3 [C usually plural] a natural ability, such as the ability to see, hear, or think: *the patient's **mental faculties***

fad /fæd/ n [C] something that is very popular for a short period of time: *the latest health fad*

fade /feɪd/ v
1 (also **fade away**) [I] to gradually disappear: *Hopes of peace are beginning to fade.* THESAURUS ▶ DISAPPEAR
2 [I,T] if material fades, or if something fades it, it becomes less bright: *The sunlight had faded the curtains.*

faeces BrE, **feces** AmE /'fi:si:z/ n [plural] formal solid waste material from your BOWELS

fag /fæg/ n [C] BrE informal a cigarette

Fahrenheit /'færənhaɪt/ n [U] (written abbreviation **F**) a temperature scale in which water freezes at 32° and boils at 212°

fail¹ /feɪl/ v
1 NOT SUCCEED [I] to not succeed in doing something that you try to do: **fail to do sth** *Doctors failed to save the girl's life.* | **[+in]** *The government has **failed in** its **attempt** to improve health services.* | *The **attempt failed**.*
2 NOT DO STH [I] to not do what is wanted, needed, or expected: **fail to do sth** *Your email failed to arrive.* | **[+in]** *teachers who **fail in** their **duty** to protect children*
3 TEST **a)** [I,T] if you fail a test, you do not pass it OPP **pass**: *I failed my driving test three times.* **b)** [T] to decide that someone has not passed a test OPP **pass**: *The examiners failed him because of poor spelling.*

Grammar
Do not say 'I failed in the test.' Say *I failed the test.*

4 STOP WORKING [I] if a machine, a part of your body etc fails, it stops working: *The engine failed after take-off.* | *his **failing** eyesight*
5 BUSINESS [I] if a business fails, it cannot continue because it has no money
6 WHEN SB TRUSTS YOU TO DO STH [T] if you fail someone, you do not do what they trusted you to do: *I felt that I had failed my parents' trust in me.* —**failed** *adj: a **failed** marriage* | *failed efforts to reform the tax laws*
PHRASES
sb's courage/nerve fails them used to say that someone suddenly loses the confidence they need to do something: *Jim's nerve failed him, and he left without asking for her phone number.*
I fail to see/understand why/how etc *formal* used to say that someone has done something annoying and you do not know why

---

THESAURUS

fail to not succeed: *She failed to get a place at university.* | *Their plan failed.*
flunk *informal especially AmE* to fail a test: *I flunked my English exam.*
not work if something does not work, it does not do what you wanted: *The treatment didn't work and he had to go back into hospital.* | *This pen doesn't work.*
go wrong if something you do goes wrong, it fails, especially after starting well: *Our chemistry experiment went wrong.*
be unsuccessful to not have the result that you wanted: *Their search was unsuccessful.* | *He applied for the job but he was unsuccessful.*
be a failure to be unsuccessful, with the result that you have wasted your efforts: *The trip was badly organized and a complete failure.*

---

fail² *n* **without fail** if you do something without fail, you always do it: *Barry rings every Friday without fail.*

failing¹ /ˈfeɪlɪŋ/ *n* [C] a fault or weakness

failing² *prep* **failing that** used to say that if one thing is not possible, there is something else you could try: *Try the specialist shops, or, failing that, the Internet.*

failure /ˈfeɪljə $ -ər/ *n*
1 [U] when someone or something does not succeed OPP **success**: *His career ended in failure.* THESAURUS ▶ FAIL
2 [C] someone or something that is not successful OPP **success**: *His last album was a total failure.*
3 **failure to do sth** the fact that someone has not done something that they should have done: *Failure to present a valid ticket will result in prosecution.*
4 [C,U] when a machine or part of your body stops working properly: **heart/kidney/liver etc failure** *He died of heart failure.* | *a power failure*

faint¹ /feɪnt/ *adj*
1 NOT CLEAR difficult to see, hear, or smell: *a faint noise* THESAURUS ▶ QUIET
2 SMALL **faint possibility/chance/hope etc** a very small possibility etc: *There's a faint hope they are still alive.*

3 WEAK if you feel faint, you feel weak and unsteady: **[+with]** *He was faint with hunger.* —**faintly** *adv*
PHRASES
not have the faintest idea (what/how etc) *informal* to not know anything at all about something

faint² *v* [I] if you faint, you become unconscious for a short time —**faint** *n* [C]

fair¹ /feə $ fer/ *adj*
1 REASONABLE reasonable, right, and accepted by most people OPP **unfair**: *It's fair to say that most scientists agree on the evolution theory.* | **not be fair on sb** *I can't work late every night – it's not fair on you.* | **to be fair** (=used to defend or excuse someone) *To be fair, she's only been in the job a week.* | **a fair deal/price/wage etc** *All we want is a fair wage.*
2 TREATING EVERYONE WELL treating everyone equally or in the right way: **[+to]** *The law is not fair to working mothers.* | *It's not fair – you always agree with Alice.* THESAURUS ▶ UNFAIR
3 AVERAGE neither very good nor very bad SYN **average**
4 LIGHT fair hair or skin is light in colour OPP **dark**
5 QUITE LARGE **a fair size/number/amount etc** quite a large size, number etc: *There's a fair chance of rain this afternoon.*
6 WEATHER fair weather is pleasant and without wind or rain —**fairness** *n* [U]
PHRASES
fair enough *BrE* used to say that what someone has said seems reasonable: *'You pay $20 and I'll pay $20.' 'Fair enough.'*
fair game if someone or something is fair game, it is reasonable and right to criticize them: *The singer's behavior made her fair game for the tabloid press.*
have more than your fair share of sth to have more problems than other people, in a way that seems unfair: *He's had more than his fair share of bad luck in his life.*

fair² *adv* **1** **fair and square** in a fair and honest way: *They won fair and square.* **2** **play fair** to play or behave in a fair and honest way

FAIR/FUNFAIR *BrE*

roller coaster

fair³ *n* [C] **1** a large outdoor event where you can buy things, get information etc: **antiques/book/computer etc fair** *an art fair* | **job/careers fair 2** (*also* **funfair** *BrE*) a form of outdoor entertainment where you can ride on exciting machines and play games to win prizes SYN **carnival** *AmE*

fairground /ˈfeəɡraʊnd $ ˈfer-/ n [C] an open space on which a fair takes place

fairly /ˈfeəli $ ˈferli/ adv
1 more than a little, but much less than very SYN **quite** BrE: She speaks English fairly well. | a fairly large room THESAURUS ▶ RATHER
2 in a way that is fair and reasonable: I felt that I wasn't treated fairly.

fair 'play n [U] when you play a game or treat people in a fair way, without cheating or being dishonest

fair 'trade n [U] the activity of obtaining goods to sell in a way that is morally good, for example to by making sure that the people who grow something are paid a fair price for it: fair trade bananas

fairway /ˈfeəweɪ $ ˈfer-/ n [C] the part of a GOLF COURSE that you hit the ball along towards the hole

fairy /ˈfeəri $ ˈferi/ n [C] (plural **fairies**) a small imaginary creature with magic powers, which looks like a very small person

fairy tale n [C] a children's story in which magical things happen

faith /feɪθ/ n
1 [U] a strong feeling of trust in someone or something: **[+in]** My faith in his ability was justified. | Everyone **had faith** in the doctor. | People will **lose faith** in the government.
2 [U] belief and trust in God: Her faith sustained her. | his faith in God
3 [C] a religion: **the Christian/Muslim/Jewish etc faith** THESAURUS ▶ RELIGION
PHRASES
good faith honest and sincere intentions: I made the offer **in good faith** (=meaning to do what I said).
keep/break faith with sb/sth to continue or stop supporting someone or something: voters who have kept faith with the Labour Party

faithful /ˈfeɪθfəl/ adj
1 remaining loyal to someone or something and continuing to support them: a **faithful friend** | **[+to]** She **remained faithful** to her principles.
2 if you are faithful to your wife, husband etc, you do not have a sexual relationship with anyone else
3 representing an event or image exactly: a faithful account of the battle | a **faithful reproduction** of the original picture —**faithfulness** n [U]

faithfully /ˈfeɪθfəl-i/ adv in a faithful way: He served us faithfully for 30 years.
PHRASES
Yours faithfully BrE the usual polite way of ending a formal letter which begins Dear Sir or Dear Madam: Yours faithfully, Miss V. Neil

fake¹ /feɪk/ adj made to look or seem like something else in order to deceive people: fake $20 bills | a fake German accent THESAURUS ▶ FALSE

fake² n [C] a copy of a valuable object that is intended to deceive people: The painting was a fake.

fake³ v **1** [T] to make something seem real in order to deceive people: He faked his father's signature on the note. **2** [I,T] to pretend to be ill, interested etc

when you are not: The doctors all thought I was **faking** it.

falcon /ˈfɔːlkən $ ˈfæl-/ n [C] a bird that eats small animals and can be trained to hunt

fall¹ /fɔːl $ fɒːl/ v (past tense **fell** /fel/, past participle **fallen** /ˈfɔːlən $ ˈfɒːl-/)
1 [I] to drop down towards the ground: Snow began to fall. | **[+out of/from]** The glass fell from his hands. | **[+down]** Something fell down the back of the fridge.
2 [I] to suddenly go down onto the ground when you are standing, walking etc: I fell and hurt my leg. | **[+down]** How did she fall down the stairs? | **[+in/into]** Pete slipped by the pool and fell in. | **fall on/to your knees** (=suddenly kneel) She fell on her knees and prayed. → see picture on page A11
3 [I] to go down to a lower level or amount OPP **rise**: The temperature fell below zero. | **[+from/to]** Profits fell from $1.3 million to $750,000. | Crime **fell sharply** (=by a large amount) last year. THESAURUS ▶ DECREASE
4 [I, linking verb] to move into a different state: I was so tired I **fell asleep** at the table. | She **fell in love with** a younger man. | Everyone **fell silent**. | **[+into]** They quickly fell into debt.
5 [I] to be part of a particular group of things: **[+into]** Both books fall into the category of historical fiction. | **[+within/under]** The matter fell within the jurisdiction of the court (=they were responsible for dealing with it).
6 [I] to hang loosely: Maria's hair fell in loose curls.
7 [I] if light or shadow falls somewhere, it appears there: **[+on/across etc]** His shadow fell across the staircase.
8 [I] to lose power: The government fell after only six months.
9 [I] to happen on a particular day or date: **[+on]** My birthday falls on a Friday this year.
10 [I] literary to be killed in a war: The monument was for all those who fell in the Great War.
PHRASES
darkness/night falls it becomes dark in the evening: We arrived just as night was beginning to fall.
sb's eyes fall on sth/sb's gaze falls on sth if your eyes fall on something, you notice it: Her eyes fell on a small object on the ground.
fall flat to fail to amuse or interest people: All my jokes fell flat.
fall into sb's hands/clutches if something falls into someone's hands, they get control over it and can use it to harm another person: These papers must not fall into the wrong hands.
fall into place if things fall into place, they become clear or start to happen as you want: Then it all fell into place and I realized what had happened.
fall into a trap to make a mistake: Don't fall into the trap of feeling guilty.
fall short to be less than is needed or less than you want: **[+of]** We fell short of our sales target this month.
fall to pieces/bits to break into many parts, especially because of being old: Her old car was falling to pieces.

| silence falls it becomes very quiet: *Silence fell on the room.*

THESAURUS – sense 2

fall (*also* **fall over/down**) to suddenly go down onto the ground when you are standing, walking etc: *She fell and cut her knee.* | *It's very slippery here. Careful you don't fall over!*
collapse to suddenly fall down because you are very tired, weak, or ill: *One of the runners collapsed during the race.*
trip on/over sth to hit your foot against something, so that you fall or almost fall: *He tripped over a rock and fell flat on his face.*
slip to slide on a smooth or slippery surface, so that you fall or almost fall: *Annie slipped on the ice and hurt her ankle.*
stumble to almost fall because you put your foot down in an awkward way: *The ground was rough and I kept stumbling.*
lose your balance to become unsteady and start to fall over: *He lost his balance when he was on top of the ladder.*

PHRASAL VERBS
fall apart
1 to break into many pieces, especially because of being old: *This house is falling apart.*
2 to stop being effective or successful: *The economy was falling apart.*
fall back on sth to use something or someone after other things or plans have failed: *If talks fail, they must fall back on the law.*
fall behind (sb/sth) to make progress more slowly than other people or than you should: *He's fallen behind at school.* | *The project has fallen behind schedule.*
fall for sb/sth
1 to be tricked into believing something that is not true: *I told him I was French and he fell for it!* **THESAURUS** ▶ BELIEVE
2 to start to love someone
fall off
1 if part of something falls off, it becomes separated from the main part: *The handle fell off.*
2 to decrease: *Demand has fallen off recently.*
fall out
1 to have a quarrel: **[+with]** *I don't want to fall out with you.*
2 if a tooth or your hair falls out, it is no longer attached to your body
fall over
1 fall over (sth) to fall to the ground: *I fell over on the ice.* | *She fell over the step* (=fell after hitting the step with her foot) *and hurt herself.*
2 fall over yourself to do sth to be very eager to do something: *They were falling over themselves to help her.*
fall through to fail to happen or be completed: *The sale fell through at the last minute.*
fall to sb/sth if an unpleasant job falls to someone, they have to do it: *It fell to me to tell them the bad news.*

fall² n
1 [DOWNWARD MOVEMENT] [C] a movement down

towards the ground: *He had a bad fall from a horse.* | *the first fall of snow that winter*
2 [DECREASE] [C] a decrease in the amount, level, or price of something [OPP] **rise**: **[+in]** *There has been a sharp fall in the temperature.* | **[+of]** *a fall of 25% in unemployment*
3 [AUTUMN] [singular, U] *AmE* the season between summer and winter, when the weather becomes colder [SYN] **autumn**: **this/that fall** *The trees were beautiful that fall.* | **in the fall** *Brad's going to college in the fall.*
4 [LOSS OF POWER] [singular] a situation when someone or something loses their power or is defeated: **[+from]** *the Prime Minister's fall from power* | **[+of]** *the rise and fall of the Roman Empire*
5 [ON RIVER] **falls** [plural] a place where a river suddenly goes straight down over a cliff [SYN] **waterfall**

fallacy /ˈfæləsi/ n [C] (*plural* **fallacies**) a false idea or belief: *the fallacy that smoking helps you concentrate*

fallen /ˈfɔːlən $ ˈfɒːl-/ v the past participle of FALL

'fall guy n [C] *informal* someone who is punished for someone else's crime or mistake

fallible /ˈfæləbəl/ *adj* able to make a mistake [OPP] **infallible**: *Humans are all fallible.*

fallout /ˈfɔːlaʊt $ ˈfɒːl-/ n [U] **1** the dangerous RADIOACTIVE dust that is in the air after a NUCLEAR explosion **2** the effects of an event: **[+from]** *We are still dealing with the fallout from his resignation.*

fallow /ˈfæləʊ $ -loʊ/ *adj* fallow land is dug but left without crops growing on it

false /fɔːls $ fɒːls/ *adj*
1 untrue or wrong: *He made false accusations.* | *Are these statements true or false?* | *The programme gave a false impression of the situation there.* **THESAURUS** ▶ WRONG
2 not real, but intended to seem real: *He adopted a false identity.* | **false teeth/eyelashes** **THESAURUS** ▶ ARTIFICIAL
3 not sincere or honest: *a false laugh* —**falsely** *adv*: *I was falsely accused.*
PHRASES
| **false alarm** a situation in which people wrongly think that something bad is going to happen: *The recent earthquake predictions were false alarms.*
| **false economy** something that is intended to save money but in fact costs more: *It's a false economy not to buy insurance.*
| **false start** an unsuccessful attempt to begin a process or event: *After two false starts, the race began.*
| **under false pretences** if you get something under false pretences, you get it by deceiving people: *He obtained the money under false pretences.*

THESAURUS

false not real – used especially about teeth, eyelashes etc. Also used about a name, address etc that someone uses to deceive people: *She was wearing false eyelashes.* | *The man used a false name.*
fake not real, and intended to deceive people. **Fake** sounds more informal than **false**: *a fake*

£20 note | a fake ID | a fake Cartier watch | a fake fur coat
forged a forged document or bank note is an illegal copy of a real one: *a forged passport*
counterfeit counterfeit money or goods are an illegal copy of the real thing: *He was arrested for trying to exchange counterfeit money.*
imitation imitation leather, fur etc is made to look like leather, fur etc, but is not real: *They're only imitation diamonds. | an imitation leather jacket*
phoney, phony *disapproving informal* not real, and intended to deceive people: *She spoke with a phoney New York accent. | phony qualifications*

falsehood /ˈfɔːlshʊd $ ˈfɒːls-/ n [C] *formal* a statement that is untrue SYN **lie**

falsify /ˈfɔːlsɪfaɪ $ ˈfɒːl-/ v [T] (**falsified, falsifying, falsifies**) to change figures, records etc so that they contain false information: *They falsified the evidence.*

falter /ˈfɔːltə $ ˈfɒːltər/ v [I] **1** to become weaker: *His determination never faltered.* **2** to stop speaking or moving because you feel weak or afraid: *She faltered for a moment.*

fame /feɪm/ n [U] the state of being known about by a lot of people because of your achievements: **win/achieve/gain/find fame** *He first won fame as a singer.* | **rise/shoot to fame** *Kate rose to fame when she was only 17.* → **claim to fame** at CLAIM²

famed /feɪmd/ *adj written* well-known SYN **famous**: **[+for]** *a region famed for its beauty*

familiar /fəˈmɪliə $ -ər/ *adj*
1 well-known to you and easy to recognize: *a familiar face* | **look/sound familiar** *The voice on the phone sounded familiar.* | **[+to]** *This problem is familiar to most teachers.*
2 be familiar with sth to know about something: *Are you familiar with this software?*
3 friendly or informal: *The waiter was a bit too familiar.* —**familiarly** *adv*: *Joseph, familiarly known as Joe*

familiarity /fəˌmɪliˈærəti/ n [U] **1** a good knowledge of something: **[+with]** *her familiarity with computers* **2** a relaxed feeling or way of behaving, because you know a person or place well: *He spoke to her with easy familiarity.*

familiarize (also **-ise** BrE) /fəˈmɪliəraɪz/ v **familiarize yourself with sth** to learn about something so that you know it well: *Familiarize yourself with the office routine.*

family /ˈfæməli/ n (plural **families**)
1 [C,U] a group of people who are related to each other, especially parents and their children: *We knew the Robertson family quite well.* | **[+of]** *a car big enough for a family of seven* | *Do you have any family in the States?* | **in sb's/the family** *I'm the only woman in our family.*
2 [C,U] children: *couples with **young families*** | *They want to **start a family** (=have a child).* | **bring up/raise a family** *Raising a family is hard work.*
3 [C] a group of related things, especially animals, plants, or languages: **the cat/dog etc family** *The tiger is a member of the cat family.* | *the Celtic family of languages*

COLLOCATIONS

adjectives
a large/big/small family *She came from a large family.*
a close family (=who spend a lot of time together and care about each other) *His family are not very close.*
the whole family/all the family *The whole family is invited.*
a one-parent/single-parent family *There are more and more one-parent families.*

noun + family
a member of sb's family *Will other members of your family need to use the computer?*

family + noun
family life (=family relationships and activities) *They have a happy family life.*
the family home (=where someone's parents or family live) *He felt it was time to leave the family home.*
a family business (=one run by members of a family) *The restaurant is a family business.*
a family holiday BrE, **a family vacation** AmE *We haven't had a family holiday for years.*

ˈfamily ˌname n [C] the name someone shares with other members of their family SYN **surname** THESAURUS NAME

ˌfamily ˈplanning n [U] the practice of controlling how many children you have, by using CONTRACEPTION

ˌfamily ˈtree n [C] a drawing that shows the names of the members of a family over a period of time and how they are related to each other

famine /ˈfæmɪn/ n [C,U] a situation in which a large number of people have little or no food for a long time and some people die

famished /ˈfæmɪʃt/ *adj* [not before noun] *informal* extremely hungry: *What's for supper? I'm famished.*

famous /ˈfeɪməs/ *adj*
1 known about by a lot of people: *a famous actor* | **[+for]** *France is famous for its wine.*
2 the famous people who are famous → **WORLD-FAMOUS**

THESAURUS

famous known about by a lot of people, often all over the world: *He's one of the most famous artists in the world.*
well-known known about by a lot of people, especially in a particular place: *In Egypt, she is very well-known.* | *a well-known restaurant*
renowned famous for something. **Renowned** is rather formal and is used mainly in writing: *The area is renowned for its beauty.* | *an internationally renowned chef*
legendary very famous and greatly admired – used about people, especially performers: *the legendary Frank Sinatra*
notorious/infamous famous in a bad way: *a notorious criminal*

famously /ˈfeɪməsli/ *adv* in a way that is very well-known: *Her cooking was famously awful.*

PHRASES

get on/along famously to get on with someone very well: *The two girls got along famously.*

FANS

fan

electric fan

fan¹ /fæn/ *n* [C]
1 someone who likes something such as a sport, type of music, or singer very much: **football/film/rock etc fan** *Thousands of football fans filled the stadium.* | **[+of]** *He was a big fan of Elvis Presley.*
2 a machine, or a thing that you wave with your hand, that cools you by making the air move

fan² *v* [T] (**fanned, fanning**) to make air move by waving a fan, piece of paper etc: *She fanned herself with a magazine.*

PHRASAL VERBS

fan out if a group of people fan out, they walk forwards while spreading over a wide area: *The soldiers fanned out across the moor.*

fanatic /fəˈnætɪk/ *n* [C] **1** someone who has extreme religious or political ideas and may be dangerous **SYN extremist**: *religious fanatics* **2** someone who likes a particular thing or activity very much: *a golf fanatic* —**fanatical** *adj* —**fanatically** /-kli/ *adv* —**fanaticism** /-tɪsɪzəm/ *n* [U]

fanciful /ˈfænsɪfəl/ *adj* imagined rather than based on facts

fancy¹ /ˈfænsi/ *v* [T] (**fancied, fancying, fancies**) *BrE informal* **1** to like or want something: *Do you fancy a drink?* | **fancy doing sth** *I don't fancy going out tonight.* **2** to feel sexually attracted to someone: *I think he fancies you.*

PHRASES

fancy!/fancy that! *spoken* used when you are surprised: *'The Petersons are getting divorced.' 'Fancy that!'*

fancy² *adj* **1** expensive and fashionable: *a fancy hotel* **THESAURUS EXPENSIVE 2** unusual and complicated, or having a lot of decoration: *I like simple food – nothing fancy.*

fancy³ *n* [singular] a feeling of liking something or someone: *He seems to have taken a fancy to you.*

PHRASES

take sb's fancy if something takes your fancy, you want to have it: *Did you see anything in the store that took your fancy?*

fancy 'dress *n* [U] *BrE* clothes that you wear, especially to parties, that make you look like a famous person, a character from a story etc: *a fancy-dress party* **THESAURUS PARTY**

fanfare /ˈfænfeə $ -fer/ *n* [C] a short loud piece of music played on a TRUMPET to introduce an important person or event

fang /fæŋ/ *n* [C] a long sharp tooth of an animal such as a snake or dog

fantasize (*also* -**ise** *BrE*) /ˈfæntəsaɪz/ *v* [I,T] to think about something that is pleasant or exciting, but unlikely to happen: **[+about]** *We all fantasize about winning the lottery.*

fantastic /fænˈtæstɪk/ *adj* **1** *informal* extremely good: *You look fantastic.* | *What a fantastic house!* | *'I got the job.' 'Fantastic!'* **THESAURUS GOOD 2** a fantastic amount is very large **3** strange or unreal: *fantastic tales of knights and dragons* —**fantastically** /-kli/ *adv*

fantasy /ˈfæntəsi/ *n* [C,U] (*plural* **fantasies**) an experience or situation that you imagine but is not real: *I had fantasies about being an artist.* **THESAURUS DREAM**

FAQ /fæk, ˌef eɪ ˈkjuː/ *n* [C] (**frequently asked questions**) a list of answers to the questions that are most often asked about a subject, especially on the Internet

far¹ /fɑː $ fɑːr/ *adv* (*comparative* **farther** /ˈfɑːðə $ ˈfɑːrðər/ *or* **further** /ˈfɜːðə $ ˈfɜːrðər/, *superlative* **farthest** /ˈfɑːðɪst $ ˈfɑːr-/ *or* **furthest** /ˈfɜːðɪst $ ˈfɜːr-/)
1 a long distance: *Have you driven far?* | *See who can throw the farthest.* | **[+from]** *I work not far from here.* | **[+away]** *Her children have all moved far away.* | **[+down/along etc]** *They live further along the street.*
2 used to ask or talk about distance: **How far** is it to the station? | *He didn't say how far he had walked.*
3 very much, or to a great degree: **far better/easier etc** *The new system is far better than the old one.* | **far more/less** *It cost far less than I expected.* | **far too much/fat/early etc** *That's far too much for one person.* | *She is by far the best athlete in the school* (=much better than anyone else). | **As far as possible** (=as much as possible), *we use fresh local ingredients.*
4 used to talk about how much progress someone makes: **How far** have you **got** with your book? | *They only **got as far as** the first course before the phone rang.* | *She's very talented and should **go far** (=be very successful).*
5 a long time: **[+ahead/back]** *We need to plan further ahead.* | *This system was being used **as far back as** 1850.* | **[+into]** *They worked far into the night.* → **as far as sth is concerned** at CONCERNED

PHRASES

as far as sth to a particular place or point, but not beyond it: *I'll come with you as far as the corner of the street.* | *The water came up as far as my knees.*
as far as I know/I can tell/I can remember etc *spoken* used to say that you think something is true, but you may be wrong: *As far as I know, Fran intends to come.*
far and wide over a large area: *His fame spread far and wide.*

far from sth used to say that something is not at all true: *The situation is far from ideal.* | *'Are you angry?' 'Far from it! I'm delighted.'*

go so far as to do sth to do something that seems surprising or extreme: *I wouldn't go so far as to call her a liar.*

go too far (*also* **take it too far**) to do something that is too extreme: *I don't mind jokes, but you've gone too far this time.*

so far until now: *We haven't had any problems so far.*

so far so good *spoken* used to say that something has been successful until now: *'How's your new job?' 'So far so good.'*

> **Grammar**
>
> Do not say 'My school is far.' Say *My school is a long way from here,* or *My school is a long way away.*
>
> **Far** is usually used in questions: *How far is it to your school?* and in negative sentences: *The school isn't very far from here.*
>
> You can also use **far** after **too**, **as**, and **so**: *It's too far to walk.* | *I ran as far as I could.* | *I wish he didn't live so far away.*

THESAURUS

far a long distance – used in negatives and questions, or after 'too', 'so', and 'as': *It's not far to the hotel.* | *Is it too far to walk?*

a long way a long distance: *It's a long way to the sea from here.*

miles *informal* a very long distance – used especially when you wish the distance was not so long: *We had to walk for miles.* | *The nearest school is miles away.*

distant *written* used about something that is a long distance from you, and often difficult to see or hear: *I could hear the distant sound of thunder.* | *the light from a distant star*

remote used about a place that is a long distance from other places: *a remote area of Alaska*

---

far² *adj* (*comparative* **farther** *or* **further**, *superlative* **farthest** *or* **furthest**)

1 a long distance away **OPP** **near**: *We can walk to the restaurant – it's not far.*

2 the far side/end/corner etc the side, end etc most distant from where you are: *the far side of the street*

PHRASES

be a far cry from sth to be very different from something: *His life as a pop star was a far cry from his childhood in Leeds.*

the far left/right people who have extreme political opinions: *Their supporters come from the far right.*

the far north/south etc the part of an area that is furthest to the north, the south etc: *They live in the far north of Scotland.*

faraway /ˈfɑːrəweɪ/ *adj* [only before noun] *literary* distant: *faraway places*

PHRASES

a faraway look an expression on your face that shows that you are not thinking about what is

around you: *Sometimes his eyes would have that faraway look.*

farce /fɑːs $ fɑːrs/ *n* **1** [singular] an event or situation that is very badly organized or not done properly: *The interview was a complete farce.* **2** [C,U] a humorous play or film with a lot of silly complicated situations —**farcical** *adj*

fare¹ /feə $ fer/ *n*

1 [C] the amount you pay to travel by train, plane, bus etc: **bus/train fare** *What's the bus fare into town?* | **air/rail fare** **THESAURUS** COST

2 [U] food, especially food served in a restaurant: *They serve traditional fare.*

fare² *v* **fare well/better/badly etc** *formal* to be successful or unsuccessful in a particular situation: *Girls fared better than boys in the tests.*

farewell /ˌfeəˈwel◄ $ ˌfer-/ *n* [C,U] the action of saying goodbye: *a party to* **bid farewell to** *their old house* | *a farewell speech*

far-'fetched *adj* very unlikely to be true: *Her story was pretty far-fetched.*

far-'flung *adj* very far away: *far-flung corners of the globe*

farm¹ /fɑːm $ fɑːrm/ *n* [C] an area of land used for growing crops or keeping animals: *a 4,000-acre farm* | **on a farm** *I grew up on a farm.* | **pig/dairy/fruit etc farm**

> **Grammar**
>
> Do not say 'She lives in a farm.' Say *She lives on a farm.*

farm² *v* [I,T] to use land for growing crops or keeping animals: *Our family has farmed here for generations.* | *They farm their land organically.* | **farmed salmon/rabbits etc** (=not wild)

farmer /ˈfɑːmə $ ˈfɑːrmər/ *n* [C] someone who owns or manages a farm: **pig/dairy/fruit etc farmer**

farmhouse /ˈfɑːmhaʊs $ ˈfɑːrm-/ *n* [C] the main house on a farm, where the farmer lives

farming /ˈfɑːmɪŋ $ ˈfɑːr-/ *n* [U] the activity of growing crops or keeping animals on a farm: **organic farming** (=without using chemicals) | **factory farming** (=when animals are kept inside in small spaces)

farmland /ˈfɑːmlænd, -lənd $ ˈfɑːrmlænd/ *n* [U] land used for farming **THESAURUS** LAND

farmyard /ˈfɑːmjɑːd $ ˈfɑːrmjɑːrd/ *n* [C] an area surrounded by farm buildings

far-'off *adj* *literary* a long distance away or a long time ago: *a far-off land*

far-'reaching *adj* having a big influence or effect: *far-reaching reforms*

farsighted /ˌfɑːˈsaɪtɪd◄ $ ˌfɑːr-/ *adj* *AmE* able to see or read things clearly only when they are far away from you **SYN** **longsighted** *BrE*

fart /fɑːt $ fɑːrt/ *v* [I] *informal* a rude word meaning to let air come out of your BOWELS —**fart** *n* [C]

farther /ˈfɑːðə $ ˈfɑːrðər/ *adj, adv* a COMPARATIVE form of FAR

> **Usage**
> In everyday English, people usually say **further**.

farthest /ˈfɑːðɪst $ ˈfɑːr-/ adj, adv a SUPERLATIVE form of FAR

> **Usage**
> In everyday English, people usually say **furthest**.

fascinate /ˈfæsɪneɪt/ v [T] to interest you very much: *The story fascinated her.*

fascinated /ˈfæsɪneɪtɪd/ adj extremely interested: **[+by]** *I am fascinated by space travel.* **THESAURUS** INTERESTED

fascinating /ˈfæsəneɪtɪŋ/ adj extremely interesting: *a fascinating subject* | *She **found** him **fascinating**.* **THESAURUS** INTERESTING

fascination /ˌfæsəˈneɪʃən/ n [singular, U] **1** the state of being very interested in something: **[+with/for]** *He had a fascination with science.* **2** the quality of being very interesting: *The sea has always **held** a **fascination** for me.*

fascism /ˈfæʃɪzəm/ n [U] an extreme RIGHT-WING political system in which people's lives are completely controlled by the state

fascist /ˈfæʃɪst/ n [C] someone who supports fascism —**fascist** adj

fashion¹ /ˈfæʃən/ n
1 [C,U] a style of clothes that is popular at a particular time, or the business of making or selling new clothes: *I'm not really interested in fashion.* | *Learn which fashions suit you.*
2 [C,U] something that is popular or thought to be good at a particular time: **[+for]** *There was a fashion for houses with big windows.* | **[+in]** *Fashions in education have changed.* | **in fashion** *Hats are in fashion again.* | **come into/go out of fashion** *Those ideas went out of fashion years ago.* | *Being very thin **is the fashion** nowadays.* **THESAURUS** FASHIONABLE
3 in a ... fashion formal in a particular way: *Can we discuss this in a civilized fashion?*

COLLOCATIONS

fashion + noun

a fashion show *She was in the audience at several Paris fashion shows.*
a fashion designer *Her favourite fashion designer is Giorgio Armani.*
a fashion model *Fashion models are usually very tall.*
a fashion magazine *She has been on the cover of every fashion magazine.*
the fashion industry *I would like a career in the fashion industry.*

adjectives

the latest fashion *She likes to wear all the latest fashions.* ⚠ Do not say 'the last fashion'. Say **the latest fashion**.

fashion² v [T] formal to shape or make something with your hands or a few tools: *He fashioned a seat from a tree stump.*

fashionable /ˈfæʃənəbəl/ adj popular or thought to be good at a particular time OPP **unfashionable**: *Black is very fashionable now.* | *It was fashionable to be thin.* | **fashionable restaurant/shop/club etc** —**fashionably** adv: *a fashionably dressed young man*

THESAURUS

fashionable popular at a particular time: *Short skirts are fashionable again.* | *Her books were fashionable in the 1980s.*
trendy informal modern and fashionable – often used about places or people that you think try too hard to be fashionable: *The area is full of smart shops and trendy restaurants.* | *His sunglasses looked very trendy.*
in fashion popular, especially for a short time – used especially about clothes: *What's in fashion this summer?*
in informal popular now: *Purple is in this year.* | *London is definitely **the in place to be**.*

fast¹ /fɑːst $ fæst/ adv
1 at a great speed, or in not much time: *You're driving too fast!* | *How fast can you get the job done?* | *a **fast-moving**, exciting film* **THESAURUS** QUICKLY
2 fast asleep sleeping very deeply: *Jim was fast asleep on the couch.*
3 be stuck/held fast to be held very firmly: *The car was stuck fast in the mud.*

fast² adj
1 moving, happening, or doing something quickly: *a fast car* | *a fast learner* | *The metro is the fastest way to get around.*
2 [not before noun] a clock that is fast shows a later time than the real time: *My watch is five minutes fast.*

THESAURUS

fast moving quickly or doing something quickly: *a fast car* | *the fastest animal in the world* | *a fast worker*
quick doing something in a short time: *I'll just have a quick wash.* | *'I'm back!' 'That was quick!'*
rapid especially written happening in a short time – used especially about changes, increases etc: *a rapid increase in the population*
high-speed designed to travel or operate very fast – used about trains and computer systems: *a high-speed train* | *high-speed Internet access*
swift written done very quickly, or after only a short time: *With a sudden swift movement, he seized the gun.*

fast³ v [I] to eat little or no food for a period of time, especially for religious reasons —**fast** n [C]

fasten /ˈfɑːsən $ ˈfæ-/ v
1 [I,T] to join together the two sides of something so that it is closed, or to become joined together: *Fasten your seat belts.* | *The skirt fastens at the back.*
2 [T] to attach something firmly to another object or surface: **fasten sth to/onto sth** *I fastened the rope to a tree.*
3 [T] to close and lock a window, gate etc

fastener /ˈfɑːsənə $ ˈfæsənər/ n [C] BrE something such as a button or pin that you use to join something together

fastening /ˈfɑːsənɪŋ $ ˈfæ-/ n [C] something that keeps a door, window etc shut

fast food n [U] food such as HAMBURGERS that is prepared and eaten quickly in a restaurant: *a fast food restaurant* **THESAURUS** ▶ **RESTAURANT**

fast-'forward v [I,T] to wind a tape or video forwards quickly without playing it —**fast forward** n [U]

fastidious /fæˈstɪdiəs/ adj very careful about small details: *He is fastidious about hygiene.* —**fastidiously** adv

fast lane n **the fast lane a)** *informal* an exciting way of life that involves expensive or dangerous activities: *She loves life in the fast lane.* **b)** the part of a big road where people drive fastest

fast track n [singular] a quick way to achieve something: *You're on the fast track to success.* —**fast-track** adj

fat¹ /fæt/ adj
1 having too much flesh on your body **OPP** thin: *You'll get fat if you eat all that.* | *a short, fat man*
2 thick or wide **OPP** thin: *a fat book*
3 [only before noun] worth a lot of money: **fat salary/paycheck/profits etc** *They wrote me a nice fat cheque.*

PHRASES

fat chance *informal* used to say that something is very unlikely to happen: *'Do you think he'll pay the money back?' 'Fat chance!'*

THESAURUS

fat having too much flesh on your body. It is rude to tell someone that they are **fat**: *I don't want to get fat.*

overweight weighing more than you should: *Her husband was very overweight.* | *I'm a few pounds overweight.*

big/large used when saying that someone has a big body: *He was a big man and I thought I'd better do what he said.*

obese extremely fat in a way that is dangerous to your health: *One third of the American population is obese.*

chubby slightly fat in a pleasant way – used especially about babies and children: *a chubby little boy in short trousers*

plump *especially written* slightly fat. **Plump** sounds gentler and nicer than **fat**: *She was a plump cheerful woman.*

fat² n
1 [U] the substance under the skin of people and animals which helps to keep them warm
2 [C,U] a substance contained in foods such as milk, cheese, butter etc: **high/low in fat** *Choose foods that are lower in fat.* | **low-fat/high-fat/full-fat** *a low-fat diet* | *full-fat milk*
3 [C,U] an oily substance taken from animals or plants and used in cooking: *Fry the onions in bacon fat.*

fatal /ˈfeɪtl/ adj **1** resulting in someone's death: **fatal accident/injury/illness etc** *a fatal heart attack* **2** having a very bad effect: **fatal mistake/error**

Treating employees badly is a fatal mistake. —**fatally** adv

fatalism /ˈfeɪtl-ɪzəm/ n [U] the belief that there is nothing you can do to prevent events from happening —**fatalist** n [C] —**fatalistic** /ˌfeɪtlˈɪstɪk◀/ adj

fatality /fəˈtæləti/ n [C] (*plural* **fatalities**) a death in an accident or a violent attack

fate /feɪt/ n
1 [C] the things that happen to someone, especially unpleasant events: **[+of]** *No one knows what the fate of the hostages will be.* | *The rest of Europe was to* **suffer** *the same* **fate.**
2 [U] a power that is believed to control what happens in people's lives: *Fate plays cruel tricks sometimes.* | **twist/quirk of fate** (=something unexpected that happens) *By a* **strange twist of fate***, we were on the same plane.*

fated /ˈfeɪtɪd/ adj [not before noun] certain to happen or to do something because a mysterious force is controlling events: **be fated to do sth** *We were fated to meet.*

fateful /ˈfeɪtfəl/ adj having an important, usually bad, effect on future events: *a fateful decision* —**fatefully** adv

father¹ /ˈfɑːðə $ -ər/ n [C]
1 a male parent: *Ask your father to help you.* | *Andrew was very excited about becoming a father.*
2 (*also* **Father**) a priest, especially in the Roman Catholic Church: *Do you know Father Vernon?*

father² v [T] to become a male parent: *He fathered five children.*

Father 'Christmas n *BrE* an imaginary man who wears red clothes, has a long white beard, and is said to bring presents to children at Christmas **SYN** **Santa Claus**

'father figure n [C] an older man who you trust and respect

fatherhood /ˈfɑːðəhʊd $ -ðər-/ n [U] the state of being a father

'father-in-law n [C] (*plural* **fathers-in-law**) the father of your husband or wife

fatherly /ˈfɑːðəli $ -ðər-/ adj typical of a kind and caring father: *fatherly advice*

'Father's Day n [C] a day on which people give cards and presents to their father → **Mother's Day**

fathom¹ /ˈfæðəm/ (*also* **fathom out**) v [T] to understand what something means after thinking about it carefully: *I still can't fathom out what she meant.*

fathom² n [C] a unit for measuring how deep water is, equal to 1.83 metres

fatigue /fəˈtiːg/ n [U] **1** extreme tiredness: *Sam's face was grey with fatigue.* **2** *technical* weakness in a substance such as metal that may cause it to break

fatten /ˈfætn/ v [T] to make an animal become fatter so that it is ready to eat

PHRASAL VERBS

fatten sb/sth ↔ **up** to make a thin person or animal fatter: *My mum's always trying to fatten me up.*

fattening /ˈfætn-ɪŋ/ adj likely to make you fat: *Avoid fattening foods like chocolate.*

fatty

fatty /ˈfæti/ *adj* containing a lot of fat: *fatty foods*

fatuous /ˈfætʃuəs/ *adj* very silly or stupid: *a fatuous remark*

faucet /ˈfɔːsɪt $ ˈfɒː-/ *n* [C] *AmE* the thing that you turn on or off in order to control the flow of water from a pipe SYN **tap** *BrE*: *a leaky faucet* → see picture at BATHROOM

fault¹ /fɔːlt $ fɒːlt/ *n*

1 RESPONSIBILITY **be sb's fault** if something bad that happens is your fault, you are responsible for it happening: *I injured my back, but it was my own fault.* | *It's your fault that we're late.* | **be sb's fault for doing sth** *It's my fault for not checking* (=I should have checked). THESAURUS ▶ BLAME

2 PROBLEM [C] something that is wrong with something: *a design fault* | **[+in]** *There's a fault in one of the loudspeakers.*

3 BAD QUALITY [C] a bad part of someone's character: *His worst fault is his arrogance.*

4 CRACK IN THE EARTH [C] a large crack in the rocks that form the Earth's surface: *the San Andreas fault* → **find fault with sb/sth** at FIND¹

PHRASES

be at fault to be responsible for something bad that has happened: *It was the other driver who was at fault.*

THESAURUS

fault something wrong with a machine, system, design etc: *The plane developed a fault in its engine.* | *a fault in the original design*

defect a fault in the way something was made: *The toy has a defect which makes it more likely to break.*

bug a fault in a computer program: *There must be some kind of bug in the system.*

flaw a mark that stops something from being perfect, or a mistake that stops an idea from being good: *The glass had one tiny flaw in it.* | *Their plan had a serious flaw.*

fault² *v* [T] to find a mistake in something: *Her performance could not be faulted.*

faultless /ˈfɔːltləs $ ˈfɒːlt-/ *adj* having no mistakes SYN **perfect**: *Yasmin spoke faultless French.*

faulty /ˈfɔːlti $ ˈfɒːlti/ *adj* **1** not working properly: *faulty wiring* **2** not correct: *faulty reasoning*

fauna /ˈfɔːnə $ ˈfɒː-/ *n* [C,U] technical all the animals living in a particular area → **flora**

faux pas /ˌfəʊ ˈpɑː, ˌfəʊ pɑː $ ˌfoʊ ˈpɑː/ *n* [C] (*plural* **faux pas** /-ˈpɑːz/) an embarrassing mistake in a social situation

favour¹ *BrE*, **favor** *AmE* /ˈfeɪvə $ -ər/ *n*

1 [C] something you do for someone in order to help them: *Could you do me a favour and tell Kelly I'm here?* | *He hired John as a favour to his father.* | *Paul, can I ask you a favour?* THESAURUS ▶ HELP

2 [U] support, approval, or agreement for something: **in favour of sth** *He spoke in favour of the proposal.* | **find/gain/win favour (with sb)** *The idea may win favour with older people.*

PHRASES

abandon/drop etc sth in favour of sth to decide not to have one thing and have something else instead: *Plans for a tunnel were rejected in favour of the bridge.*

in favour/out of favour if someone or something is in favour, people like them and approve of them: *Thompson was soon back in favour.* | **fall/go out of favour** (=become unpopular) *The custom fell out of favour at the beginning of the century.*

in sb's favour to someone's advantage, or so that someone wins: *The new rules should actually work in your favour.* | *The final score was 2–1 in Algeria's favour.*

favour² *BrE*, **favor** *AmE* *v* [T] **1** to prefer something or someone to other things or people: *Both countries seemed to favour the agreement.* **2** to treat someone better than someone else in an unfair way: *tax cuts that favour the rich*

favourable *BrE*, **favorable** *AmE* /ˈfeɪvərəbəl/ *adj* **1** showing that you like or approve of someone or something: *The film received favourable reviews.* **2** suitable and likely to make something happen or succeed: *The disease spreads quickly under favourable conditions.* **3** **make a favourable impression** to make people like or approve of you: *Try to make a favourable impression on the interviewer.* —**favourably** *adv*

favourite¹ *BrE*, **favorite** *AmE* /ˈfeɪvərət/ *adj* [only before noun] your favourite person or thing is the one you like most: *a child's favourite toy* | *What's your favourite colour?*

favourite² *BrE*, **favorite** *AmE* *n* [C] **1** something that you like more than others of the same kind: *a sweater that's an old favourite* **2** someone who is liked and treated better than others by a teacher or parent: *She was always Dad's favourite.* **3** the team, player etc that is expected to win a race or competition: *Brazil were the favorites to win the World Cup.*

favouritism *BrE*, **favoritism** *AmE* /ˈfeɪvərətɪzəm/ *n* [U] when one person or group is treated better than another in an unfair way

fawn¹ /fɔːn $ fɒːn/ *n* **1** [C] a young DEER **2** [U] a pale yellow-brown colour

fawn² *v* [I] to praise someone and be friendly to them because you want something: **[+on/over]** *journalists who fawn over celebrities*

fax /fæks/ *n*

1 [C] a document that is sent down a telephone line and then printed using a special machine: *Did you get my fax?*

2 (*also* **fax machine**) [C] a machine used for sending and receiving faxes: *What's your fax number?*

3 [U] the system of sending documents using a fax machine: **by fax** *You can book tickets by fax.* —**fax** *v* [T]: *Can you fax me the details?*

faze /feɪz/ *v* [T] informal to make you feel confused or embarrassed, so that you do not know what to do: *Nothing seemed to faze him.*

FBI /ˌef biː ˈaɪ/ *n* **the FBI** (**the Federal Bureau of Investigation**) the US police department that is controlled by the government and is concerned with crimes that happen in more than one state

fear¹ /fɪə $ fɪr/ n [C,U] the feeling you get when you are afraid or worried that something bad will happen: *His voice was full of fear.* | **[+of]** *a fear of flying* | **[+that]** *fears that prices might continue to rise* | **[+for]** *She expressed fears for her daughter's safety.* | **with fear** *The prisoner was shaking with fear.*

PHRASES

for fear (that)/for fear of sth because you are worried that something bad will happen: *They travelled at night, for fear of being seen.*

No fear! *BrE spoken informal* used humorously to say that you are definitely not going to do something: *'Do you want to come with us?' 'No fear!'*

COLLOCATIONS

adjectives

sb's greatest/worst/biggest fear *Her worst fear was making a complete fool of herself.*

an irrational fear (=one that is not reasonable) *She has an irrational fear of birds.*

frozen/paralysed with fear (=so afraid that you cannot move) *I just stood on the diving board, paralysed with fear.*

verbs

to have a fear of sth *He's always had a fear of heights.*

to show fear *I tried not to show any fear.*

to shake/tremble with fear *She was crying and trembling with fear.*

to conquer/overcome your fear (=to stop being afraid of something) *He overcame his fear of water and learned to swim.*

Word Choice: fear or fright?

Fear is the usual word to use when talking about the feeling of being afraid of something: *She has a fear of spiders.* | *Losing a child is every parent's greatest fear.*

You use **fright** when talking about something that suddenly frightens you, especially in the following phrases: *The snake gave me a fright.* | *The two boys ran off in fright.*

---

fear² v

1 [I,T] to feel afraid or worried that something bad will happen or has happened: **[+(that)]** *Police fear there may be further attacks.* | *Hundreds of people are feared dead.* | *When he didn't come home, we feared the worst* (=were afraid something very bad had happened). | **[+for]** *We left because we feared for our lives.*

2 [T] to be afraid of someone: *As a leader, he was feared by his people.*

fearful /ˈfɪəfəl $ ˈfɪr-/ adj **1** formal afraid: **[+of]** *People are fearful of rising crime.* **2** BrE extremely bad: *The room was in a fearful mess.* —**fearfully** adv

fearless /ˈfɪələs $ ˈfɪr-/ adj not afraid of anything: *a fearless explorer* —**fearlessly** adv —**fearlessness** n [U]

fearsome /ˈfɪəsəm $ ˈfɪr-/ adj very frightening: *a fearsome sight*

feasible /ˈfiːzəbəl/ adj possible, and likely to work: *a feasible solution*

feast¹ /fiːst/ n [C] **1** a large meal for a lot of people to celebrate a special occasion: *a wedding feast* **THESAURUS** MEAL **2** *informal* a good large meal: *That was a real feast!* **3** a religious holiday

feast² v [I] to eat a large meal to celebrate something

PHRASES

feast your eyes on sb/sth to look at someone or something with great pleasure: *If you like luxury cars, feast your eyes on these.*

feat /fiːt/ n [C] an impressive achievement needing a lot of strength or skill: **[+of]** *an amazing feat of engineering* | **be no mean feat** (=be difficult to do) *Getting a doctorate is no mean feat!*

feather¹ /ˈfeðə $ -ər/ n [C] one of the soft light things that cover a bird's body: *an ostrich feather →* see picture on page A3

feather² v **feather your nest** to get money by dishonest methods

feathery /ˈfeðəri/ adj soft and light like feathers: *a fern with feathery leaves*

feature¹ Ac /ˈfiːtʃə $ -ər/ n [C]

1 an important, interesting, or typical part of something: **[+of]** *An important feature of his paintings is their colours.* | *Striped tails are a common feature of many animals.*

2 a piece of writing about a subject in a newspaper or a magazine, or a special report on television or on the radio: **[+on]** *a special feature on holidaying with your dog*

3 [usually plural] a part of someone's face, such as their eyes, nose etc: *Her eyes are her best feature.*

feature² Ac v [I,T] to include something as a special or important part, or to be included: *a new movie featuring Meryl Streep* | *Blake's name did not feature in the report.*

ˈfeature ˌfilm n [C] a film of normal length made for the cinema

February /ˈfebruəri, ˈfebjʊri $ ˈfebjueri/ n [C,U] (*written abbreviation* **Feb.**) the second month of the year, between January and March: **next/last February** *Mum died last February.* | **in February** *We can do it in February.* | **on February 6th** *He arrives on February 6th.*

feces /ˈfiːsiːz/ n the American spelling of FAECES

feckless /ˈfekləs/ adj a feckless person is not determined, effective, or successful

fed /fed/ v the past tense and past participle of FEED

federal Ac /ˈfedərəl/ adj **1** consisting of a group of states that make some of their own decisions but are controlled by a central government: *Switzerland is a federal republic.* **2** relating to the national government of a country which consists of several states: *federal laws*

federation Ac /ˌfedəˈreɪʃən/ n [C] a group of states or organizations that have joined together to form a larger group: *the International Boxing Federation*

fed up

ˌfed ˈup *adj* [not before noun] *informal* annoyed or bored and wanting change: **[+with]** *I'm fed up with this constant rain.*

fee Ac /fiː/ *n* [C] an amount of money that you pay for professional services or that you pay to do something: *medical fees | college fees | The museum charges an* **entrance fee.** **THESAURUS** COST

feeble /ˈfiːbəl/ *adj* **1** extremely weak: *His voice sounded feeble.* **THESAURUS** WEAK **2** not good or effective: *a feeble excuse*

feed¹ /fiːd/ *v* (*past tense and past participle* **fed** /fed/)
1 GIVE FOOD [T] to give food to a person or animal: *Have you fed the cats?* | **feed sth to sb** *Children were feeding bread to the ducks.* | **feed sb on/with sth** *Her mum fed her on stews and meat pies.*
2 EAT [I] if animals or babies feed, they eat: **[+on]** *In winter, the birds feed on berries.* **THESAURUS** EAT
3 GIVE PLANT FOOD [T] to give a substance to a plant to help it grow
4 PROVIDE MONEY FOR FOOD [T] to provide enough food for a group of people: *money with which to feed and clothe their families*
5 SUPPLY [T] to supply something, or to put something into something else: **feed sth to sth** *The sound is fed directly to the headphones.* → **BREAST-FEED, SPOON-FEED**

feed² *n* **1** [C] *BrE* when milk is given to a small baby: **Has he had his feed yet? 2** [U] food for animals: *cattle feed*

feedback /ˈfiːdbæk/ *n* [U] advice, criticism etc about how successful or useful something is: **[+on]** *Try to* **give** *the students some* **feedback** *on the task.*

feel¹ /fiːl/ *v* (*past tense and past participle* **felt** /felt/)
1 [linking verb, T] to experience a particular physical feeling or emotion: *Do you still feel hungry? | Marie immediately felt guilty. | Stop exercising if you feel any pain. | 'How do you feel?' 'Better.' |* **[+as if/as though/like]** *I felt as though I'd won a million dollars.*
2 [T] to notice something that is touching you or happening to you: *He felt her breath on his cheek.* | **feel sb/sth do sth** *She felt his arms go round her.* | **feel yourself doing sth** *I felt myself blushing.*
3 [linking verb] to seem to have a particular quality when touched or experienced by someone: **feel smooth/cold/damp etc** *Her hands felt rough.* | *The house felt hot and stuffy.* | *Seeing him again felt strange.* | *How does* **it** *feel to be 40?* | **[+like]** *It was a year ago, but it still feels like yesterday.*
4 [I,T] to have an opinion based on your feelings rather than on facts: **[+(that)]** *I feel that I should do more to help.* | **[+about]** *How would you feel about working with Nicole?* | **feel sure/certain** *She felt sure she'd made the right decision.* **THESAURUS** THINK
5 [T] to touch something with your fingers to find out about it: *Mum, feel this stone. Isn't it smooth?* **THESAURUS** TOUCH
6 feel around/in sth etc (for sth) to try to find something by using your fingers: *She felt in her bag for a pencil.*
7 feel the force/effect/benefits etc of sth to experience the good or bad results of something: *They're beginning to feel the effects of the recession.*

PHRASES
feel like (doing) sth to want to have something or do something: *Do you feel like another drink?* **THESAURUS** WANT
feel your way 1 to move carefully with your hands out in front of you because you cannot see well: *He felt his way across the room.* **2** to do things slowly and carefully, because you are unsure about a new situation: **[+towards]** *The government is feeling its way towards a new policy.*

PHRASAL VERBS
feel for sb to feel sympathy for someone: *It was awful. I really felt for her.*

feel² *n* [singular]
1 the way that something seems to people: **[+about]** *The restaurant has a nice, relaxed feel about it.*
2 the way something feels when you touch it: **[+of]** *I like the feel of this cloth.* | *a soft feathery feel*
PHRASES
have/get a feel for sth *informal* to have or develop an understanding of something or ability with something: *Pete has a real feel for languages.*

feeling /ˈfiːlɪŋ/ *n*
1 [C,U] something that you feel in your mind, for example happiness or sadness: *Don't try to hide your feelings.* | **[+of]** *terrible feelings of guilt*
2 sb's feelings [plural] whether someone is upset or not: *He doesn't care about my feelings.*
3 [C] something that you feel physically and that affects your body: **[+of]** *feelings of dizziness | a sudden feeling of nausea*
4 [C] a belief or opinion about something: **[+on/about]** *She has* **strong feelings** *on the issue of abortion.* | *My own feeling is that we should wait.* | **[+(that)]** *I had a* **feeling** *that he'd refuse. | Leslie* **got the feeling** *that she was being watched.*
5 [U] people's attitude about a subject: *anti-American feeling |* **[+against/in favour of]** *the* **depth of feeling** *against nuclear weapons*
6 [U] the ability to feel pain, heat, cold etc in your body: *He lost all feeling in his legs.* → **gut feeling** at **GUT¹**
PHRASES
bad/ill feeling anger or lack of trust between people: *The changes have caused ill feeling in the workforce.*
have a bad feeling about sth to feel that there is something wrong about a situation, or that something bad is going to happen: *I had a bad feeling about this job from the start.*
I know the feeling *spoken* said when you understand how someone feels because you have had the same experience: *'It's embarrassing when you can't remember someone's name.' 'I know the feeling.'*

COLLOCATIONS
verbs

to have a feeling *Stephen had a sudden feeling of panic.*
to give sb a feeling *The money gave her a feeling of security.*

to hide your feelings *She could no longer hide her feelings.*
to show your feelings *Don't be afraid to show your feelings.*
to hurt sb's feelings (=to make someone feel upset) *I didn't want to hurt their feelings.*

adjectives
a deep/strong feeling *A deep feeling of sadness came over her.*
a good/great/wonderful feeling *It was a wonderful feeling to be home again.*
mixed feelings (=different kinds of feelings at the same time) *I had mixed feelings about starting my new school.*

THESAURUS

feeling something that you feel in your mind, for example happiness or sadness: *I had a feeling of regret.*
emotion a strong feeling such as love, hate, or anger: *His voice was shaking with emotion.*
instinct a natural feeling that people and animals have that helps them to know something, or to protect themselves: *My instinct told me that I shouldn't trust him.* | *the natural instinct for survival*
intuition the feeling that you know something is correct or true although you do not know the facts: *In business, you should never rely on intuition.*

feet /fiːt/ n the plural of FOOT

feign /feɪn/ v [T] *formal* to pretend to have a feeling, be ill, be asleep etc: *Feigning a headache, I went to my room.*

feisty /ˈfaɪsti/ adj having a strong determined character and a lot of energy

feline /ˈfiːlaɪn/ adj like a cat or relating to a cat

fell¹ /fel/ v the past tense of FALL

fell² v [T] **1** to cut down a tree **2** *written* to knock someone down

fellow¹ /ˈfeləʊ $ -loʊ/ n [C] **1** *old-fashioned* a man: *What a strange fellow he is!* **2** *BrE* a member of an important society or college: *a Fellow of the Royal College of Surgeons*

fellow² adj **fellow workers/students/passengers etc** people who work, study, travel etc with you

fellowship /ˈfeləʊʃɪp $ -loʊ-/ n **1** [U] a feeling of friendship that people have because they have the same interests or experiences **2** [C] a group of people with the same beliefs or interests, who have meetings together: *a Christian youth fellowship* **3** [C] a job in a university that includes detailed study of a subject

felon /ˈfelən/ n [C] *law* someone who is guilty of a serious crime: *a convicted felon*

felony /ˈfeləni/ n [C,U] (*plural* **felonies**) *law* a serious crime such as murder

felt¹ /felt/ v the past tense and past participle of FEEL

felt² n [U] a soft thick cloth made from wool or other material that has been pressed flat

,felt tip 'pen (*also* **'felt tip** *BrE*) n [C] a pen that has a hard piece of felt at the end that the ink comes through → see picture at PEN¹

female¹ /ˈfiːmeɪl/ adj
1 belonging to the sex that can have babies or produce eggs [OPP] **male** → **feminine**: *a female monkey* | *female workers* | *the female sex*
2 typical of this sex [OPP] **male**: *female qualities such as patience and kindness*
3 a female plant or flower produces fruit [OPP] **male**

female² n [C] a person or animal that belongs to the sex that can have babies or produce eggs [OPP] **male**: *The female is smaller than the male.*

feminine /ˈfemɪnɪn/ adj
1 having qualities that are thought to be typical of women, especially the qualities of being gentle, delicate, or pretty → **masculine**: *It was a very feminine room.*
2 in grammar, a feminine noun, adjective etc belongs to a class of words that have different INFLECTIONS from MASCULINE and NEUTER words → **masculine**

femininity /ˌfeməˈnɪnəti/ n [U] qualities that are thought to be typical of women → **masculinity**

feminism /ˈfemənɪzəm/ n [U] the belief that women should have the same rights and opportunities as men —**feminist** n, adj: *a feminist writer* | *militant feminists*

fence¹ /fens/ n [C]
1 a line of upright wooden posts with wire or wood between that surrounds an area of land: *the garden fence* | *a wooden fence*
2 a structure that horses jump over in a race or competition
3 *informal* someone who buys and sells stolen goods

fence² v [I] to fight with a sword as a sport
PHRASAL VERBS
fence sth ↔ in to surround a place with a fence
fence sth ↔ off to separate one area from another with a fence: *We fenced off part of the field.*

FENCING

sabre *BrE*/saber *AmE*

fencing /ˈfensɪŋ/ n [U] **1** the sport of fighting with a long thin sword **2** fences, or the material used to make them

fend /fend/ v **fend for yourself** to look after yourself without help from other people: *The kids had to fend for themselves while their parents were away.*
PHRASAL VERBS
fend sb/sth ↔ **off** to defend yourself when you are

being attacked, asked unwelcome questions etc: *She managed to fend off her attacker.*

fender /'fendə $ -ər/ n [C] **1** *AmE* the side part of a car that covers the wheels $\boxed{\text{SYN}}$ **wing** *BrE* → see picture at **CAR 2** *BrE* a low wall or bar around a FIREPLACE to prevent wood or coal from falling out

ferment¹ /fə'ment $ fər-/ v [I,T] if fruit, wine etc ferments, or if it is fermented, the sugar in it changes to alcohol —**fermentation** /ˌfɜːmen'teɪʃən $ ˌfɜːrmən-/ n [U]

ferment² /'fɜːment $ 'fɜːr-/ n [U] excitement or trouble in a country, caused especially by political change: **in ferment** *In the 1960s, American society was in ferment.*

fern /fɜːn $ fɜːrn/ n [C] a plant with green leaves shaped like large feathers but no flowers

ferocious /fə'rəʊʃəs $ -'roʊ-/ adj violent, dangerous, and frightening: *a ferocious-looking dog | a ferocious battle* —**ferociously** adv

ferocity /fə'rɒsəti $ fə'rɑː-/ n [U] extreme violence: *Police were shocked by the ferocity of the attack.*

ferret¹ /'ferɪt/ n [C] a small animal, used for hunting rats and rabbits

ferret² v

PHRASAL VERBS

ferret sth ↔ **out** *informal* to succeed in finding something, especially information: *She finally managed to ferret out the truth.*

ferry¹ /'feri/ n [C] (*plural* **ferries**) a boat that regularly carries people, often with their cars, across a narrow area of water: *a car ferry* → see picture at TRANSPORT¹

ferry² v [T] (**ferried, ferrying, ferries**) to regularly carry people or goods a short distance from one place to another: *a bus that ferries tourists from the hotel to the beach*

fertile /'fɜːtaɪl $ 'fɜːrtl/ adj **1** fertile soil is able to produce good crops: *fertile land* **2** able to become PREGNANT or make someone pregnant $\boxed{\text{OPP}}$ **infertile 3 fertile imagination/mind** an imagination or mind that produces lots of interesting and unusual ideas —**fertility** /fɜː'tɪləti $ fər-/ n [U]

fertilize (*also* **-ise** *BrE*) /'fɜːtəlaɪz $ 'fɜːrtl-aɪz/ v [T] **1** if an egg is fertilized, the egg and a SPERM join together so that a baby can start to develop **2** to put fertilizer on the soil to help plants grow —**fertilization** /ˌfɜːtəlaɪ'zeɪʃən $ ˌfɜːrtl-ə'zeɪ-/ n [U]

fertilizer (*also* **-iser** *BrE*) /'fɜːtəlaɪzə $ 'fɜːrtl-aɪzər/ n [C,U] a substance that is put on the soil to help plants grow

fervent /'fɜːvənt $ 'fɜːr-/ adj believing or feeling something very strongly: *a fervent supporter of human rights* —**fervently** adv

fervour *BrE*, **fervor** *AmE* /'fɜːvə $ 'fɜːrvər/ n [U] very strong belief or feeling: *religious fervour*

fest /fest/ n **beer/song/food etc fest** an informal occasion when a lot of people drink, sing, eat etc together

fester /'festə $ -ər/ v [I] **1** if an unpleasant feeling or problem festers, it gets worse because it has not

been dealt with: *Don't allow resentment to fester.* **2** if a wound festers, it becomes infected

festival /'festəvəl/ n [C]
1 an occasion when there are performances of many films, plays, pieces of music etc: *the Cannes Film Festival* | **[+of]** *a festival of Irish music*
2 a special occasion when people celebrate something such as a religious event: *the Muslim religious festival of Ramadan*

COLLOCATIONS

verbs

to have a festival *Tucson had a film festival last month.*

to hold a festival *The festival is held once a year.*

to go to a festival (*also* **to attend a festival** *formal*) *Have you ever been to a rock festival?*

to appear/play at a festival (=to perform there) *Kylie will be appearing at the festival.*

a festival takes place *The city's jazz festival takes place in July.*

types of festival

an international festival *an international festival of drama and dance*

a film/drama/dance festival *The movie won an award at the Cannes Film Festival.*

a music/rock/folk/jazz festival *He's appeared at folk festivals all over Europe.*

festive /'festɪv/ adj happy and special, because people are celebrating something: *festive occasions* | **the festive season** (=Christmas)

festivity /fe'stɪvəti/ n **1 festivities** [plural] things such as eating, drinking, or dancing that people do to celebrate something: *We spent the day preparing for the Christmas festivities.* **2** [U] a happy feeling that exists when people celebrate something: *There was an air of festivity at the fair.*

festoon /fe'stuːn/ v [T usually passive] to cover something with flowers, long pieces of cloth etc, as a decoration: *streets festooned with flags*

fetal /'fiːtl/ adj the usual American spelling of FOE-TAL

fetch /fetʃ/ v [T]
1 especially *BrE* to go and get something or someone and bring them back: **Go and fetch** *your dad.* | **fetch sb/sth from sth** *He fetched a blanket from upstairs.* | **fetch sb/sth/fetch sth for sb** *Could you fetch me a drink?* $\boxed{\text{THESAURUS}}$ **BRING**
2 to be sold for a particular amount of money: *The painting fetched $1.2 million.*

fetching /'fetʃɪŋ/ adj attractive: *She looks very fetching in that dress.*

fête¹ /feɪt/ n [C] **1** *BrE* an outdoor event with games, competitions, and things for sale **2** *AmE* a special occasion to celebrate something

fête² v [T usually passive] to honour someone by holding public celebrations for them: *The team was fêted from coast to coast.*

fetish /'fetɪʃ/ n [C] **1** something unusual that someone gets sexual pleasure from: *a leather fetish*

2 something that someone does too much or thinks about too much

fetus /ˈfiːtəs/ n the usual American spelling of FOETUS

feud /fjuːd/ n [C] hatred or violence between two people or groups that continues for a long time: *a feud between rival gangs* —**feud** v [I]

feudal /ˈfjuːdl/ adj the feudal system was the social system in the Middle Ages, in which people received land and protection from a lord, in return for working and fighting for the lord —**feudalism** n [U]

fever /ˈfiːvə $ -ər/ n
1 [C,U] an illness in which you have a very high temperature: **have/run a fever** *She's had a fever since last night.* | *Nick was ill with a* **high fever**.
2 [singular, U] a situation in which people feel very excited or anxious: *election fever* | **[+of]** *In a fever of excitement, Kay flew to Rome.* | **fever pitch** (=when people's excitement or anxiety is very great) *BrE: By 1918, these fears had* **reached fever pitch**. → HAY FEVER

feverish /ˈfiːvərɪʃ/ adj **1** suffering from a fever: *I'm still slightly feverish.* **THESAURUS** HOT **2** done extremely quickly because the situation is urgent: *feverish activity* **3** very excited or worried: *feverish anxiety* —**feverishly** adv

few /fjuː/ determiner, pron, adj
1 a small number of things or people: **a few** *Let's go away for a few days.* | *A few people were staring.* | 'Are there any biscuits left?' 'A few.' | **[+of]** *I've read a few of her books.* | **the last/past/next few** *the last few weeks*
2 not many things or people **OPP** many: *low-paid jobs that few people want* | **[+of]** *Very few of my friends still live here.* | *Women are having fewer children.* | *the candidate with the fewest votes* | *It is* **one of the few** *programmes I enjoy.* → LESS², LITTLE²

PHRASES
be few and far between to not happen often or not be found often: *Good jobs were few and far between.*
no fewer than used to emphasize that a number is large: *He was arrested no fewer than seven times.*
quite a few/a good few a fairly large number of things or people: *He's a good few years older than me.* | 'How many girlfriends have you had?' 'Quite a few.' | **[+of]** *Quite a few of our residents have pets.*

> **Grammar**
> Use **few** when you mean 'not many' or 'not enough': *Very few people came to the meeting.*
> Use **a few** when you mean 'some' or 'a small number': *There are still a few bottles of beer left.*
> **Few** and **a few** are always used with plural nouns.

fiancé /fiˈɒnseɪ $ ˌfiːɑːnˈseɪ/ n [C] the man whom a woman is going to marry

fiancée /fiˈɒnseɪ $ ˌfiːɑːnˈseɪ/ n [C] the woman whom a man is going to marry

fiasco /fiˈæskəʊ $ -koʊ/ n [C] (plural **fiascoes** or **fiascos**) an event that is completely unsuccessful, in a way that is very embarrassing or disappointing: *He tried to blame the whole fiasco on me.*

fib /fɪb/ n [C] spoken a small unimportant lie: *You shouldn't* **tell fibs**. —**fib** v [I] —**fibber** n [C]

fibre *BrE*, **fiber** *AmE* /ˈfaɪbə $ -ər/ n **1** [U] the parts of plants that you eat but cannot DIGEST, which help food to move through your body: *food that is high in* **dietary fibre 2** [C,U] a mass of threads used to make rope, cloth etc: *Nylon is a man-made fibre.* **3** [C] a thin thread, or one of the thin parts like threads that form natural materials such as wood —**fibrous** adj

fibreglass *BrE*, **fiberglass** *AmE* /ˈfaɪbəglɑːs $ -bərglæs/ n [U] a light material made from small glass threads pressed together

fickle /ˈfɪkəl/ adj **1** disapproving someone who is fickle is always changing their opinion about people or things: *Voters are fickle.* **2** something that is fickle, such as the weather, often changes suddenly

fiction /ˈfɪkʃən/ n
1 [U] books and stories about imaginary people and events **OPP** non-fiction: *She writes children's fiction.* **THESAURUS** BOOK
2 [C,U] something that people want you to believe is true but which is not true: *'The idea that organic food is better for you is a fiction,' he said.* → SCIENCE FICTION

fictional /ˈfɪkʃənəl/ adj fictional people or events are from a book or story, and are not real

fictitious /fɪkˈtɪʃəs/ adj not true, or not real: *a fictitious address*

fiddle¹ /ˈfɪdl/ n [C] **1** a VIOLIN **2** *BrE informal* a dishonest way of getting money: *an insurance fiddle*

fiddle² v [T] *BrE informal* to give false information about something, in order to avoid paying money or to get extra money: *Bert had been fiddling his income tax for years.*

PHRASAL VERBS
fiddle with sth **1** to keep moving and touching something, especially because you are bored or nervous: *She began fiddling with her necklace.* **2** (also **fiddle around/about with** sth *BrE*) to keep moving parts of a machine in order to make it work, without knowing exactly what you should do: *He fiddled with the controls until he had produced a clear sound.*

fiddler /ˈfɪdlə $ -ər/ n [C] someone who plays the VIOLIN

fiddly /ˈfɪdli/ adj difficult to use or do because you have to move very small objects: *a fiddly little switch*

fidelity /fɪˈdeləti/ n [U] *formal* loyalty, especially to your wife or husband by not having sex with other people **OPP** infidelity

fidget /ˈfɪdʒɪt/ v [I] to keep moving your hands or feet, especially because you are bored or nervous: *Stop fidgeting!* **THESAURUS** MOVE —**fidgety** adj

field¹ /fiːld/ n
1 an area of land in the country, where crops are grown or animals feed on grass: *the fields around the village* | **[+of]** *a field of wheat* | **corn/rice/wheat etc field**
2 an area of ground where sports are played: **baseball/football etc field** → see picture at FOOTBALL
3 a subject that people study or a type of work that

they are involved in: **[+of]** *experts in the field of psychology* | *economists **working in** this field*
4 the field all the people, companies, or horses that are competing against each other: *Troke was **leading the field** (=was the most successful) after the first round of the competition.*
5 magnetic/gravitational/force field the area in which a natural force has an effect
6 coal/oil/gas field an area where there is a lot of coal, oil, or gas under the ground → **PLAYING FIELD, TRACK AND FIELD**

PHRASES

field of view/vision the whole area that you can see without turning your head
have a field day to have a chance to do a lot of something that you enjoy, especially a chance to criticize someone: *The press had a field day when Tom left his wife.*

field² v **1** [T] if you field a team, an army etc, they represent you or fight for you in a competition, election, or war: *The Ecology Party **fielded** 109 **candidates**.* **2** [T] to answer questions, telephone calls etc, especially when there are a lot of them or they are difficult **3 be fielding** the team that is fielding in a game of CRICKET, baseball etc is the one that is throwing and catching the ball, rather than the one hitting it

fielder /ˈfiːldə $ -ər/ *n* [C] one of the players who tries to catch the ball in CRICKET, baseball etc

ˈfield ˌhockey *n* [U] *AmE* HOCKEY played on grass

ˈfield ˌmarshal *n* [C] an officer of the highest rank in the British army

ˈfield ˌtrip *n* [C] when students go somewhere to learn about a subject: *a geography field trip to Italy*

fieldwork /ˈfiːldwɜːk $ -wɜːrk/ *n* [U] study which involves going somewhere, rather than working in a class or LABORATORY

fiend /fiːnd/ *n* [C] **1** *literary* an evil person: *a sex fiend* **2** someone who is very interested in something and does it a lot: *a crossword fiend*

fiendish /ˈfiːndɪʃ/ *adj* **1** very clever in an unpleasant way: *a fiendish plot* **2** very difficult: *a fiendish puzzle* —**fiendishly** *adv*

fierce /fɪəs $ fɪrs/ *adj*
1 done with a lot of energy and strong feelings: *fierce fighting in the city* | *the **fierce competition** between the two companies* | *The proposal came under **fierce attack**.*
2 a fierce person or animal looks very violent or angry and likely to attack people: *a fierce dog* | *a fierce look* THESAURUS ▶ **VIOLENT**
3 fierce heat, cold, wind etc is very extreme or severe: *the fierce afternoon sun* —**fiercely** *adv* —**fierceness** *n* [U]

fiery /ˈfaɪəri $ ˈfaɪri/ *adj* **1** full of strong or angry emotion: *a fiery speech* | *her fiery temper* **2** looking like fire or involving fire: *a fiery sunset*

fiesta /fiˈestə/ *n* [C] a religious holiday with dancing, music etc, especially in Spain and South America

fifteen /ˌfɪfˈtiːn◂/ *number* the number 15: *a village fifteen miles south of Tourane* | *They met when she was*

fifteen (=15 years old). —**fifteenth** *adj, pron: her fifteenth birthday* | *I'm planning to leave on **the fifteenth** (=the 15th day of the month).*

fifth¹ /fɪfθ/ *adj* coming after four other things in a series: *her fifth birthday* —**fifth** *pron: I'm planning to leave on **the fifth** (=the fifth day of the month).* —**fifthly** *adv*

fifth² *n* [C] one of five equal parts of something

fifty /ˈfɪfti/ *number*
1 the number 50
2 the fifties (*also* **the '50s, the 1950s**) [plural] the years from 1950 to 1959: **the early/mid/late fifties** *The play was written in the late fifties.* —**fiftieth** *adj: her fiftieth birthday*

PHRASES

be in your fifties to be aged between 50 and 59: **early/mid/late fifties** *He's in his early fifties.*
in the fifties if the temperature is in the fifties, it is between 50 degrees and 59 degrees F: *The temperature is likely to be in the fifties tomorrow.*

ˌfifty-ˈfifty *adj, adv spoken* **1** divided equally between two people: *Let's divide the profits fifty-fifty.* **2 a fifty-fifty chance** an equal chance that something will happen or will not happen: *The operation has a fifty-fifty chance of success.*

fig /fɪɡ/ *n* [C] a small soft sweet fruit that is often eaten dried, or the tree on which this grows → see picture on page A4

fig. the written abbreviation of **figure**

fight¹ /faɪt/ *v* (*past tense and past participle* **fought** /fɔːt $ fɒːt/)
1 BE IN WAR [I,T] to take part in a war or battle: **[+in]** *Her father fought in World War I.* | **[+against]** *rebels fighting against the Russians* | *Neither country is capable of **fighting** a long war.*
2 HIT EACH OTHER [I,T] if people fight, they hit each other: *Will you two boys stop fighting!* | **[+with]** *Fans fought with police.*
3 TRY TO GET STH [I] to try hard to do or get something: **[+for]** *We will continue to fight for equal rights.* | *The boy is in hospital **fighting for** his life (=he may die).* | **fight to do sth** *Parents are fighting to save the school.*
4 TRY TO PREVENT STH [I,T] to try hard to prevent something or to get rid of something: **[+against]** *He fought against racism all his life.* | *Protesters are fighting the plans.*
5 ELECTION [T] to try to win an election or a court CASE: *Together they **fought** the general **election** of 1974.*
6 ARGUE [I] to argue: *Rachel and her boyfriend are always fighting.* | **[+with]** *She didn't want to fight with her mother.* | **[+about/over]** *We used to fight over money.*

PHRASES

fight it out to fight physically, argue, or compete until one person wins: *We left them to fight it out.*

PHRASAL VERBS
fight back
1 to work hard to achieve or oppose something, especially in a situation where you are losing: *Lewis fought back to win the match.*

2 to use violence or arguments against someone who has attacked you or criticized you: *She fought back, grabbing at his throat.*
3 fight sth ↔ back to try hard not to have or show a feeling: *'Go away,' said Julia, **fighting back** the tears.*
fight sb/sth ↔ **off**
1 to keep someone away, or to stop them doing something to you, by fighting or opposing them: *He managed to fight off his attacker.*
2 to succeed in stopping other people getting something, and to get it for yourself: *He **fought off** tough competition to get a place in the final.*

fight² n
1 [C] a situation in which two people or groups hit each other: **[+with]** *I didn't want to have a fight with him.* | **[+between]** *fights between rival groups of fans*
2 [singular] the process of trying very hard to achieve something or prevent something: **[+for]** *We support the people's fight for democracy.* | **[+against]** *More money is needed to continue the fight against AIDS.* | **fight to do sth** *They won their fight to remain in the UK.*
3 [C] an argument: **[+with]** *They've **had a big fight** with their neighbours.* | **[+over/about]** *There were often fights over money.* THESAURUS ▶ ARGUMENT
4 [C] a battle between two armies: **[+for]** *the fight for Bunker Hill*

COLLOCATIONS

verbs

to have a fight *He had a fight with another boy at school.*
to start a fight *If anyone tries to start a fight with me, they'll regret it.*
to get into a fight (=to become involved in a fight) *The men got into a fight about a girl.*
to break up a fight (=stop it) *A teacher managed to break up the fight.*
a fight breaks out (=it suddenly starts) *A fight broke out among the fans.*

types of fight

a big fight *They ended up having a big fight.*
a street fight *street fights between rival gangs*
a knife fight *He almost died in a knife fight.*
a fist fight (=in which people punch each other) *A fist fight broke out after the game.*

THESAURUS

fight a situation in which two people or groups hit and try to hurt each other: *The boys were always having fights when they were young.*
scuffle a short and not very serious fight: *There was a scuffle outside the cinema.*
riot a situation in which a crowd of people behave violently in a public place, especially in order to protest against something: *The demonstration turned into a riot and several police officers were hurt.*
brawl a noisy fight between a small group of people in a public place: *He was injured in a drunken brawl outside a pub.*
punch-up *BrE informal* a fight between two or more people, especially because of an argument: *The game ended in a punch-up between the players.*

fighter /ˈfaɪtə $ -ər/ n [C] **1** (*also* **ˈfighter plane**) a small fast military plane that can destroy other planes **2** someone who fights, especially as a sport **3** someone who keeps trying to achieve something in difficult situations → FIREFIGHTER

fighting /ˈfaɪtɪŋ/ n [U] when people or groups fight each other in a war, in the street etc: *seven days of heavy fighting*

figment /ˈfɪɡmənt/ n **a figment of sb's imagination** something that someone imagines is real, but which does not exist

figurative /ˈfɪɡjərətɪv, -ɡə-/ adj a figurative use of a word is one where it does not have its normal or basic meaning. For example, in 'a mountain of debt', 'mountain' is used in a figurative way and means 'a large amount' not 'a high hill'. —**figuratively** adv

figure¹ /ˈfɪɡə $ ˈfɪɡjər/ n [C]
1 NUMBER **a)** [usually plural] a number representing an amount, especially an official number: **unemployment/sales/crime etc figures** *the latest unemployment figures* | *Figures show that violent crime is increasing.* **b)** a number from 0 to 9, written as a sign, not as a word: *Write the amount in words and figures.* | **four-/five-/six- etc figure** (=in the 1,000s, 10,000s, 100,000s etc) *six-figure salaries* | **double figures** (=the numbers from 10 to 99) *Inflation was in double figures.* | **single figures** (=the numbers 1 to 9)
2 AMOUNT OF MONEY a particular amount of money: **[+of]** *A figure of $35m was apparently paid.*
3 PERSON **a)** someone who is important or famous in some way: *leading figures in the art world* **b)** someone with a particular type of appearance or character, especially when they are difficult to see: *I could see a dark figure in the distance.* **c)** a person in a picture
4 BODY SHAPE the shape of someone's body, especially a woman: *She **had a good figure**.*
5 ADDING NUMBERS **figures** [plural] *BrE* the activity of adding, multiplying etc numbers: *Ray's **good at figures**.*
6 SHAPE a shape in mathematics: *a six-sided figure*
7 PICTURE (*written abbreviation* **fig.**) a numbered drawing in a book → FATHER FIGURE, PUBLIC FIGURE

figure² v **1** [I] to be included as an important part of something: **[+in]** *Marriage didn't really figure in their plans.* **2** [T] *informal* to have a particular opinion after thinking about a situation: **[+(that)]** *I figured it was time to leave.*
PHRASES

that figures/it figures *especially AmE spoken* used to say that something that happens is expected or typical, especially something bad: *'It rained the whole weekend.' 'That figures.'*

PHRASAL VERBS
figure sb/sth ↔ **out** to understand something or someone after thinking about them: **[+how/why etc]** *Can you figure out how to do it?* | *Women. I just can't figure them out.*

figurehead /ˈfɪɡəhed $ ˈfɪɡjər-/ n [C] a leader who has no real power

figure of ˈeight BrE, **figure ˈeight** AmE n [C] the pattern or shape of the number 8

figure of ˈspeech n [C] a word or phrase that does not have its normal or basic meaning

filament /ˈfɪləmənt/ n [C] a very thin thread or wire

file¹ Ac /faɪl/ n [C]
1 SET OF PAPERS a set of papers, records etc that contain information about a particular person or subject: **[+on]** The school **keeps files** on all students. | **on file** (=kept in an official file) All the details are on file. | patients' medical files
2 CONTAINER FOR PAPERS a box or folded piece of thick stiff paper in which you keep loose papers → see picture at **CLASSROOM**
3 COMPUTER STORE information on a computer that you store under a particular name: **open/close a file** Click on the icon to open the file. | **create/copy/save/delete a file**
4 TOOL a metal tool with a rough surface that you rub on something to make it smooth → **NAIL FILE**
PHRASES
| **in single file** moving in a line, with one person behind another: The path was so narrow we had to walk in single file.

file² Ac v **1** [T] to store papers or information in a particular order or a particular place: The letters are **filed alphabetically**. **THESAURUS** KEEP **2** [I,T] law to give a document to a court or other organization so that it can be officially recorded and dealt with: I intend to **file** a formal **complaint**. **3** [I] if people file somewhere, they walk in a line, one behind the other: **[+into/out of etc]** The jury filed into the courtroom. **4** [T] to rub something with a metal tool to make it smooth or cut it: She sat **filing her nails**.

file ˌsharing n [U] the act of sharing computer files, such as music files, with other people using the Internet

filet /ˈfɪlɪt $ ˈfɪlət, -leɪ, fɪˈleɪ/ n, v the usual American spelling of FILLET

filing ˌcabinet BrE, **file ˌcabinet** AmE n [C] a piece of office furniture with drawers for storing important papers

fill¹ /fɪl/ v
1 a) (also **fill up**) [I,T] to make something become full, or to become full: She filled the kettle. | He kept filling our glasses up. | **fill (sth) with sth** Her **eyes filled with tears**. **b)** [T] to be in all or most of the space somewhere: the expensive ornaments that filled the apartment | **be filled with sth** The theatre was filled with smoke. **THESAURUS** FULL
2 [T] if a sound, smell, or light fills a place, you notice it because it is very loud or strong: The smell of cooking filled the kitchen. | **be filled with sth** The air was filled with the sound of birds.
3 [T] if you are filled with an emotion, you feel it very strongly: **be filled with sth** Elaine was suddenly filled with fear. | **fill sb with sth** The idea filled me with excitement.
4 [T] to provide something that is needed or wanted: **fill a need/demand** His book undoubtedly fills a need. | The company is **filling a gap** in the market.
5 [T] if you fill a period of time with a particular activity, you spend that time doing it: **fill your time/the days etc (with sth)** How do you fill your days?
6 [T] to perform a particular job, activity, or purpose in an organization, or to find someone or something to do this: **fill a post/position/vacancy etc** We need someone to fill the position of Editor. | The post has already been filled.
7 (also **fill in**) [T] to put a substance into a hole, crack etc to make a surface level: Fill any cracks in the wall before you paint.
PHRASAL VERBS
fill sb/sth **in**
1 to write all the necessary information on an official document, form etc: You'll have to fill in an application form. **THESAURUS** WRITE
2 to tell someone about recent events: **[+on]** I'll fill you in on all the news later.
fill out
1 fill sth ↔ **out** to write all the necessary information on an official document, form etc **THESAURUS** WRITE
2 to get fatter: Her **face** is beginning to **fill out**.

fill² n **your fill** as much of something as you want, or can deal with: I've **had** my **fill of** screaming kids today!

fillet¹ BrE, **filet** AmE /ˈfɪlɪt $ ˈfɪlət, -leɪ, fɪˈleɪ/ n [C,U] a piece of meat or fish without bones

fillet² BrE, **filet** AmE v [T] to remove the bones from a piece of meat or fish

filling¹ /ˈfɪlɪŋ/ adj food that is filling makes your stomach feel full

filling² n **1** [C] a small amount of metal that is put into a hole in your tooth **2** [C,U] the food that is put inside a PIE, SANDWICH etc: apple pie filling

ˈfilling ˌstation n [C] a place where you can buy petrol for your car

film¹ /fɪlm/ n
1 MOVIE [C] a story that is told using moving pictures, shown at a cinema or on television **SYN** movie: I saw a great film last night. | **[+about]** a film about a young dancer | The film will be shown on Channel 4.
2 FILM-MAKING [U] the work of making films, considered as an art or a business: I'd like to work in film. | the film industry
3 MOVING PICTURES [U] moving pictures of real events that are shown on television or at a cinema: **film footage** (=pictures) of the riot
4 IN CAMERA [C,U] the thin plastic used in a camera for taking photographs or recording moving pictures: a **roll of film**
5 THIN LAYER [singular] a very thin layer of liquid, powder etc on the surface of something: **[+of]** a film of sweat

COLLOCATIONS

verbs
to watch a film We were watching a film on TV.
to see a film I've seen all his films.
to make a film She is currently making a film in the UK.

to direct a film *The film was directed by Mike Nichols.*

to show a film *The film is being shown in cinemas all across the country.*

a film is on (=it is being shown) *There's a good film on at the cinema.*

a film stars sb *The film starred Brad Pitt.*

types of film

a war/horror/science fiction etc film *They liked watching gangster films.*

a documentary film *She made a documentary film about her own family.*

a feature film (=a full-length film shown in the cinema) *This is the young director's first feature film.*

film + noun

a film star *She looked like a film star.*

a film director *Scorsese is one of the world's most famous film directors.*

a film crew (=a group of people working to make a film) *A television film crew arrived.*

the film industry *This was a great time for the French film industry.*

film² *v* [I,T] to make a film of something for the cinema or television: *The movie was filmed in China.*

'film-,maker *n* [C] someone who makes films for the cinema or television

filter¹ /ˈfɪltə $ -ər/ *n* [C] a piece of equipment that you put gas or liquid through in order to remove solid substances that are not wanted: *a water filter*

filter² *v* **1** [T] to clean a liquid or gas using a filter: *filtered drinking water* **2** [I] if people filter somewhere, they gradually move there: *The audience began to filter into the hall.* **3** [I] if information filters somewhere, people gradually hear about it: *The news slowly filtered through to everyone in the office.*

filth /fɪlθ/ *n* [U] **1** dirt: *Wash that filth off your shoes.* **2** very offensive language, or pictures about sex

filthy /ˈfɪlθi/ *adj* **1** extremely dirty: *Doesn't he ever wash that jacket? It's filthy.* **THESAURUS** DIRTY **2** very rude or offensive, especially about sex: *filthy language*

fin /fɪn/ *n* [C] **1** one of the thin parts on the side of a fish's body that it uses to swim → see picture on page A3 **2** part of a plane that sticks up at the back and helps it to fly smoothly

final¹ Ac /ˈfaɪnəl/ *adj* **1** [only before noun] last in a series: *the final chapter of the book* | *students preparing for their final examinations* | *the **final stages** in their relationship* **THESAURUS** LAST **2** if a decision, order, or agreement is final, it cannot be changed: *Is that your final decision?* | *£300 is my final offer.* **3** [only before noun] happening at the end of a long process: *I can't wait to see the final product.*

final² Ac *n* [C] **1** the last and most important game, race etc in a competition: *the World Cup Final* | *He didn't get through to **the finals**.* **2 finals** [plural] *BrE* the examinations that students take at the end of their last year at university **3** *AmE* an important test that you take at the end of a class in high school or college → **SEMI-FINAL**

finale /fɪˈnɑːli $ fɪˈnæli/ *n* [C] the last part of a piece of music or a show, which is often the most exciting part: *Everyone was on stage for the **grand finale**.* **THESAURUS** END

finalist /ˈfaɪnəl-ɪst/ *n* [C] one of the people or teams that reaches the last part of a competition

finality Ac /faɪˈnæləti/ *n* [U] when something is finished and cannot be changed: *the finality of death*

finalize Ac (also **-ise** *BrE*) /ˈfaɪnəl-aɪz/ *v* [T] to decide firmly on the details of a plan or arrangement: *Can we finalize the details of the deal?* **THESAURUS** FINISH

finally Ac /ˈfaɪnəl-i/ *adv* **1** after a long time **SYN** **eventually**: *After several delays, the plane finally took off at six o'clock.* **2** used when you are introducing the last of a series of things **SYN** **lastly**: *And finally, I'd like to thank my teachers for all their help.* **3** in a way that does not allow changes: *It's not finally settled yet.*

THESAURUS

finally after a long time: *The train finally arrived and we all got on.*

eventually finally – used especially when you have been waiting for something for a very long time: *Eventually, the lights came back on again.*

in the end finally – used especially in spoken English: *He answered his phone in the end.*

at last used when something good happens after you have waited a long time: *At last the sun came out and we went for a swim.*

finance¹ Ac /ˈfaɪnæns, fəˈnæns $ fəˈnæns, ˈfaɪnæns/ *n* **1** [U] the control of how money should be spent, especially in a company or government: *the finance department* **2** [U] money provided by a bank to help you to pay for something: *How will you get the finance to start your business?* **3 finances** [plural] the money that a person or organization has: *The school's finances are limited.*

finance² Ac *v* [T] to provide money to pay for something **SYN** **fund**: *The organization is partly financed by the government.*

financial Ac /fəˈnænʃəl, faɪ-/ *adj* relating to money or the management of money: *a financial adviser* | *financial aid* | *The film was not a financial success* (=it did not make much money). —**financially** *adv*: *He was successful and financially secure.*

financier Ac /fəˈnænsɪə, faɪˈnæn- $ ˌfɪnənˈsɪr/ *n* [C] someone who controls or lends large sums of money

finch /fɪntʃ/ *n* [C] a small wild bird with a short beak

find¹ /faɪnd/ *v* [T] (*past tense and past participle* **found** /faʊnd/) **1 BY SEARCHING** to get something that you have been looking for: *Will you help me find my bag?* | *I can't find* *my keys.* | *I have to find somewhere to live.* | **find sb sth** (=find something for someone) *I think we can find you a job.*

2 BY CHANCE to discover something by chance: *She found a purse in the street.* | *We found a really good bar near the hotel.*

3 SEE to see or notice something: **find sb doing sth** *When the police arrived, they found him lying on the floor.* | **[+(that)]** *Michael woke up to find that the bedroom was flooded.*

4 NEW INFORMATION to discover or learn new information: *Scientists are still trying to find a cure for AIDS.* | **[+that]** *They found that men are better at reading maps than women.*

5 HAVE AN OPINION to have an opinion or feeling about someone or something: *I don't find his jokes at all funny.* | *She found the work very dull.* | **find it hard/easy etc to do sth** *I found it hard to understand her.*

6 LEARN BY EXPERIENCE to learn or know something by experience: **[+(that)]** *I soon found that it was quicker to go by bus.*

7 HAVE TIME/MONEY ETC to have enough time, money, energy etc to be able to do what you want to do: *When do you find the time to read?*

8 EXIST SOMEWHERE be found to live or exist somewhere: *This species is only found in West Africa.*

9 UNEXPECTEDLY find yourself somewhere to be in a place although you did not plan to be there: *At the end of the evening I found myself in the city centre.*

10 IN A COURT find sb guilty/not guilty (of sth) *law* to officially decide that someone is guilty or not guilty of a crime: *He was found guilty of murder.*

PHRASES

find fault with sb/sth to criticize someone or something, especially in a way that is unfair and too critical: *The teacher would always find fault with my work.*

find your feet to become confident in a new situation: *Matt's only been at the school two weeks and he hasn't found his feet yet.*

find your way (somewhere) to arrive at a place by discovering the way to get there: *Can you find your own way, or do you need a map?*

PHRASAL VERBS

find out

1 to get information about something or someone: **find sth ↔ out** *We never found out her name.* | **[+what/how/where etc]** *He hurried off to find out what the problem was.* | **[+about]** *If Dad finds out about this, he'll go crazy.* | **[+(that)]** *I found out that my parents had never been married.*

2 **find sb out** to discover that someone has been doing something dishonest or illegal: *What happens if we get found out?*

THESAURUS

find to get something that you have been looking for: *Have you found your passport yet?*

discover to find something that was hidden or that people did not know about before: *Scientists may have discovered a new planet.* | *The painting was discovered in an attic.*

detect to find something, especially something that is very difficult to notice: *The equipment can detect tiny changes in body temperature.*

come across sth to find something when you are not looking for it: *I came across some old photos of our house.*

track sb/sth down to find someone or something that is difficult to find, by searching in different places: *He promised they would track down the terrorists.*

locate *formal* to find the exact position of something: *They finally managed to locate the plane.*

find² *n* [C] something good or useful that you discover by chance: *That little Greek restaurant was a real find.*

findings /ˈfaɪndɪŋz/ *n* [plural] the information that people have learned as a result of their study, work etc: *The Commission's findings are presented in a report.*

fine¹ /faɪn/ *adj*

1 ACCEPTABLE satisfactory or acceptable: *'We're meeting at 8.30.' 'Okay, fine.'* | *In theory, the plan sounds fine.* | **[+by]** *If you want to meet up with us later, that's fine by me.*

2 HEALTHY/HAPPY healthy or reasonably happy: *'How are you?' 'I'm fine, thanks.'* THESAURUS HEALTHY

3 VERY GOOD very good: *a fine performance by William Hurt* | *a selection of fine wines* THESAURUS GOOD

4 SMALL PIECES/NARROW very thin or narrow, or made of very small pieces: *a fine layer of dust* | *a fine thread* | *fine sand*

5 DETAILS/DIFFERENCES fine details or differences are small or exact and difficult to see: *I didn't understand some of the finer points in the argument.*

6 WEATHER fine weather is bright and sunny THESAURUS GOOD

fine² *adv informal* well: *'How's everything going?' 'Fine.'* | *The car's working fine now.*

fine³ *n* [C] money that you have to pay as a punishment for breaking a law or rule: *a parking fine* THESAURUS PUNISHMENT —**fine** *v* [T]: *He was fined £100 for speeding.*

finely /ˈfaɪnli/ *adv* **1** into very small pieces: *finely chopped onion* **2** very exactly: *finely tuned instruments*

fine 'print *n* [U] SMALL PRINT

finesse /fəˈnes/ *n* [U] if you do something with finesse, you do it with a lot of skill and style

fine-'tune *v* [T] to make very small changes to something such as a machine or a plan, so that it works as well as possible: *We fine-tuned the scheme and made some useful improvements.* —**fine tuning** *n* [U]

finger¹ /ˈfɪŋɡə $ -ər/ *n* [C] one of the four long thin parts on your hand, not including your thumb: *We ate with our fingers.* → INDEX FINGER, LITTLE FINGER

PHRASES

keep your fingers crossed *spoken* to hope that something will happen in the way you want it to: *We're keeping our fingers crossed that she's going to be OK.*

not lift a finger *spoken* to not make any effort to

help someone: *I do all the work – Frank never lifts a finger.*

put your finger on sth to realize exactly what is wrong, different, or unusual about something: *There's something strange about him, but I can't put my finger on it.*

finger² v [T] to touch or feel something with your fingers

fingernail /ˈfɪŋgəneɪl $ -gər-/ n [C] the hard flat part that covers the top end of your finger → see picture at **HAND¹**

FINGERPRINT

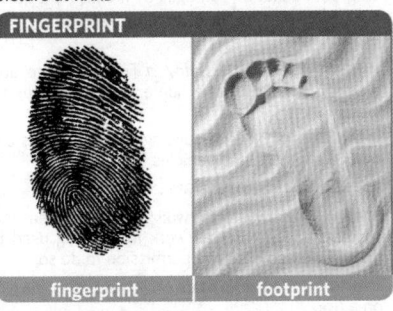

fingerprint   footprint

fingerprint /ˈfɪŋgəprɪnt $ -gər-/ n [C] the mark made by the pattern of lines at the end of someone's finger **THESAURUS** MARK

fingertip /ˈfɪŋgətɪp $ -gər-/ n [C] the end of your finger

PHRASES

have sth at your fingertips to have information easily available and ready to use: *We have all the facts and figures at our fingertips.*

finicky /ˈfɪnɪki/ adj disapproving too concerned with small details and only approving of things that are correct in every way SYN **fussy**: *She's finicky about what she eats.*

finish¹ /ˈfɪnɪʃ/ v

1 (also **finish off**) [I,T] to come to the end of doing or making something OPP **start**: *Have you finished your homework?* | **finish doing sth** *Let me just finish typing this report.* | *I've done most of the work – I'll finish it off tomorrow.* | **finish (sth) with sth** (=do something as the last thing) *He used to finish his act with a song.*

2 [I] *especially spoken BrE* if an event or activity finishes, it stops happening: *What time does the concert finish?* **THESAURUS** END

3 (also **finish up/off**) [T] to eat, drink, or use all the rest of something: *Finish your breakfast before it gets cold, Tom.* | *Who finished off the cake?*

4 finish second/third etc to be in second, third etc position at the end of a race, competition etc: *He finished second in the 100 metres.*

PHRASAL VERBS

finish up *BrE informal* to arrive at a particular place, after going to other places first: *We finished up in Rome after a three-week tour.*

finish with sb/sth

1 have/be finished with sth to no longer need to use something: *Have you finished with the scissors?*

2 *BrE* to end a romantic or sexual relationship with someone: *He's finished with Elise after all these years.*

THESAURUS

to finish doing something

finish: *I've finished my work for today.* | *Let me know when you've finished.*

complete to finish making, writing, or doing something, especially when this takes a long time. **Complete** sounds more formal than **finish**: *The building will be completed in two years' time.*

finalize to finish all the arrangements for something to happen: *They're still finalizing all the preparations for the wedding.* | *The deal was finalized late last night.*

have done *especially spoken* if you have done your work, you have finished it: *Have you done your homework yet?*

get sth over with *informal* to finish something that you do not want to have to do: *It's good to get the exams over with.*

finish² n **1** [singular] the end of something, especially a race: *It was a **close finish** (=the race ended with the competitors close together), but Jarrett won.* **THESAURUS** END **2** [C] the way a surface looks after it has been painted or polished: *a table with a glossy finish* → **PHOTO FINISH**

finished /ˈfɪnɪʃt/ adj **1** [only before noun] completed: *the finished product* **2** [not before noun] if you are finished, you have finished doing something: *I'm almost finished.* **3** [not before noun] *informal* no longer able to continue successfully: *If the bank doesn't lend us the money, we're finished.*

finite Ac /ˈfaɪnaɪt/ adj having an end or a limit: *Earth's finite resources*

fir /fɜː $ fɜːr/ (also **fir tree**) n [C] a tree with leaves shaped like needles that do not fall off in autumn

fire¹ /faɪə $ faɪr/ n

1 [C,U] uncontrolled flames and heat that destroy and damage things: *Fire destroyed part of the building.* | *Her father died in a fire.* | **on fire** (=burning) *The house is on fire!* **THESAURUS** BURN

2 [C] a pile of burning wood or coal used to heat a room or cook food: *a camp fire* | *a coal fire* | *Come and sit in front of the fire.*

3 [C] *BrE* a piece of equipment that uses gas or electricity to heat a room: *an **electric fire*** | *Could you turn the **fire on**, please?*

4 [U] when guns are fired: *Troops **opened fire** on the demonstrators* (=started shooting at them). | *Their car **came under fire** (=it was shot at).* | *Hold your fire* (=stop firing)!

PHRASES

catch fire to start burning: *One of the plane's engines caught fire.*

be/come under fire to be criticized: *The plan quickly came under fire from the Democrats.*

set fire to sth (also **set sth on fire**) to make something start burning: *The crowd set fire to several vehicles.*

COLLOCATIONS

verbs

to start a fire *The police think that the fire was started deliberately.*

to put out a fire (=to stop a fire burning) *It took firefighters two days to put out the fire.* ⚠ Do not say 'put off a fire'. Say **put out a fire**.

to fight a fire (=try to make a fire stop burning) *There was no one to fight the fire.*

a fire burns *The fire burned for several hours.*

a fire goes out (=it stops burning) *It took days for the fire to go out.*

a fire breaks out (=it starts suddenly) *A fire broke out in the kitchen.*

a fire spreads *The fire spread to the house next door.*

sth is damaged/destroyed by fire *The school was badly damaged by fire.*

noun + fire

a forest fire *Forest fires have spread to the edge of the city.*

a house fire *Every year, hundreds of people die in house fires.*

fire² v

1 **SHOOT** [I,T] to shoot bullets from a gun: **[+at/on/ into]** *Soldiers fired on the crowd.* | *He fired three shots.* **THESAURUS** ▶ SHOOT

2 **JOB** [T] to make someone leave their job **SYN** sack *BrE*: *She didn't want to get fired.* | **fire sb from sth** *I've just been fired from my job.*

3 **EXCITE** (also **fire up**) [T] to make someone very excited or interested in something: *exciting stories that fired our imagination*

4 **QUESTIONS** **fire questions at sb** to ask someone a lot of questions very quickly: *The reporters fired non-stop questions at him.*

5 **USING OIL/GAS** **oil-fired/gas-fired etc** *BrE* using oil, gas etc to produce heat or energy: *a coal-fired power station*

PHRASAL VERBS

fire away *spoken* used to tell someone that you are ready to answer questions: *'Do you mind if I ask you something?' 'Fire away.'*

'fire a,larm *n* [C] a piece of equipment that makes a loud noise to warn people of a fire in a building

firearm /ˈfaɪərɑːm $ ˈfaɪrɑːrm/ *n* [C] *formal* a gun

'fire bri,gade *BrE*, **'fire de,partment** *AmE n* [C] the FIRE SERVICE

firecracker /ˈfaɪəˌkrækə $ ˈfaɪrˌkrækər/ *n* [C] a small FIREWORK that makes a loud noise when it explodes

,fired-'up *adj* very excited, interested, or angry about something: *The crowd began to get all fired-up.*

'fire ,engine *n* [C] a large vehicle that carries FIREFIGHTERS and their equipment

'fire es,cape *n* [C] metal stairs on the outside of a building that people can use to escape if there is a fire

'fire ex,tinguisher *n* [C] a piece of equipment used for stopping small fires

firefighter /ˈfaɪəˌfaɪtə $ ˈfaɪrˌfaɪtər/ *n* [C] someone whose job is to stop fires burning

'fire ,hydrant *n* [C] a water pipe in the street used to get water for stopping fires burning

firelight /ˈfaɪəlaɪt $ ˈfaɪr-/ *n* [U] the light produced by a small fire: *The room glowed in the firelight.*

fireman /ˈfaɪəmən $ ˈfaɪr-/ *n* [C] (*plural* **firemen** /-mən/) a man whose job is to stop fires burning

fireplace /ˈfaɪəpleɪs $ ˈfaɪr-/ *n* [C] an open place in the wall of a room, where you can make a fire to heat the room

fireproof /ˈfaɪəpruːf $ ˈfaɪr-/ *adj* something that is fireproof cannot be damaged by fire: *a fireproof door*

'fire ,service *n* [C] an organization that works to stop fires

fireside /ˈfaɪəsaɪd $ ˈfaɪr-/ *n* [singular] the area around a small fire in a home: *a cat dozing by the fireside*

'fire ,station *n* [C] a building for FIREFIGHTERS and their equipment and vehicles

'fire truck *n* [C] *AmE* a FIRE ENGINE

firewall /ˈfaɪəwɔːl $ ˈfaɪrwɔːl/ *n* [C] a system that protects a computer network from being used by people who do not have permission to do so

firewood /ˈfaɪəwʊd $ ˈfaɪr-/ *n* [U] wood for burning on a fire

firework /ˈfaɪəwɜːk $ ˈfaɪrwɜːrk/ *n* [C usually plural] an object that burns or explodes to produce coloured lights and noise in the sky: *a Fourth of July fireworks display*

'firing squad *n* [C] a group of soldiers whose duty is to shoot and kill a prisoner

firm¹ /fɜːm $ fɜːrm/ *adj*

1 **NOT SOFT** not soft, and not easy to bend into a different shape: *a bed with a firm mattress* | *Choose the firmest tomatoes.* **THESAURUS** ▶ HARD

2 **DEFINITE** [only before noun] definite and not likely to change: *No firm decision has been reached.* | *They remained firm friends.*

3 **IN CONTROL** strong and in control: *This country needs firm leadership.* | **[+with]** *You need to be firm with children.* **THESAURUS** ▶ DETERMINED

4 **NOT LIKELY TO MOVE** strongly fixed in position, and not likely to move: *Make sure the ladder feels firm before you climb up.*

5 **WAY OF HOLDING STH** **a firm grip/grasp/hold etc** a way of holding something tightly and strongly: *Joe took her hand in his firm grip.* —**firmly** *adv* —**firmness** *n* [U]

firm² *n* [C] a business or company: *an engineering firm* | *a law firm* **THESAURUS** ▶ COMPANY

firm³ *v* [T]

PHRASAL VERBS

firm sth ↔ **up** **1** to make arrangements more definite: *We hope to firm up the deal next week.* **2** to make the muscles of your body harder and firmer

first¹ /fɜːst $ fɜːrst/ *number, adv, pron, adj*

1 before anyone or anything else: *the first name on the list* | *My sister said I'd be the first to get married.* *Cindy arrived first.* | *Welles made his first film at the age of 25.* | **the first thing/time/day etc** *The first time I flew on a plane I was really nervous.* | **come/finish**

first (=win a race or competition) *Jane came first in the 100 metres race.* **THESAURUS ▶ WIN**
2 before anything else happens, or before doing anything else: *I always read the sports page first.* | *Do your homework first, then you can go out.*
3 when you first do something, it is new to you and you have not done it before: *I first met him in Paris.*
4 most important: *Our first priority must be to restore peace.* | *Ron's kids always **come first** (=are most important).*
5 first prize the prize for the person who wins a competition: *She won first prize in the poetry competition.*
6 first/first of all a) before doing anything else: *First, I'd like to thank everyone for coming.* **b)** used before saying the first of several things you want to say: *I don't think Helen should go – first of all, she's too young.*
7 your first choice the thing or person you like best: *Champagne is the first choice for most wedding celebrations.* → **HEAD-FIRST**

PHRASES

at first in the beginning: *At first, Gregory was shy and hardly spoke.*
at first glance/sight the first time that you look at someone or something, before you notice any details: *At first sight, there didn't appear to be much damage.*
first thing as soon as you wake up or start work in the morning: *I'll call you first thing tomorrow, okay?*
for the first time used to say that something has never happened or been done before: *For the first time in his life, he felt truly happy.*
in the first place 1 used to give the first in a list of reasons: *Quinn couldn't have committed the crime. In the first place, he's not a violent man.* **2** used to talk about the beginning of a situation: *Why did you agree to meet her in the first place?*

first² *n* **1 a first** something that has never happened before: **[+for]** *The 3–0 defeat was a first for the team.* **2** [C] the highest form of university degree you can get in Britain: *Helen **got a first** in law.*

first 'aid *n* [U] simple medical treatment that is given as soon as possible to someone who is injured or who suddenly becomes ill

first-'class *adj* **1** excellent: *Eric has proved himself a first-class performer.* **2** a first-class ticket is a ticket for the most expensive type of seats on a plane or train —**first class** *adv*: *passengers travelling first class*

first 'floor *n* [singular] **1** *BrE* the floor of a building just above the one at the bottom level **2** *AmE* the floor of a building at the bottom level, where you go into the building **SYN** **ground floor** *BrE*

firsthand /ˈfɜːstˈhænd $ ˈfɜːrst-/ *adj* [only before noun] used to describe knowledge, experience etc that you get from doing something yourself, not from other people: *officers with firsthand experience of war* —**firsthand** /ˌfɜːstˈhænd $ ˌfɜːrst-/ *adv*: *experience you have gained firsthand*

first 'language *n* [C] the language that you first learn as a child

firstly /ˈfɜːstli $ -ɜːr-/ *adv* used before saying the first of several things: *Firstly, I would like to thank everyone who has contributed to this success.*

first name *n* [C] a name that comes before your family name → **last name**, **middle name**: *My teacher's first name is Caroline.* **THESAURUS ▶ NAME**

first 'person *n* **the first person** the form of the verb that you use with 'I' and 'we' → **second person**, **third person**

first-'rate *adj* excellent: *a first-rate show*

fiscal /ˈfɪskəl/ *adj* relating to money and taxes that are managed by the government: *the city's fiscal policies*

fish¹ /fɪʃ/ *n* (*plural* **fish** *or* **fishes**)
1 [C] an animal that lives, breathes, and swims in water: *How many **fish** did you **catch**?* → see picture on page A3
2 [U] the flesh of a fish used as food: *We had fish for dinner.*

fish² *v* **1** [I] to try to catch fish: **[+for]** *Dad's fishing for salmon.* **2** [I,T] to search for something in a bag, pocket etc, or to bring it out when you have found it: **[+about/around]** *She fished around in her purse and pulled out a photo.* | **fish sth out** *Sally opened her briefcase and fished out a small card.*

fishcake /ˈfɪʃkeɪk/ *n* [C] cooked fish mixed with cooked potato, made into a flat round shape and fried

fisherman /ˈfɪʃəmən $ -ʃər-/ *n* [C] (*plural* **fishermen** /-mən/) a man who catches fish as a job or a sport

fishing /ˈfɪʃɪŋ/ *n* [U] the sport or job of catching fish: *Do you want to **go fishing**?*

fishing rod (*also* **fishing pole** *AmE*) *n* [C] a long stick with a string and a hook tied to it, used for catching fish

fishmonger /ˈfɪʃmʌŋɡə $ -mɑːŋɡər, -mʌŋ-/ *n* [C] *especially BrE* **1** someone who sells fish **2** (*also* **fishmonger's**) a shop that sells fish

fishy /ˈfɪʃi/ *adj* **1** *informal* seeming bad or dishonest: *There's something fishy about this business.* **2** tasting or smelling like fish

fist /fɪst/ *n* [C] a hand closed with all the fingers curled inwards: *She shook her fist angrily.*

fistful /ˈfɪstfʊl/ *n* [C] the amount that you can hold in your hand: **[+of]** *a man waving a fistful of cash*

fit¹ /fɪt/ *v* (**fitted**, **fitting** *BrE*, **fit** *or* **fitted**, **fitting** *AmE*)
1 [I,T] to be the right size and shape for someone or something: *I wonder if my wedding dress still fits me?* | *This lid doesn't fit very well.*
2 [T] to put or fix something in the place where it will be used: **fit sth on/in etc sth** *We're having new locks fitted on all the main doors.*
3 [I,T] if something fits into a place, there is enough space for it: **[+in/into]** *Will the cases fit in the back of your car?* | **fit sth in/into sth** *I can't fit anything else into this suitcase.*
4 [T] to be suitable for something: *The music fits the words perfectly.* | *The punishment should fit the crime.*

F

PHRASAL VERBS
fit in
1 if someone fits in, they are accepted by the other people in a group: *The new students all had a hard time fitting in.*
2 fit sb/sth ↔ in to manage to see someone or do something, even though you have a lot of other things to do: *Dr. Tyler can fit you in on Monday at 3:30.*
3 if something fits in with other things, it is similar to them or goes well with them: **[+with]** *A new building must fit in with its surroundings.*
fit sb/sth ↔ out to provide a person or place with the equipment, furniture, or clothes that they need: *The office had been fitted out in style.*

> **Word Choice: fit or suit?**
> If a piece of clothing **fits** you, it is the correct size and shape: *This jacket fits me perfectly.*
> If clothes, colours etc **suit** you, they make you look attractive: *Your new hairstyle really suits you.*

fit² *adj*
1 suitable or good enough: **[+for]** *This book is not fit for publication!* | *After the party he was not in a fit state to drive.*
2 especially *BrE* healthy and strong, especially because you exercise regularly OPP **unfit**: *Jogging helps me keep fit.* | *He was young and physically fit.* → **KEEP FIT** THESAURUS **HEALTHY**
PHRASES
| **see/think fit to do sth** to decide that it is right to do something, even though other people may disagree: *Do whatever you think fit.*

fit³ *n* **1** [C] a short time during which you laugh or cough a lot, or become very angry, in a way that you cannot control: *a coughing fit* | *a fit of rage* **2** [C] a short period of time when someone loses consciousness and cannot control their body because their brain is not working properly: *an epileptic fit* **3** be a good/tight/perfect etc fit to fit a person or a particular space well, tightly, perfectly etc: *The skirt's a perfect fit.*
PHRASES
| **have/throw a fit** *informal* to become very angry: *If your mother finds out about this, she'll have a fit.*

fitful /ˈfɪtfəl/ *adj* something that is fitful is not continuous or regular: *a fitful sleep*

fitness /ˈfɪtnəs/ *n* [U] **1** when you are healthy and strong enough to play sports or do physical work: *physical fitness* **2** when someone or something is suitable: **[+for]** *He had doubts about her fitness for the job.*

fitted /ˈfɪtɪd/ *adj* **1 be fitted with sth** to have something as a permanent part: *Is your car fitted with an alarm?* **2** [only before noun] *BrE* made to fit a space exactly: *a fitted kitchen* | *a fitted carpet* | *fitted cupboards*

fitting¹ /ˈfɪtɪŋ/ *n* [C usually plural] *BrE* a piece of equipment in a house that seems to be attached to the house but can be removed so that you can take it with you if you sell the house → **fixture**: *I like these light fittings.*

fitting² *adj formal* suitable: *The statue is a fitting tribute to the President.*

fitting room *n* [C] a place in a shop where you can put on clothes to see how they look before you buy them

five /faɪv/ *number* the number 5: *The town is five miles away.* | *I'll be back by five* (=five o'clock). | *He is five* (=five years old). → **NINE-TO-FIVE**

fiver /ˈfaɪvə $ -ər/ *n* [C] *BrE informal* a piece of paper money worth five pounds

fix¹ /fɪks/ *v* [T]
1 REPAIR to repair something: *I've fixed your bike.* | *She fixed the problem.* THESAURUS **REPAIR**
2 DECIDE ON STH to decide on an exact time, place, price etc: *Have you fixed a date for the wedding yet?* | *The interest rate was fixed at 6.5%.*
3 FASTEN STH TO STH *BrE* to fasten something to something else so that it will not come off: **fix sth to/onto sth** *She fixed the shelf to the wall.*
4 MEAL/DRINK *AmE* to prepare a meal or drink: *Mom was fixing dinner.*
5 HAIR/MAKE-UP *AmE* to make your hair or MAKE-UP look neat and attractive: *I need to fix my hair.*
6 DISHONESTLY ARRANGE STH to arrange an election or game dishonestly so that you get the result you want: *The deal was fixed in advance.*
PHRASAL VERBS
fix sb/sth ↔ up
1 *BrE* to arrange an event or trip: *We need to fix up a meeting.*
2 to decorate or repair a room or building: *We fixed up the guest bedroom.*
3 to provide someone with something they want: **[+with]** *Can you fix me up with a bed for the night?*

fix² *n* **1 (be) in a fix** to have a problem that is difficult to solve: *We'll be in a fix if we miss the bus.* **2** [singular] an amount of an illegal drug that someone takes and needs regularly **3** [singular] a result of a game or election that has been arranged in a dishonest way: *The election was a fix.*
PHRASES
| **quick fix** something that solves a problem quickly but is only a temporary solution

fixation /fɪkˈseɪʃən/ *n* [C] a very strong interest in someone or something that is not natural or healthy: **[+with/on/about]** *He had a fixation with guns.* —**fixated** /-ˈseɪtɪd/ *adj*

fixed /fɪkst/ *adj* **1** firmly fastened in a particular position: **to/in/on** *a mirror fixed to the wall* **2** a fixed time or amount cannot be changed: *The classes begin and end at fixed times.* | *fixed prices* **3 have fixed ideas/opinions** *disapproving* to have ideas or opinions that you will not change: *She had fixed opinions on the importance of teaching grammar.*

fixedly /ˈfɪksɪdli/ *adv* without looking at or thinking about anything else: **stare/gaze/look fixedly at sth** *Ann stared fixedly at the screen.*

fixture /ˈfɪkstʃə $ -ər/ *n* [C] **1** *BrE* a sports event that has been arranged **2** [usually plural] a piece of equipment that is fixed inside a house and is sold as part of the house → **fitting**

fizz /fɪz/ n [singular, U] the BUBBLES of gas in some drinks, and the sound they make: *The mineral water has lost its fizz.* —**fizz** v [I] → see picture on page A7

fizzle /ˈfɪzəl/ v
PHRASAL VERBS
fizzle out to gradually end in a weak or disappointing way: *Their relationship fizzled out.*

fizzy /ˈfɪzi/ adj a fizzy drink contains gas

flab /flæb/ n [U] informal soft loose fat on a person's body

flabbergasted /ˈflæbəɡɑːstɪd $ -bərɡæs-/ adj informal very surprised

flabby /ˈflæbi/ adj a part of your body that is flabby has too much soft loose fat: *flabby arms*

flag¹ /flæɡ/ n [C]
1 a piece of cloth with a picture or pattern that is used as the sign of a country or organization: *the French flag* | *Children **waving flags** greeted the Russian leader.*
2 a piece of coloured cloth used in some sports as a sign or signal: *The flag went down and the race began.*

flag² v [I] (**flagged, flagging**) to become tired or weak: *By the end of the meeting we had begun to flag.* —**flagging** adj
PHRASAL VERBS
flag sb/sth ↔ **down** to make the driver of a vehicle stop by waving at them: *I flagged down a taxi.*

flagpole /ˈflæɡpəʊl $ -poʊl/ n [C] a tall pole for a flag

flagrant /ˈfleɪɡrənt/ adj a flagrant action is shocking because it is done in a very noticeable way and shows no respect for the law, the truth etc: **flagrant abuse/violation/breach etc** *a flagrant abuse of power* —**flagrantly** adv

flagship /ˈflæɡʃɪp/ n [C usually singular] a company's best and most important product, building etc: *the flagship of the Ford range*

flagstone /ˈflæɡstəʊn $ -stoʊn/ n [C] a smooth flat piece of stone used for floors, paths etc

flail /fleɪl/ v [I,T] to move your arms and legs about in an uncontrolled way: *He flailed wildly as she held him down.*

flair /fleə $ fler/ n [singular, U] a natural ability to do something well: *He has a **flair** for languages.* | **artistic/creative flair** *a job that requires artistic flair*

flak /flæk/ n [U] informal criticism: *She got a lot of flak for that decision.*

flake¹ /fleɪk/ n [C] a small flat thin piece of something: *The paint was coming off the door in flakes.* —**flaky** adj

flake² v [I] to break off in small thin pieces: *The paint is flaking off.*
PHRASAL VERBS
flake out BrE informal to fall asleep because you are very tired: *He flaked out on the sofa.*

flamboyant /flæmˈbɔɪənt/ adj **1** behaving in a confident or exciting way that makes people notice you: *a **flamboyant gesture*** **2** brightly coloured: *flamboyant clothes*

flame¹ /fleɪm/ n
1 [C,U] a bright moving yellow or orange light that you see when something is burning: *Flames poured out of the building.* | *They **doused** the **flames** (=poured water on them to stop them burning).*
2 in flames burning in a way that is difficult to control: *The house was in flames.* | **go up in flames/ burst into flames** *The plane burst into flames.*
THESAURUS BURN → OLD FLAME

flame² v [I,T] to send someone an angry or rude message on the Internet

flaming /ˈfleɪmɪŋ/ adj [only before noun] **1 a flaming row/temper** a very angry argument or temper **2** BrE informal used to emphasize what you are saying when you are annoyed: *You flaming idiot!* **3** burning brightly: *flaming torches*

flamingo /fləˈmɪŋɡəʊ $ -ɡoʊ/ n [C] (plural **flamingos** or **flamingoes**) a large pink tropical bird with long thin legs and a long neck

FLAMINGO

flammable /ˈflæməbəl/ adj materials or substances that are flammable burn very easily
SYN inflammable
OPP non-flammable

flan /flæn/ n [C] a PIE or cake without a top that is filled with fruit, cheese etc

flank¹ /flæŋk/ n [C] **1** the side of an animal's or person's body between the chest and the HIP → see picture on page A3 **2** the side of an army in a battle

flank² v [T] to be on both sides of someone or something: *The gate is flanked by statues.*

flannel /ˈflænl/ n **1** [C] BrE a piece of cloth that you use to wash yourself **2** [U] a type of soft warm cloth

flap¹ /flæp/ n **1** [C] a flat piece of cloth or paper that is fastened by one edge to something: *the flap of the envelope* **2 a flap** informal a situation in which people feel very worried about something: **be/get in a flap** *She's in a flap over moving house.*

flap² v (**flapped, flapping**) **1** [I,T] if a bird flaps its wings, it moves them up and down **2** [I] if a piece of cloth flaps, it moves backwards and forwards: *The curtains flapped in the wind.* **3** [I] BrE informal to behave in an excited or nervous way: *There's no need to flap.*

flare¹ /fleə $ fler/ (also **flare up**) v [I] **1** to suddenly begin to burn very brightly: *The fire flared up.* **2** if trouble or anger flares, it suddenly starts or becomes more violent: **Tempers flared** *during the debate.*

flare² n [C] **1** a thing that produces a bright light and that someone shoots into the air as a sign that they need help **2** a sudden bright flame

flared /fleəd $ flerd/ adj flared trousers or skirts become wider towards the bottom

'flare-up n [C] a situation in which people suddenly become very angry or violent: *an angry flare-up during the match*

flash¹ /flæʃ/ v

1 SHINE [I,T] to shine brightly for a short time, or to make a light shine in this way: *Lightning flashed overhead.* | **flash sth at/towards sb/sth** *Why is that man flashing his headlights at me?* THESAURUS ➤ SHINE

2 MOVE QUICKLY [I] to move very quickly: **[+by/past/through etc]** *A police car flashed by.* | *Images of the war flashed across the TV screen.*

3 THOUGHTS **flash through sb's mind/head/brain** if thoughts flash through your mind, you suddenly think of them: *The possibility that he was lying flashed through my mind.*

4 SMILE/LOOK **flash a smile/glance/look etc** to smile or look at someone quickly: *'I love this city,' he said, flashing a big smile.*

5 SHOW STH QUICKLY [T] to show something to someone quickly: *He flashed his I.D. card.*

6 NEWS/INFORMATION [T] to send information somewhere quickly by radio, computer, or SATELLITE: **flash sth across/to sth** *The news was flashed across the globe.*

flash² n

1 [C] a sudden quick bright light: **[+of]** *a flash of lightning*

2 [C,U] a bright light on a camera that you use to take photographs indoors

3 flash of inspiration/brilliance/anger etc a sudden clever idea or strong feeling: *His work shows occasional flashes of brilliance.*

PHRASES

a flash in the pan someone or something that is successful only for a very short time: *Beene's new novel proves that he isn't just a flash in the pan.*

in/like a flash (also **(as) quick as a flash**) very quickly: *I'll be back in a flash.*

flash³ adj **1** BrE informal looking very new, bright, and expensive – used to show disapproval: *a big flash car* **2** BrE informal liking to have expensive clothes and possessions so that other people notice you – used to show disapproval: *Chris didn't want to seem flash in front of his mates.*

PHRASES

flash flood/fire a flood or fire that happens very quickly or suddenly, and continues for only a short time: *Flash fires swept through the Los Angeles foothills last night.*

flashback /'flæʃbæk/ n **1** [C,U] part of a film, play, book etc that shows something that happened earlier **2** [C] a sudden very clear memory of a past event

flashlight /'flæʃlaɪt/ n [C] AmE a small electric light that you carry in your hand SYN **torch** BrE → see picture at **LIGHT¹**

flashpoint /'flæʃpɔɪnt/ n [C] a place where trouble or violence might easily develop suddenly

flashy /'flæʃi/ adj very big, bright, or expensive: *a flashy car*

FLASKS

flask   Thermos™ flask

flask /flɑːsk $ flæsk/ n [C] **1** BrE a type of bottle for keeping liquids hot or cold: *a flask of coffee* **2** a type of bottle with a wide base, used in chemistry **3** a small flat bottle for carrying alcoholic drinks

flat¹ /flæt/ adj (comparative **flatter**, superlative **flattest**)

1 SURFACE not sloping and with no raised parts, or with no hills or mountains: *a flat surface* | *Holland is very flat.*

2 PRICE/RATE a flat rate or price is fixed and does not change: *They charge a flat rate for delivery.*

3 TYRE a flat tyre does not have enough air inside it

4 NOT DEEP not very thick, deep, or high: *a flat box*

5 DRINK a drink that is flat has lost its gas: *This soda water has gone flat.*

6 NOT INTERESTING a performance, book etc that is flat is not very interesting or exciting

7 BATTERY BrE a flat BATTERY has lost its electrical power SYN **dead** AmE: *The batteries have gone flat.*

8 MUSICAL NOTE **a)** **E flat/B flat etc** a musical note that is slightly lower than E, B etc → **sharp b)** if a musical note is flat, it is played or sung slightly lower than it should be

9 REFUSAL **flat refusal/denial etc** a refusal etc which someone will not change

THESAURUS

flat not sloping and with no raised parts, or with no hills or mountains: *The house has a flat roof.* | *The land on the coast is mostly flat.*

level not sloping up or down, so that every part is at the same height: *The shelf looks level to me.*

smooth very flat and not rough, in a way that feels or looks good: *Your skin feels really smooth.* | *Our cat has lovely smooth fur.*

even without any holes or raised areas that might cause a problem: *Make sure the walls are even before you start painting them.* | *Be careful – the path is not very even.*

horizontal going straight across and not sloping: *Draw a horizontal line.* | *Your arms should be horizontal.*

flat² n [C]

1 PLACE TO LIVE BrE a set of rooms for someone to live in that is part of a larger building SYN **apartment** AmE: *a two-bedroom flat* | *a block of flats* (=a large building with many flats in it) THESAURUS ➤ HOUSE

2 TYRE a tyre that does not have enough air inside: *The car has a flat.*

3 MUSIC a musical note that is slightly lower than the usual note, or the sign (♭) used in written music to show this note

4 LAND **flats** [plural] an area of land that is at a low level, especially near water: *mud flats*

5 FLAT PART **the flat of sth** the flat part or side of something: *He hit the desk with the flat of his hand.*

flat³ *adv*

1 in a position in which someone or something is smooth and level, with no parts that are raised or standing up: *The bed can be folded flat for storage.* | *He lay flat on his back.* → **fall flat** at FALL¹

2 in ten seconds/two minutes etc flat *informal* very quickly, in ten seconds, two minutes etc: *He did his homework in ten minutes flat.*

PHRASES

flat out *informal* **1** as fast as possible: *We've been working flat out.* **2** *AmE* in a direct and complete way: **ask/tell sb flat out** *She asked him flat out if he was seeing another woman.*

flatly /ˈflætli/ *adv* **1 flatly refuse/deny etc** to say something in a very firm strong way: *She flatly refused to let me borrow her car.* **2** without showing any emotion: *'It's hopeless,' he said flatly.*

flatmate /ˈflætmeɪt/ *n* [C] *BrE* someone who shares a flat with other people SYN **roommate** *AmE*

'flat-pack (*also* **flat pack**) *n* [C] *BrE* furniture that is sold in a box and has to be put together

flatten /ˈflætn/ *v* [I,T] to make something flat, or to become flat: *Use a rolling pin to flatten the dough.*

flatter /ˈflætə $ -ər/ *v* [T] **1** to say nice things about someone or show that you admire them, sometimes when you do not really mean it: *He flattered her, saying how nice she looked.* THESAURUS ▶ PRAISE **2 be/feel flattered** to feel pleased because someone has shown that they like or admire you: *When they asked me to come, I felt flattered.* **3** to make someone look as attractive as they can: *That dress flatters your figure.* **4 flatter yourself** to believe that your abilities or achievements are better than they really are: **[+that]** *She flatters herself that she could have been a model.* —**flatterer** *n* [C] —**flattering** *adj*: *a flattering photograph*

flattery /ˈflætəri/ *n* [U] nice things that you say about someone or something, but which you do not really mean: *She uses flattery to get what she wants.*

flaunt /flɔːnt $ flɒːnt, flɑːnt/ *v* [T] if you flaunt your money, success, beauty etc, you try to make other people notice it and admire you for it: *The rich flaunted their wealth.*

flautist /ˈflɔːtɪst $ ˈflɒː-/ *n* [C] *BrE* someone who plays the FLUTE SYN **flutist** *AmE*

flavour¹ *BrE*, **flavor** *AmE* /ˈfleɪvə $ -ər/ *n*

1 [C] the taste that a food or drink has: *Which flavour do you want – chocolate or vanilla?* | **[+of]** *a dry wine with a slight flavor of honey* | *the rich flavour of the meat*

2 [U] a strong and pleasant taste: *The beef was full of flavour.*

3 [singular] a quality or feature that makes something have a particular style or character: *The stories have a regional flavour.*

adjectives

a delicious flavour *This type of tomato has a delicious flavour.*

a sweet/spicy/bitter/salty flavour *The flavour of the leaves is slightly bitter.*

a strong flavour *The fish has a very strong flavour.*

a mild/delicate/subtle flavour (=not strong) *a cheese with a mild flavour*

chocolate/strawberry/vanilla etc flavour *strawberry flavour ice cream*

verbs

to have a flavour *This vegetable has a similar flavour to celery.*

to add/give flavour *Mustard adds flavour to a sandwich.*

Word Choice: flavour or taste?

Flavour and **taste** are both used about the feeling produced in your mouth by food and drink.

If something tastes bad or strange, you use **taste**: *The soup had a funny taste.*

You use **flavour** especially when something has a pleasant or interesting taste: *Each wine has its own unique flavour.* | *The cheese has a delicate flavour.*

You also use **flavour** when something is added to food to make it have a particular taste: *chocolate flavour ice cream*

flavour² *BrE*, **flavor** *AmE v* [T] to give food or drink a particular taste: *The sauce is flavoured with herbs.* | **orange-flavoured/chocolate-flavoured etc** *almond-flavored cookies*

flavouring *BrE*, **flavoring** *AmE* /ˈfleɪvərɪŋ/ *n* [C,U] something used to give food or drink a particular taste

flaw /flɔː $ flɒː/ *n* [C] **1** a mistake, mark, or weakness that stops something from being perfect: **[+in]** *a flaw in the glass* | *a flaw in his argument* THESAURUS ▶ FAULT **2** a bad part of someone's character

flawed /flɔːd $ flɒːd/ *adj* something that is flawed has mistakes or weaknesses and so is not perfect: *His theory is badly flawed.*

flawless /ˈflɔːləs $ ˈflɒː-/ *adj* something that is flawless has no mistakes, marks, or weaknesses SYN **perfect**: *Sue's flawless French* —**flawlessly** *adv*

flea /fliː/ *n* [C] a very small jumping insect that bites animals and drinks their blood

'flea ˌmarket *n* [C] a market where old or used goods are sold

fleck /flek/ *n* [C] a small mark or spot: **[+of]** *a black beard with flecks of gray*

flecked /flekt/ *adj* having small marks or spots: *red flowers flecked with white*

fled /fled/ *v* the past tense and past participle of FLEE

fledgling /ˈfledʒlɪŋ/ *adj* a fledgling country, organization etc is new and still developing: *a fledgling republic*

flee /fli:/ v [I,T] (past tense and past participle **fled** /fled/) formal to leave a place very quickly in order to escape from danger: She **fled** the **country**.
THESAURUS ESCAPE

fleece /fli:s/ n 1 [C,U] the wool that covers a sheep 2 [U] an artificial soft material used to make warm jackets —**fleecy** adj

fleet /fli:t/ n [C] a group of ships or vehicles: the US seventh fleet | [+of] a fleet of taxis

fleeting /'fli:tɪŋ/ adj happening for only a moment: a fleeting smile

flesh¹ /fleʃ/ n [U]
1 the soft part of your body, between your skin and your bones: a fish with white flesh
2 the skin of the human body: naked flesh
3 the soft part inside a fruit or vegetable: Cut the melon in half and scoop out the flesh. → see picture on page A4
PHRASES
in the flesh if you see someone in the flesh, you see them in real life, not in a picture: I was thrilled to meet him in the flesh.
make sb's flesh creep/crawl to make someone feel frightened or nervous: The way he stared at her made her flesh creep.
your own flesh and blood someone who is part of your family: He raised those kids like they were his own flesh and blood.

flesh² v
PHRASAL VERBS
flesh sth ↔ **out** to add more details to something: You need to flesh out your essay with more examples.

fleshy /'fleʃi/ adj having a lot of flesh: the fleshy part of your hand

flew /flu:/ v the past tense of FLY

flex¹ /fleks/ v [T] to bend part of your body so that your muscles stretch and become tight

flex² n [C] BrE a wire covered with plastic, used to connect electrical equipment SYN **cord** AmE

flexible Ac /'fleksəbəl/ adj 1 able to change easily OPP **inflexible**: flexible working hours | Teachers have to be flexible. 2 easy to bend: a flexible tube —**flexibility** /ˌfleksə'bɪləti/ n [U]: We need **greater flexibility** in how we use resources.

flick /flɪk/ v 1 [T] to send something small through the air with a quick movement of your finger or hand: He flicked the fly off his sleeve. → see picture on page A10 2 [I,T] to move with a quick sudden movement, or to make something move in this way: [+from/up/down etc] The cow's tail flicked from side to side. | She flicked her hair back from her face. 3 [T] to press a switch in order to start or stop electrical equipment: He **flicked** the light **switch** on. —**flick** n [C]
PHRASAL VERBS
flick through sth to look at a book, magazine etc quickly: She was flicking through a magazine.
THESAURUS READ

flicker¹ /'flɪkə $ -ər/ v [I] 1 to burn or shine with an unsteady light: The candle flickered. **THESAURUS** SHINE 2 written if an expression flickers across your

face, it appears for a moment: [+across/through/on etc] A smile flickered across her face.

flicker² n [C] 1 an unsteady light that goes on and off quickly: [+of] the flicker of the firelight 2 **a flicker of emotion/uncertainty/excitement etc** a feeling or an expression that continues for a very short time: She saw a flicker of doubt in his eyes.

flier /'flaɪə $ -ər/ n another spelling of FLYER

flies /flaɪz/ n the plural of FLY²

flight /flaɪt/ n
1 [C] a journey in a plane, or the plane making a particular journey: It had been a long, tiring flight. | They caught the next flight home. | Flight 453 **THESAURUS** JOURNEY
2 [U] when something flies through the air: **in flight** You can unfasten your seat belt once the plane is in flight.
3 **flight of stairs/steps** a set of stairs: She ran up two flights of stairs.
4 [U] formal when you leave a place in order to escape from a dangerous situation: [+from] his flight from South Africa → **IN-FLIGHT**

COLLOCATIONS
verbs
to book a flight (=to reserve a seat on a plane) You can book flights online.
to get a flight I'll try to get a flight home tomorrow.
to catch/take a flight He planned to catch the 6 pm flight back to Munich.
to miss a flight Hurry, or you'll miss your flight.
a flight is cancelled/delayed All flights have been cancelled because of fog.

adjectives
a good/smooth flight Did you have a good flight?
a long-haul flight (=over a long distance) a long-haul flight to Australia
a direct flight (=going straight from one place to another) I couldn't get a direct flight to Cairo.
an international flight (=to another country) All international flights have been cancelled.
a domestic/internal flight (=between two places in the same country) The plane was on a domestic flight.

'flight at,tendant n [C] someone whose job is to look after passengers on a plane

'flight deck n [C] the area of a plane where the pilot sits

flimsy /'flɪmzi/ adj 1 thin and light, and not thick or strong: a flimsy cotton dress | a flimsy table **THESAURUS** WEAK 2 a flimsy argument or excuse is not good enough for you to believe: The evidence against him is very flimsy.

flinch /flɪntʃ/ v [I] 1 to move backwards suddenly because you are afraid or hurt: The child flinched as she touched him. 2 **not flinch from (doing) sth** to do something even though it is difficult or unpleasant: She never flinches from the truth.

fling¹ /flɪŋ/ v [T] (past tense and past participle **flung** /flʌŋ/) to throw or put something somewhere with a lot of force or in a careless way: **fling sth at/into/on etc sth/sb** *Mike flung his coat down on the chair.* | *Val flung her arms around my neck.* | **fling yourself down/through etc** *He flung himself down on the bed.* **THESAURUS** THROW

fling² *n* [C] **1** a short and not very serious sexual relationship: *They **had** a brief **fling** last year.* **2** a short period of time when you enjoy yourself a lot

flint /flɪnt/ *n* [C,U] a type of very hard stone that makes a small flame when you strike it with steel

flip /flɪp/ *v* (**flipped, flipping**)
1 MOVE STH [T] to move something or turn it over with a quick movement: **flip sth over** *She flipped the book over and looked on the back.* | *He **flipped** the lid **open** with his thumb.*
2 TURN IN THE AIR [T] to throw something flat up into the air so that it turns over: *Let's **flip a coin** to see who goes first.*
3 BECOME ANGRY [I] *informal* to suddenly become very angry: *I just flipped and started screaming at them.*
4 A SWITCH/A CONTROL [T] to move a control to start or stop electrical equipment: *You just **flip** a **switch** and the machine does everything for you.*
PHRASAL VERBS
flip through sth to look at a book or magazine quickly **THESAURUS** READ

'flip chart *n* [C] large sheets of paper that are joined at the top so that you can turn the pages over to present information to people

'flip-flops *n* [plural] *especially BrE* summer shoes held on your feet by a V-shaped band that goes between your toes **SYN** thongs *AmE*

flippant /ˈflɪpənt/ *adj* not serious enough about something, in a way that shows a lack of respect: *You shouldn't be flippant about such things.* —**flippantly** *adv* —**flippancy** *n* [U]

flipper /ˈflɪpə $ -ər/ *n* [C] **1** a flat part of the body that some sea animals, for example SEALS, use for swimming → see picture on page A3 **2** a large flat rubber shoe that you use for swimming under water

flipping /ˈflɪpɪŋ/ *adj BrE informal* used to emphasize that you are annoyed: *Where's my flipping pen?*

'flip side *n* [singular] *informal* the bad effects of something that also has good effects: *The flip side is that the medicine may cause hair loss.*

flirt¹ /flɜːt $ flɜːrt/ *v* [I] to behave as if you are sexually attracted to someone, but not in a serious way: **[+with]** *He's always flirting with the women in the office.*
PHRASAL VERBS
flirt with sth **1** to think about doing something, but not be very serious about it: *I've been flirting with the idea of moving to Greece.* **2 flirt with danger/disaster** to do something that might be dangerous or have a very bad effect

flirt² *n* [C] someone who flirts with people: *Dave is such a flirt!*

flirtation /flɜːˈteɪʃən $ flɜːr-/ *n* **1** [C] when someone is interested in something for a short time: **[+with]** *his brief flirtation with photography*

2 [U] when you behave as if you are sexually attracted to someone, but not in a serious way

flirtatious /flɜːˈteɪʃəs $ flɜːr-/ *adj* behaving as if you are sexually attracted to someone, but not in a serious way

flit /flɪt/ *v* [I] (**flitted, flitting**) to move quickly from one place to another: *Small birds flitted from branch to branch.*

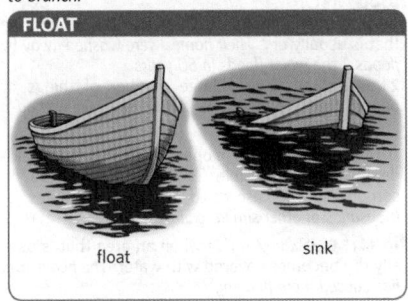
FLOAT

float   sink

float¹ /fləʊt $ floʊt/ *v*
1 [I,T] to stay on the surface of a liquid without sinking, or to make something do this: **[+on]** *Oil floats on water.* | **[+in]** *I spotted a fly floating in my drink.* | **[+down/along/past]** *leaves floating down the river* | **float sth down/along etc** *The huge logs are floated down the river.*
2 [I] to stay in the air or move slowly through the air: *The balloon floated up into the sky.*
3 [T] to sell SHARES in a company to the public for the first time: *The company was floated on the stock market last month.*

float² *n* [C] a large vehicle that is decorated to be part of a PARADE

flock¹ /flɒk $ flɑːk/ *n* [C] **1** a group of sheep, goats, or birds: **[+of]** *a flock of geese* **THESAURUS** GROUP **2** a large group of people **SYN** crowd: **[+of]** *a flock of tourists*

flock² *v* [I] if people flock to a place, a lot of them go there: *People have been flocking to see the play.*

flog /flɒg $ flɑːg/ *v* [T] (**flogged, flogging**) to beat someone with a whip or stick as a punishment —**flogging** *n* [C]

flood¹ /flʌd/ *v*
1 WATER [I,T] to cover a place with water, or to become covered with water: *The river floods the valley every spring.* | *The basement flooded and everything got soaked.*
2 ARRIVE/GO SOMEWHERE [I] to arrive or go somewhere in large numbers: **[+in/into/across]** *Refugees flooded across the border.*
3 RECEIVE A LOT **be flooded with sth** to receive so many letters, complaints etc that you cannot deal with them all: *After the show, they were flooded with calls from angry viewers.*
4 FEELING/MEMORY [I] if a feeling or memory floods over you or floods back, you feel it or remember it very strongly: **[+over]** *A feeling of relief flooded over me.* | **[+back]** *I saw her picture the other day, and it all came flooding back.*
5 LIGHT [I] if light floods into a place, it becomes

full of light: **[+in/into]** *Sunlight flooded in through the kitchen window.*

PHRASES

flood the market to sell something in very large quantities, so that the price goes down: *Manufacturers have been accused of flooding the market with cheap cars.*

flood² *n* [C]

1 a very large amount of water that covers an area that is usually dry: *Their homes were washed away by floods.* | *the worst floods in 50 years*
2 flood of sth a very large number of things or people that arrive at the same time: *We've had a flood of inquiries.*

floodgate /ˈflʌdɡeɪt/ *n* **open the floodgates** to suddenly make it possible for a lot of people to do something: *The case could open the floodgates for thousands of other similar claims.*

flooding /ˈflʌdɪŋ/ *n* [U] when an area that is usually dry becomes covered with water: *The heavy rain has caused more flooding.*

floodlight /ˈflʌdlaɪt/ *n* [C] a large bright light, used for lighting sports fields or public buildings

floodlit /ˈflʌdlɪt/ *adj* surrounded by floodlights

floor¹ /flɔː $ flɔːr/ *n* [C]

1 the surface that you walk on when you are inside a building: *a cold stone floor* | **on the floor** *water spilt on the kitchen floor* **THESAURUS** ▶ GROUND
2 one of the levels in a building: **on the first/third/top etc floor** *My office is on the third floor.* | *a **ground floor** flat*
3 an area where people work or do an activity: *workers on the **factory floor*** | *the **dance floor***
4 ocean/forest etc floor the ground at the bottom of the ocean or in a forest → SHOP FLOOR

> **Usage**
> In British English, the part of a building that is at the same level as the ground is called **the ground floor**. In American English, it is usually called **the first floor**.

floor² *v* [T] **1** to surprise or shock someone so much that they do not know what to say: *At first she was completely floored by his question.* **2** *AmE* to make a car go very fast

floorboard /ˈflɔːbɔːd $ ˈflɔːrbɔːrd/ *n* [C] a board in a wooden floor

flooring /ˈflɔːrɪŋ/ *n* [U] a material used to cover floors

floor plan *n* [C] a drawing of a room or the inside of a building, as seen from above

flop¹ /flɒp $ flɑːp/ *v* [I] (**flopped, flopping**) **1** to sit or lie down heavily, especially because you are tired: **[+into/onto etc]** *Sarah flopped down into an armchair.* **2** if a film, show, plan, or product flops, it is not successful: *The musical flopped on Broadway.* **3** to hang down loosely: *Her hair flopped across her face.*

flop² *n* [C] **1** a film, show, plan, or product that is not successful: *The show's first series was a complete flop.* **2** the noise or movement that something

makes when it falls down heavily: *He fell with a flop into the water.*

floppy /ˈflɒpi $ ˈflɑːpi/ *adj* soft and hanging down loosely: *a floppy hat*

floppy 'disk (*also* **floppy**) *n* [C] a small flat piece of plastic, used for storing information from a computer

flora /ˈflɔːrə/ *n* [U] *technical* all the plants that grow in a particular place: *the **flora and fauna** (=plants and animals) of the island*

floral /ˈflɔːrəl/ *adj* made of flowers or decorated with flowers: *a floral pattern* → see picture at **PATTERN**

florid /ˈflɒrɪd $ ˈflɔː-, ˈflɑː-/ *adj literary* **1** florid skin is red: *his florid complexion* **2** florid language, art, or music contains too many unnecessary details

florist /ˈflɒrɪst $ ˈflɔː-/ *n* [C] **1** (*also* **florist's**) a shop that sells flowers **2** someone who works in a shop that sells flowers

floss /flɒs $ flɑːs, flɔːs/ *v* [I,T] to clean between your teeth with special string

flotation /fləʊˈteɪʃən $ floʊ-/ *n* [C,U] when SHARES in a company are made available for people to buy for the first time

flotilla /fləˈtɪlə $ floʊ-/ *n* [C] a group of small ships

flounce /flaʊns/ *v* [I] to walk in a way that shows you are angry: **[+out/off]** *She flounced out of the room.*

flounder /ˈflaʊndə $ -ər/ *v* [I] **1** to not know what to do or say, because you are confused or upset: *She floundered helplessly, unable to answer his question.* **2** to move with difficulty because you are in deep water or mud

flour /flaʊə $ flaʊr/ *n* [U] powder made from grain, used for making bread and cakes

flourish¹ /ˈflʌrɪʃ $ ˈflɜːrɪʃ/ *v* **1** [I] to develop or grow and be successful: *conditions in which businesses can flourish* | *Herbs flourished in her tiny garden.* **2** [T] to wave something in your hand to make people notice it: *Henry came out flourishing a $100 bill.*

flourish² *n* **with a flourish** with a large confident movement that makes people notice you: *He opened the door with a flourish.*

flout /flaʊt/ *v* [T] *formal* to deliberately disobey a rule or law: *companies who flout the rules on child labour*

flow¹ /fləʊ $ floʊ/ *n*

1 [C usually singular] a smooth steady movement of something such as a liquid, people, traffic, or information: **[+of]** *They tried to stop the flow of blood.* | *a **steady flow** of people leaving the area* | *the **free flow** of information* | *measures to help **traffic flow***
2 [U] when ideas or a conversation can continue easily without stopping: *Sorry, I didn't mean to **interrupt** your flow.* → CASH FLOW

PHRASES

go with the flow *spoken* to decide to do the same as other people, and not try to do something different: *If you want to get along here, just go with the flow.*

flow² v [I]

1 if something flows, it moves in a smooth steady way: **[+over/down/through etc]** *The River Elbe flows through the Czech Republic.* | *A steady stream of cars flowed past her window.*

2 if words, ideas, or conversations flow, they continue easily without stopping: *After dinner, the conversation **flowed freely**.*

3 if clothing or hair flows, it hangs down loosely in an attractive way: *Her hair flowed down her back.* —**flowing** *adj*: *a fast-flowing river* | *long flowing hair*

'flow chart *n* [C] a drawing that uses lines and ARROWS to show how a series of actions or parts of a system are connected with each other

flower¹ /'flaʊə $ -ər/ *n* [C] the coloured part of a plant that produces the seeds or fruit: *a tree with beautiful pink flowers* | *wild flowers* | *The **flowers grow** mainly near rivers.* | *They **picked** some **flowers** to take home.*

PHRASES

in flower if a plant is in flower, it has flowers on it: *It was May, and the apple trees were all in flower.*

flower² v [I] if a plant or tree flowers, it produces flowers

flowerbed /'flaʊəbed $ -ər-/ *n* [C] an area of ground in which you grow flowers

flowered /'flaʊəd $ -ərd/ *adj* decorated with pictures of flowers: *a flowered dress*

flowerpot /'flaʊəpɒt $ -ərpɑːt/ *n* [C] a pot in

which you grow plants → see picture at **GARDEN**

flowery /'flaʊəri/ *adj* **1** decorated with pictures of flowers: *a flowery pattern* **2** flowery speech or writing uses complicated and unusual words

flown /fləʊn $ floʊn/ *v* the past participle of FLY¹

fl oz *BrE*, **fl.oz.** *AmE* the written abbreviation of **fluid ounce**

flu /fluː/ *n* [U] a common disease which is like a bad cold but is more serious SYN **influenza**: *The whole team **has got flu**.*

fluctuate Ac /'flʌktʃueɪt/ *v* [I] if an amount fluctuates, it keeps changing from a higher to a lower level and back again: *The price of copper fluctuated wildly.* —**fluctuation** /ˌflʌktʃu'eɪʃən/ *n* [C]: *fluctuations in temperature*

flue /fluː/ *n* [C] a pipe through which smoke or heat from a fire can go out of a building

fluent /'fluːənt/ *adj* able to speak or write a language very well, without stopping or making mistakes: *Jem can speak fluent Japanese.* | **[+in]** *Candidates must be fluent in two European languages.* —**fluently** *adv*: *She speaks Arabic fluently.* —**fluency** *n* [U]

fluff¹ /flʌf/ *n* [U] small light pieces of wool, fur, or feathers: *She picked the fluff off her sweater.*

fluff² v [T] **1** (*also* **fluff up/out**) to make something soft appear larger by shaking it: *The bird fluffed out its feathers.* **2** *informal* to make a mistake or do

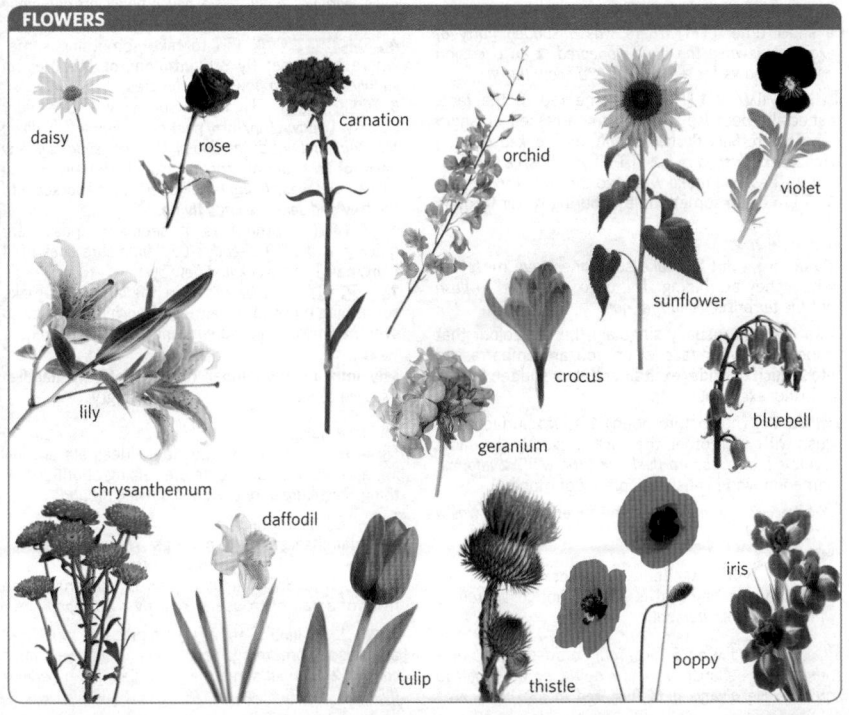

FLOWERS

daisy

rose

carnation

orchid

violet

lily

sunflower

crocus

bluebell

geranium

chrysanthemum

daffodil

iris

tulip

thistle

poppy

something badly: *Ricky fluffed the catch and we lost the game.*

fluffy /ˈflʌfi/ *adj* very soft and light to touch: *a fluffy kitten*

fluid¹ /ˈfluːɪd/ *n* [C,U] *technical* a liquid: *My doctor told me to rest and drink plenty of fluids.*

fluid² *adj* **1** a situation that is fluid is likely to change **2** fluid movements are smooth and graceful

,fluid 'ounce *n* [C] a unit for measuring liquid. There are 20 fluid ounces in a British PINT, and 16 in an American pint.

fluke /fluːk/ *n* [C] something that only happens because of luck: *The goal was a fluke.*

flung /flʌŋ/ *v* the past tense and past participle of FLING

flunk /flʌŋk/ *v* [I,T] *AmE informal* to fail a test or course: *I flunked my history exam.* **THESAURUS** FAIL

PHRASAL VERBS
flunk out *AmE informal* to have to leave a school or college because your work is not good enough: **[+of]** *Tim flunked out of Yale.*

fluorescent /fluəˈresənt $ flʊ-, flɔː-/ *adj* **1** fluorescent colours are very bright and can be seen easily, even in the dark **2** a fluorescent light is made of a long glass tube filled with a special gas that produces a very bright light

fluoride /ˈfluəraɪd $ ˈflʊr-/ *n* [U] a chemical that helps to protect teeth against decay

flurry /ˈflʌri $ ˈflɜːri/ *n* [C] (*plural* **flurries**) **1** an occasion when there is suddenly a lot of activity for a short time: **[+of]** *There was a sudden flurry of excitement when the band appeared.* **2** an occasion when it snows for a short time: *a snow flurry*

flush¹ /flʌʃ/ *v* **1** [I] to become red in the face, especially because you are embarrassed or angry **SYN** blush: *Billy flushed deeply and looked down.* | *Her cheeks flushed red.* **2** [I,T] if you flush a toilet, or if it flushes, you make water go through it to clean it **3** [T] to clean something by pouring water through it

PHRASAL VERBS
flush sb ↔ **out** to make someone leave the place where they are hiding: *The police managed to flush out the terrorists using tear gas.*

flush² *n* **1** [C usually singular] the red colour that appears on your face when you are embarrassed etc **2** flush of pride/excitement etc a sudden feeling of pride, excitement etc

flush³ *adj* [not before noun] **1** if two surfaces are flush with each other, they are at exactly the same level: *Is that cupboard flush with the wall?* **2** *informal* someone who is flush has plenty of money

flushed /flʌʃt/ *adj* red in the face: *Her face was a little flushed.*

PHRASES
flushed with excitement/success excited or pleased in a way that is easy to notice: *Jill ran in, flushed with excitement.*

flustered /ˈflʌstəd $ -ərd/ *adj* confused and nervous, often because you are doing something too quickly: *He always gets flustered in job interviews.*

—**fluster** *v* [T]: *Don't fluster me, or I'll never be ready.*

flute /fluːt/ *n* [C] a musical instrument like a thin pipe that you play by holding it across your lips and blowing over a hole → **flautist** → see picture on page A6

flutist /ˈfluːtɪst/ *n* [C] *AmE* someone who plays the flute **SYN** flautist *BrE*

flutter¹ /ˈflʌtə $ -ər/ *v* **1** [I] to wave or move gently in the air: *Flags fluttered in the wind.* **2** [I,T] if a bird or insect flutters its wings, it moves them quickly up and down **3** [I] if your heart or your stomach flutters, you feel very excited or nervous

flutter² *n* [C usually singular] **1** *BrE informal* if you have a flutter, you try to win money by GAMBLING **2** a fluttering movement

flux /flʌks/ *n* **be in (a state of) flux** to be changing a lot, so that you cannot be sure what will happen: *The fashion world is in a state of constant flux.*

fly¹ /flaɪ/ *v* (*past tense* **flew** /fluː/, *past participle* **flown** /fləʊn $ floʊn/, *third person singular* **flies**)
1 **TRAVEL BY PLANE** [I] to travel somewhere by plane: **[+to]** *They flew to Paris for their honeymoon.* | **[+from/out of]** *The team is flying out of Heathrow airport this afternoon.* **THESAURUS** TRAVEL
2 **BIRD/PLANE/INSECT MOVES** [I] if a bird, plane, or insect flies, it moves through the air: *A helicopter flew overhead.* | *Something frightened the bird and it flew off.*
3 **CONTROL A PLANE** [I,T] to be the pilot of a plane: *Bill's learning to fly.* | *I've never flown an aeroplane before.*
4 **SEND STH BY PLANE** [T] to take something somewhere by plane: **fly sth into/out of sth** *Medical supplies are being flown into the area.*
5 **MOVE QUICKLY** [I] **a)** to suddenly move very quickly: **[+down/up/into/past etc]** *Timmy flew down the stairs and out of the door.* | *The door suddenly flew open.* **b)** to suddenly move through the air: *Helena tripped and went flying* (=fell over). | *He knocked into the tray and sent the cups flying.*
6 **TIME** [I] if time flies, it seems to pass very quickly: *Is it 5:30 already? Boy, time sure does fly!* | **[+by/past]** *Last week just flew by.*
7 **FLAG/KITE** [I,T] to move in the air, or to make something move in the air: *The French flag was flying over the Embassy.* | *children flying kites in the park*

PHRASES
fly into a rage/temper (*also* **fly off the handle**) *spoken* to suddenly become very angry

PHRASAL VERBS
fly around/about if suggestions, ideas etc are flying around, a lot of people are talking about something: *There are a lot of rumours flying around.*

fly² *n* [C] (*plural* **flies**)
1 a small insect with two wings: *There were flies all over the food.* → see picture at INSECT
2 (*also* **flies** *BrE*) the ZIP or row of buttons at the front of a pair of trousers: *Your fly is unzipped.*

flyer, flier /ˈflaɪə $ -ər/ *n* [C] **1** a piece of paper that advertises something: *people giving out flyers for a concert* **2** *informal* someone who flies: *I'm a nervous flyer.*

flying¹ /ˈflaɪ-ɪŋ/ n [U] when you travel by plane: *I'm nervous about flying.*

flying² adj able to fly: *a type of flying insect*
PHRASES

flying visit a quick visit, because you do not have much time: *It was just a flying visit – I could only stay a couple of hours.*

get off to a flying start to begin something such as a job or a race very well: *The U.S. has gotten off to a flying start in the Olympics, winning four gold medals on day one.*

with flying colours if you pass a test with flying colours, you are very successful in it: *She passed the exam with flying colours.*

flying 'saucer n [C] an object that some people say they have seen in the sky, which comes from space SYN **UFO**

flyover /ˈflaɪ-əʊvə $ -oʊvər/ n [C] BrE a bridge that carries one road over another road SYN **overpass** AmE

FM /ˌef ˈem◂/ n [U] a system used for broadcasting radio programmes

foal /fəʊl $ foʊl/ n [C] a very young horse

foam¹ /fəʊm $ foʊm/ n [U] **1** (also ˌfoam ˈrubber) soft rubber with lots of air in it, used in furniture: *a foam mattress* **2** a lot of very small BUBBLES on the surface of liquid: *white foam on the tops of the waves* **3** a thick substance with a lot of BUBBLES in it: *shaving foam* —**foamy** adj

foam² v [I] to produce foam
PHRASES

be foaming at the mouth informal to be very angry: *Some senators are foaming at the mouth over what they say is obscene art.*

fob /fɒb $ fɑːb/ v (**fobbed, fobbing**) informal
PHRASAL VERBS

fob sb ↔ off 1 to tell someone something that is not true in order to stop them from complaining: [+with] *She fobbed him off with a promise to pay him the money next week.* **2** to give someone something that is not very good instead of the thing they really want: [+with] *They tried to fob me off with a cheap camera.*

focal point /ˈfəʊkəl pɔɪnt $ ˈfoʊ-/ n [C] the thing that people pay the most attention to: *the focal point of the picture*

focus¹ Ac /ˈfəʊkəs $ ˈfoʊ-/ v (**focused** or **focussed, focusing** or **focussing**) **1** [I,T] to give all your attention to a particular thing: [+on] *In his speech he focused on the economy.* | **focus (your/sb's attention/mind) on sth** *She tried to focus her mind on her work.* **2** [T] to move the controls on a camera or TELESCOPE so that you can see something clearly **3** [I,T] if you focus your eyes, or if your eyes focus, you are able to see clearly: *All eyes were focused on Maria.* —**focused** adj

focus² Ac n **1** [singular] the person or subject that people pay special attention to: [+of] *the main focus of his speech* | **focus of attention/interest** *His private life became the focus of media attention.* | [+for] *The town became the focus for new development in the*

area. **2** [U] if your focus is on something, it is what you give most attention to: [+on] *The school's focus is on basic reading and writing skills.*
PHRASES

in focus if a photograph is in focus, you can see the picture clearly: *Everything is nicely in focus in this shot.*

out of focus if a photograph is out of focus, you cannot see the picture clearly: *Unfortunately, large areas of the photograph are out of focus.*

'focus group n [C] a small group of people who are asked questions by a company, political party etc in order to find out what they think of its products, actions etc

fodder /ˈfɒdə $ ˈfɑːdər/ n [U] food for farm animals

foe /fəʊ $ foʊ/ n [C] literary an enemy

foetus, fetus /ˈfiːtəs/ n [C] a baby before it is born —**foetal** adj: *foetal abnormalities*

fog /fɒg $ fɑːg, fɔːg/ n [C,U] cloudy air near the ground, which is difficult to see through: **thick/dense/heavy/freezing fog** *The accident happened in thick fog.*

fogey /ˈfəʊgi $ ˈfoʊ-/ n [C] (plural **fogeys** or **fogies**) someone who is old-fashioned and does not like change: *a couple of old fogies*

foggy /ˈfɒgi $ ˈfɑːgi, ˈfɔːgi/ adj if the weather is foggy, there is fog: *a foggy day*
PHRASES

not have the foggiest (idea) informal to not know something at all: *I haven't the foggiest idea where they are.*

foible /ˈfɔɪbəl/ n [C] a slightly strange habit that someone has: *It's just one of his little foibles.*

foil¹ /fɔɪl/ n [U] very thin metal, used for wrapping food: *aluminium foil*

foil² v [T] to prevent something bad that someone is planning to do: *A bank robbery has been foiled by police.*

foist /fɔɪst/ v
PHRASAL VERBS

foist sth on/upon sb to make someone accept something that they do not want: *These poor-quality products are being foisted on the public.*

FOLD

fold paper   fold your arms

fold¹ /fəʊld $ foʊld/ v
1 [T] to bend a piece of paper or cloth by pressing one part over another: *He folded his clothes*

fold

carefully. | **Fold** the paper **in half**. | **fold sth up/over/back etc** She folded back the sheets.

2 [I,T] if something folds, or if you fold it, you bend part of it so that it is smaller: Vic folded his sunglasses and put them in his pocket. | The table folds flat for easy storage. | a folding chair | **fold (sth) away/up/down etc** a bed that you can fold away

3 [T] to cover something by wrapping something around it: **fold sth in sth** a plant pot folded in newspaper

4 [I] if an organization folds, it closes because it does not have enough money to continue

PHRASES

fold your arms to bend your arms, so that they rest together against your body: Grant stood by her desk with his arms folded.

fold² n [C] **1** a line in paper or cloth where you have folded it **2** [usually plural] folds in cloth or skin are parts that hang down over other parts: the folds of her skirt **3** **the fold** the group of people that you come from and belong to: a former Republican who has **returned to the fold 4** a small enclosed area in a field, where sheep are kept

-fold /fəʊld $ foʊld/ suffix **1** of a particular number of kinds: The purpose of a window is twofold: to let light in, and to let people see out. **2** a particular number of times: The value of the house has increased fourfold (=it is now worth four times as much as before).

folder /ˈfəʊldə $ ˈfoʊldər/ n [C] **1** a container for keeping papers in, made of folded card or plastic → see picture at **STATIONERY 2** a group of related documents that you store together on a computer

foliage /ˈfəʊli-ɪdʒ $ ˈfoʊ-/ n [U] formal the leaves of a plant

folk¹ /fəʊk $ foʊk/ n **1** (also **folks** especially AmE) [plural] people: Some folk will do anything for money. | ordinary folk | the old folk in the village **2** **folks** [plural] **a)** especially AmE your parents and family: Is it OK if I call my folks? **b)** used when talking to a group of people in a friendly way: OK folks, it's time to go home. **3** [U] FOLK MUSIC

folk² adj folk music, art, dancing etc is traditional and typical of a particular place: an Irish folk song

folklore /ˈfəʊklɔː $ ˈfoʊklɔːr/ n [U] the traditional stories, customs etc of a particular place

ˈfolk ˌmusic (also **folk**) n [U] traditional music from a particular place

folksy /ˈfəʊksi $ ˈfoʊ-/ adj informal friendly and informal, especially in a way that is typical of the countryside: a small town with a folksy charm

follicle /ˈfɒlɪkəl $ ˈfɑː-/ n [C] one of the small holes in your skin that hair grows from

follow /ˈfɒləʊ $ ˈfɑːloʊ/ v

1 WALK/DRIVE BEHIND [I,T] to walk or drive behind someone: If you follow me, I'll show you to your room. | She thought someone was following her. | **follow sb into/to etc sth** She followed me into the kitchen. | **followed by sb/sth** A woman came in, closely followed by three children. → see picture at **CHASE**

2 HAPPEN AFTER [I,T] to happen immediately after something else: The agreement followed months of negotiations. | In the years that followed, their friendship turned to love. | **followed by sth** a meeting followed by lunch | **there follows sth** After years of fighting, there followed a period of peace.

3 DO WHAT SB SAYS [T] to do something in the way that someone has told or advised you: I **followed** his advice. | Did you **follow** the instructions? **THESAURUS** OBEY

4 DO THE SAME THING [I,T] to do the same thing as someone else: Budget airlines have been so successful that other airlines have been forced to **follow suit** (=do the same thing) and lower their fares. | **follow sb's example/lead** Other countries should follow their lead. | Jane **followed in** her father's **footsteps** (=did the same job as her father) by becoming a doctor.

5 BE INTERESTED [T] to be interested in the progress of something: Have you been following that crime series on television?

6 ROAD/PATH/RIVER [T] to continue on a road or path, or beside a river: Follow the road for about 600m. | The road follows the river for six miles.

7 UNDERSTAND [I,T] informal to understand something: Sorry, I don't follow you. | **easy/difficult to follow** The recipes are easy to follow. **THESAURUS** UNDERSTAND

8 BE TRUE [I] if something follows, it is true because of something else that is true: **[+from]** Two conclusions follow from this. | **It** doesn't necessarily **follow that** you will earn a lot of money if you're a graduate.

PHRASES

as follows used to introduce a list of things: The winners are as follows: in first place, Tony Gwynn; in second place ...

PHRASAL VERBS

follow sb **around** to follow someone everywhere they go: He followed them around with a camera.

follow through to do what needs to be done to complete something or make it successful: **follow sth ↔ through** Harry started training as an actor, but he never followed it through.

follow sth ↔ **up**

1 to find out more about something: I saw an advert in the paper and I decided to follow it up.

2 to do something in addition to what you have already done: If you don't get any response to your letter, follow it up with a phone call.

THESAURUS

follow to walk or drive behind someone: I followed him downstairs. | I think that car's following us.

chase to run or drive fast after someone in order to catch them when they are trying to escape: The boy ran off but I chased him and caught him.

run after sb to run in order to stop or talk to someone who has just left: Sarah ran after him and begged him to come back home.

pursue to follow someone in a very determined way in order to catch or attack them. **Pursue** sounds rather formal: He said he would pursue the men until they were caught.

tail to follow someone secretly in order to see what they do and where they go: *The police had been tailing the robbers in an unmarked car.*
stalk to follow a person or animal quietly and secretly in order to attack or kill them: *She thought that the man was stalking her.*

follower /ˈfɒləʊə $ ˈfɑːloʊər/ *n* [C] **1** someone who supports a person or believes in a set of ideas: **[+of]** *a follower of Karl Marx* **2** someone who looks at the messages sent by a particular person using the SOCIAL NETWORKING service Twitter

following¹ /ˈfɒləʊɪŋ $ ˈfɑːloʊ-/ *adj* **1 the following day/year/chapter etc** the day, year etc after the one you have just mentioned: *The letter arrived the following day.* **2 the following details/questions etc** the details, questions etc that will be mentioned next: *Payment can be made in the following ways: cash, cheque, or credit card.*

following² *n* **1** [singular] a group of people who support or admire someone: *The band has a huge following in the US.* **2 the following** the people or things that you are going to mention: *The following have been selected to play: Ann Smith, Yuri Tsumoto ...*

following³ *prep* immediately after something, or as a result of something: *Following the success of his latest movie, he has had several offers of work.*

follow-up *n* **1** [C,U] something that is done to make sure that earlier actions have been successful or effective: *The hospital offers follow-up and support for all patients.* | *follow-up treatment* **2** [C] a film, book, event etc that is based on an earlier one: *The follow-up wasn't as good as the original film.* | **[+to]** *a follow-up to last year's hugely successful concert*

folly /ˈfɒli $ ˈfɑːli/ *n* [C,U] (*plural* **follies**) *formal* a very stupid thing to do: *It would be sheer folly to ignore the warnings.*

fond /fɒnd $ fɑːnd/ *adj*
1 be fond of sb/sth to like someone or something very much: *The children are very fond of each other.* | *She had grown fond of Bernard.* | *He's very fond of reading.* **THESAURUS ▶ LIKE**
2 [only before noun] showing that you like someone very much: *a fond gesture* | *As they parted, they said a fond farewell.*
3 fond memory someone or something that you remember with great pleasure: **[+of]** *I have fond memories of my time at Oxford.*
4 fond hope/belief/wish a hope, belief etc that something will happen, which seems silly because it probably will not happen —**fondness** *n* [U]

fondle /ˈfɒndl $ ˈfɑːndl/ *v* [T] to touch someone's body in a way that shows love or sexual desire

fondly /ˈfɒndli $ ˈfɑːndli/ *adv* **1** in a way that shows you like someone or something very much: *Greta smiled fondly.* | *He is still fondly remembered by people who knew him.* **2 fondly imagine/believe/hope** to wrongly think that something is true or that something will happen: *He fondly imagined that things would improve.*

font /fɒnt $ fɑːnt/ *n* [C] **1** *technical* a set of letters of a particular size and style, used in printing or on a computer screen **2** a stone container in a church that holds the water used for the ceremony of BAPTISM

food /fuːd/ *n* [C,U] things that you eat: *a hotel that is famous for its good food* | *We sell a wide range of frozen foods.* → **CONVENIENCE FOOD, HEALTH FOOD**
PHRASES
food for thought something that makes you think carefully: *His talk gave us much food for thought.*

COLLOCATIONS

adjectives
good/excellent food *The food here is excellent.*
delicious/tasty food *Your food is always delicious!*
spicy food (=with a hot taste) *I'm not used to spicy food.*
plain/simple food *Stick to plain food, such as toast or rice.*
hot/cold food *She wanted a rest and some hot food.*
fatty foods *I don't like fatty foods.*
Italian/French/Chinese etc food *I love Chinese food.*
fresh food *Try to eat as much fresh food as possible.*
organic food (=grown without artificial chemicals) *Is organic food better for you?*
junk food (=unhealthy and containing a lot of fat, sugar etc) *Students often just eat junk food.*
fast food (=food such as hamburgers that you can take away and eat quickly) *The street is full of fast food restaurants.*

verbs
to have/eat food *I haven't had any food all morning.*
to cook/prepare food *The food must be properly cooked.*
to serve food *The restaurant serves traditional British food.*
food tastes delicious/terrible etc *The food tasted better than it looked.*

---

food bank *n* [C] *AmE* a place that gives food to poor people

food chain *n* **the food chain** animals and plants considered as a group, in which a plant is eaten by an insect or animal which is then eaten by another animal etc

food miles *n* [plural] the distance between the place where food is produced and the place where it is eaten: *shoppers' concerns over food miles*

food poisoning *n* [U] a stomach illness caused by eating food that contains harmful BACTERIA

food processor *n* [C] a piece of electrical equipment used to prepare food by cutting and mixing it → see picture at **KITCHEN**

food stamp *n* [C] an official piece of paper that the US government gives to poor people so they can buy food

foodstuff /ˈfuːdstʌf/ *n* [C usually plural, U] something that you can eat: *There is now a shortage of basic foodstuffs.*

fool¹ /fuːl/ n [C] a stupid person: *I felt such a fool, locking my keys in the car.* | *Like a fool, I accepted his offer.*

PHRASES

any fool can do sth *informal* used to say that it is very easy to do something: *Any fool could see the plan wouldn't work.*

make a fool of sb to deliberately try to make someone seem stupid: *She didn't like being made a fool of.*

make a fool of yourself to do something silly or embarrassing: *He worried that he might make a fool of himself.*

be no/nobody's fool to be difficult to trick because you have a lot of knowledge and experience

fool² v [T] to make someone believe something that is not true: **fool sb into doing sth** *Don't be fooled into thinking it's easy to lose weight.* | **be fooled by sth** *Don't be fooled by appearances.* **THESAURUS** ▶ TRICK

PHRASES

you could have fooled me *spoken* used to say that you do not believe what someone has told you: *'I'm not scared.' 'You could have fooled me!'*

PHRASAL VERBS

fool around (*also* **fool about** *BrE*) to behave in a silly way: *He's been fooling around in class.*

fool (around) with sth to use something in a careless or dangerous way: *You shouldn't fool around with fireworks.*

foolhardy /ˈfuːlhɑːdi $ -ɑːr-/ adj taking stupid and unnecessary risks

foolish /ˈfuːlɪʃ/ adj not sensible: *It would be foolish to ignore his advice.* | *a foolish idea* —**foolishly** adv —**foolishness** n [U]

> **Word Choice**: foolish, silly, or stupid?
> **Foolish** sounds rather formal and is mainly used in written English. In everyday English, people usually say **silly** or **stupid**.
> **Silly** sounds more gentle and less critical than **stupid**: *I'm sorry – it was a silly thing to say.*
> You use **stupid** especially when you are annoyed with someone: *That was a really stupid thing to do!*

foolproof /ˈfuːlpruːf/ adj a foolproof plan is certain to be successful

foot¹ /fʊt/ n [C]

1 (*plural* **feet** /$ fiːt/) the part of your body that you stand on: *He kicked the ball with his right foot.* | **on foot** (=walking) *It's easier to explore the city on foot.* | **on your feet** (=standing) *It's tiring being on your feet all day.* → see picture on page A2 **THESAURUS** ▶ STAND

2 (*plural* **foot** *or* **feet**) (*written abbreviation* **ft**) a unit for measuring length, equal to 0.3048 metres: *He's six feet tall.*

3 the foot of sth the bottom of something: *the foot of the stairs* | *the foot of the bed* | *the foot of the page* | *the foot of a hill*

4 a) left-footed/right-footed using your left or right foot when you kick a ball **b) flat-footed/four-footed** having a particular type or number of feet → **drag**

your feet at DRAG¹, **have/get cold feet** at COLD¹, **set foot in sth** at SET¹, **stand on your own two feet** at STAND¹

PHRASES

back on your feet/on your feet again healthy or successful again after being ill or having problems: *It's good to see you on your feet again.*

fall/land on your feet to get into a good situation because you are lucky: *Jim always lands on his feet.*

get/keep/have a foot in the door to get your first opportunity to work in an organization: *It's hard for a young person to get a foot in the door of theater these days.*

get to your feet to stand up: *He got to his feet and began to speak.* **THESAURUS** ▶ STAND

have/keep your feet on the ground to have a sensible attitude to life: *He portrays himself as a leader with his feet on the ground.*

jump to your feet to stand up quickly: *She jumped to her feet and ran out.*

put a foot wrong *BrE* to make a mistake, especially in your job: *She hardly put a foot wrong in 40 years of doing the job.*

put your feet up to relax, especially by sitting with your feet supported on something: *Go and put your feet up!*

put your foot down 1 to say very firmly that someone must or must not do something: *You've got to put your foot down! Don't let him treat you like that!* **2** to make a car go faster

put your foot in it to accidentally say something that embarrasses or upsets someone: *I think I may have put my foot in it.*

be rushed/run off your feet to be very busy: *I've been rushed off my feet today, getting everything ready for the holiday.* **THESAURUS** ▶ BUSY

under your feet if someone is under your feet, they are annoying you by being in the same place as you, and preventing you doing what you want: *The children were getting under my feet.*

foot² v **foot the bill** *informal* to pay for something expensive or something that someone else should pay for: *It's the public who are being forced to foot the bill.*

footage /ˈfʊtɪdʒ/ n [U] film showing a particular event: *They showed some old footage of the war.*

football /ˈfʊtbɔːl $ -bɑːl/ n

1 [U] **a)** *BrE* a game played by two teams of 11 players who try to kick a ball into the other team's GOAL **SYN** **soccer**: *The children were playing football.* | *Which football team do you support?* | *a football match* | *a football pitch* **b)** *AmE* a game played by two teams of 11 players who try to carry or kick a ball into the other team's GOAL **SYN** **American football** *BrE*: *college football games* | *a football field* → see picture on p. 349

2 [C] a ball used to play the game of football —**footballer** n [C]: *a professional footballer*

footbridge /ˈfʊtbrɪdʒ/ n [C] a narrow bridge used by people who are walking → see picture at BRIDGE¹

foothills /ˈfʊthɪlz/ n [plural] the smaller hills below a group of mountains: *the foothills of the Alps* **THESAURUS** ▶ MOUNTAIN

foothold /'fʊthəʊld $ -hoʊld/ n [C] **1** a position from which you can start trying to get what you want: *The company has struggled to **gain** a **foothold** in Europe.* **2** a small hole or crack where you can safely put your foot when climbing a rock

footing /'fʊtɪŋ/ n [singular] **1** the conditions or arrangements on which something is based: **put/ place sth on a … footing** *plans to put the business back on a firm financial footing* | *The companies are now able to compete **on a** more **equal footing** (=with the same advantages and disadvantages).* **2** a firm hold with your feet when you are standing on a dangerous surface: **lose/miss your footing** *She lost her footing and fell into the water.*

footnote /'fʊtnəʊt $ -noʊt/ n [C] a note at the bottom of a page, which gives more information about something

footpath /'fʊtpɑːθ $ -pæθ/ n [C] *especially BrE* a path for people to walk along, especially in the countryside **SYN trail** *AmE: public footpaths*

footprint /'fʊtprɪnt/ n [C] a mark made by a foot or shoe: *footprints in the snow* → see picture at **FINGERPRINT**

footstep /'fʊtstep/ n [C] the sound of each step when someone is walking: *He heard footsteps in the hall.*

footstool /'fʊtstuːl/ n [C] a piece of furniture used to support your feet when you are sitting down

footwear /'fʊtweə $ -wer/ n [U] things you wear on your feet, such as shoes or boots

for¹ /fə; *strong* fɔː $ fər; *strong* fɔːr/ *prep*
1 used to say who will get something, or where something will be used: *That piece of cake is for Jane.* | *There's a letter for you.* | *We need a new battery for the radio.*
2 in order to help someone: *Let me carry the bag for you.* | *We looked after the house for them.*
3 used to say what the purpose of something is: *What's this button for?* | **for doing sth** *a knife for cutting bread* | *What did you do that for (=why did you do it)?*
4 in order to get or do something: *I paid $3 for a ticket.* | *We were waiting for the bus.*
5 used to say how long an action or situation continues: *Bake the cake for 40 minutes.* | *I've known Kim for a long time.*
6 used to show the time when something is planned to happen: *an appointment for 3:00*
7 because of something: **for doing sth** *an award for saving someone's life* | *For some reason he felt very tired.*
8 used to say where a person or vehicle is going: *Is this train for London?* | *I set off for work.*
9 used to talk about distance: *We walked for miles.*
10 used to show a price or amount: *a check for $100* | *an order for 200 copies of the book*
11 for Christmas/sb's birthday etc in order to celebrate Christmas, someone's birthday etc: *I gave him a watch for his birthday.* | *We went to my aunt's for Thanksgiving.*

F

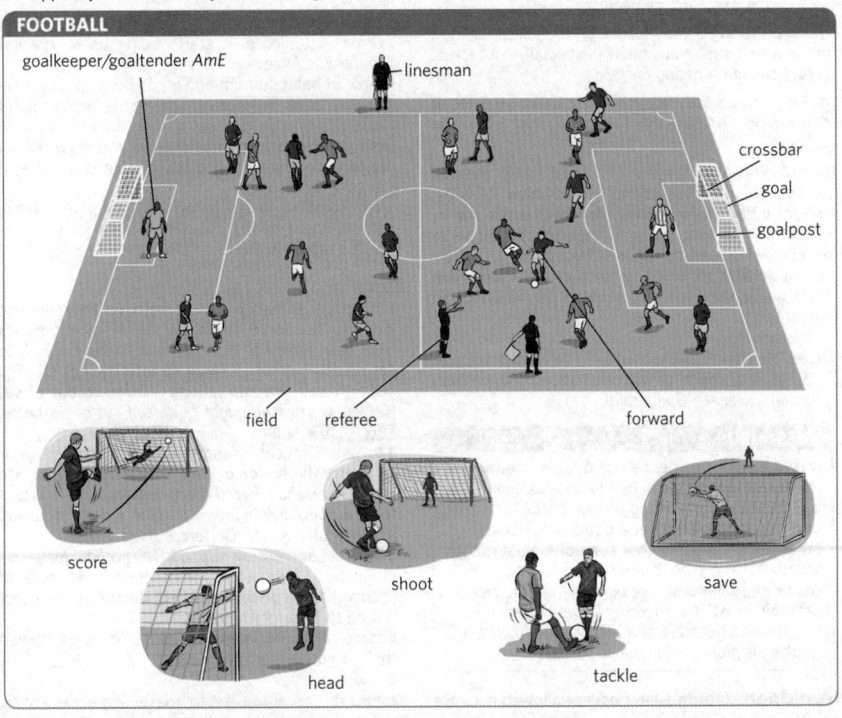

FOOTBALL

goalkeeper/goaltender *AmE* — linesman — crossbar — goal — goalpost

field — referee — forward

score — shoot — save — head — tackle

for

12 for breakfast/lunch/dinner used to say at which meal you eat something: *We had steak for dinner last night.* | *'What's for lunch?' 'Hamburgers.'*

13 used to say which person you are talking about: *It's the ideal job for me.* | *It's difficult for me to take time off work.* | *I'm really happy for you.*

14 used to say which company, team etc you belong to: *Lou works for a small publishing company.* | *He plays for the Boston Red Sox.*

15 supporting or agreeing with someone or something: *How many people voted for Mulhoney?* | *He explained the arguments for and against nuclear power.* | *Jane was all for the idea* (=she supported it completely).

16 used to say what a word or sign means: *What's the Spanish word for oil?*

17 when you consider a particular fact: *Libby's very tall for her age.* | *It's cold for July.*

PHRASES

for all sth in spite of something: *For all his faults, he's very organized.*

Grammar

When talking about the purpose of doing something, do not say 'for to do something'. Say **in order to do sth**, or just **to do sth**. For example, do not say 'He ran for to catch the bus.' Say *He ran to catch the bus.*
In order to sounds more formal than **to** and is used mainly in written English.

---

for² *linking word, literary* because

forage /ˈfɒrɪdʒ $ ˈfɑː-, ˈfɔː-/ *v* [I] to search for food or other things you need, especially outdoors: **[+for]** *animals foraging for food*

foray /ˈfɒreɪ $ ˈfɔː-, ˈfɑː-/ *n* [C] a short attempt at doing a job or activity: **[+into]** *a brief foray into politics*

forbid /fəˈbɪd $ fər-/ *v* [T] (*past tense* **forbade** /-ˈbæd, -ˈbeɪd/, *past participle* **forbidden** /-ˈbɪdn/, *present participle* **forbidding**) *formal* to order someone not to do something OPP **permit**: **forbid sb to do sth** *He forbade her to see Philip again.* | *The law strictly forbids racial discrimination.* | **be forbidden from doing sth** *He was forbidden from leaving the country.*

PHRASES

God/Heaven forbid *spoken* used to emphasize that you hope something will not happen: *'Supposing I had an accident.' 'God forbid!'*

THESAURUS

forbid to order someone not to do something: *His doctor has forbidden him to drink alcohol.* | *She was forbidden from telling anyone about her work.*
ban to say officially that a book, film, activity etc is not allowed, or that someone must not go somewhere: *The book was banned in many countries.* | *Journalists are banned from the area.*
prohibit *formal* if something is prohibited, it is not allowed because of a law or rule: *In Britain, smoking is prohibited in public places.*

---

forbidden /fəˈbɪdn $ fər-/ *adj* not allowed because

of a rule or law: *Alcohol is **strictly forbidden** in Saudi Arabia.* | **It is forbidden to** *smoke in the hospital.*

forbidding /fəˈbɪdɪŋ $ fər-/ *adj* looking frightening or unfriendly: *large forbidding buildings*

force¹ /fɔːs $ fɔːrs/ *n*

1 [C] a group of people who have been trained to do something, especially military or police work: *the **police force** | the company's **sales force** | **the forces** BrE* (=the army, navy, and air force) *Both sons are in the forces.*

2 [U] physical strength or violence: *The police **used force** to end the demonstration.* | **by force** *He had to be removed from the building by force.*

3 [U] the physical power of something: **[+of]** *The force of the explosion threw her backwards.* | *The building took the **full force** of the blast.* | *The waves were hitting the rocks **with great force**.*

4 [C] something or someone that has a very powerful effect: *Jones was **the driving force behind** the project* (=the person who made it happen). | **force for change/peace/democracy etc** (=someone or something that makes change etc more likely to happen)

5 [U] the powerful effect that someone or something has: *The village is now beginning to feel the **full force** of the tragedy.*

6 [C,U] a natural power or event: *the **forces of nature** | the force of gravity*

7 [C usually singular] a measure of wind strength: *gale force winds* → **TASK FORCE**

PHRASES

come into force/bring sth into force if a new law comes into force, it starts being used: *The law comes into force next year.*

force of habit something you do because you have always done it: *Force of habit made him get up at 6:30.*

in force 1 in large numbers: *Local people **turned out in force** to protest.* **2** if a law or rule is in force, it already exists

join/combine forces to work together to achieve something: **[+with]** *The company has joined forces with a Japanese firm.*

force² *v* [T]

1 to make someone do something they do not want to do: **force sb to do sth** *Many companies have been forced to close.* | *I had to force myself to get up this morning.* | **force sb into (doing) sth** *Bad health forced him into retiring.* | **force sb out of sth** *He was worried he might be forced out of his home.* THESAURUS **MUST**

2 to use physical strength to move something or go somewhere: **force your way through/into etc sth** *Burglars had forced their way into the house.* | **force a door/lock/window** (=open a door etc using physical strength) | *He forced open the box.*

3 to make something happen: *The scandal forced his resignation.* | *an event which **forced the pace** of change* | **force prices/rates etc down/up** *The effect will be to force down wages.*

4 force a smile/laugh to smile or laugh even though you are angry or upset

PHRASAL VERBS

force sth on/upon sb to make someone accept

something that they do not want: *I hate it when people try to force their views on me.*

THESAURUS

force sb to do sth to make someone do something they do not want to do – used when a person or a situation does this: *She was forced to marry him.* | *The bad weather forced us to stay indoors.*

make sb do sth to force someone to do something, especially using threats or violence: *The men made us lie down on the floor.*

put pressure on sb to keep trying to force someone to do something by making them feel that they should do it: *Don't put pressure on your child to study all the time.*

compel to make you feel that you must do something, or to officially force someone to do something: *I felt compelled to leave.* | *No one can compel you to do it.*

---

forced /fɔːst $ fɔːrst/ *adj* **1** a forced smile or laugh is not natural or sincere: *a mood of forced cheerfulness* **2** done suddenly because a situation makes it necessary or because someone makes you do it: *The plane had to make a **forced landing**.*

forceful /ˈfɔːsfəl $ ˈfɔːrs-/ *adj* expressing opinions strongly and clearly: *a forceful personality* | *forceful arguments* —**forcefully** *adv*

forceps /ˈfɔːseps, -səps $ ˈfɔːr-/ *n* [plural] a medical instrument for picking up and holding things

forcible /ˈfɔːsəbəl $ ˈfɔːr-/ *adj* using physical force: *There were signs of forcible entry into the building.* —**forcibly** *adv*: *He was forcibly removed.*

ford /fɔːd $ fɔːrd/ *n* [C] a place where a river is not deep, so you can drive or walk across it

fore /fɔː $ fɔːr/ *n* **to the fore** into a position of importance: *Environmental issues **came to the fore** in the 1980s.*

forearm /ˈfɔːrɑːm $ -ɑːrm/ *n* [C] the part of your arm between your hand and your elbow

forebears /ˈfɔːbeəz $ ˈfɔːrberz/ *n* [plural] *formal* the members of your family who lived in the past **SYN** ancestors

foreboding /fɔːˈbəʊdɪŋ $ fɔːrˈboʊ-/ *n* [C,U] a feeling that something bad will happen soon: *We waited with a **sense of foreboding**.*

forecast[1] /ˈfɔːkɑːst $ ˈfɔːrkæst/ *n* [C] a description of what is likely to happen: *the **weather forecast***

forecast[2] *v* [T] (*past tense and past participle* **forecast** *or* **forecasted**) to say what is likely to happen: *Rain is forecast for the weekend.* | **[+(that)]** *They forecast that profits will increase next year.* **THESAURUS** ▶ PREDICT —**forecaster** *n* [C]

forecourt /ˈfɔːkɔːt $ ˈfɔːrkɔːrt/ *n* [C] *BrE* an open area in front of a large building: *the hotel forecourt*

forefather /ˈfɔːfɑːðə $ ˈfɔːrˌfɑːðər/ *n* [C usually plural] your forefathers are the people who were part of your family a long time ago

forefinger /ˈfɔːfɪŋɡə $ ˈfɔːrˌfɪŋɡər/ *n* [C] the finger next to your thumb

forefront /ˈfɔːfrʌnt $ ˈfɔːr-/ *n* **1 in/at the forefront**

of sth in a leading position in an activity: *The Institute has been at the forefront of research into AIDS.* **2 in/at the forefront of sb's mind** if something is at the forefront of your mind, you are thinking about it a lot: *The world championships are in the forefront of my mind.*

forego /fɔːˈɡəʊ $ fɔːrˈɡoʊ/ *v* another spelling of FORGO

foregone con'clusion *n* **be a foregone conclusion** if a result is a foregone conclusion, it is certain to happen: *The election result was a foregone conclusion.*

foreground /ˈfɔːɡraʊnd $ ˈfɔːr-/ *n* **the foreground** the part of a picture that is nearest to you **OPP** background

forehand /ˈfɔːhænd $ ˈfɔːr-/ *n* [singular] a way of hitting the ball in tennis, with the flat part of your hand facing the direction of the ball → **backhand**

forehead /ˈfɒrəd, ˈfɔːhed $ ˈfɔːrəd, ˈfɑː-, ˈfɔːrhed/ *n* [C] the part of your face above your eyes → see picture on page A2

foreign /ˈfɒrɪn $ ˈfɔː-, ˈfɑː-/ *adj* **1** from or relating to a country that is not your own: *She spoke with a foreign accent.* | *foreign students* | *Do you speak any foreign languages?* **2** [only before noun] involving other countries, not just your own country **OPP** domestic: *the government's foreign policy* | *the Minister for Foreign Affairs* **3 be foreign to sb** to be strange or difficult for someone to understand: *Their way of life was completely foreign to her.* **4 foreign body/matter/object** something such as a piece of dirt that has got into a place where it does not belong, especially someone's body

foreigner /ˈfɒrənə $ ˈfɔːrənər, ˈfɑː-/ *n* [C] someone who comes from a different country → see Word Choice at STRANGER

Usage

A **foreigner** is someone from a different country. It is often used in a disapproving way: *The town is full of foreigners.* | *The local people feel that foreigners are taking their jobs.*

It sounds friendlier and more polite to talk about **people from other countries**: *I like meeting people from other countries.* | *People from other countries may find some English customs rather strange.*

Alien is used in official and legal contexts when talking about people from other countries: *The number of illegal aliens has increased.* | *I had to fill out an alien registration form.*

---

foreign ex'change *n* [U] the system of buying and selling foreign money, or foreign money itself

foreleg /ˈfɔːleg $ ˈfɔːr-/ *n* [C] a front leg of an animal

foreman /ˈfɔːmən $ ˈfɔːr-/ *n* [C] (*plural* **foremen** /-mən/) the worker in charge of a group of workers

foremost /ˈfɔːməʊst $ ˈfɔːrmoʊst/ *adj* [only before noun] the most famous or important: *the foremost novelist of her time*

forensic /fə'rensɪk, -zɪk/ *adj* [only before noun] using scientific methods to solve crimes: *forensic evidence*

forerunner /'fɔːˌrʌnə $ -ər/ *n* [C] a type of something that existed at an earlier time: **[+of]** *Babbage's machine was the forerunner of the modern computer.*

foresee /fɔː'siː $ fɔːr-/ *v* [T] (*past tense* **foresaw** /-'sɔː $ -'sɒː/, *past participle* **foreseen** /-'siːn/) to expect that something will happen in the future **SYN predict**: *No one could have foreseen such a disaster.* **THESAURUS PREDICT**

foreseeable /fɔː'siːəbəl $ fɔːr-/ *adj* **for/in the foreseeable future** continuing for as long as you can imagine: *I'll be in London for the foreseeable future.*

foreshadow /fɔː'ʃædəʊ $ fɔːr'ʃædəʊ/ *v* [T] if one event foreshadows another, it shows people that the second one will happen

foresight /'fɔːsaɪt $ 'fɔːr-/ *n* [U] the ability to imagine what might happen in the future, and consider this in your plans: *Luckily, I had the foresight to take an umbrella.*

foreskin /'fɔːˌskɪn $ 'fɔːr-/ *n* [C] the loose skin covering the end of a man's PENIS

forest /'fɒrɪst $ 'fɔː-, 'fɑː-/ *n* [C,U] a large area of land covered with trees → **wood**: *a tropical forest* —**forested** *adj*: *a thickly forested landscape* → **RAIN FOREST**

forestall /fɔː'stɔːl $ fɔːr'stɒːl/ *v* [T] to prevent something from happening

forestry /'fɒrɪstri $ 'fɔː-, 'fɑː-/ *n* [U] the science of planting and taking care of trees in forests

foretaste /'fɔːteɪst $ 'fɔːr-/ *n* **be a foretaste of sth** to be a sign of what will happen in the future: *The riots were a foretaste of what was to come.*

foretell /fɔː'tel $ fɔːr-/ *v* [T] (*past tense and past participle* **foretold** /-'təʊld $ -'toʊld/) *formal* to say what will happen in the future

forethought /'fɔːθɔːt $ 'fɔːrθɒːt/ *n* [U] careful thought or planning before you do something

forever /fər'evə $ -ər/ *adv*
1 for all future time: *I'll remember you forever.* **THESAURUS ALWAYS**
2 *spoken* for a very long time: *It took forever to get to the airport.*
3 be forever doing sth *spoken* to do something often, especially in a way that annoys people: *He's forever making comments about my weight.*

forewarn /fɔː'wɔːn $ fɔːr'wɔːrn/ *v* [T] to warn someone about something bad that might happen: **forewarn sb of sth** *We'd been forewarned of the dangers.*

forewent /fɔː'went $ fɔːr-/ *v* the past tense of FOREGO

foreword /'fɔːwɜːd $ 'fɔːrwɜːrd/ *n* [C] a short piece of writing at the beginning of a book about the book or its writer

forfeit /'fɔːfɪt $ 'fɔːr-/ *v* [T] to give something up or have it taken away from you, usually because you have broken a rule: *Violent criminals have forfeited the right to freedom.* —**forfeit** *n* [C]

forgave /fə'geɪv $ fər-/ *v* the past tense of FORGIVE

forge¹ /fɔːdʒ $ fɔːrdʒ/ *v* [T] **1** to develop a strong relationship with other groups: **forge a relationship/alliance/link (with sb)** *In 1776 the United States forged an alliance with France.* **2** to illegally copy something to make people think it is real: *a forged passport*

PHRASAL VERBS
forge ahead to do something successfully and confidently: *The team has forged ahead this season.*

forge² *n* [C] a place where metal is heated and shaped into objects

forger /'fɔːdʒə $ 'fɔːrdʒər/ *n* [C] someone who illegally copies documents, paintings etc to make people think they are real

forgery /'fɔːdʒəri $ 'fɔːr-/ *n* (*plural* **forgeries**) **1** [C] something such as a document or painting that has been illegally copied **SYN fake 2** [U] the crime of illegally copying something

forget /fə'get $ fər-/ *v* [I,T] (*past tense* **forgot** /-'gɒt $ -'gɑːt/, *past participle* **forgotten** /-'gɒtn $ -'gɑːtn/, *present participle* **forgetting**)
1 to not remember something: *I'm sorry, I've forgotten your name.* | **[+(that)]** *Don't forget that Linda's birthday is on Friday.* | **[+about]** *He completely forgot about the meeting.* | **[+what/how/where etc]** *I've forgotten what I was going to say!*
2 to not remember to do something that you should do: **forget to do sth** *I'm sorry – I forgot to post your letter.* | **[+(that)]** *Dan forgot he was supposed to pick us up from school.* | *Give me your phone number **before I forget** (=forget to get it).*
3 to not remember to bring something that you need with you: *Oh no, I've forgotten my wallet.*
4 to stop thinking about someone or something: *I'll never forget him.* | **[+about]** *Just forget about work and relax.*

PHRASES
don't forget used to remind someone about something: *Don't forget I'll be late home.* | **don't forget to do sth** *Don't forget to lock the door.*
forget it used to tell someone that something is not important: *'I'm sorry I broke your mug.' 'Forget it.'*

THESAURUS

forget to not remember something or someone: *I've forgotten their number.*
sth slips your mind if something slips your mind, you forget to do it because you are busy or thinking about other things: *I said I'd call her, and then it completely slipped my mind.*
your mind goes blank used to say that you are suddenly unable to remember something, especially the answer to a question: *In the interview, he asked me a question and my mind just went blank.*
take your mind off sth to stop thinking about a problem or a bad situation, especially by doing something else: *You should have a holiday – it will help you take your mind off things.*

Word Choice: forget or leave?
You use **forget** when you do not remember to bring something with you: *I've forgotten my passport!*

You use **leave** when talking about the place where this thing is now: *I've left my passport at home.*
Do not say 'I've forgotten my passport at home.'

forgetful /fə'getfəl $ fər-/ *adj* someone who is forgetful often forgets things: *Grandpa's getting a bit forgetful.*

forgive /fə'gɪv $ fər-/ *v* [I,T] (*past tense* **forgave** /-'geɪv/, *past participle* **forgiven** /-'gɪvən/) to decide not to be angry or punish someone who has done something wrong: *I knew that my mother would forgive me.* | **forgive myself/yourself etc** *If anything happened to the kids, she'd never forgive herself.* | **forgive sb for (doing) sth** *She never forgave him for losing her ring.*
PHRASES

sb could be forgiven for thinking/believing etc used to say that you understand why someone would think or do something: *You could be forgiven for thinking that nobody lives here.*
forgive me for asking/saying sth etc *spoken* used before you say or ask something that might seem rude: *Forgive me for saying so, but I don't think that's right.*

forgiveness /fə'gɪvnəs $ fər-/ *n* [U] when someone forgives another person: *She begged for forgiveness.*

forgiving /fə'gɪvɪŋ $ fər-/ *adj* willing to forgive: *a kind and forgiving man*

forgo, forego /fɔː'gəʊ $ fɔːr'goʊ/ *v* [T] (*past tense* **forwent** or **forewent** /-'went/, *past participle* **forgone** or **foregone** /-'gɒn $ -'gɔːn/) *formal* to not do or have something that you want: *They had to forgo a pay rise.*

forgot /fə'gɒt $ fər'ɡɑːt/ *v* the past tense of FORGET

forgotten¹ /fə'gɒtn $ fər'gɑːtn/ *v* the past participle of FORGET

forgotten² *adj* a forgotten place or person is one that people have forgotten about: *He became the forgotten man of English football.*

fork¹ /fɔːk $ fɔːrk/ *n* [C]
1 a small tool that you use for picking up and eating food, with a handle and three or four points: *Put the **knives and forks** on the table.*
2 a tool used for digging and breaking up soil, with a handle and three or four points → see picture at GARDEN
3 a place where a road or river divides into two parts: *Turn left at the fork in the road.*

fork² *v* [I] **1** if a road or river forks, it divides into two parts: *The path forked in two directions.* **2 fork left/right** to go left or right when a road divides into two parts: *Fork left at the bottom of the hill.*
PHRASAL VERBS
fork out (also **fork over** *AmE*) *informal* to spend a lot of money: *We had to fork out nearly £300.*

forked /fɔːkt $ fɔːrkt/ *adj* with one end that divides into two parts: *Snakes have forked tongues.*

forlorn /fə'lɔːn $ fər'lɔːrn/ *adj* **1** sad and lonely: *a forlorn figure sitting by herself* **2** a forlorn hope, attempt, or struggle is not going to be successful

form¹ /fɔːm $ fɔːrm/ *n*
1 TYPE [C] one type of something: **[+of]** *The bicycle is a very economical form of transport.*
2 WAY STH IS [C] the way something is or appears to be: *The medicine can be taken **in** liquid or tablet **form**.* | *The novel is written **in the form of** a series of letters.*
3 DOCUMENT [C] an official document with spaces where you give information: **fill in/fill out a form** *Fill in the form using black ink.* | *I sent off for an **application form**.*
4 SHAPE [C] a shape: *The building is **in the form of** an L.*
5 GRAMMAR [C] a way of writing or saying a word that shows its number, tense etc: *'Men' is the plural form of 'man'.*
6 WAY SB IS PERFORMING [U] *BrE* how well or badly someone is performing: *He's **in good form** (=playing well) at the moment.* | *He's been **off form** (=playing badly) lately.*
7 SCHOOL CLASS [C] *BrE old-fashioned* a class in a school

form² *v*
1 ORGANIZATION/BUSINESS [T] to start an organization or business: *The United Nations was formed in 1945.*
2 BE STH [linking verb] to be something: *The river forms the boundary between Texas and Mexico.* | *Rice forms a large **part** of their diet.*
3 START TO EXIST [I] to start to exist: *Ice had begun to form on the roads.* | *A queue quickly began to form.*
4 MAKE [T] to make something: *These rocks were formed over 4,000 million years ago.* | *Fold the paper in two to form a triangle.* | *In English the past tense is usually formed by adding '-ed'.* THESAURUS ▶ MAKE
PHRASES
form an opinion to develop an opinion based on information that you have: *He had not had time to form an opinion.*

formal /'fɔːməl $ 'fɔːr-/ *adj*
1 suitable for official or serious occasions OPP **informal**: *I only wear a suit on formal occasions.* | *'How do you do?' is a formal expression.*
2 made or done officially: *We made a formal complaint.* | *We haven't reached a formal agreement yet.*
3 formal education/training/qualifications education, training etc that you get in a school or college
—**formally** *adv*

formality /fɔː'mæləti $ fɔːr-/ *n* (*plural* **formalities**) **1** [C] a formal or official part of a process that has to be done: *the legal formalities* | **just/only a formality** (=having to be done but not important) **2** [U] very polite formal behaviour

formalize (also **-ise** *BrE*) /'fɔːməlaɪz $ 'fɔːr-/ *v* [T] to make a plan or decision official: *The contract has not yet been formalized.*

format¹ Ac /'fɔːmæt $ 'fɔːr-/ *n* [C] the way something is organized or designed: *Next week's show will be in the new format.* | *a large format paperback*

format² Ac *v* [T] (**formatted, formatting**) **1** to organize the space on a computer DISK so that information can be stored on it **2** to arrange the pages of a book or the information on a computer into a particular design —**formatting** n [U] —**formatted** adj

formation /fɔːˈmeɪʃən $ fɔːr-/ n **1** [U] the process by which something starts or develops: **[+of]** the formation of a new government **2** [C,U] the shape in which something is made or exists: rock formations | aircraft flying **in formation** (=in a pattern)

formative /ˈfɔːmətɪv $ ˈfɔːr-/ adj [only before noun] having an important influence on the way someone or something develops: a child's formative years

former[1] /ˈfɔːmə $ ˈfɔːrmər/ adj [only before noun] happening, existing, or true in the past, but not now → **present**, **previous**: former US president, George Bush | the former Yugoslavia THESAURUS PREVIOUS

> **Word Choice**: former or previous?
> **Former** sounds rather formal. It is used about someone who had a position in the past, for example someone who used to be a leader, or someone's husband: the former president of the Philippines | the former head of the CIA | the Princess's former husband
> You also use **former** when the name of a country or organization has changed: the former Soviet Union
> **Previous** means 'the one before the present one'. It is used about people, things, or periods of time: her previous husband | the previous day | Our previous house was much bigger.

former[2] n **the former** formal the first of two things that you have just mentioned OPP **latter**: Of the two theories, the former seems more likely.

formerly /ˈfɔːməli $ ˈfɔːrmərli/ adv in the past: Kiribati, **formerly known as** the Gilbert Islands THESAURUS BEFORE

formidable /ˈfɔːmədəbəl, fəˈmɪd- $ ˈfɔːr-/ adj **1** powerful, impressive, and frightening: a **formidable opponent 2** difficult and needing a lot of hard work or skill: a formidable task

formula Ac /ˈfɔːmjələ $ ˈfɔːr-/ n [C] (plural **formulas** or **formulae** /-liː/) **1** a method used to make something successful: **[+for]** There's no magic formula for success. | We're still searching for a **peace formula**. **2** a group of numbers or letters that show a mathematical or scientific rule **3** a list of the different substances in a mixture

formulate Ac /ˈfɔːmjəleɪt $ ˈfɔːr-/ v [T] **1** to develop a plan or idea and decide all the details: The government is formulating a new policy. **2** to think about what you want to say and say it clearly: McLeish took a minute to **formulate** his **reply**. —**formulation** /ˌfɔːmjəˈleɪʃən $ ˌfɔːr-/ n [C,U]

forsake /fəˈseɪk $ fər-/ v [T] (past tense **forsook** /-ˈsʊk/, past participle **forsaken** /-ˈseɪkən/) formal **1** to leave a person or place SYN **abandon 2** to stop doing or having something: I won't forsake my principles.

fort /fɔːt $ fɔːrt/ n [C] a strong building used by soldiers for defending a place

forte /ˈfɔːteɪ $ fɔːrt/ n **be sb's forte** if an activity is

your forte, you are very good at it: Cooking isn't really my forte.

forth /fɔːθ $ fɔːrθ/ → **back and forth** at BACK[2], **and so on/forth** at SO[1]

forthcoming Ac /ˌfɔːθˈkʌmɪŋ◂ $ ˌfɔːrθ-/ adj **1** [only before noun] happening soon: the forthcoming election **2** [not before noun] willing to give information: **[+about]** Mike wasn't very forthcoming about his plans. **3** [not before noun] if something is forthcoming, it is given or offered to someone: When no reply was forthcoming, she wrote again.

forthright /ˈfɔːθraɪt $ ˈfɔːrθ-/ adj approving saying what you think honestly and directly: Bill answered in his usual forthright manner.

forthwith /fɔːθˈwɪð, -ˈwɪθ $ fɔːrθ-/ adv formal immediately: This sum is payable forthwith.

fortification /ˌfɔːtɪfɪˈkeɪʃən $ ˌfɔːr-/ n **1 fortifications** [plural] towers and walls built to protect a place **2** [U] the process of making something stronger

fortify /ˈfɔːtɪfaɪ $ ˈfɔːr-/ v [T] (**fortified**, **fortifying**, **fortifies**) **1** to build towers and walls around a place to defend it: a fortified city **2** to make someone feel physically or mentally stronger: We fortified ourselves with a hearty breakfast.

fortitude /ˈfɔːtɪtjuːd $ ˈfɔːrtɪtuːd/ n [U] formal courage

fortnight /ˈfɔːtnaɪt $ ˈfɔːrt-/ n [C usually singular] BrE two weeks: The meetings take place once a fortnight. | a fortnight's holiday | a fortnight ago

fortnightly /ˈfɔːtnaɪtli $ ˈfɔːrt-/ adj BrE happening once a fortnight: fortnightly meetings —**fortnightly** adv

fortress /ˈfɔːtrɪs $ ˈfɔːr-/ n [C] a big strong building used for defending a place

fortuitous /fɔːˈtjuːɪtəs $ fɔːrˈtuː-/ adj formal something that is fortuitous is lucky and happens by chance

fortunate /ˈfɔːtʃənət $ ˈfɔːr-/ adj lucky OPP **unfortunate**: **fortunate (enough) to do sth** We were fortunate enough to get tickets for the last show. | **fortunate in (doing) sth** I was fortunate in finding a job immediately. | **[+(that)]** It was fortunate that no one was hurt. THESAURUS LUCKY

fortunately /ˈfɔːtʃənətli $ ˈfɔːr-/ adv happening because of good luck SYN **luckily** OPP **unfortunately**: Fortunately, the weather was excellent.

fortune /ˈfɔːtʃən $ ˈfɔːr-/ n **1** [C] a very large amount of money: He **made a fortune** buying and selling property. | That dress must have **cost a fortune**! | We **spent a fortune** on holiday. THESAURUS EXPENSIVE **2** [U] chance or luck: I've **had the good fortune to** work with some brilliant people. **3** [C usually plural] the good and bad things that happen to you: The win marked a change in the team's fortunes.
PHRASES
tell sb's fortune to tell someone what will happen to them in the future: The old woman offered to tell my fortune.

'fortune ,teller n [C] someone who tells you what will happen to you in the future

forty /'fɔːti $ 'fɔːrti/ number
1 the number 40
2 the forties (also **the '40s, the 1940s**) [plural] the years from 1940 to 1949: **the early/mid/late forties** He spent several years in Paris in the late forties. —**fortieth** adj: her fortieth birthday
PHRASES
| **be in your forties** to be aged between 40 and 49: **early/mid/late forties** She was in her mid forties.
| **in the forties** if the temperature is in the forties, it is between 40 degrees and 49 degrees F: In May, the temperature is usually somewhere in the high forties.

forum /'fɔːrəm/ n [C] an occasion or place where people can discuss an important subject: **[+for]** The meeting provides a forum for debate.

forward[1] /'fɔːwəd $ 'fɔːrwərd/ (also **forwards**) adv
1 towards a place in front of you OPP **backwards**: He **leaned forward** to hear what they were saying. | The crowd moved forwards.
2 towards greater progress or development: The project cannot **go forward** without more money.
3 towards the future OPP **backwards**: Successful companies are always **looking forwards**.
4 go forward to/into to successfully complete one stage of a competition so that you can compete in the next stage: Germany go forward into the next round. → **FAST-FORWARD**, **look forward to sth** at **LOOK**[1]

forward[2] adj **1** [only before noun] closer to a place that is in front of you OPP **backward**: Further **forward movement** was impossible. **2 forward planning/thinking etc** plans or ideas that are helpful for the future: Forward planning is essential. **3** disapproving too confident and friendly with people you do not know very well

forward[3] v [T] **1** to send letters or goods to someone at another address: I forwarded the letter to my manager. **2** to help something become successful: I see this as a good chance to forward my career.

forward[4] n [C] an attacking player in a sport such as football → **defender** → see picture at **FOOTBALL**

'forwarding ad,dress / $ '... ,../ n [C] a new address to which your mail is sent

'forward-,looking adj planning for the future by trying new ideas: a forward-looking company

forwards /'fɔːwədz $ 'fɔːrwərdz/ adv FORWARD

forwent /fɔː'went $ fɔːr-/ v the past tense of FORGO

fossil /'fɒsəl $ 'fɑː-/ n [C] the shape of an animal or plant that lived a very long time ago, preserved in rock

'fossil ,fuel n [C,U] a FUEL such as coal or oil that is produced by animals or plants decaying over millions of years

fossilized (also **-ised** BrE) /'fɒsəlaɪzd $ 'fɑː-/ adj preserved in rock: fossilized dinosaur bones

foster[1] /'fɒstə $ 'fɑːstər/ v [T] **1** to encourage a feeling or skill to develop: Training helps to foster team spirit. **2** to take care of someone else's child for a period of time, without becoming their legal parent → **adopt**: In the last ten years, she fostered six children.

foster[2] adj **1 foster parents/family/mother etc** the people who foster a child **2 foster child** a child who is fostered

fought /fɔːt $ fɒːt/ v the past tense and past participle of FIGHT

foul[1] /faʊl/ adj **1** a foul taste or smell is very unpleasant SYN **disgusting**: The soup tasted foul. **2** especially BrE very bad: The weather's been foul all week. | She came home from work **in a foul mood**. **3 foul language** rude and offensive words: You should never use foul language in front of a customer.

foul[2] v [T] **1** if a sports player fouls another player, they do something that is against the rules: Berger was fouled in the penalty area. **2** (also **foul up**) to make something very dirty
PHRASAL VERBS
foul up informal to do something very badly: **foul sth ↔ up** He really fouled that shot up.

foul[3] n [C] an action in sport that is against the rules

,foul 'play n [U] violence or a crime that leads to someone's death: The police do not **suspect foul play**.

found[1] /faʊnd/ v the past tense and past participle of FIND

found[2] Ac v [T] **1** to start an organization: The Academy was founded in 1666. **2 be founded on/upon sth** to be based on a set of ideas or beliefs: The US was founded on the idea of religious freedom.

foundation Ac /faʊn'deɪʃən/ n
1 BUILDING [C] the solid base under the ground that supports a building: It took the builders three weeks to **lay** the foundations.
2 BASIC IDEA [C] a basic idea or belief that something is based on: **[+of]** Justice and equality are the foundation of democracy. | This agreement will **lay** the foundations for peace. | The course gives students a **solid foundation** in computing.
3 ORGANIZATION [C] an organization that gives money for special purposes: the National Foundation for the Arts
4 ORGANIZATION'S START [singular] when an organization is first started
PHRASES
| **be without foundation/have no foundation** formal to not be true: These rumours are without foundation.

founder Ac /'faʊndə $ -ər/ n [C] someone who starts an organization

,founder 'member n [C] BrE someone who helps to establish a new organization or club SYN **charter member** AmE

foundry /'faʊndri/ n [C] (plural **foundries**) a place where metals are melted and made into things

fountain

fountain /ˈfaʊntɪn $ ˈfaʊntn̩/ n [C] a structure that sends water up into the air

FOUNTAIN

ˈfountain pen n [C] a pen that you fill with ink → see picture at **PEN**[1]

four /fɔː $ fɔːr/ number the number 4: *She is married with four children.* | *They arrived just after four* (=four o'clock). | *Luke will soon be four* (=four years old).

PHRASES

on all fours supporting your body with your hands and knees: *He was down on all fours playing with the puppy.*

ˌfour-by-ˈfour, **4x4** n [C] a FOUR-WHEEL DRIVE car, suitable for driving on rough ground

fourfold /ˈfɔːfəʊld $ ˈfɔːrfoʊld/ adj, adv four times as much or as many: *a fourfold increase in price*

ˌfour-letter ˈword n [C] a very rude word **SYN** swear word

ˌfour-poster ˈbed (also **four-ˈposter**) n [C] a bed with four tall posts at the corners, a cover fixed at the top of the posts, and curtains around the sides

foursome /ˈfɔːsəm $ ˈfɔːr-/ n [C] a group of four people doing something together: *I'll invite Jo so* **make up a foursome.**

fourteen /ˌfɔːˈtiːn◂ $ ˌfɔːr-/ number the number 14: *He used to work fourteen hours a day.* | *I started playing the guitar when I was fourteen* (=14 years old). —**fourteenth** adj, pron: *my fourteenth birthday* | *I'm planning to leave on* **the fourteenth** (=the 14th day of the month).

fourth /fɔːθ $ fɔːrθ/ adj coming after three other things in a series: *her fourth birthday* —**fourth** pron: *the fourth of July* —**fourthly** adv

ˌfour-wheel ˈdrive n [C,U] a system which gives the power of the engine to all four wheels in a vehicle, or a vehicle that has this type of system

fowl /faʊl/ n [C] (plural **fowl** or **fowls**) a bird such as a chicken that is kept for its meat and eggs

fox[1] /fɒks $ fɑːks/ n [C] a wild animal like a dog with red-brown fur and a thick tail → see picture on page A3

fox[2] v [T] BrE if something foxes you, it is too difficult for you to understand

foyer /ˈfɔɪeɪ $ ˈfɔɪər/ n [C] a room at the entrance to a public building **SYN** lobby

fracas /ˈfræka: $ ˈfreɪkəs/ n [singular] a short noisy fight

fraction /ˈfrækʃən/ n **1** [C] a part of a whole number, for example ½ or ¾ **2** [singular] a very small amount of something: **[+of]** *She paused for a fraction of a second.*

fractional /ˈfrækʃənəl/ adj very small: *a fractional increase* —**fractionally** adv

fracture[1] /ˈfræktʃə $ -ər/ v [I,T] if something hard

cracks or breaks: *He fell and fractured his arm.* | *a fractured skull* **THESAURUS** BREAK

fracture[2] n [C] a crack in a bone or other hard substance **THESAURUS** INJURY

fragile /ˈfrædʒaɪl $ -dʒəl/ adj easily broken or damaged: *fragile glassware* | *The ceasefire is fragile.* **THESAURUS** WEAK

fragment[1] /ˈfrægmənt/ n [C] a small piece of something that has broken off: **[+of]** *fragments of glass* **THESAURUS** PIECE

fragment[2] /frægˈment $ ˈfrægment, frægˈment/ v [I,T] to break something into many small parts, or to be broken in this way: *Social changes have fragmented our communities.* —**fragmented** adj: *an increasingly fragmented society*

fragrance /ˈfreɪɡrəns/ n [C,U] a pleasant smell **THESAURUS** SMELL

Word Choice: fragrance or smell?
Fragrance is more formal than **smell**, and is used in written descriptions of a pleasant smell, especially from flowers or fruit: *The fragrance of the roses filled the air.*
Smell is used about both good and bad smells: *What's that funny smell?* | *I love the smell of old furniture.*

fragrant /ˈfreɪɡrənt/ adj smelling pleasant: *a fragrant flower*

frail /freɪl/ adj thin and weak: *a frail old man* **THESAURUS** WEAK

frailty /ˈfreɪlti/ n [C,U] (plural **frailties**) a physical or moral weakness: *human frailty*

frame[1] /freɪm/ n [C]
1 the wood or metal part around something such as a picture or window: *a picture in a wooden frame* | *door/window/picture frame*
2 the main structure of a building, vehicle, or piece of furniture: *a bicycle frame* → see picture at **BICYCLE**
3 the shape of someone's body: *her slender frame*
4 frames [plural] the part of a pair of GLASSES that holds the LENSes → **TIME FRAME**

PHRASES

frame of mind the way you feel: *I'll wait until she's in a more positive frame of mind.*

frame[2] v [T] **1** to surround something or someone and make them look attractive: *Her hair was cut so that it framed her face.* **2** to put a picture or photograph into a frame: *a framed portrait* **3** to deliberately make someone seem guilty of a crime when they are not: *Murphy claims he was framed by his partner.*

framework [Ac] /ˈfreɪmwɜːk $ -wɜːrk/ n [C] **1** a set of rules, facts, or beliefs that people use to make plans or decisions: **[+of/for]** *We must work within the framework of our budget.* | *theoretical/legal/ethical etc framework* *the theoretical framework for our research* **2** the main structure that supports something such as a building or vehicle

franchise /ˈfræntʃaɪz/ n **1** [C,U] permission given by a company to sell its products or services: *beer* *brewed in Britain* **under franchise 2** [C] a business that operates as a franchise: *a fast food franchise* **3** [U] *formal* the legal right to vote in an election

frank /fræŋk/ *adj* honest and direct: *I'll be frank with you – it's not good enough.* | *a frank discussion* **THESAURUS** HONEST —**frankly** *adv*

PHRASES
to be frank *spoken* used when you are saying what you really think: *To be frank, I don't care.*

frankfurter /ˈfræŋkfɜːtə $ -fɜːrtər/ *n* [C] a long SAUSAGE **SYN** hot dog

frantic /ˈfræntɪk/ *adj* **1** extremely worried or upset: **[+with]** *Her parents were frantic with worry.* **2** hurrying in an anxious and disorganized way: *a frantic rush for tickets* —**frantically** /-kli/ *adv*

fraternal /frəˈtɜːnl $ -ɜːr-/ *adj formal* **1** showing the friendly relationship between people who have the same interest or aim: *fraternal support and cooperation* **2** relating to brothers **SYN** brotherly: *fraternal love*

fraternity /frəˈtɜːnəti $ -ɜːr-/ *n* (*plural* **fraternities**) **1 the teaching/hunting/criminal etc fraternity** people who are involved in an activity **2** [C] a club of male students at a US university → **sorority 3** [U] *formal* a feeling of friendship among a group of people

fraternize (*also* **-ise** *BrE*) /ˈfrætənaɪz $ -ər-/ *v* [I] to be friendly with someone, used especially to say that you disapprove of this: **[+with]** *Soldiers who fraternize with the enemy will be shot.*

fraud /frɔːd $ frɒːd/ *n* **1** [C,U] the crime of deceiving people in order to get money: *She was found guilty of fraud.* | **tax/insurance/benefit fraud** **THESAURUS** CRIME **2** [C] someone or something that is not what they claim to be: *He wasn't a real doctor – he was a fraud.*

fraudulent /ˈfrɔːdjələnt $ ˈfrɒːdʒə-/ *adj* dishonest and illegal: *fraudulent insurance claims* —**fraudulently** *adv*

fraught /frɔːt $ frɒːt/ *adj* **1 fraught with problems/ difficulty/danger** full of problems, difficulty etc **2** very anxious or worried

fray¹ /freɪ/ *v* [I,T] if cloth frays, or if something frays it, its threads become loose at the edge **2** [I] if someone's temper frays, they become annoyed: *As we waited, tempers began to fray.* —**frayed** *adj*

fray² *n* **the fray** a fight or argument: *More protesters soon entered the fray.*

freak¹ /friːk/ *n* [C] **1** *informal* someone who is extremely interested in something: **a health/ fitness/computer freak 2** a person or animal that is very strange: *He looks like a freak with that hair.*

freak² *adj* [only before noun] very unusual and unexpected: *a freak result* | **a freak accident/storm/wave** **THESAURUS** UNUSUAL

freak³ (*also* **freak out**) *v* [I,T] *spoken* to suddenly become very anxious, upset, or afraid, or to make someone do this: *When she heard the news, she just freaked.* | *Horror films always freak me out.*

freckle /ˈfrekəl/ *n* [C usually plural] freckles are

small light brown spots on someone's skin **THESAURUS** MARK —**freckled** *adj*

free¹ /friː/ *adj, adv*
1 NO COST if something is free, it does not cost any money: *There's a **free gift** with this month's magazine.* | *Entrance to the club is free.* | *Pregnant women can get dental treatment **free of charge**.* | *Children under 5 travel free.* | **for free** *He fixed the car for free.*
2 NOT A PRISONER not tied up or kept somewhere as a prisoner: *The UN demanded that the hostages be **set free**.* | *The bear **broke free** from its cage.* | *He walked from court a free man.*
3 NOT CONTROLLED not controlled or restricted by rules, laws, or the government → **freely**: *The government cannot restrict **free speech** (=the freedom to say what you believe).* | *The country held **free elections** last year.* | *a **free press*** | **free to do sth** *You're free to say no.* | **[+from]** *The Bank of England should be free from political control.*
4 NOT BUSY not busy working or doing other things: *Yes, I'm free next weekend.* | *I never have any **free time**.*
5 NOT BEING USED not being used by anyone else: *Excuse me, is this seat free?* **THESAURUS** EMPTY
6 NOT FIXED not fixed or held in a particular position: *She undid her hair, letting it fall free.*
7 NOT CONTAINING STH without something, especially something harmful or unpleasant: **[+of/from]** *drinks that are free from artificial sweeteners* | *fat-free yoghurt* | **tax-free/duty-free**

PHRASES
feel free *spoken* used to tell someone that they are allowed to do something: *Feel free to ask questions.*
a free hand permission to do something the way you want to: *We **gave** the design team **a free hand**.*

free² *v* [T]
1 to allow someone to leave a prison or somewhere they have been forced to stay: *The terrorists have refused to free the hostages.* | **free sb from sth** *Atkins was freed from jail yesterday.*
2 to remove something unpleasant that is affecting someone: **free sb from sth** *drugs that can free people from pain*
3 to move someone or something so that they are no longer held, fixed, or trapped: *Firefighters freed two men trapped in the burning building.*

PHRASAL VERBS
free sb/sth ↔ **up** to make something or someone available, so that they can be used: *Hiring an assistant will **free up** your **time** to do other things.*

free 'agent *n* [C] someone who is free to do what they want, and is not legally responsible to anyone else

freebie /ˈfriːbi/ *n* [C] *informal* something you are given that you do not have to pay for

freedom /ˈfriːdəm/ *n*
1 [C,U] when you are allowed to do what you want without being stopped or controlled by anyone → **liberty**: *Kids have too much freedom nowadays.* | **freedom of speech/expression/religion etc** (=the legal right to say what you want or choose your religion) | **freedom to do sth** *We want the freedom to live our lives as we please.* | *The new TV satellite*

channels offer viewers greater **freedom of choice**.
2 [U] when someone is not in prison
3 freedom from sth when you are not affected by something bad: *freedom from fear and hunger*

Word Choice: freedom or liberty?
Freedom is the right or the ability to do what you want: *Her parents gave her a lot of freedom.* | *Satellite television offers viewers greater freedom of choice.*
Liberty is more formal and is used about people's right to live, work etc without government or official restrictions: *We need to protect individual liberty at all times.* | *He sees the new law as an attack on civil liberties.*

'freedom ,fighter n [C] *approving* someone who fights against the government or army that controls their country → **terrorist**

free 'enterprise n [U] when people can own and operate a business without much government control

,free-for-'all n [C usually singular] *informal* a fight or argument involving a lot of people

freehand /'fri:hænd/ *adj, adv* a freehand drawing is drawn by hand without using any special tools

,free 'kick n [C] an occasion during a football game when a REFEREE allows a player to kick the ball freely, because the other team has broken the rules

freelance /'fri:lɑːns $ -læns/ *adj, adv* working independently for several different organizations: *a freelance journalist* | *I work freelance from home.* —**freelance** v [I] —**freelancer, freelance** n [C]

freely /'fri:li/ *adv* **1** without anyone trying to control you or prevent you doing something: *We encourage our students to **speak freely**.* | *People can now **travel freely** across the border.* | *a **freely elected** government* **2 freely available** very easy to obtain: *The information is freely available to the public.* **3 freely admit/ acknowledge** to say that something bad about yourself or your company is true: *He freely admits using drugs.* **4** in large amounts: *Her tears **flowed freely**.*

,free 'market n [C] a system in which the buying and selling of goods is not controlled by the government

Freemason /'fri:,meɪsən, ,fri:'meɪsən/ n [C] a man who belongs to a secret society in which members help other members to be successful

,free-'range *adj* free-range eggs or meat are from animals that are allowed to move around outside and are not kept in small rooms or cages

,free-'standing, freestanding /,fri:'stændɪŋ/ *adj* a free-standing object is not fixed to a frame, wall, or other support: *a free-standing cooker*

,free-to-'air *adj BrE* free-to-air television programmes do not cost extra money to watch

,free 'trade n [U] when goods coming into or going out of a country are not controlled or taxed

freeway /'fri:weɪ/ n [C] *AmE* a wide road on which cars can travel at a fast speed $\boxed{SYN}$ **motorway** *BrE* → **expressway, highway**

,free 'will n [U] the ability to make your own decisions about what to do, rather than being controlled by God or FATE
PHRASES
| **do sth of your own free will** to do something because you want to, not because you have to: *She went of her own free will.*

freeze¹ /fri:z/ v (past tense **froze** /frəʊz $ froʊz/, past participle **frozen** /'frəʊzən $ 'froʊ-/)
1 $\boxed{LIQUID}$ [I,T] if a liquid freezes, it becomes solid and hard because the temperature is very cold → **melt, thaw**: *The lake had frozen overnight.*
2 $\boxed{FOOD}$ [T] to make food very cold, usually by putting it in a freezer, so that it stays in good condition for a long time: *I'm going to freeze some of this bread.*
3 $\boxed{FEEL COLD}$ [I] to feel very cold: *You'll freeze if you don't wear a coat.*
4 $\boxed{WEATHER}$ it freezes if it freezes, the temperature drops below FREEZING POINT: *It's going to freeze tonight.* → see picture at **MELT**
5 $\boxed{STOP MOVING}$ [I] to suddenly stop moving and stay very still: *Hugh froze when he saw the snake.*
6 $\boxed{MONEY/PRICES/WAGES}$ [T] to officially prevent money from being spent, or stop prices, wages etc from increasing: *Our budget for next year has been frozen.*

freeze² n **1** [C] when prices or wages are not allowed to increase: **price/pay/wage freeze** | **[+on]** *a freeze on pay rises* **2** [C usually singular] when an activity or process is stopped for a period of time: **[+on]** *There's a freeze on recruitment at the moment.* **3** [singular] a period of time when the weather is extremely cold

freezer /'fri:zə $ -ər/ n [C] a piece of electrical equipment in which food is kept frozen → **fridge** → see picture at **KITCHEN**

freezing¹ /'fri:zɪŋ/ n **above/below freezing** above or below the temperature at which water freezes

freezing² *adj informal* extremely cold: *It's freezing in here!* | *We were freezing last night.*

'freezing ,point n [C,U] the temperature at which a liquid freezes

freight /freɪt/ n [U] goods carried by ship, train, or aircraft

'freight car n [C] *AmE* part of a train that carries goods $\boxed{SYN}$ **wagon** *BrE*

freighter /'freɪtə $ -ər/ n [C] a ship or aircraft that carries goods

French fries /,frentʃ 'fraɪz/ n [plural] *especially AmE* long thin pieces of potato cooked in hot oil $\boxed{SYN}$ **chips** *BrE* → see picture at **CHIP¹**

,French 'windows n [plural] large glass doors → see picture at **WINDOW**

frenetic /frə'netɪk/ *adj* frenetic activity is fast and not very organized: *She rushes around at a frenetic pace.*

frenzied /'frenzid/ *adj* wild and uncontrolled: *He was killed in a frenzied attack.*

frenzy /'frenzi/ *n* [singular, U] a state of great anxiety or excitement, when you cannot control your behaviour: **in/into a frenzy** *He worked the fans up into a frenzy.* | **[+of]** *a frenzy of excitement*

frequency /'fri:kwənsi/ *n* (plural **frequencies**) **1** [U] the number of times that something happens: **[+of]** *The frequency of his asthma attacks was increasing.* | *He misses school* **with** alarming **frequency** (=very often). **2** [C,U] the number of radio waves or sound waves that go past a point each second: *sounds of very high frequency*

frequent¹ /'fri:kwənt/ *adj* happening often **OPP infrequent**: *Her headaches became more frequent.* | *Buses leave for the airport* **at frequent intervals.** | *He was a* **frequent visitor** *to our house.*

frequent² /frɪ'kwent $ frɪ'kwent, 'fri:kwənt/ *v* [T] to go to a place often: *a café frequented by artists*

frequently /'fri:kwəntli/ *adv* often: *Trains are frequently late.* **THESAURUS OFTEN**

fresh /freʃ/ *adj*
1 NEW AND DIFFERENT new and different from what was done or used before: *Start again on a fresh sheet of paper.* | *We need some* **fresh ideas.** | *They decided to move to Australia and* **make a fresh start. THESAURUS NEW**
2 FOOD/FLOWERS recently picked or prepared, and not dried, tinned, frozen etc: **fresh fruit/vegetables/ fish/bread etc** *Make sure the fish is fresh.* | *fresh flowers from the garden*
3 RECENT done or experienced recently: *fresh animal tracks* | **be fresh in sb's mind/memory** *The incident was still fresh in my mind.*
4 WATER fresh water contains no salt and comes from rivers and lakes **OPP saltwater**
5 CLEAN/COOL pleasantly clean or cool: *a fresh minty taste* | *Let's go and get some* **fresh air** (=from outside a building). | *You'll feel nice and fresh after a shower.* —**freshness** *n* [U]
PHRASES
fresh from/out of sth having just left a place, especially a college or school: *a new teacher fresh from university*

freshen /'freʃən/ *v*
PHRASAL VERBS
freshen up *spoken* to wash your hands and face, so that you feel clean and comfortable: *I'd like to freshen up before dinner.*

fresher /'freʃə $ -ər/ *n* [C] *BrE* a student who has just started at a college or university

freshly /'freʃli/ *adv* **freshly made/picked/dug etc** made, picked etc very recently: *freshly ground pepper* **THESAURUS RECENTLY**

freshman /'freʃmən/ *n* [C] (plural **freshmen** /-mən/) *AmE* a student in the first year of HIGH SCHOOL or university

freshwater /'freʃwɔːtə $ -wɔːtər, -wɑː-/ *adj* [only before noun] having water that contains no salt or living in water that contains no salt: *a freshwater lake* | *freshwater fish*

fret /fret/ *v* [I] (**fretted**, **fretting**) to worry: **[+over/ about]** *She frets about her son's health.*

fretful /'fretfəl/ *adj* anxious and complaining: *a fretful child*

Fri. (also **Fri** *BrE*) the written abbreviation of **Friday**

friar /'fraɪə $ -ər/ *n* [C] a MONK who travelled around teaching about Christianity in the past

friction /'frɪkʃən/ *n* [U] **1** disagreement or angry feelings between people: **[+between]** *Money can cause friction between friends.* **2** when one surface rubs against another: *the heat produced by friction*

Friday /'fraɪdi, -deɪ/ *n* [C,U] (written abbreviation **Fri.**) the day between Thursday and Saturday → see examples at **MONDAY**

fridge /frɪdʒ/ *n* [C] a piece of electrical equipment for storing food and keeping it cool → **freezer**: *There's more milk in the fridge.* → see picture at **KITCHEN**

fried /fraɪd/ *adj* cooked in hot oil: *fried chicken* → see picture at **EGG¹**

friend /frend/ *n* [C]
1 someone you know well and enjoy spending time with: *This is my friend Kate.* | *Lee is an old friend of mine.*
2 be friends to be someone's friend: **[+with]** *I'm friends with his sister.* | *Helen and I are old friends.*
3 someone who has made a link with you on a SOCIAL NETWORKING SITE such as Facebook → **PEN FRIEND**
PHRASES
just good friends used when saying that two people like each other but are not having a romantic relationship: *She's not my girlfriend or anything – we're just good friends.*
make friends to start a friendly relationship: *He finds it hard to make friends.* | **[+with]** *I made friends with lots of people in college.*

COLLOCATIONS

adjectives

sb's best friend (=the friend they like the most) *Joe was my best friend.*

a good/close friend (=one of the friends you like the most) *We're only inviting a few close friends.* ⚠ Do not say 'a big friend'. Say **a good friend** or **a close friend**.

an old friend (=someone who has been your friend for a long time) *She doesn't forget her old friends.*

a lifelong friend (=someone who has been or will be your friend for a very long time) *Here he met George Wood, who became a lifelong friend.*

noun + friend

a school/college/university friend *She's gone shopping with some school friends.*

a childhood friend (=someone who was your friend when you were a child) *Louis and Rosa were childhood friends.*

a family friend *The doctor was an old family friend.*

verbs

to **have a friend** *Does he have a lot of friends?*
to **become friends** *We soon became friends.*
to **remain friends** *Can you remain friends with an ex-boyfriend?*

noun + friends

sb's **circle of friends** (=all the friends someone has) *He was not really part of my circle of friends.*

friendly /'frendli/ *adj*
1 behaving towards people in a way that shows you like them and want to talk to them or help them OPP **unfriendly**, **hostile**: *a friendly smile* | *a school with a friendly atmosphere* | **[+to/towards]** *The locals are very friendly towards tourists.*
2 be friendly with sb to be someone's friend: *My parents are friendly with his parents.* → ENVIRONMENTALLY FRIENDLY, USER-FRIENDLY —**friendliness** *n* [U]

THESAURUS

friendly behaving towards people in a way that shows you like them and want to talk to them or help them: *She's always very friendly and wants to know what I've been doing.* | *It's good to see a friendly face.*
nice *especially spoken* friendly and kind. **Nice** is very common in everyday conversation: *Chris is such a nice guy.*
warm a warm welcome or smile is very friendly: *The singer received a warm welcome from her fans.* | *He greeted us with a warm smile.*
welcoming friendly to people who have just arrived somewhere: *Everyone in the book club was very welcoming.*
hospitable friendly and generous to someone who is visiting your home or country: *Most of the people I met in Scotland were very hospitable and kind.*
easy to get on with *BrE informal*, **easy to get along with** *AmE informal* friendly and easy to work or live with: *My father wasn't always very easy to get on with.*

friendship /'frendʃɪp/ *n*
1 [C] a relationship between friends: *Josh and I have a close friendship.* | **[+between/with]** *The friendship between the three girls began at school.*
2 [U] the feelings and behaviour of a friend: *I needed some friendship and support.*

fries /fraɪz/ *n* [plural] *AmE* long thin pieces of potato cooked in hot oil SYN **chips** *BrE* → see picture at CHIP[1]

frieze /friːz/ *n* [C] a decorated border along the top of a wall

frigate /'frɪɡət/ *n* [C] a small fast ship used in a war to protect other ships

fright /fraɪt/ *n* [singular, U] a sudden feeling of fear: *The noise gave me a fright.* | *They both ran off in fright.*

frighten /'fraɪtn/ *v* [T] to make someone feel afraid: *Don't shout – you'll frighten the baby.* | *She was frightened by his threats.*

PHRASAL VERBS
frighten sb ↔ **away/off** to make a person or animal afraid or nervous so that they go away: *A scarecrow frightens birds away.* | *The violence has frightened off tourists.*
frighten sb **into** sth to make someone do something by frightening them: **frighten sb into doing sth** *They frightened him into confessing.*

frightened /'fraɪtnd/ *adj* feeling very nervous and worried because something bad might happen: *Don't be frightened. I won't hurt you.* | **[+of]** *Are you frightened of the dark?* | **[+that]** *She is frightened that her father will find out.* | **frightened to do sth** *Some people are frightened to fly.*

THESAURUS

frightened feeling very nervous and worried because you might get hurt or something bad might happen: *I was frightened that he might hit me.* | *Many animals are frightened of loud noises.*
scared frightened. **Scared** is less formal than **frightened**, and is very common in everyday English: *I'm scared of spiders.* | *You don't need to be scared.*
afraid frightened. **Afraid** sounds more formal than **frightened** or **scared**, and is used especially in written English: *Small children are often afraid of the dark.*
terrified very frightened: *The woman was screaming and clearly terrified.*

frightening /'fraɪtn-ɪŋ/ *adj* making you feel frightened: *a frightening experience* | **It is frightening to** *realize that I could have been killed.* —**frighteningly** *adv*

THESAURUS

frightening making you feel frightened: *The car was travelling at a frightening speed.*
scary frightening. **Scary** is less formal than **frightening** and is very common in everyday English: *a scary movie* | *a scary situation*
terrifying very frightening: *Both men had guns and it was absolutely terrifying.*
spooky *informal* frightening, especially because something makes you think of GHOSTS or powers that no one understands: *The old house was dark and spooky and no one ever went near it.*

frightful /'fraɪtfəl/ *adj BrE old-fashioned* very bad SYN **awful**: *Her hair was a frightful mess.*

frightfully /'fraɪtfəli/ *adv BrE old-fashioned* very: *I'm frightfully sorry.*

frigid /'frɪdʒɪd/ *adj* **1** a woman who is frigid gets no pleasure from sex **2** *literary* not friendly

frill /frɪl/ *n* [C] **1** a narrow piece of cloth with many folds, attached to something as a decoration **2 frills** [plural] attractive but unnecessary features: *a basic, comfortable apartment with no frills*

frilly /'frɪli/ *adj* frilly clothes are decorated with lots of frills

fringe¹ /frɪndʒ/ *n* [C] **1** *BrE* the part of your hair that hangs down above your eyes SYN **bangs** *AmE*: *She has long hair with a fringe.* → see picture at HAIR

2 a decorative edge of hanging threads on a curtain or piece of clothing

PHRASES

the fringe/fringes of sth 1 a small part of a group of people that is different from and not completely accepted by the rest of the group: **on the fringe/ fringes** *an extremist who is on the fringes of politics* **2** the edge of something: **on the fringe/fringes** *people living on the fringes of big cities*

fringe² *adj* [only before noun] not accepted by most people in a group: *a fringe organization*

fringe³ *v* [T] to be along the edge of something: *Palm trees fringe the shore.*

ˈfringe ˌbenefit *n* [C usually plural] something extra that you get with your job in addition to wages: *The company provides childcare, an important fringe benefit.*

frisk /frɪsk/ *v* [T] to search someone for hidden weapons, drugs etc by feeling their body

frisky /ˈfrɪski/ *adj* full of energy and fun: *frisky lambs*

fritter /ˈfrɪtə $ -ər/ *v*

PHRASAL VERBS

fritter sth ↔ **away** to waste money or time on unimportant things: **[+on]** *Don't fritter your money away on clothes.*

frivolity /frɪˈvɒləti $ -ˈvɑː-/ *n* [C,U] (*plural* **frivolities**) something that is not serious or sensible

frivolous /ˈfrɪvələs/ *adj* not serious or sensible, especially in a way that is not suitable: *a frivolous remark* | *Don't be so frivolous.*

frizzy /ˈfrɪzi/ *adj* frizzy hair is very tightly curled

fro /frəʊ $ froʊ/ *adv* → **to and fro** at TO³

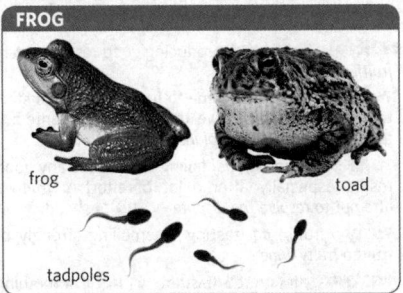

FROG

frog

toad

tadpoles

frog /frɒg $ frɑːg, frɔːg/ *n* [C] a small green animal that lives near water and has long legs for jumping → **toad**

frogman /ˈfrɒgmən $ ˈfrɑːg-, ˈfrɔːg-/ *n* [C] (*plural* **frogmen** /-mən/) *BrE* someone whose job is to swim under water using special equipment to help them breathe

frolic /ˈfrɒlɪk $ ˈfrɑː-/ *v* [I] (**frolicked, frolicking**) *literary* to play happily

from /frəm; *strong* from $ frəm; *strong* frʌm, frɑːm/ *prep*

1 starting at a particular place, time, or level: *He drove all the way from Colorado.* | **from ... to ...** *the road from here to the airport* | *I have classes from 9.30 to*

1.30. | *Tickets cost from $8 to $25.* | *I will be teaching you **from now on** (=starting now and continuing). | We'll be in Spain two hours **from now** (=in two hours, starting now).* **THESAURUS** ▶ **AFTER**

2 used when you are saying how far away something is: *We live about ten miles from the airport.* | *It landed a few inches from my head.*

3 used to say who gave or sent something: *Who is the letter from?* | *I got the idea from Colin.* | *We buy our cheese from the market.* | *Get permission from your parents first.*

4 used to say where something is before it is removed: *She took a key from inside the drawer.*

5 used to say where someone was born, or where they usually live or work: *'Where are you from?' 'I'm from South Africa.'*

6 used to say what someone or something was like before they changed: **from ... to/into ...** *She changed from a shy child to a confident young woman.* | *It was translated from Latin into English.*

7 used to say where you are when you see something: *We could see the house from the road.*

8 used to state the cause of something: *She's exhausted from the worry.* | *deaths from cancer*

9 used to state the reason for your opinion: *From what I've seen, he seems a nice man.*

10 used to say what something has been made of: *Beer is made from hops.*

11 used when you are comparing things: *He's quite different from his brother.*

frond /frɒnd $ frɑːnd/ *n* [C] a leaf of a FERN or PALM

front¹ /frʌnt/ *n*

1 **PART FURTHEST FORWARD** **the front a)** the part of something that is furthest forward **OPP back: at/in the front (of sth)** *We got on the bus and sat at the front.* | *Can I ride in the front (=of a car)?* | **[+of]** *At last I got to the front of the queue.* **b)** the side or surface of something that faces forward: **[+of]** *the controls on the front of the machine* | *a shirt with stains down the front* | *He lay **on his front** (=the front of his body).* **c)** the most important side or surface of something, which you look at first **OPP back:** *a magazine with a picture of Elvis **on the front*** | **[+of]** *The front of the house was painted white.*

2 **WEATHER** [C] a line where an area of warm air meets an area of cold air: **warm/cold front**

3 **ILLEGAL ACTIVITIES** [C] a legal business that is used to hide illegal activity: **[+for]** *The casino was a front for their drugs operation.*

4 **HIDE FEELINGS** [singular] a way of behaving that hides how you really feel: *She was worried, but **put on a brave front.***

5 **WAR** **the front** (*also* **the front line**) a line along which fighting takes place during a war: *More troops were **sent to the front.*** | *front-line troops* → **UPFRONT¹**

PHRASES

in front 1 further forward than someone or something else **SYN ahead OPP behind:** *The car in front braked suddenly.* | **[+of]** *Louise was in front of me in the queue.* **2** winning in a game or competition **SYN ahead OPP behind:** *Leeds are back in front.*

in front of sb/sth 1 facing something **OPP behind:** *She stood in front of the mirror.* | *I spend hours in front of my computer (=using it).* **2** near the entrance to a building, facing the street **OPP behind:** *You can*

front

park in front of the store. **3** where someone can see or hear you: *Don't swear in front of the children.*

on the business/political/sporting etc front in a particular area of activity: *We've had some good news on the business front.*

out front in the area near the entrance to a building: *The taxi is waiting out front.*

front² *adj* [only before noun] at or in the front of something OPP **back**: *His front teeth fell out.* | *She's on the front cover of every magazine.* | *The front door is red.* | *front row tickets*

front³ *v* [T] **1** *especially BrE* to be the person in something such as a band or television programme who leads it and is most well-known to the public: *He fronted his own band.* **2** to face something: *hotels fronting the lake*

frontal /'frʌntl/ *adj* at or relating to the front part of something: *a frontal attack on their troops* | *the frontal lobe of the brain*

frontier /'frʌntɪə $ frʌn'tɪr/ *n* [C] **1** *especially BrE* the border of a country: **[+between/with]** *a town on the frontier* between France and Spain **2 the frontiers of knowledge/science etc** the limits of what is known about something

front 'line *n* [C usually singular] the place where fighting happens in a war SYN **the front** —**front-line** *adj*: *front-line troops*

'front-page *adj* **front-page news/article/story etc** news that is important enough to be on the front page of a newspaper

front-'runner *n* [C] the person, company etc that is most likely to win or succeed: *the front-runner in the presidential election*

frost¹ /frost $ frɒːst/ *n* **1** [C,U] very cold weather, when water freezes: *There was a hard frost last night* (=it was extremely cold). | *plants killed by frost* **2** [U] a white powder of ice that covers things when the weather is very cold: *trees covered with frost* THESAURUS ▶ SNOW

frost² *v* [T] *AmE* to cover a cake with FROSTING SYN **ice** *BrE*

frostbite /'frostbaɪt $ 'frɒːst-/ *n* [U] a condition in which your fingers, toes etc become frozen and are badly damaged —**frostbitten** /-bɪtn/ *adj*

frosted /'frostɪd $ 'frɒːstɪd/ *adj* **frosted glass/ window etc** glass that has a rough surface, so that you cannot see through it clearly

frosting /'frostɪŋ $ 'frɒːstɪŋ/ *n* [U] *AmE* a sweet substance put on cakes, made from sugar and liquid SYN **icing** *BrE*

frosty /'frosti $ 'frɒːsti/ *adj* **1** very cold or covered with FROST: *a frosty morning* | *frosty ground* **2** unfriendly: *a frosty stare* THESAURUS ▶ UNFRIENDLY

froth¹ /frɒθ $ frɒːθ/ *n* [singular, U] a mass of small BUBBLES on top of a liquid —**frothy** *adj*: *frothy coffee*

froth² *v* [I] to produce a lot of froth

frown¹ /fraʊn/ *v* [I] to make an angry or unhappy expression by moving your EYEBROWS together: **[+at]** *Mel frowned at me.*

PHRASAL VERBS

frown on/upon sth to disapprove of something:

Smoking is allowed, but frowned upon.

frown² *n* [C] the expression on your face when you frown: *He looked at her* **with a** *puzzled* **frown**.

froze /frəʊz $ froʊz/ *v* the past tense of FREEZE

frozen¹ /'frəʊzən $ 'froʊ-/ *v* the past participle of FREEZE

frozen² *adj*

1 FOOD frozen food has been stored at very low temperatures to preserve it → **freeze**: *frozen peas*

2 FEELING COLD *spoken* feeling very cold: *You look frozen!*

3 WATER/EARTH changed into ice or made very hard because of very cold weather: *The ground was frozen.* | *a frozen lake*

4 UNABLE TO MOVE unable to move, usually because of fear: *She stood there frozen with terror.*

frugal /'fruːɡəl/ *adj* careful to buy or use only what is necessary OPP **extravagant**: *He led a frugal existence.* —**frugally** *adv*

fruit /fruːt/ *n* (plural **fruit** or **fruits**)

1 [C,U] something such as an apple or orange, which grows on a plant, tree, or bush, and contains seeds: *a bowl of fruit* | *Eat plenty of* **fresh fruit**. | **fruit juice/yoghurt/salad etc**

2 the fruits of sth the good results from something, after you have worked hard: *He was able to enjoy the fruits of his labours.* → **bear fruit** at BEAR¹

> **Grammar**
>
> **Fruit** (=apples, oranges etc) is usually uncountable in everyday English. Do not say 'I bought some fruits in the market.' Say *I bought some fruit in the market.*
>
> **Fruit** is used as a countable noun in formal or technical English: *It is difficult to grow oranges and other citrus fruits outside in the UK.*

fruitful /'fruːtfəl/ *adj* producing good results: *a very fruitful meeting*

fruition /fruː'ɪʃən/ *n* **come to fruition** *formal* to start to be successful or have the effect you wanted: *It took many years for his plans to come to fruition.*

fruitless /'fruːtləs/ *adj* failing to produce any good result, especially after a lot of effort: *a fruitless attempt to resolve the dispute* —**fruitlessly** *adv*

fruity /'fruːti/ *adj* tasting or smelling strongly of fruit: *a fruity wine*

frustrate /frʌ'streɪt $ 'frʌstreɪt/ *v* [T] **1** if something frustrates you, it makes you feel impatient or angry because you are unable to do what you want: *The slow pace of his learning frustrates him.* **2** to prevent someone's plans or efforts from succeeding: *Her plans were frustrated by her parents.*

frustrated /frʌ'streɪtɪd $ 'frʌstreɪtɪd/ *adj* **1** feeling impatient or angry because you are unable to do what you want: **[+with/at]** *I* **get** *really* **frustrated** with my computer sometimes. **2 a frustrated poet/ artist/actor etc** someone who would like to develop a particular skill but has not been able to

frustrating /frʌ'streɪtɪŋ $ 'frʌstreɪtɪŋ/ *adj* making you feel impatient or angry because you are unable to do what you want: *a frustrating experience* | *It's frustrating when nobody listens.*

frustration /frʌ'streɪʃən/ n [C,U] the feeling of being impatient or angry because you are unable to do what you want

fry /fraɪ/ v [I,T] (**fried, frying, fries**) to cook something in hot oil, or be cooked in hot oil: *Do you want me to fry some eggs?* | *I could smell bacon frying.* | *fried mushrooms* → see picture at **COOK¹** **THESAURUS** **COOK**

'frying ,pan n [C] a round flat pan with a long handle, used for frying food → see picture at **PAN¹**

ft the written abbreviation of **foot**

fudge¹ /fʌdʒ/ n [U] a soft creamy sweet food

fudge² v [I,T] to avoid giving exact details or a clear answer about something: *The President tried to fudge the tax issue.*

fuel¹ /'fjuːəl/ n [C,U] a substance such as coal, gas, or oil, which can be burned to produce heat or power: *The plane was running low on fuel.* | *We compared the **fuel consumption** of several cars.* → **FOSSIL FUEL**

fuel² v [T] (**fuelled, fuelling** BrE, **fueled, fueling** AmE) to make a situation worse, or make someone's feelings stronger: *The photo fuelled the rumour that they had split up.* | *inflation fuelled by government spending*

fugitive /'fjuːdʒətɪv/ n [C] someone who is trying to avoid being caught by the police

fulfil BrE, **fulfill** AmE /fʊl'fɪl/ v [T] (**fulfilled, fulfilling**) **1** **fulfil a promise/commitment/obligation etc** to do something that you have promised to do, or do something that you should do: *He fulfilled his promise to cut taxes.* | *Britain is not fulfilling the requirements of the treaty.* **2** **fulfil a hope/wish/aim etc** to achieve the thing that you hoped for, wished for etc: *She never fulfilled her dream of becoming a dancer.* | *This merger will help the company fulfil its strategic aims.* **3** **fulfil a role/function/need etc** to do or provide something that is needed: *Does the church still fulfil a need in society?* **4** **fulfil your potential** to be as successful as you can be: *We want all our students to fulfil their potential.* **5** to make you feel satisfied because you are using all your skills and qualities: *Motherhood alone did not fulfil her.*

fulfilled /fʊl'fɪld/ adj satisfied that you are doing interesting and important things in your life or job

fulfilling /fʊl'fɪlɪŋ/ adj making you feel satisfied because you are doing interesting and important things: *Teaching is a very fulfilling career.*

fulfilment BrE, **fulfillment** AmE /fʊl'fɪlmənt/ n [U] **1** the feeling of being satisfied, especially because you are doing interesting, useful, or important things: *Ann's work gives her a real **sense of fulfilment**.* **2** when someone does what they have promised to do, what they should do, or what they have always wanted to do: [+of] *The trip was the fulfilment of a childhood dream.*

full¹ /fʊl/ adj
1 **WITH NO EMPTY SPACE** containing as many things or people as possible, so there is no space left **OPP** empty: *The train was completely full.* | *We started with a full tank of petrol.* | [+of] *The garage is crammed full of junk.* | *The bottle was only half full.* |

The hotel is full up. → see picture at **EMPTY¹**
2 **COMPLETE** [only before noun] complete and including all parts or details: *Please give your full name and address.* | *He has my full support.* | *Read the full story in today's paper!* | *We will pay the full cost of repairs.*
3 **HIGHEST LEVEL/AMOUNT** [only before noun] as high in level or great in amount as possible: *The government's goal is full employment.* | *at full speed/power/volume etc He plays his stereo at full volume.*
4 **HAVING A LOT OF STH** **be full of sth/sb** a) to contain many things or people of the same kind: *a garden full of flowers* | *Eric's essay is full of mistakes.* b) feeling or showing a lot of a particular quality: *We were full of excitement.*
5 **WITH FOOD** (also **full up** BrE informal) having eaten so much food that you do not want to eat any more: *No more, thanks. I'm full.*
6 **EMPHASIZING AN AMOUNT** **a full ten days/six inches etc** (also **ten full days/six full inches etc**) used to emphasize a quantity or amount: *I told him about it a full three weeks in advance.*
7 **HAVING ALL RIGHTS** [only before noun] having all the rights that someone can have: *a full driving licence* | *a full member*
8 **BUSY** **a full life/day etc** a life or day in which you are very busy or active: *I have a full day tomorrow.*
9 **CLOTHES** made with a lot of material and fitting loosely: *a full skirt*
10 **BODY SHAPE** large and rounded in an attractive way: *a full figure*
11 **TASTE** a full flavour is pleasantly strong: *The coffee beans are roasted for a fuller flavour.*
PHRASES
be full of yourself spoken disapproving to have a high opinion of yourself: *He was too full of himself to care about anyone else.*
be in full swing if an event such as a party is in full swing, it has reached its highest level of activity: *The party was in full swing when we arrived.*
in full view of sb in a place where someone can easily see you: *She hit him in full view of the neighbours.*

THESAURUS

full containing as many things or people as possible, so there is no space left: *My suitcase was already full of clothes.* | *The theatre was completely full.*
filled with sth full of something – use this about a container when a lot of things have been put in it: *The vase was filled with flowers.*
packed completely full of people – used about a room, train etc: *The bus was packed and I couldn't get a seat.* | *a packed restaurant*
bursting with sth extremely full of something: *In summer the garden is bursting with flowers.*
overflowing if a container is overflowing, it is so full that the liquid or things inside are coming over the top: *Turn the tap off – the bath's overflowing.*

---

full² n **1** **in full** including the whole of something: *The debt must be paid in full.* **2** **to the full** as completely as possible: *My mother lived life to the full.*

full³ adv directly: [+on/in] She kissed him full on the mouth.

fullback /'fʊlbæk/ n [C] a player in a football team who plays in defence SYN **defender**

'full-blown adj at the most complete or advanced stage: full-blown AIDS

,full-'fledged adj AmE completely developed, trained, or established SYN **fully-fledged** BrE

,full-'grown adj a full-grown animal, plant, or person has developed to their full size and will not grow any bigger

,full 'house n [C] an occasion at a theatre, concert hall etc when there are no empty seats

'full-length adj **1 full-length skirt/coat etc** a skirt etc that is long or reaches the ground **2 full-length play/film/novel etc** a play etc that is not shorter than the normal length

,full 'marks n [plural] if you give someone full marks, you praise them for doing something very well: He failed, but he deserves full marks for bravery.

,full 'moon n [singular] the moon when it looks completely round

,full-'on adj as powerful, INTENSE, or extreme as possible: a full-on performance

,full-'page adj [only before noun] covering all of one page in a newspaper or magazine: a full-page advert

,full-'scale adj [only before noun] **1** as complete or thorough as possible: the threat of full-scale nuclear war | We will conduct a full-scale inquiry. **2** a full-scale drawing, model etc is the same size as the thing it represents

,full 'stop n [C] BrE a mark (.) that shows the end of a sentence or the short form of a word SYN **period** AmE

,full-'time adj, adv for all the hours of the week during which it is usual for people to work, study etc → **part-time**: Both her parents **work full-time**. | a full-time job

fully /'fʊli/ adv completely: The restaurant is **fully booked**. | I'd like to discuss this more fully with you.

,fully-'fledged adj BrE completely developed, trained, or established SYN **full-fledged** AmE: She's now a fully-fledged star.

fumble /'fʌmbəl/ v [I] to try to hold or find something, using your hands in an awkward way: [+for/in/with] I fumbled for the light switch.

fume /fju:m/ v [I] to be very angry: She was fuming.

fumes /fju:mz/ n [plural] strong-smelling gas or smoke that is unpleasant to breathe in: paint fumes

fumigate /'fju:mɪgeɪt/ v [T] to use special chemicals in order to get rid of infection or insects from a place —**fumigation** /ˌfju:mə'geɪʃən/ n [U]

fun¹ /fʌn/ n [U] enjoyment, or something that is enjoyable: Did you have fun with your friends? | The picnic was great fun. | **it is fun doing sth** It was fun dressing up as somebody else. | **(just) for fun** The quiz is just for fun, so don't take it seriously.

PHRASES
make fun of sb/sth to make unkind jokes about someone or something: They made fun of him because he was fat.

fun² adj **1** [only before noun] enjoyable: It'll be a fun day out. THESAURUS → NICE **2** a fun person is amusing and enjoyable to be with

function¹ Ac /'fʌŋkʃən/ n [C] **1** the purpose that something has, or the job that someone does: Lighting **performs** several **functions** in the home. | What is the function of a treasurer? **2** a large party or official event: The mayor was attending an official function. **3** one of the basic operations performed by a computer

function² Ac v [I] **1** to work in the correct or intended way: Rail services are now **functioning normally** again. **2** to work in a particular way: an understanding of how the economy functions
PHRASAL VERBS
function as sth to be used as another thing or to do what another thing usually does: a phrase that functions as an adverb

functional Ac /'fʌŋkʃənəl/ adj **1** designed to be useful rather than attractive: office furniture that is **purely functional 2** working correctly: The new system is now **fully functional**.

'function key n [C] one of the keys on a computer KEYBOARD, for example F1 or F2, that tell the computer to do something

fund¹ Ac /fʌnd/ n [C]
1 an amount of money that is kept for a particular purpose: donations to the church restoration fund | the staff pension fund
2 funds [plural] the money that an organization needs or has: We're trying to **raise funds** for a new sports hall. | The project was abandoned due to **lack of funds**.

fund² Ac v [T] to provide money for an activity, organization, event etc: a project funded by the EU

fundamental Ac /ˌfʌndə'mentl/ adj relating to the most basic and important parts of something: the fundamental cause of the problem | fundamental changes to the law —**fundamentally** adv: Their conclusions are fundamentally wrong.

fundamentalist /ˌfʌndə'mentəlɪst/ n [C] someone who follows religious laws very strictly —**fundamentalist** adj —**fundamentalism** n [U]

fundamentals /ˌfʌndə'mentlz/ n **the fundamentals of sth** the most important ideas, rules etc that something is based on: the fundamentals of computer programming

funding Ac /'fʌndɪŋ/ n [U] money provided by an organization for a particular purpose: government funding for universities

'fund-ˌraising n [U] the activity of collecting money for a particular purpose, especially in order to help people —**fund-raiser** n [C]

funeral /'fju:nərəl/ n [C] a ceremony for someone who has just died: The **funeral** will be **held** on Friday. | His ex-wife did not **attend** the funeral. | **funeral procession/service/mass etc**

'funeral di,rector n [C] someone who is paid to organize a funeral SYN **undertaker** BrE

'funeral home (also **'funeral ,parlour**) n [C] the place where a body is kept before a funeral

funfair /ˈfʌnfeə $ -fer/ n [C] BrE an outdoor event where you can ride on machines or play games to win prizes SYN **fair**

fungus /ˈfʌŋgəs/ n [C,U] (plural **fungi** /-dʒaɪ, -gaɪ/ or **funguses**) a simple type of plant that has no leaves or flowers and grows on wood or other surfaces. MUSHROOMS and MOULD are types of fungus.

funk /fʌŋk/ n [U] a style of popular music with a strong beat, based on JAZZ and African music

funky /ˈfʌŋki/ adj informal **1** funky music has a strong beat and is good to dance to **2** modern, fashionable, and interesting: a funky Mexican restaurant

funnel /ˈfʌnl/ n [C] **1** a tube with a wide top that you use for pouring a liquid into a narrow opening **2** BrE a metal CHIMNEY on top of a steam ship or train

funnily /ˈfʌnəli/ adv **funnily enough** spoken used to say that something is unexpected or strange: Funnily enough, I was just going to call you.

funny /ˈfʌni/ adj
1 making you laugh: You look funny in that hat. | **funny story/joke/film etc** Some of their jokes are **hysterically funny** (=extremely funny). | I don't **find** him **funny** at all. | **It's not funny** (=don't laugh) – I could have been hurt!
2 strange or unusual: I had a **funny feeling** I'd see you here. | **it's funny how/that** It's funny how I can never remember his name. | **That's funny!** I was just thinking about you when you called. | **look/feel funny** Are you OK? You look funny. THESAURUS **STRANGE**
3 dishonest, illegal, or wrong: There's **something funny** about this. | Remember, **no funny business** while I'm away.

THESAURUS

funny making you laugh: John told me a really funny joke. | She can be very funny.
amusing funny and enjoyable. **Amusing** is more formal than **funny**. It is often used when something makes you smile rather than laugh: There was an amusing article in the paper.
humorous a humorous story, poem, description etc is intended to be funny. **Humorous** is more formal than **funny**: a book of humorous poems | a humorous birthday card
witty a witty person, remark etc uses words in a funny and clever way: Sam was witty and fun to be with. | Everyone laughed at his witty remarks.
hilarious extremely funny: The movie was hilarious.

fur /fɜː $ fɜːr/ n
1 [U] the thick soft hair that covers the bodies of some animals such as cats and rabbits
2 [C,U] the fur-covered skin of an animal, used especially for making clothes, or a piece of clothing made from furs: She wore a fur coat.

furious /ˈfjʊəriəs $ ˈfjʊr-/ adj **1** very angry: [+at/about] He is furious at the court's decision. | [+with] She was furious with me. | [+that] I'm **absolutely furious** that nothing has been done. THESAURUS **ANGRY 2** done with a lot of speed, violence, or effort: He worked **at a furious pace**. —**furiously** adv

furl /fɜːl $ fɜːrl/ v [T] to roll or fold something such as an UMBRELLA or sail OPP **unfurl**

furlong /ˈfɜːlɒŋ $ ˈfɜːrlɔːŋ/ n [C] a unit of distance, used in horse racing, equal to 1/8 of a mile, or 201 metres

furnace /ˈfɜːnɪs $ ˈfɜːr-/ n [C] an enclosed space with a very hot fire in it, used for melting metals or producing power or heat

furnish /ˈfɜːnɪʃ $ ˈfɜːr-/ v [T] **1** to put furniture into a house or room: They furnished the house with antiques. **2** to provide someone with something that they need: We can furnish you with a list of local solicitors. —**furnished** adj: a **fully furnished** flat

furnishings /ˈfɜːnɪʃɪŋz $ ˈfɜːr-/ n [plural] the furniture, and other things such as curtains, in a room

furniture /ˈfɜːnɪtʃə $ ˈfɜːrnɪtʃər/ n [U] large objects in a room, such as chairs, tables, and beds

Grammar

Furniture is uncountable and is not used in the plural. It is used with a singular verb. Do not say 'The furnitures were expensive.' Say The furniture was expensive.
When talking about a single chair or table, you say **a piece of furniture**: The desk was the only piece of furniture in the room.

furore BrE, **furor** AmE /fjʊˈrɔːri, ˈfjʊərɔː $ ˈfjʊrɔːr/ n [singular] formal a sudden expression of anger among a large group of people: Darwin's theories caused a furore.

furrow¹ /ˈfʌrəʊ $ ˈfɜːroʊ/ n [C] **1** a deep line in the skin of someone's face **2** a wide deep line made in the ground, especially one in which to plant seeds

furrow² v [I,T] literary to make lines appear on someone's FOREHEAD: Her brow furrowed in concentration. —**furrowed** adj

furry /ˈfɜːri/ adj covered with fur or short threads: small furry animals

further¹ /ˈfɜːðə $ ˈfɜːrðər/ adv
1 more, or to a greater degree or level: I have nothing further to say. | His career had not progressed any further. | **go further/take sth further** Should we go further and ban smoking in the whole building?
2 (also **farther**) at or to a longer distance away: I can't walk any further. | [+down/along etc] They live further down the street.
3 into the past or future: [+back/on/ahead] Ten years further on, we still haven't found a cure.

further² adj [only before noun] additional: Are there any further questions? | Visit our website for **further details**.

further³ v [T] formal to help something to succeed: efforts to further the cause of peace

,further edu'cation n [U] BrE education for adults after leaving school, that is not at a university

furthermore Ac /ˌfɜːðəˈmɔː $ ˈfɜːrðərmɔːr/ adv
formal in addition to what has already been said

furthest /ˈfɜːðɪst $ ˈfɜːr-/ adj, adv at the greatest
distance from a place or point in time: He sat on the
chair furthest from me.

furtive /ˈfɜːtɪv $ ˈfɜːr-/ adj behaving as if you want
to keep something secret: a furtive glance
—**furtively** adv

fury /ˈfjʊəri $ ˈfjʊri/ n [singular, U] extreme anger:
She shook with fury.

fuse[1] /fjuːz/ n [C] **1** a short wire inside a piece of
electrical equipment or an electrical system that
melts if too much electricity passes through it,
preventing damage **2** a part that is connected to a
bomb, FIREWORK etc that delays or starts the explosion → **blow a fuse** at BLOW[1]

fuse[2] v [I,T] **1** to join together and become one
thing, or to join two things together: The bones of the
spine had fused together. | His style fuses Indian music
and hip-hop. **2** BrE if an electrical system fuses, or if
you fuse it, it stops working because the fuse has
melted: The lights had fused.

fuselage /ˈfjuːzəlɑːʒ $ -sə-/ n [C] the main part of a
plane → see picture at AEROPLANE

fusion /ˈfjuːʒən/ n [C,U] when two things are
joined together or combined: the fusion of hydrogen
atoms

fuss[1] /fʌs/ n **1** [singular, U] anxious or excited
behaviour or activity, usually about unimportant
things: I don't see **what all the fuss is about**. | They
wanted a quiet wedding without any fuss. **2 make a
fuss/kick up a fuss** to complain angrily or noisily
about something: One customer made a big fuss
because his food was cold.

PHRASES

> **make a fuss of sb** BrE, **make a fuss over sb** AmE to
> pay a lot of attention to someone and try to make
> them comfortable: Grandma always makes a fuss of
> me.

fuss[2] v [I] to behave in an anxious way, worrying
over unimportant things: Stop fussing! We'll be home
soon!

PHRASAL VERBS

fuss over sb to pay a lot of attention to making
someone comfortable: Don't fuss over me, Mom. I'm
fine.

fussy /ˈfʌsi/ adj someone who is fussy is very
careful about what they choose and is difficult to
please: **[+about]** He's very fussy about what he
wears. | I'm not fussy about where we go tonight (=I
don't mind). | She's a fussy eater.

futile /ˈfjuːtaɪl $ -tl/ adj certain to be unsuccessful:
a **futile attempt** to put out the fire —**futility**
/fjuːˈtɪləti/ n [U]: the futility of war

futon /ˈfuːtɒn $ -tɑːn/ n [C] a MATTRESS that can be
used as a bed or folded into a seat → see picture
at BED

future[1] /ˈfjuːtʃə $ -ər/ adj [only before noun]
1 likely to happen or exist in the future: future pat-
terns of climate change | We will preserve this forest for
future generations. | **future wife/husband/son-in-
law etc** (=someone who will be your wife, husband
etc) He met his future wife at college.
2 the future tense in grammar, the form of a verb
that is used for things that will happen in the future

future[2] n
1 the future the time after now: What are your plans
for the future? | **in the future** In the future, people will
be able to travel to other planets. | It may be useful at
some time in the future. THESAURUS ▶ SOON
2 [C] what someone will do, or what will happen to
someone or something in the future: My parents
have already planned out my whole future. | She had a
great future ahead of her. | **[+of]** He is optimistic about
the future of the business.
PHRASES

> **in future** BrE from now: In future, staff must wear
> identity badges.

COLLOCATIONS

adjectives

in the near future (=soon) I'm hoping to go to
London in the near future.

in the immediate future (=very soon) There will
be no major changes in the immediate future.

the distant future (=a long time from now) At
that time, television still belonged to the distant
future.

for the foreseeable future (=as far into the
future as you can know or imagine) He expects
to stay in the job for the foreseeable future.

verbs

to plan for the future Because of my illness, I can't
plan for the future.

to predict the future (also **to see into the future**)
It's impossible to predict the future.

what the future holds (=what will happen) I
don't know what the future holds.

the future looks good/bright etc The future looks
bright for his team.

---

future ˈperfect n the future perfect in grammar,
the form of a verb that is used to show that an
action will be completed before a particular time in
the future: I will have finished by tomorrow.

futuristic /ˌfjuːtʃəˈrɪstɪk◂/ adj something that is
futuristic looks unusual and modern, as if it belongs
in the future instead of the present: a futuristic sports
stadium

fuzz /fʌz/ n [U] short soft hair or fur

fuzzy /ˈfʌzi/ adj **1** unclear: Some of the photos are a
little fuzzy. **2** fuzzy hair is soft and curly

FYI the written abbreviation of **for your information**,
used especially in emails when you are telling
someone something they need to know

Gg

G, g /dʒiː/ *n* [C,U] (*plural* **G's, g's**) **1** the seventh letter of the English alphabet **2** the fifth note in the musical SCALE of C MAJOR, or the musical KEY based on this note

g a written abbreviation of **gram**

gabble /ˈɡæbəl/ *v* [I,T] to talk so quickly that people cannot understand what you are saying

gable /ˈɡeɪbəl/ *n* [C] the top part of a wall of a house where it joins a roof, making a shape like a TRIANGLE

gadget /ˈɡædʒɪt/ *n* [C] a small tool or machine that helps you do something: *a neat gadget for sharpening knives* **THESAURUS** ▶ **MACHINE**

gaffe /ɡæf/ *n* [C] an embarrassing mistake

gag¹ /ɡæɡ/ *v* (**gagged, gagging**) **1** [I] to be unable to swallow and feel as if you are about to bring up food from your stomach **2** [T] to cover someone's mouth with a piece of cloth so that they cannot talk: *They gagged her and tied her to a chair.* **3** [T] to stop people expressing their opinions: *an attempt to gag political activists*

gag² *n* [C] **1** *informal* a joke or funny story **2** a piece of cloth used to gag someone

gaggle /ˈɡæɡəl/ *n* **1 a gaggle of tourists/children etc** a noisy group of people: *a gaggle of schoolchildren* **2 a gaggle of geese** a group of GEESE

gaiety /ˈɡeɪəti/ *n* [U] *old-fashioned* a feeling of fun and happiness

gaily /ˈɡeɪli/ *adv* in a happy cheerful way

gain¹ /ɡeɪn/ *v*
1 [T] to get or achieve something: *The country gained independence in 1957.* | **gain control/power** *The army gained control of enemy territory.* **THESAURUS** ▶ **GET**
2 [I,T] to get an advantage from something: **gain (sth) from (doing) sth** *There is much to be gained from getting expert advice.* | *Who really stands to gain* (=will get an advantage) *from these tax cuts?*
3 [T] to increase in size or weight: *I've gained a lot of weight recently.*
4 [I] if a clock gains, it works too quickly and shows a later time than the real time

PHRASES

gain ground to become more popular or stronger: *The anti-smoking lobby is gaining ground.*

PHRASAL VERBS

gain on sb to start getting closer to someone you are chasing

Word Choice: gain or earn?
You use **earn** to talk about being paid money for the work that you do: *He earns over £40,000 a year.*

Do not use **gain** in this meaning. Do not say 'He gains over £40,000 a year.'

gain² *n*
1 [C] an advantage or an improvement: **[+in]** *substantial gains in efficiency* | **[+to/for]** *There are obvious gains for the student.* | *The party made considerable gains at local elections.*
2 [C,U] an increase in the amount or level of something: **[+in]** *a gain in weekly output* | *Try to avoid too much weight gain.*

gait /ɡeɪt/ *n* [singular] the way that someone walks: *He had a slow ambling gait.*

gala /ˈɡɑːlə $ ˈɡeɪlə, ˈɡælə/ *n* [C] a special public performance or competition: *a charity gala evening* | *a swimming gala*

galaxy /ˈɡæləksi/ *n* [C] (*plural* **galaxies**) one of the large groups of stars that make up the universe

gale /ɡeɪl/ *n* [C] a very strong wind: *Our fence blew down in the gale.* **THESAURUS** ▶ **WIND**

gall /ɡɔːl/ *n* **have the gall to do sth** to do something rude and unreasonable: *He had the gall to blame Lucy.*

gallant /ˈɡælənt/ *adj old-fashioned* **1** a gallant man is kind and polite towards women **2** brave: *a gallant attempt to save lives* —**gallantly** *adv* —**gallantry** *n* [U]

'gall ,bladder *n* [C] the organ in your body in which BILE is stored

gallery /ˈɡæləri/ *n* [C] (*plural* **galleries**) **1** a room or building where you can look at famous paintings and other types of art: *the Uffizi Gallery in Florence* → see Word Choice at **MUSEUM 2** an upper floor inside a large room, where you can sit and watch what is happening in the room below

galley /ˈɡæli/ *n* [C] **1** a kitchen on a ship or a plane **2** an ancient warship that was rowed by SLAVES

galling /ˈɡɔːlɪŋ $ ˈɡɒː-/ *adj* something that is galling makes you feel upset and angry because it is unfair

gallon /ˈɡælən/ *n* [C] a unit for measuring liquid, equal to 4.55 litres in Britain or 3.79 litres in the US

gallop /ˈɡæləp/ *v* [I] if a horse gallops, it runs very quickly —**gallop** *n* [singular]

gallows /ˈɡæləʊz $ -loʊz/ *n* [C] (*plural* **gallows**) a structure used for killing criminals by hanging them from a rope

galore /ɡəˈlɔː $ -ˈlɔːr/ *adj* [only after noun] in large amounts: *There are bargains galore in the sales.*

galvanize (*also* **-ise** *BrE*) /ˈɡælvənaɪz/ *v* [T] to shock or surprise someone so much that they do something: *The letter galvanized us into action.*

galvanized (*also* **-ised** *BrE*) /ˈɡælvənaɪzd/ *adj* galvanized metal has been treated in a special way so that it does not RUST

gambit /ˈɡæmbɪt/ *n* [C] something you do or say to get an advantage for yourself

gamble¹ /ˈɡæmbəl/ *v* [I,T]
1 to try to win money by playing cards or other games, or guessing the result of a race **SYN** **bet**: *He gambled away all his money.* | **[+on]** *My father was fond of gambling on horses.*

G

2 to do something that involves a risk and might not succeed: *They're gambling on all the team being fit by Saturday.* —**gambling** *n* [U]: *Gambling is illegal in some states.* —**gambler** *n* [C]

gamble² *n* [singular] an action or plan that involves a risk but that you hope will succeed: **[+on]** *We cannot afford to take a gamble on a new product.*

game¹ /geɪm/ *n*
1 [C] an activity or sport in which people compete with each other according to agreed rules: *We used to play games like chess.*
2 [C] an occasion when two teams or people play a sport or game: **[+of]** *How about a game of cards?*
3 games [plural] **a)** an organized sports event: *The Olympic Games are held once every four years.* **b)** *BrE* a lesson at school in which children do sport SYN PE: *We've got games this afternoon.*
4 [C] an activity in which children play: **[+of]** *a game of hide-and-seek* | *The children are playing a game in the backyard.*
5 sb's game how well someone plays a game or sport: *improve/raise your game He's taking lessons to improve his game.*
6 [U] wild animals and birds that are hunted for food or as a sport → **BALL GAME**

PHRASES
be a game if something is a game, it is done for fun, not for serious reasons: *He doesn't care about money – it's all just a game to him.*
ahead of the game if you are ahead of the game, you are more likely to be successful than the other people, organizations etc that you are competing with: *Companies like to stay ahead of the game by finding out what their competitors are doing.*
give the game away to accidentally say something that lets someone guess a secret: *You'd better not say any more, or you will give the game away.*
play games to behave in a way that is dishonest or not serious: *We want a deal. We're not interested in playing games.*

COLLOCATIONS
verbs
to play a game *Have you ever played this game before?*
to have a game *BrE Let's have a game of football.*
to see/watch a game *I saw the game on television.*
to win/lose a game *They've won their last three games.*

types of game
a computer/video game *He spends hours playing computer games.*
a card game *I never play card games for money.*
a board game *If it's wet, we could play cards or a board game.*
a team game *Cricket is a team game.*
a party game *The children enjoyed the party games.*
a basketball/baseball etc game *He was watching a baseball game on TV.*

---

game² *adj* [not before noun] willing to try something: *I'm game if you are.*

gamekeeper /ˈgeɪmkiːpə $ -ər/ *n* [C] someone whose job is to look after wild animals and birds that will be hunted

'game plan *n* [C] a plan for achieving success, especially in business or sport

'games ˌconsole (*also* **game console**) *n* [C] an electronic machine that is used for playing games on a screen → see picture on page A12

'game show *n* [C] a television programme in which people play games in order to win prizes

gaming /ˈgeɪmɪŋ/ *n* [U] *informal* the activity of playing computer games: *online gaming*

gammon /ˈgæmən/ *n* [U] *BrE* meat from a pig that has been preserved using salt

gamut /ˈgæmət/ *n* [singular] the complete range of possibilities: **[+of]** *College opened up a whole gamut of new experiences.*

gang¹ /gæŋ/ *n* [C] **1** a group of young people, especially a group that often causes trouble and fights: *two rival street gangs* | **[+of]** *a gang of kids* | **in a gang** *Do you want to be in our gang?* THESAURUS GROUP **2** a group of criminals who work together: **[+of]** *a gang of smugglers* **3** *informal* a group of friends: *All the gang will be there.*

gang² *v*
PHRASAL VERBS
gang up on/against sb to join together in order to criticize or attack someone: *Helen thinks everyone's ganging up on her.*

gangland /ˈgæŋlænd, -lənd/ *adj* **gangland killing/ murder/shooting etc** a killing etc relating to the world of organized and violent crime

gangling /ˈgæŋglɪŋ/ (*also* **gangly** /ˈgæŋgli/) *adj* unusually tall and thin and not very graceful: *a gangly teenager*

gangrene /ˈgæŋgriːn/ *n* [U] a medical condition in which a person's flesh in part of their body starts to decay

gangster /ˈgæŋstə $ -ər/ *n* [C] a member of a group of violent criminals: *Al Capone was a Chicago gangster.*

gangway /ˈgæŋweɪ/ *n* [C] **1** *BrE* the space between two rows of seats in a theatre, bus, or train **2** a board or steps between a boat and the shore for people to walk up and down

gaol /dʒeɪl/ a British spelling of JAIL

gaoler /ˈdʒeɪlə $ -ər/ *n* [C] a British spelling of JAILER

gap /gæp/ *n* [C]
1 a space between two things: **[+in]** *a gap in the traffic* | **[+between]** *the gap between two rows of seats* THESAURUS **HOLE**
2 a big difference between two things: **[+between]** *the widening gap between the rich and the poor* | *His films try to bridge the gap between tradition and modern life.*
3 something that is missing that stops something else from being good or complete: **[+in]** *His death has left a huge gap in my life.* | *Murphy will fill the gap left by Hurst's departure from the team.*
4 a period of time in which nothing happens or

nothing is said: *I went back to university after a gap of two years.* | **[+in]** *an awkward gap in the conversation* → **GENERATION GAP**

gape /geɪp/ *v* [I] to look at something or someone in surprise, with your mouth open: **[+at]** *What are all these people gaping at?*

gaping /ˈgeɪpɪŋ/ *adj* [only before noun] a gaping hole, wound, or mouth is wide and open

'gap year *n* [C] *BrE* a year between leaving school and starting university, in which someone travels or works

garage /ˈgærɪdʒ, -ɑːʒ $ gəˈrɑːʒ/ *n* [C]
1 a building for keeping a car in: *I'll put the car in the garage.*
2 a place where cars are repaired: *My car's at the garage.* | *I'll take the car to the garage tomorrow.*
3 *BrE* a place where you buy petrol [SYN] **gas station** *AmE*

garb /gɑːb $ gɑːrb/ *n* [U] *formal* a particular style of clothing

garbage /ˈgɑːbɪdʒ $ ˈgɑːr-/ *n* [U] *especially AmE*
1 waste material, such as paper, empty containers, and food thrown away [SYN] **rubbish** *BrE*: *Can you take out the garbage?*
2 stupid words or ideas: *He's talking garbage!*

'garbage ,can *n* [C] *AmE* a container that you put waste in [SYN] **dustbin** *BrE* → see picture at **BIN**

'garbage col,lector *n* [C] *AmE* someone whose job is to collect waste from garbage cans [SYN] **dustman** *BrE*

garbled /ˈgɑːbəld $ ˈgɑːr-/ *adj* garbled speech or writing is very unclear and confusing: *a garbled phone message*

garden /ˈgɑːdn $ ˈgɑːr-/ *n* [C]
1 *BrE* an area of land next to a house, where there are flowers, grass, and other plants [SYN] **yard** *AmE*: *Our house has a small garden.* | *He's in the garden cutting the grass.* | **back/front garden**
2 *AmE* a part of the area next to your house, where you grow plants of a particular kind: *a herb garden*
3 gardens [plural] a large area of land where plants are grown for the public to see: *Thousands of visitors come to the gardens each year.*

'garden ,centre *n* [C] *BrE* a place that sells plants and equipment for gardens [SYN] **nursery** *AmE*

gardener /ˈgɑːdnə $ ˈgɑːrdnər/ *n* [C] someone who works in a garden, as a job or for pleasure

gardening /ˈgɑːdnɪŋ $ ˈgɑːr-/ *n* [U] work that you do in a garden: *I'll do some gardening this afternoon.* —**garden** *v* [I]

gargantuan /gɑːˈgæntʃuən $ gɑːr-/ *adj literary* extremely large

gargle /ˈgɑːgəl $ ˈgɑːr-/ *v* [I] to hold a liquid in your throat and blow air through it without swallowing it

garish /ˈgeərɪʃ $ ˈger-/ *adj* very brightly coloured and unpleasant to look at: *a garish carpet*

garland /ˈgɑːlənd $ ˈgɑːr-/ *n* [C] a ring of flowers or leaves

garlic /ˈgɑːlɪk $ ˈgɑːr-/ *n* [U] a small plant like an onion with a very strong taste, used in cooking: *Add*

GARDEN EQUIPMENT

wheelbarrow

watering can

rake

gardening gloves

lawn mower

trowel

fork

shears

flowerpot

spade

a clove of garlic (=a piece of garlic). → see picture on page A5

garment /ˈgɑːmənt $ ˈgɑːr-/ *n* [C] *formal* a piece of clothing: *Wash delicate garments by hand.* [THESAURUS] **CLOTHES**

garnish /ˈgɑːnɪʃ $ ˈgɑːr-/ *v* [T] to decorate food with small pieces of fruit or vegetables —**garnish** *n* [C]

garret /ˈgærɪt/ *n* [C] a small room at the top of a house just under the roof

garrison /ˈgærəsən/ *n* [C] a group of soldiers who live in a building or town and defend it

garters /ˈgɑːtəz $ ˈgɑːrtərz/ *n* [plural] pieces of ELASTIC fixed to a woman's underwear and to her STOCKINGS to hold them up [SYN] **suspenders** *BrE*

gas¹ /gæs/ *n* (*plural* **gases** *or* **gasses**)
1 [C,U] a substance such as air, which is not solid or liquid: *hydrogen gas* | *a cloud of toxic gas*
2 [U] a clear substance like air that is burned to give heat for cooking and heating: *a gas stove*
3 (*also* **gasoline**) [U] *AmE* a liquid that is used for producing power in car engines [SYN] **petrol** *BrE*: *I spend over $200 a month on gas.* → **NATURAL GAS**

gas² *v* [T] (**gassed**, **gassing**) to attack or kill someone with poisonous gas

'gas ,chamber n [C] a large room in which people or animals are killed with poisonous gas

gash /gæʃ/ n [C] a deep cut —gash v [T]

'gas mask n [C] a piece of equipment that you wear over your face to protect you from breathing poisonous gases → see picture at MASK¹

gasoline /'gæsəliːn/ n [U] AmE a liquid that is used for producing power in car engines SYN gas AmE, petrol BrE

gasp /gɑːsp $ gæsp/ v [I] 1 to breathe in suddenly because you are surprised or in pain: [+in/with] Ollie gasped with pain and fell to the ground. 2 to quickly breathe in a lot of air because you are having difficulty breathing normally: Brendan was gasping for breath. THESAURUS BREATHE —gasp n [C]: a gasp of surprise

'gas ,station n [C] AmE a place that sells petrol SYN petrol station BrE

gastric /'gæstrɪk/ adj technical relating to your stomach: a gastric ulcer

gastronomic /ˌgæstrə'nɒmɪk◂ $ -'nɑː-/ adj [only before noun] formal relating to cooking and eating good food

gate /geɪt/ n [C]
1 a door in a fence or outside wall → door: open/close/shut a gate I ran back to close the gate. | front/back/main gate Make sure the back gate is locked.
2 the place where you leave an airport building to get on the plane: Please go to gate 4.

gâteau /'gætəʊ $ gɑː'toʊ/ n [C,U] (plural gâteaux /-təʊz $ -'toʊz/) BrE a large cake decorated with cream, fruit, chocolate etc → see picture at DESSERT

gatecrash /'geɪtkræʃ/ v [I,T] to go to a party when you have not been invited —gatecrasher n [C]

gateway /'geɪt-weɪ/ n 1 [C] an opening in a fence or wall where there is a gate 2 the gateway to sth a place, especially a city, that you go through in order to reach another place: St. Louis is the gateway to the West.

gather /'gæðə $ -ər/ v
1 [I,T] if people gather somewhere, or if someone gathers them, they come together in the same place: A crowd gathered to watch the fight. | [+round/around] Can you gather round so I can show you how it works? | If you gather the kids, I'll start the car. | be gathered Dozens of photographers were gathered outside Jackson's hotel.
2 [T] to believe that something is true based on the information you have: [+(that)] I gather you've had some problems with the computer. | You two know each other, I gather.
3 [T] to bring things from different places together: My job is to gather information on the subject. | gather sth up/together Anna gathered up her books.
4 gather speed/force/momentum etc to move faster, become stronger, get more support etc: The cart gathered speed as it rolled down the hill.

gathering /'gæðərɪŋ/ n [C] a party or meeting when a large number of people spend time together: a family gathering

gauche /gəʊʃ $ goʊʃ/ adj someone who is gauche says or does things that are considered impolite because they do not know the right way to behave

gaudy /'gɔːdi $ 'gɒːdi/ adj unpleasantly bright and cheap: gaudy jewellery

gauge¹ /geɪdʒ/ n [C] 1 an instrument that measures the amount or size of something: a fuel gauge 2 a measurement of the width or thickness of something: heavy gauge black polythene 3 a gauge of sth something that helps you make a judgment about a person or situation: Sales are a gauge of consumer spending.

gauge² v [T] 1 to judge what someone is likely to do or how they feel: I looked at Chris, trying to gauge his reaction. | [+whether/what/how etc] It is difficult to gauge what her next move will be. 2 to calculate the size or amount of something

gaunt /gɔːnt $ gɒːnt/ adj very thin, pale, and unhealthy

gauntlet /'gɔːntlɪt $ 'gɒːnt-/ n [C] a long thick GLOVE that you wear to protect your hand

PHRASES
run the gauntlet to be criticized or attacked by a lot of people: The minister ran the gauntlet of demonstrators.
throw down the gauntlet to invite someone to fight, argue, or compete with you: The girls threw down the gauntlet and challenged the boys to a basketball game.

gauze /gɔːz $ gɒːz/ n [U] thin light cloth with small holes in it, often used for covering wounds

gave /geɪv/ v the past tense of GIVE

gawk /gɔːk $ gɒːk/ v [I] informal to look at someone or something for a long time, in a way that looks stupid: [+at] Don't just stand there gawking at those girls.

gawky /'gɔːki $ 'gɒːki/ adj someone who is gawky is tall and not graceful: a gawky teenager

gawp /gɔːp $ gɒːp/ v [I] BrE informal to look at something for a long time, especially with your mouth open because you are surprised: [+at] What are you gawping at?

gay¹ /geɪ/ adj 1 a gay person is sexually attracted to people of the same sex SYN homosexual → lesbian: My son's just told me he's gay. 2 old-fashioned bright or attractive: gay colours 3 old-fashioned happy and excited: gay laughter

gay² n [C] someone, especially a man, who is sexually attracted to people of the same sex SYN homosexual

gaze /geɪz/ v [I] to look at someone or something for a long time: [+at/into etc] She sat gazing out of the window. THESAURUS LOOK —gaze n [singular]: Judith tried to avoid his gaze.

GB, Gb the written abbreviation of gigabyte

GCSE /ˌdʒiː siː es 'iː/ n [C] (General Certificate of Secondary Education) an examination that is taken by students aged 15 or 16 in Britain

GDP /ˌdʒiː diː 'piː/ n [U] (gross domestic product) the total value of all the goods and services produced in a country in one year, except for income received from abroad → GNP

gear¹ /gɪə $ gɪr/ *n*
1 [C,U] the machinery in a vehicle such as a car, truck, or bicycle that you use to go at different speeds: *The car has five gears.* | **in first/second etc gear** *We drove along in first gear.* | *I had to* **change gear** *halfway up the hill.* → see picture at **BICYCLE**
2 [U] special equipment, clothing etc that you need for a particular activity: *camping gear*

gear² *v*
PHRASAL VERBS
be geared to/towards sb/sth to be organized in order to achieve a particular purpose or be suitable for a particular person or situation: *All his training was geared to winning an Olympic medal.* | *advertisements that are geared towards children*
gear up to prepare for something: **[+for]** *They are gearing up for a conference in May.*

gearbox /ˈgɪəbɒks $ ˈgɪrbɑːks/ *n* [C] the system of gears in a vehicle

ˈgear stick *BrE* (*also* **ˈgear ˌlever** *BrE*, **ˈgear shift** *AmE*) *n* [C] a stick that you move to change gears in a vehicle

GED /ˌdʒiː iː ˈdiː/ *n* **the GED** (**the General Equivalency Diploma**) a document that is given to someone in the US who did not finish their HIGH SCHOOL education but has studied and passed an examination later

gee /dʒiː/ *spoken informal especially AmE* used to show that you are surprised or annoyed

geek /giːk/ *n* [C] *informal* someone who is not popular because they wear unfashionable clothes and do not know how to behave in social situations: *a computer geek* —**geeky** *adj*

geese /giːs/ *n* the plural of GOOSE

geezer /ˈgiːzə $ -ər/ *n* [C] *informal* **1** *BrE* a man **2** *AmE* an old man

gel¹ /dʒel/ *n* [C,U] a thick liquid, especially one for cleaning or for arranging your hair: *hair gel* | *shower gel*

gel² (*also* **jell** *especially AmE*) *v* [I] (**gelled, gelling**) **1** if an idea gels, it becomes clearer or more definite: *Don't start writing until the idea has gelled in your mind.* **2** if people gel, they begin to work together well as a group **3** if a liquid gels, it becomes firmer and thicker

gelatine /ˈdʒelətiːn $ -tn/ *BrE*, **gelatin** /-tɪn $ -tn/ *AmE* *n* [U] a clear substance used when cooking liquid food, to make it thicker

gelignite /ˈdʒelɪgnaɪt/ *n* [U] a very powerful explosive

gem /dʒem/ *n* [C] **1** a valuable stone that has been cut into a particular shape to make a piece of jewellery → **jewel 2** *informal* someone or something that is very special

Gemini /ˈdʒemənaɪ $ -ni/ *n* **1** [U] the sign of the Zodiac of people born between May 22 and June 21 **2** [C] someone who has this sign

gender Ac /ˈdʒendə $ -ər/ *n* **1** [C,U] the fact of being male or female: *discrimination* **on the grounds of gender** (=because someone is male or female) | *society's traditional* **gender roles 2** [U] the system in

some languages of dividing nouns, adjectives, and PRONOUNS into MASCULINE, FEMININE, or NEUTER

gene /dʒiːn/ *n* [C] a part of a CELL in a living thing that controls how it develops. Parents pass genes on to their children.

genera /ˈdʒenərə/ *n* the plural of GENUS

general¹ /ˈdʒenərəl/ *adj*
1 relating to the whole of something or its main features, not the details **OPP specific**: **in general** *What are your hopes for the future, in general?* | *I've a* **general idea** *of what to say.* | *His general health is good.*
2 including most people or situations: **in general** *In general, women are paid less.* | *The gardens are open to* **the general public** (=most ordinary people). | **As a general rule**, *I pay in cash.* | *The drug is not yet available for* **general use**.
3 [only before noun] not limited to one subject or type: *a* **general knowledge** *quiz* | *Watford* **General Hospital**
4 used in the job title of someone who has complete responsibility for a particular area of work: *the* **general manager**

general², **General** *n* [C] an officer with a high rank in an army or air force

ˌgeneral anaesˈthetic *BrE*, **general anesthetic** *AmE* *n* [C,U] a substance used to make a patient who is having an operation unconscious so that they do not feel anything

ˌgeneral eˈlection *n* [C] an election in which all the voters in a country elect a new government

generalization (*also* **-isation** *BrE*) /ˌdʒenərəlaɪˈzeɪʃən $ -lə-/ *n* [C] *disapproving* a statement that may be true for some people or situations, but that is not true for all of them: **sweeping/broad generalization** *Don't* **make** *sweeping* **generalizations**. —**generalize** /ˈdʒenərəlaɪz/ *v* [I]

generally /ˈdʒenərəli/ *adv*
1 considering something as a whole, rather than its details: *The arrangements have generally worked well.* | **Generally speaking**, *cars are cheaper in Europe.* **2** by or to most people: *It's* **generally accepted** *that the story is true.*
3 usually: *I generally get to work early.*

ˌgeneral pracˈtitioner *n* [C] a GP

ˌgeneral ˈstrike *n* [C] a situation when most of the workers in a country refuse to work

generate Ac /ˈdʒenəreɪt/ *v* [T] **1** to make something happen or start to exist: *Our discussion generated a lot of ideas.* | *Tourism* **generates** *a lot of* **income** *for the town.* **2** to produce energy, power, heat etc **THESAURUS MAKE**

generation Ac /ˌdʒenəˈreɪʃən/ *n*
1 [C also + plural verb *BrE*] all the people in a society or family who are about the same age: **[+of]** *Three generations of the Lambe family have lived here.* | **younger/older generation** *The younger generation know more about computers than their parents.* | **first-generation/second-generation etc** (=being a member of the first people to live or be born in a particular country) *first-generation immigrant families* | *Our generation has never known a war.*

G

2 [C] the average period of time between your birth and the birth of your children: *A generation ago, no one had home computers.* | *Some families have lived here for generations.*

3 [C] machines that are at the same stage of development: **[+of]** *a new generation of cell phones* | *first-generation nuclear reactors* (=the first ones built or made)

4 [U] the process of producing power or energy: **[+of]** *the generation of solar power*

,gene'ration ,gap *n* [singular] a lack of understanding between older and younger people

generator /'dʒenəreɪtə $ -ər/ *n* [C] a machine that produces electricity

generic /dʒə'nerɪk/ *adj* **1** relating to a whole group of similar things, rather than just one of them **2** a generic product does not have a BRAND NAME (=a name showing it is made by a particular company) —**generically** /-kli/ *adv*

generosity /,dʒenə'rɒsəti $ -'rɑː-/ *n* [U] a generous attitude, or generous behaviour: **[+to/towards]** *I never forgot the generosity he showed to my parents.*

generous /'dʒenərəs/ *adj*

1 someone who is generous is kind and enjoys giving people things or helping them **OPP** mean: **[+to/towards]** *Billy was extraordinarily generous to his friends.* | **[+with]** *Jim is always generous with his time* (=is willing to spend time helping people). | *It was generous of you to offer to help.* | **generous offer/gesture/donation etc** *a very generous gift* **THESAURUS** KIND

2 more than the usual amount: **generous amount/helping/portion etc** *a generous slice of cake* —**generously** *adv*: *Please give generously to Cancer Research.*

genesis /'dʒenɪsɪs/ *n* [singular] *formal* the beginning of something

genetic /dʒə'netɪk/ *adj* relating to GENES or GENETICS: *genetic research* | *genetic defects* —**genetically** /-kli/ *adv*

ge,netically 'modified *adj* (*abbreviation* **GM**) genetically modified food, crops etc have been changed so that their GENE structure is different from the one they have naturally

ge,netic engin'eering *n* [U] the science of changing the GENES of a living thing

ge,netic 'fingerprinting *n* [U] the process of examining the pattern of someone's GENES, for example to find out whether blood, hair etc found where a crime was committed is theirs **SYN** DNA fingerprinting

genetics /dʒə'netɪks/ *n* [U] the study of how GENES affect the development of living things —**geneticist** /-tɪsɪst/ *n* [C]

genial /'dʒiːniəl/ *adj* friendly, happy, and kind —**geniality** /,dʒiːni'æləti/ *n* [U] —**genially** *adv*

genie /'dʒiːni/ *n* [C] a magical creature in old Arabian stories that will do what you want when you call it

genitals /'dʒenətlz/ (*also* **genitalia** /,dʒenə'teɪliə/) *n* [plural] *formal* the sex organs that are outside your body —**genital** *adj* [only before noun]

genius /'dʒiːniəs/ *n* **1** [C] someone who has an unusually high level of intelligence, ability, or skill in a particular subject: **musical/artistic etc genius** *Newton was a mathematical genius.* **THESAURUS** SKILL

2 [U] very great and unusual intelligence, ability, or skill: *a work of pure genius* | *Only a man of genius could have thought of that.* | *His solution to the problem was a stroke of genius* (=a very clever idea).

genocide /'dʒenəsaɪd/ *n* [U] the murder of a whole race of people

genome /'dʒiːnəʊm $ -noʊm/ *n* [C] *technical* all the GENES in one cell of a living thing: *the human genome*

genre /'ʒɒnrə $ 'ʒɑːnrə/ *n* [C] *formal* a type of art, music, literature etc that has a particular style or feature: *a fashionable literary genre*

gent /dʒent/ *n* [C] *BrE informal* **1** a gentleman **2 the gents** a public toilet for men **SYN** men's room *AmE*

genteel /dʒen'tiːl/ *adj* polite in a way that was typical of people in the past who had a high social position

gentle /'dʒentl/ *adj*

1 kind and careful not to hurt anyone or anything **OPP** rough: *Arnold is a gentle, caring person.* | **gentle voice/smile**

2 not strong, extreme, or violent: **gentle exercise/walk etc** *We broke into a gentle run.* | *Melt the butter over a gentle heat.* | *a gentle breeze* —**gentleness** *n* [U] —**gently** *adv*: *a gently sloping hill*

Word Choice: gentle, kind, or helpful?

If you are **gentle**, you are careful not to hurt or upset people: *Be gentle with the baby.*

If you are **kind**, you behave in a way that shows you care about people and want to help them: *The family were very kind and offered to let me stay in their home.*

If you are **helpful**, you give someone good advice and help them to do something: *My new teachers were very helpful.* Do not use **gentle** in this meaning. Do not say 'My new teachers were very gentle.'

---

gentleman /'dʒentlmən/ *n* [C] (*plural* **gentlemen** /-mən/)

1 a polite word used for a man you do not know → **lady**: *Good evening, ladies and gentlemen* (=used to begin a speech). **THESAURUS** MAN

2 a man who is polite and behaves well → **lady**: *Roy is a perfect gentleman.* —**gentlemanly** *adj*

gentrification /,dʒentrɪfɪ'keɪʃən/ *n* [U] when a poor area improves after people who have money move there

gentry /'dʒentri/ *n* [plural] *old-fashioned* people of a high social class

genuine /'dʒenjuɪn/ *adj*

1 if something is genuine, it really is what it seems to be: *genuine diamonds*

2 a genuine feeling or desire is one that you really feel, not one that you pretend to feel **SYN** sincere: *There was genuine affection in his voice.* | *The killer showed genuine remorse.* | *Her enthusiasm seemed quite genuine.*

3 *approving* someone who is genuine is honest and sincere OPP **false**: *She's a charming girl, and far more genuine than her sister.* —**genuinely** *adv*

THESAURUS

genuine if something is genuine, it really is what it seems to be – used especially about valuable things: *Is this painting a genuine Van Gogh?* | *The pearls were genuine.*

real not false or artificial: *Is that his real name?* | *The ceilings were decorated with real gold.* | *Are those flowers real or artificial?*

authentic correct for the style of a particular country or period in history – used about food, clothes, music etc: *The restaurant serves authentic Indian food.* | *an authentic 19th-century design*

true having the good qualities that a particular type of person or thing should have: *She's a true friend.*

---

genus /'dʒiːnəs, 'dʒen-/ *n* [C] (*plural* **genera** /'dʒenərə/) *technical* a group of animals or plants of the same general type → **species**

geography /dʒi'ɒgrəfi, 'dʒɒg- $ dʒi'ɑːg-/ *n* [U] the study of the countries, oceans, cities, populations etc of the world or of a particular area: **[+of]** *the geography of Asia* —**geographer** *n* [C] —**geographical** /ˌdʒiːə'græfɪkəl◂/, **geographic** *adj*

geology /dʒi'ɒlədʒi $ -'ɑːl-/ *n* [U] the study of rocks, soil, minerals etc, and how they have changed over time —**geologist** *n* [C] —**geological** /ˌdʒiːə'lɒdʒɪkəl $ -'lɑː-/ *adj*

geometric /ˌdʒiːə'metrɪk◂/ (*also* **geometrical** /-trɪkəl/) *adj* **1** having a regular pattern of shapes and lines **2** relating to geometry

geometry /dʒi'ɒmətri $ -'ɑːm-/ *n* [U] the mathematical study of angles, shapes, lines etc

Georgian /'dʒɔːdʒən, -dʒiən $ 'dʒɔːrdʒən/ *adj* Georgian buildings, furniture etc were built or made in Britain in the 18th century

geranium /dʒə'reɪniəm/ *n* [C] a plant with red, pink, or white flowers and round leaves → see picture at **FLOWER¹**

geriatric /ˌdʒeri'ætrɪk◂/ *adj* [only before noun] relating to the medical care of old people: *geriatric medicine*

germ /dʒɜːm $ dʒɜːrm/ *n*
1 [C usually plural] a very small living thing that can make you ill SYN **bacteria**: *Sneezing spreads germs.* | *Kitchen cloths can harbour (=contain) germs.* | *fears of germ warfare (=the use of germs to harm or kill people in a war)*
2 [C usually singular] the early stages of something or a very small amount of an idea, feeling etc: **germ of an idea/theory etc** *The germ of the idea goes back to Ancient Rome.* | *There's a **germ of truth** in what he says.*

German measles /ˌdʒɜːmən 'miːzəlz $ ˌdʒɜːr-/ *n* [U] RUBELLA

germinate /'dʒɜːməneɪt $ 'dʒɜːr-/ *v* **1** [I,T] if a seed germinates, or if it is germinated, it begins to grow
2 [I] if an idea or feeling germinates, it starts to

develop —**germination** /ˌdʒɜːmə'neɪʃən $ ˌdʒɜːr-/ *n* [U]

gerund /'dʒerənd/ *n* [C] *technical* a noun formed from the PRESENT PARTICIPLE of a verb, for example 'shopping' in the sentence 'I hate shopping.'

gestation /dʒe'steɪʃən/ *n* [U] *technical* the process during which a baby grows inside its mother's body

gesticulate /dʒe'stɪkjəleɪt/ *v* [I] to make movements with your arms and hands while speaking, usually because you are excited or angry

gesture¹ /'dʒestʃə $ -ər/ *n* [C] **1** a movement of your head, arm, or hand to express your feelings: **[+of]** *Jim raised his hand in a gesture of despair.* | *He's **making rude gestures** at us.* **2** something you do or say to show that you care about someone: **[+of]** *As a **gesture of goodwill**, the wine is free.* | *Sending flowers was a **nice gesture**.*

gesture² *v* [I] to move your head, arm, or hand in order to tell someone something: *Tom gestured for me to move.*

get /get/ *v* (*past tense* **got** /gɒt $ gɑːt/, *past participle* **got** *BrE*, **gotten** /'gɒtn $ 'gɑːtn/ *AmE*, *present participle* **getting**)
1 RECEIVE/OBTAIN [T] to receive, find, or buy something: **get sth from sb** *I got an email from Chris.* | **get sb sth** *Dad got him a job at the factory.* | **get sth for sb** *Could you get some information for me?* | **get sth from sb** *She got the jacket from a friend.* | **get sth for £5/$9 etc** *You can get a laptop for under £500.* | **get yourself sth** *He's gotten himself a new girlfriend already.* | **get £5/£45,000 etc** (=receive £5 etc as payment for something) *Hospital porters get £6.50 an hour.* | **get 90%/a good mark etc** (=receive 90% etc for a test, competition etc) *Who got the highest score?* THESAURUS **BUY**
2 BRING [T] to bring someone or something back from somewhere SYN **fetch**: **get sb sth** *Carrie, go and get me a towel.* | **get sth for sb** *He went to get cigarettes for his mom.* | **get sb/sth from sth** *I'll get the kids from school later.* THESAURUS **BRING**
3 EXPERIENCE [T] to experience something: **get pleasure/a shock/a surprise etc** | *I got the impression she didn't like me.*
4 BECOME [I, linking verb] to change to a new state, feeling, or situation SYN **become**: **get bored/angry/upset etc** *Children get bored very quickly.* | *Helen got drunk, as usual.* | **get cold/dark/late etc** *We should go – it's getting late.* | **get hurt/broken/stolen etc** | *I got lost in the wood.* | **get married/divorced/engaged** *When are you getting married?* | **get washed/dressed** *Isn't it time you got dressed?* THESAURUS **BECOME**
5 ARRIVE/GO [I] to arrive, go, or move somewhere: *When did you get home?* | **[+to]** *How do I get to the station?* | *They somehow had to get past the guards.* | *The thieves **got away** (=escaped).* | *Liam **got** slowly **to** his feet (=stood up).* THESAURUS **ARRIVE**
6 HAVE OPPORTUNITY **get to do sth** to have the opportunity to do something: *She's nice once you get to know her.* | *I never get a chance to see you anymore.*
7 BUS/TRAIN [T] if you get a bus, train etc, you travel on a bus etc: *Pete always gets the bus to work.*
8 ILLNESS [T] to begin to have an illness: **get a cold/the flu/cancer etc** *I think I'm getting a cold.*
9 START **get doing sth** to begin doing something:

get

We got talking about the old days. | **get going/moving** (=start doing something that you must do) *It's late, we'd better get going.*

10 UNDERSTAND [T] *informal* to understand or hear something: *Tracy didn't **get** the joke.* | *I just **don't get it** (=do not understand). | Sorry, I didn't quite get what you said.*

11 MOVE [T] to move something to a different position: **get sth into/through/across etc** *Father got his gun down from the shelf.*

12 PROGRESS [I] to reach a particular stage in a process successfully: *She didn't **get far** with her studies.* | *I'm **not getting anywhere** (=not progressing successfully) with this job.*

13 MAKE STH HAPPEN [T] to make something happen: **get sth to do sth** *I couldn't get the car to start.*

14 MAKE SB DO STH [T] to persuade or force someone to do something: **get sb to do sth** *We couldn't get him to agree.* THESAURUS PERSUADE

15 HAVE DONE [T] to arrange for someone to do a particular job: **get sth done/fixed etc** *We'll have to get the roof mended.*

16 PUNISHMENT [T] to receive a punishment: *He got ten years for robbery.*

17 MEAL [T] *informal* to prepare a meal: *Can I get you anything for lunch?*

18 PUNISH [T] *informal* to attack, hurt, or catch someone: *I'll get you for this!*

19 DOOR/TELEPHONE [T] *informal* to answer the door or telephone: *Can you **get the door** for me, please?*

THESAURUS

get to receive, find, or buy something: *Where did you get those jeans?* | *I got an email from her yesterday.*

obtain *formal* to get something, especially information or something that you need for a particular purpose: *The information can be obtained from any local government office.* | *We managed to obtain a copy of the agreement.*

acquire *formal* to get knowledge, skills, or something big or expensive: *The course will help you to acquire the skills you need to find a job.* | *The firm was acquired by a Dutch company.*

gain to get something, especially experience, knowledge, control, or an advantage. **Gain** is more formal than **get**: *I gained a lot of useful experience.* | *The island gained its independence in 1960.*

inherit to get money or property from someone after they die: *Jo inherited a lot of money from her mother.*

get hold of sth *informal* to get something that is difficult to find: *Where can I get hold of their address?*

PHRASAL VERBS

get about *BrE*
1 to move or travel to different places
2 if news or information gets about, many people hear about it

get across to be understood, or to make someone understand something: **[+to]** *The message isn't getting across to youngsters.* | **get sth ↔ across** *What's the best way to get your ideas across?*

get ahead to be successful in your job, work etc

get along if people get along, they have a friendly relationship: **[+with]** *Do you get along well with your colleagues?* THESAURUS FRIENDLY

get around
1 get around (sth) to go to different places
2 if news or information gets around, many people hear about it
3 get around sth to avoid something that will cause problems: *There are ways of getting around the law.* THESAURUS AVOID

get around to sth to do something you have been intending to do for a long time: *I must get around to writing some cards.*

get at sb/sth
1 to be able to reach something: *We took up the carpet to get at the wiring.*
2 be getting at sth to be trying to explain an idea: *Just what are you getting at?*
3 to discover information about something: *They were determined to **get at the truth**.*
4 *informal* to keep criticizing someone

get away *informal*
1 to leave a place: **[+from]** *I didn't get away from work until late.* | *I'd love to **get away from it all** (=leave your work, duties etc for a holiday).*
2 to escape from someone who is chasing you or trying to catch you: **[+from]** *He managed to get away from the attacker.* THESAURUS ESCAPE

get away with sth to not be caught or punished for something: *He'll cheat if he thinks he can get away with it.*

get back
1 to return to a place: *It's time we were getting back.* | **[+to]** *When did you get back to London?*
2 get sth ↔ back to have something again after you had lost it or given it to someone: *Did you get your purse back?*
3 get sb back (*also* **get back at sb**) to hurt someone because they have hurt you: **[+for]** *I'll get you back for this!*

get back to sb/sth
1 to return to a previous state, condition, or activity: *Life is beginning to **get back to normal**.*
2 *informal* to return a telephone call by speaking to the person who made the call THESAURUS ANSWER

get behind if you get behind with work or a regular payment, you fail to do the work or pay the money in time: **[+with]** *Whatever you do, don't get behind with your rent.*

get by to have only just enough of something to be able to do the things you need to do: **[+on]** *She gets by on just £80 a week.* | *I know enough Italian to get by.*

get sb/sth **down**
1 *informal* to make someone feel unhappy: *Her illness gets her down.*
2 get sth ↔ down to quickly write down what someone says or what you think: *Let me get down your address.*

get down to sth to start doing something that needs time or energy: *Isn't it time you got down to some work?* THESAURUS START

get in
1 to be allowed or able to go into a place: *I applied to college but didn't get in.*

2 when a train, bus etc gets in, it arrives: *My train gets in at 10.*

3 to arrive somewhere: *What time did you get in?*

4 to be elected: *Do you think Labour will get in again?*

get in on sth *informal* to become involved in something that other people are doing: *We began a delivery service and now others want to get in on the act.*

get into sth

1 to be accepted by an organization, team etc: *Do you think he'll get into the squad?*

2 to enter or arrive at a place

3 to start being involved in a situation: **get into trouble/debt/difficulties etc** | *He got into the habit of arriving late.*

4 *informal* to start being interested in something: *I got heavily into rap music.*

5 what's got into sb? *spoken* used to say that someone is behaving very differently from usual

get off

1 get (sb) off (sth) *informal* to leave a place, or to help someone leave: *It's time we got off.* | *What time do you get off work?* | **[+to]** *I must get the kids off to school.*

2 get sth off to send a letter, package etc

3 get sth off to remove a piece of clothing you are wearing: *You'd better get those wet shoes off.*

4 get (sb) off to receive little or no punishment for a crime, or to help someone do this: *He got off lightly* (=received a very small punishment). | **[+on]** *His attorney got him off on a technicality* (=using a legal detail).

5 *informal* to go to sleep: *I couldn't get off to sleep last night.*

6 get off to a good/bad start to begin something well or badly

7 get (sth) off (sb/sth) *informal* to stop touching something or someone: *Get your hands off me!*

get off with sb *BrE informal* to start a romantic relationship with someone

get on

1 *BrE* if people get on, they have a friendly relationship: **[+with]** *She doesn't get on with my mum very well.* THESAURUS FRIENDLY

2 to continue or make progress with a job, work etc: **[+with]** *Stop talking and get on with it!*

3 to be successful in your work, job etc

4 be getting on *informal* **a)** if time is getting on, it is quite late **b)** if someone is getting on, they are quite old THESAURUS OLD

5 be getting on for sth *BrE*, **be getting on toward sth** *AmE* almost a particular age, time, or amount: *Mrs McIntyre must be getting on for 90 by now.* THESAURUS ALMOST

get onto sb/sth

1 *informal* to write or speak to someone because you want them to help you: *We got onto the landlord about the damp.*

2 to be elected to a committee, political organization etc

3 to start talking about a particular subject: *How did we get onto the war?*

get out

1 get (sb) out to leave or escape from a place, or to help someone do this: **[+of]** *The Embassy advised tourists to get out of the country.* | *Firefighters tried to get them out.* THESAURUS ESCAPE

2 get sth ↔ out to take something from the place where it is kept or hidden: *He got out a knife and pointed it at me.*

3 if secret information gets out, people find out about it

get out of sth

1 to avoid doing something that you should do: **get out of doing sth** *I'm afraid I can't get out of going to the meeting.* THESAURUS AVOID

2 get sth out of sb to persuade someone to tell or give you something

3 get sth out of sth to enjoy an activity and feel you have gained something from it: **get sth out of doing sth** *Do you get a lot out of playing the violin?*

get over

1 get over sth to feel better after an illness or bad experience: *It takes weeks to get over the flu.* | *You feel bad now, but you'll get over it.*

2 get sth over (with) to finish something difficult or unpleasant: *I'll feel better when I've got the test over with.* THESAURUS FINISH

3 get sth ↔ over to succeed in making people understand your ideas: *You'll get your message over if you stick to the point.*

get round *BrE* → GET AROUND

get round to sth *BrE* → GET AROUND TO STH

get through

1 get through sth *informal* to use or deal with a particular amount of something: *I get through about 20 cigarettes a day.* | *I've got through a lot of work this month.*

2 get (sb) through sth to reach the end of an unpleasant experience, test etc, or to help someone do this: *Her love got me through the death of my son.*

3 to succeed in telephoning someone: *I tried phoning, but I couldn't get through.*

get (sth) through to sb to succeed in making someone understand you: *How can I get through to you that I love you?*

get to sb *informal* to upset someone

get together

1 if people get together, they meet in order to do something nice: *We must get together for a drink.*

2 get sth/sb ↔ together to bring or collect several things or people so that they are in one place: *He got some residents together to form an action group.*

3 get it/your life/yourself together to change the way you live so that you are better organized, happier etc

get up

1 get (sb) up to get out of your bed after sleeping, or to make someone do this: *Get me up at 8.*

2 to stand up THESAURUS STAND

get up to sth *informal* to do something that might be slightly bad: *What are the kids getting up to, I wonder?*

getaway /ˈɡetəweɪ/ *n* [C] an escape from a place after doing something wrong: *The gunmen made their getaway in a stolen car.*

get-to·geth·er *n* [C] an informal meeting or party: *a family get-together* THESAURUS PARTY

ghastly /ˈɡɑːstli $ ˈɡæstli/ *adj* very bad or unpleasant: *a ghastly mistake* | *a ghastly woman*

ghetto /ˈgetəʊ $ -toʊ/ n [C] (plural **ghettos** or **ghettoes**) a part of a city where poor people of a particular race or class live

ghost /gəʊst $ goʊst/ n [C] the SPIRIT of a dead person that people think they can see: **[+of]** *The ghost of Marie Antoinette haunts* (=often appears in) *the palace.* | *Do you believe in ghosts?* | *a scary ghost story* —**ghostly** adj

'ghost town n [C] a town that is empty because the people who lived there have left

ghostwriter /ˈgəʊstˌraɪtə $ ˈgoʊstˌraɪtər/ n [C] someone whose job is to write a book, speech etc for another person, who then presents it as their own work

ghoul /guːl/ n [C] an evil SPIRIT in films, stories etc that steals and eats dead bodies

ghoulish /ˈguːlɪʃ/ adj getting pleasure from death, accidents etc

GI /ˌdʒiː ˈaɪ/ n [C] a soldier in the US army

giant¹ /ˈdʒaɪənt/ adj [only before noun] much bigger than usual: *a giant TV screen*

giant² n [C] **1** a very tall strong man in stories **2** a very large successful company: *the music industry giant*

gibberish /ˈdʒɪbərɪʃ/ n [U] something that you write or say that has no meaning or is difficult to understand

gibe /dʒaɪb/ n another spelling of JIBE

giddy /ˈgɪdi/ adj feeling slightly sick and unable to stand up properly because everything seems to be spinning around SYN **dizzy**

gift /gɪft/ n [C]
1 something that you give to someone: *He thanked them for all their gifts.* | **[+of]** *a generous gift of £50* | **[+from]** *The watch was a gift from a friend.*
2 a natural ability to do something: **[+for]** *a gift for languages*

COLLOCATIONS

verbs

to give sb a gift *The students give their teachers gifts at the end of term.*
to buy sb a gift *Her husband did not often buy her gifts.*
to get/receive a gift *Every child will receive a small gift.*
to accept a gift *She wasn't sure whether to accept the gift.*
to exchange gifts (=to give each other a gift) *People exchange gifts at Christmas.*

types of gift

a birthday/wedding/Christmas gift *The bedspread was a wedding gift.*
a small gift *Please accept this small gift.*
an expensive gift *He gave his friends expensive gifts.*
a perfect/ideal gift *This book would make a perfect gift.*
a free gift (=something that a shop, company etc gives its customers) *The magazine came with a free gift.*

Word Choice: gift or present?
Gift sounds rather formal. In everyday English, you usually say **present** when talking about something that you give to someone for their birthday or on another special occasion: *I got a lot of presents for my birthday.*

---

gifted /ˈgɪftɪd/ adj having a natural ability to do one or more things extremely well: **gifted musician/artist/teacher etc** *She is a gifted poet.* | **gifted child** (=one who is extremely intelligent) **THESAURUS** INTELLIGENT

'gift ˌtoken BrE, **'gift ˌvoucher** BrE, **'gift cerˌtificate** AmE n [C] a special piece of paper that is worth a particular amount of money when it is exchanged for goods in a shop

'gift wrap v [T] to wrap a present with attractive coloured paper

gig /gɪg/ n [C] a concert at which musicians play popular music or JAZZ

gigabyte /ˈgɪgəbaɪt/ n [C] (written abbreviation **GB**, **Gb**) a unit for measuring computer information, equal to 1,024 MEGABYTES

gigantic /dʒaɪˈgæntɪk/ adj extremely big: *a gigantic skyscraper* **THESAURUS** BIG

giggle /ˈgɪgəl/ v [I] to laugh quickly in a high voice, especially because you are nervous or embarrassed **THESAURUS** LAUGH —**giggle** n [C]

gild /gɪld/ v [T] to cover the surface of something with a thin layer of gold or gold-coloured paint

gill /gɪl/ n [C] one of the organs on the sides of a fish, through which it breathes → see picture on page A3

gilt /gɪlt/ adj covered with a thin layer of gold or gold-coloured paint: *a gilt chair* —**gilt** n [U]

gimme /ˈgɪmi/ informal a way of saying 'give me': *Gimme the ball!*

gimmick /ˈgɪmɪk/ n [C] disapproving something unusual that is used to make people notice something: *advertising gimmicks* —**gimmicky** adj

gin /dʒɪn/ n [C,U] a strong clear alcoholic drink made from grain

ginger¹ /ˈdʒɪndʒə $ -ər/ n [U] a light brown root with a strong hot taste that is used in cooking

GINGER

ginger² adj BrE hair or fur that is ginger is bright orange-brown in colour: *a ginger cat*

gingerly /ˈdʒɪndʒəli $ -ər-/ adv if you do something gingerly, you do it in a slow careful way, because you are afraid it will be dangerous or painful: *Jack lowered himself gingerly onto the bed.*

gipsy /ˈdʒɪpsi/ n a British spelling of GYPSY

giraffe /dʒəˈrɑːf $ -ˈræf/ n [C] a tall African animal with a very long neck and legs and dark spots on its yellow-brown fur → see picture on page A3

girder /'gɜːdə $ 'gɜːrdər/ *n* [C] an iron or steel beam that supports a floor, roof, or bridge

girdle /'gɜːdl $ 'gɜːr-/ *n* [C] a piece of women's underwear that fits tightly around the waist and HIPS

girl /gɜːl $ gɜːrl/ *n* [C]
1 a female child → **boy**: *Both boys and girls can join the choir.* | *a teenage girl* | **five-year-old girl/girl of ten etc** *The patient was a girl of twelve.* **THESAURUS** **WOMAN**
2 a daughter → **boy**: *Karen has two boys and a **little girl*** (=young daughter).
3 a young woman: *Steve's married to a Dutch girl.*
4 the girls *informal* a woman's female friends → **the lads**: *I'm going out with the girls tonight.* —**girlish** *adj*: *a peal of girlish laughter* → **PAPER GIRL**

girlfriend /'gɜːlfrend $ 'gɜːrl-/ *n* [C]
1 a girl or woman with whom you have a romantic relationship: *Do you **have** a **girlfriend**?*
2 *especially AmE* a woman's or girl's female friend

girlhood /'gɜːlhʊd $ 'gɜːrl-/ *n* [U] the period of her life when a woman is a girl

girth /gɜːθ $ gɜːrθ/ *n* [C,U] the distance around something that is big and round: *the girth of the tree's trunk*

gist /dʒɪst/ *n* **the gist** the main idea and meaning of what someone has said or written: **[+of]** *The gist of his argument is that full employment is impossible.*

give¹ /gɪv/ *v* (*past tense* **gave** /geɪv/, *past participle* **given** /'gɪvən/)
1 [I,T] to let someone have something as a present, or to provide something for someone: **give sb sth** *What did Bob give you for your birthday?* | *Researchers were given a grant to continue their work.* | *I've got some jewellery that my grandmother gave me.* | **give sth to sb** *a ring which was given to him by his mother* | *Most people are willing to **give to charity**.*

> **Grammar**
> Do not say 'He gave to me the book.' Say *He gave me the book.* or *He gave the book to me.*

2 [T] to put something in someone's hand: **give sb sth** *Give me the letter, please.* | **give sth to sb** *He poured a cup of coffee and gave it to her.* | *She gave a spare key to her neighbour.*
3 [T] to allow or make it possible for someone to do something: **give sb sth** *He **gave** us **permission** to leave.* | *Everyone will be **given a chance** to speak.* | *I asked him to **give** me more **time** to finish my essay.* | *Women were given the vote in the early 1900s.* | **give sth to sb** *This bill will give more power to local authorities.*
4 [T] to tell someone information or details about something, or tell someone to do something: *Let me **give** you some **advice**.* | **give orders/instructions** *They were given orders not to tell anyone.* | *Can you **give** me **directions** to the station* (=tell me how to get there)? | *He gives us jobs to do around the house.* | **give an account/description** *Today's newspaper gives an account of the murder.* **THESAURUS** **ORDER**
5 [T] to perform an action: *Don't move until I give the signal.* | **give a speech/performance etc** *He's giving a talk on early Roman pottery.* | **give sb sth** *Joel gave me a smile as I walked in.* | **give sb a call** (*also* **give sb a ring** *BrE*) (=telephone someone) *Give me a call around 8:00.* **THESAURUS** **DO**
6 [T] to make someone have or feel something: **give sb sth** *He **gave** us quite a **shock**.* | *That noise is **giving** me a **headache**.* | *The course has **given** me more confidence.* | **give sb problems/troubles/difficulties** *The new software has been giving us problems.* | **give sth to sb** *Their music has given a lot of pleasure to people.*
7 [T] to pay a particular amount of money for something: **give sb sth for sth** *They gave us £700 for our old car.*
8 give (sb) an impression/sense etc to make someone think about something in a particular way: *I didn't want to give him the wrong idea about the job.*
9 give a party to organize a party: *We're giving a small party for Dad's birthday next week.*
10 give sth thought/attention/consideration etc to spend some time thinking about something carefully: *I'll give the matter some thought.* **THESAURUS** **THINK**
11 [I] if something gives, it bends or stretches when pressure or weight is put on it: *The leather will give slightly as you wear the boots.*
PHRASES
give sb a hand *spoken* to help someone: **[+with]** *Can I give you a hand with that bag?*
give way 1 if a structure gives way, it falls down because it cannot support the weight on it: *The bridge gave way under the weight of the lorry.* **2** to stop or slow down when driving, in order to allow other vehicles to go first **SYN yield** *AmE*: *At the junction, you have to give way to traffic on the main road.* **3** to be replaced by something: **[+to]** *My sadness soon gave way to anger.*
not give sth another/a second thought to not think or worry about something: *The matter didn't seem important and I hardly gave it a second thought.*

THESAURUS

give to let someone have something as a present, or to provide something for someone to use: *Rob gave me a book I wanted.* | *Could you give me their address?*

hand sth out to give something to each of the people in a group: *The teacher handed out the test papers.*

present to give something to someone by putting it in their hands at a formal occasion in front of other people: *The class presented her with some beautiful flowers.* | *Who is going to present the awards?*

award to give someone a prize, medal, grade etc: *Mark entered the competition and was awarded a silver medal.*

donate to give something in order to help people. You donate money to CHARITY. You also donate your blood or part of your body to save someone's life: *They will donate some of their profits to Cancer Research.*

contribute to give money, help, ideas etc to something that a group of people are doing: *We're thinking of buying her a leaving present. Would you like to contribute?*

G

leave to officially arrange for someone to have something that you own after you die: *She left most of her money to her children.*

PHRASAL VERBS

give sb/sth **away**

1 give sth ↔ **away** to give something you own to someone without asking for money: [+to] *Give your old clothes away to charity.* | *We're giving away a free diary with tomorrow's paper.*

2 to show or say something about someone that should be kept secret → **giveaway**: *Don't worry, I won't give you away.* | *The look on his face gave the game away* (=showed something he wanted to keep secret).

give (sb) sth ↔ **back** to return something to its owner: *You'll have to give the money back.* | *I have to give Rick his car back by 3.00.*

give in

1 to finally agree to do something that you did not want to do: *Eventually I gave in and said yes.* | [+to] *The government refused to give in to the union's demands.*

2 to accept that you have lost a fight, game etc: *The rebels were eventually forced to give in.*

3 give sth ↔ **in** *BrE* to give something such as an official paper or a piece of work to someone: *You were supposed to give in this work yesterday.*

give off sth to produce a smell, light, heat etc: *The burning wood gave off a sweet smell.*

give out

1 give sth ↔ **out** to give something to each person in a group: *Can you give the drinks out, please?* | [+to] *Students were giving out leaflets to everyone in the street.*

2 to stop working correctly: *My voice gave out halfway through the song.*

give up

1 give sth ↔ **up** to stop doing something, especially something that you do regularly: *Why don't you give up smoking?* | **give up doing sth** *I gave up going to the theatre after that.* **THESAURUS** STOP

2 to stop trying to do something: *You shouldn't give up so easily.* | **give** sth ↔ **up** *She has still not given up the search.*

3 give yourself/sb up to allow yourself or someone else to be caught by the police or enemy soldiers: [+to] *In the end, his family gave him up to the police.*

give up on sb/sth to stop hoping that someone or something will change or improve: *At that point, I hadn't completely given up on the marriage.*

give² *n* [U] the ability of a material to bend or stretch when it is under pressure

give and take *n* [U] if there is give and take between two people, each person agrees to do some of the things that the other person wants: *In any relationship, there has to be some give and take.*

giveaway¹ /ˈɡɪvəweɪ/ *n* **be a giveaway** to make it easy to guess something: *His glazed eyes are a dead giveaway* (=make it very easy to guess) *that he's been taking drugs.*

giveaway² *adj* [only before noun] giveaway prices are extremely cheap

given¹ /ˈɡɪvən/ *v* the past participle of GIVE

given² *adj* **any given day/time/situation etc** any particular day, time, situation etc: *They could arrive at any given moment.* | *In any given situation, there will be winners and losers.*

given³ *prep* taking something into account: *Given the circumstances, you've coped well.*

given name *n* [C] *AmE* someone's FIRST NAME **THESAURUS** NAME

glacier /ˈɡlæsiə $ ˈɡleɪʃər/ *n* [C] a large mass of ice that moves slowly down a mountain valley —**glacial** /ˈɡleɪʃəl/ *adj*

glad /ɡlæd/ *adj*

1 [not before noun] pleased and happy about something: *'I've decided to accept his offer.' 'I'm glad.'* | **glad to do sth** *I'm glad to be back home.* | [+(that)] *We're so glad you came.* | [+when] *I'll be glad when the conference is over.* **THESAURUS** HAPPY

2 be glad of sth to be grateful for something: *Thanks, I'll be glad of the help.* | **be glad of the opportunity/chance/excuse to do sth** *They were glad of the chance to get some sleep.*

3 be glad to do sth to be willing and eager to do something: *We'd be glad to send you any information you need.*

glade /ɡleɪd/ *n* [C] *literary* a small open space in a wood or forest

gladiator /ˈɡlædieɪtə $ -ər/ *n* [C] a man who had to fight other men or animals as entertainment in ancient Rome

gladly /ˈɡlædli/ *adv* used to say politely that you are willing to do something: *She said she'd gladly pay for any damages.*

glamorize (*also* **-ise** *BrE*) /ˈɡlæməraɪz/ *v* [T] to make something appear more attractive than it really is: *TV has been accused of glamorizing crime.*

glamorous /ˈɡlæmərəs/ *adj* attractive, exciting, and related to wealth or success

glamour *BrE*, **glamor** *AmE* /ˈɡlæmə $ -ər/ *n* [U] the attractive and exciting quality of being connected with wealth and success: [+of] *the glamour of television*

glance¹ /ɡlɑːns $ ɡlæns/ *v* [I] **1** to look at someone or something for a short time: [+at/up/down etc] *I glanced at my watch.* | *Emily glanced over her shoulder.* **THESAURUS** LOOK **2** to read something very quickly: [+at/through etc] *Can you glance through these figures for me?*

glance² *n* [C] a quick look: *Jim gave him a quick glance and smiled.*

PHRASES

at a glance if you know something at a glance, you know it as soon as you see it: *Beth saw at a glance what had happened.*

glancing /ˈɡlɑːnsɪŋ $ ˈɡlæn-/ *adj* **glancing blow** a hit that partly misses so that it does not have its full force

gland /ɡlænd/ *n* [C] an organ in the body that produces a substance such as a HORMONE, SWEAT, or SALIVA —**glandular** /ˈɡlændjələ $ -dʒələr/ *adj*

glandular 'fever n [U] *BrE* an infectious illness that makes you feel weak and tired for a long time afterwards SYN **mono** *AmE*

glare¹ /gleə $ gler/ v [I] **1** to look angrily at someone or something for a long time: [+at] *She glared at him accusingly.* THESAURUS ► LOOK **2** to shine with a strong bright light that hurts your eyes: *The sun glared down on us.*

glare² n **1** [singular, U] a strong bright light that hurts your eyes: **the glare of sth** *the glare of the sun* **2** [C] a long angry look: *She gave him an icy glare.*

glaring /ˈgleərɪŋ $ ˈgler-/ adj **1** bad and very noticeable: *a glaring example of corruption* **2** too bright to look at: *a glaring light*

GLASSES

reading glasses

a glass

sunglasses

glass /glɑːs $ glæs/ n
1 [U] a hard transparent material that is used for making windows, bottles etc: *a glass bowl* | *a piece of broken glass* | **pane/sheet of glass** (=flat piece of glass with straight edges) *Double-glazed windows have two panes of glass.* → see picture at **MATERIAL¹**
2 [C] a container made of glass used for drinking, or the drink in it → **cup**: *I'll just fetch some wine glasses.* | [+of] *She poured me a glass of water.*
3 glasses [plural] two pieces of specially cut glass or plastic in a frame, which you wear in order to see more clearly SYN **spectacles**: *Tom wears glasses.*
4 [U] objects made of glass: *a collection of Venetian glass* → **MAGNIFYING GLASS, STAINED GLASS**

COLLOCATIONS - sense 3

verbs

to wear glasses *He has to wear glasses for reading.*

to have your glasses on *I didn't recognize him because I didn't have my glasses on.*

to put on your glasses *She put on her glasses to read the sign.*

to take off your glasses (*also* **to remove your glasses** *formal*) *He took off his glasses and wiped them again.*

noun + glasses

a pair of glasses *I need a new pair of glasses.*

glass 'ceiling n [singular] the fact that women are not given jobs at the highest level in a company

glass 'fibre n [U] FIBREGLASS

glasshouse /ˈglɑːshaʊs $ ˈglæs-/ n [C] *BrE* a glass building used for growing plants SYN **greenhouse**

glassware /ˈglɑːsweə $ ˈglæswer/ n [U] glass objects, especially ones used for drinking and eating

glassy /ˈglɑːsi $ ˈglæsi/ adj **1** smooth and shining, like glass: *the glassy surface of the lake* **2** glassy eyes show no feeling or understanding

glaze¹ /gleɪz/ v **1** (*also* **glaze over**) [I] if your eyes glaze over, they show no expression because you are bored or tired **2** [T] to cover clay pots, bowls etc with a thin liquid that gives them a shiny surface **3** [T] to put glass into a window frame —**glazed** adj

glaze² n [C] a liquid that is put on clay pots, bowls etc to give them a shiny surface

gleam¹ /gliːm/ v [I] **1** to shine softly and pleasantly: *The table was gleaming with wax polish.* THESAURUS ► SHINE **2** if your eyes or face gleam with a feeling, they show it: *His green eyes gleamed with pleasure.*

gleam² n [C] **1** a soft light: *a sudden gleam of light* **2** an emotion or expression that appears on someone's face for a short time: *She saw a gleam of amusement in his eyes.*

glean /gliːn/ v [T] to find out information slowly and with difficulty: **glean sth from sb** *We gleaned more information from other sources.*

glee /gliː/ n [U] a feeling of satisfaction and excitement: *The children laughed with glee.* —**gleeful** adj —**gleefully** adv

glen /glen/ n [C] a deep narrow valley in Scotland or Ireland

glib /glɪb/ adj disapproving said in a way that makes something sound simple, easy, or true when it is not: *Her answer sounded too glib.* —**glibly** adv

glide /glaɪd/ v [I] to move smoothly and quietly, as if without effort: [+across/over/down etc] *Couples glided over the dance floor.* —**glide** n [C]

glider /ˈglaɪdə $ -ər/ n [C] a light plane that flies without an engine

gliding /ˈglaɪdɪŋ/ n [U] the sport of flying a glider

glimmer¹ /ˈglɪmə $ -ər/ n [C] **1** a small sign of something such as hope or understanding: [+of] *a glimmer of hope* for the future **2** a light that is not very bright

glimmer² v [I] to shine with a light that is not very bright

glimpse¹ /glɪmps/ n [C] **1** a quick look at someone or something that does not allow you to see them clearly: [+of] *They caught a glimpse of a green car.* THESAURUS ► SEE **2** a short experience of something that helps you to understand it: *a glimpse into the future*

glimpse² v [T] to see someone or something for a moment without getting a complete view of them: *I glimpsed a figure at the window.*

glint /glɪnt/ v [I] **1** if a shiny surface glints, it gives out small flashes of light: *His white teeth glinted in his brown face.* **2** if your eyes glint with pleasure, anger etc, they show pleasure, anger etc —**glint** n [C]

glisten /ˈglɪsən/ v [I] to shine because of being wet or oily: **[+with]** *His back was glistening with sweat.*

glitch /glɪtʃ/ n [C] a small fault in a machine or piece of equipment that stops it working: *a computer glitch*

glitter¹ /ˈglɪtə $ -ər/ v [I] to shine brightly with flashing points of light: *The river glittered in the sunlight.*

glitter² n [U] **1** brightness consisting of many flashing points of light: *the glitter of her diamond ring* **2** the attractiveness and excitement connected with rich and famous people or places: *the glitter of Las Vegas*

glittering /ˈglɪtərɪŋ/ adj **1** glittering objects shine with small flashes of light: *glittering jewels* **2** successful and impressive: *a glittering career in motor racing* | *a glittering Hollywood premiere*

glitzy /ˈglɪtsi/ adj exciting and attractive because of being connected with rich, famous, and fashionable people —**glitz** n [U]

gloat /gləʊt $ gloʊt/ v [I] to show in an annoying way that you are proud of your success or someone else's failure: *Dick was still gloating over his team's win.*

global /ˈgləʊbəl $ ˈgloʊ-/ adj affecting or including the whole world: *the global economy* —**globally** adv

globalization Ac (*also* **-isation** *BrE*) /ˌgləʊbəlaɪˈzeɪʃən $ ˌgloʊbələ-/ n [U] when something such as a business operates or starts to operate in countries all over the world

global ˈwarming n [U] an increase in world temperatures, caused by an increase in CARBON DIOXIDE around the Earth

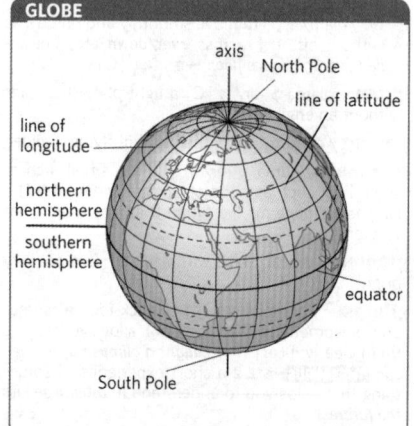

GLOBE

axis
North Pole
line of latitude
line of longitude
northern hemisphere
southern hemisphere
equator
South Pole

globe Ac /gləʊb $ gloʊb/ n **1** [C] a round object with a map of the Earth drawn on it **2 the globe** the

world: *Our company has offices all over the globe.* **3** [C] an object shaped like a ball

ˈglobe-ˌtrotting n [U] when someone spends a lot of time travelling to many different countries —**globe-trotting** adj

globule /ˈglɒbjuːl $ ˈglɑː-/ n [C] a small drop of a liquid or of a melted substance: *globules of fat*

gloom /gluːm/ n [singular, U] **1** *literary* almost complete darkness **2** a feeling of great sadness and lack of hope

gloomy /ˈgluːmi/ adj **1** making you feel that a situation will not improve: *The report paints a gloomy picture of the economy.* **2** sad because you think the situation will not improve: *the gloomy faces of the rescue workers* **THESAURUS** SAD **3** dark, especially in a way that seems sad: *a gloomy room with one small window* **THESAURUS** DARK —**gloomily** adv

glorified /ˈglɔːrɪfaɪd/ adj [only before noun] made to seem like something more important: *Many people still think of computers as glorified typewriters.*

glorify /ˈglɔːrɪfaɪ/ v [T] (**glorified, glorifying, glorifies**) **1** to make something seem more important or better than it really is: *films which glorify violence* **2** to praise someone, especially God —**glorification** /ˌglɔːrɪfɪˈkeɪʃən/ n [U]

glorious /ˈglɔːriəs/ adj **1** having or deserving praise and honour: *a glorious achievement* **2** very beautiful or impressive: *glorious views of the coast* —**gloriously** adv

glory¹ /ˈglɔːri/ n (*plural* **glories**) **1** [U] the importance, honour, and praise that people give someone they admire a lot: *The team finished the season covered in glory.* **2** [C] the things about a place or way of life which are beautiful or make people feel proud: *the glories of ancient Greece*

glory² v (**gloried, glorying, glories**)
PHRASAL VERBS
glory in sth to enjoy or be proud of something: *They gloried in their new freedom.*

gloss¹ /glɒs $ glɔːs, glɑːs/ n [singular, U] a bright shine on a surface: *a shampoo that adds gloss to your hair* | *gloss paint*

gloss² v [T] to give a short explanation for a difficult word or idea
PHRASAL VERBS
gloss over sth to avoid talking about something unpleasant, or to say as little as possible about it

glossary /ˈglɒsəri $ ˈglɔː-, ˈglɑː-/ n [C] (*plural* **glossaries**) a list of explanations of technical or unusual words, printed at the end of a book

glossy /ˈglɒsi $ ˈglɔːsi, ˈglɑːsi/ adj **1** shiny and smooth: *her glossy black hair* **2 glossy magazine/ brochure etc** a magazine etc that is printed on good-quality shiny paper, usually with lots of colour pictures

GLOVES

leather gloves

boxing gloves

mittens

oven mitts

rubber gloves

glove /glʌv/ n [C] a piece of clothing worn on your hand, with separate parts for the thumb and each finger: *a pair of gloves*

'glove com,partment n [C] a small cupboard in a car in front of the passenger seat

glow¹ /gləʊ $ gloʊ/ n [singular] **1** a soft steady light: **[+from]** *the glow from the dying fire* **2** the bright colour your face has when you exercise or are healthy **3 a glow of pleasure/pride/satisfaction etc** a strong feeling of pleasure, pride etc: *A glow of pride came over him.*

glow² v [I] **1** to shine with a soft steady light: *The red tip of his cigarette was glowing in the dark.* **THESAURUS** SHINE **2** if your face glows, it is bright or hot because you have been doing exercise, or are feeling a strong emotion: *She was **glowing with health**.* **3 glow with happiness/pride/pleasure etc** to show in your expression that you are very happy, proud etc: *She glowed with happiness.* | *Their young faces glowed with interest.*

glower /ˈglaʊə $ -ər/ v [I] to look at someone in an angry way: **[+at]** *Jill glowered at her husband but said nothing.*

glowing /ˈgləʊɪŋ $ ˈgloʊ-/ adj **glowing report/description etc** a report etc that praises someone or something

glucose /ˈgluːkəʊs $ -koʊs/ n [U] a natural form of sugar that exists in fruits

glue¹ /gluː/ n [C,U] a sticky substance used for joining things together: *Stick the ribbon on with glue.* → see picture at **CLASSROOM**

glue² v [T] (*present participle* **gluing** *or* **glueing**)
1 to join things together using glue: **glue sth (back) together** *Cut out the pieces and glue the edges together.*
2 be glued to sth *informal* to be looking at something with all your attention: *He was glued to the TV when the Olympics was on.*

glum /glʌm/ adj unhappy: *She looked glum.* | *a glum silence* —**glumly** adv

glut /glʌt/ n [C usually singular] a bigger supply of

something, especially a product or crop, than is needed **OPP** **shortage**: **[+of]** *a glut of oil on the world market*

glutinous /ˈgluːtɪnəs $ -tn-əs/ adj very sticky

glutton /ˈglʌtn/ n [C] someone who eats too much
PHRASES
glutton for punishment someone who seems to enjoy working very hard or doing something unpleasant: *Exercising again? You're a glutton for punishment!*

gluttony /ˈglʌtəni/ n [U] *formal* the bad habit of eating too much

gm a written abbreviation of **gram**

GM /ˌdʒiː ˈem/ adj *BrE* (**genetically modified**) GM crops have had their GENETIC structure changed

GMT /ˌdʒiː em ˈtiː/ n [U] (**Greenwich Mean Time**) the time as measured at Greenwich in London, used as an international standard for measuring time

gnarled /nɑːld $ nɑːrld/ adj rough and twisted: *a gnarled branch*

gnat /næt/ n [C] a small flying insect that bites

gnaw /nɔː $ nɒː/ v [I,T] to keep biting something hard: *A rat had gnawed a hole in the box.* | **[+at/on]** *a dog gnawing on a bone* **THESAURUS** BITE
PHRASAL VERBS
gnaw (away) at sb to make someone feel worried or anxious over a period of time: *Guilt had been gnawing at me all day.*

gnawing /ˈnɔːɪŋ $ ˈnɒː-/ adj [only before noun] making someone feel worry or pain for a long period of time: *gnawing doubts*

gnome /nəʊm $ noʊm/ n [C] a creature in children's stories like a little old man with a pointed hat

GNP /ˌdʒiː en ˈpiː/ n [U] (**Gross National Product**) the total value of all the goods and services produced in a country, usually in a single year → **GDP**

go¹ /gəʊ $ goʊ/ v (*past tense* **went** /went/, *past participle* **gone** /gɒn $ gɒːn/, *third person singular* **goes**)
1 [I] to leave somewhere and move or travel somewhere else → **come**: *Should I stay or go?* | *Where are you going?* | **[+to/into/inside etc]** *Mom went into the kitchen.* | *Let's go home.* **THESAURUS** LEAVE
2 [I,T] to travel: *It took an hour to go ten miles.* | *You're going too fast.* | **go by bus/plane/bike etc** *It's easier to go by train.* **THESAURUS** TRAVEL
3 [I] to move or travel somewhere in order to do something or be at an event: **go for a walk/drink/meal etc** *Shall we go for a swim?* | **go shopping/swimming/skiing etc** *Lucy and Paul have gone shopping.* | **go to do sth** *Mick's gone to buy a paper.* | **go (and) do sth** *Go see who's at the door.* | *He had a party but not many people went.* | **[+to]** *She goes to a lot of meetings.*
4 go flying/rushing/crashing etc to move somewhere in a particular way: *The ball went flying over my head.*
5 be going to do sth used to talk about what will happen or what someone intends to do in the future: *It's going to rain.* | *I'm going to tell him what you did.* **THESAURUS** INTEND

6 [I] to reach or lead to a particular place: **[+to/down etc]** *Does this road go to the airport?*

7 [linking verb] to become: *The company went bankrupt.* | **go bad/sour etc** *The milk has gone sour.* | **go grey/red/brown etc** *My hair's going grey.* | **go deaf/blind/mad etc** *I think she's going deaf.*
THESAURUS BECOME

8 [I] to happen or develop in a particular way: *How did your interview go?* | **go well/fine/wrong etc** *Everything started to go wrong.* | **how are things going?/how's it going?** (=used to ask about someone's life, work, or progress)

9 [I] to belong or fit in a particular place or position: **[+in/on]** *Dictionaries go on the bottom shelf.* | *It won't all go in one suitcase.*

10 [I] to be sent or passed on: **[+to/by/through etc]** *The e-mail went to everyone in the company.*

11 [linking verb] to be or remain in a particular state: **go unheard/unanswered/unnoticed etc** *Her cries for help went unheard.* | *Many people went hungry* (=did not have enough to eat) *during the war.*

12 [I] if a machine goes, it works: *My car won't go.*

13 [I,T] to make a sound: *The balloon went pop.* | *A bell goes at the end of break.*

14 [I] used when you are showing or describing what someone did or what something is like: *She went like this with her hand.* | *I can't remember how the story goes.*

15 [T] *spoken informal* to say something: *She went, 'Are you coming?' and I went, 'No.'*

16 [I] to disappear: *Has your headache gone yet?*

17 [I] to become weak or damaged, or stop working: *Dad's hearing is starting to go.* | *One of the lights has gone.*

18 [I] if money goes, it is spent: **[+on]** *Most of her money goes on rent.*

19 [I] if time goes, it passes: *The hours go so slowly at work.*

20 [I] to look or taste good together: *Pink and yellow just don't go.* | **[+with/together]** *This wine would go well with fish.* → NO-GO AREA

PHRASES

don't go doing sth *informal* used to tell someone not to do something: *Don't go making a mess.*

have gone and done sth *informal* used when you are annoyed by what someone has done: *He's gone and broken it!*

here/there sb goes again *informal* used when someone has annoyed you by doing something several times: *There you go again, blaming me!*

to go 1 still remaining: *Only two weeks to go before the holidays!* **2** used to say that you want to take food away from a restaurant to eat it: *I'll have large fries to go.*

Word Choice: have gone or have been?
If someone **has gone** somewhere, they are still there now: *He has gone to his sister's house* (=he is there now).
If someone **has been** somewhere, they have visited that place at some time in their life: *'Have you ever been to Tokyo?' 'Yes, I have.'*
You use **went** if you mention the time or date when someone visited a place: *I went there when I was six/last year/in 2004 etc.* Do not say *'I have been there when I was six/last year etc.'*

---

go to move or travel to another place: *She's gone to the bank.*

make your way to go somewhere slowly, carefully, or with difficulty: *I made my way to the front of the audience.*

head to go in a particular direction – used especially about ships, planes, cars etc: *The ship was heading for South America.*

proceed *formal* to go to a particular place – used especially in announcements telling people where to go: *Passengers for Miami should proceed to Gate 15.*

be off to sth *informal* to be going to go somewhere now or very soon – used to tell someone where you are going: *I'm off to school now – see you later!*

PHRASAL VERBS

go about sth to do something or begin doing something: *You're going about this the wrong way.* | **go about doing sth** *How do you go about finding work?*

go after sb/sth to try to catch someone or get something: *They both went after the same job.*

go against sb/sth
1 to be or do the opposite of what someone believes, wants, advises etc: *Lying to him goes against all my principles.*
2 if a decision, vote etc goes against you, you do not get the result that you wanted: *His lawyer is afraid the case will go against him.*

go ahead to happen or continue to do something as planned: *The railway strike looks likely to go ahead.* | **[+with]** *Are you going ahead with the conference?*

go along as you go along while doing something, without previous planning or preparation: *I made the story up as I went along.*

go along with sb/sth to agree with or support someone or something: *I'm happy to go along with your suggestion.*

go around (*also* **go round** *BrE*)
1 to behave or dress in a particular way: **go around doing sth** *You can't go around accusing people like that.* | **[+with/in etc]** *She goes around in a T-shirt all the time.*
2 if an illness or a piece of news is going around, it is being passed from one person to another: *There's a rumour going around that they're engaged.*
3 **go around with** sb/**go around together** to be friends and spend a lot of time with someone
4 **enough/plenty to go around** enough for everyone

go at sth to start to do something with a lot of energy: *She went at the task with enthusiasm.*

go away
1 to leave a place or a person: *Go away! Leave me alone!*
2 to spend some time away from home, especially on holiday: **[+for/to/on]** *We went away for the weekend.*
3 to disappear: *My headache still hasn't gone away.* | *Ignoring the problem won't make it go away.*
THESAURUS DISAPPEAR

go back
1 to return to a place: *We'd better go back.* | **[+to/into/inside]** *I'll never go back to my old school.*

2 to have started at some time in the past: *a tradition that goes back 200 years* | **[+to]** *The building goes back to Roman times.*

go back on sth **go back on your word/promise/decision etc** to not do what you have promised or agreed to do

go back to sth to start doing something again: *Go back to sleep!* | **go back to doing sth** *She went back to watching TV.*

go by

1 if time goes by, it passes: *Two weeks went by before Tony called.* | **As** the years **went by**, he forgot him.

2 go by sth to use information, rules etc to help you decide or judge something: *Going by her usual behaviour, she'll be back late.*

go down

1 DECREASE to become lower in level, amount etc: **[+to/by/from]** *The temperature went down to zero.* | **[+in]** *Computers have gone down in price.* THESAURUS DECREASE

2 JOKE/IDEA **go down well/badly etc** to get a good or bad reaction from people: *His jokes didn't go down very well.*

3 SHIP if a ship goes down, it sinks

4 PLANE if a plane goes down, it crashes

5 TYRE if something such as a tyre goes down, air comes out of it and it becomes soft

6 COMPUTER if a computer goes down, it stops working

7 SUN when the sun goes down, it goes below the HORIZON at the end of the day

go for sb/sth

1 to try to get or win something: *We're going for the gold medal.*

2 *BrE* to attack or criticize someone: *She went for him with a knife.*

3 to choose or prefer something or someone: *I'll go for the soup.*

4 that goes for/the same goes for sb/sth *spoken* used to say that something is also true about someone or something else THESAURUS CHOOSE

go in for sth

1 to take part in an examination or competition

2 to like doing something: *I've never gone in for gambling.*

go into sth

1 to start working in a particular profession: *He wants to go into teaching.*

2 to be spent or used in doing something: *Years of research went into this book.*

3 to describe or explain something thoroughly: *I don't want to go into details right now.*

go off

1 to leave in order to do something: *He went off to find Joe.*

2 to explode: *Suddenly a bomb went off.* THESAURUS EXPLODE

3 to make a loud noise: *My alarm clock didn't go off!*

4 go off sb/sth *BrE* to stop liking someone or something: *I've gone off coffee.* THESAURUS DISLIKE

5 to stop working: *All the lights went out.*

6 go off well/badly/perfectly etc to happen in a particular way

go off with sth to leave with something that belongs to someone else: *She's gone off with my pen.*

go on

1 to continue: *The meeting went on longer than expected.* | **go on doing sth** *We can't go on fighting like this!* | **[+with]** *He went on with his meal.* THESAURUS CONTINUE

2 to happen: *What's going on down there?*

3 to do something after finishing something else: **[+to]** *Shall we go on to the next topic?* | **go on to do sth** *She went on to become a successful surgeon.*

4 to continue speaking after you have stopped for a while: *'But,' he went on, 'it's not that simple.'*

5 *informal* to talk too much about something: *I got tired of him going on about all his problems.* THESAURUS TALK

6 *spoken* used to encourage someone to do something: *Go on, have some more.*

7 if time goes on, it passes: *As time went on, it got easier.*

go out

1 to leave your house, especially in order to enjoy yourself: *Are you going out tonight?* | **[+for/to]** *We went out for lunch.*

2 to have a romantic relationship with someone: *How long have you two been going out?* | **[+with]** *Lisa used to go out with Todd.*

3 to stop shining or burning: *All the lights went out.*

4 to be sent to a number of people: *A copy of the memo went out to all staff.*

5 to leave a competition because you have been defeated: *Our team went out in the first round.*

6 to stop being fashionable or used: *Hats like that went out years ago.*

7 when the TIDE goes out, the sea moves back from the land

go over sth to look at or repeat something carefully so that it is all correct or clear: *Let's go over your speech one more time.*

go round *BrE* → GO AROUND

go through

1 go through sth to have a difficult or upsetting experience: *She's just gone through a divorce.*

2 go through (sth) if a deal, agreement, or law goes through, it is officially accepted: *My loan application has finally gone through.* | *The law went through Parliament last year.*

3 go through sth to practise, read, or explain something carefully to make sure it is correct: *She went through my homework for me.*

4 go through sth to search a container or place: *A customs man went through my bags.*

5 go through sth to explain something carefully to make sure that people understand it: *Could you go through the instructions one more time?* THESAURUS EXPLAIN

go through with sth to do something you had planned or promised to do: *She couldn't go through with the wedding.*

go to sb/sth to be given to someone: *The Oscar went to Nicole Kidman.*

go under if a business goes under, it has serious problems and fails

go up

1 to increase in number or amount: *Unemployment went up again.* | **[+by/from/to]** *Fares have gone up by almost 50%.* THESAURUS INCREASE

2 to be built or put in place: *A lot of new houses have gone up.*

3 to explode or be destroyed by fire: *The entire factory went up in flames.*

go with sb/sth

1 to be included as part of something: *The car goes with the job.* | **go with doing sth** *the responsibilities that go with having a family*

2 to accept someone's idea or plan: *Let's go with John's original idea.*

go without

1 **go without (sth)** to not have something that you usually have: *She went without food for several days.*

2 **it goes without saying (that)** used to say that something is very obvious

go² *n* [C] (*plural* **goes**) **1** an attempt to do something: *'I can't get the lid off.' 'Here, let me have a go.'* | *Why not have a go at making your own pasta?* | **at/in one go** *She blew out all the candles in one go.*

2 *especially BrE* someone's turn to play in a game or to use something: *Whose go is it?* | *Can I have a go with the camera?* **THESAURUS** TRY

PHRASES

> **have a go at sb** *BrE informal* to criticize someone: *Mum had a go at me for not doing my homework.*
>
> **make a go of sth** to make something succeed, especially a business or marriage: *Nick was determined to make a go of the business.*
>
> **on the go 1** very busy: *I've been on the go all day.* **2** being used or worked on: *I've got two projects on the go.*

goad /gəʊd $ goʊd/ *v* [T] to make someone do something by annoying them until they do it: *Friends goaded him into asking her for a date.*

'go-ahead¹ *n* **give/get the go-ahead** to give or be given permission to start doing something: *We were given the go-ahead to start building.*

go-ahead² *adj BrE* a go-ahead company or person uses new methods and is eager to be successful

goal Ac /gəʊl $ goʊl/ *n* [C]

1 something that you hope to achieve in the future **SYN** aim: *Their goal is to be the number one team.* | **achieve/reach a goal** *They achieved their goal of a 50% increase in sales.* **THESAURUS** AIM

2 the area where a ball must go in order to score a point in games such as soccer or HOCKEY: *He managed to keep the ball out of the goal.* | *I was in goal* (=I was the goalkeeper).

3 the action of making the ball go into the goal, or the point scored by doing this: *Walcott scored a brilliant goal.* → see picture at **FOOTBALL** → **OWN GOAL**

goalie /'gəʊli $ 'goʊ-/ *n* [C] *informal* a goalkeeper

goalkeeper /'gəʊlˌkiːpə $ 'goʊlˌkiːpər/ (*also* **goaltender** /'gəʊlˌtendə $ 'goʊlˌtendər/ *AmE*) *n* [C] the player in a sports team whose job is to stop the ball going into their team's goal → see picture at **FOOTBALL**

goalpost /'gəʊlpəʊst $ 'goʊlpoʊst/ *n* [C usually plural] one of the two posts with a bar between them that form the sides of a GOAL in games such as football or HOCKEY → see picture at **FOOTBALL**

goat /gəʊt $ goʊt/ *n* [C] an animal with horns and long hair under its chin. Goats live on farms or wild in mountains.

goatee /gəʊ'tiː $ goʊ-/ *n* [C] a short BEARD on the end of a man's chin

gob /gɒb $ gɑːb/ *n* [C] *BrE informal* an impolite word for someone's mouth

gobble /'gɒbəl $ 'gɑː-/ (*also* **gobble up/down**) *v* [T] *informal* to eat something very quickly: *She gobbled up the whole pizza.*

gobbledygook, **gobbledegook** /'gɒbəldiguːk $ 'gɑːbəldɪgʊk, -guːk/ *n* [U] *informal disapproving* complicated language, especially in official documents, that ordinary people cannot understand

'go-between *n* [C] someone who takes messages between people who cannot meet or do not want to meet

goblet /'gɒblɪt $ 'gɑːb-/ *n* [C] a cup made of glass or metal, with a base and a stem but no handle

goblin /'gɒblɪn $ 'gɑːb-/ *n* [C] a small ugly creature in children's stories who tricks people

gobsmacked /'gɒbsmækt $ 'gɑːb-/ *adj BrE spoken informal* very surprised

'go-cart *n* another spelling of GO-KART

God, **god** /gɒd $ gɑːd/ *n*

1 God the BEING who Christians, Jews, and Muslims pray to, and who they believe created everything: *We asked God to protect us.*

2 [C] a male BEING who is believed to control some part of the world or to represent a particular quality → **goddess**: **[+of]** *Mars, the Roman god of war* → **thank God** at **THANK**

PHRASES

> **for God's sake** *spoken* used to emphasize what you are saying, when you are angry: *For God's sake, shut up!*
>
> **God forbid** *spoken* used to say that you hope that something does not happen: *God forbid that he should find out.*
>
> **God (only) knows** *spoken* **1** used to show that you are annoyed because you do not know or understand something: *God knows where she is now!* **2** used to emphasize what you are saying: *God knows I've tried.*
>
> **I swear/hope/wish to God** *spoken* used to emphasize a statement, hope, or wish: *I swear to God I didn't do it.*
>
> **sb thinks they're God's gift (to sb/sth)** *disapproving* used to say that someone thinks they are perfect in some way: *He thinks he's God's gift to women* (=he behaves as if women find him very attractive).

COLLOCATIONS

verbs

to believe in God *Do you believe in God?*

to pray to God *We have prayed to God for her recovery.*

to worship God (=to show love and respect for God) *They worship God in their own way.*

God exists *How can you prove that God exists?*

noun + God

belief/faith in God *When her son died, she lost her belief in God.*

the will of God (*also* God's will) (=what God wants to happen) *They believe it was God's will that they were on the island.*

a gift from God *I felt my baby was a gift from God.*

godchild /'gɒdtʃaɪld $ 'gɑ:d-/ n [C] (plural **godchildren** /-tʃɪldrən/) a child that a GODPARENT promises to help and to teach Christian values to

goddess /'gɒdɪs $ 'gɑ:-/ n [C] a female BEING who is believed to control some part of the world, or to represent a particular quality → **god**: [+of] *Venus, the Roman goddess of love*

godfather /'gɒd,fɑ:ðə $ 'gɑ:d,fɑ:ðər/ n [C] a male GODPARENT

godforsaken /'gɒdfəseɪkən $ 'gɑ:dfər-/ adj a godforsaken place is far from other places and has nothing interesting or cheerful in it

godmother /'gɒd,mʌðə $ 'gɑ:d,mʌðər/ n [C] a female GODPARENT

godparent /'gɒd,peərənt $ 'gɑ:d,per-/ n [C] someone who promises at a BAPTISM ceremony to help a child and to teach Christian values

godsend /'gɒdsend $ 'gɑ:d-/ n **be a godsend (for/to sb)** to be a good thing that happens when you really need it: *The rain has been a godsend for gardeners.*

go-'getter / $ '. ,.-/ n [C] someone who is likely to be successful because they are very determined

goggle-'eyed adj informal with your eyes wide open in surprise

goggles /'gɒgəlz $ 'gɑ:-/ n [plural] a pair of glasses that protect your eyes, with an edge that fits against your skin: *a pair of swimming goggles*

going¹ /'gəʊɪŋ $ 'goʊ-/ n [U] informal the difficulty or speed with which something is done: **be good/hard/slow etc going** *We got there in four hours, which is good going.* | *I'm finding this work hard going.*

PHRASES

while the going's good before a situation becomes difficult or impossible: *Let's get out while the going's good.*

going² adj [not before noun] available: *Are there any jobs going?* | **the best/biggest etc going** *We make the best computers going.*

PHRASES

a going concern a successful business: *The restaurant has developed into a going concern.*

the going rate (for sth) the usual amount you pay or receive for something: *£25 an hour is the going rate for private lessons.*

have a lot going for you to have many advantages and good qualities: *You're young and you're smart – you have a lot going for you.*

going-'over n [singular] **1** a thorough examination of something **2** when you clean something thoroughly: *My car needs a good going-over with a vacuum.*

goings-'on n [plural] informal events or activities that are strange, interesting, or illegal

'go-kart, **go-cart** n [C] a small car made of an open frame on four wheels, used in races

gold¹ /gəʊld $ goʊld/ n

1 [U] a valuable soft yellow metal, or things such as coins or jewellery made from this metal: **pure/solid gold** *His watch was solid gold.* | *She was wearing lots of gold.*

2 [C,U] the colour of gold: *a room painted in cream and gold*

3 [C] informal a GOLD MEDAL

gold² adj

1 made of gold: *a gold necklace*

2 having the colour of gold: *a gold dress*

golden /'gəʊldən $ 'goʊl-/ adj

1 having a bright yellow colour: *golden hair*

2 **golden age/years/days** a time of great happiness or success: *the golden age of film*

3 literary made of gold: *a golden crown*

PHRASES

golden anniversary (*also* golden wedding BrE) the date that is exactly 50 years after a wedding

golden boy/girl someone who is popular and successful: *She's Hollywood's current golden girl.*

golden opportunity a rare chance to get something valuable or to be very successful: *Don't miss this golden opportunity to make some cash.*

goldfish /'gəʊldfɪʃ $ 'goʊld-/ n [C] (plural **goldfish**) a small orange fish often kept as a pet

gold 'medal n [C] a prize, especially a round piece of gold, that is given to someone who wins a race or competition

goldmine /'gəʊldmaɪn $ 'goʊld-/ n [C] **1** informal a business or activity that produces large profits **2** a place where gold is dug out from under the ground

golf /gɒlf $ gɑ:lf, gɔ:lf/ n [U] a game in which players hit a small white ball into holes in the ground using a CLUB (=special stick): *Do you **play golf**?* —**golfer** n [C]

'golf club n [C] **1** a long stick that you use to hit the ball in a game of golf **2** a place where people can go to play golf

'golf course n [C] an area of land that golf is played on

gone¹ /gɒn $ gɔ:n/ v the past participle of GO

gone² adj **be gone a)** to no longer be in a place: *He waved and was gone.* **b)** to be dead or no longer exist: *The factory is gone now.*

gone³ prep BrE informal later than a particular time or older than a particular age: *It's gone midnight.* | *He's gone 60.*

gong /gɒŋ $ gɔ:ŋ, gɑ:ŋ/ n [C] a round piece of metal that you hit with a stick to make a loud sound

gonna /'gɒnə, gənə $ 'gɔ:nə, gənə/ informal a way of saying 'going to'. Some people consider this use to be incorrect: *I'm gonna try it.*

goo /gu:/ n [U] an unpleasantly sticky substance

good¹ /gʊd/ adj (comparative **better** /'betə $ -ər/, superlative **best** /best/)

1 OF A HIGH STANDARD/QUALITY of a high standard or quality: *a good hotel* | *a very good book*

2 NICE/ENJOYABLE pleasant or enjoyable: *Did you have a good holiday?* | *We had a really good time.* | *It's good to see you.* | *That's good news!*

3 SKILFUL able to do something well: *a good teacher* | *I'm not good enough to get into the team.* | **[+at]** *Gill's good at sports.* | **good at doing sth** *She's good at swimming.* | **[+with]** *He's very good with animals* (=able to deal with animals well).

> **Grammar**
> Do not say 'Mick's good in tennis.' Say *Mick's good at tennis*.

4 LIKELY TO SUCCEED likely to be successful: *That's a good idea.* | *What's the best way to do this?* | **good practice** (=a good way of doing something, which avoids problems) *It's good practice to save your files every few minutes.*

5 SUITABLE suitable or convenient: *Is this a good time to talk?* | **[+for]** *The beach is good for families.*

6 HAVING A GOOD EFFECT **be good for sb/sth** likely to improve someone's health or the condition of something: *Exercise is good for you.* | *products that are good for the environment*

7 WELL-BEHAVED a good child behaves well: *Hurry up, be a good boy.*

8 NICE kind and nice: *He's a good man.* | *It was good of you to come.*

9 LARGE large in amount or size: *a good harvest*

10 THOROUGH complete or thorough: *The car needs a good wash.* | *Take a good look.*

11 WHEN YOU ARE PLEASED spoken used when you are pleased about something: *'Tom's here.' 'Oh, good.'* | *Good. I'm glad that's finished.* → **a good deal** at DEAL¹

PHRASES

a good few/many quite a lot: *There were a good few people there.*

a good while quite a long time: *We had to wait a good while.*

as good as very nearly: *The job's as good as done.*

as good as new used when something looks in good condition, especially after it has been repaired: *The car looks as good as new.*

good for sb spoken used to say that you approve of something that someone has done: *'I'm getting married.' 'Good for you!'*

good grief/God/lord/heavens/gracious! spoken used to express surprise or anger: *Oh, good heavens! What happened to you?*

(that's a) good idea/point/question spoken used to say that someone has just said or suggested something interesting or important: *'I'll pick you up on the way there.' 'That's a good idea.'*

good job AmE spoken used to praise someone when you think they have done something well SYN **well done**

good luck spoken used to say that you hope that someone is successful: *Good luck with the new job!*

in good time BrE early enough to be ready for a particular time or event: *I arrived in good time.*

it's a good thing (*also* **it's a good job** BrE) spoken used when you are glad that something has happened: *It's a good thing I brought the map.* THESAURUS LUCKY

THESAURUS

good used about something that you like, enjoy, or think is of a high standard: *It's a really good book.* | *My French is not very good.*

nice good, pleasant, or enjoyable. Nice is very common in spoken English. In written English, it is better to use other words: *You look really nice.* | *Have a nice time!* | *It's such a nice day.*

wonderful extremely good: *a wonderful poem*

excellent extremely good – used especially when you are very pleased with something: *Sam's progress this term has been excellent.*

great/terrific/fantastic informal extremely good: *That was a great film.* | *Her cooking is fantastic.*

neat AmE informal good – used when you like something: *That's a really neat idea!* | *a neat little gadget*

attractive an attractive idea, offer, or suggestion seems good and you feel that you want to do it: *A day by the sea sounded like an attractive suggestion.*

fine fine food, drink, clothes etc are of good quality. Fine weather is sunny: *People come here to enjoy fine food and wines.* | *If it's fine tomorrow, we'll go for a walk.*

good² n [U] behaviour, attitudes, forces etc that are morally right: *the battle between good and evil* → GOODS

PHRASES

do some good/do sb good to have a useful effect: *It won't do any good arguing.* | *A rest would do you good.*

for good permanently: *Is he back home for good?* THESAURUS ALWAYS

for the good of sb/sth in order to help someone or improve a situation: *working for the good of the community* | *I'm doing this for your own good*

it's no good (doing sth) used to say that an action will not achieve what you want: *It's no good crying.*

no good/not much good/not any good 1 not useful or suitable: *One lesson's no good – you'll need more.* **2** of a low standard or level of ability: *The movie wasn't much good.* | **no good at (doing) sth** *I'm no good at math.*

what's the good of ... ?/what good is ... ? used to say that it is not worth doing or having something in a particular situation: *What's the good of a car if you can't drive?*

good ,after'noon used to say hello when greeting someone in the afternoon

> **Usage**
> In everyday English, people usually just say **Afternoon** to each other. **Good afternoon** sounds rather formal.

goodbye /gʊd'baɪ/ used when you are leaving someone, or when they are leaving: *Goodbye, Jo.* | *I just want to **say goodbye** to Pete.* | *We **said our goodbyes** (=said goodbye to everyone) and left.*

good 'evening used to say hello when greeting someone in the evening → **good night**

> **Usage**
> In everyday English, people usually just say **Evening** to each other. **Good evening** sounds rather formal.

,good-for-'nothing *adj* a good-for-nothing person is lazy and useless —**good-for-nothing** *n* [C]

,Good 'Friday *n* [C,U] the Friday before the Christian holiday of Easter, which Christians remember as the day Jesus Christ died

,good-'humoured *BrE*, good-humored *AmE adj* happy and friendly

goodie, goody /'gudi/ *n* [C] *BrE informal* a good person in a film or book **OPP** **baddie**

goodies /'gudiz/ *n* [plural] *informal* nice things, especially nice food: *a bag of goodies*

,good-'looking *adj* someone who is good-looking looks attractive **THESAURUS** BEAUTIFUL

good 'looks *n* [plural] the attractive appearance of someone's face

good 'morning used to say hello when greeting someone in the morning

> **Usage**
> In everyday English, people usually just say **Morning** to each other. **Good morning** sounds rather formal.

good-natured /ˌgud 'neɪtʃəd $ -ərd/ *adj* kind, helpful, and not easily made angry

goodness /'gudnəs/ *n* [U] **1 goodness (me)!/my goodness!** said when you are surprised **2** when someone or something is morally good: *No one can doubt his moral goodness.*

PHRASES

for goodness' sake said when you are annoyed: *For goodness' sake stop arguing!*

good 'night used to say goodbye at night, or when someone is going to bed → **good evening**

goods /gudz/ *n* [plural]
1 things that are produced in order to be sold: *The shop sells a wide range of goods.* | *How do we pay for the goods and services we need?*
2 stolen goods things that have been stolen: *He had hidden the stolen goods in a closet.*
3 *BrE* things that are carried by road, train etc **SYN** **freight**: *a goods train*

PHRASES

come up with the goods (*also* **deliver the goods**) *informal* to do what is needed or expected: *He promised so much but didn't deliver the goods.*

> **COLLOCATIONS**
> **types of goods**
>
> **electrical goods** *Second-hand electrical goods can be dangerous.*
> **household goods** *They sell a variety of household goods.*

consumer goods (=televisions, washing machines etc) *Prices of consumer goods have dropped.*
luxury goods *The government increased the tax on luxury goods.*

> **verbs**
>
> **to produce goods** *China produces more goods than any other country.*
> **to manufacture goods** *They manufacture high-quality goods.*
> **to import/export goods** *British goods were exported to Africa.*

goodwill /ˌgud'wɪl◂/ *n* [U] kind feelings between people: *We invited the neighbours as a gesture of goodwill.*

goody /'gudi/ *n* another spelling of GOODIE

'goody-,goody (*also* ,goody-'two-shoes *AmE*) *n* [C] (*plural* **goody-goodies**) a child who tries too hard to be good and helpful, in a way that others think is annoying

gooey /'guːi/ *adj informal* sticky and soft: *gooey cakes*

goof¹ /guːf/ (*also* **goof up**) *v* [I] *AmE informal* to make a silly mistake

PHRASAL VERBS
goof around *AmE informal* to spend time doing silly things
goof off *AmE informal* to waste time or avoid work

goof² *n* [C] *especially AmE informal* **1** a silly mistake **2** a silly person

goofy /'guːfi/ *adj informal* stupid or silly: *a goofy grin*

Google /'guːgəl/ *trademark* a SEARCH ENGINE (=computer program that helps you search for information on the Internet)

goop /guːp/ *n* [U] *AmE informal* a thick slightly sticky substance

goose /guːs/ *n* [C,U] (*plural* **geese** /giːs/) a bird like a large duck, or the meat from this bird: *roast goose* → see picture on page A3

gooseberry /'guzbəri, 'guːz-, 'guːs- $ 'guːsberi/ *n* [C] (*plural* **gooseberries**) a small round green fruit with a sour taste

PHRASES
play gooseberry *BrE informal* to be with two people who want to be alone and romantic together: *I don't want to play gooseberry at their romantic dinner.*

'goose ,pimples (*also* **goose bumps** *especially AmE*) *n* [plural] small raised spots on your skin that you get when you are cold or frightened

gore¹ /gɔː $ gɔːr/ *v* [T] if an animal gores someone, it wounds them with its horns

gore² *n* [U] *literary* thick dark blood from a wound

gorge¹ /gɔːdʒ $ gɔːrdʒ/ *n* [C] a deep narrow valley with steep sides

gorge² *v* **gorge yourself on sth** to eat something until you are too full to eat any more: *We gorged ourselves on cake.*

gorgeous /ˈgɔːdʒəs $ ˈgɔːr-/ *adj informal* **1** very beautiful or attractive: *He's gorgeous!* | *a gorgeous sunny day* **2** very pleasant or enjoyable

gorilla /gəˈrɪlə/ *n* [C] the largest kind of APE (=animal like a large monkey) → see picture at **APE**

gorse /gɔːs $ gɔːrs/ *n* [U] a bush with sharp points and yellow flowers

gory /ˈgɔːri/ *adj* involving a lot of violence and blood: *a gory film* **THESAURUS** ▶ **VIOLENT**

gosh /gɒʃ $ gɑːʃ/ *spoken informal* used when you are surprised

gosling /ˈgɒzlɪŋ $ ˈgɑːz-, ˈgɔːz-/ *n* [C] a very young GOOSE

gospel /ˈgɒspəl $ ˈgɑːs-/ *n* **1** [C] one of the four books in the Bible that tell the story of Christ's life **2 the gospel** the life of Christ and the ideas that he taught: *He travelled around **preaching the gospel** (*=telling people about it). **3** (*also* **gospel truth**) [U] something that is completely true: *Don't take what she says as gospel.* **4** (*also* **gospel music**) [U] a type of Christian music

gossip¹ /ˈgɒsɪp $ ˈgɑː-/ *n* **1** [U] informal talk about other people's behaviour and private lives: *She told me all **the latest gossip**.* **2** [C] someone who likes talking about other people's private lives

gossip² *v* [I] to talk about other people's behaviour and private lives: **[+about]** *People were gossiping about his wife.* **THESAURUS** ▶ **TALK**

ˈgossip ˌcolumn *n* [C] a regular article in a newspaper or magazine about the behaviour and private lives of famous people

got /gɒt $ gɑːt/ *v* the past tense and a past participle of GET

> **Usage**: got or have got?
> Do not say 'They got three children.' Say *They have got three children.*

gotta /ˈgɒtə $ ˈgɑːtə/ *informal* a way of saying 'have got to', 'has got to', 'have got a', or 'has got a'. Some people consider this use to be incorrect: *I gotta go.*

gotten /ˈgɒtn $ ˈgɑːtn/ *AmE* the past participle of GET

gouge /gaʊdʒ/ *v* [T] to make a deep hole or cut in the surface of something

PHRASAL VERBS

gouge sth ↔ **out** to remove something by making a deep hole or cut

gourmet¹ /ˈgʊəmeɪ $ ˈgʊr-, gʊrˈmeɪ/ *adj* [only before noun] relating to good food and drink: *a gourmet meal*

gourmet² *n* [C] someone who enjoys good food and wine

govern /ˈgʌvən $ -ərn/ *v*
1 [I,T] to legally control a country and make all the decisions about its laws, public services etc: *when the Belgians governed the Congo*
2 [T] if rules or principles govern a system or situation, they control how the system works or what happens: *the laws that govern the universe*

governess /ˈgʌvənəs $ -ər-/ *n* [C] a female teacher in the past, who lived with a rich family and taught their children at home

government /ˈgʌvəmənt, ˈgʌvənmənt $ ˈgʌvərn-/ *n*
1 (*also* **Government**) [C usually singular, also + plural verb *BrE*] the group of people who govern a country: *The Government is not doing enough.* | *The Government have promised to increase public expenditure.* | *the Chinese government*
2 [U] the process of governing a country: **in government** (=governing a country) *when the Conservatives were in government* | *the fight for democratic government*

COLLOCATIONS

verbs

to elect a government *A new government is elected every four years.*
a government comes to power (=it takes control of a country) *The economic situation has got worse since the government came to power.*
to overthrow/bring down a government (=to force it to lose power) *He was charged with plotting to overthrow the government.*

types of government

national government (=of the whole country) *The people elected a new national government.*
local government *She works in local government.*
federal government (=of the whole country, in a country such as the US) *The federal government has provided another $4 million.*
state government (=of a state) *The state government has introduced strict laws about pollution from cars.*
a left-wing/right-wing government *There was an attempt to overthrow the country's left-wing government.*
a military government *Pakistan was ruled by a military government.*

THESAURUS

government the people who govern a country: *The Indian government refused to sign the agreement.*
administration the government – used especially in American English about a government led by a president: *the US administration*
the authorities *formal* the people or organizations that are in charge of a country or area: *The authorities gave a warning to people to stay indoors.*
regime a government – used to show disapproval, especially because it was not elected fairly: *Most people opposed the regime.*
dictatorship a country that has a DICTATOR (=a leader with complete power who has not been elected): *Argentina was a military dictatorship until 1983.*

governor, Governor /ˈgʌvənə $ -vərnər/ *n* [C] the person in charge of an organization or place: **[+of]** *the Governor of Texas*

gown /gaʊn/ n [C] **1** a long dress that a woman wears on very formal occasions: *a wedding gown* **2** a long loose piece of clothing that you wear for a special ceremony: *a graduation gown*

GOWN

a graduation gown

GP /ˌdʒiː ˈpiː/ n [C] BrE (**general practitioner**) a doctor who treats all kinds of patients when they first become ill, and sends them to special doctors in hospitals if they have a serious illness **THESAURUS** DOCTOR

GPA /ˌdʒiː piː ˈeɪ/ n [C] AmE (**grade point average**) the average of a student's marks over a period of time

GPS /ˌdʒiː piː ˈes/ n [U] (**Global Positioning System**) a system that uses radio signals from SATELLITES to show your exact position on the Earth

grab¹ /græb/ v [T] (**grabbed, grabbing**)
1 to take hold of someone or something suddenly or violently: *He grabbed my bag and ran.* **THESAURUS** HOLD
2 informal to get some food or sleep quickly because you are busy: *Let's grab some lunch.*
3 grab a chance/opportunity informal to quickly take advantage of an opportunity: *Grab the opportunity to travel while you can.*
4 to get someone's attention: *That should grab her attention.* | *a story which has grabbed the headlines* (=has been reported in the newspapers)
PHRASAL VERBS
grab at/for sth to suddenly put out your hand to try to take hold of something

grab² n
PHRASES
make a grab for/at sth to suddenly try to take hold of something: *I made a grab for the gun.*
be up for grabs informal if something is up for grabs, it is available for anyone who wants to try to get it: *More than $1,000 in prizes is up for grabs.*

grace¹ /greɪs/ n [U]
1 SMOOTH MOVEMENT a smooth way of moving that appears natural, relaxed, and attractive: *the grace of a dancer*
2 POLITENESS polite and pleasant behaviour: *At least he had the grace to apologize.* | *Len accepted his defeat with good grace* (=willingly and cheerfully).
3 EXTRA TIME more time that is allowed to someone to finish a piece of work, pay a debt etc: **a week's/month's etc grace** *I got a few days' grace to finish my essay.*
4 PRAYER a short prayer that people say before a meal: *Who'll say grace?*

grace² v [T] formal to make a place or an object look more attractive: *the pictures that grace the walls*

PHRASES
grace us with your presence to come and spend time with a group of people – said humorously to emphasize how rarely someone does this: *Perhaps Amy will grace us with her presence for once.*

graceful /ˈgreɪsfəl/ adj
1 moving in a smooth and attractive way, or having an attractive shape: *a graceful movement* | *the graceful curve of the swan's neck*
2 behaving in a polite and pleasant way: *a graceful and quiet man* —**gracefully** adv: *She rose gracefully to her feet.*

gracious /ˈgreɪʃəs/ adj **1** polite, kind, and generous: *a gracious host* **2** comfortable and wealthy: *a gracious country lifestyle* **3 gracious (me)!/good gracious!/goodness gracious!** old-fashioned used to express surprise: *Gracious! What a thing to say!* —**graciously** adv

gradation /grəˈdeɪʃən/ n [C] formal a small change or difference between points on a scale: *gradations of colour*

grade¹ Ac /greɪd/ n [C]
1 LEVEL OF QUALITY a level of quality that a product, material etc has: *different grades of wood* | **high/low grade** *low grade farmland*
2 LEVEL OF JOB a level of job: *He joined the company on the bottom grade.*
3 MARK/SCORE a letter or number given by a teacher to show how good a student's work is: *I got a grade A in maths.*
4 YEAR AT SCHOOL one of the 12 years students are at school in the US, or the students in a particular year: *He's in third grade.*
PHRASES
make the grade to succeed or reach the necessary standard: *players who fail to make the grade*

grade² Ac v [T] **1** to say what level of a quality something has, or what standard it is: *All hotels are regularly checked and graded.* **2** especially AmE to give a mark to an examination paper or a piece of school work SYN **mark**: *The teacher hasn't graded the papers yet.*

grade crossing n [C] AmE a place where a road and railway cross each other SYN **level crossing** BrE

grade point average n [C] AmE → **GPA**

grade school n [C] AmE an ELEMENTARY SCHOOL

gradient /ˈgreɪdiənt/ n [C] a slope in a road or railway: *a steep gradient*

gradual /ˈgrædʒuəl/ adj happening slowly over a long period of time OPP **sudden**: *a gradual increase in price*

gradually /ˈgrædʒuəli/ adv slowly, over a long period of time OPP **suddenly**: *Gradually, she grew calmer.* | *The truth is gradually emerging.* **THESAURUS** SLOWLY

graduate¹ /ˈgrædʒuət/ n [C]
1 someone who has completed a university degree → **undergraduate, postgraduate**: [+of] *a graduate of Leeds University* | *a history graduate*
2 AmE someone who has completed a course at a college, school etc: *high-school graduates*

G

graduate² /'grædʒueɪt/ v [I]
1 to obtain a degree from a college or university: [+from] *He graduated from Harvard last year.*
THESAURUS LEAVE
2 *AmE* to complete your education at HIGH SCHOOL: [+from] *when I graduate from high school*
3 graduate (from sth) to sth to start doing something better, more important, or more difficult: *She wants to graduate to serious drama.*

> **Grammar**
> You **graduate from** a university. Do not say 'She graduated university.'
> You **graduate from** a college. In American English, you can also say **graduate** college or high school: *He graduated high school last May.*

graduate³ /'grædʒuət/ *adj* [only before noun] *especially AmE* relating to studies done at a university after a first degree SYN **postgraduate** *BrE*: *a graduate student*

graduated /'grædʒueɪtɪd/ *adj* divided into different levels: *graduated rates of tax*

graduation /ˌgrædʒu'eɪʃən/ n [U] when you complete a university degree or your education at an American HIGH SCHOOL: *After graduation, I left Cambridge.*

graffiti /græ'fi:ti, grə-/ n [U] writing and pictures that are drawn illegally on the walls of buildings, trains etc

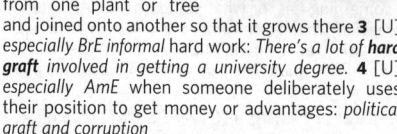
GRAFFITI

graft¹ /grɑːft $ græft/ n
1 [C] a piece of skin or bone that is taken from a healthy part of someone's body and attached to a damaged part: *a skin graft* **2** [C] a piece cut from one plant or tree and joined onto another so that it grows there **3** [U] *especially BrE informal* hard work: *There's a lot of hard graft involved in getting a university degree.* **4** [U] *especially AmE* when someone deliberately uses their position to get money or advantages: *political graft and corruption*

graft² v [T] **1** to put a piece of skin or bone from a healthy part of someone's body onto a damaged part **2** to join a part of a plant or tree onto another plant or tree

grain /greɪn/ n
1 a) [U] the seeds of crops such as corn, wheat, or rice that are gathered for food, or these crops themselves: *sacks of grain* | *the grain harvest* **b)** [C] a single seed of corn, wheat etc: [+of] *a few grains of rice*
2 the grain the natural lines that you can see in things such as wood, rock, or cloth: *Split the wood along the grain.*
3 [C] a very small piece or amount of something: [+of] *some grains of sand* | *There was a grain of truth in what he said.*

PHRASES

go **against the grain** if something goes against the grain, you do not like doing it because it is not what you would normally do: *It goes against the grain to throw food away.*

gram (*also* **gramme** *BrE*) /græm/ n [C] (*written abbreviation* **g, gm**) the basic unit for measuring weight in the METRIC system

grammar /'græmə $ -ər/ n
1 [U] the rules by which words change their form and are combined into sentences: *English grammar* | *Check your spelling and grammar.*
2 [C] a book that describes grammar rules: *a Latin grammar*

'grammar ˌschool n [C] a school in Britain for children over the age of 11, who have to pass an examination to go there

grammatical /grə'mætɪkəl/ *adj* **1** [only before noun] relating to grammar: *a grammatical error* **2** correct according to the rules of grammar: *a grammatical sentence* —**grammatically** /-kli/ *adv*

gramophone /'græməfəʊn $ -foʊn/ n [C] *old-fashioned* a RECORD PLAYER

gran /græn/ n [C] *BrE informal* a GRANDMOTHER

granary /'grænəri $ 'greɪ-, 'græ-/ n [C] (*plural granaries*) a place where grain, especially wheat, is stored

grand¹ /grænd/ *adj*
1 big and very impressive: *the grand hall* | *This was opera on a grand scale.*
2 intended to achieve something impressive: *a grand plan*
3 important and rich: *He thinks he's too grand to talk to us.*
4 a) used in the titles of buildings or places that are big and impressive: *the Grand Hotel* **b)** used in the titles of some people who belong to the highest social class: *the Grand Duke of Baden* —**grandly** *adv*
PHRASES

grand total the final total you get when you add up several numbers or amounts: *We raised a grand total of £250,000.*

grand² n [C] (*plural* **grand**) *informal* a thousand pounds or dollars: *The wedding cost ten grand.*

grandad, granddad /'grændæd/ n [C] *especially BrE informal* a GRANDFATHER

grandchild /'græntʃaɪld/ n [C] (*plural* **grandchildren** /-tʃɪldrən/) the child of your son or daughter

granddaughter /'grænˌdɔ:tə $ -ˌdɔ:tər/ n [C] the daughter of your son or daughter

grandeur /'grændʒə $ -ər/ n [U] impressive beauty, power, or size: *the grandeur of the mountains*

grandfather /'grænˌfɑːðə $ -ər/ n [C] the father of your mother or father

'grandfather ˌclock n [C] an old-fashioned tall clock which stands on the floor → see picture at CLOCK¹

grandiose /'grændiəʊs $ -oʊs/ *adj* grandiose plans sound very important or impressive, but are not practical

ˌgrand 'jury n [C] *law* a group of people in the US who decide whether someone should be judged in a court of law

grandma /'grænmɑː/ n [C] informal a GRAND-MOTHER

grandmother /'græn,mʌðə $ -ər/ n [C] the mother of your mother or father

grandpa /'grænpɑː/ n [C] informal a GRANDFATHER

grandparent /'græn,peərənt $ -,per-/ n [C usually plural] your grandparents are the parents of your mother or father: *My grandparents live in Kent.*

grand pi'ano n [C] the type of large piano often used in concerts

grandson /'grænsʌn/ n [C] the son of your son or daughter

grandstand /'grændstænd/ n [C] a large structure with rows of seats and a roof, where people sit to watch sports

granite /'grænət/ n [U] a type of very hard grey rock, often used in building

granny /'græni/ n [C] (plural **grannies**) informal a GRANDMOTHER

granola /grə'nəʊlə $ -'noʊ-/ n [U] AmE breakfast food made from nuts, grains, and seeds

grant¹ Ac /grɑːnt $ grænt/ v [T] **1** formal to give someone something or allow them to have something that they have asked for: **grant sb sth** *Ms. Chung was granted American citizenship last year.* **2** to admit that something is true although it does not make much difference to your opinion: *He's not a natural athlete, **I grant you**, but he does work hard.*
PHRASES
> **take sb/sth for granted** to expect that someone or something will always be there when you need them and never think how important or useful they are: *He spends all his time at work and takes his family for granted.*
> **take it for granted (that)** to believe that something is true without making sure: *He took it for granted that Claire would marry him.*

grant² Ac n [C] an amount of money given to someone by an organization for a particular purpose: *a research grant*

granule /'grænjuːl/ n [C] a small hard piece of something: *instant coffee granules* —**granular** /-jələ $ -ər/ adj —**granulated** adj: *granulated sugar*

grape /greɪp/ n [C] one of a number of small round green or purple fruits that grow together on a VINE. Grapes are often used for making wine: *a bunch of grapes* → see picture at **BUNCH¹**

grapefruit /'greɪpfruːt/ n [C] a round yellow CITRUS fruit with a thick skin and a sour taste → see picture on page A4

grapevine /'greɪpvaɪn/ n **hear sth on/through the grapevine** to hear news because it has been passed from one person to another in conversation

graph /grɑːf $ græf/ n [C] a drawing that uses a line or lines to show how two or more sets of measurements are related to each other: *a sales graph*

graphic /'græfɪk/ adj **1** a graphic account or description of an event is very clear and gives a lot of details, especially unpleasant ones: *She gave a graphic account of her unhappy childhood.* **2** [only before noun] related to DRAWINGS, pictures etc: **graphic art** —**graphically** /-kli/ adv: *She described the scene graphically.*

graphic de'sign n [U] the art of combining pictures and words in the production of books, magazines etc —**graphic designer** n [C]

graphics /'græfɪks/ n [plural] pictures or images, especially those produced on a computer

graphite /'græfaɪt/ n [U] a soft black substance that is a type of CARBON and is used in pencils

grapple /'græpəl/ v [I] to fight or struggle with someone, holding them tightly: **[+with]** *He tried to grapple with the guard.*
PHRASAL VERBS
grapple with sth to try hard to deal with or understand something difficult: *Molly's upstairs, grappling with her maths homework.*

grasp¹ /grɑːsp $ græsp/ v [T] **1** to take and hold something firmly in your hands: *Grasp the rope with both hands.* **THESAURUS** HOLD **2** to understand something completely: *At the time, I didn't fully grasp what he meant.* **THESAURUS** UNDERSTAND
PHRASAL VERBS
grasp at sth to try to hold onto something

grasp² n [singular] **1** the ability to understand a subject or a situation completely: **[+of]** *Her grasp of the issues was impressive.* | **a good/poor etc grasp of sth** *a good grasp of spoken English* **2** your ability to achieve or gain something: **within sb's grasp** *Eve felt that success was finally within her grasp.* | **beyond sb's grasp** *For many people, buying a house is beyond their grasp.* **3** the way you hold something, or your ability to hold it: *The bottle slipped out of his grasp and smashed on the floor.*

grasping /'grɑːspɪŋ $ 'græs-/ adj disapproving very eager to get money and unwilling to give any of it away or spend it: *a hard, grasping man*

grass /grɑːs $ græs/ n
1 [U] a very common plant with thin leaves that covers the ground in fields and gardens and is often eaten by animals: *a lion lying in the long grass* | *Please keep off the grass.* | *a blade of grass* (=a single leaf)
2 [C] a particular kind of grass: *mountain grasses*
3 [U] informal MARIJUANA —**grassy** adj: *a grassy bank*

grasshopper /'grɑːs,hɒpə $ 'græs,hɑːpər/ n [C] an insect that has long back legs for jumping and that makes short loud noises → see picture at **INSECT**

grassland /'grɑːslænd $ 'græs-/ n [U] (also **grasslands** [plural]) a large area of land covered with wild grass

grass 'roots n **the grass roots** the ordinary people in an organization, not the leaders —**grass-roots** adj: *grass-roots support*

grate¹ /greɪt/ v **1** [T] to rub cheese, vegetables etc against a GRATER (=a kitchen tool with a rough or sharp surface) in order to break them into small pieces: *grated carrot* → see picture at **CUT¹** **2** [I] to annoy someone: **[+on]** *His voice grated on her ears.* **3** [I,T] to make an unpleasant sound by rubbing against something: *The stones beneath her shoes grated harshly.*

grate² n [C] the metal frame that holds wood, coal etc in a FIREPLACE

grateful /'greɪtfəl/ adj feeling or showing thanks OPP **ungrateful**: grateful (to sb) for sth *Mona was very grateful to Peter for his advice.* | [+(that)] *I'm grateful that the kids help around the house.* | *Our grateful thanks go to all who participated.* —**gratefully** adv: *We gratefully accepted their offer of help.*
PHRASES
| **I would be grateful if you could/would ...** *formal* used to ask something in a formal situation or a letter: *I would be grateful if you would allow me to visit your school.*

grater /'greɪtə $ -ər/ n [C] a kitchen tool with a rough or sharp surface, used for grating food: *a cheese grater*

gratify /'grætɪfaɪ/ v [T] (**gratified, gratifying, gratifies**) *formal* to make someone pleased or satisfied: *She was gratified by the result.* —**gratifying** adj: *It was gratifying to know that I had won.* —**gratification** /ˌɡrætɪfɪ'keɪʃən/ n [U]

grating¹ /'greɪtɪŋ/ n [C] a metal frame with bars across it, used to cover a window or hole

grating² adj a grating sound is hard and unpleasant: *a harsh grating laugh*

gratitude /'grætɪtjuːd $ -tuːd/ n [U] the feeling of being grateful OPP **ingratitude**: *Tears of gratitude filled her eyes.*

gratuitous /grə'tjuːɪtəs $ -'tuː-/ adj said or done without a good reason, in a way that offends someone SYN **unnecessary**: *gratuitous violence in films*

gratuity /grə'tjuːɪti $ -'tuː-/ n [C] (plural **gratuities**) *formal* a small gift of money given to someone for a service they provided SYN **tip**

grave¹ /greɪv/ n [C] the place where a dead body is buried: *We visited my grandfather's grave.*

grave² adj 1 very serious and worrying: *I have grave doubts about her ability.* | *His life is in grave danger.* THESAURUS SERIOUS 2 looking or sounding very serious: *Dr Fry looked grave. 'I have some bad news,' he said.* —**gravely** adv

gravel /'grævəl/ n [U] small stones used to make a surface for paths or roads —**gravelled** BrE, **graveled** AmE adj: *a gravelled driveway*

gravelly /'grævəli/ adj a gravelly voice sounds low and rough

gravestone /'greɪvstəʊn $ -stoʊn/ n [C] a stone on a GRAVE that shows the name of the person buried there and the dates when they were alive

graveyard /'greɪvjɑːd $ -jɑːrd/ n [C] an area of ground where people are buried, often near a church → **cemetery**

gravitate /'grævɪteɪt/ v [I] *formal* to be attracted to something and move towards it or become involved with it: [+to/towards] *Students gravitate towards others with similar interests.*

gravitational /ˌɡrævɪ'teɪʃənəl◂/ adj relating to gravity: *the Earth's gravitational pull*

gravity /'grævəti/ n [U] 1 the force that makes objects fall to the ground: *the laws of gravity* 2 *formal* seriousness: [+of] *We were soon made aware of the gravity of the situation.*

gravy /'greɪvi/ n [U] a sauce made from the juice that comes from meat as it cooks, mixed with flour and water

gray /greɪ/ adj, n the usual American spelling of GREY

graying /'greɪ-ɪŋ/ adj, n the usual American spelling of GREYING

graze¹ /greɪz/ v 1 [I,T] if an animal grazes, it eats grass: *cattle grazing in the field* 2 [T] to break the surface of your skin by accidentally rubbing it against something rough: *Billy grazed his knee when he fell.* 3 [T] to touch something lightly while passing it: *A bullet grazed his cheek.*

graze² n [C] a slight wound that breaks the surface of your skin: *minor cuts and grazes* THESAURUS INJURY

grease¹ /griːs/ n [U] 1 oil or fat from food that has been cooked 2 thick oil that you put on the moving parts of a machine to make them move smoothly

grease² v [T] to put butter or oil in a pan to prevent food from sticking to it: *Grease the tin lightly with butter.*

greasy /'griːsi, -zi/ adj covered with or containing a lot of grease or oil: *greasy food* | *a shampoo for greasy hair* | *greasy skin* THESAURUS DIRTY

great¹ /greɪt/ adj
1 very large in amount or degree: *We had great fun.* | *The great majority of people are against the war.* | *A great many people died in the flood.* | *a great deal of sth We spent a great deal of time and effort decorating the house.*
2 *spoken* very good: *It's great to see you again!* | *We had a great time in Rio.* | *sound/taste/look/feel etc great You look great in that dress.* | [+for] *Our holiday villas are great for families with children.* THESAURUS GOOD
3 [only before noun] very important, successful, or famous: *the great civilizations of the past* | *the greatest movie star of them all* | *The play was a great success.* THESAURUS BIG
4 *spoken* used when you are disappointed or annoyed about something: *'Your car won't be ready until next week.' 'Oh, great!'*
5 great-grandfather/great-aunt etc the grandfather, AUNT etc of one of your parents
6 great-nephew/great-granddaughter etc the NEPHEW, GRANDDAUGHTER etc of your child
7 Greater London/Boston etc used to talk about a large city, including all the parts on the edge —**greatly** adv: *Your chances of getting cancer are greatly increased if you smoke.* —**greatness** n [U]
PHRASES
| **great big** very big

great² n [C usually plural] someone who is very successful in a particular sport, profession etc: *Jack Nicklaus is one of golf's all-time greats.*

greed /griːd/ n [U] a strong desire for more food,

money, power, possessions etc than you need: *Burning the rainforest is motivated by greed.*

greedy /ˈɡriːdi/ *adj* wanting more food, money, power, possessions etc than you need: *a greedy and selfish society* | **[+for]** *They are greedy for profit.* —**greedily** *adv* —**greediness** *n* [U]

green¹ /ɡriːn/ *adj*
1 having the colour of grass: *green eyes* | *a dark green dress*
2 covered with grass, trees, bushes etc: *green fields*
3 related to protecting the environment: *green issues such as global warming*
4 *informal* young and lacking experience: *The trainees are still pretty green.*
PHRASES
> **give sb/get the green light** if someone gives you the green light, they give permission for you to start a project, a new system etc: *Our research project has just been given the green light.*
> **be green with envy** to wish very much that you had something that someone else has: *You'll be green with envy when you see the apartment.*
> **have green fingers** *BrE*, **have a green thumb** *AmE* to be good at making plants grow: *You certainly have green fingers. The garden looks amazing.*

green² *n*
1 [C,U] the colour of grass: *different shades of green*
2 [C] the smooth flat area of grass around a hole on a golf course
3 [C] *BrE* an area of grass in the middle of a village: *the **village green***
4 greens [plural] vegetables with large green leaves: *Eat your greens.*

greenback /ˈɡriːnbæk/ *n* [C] *AmE informal* an American BANK NOTE

ˈgreen belt *n* [C,U] an area of land around a city where building is not allowed, in order to protect fields and woods

ˌgreen ˈcard *n* [C] a document that a foreigner must have in order to work legally in the US

greenery /ˈɡriːnəri/ *n* [U] green leaves and plants

greenfield site /ˈɡriːnfiːld ˌsaɪt/ *n* [C] *BrE* a piece of land that has never been built on before → **brownfield site**

greengrocer /ˈɡriːnˌɡrəʊsə $ -ˌɡroʊsər/ *n* [C] *BrE*
1 someone who owns or works in a shop selling fruit and vegetables **2 the greengrocer's** a greengrocer's shop

greenhouse /ˈɡriːnhaʊs/ *n* [C] a glass building used for growing plants that need warmth, light, and protection

ˈgreenhouse efˌfect *n* **the greenhouse effect** the warming of the air around the Earth as a result of the Sun's heat being trapped by POLLUTION → **global warming**

Greenwich Mean Time /ˌɡrenɪtʃ ˈmiːn taɪm, ˌɡrɪ-, -nɪdʒ-/ *n* → **GMT**

greet /ɡriːt/ *v* [T] **1** to say hello to someone or welcome them: *The children came rushing out to greet me.* **2** to react to something in a particular way: **be**

greeted with sth *The speech was greeted with cheers and laughter.*

greeting /ˈɡriːtɪŋ/ *n* [C,U] something you say or do when you meet someone: **in greeting** *She raised her hand in greeting.* | *The two cousins **exchanged greetings** (=greeted each other).*

gregarious /ɡrɪˈɡeəriəs $ -ˈɡer-/ *adj* someone who is gregarious enjoys being with other people → **sociable**

grenade /ɡrəˈneɪd/ *n* [C] a small bomb that can be thrown or fired from a gun: *a hand grenade*

grew /ɡruː/ *v* the past tense of GROW

grey¹ *especially BrE*, **gray** *AmE* /ɡreɪ/ *adj*
1 COLOUR having the colour of dark clouds, neither black nor white: *grey rain clouds* | *dark grey trousers*
2 HAIR having grey hair: *My father **went grey** in his forties.*
3 WEATHER weather that is grey is dull and cloudy: *It was a grey Sunday morning.*
4 BORING PERSON boring and unattractive: *grey businessmen*
5 OLD PEOPLE [only before noun] *BrE* relating to old people: *the grey vote*
PHRASES
> **grey area** a part of a subject such as law or science that is hard to deal with because the rules are not clear: *He believed that there was good and evil with no grey area in the middle.*

grey² *especially BrE*, **gray** *AmE* *n* [C,U] the colour of dark clouds, neither black nor white: *dull greys and browns* —**greyness** *n* [U]

greyhound /ˈɡreɪhaʊnd/ *n* [C] a type of thin dog that can run very fast and is used in races

greying¹ *BrE*, **graying** *AmE* /ˈɡreɪ-ɪŋ/ *adj* greying hair is starting to become grey

greying² *BrE*, **graying** *AmE* *n* **the greying of sth** the situation in which the average age of a population increases, so that there are more old people than there were in the past

grid /ɡrɪd/ *n* [C] **1** a pattern of straight lines that cross each other and form squares **2** the system of numbered squares printed on a map that helps you find exactly where something is **3** *BrE* a network of CABLES that supply an area with electricity

GRIDLOCK

TRUCKS USE RIGHT LANES

SPEED LIMIT 50

gridlock /ˈɡrɪdlɒk $ -lɑːk/ *n* [U] when the main roads in a city have so many cars etc using them that the traffic stops moving —**gridlocked** *adj*

G

grief

grief /ɡriːf/ n [U] extreme sadness, especially because someone you love has died: *His grief was obvious from the way he spoke.* | **[+at/over]** *The grief she felt over Helen's death was almost unbearable.*

PHRASES

come to grief to fail, or to be harmed or destroyed in an accident: *Their business came to grief after only six months.*

good grief! *spoken* said when you are slightly surprised or annoyed: *Good grief! What a mess!*

grievance /ˈɡriːvəns/ n [C,U] a belief that you have been treated unfairly, or an unfair situation or event that affects and upsets you: **[+against]** *He has a grievance against his former employer.*

grieve /ɡriːv/ v **1** [I,T] to feel extremely sad, especially because someone you love has died: **[+over/for]** *Sue's grieving over the death of her mother.* | *We are still grieving the loss of our mother.* **2** [T] *formal* if something grieves you, it makes you feel very unhappy: *My aunt, it grieves me to say, gets things confused.*

grievous /ˈɡriːvəs/ adj formal very serious and causing great pain or suffering: *a grievous error* | *The death of his father was a grievous blow.* —**grievously** adv

grill¹ /ɡrɪl/ v **1** [I,T] if you grill food, or if food grills, you cook it by putting it close to a strong heat coming from above **SYN broil** AmE: *Grill the bacon until crisp.* **THESAURUS COOK** **2** [T] *informal* to ask someone a lot of questions about something: *They let the man go after grilling him for several hours.*

grill² n [C] **1** BrE a part of a COOKER which cooks food on a metal shelf, using strong heat from above **2** a metal frame on which food can be cooked over a fire **3** (*also* **grille**) a frame with metal bars or wire across it that is put in front of a window or door for protection

grim /ɡrɪm/ adj **1** making you feel worried and unhappy: *grim economic news* | *When he lost his job, his future looked grim.* **2** looking or sounding very serious: *a grim-faced judge* **3** BrE informal bad, ugly, or unpleasant: *grim industrial towns* —**grimly** adv —**grimness** n [U]

grimace /ɡrɪˈmeɪs, ˈɡrɪməs/ v [I] to twist your face in an ugly way because you feel pain or do not like something: **[+at]** *I grimaced at my reflection in the mirror.* —**grimace** n [C]

grime /ɡraɪm/ n [U] a lot of dirt

grimy /ˈɡraɪmi/ adj covered with dirt: *grimy windows* **THESAURUS DIRTY**

grin /ɡrɪn/ v [I] (**grinned**, **grinning**) to smile with a very wide smile: **[+at]** *Sally was grinning at me from across the room.* **THESAURUS SMILE** —**grin** n [C]: *a friendly grin*

grind¹ /ɡraɪnd/ v [T] (*past tense and past participle* **ground** /ɡraʊnd/) **1** to press and break something such as coffee beans into small pieces or powder: **grind sth into sth** *Grind the rice into a powder.* **2** to press and rub something onto a surface: *He ground his cigarette onto the floor.* **3** to make something such as a knife sharp by rubbing it against a rough hard surface

PHRASES

grind to a halt if something grinds to a halt, it stops moving or making progress: *Traffic slowly ground to a halt.* | *After two days, the talks had ground to a halt.*

grind your teeth to rub your upper and lower teeth together, making a noise: *My husband grinds his teeth when he's asleep.*

PHRASAL VERBS

grind sb ↔ **down** to treat someone in a cruel way for such a long time that they lose all courage and hope: *She had been ground down by years of poverty and hardship.*

grind² n [singular] *informal* something that is hard work and physically or mentally tiring: *It's Monday again – back to the grind.*

grinder /ˈɡraɪndə $ -ər/ n [C] a machine for crushing coffee beans etc into powder: *a coffee grinder*

grinding /ˈɡraɪndɪŋ/ adj **grinding poverty** extreme POVERTY

grip¹ /ɡrɪp/ n

1 [singular] a tight hold on something, or your ability to hold it: *Don't **loosen** your **grip** on the rope or you'll fall.*

2 [singular] power and control over someone or something: **have/keep a (tight/firm etc) grip on sth** *Stalin's determination to keep an iron grip on Eastern Europe*

3 [singular, U] the ability of something to stay on a surface without slipping: *I want some tennis shoes with a good grip.*

PHRASES

come/get to grips with sth to understand or deal with something difficult: *Have you got to grips with your new job yet?*

get/take a grip on yourself to start to control your emotions: *Stop being hysterical and get a grip on yourself.*

grip² v [T] (**gripped**, **gripping**)

1 to hold something very tightly: *I gripped his hand in fear.* **THESAURUS HOLD**

2 to have a strong effect on someone or something: *a country gripped by economic problems*

3 to keep your attention completely: *a story that really grips you*

4 if something grips a surface, it stays on it without slipping

gripe /ɡraɪp/ v [I] *informal* to complain continuously —**gripe** n [C]

gripping /ˈɡrɪpɪŋ/ adj a gripping film, story etc is very exciting and interesting: *a gripping drama* **THESAURUS EXCITING**

grisly /ˈɡrɪzli/ adj extremely unpleasant because death or violence is involved: *a series of grisly murders*

gristle /ˈɡrɪsəl/ n [U] the part of a piece of meat that is not soft enough to eat —**gristly** adj

grit¹ /ɡrɪt/ n [U] **1** very small pieces of stone or sand **2** *informal* determination and courage

grit² v [T] (**gritted**, **gritting**) to put grit on a frozen road to make it less slippery

PHRASES

grit your teeth to use all your determination to continue in spite of difficulties: *Just grit your teeth and hang on – it'll be over soon.*

gritty /ˈgrɪti/ *adj* **1** determined and brave **2** showing an unpleasant situation as it really is: *a gritty police drama* **3** containing or covered in sand

grizzled /ˈgrɪzəld/ *adj literary* having grey hair

groan /grəʊn $ groʊn/ *v* [I] to make a long deep sound because you are in pain, or are not happy about something: *Captain Marsh was holding his arm and groaning.* | *The kids groaned when I turned off the television.* —**groan** *n* [C]

grocer /ˈgrəʊsə $ ˈgroʊsər/ *n* [C] **1** someone who owns or works in a shop that sells food and other things used in the home **2 the grocer's** *BrE* a grocer's shop

grocery /ˈgrəʊsəri $ ˈgroʊ-/ *n* (*plural* **groceries**) **1 groceries** [plural] things that you buy in a grocer's shop or a SUPERMARKET **2** (*also* **grocery store** *AmE*) [C] a shop where you buy groceries

groggy /ˈgrɒgi $ ˈgrɑːgi/ *adj* feeling weak and ill —**groggily** *adv*

groin /grɔɪn/ *n* [C] where your legs join at the front of your body

groom¹ /gruːm, grʊm/ *v* [T] **1** to train someone for an important job: **groom sb for sth** *Chris is clearly being groomed for the job of manager.* **2** to clean and brush the fur of an animal —**grooming** *n* [U]

groom² *n* [C] **1** (*also* **bridegroom**) a man who is getting married, or has just been married **2** someone whose job is to take care of horses

groove /gruːv/ *n* [C] a line cut into a surface

grope /grəʊp $ groʊp/ *v* **1** [I,T] to try to find something or go somewhere, using your hands because you cannot see: **[+for/around]** *He groped for the light switch.* | *I groped my way downstairs.* **2** [I] to have difficulty in finding the right words to say or the right solution to a problem: **[+for]** *He groped for something to say.* **3** [T] *informal* to touch someone sexually, when they do not want you to

gross¹ /grəʊs $ groʊs/ *adj* **1** [only before noun] a gross sum of money is the total amount before any tax or costs are taken away → **net**: *a gross profit of $5 million* **2** [only before noun] *formal* seriously wrong and unacceptable: *He was dismissed for gross misconduct.* **3** *spoken* very unpleasant: *There was one really gross part in the movie.* **4** *informal* very fat —**grossly** *adv*: *He's grossly overweight.* —**grossness** *n* [U]

gross² *v* [T] to gain an amount of money as a total profit, or earn it as a total amount, before tax is taken away

PHRASAL VERBS

gross sb ↔ **out** *AmE spoken* if something grosses you out, it is so unpleasant that it makes you feel sick: *Dirty fingernails gross me out.*

gross do,mestic 'product *n* [U] GDP

gross ,national 'product *n* [U] GNP

grotesque /grəʊˈtesk $ groʊ-/ *adj* ugly in a strange frightening way **THESAURUS** UGLY —**grotesquely** *adv*

grotto /ˈgrɒtəʊ $ ˈgrɑːtoʊ/ *n* [C] (*plural* **grottos** or **grottoes**) a small CAVE

grotty /ˈgrɒti $ ˈgrɑːti/ *adj BrE informal* nasty, dirty, or unpleasant

grouch /graʊtʃ/ *n* [C] *informal* **1** someone who is always complaining **2** something unimportant that you complain about

grouchy /ˈgraʊtʃi/ *adj informal* in a bad temper —**grouchiness** *n* [U]

ground¹ /graʊnd/ *n*

1 EARTH'S SURFACE [singular, U] the surface of the earth: **on the ground** *She was lying asleep on the ground.* | *The ground was frozen solid.* | **above/below/under ground** *1,000 feet below ground*

2 AREA OF LAND a) [C,U] an area of land or water, especially one that is used for a special purpose: *These are safe breeding grounds for seals.* | *an expanse of open ground* (=land with no houses, trees etc on it) **b) grounds** [plural] the land or gardens surrounding a large building: *Smoking is not allowed on school grounds.* **THESAURUS** LAND

3 REASON **grounds** [plural] a good reason for doing something: **grounds for (doing) sth** *That's not grounds for divorce.* | **on moral/legal/medical etc grounds** *The proposal was rejected on environmental grounds.* | **on (the) grounds of sth** *discrimination on the grounds of race* | **on the grounds that** *You can't fire a woman on the grounds that she's pregnant.*

4 SUBJECT [U] a subject or area of knowledge: *We keep going over the same ground* (=talking about the same things). | *The movie **breaks new ground** (=introduces new and exciting ideas).*

5 ATTITUDES [U] a general opinion or set of attitudes: *Often parents and teenagers find they have little **common ground** (=they do not share the same attitudes etc).*

6 FOR SPORT [C] a place where a sport is played: *a football ground* | *Old Trafford is Manchester United's **home ground** (=the ground that belongs to them).*

7 ELECTRICAL [singular] *AmE* a wire that connects a piece of electrical equipment to the ground for safety **SYN** **earth** *BrE* → **BREEDING GROUND**, **have/keep your feet on the ground** at **FOOT¹**, **be thin on the ground** at **THIN¹**

PHRASES

gain/lose ground to become more or less successful than someone or something you are competing with: *The Democrats have gained ground since the last election.*

get off the ground to start to be successful: *His new business is slow getting off the ground.*

hold/stand your ground to refuse to move from where you are standing or to change your opinion, even though other people are trying to make you: *The rebels succeeded in holding their ground for a brief time.* | *You need to know when to stand your ground, and when to give in.*

THESAURUS

the ground the surface of the earth: *It had been raining and the ground was very muddy.* | *He*

G

collapsed and fell to the ground.
the floor the surface that you walk on when you are inside a building: *The kitchen floor was covered in dust.*
land an area of ground that someone owns, or that is used for a particular purpose: *That's private land.* | *land for housing*
earth/soil the substance that plants grow in: *The soil here is good for growing vegetables.*

ground² v
1 PLANE [T] to stop an aircraft or pilot from flying: *All planes are grounded until the fog clears.*
2 BE BASED ON STH **be grounded in/on sth** to be based on something: *His ideas are grounded in his Christian faith.*
3 CHILD [T] *informal* to stop a child going out with their friends as a punishment: *If you stay out late again, you'll be grounded for a week.*
4 ELECTRICAL EQUIPMENT [T] *AmE* to make a piece of electrical equipment safe by connecting it to the ground with a wire SYN **earth** *BrE*

ground³ v the past tense and past participle of GRIND

,ground 'beef *n* [U] *AmE* BEEF that has been cut into very small pieces SYN **mince** *BrE*

groundbreaking /'graʊnd,breɪkɪŋ/ *adj* involving the use of new discoveries, new methods, or new ideas: *groundbreaking medical research*

,ground 'floor *n* [C] the part of a building that is on the same level as the ground SYN **first floor** *AmE*

grounding /'graʊndɪŋ/ *n* [singular] training in the basic parts of a subject or skill: **[+in]** *a basic grounding in maths*

groundless /'graʊndləs/ *adj* not based on facts or reason: *My suspicions **proved groundless**.*

'ground rules *n* [plural] the basic rules or principles on which future actions should be based: *There are a few ground rules you should follow.*

groundswell /'graʊndswel/ *n* **a groundswell of support/opinion/enthusiasm** a sudden increase in how strongly people feel about something

groundwork /'graʊndwɜːk $ -wɜːrk/ *n* [U] something that has to happen before an activity or plan can be successful: *His speech laid the **groundwork** for the peace talks.*

group¹ /gruːp/ *n* [C, also + plural verb *BrE*]
1 several people or things that are together in the same place: **[+of]** *a group of islands* | *Please get into groups of three* (=groups of three people). | **in groups** *Dolphins swim in small groups.*
2 several people or things that are connected with each other or that do things together: *He **belonged to** a terrorist **group**.* | **[+of]** *She is one of a group of women who have suffered side-effects from the drug.* | *a group of major companies*
3 several musicians who play and sing popular music together SYN **band**: *a rock group* | *The group are currently on tour.*
4 several companies that all have the same owner: *the Savoy hotel group* → BLOOD GROUP

THESAURUS

of people

group several people who are together in the same place, or who do things together: *A group of old men were playing cards.*

crowd a large number of people in the same place, especially outside: *A crowd gathered outside the US embassy.*

gang a group of people, especially a group that causes trouble and fights: *a gang of thieves*

crew a group of people who work together on a ship or plane: *the ship's crew*

of animals

herd a large group of cows, deer, or elephants: *a herd of cows*

flock a large group of sheep or birds: *A flock of birds flew over us.*

pack a group of dogs or wolves (WOLF): *a pack of wild dogs*

shoal (*also* **school**) a group of fish or DOLPHINS: *The tiny fish swim in large shoals.*

of things

bunch a group of keys, flowers, or fruit that are held or tied together: *Her husband gave her a bunch of roses.*

bundle a group of things such as papers, clothes, or sticks that are held or tied together: *There was a big bundle of newspapers outside the door.*

heap a lot of things lying on top of each other in an untidy way: *He'd left his dirty clothes in a heap on the floor.*

pile several things of the same kind placed one on top of the other: *a pile of old books*

group² *v* [I,T] to arrange things in a group: **group (sth) together/round/into etc** *Four men were grouped around a jeep.*

grouping /'gruːpɪŋ/ *n* [C] a set of people or things that have the same aims, qualities, or features: *political groupings*

grouse¹ /graʊs/ *n* [C,U] (*plural* **grouse**) a small fat bird that is hunted for food, or the meat from this bird

grouse² *v* [I] *informal* to complain

grove /grəʊv $ groʊv/ *n* [C] an area of land where a particular type of tree grows: *a lemon grove*

grovel /'grɒvəl $ 'grɑː-, 'grʌ-/ *v* [I] (**grovelled, grovelling** *BrE*, **groveled, groveling** *AmE*) **1** to try very hard to please someone because you are frightened of them or you have upset them: *She's always grovelling to the boss.* **2** to move around on your hands and knees, looking for something: *I saw him grovelling in the road for his hat.*

grow /grəʊ $ groʊ/ *v* (*past tense* **grew** /gruː/, *past participle* **grown** /grəʊn $ groʊn/)
1 [I] to get bigger in size or amount: *Babies grow quickly in their first year.* | **[+by]** *Sales grew by 10%.* | *A **growing number** of people work from home.* | **grow rapidly/slowly/steadily** *The economy has grown steadily.* | **[+in]** *Skiing has grown in popularity.*
THESAURUS INCREASE

2 [I,T] if plants grow, or if you grow plants, they develop and become big bigger: *Weeds were growing everywhere.* | *We grow our own vegetables.*

3 [I,T] if your hair or nails grow, or if you grow them, they get longer because you do not cut them: *I've decided to **grow** my hair **long**.*

4 grow old/bored/strong etc to become old, bored etc: *He was growing old, and becoming forgetful.* | *We were lost, and it was growing dark.* **THESAURUS** BECOME

PHRASAL VERBS

grow into sb/sth

1 to develop and become a particular kind of person or thing: *Joe grew into a handsome young man.*

2 if children grow into clothes, they become big enough to wear them

grow on sb if something grows on you, you gradually like it more and more: *The CD grows on you.*

grow out of sth

1 if children grow out of clothes, they become too big to wear them

2 to stop doing something as you become older: *Sarah still sucks her thumb, but she'll grow out of it.*

grow up

1 to gradually change from being a child to being an adult: *What do you want to be when you grow up?* | *I grew up in Paris* (=I lived in Paris when I was a child). **THESAURUS** LIVE

2 to start to exist or develop gradually: *Villages grew up along the river.*

> **Word Choice: grow or grow up?**
> **Grow** means to become bigger or taller. **Grow up** means to develop from being a child to being an adult.
> Do not say 'I was born and grew in Tokyo.' Say *I was born and grew up in Tokyo.*

grower /'grəʊə $ 'groʊər/ n [C] a person or company that grows fruit or vegetables in order to sell them

growl /graʊl/ v [I] if a dog, bear etc growls, it makes a deep angry sound: **[+at]** *The dog growled at me.* —**growl** n [C]

grown¹ /grəʊn $ groʊn/ v the past participle of GROW

grown² adj **grown man/woman** an adult man or woman – used especially when you think someone is not behaving as an adult should: *Whoever heard of a grown man being afraid of the dark?*

'grown-up¹ n [C] an adult – used by or to children: *Ask a grown-up to help you.*

'grown-up² adj someone who is grown-up is an adult: *She has a grown-up son.*

growth /grəʊθ $ groʊθ/ n **1** [singular, U] when something gets bigger or develops: **[+in/of]** *the growth in population* | *the growth of television* | *economic growth* | *Vitamins are necessary for healthy growth.* | *growth area/industry* (=a business or activity that is growing) *Computing remains a growth area.* **2** [U] the development of someone's character: *personal growth* **3** [C] something that grows in your body or on your skin, caused by a disease

4 [C,U] something that has grown: *His chin bore a thick growth of stubble.*

grub /grʌb/ n **1** [U] informal food **2** [C] a young insect in the form of a small white WORM

grubby /'grʌbi/ adj dirty: *grubby hands*

grudge¹ /grʌdʒ/ n [C] an unfriendly feeling towards someone because of something they did in the past: *He **has** a **grudge against** her.*

grudge² v [T] to do or give something even though you do not want to: **grudge sb sth** *I don't grudge him his success.* —**grudging** adj: *a grudging apology* —**grudgingly** adv: *He grudgingly admitted his mistake.*

gruelling BrE, **grueling** AmE /'gruːəlɪŋ/ adj very difficult and tiring: *a gruelling journey*

gruesome /'gruːsəm/ adj relating to violence or death: *a gruesome murder*

gruff /grʌf/ adj speaking in a rough unfriendly voice: *a gruff reply* —**gruffly** adv

grumble /'grʌmbəl/ v [I] to complain: **[+about]** *He kept grumbling about the food.* **THESAURUS** COMPLAIN —**grumble** n [C]

grumpy /'grʌmpi/ adj slightly angry and easily annoyed: *She's always grumpy in the morning.* —**grumpily** adv —**grumpiness** n [U]

grunge /grʌndʒ/ n [U] AmE informal unpleasant dirt **SYN** grime —**grungy** adj

grunt /grʌnt/ v **1** [I,T] to make a short low sound to show that you are not interested in something: *I asked him, but he just grunted.* **2** [I] if a pig grunts, it makes a low rough sound —**grunt** n [C]

guarantee¹ [Ac] /ˌgærən'tiː/ v [T]

1 to promise something: **[+(that)]** *I guarantee you'll love this film.* **THESAURUS** PROMISE

2 to make a formal written promise to repair or replace a product if it breaks: *Our products are **fully guaranteed**.*

3 to make it certain that something will happen: *Talent doesn't always guarantee success.*

guarantee² [Ac] n [C]

1 a formal written promise by a company to repair or replace a product if it breaks: *The phone has a one-year guarantee.* | **under guarantee** (=protected by a guarantee that has not finished yet) *Is the TV still under guarantee?*

2 a formal promise that something will be done: **[+that]** *I can't **give** a **guarantee** that there'll be no redundancies.*

guard¹ /gɑːd $ gɑːrd/ n

1 [C] someone whose job is to protect people or a place, or to make sure that a person does not escape: *a **security guard** | a **prison guard** | regular patrols by **armed guards***

2 [U] the act of protecting a place or person, or preventing a prisoner from escaping: **be on guard/ stand guard** *Soldiers are on guard outside the palace.* | *Gunmen stood guard at the camp entrance.* | **be (held/ kept) under guard** *The men were **under armed guard** at a military camp.*

3 [singular] a group of soldiers who guard someone or something

4 [C] something that is used to protect someone or

something from damage or injury: *a face guard* | *a fire guard*

5 [C] *BrE* someone whose job is to collect tickets on a train, help the passengers etc SYN **conductor** *AmE*
→ COAST GUARD, LIFE GUARD

PHRASES

catch/throw sb off guard to surprise someone by doing something that they were not expecting: *His question caught me off guard.*

be on your guard (against sth) to be very careful because you may have to deal with a bad situation: *These men are dangerous, so you must be on your guard.*

THESAURUS

guard someone whose job is to protect people or a place, or to make sure that a person does not escape: *There were two security guards outside the building.*

sentry a soldier who stands outside a building in order to guard it: *In front of the palace, a sentry was marching up and down.*

bodyguard someone whose job is to protect an important person by going everywhere with them: *the President's bodyguard*

bouncer someone whose job is to keep people who behave badly out of a club or bar: *He was thrown out of the club by a bouncer.*

---

guard² v [T]

1 to watch someone or something so that they do not escape, or get damaged or stolen: *Two men were guarding the prisoner.* | **guard sb/sth against sth** *The village must be guarded against attack.* THESAURUS▸ PROTECT

2 to protect something such as a right or secret by preventing other people from taking it away, discovering it etc: *a closely guarded secret*

PHRASAL VERBS

guard against sth to try to prevent something from happening: *Exercise can guard against illness.*

guarded /'gɑːdɪd $ 'gɑːr-/ *adj* careful not to give very much information or show your feelings: *The minister was very guarded in his comments.* | *He gave the idea a guarded welcome.*

guardian /'gɑːdiən $ 'gɑːr-/ n [C] **1** a child's guardian is someone who is legally responsible for them, but who is not their parent: *His aunt is his legal guardian.* **2** *formal* someone who guards or protects something —**guardianship** n [U]

guardian 'angel n [C] a SPIRIT or person who looks after and protects someone

guerrilla /gəˈrɪlə/ n [C] a member of an unofficial army that is fighting for political reasons: *guerrilla warfare*

guess¹ /ges/ v [I,T] to answer a question or decide something without being sure whether you are right: **guess right/correctly/wrong** *I guessed her age correctly.* | **guess how/what/whether/if etc** *Guess how much the dress cost.* | **[+(that)]** *The teacher guessed that the boys had been smoking.* | **[+at]** *I couldn't even guess at the cost.* → SECOND-GUESS

PHRASES

guess what/you'll never guess who/what etc *spoken* used to tell someone some surprising news: *Guess what! Dan's resigned.* | *You'll never guess who I saw today.*

I guess *spoken* used when you think that something is true or likely: *His light's on, so I guess he's still up.*

I guess so/not *spoken* used to agree or disagree with a statement or question: *'I don't have any choice, do I?' 'I guess not.'* | *'Is her dad rich?' 'I guess so.'*

guess² n [C] an attempt to guess something: **[+at]** *Have a guess at what the word might mean.* | *My guess is that there won't be many people at the party.* | **at a guess** *spoken* (=used to say that something is just a guess) *At a guess, I'd say it would cost about £50.*

PHRASES

be anyone's/anybody's guess *informal* to be something that no one can be certain about: *It's anyone's guess who'll win the match.*

your guess is as good as mine *spoken* used to tell someone that you do not know any more than they do about something: *'When's the next bus?' 'Your guess is as good as mine.'*

COLLOCATIONS

verbs

to make a guess *If you don't know the answer, you can always make a guess.*

to have a guess *BrE*, **to take a guess** *AmE* *How much do you think it cost? Have a guess.*

adjectives

a rough guess (=one that is not exact) *At a rough guess, we should have about 50 people coming.*

a wild guess (=one made without much thought or information) *I'd say it's worth £50,000, but that's just a wild guess.*

a lucky guess *'How did you know?' 'It was just a lucky guess.'*

a good guess (=right or almost right) *'I'd say you're twenty-three.' 'That's a good guess.'*

---

guesswork /'gesw3ːk $ -w3ːrk/ n [U] when you try to find the answer to something by guessing: *I got the right answer, but it was pure guesswork.*

guest /gest/ n [C]

1 someone who you invite to stay in your home or to go to an event: *How many guests are coming to your party?* | **as sb's guest** *You're here as my guest.*

2 someone who is staying in a hotel: *The hotel car park is for guests only.* THESAURUS▸ CUSTOMER

3 a famous person who is invited to take part in a television programme, concert etc: *He appeared as a guest on the show.* | *a guest appearance by Jack Nicholson* | **guest star/speaker etc**

PHRASES

be my guest *spoken* used to give someone permission: *'Could I use your phone?' 'Be my guest!'*

Usage
When talking about people who come to your house, in everyday English you usually say **friends**, **visitors**, or just **someone/people**: *We're having some friends over for dinner this evening.* | *I didn't realise you had someone staying with you.* **Guest** sounds rather formal in this meaning. You also use **guest** about someone who pays to stay in a hotel. Do not confuse **guest** with **customer** (=someone who buys goods or services from a shop or company).

guesthouse /'gesthaʊs/ n [C] **1** BrE a small hotel that is also the hotel owner's private home **THESAURUS** HOTEL **2** AmE a separate building next to someone's home, where visiting family or friends can stay

guidance /'gaɪdəns/ n [U] helpful advice: *Your teacher can give you guidance on your career choice.*

guide¹ /gaɪd/ n [C]
1 something that helps you to make a decision: *As a **rough guide**, you need about 100 grams of meat per person.*
2 someone whose job is to show a place to tourists: *a **tour guide***
3 a) a book that has information and advice on a particular subject: **[+to]** *a guide to African birds* **b)** a guidebook
4 BrE **a) the Guides** (also **the Girl Guides**) an organization that teaches girls practical skills such as camping, and teaches them to be good members of society **b)** a member of this organization → **scout**

guide² v [T]
1 to help someone to go somewhere, for example by showing them the right direction: **guide sb to/through/across etc sth** *He took the old lady's arm and guided her across the road.* | *We were guided through the mountains by a local villager.* **THESAURUS** TAKE
2 to influence someone's behaviour or ideas: *Teenagers need adults to guide them.*
3 to show someone the right way to do something difficult or complicated: **guide sb through sth** *Guide your students through the program one section at a time.*

guidebook /'gaɪdbʊk/ n [C] a book that gives tourists information about a place **THESAURUS** BOOK

'guide dog n [C] BrE a specially trained dog that blind people use to help them to go to places **SYN** Seeing Eye dog AmE

guideline Ac /'gaɪdlaɪn/ n [C usually plural] rules or advice about the best way to do something: **[+on]** *guidelines on writing essays*

guild /gɪld/ n [C] an organization of people who do the same job or have the same interests: *the Writers' Guild*

GUIDE DOG

guide dog BrE/
Seeing Eye dog™ AmE

guile /gaɪl/ n [U] formal the use of clever but dishonest methods to deceive people

guillotine /'gɪləti:n/ n [C] a piece of equipment used in the past to cut off criminals' heads —**guillotine** v [T]

guilt /gɪlt/ n [U]
1 a sad feeling you have when you have done something wrong: **feeling/sense of guilt** *a terrible sense of guilt and shame* **THESAURUS** SHAME
2 when someone has broken a law **OPP** innocence: *The police couldn't prove his guilt.*
3 when you are responsible for something bad that has happened

Word Choice: guilt or shame?
Guilt is the feeling you have when you know that you have done something wrong, even if other people do not know about it: *Many parents suffer feelings of guilt if something happens to their children.*
Shame is the feeling that you have when people know that you have done something wrong, and this makes you feel very embarrassed and unhappy: *If my friends ever heard about this, I would die of shame.*

'guilt-ˌridden adj feeling so guilty about something that you cannot think about anything else

guilty /'gɪlti/ adj
1 unhappy and ashamed because you have done something wrong: **[+about/at]** *He felt guilty about stealing the pen.* | *You should have a guilty conscience!* **THESAURUS** ASHAMED
2 having done something that is a crime **OPP** innocent: **[+of]** *The jury found her guilty of murder.* | *He pleaded guilty to two charges of theft.* —**guiltily** adv —**guiltiness** n [U]

THESAURUS - sense 2
guilty if someone is guilty of a crime, they did it: *His family never believed he was guilty of murder.*
innocent if someone is innocent of a crime, they did not do it: *In court, he told the jury he was innocent.*
responsible used when saying who caused something bad that has happened: *The other driver was responsible for the accident.*
be to blame if someone is to blame for a bad situation, they caused it and they deserve to be criticized: *The government is to blame for the economic crisis.*

'guinea pig n [C] **1** a small furry animal with no tail that is often kept as a pet **2** informal someone who is used in a scientific test to see how successful or safe a new product, system etc is

guise /gaɪz/ n [C] formal the way someone or something appears to be: *It's the same idea in a different guise.*

guitar /gɪ'tɑː $ -'tɑːr/ n [C] a musical instrument with six strings that you play by pulling the strings —**guitarist** n [C]

G

gulf /gʌlf/ n [C] **1** a large area of sea partly surrounded by land: *the Gulf of Mexico* **2** a great difference and lack of understanding between two groups of people: **[+between]** *the gulf between the rich and the poor*

gull /gʌl/ n [C] a SEAGULL

gullible /'gʌləbəl/ adj disapproving a gullible person is easy to trick because they always believe what people say —**gullibility** /,gʌlə'bɪləti/ n [U]

gully /'gʌli/ n [C] (plural **gullies**) a small narrow valley

gulp /gʌlp/ v **1** (also **gulp down**) [T] to swallow food or drink quickly: *Sip your drink – don't gulp it.* **THESAURUS** DRINK **2** [I] to swallow suddenly because you are surprised or nervous: *I gulped when I saw the bill.* **3** (also **gulp in**) [T] to breathe large amounts of air quickly: *He gulped in the night air.* —**gulp** n [C]

gum¹ /gʌm/ n **1** [C usually plural] the pink parts inside your mouth that your teeth grow out of **2** [U] CHEWING GUM

gum² v [T + adv/prep] (**gummed**, **gumming**) BrE old-fashioned to stick things together using glue

gumption /'gʌmpʃən/ n [U] informal the ability and determination to decide what needs to be done and to do it: *At least she had the gumption to phone.*

gun¹ /gʌn/ n [C]
1 a weapon that fires bullets: *I've never **fired** a **gun** in my life.* | **have/hold/carry a gun**
2 a tool that forces out small objects or a liquid by pressure: *a nail gun* → **jump the gun** at JUMP¹, MACHINE GUN

gun² v [T] (**gunned**, **gunning**) AmE informal to make a car go very fast by pressing the ACCELERATOR very hard

PHRASAL VERBS
gun sb ↔ **down** to shoot someone, killing or injuring them badly: *He was gunned down outside his home.*
be gunning for sb informal to be trying to find an opportunity to criticize or harm someone: *Why is she always gunning for me?*

gunboat /'gʌnbəʊt $ -boʊt/ n [C] a small ship that carries several large guns

gunfire /'gʌnfaɪə $ -faɪr/ n [U] shots fired from a gun: *the sound of gunfire*

gunge /gʌndʒ/ n [U] BrE informal a dirty, sticky, or unpleasant substance —**gungy** adj

gunman /'gʌnmən/ n [C] (plural **gunmen** /-mən/) a criminal who uses a gun

gunner /'gʌnə $ -ər/ n [C] a soldier or sailor whose job is to aim and fire a large gun

gunpoint /'gʌnpɔɪnt/ n **at gunpoint** if someone does something to you at gunpoint, they do it while threatening to shoot you: *We were held at gunpoint throughout the robbery.*

gunpowder /'gʌn,paʊdə $ -ər/ n [U] an explosive substance

gunrunning /'gʌn,rʌnɪŋ/ n [U] when guns are taken into a country secretly and illegally —**gunrunner** n [C]

gunshot /'gʌnʃɒt $ -ʃɑːt/ n **1** [C] the sound made by a gun: *We heard gunshots.* **2** [U] the bullets fired from a gun: *a **gunshot** wound*

gun-toting /'gʌn ,təʊtɪŋ $ -,toʊ-/ adj [only before noun] carrying a gun: *gun-toting street-gangs*

gurgle /'gɜːgəl $ 'gɜːr-/ v [I] to make a sound like flowing water: *The baby gurgled with pleasure.* —**gurgle** n [C]

guru /'gʊruː/ n [C] **1** informal someone that people respect because they are very wise or skilful in a particular subject: *a management guru* **2** a Hindu religious teacher

gush /gʌʃ/ v **1** [I] if a liquid gushes somewhere, a large amount of it flows there: **[+out of/from etc]** *Water gushed out of the pipe.* **2** [I,T] to express your praise or pleasure in a way that other people think is too strong: *'I love your dress,' she gushed.* —**gush** n [C]

gust /gʌst/ n [C] a sudden strong movement of wind: **[+of]** *A gust of wind blew our tent over.* —**gust** v [I]: *The forecast is for winds gusting at up to 45 miles per hour.* —**gusty** adj

gusto /'gʌstəʊ $ -toʊ/ n **with gusto** with a lot of energy and enjoyment

gut¹ /gʌt/ n **1 guts** [plural] informal courage and determination to do something difficult: *It takes a lot of guts to admit that you're wrong.* **2 a) guts** [plural] the stomach and the organs around it inside someone's body: *I've got a pain in my guts.* | *Remove the guts of the fish.* **b)** [C] the tube in your body that food passes through: *a blockage of the lower gut* → **hate sb's guts** at HATE¹
PHRASES
gut feeling/reaction/instinct informal a feeling that you are sure is right, although you cannot give a reason for it: *I had a gut feeling that he was a dangerous man.*
work/slog your guts out informal to work very hard: *We'll have to work our guts out to finish in time.*

gut² v [T] (**gutted**, **gutting**) **1** to destroy the inside of a building completely: *The school was completely gutted by fire.* **2** to remove the organs from inside a fish or animal before cooking it

gutsy /'gʌtsi/ adj informal brave and determined

gutted /'gʌtɪd/ adj [not before noun] BrE informal very disappointed: *I was gutted when I lost my job.*

gutter /'gʌtə $ -ər/ n [C] the low part at the edge of a road, or a pipe fixed to a roof, which carries away water

guttering /'gʌtərɪŋ/ n [U] BrE pipes fixed to a roof to carry away rainwater

guttural /'gʌtərəl/ adj a guttural sound is produced deep in your throat

guy /gaɪ/ n [C] informal
1 a man or a boy: *He's a really nice guy.* **THESAURUS** MAN
2 guys [plural] especially AmE informal people: *We'll see you guys Sunday, okay?*

guzzle /'gʌzəl/ v [I,T] *informal* to eat or drink a lot of something quickly: *They've been guzzling beer all evening.*

gym /dʒɪm/ n **1** [C] a large room that has equipment for doing physical exercise **2** [U] sports and exercises that you do indoors: *a gym class*

gymnasium /dʒɪm'neɪziəm/ n [C] *formal* a GYM

gymnast /'dʒɪmnæst, -nəst/ n [C] someone who does gymnastics

gymnastics /dʒɪm'næstɪks/ n [U] a sport in which you do skilful physical exercises and movements, often in competitions: *a gymnastics display*

Grammar
Do not say 'I did gymnastic when I was at school.' Say *I did gymnastics when I was at school.*

gynaecology *BrE*, **gynecology** *AmE* /ˌɡaɪnə'kɒlədʒi $ -'kɑː-/ n [U] the study and treatment of medical conditions that affect only women —**gynaecologist** n [C] —**gynaecological** /ˌɡaɪnəkə'lɒdʒɪkəl◂ $ -'lɑː-/ adj

gypsy (*also* **gipsy** *BrE*) /'dʒɪpsi/ n [C] (*plural* **gypsies**) a member of a race of people who live and travel around in CARAVANS → **traveller**

gyrate /dʒaɪ'reɪt $ 'dʒaɪreɪt/ v [I] to turn around fast in circles: *dancers gyrating wildly*

G

Hh

H, h /eɪtʃ/ n [C,U] (*plural* **H's, h's**) the eighth letter of the English alphabet

ha /hɑː/ *spoken* used to show that you are surprised or pleased about something: *Ha! I knew I was right.*

habit /ˈhæbɪt/ n
1 [C,U] something that you do regularly or usually, often without thinking about it because you have done it so many times before: *Biting your nails is a very bad habit.* | **out of habit/from habit** (=because you have always done this in the past) *After he left home, I was still cleaning his room out of habit.* | **be in the habit of doing sth** *On Friday evenings Carrie was in the habit of visiting her parents.*
2 [C] a strong physical need to keep taking a drug regularly: *Drug users often find it very difficult to give up their habit.* → **force of habit** at FORCE[1]
PHRASES

break/change the habit of a lifetime to stop doing something you have done for many years: *He broke the habit of a lifetime and came with us to the church.*

COLLOCATIONS
verbs
to have a habit (of doing sth) *He has a habit of being late.*
to get into a habit (=to start doing something regularly or often) *I got into the habit of going to bed early.*
to get out of a habit (=to stop doing something regularly or often) *She couldn't get out of the habit of saying 'sorry'.*
to break/kick a habit (=to stop doing something that is bad for you) *I've smoked for years, but I really want to kick the habit.*

adjectives
a bad habit *My sister has lots of bad habits.*
an annoying habit *He had an annoying habit of interrupting people.*
a strange/peculiar/odd habit *Some people have very odd habits.*

habitable /ˈhæbətəbəl/ adj a place that is habitable is suitable for people to live in OPP **uninhabitable**

habitat /ˈhæbətæt/ n [C] the natural environment in which a plant or animal lives: *It was great to see monkeys in their **natural habitat**.*

habitation /ˌhæbɪˈteɪʃən/ n [U] when people live in a place: *There was no sign of habitation on the island.*

habitual /həˈbɪtʃuəl/ adj formal **1** [only before noun] usual or typical of someone: *Jane was in her habitual bad temper this morning.* **2** done as a habit that you cannot stop: *a habitual smoker*

hack¹ /hæk/ v [I,T] **1** to cut something into pieces roughly: *All of the victims had been **hacked to death**.* **2** to secretly find a way of getting information from someone else's computer or changing information on it: **[+into]** *Somebody hacked into the company's central database.*

hack² n [C] a writer who does a lot of low quality work, especially writing newspaper articles

hacker /ˈhækə $ -ər/ n [C] informal someone who secretly uses or changes the information in other people's computer systems —**hacking** n [U]

hackles /ˈhækəlz/ n [plural] **sb's hackles rise** if your hackles rise, you begin to feel very angry, because of what someone has said or done

hackneyed /ˈhæknid/ adj a hackneyed phrase does not have much meaning because it has been used so often

hacksaw /ˈhæksɔː $ -sɒː/ n [C] a cutting tool with small teeth on its blade, used for cutting metal

had¹ /d, əd, həd; strong hæd/ v the past tense and past participle of HAVE → **-'d**

had² /hæd/ adj **be had** informal to be tricked: *She had the feeling she'd been had.*

haddock /ˈhædək/ n [C,U] (*plural* **haddock**) a fish that lives in northern seas, and is caught for food

hadn't /ˈhædnt/ the short form of 'had not'

haemophilia BrE, **hemophilia** AmE /ˌhiːməˈfɪliə/ n [U] a serious disease in which the flow of blood from someone's body when they are injured cannot be stopped —**haemophiliac** /-liæk/ n [C]

haemorrhage BrE, **hemorrhage** AmE /ˈhemərɪdʒ/ n [C,U] a serious medical condition in which a person is injured inside their body and a lot of blood comes out

haemorrhoids BrE, **hemorrhoids** AmE /ˈhemərɔɪdz/ n [plural] technical painful swollen BLOOD VESSELS near a person's ANUS SYN **piles**

hag /hæg/ n [C] an ugly or unpleasant old woman

haggard /ˈhægəd $ -ərd/ adj looking tired, thin, and ill: *She arrived home looking pale and haggard.*

haggle /ˈhægəl/ v [I] to argue about the amount that you will pay for something: **[+over]** *We were haggling over the price for an hour.*

hah /hɑː/ another spelling of HA

ha 'ha used in writing to show that someone is laughing

hail¹ /heɪl/ v **1** [T] to describe someone or something as being very good: **hail sb/sth as sth** *Lang's first film was immediately hailed as a masterpiece.* **2** [T] to call or wave to someone: **hail a cab/taxi** (=wave at a taxi to make it stop) **3** [I] if it hails, frozen rain falls from the sky
PHRASAL VERBS

hail from sth old-fashioned to come from a particular place: *He hails from Massachusetts.*

hail² n **1** [U] small hard drops of frozen rain that fall from the sky THESAURUS ▶ RAIN **2 a hail of bullets/stones etc** a lot of bullets, stones etc that come through the air at the same time: *a hail of gunfire*

hailstone /ˈheɪlstəʊn $ -stoʊn/ n [C usually plural] a small hard drop of frozen rain

hair /heə $ her/ n
1 [U] the mass of thin threads that grows on your head: *a young woman with short blonde hair* → see picture on p. 404

> **Grammar**
> In this meaning, hair is an uncountable noun.Do not say 'He has black hairs.' Say *He has black hair.*

2 [C,U] one of the thin threads that grows on a person's or animal's skin → **fur**: *The sofa was covered in dog hairs.* → **split hairs** at **SPLIT**[1]
PHRASES
let your hair down *informal* to stop being serious and enjoy yourself: *The party will be a good chance for everybody to let their hair down.*
be pulling/tearing your hair out *informal* to be very worried: *She's been tearing her hair out about her son's bad behaviour at school.*

COLLOCATIONS

adjectives
short/long hair *I like your hair when it's long.*
medium-length hair *Police say the man has medium-length hair.*
brown/black/dark hair *a woman with dark hair and blue eyes*
blonde/fair hair *a beautiful girl with long blonde hair*
white hair *an old man with white hair*
grey hair *BrE*, **gray hair** *AmE Her hair was starting to go grey.*
red hair (also **ginger hair** *BrE*) *a cheeky little boy with ginger hair*
straight hair *She has long straight hair.*
curly/wavy hair *When he was young, his hair was thick and curly.*

verbs
to have long/dark etc hair *She had beautiful long blonde hair.*
to have your hair cut (=by a hairdresser) *I need to get my hair cut.* ⚠ Do not say 'I cut my hair' if another person cuts your hair for you. Say **I had my hair cut.**
to wash/brush/comb your hair *He cleaned his teeth and brushed his hair.*
to dye your hair (=to change its colour) *Craig has dyed his hair black.*

---

hairbrush /ˈheəbrʌʃ $ ˈher-/ n [C] a brush that you use to make your hair tidy → see picture at **BRUSH**[1]

haircut /ˈheəkʌt $ ˈher-/ n **1** [C usually singular] when you have your hair cut by someone: *I must have a haircut.* **2** [C] the style in which your hair has been cut: *I like your new haircut.*

hairdo /ˈheədu: $ ˈher-/ n [C] (plural **hairdos**) *informal* the style in which your hair is cut or shaped

hairdresser /ˈheəˌdresə $ ˈherˌdresər/ n [C] **1** a person who cuts and arranges people's hair in particular styles **2 the hairdresser's** a hairdresser's shop: *I have an appointment at the hairdresser's.*

hairdryer /ˈheəˌdraɪə $ ˈherˌdraɪər/ n [C] a machine that blows out hot air for drying your hair

-haired /heəd $ herd/ *suffix* used to say that a person or animal has hair of a particular length, colour etc: *a fair-haired girl* | *long-haired cats*

hairgrip /ˈheəgrɪp $ ˈher-/ n [C] *BrE* a small piece of metal that holds your hair in place **SYN bobby pin** *AmE*

hairline /ˈheəlaɪn $ ˈher-/ n **1** [C] the place at the front of your head where your hair starts growing **2 hairline crack/fracture** a very thin crack: *She suffered a hairline fracture in the leg.*

hairpin /ˈheəpɪn $ ˈher-/ n [C] a U-shaped piece of metal that holds your hair in place

hairpin ˈbend *BrE*, **hairpin ˈturn** *AmE* n [C] a U-shaped bend on a steep road

ˈhair-ˌraising *adj* frightening in an exciting way: *hair-raising adventures*

hairstyle /ˈheəstaɪl $ ˈher-/ n [C] the style in which your hair has been cut or shaped

hairstylist /ˈheəˌstaɪlɪst $ ˈher-/ n [C] a HAIRDRESSER

hairy /ˈheəri $ ˈheri/ *adj* **1** covered in hair: *a hairy chest* **2** *spoken* dangerous or frightening

halal /hɑːˈlɑːl/ *adj* halal meat is meat from an animal that has been killed in a way that is approved by Muslim law

hale /heɪl/ *adj* **hale and hearty** *humorous* healthy and full of energy

half[1] /hɑːf $ hæf/ (plural **halves** /hɑːvz $ hævz/) n [C], determiner
1 one of two equal parts of something: *Two halves make a whole.* | *Over half the people in this area are unemployed.* | *Their son is two and a half.* | **[+of]** *I only saw the first half of the film.* | **half an hour/mile etc** *I got to work half an hour late.* | **in half** *Cut the tomatoes in half.* | **cut/reduce sth by half** (=make it 50% smaller) *Profits have been cut by half.* | **the first/second half** *Beckham scored in the first half of the match.*
2 the largest part of something: *She seems to be asleep half the time.*
PHRASES
> **go halves (on sth)** to share something, especially the cost of something, equally between two people: *Do you want to go halves on a pizza?*
> **half a dozen 1** six: *half a dozen eggs* **2** a few: *There were only half a dozen people there.*
> **half (past) one/two/three etc** *especially BrE* 30 minutes after one o'clock, two o'clock etc: *We're meeting at half past seven.* | *I phoned about half six.*
> **not half as/so good/interesting etc (as sb/sth)** much less good, interesting etc than someone or something else: *The movie wasn't half as good as the book.*

half[2] *adv* partly but not completely: *He shouldn't be allowed to drive – he's half blind!* | *I half expected her to shout at me.* | *a half-empty bottle*

ˌhalf-ˈbaked *adj informal* a half-baked idea is not sensible and has not been thought about carefully

ˌhalf ˈboard n [U] *especially BrE* the price of a room in a hotel including breakfast and dinner

H

'half-,brother n [C] a brother who is the child of only one of your parents

half-hearted /,hɑːf 'hɑːtɪd◄ $ 'hæf 'hɑːr-/ adj done without any real effort or interest: He made a **half-hearted attempt** to tidy his room. —**half-heartedly** adv

,half-'hour, half hour n [C] a period of 30 minutes: We waited for a good **half-hour** (=at least 30 minutes, usually more). —**half-hour** adj: a half-hour TV show

,half-'hourly adj, adv BrE done or happening every half-hour: Trains depart at half-hourly intervals from 10.30 am until 4.00 pm.

,half-'mast n **fly/be at half-mast** if a flag is flying at half-mast, it is lowered to the middle of its pole because someone important has died

'half-,sister n [C] a sister who is the child of only one of your parents

,half 'term n [C,U] BrE a short holiday in the middle of a school TERM

,half-'time n [U] a period when the players rest between two parts of a game such as football

halfway /,hɑːf'weɪ◄ $ 'hæf-/ adj, adv at a middle point: **[+between]** We live halfway between London and Manchester. | **[+through/down/up etc]** Halfway through the meal, Dan got up. | We had reached the halfway point of the walk.

'half-wit n [C] a stupid person

hall /hɔːl $ hɒːl/ n [C]
1 the area just inside the door of a building, that leads to other rooms: The bathroom's just down the hall on the right.
2 a building or large room for public events such as meetings or dances: a dance hall | Carnegie Hall → **TOWN HALL**

hallmark /'hɔːlmɑːk $ 'hɒːlmɑːrk/ n [C]
1 something that is typical of a particular person or thing: **[+of]** The explosion **had all the hallmarks** of a terrorist attack. **2** a mark put on silver or gold that shows the quality of the metal, and where and when it was made

hallo /hə'ləʊ, hæ- $ -'loʊ/ a British spelling of HELLO

,hall of 'residence n [C] BrE a college or university building where students live **SYN dormitory** AmE

hallowed /'hæləʊd $ -loʊd/ adj **1** respected and important: the hallowed halls of government **2** holy: hallowed ground

Halloween /,hæləʊ'iːn◄ $ -loʊ-/ n [U] the night of October 31, when children dress as WITCHES, GHOSTS etc → see picture at **MASK¹**

hallucinate /hə'luːsəneɪt/ v [I] to see, feel, or hear things that are not really there —**hallucination** /hə'luːsə'neɪʃən/ n [C,U]: The patients suffered hallucinations caused by the drug. —**hallucinatory** /hə'luːsənətəri $ -tɔːri/ adj: hallucinatory drugs

hallway /'hɔːlweɪ $ 'hɒːl-/ n [C] the area just inside

HAIR

straight hair

bun

curly hair

receding hair

spiky hair

plait BrE/braid AmE

fringe BrE/ bangs AmE

ponytail

bald

pigtails

wavy hair

dreadlocks

bobbed hair

the door of a building that leads to other rooms **SYN** **hall**

halo /ˈheɪləʊ $ -loʊ/ n [C] (plural **halos**) a golden circle that is shown in paintings above the head of a holy person

halt /hɔːlt $ hɒːlt/ n [singular] when something stops happening or moving for a period of time: **come/grind to a halt** The bus slowly ground to a halt. | They decided to **call a halt to** the strike (=make it stop). **THESAURUS** STOP —**halt** v [I,T] formal: The city council has halted repair work on the subways.

halter /ˈhɔːltə $ ˈhɒːltər/ n [C] a piece of rope or leather that is fastened around a horse's head to lead it along

halting /ˈhɔːltɪŋ $ ˈhɒːl-/ adj stopping a lot when you move or speak, especially because you are nervous: She spoke in a halting voice.

halve /hɑːv $ hæv/ v [T] **1** to reduce the amount of something by half: Food production was almost halved during the war. **2** to cut or divide something into two equal pieces: Wash and halve the mushrooms.

halves /hɑːvz $ hævz/ n the plural of HALF

ham /hæm/ n [C,U] preserved meat from a pig: a **slice of ham** | a **ham sandwich**

hamburger /ˈhæmbɜːgə $ -bɜːrgər/ n **1** [C] BEEF that is made into a round shape, cooked, and eaten inside a round piece of bread **2** [U] AmE BEEF that is cut into very small pieces **SYN** **mince** BrE

hamlet /ˈhæmlɪt/ n [C] a very small village

hammer¹ /ˈhæmə $ -ər/ n [C] a tool with a heavy metal part on a long handle, used for hitting nails into wood → see picture at TOOL

hammer² v **1** [I,T] to hit something with a hammer **2** [I] to hit something several times, making a lot of noise: Mike was hammering on the door with his fists. **PHRASAL VERBS**
hammer sth **into** sb to continue repeating something in order to force people to remember it: Mom hammered the message into us: don't talk to strangers!
hammer sth ↔ **out** to finally agree about the details of something: It took several days to hammer out an agreement.

hammering /ˈhæmərɪŋ/ n **1** [U] the sound of someone hitting something with a hammer or with their hands **2** [C] a very bad defeat

hammock /ˈhæmək/ n [C] a large piece of material used for sleeping on that hangs between two trees or poles

hamper¹ /ˈhæmpə $ -ər/ v [T] to make something difficult: The search for the men was hampered by bad weather.

hamper² n [C] a large basket for carrying food: a picnic hamper

hamster /ˈhæmstə $ -ər/ n [C] a small animal with soft fur and no tail that is often kept as a pet → see picture at PET¹

hamstring¹ /ˈhæmˌstrɪŋ/ n [C] a TENDON behind your knee

hamstring² v [T] (past tense and past participle **hamstrung** /-ˌstrʌŋ/) to make it difficult for someone to do or achieve something

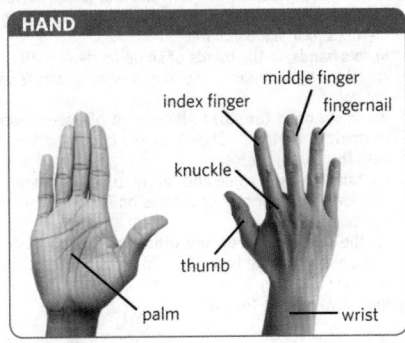

HAND

middle finger
index finger
fingernail
knuckle
thumb
palm
wrist

hand¹ /hænd/ n [C]
1 **BODY PART** the part of your body at the end of your arm, including your fingers and thumb: Tom stood in the doorway with his hands in his pockets. | **in sb's hand** He had a suitcase in his hand.

2 **USING YOUR LEFT OR RIGHT HAND** **right-handed/left-handed** always using the right hand or left hand to do things such as write, use tools etc: My sister is left-handed.

3 **HELP** **a hand** help with something: **give/lend sb a hand** Can you give me a hand moving this box? | [+with] Do you **need a hand** with the cooking? **THESAURUS** HELP

4 **ON A CLOCK** one of the long things that point to the numbers on a clock: The hour hand was pointing to 6. → see picture at WATCH²

PHRASES
at the hands of sb if you suffer at the hands of someone, they treat you badly: She suffered at the hands of her old boss.
by hand using your hands, not a machine: She does all her washing by hand.
change hands if something changes hands, it is given or sold by one person to another person: The house has changed hands three times in the last two years.
close/near at hand near: Nurses are always close at hand in case of emergency.
get/lay your hands on sth to manage to get or find something: I read every book I could get my hands on.
get out of hand to become impossible to control: Todd's behaviour is getting totally out of hand.
go hand in hand to be closely connected: Wealth and power go hand in hand.
hand in hand holding each other's hands: They walked hand in hand through the park.
hands off spoken used to warn someone not to touch something that is yours: Hands off my cookies!
have a hand in sth to influence or be involved in something: He scored one goal and had a hand in two others.
have your hands full to be very busy: You're going to have your hands full once you have the baby!

H

hand

have sth/sb on your hands to have a difficult job, problem, situation etc to deal with: *I'm afraid we have a murder on our hands, Inspector.*

in hand being dealt with now: **the job/task/matter in hand** *We need to discuss the most suitable working methods for the job in hand.*

in sb's hands/in the hands of sb being dealt with or cared for by someone: *The matter is in the hands of the police.*

be an old hand (at sth) to have a lot of experience of doing something: *Chris is an old hand at dealing with this sort of problem.*

on hand/to hand close and ready to be used when needed: *Keep a supply of candles on hand in case of power cuts.*

on the one hand ... on the other hand used when you are comparing two different facts or ideas: *On the one hand, they work slowly, but on the other hand they always finish the job.*

> **Grammar**
>
> Do not say 'in the other hand' when you mean **on the other hand**.

with your bare hands without using a weapon or tool: *He forced the doors apart with his bare hands.*

COLLOCATIONS

adjectives

sb's right/left hand *He writes with his left hand.*
big/small/tiny hands *The baby's hands were tiny.*
clean/dirty hands *Make sure that your hands are clean.*

verbs

to have/hold sth in your hand *He already had the money in his hand.*
to wash/dry your hands *You should always wash your hands before eating.*
to shake hands (=when meeting or leaving someone) *'Nice to meet you,' he said, as they shook hands.*
to clap your hands (=to hit them together to show that you think something is good) *The crowd were all singing and clapping their hands.*
to put up your hand (also **raise your hand** *formal*) (=to lift it up) *If you think you know the answer, put up your hand.*
to hold hands *Joanne and Kevin held hands on the sofa.*
to take sb's hand *He reached across the table and took her hand.*

nouns + hand

the palm of your hand (=the surface of your hand that your fingers can bend towards) *He held the coin in the palm of his hand.*
the back of your hand (=the other side from the palm) *She wrote the number on the back of her hand.*

hand² v [T] to give something to someone: **hand sth to sb** *She handed the letter to her father.* | **hand sb sth** *Can you hand me a towel?*

you have to hand it to sb *spoken* used to show that you admire someone: *You have to hand it to Liz – she's a great cook!*

PHRASAL VERBS

hand sth ↔ **around** (also **hand** sth ↔ **round** *BrE*) to offer something to each person in a group: *Could you hand the sandwiches around please, Mike?*

hand sth ↔ **back** to give something back to the person who gave it to you: **[+to]** *Mr Evans handed our essays back to us today.*

hand sth ↔ **down** to give something to a younger relation, or to people who live after you: *traditions that were handed down from generation to generation*

hand sth ↔ **in** to give something to someone in authority: *Please hand in your application by September 30.*

hand sth ↔ **out** to give something to each person in a group: *They were handing out free T-shirts at the club.* **THESAURUS** GIVE

hand sb/sth ↔ **over** to give someone or something to the person who wants to deal with them: **[+to]** *The thief was caught and handed over to the police.*

handbag /'hændbæg/ n [C] *especially BrE* a small bag that a woman uses to carry money and personal things **SYN** **purse** *AmE* → see picture at **BAG¹**

handbook /'hændbʊk/ n [C] a short book that gives information or instructions about something

handbrake /'hændbreɪk/ n [C] *BrE* a BRAKE in a car that you pull up with your hand to stop the car from moving when it is parked **SYN** **emergency brake** *AmE*

handcuffs /'hændkʌfs/ n [plural] a pair of metal rings that are put over a prisoner's wrists to hold their hands together —**handcuff** v [T]

handful /'hændfʊl/ n [C] **1** an amount that you can hold in your hand: **[+of]** *a handful of nuts* **2 a handful of sb/sth** a small number of people or things: *Only a handful of people came to the meeting.* **3 be a handful** *informal* if a child is a handful, they behave badly and are difficult to control: *She's a lovely child, but she can be a handful sometimes.*

handgun /'hændgʌn/ n [C] a small gun you hold in one hand when you fire it

hand-'held *adj* a hand-held machine is small enough to hold in your hand when you use it: *a hand-held camera*

handicap /'hændikæp/ n [C] **1** *old-fashioned* if someone has a handicap, a part of their body or their mind has been permanently injured or damaged. Many people think that this word is offensive: *a child with a severe physical handicap* **2** something that makes it difficult for you to do or achieve something: *Not being able to speak French was a real handicap.*

handicapped /'hændikæpt/ *adj* if someone is handicapped, a part of their body or their mind has been permanently injured or damaged. Many people think that this word is offensive: *a mentally handicapped child*

handicraft /'hændikrɑːft $ -kræft/ n **1** [C] an activity in which you use your hands in a skilful way to make things **2 handicrafts** [plural] things that someone has made in a skilful way using their hands

handiwork /ˈhændiwɜːk $ -wɜːrk/ n [U] if something is your handiwork, you have done it or made it using your hands

handkerchief /ˈhæŋkətʃɪf $ -kər-/ n [C] a piece of cloth or paper that you use for drying your nose or eyes SYN **hankie**

handle¹ /ˈhændl/ v [T]
1 to deal with something: *Computers can handle huge amounts of data.* | *Ms Lee handled all of our travel arrangements.* | *The job was so stressful, he couldn't handle it any longer.* THESAURUS DEAL
2 to pick up or touch something: *Handle all packages with care.*
3 to buy or sell goods: *Upton was charged with **handling stolen goods**.*

handle² n [C] the part of something that you hold when you use it: *a pan with a broken handle* | *a door handle*

handlebars /ˈhændlbɑːz $ -bɑːrz/ n [plural] the bars above the front wheel of a bicycle or MOTORCYCLE, that you turn to control the direction you go in
→ see picture at **BICYCLE**

handler /ˈhændlə $ -ər/ n [C] someone whose job is to deal with or look after a particular kind of thing: *baggage handlers* | *a police dog and its handler*

ˈhand ˌluggage n [U] small bags that you carry with you when you travel on a plane

handmade /ˌhændˈmeɪd◂/ adj made by a person and not a machine: *handmade shoes*

handout /ˈhændaʊt/ n [C] **1** money or food that is given to someone because they are poor: *a cash handout* **2** a piece of paper with information on it that is given to people in a class or meeting

handover /ˈhændəʊvə $ -oʊvər/ n [singular] **1** the act of formally giving someone else control of a place or business: **[+of]** *Troops will stay in the country to ensure a smooth **handover of power**.* **2** the act of giving something to someone: **[+of]** *His lawyer demanded the immediate handover of all relevant documents.*

handpicked /ˌhændˈpɪkt◂/ adj carefully chosen: *a handpicked team*

handset /ˈhændset/ n [C] **1** the part of a telephone that you hold near your ear and mouth **2** the part of a MOBILE PHONE that you hold in your hand

ˌhands-ˈfree adj [only before noun] a hands-free machine is one that you can use without using your hands: *a hands-free phone*

handshake /ˈhændʃeɪk/ n [C] an action in which two people take each other's right hand when they meet or leave each other, or when they make an agreement: *He greeted me with a firm handshake.*

handsome /ˈhænsəm/ adj
1 attractive – used especially about men: *a tall handsome young officer* | *Sam was **tall, dark, and handsome**.* THESAURUS BEAUTIFUL

2 [only before noun] a handsome amount of money is large: *He managed to make a **handsome profit** out of the deal.*

> **Word Choice**: handsome or good-looking?
> **Handsome** is used especially in written English. In everyday spoken English, people usually say **good-looking**: *Do you think he's good-looking?* **Handsome** is usually used about men. It is also sometimes used in literature to describe a woman who has strong-looking features: *Mrs Castle was a tall handsome woman in her late thirties.*

ˈhands-on adj doing something yourself rather than just talking about it or telling other people to do it: *a chance to get some **hands-on experience** of the job*

ˌhand-to-ˈmouth adj, adv if you have a hand-to-mouth existence, or if you live hand-to-mouth, you have only just enough money and food to live

handwash /ˈhændwɒʃ $ -wɒːʃ, -wɑːʃ/ v [T] if you handwash clothes, you wash them by hand, not in a washing machine

handwriting /ˈhændˌraɪtɪŋ/ n [U] the style of someone's writing: *She has very neat handwriting.*

handwritten /ˌhændˈrɪtn◂/ adj written by hand, not printed: *a handwritten letter*

handy /ˈhændi/ adj **1** useful: *a handy little tool* | *The extra key may **come in handy** (=be useful in the future).* THESAURUS USEFUL **2** informal near and easy to reach: *Make sure you **have** your passport **handy**.* **3 be handy with sth** to be good at using something, especially a tool: *Terry's very handy with a needle and thread.*

handyman /ˈhændimæn/ n [C] (plural **handymen** /-men/) someone who is good at making and repairing things

hang¹ /hæŋ/ v (past tense and past participle **hung** /hʌŋ/)
1 (also **hang up**) [I,T] to put something somewhere so that its top part is fixed but its bottom part is free to move, or to be in this position: **hang sth above/on/over etc sth** *He hung his coat on the back of the door.* | **[+from/on/over etc]** *Her portrait was hanging on the wall.* | *The shirt hung down to his knees.*
2 [I,T] (past tense and past participle **hanged**) to kill someone by dropping them with a rope around their neck, or to die in this way, as a punishment for a crime: **be hanged for sth** *He was hanged for murder.* | *Corey hanged himself in his prison cell.*
3 [I] to stay in the air in the same place for a long time: *Dark clouds hung over the valley.*
PHRASES
hang in the balance if something hangs in the balance, it is not certain what will happen to it: *Our whole future is hanging in the balance.*
hang your head to look ashamed and embarrassed: *Lewis hung his head and refused to answer.*
leave sb/sth hanging to not finish something or not tell someone your decision about something: *The investigation should not be left hanging.*

H

hang

PHRASAL VERBS

hang around (also **hang round/about** BrE) informal
1 hang around (sth) to stay in one place without doing very much: *We hung around outside school for about an hour.* **THESAURUS** WAIT
2 hang around with sb to spend a lot of time with someone: *I don't like the people she hangs around with.*

hang back to not want to move forward or speak, often because you are shy: *Joe tends to hang back and let the others do the talking.*

hang on
1 hang on! spoken used to tell someone to wait for you: *Hang on, I'll be with you in a minute!* **THESAURUS** WAIT
2 informal to hold something tightly: *Hang on everybody, the road's pretty bumpy.* | **[+to]** *She hung on tightly to the reins as they trotted along.* **THESAURUS** HOLD

hang onto sb/sth informal to keep something: *Hang onto that letter – you might need it later.*

hang out
1 informal to spend a lot of time at a particular place or with particular people: *Where does he usually hang out?*
2 hang sth ↔ out to hang clothes outside in order to dry them

hang up
1 to finish a telephone conversation by putting the telephone down: *She said good night and hung up.* | **[+on]** *Don't hang up on me* (=put the phone down during a conversation because you are angry)!
2 hang sth ↔ up to hang clothes on a hook etc

hang² n **get the hang of (doing) sth** informal to learn how to do something: *You'll soon get the hang of using the computer.* **THESAURUS** LEARN

hangar /'hæŋə $ -ər/ n [C] a very large building where aircraft are kept

hanger /'hæŋə $ -ər/ (also **coat hanger**) n [C] a curved piece of plastic, wood, or metal with a hook on top, used for hanging clothes on

hanger-'on n [C] (plural **hangers-on**) someone who spends a lot of time with important or rich people for their own advantage

'hang ,glider n [C] a large frame covered with cloth that you hold on to and fly slowly through the air on —**hang gliding** n [U]

hangout /'hæŋaʊt/ n [C] informal a place that you often go to

hangover /'hæŋəʊvə $ -oʊvər/ n [C] an ill feeling that you have when you have drunk too much alcohol the evening before

'hang-up n [C] informal if you have a hang-up about something, you feel worried or embarrassed about it: *Cindy has a hang-up about her nose.*

hanker /'hæŋkə $ -ər/ v **hanker after/for sth** informal to feel strongly that you want something: *She's always hankered after a place of her own.*

hankie, hanky /'hæŋki/ n [C] informal a HANDKERCHIEF

hanky-panky /,hæŋki 'pæŋki/ n [U] informal humorous sexual activity

Hanukkah /'hɑːnəkə $ 'kɑːnəkə, 'hɑː-/ n [C,U] an eight-day Jewish holiday in November or December

haphazard /,hæp'hæzəd◄ $ -ərd◄/ adj not planned or organized: *a haphazard way of working*

hapless /'hæpləs/ adj literary unlucky

happen /'hæpən/ v [I]
1 if an event happens, it exists and continues for a period of time, usually without being planned: *When did the accident happen?* | *Did anything exciting happen while I was away?* | *We waited for half an hour, but* **nothing happened.** | **Something** terrible **has happened.**
2 happen to do sth to do something by chance: *I happened to see Hannah at the store today.*
PHRASES
as it happens/it (just) so happens used to tell someone something that is surprising, interesting, or useful: *It just so happened that Mike and I went to the same school.*

PHRASAL VERBS
happen on/upon sb/sth literary to find something or meet someone by chance: *I happened on the restaurant by chance.*
happen to sb/sth to affect someone or something: *Strange things have been happening to me lately.* | *He should be here by now – something must have happened to him.*

THESAURUS

happen used especially about events that have not been planned: *The accident happened in the early hours of Friday morning.*
take place to happen – used especially about events that have been planned: *The festival takes place every year in July.*
there is/are used when saying that an event happens, either one that is planned or unplanned: *There are more floods now than in the past.* | *There's a concert at the school next Saturday.*
come up to happen – used about problems or opportunities: *Something came up at the office and I had to work late.* | *A job came up in New York, so I took it.*
occur formal to happen – used about events that have not been planned: *The incident occurred at the bus station at around 9 pm.* | *Major earthquakes like this occur very rarely.*

---

happening /'hæpənɪŋ/ n [C] a strange or unusual event

happily /'hæpəli/ adv **1** in a happy way: *They're very* **happily married.** **2** fortunately: *Happily, no one was hurt in the fire.* **3** very willingly: *I'll happily look after the kids while you're out.*

happiness /'hæpinəs/ n [U] when someone is happy: *Her eyes shone with happiness.*

happy /'hæpi/ adj (comparative **happier**, superlative **happiest**)
1 **FEELING GOOD** having feelings of pleasure, for example because something good has happened to you or because you are satisfied with your life **OPP** **sad, unhappy**: *Sam's been looking very happy*

recently. | **be happy to do sth** *John will be so happy to see you.* | **[+for]** *Congratulations! I'm very happy for you.*

2 `MAKING YOU FEEL GOOD` a happy time or event is one that makes you feel happy: *Those were the happiest years of my life.* | *They have a very happy marriage.* | *the film has a happy ending*

3 `WILLING` **be happy to do sth** to be willing to do something: *Our team of experts will be happy to answer any questions.*

4 `SATISFIED` [not before noun] satisfied: **[+about]** *I'm not very happy about this.* | **[+with]** *Are you happy with their decision?*

PHRASES

Happy Birthday/Happy New Year etc used as a way of greeting someone on a special occasion: *Happy Birthday, Michael!*

THESAURUS

happy: *I'm happy to be here with you.* | *She had a very happy childhood.*

cheerful looking and behaving in a way that shows you are happy: *Sally's always very cheerful.* | *a cheerful smile*

be in a good mood to be feeling happy and behaving in a relaxed way: *It was the end of term and everyone was in a good mood.*

pleased happy because something good has happened, or someone has done something well: *I'm pleased that I've got the job.* | *Ben's teachers are very pleased with his work.*

delighted very happy because something good has happened. **Delighted** is more formal than **pleased**: *The doctors say they are delighted with her progress.*

glad happy because something good has happened, especially when a situation has improved, or because something bad did not happen: *I'll be so glad when the exams are over.* | *We're glad that you're safe.*

thrilled very happy and excited about something that happens: *We're thrilled that they're getting married.*

satisfied feeling that something is as good as you hoped, or that something happens the way you want: *Most patients said that they were satisfied with the treatment they had received.*

contented *written* feeling happy with your life, job, situation etc and not wanting anything different: *She was contented with her life in the village.* | *He had a contented expression.*

,happy-go-'lucky *adj* not caring or worrying about what happens

,happy 'slapping *n* [C,U] the act of deliberately attacking someone and filming the attack on a MOBILE PHONE

harangue /həˈræŋ/ *v* [T] to speak angrily to someone, often for a long time, to try to persuade them that you are right

harass /ˈhærəs, həˈræs/ *v* [T] to deliberately annoy or threaten someone: *They claim that they are being harassed by the police.*

harassed /ˈhærəst, həˈræst/ *adj* anxious and tired: *He looked pale and harassed.*

harassment /ˈhærəsmənt, həˈræsmənt/ *n* [U] threatening or offensive behaviour: *racial harassment* | *Tina accused her boss of sexual harassment.*

harbour¹ *BrE*, **harbor** *AmE* /ˈhɑːbə $ ˈhɑːrbər/ *n* [C] an area of water next to the land where ships can stay safely: *They sailed into Portsmouth Harbour.*

Word Choice: harbour or port?
You use **harbour** about an area that is protected from the sea by a surrounding wall, where ships can shelter from storms.
You use **port** about a city or town with a large harbour where ships can be loaded and unloaded. You can also use **port** about a large harbour which is part of a city or town.

---

harbour² *BrE*, **harbor** *AmE* *v* [T] *formal* **1** to keep bad feelings or thoughts in your mind for a long time: *She began to harbour doubts over the wisdom of their journey.* **2** to protect someone by hiding them from the police: *She was accused of harbouring deserters.*

HARD

hard   soft

---

hard¹ /hɑːd $ hɑːrd/ *adj*

1 `NOT SOFT` not soft, and difficult to press down, cut, or break `OPP` **soft**: *a hard mattress* | *The plums are still too hard to eat.*

2 `DIFFICULT` difficult to do or understand `OPP` **easy**: *The exam was quite hard.* | **hard (for sb) to do sth** *Your question is hard for me to answer.* | *It's hard to say when Glenn will be back.* `THESAURUS` DIFFICULT

3 `INVOLVING EFFORT/SUFFERING` involving a lot of physical or mental effort or suffering: *a long hard climb to the top of the hill* | *Poor Mary, she's had a hard life.* | *Bringing up children on your own is hard work.* `THESAURUS` TIRING

4 `NOT KIND` showing no kindness or sympathy: *Mr. Katz is a hard man to work for, but he's fair.* | **be hard on sb** *She's too hard on those kids.*

5 `PROOF` **hard facts/evidence** facts etc that are true and can be proved: *The police have no hard evidence to prove that he is guilty.*

6 `DRUGS` **hard drugs** very strong illegal drugs such as HEROIN

7 `WINTER` **a hard winter** a very cold winter: *Many people suffered during the long hard winter.* —**hardness** *n* [U]

H

PHRASES

do/learn sth the hard way to make a lot of mistakes or have a lot of difficulty before learning something: *I learned this lesson the hard way.*

give sb a hard time *informal* to criticize someone a lot or make things difficult for them: *The guys were giving him a hard time about being late.*

hard cash paper money and coins: *He insisted on being paid with hard cash.*

hard currency money from a country that has a strong ECONOMY, that is unlikely to lose its value: *The country aims to export more to the West for hard currency.*

no hard feelings *spoken* used to tell someone that you do not feel angry with them any more

THESAURUS

hard not soft, and difficult to press down, break, or cut: *They slept on the cold hard floor.* | *Diamond is the hardest substance known to man.*

firm something that is firm does not feel soft when you press it – used especially when something feels right: *I like to sleep on a firm mattress.* | *Make sure the tomatoes are ripe but firm.*

stiff difficult to bend – used especially about things made from paper or cloth: *I stuck the photos on a piece of stiff card.*

tough meat that is tough is too hard and is difficult to cut or eat: *The steak was very tough.*

crisp/crispy food that is crisp is pleasantly firm and makes a noise when you bite it – used especially about lettuce and bacon: *a nice crisp lettuce* | *crispy fried bacon*

hard² *adv* using a lot of effort or force: *She'd been working hard all day.* | *Come on, push harder!*

PHRASES

be hard pressed/put/pushed to do sth to have difficulty doing something: *They'll be hard pushed to pay back the money.*

take sth hard to feel very upset about something: *Joe took the news very hard.*

hard-and-'fast *adj* hard-and-fast rules are clear and definite, and always used: *a hard-and-fast rule*

hardback /'hɑːdbæk $ 'hɑːrd-/ *n* [C] *BrE* a book that has a strong stiff cover SYN **hardcover** *AmE* → **paperback** THESAURUS► BOOK

hardball /'hɑːdbɔːl $ 'hɑːrdbɒːl/ *n* **play hardball** *AmE informal* to be very determined to get what you want, especially in business or politics

hardboard /'hɑːdbɔːd $ 'hɑːrdbɔːrd/ *n* [U] a kind of wood made out of smaller pieces of wood that have been pressed together

hard-'boiled *adj* a hard-boiled egg has been boiled until it becomes solid

hard ,copy *n* [U] information from a computer that is printed onto paper

hardcore, **hard-core** /'hɑːdkɔː $ 'hɑːrdkɔːr/ *adj* [only before noun] **1** having very strong beliefs or opinions that are unlikely to change: *hardcore opposition to abortion* **2 hard-core pornography** pictures

and films that show details of sexual behaviour, often in an unpleasant way

'hard core *n* [singular] *BrE* **1** the small group of people that are most active within a group or organization: *the hard core of the Communist Party* **2** a small group of people who refuse to change their behaviour or beliefs: *the hard core of drivers who carry on drinking and driving*

hardcover /'hɑːdkʌvə $ 'hɑːrdkʌvər/ *n* [C] *AmE* HARDBACK THESAURUS► BOOK

,hard 'disk *n* [C] a stiff DISK inside a computer that is used for permanently storing information

harden /'hɑːdn $ 'hɑːrdn/ *v* [I,T] **1** to become firm or stiff, or to make something firm or stiff: *It will take about 24 hours for the glue to harden.* **2** if your attitude hardens, or if something hardens it, you become more strict and determined and less sympathetic: *Attitudes towards the terrorists have hardened even more since the attack.* —**hardened** *adj* [only before noun]: *a hardened criminal*

,hard-'headed *adj* able to make difficult decisions without being influenced by your emotions

hard-hearted /,hɑːd 'hɑːtɪd $,hɑːrd 'hɑːr-/ *adj* not caring about other people's feelings THESAURUS► UNKIND

,hard-'hitting *adj* criticizing someone or something in a strong and effective way: *a hard-hitting TV documentary*

,hard-'line *adj* having extreme political beliefs, and refusing to change them: *hard-line conservatives* —**hard-liner** *n* [C]

hardly /'hɑːdli $ 'hɑːrdli/ *adv*
1 almost not or almost none → **barely**: *I hardly know the people I'm working with* (=do not know them very well). | *I* **can hardly** *believe it.* | *We* **hardly ever** (=almost never) *go out in the evening.* | **hardly any/anything/anyone** (=almost nothing or no one) *She'd eaten hardly anything all day.* THESAURUS► RARELY
2 used to say that something is not at all true: *This is hardly the ideal time to buy a house.*
3 used to say that something has only just happened: *The serious building work has hardly begun.*

,hard-'nosed *adj* not affected by your emotions, and determined to get what you want: *a hard-nosed businessman*

,hard of 'hearing *adj* unable to hear well → **deaf**

,hard-'pressed *adj* having a lot of problems and not much money or time: *help for hard-pressed families*

,hard 'sell *n* [singular] when the person or company selling something puts a lot of pressure on people to buy it

hardship /'hɑːdʃɪp $ 'hɑːrd-/ *n* [C,U] something that makes your life difficult, especially not having enough money: *Many families were* **suffering hardship**. | **[+of]** *the hardships of war*

,hard 'shoulder *n* [singular] *BrE* the area at the side of a big road where you are allowed to stop if you have a problem with your car SYN **shoulder** *AmE*

hard 'up adj informal not having enough money: I'm very hard up this month. **THESAURUS** POOR

hardware /'hɑːdweə $ 'hɑːrdwer/ n [U]
1 computer machinery and equipment → **software**
2 equipment and tools for your home and garden: a hardware store

hard-'wearing adj BrE clothes and materials that are hard-wearing will stay in good condition for a long time [SYN] **long-wearing** AmE

hard-'wired adj **1** technical computer systems that are hard-wired are controlled by HARDWARE and cannot be easily changed **2** if an attitude, way of behaving etc is hard-wired, you are born with it and cannot change it: The desire to communicate seems to be hard-wired into our brains.

hardwood /'hɑːdwʊd $ 'hɑːrd-/ n [C,U] strong heavy wood used for making furniture

hard-'working adj working with a lot of effort: a hard-working student

hardy /'hɑːdi $ 'hɑːrdi/ adj plants and animals that are hardy are strong and able to live in difficult conditions: hardy mountain goats

hare /heə $ her/ n [C] (plural **hare** or **hares**) an animal like a large rabbit, which can run very quickly

harem /'hɑːriːm, hɑːˈriːm $ 'hærəm, 'her-/ n [C] the group of wives or women who lived with a rich or powerful man in some Muslim societies in the past

hark /hɑːk $ hɑːrk/ v
PHRASAL VERBS
hark back to sth to keep talking about things that happened in the past: He's always harking back to his days in Hollywood.

harlot /'hɑːlət $ 'hɑːr-/ n [C] literary a PROSTITUTE

harm¹ /hɑːm $ hɑːrm/ n [U] damage, hurt, or injury: We must protect our children from harm.
PHRASES
do more harm than good to make a situation worse rather than better: Criticizing people's work often does more harm than good.
no harm done spoken used to tell someone not to worry about something they have done, because it did not have a bad effect: It's OK, I'll clean it up. No harm done.
not mean any harm/mean no harm to have no intention of hurting or upsetting anyone: I was only kidding – I didn't mean any harm.
out of harm's way in a safe place: She was glad the children were at home, out of harm's way.
there's no harm in doing sth used to suggest that it might be useful to do something: There's no harm in asking.

COLLOCATIONS
verbs
to do/cause harm A little soap won't do any harm. ⚠ Do not say 'give harm' or 'make harm'. Say **do harm** or **cause harm**.
to protect sb from harm It's natural to want to protect your children from harm.
to come to harm (=to be harmed) They got lost in the fog, but luckily they came to no harm.

adjectives
great/serious harm Smoking causes serious harm.
little harm The disease causes very little harm to the tree.
physical/psychological harm Is she at risk of physical harm?

harm² v [T] to damage or hurt someone or something: Too much sun can harm your skin. **THESAURUS** DAMAGE

harmful /'hɑːmfəl $ 'hɑːrm-/ adj causing harm: the harmful effects of smoking

harmless /'hɑːmləs $ 'hɑːrm-/ adj **1** unable or unlikely to cause any harm: Their dog barks a lot but it's harmless. **2** not likely to upset or offend anyone: a bit of harmless fun —**harmlessly** adv

harmonica /hɑːˈmɒnɪkə $ hɑːrˈmɑː-/ n [C] a small musical instrument that you hold to your mouth and blow into, moving it from side to side → see picture on page A6

harmonious /hɑːˈməʊniəs $ hɑːrˈmoʊ-/ adj **1** harmonious relationships are ones in which people are friendly and helpful to one another **2** sounds that are harmonious are very pleasant —**harmoniously** adv

harmonize (also **-ise** BrE) /'hɑːmənaɪz $ 'hɑːr-/ v [I,T] **1** if two or more things harmonize, they work well together or look good together: **[+with]** The new offices must harmonize with the other buildings in the area. **2** to sing or play musical notes that make a pleasant sound with the main tune

harmony /'hɑːməni $ 'hɑːr-/ n (plural **harmonies**) **1** [U] when people are not arguing, fighting, or disagreeing: People of many races **live** here **in harmony with** each other. **2** [C,U] notes of music combined together in a pleasant way: **in harmony** a choir singing in perfect harmony

harness¹ /'hɑːnəs $ 'hɑːr-/ n **1** [C,U] a set of leather bands used to fasten a horse to a vehicle so that it can pull it along **2** [C] a set of bands that you put round your body to hold you still or stop you falling: a safety harness

harness² v [T] **1** to control and use the natural power of something: We can harness the power of the wind to generate electricity. **2** to fasten two animals together, or to fasten an animal to a vehicle using a harness

harp¹ /hɑːp $ hɑːrp/ n [C] a large musical instrument with strings stretched across a frame with three corners, which you play with your fingers → see picture on page A6 —**harpist** n [C]

harp² v
PHRASAL VERBS
harp on informal disapproving to talk about something all the time, in a way that is annoying or boring: **[+about]** I wish they'd stop harping on about the fact that they're vegetarians.

harpoon /hɑːˈpuːn $ hɑːr-/ n [C] a weapon like a SPEAR used for hunting WHALES —**harpoon** v [T]

harrowing /'hærəʊɪŋ $ -roʊ-/ adj very shocking and upsetting: a **harrowing experience**

H

harry /ˈhæri/ v [T] (**harried, harrying, harries**) **1** to keep attacking an enemy **2** to keep asking someone for something in a way that is upsetting or annoying —**harried** adj

harsh /hɑːʃ $ hɑːrʃ/ adj **1** harsh conditions are difficult to live in and are very uncomfortable: The winters here are very harsh. **2** unpleasantly bright, loud, or rough OPP **soft**: harsh lighting **3** unkind, cruel, or strict: We need harsher laws to deal with drunk drivers. | a harsh regime —**harshly** adv

harvest /ˈhɑːvɪst $ ˈhɑːr-/ n [C,U] the time when crops are gathered from the fields, or the crops that are gathered: July is the time for the wheat harvest. | We've had a good harvest this year. —**harvest** v [T]

has /z, əz, həz; strong hæz/ v the third person singular of the present tense of HAVE

'has-been n [C] informal someone who was important or popular in the past but who has now been forgotten

hash /hæʃ/ n [C] **1** the symbol (#) **2** informal hashish

PHRASES

| **make a hash of sth** informal to do something very badly: I made a real hash of my exams.

hashish /ˈhæʃɪʃ, -iːʃ/ n [U] an illegal drug that some people smoke

hasn't /ˈhæzənt/ the short form of 'has not'

hassle¹ /ˈhæsəl/ n [C,U] spoken a situation that is annoying because it causes problems: It's such a hassle not having a washing machine.

hassle² v [T] informal to continuously ask someone to do something, in a way that is annoying: Just stop hassling me, will you?

haste /heɪst/ n [U] when you hurry to do something, because you do not have enough time: In her haste, Pam forgot the tickets.

hasten /ˈheɪsən/ v [T] formal **1** to make something happen faster or sooner SYN **hurry**: Resting will hasten recovery. **2 hasten to do sth** to do or say something quickly or without delay: Gina hastened to assure him that everything was fine.

hasty /ˈheɪsti/ adj if you are hasty, you do something quickly and not very carefully because you are in a hurry: Don't be so hasty. | a hasty decision THESAURUS QUICK —**hastily** adv: A meeting was hastily organized.

hat /hæt/ n [C] something that you wear to cover or protect your head: a big straw hat | **in a hat** a man in a fur hat → **old hat** at OLD

PHRASES

| **keep sth under your hat** informal to keep something secret: Keep this under your hat, but I've heard that James is going to resign.
| **throw/toss your hat into the ring** to say in public that you will compete in an election or for a job

hatch¹ /hætʃ/ v **1** [I,T] if an egg hatches, or if it is hatched, it breaks and a baby bird, fish, or insect comes out **2** (also **hatch out**) [I] to break through an egg in order to be born: All the chicks have hatched out. **3 hatch a plot/plan/deal etc** to form a plan etc in secret

HATS

woolly hat BrE/
wooly hat AmE

beret

hard hat

sun hat

baseball cap

top hat

hatch² n [C] a small door on a ship or aircraft

hatchback /ˈhætʃbæk/ n [C] a car with a door at the back that opens upwards

hatchet /ˈhætʃɪt/ n [C] a small AXE with a short handle

hate¹ /heɪt/ v [T] to dislike someone or something very much OPP **love**: Mary really hated him after that. | I've always hated tomatoes. | **hate doing sth** Pam hates having her photo taken. | **hate to do sth** I hate to see you so unhappy. | **hate sb's guts** informal (=hate someone very much) —**hated** adj: a hated dictator

PHRASES

I hate to do sth spoken used to say that you are sorry you have to do something: I hate to tell you this, but the match has been cancelled again. | I hate to ask, but could I borrow some money?
I hate to think what/how spoken used when you feel sure that something would have a bad result: I hate to think what Dad would say about this!

THESAURUS

hate to dislike someone or something very much: At school, she always hated sport. | He treated me badly and I hated him.
can't stand/can't bear especially spoken to hate someone or something very much: Maria's nice but I can't stand her husband. | I can't bear that song!
loathe/detest to hate something or someone very much. **Loathe** and **detest** sound much stronger and a little more formal than **hate**: My father detested racism in any form. | She absolutely loathed Shakespeare.
despise to hate someone or something and have no respect for them: She despised herself for being so selfish. | His books were despised by the critics.

hate² n [U] an angry feeling that someone has when they dislike someone very much OPP **love**: a look of hate

hateful /'heɪtfəl/ *adj* very unpleasant or unkind: *What a hateful thing to say!*

hatred /'heɪtrɪd/ *n* [C,U] an angry feeling that someone has when they dislike someone or something very much OPP **love**: *eyes full of hatred* | [+of/for] *an intense hatred of authority*

'hat trick *n* [C] three successes coming one after the other, for example three GOALS by one player

haughty /'hɔːti $ 'hɒː-/ *adj* proud and unfriendly: *her haughty manner* —**haughtily** *adv*

haul¹ /hɔːl $ hɒːl/ *v* [I,T] to pull something heavy: *We managed to haul him out of the water.* THESAURUS PULL

haul² *n* [C] **1** a large amount of things that have been stolen, or found by the police: *a big drugs haul* **2** the amount of fish caught in a net
PHRASES
| **long haul** something that takes a lot of time and effort: *the long haul back to fitness*

haulage /'hɔːlɪdʒ $ 'hɒːl-/ *n* [U] the business of carrying things by road or railway

haunches /'hɔːntʃɪz $ 'hɒːn-/ *n* [plural] your bottom and the tops of your legs: *He sat on his haunches by the fire.*

haunt¹ /hɔːnt $ hɒːnt/ *v* [T] **1** if the SPIRIT of a dead person haunts a place, it appears there often: *His ghost still haunts the castle.* **2** if something unpleasant haunts you, you keep remembering it or being affected by it: *ex-soldiers still haunted by memories of the war*

haunt² *n* [C] a place that someone likes to go to often: *The café was a favourite haunt of artists.*

haunted /'hɔːntɪd $ 'hɒːn-/ *adj* a haunted building is believed to be visited regularly by the soul of a dead person

haunting /'hɔːntɪŋ $ 'hɒːn-/ *adj* beautiful, sad, and staying in your thoughts for a long time: *haunting landscapes* —**hauntingly** *adv*: *hauntingly beautiful music*

have¹ /v, əv, həv; *strong* hæv/ *auxiliary verb* (*past tense and past participle* **had** /d, əd, həd; *strong* hæd/, *present participle* **having**, *third person singular* **has** /z, əz, həz; *strong* hæz/) used with the past participle of a verb to make perfect tenses: *Have you seen the new Disney movie?* | *She had lived in Peru for thirty years.* | *Julia hasn't skied before, has she?*
PHRASES
| **had better** used to say what is the best thing to do: *You'd better take the cake out of the oven.* | *We'd better not tell Angela just yet.*

have² /hæv/ *v* [T not in passive]
1 (*also* **have got**) used to say what someone or something looks like, or what features or qualities they possess: *He's got brown eyes and dark hair.* | *You need to have a lot of patience to be a teacher.* | *Japan has a population of over 120 million.*
2 (*also* **have got**) to own something, or be able to use something: *They've got a flat in the city centre.* | *Does she have a CD player?* | *I'd like to come, but I don't have the money.* THESAURUS OWN
3 to experience or do something: **have problems/**

trouble etc *I'm having problems using this fax machine.* | *Helen's* **had** *an* **accident** *at work.* | *The kids* **had** *great* **fun** *at the theme park.* | **have a meeting/party** *Let's have a party!* | **have a bath/wash etc** *I can't wait to get home and have a bath.* | **have sth stolen/taken etc** *She had all her jewellery stolen.*
4 to eat, drink, or smoke something: *Let's go and have a beer.* | *We're having steak tonight.* | **have lunch/breakfast etc** *What time do you usually have lunch?* THESAURUS EAT
5 (*also* **have got**) to be carrying or holding something: *Watch out! He's got a gun!* | **have sth on/with you** *Do you have a pen on you?*
6 (*also* **have got**) to think of something or experience a feeling: **Have** *you got any* **ideas** *for presents for Tom?* | *I* **had** *the* **feeling** *I'd seen him before.*
7 *BrE* to receive something such as a letter, information, or advice: *Have you had any news from Michael?*
8 (*also* **have got** *BrE*) to know or be related to someone: *Julie had six brothers.* | *I've got a friend who works for the UN.*
9 (*also* **have got**) to keep something in a particular position or state: **have sth open/closed/on etc** *He had his eyes closed.* | *You've always got the TV on so loud.*
10 **may I have/can I have/I'll have** *spoken* used when you are asking for something: *I'll have two hot dogs, please.*
11 (*also* **have got**) if you have an amount of time to do something, it is available for you: *You have 30 minutes to finish the test.* | *I'm sorry, I haven't got time to stop now.*
12 (*also* **have got**) to be ill or injured in a particular way: *Sheila's had the flu for a week.* | *He's got a broken leg.*
13 **have sth ready/done etc** to make something ready, or finish something: *They promised to have the job done by Friday.*
14 if a woman has a baby, she gives birth to it: *Sasha's had twins!*
15 **have your hair cut/have your house painted etc** to pay someone to cut your hair, paint your house etc
16 (*also* **have got** *BrE*) to be visited by someone: *Sorry, I didn't realize you had guests.* | *We're having people to dinner.* → **be had** at HAD²
PHRASAL VERBS
have (got) sth against sb/sth to dislike someone or something for a particular reason: *I can't see what you've got against the idea.* | *I* **have nothing against** *Tim personally, but he's not right for the job.*
have sth/sb **on**
1 have (got) sth ↔ on to be wearing something: *Mark had on a denim jacket.*
2 be having sb on *BrE* to be trying to make someone believe something that is not true: *Are you having me on?*
have sth **out**
1 to have something removed from your body by a medical operation: *She had her appendix out last year.*
2 have it out with sb *informal* to talk to someone directly and honestly about something bad they have done: *I think it's time you had it out with Richard.*

have³, have (got) to do *modal verb*
1 if you have to do something, you must do it because someone makes you do it, or because it is

haven

necessary: *Susan hates having to get up early.* | *You don't have to answer all the questions.* **THESAURUS** MUST

2 used to say that it is important that something happens: *You have to believe me!* | *There has to be an end to all this violence.*

3 used to tell someone how to do something: *First you have to take the wheel off.*

4 used to say that you are sure that something will happen or is true: *This has got to be a mistake.* | *Prices will have to come down eventually.*

haven /ˈheɪvən/ *n* [C] a safe or peaceful place: **[+for]** *The area is a haven for wildlife.*

haven't /ˈhævənt/ the short form of 'have not'

havoc /ˈhævək/ *n* [U] a very confused situation in which there is a lot of damage: *The storm **caused havoc** everywhere.* | *The war will **wreak havoc on** the country's economy.*

hawk /hɔːk $ hɒːk/ *n* [C] a large wild bird that eats small birds and animals

hay /heɪ/ *n* [U] grass that has been cut and dried and is used as food for animals

ˈhay ˌfever *n* [U] a medical condition like a bad COLD, caused by breathing in dust from plants

haystack /ˈheɪstæk/ *n* [C] a large pile of stored hay

haywire /ˈheɪwaɪə $ -waɪr/ *adj* **go haywire** *informal* to start working in completely the wrong way: *My computer's going haywire again.*

hazard¹ /ˈhæzəd $ -ərd/ *n* [C] something that may be dangerous or cause accidents: **[+to]** *Plastic bags can be a hazard to wildlife.* | **health/safety/fire hazard** *That old furniture is a fire hazard.*

hazard² *v* **hazard a guess** to say something that is only a guess: *I don't know how much he earns, but I could hazard a guess.*

hazardous /ˈhæzədəs $ -ər-/ *adj* dangerous or likely to cause accidents: **[+to]** *chemicals which may be hazardous to health* | *the disposal of **hazardous waste*** **THESAURUS** DANGEROUS

haze /heɪz/ *n* [singular, U] smoke, dust, or mist in the air: *a heat haze*

hazel¹ /ˈheɪzəl/ *adj* hazel eyes are light greenish-brown

hazel² *n* [C,U] a small tree that produces nuts

hazy /ˈheɪzi/ *adj* **1** air that is hazy is not clear because there is smoke, dust, or mist in it: *a hazy summer morning* **2** not clear or exact: *My memories of that night are a little hazy.*

HD /ˌeɪtʃ ˈdiː◂/ *adj* (**high-definition**) HD television or video produces very clear pictures

he /i, hi; *strong* hiː/ *pron* used to talk about a male person or animal that has already been mentioned: *'How's Josh?' 'Oh, he's fine.'*

head¹ /hed/ *n*

1 TOP PART OF BODY [C] the top part of your body that has your eyes, mouth, brain etc in it: *She raised her head to see what was happening.* → see picture on page A2

2 MIND [C] your mind: *I just said the first thing that came into my head* (=I thought of). | *I wish I could get it into his head* (=make him understand) *that school*

is important. | *Angela had **taken it into** her **head** (=suddenly decided) to go for a walk.* | **do sth in your head** (=calculate something in your mind) *You have to work out the answer in your head.*

3 LEADER [C] the leader or most important person in a group or organization: **[+of]** *the former head of the FBI* | *a meeting of **heads of state*** | **head waiter/chef/gardener etc** **THESAURUS** BOSS

4 HEAD TEACHER [C] the person in charge of a school **SYN** **head teacher** *BrE*, **principal** *AmE*: *Any student caught smoking will have to see the head.*

5 FRONT [singular] the front or the most important position: **(at) the head of sth** *the man at the head of the queue*

6 ON COIN **heads** [U] the side of a coin that has a picture of someone's head on it **OPP** **tails**

PHRASES

a head/per head for each person: *The meal worked out at £15 a head.*

be banging your head against a brick wall to be making no progress at all when trying to do something: *I'm tired of banging my head against a brick wall.*

sb can't make head nor/or tail of sth used to say that someone cannot understand something at all: *I can't make head nor tail of these instructions.*

come to a head if a problem comes to a head, it becomes worse and you have to do something about it immediately: *The situation came to a head when the workers went on strike.*

go over sb's head to be too difficult for someone to understand: *I could see that the discussion was going over their heads.*

go to sb's head if success goes to someone's head, it makes them feel more important than they are: *She never let fame go to her head.*

have a (good) head for business/figures to be naturally good at business or calculations: *My youngest sister had a good head for figures.*

keep/lose your head to behave in a sensible or stupid way in a difficult situation: *She had the ability to keep her head under pressure.*

keep your head above water to succeed in continuing, even though you have a lot of problems with money: *For years they struggled to keep their heads above water.*

keep your head down to try to avoid being noticed or getting involved: *Just get on with your job and keep your head down.*

laugh/shout/scream your head off *informal* to laugh, shout etc a lot: *Fans were screaming their heads off.*

need your head examined/be off your head used when saying that someone is crazy or stupid: *He must be off his head to go running in this weather.*

put your heads together to discuss a difficult problem together: *The next morning, we all put our heads together to decide what should be done.*

COLLOCATIONS
verbs

to turn your head *Everyone turned their heads to see.*

to shake your head (=showing disagreement) *She shook her head and said firmly, 'No.'*

to nod your head (=showing agreement) *He nodded his head sympathetically as I talked.*
to raise/lift your head (=to look upwards) *Dad briefly lifted his head from his newspaper.*
to bend/lower your head (=to look down) *He bent his head and kissed her.*
sb's head hurts/aches *My head hurts – I need to lie down.*

head² v

1 **GO IN A DIRECTION** [I] to go in a particular direction: **[+for/towards/up etc]** *a boat heading for the shore | It's time we **headed** home.* **THESAURUS** GO

2 **BE IN CHARGE** [T] to be in charge of a government, organization, or group: *Most one-parent families are headed by women.*

3 **BE LIKELY TO EXPERIENCE STH** **be heading for sth** (also **be headed for sth** *AmE*) if you are heading for a situation, it is likely to happen: *The company was heading for disaster.*

4 **LIST/PAGE** [T] to be at the top of a list, page, or group of words: *The longest list was headed 'Problems.'*

5 **FOOTBALL** [T] to hit the ball with your head in football → see picture at **FOOTBALL**

PHRASAL VERBS

head sb/sth ↔ **off**

1 to stop someone moving in a particular direction by moving in front of them: *The police headed them off at the crossroads.*

2 to prevent something bad from happening

headache /'hedeɪk/ n [C]

1 a pain in your head: *The noise was making my headache worse.* **THESAURUS** PAIN

2 a serious problem that you worry about: *money and other headaches*

> **Grammar**
> Headache is a countable noun. Do not say 'I had headache.' Say *I had a headache.*

COLLOCATIONS

adjectives

a bad/terrible/severe headache *I've got a really bad headache.* ⚠ Do not say 'a strong/heavy headache'. Say **a bad headache.**

a splitting headache (=a very bad headache) *She woke up with a splitting headache.*

a slight headache (also **a bit of a headache** *spoken*) *It's not serious. It's just a slight headache.* ⚠ Do not say 'a little headache'. Say **a slight headache** or **a bit of a headache.**

verbs

to have a headache (also **have got a headache** *spoken*) *If you have a headache you should take some aspirin.*

to get headaches/suffer from headaches (=regularly have a headache) *I used to get headaches a lot.*

to give sb a headache *Too much coffee gives me a headache.*

'**head count** n [C] the act of counting how many people are present in a particular place at one time:

*Teachers **did a head count** to check that none of the kids were missing.*

headdress /'hed-dres/ n [C] something that someone wears on their head for decoration at a ceremony or special occasion: *a feathered headdress*

head-first /ˌhed'fɜːst◂ $ -'fɜːrst◂/ adv with your head going first, before the rest of your body: *He dived head-first into the pool.*

headgear /'hedgɪə $ -gɪr/ n [U] hats and other things that you wear on your head: *Protective headgear must be worn.*

headhunter /'hedˌhʌntə $ -ər/ n [C] someone whose job is to find people for particular jobs and persuade them to leave their present jobs —**headhunt** v [T]

heading /'hedɪŋ/ n [C] the title at the top of a piece of writing

headland /'hedlənd/ n [C] an area of land that sticks out into the sea

headlight /'hedlaɪt/ (also **headlamp** /'hedlæmp/) n [C] one of the large lights at the front of a vehicle → see picture at **CAR THESAURUS** LIGHT

headline /'hedlaɪn/ n [C] 1 the title of a newspaper report, printed in large letters: *a front-page headline* 2 **the headlines** the important news stories on radio or television, read out together before the rest of the programme begins

headlong /'hedlɒŋ $ -lɔːŋ/ adv 1 **rush headlong into sth** to do something important without thinking carefully about it first: *Fran isn't the type to rush headlong into marriage.* 2 with your head going first: *Ben went tumbling headlong down the hill.*

headmaster /ˌhed'mɑːstə $ 'hedˌmæstər/ n [C] *BrE* a male teacher who is in charge of a school **SYN** head teacher, principal *AmE*

headmistress /ˌhed'mɪstrɪs $ 'hedˌmɪs-/ n [C] *BrE* a female teacher who is in charge of a school **SYN** head teacher, principal *AmE*

,**head-'on** adv 1 if someone deals with a problem head-on, they deal with it in a direct way: *She decided to face her difficulties head-on.* 2 **meet/crash/hit head-on** if two vehicles meet head-on, the front part of one vehicle hits the front part of the other: *A car and a truck had collided head-on.* —**head-on** adj: *a head-on collision*

headphones
/'hedfəʊnz $ -foʊnz/ n [plural] a piece of equipment that you wear over your ears to listen to a radio, CD PLAYER etc

HEADPHONES

headquarters
/'hedˌkwɔːtəz, ˌhed'kwɔːtəz $ -ɔːrtərz/ n [plural] (abbreviation **HQ**) the main office of a large company or organization, or the place from which military action is controlled: **[+of]** *the headquarters of the UN*

H

headrest /'hed-rest/ n [C] the top part of a chair, that supports the back of your head

headroom /'hed-rʊm, -ruːm/ n [U] the amount of space above your head inside a car, or above a car when it is under a bridge

head 'start n [C] an advantage that helps you to be successful: His education **gave** him **a head start**.

headstone /'hedstəʊn $ -stoʊn/ n [C] a piece of stone on a GRAVE, with the dead person's name on it

headstrong /'hedstrɒŋ $ -strɔːŋ/ adj very determined to do what you want SYN **stubborn**: a headstrong child

head 'teacher n [C] BrE the teacher who is in charge of a school SYN **head** BrE, **principal** AmE

head-to-'head adv, adj competing directly with another person or group: New courier companies will be **going head-to-head** with the Post Office. | a head-to-head contest

headway /'hedweɪ/ n **make headway** to come closer to achieving something: [+towards/with/in etc] We have made little headway towards a solution.

headwind /'hed,wɪnd/ n [C,U] a wind that blows directly towards you when you are moving

heady /'hedi/ adj making you feel excited, or as if you are drunk: the heady days of their youth

heal /hiːl/ (also **heal up**) v [I,T] if an injury or broken bone heals, or if someone heals it, it becomes healthy again: The scratch on her finger healed quickly. —**healer** n [C]

health /helθ/ n [U]
1 the general condition of your body, and how healthy you are: Doing more exercise will improve your health.
2 how successful an economic system or organization is: the health of the economy

COLLOCATIONS

adjectives

good/excellent health If your health is good, there's no reason why you can't exercise.
bad/poor health His mother suffers from poor health.
ill health He retired early due to ill health.

verbs

to damage sb's health Pollution can seriously damage your health.
to be in good/poor health (=to be healthy or unhealthy) He is now elderly and in bad health.
to be good/bad for your health I believe laughter is good for your health.

health + noun

health problems He's had a lot of health problems.
a health warning (=a warning printed on a product that could harm you) All cigarette packets must carry a health warning.

'health care n [U] the activity or work of looking after people's health: the promise of free health care for everyone | health care workers

'health ,centre n [C] BrE a place where there are

several doctors and nurses, where you can go for medical treatment

'health food n [C,U] food that contains only natural substances: a health food shop

healthful /'helθfəl/ adj AmE good for your body: healthful eating habits

'health ,service n [C] a public service that is responsible for providing people with medical care → **NATIONAL HEALTH SERVICE**

healthy /'helθi/ adj
1 if you are healthy, your body is in good condition and you do not feel ill or weak OPP **unhealthy**: a healthy baby girl | How do you manage to stay so healthy?
2 good for your body or your mind OPP **unhealthy**: a **healthy diet** | a campaign to encourage **healthy eating** | It's not healthy for her to depend on him like that.
3 strong and successful: The economy is in a healthy state. —**healthily** adv: Make sure that you eat healthily.

THESAURUS

healthy: I feel much healthier now that I've lost weight. | healthy foods | a healthy lifestyle
well healthy – used especially when talking about how someone feels or looks: I don't feel well. | You look well! Have you been on holiday?
fine spoken used especially when replying to someone's question, when saying that you feel good or another person feels good: 'Hi, Chris, how are you?' 'Fine, thanks.'
better less ill than you were, or no longer ill: My cold's almost gone and I'm feeling a lot better.
fit healthy and strong, especially because you exercise regularly: I wanted to keep fit so I started doing aerobics classes.
nutritious nutritious food contains a lot of the things that your body needs to stay healthy: Beans are very nutritious. | a nutritious meal

heap¹ /hiːp/ n [C] **1** a large untidy pile of things: [+of] a heap of newspapers | **in a heap** His clothes lay in a heap by the bed. THESAURUS ▸ GROUP **2 heaps/a heap (of sth)** informal a lot of something: We've got heaps of time.

heap² v **1** (also **heap up**) [T] to put a lot of things on top of each other in an untidy way: plates heaped with food **2 heap praise/criticism/insults on sb** to praise, criticize etc someone a lot: The manager heaped praise on his players.

heaped /hiːpt/ adj **heaped teaspoon/bowl/plate etc** BrE an amount of something that is as much as a spoon, plate etc can hold

hear /hɪə $ hɪr/ v [I,T] (past tense and past participle **heard** /hɜːd $ hɜːrd/)
1 to know that a sound is being made, using your ears: Can you hear that noise? | She called his name but he didn't hear. | **hear sb doing sth** I thought I heard someone knocking. | **hear sb do sth** Did you hear them leave?
2 to be told or to find out some information: [+(that)] We were sorry to hear that you were ill. | You'll **be pleased to hear** that it's nearly finished. |

[+about/of] *Where did you hear about the job?* | *Have you heard the news?*

3 hear a case to listen to all the facts of a case in a court of law in order to make a legal decision: *The case will be heard on July 16th.*

PHRASES

sb won't/wouldn't hear of it used when someone says very definitely that they do not want another person to do something: *I offered to pay, but he wouldn't hear of it.*

(do) you hear (me)? *spoken* used to emphasize an order, when you want someone to say 'yes' and agree to do what you say: *Be home by ten, do you hear?*

PHRASAL VERBS

hear from sb to get news or information from someone, usually in a letter or by telephone: *Have you heard from Jane?* | *I look forward to hearing from you* soon.

have heard of sb/sth to know that someone or something exists, because you have been told about them, read about them etc: *Phil Merton? I've never heard of him.*

hear sb **out** to listen to someone's explanation for something, without interrupting: *I know you're angry, but just hear me out.*

THESAURUS

hear to know that a sound is being made, using your ears: *I heard someone open the door.*
listen to pay attention to something, using your ears: *She was listening to the news on the radio.*
overhear to accidentally hear another person's conversation: *We were in the next room and we overheard them talking about Steven.*
I didn't catch sth *spoken* used when saying that you did not hear what someone said: *Sorry, I didn't catch the last line of the address.*
eavesdrop to deliberately listen secretly to other people's conversations: *Mandy was eavesdropping outside the bedroom door.*

hearing /'hɪərɪŋ $ 'hɪr-/ n **1** [U] the sense that you use to hear sounds: *My hearing's not as good as it used to be.* **2** [C] a meeting of a court or committee to find out the facts about something: *a court hearing*

PHRASES

a (fair) hearing an opportunity for someone to explain their actions or ideas: *We must give both sides a fair hearing.*

'hearing aid n [C] a small thing that you put in your ear to make sounds louder if you cannot hear well

'hearing im,paired adj unable to hear well

hearsay /'hɪəseɪ $ 'hɪr-/ n [U] something that other people have told you but which may not be true SYN rumour: *Don't believe it – it's just hearsay.*

hearse /hɜːs $ hɜːrs/ n [C] a large car for carrying a dead body in a COFFIN at a funeral

heart /hɑːt $ hɑːrt/ n [C]
1 the organ inside your chest that pushes blood around your body: *Tom could feel his heart beating*

faster. | *She suffers from heart problems.* → see picture on page A2

2 the part of you that feels emotions: *He's strict, but he has a kind heart.* | *It would break her heart* (=make her very sad) *if he left now.* | **in your heart** *I knew in my heart that he was right.* | *She wished* **with all** her **heart** *that she had never met him.* | *Michael was speaking* **from the heart**. | *She had* **a heart of gold** (=a kind nature).* | **kind-hearted/cold-hearted/ hard-hearted etc** (=having a kind, unkind, cruel etc nature)

3 a shape used to mean a heart or love

4 the heart of sth the centre or most important part of something: *deep in the heart of the countryside* | **the heart of the matter/problem etc** *Let's get to the heart of the matter.* → **change of heart** at CHANGE[2]

PHRASES

hearts [plural] in card games, the cards with red heart shapes on them: *the queen of hearts* → see picture at PLAYING CARD

be sth at heart if you are a particular kind of person at heart, that is the kind of character you really have: *I'm just a kid at heart.*

close/dear to sb's heart very important to someone: *It was obviously a matter close to his heart.*

do sth to your heart's content to do something as much as you want to: *You can run around here to your heart's content.*

have sb's interests at heart to want to do what is best for someone: *They have your best interests at heart.*

sb's heart goes out to sb used to say that someone feels a lot of sympathy for someone: *Our hearts go out to the victim's family.*

sb's heart sinks used to say that someone suddenly becomes very sad or disappointed: *Bert's heart sank when he saw the mess.*

know/learn sth by heart to remember or learn all of a piece of writing: *We had to learn the poem by heart.*

not have the heart to do sth *spoken* to not do something because you do not want to make someone unhappy: *I didn't have the heart to tell her the truth.*

take/lose heart to begin to have more hope or to stop having hope: *I've failed my driving test so many times I'm beginning to lose heart.*

take sth to heart to treat what someone says as important, especially when it upsets you: *Diana took the criticism to heart.*

COLLOCATIONS

verbs

sb's heart beats *My heart beat faster at the sound of his voice.*
sb's heart is pounding/thumping (=beating very strongly) *He could feel his heart pounding.*

heart + noun

heart trouble/problems *Jack has a history of heart trouble.*
a heart condition (=something wrong with your heart) *He was being treated for a heart condition.*
sb's heart rate (=the number of times someone's heart beats each minute) *Your heart rate increases as you exercise.*

H

adjectives

a bad/weak heart (=an unhealthy heart) *She didn't work because she had a bad heart.*

Usage

In everyday English, you usually say that someone is **a nice/kind/understanding etc person.** You do not usually say that someone has 'a kind heart' or 'an understanding heart'. It is possible to say this, but it is much less common.
Phrases such as **warm-hearted, kind-hearted, cold-hearted** or **hard-hearted** are used especially when describing people in written English: *A kind-hearted shopkeeper offered to lend him the money.*

heartache /ˈhɑːteɪk $ ˈhɑːrt-/ n [U] a feeling of great sadness

ˈheart atˌtack n [C] a serious medical condition in which your heart suddenly stops working normally: *He had a heart attack and was rushed to hospital.*

heartbeat /ˈhɑːtbiːt $ ˈhɑːrt-/ n [C,U] the action or the sound of your heart as it pushes blood around your body: *The doctor listened to the baby's heartbeat.*

heartbreak /ˈhɑːtbreɪk $ ˈhɑːrt-/ n [U] a strong feeling of sadness, especially about a person you love

heartbreaking /ˈhɑːtˌbreɪkɪŋ $ ˈhɑːrt-/ adj making you feel very sad: *heartbreaking pictures of starving children*

heartbroken /ˈhɑːtˌbrəʊkən $ ˈhɑːrtˌbroʊ-/ adj very sad because of something that has happened
THESAURUS SAD

heartburn /ˈhɑːtbɜːn $ ˈhɑːrtbɜːrn/ n [U] a burning feeling in your stomach or chest caused by acid from your stomach → **indigestion**

ˈheart disˌease n [U] a medical condition which prevents your heart from working normally

heartened /ˈhɑːtnd $ ˈhɑːr-/ adj feeling happier and more hopeful OPP **disheartened** —**hearten** v [T] —**heartening** adj: *heartening news*

ˈheart ˌfailure n [U] a serious medical condition in which your heart stops working

heartfelt /ˈhɑːtfelt $ ˈhɑːrt-/ adj felt very strongly and sincerely: *heartfelt thanks*

hearth /hɑːθ $ hɑːrθ/ n [C] the part of the floor around a FIREPLACE

heartily /ˈhɑːtəli $ ˈhɑːr-/ adv 1 loudly and cheerfully → **hearty**: *He laughed heartily.* 2 very much or completely: *I'm heartily sick of hearing about her problems.*

heartland /ˈhɑːtlənd $ ˈhɑːrt-/ n [C] the part of a country where an activity or belief is based or is strongest: *the industrial heartland of England*

heartless /ˈhɑːtləs $ ˈhɑːrt-/ adj cruel or not feeling any sympathy: *How can you be so heartless?*
THESAURUS CRUEL —**heartlessly** adv

heartrending /ˈhɑːtˌrendɪŋ $ ˈhɑːrt-/ adj literary making you feel a lot of sympathy for someone: *a heartrending story*

ˈheart-ˌstopping adj very exciting or frightening

ˌheart-to-ˈheart n [C] a conversation in which two people say honestly what they think or feel: *It's time you and I had a heart-to-heart.* —**heart-to-heart** adj

heartwarming /ˈhɑːtˌwɔːmɪŋ $ ˈhɑːrtˌwɔːr-/ adj something that is heartwarming makes you feel happy: *a heartwarming story*

hearty /ˈhɑːti $ ˈhɑːrti/ adj 1 friendly and full of energy: *a hearty welcome* 2 a hearty meal is very large

heat¹ /hiːt/ n

1 **WARMNESS** [U] the quality of being warm or hot: **[+of]** *the heat of the sun* | *a material that withstands intense heat*

2 **HOT WEATHER** the heat very hot weather: *the summer heat*

3 **COOKING/HEATING TEMPERATURE** [singular, U] the temperature used when cooking or heating something: **low/medium/high heat** *Melt the butter over a low heat.*

4 **STRONG FEELINGS** [U] strong feelings, especially anger or excitement: **In the heat of the moment** (=when feelings were strong), *I said things I didn't mean.*

5 **PART OF COMPETITION** [C] one part of a race or competition, which decides who will be in the next part

6 **BUILDING'S HEATING SYSTEM** [U] *AmE* the system in a building that keeps it warm **SYN** heating *BrE* → **DEAD HEAT**

heat² (also **heat up**) v [I,T] to become warm or hot, or to make something warm or hot: *Let the oven heat up.* | *Heat the milk until it boils.*

heated /ˈhiːtɪd/ adj 1 made warm using a heater: *a heated swimming pool* 2 **heated debate/argument/discussion etc** an argument etc in which people become very angry and excited: *A heated argument broke out between the two men.*

heater /ˈhiːtə $ -ər/ n [C] a machine for heating air or water

heath /hiːθ/ n [C] an area of wild land where grass and bushes grow

heathen /ˈhiːðən/ adj old-fashioned disapproving not belonging or relating to the Christian religion —**heathen** n [C]

heather /ˈheðə $ -ər/ n [U] a small plant with purple, pink, or white flowers that grows on hills

heating /ˈhiːtɪŋ/ n [U] *BrE* the system in a building that keeps it warm **SYN** heat *AmE*: *I've turned the heating up.*

heatwave /ˈhiːtweɪv/ n [C] a period of unusually hot weather

heave /hiːv/ v 1 [I,T] to pull or lift something heavy using a lot of effort: **heave sb/sth out of/onto etc sth** *He heaved himself out of the chair.* **THESAURUS** PULL 2 [I] to move up and down with strong regular movements: **[+with]** *His shoulders heaved with laughter.* 3 **heave a sigh** to breathe out loudly: *Roz heaved a sigh of relief when he'd gone.* —**heave** n [C]

heaven /ˈhevən/ n

1 (also **Heaven**) the place where some people

believe that good people go after they die → **hell**

2 [U] *informal* a very pleasant situation or experience: *It's **heaven** to lie back in a hot bath.*

3 *spoken* used in some expressions to emphasize something you think or feel: **Heaven knows** (=I do not know) *how I would have coped without her.* | *Me, get married? **Heaven forbid** (=I very much hope not)!*

4 the heavens *literary* the sky

PHRASES

for heaven's sake *spoken* used when you are annoyed or angry: *For heaven's sake, what do you want?*

(Good) Heavens! *spoken* used when you are surprised: *Good Heavens! What's happened?*

heavenly /'hevənli/ *adj* **1** [only before noun] *literary* relating to heaven or the sky: *God's heavenly kingdom* **2** *old-fashioned* very pleasant: *a heavenly smell*

heavily /'hevəli/ *adv* **1** very much or a lot: *He became **heavily involved** in the project.* | *It rained heavily all night.* | **drink/smoke heavily** **2** slowly and in a way that shows you are sad or tired: *Emma sighed heavily.* **3 heavily-built** someone who is heavily-built has a large body that looks strong

heavy /'hevi/ *adj*

1 OF GREAT WEIGHT weighing a lot OPP **light**: *I can't lift this box – it's too heavy.* | *a heavy suitcase* | *How **heavy** is this parcel (=how much does it weigh)?*

2 A LOT OF large in amount or degree: **Heavy traffic** is causing delays. | *There are reports of **heavy fighting** in the town.* | *the dangers of **heavy drinking*** | **heavy rain/snow** | **a heavy meal/lunch etc** (=making your stomach feel very full)

3 NEEDING STRENGTH needing a lot of physical strength: *A gardener does the **heavy work** for me.*

4 DIFFICULT/SERIOUS difficult and serious: *Their relationship was **getting heavy**.* | *I found the course **heavy going** (=difficult).*

5 SOLID/THICK solid or thick: *heavy boots* | *heavy soil*

6 USING FORCE using or happening with a lot of force: *a heavy blow* | *heavy footsteps*

7 BUSY **heavy day/schedule etc** a day etc when you have a lot to do: *As a lecturer, he has an especially heavy schedule at the beginning of each term.* —**heaviness** *n* [U]

PHRASES

make heavy weather of sth *BrE disapproving* to make something that you are doing seem more complicated than it really is

with a heavy heart feeling very sad

heavy-'duty *adj* heavy-duty materials, pieces of equipment etc are very strong and not easily damaged: *heavy-duty plastic*

heavy-'handed *adj* using too much force in the way you deal with people: *a heavy-handed style of management*

heavy 'industry *n* [U] industry that produces large goods such as cars and machines, or materials such as coal, steel, or chemicals

heavy 'metal *n* [U] a type of very loud modern music with a strong beat

heavyweight /'heviweɪt/ *n* [C] **1** someone or

something that has a lot of influence: *a **political heavyweight*** **2** a BOXER from the heaviest weight group —**heavyweight** *adj*

heck /hek/ *spoken informal* used when you are annoyed

heckle /'hekəl/ *v* [I,T] to shout at someone who is making a speech or performing, in order to embarrass them —**heckler** *n* [C] —**heckling** *n* [U]

hectare /'hekta:, -teə $ -ter/ *n* [C] a unit for measuring an area of land, equal to 10,000 square metres

hectic /'hektɪk/ *adj* very busy, or full of activity: *a hectic day* THESAURUS ▶ BUSY

he'd /id, hid; *strong* hi:d/ the short form of 'he would' or 'he had': *I'm sure he'd help you.* | *He'd never liked her.*

hedge¹ /hedʒ/ *n* [C] a row of bushes that separates gardens or fields

hedge² *v* [I,T] to avoid giving a direct answer: *'I'm not sure where she is,' he hedged.*

PHRASES

hedge your bets to reduce your chances of failing by doing several different things: *I hedged my bets by applying to six colleges.*

hedgehog /'hedʒhɒg $ -ha:g, -hɔ:g/ *n* [C] a small animal with sharp points covering its body

HEDGEHOG

hedgerow /'hedʒrəʊ $ -roʊ/ *n* [C] *BrE* a row of bushes along the edge of a field or road

hedonism /'hi:dənɪzəm/ *n* [U] the belief that pleasure is the most important thing —**hedonist** *n* [C]

heed¹ /hi:d/ *v* [T] *formal* to pay attention to someone's advice or warning: *The company failed to **heed** warnings about safety.*

heed² *n* **take heed of sth/pay heed to sth** *formal* to pay attention to something, especially something that someone says

heedless /'hi:dləs/ *adj* **heedless of sth** *literary* not paying attention to something

heel /hi:l/ *n* [C]

1 the back part of your foot → **toe**

2 the part under a shoe that makes it higher: *boots with high heels* | **high-heeled/low-heeled/flat-heeled** *flat-heeled walking shoes* → see picture at **SHOE¹**

hefty /'hefti/ *adj* big, heavy, or strong: *a tall hefty man* | *a hefty fine*

heifer /'hefə $ -ər/ *n* [C] a young female cow

height /haɪt/ *n*

1 [C,U] how tall someone or something is: *The boys are about the same height.* | **6 feet/10 metres etc in height** *mountains over 300 m in height* | **a height of 6 feet/10 metres etc** *The plant grows to a height of 25 cm.* → see picture at **DIMENSION**

2 [C,U] the distance something is above the

H

ground: *A fall from that height would kill you.* | a **height of 2,500 feet/10,000 metres etc** *The aircraft was flying at a height of 10,000 metres.* | **gain/lose height** (=move higher or lower in the sky) *The plane was rapidly losing height.*

3 [C] a high place or position: *From a height, the town seemed to spread for miles.* | *She'd always been scared of heights.*

4 new/great/dizzy heights extremely high levels: *Prices had reached absurd heights.*

5 [singular] the busiest, most successful etc time for something: *It was the height of the tourist season.* | *Miniskirts were the height of fashion* (=very fashionable). | **at its height** *Demand for home computers was at its height.*

heighten /ˈhaɪtn/ v [I,T] if a feeling, effect etc heightens, or if something heightens it, it increases or becomes stronger: *Television has heightened awareness of the issue.* | *The effect of the drug is heightened by alcohol.*

heinous /ˈheɪnəs/ adj formal extremely shocking and bad: *a heinous crime*

heir /eə $ er/ n [C] someone who will receive money, property, or a title when another person dies: **[+to]** *She was the heir to a fortune.*

heiress /ˈeərəs, ˈeəres $ ˈer-/ n [C] a woman who will receive money, property, or a title when someone dies

heirloom /ˈeəluːm $ ˈer-/ n [C] a valuable object that the same family has owned for many years: *a family heirloom*

held /held/ v the past tense and past participle of HOLD

helicopter /ˈhelɪkɒptə $ -kɑːptər/ n [C] an aircraft with long metal parts on top which turn around very quickly to make it fly → see picture at **TRANSPORT¹**

helium /ˈhiːliəm/ n [U] a gas that is lighter than air

hell /hel/ n
1 (*also* **Hell**) [U] the place where some people believe bad people go when they die
2 [singular, U] a very difficult or unpleasant situation or experience: *He made my life hell.* | *She's been through hell this last year.*
3 *spoken* used when you are surprised or angry, or to emphasize what you are saying. Some people consider this use offensive: *Oh hell! I've lost my keys.* | **what/why/where etc the hell?** *Where the hell have you been?*
PHRASES
a/one hell of a sth *informal* used to emphasize that something or someone is very bad or good: *The room was a hell of a mess.* | *It was one hell of a party!*
all hell broke loose *informal* used to say that people suddenly became very noisy or angry: *All hell broke loose when Aaron Lennon scored.*
(just) for the hell of it *spoken* for fun, not for any other reason: *He stole things just for the hell of it.*
like hell *informal* very much, very fast etc: *It hurt like hell.* | *He ran like hell.*
the sb/sth from hell *informal* used to say that someone or something is the worst you can imagine: *the teenager from hell*

he'll /il, hil; *strong* hiːl/ the short form of 'he will' or 'he shall'

hell-'bent adj [not before noun] very determined to do something, especially something that other people do not approve of: **hell-bent on (doing) sth** *young people who are hell-bent on having a good time*

hellish /ˈhelɪʃ/ adj informal extremely bad or difficult: *I've had a hellish day at work.* —**hellishly** adv

hello /həˈləʊ, he- $ -ˈloʊ/ (*also* **hallo, hullo** *BrE*) spoken used as a greeting when you meet someone or start speaking on the telephone: *Hello, how are you?* | *Hello, can I speak to Paul please?*
PHRASES
say hello to have a quick conversation with someone: *I just called to say hello.*

helm /helm/ n [C] the wheel or control that guides a boat
PHRASES
at the helm in charge of something: *There's a new manager at the helm.*

helmet /ˈhelmɪt/ n [C] a hard hat that protects your head: *a motorcycle helmet*

help¹ /help/ v [I,T]
1 to make it easier for someone to do something, especially by doing something for them: *How can I help?* | **help sb (to) do sth** *I helped him clear the table.* | *a course that helps students to develop confidence* | **help sb with sth** *Dad helped me with my homework.* | **help (to) do sth** *A good diet can help prevent heart disease.* | **help sb up/across etc sth** (=help someone go somewhere) *She helped her grandmother across the road.*
2 to improve a situation: *Crying won't help.* | **[+to]** *It helped to know that I had someone to talk to.*
PHRASES
Help! *spoken* used to call someone when you are in danger: *Help! Somebody call the police!*
sb can't help (doing) sth used to say that someone cannot stop doing or feeling something: *'Stop biting your nails.' 'I can't help it.'* | **can't help feeling/thinking/wondering** *I couldn't help feeling a bit jealous.*
help yourself (to sth) to take something when you want it, especially food that is offered to you: *Help yourself to more cake.*
PHRASAL VERBS
help out to help someone when they are busy or have problems: **[+with]** *My Mum helps out with the kids.* | **help sb ↔ out** *Thanks for helping me out.*

THESAURUS

help to make it easier for someone to do something, especially by doing something for them: *She helped him take off his coat.* | *Can you help me with my homework?*
give sb a hand *informal* to help someone to carry something, or do physical work: *Can you give me a hand with these bags?*
do sb a favour *BrE*, **do sb a favor** *AmE* to do something for someone you know well, in order to help them: *Could you do me a favour and post these letters?*

assist *formal* to help someone, especially by doing part of their work: *We require someone to assist us in our research.*

aid *formal* to help something to happen, or to help someone to do something: *Drinking Japanese tea aids the digestion.* | *The purpose of this book is to aid the reader.*

help² *n*

1 [U] things someone does that make it easier for someone else: *Thanks for all your help.* | **[+with]** *Do you want any help with the cooking?*
2 [singular, U] someone or something that is useful and makes it easier for you to do something: *The instructions weren't much help.* | **with the help of sth** *We got there with the help of a map.* | **be a (great/big etc) help (to sb)** *Annie was a great help.* | **be of some/great/no etc help (to sb)** *Let me know if I can be of any help to you.* → SELF-HELP

COLLOCATIONS

verbs

to give sb some help/lots of help etc *I'll give you all the help I can.*
to get help *I sometimes get help from my neighbour.*
to ask for help *She keeps asking me for help with her homework.*
to need help *Do you need help carrying your bags?*

helper /'helpə $ -ər/ *n* [C] someone who helps another person

helpful /'helpfəl/ *adj* **1** useful: *helpful advice* | *It's helpful to talk about it.* THESAURUS USEFUL **2** willing to help: *The staff were very helpful.* —**helpfully** *adv* —**helpfulness** *n* [U]

helping /'helpɪŋ/ *n* [C] an amount of food for one person: *a generous helping of pasta*

'helping ,verb *n* [C] an AUXILIARY VERB

helpless /'helpləs/ *adj* unable to look after or defend yourself: *a helpless victim* —**helplessly** *adv* —**helplessness** *n* [U]

helpline /'helplaɪn/ *n* [C] a telephone number you can call for advice or information

hem¹ /hem/ *n* [C] the edge of a piece of clothing that is turned under and sewn down

hem² *v* (**hemmed, hemming**)

PHRASAL VERBS

hem sb/sth ↔ **in** to surround someone or something closely: *a street hemmed in by tall buildings*

hemisphere /'hemɪsfɪə $ -fɪr/ *n* [C] one half of the Earth: *the northern hemisphere* → see picture at GLOBE

hemophilia /ˌhiːməˈfɪliə/ *n* the American spelling of HAEMOPHILIA

hemorrhage /'hemərɪdʒ/ *n* the American spelling of HAEMORRHAGE

hemorrhoids /'hemərɔɪdz/ *n* the American spelling of HAEMORRHOIDS

hemp /hemp/ *n* [U] a plant used to make rope and to produce the drug CANNABIS

hen /hen/ *n* [C] an adult female bird, especially a chicken → see picture at CHICKEN¹

hence Ac /hens/ *adv formal* **1** for this reason: *Her family are Welsh – hence the accent.* **2 two weeks/six months etc hence** two weeks, six months etc from now

henceforth /ˌhensˈfɔːθ, ˈhensfɔːθ $ -ɔːrθ/ (also **henceforward** /-ˈfɔːwəd $ -ˈfɔːrwərd/) *adv formal* from this time

henchman /'hentʃmən/ *n* [C] (*plural* **henchmen** /-mən/) someone who supports a powerful person and is willing to do illegal things for them

'hen ,party (also **'hen night**) *n* [C] *BrE informal* a party for women only, that happens before one of them gets married

henpecked /'henpekt/ *adj* a man who is henpecked is always being told what to do by his wife

hepatitis /ˌhepəˈtaɪtɪs/ *n* [U] a disease of the LIVER that makes your skin yellow

her /ə, hə; *strong* hɜː $ ər, hər; *strong* hɜːr/ *determiner, pron*
1 belonging or relating to a woman or girl who has already been mentioned: *That's her new car.* | *She makes all her own clothes.*
2 used when talking about a woman or girl who has already been mentioned: *Chris saw her last week.*

herald¹ /'herəld/ *v* [T] **1** to be a sign that something is going to happen soon: *flowers heralding the start of spring* **2** to publicly praise someone or something: **be heralded as sth** *The event was heralded as a great success.*

herald² *n* **herald of sth** *literary* a sign that something will happen soon: *dark clouds – the heralds of another storm*

herb /hɜːb $ ɜːrb, hɜːrb/ *n* [C] a plant used to improve the taste of food, or to make medicine —**herbal** *adj*: *herbal remedies*

herbivore /'hɜːbəvɔː $ 'hɜːrbəvɔːr, 'ɜːr-/ *n* [C] an animal that only eats plants → **carnivore** —**herbivorous** /hɜːˈbɪvərəs $ hɜːr-, ɜːr-/ *adj*

herd¹ /hɜːd $ hɜːrd/ *n* [C] a large group of animals of one type: **[+of]** *a herd of cows* THESAURUS GROUP

herd² *v* [T] to make people or animals move somewhere in a large group: **herd sb into sth** *We were herded into a small room.*

here /hɪə $ hɪr/ *adv*
1 in, to, or at this place: *I've lived here all my life.* | *Come here, please.* | **up/down/in/out here** *It's very cold out here.* | **two miles/six kilometres etc from here** *The hospital's about five miles from here.*
2 used when you are giving or showing something to someone: *Here, have my chair.* | **here is/are sth** *Here's the money you lent me.* | *Here are some photos of John.* | **here you are/go** *'Here you go.' John handed her a drink.*
3 at this point in a process or discussion: *Spring will soon be here.* | *The subject is too difficult to explain here.*
4 used when you suddenly see or find someone or something: *Here comes the bus.* | *Look, here's Jane!* | **here you are/here he is etc** *Here you are – where have you been?* | **here we are** (=used when you finally arrive somewhere) *Here we are – home at last.*

PHRASES
here and there in several different places: *He added a few details here and there.*

here goes (*also* **here we go**) *spoken* used when you are going to do something and are not sure whether you will succeed: *Ready? OK, here goes.*

here's to sb/sth *spoken* used to wish someone success, especially while you have a drink together: *Here's to your new job!*

hereabouts /ˌhɪərəˈbaʊts, ˈhɪərəbaʊts $ ˌhɪr-, ˈhɪr-/ *adv* near the place where you are: *We all live hereabouts.*

hereafter /ˌhɪərˈɑːftə $ ˌhɪrˈæftər/ *adv formal* from this time

hereby /ˌhɪəˈbaɪ, ˈhɪəbaɪ $ ˌhɪr-, ˈhɪr-/ *adv formal* as a result of this statement

hereditary /həˈredətəri $ -teri/ *adj* a hereditary quality or disease passes from a parent to a child before the child is born

heredity /həˈredəti/ *n* [U] the process by which physical or mental qualities pass from a parent to a child

herein /ˌhɪərˈɪn $ ˌhɪr-/ *adv formal* in this place, situation, document etc

heresy /ˈherəsi/ *n* [C,U] (*plural* **heresies**) a belief that is different from the official beliefs of a particular religion

heretic /ˈherətɪk/ *n* [C] someone who is considered immoral or evil because of their beliefs —**heretical** /həˈretɪkəl/ *adj*

heritage /ˈherətɪdʒ/ *n* [singular, U] the traditional customs, buildings, arts etc that are important to a country: *our national heritage*

hermit /ˈhɜːmɪt $ ˈhɜːr-/ *n* [C] someone who prefers to live away from other people

hernia /ˈhɜːniə $ ˈhɜːr-/ *n* [C] a medical condition in which an organ pushes through the muscles that should cover it

hero /ˈhɪərəʊ $ ˈhɪroʊ/ *n* [C] (*plural* **heroes**)
1 a man who is admired for doing something very brave or good → **heroine**: *national/local hero He became the world champion and a national hero.* | [+of] *a hero of the Great War*
2 the man who is the main character in a book, film, play etc → **heroine**

heroic /hɪˈrəʊɪk $ -ˈroʊ-/ *adj* extremely brave or determined: *India's heroic effort against Australia*

heroics /hɪˈrəʊɪks $ -ˈroʊ-/ *n* [plural] brave actions or words, often intended to IMPRESS people

heroin /ˈherəʊɪn $ -roʊ-/ *n* [U] a very strong illegal drug: *heroin addicts*

heroine /ˈherəʊɪn $ -roʊ-/ *n* [C] **1** a woman who is admired for doing something very brave or good → **hero 2** the woman who is the main character in a book, film, play etc → **hero**

heroism /ˈherəʊɪzəm $ -roʊ-/ *n* [U] great courage: *acts of heroism*

heron /ˈherən/ *n* [C] a large bird with long legs and a long beak, that lives near water

herring /ˈherɪŋ/ *n* [C,U] (*plural* **herring** *or* **herrings**) a small thin silver sea fish

hers /hɜːz $ hɜːrz/ *pron* the POSSESSIVE form of 'she': *That's my car. This is hers.* | *Paul is a friend of hers.*

herself /əˈself, hə-; *strong* hɜː- $ ər-, hər-; *strong* hɜːr-/ *pron*
1 the REFLEXIVE form of 'she': *She cut herself on some glass.*
2 used to emphasize that you are talking about a particular woman or girl: *She's leaving – she told me so herself.*
PHRASES
(all) by herself alone or without help from anyone: *Katy lives by herself.* | *She painted the house all by herself.*
have sth (all) to herself to not have to share something: *Alison had the house to herself that night.*
not be/feel/seem herself to not feel well or not behave in the usual way: *Sophie didn't seem herself that morning.*

he's /ɪz, hiz; *strong* hiːz/ the short form of 'he is' or 'he has': *He's my brother.* | *He's lost his keys.*

hesitant /ˈhezɪtənt/ *adj* uncertain about what to do or say, for example because you are nervous: *a hesitant smile* | **hesitant about (doing) sth** *She was hesitant about joining the group.* —**hesitantly** *adv*

hesitate /ˈhezɪteɪt/ *v* [I]
1 to pause before doing or saying something because you are nervous or not sure: *She hesitated before answering.* | [+over/about] *He hesitated over whether to follow her.*
2 don't hesitate to do sth used to encourage someone to do something and not worry about offending anyone: *Don't hesitate to call if you need any help.*

hesitation /ˌhezɪˈteɪʃən/ *n* [C,U] when you hesitate: **without hesitation** *He agreed without hesitation.* | *I have no hesitation in recommending him for the job (=I am very willing to recommend him).*

heterogeneous /ˌhetərəʊˈdʒiːniəs $ -roʊ-/ (*also* **heterogenous** /ˌhetəˈrɒdʒənəs◂ $ -ˈrɑː-/) *adj formal* having parts or members that are very different from each other

heterosexual /ˌhetərəˈsekʃuəl◂/ *adj* sexually attracted to people of the opposite sex → **bisexual**, **homosexual** —**heterosexual** *n* [C]

het up /ˌhet ˈʌp/ *adj* [not before noun] *BrE informal* anxious or upset: [+about/over] *There's no point in getting het up about it.*

hexagon /ˈheksəgən $ -gɑːn/ *n* [C] a flat shape with six sides —**hexagonal** /hekˈsægənəl/ *adj*

hey /heɪ/ *spoken* used to get someone's attention or to show you are surprised or annoyed: *Hey! Look who's here!*

heyday /ˈheɪdeɪ/ *n* [C] the time when someone or something was most popular or successful: **in sb's/sth's heyday** *a photo of Greta Garbo in her heyday*

HGV /ˌeɪtʃ dʒiː ˈviː/ *n* [C] *BrE* (**heavy goods vehicle**) a large truck

hi /haɪ/ *spoken informal* hello: *Hi! How are you?*

hiatus /haɪˈeɪtəs/ *n* [singular] *formal* a short pause

hibernate /'haɪbəneɪt $ -ər-/ v [I] if an animal hibernates, it sleeps through the winter —**hibernation** /ˌhaɪbə'neɪʃən $ -bər-/ n [U]

hiccup¹, hiccough /'hɪkʌp, -kəp/ n [C] **1** [usually plural] if you get hiccups, you make short sounds in your throat that you cannot control: I've **got the hiccups**. **2** a small problem: a hiccup in the negotiations

hiccup² v [I] (**hiccupped, hiccupping**) to have hiccups

hidden /'hɪdn/ adj difficult to see or find: hidden cameras

hide¹ /haɪd/ v (past tense **hid** /hɪd/, past participle **hidden** /'hɪdn/, present participle **hiding**)
1 [T] to put something or someone in a place so that they are difficult to see: **hide sth in/under/ behind etc** Jane hid the presents under the bed. | **hide sb/sth from sb** She had to hide her children from the soldiers. | She **keeps** sweets **hidden** in her desk.
2 [I] if you hide, you go to a place where no one can see you or find you → **hiding**: [+in/under/behind etc] The rebels hid in caves. | [+from] He was hiding from the police.
3 [T] if you hide a fact or feeling, you keep it secret: She laughed to hide her embarrassment. | He had **hidden the fact that** he was married. | **hide sth from sb** She tried to hide the truth from us.
4 [T] to cover something so that it cannot be seen clearly: The sun was hidden by clouds.

THESAURUS

hide to put something or someone in a place where they are difficult to see or find: I've hidden all the presents under the bed.
conceal formal to hide something carefully: The drugs were concealed in the bottom of the suitcase.
cover up to hide something that is unattractive or embarrassing: You can use make-up to cover up spots on your skin. | The government tried to cover up the scandal.
disguise sb/sth as sth to make someone or something look like another person or thing, so that other people will not recognize them: He disguised himself as one of the security guards.

---

hide² n **1** [C,U] the skin of an animal, used for making leather **2** [C] BrE a small building where you hide in order to watch wild animals **SYN** **blind** AmE

hide-and-'seek BrE, **hide-and-go-'seek** AmE n [U] a game in which a child tries to find other children who are hiding

hideaway /'haɪdəweɪ/ n [C] a place where you can go to be alone

hideous /'hɪdiəs/ adj very ugly or unpleasant: a hideous building **THESAURUS** UGLY —**hideously** adv

hideout /'haɪdaʊt/ n [C] a place where you can hide

hiding /'haɪdɪŋ/ n [U] if someone is in hiding, they are in a secret place because they do not want anyone to find them: Some men **went into hiding** to avoid conscription.

hierarchy Ac /'haɪrɑːki $ -ɑːr-/ n (plural **hierarchies**) **1** [C,U] a system of organizing people or things according to their importance **2** [C] the most powerful members of an organization: the church hierarchy —**hierarchical** /haɪ'rɑːkɪkəl $ -ɑːr-/ adj

hieroglyphics /ˌhaɪrə'glɪfɪks/ n [plural] a writing system that uses pictures to represent ideas

hi-fi /'haɪ faɪ, ˌhaɪ 'faɪ/ n [C] (plural **hi-fis**) old-fashioned a piece of equipment used to play recorded music **SYN** **stereo**

higgledy-piggledy /ˌhɪgəldi 'pɪgəldi/ adj, adv lying or arranged together in an untidy way: The books had been put back all higgledy-piggledy.

high¹ /haɪ/ adj
1 **TALL** used about things that are a long way from the bottom to the top, or a long way above the ground → **height, tall**: a high mountain | high buildings | How high is the Eiffel Tower? | Look how **high up** the windows are. | **100 metres/30 ft etc high** a wall five metres high | **knee-/chest- etc high** (=reaching from the ground to your knees, chest etc) The grass was **waist-high**. | a woman in **high-heels** (=shoes with high heels)
2 **GREAT** greater than usual: Petrol prices are quite high at the moment. | a **high temperature** | a **high speed** train | The caves are not safe at **high tide** (=when the sea is at a high level). | I have a **high opinion** of her (=a good opinion). **THESAURUS** EXPENSIVE
3 **OF GOOD QUALITY** of very good quality **OPP** low: The standard of his work is very high.
4 **IMPORTANT** more advanced, powerful, or important than other people or things: He rose to quite a high rank in the Navy. | Security is a high priority.
5 **SOUND** a sound that is high is near the top of the range of sounds that humans can hear **OPP** low: I couldn't sing the very high notes. | a **high-pitched** scream
6 **DRUGS** [not before noun] informal someone who is high is behaving strangely because they have taken drugs: [+on] They were all high on cocaine.
7 **CONTAINING A LOT** high in sth containing a lot of something: foods that are high in fat

PHRASES
begin/end/finish on a high note to begin, end etc very successfully: The day ended on a high note when Great Britain won the last race.

THESAURUS

high measuring a long way from the bottom to the top – used about a mountain, wall, building, or fence. Do not use **high** about people: Mount Everest is the highest mountain in the world. | a high cliff
tall high – used about a person, or about a tree, plant, building etc that is tall and narrow: He's very tall for his age. | a tall tower | tall trees
high-rise a high-rise building is tall and modern, with a lot of floors containing apartments or offices: high-rise apartment buildings | a high-rise office block
majestic big, tall, and very impressive – used about mountains, buildings, trees, and animals: The city is surrounded by majestic mountains. | a majestic herd of elephants

---

H

high² *adv*
1 at or to a level that is a long way from the ground OPP **low**: **[+above/up]** *I could see a plane high up in the sky.* | *She held the trophy high above her head.*
2 at or to a value, amount, or level that is above the normal one OPP **low**: *Prices are expected to go even higher.*

PHRASES
high and low everywhere: *I've searched high and low for my keys.*

high³ *n* [C] **1** the greatest price, level etc that has been recorded: *Last month temperatures reached an all-time high* (=the highest that has ever been known). **2** *informal* a feeling of great happiness: *She's been on a high since meeting Joe.* | *the highs and lows of a Hollywood career*

highbrow /'haɪbraʊ/ *adj* a highbrow book, film etc is very serious and difficult to understand

highchair /ˌhaɪtʃeə $ 'haɪtʃer/ *n* [C] a special tall chair for a young child to sit in while eating

high-'class *adj* of very good quality: *a high-class restaurant*

High 'Court *n* [singular] a court of law that can change the decisions made in a lower court

higher edu'cation *n* [U] education at a college or university rather than a school → **further education**

high-'flyer *n* [C] someone who is very successful in their job or studies

high-'handed *adj* using your authority in an unreasonable way: *I didn't like her high-handed manner.*

high jump *n* [singular] a sport in which you jump over a high bar

PHRASES
be for the high jump *BrE informal* if someone is for the high jump, they will be punished for something that they have done: *He'll be in for the high jump if he doesn't get that report written soon.*

highlands /'haɪləndz/ *n* [plural] an area of a country where there are a lot of mountains: *the Scottish Highlands*

high-'level *adj* [only before noun] involving people with a lot of power or importance: *high-level peace talks*

highlight¹ Ac /'haɪlaɪt/ *v* [T] **1** to make a subject or problem noticeable so that people will pay attention to it: *The chief of police highlighted the problem of car theft.* **2** to mark words on paper or on a computer SCREEN, using a colour so that they are noticed more easily

highlight² *n* [C] **1** the most important, interesting, or enjoyable part of something: **[+of]** *the highlights of today's cricket* **2 highlights** [plural] parts of someone's hair that have been made a lighter colour than the rest

highlighter /'haɪlaɪtə $ -ər/ (also **highlighter pen**) *n* [C] a thick coloured pen, used to mark words on paper → see picture at **STATIONERY**

highly /'haɪli/ *adv*
1 very: *a highly successful businessman* | *a highly intelligent woman* | *It is highly unlikely that he will pass the test.*
2 to a very good level or standard: *a highly skilled builder* | *All our staff are highly trained.*
3 with approval or respect: *She speaks very highly of your work.*

highly-'strung *BrE*, **high-strung** *AmE adj* nervous and easily upset THESAURUS **NERVOUS**

Highness /'haɪnəs/ *n* **Her/His/Your Highness** used to speak to or about a member of a royal family

high-per'formance *adj* [only before noun] a high-performance car, computer, aircraft etc is better and faster than normal ones

high-'pitched *adj* a high-pitched sound is very high

high-'powered *adj* **1** a high-powered machine or piece of equipment is very powerful **2** very important and successful: *a high-powered businessman*

high-'pressure *adj* [only before noun] **1** a high-pressure job or situation is one in which you must work very hard to succeed **2** using a lot of pressure: *a high-pressure water hose*

high-'profile *adj* [only before noun] attracting a lot of public attention: *a high-profile court case*

high-'ranking *adj* having a high position in an organization: *high-ranking officials*

high-rise *adj* [only before noun] high-rise buildings are very tall THESAURUS **HIGH**

high school *n* **1** [C,U] *AmE* a school in the US and Canada for students between the ages of 14 and 18: *high school graduates* **2** [singular] *BrE* used in the names of some schools for students between the ages of 11 and 18

high-'spirited *adj* having a lot of energy and a sense of fun: *John was in a high-spirited mood.*

high street *n* [C] *BrE* the main street in a town where the shops and businesses are: **in/on the high street** *A new bookshop has opened on the high street.* | *the high street shops* | *your local high street bank* THESAURUS **ROAD**

high-'strung *adj AmE* HIGHLY-STRUNG THESAURUS **NERVOUS**

high-tech, hi-tech /ˌhaɪ 'tek◄/ *adj* using the most modern machines, equipment, and methods: *high-tech weapons* THESAURUS **MODERN**

highway /'haɪweɪ/ *n* [C] *AmE* a main road between two cities → **expressway, freeway, motorway** THESAURUS **ROAD**

hijab /hɪˈdʒɑːb/ *n* [C] a piece of cloth covering the head and neck, which some Muslim women wear

hijack /'haɪdʒæk/ *v* [T] to use violence or threats to take control of a plane or vehicle: *Terrorists tried to hijack the plane in mid-flight.* —**hijacker** *n* [C] —**hijacking** *n* [C,U]: *an attempted hijacking*

hike /haɪk/ *v* **1** [I,T] to go for a long walk in the countryside: *Utah is a great place to go hiking.* **2** (also **hike up**) [T] to increase prices, taxes etc by a large amount —**hike** *n* [C]: *a hike across the Malvern Hills* | *a 4% hike in interest rates*

hiker /ˈhaɪkə $ -ər/ n [C] someone who enjoys long walks in the countryside

hilarious /hɪˈleəriəs $ -ˈler-/ adj very funny: a hilarious comedy act **THESAURUS** FUNNY —**hilariously** adv

hilarity /hɪˈlærəti/ n [U] formal laughter and fun

hill /hɪl/ n [C] an area of high land, like a small mountain → **downhill, uphill**: Their house is on a hill overlooking the sea. **THESAURUS** MOUNTAIN

PHRASES

| **over the hill** informal someone who is over the hill is not young any more: Many employers regard people over 45 as being over the hill.

COLLOCATIONS

verbs

to climb/go up a hill (=to walk or drive up a hill) Slowly the bus climbed the hill.
to go down a hill (also **to descend a hill** formal) We went back down the hill to get help.

adjectives

a steep hill The hills here are too steep for cycling.
a small/low hill The house stood on top of a low hill.

noun + hill

the top of a hill There is a church right on top of the hill.
the bottom/foot of a hill The village was at the bottom of a hill.

hillside /ˈhɪlsaɪd/ n [C] the sloping part of a hill

hilly /ˈhɪli/ adj having many hills: a hilly area

hilt /hɪlt/ n [C] the handle of a sword or knife
PHRASES
| **to the hilt** completely: She'll defend him to the hilt.

him /ɪm; strong hɪm/ pron the OBJECT form of 'he': That's Alan. Do you know him?

himself /ɪmˈself; strong hɪmˈself/ pron
1 the REFLEXIVE form of 'he': Bill looked at himself in the mirror. | Did he enjoy himself at the party? | **(all) by himself** (=alone or without help) He lives by himself. | **(all) to himself** (=for his own use) At last he had some time to himself.
2 used to emphasize that you are talking about a particular man or boy: It was the King himself who opened the door.
PHRASES
| **not be/feel/seem himself** if a man is not himself, he is not behaving or feeling as he usually does: He hasn't been himself all day.

hind /haɪnd/ adj [only before noun] relating to the back part of an animal with four legs: The dog stood up on its **hind legs**.

hinder /ˈhɪndə $ -ər/ v [T] to make it difficult for something to happen: The bad weather hindered our progress.

hindrance /ˈhɪndrəns/ n [C] someone or something that makes it difficult for you to do something: **[+to]** Marriage would be a hindrance to her career.

hindsight /ˈhaɪndsaɪt/ n [U] the ability to understand a situation only after it has happened: **with hindsight** With hindsight, I should have warned you to expect trouble.

Hindu /ˈhɪnduː, ˌhɪnˈduː◂/ n [C] (plural **Hindus**) someone whose religion is Hinduism —**Hindu** adj: a Hindu temple

Hinduism /ˈhɪnduː-ɪzəm/ n [U] the main religion in India, which includes belief in REINCARNATION

hinge¹ /hɪndʒ/ n [C] a piece of metal fastened to a door, lid etc that allows it to swing open or shut

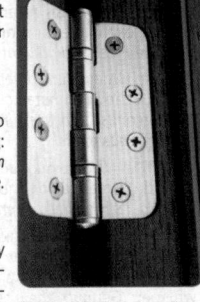

HINGE

hinge² v
PHRASAL VERBS
hinge on/upon sth to depend on something: The case against him hinged on Laura's evidence.

hint¹ /hɪnt/ n [C]
1 INDIRECT SUGGESTION something that you say or do to suggest something to someone without telling them directly: **[+about]** Sue has been **dropping hints** about her birthday. | He **gave** me some strong **hints** about getting married. | If he won't **take a hint** (=understand a hint), you'll have to be honest. | Her remark was probably a **subtle hint** for us to leave.
2 SMALL AMOUNT a small amount of something: **[+of]** A hint of perfume drifted in the air.
3 ADVICE a useful piece of advice SYN **tip**: **[+on/about]** He gave us a few **handy hints** (=useful hints) on gardening.

hint² v [I,T] to suggest something to someone without saying it directly: **[+at]** What are you hinting at? | **[+(that)]** Peg has been hinting she wants a baby.

hinterland /ˈhɪntəlænd $ -ər-/ n [singular] an area of land that is far from the coast and not near any towns or cities

hip¹ /hɪp/ n [C] one of the two parts on each side of your body between the top of your legs and your waist: a lady with a broken hip → see picture on page A2

hip² adj informal modern and fashionable SYN **cool**

'hip-hop n [U] a type of modern popular music with a strong beat that people dance to

hippie /ˈhɪpi/ n another spelling of HIPPY

hippo /ˈhɪpəʊ $ -poʊ/ n [C] (plural **hippos**) informal a hippopotamus

hippopotamus /ˌhɪpəˈpɒtəməs $ -ˈpɑː-/ n [C] (plural **hippopotamuses** or **hippopotami** /-maɪ/) a large grey African animal with a big head that lives near water → see picture on page A3

hippy, hippie /ˈhɪpi/ n [C] (plural **hippies**) someone who opposes violence and the values of western society, and believes in peace and love: the hippies of the 1960s peace movement

H

hire¹ /haɪə $ haɪr/ v [T]
1 *BrE* to pay money to borrow something for a short time **SYN** **rent** *AmE*: *It's best to hire a car when you arrive.*
2 a) to employ someone to do something for a period of time: **hire sb to do sth** *We've hired a childminder to look after Carole.* **b)** *AmE* to employ someone: *He couldn't find anyone who would hire him.*
PHRASAL VERBS
hire sth ↔ **out** *BrE* to allow someone to borrow something in return for money: *His company hires out boats to tourists.*

hire² n [U] *BrE* an arrangement to borrow something in exchange for money: *a car hire company* | **for hire** *Are these fishing boats for hire?*

his /ɪz; strong hɪz/ determiner, pron the POSSESSIVE form of 'he': *Leo hates cleaning his room.* | *His own mother refused to see him.* | *Gary introduced me to some **friends of his**.*

Hispanic /hɪˈspænɪk/ adj from or relating to Spain or Latin America, or the languages spoken there: *New York's Hispanic community* —**Hispanic** n [C]

hiss /hɪs/ v [I] **1** to make a noise that sounds like 'ssss': *Snakes only hiss at you when they're afraid.* → see picture on page A7 **2** to say something in a loud whisper: *'Get out!' she hissed furiously.* —**hiss** n [C]

historian /hɪˈstɔːriən/ n [C] someone who studies history

historic /hɪˈstɒrɪk $ -ˈstɔː-, -ˈstɑː-/ adj a historic place or event is famous or important in history: *He told journalists it was a **historic moment**.* | *funds to restore Spain's historic monuments* **THESAURUS** **IMPORTANT**

> **Word Choice: historic or historical?**
> You use **historic** about places and events that are an important part of the history of a country or area: *The city has many historic buildings.* | *a historic moment*
> You use **historical** about a book, film, person etc that is connected with history: *a historical novel* | *Dick Turpin was a real historical character.*

historical /hɪˈstɒrɪkəl $ -ˈstɔː-, -ˈstɑː-/ adj relating to people or things that happened or existed in the past: *a mixture of **historical facts** and fiction* | *a town of great **historical interest*** —**historically** /-kli/ adv: *a historically significant discovery*

history /ˈhɪstəri/ n (plural histories)
1 [U] the things that happened or existed in the past: **[+of]** *the history of post-war Europe* | *the **early history** of Peru* | **American/Chinese/European etc history** *The war was a turning point in Russian history.* | **recent/modern/ancient etc history** *He's very interested in ancient history.* | *Why don't you do a course on **local history** (=the history of the place where you live)?* | *She's studying **economic history** at university.* | *Venice is a city that **is steeped in history** (=has a long and interesting history).*
2 [singular] all the events in the development of a particular place, activity, institution etc: **[+of]** *the worst accident in the history of space travel* | *It is the first time this has happened in the college's 90-year history.*

3 [C] a written account of past events: **[+of]** *She has just written a history of Britain.*
4 [C,U] a record of something that someone has experienced in the past: *They asked about my **medical history**.* | *Does your family **have a history of** heart trouble?* → **NATURAL HISTORY**

hit¹ /hɪt/ v (past tense and past participle **hit**, present participle **hitting**)
1 **WITH YOUR HAND/A STICK ETC** [T] to move your hand, a stick etc quickly against someone or something with a lot of force: *Please don't hit me!* | **hit sb/sth with sth** *He used to hit the kids with a belt.* | *He hit the ball as **hard** as he could.* → see picture on page A11
2 **BANG/STRIKE** [T] to move into or against someone or something quickly: *The bullet hit him in the chest.* | **hit sth on/against sth** *I hit my knee on the desk.*
3 **AFFECT SB BADLY** [I,T] to affect someone badly: *His mother's death hit him very **hard**.* | *A lot of small companies have been hit by the rise in oil prices.*
4 **REACH** [T] *written* to reach a particular number or level: *Unemployment hit 2 million last month.*
5 **SUDDENLY NOTICE/REALIZE** [T] if something hits you, you suddenly notice or realize it: *The smell of smoke hit me as soon as I came in.* | *It hit me **that** he'd left me for good this time.*
6 **EXPERIENCE** [T] to experience a problem: *The business hit a bad patch in the '70s.*
PHRASES
hit it off (with sb) *informal* to like someone as soon as you meet them: *She seemed to hit it off with John, didn't she?*
hit the headlines to be reported in many newspapers, on television etc: *The couple hit the headlines last month following their break-up.*
hit the nail on the head *informal* if someone hits the nail on the head, what they have said is exactly right or true: *The moment she said it, she knew she'd hit the nail on the head.*
hit the roof/ceiling *informal* to become very angry
PHRASAL VERBS
hit back to attack or criticize someone who has attacked or criticized you: **[+at]** *Yesterday the President hit back at his critics.*
hit on/upon sth to suddenly have a good idea: *Phil has hit on a good way of raising money.*
hit out at/against sb/sth to criticize someone or something

> **THESAURUS**
> **to hit someone**
>
> **hit**: *She hit him on the head with a frying pan.*
> **beat** to hit a person or animal many times, especially very hard: *A boy was beating the donkey with a stick.*
> **punch** to hit someone hard with your closed hand, especially in a fight: *Someone punched me in the stomach.*
> **slap** to hit someone with your open hand because you are angry with them: *I wanted to slap him and tell him to shut up.*
> **smack/spank** to hit a child with your open hand in order to punish them: *I don't agree with smacking children.*

H

strike *formal* to hit someone hard: *He struck him with his rifle.*

to hit something

hit: *Jack hit the ball and it flew over the fence. | A big wave hit the ship.*

knock to hit a door or window with your closed hand to attract the attention of the people inside: *Someone was knocking on the door of her office.*

tap to hit something gently, especially in order to get someone's attention: *She tapped on the window.*

bang to suddenly hit something hard, in a way that makes a loud noise: *The man banged his glass down on the table. | The door suddenly banged shut.*

strike *formal* to hit something hard: *The tree was struck by lightning.*

hit² *n* [C]
1 a very successful and popular film, song, play etc: *The show was a huge hit in London. | Which band had a hit with 'Bohemian Rhapsody'? | a hit musical | his first **hit single***
2 an occasion when something touches the thing it was aimed at: *The ship **took a hit** and sank.*
3 a visit to a website: *The site gets 20,000 hits a day.*

hit-and-'miss (*also* ,hit-or-'miss) *adj* done in a way that is not planned or organized

hit-and-'run *adj* [only before noun] a hit-and-run accident is one in which a car hits someone and the driver does not stop to help

hitch¹ /hɪtʃ/ *v*
1 TRAVEL WITHOUT PAYING [I,T] *informal* if you hitch somewhere, you travel there without paying by asking people who are driving past to take you in their vehicle SYN hitchhike: [+across/around/to etc] *We hitched across Europe. | They hitched a lift to Paris.*
2 FASTEN [T] to fasten one thing to another: **hitch sth to sth** *Dad hitched the boat to the car.*
3 PULL UP (*also* hitch up) [T] to pull up a piece of clothing you are wearing: *She hitched her skirt above her knees.*

hitch² *n* [C] a small problem: *a couple of small technical hitches* | **without a hitch** *The concert went off without a hitch.*

hitchhike /'hɪtʃhaɪk/ *v* [I] to travel to places without paying by asking people who are driving past to take you in their vehicle SYN hitch: [+across/around etc] *They hitchhiked around France.* —**hitchhiker** *n* [C]: *A hitchhiker raised his thumb as we approached.* —**hitchhiking** *n* [U]

hi-tech /,haɪ'tek◂/ *adj* another spelling of HIGH-TECH

hitherto /,hɪðə'tuː◂ $ -ər-/ *adv formal* until now

'hit list *n* [C] *informal* a list of people or organizations that someone intends to harm: **on sb's hit list** *He says he's on the terrorists' hit list.*

'hit man *n* [C] *informal* a criminal who is employed to kill someone

HIV /,eɪtʃ aɪ 'viː◂/ *n* [U] a VIRUS that can develop into the disease AIDS

hive /haɪv/ (*also* **beehive**) *n* [C] a wooden box where BEES are kept
PHRASES
a hive of activity/industry *BrE* a place where everyone is busy: *The kitchen was a hive of activity.*

hiya /'haɪjə/ *spoken informal* used to say hello

h'm, hmm /m, hm/ *spoken* a sound that expresses doubt or disagreement

HMS /,eɪtʃ em es/ *n* (**His/Her Majesty's Ship**) used before the name of a ship in the British navy

hoard /hɔːd $ hɔːrd/ *n* [C] a set of things that someone hides so that they can use them later: **[+of]** *a hoard of gold* THESAURUS ▶ KEEP —**hoard** *v* [T]: *She had hoarded the money she inherited.*

hoarding /'hɔːdɪŋ $ 'hɔːr-/ *n* [C] *BrE* a large board fixed to the side of a building, used to show advertisements SYN **billboard**

hoarse /hɔːs $ hɔːrs/ *adj* if you or your voice is hoarse, you speak in a low rough voice —**hoarsely** *adv*

hoax /həʊks $ hoʊks/ *n* [C] a false warning about something: *a bomb hoax | The police received over 300 **hoax calls** (=telephone calls giving false warnings).*

hob /hɒb $ hɑːb/ *n* [C] *BrE* the top of a COOKER

hobble /'hɒbəl $ 'hɑː-/ *v* [I] to walk with difficulty: *He hobbled across the kitchen.*

hobby /'hɒbi $ 'hɑː-/ *n* [C] (*plural* **hobbies**) an activity that you enjoy in your free time: *My hobbies are gardening and reading.*

> **Usage**
> The word **hobby** often sounds a little old-fashioned. When talking about hobbies in everyday spoken English, you usually say things like: *What do you like to do **in your free time**?* or *When I'm not working, I like to play football with my friends.*

hobo /'həʊbəʊ $ 'hoʊboʊ/ *n* [C] (*plural* **hobos**) *AmE informal* someone without a home or job SYN **tramp** *BrE*

hockey /'hɒki $ 'hɑːki/ *n* [U] **1** *BrE* a game played on grass between two teams who use long curved sticks to hit a ball SYN **field hockey** *AmE* **2** *AmE* a game played on ice in which two teams use long sticks to hit a PUCK (=a hard flat object) SYN **ice hockey**

hodgepodge /'hɒdʒpɒdʒ $ 'hɑːdʒpɑːdʒ/ *n* another spelling of HOTCHPOTCH

hoe /həʊ $ hoʊ/ *n* [C] a garden tool with a long handle that you use to prepare soil before you plant things —**hoe** *v* [I,T]

hog¹ /hɒg $ hɑːg, hɔːg/ *n* [C] *AmE* a large pig
PHRASES
go the whole hog *informal* to do something very thoroughly: *Let's go the whole hog and have champagne.*

hog² *v* [T] (**hogged, hogging**) *informal* to use something yourself when you should share it: *How much longer are you going to hog the bathroom?*

H

hoist

hoist¹ /hɔɪst/ n [C] a piece of equipment used to lift heavy things SYN **crane**

hoist² v [T] to lift something heavy THESAURUS **LIFT**

hold¹ /həʊld $ hoʊld/ v (past tense and past participle **held** /held/)

1 HAVE STH IN YOUR HANDS [T] to have something in your hands: **hold sb/sth in your hands/arms** She held a baby in her arms. | two lovers **holding hands** (=holding each other's hands) | **hold sb/sth close/ tightly etc** He held her tightly. → see picture on page A11

2 KEEP STH IN POSITION [T] to make something stay in a particular position: **hold sth up/out etc** He held out his hand in greeting. | The police tried to hold the crowd back. | We used a brick to **hold** the door **open**. | I used glue to **hold** the photos **in place**.

3 MEETING/ELECTION [T] to have a meeting, ceremony, election etc: The President will hold talks with the Russian leader.

4 HAVE/POSSESS [T] to have or possess something: Do you hold a British passport? | Sheila held the post of Director for three years. | Who holds the world record?

5 KEEP FOR LATER USE [T] to keep something so that it can be used or made available later: We can hold your flight reservations for three days. | Our records are *held on computer*.

6 KEEP SB PRISONER [T] to keep someone in a place so they cannot leave: **hold sb prisoner/hostage/ captive** A journalist is being held hostage.

7 HAVE ENOUGH SPACE [T] to have enough space to contain a particular amount: The hall holds up to 800 guests.

8 SUPPORT [I,T] to be strong enough to support something: The bridge might not **hold** our **weight**.

9 OPINION/VIEW **hold an opinion/view** formal to have an opinion: I hold the view that all children should learn a foreign language.

10 WAIT (also **hold the line**) [I] if you ask someone on the telephone to hold, you are asking them to wait until the person they want to speak to is available THESAURUS **WAIT**

11 STILL BE TRUE [I] if something still holds, it is still true: Does your invitation for lunch still hold? → **hold sb to ransom** at **RANSOM**

PHRASES

hold sb's attention/interest to make someone feel interested: She didn't manage to hold the children's interest.

hold your breath to deliberately not breathe for a short time: How long can you hold your breath underwater?

hold your fire to not attack or criticize someone, when you had planned to: The army held fire until the enemy was about 200 yards away.

hold it/hold on spoken used to tell someone to wait: Hold on a minute, I'm just coming!

hold your own (against sb) to be as good at something as other people: Although I'm nearly 50, I can still hold my own against many younger cyclists.

hold sb responsible/liable (for sth) to believe that someone is responsible for something: The retailer will be held responsible for any faults in the product.

hold water if a reason or argument does not hold water, it does not seem true or reasonable: His

explanation of where the money came from just doesn't hold water.

be left holding the baby BrE, **be left holding the bag** AmE if you are left holding the baby, you have to deal with a difficult situation alone: My boss just went off on holiday, and as usual I was left holding the baby.

THESAURUS

hold to have something in your hands or arms: He was holding a bunch of flowers. | Do you want to hold the baby?

grip to hold something very tightly: He gripped the back of the chair.

clutch to hold something tightly, especially because you do not want to drop or lose it: The little girl clutched onto his hand.

grab to take something in your hand very quickly and suddenly: He grabbed his coat and ran out of the door. | Someone grabbed my wallet.

hang on (to sth/sb) to hold something or someone tightly to support yourself: Lucy hung on to the back of the motorbike.

get/take hold of sth to put your hand or hands around something and hold it: I took hold of the handle and pulled as hard as I could.

grasp written to put your hand or hands firmly around something in a determined way: She grasped the lowest branch and pulled herself up into the tree.

hug to put your arms around someone to show that you like them very much: They hugged each other and then said goodbye.

PHRASAL VERBS

hold sth **against** sb to not forgive someone for something they did in the past

hold sb/sth ↔ **back**

1 to stop yourself from showing a particular feeling: She struggled to **hold back** the **tears**.

2 to prevent someone from being successful or making progress: He was held back by his lack of English.

hold sth ↔ **down**

1 to keep something at a low level: We are holding down prices until 2012.

2 hold down a job to manage to remain in a job for a period of time: He's never held down a job for more than a month.

hold off

1 to delay doing something: **hold off doing sth** We held off making a decision.

2 hold sb ↔ **off** to prevent someone from attacking you or coming near you: Police held off reporters while the singer left the hall.

hold on

1 spoken to wait for a short time: Hold on, I won't be long.

2 to manage in a difficult or dangerous situation: They had to hold on until the rescue team arrived.

hold onto sth to keep something and not give it to anyone: Most investors are holding onto their shares.

hold out

1 to continue to defend yourself or refuse to do

something: **[+against]** *The rebels held out against the army for three weeks.*
2 if a supply of something holds out, there is some left: *Water supplies won't hold out much longer.*
hold out for sth to refuse to accept less than you asked for: *Workers are holding out for more money.*
hold sth **over** sb to use secret information that you have about someone to control or threaten them
hold sb **to** sth to make someone do what they promised: *He offered to help, and I'm going to hold him to it.*
hold together if a group holds together, or if something holds it together, it stays strong and united: **hold** sth ↔ **together** *It's the bad times that have held this family together.*
hold up sb/sth
1 hold sb/sth ↔ up to delay someone or something: *Sorry we're late – we were held up in traffic.*
2 to try to steal money from a shop, bank etc by threatening someone: *The clerk is recovering after he was held up at gunpoint.*

hold² n

1 HOLDING ACTION [singular, U] the action of holding something with your hand SYN **grip**: **[+on/of]** *I kept a tight hold on the fence.* | *Keep hold of my hand as we cross.* | *I took hold of her arm.* THESAURUS ▶ HOLD
2 CONTROL [singular] control, power, or influence over someone or something: **[+over]** *He seemed to have a hold over her.* | *He had learned to keep a tight hold on his emotions.*
3 STORE [C] the part of a ship or aircraft where goods are stored
PHRASES
  get hold of sb/sth to find someone or get something: *I need to get hold of Graham quickly.* | *It won't be easy getting hold of these materials.* THESAURUS ▶ GET
  on hold 1 if something is on hold, it is delayed and may not take place until later: *The project has been put on hold.* **2** if you are on hold, you are waiting to speak to someone on the telephone: *I hate the music they play when they put you on hold.*
  take (a) hold to start to have a definite effect: *Once the disease takes hold, it's difficult to treat.*

holdall /'həʊldɔːl $ 'hoʊldɔːl/ n [C] BrE a bag for clothes, tools, or sports equipment SYN **carryall** AmE → see picture at BAG¹

holder /'həʊldə $ 'hoʊldər/ n [C] **1** someone who has something: **[+of]** *the holder of the world record* | *The concert is for ticket holders only.* **2** something that holds an object: *a candle holder*

holding /'həʊldɪŋ $ 'hoʊl-/ n [C] a part of a company that someone owns

holdover /'həʊld,əʊvə $ 'hoʊld,oʊvər/ n [C] AmE an action, feeling, or idea that has continued from the past into the present SYN **hangover**

'hold-up n [C] **1** a delay, especially one caused by traffic: *There was a hold-up on the way to the office.* **2** when people try to steal money from a shop or bank, using a gun

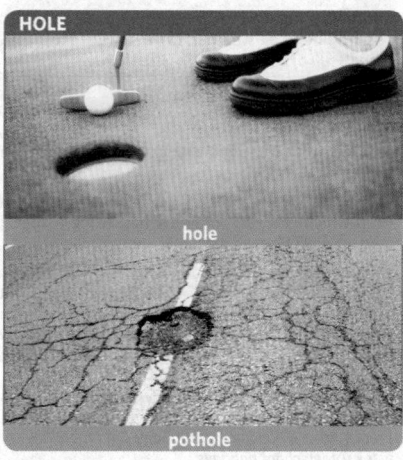

HOLE

hole

pothole

hole¹ /həʊl $ hoʊl/ n [C]

1 an empty space: **[+in]** *There's a hole in my shoe.* | *They climbed through a hole in the fence.* | *You'll need to dig a nice big hole.* | *These socks are full of holes.*
2 in golf, one of the holes that you try to hit the ball into
3 a hole in the ground that an animal lives in
4 if there is a hole in something, it is not right, usually because something or someone is missing: **[+in]** *His death left a big hole in her life.* | *Their theory is full of holes.*
5 *informal* an unpleasant place
6 *informal* a difficult situation: *We're in a bit of a hole now.* → BLACK HOLE
PHRASES
  hole in one an occasion when you get the golf ball into the hole with your first hit
  make a big hole in sth *informal* to use a large part of something, especially money: *The holiday had made a big hole in her savings.*

THESAURUS

hole an empty space in the ground, or in something that is torn or broken: *There's a hole in my jeans.* | *Dig a hole wide enough for the plant's roots.*
gap an empty area between two things or two parts of something, especially one that should not be there: *He has a gap between his two front teeth.* | *There was a gap in the fence.*
opening a hole that something can pass through or that you can see through: *The train disappeared into the dark opening of the tunnel.* | *There was no chimney, just an opening in the roof.*
leak a small hole where something has been damaged, where liquid or gas flows in or out: *There's a leak in the pipe.*
puncture *especially BrE* a small hole in a tyre which lets the air out: *My bike's got a puncture.*
slot a straight narrow hole that you put a coin, card etc into: *Put a coin in the slot before you dial the number.*

H

pothole a hole in the surface of a road caused by traffic or bad weather: *Drive slowly – the road's full of potholes.*

hole² v

PHRASAL VERBS

hole up (*also* **be holed up**) *informal* to hide or be hiding somewhere

hole-in-the-'wall *n* [C] *BrE informal* a machine from which you can obtain money, using a special card **SYN** **ATM**, **cash machine**

holiday¹ /ˈhɒlədi, -deɪ $ ˈhɑːlədeɪ/ *n*
1 (*also* **holidays**) [C,U] *BrE* a period when you travel to another place for pleasure **SYN** **vacation** *AmE*: *Did you have a nice holiday?* | *Where are you going for your holidays?* | **on holiday** *They're on holiday in Greece.*
2 (*also* **holidays**) [C,U] *BrE* a period when you rest and do not go to work or school **SYN** **vacation** *AmE*: *I really need a holiday.* | **on holiday** *I'm on holiday this week.* | *the* **school holidays**
3 [C] a day on which people do not have to go to work or school: *Monday's a* **public holiday**. → **BANK HOLIDAY**, **NATIONAL HOLIDAY**

COLLOCATIONS

verbs

to have a holiday *They seem to have lots of holidays.*
to go on holiday *I can't wait to go on holiday.*
to book a holiday *He's already booked his summer holiday.*

types of holiday

a skiing/camping/walking holiday *The kids love camping holidays.*
a family holiday *This is a great place for a family holiday.*
a summer/winter holiday *We're going to Cornwall for our summer holidays.*

holiday + noun

holiday photos (*also* **holiday snaps** *informal*) *She wanted to show me her holiday photos.*
the holiday season *The town gets very crowded during the holiday season.*
a holiday resort (=a place where a lot of people go on holiday) *Benidorm is a popular holiday resort.*

holiday² *v* [I] *BrE* to go somewhere for a holiday **SYN** **vacation** *AmE*: *The couple are holidaying in Majorca.*

'holiday-,maker *n* [C] *BrE* someone who goes to a place for a holiday **SYN** **vacationer** *AmE*

holiness /ˈhəʊlinəs $ ˈhoʊ-/ *n* [U] **1** the quality of being holy **2** **Your/His Holiness** a title used for an important religious leader, especially the POPE

holistic /həʊˈlɪstɪk $ hoʊ-/ *adj* considering a person or thing as a whole, rather than as separate parts: *a* **holistic approach** *to treating illnesses*

holler /ˈhɒlə $ ˈhɑːlər/ *v* [I,T] *AmE informal* to shout loudly —**holler** *n* [C]

hollow¹ /ˈhɒləʊ $ ˈhɑː-/ *adj*
1 having an empty space inside: *a hollow tree* **THESAURUS** **EMPTY**
2 having a surface that sinks inwards: *Tears ran down her* **hollow cheeks**.
3 without any meaning or emotion: *His words* **had a hollow ring**. | *They won, but it was a* **hollow victory**.

hollow² *n* [C] an area that is lower than the surrounding surface

hollow³ v

PHRASAL VERBS

hollow sth ↔ **out** to remove the inside of something

holly /ˈhɒli $ ˈhɑːli/ *n* [U] a tree with sharp leaves and red BERRIES, used as a decoration at Christmas

holocaust /ˈhɒləkɔːst $ ˈhɑːləkɔːst/ *n* [C] **1 the Holocaust** the killing of Jews and other people by the Nazis during the Second World War **2** a situation in which there is great destruction and death

hologram /ˈhɒləgræm $ ˈhoʊl-, ˈhɑːl-/ *n* [C] a picture made with a LASER, which looks as if it is not flat

holster /ˈhəʊlstə $ ˈhoʊlstər/ *n* [C] a container for a gun that someone wears

holy /ˈhəʊli $ ˈhoʊ-/ *adj*
1 connected with God or religion: *the holy city of Jerusalem* | *a holy war*
2 very religious: *a holy man*

> **Word Choice**: holy or sacred?
> **Holy** and **sacred** are very similar in meaning. Which word you use often depends on the phrase. Here are some examples:
> *the Holy Bible* | *the holy city of Mecca* | *a Hindu holy man* | *a holy war* | *holy water*
> *This place is* **sacred to** *both Jews and Muslims.* | *In India, cows are considered sacred.* | *sacred music* | *a sacred place*

homage /ˈhɒmɪdʒ $ ˈhɑː-/ *n* [U] something you do or say to show respect for a person or achievement: *With this memorial, we* **pay homage to** *those who defended us.*

home¹ /həʊm $ hoʊm/ *n*
1 **YOUR HOUSE** [C,U] the house or flat where you live: **at home** *I stayed at home all evening.* | **away from home** *He was away from home for six weeks.* | *He* **left home** (=stopped living with his family) *when he was 15.*
2 **YOUR COUNTRY** [C,U] the area or country that you come from or that you usually live in: *She's* **made** *Charleston her* **home**.
3 **PLACE STH COMES FROM** **the home of sth** the place where something comes from, or which is famous for something: *Chicago is known as the home of the blues.*
4 **CHILDREN'S/OLD PEOPLE'S INSTITUTION** [C] a place where people live and are looked after, for example old people or children who have no parents → **MOBILE HOME**, **NURSING HOME**, **REST HOME**, **STATELY HOME**

PHRASES

at home 1 at the place where a team usually plays OPP **away**: *Barcelona lost 2–0 at home.* **2** in someone's own country, not in other countries: *He is popular at home and abroad.*

be/feel at home to feel comfortable somewhere, or feel confident doing something: *He seemed very at home using the computer.* | *They always try to* **make** *their guests* **feel at home**.

make yourself at home spoken used to tell someone to relax when they are visiting your home

home² adv to or at the place where you live: *Mike* **got home** (=arrived home) *at five o'clock.* | *I want to* **go home**. | [+from] *Is Mum home from work?*

> **Grammar**
> Do not say 'I went to home.' Say *I went home.*
> Do not say 'I went back my home.' Say *I went back to my home.* or *I went back home.*

PHRASES

bring/drive sth home to make someone understand or realize something: *We really need to drive this message home.*

be home and dry BrE to have succeeded in doing something: *Barcelona must have thought they were home and dry after scoring three goals.*

take home £120/$600 etc used to say how much someone earns, not counting the money which is kept for tax: *I take home about $200 a week.*

home³ adj [only before noun] **1** connected with your home or family: *Their* **home life** *isn't very good.* | *good old-fashioned* **home cooking 2** playing at your team's own sports field OPP **away**: *The home team won.* | *They have won their last three home games.* **3** relating to a particular country, as opposed to foreign countries: *Most of their sales are in the home market.*

PHRASES

home truths unpleasant facts about someone or something: *I decided it was time I told him a few home truths.*

home⁴ v

PHRASAL VERBS

home in on sth **1** to move directly towards something **2** to give all your attention to something

homecoming /'həʊm,kʌmɪŋ $ 'hoʊm-/ n [C] when someone comes home after a long absence

home eco'nomics n [U] old-fashioned the study of cooking, sewing, and other skills used at home

homegrown /,həʊm'grəʊn◄ $,hoʊm'groʊn◄/ adj **1** from your own country or area: *homegrown rock stars* **2** grown in your own garden: *homegrown vegetables*

homeland /'həʊmlænd, -lənd $ 'hoʊm-/ n [C] **1** the country where you were born **2** an area with its own system of government

homeless /'həʊmləs $ 'hoʊm-/ adj **1** without a place to live: *Thousands of people were* **made homeless**. **2** the **homeless** [plural] people who do not have a place to live —**homelessness** n [U]

homely /'həʊmli $ 'hoʊm-/ adj **1** BrE pleasant and ordinary in a comfortable way: *The hotel has a warm, homely atmosphere.* **2** AmE not very attractive SYN **plain** BrE: *his homely appearance*

homemade /,həʊm'meɪd◄ $,oʊm-/ adj made at home: *homemade jam*

homemaker /'həʊm,meɪkə $ 'hoʊm,meɪkər/ n [C] especially AmE someone who works at home, cooking, cleaning, and looking after children

homeopathy /,həʊmi'ɒpəθi $,hoʊmi'ɑːp-/ n [U] a system of medicine in which someone is given very small amounts of a substance that causes their illness —**homeopathic** /,həʊmiə'pæθɪk◄ $,hoʊ-/ adj —**homeopath** /'həʊmiə,pæθ $ 'hoʊ-/ n [C]

homeowner /'həʊm,əʊnə $ 'hoʊm,oʊnər/ n [C] someone who owns their own home

'home-page n [C] the first page of a website

,home 'run n [C] a long hit in baseball, from which you score a point

,Home 'Secretary n [C] the British government minister who is in charge of dealing with crime, TERRORISM, IMMIGRATION etc

homesick /'həʊm,sɪk $ 'hoʊm-/ adj sad, because you are away from home THESAURUS SAD

homestead /'həʊmsted, -stəd $ 'hoʊm-/ n [C] a farm and the land around it

,home 'town especially BrE (also **hometown** /'həʊmtaʊn $ 'hoʊm-/ especially AmE) n [C] the place where you were born or spent your childhood

homeward /'həʊmwəd $ 'hoʊmwərd/ (also **homewards** BrE) adv towards home: *He drove homewards.* —**homeward** adj: *the homeward journey*

homework /'həʊmwɜːk $ 'hoʊmwɜːrk/ n [U] work for school that students do at home → **housework**: *Have you finished your maths homework?* THESAURUS WORK

> **Grammar**
> **Homework** is an uncountable noun and has no plural form. Do not say 'I must do my homeworks.' Say *I must do my homework.*

PHRASES

do your homework to prepare for something by getting information about it: *It was clear that the first applicant had really done her homework.*

COLLOCATIONS

verbs

to do your homework *You can watch TV when you've done your homework.* ⚠ Do not say 'make/write your homework'. Say **do your homework**.

to give sb homework (also **to set sb homework** BrE) *The teacher forgot to give us any homework.*

to help sb with their homework *Dad, will you help me with my homework?*

to hand in your homework (=to give homework you have done to your teacher) *He always hands his homework in on time.*

noun + homework

biology/history/French etc homework *I have to write an essay for my French homework.*

homicidal /ˌhɒməˈsaɪdl◂ $ ˌhɑː-/ *adj* likely to murder someone

homicide /ˈhɒmɪsaɪd $ ˈhɑː-/ *n* [C,U] the crime of killing someone

homogeneous /ˌhəʊməˈdʒiːniəs◂ $ ˌhoʊ-/ (*also* **homogenous** /həˈmɒdʒɪnəs $ -ˈmɑː-/) *adj formal* consisting of parts or members that are all the same → **heterogeneous**: *a homogeneous group of students*

homophobia /ˌhəʊməˈfəʊbiə $ ˌhoʊməˈfoʊ-/ *n* [U] hatred and fear of homosexuals —**homophobic** *adj*

homosexual /ˌhəʊməˈsekʃuəl, ˌhɒmə- $ ˌhoʊ-/ *n* [C] someone who is sexually attracted to people of the same sex SYN **gay** —**homosexual** *adj* —**homosexuality** /ˌhəʊməsekʃuˈæləti, ˌhɒ- $ ˌhoʊ-/ [U]

hone /həʊn $ hoʊn/ *v* [T] **1** to improve a skill **2** to make a knife or sword sharp

honest /ˈɒnɪst $ ˈɑːn-/ *adj*
1 someone who is honest does not lie, cheat, or steal OPP **dishonest**: *He seems a good, honest man.*
2 sincere or telling the true facts about something: *Give me an honest answer.* | *Do you want my honest opinion?* | [+with] *At least he was honest with you.* | [+about] *She was always honest about her feelings.*
PHRASES
to be honest (with you) *spoken* used when you are saying what you really think: *To be honest, I think she'll win.*

> ### THESAURUS
> **honest** someone who is honest does not lie, cheat, or steal: *You can trust Alan – he's totally honest.* | *I want you to give me an honest answer.*
> **sincere** someone who is sincere really feels or believes something, and does not pretend to feel or believe it: *He said he loved me and I thought he was sincere.* | *a sincere apology*
> **frank** speaking honestly and openly about something that people often find difficult to discuss: *She was always completely frank about her illness.* | *a frank discussion about sex*
> **reliable** if someone is reliable, you can depend on them to do what they say they will do: *I need someone reliable to look after the kids while I'm working.*
> **above board** if something is above board, it is done in an honest and legal way: *The deal was entirely above board.*

honestly¹ /ˈɒnəstli $ ˈɑːn-/ *adv* **1** *spoken* used to emphasize that what you are saying is true: *I honestly don't know.* **2** in an honest way: *She spoke honestly about her problems.*

honestly² *spoken* used when you are surprised and annoyed: *Honestly! What a stupid thing to do!*

honesty /ˈɒnəsti $ ˈɑːn-/ *n* [U] when someone is honest OPP **dishonesty**: *We never doubted his honesty.*
PHRASES
in all honesty *spoken* used to tell someone what you really think is true: *In all honesty, we did make mistakes.*

honey /ˈhʌni/ *n* [U] **1** a sweet substance made by BEES, used as food **2** *spoken* used to talk to someone you love: *Hi, honey!*

honeycomb /ˈhʌnikəʊm $ -koʊm/ *n* [C,U] the structure with many cells in which BEES store honey

honeymoon /ˈhʌnimuːn/ *n* [C] **1** a holiday after your wedding: **on a honeymoon** *We went to Italy on our honeymoon.* **2** (*also* **honeymoon period**) a period at the start of a new job or situation, when everyone is happy —**honeymooner** *n* [C]

honk /hɒŋk $ hɑːŋk, hɔːŋk/ *v* [I,T] to make a noise using the horn of a car

honor /ˈɒnə $ ˈɑːnər/ *n* the American spelling of HONOUR

honorable /ˈɒnərəbəl $ ˌɑːn-/ *adj* the American spelling of HONOURABLE

honorary /ˈɒnərəri $ ˈɑːnəreri/ *adj* an honorary title, rank, or university degree is given to show respect or admiration for someone

honour¹ *BrE*, **honor** *AmE* /ˈɒnə $ ˈɑːnər/ *n*
1 [U] when someone is honest, and behaves in a way that makes people respect and trust them: *He was a man of honour.* | *He had a deep sense of honor.* | *He wished to protect his family's honour.*
2 [singular, U] something that makes you feel proud and glad: *It's a great honour to receive this award.* | *I had the honour of meeting the President.* | *Will you do me the honour of becoming my wife?*
3 [C,U] something that is given to a person to show that people respect them and admire their achievements: *The medal is the highest honour that the association can bestow (=give).*
4 Your Honour used to speak to a judge
5 honours [plural] *BrE* a university degree in which you achieve more than the most basic level: *He graduated with first-class honours (=the best possible degree).*
PHRASES
in honour of sb/in sb's honour in order to show respect to someone: *a party given in honour of the prince*
in honour of sth in order to celebrate an event: *An oak tree was planted in honor of the occasion.*

honour² *BrE*, **honor** *AmE* *v* [T] **1** to do what you have agreed or promised to do: *You must honour this agreement.* | *We intend to honour our commitments.* **2** to publicly praise someone, or to give them a special title or AWARD for their achievements: **honour sb with sth** *He was honoured with the Nobel Prize for Medicine.* | **honour sb for sth** *They have been honoured for their courage.* **3** to treat someone with special respect: *I was treated like an honored guest.*
PHRASES
be/feel honoured (to do sth) to feel very proud and glad about something: *I'm very honoured to be here.*

honourable *BrE*, **honorable** *AmE* /ˈɒnərəbəl $ ˌɑːn-/ *adj* **1** deserving respect: *an honourable tradition* **2** having high moral standards: *an honourable man* —**honourably** *adv*

H

hood /hʊd/ n [C] **1** the part of a coat or jacket that you pull up to cover your head **2** AmE the metal cover over the engine on a car SYN bonnet BrE → see picture at CAR **3** especially AmE informal a HOODLUM

HOOD

hood

hooded /ˈhʊdɪd/ adj having or wearing a hood: a hooded jacket

hoodie /ˈhʊdi/ n [C] informal **1** a loose jacket or top made of soft material, which has a hood **2** BrE a young person who wears a hoodie

hoodlum /ˈhuːdləm/ n [C] especially AmE a violent criminal

hoodwink /ˈhʊdˌwɪŋk/ v [T] to trick someone in a clever way

hoof /huːf $ hʊf, huːf/ n [C] (plural **hoofs** or **hooves** /huːvz $ hʊvz, huːvz/) the hard foot of an animal such as a horse or cow → see picture at DEER

PHRASES

on the hoof BrE if you do something on the hoof, you deal with it when it happens, without any preparation: The government are making policy on the hoof.

hook¹ /hʊk/ n [C]
1 a curved piece of metal or plastic, used for hanging things on: Tom hung his coat on the hook.
2 a curved piece of metal, for example for catching fish
3 a way of hitting your opponent in BOXING, with your elbow bent: left/right hook

PHRASES

let/get sb off the hook to allow or help someone to get out of a difficult situation: It's not fair if they let the others off the hook now.

off the hook if the telephone is off the hook, the part that you speak into is not in its correct position, and people cannot call you: I tried to call, but your phone must have been off the hook.

hook² v [T] **1** to fasten or hang something onto or around something else: **hook sth onto/to etc sth** Hook the bucket onto the rope and lower it down. **2** to bend your finger, arm, or leg around something, so that you are holding or pulling it: **hook sth through/in/over etc sth** Ruth hooked her arm through Tony's. **3** to catch a fish: He hooked a 20-lb salmon.

PHRASAL VERBS

hook up 1 hook sb/sth ↔ up to connect someone or something to a machine or piece of equipment: [+to] Millions of people are now hooked up to the Internet. **2** AmE informal if people hook up, they meet, start having a relationship, or start working together: [+with] He'd just hooked up with Angela.

hooked /hʊkt/ adj [only before noun] **1** if you are hooked on something, you like it a lot and want to

continue doing it: children who are hooked on computer games **2** if you are hooked on a drug, you cannot stop using it

hooker /ˈhʊkə $ -ər/ n [C] especially AmE informal a PROSTITUTE

hooky /ˈhʊki/ n **play hooky** AmE informal to stay away from school without permission

hooligan /ˈhuːləgən/ n [C] someone who is violent and noisy in public places —**hooliganism** n [U]

hoop /huːp $ hʊp, huːp/ n [C] a large ring made of metal, plastic, or wood: Throw the ball through the hoop.

PHRASES

jump/go through hoops to do difficult things before you can do what you want: He had to fill out forms and jump through hoops to get the licence.

hooray /hʊˈreɪ/ another spelling of HURRAY

hoot¹ /huːt/ n [C] **1** a shout or laugh that shows you think something is funny or stupid **2** the sound made by an OWL **3** the sound made by a vehicle's horn

PHRASES

be a hoot spoken informal to be very amusing
not give a hoot/two hoots spoken informal to not care about someone or something: Nobody seems to give a hoot about recycling.

hoot² v [I,T] **1** to laugh loudly: [+with] He hooted with laughter. **2** if an OWL hoots, it makes a loud noise **3** if a vehicle hoots, it makes a loud noise with its horn

hoover /ˈhuːvə $ -ər/ v [I,T] BrE to clean the floor with a VACUUM CLEANER

Hoover n [C] trademark BrE a VACUUM CLEANER

hooves /huːvz $ hʊvz, huːvz/ n a plural of HOOF

hop¹ /hɒp $ hɑːp/ v [I] (**hopped, hopping**) **1** informal to move somewhere quickly: [+in/on etc] Hop in and I'll give you a ride. THESAURUS ▶ JUMP **2 a)** to jump or move on one leg: He hopped from one foot to the other. → see picture at JUMP¹ **b)** if a bird or animal hops, it moves by jumping along

hop² n [C] **1 a (short) hop** a short journey, especially by plane: It's a short hop from here by cab. **2** a short jump, or a jump on one foot

PHRASES

hops [plural] the flowers from which beer is made
catch sb on the hop to do something when someone is not expecting it: Sorry about the mess, but you caught me on the hop.

hope¹ /həʊp $ hoʊp/ v [I,T]
1 to want something to happen or be true, and to believe that it is possible: [+(that)] I hope you feel better soon. | **hope to do sth** He's hoping to go to Africa next year. | [+for] We're hoping for better weather tomorrow.
2 I hope so spoken used to say that you hope something that has been mentioned happens or is true: 'Will Grandma be there?' 'I hope so.'
3 I hope not spoken used to say that you hope

something that has been mentioned does not happen or is not true: *'Do you think it's going to rain?' 'I hope not.'*

hope² n

1 [C,U] the feeling of wanting something to happen or be true, and believing that it is possible: **[+of]** *I had given up hope of getting a reply to my letter.* | **in the hope that/of doing sth** (=because you hope something will happen) *She came in the hope of seeing him.*

2 [C,U] a chance that something will happen in the way that you want: **no/not much/little hope (of sth)** *There's no hope of getting the money back.* | **[+that]** *There's a **faint hope** that he'll recover.* | **sb's only/best/last hope** *Please help me - you're my only hope.*

3 [C] something that you hope will happen: *We talked about her **hopes and fears** for the future.*

COLLOCATIONS

verbs

to have hope *We still have hope that he will recover.*

to lose hope/give up hope (=to stop hoping) *She had almost given up hope of seeing him again.*

to give/offer hope *The news gave us some hope.*

to raise sb's hopes (=to make someone feel hopeful) *It would be wrong to raise their hopes too much.*

to dash/shatter sb's hopes *His hopes of winning the championship have been dashed.*

adjectives

high hopes (=a lot of hope that someone or something will be successful) *They had high hopes for their children.*

nouns + hope

a glimmer/ray of hope (=a little hope) *The peace talks offer a glimmer of hope.*

hopeful¹ /ˈhəʊpfəl $ ˈhoʊp-/ *adj* **1** believing that something good is likely or possible: **[+that]** *We're hopeful that we can find a solution.* **2** making you feel that things will happen in the way that you want: *Things don't look very hopeful.* —**hopefulness** *n* [U]

hopeful² *n* [C usually plural] someone who is hoping to be successful, especially in acting, sports, politics etc

hopefully /ˈhəʊpfəli $ ˈhoʊp-/ *adv* **1** used when you are saying what you hope will happen: *Hopefully, I'll be home on Monday.* **2** in a hopeful way: *'Is there anything to eat?' he asked hopefully.*

hopeless /ˈhəʊpləs $ ˈhoʊp-/ *adj* **1** CERTAIN TO FAIL if something you try to do is hopeless, it is certain to fail: *It was a hopeless task.* **2** VERY BAD very bad and not likely to get better: *The situation seemed hopeless.* **3** VERY BAD AT STH especially BrE informal very bad at doing something: **[+at]** *I'm hopeless at spelling.* | **[+with]** *He's hopeless with machinery.* **4** WITHOUT HOPE feeling that you have no hope: *a hopeless look on her face* —**hopelessly** *adv*

horde /hɔːd $ hɔːrd/ *n* [C] a very large crowd of people: **[+of]** *hordes of football fans*

horizon /həˈraɪzən/ *n* **1 the horizon** the place where the land or sea seems to meet the sky: **on the horizon** *We could see a ship on the horizon.* | *The sun dropped below the horizon.* **2 be on the horizon** to be likely to happen soon **3 horizons** [plural] the limit of your ideas, knowledge, and experience: *a trip that will **broaden** your **horizons***

horizontal /ˌhɒrəˈzɒntl◂ $ ˌhɔːrəˈzɑːntl◂/ *adj* a horizontal line remains the same distance from the ground or from the bottom of the page → **vertical**
THESAURUS FLAT —**horizontally** *adv*

hormone /ˈhɔːməʊn $ ˈhɔːrmoʊn/ *n* [C] a chemical in your body —**hormonal** /hɔːˈməʊnəl $ hɔːrˈmoʊ-/ *adj*

horn /hɔːn $ hɔːrn/ *n* **1 a)** [C] one of the two hard pointed parts on the heads of cows, goats etc → **antler** → see picture on page A3 **b)** [U] the substance that animals' horns are made of: *ornaments made of rhino horn* **2** [C] the thing in a vehicle that you use to make a sound as a warning or signal: *He **sounded** his **horn** angrily.* **3** [C] a musical instrument made of metal, that you play by blowing

horoscope /ˈhɒrəskəʊp $ ˈhɑːrəskoʊp, ˈhɔː-/ *n* [C] information about your life, according to the stars and PLANETS

horrendous /hɒˈrendəs, hə- $ hɑː-, hɔː-/ *adj* extremely bad —**horrendously** *adv*

horrible /ˈhɒrəbəl $ ˈhɔː-, ˈhɑː-/ *adj* very unpleasant or upsetting: *What a horrible thing to say!* | *a horrible smell* THESAURUS TASTE —**horribly** *adv*: *The whole plan had gone horribly wrong.*

horrid /ˈhɒrɪd $ ˈhɔː-, ˈhɑː-/ *adj* horrible: *Don't be so horrid to your sister.* | *a horrid smell*

horrific /hɒˈrɪfɪk, hə- $ hɔː-, hɑː-/ *adj* very bad and shocking —**horrifically** /-kli/ *adv*

horrified /ˈhɒrɪfaɪd $ ˈhɔː-, ˈhɑː-/ *adj* very shocked and upset: *She was horrified to see that he was crying.*
THESAURUS SHOCKED

horrify /ˈhɒrɪfaɪ $ ˈhɔː-, ˈhɑː-/ *v* [T] (**horrified, horrifying, horrifies**) to make someone feel very shocked and upset —**horrifying** *adj*

horror /ˈhɒrə $ ˈhɔːrər, ˈhɑː-/ *n* **1** [U] a strong feeling of shock and worry: **in horror** *She stared at him in horror.* | **to sb's horror** *To my horror, I saw he was bleeding.* **2** [C,U] something that is very terrible, shocking, or frightening: **[+of]** *We soon realized the **full horror** of the attack.*
PHRASES
horror movie/film a film about strange and frightening things

'horror ˌstory *n* [C] **1** bad experiences or conditions that you hear about **2** a story about strange and frightening things

horse /hɔːs $ hɔːrs/ *n* [C] a large animal that people ride and use for pulling things → **equestrian, pony**: *I've never ridden a horse before.* → see picture on page A3

horseback /ˈhɔːsbæk $ ˈhɔːrs-/ *n* **1 on horseback** riding a horse **2 horseback riding** AmE the activity of riding a horse SYN **horse-riding** BrE

horse 'chestnut / $ '. ,../ *n* [C] a tree which has large round brown nuts, which cannot be eaten, inside cases with sharp points

'**horse-drawn** *adj* pulled by a horse

horseman /'hɔːsmən $ 'hɔːrs-/ *n* [C] (*plural* **horsemen** /-mən/) a man who rides a horse

horseplay /'hɔːspleɪ $ 'hɔːrs-/ *n* [U] rough noisy play, with a lot of hitting or pushing

horsepower /'hɔːsˌpaʊə $ 'hɔːrsˌpaʊr/ *n* [C,U] (*plural* **horsepower**) (*abbreviation* **hp**) a unit for measuring the power of an engine

'**horse-riding** *n* [U] *BrE* the activity of riding a horse SYN **horseback riding** *AmE*

horseshoe /'hɔːʃʃuː, 'hɔːs- $ 'hɔːr-/ *n* [C] a curved piece of metal fixed to a horse's foot

horsewoman /'hɔːsˌwʊmən $ 'hɔːrs-/ *n* [C] (*plural* **horsewomen** /-ˌwɪmɪn/) a woman who rides a horse

horticulture /'hɔːtəˌkʌltʃə $ 'hɔːrtəˌkʌltʃər/ *n* [U] the activity or science of growing plants —**horticultural** /ˌhɔːtəˈkʌltʃərəl◂ $ ˌhɔːr-/ *adj* —**horticulturalist** *n* [C]

hose¹ /həʊz $ hoʊz/ *n* **1** (*also* **hosepipe** /'həʊzpaɪp $ 'hoʊz-/) [C,U] *BrE* a long rubber or plastic tube that you use to put water onto fires, gardens etc → see picture at **NOZZLE 2** [U] *AmE* PANTYHOSE

hose² *v* [T] to pour water over something or someone, using a hose: **hose sth/sb down** *Would you hose down the car for me?*

hosiery /'həʊzjəri $ 'hoʊʒəri/ *n* [U] a word for socks, TIGHTS, and STOCKINGS – used in shops

hospice /'hɒspɪs $ 'haː-/ *n* [C] a special hospital for people who are dying

hospitable /'hɒspɪtəbəl, hɒ'spɪ- $ haː'spɪ-, 'haːspɪ-/ *adj* friendly and welcoming to visitors OPP **inhospitable** THESAURUS FRIENDLY —**hospitably** *adv*

hospital /'hɒspɪtl $ 'haː-/ *n* [C,U] a building where sick or injured people receive medical treatment: **in (the) hospital** *Rick's dad is still in hospital.* | **out of (the) hospital** *Your mother should be out of hospital within three days.*

> **Usage**
> In British English, people say **go to hospital, stay in hospital** etc. In American English, people say **go to the hospital, stay in the hospital** etc.

COLLOCATIONS

verbs

to go to (the) hospital *She went to the hospital for an X-ray.*
to go into (the) hospital (=to go to hospital to stay for at least one night) *He's had to go into hospital for an operation.*
to be taken/rushed to (the) hospital *Three people were taken to hospital after a crash on the motorway.*
to be admitted to (the) hospital (=to go into hospital) *Her father was admitted to hospital with chest pains.*
to leave/come out of (the) hospital *When are you coming out of hospital?*

hospital + noun

a hospital bed *There is a shortage of hospital beds.*
a hospital ward (=a large room where people stay in hospital) *She works as a nurse on a busy hospital ward.*
hospital treatment *He cut his hand, but didn't need hospital treatment.*

types of hospital

a children's hospital *Her son spent three months in a children's hospital.*
a maternity hospital *BrE* (=for women having babies) *They were born in the same maternity hospital.*
a psychiatric hospital (*also* **a mental hospital** *old-fashioned*) (=for people with mental illness) *He was admitted to a secure psychiatric hospital.*

hospitality /ˌhɒspəˈtæləti $ ˌhaː-/ *n* [U] friendly and welcoming behaviour towards visitors

hospitalize (*also* **-ise** *BrE*) /'hɒspɪtl-aɪz $ 'haː-/ *v* **be hospitalized** if someone is hospitalized, they are taken into hospital for treatment

host /həʊst $ hoʊst/ *n* [C]
1 the person at a party, meal etc who organized it and invited the guests → **hostess**: *Our host greeted us at the door.*
2 someone who introduces the guests on a television or radio show: *a game show host*
3 a country, city, or organization that provides the space, equipment etc for a special event: **host country/government/city etc** *the host city for the next Olympic Games*
4 a (whole) host of people/things a large number of people or things: *a host of possibilities* —**host** *v* [T]: *Which country is hosting the next World Cup?*

hostage /'hɒstɪdʒ $ 'haː-/ *n* [C] someone who is kept as a prisoner by an enemy, and may be hurt or killed in order to force other people to do something → **kidnap**: **take/hold sb hostage** *The group are holding two western tourists hostage.* | *Two days later, the* **hostages** *were* **freed**.

hostel /'hɒstl $ 'haː-/ *n* [C] a cheap place for people to stay when they are away from home, or a place for people who have no home: *a student hostel* THESAURUS HOTEL

hostess /'həʊstɪs $ 'hoʊ-/ *n* [C] **1** the woman at a party, meal etc who organized it and invited the guests → **host 2** a woman who introduces the guests on a television or radio show

hostile /'hɒstaɪl $ 'haːstl, 'haːstaɪl/ *adj* **1** unfriendly or angry, and opposed to someone or something: *a hostile crowd* | **[+to]** *Public opinion was hostile to the war.* THESAURUS UNFRIENDLY **2** used to describe conditions that are difficult to live in: *animals that can survive in such a* **hostile environment 3** belonging to an enemy: *hostile territory*

hostility /hɒ'stɪləti $ haː-/ *n* **1** [U] unfriendly feelings or behaviour: **[+to/towards]** *hostility towards foreigners* **2** [U] strong or angry opposition to something: **[+to/towards]** *local hostility to the scheme*

H

3 hostilities [plural] *formal* fighting in a war: *efforts to end hostilities in the region*

hot¹ /hɒt $ hɑːt/ *adj*

1 having a high temperature OPP **cold**: *The soup's really hot.* | *the hottest day of the year* | *I was hot and tired after the journey.* | *The bar serves* **hot food** (=rather than cold). | *a* **boiling hot** *day* | *It's hot in here – can I open a window?* | *people who live in* **hot countries** (=where the weather is very hot) | *The office gets* **unbearably hot** *in summer.*

2 having a burning taste → **spicy** OPP **mild**: *a hot curry* THESAURUS **TASTE**

3 *informal* very good, popular, exciting, or attractive: *a hot new band* | *His new film is* **hot stuff**. | *The boys all think she's really hot.* → **RED-HOT**

PHRASES

hot favourite the person, party etc that most people expect to win: *He's hot favourite for a semi-final place.*

hot potato *informal* a difficult subject or problem that no one wants to deal with: *The issue has become a political hot potato.*

hot topic/issue a subject that a lot of people are discussing, especially one that causes a lot of disagreement: *Abortion is a hot topic in the US.*

in hot pursuit following someone quickly and closely because you want to catch them: *The police were in hot pursuit of the thief.*

in the hot seat in an important position and responsible for making difficult decisions: *A week of protests has put local politicians in the hot seat.*

THESAURUS

hot having a high temperature: *It's really hot today.* | *a hot drink* | *I'm too hot!*

warm a little hot, especially in a way that is pleasant: *a warm summer's evening* | *The bread was still warm from the oven.*

boiling (hot) *informal* very hot: *It's boiling hot in here!* | *I'm boiling.*

humid if the weather or a place is humid, it is hot and the air feels wet and uncomfortable: *Hong Kong gets very humid at this time of year.* | *humid weather*

lukewarm slightly warm, but not warm enough – used about a liquid that you would like to be hotter: *a cup of lukewarm coffee*

like an oven extremely hot and uncomfortable – used about the inside of rooms, buildings, and cars: *It was like an oven in the car.*

feverish if someone is feverish, their skin feels hot because they are ill: *His forehead felt all feverish.*

---

hot² *v* (**hotted, hotting**)

PHRASAL VERBS

hot up *especially BrE informal* if something hots up, there is more activity or excitement: *The election campaign is hotting up.*

hot 'air *n* [U] things that someone says that sound important, but are not sensible or true

hot 'air bal,loon *n* [C] a very large BALLOON that can carry people in the air → see picture at **BALLOON¹**

hotbed /'hɒtbed $ 'hɑːt-/ *n* [C] a place where there is a lot of a particular kind of activity: **[+of]** *The university was a hotbed of protest.*

hotchpotch /'hɒtʃpɒtʃ $ 'hɑːtʃpɑːtʃ/ *especially BrE*, **hodgepodge** *n* [singular] *informal* a strange mixture of different things

hot 'dog / $ '../ *n* [C] a hot SAUSAGE, eaten in a long piece of bread

hotel /həʊˈtel $ hoʊ-/ *n* [C] a building where you pay to sleep and eat when you are travelling or on holiday

---

COLLOCATIONS

verbs

to stay at/in a hotel *We stayed in a hotel near the airport.*

to check into a hotel (*also* **to book into a hotel** *BrE*) (=to tell the staff you have arrived, get your key etc) *He checked into the hotel a little after 2 pm.*

to check out of a hotel (=to leave a hotel) *We packed our bags and checked out of the hotel.*

adjectives

a luxury hotel (=an expensive and comfortable hotel) *a luxury hotel in central London*

a two-star/three-star etc hotel (=a hotel of a particular standard) *On our honeymoon, we stayed in a four-star hotel in Paris.*

hotel + noun

a hotel room *She was watching TV in her hotel room.*

a hotel guest *Hotel guests have free use of the gym and pool.*

the hotel manager *I'd like to speak to the hotel manager.*

THESAURUS

hotel a building where people pay to stay and eat meals: *I stayed at the Chelsea Hotel.*

motel a hotel for people travelling by car, usually with a place for the car near each room: *We needed a break from driving, so we checked into a motel for the night.*

inn a small hotel, especially an old one in the countryside. Also used in the names of some big modern hotels: *There's an inn in the village.* | *the Holiday Inn*

bed and breakfast (*also* **B & B**) a private house or small hotel, where you can sleep and have breakfast: *The lady at the B & B was very friendly and cooked us a lovely breakfast.*

guesthouse a private house where people can pay to stay and have meals: *The road next to the sea is full of guesthouses.*

hostel/youth hostel a very cheap hotel where people can stay for a short time while they are travelling: *We stayed in youth hostels to keep the cost down.*

---

hotelier /həʊˈteliər, -liə $ ˌoʊtəlˈjeɪ, ˌhoʊ-/ *n* [C] someone who owns or manages a hotel

hothead /'hɒthed $ 'hɑːt-/ *n* [C] someone who

does things too quickly without thinking
—**hotheaded** /ˌhɒtˈhedɪd◂ $ ˌhɑːt-/ adj

hotline /ˈhɒtlaɪn $ ˈhaːt-/ n [C] a special telephone number that people can call for information or advice

hotly /ˈhɒtli $ ˈhaːtli/ adv **1** in an excited or angry way: **hotly debated/disputed/denied etc** a hotly debated issue **2** done with a lot of energy and effort: the **hotly contested** race for governor

'hot spot n [C] **1** a place where there is likely to be a lot of activity or fighting: Soldiers were moved to hot spots along the border. **2** a part of a computer image on the screen that you CLICK on to make other pictures, words etc appear

ˌhot-'tempered adj becoming angry very easily

hot-'water ˌbottle n [C] a rubber container that you fill with hot water, used to make a bed warm

hound¹ /haʊnd/ n [C] a dog used for hunting

hound² v [T] to follow someone all the time and ask them questions in an annoying or threatening way: She's constantly hounded by reporters.

hour /aʊə $ aʊr/ n

1 60 MINUTE PERIOD [C] a period of 60 minutes: The meeting lasted an hour. | **in one/two/three etc hours** I'll be home in two hours. | **quarter of an hour/half an hour/three quarters of an hour** (=15, 30, 45 minutes) He was quarter of an hour late. | **[+of]** The meeting ended after four hours of talks. | It's **an hour's drive** to the airport. | a top speed of 120 **miles an hour** | **a two-hour/three-hour etc sth** a five-hour delay

2 TIME STH HAPPENS [C] a fixed period of time in the day when a particular activity, business etc happens: **office/opening/working etc hours** Our business hours are 9.00 to 5.00. | I could meet you in my **lunch hour** (=when I stop working to have lunch). | The key is kept with the caretaker **after hours** (=after the time a company, shop etc closes).

3 LONG TIME **hours** [plural] informal a long time: She spends hours on the phone.

4 TIME [C] a particular time during the day or night: The buses don't run at this hour of the night. | The baby keeps them awake **at all hours** (=at any time, even very late at night). → **RUSH HOUR**

5 12 O'CLOCK/1 O'CLOCK ETC **the hour** the exact time when a new hour starts, for example one o'clock, two o'clock etc: **on the hour** Classes begin on the hour. | Buses go at ten minutes past the hour.

hourglass /ˈaʊəɡlaːs $ ˈaʊrɡlæs/ n [C] a glass container for measuring time, with sand moving slowly from the top half to the bottom in one hour

hourly /ˈaʊəli $ ˈaʊrli/ adj **1** happening every hour: an hourly news bulletin **2** for one hour: I get an **hourly rate** of £8.

house¹ /haʊs/ n (plural houses /ˈhaʊzɪz/)

1 HOME **a)** [C] a building that someone lives in: I'm going over to Dean's house. | a four-bedroom house | **at sb's house** She's staying at Alex's house. **b)** [singular] all the people who live in a house: Be quiet or you'll wake **the whole house!**

2 BUILDING [C] a building used for a particular purpose: the Opera House | a hen house

3 LAW-MAKERS [C] a group of people who make the laws of a country: The President will address both

HOUSES

detached house *BrE*

bungalow

cottage

terraced house *BrE*/
row house *AmE*

semi-detached house *BrE*

houses of Congress. | the House of Commons

4 COMPANY [C] a company involved in a particular area of business: a famous Italian fashion house | a publishing house

5 AT SCHOOL [C] *BrE* one of the groups that the children in a school are put into, for the purposes of competing in sports etc

6 DANCE MUSIC [U] HOUSE MUSIC → **FULL HOUSE, OPEN HOUSE, PUBLIC HOUSE**

PHRASES

be on the house *spoken* if drinks or meals in a restaurant are on the house, they are free: These drinks are on the house.

THESAURUS

house a building that someone lives in, especially one that has more than one floor and is used by one family, person etc: Annie and Rick have just bought their first house.
detached house *BrE* a house that is not joined to another house: a detached four-bedroomed house
semi-detached house *BrE* a house that is joined to another house on one side
terraced house *BrE*, **row house** *AmE* one of a row of houses that are joined together
cottage a small house in the country – used

H

especially about houses in the UK: *a little cottage in the country*

bungalow a small house that is all on one level: *Bungalows are suitable for many elderly people.*

mansion a very large house: *the family's Beverly Hills mansion*

an apartment

apartment *especially AmE*, **flat** *BrE* a set of rooms where someone lives that is part of a house or bigger building: *His apartment is on the eighth floor.* | *In London, I shared a flat with some other students.*

condominium (*also* **condo** *informal*) *AmE* one apartment in a building with several apartments, owned by the people who live in them: *a ten-unit condominium complex*

house² /haʊz/ *v* [T] **1** to provide someone with a place to live: *a program to house the homeless* **2** if a building houses something, it is kept there: *The new building will house the art collection.*

'house ar,rest *n* **be under house arrest** to be kept as a prisoner by a government, inside your own house

houseboat /'haʊsbəʊt $ -boʊt/ *n* [C] a river boat that you can live in

housebound /'haʊsbaʊnd/ *adj* unable to leave your house because you are ill or old

household¹ /'haʊshəʊld $ -hoʊld/ *adj* [only before noun] relating to your home **SYN** **domestic**: *washing powder and other* **household products** | *household chores*

PHRASES

be a household name/word to be very well known: *Nelson Mandela is a household name around the world.*

household² *n* [C] all the people who live together in one house: *Many households have at least one computer.*

householder /'haʊs,həʊldə $ -,hoʊldər/ *n* [C] *formal* someone who owns or is in charge of a house → **homeowner**

'house ,husband *n* [C] a married man who works at home doing the cooking, cleaning etc

housekeeper /'haʊs,kiːpə $ -ər/ *n* [C] someone whose job is to organize the cooking, cleaning etc in a house or hotel

housekeeping /'haʊs,kiːpɪŋ/ *n* [U] the work and organization involved in looking after a house, hotel etc, for example cooking and cleaning

houseman /'haʊsmən/ *n* [C] (*plural* **housemen** /-mən/) *BrE* someone who has almost finished training as a doctor and is working in a hospital **SYN** **intern** *AmE*

housemate /'haʊsmeɪt/ *n* [C] *BrE* a person who you share a house with who is not a member of your family **SYN** **roommate** *AmE* → **flatmate**

'house ,music (*also* **house**) *n* [U] a popular type of dance music

,House of 'Commons *n* **the House of Commons**

the part of the British Parliament whose members are elected by the people

,House of 'Lords *n* **the House of Lords** the part of the British Parliament whose members have positions because of their rank or title

,House of Repre'sentatives *n* **the House of Representatives** the larger of the two parts of the US Congress or of the Parliament of Australia or New Zealand → **senate**

houseproud /'haʊspraʊd/ *adj* someone who is houseproud spends a lot of time cleaning and taking care of their home

,Houses of 'Parliament *n* **the Houses of Parliament** the buildings where the British Parliament meets, or the Parliament itself

house-to-'house *adj* **house-to-house collections/searches/inquiries etc** when people go to all the houses in an area to collect something or to find out about something

'house-,warming *n* [C] a party that you have to celebrate moving into a different house **THESAURUS** **PARTY**

housewife /'haʊswaɪf/ *n* [C] (*plural* **housewives** /-waɪvz/) a woman who stays at home doing the cooking, cleaning etc for her family, rather than doing a paid job → **homemaker**

housework /'haʊswɜːk $ -wɜːrk/ *n* [U] work that you do to look after a house, for example cleaning and washing **THESAURUS** **WORK**

housing /'haʊzɪŋ/ *n* [U] **1** the houses that people live in: *a shortage of good housing* **2** the work of providing houses for people to live in: *government housing policy*

'housing es,tate *BrE*, **'housing de,velopment** *AmE* *n* [C] a large number of similar houses that have been built together in the same place

hovel /'hɒvəl $ 'hʌ-, 'hɑː-/ *n* [C] a small dirty place where someone lives

hover /'hɒvə $ 'hʌvər, 'hɑː-/ *v* [I] **1** if a bird, insect, or HELICOPTER hovers, it stays in one place in the air: *A helicopter hovered above the crowd.* **2** to stay in one place, waiting for something: *Rick was hovering by the door, hoping to talk to me.*

hovercraft /'hɒvəkrɑːft $ 'hʌvərkræft, 'hɑː-/ *n* [C] (*plural* **hovercraft** *or* **hovercrafts**) a vehicle that travels over land or water on a strong current of air that the engines produce beneath it

how /haʊ/ *adv, linking word*
1 used to ask or talk about the way something happens or is done: *How do you spell your name?* | *He explained how the system worked.* | *We both work at the airport – that's how we met.* | **how to do sth** *Do you know how to get to her house?*
2 used to ask about amount, size, age etc: *How many children do you have?* | **how much?** (=used to ask the price of something) *How much are those peaches?* | *How old is Debbie?* | *How long have you been here?*
3 a) used to ask about someone's health or happiness, especially when you meet them: *'Hi Laurie, how are you?' 'Fine, thanks.'* | *How's she feeling today?*
b) used to ask someone for news about their life,

work etc: *So **how's it going** at work?* | ***How are you doing?***
4 used to ask someone their opinion: *'How do I look?' 'Great!'*
5 used to emphasize the quality you are mentioning: **how good/well/hot/quickly etc** *He was impressed at how well she could read.* → **KNOW-HOW**

PHRASES

how about ...? *spoken* used to suggest doing something: *How about a drink after work?*

how come? *spoken* used to ask why, especially when you are surprised about something: *How come Dave's home already?*

how do you do? *spoken formal* used when you meet someone new for the first time: *"This is my wife." "How do you do?"*

however /hauˈevə $ -ər/ *adv, linking word*
1 used to introduce an idea, fact etc that is surprising or unexpected after what you have just said: *It's an unpleasant disease. However, it's easy to treat.*
2 however difficult/expensive/hot etc used to say that even if something is very difficult etc, it does not change the situation: *We'll finish the job, **however long it takes** (=even if it takes a very long time).* | **however much/many** *I want that car, however much it costs.*
3 in any way: *You can travel however you like.*

howl /haul/ *v* [I] **1** if a dog or WOLF howls, it makes a long crying sound **2** to cry very loudly **3** if the wind howls, it makes a high loud sound —**howl** *n* [C]

howler /ˈhaulə $ -ər/ *n* [C] *informal* a stupid mistake that makes people laugh [SYN] **blunder**

HQ /ˌeɪtʃ ˈkjuː/ *n* [C,U] the abbreviation of **headquarters**

hr the written abbreviation of **hour**

HR /ˌeɪtʃ ˈɑː $ -ˈɑːr/ *n* [U] the abbreviation of HUMAN RESOURCES

HRH the written abbreviation of **His Royal Highness** or **Her Royal Highness**

hub /hʌb/ *n* [C] **1** the central and most important part of an area, system etc → **centre**: **[+of]** *The local school was the hub of the community.* **2** the central part of a wheel

hubbub /ˈhʌbʌb/ *n* [singular, U] a lot of noise, excitement etc that you can hear: *the hubbub of the crowd*

hubcap /ˈhʌbkæp/ *n* [C] a metal cover for the centre of a wheel on a vehicle

huddle /ˈhʌdl/ (*also* **huddle together/up**) *v* [I] if a group of people huddle together, they stay very close to each other because they are cold or frightened: *We all **huddled together** for warmth.* —**huddle** *n* [C]

hue /hjuː/ *n* [C] *literary* a colour: *a golden hue*

huff[1] /hʌf/ *n* **in a huff** angry because someone has offended you: *Ray walked out in a huff.*

huff[2] *v* **huff and puff** to breathe in a noisy way, especially because you are doing something tiring

hug /hʌg/ *v* (**hugged, hugging**) **1** [I,T] to put your arms around someone and hold them, because you

like or love them: *We hugged and said good night.* [THESAURUS] HOLD **2** [T] to move along the side, edge, top etc of something, staying very close to it: *The road to Barcelona hugs the Mediterranean coast.* —**hug** *n* [C]: *Give me a hug before you go.*

huge /hjuːdʒ/ *adj* very large [SYN] **enormous**: *Your room's huge compared to mine.* | *a huge dog* | **a huge amount/sum/quantity etc** *huge numbers of tourists* [THESAURUS] BIG

Grammar
Do not use **very** with **huge**. Do not say 'a very huge cake'. Just say *a huge cake*.

hugely /ˈhjuːdʒli/ *adv* extremely: *a hugely talented musician*

huh /hʌh, hʌ/ *spoken* used when you are asking a question or are slightly annoyed about something: *Not a bad restaurant, huh?*

hulk /hʌlk/ *n* [C] **1** a large heavy person or thing **2** an old ship, plane, or vehicle that is not used any more

hull /hʌl/ *n* [C] the main part of a ship that goes in the water

hullabaloo /ˌhʌləbəˈluː, ˈhʌləbəluː/ *n* [singular] *informal* a lot of noise or excitement: *There's been a big hullabaloo over his new book.*

hullo /hʌˈləu $ -ˈlou/ a British spelling of HELLO

hum /hʌm/ *v* (**hummed, humming**) **1** [I,T] to sing a tune by making a continuous sound with your lips closed: *If you don't know the words, just hum.* **2** [I] to make a low continuous sound: *insects humming in the sunshine* **3 be humming** *approving* if a place is humming, there is a lot of activity: *By nine o'clock, the restaurant was humming.* —**hum** *n* [singular]: *the hum of traffic*

human[1] /ˈhjuːmən/ *adj* belonging or relating to people: **the human body** | *the power of **the human mind*** | *The accident was a result of **human error** (=a mistake made by a person, not a machine).* | **human weakness/failing** (=a weakness that is typical of people) *Jealousy's one of the worst human failings.*

PHRASES

human interest a quality that makes a story in a newspaper interesting because it is about someone's life, relationships etc: *The story lacks any kind of human interest.*

sb is only human used to say that someone should not be blamed for what they have done: *Referees are only human. Sometimes they make mistakes.*

human[2] (*also* **human being**) *n* [C] a person

humane /hjuːˈmeɪn/ *adj* treating people or animals in a way that is not cruel or likely to cause suffering [OPP] **inhumane** —**humanely** *adv*

humanism /ˈhjuːmənɪzəm/ *n* [U] the belief that human problems can be solved through science rather than religion —**humanist** *n* [C] —**humanistic** /ˌhjuːməˈnɪstɪk◂/ *adj*

humanitarian /hjuːˌmænəˈteəriən $ -ˈter-/ *adj* concerned with improving people's living conditions and preventing unfair treatment: *The UN sent* *humanitarian aid* to help the refugees. —**humanitarian** *n* [C]

humanity /hjuːˈmænəti/ *n* [U] **1** kindness, respect, and sympathy towards other people OPP **inhumanity**: *a man of great humanity* **2** people in general, or the state of being human: *the importance of religion to humanity* **3 the humanities** subjects such as literature, history, and languages rather than mathematics and sciences

humankind /ˌhjuːmənˈkaɪnd/ *n* [U] people in general THESAURUS ▶ **PEOPLE**

humanly /ˈhjuːmənli/ *adv* **humanly possible** possible to do if you try very hard: *We'll finish it as fast as is humanly possible.*

ˌhuman 'nature *n* [U] the qualities and behaviour that are natural to most people

ˌhuman 'race *n* **the human race** all people → **mankind** THESAURUS ▶ **PEOPLE**

ˌhuman re'sources / $ ˌ.. '.../ *n* [U] the department in a company that deals with employing, training, and helping people SYN **personnel**

ˌhuman 'rights *n* [plural] the basic rights that everyone has to say what they think, vote, be treated fairly etc

humble¹ /ˈhʌmbəl/ *adj* **1** *approving* not thinking yourself better or more important than other people OPP **proud** **2** having a low social class or position: *the senator's* **humble beginnings** *on a farm in Iowa* —**humbly** *adv*

humble² *v* [T usually passive] to make someone realize that they are not as important, good etc as they thought: *You are humbled when you enter this magnificent cathedral.* —**humbling** *adj*: *a humbling experience*

humdrum /ˈhʌmdrʌm/ *adj* boring and ordinary: *a humdrum job*

humid /ˈhjuːmɪd/ *adj* humid air, weather etc feels hot and wet: *the humid heat of a tropical forest* THESAURUS ▶ **DAMP**

humidity /hjuːˈmɪdəti/ *n* [U] the amount of water that is in the air: *The plants prefer* **high humidity**.

humiliate /hjuːˈmɪlieɪt/ *v* [T] to make someone feel ashamed or stupid: *She humiliated me in front of the whole class.* —**humiliating** *adj*: *a humiliating defeat* —**humiliated** *adj* —**humiliation** /hjuːˌmɪliˈeɪʃən/ *n* [C,U]

humility /hjuːˈmɪləti/ *n* [U] *approving* the quality of not being too proud of yourself → **humble**

humorous /ˈhjuːmərəs $ ˈhjuː-, ˈjuː-/ *adj* funny – used especially about stories, books, and films that are a little funny, but which do not make you laugh loudly: *a collection of humorous short stories* THESAURUS ▶ **FUNNY** —**humorously** *adv*

humour¹ *BrE*, **humor** *AmE* /ˈhjuːmə $ ˈhjuːmər, ˈjuː-/ *n* [U]

1 the ability to think that things are funny and to laugh: *I don't like her – she's got no* **sense of humour**.

2 the quality in something that makes it funny: *There's a lot of humour in his songs.*

3 good humour a cheerful friendly attitude: *his charm and good humour*

humour² *BrE*, **humor** *AmE* *v* [T] to do what someone wants or to pretend to agree with them so that they do not become upset: *'Of course,' he said, humouring her.*

humourless *BrE*, **humorless** *AmE* /ˈhjuːmələs $ ˈhjuːmər-, ˈjuː-/ *adj* unable to laugh at things that are funny

hump¹ /hʌmp/ *n* [C] **1** a round raised area on the ground, a road etc: **speed/traffic humps** *BrE* (=a series of humps in the road to make traffic go more slowly) **2** a raised part on a CAMEL's back

hump² *v* [T] *BrE informal* to carry something heavy somewhere

hunch¹ /hʌntʃ/ *n* [C] a feeling you have that something is true or that something will happen, even if you have no information or proof: *I* **had a hunch** *you'd call today.*

hunch² *v* [I] to bend down and forward so that your back forms a curve: **hunched over sth** *He was sitting in his study, hunched over his books.* —**hunched** *adj*: *hunched shoulders*

hunchback /ˈhʌntʃbæk/ *n* [C] an offensive word for someone who cannot stand up straight and has a large raised part on their back

hundred /ˈhʌndrɪd/ *number* (*plural* **hundred** *or* **hundreds**)

1 the number 100: *The tree was probably a hundred years old.* | **two/three/four etc hundred** *I make six hundred pounds a week.* | **hundreds of pounds/dollars etc**

2 an extremely large number of things or people: **a hundred** *They've had this argument a hundred times before.* | **hundreds of sth** *He's had hundreds of girlfriends.* —**hundredth** *adj*: *her hundredth birthday* —**hundredth** *n* [C]: *four-hundredths of a second*

hundredweight /ˈhʌndrədweɪt/ *n* [C] (*plural* **hundredweight**) (*written abbreviation* **cwt**) a unit for measuring weight equal to 112 pounds or 50.8 kilograms in Britain and 100 pounds or 45.36 kilograms in the US

hung /hʌŋ/ *v* the past tense and past participle of HANG

hunger /ˈhʌŋɡə $ -ər/ *n* [U]

1 the feeling you have when you need to eat: *The baby was crying with hunger.*

2 a severe lack of food, especially for a long period of time → **thirst**: *Hundreds of people are* **dying of hunger** *every day.*

'hunger strike *n* [C] when someone, especially a prisoner, refuses to eat as a way of protesting about something

hungover /hʌŋˈəʊvə $ -ˈoʊvər/ *adj* feeling ill because you drank too much alcohol the day before

hungry /ˈhʌŋɡri/ *adj*

1 if you are hungry, you want to eat → **thirsty**: *I'm getting hungry, let's eat!*

2 ill or weak as a result of not having enough to eat for a long time → **starving**: *We shouldn't waste food when half the world is hungry.* | *Many people in our city* **go hungry** (=do not have enough food) *every day.*

3 if you are hungry for something, you want it very

much: **[+for]** *Rick was hungry for a chance to work.*
—**hungrily** *adv*

> ### THESAURUS
>
> **hungry** if you are hungry, you want to eat: *You must be hungry after your long journey.*
> **starving/ravenous** (also **starved** *AmE*) *informal* very hungry and wanting to eat as soon as possible: *We hadn't eaten all day and we were absolutely starving!*
> **peckish** *BrE informal* a little hungry: *I'm feeling a bit peckish – I think I might have an ice cream.*
> **I could eat a horse!** *informal* used when saying that you are very hungry: *I hope there's plenty to eat – I could eat a horse!*

hung-'up *adj informal* worrying too much about something

hunk /hʌŋk/ *n* [C] **1** a thick piece of something: **[+of]** *a hunk of bread* **2** *informal* an attractive man who has a strong body

hunker /'hʌŋkə $ -ər/ *v*
PHRASAL VERBS
hunker down to sit on your heels with your knees bent in front of you

hunt /hʌnt/ *v* [I,T]
1 to chase wild animals in order to catch or kill them: *These dogs have been trained to hunt.* | *They hunt rabbits and other wild animals.*
2 to look for someone or something very carefully [SYN] **search**: *The police are still hunting the killer.* | **[+for]** *Detectives are busy hunting for clues.* —**hunt** *n* [C]: *The hunt for the missing child continues today.*
PHRASAL VERBS
hunt sb/sth ↔ **down** to search for a person or animal until you catch them, especially in order to punish or kill them: *These murderers will be hunted down and brought to justice.*

hunter /'hʌntə $ -ər/ *n* [C] someone who hunts wild animals

hunting /'hʌntɪŋ/ *n* [U] **1** chasing and killing animals for food or sport **2 job-hunting/house-hunting etc** a search for a job, a house to live in etc

hurdle¹ /'hɜːdl $ 'hɜːr-/ *n* [C] **1** a problem or difficulty that you must deal with before you can achieve something: *Finding enough money for the project was the first hurdle.* **2** a small fence that a person or horse jumps over during a race

hurdle² *v* [I,T] to jump over something while you are running —**hurdler** *n* [C]

hurl /hɜːl $ hɜːrl/ *v* [T] to throw something with a lot of force: *Someone hurled a brick through the window.* [THESAURUS] **THROW**
PHRASES
> **hurl abuse/insults etc at sb** to shout angrily at someone: *He was accused of hurling abuse at the referee.*

hurray, hooray /hʊ'reɪ/ *spoken* something that you shout when you are very glad about something

hurricane /'hʌrɪkən $ 'hɜːrəkeɪn/ *n* [C] a violent storm with very strong fast winds → **tornado** [THESAURUS] **STORM**

hurry¹ /'hʌri $ 'hɜːri/ *v* [I,T] (**hurried, hurrying, hurries**) to go somewhere or do something quickly, or to make someone do this: *If we hurry we'll be in time.* | *I hate having to hurry a meal.* | **[+along/across/down etc]** *She hurried along as fast as she could.* | **hurry to do sth** *They were hurrying to catch their train.* | *Don't hurry me, I'm going as fast as I can.* —**hurried** *adj*: *a hurried breakfast* —**hurriedly** *adv*: *They left hurriedly.*
PHRASAL VERBS
hurry up
1 hurry up! *spoken* used to tell someone to do something more quickly: *Hurry up! We're late.*
2 hurry sb/sth ↔ **up** to make someone do something more quickly or make something happen more quickly: *Try to hurry the kids up or they'll be late for school.*

> ### THESAURUS
>
> **hurry** to go somewhere quickly or do something quickly, because you do not have much time: *He was hurrying to get to a meeting.*
> **rush** to go somewhere very quickly, or to do something very quickly and without being careful enough: *I rushed downstairs to answer the door.* | *It's always best not to rush through your exam.*
> **dash** to go somewhere very quickly because there is something urgent you must do or get: *She had to dash off and collect the kids from school.*
> **in a hurry** if you do something in a hurry, you do it quickly because you do not have much time: *I left the house in a hurry and forgot my keys.*
> **get a move on** *informal* to start to do something or go somewhere more quickly because you do not have much time: *You'd better get a move on if you want to catch that train!*

hurry² *n*
1 be in a hurry if you are in a hurry, you need to do things quickly because you do not have much time: *I can't talk now – I'm in a hurry.* | **be in a hurry to do sth** *Why are you in such a hurry to leave?* [THESAURUS] **HURRY**
2 (there's) no hurry *spoken* used to tell someone that they do not have to do something immediately: *You can pay me back next week – there's no hurry.*
3 not be in any hurry/be in no hurry (to do sth) to be able to wait because you have a lot of time in which to do something: *Take your time, I'm not in any hurry.*

hurt¹ /hɜːt $ hɜːrt/ *v* (past tense and past participle **hurt**)
1 [T] to cause someone to feel pain, or to damage part of your body so that it feels painful: *Careful you don't hurt yourself with that knife.* | *She hurt her shoulder playing baseball.* | *Careful you don't hurt each other.* | *Ow, you're hurting me!*
2 [I,T] if a part of your body hurts, or if something hurts it, you can feel pain in it: *My feet really hurt after all that walking!* | **It hurts when** *I breathe.* | *The sun's hurting my eyes.* [THESAURUS] **PAINFUL**
3 [I,T] to make someone feel upset or unhappy: *His comments weren't true, but they hurt.* | *I'm sorry, I didn't mean to **hurt** your **feelings**.*

H

hurt

PHRASES

sth won't/doesn't hurt (sb) *informal* used when you think someone should do something: *It won't hurt him to make his own dinner for once.*

THESAURUS

to hurt someone

hurt to cause someone to feel pain: *I fell off a ladder and hurt myself.* | *Don't hold me so tight – you're hurting me!*

injure to hurt someone badly: *The driver was seriously injured.* | *Careful you don't injure yourself.*

wound to deliberately hurt someone with a weapon such as a knife or gun: *Three soldiers were wounded in the attack.*

to hurt part of your body

hurt to do something that makes part of your body feel painful: *I hurt my back when I was lifting a heavy box.*

injure to hurt part of your body badly: *Tom injured his leg in a motorcycle accident.*

break to hurt a part of your body by breaking a bone in it: *Nicky went skiing and broke her leg.*

cut to hurt part of your body by touching a sharp object: *I cut myself on some broken glass.*

bruise to hurt your body when you fall or are hit, in a way that makes a dark mark appear on your skin: *I bruised my forehead on the doorway.*

twist/sprain to hurt your knee, wrist, shoulder etc by suddenly twisting it while you are moving: *Tony sprained his knee when he was playing soccer.*

---

hurt² *adj* [not before noun]
1 suffering pain or injury: **badly/seriously/slightly hurt** *Fortunately, no one was seriously hurt.*
2 very upset or offended: *I was very hurt by what you said.* —**hurt** *n* [U]

hurtful /'hɜːtfəl $ 'hɜːrt-/ *adj* making you feel upset or offended → **unkind**: *a hurtful remark* **THESAURUS** UNKIND

hurtle /'hɜːtl $ 'hɜːr-/ *v* [I] to move or fall very fast: **[+down/along/through etc]** *A huge rock came hurtling down the mountainside.*

husband /'hʌzbənd/ *n* [C] the man that a woman is married to → **wife**: *Have you met my husband Roy?* → **HOUSE HUSBAND**

hush¹ /hʌʃ/ *v* **hush** *spoken* used to tell someone to be quiet, or to comfort a child who is crying

PHRASAL VERBS

hush sth ↔ **up** to prevent people from knowing about something dishonest or immoral: *The bank tried to hush the whole thing up.*

hush² *n* [singular] a peaceful silence

hushed /hʌʃt/ *adj* quiet because people are listening, waiting to hear something, or talking quietly: *The courtroom was hushed.* | *people speaking in hushed voices*

hush-'hush / $ '../ *adj* informal secret: *The project's very hush-hush.*

husk /hʌsk/ *n* [C,U] the dry part that covers some grains or seeds

husky¹ /'hʌski/ *adj* **1** a husky voice is deep and sounds rough but attractive **2** *AmE* a husky man is big and strong —**huskily** *adv*

husky² *n* [C] (*plural* **huskies**) a large strong dog that is used for pulling SLEDGES over snow

hustle¹ /'hʌsəl/ *v* **1** [T] to make someone go somewhere by pushing them: *Jackson was hustled into his car by bodyguards.* **2** [I] *AmE* to hurry: *We've got to hustle or we'll be late!* **3** [I,T] *AmE informal* to buy or sell things illegally: *Young boys were hustling stolen goods on the street.*

hustle² *n* **hustle and bustle** busy and noisy activity

hustler /'hʌslə $ -ər/ *n* [C] *especially AmE* someone who tries to trick people into giving them money

hut /hʌt/ *n* [C] a small simple building with only one or two rooms: *a wooden hut*

hutch /hʌtʃ/ *n* [C] a wooden box that pet rabbits are kept in

hybrid /'haɪbrɪd/ *n* [C] **1** an animal or plant that is produced from two different types of animal or plant **2** something that is a mixture of two or more things —**hybrid** *adj*

'hybrid car *n* [C] a car that has both a petrol or DIESEL engine and an electric motor

hydrant /'haɪdrənt/ *n* [C] a FIRE HYDRANT

hydraulic /haɪ'drɒlɪk, -'drɔː- $ -'drɒː-/ *adj* a hydraulic machine or system works by the pressure of water or another liquid: *hydraulic brakes*

hydroelectric /ˌhaɪdrəʊɪ'lektrɪk◂ $ -droʊ-/ *adj* using water power to produce electricity: *a hydro-electric dam*

hydrogen /'haɪdrədʒən/ *n* [U] a gas that is lighter than air and that combines with oxygen to form water

hyena /haɪ'iːnə/ *n* [C] a wild animal like a dog that makes a loud laughing sound

HYENA

hygiene /'haɪdʒiːn/ *n* [U] when you keep yourself and the things around you clean in order to prevent diseases: *the importance of* ***personal hygiene*** | *We learnt the principles of* ***food hygiene***.

hygienic /haɪ'dʒiːnɪk $ -'dʒe-, -'dʒiː-/ *adj* clean and likely to prevent diseases from spreading: *Food must be prepared in hygienic conditions.* **THESAURUS** CLEAN

hymn /hɪm/ *n* [C] a song sung in Christian churches

hype¹ /haɪp/ *n* [U] *disapproving* when something is talked about a lot on television, in the newspapers etc, to make it seem good or important: *There's been a lot of* ***media hype*** *surrounding this movie.*

hype² (*also* **hype up**) *v* [T] to try to make people think something is good or important by talking about it a lot on television, in the newspapers etc:

The director is just using the controversy to hype his movie.

hyper /'haɪpə $ -ər/ *adj informal* too excited, or with too much energy

hyperactive /ˌhaɪpər'æktɪv◄/ *adj* a hyperactive child cannot keep still or quiet for very long —**hyperactivity** /ˌhaɪpəræk'tɪvəti/ *n* [U]

hyperbole /haɪ'pɜːbəli $ -ɜːr-/ *n* [U] a way of describing something by saying that it is much bigger, better, worse etc than it really is

hyperlink /'haɪpəlɪŋk $ -pər-/ *n* [C] a word or picture on a WEBSITE or in computer document that will take you to another page or document if you CLICK on it

hypermarket /'haɪpəˌmɑːkɪt $ -pərˌmɑːr-/ *n* [C] *BrE* a very large SUPERMARKET outside a town

hypersensitive /ˌhaɪpə'sensətɪv◄ $ -pər-/ *adj* very easily offended or upset

hypertension /ˌhaɪpə'tenʃən $ -pər-/ *n* [U] *technical* a medical condition in which your BLOOD PRESSURE is too high

hypertext /'haɪpəˌtekst $ -pər-/ *n* [U] *technical* a way of writing computer documents that makes it possible to move from one document to another by CLICKing on words or pictures, especially on the Internet

hyphen /'haɪfən/ *n* [C] a short line (-) used to join parts of words together, or to show that a word has been divided and continues on the next line —**hyphenated** *adj*

hypnosis /hɪp'nəʊsɪs $ -noʊ-/ *n* [U] when someone is put into a state like a deep sleep, so that another person can control or influence their thoughts and actions: **under hypnosis** *He remembered details of his childhood under hypnosis.*

hypnotic /hɪp'nɒtɪk $ -'nɑː-/ *adj* **1** making you feel tired or unable to pay attention to anything else, especially because of a regularly repeated sound or movement: *hypnotic music* **2** relating to hypnosis: *a hypnotic trance*

hypnotize (*also* **-ise** *BrE*) /'hɪpnətaɪz/ *v* [T] to produce a sleep-like state in someone so that you can influence their thoughts and actions —**hypnotist** *n* [C] —**hypnotism** /-tɪzəm/ *n* [U]

hypochondriac /ˌhaɪpə'kɒndriæk $ -'kɑːn-/ *n* [C] someone who worries all the time about their health, even when they are not ill —**hypochondria** /-driə/ *n* [U]

hypocrisy /hɪ'pɒkrəsi $ -'pɑː-/ *n* [U] *disapproving* when someone pretends to be a good person and have moral beliefs that they do not really have OPP **sincerity** —**hypocrite** /'hɪpəkrɪt/ *n* [C]

hypocritical /ˌhɪpə'krɪtɪkəl◄/ *adj* pretending to be a good person and have moral beliefs that you do not really have OPP **sincere**: *It would be hypocritical to get married in church when we don't believe in God.*

hypodermic /ˌhaɪpə'dɜːmɪk◄ $ -ɜːr-/ *n* [C] a piece of medical equipment with a very thin hollow needle, used for putting drugs into someone's body through the skin SYN **syringe** —**hypodermic** *adj*

hypothermia /ˌhaɪpəʊ'θɜːmiə $ -poʊ'θɜːr-/ *n* [U] *technical* a serious medical condition in which a person's body becomes too cold

hypothesis Ac /haɪ'pɒθəsɪs $ -'pɑː-/ *n* [C] (*plural* **hypotheses** /-siːz/) a suggested explanation for something which has not yet been proved → **theory**

hypothetical Ac /ˌhaɪpə'θetɪkəl◄/ *adj* based on a situation that is not real but might happen: *Students were given a hypothetical law case to discuss.* | *The question is purely hypothetical.* —**hypothetically** /-kli/ *adv*

hysterectomy /ˌhɪstə'rektəmi/ *n* [C,U] (*plural* **hysterectomies**) a medical operation to remove a woman's UTERUS

hysteria /hɪ'stɪəriə $ -'steriə/ *n* [U] extreme excitement, anger, fear etc that you cannot control: *The incident provoked mass hysteria.*

hysterical /hɪ'sterɪkəl/ *adj* **1** unable to control your behaviour or emotions because you are very excited, angry, afraid etc: *When she heard the explosion she became hysterical.* **2** *informal* extremely funny: *a hysterical new comedy* —**hysterically** /-kli/ *adv*

hysterics /hɪ'sterɪks/ *n* [plural] when you cannot control your behaviour or emotions because you are very excited, angry, afraid etc

PHRASES

be in hysterics *informal* to be laughing and not able to stop: *We were all in hysterics!*

I i

I, i /aɪ/ n [C,U] (plural **I's**, **i's**) the ninth letter of the English alphabet

I /aɪ/ pron used by the person speaking or writing to refer to himself or herself: *I saw Mike yesterday.* | *My husband and I are going to Mexico.* | *I'm not late again, am I?*

> **Word Choice: and I or and me?**
> **And I** is the grammatically correct form, but it sounds formal: *My husband and I will be having a small celebration.*
> **And me** is not grammatically correct, but it is very commonly used in everyday conversation between people who know each other well: *My sister and me are very different.*

ice¹ /aɪs/ n [U] water that has frozen and become solid: *Do you want some ice in your drink?* → **break the ice** at BREAK¹

PHRASES

put sth on ice to do nothing about a plan or suggestion for a period of time: *I'm putting my plans for a new car on ice until I finish college.*

COLLOCATIONS

adjectives

thick ice *They had to use an axe to break the thick ice.*

thin ice *The ice is thinner in the centre of the lake.*

black ice (=a thin layer of ice on a road which is difficult to see) *Drivers are being warned of black ice this morning.*

verbs

ice melts *The ice had all melted by lunchtime.*

ice forms *Ice had formed on the inside of the windows.*

ice + noun

an ice cube (=ice made in a small square shape) *She filled a jug with ice cubes and water.*

---

ice² v [T] *BrE* to cover a cake with ICING **SYN** **frost** *AmE*

PHRASAL VERBS

ice over/up to become covered with ice: *The lake iced over during the night.*

iceberg /'aɪsbɜːg $ -bɜːrg/ n [C] a very large piece of ice floating in the sea

ice cap n [C] an area of thick ice that permanently covers the North and South Poles

ice-'cold adj very cold: *an ice-cold drink*

ice 'cream / $ '../ n [C,U] a frozen sweet food with fruit, nuts, chocolate etc sometimes added to it: *strawberry ice cream*

ice cube n [C] a small block of ice that you put in a drink to make it cold → see picture at PIECE¹

ice hockey n [U] *BrE* HOCKEY played on ice → see picture on page A9

ice lolly n [C] *BrE* a piece of sweet-tasting ice on a stick that you suck **SYN** **Popsicle** *AmE*

ice pack n [C] a bag containing ice that is put on injured or painful parts of your body

ice rink n [C] a specially prepared surface of ice inside a building where you can ICE SKATE

ice skate¹ v [I] to slide on ice wearing ice skates —**ice skating** n [U] —**ice skater** n [C]

ice skate² n [C] a special boot with thin metal blades on the bottom that allows you to move quickly on ice → see picture at SKATE¹

icicle /'aɪsɪkəl/ n [C] a thin pointed piece of ice that hangs down, for example from a roof

ICICLE

icing /'aɪsɪŋ/ n [U] a sweet substance used to cover cakes. Icing is a mixture of sugar, a liquid, and sometimes butter **SYN** **frosting** *AmE*

icon /'aɪkɒn $ -kɑːn/ n [C]
1 ON A COMPUTER a small sign or picture on a computer screen that you choose when you want the computer to do something: *To send a fax, click on the telephone icon.*
2 ADMIRED PERSON someone famous who is admired by many people and is thought to represent an important idea: *a feminist icon*
3 RELIGIOUS PICTURE/FIGURE (also **ikon**) a picture or figure of a holy person —**iconic** /aɪˈkɒnɪk $ -ˈkɑː-/ adj

icy /'aɪsi/ adj (comparative **icier**, superlative **iciest**)
1 extremely cold: *an icy wind* **THESAURUS** ▶ COLD
2 covered in ice: *icy roads*

I'd /aɪd/ the short form of 'I had' or 'I would'

ID /ˌaɪ 'diː/ n [C,U] something official that shows your name, address etc, usually with a photograph **SYN** **identification**: *May I see some ID, please?* | *You'll need to show your ID card at reception.*

idea /aɪˈdɪə/ n
1 PLAN/SUGGESTION [C] something that you think of, especially a plan or suggestion: *I knew it was a bad idea to leave him on his own.* | *I have an idea – let's go to the beach.* | **[+for]** *Where did you get the idea for the book?*
2 KNOWLEDGE [singular, U] understanding or knowledge of something: **[+of]** *This book gives you an idea of what life was like during the war.* | *I want to get an idea of what the building will look like.* | *Give me a rough idea* (=not exact) *of how much it will cost.* | *Richard had no idea* (=he did not know at all) *where Celia had gone.* | *I don't have the faintest idea* (=I don't know at all) *what to get Rachel for her birthday.*
3 PURPOSE **the idea of sth** the aim or purpose of

doing something: *The idea of the game is to hit the ball into the holes.*
4 OPINION [C] an opinion: [+about] *Bill has some strange ideas about women.*

COLLOCATIONS

verbs

to have an idea *I've just had an idea.*
to get an idea *She got the idea from an article in a magazine.*
to give sb an idea *The story gave him an idea for a film.*
to come up with an idea (=to think of an idea) *If you come up with any ideas, let me know.*

adjectives

a good/great/brilliant idea *What a great idea!*
a bad idea *Inviting Katie was a really bad idea.*
a bright idea (=a very good idea – people often use this humorously when talking about a bad idea) *Whose bright idea was it to buy him a drum?*
a stupid/ridiculous/crazy idea *The idea sounded crazy to me.*

THESAURUS

idea something that you think of, especially a plan or suggestion that you tell someone about: *It sounds like a really good idea. | Do you have any ideas for presents?*
thought something that comes into your mind when you think about something: *My mind was full of strange thoughts. | He had a sudden thought.*
impression an idea in your mind about what someone or something is like: *It rained all the time, so I have a bad impression of the place.*
inspiration the idea that you use for doing or creating something: *The inspiration for her designs comes from the natural world.*
brainwave *BrE*, **brainstorm** *AmE* a sudden clever idea, especially one that solves a problem: *Then he had a brainwave – why not get someone else to do all the work?*
concept our idea about what something is like, or how something should be: *the traditional concept of marriage | Concepts of beauty are different in different cultures.*
theory a set of ideas that are used in order to explain why something happens: *a scientific theory | There are a lot of theories about what really happened that night.*

ideal¹ /aɪˈdɪəl◀/ *adj*
1 the best or most suitable: *an ideal place for a picnic | an ideal opportunity |* [+for] *This film is ideal for young children.* THESAURUS ▶ PERFECT
2 perfect, but not likely to exist: *In an ideal world there would be no war.*

ideal² *n* [C] **1** a standard that you would like to achieve: *We must work towards this ideal.* **2** a perfect example of something:* [+of]* *our ideals of beauty*

idealism /aɪˈdɪəlɪzəm/ *n* [U] the belief that you should live according to high standards or principles, even if it is difficult —**idealist** *n* [C]

—**idealistic** /ˌaɪdɪəˈlɪstɪk◀/ *adj*: *an idealistic young doctor*

idealize (*also* **-ise** *BrE*) /aɪˈdɪəlaɪz/ *v* [T] to imagine that something is perfect or better than it really is: *an idealized view of marriage*

ideally /aɪˈdɪəli/ *adv* **1** used to say how you would like things to be, even if it is not possible: *Ideally, I'd like to live in the country.* **2** perfectly: *The hotel is ideally situated next to the beach. | He's ideally suited for the job.*

identical Ac /aɪˈdentɪkəl/ *adj* exactly the same: *The two pictures looked identical. |* [+to] *Your shoes are identical to mine. |* **identical twins** (=two babies that are born together and look exactly the same) THESAURUS ▶ SAME —**identically** /-kli/ *adv*

identifiable Ac /aɪˈdentəfaɪəbəl/ *adj* easy to recognize

identification Ac /aɪˌdentɪfɪˈkeɪʃən/ *n* [U]
1 something official that shows your name, address etc, usually with a photograph SYN ID: *You can use a passport as identification.* **2** when you say that you recognize someone or something: *The bodies are awaiting identification.*

identify Ac /aɪˈdentɪfaɪ/ *v* [T] (**identified, identifying, identifies**)
1 to recognize someone or something and say correctly who or what they are: *She was unable to identify her attacker.*
2 to recognize something or discover exactly what it is: *Scientists have identified the gene that causes abnormal growth.*

PHRASAL VERBS
identify with sb to feel sympathy with someone or be able to share their feelings: *It was easy to identify with the novel's main character.*

identity Ac /aɪˈdentəti/ *n* (*plural* **identities**)
1 [C,U] who someone is: *The identity of the killer is still unknown. | The police officer asked to see my* **identity card.** **2** [U] the qualities that someone has that make them different from other people: *our cultural identity | Many people's* **sense of identity** *comes from their job.*

ideology Ac /ˌaɪdiˈɒlədʒi $ -ˈɑːl-/ *n* [C,U] (*plural* **ideologies**) a set of beliefs or ideas about politics: *Marxist ideology* —**ideological** /ˌaɪdiəˈɒdʒɪkəl $ -ˈlɑː-/ *adj*: *They have ideological differences.*

idiocy /ˈɪdiəsi/ *n* [U] extremely stupid behaviour

idiom /ˈɪdiəm/ *n* [C] a group of words that have a different meaning from the usual meaning of the separate words. For example, 'under the weather' is an idiom meaning 'ill'. THESAURUS ▶ PHRASE

idiomatic /ˌɪdiəˈmætɪk◀/ *adj* **1** idiomatic language is typical of the way people usually talk and write **2 idiomatic expression/phrase** an idiom: *Most idiomatic phrases can't be translated literally into another language.*

idiosyncrasy /ˌɪdiəˈsɪŋkrəsi/ *n* [C] (*plural* **idiosyncrasies**) an unusual habit or way of behaving that a person has —**idiosyncratic** /ˌɪdiəsɪŋˈkrætɪk◀/ *adj*

idiot /ˈɪdiət/ *n* [C] a stupid person: *Some idiot drove into the back of my car.* —**idiotic** /ˌɪdiˈɒtɪk◀ $ -ˈɑːt-/ *adj* —**idiotically** /-kli/ *adv*

idle¹ /ˈaɪdl/ adj **1** lazy: *That boy is **bone idle*** (=extremely lazy). **2** not working or being used: *The machines are now **standing idle** in the factory.* **3** not serious: *an idle threat* | *This is just idle gossip.* —**idleness** n [U] —**idly** adv

---

Word Choice: idle or lazy?

Lazy is the normal word to use in everyday English: *He's too lazy to cook for himself.* | *a lazy student*

Idle sounds more formal and a little old-fashioned. It is used mainly in written English: *her idle husband* | *the idle rich* (=lazy rich people)

---

idle² v **1** [I] if an engine idles, it runs slowly while the vehicle is not moving **2** [I,T] to spend time doing nothing: *Don't just idle your time away.*

idol /ˈaɪdl/ n [C] **1** someone that you admire very much: *a pop idol* **2** a picture or object that people WORSHIP as a god

idolize (also **-ise** BrE) /ˈaɪdəl-aɪz/ v [T] to admire someone so much that you think they are perfect: *They idolize their little boy.* **THESAURUS ▶ ADMIRE**

idyllic /ɪˈdɪlɪk, aɪ- $ aɪ-/ adj very pleasant and peaceful: *an idyllic country scene*

i.e. /ˌaɪ ˈiː/ written before a word or phrase that gives the exact meaning of something you have just written or said: *The movie is only for adults, i.e. those over 18.*

if /ɪf/ linking word

1 a) used when talking about the possibility that something might happen or be true: *If you finish first, you'll get a prize.* | *Add more salt **if necessary**.* | *I want to leave by 5 o'clock **if possible**.* | *I wouldn't tell you, **even if** I knew.* | *Are you coming to see us, and **if so** (=if you are coming), when?* | *Does he know? **If not**, what shall I tell him?* **b)** used to talk about something that sometimes happens: *If I don't go to bed by 10, I'm exhausted the next day.*

2 used to mention a fact, situation, or event that someone asks about, or is not certain about: *He **asked** me **if** I was all right.* | *I **wonder if** John's home yet.* | *I'm **not sure if** she's coming.* | *I don't know **if** he's here **or not**.*

3 used to ask something politely: *I **wonder if** you could help me?* | ***Would you mind if** I open the window?*

4 used to add to what you have just said and make it stronger: *He rarely, **if ever**, swears.* | *The snow made it difficult, **if not** impossible, to go out.* | *He wasn't unpleasant – **if anything** (=in fact), he was nicer than before.*

PHRASES

if I were you used when giving someone advice: *I'd leave if I were you.*

if only used to express a strong wish: *If only he'd agree!*

THESAURUS

if used when talking about the possibility that something might happen or be true: *If it rains, we'll have the party indoors.* | *You can always bring it back if there's a problem.*

unless if something does not happen, or if someone does not do something: *They'll be here soon, unless their flight's been delayed.*

otherwise used when saying that there will be a bad result if someone does not do something: *Hurry up – otherwise you'll be late.*

whether or not used when saying that it does not matter if something happens or if someone does something, because the result is the same: *People often get better on their own, whether or not they see a doctor.*

in case so that you are ready to deal with something that might happen: *I don't think it will rain, but I'll take my umbrella just in case.*

as long as only if something else happens or is true: *You're welcome to come, as long as you don't mind sleeping on the sofa.*

---

iffy /ˈɪfi/ adj informal **1** BrE not good: *The weather looks **a bit iffy**.* **2** not certain or approving: *She sounded a bit iffy about the idea of a party.*

igloo /ˈɪgluː/ n [C] (plural **igloos**) a house made from blocks of snow or ice

ignite /ɪgˈnaɪt/ v formal **1** [I,T] to start burning, or to make something start burning **2** [T] to start a dangerous situation, angry argument etc: *actions that could ignite a war*

ignition /ɪgˈnɪʃən/ n [singular] the electrical part of a car engine that makes it start working: *Turn the key in the ignition.*

ignominious /ˌɪgnəˈmɪniəs/ adj formal making you feel ashamed or embarrassed —**ignominiously** adv

ignorance Ac /ˈɪgnərəns/ n [U] lack of knowledge or information: **[+of]** *Ignorance of the law is no excuse.* | **in ignorance** *She remained in blissful **ignorance** of the problem* (=was not worried, because she did not know).

ignorant Ac /ˈɪgnərənt/ adj not knowing facts or information: **[+of]** *We went on, ignorant of the dangers.*

ignore Ac /ɪgˈnɔː $ -ˈnɔːr/ v [T] to deliberately not pay attention to something or someone: *They can't **ignore the fact** that he's here.* | *She **completely ignores** her husband.* | ***ignore sb's advice/warning***

Word Choice: ignore or not know about sth?

Do not use **ignore** when you mean 'not know about'.

If you **ignore** something, you deliberately do not pay any attention to it: *Drivers are ignoring the speed limits.* | *She chose to ignore his advice.*

If you do **not know about** something, you do not realize that it exists or has happened: *I didn't know about the new rules.*

You can also say *I **was unaware of** the new rules* in the same meaning.

---

ikon /ˈaɪkɒn $ -kɑːn/ n another spelling of ICON

ill¹ /ɪl/ adj

1 suffering from a disease or not feeling well: *Jenny can't come – she's ill.* | *I was **feeling ill**.* | *She was **taken ill** (=became ill) at school.* | *He's **mentally ill**.* | ***terminally ill** patients* (=patients who are going to die) | ***seriously/critically ill***

2 [only before noun] bad or harmful: *He was unable to attend because of* ***ill health.*** *| I ate the same thing, but suffered no* ***ill effects***.
PHRASES
| **ill at ease** nervous, uncomfortable, or embarrassed: *Sam looked ill at ease in his suit.*

> **THESAURUS**
>
> **ill** *especially BrE* suffering from a disease or not feeling well: *I feel really ill.* | *He was so ill he could hardly get out of bed.*
> **sick** *especially AmE* ill: *What's the matter? Are you sick?* | *The boss is off sick today* (=he cannot come to work because he is ill).
> **not very well** *especially spoken* ill, but not seriously ill: *She can't come – she's not very well.*
> **unwell** *formal* ill: *Her father had been unwell for some time.*
> **poorly** *BrE informal* ill: *He is very poorly and he may not have long to live.*
> **sickly** a sickly child is often ill: *My brother was a sickly child who was always in and out of hospital.*
> **under the weather/off colour** *informal* slightly ill: *Joe's been feeling a bit under the weather lately.*

ill² *adv* badly: *We were* ***ill prepared*** *for the shock.* | **think/speak ill of sb** (=think or say bad things about someone)
PHRASES
| **sb can ill afford (to do) sth** used to say that an action or thing will make someone's situation worse: *The senator can ill afford another scandal.*

ill³ *n* **1** ills [plural] problems: *a cure for the ills of old age* | **social/economic ills 2** [U] harm or bad luck: *She* ***wished*** *him no* ***ill***.

ill- /ɪl/ *prefix* badly or bad: *ill-concealed boredom* | *They are ill-equipped to cope.* | *ill-mannered children*

I'll /aɪl/ the short form of 'I will' or 'I shall'

ill-ad'vised *adj* not sensible —**ill-advisedly** /-əd'vaɪzdəli/ *adv*

ill-con'ceived *adj* not planned well and not having an aim that is likely to be achieved: *The ill-conceived scheme was later abandoned.*

illegal Ac /ɪ'liːgəl/ *adj* not allowed by law: *It's illegal to park here.* | **illegal drugs/substances** —**illegally** *adv* —**illegality** /ˌɪlɪ'gæləti/ *n* [U]

il,legal 'immigrant (*also* **il,legal 'alien** *AmE*) *n* [C] someone who comes into a country to live or work without official permission

illegible /ɪ'ledʒəbəl/ *adj* impossible to read: *His handwriting's illegible.*

illegitimate /ˌɪlə'dʒɪtəmət◂/ *adj* **1** *old-fashioned* born to parents who are not married **2** not allowed or not acceptable: *an illegitimate use of public money* —**illegitimacy** *n* [U]

ill-'fated *adj* unlucky and resulting in serious problems or death: *an ill-fated venture*

ill-'fitting *adj* ill-fitting clothes do not fit the person who is wearing them: *ill-fitting shoes*

ill-gotten 'gains *n* [plural] money that is obtained in an unfair or dishonest way

illicit /ɪ'lɪsɪt/ *adj* illegal or not approved of: *an illicit love affair* —**illicitly** *adv*

illiterate /ɪ'lɪtərət/ *adj* unable to read or write —**illiteracy** *n* [U]

illness /'ɪlnəs/ *n* [C,U] something wrong with your health that makes you feel ill, or the state of having something wrong with you → **disease**: *She died after a long illness.* | *How many days have you had off work because of illness?*

> **COLLOCATIONS**
>
> **verbs**
> **to have an illness** *We found out he had a serious illness.*
> **to suffer from an illness** *Tell the instructor if you are suffering from any illness.*
> **to recover from an illness** *She is recovering from an illness and needs a lot of rest.*
>
> **adjectives**
> **a serious/severe illness** *He's never had any serious illnesses.* ⚠ Do not say 'a heavy illness'. Say **a serious illness** or **a severe illness**.
> **a terminal illness** (=one that causes death and cannot be cured) *He knew he had a terminal illness.*
> **a long/short illness** *Ann died following a short illness.*
> **mental illness** *The man had a history of mental illness.*

> **THESAURUS**
>
> **illness** something wrong with your health which makes you feel ill, especially a serious health problem which lasts for a long time: *Because of her illness, she has to be very careful about what she eats.*
> **disease** an illness that is passed from one person to another, or that affects a particular part of the body: *The disease is spread by mosquitoes.* | *heart disease*
> **bug** *informal* an illness that is not serious and that spreads to other people very easily: *I got a stomach bug and had to take a day off work.*
> **condition** a serious health problem which affects part of your body, especially permanently: *He has a heart condition.* | *She has a rare skin condition.*

illogical Ac /ɪ'lɒdʒɪkəl $ ɪ'lɑː-/ *adj* not sensible or reasonable: *illogical behaviour* —**illogically** /-kli/ *adv*

ill-'treat *v* [T] to be cruel to a person or animal —**ill-treatment** *n* [U]

illuminate /ɪ'luːməneɪt, ɪ'ljuː- $ ɪ'luː-/ *v* [T] to make light shine on something, or to fill a place with light —**illumination** /ɪˌluːmə'neɪʃən/ *n* [U]

illuminating /ɪ'luːməneɪtɪŋ, ɪ'ljuː- $ ɪ'luː-/ *adj* making something easier to understand: *a very illuminating book*

illusion /ɪ'luːʒən/ *n* [C] **1** something that seems to be different from the way it really is: *The mirrors create an illusion of space.* **2** a false idea or belief: *be*

under an illusion *Terry is under the illusion that all women love him.* | *We **have no illusions about** the hard work ahead.*

illusory /ɪˈluːsəri/ *adj formal* false, but seeming to be real or true

illustrate Ac /ˈɪləstreɪt/ *v* [T] **1** to make something clear by providing an example: *A chart might help to **illustrate** this **point**.* | [+how/what] *The following examples illustrate how the system works.* | [+that] *The dispute illustrates that the regime is deeply divided.* **2** to CREATE or provide pictures for a book **THESAURUS ▷ DRAW**

illustration Ac /ˌɪləˈstreɪʃən/ *n* **1** [C] a picture in a book **THESAURUS ▷ PICTURE 2** [C,U] an example that helps you to understand something: [+of] *a **vivid illustration** of the problem*

illustrator /ˈɪləstreɪtə $ -ər/ *n* [C] someone who draws pictures for books

illustrious /ɪˈlʌstriəs/ *adj formal* famous and admired: *her **illustrious career***

ill 'will *n* [U] unfriendly feelings towards someone

im- /ɪm, ɪ/ *prefix* not – used before words beginning with 'm' or 'p': *immature* | *impossible*

I'm /aɪm/ the short form of 'I am'

image Ac /ˈɪmɪdʒ/ *n* [C]
1 the way that people consider someone or something to be: *The party is trying to **improve** its **image**.* | *It's important to **project** the right **image**.* | [+of] *the **public image** of the police*
2 a picture that you have in your mind: *She had a clear image of how he would look.*
3 a picture that you see through a camera, on a television or computer screen, in a mirror etc
4 a picture of a person or thing that is drawn, painted etc on a surface → SELF-IMAGE
PHRASES
  be the (very/living/spitting) image of sb to look exactly like someone else: *He's the spitting image of his father.*

Word Choice: image or imagine?
Image is a noun. Do not use it as a verb. Do not say 'Chicago was just how I imaged.' Say *Chicago was just how I imagined.*

imagery Ac /ˈɪmɪdʒəri/ *n* [U] the use of words or pictures to describe ideas or actions in poems, books, films etc

imaginable /ɪˈmædʒənəbəl/ *adj* used to emphasize what you are saying: *It was **the most** wonderful holiday **imaginable**.* | *They covered **every imaginable** subject.*

imaginary /ɪˈmædʒənəri $ -neri/ *adj* not real, but imagined: *imaginary creatures*

imagination /ɪˌmædʒəˈneɪʃən/ *n* [C,U]
1 the ability to form pictures or ideas in your mind: *His **fertile imagination** is shown in his stories for children.*
2 sth is sb's imagination used to say that something that someone thinks is real is not real: *Is there a humming noise, or is it my imagination?*

PHRASES
capture/catch sb's imagination to make someone feel interested or excited: *Rugby really captured the public imagination during the World Cup.*
sb's imagination runs wild (*also* **sb's imagination runs riot** *BrE*) used to say that someone imagines many strange or interesting things: *Let your imagination run riot.*

COLLOCATIONS
verbs
to have (an) imagination *These children have lots of imagination.*
to use your imagination *Use your imagination and try to guess how the story might end.*
to show imagination *All the competition entries showed imagination.*

adjectives
a good imagination *Her stories show a good imagination.*
a vivid/fertile imagination (=an ability to think of a lot of unusual or strange things) *He's not a liar, he just has a very vivid imagination.*

imaginative /ɪˈmædʒənətɪv/ *adj* **1** good at thinking of interesting ideas **2** containing new and interesting ideas —**imaginatively** *adv*

imagine /ɪˈmædʒɪn/ *v* [T]
1 to think of what something would be like if it happened: [+(that)] *Imagine you're lying on a beach.* | [+what/how] *Can you imagine what it's like?*
2 to think that something is true when it is not: *There's no one here – you're **imagining things**.*
3 to think that something is probably true: [+(that)] *I imagine Kathy will be there.*
PHRASES
you can/can't imagine sth *BrE spoken* used to emphasize that something is very good, bad etc: *You can imagine how peaceful it was.*

imbalance /ɪmˈbæləns/ *n* [C,U] when two things are not equal in size, or not the right size in relation to each other

imbecile /ˈɪmbəsiːl $ -səl/ *n* [C] a very stupid person

imbibe /ɪmˈbaɪb/ *v formal* **1** [I,T] to drink something, especially alcohol **2** [T] to be influenced by ideas

imbue /ɪmˈbjuː/ *v formal* to make someone or something have a feeling or quality
PHRASAL VERBS
imbue sb/sth **with** sth *formal*: *The ancient city is imbued with a sense of history.*

imitate /ˈɪmɪteɪt/ *v* [T] to copy the way that someone does something: *Children often imitate their parents' behaviour.* —**imitator** *n* [C]

imitation /ˌɪmɪˈteɪʃən/ *n* **1** [C,U] when you copy the way that someone talks, behaves etc: **by imitation** *Children learn by imitation.* | [+of] *Harry can **do** an excellent **imitation** of Elvis.* **2** [C] something that is a copy of something else **3 imitation leather/fur/pearls etc** something that is made to look like leather, fur etc **THESAURUS ▷ ARTIFICIAL**

immaculate /ɪˈmækjələt/ adj extremely tidy and clean **THESAURUS** TIDY —**immaculately** adv: She was immaculately dressed.

immaterial /ˌɪməˈtɪəriəl◂ $ -ˈtɪr-/ adj formal not important: The details are immaterial.

immature Ac /ˌɪməˈtʃʊə $ -ˈtʃʊr/ adj 1 disapproving behaving like a younger person: He's very immature. 2 not fully formed or developed: immature fish —**immaturity** n [U]

immeasurable /ɪˈmeʒərəbəl/ adj extremely great —**immeasurably** adv

immediacy /ɪˈmiːdiəsi/ n [U] formal when something seems important, urgent, or interesting because it is concerned with things happening now

immediate /ɪˈmiːdiət/ adj
1 happening or done without delay: **immediate action/response/reaction** a situation that requires immediate action
2 [only before noun] needing to be dealt with quickly: Our **immediate concern** was to stop the fire. | the most **immediate problem**
3 [only before noun] very near to a place: people living in the **immediate area**
4 happening just after or just before something else: plans for the **immediate future**
PHRASES
sb's immediate family your parents, children, brothers, and sisters: I contacted everyone in my immediate family.

immediately /ɪˈmiːdiətli/ adv
1 quickly and without any delay: Open this door immediately!
2 immediately before/after/following sth very soon before or after something: We spoke immediately after the meeting.
3 immediately behind/above/below etc sth in the closest position behind, above etc something: They live immediately above us.

THESAURUS

immediately quickly and without any delay: Sam immediately offered to help.
at once immediately, especially because something is urgent: The head teacher wants to see you at once.
right away (also **straightaway** BrE) especially spoken immediately, especially because something is urgent: I'll come right away. | She apologized straightaway.
instantly immediately – used when something happens at almost the same time as something else: He died instantly. | I realised instantly that I had made a mistake.

immense /ɪˈmens/ adj extremely large or great: **immense amount/value/size** They do an immense amount of work. | **immense importance/power** —**immensity** n [U]

immensely /ɪˈmensli/ adv very much: He **enjoyed** it **immensely**. | She was **immensely popular**.

immerse /ɪˈmɜːs $ -ɜːrs/ v [T] **1** to put something completely in a liquid **2 be immersed in sth** to be completely involved in something: He was immersed in his work. | **immerse yourself in sth** (=become completely involved) She has immersed herself in local politics. —**immersion** /ɪˈmɜːʃən, -ʒən $ ɪˈmɜːrʒən/ n [U]

immigrant Ac /ˈɪmɪgrənt/ n [C] someone who comes to live in a country from another country

immigration Ac /ˌɪmɪˈgreɪʃən/ n [U] **1** when people come to a country in order to live there **2** the place where officials check your documents when you enter a country

imminent /ˈɪmɪnənt/ adj going to happen soon → **eminent** —**imminence** n [U] —**imminently** adv

immobile /ɪˈməʊbaɪl $ ɪˈmoʊbəl/ adj not moving, or not able to move: Mark stood immobile. —**immobility** /ˌɪməˈbɪləti/ n [U]

immobilize (also **-ise** BrE) /ɪˈməʊbəlaɪz $ ɪˈmoʊ-/ v [T] to stop someone or something from moving

immoral /ɪˈmɒrəl $ ɪˈmɔː-/ adj morally wrong: It's immoral to treat people like that. —**immorality** /ˌɪməˈræləti/ n [U]

immortal /ɪˈmɔːtl $ -ɔːr-/ adj **1** living or continuing for ever: Nobody is immortal. **2** the **immortal words/line** used to refer to famous or amusing words said or sung by someone: In the immortal words of James Brown, 'I feel good!' —**immortality** /ˌɪmɔːˈtæləti $ -ɔːr-/ n [U]

immortalize (also **-ise** BrE) /ɪˈmɔːtəlaɪz $ -ɔːr-/ v [T] to make someone or something famous for a long time by writing about them, painting them etc

immovable /ɪˈmuːvəbəl/ adj impossible to move or change

immune /ɪˈmjuːn/ adj [not before noun] **1** not affected or not able to be affected by something unpleasant that affects other people: **[+to]** Their business seems to be immune to economic pressures. | **[+from]** He is immune from prosecution. **2** someone who is immune to a disease cannot get it

im'mune ˌsystem n [C] the system in your body that protects it against illness

immunity /ɪˈmjuːnəti/ n [U] **1** when people are protected from particular laws or from unpleasant things: **[+from]** They were **granted immunity** from prosecution. **2** when someone cannot get a disease: **[+to]** immunity to infection

immunize (also **-ise** BrE) /ˈɪmjənaɪz/ v [T] to give someone a substance that will prevent them from getting a disease **SYN** vaccinate, inoculate: Get your baby immunized against measles. —**immunization** /ˌɪmjənaɪˈzeɪʃən $ -nə-/ n [C,U]

immutable /ɪˈmjuːtəbəl/ adj formal never changing, or impossible to change

imp /ɪmp/ n [C] a small creature in stories who has magic powers and behaves badly

impact¹ Ac /ˈɪmpækt/ n **1** [C,U] the effect or influence that something or someone has: **[+of]** the environmental impact of car use | **[+on/upon]** He had a big **impact** on my life. **THESAURUS** EFFECT **2** [singular, U] the force of one object hitting another, or the moment when they touch: The impact of the crash spun the car round. | **on impact** The plane's wing was damaged on impact.

impact

impact² Ac /ɪmˈpækt/ v [I,T] *especially AmE* to have an effect on someone or something: **[+on/ upon]** *How will the changes impact on us?*

impair /ɪmˈpeə $ -ˈper/ v [T] *formal* to make something less good

impaired /ɪmˈpeəd $ -ˈperd/ adj **1** damaged or made weaker: *impaired vision* **2** visually/hearing impaired used to describe people who cannot see or hear properly: *visually impaired patients* —**impairment** n [U]

impale /ɪmˈpeɪl/ v [T] to put a long pointed object through something

impart /ɪmˈpɑːt $ -ɑːrt/ v [T] *formal* **1** to give information, knowledge etc to someone **2** to give a particular quality to something: *Garlic imparts a delicious flavour to the sauce.*

impartial /ɪmˈpɑːʃəl $ -ɑːr-/ adj able to be fair, because of not being involved or having a particular opinion: *We offer **impartial advice**.* —**impartially** adv —**impartiality** /ˌɪmpɑːʃiˈæləti $ -ɑːr-/ n [U]

impassable /ɪmˈpɑːsəbəl $ ɪmˈpæ-/ adj impossible to travel along or through

impasse /æmˈpɑːs $ ˈɪmpæs/ n [singular] when it is impossible to reach an agreement: *We were at an impasse.*

impassioned /ɪmˈpæʃənd/ adj full of emotion: *an impassioned plea*

impassive /ɪmˈpæsɪv/ adj not showing any emotion: *his impassive face* —**impassively** adv

impatient /ɪmˈpeɪʃənt/ adj **1** annoyed because of delays or mistakes that make you wait: *The passengers were **becoming impatient**.* | **[+with]** *He gets impatient with the kids.* **2** wanting to do something as soon as possible: **impatient to do sth** *Gary was impatient to leave.* —**impatience** n [U] —**impatiently** adv

impeach /ɪmˈpiːtʃ/ v [T] *law* if a government official is impeached, he or she is charged with a serious crime —**impeachment** n [U]

impeccable /ɪmˈpekəbəl/ adj without any faults: *impeccable manners* —**impeccably** adv

impede /ɪmˈpiːd/ v [T] *formal* to make it difficult for something to happen: *problems that **impede** students' progress*

impediment /ɪmˈpedəmənt/ n [C] **1** a situation or event that makes it difficult or impossible for something to happen: **[+to]** *Debt has been an impediment to development.* **2** a physical problem that makes speaking, hearing, or moving difficult: *a **speech impediment***

impel /ɪmˈpel/ v [T] (**impelled, impelling**) *formal* to make you feel that you must do something

impending /ɪmˈpendɪŋ/ adj [only before noun] going to happen soon: **impending danger/death/ disaster etc**

impenetrable /ɪmˈpenətrəbəl/ adj **1** impossible to get through or see through: *impenetrable fog* **2** very difficult to understand: *impenetrable jargon*

imperative¹ /ɪmˈperətɪv/ adj **1** *formal* extremely important: *It is **imperative that** you attend.* | *It was*

imperative to be prepared. **2** in grammar, an imperative verb expresses an order

imperative² n [C] **1** something that must be done: *Reducing pollution has become an imperative.* **2** the form of a verb that expresses an order. In 'Do it now', the verb 'do' is an imperative.

imperceptible /ˌɪmpəˈseptəbəl $ -pər-/ adj impossible to notice: *an **almost imperceptible** nod* —**imperceptibly** adv

imperfect¹ /ɪmˈpɜːfɪkt $ -ɜːr-/ adj not perfect —**imperfection** /ˌɪmpəˈfekʃən $ -pər-/ n [C,U]

imperfect² n the imperfect the form of a verb that shows an incomplete action in the past. In 'We were walking home', the verb is in the imperfect.

imperial /ɪmˈpɪəriəl $ -ˈpɪr-/ adj [only before noun] **1** relating to an EMPIRE or to its ruler **2** related to the system of weights and measurements based on INCHES, YARDS, MILES etc

imperialism /ɪmˈpɪəriəlɪzəm $ -ˈpɪr-/ n [U] when one country rules a number of other countries, or has great influence over them —**imperialist** n [C], adj

impersonal /ɪmˈpɜːsənəl $ -ɜːr-/ adj not showing any sympathy, friendliness etc: *an impersonal letter* —**impersonally** adv

impersonate /ɪmˈpɜːsəneɪt $ -ɜːr-/ v [T] to copy the way someone talks, behaves etc in order to pretend that you are that person, or in order to make people laugh **THESAURUS▶ PRETEND** —**impersonator** n [C] —**impersonation** /ɪmˌpɜːsəˈneɪʃən $ -ɜːr-/ n [C,U]

impertinent /ɪmˈpɜːtɪnənt $ -ɜːr-/ adj not respectful **SYN** rude —**impertinently** adv —**impertinence** n [U]

impervious /ɪmˈpɜːviəs $ -ɜːr-/ adj *formal* **1** not affected by something: **[+to]** *He seemed impervious to criticism.* **2** not allowing liquid to pass through: *impervious rock*

impetuous /ɪmˈpetʃuəs/ adj doing or saying things quickly, without thinking: *She was very impetuous in her youth.* —**impetuously** adv

impetus /ˈɪmpɪtəs/ n [U] **1** an influence that makes something happen, or happen more quickly: **[+for]** *The report **provided** the impetus for reform.* **2** *technical* a force that makes an object start moving, or keeps it moving

impinge /ɪmˈpɪndʒ/ v

PHRASAL VERBS

impinge on/upon sb/sth *formal* to have an effect, usually a bad effect, on someone or something

impish /ˈɪmpɪʃ/ adj not showing enough respect or not being serious enough, but in a way that people find funny: *an impish grin*

implacable /ɪmˈplækəbəl/ adj very determined to continue opposing something —**implacably** adv

implant¹ /ɪmˈplɑːnt $ ɪmˈplænt/ v [T] **1** to fix an idea in someone's mind so that they cannot forget it **2** to put something into someone's body by doing a medical operation —**implantation** /ˌɪmplɑːnˈteɪʃən $ -plæn-/ n [U]

implant² /ˈɪmplɑːnt $ -plænt/ n [C] something

artificial that has been put into someone's body in a medical operation: *breast implants*

implausible /ɪmˈplɔːzəbəl $ -ˈplɑː-/ *adj* not likely to be true: *an implausible excuse* —**implausibly** *adv*

implement¹ Ac /ˈɪmpləmənt/ *v* [T] if you implement a plan or process, you begin to make it happen: *Airlines were required to implement new safety recommendations.* —**implementation** /ˌɪmpləmenˈteɪʃən/ *n* [U]

implement² Ac /ˈɪmpləmənt/ *n* [C] a tool: *farming implements*

implicate Ac /ˈɪmplɪkeɪt/ *v* [T] to suggest or show that someone or something is involved in something bad or illegal: **implicate sb in sth** *Two people have been implicated in the robbery.*

implication Ac /ˌɪmplɪˈkeɪʃən/ *n* **1** [C] something that may happen as a result of a plan, action etc: **[+of]** *the implications of the decision* | **[+for]** *This ruling will **have implications** for many people.* | **political/financial/social implications** **2** [C,U] something that you suggest is true, without saying it directly: **[+that]** *I resent your implication that I was lying.* | **by implication** *She blamed the hospital, and – by implication – the doctor who examined her son.*

implicit Ac /ɪmˈplɪsɪt/ *adj* **1** not stated directly → **explicit**: **implicit threat/criticism/assumption** *There was implicit criticism in what she said.* **2** complete and containing no doubts: *He had **implicit faith** in me.* —**implicitly** *adv*

implode /ɪmˈpləʊd $ -ˈploʊd/ *v* [I] *formal* to explode inwards —**implosion** /ɪmˈpləʊʒən $ -ˈploʊ-/ *n* [C,U]

implore /ɪmˈplɔː $ -ɔːr/ *v* [T] *formal* to ask someone in a very emotional way to do something SYN **beg**: **implore sb to do sth** *Jan implored him to stay.*

imply Ac /ɪmˈplaɪ/ *v* [T] (**implied, implying, implies**) to suggest that something is true without saying or showing it directly → **infer**: **[+(that)]** *He implied that the money had been stolen.* | *High profits do **not necessarily imply** efficiency.*

impolite /ˌɪmpəˈlaɪt◂/ *adj formal* not polite THESAURUS **RUDE**

import¹ /ˈɪmpɔːt $ -ɔːrt/ *n* [C,U] something that is brought into a country in order to be sold, or the process of doing this OPP **export**: *Car imports have risen.* | *the import of luxury goods* | **import restrictions/controls etc**

import² /ɪmˈpɔːt $ -ɔːrt/ *v* [T]
1 to bring something into a country in order to sell it OPP **export**: **import sth from sth** *Oil was imported from the Middle East.*
2 to move information to your computer from another computer —**importer** *n* [C] —**importation** /ˌɪmpɔːˈteɪʃən $ -ɔːr-/ *n* [U]

importance /ɪmˈpɔːtəns $ -ɔːr-/ *n* [U] the quality of being important: **[+of]** *She stresses the **importance** of exercise.* | *They **attach** great **importance** to family life.* | **of great/paramount/particular importance** *Safety is of paramount importance.* | **of no/little importance** *formal* (=not important, or not very*

important) *The matter was of no importance to her.*
THESAURUS **UNIMPORTANT**

important /ɪmˈpɔːtənt $ -ɔːr-/ *adj*
1 something that is important has a big effect on what happens: *It is important to write clearly.* | *It's important that he understands.* | **important part/role/factor** *You play a very important role.* | *a very important meeting*
2 important people have a lot of power or influence: *an important customer* | *It makes them **feel important.***
3 **be important to sb** if someone or something is important to you, you care a lot about them: *It is important to tell your children that you are proud of them.* → **SELF-IMPORTANT**

THESAURUS

important something that is important has a big effect on what happens: *an important announcement* | *It's important to wear gloves.*
big important or serious – used especially about a problem, decision, or event: *Getting married is a big decision.* | *Knife crime is a big problem.*
major a major problem, change, cause, reason etc is one of the most important or serious ones: *Alcohol is a major cause of accidents.* | *There have been several major changes in my life.*
key extremely important – used when emphasizing that someone or something is much more important than other things: *He played a key role in the team's success.* | *the key objective*
main/chief/principal more important than all the others: *What is your main aim?* | *This was the principal reason for their decision.*
essential very important, especially for the success, health, or safety of someone or something: *Fresh vegetables are an essential part of a healthy diet.* | *It is essential to use the right equipment.*
vital/crucial extremely important and necessary in order to avoid problems or failure: *His evidence was vital to the case.* | *Timing is crucial.*
historic a historic event, moment etc brings important changes and is remembered as part of history: *the historic moment when man first walked on the Moon*

---

importantly /ɪmˈpɔːtəntli $ -ɔːr-/ *adv* **more/most importantly** used before mentioning something more important or the most important thing: *Ask them questions and, more importantly, listen to their answers.*

impose Ac /ɪmˈpəʊz $ -ˈpoʊz/ *v* **1** [T] to force people to accept something: **impose sth on sb** *The government imposed a ban on all imports.* **2** [I] *formal* to expect or ask someone to do something for you when this is not convenient for them: **[+on/upon]** *I didn't want to impose on Martin.*

imposing /ɪmˈpəʊzɪŋ $ -ˈpoʊ-/ *adj* large and impressive: *an imposing building*

imposition Ac /ˌɪmpəˈzɪʃən/ *n* **1** [U] the introduction of a rule, punishment, tax etc: **[+of]** *the imposition of VAT* **2** [C] *formal* something that someone expects you to do for them, which is not convenient for you

impossible /ɪmˈpɒsəbəl $ ɪmˈpɑː-/ *adj*
1 something that is impossible cannot happen or be done: *It is impossible to predict what will happen.* | *The noise* **made** *sleep* **impossible.** | **almost/virtually/practically etc impossible** *It would be virtually impossible for us to win.*
2 an impossible situation is very difficult to deal with: *He's put me in an* **impossible position.**
3 someone who is impossible is unreasonable and very annoying: *You're impossible!*
4 the impossible something that cannot be done: *You can't* **do the impossible.** | *You're* **asking the impossible** *of me.* —**impossibility** /ɪmˌpɒsəˈbɪləti $ -ˌpɑː-/ *n* [C,U]

THESAURUS

impossible something that is impossible cannot happen or be done: *It's impossible to hear what you're saying.* | *an impossible task*
out of the question if something is out of the question, it is completely impossible or it cannot be allowed: *It was out of the question for them to get married.*
there's no way *informal* used when saying that you feel sure something is impossible: *There's no way you can get lost.*

---

impossibly /ɪmˈpɒsəbli $ -ˈpɑː-/ *adv* extremely: *an impossibly difficult task*

impostor (*also* **imposter** *AmE*) /ɪmˈpɒstə $ -ˈpɑːstər/ *n* [C] someone who pretends to be someone else in order to trick people

impotent /ˈɪmpətənt/ *adj* **1** without enough power, strength, or control to influence a situation: *an impotent city council* **2** a man who is impotent cannot have sex because he cannot get an ERECTION —**impotence** *n* [U]

impound /ɪmˈpaʊnd/ *v* [T] *law* if the police or the courts impound something, they take it and keep it until they decide that its owner can have it back: *His car was impounded for four days.*

impoverished /ɪmˈpɒvərɪʃt $ -ˈpɑː-/ *adj* very poor: *impoverished villages*

impractical /ɪmˈpræktɪkəl/ *adj* impractical plans or ideas are unlikely to succeed: *The designs were totally impractical.*

imprecise Ac /ˌɪmprɪˈsaɪs◄/ *adj* not exact: *She could only give a vague and imprecise description of her attacker.*

impregnable /ɪmˈpregnəbəl/ *adj* a place that is impregnable is so strong and well-protected that it cannot be entered by force: *an impregnable castle*

impregnate /ˈɪmpregneɪt $ ɪmˈpreg-/ *v* [T] **1** to make a substance spread completely through something: *The paper has been impregnated with perfume.* **2** *technical* to make a woman or female animal PREGNANT

impress /ɪmˈpres/ *v*
1 [I,T] to make someone feel admiration and respect for you: *He was trying to impress me.* | **be impressed with/by sth** *I was impressed by her singing.*

2 impress sth on sb to make someone realize that something is very important: *Dad always impressed on us the need to work hard.*

impression /ɪmˈpreʃən/ *n* [C]
1 OPINION/FEELING the opinion or feeling you have about someone or something because of the way they seem: *I* **had the impression that** *she wasn't very happy.* | *What* **impression** *did you* **get** *of the new headmaster?* | *He* **gave** *the* **impression** *of being very shy.* | *Ruth was keen to* **make a good impression** *on us all.* | **be under the impression (that)** (=to believe that something is true when it is not) *Sorry, I was under the impression you were the manager.*
THESAURUS ▶ IDEA
2 IMITATION when someone copies the way a famous person talks or behaves, in order to make people laugh: *She* **does** *a great* **impression of** *Madonna.*
3 MARK the mark left by pressing something into a soft surface

impressionable /ɪmˈpreʃənəbəl/ *adj* easy to influence: *an impressionable young child*

impressionistic /ɪmˌpreʃəˈnɪstɪk◄/ *adj* based on a general feeling of what something is like: *an impressionistic account of the war*

impressive /ɪmˈpresɪv/ *adj* something that is impressive makes you admire it because it is very good, big, important etc: *The view was impressive.* | *a very impressive achievement* —**impressively** *adv*: *an impressively tall oak*

imprint¹ /ˈɪmprɪnt/ *n* [C] the mark left by an object that has been pressed onto something: [+of] *the imprint of his hand on the clay*

imprint² /ɪmˈprɪnt/ *v* **1 be imprinted on your mind/memory/brain** if something is imprinted on your mind etc, you can never forget it: *That morning was imprinted on her mind forever.* | *She stared wide-eyed at his face, as if imprinting it on her brain.* **2** [T] to print or press a mark on something

imprison /ɪmˈprɪzən/ *v* [T] to put someone in prison or keep them in a place they cannot escape from: *He was imprisoned for 18 months.* —**imprisonment** *n* [U]

improbable /ɪmˈprɒbəbəl $ -ˈprɑː-/ *adj* not likely to happen or be true: *It is* **highly improbable** *that humans ever lived here.*

impromptu /ɪmˈprɒmptju: $ ɪmˈprɑːmptu:/ *adj* done without preparation or planning: *He stood up and made an impromptu speech.*

improper /ɪmˈprɒpə $ -ˈprɑːpər/ *adj* **1** dishonest, illegal, or morally wrong: *Three police officers have been accused of* **improper conduct.** **2** not sensible, right, or fair in a particular situation: *It would be* **improper** *to comment on the case until after the investigation.* **3** wrong or not correct: *improper labelling* —**improperly** *adv*: *improperly dressed*

impropriety /ˌɪmprəˈpraɪəti/ *n* [C,U] (*plural* **improprieties**) *formal* something that is unacceptable according to moral, social, or professional standards

improve /ɪmˈpruːv/ *v* [I,T] to become better, or to make something better: *Her German is improving.* |

The school needs to improve its exam results. | **greatly/significantly/dramatically improve** *The situation improved dramatically.* —**improved** *adj: new improved materials*

PHRASAL VERBS

improve on/upon sth to do something better than before: *I improved on my 2:17:22 time from last year.*

improvement /ɪmˈpruːvmənt/ *n* [C,U] when something becomes better than it was: **[+in]** *There was a steady improvement in efficiency.* | **dramatic/significant improvement** *There has been a significant improvement in our profits.* | *Ben's schoolwork is showing **signs of improvement**.* | *The new version **is an improvement on** (=is better than) the old model.* | *His playing has made progress, but **there's still room for improvement** (=it could be even better).*

improvise /ˈɪmprəvaɪz/ *v* [I,T] to make or do something without any preparation, using things that are available: *I forgot to bring my notes, so I had to improvise.* —**improvisation** /ˌɪmprəvaɪˈzeɪʃən $ ɪmˌprɑːvə-/ *n* [C,U]

impudent /ˈɪmpjədənt/ *adj formal* behaving in a rude way and not showing respect —**impudence** *n* [U] —**impudently** *adv*

impulse /ˈɪmpʌls/ *n* **1** [C,U] a sudden desire to do something before thinking about whether it is sensible: **impulse to do sth** *I resisted the impulse to hit him.* | **on impulse** (=because of an impulse) *Don't buy things on impulse.* **2** [C] *technical* a short electrical signal that travels in one direction along a nerve or wire

impulsive /ɪmˈpʌlsɪv/ *adj* doing things without thinking about the possible dangers or problems: *an impulsive young man* —**impulsively** *adv*

impunity /ɪmˈpjuːnəti/ *n* **with impunity** without risk of punishment: *Human rights were violated with impunity.*

impure /ɪmˈpjʊə $ -ˈpjʊr/ *adj* not pure or clean: *impure gold*

impurity /ɪmˈpjʊərəti $ -ˈpjʊr-/ *n* [C] (*plural* **impurities**) a part of an almost pure substance that is of a lower quality: *There were some impurities in the metal.*

in¹ /ɪn/ *prep*

1 used to say the place or container where someone or something is: *The cheese is in the fridge.* | *I live in Spain.* | *a hole in the ground*

2 into a container or place: *Lou looked in her bag.*

3 used to say how something is done: *She performed in a confident manner.* | *I write to Luca in Italian.* | *He spoke in a low voice.*

4 used with the names of months, years, seasons etc to say when something happens: *She retired in April.* | *Insects are most active in summer.*

5 during a period of time: *I earned £75 in a day.*

6 at the end of a period of time: *We'll be back in a week.* **THESAURUS** AFTER

7 doing a particular kind of job: *He's in marketing.*

8 wearing something: *a man in a suit* | *Lucy was dressed in black.*

9 used to describe the condition of something or someone: *The company was in trouble.* | *You may be in danger.*

10 arranged in a particular way: *We stood in a line.* | *Entries are in alphabetical order.*

11 used to say how common or how likely something is: *One in ten homes now has cable TV.*

in² *adv*

1 into or inside a container or place **OPP** out: *He walked to his car and got in.*

2 inside or into a building or room, especially the one where you live or work: *You're never in when I call.* | *Come in!*

3 if a train, plane, boat etc is in, it has arrived at the station, airport etc: *Our train's not in yet.*

4 received by a person or organization to be dealt with by them: *Applications must be in by June 1.*

PHRASES

be in for sth if someone is in for something unpleasant, it is going to happen to them: *Dana is in for a shock.*

be/get in on sth to be or become involved in something that is happening: *They were both in on the decision.*

in³ *adj informal* fashionable: *Long hair is in again.* | *Jeans are **the in thing** this year.* **THESAURUS** FASHIONABLE

in- /ɪn/ *prefix* not: *inactive* | *inattention* (=lack of attention)

inability /ˌɪnəˈbɪləti/ *n* [singular, U] when someone is unable to do something: *his inability to read*

inaccessible Ac /ˌɪnəkˈsesəbəl◂/ *adj* impossible to reach: *In winter, the village is often inaccessible.*

inaccuracy Ac /ɪnˈækjərəsi/ *n* (*plural* **inaccuracies**) **1** [C] a statement that is not completely correct: *The report contains several inaccuracies.* **2** [U] a lack of correctness: *the inaccuracy of the data*

inaccurate Ac /ɪnˈækjərət/ *adj* not correct: *The figures were inaccurate.* **THESAURUS** WRONG —**inaccurately** *adv*

inaction /ɪnˈækʃən/ *n* [U] the fact that someone is not doing anything: *The government was criticized for inaction.*

inactive /ɪnˈæktɪv/ *adj* not doing anything, not working, or not moving **OPP** active

inactivity /ˌɪnækˈtɪvəti/ *n* [U] when you are not doing anything, not working, or not moving **OPP** activity: *I was getting bored with all this inactivity.*

inadequacy Ac /ɪnˈædəkwəsi/ *n* (*plural* **inadequacies**) **1** [U] a feeling that you are not as good, clever, skilled etc as other people: *He suffers from **feelings of inadequacy**.* **2** [U] when something is not good enough in quality, ability, size etc: **[+of]** *the inadequacy of public transport* **3** [C usually plural] a fault or weakness: *I am quite aware of my own inadequacies.*

inadequate Ac /ɪnˈædəkwət/ *adj* **1** not good enough, big enough, skilled enough etc: *The school has inadequate computer facilities.* **2** someone who feels inadequate thinks other people are better, more skilful, more intelligent etc than they are —**inadequately** *adv*

inadmissible /ˌɪnəd'mɪsəbəl◂/ adj law inadmissible information cannot be used in a court of law: *The judge ruled that his evidence was inadmissible.*

inadvertently /ˌɪnəd'vɜːtəntli $ -ɜːr-/ adv without realizing what you are doing: *I inadvertently left without paying.* —**inadvertent** adj

inadvisable /ˌɪnəd'vaɪzəbəl◂/ adj not sensible: *Strong winds made driving inadvisable.*

inalienable /ɪn'eɪliənəbəl/ adj formal an inalienable right cannot be taken away from you

inane /ɪ'neɪn/ adj very stupid or without much meaning: *the children's inane chatter*

inanimate /ɪn'ænəmət/ adj not living: *an **inanimate** object*

inappropriate Ac /ˌɪnə'prəʊpri-ət $ -'proʊ-/ adj not suitable: *His behaviour was totally inappropriate.* —**inappropriately** adv

inarticulate /ˌɪnɑː'tɪkjələt◂ $ -ɑːr-/ adj not able to express yourself well when you speak

inasmuch as /ˌɪnəz'mʌtʃ əz/ linking word, formal used to explain why what you are saying is true: *Ann is guilty, inasmuch as she knew what the others were planning.*

inaudible /ɪn'ɔːdəbəl $ -'ɒː-/ adj too quiet to be heard: *Her reply was inaudible.*

inaugurate /ɪ'nɔːgjəreɪt $ -'nɒː-/ v [T] **1** to hold an official ceremony when someone starts doing an important job in government: *The President was inaugurated March 4.* **2** to open a building or start an organization, event etc for the first time: *The Turner Prize was inaugurated in 1984.* —**inaugural** adj: *the club's inaugural meeting* —**inauguration** /ɪˌnɔːgjə'reɪʃən $ ɪˌnɒː-/ n [C,U]

inauspicious /ˌɪnɔː'spɪʃəs◂ $ ˌɪnɒː-/ adj formal seeming to show that something will not be successful

inborn /ˌɪn'bɔːn◂ $ -ɔːrn◂/ adj an inborn quality is one that you have had since birth: *inborn instincts*

inbox /'ɪnbɒks $ -bɑːks/ n [C] the place in a computer email program where new messages arrive

Inc. /ɪŋk/ the written abbreviation of **Incorporated**: *General Motors Inc.*

incalculable /ɪn'kælkjələbəl/ adj too great to be calculated: *The scandal has done **incalculable damage** to her reputation.*

incandescent /ˌɪnkæn'desənt◂ $ -kən-/ adj formal **1** giving a bright light when heated **2** extremely angry —**incandescence** n [U]

incantation /ˌɪnkæn'teɪʃən/ n [C] a set of special words that are used in magic

incapable Ac /ɪn'keɪpəbəl/ adj not able to do something: [+of] *He was incapable of controlling his temper.*

incapacitate Ac /ˌɪnkə'pæsɪteɪt/ v [T] to make you too ill or weak to live normally: *He was incapacitated by illness in 1993.*

incapacity /ˌɪnkə'pæsəti/ n [U] formal lack of ability or strength to do something, especially because you are ill

incarcerate /ɪn'kɑːsəreɪt $ -ɑːr-/ v [T] formal to put someone in prison —**incarceration** /ɪnˌkɑːsə'reɪʃən $ -ˌkɑːr-/ n [U]

incarnate /ɪn'kɑːnət $ -ɑːr-/ adj **1 be beauty/evil/ greed etc incarnate** to be extremely beautiful, evil etc: *She is patience incarnate.* **2** having taken human form: **God/the Devil etc incarnate** *the belief that Jesus was God incarnate*

incarnation /ˌɪnkɑː'neɪʃən $ -ɑːr-/ n **1** [C] one of the different lives that, according to some religions, people have: *He felt he had met her before, **in a previous incarnation**.* **2 be the incarnation of goodness/evil etc** having a lot of goodness etc: *He is the incarnation of wisdom.*

incendiary /ɪn'sendiəri $ -dieri/ adj **incendiary bomb/device etc** a bomb etc designed to cause a fire

incense /'ɪnsens/ n [U] a substance that has a pleasant smell when you burn it

incensed /ɪn'senst/ adj very angry

incentive Ac /ɪn'sentɪv/ n [C,U] something that encourages you to work harder or to start a new activity: **incentive (for sb) to do sth** *an incentive for children to work hard*

inception /ɪn'sepʃən/ n [singular] formal the start of an organization: *since the club's inception in 1905*

incessant /ɪn'sesənt/ adj never stopping: *her incessant chatter* —**incessantly** adv

incest /'ɪnsest/ n [U] illegal sex between people who are closely related, for example a brother and sister —**incestuous** /ɪn'sestʃuəs/ adj

inch[1] /ɪntʃ/ n [C] a unit for measuring length, equal to 2.54 centimetres: *The fish was 48 inches long.* | **a one-/two- etc inch sth** *a six-inch nail*

PHRASES

not give/budge an inch to completely refuse to change your decision or opinion: *Neither side is prepared to give an inch.*

inch[2] v [I,T] to move very slowly and carefully: *I **inched** my way along the wall.*

incidence Ac /'ɪnsɪdəns/ n [singular] formal how often something happens: [+of] *The area has a high incidence of cancer.*

incident Ac /'ɪnsɪdənt/ n [C] an event, especially one that is unusual, important, or violent: *One man was arrested following the incident.*

incidental /ˌɪnsɪ'dentl◂/ adj happening or existing in connection with something else that is more important: [+to] *Where the story is set is incidental to the plot.*

incidentally Ac /ˌɪnsə'dentli/ adv used to add more information to what you have just said, or to introduce a new subject that you have just thought of: *Incidentally, how old is Mary?*

incinerate /ɪn'sɪnəreɪt/ v [T] to burn something in order to destroy it

incinerator /ɪn'sɪnəreɪtə $ -ər/ n [C] a machine that burns things in order to destroy them

incipient /ɪn'sɪpiənt/ adj [only before noun] formal just starting to happen or exist: *a sign of incipient illness*

incision /ɪnˈsɪʒən/ n [C] a neat cut made into something, especially during a medical operation

incisive /ɪnˈsaɪsɪv/ adj showing intelligence and a clear understanding of something: *He made some very incisive remarks.*

incite /ɪnˈsaɪt/ v [T] to deliberately encourage people to be violent, hate other people, or commit a crime: *He was accused of **inciting racial hatred**.* —**incitement** n [C,U]

inclement /ɪnˈklemənt/ adj formal inclement weather is unpleasantly cold and wet

inclination Ac /ˌɪnkləˈneɪʃən/ n [C,U] a feeling that makes you want to do something: **inclination to do sth** *He showed no **inclination** to leave.*

incline¹ Ac /ɪnˈklaɪn/ v **1** [I] formal to think that a particular belief or opinion is probably right: **[+to]** *I incline to the view that the child was telling the truth.* **2** [I,T] to slope at a particular angle, or to make something do this: *The slope inclines at an angle of 36°.* **3 incline sb to do sth** formal to influence someone or make them do something: *The accident inclined him to reconsider his career.* **4 incline your head** formal to bend your neck so that your head is lowered

incline² Ac /ˈɪnklaɪn/ n [C] a slope: *a steep incline*

inclined /ɪnˈklaɪnd/ adj **1 be inclined to agree/ think/believe etc** to have a particular opinion, but not very strongly: *I'm inclined to think Ed is right.* **2 be inclined to do sth/be inclined to sth** to be likely to do something: *Children are inclined to get lost.* **3 be/feel inclined (to do sth)** to want to do something, but without having a strong desire: *I didn't feel inclined to explain my behaviour to anyone.*

include /ɪnˈkluːd/ v [T]
1 if one thing includes another, the second thing is part of the first: *The price includes lunch.* | **be included in sth** *Service is included in the bill.*
2 to allow someone to be part of a group or activity OPP **exclude**: *The other children refused to include her in their games.*

including /ɪnˈkluːdɪŋ/ prep used to introduce someone or something that is part of the thing that you have just mentioned OPP **excluding**: *He trained many jockeys, including John Watts.* | *The price is £3, including postage.* THESAURUS **EXCEPT**

inclusion /ɪnˈkluːʒən/ n [C,U] when you include someone or something in a larger group or set: **[+in]** *I am surprised at his inclusion in the team.* | *Are there any new inclusions on the list?*

inclusive /ɪnˈkluːsɪv/ adj **1** an inclusive price or cost includes everything: **[+of]** *The cost is £200, inclusive of meals.* **2 Monday to Friday inclusive/ 15-20 inclusive etc** including Monday and Friday and all the days between them, 15 and 20 and all the numbers between them etc: *I will be away from 1-5 May inclusive.*

incognito /ˌɪnkɒgˈniːtəʊ $ ˌɪnkɑːgˈniːtoʊ/ adv hiding who you really are: *The prince travelled incognito.*

incoherent Ac /ˌɪnkəʊˈhɪərənt◄ $ -koʊˈhɪr-/ adj confused and not expressing ideas clearly: *a rambling incoherent speech* —**incoherently** adv

income /ˈɪŋkʌm, ˈɪn-/ n [C,U] the money that you earn or receive regularly, for example from your work: *Their **annual income** is less than $24,000.* | **on a good/bad/high etc income** (=earning a particular amount) *families that are on a low income* | **high-income/low-income** *high-income households* | **[+from]** *He gets a small income from savings.* | *an elderly couple living on a **fixed income** (=an income that does not change or grow)* THESAURUS **SALARY** → DISPOSABLE INCOME

ˈincome tax n [U] tax that you pay on the money that you earn

incoming /ˈɪnkʌmɪŋ/ adj [only before noun] **1** arriving at or coming to a place → **outgoing**: *incoming flights* | *incoming phone calls* **2** an incoming president, government etc has just been elected or chosen → **outgoing**

incommunicado /ˌɪnkəmjuːnɪˈkɑːdəʊ $ -doʊ/ adj, adv if you are held incommunicado, you are kept in a place where other people cannot speak to you

incomparable /ɪnˈkɒmpərəbəl $ -ˈkɑːm-/ adj so impressive, beautiful etc that nothing or no one is better: *an incomparable view*

incompatible Ac /ˌɪnkəmˈpætəbəl◄/ adj too different to be used together, or work or live together happily: *two incompatible computer systems* | *Roy and I have always been incompatible.* | **[+with]** *Going to war is incompatible with his religious beliefs.* —**incompatibility** /ˌɪnkəmpætəˈbɪləti/ n [U]

incompetence /ɪnˈkɒmpətəns $ -ˈkɑːm-/ n [U] when someone does not do their job properly

incompetent /ɪnˈkɒmpɪtənt $ -ˈkɑːm-/ adj not doing your job properly: *an incompetent teacher* —**incompetently** adv

incomplete /ˌɪnkəmˈpliːt◄/ adj not having all its parts, or not finished: *an incomplete sentence* | *The report is still incomplete.* —**incompletely** adv

incomprehensible /ɪnˌkɒmprɪˈhensəbəl $ -ˌkɑːm-/ adj impossible to understand: *His speech was incomprehensible.*

incomprehension /ɪnˌkɒmprɪˈhenʃən $ -ˌkɑːm-/ n [U] when you do not understand something: *He gave me a look of complete incomprehension.*

inconceivable Ac /ˌɪnkənˈsiːvəbəl/ adj too strange to seem possible: **It is inconceivable that** *her husband didn't know what she was doing.*

inconclusive Ac /ˌɪnkənˈkluːsɪv◄/ adj not leading to a clear decision or result: *The evidence was inconclusive.*

incongruous /ɪnˈkɒŋɡruəs $ -ˈkɑːŋ-/ adj formal strange, unexpected, or unsuitable in a particular situation: *He looked incongruous in his new suit.*

inconsequential /ɪnˌkɒnsəˈkwenʃəl◄ $ -ˌkɑːn-/ adj formal not important: *the children's inconsequential chatter*

inconsiderate /ˌɪnkənˈsɪdərət◄/ adj not caring about other people's needs or feelings OPP **considerate**: *It was inconsiderate of you not to call.* THESAURUS **UNKIND**

inconsistency Ac /ˌɪnkənˈsɪstənsi/ n (plural **inconsistencies**) 1 [U] when someone keeps changing their behaviour, reactions etc so that other people become confused OPP **consistency** 2 [C,U] a situation in which two statements are different and cannot both be true: *There are some inconsistencies in her statement.*

inconsistent Ac /ˌɪnkənˈsɪstənt◂/ adj 1 two statements that are inconsistent cannot both be true: [+with] *His story was inconsistent with the evidence.* 2 not right according to a set of principles or standards: [+with] *This approach is inconsistent with Section 38 of the Act.* 3 inconsistent behaviour, work etc changes too often from good to bad: *The team's performance has been very inconsistent this season.*

inconsolable /ˌɪnkənˈsəʊləbəl◂ $ -ˈsoʊ-/ adj so sad that you cannot be comforted

inconspicuous /ˌɪnkənˈspɪkjuəs◂/ adj not easily noticed OPP **conspicuous**: *She tried to look inconspicuous.*

incontinent /ɪnˈkɒntɪnənt $ -ˈkɑːn-/ adj unable to control the passing of liquid or solid waste from your body —**incontinence** n [U]

incontrovertible /ˌɪnkɒntrəˈvɜːtəbəl $ ɪnˌkɑːntrəˈvɜːr-/ adj formal facts that are incontrovertible are definitely true and cannot be proved false: *The evidence against him is incontrovertible.*

inconvenience¹ /ˌɪnkənˈviːniəns/ n 1 [U] when something causes problems for you: *We apologise for the delay and any inconvenience caused.* 2 [C] something or someone that causes you problems: *His injury was an inconvenience rather than a disaster.*

inconvenience² v [T] to cause problems for someone

inconvenient /ˌɪnkənˈviːniənt◂/ adj causing problems, often in a way that is annoying: *Monday's a bit inconvenient. How about Tuesday?* —**inconveniently** adv

incorporate Ac /ɪnˈkɔːpəreɪt $ -ɔːr-/ v [T] to include something as part of a group, system, plan etc: **incorporate sth into/in sth** *These exercises can easily be incorporated into your daily routine.* —**incorporation** /ɪnˌkɔːpəˈreɪʃən $ -ɔːr-/ n [U]

Incorporated /ɪnˈkɔːpəreɪtɪd $ -ɔːr-/ adj (written abbreviation **Inc.**) used after the name of a company to show that it is a CORPORATION

incorrect /ˌɪnkəˈrekt◂/ adj not correct: *The advice given was incorrect.* THESAURUS WRONG —**incorrectly** adv

incorrigible /ɪnˈkɒrədʒəbəl $ -ˈkɔː-/ adj someone who is incorrigible has a fault that cannot be changed: *He's an incorrigible liar.*

increase¹ /ɪnˈkriːs/ v [I,T] if you increase something, or if it increases, it becomes bigger in number, amount, or degree OPP **decrease**, **reduce**: *Regular exercise increases your chances of living longer.* | *The number of prisoners has increased dramatically.* | **increase in value/price/size etc** *The waves were increasing in size.* | **increase (sth) by sth** *Food prices increased by 3% last year.* —**increasing** adj: *the increasing use of nuclear power* —**increased** adj: *an increased risk of cancer*

THESAURUS

to increase

increase to become bigger in number, amount, or level: *The number of students has increased by 50%.*

rise to increase. **Rise** sounds rather formal and is used especially about the temperature, level, or standard of something: *The temperature could rise to 40 degrees.* | *Unemployment rose to its highest ever level.*

go up to increase. **Go up** is less formal than **increase** or **rise**, and is very common in everyday English: *My rent's gone up again.*

grow to increase, especially gradually over a period of time: *Support for him is growing.* | *The number of people who work from home is growing.*

double to become twice as much: *The town's population has doubled.*

shoot up to increase very quickly and suddenly: *House prices shot up.*

to make something increase

increase to make something larger in number, amount, or level: *You need to increase the amount of exercise you do each day.* | *All they want to do is increase their profits.*

put sth up to increase prices, taxes, rents etc **Put sth up** is less formal than **increase**, and is very common in everyday English: *They've put up the price of their clothes.*

raise to increase prices, taxes, or standards: *No one wants the government to raise taxes.* | *Our aim is to raise students' levels of achievement.*

double to make the number, amount, size etc of something twice as large: *The company has doubled the number of its staff.*

expand to increase something so that it includes a wider range of things, or to increase the size of a business: *Many colleges have expanded the range of their courses.*

increase² /ˈɪnkriːs/ n [C,U] a rise in amount, number, or degree OPP **decrease**: [+in] *There has been a massive increase in unemployment.* | **tax/wage/price etc increase** *There may be further price increases later in the year.* | *Crime in the city is on the increase* (=is increasing).

increasingly /ɪnˈkriːsɪŋli/ adv more and more: *His music is becoming increasingly popular.*

incredible /ɪnˈkredəbəl/ adj 1 extremely good, large, or great: *The view was incredible.* | *She moved with incredible speed.* 2 too strange to be believed, or very difficult to believe: **It's incredible that** *he survived the fall.* | *I find it almost incredible that no one noticed these errors.*

incredibly /ɪnˈkredəbli/ adv 1 extremely: *Nicotine is incredibly addictive.* 2 in a way that is difficult to believe: *Incredibly, he was not injured.*

incredulous /ɪnˈkredjələs $ -dʒə-/ adj unable or unwilling to believe something: *She gave him an incredulous look.* —**incredulously** adv

increment /ˈɪŋkrəmənt/ n [C] a regular increase in an amount: *an annual salary increment of 2%*

incriminate /ɪnˈkrɪməneɪt/ v [T] to make someone seem guilty of a crime: **incriminate yourself** He refused to incriminate himself by answering questions. —**incriminating** adj: Police found some incriminating evidence at his home.

incubate /ˈɪŋkjəbeɪt/ v [I,T] if a bird incubates its eggs, or if the eggs incubate, they are kept warm until the young birds are born —**incubation** /ˌɪŋkjəˈbeɪʃən/ n [U]

incubator /ˈɪŋkjəbeɪtə $ -ər/ n [C] **1** a machine used in hospitals for keeping very small babies alive **2** a machine for keeping eggs warm until the young birds come out

inculcate /ˈɪnkʌlkeɪt $ ɪnˈkʌl-/ v [T] formal to fix an idea into someone's mind

incumbent¹ /ɪnˈkʌmbənt/ n [C] someone who has an official job for which they have been elected

incumbent² adj formal **it is incumbent on/upon sb to do sth** it is the duty or responsibility of someone to do something

incur /ɪnˈkɜː $ -ˈkɜːr/ v [T] (**incurred, incurring**) to experience something unpleasant: We do not want to **incur** any further **costs**. | The company has **incurred** heavy financial **losses**. | I hope I won't **incur** his **anger**.

incurable /ɪnˈkjʊərəbəl $ -ˈkjʊr-/ adj impossible to cure [OPP] **curable**: an incurable disease

incursion /ɪnˈkɜːʃən, -ʒən $ ɪnˈkɜːrʒən/ n [C] formal a sudden attack into an area that belongs to other people

indebted /ɪnˈdetɪd/ adj **be indebted to sb** formal to be very grateful to someone: I am indebted to you for your help.

indecent /ɪnˈdiːsənt/ adj likely to offend or shock people: indecent photographs —**indecency** n [C,U]

indecision /ˌɪndɪˈsɪʒən/ n [U] when you are unable to make a decision: After a week of indecision, the jury finally gave its verdict.

indecisive /ˌɪndɪˈsaɪsɪv◂/ adj unable to make decisions: a weak indecisive leader

indeed /ɪnˈdiːd/ adv
1 used to emphasize something that you are saying: The test proved that Vince was indeed the father. | 'Would it help if you had an assistant?' 'It would, indeed.'
2 formal used to add something extra to support what you have said: I didn't mind at all. Indeed, I was pleased.
3 especially BrE used with 'very' to emphasize what you are saying: The essay was very good indeed. | Thank you very much indeed.
4 especially BrE spoken used to show that you are surprised or annoyed by something: 'He said he was too busy to see you.' 'Did he indeed?'

indefatigable /ˌɪndɪˈfætɪɡəbəl/ adj formal determined and never giving up

indefensible /ˌɪndɪˈfensəbəl◂/ adj too bad to be excused: indefensible behaviour

indefinable /ˌɪndɪˈfaɪnəbəl◂/ adj difficult to describe or explain: She felt a sudden indefinable sadness.

indefinite [Ac] /ɪnˈdefənət/ adj happening for a period of time that has no definite end: He was away in Alaska for an indefinite period.

in,definite 'article n [C] in grammar, the words 'a' or 'an' → **definite article**

indefinitely [Ac] /ɪnˈdefənətli/ adv until a time in the future that has not yet been arranged: The meeting has been postponed indefinitely.

indelible /ɪnˈdeləbəl/ adj impossible to forget or remove: The film left an indelible impression on me. | indelible ink

indelicate /ɪnˈdeləkət/ adj formal slightly rude or offensive: an indelicate question

indemnity /ɪnˈdemnəti/ n (plural **indemnities**) law **1** [U] protection that someone gives you by promising to pay for any damage or loss that you suffer **2** [C] a payment for the loss of money, goods etc

indent /ɪnˈdent/ v [T] if you indent a line when you are writing, you start it further into the page than the other lines

indentation /ˌɪndenˈteɪʃən/ n [C] a cut or small hole in the surface of something

independence /ˌɪndəˈpendəns/ n [U]
1 political freedom from control by another country: **[+from]** Nigeria gained independence from Britain in 1960.
2 the freedom and ability to make your own decisions in life, without having to ask other people for permission, help, or money: Many old people want to maintain their independence. | Having a job gives you **financial independence**.

COLLOCATIONS

verbs

to get independence We got our independence in 1961.

to gain/achieve/win independence Swaziland gained independence in 1968.

to declare independence (=to say that you are now independent) They threatened war if the region declared independence.

to grant a country independence (=to allow a country to become independent) India was granted independence in 1947.

adjectives

full/complete independence We will accept nothing less than full independence.

independence + noun

Independence Day (=the day on which a country's independence is celebrated) July 4th is American Independence Day.

independent /ˌɪndəˈpendənt◂/ adj
1 not owned or controlled by another government or organization: a small independent bookshop | **[+of]** a central bank that is independent of the government
2 not involved in a particular situation, and therefore trusted to be fair in judging it: an independent panel of scientists | Parents have called for an **independent inquiry** (=one organized by independent people).
3 confident, free, and not needing to ask other

people for help, money, or permission to do something: *Jo is an independent young woman.* | *He helps disabled people to lead independent lives.* —**independently** *adv*

'in-depth *adj* **in-depth study/report etc** a study, report etc that is thorough, complete, and considers all the details

indescribable /ˌɪndɪˈskraɪbəbəl◂/ *adj* something that is indescribable is so good, strange, frightening etc that it is hard to describe: *a feeling of indescribable joy*

indestructible /ˌɪndɪˈstrʌktəbəl◂/ *adj* too strong to be destroyed: *an indestructible toy* THESAURUS **STRONG**

indeterminate /ˌɪndɪˈtɜːmənət◂ $ -ɜːr-/ *adj* impossible to know exactly: *a woman of indeterminate age*

index¹ Ac /ˈɪndeks/ *n* [C] **1** (*plural* **indexes**) an alphabetical list of names, subjects etc at the back of a book, with the numbers of the pages where they can be found THESAURUS **LIST 2** (*plural* **indexes**) a set of cards or a DATABASE with information in alphabetical order **3** (*plural* **indexes** *or* **indices** /ˈɪndɪsiːz/) something you can use to compare prices, costs etc or to measure changes: *an index of economic growth*

index² Ac *v* [T] to make an index for something

'index ˌfinger *n* [C] the finger next to your thumb SYN **forefinger** → see picture at HAND¹

Indian /ˈɪndiən/ *n* [C] **1** someone from India **2** a NATIVE AMERICAN —**Indian** *adj*

indicate Ac /ˈɪndɪkeɪt/ *v* **1** [T] to show that something exists or that it is likely to be true: [+(that)] *Research indicates that women live longer than men.* **2** [T] to say or do something that shows what you want or intend to do: [+(that)] *Ralph patted the sofa to indicate that she should join him.* **3** [T] to direct someone's attention to something or someone, for example by pointing: *'That's her,' he said, indicating a girl in a red skirt.* **4** [I,T] *BrE* to show which way you are going to turn in a vehicle SYN **signal**: *I indicated left.*

indication Ac /ˌɪndɪˈkeɪʃən/ *n* [C,U] a sign that something exists or is likely to be true: [+of] *Dark green leaves are an indication of healthy roots.*

indicative Ac /ɪnˈdɪkətɪv/ *adj* **1 be indicative of sth** to show that something exists or is likely to be true: *His reaction is indicative of how frightened he is.* **2** in grammar, an indicative verb expresses a statement

indicator Ac /ˈɪndəkeɪtə $ -ər/ *n* [C] **1** something that can be regarded as a sign of something else: *The main economic indicators suggest that trade is improving.* **2** *BrE* one of the lights on a car that show which way it is going to turn SYN **turn signal** *AmE* → see picture at CAR

indices /ˈɪndɪsiːz/ *n* a plural of INDEX

indict /ɪnˈdaɪt/ *v* [I,T] *especially AmE law* to officially charge someone with a crime: [+for] *He has been indicted for murder.* —**indictment** *n* [C,U] —**indictable** *adj*: *an indictable offense*

indie /ˈɪndi/ *adj* used to refer to popular music that

is produced by small independent companies: *an indie band*

indifference /ɪnˈdɪfərəns/ *n* [U] lack of interest or concern: [+to] *his apparent indifference to material luxuries*

indifferent /ɪnˈdɪfərənt/ *adj* **1** not interested in something, and not caring about it: [+to] *an industry that seems indifferent to environmental concerns* **2** not particularly good: *a rather indifferent meal*

indigenous /ɪnˈdɪdʒənəs/ *adj* indigenous plants and animals grow or live naturally in a place

indigestible /ˌɪndɪˈdʒestəbəl◂/ *adj* food that is indigestible is difficult for your stomach to deal with

indigestion /ˌɪndɪˈdʒestʃən/ *n* [U] pain that you get when your stomach cannot break down food that you have eaten

indignant /ɪnˈdɪɡnənt/ *adj* angry because you feel insulted or unfairly treated: [+at/about] *Liz was indignant at the school's attitude.* —**indignantly** *adv* —**indignation** /ˌɪndɪɡˈneɪʃən/ *n* [U]

indignity /ɪnˈdɪɡnəti/ *n* [C,U] (*plural* **indignities**) a situation that makes you feel ashamed and not respected: *Two diplomats* **suffered the indignity of** *being arrested.*

indigo /ˈɪndɪɡəʊ $ -ɡoʊ/ *n* [U] a dark purple-blue colour —**indigo** *adj*

indirect /ˌɪndəˈrekt◂/ *adj* **1** caused by something, but not in a direct or clear way: *the* **indirect effects** *of climate change* **2** an indirect way to a place is not the straightest way: *an indirect route* **3** not saying or showing something in a clear definite way —**indirectly** *adv*

ˌindirect 'object *n* [C] in grammar, the person that something is given to, said to, made for etc. For example, in the sentence 'I asked him a question', the indirect object is 'him'. → **direct object**

ˌindirect 'speech *n* [U] REPORTED SPEECH

indiscreet /ˌɪndɪˈskriːt◂/ *adj* saying things in an open way when you should be more careful to keep them secret: *Try to stop him from saying something indiscreet.*

indiscretion Ac /ˌɪndɪˈskreʃən/ *n* [C,U] behaviour that shows a lack of good judgment and often seems immoral to other people: *We can forgive him his youthful indiscretion.*

indiscriminate /ˌɪndɪˈskrɪmənət◂/ *adj* indiscriminate actions are done without considering what harm they might cause: *indiscriminate killings by terrorists* —**indiscriminately** *adv*

indispensable /ˌɪndɪˈspensəbəl◂/ *adj* someone or something that is indispensable is so important or useful that you cannot manage without them: [+to] *The book is indispensable to anyone learning maths.*

indisputable /ˌɪndɪˈspjuːtəbəl◂/ *adj* an indisputable fact is definitely true: *The evidence was indisputable.*

indistinct Ac /ˌɪndɪˈstɪŋkt◂/ *adj* difficult to see, hear, or remember clearly: *She muttered something indistinct.* —**indistinctly** *adv*

indistinguishable /ˌɪndɪˈstɪŋɡwɪʃəbəl/ *adj* if one thing is indistinguishable from another, it is so similar that you cannot see the difference between them: **[+from]** *This material is indistinguishable from real silk.*

individual¹ Ac /ˌɪndəˈvɪdʒuəl◂/ adj
1 [only before noun] an individual person or thing is just one, considered separately from other people or things: *Each individual drawing is slightly different. | We try to meet the needs of the individual customer.*
2 belonging to or intended for one person rather than a group: *The children get individual attention. | We divided the food into individual portions.*
3 an individual way of doing things is different from anyone else's: *She's got a very individual way of dressing.*

individual² Ac n [C] one person, considered separately from the rest of the group or society that they live in: *the rights of the individual | donations from **private individuals** (=people, not organizations)*

individualism Ac /ˌɪndəˈvɪdʒuəlɪzəm/ n [U] when someone does things in their own way without being influenced by other people

individualist Ac /ˌɪndəˈvɪdʒuəlɪst/ n [C] someone who does things in their own way without being influenced by other people —**individualistic** /ˌɪndəvɪdʒuəˈlɪstɪk◂/ adj: *a highly individualistic approach to life*

individuality Ac /ˌɪndəvɪdʒuˈæləti/ n [U] the quality that makes someone different from everyone else: *work that allows children to express their individuality*

individually Ac /ˌɪndəˈvɪdʒuəli/ adv separately, not together in a group: *He thanked everyone individually.*

indoctrinate /ɪnˈdɒktrəneɪt/ v [T] to train someone to accept one set of beliefs and not consider any others: *They were indoctrinated not to question their leaders.* —**indoctrination** /ɪnˌdɒktrəˈneɪʃən $ ɪnˌdɑːk-/ n [U]

indomitable /ɪnˈdɒmətəbəl $ ɪnˈdɑː-/ adj formal very brave and determined

indoor /ˈɪndɔː $ -ɔːr/ adj [only before noun] used or happening inside a building OPP **outdoor**: *an indoor swimming pool | indoor plants*

indoors /ˌɪnˈdɔːz◂ $ -ɔːrz◂/ adv inside a building OPP **outdoors**: *It's raining – let's go indoors. | He stayed indoors all morning.*

induce Ac /ɪnˈdjuːs $ ɪnˈduːs/ v [T]
1 PERSUADE formal to make someone decide to do something: **induce sb to do sth** *Nothing would induce me to vote for him again.*
2 BABY to make a woman give birth to her baby by giving her a special drug
3 CAUSE formal to cause a physical feeling or condition: *This drug may induce drowsiness.*

inducement /ɪnˈdjuːsmənt $ ɪnˈduːs-/ n [C,U] formal something that you are offered to persuade you to do something

induct /ɪnˈdʌkt/ v [T] especially AmE to officially introduce someone into a group or organization

induction Ac /ɪnˈdʌkʃən/ n [C,U] the process of officially introducing someone into a group or organization: *a two-day **induction course** for the new employees*

indulge /ɪnˈdʌldʒ/ v **1** [I,T] to let yourself do something that you enjoy, especially something that is considered bad for you: **[+in]** *From time to time, we indulge in a little lunchtime drinking.* | **indulge yourself** *Go on, indulge yourself for a change!* **2** [T] to let someone do or have whatever they want, even if it is bad for them: *Ralph indulges his children terribly.*

indulgence /ɪnˈdʌldʒəns/ n **1** [U] the habit of eating too much, drinking too much etc: *a life of indulgence* **2** [C] something that you do or have for pleasure, not because you need it: *Chocolate is my only indulgence.*

indulgent /ɪnˈdʌldʒənt/ adj willing to let someone have whatever they want, even if it is bad for them: *indulgent parents*

industrial /ɪnˈdʌstriəl/ adj
1 relating to industry or the people working in it: *industrial development | an industrial dispute | an industrial accident*
2 an industrial country or area has a lot of industries: *the industrial nations of the world | an **industrial society** —***industrially** adv

in,dustrial 'action n [U] BrE an action such as a STRIKE (=stopping work) taken by workers involved in a disagreement with their employer

in,dustrial es'tate BrE, **in,dustrial 'park** AmE n [C] an area of land that has businesses and small factories on it

industrialist /ɪnˈdʌstriəlɪst/ n [C] someone who owns or runs a factory or industrial company

industrialized (also **-ised** BrE) /ɪnˈdʌstriəlaɪzd/ adj an industrialized country or area has a lot of industry —**industrialization** /ɪnˌdʌstriəlaɪˈzeɪʃən $ -lə-/ n [U]

in,dustrial re'lations n [plural] the relationship between workers and employers

industrious /ɪnˈdʌstriəs/ adj formal always working hard: *industrious young women* —**industriously** adv

industry /ˈɪndəstri/ n (plural **industries**)
1 [U] the production of goods: *Most of these men work in the construction industry. | The software is widely used in industry.*
2 [C] all the companies that work in one particular type of trade or service: *the coal industry*

COLLOCATIONS
types of industry

manufacturing industry (=industries in which goods are produced in factories) *Fewer people are employed in manufacturing industry than 25 years ago.*
service industries (=businesses that provide a service, such as banking and tourism) *There has been a rapid growth in service industries.*
the construction/car/textile etc industry *Hundreds of jobs have been lost in the car industry.*
the tourist/travel industry *The tourist industry earns billions of dollars per year.*
the film/music/entertainment industry *She hoped to work in the music industry.*

---

inebriated /ɪˈniːbrieɪtɪd/ adj formal drunk

inedible /ɪnˈedəbəl/ *adj* something that is inedible cannot be eaten: *inedible mushrooms*

ineffective /ˌɪnəˈfektɪv◂/ *adj* not achieving the correct effect or result: *The treatment was completely ineffective.*

ineffectual /ˌɪnəˈfektʃuəl◂/ *adj* not having the ability, confidence, or personal authority to get things done: *an ineffectual leader*

inefficient /ˌɪnəˈfɪʃənt◂/ *adj* not using time, money, energy etc in the best way: *an inefficient use of resources* —**inefficiently** *adv* —**inefficiency** *n* [C,U]

inelegant /ɪnˈelɪɡənt/ *adj* not graceful or attractive: *She was sitting in a rather inelegant position.*

ineligible /ɪnˈelədʒəbəl/ *adj* not allowed to do or to have something: *People under 18 are ineligible to vote.*

inept /ɪˈnept/ *adj* not good at doing something: *an inept driver* —**ineptly** *adv*

inequality /ˌɪnɪˈkwɒləti $ -ˈkwɑː-/ *n* [C,U] (*plural* **inequalities**) an unfair situation, in which some groups in society have more money, opportunities, power etc than others: **[+in]** *a new attempt to tackle inequalities in the education system* | **[+of]** *There is still inequality of opportunity.*

inequity /ɪnˈekwəti/ *n* [C,U] (*plural* **inequities**) *formal* lack of fairness, or something that is unfair

inert /ɪˈnɜːt $ -ɜːrt/ *adj* **1** *technical* an inert substance does not produce a chemical reaction when it is combined with other substances: *an inert gas* **2** *formal* not moving: *He lay, inert, in his bed.*

inertia /ɪˈnɜːʃə $ -ɜːr-/ *n* [U] **1** when no one wants to do anything to change a situation: *There is a feeling of political inertia in the country.* **2** *technical* the force that keeps an object in the same position until it is moved, or that keeps it moving until it is stopped **3** a feeling that you have no energy and do not want to do anything

inescapable /ˌɪnɪˈskeɪpəbəl◂/ *adj formal* an inescapable fact is one that cannot be ignored: *The inescapable conclusion is that Reynolds killed himself.*

inevitable Ac /ɪˈnevətəbəl/ *adj* **1** if something is inevitable, it will definitely happen and you cannot avoid it: *Death is inevitable.* | *It is inevitable that you will be caught.* **2 the inevitable** something that will definitely happen: *Finally, the inevitable happened and he lost his job.* —**inevitably** *adv*: *Inevitably, his alcohol problem affected his work.* —**inevitability** /ɪˌnevətəˈbɪləti/ *n* [U]

inexact /ˌɪnɪɡˈzækt◂/ *adj formal* not exact: *Psychology is an inexact science.*

inexcusable /ˌɪnɪkˈskjuːzəbəl◂/ *adj* inexcusable behaviour is too bad to be excused

inexhaustible /ˌɪnɪɡˈzɔːstəbəl◂ $ -ˈzɒːs-/ *adj* an inexhaustible amount of something is so large that it will never be finished or used up: *She has an **inexhaustible supply** of funny stories.*

inexorable /ɪnˈeksərəbəl/ *adj formal* an inexorable process cannot be stopped: *the seemingly inexorable rise in crime*

inexpensive /ˌɪnɪkˈspensɪv◂/ *adj* cheap but good: *an inexpensive vacation* THESAURUS CHEAP —**inexpensively** *adv*

inexperienced /ˌɪnɪkˈspɪəriənst◂ $ -ˈspɪr-/ *adj* not having very much experience or knowledge: *an inexperienced driver* —**inexperience** *n* [U]

inexplicable /ˌɪnɪkˈsplɪkəbəl◂ $ ɪnˈeksplɪkəbəl, ˌɪnɪkˈsplɪk-/ *adj* something that is inexplicable is so unusual or strange that you cannot explain it: *the inexplicable disappearance of a young woman* —**inexplicably** *adv*

inextricably /ˌɪnɪkˈstrɪkəbli, ɪnˈekstrɪk-/ *adv formal* things that are inextricably connected cannot be separated from each other: *Poverty and bad health are inextricably linked.*

infallible /ɪnˈfæləbəl/ *adj* **1** always right and never making mistakes: *No expert is infallible.* **2** something that is infallible always works correctly: *an infallible cure for hiccups*

infamous /ˈɪnfəməs/ *adj* well known for being bad or evil: *an infamous killer* THESAURUS FAMOUS

infancy /ˈɪnfənsi/ *n* [U] **1** the period in a child's life before he or she can walk or talk: **in infancy** *Their son died in infancy.* **2** the time when something is just starting to be developed: *Genetic engineering is still **in its infancy**.*

infant /ˈɪnfənt/ *n* [C] *formal* a baby or very young child

infantile /ˈɪnfəntaɪl/ *adj formal* infantile behaviour seems silly in an adult because it is more suitable to a child: *infantile jokes*

infantry /ˈɪnfəntri/ *n* [U] soldiers who fight on foot

infatuated /ɪnˈfætʃueɪtɪd/ *adj* having strong feelings of love for someone: **[+with]** *He's infatuated with her.* —**infatuation** /ɪnˌfætʃuˈeɪʃən/ *n* [C,U]

infect /ɪnˈfekt/ *v* [T] **1** to give someone a disease: *People can feel well but still infect others.* | **infect sb with sth** *Thousands of people have been infected with the virus.* **2** to make food, water etc likely to spread disease: *The eggs were infected with bacteria.* **3** if a feeling that you have infects other people, it makes them feel the same way: *His cynicism seems to have infected the whole team.*

infected /ɪnˈfektɪd/ *adj* **1** a wound that is infected has harmful BACTERIA in it which prevent it from getting better **2** food, water etc that is infected contains BACTERIA that spread disease

infection /ɪnˈfekʃən/ *n* [C,U] a disease in part of your body, caused by BACTERIA or a VIRUS: *Wash the cut thoroughly to protect against infection.* | *She's off school with a throat infection.*

COLLOCATIONS

verbs

to have an infection *A fever is usually a sign that you have an infection.*

to suffer from an infection *He was suffering from a kidney infection.*

to get/develop an infection *She cut her finger and developed an infection.*

infectious /ɪnˈfekʃəs/ *adj*
1 an infectious disease can be passed from one person to another: *Flu is **highly infectious**.*
2 someone who is infectious has a disease that could be passed to other people: *Some people with HIV may feel well but will still be infectious.*
3 infectious feelings or laughter spread quickly from one person to another: *She's got an infectious laugh.* | *his infectious enthusiasm*

infer [Ac] /ɪnˈfɜː $ -ɜːr/ *v* [T] (**inferred, inferring**) *formal* to decide that something is probably true because of other information that you already have: **infer sth from sth** *I inferred from his letter that he was still angry with me.*

inference [Ac] /ˈɪnfərəns/ *n* [C,U] *formal* a fact that you think is true, based on information that you already know, or the process of deciding this

inferior¹ /ɪnˈfɪəriə $ -ˈfɪriər/ *adj* not good, or not as good as someone or something else → **superior**: *wine of inferior quality* | **[+to]** *I always felt slightly inferior to her.* —**inferiority** /ɪnˌfɪəriˈɒrəti $ ɪnˌfɪriˈɔːr-/ *n* [U]: *She suffers from feelings of inferiority.*

inferior² *n* [C] someone who has a lower position or rank than you in an organization → **superior**

inferno /ɪnˈfɜːnəʊ $ -ɜːrnoʊ/ *n* [C] (*plural* **infernos**) *literary* a very large and dangerous fire: *a raging inferno*

infertile /ɪnˈfɜːtaɪl $ -ˈfɜːrtl/ *adj* **1** unable to have babies **2** infertile land is not good enough to grow plants in —**infertility** /ˌɪnfəˈtɪləti $ -fər-/ *n* [U]

infest /ɪnˈfest/ *v* [T] if insects, rats etc infest a place, there are a lot of them and they usually cause damage: **be infested with sth** *The kitchen was infested with cockroaches.* —**infestation** /ˌɪnfeˈsteɪʃən/ *n* [C,U]: *an infestation of rats*

infidelity /ˌɪnfəˈdeləti/ *n* [C,U] (*plural* **infidelities**) when someone has sex with someone who is not their wife, husband, or partner

infighting /ˈɪnfaɪtɪŋ/ *n* [U] unfriendly disagreement between members of the same group or organization: *There has been a lot of political infighting in the party.*

infiltrate /ˈɪnfɪltreɪt $ ɪnˈfɪltreɪt, ˈɪnfɪl-/ *v* [I,T] to secretly join an organization to find out information about it: *Police attempts to infiltrate neo-Nazi groups have been unsuccessful.* | *Militant groups have been infiltrating into the north of the country.*

infinite [Ac] /ˈɪnfənət/ *adj* **1** very great in amount or degree: *a teacher with infinite patience* **2** without limits in space or time: *an infinite universe*

infinitely [Ac] /ˈɪnfənətli/ *adv* very much: *someone with infinitely more experience*

infinitesimal /ˌɪnfɪnəˈtesəməl◂/ *adj* extremely small: *infinitesimal changes in temperature*

infinitive /ɪnˈfɪnətɪv/ *n* [C] in grammar, the basic form of a verb, used with 'to'. In the sentence 'I forgot to buy milk', 'to buy' is an infinitive.

infinity /ɪnˈfɪnəti/ *n* **1** [U] a space or distance without limits or an end **2** [singular, U] a number that is too large to be calculated

infirm /ɪnˈfɜːm $ -ɜːrm/ *adj* someone who is infirm is old, ill, and weak

infirmary /ɪnˈfɜːməri $ -ɜːr-/ *n* [C] (*plural* **infirmaries**) a hospital – used in the names of some hospitals

infirmity /ɪnˈfɜːməti $ -ɜːr-/ *n* [C,U] (*plural* **infirmities**) *formal* an illness

inflame /ɪnˈfleɪm/ *v* [T] to make someone's feelings of anger or excitement much stronger

inflamed /ɪnˈfleɪmd/ *adj* a part of your body that is inflamed is red and painful

inflammable /ɪnˈflæməbəl/ *adj* materials or substances that are inflammable burn very easily **SYN** flammable **OPP** non-flammable: *Petrol is highly inflammable.*

inflammation /ˌɪnfləˈmeɪʃən/ *n* [C,U] pain and swelling in a part of your body

inflammatory /ɪnˈflæmətəri $ -tɔːri/ *adj* *formal* an inflammatory speech or piece of writing is likely to make people angry

INFLATABLE

an inflatable boat

inflatable /ɪnˈfleɪtəbəl/ *adj* an inflatable object is one that you fill with air before you use it: *an inflatable boat*

inflate /ɪnˈfleɪt/ *v* **1** [I,T] to fill something such as a ball or tyre with air **2** [T] to make a price or number higher than it should be: *Hotels inflate prices at this time of year.*

inflated /ɪnˈfleɪtɪd/ *adj* **1** inflated prices or costs are higher than they should be: **grossly/vastly/hugely inflated** *hugely inflated prices for tickets* **2** filled with air: *an inflated life-jacket*

inflation /ɪnˈfleɪʃən/ *n* [U]
1 when the price of things you buy keeps increasing: **high/low inflation** *The 1990s was a period of high inflation.* | *What is the current **rate of inflation**?* | *the government's attempts to control inflation*
2 when you fill something with air

inflationary /ɪnˈfleɪʃənəri $ -ʃəneri/ *adj* causing prices to keep increasing

inflection, **inflexion** /ɪnˈflekʃən/ n [C,U]
1 technical the way the ending of a word changes to show that it is plural, in the past tense etc **2** the way the sound of your voice goes up and down when you are speaking

inflexible Ac /ɪnˈfleksəbəl/ adj **1** not willing to change your opinions or ideas **2** something that is inflexible is stiff and will not bend —**inflexibility** /ɪnˌfleksəˈbɪləti/ n [U]

inflict /ɪnˈflɪkt/ v [T] to make a person or place suffer something unpleasant: **inflict sth on/upon sb/sth** The earthquake inflicted a lot of damage on the area.

in-flight adj [only before noun] provided during a plane journey: in-flight movies

influence¹ /ˈɪnfluəns/ n
1 [C,U] if someone has influence, they have the power to change how things develop or how people behave: Kate used her influence to get her friend a job. | **[+on]** Your mood can have an influence on your health. | **under sb's/sth's influence** (also **under the influence of sb/sth**) They had come under the influence of a religious sect. **THESAURUS** EFFECT
2 [C] someone or something that has an effect on other people or things: **[+on]** She was a bad influence on him. | The country remains untouched by **outside influences**.
PHRASES
under the influence (of drink/alcohol/drugs etc) drunk, or feeling the effects of an illegal drug: She was convicted of driving under the influence of alcohol.

COLLOCATIONS

verbs
to have/be an influence My English teacher was a big influence on me.
to exert an influence formal (=to have an influence) Your family will always exert some influence over you.
to use your influence He used his influence with local politicians to try to get the decision changed.

adjectives
a good/positive influence I try to be a good influence on my students.
a bad influence His wife thought his brother was a bad influence.
a strong/powerful/profound influence The book had a very profound influence on me as a child.
a big/great influence His music had a great influence on all of us.

influence² v [T] to change how something develops, or how someone behaves: His advice **strongly influenced** my decision. **THESAURUS** PERSUADE

influential /ˌɪnfluˈenʃəl◂/ adj able to influence what happens or what people think: He has some very influential friends.

influenza /ˌɪnfluˈenzə/ n [U] technical FLU

influx /ˈɪnflʌks/ n [C] the arrival of large numbers of people or things: **[+of]** an influx of tourists

info /ˈɪnfəʊ $ -foʊ/ n [U] informal information

inform /ɪnˈfɔːm $ -ɔːrm/ v [T] formal to formally tell someone about something: **inform sb about/of sth** No one informed me about the change of plan. | She was informed of the accident by the police. | **inform sb (that)** The college informed me that I had been accepted. **THESAURUS** TELL

PHRASAL VERBS
inform on/against sb to secretly give information about someone to the police

informal /ɪnˈfɔːməl $ -ɔːr-/ adj
1 relaxed and friendly: an informal party
2 suitable for ordinary situations: informal clothes —**informally** adv —**informality** /ˌɪnfɔːˈmæləti $ -fɔːr-/ n [U]

Word Choice: informal or casual?
You use **informal** especially in the phrase **informal dress** (=informal clothes). You do not talk about 'an informal shirt/jacket etc'.
You use **casual** about clothes, or about a shirt, a jacket, a pair of shoes, or trousers: He was wearing a casual shirt.

informant /ɪnˈfɔːmənt $ -ɔːr-/ n [C] someone who secretly gives information about someone to the police

information /ˌɪnfəˈmeɪʃən $ -fər-/ n [U] facts or details about a situation, person, or event: **[+about/on]** The book contains information about many subjects. | For further information, call the number below.

Grammar
Information is an uncountable noun and is never plural.
Do not say 'some informations'. Say **some information**.
Do not say 'a useful information'. Say **a useful piece/bit of information**.

COLLOCATIONS

adjectives
useful/valuable information The guidebook is full of useful information.
correct/accurate information Not all the information you find on the Internet is correct.
false/wrong information The information about train times was wrong.

verbs
to have information He said he had some information about my family.
to contain information Unfortunately, the article contained some false information.
to get information Get as much information as you can about the company.
to give/provide information We weren't given enough information to make a decision.

nouns + information
a piece/bit of information Here's an interesting piece of information.

information superhighway /ˌɪnfəmeɪʃən ˌsuːpəˈhaɪweɪ $ -fərmeɪʃən ˌsuːpər-/ n **the information superhighway** the Internet

infor'mation tech,nology n [U] (abbreviation **IT**) the use of computers to store information and make it available

informative /ɪnˈfɔːmətɪv $ -ɔːr-/ adj providing useful information: *The lecture was very informative.*

informed /ɪnˈfɔːmd $ -ɔːr-/ adj having plenty of knowledge and information about something: **well-informed/ill-informed** *He's very **well-informed** about this subject.* | *I want to learn as much as I can so that I can make an **informed decision**.*

informer /ɪnˈfɔːmə $ -ɔːrmər/ n [C] someone who secretly gives information about someone to the police

infraction /ɪnˈfrækʃən/ n [C,U] formal when someone breaks a rule or law

infra-red /ˌɪnfrə ˈred◂/ adj infra-red light gives out heat but cannot be seen

infrastructure [Ac] /ˈɪnfrəˌstrʌktʃə $ -ər/ n [C,U] the basic systems and structures that a country or organization needs in order to work properly, for example roads, railways, banks etc

infrequent /ɪnˈfriːkwənt/ adj not often: *The buses into town are quite infrequent.* | *He was an infrequent visitor to our house.* —**infrequently** adv

infringe /ɪnˈfrɪndʒ/ v [T] to do something that is against the law or someone's legal rights: *Making photocopies of a book **infringes** the **copyright**.* —**infringement** n [C,U]

PHRASAL VERBS

infringe on/upon sth to limit someone's freedom in some way: *The rule infringes on our right to free speech.*

infuriate /ɪnˈfjʊərieɪt $ -ˈfjʊr-/ v [T] to make someone very angry: *His attitude infuriated me.*

infuriating /ɪnˈfjʊərieɪtɪŋ $ -ˈfjʊr-/ adj very annoying: *an infuriating delay*

infuse /ɪnˈfjuːz/ v **1** [T] formal to fill something or someone with a feeling or quality: **be infused with sth** *Her books are infused with humour.* **2** [I,T] if you infuse tea or HERBS, you leave them in very hot water while their taste passes into the water —**infusion** /-ˈfjuːʒən/ n [C,U]

ingenious /ɪnˈdʒiːniəs/ adj extremely clever: *an ingenious plan* | *an ingenious device for getting frost off your car window* | *He was an ingenious inventor.* —**ingeniously** adv

ingenuity /ˌɪndʒəˈnjuːəti $ -ˈnuː-/ n [U] skill at inventing things and thinking of new ideas

ingest /ɪnˈdʒest/ v [T] technical to eat or drink something

ingrained /ɪnˈɡreɪnd/ adj **1** ingrained attitudes or behaviour are firmly established and difficult to change **2** ingrained dirt is under the surface of something and difficult to remove

ingratiate /ɪnˈɡreɪʃieɪt/ v **ingratiate yourself (with sb)** disapproving to try very hard to get someone's approval: *He tried to ingratiate himself with the boss.* —**ingratiating** adj

ingratitude /ɪnˈɡrætɪtjuːd $ -tuːd/ n [U] when someone is not grateful for something

ingredient /ɪnˈɡriːdiənt/ n [C] **1** one of the things you use to make a particular kind of food: *Mix the ingredients together in a bowl.* **2** one of the qualities that you need to achieve something: *AI **has all the ingredients of** a great player.*

inhabit /ɪnˈhæbɪt/ v [T] formal to live in a place: *The woods are inhabited by deer.* **THESAURUS** ▶ LIVE

inhabitant /ɪnˈhæbɪtənt/ n [C] formal the inhabitants of a place are the people who live there

inhale /ɪnˈheɪl/ v [I,T] formal to breathe in air, smoke, or gas: *Ed lit a cigarette and **inhaled deeply**.* —**inhalation** /ˌɪnhəˈleɪʃən/ n [U]

inhaler /ɪnˈheɪlə $ -ər/ n [C] a small plastic tube containing medicine that you breathe in if you suffer from ASTHMA

inherent [Ac] /ɪnˈhɪərənt, -ˈher- $ -ˈhɪr-, -ˈher-/ adj a quality that is inherent in something is a natural part of it and cannot be separated from it: **[+in]** *The problem is inherent in our education system.* —**inherently** adv

inherit /ɪnˈherɪt/ v

1 **MONEY/PROPERTY** [I,T] to receive money or property from someone when they die: **inherit sth from sb** *He inherited £10,000 from his aunt.* **THESAURUS** ▶ GET

2 **CHARACTER/APPEARANCE** [T] to have the same character or appearance as your parents: *I inherited my mother's curly hair.*

3 **SITUATION** [T] if you inherit a difficult situation, you have to deal with problems that were caused by other people in the past: *The government inherited many problems.*

inheritance /ɪnˈherɪtəns/ n [C,U] money or property that you receive from someone when they die

inhibit [Ac] /ɪnˈhɪbɪt/ v [T] **1** to prevent something from growing or developing well: *An unhappy family life may inhibit children's learning.* **2** to make someone feel embarrassed or nervous so that they cannot do or say what they want

inhibited /ɪnˈhɪbɪtɪd/ adj too embarrassed or nervous to do or say what you want

inhibition [Ac] /ˌɪnhɪˈbɪʃən/ n [C,U] shyness or embarrassment that stops you doing or saying what you want: *He's got a lot of inhibitions.* | *People **lose their inhibitions** when they drink alcohol.*

inhospitable /ˌɪnhɒˈspɪtəbəl $ -hɑː-/ adj **1** an inhospitable place is unpleasant and difficult to live in **2** an inhospitable person is unfriendly to visitors

in-'house adj, adv within a company or organization: *in-house training*

inhuman /ɪnˈhjuːmən/ adj **1** very cruel and bad: *inhuman acts of terrorism* **2** lacking any human qualities in a way that seems strange or frightening: *a strange inhuman sound*

inhumane /ˌɪnhjuːˈmeɪn/ adj if you treat someone in an inhumane way, you are very cruel to them: *the inhumane treatment of prisoners* —**inhumanely** adv

inhumanity /ˌɪnhjuːˈmænəti/ n [U] very cruel behaviour: *man's inhumanity to man*

inimitable /ɪˈnɪmətəbəl/ adj too good or skilful for anyone else to copy with the same high standard: *the inimitable Elvis*

iniquity /ɪˈnɪkwəti/ n [C,U] (plural **iniquities**) *formal* something that is very unfair: **[+of]** *the iniquities of the tax system* —**iniquitous** adj

initial¹ Ac /ɪˈnɪʃəl/ adj [only before noun] happening at the beginning: *an initial period of training* | *the initial stages of the disease* —**initially** adv: *Initially, I didn't like him.*

initial² n [C usually plural] the first letter of a name: *His initials are W.G. – for William Grout.*

initial³ v [T] (**initialled**, **initialling** BrE, **initialed**, **initialing** AmE) to write your initials on a document: *The two countries have initialled the agreement.*

initiate Ac /ɪˈnɪʃieɪt/ v [T] **1** *formal* to arrange for something important to start: *He initiated legal proceedings against the newspaper.* **2** to tell someone about something or show them how to do something **3** to introduce someone into an organization, often with a special ceremony —**initiation** /ɪˌnɪʃiˈeɪʃən/ n [C,U]

initiative Ac /ɪˈnɪʃətɪv/ n **1** [U] when you make decisions and do things without waiting for someone to tell you what to do: *You need to **have** a lot of initiative to do this job.* | *I wish he would **show** more initiative.* **2** [C] an important new plan or process to achieve an aim or solve a problem: *a new government initiative to reduce car crime* **3 have/take the initiative** if you have or take the initiative, you are in a position to control a situation and decide what to do next: *Students took the initiative to raise money for a music program.*

inject /ɪnˈdʒekt/ v [T] **1** to put a drug into someone's body by using a special needle: **inject sth into sb/sth** *The vaccine is injected into your arm.* **2** to improve something by adding excitement or interest to it: **inject sth into sth** *The company is injecting more fun into their designs.*

injection /ɪnˈdʒekʃən/ n
1 [C,U] when a drug is put into your body, using a special needle: *The nurse **gave** me an **injection**.* | **[+of]** *an injection of insulin*
2 [C] the addition of money to something in order to improve it: **[+of]** *The firm received a **cash injection** of $6 million.*

'in-joke n [C] a joke that is only understood by a particular group of people

injunction /ɪnˈdʒʌŋkʃən/ n [C] *law* an order given by a court which tells someone not to do something

injure Ac /ˈɪndʒə $ -ər/ v [T] to hurt someone and damage part of their body: *He injured his leg playing rugby.* | **be badly/seriously/critically injured** *She was badly injured in the accident.* **THESAURUS** HURT

injured Ac /ˈɪndʒəd $ -ərd/ adj **1** an injured person or animal has been hurt: *The injured passengers were taken to hospital.* **2 the injured** [plural] people who have been hurt: *Many of the injured are still in a serious condition*

injury Ac /ˈɪndʒəri/ n [C,U] (plural **injuries**) damage to part of your body that you get in an accident or attack: *She was taken to hospital with serious head injuries.*

COLLOCATIONS

verbs

to suffer an injury *Four of the passengers suffered serious injuries.*

to be treated for an injury *A woman was treated for head injuries.*

to recover from an injury *It only took her a few days to recover from the injury.*

types of injury

a head/leg/shoulder etc injury *His football career was ended by a knee injury.*

a serious/bad injury *Thank goodness the injury wasn't serious.*

a fatal injury (=one that kills you) *He was taken to hospital, but his injuries proved fatal.*

a minor injury (=not serious) *Amazingly, the driver had only minor injuries.*

THESAURUS

injury damage to part of your body that you get in an accident or attack: *The driver had serious injuries.* | *a head injury*

wound an injury caused by a weapon such as a knife, gun, or bomb: *He died from a bullet wound in his chest.* | *a knife wound*

cut a hole in your skin caused by a sharp object, from which blood comes out: *I had a big cut on my arm.*

bruise a dark mark on your skin that you get when you fall or get hit: *After the fight, his arms were covered in bruises.*

graze an area of skin that is a little damaged, for example when you fall over: *Kids are always getting grazes on their legs and knees.*

fracture a crack in a bone: *He suffered a small fracture of the skull.*

---

injustice /ɪnˈdʒʌstɪs/ n [C,U] when people are treated in a bad and unfair way: *There's so much injustice in the world.*

ink /ɪŋk/ n [C,U] a coloured liquid used for writing, printing, or drawing: **in ink** *a message written in black ink*

inkling /ˈɪŋklɪŋ/ n [C] a slight idea about something: *I **had an inkling** that she was pregnant.*

inland /ˈɪnlənd/ adj, adv away from the coast: *an inland village* | *Lake Sabaya lies six miles inland.*

'in-laws n [plural] *informal* the relatives of your husband or wife

inlet /ˈɪnlet, ˈɪnlɪt/ n [C] **1** a narrow area of water that goes into the land from the sea or a lake **2** a tube through which liquid or gas flows into a machine

inmate /ˈɪnmeɪt/ n [C] someone who is kept in a prison

inn /ɪn/ n [C] a small hotel or PUB **THESAURUS** HOTEL

innards /ˈɪnədz $ -ərdz/ n [plural] *informal* the parts inside your body

innate /ɪ'neɪt◂/ adj an innate quality or ability is something you are born with: an innate ability to learn languages —**innately** adv

inner /'ɪnə $ -ər/ adj
1 on the inside or near the centre of something: the castle's inner walls
2 inner thoughts or feelings are ones that you feel strongly but do not always show to other people

,inner 'city n [C] the part of a city that is near the centre, especially the part where the buildings are in a bad condition and the people are poor: the problem of crime in our inner cities —**inner city** adj: an inner city housing estate

innermost /'ɪnəməʊst $ -nərmoʊst/ adj [only before noun] **1** your innermost feelings, desires etc are your most personal and secret ones **2** formal furthest inside or nearest to the centre

inning /'ɪnɪŋ/ n [C] one of the nine periods of play in a game of baseball

innings /'ɪnɪŋz/ n [C] (plural **innings**) one of the periods of play in a game of CRICKET

innkeeper /'ɪn,kiːpə $ -ər/ n [C] old-fashioned someone who owns or manages an INN

innocence /'ɪnəsəns/ n [U]
1 the fact that someone is not guilty of a crime OPP guilt: Can you prove your **innocence**?
2 when someone has not had much experience of life: the innocence of a child

innocent /'ɪnəsənt/ adj
1 someone who is innocent has not done anything wrong OPP guilty: Nobody believed that I was innocent. | [+of] He's innocent of the murder. | The court found him innocent. THESAURUS GUILTY
2 innocent victims/bystanders/people etc people who get hurt or killed in a war or crime although they are not directly involved in it: Many innocent civilians were killed.
3 done or said without intending to harm or offend anyone: an innocent remark
4 someone who is innocent does not know about the bad things in life: an innocent child —**innocently** adv

innocuous /ɪ'nɒkjuəs $ ɪ'nɑːk-/ adj not likely to harm anyone or cause trouble: an innocuous remark

innovation Ac /,ɪnə'veɪʃən/ n **1** [C] a new idea, method, or invention: [+in] innovations in teaching **2** [U] the introduction of new ideas or methods —**innovate** /'ɪnəveɪt/ v [I,T] —**innovative** adj —**innovator** n [C]

innuendo /,ɪnju'endəʊ $ -doʊ/ n [C,U] (plural **innuendoes** or **innuendos**) a remark that suggests something sexual or unpleasant without saying it directly

innumerable /ɪ'njuːmərəbəl $ ɪ'nuː-/ adj very many

inoculate /ɪ'nɒkjəleɪt $ ɪ'nɑː-/ v [T] to protect someone against a disease by putting a weak form of the disease into their body using a needle → **immunize**, **vaccinate**: Have you been inoculated against hepatitis? —**inoculation** /ɪ,nɒkjə'leɪʃən $ ɪ,nɑːk-/ n [C,U]

inoffensive /,ɪnə'fensɪv◂/ adj unlikely to offend anyone: an inoffensive little man

inordinate /ɪ'nɔːdənət $ -ɔːr-/ adj far more than you would normally expect: an **inordinate amount** of time —**inordinately** adv

inorganic /,ɪnɔː'gænɪk◂ $ -ɔːr-/ adj not consisting of anything that is living or has lived in the past: an inorganic fertilizer

inpatient /'ɪn,peɪʃənt/ n [C] someone who stays in hospital while they receive treatment

input Ac /'ɪnpʊt/ n **1** [U] information that is put into a computer **2** [C,U] the ideas and things that you do to make something succeed: Teachers contributed most of the input into the survey. **3** [C,U] technical electrical power that is put into a machine —**input** v [T]

inquest /'ɪnkwest/ n [C] an official process to discover why someone has died

inquire, enquire /ɪn'kwaɪə $ -'kwaɪr/ v [I,T] formal to ask someone for information: 'Why are you doing that?' he inquired. | [+about] I am writing to inquire about your advertisement in 'The Times'. THESAURUS ASK

PHRASAL VERBS
inquire into sth to ask questions in order to get more information about something: The investigation inquired into the company's financial dealings.

inquiring (also **enquiring** BrE) /ɪn'kwaɪərɪŋ $ -'kwaɪr-/ adj **1** an inquiring look or expression shows that you want to ask about something **2 inquiring mind** someone who has an inquiring mind wants to learn new things: a child's inquiring mind —**inquiringly** adv

inquiry, enquiry /ɪn'kwaɪəri $ ɪn'kwaɪri, 'ɪŋkwəri/ n [C] (plural **inquiries**)
1 a question you ask in order to get information: [+about] We're getting a lot of inquiries about our new bus service. | I'll **make** some **inquiries**. THESAURUS QUESTION
2 an official process to discover why something bad happened: [+into] a government inquiry into the causes of the disaster | launch/set up/hold an inquiry The police have launched a **murder inquiry**.

inquisition /,ɪnkwə'zɪʃən/ n [C] a series of questions that someone asks in a threatening or unpleasant way

inquisitive /ɪn'kwɪzətɪv/ adj an inquisitive person or animal is very interested in everything: Cats are inquisitive animals. —**inquisitively** adv

inroads /'ɪnrəʊdz $ -roʊdz/ n **make inroads into/on** sth to start being more successful in something: The company has made inroads into the European market.

,ins and 'outs n [plural] all the details of a complicated situation or problem: [+of] the ins and outs of the matter

insane /ɪn'seɪn/ adj **1** informal very stupid: an insane idea | You're taking an insane risk. THESAURUS CRAZY **2** seriously mentally ill —**insanely** adv

insanity /ɪn'sænəti/ n [U] **1** when someone is seriously mentally ill **2** very stupid actions that may cause you serious harm

insatiable /ɪnˈseɪʃəbəl/ *adj* always wanting more of something: *his **insatiable appetite** for power* | *an **insatiable demand** for new products*

inscribe /ɪnˈskraɪb/ *v* [T] to write or cut words on something: **be inscribed in/on sth** *His name is inscribed on the trophy.* —**inscription** /-ˈskrɪpʃən/ *n* [C]

inscrutable /ɪnˈskruːtəbəl/ *adj* someone who is inscrutable shows no emotion on their face so that it is impossible to know what they are thinking

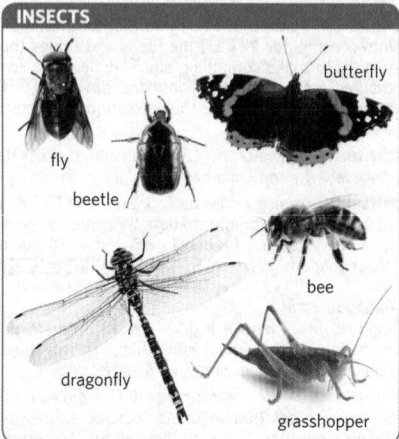

INSECTS

butterfly
fly
beetle
bee
dragonfly
grasshopper

insect /ˈɪnsekt/ *n* [C] any small creature that has six legs, for example a fly

insecticide /ɪnˈsektɪsaɪd/ *n* [U] a chemical substance for killing insects

insecure $\boxed{\text{Ac}}$ /ˌɪnsɪˈkjʊə◂ $ -ˈkjʊr◂/ *adj* **1** if you are insecure, you do not feel confident about yourself: **[+about]** *She's very insecure about her appearance.* **2** if something such as a job is insecure, it could be taken away or lost at any time —**insecurity** *n* [C,U]

insemination /ɪnˌseməˈneɪʃən/ *n* [U] *technical* the act of putting SPERM into a woman or female animal in order to make her have a baby: **artificial insemination** (=done by medical treatment, not sex)

insensitive /ɪnˈsensətɪv/ *adj* **1** someone who is insensitive does not notice other people's feelings and often does or says things that upset them: *Sometimes he can be rather insensitive.* | *an insensitive remark* **2** [not before noun] not affected by physical effects or changes —**insensitively** *adv* —**insensitivity** /ɪnˌsensəˈtɪvəti/ *n* [U]

inseparable /ɪnˈsepərəbəl/ *adj* **1** people who are inseparable are always together and are very friendly with each other: *My brother and I were inseparable.* **2** *formal* things that are inseparable cannot be considered separately: **[+from]** *Britain's economic fortunes are inseparable from the world situation.*

insert¹ $\boxed{\text{Ac}}$ /ɪnˈsɜːt $ -ɜːrt/ *v* [T] to put something inside something else: **insert sth in/into/between sth** *Insert the coins in the machine.*

insert² /ˈɪnsɜːt $ -ɜːrt/ *n* [C] **1** printed pages that

are put inside a newspaper or magazine in order to advertise something **2** something that is designed to be put inside something else: *Dave wore special inserts in his shoes to make him look taller.*

inside¹ /ɪnˈsaɪd/ *adv, prep*
1 in or into a container $\boxed{\text{OPP}}$ **outside**: *Is there anything inside the box?*
2 in or into a building or room $\boxed{\text{OPP}}$ **outside**: *The rooms inside the building have just been painted.* | *Let's go inside – it's cold.* → see picture on page A8
3 if someone is inside a group or organization, they are part of it $\boxed{\text{OPP}}$ **outside**: *The information comes from sources inside the company.*
4 in a country or area $\boxed{\text{OPP}}$ **outside**: *Little is known of events inside this mysterious country.*
5 if you have a feeling or thought inside your head, you feel or think it without telling anyone: *You just don't understand how I feel inside.* | *Joe's a strange guy – you never know what's going on inside his head.*
6 in less than a particular amount of time: *We'll be there inside an hour.*

inside² /ɪnˈsaɪd, ˈɪnsaɪd/ *n*

INSIDE OUT

1 the inside the inner part of something $\boxed{\text{OPP}}$ **the outside**: **[+of]** *The inside of the car was filthy.* | **on the inside** *The apple's rotten on the inside.*
2 sb's inside/insides *informal* someone's stomach

PHRASES
inside out with the usual outside parts on the inside: *Your jumper's inside out.*
know sth inside out *BrE*,
know sth inside and out *AmE* to know something in great detail: *She knows the business inside out.*

inside³ /ˈɪnsaɪd/ *adj* **1** on the inside of something: *the inside pages of the newspaper* | *the inside pocket of his jacket* **2 inside information/the inside story etc** information that is available only to people who are part of a group or organization: *His book tells the inside story of the terrorist group.*

insider /ɪnˈsaɪdə $ -ər/ *n* [C] someone who knows a lot about an organization because they are part of it

insidious /ɪnˈsɪdiəs/ *adj* *formal* happening gradually without being noticed, but causing a lot of harm: *the insidious effects of pollution* —**insidiously** *adv*

insight $\boxed{\text{Ac}}$ /ˈɪnsaɪt/ *n* [C,U] a clear understanding of a complicated situation, idea etc: **[+into]** *The article gives us an insight into Chinese culture.*

insignia /ɪnˈsɪɡniə/ *n* [C] (*plural* **insignia**) a BADGE or sign that shows which organization someone belongs to, or the rank they have

insignificant $\boxed{\text{Ac}}$ /ˌɪnsɪɡˈnɪfɪkənt◂/ *adj* small and unimportant: *insignificant effects* —**insignificance** *n* [U]

insincere /ˌɪnsɪnˈsɪə◂ $ -ˈsɪr◂/ adj pretending to feel or think something: an insincere smile —**insincerely** adv —**insincerity** /ˌɪnsɪnˈserəti/ n [U]

insinuate /ɪnˈsɪnjueɪt/ v [T] to suggest that something bad is true, without saying it directly: [+that] He insinuated that she had lied. —**insinuation** /ɪnˌsɪnjuˈeɪʃən/ n [C,U]

insipid /ɪnˈsɪpɪd/ adj not strong or interesting: insipid colors

insist /ɪnˈsɪst/ v [I,T]
1 to demand that something should happen: I didn't want to go but Jane insisted. | **insist on (doing) sth** He insisted on paying the bill. | [+(that)] I insisted that he leave. | I'll call her tomorrow, **if you insist**.

> **Grammar**
> Do not say 'She insisted to come with us.' Say She insisted on coming with us.

2 to say firmly and often that something is true, especially when other people do not believe you: [+(that)] He insisted he had done nothing wrong. | [+on] She always insisted on her innocence.

insistence /ɪnˈsɪstəns/ n [U] **1** when you demand that something should happen: [+on] an insistence on high standards | [+that] an insistence that safety checks should be done properly **2** when you say firmly that something is true, especially when other people think it may not be true: [+that] the government's insistence that the drug is safe

insistent /ɪnˈsɪstənt/ adj **1** saying firmly that something should happen or that something is true: his father's insistent voice | [+(that)] He was insistent that I should come. **2** continuing for a long time in a way that is difficult to ignore: an insistent ringing sound —**insistently** adv

insofar as, **in so far as** /ˌɪnsəʊˈfɑːr əz $ -soʊ-/ linking word, formal to the degree that: The report was relevant only insofar as it provided financial information.

insolent /ˈɪnsələnt/ adj formal rude and not showing any respect: an insolent stare —**insolence** n [U] —**insolently** adv

insoluble /ɪnˈsɒljəbəl $ ɪnˈsɑːl-/ adj **1** (also **insolvable** /ɪnˈsɒlvəbəl $ -ˈsɑːl-/ AmE) impossible to solve: insoluble problems **2** an insoluble substance does not DISSOLVE when you put it in liquid OPP **soluble**

insolvent /ɪnˈsɒlvənt $ ɪnˈsɑːl-/ adj formal not having enough money to pay what you owe SYN **bankrupt**

insomnia /ɪnˈsɒmniə $ ɪnˈsɑːm-/ n [U] the problem of not being able to sleep —**insomniac** [C]

inspect **Ac** /ɪnˈspekt/ v [T]
1 to examine something carefully: **inspect sth carefully/closely** She bent down to inspect the plant more closely. | **inspect sth for sth** He inspected the car for damage.
2 to visit a building or organization officially in order to make sure that everything is satisfactory and that rules are being obeyed: The building was inspected by fire officers. —**inspection** /-ˈspekʃən/ n [C,U]: An inspection was carried out at the school.

inspector **Ac** /ɪnˈspektə $ -ər/ n [C]
1 someone whose job is to check that something is satisfactory and that rules are being obeyed: school inspectors
2 a police officer of middle rank

inspiration /ˌɪnspəˈreɪʃən/ n [C,U] **1** a good idea about what you should say, do, write etc, or the person or thing which gives you this: an artist who **drew inspiration from** Monet's work | [+for] His time in Mexico provided the **inspiration** for this novel. | Libraries are a good **source of inspiration**. THESAURUS▶ **IDEA 2 be an inspiration to sb** to be so good or successful that people admire you and want to achieve something themselves: At 87, he's an inspiration to us all. —**inspirational** adj

inspire /ɪnˈspaɪə $ -ˈspaɪr/ v [T] **1** to encourage someone and make them want to do something: **inspire sb to do sth** She inspired many young people to take up the sport. **2** to make someone have a particular feeling or react in a particular way: **inspire sth in sb/inspire sb with sth** A good teacher **inspires confidence** in students. —**inspiring** adj

inspired /ɪnˈspaɪəd $ -ˈspaɪrd/ adj good and impressive: It was an inspired choice.

instability **Ac** /ˌɪnstəˈbɪləti/ n [U] when a situation or someone's behaviour is likely to change suddenly → **unstable**: political instability | mental instability

install /ɪnˈstɔːl $ -ˈstɒːl/ v [T]
1 EQUIPMENT to put a piece of equipment somewhere and connect it so that you can use it: The company has installed security cameras.
2 SOFTWARE to add new software to a computer
3 PERSON to give someone an important job or position: She was installed as Chancellor of the university. —**installation** /ˌɪnstəˈleɪʃən/ n [C,U]

instalment BrE, **installment** AmE /ɪnˈstɔːlmənt $ ɪnˈstɒːl-/ n [C] **1** a payment that you make every week, month etc in order to pay for something: We're **paying** for the car **by** monthly **instalments**. **2** one of several parts of a story that are PUBLISHED or shown at different times

instance **Ac** /ˈɪnstəns/ n [C] an example of a particular kind of situation: [+of] instances of violence | **In this instance** I think she was mistaken.
PHRASES
 for instance for example: In many countries, for instance Japan, fish is an important part of the diet.

instant¹ /ˈɪnstənt/ adj
1 happening immediately: The band became an instant success.
2 [only before noun] instant food can be prepared quickly by adding hot water: instant coffee

instant² n [singular] a moment: He paused for an instant before replying. | He disappeared **in an instant** (=immediately).

instantaneous /ˌɪnstənˈteɪniəs◂/ adj happening immediately: an instantaneous reaction —**instantaneously** adv

instantly /ˈɪnstəntli/ adv immediately: Both victims died instantly. THESAURUS▶ **IMMEDIATELY**

instant 'replay n [C] AmE an exciting moment in

a sports game that is shown again on television immediately after it happens SYN **action replay** BrE

instead /ɪnˈsted/ adv used to say that something is done, used etc when something else is not done or used: If Jane can't go, I'll go instead. | [+of] Can I have cheese instead of ham?

instigate /ˈɪnstɪɡeɪt/ v [T] formal to make something start to happen: The government instigated a programme of reforms. —**instigator** n [C] —**instigation** /ˌɪnstɪˈɡeɪʃən/ n [U]

instil BrE, **instill** AmE /ɪnˈstɪl/ v [T] (**instilled**, **instilling**) to make someone think, feel, or behave in a particular way: **instil sth into sb** Her parents had instilled a sense of duty into her.

instinct /ˈɪnstɪŋkt/ n [C,U] a natural ability or feeling that makes people or animals know something or behave in a particular way: **Instinct told** me something was wrong. | [+for] Animals have a natural instinct for survival. | **instinct to do sth** a cat's instinct to kill birds THESAURUS FEELING —**instinctive** /ɪnˈstɪŋktɪv/ adj: an instinctive reaction —**instinctively** adv

institute[1] Ac /ˈɪnstɪtjuːt $ -tuːt/ n [C] an organization that does scientific or educational work: a research institute | [+of/for] the Institute for Space Studies

institute[2] Ac v [T] formal to start a system, rule, legal process etc: New taxes have been instituted.

institution Ac /ˌɪnstɪˈtjuːʃən $ -ˈtuː-/ n [C]
1 a large important organization such as a university, church, or bank: **financial/political/educational etc institution** banks and other financial institutions THESAURUS ORGANIZATION
2 an important custom that has existed for a long time: **social institutions** such as the family and religion | [+of] the institution of marriage
3 a place where people are sent to be looked after, for example old people or children with no parents

institutional Ac /ˌɪnstɪˈtjuːʃənəl $ -ˈtuː-/ adj
1 relating to an institution: institutional care
2 institutionalized: He claims that there is institutional racism in the police force.

institutionalized Ac (also **-ised** BrE) /ˌɪnstɪˈtjuːʃənəlaɪzd $ -ˈtuː-/ adj institutionalized attitudes and behaviour have existed for so long in an organization that they seem normal even though they are bad: There is institutionalized corruption throughout the system.

instruct Ac /ɪnˈstrʌkt/ v [T] **1** to officially tell someone what to do: **instruct sb to do sth** The doctor instructed me to change my diet. THESAURUS ORDER
2 formal to teach someone something: **instruct sb in sth** Greater effort is needed to instruct children in road safety.

instruction Ac /ɪnˈstrʌkʃən/ n
1 instructions [plural] printed information that tells you how to do or use something: [+on] Are there any instructions on how to make the model? | [+for] The equipment comes with detailed instructions for use.
2 [C usually plural] an order telling you what you must do: **instructions to do sth** We were given strict instructions not to leave the building. | [+that] She left

instructions that her paintings should not be sold. THESAURUS ORDER
3 [U] formal training in a particular skill or subject: [+in] The trainees were **given instruction** in the use of computers. —**instructional** adj

COLLOCATIONS

verbs

to follow the instructions (=to do what the instructions tell you to do) I followed the instructions but the printer still didn't work.
to read the instructions Did you read the instructions on the packet?
the instructions say The instructions say it should be washed in cool water.

adjectives

clear instructions His instructions weren't very clear.
detailed instructions For detailed instructions, see our website.
full instructions (=detailed and complete) Full installation instructions are provided.
step-by-step instructions (=giving details of each thing you should do in order) This book gives step-by-step instructions on how to create a vegetable garden.

instruction + noun

an instruction book/manual/leaflet I've lost the instruction manual for my phone.

instructive Ac /ɪnˈstrʌktɪv/ adj giving useful information: an instructive experience

instructor Ac /ɪnˈstrʌktə $ -ər/ n [C] someone who teaches an activity or sport: **driving/flying/ski etc instructor** THESAURUS TEACHER

instrument /ˈɪnstrəmənt/ n [C]
1 a special tool or piece of equipment, especially one used in science or medicine: scientific instruments | navigation instruments
2 an object for producing music, such as a piano or VIOLIN: Can you play any **musical instruments**? | **wind/percussion/stringed instrument**
3 formal someone or something that is used to achieve a particular result: [+of] an instrument of social change

instrumental /ˌɪnstrəˈmentl◂/ adj **1** be **instrumental in (doing) sth** formal to be important in making something happen: He was instrumental in developing the program. **2** instrumental music is for instruments, not voices

insubordination /ˌɪnsəbɔːdəˈneɪʃən $ -ˌbɔːrdnˈeɪ-/ n [U] formal when someone refuses to obey a person in authority —**insubordinate** /ˌɪnsəˈbɔːdənət $ -ˈɔːr-/ adj

insubstantial /ˌɪnsəbˈstænʃəl◂/ adj formal not strong or large: insubstantial changes

insufferable /ɪnˈsʌfərəbəl/ adj very annoying

insufficient Ac /ˌɪnsəˈfɪʃənt◂/ adj not enough: [+for] Her salary was insufficient for their needs. | **insufficient to do sth** The heating was insufficient to kill the bacteria. —**insufficiently** adv —**insufficiency** n [singular, U]

insular /'ɪnsjələ $ 'ɪnsələr, 'ɪnfə-/ adj disapproving not interested in other groups, countries, ways of life etc —**insularity** /ˌɪnsjə'lærəti $ -sə-, -fə-/ n [U]

insulate /'ɪnsjəleɪt $ 'ɪnsə-, 'ɪnfə-/ v [T] to cover something with a material that stops electricity, sound, heat etc from getting in or out: Insulate the pipes so they don't freeze. —**insulation** /ˌɪnsjə'leɪʃən $ ˌɪnsə-/ n [U]

insulin /'ɪnsjəlɪn $ 'ɪnsə-/ n [U] a substance that controls the level of sugar in your blood

insult¹ /'ɪnsʌlt/ n [C] a remark or action that is offensive or shows a lack of respect: He started **shouting insults** at her. | [+to] The plan is an insult to teachers.

insult² /ɪn'sʌlt/ v [T] to say or do something that offends someone: You should apologize for insulting her. | John would be insulted if we didn't go. —**insulting** adj: comments that are insulting to women

> **Word Choice: insult or offend?**
> If you **insult** someone, you say or do something very rude to them that shows a lack of respect: The man started insulting me and my family. | They claim that the advertisement insults women.
> If you **offend** someone, you make them feel annoyed or upset by saying something that they think is unkind or shows a lack of respect: I hope I haven't offended you. | Religious groups were offended by the film.

insuperable /ɪn'sjuːpərəbəl◂ $ ɪn'suː-/ adj formal an insuperable difficulty or problem is impossible to solve

insurance /ɪn'ʃʊərəns $ -'ʃʊr-/ n [U] an arrangement in which you pay a company money and they pay the costs if you become ill, have an accident etc: an **insurance policy** | **insurance companies** | [+against] He **took out insurance** against unemployment. | **health/car/travel etc insurance** → LIFE INSURANCE

insure /ɪn'ʃʊə $ -'ʃʊr/ v **1** [I,T] to buy or provide insurance for someone or something: Are the paintings insured? | **insure (sb/sth) against/for sth** Make sure you're insured against flood damage. **2** an American spelling of ENSURE

insurmountable /ˌɪnsə'maʊntəbəl◂ $ -sər-/ adj formal an insurmountable difficulty or problem is impossible to solve

insurrection /ˌɪnsə'rekʃən/ n [C,U] formal a violent attempt by a group of people to take control of their country

intact /ɪn'tækt/ adj [not before noun] not broken or damaged: Fortunately, the glass **remained intact**.

intake /'ɪnteɪk/ n **1** [singular, U] the amount of food, drink etc that you take into your body: [+of] Try to reduce your intake of fat. | **food/alcohol/calorie etc intake 2** [C,U] the number of people who join a school, profession etc at a particular time: [+of] a yearly intake of 300 students

PHRASES
intake of breath when you suddenly breathe in, especially when you are shocked: He gave a sharp intake of breath.

intangible /ɪn'tændʒəbəl/ adj an intangible quality or feeling is difficult to describe exactly

integral Ac /'ɪntəgrəl/ adj forming part of something, especially a very important part: Training is an **integral part of** any team's preparation. | [+to] Music is integral to the island's culture. —**integrally** adv

integrate Ac /'ɪntɪgreɪt/ v **1** [T] to combine things in a way that makes something more effective: **integrate sth with/into sth** Pictures are integrated into the text. **2** [I,T] to become part of a group or society, or to help someone do this: **integrate (sb) with/into sth** Students with learning difficulties can be integrated into ordinary schools. —**integrated** adj —**integration** /ˌɪntɪ'greɪʃən/ n [U]

integrity Ac /ɪn'tegrəti/ n [U] the quality of being honest and having high moral standards: a man **of great** professional **integrity**

intellect /'ɪntəlekt/ n [C,U] the ability to understand things and think intelligently: human intellect

intellectual /ˌɪntə'lektʃuəl◂/ adj **1** relating to the ability to understand things and think intelligently: children's intellectual development **2** well-educated and interested in serious subjects and ideas —**intellectual** n [C] —**intellectually** adv

intelligence Ac /ɪn'telədʒəns/ n [U]
1 the ability to learn and understand things: You need a reasonable level of intelligence to be good at the game. | **low/high intelligence** a man of low intelligence
2 information about the secret activities of criminals or foreign governments: the British **intelligence services** | intelligence gathering → ARTIFICIAL INTELLIGENCE

intelligent Ac /ɪn'telədʒnət/ adj
1 having a high level of mental ability and good at learning and understanding ideas: **highly intelligent** students
2 an intelligent comment, question etc shows that you have thought about something carefully and understand it well: The students asked a lot of intelligent questions. —**intelligently** adv

> **THESAURUS**
> **intelligent** having a high level of mental ability and good at learning and understanding ideas: Some dogs are quite intelligent. | You have to be very intelligent to be a doctor.
> **clever** especially BrE, **smart** especially AmE able to think and learn quickly and find ways to solve problems: You're so clever! How did you think of that? | A smart lawyer spotted a mistake in the police evidence.
> **bright** intelligent – used especially about children and young people: She's a bright kid.
> **brilliant** extremely intelligent and good at the work you do: a brilliant scientist
> **gifted** a gifted child is much more intelligent than most children of the same age: a special school for gifted children

wise able to make good decisions and give sensible advice, especially because you have a lot of experience of life: *a wise old man*
cunning good at getting what you want, often by making secret plans or tricking people: *He was a cunning politician who knew how to use the situation to his advantage.*

intelligible /ɪnˈtelədʒəbəl/ *adj* clear enough to understand: **[+to]** *The instructions should be intelligible to users.* —**intelligibly** *adv*

intend /ɪnˈtend/ *v* [T]
1 to have something in your mind as a plan or purpose: *The work took much longer than we intended.* | **intend to do sth** *I intend to move house next year.* | **intend doing sth** *I intended staying two nights.* | **intend sth as sth** *It was intended as a joke.*
2 be intended for sb/sth to be provided or designed for a particular person or purpose: *a book intended for children aged 5–7*

THESAURUS

intend to do sth to have decided that you want to do something in the future: *Please let us know if you intend to accept our offer.*
be going to do sth to intend to do something, especially something you have already arranged: *She's going to start art classes next week.*
mean to do sth *especially spoken* to intend to do something – used especially when you forgot to do something, or you did not have a chance to do it: *I didn't mean to hurt your feelings.* | *I've been meaning to talk to you about it.*
be thinking of doing sth to have an idea in your mind that you are considering doing, although you have not decided yet: *We're thinking of going to Thailand in the summer.*
set out to do sth to decide to do something and make plans to achieve it, in a very determined way: *He set out to win the championship.*

intense Ac /ɪnˈtens/ *adj* **1** extreme or very great: *Students are under intense pressure to succeed.* | *the intense heat of the desert* **2** *disapproving* someone who is intense is serious and has very strong feelings —**intensely** *adv* —**intensity** *n* [U]

intensify Ac /ɪnˈtensɪfaɪ/ *v* [I,T] (**intensified, intensifying, intensifies**) to increase in degree or strength, or to make something do this: *The campaign has intensified.* —**intensification** /ɪnˌtensɪfɪˈkeɪʃən/ *n* [U]

intensive Ac /ɪnˈtensɪv/ *adj* involving a lot of work or effort in a short time: *an intensive language course* —**intensively** *adv*

inˌtensive ˈcare *n* [U] a hospital department for people who are very seriously ill or injured: *She died in intensive care.*

intent¹ /ɪnˈtent/ *adj* **1 be intent on (doing) sth** to be determined to do something: *She was intent on winning.* **2** giving careful attention to something: *an intent look*

intent² *n* [C,U] *formal or law* an intention: *the offence of possessing a firearm with intent to endanger life*
PHRASES
to/for all intents and purposes not exactly but in all the most important ways: *To all intents and purposes, a baby is helpless.*

intention /ɪnˈtenʃən/ *n* [C,U] something you plan to do: **have no/every intention of doing sth** *I have no intention of getting married.* | *She went to the US with the intention of getting a job.* | **intention to do sth** *He announced his intention to resign.*

intentional /ɪnˈtenʃənəl/ *adj* done deliberately SYN **deliberate**: *I'm sorry I upset you – it wasn't intentional.* —**intentionally** *adv*

inter- /ɪntə $ -tər/ *prefix* between or involving two or more things or people: *intermarriage* (=marriage between people of different races, religions etc)

interact Ac /ˌɪntərˈækt/ *v* [I] **1** if things interact, they have an effect on each other: **[+with]** *drugs that interact with each other* **2** to talk to people and do things with them: **[+with]** *the limited time teachers have to interact with each child* —**interaction** /-ˈækʃən/ *n* [C,U]

interactive Ac /ˌɪntərˈæktɪv/ *adj* **1** involving communication between a computer, television etc and the person using it: *interactive software* **2** involving talking to people and working together —**interactively** *adv*

intercept /ˌɪntəˈsept $ -ər-/ *v* [T] to stop someone or something that is going from one place to another: *Police intercepted his letters.* —**interception** /-ˈsepʃən/ *n* [C,U]

interchangeable /ˌɪntəˈtʃeɪndʒəbəl $ -tər-/ *adj* things that are interchangeable can be used instead of each other: *interchangeable camera lenses* —**interchangeably** *adv*

intercom /ˈɪntəkɒm $ ˈɪntərkɑːm/ *n* [C] a system used for speaking to people in different parts of a building, aircraft etc

interconnect /ˌɪntəkəˈnekt $ -tər-/ *v* [I,T] if two things are interconnected, or if they interconnect, they are related and one is affected or caused by the other: *a number of separate but interconnected issues*

intercontinental /ˌɪntəkɒntɪˈnentl $ -tərkɑːn-/ *adj* going between or involving CONTINENTS: *an intercontinental flight*

intercourse /ˈɪntəkɔːs $ ˈɪntərkɔːrs/ *n* [U] *formal* when two people have sex

interdependent /ˌɪntədɪˈpendənt◂ $ -tər-/ *adj* interdependent people or things depend on each other —**interdependence** *n* [U]

interest¹ /ˈɪntrɪst/ *n*
1 [singular, U] the feeling that you want to know more about something or someone: **[+in]** *We both have an interest in music.* | *He began to take an interest in politics.* | *She's never shown any interest in me.* | *After a while, I lost interest.*
2 [C] something you enjoy doing: *His main interests are reading and golf.*

3 [U] money charged or paid by a bank when you borrow or save money: **[+on]** *You pay 9% interest on the loan.* | *an interest-free* (=with no interest) *loan*
4 [U] the quality of being interesting: *museums, parks, and other places of interest* | *a book that will be of interest to parents*
5 [C,U] someone's success, happiness etc, which may be helped or harmed: *a policy designed to protect the interests of farmers* | *be in sb's (best) interest(s)* (=be the best thing for someone) *It's in your interests to provide the information.* | *changes that are in the public interest* (=will help the public) → SELF-INTEREST, VESTED INTEREST

PHRASES

in the interest(s) of justice/safety/efficiency etc in order to make something fair, safe etc: *The race was cancelled in the interests of safety.*

interest² v [T] to make someone want to know more about something: *Here's a book that might interest you.* | *What interests me is the history of the place.*

PHRASES

can/could I interest you in sth? *spoken* used as a polite way of persuading someone to try or buy something: *Can I interest you in a cake?*

interested /ˈɪntrɪstɪd/ *adj*
1 [not before noun] if you are interested in something, you want to know more about it and you give it your attention OPP **uninterested, bored: [+in]** *She's very interested in computers.* | *be interested to hear/know/learn etc* *I'd be interested to know what you think about it.*
2 [not before noun] wanting to do or have something: *be interested in doing sth* *Would you be interested in coming to London with me?* THESAURUS WANT
3 interested parties/groups the people or groups who will be affected by something OPP **disinterested**: *All interested parties are invited to attend the meeting.*

THESAURUS

interested if you are interested in something, you want to know more about it and you give it your attention: *I was interested in what he had to say.*
fascinated very interested by something you see, read, or hear about: *Many people are fascinated by ancient Egypt.*
be into sth *informal* used when talking about the things you are interested in and enjoy: *He's into Japanese films at the moment.*
gripped/riveted very interested in a story, film, event etc, so that you cannot stop reading, watching, listening etc: *It's a great book – I was gripped from the very first page.*
absorbed very interested in something you are doing, especially so that you do not notice anything else: *She was so absorbed in her work that she didn't hear the phone ringing.*
be obsessed with sth to be too interested in something, so that you cannot stop thinking about it, often in an unhealthy way: *Some young girls are obsessed with losing weight.*

Word Choice: not interested, uninterested, or disinterested?
The opposite of **interested** is **not interested**: *The boys aren't interested in football at all.*
You use **uninterested** especially when someone does not think that something is important: *She seems uninterested in becoming famous.* | *The government is uninterested in ordinary people's problems.*
You use **disinterested** about someone who is able to judge a situation fairly, because they will not get an advantage from it, or they do not support one particular person, group etc: *The researcher should be a disinterested observer.* | *disinterested advice*

interesting /ˈɪntrəstɪŋ/ *adj* if something is interesting, it keeps your attention because it is unusual or exciting, or it contains information that you did not know about: *I found the talk very interesting.* | *It's interesting to compare them.* | *It's interesting that she married someone similar to her father.* | *He's an interesting character.* —**interestingly** *adv*

THESAURUS

interesting if something is interesting, it keeps your attention because it is unusual or exciting, or it contains information that you did not know about: *I saw an interesting programme about Japan.*
fascinating extremely interesting: *Istanbul is a fascinating city.*
gripping/riveting used about a very interesting and exciting story, film etc that you do not want to stop reading or watching: *This gripping movie will keep you on the edge of your seat.*
absorbing interesting and enjoyable to do, read etc in a way that keeps your attention completely: *The book is an absorbing account of the singer's life.*
intriguing interesting because it is different from what you expected, or you are not sure what it means: *It sounded like an intriguing idea.*
I couldn't put it down *spoken* you say this when a book was so interesting that you could not stop reading it: *It's a great book – I couldn't put it down.*

'interest ,rate *n* [C] the PERCENTAGE (=3%, 4% etc) charged by a bank when you borrow money, or paid to you when you have money in an account there

interface /ˈɪntəfeɪs $ -ər-/ *n* [C] the way in which you see the information from a computer program on the screen, or how you type information into the program

interfere /ˌɪntəˈfɪə $ -tərˈfɪr/ *v* [I] to try to become involved in a situation when people do not want you to: **[+in]** *I wish he'd stop interfering in my life.*

PHRASAL VERBS

interfere with sth to prevent something from continuing or developing successfully: *Don't let sports interfere with your schoolwork.*

interference /ˌɪntəˈfɪərəns $ -tərˈfɪr-/ *n* [U] **1** when someone interferes in something: **[+in]** *I resented his interference in my work.* **2** unwanted noise on the radio, telephone etc, or faults in a television picture

interim[1] /'ɪntərɪm/ *adj* temporary until something or someone final can be made or found: *an interim report*

interim[2] *n* **in the interim** in the period of time between two events

interior /ɪn'tɪəriə $ -'tɪriər/ *n* [C] the inside part of something OPP **exterior**: *a car with a spacious interior* —**interior** *adj*

in,terior de'sign *n* [U] the job of choosing colours, materials, furniture etc for the inside of people's houses —**interior designer** *n* [C]

interject /ˌɪntə'dʒekt $ -ər-/ *v* [I,T] *formal* to interrupt someone with a remark: *'I don't agree,' Kim interjected.*

interjection /ˌɪntə'dʒekʃən $ -ər-/ *n* [C] in grammar, a word or phrase used to express surprise, shock, pain etc

interlude /'ɪntəluːd $ -ər-/ *n* [C] a period of time between events or situations: *a brief interlude*

intermarriage /ˌɪntə'mærɪdʒ $ -ər-/ *n* [U] marriage between people of different races, religions etc —**intermarry** *v* [I]

intermediary /ˌɪntə'miːdiəri $ ˌɪntər'miːdieri/ *n* [C] (*plural* **intermediaries**) someone who tries to help two people or groups to agree with each other

intermediate Ac /ˌɪntə'miːdiət◂ $ -ər-/ *adj* **1** between the basic and advanced levels in a subject: *an intermediate English class* **2** between two stages, levels, places etc

interminable /ɪn'tɜːmənəbəl $ -ɜːr-/ *adj* long and boring: *interminable speeches* THESAURUS **LONG** —**interminably** *adv*

intermission /ˌɪntə'mɪʃən $ -tər-/ *n* [C] *especially AmE* a short period between the parts of a play, concert etc SYN **interval** *BrE*

intermittent /ˌɪntə'mɪtənt◂ $ -tər-/ *adj* happening sometimes but not continuously: *intermittent rain* —**intermittently** *adv*

intern[1] /ɪn'tɜːn $ -ɜːrn/ *v* [T] to put someone in prison for political reasons —**internment** *n* [C,U]

intern[2] /'ɪntɜːn $ -ɜːrn/ *n* [C] *AmE* **1** someone who has almost finished training as a doctor and is working in a hospital SYN **houseman** *BrE* **2** a student who does a job for a short time to get experience

internal Ac /ɪn'tɜːnl $ -ɜːr-/ *adj* inside something such as your body or a country OPP **external**: *internal bleeding* | *internal flights* —**internally** *adv*

international /ˌɪntə'næʃənəl $ -tər-/ *adj* relating to or involving more than one country → **national**: *international trade* —**internationally** *adv*
PHRASES
the international community the powerful countries of the world and their government leaders: *The international community is becoming increasingly worried about the possibility of war breaking out.*

Internet, internet /'ɪntənet $ -tər-/ *n* **the Internet** a system that allows people using computers around the world to exchange information → **the Net, the Web**: **on the Internet** *I bought it on the internet.* | *She's always on the Internet* (=using the Internet).

Grammar
Do not say 'You can get the information by the Internet.' Say *You can get the information on the Internet.*

COLLOCATIONS
verbs

to use the Internet *You can use the Internet to look for jobs.*
to go on the Internet *I went on the Internet to find out more about him.*
to surf the Internet (=to look at different websites) *She spends hours surfing the Internet every evening.*
to buy/book sth on the Internet *He bought the chairs on the Internet.*

Internet + noun

an Internet user *Internet users need to be aware of a few safety issues.*
Internet access *Do you have Internet access at home?*
an Internet connection *Our classroom is equipped with a high-speed Internet connection.*
an Internet service provider (=a company that allows you to connect to the Internet) *If you have trouble connecting, call your Internet service provider.*
Internet shopping/banking *Internet banking saves customers a lot of time.*

interpersonal /ˌɪntə'pɜːsənəl◂ $ -tər'pɜːr-/ *adj* involving relationships between people

interplay /'ɪntəpleɪ $ -ər-/ *n* [U] the way that people or things affect each other: **[+of]** *the interplay of mental and physical factors*

interpret Ac /ɪn'tɜːprɪt $ -ɜːr-/ *v* **1** [T] to explain or decide what something means: **interpret sth as sth** *His silence was interpreted as guilt.* **2** [I,T] to translate spoken words into another language

Word Choice: interpret or translate?
Interpret means to translate what someone is saying immediately, so that people who speak different languages can talk to each other: *She can't speak English, so her daughter has to interpret for her.*
You use **translate** about changing both spoken and written language into another language: *The book has been translated into over 60 languages.* | *Can you translate what he just said?*

interpretation Ac /ɪn,tɜːprɪ'teɪʃən $ -ɜːr-/ *n* [C,U] **1** a way of explaining or understanding something: **[+of]** *a different interpretation of events* **2** the way someone performs a play, piece of music etc

interpreter /ɪnˈtɜːprɪtə $ -ˈtɜːrprɪtər/ n [C] someone who translates spoken words into another language

interrelated /ˌɪntərɪˈleɪtɪd◂/ adj things that are interrelated are related and affect each other

interrogate /ɪnˈterəɡeɪt/ v [T] to ask someone a lot of questions, often in a threatening way **THESAURUS** ASK —**interrogator** n [C] —**interrogation** /ɪnˌterəˈɡeɪʃən/ n [C,U]

interrogative /ˌɪntəˈrɒɡətɪv◂ $ -ˈrɑː-/ n [C] in grammar, a word or sentence that is used to ask a question —**interrogative** adj

interrupt /ˌɪntəˈrʌpt/ v
1 [I,T] to stop someone while they are speaking or doing something by suddenly speaking to them, making a noise etc: Sorry to interrupt, but I need some help. | He was interrupted by the telephone.
2 [T] to stop something happening for a short time: His career was interrupted by the war. —**interruption** /-ˈrʌpʃən/ n [C,U]

intersect /ˌɪntəˈsekt $ -ər-/ v [I,T] if two roads, lines etc intersect, they meet or cross each other

INTERSECTION

intersection

T-junction BrE

intersection /ˌɪntəˈsekʃən, ˈɪntəsekʃən $ -tər-/ n [C] a place where two roads, lines etc meet or cross each other

interspersed /ˌɪntəˈspɜːst $ -tərˈspɜːrst/ adj be interspersed with sth if something is interspersed with something else, there is sometimes one thing and sometimes the other: sunny periods interspersed with showers

interstate¹ /ˈɪntəsteɪt $ -tər-/ n [C] AmE a wide road that goes between states, on which cars can travel very fast

interstate² adj [only before noun] involving different states, especially in the US: interstate commerce

intertwined /ˌɪntəˈtwaɪnd $ -tər-/ adj twisted together or closely related

interval Ac /ˈɪntəvəl $ -tər-/ n [C] **1** a period of time between two events or activities: [+between] the interval between arrival and departure **2** BrE a

short period between the parts of a play, concert etc SYN **intermission** AmE
PHRASES
at ... intervals 1 used to say how often something happens: Payments are made **at regular intervals**. | **at weekly/monthly etc intervals** inspections at monthly intervals **2** used to talk about the distance between objects: **at regular/3m/5m etc intervals** trees planted at regular intervals

intervene Ac /ˌɪntəˈviːn $ -tər-/ v [I] **1** to do something to try to influence or stop an argument, problem, war etc: [+in] He didn't want to intervene in the debate. **2** to happen between two events, especially in a way that interrupts or prevents something: They had planned to marry, but the war intervened. —**intervention** /-ˈvenʃən/ n [C,U]

intervening Ac /ˌɪntəˈviːnɪŋ $ -tər-/ adj **the intervening years/months/decades etc** the time between two events: Not much has changed in the intervening years.

interview¹ /ˈɪntəvjuː $ -ər-/ n [C]
1 a meeting in which someone asks you questions, especially to find out if you are suitable for a job: [+for] She had an interview for a teaching job.
2 an occasion when someone famous is asked questions: [+with] an exclusive interview with the President | He refused to **give** any **interviews** (=he refused to answer any questions).

COLLOCATIONS

verbs
to have an interview He had a job interview on Monday.
to get an interview I applied for the job but I didn't even get an interview.
to go for an interview (also **to attend an interview** formal) She went for an interview at a publishing company.

noun + interview
a job interview Do you know how to dress when going for a job interview?

interview² v [T] to ask someone questions in an interview: Police have named four suspects they want to interview. | **interview sb for sth** He was interviewed for the manager's job.

interviewee /ˌɪntəvjuːˈiː $ -tər-/ n [C] the person who answers the questions in an interview

interviewer /ˈɪntəvjuːə $ -tərvjuːər/ n [C] the person who asks the questions in an interview

intestine /ɪnˈtestɪn/ n [C] the tube in your body that carries food from your stomach → see picture on page A2 —**intestinal** adj

intimate¹ /ˈɪntəmət/ adj **1** having a very close relationship: They became intimate friends. **2** very private or personal: an interview revealing **intimate details** of his life **3** private and friendly in a way that makes you feel comfortable: a hotel with an intimate atmosphere **4** intimate knowledge/understanding of sth a knowledge or understanding of all the details of something: She has an intimate knowledge of the business. —**intimately** adv —**intimacy** n [U]

intimate² /ˈɪntɪmeɪt/ v [T] *formal* to make someone understand what you mean without saying it directly: **[+that]** *The President has strongly intimated that he will not sign the treaty.* —**intimation** /ˌɪntəˈmeɪʃən/ n [C,U]

intimidate /ɪnˈtɪmədeɪt/ v [T] to frighten someone or make them feel nervous: *She refused to let him intimidate her.* **THESAURUS ▶ THREATEN** —**intimidating** *adj*: *I found the interview quite intimidating.* —**intimidated** *adj*: *She felt intimidated by the crowd.* —**intimidation** /ɪnˌtɪməˈdeɪʃən/ n [U]

into /ˈɪntə; before vowels ˈɪntu; strong ˈɪntuː/ *prep*
1 towards the inside of a place or container: *He went back into the house.* | *Lucy got into bed.* → see picture on page A8
2 involved in a situation or activity: *He was always getting into trouble.* | *I'd like to go into teaching.*
3 making a shape: *She made the clay into a ball.* | *Cut the cake into pieces.*
4 moving towards something and hitting it: *The car ran into a wall.*
5 trying to find out information about something: *They are doing research into the causes of depression.*
PHRASES
be into sth *informal* to be interested in something: *Dave's really into music.* **THESAURUS ▶ LIKE**

intolerable /ɪnˈtɒlərəbəl $ -ˈtɑː-/ *adj* extremely bad, annoying, or painful: *The situation has become intolerable.* | *The exams will put intolerable pressure on students.*

intolerant /ɪnˈtɒlərənt $ -ˈtɑː-/ *adj* not willing to accept people who have different opinions or ways of behaving: **[+of]** *He's very intolerant of other people.* —**intolerance** n [U]

intonation /ˌɪntəˈneɪʃən/ n [C,U] the way in which the level of your voice changes as you speak

intoxicated /ɪnˈtɒksɪkeɪtɪd $ -ˈtɑːk-/ *adj formal*
1 drunk **2** very happy or excited: **[+by/with]** *He was intoxicated by his own success.* —**intoxicating** *adj*

intractable /ɪnˈtræktəbəl/ *adj formal* very difficult to control or solve: *an intractable problem*

intranet /ˈɪntrənet/ n [C] a computer system for sending or looking at information within a company → **Internet**

intransigent /ɪnˈtrænsədʒənt/ *adj formal* not willing to change your opinions or behaviour —**intransigence** n [U]

intransitive /ɪnˈtrænsətɪv/ *adj* in grammar, an intransitive verb does not have an object. In the sentence 'She cried', 'cry' is intransitive. → **transitive**

intravenous /ˌɪntrəˈviːnəs◂/ *adj* put into your VEINS: *an intravenous drug* —**intravenously** *adv*

intray /ˈɪntreɪ/ n [C] a container on your desk, containing work that you have to do

intrepid /ɪnˈtrepɪd/ *adj* willing to do dangerous things or go to dangerous places: *intrepid explorers*

intricate /ˈɪntrɪkət/ *adj* involving a lot of small parts or details: *an intricate pattern* —**intricacy** n [C,U] —**intricately** *adv*

intrigue¹ /ɪnˈtriːg/ v [T] if something intrigues you, it interests you a lot because it is unusual or mysterious: *He was intrigued by the woman next to him.*

intrigue² /ˈɪntriːg/ n [C,U] secret plans to harm or deceive someone: *political intrigue*

intriguing /ɪnˈtriːgɪŋ/ *adj* something that is intriguing is interesting because it is unusual or mysterious: *an intriguing story*

intrinsic Ac /ɪnˈtrɪnsɪk, -zɪk/ *adj* part of the nature or character of something: *Steel is a useful material because of its intrinsic strength.* —**intrinsically** /-kli/ *adv*

intro /ˈɪntrəʊ $ -troʊ/ n [C] (*plural* **intros**) *informal* a short part at the beginning of a song, piece of writing etc SYN **introduction**

introduce /ˌɪntrəˈdjuːs $ -ˈduːs/ v [T]
1 to bring a system, plan, or product into use for the first time: *The store has introduced a new range of food.* | *A no-smoking policy was introduced last year.*
2 to bring something such as an animal or plant to a place for the first time: **introduce sth into sth** *The animal was introduced into Britain from Canada.*
3 if you introduce people who are meeting for the first time, you tell them each other's names: **introduce sb to sb** *Alice, let me introduce you to Jane.* | **introduce yourself** (=formally tell someone who you are) *Please allow me to introduce myself.*
4 introduce sb to sth to tell someone about something or give them an opportunity to try it for the first time: *Mary introduced us to Thai food.*
5 to announce who is going to speak or perform on a television or radio programme or at an event: *Jim Yeo will introduce the show.*

introduction /ˌɪntrəˈdʌkʃən/ n
1 [U] when people start using something for the first time: **[+of]** *the recent introduction of new laws*
2 [U] when people bring something to a place for the first time: **[+of]** *the introduction of plants such as the tomato from South America* | *the introduction of Buddhism to China*
3 [C] when you tell someone another person's name when they meet for the first time: *When everyone had arrived, she **made the introductions**.*
4 [C] a short explanation at the beginning of a book or speech: *In the introduction, she explains why she wrote the book.*
5 [C] something that explains the basic facts of something: **[+to]** *The book is a useful introduction to French history.*
6 [singular] your first experience of something: **[+to]** *My introduction to watersports came when we moved to Italy.*

introductory /ˌɪntrəˈdʌktəri◂/ *adj* [only before noun] **1** said or written at the beginning of a book or speech in order to explain what it is about: *a short introductory paragraph* **2** intended for people who have never done something before: *an **introductory course** in French* **3 introductory price/offer** a special low price that is intended to encourage people to buy a new product: *The product will be available at an introductory price of $75.*

introspective /ˌɪntrəˈspektɪv◂/ *adj* thinking a lot about your own thoughts and feelings

introvert /ˈɪntrəvɜːt $ -ɜːrt/ n [C] someone who is quiet and shy, and does not enjoy being with other people OPP **extrovert** —**introverted** adj

intrude /ɪnˈtruːd/ v [I] to go into a place or become involved in a situation where you are not wanted: **[+on/upon/into]** I'm sorry to intrude on your meal, but I need to talk to you. —**intrusion** /-ˈtruːʒən/ n [C,U] —**intrusive** /-sɪv/ adj

intruder /ɪnˈtruːdə $ -ər/ n [C] someone who goes into a place where they should not be, especially in order to steal something

intuition /ˌɪntjuˈɪʃən $ -tu-, -tju-/ n [C,U] the feeling that you know something is correct or true, although you do not know why: Trust your intuition.

intuitive /ɪnˈtjuːətɪv $ -ˈtuː-, -ˈtjuː-/ adj based on feelings rather than facts: an intuitive judgment —**intuitively** adv

Inuit /ˈɪnjuɪt, ˈɪnuɪt $ ˈɪnuɪt/ n the Inuit a group of people who live in the very cold northern areas of North America —**Inuit** adj

inundate /ˈɪnəndeɪt/ v be inundated (with/by sth) to receive so much of something that you cannot easily deal with it all: We were inundated with offers of help.

invade /ɪnˈveɪd/ v
1 [I,T] to enter a place with an army, in order to take control of it: The Romans invaded Britain.
2 [T] to go into a place in large numbers, especially when you are not wanted: Every summer the town is invaded by tourists. —**invader** n [C]

invalid¹ /ɪnˈvælɪd/ adj **1** not acceptable because of a law or rule: The contract was invalid. **2** not based on true facts or good judgment: an invalid argument **3** not recognized or accepted by a computer: an invalid password —**invalidity** /ˌɪnvəˈlɪdəti/ n [U]

invalid² /ˈɪnvəliːd, -lɪd $ -lɪd/ n [C] someone who is ill and needs to be looked after

invalidate Ac /ɪnˈvælɪdeɪt/ v [T] formal **1** to make a document, claim etc no longer officially acceptable: Failure to follow the instructions will invalidate the guarantee. **2** to show that something such as a belief or explanation is wrong

invaluable /ɪnˈvæljuəbəl, -jəbəl $ -ˈvæljəbəl/ adj extremely useful: invaluable help | **[+for/to]** a service that's invaluable for elderly people

invariably Ac /ɪnˈveəriəbli $ -ˈver-/ adv always: Visitors to the school invariably comment on its relaxed atmosphere. —**invariable** adj

invasion /ɪnˈveɪʒən/ n [C,U] when the army of one country enters another country, in order to take control of it: **[+of]** the invasion of Normandy
PHRASES
invasion of privacy a situation in which someone tries to find out things about you or watches you, when you do not want this

invent /ɪnˈvent/ v [T]
1 to think of an idea for a new product, machine etc, and design it or make it: Alexander Bell invented the telephone.
2 to think of an idea or story that is not true, usually

in order to deceive someone: You'll have to invent a better excuse!

THESAURUS

invent to think of an idea for a new product, machine etc, and design it or make it: He invented the light bulb.
discover to find a new substance, fact, way of doing something etc that no one has ever found or thought of before: Scientists may have discovered a cure for the disease. | Pierre and Marie Curie discovered radium.
create to make something completely new using your imagination, for example a new design or character: Mickey Mouse was created by Walt Disney. | He created a whole new range of simple recipes.
think of sth/come up with sth to produce a new idea, name, method etc by thinking carefully about it: Together they came up with the idea for the business. | See if you can think of a better name for the book.
make sth up to invent a story, song, game etc: Mum used to make up stories for us at bedtime.

---

invention /ɪnˈvenʃən/ n
1 [C] a machine, tool, system etc that someone has invented: The computer was one of the most important inventions of the twentieth century.
2 [U] when someone invents something: **[+of]** the invention of television
3 [C,U] a story or explanation that is not true: The story is just a media invention.

inventive /ɪnˈventɪv/ adj using new and interesting ideas: an inventive writer | inventive solutions to problems

inventor /ɪnˈventə $ -ər/ n [C] someone who has invented something: the inventor of the bicycle

inventory /ˈɪnvəntri $ -tɔːri/ n [C] (plural **inventories**) a list of all the things in a place: **[+of]** They made an **inventory** of the museum.

invert /ɪnˈvɜːt $ -ɜːrt/ v [T] formal to put something in the opposite position to the one it was in before, especially by turning it upside down —**inversion** /-ˈvɜːʃən $ -ˈvɜːrʒən/ n [C,U]

in,verted 'commas n [plural] BrE QUOTATION MARKS

invest Ac /ɪnˈvest/ v
1 [I,T] to buy shares, goods, or property because you hope you can make a profit: **invest (sth) in sth** He made a lot of money investing in property. | She invested all her money in shares.
2 [I,T] to spend money on something in order to improve it or make it succeed: **invest (sth) in sth** The government needs to invest more in our schools. | The company invested £10 million in the project.
3 [T] to use a lot of time, effort, or money to make something succeed: **invest sth in sth** She invested all her energy in her job. —**investor** n [C]
PHRASAL VERBS
invest in sth to buy something because it will be useful: I've invested in a new computer.

investigate Ac /ɪnˈvestɪgeɪt/ v [I,T] to try to find

out about something, especially a crime or accident: *The cause of the fire is being investigated.* —**investigator** *n* [C] —**investigative** /-gətɪv $ -geɪtɪv/ *adj*: *an investigative journalist*

investigation Ac /ɪnˌvestɪˈgeɪʃən/ *n* [C,U] an official attempt to find out about something, especially a crime or accident: *a murder investigation* | **[+into]** *Police have **launched** an **investigation** into the tragedy.* | **under investigation** (=being investigated) *The case is still under investigation.*

investment Ac /ɪnˈvestmənt/ *n* **1** [C,U] the use of money to make a profit or make a business successful, or the money that is used: *a £50,000 investment* | **[+in]** *We have **made** a big **investment** in technology.* **2** [C] something that you buy because it will be useful: *A comfortable bed is a **good investment**.*

inveterate /ɪnˈvetərət/ *adj* [only before noun] doing something a lot, and not likely to stop doing it: *He's an inveterate traveller.*

invigilate /ɪnˈvɪdʒəleɪt/ *v* [I,T] *BrE* to watch people who are taking an examination and make sure that they do not cheat —**invigilator** *n* [C]

invigorating /ɪnˈvɪgəreɪtɪŋ/ *adj* making you feel more active and healthy: *an invigorating swim* —**invigorate** *v* [T]

invincible /ɪnˈvɪnsəbəl/ *adj* too strong to be defeated or destroyed

invisible Ac /ɪnˈvɪzəbəl/ *adj* impossible to see: **[+to]** *a plane that's invisible to enemy radar* —**invisibility** /ɪnˌvɪzəˈbɪləti/ *n* [U]

invitation /ˌɪnvɪˈteɪʃən/ *n*
1 [C,U] a written or spoken request that invites someone to do something: **[+to]** *I've had an invitation to John's party.* | **invitation to do sth** *He accepted an invitation to speak at the conference.* | **at the invitation of sb** *He visited the country at the invitation of the President.* | **by invitation** *Entry is by invitation only* (=only people who have been invited can go). **2** [singular] a situation that encourages something else to happen, especially something unpleasant: **[+to]** *An unlocked door is an **open invitation** to thieves.*

COLLOCATIONS
verbs
to get an invitation (*also* **to receive an invitation** *formal*) *She didn't get an invitation to the wedding.*
to have an invitation *I had an invitation to drinks at my boss's house.*
to accept an invitation *He accepted their invitation to stay for dinner.*

types of invitation
a party/wedding invitation *We've sent out all the wedding invitations.*
a formal/official invitation *We got a formal invitation to the gallery opening.*

invite¹ /ɪnˈvaɪt/ *v* [T]
1 to ask someone to come to a party, meal etc: **invite sb to (do) sth** *I was invited to their wedding.* | **invite sb for sth** *They've invited us for lunch.*

2 to officially ask someone to do something: **invite sb to do sth** *She was invited to give a speech.*
3 to encourage something bad to happen: *a policy that invites criticism*

PHRASAL VERBS
invite sb **along** to ask someone to come with you when you go somewhere: *Why don't we invite Jane along?*
invite sb **in** to ask someone to come into your home
invite sb **over** (*also* **invite** sb **round** *BrE*) to ask someone to come to your home: **[+for]** *Let's invite Rob over for a meal.*

invite² /ˈɪnvaɪt/ *n* [C] *informal* an invitation to a party, meal etc

inviting /ɪnˈvaɪtɪŋ/ *adj* something that is inviting is attractive and pleasant: *The room was warm and inviting.* —**invitingly** *adv*

invoice /ˈɪnvɔɪs/ *n* [C] a list of goods that have been supplied or work that has been done, and how much money you owe —**invoice** *v* [T]

invoke Ac /ɪnˈvəʊk $ -ˈvoʊk/ *v* [T] *formal* to use a law or rule to support something that you are saying or doing

involuntary /ɪnˈvɒləntəri $ ɪnˈvɑːlənteri/ *adj* an involuntary movement is one you make suddenly in a way you cannot control: *She gave an involuntary gasp of surprise.* —**involuntarily** *adv*

involve Ac /ɪnˈvɒlv $ ɪnˈvɑːlv/ *v* [T]
1 if an activity or situation involves something, that thing is a part of it: *The job involves a lot of travelling.* | **involve doing sth** *The project will involve working abroad.*
2 to include or affect someone or something: *an accident involving five cars*
3 to ask or allow someone to take part in something: **involve sb in (doing) sth** *Schools are trying to involve parents in their children's education.*

involved /ɪnˈvɒlvd $ ɪnˈvɑːlvd/ *adj* **1** be/get involved to take part in something, or be related to it in some way: **[+in]** *Several companies were involved in the project.* | **[+with]** *If you'd like to get involved with the group, call this number.* | **closely/actively/heavily involved** *He was closely involved with training the team.* **2** be involved with sb to have a relationship with someone, especially a romantic or sexual one: *She was involved with an older man.* **3** complicated: *a long involved story* —**involvement** *n* [U]

inward /ˈɪnwəd $ -wərd/ *adj* **1** [only before noun] an inward feeling or thought is one that you have but do not show to other people: *an inward feeling of despair* **2** towards the inside or centre of something —**inwardly** *adv*

inwards /ˈɪnwədz $ -wərdz/ *especially BrE*, **inward** *especially AmE adv* towards the inside of something OPP **outwards**: *The door opened inwards.*

in-your-ˈface *adj informal* intended to shock and insult: *in-your-face comedy*

iodine /ˈaɪədiːn $ -daɪn/ *n* [U] a chemical that is used on wounds to prevent infection

IOU /ˌaɪ əʊ ˈjuː $ -oʊ-/ n [C] *informal* a note you sign to say that you owe money to someone

IPA /ˌaɪ piː ˈeɪ◂/ n [singular] (**International Phonetic Alphabet**) a system of signs used to represent speech sounds

iPod /ˈaɪpɒd $ -pɑːd/ n [C] *trademark* a piece of electronic equipment for storing and playing music, which you can carry around with you

IQ /ˌaɪ ˈkjuː/ n [C] (**Intelligence Quotient**) your level of intelligence, measured by a special test: *She has an IQ of 120.*

ir- /ɪ/ *prefix* not – used before words beginning with 'r': *irregular* | *irreligious*

irate /aɪˈreɪt◂/ adj *formal* very angry: *irate customers*

iris /ˈaɪərɪs $ ˈaɪrɪs/ n [C] **1** a tall plant with purple, yellow, or white flowers and long thin leaves → see picture at **FLOWER**[1] **2** the coloured part of your eye → see picture at **EYE**[1]

irk /ɜːk $ ɜːrk/ v [T] to annoy someone

iron[1] /ˈaɪən $ ˈaɪərn/ n
1 [U] a hard metal that is used to make steel, and is in food and blood in small quantities: *iron gates* | *I'm taking iron tablets.*
2 [C] a piece of equipment you use for making clothes smooth

iron[2] v [T] to make clothes smooth using an iron: *I need to iron my shirt.* —**ironing** n [U]: *I hate doing the ironing.*
PHRASAL VERBS
iron sth ↔ **out** to solve a small problem: *There are still a few problems to iron out.*

iron[3] adj very determined, strict, or severe: *He has an iron will.*

ironic /aɪˈrɒnɪk $ aɪˈrɑː-/ adj **1** an ironic situation is strange or amusing because it is completely different from what you expect: *It's ironic that your car was stolen outside the police station.* **2** saying the opposite of what you mean, especially in order to be funny: *I think he was being ironic.* —**ironically** /-kli/ adv: *Ironically, a lot of crimes are committed quite close to police stations.*

'ironing ˌboard n [C] a narrow table that you iron clothes on → see picture at **BOARD**[1]

irony /ˈaɪərəni $ ˈaɪrə-/ n (plural **ironies**) **1** [U] when you say the opposite of what you mean, especially in order to be amusing: *'You seem interested,' he said with **a touch of irony**.* → see Word Choice at **SARCASM 2** [C,U] a situation that is strange or amusing because it is completely different from what you expect: *The irony is that traffic congestion is worse despite new transport policies.*

irrational Ac /ɪˈræʃənəl/ adj not based on sensible reasons or thoughts: *irrational fears* —**irrationally** adv

irreconcilable /ɪˌrekənˈsaɪləbəl◂/ adj *formal* irreconcilable attitudes or opinions are so different that it is impossible to reach an agreement: *There are still some **irreconcilable differences** between them.*

irregular /ɪˈregjələ $ -ər/ adj **1** not happening at regular times: *an irregular heartbeat* | *He returned to Britain **at irregular intervals**.* **2** an irregular shape or

surface is not smooth, even, or straight **3** not following the usual rules in grammar: *irregular verbs* **4** *formal* not obeying legal or moral rules: *financially irregular practices* —**irregularly** adv —**irregularity** /ɪˌregjəˈlærəti/ n [C,U]

irrelevant Ac /ɪˈreləvənt/ adj not useful or important in a particular situation: *I won't bore you with all the irrelevant details.* | *His age is completely irrelevant.* | **[+to]** *topics that are irrelevant to students* —**irrelevance** n [C,U]

irreparable /ɪˈrepərəbəl/ adj irreparable damage or harm is so bad that it can never be repaired or made better —**irreparably** adv

irreplaceable /ˌɪrɪˈpleɪsəbəl◂/ adj too valuable or rare to be replaced: *irreplaceable books*

irrepressible /ˌɪrɪˈpresəbəl◂/ adj always confident, happy, and full of energy

irreproachable /ˌɪrɪˈprəʊtʃəbəl◂ $ -ˈproʊtʃ-/ adj *formal* very good and impossible to criticize: *His behaviour was irreproachable.*

irresistible /ˌɪrɪˈzɪstəbəl◂/ adj **1** if something is irresistible, it is so good or nice that you want it: **[+to]** *The offer of so much money would be irresistible to most people.* **2** too strong or powerful to be stopped: *I had an **irresistible urge** to laugh.*

irrespective /ˌɪrɪˈspektɪv/ adv **irrespective of sth** used to say that something does not affect a situation at all: *Anyone can join, irrespective of age.*

irresponsible /ˌɪrɪˈspɒnsəbəl◂ $ -ˈspɑːn-/ adj doing things that are not sensible, without thinking about the possible bad results: *He's got a very irresponsible attitude to his work.* | **highly/totally irresponsible** *He's unreliable and totally irresponsible.* —**irresponsibly** adv

irreverent /ɪˈrevərənt/ adj showing no respect for something that most people respect

irreversible Ac /ˌɪrɪˈvɜːsəbəl◂ $ -ˈvɜːr-/ adj irreversible damage or change cannot be changed back to how it was before

irrevocable /ɪˈrevəkəbəl/ adj *formal* impossible to change or stop: *an irrevocable decision*

irrigate /ˈɪrɪgeɪt/ v [T] to supply land or crops with water —**irrigation** /ˌɪrəˈgeɪʃən/ n [U]

irritable /ˈɪrɪtəbəl/ adj becoming annoyed very easily —**irritably** adv —**irritability** /ˌɪrɪtəˈbɪləti/ n [U]

irritant /ˈɪrɪtənt/ n [C] *formal* **1** something that annoys you: *It was a minor irritant for the government.* **2** something that makes part of your body painful and sore: *a skin irritant*

irritate /ˈɪrɪteɪt/ v [T] **1** to annoy someone: *Her attitude irritated me.* **2** to make a part of your body sore: *Wool irritates my skin.* —**irritated** adj: *He was getting irritated.* —**irritating** adj: *an irritating habit* —**irritatingly** adv —**irritation** /ˌɪrɪˈteɪʃən/ n [C,U]

is /s, z, əz; strong ɪz/ the third person singular of the present tense of **BE**

-ish /ɪʃ/ *suffix* **1** quite or fairly: *youngish* (=not very young, but not old either) | *tallish* | *reddish hair* **2** *spoken* about: *We'll expect you eightish* (=at about 8 o'clock). | *He's fortyish* (=about 40 years old).

Islam /'ɪslɑːm, 'ɪz-, ɪs'lɑːm/ n [U] the Muslim religion, which was started by Muhammad and whose holy book is the Quran (Koran) —**Islamic** /ɪz'læmɪk, ɪs-/ adj

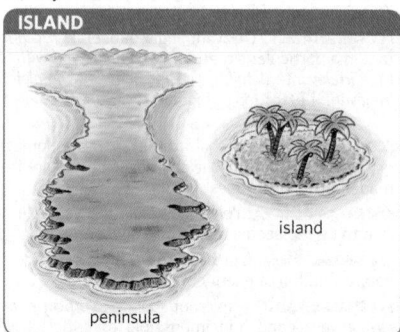

ISLAND

island

peninsula

island /'aɪlənd/ n [C] a piece of land surrounded by water: *the Cayman Islands* | **on an island** *a holiday on the Greek island of Crete* → **DESERT ISLAND**

> **Grammar**
> Do not say 'Jim lived in an island.' Say *Jim lived on an island.*

islander /'aɪləndə $ -ər/ n [C] someone who lives on an island

isle /aɪl/ n [C] an island, used in poems or in names of islands

isn't /'ɪzənt/ the short form of 'is not': *He isn't here.*

isolate Ac /'aɪsəleɪt/ v [T] to separate one person or thing from other people or things: **isolate sb/sth from sb/sth** *Presley's success isolated him from his friends.*

isolated Ac /'aɪsəleɪtɪd/ adj **1** far away from other places: *an isolated farm* **2** lonely and unable to meet other people: *Young mothers often feel isolated.* **THESAURUS** LONELY **3** happening only once, or existing in only one place: *The violence was an isolated incident.*

isolation Ac /ˌaɪsə'leɪʃən/ n [U] **1** when one person, place, or thing is separate from others: **geographical/political etc isolation** *the island's geographical isolation* | **in isolation (from sb/sth)** (=separately from other people or things) *He works in complete isolation.* | *You can't consider the facts in isolation from each other.* **2** a feeling of being lonely: *the isolation of old people*

ISP /ˌaɪ es 'piː/ n [C] (**Internet service provider**) a business that provides a connection to the Internet for people's computers

issue¹ /'ɪʃuː, 'ɪsjuː $ 'ɪʃuː/ n [C]
1 a subject or problem that people discuss: *This is a very important political issue.* | **[+of]** *We discussed the issue of teachers' pay.* | **I'd like to raise the issue** (=start to discuss the issue) *of safety.* | **important/key/major issue** *This is one of the key issues for the government.* **THESAURUS** SUBJECT
2 a magazine or newspaper that is printed at one particular time: **[+of]** *the latest issue of 'Vogue'*

make an issue of sth to start an argument or discussion about something that is not important: *Jim was upset by Eleanor's remarks, but didn't make an issue of it.*
take issue with sb/sth to disagree or argue with someone or something: *He took issue with the decision.*

issue² Ac v [T] **1** to officially make a statement or give an order, warning etc: *The government has issued a warning to people travelling to this area.* | *a statement issued by the White House* **2** to officially give people documents, equipment etc: *Thousands of passports are issued each year.* | **issue sb with sth** *Staff are issued with special clothing.*

it /ɪt/ pron
1 used to refer to something that has already been mentioned: *'Where's the bread?' 'It's on the shelf.'* | *Don't blame me. It wasn't my idea.*
2 the situation that someone is in now: *How's it going, Bob* (=how are you)? | *I like it here in Rio.*
3 used as the subject or object of a sentence when the real subject or object is later in the sentence: *It costs less to drive than to take the bus.*
4 used when talking about the weather, time, distance etc: *It's raining.* | *What time is it?*
5 used to emphasize a piece of information in a sentence: *It's John you should talk to, not me.*
6 used to say who a person is: *'Who's on the phone?' 'It's Jill.'*

IT /ˌaɪ 'tiː/ n [U] (**information technology**) the study or use of computers to store and manage information

italics /ɪ'tælɪks/ n [plural] a style of printed letters that slope to the right —**italic** adj

itch¹ /ɪtʃ/ v [I] **1** to have an unpleasant feeling on your skin that makes you want to rub it: *Her leg was itching.* **2 be itching to do sth/be itching for sth** *informal* to want to do something very much: *He was itching to go home.*

itch² n [singular] an unpleasant feeling on your skin that makes you want to rub it

itchy /'ɪtʃi/ adj if part of your body is itchy, it feels unpleasant and you want to rub it: *an itchy nose* —**itchiness** n [U]

it'd /'ɪtəd/ the short form of 'it would' or 'it had': *It'd be nice to go to the beach.* | *It'd been raining all day.*

item Ac /'aɪtəm/ n [C]
1 a single thing of a particular type or in a set or list: **item of clothing/furniture/equipment etc** *What was the last item of clothing you bought?* | **item on a list/menu/agenda** *the second item on my list*
2 a piece of news in a newspaper or magazine, or on television: *There was an item about the kidnapping in the paper.* | *a news item*

itemize (also **-ise** BrE) /'aɪtəmaɪz/ v [T] to make a list with details about each thing on the list

itinerant /aɪ'tɪnərənt/ adj formal travelling from place to place: *an itinerant musician*

itinerary /aɪ'tɪnərəri $ -nəreri/ n [C] (plural **itineraries**) a plan or list of the places you will visit on a trip

it'll /ˈɪtl/ the short form of 'it will': *It'll never work.*

it's /ɪts/ the short form of 'it is' or 'it has': *It's snowing!* | *It's been a great year.*

its /ɪts/ *determiner* the POSSESSIVE form of 'it': *The tree has lost all of its leaves.* | *The hotel has **its own** pool.*

> **Grammar**
> You use **its** in possessives, for example: *The dog has hurt its leg.* | *The company has changed its address.* Do not say 'The dog has hurt it's leg.' or 'The company has changed it's address.'
> You use **it's** as a short way of saying **it is** or **it has**, for example *It's cold* (=it is cold) *today.* | *It's been raining* (=it has been raining).

itself /ɪtˈself/ *pron* the REFLEXIVE form of 'it': *The cat was washing itself.*

PHRASES

in/of itself considered separately from other things or facts: *This might seem a small change in itself, but it is an important step.*

IV /ˌaɪ ˈviː/ *n* [C] *AmE* a piece of hospital equipment used for putting liquids directly into your blood [SYN] **drip** *BrE*

I've /aɪv/ the short form of 'I have': *I've seen you somewhere before.*

IVF /ˌaɪ viː ˈef/ *n* [U] *technical* (**in vitro fertilization**) a process in which a human egg is FERTILIZEd outside the woman's body

ivory /ˈaɪvəri/ *n* [U] **1** the hard smooth yellow-white substance from the TUSK of an ELEPHANT **2** a pale yellow-white colour —**ivory** *adj*

ivy /ˈaɪvi/ *n* [U] a climbing plant with dark green shiny leaves

I

J, j /dʒeɪ/ n [C,U] (plural **J's**, **j's**) the tenth letter of the English alphabet

jab¹ /dʒæb/ v [I,T] (**jabbed**, **jabbing**) to push something into or towards something else with short quick movements: *He angrily jabbed a finger into my chest.*

jab² n [C] **1** a sudden hard push, especially with a pointed object **2** *BrE informal* an INJECTION: *a tetanus jab*

jabber /dʒæbə $ -ər/ v [I] to talk quickly but not very clearly: *Franco jabbered away about football.*

jack¹ /dʒæk/ n [C] **1** a piece of equipment used for lifting something heavy, such as a car **2** a card used in card games which has a young man's picture on it: *the jack of hearts* → see picture at **PLAYING CARD**

jack² v

PHRASAL VERBS

jack sth ↔ **in** *BrE informal* to stop doing something such as your job: *I'm seriously thinking about jacking it all in.*

jack sth ↔ **up 1** to lift something heavy using a jack: *Dad jacked the car up so I could change the tyre.* **2** *informal* to increase prices, sales etc by a large amount: *Airlines always jack up fares at Christmas.*

jackal /dʒækɔːl, -kəl $ -kəl/ n [C] a wild animal like a dog that lives in Africa and Asia

jacket /dʒækɪt/ n [C] a short light coat: *denim/leather etc jacket He was wearing jeans and a leather jacket.* → see picture at **CLOTHES** → **DINNER JACKET, LIFE JACKET**

jacket po'tato n [C] *BrE* a potato baked with its skin on

jack-knife v [I] if a large vehicle with two parts jack-knifes, the back part swings towards the front part because the driver cannot control it

jackpot /dʒækpɒt $ -pɑːt/ n [C] a large amount of money that you can win

PHRASES

hit the jackpot 1 to win a lot of money **2** to be very successful or lucky: *The National Theatre hit the jackpot with its first musical.*

Jacuzzi /dʒəˈkuːzi/ n [C] *trademark* a large bath for one or more people, with hot water full of bubbles

jade /dʒeɪd/ n [U] a hard green stone used for making jewellery

jaded /dʒeɪdɪd/ adj no longer feeling interested or excited: *She seemed jaded and in need of a break.*

jagged /dʒægɪd/ adj having a rough edge with sharp points: *jagged rocks | the jagged edge of an old tin can*

jaguar /dʒægjuə $ dʒægwɑːr/ n [C] a large wild cat with black spots that lives in Central and South America

jail¹ (also **gaol** *BrE*) /dʒeɪl/ n [C,U] a place where criminals are kept as a punishment SYN **prison: in jail** *He was sentenced to six years in jail.*

jail² (also **gaol** *BrE*) v [T] to put someone in prison: *He was jailed for tax evasion.*

jailer (also **gaoler** *BrE*) /dʒeɪlə $ -ər/ n [C] *old-fashioned* someone who guards prisoners in a prison

jam¹ /dʒæm/ n

1 [C,U] a thick sticky sweet food made from fruit: *raspberry jam | a jam sandwich*

2 [C] a situation in which it is difficult to move because there are too many people, cars etc → **TRAFFIC JAM**

jam² v (**jammed**, **jamming**)

1 PUSH [T] to push something somewhere using a lot of force until it cannot move any further: *I managed to jam everything into one suitcase. | A chair had been jammed up against the door.*

2 STOP WORKING/MOVING [I,T] if a machine, door etc jams, or if you jam it, it no longer works properly because something is stopping one of its parts from moving: *Every time I try to use the fax, it jams.*

3 FILL A PLACE [T] if a lot of people or things jam a place, they fill it so that no one or nothing can move: *Excited football fans jammed the streets.*

4 MUSIC [I] to play music with other people in an informal way

5 RADIO SIGNALS [T] to deliberately block radio signals —**jammed** adj: *The door is jammed again.*

jamboree /ˌdʒæmbəˈriː/ n [C] a big noisy party or celebration

jam-'packed adj *informal* completely full of people or things: [+with] *The slopes were jam-packed with skiers.*

jangle /dʒæŋɡəl/ v [I,T] if small metal objects jangle, they make a noise as they hit against each other: *Her jewellery jangled when she moved.* —**jangle** n [singular]

janitor /dʒænɪtə $ -ər/ n [C] *especially AmE* someone whose job is to clean and look after a large building SYN **caretaker** *BrE*: *the school janitor*

January /dʒænjuəri, -njʊri $ -njueri/ n [C,U] (written abbreviation **Jan.**) the first month of the year, between December and February: *next/last January I haven't heard from him since last January. | in*

January *My birthday's in January.* | **on January 6th** *The meeting will be on January 6th.*

jar¹ /dʒɑː $ dʒɑːr/ *n* [C] a round glass container with a lid, used for storing food: *a jam jar* | **[+of]** *a small jar of pickles* → see picture at **CONTAINER**

jar² *v* [I,T] (**jarred, jarring**) **1** to damage something by a sudden shock or pressure: *Alice landed badly and jarred her knee.* **2** to make someone feel uncomfortable or annoyed: *The noise of the drill was starting to jar on my nerves.*

jargon /ˈdʒɑːgən $ ˈdʒɑːrgən, -gən/ *n* [U] words and phrases used by people in the same profession that are difficult for other people to understand: **technical/medical/legal etc jargon** THESAURUS **WORD**

jaundice /ˈdʒɔːndɪs $ ˈdʒɒːn-, ˈdʒɑːn-/ *n* [U] an illness in which your skin becomes yellow

jaundiced /ˈdʒɔːndɪst $ ˈdʒɒːn-, ˈdʒɑːn-/ *adj* if you have a jaundiced attitude to something, you think it is bad because of your past experience: *a jaundiced view of the world*

jaunt /dʒɔːnt $ dʒɒːnt, dʒɑːnt/ *n* [C] a short journey for pleasure

jaunty /ˈdʒɔːnti $ ˈdʒɒːnti, ˈdʒɑːnti/ *adj* showing that you feel confident and happy: *his jaunty air of self-confidence* —**jauntily** *adv*

javelin /ˈdʒævəlɪn/ *n* [C] a long pointed stick thrown as a sport

jaw /dʒɔː $ dʒɒː/ *n* [C]
1 one of the two bones in your face that contain your teeth: *She suffered a broken jaw in the accident.* | **upper/lower jaw** → see picture on page A2
2 the bottom part of your face, below your mouth
PHRASES

> **sb's jaw dropped** used to say that someone looked very surprised or shocked: *His jaw dropped when he saw her.*

jaywalking /ˈdʒeɪˌwɔːkɪŋ $ -ˌwɒː-/ *n* [U] when you walk across a street in a careless or dangerous way

jazz¹ /dʒæz/ *n* [U] a type of music with a strong beat, in which musicians often play in a way that is not planned: *modern jazz* | *a singer in a jazz band*

jazz² *v*
PHRASAL VERBS
jazz *sth* ↔ **up** to make something more exciting and interesting: *Jazz up your bathroom by replacing the tiles.*

jealous /ˈdʒeləs/ *adj*
1 unhappy because someone else has something that you wish you had: **[+of]** *You're just jealous of me because I got better grades.*
2 unhappy because someone you like or love is showing interest in another person: *I only went out with him to* **make** *Steve* **jealous.** | **jealous husband/lover/wife etc**

> **Word Choice**: jealous or envious?
> Both these words are used about wishing that you had something that someone else has. **Jealous** sounds stronger than **envious**, and sometimes means that you have unkind feelings towards the other person.

Compare these sentences: *You're jealous of him because he's a better player than you are* (=you have strong and bitter feelings towards him because he is better than you). | *I'm really envious of their new house* (=I wish I had a house like theirs).

jealously /ˈdʒeləsli/ *adv* **1** if you jealously guard or protect something, you try very hard to keep or protect it: *a jealously guarded secret* **2** while feeling jealous

jealousy /ˈdʒeləsi/ *n* [C,U] (*plural* **jealousies**) the feeling you have when you are jealous: *She felt a stab* (=sudden strong feeling) *of jealousy.*

jeans /dʒiːnz/ *n* [plural] a popular type of trousers made from DENIM: *a new* **pair of jeans** → see picture at **CLOTHES**

Jeep /dʒiːp/ *n* [C] *trademark* a vehicle made for travelling over rough ground

jeer /dʒɪə $ dʒɪr/ *v* [I,T] to say rude things to someone or laugh at them: *Fans jeered at the referee.* —**jeer** *n* [C]

Jell-O, jello /ˈdʒeləʊ $ -loʊ/ *n* [U] *trademark AmE* JELLY

jelly /ˈdʒeli/ *n* (*plural* **jellies**) **1** [C,U] *BrE* a sweet food made with fruit juice that is solid but shakes when you move it SYN **Jell-O** *AmE*: *strawberry jelly and ice cream* **2** [U] *especially AmE* a thick sweet food made from fruit SYN **jam** *BrE*: *a peanut butter and jelly sandwich*

jellyfish /ˈdʒelifɪʃ/ *n* [C] (*plural* **jellyfish**) a transparent sea animal with long parts that hang down from its body → see picture on page A3

jeopardize (*also* **-ise** *BrE*) /ˈdʒepədaɪz $ -ər-/ *v* [T] to risk losing or destroying something valuable or important: *He didn't want to jeopardize his career by complaining about his boss.*

jeopardy /ˈdʒepədi $ -ər-/ *n* **in jeopardy** in danger of being lost or harmed: *The peace talks are in jeopardy.*

jerk¹ /dʒɜːk $ dʒɜːrk/ *v* [I,T] to move with a sudden quick movement, or to make something move in this way: *Sara jerked her head up to look at him.* | *He suddenly jerked open the car door.*

jerk² *n* [C] **1** a sudden quick movement: *a jerk of her head* | *She sat up with a jerk.* **2** *AmE informal* someone who is stupid or very annoying

jerky /ˈdʒɜːki $ -ɜːr-/ *adj* jerky movements are rough, with many starts and stops: *The elevator's jerky movements alarmed me.* —**jerkily** *adv*

jersey /ˈdʒɜːzi $ -ɜːr-/ *n* **1** [C] a shirt made of soft material, worn for playing sports: *a football jersey* **2** [C] *BrE* a SWEATER **3** [U] a soft material made of cotton or wool

jest /dʒest/ *n* **in jest** something you say in jest is meant to be funny, not serious —**jest** *v* [I]

jester /ˈdʒestə $ -ər/ *n* [C] a man employed in the past by a king to entertain people with jokes, stories etc

Jesus /'dʒiːzəs/ (also ˌJesus 'Christ) *n* the man who Christians believe was the son of God, and on whose life and ideas Christianity is based

jet¹ /dʒet/ *n* [C]
1 a very fast plane: *He travels in his own **private jet**.* | **jet fighter/aircraft** → JUMBO JET
2 a thin stream of gas, liquid etc that is forced out of a small hole: **[+of]** *a strong jet of water*

jet² *v* [I] (**jetted, jetting**) *informal* to travel somewhere by plane: **[+off]** *You could be jetting off for a week in the Caribbean.*

jet-'black *adj* very dark black: *jet-black hair*

jet 'engine *n* [C] a powerful engine used in planes

'jet lag *n* [U] the feeling of being very tired after a long journey in a plane —**jet-lagged** *adj*

jettison /'dʒetəsən, -zən/ *v* [T] **1** to get rid of something that you do not need or want: *The scheme was jettisoned as it was too costly.* **2** to throw something away from a moving plane, ship, or vehicle

jetty /'dʒeti/ *n* [C] (*plural* **jetties**) a wide stone or wooden structure used for getting on and off boats

Jew /dʒuː/ *n* [C] someone whose religion is Judaism → **Jewish**

jewel /'dʒuːəl/ *n* [C] a valuable stone, such as a DIAMOND

jewelled *BrE*, **jeweled** *AmE* /'dʒuːəld/ *adj* decorated with valuable stones: *a jewelled box*

jeweller *BrE*, **jeweler** *AmE* /'dʒuːələ $ -ər/ *n* [C] someone who sells, makes, or repairs jewellery

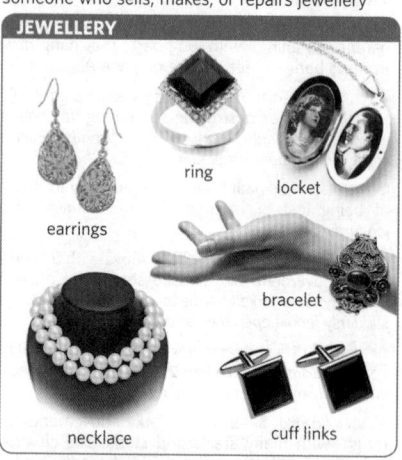

JEWELLERY

ring

locket

earrings

bracelet

necklace

cuff links

jewellery *BrE*, **jewelry** *AmE* /'dʒuːəlri/ *n* [U] small things that you wear for decoration, such as rings and NECKLACES: *a piece of gold jewellery*

> **Grammar**
> Jewellery is uncountable and is not used in the plural. It is used with a singular verb. Do not say 'All her jewelleries were stolen.' Say *All her jewellery was stolen.*
> When talking about a single ring or necklace, you say **a piece of jewellery**.

Jewish /'dʒuːɪʃ/ *adj* relating to Jews or Judaism

jibe, gibe /dʒaɪb/ *n* [C] something that you say to make someone else seem silly

jig /dʒɪg/ *n* [C] a type of quick dance, or the music for this dance

jiggle /'dʒɪgəl/ *v* [I,T] to move from side to side with short quick movements, or to make something move this way

jigsaw /'dʒɪgsɔː $ -sɒː/ (also 'jigsaw ˌpuzzle) *n* [C] a picture that has been cut up into many small pieces that you try to fit together again

jilt /dʒɪlt/ *v* [T] *old-fashioned* to suddenly end a romantic relationship with someone

jingle¹ /'dʒɪŋgəl/ *v* [I,T] if small metal objects jingle, or if you jingle them, they make a noise when you shake them together: *Tom nervously jingled the coins in his pocket.*

jingle² *n* **1** [C] a short song used in television or radio advertisements **2** [singular] the sound of small metal objects being shaken together

jinx /dʒɪŋks/ *n* [singular] someone or something that brings bad luck: *There's some kind of jinx on the team.* —**jinxed** *adj* —**jinx** *v* [T]

jitters /'dʒɪtəz $ -ərz/ *n* [plural] a feeling of being nervous and anxious: *her last-minute jitters before the wedding*

jittery /'dʒɪtəri/ *adj* worried and nervous: *She was so jittery about seeing him she couldn't keep still.*
THESAURUS NERVOUS

Jnr *BrE* the written abbreviation of **Junior**, used after someone's name SYN **Jr.** *AmE*

job Ac /dʒɒb $ dʒɑːb/ *n* [C]
1 the work that you do regularly to earn money: *She applied for a job at a bank.* | **out of a job** (=unemployed) *He found himself out of a job.*
2 something that needs doing: **the job of doing sth** *Let's get on with the job of finding Jenny.* | **difficult/easy etc job** *It's not going to be an easy job.* | *I **do** some **jobs** around the house.*
3 something you are responsible for doing: **it is sb's job to do sth** *It's my job to make sure everyone gets there on time.*
PHRASES
> **do a good/bad etc job** (also **make a good/bad etc job of sth** *BrE*) to do something well or badly: *They've done an excellent job of marketing the product.*
> **do the job** *informal* to have the effect or result you want: *A little more glue should do the job.*
> **have a job doing sth/to do sth** *spoken* to have difficulty doing something: *We had a job finding somewhere to park.* | *You'll have a job to see anything.*
> **it's a good job (that)** *BrE spoken* used to say that it is lucky something happened: *It's a good job you were wearing your seat belt.*
> **be just the job** *BrE spoken* to be exactly what is needed or wanted: *This bag is just the job for carrying your sports gear.*
> **on the job** while doing work or at work: *All our employees get on-the-job training.*

COLLOCATIONS

verbs

to have a job *He's never had a job.*

to apply for a job *Over 200 people applied for the job.*

to offer sb a job *They called and offered me the job.*

to take a job (=accept a job you are offered) *She decided to take the job.*

to get/find a job *Maybe you could get a job in a shop.*

to lose your job *Hundreds of people could lose their jobs at the factory.*

to leave/quit your job *Why did you leave your job?*

adjectives

a temporary/permanent job *I'm hoping to find a permanent job after college.*

a part-time/full-time job *I got a part-time job in a café.*

a Saturday job (=a job working only on Saturdays, for example in a shop) *She had a Saturday job while she was still at school.*

THESAURUS

job the work that you do regularly to earn money, especially when you work for a company or a public organization: *My first job was in a record store.* | *She sometimes wished she had a different job.*

work activities that you do to earn money: *Thousands of men are looking for work.* | *He started work when he was 15.*

profession a job that needs special education and training, for example being a teacher, doctor, or lawyer: *He wants to go into the medical profession* (=become a doctor). | *She works in the legal profession* (=she is a lawyer).

occupation *formal* a job or type of job – often used on official documents: *Give details of your current occupation.*

career the work you do or plan to do for most of your life: *Have you thought about your future career?*

position *formal* a particular job in an organization: *I am writing to apply for the position of sales manager.*

vacancy a job that is available for someone to do: *I'm afraid that the vacancy has already been filled.*

what you do (for a living) the usual way of talking or asking about someone's job: *'What do you do for a living?' 'I'm a teacher.'*

'job ,centre *n* [C] a place run by the British government where jobs are advertised and help is provided for people who are looking for work

'job de,scription *n* [C] an official list of the work and responsibilities that you have in your job

jobless /ˈdʒɒbləs $ ˈdʒɑːb-/ *adj* without a paid job **SYN** unemployed: *Ten percent of the town's workers are jobless.*

'job ,seeker *n* [C] *BrE* someone who does not have a job and is looking for one

jockey¹ /ˈdʒɒki $ ˈdʒɑːki/ *n* [C] someone who rides horses in races

jockey² *v* [I] to compete strongly to get into the best position or situation, or to get the most power: **[+for]** *photographers **jockeying for position** at the bar* | *After the war, rival politicians began to **jockey for power**.*

jocular /ˈdʒɒkjələ $ ˈdʒɑːkjələr/ *adj formal* happy and making jokes

jog /dʒɒg $ dʒɑːg/ *v* (**jogged, jogging**) **1** [I,T] to run slowly, especially for exercise: *Julie jogs three miles every morning.* → see picture on page A11 **THESAURUS** RUN **2** [T] to knock or push something lightly by mistake: *Someone jogged her elbow, and she spilt her drink.* —**jog** *n* [singular]

PHRASES

jog sb's memory to make someone remember something: *This photo might jog your memory.*

jogging /ˈdʒɒgɪŋ $ ˈdʒɑː-/ *n* [U] the activity of running for exercise: *He goes jogging regularly.* **THESAURUS** RUN —**jogger** *n* [C]

join¹ /dʒɔɪn/ *v*

1 ORGANIZATION/CLUB [T] to become a member of an organization, society, or group: *Trevor joined the BBC in 1969.* | *Have you joined any clubs?*

2 OTHER PEOPLE [T] to go somewhere in order to be with someone else: *Shall we join the others in the garden?*

3 DO STH TOGETHER **a)** [I,T] to do something together with someone else: **join sb for sth** *Why don't you join us for dinner?* | **join (with) sb in doing sth** *Please join with me in welcoming tonight's speaker.* **b)** [T] to begin to take part in an activity that other people are already doing: *Local people joined the hunt for the missing girl.*

4 CONNECT [T] to connect or fasten things together: *Join the two pieces of wood with strong glue.* | **join sth together** *the corridor that joins the three buildings together*

5 ROADS/RIVERS [I,T] if two roads, rivers etc join, they come together and are connected at a particular place: *the point where the two rivers join*

6 QUEUE **join a queue/line** to go and stand at the end of a line of people: *He joined the queue for the bus.*

PHRASES

join hands if two people join hands, they hold each other's hands: *They joined hands and danced round.*

PHRASAL VERBS

join in (sth) to begin to take part in something that other people are doing: *The other children wouldn't let Sam join in.* | *Everyone joined in the conversation.*

join up

1 to meet with other people to do something, or to take part in an activity with other people: *We can all join up for a drink later.* | **[+with]** *They've joined up with local environmentalists.*

2 *BrE* to become a member of the army, navy etc

THESAURUS – sense 4

join to make two things become connected together, especially permanently so that they form a single thing: *Doctors used a metal rod to*

join the two pieces of bone together. | If you join the two words together, you get 'shan't'.
attach to join one thing to another, so that it stays in position. **Attach** is often used when you can separate the two things later: *She attached the photo to the letter with a paper clip.*
connect (*also* **connect up**) to join pieces of equipment together, especially with a wire or pipe, so that electricity, gas, water etc can pass from one to another: *A pipe connects the two gas tanks.*
link (*also* **link up**) to connect machines, systems, computers etc, so that electronic signals can pass from one to another: *All the office PCs are linked to the main server.*

join² n [C] a place where two parts of an object are connected or fastened together

'joined-up adj [only before noun] BrE **1** joined-up writing has all the letters in each word connected to each other **2** joined-up systems, institutions etc combine different groups, ideas, or parts in a way that works well: ***joined-up government*** | *the need for **joined-up thinking** between departments*

joiner /'dʒɔɪnə $ -ər/ n [C] BrE someone who makes wooden doors, window frames etc

joint¹ /dʒɔɪnt/ adj shared by or involving two or more people: *They have to reach a joint decision.* | *a joint bank account* | *The research was a **joint effort** by the two groups.* —**jointly** adv: *Sam and I are jointly responsible for the project.*

joint² n [C]
1 BODY PART a part of the body where two bones meet: **hip/knee/elbow etc joint**
2 PLACE WHERE PARTS JOIN a place where two things or parts of an object are joined together: *One of the joints between the pipes was leaking.*
3 MEAT BrE a large piece of meat with a bone in it: [+of] *a joint of beef*
4 BAR/CLUB/RESTAURANT informal a place such as a bar, club, or restaurant: *a fast-food joint*
5 CIGARETTE informal a cigarette that contains CANNABIS

joint 'venture n [C] a business arrangement in which two or more companies work together

joke¹ /dʒəʊk $ dʒoʊk/ n [C] something funny that you say or do to make people laugh: *Ed loves telling jokes.* | [+about] *kids' jokes about their teachers* | *I only did it as a joke.* → IN-JOKE
PHRASES
be a joke informal to be completely useless, stupid, or unreasonable: *Public transport here is a joke.*
get beyond a joke to become serious and worrying: *All this junk mail is getting beyond a joke.*
make a joke (out) of sth to treat something serious as if it were funny: *It was so bad she tried to make a joke of it.*
be no joke used to emphasize that a situation is serious or difficult: *Looking after three kids on your own is no joke.*

COLLOCATIONS

verbs
to tell a joke (=to repeat a funny story) *Sam told me a joke.* ⚠ Do not say 'say a joke'. Say **tell a joke.**
to make/crack a joke (=to say something intended to be funny) *They were all laughing and cracking jokes.*
to play a joke on sb (=to trick someone to make people laugh) *John's always playing jokes on his brothers.*
to get a joke (=to understand a joke and find it funny) *I didn't get the joke.*

adjectives
a good/funny joke *Do you know any good jokes?*
a sick joke (=very unpleasant and often about death or suffering) *Within days of the disaster, people were making sick jokes about it.*
a practical joke (=one that involves tricking someone) *His friend had sent him the card as a practical joke.*

joke² v [I] **1** to say things that are funny or that you do not really mean: [+about] *The guys laughed and joked about it later.* | [+with] *He was relaxed, joking with the reporters.* | [+that] *His students joked that he should go into politics.* | *Hey, calm down – I'm **only joking**!* —**jokingly** adv
PHRASES
you're joking/you must be joking spoken used when you are surprised by what someone has said because it seems strange or silly: *Buy a house, on my salary? You must be joking!*

joker /'dʒəʊkə $ 'dʒoʊkər/ n [C] **1** someone who likes to say or do funny things **2** a card used in some card games that has no fixed value

jolly¹ /'dʒɒli $ 'dʒɑːli/ adj happy: *a jolly atmosphere*

jolly² adv BrE spoken old-fashioned very: *It's jolly cold outside!*

jolt¹ /dʒəʊlt $ dʒoʊlt/ n [C] **1** a sudden shock: *It **gave me a jolt** to see her looking so ill.* | *Sam woke **with a jolt.*** **2** a sudden strong movement: *There was a terrific jolt as the lift stopped.*

jolt² v [I,T] to move suddenly and strongly, or to make someone or something do this: *The train jolted to a halt.*

jostle /'dʒɒsəl $ 'dʒɑː-/ v [I,T] to push against other people in a crowd: [+for] *Spectators jostled for a better view.*

jot /dʒɒt $ dʒɑːt/ v (**jotted, jotting**)
PHRASAL VERBS
jot sth ↔ **down** to write something quickly on a piece of paper: *Let me jot down your phone number.*
THESAURUS WRITE

journal Ac /'dʒɜːnl $ -ɜːr-/ n [C] **1** a serious magazine about a particular subject: *a scientific journal* **2** a written account of the things that happen to you each day SYN diary

journalism /'dʒɜːnəl-ɪzəm $ -ɜːr-/ n [U] the job of writing reports for newspapers, magazines, television, or radio

journalist /ˈdʒɜːnəl-ɪst $ -ɜːr-/ n [C] someone who writes reports for newspapers, magazines, television, or radio → **reporter**

journey /ˈdʒɜːni $ -ɜːr-/ n [C] especially BrE an occasion when you travel from one place to another, especially over a long distance: **[+to/from/through]** My journey to work takes about an hour. | **on a journey** She met some interesting people on her journey.

COLLOCATIONS

verbs

to make a journey He makes a hundred-mile journey to see his mother every week.
to go on a journey (=to make a long journey) He explained that he had to go on a journey.
to set out/set off on a journey (=to start a long journey) Before setting off on a journey, look at maps and guidebooks.

noun + journey

a car/plane/bus etc journey It's a six-hour bus journey from here.

adjectives

a long journey The journey was long and tiring.
a safe journey (=used especially to wish someone a good journey) Have a safe journey.
a wasted journey (=one that did not achieve the result you wanted) I'm sorry you had a wasted journey – he's not here.

THESAURUS

journey especially BrE an occasion when you travel from one place to another – used especially about travelling a long distance, or travelling somewhere regularly: The journey to Chicago can take up to 8 hours. | How was your journey to work?
trip a journey to visit a place: Did you enjoy your trip to the zoo?
expedition a long and carefully organized journey, especially to a dangerous or unfamiliar place: They were on an expedition to the North Pole.
pilgrimage a journey to a holy place for religious reasons: Thousands of people make the annual pilgrimage to Mecca.
flight a journey by air: The flight was delayed because of bad weather.
voyage a long journey over the sea: He completed a three-year round-the-world voyage.
drive a journey in a car, often for pleasure: Do you want to go for a drive along the coast?
ride a journey on a bicycle, motorcycle, or horse, or in someone's car: We went for a bike ride in the park. | a short taxi ride

jovial /ˈdʒəʊviəl $ ˈdʒoʊ-/ adj friendly and cheerful: a jovial manner

joy /dʒɔɪ/ n [C,U] a feeling of great happiness and pleasure, or something that gives you this feeling: **for/with joy** She cried with joy when she heard the news. | **[+of]** the joys of travel | The garden is her **pride**

and joy. | **be a joy to teach/watch etc** The Jaguar's a joy to drive.

PHRASES

no/not any joy BrE spoken if you have no joy, you do not succeed in getting something: I've looked everywhere but I haven't **had any joy**.

joyful /ˈdʒɔɪfəl/ adj very happy, or making people very happy: a joyful reunion —**joyfully** adv

joyless /ˈdʒɔɪləs/ adj without any happiness: a joyless childhood

joyous /ˈdʒɔɪəs/ adj literary very happy, or making people very happy SYN **joyful**: a joyous occasion —**joyously** adv

joyriding /ˈdʒɔɪˌraɪdɪŋ/ n [U] the crime of stealing a car and driving it in a fast and dangerous way for fun —**joyride** v [I] —**joyrider** n [C]

joystick /ˈdʒɔɪˌstɪk/ n [C] a handle used to control an aircraft or a computer game

JP /ˌdʒeɪ ˈpiː/ n [C] a JUSTICE OF THE PEACE

Jr. AmE the written abbreviation of **Junior**, used after someone's name SYN **Jnr** BrE

jubilant /ˈdʒuːbələnt/ adj extremely happy because of a success: a jubilant crowd —**jubilation** /ˌdʒuːbəˈleɪʃən/ n [U]

jubilee /ˈdʒuːbəliː, ˌdʒuːbəˈliː/ n [C] a date that is celebrated because it is an exact number of years after an important event: **silver/golden/diamond jubilee** (=25, 50, 60 years after something) Queen Victoria's diamond jubilee

Judaism /ˈdʒuːdeɪ-ɪzəm, ˈdʒuːdə- $ ˈdʒuːdə-, ˈdʒuːdi-/ n [U] the Jewish religion

judge¹ /dʒʌdʒ/ n [C]
1 the person who controls a court of law and decides how criminals should be punished: the sentence imposed by the judge | **federal/high court/district etc judge** (=a judge in a particular court)
2 someone who decides who has won a competition: a **panel** (=group) **of judges**

PHRASES

a good/bad judge of sth someone whose opinion of something is usually right or wrong: She's a good judge of character.

> **Word Choice**: referee, umpire, or judge?
> You use **referee** about sports such as football, rugby, basketball, or boxing.
> You use **umpire** about sports such as cricket, baseball, and tennis.
> You use **judge** about sports competitions where a team of judges decide who has got the most points, for example gymnastics, ice skating, or diving.

judge² v
1 FORM AN OPINION [I,T] to form or give an opinion about someone or something using the information you have: **judge sb/sth on/by sth** Never judge a person by their looks. | Employees should be judged on the quality of their work. | **[+whether/what/how]** It's **difficult to judge** whether he was telling the truth. | **[+that]** By then, **it was judged that** the crisis was over.

2 CHOOSE WINNER [I,T] to decide who has won a competition: *Who's judging the talent contest?*

3 CRITICIZE [I,T] to form an opinion about someone in a CRITICAL or unfair way: *You have no right to judge other people's lifestyles.*

4 IN A COURT OF LAW [T] to decide in a court of law whether someone is guilty of a crime

PHRASES

judging by/from sth used when giving the reason why you think something is true: *Judging by his performance, he has a good chance of winning.*

judgment (*also* **judgement** *BrE*) /ˈdʒʌdʒmənt/ *n*
1 OPINION [C,U] your opinion about something, based on the information you have: *We must make a judgment about whether it's worth the risk.*
2 ABILITY TO DECIDE [U] the ability to make sensible decisions about situations or people: *I trust your professional judgement.* | *a serious error of judgment*
3 LEGAL DECISION [C,U] a legal decision made by a judge or a court of law

judgmental (*also* **judgemental** *BrE*) /dʒʌdʒˈmentl/ *adj disapproving* criticizing people unfairly

judicial /dʒuːˈdɪʃəl/ *adj* relating to the law, judges etc: *the judicial system*

judiciary /dʒuːˈdɪʃəri $ -ʃieri, -ʃəri/ *n* **the judiciary** *formal* all the judges in a country who, together, form part of the system of government

judicious /dʒuːˈdɪʃəs/ *adj formal* sensible and careful: *a judicious choice*

judo /ˈdʒuːdəʊ $ -doʊ/ *n* [U] a sport from Japan in which you try to throw your opponent onto the ground

jug /dʒʌg/ *n* [C] a container with an opening at the top and a handle, used for pouring or holding liquids

juggle /ˈdʒʌgəl/ *v* **1** [I,T] to keep three or more balls, plates etc moving through the air by throwing and catching them very quickly **2** [T] to fit two or more activities into your life, especially with difficulty: **juggle sth and/with sth** *It's hard work trying to juggle family life and a career.*

juggler /ˈdʒʌglə $ -ər/ *n* [C] someone who juggles balls, plates etc to entertain people

juice /dʒuːs/ *n*
1 [C,U] the liquid from fruit or vegetables, or a drink made from this: *a carton of juice* | *an orange juice, please*
2 [C usually plural, U] the liquid that comes out of meat when it is cooked

juicy /ˈdʒuːsi/ *adj* **1** containing a lot of juice: *a juicy peach* **2** **juicy gossip/details etc** *informal* interesting or shocking information about someone or something: *The media are always looking for a juicy story.*

jukebox /ˈdʒuːkbɒks $ -baːks/ *n* [C] a machine, usually in bars, that plays music when you put money in

July /dʒʊˈlaɪ/ *n* [C,U] (*written abbreviation* **Jul.**) the seventh month of the year, between June and August: **next/last July** *She came over to England last July.* | **in July** *We usually go on holiday in July.* | **on July 6th** *The meeting will be on July 6th.*

jumble¹ /ˈdʒʌmbəl/ *n* **1** [singular] an untidy group of things: **[+of]** *a jumble of pots and pans* **2** [U] *BrE* things that are sold at a JUMBLE SALE

jumble² (*also* **jumble up**) *v* [T] to mix things together so that they become untidy: *Don't jumble all my papers up.* THESAURUS MIX

jumble sale *n* [C] *BrE* a sale of used clothes, books etc to get money for a local church, school etc SYN **rummage sale** *AmE*

jumbo /ˈdʒʌmbəʊ $ -boʊ/ *adj* [only before noun] *informal* larger than other things of the same type: *a jumbo sausage*

jumbo jet (*also* **jumbo**) *n* [C] a very big plane that carries passengers

JUMP

bounce

hop

jump

skip *BrE*/skip rope *AmE*

jump¹ /dʒʌmp/ *v*
1 [I,T] to push yourself up into the air, or over or off something, using your legs: **[+into/off/down etc]** *Boys were jumping off the bridge into the river.* | *Fans were cheering and jumping up and down.* | *His horse jumped the final fence.*
2 [I] to move quickly or suddenly in a particular direction: **[+up/into/out etc]** *Paul jumped up to answer the door.* | *We all jumped in a taxi.* | *Robert jumped to his feet.*
3 [I] to make a sudden movement because you are surprised or frightened: *I didn't hear you come in – you made me jump!*
4 [I] to increase or improve suddenly and a lot: **[+by]** *Profits have jumped by 20%.* | **jump (from sth) to sth** *Norway jumped from ninth to third place.*
5 [I] to change quickly from one subject to another: **jump from sth to sth** *The story jumps from Tom's childhood to his wartime adventures.*

PHRASES

jump down sb's throat to suddenly speak angrily to someone: *It was just a suggestion. You don't have to jump down my throat.*

jump for joy to be extremely happy about something: *We heard the news and everyone in the room was jumping for joy.*

jump the gun to start doing something too soon without thinking about it carefully: *We don't know all the facts, so let's not jump the gun.*

jump the queue *BrE disapproving* to go ahead of other people who are already waiting in a line: *There were angry shouts as a woman tried to jump the queue.*

jump to conclusions to form an opinion about something before you have all the facts: *There may be a simple explanation. Let's not jump to conclusions.*

PHRASAL VERBS

jump at sth to eagerly accept an opportunity to do something: *Ruth **jumped at the chance** to study in Paris.*

THESAURUS

jump to push yourself up into the air, or over or off something, using your legs: *He jumped up onto the ledge.* | *The boys jumped across the stream.*

skip to run while making little jumps between your steps: *The children were skipping down the street.*

hop to move around on one leg. Also used when saying that frogs, insects, rabbits etc suddenly jump somewhere: *He was hopping around because he'd injured his foot.* | *The frog hopped into the pond.*

leap to jump up high or a long way: *The horse leapt over the gate.*

spring *especially written* to jump or move somewhere suddenly: *The cat sprang up onto the sofa.* | *She sprang out of bed and ran downstairs.*

dive to jump into water with your head and arms first: *Always be careful when you're diving into the swimming pool.*

---

jump² n

1 MOVEMENT UP/DOWN [C] when you push yourself into the air using your legs, or let yourself drop from something: *the best jump of the competition* | **parachute/bungee jump** *I'd love to **do** a parachute jump.*

2 INCREASE [singular] a sudden increase in an amount or value: **[+in]** *a big jump in house prices*

3 STH YOU JUMP OVER [C] something that a person or horse jumps over in a competition → **HIGH JUMP, LONG JUMP**

jumper /ˈdʒʌmpə $ -ər/ n [C] **1** *BrE* a piece of clothing made of wool that covers the upper part of your body and your arms SYN **sweater** → see picture at **CLOTHES 2** *AmE* a dress without sleeves, usually worn over a shirt SYN **pinafore** *BrE*

ˈjump rope n [C] *AmE* a long piece of rope that children use for jumping over SYN **skipping rope** *BrE*

jumpy /ˈdʒʌmpi/ *adj informal* nervous or anxious THESAURUS NERVOUS

junction /ˈdʒʌŋkʃən/ n [C] a place where one road, railway line etc joins another: *the junction of Abbot Road and New Street*

juncture /ˈdʒʌŋktʃə $ -ər/ n [singular] *formal* a particular point in an activity or period of time: *At this juncture, we'll take a break.*

June /dʒuːn/ n [C,U] (*written abbreviation* **Jun.**) the sixth month of the year, between May and July: **next/last June** *He died last June.* | **in June** *My birthday's in June.* | **on June 6th** *We met on June 6th.*

jungle /ˈdʒʌŋɡəl/ n [C,U] a large tropical forest with trees and large plants growing very close together

Junior /ˈdʒuːniə $ -ər/ (*written abbreviation* **Jnr** *BrE*, **Jr.** *AmE*) used after the name of a man who has the same name as his father: *John J. Wallace Junior*

junior¹ *adj*

1 having a low rank in an organization or profession → **senior**: *a junior executive*

2 for young people below a particular age: *the junior football club*

junior² n [C] **1** a young person who takes part in sport for people below a particular age **2** *especially BrE* someone who has a low rank in an organization or profession **3 a)** *AmE* a student in the third year of HIGH SCHOOL or college **b)** *BrE* a child at a junior school

PHRASES

be ten years/six months etc sb's junior to be ten years, six months etc younger than someone: *His wife is ten years his junior.*

junior ˈcollege n [C,U] a college in the US and Canada where students do a course for two years

junior ˈhigh school (*also* **junior ˈhigh**) n [C,U] a school in the US and Canada for students between the ages of 12 and 14 or 15

ˈjunior ˌschool n [C,U] a school in Britain for children between the ages of 7 and 11 → **primary school**

junk /dʒʌŋk/ n [U] old or unwanted things that have no use or value: *a cupboard full of junk*

ˈjunk food n [U] food that is not healthy because it contains a lot of fat or sugar

junkie /ˈdʒʌŋki/ n [C] *informal* **1** someone who takes dangerous drugs and is dependent on them **2 TV/sports etc junkie** someone who likes something and does it a lot

ˈjunk mail n [U] *disapproving* letters or emails, especially advertisements, sent to a large number of people THESAURUS ADVERTISEMENT

junta /ˈdʒʌntə, ˈhʊntə/ n [C] a military government that has gained power by using force

Jupiter /ˈdʒuːpɪtə $ -ər/ n the fifth PLANET from the Sun

jurisdiction /ˌdʒʊərəsˈdɪkʃən $ ˌdʒʊr-/ n [U] the legal power to make decisions about something: *the court's jurisdiction*

juror /ˈdʒʊərə $ ˈdʒʊrər/ n [C] a member of a jury

jury /ˈdʒʊəri $ ˈdʒʊri/ n [C] (*plural* **juries**)

1 a group of twelve ordinary people in a court who decide whether someone is guilty: *the **members of the jury***

2 a group of people who choose the winner of a competition → **GRAND JURY**

just

[Ac] = words from the Academic Word List

just¹ /dʒəst; *strong* dʒʌst/ *adv*

1 exactly: *You look **just like** your dad.* | *The temperature was **just right**.* | *The phone rang **just as** (=at the exact moment when) we were leaving.* | ***Just then*** (=at exactly that moment), *Anne ran in from the garden.* **THESAURUS** EXACTLY

2 only: *'Who was there?' 'Just me and Elaine.'* | *It's not serious – just a small cut.* | *I just want to go to bed* (=that is all I want to do). | ***just a minute/second*** (=used to ask someone to wait for a short time)

3 only a short time ago: *She's just got married.* | *I've just had a really good idea.* **THESAURUS** RECENTLY

4 now or very soon: *Hang on, I'm just coming.* | *He's just leaving.* | **be just about to do sth** (=be going to do something very soon) *I was just about to phone you.*

5 just before/after/outside/over etc sth a small amount of time, distance, etc: *Lucy got home just after us.* | *They live just outside Paris.*

6 (only) just used to show that something happens with difficulty or almost does not happen: *They just managed to get to the station in time.* | *It only just fits through the door.* | *We had **just enough** (=enough but no more) money.*

7 *spoken* used to emphasize something you are saying: *I just couldn't believe the news.* | *That's just wonderful!* | *I didn't realise **just how** rich they were.*

8 *spoken* used to politely ask or tell someone something: *Could I just use your phone?*

PHRASES

it's just as well *spoken* used to say that it is lucky that something happened: *It's just as well you were there to help.*

just about almost: *We're just about finished.* | *Just about everyone replied.* **THESAURUS** ALMOST

just as good/important/much etc equally as good, important etc: *The $250 TV is just as good as the $300 one.*

just in case *spoken* in order to be prepared for something that might happen: *I'll take my umbrella, just in case.*

just now *spoken* **1** a short time ago: *He was here just now.* **2** at this moment: *I'm busy just now. Can I call you back?*

just² /dʒʌst/ *adj formal* morally right and fair **OPP** unjust: *a just punishment*

justice /'dʒʌstɪs/ *n* [U]

1 the system by which people are judged in courts of law and criminals are punished: *the criminal justice system* | *The killers must be **brought to justice*** (=caught and punished).

2 fairness in the way people are treated **OPP** injustice: *Children have a strong **sense of justice**.*

PHRASES

do sb/sth justice to show or talk about someone in a way that makes them seem as attractive, good etc as they really are: *This picture doesn't do you justice.*

Justice of the 'Peace *n* [C] (*abbreviation* **JP**) someone who decides whether a person is guilty of a crime in a small local court

justifiable [Ac] /'dʒʌstəfaɪəbəl/ *adj* done for good reasons: *a justifiable decision* —**justifiably** *adv*

justification [Ac] /,dʒʌstɪfɪ'keɪʃən/ *n* [C,U] a good reason for doing something: *There's **no justification for** upsetting her like that.* **THESAURUS** REASON

justified [Ac] /'dʒʌstɪfaɪd/ *adj* having an acceptable explanation or reason **OPP** unjustified: *Your complaints are certainly justified.*

justify [Ac] /'dʒʌstɪfaɪ/ *v* [T] (**justified, justifying, justifies**) to give a good reason for doing something that other people think is unreasonable: **justify (doing) sth** *How can you justify spending so much money on a coat?*

jut /dʒʌt/ (*also* **jut out**) *v* [I] (**jutted, jutting**) to stick out further than the surrounding things: *a point of land that juts out into the ocean*

juvenile /'dʒuːvənaɪl $ -nəl, -naɪl/ *adj* **1** *law* relating to young people who are not yet adults: *juvenile crime* **2** *disapproving* silly and typical of a child rather than an adult: *a juvenile sense of humour* —**juvenile** *n* [C]

juvenile de'linquent *n* [C] *formal* a child or young person who behaves in a criminal way

juxtapose /,dʒʌkstə'pəʊz $ 'dʒʌkstəpoʊz/ *v* [T] *formal* to put together things that are very different, especially in order to compare them —**juxtaposition** /,dʒʌkstəpə'zɪʃən/ *n* [C,U]

Kk

K¹, k /keɪ/ n [C,U] (plural **K's, k's**) the 11th letter of the English alphabet

K², k **1** informal an abbreviation of **thousand**, used when talking about money: *He earns £50K a year.* **2** a written abbreviation of **kilobyte**

kaleidoscope /kəˈlaɪdəskəʊp $ -skoʊp/ n **1** [singular] a large number of very different things: **[+of]** *a kaleidoscope of cultures* **2** [C] a tube with mirrors and pieces of coloured glass at one end that shows different coloured patterns when you turn it

KANGAROO

kangaroo /ˌkæŋɡəˈruː/ n [C] (plural **kangaroos**) a large Australian animal that jumps and carries its babies in a pocket on its stomach

karaoke /ˌkæriˈəʊki $ ˌkɑːrɑːˈoʊ-/ n [U] when someone sings popular songs while a machine plays the music, for entertainment

karat /ˈkærət/ n [C] AmE a unit for measuring how pure a piece of gold is SYN **carat** BrE

karate /kəˈrɑːti/ n [U] a sport from Japan in which you fight using your hands and feet → see picture on page A9

karma /ˈkɑːmə $ -ɑːr-/ n [U] the belief that the good and bad things you do in your life will affect you in the future, according to some religions

kayak /ˈkaɪæk/ n [C] a small boat, usually for one person → **canoe** → see picture on page A9 —**kayaking** n [U]

KB, Kb a written abbreviation of **kilobyte**

kebab /kəˈbæb $ kəˈbɑːb/ n [C] BrE **1** thin pieces of meat and pieces of vegetables wrapped in thin bread **2** small pieces of meat and vegetables, cooked on a stick

keel¹ /kiːl/ n [C] a bar along the bottom of a boat that keeps it steady

PHRASES

on an even keel continuing in a steady way: *I'd just got my life back on an even keel after the break-up.*

keel² v

PHRASAL VERBS

keel over to fall over suddenly: *Several soldiers keeled over in the heat.*

keen /kiːn/ adj

1 wanting to do something very much SYN **eager**: **keen to do sth** *US companies are keen to enter the Chinese market.* | **keen on doing sth** *They're keen on getting more young people to apply.* | *The students all seem very keen* (=they want to learn).

2 especially BrE liking someone or something very much, or being very interested in them: **[+on]** *I'm not very keen on their music.* | *She takes **a keen interest in** politics.* THESAURUS ► LIKE

3 a keen sense or feeling is very strong: *Sarah felt a keen sense of loss.* | *his keen eye for talent* —**keenly** adv

keep¹ /kiːp/ v (past tense and past participle **kept** /kept/)

1 STAY/MAKE SB OR STH STAY [linking verb] to stay in the same state or position, or to make someone or something do this: **keep (sb/sth) warm/safe/alive etc** *This blanket should help keep you warm.* | **keep (sb) awake/calm/happy etc** *activities to keep everyone happy* | ***Keep still** for a moment.* | *Try to keep the place **tidy**.* | **keep (sb/sth) away/back/out etc** *high fences to keep intruders out* | **keep sb busy/occupied/amused etc** *My work's been keeping me very busy.* | *They **kept** their plans **secret**.*

2 CONTINUE **keep (on) doing sth** to continue doing something, or to do the same thing many times: *Food prices keep on rising.* | **keep saying/telling/repeating etc** *I keep telling him, but he won't listen!* | **keep going** (=used to tell someone to continue doing something or going somewhere) *Keep going – we're nearly there.*

3 NOT SELL/GIVE STH [T] to continue to have something and not give it back, sell it etc: *You can keep the book. I don't need it.* | *We've decided to keep this car for another year.*

4 STORE STH [T] to leave something in a particular place, so that you can find it: *Where do you keep your teabags?* | **[+in/on/under etc]** *The information is kept on computer.*

5 IN PRISON/HOSPITAL ETC [T] to make someone stay in prison, a hospital etc: *They kept him in jail for two weeks.*

6 DELAY SB [T] to delay someone: *I don't know what's keeping her. It's 8:00 already.* | *Sorry to keep you waiting* (=make you have to wait).

7 PROMISE/ARRANGEMENT [T] to do something you have promised or arranged to do: *She had to rush off to keep an appointment.* | **keep your promise/word**

8 WRITE DOWN INFORMATION **keep a record/diary etc** to regularly write down information about something: *Keep a record of what you spend.*

9 SECRET **keep a secret** to not tell anyone about a secret: *Can you keep a secret?*

10 PROVIDE NECESSARY THINGS [T] to provide someone with the money, food etc they need: *I don't earn enough to keep a family.* | **keep sb going** (=to be enough for what is needed for a short time) *Have a biscuit to keep you going.*

11 FOOD [I] if food keeps, it stays fresh: *That yoghurt won't keep much longer.*

12 ANIMALS [T] to have animals and look after them: *We used to keep chickens.*

THESAURUS – sense 4

keep to leave something in a particular place so that you can find it: *Where do you keep the scissors?*

store to put things in a place and keep them until you need them: *Food should be stored in a cool dry place.*

save to keep something so that you can use or enjoy it later: *He had been saving the bottle of champagne for a special occasion.*

file to store papers or information in a particular order or in a particular place: *All the students' records are filed alphabetically.*

hoard to keep a lot of something because you think you may not be able to get it in the future: *People have been hoarding food and fuel in case there is another attack.*

PHRASAL VERBS

keep at sth to continue to do something although it is difficult: *It's hard work, but keep at it!*

keep away to not go near someone or something: **[+from]** *Keep away from the fire.* **THESAURUS▶** AVOID

keep sth ↔ **back** to not tell someone about something: *She was keeping something back from me.*

keep sth ↔ **down** to prevent something from increasing too much: *I hope they keep the rents down.* | *Please keep the noise down* (=be quieter)!

keep sb **in** to make someone stay in hospital, or to make a child stay inside as a punishment

keep from

1 keep sth **from** sb to not tell someone about something: *He kept the news from his family for days.*

2 keep (sb/sth) from (doing) sth to prevent someone from doing something or prevent something from happening: *Am I keeping you from your work?* | *I bit my lip to keep from crying.*

keep off

1 keep sth **off (sth)** to prevent something from touching or damaging something else: *A hat will keep the sun off your head.*

2 keep off sth to avoid using, eating, touching etc something: *You should keep off alcohol.* | *Keep off the grass.*

keep on

1 keep on doing sth to continue doing something, or to do something many times: *Just keep on trying.* **THESAURUS▶** CONTINUE

2 keep sb **on** to continue to employ someone: *If he's good, they might keep him on.*

3 *informal disapproving* to talk about something a lot, or tell someone to do something many times, in an annoying way: **[+about]** *She kept on about the wedding all the time.* | **[+at]** *Don't keep on at me!*

keep out of sth to not become involved with something: *You keep out of this, Campbell.*

keep to sth

1 to do what you should do or agreed to do: *They failed to keep to the agreement.*

2 to stay on a particular road, path etc: *Keep to the main roads.*

3 keep sth **to a minimum** to prevent the amount or level of something getting too high

4 keep sth **to yourself** to not tell anyone about something: *Kim kept Gina's secret to herself.*

5 keep (yourself) to yourself to live in a very quiet, private way

keep up

1 keep sth ↔ **up** to continue doing something, or to make something continue: *Keep up the good work.* | *It's exhausting and I don't know how long she can keep it up.*

2 to do something as well or as quickly as other people: **[+with]** *Dave isn't keeping up with the rest of the class.*

3 to move as quickly as someone: *Wait, I can't keep up!*

4 to know about the latest facts, information, and products in a particular area: **[+with]** *It's hard to keep up with all the changes in computer technology.*

5 if one process keeps up with another, it increases at the same speed and by the same amount: **[+with]** *Food production is not keeping up with population growth.*

6 keep sb **up** to prevent someone from sleeping: *The baby kept us up all night.*

keep² n **1 earn your keep** to do enough work to pay for your food, clothes etc **2 for keeps** *informal* for ever: *It's yours for keeps.*

keeper /'kiːpə $ -ər/ n [C] **1** someone who looks after animals or a place and the things that are in it: *cattle keepers* | **[+of]** *the keeper of Egyptian Antiquities at the British Museum* **2** a GOALKEEPER → GAMEKEEPER, ZOO-KEEPER

keep 'fit n [U] *BrE* a class in which you do exercises to keep yourself healthy

keeping /'kiːpɪŋ/ n **in keeping/out of keeping (with sth)** suitable or not suitable for a particular style or situation: *The modern furniture wasn't really in keeping with the rest of the house.* → SAFEKEEPING

keepsake /'kiːpseɪk/ n [C] a small object that you keep to remind you of someone

keg /keg/ n [C] a large container used for storing beer

kennel /'kenl/ n [C] **1** a small outdoor building for a dog to sleep in **2** (*also* **kennels** [plural] *BrE*) a place where dogs are looked after while their owners are not at home

kept /kept/ v the past tense and past participle of KEEP

kerb *BrE*, **curb** *AmE* /kɜːb $ kɜːrb/ n [C] the edge of the PAVEMENT at the side of the road

kernel /'kɜːnl $ 'kɜːr-/ n [C] the centre part of a nut or seed

kerosene /'kerəsiːn/ n [U] *especially AmE* a type of oil that is burned for heat and light **SYN** paraffin *BrE*

ketchup /'ketʃəp/ n [U] a cold red sauce made from tomatoes that you put on food

kettle /'ketl/ n [C] a container used for boiling water: *I'll put the kettle on for a cup of tea.* → see picture at KITCHEN

key¹ /kiː/ n [C]

1 FOR A LOCK something that you put into a lock in order to open a door, start a car etc: **house/car keys** *I lost my car keys.* | *A bunch of keys hung from his belt.*

2 ON A COMPUTER/PIANO one of the things you press to produce letters and numbers on a computer, or sounds on a piano

3 IMPORTANT PART **the key (to sth)** the part of a plan, action etc that will make it possible for it to succeed: **[+to]** *Preparation is the key to success.* | *a discovery that may* **hold the key** *to our understanding of the universe*

4 MUSICAL NOTES a set of musical notes that is based on one particular note: *the key of C major*

5 ON A MAP/DRAWING a list of the signs, colours etc used on a map, technical drawing etc that explains what they mean

6 PRINTED ANSWERS the printed answers to a test or set of questions in a book

key² *adj* [only before noun] very important or necessary: *a key witness* | *a* **key decision** THESAURUS **IMPORTANT**

key³ *v*

PHRASAL VERBS

key sth ↔ **in** to put information into a computer THESAURUS **WRITE**

keyboard /ˈkiːbɔːd $ -bɔːrd/ *n* [C] **1** a set of keys on a computer, a piano etc that you press to produce letters or sounds **2** (*also* **keyboards** [plural]) an electronic musical instrument similar to a piano that can make sounds like many different instruments

KEYBOARDS

computer keyboard

electronic keyboard

keyed 'up *adj* [not before noun] worried or excited

keyhole /ˈkiːhəʊl $ -hoʊl/ *n* [C] the hole in a lock that you put the key in

keynote /ˈkiːnəʊt $ -noʊt/ *adj* **keynote speech/ address/lecture** the most important speech etc at a formal meeting

keypad /ˈkiːpæd/ *n* [C] a small box with buttons on it that you press to put information into a computer, telephone etc

'key ring *n* [C] a metal ring that you keep keys on

keyword /ˈkiːwɜːd $ -wɜːrd/ *n* [C] a word that you type into a computer so that it will search for that word on the Internet: *You can find the site by entering the keyword 'Quark'.*

kg the written abbreviation of **kilogram**

khaki /ˈkɑːki $ ˈkæki, ˈkɑːki/ *n* [U] a dull greenbrown or yellow-brown colour —**khaki** *adj*

kick¹ /kɪk/ *v*

1 [T] to hit or move something with your foot: **kick sth into/out of/around etc sth** *Billy was* **kicking a ball** *around the yard.* | **kick sth down** *The police kicked the door down.* → see picture on page A11

2 [I,T] to move your legs quickly forwards or backwards: *a baby kicking its legs* | *He* **kicked off** *his shoes and lay on the bed.*

3 kick yourself *spoken* to be annoyed with yourself because you have done something silly, made a mistake etc: *You'll kick yourself when I tell you the answer.*

PHRASES

kick the habit to stop doing something such as smoking, taking drugs etc: *smokers who want to kick the habit*

kick up a fuss *informal* to complain loudly about something: *People are kicking up a fuss about the noise from the airport.*

PHRASAL VERBS

kick in *informal* to begin to have an effect: *Those pills should kick in any time now.*

kick off *informal* to start: **[+with]** *The festivities will kick off with a barbecue dinner.*

kick sb ↔ **out** *informal* to make someone leave a place, job etc: **[+of]** *He was kicked out of the club for fighting.*

kick² *n* [C]

1 an action of hitting something with your foot: *Brazil scored with the last kick of the match.* | *If the gate won't open, just* **give** *it* **a** *good* **kick.**

2 *informal* a feeling of pleasure and excitement: *Alan* **gets a real kick out of** *skiing.* | **do sth for kicks** *She started stealing for kicks.* → **FREE KICK**

kickback /ˈkɪkbæk/ *n* [C,U] *informal* money that a person gets for secretly and dishonestly helping someone SYN **bribe**

kickoff /ˈkɪkɒf $ -ɒːf/ *n* [C,U] the time when a football game starts, or the first kick of the game: *Kickoff is at midday.*

'kick-start *v* [T] to do something to help a process or activity start or develop more quickly: *A cut in interest rates might kick-start the economy.*

kid¹ /kɪd/ *n*

1 [C] *informal* a child: *How many kids do you have?* | *when I was a* **little kid**

2 [C] *informal* a young person: *Kids these days spend a fortune on CDs.* | *college kids*

3 [C,U] a young goat, or the leather made from its skin

PHRASES

kid brother/sister *especially AmE informal* a younger brother or sister SYN **little brother/sister** *BrE: My kid sister always follows me around.*

kid² *v* (**kidded, kidding**) *informal* **1** [I,T] to make a joke, especially by saying something that is not true: *Don't worry, I was* **just kidding**. **2** [T] to make yourself or someone else believe something that is untrue or unlikely: **kid yourself (that)** *Don't kid yourself he'll ever change.*

PHRASES

no kidding/you're kidding *spoken informal* said when you are surprised by what someone has said: *Carlotta's 39? No kidding!*

kiddie, kiddy /ˈkɪdi/ *n* [C] *especially BrE informal* a young child: *Is the film suitable for kiddies?*

kidnap /ˈkɪdnæp/ *v* [T] (**kidnapped, kidnapping** *BrE,* **kidnaped, kidnaping** *AmE*) to take someone somewhere by force, especially in order to get

K

money for returning them —**kidnapper** *n* [C] —**kidnapping** (*also* **kidnap**) *n* [C,U]

kidney /'kɪdni/ *n* [C] one of the two organs in your lower back that separate waste liquid from blood → see picture on page A2

kill¹ /kɪl/ *v*
1 [I,T] to make a person or animal die: *He's in jail for killing a policeman.* | **kill yourself** *She tried to kill herself.* | *Smoking kills.* **THESAURUS** ▶ **DIE**
2 [T] to make something stop, or prevent it from happening: *They gave her drugs to kill the pain.*
3 my head/back etc is killing me *spoken* used to say that part of your body is hurting a lot: *I've walked miles and my feet are killing me.*
PHRASES
kill yourself laughing to laugh a lot about something: *He killed himself laughing when he saw me.*
kill time/an hour etc *informal* to spend time doing something that is not important while you are waiting for something else to happen: *She read a magazine to kill time.*
kill two birds with one stone to achieve two things with one action: *I need to go and see Annie, so I thought I'd visit you on the way – kill two birds with one stone.*
sb will kill/could have killed sb *spoken* used to say that someone will be or was very angry with someone: *My wife will kill me if she finds out.*

PHRASAL VERBS
kill sb/sth ↔ **off** to stop someone or something from existing any more: *Pollution is rapidly killing off the plant life.*

THESAURUS

kill to make someone die: *She wanted to kill them for what they had done.* | *Eleven soldiers were killed in the attack.*
murder to deliberately kill someone – used when talking about this as a crime: *The police think that he was murdered.*
assassinate to deliberately kill an important person, especially a politician: *President Kennedy was assassinated in 1963.*
execute to kill someone as a punishment for a crime: *If he is found guilty, he will be executed.*
commit suicide to deliberately kill yourself: *She became depressed and later committed suicide.*
massacre to kill a lot of people in a violent way: *The soldiers massacred hundreds of innocent women and children.*
slaughter to kill animals for food: *The sheep are taken away to be slaughtered.*

kill² *n* [singular] the act of killing a hunted animal
PHRASES
move in/close in for the kill to get nearer to killing or defeating someone: *His opponent was moving in for the kill.*

killer /'kɪlə $ -ər/ *n* [C] a person, animal, or thing that kills: *The police are still looking for the girl's killer.* | *weed killer*

killing /'kɪlɪŋ/ *n* [C] a murder: *a series of **brutal killings***

PHRASES
make a killing *informal* to make a lot of money very quickly: *The property developers are making a killing.*

kiln /kɪln/ *n* [C] a special OVEN for baking clay pots, bricks etc

kilo /'kiːləʊ $ -loʊ/ *n* [C] (*plural* **kilos**) a kilogram: *I weigh 65 kilos.*

kilobyte /'kɪləbaɪt/ *n* [C] (*written abbreviation* **K**, **KB**) a unit for measuring computer information, equal to 1,024 BYTES

kilogram, **kilogramme** /'kɪləgræm/ (*also* **kilo**) *n* [C] (*written abbreviation* **kg**) a unit for measuring weight, equal to 1,000 grams

kilometre *BrE*, **kilometer** *AmE* /'kɪləmiːtə, kɪ'lɒmɪtə $ kɪ'lɑːmɪtər/ *n* [C] (*written abbreviation* **km**) a unit for measuring length, equal to 1,000 metres

kilowatt /'kɪləwɒt $ -wɑːt/ *n* [C] (*written abbreviation* **kW**) a unit for measuring electrical power, equal to 1,000 WATTS

kilt /kɪlt/ *n* [C] a skirt traditionally worn by Scottish men

kimono /kɪ'məʊnəʊ $ -'moʊnoʊ/ *n* [C] (*plural* **kimonos**) a loose piece of clothing traditionally worn in Japan

kin /kɪn/ *n* [plural] *old-fashioned* your family
PHRASES
next of kin *formal* the person in your family who you are most closely related to: *The police will have to inform the next of kin about his death.* **THESAURUS** ▶ **RELATIVE**

kind¹ /kaɪnd/ *n* [C] a type of person or thing → **sort**: **[+of]** *What kind of pizza do you want?* | *We sell **all kinds** of hats.* | *I think they're having **some kind** of party upstairs.* | **of its kind** *The course is the only one of its kind.* | *Ted just isn't **the marrying kind** (=the type of person who gets married).*
PHRASES
a kind of (a) sth *spoken* used to say that your description of something is not exact: *a kind of reddish-brown colour*
kind of *spoken* slightly, or in some ways SYN **sort of**, **kinda** *AmE*: *He looks kind of weird to me.* | *I'm kind of glad I didn't win.*
nothing/anything of the kind *spoken* used to emphasize that what has been said is not true: *I never said anything of the kind!*
of a kind *disapproving* used to say that something is not as good as it should be: *I think it's chicken – of a kind.*
one of a kind the only one of a particular type of thing: *Each vase is handmade and one of a kind.*

kind² *adj* someone who is kind shows that they care about other people and wants to help them OPP **unkind**: *She's a kind and generous person.* | **[+to]** *Everyone's been so kind to me.* | *Thank you for your **kind offer**.* | **it's kind of sb (to do sth)** *It was kind of him to call.*

PHRASES

kind regards *formal* used to end a formal but friendly letter: *I look forward to working with you again. Kind regards, Beth Jones.*

THESAURUS

kind showing that you care about other people and want to help them: *It's kind of you to offer to help. | a kind old lady*

nice *especially spoken* friendly and kind: *All the teachers are really nice.*

generous kind because you give people money, presents etc: *Her father was very generous and was always buying her things.*

thoughtful thinking of things you can do to make other people happy or feel good: *It was thoughtful of you to send him a card.*

considerate thinking about other people's feelings and careful not to do anything that will upset them: *Our neighbours are very considerate and keep their TV turned down.*

sympathetic saying kind things to someone who has problems, and showing that you care about them: *My friends were very sympathetic when my dog died.*

---

kinda /'kaɪndə/ *adv AmE spoken* a way of writing or saying 'kind of' which many people think is incorrect SYN **slightly**: *I'm kinda tired.*

kindergarten /'kɪndəgɑːtn $ -dərgɑːrtn/ *n* [C,U] **1** *BrE* a school for children aged two to five SYN **nursery school 2** *AmE* a school or class for children aged 5

kind-hearted /ˌkaɪnd 'hɑːtɪd◂ $ -ɑːr-/ *adj* kind and generous

kindle /'kɪndl/ *v* [I,T] **1** if you kindle a fire, or if it kindles, it starts to burn **2** to make someone feel interested, excited, hopeful etc: **kindle sth in sb** *A love of poetry was kindled in him by his mother.*

kindling /'kɪndlɪŋ/ *n* [U] small pieces of dry wood, leaves etc that you use for starting a fire

kindly¹ /'kaɪndli/ *adv* **1** in a kind way: *Miss Havisham looked kindly at Joe. | kindly offer/agree/give etc Dad's kindly offered to lend us his car.* **2** *spoken formal* used to mean 'please', especially when you are annoyed: *Kindly go away.*

PHRASES

not take kindly to sth to be unwilling to accept a situation because it annoys you: *He didn't take kindly to being told what to do.*

kindly² *adj old-fashioned* kind

kindness /'kaɪndnəs/ *n* [U] kind behaviour: *Sam never forgot her kindness.*

kindred /'kɪndrɪd/ *adj* **kindred spirit** someone who thinks and feels the way you do

king /kɪŋ/ *n* [C]

1 ROYAL RULER a man from a royal family who rules a country → **queen**: **[+of]** *the King of Spain | Leopold was crowned king in October.*

2 MOST IMPORTANT/BEST **the king of sth** the most important or best person or thing in a particular area, activity etc: *The lion is the king of the jungle.*

3 IN CHESS the most important piece in a game of CHESS

4 IN CARD GAMES a playing card with a picture of a king on it

kingdom /'kɪŋdəm/ *n* [C] a country that is ruled by a king or queen: **[+of]** *the Kingdom of Nepal*

PHRASES

the animal/plant kingdom all animals or plants considered together as a group: *Bacteria belong to the plant kingdom.*

kingfisher /'kɪŋˌfɪʃə $ -ər/ *n* [C] a small brightly coloured bird that catches fish in rivers

'king-size (*also* **'king-sized**) *adj* very big: *a king-size bed*

kink /kɪŋk/ *n* [C] a twist in something that is normally straight

kinky /'kɪŋki/ *adj informal* kinky sexual activities are strange and unusual: *kinky sex videos*

kinship /'kɪnʃɪp/ *n* **1** [U] *literary* family relationships **2** [singular, U] a strong connection between people: *He **felt a kinship** with the only other American on the base.*

kiosk /'kiːɒsk $ -ɑːsk/ *n* [C] a small building in the street where newspapers, sweets etc are sold

kip /kɪp/ *n* [singular, U] *BrE informal* a short period of sleep —**kip** *v* [I]

kipper /'kɪpə $ -ər/ *n* [C] a type of fish that has been preserved using smoke and salt

kiss¹ /kɪs/ *v* [I,T] to touch someone with your lips as a greeting or to show them love: **kiss sb on sth** *She kissed me on the cheek. | Matt **kissed** her **good night** and left the room. | As they parted, John and Mary kissed.*

kiss² *n* [C] an act of kissing: *a passionate kiss*

PHRASES

give sb the kiss of life *BrE* to breathe air into someone's lungs in order to make them start breathing again: *A passer-by gave him the kiss of life.*

COLLOCATIONS

verbs

to give sb a kiss *Give your grandma a kiss.*

to blow sb a kiss (=to kiss your hand and then blow across it towards someone) *She blew him a kiss from the train.*

types of kiss

a big/little kiss *I'm going to give him a big kiss when I see him.*

a quick kiss *He gave her a quick kiss on the cheek.*

a goodnight kiss (=when saying good night to someone) *Mum will come up and give you a goodnight kiss.*

---

kit /kɪt/ *n* [C] **1** a set of tools, clothes etc that you use for a particular purpose or activity: *a bike repair kit | my football kit* **2** something that you buy in parts and put together yourself: *I built the boat **from a kit**.*

kitchen /'kɪtʃɪn/ *n* [C] the room where you prepare and cook food: *She's in the kitchen making the dinner. | kitchen cupboards*

K

kite /kaɪt/ n [C] a toy made of paper or cloth that flies in the air on the end of a long string

kitsch /kɪtʃ/ n [U] things such as decorations that are cheap, ugly, or unfashionable: *Her house was full of 1970s kitsch.*

kitten /'kɪtn/ n [C] a young cat

kitty /'kɪti/ n [C usually singular] (*plural* **kitties**) the money that people have collected for a particular purpose

'kitty-,corner adv AmE informal on the opposite corner of a street from a particular place

kiwi fruit /'kiːwiː fruːt/ (*also* **kiwi**) n [C] a small brown fruit which is green inside with black seeds → see picture on page A4

Kleenex /'kliːneks/ n [C,U] (*plural* **Kleenex**) *trademark* a TISSUE

klutz /klʌts/ n [C] AmE informal someone who drops things or falls easily —**klutzy** adj

km the written abbreviation of **kilometre**

knack /næk/ n [singular] informal a natural skill or ability: **knack for/of doing sth** *Harry has the knack of making friends wherever he goes.*

knackered /'nækəd $ -ərd/ adj [not before noun] BrE informal extremely tired

knapsack /'næpsæk/ n [C] AmE a bag that you carry on your back SYN **backpack**

knead /niːd/ v [T] to press a mixture of flour and water many times with your hands, for example to make bread: *Knead the dough for three minutes.*

knee /niː/ n [C]
1 the middle part of your leg, where it bends: **on your knees** *She was on her knees, weeding the garden.* | *a painful knee injury* → see picture on page A2
2 the part of your trousers that covers your knee: *His jeans had holes in both knees.*
PHRASES
bring sb/sth to their knees to defeat or destroy someone or something, so that they cannot continue: *The recession brought many companies to their knees.*

kneecap /'niːkæp/ n [C] the bone at the front of your knee → see picture on page A2

knee-'deep adj **1** deep enough to reach your knees: *The snow was almost knee-deep.* **2** [not before noun] having a lot of something to deal with: **[+in]** *We ended up knee-deep in debt.*

knee-'high adj tall enough to reach your knees: *knee-high grass*

'knee-jerk adj **knee-jerk reaction/response** something you say or feel as an immediate reaction, without thinking about it

kneel /niːl/ (*also* **kneel down**) v [I] (*past tense and past participle* **knelt** /nelt/ *also* **kneeled** AmE) to be in or move into a position where your body is resting on your knees: *She knelt down and began to pray.* → see picture on page A11

knew /njuː $ nuː/ v the past tense of KNOW

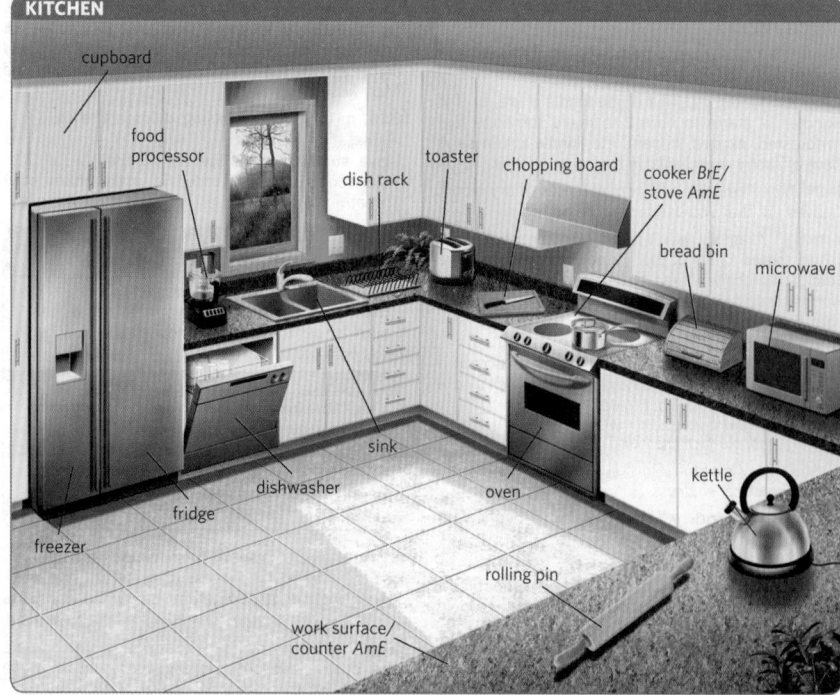

KITCHEN

cupboard

food processor

dish rack

toaster

chopping board

cooker BrE/ stove AmE

bread bin

microwave

sink

dishwasher

fridge

freezer

oven

kettle

rolling pin

work surface/ counter AmE

knickers /'nɪkəz $ -ərz/ n [plural] BrE women's underwear that covers the area between the waist and the top of the legs SYN **panties** AmE: *a pair of black knickers* → see picture at CLOTHES

knick-knack /'nɪk næk/ n [C] a small object used as a decoration

knife /naɪf/ n [C] (plural **knives** /naɪvz/) a tool used for cutting or as a weapon: *a knife and fork | gangs of young boys carrying knives | a sharp knife* —**knife** v [T]: *She had been knifed to death.* → POCKET KNIFE

knight /naɪt/ n [C] **1** a man with a high rank in the past, who was trained to fight while riding a horse **2** in Britain, a man who has received a special honour from the king or queen and can use 'Sir' before his name → **dame** —**knight** v [T]: *He was knighted in 2001.*

knighthood /'naɪthʊd/ n [C,U] a British rank and title given to a man as an honour for doing good things

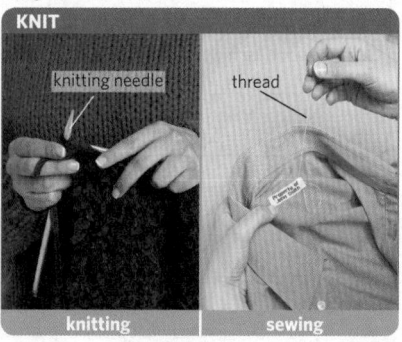

KNIT

knitting needle

thread

knitting   sewing

knit /nɪt/ v [I,T] (past tense and past participle **knitted** or **knit**, present participle **knitting**) to make clothes out of wool using two long needles or a special machine: *She's knitting a sweater.* —**knitting** n [U]

'knitting ˌneedle n [C] one of the two long needles that you use to knit clothes out of wool → see picture at KNIT

knitwear /'nɪt-weə $ -wer/ n [U] knitted clothes such as SWEATERS, sold in shops

knives /naɪvz/ n the plural of KNIFE

knob /nɒb $ nɑːb/ n [C] a round handle or button that you turn to open a door, turn on a radio etc

knobbly /'nɒbli $ 'nɑːbli/ BrE, **knobby** /'nɒbi $ 'nɑːbi/ AmE adj not smooth, with hard parts sticking out from the surface: *knobbly knees*

KNOCK

knock¹ /nɒk $ nɑːk/ v
1 [I] to hit a door or window with your hand to attract the attention of people inside: **[+on/at]** *There's someone knocking on the front door.*
THESAURUS HIT

Grammar
Do not say 'Terry knocked the door.' Say *Terry knocked at the door.* or *Terry knocked on the door.*

2 [T] to hit someone or something so that they move or fall down: **knock sth out of/from/off sth** *Tim knocked the glass out of my hand. | Two boys knocked him to the ground. | A blow like that could knock you unconscious.* | **knock sth over** *I'm afraid I've knocked over a vase.*
3 [T] to hit part of your body on something and hurt it: **knock sth on sth** *She knocked her head on a stone.*
4 [T] *informal* to criticize someone or something, especially unfairly: *'I hate this job.' 'Don't knock it – it could be worse!'*

PHRASES

knock on wood AmE used to say that you do not want your good luck to end SYN **touch wood** BrE: *The kids are all healthy, knock on wood.*

knock some sense into sb to make someone learn to behave in a more sensible way: *Maybe his teachers can knock some sense into him.*

PHRASAL VERBS

knock sth ↔ **back** *informal* to drink a lot of alcohol very quickly: *We knocked back another bottle.*
knock sb/sth ↔ **down**
1 to hit someone and make them fall down to the ground: *A mother of two has been knocked down by a bus and killed.*
2 *informal* to reduce the price of something: *The chair was knocked down from $800 to $550.*
3 to destroy a building or part of a building: *Workers began to knock down the wall.* THESAURUS DESTROY
knock off *informal*
1 knock off (sth) to stop working: *We knocked off at 5 o'clock.*
2 knock sth ↔ off to reduce the price of something by a particular amount: *I got him to knock $10 off the regular price.*
knock sb/sth ↔ **out**
1 to make someone become unconscious, especially by hitting them: *Ali knocked out his opponent in the fifth round.*
2 to defeat a person or team so that they cannot continue in a competition: *Indiana got knocked out in the first round.*
knock sb ↔ **over** to hit someone with a moving vehicle and hurt or kill them: *The elderly man was knocked over while crossing the road.*
knock sth ↔ **up** *spoken* to make something quickly and without using much effort: *I'm sure I can knock up some pasta.*

knock² n [C]
1 the sound of someone or something hitting a hard surface: *There was a loud knock at the door.*
2 the action of something hard hitting your body: **[+on]** *He got a knock on the head.*

knocker /'nɒkə $ 'nɑːkər/ n [C] a piece of metal on a door that you use to knock on the door

'knock-on adj BrE **have a knock-on effect (on sth)** to start a process in which one thing that happens will have an effect on another thing: *The price rises will have a knock-on effect on the economy.*

K

knockout

knockout /'nɒk-aʊt $ 'nɑːk-/ *n* [C] when a BOXER hits his opponent so hard that he falls down and cannot get up again

knot¹ /nɒt $ nɑːt/ *n* [C]

1 [IN STRING/ROPE/CLOTH ETC] a place where pieces of string, rope, cloth etc have been tied together: *He put some string round the parcel and **tied a knot**.*

2 [SHIP'S SPEED] a unit for measuring the speed of a ship

3 [IN WOOD] a hard round place in a piece of wood where a branch once joined the tree

knot² *v* [T] (**knotted, knotting**) to fasten something by tying together pieces of string, rope etc

know¹ /nəʊ $ noʊ/ *v* (*past tense* **knew** /njuː $ nuː/, *past participle* **known** /nəʊn $ noʊn/)

1 [I,T] to have knowledge or information about something: *Who knows the answer?* | **know (something/nothing etc) about sth** *He knows a lot about cars.* | **know (something/nothing etc) of sth** *Do you know of any good restaurants in the area?* | [**+(that)**] *We know that greenhouse gases can affect the climate.* | [**+how/what/where etc**] *Nobody knows where she's gone.* | **know how to do sth** (=have learned how to do something) *Do you know how to make risotto?* | **Let me know** (=tell me) *what time you will arrive.* **THESAURUS** TELL

2 [I,T] to be or feel sure about something: *'Are you seeing Jim tomorrow?' 'I don't know yet.'* | [**+(that)**] *I know I won't get the job.* | [**+if/whether**] *I don't know if I'll be able to come.* | **How do you know** (=what makes you say it, do it again? | *Gail left at 6.00,* **as far as I know** (=I think, but I'm not sure).

3 [T] to be or become familiar with a person, place etc: *I knew Hilary in high school.* | *a chance for students to **get to know** each other* | *Jean **knows** Paris **well**.* | *Luckily, Jo **knew the way** to the hospital* (=knew how to get there). | *You should **know** the system **inside out** (=be very familiar with it). | *I grew up here; I **know** the place **like the back of my hand**** (=know it very well).

4 [T] to realize or understand something: *She knew the risks involved.* | *'I felt so tired.' 'Yes, I **know what you mean**.'* | [**+(that)**] *Suddenly, she knew that something was terribly wrong.* **THESAURUS** PREDICT

5 [T] to have experience of something: *I don't think he ever knew true happiness.* | *I **have never known** a case quite like this one.*

PHRASES

Heaven/goodness/who knows *spoken* used to emphasize that you do not know something: *Who knows what will happen?*

I know *spoken* **1** used to agree with someone: *'We have to talk about it, Rob.' 'Yeah, I know.'* **2** used when you suddenly think of an idea: *I know. Let's ask Michael.*

know better (than to do sth) to be wise and experienced enough to not do something: *I thought you knew better than to tell Mum.*

know sb/sth as sth to think of someone as having particular qualities, or to give them a particular name: *I knew him as a hard-working and honest politician.* | *Diana became known as 'the people's Princess'.*

you know *spoken* **1** used to make sure that someone understands what, who etc you are talking about: *I felt very upset, you know?* | *that girl, you know, with long blonde hair* **2** used to emphasize a statement: *There's no excuse, you know.* **3** used to pause while you think of what to say next: *Well, you know, that's not entirely true.* **4** used to start talking about something or to make someone listen: *You know, he's going to be taller than his dad.*

you never know *spoken* used to say that something might happen, although it seems unlikely: *You never know. You might be lucky and win!* **THESAURUS** MAYBE

THESAURUS

know to have knowledge or information about something: *Did you know that they're getting married?*

realize (*also* **realise** *BrE*) to know that something is true or that a situation exists, especially when this could have an important effect: *None of us realized the danger we were in.* | *Do you realize how much this will cost?*

can tell *especially spoken* to know from something is true because you can see signs that show this: *His eyes were red and I could tell he'd been crying.*

be aware *formal* to know that a situation or a problem exists: *Many people are not aware that the disease can kill you.*

---

know² *n* **in the know** having more information about something than most people: *People in the know go to beaches on the south of the island.*

'know-all *n* [C] *BrE disapproving* someone who behaves as if they know everything [SYN] **know-it-all** *AmE*

'know-how *n* [U] *informal* knowledge, practical ability, or skill: *technical know-how*

knowing /'nəʊɪŋ $ 'noʊ-/ *adj* [only before noun] showing that you know all about something, especially something secret: *He gave us a **knowing look**.*

knowingly /'nəʊɪŋli $ 'noʊ-/ *adv* **1** in a way that shows you know about something secret or embarrassing: *Brenda smiled knowingly at me.* **2** deliberately: *He'd never knowingly hurt you.*

'know-it-all *n* [C] *AmE disapproving* someone who behaves as if they know everything [SYN] **know-all** *BrE*

knowledge /'nɒlɪdʒ $ 'nɑː-/ *n* [U]

1 the information, skills, and understanding that you have got through learning or experience: *You don't need to have any special knowledge to do this job.* | [**+of**] *His knowledge of American history is impressive.* | [**+about**] *our knowledge about the functioning of the brain*

2 when you know about a particular situation or event, or the information you have about it: *Evans **denied all knowledge** of the robbery.* | **to (the best of) sb's knowledge** (=used to say that someone may not know all the facts) *To the best of my knowledge, the new project will be starting in June.* | **without sb's knowledge** *The contract had been signed without his knowledge.* → **common knowledge** at COMMON¹

Grammar

Knowledge is uncountable and is not used in the plural. It is used with a singular verb. Do not say 'His knowledges are impressive.' Say *His knowledge is impressive.*

You say **knowledge of** a subject. Do not say 'Her knowledge in history is very good.' Say *Her knowledge of history is very good.*

COLLOCATIONS

verbs

to have knowledge of sth *Candidates must have some knowledge of databases.*

to get knowledge (*also* **to gain/acquire knowledge** *formal*) *There are some types of knowledge you can't get from a book.* ⚠ Do not say 'learn knowledge'. Say **get knowledge**, **gain knowledge**, or **acquire knowledge**.

to increase/improve your knowledge *I wanted to improve my knowledge of music.*

to show/demonstrate your knowledge *This is a chance for you to demonstrate your knowledge of Spanish.*

adjectives

general knowledge (=knowledge about a lot of different subjects) *Reading newspapers will improve your general knowledge.*

basic knowledge *A basic knowledge of German would be helpful.*

detailed knowledge *You need a lawyer with a detailed knowledge of tax legislation.*

specialist/expert knowledge *You don't need any specialist knowledge to understand the book.*

knowledgeable /ˈnɒlɪdʒəbəl $ ˈnɑː-/ *adj* knowing a lot: [+about] *Steve's very knowledgeable about politics.*

known¹ /nəʊn $ noʊn/ *v* the past participle of KNOW

known² *adj* known about, especially by a lot of people → **well-known**: *a known criminal* | **be known for sth** *The region is known for its fine wines.*

knuckle¹ /ˈnʌkəl/ *n* [C] the bones where your fingers join the rest of your hand → see picture at HAND¹

knuckle² *v*

PHRASAL VERBS

knuckle down *informal* to start working hard

knuckle under *informal* to do what you are told to do, even though you do not want to

koala /kəʊˈɑːlə $ koʊ-/ (*also* ko,ala ˈbear / $ ˌ.. ,./) *n* [C] an Australian animal like a small grey bear that climbs trees → see picture on page A3

Koran (*also* Quran, Qur'an) /kɔːˈrɑːn, kə- $ kəˈræn, -ˈrɑːn/ *n* the Koran the holy book of the Muslims

kosher /ˈkəʊʃə $ ˈkoʊʃər/ *adj* kosher food is prepared according to Jewish law

kowtow /ˌkaʊˈtaʊ/ *v* [I] to be very eager to obey or be polite to someone in authority: [+to] *I refuse to kowtow to that man.*

kph the written abbreviation of **kilometres per hour**

kudos /ˈkjuːdɒs $ ˈkuːdɑːs/ *n* [U] admiration and respect that you get for something you do

kung fu /ˌkʌŋ ˈfuː/ *n* [U] a Chinese sport in which people fight with their feet and hands

kW the written abbreviation of **kilowatt**

K

L l

L, l /el/ *n* [C,U] (*plural* **L's, l's**) the 12th letter of the English alphabet

L 1 the written abbreviation of **large**, used on clothes to show the size **2** the written abbreviation of **lake**, used on maps **3** the written abbreviation of **learner**, used on cars to show that the driver is a learner → **L-PLATE**

l the written abbreviation of **litre**

lab /læb/ *n* [C] *informal* a LABORATORY

label¹ Ac /'leɪbəl/ *n* [C]
1 a piece of paper or cloth that is attached to something and gives information about it: **on a label** *Always read the instructions on the label.*
2 (*also* **record label**) a company that makes records: *the EMI label*
3 a word or phrase that is used to describe someone or something: *She doesn't like being given the label 'feminist writer'.*

label² Ac *v* [T] (**labelled, labelling** *BrE*, **labeled, labeling** *AmE*) **1** to fasten a label to something, or write information on something to show what it is: *Label the diagram clearly.* | **label sth sth** *The file was labelled 'Top Secret'.* **2** to use a word or phrase to describe someone: **label sb/sth (as) sth** *He was labelled a troublemaker.*

labor Ac /'leɪbə $ -ər/ *n, v* the American spelling of LABOUR

laboratory /lə'bɒrətri $ 'læbrətɔːri/ *n* [C] (*plural* **laboratories**) a special room or building used for scientific work: *a research laboratory*

labored Ac /'leɪbəd $ -berd/ *adj* the American spelling of LABOURED

laborer /'leɪbərə $ -bərər/ *n* the American spelling of LABOURER

laborious /lə'bɔːriəs/ *adj* taking a lot of time and effort: *Sorting the books was a **laborious task**.*

'labor ˌunion *n* [C] *AmE* an organization that represents workers who do the same kind of job SYN **trade union** *BrE*

Labour /'leɪbə $ -ər/ *n* the LABOUR PARTY: *We've always **voted Labour**.* | *a Labour MP*

labour¹ Ac *BrE*, **labor** *AmE n* **1** [U] work, especially hard physical work: *The job involves hard **manual labour** (=hard work that you do with your hands).* **2** [U] people who work in an industry or country: *There is a shortage of **skilled labour** (=trained workers).* | *These countries can provide **cheap labour**.* | **labour force** (=all the people who work in a company or country) *the number of women in the labour force* | **labour-intensive** (=needing a lot of workers) *labour-intensive farming methods* **3** [singular, U] the process of giving birth to a baby: **in labour** *Meg was in labour for six hours.*

labour of love something that you do because you enjoy it, not for money: *The movie is clearly a labor of love.*

labour² Ac *BrE*, **labor** *AmE v* [I] **1** to work hard: *Farmers were laboring in the fields.* | **[+over]** *I laboured over that report for days.* **2** to move slowly and with difficulty: *The bus was labouring up the steep, windy road.*

laboured Ac *BrE*, **labored** *AmE* /'leɪbəd $ -bərd/ *adj* done with difficulty: *His breathing sounded rather laboured.*

labourer *BrE*, **laborer** *AmE* /'leɪbərə $ -ər/ *n* [C] someone whose job involves hard physical work, especially outside: *a farm labourer*

'labour ˌmarket *BrE*, **labor market** *AmE n* [C] used to talk about all the people looking for work and the jobs that are available: *married women re-entering the labour market*

'Labour ˌParty *n* **the Labour Party** one of the main political parties in Britain

'labour-ˌsaving *BrE*, **labor-saving** *AmE adj* [only before noun] labour-saving equipment makes it easier for you to do a job

labrador /'læbrədɔː $ -ɔːr/ *n* [C] a large dog with short fur

labyrinth /'læbərɪnθ/ *n* [C] a network of paths or passages from which it is difficult to find your way out SYN **maze**: **[+of]** *a labyrinth of narrow streets*

lace¹ /leɪs/ *n* **1** [U] a delicate cloth made with patterns of very small holes: *lace curtains* **2** [C] a string that is used to fasten a shoe SYN **shoelace** → see picture at SHOE¹

lace² (*also* **lace up**) *v* [T] to fasten clothes or shoes by tying the laces: *Paul laced up his boots.*

lack¹ /læk/ *n* [singular, U] when there is not enough of something SYN **shortage**: **[+of]** *She suffers from a lack of confidence.* | **for lack of sth** *The museum may be forced to close for lack of funds.*

lack² *v* [T] to not have something or not have enough of something: *The only thing she lacks is experience.*

lacking /'lækɪŋ/ *adj* [not before noun] **1** not having enough of something: **[+in]** *He is completely lacking in confidence.* **2** not existing or available: *The information they need is lacking.*

lacklustre *BrE*, **lackluster** *AmE* /'læk,lʌstə $ -ər/ *adj* not very good or exciting SYN **dull**: *a lacklustre performance*

laconic /lə'kɒnɪk $ -'kɑː-/ *adj* using only a few words

lacquer /'lækə $ -ər/ *n* [U] a liquid painted on wood or metal to give it a hard shiny surface —**lacquered** *adj*

lacy /'leɪsi/ *adj* made of LACE, or looking like lace

lad /læd/ *n* **1** [C] *old-fashioned* a boy or young man THESAURUS ▶ MAN **2 the lads** *BrE spoken* [plural] a group of male friends → **the girls**: *a night out with the lads*

ladder /ˈlædə $ -ər/ n [C]

1 a piece of equipment used for climbing up to high places. A ladder has two long bars connected by RUNGS (=short bars that you use as steps).

2 a series of levels within an organization, profession, or society: *Women have had to fight to **climb** the career **ladder**.*

3 *BrE* a long hole in STOCKINGS or TIGHTS **SYN** **run** *AmE*

LADDER

ladder

rung

stepladder

laden /ˈleɪdn/ adj heavily loaded with something, or containing a lot of something: [+with] *The table was laden with food.* | *a fully laden truck*

ˈladies' room n [C] *AmE* a women's toilet **SYN** **the ladies** *BrE*

ladle /ˈleɪdl/ n [C] a large round deep spoon with a long handle, used for serving soup —**ladle** (also **ladle out**) v [T]: *He ladled soup into the bowls.*

lady /ˈleɪdi/ n [C] (plural **ladies**)

1 a polite word for a woman → **gentleman**: *Good afternoon, ladies.* | *young/old/elderly etc lady The young lady at reception sent me up here.* | *the ladies' hockey team* **THESAURUS** **WOMAN**

2 a woman who is polite and behaves well → **gentleman**: *A lady never swears.*

3 the ladies *BrE* a public toilet for women **SYN** **ladies' room** *AmE*

4 Lady a title used before the name of a British woman of high social rank: *Lady Helen Windsor*

Word Choice: lady or woman?

In everyday English, the usual word to use is **woman**: *Who is that woman over there?* | *Most of our customers are women.*

You use **lady** when you want to be polite: *Are you the lady I spoke to on the phone?*

Lady is also used in written descriptions, for example in novels: *The door was answered by an elderly lady.*

ladybird /ˈleɪdibɜːd $ -bɜːrd/ *BrE*, **ladybug** /ˈleɪdibʌɡ/ *AmE* n [C] a small insect that is red with black spots

ladylike /ˈleɪdilaɪk/ adj old-fashioned very polite or quiet in the way that people in the past thought was suitable for women: *ladylike behaviour*

lag¹ /læɡ/ v (**lagged**, **lagging**)

PHRASAL VERBS

lag behind (sb) to move or develop more slowly than others: *She stopped to wait for Ian, who was lagging behind.*

lag² n [C] a delay between two events **SYN** **time lag** → **JET LAG**

lager /ˈlɑːɡə $ -ər/ n [C,U] *BrE* a light beer, or a glass of this beer: *a glass of lager* | *Two lagers, please.*

lagoon /ləˈɡuːn/ n [C] an area of sea water that is separated from the sea by sand, rocks etc

laid /leɪd/ v the past tense and past participle of LAY

ˌlaid-ˈback adj relaxed and not seeming to worry about anything: *He has a very laid-back approach to life.* **THESAURUS** **RELAXED**

lain /leɪn/ v the past participle of LIE¹

lair /leə $ ler/ n [C] the place where a wild animal hides and sleeps **SYN** **den**

lake /leɪk/ n [C] a large area of water surrounded by land: *Lake Michigan* | **in a lake** *There were some boys swimming in the lake.* | **on a lake** *There were some small boats on the lake.*

THESAURUS

lake a large area of water surrounded by land: *The town lies on the edge of a big lake.*

reservoir a lake where water is stored before it is supplied to people's houses: *They built two reservoirs to supply water to the city.*

pond a small area of water, especially one that is made in a field or garden: *There were several ducks on the village pond.*

pool a small area of still water in a hollow place: *The tide went out, leaving pools of water on the shore.*

puddle a very small area of water on the ground, especially after it has been raining: *The children enjoyed splashing in the puddles.*

LAMB

lamb

sheep

lamb /læm/ n [C,U] a young sheep, or the meat of a young sheep → **mutton**: *roast lamb*

lambast /læmˈbæst/ v [T] formal to criticize someone or something very severely, especially in public

lame /leɪm/ adj **1** unable to walk properly – used mainly about animals **2** a lame excuse or explanation is weak and difficult to believe: *She gave some lame excuse about missing the bus.*

ˌlame ˈduck n [C] **1** a person, business etc that is having problems and needs help **2 lame duck president/governor etc** informal a president etc with no real power because he or she will soon stop being president

lamely /ˈleɪmli/ adv if you say something lamely, you do not sound confident and other people find it difficult to believe you

lament /ləˈment/ v [I,T] formal to express feelings

lamentable

of sadness or disappointment about something —**lament** n [C]

lamentable /ˈlæməntəbəl, ləˈmentəbəl/ adj formal very unsatisfactory or disappointing

laminated /ˈlæmɪneɪtɪd/ adj **1** laminated material is made stronger by joining several thin layers on top of each other: laminated glass **2** covered with a thin layer of plastic for protection: a laminated ID card —**laminate** / $ -nət/ n [C]

lamp /læmp/ n [C] an object that produces light by using electricity, oil, or gas: a desk lamp | a bedside lamp → see pictures at **BICYCLE**, **LIGHT**[1] **THESAURUS LIGHT**

lampoon /læmˈpuːn/ v [T] to criticize someone such as a politician in a funny way that makes them seem stupid

lamp-post /ˈlæmp-pəʊst $ -poʊst/ n [C] a tall pole that supports a light over a street or public area

lampshade /ˈlæmpʃeɪd/ n [C] a cover fixed over a light to make it less bright

land[1] /lænd/ n

1 [U] an area of ground: He owns 5,000 acres of agricultural land. **THESAURUS GROUND**
2 [U] the solid dry part of the Earth's surface **OPP** sea: **on land** Frogs live on land and in the water. | **by land** They travelled by sea and by land. | They were glad to be back on **dry land**.
3 [C] literary a country or area: **distant/foreign lands** He had travelled to many foreign lands. | He longed to return to his **native land** (=the land where he was born). **THESAURUS COUNTRY**

COLLOCATIONS

noun + land

a piece/plot of land (=an area of land) They own a small piece of land.
an acre/a hectare of land She has ten acres of land.

adjectives

good/fertile land (=good for growing crops) The land here is very fertile.
agricultural land The factory is polluting nearby agricultural land.
industrial land There is plenty of industrial land available.
open land (=without buildings, fences etc) London was once surrounded by open land.
private land (=land that is owned by someone) Do you know you're on private land?

THESAURUS

land an area of ground: The land could be used for building houses.
farmland land that is used for farming: The village is surrounded by farmland.
territory land that belongs to a country, or that a country or group controls during a war: US territory | The army was advancing into enemy territory.
the grounds the gardens and land around a big building such as a castle, school, or hospital: They went for a walk in the palace grounds.

land[2] v

1 [I,T] to come onto the ground after being in the air or on water: Has her flight landed yet? | We will be landing in Rome in fifteen minutes. | One bird landed right in front of us. | [+in/on/under etc] Chris slipped and landed on a nail. | The pilot managed to land the aircraft safely. | Two thousand troops were landed on the beach.
2 [T] informal to succeed in getting an important job, contract, or deal: Kelly's landed a job with a big law firm. → **CRASH-LAND**

PHRASAL VERBS

land sb in sth to cause someone to be in a difficult situation or have serious problems: She developed pneumonia, which landed her in hospital.
be landed with sth informal to have to deal with or pay for something, when you do not want to have to do this: I've been landed with the job of clearing up the mess.

landed /ˈlændɪd/ adj [only before noun] **1 landed gentry/family/nobility** a family or group that has owned a lot of land for a long time **2** including a lot of land: farms and landed estates

landfill /ˈlændfɪl/ n **1** [U] the practice of burying waste under the ground, or the waste buried in this way **2** [C] a place where waste is buried under the ground

landing /ˈlændɪŋ/ n **1** [C,U] the action of bringing a plane down to the ground after flying → **take-off**: **emergency/forced/crash landing** The pilot had to make an emergency landing. **2** [C] the floor at the top of a set of stairs

landlady /ˈlændˌleɪdi/ n [C] (plural **landladies**) **1** a woman that you rent a room or house from **2** BrE a woman who owns or manages a PUB

landline /ˈlændˌlaɪn/ n [C] a telephone connection that uses wires, as opposed to a MOBILE PHONE

landlocked /ˈlændlɒkt $ -lɑːkt/ adj a landlocked country, state etc is surrounded by other countries and has no coast

landlord /ˈlændlɔːd $ -lɔːrd/ n [C] **1** a man that you rent a room or house from **2** BrE a man who owns or manages a PUB

landmark /ˈlændmɑːk $ -mɑːrk/ n [C] **1** something that helps you recognize where you are, such as a famous building **2** a very important event, change, or discovery in the development of something: [+in] a landmark in the history of aviation

landmass /ˈlændmæs/ n [C] technical a large area of land such as a CONTINENT

landmine /ˈlændmaɪn/ n [C] a bomb hidden in the ground that explodes when someone walks or drives over it

landowner /ˈlændˌəʊnə $ -ˌoʊnər/ n [C] someone who owns a large amount of land

landscape[1] /ˈlændskeɪp/ n [C] **1** a view across an area of land: **rural/industrial/urban landscape 2** a picture of an area of countryside: a landscape painter → see picture at **PAINTING** **THESAURUS PICTURE**

landscape[2] v [T] to make an area of land look more attractive by changing its design and putting in new plants

landslide /'lændslaɪd/ n [C] **1** a victory in an election in which one person or party gets a lot more votes than all the others: *a landslide victory* **2** a sudden fall of a lot of earth or rocks down a hill, cliff, or mountain

lane /leɪn/ n [C] **1** a narrow road in the countryside: *a quiet country lane* **THESAURUS** ROAD **2** a road in a town – used in the names of streets: *They live in Turnpike Lane.* **3** one of the parts of a road that vehicles travel along: **inside/middle/outside lane** *He was doing 100 mph in the outside lane.* **4** one of the narrow areas that a competitor in a race runs or swims along: *Radcliffe is running in lane eight.* **5** a course along which ships or aircraft regularly travel: *The accident happened in a busy shipping lane.*

language /'læŋgwɪdʒ/ n
1 [C] the words that people use to speak or write to each other: *Do you speak any foreign languages?*
2 [U] the use of written or spoken words to communicate: *a new theory about the origins of language*
3 [U] the kind of words that a person uses, or that are used when talking or writing about a particular subject: **[+of]** *the language of business* | *He never used bad language* (=rude words). | **legal/medical/scientific etc language**
4 [C,U] a system of instructions used in computer programs
5 [C,U] any system of signs, movements, or sounds that are used to express meanings or feelings: *the language of music* → BODY LANGUAGE, SIGN LANGUAGE

COLLOCATIONS

verbs
to speak a language *She speaks several languages.*
to talk/speak in a language *What language were they talking in?*
to use a language *They use two languages at home.*
to learn a language *I'd like to learn another language.*

adjectives
a foreign language *The men were talking in a foreign language.*
the English/Japanese/Spanish etc language *He spent years studying the Russian language.*
sb's first/native language (=the language someone first learned as a child) *His first language was Spanish.*
a second language (=a language you speak that is not your first language) *Most of the students learn English as a second language.*
the official language (=the language used in politics, the law etc) *The official language of Ghana is English.*

language + noun
a language student/learner *Language learners need to know how to use these phrases.*
a language teacher *a book for language teachers*

THESAURUS

dialect a form of a language that is spoken in one part of a country: *Mandarin and Cantonese are two of the Chinese dialects.*

accent the way that someone pronounces words, because of where they were born or live, or because of their social class: *She has a strong New Jersey accent.*

slang very informal spoken language, used especially by people who belong to a particular group, for example young people: *'Fierce' is slang for 'good'.*

terminology the technical words that are used in a subject: *Patients are often unfamiliar with medical terminology.*

jargon *especially disapproving* words and phrases used by people in the same profession that are difficult for other people to understand: *The instructions were written in complicated technical jargon.*

language laboratory / $ '.. ,....,/ n [C] (plural **language laboratories**) a room in a school or college where you can practise a foreign language by listening to tapes and recording your own voice

languid /'læŋgwɪd/ adj literary moving or speaking slowly and with very little effort or energy

languish /'læŋgwɪʃ/ v [I] to remain in a difficult situation for a long time: **[+in/at]** *United are currently languishing at the bottom of the league.*

lanky /'læŋki/ adj very tall and thin

lantern /'læntən $ -ərn/ n [C] a type of lamp that you can carry consisting of a glass or metal container with a light inside → see picture at LIGHT¹ **THESAURUS** LIGHT

lap¹ /læp/ n [C] **1** the upper part of your legs when you are sitting down: **on/in sb's lap** *Paul was sitting on his mother's lap.* **2** one journey around a race track or swimming pool: *Hill overtook Schumacher on the last lap.*

lap² v (**lapped, lapping**) **1** [I,T] if water laps against something, it moves gently against it: **[+against/at/over]** *Waves were lapping against the shore.* **2** (*also* **lap up**) [T] if an animal laps a drink, it drinks with quick movements of its tongue: *The cat started to lap up the milk.*
PHRASAL VERBS
lap sth ↔ **up** to accept something very eagerly in a way that shows you like it a lot: *She is lapping up all the attention.*

lapel /lə'pel/ n [C] the part at the front of a coat or JACKET that is joined to the collar and folds back on both sides

lapse¹ /læps/ n [C] **1** a short period of time during which you do not do something well or properly: **[+of/in]** *a brief lapse of concentration* **2** [usually singular] a period of time between two events: **[+of]** *They returned after a considerable lapse of time.*

lapse² v [I] if a contract or agreement lapses, it comes to an end: *Your membership of the tennis club has lapsed.*
PHRASAL VERBS
lapse into sth **1** to change into another state or condition, especially one that is worse or less active than before: *They lapsed into silence.* | *The Empire lapsed into chaos.* **2** to start behaving or speaking in

a way that you did before: *Without thinking, he lapsed into French.*

laptop /'læptɒp $ -tɑːp/ n [C] a small computer that you can carry with you → see picture on page A12

lard /lɑːd $ lɑːrd/ n [U] thick white fat used in cooking

larder /'lɑːdə $ 'lɑːrdər/ n [C] a large cupboard or small room used for storing food

large /lɑːdʒ $ lɑːrdʒ/ adj big in size, number, or amount **OPP small**: *a large pizza* | *Birmingham is the second largest city in Britain.* | **large number/amount/ quantity** *They spent large amounts of money on gambling.* | *The T-shirt comes in Small, Medium, and Large.* | *Frank was a very large man.* **THESAURUS** BIG
PHRASES
   be at large if a criminal or wild animal is at large, they have escaped from somewhere: *Two of the escaped prisoners are still at large.*
   by and large generally: *By and large, the show was a success.*
   larger than life more exciting or interesting than other people or things: *She was an extrovert, larger than life and very self-confident.*
   the population/public etc at large people in general: *The population at large has become more mobile.*

largely /'lɑːdʒli $ 'lɑːr-/ adv mostly or mainly: *The delay was largely due to bad weather.*

large-'scale adj [only before noun] using or involving a lot of people or things **OPP small-scale**: *large-scale unemployment* | *a large-scale police operation*

lark /lɑːk $ lɑːrk/ n [C] a small brown bird that has a beautiful song

larva /'lɑːvə $ 'lɑːrvə/ n [C] (plural **larvae** /-viː/) a young insect with a soft body, before it becomes an adult

laryngitis /ˌlærɪnˈdʒaɪtɪs/ n [U] an illness that makes your throat swell, so that it is difficult to talk

larynx /'lærɪŋks/ n [C] (plural **larynges** /ləˈrɪndʒiːz/ or **larynxes**) technical the part of your throat where your voice is produced

lasagne BrE, **lasagna** AmE /ləˈsænjə, -ˈzæn- $ -ˈzɑːn-/ n [C,U] a type of Italian food made with flat pieces of PASTA, meat or vegetables, and cheese

laser /'leɪzə $ -ər/ n [C] a piece of equipment that produces a powerful narrow beam of light, or the beam of light itself: *laser surgery*

lash¹ /læʃ/ v **1** [I,T] if rain, waves, or wind lash against something, they hit it hard or blow hard against it: **[+against/down]** *The rain was lashing down outside.* **2** [T] to hit someone very hard with a whip or stick **SYN** beat **3** [T] to tie something tightly to something else, using a rope: **lash sth to sth** *The oars were lashed to the sides of the boat.*
PHRASAL VERBS
lash out to suddenly attack someone or speak angrily to them: **[+at]** *Olson lashed out at the media.*

lash² n [C usually plural] **1** one of the hairs that grow around the edges of your eyes **SYN** eyelash **2** a hit with a whip as a punishment: *He was given fifty lashes.*

lass /læs/ n [C] BrE a girl or young woman – used in Scotland and the north of England

lasso /ləˈsuː, ˈlæsəʊ $ -soʊ/ n [C] (plural **lassos** or **lassoes**) a rope with one end tied in a circle, used for catching cattle and horses —**lasso** v [T]

last¹ /lɑːst $ læst/ determiner, adj
1 most recent: *My last boyfriend was crazy about football.* | *When was **the last time** you were here?* | **last night/week/Sunday etc** *Did you go out last night?* | **the last few months/ten years etc** (=the period until now) *The town has changed a lot in the last few years.* **THESAURUS** PREVIOUS

Grammar
Do not say 'I went there on last Monday/Friday etc.' Say *I went there last Monday/Friday etc.*

2 happening or coming at the end, after all the others: *What time does the last bus leave?* | *the last chapter of the book* | **last but one/two etc** (=the one before the last one, two etc) *He escaped with his family on the last but one ship to leave.* | **second/next to last** (=the one before the last one)
3 the last person or thing is the only one that remains: *Is it all right if I have the last piece of cake?* | *He was the last great explorer.*
PHRASES
   have the last word to say the last thing in a discussion or argument, or make the final decision about something: *She always has to have the last word!*
   the last minute/moment the latest possible time before something happens: *The concert was cancelled at the last minute.*
   the last person/thing the person or thing you did not expect at all, or the one that you want least of all: *You're the last person I expected to see.* | *The last thing she wanted was to upset him.*

THESAURUS – sense 2

last happening or existing at the end, with no others after: *The last train leaves at 10 p.m.*
final last in a series of actions, events, parts of a story etc: *the final scene of the film* | *the final day of the trial*
closing used about the last part of a long period of time, or of an event, book etc that has been exciting or interesting: *He scored a goal in the closing minutes of the game.*
penultimate the one before the last one: *the penultimate chapter of the book*

last² adv
1 most recently before now: *When did you last go shopping?*
2 after everything or everyone else **OPP** first: *Add the flour last.* | *Last of all, I'd like to thank you all for coming.*
PHRASES
   last but not least used before mentioning the last person or thing in a list, to emphasize that they are

still important: *Last but not least, I'd like to thank my mother.*

last³ n, pron

1 the last the person or thing that comes after all the others OPP the first: **the last to do sth** *Lee was the last to go to bed.*

2 the last of sth the only part of something that remains: *Is this the last of the bread?*

PHRASES

at (long) last used when something happens after people have waited a long time for it: *At last, dinner was ready.* THESAURUS FINALLY

the day/week/year etc before last the day, week etc before the one that has just finished: *I saw her the night before last.*

last⁴ v [I,T]

1 to continue for a particular length of time: **[+for/ until/through etc]** *The hot weather lasted for two weeks.* | *The petrol should last until we get to London.* | **last an hour/ten minutes etc** *Each lesson lasts an hour.* THESAURUS CONTINUE

2 to continue to exist, be effective, or remain in good condition: *The batteries will last for up to eight hours.* | **last (sb) two days/three weeks etc** *A good coat should last you ten years.*

3 to be enough for someone for a period of time: **last (sb) two days/three weeks etc** *We had $50 to last us the rest of the month.*

last-'ditch adj **last-ditch effort/attempt etc** a final attempt to achieve something before it is too late: *a last-ditch effort to free the hostages*

lasting /'lɑːstɪŋ $ 'læs-/ adj continuing for a long time: *The incident made a **lasting impression** on me.*

lastly /'lɑːstli $ 'læst-/ adv used to say that the next thing you mention will be the last thing OPP firstly: *And lastly, I'd like to thank my producer.*

> **Word Choice: lastly or at last?**
> You use **lastly** before mentioning the last thing that you want to say: *Lastly, thanks to everyone for all their help.*
> You use **at last** when you are pleased because something happens that you have been waiting for: *At last, they're here!* | *The exams were over at last.*

last-'minute adj happening or done as late as possible: *I was out doing some last-minute Christmas shopping.*

'last name n [C] a SURNAME THESAURUS NAME

latch¹ /lætʃ/ n [C] **1** a small metal bar used for fastening a door, gate, or window **2** a type of lock for a door that needs a key when being opened from outside: *She left the door **on the latch** (=closed but not locked).*

latch² v

PHRASAL VERBS

latch on to sth *BrE informal* to become very interested in something

late /leɪt/ adj, adv

1 arriving, happening, or done after the time that was expected or arranged OPP early: *Sorry I'm late!* |

ten minutes/two hours etc late *Our flight arrived two hours late.* | **[+for]** *Abi was late for school.*

2 near the end of a period of time OPP early: *We should be there by late afternoon.* | *music that was popular in the late 1970s* | *St Mary's Church was built in the late 18th century.* | *He's in his late forties.*

3 near the end of the day OPP early: *It's getting late. We'd better go home.*

4 [only before noun] *formal* dead: *the late Sir William Russell*

PHRASES

too late after the time when something could have been done: *It's too late to change things now.*

> **THESAURUS**
>
> **late** arriving, happening, or done after the time that was expected or arranged: *The bus was late, so I missed the start of the film.*
> **overdue** not paid, returned, or happening by the expected time: *My library books were all overdue.*
> **behind with/on sth** late in doing something that you have to do: *She's behind with her homework.* | *We got behind on our rent (=we did not pay it on time).*

latecomer /'leɪtˌkʌmə $ -ər/ n [C] someone who arrives late

lately /'leɪtli/ adv recently: *I've been feeling very tired lately.* THESAURUS RECENTLY

> **Grammar**
> You always use **lately** with the present perfect. Do not say 'I was busy lately.' Say *I've been very busy lately.*

'late-night adj [only before noun] happening late at night, or later than usual: *late-night television* | *late-night shopping*

latent /'leɪtənt/ adj *formal* something that is latent is present but hidden, and may develop or become more noticeable in the future: *latent aggression*

later¹ /'leɪtə $ -ər/ (also ˌlater 'on) adv after the present time or a time you are talking about: *I'm going out – I'll see you later.* | *We can talk about that later on.* | **a year/three weeks etc later** *He became senator two years later.* | **later that day/morning etc** *The baby died later that night.* THESAURUS AFTER

later² adj [only before noun] happening or coming in the future, or after something else: *The rules are dealt with in a later chapter.* | *The party was postponed to a later date.* | *Later models of the car are much improved.*

lateral /'lætərəl/ adj *formal* **1** relating to the sides of something: *The wall is weak and needs lateral support.* **2** relating to positions, jobs etc that are at the same rank: *Employees can expect lateral moves to different departments.* —**laterally** adv

latest¹ /'leɪtɪst/ adj [only before noun] the most recent or the newest: *all the latest gossip* THESAURUS NEW

latest² n **1** the latest the most recent or newest thing: **[+in]** *the latest in a series of meetings* **2** at the latest no later than the time mentioned: *I'll be home by 11 o'clock at the latest.*

latex /ˈleɪteks/ *n* [U] a thick white liquid produced by some plants, used in making rubber, paint, glue etc

lather /ˈlɑːðə $ ˈlæðər/ *n* [singular, U] a white mass of bubbles produced by mixing soap in water

Latin[1] /ˈlætɪn $ ˈlætn/ *n* [U] the language used in ancient Rome

Latin[2] *adj* **1** written in Latin **2** from or relating to a country whose language developed from Latin

Latin A'merican *adj* relating to South or Central America

latitude /ˈlætɪtjuːd $ -tuːd/ *n* [C,U] *technical* the distance north or south of the EQUATOR, measured in degrees → **longitude** → see picture at **GLOBE**

latter[1] /ˈlætə $ -ər/ *n* **the latter** *formal* the second of two people or things just mentioned → **former**

latter[2] *adj formal* **1** being the second of two people or things → **former 2** the latter part of a period of time is nearest to the end of it: *the latter part of November*

latterly /ˈlætəli $ -ər-/ *adv BrE formal* recently

laudable /ˈlɔːdəbəl $ ˈlɔːd-/ *adj formal* deserving praise

laugh[1] /lɑːf $ læf/ *v* [I] to make sounds with your voice because you think something is funny: **[+at]** *She was laughing at the memory.* | *Tony* **laughed so hard** *he nearly fell over.* | *Jill* **burst out** (=suddenly started) **laughing**.

PHRASAL VERBS

laugh at sb/sth to make unkind or funny remarks about someone, because you think they are stupid or look silly: *The other kids laughed at him when he didn't understand.*

laugh sth ↔ **off** to pretend that something is not very serious by joking about it: *He laughed off suggestions that he would resign.*

THESAURUS

laugh to make sounds with your voice because you think something is funny: *His jokes always make me laugh.*
giggle to laugh quickly in a high voice, especially because you are nervous or embarrassed: *A group of girls were giggling at the back of the class.*
chuckle to laugh quietly, especially because you are thinking about or reading something funny: *He chuckled to himself as he read the letter.*
snigger *BrE*, **snicker** *AmE* to laugh quietly in an unkind way, for example when someone is hurt or embarrassed: *Billy stood up and started to sing, and one or two people sniggered.*
roar with laughter to laugh very loudly: *The audience were all roaring with laughter.*

---

laugh[2] *n* [C]

1 the act of laughing or the sound you make when you laugh: **with a laugh** *'What a mess!' she said, with a laugh.*
2 an enjoyable time: *a great holiday with lots of laughs*

PHRASES

be a (good) laugh *BrE* to be amusing: *I like Peter – he's a good laugh.*
for a laugh *BrE* for fun: *We went to the casino, just for a laugh.*
have the last laugh to be successful, after other people have criticized you or thought that you could not succeed: *Men make jokes about women drivers, but women have the last laugh – their insurance rates are cheaper.*

COLLOCATIONS

verbs

to give a laugh (=to laugh) *He gave a short laugh.*
to have a laugh (=to laugh about something) *We had a good laugh about the mistake.*
to get a laugh (=to be laughed at) *That joke always gets a laugh.*

adjectives

a good laugh *I'm sure he'll have a good laugh about it.*
a little/small/short laugh *Rachel gave a nervous little laugh.*
a loud/soft laugh *There were loud laughs from the audience.*

---

laughable /ˈlɑːfəbəl $ ˈlæ-/ *adj* something that is laughable is so bad, silly etc that you cannot be serious about it

'laughing stock *n* [singular] someone who has done something so silly that people have no respect for them

laughter /ˈlɑːftə $ ˈlæftər/ *n* [U] when people laugh, or the sound of people laughing: *Tom* **burst into laughter** (=started laughing). | *The audience* **roared with laughter**. **THESAURUS** **LAUGH**

launch[1] /lɔːntʃ $ lɑːntʃ/ *v* [T] **1** to start something big or important: *We have launched a campaign to raise $50,000.* **THESAURUS** **SHOOT 2** to make a new product or book available to be sold: *Jaguar is planning to launch a new sports car.* **3** to put a boat into the water or to send a spacecraft into space

PHRASAL VERBS

launch into sth to suddenly start describing or criticizing something

launch[2] *n* [C] when something is launched

launder /ˈlɔːndə $ ˈlɔːndər/ *v* [T] to hide illegally obtained money by putting it into legal businesses

launderette /ˌlɔːndəˈret $ ˌlɔːn-/ *BrE*, **Laundromat** /ˈlɔːndrəmæt $ ˈlɔːn-/ *trademark AmE n* [C] a place where you pay to wash your clothes in a machine

laundry /ˈlɔːndri $ ˈlɔːn-/ *n* (*plural* **laundries**) **1** [U] clothes, sheets etc that need to be washed, or that have been washed **THESAURUS** **WASH 2** [C] a place where clothes are washed

laurel /ˈlɒrəl $ ˈlɔː-, ˈlɑː-/ *n* [C,U] a small tree with big smooth shiny leaves

PHRASES

rest on your laurels to stop trying to achieve things, after achieving something good: *You should never rest on your laurels.*

lava /ˈlɑːvə/ n [U] hot melted rock that flows from a VOLCANO → see picture at **VOLCANO**

lavatory /ˈlævətəri $ -tɔːri/ n [C] (plural **lavatories**) formal a toilet THESAURUS ▸ **TOILET**

lavender /ˈlævəndə $ -ər/ n [U] a plant that has purple flowers with a strong pleasant smell

lavish[1] /ˈlævɪʃ/ adj **1** expensive or impressive: a **lavish lifestyle 2** very generous: [+with/in] Her mother was lavish with advice. —**lavishly** adv

lavish[2] v [T] to give someone a lot of love, praise, money etc: **lavish sth on sb** He lavished attention on her.

law /lɔː $ lɒː/ n
1 [U] the system of rules that people in a country or area must obey → **legal**: People are punished for breaking the law. | **by law** By law, seat belts must be worn by all passengers. | **against the law** In Sweden, it is against the law to hit a child. | I want to study law. THESAURUS ▸ **RULE**
2 [C] a rule that people in a country or place must obey: the anti-terrorism laws | [+against] the laws against drug use | [+on] European laws on equal opportunities
3 **the law** the police: She may be in trouble with the law.
4 [C] the PRINCIPLE that explains why something happens, especially in science or economics: the law of gravity → **MARTIAL LAW**
PHRASES
law and order when people obey the law, and crime is controlled by the police and the courts of law: The breakdown of law and order is a great cause for concern.

COLLOCATIONS

verbs

to obey the law I have always obeyed the law.
to break the law (=to do something illegal) The company denied breaking the law.
to pass/introduce a law Hong Kong passed laws against killing rare animals for food.
to become law His proposals failed to become law.
the law says The law says you can marry at 16.

types of law

tax/divorce/employment law There will be changes in tax law.
international law The bombings were illegal under international law.
criminal law (=laws concerning crimes) He proposed reform of the criminal law.
a strict/tough law The country has strict environmental laws.

---

law-a·bid·ing adj obeying laws: a **law-abiding citizen**

lawful /ˈlɔːfəl $ ˈlɒː-/ adj formal allowed or recognized by law: a lawful arrest

lawless /ˈlɔːləs $ ˈlɒː-/ adj formal not obeying the law, or not controlled by law

lawn /lɔːn $ lɒːn/ n [C] an area of grass that is kept cut short

lawn mower n [C] a machine used for cutting grass → see picture at **GARDEN**

lawsuit /ˈlɔːsuːt, -sjuːt $ ˈlɒːsuːt/ n [C] a problem or complaint that a person or organization brings to a court of law to be settled

lawyer /ˈlɔːjə $ ˈlɒːjər/ n [C] someone whose job is to advise people about the law or speak for them in court

lax /læks/ adj not strict: lax security

laxative /ˈlæksətɪv/ n [C] a medicine or something that you eat that makes your BOWELS empty easily —**laxative** adj

lay[1] /leɪ/ v the past tense of LIE[1] THESAURUS ▸ **PUT**

lay[2] v (past tense and past participle **laid** /leɪd/)
1 [T] to put something down in a flat position: **lay sth on sth** He laid his hand on my shoulder. | Lay the material flat on the table.
2 **lay bricks/carpet/cables etc** to put bricks, a CARPET etc in the correct place, especially on the ground or floor
3 **lay the foundations/groundwork/base** to provide the conditions that make it possible for something to happen or be successful
4 [I,T] if a bird, insect etc lays eggs, it produces them from its body
5 [T] BrE to put knives, forks, plates etc on a table before a meal: Can you **lay the table** for dinner?
PHRASES
lay a hand/finger on sb to hurt someone by hitting them: If you lay a hand on her, I'll call the police.
lay claim to sth to say officially that something belongs to you: The prince had come to lay claim to his father's kingdom.
lay (your) hands on sth to find something: I wish I could lay my hands on that book.
lay sb open to sth to do something that makes it possible that someone will be blamed, criticized etc: Such behaviour could lay her open to criticism.
lay a trap to prepare a trap to catch someone or something: The thieves were unaware that the police had laid a trap for them.

PHRASAL VERBS
lay down sth
1 to say officially what rules or methods must be obeyed or used: strict safety regulations laid down by the government
2 **lay down the law** to tell other people what to do in an unpleasant way
lay into sb informal to attack or criticize someone: Two men were laying into each other.
lay off
1 **lay sb ↔ off** to stop employing a worker because there is not enough work to do
2 **lay off (sb/sth)** informal to stop doing or using something, or treating someone unkindly
lay sth **↔ on** to provide food, entertainment etc: Lola laid on a great meal for us.
lay sth **↔ out**
1 to spread something out: Let's lay the map out on the table.
2 to arrange a building, town, garden etc: The gardens were attractively laid out.

L

lay up **be laid up** to have to stay in bed because you are ill or injured: **[+with]** *She's laid up with flu.*

lay³ *adj* [only before noun] **1** not having special training or knowledge: *lay witnesses* **2** not having an official position in the church: *a lay preacher*

layabout /ˈleɪəbaʊt/ *n* [C] *BrE informal* a lazy person who avoids work

'lay-by *n* [C] (*plural* **lay-bys**) *BrE* an area at the side of a road where vehicles can stop

layer Ac /ˈleɪə $ -ər/ *n* [C]
1 an amount or piece of a substance that covers a surface or that is between two other things: **[+of]** *a layer of dust* | **thin/thick layer** | **top/bottom layer**
2 one of several levels in a complicated system: **[+of]** *We have fewer layers of management.* → OZONE LAYER

layman /ˈleɪmən/ *n* [C] (*plural* **laymen** /-mən/) someone who is not trained in a particular subject or type of work

'lay-off *n* [C usually plural] when a worker's job is stopped because there is not enough work

layout /ˈleɪaʊt/ *n* [C] the way in which the different parts of something are arranged: *He described the layout of the building.*

laze /leɪz/ *v* [I] to relax and not do very much: **[+around/about]** *We lazed around, gazing at the views.*

lazy /ˈleɪzi/ *adj*
1 someone who is lazy does not like working or doing things that need effort: *the laziest girl in the class* | *He felt too lazy to get out of bed.*
2 a lazy period of time is spent relaxing: *lazy summer afternoons*

lb. the written abbreviation of **pound**

lead¹ /liːd/ *v* (*past tense and past participle* **led** /led/)
1 **TAKE SB SOMEWHERE** [T] to take someone to a place by going with them or in front of them: *The manager led the way through the office.* | **lead sb to/into etc sth** *The horses were led to safety.*
2 **GO AT THE FRONT** [I,T] to go in front of a line of people or vehicles: *A jazz band was leading the parade.*
3 **BE IN CHARGE** [T] to be in charge of something: *He has led the party for over twenty years.* | *Beckham led his team to victory.*
4 **CAUSE STH** [I,T] to cause something to happen, or to cause someone to do something: **[+to]** *a degree that could lead to a career in journalism* | **lead sb to do sth** *He led everyone to believe that he was wealthy.* **THESAURUS** CAUSE
5 **BE MORE SUCCESSFUL** [T] to be more successful than other people, companies, or countries: *US companies lead the world in biotechnology.*
6 **BE WINNING** [I,T] to be winning a game or competition: *At half-time, Brazil led 1-0.* **THESAURUS** WIN
7 **PATH/DOOR ETC** [I] used to say where you can get to using a path, door etc: **[+to/towards]** *The path led down to a lake.*
8 **LIFE** **lead a ... life** to have a particular kind of life: *I lead a quiet life.*

PHRASES
lead sb astray to encourage someone to do bad or immoral things: *Older boys were leading him astray.*

PHRASAL VERBS
lead off (sth) if a road or room leads off a place, it is directly joined to that place: *A small track led off the main road.*

lead sb **on** to make someone believe that you love them when you do not

lead up to sth to come before something and often be a cause of it: *the events leading up to the trial*

THESAURUS

lead to take someone to a place by going with them or in front of them: *She led me into the kitchen.*

take to take someone to a place when you are paying or when you are responsible for them: *I took the children to see a film.*

show to take someone to a place such as a table in a restaurant or a hotel room and leave them there: *A waitress showed us to our table.*

guide to show someone around or to a place that you know well, especially to show them interesting things: *He guided them around the museum.*

escort to take someone somewhere, especially in order to protect or guard them: *Armed guards escorted the President to his car.*

---

lead² *n*
1 **the lead** the first position in a race or competition: **in/into the lead** *She was in the lead from start to finish.* | *The Canadians went into the lead immediately.* | *The Bears took the lead for the first time this season.* **THESAURUS** WIN
2 [singular] the amount or distance by which one team or player is ahead of another: *Italy has a 2-0 lead.*
3 [singular] if someone follows someone's lead, they do the same as the other person has done: *Other countries are likely to follow Germany's lead.*
4 **take the lead (in doing sth)** to be the first, or the most active, in doing something: *The US took the lead in the war against terrorism.*
5 [C] a piece of information that may help you to solve a crime or problem: *The police have investigated several leads.*
6 (*also* **lead role**) [C] the main acting part in a play or film: *Brad Pitt will play the lead.* **THESAURUS** ACTOR
7 **lead singer/guitarist** the main singer or GUITARIST in a group: *She's the lead singer in a band.*
8 [C] *BrE* a piece of rope, leather etc fastened to a dog's collar to control it **SYN** leash especially AmE
9 [C] *BrE* a wire used to connect a piece of electrical equipment to a power supply **SYN** cord AmE

lead³ /led/ *n* **1** [U] a heavy soft grey metal **2** [C,U] the dark grey substance in the centre of a pencil

leader /ˈliːdə $ -ər/ *n* [C]
1 the person who is in charge of a group, organization, country etc: **[+of]** *leaders of the black community* | *a gathering of world leaders*
2 the person or group that is ahead of all the others in a race or competition

THESAURUS

leader the person who is in charge of a group, organization, country etc: *Party members will vote to elect a new leader.*

ruler someone who has official power over a country, for example a king or queen: *Cleopatra was an ancient Egyptian ruler.* | *the country's military rulers*

head of state the person who is officially in charge of a country. The head of state is not necessarily the head of the government. For example, in Britain, the Queen is the official head of state: *Twenty-one heads of state will meet at the annual World Trade Summit.*

ringleader the leader of a group of people who are doing something illegal or bad: *Police believe that they have caught the ringleaders of the gang.*

leadership /ˈliːdəʃɪp $ -ər-/ *n* **1** [U] when someone is the leader of a team, organization etc: **[+of]** *He took over the leadership of the Republican Party.* **2** [U] the quality of being good at leading a team, organization, country etc: *someone with vision and leadership* **3** [singular] the people who are in charge of a country, organization etc

leading /ˈliːdɪŋ/ *adj* [only before noun] best, most important, or most successful: ***leading members*** *of the government* | *He played a **leading role** in the development of radio.*
PHRASES

leading question a question that tricks someone into giving you the answer you want: *keen reporters asking leading questions*

leading edge /ˌliːdɪŋ ˈedʒ/ *n* CUTTING EDGE

leaf¹ /liːf/ *n* [C] (*plural* **leaves** /liːvz/) one of the flat green parts of a plant that are joined to its stem or branches → see picture at **PLANT¹**
PHRASES

take a leaf out of sb's book to behave like someone else who behaves well: *They are committing $3 million to research. We could take a leaf out of their book.*

turn over a new leaf to start to behave in a much better way: *He's decided to turn over a new leaf and give up gambling.*

leaf² *v*
PHRASAL VERBS
leaf through sth to turn the pages of a book or magazine quickly, without reading it carefully

leaflet /ˈliːflɪt/ *n* [C] a piece of printed paper that gives information or advertises something

leafy /ˈliːfi/ *adj* **1** having a lot of leaves: *leafy vegetables* **2** having a lot of trees and plants: *a leafy suburb*

league /liːg/ *n* [C] **1** a group of sports teams or players who play games against each other: *the Football League* | **top/bottom of the league 2** a group of people or countries that join together because they have similar aims or beliefs

PHRASES
be in league with sb to be working with someone secretly, especially for a bad purpose: *He is suspected of being in league with terrorists.*

not be in the same league (as sb/sth) to not be nearly as good or important as someone or something else: *It's quite a good movie but it's not in the same league as 'The Matrix'.*

leak¹ /liːk/ *v*
1 [I,T] if a container, pipe, roof etc leaks, there is a small hole or crack in it that lets liquid or gas flow through: *The roof is leaking.* | *My car's leaking oil.* → see picture at **DRIP¹**
2 [I] if a liquid or gas leaks somewhere, it gets through a hole in something: **[+into/from/out]** *Gas was leaking out of the pipes.*
3 [T] to deliberately give secret information to newspapers, television etc: *The report's findings had been leaked.* | **leak sth to sb** *She leaked information to the press.*
PHRASAL VERBS
leak out if secret information leaks out, a lot of people find out about it

leak² *n* [C]
1 a small hole that liquid or gas gets out through: *There's a leak in the roof.* **THESAURUS** HOLE
2 gas/oil/water etc leak when liquid or gas gets out through a hole: *The explosion was caused by a gas leak.*
3 when secret information is deliberately given to newspapers, television etc: *security leaks*

leakage /ˈliːkɪdʒ/ *n* [C,U] when liquid or gas gets out through a hole

leaky /ˈliːki/ *adj* having a hole or crack that liquid or gas can pass through: *a leaky roof*

lean¹ /liːn/ *v* (*past tense and past participle* **leaned** or **leant** /lent/ *especially BrE*)

LEAN

1 [I] to move or bend your body in a particular position: **[+forward/back/over etc]** *Lean back and enjoy the ride.* | *She leant towards him and listened.*
2 [I,T] to be supported in a sloping position by a wall or surface, or to put something in this position: **lean (sth) on/against sth** *She was leaning on the fence.* | *He leant his bicycle against the wall.*
PHRASAL VERBS
lean on sb to depend on someone for support or encouragement

lean² *adj* **1** thin in a healthy and attractive way: *Mike was tall and lean.* **2** lean meat does not have much fat on it **3** not producing good results: *a lean year for small businesses*

leaning /ˈliːnɪŋ/ *n* [C] a tendency to agree with a particular set of ideas or beliefs: *his political leanings*

leap¹ /liːp/ v [I] (past tense and past participle **leapt** /lept/ especially BrE or **leaped** especially AmE) **1** to jump up high or a long way: **[+over/from/into etc]** She leapt over the fence. **THESAURUS** JUMP 2 to move very quickly and with a lot of energy: **[+up/out of etc]** He leapt up the stairs.
PHRASES
| **leap at the opportunity/chance** to accept an opportunity very eagerly: He leapt at the opportunity to study art in Paris.

leap² n [C] **1** a big jump **2** a large increase or change: a leap in pre-tax profits | He improved **in leaps and bounds** (=very much, very quickly).

leapfrog /ˈliːpfrɒg $ -frɔːg, -frɑːg/ n [U] a children's game in which someone bends over and someone else jumps over them —**leapfrog** v [I,T]

LEAPFROG

leap year n [C] a year when February has 29 days instead of 28

learn /lɜːn $ lɜːrn/ v (past tense and past participle **learned** or **learnt** /lɜːnt $ lɜːrnt/ especially BrE)
1 [I,T] to get knowledge of a subject or skill by studying, doing it, or being taught: What's the best way to learn a language? | **learn (how) to do sth** I learned to drive when I was 17. | **learn (sth) from sb/sth** I learnt a lot from my father.
2 [I,T] formal to find out information or news by hearing it from someone or reading it: **[+of/about]** He learned about his new job by telephone. | **[+(that)]** When did she learn that she was pregnant? | **[+whether/who/why]** I had yet to learn whether I had a college place.
3 [T] to get to know something so well that you can easily remember it: The actors are still **learning** their lines.
4 [I,T] to gradually understand a situation and start behaving in the way that you should: **[+(that)]** They have to learn that they can't do whatever they like. | **learn to do sth** These lads must learn to accept orders. | I think he's **learned** his **lesson**. —**learner** n [C]: a slow learner

THESAURUS

learn to get knowledge of a subject or skill by studying, doing it, or being taught: She has been learning English for six years.
pick sth up to learn something without much effort, by watching or listening to other people: The rules of the game are easy – you'll soon pick them up.
get the hang of sth informal to learn how to do or use something that is quite complicated, especially by practising: Driving a car is easy once you've got the hang of it.
master to learn something so well that you have no difficulty with it, especially a skill, a musical instrument, or a language: It can take

years to master the violin. | She soon mastered the local language.

learned /ˈlɜːnɪd $ ˈlɜːr-/ adj formal having a lot of knowledge because you have read and studied a lot

learning /ˈlɜːnɪŋ $ ˈlɜːr-/ n [U] knowledge gained by reading and studying

learning curve n [C] the rate at which you learn a new skill: Everyone in the centre has been through a **steep learning curve** (=they had to learn very quickly).

learnt /lɜːnt $ lɜːrnt/ v a past tense and past participle of LEARN

lease /liːs/ n [C] a legal agreement by which you pay rent in order to use a building, car etc for a period of time: a two-year lease on the apartment —**lease** v [T]
PHRASES
| **a new lease of life** BrE, **a new lease on life** AmE a further period of being useful or healthy, after becoming damaged, ill etc: Changing jobs has given me a new lease of life.

leash /liːʃ/ n [C] especially AmE a piece of rope or leather fastened to a dog's collar in order to control it **SYN** **lead** BrE

least¹ /liːst/ determiner, pron **the least** the smallest amount: Women get jobs which pay the least. | What would cause the least damage to the environment?
PHRASES
| **at least 1** not less than a particular number or amount: It will take at least 20 minutes to get there. | He had at least $100,000 in savings. **2** even if something better is not true or is not done: At least he didn't lie to me. | Well, at least the roof is fixed. **3** used before correcting or changing something that you have just said: He's gone home – at least I think he has.
| **not (in) the least (bit)** not at all, or none at all: I wasn't in the least worried.
| **to say the least** used to show that something is worse or more serious than you are actually saying: His teaching methods were strange, to say the least.

least² adv less than anything or anyone else **OPP** **most**: It's amazing what happens when you least expect it. | The tax affected those who could least afford to pay it.
PHRASES
| **not least** formal used when mentioning an important example, reason etc: Many other problems remain, not least the shortage of engineers.

leather /ˈleðə $ -ər/ n [U] animal skin used for making shoes, bags etc: a leather belt → see picture at MATERIAL¹

leathery /ˈleðəri/ adj hard and stiff like leather, rather than soft or smooth: leathery brown skin

leave¹ /liːv/ v (past tense and past participle **left** /left/)
1 [I,T] to go away from a place or person: Frances left work early to meet her mother. | **[+at]** The plane

leaves at 12.30. | **[+for]** *I'm sorry, he's already left for work.*

2 [I,T] if you leave your job, home, school etc, you permanently stop doing that job, living at home etc: *My daughter got a job as a hairdresser after she **left** school.* | *Next year the President **leaves** office.*

3 [T] if you leave someone or something in a place when you go away, they remain there: **leave sth/sb in/on etc sth** *I left the car keys in the house* (=by accident). | *Just leave those letters on my desk, please.*

4 [T] to let something stay in a particular state or condition: **leave sth on/off/out etc** *You've left your lights on.* | **leave sth doing sth** *He'd **left** the tap **running**.*

5 [T] if an event leaves someone or something in a particular condition, they are in that condition because of it: **leave sb/sth with sth** *After the infection, she was left with a nasty cough.* | **leave sb doing sth** *The incident left her feeling confused and hurt.*

6 if something is left, it remains after everything else has gone, been taken away, or used: *There's never much money **left** over at the end of the week.* | *We don't **have** much time **left**.*

7 [T] to delay doing something: *Leave the dishes. I'll do them later.*

8 [T] to not eat or use part of something: *Hey, leave some cake for me!*

9 [T] to let someone decide something or be responsible for something: **leave sth to sb** *I'll leave the decision to you.*

10 [I,T] to end a relationship with a husband, partner etc: **leave sb for sb** *He left his wife for a younger woman.*

11 [T] to give something to someone after you die: **leave sb sth** *Hugo left me his mother's ring.*
THESAURUS GIVE

PHRASES

> **leave sb alone** to stop annoying or upsetting someone: *Oh, just leave me alone, will you?*
> **leave sth alone** to stop touching something: *Leave the joystick alone – you'll break it.*

PHRASAL VERBS

leave sb/sth ↔ **behind**
1 to not take something or someone with you when you leave a place
2 to make more progress than someone else
leave off *informal* to stop doing something: *Let's start from where we left off yesterday.*
leave sb/sth ↔ **out** to not include someone or something: **[+of]** *Kidd has been left out of the team.*

THESAURUS

leave a place

leave to go away from a place or person: *Just as I was leaving the house, the phone rang.*
go *especially spoken* to leave somewhere: *Come on, boys, it's time to go.* | *They've already gone.*
set off *especially BrE* to leave somewhere and begin a journey: *The following day we set off for Vienna.*
take off when a plane takes off, it leaves the ground: *Our plane took off late because of the fog.*
emigrate to leave your own country in order to live permanently in another country: *In 2005, his family emigrated to New Zealand.*

depart *formal* to leave – used especially about trains, buses, planes etc: *The train for London will depart from platform 3.*

leave school/college

leave *especially BrE* to finish studying at school or college: *She found it difficult to get a job after leaving university.*
graduate to successfully finish your studies at a college or university, or at an American high school: *Kelly graduated from Oxford University with a degree in English.* | *Approximately 80% of Americans graduate from high school.*
drop out to leave school, college, or university before you have finished your studies: *He dropped out of college after the first year.*

leave your job

leave to stop doing a job: *Why did you leave your last job?*
quit to leave your job because you are not happy with it: *After enduring months of harassment, Mrs Collins decided to quit her job.*
resign to officially announce that you are going to leave your job: *The company director was forced to resign over the scandal.*
retire to leave your job because you have reached the age when most people stop working: *Ken's 65 and is hoping to retire in May.*

leave² *n* [U] **1** time that you are allowed to spend away from your job: **on leave** *soldiers home on leave* | **sick/maternity leave** (=time away from work because you are ill or have had a baby) **2** *formal* permission

leaves /liːvz/ *n* the plural of LEAF

lecherous /ˈletʃərəs/ *adj* showing sexual desire in a way that is unpleasant or annoying —**lechery** *n* [U] —**lecher** *n* [C]

lectern /ˈlektən $ -ərn/ *n* [C] a high desk that you stand behind when you make a speech

lecture¹ /ˈlektʃə $ -ər/ *n* [C] **1** a long talk about a subject, especially a talk given by a teacher to college students: **[+on/about]** *He gave a series of lectures on French literature.* **THESAURUS** SPEECH **2** a long serious talk that criticizes someone or warns them about something: **[+on/about]** *Dad **gave** me a long **lecture** about school.*

COLLOCATIONS

verbs

to give a lecture (*also* **to deliver a lecture** *formal*) *He will give a lecture on Greek art.*
to go to a lecture (*also* **to attend a lecture** *formal*) *Some of the students don't go to any lectures.*

lecture + noun

a lecture hall/room (*also* **a lecture theatre** *BrE*) *I sat at the back of the lecture hall.*
lecture notes (=written by the speaker or by a listener) *Read through your lecture notes.*

lecture² Ac *v* **1** [T] to talk angrily to someone for a long time, criticizing them or warning them about something: **lecture sb about/on sth** *He was lecturing us about making too much noise.* **2** [I] to teach a group of people about a subject, especially at a college —**lecturer** *n* [C]

led /led/ *v* the past tense and past participle of LEAD

ledge /ledʒ/ *n* [C] a flat surface that sticks out from the side of a mountain or a wall

ledger /ˈledʒə $ -ər/ *n* [C] a book in which the financial records of a company are kept

leech /liːtʃ/ *n* [C] a small creature that sticks to your skin and drinks your blood

leek /liːk/ *n* [C] a tall thin vegetable that tastes similar to an onion → see picture on page A5

leer /lɪə $ lɪr/ *v* [I] to look at someone in an unpleasant way that shows you think they are sexually attractive —**leer** *n* [C]

leeway /ˈliːweɪ/ *n* [U] freedom to do what you want: *We didn't give him much leeway.*

left¹ /left/ *adj* [only before noun]
1 on the side of your body that contains your heart OPP **right**: *the left side of his face* | **left leg/arm/ knee etc** *Jim's broken his left leg.*
2 on the same side of something as your left side OPP **right**: *Take a left turn at the lights.*

left² *adv* towards the left side OPP **right**: *Turn left at the church.*

left³ *n* [singular]
1 the left side or direction OPP **right**: **on/to the/your left** *It's the second door on your left.* | *Also pictured are, from left to right, brothers Tom, Sam, and Jack.*
2 a left turn OPP **right**: *Take the next left.*
3 **the left/the Left** political parties or groups whose beliefs are typical of, or similar to, SOCIALISM: *He has support from the left.*

left⁴ *v* the past tense and past participle of LEAVE

left-'hand *adj* [only before noun] on the left side of something: *the top left-hand drawer*

left-'handed *adj* someone who is left-handed uses their left hand to write, throw etc

left 'luggage ,office *n* [C] *BrE* a place at a station, airport etc where you can pay to leave your bags and collect them later

leftovers /ˈleftəʊvəz $ -oʊvərz/ *n* [plural] food that has not been eaten during a meal —**leftover** *adj*: *leftover food*

left-'wing *adj* having beliefs that are typical of, or similar to, SOCIALISM: *a left-wing newspaper* —**left- winger** *n* [C] —**left wing** *n* [singular]: *the left wing of the party*

leg /leg/ *n* [C]
1 one of the long parts of your body that your feet are joined to, or a similar part on an animal or insect
2 one of the parts that support a table, chair etc
3 the part of your trousers that covers your leg
4 one part of a journey, race, or competition: **[+of]** *the second leg of the World Championship*
PHRASES
not have a leg to stand on *informal* to be unable to prove or legally support something: *If you don't sign a contract, you won't have a leg to stand on.*

legacy /ˈlegəsi/ *n* [C] (*plural* **legacies**) **1** a situation, especially a bad one, that exists as a result of things that happened before: **[+of]** *the legacy of the war*
2 money or property that you receive from someone after they die SYN **inheritance**

legal Ac /ˈliːgəl/ *adj*
1 allowed or done according to the law OPP **illegal**: *It's perfectly legal to charge a fee.* | *He had twice the legal limit of alcohol in his blood.*
2 relating to the law: *free legal advice* | *the Scottish legal system* | *She threatened to take legal action against them.* —**legally** *adv* —**legality** /lɪˈgæləti/ *n* [U]

legalize (*also* **-ise** *BrE*) /ˈliːgəlaɪz/ *v* [T] to make something legal: *a campaign to legalize cannabis* —**legalization** /ˌliːgəlaɪˈzeɪʃən $ -lə-/ *n* [U]

legend /ˈledʒənd/ *n* **1** [C,U] an old well-known story about adventures or magical events: **[+of]** *the legend of King Arthur* | **According to legend**, *her tears formed a lake.* → see Word Choice at MYTH **2** [C] someone who is famous for being very good at something: *He was a legend in his own lifetime.* **3** [C] *formal* a phrase or word written on a sign, coin etc

legendary /ˈledʒəndəri $ -deri/ *adj* **1** very famous and admired: *the legendary baseball player Babe Ruth*
THESAURUS FAMOUS **2** [only before noun] appearing in legends

leggings /ˈlegɪŋz/ *n* [plural] a piece of women's clothing that fits tightly around the legs

legible /ˈledʒəbəl/ *adj* written clearly enough to be read OPP **illegible** —**legibly** *adv*

legion¹ /ˈliːdʒən/ *n* [C] a large group of soldiers, especially in the ancient Roman army

legion² *adj* [not before noun] *formal* very many: *Examples of this are legion.*

legislate Ac /ˈledʒəsleɪt/ *v* [I] to make a law about something: **[+against/for/on]** *The government has no plans to legislate against smoking in public.* —**legislator** *n* [C]

legislation /ˌledʒəˈsleɪʃən/ *n* [U] a law or set of laws: **[+on]** *The government has introduced new legislation on taxation.*

legislative Ac /ˈledʒəslətɪv $ -leɪtɪv/ *adj* relating to the making of laws: *legislative powers*

legislature Ac /ˈledʒəsleɪtʃə, -lətʃə $ -ər/ *n* [C] an institution that makes or changes laws

legitimate /ləˈdʒɪtəmət/ *adj* **1** reasonable: *a perfectly legitimate question* **2** not illegal: *legitimate business activities* —**legitimacy** *n* [U]

leisure /ˈleʒə $ ˈliːʒər/ *n* [U] time when you are not working and can do things you enjoy: **leisure activities** *such as sailing and swimming* | *They want better leisure facilities.*
PHRASES
at your leisure without hurrying or at a suitable time: *Read it at your leisure.*

'leisure ,centre *n* [C] *BrE* a place where you can do sports, exercise classes etc

leisurely /ˈleʒəli $ ˈliːʒərli/ *adj* done in a slow relaxed way: *a leisurely walk around the park*

lemon /'lemən/ n [C,U] a yellow fruit that tastes sour: *a slice of lemon* | *lemon juice* → see picture on page A4

lemonade /ˌleməˈneɪd◂/ n [U] **1** *BrE* a sweet drink with bubbles that tastes of lemons **2** a drink made with lemon juice, sugar, and water

lend /lend/ v (*past tense and past participle* **lent** /lent/)
1 [T] to let someone borrow money or something that belongs to you: **lend sb sth** *Could you lend me £10?* | **lend sth to sb** *I've lent my bike to Tom.*
2 [I,T] if a bank lends you money, it lets you have money that you must pay back with INTEREST
3 [T] *formal* to give something a particular quality: *The Prime Minister's presence lent a degree of importance to the occasion.* —**lender** n [C] —**lending** n [U]
PHRASES
lend (sb) a hand to help someone do something: *Lend me a hand with this box.*
lend itself to sth to be suitable for being used in a particular way: *Fish does not lend itself well to reheating.*
lend (your) support (to sb/sth) *formal* to support someone or something: *The government is lending its support to the campaign.*

length /leŋθ/ n
1 [C,U] the distance from one end of something to the other end → **breadth**, **width**: **[+of]** *What's the length of the room?* | **2** feet/8 metres etc in length *The whale measured three metres in length.* | *She walked* **the full length of** *the train* (=all the way along the train). → see picture at **DIMENSION**
2 [C,U] the amount of time that something continues for: **[+of]** *the average length of prison sentences*
3 **shoulder-length/knee-length etc** reaching as far as your shoulders, knees etc: *knee-length shorts*
4 [C] a piece of something that is long and thin: **[+of]** *two lengths of rope* → **FULL-LENGTH**
PHRASES
at length 1 for a long time: *He spoke at length about his experiences.* **2** *literary* after a long time: *'I think not,' he said at length.*
go to great/some/any etc lengths (to do sth) to try very hard or to do whatever is necessary to achieve something: *She went to great lengths to help us.*

lengthen /'leŋθən/ v [I,T] to become longer, or to make something longer

lengthwise /'leŋθwaɪz/ (*also* **lengthways** /-weɪz/ *BrE*) adv in the direction of the longest side: *Fold the cloth lengthwise.*

lengthy /'leŋθi/ adj continuing for a long time: *a lengthy process* **THESAURUS** LONG

lenient /'liːniənt/ adj not strict when dealing with people: *The judge was too lenient.* —**leniency** n [U]

lens /lenz/ n [C] **1** a piece of glass or plastic that makes things look different, for example in a camera or pair of glasses **2** the part inside your eye that bends the light to produce an image → **CONTACT LENS**

lent /lent/ v the past tense and past participle of LEND

Lent n [U] the 40 days before Easter, when people sometimes stop eating some types of food

lentil /'lentl, -təl/ n [C usually plural] a small round seed used as food

Leo /'liːəʊ $ 'liːoʊ/ n (*plural* **Leos**) **1** [U] the sign of the Zodiac of people born between July 24 and August 23 **2** [C] someone who has this sign

leopard /'lepəd $ -ərd/ n [C] a large wild cat with yellow fur and black spots → see picture at **TIGER**

leotard /'liːətɑːd $ -ɑːrd/ n [C] a tight piece of clothing that does not cover the arms or legs, worn for dancing

leper /'lepə $ -ər/ n [C] someone who has leprosy

leprosy /'leprəsi/ n [U] a serious disease in which the flesh is destroyed

lesbian /'lezbiən/ n [C] a woman who is sexually attracted to other women —**lesbian** adj

less¹ /les/ adv not so much, or to a smaller degree OPP **more**: *I definitely walk less since I've had the car.* | **less .... than ...** *The tickets were* **much less** *expensive than I expected.* | *Our trips became* **less and less** *frequent.*

less² determiner, pron a smaller amount OPP **more**: *Most single parents earned £200 a week or less.* | *engines which use less fuel* | **[+than]** *I live less than a mile from here.* | **[+of]** *She spends less of her time abroad now.* | *I saw* **less and less** *of each other.*
PHRASES
no less used to emphasize that the person or thing you are talking about is impressive: *The award was presented by the mayor, no less.*
no less than sth used to emphasize that a number is surprisingly large: *The USA was importing no less than 45% of its oil.*

> **Word Choice: less or fewer?**
> You use **less** before an uncountable noun: *We've had less rain this year.* | *The journey takes less time.*
> You use **fewer** before a countable noun that is used in the plural: *In those days, there were fewer cars on the streets.*

-less /ləs/ suffix not having or doing something: *childless couples* | *a windowless room*

lessen /'lesən/ v [I,T] to become less, or to make something become less **SYN** **reduce**: *Exercise lessens the risk of heart disease.* —**lessening** n [singular]

lesser /'lesə $ -ər/ adj [only before noun] *formal* not as large or important as something else: *a* **lesser sum** | *The major critics were Italy and,* **to a lesser extent**, *Germany.* —**lesser** adv: *a lesser known French poet*
PHRASES
the lesser of two evils the less unpleasant or harmful of two bad choices: *Neither candidate for the presidency was ideal, but Wilson was the lesser of two evils.*

lesson /ˈlesən/ n [C]
1 a period of time in which someone is taught a subject or skill: **have/take lessons** *Hannah is taking guitar lessons.* | **[+in/on]** *lessons in first aid*
2 *BrE* a period of time in which school students are taught a particular subject SYN **class** *AmE*: **French/physics/art etc lesson**
3 experience or information that you can use in the future: *Important lessons were learned from the accident.*

lest /lest/ *linking word, literary* in order to make sure that something does not happen: *He turned away lest his annoyance be seen.*

let /let/ v [T] (*past tense and past participle* **let**, *present participle* **letting**)
1 to allow someone to do something : *I'll come if my dad lets me.* | **let sb do sth** *'Let him go,' said Ralph.* | **let sb in/through/out etc** *Let me through – I'm a doctor!* | **let yourself do sth** *She was afraid to let herself believe it.* THESAURUS ALLOW

> **Grammar**
> Do not say 'My father won't let me to go dancing.' Say *My father won't let me go dancing.*

2 to not try to stop something from happening: **let sth do sth** *She let the book fall down onto the floor.*
3 (*also* **let out**) to allow someone to use a room or building in return for money: **let sth (out) to sb** *They let the flat to students.*
PHRASES
let alone used to say that one thing is not true or does not happen, so another thing cannot possibly be true or happen: *The baby can't even crawl yet, let alone walk!*
let go to stop holding someone or something: **[+of]** *'Let go of me!' Ben shouted.*
let sth go 1 to not criticize or punish someone for something: *I'll let it go today, but don't be late again.* **2** to stop worrying about something: *Let it go. It's not worth worrying about.*
let yourself go 1 to relax completely and enjoy yourself: *We'd never seen the teachers let themselves go like this.* **2** to allow yourself to become unhealthy or unattractive: *He let himself go over the years.*
let yourself in for sth to do something that will cause you trouble: *Now what's she let herself in for?*
let sb know to tell someone something: *Let me know when you're ready.* | *If there are any problems, I'll let you know.* THESAURUS TELL
let me do sth *spoken* used when you are offering to help someone: *Let me carry that for you.*

PHRASAL VERBS
let sb ↔ **down** to disappoint someone, especially by not doing what you promised: *You won't let me down, will you?* THESAURUS DISAPPOINTED
let sb **in on** sth to tell someone a secret
let sb **off** to not punish someone or not make them do something: *I'll let you off this time, but don't be late again.*
let on to show that you know a secret: **[+(that)]** *I won't let on I know anything.*
let out sth **let out a scream/cry etc** to suddenly shout or make a noise

let up to become less extreme or severe: *The rain never let up.*

letdown /ˈletdaʊn/ n [singular] *informal* something that disappoints you because it is not as good as you expected

lethal /ˈliːθəl/ adj able to cause death: *a lethal dose of the drug* | *a lethal weapon*

lethargic /ləˈθɑːdʒɪk $ -ˈθɑːr-/ adj having no energy, so that you feel lazy or tired —**lethargy** /ˈleθədʒi $ -ər-/ n [U]

let's /lets/ *spoken* the short form of 'let us', used to suggest to someone that you should do something together: *I'm hungry – let's eat.* | *Let's not argue.*
PHRASES
let's see *spoken* used when you are trying to remember or find something: *Now let's see, where did I put it?*

letter /ˈletə $ -ər/ n [C]
1 a written message that you put into an envelope and send to someone: **[+from/to]** *The school had written several letters to his parents.*
2 a symbol used in writing to represent a sound: *the letter 'A'* → **COVERING LETTER**
PHRASES
follow/obey sth to the letter to do exactly what someone tells you to do: *He followed their instructions to the letter.*
the letter of the law the exact words of a law or agreement, rather than the intended or general meaning: *The builders adhered to the letter of the law, but not to its spirit.*

COLLOCATIONS

verbs

to get/have a letter (*also* **to receive a letter** *formal*) *I had a letter from Kim a few days ago.*
to write a letter *He wrote a letter complaining about the service.*
to send sb a letter *She sent me a lovely letter.*
to post a letter *BrE*, **to mail a letter** *AmE I'm going out to post some letters.*
to answer a letter/reply to a letter *The company didn't answer my letter.*
a letter comes/arrives *A letter came for you today.*

types of letter

a long/short letter *She wrote a long letter to her brother.*
a business letter *Do you know how to write a business letter?*
an official letter *I got an official letter from the university.*
a love letter *I found a bundle of old love letters.*
a thank-you letter *You ought to send Aunt Jane a thank-you letter.*
a letter of thanks/apology/complaint *She received a letter of apology from the hospital.*

---

letterbox /ˈletəbɒks $ ˈletərbɑːks/ n [C] *BrE* **1** a hole in a door through which letters are delivered SYN **mailbox** *AmE* **2** a box in a post office or in the street, where you post letters SYN **postbox** *BrE*, **mailbox** *AmE*

lettering /'letərɪŋ/ n [U] letters that are written or drawn in a particular style: *ornate gold lettering*

lettuce /'letɪs/ n [C,U] a green vegetable with thin leaves, eaten raw in SALADS → see picture on page A5

letup /'letʌp/ n [singular, U] a pause or reduction in a difficult or unpleasant activity: *There has been no letup in the fighting.*

leukemia (also **leukaemia** *BrE*) /luːˈkiːmiə/ n [U] a form of CANCER that affects the blood

level¹ /'levəl/ n [C]
1 AMOUNT an amount, degree, or number of something: **high/low level** *high levels of pollution* | *Try to reduce your **stress levels**.*
2 HEIGHT the height of something above or below something else: *The **water level** was rising.* | *The whole area is below **ground level**.* | **eye/knee/shoulder etc level** (=the same height as your eyes etc) *The picture was hung at eye level.*
3 STANDARD a particular standard, for example in sport or education: **at ... level** *Few athletes compete at international level.* | *the advanced-level course*
4 RANK a position or rank within an organization or system: *Employees at all levels were affected.*
5 IN A BUILDING a floor in a building that has several floors: *Her office is on Level 3.*
6 WAY OF CONSIDERING a way of considering something or of dealing with something: *On a **personal level**, I find this very upsetting.* → HIGH-LEVEL, LOW-LEVEL, SEA LEVEL

level² adj
1 flat, with no part higher than the rest: *The floor was not completely level.* THESAURUS FLAT
2 at the same height or in the same position as something else: **[+with]** *His face was level with hers.*
3 having the same number of points: *They **finished level**.*
PHRASES
a level playing field a situation in which different people, companies etc can compete fairly because no one has special advantages: *Small businesses want to compete on a level playing field with larger ones.*

level³ v (**levelled, levelling** *BrE*, **leveled, leveling** *AmE*) **1** (also **level off**) [T] to make a surface flat **2** [T] to knock something down to the ground and destroy it: *The earthquake leveled several buildings.* **3** [I,T] *BrE* to score a point in a competition, so that both sides are equal **4 level criticism/charges against/at sb** to say that you think someone has done something wrong: *Similar accusations have been leveled at other organizations.*
PHRASAL VERBS
level off/out to stop rising or falling, and continue at the same height or amount: *The plane levelled off at 30,000 feet.*
level with sb *informal* to tell someone the truth or what you really think

level 'crossing n [C] *BrE* a place where a railway crosses a road SYN **grade crossing** *AmE*

level-'headed adj calm and sensible

lever¹ /'liːvə $ 'levər/ n [C] **1** a bar that you put under a heavy object in order to lift the object up **2** a handle on a machine that you move to make the machine work

lever² v [T] **1** to move something using a lever: *He levered the door open with a crowbar.* **2 lever yourself up/out of etc sth** to move your body by pushing on something with your arms: *He levered himself out of the hole.*

leverage /'liːvərɪdʒ $ 'le-, 'liː-/ n [U] **1** influence that you use to make people do what you want: *Small businesses have less leverage when dealing with banks.* **2** the action, use, or power of a lever

levitate /'levɪteɪt/ v [I] to rise and float in the air as if by magic —**levitation** /ˌlevɪˈteɪʃən/ n [U]

levy Ac /'levi/ v (**levied, levying, levies**) **levy a tax/charge etc (on sth)** to officially make people pay a tax etc: *a tax levied on electrical goods* —**levy** n [C]

lewd /luːd/ adj using rude words or movements that make you think of sex: *lewd comments*

lexical /'leksɪkəl/ adj technical relating to words

lexicon /'leksɪkən $ -kɑːn, -kən/ n [C] all the words used in a language or by a group of people

liability /ˌlaɪəˈbɪləti/ n (plural **liabilities**) **1** [C,U] legal responsibility for something, especially for injury, damage, or a debt: **[+for]** *They have **admitted liability** for the accident.* **2** [singular] something that causes problems or is likely to be dangerous: *That car is a liability!*

liable /'laɪəbəl/ adj **1 be liable to do sth** to be likely to do something: *The car's liable to overheat.* **2** legally responsible for something: **[+for]** *The company is not liable for any damage.* **3 be liable to sth** to be likely to be affected by something bad: *You're more liable to injury when you don't get regular exercise.*

liaise /liˈeɪz/ v [I] to work with other people and exchange information with them: **[+with]** *She liaises with local schools.*

liaison /liˈeɪzən $ 'liːəzɑːn, liˈeɪ-/ n **1** [singular, U] the way two groups of people work together: **[+between/with]** *close liaison between the army and police* **2** [C] a sexual relationship, especially a secret one

liar /'laɪə $ -ər/ n [C] someone who tells lies

libel /'laɪbəl/ n [C,U] when someone writes or prints untrue statements about someone → **slander**: *He sued the magazine for libel.* —**libel** v [T] —**libellous** *BrE*, **libelous** *AmE* adj

Word Choice: libel or slander?
You use **libel** about the crime of writing something untrue about someone, for example in a newspaper.
You use **slander** about the crime of saying something untrue about someone in public.

liberal¹ Ac /'lɪbərəl/ adj **1** willing to understand or respect other people's ideas and behaviour: *a liberal attitude towards sex* **2** supporting changes in political, social, or religious systems that give people more freedom **3** giving or using a lot of something: *Don't be too liberal with the salt.*

L

liberal² Ac n [C] someone with liberal opinions or principles

Liberal 'Democrats n [plural] (*abbreviation* **Lib Dems**) a British political party —**Liberal Democrat** *adj*

liberalize Ac (*also* **-ise** *BrE*) /'lɪbərəlaɪz/ v [T] to make a system, law, or attitude less strict —**liberalization** /ˌlɪbərəlaɪˈzeɪʃən $ -rələ-/ n [U]

liberally Ac /'lɪbərəli/ adv in large amounts

liberate Ac /'lɪbəreɪt/ v [T] to free someone or something from restrictions or someone's control: *The city was liberated by the Allies in 1944.* | **liberate sb from sth** *They need to liberate themselves from the past.* —**liberating** *adj*: *a very liberating experience* —**liberator** n [C] —**liberation** /ˌlɪbəˈreɪʃən/ n [U]

liberated Ac /'lɪbəreɪtɪd/ adj behaving in a free modern way

liberty /'lɪbəti $ -ər-/ n (plural **liberties**) **1** [C,U] the freedom and the right to do whatever you want without asking permission or being afraid of authority: *principles of liberty and democracy* → see Word Choice at **FREEDOM** **2** [C] something that you do, although you do not have permission: *I took the liberty of inviting him to join us.*

PHRASES

at liberty *formal* not in prison or not kept in an enclosed space **SYN** **free**: *Only two of the original gang are still at liberty.*

be at liberty to do sth *formal* to have permission to do something: *The reporter said that he was not at liberty to reveal his source.*

libido /lɪˈbiːdəʊ $ -doʊ/ n [C,U] (plural **libidos**) sexual desire

Libra /'liːbrə/ n **1** [U] the sign of the Zodiac of people born between September 24 and October 23 **2** [C] someone who has this sign

librarian /laɪˈbreəriən $ -'brer-/ n [C] someone who works in a library

library /'laɪbrəri, -bri $ -breri/ n [C] (plural **libraries**)
1 a room or building containing books that can be looked at or borrowed: *a library book*
2 a group of books, CDs etc collected by one person

lice /laɪs/ n the plural of LOUSE

licence *BrE*, **license** *AmE* /'laɪsəns/ n
1 [C] an official document that gives you permission to do or own something: *a pilot's licence* | **licence to do sth** *He has lost his licence to sell alcohol.*
2 [U] *formal* freedom to do or say whatever you want → **OFF-LICENCE**

PHRASES

under licence if a product is made or sold under licence, it is made or sold by a company that has an official agreement with the owner of the product that allows them to do this: *The car is built under licence in the UK.*

COLLOCATIONS
verbs

to have a licence (*also* **to hold a licence** *BrE*) *They didn't have a television licence.*

to get a licence (*also* **to obtain a licence** *formal*) *He got his pilot's licence last week.*
to apply for a licence *Companies will have to apply for a licence to import these chemicals.*
to lose your licence (=to have it taken away as a punishment) *Drivers who drink risk losing their licences.*

types of licence

a driving licence *BrE*, **a driver's license** *AmE* *The police officer asked to see my driver's license.*
a pilot's licence (=a licence to fly a plane) | **a television licence** *BrE* (=one that allows you to use your television and pays for public television programmes)

license Ac /'laɪsəns/ v [T] to give official permission for someone to do something: **be licensed to do sth** *Is he licensed to carry a gun?* —**licensed** *adj* [only before noun]: *licensed drivers*

'license plate n [C] *AmE* a sign on the front and back of a car that shows its official number **SYN** **number plate** *BrE* → see picture at **CAR**

'licensing ,laws n [plural] the British laws that say when and where you can sell alcohol

lichen /'laɪkən, 'lɪtʃən/ n [C,U] a plant that spreads over the surface of stones and trees

lick¹ /lɪk/ v [T] to move your tongue across the surface of something: *The dog jumped up and licked her face.*

lick² n [C usually singular] when you move your tongue across the surface of something

PHRASES

a lick of paint *informal* some paint put on something to improve its appearance: *The room will look better with a lick of paint.*

licorice /'lɪkərɪs, -rɪʃ/ n the American spelling of LIQUORICE

lid /lɪd/ n [C]
1 a cover for a pot, box, or other container: *Put the lid on the pan.* **THESAURUS** **CLOSE**
2 an EYELID

lie¹ /laɪ/ v [I] (past tense **lay** /leɪ/, past participle **lain** /leɪn/, present participle **lying**, third person singular **lies**)
1 to be in a position in which your body is flat on the floor, a bed etc, or to put yourself in this position: **[+on/in]** *We lay on the beach all morning.* | **[+back]** *I love to lie back in a nice hot bath and relax.* | *My mom used to lie awake worrying.*
2 to be in a flat position on a surface: **[+on/in etc]** *His letter was lying on her desk.*
3 if a city, town etc lies in a particular position, it is in that position: *The town lies to the east of the lake.*
4 if a problem lies somewhere, it is caused by that thing, person, or situation: **[+in/with etc]** *The fault lies with the computer system.*
5 [linking verb] to be in a particular condition or state: *The boats in this once-busy fishing village now lie idle* (=are not busy working). | *The city lay in ruins.*
6 if something lies in the future, it is going to happen to you in the future: *the difficulties that lie ahead*

for the refugees | *Who knows what **lies in store** for any of us?*

PHRASES

lie in wait (for sb/sth) to remain hidden in a place and wait for someone so that you can attack them: *The mugger lay in wait for his victim.*

lie low to remain hidden because someone is trying to find you: *We'll have to lie low until tonight.*

PHRASAL VERBS

lie around (*also* **lie about** *BrE*)

1 lie around (sth) if something is lying around, it has been left somewhere in an untidy way, not in the place where it should be: *Stop **leaving** your clothes **lying around**.*

2 to spend time lying somewhere, not doing anything: *We just lay around on the beach the whole time.*

lie behind sth to be the real reason for an action, even though this may be hidden: *What really **lay behind** her question?*

lie down

1 to put yourself in a position in which your body is flat on the floor, a bed etc: *I'm going upstairs to lie down.*

2 not take sth lying down *informal* to refuse to accept bad treatment without complaining

lie² v [I] (**lied, lying, lies**) to tell someone something that you know is not true: **[+to]** *I would never lie to you.* | **[+about]** *Have you ever lied about your age?*

lie³ n [C] something that you say or write that you know is not true: *That's a lie!*

COLLOCATIONS

verbs

to tell a lie *I always know when she's telling lies.*
⚠ Do not say 'say a lie'. Say **tell a lie**.
to believe a lie *People believed her lies.*

adjectives

a complete/total lie *I said I'd never met her, which was a complete lie.*
a big/little lie *The whole story is a big lie.*
a white lie (=a little lie that you tell to avoid upsetting someone) *Sometimes it is kinder to tell a white lie.*
a blatant lie (=an obvious lie) *How could they tell such blatant lies?*

noun + lies

a pack of lies *informal* (=a lot of lies) *He admitted he had told us a pack of lies.*

'lie de,tector n [C] a piece of equipment used to check whether someone is telling the truth or not, by measuring sudden changes in their heart rate

'lie-down n [singular] *BrE* a short rest: *I'm going to have a lie-down.*

'lie-in n [singular] *BrE* when you stay in bed longer than usual in the morning: *I always have a lie-in on a Sunday.*

lieu /ljuː, luː $ luː/ n **in lieu (of sth)** instead of something: *time off in lieu of payment*

lieutenant /lefˈtenant $ luːˈten-/ n [C] an officer with a fairly low rank in the army, navy, or AIR FORCE, or a fairly high rank in the US police

life /laɪf/ n (plural **lives** /laɪvz/)

1 [C,U] the period of time when you are alive: *sb's life This is the happiest **day of** my **life**. | He spent the **rest of** his **life** in France. | For the first time **in** my **life**, I felt old. | The accident left him crippled **for life** (=badly injured for the rest of his life).* **THESAURUS** ▶ ALWAYS

2 [C,U] the state of being alive → **alive, dead, live, death**: *He lost his life in a helicopter crash.*

3 [C,U] all the experiences and activities that are typical of a particular job, situation, or activity → **lifestyle**: *Life in London is so hectic. | **family/home/married life** | **private/social/sex/love etc life** I don't want any advice about my love life! | Having a baby **changes** your **life**. | the American **way of life** | a life of crime/poverty etc*

4 [U] living things such as people, animals, or plants: *Is there life on other planets?* | **plant/animal/bird etc life** *the island's plant life*

5 [U] activity or movement: *She was so young and **full of life**. | There were no **signs of life** in the house.*

6 [C usually singular] the period of time that something continues to exist or be good enough to use **SYN** lifespan: **[+of]** *What's the average life of a family car?*

7 (*also* **life im'prisonment**) [U] when someone is put in prison for the rest of their life: *I think murderers should **get life**. → DOUBLE LIFE, STILL LIFE, WAY OF LIFE*

PHRASES

bring sth to life/come to life to make something more exciting, or to become more exciting: *The game really came to life in the second half.*

get a life! *spoken* used to tell someone that they are boring and should find more exciting things to do: *Just stop complaining and get a life!*

real life what really happens, rather than what happens in stories or in your imagination: *Real life is likely to be more complicated than that.* | **in real life** *Things like that don't happen in real life.*

that's life *spoken humorous* said when something bad happens, to show that you accept it could happen to anyone: *All our efforts were wasted, but I guess that's life.*

COLLOCATIONS – sense 2

verbs

to save sb's life *Wearing a seat belt can save your life.*
to risk your life *He risked his life to save his dog from drowning.*
to lose your life (=to die) *We remember those who lost their lives in the war.*
to take your own life (=to kill yourself) *He had no reason to take his own life.*
to spare sb's life (=to not kill someone, when you could kill them) *She begged him to spare the life of her son.*
to cost sb their life/cost lives (=to result in someone's death) *That decision may have cost him his life.*
to owe sb your life (=to be still alive because of someone's actions) *I owe these doctors my life.*

lifebelt /ˈlaɪfbelt/ n [C] **1** *BrE* a LIFEBUOY **2** *AmE* a special belt you wear in water to prevent you from sinking

lifeboat /ˈlaɪfbəʊt $ -boʊt/ n [C] a boat that is used to help people who are in danger at sea

lifebuoy /ˈlaɪfbɔɪ $ -buːi, -bɔɪ/ n [C] a large ring made from material that floats, which you throw to someone who has fallen in the water to prevent them from sinking

'life ˌcycle n [C] the stages of development that a living thing goes through

ˌlife exˈpectancy n [C,U] the length of time that someone is likely to live

'lifeguard /ˈlaɪfɡɑːd $ -ɡɑːrd/ n [C] someone whose job is to help swimmers who are in danger at a beach or swimming pool

'life inˌsurance n [U] a type of insurance that someone buys so that when they die their family will receive money

'life ˌjacket n [C] a piece of clothing that you wear around your chest so that you will float if you fall into water

lifeless /ˈlaɪfləs/ adj **1** literary dead or seeming to be dead **2** not at all interesting or exciting: a lifeless performance

lifelike /ˈlaɪflaɪk/ adj a lifelike picture, model etc looks like a real person or thing: a lifelike statue

lifeline /ˈlaɪflaɪn/ n [C] something that someone depends on completely: The phone is her lifeline.

lifelong /ˈlaɪflɒŋ $ -lɔːŋ/ adj [only before noun] continuing all through your life: a **lifelong friend**

lifesaver /ˈlaɪfseɪvə $ -ər/ n [C] someone or something that helps you in a very important way

life-saving¹ /ˈlaɪfˌseɪvɪŋ/ adj [only before noun] life-saving medical treatment or equipment is used to help save people's lives: a life-saving heart operation

life-saving² n [U] the skills necessary to save a person who cannot swim: a life-saving certificate

'life-size (also **'life-sized**) adj a life-size picture, model etc of something or someone is the same size as they really are

lifespan /ˈlaɪfspæn/ n [C] the length of time that someone will live or something will work

lifestyle /ˈlaɪfstaɪl/ n [C,U] the way that someone lives, including their work and activities, and what things they own: Regular exercise is part of a **healthy lifestyle**.

'life support ˌsystem n [C] medical equipment that keeps someone alive when they are extremely ill

'life-ˌthreatening adj a life-threatening illness, injury etc can kill you

lifetime /ˈlaɪftaɪm/ n [C usually singular] the period of time during which someone is alive

'life vest n [C] AmE a LIFE JACKET

lift¹ /lɪft/ v

1 (also **lift up**) [T] to move something or someone to a higher position: Can you help me lift this box? | He lifted his hand to wave. | **lift sb/sth onto/into etc sth** Dad lifted me onto his shoulders. → see picture on page A11

2 [T] to remove a rule or law that stops something

happening: The US plans to **lift** its **ban** on Cuban cigars.

3 [I] if cloud or MIST lifts, it starts to get sunny or bright

PHRASES

lift sb's spirits/sb's spirits lift to make someone feel happier, or to begin to feel happier: Ed tried hard to lift her spirits.

not lift a finger informal to do nothing to help: My husband never lifts a finger in the house.

PHRASAL VERBS

lift off if a SPACECRAFT lifts off, it leaves the ground and goes up into the air → **take off**

THESAURUS

lift (up) to move something or someone to a higher position: I can't lift this bag – it's too heavy. | She lifted the cat up onto her knee.

raise to lift something to a higher position before lowering it again. **Raise** is more formal than **lift**: We all raised our glasses. | The bridge can be raised to allow ships to pass under it.

pick up to lift something up from the ground, from a table etc, especially something small or light: He picked up the letter and put it in his pocket.

hoist to lift up something which is heavy and difficult to carry: He hoisted the sack over his shoulder.

put your hand up to lift your arm into the air, for example because you want to speak in a class or when voting: Put your hand up if you know the answer.

---

lift² n [C]

1 BrE a machine that takes you up and down between floors in a building SYN elevator AmE: **take/use a lift**

2 especially BrE if you give someone a lift, you take them somewhere in your car: Could anybody **give** Sue **a lift** home? | Do you want a lift?

PHRASES

give sb/sth a lift to make someone more cheerful or confident: A win would really give the team a lift.

'lift-off n [C,U] the moment when a space vehicle leaves the ground

ligament /ˈlɪɡəmənt/ n [C] a band of strong material in your body that joins bones together

light¹ /laɪt/

1 [U] the energy from the Sun, a lamp etc that allows you to see things: Light poured in through the window.

2 [C] something such as a lamp that produces light, using electricity: **turn/switch/put a light on/off** Can you turn the light on, please? | The lights of the other traffic dazzled him.

3 [C usually plural] a set of red, green, and yellow lights that control the movement of traffic SYN traffic lights: **at the lights** Turn left at the lights. | Wait for the **lights** to **change** to green.

4 a light something such as a match, used to light a cigarette: Excuse me, do you have a light?

LIGHT

lantern

candle

lamp

torch BrE/
flashlight AmE

PHRASES

come to light/be brought to light to become known: *The new evidence did not come to light until after the trial.*

first light the time when it first gets light in the morning: *We set out at first light.*

in a new/different/bad etc light if someone or something is seen or shown in a new, different, bad etc light, people have a new, different, bad etc opinion about them: *I suddenly saw my father in a different light.*

in the light of sth BrE, **in light of sth** AmE after considering something: *In light of the tragic events, tonight's concert has been cancelled.*

light at the end of the tunnel something that gives you hope that a bad situation will end soon: *After a very difficult year, we are starting to see light at the end of the tunnel.*

see the light to finally realize or understand something: *I am hoping that the government will see the light and change this policy.*

shed/throw/cast light on sth to provide new information about something that makes it easier to understand: *These discoveries may shed new light on the origins of the universe.*

COLLOCATIONS

adjectives

bright/strong light *The light was so bright I could hardly see.*

dim light (=not bright) *She could only just see his face in the dim light.*

good/bad light (=bright enough or not bright enough) *The light in here isn't very good.*

natural light (=from the Sun) *There was no natural light, just a bare light bulb.*

artificial light (=from lamps) *The colour of the carpet looks different in artificial light.*

verbs

light shines *The morning light was shining through the window.*

light comes from sth *The only light came from the fire.*

light falls on/across sth (=appears on it) *He moved forward, and the light fell on his face.*

to reflect light *Snow reflects a lot of light.*

noun + light

a beam/ray of light (=a thin line of light) *the beam of light from the torch*

a flash of light (=a sudden bright light that appears for a very short time) *The sky was lit up by flashes of light.*

the morning/evening light *His hair shone like gold in the morning light.*

THESAURUS – sense 2

light something that produces light using electricity: *The lights in the house were all on.*

lamp an object that produces light using electricity, oil, or gas – often used in names of lights: *a table lamp | a street lamp | a reading lamp*

torch BrE, **flashlight** AmE a small electric lamp that you carry in your hand: *We shone our torches around the cave.*

headlight (*also* **headlamp**) one of the two large lights at the front of a vehicle: *I could see car headlights coming towards me.*

lantern a lamp you can carry, consisting of a glass or metal container with a light inside: *The miners used lanterns which were lit by candles.*

light² adj

1 COLOUR a light colour is pale, not dark OPP **dark**: **light blue/green/brown etc** *a light blue dress*

2 ROOM if a room is light, a lot of light from the Sun gets into it OPP **dark**: *The kitchen is light and roomy.*

3 SKY IS NOT DARK it is light used to say that there is enough light to see by OPP **dark**: *It was still light when we got home.*

4 NOT HEAVY not heavy: *Your bag's a lot lighter than mine.* | *It's **as light as a feather** (=very light).*

5 GENTLE not having or using much force or power SYN **gentle**: *a light wind | a light tap on the door | Try some light exercise.*

6 CLOTHES light clothes are thin and not very warm: *a light sweater*

7 FOOD light food does not make you feel too full OPP **rich**: *a light snack*

8 FOR ENTERTAINMENT not serious or difficult, and intended to entertain people: *It's the perfect book if you want some **light reading**.* | **light entertainment** (=programmes, shows etc that are very easy to watch or listen to, especially comedy)

9 NOT MUCH small in amount: *Traffic is much lighter on Sundays.*

10 SLEEP **a) light sleep** sleep from which you wake up easily: *I fell into a light sleep.* **b) light sleeper** someone who wakes up easily: *My roommate is a very light sleeper.* —**lightness** n [U]

PHRASES

make light of sth to joke about something or treat it as if it were not important: *She tried to make light of the situation, but I knew she was upset.*

light³ v (*past tense and past participle* **lit** /lɪt/ *or* **lighted**)

1 [I,T] to start to burn, or to make something start burning: *I lit another cigarette.* | *The fire won't light because the wood's wet.*

2 [T] to produce light in a room etc: *The room was warm and brightly lit.* | *well-lit streets*

PHRASAL VERBS

light up

1 light sth ↔ up to make a place or thing become light or bright: *The fireworks lit up the sky.* | *The fountain is lit up at night.*

2 if someone's face or eyes light up, they suddenly look happy or excited

3 *informal* to light a cigarette

light⁴ *adv* **travel light** to not take too many clothes etc with you when you travel

'light bulb *n* [C] the glass part of an electric light, where the light shines from

lighted /'laɪtɪd/ *adj* **1** a lighted window, room etc has a light on inside **2** a lighted CANDLE, match etc is burning

lighten /'laɪtn/ *v* **1** [T] to reduce the amount of work, worry, debt etc that someone has: *The new computers should lighten our workload.* **2** [I,T] to become brighter, or to make something become brighter: *As the sky lightened, we could see where we were.*

PHRASAL VERBS

lighten up *informal* to become less serious or strict

lighter /'laɪtə $ -ər/ *n* [C] a small object that produces a flame to light a cigarette

'light-'headed *adj* unable to think clearly or move steadily, for example because you are ill or have drunk some alcohol

light-hearted /,laɪt 'hɑːtɪd $ -ɑːr-/ *adj* **1** not intended to be serious: *a light-hearted remark* **2** cheerful and not worried

lighthouse /'laɪthaʊs/ *n* [C] a tower with a bright light that warns ships of danger

LIGHTHOUSE

lighting /'laɪtɪŋ/ *n* [U] the lights in a place, or the quality of the light: *Better street lighting might help prevent crime.*

lightly /'laɪtli/ *adv* **1** with only a small amount of weight or force **SYN gently**: *He touched her lightly on the shoulder.* **2** using or having only a small amount of something: *a lightly greased pan*

3 take/treat/approach sth lightly to do something without serious thought: *We did not take this decision lightly.*

PHRASES

get off lightly (*also* **be let off lightly**) to be punished in a way that is less severe than you deserve: *They got off lightly considering the seriousness of the crime.*

lightning¹ /'laɪtnɪŋ/ *n* [U] a bright flash of electrical light in the sky during a storm: *Several trees were* **struck** (=hit) **by lightning.** | **thunder and lightning**

LIGHTNING

lightning² *adj* [only before noun] very fast: *a lightning attack*

lightweight /'laɪt-weɪt/ *adj* weighing very little: *a lightweight jacket*

'light year *n* [C] the distance that light travels in one year (about 9,460,000,000,000 kilometres), used for measuring distances between stars

PHRASES

light years ahead of sth/better than sth etc *informal* more advanced, much better etc than someone or something else: *This product is light years ahead of its competitors.*

likable /'laɪkəbəl/ *adj* another spelling of LIKEABLE

like¹ /laɪk/ *prep*

1 similar to something else, or happening in the same way: *Her hair is dark brown, like mine.* | **look/sound/feel etc like** *The garden looked like a jungle.* | *He's* **very like** *his brother.* | *Sometimes you sound* **just like** (=exactly like) *my mum.* | *He looked* **nothing like** (=not at all like) *the man in the photo.*
THESAURUS SAME

2 used to give an example of something: *Things like glass and paper can be recycled.*

3 typical of a person: *It's not like Dad to be late.*

4 like this/that/so *spoken* used when you are showing someone how to do something: *You have to fold the corners back, like this.*

PHRASES

just like that if you do something just like that, you do it without thinking about it or planning it carefully: *You can't give up your job just like that!*

more like nearer to a particular amount: *The real figure may be more like ninety.*

nothing like *BrE* not at all: *This will be* **nothing like enough** *money.*

something like not much more or less than a particular amount: *Seats cost something like $50 each.*

what is sb/sth like? *spoken* used to ask someone to describe or give their opinion of a person or thing: *What's their house like inside?*

Usage

Many teachers think that using **like** before giving an example is wrong. It is better to use **such as**, especially in written English.
It is better to write *Games* **such as** *chess take a long time to learn.* rather than 'Games like chess take a long time to learn.'

like² *v* [T]

1 to enjoy something or think that someone or something is nice, good, or right **OPP dislike**: *Do you* *like this colour?* | *I don't* **like** *it when you get angry.* | **like doing sth** *I don't like making speeches.* | **like to do sth** *I like to see people enjoying themselves.* | *I* **quite** **like** *their new CD.* | *We* **really liked** *the film.* | *She* **likes** *John* **very much.** THESAURUS ▶ DISLIKE

2 to prefer to do something or have something happen in a particular way: **like to do sth** *I like to get up early.* | **like sb to do sth** *We like our students to take part in sports.*

3 would like used to say what you want or to ask someone what they want: *I'd like a cheeseburger, please.* | **would like to do sth** *I'd like to visit Australia someday.* | *I'd* **just like** *to say how grateful we are.* | *Would you like a drink?* | **would you like (sb) to do sth?** *Would you like to come with us?* THESAURUS ▶ WANT

PHRASES

as long/as much etc as you like as long, as much etc as you want: *Take as many as you like.*

I'd like to think/believe (that) used to say that you wish or hope something is true, when you are not sure that it is: *I'd like to think that we offer a good service to everyone.*

if you like *BrE spoken* **1** used to suggest or offer something: *We could watch a video this evening if you like.* **2** used to agree to something: *'Shall we get a takeaway?' 'If you like.'*

(whether something) like it or not used to emphasize that something will happen or is true and cannot be changed: *Like it or not, people are often judged by their appearance.*

whatever/wherever/anything etc you like whatever thing you want, in whatever place you want etc: *You can sit wherever you like.*

Grammar

Like is not used in the progressive. Do not say *'I am liking their music.'* Say *I like their music.*

THESAURUS

like to enjoy something or think that someone or something is nice, good, or right: *I like Japanese food.*

be fond of sb/sth *especially BrE* to like someone or something, especially something you have had for a long time or someone you have known for a long time: *Over the years, I've become quite fond of him.*

be keen on sb/sth *especially BrE* to like someone, or to feel very enthusiastic about something: *He isn't very keen on the idea.*

be into sth *informal* to like doing something or be interested in a particular subject: *She's really into folk music.* | *Are you into cooking?*

to like something very much

love/adore to like something very much. **Adore** is stronger than **love** and is more formal: *I love your dress!* | *The critics adored the play.*

be crazy about sth (*also* **be mad about sth** *BrE*) *informal* to be extremely interested in an activity and spend a lot of time doing it or watching it: *He's crazy about football.*

be addicted to sth to like doing something so much that you spend all your free time doing it: *My brother's addicted to computer games.*

---

like³ *n*
PHRASES

sb's likes and dislikes the things that someone likes and does not like

and the like and similar things: *social problems such as poverty, unemployment, and the like*

the likes of sb *spoken* used to talk about a particular type of person: *He thinks he's too good for the likes of us.*

like⁴ *adv spoken* used while you are thinking what to say next: *The water was, like, really cold.*
PHRASES

I'm like/he's like etc used to say what someone said: *I was like 'What?'*

like⁵ *linking word, spoken informal* **1** in the same way as someone or something: *No one can score goals like he can.* **2** as if: *It looks like it's going to rain.*
PHRASES

like I say/said used to repeat something that you have already said: *I'm sorry, but, like I say, she's not here right now.*

-like /laɪk/ *suffix* similar to or typical of a thing or person: *a jelly-like substance* | *ladylike behaviour*

likeable, likable /ˈlaɪkəbəl/ *adj* likeable people are nice and easy to like THESAURUS ▶ NICE

likelihood /ˈlaɪklihʊd/ *n* [singular, U] the degree to which something can be expected to happen: **[+of]** *Using a seat belt reduces the likelihood of injury in a car accident.*
PHRASES

in all likelihood almost certainly: *The president will, in all likelihood, have to resign.*

likely¹ /ˈlaɪkli/ *adj* probably true or probably going to happen OPP **unlikely**: *Snow showers are likely tomorrow.* | *the most* **likely cause** *of the problem* | **likely to do/be sth** *Young drivers are more likely to have accidents than older drivers.* | *It is* **more than likely** (=almost certain) *the votes will have to be recounted.*

likely² *adv* probably: **most/very likely** *I'd very likely have done the same thing.* THESAURUS ▶ PROBABLY
PHRASES

not likely *especially BrE spoken* used to say that you definitely will not do something: *'Are you inviting Mary to the party?' 'Not likely!'*

like-'minded *adj* like-minded people have similar interests and opinions

liken /ˈlaɪkən/ *v*
PHRASAL VERBS

liken sb/sth **to** sb/sth to say that two people or things are similar: *Critics likened the new theatre to a supermarket.*

likeness /ˈlaɪknəs/ *n* **1** [C,U] the quality of being similar in appearance to someone or something: **[+to]** *Hugh's likeness to his father* **2** [C] a picture of someone, especially one that looks very like them

likewise Ac /ˈlaɪk-waɪz/ *adv formal* in the same way: *The dinner was superb. Likewise the concert.*

liking /ˈlaɪkɪŋ/ n [singular] *formal* when you like someone or something: [+for] *She had a liking for champagne.*

PHRASES

take a liking to sb/sth to begin to like someone or something

be to sb's liking *formal* to be just what someone wanted: *I hope everything was to your liking, Sir.*

too bright/strong/quiet etc for sb's liking brighter, stronger etc than someone likes: *This weather's too hot for my liking.*

lilac /ˈlaɪlək/ n **1** [C,U] a small tree with pale purple or white flowers **2** [U] a pale purple colour —**lilac** *adj*

Lilo /ˈlaɪləʊ $ -loʊ/ n [C] (*plural* **Lilos**) *trademark BrE* a rubber MATTRESS filled with air and used as a bed or for floating on water

lilt /lɪlt/ n [singular] a pleasant pattern of rising and falling sound in someone's voice or in music —**lilting** *adj*

lily /ˈlɪli/ n [C] (*plural* **lilies**) a plant with large white or coloured flowers → see picture at **FLOWER**[1]

limb /lɪm/ n [C] **1** an arm or leg **2** a large branch of a tree

PHRASES

out on a limb alone and without help or support: *By voting for Wiesner we'd gone out on a limb.*

limbo /ˈlɪmbəʊ $ -boʊ/ n **be in limbo** to be in an uncertain situation because you are waiting for something to happen: *I'm in limbo until I get my exam results.*

lime /laɪm/ n **1** [C,U] a bright green fruit with a sour taste, or the tree that this fruit grows on → see picture on page A4 **2** [U] a white powdery substance used for making CEMENT

limelight /ˈlaɪmlaɪt/ n [singular, U] a situation in which someone has the attention of a lot of people: **in/out of the limelight** *Ted loves being in the limelight.*

limerick /ˈlɪmərɪk/ n [C] a short humorous poem with five lines

limestone /ˈlaɪmstəʊn $ -stoʊn/ n [U] a type of rock that contains CALCIUM

limit[1] /ˈlɪmɪt/ n [C]

1 the greatest or least amount, number etc that is allowed or possible: [+to/on] *There is a limit on the time you have to take the test.* | [+of] *the limits of human knowledge* | **within a limit** *He finished within the time limit.*

2 the border or edge of a place: *Los Angeles* **city limits**

PHRASES

off limits beyond the area where someone is allowed to go: *The beach is off limits after midnight.*

be over the limit to have drunk more than the legal amount of alcohol for driving: *I knew that if I had another drink, I would be over the limit.*

within limits within the time, level, amount etc considered acceptable: *You can come and go as you want – within limits.*

COLLOCATIONS

verbs

to set a limit *Set yourself a time limit of 30 minutes for dealing with email.*

to put a limit on sth *The diet doesn't put any limit on fresh fruit or vegetables.*

to go over a limit (*also* **to exceed a limit** *formal*) *He was stopped by police for going over the speed limit.*

to reach a limit *He had reached the limit of his patience.*

types of limit

an upper/lower limit (=the highest or lowest amount allowed) *She was at the upper limit of the healthy weight range for her height.*

a legal limit (=a limit set by law) *Pesticide levels are already above legal limits in many areas.*

an age limit *There is no age limit for applicants.*

a weight/height limit *The weight limit per bag is 20 kilos.*

a time limit | **a speed limit**

limit[2] v [T]

1 to stop something from increasing beyond a particular point: *a decision to limit imports of foreign cars* | **limit sth to sth** *Seating is limited to 500.*

2 to stop someone from doing something or developing: *A lack of education will limit your job opportunities.* | **limit yourself to sth** *I limit myself to two cups of coffee a day.*

3 **be limited to sth** to exist or happen only in a particular place, group etc: *The damage was limited to the roof.* —**limiting** *adj*

limitation /ˌlɪmɪˈteɪʃən/ n **1** [C,U] when something is kept below a particular amount: *a nuclear limitation treaty* **2** [C usually plural] something that limits how good or effective someone or something can be: *It's a nice car, but it* **has** *its* **limitations**.

limited /ˈlɪmɪtɪd/ *adj* not much or not many: *My knowledge of the business is limited.*

limited 'company n [C] a British company whose owners have to pay only a limited amount if the company gets into debt

limitless /ˈlɪmɪtləs/ *adj* without a limit or end

limousine /ˈlɪməziːn, ˌlɪməˈziːn/ (*also* **limo** /ˈlɪməʊ $ -moʊ/ *informal*) n [C] a large expensive comfortable car, driven by someone who is paid to drive

limp[1] /lɪmp/ *adj* not firm or strong: *a limp handshake* —**limply** *adv*

limp[2] v [I] to walk with difficulty because one leg is hurt: *He limped to the chair and sat down.* **THESAURUS** WALK —**limp** n [singular]: *Brody walks with a limp.*

linchpin /ˈlɪntʃpɪn/ n **the linchpin of sth** the most important person or thing in a system or group, on which others depend: *My uncle was the linchpin of the family.*

line[1] /laɪn/ n [C]

1 **LONG MARK** a long thin mark on a surface: *Draw a* **straight line** *across the top of the page.* | *Marty raced towards* **the finishing line**. | *There were* **fine lines** *around her eyes.*

2 OF PEOPLE/THINGS **a)** a row of people or things next to each other: **[+of]** *a line of trees at the side of the road* | *The men were **standing in a line**.* **b)** *especially AmE* a number of people, cars etc that are waiting one behind the other SYN queue *BrE:* **[+of]** *a line of vehicles waiting to get into the car park* | **in line** *Three times a day we **stood in line** for food.*

3 BORDER the place where one area stops and another one starts: **state/county line** *AmE: He was born just across the state line.*

4 DIRECTION the direction in which something travels between two places: *Light travels **in a straight line**.*

5 TELEPHONE a telephone wire or connection: *I'm sorry, **the line is busy** (=someone is using it).* | **on the line** (=telephoning) *Harry is on the line from New York.* | *I **got on the line to** (=telephoned) the hospital this morning.*

6 FOR TRAINS a track that a train travels along: *the London to Glasgow line* | **railway line** *BrE,* **railroad line** *AmE*

7 BETWEEN TWO TYPES OF THING [usually singular] the point at which something becomes something else: **[+between]** *There is a **fine line** between religion and superstition.*

8 SHAPE [usually plural] the outer shape of something long or tall: *the car's elegant lines*

9 ROW OF WORDS a row of words in a poem, document etc: *the opening line of the song*

10 WORDS FOR A PLAY **lines** [plural] the words that someone learns and says in a play: *I haven't **learnt** my **lines** yet.*

11 WAY OF THINKING/BEHAVING a way of thinking about or doing something: **[+on]** *the government's line on immigration* | **take a tough/firm/hard line on sth** *The school takes a tough line on drugs.* | **line of argument/reasoning/enquiry etc** *This line of questioning wasn't going to succeed.*

12 PIECE OF ROPE/STRING/WIRE a piece of rope, string, or wire that has a particular purpose: *Could you hang the washing on the line?* | *a fishing line*

13 PRODUCTS a type of goods for sale in a shop: *a line of low-priced computers* → ASSEMBLY LINE, DOTTED LINE, FRONT LINE, MAIN LINE, **somewhere along the line** at SOMEWHERE

PHRASES

along those/these lines similar to something else: *a trip to the beach, or **something along those lines***

drop sb a line *informal* to write a short letter or email to someone: *Drop me a line when you get there.*

be in line for sth to be likely to be given something: *He's in line for promotion.*

be in line with sth to be what is expected or ordered, or to match something: *The figures were in line with economists' forecasts.*

on line connected to or using a computer system: *You can book tickets on line.*

be out of line *informal* to be behaving in a way that is not acceptable: *I thought what Kenny said was out of line.*

be/put sth on the line if something such as your job is on the line, you may lose it: *From now on, all our jobs are on the line.*

THESAURUS

line a long thin mark on a surface: *If the ball goes over the line, it's out of play.*
stripe a line of colour, especially one of several lines of colour: *The French flag has red, white, and blue stripes.*
crease a line on a piece of clothing or paper where it has been folded or crushed: *She was trying to smooth out the creases in her dress.*
wrinkle a line on someone's face because they are old: *The cream helps get rid of wrinkles.*

line² *v* [T] **1** to sew a piece of material onto the inside or back of another piece: *a coat lined with silk* **2** to form rows along the edges of something: *Thousands of spectators lined the route.* | *a wide avenue lined with trees*

PHRASAL VERBS

line up 1 to stand in a row or line, or to make people do this: *Line up, everybody.* | **line sb ↔ up** *He lined us up in the corridor.* **2 line sth ↔ up** to arrange things in a row **3 line sb/sth ↔ up** to arrange for someone to be available, or for something to happen: *We've lined up a good speaker for tonight.*

linear /ˈlɪniə $ -ər/ *adj* **1** consisting of lines, or in the form of a straight line: *a linear drawing* **2** involving a series of events, ideas etc that develop from one stage to the next

lined /laɪnd/ *adj* **1** a skirt, coat etc that is lined has a piece of material covering the inside: *a fur-lined coat* **2** lined paper has straight lines printed on it

'line ˌmanager *n* [C] *BrE* **sb's line manager** someone who has a higher rank than you in a company and is in charge of your work THESAURUS BOSS

linen /ˈlɪnɪn/ *n* [U] **1** sheets, TABLECLOTHS etc: *bed linen* **2** a strong high-quality cloth

liner /ˈlaɪnə $ -ər/ *n* [C] **1** a large ship for passengers: *an ocean liner* **2** a piece of material used inside something: *a dustbin liner*

linesman /ˈlaɪnzmən/ *n* [C] (*plural* **linesmen** /-mən/) an official in a sport who decides when a ball has gone out of the playing area → see picture at FOOTBALL

'line-up *n* [C usually singular] **1** the group of performers, players, or activities that will be part of an event **2** *especially AmE* a group of people arranged in a row by the police so that a person who saw a crime can try to recognize the criminal

linger /ˈlɪŋɡə $ -ər/ *v* [I] **1** (*also* **linger on**) if a smell, memory etc lingers, it does not disappear for a long time: *a taste that lingers in your mouth* **2** to stay somewhere or continue something for longer than usual: **[+over]** *They lingered over their coffee.*

lingerie /ˈlænʒəri $ ˌlɑːnʒəˈreɪ, ˈlænʒəri/ *n* [U] women's underwear

lingering /ˈlɪŋɡərɪŋ/ *adj* continuing for a long time: *a lingering kiss*

lingo /ˈlɪŋɡəʊ $ -ɡoʊ/ *n* (*plural* **lingos**) *informal* **1** [C usually singular] a language **2** [singular, U] words and phrases used by a particular group of people: *medical lingo*

linguist /ˈlɪŋɡwɪst/ *n* [C] **1** someone who is good

at languages **2** someone who studies linguistics

linguistic /lɪŋˈgwɪstɪk/ *adj* relating to language or linguistics: *a child's linguistic development*

linguistics /lɪŋˈgwɪstɪks/ *n* [U] the study of language and languages: *I did linguistics for two years at university.*

lining /ˈlaɪnɪŋ/ *n* [C,U] a piece of material that covers the inside of something: *a jacket with a silk lining*

link¹ Ac /lɪŋk/ *v* [T]
1 to make or show a connection between two or more situations, things, or people: **link sth to/with sth** *Lung cancer has been linked to cigarette smoking.*
2 be linked (to/with sth) if two things are linked, they are related in some way: *Are the deaths linked?*
3 to physically join two or more things or places: **link sth to/with sth** *A bridge links Venice to the mainland.* | *The PC is linked to the server.* **THESAURUS** ▶
JOIN

link² Ac *n* [C]
1 a relationship or connection between two or more events, people, or ideas: **[+between]** *the link between drug use and crime* | **the close links** *between students and teachers* | **[+with]** *The company has* **strong links** *with investors in France and Italy.*
2 rail/road/telephone etc link something that makes communication or travel between two places possible: *a direct computer link*
3 one of the rings that make up a chain

linkage Ac /ˈlɪŋkɪdʒ/ *n* [C,U] *formal* a connection or relationship between two things

'linking ˌverb *n* [C] a verb that connects the subject of a sentence to its COMPLEMENT, for example 'seems' in the sentence 'The house seems big.'

'linking ˌword *n* [C] a word such as 'but', 'and', or 'while' that connects phrases or parts of sentences **SYN** conjunction

'link-up *n* [C] a connection between two things, especially organizations or communication systems

linoleum /ləˈnəʊliəm $ -ˈnoʊ-/, **lino** /ˈlaɪnəʊ $ -noʊ/ *n* [U] a smooth material used to cover floors

lint /lɪnt/ *n* [U] *especially AmE* soft light pieces of thread or wool that come off a material **SYN** fluff *BrE*

lion /ˈlaɪən/ *n* [C] a large brown wild cat from Africa or Asia. A male lion has a MANE (=long thick hair on its neck): *lion cubs* (=baby lions)
PHRASES
the lion's share (of sth) the largest share of something: *He had risked the lion's share of his savings on the stock market.*

lioness /ˈlaɪənes, -nəs/ *n* [C] a female lion → see picture at LION

lip /lɪp/ *n* [C]
1 the edge of your mouth where your skin is red or darker: *a kiss on the lips* | **top/bottom lip** *His bottom lip swelled up.* → see picture on page A2
2 [usually singular] the edge of a container used to hold or pour liquid

LION

mane

lion

lioness   cub

'lip balm (*also* **'lip salve** *BrE*) *n* [C,U] a soft substance used to protect your lips

lip-read /ˈlɪp riːd/ *v* [I,T] (*past tense and past participle* **lip-read** /-red/) to understand what someone says by watching their lips move, especially because you cannot hear —**lip-reading** *n* [U]

'lip ˌservice *n* **pay lip service to sb/sth** to say that you support or agree with something without doing anything to prove it

lipstick /ˈlɪpˌstɪk/ *n* [C,U] a substance you put on your lips to make them a different colour

liqueur /lɪˈkjʊə $ lɪˈkɜːr/ *n* [C,U] a strong sweet alcoholic drink

liquid /ˈlɪkwɪd/ *n* [C,U] a substance that is not solid or a gas, such as water or milk: *Add a little more liquid to the sauce.* —**liquid** *adj*: *liquid fuel*

liquidation /ˌlɪkwəˈdeɪʃən/ *n* [C,U] when a business is forced to close and sell everything in order to pay its debts: *The company has* **gone into liquidation**. —**liquidate** /ˈlɪkwədeɪt/ *v* [I,T]

liquidizer (*also* **-iser** *BrE*) /ˈlɪkwədaɪzə $ -ər/ *n* [C] a small electric machine that makes solid foods into liquids **SYN** blender —**liquidize** *v* [T]

liquor /ˈlɪkə $ -ər/ *n* [C,U] *especially AmE* a strong alcoholic drink such as WHISKY

liquorice *BrE*, **licorice** *AmE* /ˈlɪkərɪs, -rɪʃ/ *n* [U] a black substance with a strong taste, used in sweets

'liquor ˌstore *n* [C] *AmE* a shop where alcohol is sold **SYN** off-licence *BrE*

lisp /lɪsp/ *n* [C usually singular] a fault in the way someone speaks that makes them pronounce 's' as 'th' —**lisp** *v* [I,T]

list /lɪst/ *n* [C] a set of things that you write down, one below the other: **[+of]** *a long list of names* | **on a list** *There are 30 people on the hospital waiting list.* —**list** *v* [T]: *The book lists more than 1,000 hotels.* →
HIT LIST, SHORT LIST

COLLOCATIONS

verbs

to make/write a list *Make a list of the things you have to do.*

to put sth on a list *I'll put your name on the list.*

to add sth to a list *Here are some questions to add to your list.*

noun + list

the top/bottom of a list *A new kitchen is at the top of my list.*

types of list

a shopping list (also **a grocery list** *AmE*) (=a list of things you want to buy) *I've forgotten my shopping list.*

a waiting list (=a list of people who are waiting for something) *There is a waiting list for this car.*

a mailing list (=a list of people that a company sends information to) *Please add me to your mailing list.*

a guest list *Can you get me on the guest list for the party?*

a price list *I've got their latest catalogue and price list.*

THESAURUS

list a set of things that you write down, one below the other: *She made a list of the people she wanted to invite to the party.*

checklist a list that helps to remind you of all the things you need to do: *The book provides a useful checklist of what to take with you when travelling.*

register an official list or record of people or things: *The club keeps a register of members.*

programme *BrE*, **program** *AmE* a list of all the activities or events that have been planned: *Because of bad weather, the programme of events has been changed slightly.*

agenda a list of the subjects that people will discuss at a meeting: *The first item on the agenda is the school roof.*

index an alphabetical list of names and subjects at the back of a book that shows which page they are mentioned on: *I looked up his name in the index.*

listen /ˈlɪsən/ v [I]
1 to pay attention to what someone is saying or to something you can hear: **[+to]** *What sort of music do you like listening to?* | **[+for]** *He stopped and listened carefully for any sound.* | *Listen, Doug. I need your help.* **THESAURUS** HEAR

> **Grammar**
> Do not say 'I like listening music.' Say *I like listening to music.*

2 to accept advice from someone: **[+to]** *I wish I'd listened to Dad.* | *She refuses to listen to reason* (=accept sensible advice).
PHRASAL VERBS
listen in to listen secretly to someone's conversation **SYN** eavesdrop: **[+on]** *The kids listen in on our phone calls.*

listen out *BrE informal* to listen carefully so that you will notice a particular sound
listen up *especially AmE spoken* used to get people's attention before you say something

listener /ˈlɪsənə $ -ər/ n [C] **1** someone who listens to the radio **2 good listener** someone who listens carefully to other people's problems, stories etc: *Being a good listener helps others have confidence in you.*

listing /ˈlɪstɪŋ/ n [C] an official or public list: *movie listings*

listless /ˈlɪstləs/ adj feeling tired and not interested in things —**listlessly** adv

lit /lɪt/ v a past tense and past participle of LIGHT

litany /ˈlɪtəni/ n [C] (plural **litanies**) *disapproving* a long list of problems, excuses etc

liter /ˈliːtə $ -ər/ n the American spelling of LITRE

literacy /ˈlɪtərəsi/ n [U] the ability to read and write

literal /ˈlɪtərəl/ adj the literal meaning of a word, phrase etc is its basic or original meaning → **figurative**: *a literal interpretation of the Bible*

literally /ˈlɪtərəli/ adv **1** according to the basic or original meaning of a word or phrase: *Your body is literally a 'machine'.* | **take sb/sth literally** (=believe the exact words someone says, rather than their general meaning) **2** used to emphasize that what you are saying is true: *We literally worked day and night.*

literary /ˈlɪtərəri $ ˈlɪtəreri/ adj [only before noun] relating to literature: *a literary prize*

literate /ˈlɪtərət/ adj **1** able to read and write **OPP** illiterate **2** well educated

literature /ˈlɪtərətʃə $ -tʃʊr/ n [U]
1 books, poems, plays etc that people think are good, serious, and important: *a major **work of literature*** | *a degree in English literature* **THESAURUS** BOOK
2 printed information about something: **[+on]** *government literature on energy conservation*

lithe /laɪð/ adj able to move your body easily and gracefully

litigation /ˌlɪtəˈɡeɪʃən/ n [U] *law* the process of taking legal action in a court of law

litre *BrE*, **liter** *AmE* /ˈliːtə $ -ər/ n [C] (written abbreviation **l**) a unit for measuring liquid in the METRIC system: **[+of]** *a litre of water* | **litre bottle/container etc** *a 3-litre oil drum*

litter[1] /ˈlɪtə $ -ər/ n **1** [U] paper, bottles, cans etc that people do not want and have left on the ground in a public place → **garbage**: *Anyone caught **dropping litter** is fined.* **2** [C] a group of baby animals born from the same mother at the same time: **[+of]** *a litter of kittens*

litter[2] v [T] if things litter a place, they are spread over it in an untidy way: **litter sth with sth** *His desk was littered with papers.*

little[1] /ˈlɪtl/ adj
1 small in size: *The little shop was very crowded.* | *a nice little town* | *a tiny little baby* | **a little bit (of sth)**

(=a small amount of something) *Add a little bit of milk to the sauce.* **THESAURUS** SMALL

2 [only before noun] short in time or distance: *He arrived **a little while** ago.* | *Let's walk **a little way** together.*

3 young or still a child: *two little girls* | *Were you naughty when you were little?* | **little brother/sister** *BrE* (=a younger brother or sister) **THESAURUS** YOUNG

4 [only before noun] not important: *You worry too much about little things.*

> **Word Choice: little or small?**
> You often use **little** when talking about your feelings about someone or something: *What a pretty little baby!* | *It's a lovely little garden.* | *You poor little thing!*
> You use **small** when you just want to talk about the size: *Can I have a small box of matches?* | *Their house is very small.*

little² *determiner, pron*

1 not much or not enough → **less**: *Little is known about his life.* | *She had **very little** money.*

2 a little a small amount: *'More coffee?' 'Just a little.'* | **a little more/less** *Let's have a little less noise, please.* | **as little as £5/three months etc** (=used to emphasize how small an amount is) *Insurance can cost as little as £2 a week.*

little³ *adv*

1 a little slightly or to a small degree **SYN** **a bit**: *She trembled a little as she spoke.* | **a little more/better/further etc** *Move your chair a little closer.*

2 not much: *She goes out very little.* | **little more/better (than sth)** *His voice was little more than a whisper.* | *a **little known** fact* (=known by only a few people)

PHRASES

| **little by little** gradually: *Little by little, she gained confidence.* **THESAURUS** SLOWLY

little 'finger *n* [C] the smallest finger on your hand

live¹ /lɪv/ *v*

1 [I] if you live in a place, your home is there: **[+in/at/near etc]** *Matt lives in Boston.* | *She **lived next door** to me.* | *Sam is 25 but he still **lives at home*** (=with his parents). | **live here/there** *Does Paul live here?*

2 [I] to be alive or to continue to stay alive: **[+in/before/at]** *He lived in the eighteenth century.* | *Plants can't live without light.* | *People are **living longer** than ever.* | **live to (be) 80/90 etc** *My grandma lived to be 84.*

3 [I,T] to have a particular kind of life, or to live in a particular way: **live in peace/poverty etc** *We live in fear of crime.* | **live peacefully/quietly etc** *Mark likes living dangerously.* | **live a quiet/active/healthy etc life** *She lives a busy life.*

4 [I] to have an exciting life: *I want to live a little before I settle down.*

PHRASES

| **live it up** *informal* to spend a lot of money doing things that you enjoy: *He enjoyed going to nightclubs and living it up.*

PHRASAL VERBS

live sth ↔ **down** to be able to stop people reminding you about something embarrassing that you did: *I'll never live it down if the boys find out.*

live for sb/sth if you live for someone or something, they are the most important thing in your life: *She lives for her children.*

live in *BrE* to live in the place where you work or study: *Many students live in during the first year.*

live off sb/sth to depend on someone or something for money, food etc: *Older people do not want to live off their savings.*

live on

1 to continue to exist: *Her memory will live on* (=people will remember her).

2 live on sth a) to have a particular amount of money to buy what you need: *I don't know how you live on only £80 a week.* **b)** to eat a lot of a particular kind of food: *Kids these days live on burgers and fries.*

live through sth to experience a difficult or dangerous situation: *She has lived through two wars.*

live together if two people live together, they share a house and have a sexual relationship but they are not married → **live with** **THESAURUS** MARRIED

live up to sth to be as good as someone expects: *Did the game **live up to** your **expectations**?*

live with sb/sth

1 to accept a difficult situation that will probably continue: *I've learned to live with stress.*

2 to live in the same house as someone and have a sexual relationship with them, without being married → **live together**

THESAURUS

live to have your home somewhere: *She lives in Los Angeles.*

be from/come from use this when talking about the country, city, or area where you usually live: *Anna comes from Italy, but she's living in London at the moment.* | *'Where are you from?' 'I'm from Poland.'*

inhabit *formal* if a group of people or animals inhabit a place, they live there: *The island is inhabited by a rare species of bird.* | *The people who inhabit this region are mostly Tibetan.*

grow up to live somewhere when you are a child: *She grew up in France.*

live² /laɪv/ *adj, adv*

1 **NOT DEAD** [only before noun] alive, not dead **SYN** **living** **OPP** **dead**: *experiments on live animals*

2 **TELEVISION/RADIO** a live television or radio programme is seen or heard by people while it is happening: *a live broadcast of the World Cup Final* | *live TV coverage* | **broadcast/show sth live** *The funeral will be shown live on TV.*

3 **MUSIC/THEATRE** live music, theatre etc is performed for people who are watching in the same place: **live music/jazz/performance etc** *We have live bands on Saturdays.* | **perform/play live** *Grandad saw the Beatles play live.*

4 **ELECTRICITY** a live wire has electricity flowing through it

5 **BOMB/BULLET** a live bomb, bullet etc has not yet exploded: *a live landmine*

PHRASES

go live if a project or system goes live, people use it for the first time: *Our website goes live next month.*

livelihood /'laɪvlihʊd/ n [C,U] the way you earn money in order to live: *Farming is their livelihood.*

lively /'laɪvli/ adj **1** happy and active: *a lively child* **2** interesting and exciting: *a lively debate* | *the city's lively nightlife* —**liveliness** n [U]

liven /'laɪvən/ v
PHRASAL VERBS
liven up to become more exciting or interesting, or to make something do this: **liven sth ↔ up** *Better music would have livened the party up.*

liver /'lɪvə $ -ər/ n **1** [C] the organ inside your body that cleans your blood → see picture on page A2 **2** [U] the liver of an animal, used as food

lives /laɪvz/ n the plural of LIFE

livestock /'laɪvstɒk $ -staːk/ n [U] animals that are kept on a farm

livid /'lɪvɪd/ adj very angry SYN **furious** THESAURUS ANGRY

living¹ /'lɪvɪŋ/ n
1 [C usually singular] the money that you earn from working: *What do you **do for a living** (=what is your job)?* | *All **earn/make a living** It's hard to make a living as an actor.* THESAURUS JOB
2 [U] the way that someone lives their life: *a guide to **healthy living***
3 the living [plural] all the people who are alive, not dead OPP **the dead** → **the cost of living** at COST¹, STANDARD OF LIVING

living² adj **1** alive now OPP **dead**: *one of our greatest living writers* | *All **living things** (=people, animals, and plants) are made of cells.* **2** still used or done now: *a **living language** (=one that people still use)* | *the worst disaster **in living memory** (=that people can still remember)*

'living room (also **sitting room** BrE) n [C] the main room in a house, where you relax, watch television etc SYN **lounge**

lizard /'lɪzəd $ -ərd/ n [C] a small animal with thick skin and a long tail that lives in hot countries → see picture at REPTILE

-'ll /l/ v the short form of 'will' or 'shall': *He'll be here soon.*

load¹ /ləʊd $ loʊd/ n [C]
1 a large quantity of something that a vehicle, person etc is carrying: **[+of]** *a ship with a **full load** of fuel* | **bus load/car load** (=the amount that a bus or car can carry) *a bus load of tourists*
2 the amount of work that a person or a machine has to do: *a **heavy work load** (=large amount of work)*
PHRASES
a load of rubbish/nonsense BrE spoken used to say that you think something is very stupid or bad: *He was talking a load of rubbish.*
a load of sth/loads of sth BrE informal a lot of something: *Don't worry, we have loads of time.* | **loads to do/see/eat etc** *There's loads to do in Tokyo.*

load² v
1 (also **load up**) [I,T] to put a large quantity of something into a vehicle or container OPP **unload**: *Have you finished loading the dishwasher?* | **load sth into/onto sth** *They loaded their baggage into the car.*
2 [T] to put something into a machine in order to use it or make it work: **load sth with sth** *Did you load the camera with 400 film?*
3 [I,T] if you load a program onto a computer, or if it loads, you put it into the computer → **download**
PHRASAL VERBS
load sb/sth ↔ **down** to make someone or something carry too many things or make someone do too much work: **[+with]** *I was loaded down with shopping.*

loaded /'ləʊdɪd $ 'loʊ-/ adj
1 a loaded gun has bullets in it
2 containing or carrying a lot of things: *a loaded truck* | **[+with]** *a table loaded with delicious desserts*
3 [not before noun] informal very rich THESAURUS RICH
PHRASES
loaded question disapproving a question that is unfair because it is meant to make you say something that you do not want to say: *He accused the reporter of asking him a loaded question.*

loaf /ləʊf $ loʊf/ n [C] (plural **loaves** /ləʊvz $ loʊvz/) bread that is baked in one large piece: *a loaf of bread* → see picture at BREAD

loan¹ /ləʊn $ loʊn/ n
1 [C] an amount of money that you borrow: **[+of]** *a loan of $6,000* | *a $25,000 **bank loan** (=from a bank)* | **business/student/personal loan** (=money you borrow for business, university, or personal costs) *We **took out** a personal **loan** to pay for our holiday.* | **pay off/repay/pay back a loan** (=give back money you have borrowed)
2 [singular] when you lend something to someone: **[+of]** *Thanks for the loan of that book.*
PHRASES
on loan (from sb/sth) if something is on loan, it has been borrowed: *The paintings are on loan from other galleries.*

loan² v [T] to lend something to someone: **loan sb sth** *Can you loan me $20?*

'loan shark n [C] disapproving someone who lends money at a very high rate of INTEREST

loath /ləʊθ $ loʊθ/ adj **be loath to do sth** formal to be unwilling to do something SYN **reluctant**

loathe /ləʊð $ loʊð/ v [T] to hate someone or something very much THESAURUS HATE —**loathing** n [U]

loathsome /'ləʊðsəm $ 'loʊθ-/ adj very unpleasant or cruel

loaves /ləʊvz $ loʊvz/ n the plural of LOAF

lob /lɒb $ laːb/ v [T] (**lobbed**, **lobbing**) to throw or hit something high into the air: **lob sth at/over etc sth** *kids lobbing stones at cars* —**lob** n [C]

lobby¹ /'lɒbi $ 'laːbi/ n [C] (plural **lobbies**)
1 a large area inside the entrance of a public building: *the hotel lobby*
2 a group of people who try to persuade

L

a government to change a particular law or situation: *the anti-war lobby*

lobby[2] v [I,T] (**lobbied, lobbying, lobbies**) to try to persuade a government to do something: [**+for/against**] *The group is lobbying for a change in the law.* —**lobbyist** n [C]

lobe /ləʊb $ loʊb/ n [C] **1** an EARLOBE **2** *technical* a round part of your brain or lung

lobster /'lɒbstə $ 'lɑːbstər/ n [C,U] a sea animal with eight legs, a shell, and large CLAWS, or the meat of this animal as food → see picture at SHELLFISH

local[1] /'ləʊkəl $ 'loʊ-/ adj
1 relating to a particular area, especially the area you live in: *Our kids go to the local school.* | *the local newspaper* | *local residents* | **local government** (*also* **local authority** *BrE*) (=the government of a particular area or city) THESAURUS ► NEAR
2 affecting only part of your body: *Local anaesthetic is used for tooth extractions.*

local[2] n [C] **1** someone who lives in the place that you are talking about: *I asked one of the locals for directions.* **2 sb's local** *BrE informal* the PUB nearest someone's home, where they usually go: *I usually have a pint or two at my local on Friday nights.* **3** *AmE* a bus or train that stops at all the stopping places

locality /ləʊ'kæləti $ loʊ-/ n [C] (*plural* **localities**) *formal* a small area of a country, city etc

localized (*also* **-ised** *BrE*) /'ləʊkəlaɪzd $ 'loʊ-/ adj *formal* happening within a small area: *localized flooding*

locally /'ləʊkəli $ 'loʊ-/ adv in the area where you are or the area you are talking about: *Do you* **live** *locally?*

local time n [U] the time of day in a particular part of the world: *We arrived in Boston at 16.40 local time.*

locate Ac /ləʊ'keɪt $ 'loʊkeɪt/ v **1** [T] to find the exact position of something: *Divers have located the shipwreck.* THESAURUS ► FIND **2 be located in/near etc sth** to be in a particular place or position: *The town is located on the shores of a lake.* **3** [I,T] to build or move a company's offices somewhere: **locate (sth) in/at etc sth** *Big retail stores are not prepared to locate in poor areas.*

location Ac /ləʊ'keɪʃən $ loʊ-/ n **1** [C] a particular place or position: [**+of**] *Draw a map showing the* **precise** *location of the accident.* | *the town's* **geographical location** THESAURUS ► PLACE **2** [C,U] a place where a film is made, away from the usual building: **on location** *The scene was shot on location in Montana.*

loch /lɒx, lɒk $ lɑːk, lɑːx/ n [C] a word for a lake in Scotland: *Loch Garten*

lock[1] /lɒk $ lɑːk/ v
1 [I,T] to fasten something with a key, or to fasten with a key OPP **unlock**: *Did you lock the car?* | *The window won't lock.*
2 [T] to put someone or something in a place and fasten the door, lid etc with a key: **lock sth in sth** *He locked the money in a drawer.* | **lock sth away** *The documents were locked away in a safe.*

3 [I,T] to become fixed in one position and impossible to move: *The wheels locked and we skidded.* | *She locked her arms around his neck.*
PHRASAL VERBS
lock sb in/out to prevent someone from leaving or entering a place by locking the door: *I turned the handle but we were locked in.*
lock up
1 to make a building safe by fastening the doors with a key: **lock sth ↔ up** *I'll lock up the garage.*
2 lock sb ↔ up to put someone in prison: *Too many kids are being locked up.*

LOCKS
bicycle lock
combination lock
padlock

lock[2] n [C]
1 something you use to fasten a door, drawer etc and that you usually open with a key: *I put my key in the lock.* | *a bicycle lock* | *Dad keeps his cigars* **under lock and key** (=somewhere fastened with a lock).
2 a group of hairs growing together on your head: [**+of**] *a lock of hair*
3 a part of a river or CANAL that you close with gates to raise or lower the level of the water → COMBINATION LOCK
PHRASES
| **lock, stock, and barrel** including every part of something: *He moved the whole company, lock, stock, and barrel, to Mexico.*

locker /'lɒkə $ 'lɑːkər/ n [C] a small cupboard that locks, used to store books, clothes etc safely in a building such as a college or office

locker room n [C] a room in a sports building, school etc where people change their clothes and leave them in lockers

locket /'lɒkɪt $ 'lɑː-/ n [C] a piece of jewellery that you wear on a chain around your neck, with a small box that can contain a picture, piece of hair etc → see picture at JEWELLERY

locksmith /'lɒkˌsmɪθ $ 'lɑːk-/ n [C] someone who makes and repairs locks

locomotive /ˌləʊkə'məʊtɪv $ ˌloʊkə'moʊ-/ n [C] *technical* a train engine

locust /'ləʊkəst $ 'loʊ-/ n [C] an insect from Africa

or Asia that flies in a large group, eating and destroying crops: *a swarm of locusts*

lodge¹ /lɒdʒ $ lɑːdʒ/ v **1** [I] to become stuck somewhere, or make something become stuck: **[+in]** *A fishbone lodged in his throat.* | **be lodged in/between/behind etc sth** *A bullet was lodged behind his heart.* **2 lodge a complaint/protest/ appeal** BrE to make a formal complaint, protest etc: **[+with/against]** *Do you wish to lodge a complaint against the club?* **3** [I + adv/prep] old-fashioned to pay to live in someone's house

lodge² n [C] **1** a small building or room at the entrance to a building: *the porter's lodge* **2** a small house in the country, especially one at the entrance to a very large house

lodger /ˈlɒdʒə $ ˈlɑːdʒər/ n [C] BrE someone who pays to live in someone's house SYN **boarder** AmE

lodging /ˈlɒdʒɪŋ $ ˈlɑː-/ n [C,U] a place where you pay to live: *I pay £90 a week for board and lodging* (=meals and a room).

loft /lɒft $ lɔːft/ n [C] **1** BrE a room or space under the roof of a house SYN **attic 2** AmE a raised area above the main part of a room

lofty /ˈlɒfti $ ˈlɔː-/ adj very high and impressive: *the lofty heights of Ben Nevis*

log¹ /lɒg $ lɒːg, lɑːg/ n [C] **1** a thick piece of wood from a tree → see picture at PLANT¹ **2** an official record of events: **[+of]** *The captain keeps a log of incidents.*

log² v [T] (**logged, logging**) to make an official record of events

PHRASAL VERBS

log in/on to do the actions on a computer that will allow you to start using it: **[+to]** *Log on to your home page.*

log out/off to stop using a computer by doing particular actions

logarithm /ˈlɒgərɪðəm $ ˈlɔː-, ˈlɑː-/ n [C] one of a set of numbers that you use to solve some mathematical problems

loggerheads /ˈlɒgəhedz $ ˈlɔːgər-, ˈlɑː-/ n **be at loggerheads (with sb)** to disagree very strongly with someone: *The two families have been at loggerheads for years.*

logging /ˈlɒgɪŋ $ ˈlɔː-, ˈlɑː-/ n [U] the activity of cutting down trees in order to sell the wood

logic /ˈlɒdʒɪk $ ˈlɑː-/ n [U] **1** a sensible reason or way of thinking: *There is no logic in releasing criminals just because prisons are crowded.* | **[+of]** *the logic of my argument* **2** a formal method of reasoning, in which ideas are based on previous ideas

logical Ac /ˈlɒdʒɪkəl $ ˈlɑː-/ adj **1** reasonable and sensible OPP **illogical**: *He seems the logical choice for the job.* | *There's only one logical conclusion.* **2** based on the rules of logic: *logical analysis* —**logically** /-kli/ adv

logistics /ləˈdʒɪstɪks $ loʊ-/ n [plural] the practical arrangements that are necessary to make a complicated plan or activity succeed: **[+of]** *the logistics of organizing an international music festival* —**logistical** adj —**logistically** /-kli/ adv

logo /ˈləʊgəʊ $ ˈloʊgoʊ/ n [C] (plural **logos**) a design that is the official sign of a company or organization

loins /lɔɪnz/ n [plural] literary the part of your body below your waist, where the sex organs are

loiter /ˈlɔɪtə $ -ər/ v [I] to stand or wait somewhere, especially in a public place, without any clear reason

LOL 1 (**laughing out loud**) used in emails, TEXT MESSAGES etc to show that you think something is funny **2** (**lots of love**) used at the end of a friendly email, TEXT MESSAGE, or letter to someone you know well

loll /lɒl $ lɑːl/ v [I] to sit or lie in a lazy or relaxed way: **[+around/in etc]** *He lolled back in his chair.*

lollipop /ˈlɒlipɒp $ ˈlɑːlipɑːp/ n (also **lolly** /ˈlɒli $ ˈlɑː-/ BrE) n [C] a hard sweet on a stick

lone /ləʊn $ loʊn/ adj [only before noun] used to talk about the only person in a place, or the only person that does something: *a lone gunman* | *the lone survivor of a shipwreck* | *a **lone parent** (=someone who lives alone with their children)*

lonely /ˈləʊnli $ ˈloʊn-/ adj
1 unhappy because you are alone or do not have any friends SYN **lonesome** AmE: *Don't you **get lonely** living on your own?* | *a lonely old man*
2 a lonely place is a long way from where people live: *a lonely country road* —**loneliness** n [U]

THESAURUS

lonely (*also* **lonesome** AmE) unhappy because you are alone or do not have any friends: *Children can feel sad and lonely.* | *I get so lonesome here with no one to talk to.*
isolated lonely because your situation makes it difficult for you to meet people: *Old people often feel very isolated.*
homesick unhappy because you are a long way from your home, your family, and your friends: *She was very homesick and called her parents every day.*
miss sb used when saying that you feel unhappy because someone is not there with you: *I missed my old friends when I changed schools.*

---

lonely ˈhearts n **lonely hearts club/page/column** a club or a page of advertisements in a newspaper, used by people who want to meet someone and have a romantic relationship with them

loner /ˈləʊnə $ ˈloʊnər/ n [C] someone who likes to be alone

lonesome /ˈləʊnsəm $ ˈloʊn-/ adj AmE very unhappy because you are alone or have no friends
THESAURUS ▶ LONELY

long¹ /lɒŋ $ lɒːŋ/ adj
1 measuring a large distance from one end to the other OPP **short**: *long hair* | *It's a long walk home from here.* | *My parents live quite **a long way** away.*
THESAURUS ▶ FAR
2 continuing for a large amount of time OPP **short**: *a long, boring meeting* | *a long period of time* | *It took a long time for the little girl to start to relax.* | *a long*

long

day/week (=a boring or tiring day or week) | *I work very **long hours*** (=more working hours than usual).
3 used to talk or ask about the distance between the ends of something, or the time between the beginning and the end of something: *The snake was at least three feet long.* | *His speech was 20 minutes long.* | *How long is your garden?*
4 a long book has a lot of pages
5 a long list has a lot of things on it

PHRASES

in the long run *informal* in the future, not immediately: *All our hard work will be worth it in the long run.*

a long shot someone or something with very little chance of success: *It's a long shot, but does anybody have a screwdriver with them?*

THESAURUS – sense 2

long continuing for a long time: *It's a long film – over two hours.*
lengthy continuing for a long time, especially longer than you want or expect: *There are lengthy delays on the roads.* | *Getting a visa is a lengthy process.*
long-running [only before noun] continuing for a long time – used especially about arguments, campaigns, or shows: *He's been involved in a long-running battle with his neighbours.*
long-lasting continuing for a long time – used especially about effects or relationships: *The crisis could have a long-lasting effect on the economy.* | *a long-lasting friendship*
interminable very long and boring: *The journey seemed interminable.*

---

long² *adv* a great amount of time: *This won't **take long.*** | *Have you been **waiting long**?* | **for long** *Have you known the Garretts for long?* | **long to do sth** *The farm was sold long before you were born.* | **long ago** *He left his home long ago.* | **long-awaited/long-lasting/long-established etc** *a long-forgotten argument*

PHRASES

as/so long as on the condition that: *You can go as long as you're back by four o'clock.*
before long soon: *It will be Christmas before long.*
THESAURUS▶ SOON
no longer/not any longer used to show that something happened in the past, but does not happen now: *Mr. Allen no longer works for the company.*

long³ *v* [I] *formal* to want something very much: [+for] *I used to long for a baby sister.* | **long to do sth** *The children longed to get outside.* —**longing** *n* [C,U]: *She had a great longing for her home country.* —**longingly** *adv*

long-ˈdistance *adj* involving places that are a long distance apart: *long-distance flights* | *a long-distance phone call* —**long-distance** *adv*

longevity /lɒnˈdʒevəti $ lɑː-, lɔːn-/ *n* [U] *formal* long life

longhand /ˈlɒŋhænd $ ˈlɔːŋ-/ *n* [U] writing by hand rather than using a machine such as a computer

ˈlong-haul *adj* **long-haul flight/route/destination etc** a long-haul flight etc is over a very long distance

longitude /ˈlɒndʒɪtjuːd $ ˈlɑːndʒɪtuːd/ *n* [C,U] *technical* a position on the Earth measured in degrees east or west of an imaginary line from the top of the Earth to the bottom → **latitude** → see picture at **GLOBE** —**longitudinal** /ˌlɒndʒɪˈtjuːdɪnəl◂ $ ˌlɑːndʒɪˈtuː-/ *adj*

ˈlong jump *n* **the long jump** a sport in which you jump as far as possible

ˌlong-ˈlife *adj* **1** long-life products continue working longer than ordinary ones: *long-life batteries* **2** *BrE* long-life foods stay fresh longer than ordinary ones: *long-life milk*

long-lived /ˌlɒŋ ˈlɪvd◂ $ ˌlɔːŋ ˈlaɪvd/ *adj* living or existing for a long time

ˌlong-ˈlost *adj* **long-lost friend/cousin/brother etc** a friend etc that you have not seen for a very long time: *He greeted me like a long-lost friend.*

ˌlong-ˈrange *adj* [only before noun] **1** able to hit something that is a long way away **OPP** **short-range**: *a long-range missile* **2** relating to a time that continues far into the future: *a long-range weather forecast*

ˌlong-ˈrunning *adj* [only before noun] used about something that has been continuing for a long time: *their long-running legal battle* **THESAURUS▶ LONG**

longshoreman /ˈlɒŋʃɔːmən $ ˈlɔːŋʃɔːr-/ *n* [C] (*plural* **longshoremen** /-mən/) *AmE* someone whose job is to load and unload ships at a DOCK **SYN** **docker** *BrE*

longsighted /ˌlɒŋˈsaɪtɪd◂ $ ˌlɔːŋ-/ *adj* *BrE* able to see or read things clearly only when they are far from your eyes **SYN** **far-sighted** *AmE* **OPP** **shortsighted**

ˌlong-ˈstanding *adj* having continued or existed for a long time: *a long-standing agreement between the two countries*

ˌlong-ˈsuffering *adj* patient in spite of problems or other people's annoying behaviour: *his **long-suffering wife***

ˌlong-ˈterm *adj* continuing for a long period of time into the future → **short-term**: *the long-term effects of smoking* → **in the long/short term** at **TERM¹**

ˈlong-time *adj* [only before noun] having existed or continued to be a particular thing for a long time: *a long-time ambition* | *a long-time friend of the family*

long ˌwave *n* [U] (*written abbreviation* **LW**) radio broadcasting using radio WAVES of 1,000 metres or more in length → **medium wave, short wave, FM**

long-winded /ˌlɒŋ ˈwɪndɪd◂ $ ˌlɔːŋ-/ *adj* talking for too long in a way that is boring: *a long-winded speech*

loo /luː/ *n* [C] (*plural* **loos**) *BrE informal* a toilet **THESAURUS▶ TOILET**

LOOK

They are looking at the paintings.

He is watching TV.

look¹ /lʊk/ v

1 USE YOUR EYES [I] to turn your eyes towards something or someone so that you can see them: *I didn't see it. I wasn't looking.* | **[+at]** *'It's time to go,' said Patrick, looking at his watch.* | **[+down/away/over etc]** *I looked down the road but she'd gone.* THESAURUS SEE

2 SEARCH [I] to try to find someone or something: **[+for]** *Brad was looking for you last night.* | **[+in/under/between etc]** *Try looking under the bed.*

3 SEEM [linking verb] to seem or appear: *You look nice in that dress.* | **look tired/happy/worried etc** *The future's looking good.* | **look good/bad etc** *The future's looking good.* | **what does sb/sth look like?** (=describe their appearance) | **[+as if/as though/like]** *He looked as if he hadn't washed for a week.* | **It looks like** *she's not coming back.* | **strange-looking/dirty-looking etc** *healthy-looking children* THESAURUS SEEM

4 GET SB'S ATTENTION **look** *spoken* **a)** used to make someone notice something: *Look! There's a fox!* **b)** used to draw attention to what you are saying, especially when you are annoyed: *Look, I've had enough of this. I'm going home.*

5 FACE STH [I] if a building looks in a particular direction, it faces that direction: *Our room looks over the harbour.*

6 WANT TO DO STH **be looking to do sth** to want or be planning to do something: *He's looking to make a lot of money from this investment.*

7 MODERN/OLD-FASHIONED **forward-looking/ backward-looking** modern or old-fashioned in your ideas, methods etc: *We have a very forward-looking management team.*

PHRASES

look sb in the eye to look directly at someone when you are speaking to them, especially to show that you are not afraid of them or that you are telling the truth: *Owen didn't dare look his father in the eye.*

look out! *spoken* used to warn someone of danger: *Look out! There's a car coming.*

look to sb for sth/to do sth to depend on someone to provide help, advice etc: *He looks to me for advice.*

THESAURUS

look to turn your eyes towards something or someone so that you can see them: *She looked at me and smiled.*

have/take a look *especially spoken* to look at something quickly, especially in order to find or check something: *Take a look at this picture!* | *He had a look at the tyre to see if it needed more air in it.*

glance to look at someone or something for a short time: *The teacher glanced up at the clock.*

peek/peep to look quickly at something – used especially when you should not look, or when you are looking through a small gap: *The door was open, so he peeked inside.* | *She peeped over the fence.*

peer to look very carefully, especially because you cannot see something clearly: *We peered through the mist, trying to see if anyone was out there.*

glare to look at someone in an angry way: *When I said sorry, he just glared at me.*

stare to look at someone or something for a long time without moving your eyes: *It's rude to stare.*

gaze to look at someone or something for a long time, often without realizing that you are doing it: *The couple were gazing at each other.* | *We sat gazing at the view for hours.*

PHRASAL VERBS

look after sb/sth to take care of someone or something: *We look after Rodney's kids until he gets home from work.*

look ahead to think about and plan for what might happen in the future

look around (*also* **look round** *BrE*)

1 to try to find something: **[+for]** *I'm looking around for a new job.*

2 look around/round (sth) to look at what is in a place such as a building, shop, town etc, especially when you are walking: *We have three hours to look around the city.*

look at sb/sth

1 to read something quickly, but not thoroughly: *Jane was looking at a magazine while she waited.*

2 to examine something and try to find out what is wrong with it: *You should get a doctor to look at that cut.*

3 to study and think carefully about something: *The government will look at the report this week.*

4 look at sb/sth *spoken* used to mention someone or something as an example: *You can get a good job without a degree – just look at your Uncle Ron.*

5 to think about something in a particular way: *It all depends how you look at the situation.*

look back to think about something that happened in the past: **[+on]** *Looking back on it, I think I was wrong to leave when I did.*

look down on sb to think that you are better than someone else

look forward to sth to be excited and happy about

L

look

something that is going to happen: **look forward to doing sth** *I'm really looking forward to going to Japan.*
look into sth to try to find out the truth about a problem, crime etc: *We are looking into the cause of the fire.*
look on
1 to watch something happening, without being involved in it: *The crowd looked on as the two men fought.*
2 look on/upon sb/sth to think about someone or something in a particular way: **[+as]** *I look on him as a good friend.*
look out for sb/sth to try to notice someone or something: *Look out for Jane at the conference.*
look sth ↔ **over** to examine something quickly: *Can you look this letter over for me before I send it?*
look round *BrE →* LOOK AROUND
look through sth
1 to look for something in a pile of papers, a drawer, someone's pockets etc: *Look through your pockets and see if you can find the receipt.*
2 to read something carefully **THESAURUS** READ
look up
1 if a situation is looking up, it is getting better: *Things are looking up since I found a job.*
2 look sth ↔ up to find information in a book, on a computer etc: *If you don't know the word, look it up in the dictionary.*
3 look sb ↔ up to visit someone you have not seen for quite a long time: *Don't forget to look me up when you come to Atlanta.*
look up to sb to admire and respect someone: *He looks up to his older brother.* **THESAURUS** ADMIRE

look² n
1 SEE STH [C usually singular] when you look at something: **have/take a look (at sb/sth)** *Let me have a look at that map again.* **THESAURUS** LOOK
2 SEARCH [singular] an attempt to find something: **[+for]** *He's **had a look** for the file but he hasn't found it.*
3 EXPRESSION [C] **a)** an expression on someone's face: *He had a worried **look on** his face.* **b)** when someone looks at you with a particular expression on their face: *She **gave** me an angry **look**.*
4 THINK ABOUT [singular] an act of examining something and thinking about it: **[+at]** *This month, **take** a long hard **look** at where your money is going.*
5 APPEARANCE [C usually singular] the appearance of someone or something: *I **don't like the look of** those rain clouds.*
6 FASHION [C] a particular fashion or style: *the nautical look*
7 ATTRACTIVENESS **looks** [plural] physical attractiveness: *Stop worrying about your looks.*

lookalike /ˈlʊkəlaɪk/ n [C] *informal* someone who looks very similar to a famous person: *a Madonna lookalike*

ˈlook-in n **get a look-in** *BrE informal* to have a chance to take part in or succeed in something: *The rest of us didn't get a look-in.*

lookout /ˈlʊkaʊt/ n [C] someone who watches carefully for danger, or the place where they do this

PHRASES
| **be on the lookout (for sth)** to pay attention to the things around you in order to find something you want or to avoid something: *Be on the lookout for snakes!*

loom¹ /luːm/ v [I] **1** to appear as a large unclear often frightening shape: **[+ahead/up etc]** *The mountain loomed up in front of us.* **2** if a problem or difficulty looms, it is likely to happen very soon: *My exams are looming.*

loom² n [C] a machine used for weaving cloth

loony /ˈluːni/ n [C] (*plural* **loonies**) *informal* someone who behaves in a crazy or strange way —**loony** *adj*: *He's full of loony ideas.*

loop¹ /luːp/ n [C] a shape like a circle in a piece of wire, string etc: *A loop of wire held the gate shut.*

PHRASES
| **be out of the loop** *AmE* to not be part of a group of people that make decisions: *Gaynor says he was out of the loop when the order was given.*

loop² v **loop sth over/around etc sth** to make a loop, or to tie something into a loop

loophole /ˈluːphəʊl $ -hoʊl/ n [C] a small mistake in a law that makes it possible to legally avoid doing what the law says: *tax loopholes*

LOOSE

loose clothes

tight clothes

loose¹ /luːs/ *adj*
1 not firmly fixed in place: *a loose tooth | The screw has **come loose**.*
2 not fastened together or kept together in a container: *She had left her hair loose. | The potatoes are sold loose.*
3 loose clothes are big and do not fit tightly
4 free, not controlled, tied up, or kept in a prison, cage etc: *Two of the prisoners **broke loose** from the guards.* | **let/turn/set sb loose** *He threatened to let his dogs loose.*
5 not exact: *a loose translation* —**loosely** *adv*

PHRASES
| **be at a loose end** to have nothing to do: *I was at a loose end, so I decided to watch a DVD.*
| **loose change** coins that you have: *Bill felt in his pocket for some loose change.*
| **loose ends** parts of something that have not been completed or correctly done: *We've nearly finished, but there are still a few **loose ends** to be **tied up** (=dealt with or completed).*

loose² *n* **be on the loose** if a criminal or animal is on the loose, they have escaped

loosen /ˈluːsən/ *v* [I,T] to become or to make something less tight or less firmly fastened: *The screws holding the shelf had loosened.* | *He loosened his tie.*

PHRASAL VERBS

loosen up to become more relaxed: *Claire loosened up after a few drinks.*

loot¹ /luːt/ *v* [I,T] to steal things during a war or RIOT: *Shops were looted and burned down.* —**looting** *n* [U] —**looter** *n* [C]

loot² *n* [U] things that have been stolen

lop /lɒp $ lɑːp/ *v* (**lopped, lopping**)

PHRASAL VERBS

lop sth ↔ **off** to cut part of something off, especially a branch from a tree

lope /ləʊp $ loʊp/ (*also* **lope off**) *v* [I] to run or walk with long slow steps: *He loped off down the corridor.* —**lope** *n* [singular]

lopsided /ˌlɒpˈsaɪdɪd $ ˌlɑːp-/ *adj* having one side that is heavier or lower than the other: *a lopsided grin*

Lord /lɔːd $ lɔːrd/ *n* [C] **1** a man in the highest social class, especially in Britain → **Lady**: *Lord Mountbatten* **2 the/our Lord** a title for God or Jesus Christ **3 the Lords** the HOUSE OF LORDS → **the Commons**

lore /lɔː $ lɔːr/ *n* [U] traditional stories, history, or knowledge about magic, nature etc

lorry /ˈlɒri $ ˈlɔːri, ˈlɑːri/ *n* [C] (*plural* **lorries**) *BrE* a large vehicle used for carrying goods SYN **truck** → see picture at **TRANSPORT¹**

lose /luːz/ *v* (*past tense and past participle* **lost** /lɒst $ lɔːst/)

1 STOP HAVING STH [T] to stop having something that is important to you or that you need → **loss**: *Tom lost his job.* | *Drunk drivers should lose their licence.* | **lose an arm/leg/eye etc** *He lost his leg in a motorcycle accident.* | *He's lost a lot of blood.* | *I lost a lot of money when the stock market crashed.*

2 STOP HAVING A QUALITY/ABILITY ETC [T] to stop having a particular attitude, quality, ability etc, or to gradually have less of it → **loss**: *You're looking slim. Have you lost weight?* | **lose your sight/hearing/ voice/balance etc** *Jim lost his balance and fell.* | **lose confidence/interest/hope etc** *Carol lost interest in ballet in her teens.* | *Try not to lose heart* (=become sad and hopeless) *– there are plenty of other jobs.* | *We must never lose sight of* (=forget) *our goals.*

3 CAN'T FIND SB/STH [T] to become unable to find someone or something: *Danny's always losing his keys.*

4 NOT WIN [I,T] to fail to win a game, argument, war etc OPP **win** → **defeat**: *They played so badly they deserved to lose.* | **[+by]** *The Democrat candidate lost by 8,000 votes.* | **[+to]** *Liverpool lost to AC Milan.*

5 DIE [T] **a) lose your life** to die: *5,000 soldiers lost their lives.* THESAURUS ▶ **DIE b)** if you lose a relative or friend, that person dies

6 CONFUSE [T] *spoken informal* to confuse someone when you are trying to explain something to them: *Explain it again – you've lost me already.*

7 WASTE [T] to waste time or an opportunity: *You lost your chance!* | *There's no time to lose!*

PHRASES

have nothing to lose if you have nothing to lose, it is worth taking a risk because you cannot make your situation any worse: *You should apply for the job – you have nothing to lose.*

lose it *informal* to become angry, confused, upset etc: *She completely lost it when I told her that the vase had been broken.*

lose your temper/cool to become angry: **[+with]** *She tried not to lose her temper with him.*

lose your way/bearings to stop knowing where you are or which direction you should go in: *I lost my way in the network of tiny streets.*

PHRASAL VERBS

lose out to not get something good, valuable etc because someone else gets it instead: **[+to/in/on]** *She lost out to Nicole Kidman for the lead role.*

loser /ˈluːzə $ -ər/ *n* [C] **1** someone who has lost a competition, game etc: **good/bad loser** (=someone who behaves well or badly when they lose) **2** *informal* someone who is never successful in life, work, or relationships: *He's such a loser!*

loss /lɒs $ lɔːs/ *n*

1 [C,U] when you do not have something any longer, or when you have less of it: **[+of]** *The loss of their home was a shock to the family.* | *a temporary loss of memory* | *severe weight loss* | *job losses*

2 [C,U] if a company makes a loss, it earns less money than it spends OPP **profit**: *The company made a loss of $250,000 last year.*

3 [C,U] the death of a person: *After heavy losses* (=many deaths), *they were forced to surrender.* | *The floods caused great damage and loss of life.*

4 [U] a feeling of sadness because someone or something is not there any more: *She felt a great sense of loss when her son left home.*

5 [singular] a disadvantage caused by someone leaving or something being taken away: **[+to]** *If she leaves, it will be a great loss to the company.* → **cut your losses** at **CUT¹**

PHRASES

be at a loss to be confused or uncertain about what to do or say: *Local people are at a loss to know how to deal with the problem.*

lost¹ /lɒst $ lɔːst/ *adj*

1 not knowing where you are or how to find your way: *We got lost driving around the city.* | *a lost child* **2** if something is lost, you cannot find it: *two boys searching for a lost ball* | *The card got lost in the post.* **3 be/feel lost** to not feel confident or happy: *He felt completely lost when his wife died.* → **LONG-LOST**

PHRASES

be lost for words to be so shocked, IMPRESSed etc that you cannot think what to say: *For once in her life, she was lost for words.*

be lost on sb if something such as a joke is lost on someone, they cannot understand it: *The joke was completely lost on Neil.*

get lost! *spoken* used to tell someone rudely to go away: *Leave me alone. Go on, get lost!*

lost cause something that will definitely not be successful: *It looked like the match was a lost cause.*

lost² *v* the past tense and past participle of LOSE

lost 'property *n* [U] things that people have accidentally left in a public place, which are kept until the owner collects them

lot /lɒt $ lɑːt/ *n*

1 a lot (*also* **lots** *informal*) a large amount, quantity, or number of something: **[+of]** *There was a lot of people at the concert last night.* | *She's got lots of money.* | 'How many CDs have you got?' 'Lots.' | **a lot to do/see etc** *There's a lot to see in London.*

2 a lot a) used to say that something happens to a great degree or often: *Things have changed a lot since I was a child.* **THESAURUS** OFTEN **b)** if someone or something is a lot better, faster etc, they are much better, faster etc: *You'll get there a lot faster if you drive.*

3 [C] *BrE informal* a group of people or things considered together: *I need to take this lot to the post office.* | **[+of]** *There's another lot of students starting next week.*

4 the lot *especially BrE* the whole of something: *He bought a huge bar of chocolate and ate the lot.*

5 [C] *AmE* an area of land used for a particular purpose: *a parking lot*

6 [C] something being sold at an AUCTION

7 [singular] the kind of life you have: *She seems happy enough with her lot.*

lotion /ˈləʊʃən $ ˈloʊ-/ *n* [C,U] a liquid mixture that you put on your skin or hair to clean, SOFTEN, or protect it: *suntan lotion*

lottery /ˈlɒtəri $ ˈlɑː-/ *n* [C] (*plural* **lotteries**) a competition in which people choose a set of numbers and win money if they have chosen the winning numbers

lotto /ˈlɒtəʊ $ ˈlɑːtoʊ/ *n* [C] (*plural* **lottos**) a game used to make money, in which people buy tickets with a series of numbers on them. If their numbers are picked by chance, they win money or a prize.

loud¹ /laʊd/ *adj*

1 making a lot of noise: *The TV's too loud!* | *a loud bang*

2 loud clothes are very brightly coloured —**loudly** *adv*

THESAURUS

loud making a lot of noise – used about sounds, voices, or music: *Joe was talking in a very loud voice.*

noisy making a lot of noise – used about people, machines, and places that are too loud, often in an annoying way: *noisy neighbours* | *The room was very noisy.*

rowdy behaving in a noisy way and likely to cause trouble: *There was a crowd of rowdy students in the bar.*

deafening extremely loud, especially so that you cannot hear anything else: *Our conversation was interrupted by the deafening roar of an aircraft taking off.*

at full volume as loudly as possible – used about sounds produced by television, radio,

---

musical equipment etc: *He played the CD at full volume.*

loud² *adv* in a way that makes a lot of noise **SYN** **loudly**: *You'll have to speak a bit louder.*

PHRASES

out loud in a way that people can hear: *Read it out loud, so we can all hear.*

loudspeaker /ˌlaʊdˈspiːkə, ˈlaʊdˌspiːkə $ -ər/ *n* [C] a piece of equipment that makes sounds louder

lounge¹ /laʊndʒ/ *n* [C]

1 a room in a hotel or airport, where people can sit and relax: *the **departure lounge***

2 *BrE* the room in your house where you sit and relax

lounge² *v* [I] to stand or sit somewhere in a relaxed way: *We were lounging by the pool.*

PHRASAL VERBS

lounge about/around *BrE* to spend time relaxing and doing nothing

louse /laʊs/ *n* [C] (*plural* **lice** /laɪs/) a very small insect that lives on the skin or hair of animals and people

lousy /ˈlaʊzi/ *adj informal* very bad: *a lousy film* **THESAURUS** BAD

lout /laʊt/ *n* [C] a loud violent man

lovable, **loveable** /ˈlʌvəbəl/ *adj* easy to love: *a lovable child*

love¹ /lʌv/ *v* [T]

1 to like someone in a romantic or sexual way: *I love you.* | *the first boy I ever really loved* **THESAURUS** LIKE

2 to care about someone a lot, especially a member of your family or a close friend: *I love my mom.* | *It can be hard to cope with the death of a **loved one*** (=person you care about).

3 to like something very much, or enjoy doing something very much: *I love chocolate.* | **love doing sth** *Tom loves going to the cinema.* | **love to do sth** *He loved to spend time here.*

4 I'd love to (do sth) *spoken* used to say that you want to do something very much: *I'd love to go to Egypt one day.* | 'Do you want to come?' 'I'd love to.' **THESAURUS** WANT

THESAURUS

love to like someone very much and care a lot about them – used about people in your family or someone who you are sexually attracted to: *He knew that his parents loved him.* | *My boyfriend told me that he loved me.*

adore to love and admire someone very much: *She adored her father.*

be in love (with sb) if two people are in love with each other, they have strong romantic feelings for each other: *They were young and very much in love.* | *I could see that she was in love with him.*

be crazy about sb *informal* to love someone very much: *She's crazy about you.*

have a crush on sb to have strong feelings of love and admiration for someone, especially a much older person, or a famous person you have never met, when you know you cannot have a relationship with them: *She had a crush on one of her teachers.*

love² n

1 [U] a strong romantic feeling for someone: **[+for]** *Their love for each other grew stronger every day.* | **in love** *a woman in love* | **[+with]** *I think I'm falling in love with you.*

2 [U] when you care very much about someone, especially a member of your family or a close friend: **[+for]** *a mother's love for her son*

3 [C] someone you love: *You were my **first love.*** | *There she met **the love of** her life* (=the person she loved most in her life).

4 [C,U] a strong feeling of liking or enjoying something very much, or something that gives you this feeling: **[+of]** *his love of the countryside* | *She **has a** great **love of** music.* | *His greatest love is football.*

5 *BrE spoken informal* **a)** used when talking to someone who you love: *Are you OK, love?* **b)** used when talking in a friendly way to someone you do not know, especially a woman

PHRASES

love at first sight a situation in which you love someone as soon as you see them: *When they met, it was love at first sight.*

love (from) sb (*also* **with love (from) sb**) used at the end of a friendly letter: *With love from Peter.* | *Hope to see you soon. **Lots of love**, Chris.*

make love (to/with sb) to have sex with someone
send/give your love (to sb) to ask someone to give your friendly greetings to someone else: *Your father sends his love.*

COLLOCATIONS

verbs

to be in love *I'm not in love with him.*
to fall in love (=to start being in love) *They became friends and eventually fell in love.*

adverbs

very much in love *We were very much in love.*
madly/deeply in love *You know he's madly in love with you.*

adjectives

true love (=real love) *Will she ever find true love?*

love + noun

a love song *He made an album of love songs.*
a love story *Romeo and Juliet is a famous love story.*
a love letter *I've kept all his old love letters.*

'love af,fair n [C] a romantic sexual relationship

lovely /'lʌvli/ adj

1 beautiful: *You **look lovely** in that dress.* | *What a lovely garden!* **THESAURUS** BEAUTIFUL

2 *especially BrE* very pleasant or enjoyable: *Thanks for a lovely evening.* | *The food was lovely.* **THESAURUS** NICE

lover /'lʌvə $ -ər/ n [C] **1** someone you have a sexual relationship with, especially who you are not married to: *They became lovers soon after they met.*

2 someone who enjoys something very much: **music/art/animal lover**

loving /'lʌvɪŋ/ adj behaving in a gentle kind way that shows you love someone: *a wonderful, loving husband* —**lovingly** adv

low¹ /ləʊ $ loʊ/ adj

1 IN HEIGHT not far above the ground **OPP** high: *a low ceiling* | *low clouds* | *Put it on the lowest shelf.*

2 IN AMOUNT/VALUE small in amount, value etc **OPP** high: *Temperatures will be lower than yesterday.* | *We try to keep our prices as low as possible.* | *families on low incomes* | **low-fat/low-salt etc** (=with very little fat, salt etc) *low-alcohol beer* **THESAURUS** CHEAP

3 IN STANDARD below an acceptable standard **OPP** high: *She got a very low grade in English.* | *low quality goods*

4 UNHAPPY [not before noun] unhappy: *Kerry's been pretty low lately.*

5 VOICE/SOUND a low voice or sound is quiet or deep **THESAURUS** QUIET

6 LIGHTS lights that are low are not bright

low² adv in a low position or at a low level **OPP** high: *The sun sank low on the horizon.* | *low-flying aircraft* | **low-paid workers** (=who do not earn much money)

low³ n [C] a low price, level etc **OPP** high: *Oil prices have dropped to an **all-time low*** (=the lowest they have ever been). | *Tomorrow's low will be 8°C.*

lowbrow /'ləʊbraʊ $ 'loʊ-/ adj disapproving a lowbrow newspaper, book etc is easy to understand and not very serious **OPP** highbrow

,low-'cut adj low-cut clothes show the top of a woman's chest: *a tight low-cut dress*

lowdown /'ləʊdaʊn $ 'loʊ-/ n **the lowdown (on sb/sth)** the important facts about someone or something: ***Give** me **the lowdown on** what happened.*

lower¹ /'ləʊə $ 'loʊər/ adj [only before noun]

1 below something else, or at the bottom of something **OPP** upper: *I injured my lower back.* | *the lower floors of the building*

2 less important than other things: *the lower levels of management*

lower² v [T] **1** to reduce something in amount, strength etc: *We're lowering prices on all our products!* | *Helen **lowered** her **voice*** (=spoke more quietly). **THESAURUS** REDUCE **2** to move something down **OPP** raise: *The flag was lowered at sunset.*

,lower 'case n [U] letters written in their small form, for example a, b, c → **upper case**, **capital**

,low-'key adj done in a way that will not attract a lot of attention: *The reception was very low-key.*

lowlands /'ləʊləndz $ 'loʊ-/ n [plural] an area of land that is lower than the land around it → **highlands**: *the Scottish lowlands* —**lowland** adj [only before noun]

,low-'level adj **1** close to the ground: *low-level bombing attacks* **2** used about positions or jobs that are not very important **OPP** high-level: *routine, low-level clerical tasks*

lowly /'ləʊli $ 'loʊ-/ adj literary low in rank or importance: *He had a very lowly job.*

low-'lying *adj* low-lying land is not much higher than the level of the sea

'low-rise *adj* [only before noun] a low-rise building does not have many levels → **high-rise**

low-tech /ˌləʊ ˈtek◄ $ ˌloʊ-/ *adj* not using the most modern machines or methods OPP **high-tech**

loyal /ˈlɔɪəl/ *adj* always supporting your friends, beliefs, country etc OPP **disloyal**: *a loyal friend* | *his loyal supporters* | **[+to]** *soldiers who remain loyal to the president*

loyalist /ˈlɔɪəlɪst/ *n* [C] someone who continues to support a government or country, especially during a period of change —**loyalist** *adj*: *loyalist troops*

loyalty /ˈlɔɪəlti/ *n* (*plural* **loyalties**) **1** [U] when someone always supports someone or something: *The company demands loyalty from its workers.* **2** [C usually plural] a feeling of support for someone or something: *My loyalties lie with my family.* | *I wasn't sure where his **political loyalties** lay.*

lozenge /ˈlɒzəndʒ $ ˈlɑː-/ *n* [C] a small SWEET containing medicine

LP /ˌel ˈpiː/ *n* [C] *old-fashioned* (**long-playing record**) a record that plays for about 25 minutes on each side SYN **album**

L-plate /ˈel pleɪt/ *n* [C] a red letter 'L' put on a car in Britain to show that the driver is learning to drive

LSD /ˌel es ˈdiː/ *n* [U] an illegal drug that makes people see things that are not really there

Ltd the written abbreviation of **limited company**, used after the names of companies → **plc**: *Barkers Tools Ltd*

lubricant /ˈluːbrɪkənt/ *n* [C,U] a substance such as oil that is put on things that rub together, making them move more smoothly

lubricate /ˈluːbrɪkeɪt/ *v* [T] to put a substance such as oil on something so that it will move more smoothly

lucid /ˈluːsɪd/ *adj* **1** clear and easy to understand: *a lucid and interesting article* **2** able to think clearly

luck /lʌk/ *n* [U]
1 good things that happen by chance: *Her success was due to a combination of hard work and good luck.* | *Have you had any luck finding a job?* | **with (any/a bit of) luck** *With any luck, he won't be home yet.*
2 the way in which good or bad things happen to people by chance: *It's just a matter of luck – there's nothing we can do.* | *He had some bad luck and lost all his money.* THESAURUS **UNLUCKY**
PHRASES
bad/hard/tough luck *spoken* used to express sympathy for someone when something bad has happened: *Oh, bad luck – that shot nearly went straight in the hole.*
good luck/best of luck *spoken* used to say that you hope someone is successful: **[+with]** *Good luck with the competition!*
be in/out of luck to be lucky or unlucky: *You're in luck – there's one ticket left.*

good/bad luck *She wished him good luck.* | *It was just bad luck that you didn't see him.*
sheer/pure luck (=chance, not skill or effort) *By sheer luck, I guessed right.*

verbs
to have good/bad etc luck *You may have better luck than I did.*
to have no luck (*also* **to not have much/any luck**) *So far, I've had no luck finding a boyfriend.*
to wish sb luck *Wish me luck for the exam.*
to bring sb luck *She believed the stone brought her luck.*

noun + luck
a bit/piece/stroke of luck (=something good that happens by chance) *Then we had an extraordinary stroke of luck.*
a matter of luck (=something that depends on chance) *Winning is a matter of luck.*

lucky /ˈlʌki/ *adj*
1 having good luck, or happening because of good luck SYN **fortunate** OPP **unlucky**: *'I just got the last bus.' 'That was lucky!'* | **be lucky to be/do/have sth** *You're lucky to have such a caring husband.* | *We're lucky to still be alive!* | *I was **lucky enough** to see them live in concert.* | **[+if]** *You'll be lucky if you get that far.* | *The boys **had a lucky escape** (=were lucky that nothing bad happened to them).* | *the **lucky winner** of $10,000*
2 something that is lucky brings you good luck: *Seven is my lucky number.* —**luckily** *adv*: *Luckily, I had my keys with me.*

THESAURUS
lucky having good luck, or happening because of good luck: *I was very lucky to survive the accident.*
fortunate lucky. **Fortunate** sounds more formal than **lucky**: *He was in the fortunate position of having two job offers.*
it is a good thing that *especially spoken* used when saying that there would have been problems if something had not happened: *It's a good thing that you brought an umbrella with you.*
it is a miracle that used when saying that it was extremely lucky that something happened or did not happen: *It's a miracle that no one was killed in the fire.*

lucrative /ˈluːkrətɪv/ *adj formal* a lucrative job or activity is one that you earn a lot of money from

ludicrous /ˈluːdɪkrəs/ *adj* stupid, wrong, and unreasonable SYN **ridiculous**: *a ludicrous suggestion* THESAURUS **STUPID** —**ludicrously** *adv*

lug /lʌg/ *v* [T] (**lugged**, **lugging**) *informal* to pull or carry something heavy: *We lugged our suitcases up to our room.*

luggage /ˈlʌgɪdʒ/ *n* [U] the bags and cases that you carry when you are travelling SYN **baggage**

'luggage rack n [C] **1** a shelf in a train, bus etc for putting luggage on **2** AmE a special frame on top of a car that you tie luggage on SYN roof rack BrE → see picture at CAR

lugubrious /luːˈguːbriəs/ adj literary very sad and serious

lukewarm /ˌluːkˈwɔːm◂ $ -ˈwɔːrm◂/ adj **1** a liquid that is lukewarm is only slightly warm: lukewarm water THESAURUS> HOT **2** not showing very much interest or excitement: a lukewarm response

lull[1] /lʌl/ v [T] **1** to make someone feel calm and SLEEPY: Singing softly, she lulled us to sleep. **2** to make someone feel safe so that they can easily be tricked: lull sb into (doing) sth She was lulled into believing that there was no danger.

lull[2] n [C] a short period when there is less activity or noise than usual: a lull in the conversation

lullaby /ˈlʌləbaɪ/ n [C] (plural lullabies) a song that you sing to children to make them sleep

lumber[1] /ˈlʌmbə $ -ər/ v **1** [I] to move slowly and heavily: [+along/towards etc] The bear lumbered towards us. **2** get/be lumbered with sth to be given a job or responsibility that you do not want: I got lumbered with looking after my brother.

lumber[2] n [U] especially AmE wood that is used for building

luminous /ˈluːmɪnəs/ adj able to shine in the dark

lump[1] /lʌmp/ n [C]
1 a small irregular piece of something: [+of] a lump of mud | a huge lump of cheese → see picture at PIECE[1] THESAURUS> PIECE
2 a hard swelling on someone's skin or in their body: She found a lump in her breast.
PHRASES
a lump in your throat a feeling that you want to cry: There was a lump in my throat and tears in my eye as he waved goodbye.

lump[2] v [T] to put two or more different people or things together and consider them as a single group: lump sth together All the costs have been lumped together.

,lump 'sum n [C] an amount of money given in a single payment: You'll receive a lump sum of £50,000.

lumpy /ˈlʌmpi/ adj with a lot of lumps: a lumpy mattress

lunacy /ˈluːnəsi/ n [U] behaviour that seems completely crazy: It would be sheer lunacy to give up college now.

lunar /ˈluːnə $ -ər/ adj relating to the Moon → solar: a lunar eclipse

lunatic /ˈluːnətɪk/ n [C] someone who behaves in a stupid or crazy way that can be dangerous —lunatic adj

lunch[1] /lʌntʃ/ n [C,U] a meal that you eat in the middle of the day: for lunch What's for lunch? | at lunch I think she's at lunch right now.

COLLOCATIONS
verbs
to have/eat lunch We had lunch before we left.
to have sth for lunch I had some soup for lunch.

to go out for/to lunch (=at a restaurant etc) Shall we go out for lunch on Sunday?
to come for/to lunch We have friends coming for lunch.
to make lunch I'll make lunch while you finish that.

types of lunch
a light lunch (=a small lunch) I usually have a light lunch.
a packed lunch BrE, a bag/sack lunch AmE (=food that you take to school, work etc for lunch) He always takes a packed lunch to work.
Sunday lunch BrE (=a hot lunch eaten on Sunday) We were cooking a chicken for Sunday lunch.

lunch + noun
a lunch break (=when you stop working to eat lunch) They have a one-hour lunch break.
the lunch hour She did some shopping in her lunch hour.

Word Choice: lunch or dinner?
Lunch is always a midday meal. **Dinner** is usually a meal that you eat in the evening, but it is also sometimes used about a meal that you eat in the middle of the day, for example on a special occasion: Christmas dinner | Thanksgiving dinner
In British English, people also refer to school lunches as **school dinners**.

lunch[2] v [I] formal to eat lunch

luncheon /ˈlʌntʃən/ n [C,U] formal lunch

lunchtime /ˈlʌntʃtaɪm/ n [C,U] the time in the middle of the day when people usually eat lunch: I'll give you a call at lunchtime.

lung /lʌŋ/ n [C] one of two organs in your body that you use for breathing → see picture on page A2

lunge /lʌndʒ/ v [I] to make a sudden movement towards someone or something, often to attack them: [+forward/at/towards] Greg lunged forward to grab her arm. —lunge n [C]

lurch[1] /lɜːtʃ $ lɜːrtʃ/ v [I] to move in an unsteady or uncontrolled way: [+across/along etc] He lurched drunkenly towards us.

lurch[2] n [singular] when something or someone moves in an unsteady or uncontrolled way
PHRASES
leave sb in the lurch to leave someone in a very difficult situation: She's still upset because that man left her in the lurch.

lure[1] /lʊə, ljʊə $ lʊr/ v [T] to persuade or trick someone into doing something by making it seem attractive or exciting: Salesmen who lure people into spending large amounts of money.

lure[2] n [singular] when something attracts people: the lure of huge profits

lurid /ˈlʊərɪd, ˈljʊərɪd $ ˈlʊrɪd/ adj **1** deliberately shocking and involving sex or violence: a lurid description of the murder **2** too brightly coloured: a lurid green dress

L

lurk /lɜːk $ lɜːrk/ v [I] to wait somewhere secretly, usually before doing something bad: *I was scared that someone might be lurking in the bushes.*

luscious /ˈlʌʃəs/ adj very good to eat or drink: *luscious ripe strawberries*

lush /lʌʃ/ adj having a lot of green and healthy plants or leaves: *lush green fields*

lust[1] /lʌst/ n [U] **1** a very strong feeling of sexual desire **2** a strong desire to have something, such as power or money: **[+for]** *his lust for glory*

PHRASES

lust for life when someone has a lot of energy and seems to enjoy life very much: *Despite his age, he still hadn't lost his lust for life.*

lust[2] v [I] **1 lust after sb** to have a strong feeling of sexual desire for someone **2 lust after/for sth** to want something very much: *politicians who lust after power*

lustre *BrE*, **luster** *AmE* /ˈlʌstə $ -ər/ n [singular, U] an attractive shiny appearance

lusty /ˈlʌsti/ adj strong and healthy

luxuriant /lʌgˈzjʊəriənt, ləgˈʒʊəriənt $ ləgˈʒʊriənt/ adj formal growing thickly and strongly: *luxuriant black hair*

luxurious /lʌgˈzjʊəriəs, ləgˈʒʊəriəs $ ləgˈʒʊriəs/ adj very comfortable, beautiful, and expensive: *a luxurious hotel* THESAURUS ▶ COMFORTABLE

luxury /ˈlʌkʃəri/ n (plural **luxuries**)
1 [U] great comfort and pleasure, especially from beautiful or expensive things: *They **lived a life of luxury**.* | **in luxury** *They now live in luxury in Switzerland.* | *We never had much money for **luxury goods**.* | **luxury car/home/hotel etc** (=large and expensive)
2 [C] something expensive that you want but do not need OPP **necessity**: *luxuries like chocolate and perfume* | *A holiday is a luxury we can't afford.*
3 the luxury of sth the ability to have or do something pleasant: *They don't **have the luxury of** choosing where to live.*

-ly /li/ suffix in a particular way: *She dressed quickly.* | *He is financially dependent on his parents.*

Lycra /ˈlaɪkrə/ n [U] trademark a material that is used especially for making sports clothes that fit tightly, because it moves with your body

lying /ˈlaɪ-ɪŋ/ v the present participle of LIE

lynch /lɪntʃ/ v [T] if a crowd of people lynches someone they think is guilty of a crime, they kill them without a TRIAL —**lynching** n [C]

lyrical /ˈlɪrɪkəl/ adj expressing feelings in a beautiful way: *lyrical poetry*

lyrics /ˈlɪrɪks/ n [plural] the words of a song: *a simple melody and great lyrics*

L

Picture dictionary

Body   A2

Animals   A3

Fruit   A4

Vegetables   A5

Musical instruments   A6

Sounds   A7

Prepositions   A8

Sports   A9

Verbs of movement (hands)   A10

Verbs of movement (body)   A11

Technology   A12

Language notes   A14

Grammar reference   A44

Body

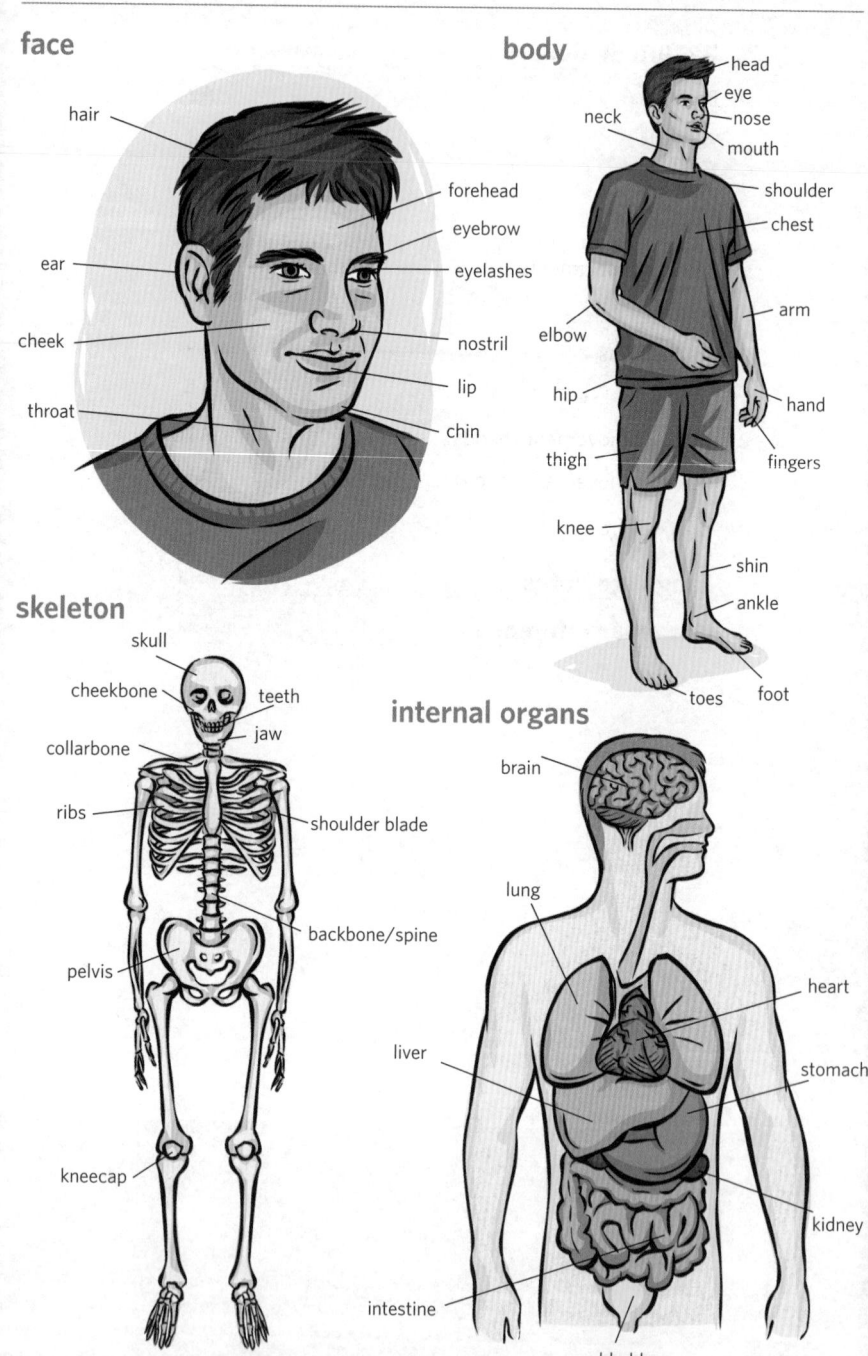

face

hair
forehead
eyebrow
eyelashes
ear
cheek
nostril
lip
throat
chin

body

head
eye
nose
mouth
neck
shoulder
chest
arm
elbow
hip
hand
thigh
fingers
knee
shin
ankle
toes
foot

skeleton

skull
cheekbone
teeth
collarbone
jaw
ribs
shoulder blade
backbone/spine
pelvis
kneecap

internal organs

brain
lung
heart
liver
stomach
kidney
intestine
bladder

beak
tail feathers
throat
breast
claw
bird
owl
talon
flipper
penguin
duck
goose
webbed foot
tail
fin
gill
fish
swordfish
shark
jellyfish
whale
fox
horn
wolf
hippopotamus
rhinoceros
cow
calf
antelope
flank
back
muzzle
shoulder
belly
knee
horse
hoof
donkey
giraffe
koala

Fruit

apple
pip *BrE*
core
apricot
avocado
skin
banana
blackberries
stalk
cherries
coconuts
blackcurrants
grapefruit
pith
segment
grapes
flesh
kiwi fruit
lemon
lime
mango
nectarine
seeds
plum
melon
strawberry
stone *BrE*/pit *AmE*
peach
pears
pineapple
raspberries
figs
rhubarb
blueberries
peel
pith
segment
oranges
watermelon

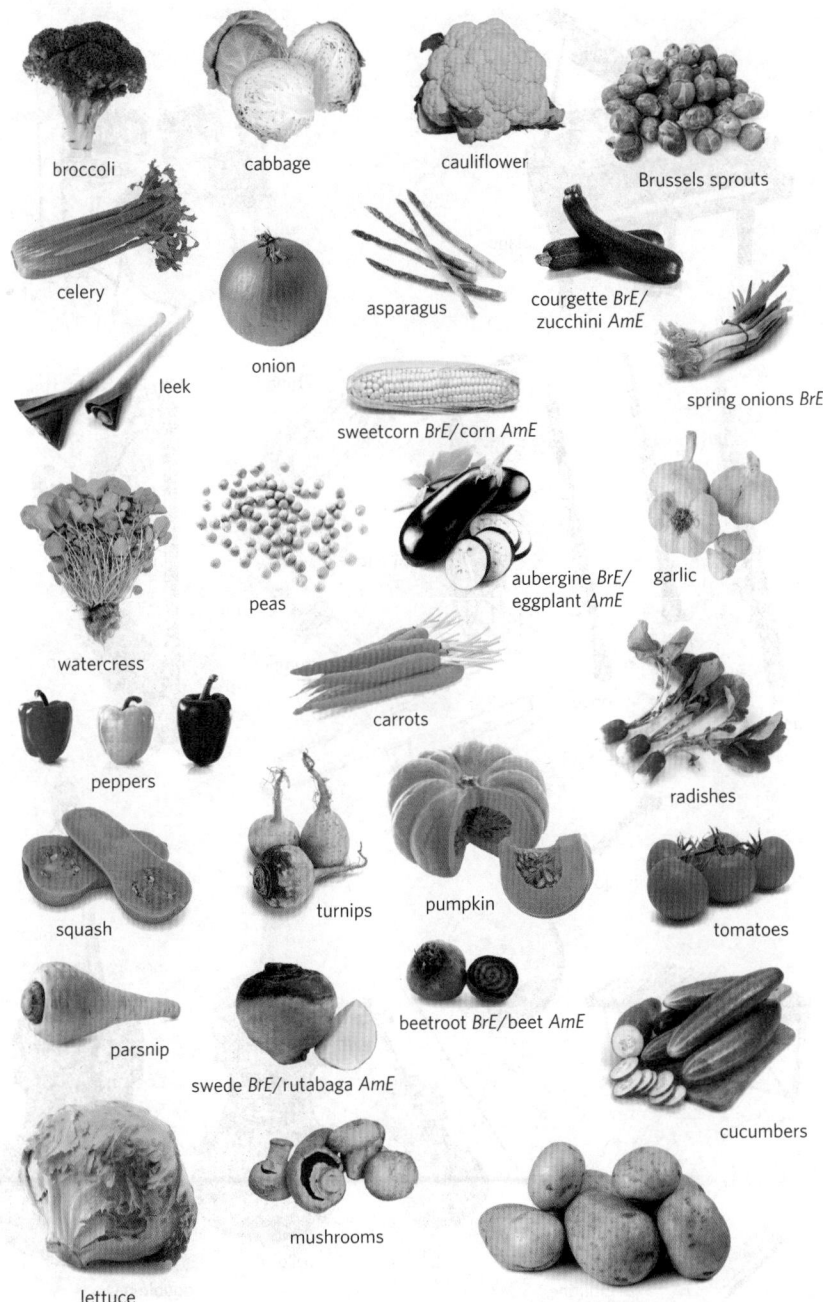

broccoli

cabbage

cauliflower

Brussels sprouts

celery

asparagus

courgette *BrE*/
zucchini *AmE*

onion

leek

sweetcorn *BrE*/corn *AmE*

spring onions *BrE*

watercress

peas

aubergine *BrE*/
eggplant *AmE*

garlic

carrots

peppers

radishes

squash

turnips

pumpkin

tomatoes

parsnip

beetroot *BrE*/beet *AmE*

swede *BrE*/rutabaga *AmE*

cucumbers

lettuce

mushrooms

potatoes

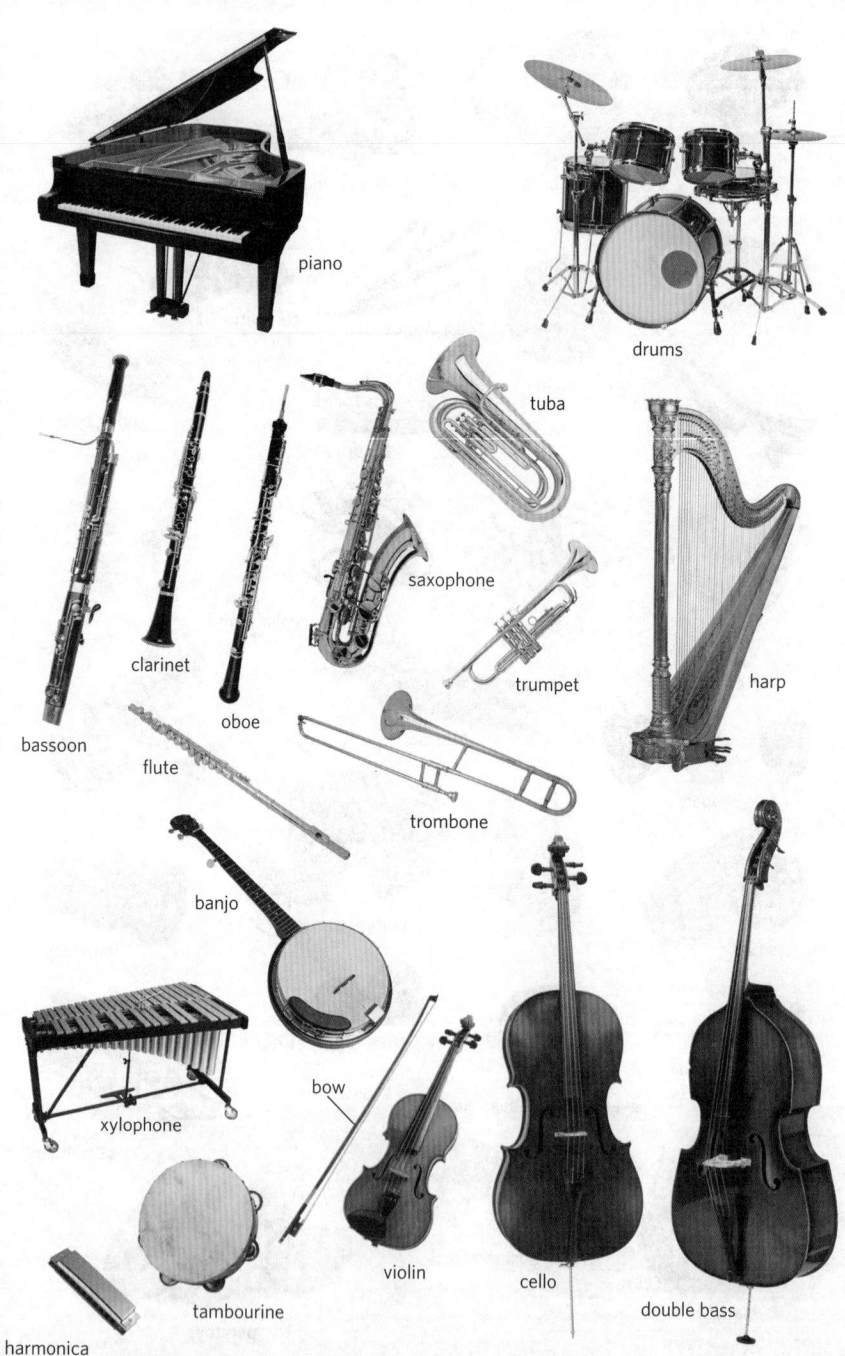

piano

drums

tuba

saxophone

trumpet

harp

clarinet

oboe

bassoon

flute

trombone

banjo

xylophone

bow

violin

cello

double bass

tambourine

harmonica

Sounds

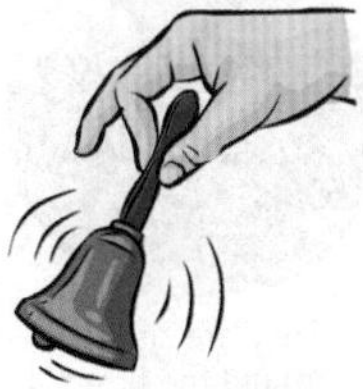
ring

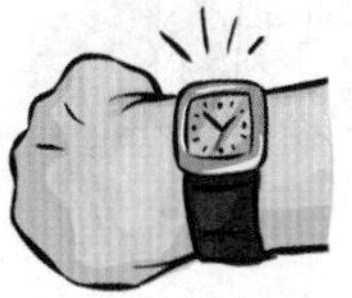
tick

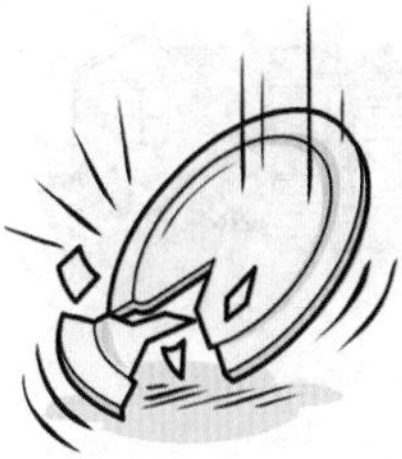
crash

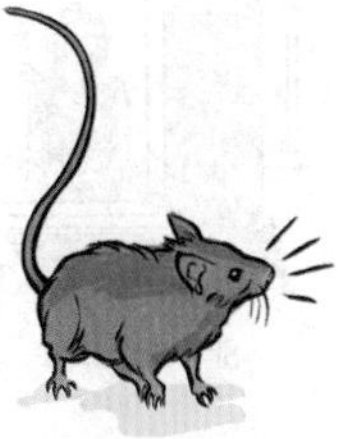
squeak

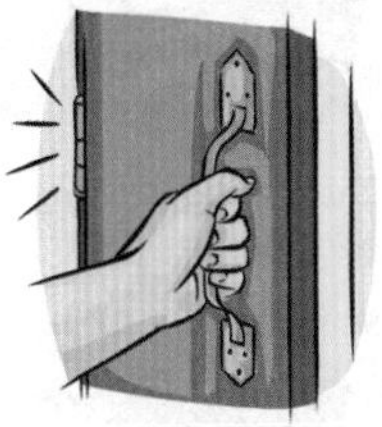
creak

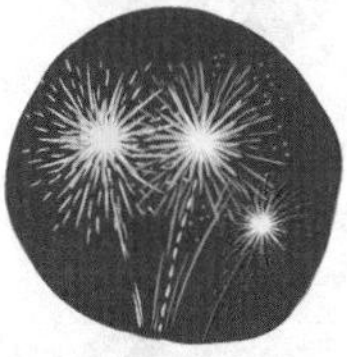
bang

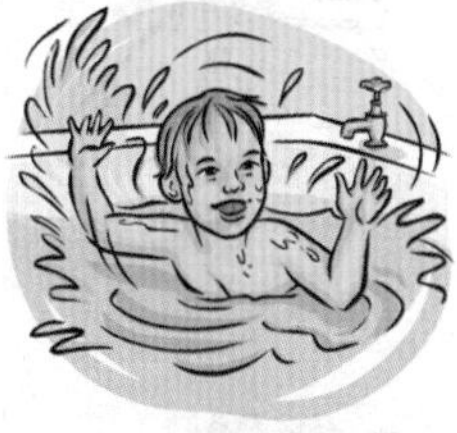
splash

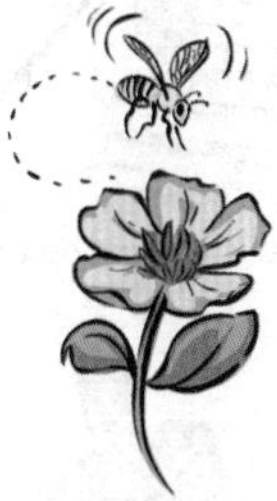
buzz

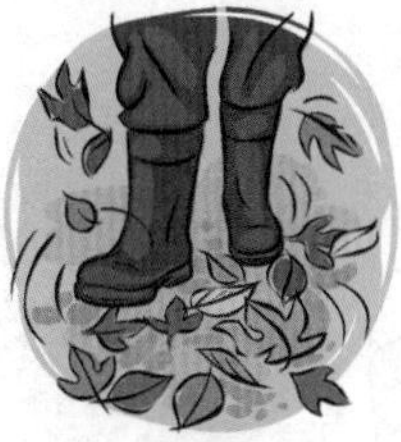
rustle

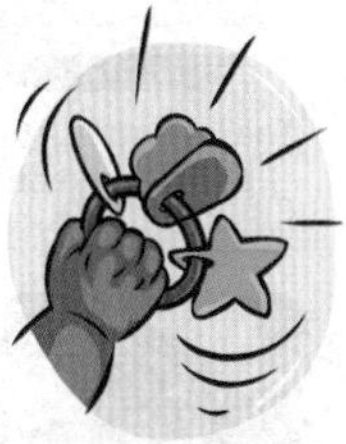
rattle

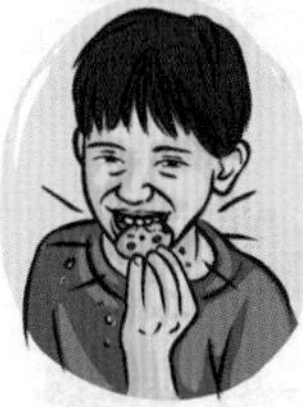
crunch

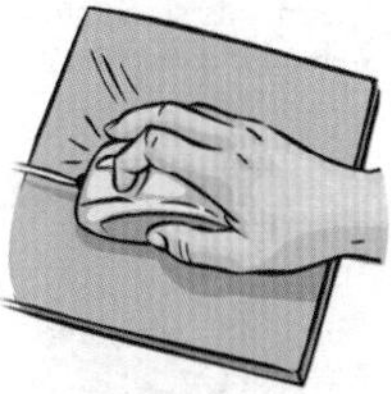
click

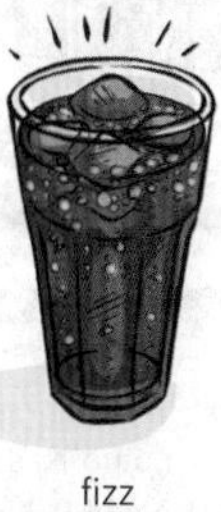
fizz

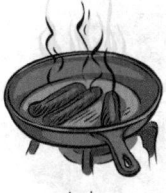

sizzle

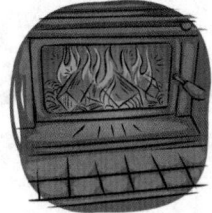

crackle

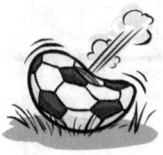

hiss

Prepositions

She is **inside** the house.

He is **outside** the house.

She is going **into** the house.

They are sitting **round** the fire.

He is walking **down** the stairs.

She is walking **up** the stairs.

The ball is rolling **towards** the goal.

There's a boy walking **across** the street.

The man is standing **behind** the woman.

The car is parked **in front of** the house.

The little girl is standing **beside** her mother.

The men are sitting **opposite** each other.

A boy is leaning **against** a wall.

There is a vase of flowers **next to** the clock.

He is sitting **between** two women on the sofa.

The train is going **through** the tunnel.

The cat is **under** the table.

She is sitting **on** the bed.

There is a bridge **over** the river.

There's a restaurant **above** the florist's./ There's a florist's **below** the restaurant.

Sports

baseball bat

baseball

racket

tennis court

tennis

table tennis

basketball

ice hockey

rugby

climbing

cycling

mountain biking

rowing

skating

speed skating

boxing

skiing

karate

kayaking

clap

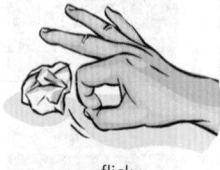

flick

tap

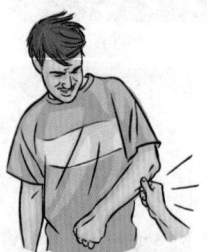

pinch

hold hands

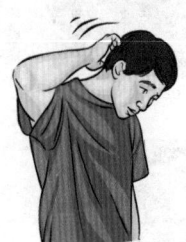

scratch

poke/prod

point

stroke

tickle

wave

pick up

put down

lift

carry

drop

stretch

bend

squat

crouch

kneel

push

pull

hold

climb

fall

run

jog

walk

sit

crawl

tiptoe

march

throw

kick

hit

punch

catch

CD

monitor

keyboard

mouse

computer

laptop

mobile phone *BrE*/cell phone *AmE*

DVD

DVD player

television

scanner

receiver

palmtop

games console

telephone

MP3 player

Memory Stick™

Language notes

A14

by Diane Schmitt, Senior Lecturer in EFL/TESOL
Nottingham Trent University

Vocabulary acquisition A14

Collocations A16

Synonyms and antonyms A20

Thesaurus A22

Phrases and idioms A24

Word families A26

Writing essays A27

Writing letters, emails, and text messages A30

Word building A35

Numbers and measurements A40

Grammar reference

A44

Articles A44

Countable and uncountable nouns A45

Verb patterns A46

Adjective patterns A47

Phrasal verbs A48

Modal verbs A50

Verb tenses A52

Language notes

The Language notes have been written for the Longman Active Study Dictionary *by Diane Schmitt, Senior Lecturer in EFL/TESOL, Nottingham Trent University. The information and statistics in this section are based on research into second language vocabulary acquisition by Diane Schmitt and Norbert Schmitt, Professor of Applied Linguistics, University of Nottingham.*

Vocabulary acquisition

There is no doubt that the more vocabulary you know, the easier you will find it to produce and understand English. But just how much vocabulary do you need? Because many English words are part of 'Word Families' (for example, *imagine verb, imagination noun, imaginary adjective*) we can consider the total vocabulary you need in terms of these word families. (See also page A26 for more information about them.)

1 How many word families do native speakers of English know?
   a 5,000   b 20,000   c 50,000   d 100,000

2 How many word families are needed to read comfortably in English?
   a 1,600   b 9,000   c 17,000   d 30,000

3 How many word families does the average English speaker use in daily conversations?
   a 6,000   b 8,000   c 12,000   d 25,000

4 How many word families would you need to study at a university in English?
   a 700   b 5,000   c 9,000   d 50,000

The amount of vocabulary you need depends on what you want to do in English. However much vocabulary you know now, you will want to learn more, and your dictionary is an important tool for achieving this goal.

Core vocabulary

The Longman Active Words are the 3,000 most common words in English. This intermediate-level vocabulary is given in red in the *Longman Active Study Dictionary* to mark its importance. These words provide you with the foundations of a very good vocabulary. If you know these words, you should be able to express many of the things you might want to say in English. However, the mark of good English usage is being able to produce the best word for each context, so the more vocabulary you know, the more precisely you will be able to express yourself.

What does it mean to know a word?

A dictionary is a book that gives a list of words in alphabetical order, with their meanings. However, it is not enough simply to know a word's meaning. The diagram on the next page shows that there are many other aspects of words that you must learn if you wish to use them appropriately.

Answers
1 20,000   2 9,000   3 6,000   4 9,000

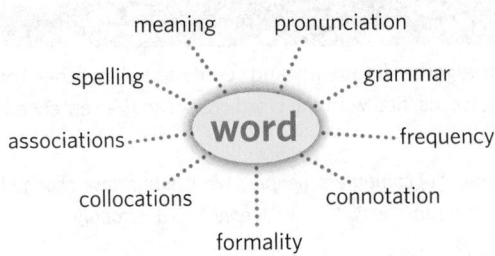

Turn to page iv in this dictionary. There you will see how each entry provides information about each of these aspects.

Because there is so much to know about individual words, you will need to see new words many times before you can really master them. You need to notice and focus on new words between 6-20 times before they really become part of your vocabulary.

Study tips

Tip 1 - which words should I study?
Each time you look up a word in your dictionary, put a pencil mark next to that word. If you notice that you have put three or four pencil marks next to a word, then this is a word you see often and need to know. Study this word.

Tip 2 - how do I study new words?
1   Read widely and listen to as much English as you can. Make a list of words you look up, guess or skip while reading or listening. Review the words in your list.
2   Put a star next to the words that were important for your understanding of this passage. Then put a star next to words that will be generally useful for future reading and listening.
3   Put the starred words into a vocabulary notebook.

Tip 3 - how do I use a vocabulary notebook?
1   First, write down the word you want to study in English. Be sure to spell it correctly.
2   Next, put down key information that will help you use the word – meaning, pronunciation and any notes about grammar (e.g. *only used before a noun*), formality and collocation.

Tip 4 - how do I make connections between words?
1   Select three categories, for example *problems, processes, solutions* or *in the home, at work, in school* or *positive things, negative things, neutral things*, and make three columns on a piece of notepaper.
2   Review the words from your notebook.
3   Select words that fit the categories you have chosen.

Collocations

Some words appear together frequently and seem natural together. For example, only one of the following words 'fits' with the word *change* in the sentence below. Do you know which one it is?

With the development of computers, people's work habits have changed _____.
  a *powerfully*   b *dramatically*   c *deeply*   d *strongly*

Although all of the four words have a similar meaning, only *dramatically* would be used in this sentence. The other words would feel awkward and unusual, and are not good 'partners' for *change*.

When you look at words in context, you can see patterns in the way they are used. These patterns are not based on rules of grammar, but on traditions of use by native speakers. Certain words tend to occur together and are 'word partners'. This partnership is called **collocation**.

> For example, we say: *tall girl* and *high mountain*
> But we do not say: *high girl* or *tall mountain*

Sometimes the link between word partners and their meaning is clear and unsurprising, for example in the collocations *bright light* or *heavy load*. Other times, the link may be unexpected as when we say: *bright child* or *heavy heart*.

Here are some typical collocation patterns:

noun + verb	*prices fall*
verb + noun	*lose hope*
adjective + noun	*a strong opinion*
verb + adverb	*breathe heavily*
noun + noun	*junk food*

Collocation partnerships

Some words in English are very frequent, and the collocations including these words can also be very common. For example, here are some common collocations made up of frequent words:

strong winds	*pretty girl*	*black coffee*	*heavy rain*

Other words are not very common, but they occur surprisingly often in combination with certain words. Here are some examples:

elder brother	*incurable disease*	*excruciating pain*	*glaringly obvious*

When you see *elder*, *incurable*, *excruciating* and *glaringly*, they are very likely to appear in these word combinations.

English includes a number of verbs which are used so much that they have lost much of their meaning. These are called *delexicalized verbs*. Some of the most common of these include:

do   get   give   have   make

The problem is that it is often difficult to decide which verb to use. Because the verbs have little meaning to help you, it may seem that there is no reason to choose one instead of another. Therefore, collocations with this type of verb are particularly tricky for learners of English. For example, consider the following possibilities:

1 *Your friend asks about what to do in a difficult situation:*
   a *You do advice.*   b *You give advice.*   c *You make advice.*

2 *Something is causing problems. You want to tell someone about this:*
   a *You do a complaint.*   b *You give a complaint.*   c *You make a complaint.*

3 *There are two things you can choose from. You choose one. Therefore:*
   a *You do a choice.*   b *You give a choice.*   c *You make a choice.*

4 *Your teacher asks you to write an essay:*
   a *You do the assignment.*   b *You get the assignment.*   c *You make the assignment.*

The correct collocations in these examples are:

1 You *give* advice. | 2 You *make* a complaint. | 3 You *make* a choice. | 4 You *do* an assignment.

Because it is often difficult to know which is the right collocation to use with a word, this dictionary gives special attention to collocations. It includes a large number of boxes which supply explanations and examples to help you understand the most important collocations. Below is an example of the COLLOCATIONS box for *test*:

COLLOCATIONS

verbs

to take a test (*also* **to do a test** *BrE*) *All students have to take a test in English.*

COMMON ERRORS

⚠ Do not say 'make a test'. Say **take a test** or **do a test**.

to give sb a test *Shall I give you a test on your vocabulary?*

to pass/fail a test (=to succeed in it, or to not succeed) *All the children passed the maths test.*

to do well/badly in a test *BrE*, **to do well/badly on a test** *AmE* *I didn't do very well in the chemistry test.*

types of test

a biology/history etc test *I got 80% in the geography test.*

a spelling/reading/listening test *Part of the exam is a listening test.*

a written test *The written test involves doing two short essays.*

a driving test *When are you taking your driving test?*

Collocations and meaning

The kind of collocations that go with a verb can tell you something about its true meaning. For example, the verb *cause* sounds neutral, but it is very often used with nouns that concern bad events. The following words are common collocations of *cause*:

problems	death	concern	alarm
trouble	damage	harm	disease
cancer	difficulties	pain	injury

Because *cause* is mainly used when talking about bad events, we can say that this word has a 'negative connotation'. Not all words have positive or negative connotations, but it is worthwhile to watch out for this possibility when learning and using collocations.

For other events, for example *changes*, *improvements*, or *developments*, you usually use the phrasal verb *bring about*:

The Internet has brought about big changes in the way we live our lives.
The treatment brought about some improvement in his condition.

For feelings, such as *interest*, *curiosity*, *concern*, *suspicion*, or *anger*, you often use the verb *arouse*, for example:

The announcement aroused concern in Washington.
The film aroused a lot of interest when it was first shown at the Cannes Film Festival.

In these last two sentences, you can use *cause* instead of *arouse*. However, if you vary the language you use, and use collocations such as *arouse* or *bring about*, your English will sound much more natural and fluent.

Collocations can also be different for words depending on their word class (part of speech). Let us consider the case of *border*. In the noun form, it has the collocations you might expect from its meaning of 'the official line that separates two countries or states':

border guards
border town
border crossing
border region
border patrol
German/Russian border

However, the verb form *(be) bordering* is different. About half of the cases of *bordering* are followed by the preposition *on*. With *bordering + on*, we find a very different type of collocation:

bordering on hysteria	bordering on arrogance	bordering on chaos
bordering on bad taste	bordering on contempt	bordering on cruelty
bordering on obsession	bordering on apathy	bordering on insanity

If we look at all of the cases of *bordering on* in a large language database, we find that about 70% of them have some kind of negative collocation, such as in the examples above. This points out that different members of a word family (e.g. noun, verb) may have different sets of common collocations.

Collocation form

Collocation partners can occur next to each other, or they can be several words apart.

> breathe + deeply

*You should **breathe deeply** and relax.*
*She forced herself to **breathe deeply**.*

*After the shock, she needed to **breathe** in **deeply**.*
*She managed to **breathe** more **deeply** after sitting down.*

*The doctor asked him to **breathe** slowly and **deeply**.*
*Yoga taught her to **breathe** softly but **deeply**.*

Collocations can also occur either before or after their partner.

> shining + stars

*Her happy eyes were **shining** like **stars**.*
*He was amazed at the number of **shining stars** in the night.*
*She tried to count all the **stars shining** in the winter sky.*
*The peaceful **stars** were **shining** overhead.*
*The **stars** are always **shining** when you are around.*

Language notes

Synonyms and antonyms

Synonyms

When you are introduced to a new word, your teacher or textbook may often link the new word to a synonym that you already know. For example, you may be told that *sad* is the same as *unhappy*. However, although synonyms are words that are similar, there are normally key differences in their meanings and how they are actually used in speech and writing.

There are several ways that synonyms might differ from one another:

- The words are not used about the same things - you say *a sad song*, not 'an unhappy song'. You say *an unhappy marriage*, not 'a sad marriage'.
- One word has a wide meaning, whereas the other word has a more specific meaning. For example, *unhappy* has a very wide meaning, but *homesick* has a much more specific meaning - you are *homesick* because you miss your family and friends.
- One word is only used in British or American English. For example, British people say *lift*, but American people say *elevator*.
- One word is more formal or informal than the other. For example, *accompany* sounds more formal than *go with*.
- One word sounds more polite than the other. For example, *elderly* sounds more polite than *old*.
- One word is used in technical or medical contexts, whereas the other is the word that ordinary people use. For example, a *contusion* is a medical word for a *bruise*.
- One word is much less frequent than the other. For example, *idle* is less frequent than *lazy*.

This means that it is important to treat synonyms with care. Try to find out how they are different from each other. The truth is that very few pairs of words can be used interchangeably in the same situations.

Exercise

Match the synonym pairs on the left with the descriptions on the right, which explain why they are not interchangeable. The first one has been done for you:

1	a apartment	b <u>flat</u>	one is British English
2	a mad	b angry	one is more informal
3	a examine	b look at	one is more formal
4	a die	b pass away	one is more polite
5	a respiration	b breathing	one is technical
6	a determined	b stubborn	one is disapproving
7	a give	b donate	one is used especially about money or blood

Answers
1b 2a 3a 4b 5a 6b 7b

Antonyms

The most common definition of **antonyms** is that they are opposites. In fact, there are three main ways that words can be antonyms.

1 Both things cannot be true at the same time. For example, you cannot be both:

> *alive and dead*   *married and single*   *male and female*

2 When two things are mentioned in the opposite order, but both describe the same relationship. In the example '*John **bought** the car from Sam.*' and '*Sam **sold** the car to John.*', both sentences describe the same event. Other examples include:
   * *parent/child, husband/wife, employer/employee*
   * *X is **below** Y/Y is **above** X*
   * *Karen **lent** Chris some money./Chris **borrowed** some money from Karen.*

3 Graded antonyms like *hot* and *cold* are opposites on a scale.

> | freezing | cold | cool | lukewarm | warm | hot | boiling |
> |---|---|---|---|---|---|---|
> ←————————————————————————————————————→

As you can see, this scale goes from *freezing* (=very cold) to *boiling* (=very hot).

Another feature of antonyms is that one word in the pair will be more common. If I want to know the size of something, I will ask, '*How big is your car?*' This does not mean I think your car is big; instead, *big* is used to represent the concept of size. I will not say, '*How small is your car?*' unless I already know that your car is small.

> **Which is more common?**
>
> 1 a How narrow is X?   b How wide is X?
>
> 2 a Is the office busy?   b Is the office quiet?
>
> 3 a How young is your sister?   b How old is your sister?

Answers
1b 2a 3b

Because words like *free* have more than one meaning, they may have more than one antonym.

free gift – expensive gift   *free movement – controlled movement*
free day – busy day   *pain-free – painful*

> **What are the opposites for *hard* and *mild*?**
>
> a hard worker   e mild shampoo
>
> b hard time   f mild weather
>
> c hard chair   g mild heart attack
>
> d hard decisions   h mild flavour

Answers
a lazy worker   b easy time   c soft chair   d easy decisions
e harsh shampoo   f cold weather   g severe heart attack   h spicy flavour

Thesaurus

One of the main benefits of building a larger vocabulary is that it will enable you to be more precise. In other words, you'll be able to say exactly what you want to say instead of being limited to simple ideas because you don't have the vocabulary you need.

A helpful tool for finding more precise words is a **thesaurus**. A thesaurus is normally a book or an online resource that provides lists of words and their synonyms. However, a list of synonyms is not very useful if you do not know the meanings of each of the words and what makes them different from one another.

This dictionary goes one step further than a normal thesaurus by including THESAURUS boxes which provide synonym lists with their meanings. Take a look at the one for *decide*.

Imagine you are writing a report about a project and you want to show that all the members of your team took part in deciding things. Look at the THESAURUS box for *decide* and choose which word best completes the sentence below.

> *After several hours of discussion, the committee finally _____ .*

The answer is *came to a decision* because this phrase often includes the idea of 'a group of people making a decision after discussing it'. *Make up your mind* also

> **THESAURUS**
>
> **decide** to make a choice to do something: *We decided to celebrate by having a party.*
> **make up your mind** *especially spoken* to decide something, especially after thinking about it for a long time: *I can't make up my mind what to wear.*
> **choose to do sth** to decide to do something – especially when this is different from what people expect or tell you to do: *She chose to ignore my advice.*
> **make a decision** to decide after thinking carefully, especially about something very important: *Have you made a decision about where you want to go to university?*
> **come to/reach a decision** to decide about something important after discussing or considering it – used especially about groups of people: *The jury took several hours to reach a decision.*

includes the idea of 'taking time over the decision', but is more commonly used in spoken conversation, so cannot be used in a written report and is usually only used about one person.

Look up the following words in your dictionary:

1 *government* – *Which synonyms are disapproving?*
2 *healthy* – *Which synonym describes someone who goes to the gym daily?*
3 *job* – *Which synonym is best if you wish to advertise a job in the newspaper?*
4 *lonely* – *Which synonym is best to describe someone who is lonely because they miss their friends?*

Language notes

Another reason synonyms are not equal to each other is because they do not share the same grammatical behaviour. Take a look at the THESAURUS box for *force*. Notice the differences in the grammatical patterns that follow each synonym.

THESAURUS

force sb to do sth to make someone do something they do not want to do - used when a person or a situation does this: *She was forced to marry him.* | *The bad weather forced us to stay indoors.*
make sb do sth to force someone to do something, especially using threats or violence: *The men made us lie down on the floor.*
put pressure on sb to keep trying to force someone to do something by making them feel that they should do it: *Don't put pressure on your child to study all the time.*
compel to make you feel that you must do something, or to officially force someone to do something: *I felt compelled to leave.* | *No one can compel you to do it.*

Complete the following sentences using the word *force* or one of its synonyms. You need to pay attention to both meaning and the grammar patterns.

5 *The woman's parents _____ on her to give up her studies and get married.*

6 *Health officials _____ the restaurant to close its doors until it improved its cleanliness.*

7 *The government was _____ to rescue the banks to prevent further damage to the economy.*

8 *Our parents always _____ us clean our plates at dinner or else we had to go straight to bed.*

When choosing a synonym you also have to be aware of register. Register concerns whether a word is formal or informal and whether it is most commonly used in spoken or written English. The THESAURUS boxes in your dictionary give you this information. For example, here is the THESAURUS box for *approximately*.

THESAURUS

approximately a little more or less than an exact number, amount etc: *Birmingham is approximately 100 miles from London.*
about/around approximately. **About** and **around** are much more common than **approximately** in everyday spoken English: *I'll be back at about 5:30.*
roughly approximately - used especially when the exact number or amount is not very important: *We're expecting roughly 100 people to come.*
or so *informal* used after a number or amount to show that it may be a little more or less: *I'm going on holiday in a month or so.*

Decide whether the sentences below are most likely to be spoken or written.

9 *The room was very crowded. I'd guess there were roughly 75 people in a room designed for 50.*

10 *The company announced that it would increase its workforce by approximately 10% by the end of the year.*

Answers
1 regime, dictatorship 2 fit 3 vacancy, position 4 homesick 5 put pressure (on sb)
6 forced (sb to do sth) 7 compelled 8 made (sb do sth) 9 spoken 10 written

Phrases and idioms

Although we think of dictionaries as focusing on single words, sometimes understanding meaning requires recognizing groups of words that go together to create one meaning. These can be **phrases** or **idioms**.

An **idiom** is a group of words that together create one meaning. What makes idioms special, though, is that the meaning of the whole idiom cannot be worked out from the meaning of the individual words.

Special meanings

The following sentences contain idioms. If you do not know the meanings, you can look each one up in the dictionary.

The birthday party was no longer a surprise because Alice accidentally **spilled** *the beans yesterday. (=told the secret)*

Use the key word and look up the phrase using that word.

Stephanie is in the **doghouse** *because she forgot to pick up the tickets for the concert.*
I can't put my **finger** *on what's wrong with Steve. He's been acting strangely all day.*
There were a lot of **raised** *eyebrows when Sharon was promoted instead of Alan.*

Fixed forms

Idioms are also different from other phrases because they often have a fixed word order, i.e. the words cannot be changed or moved around as easily as they can be in phrases that are not idioms.

We searched high and low, but we couldn't find Emma's doll.
⚠ We can't say 'low and high' or 'tall and low'.

Annie asked me to keep the news of her engagement under my hat *until she had told her parents.*
⚠ We can say *keep something under your hat*; we don't say 'keep something <u>in</u> your hat' or '<u>put</u> something under your hat'. If we changed these words, the phrase would lose its idiomatic meaning.

Some idioms, however, do have some flexibility. One part of the idiom sometimes uses different words. *Have something up your sleeve* can also be *have a trick up your sleeve* or *have an ace up your sleeve*. All of these mean 'to have a secret plan that you will use later'.

We might say something expensive *costs the earth*. But we can also say *I paid the earth* or *I was charged the earth*.

Frequency

The biggest difference between idioms and single words is how often they occur. Taken as a group, there are a lot of idioms in the English language; however, any single idiom is not very frequent. Therefore, although idioms are fun to study, you need to take care about when to use them. Learning to use idioms requires paying attention to the same aspects of word knowledge that you saw for single words.

For example, *to sit on the fence*, which means you avoid saying which side of an argument you support or what you think is the best thing to do, is normally used to describe someone in a negative way. This is connotation.

Idioms are more common in informal conversation and newspaper language (especially tabloid newspapers) than in other areas of language use. *To get the sack* is an informal way of saying someone has lost his or her job. They are much less common in formal writing, for example in essays and formal academic writing.

Put the idioms you want to learn into your vocabulary notebook and follow the same tips as for learning single words.

Other types of phrases

Many phrases are useful for building sentences and organizing talk and writing. The following phrases and others like them are very commonly used and so are useful to learn.

Functional phrases

To introduce a new topic or idea: *Guess what?, First of all, ...*
To show agreement: *I see what you mean, That's a good point.*
To clarify: *What I mean is, What I'm trying to say is, How shall I put it?*
To summarize: *To make a long story short, In a nutshell, On the whole, ...*
To end a conversation: *That's about it/all there is to it, I've got to run now, It's been great talking to you.*

Sentence frames

These are different ways of starting a sentence and make you sound more fluent:

It's amazing how ...	*I think that ...*	*I want to make it clear that ...*
It seems to me ...	*What I mean is ...*	*Let's see ...*

Fluency markers

These hold your place in a conversation and make you sound more fluent:

you know	*by and large*	*if you see what I mean*
and so on	*at any rate*	*as I was saying*

Word families

Most words are part of a 'family' of words that share a core meaning. For example, the words *agree* (verb) and *agreement* (noun) are related. When reading and listening, it is important to recognize that words such as *permit* (noun) and *permission* (adjective) represent the same meaning. When choosing which word to use, it is important to know whether an idea can be expressed as a noun, verb, adjective, or adverb, because using a different word family member creates a different emphasis and enables greater flexibility of expression. For example:

> She spent two weeks in London **promoting** her new book. (the emphasis is on 'she')
> The **promotional** tour for her new book included two weeks in London. (the emphasis is on the tour)

When looking up words from the same family in your dictionary, look at the words above and below your key word. Sometimes word family members will not be next to each other in the dictionary because of their spelling. For example, *habitual* is separated from *habit* by three words. Be careful, some words that are near to your key word and share a similar spelling may not be part of the same word family, because they do not have a shared meaning. *Hardly* means something very different from *hard*.

The beginning of each word in a family is the same (we call this the **root**) and it is the endings that change. The spelling of word families changes by adding or dropping a suffix from the root. Common suffixes that change the part of speech include **-ize**, **-ness**, and **-ly**:

verb	→	noun	suffix	adj	→	verb	suffix	noun	→	adj	suffix
appear		appearance	-ance	stable		stabilize	-ize	plenty		plentiful	-ful
describe		description	-tion	dominant		dominate	-ate	economy		economic	-ic
assess		assessment	-ment	intense		intensify	-ify	industry		industrial	-al

Look at the table below and fill in the missing parts of the word family for each word. The first word family has been done for you.

	noun	adjective	verb	adverb
1	explosion	explosive	**explode**	✗
2	....	**possible**	✗	....
3	....	....	**satisfy**	....
4	**nation**	....	....	....
5	**memory**	....	....	....
6	....	**popular**	....	....

Answers

1 possibility, **possible**, possibly   3 satisfaction, satisfactory, **satisfy**, satisfactorily   4 nation, national, nationalize, nationally   5 **memory**, memorable, memorize, memorably   6 popularity, **popular**, popularize, popularly   2 possibility, possibly

Writing essays

Starting the essay

In your introduction you can:

Emphasize that this is an important subject

*Climate change is **one of the most important issues** facing the world today.*

*Terrorism is **probably the biggest** threat to our democracy.*

Make a general statement about this subject

***It is a well-known fact** that smoking causes cancer.*

***There is no doubt that** digital technology has had a big effect on our lives.*

Say what many people think

***For many people**, their car is not a luxury but a necessity.*

***Most scientists would agree that** alcohol is bad for your health.*

***It is often claimed that** the best things in life are free.*

Quote the opinion of a famous person

It is often a good idea to begin with a quotation, which tells the reader more about an important theme of your essay.

*John F Kennedy **once said that** although he was born in America, he had always been a citizen of the world.*

***In the words of** Barack Obama, 'Change does not happen overnight.'*

Mention the overall theme of your essay

***In this essay, I will argue that** we need to deal with the causes of terrorism, as well as the terrorists themselves.*

***In this essay, I will examine** the relationship between violence in films and in real life.*

Organizing the essay

Ordering

It is important to present your points in a clear logical order, so that the reader can understand your argument.

In your essay, you can order the points using numbers, for example:

There are many reasons for reducing our dependence on cars.

***Firstly/First of all**, cars cause huge amounts of pollution. Almost a third of all atmospheric pollution comes from road transport.*

***Secondly**, you can get much more exercise if you leave your car at home. Many regular car users are very unfit.*

***Thirdly**, our roads are becoming full with cars. It is often quicker to use public transport.*

Be careful not to use too many numbers. This looks repetitive. Do not say 'fourthly' or 'fifthly'. Other phrases you can use are:

> **To begin with**, *driving may seem like a cheap form of transport, but there are also big environmental costs.*

> **In addition/Furthermore/Moreover**, *studies have shown that there is a link between pollution from cars and childhood illnesses such as asthma.*

> **Finally/Lastly**, *it is becoming impossible to escape noise pollution from cars.*

Give both sides of the argument

It is important to give a balanced view of the subject. When giving the other side of the argument you can use the following phrases:

> **However/Nevertheless/On the other hand**, *cars have also brought many benefits.*

> **It is also true that** *cars are an important part of our lives.*

> **Another way of looking at this issue** *is to imagine what the world would be like without cars.*

> **There is more than one way of looking at this problem.**

> *People say that driving brings people together. However,* **the opposite is also true**.

Other ways of mentioning important points

> **It should be noted/stressed that** *a lot of people's jobs depend on cars.*

> **This brings us to the question of** *whether there are any real alternatives to road transport in today's world.*

Writing a conclusion

In your conclusion, you should give a summary of the points you have made. You can use the following phrases:

> **In conclusion**, *there are many reasons for thinking that we need to move away from using cars.*

> **To sum up/summarize**, *cars have both good and bad points.*

> **On balance**, *although cars have many disadvantages, it is difficult to imagine a world without them.*

You can also end by giving your own personal opinion (see next section).

Expressing your personal opinion

You often give your own personal opinion at the end of the essay, after you have presented your arguments. In essays, you should avoid spoken expressions such as 'I think that'. Instead, it is better to use phrases such as:

> **In my opinion/view** (do not say 'according to my opinion'), *people should try to use their cars less, for the sake of the future of our planet.*

> **My (own) personal opinion/view** *is that there is no alternative to the car.*

> **It seems to me that** *driving has too big a cost to the environment.*

Sample essay

The common phrases have been highlighted, so that you can see how they are used.

Discuss the advantages and disadvantages of nuclear energy.

James Lovelock **once said that** nuclear power is 'the only green solution' to the problem of climate change. Considering the possible harmful effects of nuclear energy, it is interesting that one of the world's leading environmental scientists would make this statement. **In this essay, I will examine some of the reasons** why some people consider nuclear power to be so useful and other people think it is so dangerous.

First of all then, why is nuclear energy so attractive at this time? **To begin with**, it is much cleaner than oil or coal, because it does not produce carbon gases. These carbon gases are responsible for global warming, which **is probably the biggest problem facing the world today**.

Secondly, nuclear energy is much more reliable than wind energy or solar power. Although these alternative sources of energy are very safe, they cannot be used to provide power 24 hours a day, for obvious reasons.

Lastly, nuclear energy does not use up large quantities of the earth's natural resources. One day, we will run out of oil. Modern nuclear reactors produce as much plutonium as they use, giving an inexhaustible supply of energy. These reactors are known as 'breeder reactors'.

On the other hand, nuclear power also has some big disadvantages. When nuclear energy was being developed, one of its first uses was for making the nuclear weapons that were dropped on Hiroshima. The horror of these events showed the destructive power of this form of energy.

In addition, there is no completely safe way of dealing with nuclear waste. This can remain radioactive for hundreds of thousands of years. Although nuclear energy may seem cheap now, it is not cheap when one takes into account the cost of storing nuclear waste. **This is the most important issue** for people who have doubts about the safety of nuclear energy.

In conclusion, although many people may not like the idea of using nuclear energy, it may be the only way of saving the planet, because of the disastrous effects of climate change. **For this reason**, nuclear energy is seen as a necessary evil. **My own personal view** is that it seems sensible to also find ways of reducing our use of energy, and to use alternative sources of energy such as wind power and solar power as much as possible.

(NB This essay is purely illustrative and does not necessarily represent the views of Pearson Longman.)

Writing letters, emails, and text messages

Informal letters and emails

Beginning an informal email	*Hi* + first name *Hi* When you are replying, you often go straight into the message, without mentioning the other person's name.
Beginning an informal letter	*Dear* + first name You write your address and the date in the top right-hand corner of the letter.
Useful phrases	*(It was) good to hear from you.* *Thanks for your letter.* *Hope you are well.* *How are you?/How are things with you?* *Sorry I haven't written/been in touch.* *It was good/great to see you* last weekend. *We're having a great time* in Paris. *I've got some (good/great) news.* *Just a quick note to* say I'll be back on Monday. *I was wondering if* you wanted to meet up some time. *Let me know when* you're free. *Hope to see you soon./Look forward to seeing you soon.* *Write soon./Keep in touch.* *It would be great to have your news.* *Give my love/regards/best wishes to* your family.
Ending an informal email or letter	*All the best/Best* *Best wishes* *Regards* (slightly more formal) *Love/Lots of love* (only to close friends and family) *See you soon* *Take care* then your first name. In informal emails, you can end by writing just the first letter of your first name, for example J (=Joanna). If you want to add after this, you use *PS*. *PS Hope you like your present.*

⊠

Hi Joanna

How are things with you? Sorry I haven't been in touch lately. I've been really busy with my exams.

I've got some news – I'm planning to start an English course in London in September. I was wondering if you wanted to meet up some time? It would be great to see you again. Let me know when you're free.

All the best

Abdul

PS Please give my best wishes to your family.

⊠

Hi. Good to hear from you. I'm OK. I've just applied for my first job – hope I get it!

It will be great to see you again. Give me a call nearer the time. My mobile number is 0555 55557. You must come and stay with us when you're here.

See you very soon

Take care

J

Formal letters and emails

Beginning a formal letter or email	Write your address and then the date, in the top right-hand corner of the letter. Write the name of the person you are writing to and their address below this on the left. **Dear Mr Jones/Dr Smith/Professor Cox** **Dear Sir or Madam** (used when you do not know the person's name) **To whom it may concern** (more formal - used when you do not know the person's name)
Useful phrases	**I am writing to enquire about** English courses at your college. **I am writing in response to** the advertisement in today's 'Times'. **I am writing to apply for the position of** sales assistant, which was advertised in yesterday's 'Guardian'. **I am writing to inform you that** I would like to accept your offer of a place at Warford College. **I am writing to complain** about the standard of service at your hotel. **I would be most grateful if you could** reserve a double room for me for the nights of Friday April 7th and Saturday April 8th. **Further to** your letter of July 20th, I am pleased to accept your invitation. **I am afraid that/I regret that** I will be unable to attend the meeting. **I enclose/Please find enclosed** a cheque for $200. **Please accept my apologies for** not having contacted you earlier. **I look forward to hearing from you soon.** **Please do not hesitate to contact me** if you require any further information. **May I take this opportunity to thank you** for your interest in our college. **Thank you for your kind attention.** **Thank you in advance for** your help. **I can be contacted at** the above address or on 0555 55557.
Ending a formal letter or email	**Yours sincerely** (*BrE*) - when you began with the person's family name **Yours faithfully** (*BrE*) - when you do not know the person's name **Sincerely (yours)/Yours truly** (*AmE*)

Tips when writing formal letters

⚠ Do not say 'Dear Mr' with no name. If you do not know a man's name, say *Dear Sir*. For a woman, say *Dear Madam*.

⚠ Do not say 'Dear Mr Tom Jones'. Say *Dear Mr Jones*.

⚠ Do not say 'Dear Mr Manager/Mrs Receptionist'. Just say *Dear* + the person's name, or *Dear Sir or Madam* if you do not know their name.

⚠ Do not use short forms such as 'don't' or 'can't'. Use the full form *do not* or *cannot*.

22 Browntree Road
Manor Green
London N63 0QT
3rd July 2009

Human Resources Department
Eatham Publishing
89 Eatham Rd
London SW29 9HQ

Dear Sir or Madam

I am writing to apply for the post of junior designer, which was advertised in yesterday's '*Independent*'. I enclose my curriculum vitae.
I have just completed a two-year course in graphic design at Warford College and I think this job would be an excellent opportunity for me to begin my career as a graphic designer.

Yours faithfully

Joanna Lucas

Joanna Lucas (Ms)

Human Resources Department
Eatham Publishing
89 Eatham Rd
London SW29 9HQ
10th July 2009

Ms Joanna Lucas
22 Browntree Road
Manor Green
London N63 0QT

Dear Ms Lucas

Thank you for your enquiry about the post of junior designer. I am pleased to inform you that you have been selected for an interview on Monday 20th July at 3 pm.
Could you let me know as soon as possible if you will be able to attend the interview?

Yours sincerely

Paul Martin

Paul Martin
Human Resources Director, Eatham Publishing

Language notes

Text messages

Text messages and some emails are written very quickly, using abbreviations for words and phrases.

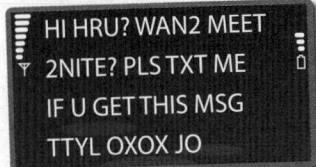

HI HRU? WAN2 MEET
2NITE? PLS TXT ME
IF U GET THIS MSG
TTYL OXOX JO

This means:
'Hi. How are you? Do you want to meet tonight? Please text me if you get this message. Talk to you later. Hugs and kisses. Jo'

Abbreviations

2 = to, too
2DAY = today
2MORO = tomorrow
2NITE = tonight
4 = for
B = be
B4 = before
BF = boyfriend or best friend
BRB = be right back
    (=I will come back soon)
BTW = by the way
CU = see you
GF = girlfriend
GR8 = great
HRU = how are you?
ILU = I love you
L8R/CUL8R = see you later
LOL = laugh out loud/lots of love
MSG = message
OMG = oh my God (=I'm very surprised)
OXOX = hugs and kisses
PLS = please

R = are
ROTFL = rolling on the floor laughing
    (=that was very funny)
SPK = speak
SUM = some
SUM1 = someone
THX or TX = thanks
TTYL = talk to you later
TXT ME = text me
U = you
U2 = you too
UR = you are
W8 = wait
WAN2 = want to
WKND = weekend
XLNT = excellent
:-) = I'm happy
:-> = I'm very happy
:-(= I'm sad
:-< = I'm very sad
:-O = I'm surprised
:-* = kiss

Word building

Prefixes and suffixes

A **prefix** is a short group of letters found at the beginning of some words, which gives the word a particular meaning. For example, **un-** is a prefix that means *not*, as in *unhealthy* (=not healthy) or *unhelpful* (=not helpful).

A **suffix** is a short group of letters found at the end of some words, which gives the word a particular meaning. A common suffix is **-less**, meaning *without*, as in *painless* (=without any pain) or *hopeless* (=without any hope).

Some words contain both a prefix and a suffix. For example, *unrecognizable* contains both the prefix **un-** (=not) and the suffix **-able** (=able to be ...), giving the meaning 'not able to be recognized'.

Often the suffix makes a word change its part of speech. For example, the noun *realization* contains the verb *realize* and the suffix **-ation** (=the act of ...), giving the meaning 'the act of realizing that something is true'. The adverb *easily* contains the adjective *easy* and the suffix **-ly** (=in a ... way), giving the meaning 'in an easy way'.

Word formation using prefixes and suffixes

The tables below show you how new meanings and new parts of speech can be created using prefixes and suffixes.

Noun formation

Noun beginnings (Prefixes)	Meaning	Examples
anti-	used to prevent something	antifreeze, antiseptic
bio-	relating to life and living things	biology, biochemistry
co-	with or together	co-worker, co-author
eco-	relating to the environment	ecology, ecosystem
ex-	former, in the past	ex-husband, ex-girlfriend
inter-	between or among	intersection, interference
mid-	middle	midday, midnight, midweek
mis-	bad or wrong	misspelling, mismanagement
non-	not	non-smoker, nonsense
over-	too much	overgrowth, overpopulation
psycho-	relating to the mind	psychology, psychotherapy
self-	of or by yourself	self-confidence, self-control
semi-	half	semi-circle, semi-detached
sub-	1 under 2 less important or smaller	submarine, subconscious, subway subcommittee, subsection

Language notes

Noun endings (Suffixes)	Meaning	Examples
-ability, -ibility	when sth is possible *(makes nouns from adjectives)*	reliability, flexibility, responsibility
-al	used to say that sb/sth does sth or sth happens *(makes nouns from verbs)*	arrival, refusal, denial
-an **-ian**	a particular person, place or subject *(makes nouns from names)*	American, Christian, historian
-ation	when sb does sth or sth happens *(makes nouns from verbs)*	creation, confirmation, hesitation, exploration
-ator	sb or sth that does or makes something *(makes nouns from verbs)*	creator, generator, administrator, investigator
-cy	used in the names of qualities *(makes nouns from adjectives)*	fluency, accuracy, decency
-er, -or, -ar, -r	1 a person who does an activity 2 a person who lives in a place 3 a thing that does something	footballer, actor, liar Londoner, New Zealander heater, cooler, computer
-ful	the amount that a container holds	spoonful, cupful, handful
-ist	1 sb who supports a particular set of ideas or beliefs 2 sb who plays a particular musical instrument 3 sb who does a particular activity or type of work	idealist, communist, leftist, environmentalist violinist, pianist, cellist, guitarist novelist, journalist, geologist, motorist, cyclist
-ity **-ty**	used in the names of qualities or types of behaviour *(makes nouns from adjectives)*	stupidity, brutality, cruelty, beauty, anxiety
-let	a small kind of a particular thing	piglet, booklet
-ment	1 an activity or way of doing sth 2 a particular quality *(makes nouns from verbs)*	development, entertainment embarrassment, amusement, contentment
-ness	used in the names of qualities *(makes nouns from adjectives)*	happiness, goodness, loudness, quietness
-ology	the science or study of sth	psychology, sociology, biology
-ship	1 a situation between people or organizations 2 a skill or ability to do sth well	friendship, partnership, relationship craftsmanship, musicianship
-ware	used in the names of particular kinds of goods	hardware, software, glassware, silverware
-y	used in the names of feelings	jealousy, sympathy

Language notes

Adjective formation

Adjective beginnings (Prefixes)	Meaning	Examples
anti-	1 opposed to 2 opposite to	antinuclear anticlockwise
cross-	going across or between	cross-country, cross-cultural
dis-	not	discontented, disapproving
eco-	relating to the environment	ecofriendly
extra-	beyond or outside, or not included in something	extracurricular, extramarital, extraordinary
in- **im-** before b, m, p **il-** before l **ir-** before r	not	inexact, incorrect impossible, imprecise illegal, illegible irregular, irresponsible
inter-	between or among	international, interpersonal
multi-	having many of something	multinational, multimedia
non-	not	nonstop, non-smoking
over-	1 too much 2 across or above	overexcited, overemotional overland, overseas, overhead
post-	after or later than	postwar, postgraduate
pre-	before or earlier than	pre-existing, prehistoric
trans-	across or on the other side of	transatlantic
ultra-	1 very, extremely sth 2 beyond	ultramodern ultrasonic
un-	not	uncomfortable, unhappy

Adjective endings (Suffixes)	Meaning	Examples
-able **-ible**	1 able to be (broken, drunk, washed etc) 2 having a particular quality *(makes adjectives from verbs)*	breakable, drinkable, washable reasonable, responsible
-al **-ial**	relating to something	political, ceremonial, facial
-an **-ian**	relating to a particular person, place, or subject	American, Christian, civilian, reptilian
-ed	1 having a particular thing 2 having a particular quality	bearded, armed big-headed, bored
-en	made of something	wooden, golden, silken
-er	makes the comparative of short adjectives	hotter, cooler, nearer, bigger, safer

Language notes

-est	makes the superlative of short adjectives	hottest, coolest, nearest, biggest
-ish	1 relating to a country, its language or its people 2 like or typical of 3 quite or slightly 4 approximately, about	British, Spanish, Swedish childish, impish, boyish smallish, greenish sixish, fortyish
-ive	used to say that sb or sth does or is able to do sth (*makes adjectives from verbs*)	creative, communicative, cooperative, supportive
-less	without	hopeless, childless, painless
-like	like or typical of (*makes adjectives from nouns*)	childlike, lifelike, godlike
-ly	1 behaving in a way that is typical of a particular kind of person 2 happening regularly	friendly, motherly, fatherly hourly, weekly, monthly
-most	makes the superlative of some adjectives	topmost, northernmost, uppermost
-ous	having a particular quality	dangerous, spacious, envious
-th	makes adjectives from numbers (apart from numbers which end in 1, 2, 3)	sixth, hundredth, ninth, fortieth
-y	covered in sth or having a lot of sth, or having a particular quality	dirty, dusty, cloudy, rainy, noisy, windy, smelly, greedy

Verb formation

Verb beginnings (Prefixes)	Meaning	Examples
de-	to remove or reduce sth	decaffeinate, devalue
dis-	1 to not do sth 2 to remove sth	disagree, disapprove, disobey disconnect, disinfect
mis-	to do sth badly or wrongly	misunderstand, misinterpret
re-	to make or do sth again	rethink, remake, redo, reinvent
trans-	1 to change sth completely 2 to move sth to a new place	translate, transform transfer, transport
un-	to remove or unfasten sth	undress, unlock, untie

Language notes

Verb endings (Suffixes)	Meaning	Examples
-en	to become or make sth become	darken, soften, lighten
-ize, -ise *(BrE)* **-ize** *(AmE)*	to become or make sth become	popularize, legalize, modernize, harmonize
-ify	to give sth a particular quality	solidify, simplify, purify

Adverb formation

Because most adverbs are formed from adjectives, they can take the same beginnings as adjectives.

Adverb endings (Suffixes)	Meaning	Examples
-er, -r	makes the comparative of adverbs	later, sooner, farther
-est, -st	makes the superlative of adverbs	latest, soonest, farthest
-ly	1 in a particular way *(makes adverbs from adjectives)* 2 happening regularly *(makes adverbs from nouns)*	carefully, slowly, easily, fully, freely, impatiently hourly, daily, weekly
-ward, -wards	in a particular direction	northward(s), backward(s)

Note that there are a small number of adverbs which do not have the same meaning as the adjectives they were formed from. You should look these up in the dictionary and learn them:

awfully ≠ awful + ly   **lately** ≠ late + ly   **terribly** ≠ terrible + ly
barely ≠ bare + ly   **shortly** ≠ short + ly   **scarcely** ≠ scarce + ly
hardly ≠ hard + ly

Numbers and measurements

How numbers are spoken

Numbers over 100

101	a hundred and one
110	a hundred (and) ten

> **Note**
> British speakers say *'a hundred and ten/eleven etc'*. American speakers often leave out the *'and'*.

200	two hundred (Do not say 'two hundreds'.)
895	eight hundred (and) ninety-five
1,001	a thousand and one
1,201	one thousand two hundred and one, or twelve hundred and one
1,538	one thousand, five hundred (and) thirty-eight, or fifteen hundred (and) thirty-eight
2,052	two thousand (and) fifty-two
100,000	a hundred thousand
1,000,000	a million
1,000,000,000	a billion

> **Note**
> You can say *'a hundred/a thousand etc'* or *'one hundred/one thousand etc'*. *'A hundred/a thousand'* is more common.

Phone numbers and credit card numbers

01279 623623   oh one two seven nine six two three six two three

> **Note**
> You say *'0'* as *'oh'* or *'zero'*.

2277766 double two treble seven double six

> **Note**
> People often say *'66'* as *'double six'*. People often say *'777'* as *'treble seven'* or *'triple seven'*.

If you phone someone's office, you often need to ask for his or her extension number: *Can I have extension 3901 (=three nine zero one)?*

Ordinal numbers

These are numbers that tell you the 'order' of things:

1st	first
2nd	second
3rd	third
4th	fourth
21st	twenty-first
100th	hundredth

Fractions and decimals

½	(a) half
2½	two and a half

> **Note**
> Do not say *'two hours and a half'*. Say *two and a half hours*.

⅓	a third/one-third
⅔	two-thirds
0.1	(nought) point one
5.86	five point eight six

Mathematical calculations

$3 + 8 = 11$	Three plus eight is eleven.
$8 - 3 = 5$	Eight minus three equals five.
$17 \times 6 = 102$	Seventeen multiplied by six is a hundred and two.
$57 \div 3 = 19$	Fifty-seven divided by three is nineteen.
3% of $200 = 6$	Three per cent of two hundred is six.

Note

'='

In everyday English, you say *'is'*.
In more technical English, you say *'equals'*.

'×'

In everyday English, you say *'times'*.
In more technical English, you say *'multiplied by'*.
When multiplying combinations of numbers up to 12, you can say, for example, *Seven sixes are forty-two.* or *Two fours are eight.*

$\sqrt{16} = 4$ The square root of sixteen is four.
$\sqrt[3]{16} = 2$ The cube root of sixteen is two.
$10^2 = 100$ Ten squared is a hundred.
$10^5 = 1,000,000$ Ten to the power (of) five is a million.

Dates

2009   two thousand and nine
2010   two thousand (and) ten *or* twenty ten
2012   two thousand and twelve *or* twenty twelve
1987   nineteen eighty-seven
1903   nineteen-oh-three
1800   eighteen hundred
the 1960s/the '60s
          the nineteen sixties/the sixties (the period between 1960 and 1969)
the 1840s
          the eighteen forties (the period between 1840 and 1849)

Times

12.00   twelve o'clock. You can also say 'midday' or 'noon', or 'midnight'.
12.30   half past twelve *or* twelve thirty
7.15   a quarter past seven. American speakers often say 'a quarter after seven'. You can also say 'seven fifteen'. This sounds more formal.

7.45   a quarter to eight. American speakers often say 'a quarter of eight'. You can also say 'seven forty-five'.
9.05   five past nine. American speakers often say 'five after nine'. You can also say 'nine-oh-five'.

Note

You do not need to say *'minutes'* with times that have 5, 10, 20, 25 etc. With other numbers, you can say *'minutes'*, for example:
7.57 three minutes to eight
2.14 fourteen minutes past two

14.30   fourteen thirty
23.55   twenty-three fifty-five
4ish/7ish **etc** fourish/sevenish etc
          (=about four o'clock/seven o'clock)

Prices

£1   a pound
50p   fifty p (pronounced 'pee')
£1.50   one pound fifty
$1.80   a dollar eighty *or* a dollar and eighty cents
€2.60   two Euros sixty *or* two Euros sixty cents

Ages

The church is over 400 years old.
The whiskey is eight years old.
I'm 22.

Note

For people's ages, you usually just say *'I'm 18.'* (rather than the full phrase *'I'm 18 years old.'*).
You can use **six-year-old/ten-year-old** etc as an adjective: *a 15-year-old boy.*
Do not say *'a 15 years old boy'.*

Language notes

If you want to say roughly what someone's age is, you can say:

He's in his twenties (=between 21 and 29).
She's in her teens (=between 13 and 19).
He's in his late forties (=between 47 and 49).
My grandfather is in his early seventies (=between 71 and 73).
I'm in my mid-thirties (=between 34 and 36).

Heights

People:
I'm 5 ft 10. (=I'm five foot ten.)
She's 1 metre 62.
He's 6 ft tall.

> **Note**
> You usually say *'five foot'* rather than *'five feet'*.
> One foot = 30.48 cm.
> One inch = 2.54 cm.

Places:
Mount Everest is 29,000 ft high.
The town is 2,032 metres above sea level.

> **Note**
> You say that a person is *'six feet tall'* (you often leave out the word *'tall'*).
> You say that a building or mountain is *'1,000 feet high'*.

Weights

People:
He's 20 stone.
She's 120 lbs.
I'm 65 kilos.

> **Note**
> One kilo = 2.2 pounds/lbs.
> One stone = 14 pounds.
> British people usually use stones and pounds. American people usually use pounds.

Things:
I bought a kilo of tomatoes.

> **Note**
> British people usually use kilos.
> American people usually use pounds.

Clothes sizes

I'm a size 8/43. (=for shoes)
She's a size 14. (=for women's clothes)
He takes a 36 inch waist/leg. (=for trousers)

> **Note**
> You can say *I take a (size) 14.* or *I'm a (size) 14.*
> For most clothes, you usually say *I take a medium/large/small/extra-large*.
> You can also say *I'm an M/L/S/XL.*

Temperatures

It's 25°C (=twenty-five degrees Celsius).
The temperature fell to -14° (=minus fourteen).
The temperature is in the mid-eighties (=between 84 and 86 degrees Fahrenheit).
I had a temperature of 101°. (=I had a fever. Normal body temperature is 98.4°F.)

> **Note**
> British people use both Celsius and Fahrenheit. American people usually use Fahrenheit.

Scores

The score was 4-4 (=four-all).
United won the game 5-0 (=five-nil *BrE*, five-zero *AmE*).
She won the first set 6-3 (=six-three).
The score was 40-0 (=forty-love. This is used in tennis.).

Speeds

The maximum speed limit is 30 mph (=miles per hour).
The plane was travelling at 410 kph (=kilometres per hour).

Words that are numbers

Some words are written as numbers. Here are some common examples:

4x4 *noun* (four-by-four) a car or truck that has a four-wheel drive: *The streets are full of big 4x4s.*

18 *noun* a film that you must be 18 or over to watch: *It's an 18.*

24/7 *adverb* (twenty-four seven) If you do something 24/7, you do it all the time, twenty-four hours a day: *We're open for business 24/7.*

(See also **Text messages**, on page A34)

Weights and measures

Length

1 inch (in) = 2.54 centimetres (cm)
12 inches = 1 foot (ft) = 0.3048 metres (m)
3 feet = 1 yard (yd) = 0.9144 metres (m)
1,760 yards = 1 mile (m) = 1.609 kilometres (km)
The tunnel is 32 miles long.
The rug measures 8' by 5' 3" (=eight feet by five feet three inches or eight foot etc).

Area

1 square inch (sq in) = 6.4516 square centimetres (cm²)
1 square foot (sq ft) = 0.0929 square metres (m²)
1 square yard (sq yd) = 0.8361 square metres (m²)
1 acre = 4,047 square metres (m²)
1 square mile (sq m) = 259 (hectares/ ha)/2.59 km² (square kilometres/km²)
The total area of the United States is approximately 3.8 million square miles.
A typical house has a floor area of 90 m².

Cubic measurement

1 cubic inch (cu in) = 16.39 cubic centimetres (cm³/cc)
1 cubic foot (cu ft) = 0.02832 cubic metres (m³)
1 cubic yard (cu yd) = 0.7646 cubic centimetres (cm³)
The car has 35 cubic feet of luggage space.
a 694cc engine

Capacity

1 fluid ounce (fl oz) = 28.41 cubic centimetres (cm³/cc)
1 pint (pt) = 0.568 litres (UK)/0.473 litres (US)
1 quart (qt) = 2 pints = 1.136 litres (UK)/0.946 litres (US)
1 gallon (gal) = 8 pints = 45.46 litres (UK)/37.85 litres (US)

> **Note**
> American pints, quarts and gallons are smaller than British ones.

Can I have two pints of lager?
Our car does about 60 miles per gallon (=of petrol).

Weight

1 ounce (oz) = 28.35 grams (g)
1 pound (lb) = 0.4536 kilograms (kg)
1 stone (st) = 14 pounds = 6.35 kilograms (kg)
1 hundredweight (cwt) = 50.8 kilograms (kg)
1 ton = 1016.04 kilograms/1.01604 metric tonnes
Melt four ounces of butter in a pan.
The ship weighed over 80,000 tons.

Articles

The articles are **a/an** ('the indefinite article') and **the** ('the definite article').

a/an

You use **a** or **an**

- when talking about something for the first time:
  *Do you want to go to **a** concert?*

- when talking about a type of person or thing:
  *She wants to be **a** lawyer.* | *Sushi is **a** traditional Japanese dish.*

- when talking about one of several things or people, when it is not important to say which one:
  ***A** woman I work with told me about the concert.* (=one of the women I work with)

> **Note**
> You use **a**
> - when the next word begins with a consonant: ***a** big car* | ***a** tall building*
> - when the next word begins with 'u', when this is pronounced 'you': ***a** university*
> You use **an**
> - when the next word begins with a vowel: ***an** elephant* | ***an** umbrella*
> - when the next word begins with an 'h' which is not pronounced: ***an** hour* | ***an** honest man*

the

You use **the**

- when you have already mentioned this thing or person:
  ***The** concert is on Saturday.* | *She's **the** woman that I was telling you about.*

- when it is clear from the situation which thing or person you mean:
  *Have you fed **the** cat?* (=we only have one cat)
  *There's **the** hotel, over there.* (=you can clearly see this hotel)

- when talking about places that you often visit:
  *She has gone to **the** bank.* | *I'm at **the** gym.*

- with singular nouns such as *the world, the sea, the sky,* or *the sun*:
  *They travelled all over **the** world.* | ***The** sun is coming out.*

- in the names of <u>some</u> places and organizations:
  *I'm from **the** United States.* | *Were you born in **the** UK?* | *He works for **the** BBC.* | *We sailed down **the** Nile.*

Do not use **a/an** or **the**

- with plural nouns when talking in general about something:
  Tigers are very fierce animals. (Not 'the tigers')

- with uncountable nouns when talking in general about something:
  There has been a big increase in crime. (Not 'the crime')

- when talking about ways of travelling, meals, and times:
  We went by bus. (Not 'by the bus') | *They stopped for lunch.* (Not 'for the lunch') |
  I'll be back before midnight. (Not 'before the midnight')

- with <u>most</u> place names:
  Last year we went to Spain. (Not 'the Spain') | *I'm from Prague.* (Not 'the Prague')

Countable and uncountable nouns

Countable nouns

A **countable noun** is one that you can count, for example *apple*, *car*, or *year*.

In this dictionary, countable nouns are shown as follows:

> **cat** S1 W3 /kæt/ *n* [C]
> **1 a)** a small animal with four legs that people often |

Uncountable nouns

An **uncountable noun** is one that you cannot count. Uncountable nouns are often general words for substances (*water*, *gold*), subjects (*mathematics*, *psychology*), emotions (*love*, *sadness*), qualities (*intelligence*, *beauty*) and other abstract things (*knowledge*, *time*).

In this dictionary, uncountable nouns are shown as follows:

> **information** /ˌɪnfəˈmeɪʃən $ -fər-/ *n* [U] facts or
> details about a situation person or event.

Differences

- A countable noun can be singular or plural: *ticket/tickets*.
  An uncountable noun cannot be used in the plural. Do not say 'informations'. Say *some information*.

- A countable noun can be followed by a singular verb: *The key is in the door.*, or a plural verb: *The keys are in the door.*
  An uncountable noun can only be followed by a singular verb: *Security is important.*

- You can use **a/an** before a countable noun: *a house* | *an elephant*
  You do not usually use **a/an** before an uncountable noun. Do not say 'an advice'. Say *some advice* or *a piece of advice*.

- You use **many** before a plural countable noun: *How many days do you need?*
  You use **much** before an uncountable noun: *How much time will it take?*

- You use **few** before a plural countable noun: *There are still a few seats left.*
  You use **little** before an uncountable noun: *There is only a little milk left.*

- You can use an uncountable noun on its own, without *the*, *some*, or *any*: *I don't eat meat.* | *Time is money.* | *English is easy.*
  You cannot use a countable noun in the singular in this way – it must be in the plural.
  You say *I like reading books.* (Not 'I like reading book.')

Nouns that are countable and uncountable

Some nouns can be used in a countable and an uncountable way, depending on their meaning. This often happens with food and drink, for example *cheese*, *wine*, or *coffee*, or with some abstract nouns, for example *trouble*, *difficulty*, *pleasure*.

Here are some examples of nouns that can be countable and uncountable:

countable [C]	uncountable [U]
Camembert is a well-known French cheese. (=a particular type of cheese)	*France produces a lot of cheese.* (=cheese in general)
Do you want a coffee? (=a cup of coffee)	*Do you want some more coffee?*
We're having a few difficulties.	*He climbed the stairs with difficulty.*
He enjoys the simple pleasures of life.	*She gets a lot of pleasure from her work.*

Verb patterns

Different verbs have different patterns. When you study a verb, it is important to learn the patterns that go with it.

For example, you **allow someone <u>to do</u> something**:

*His boss **allowed him to go** home early.*

But, you **let someone <u>do</u> something**:

*His boss **let him go** home early.*

Do not say 'My father won't let me to go dancing.'

Say *My father won't let me <u>go</u> dancing.*

Patterns for verbs are shown in this dictionary as follows:

> **let** /let/ v [T] (*past tense and past participle* **let**, *present participle* **letting**)
> **1** to allow someone to do something : *I'll come if my dad lets me.* | **let sb do sth** *'Let him go,' said Ralph.* | **let sb in/through/out etc** *Let me through – I'm a doctor!* | **let yourself do sth** *She was afraid to let herself believe it.* **THESAURUS** ➤ ALLOW
>
> **Grammar**
> Do not say ' My father won't let me to go dancing.' Say *My father won't let me go dancing.*

Exercise

Choose the right pattern to use with the verb in these sentences. You can look up the verb in your dictionary, to check that you have chosen the right pattern. The first sentence has been done for you.

1 She wants (become) _____ a doctor.
   She wants <u>to become</u> a doctor.

2 Have you finished (do) _____ your homework?

3 He explained (use) _____ the phone.

4 The government prevented the men (leave) _____ the country.

5 The teacher made him (do) _____ the test again.

6 I think it's starting (rain) _____ .

7 They promised (lend) _____ us the money.

8 The team succeeded (win) _____ the championship.

9 I thanked him for (help) _____ me.

10 Joe admitted (steal) _____ the money.

11 I remember (go) _____ there when I was a child.

12 Some people will do anything to avoid (pay) _____ taxes.

Answers

11 going 12 paying
7 to lend/that they would lend 8 in winning 9 helping 10 stealing/that he had stolen
1 to become 2 doing 3 how to use 4 from leaving 5 do 6 to rain

Grammar reference

Adjective patterns

Different adjectives are followed by different patterns. When you study an adjective, it is important to learn the patterns that go with it, especially which preposition you need to use.

For example, you say:

*I'm **interested in** golf.*

*She's very **keen on** golf.*

*Mick's **good at** golf.*

Do not say 'I'm good in English.'
Say *I'm **good at** English.*

You can also use good with *v+ing*, for example:

*She's **good at** asking difficult questions.*

You use interested and keen with *to+infinitive*, for example:

*I'll be **interested to** see who wins the game.*

*We were **keen to** get started.*

Patterns for verbs are shown in this dictionary as follows:

good¹ /gʊd/ *adj* (comparative **better** /ˈbetə $ -ər/, superlative **best** /best/)

3 SKILFUL able to do something well: *a good teacher* | *I'm not good enough to get into the team.* | **[+at]** *Gill's very good at sports.* | **good at doing sth** *She's good at swimming.* | **[+with]** *He's very good with animals* (=able to deal with animals well).

Grammar
Do not say 'Mick's good in tennis.' Say *Mick's good at tennis.*

Exercise

Choose the right pattern to use with the adjective in each of these sentences. You can look up the adjective in your dictionary, to check that you have chosen the right pattern. The first sentence has been done for you.

1 I was bored _____ the movie.
   I was bored *with* the movie.

2 People are tired _____ seeing the same programmes on TV.

3 He felt angry _____ them _____ the way he had been treated.

4 We're hopeful _____ we can find a solution soon.

5 Your parents must be very proud _____ you.

6 She was worried _____ her father would be angry with her.

7 I'm delighted _____ inform you that you have won first prize.

8 There's no need to be embarrassed _____ it.

9 I was disappointed _____ the result.

10 My brother is terrible _____ languages.

11 The team are confident _____ success.

12 The boy looked so miserable that I felt sorry _____ him.

Phrasal verbs

What is a phrasal verb?

A **phrasal verb** usually consists of a verb and a preposition or an adverb, which are used together in a particular meaning, for example *get up* (=leave your bed) or *look after* (=take care of someone or something). Some phrasal verbs consist of three words, for example *put up with* (=tolerate) or *look forward to* (=feel pleased because something is going to happen).

Sometimes it is possible to guess the meaning of the phrasal verb from the individual words. For example, *come in* means 'come into' or 'enter' a room. Often, though, the phrasal verb has its own special meaning, which is independent from the individual words, for example: *She **made up** an excuse* (=she invented one). | *The game has been **put off** till next Saturday* (=postponed).

Phrasal verbs and formality

Phrasal verbs are very common in everyday spoken English. They are less common in more formal or academic English.

For example, in everyday spoken English, instead of saying:

> *I've decided to **accept** their offer.*

it is more natural to say:

> *I've decided to **take up** their offer.*

Instead of saying:

> *People often try to **avoid** paying taxes.*

it is more natural to say:

> *People often try to **get out of** paying taxes.*

Exercise

Choose the right phrasal verb from the list for each sentence. You can look up the meanings of the phrasal verbs in your dictionary if you are not sure. The first sentence has been done for you.

get together | get over | get in | take off | go off | put out | get down to | eat up

1 Is it alright if I (remove) _____ my jacket?
   Is it alright if I _take off_ my jacket?

2 The firefighters managed to (extinguish) _____ the fire.

3 You'd better (finish) _____ your dinner before it gets cold.

4 The bomb (exploded) _____ in a busy street.

5 What time does your flight (arrive) _____ ?

6 I've finally (recovered from) _____ my illness.

7 Would you like to (meet) _____ for a meal some time?

8 It's time to (start) _____ some work.

Answers

1 take off 2 put out 3 eat up 4 went off 5 get in 6 got over 7 get together 8 get down to

Grammar reference

The five types of phrasal verb

1 Phrasal verbs that do not have an object	**get up** to get out of bed: *What time do you normally get up?* **come out** to appear in the sky: *Finally the sun came out.*
2 Separable phrasal verbs These phrasal verbs have an object which can come before or after the particle (*on, off, in* etc). If the object is a pronoun (*it, them, him* etc), the pronoun must come before the particle. In this dictionary, this type of phrasal verb is shown with a special symbol '↔'.	**take sth ↔ off** to remove something: *Can I take off my sweater?* | *She unscrewed the lid and took it off.* **turn sth ↔ on** to make something start working: *He turned on the radio.* | *The computer makes a funny noise when you turn it on.*
3 Phrasal verbs whose object must come in a fixed position Some phrasal verbs must have an object **after** the particle. Other phrasal verbs must have an object **before** the particle.	**get through sth** to use a particular amount of something: *We get through a lot of milk.* **get sb down** to make someone unhappy: *His illness is getting him down.*
4 Phrasal verbs that can be used with or without an object	**join in** to start taking part in something that other people are already doing: *We all joined in the game.* | *I want you all to join in.*
5 Three-part phrasal verbs These phrasal verbs consist of a verb and two particles.	**put up with sth** to accept a bad situation without complaining: *I don't know how you put up with all that noise.* **get sth out of sb** to persuade someone to tell or give you something: *I managed to get the truth out of him.*

Phrasal verbs in the *Longman Active Study Dictionary*:

PHRASAL VERBS
get through
1 get through sth *informal* to use or deal with a particular amount of something: *I get through about 20 cigarettes a day.* | *I've got through a lot of work this month.*
2 get (sb) through sth to reach the end of an unpleasant experience, test etc, or to help someone do this: *Her love got me through the death of my son.*
3 to succeed in telephoning someone: *I tried phoning, but I couldn't get through.*

Modal verbs

The main modal verbs are **can, could, must, will, would, should, may, shall**, and **might**. **Need to, ought to, have to**, and **have got to** are also used as modal verbs.

You use a modal verb before a main verb when you are doing the following things:

Making requests: can, will, could, would
Can you open the window?
Could you pass the sugar? (**Could** is more polite than **can**.)
Would you give him a message? (**Would** is more polite than **can**.)
Will you repeat that, please? (**Will you** sounds very direct.)

Asking for and giving permission: can, may, could
'*Can* we go home now?' 'Yes, you *can*.'
May I ask you a personal question? (**May** is more polite or more formal than **can**.)
You *may* start the test.
Could we have a break? (**Could** is more polite than **can**.)

Saying that something is not allowed: must not, can't
You *mustn't* tell anyone about this.
You *can't* eat in class.

Offering to help: can, may, shall, will
Can I give you a hand?
May I help you? (**May** is more formal than **can**.)
Shall I take you to the station? (**Shall I** is used especially in British English.)
I'*ll* lend you some money.

Making suggestions and giving advice: should, ought to, shall, must
He *should* go and see a doctor.
You *ought to* put on some warm clothes. (**Ought to** sounds stronger than **should**.)
Shall we go home?
If you're in London, you *must* go to the British Museum. (You use **must** when strongly recommending something to someone.)

Talking about ability: can, could
He *can* speak three languages.
I *couldn't* hear what she was saying.

Talking about necessity and obligation: must, have to, have got to, need to
You *must* tell him the truth.
We *must* go now.
I *have to* get up early tomorrow. (You use **have to** especially when you have arranged to do something, or when the situation forces you to do something.)
We've *got to* be back by 6 o'clock. (**Have got to** is used in British English. It means the same as **have to**, and is only used in the present tense.)
The plane leaves at 8.30, so you *will need to* get ready soon.
There's still plenty of time, so you *don't need to worry/needn't worry*.

Saying that you are certain about something: must, can't, will, shall

'They're 20 minutes late.' 'They **must** be stuck in traffic.'

You **can't** be serious! (You use **can't** when saying that something is definitely not true.)

It **will** soon be summer. (You use **will** when talking about things that will definitely happen.)

The men **won't** be here for long.

We **shall** never surrender. (**I/we shall** is used especially in more formal British English, when saying that you will definitely do something.)

I **shan't** forget what you've done.

Saying that something will probably happen: should, ought to

We **should** be there in half an hour.

The film **ought to** finish soon.

Saying that it is possible that something is true: may, could, might

Her phone **may** be switched off.

The journey **could** take up to four hours. (**Could** means the same as **may**.)

He **might** be in his office. (**Might** sounds less sure than **may**.)

Points to watch with modal verbs

- Modal verbs are usually followed by an infinitive without 'to':

  Cats can see in the dark. (Not 'Cats can ~~to~~ see in the dark.')

  You must stay in bed. (Not 'You must ~~to~~ stay in bed.')

  You needn't get up early tomorrow. (Not 'You needn't ~~to~~ get up early.')

- In spoken English, the following negative short forms are often used:

  can't (=cannot) | **couldn't** (=could not) | **mustn't** (=must not) | **won't** (=will not) | **shouldn't** (=should not) | **wouldn't** (=would not) | **shan't** (=shall not) | **needn't** (=need not) | **mightn't** (=might not)

- **Must** is only used in the present tense. When talking about the past you use **had to**, and when talking about the future you use **will have to**:

  He says I will have to have an operation. (Not 'I ~~will must~~ have an operation.')

- When saying that the situation forces you to do something, you usually use **have to** rather than **must**:

  The students have to work very hard. (rather than 'The students must work very hard.')

- **Must not** and **need not/do not need to** are used in different ways. Compare these sentences:

  You mustn't tell her. (='I forbid you to do this.')

  You needn't tell her. (='It is not necessary to tell her.')

Verb tenses

Talking about the present

The present progressive

This is used

- when talking about things that are happening now, especially when this will stop or change soon: *It's raining outside.* | *She is watching television.* | *I'm staying with some friends until I can find somewhere to live.*

- when talking about your studies: *I'm studying English at an evening class.*

- when saying that someone does something often, especially something annoying: *He's always criticizing my work.*

The simple present

This is used

- when talking about things that are happening now and will continue to happen in the future: *She lives in a big house.* | *He works in an office.*

- when stating facts: *Water boils at about 100°C.* | *Cats don't normally eat fruit.*

- when saying that something happens regularly, especially with always, often, usually, sometimes, never etc, or with a time phrase: *He always drives to work.* | *I go to my guitar class on Mondays.* Compare these sentences:

    I usually stay with my sister. (=I do this regularly)

    I'm staying with my sister. (=I am staying there now)

- when describing a series of actions that are happening now, for example in a sports commentary: *Ronaldo passes to Rooney. He shoots! He scores!*

- with the following verbs: *agree, be, believe, belong, deserve, disagree, hate, have, like, love, know, mean, need, prefer, recognize, remember, see, understand, want, wish.* Do not use these verbs in the progressive: *I love Japanese food.* | *She hates arguments.* | *You remember his face.*

> ⚠ **Common errors**
>
> Do not say 'I'm liking their music.' Say *I like their music.*
>
> Do not use the progressive tense to talk about things you do regularly. Do not say 'I am going to school by train every morning.' Say *I go to school by train every morning.*
>
> Do not say 'I study English literature.' Say *I'm studying English literature.*

Talking about the future

There are several different ways of talking about the future in English. The most common ways are will and going to.

Will

This is used

- when saying that something will definitely happen: *The next meeting will be on Monday.* | *You won't be late, will you?*

- when saying that you think, expect, doubt, feel sure etc that something will happen. It is also used when saying that something will probably, definitely, perhaps/maybe etc happen: *I think* she'll be pleased. | I doubt they'll believe you. | The game will probably be cancelled. | Perhaps it will do him good.

- when saying that you have just decided to do or have something: I'll have the cheesecake. | We'll call you later.

Going to
This is used

- when saying what you plan or intend to do: What are you going to do when you leave college? | I'm going to ask if I can have some time off.
- when you think that something will happen soon, especially because you can see or feel signs of this: The sky's getting dark - it's going to rain. | I'm going to be sick.

About to
This is used when saying that something will happen very soon: The plane is about to take off. | The concert is about to start.

The present continuous
This is used when saying that you have arranged to do something at a particular time: We're going to Jamaica for our holiday this year. | What are you doing this evening?

The simple present
This is used

- when talking about things that are officially arranged to happen: The meeting starts at 4 o'clock. | The plane leaves at 9 a.m.
- in clauses that begin with when, if, unless, before, after, until, as soon as: We'll tell you when we're ready. | Let me know if you need any help. | Don't do anything until I say.

> ⚠ **Common errors**
> Do not say 'I'll call you when I will get back.' Say I'll call you when I get back.

The future perfect
This is used when saying that something will be finished or reach a total by a particular time in the future: We will have finished the work by Friday. | By 2050 the world's population will have reached 9 billion. | In June I will have been here for 5 years.

Shall
This is used in British English

- when making suggestions about what to do, or when offering to do something:
  Shall we go? | Shall I tell him?
- when saying very firmly and definitely that you will do something:
  We shall never surrender. | I shan't (=shall not) forget what you have done.

Talking about the past

The simple past
This is used when saying that something happened in the past. You often say the time, day, year etc when it happened: *I saw him last week.* | *We went there two years ago.* | *He kicked the ball into the back of the net.*

The past progressive
This is used
- when you want to talk about something that continued to happen in the past, for a limited period of time: *We were living in France at that time.* | *I was trying to get the waiter's attention.*
- when you want to talk about something that continued to happen for a period of time, during which another thing happened: *I was having a bath when I heard someone at the door.* | *They met each other while they were studying at college.*

> ⚠ **Common errors**
> Some verbs (*agree, be, believe, belong, deserve, disagree, hate, have, like, love, know, mean, need, prefer, recognize, remember, see, understand, want, wish*) are not used in the progressive. Do not say 'I was not believing him.' Say *I didn't believe him.*

The present perfect
This is used
- when saying that something started to happen in the past and has continued to happen until now: *We've lived here for 5 years.* | *I've always wanted to go to Egypt.*
  Compare these sentences:
  I've studied English for many years. (=I'm still studying it now)
  I studied English for many years. (=I am not studying it now)
- when saying that something happened in the past, but it has an effect on the situation now:
  Someone has broken the window. (=it needs to be repaired)
  The taxi has arrived. (=you need to get in the taxi)
  He can't play today – he's hurt his leg. (=his leg is preventing him from playing)

  This use is also very common in news reports: *There has been a big earthquake in Japan.* | *There has been a sharp rise in unemployment.*

  British speakers often use the present perfect with just, already, and yet in this meaning. American speakers use the simple past tense.
  Compare these examples:

British English	American English
I've just seen Carol.	*I just saw Carol.*
You've already told me that.	*You already told me that.*
Have they come home yet?	*Did they come home yet?*

- when saying that something happened at some time in the past, when it is not important to say when it happened: *Have you had this kind of illness before?*
  Compare these sentences:
  Have you been to Paris? (=at any time in your life)
  I went to Paris last summer.

> ⚠ **Common errors**
> Do not say 'I have been to London last year.' Say *I went to London last year*.
> If you mention the time when something happens, you should not use the present perfect tense.

The present perfect progressive

This is used instead of the present perfect, when you want to emphasize the period of time. You use it

- when you want to talk about something that has continued to happen for a period of time and is still happening now. It is often used with for and since: *I've been studying English for 8 years.* | *We've been living here since 2008.* | *I've been thinking of getting a new car.*

- when you want to talk about something that has been happening recently, which affects the situation now: *'You look tired.' 'I've been working really hard.'* | *It's been raining all week, so the ground is really wet.*

> ⚠ **Common errors**
> Some verbs (see list at the end of **Talking about the present**) are not used in the progressive.
> Do not say 'I've been knowing him for a long time.' Say *I've known him for a long time*.

The past perfect

This is used when you want to talk about a past action, which happened before another past action: *After they had all gone home, I went to bed.* | *He said that he had got stuck in traffic.*

The past perfect continuous

This is used instead of the past perfect, when you want to emphasize that the past action continues for a period of time: *By the time the meal arrived, we had already been waiting for over an hour.*

Used to

This is used when you want to say that something happened in the past, but it no longer happens now: *I used to play football when I was at school.* | *I didn't use to like spicy food.* | *What did you use to do in the evenings?*

Conditionals

with will

This is used when talking about a possible situation that could really happen. You use the simple present tense in the clause that begins with if or unless: *If she works hard, she will pass her exam.* | *She won't pass her exam unless she works hard.* (=if she doesn't work hard)

> ⚠ **Common errors**
> Do not say 'If she will work hard.'

with would, might, or could

This is used when talking about an imaginary situation, or one that is very unlikely. You use the simple past tense in the if clause: *What would you do if you won the lottery?* | *I would lend you the money if I had it.* | *If I could live anywhere, I would live in Morocco.*

> ⚠ **Common errors**
> Do not say 'If I would win the lottery.'

When talking about the past, you use would have, might have, or could have: *If I had known, I would have offered to help.* | *None of this might have happened, if you had been more careful.* | *If you had told us, we could have lent you the money.*

if I _were_ or if I _was_?

If I were/if he were is the correct form: _If I were president, I would cut taxes._ | _Grandma would be really pleased if she were here now._

If I was/if he was is used in informal spoken English: _If I was older, would you still love me?_ | _If he was my son, I would make him clear up the mess._

People usually say if I were you or if I were him/her in both formal and informal English: _If I were you, I would give up smoking._ | _If I were her, I'd leave him._

with the simple present

This is used when saying that something always happens: _If you mix hydrogen and oxygen, you get water._

Regular verb forms for each tense

Present simple

| I/you/we/they play | do not/don't play | Do you play? |
| he/she/it plays | does not/doesn't play | Does he play? |

Present continuous

I am playing	am not playing	Am I playing?
he/she/it is playing	is not/isn't playing	Does she play?
you/we/they are playing	are not/aren't playing	Do you play?

Future with 'will'

| I/you/he/she/it/we/they will play | will not/won't play | Will she play? |

Future perfect

| I/you/he/she/it/we/they will have played | will not have/won't have played | Will she have played? |

Future perfect continuous

| I/you/he/she/it/we/they will have been playing | will not have/won't have been playing | Will she have been playing? |

Simple past

| I/you/he/she/it/we/they played | did not/didn't play | Did he play? |

Past continuous

| I/he/she/it was playing | was not/wasn't playing | Was she playing? |
| you/we/they were playing | were not/weren't playing | Were you playing? |

Present perfect

| I/you/we/they have played | have not/haven't played | Have you played? |
| he/she/it has played | has not/hasn't played | Has he played? |

Present perfect continuous

| I/you/we/they have been playing | have not/haven't been playing | Have you been playing? |
| he/she/it has been playing | has not/hasn't been playing | Has he been playing? |

Past perfect

| I/you/he/she/it/we/they had played | had not/hadn't played | Had he played? |

Past perfect continuous

| I/you/he/she/it/we/they had been playing | had not/hadn't been playing | Had she been playing? |

Mm

M, m /em/ *n* [C,U] (*plural* **M's, m's**) the 13th letter of the English alphabet

m 1 the written abbreviation of **metre 2** the written abbreviation of **medium**, used on clothes to show the size **3** the written abbreviation of **mile 4** the written abbreviation of **million**

MA, M.A. /ˌem ˈeɪ/ *n* [C] (**Master of Arts**) a higher university degree → **MSc**

ma'am /mæm, mɑːm, məm $ mæm/ *n AmE spoken* a polite word you use to talk to a woman you do not know

mac /mæk/ *n* [C] *BrE* a coat you wear to keep out the rain SYN **mackintosh**

macabre /məˈkɑːbrə, -bə $ -brə, -bər/ *adj* strange and frightening

macaroni /ˌmækəˈrəʊni $ -ˈroʊ-/ *n* [U] a type of PASTA in the shape of small tubes

machete /məˈʃeti, məˈtʃeti/ *n* [C] a large knife with a wide heavy blade

machine /məˈʃiːn/ *n* [C] a piece of equipment that uses power, usually from electricity, to do a job: **washing/sewing etc machine** (=a machine that washes, sews etc) | *There was a message on the answering machine* (=a machine for recording telephone messages). | **[+for]** *a machine for sorting the mail* | *Some of these new computers are very powerful machines.* | **by machine** *The cloth is cut by machine.* → **CASH MACHINE, SLOT MACHINE, VENDING MACHINE**

THESAURUS

machine a piece of equipment that uses power, usually from electricity, to do a job: *Can you put the clothes in the washing machine?* | *They make machines for printing newspapers.*
gadget a small useful piece of equipment that you can use for doing something: *a gadget that you can use for making popcorn*
device a small piece of equipment, especially an electronic one, that you use for doing something: *Electronic devices such as iPods are very attractive to thieves.* | *labour-saving devices*
contraption a machine that looks strange or complicated: *There was a strange contraption that looked as if it might be some kind of heater.*

ma'chine gun *n* [C] a gun that fires a lot of bullets very quickly

machinery /məˈʃiːnəri/ *n* [U] **1** large machines: *agricultural machinery* **2** a system for doing something: *the machinery of the government*

macho /ˈmætʃəʊ $ ˈmɑːtʃoʊ/ *adj informal* behaving in a way that is typical of men, for example being strong or brave, or not showing your feelings

mackintosh /ˈmækɪntɒʃ $ -tɑːʃ/ *n* [C] *BrE old-fashioned* a coat you wear to keep out the rain SYN **mac**

macro /ˈmækrəʊ $ -roʊ/ *n* [C] (*plural* **macros**) a set of instructions for a computer, stored and used as a unit

macrocosm /ˈmækrəʊˌkɒzəm $ -kroʊˌkɑː-/ *n* [C] a large group or system, considered as a single unit OPP **microcosm**

mad /mæd/ *adj*
1 ANGRY *informal* angry: *You make me so mad!* | **[+at]** *Lisa was really mad at me for telling Dad.* | **go mad** *BrE* (=become very angry) *Mum will go mad when she finds out.* THESAURUS ANGRY
2 CRAZY *BrE informal* crazy or very silly: *You're mad to get involved with someone like him!* | *a mad idea* THESAURUS CRAZY
3 MENTALLY ILL *old-fashioned* mentally ill: *Van Gogh went mad* (=became mentally ill).
4 EXCITED behaving in an excited or uncontrolled way: *The crowd went mad when Liverpool scored.*
5 DONE QUICKLY **a mad dash/rush/panic** *informal* when you try to do something very quickly because you do not have much time: *It was a mad rush to get ready on time.*
PHRASES
drive sb mad if something or someone drives you mad, you find them very annoying: *The flies are driving me mad.*
like mad *informal* very quickly: *Everyone was working like mad.*
be mad about sb/sth *BrE informal* to like someone or something very much: *The kids are mad about football.* THESAURUS LIKE

madam /ˈmædəm/ *n* a polite word used to talk to a woman who is a customer in your shop, restaurant etc → **sir**: *Can I help you, madam?*
PHRASES
Dear Madam used to begin a formal letter to a woman whose name you do not know: *Dear Madam, I am writing in connection with my letter of 16th November.*

mad 'cow dis,ease *n* [U] *informal* BSE

madden /ˈmædn/ *v* [T] to make someone very angry —**maddening** *adj*: *Things moved with maddening slowness.*

made¹ /meɪd/ *v* the past tense and past participle of MAKE

made² *adj* → **MAN-MADE, READY-MADE**
PHRASES
have (got) it made *informal* to have everything you need to be happy or successful: *If you can get this job, you've got it made.*
be made for sb/sth to be perfectly suitable for a person, group, or situation: *I think Anna and Juan were made for each other.*

madhouse /ˈmædhaʊs/ *n* [C] a place that is very busy and noisy

madly /ˈmædli/ *adv* in a wild uncontrolled way: *Allen was beating madly on the door.*
PHRASES
madly in love very much in love: *John and Sue are madly in love.*

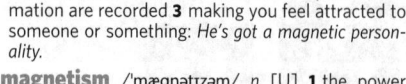

madman /'mædmən/ *n* [C] (*plural* **madmen** /-mən/) **1** a man who behaves in a very dangerous or stupid way: *He drives like a madman.* **2** *old-fashioned* a man who is mentally ill

madness /'mædnəs/ *n* [U] **1** very stupid and often dangerous behaviour: *It would be madness to go cycling in this weather.* **2** *BrE old-fashioned* severe mental illness **SYN** **insanity**

maestro /'maɪstrəʊ $ -roʊ/ *n* [C] (*plural* **maestros**) someone who can do something very well, especially a musician

mafia /'mæfiə $ 'mɑː-, 'mæ-/ *n* **the Mafia** a large organization of criminals

magazine /ˌmægə'ziːn $ 'mægəziːn/ *n* [C] **1** a large thin book with a paper cover, which is sold every week or every month: **in a magazine** *an article in a women's magazine* | *a fashion magazine* **2** the part of a gun that holds the bullets

maggot /'mægət/ *n* [C] a young insect with a soft body that grows into a FLY

magic¹ /'mædʒɪk/ *n* [U] **1** a special power that can make strange or impossible things happen in stories: *Do you believe in magic?* **2** when someone does tricks that look like magic: *a magic show* **3** a special attractive quality: **[+of]** *the magic of the East* → **BLACK MAGIC**

magic² *adj* [only before noun] having magic powers or used in magic: *magic spells* | *a magic carpet*

magical /'mædʒɪkəl/ *adj* **1** very enjoyable and exciting, in a strange or special way: *a magical evening beneath the stars* **2** having magic powers or done using magic —**magically** /-kli/ *adv*

magician /mə'dʒɪʃən/ *n* [C] **1** someone who does magic tricks to entertain people **2** a man in stories who has magic powers

magistrate /'mædʒəstreɪt, -strət/ *n* [C] someone who decides if people are guilty of less serious crimes in a court of law

magnanimous /mæg'nænɪməs/ *adj formal* kind and generous towards other people, especially someone you have just defeated

magnate /'mægneɪt, -nət/ *n* [C] **steel/oil/shipping etc magnate** a rich and powerful person who owns a company that produces steel, oil etc

magnesium /mæg'niːziəm/ *n* [U] a silver-white metal that burns with a bright white flame

magnet /'mægnɪt/ *n* [C] **1** a piece of iron or steel that makes other metal objects move towards it **2** a person or place that attracts a lot of people: *Darlington has recently become a magnet for new companies.* —**magnetize** (*also* **-ise** *BrE*) *v* [T]

MAGNET

magnetic /mæg'netɪk/ *adj* **1** something that is magnetic has the power of a magnet **2** **magnetic tape/disks/media** tape or DISKS on which sound, pictures, or computer information are recorded **3** making you feel attracted to someone or something: *He's got a magnetic personality.*

magnetism /'mægnətɪzəm/ *n* [U] **1** the power that a magnet has to attract things **2** a quality that makes people feel attracted to someone or something

magnificent /mæg'nɪfəsənt/ *adj* very good or beautiful, and very impressive: *He gave a magnificent performance.*

magnify /'mægnɪfaɪ/ *v* [T] (**magnified**, **magnifying**, **magnifies**) **1** to make something appear bigger **2** to make something become, or seem, more important or serious: *The report magnifies the risks.* —**magnification** /ˌmægnɪfɪ'keɪʃən/ *n* [C,U]

MAGNIFY

magnifying glass

'magnifying ˌglass *n* [C] a round piece of glass with a handle, that makes things look bigger when you look through it

magnitude /'mægnɪtjuːd $ -tuːd/ *n* [U] how large or important something is: **the magnitude of sth** *He was surprised by the magnitude of the task.*

magnolia /mæg'nəʊliə $ -'noʊ-/ *n* [C] a bush with large white or pink flowers

magpie /'mægpaɪ/ *n* [C] a black and white bird with a long tail

mahogany /mə'hɒɡəni $ mə'hɑː-/ *n* [U] a hard dark wood, often used for making furniture

maid /meɪd/ *n* [C] **1** a female servant, especially in a large house **2** *literary* a maiden

maiden¹ /'meɪdn/ *n* [C] *literary* a girl or young woman who is not married

maiden² *adj* **maiden flight/voyage** the first trip that a plane or ship makes

'maiden ˌname *n* [C] a woman's family name before she gets married **THESAURUS** ▶ **NAME**

mail¹ /meɪl/ *n* [U] **1** the letters and packages that are delivered to you **SYN** **post** *BrE*: *What time does the mail come?* | *They promised to forward my mail to my new address.* **2** **the mail** *especially AmE* the system of collecting and delivering letters and packages **SYN** **the post** *BrE*: **in the mail** *I just put the letter in the mail.* **3** messages that are sent and received on a computer **SYN** **email**: *Check your mail every day.* → **JUNK MAIL**

PHRASES
hate mail letters that say bad things about the person they are sent to: *The politician had received a lot of hate mail.*

mail² *v* [T]
1 to send a message or document to someone using a computer **SYN** **email**: **mail sth to sb** *Did you mail those pictures to me?* | *I'll mail you.*

2 *especially AmE* to send a letter or package to someone SYN **post** *BrE*: *I'll mail it to you tomorrow.*

mailbox /'meɪlbɒks $ -bɑːks/ *n* [C] **1** *AmE* a box, usually outside your house, where your letters are delivered or collected **2** *AmE* a container where you post letters SYN **postbox** *BrE* **3** in a computer, the part where email messages are stored

'mailing list *n* [C] a list of names and addresses, used by an organization when it sends information to people

mailman /'meɪlmæn/ *n* [C] (*plural* **mailmen** /-men/) *AmE* a man who delivers letters and packages to people's houses SYN **postman** *BrE*

mail 'order *n* [U] a system of buying goods in which you choose them at home and they are delivered to you

maim /meɪm/ *v* [T] to wound or injure someone very seriously and often permanently: *Landmines continue to kill and maim people.*

main¹ /meɪn/ *adj* [only before noun] bigger or more important than other things: *the main meal of the day* | *The main problem is the cost.* | *the main reason for his decision* THESAURUS **IMPORTANT**

PHRASES

the main thing *spoken* used to say that something is the most important thing in a situation: *You're safe, that's the main thing.*

main² *n* [C] **1** a large pipe carrying water or gas, which is connected to people's houses by smaller pipes: *a water main* **2 the mains** *BrE* **a)** the place on a wall where you connect equipment to the electricity supply **b)** electricity that is supplied through wires, or water or gas that is supplied through pipes: *mains electricity/water/gas Some of the older houses do not have mains electricity.*

PHRASES

in the main *spoken* generally: *The weather was very good in the main.*

main 'clause *n* [C] in grammar, a group of words that can stand alone as a complete sentence → **subordinate clause**

main 'course *n* [C] the main part of a meal

mainframe /'meɪnfreɪm/ *n* [C] a large computer that can work very fast and that a lot of people can use at the same time

mainland /'meɪnlənd, -lænd/ *n* **the mainland** the main part of an area of land, not the islands that are near it —**mainland** *adj*: *mainland Europe*

main 'line *n* [C] an important railway that connects two cities: *the main line between Belfast and Dublin*

mainly /'meɪnli/ *adv* used to mention the main part of something: *The workforce consists mainly of women.* | *I don't go out much, mainly because of the kids.*

mainstay /'meɪnsteɪ/ *n* [C] the most important part of something that allows it to continue or succeed: **[+of]** *Farming was the mainstay of the economy.*

mainstream /'meɪnstriːm/ *n* **the mainstream** the

most usual ideas or ways of doing something that are accepted by most people: **[+of]** *the mainstream of religious opinion* —**mainstream** *adj*: *mainstream education*

'Main Street *n* [C] *AmE* the most important street in a town, with many shops and businesses on it SYN **high street** *BrE* THESAURUS **ROAD**

maintain **Ac** /meɪn'teɪn, mən-/ *v* [T]
1 to make something continue in the same way or at the same standard as before: *We need to maintain good relations with our customers.* | *It is important to maintain a reasonable level of fitness.*
2 to keep something in good condition by taking care of it: *It costs a lot of money to maintain a big house.*
3 to say that you are sure that something is true: **[+that]** *She always maintained that her son was alive.* | *He has always **maintained** his **innocence** (=said that he is innocent).*

maintenance **Ac** /'meɪntənəns/ *n* [U] **1** the work that is necessary to keep something in good condition: *He was carrying out routine **maintenance work**.* **2** when people make a situation continue: **[+of]** *the maintenance of international peace and security* **3** *BrE* payments that are made to a former wife or husband after a marriage ends

maisonette /ˌmeɪzə'net/ *n* [C] *BrE* an apartment that is part of a building like a large house

maize /meɪz/ *n* [U] *BrE* a tall plant with yellow seeds that are used for food SYN **corn** *AmE*

majestic /mə'dʒestɪk/ *adj* very big, impressive, or beautiful: *majestic mountain scenery* THESAURUS **HIGH**

majesty /'mædʒəsti/ *n* [U] **1 Your/Her/His Majesty** used when talking to or about a king or queen **2** *formal* when something is powerful, impressive, or beautiful: *the majesty of the hills*

major¹ **Ac** /'meɪdʒə $ -ər/ *adj*
1 very large, serious, or important → **minor**: *Traffic is a major problem.* | *He played a major part in the negotiations.* THESAURUS **BIG**
2 a major key is one of the two main sets of musical notes → **minor**: *a symphony in A major*

major² *n* [C] **1** (*also* **Major**) an officer of middle rank in the army **2** *AmE* **a)** the main subject that you study at college or university **b) English/history etc major** a student at college or university whose main subject is English, history etc

major³ *v*
PHRASAL VERBS
major in sth *AmE* to study something as your main subject at college or university → **minor** THESAURUS **STUDY**

majority **Ac** /mə'dʒɒrəti $ mə'dʒɔː-, mə'dʒɑː-/ *n* (*plural* **majorities**)
1 [singular, also + plural verb *BrE*] most of the people or things in a group → **minority**: **[+of]** *Money is a problem for the majority of students.* | *The majority of people support the idea.* | **great/vast/ overwhelming majority** (=almost all of a group) *In the vast majority of cases, the disease is fatal.* | **be in the majority** (=form the largest group) *Boys were in*

the majority. | **majority vote/decision/verdict etc** (=when more people vote for something than against it) *He was found guilty by majority verdict.*
2 [C usually singular] if one person or group wins a majority in an election, they win more votes than other people or groups: **[+of]** *He won by a majority of 500.* | **clear/overall/absolute majority** (=when one party wins more votes than all the others)

M make¹ /meɪk/ v (*past tense and past participle* **made** /meɪd/)
1 PRODUCE/BUILD [T] to produce or build something: *She makes all her own clothes.* | *The furniture was made by a Swedish firm.* | **make sth from/out of sth** *She made the skirt out of some old fabric.* | **be made from/of/out of sth** *Paper is made from wood.* | **make sb sth** *He made me a beautiful card.*
2 DO [T] used with some nouns to say that someone does something: *You've made a mistake.* | *Could I make a suggestion?* | *He made a speech.* | *The decision has already been made.* THESAURUS DO
3 COOK [T] to cook something: *I've made a cake.* | *She made lunch for everyone.* THESAURUS COOK
4 CAUSE STH TO HAPPEN [T] to cause something to happen, or cause someone to do something: **make sb/sth do sth** *Sarah always makes me laugh.* | **make sb sad/happy/excited etc** *He's made me so happy.* | **make sth difficult/easy/possible etc** *Heavy rain made driving very difficult.* THESAURUS CAUSE
5 CAUSE STH TO APPEAR [T] to cause something to appear: *Make a hole in the paper.*
6 FORCE SB TO DO STH **make sb do sth** to force someone to do something: *He made me stand against the wall.* THESAURUS FORCE
7 GIVE SB A JOB **make sb sth** to give someone a particular job or title: *They made him the manager.*
8 EARN MONEY [T] to earn or get money: *Irene makes about $60,000 a year.* THESAURUS EARN
9 ADD UP TO STH [linking verb] to be a particular number or amount when added together: *2 and 2 make 4.*
10 RESULT OF A CALCULATION [T] used to say what you have calculated a number to be: *I make that 54.*
11 ACHIEVE STH [T] to succeed in achieving something: *He didn't make the team* (=he wasn't good enough to be in the team). | *The story made the front page of the newspapers.*
12 GO TO AN EVENT [T] *informal* to be able to go to something that has been arranged: *I'm afraid I can't make the meeting next week.*
13 BE SUITABLE [linking verb] to be suitable for a job or purpose, because you have the right qualities: *John will make a good father.* → **be made for sb/sth** at MADE²
PHRASES
make do to use the things you have, although you really want other things: **[+with]** *You'll have to make do with some toast.*
make it 1 to succeed in arriving somewhere: *We made it to the station just in time.* **2** to achieve a high level of success, for example in your work: *He really felt he'd made it.* THESAURUS SUCCEED **3** to continue to live after being ill or after a difficult experience: *They didn't think he'd make it.* **4** if you

make it a particular time, your watch says that time: *I make it ten past two.*
make it Friday/ten o'clock etc *spoken* used to arrange a day or time to meet someone: *Let's make it Saturday morning.*
make or break sth to make someone or something be very successful, or make them fail completely: *Critics can make or break a young performer.*
that makes two of us *spoken informal* used to say that you feel the same as someone else: *'I'm so tired!' 'Yeah, that makes two of us.'*

Word Choice: make or cook?
You **make** or **cook** a meal: *Do you want to make breakfast?* | *I was cooking dinner when the phone rang.*
You **cook** food using a pan or oven to heat it: *Cook the potatoes in boiling water.*
You **make** a particular type of food using other foods: *Shall I make a salad?* | *Do you know how to make an omelette?* | *She makes lovely cakes.*

THESAURUS

make to make things yourself, or in a factory: *He makes all his own furniture.* | *The company makes cars.*
produce to make something in large quantities to be sold, or to make something as the result of a natural process: *Most of the goods we buy are produced in China.* | *The body produces a substance called insulin.*
manufacture to make things in factories: *The company manufactures aircraft parts.*
create to make something new and original: *They created a new type of music.* | *Harry Potter was created by J.K.Rowling.*
build to make a house, road, bridge, tunnel etc: *They wanted to build a road through the village.*
form to make something as the result of a chemical reaction or natural process: *Hydrogen and oxygen combine to form water.* | *The research will help us understand how planets are formed.*
generate to make electricity, power, or heat: *Wind can be used to generate electricity.*

PHRASAL VERBS
make for sth
1 to go towards a place: *He made for the door.*
2 to have a particular result or effect: *It should make for an interesting day.*
make sth **into** sth to change something into something else: *We made his room into a study.*
make sth **of** sb/sth
1 to have a particular opinion or understanding of someone or something: ***What do you make of** this letter?* | *I **don't know what to make of** her.*
2 make too much of sth to treat something as if it is more important than it really is
3 make sth of your life/of yourself to use the opportunities that you have to become successful
make off with sth *informal* to steal something
make out
1 make sth ↔ **out** to be able to hear, see, or understand something: *He could just make out a dark*

shape. | [+make out what/who etc] *I can't make out what the sign says.*

2 make a cheque out (to sb) to write a cheque so that money is paid to someone

3 make out sth *informal* to say that something is true when it is not: [+make out (that)] *Brian was making out he'd won.*

4 *AmE informal* to kiss and touch in a sexual way

make up

1 make sth ↔ up to invent a story or an excuse: *Ron made up an excuse.* **THESAURUS** INVENT

2 make up sth to combine together to form something: *the rocks and minerals that make up the Earth's outer layer*

3 make it up to sb to do something good for someone because you feel responsible for something bad that happened to them

4 to become friends with someone again, after an argument

5 make sb up to put coloured substances on someone's face, in order to improve or change their appearance

make up for sth

1 to replace something that is lost or missing, or to make a bad situation seem better: *He ate a big lunch, to make up for missing breakfast.*

2 to have so much of one quality that it does not matter that you do not have others: *Jay lacks experience, but he makes up for it with hard work.*

3 make up for lost time to do something quickly because you started late or worked too slowly

make² *n* [C] a type of product made by a company: [+of] *a very popular make of washing machine* | *What make is your car?*

PHRASES

be on the make *disapproving* to try to get money or power for yourself: *He was just a salesman on the make.*

Word Choice: make or brand?
You use **make** about the name of the company that makes a product, especially a car or a machine: *'What make is your car?' 'It's a Renault.'* You use **brand** about the name that a company has given to one of its products, especially a type of food or a cleaning product: *'What brand of soap do you use?' 'Palmolive.'*

'make-be,lieve *n* [U] when you imagine or pretend that something is real

makeover /'meɪkəʊvə $ -oʊvər/ *n* [C] **1** when you change the way you look completely by buying new clothes, getting your hair cut etc **2** when you change the way a building, room etc looks: *Let's give this room a makeover.*

maker /'meɪkə $ -ər/ *n* [C] **1** a person or company that produces something: [+of] *the makers of the car* | *the film maker Steven Spielberg* **2** a piece of equipment that makes something: *a bread maker* **3 decision/policy etc maker** someone who makes decisions etc: *Who's the decision maker in this department?*

makeshift /'meɪkʃɪft/ *adj* [only before noun] made to be used for a short time only, when nothing

better is available: *They slept in makeshift tents.*

'make-up, makeup /'meɪkʌp/ *n* **1** [U] coloured substances that you put on your face to improve or change your appearance: *I don't wear much make-up.* | *It always takes her ages to put on her make-up.* **2** [singular] the combination of different people in a group: [+of] *I don't think we should change the make-up of the team.* **3** [singular, U] the different qualities that make someone or something the way they are: *They have the same genetic make-up.*

making /'meɪkɪŋ/ *n* [U] the process or business of making something: *the art of rug making* | *the people involved in decision making* | *a book that was ten years in the making* (=took ten years to make)

PHRASES

be the making of sb to make someone a better or more successful person: *This job will be the making of him.*

have the makings of sth to have the qualities needed to become a particular kind of person or thing: *Sandy has the makings of a good doctor.*

sth in the making a person or thing that will develop into something: *He is certainly a star in the making.*

of your own making done or caused by you, and not by anyone else: *These problems are all of his own making.*

malaise /mə'leɪz, mæ-/ *n* [singular, U] *formal* a problem or illness that is difficult to describe exactly: *the general economic malaise*

malaria /mə'leəriə $ -'ler-/ *n* [U] a serious tropical disease that is spread by MOSQUITOes

male¹ /meɪl/ *adj*
1 belonging to the sex that cannot have babies OPP **female** → **masculine**: *a male lion*
2 typical of this sex OPP **female**: *his male pride*

male² *n* [C] a male person or animal OPP **female**

,male 'chauvinist *n* [C] a man who has fixed traditional ideas about the position of women in society, and thinks that men are better or more important than women —**male chauvinism** *n* [U]

malevolent /mə'levələnt/ *adj formal* wanting to cause harm to someone

malfunction /mæl'fʌŋkʃən/ *n* [C] a fault in the way something works —**malfunction** *v* [I]

malice /'mælɪs/ *n* [U] when you want to hurt, upset, or embarrass someone: *He didn't do it out of malice.*

malicious /mə'lɪʃəs/ *adj* intended to hurt, upset, or embarrass someone: *malicious gossip* —**maliciously** *adv*

malign¹ /mə'laɪn/ *v* [T] *formal* to say or write unpleasant and untrue things about someone: *He was much maligned by the press.*

malign² *adj formal* harmful OPP **benign**: *He is a malign influence on the children.*

malignant /mə'lɪgnənt/ *adj* containing CANCER cells → **benign**: *a malignant tumour*

mall /mɔːl, mæl $ mɔːl/ *n* [C] a large covered area containing a lot of shops: *a shopping mall*

malleable /ˈmæliəbəl/ *adj* **1** easy to press or bend into a new shape: *Clay is a malleable material.* **2** *formal* someone who is malleable is easy to influence

mallet /ˈmælɪt/ *n* [C] a wooden hammer

malnourished /ˌmælˈnʌrɪʃt $ -ˈnɜː-, -ˈnʌ-/ *adj* ill or weak because of not eating enough good food

malnutrition /ˌmælnjʊˈtrɪʃən $ -nʊ-/ *n* [U] a serious medical condition caused by not eating enough good food

malpractice /mælˈpræktɪs/ *n* [C,U] when someone such as a doctor or lawyer does not do their job properly

malt /mɔːlt $ mɒːlt/ *n* **1** [U] grain, usually BARLEY, that is used for making beer, WHISKY etc **2** [C] *AmE* a drink made from milk, malt, and ICE CREAM

maltreatment /mælˈtriːtmənt/ *n* [U] *formal* when someone is treated cruelly —**maltreat** *v* [T]

mama /ˈmɑːmə/, **momma** *n* [C] *AmE* mother – used by or to children

mammal /ˈmæməl/ *n* [C] an animal that can feed its young with milk from its body, for example a dog, cow, or human

mammoth¹ /ˈmæməθ/ *adj* extremely large: *a mammoth task*

mammoth² *n* [C] a creature like an ELEPHANT that existed a long time ago

man¹ /mæn/ *n* (*plural* **men** /men/)
1 [C] an adult male person: *This rule applies to both men and women.* | *a middle-aged man*
2 [C] *old-fashioned* a person, either male or female: *All men are equal.*
3 [U] people as a group: *This is one of the worst diseases known to man.* → **BEST MAN, HIT MAN, RIGHT-HAND MAN, STUNT MAN**
PHRASES
| **the man in the street** ordinary people: *How will the legislation affect the man in the street?*

Word Choice: man, mankind, or humankind?
You can use any of these three words when talking about all humans as a group. Some people prefer to use **humankind**, because they want to make it clear that this includes both men and women and not just men.

THESAURUS

man an adult male person: *Is your driving instructor a man or a woman?*
guy (*also* **bloke** *BrE*) *informal* a man – used especially in spoken English: *He's such a nice guy.* | *Who's that bloke with the blond hair?*
gentleman *formal* a man – used when you want to be polite: *Please could you serve this gentleman?*
lad *informal* a young man, especially one of a group of friends: *He's going out with the lads tonight.*
youth a teenage boy or young man – used especially in a disapproving way: *She was attacked by a gang of youths.*

---

man² *v* [T] (**manned**, **manning**) to work with a machine or system, or to work in a place: *The phones were manned by volunteers.* —**manned** *adj*: *a manned rocket*

man³ *especially AmE spoken informal* used to emphasize what you are saying: *Man, was she angry!*

manage /ˈmænɪdʒ/ *v*
1 [I,T] to succeed in doing something difficult or in dealing with problems: **manage to do sth** *I finally managed to open the door.* | *How do you manage to stay so slim?* | *I don't know how I'll manage it, but I'll be there.* | [+**without**] *How do you manage without a washing machine?* | *Can you manage that suitcase* (=can you carry it)? **THESAURUS** ▸ **SUCCEED**
2 [I] to succeed in buying the things that you need, even though you do not have much money: *I don't know how we'll manage now you've lost your job.*
3 [T] to be in charge of a business: *The hotel has been owned and managed by the same family for 200 years.*
4 [T] to use time, money, or other things sensibly, without wasting them: *You need to learn to manage your time more effectively.*

manageable /ˈmænɪdʒəbəl/ *adj* easy to control or deal with: *Divide the task into manageable sections.*

management /ˈmænɪdʒmənt/ *n*
1 [U] the job of controlling and organizing the work of a company or organization: *I don't enjoy management.* | **in management** *He works in management.* | *She's a management consultant.* | *You will need to learn management skills.*
2 [singular, U] the people who are in charge of controlling and organizing a company or organization: *Management will discuss this issue next week.* | *The factory is under new management.* | **senior/middle management**
3 [U] the way that a situation or event is controlled or organized: [+**of**] *careful management of the economy*

manager /ˈmænɪdʒə $ -ər/ *n* [C]
1 someone who is in charge of a business or of part of a business: [+**of**] *the manager of the factory* | *our new sales manager* | *the general manager* **THESAURUS** ▸ **BOSS**
2 someone who is in charge of training and organizing a sports team: *the England manager* | [+**of**] *the manager of Lazio*
3 someone who is in charge of the business affairs of a singer, actor etc → **LINE MANAGER, STAGE MANAGER**

manageress /ˌmænɪdʒəˈres $ ˈmænɪdʒərɪs/ *n* [C] *BrE old-fashioned* a woman who is in charge of a shop, restaurant etc

managerial /ˌmænəˈdʒɪəriəl $ -ˈdʒɪr-/ *adj* connected to the job of a manager: *She's got good managerial skills.*

managing diˈrector *n* [C] *BrE* a person who is in charge of a large company **THESAURUS** ▸ **BOSS**

mandarin /ˈmændərɪn/ *n* [C] a kind of small orange

mandate¹ /ˈmændeɪt/ *n* [C] **1** the authority to do something, because people have voted for it: **mandate to do sth** *The President has a clear mandate to* *tackle crime.* | **[+for]** *a mandate for reform* **2** *formal* an official instruction

mandate² /ˈmændeɪt/ v [T] *especially AmE formal* to officially order or allow someone to do something: *Teachers are mandated by law to give this information.*

mandatory /ˈmændətəri $ -tɔːri/ adj *formal* something that is mandatory must be done because of a rule or law: *mandatory safety inspections*

mane /meɪn/ n [C] the long hair on the neck of a horse or lion → see picture at **LION**

maneuver /məˈnuːvə $ -ər/ n, v the American spelling of MANOEUVRE

maneuverable /məˈnuːvərəbəl/ adj the American spelling of MANOEUVRABLE

manger /ˈmeɪndʒə $ -ər/ n [C] a container from which horses and cattle eat

mangled /ˈmæŋɡəld/ adj twisted and crushed: *the mangled remains of the vehicle*

mango /ˈmæŋɡəʊ $ -ɡoʊ/ n [C] (plural **mangos**) a tropical fruit with sweet yellow flesh → see picture on page A4

manhandle /ˈmænhændl/ v [T] to move someone or something roughly, using force: *They manhandled him out of the house.*

manhole /ˈmænhəʊl $ -hoʊl/ n [C] a covered hole on the surface of a road, which people go down to check pipes, wires etc

manhood /ˈmænhʊd/ n [U] being a man: *He had not yet **reached manhood**.* | *He felt he had to **prove** his **manhood**.*

manhunt /ˈmænhʌnt/ n [C] an organized search for a criminal

mania /ˈmeɪniə/ n [C,U] **1** a very strong interest in something: **[+for]** *her mania for cleanliness* **2** *technical* a mental illness that makes someone extremely excited or violent

maniac /ˈmeɪniæk/ n [C] *informal* someone who behaves in a stupid or dangerous way: *He drives like a maniac.*

manic /ˈmænɪk/ adj behaving in a very excited way: *He seemed full of manic energy.* | *She suffers from **manic depression** (=a mental illness in which you are sometimes very excited and sometimes very sad).*

manicure /ˈmænəkjʊə $ -kjʊr/ n [C,U] a treatment in which someone cuts and shapes your fingernails —**manicure** v [T]

manifest¹ /ˈmænəfest/ v [T] *formal* to show something or be seen clearly: **manifest itself** *The disease manifests itself in many ways.*

manifest² adj *formal* easy to see: *his manifest reluctance to discuss the matter* —**manifestly** adv

manifestation /ˌmænəfeˈsteɪʃən $ -fə-/ n [C,U] *formal* a sign that something happens or that something exists: **[+of]** *a manifestation of the greenhouse effect*

manifesto /ˌmænəˈfestəʊ $ -toʊ/ n [C] (plural **manifestos**) a written statement by a political group, saying what they intend to do: *the party's election manifesto*

manipulate Ac /məˈnɪpjəleɪt/ v [T] **1** to make someone do what you want by skilfully influencing them: *Don't try to manipulate me!* **2** to skilfully control or move something: *You can manipulate the graphic images.* —**manipulation** /məˌnɪpjəˈleɪʃən/ n [U]

manipulative Ac /məˈnɪpjələtɪv $ -leɪ-/ adj *disapproving* clever at influencing people to get what you want

mankind /ˌmænˈkaɪnd/ n [U] all humans, considered as a group **SYN** **humankind**: *the evolution of mankind* **THESAURUS** PEOPLE

manly /ˈmænli/ adj having qualities that people expect and admire in a man: *a deep manly voice* —**manliness** n [U]

man-'made adj not made naturally, or not made of natural materials: **man-made fabrics** | *a man-made lake* **THESAURUS** ARTIFICIAL

mannequin /ˈmænəkɪn/ n [C] a model of the human body used for showing clothes

manner /ˈmænə $ -ər/ n
1 [singular] *formal* the way in which something is done or happens: **the manner of (doing) sth** *The manner of his death was surprising.* | **in a manner** *It will be decided in a manner that is fair.*
2 [singular] the way in which someone behaves with other people: *She has a calm relaxed manner.* | **[+towards]** *Beth's manner towards him had changed.*
3 manners [plural] polite ways of behaving in social situations: **good/bad manners** *Her children all **had good manners**.* | *Dad gave us a lecture about **table manners** (=behaviour when eating a meal).*
THESAURUS POLITE
PHRASES
all manner of sth *formal* many different kinds of things or people: *We discussed all manner of subjects.*
in a manner of speaking in some ways, though not exactly: *I'm in charge here now, in a manner of speaking.*

mannered /ˈmænəd $ -ərd/ adj **well-mannered/bad-mannered/mild-mannered etc** polite, impolite etc in the way you behave

mannerism /ˈmænərɪzəm/ n [C,U] a way of speaking or behaving that is typical of a particular person: *He has the same mannerisms as his father.*

manoeuvrable *BrE*, **maneuverable** *AmE* /məˈnuːvərəbəl/ adj easy to move or turn

manoeuvre¹ *BrE*, **maneuver** *AmE* /məˈnuːvə $ -ər/ n [C] **1** a movement that needs skill or care: *a complicated manoeuvre* **2** a clever action done to get an advantage for yourself: *political maneuvers* **3 manoeuvres** [plural] military activities that are done as practice or training

manoeuvre² *BrE*, **maneuver** *AmE* v [I,T] to move, or to move something, into a different position, especially something heavy: *Small boats are easier to manoeuvre.*

manor /ˈmænə $ -ər/ n (also **'manor house**) n [C] a big old house with a large area of land around it

manpower /ˈmænˌpaʊə $ -ˌpaʊr/ n [U] all the people available to do a particular kind of work: *a lack of trained manpower*

mansion /'mænʃən/ n [C] a very large house
THESAURUS HOUSE

manslaughter /'mæn,slɔːtə $ -,slɔːtər/ n [U] law the crime of killing someone, but without intending to kill them → **murder**

mantelpiece /'mæntlpiːs/ (also **mantel** /'mæntl/ AmE) n [C] the shelf above a FIREPLACE

mantle /'mæntl/ n **take on/assume/wear the mantle of sth** formal to accept or have an important job or position: Callaghan took on the mantle of party leader.

mantra /'mæntrə/ n [C] a word or phrase that is repeated many times, for example while praying

manual¹ Ac /'mænjuəl/ adj **1** manual work involves using your hands or physical strength: manual jobs | manual workers **2** operated or done by hand: a manual typewriter —**manually** adv

manual² Ac n [C] a book that tells you how to do something, especially how to use a machine: a **computer manual**

manufacture /,mænjə'fæktʃə $ -ər/ v [T] to use machines to make goods, usually in large numbers or amounts: The company manufactures chemicals. | manufactured goods **THESAURUS** MAKE —**manufacture** n [U]: the manufacture of high-technology equipment

manufacturer /,mænjə'fæktʃərə $ -ər/ n [C] a company that makes goods: a paint manufacturer

manufacturing /,mænjə'fæktʃərɪŋ/ n [U] the business of producing goods in factories: the manufacturing industry

manure /mə'njʊə $ mə'nʊr/ n [U] solid waste from animals, put into the soil to improve it and help plants grow

manuscript /'mænjəskrɪpt/ n [C] **1** a book or piece of writing before it is printed **2** an old book or document written by hand: a medieval manuscript

many /'meni/ determiner, pron, adj
1 a large number of people or things – used especially in negative sentences or questions OPP **few**: I don't have many friends. | Were there many people at the party? | Some of the houses have bathrooms but many do not. | **[+of]** Many of our staff work part-time. | There are **so many** I want. | You've been reading **too many** romantic novels (=more than you should). | **a great many/a good many/very many** (=a very large number) It happened a good many years ago.
2 **how many** used to ask or talk about how large a number is: How many sisters do you have? | I don't know how many tickets to buy.
3 **many a sth** formal or old-fashioned a large number of people or things: I've sat here **many a time** (=often) and wondered about it. → **LOT**
PHRASES

as many used to talk about a number of people or things compared to another number: **as many ... as** I don't have as many lessons as I did last year. | **twice/three times etc as many** They now employ twice as many women as men.
as many as 50/100 etc used to emphasize that a number is surprisingly large: As many as 2,000 jobs could disappear.

many thanks written used in letters to thank someone for something: Many thanks for your letter.

Maori /'maʊri/ n [C] someone who belongs to the race of people that first lived in New Zealand —**Maori** adj

map¹ /mæp/ n [C] a drawing of a particular area that shows its roads, rivers, mountains etc: **[+of]** a street map of Mexico City | **on a map** The theatre isn't on this map. → see picture at CLASSROOM

COLLOCATIONS

verbs
to look at a map We'd better stop and look at the map.
to study a map (=to look carefully at a map) Two walkers were studying a map.
to read a map (=to look at a map and understand the information on it) Are you any good at reading maps?
to find sth on a map I couldn't find the lake on the map.
to draw a map I'll draw you a map of the village.
to be marked on a map (=to be shown on a map) The bridge should be marked on the map.

adjectives
a detailed map We need a detailed map of the area.
a large-scale map (=showing a small area in a lot of detail) a large-scale map of Paris

noun + map
a road/street map They bought a road map of the USA.

---

map² v [T] (**mapped**, **mapping**) to make a map of an area
PHRASAL VERBS
map sth ↔ **out** to plan carefully how something will happen: Her parents had already mapped out her future.

maple /'meɪpəl/ n [C,U] a tree with leaves that have five points and that turn red or gold in autumn

mar /mɑː $ mɑːr/ v [T] (**marred**, **marring**) to make something less attractive or enjoyable SYN **spoil**: The election day was marred by violence.

marathon /'mærəθən $ -θɑːn/ n [C] **1** a race in which people run about 26 miles or 42 kilometres **2** an activity that continues for a long time and needs determination or patience: a marathon journey lasting 56 hours

marauding /mə'rɔːdɪŋ $ -'rɒː-/ adj [only before noun] written searching for something to kill, steal, or destroy: **marauding gangs**

marble /'mɑːbəl $ 'mɑːr-/ n **1** [U] a type of hard rock that becomes smooth when polished, used for making buildings, STATUES etc **2** [C] a small coloured glass ball, used to play a children's game

march¹ /mɑːtʃ $ mɑːrtʃ/ v [I]
1 if soldiers march, they walk with firm regular steps: **[+across/along/past etc]** Troops marched into the capital. → see picture on page A11 **THESAURUS** WALK

2 to walk together in a large group to protest about something: **[+along/down/through etc]** *Five thousand demonstrators marched through the city.*
3 to walk quickly because you are angry or determined: **[+off/out etc]** *He marched out of the room without a word.*

march² *n* [C]
1 an organized event in which a lot of people walk together to protest about something: *a peace march* (=demanding peace not war)
2 a journey made by soldiers who are walking from one place to another: *the long march south*
3 a piece of music with a regular beat for people to march to

March *n* [C,U] (*written abbreviation* **Mar.**) the third month of the year, between February and April: **next/last March** *She started work here last March.* | **in March** *The theater opened in March.* | **on March 6th** *There's a meeting on March 6th.*

mare /meə $ mer/ *n* [C] a female horse

margarine /ˌmɑːdʒəˈriːn, ˌmɑːgə- $ ˈmɑːrdʒərɪn/ *n* [U] a food used instead of butter, made from animal or vegetable fat

margin Ac /ˈmɑːdʒɪn $ ˈmɑːr-/ *n* [C] **1** the empty space at the side of a page: **in the margin** *Write your marks in the margin.* **2** the difference between the number of votes, points etc that the winners and the losers get in an election or competition: *They won by a wide margin* (=by a lot of votes etc). **3** *technical* the difference between what it costs a business to buy or produce something and how much they sell it for: *a profit margin of 30%*

PHRASES
margin of error the degree to which a calculation might or can be wrong: *The poll has a margin of error of three percent.*

marginal Ac /ˈmɑːdʒɪnəl $ ˈmɑːr-/ *adj* very small or unimportant: *a marginal improvement*

marginalize (*also* **-ise** *BrE*) /ˈmɑːdʒənəlaɪz $ ˈmɑːr-/ *v* [T] to make a person or group unimportant and powerless in an unfair way: *Some employees complained of being marginalized.*

marginally Ac /ˈmɑːdʒənəli $ ˈmɑːr-/ *adv* very slightly: *The other car was marginally cheaper.*

marijuana /ˌmærəˈwɑːnə, -ˈhwɑːnə/ *n* [U] an illegal drug that is smoked SYN **cannabis**

marina /məˈriːnə/ *n* [C] a small area of water where people keep boats used for pleasure

marinate /ˈmærəneɪt/ (*also* **marinade** /ˌmærəˈneɪd/) *v* [T] to put food into a mixture of oil and spices before you cook it —**marinade** *n* [C,U]

marine /məˈriːn/ *adj* [only before noun] **1** relating to the sea and the creatures that live there: *marine life* **2** relating to ships or the navy

Marine *n* [C] a soldier who serves on a ship, especially a member of the Royal Marines or the US Marine Corps

mariner /ˈmærənə $ -ər/ *n* [C] *literary* a SAILOR

marital /ˈmærətl/ *adj* [only before noun] relating to marriage: *marital problems* | *your marital status* (=whether you are married or not)

maritime /ˈmærətaɪm/ *adj* [only before noun] relating to the sea or ships

mark¹ /mɑːk $ mɑːrk/ *n* [C]
1 a small area of dirt or damage on something: **[+on]** *His feet left dirty marks on the carpet.* | **burn/scratch/bite etc mark** *burn marks on the kitchen table*
2 a small area of different colour on a person's skin or an animal's fur → **birthmark**: *a black cat with a white mark on its chest*
3 a sign or shape that is written or printed: *Make a mark in the centre of the circle.* | *punctuation marks*
4 a particular level, number etc that something reaches: *Unemployment passed the one million mark.* | *The temperature should reach the 20 degree mark tomorrow.*
5 *especially BrE* a letter or number given by a teacher to show how good a student's work is SYN **grade** *AmE*: **good/high/top mark** *She always gets good marks.* | **pass mark** (=the mark needed to pass an exam) | **get full marks** (=get everything correct)
6 a mark of sth a sign of a particular quality or feeling: *The 2-minute silence was a mark of respect for the dead.*
PHRASES
make/leave your mark to become successful or famous: **[+as]** *Dorsey made his mark as a pianist.*
off the mark/wide of the mark not correct: *Our estimate was way off the mark* (=completely wrong).
on your marks, get set, go! *spoken* said in order to start a race
be quick/slow etc off the mark to be quick, slow etc to understand or react to something: *You'll have to be quick off the mark if you want to find a job around here.*

THESAURUS

mark a small area of dirt or damage on something: *How can I get those dirty marks off the wall?*
stain a mark that is difficult to remove, especially one made by a dark liquid: *Is that a wine stain on the carpet?* | *a blood stain*
blemish a mark that spoils the appearance of a surface or someone's skin: *Choose fresh fruit, with no blemishes.*
fingerprint a mark made by someone's fingers: *The glass was covered with greasy fingerprints.*
scar a permanent mark on your skin, caused by an injury or operation: *It was a bad cut that would leave a thick scar.*
bruise a mark on your skin that you get when you have fallen or been hit: *He fell off his bike and came home covered in bruises.*
pimple a small red or yellow mark on your skin that teenagers often have: *There was a pimple on his nose.*
freckle one of several small brown marks on someone's face or arms: *The sun gives me freckles.*
mole a small raised dark brown mark on your skin: *She had a mole on her left arm.*

mark² v [T]

1 to write or draw on something, for someone else to see: **mark sth on sth** *The price is marked on the bottom.* | **mark sth personal/fragile/urgent etc** *a document marked 'private and confidential'*

2 to leave an area of dirt or damage on something: *The front of the car was marked where a truck had hit it.*

3 to celebrate an important event: **mark sth with sth** *They're planning to mark their anniversary with a big party.* | *She was given a gold watch to **mark** the **occasion**.*

4 to show where something is: *He marked the route on the map in red.*

5 to be a sign of an important change or development: *The move **marks a change** in government policy.* | *These elections **mark the end of** an era.*

6 *especially BrE* to read a piece of a student's work and give a number or letter that shows how good it is SYN **grade** *AmE*

7 *especially BrE* to stay close to someone from the opposing team in a sports game SYN **guard** *AmE*

PHRASAL VERBS

mark sth ↔ **down**

1 to write something on paper, especially in order to keep a record: **[+as]** *The teacher marked him down as absent.*

2 to reduce the price of something: **[+from/to]** *Coats have been marked down from $80 to $50.*

mark sth ↔ **out** to show the shape or position of something by drawing lines around it: *A volleyball court was marked out on the grass.*

mark sth ↔ **up** to increase the price of something: *CDs may be marked up as much as 80%.*

marked /maːkt $ maːrkt/ *adj* very easy to notice: *a marked lack of enthusiasm* —**markedly** /'maːkɪdli $ 'maːr-/ *adv*

marker /'maːkə $ 'maːrkər/ *n* [C] **1** an object, sign etc that shows the position of something **2** (*also* **marker pen** *BrE*) a large pen with a thick point → see picture at **CLASSROOM**

market¹ /'maːkɪt $ 'maːr-/ *n*

1 [C] an outside area or large building where people buy and sell goods, food etc: *We buy all our vegetables from the market.* | **fish/fruit and vegetable/ flower etc market** *an antiques market* | *a **street market** (=where people sell things from tables in the street)* | *a **market stall** (=big table on which you put things you want to sell)*

2 the market the STOCK MARKET: *Analysts are forecasting a downturn in the market.*

3 [C] business or trade in a particular type of goods or service: *The company has 50% of the market.* | **the housing/property etc market** *the European car market*

4 [C] a country or area where a company sells its goods: *Our main overseas market is Japan.*

5 [singular] the number of people who want to buy something: **[+for]** *The market for academic books is small.* THESAURUS CUSTOMER → **BLACK MARKET, FLEA MARKET, FREE MARKET, LABOUR MARKET**

PHRASES

on the market available for people to buy: *The new game will be on the market in May.* | *We're **putting** our house **on the market** (=offering it for sale).*

market² *v* [T] to advertise something in a particular way in order to sell it: **market sth as sth** *The book is being marketed as a sophisticated comedy.*

marketable /'maːkətəbəl $ 'maːr-/ *adj* marketable goods or skills are easy to sell

market e'conomy *n* [C] an economic system in which companies are not controlled by the government

market 'forces *n* [plural] the way things affect the levels of prices and wages, for example how many people want to buy a particular product and how much is available

marketing /'maːkətɪŋ $ 'maːr-/ *n* [U] the activity of deciding how to advertise a product, what price to charge for it etc: *He works in **sales and marketing**.* | *a **marketing campaign***

marketplace /'maːkətpleɪs $ 'maːr-/ *n* [C] **1** an area in a town where there is a market **2 the marketplace** the business of competing with other companies to buy and sell goods: *The changes should increase our ability to compete in the marketplace.*

market re'search *n* [U] the business activity of finding out what goods people buy and why they buy them

marking /'maːkɪŋ $ 'maːr-/ *n* [C usually plural] things painted or written on something, or the colours and patterns on something such as an animal's fur: *strange markings on the walls of the cave*

marksman /'maːksmən $ 'maːrks-/ *n* [C] (*plural* **marksmen** /-mən/) someone who can shoot a gun very well

'mark-up *n* [C] the amount by which a shop increases the price of its goods from what they paid for them to what they sell them for: *The usual mark-up is 20%.*

marmalade /'maːmədeɪd $ 'maːr-/ *n* [U] a JAM made from fruit such as oranges or LEMONS

maroon¹ /mə'ruːn/ *n* [U] a dark brownish-red colour —**maroon** *adj*

maroon² *v* **be marooned** to be left somewhere in a difficult situation, where there is no one to help you: *The car broke down and we were marooned.*

marquee /maː'kiː $ maːr-/ *n* [C] **1** *BrE* a large tent used at an outdoor event or for a party **2** *AmE* a large sign above the door of a theatre or cinema that gives the name of the play or film

marriage /'mærɪdʒ/ *n*

1 [C,U] a relationship between two people who are married, or the state of being married: *They have a very happy marriage.* | **[+to]** *the breakup of his marriage to Marilyn Monroe*

2 [C] a wedding ceremony: *The **marriage took place** at St John's Church.* | **[+to]** *after his marriage to Anne Boleyn*

COLLOCATIONS

adjectives

a happy/unhappy marriage *My parents had a very happy marriage.*

a good/bad marriage *A good marriage is not something one person can create on their own.*

sb's first/second etc marriage *His first marriage ended in divorce.*
an arranged marriage (=when your parents choose the person you will marry) *Arranged marriages are common in India.*
a mixed marriage (=between people of different races or religions) *Her parents disapproved of mixed marriages.*

verbs

to have a long/happy/good etc marriage *We had a long and happy marriage.*
to save your marriage (=to stop your marriage from ending) *If you really want to save your marriage, go home.*
a marriage breaks down/up (=ends because of disagreements) *He was very depressed when his marriage broke up.*

noun + marriage

the breakdown/breakup of sb's marriage (=the end of it) *What was the reason for the breakup of your marriage?*

married /'mærɪd/ *adj* having a husband or a wife: *Are you married or single?* | **[+to]** *Nicole is married to my brother.* | *We're getting married next month.*

Grammar
Do not say 'He got married with an actress.' Say *He got married to an actress.*

THESAURUS

married someone who is married has a husband or wife: *My parents have been happily married for 20 years.* | *a married couple*
single not married: *She prefers being single.* | *a single mother*
be living together to be sharing a home with someone, but not be married to them: *They'd been living together for many years, but had never married.*
engaged someone who is engaged has formally agreed to marry another person in the future: *David and Sarah announced that they were getting engaged.*
divorced no longer married because you have legally ended your marriage: *It can be hard for kids when their parents get divorced.*
separated if a husband and wife are separated, they are no longer living together, because of problems with their marriage: *The couple had been separated for some time before the divorce.*
widowed if you are widowed, your husband or wife has died: *She was widowed when she was 52.*

marrow /'mærəʊ $ -roʊ/ *n* **1** [U] the soft substance in the middle of bones **2** [C] *BrE* a large long green vegetable

marry /'mæri/ *v* (**married, marrying, marries**)
1 [I,T] if you marry someone, you become their husband or wife → **married**: *I've asked her to marry me.* | *She married young* (=at a young age). | *They got married last year.*
2 [T] to officially make two people husband and wife at a special ceremony

Mars /mɑːz $ mɑːrz/ *n* a small red PLANET, fourth from the Sun

marsh /mɑːʃ $ mɑːrʃ/ *n* [C,U] an area of soft wet land —**marshy** *adj*

marshal[1] /'mɑːʃəl $ 'mɑːr-/ *n* [C] **1** an officer of the highest rank in the army or air force of some countries **2** someone who helps to organize or control a large public event

marshal[2] *v* [T] (**marshalled, marshalling** *BrE*, **marshaled, marshaling** *AmE*) to organize something so that you can use it in an effective way: *She paused a moment to **marshal** her **thoughts**.*

marshmallow /ˌmɑːʃˈmæləʊ $ 'mɑːrʃmeloʊ/ *n* [C,U] a soft white or pink sweet made of sugar

marsupial /mɑːˈsuːpiəl $ mɑːr-/ *n* [C] an animal such as a KANGAROO that carries its babies in a pocket of skin on its body

mart /mɑːt $ mɑːrt/ *n* [C] *AmE* a place where goods are sold

martial /'mɑːʃəl $ 'mɑːr-/ *adj* [only before noun] relating to war or fighting

martial 'art *n* [C] a sport such as KARATE in which you fight using your hands and feet

martial 'law *n* [U] a situation in which the army controls a city, country etc

Martian /'mɑːʃən $ 'mɑːr-/ *n* [C] an imaginary creature from the PLANET Mars —**Martian** *adj*

martyr /'mɑːtə $ 'mɑːrtər/ *n* [C] **1** someone who dies for their religious or political beliefs **2** someone who tries to get other people's sympathy by complaining about their life —**martyrdom** *n* [U]

marvel[1] /'mɑːvəl $ 'mɑːr-/ *v* [I,T] (**marvelled, marvelling** *BrE*, **marveled, marveling** *AmE*) to feel or express great surprise or admiration for something: **[+at]** *I marvelled at her ingenuity.* | *I marvelled that anyone could be so stupid.*

marvel[2] *n* [C] something or someone that is extremely good or skilful: **[+of]** *the marvels of modern science*

marvellous *BrE*, **marvelous** *AmE* /'mɑːvələs $ 'mɑːr-/ *adj* extremely good or enjoyable: *a marvellous book*

Marxism /'mɑːksɪzəm $ 'mɑːr-/ *n* [U] a system of political ideas based on the writings of Karl Marx

Marxist /'mɑːksɪst $ 'mɑːr-/ *adj* relating to Marxism —**Marxist** *n* [C]

marzipan /'mɑːzəpæn $ 'mɑːrtsə-, 'mɑːrzə-/ *n* [U] a sweet food made with ALMONDs and used to cover cakes

mascara /mæˈskɑːrə $ mæˈskærə/ *n* [U] something you can put on your EYELASHes to make them look darker and longer

mascot /'mæskət, -kɒt $ -kɑːt/ *n* [C] an animal, toy etc that a team or organization thinks will bring them good luck

masculine /'mæskjələ̩n/ *adj*
1 having qualities that people think are typical of men: *a masculine voice*
2 in some languages, belonging to a group of nouns,

PRONOUNS etc that is different from the FEMININE and NEUTER groups → **feminine**

masculinity /ˌmæskjəˈlɪnəti/ n [U] the qualities that are considered to be typical of men → **femininity**

mash /mæʃ/ v [T] to crush food until it is soft: *Mash the potatoes in a bowl.* —**mashed** adj

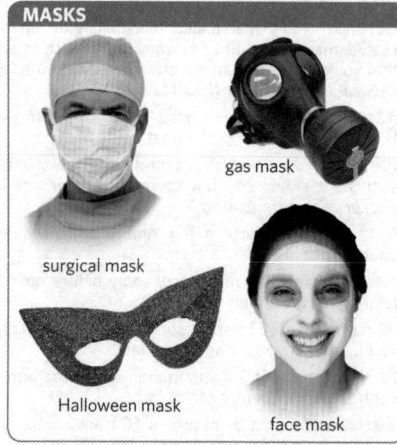

MASKS

gas mask

surgical mask

Halloween mask

face mask

mask¹ /mɑːsk $ mæsk/ n [C] something that covers all or part of your face in order to protect or hide it: *He was robbed by two men wearing masks.*

mask² v [T] to prevent a smell, taste, sound etc from being noticed: *The sugar masks the taste of the medicine.*

masked /mɑːskt $ mæskt/ adj wearing a mask

'masking tape n [U] paper that is sticky on one side, used to protect the edge of an area you are painting

masochism /ˈmæsəkɪzəm/ n [U] when someone gets pleasure from being hurt, for example sexual pleasure —**masochist** n [C] —**masochistic** /ˌmæsəˈkɪstɪk◀/ adj

mason /ˈmeɪsən/ n [C] 1 a person who makes things using stone 2 a FREEMASON

masonry /ˈmeɪsənri/ n [U] bricks or stones that a building or wall is made from

masquerade /ˌmæskəˈreɪd/ v [I] to pretend to be someone or something different: **[+as]** *He masqueraded as a doctor.*

mass¹ /mæs/ n

1 LARGE AMOUNT **a)** [C usually singular] a large amount or number of something all together: *a great/solid/dense etc mass (of sth) a dense mass of forest | a seething mass of people* **b)** masses (of sth) BrE informal a lot of something: *I've got masses of homework.*

2 RELIGIOUS CEREMONY (also **Mass**) [C,U] the main religious ceremony in the Roman Catholic Church and some other Christian churches

3 IN PHYSICS [U] technical the amount of material in

something – used in physics: **[+of]** *the mass of the sun*

4 ORDINARY PEOPLE **the masses** [plural] all the ordinary people in a society

mass² adj involving a large number of people: *mass communication | weapons of mass destruction*

mass³ v [I,T] to come together, or to make people or things come together, in a large group: *Troops are massing at the border.*

massacre /ˈmæsəkə $ -ər/ n [C,U] when a lot of INNOCENT people are killed violently: *the massacre of women and children* THESAURUS KILL —**massacre** v [T]

massage /ˈmæsɑːʒ $ məˈsɑːʒ/ n [C,U] when you press and rub someone's body to reduce pain or help them relax: *He gave me a back massage.* —**massage** v [T]

masseur /mæˈsɜː $ -ˈsɜːr/ n [C] someone who gives massages

masseuse /mæˈsɜːz $ mæˈsuːz/ n [C] a woman who gives massages

massive /ˈmæsɪv/ adj very big: *a massive dog | He had a massive heart attack.* THESAURUS BIG —**massively** adv

'mass-ˌmarket adj [only before noun] designed to be bought by a very large number of people: *mass-market paperbacks*

ˌmass 'media n **the mass media** television, radio, and newspapers

ˌmass 'murderer n [C] someone who has murdered a lot of people

ˌmass-proˈduced adj things that are mass-produced are made cheaply and in large numbers, using machines: *mass-produced cars* —**mass production** n [U]

mast /mɑːst $ mæst/ n [C] **1** a tall pole used to hold up the sails of a ship **2** BrE a metal pole that sends out radio signals

master¹ /ˈmɑːstə $ ˈmæstər/ n [C]
1 SKILLED PERSON someone who is very skilled at something: **[+of]** *a master of kung fu*
2 CONTROLLER old-fashioned the man who has control over servants, animals, or workers → **mistress**
3 DOCUMENT/RECORDING a document or recording that you use to make copies
4 UNIVERSITY QUALIFICATION **Master of Arts/Science etc** a QUALIFICATION that you study for at university after you have got your first DEGREE
5 TEACHER BrE old-fashioned a male teacher

master² v [T] **1** to learn a subject or skill very well: *I never mastered the violin.* THESAURUS LEARN **2** to learn to control a feeling or situation: *I finally mastered my fear of water.*

master³ adj [only before noun] a master document or recording is the one you use to make copies

masterful /ˈmɑːstəfəl $ ˈmæstər-/ adj done with great skill: *a masterful performance*

mastermind /ˈmɑːstəmaɪnd $ ˈmæstər-/ n [C usually singular] someone who organizes a complicated plan, especially a criminal plan: **[+behind]** *the mastermind behind the hijacking* —**mastermind** v [T]

M

masterpiece /'mɑːstəpiːs $ 'mæstər-/ n [C] a very good work of art or piece of writing

'master's de,gree (also **master's** informal) n [C] a QUALIFICATION that you study at university after you have got your first DEGREE

mastery /'mɑːstəri $ 'mæ-/ n [U] **1** great skill or understanding of something: a pianist with total mastery of her instrument **2** complete control over someone or something: [+of/over] They fought for mastery of the area.

masturbate /'mæstəbeɪt $ -tər-/ v [I,T] to rub your sex organs for sexual pleasure —**masturbation** /,mæstə'beɪʃən $ -tər-/ n [U]

mat¹ /mæt/ n [C] **1** a piece of thick material that covers part of a floor: a prayer mat (=used to kneel on to pray) → see picture at BATHROOM **2** a small piece of thick material that you put on a table: Put that hot dish on a mat. | a mouse mat (=used with a computer mouse)

mat² adj another spelling of MATT

match¹ /mætʃ/ n
1 [C] especially BrE a game or sports event between two teams or players: [+against/between/with] Did you watch the match between Kenya and Ireland? | **tennis/cricket/football match** Who won the football match? | **boxing/wrestling match**
2 [C] a small wooden stick with a coloured substance at one end that produces a flame when you rub it quickly against something rough: **strike/light a match** He lit a match so we could see. | a box of matches
3 [singular] something that is the same colour or pattern as something else, or looks attractive with it: [+for] These shoes are a perfect match for your bag.
4 [singular] someone who is as strong, as clever, as fast etc as an opponent: [+for] I don't think he'll be a match for the champion.

> **Word Choice: match or game?**
> A **match** is an organized game, especially one that has been arranged as part of a competition and that people go to watch. **Match** is used especially in British English: Liverpool have won every match this season. | a school cricket match
> A **game** is used about any occasion when people play sport, chess, cards etc together. **Game** is used in both British and American English: a baseball game | I was having a game of Scrabble with my brother.

match² v
1 [I,T] if one thing matches another, or if two things match, they look good together because they are the same or similar: The carpet matches the curtains. | Your socks don't match.
2 [I,T] if two pieces of information match, or if one matches the other, they are connected and are not different from each other: The suspect matches the eye-witness description.
3 [T] to put two people or things together because they are similar, connected, or suitable for each other: **match sb/sth to/with sb/sth** Match the words on the right with the pictures on the left.
4 [T] to be as good as someone or something else:

No one can match his speed on the field. | **equally/evenly matched** The two candidates are evenly matched.
PHRASAL VERBS
match up
1 match sb/sth ↔ up to put people or things together because they are connected or suitable for each other: We match up graduates and employers. | [+with] Annie tried to match me up with her cousin.
2 if two pieces of information match up, they are the same: [+with] The evidence does not match up with his statement.
3 match up to sb's expectations/hopes etc to be as good as someone expected, wanted etc

matchbox /'mætʃbɒks $ -bɑːks/ n [C] a small box containing matches

matching /'mætʃɪŋ/ adj [only before noun] in the same colour, style, pattern etc as something else: a necklace with matching earrings **THESAURUS** SAME

matchless /'mætʃləs/ adj literary better than anything else

mate¹ /meɪt/ n [C] **1** someone that you do things with, such as a job or sport: His **team mates** congratulated him. | an evening out with her **work mates** | her **school mates 2** BrE informal a friend **3** the sexual PARTNER of an animal **4** an officer on a ship → CLASSMATE, ROOMMATE

mate² v [I] when animals mate, they have sex to produce babies: [+with] The male mates with several females.

material¹ /mə'tɪəriəl $ -'tɪr-/ n
1 [C,U] cloth used to make clothes, curtains etc **SYN** fabric: a dress made of light cotton material | a selection of woollen materials
2 [C,U] a solid substance that you can use to make things: They sell all sorts of **building materials**. | Most of our **raw materials** (=natural materials that have not been changed) are imported. | a lorry transporting **radioactive material** → see picture on page 550
3 [U] information or ideas that are used in books, films etc: Does his book contain any new material?

> **THESAURUS – sense 2**
> **material** a solid substance used for making things: Their products are made from recycled materials.
> **substance** a type of liquid or solid, such as a chemical, mineral, or something produced by your body, a plant etc: The tree was covered in a sticky substance. | Diamond is the hardest substance known to man.
> **stuff** informal a substance – used especially when you do not know exactly what something is: What's that stuff you clean the floor with?

material² adj **1** relating to money or possessions, rather than religion, moral beliefs etc **OPP** spiritual: We are not interested in material wealth. **2** formal important and having an effect on a result: No material evidence was presented in court.

materialism /mə'tɪəriəlɪzəm $ -'tɪr-/ n [U] disapproving the belief that money and possessions are more important than religion, moral beliefs etc —**materialistic** /mə,tɪəriə'lɪstɪk◀ $ -,tɪr-/ adj

materialize

MATERIALS

silver bracelet

concrete block

woolly glove BrE/ wooly glove AmE

wooden barrel

rubber boots

leather belt

glass jar

plastic mixing bowl

materialize (also **-ise** BrE) /mə'tɪəriəlaɪz $ -'tɪr-/ v [I] if a possible event or plan materializes, it happens: His dream failed to materialize.

maternal /mə'tɜːnl $ -ɜːr-/ adj 1 typical of the way a good mother behaves: Looking after the twins awakened her **maternal instincts**. 2 [only before noun] technical relating to your mother → **paternal**: my maternal grandfather

maternity /mə'tɜːnəti $ -ɜːr-/ adj [only before noun] relating to a woman who is going to have a baby soon → **paternity**: maternity clothes | **maternity leave** (=time that a woman has away from her job because she has just had a baby)

math /mæθ/ n [U] AmE mathematics SYN **maths** BrE

mathematical /ˌmæθə'mætɪkəl◂/ adj connected with mathematics: a mathematical equation

mathematician /ˌmæθəmə'tɪʃən/ n [C] someone who studies or teaches mathematics

mathematics /ˌmæθə'mætɪks/ n [U] the science of numbers and shapes

maths /mæθs/ n [U] BrE mathematics SYN **math** AmE

matinée /'mætəneɪ $ ˌmætn'eɪ/ n [C] a performance of a play or film in the afternoon

matriarch /'meɪtriɑːk $ -ɑːrk/ n [C] an older woman who has the most power and influence in her family

matrimony /'mætrəməni $ -moʊni/ n [U] formal being married —**matrimonial** /ˌmætrə'məʊniəl $ -'moʊ-/ adj

matron /'meɪtrən/ n [C] BrE old-fashioned a nurse who is in charge of other nurses in a hospital

matt, **matte**, **mat** /mæt/ adj a matt paint, colour, or photograph is not shiny OPP **gloss**

matted /'mætɪd/ adj matted hair or fur is twisted and stuck together

matter¹ /'mætə $ -ər/ n
1 [C] a subject or situation that you must deal with: We have some important matters to discuss. | [+for] This is a matter for the police. THESAURUS **SUBJECT**
2 matters [plural] the situation you are talking about: If you say anything, it will **make matters worse**.
3 the matter spoken used in phrases when you are saying that there is a problem of some sort: **What's the matter?** You look upset. | Is there **something the matter with** Jane? | **Nothing's the matter**, leave me alone. | **There's something the matter with** my computer (=it isn't working properly).
4 [U] **a)** technical the material that everything in the universe is made of **b)** formal a particular substance or type of thing: **waste/solid/organic etc matter** The insects eat vegetable matter. | **reading/printed etc matter** Take some reading matter for the trip. → **SUBJECT MATTER**

PHRASES
be a matter of (doing) sth used to say what something involves: Driving is just a matter of practising. | Whether he has any talent is **a matter of opinion** (=it depends on your views).
a matter of seconds/days/inches etc only a few seconds, days etc: An ambulance came in a matter of minutes.
as a matter of sth because of a particular belief or quality: **As a matter of interest** (=because I am interested), where are you from?
as a matter of course as part of the normal process or system: They checked the rest of the house as a matter of course.
as a matter of fact spoken used to add details to something you have just said, especially when these are surprising or unexpected: 'Do you know Liz?' 'As a matter of fact, we were in school together.'
for that matter used to say that what is true about one thing is also true of another: I don't like him, or his sister for that matter.
no matter how/where/what etc spoken used to say that a situation stays the same whatever happens: No matter how hard she tried, she couldn't open it.

COLLOCATIONS
adjectives
a serious/an important matter Don't laugh – it's a serious matter.

a small/trivial matter (=a matter that is not important) *She loses her temper over trivial matters.*

a simple/an easy matter (=something that is easy to do) *Fixing the problem is not a simple matter.*

a personal/private matter *May I talk to you about a personal matter?*

verbs

to discuss the matter *I will discuss the matter with my wife.*

to raise the matter (=to mention a matter to someone) *I've raised the matter with my boss several times.*

to settle/resolve the matter (=to decide or deal with a matter) *They are meeting tonight to settle the matter.*

matter + noun

a matter of importance (=something important) *He consulted her on all matters of importance.*

a matter of concern (=something that concerns people) *This is a matter of deep concern to many people.*

matter² v [I] to be important: **it doesn't/won't etc matter if** *It doesn't matter if you're late.* | **matter what/which/how** *I don't think it matters what you do.* | **[+that]** *Does it matter that the covers don't match?* | **[+to]** *Money is the only thing that matters to him.* | *The environment really matters* (=it matters a lot). | *Age doesn't matter much in this job.*

matter-of-ʹfact *adj* showing no emotion when you talk about something: **[+about]** *Jan was matter-of-fact about her divorce.*

matting /ˈmætɪŋ/ n [U] strong rough material

mattress /ˈmætrɪs/ n [C] the soft thick part of a bed that you lie on: *I sleep better on a firm mattress.* | *a soft mattress* → see picture at BED

mature Ac /məˈtʃʊə $ -ˈtʃʊr/ adj
1 SENSIBLE behaving in a reasonable way like an adult OPP **immature**: *She's very mature for her age.*
2 FULLY GROWN fully grown or developed: *a mature cherry tree* | *Cats are sexually mature at a young age.*
3 OLDER [only before noun] a polite way of referring to someone who is older than other people who are doing the same thing: *fashions for mature brides* | **mature student** *BrE* (=a student who is over 25 years old)
4 CHEESE/WINE mature cheese or wine tastes strong because it has developed for a long time —**mature** v [I,T]: *Pat's matured since going to college.*

maturity Ac /məˈtʃʊərəti $ -ˈtʃʊr-/ n [U] **1** when someone behaves sensibly and like an adult OPP **immaturity**: *He showed a lack of maturity for his age.* **2** the time when someone or something is fully developed: *Rabbits reach maturity in only five weeks.*

maudlin /ˈmɔːdlɪn $ ˈmɒː-/ adj talking in a sad and silly way: *He gets maudlin after a few drinks.*

maul /mɔːl $ mɒːl/ v [T] **1** if an animal mauls someone, it injures them by tearing their flesh: *He was mauled by a lion.* **2** disapproving to touch someone in a rough sexual way

mausoleum /ˌmɔːsəˈliːəm $ ˌmɒː-/ n [C] a stone building containing the dead bodies of important people

mauve /məʊv $ moʊv/ n [U] a pale purple colour —**mauve** adj

maverick /ˈmævərɪk/ n [C] someone whose ideas or opinions are different from those of most people: *a political maverick*

max /mæks/ adj the abbreviation of **maximum** —**max** adv: *It'll cost $50 max.* —**max** n [C usually singular]

maxim /ˈmæksɪm/ n [C] a phrase that gives advice on sensible behaviour

maximize Ac (also **-ise** BrE) /ˈmæksəmaɪz/ v [T] to increase something as much as possible OPP **minimize**: *Reduce costs and maximize profits.*

maximum Ac /ˈmæksəməm/ adj [only before noun] the maximum amount, speed, number etc is the biggest that is possible OPP **minimum**: *a maximum speed limit of 70 mph* —**maximum** n [C usually singular]: *He now faces a maximum of 10 years in jail.* —**maximum** adv: *It's worth £10, maximum.*

may /meɪ/ modal verb
1 if something may happen, it is possible that it will happen, but not certain → **might**, **can**: *Your job may involve travel.* | *I may not have enough money.*
2 formal used to say that someone is allowed to do something: *Students may borrow CDs from the library.*
3 spoken used to ask or suggest something politely: *May I ask your name?* → see Word Choice at CAN
4 used to say that you accept that one thing is true but that something else connected to it is more important: *Exercise may be dull but we all need it.*
PHRASES

may as well spoken used to say that someone should do something because there is no reason not to: *We may as well go to bed.*

Grammar

May is not used in questions about possible events or situations. Use **might** instead: *Might there be problems?*

May n [C,U] the fifth month of the year, between April and June: **next/last May** *I haven't heard from her since last May.* | **in May** *The work began in May.* | **on May 6th** *We don't have any meetings on May 6th, do we?*

maybe /ˈmeɪbi/ adv
1 used to say that something could be true or could happen, but you are not sure SYN **perhaps**: *Maybe Ann has already left.* | *Maybe you're right and maybe not.*
2 spoken used to answer a question when you are not sure whether to answer yes or no: *'Are you going to accept?' 'Maybe. I don't know.'*
3 used to make a suggestion: *Maybe you should complain.*
4 used to show that you are not sure about a number or amount: *He was 30, maybe 35 years old.*

THESAURUS

maybe used when saying that something may be true or may happen, but that you are not

sure: *Maybe you're right.* | *'Are you going to Kate's party?' 'Maybe. I don't know.'*
perhaps maybe. **Perhaps** is slightly more formal than **maybe** and is more common in written English: *This is perhaps his funniest novel.*
possibly used when saying that it is possible that something is true or might happen **Possibly** sounds a little less likely than **maybe** or **perhaps**: *'Do you think you'll go back there?' 'Possibly, but it won't be for a long time.'*
may/might/could used when you have some reason to believe that something will happen, but you are not sure: *I may still have the instruction book.* | *'Do you think they'll win?' – 'They might.'* | *He could be stuck in a traffic jam.*
you never know used when telling someone that something good might happen unexpectedly, although it is very unlikely: *He might change his mind – you never know.*

mayday /ˈmeɪdeɪ/ *n* [singular] a radio signal that a ship or plane uses to ask for help → **SOS**

mayhem /ˈmeɪhem/ *n* [U] a very confused situation in which people are frightened or excited: *A scene of **complete mayhem** followed the blast.*

mayonnaise /ˌmeɪəˈneɪz $ ˈmeɪəneɪz/ *n* [U] a thick cold white SAUCE made with eggs and oil

mayor /meə $ ˈmeɪər/ *n* [C] **1** the person who is elected to lead the government of a town or city **2** BrE someone who is chosen to represent a town or city at official ceremonies

maze /meɪz/ *n* [C] a complicated system of roads or paths where you might get lost: **[+of]** *a maze of corridors*

MB, Mb the written abbreviation of **megabyte**

MBA (also **M.B.A.** AmE) /ˌem biː ˈeɪ/ *n* [C] (**Master of Business Administration**) a university degree in the skills needed to be in charge of a business, that you can get after your first degree

McCoy /məˈkɔɪ/ *n* **the real McCoy** informal something that is real, not a copy

MD BrE, **M.D.** AmE /ˌem ˈdiː/ *n* **1** (**Doctor of Medicine**) a university degree in medicine that you can get after your first degree **2** [C] BrE a MANAGING DIRECTOR

me /mi; strong miː/ *pron* the object form of 'I': *Give me a kiss.* | *'Who's that in the photo?' 'It's me!'*
PHRASES
me neither (also **nor me**) spoken used to agree with a negative statement: *'I don't like coffee.' 'Nor me.'*
me too spoken used to agree with someone: *'I'm hungry!' 'Me too.'*

ME /ˌem ˈiː/ *n* [U] BrE (**myalgic encephalomyelitis**) an illness that makes you feel very tired and weak and can last for a long time

meadow /ˈmedəʊ $ -doʊ/ *n* [C] a field with wild grass and flowers

meagre BrE, **meager** AmE /ˈmiːgə $ -ər/ *adj* very small in amount: *his meagre wages* | *a school with meagre resources*

meal /miːl/ *n* [C] when you sit down to eat food, or the food that you eat

COLLOCATIONS
verbs
to have/eat a meal *We had a meal at our local Italian restaurant.* ⚠ Do not say 'take a meal'. Say **have a meal**.
to cook/make a meal (also **to prepare a meal** formal) *She cooked him his favourite meal.*
to serve a meal *We do not serve meals after 9.30 pm.*
to go out for a meal *Shall we go out for a meal tonight?*
to take sb out for a meal *James is taking me out for a meal tomorrow.*

types of meal
a big/large meal *We don't have a big meal at lunchtime.*
a light meal (=with not a lot of food) *Breakfast is usually a light meal.*
sb's main meal *We usually have our main meal in the evening.*
a three-course/five-course etc meal (=a meal with several separate parts) *Who has time to prepare a three-course meal every evening?*
a square meal (also **a proper meal** BrE) (=big meal, especially a cooked meal) *How long is it since you had a square meal?*
a good/decent meal (=a meal that is large enough and tastes good) *You can get a good meal there for under £10.*

THESAURUS
meal an occasion when you sit down and eat food at a particular time of the day, or the food that you eat: *Breakfast is the most important meal of the day.* | *a tasty meal*
feast a large meal for a lot of people, especially to celebrate an event: *a wedding feast* | *They held a feast in his honour.*
banquet a formal official meal for a lot of people on an important occasion: *The main hall is used for royal banquets.*
snack a small amount of food eaten between main meals: *I'll take a snack to eat on the train.*
something to eat a meal, especially a small or quick one: *Can I get you something to eat?*
picnic a meal that you eat outdoors, consisting of food that you prepared earlier: *sandwiches, and other picnic food*
takeaway BrE, **takeout** AmE a meal that you buy from a restaurant and eat at home: *I don't feel like cooking – let's get a takeaway.*

mealtime /ˈmiːltaɪm/ *n* [C] the usual time that you eat a meal: **at mealtimes** *I only see my boys at mealtimes.*

mealy-mouthed *adj* not brave or honest enough to say what you really think

mean¹ /miːn/ *v* [T] (past tense and past participle **meant** /ment/)
1 to have a particular meaning or idea: *What does*

that word mean? | **[+(that)]** *The red light means the battery is flat.*

2 to intend to express a particular idea or feeling when you say something: **[+(that)]** *I meant we'd be coming later.* | *I don't quite **see what you mean** (=I don't understand what you are trying to say).* | **(do) you mean ...?** (=used to check that you understand what someone intended to say) *Do you mean I should go?* | *He didn't **really mean it** when he said he loved me.* | *I **meant what I said**.* | *Julie seems rude but she **means well** (=intends to be kind and helpful).*

3 to intend to do something or make something happen: **mean to do sth** *I've been meaning to call you.* | *I **didn't mean to upset you**.* | **mean sb/sth to do sth** *I never meant this to happen.* | *It **was meant to be** a joke.* | **mean (for) sb to do sth** *especially AmE: I didn't mean for her to get hurt.* **THESAURUS** ▶ INTEND

4 to cause something or make it likely to happen: **[+(that)]** *Those clouds mean that it will snow.* | **mean doing sth** *The job will mean travelling.*

5 used to say how important something is to you: **mean sth to sb** *That medal **meant a lot** to Dad.*

PHRASES

I mean *spoken* used to correct or explain more about something you have just said: *She plays the violin, I mean the viola.* | *She's just so nice. I mean, she's a kind person.*

mean business *informal* if you mean business, you are very determined to do something: *He knocked firmly on the door to show he meant business.*

be meant for sb/sth to be intended for a particular person or purpose: *The chocolate was meant for Mum.*

be meant to be sth if something is meant to be good, exciting etc, people say that it is good, exciting etc: *His latest book is meant to be really good.*

be meant to do sth if you are meant to do something, you should do it: *The police are meant to protect us.* | *You're meant to inform the school if you change your address.*

what do you mean ...? *spoken* **1** used when you do not understand what someone is trying to say: *What did you mean when you wrote that?* **2** used when you are surprised and annoyed by what someone has just said: *What do you mean, you sold the car?*

mean² *adj*

1 cruel and not kind: **[+to]** *Don't be so mean to your sister.* | *It **was mean of** you not to ask her.* **THESAURUS** ▶ UNKIND

2 *BrE* not willing to spend money **SYN** cheap *AmE,* stingy *BrE: He's too mean to offer us a lift.* | **[+with]** *She's very mean with money.*

3 a mean sth *informal* used to say that something is very good: *Ray plays a mean game of tennis.*

4 [only before noun] *technical* average: *What is the mean annual rainfall of Brazil?*

PHRASES

no mean achievement/performance/feat used to say that what someone has done is very impressive: *Winning was no mean feat.*

mean³ *n* [C usually singular] *technical* an average amount, figure, or value

meander /miˈændə $ -ər/ *v* [I] to move slowly and not in a straight line: *a meandering stream*

meaning /ˈmiːnɪŋ/ *n*

1 [C,U] the idea that is expressed or represented by something you read, see, or hear: **[+of]** *What's the meaning of this word?* | **[+behind]** *I guessed the meaning behind his speech.*

2 [U] the importance or purpose something has: **[+of]** *the meaning of life* | *After she died, my life **had no meaning**.*

COLLOCATIONS

verbs

to have a meaning *This word has two meanings.*
to understand the meaning *She understood the meaning of his smile.*
to know the meaning *I didn't know the meaning of the word 'dilemma'.*
to explain the meaning *Could you explain the meaning of this phrase, please?*

adjectives

the original meaning *The original meaning of 'terrible' is 'causing terror'.*
the exact/precise meaning *There may be confusion about the precise meaning of a word.*
sth's true/real meaning *Children understand the true meaning of these stories.*
a hidden meaning *Does the poem have a hidden meaning?*
a double meaning (=two meanings at the same time) *The book's title, 'Weaving', has a double meaning.*
the literal meaning *The literal meaning of 'telephone' is 'faraway sound'.*

meaningful /ˈmiːnɪŋfəl/ *adj* **1** having a clear meaning that people can understand: *data that is meaningful only to scientists* **2 meaningful look/smile etc** a look etc that clearly expresses the way someone feels: *We exchanged meaningful glances.* **3** serious, useful, or important: *I want to do something meaningful with my life.*

meaningless /ˈmiːnɪŋləs/ *adj* without purpose or meaning: *Life felt meaningless.*

means /miːnz/ *n* (plural **means**)

1 [C] a way of doing something: **[+of]** *The window is the only means of escape.* | **means of communication/transport** *Email is the best means of communication.* | **a means of doing sth** *I had no means of getting home.* **THESAURUS** ▶ WAY

2 [plural] the money or income you have: **have the means to do sth** *We don't have the means to pay for private education.* | *A holiday is **beyond my means** (=I cannot afford it).*

PHRASES

by all means used to agree or give permission **SYN** of course: *'Can I bring Alan?' 'By all means!'*
by no means/not by any means not at all: *He was not rich by any means.*
a means to an end something that you do only to achieve a particular result: *My job is just a means to an end.*

'means-tested *adj* means-tested income is

money you can receive from the government only after an official check has proved that you need it

meant /ment/ v the past tense and past participle of MEAN

meantime /'miːntaɪm/ n **in the meantime** until something happens, or in the time between two events: *Dinner's nearly ready. Would you like a drink in the meantime?*

meanwhile /'miːnwaɪl/ adv while something else is happening, or in the time between two events: *Bill took the dogs out. Meanwhile, I fed the cats.*

measles /'miːzəlz/ n [U] an infectious illness that produces a fever and small red spots on your body

measly /'miːzli/ adj informal very small and disappointing in size or amount: *a measly gift*

measurable /'meʒərəbəl/ adj big enough to be measured or have an effect: *There has been a measurable improvement in your work.* —**measurably** adv

measure¹ /'meʒə $ -ər/ v

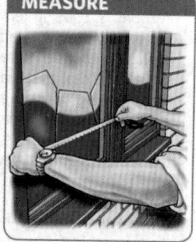
MEASURE

1 [I,T] to find out the size, weight, or quantity of something: **measure sth with sth** *I measured it with a ruler.* | **measure sth in inches/kilos etc** *The instrument measures depth in metres.* | **measure the height/weight/amount etc of sth** *How can we measure the amount of rainfall?*

2 [linking verb] to be a particular size, length, or amount: *The room measures 4 metres by 6 metres.* | *The earthquake measured 6.5 on the Richter scale.*

3 [T] to decide how important or good something is: **measure sth by sth** *Success is not only measured by exams.*

PHRASAL VERBS

measure sb/sth **against** sb/sth to judge someone or something by comparing them with another person or thing

measure up to be good enough for a particular job or to reach a particular standard: **[+to]** *Does college measure up to your expectations?*

measure² n [C]

1 an official action that is meant to deal with a problem: *New safety measures are needed.* | *The government must take measures to reduce crime.*

2 **be a measure of sth** formal to be a sign of how important something is: *It's a measure of our trust that we let you go.*

3 **a measure of sth** formal a reasonable amount of something: *He achieved a measure of success with his first book.*

4 [C,U] an amount or unit in a measuring system: *a table of weights and measures* → **TAPE MEASURE**

PHRASES

for good measure in addition to what has already been done: *Add a bit more salt for good measure.*

half measures things done to deal with a problem

that are not firm or effective enough: *The government has only taken half measures to solve the problem.*

measurement /'meʒəmənt $ -ʒər-/ n
1 [C] the length, height, level etc of something, or the process of measuring it: *What's your chest measurement?* | *Do you know the measurements of the room?* | *I need to take a few measurements.*
2 [U] when you measure something: *After careful measurement, we felt sure the furniture would fit in.*

meat /miːt/ n [U] the flesh of animals and birds that people eat: *I don't eat meat.* | *a meat pie* | **red meat** (=dark meat, such as beef) | **white meat** (=pale meat, such as chicken)

meaty /'miːti/ adj **1** containing a lot of meat, or tasting of meat **2** interesting or important: *his first meaty role as an actor*

mecca /'mekə/ n **1** [singular] a place that many people want to visit because they are interested in something: **[+for]** *The island is a mecca for windsurfers.* **2 Mecca** a city in Saudi Arabia that is a holy place for Muslims. It is now often called Makkah.

mechanic /mɪ'kænɪk/ n **1** [C] someone whose job is to repair vehicles and machinery **2 the mechanics of (doing) sth** the way in which something works or is done: *the mechanics of grammar* **3 mechanics** [U] the science of how forces affect objects

mechanical /mɪ'kænɪkəl/ adj **1** relating to machines, or using power from a machine: *Mechanical failure caused the accident.* | *mechanical toys* **2** saying or doing something without thinking, because you have said or done it so often before: *a mechanical smile* —**mechanically** /-kli/ adv

mechanism Ac /'mekənɪzəm/ n [C] **1** the part of a machine that does a particular job: *the brake mechanism* **2** a system for doing something: **mechanism for (doing) sth** *We need an effective mechanism for dealing with enquiries.*

mechanized (also **-ised** BrE) /'mekənaɪzd/ adj using machines instead of people: *mechanized farming*

medal /'medl/ n [C] a round flat piece of metal given to someone who has been successful in a competition or done something brave: **gold/silver/bronze medal** *She won a gold medal at the Olympics.*

medallion /mə'dæliən/ n [C] a piece of metal like a large coin, worn on a chain around someone's neck

medallist BrE, **medalist** AmE /'medl-ɪst/ n [C] someone who has won a medal in a competition: **gold/silver/bronze medallist** *an Olympic silver medallist*

meddle /'medl/ v [I] to try to influence a situation that does not involve you or that you do not understand: **[+in]** *I don't want him meddling in our affairs.*

media Ac /'miːdiə/ n
1 the media television, radio, newspapers, and magazines: **in the media** *The story was reported in the media.* | **media coverage/attention/interest** *The trial created huge media interest.* **THESAURUS** ▶ **NEWSPAPER**

2 the plural of MEDIUM → **MASS MEDIA**

> **Grammar**
> Do not say 'the medias'. Say **the media**.
> **Media** can be followed by a singular or a plural verb.

mediaeval /ˌmediˈiːvəl◂ $ ˌmiː-/ adj a British spelling of MEDIEVAL

median /ˈmiːdiən/ n [C] AmE a narrow piece of land that separates the two sides of a big road **SYN** central reservation BrE

mediate Ac /ˈmiːdieɪt/ v [I,T] to try to end an argument between people: **[+between]** UN officials mediated between the two countries. —**mediator** n [C] —**mediation** /ˌmiːdiˈeɪʃən/ n [U]

medic /ˈmedɪk/ n [C] informal **1** BrE a doctor or medical student **2** AmE someone in the army who is trained to give medical treatment

medical¹ Ac /ˈmedɪkəl/ adj relating to medicine and the treatment of diseases or injuries: medical treatment | medical students | **the medical profession** (=doctors, nurses etc) —**medically** /-kli/ adv

medical² n [C] BrE an examination by a doctor to see if you are healthy **SYN** physical AmE

medicated /ˈmedɪkeɪtɪd/ adj containing a substance that helps skin or hair problems: medicated shampoo

medication /ˌmedɪˈkeɪʃən/ n [C,U] drugs given to people who are ill: **be on medication (for sth)** He's on medication for depression.

medicinal /məˈdɪsənəl/ adj used for treating illnesses: plants with **medicinal properties** (=containing things that can cure illnesses)

medicine /ˈmedsən $ ˈmedəsən/ n
1 [C,U] a substance for treating an illness, especially one that you drink: Have you **taken** your **medicine**? | a medicine bottle | cough medicine
2 [U] the treatment and study of illnesses and injuries: Sarah is studying medicine. | **alternative/ traditional/modern medicine** advances in modern medicine → **COMPLEMENTARY MEDICINE**

> **Word Choice: a medicine or medication?**
> **Medicine** is a general word that you use about any substance that is used to treat an illness: The medicine tasted horrible. | The plant is used for making medicines.
> You use **medication** especially about drugs that someone has to take regularly, especially for a serious health problem that lasts a long time: Has she taken her medication? | He is **on medication** (=taking medication) for his heart.

medieval (also **mediaeval** BrE) /ˌmediˈiːvəl◂ $ ˌmiː-/ adj relating to the MIDDLE AGES (=the time between about AD 1100 and 1500): a medieval castle

mediocre /ˌmiːdiˈəʊkə◂ $ -ˈoʊkər◂/ adj not very good: a mediocre performance

meditate /ˈmedɪteɪt/ v [I] **1** to be silent and calm for a period of time as part of your religion or to help you relax **2** formal to think seriously about something: **[+on]** She sat meditating on the day's

events. —**meditation** /ˌmedɪˈteɪʃən/ n [U]

Mediterranean /ˌmedɪtəˈreɪniən◂/ n **the Mediterranean** the sea that has the countries of southern Europe, North Africa, and the Middle East around it, or the area of southern Europe around this sea —**Mediterranean** adj

medium¹ Ac /ˈmiːdiəm/ adj of middle size or amount: What size do you want – small, medium, or large? | **(of) medium height/length/size etc** a man of medium height

medium² Ac n [C] **1** (plural media /-diə/ or mediums) a way of communicating information or ideas → **media**: Advertising is a powerful medium. | **[+of]** Language is a medium of communication. | **[+for]** Sport is the perfect medium for publicity. **2** (plural mediums) someone who says they receive messages from dead people

ˈmedium-sized (also **ˈmedium-size**) adj not small or large: a medium-size business

ˈmedium ˌwave n [U] (written abbreviation **MW**) radio broadcasting using radio WAVES between 100 and 1,000 metres in length → **long wave**, **short wave**, **FM**

medley /ˈmedli/ n [C] **1** a piece of music with several different songs in it: **[+of]** a medley of Beatles songs **2** a mixture of different things: **[+of]** a medley of smells

meek /miːk/ adj very quiet and always doing what other people want —**meekly** adv

meet /miːt/ v (past tense and past participle **met** /met/)
1 BY ARRANGEMENT [I,T] to be at the same place as someone else because you have arranged it: I'll meet you at 8 o'clock. | We'll meet at the theatre. | **meet (sb) for sth** Let's meet for lunch.
2 BY CHANCE [I,T] to see and speak to someone without planning it: Guess who I just met? | We met while we were both shopping in town, and decided to go for a coffee.
3 FOR THE FIRST TIME [I,T] to see and talk to someone for the first time: We first met at a party. | I met my husband at school. | **nice/pleased to meet you** spoken (=used when you meet someone for the first time) 'This is my sister Jane.' 'Pleased to meet you.'
4 AT AN AIRPORT/STATION ETC [T] to be waiting for someone when they arrive at an airport, station etc: Dad came to meet us at the station. | **meet sb off a train/plane etc** A friend's meeting her off the boat.
5 JOIN [I,T] if two things meet, they join or touch: the place where the path meets the road | His eyebrows meet in the middle.
6 GROUP OF PEOPLE [I] if a group of people meet, they come together to do something: The chess club meets every Tuesday.
7 IN A COMPETITION [I,T] to play against someone in a competition: Leeds will meet Liverpool on Saturday. | The two teams haven't met since last season.
8 BE GOOD ENOUGH **meet a need/demand/ requirement etc** to be good enough to do what someone needs, wants, or expects: She didn't meet the requirements for the job. | beaches that **meet** European **standards** of cleanliness

M

9 PROVIDE MONEY **meet a cost/expense etc** to provide the money for something: *Many families have difficulty meeting the cost of university education.*

PHRASAL VERBS

meet up to meet someone in order to do something together: *Let's meet up later.* | **[+with]** *I'm planning to meet up with my brother.*

meet with sb/sth

1 to have a meeting with someone: *The President met with European leaders today.*

2 to get a particular reaction or result: *The plans have met with widespread opposition.* | *Our efforts have so far met with little success.*

meeting /ˈmiːtɪŋ/ n [C]

1 an event where people meet to discuss something: *I've got an important meeting this afternoon.* | **at/in a meeting** *She's in a meeting at the moment.* | **[+with]** *a meeting with my tutor*

2 when you meet someone: *She had disliked him since their first meeting.* | *A **chance meeting** (=a meeting that was not planned) in 1985 changed his life.*

COLLOCATIONS

verbs

to have a meeting (*also* **to hold a meeting** *formal*) *We had a meeting to discuss the problem.*
to go to a meeting (*also* **to attend a meeting** *formal*) *I have to go to a meeting now.*
to call a meeting (=to arrange a meeting) *The head teacher called a meeting of parents.*

types of meeting

a monthly/weekly/annual meeting *On Wednesday, there's our weekly staff meeting.*
a committee/staff/board etc meeting *The next committee meeting is on 9th January.*
a business meeting *She will be in business meetings all morning.*
a public meeting *He gave a speech at a public meeting.*
a summit meeting (=between government leaders) *The Prime Minister is in Paris for a summit meeting.*
a protest meeting *Anti-road campaigners are holding a protest meeting today.*

THESAURUS

meeting an occasion when people meet in order to discuss something: *He has gone to a business meeting.*
appointment a meeting arranged for a particular time: *I have an appointment with Dr Hanson at 3.15.*
conference an event that continues for several days at which a lot of people meet to discuss a particular subject and hear speeches about it: *She often has to give talks at conferences.*
rally a large public meeting, especially one held outdoors to support or protest about something: *More than a thousand people held a peace rally in London.*
get-together an informal meeting or party: *We're having a small get-together for my birthday.*
date an occasion when you go out socially with someone you are hoping to have a romantic relationship with: *Why don't you ask her out on a date?*

mega /ˈmegə/ adj informal very big and impressive: *Their first single was a mega hit.*

megabyte /ˈmegəbaɪt/ n [C] (written abbreviation **MB**) a unit for measuring computer information, equal to just over a million BYTES

megalomania /ˌmegələʊˈmeɪniə $ -loʊ-/ n [U] when someone wants a lot of power and enjoys controlling people —**megalomaniac** /-niæk/ n [C]

megaphone /ˈmegəfəʊn $ -foʊn/ n [C] a piece of equipment you talk through to make your voice louder when speaking to a crowd

melancholy /ˈmelənkəli $ -kɑːli/ n [U] formal a feeling of sadness

melee /ˈmeleɪ $ ˈmeɪleɪ, meˈleɪ/ n [C] a confusing and noisy situation involving a lot of people

mellow¹ /ˈmeləʊ $ -loʊ/ adj **1** pleasant and not too loud, bright, strong etc: *mellow music* | *a mellow flavor* **2** calm, relaxed, and gentle: *He was in a mellow mood.*

mellow² v [I,T] if you mellow, or if something mellows you, you become more gentle and sympathetic: *Age had not mellowed her.*

melodic /məˈlɒdɪk $ -ˈlɑː-/ (also **melodious** /məˈləʊdiəs $ -ˈloʊ-/) adj pleasant to listen to: *a melodic voice*

melodrama /ˈmelədrɑːmə $ -drɑːmə, -dræmə/ n [C,U] a story or play in which a lot of exciting things happen, and the characters show a lot of strong feelings

melodramatic /ˌmelədrəˈmætɪk◂/ adj behaving in a way that makes a situation seem much worse or much more important than it really is

melody /ˈmelədi/ n [C,U] (plural **melodies**) a tune

melon /ˈmelən/ n [C,U] a large sweet fruit with yellow or green skin and a lot of flat seeds → see picture on page A4

MELT

frozen | melted

melt /melt/ v

1 [I,T] to change from solid to liquid, or to make something do this by heating it → **freeze**, **thaw**: *The snow's melting.* | *Melt the chocolate in a pan.*

2 (also **melt away**) [I] to gradually disappear: *His anger slowly melted away.*

3 [I,T] to feel or make someone feel a lot of love or sympathy: *My **heart melted** when I saw her crying.*

PHRASAL VERBS

melt sth ⟷ **down** to heat a metal object until it becomes liquid

meltdown /'meltdaʊn/ n [C,U] an accident in which material inside a NUCLEAR REACTOR melts and burns through its container

'melting pot n [singular] a place where people from different races, countries, or social classes come to live together

member /'membə $ -ər/ n [C]
1 someone who belongs to a group or organization: **[+of]** He's a member of the tennis club.
2 something that is part of a group: Cats and tigers are members of the same species.

COLLOCATIONS

types of member

a team/committee/staff etc member Other team members began complaining.

a leading/senior member (=an important member) She was a leading member of an animal rights organization.

an active member (=one who takes part in many activities of an organization) My father was an active member of the church.

a new member The chess club always welcomes new members.

a founder member BrE, **a charter member** AmE (=one who helped start a group or organization) He was one of the band's founder members.

member + noun

a member of staff BrE I'd like to welcome a new member of staff.

a member of the public The building is open to members of the public.

a member of society (=a citizen) Many ex-prisoners have become useful members of society.

‚Member of 'Parliament n [C] (plural **Members of Parliament**) an MP **THESAURUS** POLITICIAN

membership /'membəʃɪp $ -ər-/ n **1** [U] when someone is a member of a group or organization: **[+of]** Greece **applied for membership** of the EU in 1975. | **[+in]** AmE: I renewed my **membership** in the club. | **membership fees** | a **membership card**
2 [singular, U] the members of an organization, or the total number of members: There has been an increase in membership this year. | The membership voted to change the rules.

membrane /'membreɪn/ n [C,U] a thin piece of skin that covers or connects parts of your body

memento /mə'mentəʊ $ -toʊ/ n [C] (plural **mementos**) a small thing that you keep to remind you of someone or something **SYN** souvenir: **[+of]** I kept the photos as a memento of our trip.

memo /'meməʊ $ -moʊ/ n [C] (plural **memos**) a short official note to someone in the same company: **[+to/from]** a memo from the manager

memoirs /'memwɑːz $ -wɑːrz/ n [plural] a book that someone writes about their life and experiences

memorabilia /‚memərə'bɪliə/ n [plural] things that you collect because they relate to a famous person or a subject you are interested in: soccer memorabilia

memorable /'memərəbəl/ adj good or enjoyable and likely to be remembered: a memorable day
—**memorably** adv

memorandum /‚memə'rændəm/ n [C] (plural **memoranda** /-də/ or **memorandums**) formal a MEMO

memorial¹ /mə'mɔːriəl/ adj [only before noun] done to remind people of someone who has died: a **memorial service** for people who died in the fire

memorial² n [C] something that is built to remind people of someone who has died: **[+to]** The stone is a permanent memorial to the victims of war. | a **war memorial**

memorize (also **-ise** BrE) /'meməraɪz/ v [T] to learn words, music etc so that you remember them perfectly **THESAURUS** REMEMBER

memory /'meməri/ n (plural **memories**)
1 [C,U] the ability to remember things: She has a very good memory. | **[+for]** My memory for names is terrible. | **from memory** (=using your memory and not notes) He recited the list from memory. | I'm afraid I forgot – I **have a memory like a sieve** (=I forget things very easily)!
2 [C usually plural] something that you remember from the past: **[+of]** I have happy memories of that summer. | My most **vivid memory** is the silence after the accident. | The smell **brought back memories** of childhood.
3 [C,U] the part of a computer where information is stored: 128 megabytes of memory

PHRASES

in memory of sb in order to remind people of someone who has died: a garden created in memory of the princess

in/within memory during the time that people can remember: the worst floods **in living memory** (=that anyone can remember)

COLLOCATIONS

adjectives

a good/excellent memory At 90, her memory is still very good.

a bad/poor/terrible memory I've got a terrible memory, so I write everything down.

a short memory (=so that you soon forget things) Some people have short memories for promises they've made.

a long memory (=so that you remember things for a long time) Those of you with long memories will remember his first film.

a photographic memory (=a memory that helps you remember every detail of things you have seen)

verbs

to lose your memory (=to become unable to remember what happened in the past) The blow to his head caused him to lose his memory.

to remain/stay/stick in sb's memory (=to be remembered for a long time) *His reply stuck in my memory.*

to refresh/jog sb's memory (=to help someone to remember) *I looked at my notes to refresh my memory.*

'Memory Stick n [C] *trademark* a card used to store information electronically that fits into computers, DIGITAL cameras etc → see picture on page A12

men /men/ n the plural of MAN

menace¹ /'menɪs/ n **1** [C] something or someone that is dangerous: **[+of]** *the growing menace of oil pollution at sea* | **[+to]** *He's a menace to society.* **2** [U] a threatening quality or feeling: *There was menace in her voice.*

menace² v [T] *formal* to threaten someone

menacing /'menəsɪŋ/ adj making you expect something unpleasant SYN **threatening**: *a menacing look* —**menacingly** adv

menagerie /mə'næedʒəri/ n [C] a group of wild animals that someone keeps

mend¹ /mend/ v [T] to repair something that is broken or damaged SYN **fix**: *We need someone to mend the roof.* THESAURUS ▶ REPAIR

MEND

mend² n **be on the mend** to be getting better after an illness

menial /'mi:niəl/ adj menial work is boring and needs no skill

meningitis /ˌmenɪn'dʒaɪtɪs/ n [U] a serious infectious disease that affects the brain

menopause /'menəpɔːz $ -pɒːz/ n **the menopause** the time when a woman stops menstruating, which usually happens around the age of 50

'men's room n [C] *especially AmE* a toilet for men SYN **gents** *BrE*

menstruate /'menstrueɪt/ v [I] *technical* when a woman menstruates every month, blood flows from her body —**menstrual** adj —**menstruation** /ˌmenstru'eɪʃən/ n [U]

mental Ac /'mentl/ adj [only before noun] relating to the mind, or happening in the mind: *Stress affects physical and **mental health**.* | **mental illness** | *a child's mental development* | *mental arithmetic* | *He **made a mental note** (=made a special effort to remember) to call her.* —**mentally** adv: *mentally ill*

mentality Ac /men'tæləti/ n [C] (*plural* **mentalities**) a particular attitude or way of thinking: *I can't understand his middle-class mentality.*

mention¹ /'menʃən/ v [T] to talk or write about something without giving many details: *Your name was mentioned in the book.* | **mention sth to sb** *I'll*

mention it to Jo and see what she says. | **[+(that)]** *He did mention he was having problems.* THESAURUS ▶ SAY

PHRASES

don't mention it *spoken* used to say politely that someone does not need to thank you: *'Thanks for the meal.' 'Don't mention it.'*

not to mention sth used to add something even more surprising: *He already owns several cars, not to mention the boat.*

mention² n [singular, U] when you mention someone or something in a conversation or piece of writing: **[+of]** *There was no mention of money.* | *He **made no mention** of his wife.* | **At the mention of** *ice cream, the child became excited.*

mentor /'mentɔː $ -tɔːr/ n [C] someone who advises and helps a less experienced person —**mentoring** n [U]

menu /'menjuː/ n [C]
1 a list of all the food you can choose in a restaurant: *Could we see the menu, please?* | **on the menu** *Is there any fish on the menu?*
2 a list of things on a computer screen that you can ask the computer to do: *Select 'Print' from the main menu.* → DROP-DOWN MENU

meow /miˈaʊ/ v, n the usual American spelling of MIAOW

MEP /ˌem iː 'piː/ n [C] (**Member of the European Parliament**) someone who has been elected as a member of the Parliament of the European Union

mercenary¹ /'mɜːsənəri $ 'mɜːrsəneri/ n [C] (*plural* **mercenaries**) a soldier who will fight for any country for money

mercenary² adj only interested in getting money for yourself

merchandise /'mɜːtʃəndaɪz, -daɪs $ 'mɜːr-/ n [U] *formal* goods that are being sold

merchandising /'mɜːtʃəndaɪzɪŋ $ 'mɜːr-/ n [U] products you can buy relating to a popular film, sports team, singer etc

merchant¹ /'mɜːtʃənt $ 'mɜːr-/ n [C] someone whose job is to buy and sell large amounts of something: *a wine merchant*

merchant² adj [only before noun] merchant ships are used for trade, not for war

merciful /'mɜːsɪfəl $ 'mɜːr-/ adj **1** kind and forgiving someone **2** a merciful death seems fortunate because it ends someone's suffering

mercifully /'mɜːsɪfəli $ 'mɜːr-/ adv fortunately, because a situation could have been much worse: *The trip was mercifully short.*

merciless /'mɜːsɪləs $ 'mɜːr-/ adj cruel and not caring if people suffer: *a merciless attack*

mercury /'mɜːkjəri $ 'mɜːr-/ n [U] a silver-coloured liquid metal, used in THERMOMETERS

Mercury n the PLANET that is nearest the Sun

mercy /'mɜːsi $ 'mɜːrsi/ n [U] kindness and willingness to forgive someone: *He **showed** no **mercy** to anyone.*

PHRASES

at the mercy of sb/sth unable to do anything to protect yourself from someone or something: *We were at the mercy of the weather.*

mere /mɪə $ mɪr/ *adj* [only before noun] used to emphasize how small or unimportant something is: *She won by a mere two points.* | *The mere thought made her furious.* | *The merest noise makes him nervous.*

merely /ˈmɪəli $ ˈmɪrli/ *adv* **1** used to emphasize that you are talking about only one thing and nothing else: *I called merely to say that I won't be able to come tomorrow.* **2** used to emphasize that something is very small or unimportant: *It was not a big problem, merely an inconvenience.*

merge /mɜːdʒ $ mɜːrdʒ/ *v* [I,T] to combine, or to join things together to form one thing: *a computer program that makes it easy to merge text and graphics* | **[+with]** *The company merged with a German electronics firm.* | **[+into]** *The village seems to merge into the landscape.* | **merge sth into sth** *The two magazines were merged into a single publication.*

merger /ˈmɜːdʒə $ ˈmɜːrdʒər/ *n* [C] when two companies join to form one larger one: **[+of/ between]** *a proposed merger between two banks* | **[+with]** *a merger with another hotel group*

meridian /məˈrɪdiən/ *n* [C] one of the imaginary lines drawn from the North Pole to the South Pole on a map

meringue /məˈræŋ/ *n* [C,U] a light sweet food made by baking a mixture of sugar and the white part of eggs

merit¹ /ˈmerɪt/ *n* [C,U] a good quality or feature: *The new scheme has several merits.* | **[+of]** *The book **has the merit** of being short yet informative.* | *There is some **merit in** this argument.* | **on merit** *Students are selected on merit* (=because they are good). | **of great/considerable/outstanding merit** *a poet of considerable merit*

merit² *v* [T] *formal* to deserve something: *an interesting question which merits attention*

mermaid /ˈmɜːmeɪd $ ˈmɜːr-/ *n* [C] in stories, a woman who has a fish's tail instead of legs, and lives in the sea

merriment /ˈmerɪmənt/ *n* [U] *literary* laughter, fun, and enjoyment: *Her eyes sparkled with merriment.*

merry /ˈmeri/ *adj literary* happy: *a merry tune* —**merrily** *adv*

PHRASES

Merry Christmas! used to greet someone at Christmas: *Merry Christmas and a Happy New Year!*

ˈmerry-go-ˌround *n* [C] a machine that turns around and around and has model cars or animals for children to sit on SYN **roundabout** *BrE*, **carousel** *AmE*

mesh¹ /meʃ/ *n* [C,U] material made of threads or wires that have been fastened together like a net: *a wire mesh fence*

mesh² *v* [I] if two ideas or things mesh, they fit well together: **[+with]** *His ideas didn't mesh with the views of the party.*

mesmerize (also **-ise** *BrE*) /ˈmezməraɪz/ *v* [T] if you are mesmerized by someone or something, you cannot stop looking at them or listening to them because they are so attractive or interesting: *He was mesmerized by her beauty.* —**mesmerizing** *adj*

mess¹ /mes/ *n* **1** [singular, U] when a place or person looks dirty and untidy: *The house was a **complete mess**.* | **in a mess** *BrE: He left the room in a terrible mess.* | *Try not to **make a mess** while you're cooking.* THESAURUS ▶ UNTIDY **2** [singular] *informal* a situation in which there are a lot of problems: **in a mess** *The whole system is in a mess.* | *She felt she'd **made a mess of** her life.*

mess² *v*

PHRASAL VERBS

mess around (also **mess about** *BrE*) *informal* **1** to do things that are silly or not useful: *Come on – we haven't got time to mess around.* **2** **mess sb around** to treat someone badly, especially by changing your mind or not being honest: *I won't let him mess me around.*

mess around with sb/sth (also **mess about with** sb/sth *BrE*) *informal* **1** to play with something or make small changes to it, especially in a way that annoys someone: *Who's been messing around with my camera?* **2** to have a sexual relationship with someone, which people do not approve of

mess up *informal* **1** **mess sth** ↔ **up** to spoil something: *I hope I haven't messed up your plans.* **2** **mess sth** ↔ **up** to make something dirty or untidy: *Who messed up the kitchen?* **3** to make a mistake and do something badly: *I messed up on the last question.* | **mess sth** ↔ **up** *I think I messed up the test.*

mess with sb/sth *informal* to get involved with someone or something that is dangerous or could cause problems: *Don't mess with this guy.*

message /ˈmesɪdʒ/ *n* [C]

1 a piece of information that you tell someone, send to them, or leave for them: *Will you give Stephen a message from me, please?*

2 [usually singular] the main idea that someone is trying to communicate in a film, book, speech etc: *The film **sends** a clear **message** about the horrors of war.* | *an effective way of **getting** your **message across** (=communicating what you want to say)* THESAURUS ▶ TELL

PHRASES

get the message *informal* to understand what someone is trying to tell you: *OK, I get the message – I'm going.*

COLLOCATIONS

verbs

to get a message (also **to receive a message** *formal*) *Didn't you get my message?*

to send a message *They send text messages to each other all day.*

to leave a message *I left a message on her voicemail.*

to give sb/pass on a message *Could you pass on a message to him for me?*

message board

to take a message (=to write down a message from someone for someone else) *Sorry, she's not home yet. Can I take a message?*

types of message

a telephone/phone message *There was a telephone message for her to call Harry.*
a text message *I use my mobile mainly for text messages.*
an email/mail message *We got an email message from some friends in Canada.*
an error message (=on a computer screen) *If you enter a date in the past, you will get an error message.*
a message of support/sympathy/ congratulations *We've had a lot of messages of support.*

message board *n* [C] a place on a website where you can read or leave messages

messenger /'mesɪndʒə, -sən- $ -ər/ *n* [C] someone who takes messages to other people

Messiah /mə'saɪə/ *n* **the Messiah** the person who some religions believe will be sent by God to save the world

Messrs the written plural of MR

messy /'mesi/ *adj* **1** dirty or untidy: *a messy room* **THESAURUS** UNTIDY **2** a messy job or activity involves making a lot of mess **3** *informal* a messy situation is complicated and unpleasant: *a messy divorce*

met /met/ *v* the past tense and past participle of MEET

metabolism /mə'tæbəlɪzəm/ *n* [C,U] the chemical processes in your body that change food into energy

metal /'metl/ *n* [C,U] a hard substance such as iron, gold, or steel: *It's made of metal.* | *a metal box*

metal de,tector *n* [C] a machine used for finding metal objects

metallic /mə'tælɪk/ *adj* containing metal, or tasting, sounding, or shining like metal: *metallic blue paint*

metamorphosis /ˌmetə'mɔːfəsɪs $ -'mɔːr-/ *n* [C,U] (plural **metamorphoses** /-siːz/) *formal* when something changes into something completely different: *the country's metamorphosis into a modern, industrialized nation*

metaphor /'metəfə, -fɔː $ -fɔːr/ *n* [C,U] a way of describing something by referring to it as something else → **simile**: *'A river of tears' is a metaphor.* —**metaphorical** /ˌmetə'fɒrɪkəl $ -'fɔː- -'fɑː-/ *adj* —**metaphorically** /-kli/ *adv*

metaphysical /ˌmetə'fɪzɪkəl/ *adj* concerned with the nature of truth, life, and reality

mete /miːt/ *v*
PHRASAL VERBS
mete *sth* ↔ **out** *formal* to give a punishment to someone

meteor /'miːtiə $ -ər/ *n* [C] a small piece of rock or metal that is moving through space

meteoric /ˌmiːti'ɒrɪk $ -'ɔːrɪk, -'ɑːrɪk/ *adj* happening very suddenly and quickly: *his meteoric rise to fame*

meteorite /'miːtiəraɪt/ *n* [C] a piece of rock or metal that has come from space and landed on Earth

meteorology /ˌmiːtiə'rɒlədʒi $ -'rɑː-/ *n* [U] the scientific study of weather —**meteorologist** *n* [C]

meter /'miːtə $ -ər/ *n* [C] **1** a piece of equipment that measures the amount of gas, electricity, water etc you have used: *A man came to read the electricity meter.* | *a parking meter* (=one that measures how long you have parked somewhere) **2** the American spelling of **metre**

methadone /'meθədəʊn $ -doʊn/ *n* [U] *technical* a drug that is often given to people who are trying to stop taking HEROIN

methane /'miːθeɪn $ 'me-/ *n* [U] a gas with no colour or smell

method Ac /'meθəd/ *n* [C] a way of doing something, especially one that a lot of people know about and use: *traditional teaching methods* | **method of/for (doing) sth** *This is the simplest method of payment.* **THESAURUS** WAY

methodical Ac /mə'θɒdɪkəl $ -'θɑː-/ *adj* careful and well-organized —**methodically** /-kli/ *adv*

Methodist /'meθədɪst/ *n* [C] someone who belongs to a Christian religious group that follows the ideas of John Wesley —**Methodist** *adj*

methodology Ac /ˌmeθə'dɒlədʒi $ -'dɑː-/ *n* [C,U] (plural **methodologies**) the set of methods used to do a job or study something

meticulous /mə'tɪkjələs/ *adj* very careful about details, with everything done correctly: *They keep meticulous records.* **THESAURUS** CAREFUL —**meticulously** *adv*

metre *BrE*, **meter** *AmE* /'miːtə $ -ər/ *n* (written abbreviation **m**)
1 [C] a unit for measuring length, equal to 100 centimetres
2 [C,U] the regular pattern of sounds made by the words of a poem

metric /'metrɪk/ *adj* using the system of weights and measures based on grams, metres, and litres → **imperial**

metro /'metrəʊ $ -troʊ/ *n* [singular] a railway system running under the ground in a city **SYN** **underground** *BrE*, **subway** *AmE*: *the Paris Metro*

metropolis /mɪ'trɒpəlɪs $ -'trɑː-/ *n* [C] a very large city, or the most important city of a country —**metropolitan** /ˌmetrə'pɒlətən $ -'pɑː-/ *adj* [only before noun]

mettle /'metl/ *n* [U] courage and determination to do something even when it is very difficult

mews /mjuːz/ *n* [plural] *BrE* a small street or area in a city where horses used to be kept, but where people now live

mg the written abbreviation of **milligram**

miaow *BrE*, **meow** *AmE* /mi'aʊ/ *v* [I] if a cat miaows, it makes a crying sound —**miaow** *n* [C]

mice /maɪs/ *n* the plural of MOUSE

mickey /ˈmɪki/ (*also* **mick** /mɪk/) *n* **take the mickey (out of sb)** *BrE informal* to make someone seem silly, for example by making jokes about them or copying them → **tease**

micro- /maɪkrəʊ, -krə $ -krəʊ, -krə/ *prefix* very small, or relating to very small things: *microcomputers* | *a microscope* (=for looking at very small things)

microbe /ˈmaɪkrəʊb $ -kroʊb/ *n* [C] an extremely small living thing that you cannot see without a MICROSCOPE

microbiology /ˌmaɪkrəʊbaɪˈɒlədʒi $ -krəʊbaɪˈɑːl-/ *n* [U] the scientific study of very small living things —**microbiologist** *n* [C]

microchip /ˈmaɪkrəʊˌtʃɪp $ -kroʊ-/ *n* [C] a very small piece of SILICON containing electronic parts, used in computers and other machines

microcosm /ˈmaɪkrəʊkɒzəm $ -kroʊkɑː-/ *n* [C] a small group that has the same qualities or features as a much larger one → **macrocosm**: *New York's mix of people is a microcosm of America.*

microorganism /ˌmaɪkrəʊˈɔːɡənɪzəm $ -kroʊˈɔːr-/ *n* [C] an extremely small living thing that you cannot see without a MICROSCOPE

microphone /ˈmaɪkrəfəʊn $ -foʊn/ *n* [C] a piece of equipment that you use to record sounds or to make sounds louder

microprocessor /ˈmaɪkrəʊˌprəʊsesə $ -kroʊˌprɑːsesər/ *n* [C] the main MICROCHIP in a computer, which controls most of its operations

microscope /ˈmaɪkrəskəʊp $ -skoʊp/ *n* [C] a scientific instrument that makes very small things look larger

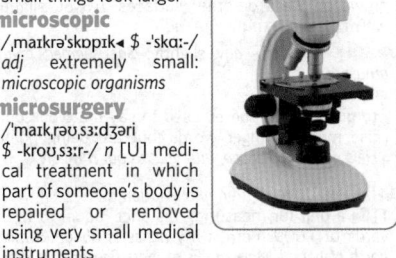
MICROSCOPE

microscopic /ˌmaɪkrəˈskɒpɪk◂ $ -ˈskɑː-/ *adj* extremely small: *microscopic organisms*

microsurgery /ˈmaɪkrəʊˌsɜːdʒəri $ -kroʊˌsɜːr-/ *n* [U] medical treatment in which part of someone's body is repaired or removed using very small medical instruments

microwave /ˈmaɪkrəweɪv/ (*also* **microwave oven**) *n* [C] a machine that cooks food very quickly, using electric waves instead of heat → *see picture at* **KITCHEN** **THESAURUS** COOK —**microwave** *v* [T]

mid- /mɪd/ *prefix* middle: *She's in her mid-20s.* | *in mid-July*

midair /ˌmɪdˈeə $ -ˈer◂/ *n* **in midair** in the air or sky: *The plane exploded in midair.* —**midair** *adj* [only before noun]

midday /ˌmɪdˈdeɪ◂ $ ˈmɪd-deɪ/ *n* [U] 12 o'clock in the middle of the day **SYN** noon → **midnight**: **at/around/by midday** *I met him at midday.*

middle¹ /ˈmɪdl/ *n*
1 the middle the centre part of something, or the part between the beginning and end of something: **[+of]** *We rowed out to the middle of the lake.* | *Go back to sleep – it's the middle of the night!* | **in the middle** *Look at this old photo – that's me in the middle.* | *Someone fainted in the middle of the ceremony.*
2 sb's middle *informal* someone's waist: *She put the scarf around her middle.*
PHRASES
be in the middle of (doing) sth to be busy doing something: *Can I call you back? I'm in the middle of cooking dinner.*
in the middle of nowhere a long way from a town: *The house was in the middle of nowhere.*

Grammar
Do not say 'on the middle of the room'. Say **in the middle** of the room.

middle² *adj* [only before noun]
1 nearest the centre: *Shall we sit in the middle row?* | *The middle lane was blocked because of an accident.* → *see picture at* **HAND¹**
2 half of the way through an event or period of time: *the middle part of the day*
3 between high and low, big and small etc: *a car in the middle price range*
PHRASES
middle ground opinions or ideas that are not extreme, and that people can agree about: *Their party has dominated the middle ground in politics for the last thirty years.*

middle-'aged *adj* between the ages of about 40 and 60: *a middle-aged businessman* —**middle age** *n* [U]

Middle 'Ages *n* **the Middle Ages** the period in European history between about 1100 and 1500 AD

middle 'class *n* [C] the social class that includes people who are educated and work in professional jobs, for example teachers or managers —**middle-class** *adj*: *middle-class families*

Middle 'East *n* **the Middle East** the area including Iran and Egypt and the countries between them

middleman /ˈmɪdlmæn/ *n* [C] (*plural* **middlemen** /-men/) someone who buys things to sell to someone else, or who arranges a business deal between two other people

middle 'name *n* [C] the name that is between your first name and your family name **THESAURUS** NAME

middle-of-the-'road *adj* middle-of-the-road opinions are not extreme or likely to cause disagreement

'middle school *n* [C] a school in Britain for children between the ages of 8 and 12, and in the US for children between 11 and 14

midfield /ˈmɪdfiːld/ *n* [U] the middle part of the area where a game such as football is played —**midfielder** *n* [C]

midget /'mɪdʒɪt/ n [C] an offensive word for a very small person

Midlands /'mɪdləndz/ n **the Midlands** the central area of England, around Birmingham

midlife crisis /ˌmɪdlaɪf 'kraɪsɪs/ n [singular] a period of worry and doubt about your life that some people experience when they are about 40 and 50 years old

midnight /'mɪdnaɪt/ n [U] 12 o'clock at night → **midday: at/around/by midnight** *We close at midnight.*

> **Word Choice: midnight or the middle of the night?**
> **Midnight** means 12 o'clock at night: *We arrived home at midnight.*
> The **middle of the night** is the period of time between about 11.30 and 3 o'clock: *I woke up in the middle of the night.* Do not say 'I woke up in the midnight.'

midriff /'mɪdrɪf/ n [C] the part of your body between your chest and your waist

midst /mɪdst/ n [singular, U] the middle of an event, situation, place, or group: *The government is **in the midst of** a major crisis.* | *We have a traitor in our midst.*

midsummer /ˌmɪd'sʌmə◂ $ -ər◂/ n [U] the middle of summer: *a lovely midsummer day*

midterm /'mɪdtɜːm $ -tɜːrm/ adj [only before noun] in the middle of one of the main periods of the school year, or in the middle of an elected government's time in power: *midterm tests* | *midterm elections*

midway /ˌmɪd'weɪ◂ $ 'mɪdweɪ/ adj, adv at the middle point between two places, or between the beginning and end of something: **midway between sth and sth** *There's a gas station midway between here and Fresno.* | **[+through]** *He collapsed midway through the performance.*

midweek /ˌmɪd'wiːk◂ $ 'mɪdwiːk/ adj, adv on one of the middle days of the week: *a midweek match against Liverpool* | *I'll be seeing him midweek.*

Midwest /ˌmɪd'west/ n **the Midwest** the central area of the US —**Midwestern** adj

midwife /'mɪdwaɪf/ n [C] (plural **midwives** /-waɪvz/) a nurse who has been trained to help women when they are having a baby

midwinter /ˌmɪd'wɪntə $ -ər/ n [U] the middle of winter

miffed /mɪft/ adj informal slightly annoyed

might¹ /maɪt/ modal verb
1 if something might happen or might be true, it is possible, but you are not certain: *I might be able to go.* | *I think he might be French.* | *Do you think she might have missed the train?* **THESAURUS** MAYBE
2 might have used to say that something was a possibility in the past although it did not actually happen: *The tiger might have killed you!*
3 especially BrE formal used to ask politely for something **SYN** may: *Might I have some water?*
4 used to suggest politely what someone should do:

You might try phoning her at home. → **may/might as well** at WELL¹

might² n [U] literary great strength and power: *She pushed **with all** her **might**.*

mightn't /'maɪtənt/ especially BrE informal the short form of 'might not'

might've /'maɪtəv/ informal the short form of 'might have'

mighty¹ /'maɪti/ adj literary very strong, big, and powerful: *the mighty Mississippi river*

mighty² adv AmE informal very: *That chicken smells mighty good.*

migraine /'miːgreɪn, 'maɪ- $ 'maɪ-/ n [C] an extremely bad HEADACHE

migrant Ac /'maɪgrənt/ n [C] **1** someone who goes to live in another area or country, especially to find work → **emigrant, immigrant**: *the flow of economic migrants* | *migrant workers* **2** a bird or animal that migrates

migrate Ac /maɪ'greɪt $ 'maɪgreɪt/ v [I] **1** if birds or animals migrate, they travel from one part of the world to another at the same time each year **2** to go to live in another area or country, especially to find work → **emigrate** —**migration** /maɪ'greɪʃən/ n [C,U] —**migratory** /maɪ'greɪtəri, 'maɪgrətəri $ 'maɪgrətɔːri/ adj

mike /maɪk/ n [C] informal a MICROPHONE

mild /maɪld/ adj
1 quite warm: *a mild climate*
2 not too severe, strong, or serious: *a mild case of flu* | *mild criticism* | *The previous recession was **relatively mild**.*
3 not having a strong taste: *mild cheddar cheese* **THESAURUS** TASTE

mildew /'mɪldjuː $ -duː/ n [U] a substance that grows on walls or other surfaces in wet, slightly warm places —**mildewed** adj

mildly /'maɪldli/ adv slightly: *She seemed mildly amused.*
PHRASES
to put it mildly spoken used to say that you could use much stronger words, but are being polite: *He's not very pleased with you, to put it mildly.*

mile /maɪl/ n (written abbreviation **m**)
1 [C] a unit for measuring distance, equal to 1,760 yards or 1,609 metres: *My house is about 15 miles north of here.* | *Mark walks at least five miles a day.* | *He was driving at 70 **miles per hour**.*
2 miles [plural] informal a very long distance: **for miles** *We walked for miles without seeing anyone.*

mileage /'maɪlɪdʒ/ n [singular, U] the number of miles that a vehicle has travelled since it was new: *a used car with a **low mileage***

milestone /'maɪlstəʊn $ -stoʊn/ n [C] a very important event in the development of something: **[+in]** *an important milestone in South African history*

milieu /'miːljɜː $ miː'ljɜː, -'ljuː/ n [C,U] (plural **milieux** /-ljɜː, -ljɜːz $ -'ljuːz, -'ljɜː, -'ljuː/ or **milieus**) formal the things and people that surround you and influence the way you live and think

militant /ˈmɪlɪtənt/ *adj* willing to use strong or violent action in order to achieve political or social change: *a militant protest group* —**militant** *n* [C] —**militancy** *n* [U]

militarism /ˈmɪlətərɪzəm/ *n* [U] the belief that a country should increase its army, navy etc and use them to get what it wants

military[1] Ac /ˈmɪlɪtəri $ -teri-/ *adj* used by or relating to the army, navy, or air force: *military aircraft* | **military forces** | *All young men had to* **do military service** (=spend a period of time in the army, navy, or air force).

military[2] Ac *n* **the military** the military forces of a country: *My father is in the military.*

militia /məˈlɪʃə/ *n* [C] a group of trained soldiers who are not part of an official army

milk[1] /mɪlk/ *n* [U] a white liquid produced by female animals and drunk by people, or produced by women and animals to feed their babies: *a glass of milk* | *Would you like milk in your coffee?* | *Breast milk is best for babies.*

milk[2] *v* [T] to take milk from a cow or goat.

PHRASES
milk sb/sth for sth to get all the money, advantages etc that you can from a person or situation: *He seemed to be milking me for information.*

milkman /ˈmɪlkmən/ *n* [C] (*plural* **milkmen** /-mən/) someone in Britain who delivers milk to houses

milk'shake / $ ../ *n* [C,U] a cold drink made from milk mixed with fruit or chocolate

milky /ˈmɪlki/ *adj* containing a lot of milk, or similar to milk: *milky coffee* | *a sweet milky flavour*

Milky 'Way *n* **the Milky Way** the pale white band of stars that can be seen across the sky at night

mill[1] /mɪl/ *n* [C] **1** a building containing a large machine for crushing grain into flour, or the machine itself **2** a factory that produces materials such as cotton, cloth, or steel: *an old cotton mill* **3** **coffee/pepper mill** a small machine for crushing coffee or pepper

mill[2] *v* [T] to crush grain, pepper etc in a mill: *freshly milled black pepper*

PHRASAL VERBS
mill around/about (sth) if a lot of people are milling around, they move around a place without a particular purpose: *Crowds of students were milling around in the streets.*

millennium /mɪˈleniəm/ *n* [C] (*plural* **millennia** /-niə/) a period of 1,000 years, or the time when a new 1,000-year period begins: *How did you celebrate* **the millennium** (=when the year 1999 became 2000)?

milligram /ˈmɪlɪɡræm/ *n* [C] (*written abbreviation* **mg**) a unit for measuring weight. There are 1,000 milligrams in one gram.

millilitre *BrE*, **milliliter** *AmE* /ˈmɪlɪliːtə $ -ər/ *n* [C] (*written abbreviation* **ml**) a unit for measuring liquids. There are 1,000 millilitres in one litre.

millimetre *BrE*, **millimeter** *AmE* /ˈmɪlɪmiːtə $ -ər/ *n* [C] (*written abbreviation* **mm**) a unit for measuring

length. There are 1,000 millimetres in one metre.

million /ˈmɪljən/ *number* (*plural* **million** *or* **millions**) **1** the number 1,000,000: **two/three/four etc million** *six million people* | **millions of pounds/dollars etc** **2** an extremely large number of people or things: **a million** *I've got a million ideas.* | **millions of sth** *She seems to have millions of friends.* —**millionth** *adj*: *The park has just received its millionth visitor.* —**millionth** *n* [C]

millionaire /ˌmɪljəˈneə $ -ˈner/ *n* [C] someone who is very rich and has at least one million dollars or pounds

millisecond /ˈmɪlɪˌsekənd/ *n* [C] a unit for measuring time. There are 1,000 milliseconds in one second.

mime /maɪm/ *n* [C,U] the use of movements to tell a story, without any words —**mime** *v* [I,T]

mimic /ˈmɪmɪk/ *v* [T] (**mimicked**, **mimicking**) to copy the way someone speaks or behaves, especially to make people laugh: *Some of the boys were mimicking the teacher.* —**mimic** *n* [C]: *He's a good mimic.* —**mimicry** *n* [U]

min. **1** the written abbreviation of **minimum 2** the written abbreviation of **minute**

mince[1] /mɪns/ *v* [T] to cut food into extremely small pieces, using a machine: *minced beef*

mince[2] *n* [U] *BrE* meat, especially BEEF, that has been cut into very small pieces in a machine SYN **ground beef** *AmE*

mincemeat /ˈmɪns-miːt/ *n* [U] a mixture of dried fruits and nuts, used to make cakes etc

mince 'pie *n* [C] a small PIE filled with mincemeat, traditionally eaten at Christmas

mind[1] /maɪnd/ *n* [C,U] **1** the part of a person that makes them able to think, feel, and imagine things → **brain**: *Relaxation is good for mind and body.* | *the complex nature of* **the human mind** | **in sb's mind** *I keep going over the problem in my mind.* **2** **technically minded/politically minded/liberal-minded etc** having a particular attitude, or interested in a particular thing: *scientifically minded students* → **at/in the back of your mind** at BACK[1], **cast your mind back** at CAST[1], **change your mind** at CHANGE[1], **frame of mind** at FRAME[1], **have an open mind** at OPEN[1], **give sb a piece of your mind** at PIECE[1], **slip your mind** at SLIP[1], **speak your mind** at SPEAK, **STATE OF MIND**

PHRASES
come/spring to mind if something comes to mind, you suddenly think of it: *A memory of last night came to mind, and he smiled.*
cross/enter your mind if a particular idea crosses your mind, you think of it: *It never crossed my mind that she was lying.*
get/put sb/sth out of your mind to stop yourself thinking about someone or something: *I just couldn't get her out of my mind.*
go/be out of your mind *informal* to be stupid or crazy: *Marry him? She must be out of her mind!*
have sth in mind to be planning to do something: *What changes do you have in mind?*

mind

keep/bear sth in mind to remember something that may be useful in the future: *It's a good idea – I'll keep it in mind.*

make up your mind to decide something: *Have you made up your mind which college to go to?* THESAURUS DECIDE

on your mind if something is on your mind, you are thinking or worrying about it a lot: *Dad seems to have something on his mind.*

put your mind to sth to decide that you want to achieve something and try very hard to do it: *Anyone can lose weight if they put their mind to it.*

put/set sb's mind at rest to make someone feel less worried about something: *See a doctor to put your mind at rest.*

take sb's mind off sth to make someone stop thinking and worrying about something: *I put some music on to take my mind off the subject.* THESAURUS FORGET

to my mind in my opinion: *To my mind, they are the better team.*

with sb/sth in mind considering someone or something when doing something: *cities designed with wildlife in mind*

mind² v

1 [I,T] to feel annoyed or upset about something: *It was raining, but we didn't mind.* | *Do you think she'd mind if we didn't come?* | **mind (sb) doing sth** *Do you mind having to work so late?*

2 [T] to look after someone or something for a short time: *Could you mind my bag?*

3 mind! *BrE spoken* used to warn someone to be careful of something: *Mind the step!* | **Mind you don't hit your head.**

PHRASES

do/would you mind? *spoken* used to ask politely if you can do something, or if someone will do something: *Do you mind if I use your phone?* | *Would you mind waiting a moment?*

I don't mind *especially BrE* used to say that you are happy to accept whatever someone else decides: *'Orange or apple juice?' 'I don't mind.'* | **[+what/who/where]** *I don't mind where we go.*

I wouldn't mind … *spoken* used to say that you would like something: *I wouldn't mind another cup of coffee.*

mind you used to add more information to what you have just said: *It's a beautiful house. Mind you, it cost enough.*

mind your own business *spoken* to not ask questions about a situation that does not involve you: *'So did he kiss you?' 'Mind your own business!'*

never mind *spoken* used to tell someone not to worry, or that something is not important: *'I'm sorry I'm so late.' 'Never mind.'*

not mind doing sth to be willing to do something: *I don't mind driving if you're tired.*

PHRASAL VERBS

mind out *BrE spoken* used to warn someone to move out of the way

'mind-,blowing *adj informal* very exciting or strange

'mind-,boggling *adj informal* very difficult to imagine because of being so big, strange, complicated

etc: *the mind-boggling distances in space*

minder /ˈmaɪndə $ -ər/ *n* [C] *BrE* someone who is employed to protect another person

mindful /ˈmaɪndfəl/ *adj* **mindful of sth** *formal* remembering a particular rule or fact when you are making decisions about what to do: *Mindful of the guide's warning, they returned before dark.*

mindless /ˈmaɪndləs/ *adj* **1** stupid and without any purpose: *mindless vandalism* **2** able to be done without using your mind: *a mindless job*

mindset /ˈmaɪndset/ *n* [C] the attitude and way of thinking that someone has: *a very old-fashioned mindset*

mine¹ /maɪn/ *pron* the POSSESSIVE form of 'I': *'Whose coat is this?' 'It's mine.'* | *His English is better than mine.* | **of mine** *He's an old friend of mine.*

mine² *n* [C]

1 a deep hole or holes in the ground that people dig to remove coal, gold etc: *a coal mine*

2 a bomb that is hidden under the ground or under water that explodes when it is touched

mine³ *v* **1** [I,T] to dig into the ground to get coal, gold etc **2** [T] to put bombs under the ground or under water

minefield /ˈmaɪnfiːld/ *n* **1** [C] an area of land or sea where bombs have been hidden **2** [singular] a situation in which there are many hidden difficulties and dangers: *Choosing the right school can be a mine-field.*

miner /ˈmaɪnə $ -ər/ *n* [C] someone who works in a mine

mineral /ˈmɪnərəl/ *n* [C]

1 a substance that is formed naturally in the earth, such as coal, salt, stone, or gold: *The area is very rich in minerals.*

2 a natural substance such as iron that is in some foods and is important for good health: *Milk is full of vitamins and minerals.*

'mineral ,water *n* [C,U] water that comes from under the ground and contains minerals that are good for you

mingle /ˈmɪŋɡəl/ *v* **1** [I,T] if smells, sounds, or feelings mingle, they mix together: *Add the wine and allow the flavours to mingle.* **2** [I] to meet and talk to a lot of different people at an event: **[+with]** *Diana enjoyed mingling with the crowds.*

mini- /mɪni, mɪnə/ *prefix* very small or short: *a minibreak (=a short holiday)*

miniature¹ /ˈmɪnətʃə $ ˈmɪniətʃər/ *adj* [only before noun] much smaller than normal: *a miniature railway* | *miniature roses* THESAURUS SMALL

miniature² *n* [C] a very small painting, especially of a person

PHRASES

in miniature exactly like someone or something else, but much smaller: *She's her mother in miniature.*

minibus /ˈmɪnibʌs/ *n* [C] *BrE* a small bus for about 12 people

M

minicab /ˈmɪnikæb/ n [C] *BrE* a taxi that you have to order by telephone, not one that you can stop in the street

minimal Ac /ˈmɪnəməl/ adj very small in degree or amount: *The storm caused only minimal damage.* —**minimally** adv

minimalism /ˈmɪnəməlɪzəm/ n [U] a style of art, design, music etc that is very simple and uses only basic shapes, colours etc —**minimalist** adj, n [C]

minimize Ac (also **-ise** *BrE*) /ˈmɪnɪmaɪz/ v [T] **1** to make the amount of something dangerous or unpleasant as small as possible: *To minimize the risk of getting heart disease, exercise daily.* **2** to make a document or program on your computer very small while you are not using it OPP **maximize**

minimum¹ Ac /ˈmɪnəməm/ adj the minimum number or amount is the smallest that is possible or needed OPP **maximum**: *The minimum age for retirement is 55.* | *the national minimum wage* —**minimum** adv: *It's worth £50, minimum.*

minimum² Ac n [singular] the smallest number or amount that is possible or needed OPP **maximum**: **a minimum of sth** *Having a horse costs a minimum of £2,000 a year.* | *Costs were kept to a minimum.*

mining /ˈmaɪnɪŋ/ n [U] the job or industry of digging coal, gold etc out of the ground

miniscule /ˈmɪnəskjuːl/ adj another spelling of MINUSCULE

miniskirt /ˈmɪniskɜːt $ -skɜːrt/ n [C] a very short skirt

minister¹ /ˈmɪnɪstə $ -ər/ n [C]
1 a politician who is in charge of a government department: **[+of]** *the Minister of Education*
2 a priest in some Christian churches

minister² v
PHRASAL VERBS
minister to sb/sth *formal* to give help to someone, especially someone sick or old: *doctors ministering to the needs of their patients*

ministerial Ac /ˌmɪnəˈstɪəriəl $ -ˈstɪr-/ adj [only before noun] relating to government ministers: *ministerial decisions*

ministry Ac /ˈmɪnəstri/ n [C] (plural **ministries**) a government department: *the Defence Ministry* | *the Ministry of Agriculture*

mink /mɪŋk/ n [C,U] (plural **mink** or **minks**) a small animal with soft brown fur, or the valuable fur from this animal: *a mink coat*

minnow /ˈmɪnəʊ $ -noʊ/ n [C] a very small fish

minor¹ Ac /ˈmaɪnə $ -ər/ adj
1 small and not very important or serious → **major**: *We made a few minor changes to the plan.* | *a minor road* | **minor injury/surgery/illness** *He escaped with only minor injuries.* THESAURUS **SMALL**
2 based on a particular type of musical SCALE → **major**: *Mahler's Symphony No. 3 in D minor*

minor² n [C] *law* someone who is below the age at which they become legally responsible for their actions

minor³ v
PHRASAL VERBS
minor in sth *AmE* to study a second subject as part of your university degree → **major**: *I'm minoring in African Studies.*

minority Ac /maɪˈnɒrəti $ məˈnɔː-, məˈnɑː-/ n (plural **minorities**)
1 [singular] a small part of a larger group of people or things → **majority**: **[+of]** *Only a minority of students get a first-class degree.*
2 [C usually plural] a group of people of a different race or religion from most people in a country: *children from ethnic minorities* | *language classes for minority groups* | *the teaching of minority languages in schools*
PHRASES
be in the/a minority to form less than half of a larger group: *Boys are very much in the minority in the dance class.*

mint¹ /mɪnt/ n **1** [U] a plant with leaves that have a strong fresh taste, used in cooking: *mint tea* **2** [C] a sweet with the strong fresh taste of PEPPERMINT **3** [C] a place where coins are officially made —**minty** adj: *a minty taste*

mint² v [T] to make a coin

minus¹ /ˈmaɪnəs/ prep **1** used to show that one number is being taken away from another → **plus**: *17 minus 5 is 12 (17 - 5 = 12).* **2** a minus number is below zero: *Temperatures tonight will fall to minus 8.* **3** without something that would normally be there: *He came back minus a couple of front teeth.*

minus² n [C] something bad about a situation → **plus**: *There are pluses and minuses to living in a big city.* | *On the minus side, there is no free back-up service if things go wrong.*

minuscule, miniscule /ˈmɪnəskjuːl/ adj very small: *a minuscule amount of food*

ˈminus ˌsign (also **minus**) n [C] the sign (-) used to show that a number is less than zero, or that one number is taken away from another

minute¹ /ˈmɪnət/ n [C]
1 a period of time equal to 60 seconds. There are 60 minutes in one hour: *Clare's train arrives in 15 minutes.* | *It's three minutes to ten.* | *a ten-minute bus ride* | *He called 20 minutes ago.*
2 a minute a very short period of time: *It'll only take me a minute to do this.* | *He was there a minute ago.* THESAURUS **TIME**
3 minutes [plural] an official written record of the things that were said during a meeting: *the minutes of the last meeting* | *Is someone taking the minutes?*
PHRASES
(at) any minute (now) very soon: *She should get here any minute now.* THESAURUS **SOON**
by the minute used to say that something is happening more and more: *She was getting angrier by the minute.*
in a minute very soon: *I'll do it in a minute.* THESAURUS **SOON**
the last minute the last possible time, just before it is too late: *He cancelled the trip at the last minute.* | *Don't leave it until the last minute to write your essay.* → **LAST-MINUTE**

the minute (that) as soon as: *I knew it was Jill the minute I heard her voice.*

this minute immediately: *Come here, this minute!*

wait/just a minute *spoken* **1** used to ask someone to wait for a short period of time: *'Are you coming with us?' 'Yes, just a minute.'* **2** used when you do not agree with someone: *Wait a minute – that can't be right!*

minute² /ˈmaɪnjuːt $ -ˈnuːt/ *adj* **1** extremely small: *minute handwriting* **THESAURUS** SMALL **2** very careful and thorough: *John explained the plan in minute detail.*

miracle /ˈmɪrəkəl/ *n [C]* **1** something very lucky or very good that you did not expect to happen or did not think was possible: *It's a miracle that no one was hurt. | The builders have worked miracles in finishing the job so quickly.* **THESAURUS** LUCKY **2** something that seems impossible and is thought to be caused by God

PHRASES

miracle cure/drug a very effective medical treatment that cures even serious diseases: *There is no miracle cure for diabetes.*

miraculous /mɪˈrækjələs/ *adj* very lucky and completely unexpected: *a miraculous recovery* —**miraculously** *adv*

mirage /ˈmɪrɑːʒ $ məˈrɑːʒ/ *n [C]* when the hot air in a desert makes you see water that is not really there

mirror¹ /ˈmɪrə $ -ər/ *n [C]* a piece of special glass made so that when you look at it you see yourself: *in a mirror He glanced at his reflection in the mirror.* → see picture at **BATHROOM**

mirror² *v [T]* to be very similar to something or to show clearly what it is like: *The excitement of the 1960s is mirrored in its music.*

mirth /mɜːθ $ mɜːrθ/ *n [U] formal* laughter and happiness

mis- /mɪs/ *prefix* bad or wrong, or badly or wrongly: *Don't misbehave. | economic mismanagement | You misunderstand me.*

misapprehension /ˌmɪsæprɪˈhenʃən/ *n [C,U] formal* a mistaken belief: **under a misapprehension** *I was under the misapprehension that Eric was still working in Germany.*

misappropriate /ˌmɪsəˈprəʊprieɪt $ -ˈproʊ-/ *v [T] formal* to dishonestly take money that you are responsible for —**misappropriation** /ˌmɪsəprəʊpriˈeɪʃən $ -proʊ-/ *n [U]: the misappropriation of funds*

misbehave /ˌmɪsbɪˈheɪv/ *v [I]* to behave badly **OPP** behave —**misbehaviour** *BrE,* **misbehavior** *AmE* /-ˈheɪvjə $ -ər/ *n [U]*

miscalculate /ˌmɪsˈkælkjʊleɪt/ *v [I,T]* **1** to make a mistake when you are calculating something: *We miscalculated how long it would take to get there.* **2** to make a wrong judgment about a situation: *The Government has miscalculated public opinion.* —**miscalculation** /ˌmɪsˌkælkjəˈleɪʃən/ *n [C,U]*

miscarriage /ˌmɪsˈkærɪdʒ, ˈmɪskærɪdʒ/ *n [C,U]* if a woman has a miscarriage, her baby is born much too early and it dies → **abortion**

PHRASES

miscarriage of justice when someone is wrongly punished by a court of law for something they did not do: *He was the victim of a serious miscarriage of justice.*

miscarry /mɪsˈkæri/ *v* (**miscarried, miscarrying, miscarries**) **1** [I,T] to give birth to a baby too early so that it dies **2** [I] *formal* to not be successful: *All our careful plans had miscarried.*

miscellaneous /ˌmɪsəˈleɪniəs◂/ *adj* of many different kinds: *a miscellaneous assortment of books*

mischief /ˈmɪstʃɪf/ *n [U]* bad behaviour by children that is annoying but causes no serious harm: *He was a lively child, and full of mischief.*

mischievous /ˈmɪstʃəvəs/ *adj* a mischievous child behaves badly, but in a way that is not serious: *a mischievous little girl* —**mischievously** *adv*

misconception /ˌmɪskənˈsepʃən/ *n [C,U]* an idea that is wrong or untrue, but that people still believe: **[+that]** *the misconception that only gay people can get AIDS*

misconduct /ˌmɪsˈkɒndʌkt $ -ˈkɑːn-/ *n [U] formal* bad or dishonest behaviour by someone in a position of authority: *Dr Patton was found guilty of serious professional misconduct.*

misconstrue /ˌmɪskənˈstruː/ *v [T] formal* to not understand correctly something that someone has said or done: *His behaviour could easily be misconstrued.*

misdeeds /ˌmɪsˈdiːdz/ *n [plural] literary* wrong or illegal actions

misdemeanour *BrE,* **misdemeanor** *AmE* /ˌmɪsdɪˈmiːnə $ -ər/ *n [C] formal* a crime that is not very serious

miser /ˈmaɪzə $ -ər/ *n [C]* someone who is not generous and does not like spending money

miserable /ˈmɪzərəbəl/ *adj* **1** very unhappy: *I felt miserable. | Why are you looking so miserable?* **THESAURUS** SAD **2** unpleasant: *The weather's been pretty miserable all summer. | They lead miserable lives.* **3** very small in amount, or very bad in quality: *Nurses tend to earn a miserable salary.* —**miserably** *adv*

misery /ˈmɪzəri/ *n [C,U]* (*plural* **miseries**) when someone is very unhappy or is suffering badly: **[+of]** *the misery of life in the refugee camps | the miseries of war*

PHRASES

put sb/sth out of their misery 1 *informal* to make someone stop feeling worried, especially by telling them something they are waiting to hear: *Come on, put us out of our misery and tell us what happened.* **2** to kill an animal that is old or ill so that it does not suffer any more: *I think you should put the poor creature out of its misery.*

misfire /ˌmɪsˈfaɪə $ -ˈfaɪr/ *v [I]* **1** to not have the result that you intended: *His attempt at a joke misfired.* **2** if a gun misfires, the bullet does not come out

misfit /'mɪsˌfɪt/ n [C] someone who seems strange because they are different from the other people in a group: *I was always a bit of a misfit at school.*

misfortune /mɪsˈfɔːtʃən $ -ɔːr-/ n [C,U] bad luck, or something that happens to you as a result of bad luck: *They **had the misfortune to** be in the wrong country when the war broke out.*

misgiving /mɪsˈɡɪvɪŋ/ n [C,U] a feeling of doubt or worry about something: *Opponents of nuclear energy **have** deep **misgivings about** its safety.*

misguided /mɪsˈɡaɪdɪd/ adj based on an idea or opinion that is wrong: *the misguided belief that it would be easier to find work in London*

mishandle /mɪsˈhændl/ v [T] to deal with something in the wrong way: *The investigation was seriously mishandled by the police.*

mishap /'mɪshæp/ n [C,U] a small accident or mistake

mishear /mɪsˈhɪə $ -ˈhɪr/ v [I,T] (past tense and past participle **misheard** /-ˈhɜːd $ -ˈhɜːrd/) to not hear properly what someone says, so that you think they said something different

mishmash /'mɪʃmæʃ/ n [singular] informal disapproving a mixture of a lot of very different things

misinform /ˌmɪsɪnˈfɔːm $ -ɔːrm/ v [T] to give someone information that is incorrect or untrue: *I'm afraid you've been misinformed – she doesn't live here any more.*

misinterpret Ac /ˌmɪsɪnˈtɜːprɪt $ -ɜːr-/ v [T] to understand something wrongly: *She had misinterpreted his silence as anger.*

misjudge /ˌmɪsˈdʒʌdʒ/ v [T] **1** to form a wrong or unfair opinion about a person or a situation: *The President had badly misjudged the mood of the voters.* **2** to guess an amount or distance wrongly: *I misjudged the speed of the car coming towards me.* —**misjudgment, misjudgement** n [C,U]

mislay /ˌmɪsˈleɪ/ v [T] (past tense and past participle **mislaid** /-ˈleɪd/) to put something somewhere and then forget where you put it: *I seem to have mislaid my gloves.*

mislead /ˌmɪsˈliːd/ v [T] (past tense and past participle **misled** /-ˈled/) to deliberately tell someone something that is not true: *Wiggins has admitted trying to mislead the police.* THESAURUS TRICK

misleading /mɪsˈliːdɪŋ/ adj likely to make someone believe something that is not true: *Statistics can be very misleading.* THESAURUS WRONG

mismanagement /mɪsˈmænɪdʒmənt/ n [U] when someone manages a company or organization badly or illegally: *He has been accused of mismanagement.* —**mismanage** v [T]

mismatch /'mɪsmætʃ/ n [C] a combination of things or people that do not work well together or are not suitable for each other: **[+between]** *There was a huge mismatch between supply and demand.*

misnomer /mɪsˈnəʊmə $ -ˈnoʊmər/ n [C] a wrong or unsuitable name: *'Silent movie' is a misnomer since the movies usually had a musical accompaniment.*

misogynist /mɪˈsɒdʒɪnɪst $ məˈsɑː-/ n [C] a man who hates women —**misogyny** n [U]

misplaced /ˌmɪsˈpleɪst◂/ adj misplaced feelings of trust, love etc are wrong and unsuitable, because the person that you have these feelings for does not deserve them

misprint /'mɪs-prɪnt/ n [C] a small spelling mistake in a book, magazine etc THESAURUS MISTAKE

mispronounce /ˌmɪsprəˈnaʊns/ v [T] to pronounce a word wrongly

misquote /ˌmɪsˈkwəʊt $ -ˈkwoʊt/ v [T] to make a mistake when you are reporting what someone else has said or written: *They insisted that the Governor had been misquoted.*

misread /ˌmɪsˈriːd/ v [T] (past tense and past participle **misread** /-ˈred/) **1** to make a wrong judgment about a situation: *The UN misread the situation.* **2** to read something wrongly: *I must have misread the date on the letter.*

misrepresent /ˌmɪsreprɪˈzent/ v [T] to deliberately give a wrong description of someone's opinions or of a situation —**misrepresentation** /ˌmɪsreprɪzenˈteɪʃən/ n [C,U]

MISS

He missed the train.

miss¹ /mɪs/ v

1 [T] to feel sad because you cannot be with someone that you like, or cannot do something that you enjoy: *I really missed Paula after she'd left.* | *What do you miss most about life in Canada?* | **miss doing sth** *I really miss talking to him on the phone.* THESAURUS LONELY

2 [T] to not go somewhere or do something, especially when you want to but cannot: *Vialli will miss tonight's game because of a knee injury.* | *She was upset at missing all the excitement.* | **miss a chance/opportunity** *I'd hate to miss the chance of meeting him.*

3 [T] to be too late for something: *By the time we got there, we'd missed the beginning of the movie.* | **miss a bus/train/plane etc** *Hurry up or we'll miss the train!*

4 [I,T] to not succeed in hitting or catching something: *She fired at the target but missed.* | *Jackson missed an easy catch.*

5 [T] to not see, hear, or notice something: *Jody found an error that everyone else had missed.* | *Maeve's sharp eyes missed nothing.* | *It's a huge hotel on the corner. You can't miss it.*

PHRASES

miss the boat/bus informal to not use an opportunity to do something: *You'll miss the boat if you don't buy shares now.*

miss

Ac = words from the Academic Word List

miss the point to not understand the most important fact about something: *I'm sorry, I think you're missing the point completely.*

miss out

1 to not have the chance to do something that you would enjoy: *Some children miss out because their parents can't afford to pay for school trips.*

2 miss sb/sth ↔ out *BrE* to not include someone or something: *I hope we haven't missed any names out from the list.*

miss² *n* [C] when you fail to hit, catch, or hold something: *The players are still talking about the penalty miss in the second half.*

PHRASES

give sth a miss *BrE informal* to decide not to do something: *As the tickets were so expensive, we decided to give the concert a miss.*

Miss *n*

1 used in front of the name of a girl or a woman who is not married → **Mrs, Ms, Mr**: *Miss Jones will see you now.*

2 *spoken* used as a polite way of talking to a young woman when you do not know her name → **madam, sir**: *Excuse me, Miss – you've dropped your umbrella.*

3 *BrE spoken* used by children when talking to a female teacher, whether she is married or not: *I know the answer, Miss.*

Word Choice: Miss or Ms?
Many unmarried women prefer to be called **Ms**. **Miss** sounds rather old-fashioned. If you do not know whether a woman is married, it is better to use **Ms**.

misshapen /ˌmɪsˈʃeɪpən, mɪˈʃeɪ-/ *adj* not the normal or natural shape

missile /ˈmɪsaɪl $ ˈmɪsəl/ *n* [C] **1** a weapon that can fly over long distances and that explodes when it hits the thing it has been aimed at: *a **nuclear missile*** **2** an object that someone throws at a person in order to hurt them

missing /ˈmɪsɪŋ/ *adj*

1 lost, or not in the usual or expected place: *Police are still searching for the missing child.* | *Two crew members survived, but two are still missing.* | **[+from]** *There's a button missing from this shirt.* | *The scissors have **gone missing** again.*

2 not included: **[+from]** *Why is my name missing from the list?*

mission /ˈmɪʃən/ *n* [C] **1** an important job that someone has been sent to a place to do: *Our mission was to find out everything about their plans.* | *a bombing mission* | *a **peacekeeping mission*** **2** a group of important people who are sent by their government to another country to discuss something or collect information: *a Canadian trade mission to Japan* **3** something that you feel you must do because it is your duty: *His mission was to help young people in his local community.*

missionary /ˈmɪʃənəri $ -neri/ *n* [C] (*plural **missionaries***) someone who goes to a foreign country in order to teach people about Christianity

misspell /ˌmɪsˈspel/ *v* [T] (*past tense and past participle* **misspelt** /-ˈspelt/ or **misspelled**) to spell a word wrongly —**misspelling** *n* [C,U]

misstep /ˈmɪs-step/ *n* [C] *AmE* a mistake, especially one that is caused by not understanding a situation correctly: *A misstep here could cost millions of dollars.*

mist¹ /mɪst/ *n* [C,U] a layer of cloud close to the ground that makes it difficult for you to see very far → **fog**: *The mist was starting to clear.*

mist² (*also* **mist over/up**) *v* [I,T] to become covered with very small drops of water, or to make something do this: *All the windows had misted over.*

mistake¹ /məˈsteɪk/ *n* [C]

1 something that is wrong or has been done in the wrong way → **error**: *Ivan's work is full of spelling mistakes.*

2 something you do that is not sensible or has a bad result: *It's your decision, but I warn you – you're **making a mistake**.* | *I **made the mistake** of giving him my phone number.* | *Marrying Julie was a **big mistake**.* | *It would **be a mistake** to underestimate Moya's ability.*

PHRASES

by mistake without intending to do something **SYN** accidentally **OPP** on purpose: *Someone must have left the door open by mistake.*

COLLOCATIONS

verbs

to make a mistake *We may have made a mistake in our calculations.* ⚠ Do not say 'do a mistake'. Say **make a mistake**.

to correct a mistake *She read through the letter, correcting his mistakes.*

to realize your mistake *I stopped as soon as I realized my mistake.*

adjectives

a little/small mistake *Even a small mistake could cause problems.*

a serious mistake *He realized he had made a serious mistake.*

a silly/stupid mistake *Your work is full of silly mistakes.*

a common mistake *This is one of the commonest mistakes learners make.*

noun + mistake

a spelling mistake *She spotted two spelling mistakes in the article.*

THESAURUS

mistake something that is wrong or has been done in the wrong way: *I made a mistake – her name is Cleo, not Chloe.* | *a spelling mistake*
error *formal* a mistake: *The report was full of errors.* | *a grammatical error* | *a computer error*
booboo *informal* a mistake when you are saying or doing something, especially an embarrassing one: *I think I just made a booboo. I forgot to save the file.*
misprint a mistake in something that is printed: *There was a misprint in the article.*

mistake² v [T] (*past tense* **mistook** /-'stʊk/, *past participle* **mistaken** /-'steɪkən/) to understand something wrongly: *I must have mistaken what he said.*

PHRASES

mistake sb/sth for sb/sth to wrongly think that one person or thing is someone or something else: *I mistook him for his brother.*

there's no mistaking sb/sth used to say that you are certain about something: *There was no mistaking the anger in her voice.*

mistaken /mə'steɪkən/ adj if you are mistaken, you are wrong about something: *I thought he said 12 o'clock, but I might have been mistaken.* | *We bought the rug in Turkey, if I'm not mistaken.* THESAURUS WRONG —**mistakenly** adv

mister /'mɪstə $ -ər/ n AmE spoken informal used to talk to a man whose name you do not know: *Hey, mister – is this your wallet?*

Mister n the full form of Mr

> **Word Choice**: Mister, Mr, or Sir?
> When talking politely to a man, you use **Mr** (pronounced 'Mister') with his surname: *Excuse me, Mr Smith!*
> Do not use **Mr** with someone's first name. Do not say 'Excuse me, Mr Chris!' Say *Excuse me, Chris!*
> In polite English, you use **Sir** when speaking to a man whose name you do not know: *How can I help you, Sir?*
> You usually use **Mister** on its own only when you are angry: *Listen, Mister! I've had just about enough of you today!*

mistletoe /'mɪsəltəʊ $ -toʊ/ n [U] a plant with small round white fruit that is often used as a decoration at Christmas

mistook /mə'stʊk/ v the past tense of MISTAKE

mistreat /ˌmɪs'triːt/ v [T] to treat a person or animal cruelly: *The hostages said they had not been mistreated.* —**mistreatment** n [U]

mistress /'mɪstrɪs/ n [C] a married man's secret lover

mistrust /mɪs'trʌst/ n [U] the feeling that you cannot trust someone or something: *He had a deep mistrust of politicians.* —**mistrust** v [T] —**mistrustful** adj

misty /'mɪsti/ adj misty weather is weather with a lot of mist: *a cold, misty morning*

misunderstand /ˌmɪsʌndə'stænd $ -ər-/ v [I,T] (*past tense and past participle* **misunderstood** /-'stʊd/) to not understand something correctly: *I think you misunderstood my question.*

misunderstanding /ˌmɪsʌndə'stændɪŋ $ -ər-/ n **1** [C,U] a problem caused by someone not understanding a question, situation, or instruction correctly: *There must have been some misunderstanding. I didn't order this.* **2** [C] a small argument or disagreement

misunderstood /ˌmɪsʌndə'stʊd $ -ər-/ adj if someone is misunderstood, people do not like them

because they do not know them or understand them

misuse /ˌmɪs'juːz/ v [T] to use something in the wrong way or for the wrong purpose: *The chairman was accused of misusing club funds.* —**misuse** /-'juːs/ n [C,U]: *a misuse of power*

mite /maɪt/ n [C] **1** a very small insect that lives in plants, animals' fur, stored food etc **2** a small child, especially one you feel sorry for **3 a mite** informal slightly: *She's a mite shy.*

mitigate /'mɪtɪgeɪt/ v [T] formal to make something less harmful or less serious —**mitigation** /ˌmɪtə'geɪʃən/ n [U]

mitigating /'mɪtəgeɪtɪŋ/ adj **mitigating circumstances/factors** facts that make a crime or mistake seem less serious

mitt /mɪt/ n [C] **1** a type of leather GLOVE used for catching a ball in BASEBALL **2** a thick GLOVE that you wear to protect your hand: *an oven mitt* → see picture at **GLOVE**

mitten /'mɪtn/ n [C] a type of GLOVE that does not have separate parts for each finger → see picture at **GLOVE**

mix¹ /mɪks/ v

1 [I,T] if you mix two or more substances, or if they mix, they combine to become a single substance: *Oil and water don't mix.* | **mix sth and sth** *You can make green by mixing blue and yellow paint.* | **mix sth with sth** *Shake the bottle well to mix the oil with the vinegar.* | **mix sth together** *First mix the butter and sugar together, then add the milk.*

2 [I,T] to combine two or more different activities, ideas, styles etc: **mix sth and sth** *Glennie's latest CD mixes classical music and rock 'n' roll.* | **mix sth with sth** *I don't like to mix business with pleasure.*

3 [I] to enjoy talking to other people and meeting new people: **[+with]** *Charlie doesn't mix well with the other children.*

PHRASAL VERBS

mix sb/sth ↔ **up**

1 to think that one person or thing is someone or something else: *I'm always mixing up the kids' names.*

2 to change the order in which things have been arranged: *Whatever you do, try not to mix those papers up.*

> **THESAURUS**
>
> **mix** to put different substances together, so that they become a single substance, or to put different styles, ideas, or other things together: *If you mix blue and red, you get purple.* | *Her books mix action with romance.*
>
> **combine** to mix things together. **Combine** is more formal than **mix**: *Combine the butter and the sugar.* | *The drug can be dangerous when combined with other drugs.*
>
> **jumble** to mix things together in an untidy way, so that they are not in any order: *Their shoes were all jumbled together next to the back door.*
>
> **dilute** to mix a liquid with water in order to make it weaker: *If you prefer, you can dilute fruit juice with water.*

mix² n **1** [singular] a combination of different things

mixed

or people: **[+of]** *There was a good mix of people at the party.* | *a complicated mix of colours and textures* **2** [C,U] a powder that is added to liquid to make something: *cake mix* **3** [C] a particular arrangement of sounds, instruments, and voices in a piece of music

mixed /mɪkst/ *adj*
1 consisting of a lot of different types of things, people, ideas etc: *mixed herbs* | *We had **mixed feelings** (=feelings of happiness and sadness at the same time) about moving so far away.*
2 mixed reaction/response/reviews etc if something gets a mixed reaction etc, some people say they like it, but others dislike it: *The film has had mixed reviews from the critics.*
3 *BrE* for both males and females → **co-ed**: *a mixed school*

PHRASES
a mixed blessing something that is good in some ways but bad in others: *Living so near my parents was a mixed blessing.*
(of) mixed race a person of mixed race has parents of different races: *He is of mixed race.*

,**mixed 'marriage** *n* [C] a marriage between people from different races or religions

,**mixed 'up** *adj* **1** (*also* **mixed-up**) confused and suffering from emotional problems: *a lonely mixed-up adolescent* **2** confused, for example because you have too many different details to remember or think about: *I got a little mixed up and went to the wrong restaurant.*

PHRASES
be/get mixed up in sth to be involved in an illegal or dishonest activity: *He was only 14 when he got mixed up in drug-dealing.*

mixer /ˈmɪksə $ -ər/ *n* [C] **1** a piece of equipment used for mixing things together: *a food mixer* **2** a drink that can be mixed with alcohol: *There are some mixers in the fridge.*

mixture /ˈmɪkstʃə $ -ər/ *n*
1 [C,U] a liquid or other substance that is made by mixing several substances together, especially in cooking: *cake mixture* | *Pour the mixture into four small dishes.*
2 [C] a combination of two or more different things: **[+of]** *The town is a mixture of the old and the new.* | *a mixture of emotions*

'**mix-up** *n* [C] *informal* a situation in which people are confused or make mistakes about arrangements: *There was a mix-up at the station and Eddie got on the wrong bus.* | **[+over]** *There was a mix-up over the hotel booking.*

ml the written abbreviation of **millilitre**

mm the written abbreviation of **millimetre**

moan /məʊn $ moʊn/ *v* [I] **1** to make a long low sound expressing pain or unhappiness: *She lay on the bed moaning with pain.* **2** to complain about something in an annoying way: *I wish you'd stop moaning all the time.* **THESAURUS** COMPLAIN —**moan** *n* [C]: *There was a moan of pain from the injured man.*

moat /məʊt $ moʊt/ *n* [C] a deep wide hole that is dug around a castle to defend it

mob¹ /mɒb $ mɑːb/ *n* [C] a large noisy crowd, especially one that is angry and violent

mob² *v* [T] (**mobbed**, **mobbing**) if people mob a famous person, they rush to get near them and form a crowd around them: *Wherever she went, she was mobbed by fans.*

mobile¹ /ˈməʊbaɪl $ ˈmoʊbəl, -biːl/ *adj* **1** able to move or be moved quickly and easily: *She's 83 and not very mobile.* | *mobile missile systems* **2** able to move from one job, area, or social class to another: *an increasingly mobile population* **3 mobile shop/library/clinic etc** *BrE* a shop etc in a vehicle, which is driven from place to place: *A mobile library visits the village once a week.*

mobile² /ˈməʊbaɪl $ ˈmoʊbiːl/ *n* [C] **1** *BrE* a MOBILE PHONE **2** a decoration made of small objects that hang down on wires or strings and move when air blows around them

,**mobile 'home** *n* [C] **1** *BrE* a large CARAVAN that always stays in the same place and is used as a house **2** *AmE* a type of house made of metal, which can be pulled by a vehicle and moved to another place **THESAURUS** HOUSE

mobile 'phone *n* [C] *BrE* a telephone that you can carry with you and use anywhere **SYN** **cell phone** *AmE* → see picture on page A12

mobility /məʊˈbɪləti $ moʊ-/ *n* [U] **1** the ability to move easily from one job, area, or social class to another: *social mobility* **2** the ability to move easily: *elderly people with limited mobility*

mobilize (*also* **-ise** *BrE*) /ˈməʊbəlaɪz $ ˌmoʊ-/ *v* **1** [T] to encourage people to support something in an active way: *a campaign to **mobilize support** for the strike* **2** [I,T] if a country mobilizes, or mobilizes its army, it prepares to fight a war —**mobilization** /ˌməʊbəlaɪˈzeɪʃən $ ˌmoʊbələ-/ *n* [C,U]

mobster /ˈmɒbstə $ ˈmɑːbstər/ *n* [C] *especially AmE* a member of a criminal group

mock¹ /mɒk $ mɑːk/ *v* [I,T] to try to make someone seem stupid, for example by copying them or saying unkind things about them: *'Are you afraid?' he mocked.* —**mockingly** *adv*

mock² *adj* [only before noun] not real, but intended to be very similar to something real: *a mock interview* | **mock surprise/horror etc** *She shook her head in mock disgust.*

mock³ *n* [C] *BrE* a school examination taken as practice for an official examination

mockery /ˈmɒkəri $ ˈmɑː-/ *n* [U] when someone laughs at someone or something or tries to make them seem stupid

PHRASES
make a mockery of sth to make a plan, system, organization etc seem useless or stupid: *His release from prison makes a mockery of the law.*

'**mock-up** *n* [C] a model of something, made before the real thing is built, or made for a film, show etc

modal verb /ˌməʊdl ˈvɜːb $ ˌmoʊdl ˈvɜːrb/ (*also* **modal**) *n* [C] *technical* a verb such as 'can', 'might', or 'must' that is used with other verbs to show ideas such as possibility, permission, or intention

mode Ac /məʊd $ moʊd/ n [C] formal a particular way of behaving, living, or doing something: [+of] different **modes of transport**

model¹ /ˈmɒdl $ ˈmɑːdl/ n [C]
1 SMALL COPY a small copy of a building, vehicle, machine etc, especially one that can be made from separate parts: [+of] a model of the Eiffel Tower | Simon spends hours making models. | a **working model** (=one with parts that move) of a steam engine
2 FASHION someone whose job is to show clothes, hair styles etc by wearing them at fashion shows or for photographs: a **fashion model**
3 TYPE OF CAR/MACHINE a particular type or design of a vehicle or machine: the **latest** (=newest) **model** from BMW
4 GOOD EXAMPLE someone or something that people want to copy because they are successful or have good qualities: [+for] This approach may **serve as a model** (=be used as a model) for projects in other cities.
5 FOR ARTISTS someone who is employed by an artist or photographer to be painted or photographed
6 DESCRIPTION OF STH a description of how a system works or what you expect something will be like, especially one made using a computer: [+of] **computer models** of climate change → ROLE MODEL

model² adj [only before noun] **1** a model student, wife etc does everything exactly as they should: a model employee **2** model aeroplane/train/car etc a small copy of a plane, train etc, especially one that you can make

model³ v [I,T] (**modelled, modelling** BrE, **modeled, modeling** AmE) to wear clothes at a fashion show or in magazine photographs in order to show them to people: She models for 'Elle' magazine.
PHRASES
be modelled on sth to be designed in a way that copies another system or way of doing something: a constitution modelled on the French system
model yourself on sb BrE, **model yourself after sb** AmE to try to be like someone because you admire them: Pete models himself on Elvis Presley.

modelling BrE, **modeling** AmE /ˈmɒdl-ɪŋ $ ˈmɑː-/ n [U] the work of a fashion model: a career in modelling

modem /ˈməʊdəm, -dem $ ˈmoʊ-/ n [C] a piece of electronic equipment used for sending information along telephone wires from one computer to another

moderate¹ /ˈmɒdərət $ ˈmɑː-/ adj **1** not very big or very small, very hot or very cold, very fast or very slow etc: Cook over a moderate heat. **2** having opinions or beliefs, especially about politics, that are not extreme: moderate Republicans —**moderately** adv

moderate² /ˈmɒdəreɪt $ ˈmɑː-/ v [I,T] formal to make something less extreme, or to become less extreme: The students moderated their demands.

moderate³ /ˈmɒdərət $ ˈmɑː-/ n [C] someone whose opinions or beliefs, especially about politics, are not extreme

moderation /ˌmɒdəˈreɪʃən $ ˌmɑː-/ n [U] formal sensible control of your behaviour and ideas

PHRASES
in moderation if you do something in moderation, you do not do it too much: He drinks only in moderation.

modern /ˈmɒdn $ ˈmɑːdərn/ adj
1 [only before noun] belonging to the present time or most recent time **SYN** contemporary: in **the modern world** | people in **modern society** | one of the greatest events of **modern times**
2 using the most recent designs, methods, ideas etc: the use of **modern technology** | advances in **modern medicine** | The school is very modern in its approach to sex education.
3 [only before noun] modern art, music, literature etc use styles that are very different from traditional styles: modern dance —**modernity** /mɒˈdɜːnəti $ məˈdɜːr-/ n [U]: a conflict between tradition and modernity

---

THESAURUS – sense 2

modern using the most recent designs, methods, ideas etc: modern farming methods | a bright modern office building
the latest the newest that is available: the latest fashions | the latest edition of the book
up-to-date using the most modern technology, ideas, or information that is available: Our equipment isn't very up-to-date. | Is your map up-to-date?
high-tech using very modern electronic equipment and machines, especially computers: Today's fire service uses high-tech equipment for fighting fires.
state-of-the-art using the newest and most advanced methods, materials, or knowledge: a state-of-the-art language laboratory
newfangled informal modern – used when you disapprove of something and do not think it as good as the things that existed before: He didn't like using newfangled gadgets such as mobile phones.

---

modern-day adj [only before noun] existing now, not in the past: modern-day Egypt

modernize (also **-ise** BrE) /ˈmɒdənaɪz $ ˈmɑːder-/ v [I,T] to make something more modern, or to become more modern: plans to modernize the factory —**modernization** /ˌmɒdənaɪˈzeɪʃən $ ˌmɑːdərnə-/ n [C,U]

modern languages n [plural] BrE languages that are spoken now, such as French or German, studied as a subject at school or university

modest /ˈmɒdɪst $ ˈmɑː-/ adj **1** approving someone who is modest does not talk in a proud way about their abilities or achievements: a quiet modest man **2** not very big in size, amount, value etc: a modest increase —**modestly** adv

modesty /ˈmɒdəsti $ ˈmɑː-/ n [U] the quality of not talking in a proud way about your abilities, achievements, etc

modicum /ˈmɒdɪkəm $ ˈmɑː-/ n **a modicum of sth** formal a small amount of something, especially something good: a modicum of success

modification Ac /ˌmɒdɪfɪˈkeɪʃən $ ˌmɑ:-/ n [C,U] a small change to something, or the process of changing something: **[+to]** We've **made** a few **modifications** to the design.

modifier /ˈmɒdəfaɪə $ ˈmɑ:dɪfaɪər/ n [C] technical an adjective, adverb, or phrase that gives additional information about another word

modify Ac /ˈmɒdɪfaɪ $ ˈmɑ:-/ v [T] (**modified**, **modifying**, **modifies**) **1** to make small changes to something in order to make it better or more suitable: The course will have to be modified for younger students. **THESAURUS** CHANGE **2** technical if an adjective, adverb etc modifies another word, it gives more information about it

module /ˈmɒdju:l $ ˈmɑ:dʒu:l/ n [C] **1** especially BrE one of the parts of a course of study: You can choose five modules in the first year. **2** a part of a spacecraft that can separate from the main part and be used for a particular purpose —**modular** /ˈmɒdjələ $ ˈmɑ:dʒələr/ adj

mogul /ˈməʊɡəl $ ˈmoʊ-/ n [C] **movie/media etc mogul** someone who has great power and influence in a particular industry

mohair /ˈməʊheə $ ˈmoʊher/ n [U] expensive wool made from the hair of a type of goat

Mohammed /məʊˈhæməd, mə- $ moʊ-/ n another spelling of MUHAMMAD

moist /mɔɪst/ adj slightly wet, especially in a pleasant way: a moist chocolate cake | Make sure the soil is moist. **THESAURUS** WET

> **Word Choice: moist or damp?**
> You use **moist** when something is slightly damp and soft in a pleasant way, or in the way that something should be: The cake was lovely and moist. | The cream helps your skin stay moist.
> You also use **moist** about someone's eyes, when they are about to cry: By the end of the film, her eyes were moist.
> **Damp** means slightly wet: a damp cloth | a damp sponge. It is often used when this seems rather unpleasant: The room felt cold and damp.
> You also use **damp** about weather or a period of time when it rains: damp weather | a damp December morning

moisten /ˈmɔɪsən/ v [T] to make something slightly wet

moisture /ˈmɔɪstʃə $ -ər/ n [U] small amounts of water in or on something: your skin's natural moisture

moisturizer (also **-iser** BrE) /ˈmɔɪstʃəraɪzə $ -ər/ n [C,U] liquid that you put on your skin to make it less dry —**moisturize** v [I,T]

molar /ˈməʊlə $ ˈmoʊlər/ n [C] one of the large teeth at the back of your mouth

molasses /məˈlæsɪz/ n [U] AmE a thick sweet black liquid that is obtained from the sugar plant and used in cooking **SYN** treacle BrE

mold /məʊld $ moʊld/ n, v the American spelling of MOULD

molding /ˈməʊldɪŋ $ ˈmoʊl-/ n the American spelling of MOULDING

moldy /ˈməʊldi $ ˈmoʊl-/ adj the American spelling of MOULDY

MOLE

mole /məʊl $ moʊl/ n [C] **1** a small dark furry animal that is almost blind. Moles live under the ground. **2** a small dark brown mark on your skin **THESAURUS** MARK **3** someone who works for an organization while secretly giving information to its enemies

molecule /ˈmɒlɪkju:l $ ˈmɑ:-/ n [C] the smallest unit into which a substance can be divided without losing its own chemical nature: Water molecules consist of two hydrogen atoms and one oxygen atom. —**molecular** /məˈlekjələ $ -ər/ adj

molest /məˈlest/ v [T] to attack or harm someone, especially a child, by touching them in a sexual way or trying to have sex with them: He was accused of molesting a 14-year-old boy. —**molester** n [C]: a child molester —**molestation** /ˌməʊleˈsteɪʃən $ ˌmoʊ-/ n [U]

mollify /ˈmɒlɪfaɪ $ ˈmɑ:-/ v [T] (**mollified**, **mollifying**, **mollifies**) formal to make someone feel less angry

mollusc BrE, **mollusk** AmE /ˈmɒləsk $ ˈmɑ:-/ n [C] a type of sea or land animal that has a soft body covered by a hard shell: snails and other molluscs

mollycoddle /ˈmɒliˌkɒdl $ ˈmɑ:liˌkɑ:dl/ v [T] disapproving to treat someone too kindly and protect them from anything unpleasant

molt /məʊlt $ moʊlt/ v the American spelling of MOULT

molten /ˈməʊltən $ ˈmoʊl-/ adj molten metal or rock is liquid because it is very hot

mom /mɒm $ mɑ:m/ n [C] AmE informal mother **SYN** mum BrE: Mom, can we go swimming? | My mom's a secretary.

moment /ˈməʊmənt $ ˈmoʊ-/ n [C]
1 a particular point in time: It was one of the most exciting moments in his life. | **at that/this moment** (=exactly then/now) At that moment, there was a knock on the door. | Do you remember **the moment when** we first met?
2 a very short period of time: He was here **a moment ago**. | **A few moments** later, the phone rang. | Would you mind **waiting a moment**? | **in a moment** (=very soon) I'll bring you some tea in a moment. | **for a moment** She was silent for a moment. **THESAURUS** TIME → **on the spur of the moment** at SPUR[1]

PHRASES

(at) any moment very soon: *It could start to rain at any moment.*

at the moment now: *We're very busy at the moment.*

for the moment used to say that something is happening or is true now but may change in the future: *For the moment, we're just friends.*

THESAURUS ▶ NOW

the last moment at the latest possible time: *As usual, she arrived at the last moment.*

the moment (that) ... as soon as someone does something or something happens: *I'll call you the moment I hear anything.*

> **Grammar**
>
> Do not say 'In that moment, Sylvia arrived.' Say **At that moment**, Sylvia arrived.

momentarily /'məʊməntərəli $,məʊmən'terəli/ *adv* **1** for a very short time **SYN** **briefly**: *Jim paused momentarily.* **2** *AmE* very soon: *I'll be with you momentarily.*

momentary /'məʊməntəri $ 'məʊmənteri/ *adj* happening for a very short time **SYN** **brief**: *There was a momentary silence.*

momentous /məʊ'mentəs, mə- $ moʊ-, mə-/ *adj* a momentous event, change, or decision is very important: *the momentous events at the end of the century*

momentum /məʊ'mentəm, mə- $ moʊ-, mə-/ *n* [U] **1** when something continues to increase, develop, or become more successful: **gain/gather momentum** *The campaign continued to gather momentum.* **2** the force that makes a moving object continue to move: **gain/gather momentum** (=move faster and faster) *The wheel rolled downhill, gathering momentum.*

momma /'mɒmə $ 'mɑːmə/ *n AmE* another spelling of MAMA

mommy /'mɒmi $ 'mɑːmi/ *n* [C] (*plural* **mommies**) *AmE* mother – used by or to young children **SYN** **mummy** *BrE*

Mon. (*also* **Mon** *BrE*) the written abbreviation of **Monday**

monarch /'mɒnək $ 'mɑːnərk, -ɑːrk/ *n* [C] a king or queen

monarchy /'mɒnəki $ 'mɑːnərki/ *n* (*plural* **monarchies**) **1** [U] the system in which a country is ruled by a king or queen **2** [C] a country that is ruled by a king or queen → **republic**

monastery /'mɒnəstri $ 'mɑːnəsteri/ *n* [C] (*plural* **monasteries**) a place where MONKs live → **convent**

monastic /mə'næstɪk/ *adj* relating to MONKs or a monastery

Monday /'mʌndi, -deɪ/ *n* [C,U] (*written abbreviation* **Mon.**) the day between Sunday and Tuesday: **on Monday** *It was raining on Monday.* | **Monday morning/afternoon etc** *Let's go out for a meal on Monday night.* | **last Monday** *They arrived last Monday.* | **next Monday** (=Monday of next week) *Shall we meet next Monday?* | **this Monday** *The UK office will open for business this Monday.* | **a Monday** (=one of the Mondays in the year) *My birthday is on a Monday this year.*

monetary /'mʌnətəri $ 'mɑːneteri/ *adj* [only before noun] relating to money, especially all the money in a particular country: *the government's monetary policy*

money /'mʌni/ *n* [U]

1 what you earn by working and use to buy things, often in the form of coins, paper notes etc → **monies**: *I didn't have enough money to pay for a room.* | *She put the money in her purse.*

2 sb's money all someone's money and the things they own: *The family **made** their **money** in the woollen trade.*

3 the money informal the amount of money that you earn for doing a job: *The money's terrible.* → **POCKET MONEY**, **be rolling in money** at ROLL¹, **SPENDING MONEY**

PHRASES

get your money's worth to get enough for the price that you paid: *We stayed right to the end, to get our money's worth.*

> **COLLOCATIONS**
>
> **verbs**
>
> **to have money** *I don't think they have very much money.*
>
> **to earn money** *He doesn't earn much money.*
>
> **to make money** (=to earn money or make a profit) *I make more money than he does.* ⚠ Do not say 'gain money'. Say **make money**.
>
> **to lose money** (=to get less money than you spend, in business) *Unfortunately, the company is still losing money.*
>
> **to spend money** *I spend a lot of money on clothes.*
>
> **to cost money** *The repairs will cost a lot of money.*
>
> **to save money** (=to use less money) *Turning your heating down will save money.*
>
> **to save (up) money** (=to not spend money you receive) *She had saved up enough money to buy a car.*
>
> **to raise money** (=to get money for a charity, school etc by doing something) *They organized events to raise money for the school.*
>
> **noun + money**
>
> **a sum/an amount of money** *He offered me a large sum of money.*
>
> **a waste of money** *The trip was a waste of money.*

> **THESAURUS**
>
> **money** what you earn by working and use to buy things: *We don't have enough money to buy a house.*
>
> **cash** money in the form of coins and notes: *You can pay in cash or by cheque.*
>
> **currency** the money used in a particular country: *The Russian currency is the rouble.*
>
> **change** money in the form of coins of low value, or the money that you get back when you are paying for something with more money than it cost: *He emptied all the change out of his pockets.* | *The sales clerk handed me my change.*
>
> **note** *BrE*, **bill** *AmE* a piece of paper money: *a £20 note* | *a $5 bill*

'money ,market n [C] all the banks and other institutions that buy, sell, lend, or borrow money in order to make a profit

'money ,order n [C] *especially AmE* an official document that you buy in a post office or bank and send to someone so that they can exchange it for money in a bank SYN **postal order** *BrE*

mongrel /'mʌŋgrəl $ 'ma:ŋ-, 'mʌŋ-/ n [C] a dog that is a mix of different breeds

monies, **moneys** /'mʌniz/ n [plural] *law* money: *a refund of all monies paid*

monitor¹ Ac /'mɒnɪtə $ 'ma:nɪtər/ v [T] to carefully watch or measure something to see how it changes over a period of time: *Your manager will* **closely monitor** *your progress.*

monitor² n [C] **1** the part of a computer with a screen, or a television screen: *the information displayed on the* **computer monitor** → see picture on page A12 **2** a piece of equipment that measures and shows the level, speed etc of something: *a heart monitor*

monk /mʌŋk/ n [C] a member of a religious group of men who live together in a MONASTERY → **nun**

monkey /'mʌŋki/ n [C] a small brown animal with a long tail, which uses its hands to climb trees and lives in hot countries

PHRASES

monkey business *informal* bad or dishonest behaviour: *We suspect some monkey business has been going on.*

'monkey wrench n [C] *especially AmE* a tool used for holding or turning things

mono /'mɒnəʊ $ 'ma:noʊ/ n [U] *AmE informal* an infectious illness that makes you feel weak and tired for a long time SYN **glandular fever** *BrE*

mono- /mɒnəʊ, -nə $ -noʊ, -nə/ prefix one: *a monolingual dictionary (=using only one language)*

monochrome /'mɒnəkrəʊm $ 'ma:nəkroʊm/ adj consisting only of the colours black, white, and grey: *a monochrome image*

monogamy /mə'nɒgəmi $ mə'na:-/ n [U] when people have only one husband or wife or only one sexual partner —**monogamous** adj: *We live in a monogamous society.*

monogram /'mɒnəgræm $ 'ma:-/ n [C] a design that is made using the first letters of someone's names, and is put on clothes and other possessions —**monogrammed** adj

monolingual /ˌmɒnəʊ'lɪŋgwəl◀ $ ˌma:nə-/ adj speaking or using only one language → **bilingual**, **multilingual**: *a monolingual dictionary*

monolithic /ˌmɒnə'lɪθɪk◀ $ ˌma:-/ adj a monolithic organization, political system etc is large, powerful, and difficult to change —**monolith** /'mɒnəlɪθ $ 'ma:-/ n [C]

monologue (also **monolog** AmE) /'mɒnəlɒg $ 'ma:nl-ɔ:g, -a:g/ n [C] a long speech by one person → **dialogue**

monopolize (also **-ise** BrE) /mə'nɒpəlaɪz $ -'na:-/ v [T] to control a situation completely so that other people cannot share it or take part in it: *The company has monopolized the drinks market.* | *He monopolized the conversation all evening.* —**monopolization** /məˌnɒpəlaɪ'zeɪʃən $ -ˌna:pələ-/ n [U]

monopoly /mə'nɒpəli $ mə'na:-/ n (plural **monopolies**) **1** [C usually singular] the complete control of an area of business or industry by a company or government, which makes it impossible for other organizations to compete: [+of] *the state* **monopoly** *of television* | [+on] *The company used to* **have a monopoly** *on telephone services.* **2** [C] a large company that controls all or most of a business activity **3** [singular] if someone has a monopoly on something, no one else can have it, share it etc: [+on] *No religion* **has a monopoly** *on truth.*

monosyllabic /ˌmɒnəsɪ'læbɪk◀ $ ˌma:-/ adj **1** someone who is monosyllabic does not say very much and does not try to be friendly **2** a monosyllabic word has only one SYLLABLE

monosyllable /'mɒnəˌsɪləbəl $ 'ma:-/ n [C] a word with only one SYLLABLE, for example 'no'

monotone /'mɒnətəʊn $ 'ma:nətoʊn/ n [singular] a way of speaking that sounds boring because your voice never changes: *He continued talking in a slow monotone.*

monotonous /mə'nɒtənəs $ mə'na:-/ adj boring and always the same: *monotonous work* | *He won every game* **with monotonous regularity**. THESAURUS▶ BORING —**monotony** n [U] —**monotonously** adv

monsoon /mɒn'su:n $ ma:n-/ n [C] the time when it rains a lot in India and other southern Asian countries

monster¹ /'mɒnstə $ 'ma:nstər/ n [C] **1** a large ugly frightening creature in stories: *a sea monster* **2** someone who is very cruel and evil: *Only a monster could kill an innocent child.*

monster² adj [only before noun] *informal* unusually big

monstrosity /mɒn'strɒsəti $ ma:n'stra:-/ n [C] (plural **monstrosities**) something that is large and ugly, especially a building

monstrous /'mɒnstrəs $ 'ma:n-/ adj **1** very wrong, immoral, or unfair: *a monstrous crime* **2** very large and often frightening: *monstrous waves* —**monstrously** adv

montage /'mɒntɑːʒ $ ma:n'tɑːʒ/ n [C,U] a picture, piece of music etc made by combining parts of different pictures, pieces of music etc, or the process of making it

month /mʌnθ/ n [C]
1 one of the 12 periods of time that a year is divided into: **this/last/next month** *She'll be ten this month.* | *The work should be finished by* **the end of the month**. | *She earns £1,000* **a month** (=each month).
2 a period of time of about four weeks: *We'll be away for four months.* | *We have an eight-month-old daughter.*
3 months [plural] a long time, especially several months: *Painting the house took months.*

Grammar

You use **in** to talk about a month, but not about a particular date in that month: *He was born in February.*

You use **on** to talk about a particular date in a month: *He was born on February 20th.* | *She finishes school on the nineteenth of July.*

Do not use **in** or **on** before **next**, **last**, and **this**.

Do not say 'The meeting is on next month.' Say *The meeting is next month.*

Do not say 'He died on last January.' Say *He died last January.*

monthly /'mʌnθli/ *adj* happening or produced once a month: *monthly meetings* | *a monthly magazine* | *a monthly salary of $2,000* —**monthly** *adv*: *All employees are paid monthly.*

monument /'mɒnjəmənt $ 'mɑː-/ *n* [C] **1** something that is built to remind people of an important event or famous person: **[+to]** *The cross is a monument to the men who died in battle.* **2** an old building or place that is important in history: *ancient monuments*
PHRASES

 be a monument to sth to show clearly the result of someone's qualities, beliefs, actions etc: *The company is a monument to his energy and determination.*

monumental /ˌmɒnjə'mentl◂ $ ˌmɑː-/ *adj* extremely large, bad, impressive, important etc: *a monumental task* | *a monumental error* | *Darwin's monumental work on evolution*

moo /muː/ *v* [I] to make the sound that a cow makes —**moo** *n* [C]

mood /muːd/ *n* [C]
1 the way someone feels at a particular time: **be in a good/bad etc mood** *You're certainly in a good mood today!*
2 technical one of the sets of verb forms in grammar such as the INDICATIVE (=expressing a fact or action) or the IMPERATIVE (=expressing a command) etc
PHRASES

 be in a mood to feel unhappy or angry: *He's been in a mood all day.*
 be/feel in the mood to feel that you want to do something: **[+for]** *We were all in the mood for a party.*
 be in no mood for sth/to do sth (=to not want to do something): *He was obviously in no mood for talking.*

COLLOCATIONS

types of mood

a good mood (=when someone feels happy) *I hope she's in a good mood today.*
a bad mood (=when someone feels angry) *Why are you in such a bad mood?*
a confident/relaxed/strange etc mood *The players are in a confident mood.*
a holiday/party/festive mood (=a happy mood in which you want to enjoy a holiday or party) *We're all getting into a party mood.*

nouns

a mood of optimism/despair/excitement etc *A mood of excitement had built up in the office.*

a change of mood *That afternoon, there was a total change of mood.*
mood swings (=large changes of mood) *Sudden mood swings can be a sign of mental illness.*

verbs

sb's mood changes *Then his mood changed, and he laughed.*
sb's mood improves *We'll just have to wait for her mood to improve.*

moody /'muːdi/ *adj* often becoming angry or unhappy: *a moody teenager* —**moodily** *adv* —**moodiness** *n* [U]

moon /muːn/ *n*
1 the moon/Moon the round object that moves around the Earth and shines in the sky at night: *the first person to land on the moon* THESAURUS ▶ STAR
2 [singular] the shape of the moon at a particular time of the month: *There's **no moon** tonight* (=it cannot be seen). | **full/half moon** (=when the moon is a complete/half circle)
3 [C] a round object that moves around another PLANET: *How many moons does Jupiter have?* → **once in a blue moon** at ONCE[1]
PHRASES

 over the moon BrE informal very happy: *She's over the moon about her new job.*

moonbeam /'muːnbiːm/ *n* [C] a line of light from the moon

moonlight[1] /'muːnlaɪt/ *n* [U] the light that comes from the moon: **in the moonlight** *The pool glistened in the moonlight.*

moonlight[2] *v* [I] informal to have a second job in addition to your main job: *He's been moonlighting as a DJ.*

moonlit /'muːnˌlɪt/ *adj* lit by the moon: *a beautiful moonlit night*

moor[1] /mʊə $ mʊr/ *n* [C usually plural] especially BrE a wild area of high land covered with rough grass or low bushes: *the North Yorkshire Moors*

moor[2] *v* [I,T] to fasten a boat to land or to the bottom of the sea

mooring /'mʊərɪŋ $ 'mʊr-/ *n* [C] **1** the place where a ship or boat is fastened to land **2** moorings [plural] the ropes, chains etc used to fasten a ship or boat to the land

moose /muːs/ *n* [C] (*plural* moose) a large wild animal like a DEER with large flat horns

moot[1] /muːt/ *adj* **1 a moot point/question** something that has not yet been decided or agreed, and that people have different ideas about: *Whether she was to blame or not is a moot point.* **2** AmE no longer likely to happen or exist: *The proposal is moot because of a lack of funds.*

moot[2] *v* **be mooted** to be suggested for people to consider

mop[1] /mɒp $ mɑːp/ *n* **1** [C] a thing for washing floors consisting of a long stick with a soft end → see picture at MOP[2] **2** [singular] informal a large amount of thick untidy hair: **[+of]** *a mop of black curly hair*

MOP

a broom

a mop

a bucket

mop | sweep

mop² v [T] (**mopped, mopping**) **1** to wash a floor with a mop **2** to dry your face or remove liquid from something using a cloth SYN **wipe**: **mop sth from sth** He mopped the sweat from his face.
PHRASAL VERBS
mop sth ↔ **up** to remove liquid from a surface, using a mop or cloth: Can you mop up the milk you've spilled?

mope /məup $ moup/ (also **mope around**) v [I] to spend time feeling unhappy and doing very little

moped /'məuped $ 'mou-/ n [C] a vehicle like a bicycle with a small engine

moral¹ /'mɒrəl $ 'mɔː-/ adj
1 [only before noun] based on principles of what is right and wrong → **ethical** OPP **immoral**: This is a moral issue, not a political one. | **moral values/ standards/principles** an emphasis on traditional moral values | **moral obligation/duty/responsibility** We have a moral duty to help the poor. | This presented him with a **moral dilemma**.
2 a moral person has high standards of behaviour based on principles of what is right and wrong OPP **immoral, amoral**: a man of high moral integrity —**morally** adv: Slavery is morally wrong.
PHRASES
moral support help and encouragement that you give to someone: I went along to offer moral support.
moral victory when you show that your beliefs are right and fair even if you do not win the argument, game etc: Although we lost the case on a technicality, we won a moral victory.

moral² n [C] **1** something you learn from a story: **[+of]** The moral of the story is that crime doesn't pay. **2** morals [plural] principles or standards of good behaviour → **ethics**: He has no morals!

morale /məˈrɑːl $ məˈræl/ n [U] the level of confidence and positive feelings that a person or group has: Talk of job losses is bad for morale. | **Morale** in the team is quite **low**.

moralistic /ˌmɒrəˈlɪstɪk◂ $ ˌmɔː-/ adj with strong beliefs about what is right and wrong and about how people should behave —**moralist** /'mɒrəlɪst $ 'mɔː-/ n [C]

morality /məˈræləti/ n [U] ideas about what is right and wrong: Are standards of morality declining? | **[+of]** a discussion on the morality of abortion

moralize (also **-ise** BrE) /'mɒrəlaɪz $ 'mɔː-/ v [I] to tell people what is the right or wrong way to behave, especially when they think this is annoying

moratorium /ˌmɒrəˈtɔːriəm $ ˌmɔː-/ n [singular] when an activity is officially stopped for a period of time: a moratorium on arms sales

morbid /'mɔːbɪd $ 'mɔːr-/ adj with a strong interest in unpleasant subjects, especially death: a morbid fascination with murder stories

more¹ /mɔː $ mɔːr/ adv
1 [used before an adjective or adverb to form a comparative] used to say that someone or something has a greater amount of a quality OPP **less**: You'll have to be more careful next time. | **more ... than** My meal was more expensive than Dan's. | That's **much** more interesting! | She's **far** more intelligent than I am. | He seems **a lot** more cheerful these days.
2 used to say that something happens a greater number of times or for longer than before OPP **less**: I promised I'd help more with the housework. | We see our grandchildren **more than** we used to. | She goes out **a lot** more now that she has a car. | I miss him **much** more than I used to.
3 used to say that something happens to a greater degree OPP **less**: She cares more about her dogs than she does about me! → **once more** at ONCE¹
PHRASES
more and more used to say that a situation gradually increases: She finds getting about more and more difficult.
more or less almost: It looks more or less flat.
THESAURUS ▶ ALMOST
not any more no longer happening or true: Sarah doesn't live here any more.

more² determiner, pron
1 a greater amount or number OPP **less**: **more ... than** There's more advertising than there used to be. | Orange juice costs **more than** beer in some bars.
2 an additional number or amount: Would you like some more coffee? | **some/a few more** I have to make a few more phone calls. | **10/20 etc more** We need five more chairs.
PHRASES
more and more an increasing number of something: These days, more and more people travel long distances to work.
more or less almost: The article says more or less the same thing as the other one.

THESAURUS – sense 2

more in addition to what is already there, has already been made or used etc: He put some more logs on the fire. | More people came into the room.
another one more: Can I have another biscuit?
extra more of something, in addition to the usual amount or number: We get an extra day's holiday this year. | You can use the pool at no extra cost.
spare a spare key, tyre, room etc is another one that you have in case you need to use it: It's always best to have a spare key.
additional formal more than the amount that was agreed or expected at the beginning:

Additional troops will be sent to the region. | additional charges

further formal more, in addition to what there is already or what has happened already: For further information, call this number. | She has gone into hospital for further tests.

moreover /mɔːrˈəʊvə $ -ˈoʊvər/ adv formal used to introduce information that adds to or supports something you have just said: The new design is not very good. Moreover, it is very expensive.

mores /ˈmɔːreɪz/ n [plural] formal the customs, social behaviour, and moral values of a particular group

morgue /mɔːɡ $ mɔːrɡ/ n [C] a room or building where dead bodies are kept before they are buried or burned SYN **mortuary**

morning /ˈmɔːnɪŋ $ ˈmɔːr-/ n [C,U]
1 the early part of the day, from when the sun rises until the middle of the day: I got a letter from Jack this morning. | **in the morning** I'll deal with it in the morning (=tomorrow morning). | Classes start at nine in the morning (=every morning). | **on Monday/Friday etc mornings** He sleeps late on Sunday mornings.
2 the part of the night that is after MIDNIGHT: The phone rang at three o'clock in the morning.
3 (good) morning spoken used when you meet someone in the morning

COLLOCATIONS

adjectives

this morning I've got a lot of things to do this morning.
yesterday/tomorrow morning I'll see you tomorrow morning.
the next/following morning Sarah was up at seven the next morning.
early/late morning We didn't set off until late morning.
a beautiful/fine/sunny etc morning Wake up – it's a beautiful morning.

noun + morning

Friday/Monday/Saturday etc morning We'll discuss it on Monday morning.
a spring/summer/autumn/winter morning It was a bright spring morning.

morning + noun

the morning sun/light/mist He strolled along, enjoying the morning sun.
sb's morning run/swim/coffee (=that someone has in the morning) She had already been for her morning run.

'morning ,sickness n [U] a feeling of sickness that some women have during the morning when they are PREGNANT, usually in the early months

moron /ˈmɔːrɒn $ -rɑːn/ n [C] informal an offensive word for someone who you think is very stupid —**moronic** /məˈrɒnɪk $ -ˈrɑː-/ adj

morose /məˈrəʊs $ -ˈroʊs/ adj unhappy, bad-tempered, and silent

morphine /ˈmɔːfiːn $ ˈmɔːr-/ n [U] a powerful drug used to stop pain

morsel /ˈmɔːsəl $ ˈmɔːr-/ n [C] literary a small piece of food: a morsel of bread

mortal[1] /ˈmɔːtl $ ˈmɔːrtl/ adj **1** not able to live for ever OPP **immortal**: All men are mortal. **2** causing death SYN **fatal**: a mortal wound **3 mortal fear/terror/danger etc** extreme fear, danger etc: He lived in mortal fear of being attacked. —**mortally** adv: He was mortally wounded.

mortal[2] n **1 lesser/ordinary/mere mortals** ordinary people, when compared with people who are more important or powerful: In Hollywood you can stay forever young, unlike us mere mortals. **2** [C] literary a human being

mortality /mɔːˈtæləti $ mɔːr-/ n [U] **1** (also **mor'tality ,rate**) the number of deaths during a particular period of time or from a particular cause: a rise in the infant mortality rate **2** the fact that you will die one day OPP **immortality**: The heart attack reminded me of my own mortality.

mortar /ˈmɔːtə $ ˈmɔːrtər/ n **1** [U] a mixture of CEMENT, sand, and water, used in building for joining bricks or stones together **2** [C] a heavy gun that fires EXPLOSIVEs high into the air

mortgage /ˈmɔːɡɪdʒ $ ˈmɔːr-/ n [C] money that you borrow in order to buy a house, and pay back over a large number of years: They're finding it difficult to **pay** their **mortgage**. —**mortgage** v [T]

mortician /mɔːˈtɪʃən $ mɔːr-/ n [C] AmE someone whose job is to arrange funerals and prepare bodies to be buried SYN **undertaker** BrE

mortified /ˈmɔːtɪfaɪd $ ˈmɔːr-/ adj extremely embarrassed or ashamed: Pete was mortified to learn of his mistake.

mortuary /ˈmɔːtʃuəri $ ˈmɔːrtʃueri/ n [C] (plural **mortuaries**) a building or room where dead bodies are kept before they are buried or burned SYN **morgue**

mosaic /məʊˈzeɪ-ɪk $ moʊ-/ n [C,U] a pattern or picture made from small pieces of coloured stone or glass

Moslem /ˈmɒzlɪm $ ˈmɑːz-/ n [C] another spelling of MUSLIM —**Moslem** adj

mosque /mɒsk $ mɑːsk/ n [C] a building where Muslims go to pray

mosquito /məˈskiːtəʊ $ -toʊ/ n [C] (plural **mosquitoes** or **mosquitos**) a small flying insect that bites and sucks blood

moss /mɒs $ mɒːs/ n [U] a very small green plant that grows in a thick soft mass on trees and rocks —**mossy** adj

most[1] /məʊst $ moʊst/ adv
1 [used before an adjective or adverb to form a superlative] used to say that someone or something has the greatest amount of a quality OPP **least**: Anna is **one of the most** beautiful women I know. | I forgot to tell you the most important thing! | easily the most popular sport in schools

2 more than anything or anyone else: *She liked the dark beer most.* | *The weaker students will benefit most of all.*

3 *AmE spoken* almost: *We eat at Joe's most every weekend.*

4 *formal* very: *It was a most pleasant evening.*

most² *determiner, pron*

1 almost all: *Most computers have a disk drive.* | **[+of]** *Most of the kids in the team live near here.* | *Most of the time* (=usually) *he's no trouble.*

2 more than anyone or anything else: **the most** *Which class has the most children?* | *Whoever scores most will win.*

3 the largest number or amount that is possible: **the most** *How can we get the most power from the engine?* | *The most I can give you is $100.*

PHRASES

at (the) most used to say that a number or amount will not be larger than you say: *The book should cost $10 at the most.*

for the most part usually or generally, but not always or not completely SYN **mostly**: *Things, for the most part, had gone smoothly.*

make the most of sth to get the greatest advantage you can from a situation: *Go out and make the most of the sunshine.*

Grammar

You use **most** immediately before a plural noun or an uncountable noun, when you are talking about something in general: *I like most animals.* | *Most modern art is really boring.*

You use **most of** before 'the', 'this', 'my' etc when you are talking about a particular group or thing: *I got most of the answers right.* | *Most of this book is easy to understand.* | *He does most of his work at home.*

---

mostly /ˈməʊstli $ ˈmoʊst-/ *adv* in most cases or most of the time: *Mostly, he travels by car.* | *The room was full of sports people, mostly footballers.*

MOT /ˌem əʊ ˈtiː $ -oʊ-/ (*also* **MOT test**) *n* [C] a test in Britain that all cars more than three years old must pass every year in order to show that they are still safe to be driven

motel /məʊˈtel $ moʊ-/ *n* [C] a hotel for people travelling by car THESAURUS ▸ HOTEL

moth /mɒθ $ mɒːθ/ *n* [C] an insect similar to a BUTTERFLY that usually flies at night

mother¹ /ˈmʌðə $ -ər/ *n* [C]

1 your female parent, or any woman who is a parent: *My mother said I have to be home by 9:00.* | **mother of two/three etc** (=with two, three etc children) *a 34-year-old mother of four*

2 an animal's female parent

PHRASES

the mother of all … *informal* used when emphasizing that something is very big, bad, or important: *I woke up with the mother of all hangovers.*

mother² *v* [T] to take care of someone as if they were a child

motherhood /ˈmʌðəhʊd $ -ðər-/ *n* [U] being a mother

mother-in-law *n* [C] (*plural* **mothers-in-law**) the mother of your husband or wife

motherly /ˈmʌðəli $ -ðər-/ *adj* a motherly woman is loving and kind

mother-of-pearl *n* [U] a smooth shiny substance on the inside of some shells, used for making buttons, jewellery etc

Mother's Day *n* [singular] a day when people give cards and gifts to their mothers → **Father's Day**

mother tongue *n* [C] the first language that you learn as a child

motif /məʊˈtiːf $ moʊ-/ *n* [C] **1** an idea or subject that is regularly repeated and developed in a book, film etc **2** a small picture used to decorate something: *a T-shirt with a butterfly motif*

motion¹ /ˈməʊʃən $ ˈmoʊ-/ *n* **1** [U] the process of moving, or the way that someone or something moves: **[+of]** *the rolling motion of the ship* **2** [C] a single movement of your head or hand: *He made a motion with his hand, to tell me to keep back.* **3** [C] a suggestion that is made formally at a meeting and then decided on by voting: *I'd like to propose a motion to change our working hours.* | *Most people opposed the motion he had put forward.* | *The motion was carried unanimously.* | *I think the motion will be defeated.* → **SLOW MOTION**

PHRASES

go through the motions (of doing sth) to do something because you have to do it, without being very interested: *I feel so bored at work, like I'm just going through the motions.*

put/set sth in motion to start a process: *The plans had been passed and already put in motion.*

motion² *v* [I,T] to tell someone to do something by moving your head or hand: **motion (for) sb to do sth** *She motioned for him to sit down.*

motionless /ˈməʊʃənləs $ ˈmoʊ-/ *adj* not moving at all: *He stood motionless in the doorway.*

motion picture *n* [C] *AmE* a film made for cinema SYN **movie**

motivate /ˈməʊtɪveɪt $ ˈmoʊ-/ *v* [T] **1** to be the reason why someone does something: *I can't understand what motivates him to do such terrible things.* **2** to make someone want to achieve something, especially by encouraging them to work harder: **motivate sb to do sth** *managers who motivate their staff to achieve targets* —**motivated** *adj*: *a racially motivated attack* | *highly motivated students* (=students who are eager to work hard)

motivation Ac /ˌməʊtɪˈveɪʃən $ ˌmoʊ-/ *n* **1** [U] when you want to do something: *Jack is smart, but he lacks motivation.* **2** [C] the reason why you want to do something: **[+for]** *What was your motivation for writing the book?*

motivational /ˌməʊtɪˈveɪʃənəl $ ˌmoʊ-/ *adj* [only before noun] motivational speeches, books etc are intended to make people eager to do something

motive Ac /ˈməʊtɪv $ ˈmoʊ-/ *n* [C] the reason why someone does something, especially something wrong or bad: **[+for]** *Jealousy was the motive for the murder.* THESAURUS ▸ REASON

motley /'mɒtli $ 'mɑːtli/ adj **motley crew/collection etc** a group of people or things that do not seem to belong together

motor[1] /'məʊtə $ 'moʊtər/ n [C] the part of a machine that uses electricity, petrol etc to make it move: *an electric motor*

motor[2] adj [only before noun] **1** using power from an engine: *a motor vehicle* **2** BrE relating to cars SYN **auto** AmE: *the motor industry*

motorbike /'məʊtəbaɪk $ 'moʊtər-/ n [C] especially BrE a MOTORCYCLE → see picture at TRANSPORT[1]

motorboat /'məʊtəbəʊt $ 'moʊtərboʊt/ n [C] a small fast boat with an engine → see picture at TRANSPORT[1]

motorcade /'məʊtəkeɪd $ 'moʊtər-/ n [C] a group of cars that surround an important person's car to protect it

'**motor car** n [C] formal a car

motorcycle /'məʊtə,saɪkəl $ 'moʊtər-/ n [C] a vehicle with two wheels and an engine SYN **motorbike**

motorcyclist /'məʊtə,saɪklɪst $ 'moʊtər-/ n [C] someone who rides a MOTORCYCLE

motoring /'məʊtərɪŋ $ 'moʊ-/ adj [only before noun] BrE relating to cars and driving: *a motoring holiday*

motorist /'məʊtərɪst/ n [C] someone who drives a car SYN **driver**

motorized (also **-ised** BrE) /'məʊtəraɪzd $ 'moʊ-/ adj having a motor: *a motorized wheelchair*

'**motor ,vehicle** n [C] formal a car, bus etc

motorway /'məʊtəweɪ $ 'moʊtər-/ n [C] BrE a wide road for driving fast over long distances SYN **freeway** AmE → **expressway, highway**: **on a motorway** *We broke down on the motorway.* THESAURUS ROAD

mottled /'mɒtld $ 'mɑː-/ adj covered with patterns of light and dark colours: *the kitten's mottled grey fur*

motto /'mɒtəʊ $ 'mɑːtoʊ/ n [C] (plural **mottos** or **mottoes**) a short statement that expresses someone's aims or principles

mould[1] BrE, **mold** AmE /məʊld $ moʊld/ n **1** [C] a container that you pour liquid into so that the liquid will take its shape when it becomes solid: *a chocolate mould* **2** [U] a green or black substance that grows on old food or on wet things: *a piece of old cheese covered in mould*

mould[2] BrE, **mold** AmE v [T] **1** to shape a soft substance by pressing it or rolling it **2** to influence the way someone's character or attitudes develop: *an attempt to mould public opinion*

moulding BrE, **molding** AmE /'məʊldɪŋ $ 'moʊl-/ n [C,U] a piece of wood, stone etc put around the edge of something as a decoration

mouldy BrE, **moldy** AmE /'məʊldi $ 'moʊl-/ adj covered with mould: *mouldy cheese* | *Some of the vegetables had* **gone mouldy**.

moult BrE, **molt** AmE /məʊlt $ moʊlt/ v [I] when an animal or bird moults, it loses hair or feathers so that new ones can grow

mound /maʊnd/ n [C] **1** a pile of earth that looks like a small hill **2** a large pile of something: **[+of]** *a mound of papers*

mount /maʊnt/ v

1 START STH [T] to organize and begin an event or course of action: *The museum is* **mounting** *an exhibition of students' art.* | **mount a campaign/challenge/attack** *They are mounting a campaign to stop the school closing.*

2 INCREASE (also **mount up**) [I] to gradually increase → **mounting**: *His debts continued to mount up.* | *Tensions in the region are mounting.*

3 HORSE/BICYCLE [I,T] formal to get on a horse or bicycle OPP **dismount**: *He mounted his horse and rode off.*

4 STEP/STAIRS [T] formal to go up something such as stairs or a step: *He mounted the steps to the stage.*

5 FASTEN [T] to fix something onto a surface: *a metal box mounted on the wall*

Mount n (written abbreviation **Mt**) used in the names of mountains: *Mount Everest*

mountain /'maʊntɪn $ 'maʊntən/ n [C]

1 a very high hill: *She is the first woman to* **climb** *this* **mountain**. | *a* **mountain range** (=line of mountains) | **in the mountains** *We went hiking up in the mountains.* **2** informal a large amount of something: **[+of]** *I've got a mountain of ironing to do.*

PHRASES

make a mountain out of a molehill to treat a small problem as if it were very serious: *She was only five minutes late! You're making a mountain out of a molehill.*

THESAURUS

mountain a very high hill: *Kilimanjaro is the highest mountain in Africa.*

hill an area of land that is higher than the land around it, and often has a rounded top: *The house has wonderful views of the surrounding hills.*

volcano a mountain that has a hole at the top, through which smoke and hot liquid rock come out: *The volcano erupted, destroying the city below.*

foothills a group of smaller hills below some high mountains: *the foothills of the Pyrenees*

cliff the steep side of an area of land, often next to the sea: *There are white cliffs all along the coast.*

peak the pointed top of a mountain: *the snow-covered peaks of the Himalayas*

summit the very highest point of a mountain: *the summit of Mount Everest*

'**mountain ,bike** n [C] a strong bicycle with wide tyres designed for riding on rough ground → see picture on page A9

mountaineering /,maʊntə'nɪərɪŋ $,maʊntn'ɪrɪŋ/ n [U] the sport of climbing mountains —**mountaineer** n [C]

mountainous /'maʊntɪnəs $ 'maʊntənəs/ adj a mountainous area has a lot of mountains

mountainside /ˈmaʊntənsaɪd $ ˈmaʊntən-/ n [C] the side of a mountain: *They walked down the mountainside.*

mounting /ˈmaʊntɪŋ/ adj [only before noun] increasing: *The government has come under mounting criticism.* | *the company's mounting debts*

mourn /mɔːn $ mɔːrn/ v **1** [I,T] to feel very sad because someone has died: *She is still mourning her son's death.* | **[+for]** *mourning for her child* **2** [T] to feel sad because something no longer exists

mourner /ˈmɔːnə $ ˈmɔːrnər/ n [C] someone who is at a FUNERAL

mournful /ˈmɔːnfəl $ ˈmɔːrn-/ adj very sad: *slow, mournful music* —**mournfully** adv

mourning /ˈmɔːnɪŋ $ ˈmɔːr-/ n [U] feelings of great sadness because someone has died: *a day of national mourning for victims of the earthquake* | **in mourning** (=feeling great sadness) *She is still in mourning for her husband.*

mouse /maʊs/ n [C]
1 (*plural* **mice** /maɪs/) a small furry animal with a long tail and a pointed nose
2 (*plural* **mouses**) a small object connected to a computer that you move with your hand to give instructions to the computer → see picture on page A12

ˈ**mouse mat** (also ˈ**mouse pad** AmE) n [C] a small piece of material that you move a computer mouse on

mousse /muːs/ n [C,U] **1** a cold sweet food made from cream, eggs, and fruit or chocolate **2** a substance that you put in your hair to hold it in position

moustache (also **mustache** AmE) /məˈstɑːʃ $ ˈmʌstæʃ/ n [C] hair a man grows on his upper lip

mousy, **mousey** /ˈmaʊsi/ adj mousy hair is light brown

mouth¹ /maʊθ/ n [C] (*plural* **mouths** /maʊðz/)
1 the part of your face that you use for speaking and eating: *She stared at me with her mouth open.* | **in/into your mouth** *The sweet left a strange taste in my mouth.* → see picture on page A2
2 the entrance to a CAVE or large hole: **[+of]** *the mouth of the tunnel*
3 the part of a river where it joins the sea
4 the open part at the top of a container: **[+of]** *the mouth of a jar*

PHRASES
| **big/loud mouth** *informal* someone who often says things that they should not say or who says things in a loud way: *He's a bit of a loud mouth who never shuts up.*
| **keep your mouth shut** *informal* to not talk about

MOUSTACHE

moustache/ mustache AmE

beard

something, especially a secret: *The party's a surprise, so keep your mouth shut about it.*
make your mouth water if food makes your mouth water, it looks so good that you want to eat it immediately → **mouth-watering**: *The smell of baking bread was making her mouth water.*

COLLOCATIONS

verbs
to open your mouth *I opened my mouth to scream.*
to close/shut your mouth *She started to speak, then closed her mouth.*
sb's mouth falls/drops open (=in surprise) *His mouth fell open when he saw who it was.*

adjectives
a big/large/wide mouth *He had a big nose and a big mouth.*
a small mouth *She stuffed the cake into her small mouth.*
sb's mouth is open *His mouth was open and he was snoring.*
sb's mouth is full (=of food) *Don't talk with your mouth full.*
sb's mouth is dry (=especially because they are nervous or ill) *My mouth was dry and my hands were shaking.*

noun + mouth
the corner/side of sb's mouth *A cigarette hung out of the corner of his mouth.*
the roof of sb's mouth (=the top inside part) *The hot stew burned the roof of his mouth.*

---

mouth² /maʊð/ v [T] to move your lips as if you are saying words, but without making any sound: *Karen was mouthing the answer to me behind the teacher's back.*
PHRASAL VERBS
mouth off *informal* to talk angrily or rudely to someone: *Mick was suspended for mouthing off to teachers.*

mouthful /ˈmaʊθfʊl/ n **1** [C] an amount of food or drink that you put into your mouth at one time: *He took a big mouthful of cake.* **2** a mouthful *informal* a long word or phrase that is difficult to say: *Her real name is quite a mouthful, so we just call her Dee.*

ˈ**mouth ˌorgan** n [C] a HARMONICA

mouthpiece /ˈmaʊθpiːs/ n [C] **1** the part of a musical instrument, telephone etc that you put in or next to your mouth **2** [usually singular] a person or newspaper that expresses the opinions of a government or political group: *'Pravda' used to be the mouthpiece of the Communist Party.*

mouthwash /ˈmaʊθwɒʃ $ -wɔːʃ, -wɑːʃ/ n [C,U] a liquid that you use to clean your mouth and make your breath smell fresh

ˈ**mouth-ˌwatering** adj mouth-watering food looks or smells extremely good **THESAURUS** ▶ DELICIOUS

movable /ˈmuːvəbəl/ adj something that is movable can be moved: *toy soldiers with movable arms*

move¹ /muːv/ v
1 [I,T] to change from one place or position to another, or to make something do this: **move (sth)**

away/back/forward etc *Move away from the door! | He moved the chair into the corner of the room. |* **[+about/around]** *She could hear someone moving around downstairs. | The traffic was still moving slowly.*
2 [I] to go to a new place to live or work: **[+to/into/ from]** *They moved to Birmingham in May. |* **move house** *BrE* (=go to live in a different house) *We're moving house next week.*
3 [I] used when saying how quickly something is progressing or changing: *Things seem to be moving very slowly. | You need to move quickly to take advantage of this opportunity.*
4 [T] to make someone feel a strong emotion, especially sadness or sympathy → **moving**: *The story* **moved** *us* **to tears** (=made us cry). | *Harry was genuinely moved by what he saw.*
5 [T] to change the time or order of something: **move sth from/to sth** *The meeting's been moved from Wednesday to Thursday.*

PHRASES

get moving *spoken* to start doing something or going somewhere quickly: *If you don't get moving, you'll miss the bus.*

PHRASAL VERBS

move away to go to live in a different area: *My best friend moved away when I was ten.*
move in
1 to start living in a new house: *When are you moving in?*
2 to start living with someone in the same house: **[+with]** *Steve's moving in with his girlfriend. |* **[+together]** *We're thinking about moving in together.*
move off if a car, train etc moves off, it moves forward to start its journey
move on
1 to stop doing or dealing with one thing, and start doing or dealing with something else: *I enjoyed my job, but it was time to move on. |* **[+to]** *I'd like to move on to the subject of education.*
2 to leave a place where you have been staying and continue on your journey: *After three days we decided it was time to move on.*
3 to develop, improve, or become more modern: *Her ideas have hardly moved on since the thirties.*
move out to permanently leave the house where you are living: *We have to move out by next Friday.*
move over to change position so that there is more space for other people or things: *Move over so Jim can sit down.*
move up
1 to change to a higher job, group, level etc: **[+to]** *He's moved up to tenth in the world rankings.*
2 *BrE* to change position so that there is more space for other people or things: *If everyone moves up a bit, you can sit here.*

THESAURUS

move to change from one place or position to another: *I wish that car would move out of the way. | Every time I move, my arm hurts.*
sway to move slowly from one side to the other: *The palm trees swayed slightly.*
rock to move repeatedly from one side to another, with small gentle movements: *I could see her rocking gently in her chair.*

wobble to move unsteadily from side to side: *The ladder began to wobble.*
fidget to keep moving or playing with your fingers, hands, feet etc, because you are bored or nervous: *The children were fidgeting in their seats all the way through the film.*
twitch to make small movements with your face, eye, hand etc that you cannot control: *His face kept twitching.*
budge to move – used when you are trying hard to make something move, often without success: *I can't get the table to budge.*

move² *n* [C]
1 something that you decide to do in order to achieve something: *She wondered what her next move should be. | Hiring Peter was definitely **a good move** (=a good decision). |* **[+to/towards]** *The talks are a definite move towards peace.*
2 a movement in a particular direction: *Arnison* **made a move** *for the door. | I knew he was* **watching** *my* **every move.**
3 when you go to live or work in a new place: *How did the move go?*
4 when you change the position of one of the pieces in a game such as CHESS: *It's your move.*

PHRASES

be on the move to be travelling to different places all the time: *I always take my mobile phone when I'm on the move.*
get a move on *spoken* used to tell someone to hurry: *Get a move on, or we'll be late!* **THESAURUS HURRY**
make a move *BrE spoken* to leave a place: *It's late – we'd better be making a move.*

movement /'mu:vmənt/ *n*
1 [C] a group of people who have the same beliefs and work together to achieve a particular aim: **civil rights/peace etc movement** *the civil rights movement of the 1960s |* **[+for]** *the movement for independence*
2 [C,U] a change of position, or when someone or something moves or is moved: *Any movement caused him a lot of pain. | She was neat and quick in all her movements. |* **[+of]** *I noticed a* **slight movement** *of the curtain.*
3 [C] a gradual change in a situation or in people's attitudes or opinions: **[+away/towards]** *a movement away from traditional values*
4 sb's movements the places where someone goes and the things they do during a particular time: *Police are trying to trace his movements over the last 48 hours.*
5 [C] one of the parts that a piece of CLASSICAL music is divided into

mover /'mu:və $ -ər/ *n* [C] **1** *especially AmE* someone whose job is to move people's furniture from one house to another **2** someone or something that moves in a particular way

movie /'mu:vi/ *n* [C]
1 *especially AmE* a film that is shown at a cinema or on television **SYN** film: *Do you want to see a movie tonight?*
2 the movies *AmE* the cinema: *How often do you* **go** *to the movies?*

moviegoer /ˈmuːviˌɡəʊə $ -ˌɡoʊər/ *n* [C] *especially AmE* someone who goes to see films at the cinema, especially regularly

'movie ,theater *n* [C] *AmE* a building where you go to see films SYN **cinema** *BrE*

moving /ˈmuːvɪŋ/ *adj* **1** making you feel strong emotions, especially sadness or sympathy: **deeply/profoundly moving** *a deeply moving experience* **2** [only before noun] changing from one position to another: *the effects of moving light* | **fast-moving/slow-moving** *fast-moving traffic* —**movingly** *adv*: *He spoke movingly about his experiences.*

mow /məʊ $ moʊ/ *v* [I,T] (*past tense* **mowed**, *past participle* **mowed** or **mown** /məʊn $ moʊn/) to cut grass with a machine: *Dan was mowing the lawn.* THESAURUS ▶ CUT

PHRASAL VERBS

mow sb ↔ **down** *informal* to kill someone by shooting them or driving into them very fast: *A driver was jailed for mowing down a nine-year-old girl.*

mower /ˈməʊə $ ˈmoʊər/ *n* [C] a machine used for cutting grass SYN **lawn mower**

MP /ˌem ˈpiː/ *n* [C] (**Member of Parliament**) someone who has been elected to a parliament to represent people from a particular area: **[+for]** *She's the MP for Liverpool North.* THESAURUS ▶ POLITICIAN

,MP'3 ,player *n* [C] a machine or computer program that plays music that has been DOWNLOADed from the Internet → see picture on page A12

mpg /ˌem piː ˈdʒiː/ (**miles per gallon**) used to describe the amount of petrol a car uses

mph /ˌem piː ˈeɪtʃ/ (**miles per hour**) used to describe the speed of a vehicle or the wind: *a speed of 180 mph*

Mr *BrE*, **Mr.** *AmE* /ˈmɪstə $ -ər/ a title used before a man's family name: *Mr Smith is the headteacher.*

Mrs *BrE*, **Mrs.** *AmE* /ˈmɪsɪz/ a title used before a married woman's family name → **Ms**, **Miss**, **Mr**: *Mrs Smith*

MRSA /ˌem ɑːr es ˈeɪ/ *n* [U] a type of BACTERIA that cannot be treated with normal ANTIBIOTIC drugs

Ms *BrE*, **Ms.** *AmE* /mɪz, məz/ a title used before the family name of a married or unmarried woman → **Mrs** → see Word Choice at MISS

MS /ˌem ˈes/ *n* [U] (**multiple sclerosis**) a serious illness that affects your nerves, and gradually makes you weak and unable to move

MSc *BrE*, **M.Sc.** *AmE* /ˌem es ˈsiː/ *n* [C] (**Master of Science**) a higher university degree in a science subject → **MA**

Mt the written abbreviation of **Mount**: *Mt Everest*

much¹ /mʌtʃ/ *adv*
1 a lot: **much better/easier/higher etc** *I'm feeling much better now.* | *This test was much more difficult.* | **much too young/big/fast etc** *He was driving much too fast.* | *'Did you enjoy it?' 'No, **not much** (=not a lot).'* | *Thank you **very much**.*
2 **much like sth** (also **much (the same) as ...**) very similar to something: *It tastes much like butter.* | *The house was much as I remembered it.*

PHRASES

not much good (at sth) not good at doing something: *I'm not much good at cooking.*

so much, how much used to emphasize the amount or degree of something: *He'd changed **so much** I didn't recognize him.* | *I know **how much** he likes Ann.*

much² *determiner, pron* a large amount of something: *Was there much traffic?* | *We don't have much time.* | *You haven't eaten much.* | **[+of]** *Much of the city was destroyed.* | **(far/much) too much** *There was much too much work for one person.* | *There's **so much** I need to do.* | *Eat **as much as** you can.* → LOT

PHRASES

how much used to talk or ask about the amount or cost of something: *How much milk do we need?* | *How much is that shirt?*

not be much of a sth to not be a good example of something, or to not be good at something: *He wasn't much of a father.*

not be up to much *BrE informal* to be of bad quality: *The hotel food wasn't up to much.*

be too much for sb to be too difficult or unpleasant for someone: *The shock was too much for him.*

muck¹ /mʌk/ *n* [U] **1** dirt or mud: *His hands were covered in muck.* **2** *BrE* solid waste from animals: *dog muck*

muck² *v*

PHRASAL VERBS

muck about/around *BrE informal* **1** to behave in a silly way, especially when you should be working: *Stop mucking about and do your homework.* **2 muck sb about/around** to cause trouble for someone by changing your mind a lot or not doing what you promised to do

muck in *BrE informal* to work together with other people in order to get a job done: *If we all muck in, we should finish the painting tomorrow.*

muck sth ↔ **up** *BrE informal* to spoil something, or do something badly: *I don't want to muck up my chances of success.*

mucky /'mʌki/ *adj informal* dirty: *mucky hands*

mucus /'mjuːkəs/ *n* [U] a thick liquid produced in your nose

mud /mʌd/ *n* [U] soft wet earth: *a vehicle that can drive through mud and water* | **covered/caked with mud** *boots caked with mud*

muddle¹ /'mʌdl/ *n* [C usually singular] a situation when people are confused about something, especially with the result that they make mistakes: *The ceremony was an embarrassing muddle.* | **be/get in a muddle** (=be or get confused) *I was in such a muddle I forgot the meeting was today.* | **[+over/about]** *There was some muddle over our hotel reservation.*

muddle² (*also* **muddle up**) *v* [T] *especially BrE* **1** to put things in the wrong order: *The papers had all been muddled up.* **2** to wrongly think that one person or thing is someone or something else: *The twins are so alike that it's easy to* **get** *them* **muddled up.** **3** to confuse someone, especially so that they make a mistake: *I've* **got** *a bit* **muddled.** *What date are we leaving?*
PHRASAL VERBS
muddle through/along to continue doing something even though it is difficult or you feel unsure about it: *The students were often left to muddle along without help.*

muddled /'mʌdld/ *adj* confused: *muddled thinking*

muddy¹ /'mʌdi/ *adj* covered with mud or containing mud: *muddy boots* | *muddy water* THESAURUS DIRTY

muddy² *v* [T] (**muddied**, **muddying**, **muddies**) to make something dirty with mud: *Try not to muddy your shoes.*
PHRASES
muddy the waters/the issue to make a situation more complicated or confusing than it was before: *These new studies merely muddy the waters.*

mudguard /'mʌdɡɑːd $ -ɡɑːrd/ *n* [C] *BrE* a curved piece of metal or plastic that covers the wheel of a bicycle or MOTORBIKE → see picture at **BICYCLE**

muesli /'mjuːzli/ *n* [U] grain, nuts, and dried fruit that you eat with milk for breakfast

muffin /'mʌfɪn/ *n* [C] **1** a small cake: *a blueberry muffin* **2** a small round type of bread that you eat hot with butter

muffle /'mʌfəl/ *v* [T] to make a sound less loud or clear: *Snow muffled the sound of the traffic.* —**muffled** *adj*: *I heard muffled voices downstairs.*

muffler /'mʌflə $ -ər/ *n* [C] **1** *old-fashioned* a SCARF **2** *AmE* a piece of equipment that makes a vehicle's engine sound quieter SYN **silencer** *BrE*

mug¹ /mʌɡ/ *n* [C] **1** a large cup with straight sides, or the liquid inside it: *a coffee mug* | **a mug of sth** *He was drinking a mug of tea.* **2** *BrE informal* someone who is stupid and easy to deceive

MUG

cup

mug

saucer

mug² *v* [T] (**mugged**, **mugging**) to attack and rob someone in a public place: *He was mugged outside the bank.* THESAURUS STEAL —**mugger** *n* [C] —**mugging** *n* [C,U]

muggy /'mʌɡi/ *adj informal* muggy weather is unpleasant because it is too warm and the air is wet SYN **humid** THESAURUS DAMP

mugshot /'mʌɡʃɒt $ -ʃɑːt/ *n* [C] *informal* a photograph of someone's face, especially a criminal's

Muhammad, Mohammed /mʊ'hæməd, mə-/ the Arab PROPHET who founded the religion of Islam

mulch /mʌltʃ/ *n* [singular, U] decaying leaves that you put on soil to improve its quality

mule /mjuːl/ *n* [C] an animal that has a DONKEY and a horse as parents

mull /mʌl/ *v*
PHRASAL VERBS
mull sth ↔ **over** to think about something carefully: *She had plenty of time to* **mull things over.**

mullah /'mʌlə, 'mʊlə/ *n* [C] a Muslim teacher of law and religion

multi- /mʌlti, mʌltə/ *prefix* many: *multicoloured posters*

multicultural /,mʌlti'kʌltʃərəl◂/ *adj* involving people or ideas from many different countries, races, or religions: *a multicultural society*

multilateral /,mʌltɪ'lætərəl◂/ *adj* involving several different countries or groups → **bilateral, unilateral**: *multilateral peace talks*

multilingual /,mʌltɪ'lɪŋɡwəl◂/ *adj* using or speaking several different languages → **bilingual, monolingual**: *multilingual communities*

multimedia /,mʌlti'miːdiə◂/ *adj* [only before noun] using a mixture of sounds, pictures etc to give information, especially on a computer: *multimedia software* —**multimedia** *n* [U]

multinational¹ /,mʌltɪ'næʃənəl◂/ *adj* based or working in many countries: *multinational companies* | *multinational workforces*

multinational² *n* [C] a large company that has offices in many different countries

multiple¹ /'mʌltəpəl/ *adj* [only before noun] many, or involving many things or people: *He suffered multiple injuries.* | *a multiple murderer*

multiple² n [C] a number that contains a smaller number an exact number of times: *20 is a multiple of 5.*

multiple 'choice adj a multiple choice examination or question shows several different answers, and you must choose the correct one

multiple sclerosis /ˌmʌltəpəl skləˈrəʊsɪs $ -ˈroʊ-/ n [U] (abbreviation **MS**) a serious illness that affects your nerves, and gradually makes you weak and unable to move

multiplex /ˈmʌltəpleks/ n [C] a large cinema with several rooms in which films are shown

multiplication /ˌmʌltɪplɪˈkeɪʃən/ n [U] when you calculate something by adding the same number to itself a particular number of times → **division**

multiplicity /ˌmʌltəˈplɪsəti/ n [singular, U] formal a large number or great variety of things

multiply /ˈmʌltəplaɪ/ v [I,T] (**multiplied, multiplying, multiplies**) **1** to do a calculation in which you add one number to itself a particular number of times → **divide**: **multiply sth by sth** *Four multiplied by five is twenty.* **2** to increase by a large amount or number, or to make something do this: *Smoking multiplies the risk of having a heart attack.*

multipurpose /ˌmʌltiˈpɜːpəs◂ $ -ˈpɜːr-/ adj having many different uses: *a multipurpose tool*

multiracial /ˌmʌltɪˈreɪʃəl◂/ adj including or involving many different races of people: *a multiracial society*

multi-'storey adj [only before noun] BrE a multi-storey building has many levels: *a **multi-storey car park***

multitasking /ˈmʌltiˌtɑːskɪŋ $ -ˌtæs-/ n [U] when a person or computer does more than one thing at the same time

multitude /ˈmʌltɪtjuːd $ -tuːd/ n **a multitude of sb/sth** formal a very large number of people or things: *a multitude of possibilities*

mum /mʌm/ n [C] BrE mother SYN **mom** AmE: *Mum, can I borrow some money? | My mum's a teacher.*

mumble /ˈmʌmbəl/ v [I,T] to say something very quietly, so that it is difficult to understand you: *Micky mumbled an apology.*

mumbo-jumbo /ˌmʌmbəʊ ˈdʒʌmbəʊ $ -boʊ ˈdʒʌmboʊ/ n [U] informal ideas or words that you think are stupid or have no meaning

mummy /ˈmʌmi/ n [C] (plural **mummies**) **1** BrE mother – used especially by or to young children SYN **mommy** AmE: *Go and ask Mummy for a drink.* **2** a dead body that has been preserved by wrapping it in cloth, especially in ancient Egypt

mumps /mʌmps/ n [U] an infectious illness that makes your neck swell and become painful

munch /mʌntʃ/ v [I,T] to eat something in a noisy way: **[+on]** *Anna sat munching on her toast.* THESAURUS **EAT**

mundane /mʌnˈdeɪn/ adj ordinary and boring: *a mundane job*

municipal /mjuːˈnɪsəpəl $ mjuˈ-/ adj relating to the government of a town or city: *municipal elections*

munitions /mjuːˈnɪʃənz $ mjuˈ-/ n [plural] military supplies such as bombs and guns

mural /ˈmjʊərəl $ ˈmjʊrəl/ n [C] a picture painted on a wall

murder¹ /ˈmɜːdə $ ˈmɜːrdər/ n [C,U] the crime of killing someone deliberately → **manslaughter**: *Police believe the **murders were committed** by the same person.* | **[+of]** *He was **charged with** the **murder** of his wife.* | *The **murder weapon** was believed to be an axe.* | *the **murder victim*** THESAURUS **CRIME**

PHRASES
get away with murder informal to do anything you want, even bad things, without being punished: *She lets the children get away with murder.*
sth is murder spoken used to say that something is very difficult or unpleasant: *The traffic was murder this morning.*

Word Choice: murder or manslaughter?
Murder is the crime of deliberately killing someone, especially when you planned to do this.
Manslaughter is the crime of accidentally killing someone when you did not plan or intend to do this.

murder² v [T] to kill someone deliberately: *He denies murdering the teenager.* THESAURUS **KILL** —**murderer** n [C]

murderous /ˈmɜːdərəs $ ˈmɜːr-/ adj dangerous and likely to kill people: *a murderous attack*

murky /ˈmɜːki $ ˈmɜːr-/ adj **1** dark and difficult to see through: *murky water* THESAURUS **DARK** **2** involving dishonest or illegal behaviour: *a man with a murky past*

murmur /ˈmɜːmə $ ˈmɜːrmər/ n [C] a soft quiet sound, especially one made by someone's voice: *She answered in a low murmur.* | *the **murmur of voices*** | **murmur of agreement/surprise etc** (=one that expresses a particular feeling) —**murmur** v [I,T]: *He softly murmured her name.*

muscle¹ /ˈmʌsəl/ n
1 [C,U] one of the pieces of flesh inside your body that you use in order to move: **leg/neck/stomach etc muscles** *exercises to strengthen your leg muscles* | **pull/strain a muscle** (=injure a muscle)
2 [U] power or influence: *financial muscle*

muscle² v

PHRASAL VERBS
muscle in disapproving to use your power to get involved in something that someone else is doing, especially in business

muscular /ˈmʌskjələ $ -ər/ adj **1** having large strong muscles: *strong muscular arms* THESAURUS **STRONG** **2** relating to the muscles: *a muscular disease*

muse /mjuːz/ v [I] formal to think about something for a long time

museum /mjuːˈziːəm $ mjuˈ-/ n [C] a building where people can go and see important objects relating to art, history, science etc: *the Museum of Modern Art* | *a military museum*

Word Choice: museum or gallery?
A **museum** shows a range of different objects that are connected with art, history, science etc: *the Natural History Museum* | *the British Museum*
A **gallery** shows works of art such as pictures or SCULPTURES: *the Tate Gallery in London*

mush /mʌʃ/ n [singular, U] an unpleasant soft substance, especially food —**mushy** adj

mushroom¹ /'mʌʃruːm, -rʊm/ n [C] one of several types of FUNGUS with a stem and a round top. Some types can be eaten. → see picture on page A5 → **toadstool**: *mushroom soup*

mushroom² v [I] to increase or develop very quickly: *Sales began to mushroom.*

music /'mjuːzɪk/ n [U]
1 a pattern of sounds made by people playing musical instruments or singing: *She listens to pop music all day.*
2 a set of written marks representing musical sounds, or paper with these marks on it: *Can you read music?* → **face the music** at FACE²

Grammar
Music is an uncountable noun. Do not say 'musics'.

COLLOCATIONS

verbs
to listen to music *I like listening to classical music.*
to play music (=as a band or on a radio, CD player etc) *The DJ plays a variety of music.*
to write/compose music *Who wrote the music for the film?*
to make music (=play or compose music) *We just wanted to make music together.*

types of music
classical music *He has a great knowledge of classical music.* ⚠ Do not say 'classic music'. Say **classical music**.
pop/rock/folk/jazz music *From her bedroom came the sound of pop music.*
live music (=played by musicians on stage) *They danced to live music.*
background music (=that you hear but do not listen to) *I hate background music in restaurants.*

noun + music
a piece of music *What's your favourite piece of music?*

musical¹ /'mjuːzɪkəl/ adj **1** [only before noun] relating to music: *a musical instrument* (=piano, GUITAR etc) **2** good at playing or singing music: *I'm not very musical.* —**musically** /-kli/ adv

musical² n [C] a play or film that includes singing and dancing

musician /mjuːˈzɪʃən $ mjʊ-/ n [C] someone who plays a musical instrument, especially as a job: *a talented musician* | *jazz musicians*

musket /'mʌskɪt/ n [C] a type of gun used in the past

Muslim /'mʊzləm, 'mʌz-, 'mʊs-/ n [C] someone whose religion is Islam —**Muslim** adj

muslin /'mʌzlɪn/ n [U] very thin cotton cloth

mussel /'mʌsəl/ n [C] a small sea animal with a black shell and a soft body that you can eat → see picture at SHELLFISH

must¹ /məst; strong mʌst/ modal verb (negative short form **mustn't**)
1 used when saying that it is necessary or very important that someone does something, especially because of a law or rule: *All passengers must wear seat belts.* | *This book must not be removed from the library* (=do not remove it).
2 used when saying that you feel strongly that you should do something: *It's getting late – I really must go.*
3 used when saying that you think something is very likely to be true: *George must be almost eighty now.* | *You must have been very upset.*
4 spoken used when suggesting that someone should do something: *You must come and visit us sometime.*

THESAURUS

must used when saying that it is necessary or very important that someone does something, especially because of a law or rule, or because you feel strongly that you should do it: *You must not copy other people's work.* | *I must get some money out of the bank.*
have to do sth to need to do something because the situation you are in makes it necessary, or there is a rule that says you must do it: *I have to be in school early tomorrow.* | *Do we have to show our passports?*
be obliged to do sth especially BrE formal to have to do something because of a rule or law: *Employers are legally obliged to provide facilities for disabled people.*
be forced to do sth (also **be compelled to do sth** formal) to have to do something that you do not want to do: *He was forced to resign.*

must² /mʌst/ n [C usually singular] something that you must do or have: *Warm clothes are a must in the mountains.*

mustache /məˈstɑːʃ $ 'mʌstæʃ/ n the usual American spelling of MOUSTACHE

mustard /'mʌstəd $ -ərd/ n [U] a yellow sauce with a strong taste, usually eaten with meat

muster /'mʌstə $ -ər/ (also **muster up**) v [T] to get enough confidence, courage etc to do something difficult: **muster (up) the support/courage/energy etc to do sth** *Finally, she mustered the courage to call him.* | *He hit the ball with as much strength as he could muster.*

mustn't /'mʌsənt/ the short form of 'must not': *You mustn't tell him what I said.*

must've /'mʌstəv/ the short form of 'must have': *He must've been tired.*

musty /'mʌsti/ adj having an unpleasant, old, or wet smell: *the musty smell of old books*

mutant /'mju:tənt/ n [C] an animal or plant that is different from others of the same kind because of a change in its GENES —**mutant** adj

mutate /mju:'teɪt $ 'mju:teɪt/ v [I] if an animal or plant mutates, it becomes different from others of the same kind because of a change in its GENES —**mutation** /mju:'teɪʃən/ n [C,U]: genetic mutation

mute¹ /mju:t/ adj written not saying anything: She stayed mute and defiant.

mute² n [C] old-fashioned someone who cannot speak

muted /'mju:tɪd/ adj 1 quieter than usual: the sound of **muted voices** 2 not expressing strong feelings: The proposal received a **muted response**. 3 a muted colour is not very bright

mutilate /'mju:təleɪt/ v [T] to violently damage someone's body, especially by cutting off part of it: Many of the bodies had been mutilated. —**mutilation** /ˌmju:tə'leɪʃən/ n [C,U]

mutineer /ˌmju:tə'nɪə $ ˌmju:tn'ɪr/ n [C] someone who is involved in a mutiny

mutinous /'mju:tɪnəs $ -tn-əs/ adj formal refusing to obey someone: mutinous soldiers

mutiny /'mju:tɪni $ -tn-i/ n [C,U] (plural **mutinies**) when a group of people, especially soldiers or SAILORS, refuse to obey the person who is in charge, and try to take control themselves —**mutiny** v [I]

mutt /mʌt/ n [C] informal a dog that is a mixture of different breeds

mutter /'mʌtə $ -ər/ v [I,T] to say something quietly, especially because you are annoyed or do not want someone to hear you: 'Stupid fool,' he muttered. —**mutter** n [singular]: 'I don't know,' he said in a low mutter.

mutton /'mʌtn/ n [U] the meat from an adult sheep → **lamb**

mutual Ac /'mju:tʃuəl/ adj 1 mutual feelings are when two or more people have the same feelings about each other: Mutual trust is important in a marriage. | I didn't like Dev and **the feeling was mutual**. | The relationship ended **by mutual agreement** (=they both agreed to it). 2 [only before noun] mutual support, help etc is support that two or more people give each other: the mutual support you get in a small community 3 a mutual friend or interest is one that two people both have —**mutually** adv: a mutually beneficial arrangement

muzzle¹ /'mʌzəl/ n [C] 1 the nose and mouth of an animal, especially a dog or horse → see picture on page A3 2 a cover you put on a dog's mouth to stop it biting people 3 the open end of a gun where the bullets come out

muzzle² v [T] 1 to put a muzzle over a dog's mouth so that it cannot bite people 2 to prevent someone from saying what they think in public

MW the written abbreviation of **medium wave**

my /maɪ/ determiner belonging or relating to me: My mother's a doctor. | I tried not to let my feelings show. | It was **my own** idea.

myriad /'mɪriəd/ n **a myriad of sth** written a large number of things: a myriad of colours —**myriad** adj: Florida's myriad attractions

myself /maɪ'self/ pron
1 the REFLEXIVE form of 'I': I **made myself** a cup of coffee. | I went over to Jane and introduced myself.
2 used to emphasize 'I': Why do I have to do everything myself? | I **myself** have never been there.
PHRASES
(all) by myself alone or without anyone else's help: I went to the movie by myself. | I painted the house all by myself.
have sth (all) to myself to not have to share something with anyone else: I've got the house to myself this weekend.

mysterious /mɪ'stɪəriəs $ -'stɪr-/ adj
1 strange or difficult to explain or understand: mysterious deaths | She disappeared **in mysterious circumstances**. | my mysterious new neighbour
THESAURUS ▶ STRANGE
2 not saying much about something, in a way that makes people want to know more: **[+about]** He's being very mysterious about his new girlfriend. —**mysteriously** adv: He had mysteriously disappeared.

mystery¹ /'mɪstəri/ n (plural **mysteries**)
1 PUZZLE [C] something that is difficult to explain or understand: There's still much about the disease that **remains a mystery**. | The way her mind worked was a mystery to him. | The police never **solved the mystery** of his death.
2 UNUSUAL QUALITY [U] a quality that makes someone or something seem strange, interesting, or difficult to understand: the **mystery surrounding** his disappearance | The dark glasses gave her **an air of mystery**.
3 STORY (also '**murder ˌmystery**) [C] a story about a murder, in which you are not told who the murderer is until the end: an Agatha Christie mystery

mystery² adj [only before noun] used to describe something or someone that people do not have full information about: a mystery illness

mystic /'mɪstɪk/ n [C] someone who tries to discover religious truth through long periods of prayer, thought etc

mystical /'mɪstɪkəl/ (also **mystic**) adj relating to religious or magic powers that people cannot understand: a mystical experience —**mystically** /-kli/ adv

mysticism /'mɪstɪsɪzəm/ n [U] when people try to discover religious truth through long periods of prayer, thought etc

mystify /'mɪstɪfaɪ/ v [T] (**mystified, mystifying, mystifies**) if something mystifies you, it is so strange or confusing that you cannot understand or explain it: Her disappearance has mystified her family. —**mystifying** adj

mystique /mɪ'sti:k/ n [U] the quality that makes someone or something seem mysterious, special, or exciting: the mystique surrounding show business

myth /mɪθ/ n [C,U] **1** an idea that many people believe, but which is not true: **[+of]** *the myth of male superiority* | **[+that]** *the myth that the disease only affects older people* **2** an ancient story, especially about gods, or that tries to explain a natural or historical event

> **Word Choice: myth or legend?**
> A **myth** is a story that is often about the gods of an ancient civilization, or is intended to explain a natural or historical event. It is usually completely untrue: *In the Greek myth, the dead travel across the River Styx.*
> A **legend** is a story that is often about a famous person or a place. It sometimes has a part that is true: *the legend of King Arthur* | *According to legend, the land of Atlantis disappeared under the ocean.*

mythical /ˈmɪθɪkəl/ adj **1** existing only in an ancient story: *mythical creatures* **2** imagined, but not real or true

mythology /mɪˈθɒlədʒi $ -ˈθɑː-/ n [U] ancient stories and the beliefs they represent: *Greek mythology* —**mythological** /ˌmɪθəˈlɒdʒɪkəl◄ $ -ˈlɑː-/ adj

M

Nn

N, n /en/ *n* [C,U] (*plural* **N's, n's**) the 14th letter of the English alphabet

N the written abbreviation of **north** or **northern**

n. (*also* **n** *BrE*) the written abbreviation of **noun**

'n' /n, ən/ *informal* a short form of 'and': *rock 'n' roll*

N/A (**not applicable**) something you write on a form to show that you do not need to answer a particular question

nab /næb/ *v* [T] (**nabbed, nabbing**) *informal* to catch someone who is doing something wrong: *The police nabbed him for speeding.*

naff /næf/ *adj BrE informal* silly and unfashionable: *a naff film*

nag /næg/ *v* [I,T] (**nagged, nagging**) to keep asking someone to do something in an annoying way: *She keeps nagging me to fix the lamp.* **THESAURUS** ASK

nagging /'nægɪŋ/ *adj* [only before noun] making you worry or feel pain all the time: *a **nagging** doubt*

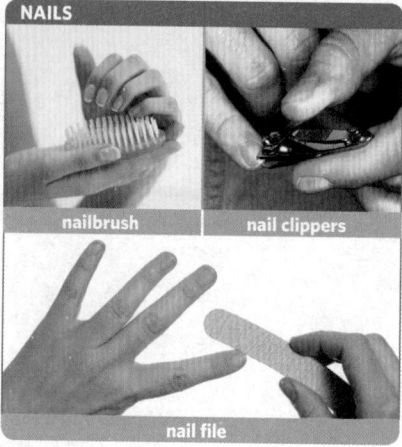

NAILS

nailbrush | nail clippers

nail file

nail¹ /neɪl/ *n* [C]
1 a thin pointed piece of metal with a flat end that you hit with a hammer: **hammer/drive a nail** *She hammered a nail into the wall.*
2 the thin hard parts on the ends of your fingers and toes: *Stop **biting** your **nails**!* → **hit the nail on the head** at **HIT¹**

nail² *v* [T] to fasten something to something else with nails: *The windows were nailed shut.*
PHRASAL VERBS
nail sth ↔ **down** to reach a definite agreement about something: *They nailed down the details of the deal.*

'nail-,biting *adj* very exciting: *a nail-biting finish to the race*

nailbrush /'neɪlbrʌʃ/ *n* [C] a small brush for cleaning your nails → see picture at **NAIL¹**

'nail file *n* [C] a thin piece of metal with a rough surface used for shaping your nails → see picture at **NAIL¹**

'nail ,polish (*also* **'nail ,varnish** *BrE*) *n* [U] coloured liquid that women put on their nails

naive /naɪˈiːv/ *adj* if someone is naive, they believe people are nicer and that things will be easier than they really are, because they have not had much experience of life: *a naive young girl* —**naively** *adv* —**naivety** /naɪˈiːvəti/ *n* [U]

naked /'neɪkɪd/ *adj*
1 not wearing any clothes **SYN** **nude** → **bare**: *a naked man* | **stark naked** (=completely naked)
2 [only before noun] naked emotions are not hidden and are shocking: *naked aggression*
3 naked flame/light a flame or light that is not covered: *Never have a naked flame near gasoline.* —**nakedness** *n* [U]
PHRASES
with/to the naked eye if you can see something with the naked eye, you can see it without the help of an instrument such as a MICROSCOPE: *These tiny creatures are barely **visible to the naked eye**.*

name¹ /neɪm/ *n*
1 [C] what someone or something is called: *Hello, my name's Ian.* | [+of] *What's the name of the street?* | [+for] *Edo was the ancient name for Tokyo.* | **by name** *He mentioned you by name.* **THESAURUS** WORD
2 [singular] the opinion that people have about a person or organization **SYN** **reputation**: *the **good name** of the company* | *This kind of incident **gives** football **a bad name**.* | **make your name/make a name for yourself** (=become famous for something) *He made a name for himself as a painter.*
3 big/famous/household name *informal* a famous person, company, or product: *the biggest names in show business* → **BRAND NAME, PLACE NAME, TRADE NAME, USER NAME**
PHRASES
call sb names to insult someone by using unpleasant words to describe them: *The other kids kept calling him names.*
be in sb's name/in the name of sb to legally belong to someone: *The house is in my husband's name.*
in the name of religion/freedom/science etc using religion, freedom etc as the reason why something is done: *experiments done in the name of science*

COLLOCATIONS
verbs

to have a name *You have such a pretty name!*
to give sb/sth a name *The new plant has not yet been given a name.*
to change your name *Robert Zimmerman changed his name to Bob Dylan.*
to sign your name *He signed his name on the contract.*

to give your name (=to tell someone, especially an official, your name) *The man refused to give his name.*

to know sb's name *I don't know the name of the person who helped me.*

to call sb's name (=to say someone's name loudly, to get their attention) *I heard someone calling my name.*

to use a name (=to tell people to call you a particular name) *She uses her maiden name at work.*

adjectives

sb's full name *Her full name is Jennifer Emily Marshall.*

sb's real name *Garcia is not his real name.*

a false name *He had given a false name and address.*

THESAURUS

name what someone or something is called: *What's your name?*

first name/Christian name/given name the name chosen for you by your parents: *His first name is Paul.*

last name/family name/surname the name that you share with your family or husband: *Does anyone know Beth's last name?*

middle name the name between your first name and your family name: *Her middle name was Maria.*

maiden name a woman's family name before she married and began using her husband's name: *My mother's maiden name was Johnson.*

nickname a name that people call you for fun that is not your real name: *We had nicknames for all the teachers.*

---

name² *v* [T] **1** to give someone or something a name → **call**: **name sb John/Ann etc** *We named our daughter Sarah.* | **name sb/sth after sb/sth** *BrE*, **name sb/sth for sb/sth** *AmE* (=give them the same name as another person or thing) *He was named after his grandfather.* **2** to say what the name of someone or something is, especially officially: *The murder victims have not yet been named.* | **name sb as sth** *The woman who was shot has been named as Mary Grey.* **3** to say that someone has been chosen for an important job or prize: **name sb/sth (as) sth** *Quinn was named as the new manager.*
PHRASES
name your price *spoken* to say how much you are willing to pay or sell something for: *So many teams are interested in the player that he can name his price.*
you name it (they've got it) *spoken* used after a list of things to mean that there are many more you could mention: *Beer, whisky, wine – you name it, we've got it!*

'name-check *n* [C] when the name of a famous person, product, organization etc is mentioned in something such as an advertisement —**namecheck** *v* [T]

namedropping /'neɪmˌdrɒpɪŋ $ -ˌdrɑː-/ *n* [U] when someone mentions the name of a famous

person to make it seem that they know them personally

nameless /'neɪmləs/ *adj* a nameless person is someone whose name is not known: *pictures by a nameless artist*
PHRASES
who shall remain nameless *spoken* used when you want to say that someone has done something wrong, but without mentioning their name: *Someone, who shall remain nameless, forgot to lock the door.*

namely /'neɪmli/ *adv* used to add more information about the people or things that you have just mentioned: *He was arrested for possessing a weapon, namely a knife.*

namesake /'neɪmseɪk/ *n* sb's namesake someone who has the same name as someone else

nan /næn/ (*also* **nanna** /'nænə/) *n* [C] *BrE informal* grandmother – used especially by children

nanny /'næni/ *n* [C] (*plural* **nannies**) a woman whose job is to take care of a family's children, usually in their own home

nanotechnology /ˌnænəʊtek'nɒlədʒi $ -noʊtek'nɑː-/ *n* [U] *technical* the science of developing and making extremely small but powerful machines

nap¹ /næp/ *n* [C] a short sleep during the day: **take/have a nap** *He's having his afternoon nap.* **THESAURUS** SLEEP

nap² *v* [I] (**napped**, **napping**) to sleep for a short time during the day
PHRASES
be caught napping *informal* to not be ready when something happens: *The goalkeeper was caught napping, and Parker scored the winning goal.*

napalm /'neɪpɑːm $ -pɑːm, -pɑːlm/ *n* [U] a substance used as a weapon to burn people or things

nape /neɪp/ *n* [singular] *literary* the back of your neck

napkin /'næpkɪn/ *n* [C] a square of cloth or paper that you use at meals to keep your clothes, hands, and mouth clean

nappy /'næpi/ *n* [C] (*plural* **nappies**) *BrE* a piece of cloth or paper that a baby wears on its bottom **SYN** **diaper** *AmE*: *His nappy needs changing.*

narcissism /'nɑːsɪsɪzəm $ 'nɑːr-/ *n* [U] *disapproving* when someone spends too much time thinking about and admiring their own appearance or abilities —**narcissistic** /ˌnɑːsə'sɪstɪk $ ˌnɑːr-/ *adj*

narcotic /nɑː'kɒtɪk $ nɑːr'kɑː-/ *n* [C] a strong drug such as HEROIN that stops pain and makes people sleep —**narcotic** *adj*

narrate /nə'reɪt $ 'næreɪt, næ'reɪt, nə-/ *v* [T] *formal* to tell a story or explain what is happening in a film, television programme etc —**narration** /nə'reɪʃən/ *n* [C,U]

narrative /'nærətɪv/ *n* [C,U] the description of events in a story —**narrative** *adj*

narrator /nə'reɪtə $ 'næreɪtər, næ'reɪtər, nə-/ *n* [C] someone who tells a story or explains what is happening in a film, television programme etc

narrow¹ /ˈnærəʊ $ -roʊ/ adj
1 something that is narrow measures a short distance from one side to the other OPP **wide** → **broad**: *the narrow streets* | *his narrow bed* | *The stairs were very narrow.*
2 limited: *a narrow view of life* | *a narrow range of subjects*
3 narrow victory/defeat etc when someone wins or loses by only a small amount: *The party suffered a narrow defeat in the elections.* —**narrowness** n [U]
PHRASES
have a narrow escape to only just avoid danger or trouble: *We had a narrow escape when a bus hit the car.*

narrow² v [I,T] to become narrower, or to make something narrower: *The road narrows here.*
PHRASAL VERBS
narrow sth ↔ down to reduce the number of people or things that you can choose from: [+to] *We've narrowed down the number of candidates to two.*

narrowly /ˈnærəʊli $ -roʊ-/ adv by only a small amount: *He narrowly avoided being killed.*

narrow-'minded / $ ˈ.. ˌ.../ adj not willing to accept ideas that are new and different from your own

nasal /ˈneɪzəl/ adj **1** [only before noun] relating to the nose: *the nasal passage* **2** a nasal sound or voice comes mainly through your nose

nasty /ˈnɑːsti $ ˈnæsti/ adj unpleasant or unkind: *a nasty accident* | *a nasty shock* | *Drivers have a nasty habit of driving too close to cyclists.* | *What a nasty thing to say!* | [+to] *Don't be so nasty to your sister* (=treat her unkindly). | **get/turn nasty** *especially BrE* (=suddenly start behaving in a threatening way) *When Tim refused, Dan turned nasty.* THESAURUS UNKIND —**nastiness** n [U] —**nastily** adv

nation /ˈneɪʃən/ n [C] a country and its people: *the world's leading industrial nations* | *The President's speech to the nation* THESAURUS COUNTRY

national¹ /ˈnæʃənəl/ adj
1 relating to the whole of a nation, not just part of it → **local**: *Drugs are a national problem.* | *national elections* | *an issue of national importance*
2 relating to or typical of a particular nation → **international**: *national dress*
3 owned or controlled by the government of a country: *Spain's national airline* → **GROSS NATIONAL PRODUCT**

national² n [C] formal a citizen of a particular country who is living in another country: *Turkish nationals*

national 'anthem n [C] a country's official song

National 'Health Service n **the National Health Service** the NHS

national 'holiday n [C] AmE a day when people in a country do not work and the shops are closed SYN **public holiday** BrE

nationalise /ˈnæʃənəlaɪz/ v a British spelling of NATIONALIZE

nationalism /ˈnæʃənəlɪzəm/ n [U] **1** when a group of people want to have their own government and be independent of another country: *Scottish nationalism* **2** the feeling of being very proud of your country and believing that it is better than other countries

nationalist /ˈnæʃənəlɪst/ n [C] **1** someone who wants to be politically independent from another country: *Welsh nationalists* **2** someone who is very proud of their country and believes that it is better than other countries —**nationalist** adj

nationalistic /ˌnæʃənəˈlɪstɪk◂/ adj disapproving believing that your country is much better than other countries: *a nationalistic speech*

nationality /ˌnæʃəˈnæləti/ n [C,U] (plural **nationalities**) when you are legally a citizen of a country: *He has British nationality.*

nationalize (also **-ise** BrE) /ˈnæʃənəlaɪz/ v [T] if a government nationalizes an organization, it takes control of it OPP **privatize** —**nationalization** /ˌnæʃənəlaɪˈzeɪʃən $ -nələ-/ n [C,U]

nationally /ˈnæʃənəli/ adv throughout a country: *nationally recognized qualifications*

national 'monument n [C] a building, area of land etc that is protected by the government for people to visit

national 'park n [C] beautiful land that is protected by the government for people to visit

national se'curity n [U] the ways a country protects its citizens by keeping its secrets safe and its army strong

national 'service n [U] the system of making all adults spend a period of time in the army, navy, or air force

nation 'state n [C] a politically independent country

nationwide /ˌneɪʃənˈwaɪd◂, ˈneɪʃənwaɪd/ adv, adj in every part of the country: *a nationwide search for the missing girl* | *It's available in department stores nationwide.*

native¹ /ˈneɪtɪv/ adj **1** [only before noun] relating to the place where you were born or have always lived: *He returned to his native Poland.* | **native Californian/New Yorker etc** | **native language/tongue** (=the language you first learned to speak) **2** a native plant or animal grows or lives naturally somewhere, and was not brought there from somewhere else: *native species of trees*

native² n [C] **1** someone who was born in a particular country: [+of] *a native of Brazil* **2** [usually plural] old-fashioned a word used in the past to refer to the people who lived in Africa, America etc before Europeans arrived. Many people now consider this use to be offensive.

Native A'merican n [C] someone who belongs to one of the races that lived in North America before Europeans arrived

native 'speaker n [C] someone who learned a particular language as their first language when they were a baby

NATO /ˈneɪtəʊ $ -toʊ/ n (**North Atlantic Treaty Organization**) a group of countries in North America and Europe that give military help to each other

natter /ˈnætə $ -ər/ v [I] BrE informal to talk about unimportant things → **chat** —**natter** n [singular]

natural¹ /ˈnætʃərəl/ adj
1 natural things are found in nature rather than being made by humans: earthquakes and other **natural disasters** | **the natural world** (=trees, rivers, animals, plants etc) | death from **natural causes** (=because of illness or old age)
2 normal or usual in a particular situation **OPP unnatural, abnormal**: it is natural (for sb) to do sth It's not natural for a child of his age to be so quiet. | **It's** only **natural that** he's worried. | Babies have a natural fear of falling.
3 having a skill or ability which you were born with, rather than one that you had to learn: a natural athlete —**naturalness** n [U]

THESAURUS

natural existing in nature and not made or caused by people: a natural lake | natural disasters such as earthquakes
wild wild flowers, plants, and animals are not grown or looked after by people. Wild areas of land have no people, houses, farms etc on them: wild flowers | a wild animal
pure pure water, JUICE, wool, cotton etc has had nothing added to it: pure orange juice | pure mountain water | pure lambswool
organic organic food or products are produced without using chemicals: organic fruit and vegetables | organic cotton
unspoiled unspoiled places are still beautiful because no one has built roads or buildings on them: unspoiled countryside

---

natural² n **be a natural** to be very good at doing something without being taught

natural 'gas n [U] gas used for cooking or heating that is taken from under the ground

natural 'history n [U] the study of plants and animals

naturalist /ˈnætʃərəlɪst/ n [C] someone who studies plants and animals

naturalize (also **-ise** BrE) /ˈnætʃərəlaɪz/ v **be naturalized** to be officially given the right to live in a country where you were not born —**naturalization** /ˌnætʃərəlaɪˈzeɪʃən $ -lə-/ n [U]

naturally /ˈnætʃərəli $ -tʃərəli, -tʃərli/ adv
1 used to say that something is normal and not surprising: Naturally, we wanted to win. | **Naturally enough**, she wanted promotion.
2 in a way that is the result of nature, not of someone's actions: My hair is naturally curly. | a naturally gifted soccer player | The tomatoes are left to dry naturally in the sun.
3 in a relaxed and normal way: Try to **act naturally**.

natural re'sources / $ ˌ.. ˈ.../ n [plural] things that exist in nature and can be used by people, for example oil, trees etc

natural se'lection n [U] technical the process by which only plants and animals that are suitable for life in their environment will continue to exist

nature /ˈneɪtʃə $ -tʃər/ n
1 [U] everything in the world that is not made or controlled by humans, such as animals, plants, and the weather: the **forces of nature** | **in nature** substances that are not found in nature
2 [C,U] someone's character, or what something is like: a child with a happy nature | **in sb's nature** It's not in Jane's nature to lie. | **by nature** She was by nature a friendly person. | Of course she's jealous – it's only **human nature** (=the feelings and ways of behaving that all people have). | **[+of]** The **exact nature** of the problem is not clear. | **of this/that nature** I never trouble myself with questions of that nature. | The support being given is of a practical nature. | Any government funding would be temporary in nature. → **GOOD-NATURED, HUMAN NATURE**

> **Word Choice**: nature, countryside, or scenery?
> **Nature** is a very general word that is used about trees, animals, and everything in the world that is not made by humans: the wonders of nature | We shared a love of nature.
> The **countryside** is the land outside the towns and cities, where there are fields, trees, and farms: We decided to go for a walk in the countryside.
> **Scenery** is the natural features in an area, such as mountains, valleys, and lakes: The US has some spectacular scenery.
> Do not say 'Japan has beautiful nature.' Say Japan has some beautiful countryside/scenery.

nature re,serve n [C] an area of land where animals and plants are protected

naught /nɔːt $ nɒːt/ n [U] a word meaning 'nothing', which was used in the past: Our plans **came to naught** (=failed).

naughty /ˈnɔːti $ ˈnɒːti, ˈnɑːti/ adj a naughty child behaves badly —**naughtiness** n [U] —**naughtily** adv

nausea /ˈnɔːziə, -siə $ ˈnɒːziə, -ʃə/ n [U] formal the feeling that you have when you are going to VOMIT

nauseate /ˈnɔːzieɪt, -si- $ ˈnɒːzi-, -ʃi-/ v [T] to cause someone to feel that they are going to VOMIT

nauseating /ˈnɔːzieɪtɪŋ, -si- $ ˈnɒːzi-, -ʃi-/ adj
1 making you feel annoyed or offended: nauseating racist remarks **2** making you want to VOMIT: a nauseating smell —**nauseatingly** adv

nauseous /ˈnɔːziəs, -siəs $ ˈnɒːziəs, -ʃəs/ adj feeling that you are going to VOMIT, or making you feel this way **SYN sick**: I felt slightly **nauseous**. | a nauseous smell

nautical /ˈnɔːtɪkəl $ ˈnɒː-/ adj relating to ships or sailing —**nautically** /-kli/ adv

naval /ˈneɪvəl/ adj [only before noun] relating to the navy: a naval battle

navel /ˈneɪvəl/ n [C] the small hole in your stomach **SYN belly button**

navigable /'nævəgəbəl/ *adj* a river, lake etc that is navigable is deep and wide enough for ships to travel on

navigate /'nævɪgeɪt/ *v* **1** [I,T] to decide which way a car or ship should go, using maps: *I'll drive – you take the map and navigate.* **2** [T] to sail across or along an area of water

navigation /ˌnævəˈgeɪʃən/ *n* [U] when you decide which direction your car or ship should go —**navigational** *adj*

navigator /'nævəgeɪtə $ -tər/ *n* [C] a person on a ship or plane whose job is to plan the direction it should be travelling

navy /'neɪvi/ *n* (*plural* **navies**) **1** [C] the people and ships that a country has for fighting a war at sea: **in the navy** *Is he still in the navy?* | *Join the navy and see the world.* **2** [U] a very dark blue colour —**navy** *adj*

navy 'blue (*also* **navy**) *adj* very dark blue

Nazi /'nɑːtsi/ *n* [C] a member of the National Socialist Party that controlled Germany from 1933 to 1945 —**Nazi** *adj* —**Nazism** *n* [U]

N.B. (*also* **NB**) *written* (*nota bene*) used to make a reader pay attention to important information

NCO /ˌen siː ˈəʊ $ -ˈoʊ/ *n* [C] (**non-commissioned officer**) an officer of low rank in the British army

NE the written abbreviation of **northeast** or **northeastern**

near¹ /nɪə $ nɪr/ *adv, prep*
1 only a short distance away from someone or something: *They live near Osaka.* | *Is there a bank near here?* | [+to] *a hotel near to the beach*
2 soon before a particular time or event: *near the end of the week* | [+to] *nearer to Christmas*
3 almost doing something or almost in a particular state: *The work is near completion.* | *a near impossible task* | *We're no nearer an agreement.* | [+to] *People fleeing the building were near to panic.* | **come/be near to doing sth** *She came near to hitting him.*

THESAURUS

near only a short distance away from something or someone: *Versailles is near Paris.* | *She moved to Boston to be near her sister.*
close very near something or someone, or almost touching them: *The houses were built very close together.* | *You're sitting too close to me.*
not far (away) not a long distance away – used when saying that a place is near enough to be easy to get to: *Let's go to my house – it's not far from here.*
nearby near here or near a particular place: *Is there a coffee shop nearby?* | *a nearby farm*
next door in the next house or building: *She lives next door to us.*
local local shops, schools etc are in the area where you live: *The local library is closed on Mondays.*
within walking distance not far away, so you can walk there easily: *There are several good restaurants within walking distance.*

---

near² *adj*
1 only a short distance away from someone or

something: *It's very near.* | *The nearest* (=closest) *beach is only a mile away.*
2 near disaster/collapse etc almost a DISASTER, COLLAPSE etc: *The election was a near disaster for the party.*
3 near miss when a bomb, plane, car etc nearly hits something but does not: *a near miss between two aircraft*

PHRASES
in the near future soon: *The school hopes to open in the near future.* **THESAURUS** SOON
near relative/relation a relative who is very closely related to you, such as a parent: *Only near relatives are allowed to visit patients.*

near³ *v* [T] to come closer to a particular place, time, or state SYN **approach**: *Jo began to feel nervous as she neared the house.* | *employees nearing retirement*

nearby /'nɪəbaɪ $ nɪr-/ *adj* not far away: *a nearby lake* **THESAURUS** NEAR —**nearby** /nɪəˈbaɪ $ nɪr-/ *adv*: *Do you live nearby?*

nearly /'nɪəli $ 'nɪrli/ *adv* especially BrE almost: *We've nearly finished.* | *It's nearly seven years since I last saw him.* | *He's nearly as tall as me.* | *He very nearly died.* **THESAURUS** ALMOST

PHRASES
not nearly used to say that something is definitely not true: *He's not nearly as nice as his brother.*

nearsighted /ˌnɪəˈsaɪtɪd◂ $ 'nɪrsaɪtɪd/ *adj* especially AmE unable to see things clearly unless they are close to you SYN **shortsighted** BrE

neat /niːt/ *adj*
1 arranged in a tidy and careful way: *neat handwriting* | *His clothes were always neat and clean.* | *Her room was neat and tidy.*
2 someone who is neat likes to keep things tidy **THESAURUS** TIDY
3 AmE spoken informal very good or enjoyable: *That's a neat idea!* **THESAURUS** GOOD
4 simple and effective: *a neat solution to the problem*
5 especially BrE a neat alcoholic drink has no ice or water or any other liquid added SYN **straight** —**neatly** *adv*: *It fits neatly into the corner.* | *The clothes were neatly folded.* —**neatness** *n* [U]

necessarily /'nesəsərəli, ˌnesəˈserəli $ ˌnesəˈserəli/ *adv* **not necessarily** used to say that something may not be true, or may not always happen: *Expensive restaurants do not necessarily have the best food.*

necessary /'nesəsəri $ -seri/ *adj* if something is necessary, you need to have it or do it: *'Do I need to bring any money with me?' 'No, that won't be necessary.'* | *The booklet provides all the necessary information.* | *The police are advising motorists to travel only if their journey is absolutely necessary.* | **it is necessary (for sb) to do sth** *It may be necessary for me to have an operation.* | **make it necessary (for sb) to do sth** *The rise in costs made it necessary to increase prices.* | **necessary for (doing) sth** *A good diet is necessary for maintaining a healthy body.* | **if/when/where necessary** *You can take the test again if necessary.*

PHRASES

necessary evil something unpleasant that you have to accept in order to achieve what you want: *He regarded work as a necessary evil.*

THESAURUS

necessary if something is necessary, you need to have it or do it: *Reservations aren't always necessary.* | *I have all the necessary documents.*
essential very important and necessary, especially in order to be healthy, successful etc: *Fresh fruit and vegetables are an essential part of a healthy diet.* | *Good timing is essential.*
vital extremely important and necessary, because there will be serious problems without it: *Tourism is vital to the local economy.* | *a vital piece of evidence*
compulsory if something is compulsory, you must do it because of a rule or law: *a compulsory training course*
obligatory *formal* if something is obligatory, you must do it because of a rule or law. **Obligatory** sounds stronger and more formal than **compulsory**: *The use of seatbelts is obligatory.*

necessitate /nɪˈsesɪteɪt/ v [T] *formal* to make something necessary: *His injuries may necessitate long-term treatment.*

necessity /nəˈsesəti/ n (*plural* **necessities**) **1** [C] something you need: **[+for]** *A car is an* **absolute necessity** *for this job.* | **[+of]** *Water is a* **basic necessity** *of life.* **2** [U] when you must do something: **necessity to do sth** *There's no necessity to pay now* (=you do not need to pay now). | **through/out of necessity** (=because you must do it) *They did it out of necessity.*

NECKS

polo neck *BrE/* turtleneck *AmE*

open-neck

V-neck

neck¹ /nek/ n [C]
1 the part of your body that joins your head to your shoulders: **around sb's neck** *She wore a gold chain around her neck.* → see picture on page A2
2 the part of a piece of clothing that goes around your neck: **V-necked/open-necked etc** *a V-necked sweater*
3 the narrow part near the top or end of something such as a bottle → **POLO NECK, V-NECK**

PHRASES

in this/sb's neck of the woods *informal* in a particular area or part of the country: *What are you doing in this neck of the woods?*

neck and neck if two people, teams etc are neck and neck during a race or competition, they are level with each other: *The two main parties are still neck and neck in the opinion polls.*
be up to your neck in sth *informal* **1** to have too much work to do: *She's up to her neck in work.* **2** to be in a very difficult situation: *He's up to his neck in debt.*

neck² v **be necking** *old-fashioned* to be kissing in a sexual way

necklace /ˈnek-lɪs/ n [C] a piece of jewellery that you wear around your neck: *a diamond necklace* → see picture at **JEWELLERY**

neckline /ˈnek-laɪn/ n [C] the edge of a piece of woman's clothing around the neck

necktie /ˈnektaɪ/ n [C] *AmE formal* a **TIE**

nectar /ˈnektə $ -ər/ n [U] the sweet liquid that BEES collect from flowers

nectarine /ˈnektəriːn $ ˌnektəˈriːn/ n [C] a juicy fruit like a PEACH → see picture on page A4

née /neɪ/ adj used to say what a married woman's family name was when she was born. 'Née' is put after her married name and before her old name: *Jo Lee, née Jones*

need¹ /niːd/ v [T]
1 if you need something, you must have it: *These plants need plenty of light and water.* | *I live in the city, so I don't really need a car.* | *How much money do you need?* | **need sth for sth** *I need glasses for reading.* | **need sb to do sth** *I need you to help me with the cooking.* | *Food and medicines are* **urgently needed.** | *This job needs a lot of patience.*
2 to feel that you want something very much: *I need a drink.*
3 **need to do sth** used to say that an action or situation is necessary: *He needs to see a doctor.* | *She didn't need to think about her decision.* | **needn't do sth** *I needn't take up any more of your time.*
4 used to say that something should have something done to it: **sth needs painting/cleaning/ cutting etc** *The house needs painting.* | **sth needs to be ...** *The car needs to be repaired.* | **need a (good) wash/clean/cut etc** *His hair needs a wash.*

PHRASES

you don't need to/you needn't used to give someone permission to not do something: *You don't need to wait for me.*

Word Choice: don't need to, don't have to, or must not?
You use **don't need to** and **don't have to** when saying it is not necessary for you to do something: *We don't need to leave yet.*
You can also say *We* **needn't** *leave yet.* Do not say 'We needn't to leave yet.'
In the past tense, you can say *We* **didn't need to** *leave so early, We* **needn't have left** *so early, or We* **didn't have to** *leave so early.*
Don't have to is also used when talking about obligation. For example, you say *The workers* **don't have to** *wear uniforms* (=there is no rule that says they must wear uniforms). This is very different from saying **must not**: *The workers*

must not wear uniforms (=they are not allowed to wear uniforms).

need² n
1 [singular, U] a situation in which something is necessary: **[+for]** *There is an **urgent need** for more nurses.* | **need to do sth** *the need to have better trained staff* | **feel the need (to do sth)** *He did not feel the need to complain.* | *I'll work all night **if need be** (=if it is necessary).*
2 [C usually plural] something you must have in order to have a normal life: **sb's needs** *a family's* **basic needs** | **meet/satisfy a need** (=provide something that people want or need) *Schools must satisfy the needs of their pupils.* → **SPECIAL NEEDS**
PHRASES
in need not having enough food or money: *families in need*
be in need of sth to need something: *We're **in urgent need of** help.*
there's no need (for sb) to do sth 1 used to say that someone does not have to do something: *There's no need to come if you don't want to.* **2** spoken used to tell someone to stop doing something: *There's no need to shout – I'm not deaf.*

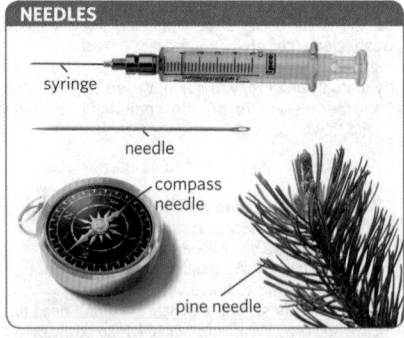

NEEDLES

syringe

needle

compass needle

pine needle

needle¹ /ˈniːdl/ n [C]
1 SEWING a small thin piece of metal that you use for sewing, with a point at one end and a hole at the other end → **pin**: *a needle and thread*
2 KNITTING a KNITTING NEEDLE
3 MEDICINE a very thin piece of metal on the end of

a SYRINGE (=hollow tube), used to put medicine or drugs into your body, or to take blood out
4 SHOWS MEASUREMENT a part on a piece of equipment that points to measurements or directions: *a compass needle*
5 ON A TREE a small thin pointed leaf, especially from a PINE tree
6 ON A RECORD PLAYER the very small part in a RECORD PLAYER that touches the record in order to play it → **PINE NEEDLE, PINS AND NEEDLES**
PHRASES
be like looking for a needle in a haystack informal used to say that something is almost impossible to find: *I can't find the file anywhere – it's like looking for a needle in a haystack.*

needle² v [T] informal to deliberately annoy someone, often in a joking way SYN **tease**: *She's always needling Jim about his weight.*

needless /ˈniːdləs/ adj not necessary, and easy to avoid: *needless suffering* —**needlessly** adv
PHRASES
needless to say used when you are telling someone something that you expect they will already know: *Needless to say, with four children we're always busy.*

needlework /ˈniːdlwɜːk $ -wɜːrk/ n [U] sewing, or things that you make by sewing

needn't /ˈniːdnt/ especially BrE spoken the short form of 'do not need to'

needy /ˈniːdi/ adj **1 a)** having very little food or money: *a needy family* **b) the needy** [plural] people who do not have enough food or money **2** someone who is needy needs a lot of love and attention

negate Ac /nɪˈɡeɪt/ v [T] formal to prevent something from having any effect: *The increase in the price of oil was negated by the fall in the value of the dollar.* —**negation** /-ˈɡeɪʃən/ n [U]

negative¹ Ac /ˈneɡətɪv/ adj
1 BAD bad or harmful OPP **positive**: *Late nights were starting to have a **negative effect** on my work.* | *Technological innovation also has a **negative side**.*
2 NOT LIKING SB/STH thinking only of the bad things about a situation, person etc OPP **positive**: *teenagers with a **negative attitude** towards authority* | **[+about]** *She's been very negative about school lately.*
3 NO/NOT **a)** a negative answer or reply means 'no' OPP **affirmative**: *We were puzzled by their negative response to our request.* **b)** a negative sentence or phrase contains a word such as 'no', 'not', or 'nothing'
4 SCIENTIFIC TEST a scientific test that is negative shows that a particular chemical or medical condition has not been found OPP **positive**: *The pregnancy test was negative.*
5 NUMBER less than zero: *negative numbers*
6 ELECTRICAL CURRENT technical a negative electrical current is carried by ELECTRONS OPP **positive** —**negatively** adv

negative² Ac n [C] **1** a word or phrase that means 'no' **2** a camera film from which you can print a photograph. A negative shows dark areas as light, and light areas as dark.

neglect¹ /nɪˈglekt/ v [T] **1** to not pay enough attention to someone or something, or not take care of them: *You mustn't neglect your family.* | *The building has been badly neglected.* **2 neglect to do sth** to not do something that you should do: *The company neglected to pay according to the contract.* —**neglected** adj —**neglectful** adj

neglect² n [U] when something or someone is not looked after well: *children suffering from neglect*

negligence /ˈneglɪdʒəns/ n [U] when someone does not do something that they are responsible for doing, with the result that something bad happens: *The boy's parents are suing the hospital for negligence.*

negligent /ˈneglɪdʒənt/ adj not doing something that you are responsible for doing, with the result that something bad happens

negligible /ˈneglɪdʒəbəl/ adj very small and unimportant: *The damage was negligible.*

negotiable /nɪˈgəʊʃiəbəl, -ʃə- $ -ˈgoʊ-/ adj prices, amounts etc that are negotiable can be discussed and changed

negotiate /nɪˈgəʊʃiert $ -ˈgoʊ-/ v **1** [I,T] to discuss something in order to make an agreement, especially in business or politics: **[+with]** *The government refuses to negotiate with terrorists.* | *UN representatives are trying to negotiate a ceasefire.* **2** [T] to succeed in going past or over a difficult place on a road, path etc: *She slowed down to negotiate the corner.* —**negotiator** n [C]

negotiation /nɪˌgəʊʃiˈeɪʃən $ -ˌgoʊ-/ n [C usually plural, U] official discussions between two groups who are trying to make an agreement: **peace/trade/wage negotiations** *Employers are facing another* **round of wage negotiations**. | **[+with]** *We refuse to enter into negotiations with the rebels.*

Negro /ˈniːgrəʊ $ -groʊ/ n [C] (*plural* **Negroes**) old-fashioned a word meaning a black person, which some people now consider offensive

neigh /neɪ/ v [I] if a horse neighs, it makes a loud noise —**neigh** n [C]

neighbour BrE, **neighbor** AmE /ˈneɪbə $ -bər/ n [C]
1 someone who lives next to you or near you: **sb's neighbours** *My neighbours often look after the kids after school.* | **next-door neighbours** (=the people who live in the house next to yours) *Our next-door neighbours complained about the noise.*
2 a person or country that is next to another person or country: **sb's/sth's neighbour** *You'll have to share a book with your neighbor.* | *Germany's neighbours*

neighbourhood BrE, **neighborhood** AmE /ˈneɪbəhʊd $ -ər-/ n [C] an area of a town, and the people who live there: *He grew up in a tough neighbourhood.* | *a neighborhood school*

neighbouring BrE, **neighboring** AmE /ˈneɪbərɪŋ/ adj [only before noun] near the place you are talking about: *neighbouring towns*

neighbourly BrE, **neighborly** AmE /ˈneɪbəli $ -ər-/ adj friendly and helpful to people who live near you: *a neighbourly visit* —**neighbourliness** n [U]

neither¹ /ˈnaɪðə $ ˈniːðər/ determiner, pron not one and not the other of two people or things → **either**,

both: *It was a boring game and neither team played well.* | **[+of]** *Neither of them can drive.*

neither² adv used to show that a negative statement is also true about another person or thing → **either**: **neither does/can/will etc sb** *'I didn't like sport at school.' 'Neither did I.'* | *'Tom can't swim yet.' 'Neither can Sam.'* | *'I haven't seen Greg in a long time.' 'Me neither* (=and I have not seen him).'

neither³ linking word **neither ... nor ...** used when mentioning two things that are not true or do not happen: *Neither his mother nor his father spoke English.* | *The equipment is neither accurate nor safe.*

neo- /niːəʊ, niːə $ niːoʊ, niːə/ prefix used to say that a style, belief etc is similar to one that existed in the past: *a neo-classical palace*

neon /ˈniːɒn $ -ɑːn/ n [U] a gas that is used in tubes in electric lights and signs: *neon lights*

nephew /ˈnefjuː, ˈnev- $ ˈnef-/ n [C] the son of your brother or sister, or the son of your husband's or wife's brother or sister → **niece**

nepotism /ˈnepətɪzəm/ n [U] when people use their power in an unfair way by giving the best jobs to their family or friends

Neptune /ˈneptjuːn $ -tuːn/ n the PLANET that is eighth in order from the Sun

nerd /nɜːd $ nɜːrd/ n [C] informal someone who is unfashionable and interested in boring things —**nerdy** adj

nerve /nɜːv $ nɜːrv/ n
1 nerves [plural] the feeling of being worried or a little frightened: *A lot of people* **suffer from nerves** *before going on stage.* | **calm/steady your nerves** (=stop yourself feeling worried or frightened) *I drank a glass of brandy to calm my nerves.* | **Exam nerves** *are part of student life.* | **be a bundle/bag of nerves** (=be very nervous)
2 [C] a thing in your body that sends information to and from your brain, for example when you feel pain, or when you want to move: *nerve damage* | *the nerves in your fingers*
3 [U] courage and confidence in a dangerous or difficult situation: **the nerve to do sth** *I didn't* **have the nerve** *to ask for a pay rise.* | **It takes nerve** *to stand up for what you believe like that.* | *I was going to jump, but I* **lost my nerve** (=became nervous and unable to do what I had intended).
4 [singular] informal disapproving a way of behaving that does not seem polite or sensitive: *'She didn't even say sorry.'* **'What a nerve!'** | **have the nerve to do sth** *And then he had the nerve to criticize my cooking!*

PHRASES
get on sb's nerves informal to annoy someone, especially by doing a particular thing a lot: *Her voice was starting to get on my nerves.*

touch/hit a (raw) nerve to say something that upsets someone: *I think I hit a nerve when I mentioned her ex-husband.*

nerve-racking, **nerve-wracking** /'nɜːv ˌrækɪŋ $ 'nɜːrv-/ *adj* very worrying or frightening: *Giving a speech is a nerve-racking experience.*

nervous /'nɜːvəs $ 'nɜːr-/ *adj*
1 worried or frightened about something and unable to relax → **anxious**: **[+about]** *Sam's very nervous about his driving test.* | *Stop watching me. You're **making** me **nervous**.* | *Most people **get nervous** before an interview.* | *By the end of the journey, I was **a nervous wreck** (=extremely nervous and frightened).* | **a nervous smile/laugh/look etc**
THESAURUS WORRIED
2 a nervous person becomes worried, frightened, or upset easily: *a nervous child*
3 [only before noun] a nervous illness is related to the nerves in your body —**nervously** *adv* —**nervousness** *n* [U]

THESAURUS
nervous worried or frightened about something and unable to relax: *Are you nervous about your exam?*
tense worried and unable to relax in a way that makes you get angry or upset easily: *I always feel tense when I've had a hard day at work.*
on edge nervous because you are worried about what might happen, so that you cannot behave in a friendly relaxed way: *He's on edge because he's waiting for the results of his interview.*
jumpy/jittery nervous so that you are easily surprised by sudden sounds or movements: *Don't keep looking back – you're making me jumpy.*
highly-strung *BrE*, **high-strung** *AmE* becoming nervous or upset easily because that is your character: *People who work in the theatre are often highly-strung.*
have butterflies in your stomach *informal* to feel nervous about something that you are going to do very soon, especially because it is important and you want to do it well: *I always have butterflies in my stomach before a concert.*

ˌnervous 'breakdown *n* [C] a mental illness in which someone becomes very worried and unhappy, and cannot live a normal life

'nervous ˌsystem *n* [C] the nerves in your body, together with your brain, which allow you to feel pain, heat etc, and which control your movements

-ness /nəs/ *suffix* used to form nouns that refer to a quality or state: *happiness* | *effectiveness*

nest /nest/ *n* [C] **1** a place that a bird makes to lay its eggs in: *a bird's nest* | *Crows **build** their **nests** high in the trees.* **2** a place where insects or small animals live: *a wasps' nest* —**nest** *v* [I]

'nest egg *n* [C] an amount of money that you have saved

nestle /'nesəl/ *v* [I,T] to be in or move into a comfortable or pleasant position, surrounded by something soft or protecting: **[+in/among/between etc]** *a village nestling among the hills* | *The little cat **nestled** its **head** in my arms.*

NETS
tennis net | basketball net
fishing net

net¹ /net/ *n*
1 INTERNET **the Net** (*also* **the net**) the system that allows computer users around the world to exchange information SYN **the Internet**, **the Web**: **on the Net** *I saw the advertisement on the Net.*
2 IN SPORTS [C] the thing that you hit the ball into in sports such as football, or that you hit the ball over in tennis → **goal**: **into the net** *The ball bounced off the post and into the net.*
3 FOR CATCHING STH [C] something that you use for catching fish, animals etc, made of pieces of string or wire joined together with spaces between them: *a **fishing net***
4 MATERIAL [C,U] material made from very fine threads with small spaces between them, or something made from this material: *net curtains* | *a mosquito net* → **SAFETY NET**, **surf the net** at **SURF¹**

net² *v* [T] (**netted**, **netting**) **1** to get a particular amount of money as profit **2** to kick the ball into the net in football → **score 3** to catch a fish in a net

net³ (*also* **nett** *BrE*) *adj* a net amount of money is the amount that remains after tax etc has been taken away → **gross**: *a net profit of $500,000*
PHRASES
net weight the weight of something without its container: *a box of cereal with a net weight of 500g*

netball /'netbɔːl $ -bɒːl/ *n* [U] a game in which two teams, usually girls or women, try to win points by throwing a ball to each other and through a high net → **basketball**

netting /'netɪŋ/ *n* [U] material made from pieces of string, wire etc joined together with spaces between → **net**

nettle /'netl/ *n* [C] a wild plant with leaves that sting your skin if you touch them

network¹ Ac /'netwɜːk $ -wɜːrk/ *n* [C]
1 SYSTEM a system of things that are connected with each other: *a high-speed European **rail network*** | *a mobile phone network*

2 COMPUTERS a number of computers that are connected to each other so that they can share information: *the university* **computer network**

3 PEOPLE/ORGANIZATIONS a large number of people, organizations etc that know and help each other, or work together: **[+of]** *Tim had a strong network of contacts in Europe.* | *the importance of the* **family network**

4 RADIO/TELEVISION a group of radio or television companies that broadcast the same programmes in different parts of a country

network² Ac *v* **1** [I] to talk to other people who do the same type of work in order to share information, help each other etc **2** [T] to connect several computers together so that they can share information —**networking** *n* [U]

neural /ˈnjʊərəl $ ˈnʊr-/ *adj technical* relating to a nerve or the NERVOUS SYSTEM

neurology /njʊˈrɒlədʒi $ nʊˈrɑː-/ *n* [U] the scientific study of the NERVOUS SYSTEM and the diseases relating to it —**neurologist** *n* [C] —**neurological** /ˌnjʊərəˈlɒdʒɪkəl◂ $ ˌnʊrəˈlɑː-/ *adj*

neurosis /njʊˈrəʊsɪs $ nʊˈroʊ-/ *n* [C,U] (*plural* **neuroses** /-siːz/) a mental illness that makes someone very worried or frightened

neurotic /njʊˈrɒtɪk $ nʊˈrɑː-/ *adj* very worried or frightened about something in a way that is not normal: *She's neurotic about her health.* —**neurotic** *n* [C]

neuter¹ /ˈnjuːtə $ ˈnuːtər/ *adj* used to describe the nouns, adjectives etc in some languages that do not belong to the FEMININE or MASCULINE groups

neuter² *v* [T] to remove part of an animal's sex organs so that it cannot produce baby animals

neutral¹ Ac /ˈnjuːtrəl $ ˈnuː-/ *adj* **1** not supporting any of the countries, groups, or people in a war, argument etc: *Switzerland* **remained neutral** *during World War II.* **2** not showing any strong feelings or opinions: *'I see,' she said in a* **neutral tone**. **3** a neutral colour is not strong or bright, for example grey

neutral² *n* [U] the position of the GEARS of a car when the engine does not turn the wheels: *Start the car in neutral.*

neutrality Ac /njuːˈtræləti $ nuː-/ *n* [U] when a country or person does not support any of the people or groups involved in a war, argument etc

neutralize Ac (*also* -**ise** *BrE*) /ˈnjuːtrəlaɪz $ ˈnuː-/ *v* [T] to prevent something from having any effect: *a substance that neutralized the smell*

neutron /ˈnjuːtrɒn $ ˈnuːtrɑːn/ *n* [C] a part of an atom that has no electrical CHARGE → see picture at **ATOM**

never /ˈnevə $ -ər/ *adv*
1 not at any time, or not once: *He never saw her again.* | *I've never been to Hawaii.* | *I'll never forgive him.* → **OFTEN, RARELY, SOMETIMES**
2 used to make a strong negative statement about the past: *She never even knew he was married!*
3 never! *BrE spoken* used when you are very surprised about something: *'He's sixty now, you know.' 'Never!'*

never mind *spoken* used to tell someone that they do not need to worry about something: *'We've missed the bus.' 'Never mind – there's another one in ten minutes.'*
you never know *spoken* used to say that something that seems unlikely may happen: *You never know, you might be lucky.* THESAURUS **MAYBE**

Grammar
You usually use **never** before a verb: *He never listens to me.* | *I never wanted to go back.*
You use **never** after the verb **to be**: *Her father was never angry.* | *She's never late.*
If there are two or more verbs, **never** comes after the first one: *I have never read any of her books.*

THESAURUS

never not at any time, or not once: *I've never been to France.*
never ever never – used for emphasis: *I have never ever seen him before in my life.* | *Never ever do that again!*
not once used when you are surprised or annoyed because someone never did something: *He didn't once offer to help me.*
not for a moment used when emphasizing that you never had a particular thought or idea: *'Did you believe him?' 'No, not for a moment.'*
not/never in a million years *informal* used when emphasizing that you are sure that something will never happen: *She won't give you the money back. Not in a million years!*

---

never-'ending *adj disapproving* seeming to continue for a very long time SYN **endless**: *The journey was never-ending.*

nevertheless Ac /ˌnevəðəˈles $ -vər-/ *adv formal* in spite of what has just been mentioned: *He's friendly enough, but nevertheless I don't trust him.*

new /njuː $ nuː/ *adj*
1 RECENTLY MADE recently made, built, or developed OPP **old**: *Have you got their new album?* | *a new leisure centre* | *technology that is completely new*
2 RECENTLY BOUGHT recently bought: *Do you like my new shoes?*
3 NOT USED BEFORE not used or owned by anyone before: *new and second-hand books for sale* | *a* **brand new** (=completely new) *car*
4 RECENTLY CHANGED different or changed from what you had or experienced before OPP **old**: *Is your new teacher OK?* | **[+to]** *a lifestyle that was completely new to me*
5 RECENTLY ARRIVED someone who is new in a place, job etc has recently arrived or started there: *information for new students* | *Are you new here?*
6 RECENTLY DISCOVERED recently discovered: *a new planet* | *important new evidence* —**newness** *n* [U]
PHRASES
as good as new (*also* **like new**) in excellent condition: *The dress is still like new because I have worn it only for important occasions.* THESAURUS **CONDITION**

THESAURUS

new recently made, produced, or bought: *Do you like my new dress?* | *the city's new hospital*
brand new completely new: *These shoes look brand new.* | *a brand new apartment*
recent made or produced a short time ago: *A recent study suggests women are more likely to get the disease than men.*
latest the most recent: *His latest book is set in Spain.* | *the latest news from China*
original new and different from what other people have done before: *His style is completely original.* | *a highly original design*
fresh fresh food has been recently made or picked. Fresh ideas or methods are new and different from previous ones: *Eat plenty of fresh fruit and vegetables.* | *We need to take a fresh look at the problem.*
revolutionary completely new in a way that has a very big effect – used especially about ideas, methods, or inventions: *Darwin's theories were revolutionary.*

New 'Age *adj* relating to religious beliefs, types of medicine, or ways of living that are not like the beliefs etc of traditional Western society

newborn /'njuːbɔːn $ 'nuːbɔːrn/ *adj* a newborn baby or animal has just been born —**newborn** *n* [C]

newcomer /'njuːkʌmə $ 'nuːkʌmər/ *n* [C] someone who has recently arrived somewhere or recently started doing an activity: **[+to]** *a newcomer to teaching*

newfangled /ˌnjuːˈfæŋɡəld◂ $ ˌnuː-/ *adj* disapproving newfangled ideas, machines etc are new or modern **THESAURUS** ▶ MODERN

'new-found *adj* [only before noun] recently obtained, found, or achieved: *He enjoyed his **new-found freedom**.*

newly /'njuːli $ 'nuːli/ *adv* **newly built/married/ qualified etc** very recently built, married etc **THESAURUS** ▶ RECENTLY

newlyweds /'njuːliwedz $ 'nuː-/ *n* [plural] a man and a woman who have recently got married

news /njuːz $ nuːz/ *n* [U]
1 information about something that has happened recently: *I have some good news for you!* | *Sit down and tell me all your news.* | **[+of/about]** *Everyone was shocked by the news of the arrests.*
2 reports of recent events in the newspapers, on the radio, or on television: *Here's the sports news from Jane Murray.* | **[+of]** *news of an explosion in the city* | **news story/report/programme etc** *a news broadcast*
3 the **news** a regular television or radio programme that gives you reports of recent events: *the ten o'clock news* | **on the news** *I heard it on the news last night.* | **watch/listen to the news** *Shall we watch the news?*

PHRASES

that's news to me *spoken* used when you are surprised or annoyed because you have not been told something earlier: *He's married? That's news to me.*

Grammar

News is an uncountable noun. You use a singular verb with it.
Do not say 'The news were good.' Say *The news was good.*

COLLOCATIONS

adjectives

good/great/wonderful news *'She got the job.' 'Oh, that is good news!'*
bad/terrible news *I'm afraid I have some bad news for you.*
the latest news *What's the latest news?*
important news *He said he had some important news to tell me.*

verbs

to have some news *Do you have any news about the baby?*
to tell sb the news *I'd better go and tell Anne the news.*
to break the news (=to tell someone some bad news) *Who's going to break the news to him about the game?*
to hear the news (=to hear about something that has happened) *Have you heard the news about Joe?*

noun + news

a piece of news (also **a bit of news** *BrE*) *I've had a rather surprising piece of news.*

'news ,agency *n* [C] a company that supplies news stories to newspapers, radio, and television

newsagent /'njuːzeɪdʒənt $ 'nuːz-/ *n* [C] *BrE*
1 newsagent's a shop that sells newspapers and magazines **2** someone who owns or works in a shop selling newspapers and magazines

'news ,bulletin *n* [C] **1** *BrE* a short news programme on radio or television **2** *AmE* a short news report about something important that has just happened, given suddenly in the middle of a television or radio programme **SYN** **newsflash** *BrE*

newscast /'njuːzkaːst $ 'nuːzkæst/ *n* [C] *AmE* a news programme on television

newscaster /'njuːzkaːstə $ 'nuːzkæstər/ *n* [C] someone who reads the news on television

newsflash /'njuːzflæʃ $ 'nuːz-/ *n* [C] *BrE* a short news report about something important that has just happened, given suddenly in the middle of a television or radio programme **SYN** **news bulletin** *AmE*

newsgroup /'njuːzgruːp $ 'nuːz-/ *n* [C] a discussion group on the Internet, with a place where people who share an interest can exchange messages

newsletter /'njuːzletə $ 'nuːzletər/ *n* [C] a printed report with news about an organization, sent regularly to its members: *our church newsletter*

newspaper /'njuːspeɪpə $ 'nuːzpeɪpər/ *n*
1 [C] a set of folded pieces of paper printed with

news, pictures, advertisements etc and sold daily or weekly SYN **paper**: **in the newspaper** *I saw his picture in the newspaper.*
2 [C] a company that produces a newspaper SYN **paper**
3 [U] pieces of paper from old newspapers: *plates wrapped in newspaper*

Grammar
Do not say 'I read it on the newspaper.' Say *I read it in the newspaper.*

COLLOCATIONS

verbs
to read a newspaper *I read the newspaper every day.*
to see/read sth in the newspaper *I saw his picture in the newspaper.*
to appear in a newspaper *The article appeared in the 'Observer' newspaper yesterday.*

types of newspaper
a national/local newspaper *She put an ad in the local newspaper.*
a daily/weekly/Sunday newspaper *Do you get a daily newspaper?*

newspaper + noun
a newspaper article/report/story *Have you seen this newspaper article?*
a newspaper column (=a regular article written by a particular journalist) *He writes a newspaper column about his family life.*
a newspaper headline *Don't believe all those frightening newspaper headlines.*
a newspaper reporter *I was once interviewed by a newspaper reporter.*

THESAURUS

newspaper a set of folded pieces of paper printed with news, pictures, advertisements etc: *His picture was in all the national newspapers.*
paper a newspaper. **Paper** is more common than **newspaper** in everyday English: *Can I borrow your paper?* | *I read about it in the paper.*
the press newspapers and news magazines in general, and the people who write for them: *the freedom of the press* | *The press were desperate to get his story.*
the media newspapers, magazines, television, radio, and the Internet, considered as a group that provides news and information: *You may have seen her in the media, talking about her new book.*
tabloid a newspaper that has small pages, a lot of photographs, short stories, and not much serious news: *The tabloids are full of gossip about the wedding.*
broadsheet *BrE* a serious newspaper printed on large sheets of paper, with news about politics, finance, and foreign affairs: *The broadsheets reported the latest news from Wall Street.*

newsprint /'njuːzprɪnt $ 'nuːz-/ n [U] the paper and ink that is used to print newspapers

newsreader /'njuːzˌriːdə $ 'nuːzˌriːdər/ n [C] *BrE* someone who reads the news on television or radio SYN **anchor** *AmE*

newsstand /'njuːzstænd $ 'nuːz-/ n [C] a place on a street where newspapers are sold

newsworthy /'njuːzˌwɜːði $ 'nuːzˌwɜːrði/ adj important or interesting enough to be reported as news: *newsworthy events*

newt /njuːt $ nuːt/ n [C] a small animal with a long body, four legs, and a tail, which lives in water and on land

New 'Testament n **the New Testament** the part of the Bible that describes the life of Jesus Christ → **Old Testament**

new 'wave n [singular] people who try to introduce new ideas in music, films, art, politics etc: *the new wave of British cinema* —**new wave** adj

New 'World n **the New World** North, Central, and South America

new year n **the new year** the first few weeks of a year: **in the new year** *Let's meet up in the new year.*

New 'Year n [U] the time when you celebrate the beginning of the year: *Happy New Year!*

New Year's 'Day n [singular, U] January 1st, the first day of the year in Western countries

New Year's 'Eve n [singular, U] December 31st, the last day of the year in Western countries

next¹ /nekst/ adj, determiner
1 the next day, time, event etc is the one that happens after the present one: *They returned to New York the next day.* | *The next flight leaves in 45 minutes.* | *Next time* (=when something happens again), *be more careful!* | **next Monday/May/year/summer etc** *See you next week.* | **the next thing sb knew** (=used when something surprising happens suddenly) *The next thing I knew, I was lying face down on the table.*

Grammar
Do not say 'on next Monday/Friday etc'. Say **next Monday/Friday etc**: *I'm going to Paris next Friday.*
Do not say 'on next week/month etc'. Say **next week/month etc**: *I've got a job interview next week.*

2 the next place is the one closest to where you are now: *Turn left at the next corner.* | *the people at the next table*
3 the next person or thing in a list, series etc is the one after the present one: *Who will be the next President?* | *Read the next chapter by Friday.* | **the next biggest/largest etc** *Jo's the next oldest in the family.*
PHRASES

the next best thing something that is almost as good as what you really want: *Talking on the phone is the next best thing to being together.*

next² adv
1 immediately afterwards: *What shall we do next?* | *Next, write your name at the top of the page.*
2 on the next occasion: *When I next saw her, she ignored me.*

N

PHRASES

next to sb/sth 1 beside someone or something: *I sat next to a really nice guy on the plane.* **2** used to give a list of things you like, hate etc, when you want to say which you like, hate etc most: *Next to soccer, I like tennis best.*

next to nothing very little: *I bought the car for next to nothing!*

THESAURUS

next to someone or something

next to very close to someone or something: *My sister's room is next to mine.*

beside next to the side of someone or something: *Come and sit beside me.*

by next to something – often used about being very close to a window, door, or the edge of an area of water: *I'd love to live by the sea.* | *He always sits by the window.*

next door in the building or room next to yours: *They have lived next door since we were children.*

alongside close to the side of something, especially a river, railway, boat, or vehicle: *The canal runs alongside the railway line.*

next³ *pron* the person or thing in a list, series etc that comes after the one you are dealing with now: *What's next on the shopping list?* | **next to do sth** *Who's next to see the doctor?*

PHRASES

the week/year etc after next the week, year etc that follows the next one: *Let's meet some time the week after next.*

next 'door *adv* **1** in the house, room, building etc that is nearest to your home: *The Simpsons live next door.* | **[+to]** *Who's next door to you?* **THESAURUS** NEXT **2** next to sth in the building that is nearest to another building: *The post office is next door to the supermarket.* **THESAURUS** NEAR —**'next-door** *adj*: *my next-door neighbour*

next of 'kin *n* [C] (*plural* **next of kin**) *formal* the person who has the closest family relationship to you, for example your husband, wife, or mother **THESAURUS** RELATIVE

NHS /ˌen eɪtʃ 'es/ *n* **the NHS (the National Health Service)** the British system that provides free medical treatment for everyone, paid for by taxes

nib /nɪb/ *n* [C] the part of a pen that puts the ink on the page

nibble /'nɪbəl/ *v* [I,T] to eat a small amount of food with very small bites **THESAURUS** EAT —**nibble** *n* [C]

NIBBLE

nice /naɪs/ *adj*

1 pleasant, attractive, or enjoyable: *Did you have a nice time?* | *That's a nice sweater.* | **look/taste/smell nice** *You look nice in that suit.* | **nice and warm/cool/sweet etc** *It's nice and warm in here.* | **a nice big/new/long etc sth** *a nice long holiday* | *It would be nice to go to Spain.* **THESAURUS** GOOD

2 friendly or kind: *They're all really nice people.* | **[+to]** *Everyone's been very nice to us since we arrived.* | **[+about]** *I said sorry and he was quite nice about it.* | **it is nice of sb (to do sth)** *It was nice of you to come.* **THESAURUS** FRIENDLY

PHRASES

(it's) nice to meet you *spoken* used when you meet someone for the first time

(it's been) nice meeting you *spoken* used when saying goodbye to someone you have met for the first time

THESAURUS

person

nice friendly or kind: *Karen's really nice, isn't she?*

charming polite and friendly in a way that makes people like you: *He was charming and witty, and the staff all loved him.*

likeable easy to like: *The new boss seemed very likeable.*

sweet *especially spoken* very kind and gentle: *How sweet of you to send me flowers!* | *a sweet little old lady*

great *especially spoken* used about someone you like and admire a lot: *I think your brother's great!*

thing, place, day etc

nice used when something seems good or enjoyable: *That's a nice dress.* | *Have a nice time!* | *It's been a really nice day.*

great (*also* **brilliant** *BrE*) *especially spoken* very good or enjoyable: *His concerts are always great.* | *It's a great car.*

pleasant a pleasant place, activity, or occasion is good or enjoyable. **Pleasant** sounds more formal than **nice**: *a pleasant little town* | *Thank you for a very pleasant evening.*

lovely used when you enjoyed something very much: *It was a lovely meal.* | *The children had a lovely time.*

enjoyable giving you pleasure: *Exercise should be an enjoyable experience.* | *We had a very enjoyable stay.*

fun *especially spoken* enjoyable. **Fun** is more informal than **enjoyable**: *Skiing is great fun.* | *It was a fun day.*

charming pleasant – used especially about places that are attractive in a simple way: *a charming little town*

nice-'looking *adj* attractive: *a nice-looking guy*

nicely /'naɪsli/ *adv* **1** in a good, satisfactory, or attractive way: *'How's your love life going?' 'Very nicely, thanks!'* | *a nicely dressed young man* **2** in a polite or pleasant way: *Don't forget to ask nicely.*

nicety /'naɪsəti/ *n* [C usually plural] (*plural* **niceties**) a small detail that is the difference between the correct and the incorrect way of doing something: *the niceties of the law*

niche /niːʃ, nɪtʃ $ nɪtʃ, niːʃ/ *n* [C] **1** a job or activity that is perfect for someone's abilities and character: *She found her niche as a fashion designer.* **2** a hollow place in a wall, often made to hold a STATUE

PHRASES

niche market *technical* a small group of people with particular needs or interests that companies try to sell specific products to: *Young women travelers are a growing niche market in the tourism industry.*

nick¹ /nɪk/ *n* [C] a very small cut on the surface or edge of something

PHRASES

in good/bad nick *BrE informal* in good or bad condition: *Our car's old but it's in good nick.*

in the nick of time at the last moment before it is too late to do something: *The doctor arrived in the nick of time.*

nick² *v* [T] **1** to accidentally make a small cut on the surface or edge of something: *I nicked my chin when I was shaving.* **2** *BrE informal* to steal something

THESAURUS STEAL

nickel /ˈnɪkəl/ *n* **1** [U] a hard silver-white metal that is an ELEMENT and is used for making other metals **2** [C] a coin used in the US and Canada that is worth five cents

nickname /ˈnɪkneɪm/ *n* [C] a short or friendly name for someone that is used by their friends or family: *His nickname was 'Curly' because of his hair.* **THESAURUS** NAME —**nickname** *v* [T]: *The puppy was soon nicknamed 'Trouble'.*

nicotine /ˈnɪkətiːn/ *n* [U] the substance in tobacco that makes you want to continue smoking

niece /niːs/ *n* [C] the daughter of your brother or sister, or the daughter of your husband's or wife's brother or sister → **nephew**

nifty /ˈnɪfti/ *adj informal* something that is nifty is good because it is effective or fast: *a nifty little gadget*

niggle /ˈnɪgəl/ *v* [T] to annoy or worry someone slightly: *Something's been niggling her all day.*

niggling /ˈnɪgəlɪŋ/ *adj* **niggling doubt/injury/ problem etc** a slight doubt, injury etc that does not go away

nigh /naɪ/ *adv literary* near

PHRASES

well nigh/nigh on *old-fashioned* almost: *It was nigh on impossible to ignore him.*

night /naɪt/ *n* [C,U]
1 the dark part of each 24-hour period, when people usually sleep [OPP] **day**: **at night** *It's very cold here at night.* | **in the night** *Did you hear the storm in the night?* | *The party went on all night.* | *She works three nights a week.*
2 the evening: **last/tomorrow night** *Did you go out last night?* | *He goes out* **every night.** | **on Monday/ Saturday etc night** *There's a party on Friday night.* | *We had a really good* **night out** (=an evening when you go to a restaurant, party etc). | *The park is open until* **late at night.** → **GOOD NIGHT, STAG NIGHT**

PHRASES

night and day/day and night all the time: *The prisoners were guarded day and night.*

COLLOCATIONS

adjectives

a dark night *The night was dark as we set off.*
a cold night *You can't spend a cold night like this outside.*
a clear night (=without clouds) *It was a clear night and the sky was full of stars.*
an early/late night (=when you go to bed early or late) *You look tired – you should have an early night.*
a sleepless night (=when you cannot sleep, usually because of worry) *Her son has caused her many sleepless nights.*

noun + night

the middle of the night *I woke up in the middle of the night.*

verbs

to spend a night somewhere (=to sleep somewhere) *He had to spend the night in his car.*
to stay the night (=to sleep at someone's house) *I stayed the night at Eric's.*
night falls *written* (=it starts to become dark) *It grew colder as night fell.*

nightclub /ˈnaɪtklʌb/ *n* [C] a place where people go late in the evening to drink and dance

nightdress /ˈnaɪtdres/ *n* [C] a piece of clothing, like a dress, that women wear in bed

'night ˌduty *n* [U] work that is done during the night, as part of someone's job: *There are three nurses on night duty each night.*

nightfall /ˈnaɪtfɔːl $ -fɔːl/ *n* [U] *literary* the time in the evening when it starts to get dark [SYN] **dusk**

nightgown /ˈnaɪtgaʊn/ *n* [C] *old-fashioned* a nightdress

nightie /ˈnaɪti/ *n* [C] *informal* a nightdress

nightingale /ˈnaɪtɪŋgeɪl/ *n* [C] a small bird that sings beautifully, especially at night

nightlife /ˈnaɪtlaɪf/ *n* [U] bars, clubs, restaurants etc that people can go to in the evening in a town or city: *Las Vegas is famous for its nightlife.*

nightlight /ˈnaɪtlaɪt/ *n* [C] a small light that you put in a child's room at night

nightly /ˈnaɪtli/ *adj, adv* happening every night: *a nightly news broadcast*

nightmare /ˈnaɪtmeə $ -mer/ *n* [C] **1** a very frightening dream: **[+about]** *I still* **have nightmares** *about the accident.* **THESAURUS** DREAM **2** [usually singular] a very unpleasant or difficult experience: *The trip was an absolute nightmare.* | *It was every teacher's* **worst nightmare** (=the worst thing that could have happened). | *a nightmare journey* —**nightmarish** *adj*

'night ˌschool *n* [U] classes that you go to in the evening: *I'm studying Spanish at night school.*

'night ˌshift *n* [C,U] a period of time at night when people regularly work: **work/do a night shift** *Doctors often have to work night shifts.* | **on (the) night shift** *Lee's on night shift this week.*

nightshirt /ˈnaɪtʃɜːt $ -ʃɜːrt/ *n* [C] a long loose shirt that someone, especially a man, wears in bed

nightstand /ˈnaɪtstænd/ n [C] AmE a small table beside a bed

nightstick /ˈnaɪtˌstɪk/ n [C] AmE a short stick carried as a weapon by police officers SYN **truncheon** BrE

'night-time n [U] the time during the night when it is dark: **at night-time** *It's quite noisy here at night-time.*

ˌnight 'watchman n [C] someone whose job is to guard a building at night

nil /nɪl/ n [U] nothing or zero: *The score was seven nil.* | *His chances of winning are almost nil.*

nimble /ˈnɪmbəl/ adj able to move quickly and skilfully: *nimble fingers* —**nimbly** adv

nine /naɪn/ number the number 9: *He's only been in this job for nine months.* | *We open at nine* (=nine o'clock). | *Tim learnt to swim when he was nine* (=nine years old).

nineteen /ˌnaɪnˈtiːn◂/ number the number 19: *It was nineteen minutes past seven.* | *I was only nineteen* (=19 years old). —**nineteenth** adj, pron: *her nineteenth birthday* | *I'm planning to leave on **the nineteenth*** (=the 19th day of the month).
PHRASES
nineteen to the dozen if someone talks nineteen to the dozen, they talk very quickly without stopping: *He was talking excitedly nineteen to the dozen.*

ˌnine-to-'five adj nine-to-five jobs or hours involve working between 9 o'clock in the morning and 5 o'clock in the afternoon: *Being a chef is not a nine-to-five job.* —**nine-to-five** adv: *If you want to work nine-to-five, don't become a nurse.*

ninety /ˈnaɪnti/ number
1 the number 90
2 the nineties (also **the '90s, the 1990s**) [plural] the years from 1990 to 1999: **the early/mid/late nineties** *The industry received a lot of bad publicity in the early nineties.* —**ninetieth** adj: *grandma's ninetieth birthday*
PHRASES
be in your nineties to be aged between 90 and 99: **early/mid/late nineties** *He was in his late nineties when he died.*
in the nineties if the temperature is in the nineties, it is between 90 degrees and 99 degrees F: *We may see temperatures in the nineties later this week.*

ninth¹ /naɪnθ/ adj coming after eight other things in a series: *her ninth birthday* —**ninth** pron: *I'm planning to leave on **the ninth*** (=the ninth day of the month).

ninth² n [C] one of nine equal parts of something

nip¹ /nɪp/ v (**nipped, nipping**) **1** [I] BrE informal to go somewhere quickly or for a short time: **[+into/to etc]** *I've got to nip into town.* **2** [I,T] to bite someone or something slightly: *The dog nipped her on the leg.*
PHRASES
nip sth in the bud to prevent something from becoming a problem by stopping it as soon as it starts: *This violence must be nipped in the bud.*

nip² n [C] a slight bite

nipple /ˈnɪpəl/ n [C] **1** one of the two dark raised circles on your chest. Babies suck their mother's nipple to get milk. **2** AmE the piece of rubber that a baby sucks to get milk from a bottle SYN **teat** BrE

nippy /ˈnɪpi/ adj informal **1** weather that is nippy is cold **2** BrE able to move quickly: *a nippy little car*

nirvana /nɪəˈvɑːnə, nɜː- $ nɪr-, nɜːr-/ n [U] the final state of complete knowledge and understanding that believers in Buddhism try to achieve

'nit-ˌpicking n [U] when someone argues about small details or criticizes small mistakes in a way that annoys you —**nit-picking** adj

nitrate /ˈnaɪtreɪt, -trət/ n [C,U] a chemical used on soil in order to make crops grow better

nitrogen /ˈnaɪtrədʒən/ n [U] a gas that is the main part of the Earth's air

nits /nɪts/ n [plural] the eggs of a small insect that are sometimes found in people's hair

nitty-gritty /ˌnɪti ˈgrɪti/ n **the nitty-gritty** informal the basic and practical facts and details of something: **[+of]** *the nitty-gritty of finding a job* | *Let's **get down to the nitty-gritty** and work out costs.*

no¹ /nəʊ $ noʊ/ spoken
1 used to give a negative reply to a question, offer, or request OPP **yes**: *'Are you Spanish?' 'No, Italian.'* | *'Do you want some more coffee?' '**No thanks.**'* | *I asked Dad if I could have a dog but he **said no**.* | *'Do you see her often?' 'Oh no, only about once a year.'*
THESAURUS **REFUSE**
2 used when you disagree with a statement: *'Gary's strange.' 'No, he's just shy.'*
3 used when you agree with a negative statement: *'He shouldn't drive so fast.' 'No, it's really dangerous.'*
4 used when you do not want someone to do something: *No, Jan, don't touch that switch.*
5 used when you are surprised, shocked, or annoyed by something: *Oh no, I've lost my keys!*

no² determiner
1 not any: *I'm sorry, there are no tickets left.* | *a house with no garage* | *'There's no need to explain,' he said.*
2 used on a sign to show that something is not allowed: *No smoking.*

no³ adv not any – used before a COMPARATIVE form: *We're inviting **no more than** thirty people.* | *I'll be back no later than 10 o'clock.*

no⁴ n [C] (plural **noes**) a negative answer or decision: *Her answer was a definite no.*

no. (plural **nos.**) the written abbreviation of **number**

nobility /nəʊˈbɪləti, nə- $ noʊ-, nə-/ n **1 the nobility** the group of people in some countries who have the highest social rank **2** [U] the quality of being morally good or generous

noble¹ /ˈnəʊbəl $ ˈnoʊ-/ adj **1** morally good or generous: *a noble ideal* **2** belonging to the nobility: *noble families* —**nobly** adv

noble² (also **nobleman** /ˈnəʊbəlmən $ ˈnoʊ-/, **noblewoman** /ˈnəʊbəlˌwʊmən $ ˈnoʊ-/) n [C] someone of the highest social rank

nobody¹ /ˈnəʊbədi $ ˈnoʊbɑːdi, -bədi/ pron NO ONE:

Nobody knows what will happen. | *I'll have the cake if **nobody else** wants it.*

nobody² *n* [C] (*plural* **nobodies**) someone who is not important, successful, or famous: *I don't know why he's interested in a nobody like me.*

no-'brainer *n* [singular] *informal* a decision that is very easy, because it is obvious what is the best thing to do: *For me, travelling by public transport is a no-brainer.*

nocturnal /nɒkˈtɜːnl $ nɑːˈktɜːr-/ *adj* **1** nocturnal animals are active at night and sleep during the day **2** *formal* happening at night

nod /nɒd $ nɑːd/ *v* [I,T] (**nodded, nodding**)
1 to move your head up and down, especially to say yes or to show that you understand something → **shake**: *'Are you Jill?' he asked. She smiled and nodded.* | *She **nodded** her **head** sympathetically.*
2 to move your head up and down once, in order to greet someone or to give them a sign: [+to/at/towards] *I nodded to the waiter.* | *'Sally's in there,' he said, nodding towards the kitchen.* —**nod** *n* [C]: *He gave a nod of agreement.*
PHRASAL VERBS
nod off *informal* to begin to sleep, often without intending to: *I kept nodding off during the lecture.*

nodule /ˈnɒdjuːl $ ˈnɑːdʒuːl/ *n* [C] a small round raised part, especially a small swelling on a plant or someone's body

noes /nəʊz $ noʊz/ *n* the plural of NO

no-'frills *adj* having only features that are basic and necessary: *a no-frills airline*

no-'go ˌarea *n* [C] an area of a city where it is not safe for people to go because of the crime or violence there

noise /nɔɪz/ *n* [C,U] a sound, especially one that is unpleasant or loud: [+of] *the noise of traffic* | *The computer is **making** a strange **noise**.* | *He heard a whistling noise outside.* | *People living near the airport have complained about **noise levels**.*

THESAURUS

noise a sound, especially one that is unpleasant or loud: *strange noises* | *She was careful not to make too much noise.*
racket/din a loud annoying noise: *The kids are making a terrible racket.*
roar a loud noise that continues for a long time, especially the noise from an engine, traffic, waves, or a crowd: *I heard the roar of the plane's engines starting up.*

noiselessly /ˈnɔɪzləsli/ *adv* written without making any sound: *Adam crept noiselessly around the house.*

'noise polˌlution *n* [U] loud or continuous noise that is unpleasant and annoying

noisy /ˈnɔɪzi/ *adj* making a lot of noise, or full of noise OPP **quiet**: *noisy children* | *The bar was too noisy.* **THESAURUS** ▶ LOUD —**noisily** *adv*

nomad /ˈnəʊmæd $ ˈnoʊ-/ *n* [C] a member of a tribe that does not live in one place, but travels from place to place, usually in order to find grass for their animals —**nomadic** /nəʊˈmædɪk $ noʊ-/ *adj*

'no-man's ˌland *n* [singular, U] land that no one owns or controls, especially an area between two opposing armies

nominal /ˈnɒmɪnl $ ˈnɑː-/ *adj* **1 nominal sum/charge/fee etc** a small amount of money, not what something would usually cost: *A nominal charge is made for use of the tennis court.* **2** officially described as something, when this is not really true: *He was the nominal leader of the campaign.*

nominally /ˈnɒmɪnəli $ ˈnɑː-/ *adv* officially described as something, when this is not really true: *a nominally independent country*

nominate /ˈnɒmɪneɪt $ ˈnɑː-/ *v* [T] to officially suggest that someone or something should be given an important position or prize: **nominate sb/sth for sth** *The film was nominated for an award.* | **nominate sb/sth as sth** *The party nominated him as presidential candidate.* **THESAURUS** ▶ SUGGEST —**nomination** /ˌnɒməˈneɪʃən $ ˌnɑː-/ *n* [C,U]

nominee /ˌnɒməˈniː $ ˌnɑː-/ *n* [C] someone who has been nominated for something: *the Democratic Party's presidential nominee*

non- /nɒn $ nɑːn/ *prefix* not: *non-British visitors* | *non-smokers* (=people who do not smoke)

ˌnon-agˈgression *n* [U] when a country or government does not use military force or threats against another

ˌnon-alcoˈholic *adj* a non-alcoholic drink does not have any alcohol in it

nonchalant /ˈnɒnʃələnt $ ˌnɑːnʃəˈlɑːnt/ *adj* not seeming worried or interested: *'Will John be at the party?' she asked, trying to sound nonchalant.* | *a nonchalant shrug* —**nonchalance** *n* [U] —**nonchalantly** *adv*

ˌnon-ˈcombatant / $ ˌ..ˈ../ *n* [C] a member of an army who does not fight, for example an army doctor

ˌnon-comˈmittal *adj* not giving a definite answer, or not showing what your intentions are: *a non-committal reply* —**non-committally** *adv*

nonconformist Ac /ˌnɒnkənˈfɔːmɪst◀ $ ˌnɑːnkənˈfɔːr-/ *adj* having different beliefs or different ways of doing something from most other people: *nonconformist writers* —**nonconformist** *n* [C]

nondescript /ˈnɒndəˌskrɪpt $ ˌnɑːndəˈskrɪpt/ *adj* disapproving not having any noticeable or interesting qualities: *a nondescript brown suit*

none¹ /nʌn/ *pron* not any of something, or not one person or thing: *'Can I have some more coffee?' 'Sorry, there's none left.'* | [+of] *None of the money was missing.* | *None of us really knew him.* | *Small improvements are better than **none at all**.*

Grammar
If you use **none of** with an uncountable noun, the verb is singular: *None of the information was true.*
If you use **none of** with a plural noun, the verb can be singular or plural: *None of my friends was there.*

none² *adv* **1 none too** not at all: *He's none too happy with the situation.* | *She put the glass down none too gently.* **2 none the worse/wiser** not any worse than before, or not knowing any more than before: **[+for]** *She seems none the worse for her terrible experience.*

nonentity /nɒˈnentəti $ nɑː-/ *n* [C] (*plural* **nonentities**) someone who is not important or special in any way

nonetheless Ac /ˌnʌnðəˈles/ *adv formal* in spite of what has just been mentioned SYN **nevertheless**: *The information was complicated but nonetheless helpful.*

non-eˈvent *n* [C usually singular] *informal* an event that is much less exciting or interesting than you expected: *My 21st birthday was a complete non-event.*

nonexistent /ˌnɒnɪɡˈzɪstənt◂ $ ˌnɑːn-/ *adj* not existing at all: **almost/virtually/practically nonexistent** *Industry in the area is virtually nonexistent.*

non-ˈfiction *n* [U] books about real facts or events OPP **fiction** THESAURUS ▶ BOOK

non-ˈflammable *adj* materials or substances that are non-flammable do not burn easily or do not burn at all OPP **flammable, inflammable**

non-interˈvention *n* [U] when a government of a powerful country does not get involved in the affairs of other countries

ˈno-no *n* [singular] *informal* something that you must not do because people think it is unacceptable: *At that time, wearing a short skirt was a definite no-no.*

no-ˈnonsense *adj* [only before noun] very practical and sensible: *a no-nonsense attitude to work*

nonpayment /ˌnɒnˈpeɪmənt $ ˌnɒːn-/ *n* [U] when you do not pay money that you owe: **[+of]** *nonpayment of rent*

nonplussed /ˌnɒnˈplʌst $ nɑːn-/ *adj* [not before noun] not knowing what to do or say because you are so surprised: *He was a little nonplussed by the question.*

non-ˈprofit (*also* ˌnon-ˈprofitmaking *BrE*) *adj* a non-profit organization uses the money it earns to help people instead of making a profit

non-prolifeˈration *n* [U] the POLICY of limiting the number of NUCLEAR or chemical weapons in the world

non-reˈnewable *adj* non-renewable types of energy such as coal or gas cannot be replaced after they have been used

non-ˈresident *n* [C] **1** someone who does not live permanently in a particular country **2** *BrE* someone who is not staying in a particular hotel: *The hotel restaurant is open to non-residents.*

nonsense /ˈnɒnsəns $ ˈnɑːnsens/ *n* [U]
1 statements or opinions that are not true or seem very stupid SYN **rubbish** *BrE*: **absolute/complete/utter nonsense** *He described the rumours as 'absolute nonsense'.* | **[+about]** *Do you believe all this nonsense about ghosts?* | *Now you're **talking nonsense**.* | *I've never heard such **a load of nonsense** (=a lot of nonsense).* | **it is nonsense to do sth** *It's nonsense to say that mistakes are never made.*

2 stupid and annoying behaviour: *I'm not putting up with any more of this nonsense!*
3 speech or writing that you cannot understand because it has no meaning —**nonsensical** /nɒnˈsensəkəl $ nɑːn-/ *adj*

non-ˈsmoker *n* [C] someone who does not smoke

non-ˈsmoking *adj* a non-smoking area or building is one where smoking is not allowed

non-ˈstandard *adj* **1** non-standard ways of speaking are considered to be incorrect by a lot of people **2** not the usual type or size: *a non-standard size*

non-ˈstarter *n* [C usually singular] *informal* something or someone that is very unlikely to succeed: *The idea is a complete non-starter.*

nonstick /ˌnɒnˈstɪk◂ $ ˌnɑːn-/ *adj* a nonstick pan has a special surface that food will not stick to

nonstop /ˌnɒnˈstɒp◂ $ ˌnɑːnˈstɑːp◂/ *adj, adv* without stopping: *Dan worked nonstop for 12 hours.* | *a nonstop flight from Vancouver to London*

nonviolence /ˌnɒnˈvaɪələns $ ˌnɑːn-/ *n* [U] when people try to make political or social changes without using violence: *a policy of nonviolence* —**nonviolent** *adj*

noodles /ˈnuːdlz/ *n* [plural] long thin pieces of food made from flour, water, and eggs, usually cooked in boiling water

nook /nʊk/ *n* [C] *literary* a small quiet place: *a shady nook*
PHRASES
every nook and cranny every part of a place: *We searched every nook and cranny.*

noon /nuːn/ *n* [U] 12 o'clock in the middle of the day SYN **midday**: **at/by/before noon** *They left at noon.* | *The wedding is at **12 noon**.*

ˈno one (*also* **nobody**) *pron* not anyone: *No one saw him arrive.* | *She whispered so that **no one else** could hear.*

noose /nuːs/ *n* [C] a circle of rope that can be pulled tight to catch animals or hang someone

nope /nəʊp $ noʊp/ *adv spoken informal* used to say 'no' when you answer someone: *'Hungry?' 'Nope, I just ate.'*

ˈno place *adv especially AmE informal* nowhere: *There's no place left to hide.*

nor /nɔː $ nɔːr/ *linking word, adv*
1 neither ... nor used to show that two things are not true or do not happen: *Julie was neither shocked nor surprised by the news.* | *They can neither read nor write.*
2 *formal* used after a negative statement and before another negative statement: *She didn't reply, nor did she look at him.*
3 nor can I/nor did he etc used after a negative statement to say that the same thing is true for someone or something else: *'I don't want to go.' 'Nor do I.'*

norm Ac /nɔːm $ nɔːrm/ *n* **1 the norm** what is usual or normal: *a country where disease and poverty are the norm* **2 norms** [plural] the usual and acceptable ways of behaving: *cultural and social norms*

normal Ac /'nɔːməl $ 'nɔːr-/ adj
1 usual, typical, and expected → **abnormal**: *He just wanted a normal life.* | *I'll be glad when things get **back to normal**.* | *The test was done **in the normal way**.* | *It's normal to feel nervous before an operation.* | **quite/perfectly normal** *His voice sounded perfectly normal.*
2 someone who is normal is mentally and physically healthy and behaves like most other people: *a perfectly normal little boy*

THESAURUS

normal usual, typical, and expected: *Is it normal to faint after you've given blood?*
ordinary (*also* **regular** *AmE*) not special, unusual, or different from normal: *It's just an ordinary house in an ordinary street.*
average around the usual level or amount: *My weight is about average.*
standard the standard size, shape, or method of doing something is the usual one: *What's the standard size for a swimming pool?*
regular a regular coffee, cola etc is the normal size, and is not big or small – used when ordering food and drink: *I'll have a regular fries.*
routine a routine check, inspection, operation etc is one that is done regularly, not for any special reason: *a routine medical examination*
everyday everyday objects are things that you use in your normal life. Everyday events are ones that happen in your normal life: *a jug, a lamp, or some other everyday object*

---

normality Ac /nɔːˈmæləti $ nɔːr-/ (*also* **normalcy** /'nɔːməlsi $ 'nɔːr-/ *AmE*) *n* [U] a situation in which everything happens in the usual way: *a return to normality after years of war*

normalize Ac (*also* **-ise** *BrE*) /'nɔːməlaɪz $ 'nɔːr-/ *v* [I,T] to become normal again, or to make a situation become normal again: *The two countries are working to **normalize relations**.* —**normalization** /ˌnɔːməlaɪˈzeɪʃən $ ˌnɔːrmələ-/ *n* [U]

normally Ac /'nɔːməli $ 'nɔːr-/ *adv*
1 usually: *I normally cycle to college.*
2 in the usual or expected way: *Try to relax and breathe normally.*

north¹, **North** /nɔːθ $ nɔːrθ/ *n* [singular, U] (*written abbreviation* **N**)
1 the direction towards the top of a map: *Which way is north?* | **from/towards the north** *The army is approaching from the north.* | **to the north (of sth)** *Santorini is about 110km to the north of Crete.*
2 **the north** the northern part of a country or area: *The north will be dry and bright.* | **[+of]** *the north of France*

north², **North** *adj* [only before noun] (*written abbreviation* **N**)
1 in the north or facing the north: *the north side of the building* | *He lives in North Wales.*
2 a north wind comes from the north

north³ *adv* (*written abbreviation* **N**) towards the north: *The birds fly north in the summer.* | **[+of]** *Chicago is four hours north of Indianapolis.*

up north *informal* to or in the north of the country: *They've moved up north.*

northbound /'nɔːθbaʊnd $ 'nɔːrθ-/ *adj* travelling or leading towards the north: *northbound traffic*

northeast¹, **Northeast** /ˌnɔːθˈiːst◂ $ ˌnɔːrθ-/ *n* [U] (*written abbreviation* **NE**) **1** the direction that is exactly between north and east **2** **the northeast** the northeastern part of a country —**northeast** *adv*: *He headed northeast across the open sea.*

northeast², **Northeast** *adj* [only before noun] (*written abbreviation* **NE**) **1** in the northeast of a place: *the northeast outskirts of Las Vegas* **2** a northeast wind comes from the northeast

northeasterly /ˌnɔːθˈiːstəli $ ˌnɔːrθˈiːstərli/ *adj* **1** towards or in the northeast: *They set off in a northeasterly direction.* **2** a northeasterly wind comes from the northeast

northeastern /ˌnɔːθˈiːstən $ ˌnɔːrθˈiːstərn/ *adj* (*written abbreviation* **NE**) in or from the northeast part of a country or area: *the northeastern states of the US*

northerly /'nɔːðəli $ 'nɔːrðərli/ *adj* **1** towards or in the north: *We set off in a northerly direction.* **2** a northerly wind comes from the north

northern, **Northern** /'nɔːðən $ 'nɔːrðərn/ *adj* (*written abbreviation* **N**) in or from the north of a country or area: *a man with a northern accent* | *northern Europe*

northerner, **Northerner** /'nɔːðənə $ 'nɔːrðərnər/ *n* [C] someone from the northern part of a country

northernmost /'nɔːðənməʊst $ 'nɔːrðərnmoʊst/ *adj* furthest north: *the northernmost tip of the island*

North 'Pole *n* **the North Pole** the most northern point on the surface of the Earth → see picture at **GLOBE**

northwards /'nɔːθwədz $ 'nɔːrθwərdz/ (*also* **northward**) *adv* towards the north: *We sailed northwards.* —**northward** *adj*: *the northward journey*

northwest¹, **Northwest** /ˌnɔːθˈwest◂ $ ˌnɔːrθ-/ *n* [U] (*written abbreviation* **NW**) **1** the direction that is exactly between north and west **2** **the northwest** the northwestern part of a country —**northwest** *adv*: *She rode northwest toward Boulder.*

northwest², **Northwest** *adj* [only before noun] (*written abbreviation* **NW**) **1** a northwest wind comes from the northwest **2** in the northwest of a place: *the northwest suburbs of the city*

northwesterly /ˌnɔːθˈwestəli $ ˌnɔːrθˈwestərli/ *adj* **1** towards or in the northwest: *They set off in a northwesterly direction.* **2** a northwesterly wind comes from the northwest

northwestern /ˌnɔːθˈwestən $ ˌnɔːrθˈwestərn/ *adj* (*written abbreviation* **NW**) in or from the northwest part of a country or area: *a town in northwestern Canada*

nos. // the written abbreviation of **numbers**

nose¹ /nəʊz $ noʊz/ *n* [C]
1 the part of your face that you use for smelling and breathing → **nasal**, **nostril**: *Breathe in through your*

nose. | *He punched me on the nose.* → see picture on page A2

2 the front end of a plane, ROCKET etc

PHRASES

get up sb's nose *informal* to annoy someone: *She always manages to get right up everyone's nose.*

keep your nose out (of sth) *informal* to avoid becoming involved in a situation that should not involve you: *Keep your nose out of my business!*

look down your nose at sb to think you are much better than someone else: *She tends to look down her nose at people.*

stick/poke your nose into sth *informal* to be too interested in a situation that should not involve you, in a way that annoys people: *I wish he'd stop poking his nose into my business.*

turn your nose up at sth to refuse to accept something because you do not think it is good enough for you: *Shoppers are turning their noses up at cheap cuts of meat.*

(right) under sb's nose so close to someone that they should notice, but do not: *The crime was committed right under the nose of a police officer.*

COLLOCATIONS

adjectives

a big/small nose *She thought her big nose was ugly.*

a long nose *He had a long, straight nose.*

a red nose (=because you are cold or drunk, or have a cold) *Her nose was red from the cold.*

a runny nose (=with clear liquid coming out) *I had a sore throat and a runny nose.*

a blocked nose (=because of a cold) *I can't breathe properly because my nose is blocked.*

verbs

to blow your nose (=to clear your nose by breathing out strongly through it) *He took out a handkerchief and blew his nose.*

to wipe your nose (=to wipe liquid away from your nose) *The boy wiped his nose on his sleeve.*

to pick your nose (=to remove substances from inside your nose with your finger) *Stop picking your nose, Freddy.*

sb's nose is running (=clear liquid is coming out) *I gave him a tissue because his nose was running.*

---

nose² *v* [I] if a vehicle noses forward, it moves forward slowly and carefully **SYN edge**: [**+forward/ out etc**] *The taxi nosed out into the traffic.*

PHRASAL VERBS

nose around (sth) (*also* **nose about** (sth) *BrE*) to look around a place in order to find something when no one else is there: *I don't like the idea of someone nosing around my house.*

nosebleed /'nəʊzbliːd $ 'noʊz-/ *n* [C] if you have a nosebleed, blood comes out of your nose

nosedive /'nəʊzdaɪv $ 'noʊz-/ *n* [C] **1** a sudden big fall in the price, value, or amount of something: *Profits took a nosedive last year.* **2** a sudden steep drop by a plane, with its front end pointing towards the ground —**nosedive** *v* [I]

nosey /'nəʊzi $ 'noʊ-/ *adj* another spelling of NOSY

nostalgia /nɒˈstældʒə $ nɑː-/ *n* [singular, U] the slightly sad feeling you have when you think about nice things that happened in the past: [**+for**] *He felt a brief nostalgia for his life on the farm.* —**nostalgic** *adj* —**nostalgically** /-kli/ *adv*

nostril /'nɒstrəl $ 'nɑː-/ *n* [C] one of the two holes at the bottom end of your nose, which you breathe through → see picture on page A2

nosy, nosey /'nəʊzi $ 'noʊ-/ *adj* always trying to find out private information about someone: *Our neighbours are really nosy.* —**nosiness** *n* [U]

not /nɒt $ nɑːt/ *adv*

1 used to make a word or statement negative → **no**: *Most stores are not open on Sundays.* | *He does not speak English.* | *There were not many people there.* | **not at all/not ... at all** (=used to emphasize what you are saying) *I was not at all surprised to see her.* | *I did not like her at all.* | **not a lot/not much** (=little) *Not much is known about the disease.*

2 used in order to make a word or expression have the opposite meaning: *Edinburgh is not far now.* | *The food is **not very** good here.* | *Not many people* (=only a few) *have read the report.* | *Most of the hotels are **not that** cheap* (=they are expensive).

3 used instead of a whole phrase to mean the opposite of what has been mentioned before it → **so**: *No one knows if the story is true **or not**.* | *'Is Mark still ill?' 'I hope not.'*

PHRASES

not a/not one not any person or thing; none: *There wasn't a cloud in the sky.* | *Not one of the students knew the answer.*

not only in addition to being or doing something: **not only ... (but) also ...** *She's not only funny, she's also clever.*

notable /'nəʊtəbəl $ 'noʊ-/ *adj* important, interesting, or unusual enough to be noticed: [**+for**] *an area notable for its forests*

notably /'nəʊtəbli/ *adv* especially, or particularly: *Some politicians, most notably the President, refused to comment.*

notation /nəʊˈteɪʃən $ noʊ-/ *n* [C,U] a system of marks and signs to show musical sounds, numbers etc

notch¹ /nɒtʃ $ nɑːtʃ/ *n* [C] **1** a level of something, for example quality or achievement: *Her new book is several notches above anything else she has written.* **2** a V-shaped cut in a surface or edge

notch² *v*

PHRASAL VERBS

notch sth ↔ **up** to achieve a victory or a particular total: *He has notched up four goals in four games.*

note¹ /nəʊt $ noʊt/ *n*

1 TO REMIND YOU [C] something that you write down in order to remember something: *I'll just make a note of your new address.* | *Keep a note of any problems that you have.* **THESAURUS** WRITE

2 FOR STUDYING notes [plural] information that a student writes down in a lesson or from a book: *Did you take notes during the lecture?* | *lecture notes*

3 LETTER [C] a short informal letter: *I wrote Jane a*

short **note** to thank her for the meal. | This is just a quick **note** to let you know that I can't come.

4 **EXTRA INFORMATION** [C] a short piece of writing that gives extra information at the end of a document or book, or at the bottom of a page → **footnote**

5 **MUSIC** [C] a particular musical sound, or the symbol that represents it: He hummed a few notes of a tune.

6 **MONEY** [C] BrE paper money **SYN** bill AmE; **bank note** → **coin**: a ten-pound note **THESAURUS** MONEY

7 **FEELING** [singular] a feeling or quality: [+of] There was a note of doubt in her voice. | She ended her speech on a personal note. → **begin/end/finish on a high note** at HIGH¹, **compare notes (with sb)** at COMPARE, **note of caution** at CAUTION¹

PHRASES

sb/sth **of note** formal someone or something that is important: a writer of note

take note (of sth) to pay careful attention to something: We must always take note of our customers' views.

note² v [T] 1 to notice or pay careful attention to something: [+that] Please note that the museum is closed on Mondays. 2 (also **note down**) to write something down so that you will remember it: He noted down my name.

notebook /'nəʊtbʊk $ 'noʊt-/ n [C] 1 a book in which you can write notes → see picture at **CLASSROOM** 2 a small computer that is about the size of a book

noted /'nəʊtɪd $ 'noʊ-/ adj well-known or famous: a noted author | [+for] an area noted for its cheeses

notepad /'nəʊtpæd $ 'noʊt-/ n [C] a group of sheets of paper fastened together at the top, used for writing notes → see picture at **PAD¹**

notepaper /'nəʊt,peɪpə $ 'noʊt,peɪpər/ n [U] paper used for writing letters

noteworthy /'nəʊt,wɜːði $ 'noʊt,wɜːr-/ adj formal important or interesting enough to deserve attention: a noteworthy event

nothing¹ /'nʌθɪŋ/ pron

1 not anything: There's nothing in the bag. | There was **nothing else** we could do. | He had **nothing more** to say. | We **know nothing about** her family. | I couldn't just **do nothing**.

2 not anything that you consider to be important or interesting: There's nothing on television tonight. | 'What did you say?' 'Oh, nothing.'

3 zero, or zero points **SYN** nil BrE: The Red Sox won the game three nothing.

PHRASES

for nothing without any result or payment: I did all that work for nothing.

have nothing against sb/sth if you have nothing against someone or something, they do not annoy or offend you: I have nothing against him personally.

have/be nothing to do with sb/sth to not be connected or involved with someone or something: I had nothing to do with the decision. | It's got nothing to do with you. **THESAURUS** RELATED

if nothing else used to emphasize that there is one good quality or feature, although it may be the

only one: If nothing else, Jack is good at making decisions.

nothing but only: We've had nothing but rain for two weeks.

there's nothing in/to sth used to say that what people are saying about someone or something is not true: It seems there's nothing in the rumours that she is going to leave.

there's nothing like sth used to say that something is very good: There's nothing like a hot bath at the end of a tiring day.

nothing² adv **be nothing like sb/sth** to have no qualities that are similar to someone or something: She's nothing like her brother.

nothingness /'nʌθɪŋnəs/ n [U] a state of complete emptiness, where nothing exists

notice¹ /'nəʊtɪs $ 'noʊ-/ v [I,T] to see, feel, or hear someone or something: I said hello, but she didn't notice. | [+(that)] Max noticed that her hands were shaking. | [+who/what/how etc] She hadn't noticed before how tired he looked. | **notice sb/sth doing sth** Did you notice him leaving the party early?

THESAURUS SEE

THESAURUS

notice to realize that something is there or that something is happening, because you can see, hear, or feel it: I noticed that she wasn't feeling very well.

detect to notice something, especially something that is difficult to notice. **Detect** is used about people and machines: The device is used to detect changes in the temperature of sea water.

spot to notice something, especially something that is difficult to see or that you see only for a short time. **Spot** is more informal than **notice**: I spotted him in the crowd. | Did you spot the deliberate mistake?

become aware to gradually begin to notice something: He became aware that he was being followed.

observe formal to notice something as a result of watching or studying it closely: Galileo observed that the Moon has mountains and valleys.

catch your eye if something catches your eye, you suddenly notice it because it is interesting or attractive: The picture caught my eye when I was in the shop.

---

notice² n

1 [U] when you notice or pay attention to someone or something: Don't **take** any **notice** of her – she's just annoyed. | I waved but she **took no notice**. | It **came to** the **notice** of the committee (=they noticed) that many members had not paid their fees.

2 [C] a written or printed statement that gives information or a warning to people → **sign**: I'll put up a notice about the meeting.

3 [U] information or a warning about something that will happen: You must **give** the bank three days' **notice** before closing your account.

PHRASES

at short notice BrE, **on short notice** AmE if you do something at short notice, you do not have much time to prepare for it: *Thanks for agreeing to see me at such short notice.* THESAURUS SUDDENLY

hand in your notice/give (your) notice to tell your employer that you will soon be leaving your job → **resign**: *She's threatening to hand in her notice.*

until further notice from now until another change is announced: *The store will be closed until further notice.*

Word Choice: notice or sign?

A **notice** shows written information and is attached to a board, door, post etc. It is often there only for a short time: *There was a notice on the door which said 'Do not disturb'.*

A **sign** shows information using symbols or writing. It is often permanent, and it sometimes stands on its own: *There was a 'No Entry' sign at the end of the street.* | *a no smoking sign*

---

noticeable /'nəʊtəsəbəl $ 'noʊ-/ *adj* easy to notice: *There's been a noticeable improvement in your work.* —**noticeably** *adv*

noticeboard /'nəʊtəsbɔːd $ 'noʊtəsbɔːrd/ *n* [C] *BrE* a board on a wall that notices can be fixed to SYN **bulletin board** *AmE* → see picture at CLASSROOM

notify /'nəʊtɪfaɪ $ 'noʊ-/ *v* [T] (**notified, notifying, notifies**) *formal* to tell someone something officially SYN **inform**: *Have you notified the police?* —**notification** /ˌnəʊtɪfɪ'keɪʃən $ ˌnoʊ-/ *n* [C,U]

notion Ac /'nəʊʃən $ 'noʊ-/ *n* [C] an idea, belief, or opinion about something, especially one that is wrong: *Where did you get the notion that I was leaving?*

notoriety /ˌnəʊtə'raɪəti $ ˌnoʊ-/ *n* [U] when someone is famous for doing something bad

notorious /nəʊ'tɔːriəs, nə- $ noʊ-, nə-/ *adj* famous for something bad: **[+for]** *The city is notorious for its rainy weather.* THESAURUS FAMOUS —**notoriously** *adv*

notwithstanding Ac /ˌnɒtwɪθ'stændɪŋ, -wɪð- $ ˌnɑːt-/ *prep, adv* *formal* in spite of something: *The team has continued to be successful, notwithstanding recent criticism.*

nought /nɔːt $ nɒːt/ *number BrE* the number 0 SYN **zero**: *A billion is 1 with 9 noughts after it.* | **nought point one/two/three etc** (=0.1, 0.2, 0.3 etc)

noun /naʊn/ *n* [C] in grammar, a word that is the name of a person (such as 'Michael' or 'teacher'), place (such as 'France' or 'school'), thing or activity (such as 'coffee' or 'football'), or quality or idea (such as 'danger' or 'happiness') → PROPER NOUN

nourish /'nʌrɪʃ $ 'nɜːrɪʃ, 'nʌ-/ *v* [T] to give a person, animal, or plant the food they need in order to live and grow: *healthy well-nourished children*

nourishing /'nʌrɪʃɪŋ $ 'nɜː-, 'nʌ-/ *adj* nourishing food makes you strong and healthy: *nourishing soup*

nourishment /'nʌrɪʃmənt $ 'nɜː-, 'nʌ-/ *n* [U] *formal* food that is needed to live, grow, and be healthy

novel¹ /'nɒvəl $ 'nɑː-/ *n* [C] a long written story about characters and events that are not real → **fiction**: *the novels of Jane Austen* | *He's written several novels.* THESAURUS BOOK

novel² *adj* new, different, and unusual: *What a novel idea!*

novelist /'nɒvəlɪst $ 'nɑː-/ *n* [C] someone who writes novels

novelty /'nɒvəlti $ 'nɑː-/ *n* (*plural* **novelties**) **1** [C] something that is new and unusual: *In the 1950s, television was still a novelty.* **2** [U] the quality of being new, different, and unusual: *the novelty of using the new type of mobile phone* **3** [C] a small cheap object often given as a present

November /nəʊ'vembə, nə- $ noʊ'vembər, nə-/ *n* [C,U] (*written abbreviation* **Nov.**) the 11th month of the year, between October and December: **next/last November** *We met last November.* | **in November** *It snowed in early November.* | **on November 6th** *The match will take place on November 6th.*

novice /'nɒvɪs $ 'nɑː-/ *n* [C] someone who has just begun learning a skill or activity: *a novice at chess*

now¹ /naʊ/ *adv*
1 at the present time: *Jean and her husband are now living in Canada.* | **right now/just now** (=at the time of speaking) *Right now, we're not really ready to decide.* | **by/before now** (=before the present time) *Steve should be home by now.* | **from now on** (=starting now) *Meetings will be held on Friday from now on.* | **for now** (=for a short time) *You can leave your bags in the hall for now.*
2 immediately: *The bell has rung - stop writing now.* | *If we leave now, we'll be there before dark.*
3 *spoken* used to get someone's attention, when you are going to ask for information, or when you pause: *Now, let's discuss payment.* | *Now, what did you say your name was?*
PHRASES
(every) now and then/now and again sometimes: *He sees her every now and then at the college.* THESAURUS SOMETIMES
three weeks/two years etc now used when saying how long ago something started: *It's been over a year now since I started working here.*

THESAURUS

now at this time: *Can I come in now?* | *It's now 10 am.*
currently *formal* now - used when describing what a situation is like: *There are currently no problems on the subway system.*
at the moment (*also* **at present** *formal*) now - used especially to say that something is happening now, but you do not expect it to continue for a long time: *At the moment, I'm reading a book by Martin Amis.* | *At present, he's in the US.*
for now (*also* **for the time being**) for a short time from now, but not permanently - used when you think the situation may change, or you may decide to change what you are doing later: *Let's leave our plans as they are for the time being.*

now² (also **'now that**) linking word because of something or as a result of something: *Now that the kids have left home, the house feels empty.* | *I'm going to relax now the school year is over.*

nowadays /ˈnaʊədeɪz/ adv now, compared to what happened in the past: *People live longer nowadays.*

no 'way adv spoken used to emphasize that you will not agree or be able to do something: *'Are you going to work over the weekend?' 'No way!'* | *No way will we be finished by five o'clock.* | **There's no way** *I'm going to pay £300 just for a weekend in Paris.*

nowhere /ˈnəʊweə $ ˈnoʊwer/ adv not in or to any place: **nowhere to go/live/sit etc** *He's got nowhere to sleep tonight.* | *There's nowhere to put anything in our new apartment.*

PHRASES
> **from nowhere** happening or appearing suddenly and without warning: *The policeman **appeared** as if **from nowhere**.*
> **get nowhere** to have no success, or to make no progress: **[+with]** *He was getting nowhere with his new play.* | *A negative attitude will **get** you **nowhere**.*
> **nowhere near** **1** far from a particular place: *Buffalo is nowhere near New York City.* **2** not at all: *The building's nowhere near finished.*
> **nowhere to be seen/found** (also **nowhere in sight**) not in a particular place: *Her husband was nowhere to be seen.*

no-'win situ,ation n [C] a situation that will end badly whatever you decide to do

noxious /ˈnɒkʃəs $ ˈnɑːk-/ adj formal harmful or poisonous: *noxious chemicals*

nozzle /ˈnɒzəl $ ˈnɑː-/ n [C] a short tube on the end of a pipe or HOSE that controls the amount of liquid coming out

nr BrE the written abbreviation of **near**

n't /nt/ the short form of 'not': *He isn't* (=is not) *here.* | *She can't* (=cannot) *see him.* | *I didn't* (=did not) *do it.*

nuance /ˈnjuːɑːns $ ˈnuː-/ n [C,U] a very small difference in meaning, colour, or feeling

nuclear Ac /ˈnjuːkliə $ ˈnuːkliər/ adj
1 relating to or involving the NUCLEUS (=central part) of an atom, or the energy produced when the nucleus of an atom is either split or joined with the nucleus of another atom: *a nuclear power station* | *France relies on **nuclear energy**.* | *nuclear physics*
2 relating to or involving the use of weapons that use nuclear energy: *a nuclear war* | *nuclear weapons* | *a nuclear bomb*

nuclear dis'armament n [U] when a country or government gets rid of its NUCLEAR weapons

nuclear 'family n [C] a family that consists of a father, mother, and children

nuclear re'actor n [C] a large machine that produces nuclear energy

nucleus /ˈnjuːkliəs $ ˈnuː-/ n [C] (plural **nuclei** /-kliaɪ/) **1** the central part of an atom or cell **2** **the nucleus of sth** the most important part of something: *Photographs by Weston **form the nucleus of** the collection.*

nude¹ /njuːd $ nuːd/ adj not wearing any clothes SYN **naked** —**nudity** n [U]

nude² n [C] a painting, photograph etc of someone who is not wearing any clothes

PHRASES
> **in the nude** not wearing any clothes: *He was standing there in the nude.*

nudge /nʌdʒ/ v [T] to push someone or something gently with your elbow: *Ken nudged me and said, 'Look!'* THESAURUS ▸ PUSH —**nudge** n [C]

nudist /ˈnjuːdɪst $ ˈnuː-/ n [C] someone who believes it is good for you to wear no clothes —**nudist** adj: *a nudist beach* —**nudism** n [U]

nudity /ˈnjuːdəti $ ˈnuː-/ n [U] when people are not wearing any clothes: *There are scenes of nudity in the play.*

nugget /ˈnʌgɪt/ n [C] a small rough piece of a valuable metal: *a gold nugget*

nuisance /ˈnjuːsəns $ ˈnuː-/ n [C usually singular] someone or something that annoys you or causes problems: *Sorry to be a nuisance, but could I use your phone?* | **what a nuisance** BrE spoken: *What a nuisance! I've forgotten my keys.*

nuke¹ /njuːk $ nuːk/ v [T] informal to attack a place using NUCLEAR weapons

nuke² n [C] informal a NUCLEAR weapon

null and void /ˌnʌl ənd ˈvɔɪd/ adj law having no legal authority: *The court declared the contract to be null and void.*

nullify /ˈnʌlɪfaɪ/ v [T] (**nullified, nullifying, nullifies**) **1** law to state officially that something has no legal force: *The Senate has voted to nullify the decree.* **2** formal to make something less powerful or effective: *Recent wage increases have been nullified by inflation.*

numb¹ /nʌm/ adj **1** not able to feel anything: *My feet were numb with cold.* **2** very shocked and unable to think or speak: *We all felt numb when we heard the news.* —**numbness** n [U] —**numbly** adv

numb² v [T] **1** to make a part of your body unable to feel anything: *The cold wind numbed my face.* **2** to make someone unable to think, feel, or react in a normal way

number¹ /ˈnʌmbə $ -bər/ n
1 [C] a word or sign that shows an amount or quantity → **figure**: *Five was her lucky number.*
2 [C] a telephone number: *My new number is 502-6155.* | *Sorry, you have the **wrong number**.*
3 [C] a number used to show the position of something in a set or list: *Look at question number 5.* | *a number 17 bus*
4 [C] a set of numbers used to recognize something: *What's your credit card number?*
5 [C,U] an amount of something that can be

NOZZLE — nozzle — hose/hosepipe BrE

counted: **the number of sth** *an increase in the number of cars on the roads* | **a number of sth** (=several) *We received a number of complaints.* | **a large/small/ significant/growing etc number of sb/sth** *a small number of people affected* | *Young people have been leaving the countryside for the towns* **in large numbers.** | *What sort of numbers* (=how many people) *are you expecting at the party?*
6 [C] a single piece of popular music out of several performed together → **CARDINAL NUMBER, ORDINAL NUMBER, PRIME NUMBER, REGISTRATION NUMBER, SERIAL NUMBER, WHOLE NUMBER**

COLLOCATIONS

adjectives

an even number (=2, 4, 6, 8 etc) *All even numbers can be divided by 2.*
an odd number (=1, 3, 5, 7 etc) *I shouldn't have an odd number of socks!*
a round number (=a number ending in zero) *A hundred is a nice round number.*
a whole number (=a number that is not a fraction) *Your answer should be the nearest whole number.*
a prime number (=a number that can be divided only by itself and 1) *After 7, what is the next prime number?*

verbs

to add numbers up/together *Add the two numbers together.*
to take away/subtract one number from another *Subtract this number from the total.*
to multiply one number by another *If you multiply a number by an even number, the answer is always even.*
to divide one number by another *This number is then divided by 20.*

number² *v* **1** [T] to give a number to something that is part of a set or list: *Number the items from one to ten.* **2** [linking verb] if people or things number a particular amount, that is how many there are: *The crowd numbered around 20,000.*

'**number ,plate** *n* [C] *BrE* the sign on the front and back of a vehicle that shows its official number [SYN] **license plate** *AmE* → see picture at **CAR**

,**Number 'Ten** *n* the official home of the British Prime Minister

numeracy /'nju:mərəsi $ 'nu:-/ *n* [U] the ability to do calculations and understand simple mathematics → **literacy**: *numeracy skills*

numeral /'nju:mərəl $ 'nu:-/ *n* [C] a written sign such as 5 or 22 used to show a number: *Roman numerals* —**numeral** *adj*

numerate /'nju:mərət $ 'nu:-/ *adj* able to understand basic mathematics

numerical /nju:'merɪkəl $ nu:-/ *adj* expressed in numbers, or relating to numbers: **in numerical order** (=numbered 1, 2, 3 etc) *The pages should be in numerical order.* —**numerically** /-kli/ *adv*

numerous /'nju:mərəs $ 'nu:-/ *adj formal* many: *We've discussed this before on* **numerous occasions.**

nun /nʌn/ *n* [C] a member of a group of religious women who live apart from other people in a CONVENT → **monk**

nurse¹ /nɜːs $ nɜːrs/ *n* [C] someone whose job is to look after people who are ill or injured: *a male nurse* | *the school nurse* | *a student nurse* (=someone who is learning to be a nurse)

nurse² *v* **1** [T] to look after someone who is ill or injured **2** [T] to rest when you have an injury so that it will get better: *Blake is nursing an ankle injury.* **3** [I,T] to BREAST-FEED a baby **4** [T] to have an idea or feeling in your mind for a long time: *Tom had always nursed an ambition to be a pilot.*

nursery /'nɜːsəri $ 'nɜːr-/ *n* (*plural* **nurseries**) **1** [C,U] a place where young children are looked after during the day [SYN] **day care center** *AmE* **2** [C] a place where plants and trees are grown and sold

'**nursery rhyme** *n* [C] a short song or poem for children

'**nursery ,school** *n* [C] a school for children between three and five years old

nursing /'nɜːsɪŋ $ 'nɜːr-/ *n* [U] the job of looking after people who are ill, injured, or very old: *the nursing profession*

'**nursing home** *n* [C] a small hospital for people who are too old or ill to take care of themselves

nurture /'nɜːtʃə $ 'nɜːrtʃər/ *v* [T] *formal* **1** to help a plan, feeling etc develop: *We will nurture closer relationships with companies abroad.* **2** to feed and look after a child, plant etc while it is growing: *children nurtured by loving parents*

NUTS

cashews
pistachios
almonds
walnuts
peanuts
chestnuts
coconuts

nut /nʌt/ *n* [C]
1 a large seed that you can eat that usually grows in a hard brown shell: *a cashew nut*
2 a small piece of metal with a hole in the middle that is screwed onto a BOLT to fasten things together
3 *informal* someone who is crazy or behaves strangely
4 golf/opera etc nut *informal* someone who is very interested in golf etc → **fanatic**

nutcracker /'nʌtˌkrækə $ -ər/ n [C] (also **nutcrackers** [plural] BrE) the thing you use for breaking the shells of nuts

nutmeg /'nʌtmeg/ n [U] a sweet brown spice made from the seed of a tropical tree

nutrient /'njuːtriənt $ 'nuː-/ n [C] a chemical or food that helps plants, animals, or people to live and grow: Plants absorb nutrients from the soil. —**nutrient** adj

nutrition /njuːˈtrɪʃən $ nuː-/ n [U] the kind of food you eat and the way it affects your health: Good nutrition is vital. —**nutritional** adj: the nutritional content of foods —**nutritionally** adv

nutritionist /njuːˈtrɪʃənɪst $ nuː-/ n [C] someone who has EXPERT knowledge about nutrition

nutritious /njuːˈtrɪʃəs $ nuː-/ adj food that is nutritious contains the substances that your body needs: a simple but **highly nutritious** meal **THESAURUS** HEALTHY

nuts /nʌts/ adj informal crazy, silly, or angry: I'll go nuts if I have to wait any longer. | That noise is **driving me nuts**. **THESAURUS** CRAZY

nutshell /'nʌtʃel/ n **(to put it) in a nutshell** spoken used when you are explaining only the main facts or details about something: The problem, in a nutshell, was money.

nutter /'nʌtə $ -ər/ n [C] BrE informal a crazy person: That woman's a complete nutter!

nutty /'nʌti/ adj **1** informal crazy **2** tasting like nuts

nuzzle /'nʌzəl/ v [I,T] to gently rub your head or nose against someone to show that you like them: The dog nuzzled its head against her knees.

NW the written abbreviation of **northwest** or **northwestern**

nylon /'naɪlɒn $ -lɑːn/ n [U] a strong artificial material used for making clothes, plastic, rope etc: nylon stockings | a carpet made of 80% wool and 20% nylon

nymph /nɪmf/ n [C] one of the SPIRITS of nature who appears as a young girl in ancient Greek and Roman stories

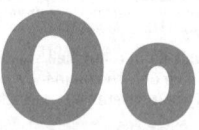

Oo

O, o /əʊ $ oʊ/ n [C,U] (plural **O's**, **o's**) **1** the 15th letter of the English alphabet **2** spoken a zero

oaf /əʊf $ oʊf/ n [C] a man who is stupid or rude

oak /əʊk $ oʊk/ n [C,U] a large tree that is common in northern countries, or the hard wood from this tree

OAP /ˌəʊ eɪ 'piː $ ˌoʊ-/ n [C] BrE an OLD AGE PENSIONER

oar /ɔː $ ɔːr/ n [C] a long pole that is wide at one end, used for rowing a boat

oasis /əʊ'eɪsɪs $ oʊ-/ n [C] (plural **oases** /-siːz/) **1** a place in a desert where there are trees and water **2** somewhere that is more pleasant and peaceful than the area that surrounds it: The park was an oasis of peace.

oath /əʊθ $ oʊθ/ n (plural **oaths** /əʊðz $ oʊðz/) **1** [C] a formal promise: **swear/take an oath** He swore an oath to support the Constitution. **2** [singular, U] law a formal promise to tell the truth in a court of law: **on/under oath** (=having promised to tell the truth) The evidence was given under oath. | Each witness must **take the oath** (=make this promise).

COLLOCATIONS

verbs

to swear/take an oath As children, they took an oath of friendship.
to break an oath (=to do something you promised not to do) I will never break my oath.

oath + nouns

an oath of loyalty/allegiance They swore an oath of allegiance to the king.
an oath of secrecy Anyone who joined the group had to swear an oath of secrecy.

adjectives

a solemn oath (=a very serious oath) He swore a solemn oath never to tell.

Word Choice: oath or vow?
You usually swear or take an oath in a court, or at a public ceremony that is part of a country's official system: The witness has to swear an oath that they will tell the truth. | The president will take the oath of office.
You usually make a **vow** at a religious ceremony: The couple made their wedding vows. You can also make a **vow** to yourself that you will definitely do or not do something in the future: I made a vow that I would never tell anyone.

oatmeal /'əʊtmiːl $ 'oʊt-/ n [U] crushed oats used for making cakes or PORRIDGE

oats /əʊts $ oʊts/ n [plural] a grain that is eaten by people and animals

obedient /ə'biːdiənt/ adj someone who is obedient does what a person, law, or rule tells them to do OPP **disobedient**: a quiet and obedient child —**obedience** n [U]: absolute obedience to the King —**obediently** adv

obese /əʊ'biːs $ oʊ-/ adj much too fat, in a way that is dangerous to your health **THESAURUS** FAT —**obesity** n [U]

obey /əʊ'beɪ, ə- $ oʊ-, ə-/ v [I,T] to do what a person, law, or rule tells you to do OPP **disobey**: Most dogs will obey simple commands. | He refused to obey his father.

THESAURUS

obey to do what a person in authority tells you to do, or what a law or rule says: I obeyed his orders. | The law must be obeyed.
do what sb says to do what someone has suggested or advised you to do: You should do what the doctor said and stay in bed.
do as you are told (also **do what you are told**) to do what your parent or teacher says you must do – used about children: He's a bad boy – he never does what he's told.
follow sb's instructions/orders/advice to do what someone tells you to do, or advises you to do: She followed the instructions on the packet. | I followed your advice and went by train.

obituary /ə'bɪtʃuəri $ -tʃueri/ n [C] (plural **obituaries**) a report of someone's death in a newspaper

object¹ /'ɒbdʒɪkt $ 'ɑːb-/ n
1 [C] a thing that you can see, hold, or touch: a small silver object | an everyday object
2 [singular] the purpose of a plan, activity etc → **aim, goal**: **[+of]** The object of the game is to improve children's skills.
3 an object of desire/pity etc someone or something that you want to have, feel sorry for etc: She was no longer an object of desire for him.
4 [C] in grammar, a noun or phrase that describes the person or thing that is affected by an action → **subject** → **DIRECT OBJECT, INDIRECT OBJECT**

object² /əb'dʒekt/ v [I,T] to say that you do not like or approve of something: If no one objects, I would like to be present. | **[+to]** I objected to having to rewrite the article. **THESAURUS** COMPLAIN —**objector** n [C]

objection /əb'dʒekʃən/ n [C] a reason you have for opposing something: **have no/any objection** I have no objection to her being invited. | **raise/make an objection** (=say you oppose something) I don't think my boss will raise any objections. | **[+to]** He had moral objections to killing animals for food.

objectionable /əb'dʒekʃənəbəl/ adj unpleasant and likely to offend people **SYN offensive**: an objectionable remark

objective¹ [Ac] /əb'dʒektɪv/ n [C] something that you are working hard to achieve: Our main objective is to raise money. **THESAURUS** AIM

objective² Ac adj not influenced by your own feelings or opinions OPP **subjective**: *It's hard to give an objective opinion about your own children.* —**objectively** adv —**objectivity** /ˌɒbdʒekˈtɪvəti $ ˌɑːb-/ n [U]

obligated /ˈɒblɪɡeɪtɪd $ ˈɑːb-/ adj **be/feel obligated to sb** especially AmE to feel that it is your duty to do something for someone

obligation /ˌɒbləˈɡeɪʃən $ ˌɑːb-/ n [C,U] a moral or legal duty to do something: **an obligation to do sth** *Employers have an obligation to provide a safe working environment.* | **be under an/no obligation to do sth** *People entering the shop are under no obligation to buy.*

obligatory /əˈblɪɡətəri $ -tɔːri/ adj formal something that is obligatory has to be done because of a law, rule etc SYN **compulsory** THESAURUS **NECESSARY**

oblige /əˈblaɪdʒ/ v **1** [T] formal if you are obliged to do something, you have to do it because the situation, the law etc makes it necessary: **be obliged to do sth** *Doctors are obliged to keep all medical records secret.* THESAURUS **MUST 2** [I,T] to do something that someone has asked you to do: *Whenever we needed help, Ed was always **happy to oblige**.*

obliged /əˈblaɪdʒd/ adj **1 feel obliged to do sth** to feel that you must do something: *I felt obliged to tell her the truth.* **2 (I'm) much obliged (to you)** spoken old-fashioned used to thank someone very politely

obliging /əˈblaɪdʒɪŋ/ adj always ready to help other people —**obligingly** adv

oblique /əˈbliːk/ adj not said or written in a direct way: *an **oblique reference** to his drinking problem*

obliterate /əˈblɪtəreɪt/ v [T] to destroy something completely: *Large areas of the city were obliterated.* —**obliteration** /əˌblɪtəˈreɪʃən/ n [U]

oblivion /əˈblɪviən/ n [U] **1** when someone or something is completely forgotten: *old movie stars who have faded into oblivion* **2** when someone does not notice what is happening around them: *He drank himself into oblivion.*

oblivious /əˈblɪviəs/ adj not noticing or not knowing about something SYN **unaware**: **[+to/of]** *Max was fast asleep, completely oblivious to the noise outside.*

oblong /ˈɒblɒŋ $ ˈɑːblɔːŋ/ n [C] a shape that has four straight sides, two of which are longer than the other two, and four angles of 90 degrees → **rectangle** —**oblong** adj: *an oblong box*

obnoxious /əbˈnɒkʃəs $ -ˈnɑːk-/ adj extremely unpleasant or rude: *What an obnoxious man!*

oboe /ˈəʊbəʊ $ ˈoʊboʊ/ n [C] a wooden musical instrument like a narrow tube that you play by blowing into it —**oboist** n [C]

obscene /əbˈsiːn/ adj **1** offensive and shocking in a sexual way: **obscene phone calls** | *He made an obscene gesture.* **2** extremely immoral or unfair, in a way that makes you angry: *obscene pay increases* —**obscenely** adv

obscenity /əbˈsenəti/ n (plural **obscenities**) **1** [C usually plural] a sexually offensive word or phrase:

kids shouting obscenities **2** [U] sexually offensive words, pictures, or actions, especially in a book, play etc: *laws against obscenity*

obscure¹ /əbˈskjʊə $ -ˈskjʊr/ adj **1** difficult to understand: *Jarrett didn't like the plan, **for some obscure reason**.* **2** not famous: *an obscure poet*

obscure² v [T] **1** to make something difficult to know or understand: *Recent successes have obscured the fact that the company is still in trouble.* **2** to prevent something from being seen: *The top of the hill was obscured by clouds.*

obscurity /əbˈskjʊərəti $ -ˈskjʊr-/ n [U] when someone is not known or remembered: *O'Brien retired from politics and died in obscurity.*

observance /əbˈzɜːvəns $ -ɜːr-/ n [U] formal when people obey a law, or do something because it is part of a religious custom: **[+of]** *strict observance of religious law*

observant /əbˈzɜːvənt $ -ɜːr-/ adj good at noticing things: *The bomb was spotted by an observant member of the public.*

observation /ˌɒbzəˈveɪʃən $ ˌɑːbzər-/ n **1** [U] when you watch someone or something carefully: **[+of]** *careful observation of the animal's behaviour* | **under observation** (=being watched carefully) *He was **kept under observation** in the hospital.* **2** [C] a spoken or written remark: *I would like to **make an observation** (=say something about what is being discussed).*

observatory /əbˈzɜːvətəri $ əbˈzɜːrvətɔːri/ n [C] (plural **observatories**) a special building from which scientists watch the sky

observe /əbˈzɜːv $ -ɜːrv/ v [T] **1** to watch someone or something carefully: *psychologists observing child behaviour* **2** formal to see or notice something: *I observed the suspect entering the house.* THESAURUS **NOTICE 3** formal to say something: *'We're already late,' Hendry observed.* **4** to obey a law, agreement, or religious custom: *Both sides are observing the ceasefire.*

observer /əbˈzɜːvə $ -ɜːrvər/ n [C] **1** someone who goes to a meeting, class, event etc to officially watch or check what is happening: *a group of UN observers in Bosnia* **2** someone who watches or notices something

obsessed /əbˈsest/ adj if you are obsessed with something, you think about it all the time and cannot think of anything else: **[+with/about]** *William is obsessed with making money.* THESAURUS **INTERESTED**

obsession /əbˈseʃən/ n [C,U] when you are obsessed with something, or the thing you are obsessed with: **[+with]** *an obsession with sex* —**obsessional** adj

obsessive /əbˈsesɪv/ adj thinking about something all the time: **[+about]** *She's obsessive about her weight.* —**obsessively** adv

obsolete /ˈɒbsəliːt $ ˌɑːbsəˈliːt/ adj no longer used or useful, because something newer or better is now available: *Our computer system will soon be obsolete.* THESAURUS **OLD-FASHIONED** —**obsolescence** /ˌɒbsəˈlesəns $ ˌɑːb-/ n [U]

obstacle /ˈɒbstəkəl $ ˈɑːb-/ n [C] **1** something that makes it difficult to do something: **[+to]** *Lack of confidence can be a big obstacle to success.* **2** something that blocks a road, path etc → see picture at **BARRIER**

obstetrician /ˌɒbstəˈtrɪʃən $ ˌɑːb-/ n [C] a doctor who deals with the birth of children

obstinate /ˈɒbstənət $ ˈɑːb-/ adj refusing to change your opinions or behaviour [SYN] **stubborn** —**obstinately** adv —**obstinacy** n [U]

obstruct /əbˈstrʌkt/ v [T] **1** to block a road, path etc: *A van was obstructing traffic.* **2** to try to prevent something from happening by making it difficult: *Maya was charged with obstructing the investigation.* —**obstructive** adj

obstruction /əbˈstrʌkʃən/ n **1** [C,U] when something blocks a road, tube etc, or the thing that blocks it: *The accident caused an obstruction on the freeway.* → see picture at **BARRIER 2** [U] when someone tries to prevent a legal or political process: *obstruction of justice*

obtain Ac /əbˈteɪn/ v [T] formal to get something: *Maps can be obtained at the tourist office.* | **obtain sth from sb/sth** *You will need to obtain permission from the principal.* [THESAURUS] **GET** —**obtainable** adj

> **Word Choice: obtain or get?**
> **Obtain** is more formal than **get**. You use **obtain** especially about something that you have to ask for officially, or try hard to get: *We have managed to obtain a copy of the original document.* | *It is difficult to obtain accurate information.*

obtrusive /əbˈtruːsɪv/ adj disapproving too noticeable [OPP] **unobtrusive**: *obtrusive lighting*

obtuse /əbˈtjuːs $ -ˈtuːs/ adj **1** formal slow to understand something **2** technical an obtuse angle is between 90 and 180 degrees

obvious Ac /ˈɒbviəs $ ˈɑːb-/ adj easy to notice or understand: *an obvious mistake* | **It was obvious that** *Gina was lying.* | **[+to]** *It might be obvious to you but it isn't to me.* | *Thornton seemed **the obvious choice** for the job.* | **The obvious thing to do** (=clearly the best thing to do) *was to ring the school.* | *The mistake was **glaringly** **obvious*** (=extremely obvious). —**obviously** adv: *She obviously didn't want to go.*

occasion /əˈkeɪʒən/ n
1 a) [C] a time when something happens: **on an occasion** *They had met on several occasions.* **b)** [singular] a suitable time or a reason to do something: *Christmas is an occasion to see old friends.*
2 [C] an important event: *We're saving the champagne for a special occasion.*
PHRASES
on occasion(s) sometimes but not often: *She can be very rude on occasion.*

COLLOCATIONS - sense 2
adjectives

a special occasion *The room is only used on special occasions.*

a big/great occasion *The cup final is a big occasion for us.*

a happy/sad occasion *A wedding is supposed to be a happy occasion.*

a formal occasion *Wear something suitable for a formal occasion.*

a social occasion *I prefer not to discuss business at social occasions.*

a historic occasion (=one that is important as part of history) *This is truly a historic occasion.*

verbs

to celebrate an occasion *We celebrated the occasion by going out for a meal.*

occasional /əˈkeɪʒənəl/ adj happening sometimes but not often: *Tomorrow will be warm, with occasional showers.* | **the occasional trip/letter/game etc** (=a few trips, letters etc, not happening or coming regularly) *I still get the occasional letter from him.*

occasionally /əˈkeɪʒənəli/ adv sometimes but not often: *We occasionally meet up for a drink.* | *The birds are seen only **very occasionally*** (=rarely) *in this country now.* [THESAURUS] **SOMETIMES**

occult /ˈɒkʌlt, əˈkʌlt $ əˈkʌlt, ˈɑːkʌlt/ n **the occult** things relating to magic, SPIRITS etc —**occult** adj

occupant Ac /ˈɒkjəpənt $ ˈɑːk-/ n [C] formal someone who lives in a building, room etc, or who is in it

occupation Ac /ˌɒkjəˈpeɪʃən $ ˌɑːk-/ n
1 [C] formal a job or profession: *Please state your name and occupation.* [THESAURUS] **JOB**
2 [U] when an army goes into another country and takes control of it using force: *the occupation of Poland*
3 [C] formal a way of spending your time

occupational Ac /ˌɒkjəˈpeɪʃənəl◂ $ ˌɑːk-/ adj relating to your job: **occupational hazard** (=a risk of a particular job)

occupied /ˈɒkjəpaɪd $ ˈɑːk-/ adj [not before noun] **1** a room, bed, seat etc that is occupied is being used: *All the apartments on the first floor are occupied.* **2** busy doing something: *I brought along some toys to **keep** the kids **occupied**.*

occupier Ac /ˈɒkjəpaɪə $ ˈɑːkjəpaɪər/ n [C] BrE formal someone who lives in or uses a place

occupy Ac /ˈɒkjəpaɪ $ ˈɑːk-/ v [T] (**occupied, occupying, occupies**) **1** to be living, working, or staying in a place: *The seventh floor of the building is occupied by Salem Press.* **2** if something occupies you or your time, you are busy doing it: *Sport occupies most of his spare time.* | **occupy yourself** (=keep busy) *How do you occupy yourself now that you're retired?* **3** to go into a place and take control of it, using military force: *Rebel forces occupied the city.* **4** if something occupies a space, it fills it: *A painting occupied the entire wall.* **5** formal to have a particular job or position: *Few women occupy senior positions.*

occur Ac /əˈkɜː $ əˈkɜːr/ v [I] (**occurred, occurring**) formal to happen or exist, especially in a particular place or situation: *Major earthquakes like this occur very rarely.* | **[+in/among]** *The disease occurs mainly in young children.* [THESAURUS] **HAPPEN**

PHRASAL VERBS

occur to sb to come into someone's mind: *It occurred to me today that no one has told John yet. | Did it never occur to you to phone?*

occurrence Ac /əˈkʌrəns $ əˈkɜː-/ *n* [C] something that happens: *Stress-related illness is now a fairly common occurrence.*

ocean /ˈəʊʃən $ ˈoʊ-/ *n*
1 the ocean the large area of salt water that covers most of the Earth's surface
2 [C] one of the five very large areas of water in the world: *the Indian Ocean* —**oceanic** /ˌəʊʃiˈænɪk◂ $ ˌoʊ-/ *adj*

> **Word Choice: the ocean or the sea?**
> When talking about the water around the coast, American speakers say **the ocean**: *They went for a swim in the ocean.* British speakers usually say **the sea**: *They went for a swim in the sea.*

o'clock /əˈklɒk $ əˈklɑːk/ *adv* **one/two/three etc o'clock** one of the times when the clock shows the exact hour as a number from 1 to 12: **at ... o'clock** *We got up at six o'clock. | 'What time is it?' 'It's almost four o'clock.'*

octagon /ˈɒktəgən $ ˈɑːktəgɑːn/ *n* [C] a flat shape that has eight sides —**octagonal** /ɒkˈtægənəl $ ɑːk-/ *adj*

octave /ˈɒktəv, -teɪv $ ˈɑːk-/ *n* [C] the set of eight musical notes from the first to the last note of a SCALE

October /ɒkˈtəʊbə $ ɑːkˈtoʊbər/ *n* [C,U] (*written abbreviation* **Oct.**) the tenth month of the year, between September and November: **next/last October** *We moved in last October.* | **in October** *His birthday's in October.* | **on October 6th** *We arrived on October 6th.*

octopus /ˈɒktəpəs $ ˈɑːk-/ *n* [C] (*plural* **octopuses** or **octopi**) a sea creature with a soft body and eight TENTACLES (=arms)

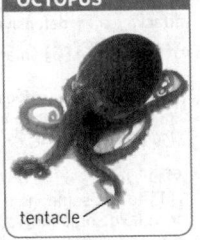

OCTOPUS

tentacle

odd Ac /ɒd $ ɑːd/ *adj*
1 STRANGE strange or different from what you expect: *Jake's an odd guy.* | **The odd thing was that** *he didn't seem to mind.* | *It's odd that she hasn't phoned.* THESAURUS STRANGE
2 NUMBER odd numbers cannot be divided exactly by two OPP **even**
3 A FEW **the odd drink/game/occasion etc** *spoken* a few drinks, games etc, but not happening regularly: *I still enjoy the odd game of tennis.*
4 APPROXIMATELY **20-odd/30-odd etc** *spoken* approximately or a little more than 20, 30 etc: *He must have worked here twenty-odd years.*
5 NOT IN A PAIR [only before noun] separated from its pair or set: *an odd sock*
PHRASES

odd jobs small practical jobs of different kinds: *He's been doing various odd jobs around the house.*

the odd man/one out someone or something that is different from the other people or things in a group: *See if you can spot the odd one out in the list.*

oddity /ˈɒdəti $ ˈɑː-/ *n* [C] (*plural* **oddities**) a strange or unusual person or thing

oddly /ˈɒdli $ ˈɑːdli/ *adv* in a strange or unusual way: *Roger's been behaving very oddly.*
PHRASES

oddly enough used when something seems strange or surprising: *Oddly enough, she didn't seem offended.*

odds Ac /ɒdz $ ɑːdz/ *n* [plural] **1** how likely it is that something will or will not happen: **[+of]** *The odds of winning the lottery are about 14 million to 1.* | **The odds are** (=probably) *you won't need it, but you never know.* **2** difficulties that make a good result seem very unlikely: *He recovered from his injury **against all the odds** (=in spite of it seeming very unlikely).*
PHRASES

at odds (with sb) disagreeing with someone: *Britain was at odds with France on the subject of nuclear testing.*

odds and 'ends *n* [plural] *informal* small things that are not important or valuable

ode /əʊd $ oʊd/ *n* [C] a poem written to or about a person or thing

odour *BrE*, **odor** *AmE* /ˈəʊdə $ ˈoʊdər/ *n* [C] a smell, especially an unpleasant one THESAURUS SMELL

odyssey /ˈɒdəsi $ ˈɑː-/ *n* [C] *literary* a long journey involving a series of experiences

oestrogen *BrE*, **estrogen** *AmE* /ˈiːstrədʒən $ ˈes-/ *n* [U] a chemical substance produced by a woman's body

of /əv, ə; *strong* ɒv $ əv, ə; *strong* ɑːv/ *prep*
1 used to show what or who something belongs to or relates to: *the colour of his eyes | a friend of Sam's | the first part of the story*
2 used when talking about amounts or groups: *two kilos of sugar | a cup of coffee | a herd of elephants*
3 used to show the size or age of something: *a rise of 9% | a child of eight*
4 used in dates: *the 23rd of January, 1998*
5 used to mention a particular thing, after describing it as something: *the city of New Orleans | the problem of unemployment*
6 used to say what something shows: *a photo of Paula's baby*
7 used to show direction: *I live just north of here.*
8 used after nouns describing an action to show who or what the action is done to or who did it: *the testing of river water for chemicals | the arrival of British troops*
9 written, made, produced etc by someone: *the novels of Charles Dickens*
10 used to say when something happened: *the floods of 1997*
11 used to show the cause of someone's death: *She died of cancer.* → **of course** at COURSE¹

off

off /ɒf $ ɒːf/ *adv, adj, prep*
1 away from something: *She waved goodbye as she drove off.* | *Turn off the motorway at junction 11.*
2 not on something, or removed from something: *A button's come off my shirt.* | *Take your coat off.* | *Keep off the grass!*
3 out of a bus, train, plane etc [OPP] **on**: *I'll get off at the next stop.*
4 not working or being used [OPP] **on**: *All the lights were off.* | *Remember to switch the computer off.*
5 not at work or school because you are ill or on holiday: *He's been off work for six weeks.* | *I'm **taking the day off** tomorrow.*
6 used to say how far away something is in distance or time: *Spring is still a long way off.* | *The mountains were far off in the distance.*
7 a) a short distance from a place: *an island off the coast of Florida* | *a hotel just off the main square* **b)** joined to a room, area, building etc: *There's a small bathroom off the main bedroom.*
8 used to talk about a reduction in price: *You get 15% off if you buy $100 worth of groceries.*
9 if an event that was arranged is off, it will not now happen [OPP] **on**: *The wedding's off!*
10 be off to have started a journey: *At last, we're off!*
11 *especially BrE* food or drink that is off is no longer fresh → **rotten, sour**: *This milk smells off.*
12 not correct: *His calculations are off by 20%.* → **BETTER OFF**

PHRASES
> **have an off day** *spoken* to have a day when you are not doing something as well as you usually do: *Every player has an off day occasionally.*
> **off and on/on and off** for short periods of time, but not regularly: *I worked as a secretary off and on for three years.*

offal /ˈɒfəl $ ˈɒː-, ˈɑː-/ *n* [U] the KIDNEYS, LIVER etc of an animal, used as food

offbeat /ˌɒfˈbiːt◂ $ ˌɒːf-/ *adj informal* unusual, especially in an interesting way: *offbeat humour*

off-'centre *BrE,* **off-center** *AmE adv, adj* not exactly in the centre of something

'off-chance *n* **on the off-chance** if you do something on the off-chance, you do it hoping that something will happen, although it is unlikely: **[+(that)]** *He only went to the party on the off-chance that Pippa might be there.*

off-'colour *adj* [not before noun] *BrE* slightly ill [THESAURUS] **ILL**

offence *BrE,* **offense** *AmE* /əˈfens/ *n*
1 [C] a crime: *Possession of stolen goods is a criminal offence.* | *If you lie to the police, you are committing an offence.*
2 [U] when you upset or offend someone by something you say or do: **cause/give offence** *The problem was how to say no without causing offence.* | *A lot of women **took offence** (=felt offended) at Rawling's speech.* | **no offence (meant)** *spoken* (=used to tell someone that you hope what you are going to say will not upset them) *No offence, John, but I'd rather get a professional opinion.*

verbs
to commit an offence *She did not realize she was committing an offence.*
to charge sb with an offence *He was arrested, but not charged with any offence.*
to be convicted of an offence (=to have a court decide you are guilty of committing it) *Have you ever been convicted of a driving offence?*

types of offence
a criminal offence *It is a criminal offence to help someone to commit suicide.*
a serious offence *Using someone else's credit card is a serious offence.*
a minor offence (=not serious) *Most of the arrests were for minor offences.*
a traffic/drug etc offence *In his youth he was convicted of drug offences.*

offend /əˈfend/ *v*
1 [T] to make someone angry or upset, by doing or saying something that they think is rude, unkind, or unacceptable: *I'm sorry, I didn't mean to offend you.* | *Anna was **deeply offended** by such a personal question.* → see Word Choice at **INSULT**
2 [I] *formal* to commit a crime

offender /əˈfendə $ -ər/ *n* [C] someone who has committed a crime: *an institution for **young offenders***

offense[1] /əˈfens/ *n* the American spelling of OFFENCE

offense[2] /əˈfens $ ˈɒːfens, ˈɑː-/ *n* [C,U] *AmE* the players in a game such as football who try to get points [OPP] **defense**

offensive[1] /əˈfensɪv/ *adj* **1** likely to upset or offend people [OPP] **inoffensive**: *Some people **found** the song **offensive**.* [THESAURUS] **RUDE 2** used or intended for attacking [OPP] **defensive**: *an offensive weapon*

offensive[2] *n* [C] an attack on a place by an army
PHRASES
> **be/go on the offensive** to attack or criticize people: *Republicans went on the offensive over soaring gasoline prices.*

offer[1] /ˈɒfə $ ˈɒːfər, ˈɑː-/ *v*
1 [T] to ask someone if they would like something, or to hold something out for them to take: **offer sb sth** *Can I offer you a drink?* | **offer sth to sb** *Simon lit a cigarette and then offered one to Ben.*
2 [I,T] to say that you are willing to do something: **offer to do sth** *Carol didn't even offer to help.*

> **Grammar**
> Do not say 'She offered me to drive to the station.' Say *She offered to drive me to the station.*

3 [T] to provide something that people want or need: *We offer a wide range of services.* | **offer advice/help/support etc** *Your doctor should be able to offer you advice on diet.*
4 [T] to say that you will pay a particular amount of money for something: **offer sb sth** *They've offered us £170,000 for the house.*

offer² n [C]
1 when you say that you will give something to someone or do something for them: **[+of]** *Thanks for your offer of help.*
2 an amount of money that someone says they will pay for something: *He made me an offer of $50 for the bike.*
3 when something is sold at a lower price than usual → **discount**: *Don't miss our special offer – two videos for the price of one.*

PHRASES
on offer *BrE* **1** available to buy, use, or do: *Activities on offer include windsurfing and water-skiing.* **2** being sold at a price that is lower than usual: *Beef is on offer this week.*

COLLOCATIONS

verbs
to make an offer *They made me a job offer.*
to get/receive an offer *She was hoping to get an offer of a place at university.*
to accept an offer *Are you going to accept their offer?*
to refuse/reject an offer (*also* **to turn down an offer**) *He refused Larry's offer of coffee.*

types of offer
a job offer *He's had a number of job offers.*
a kind/generous offer *Thank you very much for your kind offer.*

offering /ˈɒfərɪŋ $ ˈɒː-, ˈɑː-/ n [C] something that you give to someone, especially to God

offhand¹ /ˌɒfˈhænd◂ $ ˌɒːf-/ adj seeming not friendly or interested: *an offhand voice*

offhand² adv immediately, without time to think: *I can't tell you offhand – I'll have to check.*

office /ˈɒfɪs $ ˈɒː-, ˈɑː-/ n
1 [C] a building that belongs to an organization, where people work: *Are you going to the office today?* | **main/head office** (=most important office) | **office worker**
2 [C] a room where you work that has a desk, telephone etc: *the manager's office*
3 [C,U] an important job or position: **in office** *The president died after only fifteen months in office.* | *Watson held office* (=had an important job) *as finance minister.* → **BOOKING OFFICE, BOX OFFICE, POST OFFICE, REGISTER OFFICE, REGISTRY OFFICE**

PHRASES
office hours the time between about 9.00 in the morning and 5.00 in the afternoon, when people in offices are working: *He can be contacted during normal office hours.*

officer /ˈɒfəsə $ ˈɒːfəsər, ˈɑː-/ n [C]
1 someone who has a position of authority in the army, navy etc: **army/naval/military officer**
2 someone who has a position of authority in an organization: *a local government officer*
3 a policeman or policewoman **SYN** **police officer**
→ **COMMANDING OFFICER, PROBATION OFFICER**

official¹ /əˈfɪʃəl/ adj
1 approved of or done by someone in authority,

especially the government: *an official inquiry into the plane crash* | *You will have to get official permission.*
2 relating to a position of authority: *Her official title is Public Safety Adviser.* | *The President began a four-day official visit to France.*
3 official reasons, information etc are what people are told, although they may not be true: *The official reason for his resignation was ill health.*

official² n [C] someone who has a position of authority in an organization, especially a government: *US Administration officials*

officially /əˈfɪʃəli/ adv
1 in an official or formal way: *The new bridge was officially opened this morning.*
2 according to the reason or information that has been given, which may not be true: *The meeting was cancelled, officially because of bad weather.*

officiate /əˈfɪʃieɪt/ v [I] *formal* to do official duties at a ceremony or important event

officious /əˈfɪʃəs/ adj *disapproving* too eager to tell people what to do: *officious bureaucrats*

offing /ˈɒfɪŋ $ ˈɒː-, ˈɑː-/ n **be in the offing** to be going to happen soon: *Big changes are in the offing.*

off-ˌkey adj sung or played slightly too high or too low → **in tune** —**off-key** adv: *He sang off-key.*

ˈoff-ˌlicence n [C] *BrE* a shop that sells alcohol **SYN** **liquor store** *AmE*

offline, off-line /ˌɒfˈlaɪn $ ˌɒːf-/ adj, adv if your computer is offline, it is not connected to the Internet **OPP** **online**: *I work offline most of the day.*

offload /ˌɒfˈləʊd $ ˌɒːfˈloʊd/ v [T] to get rid of something that you do not want by giving it or selling it to someone else: *He tried to offload some of his work onto me.*

ˌoff-ˈmessage adj if a politician is off-message, he or she says things that do not follow the ideas of their political party → **on-message**

ˌoff-ˈpeak adj, adv *BrE* off-peak travel, electricity etc is cheaper because it is done or used at less busy times: *off-peak rail services*

ˈoff-ˌputting adj *BrE* if a feature of something is off-putting, it makes you not want to do or have it: *I found the style of the book very off-putting.*

ˈoff-ramp n [C] *AmE* a road for driving off a HIGH-WAY or FREEWAY **SYN** **slip road** *BrE* **OPP** **on-ramp**

offset **Ac** /ˈɒfset, ˌɒfˈset $ ˈɒːfset, ˌɒːfˈset/ v [T] (*past tense and past participle* **offset**, *present participle* **offsetting**) if one thing offsets another, it has an opposite effect so that the final result is less expensive, less noticeable etc: *The cost of the flight was offset by the cheapness of the hotel.*

offshoot /ˈɒfʃuːt $ ˈɒːf-/ n [C] something that has developed from something bigger: *The company was an offshoot of Bell Telephones.*

offshore /ˌɒfˈʃɔː $ ˌɒːfˈʃɔːr◂/ adj **1** in the sea, not far from the coast: *America's offshore oil reserves*
2 offshore **bank/account/company** a bank, bank account etc that is not in your home country but in another country where you pay less tax: *He keeps his money in an offshore bank.*

offside /ˌɒfˈsaɪd◂ $ ˌɔːf-/ *adj, adv* in a position in FOOTBALL or HOCKEY where you are not allowed to touch the ball

offspring /ˈɒfˌsprɪŋ $ ˈɔːf-/ *n* [C] (*plural* **offspring**) someone's child

offstage /ˌɒfˈsteɪdʒ◂ $ ˈɔːf-/ *adj, adv* just behind or at the side of a stage in a theatre: *There was a loud crash offstage.*

ˌoff-the-ˈcuff *adj* an off-the-cuff remark or comment is one that you make without thinking about it first

ˌoff-the-ˈwall *adj informal* very strange

ˌoff-ˈwhite *adj* greyish-white or yellowish-white

often /ˈɒfən, ˈɒftən $ ˈɔːf-/ *adv*
1 many times or regularly: *I often work at the weekend.* | *We should go out more often.* | *How often do you see your parents?* | *She's quite often late for school.* | *This kind of accident happens all too often.*
2 in many situations or at many times: *Headaches are often caused by stress.*
PHRASES

> **every so often** sometimes but not very frequently: *I see him every so often.*
> **not very often** used when saying that something happens rarely: *It's not very often that he visits us.*
> **THESAURUS** ▶ RARELY

> **Grammar**
> You usually use **often** before a verb: *He often gets home late.*
> You use **often** after the verb **to be**: *The trains are often crowded.*
> If there are two or more verbs, **often** comes after the first one: *I don't often watch TV.*

THESAURUS

often many times or regularly: *The weather's often rainy at this time of year.* | *We often meet for a drink after work.*
a lot often – used especially in informal English: *I think she likes him – she talks about him a lot.*
frequently often – used especially in more formal English: *Passengers complain that trains are frequently late.*
regularly often and at regular times: *Buses run regularly every ten minutes.*
again and again used to emphasize that someone does something many times, or the same thing happens many times: *I've tried phoning again and again but there's no answer.* | *This washing machine has gone wrong again and again.*
repeatedly used to emphasize that someone does something many times. **Repeatedly** sounds more formal than **again and again**: *His doctor repeatedly told him to take more exercise.*
constantly very often, especially when this is annoying or causes problems: *I'm constantly being asked that question.*

ogle /ˈəʊɡəl $ ˈoʊ-/ *v* [I,T] to look at someone in a way that shows you think they are sexually attractive

ogre /ˈəʊɡə $ ˈoʊɡər/ *n* [C] **1** someone who is cruel and frightening **2** a large ugly man in children's stories

oh /əʊ $ oʊ/ *spoken* **1** used before saying something or replying to a question: *Oh, hello.* | *'What time did he leave?' 'Oh, about ten.'* **2** used to express a strong emotion or to emphasize your opinion: *Oh, how annoying!* | *Oh good, Ted's here.*

ohm /əʊm $ oʊm/ *n* [C] a unit for measuring electrical RESISTANCE

oil¹ /ɔɪl/ *n* [U]
1 a thick dark liquid from under the ground, used to make petrol: *the price of oil* | *oil companies*
2 a thick liquid used to make the parts of machines move more easily: *engine oil*
3 a liquid that comes from plants or animals, used especially in cooking: *cooking oil* | *vegetable/olive/sunflower oil* *tuna in olive oil* → CRUDE OIL, ESSENTIAL OIL

oil² *v* [T] to put oil onto something

oilfield /ˈɔɪlfiːld/ *n* [C] an area of land or sea under which there is oil

ˈoil ˌpainting *n* [C] a picture painted with paint that contains oil

OIL RIG

ˈoil rig *n* [C] a large structure with equipment for getting oil out of the ground

ˈoil slick *n* [C] a large area of oil floating on the sea or a river

ˈoil well *n* [C] a deep hole made to get oil out of the ground

oily /ˈɔɪli/ *adj* **1** covered with oil, or containing a lot of oil: *oily fish* **2** similar to oil: *an oily substance*

ointment /ˈɔɪntmənt/ *n* [C,U] a substance that you rub into your skin as a medical treatment

OK¹, okay /ˌəʊ ˈkeɪ $ ˌoʊ-/ *spoken*
1 used to say that you agree, or to ask someone if they agree: *'Can I borrow your bike?' 'Okay.'* | *We have to leave early, OK?*
2 used when you start talking, or continue to talk after a pause: *OK, any questions?*

OK², okay *adj spoken*
1 if you are OK, you are not ill, injured, or sad **SYN** **all right**: *Is everybody OK? | Do you feel OK now?*
2 something that is OK is acceptable: *Does my hair look OK? | 'Sorry I'm late.' 'That's OK.' | Is it OK if Lisa comes?*

3 not bad, but not very good: *'Was the food good?' 'It was OK.'* THESAURUS> SATISFACTORY —**OK** *adv*: *Is your computer working OK?*

OK³, **okay** *v* [T] (**OK'd**, **OK'ing**, **OK's**) *informal* to agree to allow something to happen: *His parents okayed the plan.*

OK⁴, **okay** *n* **give/get the OK** *informal* to give or get permission to do something

old /əʊld $ oʊld/ *adj*
1 a) someone or something that is old has lived or existed for a long time OPP young, new: *an old man* | *Her car is really old.* | *Wear old clothes for exercising.* | *one of the oldest houses in the village* **b) the old** old people
2 used to talk about the age of someone or something: **be 3/50/300 etc years old** *Our dog is three years old.* | **How old** are you? | *My sister is older than me.* | **ten-year-old/six-week-old etc** *a ten-year-old boy*
3 [only before noun] your old house, job, car etc is one that you had before but do not have now SYN former: *one of her old boyfriends* THESAURUS> PREVIOUS
4 [only before noun] old things are familiar because you have experienced or heard them many times before: *He always gives the same old excuse.*
5 old friend/enemy/colleague etc someone who has been your friend, enemy etc for a long time: *He's an old friend of my father's.*
6 good/poor/silly etc old *spoken* used to talk about someone you like: *Good old Liz! She's so smart.*
PHRASES
any old thing/place/way etc *spoken* used to say that it does not matter which thing, place etc you choose: *Do it any old way you like.*
old hat not new or interesting: *The movie's special effects now seem old hat.*
the old days times in the past: *Things were much better in the old days.*

THESAURUS
person
old someone who is old has lived for a long time: *an old man*
elderly a polite word for old: *An elderly lady got on the bus.*
aging (*also* **ageing** *BrE*) becoming old: *the problems of an ageing population* | *his aging parents*
elder brother/sister *especially BrE* a brother or sister who is older than you. **Elder** sounds more formal than **older**: *His elder brother worked in a bank.*
be getting on (in years) *informal* to be quite old: *He's 54 now, so he's getting on.*
thing
old something that is old has existed for a long time: *The house is very old.* | *an old proverb*
ancient very old – used about things that existed thousands of years ago, or things that look very old: *ancient civilisations* | *an ancient Rolls Royce*
antique antique furniture, clocks, jewellery etc are old and often valuable: *an antique ring*

old 'age *n* [U] the time in your life when you are old

old age 'pensioner *n* [C] *BrE* (*abbreviation* **OAP**) an old person who does not work any more and receives a PENSION (=money from a company or from the government)

olden /'əʊldən $ 'oʊld-/ *adj* **in the olden days/in olden times** a long time ago

old-'fashioned *adj* not modern or fashionable any more: *old-fashioned ideas about women* | *All her clothes look old-fashioned.*

THESAURUS
old-fashioned not modern or fashionable any more: *Their music sounds rather old-fashioned.* | *an old-fashioned sewing machine*
out-of-date out-of-date books, maps etc do not contain the most recent information and are not useful: *Our map was completely out-of-date.*
outdated outdated machines, equipment, or methods are not modern and need to be changed: *outdated farming methods* | *They still use outdated technology.*
dated something that is dated has a style that was fashionable until recently, but now seems old-fashioned: *The hotel now looks rather dated.* | *His films seem rather dated these days.*
obsolete machines, equipment, and technology that are obsolete have been replaced by much better ones: *These days, you buy a computer and it's almost immediately obsolete.*

old 'flame *n* [C] *informal* someone who was your boyfriend or girlfriend in the past

oldie /'əʊldi $ 'oʊldi/ *n* [C] *informal* an old thing or person, especially a song or film

old 'man *BrE spoken informal* **1** your husband **2** your father

Old 'Testament *n* **the Old Testament** the part of the Bible that is about the time before the birth of Christ → **New Testament**

old-time *adj* [only before noun] of the sort that used to exist or be done in the past: *old-time remedies*

old 'wives' tale *n* [C] an old belief that is now considered to be untrue

Old 'World *n* **the Old World** Europe, Asia, and Africa

olive /'ɒlɪv $ 'ɑː-/ *n* **1** [C] a small black or green fruit, used as food or for making oil: *olive oil* **2** (*also* **olive green**) [U] a pale green colour —**olive** *adj*

Olympic Games /ə,lɪmpɪk 'ɡeɪmz/ (*also* **Olympics**) *n* **the Olympic Games/the Olympics** an international sports event held every four years —**Olympic** *adj*

ombudsman /'ɒmbʊdzmən $ 'ɑːm-/ *n* [C] (*plural* **ombudsmen**) someone who deals with complaints made by ordinary people against companies, newspapers, the government etc

omelette *BrE*, **omelet** *AmE* /'ɒmlət $ 'ɑːm-/ *n* [C] eggs mixed together and cooked in hot fat: *a cheese omelette*

omen /'əʊmən $ 'oʊ-/ *n* [C] a sign of what will happen in the future: **a good/bad omen**

ominous /'ɒmɪnəs $ 'ɑː-/ *adj* making you feel that something bad is going to happen: *ominous black clouds* —**ominously** *adv*

omission /əʊ'mɪʃən, ə- $ oʊ-, ə-/ *n* [C,U] when something is not included or not done: *the omission of his name from the report*

omit /əʊ'mɪt, ə- $ oʊ-, ə-/ *v* [T] (**omitted**, **omitting**) **1** to not include something $\boxed{\text{SYN}}$ **leave out**: *Important details had been omitted.* **2 omit to do sth** *formal* to not do something: *She omitted to tell me she was married.*

omnipotent /ɒm'nɪpətənt $ ɑːm-/ *adj formal* powerful enough to be able to do anything —**omnipotence** *n* [U]

on¹ /ɒn $ ɑːn, ɒːn/ *prep*
1 touching something or being supported by something: *She sat on the bed.* | *the picture on the wall* | *You've got mud on your face.* → see picture on page A8
2 in a place or position: *Henry grew up on a farm.* | *a restaurant on Main Street* | **on the left/right** *That's Jill on the left.*
3 written, shown, or broadcast somewhere: *the picture on page 25* | **on television/TV/the radio** *Is there anything good on TV?*
4 during a particular day: *See you on Monday.* | *I was born on June 15th.*
5 using a machine, instrument, or piece of equipment: *Did you do this on a computer?* | *Anna's* **on the phone**. | **on the piano/violin etc** *Play me something on the piano.*
6 about a subject: *a book on China* | *information on hotels* $\boxed{\text{THESAURUS}}$ **ABOUT**
7 used to say that a person or thing is affected by something: *a tax on cigarettes*
8 travelling using something: **on a bus/plane/train/boat** *I came on the bus.* | **on a bike/horse** *He likes riding around on his bike.*
9 used for saying how information is stored or recorded: **on disk/tape/video/DVD** *Keep a back-up copy on disk.*
10 receiving money for a job or as a regular payment: *He's on quite a good salary now.* $\boxed{\text{THESAURUS}}$ **EARN**
11 taking a medicine or drugs: *She's on antibiotics.*
12 during a trip, holiday etc: *They met on a trip to Spain.*
13 included in a group or a list: *You're on my team.*
14 immediately after something happens: *Go to the reception desk on arrival.*
15 have sth on you to have something with you now: *Do you have a pen on you?*
16 sth is on me/us etc used to say that you will pay for someone's meal, drinks etc: *The drinks are on me.* $\boxed{\text{THESAURUS}}$ **PAY**

on² *adj, adv*
1 used to say that someone continues to do something, or that something continues to happen: *The meeting went on for hours.* | *Let's drive on a little further.* | *He talked* **on and on** *about his job.*
2 if a machine is on, it is operating or working $\boxed{\text{OPP}}$ **off**: *The lights are still on in her office.* | *How do you switch the computer on?*
3 if you have a piece of clothing on, you are wearing it: *Put your coat on – it's cold.*
4 into a bus, plane, train, or ship: *I got on at Vine Street.*
5 attached to something: *Put the lid on properly.* | *a box with a label on*
6 being broadcast or shown: *The news will be on in a minute.* | *What's on at the cinema?*
7 if an event is on, it has been planned and is happening: *There's a festival on this weekend.* → **off** **and on/on and off** at **OFF**

PHRASES
from then on/from that day on after that time into the future: *From that day on, they were friends.*
have sth on *informal* to have something that you must do: *I've got a lot on at the moment.*

once¹ /wʌns/ *adv*
1 one time: *We only met once.* | *I've been here* **once before**. | **once a week/year etc** (=one time every week, year etc) *She goes to the gym once a week.*
2 in the past, but not now: *They were once close friends.*

PHRASES
all at once *literary* suddenly: *All at once, there was a loud bang.*
at once 1 at the same time: *I can't do two things at once!* **2** immediately: *I recognised him at once.* $\boxed{\text{THESAURUS}}$ **IMMEDIATELY**
for once *spoken* used to say that something should happen more often: *Will you listen for once?*
once again/more 1 again, after happening several times before: *He asked the question once more.* **2** used to say that a situation returns to a previous state: *Everything was peaceful once again.*
once and for all definitely and finally: *Let's settle this once and for all.*
once in a blue moon very rarely: *She only sees him once in a blue moon.*
(every) once in a while sometimes, but not often: *I see my ex-boyfriend every once in a while.* $\boxed{\text{THESAURUS}}$ **SOMETIMES**
once upon a time a long time ago – used in children's stories: *Once upon a time, there was a princess.*

once² *linking word* from the time something happens: *Once she started crying, she couldn't stop.*

oncoming /'ɒnkʌmɪŋ $ 'ɑːn-, 'ɒːn-/ *adj* oncoming cars are coming towards you

one¹ /wʌn/ *number* the number 1: *They have one child.* | *one hundred and twenty-one pounds* | *Come back at one* (=one o'clock). | *Katie's about one* (=one year old).

PHRASES
one or two a small number of people or things: *We've made one or two changes.*

one² *pron* (*plural* **ones**)
1 used when you are talking about someone or something of the kind that has already been mentioned: *'Do you have a DVD player?' 'No, but I'm*

getting one.' | He ate his sandwich and took **another one**. | That winter was **a cold one**.

2 used to talk about a particular person or thing from a group: He has two sisters. One is a doctor. | I'm **the one** on the left of the picture. | **[+of]** One of my CDs is missing. | **this/that one** I like that one best.

3 formal used to mean people in general, including yourself: One never knows what may happen. → **NO ONE**

PHRASES

(all) in one if something is several different things all in one, it is all of those things: a garage and workshop in one

one after the other (also **one after another**) happening without much time in between: He scored three goals, one after another.

one by one if people do something one by one, first one person does it, then the next etc: One by one, people sat down.

one³ determiner, adj

1 used to emphasize a particular person or thing: One person she really likes is Kim. | I know **one thing** for sure – he's lying.

2 one day/morning etc a) on a particular day etc in the past: I saw him one day in town. **b)** at some time in the future: Let's go out one evening.

3 only: Our one worry is it's very expensive.

PHRASES

for one thing spoken used when giving a reason: You can't go. You're not old enough, for one thing.

,one an'other pron each other: They shook hands with one another.

,one-'liner n [C] a very short joke or funny remark

'one-man adj [only before noun] performed or controlled by one person: a one-man show

,one-night 'stand n [C] informal an occasion when two people have sex, but do not meet again

,one-'off adj [only before noun] happening only once: a one-off payment —**one-off** n [C]

onerous /'ɒnərəs, 'əʊ- $ 'ɑː-, 'oʊ-/ adj formal difficult and tiring: onerous duties

oneself /wʌn'self/ pron formal the REFLEXIVE form of 'one', used when you are talking about people in general, including yourself

,one-'sided adj **1** disapproving considering or showing only one opinion in an argument, in a way that is unfair: a one-sided view of the problem **2** a one-sided competition is not equal because one team is much stronger

'one-time adj [only before noun] former: the one-time captain of the US team

,one-to-'one (also one-on-one) adj between only two people: tuition on a one-to-one basis

,one-track 'mind n [C] if you have a one-track mind, you are always thinking about one thing, especially sex

one-upmanship /wʌn'ʌpmənʃɪp/ n [U] attempts to make yourself seem better than other people

,one-'way adj **1** a one-way street is one on which cars can travel in only one direction **2** a one-way

ticket is for travelling to a place, but not for coming back SYN single BrE OPP **return, round trip**

'one-woman adj [only before noun] performed by one woman: a one-woman show

ongoing Ac /'ɒnˌɡəʊɪŋ $ 'ɑːnˌɡoʊɪŋ, 'ɔːn-/ adj continuing to happen: ongoing discussions

onion /'ʌnjən/ n [C,U] a round white vegetable, usually with brown skin, which has a strong smell and taste: Chop the onions finely. | onion soup → see picture on page A5 → **SPRING ONION**

online, on-line /,ɒn'laɪn $,ɑːn-, ,ɔːn-/ adj, adv connected to or using a computer or network of computers OPP **offline**: online banking facilities (=available using the Internet) | Our school **went online** (=started to be online) this year.

onlooker /'ɒnˌlʊkə $ 'ɑːn-, 'ɔːn-/ n [C] someone who watches something happening without being involved in it

only¹ /'əʊnli $ 'oʊn-/ adv

1 not more than a particular amount, number etc: Tina left home when she was only 16. | He only has one pair of shoes. | It took only a few minutes.

2 not anyone or anything else: Only you know the truth. | Parking is for customers only. | We can **only hope** (=all we can do is hope) she never finds out.

3 not in any other situation, or not for any other reason: You can only get to the beach by boat. | You can come, but **only if** you don't interfere. | I **only** invited him **because** I felt sorry for him.

4 used to say that someone or something is not important: It's only a piece of paper.

5 used to say that something happened very recently: **only last week/last year/yesterday** I saw him only yesterday and he looked fine.

PHRASES

if only used to say that you wish something was true: If only I'd brought my camera. | If only she would listen!

not only ... (but) used to say that one thing is true, and another thing is also true: He's not only great-looking, he's also a nice guy.

only just 1 a very short time ago: They only just left. **2** almost not SYN **barely**: I only just finished in time.

only too very: She was only too glad to help.

only² adj used to say that there are no other people or things of the same kind: She's the only girl in the class. | I was **the only one** who disagreed.

PHRASES

an only child a child with no brothers or sisters: My husband had been an only child.

the only thing is ... spoken used when you are going to mention a problem: I'd like to come – the only thing is I've got a lot of homework.

only³ linking word used to mean 'but' when you are giving the reason why something did not or will not happen: I would help you, only I'm too busy.

,on-'message adj if a politician is on-message, he or she says things that agree with the ideas of their political party → **off-message**

,on-'off adj [only before noun] happening sometimes and not at other times: an on-off romantic relationship

on-ramp

'on-ramp n [C] AmE a road for driving onto a HIGHWAY or FREEWAY SYN **slip road** BrE OPP **off-ramp**

'on-screen adj shown on a computer screen, or on a television or cinema screen: Click 'Yes', then follow the on-screen instructions.

onset /'ɒnset $ 'ɑːn-, 'ɔːn-/ n **the onset of sth** the beginning of something: the onset of winter

onslaught /'ɒnslɔːt $ 'ɑːnslɔːt, 'ɔːn-/ n [C] a very strong attack or criticism

onto /'ɒntə; before vowels 'ɒntu; strong 'ɒntuː $ 'ɑːn-, 'ɔːn-/ prep used to say that someone or something moves to a position on a surface: The cat jumped onto the table. | **get onto a bus/plane/train** (=get into it) Two girls got onto the bus.
PHRASES
be onto sb informal to know who did something wrong or illegal: The police are onto him.
be onto sth informal to have discovered or produced something important or interesting: He seems to be onto something with his latest ideas.

onus /'əʊnəs $ 'oʊ-/ n **the onus is on sb to do sth** it is someone's responsibility to do something: The onus is on you to check the equipment is safe.

onward /'ɒnwəd $ 'ɑːnwərd, 'ɔːn-/ adj [only before noun] moving forward or continuing: the onward journey

onwards /'ɒnwədz $ 'ɑːnwərdz, 'ɔːn-/ especially BrE, **onward** especially AmE adv **from ... onwards** starting at a particular time and continuing: The cafeteria is open from 8.30 onwards.

oops /ʊps/ spoken used when you have made a small mistake, dropped something etc: Oops, sorry about that!

ooze /uːz/ v **1** [I,T] to flow slowly from somewhere: Blood oozed from the wound. **2** [T] informal to show a lot of a particular quality: He oozes charm.

opal /'əʊpəl $ 'oʊ-/ n [C,U] a white stone used in jewellery

opaque /əʊ'peɪk $ oʊ-/ adj **1** difficult or impossible to see through OPP **transparent**: opaque glass **2** formal hard to understand

open¹ /'əʊpən $ 'oʊ-/ adj
1 NOT CLOSED if something is open, it has been moved so that there is a space between different parts of it OPP **closed, shut**: Come in – the door's open. | I could barely keep my eyes open. | A book lay **open** on the table. | All the windows were **wide open**. | His shirt was **open** at the neck.
2 BUSINESS/BUILDING ready for business and allowing customers, visitors etc to enter OPP **closed**: We're open until six. | When will the new library be open? | The firm will be **open for business** next week.
3 AVAILABLE FOR ANYONE available for anyone to do or take part in: **[+to]** Few jobs were open to women in those days. | an open competition
4 NOT SURROUNDED not surrounded by buildings, walls etc: the open countryside
5 NOT COVERED not covered: an open fire
6 HONEST honest and not keeping anything secret → **openly, openness**: We try to be open with each other.

7 NOT HIDDEN open hostility/impatience/curiosity etc hostility, impatience etc that is not hidden or secret: open hostility between the two nations
PHRASES
in the open air outside: The concert will take place in the open air. THESAURUS OUTSIDE
keep/have an open mind (about/on sth) to not decide about something until you have found out more: I'm trying to keep an open mind about her suggestion.
keep your eyes/ears open spoken to keep looking or listening carefully so that you notice anything that may be important: Keep your eyes open for mushrooms.
be open to doubt/question/criticism etc used when saying that something can be doubted, questioned, criticized etc: His analysis is open to question.
be open to suggestions/comments etc to be willing to consider or accept something new: The committee is open to suggestions.
welcome/greet sb/sth with open arms to be very pleased to see someone or something: They welcomed us with open arms.

open² v
1 DOOR/WINDOW/EYES ETC [I,T] to become open, or to make something open OPP **shut**: The doors open automatically. | Can you open the window? | She opened her eyes. | Louise opened a bottle of wine.
2 SHOP/BANK ETC [I] if a shop, bank etc opens at a particular time, people can use it after that time: What time does the bookstore open on Sundays?
3 FILM/PLAY/PUBLIC BUILDING ETC [I,T] if a film, play, public building etc opens, or if it is opened, people can start to see it or use it: A new play opens next week on Broadway. | The restaurant first opened in 1986. | Parts of the White House will be opened to the public. THESAURUS START
4 SPREAD OUT [I,T] to spread something out, or to become spread out: I can't open my umbrella. | The flowers are starting to open.
5 COMPUTER PROGRAM [T] to make a computer program ready to use: I can't open the file.
6 BANK ACCOUNT [T] if you open a bank account, you arrange for it to start: Why don't you open a new account?
PHRASES
open fire (on sb/sth) to start shooting at someone or something: Troops opened fire on the protesters. THESAURUS SHOOT

PHRASAL VERBS
open into/onto sth to lead directly into a place: The kitchen opens onto the back yard.
open up
1 to become available or possible, or to make something available or possible: New business opportunities are opening up all the time. | **open sth ↔ up** They decided to open up their home to young people.
2 to stop being shy and say what you really think: It takes a long time for him to open up.

THESAURUS

open to make something open – used about a door, window, container etc, or about your eyes or mouth: *I opened the door slowly.* | *Open your eyes!*

unlock to open a door, drawer etc with a key: *She unlocked the car door and got in.*

unscrew to open a lid on a bottle, container etc by turning it: *Can you unscrew this lid for me?*

unwrap to open a package by removing the paper that covers it: *The children began unwrapping their Christmas presents.*

unfasten/undo to make a belt, button, piece of clothing etc open instead of fastened or tied: *He unfastened his jacket.* | *Don't undo your seat belt till the plane stops.*

open[3] *n* **out in the open a)** outdoors: *It's fun to eat out in the open.* **b)** not hidden or secret: *The truth is finally out in the open.*

,open-'air *adj* not inside a building: *open-air concerts*

'open day *n* [C] *BrE* a day when people can visit a school, company etc and see what is done there **SYN** **open house** *AmE*

,open-'ended *adj* without a fixed ending time: *an open-ended contract*

OPENERS

bottle opener

can opener/ tin opener *BrE*

cork

corkscrew

---

opener /'əʊpənə $ 'oʊpənər/ *n* [C] **can/tin/bottle opener** something you use to open cans or bottles

,open-heart 'surgery *n* [U] when doctors cut open someone's chest to do an operation on their heart

,open 'house *n* [C] *AmE* a day when people can visit a school, company etc and see what is done there **SYN** **open day** *BrE*

opening[1] /'əʊpənɪŋ $ 'oʊ-/ *n* [C] **1** a ceremony to celebrate the first time that a new public building, road etc is available for people to use: *the opening of the new art gallery* **2** the beginning of something: *a speech at the opening of the conference* **3** a job or opportunity that is available: *Are there any openings for gardeners?* **4** a hole or space in something: *an opening in the fence* **THESAURUS** → **HOLE**

opening[2] *adj* [only before noun] first or happening at the beginning of something: *the President's opening remarks* | *the opening match of the season* | **opening night** (=the first night of a new play, film etc)

PHRASES

opening hours the time each day when a shop, library etc is open: *Opening hours are Monday to Friday from 9 am to 5 pm.*

openly /'əʊpənli $ 'oʊ-/ *adv* honestly and without keeping anything secret: *a chance to talk openly about your problems*

,open-'minded *adj* willing to consider new ideas, opinions, or ways of doing things: *their sympathetic, open-minded attitudes to young people* —**open-mindedness** *n* [U]

,open-'mouthed *adj, adv* with your mouth wide open, because you are surprised or shocked: *We stared open-mouthed at the images on the screen.*

openness /'əʊpənnəs $ 'oʊ-/ *n* [U] when someone is honest and does not keep things secret

'open ,plan *adj* an open plan office, school etc does not have walls dividing it into separate rooms

opera /'ɒpərə $ 'ɑː-/ *n* [C,U] a musical play in which all of the words are sung: *an opera singer* → **SOAP OPERA** —**operatic** /,ɒpə'rætɪk◀ $,ɑː-/ *adj*

operate /'ɒpəreɪt $ 'ɑːp-/ *v*
1 [I,T] to work, or to make something work: *The machine seems to be operating smoothly.* | *He doesn't know how to operate the equipment.* | *Most freezers operate at below −18°C.*
2 [I] to cut into someone's body in order to remove or repair a part that is damaged: *Doctors had to operate to remove the bullet.* | **[+on]** *Surgeons operated on him for eight hours.*
3 [I,T] to do business, or to manage and control something: *She operated her business from a large house in Brighton.* | *The bakery operates all day.* | *Volunteers are operating an emergency hospital.*
4 [I] to have a particular effect: **[+as]** *The foam operates as a filter.*

'operating room *n* [C] *AmE* a part of a hospital where doctors do operations **SYN** **operating theatre** *BrE*

'operating ,system *n* [C] a system in a computer that helps all the programs to work

'operating ,theatre *n* [C] *BrE* a part of a hospital where doctors do operations **SYN** **operating room** *AmE*

operation /,ɒpə'reɪʃən $,ɑːp-/ *n*
1 **IN HOSPITAL** [C] when doctors cut into someone's body in order to remove or repair a part that is damaged: **[+on]** *He's recovering from an operation on his shoulder.*
2 **ACTION TO DO STH** [C] when people work together in a planned way in order to do something: *a rescue operation*
3 **BUSINESS/ORGANIZATION** [C,U] the work of a business or organization, or one of the parts of a company or organization: *Many small businesses fail in the first year of operation.* | *the company's property development operation*

4 MACHINES/EQUIPMENT [U] the way in which something works, or when someone makes something work: *The job involves the operation of heavy machinery.*

5 COMPUTER ACTION [C] *technical* an action done by a computer: *The computer can do several operations at one time.*

PHRASES

in operation if a system or machine is in operation, it is working: *Video cameras were in operation.*

come into operation to start working or being used: *The new system came into operation in 1999.*

COLLOCATIONS

verbs

to have an operation *She's having her operation today.* ⚠ Do not say 'take an operation'. Say **have an operation**.

to do/carry out an operation (*also* **to perform an operation** *formal*) *I've done this operation hundreds of times.* ⚠ Do not say 'make an operation'. Say **do an operation** or **carry out an operation**.

to recover from an operation *It may take her weeks to recover from the operation.*

types of operation

a knee/heart/stomach etc operation *He went into hospital yesterday for a knee operation.*

a major/minor operation *The doctor told him he needed a major operation.*

an emergency operation *Surgeons performed an emergency operation to save his sight.*

operational /ˌɒpəˈreɪʃənəl◄ $ ˌɑːp-/ *adj* **1** working and ready to be used: *The new airport will soon be operational.* **2** relating to the work of a business, government etc: *operational costs*

operative /ˈɒpərətɪv $ ˈɑːpərə-, ˈɑːpəreɪ-/ *adj formal* working and able to be used: *The law will become operative in a month.*

operator /ˈɒpəreɪtər $ ˈɑːpəreɪtər/ *n* [C] **1** someone who works on a telephone SWITCHBOARD: *Ask the operator to help you with the call.* **2** someone whose job is to use a machine or piece of equipment: *a crane operator* **3** a company that does a particular type of business: *a tour operator*

opinion /əˈpɪnjən/ *n* [C,U] what you think about something or someone: [+on/of/about] *We have very different opinions on education.* | *What is your opinion of the band?* | **in my opinion** (=used when giving your opinion) *In my opinion, he made the right decision.* | **be of the opinion that** *formal:* *Otto was of the opinion that the situation would improve soon.* THESAURUS AGREE → **difference of opinion** at DIFFERENCE, **matter of opinion** at MATTER

Grammar
Do not say 'according to my opinion'. Say **in my opinion**.

COLLOCATIONS

verbs

to have/hold an opinion *Do you have any opinions about this?*

to give/express an opinion *Everyone has the right to express an opinion.* ⚠ Do not say 'say your opinion'. Say **give your opinion** or **express your opinion**.

to ask sb's opinion (*also* **to ask for sb's opinion**) *Nobody asked your opinion.*

to form an opinion (=to decide what your opinion is) *I didn't have enough information to form an opinion.*

adjectives

sb's personal opinion (=what one particular person thinks) *You have to respect the other person's views, whatever your own personal opinion.*

a high/low opinion (=the opinion that someone or something is good or bad) *Her boss has a high opinion of her work.*

strong opinions *People have strong opinions about this subject.*

public/popular opinion (=what most people think) *Politicians have to listen to public opinion.*

a second opinion (=advice from a second doctor) *My doctor says I need an operation, but I've asked for a second opinion.*

opinionated /əˈpɪnjəneɪtɪd/ *adj disapproving* an opinionated person has very strong opinions: *an opinionated old fool*

o'pinion poll *n* [C] when a lot of people are asked what they think about a subject, especially about politics

opium /ˈəʊpiəm $ ˈoʊ-/ *n* [U] a very strong illegal drug made from POPPY seeds

opponent /əˈpəʊnənt $ əˈpoʊ-/ *n* [C] **1** someone who is competing against you in a sport or competition: *His opponent is twice as big as he is.* **2** someone who disagrees with a plan, idea etc: [+of] *opponents of Darwin's theory*

opportune /ˈɒpətjuːn $ ˌɑːpərˈtuːn/ *adj* **an opportune moment/time etc** *formal* a good time for doing something

opportunist /ˌɒpəˈtjuːnɪst $ ˌɑːpərˈtuː-/ *n* [C] someone who uses every chance to get power or advantages —**opportunism** *n* [U] —**opportunist** (*also* **opportunistic** /ˌɒpətjuːˈnɪstɪk $ ˌɑːpərtuː-/) *adj*

opportunity /ˌɒpəˈtjuːnəti $ ˌɑːpərˈtuː-/ *n* [C,U] (*plural* **opportunities**) a chance to do something: **opportunity to do sth** *He wasn't given the opportunity to defend himself.* | **at the first/earliest opportunity** *I left school at the earliest opportunity.* → PHOTO OPPORTUNITY

COLLOCATIONS

verbs

to have/get an opportunity *The children will have the opportunity to visit a farm.*

to be given an opportunity *I hope I'll be given an opportunity to play for England.*

to take/use an opportunity (=to do something you have a chance to do) *I would like to take this opportunity to say thank you.*

to miss/lose/waste an opportunity (=to not do something you have a chance to do) *Don't waste this opportunity to learn something new.*
an opportunity comes/arises (=it happens) *Perhaps she would explain later, if the opportunity arose.*

adjectives

a good/great/wonderful etc opportunity *This is a great opportunity for me.*
the ideal/perfect opportunity *It's the ideal opportunity to tell him what you think.*
a golden opportunity (=a very good one) *They missed a golden opportunity to score a winning goal.*
a rare/unique opportunity *a unique opportunity to stay in a real castle*

noun + opportunity

job/employment opportunities *There aren't many job opportunities at the moment.*

oppose /ə'pəʊz $ ə'poʊz/ v [T] to disagree with something and try to change or stop it: *They oppose any changes to the present system.*

opposed /ə'pəʊzd $ ə'poʊzd/ adj
1 be opposed to sth to believe that something is wrong and should not be allowed: *Most people are opposed to the death penalty.*
2 as opposed to sth used when mentioning two different things, when only one is involved, acceptable etc: *Students discuss ideas, as opposed to just copying from books.*

> **Word Choice: opposed to or against?**
> **Opposed to** sounds rather formal. In everyday English, people usually say that they are **against** something: *I'm against fox-hunting. I think it's a very cruel sport.*

opposing /ə'pəʊzɪŋ $ ə'poʊ-/ adj [only before noun] **1** opposing teams, groups etc are competing or arguing with each other **2** opposing ideas, opinions etc are completely different from each other

opposite¹ /'ɒpəzət $ 'ɑːp-/ adj
1 completely different: *I thought the music would relax me, but it had the opposite effect.*
2 facing something, or directly across from something: *a building on the opposite side of the river*

PHRASES

your opposite number someone who does the same job as you for a different organization, a different country etc: *a speech by his opposite number in the Labour Party*
the opposite sex people who are of a different sex: *She finds it hard to talk to members of the opposite sex.*

opposite² prep, adv if one thing or person is opposite another, they are facing each other: *Put the piano opposite the sofa.* | *He's moved into the house opposite.* → see picture on page A8

opposite³ n [C] something that is completely different from something else: *I didn't feel sleepy – just the opposite.* | *'What is the opposite of happiness?' 'Sadness.'*

opposition /ˌɒpə'zɪʃən $ ˌɑːp-/ n
1 [U] when people disagree strongly with something: **[+to]** *opposition to the war* | **strong/fierce/stiff opposition** *The proposals met with strong opposition.* | **in opposition to sb/sth** *They were united in opposition to a common enemy.*
2 [C,U also + plural verb BrE] the person, team, company etc that you are competing against: *They played well against good opposition.* | *The opposition were beginning to dominate the game.*

Opposition n the **Opposition** in some countries such as Britain, the main political party in the parliament that is not part of the government: *the leader of the Opposition*

oppress /ə'pres/ v [T] to treat people in an unfair and cruel way —**oppressed** adj: *an oppressed minority* —**oppression** /ə'preʃən/ n [U]

oppressive /ə'presɪv/ adj **1** cruel and unfair: *an oppressive military government* **2** making you feel uncomfortable: *oppressive heat*

oppressor /ə'presə $ -ər/ n [C] a person or group that treats people in a cruel and unfair way

opt /ɒpt $ ɑːpt/ v **opt for sth/to do sth** to choose one thing or do one thing instead of another: *We've opted for a smaller car.* | *More students are opting to go to college.* **THESAURUS ▶ CHOOSE**

PHRASAL VERBS
opt out to choose not to join in a group or system: **[+of]** *Several countries may opt out of the agreement.*

optic /'ɒptɪk $ 'ɑːp-/ adj technical relating to the eyes: *the optic nerve*

optical /'ɒptɪkəl $ 'ɑːp-/ adj **1** relating to the way light is seen, or relating to the eyes: *an optical instrument* **2** using light to record and store information, especially in computer systems —**optically** /-kli/ adv

optical il'lusion n [C] a picture or image that tricks your eyes and makes you see something that is not actually there

optician /ɒp'tɪʃən $ ɑːp-/ n [C] **1** BrE someone who tests people's eyes and sells them glasses in a shop **2** AmE someone who makes glasses

optimal /'ɒptɪməl $ 'ɑːp-/ adj formal OPTIMUM

optimism /'ɒptɪmɪzəm $ 'ɑːp-/ n [U] the belief that good things will happen OPP **pessimism**: *optimism about the country's economic future*

optimist /'ɒptɪmɪst $ 'ɑːp-/ n [C] someone who believes that good things will happen OPP **pessimist**

optimistic /ˌɒptə'mɪstɪk◂ $ ˌɑːp-/ adj believing that good things will happen in the future OPP **pessimistic**: **[+about]** *Tom's optimistic about finding a job.* | **[+that]** *I'm optimistic that things will improve.* —**optimistically** /-kli/ adv

optimize (also -ise BrE) /'ɒptɪmaɪz $ 'ɑːp-/ v [T] to do or use something in a way that is as effective as possible

optimum /'ɒptɪməm $ 'ɑːp-/ adj [only before noun] formal best or most suitable for a particular purpose: *optimum use of space*

option [Ac] /ˈɒpʃən $ ˈɑːp-/ n [C] **1** something that you can choose to do [SYN] **choice**: *It's the only option we have left.* | *You have the option of walking or going on the bus.* **2 have no option (but to do sth)** to have to do something, especially when you do not want to do it: *They had no option but to cut jobs.*

PHRASES

keep/leave your options open to not make a definite decision so that you have more possibilities to choose from: *Leave your options open until you have the results of the test.*

optional [Ac] /ˈɒpʃənəl $ ˈɑːp-/ adj if something is optional, it is available but you do not have to choose it [OPP] **compulsory**: *The sunroof is optional.*

optometrist /ɒpˈtɒmɪtrɪst $ ɑːpˈtɑː-/ n [C] someone who examines people's eyes and orders glasses for them —**optometry** n [U]

opulent /ˈɒpjələnt $ ˈɑːp-/ adj decorated in an expensive way: *an opulent hotel* —**opulence** n [U] —**opulently** adv

or /ə; strong ɔː $ ər; strong ɔːr/ linking word
1 used between two possibilities, or before the last in a series of possibilities → **either**: *Coffee or tea?* | *You can go by bus, by train, or by plane.*
2 used after a negative verb when you mean not one thing and not another thing: *They don't eat meat or fish.*
3 (also **or 'else**) used to warn someone that something bad will happen if they do not do something: *Hurry, or you'll miss your plane.*
4 two or three/20 or 30 etc about or between the numbers you mention: *'How many people were there?' 'Oh, 30 or 40.'*
5 used to further explain something that you have just said: *biology, or the study of living things*

PHRASES

or anything/something spoken used to talk or ask about something similar to the thing you have just mentioned: *Do you want to go out for a drink or something?*

or so used after a number, time, distance etc to show that it is not exact: *There's a gas station a mile or so down the road.*

oral¹ /ˈɔːrəl/ adj
1 spoken, not written: *an oral report*
2 relating to the mouth: *oral hygiene* —**orally** adv

oral² n [C] a test in which questions and answers are spoken rather than written [THESAURUS] **TEST**

orange /ˈɒrəndʒ $ ˈɔːr-, ˈɑːr-/ n
1 [C] a juicy round fruit with a thick skin that is a colour between red and yellow → see picture on page A4
2 [U] a colour that is between red and yellow —**orange** adj: *an orange shirt*

orangutang /ɔːˈræŋuːtæŋ $ əˈræŋətæŋ/, **orangutan** /-tæn/ n [C] a large animal like a monkey that has long arms and long orange hair → see picture at **APE**

orator /ˈɒrətə $ ˈɔːrətər, ˈɑː-/ n [C] someone who is good at making political speeches

orbit¹ /ˈɔːbɪt $ ˈɔːr-/ n [C] the circle that something moves in when it is going around the Earth, the Sun etc

orbit² v [I,T] to travel in space around a larger object such as the Earth, the Sun etc: *a satellite that orbits the Earth*

orchard /ˈɔːtʃəd $ ˈɔːrtʃərd/ n [C] a place where fruit trees are grown

orchestra /ˈɔːkəstrə $ ˈɔːr-/ n [C also + plural verb BrE] a large group of musicians who play CLASSICAL music together —**orchestral** /ɔːˈkestrəl $ ɔːr-/ adj

orchestrate /ˈɔːkəstreɪt $ ˈɔːr-/ v [T] to organize an important event or a complicated plan, especially secretly: *a carefully orchestrated campaign*

orchid /ˈɔːkɪd $ ˈɔːr-/ n [C] a flower that is often very beautiful and unusual → see picture at **FLOWER¹**

ordain /ɔːˈdeɪn $ ɔːr-/ v [T] to officially make someone a priest → **ordination**

ordeal /ɔːˈdiːl, ˈɔːdiːl $ ɔːrˈdiːl, ˈɔːrdiːl/ n [C] a very unpleasant experience: *School can be an ordeal for some children.*

order¹ /ˈɔːdə $ ˈɔːrdər/ n
1 [C,U] the way that several things are arranged in relation to each other → **sequence**: **in the right/ wrong/same order** *Can you keep the pictures in the same order?* | *Are all the slides in order?* | *The names were written **in alphabetical order** (=with 'a' names first, then 'b' names etc).* | *State the main points **in order of importance**.*
2 [C] when a customer asks for a particular kind of food or drink in a restaurant: *Can I **take your order** (=write down what you want to eat)?*
3 [C] when a customer asks a company to make or send goods: **[+for]** *The school has just put in an order for ten new computers.* | **on order** *Hundreds of the aircraft are on order.*
4 [C] an official instruction from someone in authority that must be obeyed: **order (for sb) to do sth** *Captain Smith gave the order to advance.* [THESAURUS] **ORDER**
5 [U] when people obey laws or rules, and do not cause trouble: *Police are working hard to maintain **law and order**.* | *Order has now been restored in the capital city.* → **MAIL ORDER, MONEY ORDER, POSTAL ORDER, STANDING ORDER**

PHRASES

in order to/for/that so that something can happen, or so that someone can do something: **in order to do sth** *Plants need light in order to live.* | **in order for sb/sth to do sth** *In order for the company to remain competitive, jobs must be shed.* | **in order that** *I must have it in writing in order that I know exactly what is happening.*

in order legally or officially correct: *Your passport seems to be in order.*

out of order 1 if a machine is out of order, it has stopped working: *The photocopier is out of order again.* [THESAURUS] **BROKEN 2** BrE informal used to say that someone's behaviour is rude or unacceptable: *That remark was out of order!*

COLLOCATIONS - sense 4
verbs

to give/issue an order Who gave the order to shoot?
to obey/disobey an order Soldiers are expected to obey orders without question.
to follow/carry out an order He had failed to carry out the order of the court.
to have orders to do sth Police had orders to search every house in the village.
to take orders from sb (=to be given orders by someone and obey them) I don't take orders from you!
to get/receive an order We got the order to stop firing.

order² v

1 **ASK FOR FOOD/DRINK** [I,T] to ask for food or drink in a restaurant, bar etc: He sat down and ordered a beer. | Are you ready to order? **THESAURUS** ASK
2 **ASK FOR GOODS** [T] to ask a company to make or send something: I've ordered a new computer from the supplier. | **order sb sth** I'll order you a taxi.
3 **TELL SB TO DO STH** [T] to officially tell someone that they must do something: 'Stay right there,' she ordered. | **order sb to do sth** Her doctor ordered her to rest for a week. | **[+that]** He ordered that his daughters be brought up as Christians.
4 **ARRANGE** [T] to arrange something in a particular way: The names are ordered alphabetically.

PHRASAL VERBS
order sb **around** (also **order** sb **about** BrE) to give someone orders in an annoying or threatening way: How dare he order her about like that?

THESAURUS - sense 3

order to tell someone that they must do something, especially using your official authority: A policeman ordered him to stop. | He ordered his men to put down their weapons.
tell to say to someone that they must do something: She told the kids to stop making so much noise.
give orders/instructions to tell other people exactly what they must do: They gave orders that no one should enter the building. | She gave us careful instructions on how to look after the cats.
command if a king, general, captain etc commands someone to do something, they order that person to do it: The general commanded the troops to attack.
instruct formal to tell someone exactly what to do in a particular situation: You will be instructed on what to do if there is a fire.

orderly¹ /ˈɔːdəli $ ˈɔːrdərli/ adj well-organized or tidily arranged: an orderly desk

orderly² n [C] (plural **orderlies**) someone who does jobs in a hospital that do not need any special training

ordinal number /ˌɔːdənəl ˈnʌmbə $ ˌɔːrdənəl ˈnʌmbər/ n [C] a number such as first, second, or third → **cardinal number**

ordinarily /ˈɔːdənərəli, ˌɔːdənˈeərəli $ ˌɔːrdənˈerəli/ adv especially AmE usually: I don't ordinarily go to movies in the afternoon.

ordinary /ˈɔːdənəri $ ˈɔːrdəneri/ adj
1 average, common, or usual, not different or special: It's just an ordinary camera. | The book is about **ordinary people**. **THESAURUS** NORMAL
2 not particularly good or impressive: I thought the paintings were pretty ordinary.
PHRASES
out of the ordinary very different from what usually happens: Anything out of the ordinary made her nervous. **THESAURUS** UNUSUAL

ordination /ˌɔːdəˈneɪʃən $ ˌɔːr-/ n [C,U] the ceremony in which someone is ORDAINed (=officially made a priest)

ore /ɔː $ ɔːr/ n [C,U] rock or earth from which metal can be obtained

organ /ˈɔːgən $ ˈɔːr-/ n [C]
1 part of the body of a human, animal, or plant that has a particular purpose: the liver and other **internal organs** | **sexual/reproductive organs** | **organ transplant** (=an operation in which an organ is put into the body of another person) | **organ donor** (=the person who gives an organ) → see picture on page A2
2 **a)** a musical instrument like a piano with large pipes that produce the sound, played especially in churches → **organist b)** an electronic instrument with a KEYBOARD like a piano → **MOUTH ORGAN**

organic /ɔːˈgænɪk $ ɔːr-/ adj
1 relating to farming or gardening without using chemicals that are harmful to the environment: **organic food/vegetables/milk etc** **THESAURUS** NATURAL
2 related to or produced by living things **OPP** inorganic: organic matter —**organically** /-kli/ adv

organism /ˈɔːgənɪzəm $ ˈɔːr-/ n [C] a living thing, usually a very small one: a microscopic organism

organist /ˈɔːgənɪst $ ˈɔːr-/ n [C] someone who plays the ORGAN

organization (also **-isation** BrE) /ˌɔːgənaɪˈzeɪʃən $ ˌɔːrgənə-/ n
1 [C] a group of people, companies, or countries that has formed for a particular purpose: the human rights organization Amnesty International | international organizations such as the UN
2 [U] the way in which something is organized, or the activity of organizing something: He was responsible for the organization of the party's election campaign. —**organizational** adj

THESAURUS

organization a group of people, companies, or countries that has formed for a particular purpose: The United Nations and other organizations are trying to end the war.
institution an organization that does educational, scientific, or financial work, especially one that is important and has existed for a long time: schools, colleges and other

academic institutions | financial institutions such as banks

association an organization for people in a particular profession, sport etc, that represents its members – used especially in names: *the College Basketball Association | the National Association of Teachers*

party an organization of people with the same political aims: *She belongs to the Labour Party. | All the main political parties supported the new law.*

club/society an organization for people who share an interest, for example a sport: *He is a member of the local golf club. | I joined the university drama society.*

union an organization formed by workers to protect their rights: *The unions are threatening strike action.*

charity an organization that collects money to help people who are poor, sick etc and does not make a profit for itself: *I think we should give the money to a charity.*

organize (also **-ise** *BrE*) /'ɔːɡənaɪz $ 'ɔːr-/ v [T] to plan or arrange something: *Who's organizing the New Year's party?* —**organizer** n [C]

organized (also **-ised** *BrE*) /'ɔːɡənaɪzd $ 'ɔːr-/ adj **1 well/badly/carefully organized** planned and arranged well, badly, or carefully: *The exhibition wasn't very well organized.* **2 well/badly organized** good or bad at planning the things that you have to do and doing them at the right time: *She's really badly organized.* **3** involving many people doing something in a planned way: *organized sports*

organized 'crime n [U] crimes committed by a large and organized group of powerful criminals

orgasm /'ɔːɡæzəm $ 'ɔːr-/ n [C,U] the moment when you have the greatest sexual pleasure during sex

orgy /'ɔːdʒi $ 'ɔːr-/ n [C] (*plural* **orgies**) **1** a party at which people behave in an uncontrolled way, for example drinking a lot of alcohol and having sex **2 an orgy of sth** when people do something a lot, especially something bad: *an orgy of violence*

Orient /'ɔːriənt, 'ɒ- $ 'ɔːr-/ n **the Orient** *old-fashioned* the eastern part of the world, especially China and Japan

Oriental /ˌɔːriˈentl◂, ˌɒri- $ ˌɔːr-/ adj *old-fashioned* relating to Asia, especially China and Japan: *Oriental culture*

orientation $\boxed{Ac}$ /ˌɔːriənˈteɪʃən, ˌɒri- $ ˌɔːr-/ n [C,U] the kind of beliefs and ideas that a group or person has: **political/religious orientation** *the group's right-wing political orientation*
PHRASES
sexual orientation whether someone is HETERO-SEXUAL or HOMOSEXUAL: *Someone's sexual orientation shouldn't prevent them from getting a job.*

oriented $\boxed{Ac}$ /'ɔːrientəd, 'ɒri- $ 'ɔːr-/ (also **orientated** /'ɔːriənteɪtəd, 'ɒri- $ 'ɔːr-/ *BrE*) adj mainly concerned with or aimed at a particular thing or group of people: *complaints that the magazine has become*

too **politically oriented | market-oriented/export-oriented etc**

origin /'ɒrɪdʒɪn $ 'ɔː-, 'ɑː-/ n [C,U]
1 the place, time, or situation in which something began to exist: **[+of]** *the origin of life on Earth |* **of Latin/German etc origin** *The word is of Latin origin. |* **in origin** *Some field boundaries are medieval in origin. | The company* **had its origins in** *France.* **THESAURUS** BEGINNING
2 the country, race, or social class from which someone comes: *He's proud of his Italian origins. |* **ethnic/racial/social origin** *| She could never forget her* **humble origins** (=the low social class she came from). *| They will be sent back to their* **country of origin**.

THESAURUS

origin/origins the place, time, or situation in which something began to exist: *What is the origin of the word 'ecology'? | the origins of modern science*
source the thing, place etc that you get something from: *The Internet is a very useful source of information. | Beans are a good source of protein.*
root the **root** of a problem is its main cause. The **roots** of a belief, musical style etc are the ideas, styles etc that it was first based on: *We need to get to the root of the problem. | the roots of Christianity*
the birthplace of sth the place where something first started to exist: *New Orleans is the birthplace of jazz.*

---

original¹ /əˈrɪdʒɪnəl, -dʒənəl/ adj
1 [only before noun] existing first, before any changes were made: *The house still has its original stone floor. | Our original plan was too expensive.*
2 completely new and different: *a* **highly original** *style of painting* **THESAURUS** NEW
3 [only before noun] an original painting, drawing etc is not a copy: *Is that an original Matisse* (=painting by Matisse)?

original² n [C] a painting, document etc that is not a copy

originality /əˌrɪdʒəˈnæləti/ n [U] the quality of being completely new and different: *The design is good but lacks originality.*

originally /əˈrɪdʒənəli, -dʒənəli/ adv in the beginning: *Her family* **originally came from** *Thailand. | We had* **originally intended** *to go by car, but in the end we took the train.*

originate /əˈrɪdʒəneɪt/ v *formal* **1** [I] to start to develop in a particular place or at a particular time: **[+in]** *The custom of having a Christmas tree originated in Germany.* **2** [T] to have the idea for something and start it: *the man who originated this technique* —**originator** n [C]

ornament /'ɔːnəmənt $ 'ɔːr-/ n [C] an object that you keep in your house as a decoration: *china ornaments*

ornamental /ˌɔːnəˈmentl◂ $ ˌɔːr-/ adj intended to be attractive rather than useful: *ornamental plants*

ornate /ɔːˈneɪt $ ɔːr-/ adj having a lot of decoration: ornate furniture —**ornately** adv

ornithology /ˌɔːnəˈθɒlədʒi $ ˌɔːrnəˈθɑː-/ n [U] the study of birds —**ornithologist** n [C]

orphan¹ /ˈɔːfən $ ˈɔːr-/ n [C] a child whose parents are dead

orphan² v **be orphaned** if a child is orphaned, both its parents die or its only remaining parent dies

orphanage /ˈɔːfənɪdʒ $ ˈɔːr-/ n [C] a place for orphans to live in, especially in past times

orthodox /ˈɔːθədɒks $ ˈɔːrθədɑːks/ adj **1** orthodox ideas or methods are traditional ones that most people think are right or normal: orthodox methods of treating disease **2** having traditional religious beliefs and practices: an orthodox Jew —**orthodoxy** n [C,U]

orthopedic (also **orthopaedic** BrE) /ˌɔːθəˈpiːdɪk◂ $ ˌɔːr-/ adj relating to the medical treatment of problems that affect people's bones or muscles

Oscar /ˈɒskə $ ˈɑːskər/ n [C] trademark a prize that is given each year in the US for the best film, performance in a film etc

oscillate /ˈɒsəleɪt $ ˈɑː-/ v [I] formal to keep changing between two things, amounts, or directions

osmosis /ɒzˈməʊsɪs $ ɑːzˈmoʊ-/ n [U] if you learn facts or ideas by osmosis, you gradually learn them by hearing them often

ostensible /ɒˈstensəbəl $ ɑː-/ adj [only before noun] an ostensible reason, aim etc is one that seems or is said to be the real one, but is not —**ostensibly** adv: She moved away, ostensibly to examine a photo on the wall.

ostentatious /ˌɒstənˈteɪʃəs◂, -ten- $ ˌɑː-/ adj done, worn etc in order to make other people notice and admire you: an ostentatious display of wealth —**ostentatiously** adv —**ostentation** n [U]

osteopath /ˈɒstiəpæθ $ ˈɑː-/ n [C] someone who treats medical problems such as back pain by moving and pressing the muscles and bones

ostracize (also **-ise** BrE) /ˈɒstrəsaɪz $ ˈɑː-/ v [T] if people ostracize a member of their group, they start treating them in an unfriendly way: There was a time when criminals would be ostracized by the whole village. —**ostracism** /-sɪzəm/ n [U]

ostrich /ˈɒstrɪtʃ $ ˈɒː-, ˈɑː-/ n [C] a big African bird with long legs that cannot fly

OSTRICH

other /ˈʌðə $ ˈʌðər/ determiner, adj, pron **1** used to refer to the rest of a group or the second thing of a pair: Anna has a job, but the other girls are still at school. | The other students are about the same age as me. | Here's one sock – where's **the other one**? | We ate one of the pizzas and froze **the other**. | Can I stay here until **the others** come back? **2** used to refer to additional things or people of the same kind → **another**: Have you any other questions? **3** used to refer to a different person or thing from the one you have just mentioned or from this one → **another**: Can we meet some other time – I'm busy right now. | Their cottage is on the other side of the lake. | I do not deny that some schools are better than others. → **EACH OTHER**

PHRASES

every other day/week etc one day, week etc in every two: Her husband cooks dinner every other day. **someone/something etc or other** used when you are not certain about the person, thing etc you are referring to: We'll get the money somehow or other. **other than** except: She has no one to talk to other than her family. **the other day/morning etc** spoken recently: I was talking to Ted the other day. **THESAURUS** RECENTLY

otherwise /ˈʌðəwaɪz $ ˈʌðər-/ adv **1 a)** used to say what will happen if something else does not happen first, usually when it is bad: You'd better go now, otherwise you'll be late. **b)** used to say what would or might have happened if the situation had been different: We had no phone then, otherwise we would have rung the police. **THESAURUS** IF **2** except for what has just been mentioned: The sleeves are a bit long, but otherwise the dress fits fine. | The weather spoiled an otherwise perfect day. **3 think/decide/pretend etc otherwise** to think, decide, or say the opposite of what someone else thinks or decides: If you're scared, it's better to pretend otherwise.

PHRASES

or otherwise or not: respect for all creatures, human or otherwise

otter /ˈɒtə $ ˈɑːtər/ n [C] a small animal with brown fur that swims and eats fish

ouch /aʊtʃ/ spoken said when you suddenly feel pain: Ouch! That hurt!

oughtn't /ˈɔːtnt $ ˈɒː-/ the short form of 'ought not'

ought to /ˈɔːt tuː $ ˈɒːt-/ modal verb **1** used to say that someone should do something SYN should: You ought to take a day off. | I ought not to be telling you this. | We ought to have invited them back with us (=but we didn't). **2** used to say that you expect something to happen or be true: The weather ought to be nice in August.

ounce /aʊns/ n **1** [C] (written abbreviation **oz**) a unit for measuring weight, equal to 1/16 of a pound or 28.35 grams **2 an ounce of sth** even a small amount of something: If you had an ounce of sense, you'd leave him.

our /aʊə $ aʊr/ determiner belonging to or relating to us: Our daughter is at college.

ours /aʊəz $ aʊrz/ pron the POSSESSIVE form of 'we': 'Whose car is that?' 'It's ours.' | They have their tickets, but ours haven't come yet.

ourselves /aʊəˈselvz $ aʊr-/ pron **1** the REFLEXIVE form of 'we': It was strange seeing ourselves on television. **2** used to emphasize the word 'we': We started this business ourselves.

(all) by ourselves alone or without help: *We found our way here all by ourselves.*

have sth (all) to ourselves to not have to share something with other people: *We'll have the house to ourselves next week.*

oust /aʊst/ v [T] to force someone out of a position of power: *an attempt to **oust** the communists **from power***

out¹ /aʊt/ adv, adj

1 a) from inside a place or container OPP **in**: *Close the door on your way out.* | **[+of]** *She tipped cereal out of the packet into her bowl.* **b)** no longer inside a place or container OPP **in**: *The kids are out in the back garden.* | *Ms Jackson is out right now* (=not at home or not in her office). | **[+of]** *He was thrilled to be out of hospital.* THESAURUS OUTSIDE

2 in or to a place far away: *The family are due to fly out to America shortly.*

3 a light or fire that is out is no longer shining or burning: *Turn the lights out when you go to bed.*

4 available to be bought: *Morrison has a new book out this month.*

5 *spoken* not possible: *Skiing's out because it costs too much.*

6 not fashionable now OPP **in**: *Bright lipstick shades are out.*

7 if a number obtained by calculating is out, it is wrong: *Their forecast of population increase was out by 5%.*

8 not allowed to continue playing a game, according to its rules

9 if flowers on a plant are out, they have opened

10 if the sun or stars are out, they can be seen in the sky

11 if a secret is out, it has become known

12 if the TIDE is out, the sea is at its lowest level

PHRASES

be out for sth/be out to do sth *informal* to intend to get or do something: *He's just out to get attention.*

be out of sth to have none of something left: *We're almost out of gas.*

8 out of 10/19 out of 20 etc used to say how many people or things in a group do something or are something: *Eight out of ten teachers* (=80 per cent of teachers) *say they have too much paperwork to do.*

out of curiosity/fear/pity etc because of curiosity, fear etc: *She gave him the job out of pity.*

out of trouble/danger/office etc not in trouble, danger etc: *Keep out of trouble.* | *The patient is now out of danger.*

out² v [T] to publicly say that someone is HOMO-SEXUAL when they do not want that fact known

out-and-'out adj [only before noun] used to emphasize your description of someone or something: *an out-and-out lie*

outback /'aʊtbæk/ n **the outback** the part of Australia far away from cities, where not many people live

outbid /aʊt'bɪd/ v [T] (*past tense and past participle* **outbid**, *present participle* **outbidding**) to offer more money for something than someone else

outbreak /'aʊtbreɪk/ n [C] when something bad such as a serious disease or a war starts: **[+of]** *an outbreak of malaria*

outburst /'aʊtbɜːst $ -bɜːrst/ n [C] when someone suddenly shows a strong emotion, especially anger: *an angry outburst*

outcast /'aʊtkɑːst $ -kæst/ n [C] someone who is not accepted by other people: *a social outcast*

outclass /aʊt'klɑːs $ -'klæs/ v [T] to be much better than someone at doing something

outcome Ac /'aʊtkʌm/ n [singular] the final result of a meeting, process etc: **[+of]** *the outcome of the election* THESAURUS RESULT

outcrop /'aʊtkrɒp $ -krɑːp/ (*also* **outcropping** /'aʊtkrɒpɪŋ $ -krɑː-/ AmE) n [C] a large piece of rock that is not covered by earth

outcry /'aʊtkraɪ/ n [singular] an angry protest by a lot of people: **[+against]** *a public outcry against nuclear weapons testing*

outdated /aʊt'deɪtɪd◂/ adj no longer useful or modern: *factories full of outdated machinery* THESAURUS OLD-FASHIONED

outdo /aʊt'duː/ v [T] (*past tense* **outdid** /-'dɪd/, *past participle* **outdone** /-'dʌn/, *third person singular* **outdoes** /-'dʌz/) to be better or more successful than someone else: *two brothers trying to outdo each other* | ***Not to be outdone**, Robson made the score 2-0 just before half-time* (=he did as well as the other player who scored).

outdoor /aʊt'dɔː◂ $ -'dɔːr◂/ adj [only before noun] existing, happening, or used outside, not inside a building OPP **indoor**: *an outdoor swimming pool*

outdoors¹ /aʊt'dɔːz $ -'dɔːrz/ adv not in a building SYN **outside** OPP **indoors**: *I prefer working outdoors.* THESAURUS OUTSIDE

outdoors² n **the (great) outdoors** the countryside

outer /'aʊtə $ -ər/ adj [only before noun] on or near the outside of something OPP **inner**: *Remove the tough outer leaves.*

outermost /'aʊtəməʊst $ -tərmoʊst/ adj [only before noun] furthest from the middle of something OPP **innermost**: *the outermost planets*

outer 'space n [U] the area outside the Earth's air where the stars and PLANETS are

outfit /'aʊtfɪt/ n [C] a set of clothes that you wear together: *She was wearing her usual outfit of white blouse and black skirt.*

outflank /aʊt'flæŋk/ v [T] to gain an advantage over an opponent, especially in politics

outgoing /aʊt'gəʊɪŋ◂ $ -'goʊ-/ adj **1** someone who is outgoing enjoys meeting and talking to people **2 the outgoing president/government etc** a person or group that is finishing a job as president, government etc **3** [only before noun] going away from a place: *outgoing phone calls*

outgoings /'aʊtgəʊɪŋz $ -goʊ-/ n [plural] *BrE* the money that you spend on rent, food etc

outgrow /aʊt'grəʊ $ -'groʊ/ v [T] (*past tense* **outgrew** /-'gruː/, *past participle* **outgrown** /-'grəʊn

$ -'groʊn/) to become too big or too old for something: *Kara's already outgrown her shoes.* | *She had outgrown her passion for horses.*

outing /'aʊtɪŋ/ *n* [C] a short trip for a group of people: *We're going on a family outing.*

outlandish /aʊt'lændɪʃ/ *adj* strange and unusual: *outlandish clothes*

outlast /aʊt'lɑːst $ -'læst/ *v* [T] to continue for longer than someone or something else: *The whole point of the game is to outlast your opponent.*

outlaw¹ /'aʊtlɔː $ -lɔː/ *v* [T] to officially say that something is illegal: *Gambling was outlawed here in 1980.*

outlaw² *n* [C] *old-fashioned* someone who is hiding from law officers

outlay /'aʊtleɪ/ *n* [C,U] an amount of money that you spend to start a new business, activity etc: *a huge initial outlay*

outlet /'aʊtlet, -lɪt/ *n* [C] **1** a way of expressing or getting rid of strong feelings: *I use judo as an outlet for stress.* **2** a place where gas or liquid can flow out of something **3** *formal* a shop that sells a company's products

outline¹ /'aʊtlaɪn/ *n* **1** [singular] the main ideas or facts about something: **[+of]** *an outline of the company's plan* **2** [C] a line around the edge of something that shows its shape

outline² *v* [T] to describe the main ideas or facts about something: *a speech outlining his work in refugee camps*

outlive /aʊt'lɪv/ *v* [T] to live longer than someone else: *She outlived her husband by ten years.*

outlook /'aʊtlʊk/ *n* **1** [C] your general attitude to life and the world: **[+on]** *a positive outlook on life* **2** [usually singular] what is expected to happen in the future: **[+for]** *The long-term outlook for the industry is worrying.*

outlying /'aʊtˌlaɪ-ɪŋ/ *adj* [only before noun] a long way from other places: *Outlying villages had been attacked.*

outmanoeuvre *BrE*, **outmaneuver** *AmE* /ˌaʊtmə'nuːvə $ -ər/ *v* [T] to cleverly achieve something when someone else does not want you to achieve it: *Alan had outmanoeuvred her with ease.*

outmoded /aʊt'məʊdɪd $ -'moʊ-/ *adj* OUTDATED

outnumber /aʊt'nʌmbə $ -ər/ *v* [T] to be greater in number than another group: *Women outnumber men in the nursing profession.*

out-of-date *adj* **1** not containing the most recent information: *The guidebook is hopelessly out-of-date.* **THESAURUS** OLD-FASHIONED **2** if a ticket, official document etc is out-of-date, the period when you are allowed to use it has ended: *an out-of-date passport* **3** if something is out-of-date, it seems old-fashioned and has been replaced by things that are more modern **SYN** outdated: *out-of-date technology*

out-of-the-way *adj* a long way from other places

out-of-town *adj* [only before noun] **1** to, from, or in another town **2** *BrE* on the edge of a town: *out-of-town shopping centres*

outpace /aʊt'peɪs/ *v* [T] to go faster, work better, or develop faster than other people or things

outpatient /'aʊtˌpeɪʃənt/ *n* [C] someone who goes to a hospital for treatment but does not stay there all night

outperform /ˌaʊtpə'fɔːm $ -pər'fɔːrm/ *v* [T] to do something better than other things or people: *Mart Stores continued to outperform other retailers.*

outplay /aʊt'pleɪ/ *v* [T] to play better than your opponent in a game

outpost /'aʊtpəʊst $ -poʊst/ *n* [C] a small town or group of buildings a long way from other places

outpouring /'aʊtpɔːrɪŋ/ *n* [C] when a lot of people suddenly start expressing an emotion: **[+of]** *the public outpouring of grief following the Princess's death*

output¹ Ac /'aʊtpʊt/ *n* [C,U] the amount of goods, energy etc that someone or something produces → **input**: *Economic output is down by 10% this year.*

output² Ac *v* [T] (*past tense and past participle* **output**, *present participle* **outputting**) if a computer outputs information, it produces it

outrage¹ /'aʊtreɪdʒ/ *n* **1** [U] a feeling of extreme anger or shock: **public outrage** *at the scandal* **2** [C] something that causes extreme anger or shock: *This is an outrage!* | *terrorist outrages*

outrage² *v* [T] to make someone feel very angry or shocked —**outraged** *adj*

outrageous /aʊt'reɪdʒəs/ *adj* very shocking or bad: *the outrageous cost of school uniform* —**outrageously** *adv*

outright¹ /'aʊtraɪt/ *adj* [only before noun] **1** complete and total: *outright victory* | *an outright ban on handguns* **2** said clearly and directly: *an outright refusal*

outright² /aʊt'raɪt/ *adv* **1** clearly and directly: *Should I ask Margaret outright?* **2** completely: *They haven't rejected the plan outright.* **3** be killed outright to be killed immediately in an accident: *He was killed outright in the car crash.*

outrun /aʊt'rʌn/ *v* [T] (*past tense* **outran** /-'ræn/, *past participle* **outrun**, *present participle* **outrunning**) **1** to run faster or further than someone else **2** to develop more quickly than something else

outset /'aʊtset/ *n* **at/from the outset** at or from the beginning: *I warned you at the outset that this wouldn't be easy.*

outshine /aʊt'ʃaɪn/ *v* [T] (*past tense and past participle* **outshone** /aʊt'ʃɒn $ -'ʃoʊn/) to be much better at something than someone else

outside¹ /aʊt'saɪd, 'aʊtsaɪd/ *prep, adv* **1** not inside a building or room, but near it **OPP** inside: *Can I go and play outside, Dad?* | *Wait outside, I want to talk to him alone.* | *He left an envelope outside my door.* → see picture on page A8 **2** further than the edge of a city, town etc: *We live just outside Leeds.* | **[+of]** *especially AmE: a field outside of Roswell* **3** further than the limits of a situation, activity etc: *Teachers can't control what students do outside* school. | **[+of]** *especially AmE: I have a lot of interests outside of football.*

THESAURUS

outside not inside a building, but near it: *They went outside to see what was happening.*
out outside – used especially before prepositions or adverbs: *We slept out under the stars. | I can hear somebody out there.*
outdoors (*also* **out of doors**) not inside buildings – used when talking about this as a healthy and enjoyable thing: *The kids are outdoors all the time in the summer.*
in the open air outside where the air is fresh: *After a day in the office, I wanted to get out in the open air.*

---

outside² /aʊt'saɪd, 'aʊtsaɪd/ n **1 the outside** the part of something that is furthest from the centre OPP **the inside**: *The outside of the building is pink.* **2 on the outside** used when describing the way someone or something seems to be: *Their marriage seemed so perfect on the outside.*

outside³ /'aʊtsaɪd/ adj [only before noun] **1** an outside wall, toilet etc is not inside a building **2** involving someone who does not belong to your group or organization: *We need some outside help.*
PHRASES

outside interests things you do or are interested in that are not connected with your work: *Does she have any outside interests?*
the outside world the rest of the world: *The city is cut off from the outside world by floods.*

outsider /aʊt'saɪdə $ -ər/ n [C] someone who does not belong to a particular group or organization: *Sometimes I feel like an outsider in my own family.*

outsize /'aʊtsaɪz/ (*also* **outsized** /'aʊtsaɪzd/) adj [only before noun] larger than normal: *her outsize handbag*

outskirts /'aʊtskɜːts $ -ɜːr-/ n **the outskirts** the parts of a city or town that are furthest from the centre: **on the outskirts (of sth)** *They have an apartment on the outskirts of Geneva.*

outspoken /aʊt'spəʊkən $ -'spoʊ-/ adj someone who is outspoken says what they think even though it may shock or offend people: *an outspoken critic of the government*

outstanding /aʊt'stændɪŋ/ adj **1** excellent and impressive: *an outstanding performance* **2** not yet done or paid: *an outstanding debt* —**outstandingly** adv: *The business has been outstandingly successful.*

outstay /aʊt'steɪ/ v → **outstay your welcome** at **WELCOME⁴**

outstretched /ˌaʊt'stretʃt◂/ adj if your arms or legs are outstretched, they are stretched out as far as possible: *I took hold of his outstretched arm.*

outstrip /aʊt'strɪp/ v [T] (**outstripped, outstripping**) to be larger or better than someone or something else: *His qualifications far outstripped those of the other candidates.*

outward /'aʊtwəd $ -wərd/ adj **1** relating to how

---

someone or something seems to be: *Amy answered with outward composure. | the car's outward appearance* **2** going away from a place or towards the outside: *an outward flight*

outwardly /'aʊtwədli $ -wərd-/ adv used when saying how someone or something seems to be, rather than how they really are: *outwardly confident people*

outwards /'aʊtwədz $ -wərdz/ *especially BrE*, **outward** *especially AmE* adv away from the centre of something OPP **inwards**: *Lie on your tummy with your elbows pointing outwards.*

outweigh /aʊt'weɪ/ v [T] to be more important than something else: *The benefits outweigh the costs.*

outwit /aʊt'wɪt/ v [T] (**outwitted, outwitting**) to use tricks or clever plans to defeat someone, escape from them etc: *He outwitted his pursuers by suddenly changing direction.*

oval /'əʊvəl $ 'oʊ-/ n [C] a shape that is like a circle, but longer than it is wide → see picture at **SHAPE¹** —**oval** adj

ovary /'əʊvəri $ 'oʊ-/ n [C] (*plural* **ovaries**) the part of a female person or animal that produces eggs

ovation /əʊ'veɪʃən $ oʊ-/ n [C] if people give someone an ovation, they CLAP their hands to show their approval: **standing ovation** (=when people stand and clap)

oven /'ʌvən/ n [C] a piece of equipment that you cook food inside. It is usually shaped like a metal box with a door → **cooker, stove**: *Bake in a hot oven for ten minutes.* | **gas/electric/microwave oven** → see picture at **KITCHEN**

over¹ /'əʊvə $ 'oʊvər/ prep
1 going from one side of something to the other, especially by jumping, climbing, or flying → **across**: *I jumped over the wall and ran along the bank. | They had to climb over piles of rubble to reach him. | the next bridge over the river* → see picture on page A8
2 above or higher than something OPP **under**: *The sign over the door said 'No Exit'.*
3 over the road/street/river etc on the opposite side of the road, street etc: *There's a supermarket over the road.*
4 on something or covering it OPP **under**: *Put this blanket over him.*
5 more than a particular amount, number, or age: *It cost over £1,000.* | **the over-30s/over-50s etc** (=people who are more than a particular age)
6 during: *I saw Julie over the summer.* | **over the past/next few months/years etc** *The situation has improved over the past ten years.*
7 down from the edge of something: *The car fell over a cliff.*
8 about: *an argument over some jewellery*
9 used to say who or what is controlled, influenced, or defeated: *the period in which Spain ruled over Portugal | their 2–1 victory over Leeds*
10 using the telephone or a radio: *The salesman explained it to me over the phone.*
PHRASES

be/get over sth to feel better after being ill or upset → **recover**: *I still haven't got over this flu.*

over² *adv, adj*

1 down from an upright position: *Kate fell over and hurt her ankle.* | *I saw him push the bike over.*

2 to a particular place: *Come over tomorrow and we'll go shopping.*

3 to or in a place on the other side of something: *I'm flying over to Sweden next week.* | *He strolled over to the window.* | **over here/there** *I'm over here!*

4 finished: *The game was nearly over.*

5 **roll/turn/flip etc (sth) over** to move, or to move something, so that another side can be seen: *He rolled over and went to sleep.*

6 above or higher than something: *You can't hear anything when the planes fly over.*

7 more than a particular amount, number, or age: *a game for children aged six and over*

PHRASES

get sth over with to do something unpleasant so that you do not have to worry about it any more: *Call her and get it over with.*

(all) over again once more from the beginning: *The computer lost all my work, and I had to do it all over again.*

over and over (again) many times: *He made us sing the song over and over until we got it right.*

over to sb used to say that it is now someone else's turn to do something: *We've raised the issue – now it's over to the government.*

over- /ˈəʊvə $ ˈoʊvər/ *prefix* too much: *You're overqualified.* | *overcrowded prisons* | *people who overeat*

overall¹ Ac /ˌəʊvərˈɔːl◂ $ ˌoʊvərˈɔːl◂/ *adj, adv* considering or including everything: *The overall cost of the trip is $500.* | *Overall, the situation looks good.*

overall² /ˈəʊvərɔːl $ ˈoʊvərɔːl/ *n* **1** [C] *BrE* a loose-fitting piece of clothing like a coat that is worn over clothes to keep them clean when you are working **2** **overalls** [plural] *BrE* a piece of clothing like a shirt and trousers joined together, that you wear over your clothes to keep them clean when you are working **3** **overalls** [plural] *AmE* trousers with a piece that covers your chest, held up by two bands that go over your shoulders SYN **dungarees** *BrE*

overate /ˌəʊvərˈet, -ˈeɪt $ ˌoʊvərˈeɪt/ *v* the past tense of OVEREAT

overawed /ˌəʊvərˈɔːd $ ˌoʊvərˈɔːd/ *adj* if you are overawed by someone or something, they IMPRESS you a lot and make you feel nervous or slightly frightened: *Our players were overawed by the large crowd.*

overbearing /ˌəʊvəˈbeərɪŋ $ ˌoʊvərˈber-/ *adj* always trying to control other people without considering their feelings: *an overbearing father*

overboard /ˈəʊvəbɔːd $ ˈoʊvərbɔːrd/ *adv* over the side of a ship into the water: *He **fell overboard** into the icy water.*

PHRASES

go overboard *informal* to do something in a way that is too extreme, for example to praise or thank someone too much: *'That was absolutely amazing!' 'OK, there's no need to go overboard.'*

overburdened /ˌəʊvəˈbɜːdnd $ ˌoʊvərˈbɜːrdnd/ *adj* having too much work to do, or too many problems: *teachers overburdened with work*

overcame /ˌəʊvəˈkeɪm $ ˌoʊvər-/ *v* the past tense of OVERCOME

overcast /ˌəʊvəˈkɑːst◂ $ ˌoʊvərˈkæst◂/ *adj* a sky that is overcast is dark and cloudy

overcharge /ˌəʊvəˈtʃɑːdʒ $ ˌoʊvərˈtʃɑːrdʒ/ *v* [I,T] to ask someone for too much money for something you are selling

overcoat /ˈəʊvəkəʊt $ ˈoʊvərkoʊt/ *n* [C] a long thick warm coat

overcome /ˌəʊvəˈkʌm $ ˌoʊvər-/ *v* [T] (*past tense* **overcame** /-ˈkeɪm/, *past participle* **overcome**) **1** to succeed in controlling a feeling or solving a problem: *I'm trying to overcome my fear of flying.* **2** **be overcome (by sth)** to be so strongly affected by an emotion that you become weak or unable to control your feelings: *Alice tried to speak but she was overcome by tears.* **3** **be overcome by fumes/smoke/gas** to become seriously ill or unconscious because of breathing smoke or gas: *Five employees were overcome by smoke.* **4** to fight against someone or something and win: *Australia overcame the Netherlands 2–1.*

overcrowded /ˌəʊvəˈkraʊdɪd◂ $ ˌoʊvər-/ *adj* a place that is overcrowded has too many people in it: *overcrowded prisons* —**overcrowding** *n* [U]

overdo /ˌəʊvəˈduː $ ˌoʊvər-/ *v* [T] (*past tense* **overdid** /-ˈdɪd/, *past participle* **overdone** /-ˈdʌn/, *third person singular* **overdoes** /-ˈdʌz/) to do or use too much of something: *Don't overdo it.*

overdone /ˌəʊvəˈdʌn◂ $ ˌoʊvər-/ *adj* cooked for too long: *This steak is overdone.*

overdose /ˈəʊvədəʊs $ ˈoʊvərdoʊs/ *n* [C] too much of a drug taken at one time: **[+of]** *She **took an overdose** of painkillers.* —**overdose** /ˌəʊvəˈdəʊs $ ˌoʊvərˈdoʊs/ *v* [I]

overdraft /ˈəʊvədrɑːft $ ˈoʊvərdræft/ *n* [C] an arrangement with your bank that allows you to spend more money than you have in your account: *a £200 overdraft*

overdrawn /ˌəʊvəˈdrɔːn $ ˌoʊvərˈdrɔːn/ *adj* **be/go overdrawn** to have spent more money than the amount you have in your bank account

overdue /ˌəʊvəˈdjuː◂ $ ˌoʊvərˈduː◂/ *adj* late in arriving or being done: *Her baby's ten days overdue.* | *an overdue gas bill* THESAURUS ▶ LATE

overeat /ˌəʊvərˈiːt $ ˌoʊ-/ *v* [I] (*past tense* **overate** /-ˈet, -ˈeɪt $ -ˈeɪt/, *past participle* **overeaten** /-ˈiːtn/) to eat too much

overestimate Ac /ˌəʊvərˈestɪmeɪt $ ˌoʊ-/ *v* [I,T] to think that someone or something is bigger, more important etc than they really are OPP **underestimate**: *The company overestimated demand for their new product.* —**overestimate** /-mət/ *n* [C]

O

overflow

overflow /ˌəʊvəˈfləʊ $ ˌoʊvərˈfloʊ/ v **1** [I,T] if a river or a container overflows, it is so full that the liquid inside flows over the edge: *The drains flooded and water overflowed down the street.* | *The river overflowed its banks.* **2** [I] if a place overflows with people or things, there are too many of them to fit into it

OVERFLOW

overgrown /ˌəʊvəˈɡrəʊn◂ $ ˌoʊvərˈɡroʊn◂/ adj covered with plants that have grown in an untidy way

overhang /ˌəʊvəˈhæŋ $ ˌoʊvər-/ v [I,T] (*past tense and past participle* **overhung** /-ˈhʌŋ/) to hang over something: *branches overhanging the path*

overhaul /ˌəʊvəˈhɔːl $ ˌoʊvərˈhɔːl/ v [T] to examine all the parts of a machine, system etc and repair or change them if necessary —**overhaul** /ˈəʊvəhɔːl $ ˈoʊvərhɔːl/ n [C]

overhead /ˌəʊvəˈhed◂ $ ˌoʊvər-/ adj, adv above your head: *overhead lights* | *A plane flew overhead.*

overheads /ˈəʊvəhedz $ ˈoʊvər-/ n [plural] BrE, **overhead** [U] AmE money that a business has to spend on rent, electricity etc

overhear /ˌəʊvəˈhɪə $ ˌoʊvərˈhɪr/ v [T] (*past tense and past participle* **overheard** /-ˈhɜːd $ -ˈhɜːrd/) to hear what people are saying when they are talking to each other and do not know you are listening: *I couldn't help overhearing bits of their conversation.*
THESAURUS ▶ HEAR

> **Word Choice: overhear or eavesdrop?**
> If you **overhear** something, you accidentally hear someone say it: *By chance, I overheard Geoff talking to Sue about the party.*
> If you **eavesdrop** on someone's conversation, you deliberately listen secretly to what they are saying: *She accused Brian of eavesdropping on her conversation with Terry.*

overheat /ˌəʊvəˈhiːt $ ˌoʊvər-/ v [I,T] to become too hot, or to make something too hot

overhung /ˌəʊvəˈhʌŋ $ ˌoʊvər-/ v the past tense and past participle of OVERHANG

overjoyed /ˌəʊvəˈdʒɔɪd $ ˌoʊvər-/ adj extremely happy

overkill /ˈəʊvəkɪl $ ˈoʊvər-/ n [U] when there is more of something than is necessary or wanted: *More television coverage of the election would be overkill.*

overland /ˌəʊvəˈlænd◂ $ ˌoʊvər-/ adj, adv across land, not by sea or air: *They are travelling overland to China.* | *an overland route*

overlap Ac /ˌəʊvəˈlæp $ ˌoʊvər-/ v [I,T] (**overlapped**, **overlapping**) **1** if two things overlap, part of one thing covers part of the other: *Roof tiles must*

overlap. **2** if two subjects, activities, ideas etc overlap, they include some but not all of the same things: *Our jobs overlap in certain areas.* —**overlap** /ˈəʊvəlæp $ ˈoʊvər-/ n [C,U]

overleaf /ˌəʊvəˈliːf $ ˈoʊvərliːf/ adv on the other side of a page: *See the chart overleaf.*

overload /ˌəʊvəˈləʊd $ ˌoʊvərˈloʊd/ v [T] (*past participle* **overloaded** or **overladen** /-ˈleɪdn/) **1** to put too many things or people on or into something: *The boat was overloaded and began to sink.* **2** to give someone too much work to do or information to deal with **3** to put too much electricity through an electrical system or piece of equipment —**overload** /ˈəʊvələʊd $ ˈoʊvərloʊd/ n [C,U]

overlook /ˌəʊvəˈlʊk $ ˌoʊvər-/ v [T] **1** to not notice something, or to not realize how important it is: *The police overlooked a key piece of evidence.* **2** if a building, room, window etc overlooks something, you can see that thing from the building, room etc: *a room overlooking the beach* **3** formal to forgive someone for a mistake, bad behaviour etc: *I am willing to overlook what you said this time.*

overly /ˈəʊvəli $ ˈoʊvər-/ adv too: *I think Kane is being overly optimistic.*

overnight /ˌəʊvəˈnaɪt $ ˌoʊvər-/ adv, adj **1** for or during the night: *She's staying overnight at a friend's house.* | *an overnight flight to Boston* **2** if something happens overnight, it happens quickly: *You can't expect to lose weight overnight.* | *The play was an overnight success.*

overpass /ˈəʊvəpɑːs $ ˈoʊvərpæs/ n [C] AmE a structure like a bridge that allows one road to go over another road SYN **flyover** BrE

overpopulated /ˌəʊvəˈpɒpjəleɪtɪd $ ˌoʊvərˈpɑːp-/ adj a country or city that is overpopulated has too many people —**overpopulation** /ˌəʊvəpɒpjəˈleɪʃən $ ˌoʊvərpɑːp-/ n [U]

overpower /ˌəʊvəˈpaʊə $ ˌoʊvərˈpaʊr/ v [T] to defeat someone because you are stronger

overpowering /ˌəʊvəˈpaʊərɪŋ◂ $ ˌoʊvərˈpaʊr-/ adj an overpowering feeling, need, smell etc is very strong: *The smell of gas was overpowering.*

overpriced /ˌəʊvəˈpraɪst◂ $ ˌoʊvər-/ adj too expensive: *overpriced restaurants* **THESAURUS** ▶ EXPENSIVE

overran /ˌəʊvəˈræn $ ˌoʊ-/ v the past tense of OVERRUN

overrated /ˌəʊvəˈreɪtɪd◂ $ ˌoʊ-/ adj not as good or important as some people think: *We thought the play was overrated.*

overreact /ˌəʊvəriˈækt $ ˌoʊ-/ v [I] to be more angry, afraid, worried etc than you should be —**overreaction** /-riˈækʃən/ n [C,U]

override /ˌəʊvəˈraɪd $ ˌoʊ-/ v [T] (*past tense* **overrode** /-ˈrəʊd $ -ˈroʊd/, *past participle* **overridden** /-ˈrɪdn/) **1** to use your power to change someone else's decision: *Congress has overridden the President's veto.* **2** to be stronger or more important than something else: *The economy often seems to override other political issues.*

overriding /ˌəʊvəˈraɪdɪŋ◄ $ ˌoʊ-/ adj [only before noun] more important than anything else: *Crime seems to be the overriding concern of voters.*

overrule /ˌəʊvəˈruːl $ ˌoʊ-/ v [T] to change an order or decision that you think is wrong, using your official power

overrun /ˌəʊvəˈrʌn $ ˌoʊ-/ v (past tense **overran** /-ˈræn/, past participle **overrun**, present participle **overrunning**) **1** [T] if unwanted things or people overrun a place, they spread over it in great numbers: *The town is being overrun by rats.* **2** [I] to take more time or money than intended: *The meeting overran by half an hour.*

overseas Ac /ˌəʊvəˈsiːz◄ $ ˌoʊvər-/ adj, adv to, in, or from a foreign country that is across the sea: *overseas students | My wife is working overseas.*

oversee /ˌəʊvəˈsiː $ ˌoʊvər-/ v [T] (past tense **oversaw** /-ˈsɔː $ -ˈsɒː/, past participle **overseen** /-ˈsiːn/) to be in charge of a group of workers and check that work is done correctly

overshadow /ˌəʊvəˈʃædəʊ $ ˌoʊvərˈʃædoʊ/ v [T] **1** to make something less enjoyable or happy: *The film festival was overshadowed by the news of the actor's death.* **2** to make someone or something else seem less important or successful: *He felt constantly overshadowed by his older brother.*

overshoot /ˌəʊvəˈʃuːt $ ˌoʊvər-/ v [I,T] (past tense and past participle **overshoot** /-ˈʃɒt $ -ˈʃɑːt/) to accidentally go a little further than you intended: *The plane overshot the runway and crashed into a ditch.*

oversight /ˈəʊvəsaɪt $ ˈoʊvər-/ n [C,U] a mistake that is caused by someone forgetting to do something or not noticing something

oversimplify /ˌəʊvəˈsɪmplɪfaɪ $ ˌoʊvər-/ v [I,T] (**oversimplified, oversimplifying, oversimplifies**) disapproving to make something seem simpler than it really is by ignoring many important facts —**oversimplification** /ˌəʊvəsɪmplɪfɪˈkeɪʃən $ ˌoʊvər-/ n [C,U]: *a gross oversimplification*

oversized /ˌəʊvəˈsaɪzd◄ $ ˌoʊvər-/ adj bigger than usual, or too big

oversleep /ˌəʊvəˈsliːp $ ˌoʊvər-/ v [I] (past tense and past participle **overslept** /-ˈslept/) to sleep for longer than you intended **THESAURUS▶ SLEEP**

overspend /ˌəʊvəˈspend $ ˌoʊvər-/ v [I,T] (past tense and past participle **overspent** /-ˈspent/) to spend more money than you can afford: *The hospital has overspent its budget.*

overstate /ˌəʊvəˈsteɪt $ ˌoʊvər-/ v [T] to talk about something in a way that makes it seem more important, serious etc than it really is

overstep /ˌəʊvəˈstep $ ˌoʊvər-/ v [T] (**overstepped, overstepping**) to behave in a way that is not acceptable or allowed: *Wilson has clearly **overstepped** his **authority**.* | **overstep the limits/bounds/boundary (of sth)** | **overstep the mark/line**

overstretch /ˌəʊvəˈstretʃ $ ˌoʊvər-/ v [T] to try to do more than you can in the time or with the money that you have available

overt /əʊˈvɜːt, əʊˈvɜːt $ ˈoʊvɜːrt, oʊˈvɜːrt/ adj done publicly, without trying to hide anything **OPP covert**: *overt discrimination* —**overtly** adv

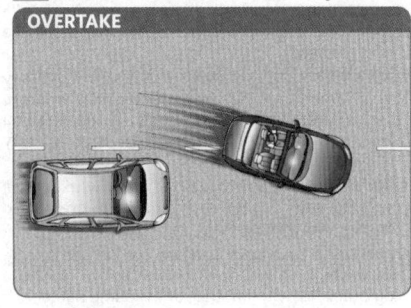

OVERTAKE

overtake /ˌəʊvəˈteɪk $ ˌoʊvər-/ v (past tense **overtook** /-ˈtʊk/, past participle **overtaken** /-ˈteɪkən/) **1** [I,T] to go past a moving vehicle or person because you are going faster than them: *The accident happened as he was overtaking a bus.* **2** [T] literary if something bad overtakes you, it happens suddenly and affects you strongly → **overcome**: *She was overtaken by exhaustion.* **3** [T] to develop and become more successful, important, or advanced than someone or something else: *Television soon overtook the cinema in popularity.*

over-the-counter adj over-the-counter drugs can be obtained without a PRESCRIPTION (=a written order) from a doctor

overthrow /ˌəʊvəˈθrəʊ $ ˌoʊvərˈθroʊ/ v [T] (past tense **overthrew** /-ˈθruː/, past participle **overthrown** /-ˈθrəʊn $ -ˈθroʊn/) to remove a leader or government from power by using force

overtime /ˈəʊvətaɪm $ ˈoʊvər-/ n [U] time that you spend working in your job in addition to your normal working hours

overtones /ˈəʊvətəʊnz $ ˈoʊvərtoʊnz/ n [plural] if something has overtones, an emotion, attitude etc is involved but not expressed directly: **political/racial/emotional etc overtones** *the murder's political overtones*

overtook /ˌəʊvəˈtʊk $ ˌoʊvər-/ v the past tense of OVERTAKE

overture /ˈəʊvətjʊə, -tʃʊə, -tʃə $ ˈoʊvərtjʊr, -tʃʊr, -tʃər/ n [C] **1** a piece of music that comes before a longer musical piece, especially an OPERA **2 overtures** [plural] an attempt to begin a friendly relationship with a person, country etc: *The new president **made overtures to** the United States.*

overturn /ˌəʊvəˈtɜːn $ ˌoʊvərˈtɜːrn/ v **1** [I,T] if something overturns, or if you overturn it, it turns upside down or falls over on its side: *The car overturned on a country road.* **2** [T] to officially change a decision made by a court: *The appeal court **overturned the decision.***

overview /ˈəʊvəvjuː $ ˈoʊvər-/ n [C] a short description of a subject or situation, giving its main features but not all the details

overweight /ˌəʊvəˈweɪt◄ $ ˌoʊvər-/ adj too heavy or too fat: *I'm ten pounds overweight.*

overwhelm /ˌəʊvəˈwelm $ ˌoʊvər-/ v [T] if a feeling overwhelms you, you feel it so strongly that you cannot think clearly: *Josh was overwhelmed with guilt.* | *She was overwhelmed by emotion when she heard the news.*

overwhelming /ˌəʊvəˈwelmɪŋ $ oʊvər-/ adj **1** very big in amount or number: *overwhelming evidence that smoking damages your health* **2** affecting you very strongly: *an overwhelming urge to cry* —**overwhelmingly** adv

overworked /ˌəʊvəˈwɜːkt◂ $ ˌoʊvərˈwɜːrkt◂/ adj made to work too much or too hard: *overworked nurses* —**overwork** n [U]

overwrite /ˌəʊvəˈraɪt $ ˌoʊvər-/ v [T] (past tense **overwrote**, past participle **overwritten**) to replace a computer FILE with another of the same name

overwrought /ˌəʊvəˈrɔːt◂ $ ˌoʊvəˈrɔːt◂/ adj very upset, nervous, and worried

ovulate /ˈɒvjˑleɪt $ ˈɑːv-/ v [I] technical when a woman or female animal ovulates, she produces eggs inside her body —**ovulation** /ˌɒvjˑˈleɪʃən $ ˌɑːv-/ n [U]

ow /aʊ/ spoken used when you suddenly feel pain: *Ow! That hurt!*

owe /əʊ $ oʊ/ v [T]
1 to have to pay someone some money they have lent you, or pay for something they gave you or did for you → **borrow**, **lend**: **owe sb money/£10 etc** *Bob owes me $20.* | **owe sth to sb** *We owe money to the bank.* | **owe sb for sth** *I still owe Conrad for dinner.* | *How much do I owe you* (=used when you want to pay for something)?
2 to feel that you should do something for someone or give someone something, for example because they have done something for you: **owe sb sth** *I owe you an apology.* | *Gary owes me a favour.*
3 to have something or have achieved something because of what someone else has done: **owe sth to sb** *I owe it all to my parents.*

THESAURUS

owe if you owe someone some money, you need to pay it back: *You still owe me $50.* | *Let me know how much I owe you for the shopping.*
be in debt to owe money, especially a lot of money that you have difficulty paying back: *Many young people are in debt when they finish university.*
be overdrawn to owe money to your bank because you have spent more money than you had in your account: *The bank sent me a letter saying I was overdrawn.*
be in the red informal to owe more money than you have: *The company is over £1,000,000 in the red.*

'owing to prep because of: *Work on the building has stopped, owing to lack of money.*

owl /aʊl/ n [C] a bird that hunts at night and has large eyes and a loud call → see picture on page A3

own¹ /əʊn $ oʊn/ determiner, pron
1 belonging to you and no one else: *She wants her own room.* | **sth of your own** *He decided to start a business of his own.* | *I can't afford a place of my own* (=my own home).
2 done by a particular person without the help of anyone else: *Luis has started writing his own songs.* | *You have to learn to make your own decisions.*

PHRASES
get your own back (on sb) informal to do something bad to someone because they have done something bad to you: *She wanted to get her own back on Liz for ruining her party.*
(all) on your own 1 alone: *Rick lives on his own.* **2** without anyone's help: *Martha raised six children all on her own.*

own² v [T] if you own something, it legally belongs to you, especially because you bought it or were given it → **possess**: *Duane and his wife own a restaurant in Atlanta.*

PHRASAL VERBS
own up to admit that you have done something wrong: **own up to (doing) sth** *No one owned up to breaking the window.*

THESAURUS

own if you own something, it legally belongs to you: *We don't own the house – we just rent it.*
have to own something, especially something ordinary that you use every day: *She has a lot of lovely clothes.* | *Most students have computers.*
belong to sb/sth used when saying who owns something: *The ring belonged to my grandmother.*
possess formal to own something: *He was charged with possessing a gun.* | *They took away everything she possessed.*

owner /ˈəʊnə $ ˈoʊnər/ n [C] someone who owns something: *a dog owner* | **[+of]** *the owner of the local hotel*

ownership /ˈəʊnəʃɪp $ ˈoʊnər-/ n [U] the state of owning something, or the fact that a particular person owns something: **[+of]** *a dispute over the ownership of the land*

ˌown 'goal n [C] BrE **1** a GOAL that you accidentally score against your own team **2** informal something you do that has bad results for you or the group you belong to

ox /ɒks $ ɑːks/ n [C] (plural **oxen** /ˈɒksən $ ˈɑːk-/) a large type of BULL (=male cow). In the past, oxen were used to pull heavy loads, especially on farms.

oxygen /ˈɒksɪdʒən $ ˈɑːk-/ n [U] a gas in the air that all living things need

oyster /ˈɔɪstə $ -ər/ n [C,U] a small sea animal that has a shell and makes a jewel called a PEARL

oz the written abbreviation of **ounce**

ozone layer /ˈəʊzəʊn ˌleɪə $ ˈoʊzoʊn ˌleɪər/ n [singular] a layer of gases around the Earth that stops harmful RADIATION from the Sun from reaching the Earth

P, p /piː/ *n* [C,U] (*plural* **P's**, **p's**) the 16th letter of the English alphabet

p. (*also* **p** *BrE*) **1** the written abbreviation of **page 2** *BrE* the abbreviation of **penny** or **pence**

p & p *BrE* the written abbreviation of **postage and packing**

p.a. the written abbreviation of **per annum**

PA /ˌpiː ˈeɪ/ *n* [C] **1** *BrE* (**personal assistant**) a secretary who works for one person **2** (**public address system**) electronic equipment that makes someone's voice loud enough to be heard by large groups of people

pace¹ /peɪs/ *n* **1** [singular] the speed at which something happens, or at which someone moves, works etc: *She heard someone behind her and quickened her pace.* | **[+of]** *the relaxed pace of life in Italy* **2** [C] a single step: *He took a pace towards the door.*
PHRASES
| **keep pace (with sb/sth)** to change as fast as something else, or to move as fast as someone else: *Supply has to keep pace with increasing demand.*

pace² *v* **1** [I,T] to walk first in one direction and then in the other many times, especially because you are worried: **[+around/up and down]** *He paced up and down the hospital corridor.* **2 pace yourself** to do something at a steady speed so that you do not get tired too quickly: *It's a long climb, so you have to pace yourself.*

pacemaker /ˈpeɪsˌmeɪkə $ -ər/ *n* [C] a small machine that is put inside someone's chest to help their heart beat regularly

pacifier /ˈpæsəfaɪə $ -faɪər/ *n* [C] *AmE* a rubber object that a baby sucks so that he or she does not cry **SYN** **dummy** *BrE*

pacifist /ˈpæsɪfɪst/ *n* [C] someone who believes that wars are wrong and who refuses to fight in them —**pacifism** *n* [U]

pacify /ˈpæsɪfaɪ/ *v* [T] (**pacified**, **pacifying**, **pacifies**) to make someone calm and quiet after they have been angry or upset

pack¹ /pæk/ *v*
1 (*also* **pack up**) [I,T] to put things into cases, bags etc ready for a journey: *Have you finished packing up yet?* | *Don't forget to pack a warm coat.*
2 [T] to put something into a container so that it can be moved, sold, or stored: *Glass must be packed carefully.* | **pack sth in/into sth** *The fish are packed in ice at sea.*
3 [I,T] to go in large numbers into a place, or to make people or animals do this, until the place is too full → **packed**: **[+into/in/onto]** *Thousands of*

people packed into the stadium. | *chickens packed together in tiny cages*
PHRASAL VERBS
pack sth ↔ **in**
1 (*also* **pack** sth **into** sth) to do a lot of things in a short time: *I don't know how we packed so much activity into one weekend.*
2 *BrE informal* to stop doing a job or activity, especially because you do not enjoy it: *Sometimes I feel like packing my job in.*
pack sb **off** *informal* to send someone to stay somewhere: *We were packed off to camp every summer.*
pack up
1 *informal* to finish work: *I think I'll pack up and go home early.*
2 *BrE informal* if a machine packs up, it stops working because something is wrong with it: *The television's packed up again.*

pack² *n* [C]
1 **THINGS PUT TOGETHER** **a)** several similar things wrapped or packed together in order to sell them or send them to someone: **[+of]** *a pack of three T-shirts* | *Send for your free **information pack**.* **b)** *AmE* a small container made of paper or plastic that something is sold in **SYN** **packet** *BrE*: **[+of]** *a pack of cigarettes*
2 **GROUP OF ANIMALS** a group of wild animals that hunt together: **[+of]** *a pack of dogs* **THESAURUS** **GROUP**
3 **BAG** a bag for equipment, clothes etc that you carry on your back, especially when climbing or walking **SYN** **backpack**, **rucksack** *BrE*
4 **GROUP OF PEOPLE** a group of the same type of people, especially a group who you do not approve of: **[+of]** *a pack of thieves*
5 **CARDS** a set of playing cards **SYN** **deck** *AmE* → **ICE PACK**

package¹ /ˈpækɪdʒ/ *n* [C]
1 something that has been packed in a box or wrapped in paper, and then sent by mail or delivered **SYN** **parcel** *BrE*
2 *AmE* the box, bag etc that food or other goods are sold in **SYN** **packet** *BrE*: *a package of cookies*
3 a set of related programs sold together for use on a computer: *a new **software package***

package² *v* [T] **1** to put food or goods in a box, bag etc ready to be sold: *food packaged in cartons* **2** to make something seem attractive so that people will become interested in it or buy it: *The band was packaged to appeal to young girls.*

'package tour (*also* **'package ˌholiday** *BrE*) *n* [C] a holiday arranged by a company for a fixed price that includes the cost of your hotel and travel

packaging /ˈpækɪdʒɪŋ/ *n* [U] the bags, boxes etc that a product is sold in

packed /pækt/ *adj* full of people: **[+with]** *The island was packed with tourists.* **THESAURUS** **FULL**

ˌpacked 'lunch *n* [C] *BrE* food such as sandwiches and fruit that you take to eat at work, school etc

packet /ˈpækɪt/ *n* [C] *BrE* a small container made of paper or plastic that something is sold in **SYN** **pack** *AmE*: **[+of]** *a packet of biscuits* → see picture at **CONTAINER**

packing /'pækɪŋ/ n [U] **1** when you put things into cases or boxes in order to send or take them somewhere: *I can* **do my packing** *on Friday night.* **2** the material used for packing things so that they can be sent somewhere

pact /pækt/ n [C] a formal agreement between two countries, groups, or people

PADS

notepad

pad of cotton wool

knee pad

pad¹ /pæd/ n [C] **1** a thick piece of soft material used to protect something or make it more comfortable: **[+of]** *a pad of cotton wool* | **knee/elbow/shin etc pad** (=worn to protect part of your body when playing a sport) **2** several sheets of paper fastened together, used for writing or drawing: *a sketch pad*

pad² v (**padded, padding**) **1** [I + adv/prep] to walk somewhere quietly **2** (*also* **pad out**) [T] to make a piece of writing longer by adding unnecessary words or information

padded /'pædɪd/ adj covered or filled with soft material in order to protect something or make something more comfortable: *a padded envelope* | *padded boots*

padding /'pædɪŋ/ n [U] material used to protect something or make something more comfortable

paddle¹ /'pædl/ n [C] **1** a short pole with a wide flat end, used for moving a small boat in water → **oar 2** [usually singular] *BrE* when you take off your shoes and socks and walk in water: *Let's go for a paddle.*

paddle² v **1** [I,T] to move a small boat in water, using a paddle → **row 2** [I] *BrE* to walk without shoes or socks in water: **[+in]** *children paddling in the stream*

paddock /'pædək/ n [C] a small field where horses are kept

paddy field /'pædi fiːld/ n [C] a field where rice is grown

padlock /'pædlɒk $ -lɑːk/ n [C] a small lock that you put on a door, bicycle etc → see picture at LOCK² —**padlock** v [T]

paediatrician *BrE*, **pediatrician** *AmE* /ˌpiːdiə'trɪʃən/ n [C] a doctor who deals with children

paediatrics *BrE*, **pediatrics** *AmE* /ˌpiːdi'ætrɪks/ n [U] the area of medicine relating to children and their illnesses —**paediatric** adj

paedophile *BrE*, **pedophile** *AmE* /'piːdəfaɪl/ n [C] someone who is sexually attracted to children

pagan /'peɪgən/ adj not belonging to any of the main world religions – used about very old religious beliefs and customs: *pagan festivals* —**pagan** n [C]

page¹ /peɪdʒ/ n [C] a piece of paper in a book, newspaper etc, or one side of it: **on page 5/the next page etc** *The test questions start on page 2.* | *The report was 50 pages long.* → **WEB PAGE**

COLLOCATIONS

adjectives

the next/previous page *She read the previous page again.*

the opposite page *A picture on the opposite page caught my attention.*

the front/back page (=of a newspaper) *The story is on the front page of every newspaper.*

a blank page (=with nothing on it) *Leave a blank page after the title.*

verbs

to turn a page *Quickly, she turned the page.*

turn to/see page 22/45 etc *For more on this story, turn to page 23.*

nouns

the top of the page *Put the date at the top of the page.*

the bottom/foot of the page *The answers are at the bottom of page 14.*

page² v [T] **1** to call someone's name in a public place using a LOUDSPEAKER **2** to call someone using a PAGER (=small machine that receives messages)

pageant /'pædʒənt/ n [C] a public show that usually tells a historical or religious story: *the annual Christmas pageant*

pageantry /'pædʒəntri/ n [U] impressive ceremonies or events, involving many people wearing special clothes: *the splendour of royal pageantry*

pager /'peɪdʒə $ -ər/ n [C] a small machine you can carry that receives telephone messages and makes a noise when one is waiting for you

paid¹ /peɪd/ v the past tense and past participle of PAY

paid² adj **1** paid work is work that you receive money for doing: *paid employment* | **highly/poorly paid** *a highly paid job* **2** used to talk about a period of time when your employer pays you even though you are not working: *paid holidays*

paid-up adj *BrE* **paid-up member** someone who has paid the money needed to be a member of a club, political party etc: *a paid-up member of the union*

pail /peɪl/ n [C] *especially AmE* a BUCKET

pain¹ /peɪn/ n

1 [C,U] the feeling you have when part of your body hurts: **[+in]** *I have a pain in my lower back.* | **in pain** *Cassie lay groaning in pain on the bed.*

2 [U] sadness and unhappiness: *the pain children feel when their parents divorce*

PHRASES

a pain (in the neck) *spoken* someone or something that is very annoying: *I find the paperwork a pain in the neck.*

be at pains to do sth/take pains to do sth to make a special effort to do something: *He was at pains to emphasize the advantages of the new system.*

COLLOCATIONS

verbs

to have a pain *He has a pain in his stomach.*
to feel pain (also **to suffer from pain**) *If you feel any pain, stop exercising.*
to cause pain *Several conditions can cause back pain.*
to relieve/ease/reduce pain (=to make it less bad) *Aspirin is used to relieve pain.*

adjectives

a bad pain *I've got a really bad pain in my leg.*
severe/terrible pain *She woke up with terrible stomach pains.* ⚠ Do not say 'big pain'. Say **terrible pain** or **severe pain**.
a sharp pain (=a short severe pain) *A sharp pain went through his leg when he stood up.*
excruciating/unbearable pain (=very severe pain) *The pain in my eye was excruciating.*

noun + pain

chest/back/stomach pain *Patients with chest pain should be seen immediately by a doctor.*

THESAURUS

pain the feeling you have when part of your body hurts: *The pain in my chest was getting worse.*
ache a continuous pain, especially one that is not very bad: *She had a fever and aches in her muscles.*
headache/stomach ache/toothache/backache/earache a continuous pain in a part of your body: *The noise is giving me a headache.* | *The next day I had a stomach ache.*
suffering great physical or mental pain, which makes someone very unhappy: *I wish there was something I could do to ease their suffering* (=reduce it).

---

pain² v **it pains sb to do sth** *formal* used to say that it is difficult and unpleasant for someone to have to do something

pained /peɪnd/ adj upset or slightly annoyed: *a pained expression*

painful /ˈpeɪnfəl/ adj

1 making you feel very unhappy or upset: *painful memories of the war* | **it is painful to do sth** *It was*

painful to leave the house where I was born. | **[+for]** *The divorce was painful for the children.*

2 making you feel physical pain: *Her ankle was swollen and painful.* | *a painful blow on the head*

THESAURUS – sense 2

painful if a part of your body or an injury is painful, you feel pain in it: *Is your back still painful?* | *When I broke my arm, it was extremely painful.*
sore painful, especially because of an infection, or because you have done a lot of exercise: *a sore throat* | *My muscles were sore after the race.*
tender painful when it is touched: *The skin around the cut is red and tender.*
stiff painful and difficult to move, for example because you have been in one position for too long: *My legs were a bit stiff after the journey.*
sth hurts used when saying that part of your body is painful: *Mum – my stomach hurts.*

---

painfully /ˈpeɪnfəli/ adv **1** very – used to emphasize a bad quality, or something that is unpleasant and upsetting: *She was painfully shy as a child.* | **painfully clear/obvious/apparent** *It was painfully obvious that he was lying.* **2** in a way that makes you feel physical pain: *Bill walked slowly and painfully to the door.*

painkiller /ˈpeɪnˌkɪlə $ -ər/ n [C] a medicine that reduces pain

painless /ˈpeɪnləs/ adj causing no pain: *a painless death*

painstaking /ˈpeɪnzˌteɪkɪŋ/ adj very careful and thorough: *painstaking research* **THESAURUS** ► CAREFUL
—**painstakingly** adv

paint¹ /peɪnt/ n

1 [C,U] a liquid that you put on walls and other surfaces using a brush to make the surface a particular colour: *a can of yellow paint* | *The kitchen needs a fresh coat of paint* (=layer of paint).

2 paints [plural] a set of small tubes or blocks of paint, used for painting pictures: *oil paints*

paint² v [I,T]

1 to put paint on a surface: *What color are you painting the house?* | **paint sth (in) blue/red/green etc** *I'm painting my bedroom yellow.*

2 to make a picture of someone or something, using paint: *He's just finished painting his wife's portrait.*

paintbox /ˈpeɪntbɒks $ -bɑːks/ n [C] a small box containing blocks of coloured paints

paintbrush /ˈpeɪntbrʌʃ/ n [C] a brush used to paint pictures or walls → see picture at **BRUSH¹**

painter /ˈpeɪntə $ -ər/ n [C]

1 someone who paints pictures **SYN** artist: *a landscape painter*

2 someone whose job is painting houses, rooms etc: *a **painter and decorator***

painting /ˈpeɪntɪŋ/ n

1 [C] a painted picture: *an exhibition of paintings and sculptures* → see picture on page 640

2 [U] the process of painting: *Van Gogh's style of painting* → **OIL PAINTING**

paintwork

PAINTINGS

landscape

still life

portrait

abstract

paintwork /'peɪntwɜːk $ -wɜːrk/ n [U] paint on a car, house etc

pair¹ /peə $ per/ n [C]
1 something made of two similar parts that are joined together: **pair of trousers/scissors/glasses etc** a pair of jeans
2 two things of the same type that are used together: **pair of socks/earrings/shoes etc** a new pair of gloves
3 two people who do something together or who know each other well → **couple**: a pair of dancers | **Work in pairs** on the next exercise. → AU PAIR

pair² v
PHRASAL VERBS
pair off if two people pair off or someone pairs them off, they come together, especially to start a romantic relationship: The guests paired off for the first dance. | **pair sb ↔ off (with sb)** She tried to pair me off with her son.
pair up if two people pair up or someone pairs them up, they work together or do something together: **[+with]** I paired up with Mike for the quiz. | **pair sb ↔ up** The children were paired up.

pajamas /pə'dʒɑːməz $ -'dʒæ-, -'dʒɑː-/ n [plural] the American spelling of PYJAMAS

pal /pæl/ n [C] informal a friend: a college pal

palace /'pælɪs/ n [C] a large house where a king or queen lives: Buckingham Palace

palatable /'pælətəbəl/ adj **1** palatable food or drink tastes quite pleasant: a very palatable wine **2** an idea, suggestion etc that is palatable is acceptable: The idea was **more palatable to** Washington than London.

palate /'pælət/ n [C] **1** the top inside part of your mouth **2** your sense of taste

palatial /pə'leɪʃəl/ adj a palatial building is big and beautifully decorated: a palatial hotel

pale¹ /peɪl/ adj
1 having a skin colour that is whiter than usual, especially because you are ill or frightened: Jan looked tired and pale. | **turn/go pale** He suddenly went pale.
2 a pale colour is a light form of a colour SYN **light** OPP **dark**: pale green walls

pale² v [I] **1** to seem unimportant, unattractive etc compared to something else: Once you've experienced sailing, other sports **pale in comparison**. **2** if you pale, your face becomes whiter than usual, especially because you are ill or frightened: Hettie paled when she heard the news.

palette /'pælət/ n [C] a board that an artist uses for mixing paints

pall¹ /pɔːl $ pɒːl/ n **a pall of smoke/dust etc** a thick dark cloud of smoke, dust etc

pall² v [I] literary to become less interesting or enjoyable: City life was beginning to pall.

pallid /'pælɪd/ adj literary pale and unhealthy: a pallid complexion

pallor /'pælə $ -ər/ n [singular] formal a pale unhealthy colour of the skin or face

palm¹ /pɑːm $ pɑːm, pɑːlm/ n [C] **1** the surface of your hand in which you hold things: He held the pebble **in the palm of** his hand. → see picture at HAND¹ **2** a palm tree

palm² v
PHRASAL VERBS
palm sth ↔ **off** to persuade someone to take or buy something that is not of good quality or is not what they really want: **[+on/onto]** My brother's always trying to palm his old clothes off on me.
palm sb **off with** sth to give someone an explanation that is not true but that you hope they will accept: She's always palming me off with excuses.

palmtop /'pɑːmtɒp $ 'pɑːmtɑːp, 'pɑːlm-/ n [C] a very small computer that you can hold in your hand → see picture on page A12

'palm tree n [C] a tall tree with large pointed leaves at the top that grows near beaches or in deserts

palpable /'pælpəbəl/ adj easy to notice: a palpable sense of relief —**palpably** adv

palpitations /ˌpælpə'teɪʃənz/ n [plural] when your heart beats in a fast irregular way, especially because you are ill or very anxious

paltry /'pɔːltri $ 'pɒːl-/ adj too small to be useful or important: a paltry pay increase

pamper /'pæmpə $ -ər/ v [T] to give someone a lot of care and attention

pamphlet /'pæmflɪt/ n [C] a thin paper book containing information about something

pan¹ /pæn/ n [C] a metal container that you use for cooking, usually with a long handle → **saucepan**: Melt the butter in a pan. | a frying pan | pots and pans

pan² v (**panned**, **panning**) **1** [T] informal to strongly criticize a film, play etc in a newspaper or on television or radio: His latest movie has been panned by the critics. **2** [I] if a film or television camera pans in a particular direction, it moves in that direction: **[+across/back etc]** The camera panned across the crowd.

PANS

saucepan

frying pan

wok

PHRASAL VERBS

pan out *informal* to happen or develop in a particular way: *Let's wait and see how things pan out.*

panacea /ˌpænəˈsɪə/ *n* [C] something that people think will solve all their problems

panache /pəˈnæʃ, pæ-/ *n* [U] a way of doing something that people admire because it makes it seem easy: **with panache** *He played with skill and panache.*

pancake /ˈpænkeɪk/ *n* [C] a thin flat food made from flour, milk, and eggs that is cooked in a pan and eaten hot

panda /ˈpændə/ *n* [C] a large black and white animal that is similar to a bear and lives in China → see picture at BEAR²

pandemonium /ˌpændəˈməʊniəm $ -ˈmoʊ-/ *n* [U] when there is a lot of noise and activity because people are angry, excited etc

pander /ˈpændə $ -ər/ *v*
PHRASAL VERBS
pander to sb/sth to give someone anything they want in order to please them, even when it is unreasonable or unnecessary: *He accused the Tories of pandering to middle-class voters.*

pane /peɪn/ *n* [C] a piece of glass in a window or door: *a window pane*

panel Ac /ˈpænl/ *n* [C] **1** a piece of wood, glass etc that is part of a door, wall, or ceiling: *an oak door with three panels* **2** a group of people who are chosen to discuss something or answer questions: **[+of]** *a panel of experts* | **on a panel** *There were several professors on the panel.* **3 instrument/control panel** the part in a car, plane, boat etc that has the controls on it: *He checked his instrument panel.*

panelled *BrE*, **paneled** *AmE* /ˈpænld/ *adj* covered with flat pieces of wood: *a panelled door*

panelling *BrE*, **paneling** *AmE* /ˈpænəl-ɪŋ/ *n* [U] flat pieces of wood, used to decorate walls: *oak panelling*

panellist *BrE*, **panelist** *AmE* /ˈpænəlɪst/ *n* [C] one of a group of people who answer questions on a radio or television programme

pang /pæŋ/ *n* [C] a sudden strong feeling of pain, sadness etc: ***hunger pangs*** | **[+of]** *She was having pangs of guilt about Pete.*

panhandle /ˈpænˌhændl/ *v* [I] *AmE informal* to ask for money in the streets **SYN beg** —**panhandler** *n* [C]

panic¹ /ˈpænɪk/ *n* [C,U] a sudden strong feeling of fear or anxiety that makes you do things without thinking carefully: *Stephen had a sudden feeling of panic.* | **in (a) panic** *People ran into the streets in a panic after the explosion.* | *There was panic on Wall Street as prices fell.*

panic² *v* [I,T] (**panicked**, **panicking**) to feel so frightened that you cannot think clearly or behave sensibly, or to make someone feel like this: *Stay where you are and don't panic!* —**panicky** *adj*

'panic-ˌstricken *adj* very frightened and unable to think clearly or behave sensibly

panorama /ˌpænəˈrɑːmə $ -ˈræmə/ *n* [C] a view over a wide area of land —**panoramic** /ˌpænəˈræmɪk◀/ *adj*: *a panoramic view of Hong Kong*

pansy /ˈpænzi/ *n* [C] (*plural* **pansies**) a small brightly coloured garden flower

pant /pænt/ *v* [I] to breathe quickly with short noisy breaths, especially after exercising or because it is hot **THESAURUS ▶ BREATHE**

panther /ˈpænθə $ -ər/ *n* [C] a large black wild animal that is a type of cat → see picture at TIGER

panties /ˈpæntiz/ *n* [plural] *especially AmE* a piece of women's underwear that covers the area between the waist and the top of the legs **SYN knickers** *BrE*

pantomime /ˈpæntəmaɪm/ *n* [C,U] **1** (*also* **panto** /ˈpæntəʊ $ -toʊ/ *BrE informal*) a type of play for children that is performed in Britain around Christmas, with a traditional story, jokes, and songs **2** *AmE* a method of performing using only actions and not words, or a play performed using this method **SYN mime**

pantry /ˈpæntri/ *n* [C] (*plural* **pantries**) a small room near or in a kitchen where food is kept

pants¹ /pænts/ *n* [plural]
1 *BrE* a piece of underwear that covers the area between your waist and the top of your legs **SYN underpants** *AmE* → **boxer shorts**, **knickers**
2 *especially AmE* a piece of clothing that covers you from your waist to your feet and has a separate part for each leg **SYN trousers** *BrE*: *young men in baggy pants*

pants² *adj* [not before noun] *BrE spoken informal* very bad: *The concert was pants.*

pantsuit /ˈpæntsuːt, -sjuːt $ -suːt/ *n* [C] *AmE* a suit for women, which consists of a jacket and trousers **SYN trouser suit** *BrE*

pantyhose /ˈpæntihəʊz $ -hoʊz/ *n* [plural] *AmE* a piece of women's clothing made of very thin material that covers the legs from the feet to the waist, usually worn under dresses or skirts **SYN tights** *BrE*

papacy /ˈpeɪpəsi/ *n* **the papacy** the position and authority of the POPE

papal /ˈpeɪpəl/ *adj* relating to the POPE

paparazzi /ˌpæpəˈrætsi $ ˌpɑːpəˈrɑː-/ *n* [plural] photographers who follow famous people in order to take photographs they can sell to newspapers

paper[1] /ˈpeɪpə $ -ər/ n

1 **FOR WRITING ON ETC** [U] thin material used for writing on, drawing on, wrapping things etc: *Have you got any coloured paper?*

Grammar
In this sense, **paper** is uncountable. Do not say 'a paper'. Say *a piece/sheet of paper*.

2 **NEWSPAPER** [C] a newspaper: *I read about it in yesterday's paper.* | *a local paper* (=the newspaper for the area you live in)* **THESAURUS** NEWSPAPER

3 **DOCUMENTS** papers [plural] important or official documents or letters: *There are several papers for you to sign.*

4 **SPEECH/PIECE OF WRITING** [C] a talk or a piece of writing on a particular subject by someone who has studied it: **[+on]** *She's giving a paper on classical architecture.*

5 **EXAMINATION** [C] an examination on a particular subject done as part of a course at school or university: *The history paper was really easy.*

PHRASES

on paper 1 if you put ideas or information on paper, you write them down: *You need to get some of your thoughts down on paper.* **2** if an idea seems good on paper, it is good as an idea, but probably not in a real situation: *It looks good on paper, but I still don't think it will work.*

COLLOCATIONS

noun + paper

a piece of paper *Here, use this piece of paper.*
a sheet of paper *The floor was covered with crumpled sheets of paper.*
a scrap/slip of paper (=a small piece) *I grabbed a pen and a scrap of paper.*

types of paper

plain paper (=with nothing printed on it) *The letter was typed on plain paper.*
recycled paper (=made from waste paper) *This leaflet is printed on recycled paper.*
writing paper/notepaper (=for writing letters on) *She always wrote on pink writing paper.*
wrapping paper (=for wrapping presents) *Try to save and reuse wrapping paper.*

---

paper[2] v [T] to cover the walls of a room with WALLPAPER

paperback /ˈpeɪpəbæk $ -ər-/ n [C] a book with a fairly stiff paper cover → **hardback**: **in paperback** *His novel is now available in paperback.* **THESAURUS** BOOK

ˈpaper boy n [C] a boy who delivers newspapers to people's houses

paperclip /ˈpeɪpəklɪp $ -ər-/ n [C] a small piece of curved wire used for holding sheets of paper together → see picture at **STATIONERY**

ˈpaper girl n [C] a girl who delivers newspapers to people's houses

paperweight /ˈpeɪpəweɪt $ -ər-/ n [C] a small heavy object that you put on top of pieces of paper to keep them in that place

paperwork /ˈpeɪpəwɜːk $ -pərwɜːrk/ n [U] **1** work

such as writing letters or reports: *The job involves a lot of paperwork.* **2** the documents that you need for a business deal, journey etc: *I've left all the paperwork in the office.*

paprika /ˈpæprɪkə, pəˈpriːkə $ pəˈpriːkə/ n [U] a red spice made from a type of sweet PEPPER

par /pɑː $ pɑːr/ n **1 be on a par (with sth)** to be at the same level or standard: *Technological developments in the US are on a par with those in Japan.* **2 be below par/not be up to par** to be not as good as the usual or expected standard: *Italy's performance in the Championships wasn't up to par.*

parable /ˈpærəbəl/ n [C] a short story that teaches a moral or religious lesson, especially one from the Bible

parabola /pəˈræbələ/ n [C] technical a curve like the course of an object that is thrown into the air and comes down a little distance away

paracetamol /ˌpærəˈsiːtəmɒl, -ˈset- $ -mɑːl, -mɒːl/ n [C,U] (plural **paracetamol** or **paracetamols**) BrE a common drug used to reduce pain, which does not contain ASPIRIN

parachute[1] /ˈpærəʃuːt/ n [C] a piece of equipment worn by people who jump out of planes, to make them fall slowly and safely to the ground

PARACHUTE

parachute[2] v [I + adv/ prep] to jump from a plane using a parachute

parade[1] /pəˈreɪd/ n [C] **1** a public celebration when musical bands, decorated vehicles etc move down the street: *a victory parade* **2** a military ceremony in which soldiers stand or march together so that important people can examine them: **on parade** *The soldiers were on parade.*

parade[2] v **1** [I] to walk in a large group to celebrate or protest about something: **[+through/around etc]** *Peace demonstrators paraded through the town.* **2** [T] to show your skill, knowledge, possessions etc in order to make people admire you: *He loves parading his wealth in front of people.*

paradigm Ac /ˈpærədaɪm/ n [C] formal a very clear or typical example of something —**paradigmatic** /ˌpærədɪɡˈmætɪk◂/ adj

paradise /ˈpærədaɪs/ n **1 Paradise** the place where some people think good people go after they die **SYN** **heaven 2** [singular, U] a place or situation that you like very much or that is very beautiful: **[+for]** *Hawaii is a paradise for wind surfers.* | **a walker's/ shopper's etc paradise**

paradox /ˈpærədɒks $ -dɑːks/ n [C] a situation or statement that seems strange because it involves two ideas or qualities that are very different: *It's a paradox that so many poor people are living in such a rich country.* —**paradoxical** /ˌpærəˈdɒksɪkəl◂ $ -ˈdɑːk-/ adj —**paradoxically** /-kli/ adv

paraffin /'pærəfɪn/ n [U] BrE oil used for heating and in lamps, made from PETROLEUM or coal SYN **kerosene** AmE

paragon /'pærəgən $ -gɑːn/ n [C] someone who is perfect or extremely brave, good etc: **[+of]** He expects me to be a **paragon of virtue** (=perfectly good, honest etc).

paragraph Ac /'pærəgrɑːf $ -græf/ n [C] a part of a piece of writing that starts on a new line

parallel¹ Ac /'pærəlel/ adj **1** two lines, roads etc that are parallel go in the same direction and are the same distance apart all the way: **[+to/with]** The street **runs parallel** to the railroad. **2** similar and happening at the same time: The British and French police are conducting parallel investigations.

parallel² Ac n [C] a relationship or similarity between two things: **[+between]** books that attempt to **draw parallels** between brains and computers (=show how they are similar)

parallel³ Ac v [T] formal to be similar to something else, or to happen at the same time as something else: Symptoms of depression often parallel those of more severe mental illnesses.

paralyse BrE, **paralyze** AmE /'pærəlaɪz/ v [T] **1** [usually passive] to make someone lose the ability to move their body or part of their body **2** to make a system or organization unable to work or continue normally: Heavy snow has paralyzed transport in several cities. —**paralysed** adj: The stroke left him paralyzed.

paralysis /pəˈrælɪsɪs/ n [U] when you lose the ability to move your body or part of your body

paramedic /,pærəˈmedɪk/ n [C] someone who usually works in an AMBULANCE and is trained to help ill or injured people, but is not a doctor or nurse

parameter Ac /pəˈræmɪtə $ -ər/ n [C usually plural] a fixed limit that controls the way that something should be done: Congress will decide on parameters for the investigation.

paramilitary /,pærəˈmɪlətəri $ -teri◂/ adj a paramilitary organization is an illegal military group that uses violence to achieve political aims: paramilitary forces —**paramilitaries** n [plural]

paramount /'pærəmaʊnt/ adj formal more important than anything else: Safety is paramount. | Good education is **of paramount importance**.

paranoia /,pærəˈnɔɪə/ n [U] an unreasonable belief that you cannot trust people or that they are trying to harm you

paranoid /'pærənɔɪd/ adj feeling anxious and worried that you cannot trust people or that they are trying to harm you: **[+about]** She's paranoid about going out at night alone.

paranormal /,pærəˈnɔːməl◂ $ -ˈnɔːr-/ adj paranormal events cannot be explained by science and seem strange and mysterious: ghosts and other paranormal phenomena

parapet /'pærəpət, -pet/ n [C] a low wall at the edge of a high roof, bridge etc

put/stick your head above the parapet BrE to take a risk: No one else was prepared to put their head above the parapet and say they were willing to support the plan.

paraphernalia /,pærəfəˈneɪliə $ -fər-/ n [U] the things that are used for a particular activity: photographic paraphernalia

paraphrase /'pærəfreɪz/ v [T] to express what someone says or writes in a shorter and clearer way —**paraphrase** n [C]

paraplegic /,pærəˈpliːdʒɪk◂/ n [C] someone who is unable to move the lower part of their body

parasite /'pærəsaɪt/ n [C] a plant or animal that lives on or in another plant or animal and gets food from it

parasol /'pærəsɒl $ -sɔːl, -sɑːl/ n [C] a type of UMBRELLA used for protection from the sun

paratrooper /'pærə,truːpə $ -ər/ n [C] a soldier who is trained to jump out of planes using a PARACHUTE

paratroops /'pærətruːps/ n [plural] a group of paratroopers that fights together as a military unit

parcel /'pɑːsəl $ 'pɑːr-/ n [C] especially BrE something that has been packed in a box or wrapped in paper, and then sent by mail or delivered SYN **package**

parched /pɑːtʃt $ pɑːrtʃt/ adj **1** spoken very thirsty **2** parched land is very dry

parchment /'pɑːtʃmənt $ 'pɑːr-/ n [U] thick yellow-white writing paper used in the past

pardon¹ /'pɑːdn $ 'pɑːrdn/ spoken used to politely ask someone to repeat something because you did not hear it: 'Your shoes are in the bedroom.' 'Pardon?' 'I said your shoes are in the bedroom.'
pardon me 1 used to say 'sorry' when you have done something that is considered rude SYN **excuse me**: Oh, pardon me. Did I interrupt? **2** AmE used to politely get someone's attention in order to ask them a question SYN **excuse me**: Pardon me, is this the way to City Hall?

pardon² v [T] to officially allow someone who is guilty of a crime to go free: Over 250 political prisoners were pardoned.

pardon³ n [C] an official order allowing someone who is guilty of a crime to go free: Tyler was later given a pardon. → **I beg your pardon** at BEG

pare /peə $ per/ v [T] to cut off the outer layer of something, especially the skin of a fruit: Pare the apples and slice them into chunks.
pare sth ↔ **down** to gradually reduce an amount or number: Production costs have had to be pared down.

parent /'peərənt $ 'per-/ n [C] someone's father or mother: My parents are coming to visit next week. → SINGLE PARENT —**parental** /pəˈrentl/ adj: parental concern

parentage /'peərəntɪdʒ $ 'per-/ n [U] used to talk about your parents, especially the country where they were born, their social class, or their religion: *an English-born man with Irish parentage*

'parent ,company *n* [C] a company that controls a smaller company or organization

parenthesis /pəˈrenθəsɪs/ *n* [C usually plural] (*plural* **parentheses** /-siːz/) one of the pair of signs ( ) put around words to show additional information **SYN** **bracket**: *in parentheses The numbers in parentheses refer to page numbers.*

parenthood /ˈpeərənthʊd $ ˈper-/ *n* [U] when someone is a parent

parenting /ˈpeərəntɪŋ $ ˈper-/ *n* [U] the skill or activity of looking after your own children: *the importance of good parenting skills*

parish /ˈpærɪʃ/ *n* [C] an area that has its own church

parishioner /pəˈrɪʃənə $ -ər/ *n* [C] someone who lives in a parish, especially someone who regularly goes to church there

parity /ˈpærəti/ *n* [U] *formal* the state of being equal, especially having equal pay, rights, or power **SYN** **equality**: [+with] *Prison workers are demanding pay parity with the police force.*

park¹ /pɑːk $ pɑːrk/ *n* [C]
1 a large area with grass and trees in a town, where people walk, play games etc
2 a large area of land in the country which has been kept in its natural state to protect the plants and animals there: **national/state/country park →** AMUSEMENT PARK, CAR PARK, NATIONAL PARK, THEME PARK, TRAILER PARK

park² *v* [I,T] to put your car somewhere for a period of time: *We couldn't find anywhere to park.* | *Tony parked the car and got out.*

parking /ˈpɑːkɪŋ $ ˈpɑːr-/ *n* [U] when you park a car somewhere, or the space where you can park it: *No Parking.* | *Free parking is available at the hotel.* | **parking space/place/spot** *Are there any parking spaces left?*

> **Word Choice: parking or car park?**
> You use **car park/parking lot** about a place where you can park your car: *There's a car park in front of the station.* Do not say 'There is a parking in front of the station.'
> You use **parking** when speaking generally about parking cars: *Parking can be a problem.* | *There is not enough parking in the city centre.*

'parking lot *n* [C] *AmE* an open area where people can park their cars **SYN** **car park** *BrE*

'parking ,meter *n* [C] a machine at the side of a road which you put money into when you park your car beside it

'parking ,ticket *n* [C] an official piece of paper that is put on your car telling you to pay money because you have parked illegally

parliament /ˈpɑːləmənt $ ˈpɑːr-/ *n*
1 (*also* **Parliament**) [C also + plural verb *BrE*] the group of people who are elected to make a country's laws and discuss important affairs → **government**, **MP**: *the Russian parliament*

2 Parliament [U also + plural verb *BrE*] the parliament of the United Kingdom: *He entered Parliament* (=was elected to Parliament) *in 1979.* | **in Parliament** *decisions taken in Parliament*

parliamentary /ˌpɑːləˈmentəri◀ $ ˌpɑːr-/ *adj* [only before noun] relating to or governed by a parliament: *a parliamentary democracy*

parlour *BrE*, **parlor** *AmE* /ˈpɑːlə $ ˈpɑːrlər/ *n* [C] **massage/ice cream/funeral etc parlour** a shop or business that provides a particular service

parochial /pəˈrəʊkiəl $ -ˈroʊ-/ *adj disapproving* only interested in things that affect your local area: *Local newspapers are very parochial.*

parody¹ /ˈpærədi/ *n* [C,U] (*plural* **parodies**) a piece of writing, music etc or an action that copies someone or something in an amusing way: [+of] *a parody of a Texas accent*

parody² *v* [T] (**parodied, parodying, parodies**) to copy someone or something in an amusing way

parole¹ /pəˈrəʊl $ -ˈroʊl/ *n* [U] when someone is allowed to leave prison early, but they will have to return if they do not behave well: **on parole** *He was released on parole.*

parole² *v* [T] to allow someone to leave prison on parole

parrot /ˈpærət/ *n* [C] a tropical bird with brightly coloured feathers that you can teach to copy human speech

'parrot ,fashion *adv BrE disapproving* if you learn something parrot fashion, you repeat what someone has just said without understanding it

parsley /ˈpɑːsli $ ˈpɑːr-/ *n* [U] a herb with curly leaves

parsnip /ˈpɑːsnɪp $ ˈpɑːr-/ *n* [C,U] a white or yellow vegetable that is the root of a plant → see picture on page A5

part¹ /pɑːt $ pɑːrt/ *n*
1 [C] one of the pieces, areas etc that form the whole of something: [+of] *the upper part of the body* | *people in other parts of the country* | *the early part of the 19th century* | *The book is divided into three parts.*
2 [C usually plural] a piece used to make a machine or vehicle: **spare parts** (=parts used to replace broken or old ones) | *a car parts factory*
3 part of sth some, but not all, of a particular thing: *Part of the problem is that we're just too busy.* | **As part of** *my job I visit local schools.*
4 [C] the words and actions of a particular character in a play or film **SYN** **role**: *Sara played the part of Cinderella.*
5 [C] *AmE* the line on your head made by dividing your hair with a comb **SYN** **parting** *BrE*
PHRASES
the best/better part of sth nearly all of something, especially a period of time: *We waited for the best part of an hour.*
for my/his etc part *formal* used when saying what a particular person thinks or does: *David, for his part, was very worried.*
for the most part mostly or usually: *For the most part, residents were thankful.*

have a part to play to have a particular job or be responsible for something: **[+in]** *We all have a part to play in making a better world.*

in part partly but not completely: *The accident was due in part to bad weather.*

on sb's part/on the part of sb used when describing a particular person's actions or feelings: *It was a mistake on her part.* | *There has never been any jealousy on my part.*

be part and parcel of sth to be a part of an activity, job etc that cannot be avoided: *Working long hours is part and parcel of being a journalist.*

play a part (in sth) to be involved in something and affect the way it happens or develops: **[+in]** *Luck certainly played a part in their success.* | **play a major/important/big etc part** *Music has always played an important part in my life.*

take part to be involved in an activity, sport, event etc with other people: **[+in]** *About 400 students took part in the protest.*

THESAURUS

part one of the pieces, areas etc that form the whole of something: *The front part of the car was badly damaged.* | *the northern part of Russia*

piece one of several parts that you divide something into, or that you join together to make something: *Would you like a piece of cake?* | *A piece of the tent is missing.*

bit *informal* a small part of something – used especially in British English: *I gave him a bit of my sandwich.*

section a part of something that is clearly different and separate from other parts: *The test is divided into two sections.* | *the reference section of the library*

chapter one of the parts that a book is divided into: *I've already read the first two chapters.*

scene one of the parts that a film or play is divided into: *The final scene of the movie was very sad.*

episode a part of a story on the television or radio, which is broadcast on different days, or every week: *I missed last night's episode of Neighbours.*

---

part² v **1** (also **part 'company**) [I] **a)** to end a romantic or working relationship with someone → **separate: [+from]** *Ben parted from his wife last year.* | *Not long after, the Beatles parted company.* **b)** to say goodbye and go in different directions: *They parted at Baker Street.* **2** [I,T] to move apart, or to make two things move apart: *Her lips parted slightly.* | *I parted the curtains and looked out.* **3 be parted from sb/sth** to be separated from someone or something that you love: *She couldn't bear to be parted from her son.* **4** [T] to separate your hair into two parts, using a comb

PHRASAL VERBS

part with sth to give or sell something to someone, although you do not want to: *I was reluctant to part with the painting.*

part³ adv partly one thing and partly another: *The exam is part written, part spoken.*

,part ex'change n [C,U] *BrE* a way of buying a new car, television etc in which you give your old car, television etc as part of the payment

partial /ˈpɑːʃəl $ ˈpɑːr-/ adj **1** not complete: *The exhibition was only a partial success.* **2 be partial to sth** to like something very much: *I'm very partial to fish.*

partially /ˈpɑːʃəli $ ˈpɑːr-/ adv not completely [SYN] **partly**: *The operation was **partially successful**.* | **partially sighted** people (=who cannot see well)

participant [Ac] /pɑːˈtɪsəpənt $ pɑːr-/ n [C] someone who takes part in an activity or event

participate [Ac] /pɑːˈtɪsəpeɪt $ pɑːr-/ v [I] to take part in an activity or event: **[+in]** *Eight schools participated in the project.* —**participation** /pɑːˌtɪsəˈpeɪʃən $ pɑːr-/ n [U]: *Participation in sport is encouraged.*

> **Grammar**
>
> Do not say 'Eight runners participated on the race.' Say *Eight runners participated in the race.*

participle /ˈpɑːtəsɪpəl, pɑːˈtɪsəpəl $ ˈpɑːr-/ n [C] the form of a verb, usually ending in '-ing' or '-ed', that is used to form verb tenses or adjectives → PAST PARTICIPLE, PRESENT PARTICIPLE

particle /ˈpɑːtɪkəl $ ˈpɑːr-/ n [C] a very small piece of something: *dust particles*

particular¹ /pəˈtɪkjələ $ pərˈtɪkjələr/ adj
1 [only before noun] a particular thing, person, or time is the one that you are talking about, and not any other [SYN] **specific**: *In this particular case, no one was injured.* | *Each writer has his **own particular** style.* | *I was very busy at that particular time.*
2 [only before noun] special or great: *Pay particular attention to your brakes.* | *The video is of **particular interest** to teachers.* | *There's **no particular reason** to worry.*
3 very careful about choosing exactly what you like, and not easily satisfied [SYN] **fussy**: **[+about]** *He's very particular about his food.*

particular² n **1 in particular** especially: *I liked Venice in particular.* | **anything/anyone/anywhere in particular** *Is there anything in particular you'd like to see?* **2 particulars** [plural] details about something, especially a job, property, or legal case: *Further particulars may be obtained from Dr Evans.*

particularly /pəˈtɪkjələli $ pərˈtɪkjələrli/ adv more than usual, or more than other people or things [SYN] **especially**: *It was particularly hot that day.* | *He's particularly popular with the students.*
PHRASES

> **not particularly** not very or not very much: *I'm not particularly religious.* | *'Are you hungry?' 'Not particularly.'*

parting¹ /ˈpɑːtɪŋ $ ˈpɑːr-/ n **1** [C,U] *formal* an occasion when two people leave each other: *an emotional parting* **2** [C] *BrE* the line on your head made by dividing your hair with a comb [SYN] **part** *AmE*

parting² adj **1 parting kiss/gift/glance etc** a kiss etc that you give someone as you leave **2 parting shot** an unpleasant remark that you make just as you are leaving, especially at the end of an argument

partisan /ˌpɑːtɪˈzæn $ ˈpɑːrtəzən, -sən/ adj strongly supporting one political party, plan, or leader, especially without enough thought: a fiercely partisan crowd —**partisan** n [C]

partition[1] /pɑːˈtɪʃən $ pər-, pɑːr-/ n **1** [C] a thin wall that separates one part of a room from another **2** [U] when a country is divided into two or more separate countries: **[+of]** the partition of India

partition[2] v [T] to divide a country, building, or room into two or more parts

PHRASAL VERBS

partition sth ↔ **off** to divide part of a room from the rest, using a partition

partly /ˈpɑːtli $ ˈpɑːr-/ adv to some degree, but not completely: They moved to France, partly to be nearer their daughter. | I was partly to blame.

partner[1] Ac /ˈpɑːtnə $ ˈpɑːrtnər/ n [C]
1 the person that you are married to, or that you live with as if you are married → **husband**, **wife**: She lives with her partner Tom.
2 one of the owners of a business: **[+in]** He's a partner in a law firm.
3 someone that you do an activity with, for example dancing or playing a game against two other people: my tennis partner
4 a country or organization that has an agreement with another: Germany's **trading partners**

partner[2] v [T] to be someone's partner in a dance, game etc

partnership Ac /ˈpɑːtnəʃɪp $ ˈpɑːrtnər-/ n **1** [C,U] a relationship between two or more people, organizations, or countries: Marriage is a partnership. | **in partnership with sb** We work in partnership with other schools. **2** [U] when you are a partner in a business: He **went into partnership with** John Kent. **3** [C] a business owned by two or more people

ˌpart of ˈspeech n [C] (plural **parts of speech**) technical one of the groups into which words are divided in grammar, for example noun, verb, or adjective

ˌpart-ˈtime adj, adv for only a part of the normal working day or week → **full-time**: a part-time job | I **work part-time**.

party[1] /ˈpɑːti $ ˈpɑːrti/ n [C] (plural **parties**)
1 a social event when a lot of people meet to eat, drink, dance etc: Are you going to Amy's birthday party?
2 [also + plural verb BrE] a political organization with particular ideas and aims that you can vote for in elections: **the Labour/Communist/Democratic etc Party** The Labour Party are demanding a change in the law. | the country's two main **political parties** | members of the **ruling party** (=the party in power) | the **opposition party** (=the party that is not in power) **THESAURUS** ORGANIZATION
3 [also + plural verb BrE] a group of people who are travelling or working together: **[+of]** a party of schoolchildren | No one in our party spoke French.
4 one of the people or groups who are involved in a legal argument or agreement → **SEARCH PARTY**, **THIRD PARTY**

party[2] v [I] (**partied**, **partying**, **parties**) informal to enjoy yourself with a group of other people by eating, drinking, dancing etc: He likes to party.

ˈparty ˌanimal n [C] informal someone who enjoys going to a lot of parties

pass[1] /pɑːs $ pæs/ v
1 GO PAST (also **pass by**) [I,T] to go past someone or something: We used to pass the shop every day. | Luke stepped aside to let me pass. | A plane passed overhead.
2 GO THROUGH/ACROSS ETC [I,T] to go through, across, around etc something, or to make something do this: **[+through/across/around etc]** We passed through the gate into the yard. | The road

passes through the town centre. | *Pass the rope around the post.*

3 GIVE STH TO SB [T] to give something to someone else, especially by putting it in their hand: **pass sb sth/pass sth to sb** *Could you pass me the salt, please?* | *I passed the letter back to her.* | *I'll pass the information to our sales department.*

4 TEST/EXAM **a)** [I,T] to succeed in an examination or test OPP **fail**: *Did you pass all your exams?* | *I passed my driving test!* | *She passed with flying colours* (=got very high marks). **b)** [T] to officially decide that someone has succeeded in an examination or test OPP **fail**

5 SPORT [I,T] to kick, throw, or hit a ball to another member of your team: **[+to]** *Why didn't he pass to Mark?* THESAURUS **THROW**

6 TIME **a)** [I] if time passes, it goes by: *The days passed slowly.* **b)** [T] to spend time, especially when you are waiting for something or are bored: *We played cards **to pass the time** (=help us stop feeling bored).*

7 LAW/SUGGESTION [T] to officially accept a law or suggestion, especially by voting: *The Act was passed in 1993.*

8 CHANGE OWNER [I] *formal* to change from being owned or controlled by one person to being owned or controlled by another person: **[+to]** *The land will pass to my son when I die.*

9 END [I] to end: *The storm soon passed.*

PHRASES

let sth pass to deliberately not say anything when someone says or does something that you do not like: *He was very rude, but I decided to **let it pass**.*

pass judgment (on sb/sth) to give your opinion about someone or something: *I'm here to help, not to pass judgment.*

pass sentence to officially decide how a criminal will be punished: *The judge asked for more psychiatric reports before passing sentence.*

pass water to URINATE: *The patient reported difficulties in passing water.*

PHRASAL VERBS

pass sth ↔ **around** (*also* **pass** sth ↔ **round** *BrE*) to offer or show something to each person in a group: *Pass the cakes around, Roy.*

pass away to die – used if you want to avoid saying the word 'die' THESAURUS **DIE**

pass by (sb/sth) to go past someone or something: *He waited until the doctor had passed by.* | *You'll pass by the Hotel Bern.*

pass sth ↔ **down** [usually passive] to give or teach something to people who are younger than you or live after you: *The skill was passed down from father to son.*

pass for sb/sth to be thought to be something that you are not: *She could easily pass for a boy.*

pass sb/sth **off as** sth to make people think that a person or thing is something that they are not: *He passed himself off as a doctor.*

pass sth ↔ **on** to give someone something, especially information that someone else has given you: **[+to]** *Can you **pass** the **message on** to Bob?*

pass out to suddenly become unconscious SYN **faint**

pass sth ↔ **up** to not use a chance to do something: **pass up a chance/opportunity/offer etc** *You shouldn't pass up the chance to go to university.*

pass² n [C] **1** an official piece of paper that shows that you are allowed to enter a building or travel on a bus or train without paying: *The guard checked our passes.* | *a **bus pass*** **2** a successful result in an examination OPP **fail**: **[+in]** *an A-level pass in English* | *The **pass mark** (=mark you need to be successful) is 55%.* **3** an action of kicking, throwing, or hitting a ball to another member of your team: *a brilliant pass* **4** a road or path through or over mountains: *a narrow **mountain pass***

passable /'pɑːsəbəl $ 'pæ-/ *adj* **1** fairly good, but not excellent: *The beer was passable.* **2** a road or river that is passable is not blocked, so you can travel along or across it OPP **impassable**

passage /'pæsɪdʒ/ *n*
1 (*also* **passageway** /'pæsɪdʒweɪ/) [C] a long narrow area with walls on either side which connects one room or place to another → **corridor**: *My office is just along the passage.* | *an underground passage*
2 [C] a short part of a book, poem, speech, piece of music etc: **[+from/of]** *a passage from the Koran*
3 [U] movement or progress from one place or stage to another: *Thousands of people have been offered **free passage** out of the war zone.*
4 [C] a tube in your body that air or liquid can pass through: *nasal passages*

PHRASES

the passage of time *literary* the passing of time: *She still missed him despite the passage of time.*

passé /'pæseɪ, 'pɑː- $ pæˈseɪ/ *adj* no longer modern or fashionable

passenger /'pæsɪndʒə, -sən- $ -ər/ *n* [C] someone who is travelling in a car, plane, train etc, but is not driving it or working on it: **Rail passengers** *are facing even longer delays.*

passerby /ˌpɑːsəˈbaɪ $ ˌpæsər-/ *n* [C] (*plural* **passersby**) someone who is walking past a place: *His shouts were heard by a passerby.*

passing¹ /'pɑːsɪŋ $ 'pæ-/ *adj* [only before noun] **1** a passing thought or feeling is short and not very serious: *a passing interest in golf* **2** going past: *A passing car stopped to help.*

passing² *n* **1 in passing** if you say something in passing, you mention it while you are talking about something else: *He did **mention** Jean, but only **in passing**.* **2 the passing of time** the process of time going by

passion /'pæʃən/ *n* **1** [C,U] a very strong feeling of love or sexual desire: *His eyes were burning with passion.* **2** [C,U] a very strong belief or feeling about something: *She writes with passion and humour.* **3** [C] a very strong liking for something: **[+for]** *Lucy's passion for music*

passionate /'pæʃənət/ *adj* **1** showing or involving very strong feelings of love or sexual desire: *a passionate kiss* **2** showing very strong feelings or ideas about something: *a passionate speech* —**passionately** *adv*

passive¹ Ac /ˈpæsɪv/ adj
1 someone who is passive accepts what happens or what people say without trying to change or influence it OPP **active**: *their passive acceptance of their fate*
2 *technical* used to describe a verb or sentence in which the subject of the verb is affected by the action rather than doing the action. In the sentence 'I was invited to the party', the verb is passive. → ACTIVE —**passively** *adv* —**passivity** /pæˈsɪvəti/ *n* [U]

passive² Ac *n* **the passive (voice)** *technical* the passive form of a verb

,passive 'smoking *n* [U] when you breathe in smoke from other people's cigarettes

Passover /ˈpɑːsəʊvə $ ˈpæsoʊvər/ (*also* **the Passover**) *n* [U] the Jewish holiday that celebrates the Jewish escape from ancient Egypt

passport /ˈpɑːspɔːt $ ˈpæspɔːrt/ *n* [C]
1 an official document with your photograph and details about you inside it that you need when you travel to other countries: **American/British etc passport** *My son holds* (=has) *an American passport.*
2 passport to success/happiness etc something that makes success, happiness etc easy to achieve: *Money is not always a passport to happiness.*

'passport con,trol *n* [U] the place where your passport is checked when you leave or enter a country

password /ˈpɑːswɜːd $ ˈpæswɜːrd/ *n* [C] a secret word that you must use before you can operate a computer system or enter a place: **Type in** *your* **password.**

past¹ /pɑːst $ pæst/ *adj*
1 [only before noun] done, used, or experienced in a time before now: *Hopefully, I have learned from past mistakes.* | *He knew from* **past experience** *that Maria had a bad temper.*
2 [only before noun] used to talk about a period of time that has just finished: *the events of the past year* | *Tim's been in Rome for the past week.*
3 finished or having come to an end: *By mid-June the danger was past.*
4 the past tense the form of a verb that is used to show a past action or state: *The past tense of 'come' is 'came'.*
5 past leader/president/champion etc a leader etc in the past: *She was the past leader of the party.*

past² *prep, adv*
1 later than a particular time: *It's ten past nine* (=ten minutes after nine). | *It was already past midnight.*
2 further than a particular place: *Our house is* **just past** (=a little further than) *the bridge.*
3 go/walk/drive etc past (sb/sth) to move towards and then beyond a person or place, without stopping: *He walked past me as though I didn't exist.* | *We drove past slowly.*
4 beyond a particular limit, stage, or age: *This yoghurt's* **past** *its* **sell-by date.** | *I'm past the age for romance.*
5 if a period of time goes past, it passes: *Weeks* **went past** *without any news.*

PHRASES
I wouldn't put it past sb (to do sth) *spoken* used to say that you would not be surprised if someone did something bad or unusual because it is typical of them: *I wouldn't put it past Neil to be violent.*
past it *BrE spoken* too old to do something or be useful: *Just because I'm retired, I'm not past it.*

past³ *n*
1 the past the time that existed before the present: **in the past** *People travel more now than in the past.* | *Good manners have become* **a thing of the past** (=no longer exist).
2 the past the form of a verb that is used to show a past action or state SYN **the past tense**: *What's the past of 'go'?*
3 [C] all the things that have happened in a person's life or in a particular place: *She never talks about her past.* | *The country has a violent past.*

pasta /ˈpæstə $ ˈpɑː-/ *n* [U] an Italian food made from flour, eggs, and water and cut into various shapes and cooked

paste¹ /peɪst/ *n* [C,U] **1 meat/fish/tomato etc paste** a soft smooth food made from crushed meat, fish etc **2** a soft wet mixture that can be easily spread **3** a type of thick glue that is used for sticking paper: **wallpaper paste**

paste² *v* **1** [T] to stick paper to a surface, using glue **2** [I,T] to move or copy words, pictures etc from one computer document to another

pastel¹ /ˈpæstl $ pæˈstel/ *adj* [only before noun] pastel colours are light and pale

pastel² *n* **1** [C,U] a small coloured stick used for drawing **2** [C usually plural] a picture drawn with pastels **3** [C usually plural] a light colour

pasteurized (*also* **-ised** *BrE*) /ˈpɑːstʃəraɪzd, -stə- $ ˈpæs-/ *adj* pasteurized milk has been specially heated to kill any BACTERIA in it

pastime /ˈpɑːstaɪm $ ˈpæs-/ *n* [C] something that you enjoy doing when you are not working SYN **hobby**

pastor /ˈpɑːstə $ ˈpæstər/ *n* [C] a priest in some Protestant churches

pastoral /ˈpɑːstərəl $ ˈpæ-/ *adj* **1** relating to the work of a priest or teacher in helping people with personal matters: **Pastoral care** *at the school is excellent.* **2** *literary* typical of peaceful country life: *pastoral scenes*

,past 'participle *n* [C] the form of a verb used in PERFECT tenses (for example 'eaten' in 'I have eaten'), or in the PASSIVE (for example 'changed' in 'it was changed'), or sometimes as an adjective (for example 'broken' in 'a broken leg')

,past 'perfect *n* **the past perfect** the form of a verb that shows that an action was completed before another event happened. In the sentence 'After I had finished my meal, I went upstairs', 'had finished' is in the past perfect.

pastry /ˈpeɪstri/ *n* (*plural* **pastries**) **1** [U] a mixture of flour, fat, and water that you roll flat then fill with other food and bake **2** [C] a small cake made with pastry

pasture /'pɑːstʃə $ 'pæstʃər/ *n* [C,U] land that is covered with grass and used for cows, sheep etc to feed on

pasty¹ /'peɪsti/ *adj* a pasty face looks pale and unhealthy

pasty² /'pæsti/ *n* [C] (*plural* **pasties**) *BrE* a type of food with meat or vegetables in the middle and pastry all around the outside

pat¹ /pæt/ *v* [T] (**patted, patting**) to touch someone or something lightly with your flat hand, in a friendly way: *She patted me on the shoulder.*

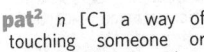

PAT

THESAURUS ▶ TOUCH

PHRASES

pat sb on the back to praise someone when they have done something well: *You can pat yourselves on the back for a job well done.*

pat² *n* [C] a way of touching someone or something lightly with your flat hand, in a friendly way: *He gave the dog a friendly pat.*

PHRASES

a pat on the back praise for something you have done well: *I think you all deserve a pat on the back for your hard work.*

pat³ *adj* [only before noun] *disapproving* a pat answer seems too quick and simple, as though it has been used many times

patch¹ /pætʃ/ *n* [C]

1 SMALL AREA a small area of something: **[+of]** *a patch of grass | a black cat with white patches | icy patches on the road | He wore a hat to cover his **bald patch**.*

2 ON CLOTHES a small piece of material that you use to cover a hole in your clothes: *old trousers with patches on the knees*

3 FOR GROWING STH a small area of land where you grow fruit or vegetables: *a vegetable patch*

4 OVER SB'S EYE a small piece of material that you use to cover one eye when it is injured

PHRASES

a bad/rough patch *especially BrE informal* a difficult or unhappy time: *I've been going through a bad patch recently.*

not be a patch on sb/sth *BrE informal* to be much less good, attractive etc than someone or something else: *His second book isn't a patch on his first.*

patch² (*also* **patch up**) *v* [T] to repair a hole in something by putting a small piece of material over it: *a pair of old patched jeans*

PHRASAL VERBS

patch sth/sb ↔ **up 1** to end an argument and become friendly with someone again: *He's patched things up with his girlfriend now.* **2** to give quick and basic medical treatment to someone who is injured: *They patched him up and sent him back to work.*

patchwork /'pætʃwɜːk $ -wɜːrk/ *n* [U] a type of sewing in which you sew a lot of different coloured pieces of cloth together to make a large piece of cloth: *a patchwork quilt*

patchy /'pætʃi/ *adj* **1** happening in some places but not everywhere: *patchy fog* **2** good in some ways but not in others: *My French is quite patchy.*

pâté /'pæteɪ $ pɑːˈteɪ, pæ-/ *n* [U] a smooth mixture made from meat, fish, or vegetables that you spread on bread: *smoked salmon pâté*

patent¹ /'peɪtnt, 'pæ- $ 'pæ-/ *n* [C] an official document that gives one person or company the right to make and sell a new product, and no one else is allowed to copy it

patent² *v* [T] to get a patent for something

patent³ *adj* [only before noun] *formal* **a patent lie/patent nonsense etc** something that is clearly not true or not sensible

patent leather /ˌpeɪtnt 'leðə◂ $ ˌpætnt 'leðər/ *n* [U] very shiny leather

patently /'peɪtntli $ 'pæ-/ *adv* in a way that is very clear and easy to see: *This is **patently untrue**.* | *It's **patently obvious** that she's lying.*

paternal /pəˈtɜːnl $ -ɜːr-/ *adj* **1** paternal feelings or behaviour are like those of a good father → **maternal**: *Dad gave me some paternal advice.* **2 paternal grandfather/uncle etc** your father's father, brother etc

paternity /pəˈtɜːnəti $ -ɜːr-/ *n* [U] *law* when someone is a father or becomes a father: *paternity leave*

path /pɑːθ $ pæθ/ *n* [C] (*plural* **paths** /pɑːðz $ pæðz/)

1 a narrow track that people walk along: *a path through the woods*

2 the direction or line along which someone or something is moving: **[+of]** *He walked straight into the path of a lorry.* | *The plane had strayed off its **flight path**.*

3 a plan or series of actions that will lead to achieving something: **[+to]** *the path to economic recovery*

COLLOCATIONS
verbs
to follow a path (=to go along it) *Keep following the path until you come to a gate.*
to take a path (=to start going along it) *I think we've taken the wrong path.*
to keep to the path (=to stay on a path) *Keep to the path so as not to disturb the wildlife.*
a path leads somewhere *The path leads down to the valley.*
adjectives
a narrow path *A narrow path takes you down to the beach.*
a steep path *Their house is at the top of a steep path.*
a winding path (=with many curves) *She set off down the winding path.*
noun + path
a garden path *A policeman was coming up the garden path.*

P

a cycle path (=for people riding bicycles) *We plan to create many more cycle paths.*

pathetic /pə'θetɪk/ *adj* **1** very bad, useless, or weak: *a pathetic excuse* | *Stop being so pathetic!* **2** making you feel sadness and sympathy: *The boy looked small and pathetic.*

pathological /ˌpæθə'lɒdʒɪkəl◄ $ -'lɑː-/ *adj* **1** pathological behaviour or feelings are extreme and unreasonable, and you cannot control them: *He's a pathological liar.* **2** *technical* relating to pathology

pathologist /pə'θɒlədʒɪst $ -'θɑː-/ *n* [C] a doctor who has studied pathology, especially one who tries to find out the causes of death

pathology /pə'θɒlədʒi $ -'θɑː-/ *n* [U] the study of diseases and causes of death

pathos /'peɪθɒs $ -θɑːs/ *n* [U] *literary* the quality in a person or a situation that makes you feel sympathy for them

pathway /'pɑːθweɪ $ 'pæθ-/ *n* [C] a PATH

patience /'peɪʃəns/ *n* [U]
1 the ability to stay calm and not get angry when you are waiting for something or doing something difficult OPP **impatience**: *I don't have the patience to be a teacher.* | [+with] *She's got no patience with children.* | *I finally lost my patience and shouted at her.* | *He was running out of patience.*
2 *BrE* a game of cards played by one person SYN **solitaire** *AmE*

patient¹ /'peɪʃənt/ *n* [C] someone who is getting medical treatment from a doctor or in hospital: *Dr Ross is very popular with his patients.*

patient² *adj* able to stay calm and not become angry when you are waiting for something or doing something difficult OPP **impatient**: *Just be patient and wait.* | [+with] *She's always very patient with her students.* —**patiently** *adv*: *He waited patiently to speak.*

patio /'pætiəʊ $ -oʊ/ *n* [C] (*plural* **patios**) a flat hard area near a house where people sit outside: *We'll eat on the patio.*

patriarchal /ˌpeɪtri'ɑːkəl◄ $ -'ɑːr-/ *adj* a patriarchal society is ruled or controlled only by men

patriot /'pætriət, -triɒt, 'peɪ- $ 'peɪtriət, -triɑːt/ *n* [C] someone who loves their country and is willing to fight to defend it

patriotic /ˌpætri'ɒtɪk◄, ˌpeɪ- $ ˌpeɪtri'ɑːtɪk◄/ *adj* having or showing great love for your country: *patriotic songs* —**patriotism** /'pætriətɪzəm, 'peɪ- $ 'peɪ-/ *n* [U]

patrol¹ /pə'trəʊl $ -'troʊl/ *n* **1** [C,U] when police, guards, or soldiers go regularly around a building or area to check that there is no trouble or danger: **on patrol** *a police officer on patrol* **2** [C] a group of police, guards, or soldiers that regularly check a particular area: *the US border patrol* | *a police patrol car*

patrol² *v* [I,T] (**patrolled, patrolling**) to regularly go around a building or area to check that there is no trouble or danger: *Officers patrol the area regularly.*

patrolman /pə'trəʊlmən $ -'troʊl-/ *n* [C] (*plural* **patrolmen** /-mən/) *AmE* a police officer who patrols a particular area

patron /'peɪtrən/ *n* [C] **1** someone who supports or gives money to an organization, artist, writer, or musical performer: [+of] *a patron of the arts* **2** *formal* someone who uses a particular shop, restaurant, or hotel

patronage /'pætrənɪdʒ 'peɪ-, 'pæ-/ *n* [U] the support or money that a patron gives: *artists who enjoyed the Prince's patronage*

patronize (*also* **-ise** *BrE*) /'pætrənaɪz $ 'peɪ-, 'pæ-/ *v* [T] **1** to talk to someone in a way that shows you think you are better than they are or know more than they do: *It's important not to patronize children.* | *Don't patronize me.* **2** *formal* to regularly go to a particular shop, restaurant etc

patronizing (*also* **-ising** *BrE*) /'pætrənaɪzɪŋ $ 'peɪ-, 'pæ-/ *adj* someone who is patronizing talks to you in a way that shows they think they are better than you or know more than you do: *patronizing remarks*

patron 'saint *n* [C] a Christian holy person who is believed to protect a particular place or particular people

patter /'pætə $ -ər/ *n* [singular] **1** the gentle sound made by light quick steps or rain hitting a surface: [+of] *the patter of rain on the roof* **2** a way of talking that is fast and continuous: *a car salesman's patter* —**patter** *v* [I]

pattern /'pætən $ 'pætərn/ *n* [C]
1 the regular way in which something happens: *Weather patterns have changed in recent years.* | [+of] *changing patterns of behaviour among students* | *Children's development does not follow a set pattern* (=always happen in the same way).
2 a regular design of shapes, colours, and lines: *a pattern of small red and white squares*
3 a shape that you copy onto cloth or paper when you are making something, especially clothes: *a skirt pattern*

patterned /'pætənd $ -ərnd/ *adj* decorated with a pattern: *a patterned carpet*

paunch /pɔːntʃ $ pɒːntʃ/ *n* [C] a man's fat stomach

pauper /'pɔːpə $ 'pɒːpər/ *n* [C] *old-fashioned* someone who is very poor

pause¹ /pɔːz $ pɒːz/ *v* [I] to stop doing something for a short time before you start again: [+for] *She paused for a moment before replying.* | *He paused for breath halfway up the stairs.* THESAURUS STOP

pause² *n* [C] a short time when you stop speaking or doing something: *'Yes,' she said, after a brief pause.* | [+in] *There was a pause in the conversation.*
PHRASES
give sb pause for thought to make someone think seriously and carefully about something: *High real estate prices have given potential buyers pause for thought.*

pave /peɪv/ *v* [T usually passive] to cover a path, road etc with a hard surface, especially of large flat stones: *a paved courtyard*

PHRASES

pave the way for sth to make it possible for something to happen in the future: *The talks could pave the way for a ceasefire agreement.*

pavement /'peɪvmənt/ n
1 [C] *BrE* the path you walk on at the side of a road **SYN** **sidewalk** *AmE*: *A policeman was standing on the pavement outside the bank.*
2 [U] *AmE* the hard surface of a road

pavilion /pə'vɪljən/ n [C] **1** a temporary building or tent that is used for public shows or other events **2** *BrE* a building at a sports field where players can change their clothes

paving stone n [C] a flat piece of stone – used with other pieces to make a hard surface to walk on

paw¹ /pɔː $ pɒː/ n [C] the foot of an animal such as a dog, cat, or lion

paw² v [I,T] if an animal paws something, it touches it several times with its paw: **[+at]** *The dog whined and pawed at the door.*

pawn¹ /pɔːn $ pɒːn/ n [C] **1** a piece in a game of CHESS that can move forward one square at a time **2** a weak person who is used or controlled by a much more powerful person

pawn² v [T] to leave something valuable with a pawnbroker in order to borrow money from them: *She pawned her wedding ring.*

pawnbroker /'pɔːnˌbrəʊkə $ 'pɒːnˌbrəʊkər/ n [C] someone who lends money to people. You leave something valuable with a pawnbroker, who sells it if you do not pay back the money.

pay¹ /peɪ/ v (*past tense and past participle* **paid** /peɪd/)
1 [I,T] to give someone money for something you buy or for a service: **[+for]** *Who's going to pay for all this?* | **pay sth for sth** *I paid £25 for that watch.* | **pay sb for sth** *I've paid him for the lessons in advance.* | *Can you **pay cash**?* | *I'll **pay by cheque**.*
2 [I,T] to give someone money for the job that they do: *They only pay £4 an hour.* | **pay sb sth** *I pay him $20 a day.* | *He **gets paid** £500 a week.* | **well/badly paid** *a well paid job* **THESAURUS** EARN
3 [T] to give money that you owe to a person, organization etc: *Don't forget to **pay** the electricity bill.* | *Can I pay you the rest next week?* | **pay a fine/pay damages/pay costs** (=give money to someone because the law says you must)
4 [I] if something pays, it is worth doing because you get an advantage from it: *Crime doesn't pay.*
5 [I,T] to suffer or be punished for something wrong you have done: **[+for]** *You'll pay for this one day!* | **pay the penalty/price** *He's paying the price for not working hard enough at school.* → **pay lip service to sb/sth** at LIP SERVICE, **pay your respects** at RESPECT¹
PHRASES

pay attention (to sb/sth) to listen to or watch someone or something carefully: *Always pay attention to the car in front.*

PATTERNS

pinstripe

plain

zigzag

stripy/striped

tartan

spotted

checked

floral

pay sb a compliment to tell someone that you think they are nice, attractive, intelligent etc: *I was just trying to pay her a compliment.*

pay your respects (to sb) *formal* to visit or speak to someone in order to be polite: *We paid our respects to the mayor.*

pay tribute to sb to publicly praise or thank someone: *He paid tribute to the firefighters who fought the blaze.*

pay sb a visit/pay a visit to sb/sth to go to see a person or place: *I'll pay you a visit when I'm in town.* | *We paid a visit to the art gallery.*

pay your way to pay for things yourself, without depending on other people: *Sophie worked to pay her way through college.*

PHRASAL VERBS
pay sb/sth ↔ **back**
1 to give someone the money that you owe them SYN **repay**: *Can I borrow $10? I'll pay you back tomorrow.*
2 to do something unpleasant to someone because they have done something unpleasant to you: *I'll pay you back for this!*
pay off
1 pay sth ↔ off to give back all the money that you owe: *I'm trying to pay off my overdraft.*
2 if something that you do pays off, it has a good result: *All that hard work finally paid off.*
pay out sth to pay a lot of money for something
pay up *informal* to pay money that you owe, especially when you do not want to

pay² n [U] money that you are given for doing your job THESAURUS ▶ SALARY

COLLOCATIONS
types of pay
low pay *I left the job because of the low pay.*
good pay *It's hard work, but the pay is good.*
higher/better pay *Farm workers deserve higher pay.*
basic pay *BrE*, **base pay** *AmE* (=not including any extra pay) *He gets a bonus in addition to his basic pay.*
holiday pay *BrE*, **vacation pay** *AmE* (=pay when you are on holiday) *Freelancers get no holiday pay.*

pay + noun
a pay rise *BrE*, **a pay raise** *AmE This is not a good time to ask for a pay rise.*
a pay increase (=for a group of workers) *Police officers got a 6% pay increase this year.*
a pay cut *Everyone had to take a pay cut.*

payable /ˈpeɪəbəl/ *adj* **1** a bill or debt etc that is payable must be paid: *The rent is payable on the first day of the month.* **2** payable to sb a cheque that is payable to someone has their name written on it and the money must be paid to them: *Cheques should be **made payable** to Granada TV.*

pay cheque *BrE*, **paycheck** *AmE* /ˈpeɪtʃek/ *n* [C] a cheque that you get each week or each month for doing your job

payday /ˈpeɪdeɪ/ *n* [U] the day each week or month when you are paid for doing your job

payee /peɪˈiː/ *n* [C] the person that a cheque must be paid to

payer /ˈpeɪə $ -ər/ *n* [C] someone who pays something: *taxpayers*

payment /ˈpeɪmənt/ *n* [C,U] an amount of money that is paid: *You can **make payments** in cash or by cheque.* | *Do you **accept payment** by credit card?* | *I **received** a **payment** of £200.* → **BALANCE OF PAYMENTS, DOWN PAYMENT**

payoff /ˈpeɪɒf $ -ɒːf/ *n* [C] **1** an advantage that you get from something that you do **2** an illegal payment that is made to someone, especially to stop them from causing you trouble

pay phone *n* [C] a public telephone that you pay to use

payroll /ˈpeɪrəʊl $ -roʊl/ *n* [C] a list of all the people who are employed by a company: **on the/its payroll** *The company has over a thousand people on its payroll.*

PC¹ /ˌpiː ˈsiː◂/ *n* [C]
1 (**personal computer**) a small computer that is used by one person at a time
2 *BrE* (**police constable**) a policeman of the lowest rank

PC² *adj* POLITICALLY CORRECT

PE /ˌpiː ˈiː/ *n* [U] (**physical education**) sport and physical activity taught as a school subject

pea /piː/ *n* [C] a small round green seed that you can cook as a vegetable → see picture on page A5

peace /piːs/ *n* [U]
1 when there is no war: **[+between]** *peace between the two nations* | **at peace (with sb)** *The country is now at peace with its neighbour.*
2 when everything is quiet and calm: *All I want is some **peace and quiet**.* | **in peace** *Just let me read in peace.* | *The children won't **leave** me **in peace**.*
3 when you feel calm, happy, and not worried: *her search for **inner peace*** | *Talking to your doctor will give you **peace of mind**.*

COLLOCATIONS
verbs
to make peace (=to agree to stop fighting) *France made peace with Britain.*
to bring peace *He has worked hard to bring peace to Northern Ireland.*
to live in peace *Hopefully, the two communities will be able to live in peace.*

peace + noun
peace talks/negotiations *Peace talks will begin on Monday.*
a peace treaty/agreement *Egypt and Israel signed a peace treaty.*
a peace plan (=proposals for achieving peace) *They rejected the peace plan.*

noun + peace
world peace *This regime is a threat to world peace.*

peaceable /ˈpiːsəbəl/ adj not wanting to argue or fight

peaceful /ˈpiːsfəl/ adj
1 quiet and calm: *The wood was cool and peaceful.* | *a peaceful afternoon* **THESAURUS** QUIET
2 not involving war or violence: *a peaceful demonstration* | *A peaceful solution to the conflict*
—**peacefully** adv: *She was sleeping peacefully.*
—**peacefulness** n [U]

peacekeeping /ˈpiːsˌkiːpɪŋ/ adj **peacekeeping troops/forces etc** soldiers who are sent to a place to stop people from fighting each other
—**peacekeeper** n [C]

peacetime /ˈpiːstaɪm/ n [U] when a country is not fighting a war

peach /piːtʃ/ n [C] a round juicy fruit with a soft yellow and red skin and a large seed inside → see picture on page A4

peacock /ˈpiːkɒk $ -kaːk/ n [C] a large bird. The male has long blue and green tail feathers that it can lift and spread out.

peak¹ /piːk/ n [C] **1** the time when someone or something is best, highest, or most successful: *The holiday season is now **at its peak**.* | *Profits this month have reached a new peak.* | *At 40 many people are **at the peak of** their careers.* **2** a mountain or the pointed top of a mountain: *the snow-covered peaks of the Alps* | *a **mountain peak*** **THESAURUS** MOUNTAIN **3** BrE the flat curved part of a hat that covers your eyes **SYN** visor AmE

peak² v [I] to reach the highest point or level: *Sales peaked in July.*

peak³ adj **1** highest or best: *Prices hit their peak level last year.* | *a new shampoo that will keep your hair **in peak condition*** **2** BrE peak times are when the largest number of people are travelling or doing something: *There are extra buses during peak times.* | *the **peak** holiday **periods***

peal /piːl/ n [C] a loud long sound of laughter, THUNDER, or bells ringing: [+of] *peals of laughter* | *a sudden peal of thunder*

peanut /ˈpiːnʌt/ n [C] **1** a small nut in a light brown shell which grows under the ground: *a packet of salted peanuts* → see picture at NUT **2** [plural] **peanuts** informal a very small amount of money: *He gets **paid peanuts**!*

peanut 'butter / $ ˈ.. ˌ../ n [U] a soft food made from crushed peanuts that you spread on bread

pear /peə $ per/ n [C] a sweet juicy fruit that is round at the bottom and thinner at the top → see picture on page A4

pearl /pɜːl $ pɜːrl/ n [C] a small white round object that forms inside an OYSTER and is a valuable jewel

'pear-shaped adj **go pear-shaped** informal if something you are doing goes pear-shaped, it fails completely

peasant /ˈpezənt/ n [C] a poor farmer who owns or rents a small amount of land, either in the past or in poor countries

peat /piːt/ n [U] a black substance formed in the ground from decaying plants that you can use to help plants grow or burn instead of coal

pebble /ˈpebəl/ n [C] a small smooth stone that you find in a river or on a beach

peck¹ /pek/ v [I,T] **1** if a bird pecks something, it hits or bites it with its beak: [+at] *pigeons pecking at breadcrumbs* **2 peck sb on the cheek/forehead etc** to kiss someone quickly and gently: *'Bye darling,' she said, pecking him on the cheek.*

peck² n [C] **1** a quick kiss: *He **gave** her a quick **peck on the cheek**.* **2** the action of a bird pecking something with its beak

peckish /ˈpekɪʃ/ adj BrE informal slightly hungry: *She was **feeling** a bit **peckish**.* **THESAURUS** HUNGRY

peculiar /pɪˈkjuːliə $ -ər/ adj **1** strange and surprising: *a peculiar smell* | *He's a rather peculiar boy.* **THESAURUS** STRANGE **2 be peculiar to sb/sth** if something is peculiar to one place, person etc, only that place or person has it: *a building style peculiar to this area*

peculiarity /pɪˌkjuːliˈærəti/ n (plural **peculiarities**) **1** [C] an unusual feature or habit that only one particular person, thing, or place has: *a peculiarity of the British legal system* **2** [U] the quality of being strange or unusual: [+of] *the peculiarity of her situation*

peculiarly /pɪˈkjuːliəli $ -ər-/ adv **1** peculiarly British/male etc typical only of British people, men etc: *a peculiarly American attitude* **2** in a strange or unusual way: *He was behaving very peculiarly.*

pedagogical /ˌpedəˈgɒdʒɪkəl $ -ˈgaː-/ adj formal pedagogical ideas and methods are about the different ways of teaching things to people

pedal¹ /ˈpedl/ n [C] **1** the part of a bicycle that you push round with your foot to make it move forward → see picture at BICYCLE **2** the part of a car or machine that you press with your foot to make it move or work: **brake/clutch pedal** | **accelerator pedal** BrE/**gas pedal** AmE

pedal² v [I,T] (**pedalled, pedalling** BrE, **pedaled, pedaling** AmE) to ride a bicycle by pushing the pedals with your feet: *He pedalled along the road.*

pedantic /pɪˈdæntɪk/ adj disapproving paying too much attention to small unimportant details or rules

peddle /ˈpedl/ v [T] to try to sell things to people, especially illegal drugs or other things that people disapprove of: *He was accused of peddling drugs.* | *The pictures were peddled around to various dealers.*

peddler /ˈpedlə $ -ər/ n [C] **1** AmE someone who walked from place to place in the past selling things **SYN** pedlar BrE **2** old-fashioned someone who sells illegal drugs **SYN** dealer

pedestal /ˈpedəstəl/ n [C] the base that a STATUE stands on
PHRASES
| **put sb on a pedestal** to admire someone very much: *She puts her husband on a pedestal.*

pedestrian¹ /pəˈdestriən/ n [C] someone who is walking, especially along a street where there are cars

pedestrian² *adj* **1** ordinary, and not very interesting, or exciting: *The whole ceremony was rather pedestrian.* **2** [only before noun] used by pedestrians: *a pedestrian precinct* (=a shopping area where cars cannot go)

pe,destrian 'crossing *n* [C] *BrE* a marked place on the road where people who are walking can safely cross SYN **crosswalk** *AmE*

pediatrician /ˌpiːdiə'trɪʃən/ *n* [C] the American spelling of PAEDIATRICIAN

pediatrics /ˌpiːdi'ætrɪks/ *n* [U] the American spelling of PAEDIATRICS

pedicure /'pedɪkjʊə $ -kjʊr/ *n* [C] a treatment for feet and toenails, to make them more comfortable or beautiful —**pedicurist** *n* [C]

pedigree¹ /'pedəgriː/ *n* [C,U] **1** the parents and other past family members of a person or animal, or an official written record of this: *a horse with a good pedigree* **2** all the things that a person or organization has achieved: *a young writer with an impressive pedigree*

pedigree² *adj* [only before noun] a pedigree animal has parents and grandparents from the same special BREED: *a pedigree Alsatian*

pedlar /'pedlə $ -ər/ *n* [C] *BrE* someone who walked from place to place in the past selling things SYN **peddler** *AmE*

pedophile /'piːdəfaɪl/ *n* the American spelling of PAEDOPHILE

pee /piː/ *n* [singular] *informal* when you go for a pee, you URINATE —**pee** *v* [I]

peek /piːk/ *v* [I] to look at something quickly, especially when you should not: *The door was open, so I peeked into the room.* THESAURUS LOOK —**peek** *n* [C]

peel¹ /piːl/ *v* **1** [T] to remove the skin of a fruit or vegetable: *Will you peel the potatoes, please?* THESAURUS CUT **2** (*also* **peel off**) [I] if skin, paint, or paper peels, it comes off, usually in small pieces: *My skin always peels when I've been in the sun.* | *The paint was beginning to peel off.* → **keep your eyes peeled** at EYE¹

PEEL

PHRASAL VERBS

peel sth ↔ **off 1** to remove a layer from the surface of something else: *Peel off the label.* **2** to take your clothes off: *Tom peeled off his wet shorts.*

peel² *n* [U] the skin of a fruit or vegetable that you remove before eating it: *orange peel* | *potato peel* → see picture on page A4

Word Choice: peel or rind?
You use **peel** or **rind** about the outside part of fruits such as oranges and lemons. You use **rind** about the outside part of bacon or cheese.

---

peep¹ /piːp/ *v* [I] **1** to look at something quickly and secretly: [+through/out/at etc] *I saw Joe peeping through the curtains.* THESAURUS LOOK **2** if something peeps from somewhere, you can just see a small amount of it: [+out/above/through etc] *The sun finally peeped out from behind the clouds.*

peep² *n* [C usually singular] **1** a quick or secret look at something: [+at/into] *She took a peep at the answers in the back of the book.* **2** *informal* a sound that someone makes: *There has not been a peep out of the children.*

peer¹ /pɪə $ pɪr/ *n* [C] **1** [usually plural] (*also* **peer group**) *formal* your peers or peer group are people who are the same age as you or who have the same type of job or social position: *Teenagers usually prefer to spend their time with their peers.* | *Kids may take drugs because of peer pressure* (=because they feel they must do the same as other people of their age). **2** someone who belongs to a family of high social rank in Britain, for example a lord

peer² *v* [I] to look very carefully, especially because it is difficult for you to see something clearly: [+at/into/through etc] *Someone was peering through the window.* THESAURUS LOOK

peerage /'pɪərɪdʒ $ 'pɪr-/ *n* [U] the rank of a British peer

peeved /piːvd/ *adj informal* annoyed: *Peeved at his silence, she left.*

peg¹ /peg/ *n* [C] **1** a short object that is fastened to a wall, used for hanging things on: *a coat peg* *BrE* a small plastic or wooden object used to fasten wet clothes to a thin rope to dry SYN **clothes peg**, **clothes pin** *AmE* **3** (*also* **tent peg**) a pointed piece of wood or metal that you push into the ground to keep a tent in the correct position

peg² *v* [T] (**pegged, pegging**) **1** to fasten wet clothes to a rope with pegs: *Peg the clothes on the washing line.* **2** to keep prices, wages etc at a particular level or value: *a currency pegged to the American dollar*

pelican /'pelɪkən/ *n* [C] a large water bird that catches fish and stores them in a deep bag of skin under its beak

pellet /'pelɪt/ *n* [C] a small hard ball made from paper, metal etc: *shotgun pellets*

pelt¹ /pelt/ *v* **1** [T] to throw a lot of things at someone: **pelt sb with sth** *Two kids were pelting each other with snowballs.* **2** [I] to be raining very hard: *It's pelting down out there.* **3** [I + adv/prep] *informal* to run somewhere very fast

pelt² *n* [C] the skin of a dead animal with the fur or hair still on it

PHRASES

(at) full pelt *BrE* as fast as possible: *Nancy ran at full pelt to the school.*

pelvis /'pelvɪs/ *n* [C] the set of large wide curved bones at the base of your SPINE, to which your legs are joined → see picture on page A2 —**pelvic** *adj*

PENS

pen   fountain pen   felt-tip pen   pencil

pen¹ /pen/ n [C,U]
1 a thing that you use for writing and drawing in ink: *a ballpoint pen* | *a felt-tip pen* | **in pen** *Please fill out the form in pen.* → **FOUNTAIN PEN**
2 a small area surrounded by a fence, used for keeping farm animals in

pen² v [T] (**penned, penning**) *literary* to write a letter, note, poem etc with a pen

penal /ˈpiːnl/ adj [only before noun] relating to the legal punishment of criminals: *the penal system*

penalize (also **-ise** BrE) /ˈpiːnəl-aɪz $ ˈpiː-, ˈpe-/ v [T] **1** to punish someone or treat them unfairly: *Two students were penalized very differently for the same offence.* **2** to punish a team or player in sports by giving an advantage to the other team: *Our team was penalized for wasting time.*

penalty /ˈpenlti/ n [C] (plural **penalties**) **1** a punishment for not obeying a law, rule, or legal agreement: *There's a penalty of £50 for not paying your bus fare.* | *I'm against* **the death penalty** (=the punishment of being killed). **THESAURUS** **PUNISHMENT**
2 something bad that happens to you because of something you have done or because of the situation you are in: *One of the penalties of being famous is the loss of privacy.* **3** a disadvantage in sports given to a team or player for not obeying a rule: *Woodson received a penalty.* **4** a chance to kick the ball into the GOAL in a game of football, given because the other team has not obeyed a rule

penance /ˈpenəns/ n [C,U] something you must do to show that you are sorry for something wrong you have done, especially in some religions

pence /pens/ n BrE (abbreviation **p**) a plural of PENNY

penchant /ˈpɒnʃɒn, ˈpentʃənt $ ˈpentʃənt/ n **a penchant for sth** if you have a penchant for something, you like it very much: *He* **has a penchant** *for fast cars.*

pencil¹ /ˈpensəl/ n [C,U] a thing that you use for writing and drawing using the black or coloured substance in the middle: *a sharp pencil* | *Remember to bring a pencil and paper.* | **in pencil** *The note was written in pencil.* → see picture at **PEN¹**

pencil² v [T] (**pencilled, pencilling** BrE, **penciled, penciling** AmE) to write or draw something using a pencil
PHRASAL VERBS
pencil sth/sb ↔ **in** to make an arrangement to meet someone or do something, although it is not very definite: *I've pencilled you in for next Tuesday.*

'pencil case n [C] a bag or box used for keeping pens, pencils etc in → see picture at **CASE**

'pencil ,sharpener n [C] a thing you use for making pencils sharp → see picture at **STATIONERY**

pendant /ˈpendənt/ n [C] a piece of jewellery that hangs from a chain around your neck

pending¹ /ˈpendɪŋ/ prep formal while waiting for something, or until something happens: *The decision has been delayed pending further medical tests.*

pending² adj formal not yet decided, agreed on, or finished: *Their divorce is still pending.*

pendulum /ˈpendjələm $ -dʒə-/ n [C] a long metal stick with a heavy part at the bottom that swings regularly from side to side to control the working of a clock

penetrate /ˈpenətreɪt/ v [I,T] to enter something or pass through it, especially when this is difficult: *bullets that can penetrate metal* | *Sunlight barely penetrated the dirty windows.* —**penetration** /ˌpenəˈtreɪʃən/ n [U]

penetrating /ˈpenətreɪtɪŋ/ adj **1 penetrating look/ stare etc** a look etc that makes you feel uncomfortable and seems to see inside your mind: *He gave her a penetrating stare.* **2** showing an ability to understand things quickly and well: *They asked a number of penetrating questions.* **3** a penetrating sound is very loud and clear: *a high penetrating voice*

'pen friend n [C] BrE a PEN PAL

penguin /ˈpeŋgwɪn/ n [C] a large black and white Antarctic sea bird, which cannot fly but uses its wings for swimming → see picture on page A3

penicillin /ˌpenɪˈsɪlɪn/ n [U] a type of medicine used to treat infections caused by BACTERIA

peninsula /pəˈnɪnsjələ $ -sələ/ n [C] a piece of land that is almost completely surrounded by water but is joined to a larger area of land: *the Malay peninsula* → see picture at **ISLAND**

penis /ˈpiːnɪs/ n [C] the male sex organ

penitent /ˈpenɪtənt/ adj formal feeling sorry because you have done something bad, and intending not to do it again **SYN** repentant —**penitence** n [U]

penitentiary /ˌpenɪˈtenʃəri/ n [C] (plural **penitentiaries**) a prison in the US

penknife /ˈpen-naɪf/ n [C] (plural **penknives** /-naɪvz/) a small knife with blades that fold into the handle, usually carried in your pocket

'pen name n [C] a name used by a writer instead of his or her real name

pennant /ˈpenənt/ n [C] a long pointed flag

penniless /ˈpenɪləs/ adj having no money

penny /ˈpeni/ n [C] (abbreviation **p**) **1** (plural **pence** or **pennies**) a coin worth 1/100 of a pound **2** (plural **pennies**) a coin worth 1/100 of a dollar → **cent**
PHRASES
every penny all of an amount of money: *Every penny that we receive goes towards famine relief.*
not a penny no money at all: *It won't cost you a penny!*

'pen pal n [C] someone you become friendly with by writing letters, especially someone who lives in another country and who you have never met

pension /'penʃən/ n [C] money that the government or a company pays regularly to someone who does not work any more because they are old or ill: *She was receiving a **state pension**. | a company **pension scheme***

pensioner /'penʃənə $ -ər/ n [C] *BrE* an old person who receives a pension

pensive /'pensɪv/ adj thinking about something and seeming slightly worried or sad: *a pensive expression* —**pensively** adv

pentagon /'pentəgən $ -gɑːn/ n [C] a flat shape with five sides and five angles

Pentagon n **the Pentagon** the building in Washington DC from which the US army, navy etc are controlled, or the people who work there

pentathlon /pen'tæθlən/ n [C] a sports competition in which you have to do five different sports

penthouse /'penthaʊs/ n [C] an expensive apartment on the top floor of a tall building

pent-up /ˌpent 'ʌp◂/ adj pent-up emotions are emotions that you have stopped yourself from showing for a long time: *pent-up anger*

penultimate /pe'nʌltəmət, pə-/ adj [only before noun] not the last, but immediately before the last: *the penultimate chapter of the book* **THESAURUS** LAST

people¹ /'piːpəl/ n
1 [plural] men, women, and children. 'People' is the usual plural of 'person': *I like the people I work with. | How many people were at the party? | I don't care what people think.*
2 the people all the ordinary people in a country or place who do not have important jobs or high social positions → **population**: *Rice was the main food of the common people.*
3 [C also + plural verb] *formal* a race or nation: **[+of]** *the peoples of Asia | the American people*
PHRASES
of all people *spoken* used to emphasize that you are very surprised that a particular person did or did not do something: *Why did he, of all people, get promotion?*

THESAURUS

people men, women, and children in general: *I met a lot of really nice people in Mexico.*
the public ordinary people who do not belong to the government, a particular organization etc: *The public has a right to know how their taxes are being spent.*
population all the people who live in a town or country – used especially when giving some facts about them: *The city has a population of 11 million. | Most of the population speaks Russian.*
the human race all the people in the world, considered as a group: *a book on the history of the human race*
mankind/humankind people in general – used especially when talking about their development: *Mankind's understanding of the*

universe has changed. | It was a great achievement for humankind.

Word Choice: people or persons?
The usual plural of **person** is **people**: *There were a lot of people at the party.*
Persons is sometimes used in formal and legal contexts, for example on official notices and documents: *This lift can carry up to 12 persons.| the 1969 Children and Young Persons Act*

people² v **be peopled with/by sb** *literary* if a country or area is peopled by people of a particular type, they live there

pepper¹ /'pepə $ -ər/ n
1 [U] a powder that is used to add a hot taste to food: *salt and pepper*
2 [C] a hollow red, yellow, or green vegetable: *green peppers* → see picture on page A5

pepper² v **be peppered with sth** to contain a lot of things of a particular type: *The article is peppered with mistakes.*

peppermint /'pepə,mɪnt $ -ər-/ n **1** [U] a plant with a strong taste and smell, often used in sweets **2** [C] a sweet with the taste of peppermint

'pep talk /'pep tɔːk $ -tɔːk/ n [C] *informal* a short speech intended to encourage people to work harder, win a game etc: *The coach **gave** the team a **pep talk**.*

per /pə; strong pɜː $ pər; strong pɜːr/ prep for each: *How much are bananas per pound? | He charges £20 per lesson.*

per annum /pər 'ænəm/ adv formal (written abbreviation **p.a.**) for each year: *a salary of $40,000 per annum*

per capita /pə 'kæpɪtə $ pər-/ adj, adv formal used to describe the average amount of something in a particular place, calculated according to the number of people who live there: *the country's per capita income*

perceive Ac /pə'siːv $ pər-/ v [T] formal **1** to understand or think about something or someone in a particular way → **perception**: **perceive sth/sb as sth** *Even as a young woman she was perceived as a future leader.* **2** to notice, hear, or see something: *Cats are not able to perceive colour.*

percent Ac /pə'sent $ pər-/ (also **per 'cent** *BrE*) n, adj, adv **5 per cent (5%)/10 per cent (10%)** etc an amount equal to five, ten etc parts out of a total of a hundred parts: *Inflation is down 2%. | There's a 10% service charge.* | **[+of]** *Only 50% of the people voted.* | **go up/down (by) 5%/10%** etc *Sales have gone up by 20%.* | *an interest rate of 5%*
PHRASES
a/one hundred per cent completely: *I agree with you a hundred per cent.*

percentage Ac /pə'sentɪdʒ $ pər-/ n [C usually singular] an amount that is expressed as if it is a part of a total that is 100: **[+of]** *What percentage of* the workers are women? | **a high/low/small percentage of sth** That figure only represents a small percentage of the total cost.

perceptible /pəˈseptəbəl $ pər-/ adj formal something that is perceptible can be noticed, although it is small OPP **imperceptible**: perceptible changes in temperature —**perceptibly** adv

perception Ac /pəˈsepʃən $ pər-/ n **1** [C] the way you think about something and your idea of what it is like: children's perceptions of the world **2** [U] the way you notice things with your senses: drugs that alter perception **3** [U] the ability to understand or notice things quickly: She shows unusual perception for a child of her age.

perceptive /pəˈseptɪv $ pər-/ adj someone who is perceptive notices things quickly and understands situations, people's feelings etc well: a perceptive young man —**perceptively** adv

perch¹ /pɜːtʃ $ pɜːrtʃ/ n [C] a branch or stick where a bird sits

perch² v **1** be perched on/above etc sth to be in a position on top of something or on the edge of something: The hotel was perched high on a cliff above the bay. **2** [I] to sit on the edge of something: She perched herself on the bar stool.

percussion /pəˈkʌʃən $ pər-/ n [U] drums and other musical instruments which you play by hitting them

perennial /pəˈreniəl/ adj continuing or existing for a long time, or happening again and again: the **perennial problem** of poverty

perfect¹ /ˈpɜːfɪkt $ ˈpɜːr-/ adj
1 not having any mistakes, faults, or damage OPP **imperfect**: a car in perfect condition | Her Spanish is perfect.
2 very good: John was in perfect health. | The jeans were a perfect fit.
3 exactly right for a particular purpose SYN **ideal**: [+for] This rug's perfect for the living room. | a perfect day for a picnic
4 used to emphasize what you are saying SYN **complete**, **total**: I felt a perfect fool! | It **makes perfect sense**. | a **perfect stranger**

THESAURUS – sense 3
perfect exactly right for a particular purpose or person: This car is perfect for a big family.
ideal very suitable and exactly what you want – often used about something or someone that you imagine, but that does not really exist: What would be your ideal job? | She still hasn't found her ideal man.
just right informal very suitable in every way: That dress is just right for you.

perfect² /pəˈfekt $ pər-/ v [T] to make something perfect: He was trying to perfect his guitar technique.

perfect³ /ˈpɜːfɪkt $ ˈpɜːr-/ n **the perfect (tense)** the form of a verb which is used when talking about time up to and including the present. In English this is formed with 'have' and the past participle, for example 'Someone has stolen my car'. SYN **present perfect** → FUTURE PERFECT, PAST PERFECT

perfection /pəˈfekʃən $ pər-/ n [U] when something is perfect: I'll do my best, but don't expect perfection. | **to perfection** The beef was cooked to perfection.

perfectionist /pəˈfekʃənɪst $ pər-/ n [C] someone who is not satisfied with anything unless it is completely perfect

perfectly /ˈpɜːfɪktli $ ˈpɜːr-/ adv
1 used to emphasize what you are saying: The sale was perfectly legal. | You know perfectly well what I mean!
2 in a perfect way: She speaks English perfectly.

perforated /ˈpɜːfəreɪtɪd $ ˈpɜːr-/ adj something that is perforated has a hole or holes in it: Store the fruit in perforated polythene bags. | a **perforated eardrum** (=damaged by having a hole in it) —**perforation** /ˌpɜːfəˈreɪʃən $ ˈpɜːr-/ n [C usually plural]

perform /pəˈfɔːm $ pərˈfɔːrm/ v
1 [I,T] to do something to entertain people such as acting in a play or playing music: We performed 'Hamlet' last year.
2 [T] to do something such as a job or piece of work: Surgeons performed an emergency operation. | **perform a function/role** software that performs a specific function THESAURUS ▶ DO
3 perform well/badly etc to work or do something well, badly etc: The car performs well on mountain roads.

performance /pəˈfɔːməns $ pərˈfɔːr-/ n
1 [C] an occasion when someone entertains people by performing a play or a piece of music: a brilliant performance of Beethoven's Fifth Symphony | The next performance is at 8 o'clock. | a **live performance** by a local band
2 [C,U] how well or badly someone or something does something: the country's economic performance | The car's performance on mountain roads was impressive.
3 [U] when someone does their job: the performance of his official duties

performer /pəˈfɔːmə $ pərˈfɔːrmər/ n [C] an actor, musician etc who performs to entertain people: a circus performer

per,forming 'arts n **the performing arts** arts such as dance, music, or DRAMA

perfume /ˈpɜːfjuːm $ ˈpɜːr-/ n [C,U]
1 a liquid with a strong pleasant smell, which you put on your skin SYN **scent**: She never wears perfume. THESAURUS ▶ SMELL
2 literary a pleasant smell —**perfumed** adj: perfumed soap

perhaps /pəˈhæps, præps $ pər-, præps/ adv
1 used to say that something may be true, but you are not sure SYN **maybe**: Sarah's late – perhaps she missed the bus. | 'Are you sure he knows?' '**Perhaps not**.' THESAURUS ▶ MAYBE
2 spoken used to politely ask or suggest something: Perhaps you'd like to join us?
3 used to say that a number is only a guess: Perhaps 200 people were there.
4 used to give your opinion, when you do not want to be too definite: This is perhaps her best novel yet.

peril /ˈperəl/ n [C,U] formal great danger: **in peril** Our soldiers were in great peril. | the perils of taking drugs

perilous /ˈperələs/ adj literary very dangerous: a perilous journey —**perilously** adv

perimeter /pəˈrɪmɪtə $ -ər/ n [C] the edge that surrounds an area of land or a shape: **[+of]** the perimeter of the airfield | Calculate the perimeter of the triangle (=the total length of its sides).

period¹ Ac /ˈpɪəriəd $ ˈpɪr-/ n [C]
1 a length of time: **[+of]** a period of six weeks | the period from Christmas until New Year | We've been studying the Civil War period.
2 the flow of blood that comes from a woman's body each month
3 AmE the mark (.) used in a piece of writing to show the end of a sentence or an abbreviation **SYN** full stop BrE
4 one of the equal parts that the school day is divided into **SYN** lesson BrE: The first period on Tuesday is history.

THESAURUS

period a length of time: the Christmas period | statues from the Roman period | Cats sleep for short periods.

time a period of years, months, days etc, when something happens: It was a time of great social change. | This is a difficult time for all of us.

age a long period of time, especially a stage in the development of civilization or technology: We live in the age of the Internet. | The temple dates from the Stone Age (= when people used tools made of stone).

era a period in history, especially one that has a particular character, or that is just beginning or ending: the modern era | the Victorian era | a new era in US foreign policy
---

period² adj **period costume/furniture** clothes or furniture in the style of a particular time in history

periodic Ac /ˌpɪəriˈɒdɪk◂ $ ˌpɪriˈɑː-/ (also **periodical**) adj happening a number of times but not frequently: periodic attacks of flu —**periodically** /-kli/ adv: The river floods periodically.

periodical Ac /ˌpɪəriˈɒdɪkəl $ ˌpɪriˈɑː-/ n [C] a magazine, especially one about a technical subject

peripheral¹ /pəˈrɪfərəl/ adj formal less important or less central than other facts, places, jobs etc: peripheral information

peripheral² n [C] a piece of equipment that is connected to a computer, for example a PRINTER

periphery /pəˈrɪfəri/ n [C usually singular] (plural **peripheries**) the outside area or edge of something: an industrial site on the periphery of the city

perish /ˈperɪʃ/ v [I] literary to die: Hundreds perished when the ship sank.

perishable /ˈperɪʃəbəl/ adj food that is perishable can quickly become bad to eat: milk and other perishable items

perjury /ˈpɜːdʒəri $ ˈpɜːr-/ n [U] the crime of not telling the truth in a law court —**perjurer** n [C]

perk¹ /pɜːk $ pɜːrk/ n [C usually plural] something that your employer gives you in addition to your pay, such as free meals or a car: Free travel is one of the perks of the job.

perk² v

PHRASAL VERBS

perk up to become happier and more interested in what is happening around you, or to make someone feel this way: Meg soon perked up when his letter arrived. | **perk sb up** A cup of tea should perk you up.

perky /ˈpɜːki $ ˈpɜːrki/ adj informal confident, happy, and active: a perky salesgirl —**perkily** adv —**perkiness** n [U]

perm /pɜːm $ pɜːrm/ n [C] a way of putting curls into straight hair, using chemicals: I've decided to **have** a perm. —**perm** v [T]

permanent /ˈpɜːmənənt $ ˈpɜːr-/ adj continuing to exist for a long time or for all future time **OPP** temporary: a permanent job | an illness that causes permanent loss of sight —**permanence** n [U]

permanently /ˈpɜːmənəntli $ ˈpɜːr-/ adv always, or for a very long time: The accident left him permanently disabled. **THESAURUS** ➤ ALWAYS

permeate /ˈpɜːmieɪt $ ˈpɜːr-/ v [I,T] formal to enter and spread through every part of something, or to be present in every part: Water had permeated through the wall. | A feeling of sadness permeates his music.

permissible /pəˈmɪsəbəl $ pər-/ adj formal allowed by law or by the rules: permissible levels of pollution

permission /pəˈmɪʃən $ pər-/ n [U] if you have permission to do something, someone in authority allows you to do it: **permission to do sth** Did your father give you permission to use his car? | **without permission** Don't take food from the fridge without permission. | **[+for]** The Department of Transport finally granted permission for the scheme. **THESAURUS** ➤ ALLOW

COLLOCATIONS

verbs

to have permission Do you have permission to be here?

to ask (for) permission (also **to request permission** formal) You have to ask permission if you want to leave early.

to give permission (also **to grant permission** formal) The authorities gave him permission to remain in the country.

to get permission We were trying to get permission to film in the church.

to obtain/receive permission formal The aircraft received permission to land.

to refuse sb permission He was refused permission to enter the base.

permissive /pəˈmɪsɪv $ pər-/ adj not strict, and allowing behaviour that many people disapprove of: the **permissive society** of the 1970s

permit¹ /pəˈmɪt $ pər-/ v [T] (**permitted**, **permitting**) formal to allow something to happen or someone to do something: Smoking is not permitted inside the building. | **permit sb to do sth** *The visa permits you to stay for three weeks.* THESAURUS ▶ ALLOW

PHRASES
weather permitting if the weather is good enough: *We'll probably go to the beach, weather permitting.*

permit² /'pɜːrmɪt $ 'pɜːr-, pər'mɪt/ *n* [C] an official written statement allowing you to do something: *You can't park here without a permit.* | *a work permit*

permutation /ˌpɜːmjʊ'teɪʃən $ ˌpɜːr-/ *n* [C] one of the different ways in which a number of things can be arranged: *We tried various permutations of the colours.*

pernicious /pə'nɪʃəs $ pər-/ *adj* formal very harmful or evil: *the **pernicious influence** of TV violence*

perpendicular /ˌpɜːpən'dɪkjələ◂ $ ˌpɜːrpən'dɪkjələr◂/ *adj* at an angle of 90 degrees to something, especially the ground → **vertical**: *a perpendicular line*

perpetrate /'pɜːpətreɪt $ 'pɜːr-/ *v* [T] *formal* to do something that is wrong or illegal —**perpetrator** *n* [C]

perpetual /pə'petʃuəl $ pər-/ *adj* continuing all the time without changing or stopping: *the perpetual noise of the machines* —**perpetually** *adv*

perpetuate /pə'petʃueɪt $ pər-/ *v* [T] *formal* to make a situation, attitude etc continue to exist for a long time, especially one that is bad: *The prison system was designed to perpetuate crime, not prevent it.*

perplexed /pə'plekst $ pər-/ *adj* confused by something that you do not understand SYN **puzzled**: *The child looked totally perplexed.* —**perplex** *v* [T]

persecute /'pɜːsɪkjuːt $ 'pɜːr-/ *v* [T] to treat someone cruelly and unfairly, especially because of their beliefs: *Christians were persecuted by the Emperor Nero.* —**persecutor** *n* [C] —**persecution** /ˌpɜːsɪ'kjuːʃən $ ˌpɜːr-/ *n* [U]

perseverance /ˌpɜːsə'vɪərəns $ ˌpɜːrsə'vɪr-/ *n* [U] determination to keep trying to do something difficult: *I admire her perseverance.*

persevere /ˌpɜːsə'vɪə $ ˌpɜːrsə'vɪr/ *v* [I] to continue trying to do something difficult in a determined way: **[+with]** *I'm not enjoying the course, but I'll persevere with it.*

persist Ac /pə'sɪst $ pər-/ *v* [I] **1** to continue to do something, even though it is difficult or other people do not approve of it: **persist in (doing) sth** *He persisted in denying the charges against him.* **2** if something bad persists, it continues to exist or happen: *If the pain persists, see a doctor.*

persistent Ac /pə'sɪstənt $ pər-/ *adj* **1** continuing for a long time or happening often, especially in a way that is unpleasant or annoying: *a persistent cough* | *persistent problems* **2** continuing to do something even when it is difficult or people tell you not to do it: *You have to be persistent if you want to get a job.* | *penalties for **persistent offenders*** —**persistently** *adv* —**persistence** *n* [U]

person /'pɜːsən $ 'pɜːr-/ *n* [C] (*plural* **people** /'piːpəl/) a man, woman, or child: *She's a very generous person.* | *Dan was the first person I met when I*

arrived. | **the sort/kind/type of person** *I'm not the sort of person who watches TV all day.* | **a city/ outdoor/cat etc person** (=someone who likes cities, outdoor activities etc) → **FIRST PERSON, SECOND PERSON, THIRD PERSON**

PHRASES
in person if you do something in person, you do it by going somewhere yourself rather than sending someone else or writing a letter etc: *You can reserve tickets either in person or by telephone.*

persona /pə'səʊnə $ pər'soʊ-/ *n* [C] (*plural* **personas** or **personae** /-niː/) the way you behave when you are with other people or in a particular situation: *His **public persona** is very different from the one his family sees.*

personable /'pɜːsənəbəl $ 'pɜːr-/ *adj* someone who is personable is attractive and pleasant

personal /'pɜːsənəl $ 'pɜːr-/ *adj*
1 [only before noun] belonging or relating to one particular person: *books, clothes, and other **personal belongings*** | *I know **from personal experience** how difficult it is to write a book.* | *a matter of **personal choice***
2 relating to the private parts of your life such as your feelings, health, relationships etc: *I don't answer questions about my **personal life**.* | *She has a few **personal problems**.* | *Can I ask you a **personal question**?*
3 criticizing someone in a rude way: *personal remarks* | *There's no need to **get personal**.* | *It's nothing **personal** (=I am not trying to offend you), I just need some time alone.*
4 involving doing something yourself rather than asking someone else to do it: *The President made a personal visit to the scene of the accident.*
5 [only before noun] relating to your body or the way you look: *personal hygiene*

ˌpersonal as'sistant *n* [C] a PA

ˌpersonal com'puter *n* [C] a PC

personality /ˌpɜːsə'næləti $ ˌpɜːr-/ *n* (*plural* **personalities**)
1 [C,U] someone's character, especially the way they behave towards other people: *She's an ambitious woman with a strong personality.* | *Childhood experiences can affect personality.*
2 [C] a famous person, especially in sport, television, films etc SYN **celebrity**: *a TV personality*
3 [U] the qualities that make someone interesting to be with: *You need personality rather than qualifications to do this job.*

personalize (*also* **-ise** *BrE*) /'pɜːsənəlaɪz $ 'pɜːr-/ *v* [T] **1** to put your name or INITIALS on something or decorate it in your own way to show that it belongs to you: *You can personalize the T-shirts with your own pictures.* **2** to design or change something so that it is suitable for a particular person: *We provide a complete beauty programme personalized to you.* —**personalized** *adj*: *personalized number plates*

personally /'pɜːsənəli $ 'pɜːr-/ *adv*
1 *spoken* used to emphasize that you are giving your own opinion: *Personally, I think it's a bad idea.*
2 doing something yourself rather than getting

someone else to do it: *I delivered the letter personally.* | *The manager has personally overseen the design of the rooms.* | *Students are **personally responsible for** the payment of their fees.*
3 as a friend or as someone you have met: *I don't* **know** *her* **personally** *but I like her work.*
PHRASES

take sth personally to get upset because you think someone's remarks or behaviour are directed at you: *Don't take it personally – she's rude to everyone.*

,personal 'organizer *n* [C] a small book with loose pages, or a very small computer, for recording addresses, meetings etc

,personal 'pronoun *n* [C] a PRONOUN such as 'I', 'you', or 'they'

,personal 'stereo *n* [C] a small machine that plays CASSETTES or CDs, which you carry around with you and listen to with HEADPHONES

,personal 'trainer *n* [C] someone whose job is to help people decide what type of exercise is best for them and show them how to do it

personify /pəˈsɒnɪfaɪ $ pərˈsɑː-/ *v* [T] (**personified, personifying, personifies**) **1** to be a typical example of something or have a lot of a particular quality: *He personifies the English gentleman.* | **be kindness/ charm/courage etc personified** *Mr Rowley was diplomacy personified.* **2** to think of or represent something as a person: **personify sth as sb** *Time is often personified as an old man.* —**personification** /pəˌsɒnɪfɪˈkeɪʃən $ pərˌsɑː-/ *n* [C,U]

personnel /ˌpɜːsəˈnel $ ˌpɜːr-/ *n* **1** [plural] the people who work in a company or organization → **staff**: *military personnel* **2** [U] the department in a company that chooses people for jobs, deals with their problems etc **SYN** **human resources**: *a personnel manager*

perspective Ac /pəˈspektɪv $ pər-/ *n* **1** [C] a way of thinking about something: **[+on]** *Working abroad gives you* **a whole new perspective** *on life.* | **from a ... perspective** *Try and approach the problem from a different perspective.* **2** [U] a sensible way of thinking about something so that you do not imagine that something is more serious than it is: **get/keep/put sth in perspective** *It's important to put things in perspective.* | *We must keep* **a sense of perspective** *about this.* **3** [U] a method of drawing a picture which makes objects look solid and makes some things look further away than others

perspiration /ˌpɜːspəˈreɪʃən $ ˌpɜːr-/ *n* [U] *formal* SWEAT

perspire /pəˈspaɪə $ pərˈspaɪr/ *v* [I] *formal* to SWEAT

persuade /pəˈsweɪd $ pər-/ *v* [T]
1 to make someone decide to do something by telling them why it is a good idea, or asking them many times: **persuade sb to do sth** *John was trying to persuade me to stay.*
2 to make someone believe something **SYN** **convince**: **[+(that)]** *She'll only take me back if I can persuade her that I've changed.* | **persuade sb of sth** *We must persuade people of the importance of protecting the environment.*

persuade to make someone decide to do something by telling them why it is a good idea, or asking them many times: *I'll try and persuade her to come to the party.*
encourage to try to persuade someone to do something you think it will be good for them: *Farmers are being encouraged to use fewer chemicals.*
influence to have an effect on what someone does or thinks, but without directly persuading them: *People are easily influenced by advertising.* | *His work influenced other writers.*
convince to succeed in persuading someone that something is true or is the right thing to do: *I finally convinced her to go to the police.*
get sb to do sth *informal* to ask or persuade someone to do something, especially something that would help or please you: *I can't get her to listen to me.* | *I'll get my Dad to drive us there.*
talk sb into (doing) sth to persuade someone to do something they do not really want to do: *Don't let other people talk you into doing silly things.*

persuasion /pəˈsweɪʒən $ pər-/ *n* **1** [U] when you persuade someone to do something: *After a little* **gentle persuasion***, Debbie agreed to come.* | *It took all his* **powers of persuasion** *(=skill at persuading people) to convince her.* **2** [C,U] *formal* a particular belief that you have: **political/religious persuasion** *people of all kinds of religious persuasion*

persuasive /pəˈsweɪsɪv $ pər-/ *adj* able to make people do or believe something: *He can be very persuasive.* | *persuasive evidence* —**persuasively** *adv*

pertain /pəˈteɪn $ pər-/ *v*
PHRASAL VERBS
pertain to sth *formal* to relate directly to something

pertinent /ˈpɜːtɪnənt $ ˈpɜːr-/ *adj formal* directly relating to something that is being considered **SYN** **relevant**: *He asked a lot of very* **pertinent questions***.*

perturbed /pəˈtɜːbd $ pərˈtɜːrbd/ *adj formal* worried or upset: **[+by/at/about]** *He didn't seem at all perturbed by the news of his father's death.* —**perturb** *v* [T]

peruse /pəˈruːz/ *v* [T] *formal* to read or look at something carefully

pervade /pəˈveɪd $ pər-/ *v* [T] *formal* if a feeling, idea, or smell pervades a place, it is in every part of the place: *A feeling of hopelessness pervaded the country.* | *The smell of tobacco pervaded the room.*

pervasive /pəˈveɪsɪv $ pər-/ *adj* existing everywhere: *the pervasive influence of television*

perverse /pəˈvɜːs $ pərˈvɜːrs/ *adj* strange or unreasonable, and not what people expect: *He takes perverse pleasure in arguing with everyone.* —**perversely** *adv*

perversion /pəˈvɜːʃən, -ʒən $ pərˈvɜːrʒən/ *n* [C,U] sexual behaviour that is considered strange and unacceptable

pervert[1] /ˈpɜːvɜːt $ ˈpɜːrvɜːrt/ n [C] someone whose sexual behaviour is considered strange and unacceptable

pervert[2] /pəˈvɜːt $ pərˈvɜːrt/ v [T] to change someone or something in a harmful way: *Violent images may pervert the minds of young children.*

perverted /pəˈvɜːtɪd $ pərˈvɜːr-/ adj strange and unacceptable, often in a sexual way: *perverted desires*

pessimism /ˈpesəmɪzəm/ n [U] the feeling that things will happen in a bad or unsuccessful way OPP optimism: [+about/over] *There is widespread pessimism over the future of the Middle East peace talks.*

pessimist /ˈpesəmɪst/ n [C] someone who always expects that bad things will happen OPP optimist

pessimistic /ˌpesəˈmɪstɪk◀/ adj expecting that bad things will happen OPP optimistic: *a pessimistic view of life* | [+about] *She was very pessimistic about the future.*

pest /pest/ n [C] **1** a small animal or insect that destroys crops or food **2** *informal* an annoying person

pester /ˈpestə $ -ər/ v [T] to annoy someone, especially by asking them many times to do something: **pester sb to do sth** *He keeps pestering me to buy him a new bike.* | **pester sb for sth** *Tourists are likely to be pestered for money.*

pesticide /ˈpestɪsaɪd/ n [C,U] a chemical used to kill insects that damage crops

PETS

cat

dog

rabbit   hamster

pet[1] /pet/ n [C] an animal that you keep at home: *Cats are popular pets.* → **TEACHER'S PET**

COLLOCATIONS

verbs

to have a pet *They have lots of pets.*
to keep a pet (=to have one in your home) *We weren't allowed to keep pets.*
to look after/care for a pet *Sometimes people don't know how to look after their pets properly.*
to feed the pets (=to give them their food) *She's feeding the pets while we're away.*

to make good pets (=to be good as pets) *Guinea pigs make good pets.*

pet + noun

a pet dog/rabbit/snake etc *Her brother had a pet rabbit.*
pet food *Where do you keep the pet food?*
a pet shop *She bought the mice from a pet shop.*

pet[2] adj **pet project/subject/theory etc** a plan, subject, or idea that you particularly like or are interested in

PHRASES

pet hate *BrE*, **pet peeve** *AmE* something that you particularly dislike
pet name a short friendly name for someone that is used especially by their friends and family SYN **nickname**: *He had pet names for all his grandchildren.*

pet[3] v [T] (**petted, petting**) to touch and move your hand gently over someone, especially an animal or a child SYN **stroke**: *Our cat loves being petted.*

petal /ˈpetl/ n [C] one of the coloured parts of a flower: *rose petals* → see picture at **PLANT**[1]

peter /ˈpiːtə $ -ər/ v

PHRASAL VERBS

peter out to gradually become smaller, quieter, less etc and then stop: *The road finally petered out.*

petite /pəˈtiːt/ adj a woman who is petite is small and attractively thin

petition[1] /pəˈtɪʃən/ n [C] a piece of paper that a lot of people have signed, asking someone in authority to do or change something: [+for/against] *More than 1,000 people signed a petition against experiments on animals.*

petition[2] v [I,T] to officially ask someone in authority to do something, especially by giving them a petition: [+for/against] *Residents are petitioning against the new road.* | **petition sb to do sth** *Many people have petitioned the government to intervene.*

petrified /ˈpetrɪfaɪd/ adj very frightened: *I'm absolutely petrified of dogs.* —**petrify** v [T]

petrol /ˈpetrəl/ n [U] *BrE* a liquid that you put in a vehicle to make the engine work SYN **gas** *AmE*: *How much petrol did you put in?* | *petrol prices*

petroleum /pəˈtrəʊliəm $ -ˈtroʊ-/ n [U] oil from under the ground that is used to make petrol and other substances

'petrol ˌstation n [C] *BrE* a place where you buy petrol for your car SYN **gas station** *AmE*

petticoat /ˈpetikəʊt $ -koʊt/ n [C] *BrE* a piece of women's underwear like a thin dress or skirt SYN **slip**

petty /ˈpeti/ adj **1** not serious or important: *petty problems* | **petty crime/theft 2** caring too much about unimportant things, especially in an unkind way: *He can be very petty.* —**pettiness** n [U]

petulant /ˈpetʃələnt/ adj behaving in an impatient and angry way, like a child —**petulance** n [U] —**petulantly** adv

P

pew /pju:/ n [C] a long wooden seat in a church

pewter /ˈpju:tə $ -ər/ n [U] a grey metal made by mixing LEAD and TIN

pH /ˌpi: ˈeɪtʃ/ n [singular] technical a number on a scale of 0 to 14 which shows how acid or ALKALINE a substance is: soil with a pH of 3.1

phantom¹ /ˈfæntəm/ n [C] literary a GHOST

phantom² adj [only before noun] imaginary and not real

pharaoh /ˈfeərəʊ $ ˈferoʊ/ n [C] a ruler of ancient Egypt

pharmaceutical /ˌfɑ:məˈsju:tɪkəl◄ $ ˌfɑ:rməˈsu:-/ adj relating to the production of drugs and medicines: pharmaceutical companies

pharmacist /ˈfɑ:məsɪst $ ˈfɑ:r-/ n [C] someone whose job is to prepare medicines in a shop or hospital

pharmacy /ˈfɑ:məsi $ ˈfɑ:r-/ n (plural pharmacies) **1** [C] a shop or a part of a shop where you can get medicines SYN chemist **2** [U] the study or preparation of drugs and medicines

phase¹ Ac /feɪz/ n [C] one part of a process: [+of] the first phase of the project | The new drug is still in the experimental phase.

phase² Ac v
PHRASAL VERBS
phase sth ↔ **in** to gradually start using a new system, law etc: Regular homework is phased in as children approach high school age.
phase sth ↔ **out** to gradually stop using or providing something: All tax relief on company cars will be phased out.

PhD /ˌpi: eɪtʃ ˈdi:/ n [C] (**Doctor of Philosophy**) the highest university DEGREE, or someone who has this degree

pheasant /ˈfezənt/ n [C,U] a large bird with a long tail, often shot for food, or the meat from this bird

phenomenal Ac /fɪˈnɒmɪnəl $ -ˈnɑ:-/ adj very great or impressive: the **phenomenal success** of computer games | a **phenomenal growth** in population —**phenomenally** adv

phenomenon Ac /fɪˈnɒmənən $ fɪˈnɑ:mənɑ:n, -nən/ n [C] (plural **phenomena** /-nə/) something that happens or exists, especially something that is unusual or difficult to understand: [+of] The phenomenon of laughter is unknown in animals. | **social/natural/cultural etc phenomenon** earthquakes and other natural phenomena

phew /fju:/ spoken used when you feel tired, hot, or happy to have avoided a difficult or unpleasant situation

philanthropist /fɪˈlænθrəpɪst/ n [C] a rich person who gives a lot of money to help people —**philanthropic** /ˌfɪlənˈθrɒpɪk◄ $ -ˈθrɑ:-/ adj

philistine /ˈfɪləstaɪn $ -sti:n/ n [C] someone who does not like or understand art, literature, music etc —**philistine** adj

philosopher Ac /fəˈlɒsəfə $ -ˈlɑ:səfər/ n [C] someone who studies and develops ideas about life, thought, and behaviour

philosophical Ac /ˌfɪləˈsɒfɪkəl◄ $ -ˈsɑ:-/ (also **philosophic** /-ˈsɒfɪk $ -ˈsɑ:-/) adj **1** relating to philosophy: a philosophical discussion **2** calmly accepting a difficult or unpleasant situation that you cannot change: [+about] He was philosophical about losing. —**philosophically** /-kli/ adv

philosophy Ac /fəˈlɒsəfi $ -ˈlɑ:-/ n (plural **philosophies**) **1** [C,U] the study of ideas about life, thought, and behaviour: She's studying philosophy at university. | the philosophy of Aristotle **2** [C] a belief about how you should live your life, do your job etc: My philosophy is enjoy life while you can!

phlegm /flem/ n [U] a thick substance produced in your nose and throat when you have a cold

phlegmatic /fleɡˈmætɪk/ adj formal calm and not easily excited or worried

phobia /ˈfəʊbiə $ ˈfoʊ-/ n [C] a strong unreasonable fear of something: [+about] He **has a phobia** about birds. —**phobic** adj

phone¹ /fəʊn $ foʊn/ n [C,U] a telephone: He rushed to answer the phone. | **by phone** You can reserve tickets by phone. | **on the phone** (=talking to someone using a telephone) Could you turn the TV down? I'm on the phone. **THESAURUS** PHONE → CELL PHONE, MOBILE PHONE, PAY PHONE

COLLOCATIONS

verbs

the phone rings The phone rang while I was in the shower.

to answer the phone (also **to pick up the phone**) His wife answered the phone.

to put the phone down (=to end the conversation) Greg said goodbye and put the phone down.

to use a phone Can I use the phone?

to talk/speak to sb on the phone They talk on the phone for hours.

phone + noun

a phone call I had a phone call from Pam this morning.

a phone number What's your phone number?

a phone line (=a telephone wire or connection) My office has a separate phone line.

a phone bill (=a bill for phone calls) Why are our phone bills so high?

---

phone² (also **phone up**) v [I,T] to speak to someone using a telephone SYN call: Carla phoned me in the middle of the night. | I'll phone and find out what time the museum opens. | For more information, phone 0296 333444. | I'm busy but I'll **phone** you **back** (=phone again) later.

Grammar
Do not say 'I phoned to Terry.' Say I phoned Terry.

THESAURUS

phone to speak to someone using a telephone. **Phone** is used especially in British English: I'll phone you tomorrow.

call to phone someone. **Call** is used in both British and American English: One of the neighbours called the police.

ring to phone someone. **Ring** is used in informal British English: *How often do you ring your parents?*

telephone *formal* to phone someone: *A lot of people telephoned the BBC to complain.*

give sb a call *informal* (*also* **give sb a ring** *BrE informal*) to phone someone: *If you ever come to Seattle, give me a call.*

be on the phone to be talking to someone using a telephone: *Just a minute – I'm on the phone.*

'phone book *n* [C] a book containing the names, addresses, and telephone numbers of people in an area SYN **telephone directory**

'phone booth (*also* **'phone box** *BrE*) *n* [C] a structure containing a public telephone

'phone call *n* [C] a situation when you telephone someone, or they telephone you: *I need to **make a phone call**.* | *There's a phone call for you.*

'phone card *n* [C] a plastic card that can be used in some public telephones instead of money

'phone-in *n* [C] a radio or television programme in which you hear people asking questions and expressing their opinions on the telephone

phonetic /fə'netɪk/ *adj technical* relating to the sounds of human speech —**phonetically** /-kli/ *adv*

phonetics /fə'netɪks/ *n* [U] the study of speech sounds

phoney (*also* **phony** *AmE*) /'fəʊni $ 'foʊ-/ *adj* **1** not real, and intended to deceive someone THESAURUS **FALSE** a *phoney American accent* **2** *disapproving* pretending to be something you are not —**phoney** *n* [C]

phosphate /'fɒsfeɪt $ 'fɑːs-/ *n* [C,U] a chemical used in industry and farming

photo /'fəʊtəʊ $ 'foʊtoʊ/ *n* [C] (*plural* **photos**) *informal* a photograph: [+of] *Will you **take a photo** of me and Anna together?* | **in the photo** *The boy in the photo is my brother.*

photocopier /'fəʊtəʊˌkɒpiə $ 'foʊtəˌkɑːpiər/ *n* [C] a machine that makes copies of documents

photocopy¹ /'fəʊtəʊˌkɒpi $ 'foʊtəˌkɑːpi/ *n* [C] (*plural* **photocopies**) a copy of a document made by a photocopier: [+of] *She made a photocopy of the map.*

photocopy² *v* [T] (**photocopied**, **photocopying**, **photocopies**) to make a copy of a document using a photocopier

photo 'finish *n* [C] the end of a race in which the runners finish very close together, so that a photograph has to be looked at to decide who won

photogenic /ˌfəʊtə'dʒenɪk◄, ˌfəʊtə- $ ˌfoʊtə-/ *adj* someone who is photogenic always looks attractive in photographs

photograph¹ /'fəʊtəɡrɑːf $ 'foʊtəɡræf/ (*also* **photo** *informal*) *n* [C] a picture that you make using a camera: [+of] *She showed me a photograph of her son.*

COLLOCATIONS

verbs

to take a photograph *He wanted to take a photograph of me.*

types of photograph

a colour photograph *BrE*, **a color photograph** *AmE The book has some great colour photographs.*

a black-and-white photograph *I found an old black-and-white photograph of my grandmother.*

a framed photograph *The walls were covered with framed photographs.*

a wedding photograph *They looked so happy in their wedding photographs.*

photograph + noun

a photograph album (=a book in which you put photographs) *We were looking through some old photograph albums.*

photograph² *v* [T] to make a picture of someone or something using a camera

photographer /fə'tɒɡrəfə $ -'tɑːɡrəfər/ *n* [C] someone who takes photographs, especially as a job

photographic /ˌfəʊtə'ɡræfɪk◄, ˌfoʊ-/ *adj* relating to photographs and photography: *photographic equipment*

photography /fə'tɒɡrəfi $ -'tɑː-/ *n* [U] the skill or process of taking photographs

'photo oppor'tunity *n* [C] a chance for someone such as a politician to be photographed for a newspaper in a way that will make them look good

phrasal 'verb *n* [C] a verb with an adverb or PREPOSITION after it, which has a different meaning from the verb used alone. 'Set off', 'look after', and 'put up with' are all phrasal verbs.

phrase¹ /freɪz/ *n* [C]

1 a group of words that together have a particular meaning: *Darwin's famous phrase 'the survival of the fittest'*

2 *technical* a group of words without a main verb, used to form part of a sentence, for example 'a piece of bread'

THESAURUS

phrase a group of words that together have a particular meaning: *a list of useful English words and phrases* | *President Obama used the phrase 'Yes we can!'*

expression a phrase, especially a fixed set of words that are often used in a language: *I'm not sure where the expression comes from.*

idiom a group of words with a special meaning that you cannot guess from each separate word in the group: *'Under the weather' is an idiom which means 'ill'.*

cliché a phrase that is boring and slightly annoying because people use it a lot: *I'm tired of hearing the same old clichés about men and women.*

saying/proverb a well-known phrase that gives advice about life: *You know the saying – 'you shouldn't judge a book by its cover.'* | *the old proverb 'a stitch in time saves nine'*

phrase² v [T] to express something in a particular way: *Ben tried to think how to phrase his next question.*

'phrase book n [C] a book that contains useful words and phrases in a foreign language that you use when you are travelling

physical¹ Ac /ˈfɪzɪkəl/ adj
1 relating to your body rather than your mind → **mental**, **emotional**: *physical strength | people with mental and physical disabilities | **Physical appearance** (=the way you look) is very important to young people. | My attraction to him was totally physical.*
2 relating to real things you can see and touch: *ways to improve the physical environment in our cities*
3 physical science is related to PHYSICS: *physical chemistry* —**physically** /-kli/ adv: *Try to keep physically fit.*

physical² n [C] especially AmE an examination of your body by a doctor to check that you are healthy

,physical edu'cation n [U] (abbreviation **PE**) sport and physical exercise that are taught as a school subject

physician /fəˈzɪʃən/ n [C] especially AmE formal a doctor THESAURUS **DOCTOR**

physics /ˈfɪzɪks/ n [U] the science that involves the study of natural forces such as light, heat, and movement —**physicist** /ˈfɪzɪsɪst/ n [C]

physiology /ˌfɪziˈɒlədʒi $ -ˈɑː-/ n [U] the science that studies the way that the bodies of living things work —**physiological** /ˌfɪziəˈlɒdʒɪkəl $ -ˈlɑː-/ adj

physiotherapy /ˌfɪziəʊˈθerəpi $ -zioʊ-/ n [U] a way of treating injuries and medical conditions using special exercises, heat etc —**physiotherapist** n [C]

physique /fəˈziːk/ n [C] the shape and size of your body: *a man with a muscular physique*

pianist /ˈpiːənɪst $ piˈænəst, ˈpiːə-/ n [C] someone who plays the piano

piano /piˈænəʊ $ -noʊ/ n [C] (plural **pianos**) a large musical instrument that you play by pressing down black and white KEYS → see picture on page A6 → **pianist**: *I'm learning to play the piano. | piano music | piano lessons* → **GRAND PIANO**

piccolo /ˈpɪkələʊ $ -loʊ/ n [C] (plural **piccolos**) a musical instrument that looks like a small FLUTE

pick¹ /pɪk/ v [T]
1 to choose something or someone: *Students have to pick three courses. | **pick sb for sth** Have you been picked for the volleyball team?* THESAURUS **CHOOSE**
2 to remove a flower or fruit from a plant or tree: *Amy picked a bunch of wild flowers. | **freshly picked** strawberries*
3 to remove something carefully from a place, especially something small: **pick sth off (sth)** *She sat nervously picking bits of fluff off her sweater.*

PHRASES
pick and choose to choose only the things or people that you like very much: *I don't have enough money to pick and choose.*
pick sb's brain(s) to ask someone for information or advice about something: *I've come to pick your brains.*

pick a fight/argument/quarrel (with sb) to deliberately start an argument or fight with someone: *Some drunk tried to pick a fight with me.*
pick a lock to open a lock using something such as a piece of wire, not a key: *The thieves must have used something to pick the lock.*
pick your nose to remove substances from inside your nose with your finger
pick sb's pocket to steal something from someone's pocket → **pickpocket**: *The boys had their pockets picked at the station.*
pick your way through/across/along etc sth to walk carefully, choosing exactly where to put your feet: *Ella picked her way carefully over the rocks.*

PHRASAL VERBS
pick at sth
1 to eat only a small amount of food because you are not hungry or do not like the food: *I was so nervous I could only pick at my lunch.* THESAURUS **EAT**
2 to pull something slightly several times with your fingers: *She was picking nervously at her skirt.*
pick on sb to criticize or blame someone in an unfair way: *The teacher's always picking on me!*
pick sb/sth ↔ **out**
1 to choose someone or something from a group: *His story was picked out as the best.*
2 to recognize someone from a group of people: *The woman was able to pick out her attacker.*
pick up
1 pick sb/sth ↔ **up** to lift someone or something: *Pick me up, Daddy! | I picked up the phone just as it stopped ringing.* → see picture on page A11 THESAURUS **LIFT**
2 pick sth ↔ **up** to buy something while you are going somewhere or doing something: *Do you want me to pick up some milk while I'm out?* THESAURUS **BUY**
3 pick sb/sth ↔ **up** to collect someone or something from a place, especially in the car: *What time should we pick you up at the airport?*
4 pick sth ↔ **up** to win or be given something: *He's already picked up three prizes this year.*
5 if a situation picks up, it improves: *Business will pick up soon.*
6 if the wind picks up, it becomes stronger
7 pick sth ↔ **up** to learn something by listening to or watching other people: *I picked up a few words of French while I was in France.* THESAURUS **LEARN**
8 pick sth ↔ **up** to notice something that is not easy to notice: *The dogs were able to pick up the scent.*
9 pick sth ↔ **up** if a machine picks up a sound or a signal, it receives it: *We can pick up French radio stations from here.*
10 pick sth ↔ **up** to get an illness: *I picked up a virus while I was in England.*
11 pick sb ↔ **up** if the police pick someone up, they take them somewhere to answer questions
12 pick sb ↔ **up** to talk to someone and try to begin a sexual relationship with them

pick² n [C] a pickaxe
PHRASES
take/have your pick if you can take or have your pick of different things, you can choose which one you want: *Take your pick from a choice of hot or cold*

dishes. | She **could take** her **pick of** any of the men in the office.

the pick of sth informal the best of a group of things or people: We'll be reviewing the pick of this month's new movies. | All the wines were good but this was **the pick of the bunch**.

pickaxe BrE, **pickax** AmE /'pɪk-æks/ n [C] a large tool used for breaking up rocks or hard ground. It has a long handle with a curved iron bar.

picker /'pɪkə $ -ər/ n **apple/cotton/mushroom etc picker** a person or machine that picks fruit or vegetables

picket¹ /'pɪkɪt/ n [C] **a)** when a group of people stand outside a building in order to protest about something or to stop people entering during a STRIKE: There were **mass pickets** (=involving a lot of people) at the factory gates. **b)** a person or group of people involved in a picket

picket² v [I,T] to stand outside a building in order to protest about something or to stop people entering during a STRIKE: Demonstrators picketed the US Embassy.

'picket ,fence n [C] AmE a fence made of a line of pointed sticks fixed into the ground

pickle¹ /'pɪkəl/ n **1** [C,U] BrE a thick cold sauce made from pieces of vegetables preserved in VINEGAR **2** [C] especially AmE a CUCUMBER that has been preserved in VINEGAR or salt water

pickle² v [T] to preserve food in VINEGAR and salt

pickled /'pɪkəld/ adj pickled vegetables, eggs etc have been preserved in VINEGAR

'pick-me-up n [C] informal a drink or medicine that makes you feel happier and gives you more energy

pickpocket /'pɪk,pɒkɪt $ -,pɑːk-/ n [C] someone who steals things from people's pockets or bags in public places THESAURUS▶ THIEF

pickup /'pɪkʌp/ (also **'pickup ,truck**) n [C] a vehicle with a large open part at the back, used for carrying goods → see picture at TRANSPORT¹

picky /'pɪki/ adj informal someone who is picky only likes a small number of things SYN fussy: a picky eater

picnic¹ /'pɪknɪk/ n [C] if you have a picnic, you take food somewhere and eat it outdoors, especially in the country: We decided to **have a picnic** down by the lake. | Shall we **take a picnic** with us? | **go on/for a picnic** THESAURUS▶ MEAL

picnic² v [I] (**picnicked, picnicking**) to have a picnic

pictorial /pɪk'tɔːriəl/ adj formal relating to or using pictures

picture¹ /'pɪktʃə $ -ər/ n

1 PAINTING/DRAWING/PHOTOGRAPH [C] a painting, drawing, or photograph: a book with pictures in it | [+of] She has a picture of her boyfriend by her bed. | **sb's picture** (=a photograph of someone) Leo's picture was in the paper yesterday.

2 ON TELEVISION [C] an image on a television or film screen: dramatic pictures of the floods in Eastern Europe

3 DESCRIPTION/IDEA [C usually singular] a description or idea of what something is like: [+of] The

report gives a **clear picture** of life in the army. | **overall/complete/accurate picture** It is difficult to get a complete picture of what happened. | **give/paint a ... picture** He painted a depressing picture of life in the city.

4 GENERAL SITUATION [singular] the general situation in a place, organization etc: The political picture has changed greatly. | **the big/bigger/wider picture** (=a situation considered as a whole) We need to step back and look at the bigger picture.

5 FILM/CINEMA **a)** [C] a film **b) the pictures** BrE the cinema: Do you want to go to the pictures on Saturday? → MOTION PICTURE

PHRASES

get the picture spoken to understand something: Yeah, okay. I get the picture.

out of/not in the picture informal if someone is out of the picture, they are no longer involved in a situation: With his brother out of the picture, Alex was getting all the attention.

put/keep sb in the picture informal to give someone the information they need to understand a situation: She promised to keep Sybil in the picture.

COLLOCATIONS

verbs

to draw/paint a picture Draw a picture of your house.

to take a picture (=to take a photograph) Do you mind if I take a picture of you?

a picture shows sth (=used to say what is in a picture) The picture shows a man on a horse.

a picture is of sth (=a picture shows something) The other picture was of a small boy.

THESAURUS

picture a painting, drawing, or photograph: a picture of a horse | He painted the picture in 1890.

sketch a drawing that you do quickly using a pencil or pen: I did a quick sketch of the bird, before it moved.

illustration a picture in a book: The book has some beautiful illustrations.

portrait a picture of a person: a portrait of the Queen

landscape a painting or photograph that shows an area of countryside: This is a 19th-century landscape.

caricature a funny drawing of someone that makes a part of their face or body look bigger, worse etc than it really is: He did a brilliant caricature of the President.

---

picture² v [T] **1** to imagine something clearly: She pictured him opening the letter and reading it. **2** to show something or someone in a photograph, painting, or drawing: The prince is pictured on every front page today.

picturesque /,pɪktʃə'resk◂/ adj a picturesque place is pretty in an old-fashioned way

pie /paɪ/ n [C,U] **a)** fruit baked inside PASTRY: an apple pie → see picture at DESSERT **b)** BrE meat, fish, or vegetables baked inside PASTRY or with potato on top: chicken and mushroom pie → MINCE PIE

piece

PHRASES

pie in the sky *informal* something that someone says will happen but which you think is very unlikely: *Hope of a cure is just pie in the sky.*

piece¹ /piːs/ n [C]

1 a part of something that has been cut, broken, or separated from the rest of it: **[+of]** *Do you want a piece of bread?* | *You'll need several small pieces of string.* | **in pieces** (=broken into many parts) *The vase lay in pieces on the floor.* | *shelves that* **come to pieces** (=separate into parts) *for easy transport* | *He had to* **take** *the clock* **to pieces** (=separate it into parts) *to repair it.* | *All my clothes are* **falling to pieces** (=are old and in bad condition). | **smash/tear/rip sth to pieces** (=break something into many parts, especially violently) THESAURUS ▶ PART

2 a single thing of a particular type, or one part of a set of things: **[+of]** *a beautiful* **piece of furniture** | *I wrote the address down on a* **piece of paper.** | *valuable* **pieces of equipment** | *a chess piece*

3 a piece of advice/information/luck etc a small amount of advice, information etc: *Let me give you a piece of advice.* | *I've had a rather surprising piece of news.*

4 something that has been written or made by an artist, musician, or writer: **[+of]** *a beautiful piece of music* | *Robert wrote a short piece on the festival for the local paper.*

5 a coin that is worth a particular amount: *a 50p piece*

PHRASES

give sb a piece of your mind *informal* to tell someone that you are very angry with them: *If I see her, I'll give her a piece of my mind!*

go to pieces to become so upset or nervous that you cannot think or behave normally: *After his wife left, he went to pieces.*

(all) in one piece not damaged or injured: *Call Mum and let her know you got here in one piece* (=arrived safely).

be a piece of cake *informal* to be very easy to do: *Learning Spanish is a piece of cake compared to learning Japanese.* THESAURUS ▶ EASY

THESAURUS

piece a part of something that has been cut, broken, or separated from the rest of it: *Would you like a piece of pizza?* | *a piece of broken glass*

bit *especially BrE* a piece. **Bit** is more informal than **piece** and is used especially about small pieces: *an old bit of metal* | *I tied them together with a bit of string.*

scrap a small piece of paper or cloth, or of food that no one wants: *I wrote her address on a scrap of paper.*

slice a thin flat piece of bread, cake, meat etc cut from a larger piece: *a slice of toast*

lump a small piece of something solid: *two lumps of sugar* | *a lump of coal*

chunk a piece of something solid that does not have a regular shape – used especially about food, rock, or metal: *He broke off a chunk of bread.*

bar a block of soap, chocolate, or gold, with straight sides: *a bar of soap* | *gold bars worth more than £26 million*

a very small piece

fragment a very small piece that has broken off something hard: *Fragments of broken glass lay on the floor.*

crumb a very small piece of bread, cake etc: *He dropped crumbs all over the floor.*

speck a very small piece of dirt or dust: *Sarah brushed a few specks of dirt off her shirt.*

drop a very small amount of a liquid: *I felt a drop of rain.*

piece² v

PHRASAL VERBS

piece sth ↔ **together 1** to use all the information you have about a situation to discover the truth about it: *Police are trying to piece together exactly what happened.* **2** to put all the parts of something into their correct position

piecemeal /ˈpiːsmiːl/ *adj* happening or done slowly and not in a planned way: *a piecemeal approach to the problem* —**piecemeal** *adv*: *The changes were introduced piecemeal.*

piecework /ˈpiːswɜːk $ -wɜːrk/ *n* [U] work for which you are paid for the amount you produce rather than for the number of hours you work

ˈpie ˌchart *n* [C] a circle divided into parts by lines coming from the centre to show how big the different parts of a total amount are

pier /pɪə $ pɪr/ *n* [C] a structure that is built out into the sea so that boats can stop next to it or people can walk along it

pierce /pɪəs $ pɪrs/ *v* [T] **1** to make a hole in or through something using an object with a sharp point: *A bullet pierced his body.* | *I'm getting my* **ears pierced** (=having holes for jewellery made in my ears). **2** *literary* if a bright light or a loud sound pierces something, you suddenly see it or hear it: *The lights from the boat pierced the fog.*

piercing /ˈpɪəsɪŋ $ ˈpɪr-/ *adj* **1** a piercing sound is very loud, high, and unpleasant: *a piercing scream* **2** a piercing wind is strong and cold **3** *literary* someone with piercing eyes is looking at you and seems to know what you are thinking

piety /ˈpaɪəti/ *n* [U] behaviour that shows respect for God and religion

pig¹ /pɪg/ n [C]

1 a farm animal with short legs, a fat body, and a curled tail SYN **hog** *AmE* → GUINEA PIG

2 *spoken* someone who eats too much, or who is dirty or unpleasant: *You ate all the pizza, you pig.*

pig² v (pigged, pigging)

PHRASAL VERBS

pig out *informal* to eat too much food all at one time: **[+on]** *We pigged out on ice cream last night.*

pigeon /ˈpɪdʒɪn/ *n* [C] a grey bird with short legs that is common in cities

pigeonhole¹ /ˈpɪdʒənhəʊl $ -hoʊl/ *n* [C] one of a set of small open boxes fixed to a wall. You leave letters, messages etc for particular people in the boxes.

pigeonhole² v [T] to decide unfairly that someone or something belongs to a particular group or type

pigeon-'toed adj someone who is pigeon-toed has feet that turn towards each other as they walk

piggyback /ˈpɪgibæk/ n [C] if you give a child a piggyback, you carry them on your back —**piggyback** adv

piggy bank /ˈpɪgi bæŋk/ n [C] a small container used by children for saving coins, often in the shape of a pig

pigheaded /ˌpɪgˈhedɪd◄/ adj determined to do things a particular way even when there are good reasons not to

piglet /ˈpɪglɪt/ n [C] a young pig

pigment /ˈpɪgmənt/ n [C,U] technical a substance that makes skin, hair, plants etc a particular colour

pigmentation /ˌpɪgmənˈteɪʃən/ n [U] technical the natural colour of living things

pigsty /ˈpɪgstaɪ/ (also **pigpen** /ˈpɪgpen/ AmE) n [C] (plural **pigsties**) 1 a place on a farm where pigs are kept 2 informal a very dirty or untidy place

pigtail /ˈpɪgteɪl/ n [C] long hair that is twisted together SYN **plait** BrE, **braid** AmE → **ponytail** → see picture at HAIR

pike /paɪk/ n [C] (plural **pike**) a large fish that eats other fish and lives in rivers and lakes

pile¹ /paɪl/ n [C]
1 a lot of similar things put one on top of the other: [+of] a pile of folded clothes | She tidied up the books and **put them in piles**. THESAURUS GROUP
2 a large amount of something arranged in a shape like a small hill: a huge pile of rubbish | piles of snow by the side of the road
3 **piles** [plural] informal painfully swollen BLOOD VESSELS near a person's ANUS SYN **haemorrhoids**

pile² (also **pile up**) v [T] to make a pile of things somewhere: They piled the boxes up in a corner of the garage. | [+with] a plate **piled high** with spaghetti
PHRASAL VERBS
pile into/out of sth informal if people pile into or out of a place or vehicle, they go in or out quickly in no particular order: We all piled into the car.
pile up to become larger in quantity or amount, and become difficult to manage: Debts from the business were piling up quickly.

'pile-up n [C] informal a traffic accident involving several vehicles: a 16-car pile-up THESAURUS ACCIDENT

pilfer /ˈpɪlfə $ -ər/ v [I,T] to steal a small amount of money or things that are not worth much

pilgrim /ˈpɪlgrɪm/ n [C] someone who travels to a holy place for a religious reason

pilgrimage /ˈpɪlgrəmɪdʒ/ n [C,U] a trip to a holy place for a religious reason THESAURUS JOURNEY

P

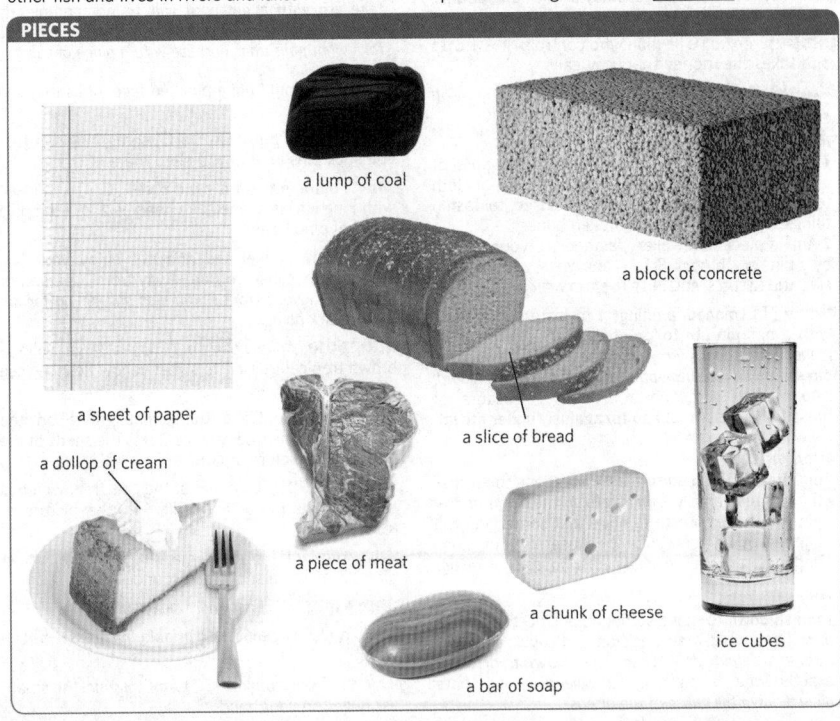

PIECES

a lump of coal

a block of concrete

a sheet of paper

a slice of bread

a dollop of cream

a piece of meat

a chunk of cheese

ice cubes

a bar of soap

pill /pɪl/ *n* [C]
1 a small solid piece of medicine that you swallow: *He has to **take pills** to control his blood pressure.* | *a bottle of **sleeping pills***
2 the Pill a pill that some women take to prevent them from having a baby: **on the Pill** *My doctor advised me to go on the Pill* (=take the Pill).

pillage /'pɪlɪdʒ/ *v* [I,T] if soldiers pillage a place in a war, they steal things from it and cause damage

pillar /'pɪlə $ -ər/ *n* [C] a tall solid piece of stone, wood etc used to support part of a building
PHRASES
| **pillar of the community/church etc** someone who is an active and important member of a group or organization: *The doctor is one of the pillars of our community.*

pillion /'pɪljən/ *n* [C] the seat for a passenger on a MOTORCYCLE —**pillion** *adv*

pillow /'pɪləʊ $ -loʊ/ *n* [C] the soft object you rest your head on when you sleep → see picture at BED

pillowcase /'pɪləʊkeɪs $ -loʊ-/ *n* [C] a cover for a pillow

pilot /'paɪlət/ *n* [C]
1 someone who flies a plane: *an **airline pilot***
2 someone who guides a ship through a difficult area of water
3 pilot study/programme etc a study etc that is done to test whether people like an idea, product etc: *They carried out a pilot study on the new perfume.* —**pilot** *v* [T]

pimp /pɪmp/ *n* [C] a man who controls PROSTITUTES and takes the money that they earn

pimple /'pɪmpəl/ *n* [C] a small raised red spot on your skin **THESAURUS** MARK —**pimply** *adj*

pin¹ /pɪn/ *n* [C]
1 a) a short thin piece of metal with a sharp point at one end, used especially for holding pieces of cloth together **b)** a thin piece of metal used to fasten things together, especially broken bones
2 *AmE* a piece of jewellery fastened to your clothes by a pin **SYN brooch** *BrE* → BOBBY PIN, DRAWING PIN, PINS AND NEEDLES, ROLLING PIN, SAFETY PIN

pin² *v* [T] (**pinned**, **pinning**) **1** to fasten something with a pin: **pin sth to/on etc sth** *There was a note pinned to the door.* | *Pin your name tag on your jacket.* | **pin sth up** *I'll pin these photos up on the notice board.*
2 to prevent someone from moving because of pressure or weight: **pin sb to/against/under etc sth** *He was pinned under the car.*
PHRASES
| **pin the blame on sb** to blame someone for something, often unfairly: *Don't try to pin the blame on me!*
| **pin your hopes on sth** to hope that something will happen or be successful, because all your plans depend on it: *She's pinned all her hopes on winning.*

PHRASAL VERBS
1 pin sb down to make someone decide something, or tell you what their decision is: *I couldn't pin him down to a definite date.* **2 pin sth ↔ down** to discover exactly what something is: *Scientists may have pinned down the cause of the disease.*

PIN /pɪn/ (also **pin ˌnumber**) *n* [C] (**personal identification number**) a number you use to take money from a machine using a plastic card

pinafore /'pɪnəfɔː $ -fɔːr/ *n* [C] *BrE* a dress that does not cover your arms, usually worn over a shirt

pinball /'pɪnbɔːl $ -bɔːl/ *n* [U] a game played on a machine in which you push buttons to try to stop a ball rolling off a sloping board

pincer /'pɪnsə $ -ər/ *n* [C] one of the pair of CLAWS (=sharp curved nails) that some insects and SHELLFISH have

pinch¹ /pɪntʃ/ *v* [T] **1** to press a part of someone's skin tightly between your finger and thumb: *He pinched her arm playfully.* **2** *informal* to steal something: *Someone's pinched my pen!*

pinch² *n* **1 a pinch of salt/pepper etc** a small amount of salt, pepper etc that you can hold between your finger and thumb: *It needs a pinch of pepper.* **2** [C] when you press someone's skin between your finger and thumb: *She gave him a playful pinch.* → see picture on page A10
PHRASES
| **at a pinch** *BrE*, **in a pinch** *AmE* used to say that you could probably do something difficult if it was really necessary or urgent: *I could get $300, maybe $400 in a pinch.*
| **feel the pinch** to have financial difficulties because you do not have enough money: *Small businesses are feeling the pinch.*
| **take sth with a pinch of salt** to not completely believe what someone says to you: *You have to take what politicians promise with a pinch of salt.*

pinched /pɪntʃt/ *adj* a pinched face looks thin and unhealthy

pincushion /'pɪnˌkʊʃən/ *n* [C] something soft that you stick pins into until you need them

pine¹ /paɪn/ *n* **1** (also **pine tree**) [C,U] a tall tree with long leaves shaped like needles **2** [U] the pale wood of pine trees

pine² *v* [I] to feel sad and not enjoy your life, especially because you are away from a person or place you love: **[+for]** *Karen was still pining for her friends back home.*

pineapple /'paɪnæpəl/ *n* [C,U] a large yellow-brown tropical fruit or its sweet yellow flesh → see picture on page A4

ˈpine ˌcone *n* [C] a thing that grows on the branches of pine trees and contains the seeds of the tree → see picture at CONE

ˈpine ˌneedle *n* [C] a leaf of the PINE tree, which is thin and sharp like a needle → see picture at NEEDLE¹

ping /pɪŋ/ *v* [I] if a bell, machine, or metal object pings, it makes a short high sound —**ping** *n* [C]

ˈping-pong *n* [U] *informal* TABLE TENNIS

pink /pɪŋk/ *adj* pale red: *a **bright pink** dress* —**pink** *n* [C,U]

pinkie, pinky /'pɪŋki/ *n* [C] *AmE informal* the smallest finger on your hand

pinnacle /ˈpɪnəkəl/ n **1** [singular] the most successful part of something: **[+of]** *She reached the pinnacle of her career at the age of 45.* **2** [C] *literary* a high mountain top

pinpoint¹ /ˈpɪnpɔɪnt/ v [T] to say exactly where something is or what something is: **[+what/how/why etc]** *I'm trying to pinpoint where we are on the map.*

pinpoint² *adj* **with pinpoint accuracy** very exactly: *Today's planes can drop bombs with pinpoint accuracy.*

pinprick /ˈpɪnˌprɪk/ n [C] a very small area or hole: *pinpricks of light*

pins and ˈneedles n [U] an uncomfortable feeling, especially in your foot or leg, that you get when you have not moved part of your body for a long time

pinstripe /ˈpɪnstraɪp/ n [U] dark cloth with thin light lines on it: *a blue pinstripe suit* → see picture at PATTERN

pint /paɪnt/ n [C] a unit for measuring liquid, equal to 0.473 litres in the US or 0.568 litres in Britain: **[+of]** *a pint of milk*

pin-up n [C] a picture of someone famous or attractive, often not wearing many clothes

pioneer¹ /ˌpaɪəˈnɪə $ -ˈnɪr/ n [C] **1** one of the first people to do something, whose work or ideas are later developed by other people: **[+of]** *the pioneers of cinema* **2** one of the first people to travel to an unknown place and begin living there

pioneer² v [T] to be the first person to do, invent, or use something new: *a technique pioneered by the Cambridge team*

pioneering /ˌpaɪəˈnɪərɪŋ◂ $ -ˈnɪr-/ adj [only before noun] introducing new or better ideas or methods for the first time: **pioneering work/research/efforts etc** *the pioneering work of NASA scientists*

pious /ˈpaɪəs/ adj having strong religious beliefs, and showing this in the way you behave → **piety** —**piously** adv

pip¹ /pɪp/ n [C] *BrE* a small seed from a fruit such as an apple or orange → see picture on page A4

pip² v [T] (**pipped**, **pipping**) *BrE* to beat someone by a small amount or at the last moment in a race or competition: **pip sb to/for sth** *Jackson just pipped him for the gold medal.* | *The Maclaren team were **pipped at the post** (=beaten at the last moment) by Ferrari.*

pipe¹ /paɪp/ n [C]
1 a tube that liquid or gas flows through: *a **water pipe** | A **pipe** had **burst** in the kitchen, flooding the floor.*
2 a thing used for smoking tobacco, consisting of a small tube with a container shaped like a bowl at one end: *My grandad used to **smoke a pipe**.*
3 a simple musical instrument like a tube that you blow through

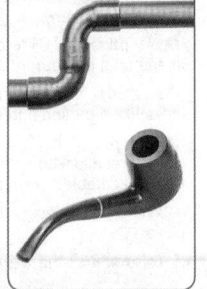
PIPES

PHRASES
pipe dream an idea, plan etc that will probably never happen: *Making it all the way to the Olympics is a pipe dream for most athletes.*

pipe² v [T] to send a liquid or gas through a pipe to another place: **pipe sth into/from/out of etc sth** *The oil is piped from Alaska.*
PHRASAL VERBS
pipe up *informal* to suddenly start speaking: *Then Dennis piped up, saying he didn't agree.*

pipeline /ˈpaɪp-laɪn/ n [C] a line of pipes used to carry gas, oil etc over long distances
PHRASES
be in the pipeline if a change, idea, or event is in the pipeline, it is being planned and will happen soon: *More job losses are in the pipeline.*

piping¹ /ˈpaɪpɪŋ/ n [U] the pipes used to carry liquid or gas in or out of a building

piping² *adv* **piping hot** very hot – used about food or drinks: *piping hot soup*

piquant /ˈpiːkənt/ adj *formal* having a pleasantly spicy taste: *a piquant sauce*

pique¹ /piːk/ v [T usually passive] to make someone feel annoyed or upset: *Privately, Zach was piqued not to get the job.*
PHRASES
pique sb's interest/curiosity to make someone interested in something: *The tour of the hospital piqued her interest in studying medicine.*

pique² n [U] *formal* a feeling of being annoyed or upset: *Greta left in a fit of pique.*

piracy /ˈpaɪərəsi $ ˈpaɪrə-/ n [U] **1** the crime of attacking and stealing from ships **2** the crime of illegally copying and selling books, videos, computer programs etc: *software piracy*

piranha /pəˈrɑːnə $ -ˈrɑːnjə, -ˈrænə/ n [C] a South American fish with sharp teeth that lives in rivers and eats flesh

pirate¹ /ˈpaɪərət $ ˈpaɪrət/ n [C] **1** someone on a ship who attacks other boats and steals things from them **2** someone who illegally copies and sells another person's work: *video pirates*

pirate² v [T] to illegally copy and sell someone else's work

Pisces /ˈpaɪsiːz/ n **1** [U] the sign of the Zodiac of people born between February 20 and March 20 **2** [C] someone who has this sign

pistachio /pəˈstɑːʃiəʊ $ pəˈstæʃioʊ/ n [C] (*plural* **pistachios**) a small green nut you can eat → see picture at NUT

piste /piːst/ n [C] *BrE* a slope covered in snow which is prepared for people to SKI on

pistol /ˈpɪstl/ n [C] a small gun you hold in one hand

piston /ˈpɪstən/ n [C] a part of an engine that moves up and down to make the other parts move

pit¹ /pɪt/ n [C] **1** a hole that has been dug in the ground: *a **deep pit*** **2** a coal mine **3** *AmE* the large hard seed in some fruits **SYN** **stone** *BrE*: *a peach pit*

→ see picture on page A4 **4 the pits** *BrE*, **the pit** *AmE* the place beside a race track where race cars come for petrol, new tyres etc

PHRASES

in the pit of your stomach if you have a feeling in the pit of your stomach, you feel very nervous, afraid etc, especially in a way that makes you feel sick: *With a feeling of panic in the pit of her stomach, she looked for the exit.*

be the pits *informal* to be very bad: *This place is the pits!*

pit² *v* [T] (**pitted**, **pitting**) *AmE* to take out the large hard seed inside some types of fruit

PHRASAL VERBS

pit sb/sth **against** sb/sth to test someone's strength, ability etc against someone or something else in a competition or fight: *This week's big game pits Houston against Miami.*

pitch¹ /pɪtʃ/ *n* **1** [C] *BrE* an area of ground used for playing a sport SYN **field: football/cricket/rugby etc pitch** *the Wembley soccer pitch* **2** [singular, U] a strong level of feeling about something: *Their excitement rose to fever pitch* (=a very excited level). **3** [singular, U] how high or low a note or other sound is **4** [C] *informal* an attempt to persuade someone to buy something or to do something: *an aggressive sales pitch* **5** [C] a throw of the ball towards the BATTER in a game of baseball

pitch² *v* **1** [T] to set a speech, examination etc at a particular level of difficulty: [+at] *The questions were pitched at a very high level.* **2** [T] to throw something with a lot of force: **pitch sth over/into etc sth** *Carl tore up the letter and pitched it into the fire.* **3** [I,T] to aim and throw the ball in a game of baseball: *Who's pitching for the Red Sox today?* **4** [I,T] to fall suddenly and heavily in a particular direction, or to make someone or something fall in this way: [+into/forward etc] *She slipped and pitched forward onto the ground.* **5** [T] to aim a product at a particular group of people: **pitch sth at sb/sth** *Their new range of PCs is pitched at the home user.* **6** [I,T] to try to persuade someone to do business with you: [+for] *Several companies are pitching for the contract.* **7** [T] to make a sound at a particular level: *Her voice was pitched low and soft.*

PHRASES

pitch a tent/pitch camp to put up a tent: *We'd better pitch the tent before it gets dark.*

PHRASAL VERBS

pitch in *informal* to join others and help with an activity: *If we all pitch in, we'll finish in no time.*

pitch ˈblack (*also* ˌpitch ˈdark) *adj* completely black or dark: *It was pitch black in the basement.*

pitcher /ˈpɪtʃə $ -ər/ *n* [C] **1** the player in baseball who throws the ball **2** *AmE* a container used for holding and pouring liquids SYN **jug** *BrE*

pitchfork /ˈpɪtʃfɔːk $ -fɔːrk/ *n* [C] a farm tool with a long handle and two long metal points

piteous /ˈpɪtiəs/ *adj literary* making you feel pity for someone: *a piteous cry* —**piteously** *adv*

pitfall /ˈpɪtfɔːl $ -fɔːl/ *n* [C usually plural] a problem or difficulty that is likely to happen in a particular situation: [+of] *the pitfalls of buying an old car*

pith /pɪθ/ *n* [U] the white substance just under the skin of fruit such as oranges → see picture on page A4

pithy /ˈpɪθi/ *adj* spoken or written in clear language, without using too many words: *pithy comments*

pitiful /ˈpɪtɪfəl/ *adj* **1** making you feel sadness and pity: *a pitiful sight* **2** extremely bad: *His performance last night was pitiful.* —**pitifully** *adv*

pitiless /ˈpɪtɪləs/ *adj* showing no pity for people who are suffering

pittance /ˈpɪtəns/ *n* [singular] a very small amount of money: *She earns a pittance.*

pitted /ˈpɪtɪd/ *adj* a pitted surface is covered in small marks or holes: *a road pitted with potholes*

pity¹ /ˈpɪti/ *n*

1 a pity spoken used when you are disappointed about a situation and wish it was different SYN **shame: it's a pity (that)** *It's a pity you can't come.* | **what a pity/that's a pity** *'We're leaving tomorrow.' 'What a pity!'*

2 [U] sadness that you feel for someone who is suffering or unhappy → **pitiful, pitiless:** *I listened to Jason's story with pity.*

PHRASES

take/have pity on sb to feel that you want to help someone who is in a bad situation: *Anna looked so upset that Jean took pity on her.*

> **Word Choice: pity or sympathy?**
> You use **pity** when you feel sad for someone because they are in a very bad situation: *She looked at him with pity.*
> You use **sympathy** when you understand how someone feels, especially so that you want to help them: *I have a lot of sympathy for the boy's parents.*

pity² *v* [T] (**pitied**, **pitying**, **pities**) to feel sympathy for someone who is in a bad situation: *Sam pitied his grandmother, living there all alone.*

pivot /ˈpɪvət/ *n* [C] **1** a fixed central point or pin that something balances or turns on **2** the most important thing about a situation which other things depend on —**pivot** *v* [I,T]

pivotal /ˈpɪvətəl/ *adj* having a very important effect on a situation, system etc: *Japan has a pivotal role in the world economy.*

pixel /ˈpɪksəl/ *n* [C] *technical* the smallest unit of an image on a computer screen

pixie /ˈpɪksi/ *n* [C] a small imaginary creature that looks like a person and has magic powers

pizza /ˈpiːtsə/ *n* [C,U] a food made of thin flat round bread, baked with tomato, cheese, and sometimes vegetables or meat on top

pizzeria /ˌpiːtsəˈriːə/ *n* [C] a restaurant that serves pizza

pl. (*also* **pl** *BrE*) the written abbreviation of **plural**

placard /'plækɑːd $ -ərd/ *n* [C] a large notice or advertisement on a piece of card, which is put up or carried in a public place

placate /pləˈkeɪt $ ˈpleɪkeɪt/ *v* [T] *formal* to make someone stop feeling angry

place¹ /pleɪs/ *n* [C]
1 POSITION/AREA/BUILDING an area, space, building, or position: *He showed me the place where the accident happened.* | **in a ... place** *Keep your passport in a safe place.* | *The place was full of screaming children.* | *Paint is coming off the wall* **in places** (=in some areas). | **[+for]** *Portugal is a great place for a holiday.* | **a place to do sth** *I couldn't find a place to park.* | *Are there any good places to eat round here?*
2 HOME *informal* a house or apartment where someone lives: **sb's place** *Shall we go back to my place for coffee?* | *They've got a big place in the country.*
3 SPACE TO SIT/PUT STH a space where you can sit, or a space where you can put something: *I might be late, so can you save me a place?* | *Put the CDs back in their place.*
4 OPPORTUNITY TO DO STH an opportunity to go somewhere or join in an activity: **[+on]** *There are a few places left on the German course.* | **[+in]** *If you don't come, you might lose your place in the team.*
5 SB'S/STH'S IMPORTANCE the importance or position that someone or something has: **[+in]** *Work has an important place in all our lives.* | *Boston's got a special* **place** *in my heart.*
6 OCCASION/SITUATION the right occasion or situation for something: *This isn't the place to discuss money.*
7 IN A BOOK/SPEECH the point that you have reached in a book or a speech: *You made me* **lose** *my* **place** (=forget the point that I had reached).
8 IN A RACE/COMPETITION **first/second/third etc place** first, second etc position in a race or competition: *Jerry* **finished in** *fifth* **place**. | *Italy* **took** *second* **place**. → **NO PLACE**, **in the first place** at **FIRST¹**
PHRASES
  all over the place *informal* everywhere: *There were policemen all over the place!*
  fall into place if things fall into place in your mind, you suddenly understand what is really happening: *The various parts of the plan fell into place in my mind.*
  in place 1 in the correct position: *The chairs for the concert were nearly all in place.* **2** existing and ready to be used: *By then the new system will be in place.*
  in sb's place used when talking about what you would do if you were in someone else's situation: *What would you do in my place?*
  in place of sb/sth instead of someone or something else: *There's football on in place of the normal programmes.*
  out of place not suitable for or comfortable in a particular situation: *He always felt out of place at parties.* THESAURUS ▶ UNSUITABLE
  put sb in their place to show someone that they are not as important or intelligent as they think they are: *I soon put him in his place!*
  take place to happen: *When did the robbery take place?* THESAURUS ▶ HAPPEN

take the place of sb/sth to exist or be used instead of someone or something else SYN **replace**: *Could computers ever take the place of teachers?*

THESAURUS

place an area, space, building etc – often used about somewhere that you visit or use for a particular purpose: *We went to a place called Fordwell.* | *This would be a good place to put the desk.*
position the exact place where someone or something is, in relation to other things: *From this position, they could see the enemy's camp.*
point a particular place on a road, river, path, line etc: *The accident happened near the point where the two motorways meet.*
spot *informal* a pleasant place where you go to relax, or a place where something happened: *I know a nice spot for a picnic.* | *It was on this spot that the Great Fire of London started.*
location the place where someone or something is – used especially when you want to be exact, or when saying how suitable the place is: *The map shows the exact location of the village.* | *The house is in a very good location, about five minutes from the shops.*
site an area of ground where something will be built, or where something important happened in the past: *a building site* | *the site of a great battle*

place² *v* [T] **1** to put something carefully somewhere SYN **put**: **place sth in/on etc sth** *She placed the bowl on the top shelf.* THESAURUS ▶ PUT **2** to put someone or something in a particular situation SYN **put**: *This places me in an embarrassing position.* **3** to consider that something has a particular level of importance: *Most people* **place a high value on** *friendship.* **4 can't place sb** to be unable to remember who someone is or where you have met them: *He looks familiar, but I can't place him.* **5** to arrange for something to be done: *You can* **place orders** *by telephone.* | *We* **placed an advertisement** *in the local paper.*

placebo /pləˈsiːbəʊ $ -boʊ/ *n* [C] (*plural* **placebos**) a harmless substance given to a sick person instead of medicine, without telling them it is not real

placement /'pleɪsmənt/ *n* **1** [C] a job that is found for someone, especially to give them experience of work: *a work experience placement* **2** [singular, U] when you find a place for someone to live, work, or study: *the placement of children in special schools*

place name *n* [C] the name of a particular place, such as a town, mountain etc

placid /'plæsɪd/ *adj* not getting angry or upset easily: *a placid baby* —**placidly** *adv*

plagiarism /'pleɪdʒərɪzəm/ *n* [U] when someone uses another person's ideas, words, or work and pretends they are their own: *She was accused of plagiarism in her thesis.* —**plagiarist** *n* [C]

plagiarize (*also* -**ise** *BrE*) /'pleɪdʒəraɪz/ *v* [I,T] to use another person's ideas, words, or work and pretend they are yours

plague¹ /pleɪg/ *n* **1** [C,U] a disease that spreads

quickly and kills a lot of people **2 a plague of sth** a sudden large increase in the numbers of a particular animal or insect that is difficult to control: *a plague of rats*

plague² v [T] to cause pain or trouble to someone for a long time: *Renee had always been plagued by ill health.*

plaice /pleɪs/ n [C,U] (*plural* **plaice**) a flat sea fish that people eat

plaid /plæd/ n [U] a pattern of crossed lines and squares, especially on cloth SYN **tartan**

plain¹ /pleɪn/ adj
1 easy to understand or recognize SYN **obvious**: *It's plain that he doesn't agree.* | *They made it plain* (=said clearly) *that they did not want us there.*
2 without anything added or without decoration SYN **simple**: *plain food* | *a plain white shirt* | *a sheet of plain paper* (=paper with no lines on it) → see picture at **PATTERN**
3 saying what you think honestly and in clear simple language: *The plain fact is that we can't afford it.* | *The document is written in plain English.*
4 a plain person is not attractive

plain² n [C] a large area of flat dry land

plain³ adv informal used to emphasize some adjectives: *They're just plain lazy.*

plain-'clothes adj plain-clothes police wear ordinary clothes so that they can work without being recognized

plainly /'pleɪnli/ adv **1** in a way that is easy to see or understand SYN **clearly**: *Mrs Gorman was plainly delighted.* | *She told him plainly that she wouldn't marry him.* **2** simply or without decoration: *a plainly furnished room*

plaintiff /'pleɪntɪf/ n [C] law someone who brings a legal action against another person in a court of law → **defendant**

plaintive /'pleɪntɪv/ adj sounding sad: *plaintive cries*

plait /plæt $ pleɪt, plæt/ v [T] BrE to twist three long pieces of hair, rope etc over and under each other to make one long piece SYN **braid** AmE → see picture at **HAIR** —**plait** n [C]

plan¹ /plæn/ n [C]
1 something you have decided to do, or an idea for doing something in an organized way: **plan to do sth** *The company has plans to create 30 more jobs.* | **[+for]** *the government's plans for economic recovery*
2 a drawing of a building, room, or machine as you would see it from above, showing its shape and measurements: *An architect is drawing up some plans for us.*
3 a map showing roads, towns, and buildings: **[+of]** *a street plan of London* → **FLOOR PLAN, GAME PLAN, OPEN PLAN**

PHRASES

| **Plan A** your first plan, which you will use if things happen the way you expect: *Plan A is to hire a car and drive along the coast.*

| **Plan B** your second plan, which you can use if things do not happen the way you expect: *It's time to put Plan B into action.*

COLLOCATIONS

verbs

to have plans *She has plans to go to college next year.*
to make plans *Helen's busy making plans for her wedding.* ⚠ Do not say 'do a plan'. Say **make a plan**.
to change your plans *They changed their plans at the last minute.*
to carry out a plan (=to do what you have planned) *The plan was never carried out.*
a plan works (=is successful) *His plan had worked perfectly.*
to go according to plan (=to happen in the way that was planned) *If things go according to plan, we'll leave on Monday.*

noun + plan

a change of plan *There's been a slight change of plan.*

THESAURUS

plan something you have decided to do, or an idea for doing something in an organized way: *What are your plans for the weekend?* | *the plan to build a new airport*
scheme BrE an official plan, especially one that is intended to help people The American word for this is **program**: *the state pension scheme* | *a scheme to build 3,000 new houses*
plot/conspiracy a secret plan to do something bad or illegal, made by a group of people: *He was involved in a plot to kill the king.*
strategy a careful plan for achieving something complicated that may take a long time: *the company's strategy for future development*
programme BrE, **program** AmE a series of activities intended to develop or improve something, especially arranged by a government or a big organization: *America's program for economic recovery* | *our staff training programme*
timetable BrE a plan of the exact times when something will happen, especially when trains or buses leave: *the bus timetable*

plan² v (**planned, planning**)
1 [I,T] to think about something you want to do, and decide how you will do it: *We've been planning our trip for months.* | *You need to plan ahead to make the best use of your money.* | **[+for]** *Talks are planned for next week.*
2 [T] to intend to do something: **plan on doing sth** *How long do you plan on staying?* | **plan to do sth** *Where do you plan to go next year?*
3 [T] to think about something you are going to make, and decide what it will be like → **design**: *We spent ages planning the garden.* —**planning** n [U]

plane /pleɪn/ n [C]
1 a vehicle with wings and an engine, which can fly: *Our plane landed in Chicago just after six.* | **by plane** *It's much quicker to go by plane.*
2 a level of thought or activity: **on a different/higher plane** *Creative people live on a different plane.*
3 a tool used for making wooden surfaces smooth

planet /'plænɪt/ n [C]
1 a very large round object in space that moves around the Sun or another star: *Mercury is the smallest planet.* **THESAURUS ▸ STAR**
2 the planet the world: *the environmental future of the planet* —**planetary** adj

planetarium /ˌplænə'teəriəm $ -'ter-/ n [C] a building where lights on a curved ceiling show the movements of planets and stars

plank /plæŋk/ n [C] a long flat piece of wood

plankton /'plæŋktən/ n [U] extremely small plants and animals that live in water and are eaten by fish

planner /'plænə $ -ər/ n [C] someone whose job is to plan something, especially the way towns develop

plant¹ /plɑːnt $ plænt/ n [C]
1 a living thing that has leaves and roots and grows in earth: *Don't forget to water the plants.* | *a tomato plant* → **LOG¹, SAPLING**
2 a factory and all its equipment: *a chemical plant*

plant² v [T] **1** to put plants or seeds in the ground to grow: *I planted the rose bush last year.* | **plant a field/an area etc with sth** *a hillside planted with pine trees* **2** informal to hide stolen or illegal goods in someone's bags, room etc in order to make that person seem guilty: **plant sth on sb** *Someone must have planted the drugs on her.* **3** to put something firmly in or on something else: **plant sth in/on etc sth** *He planted a kiss on her cheek.* **4 plant a bomb** to put a bomb somewhere: *Two men are accused of planting the bomb on the plane.*

plantation /plæn'teɪʃən, plɑː- $ plæn-/ n [C] **1** a large area of land in a hot country where crops such as tea, cotton, or sugar are grown: *a rubber plantation* **2** a large group of trees that are grown to produce wood

plaque /plɑːk, plæk $ plæk/ n **1** [C] a piece of flat metal or stone with writing on it, attached to a building to remind people of a famous event or person: *The plaque read: Samuel Johnson was born here.* **2** [U] a harmful substance that forms on your teeth

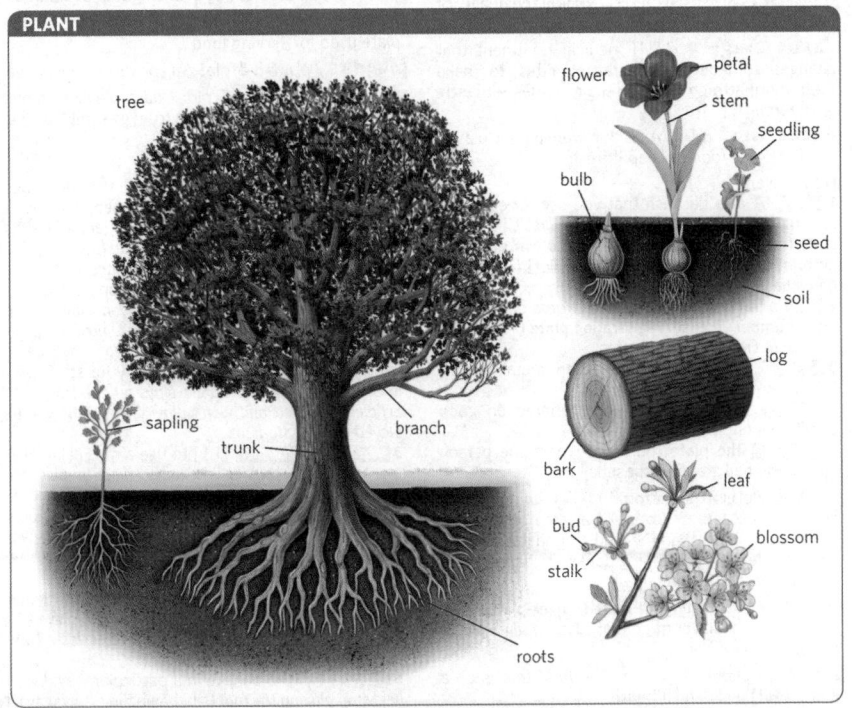

PLANT

tree, flower, petal, stem, seedling, bulb, seed, soil, log, bark, leaf, bud, blossom, stalk, sapling, branch, trunk, roots

plasma /ˈplæzmə/ n [U] the liquid part of your blood that contains the blood cells

plasma screen n [C] a special very thin television or computer screen

plaster¹ /ˈplɑːstə $ ˈplæstər/ n **1** [U] a substance used to cover walls and ceilings and give them a smooth surface **2** [C] BrE a piece of special material that you stick on your skin to cover small wounds SYN **Band-Aid** trademark AmE **3 in plaster** BrE if your leg, arm etc is in plaster, it has a PLASTER CAST around it because a bone is broken: She had her arm in plaster for weeks.

plaster² v [T] **1** to completely cover a surface with something: **plaster sth with sth** The walls were plastered with posters. **2** [usually passive] to make your hair lie flat or stick to your head: **plaster sth to sth** His hair was plastered to his forehead with sweat. **3** to put plaster on a wall or ceiling in order to make it smooth

plaster cast n [C] a cover made from plaster, used to protect a broken bone

plaster of Paris /ˌplɑːstər əv ˈpærɪs $ ˌplæs-/ n [U] a mixture of white powder and water, used especially for making plaster casts

plastic¹ /ˈplæstɪk/ n [C,U] a cheap light material that is produced by a chemical process and used for making many different objects: toys made of plastic

plastic² adj made of plastic: a **plastic bag** | plastic spoons

plasticity /plæˈstɪsəti/ n [U] technical the quality of being easily made into any shape

plastic surgery n [U] medical treatment that changes someone's appearance, either to make them more attractive or to repair injuries —**plastic surgeon** n [C]

plastic wrap n [U] AmE thin transparent plastic used to cover food to keep it fresh

plate /pleɪt/ n [C]
1 FOR FOOD a) a flat dish that you use for eating or serving food: Take a plate and help yourself. | a **dinner plate** (=a large round plate) **b)** (also **plateful**) the amount of food that is on a plate: **[+of]** I've already had a huge plate of spaghetti.
2 SIGN a flat piece of metal with words or numbers on it: **number/license/registration plate** (=on a car) a car with French number plates
3 METAL COVERING gold/silver plate metal with a thin covering of gold or silver
4 PICTURE a picture in a book, printed on good quality paper
5 BASEBALL the plate the place where the person hitting the ball stands in baseball

plateau /ˈplætəʊ $ plæˈtoʊ/ n [C] (plural **plateaus** or **plateaux** /-təʊz $ -ˈtoʊz/) **1** a large area of flat land that is higher than the land around it **2** a period when the level of something does not change: Inflation has **reached a plateau**.

plated /ˈpleɪtɪd/ adj **gold-plated/silver-plated** covered with a thin layer of gold or silver: a silver-plated spoon

plateful /ˈpleɪtfʊl/ n [C] all the food that is on a plate: **[+of]** a plateful of toast

plate glass n [U] glass made in large thick sheets, used especially in shop windows

platform /ˈplætfɔːm $ -fɔːrm/ n [C]
1 FOR TRAINS especially BrE the area at a station where you get on and off a train: The Edinburgh train will depart from platform six.
2 FOR SPEECHES/PERFORMANCES a raised structure for people to stand on when they are speaking or performing → **stage**: He climbed onto the platform and began to address the crowd.
3 IN POLITICS a) the main ideas and aims of a political party, especially the ones that they state just before an election: **[+of]** The government was elected on a platform of reform. **b)** a chance for someone to express their opinions, especially political opinions: **[+for]** He used the interview as a platform for his views on education.
4 TALL STRUCTURE a tall structure that people can stand or work on: an oil exploration platform
5 COMPUTER SYSTEM the type of computer system or software that someone uses: a multimedia platform

platinum /ˈplætənəm/ n [U] a silver-grey metal that is used to make expensive jewellery and in industry

platitude /ˈplætɪtjuːd $ -tuːd/ n [C] disapproving a statement that has been made many times before and is not interesting: a speech full of platitudes

platonic /pləˈtɒnɪk $ -ˈtɑː-/ adj a platonic relationship is friendly and not sexual

platoon /pləˈtuːn/ n [C] a small group of soldiers

platter /ˈplætə $ -ər/ n [C] especially AmE a large plate used for serving food

plaudits /ˈplɔːdəts $ ˈplɒː-/ n [plural] formal praise

plausible /ˈplɔːzəbəl $ ˈplɒː-/ adj a plausible story, reason etc seems likely to be true OPP **implausible**: a plausible explanation

play¹ /pleɪ/ v
1 CHILDREN [I,T] when children play, they do things that they enjoy, often with other people or with toys: Kids were playing outside in the street. | **[+with]** Why don't you go and play with your friends? | The children were playing cowboys and Indians.
2 SPORT/GAME [I,T] to take part in a sport or game: The guys are playing basketball. | Do you know how to play chess? | **[+against]** Manchester United are playing against Liverpool on Saturday. | Who is she playing (=playing against) in the final? | **play for sth** (=play in a particular team) Garcia plays for the Hornets. | Scholes is injured and won't play. | The game will be played at Shea stadium.
3 MUSICAL INSTRUMENT [I,T] to use a musical instrument to produce music: I'm learning to play the piano. | You play very well.
4 CD/RADIO ETC [I,T] if a CD, radio etc plays, or if you play it, it produces music or sounds: A radio was playing softly. | **play sb sth** Let me play you my new CD.
5 FILM/THEATRE [T] to act the part of a particular character in a film, play etc: The hero is played by Sean Penn. | **play a role/part/character** Josie Lawrence plays the part of Lottie.
6 BEHAVE [I,T] to behave in a particular way: I wish he'd stop **playing the fool** (=behaving in a silly way). |

*Always **play safe** (=avoid risks) by telling someone where you are going.* → **play hooky** at HOOKY, **play truant** at TRUANT

PHRASES

play ball *informal* to agree to do what someone wants you to do: *Do you think he'll play ball?*

play the game to do things in the usual or expected way: *If you don't play the game, you won't survive.*

play games *disapproving* to cause problems or annoy people by not being completely honest with them: *She's playing games with his emotions.*

play it by ear to wait until you know more about a situation before you make any definite plans: *'Shall we take a picnic?' 'Well, let's play it by ear.'*

play a trick/joke on sb to do something to surprise or trick someone: *The kids in the class decided to play a joke on their teacher.*

play a part/role to have an effect on something: *A good diet plays an important part in keeping healthy.*

What is sb playing at? *BrE spoken* used when you do not understand what someone is doing or why they are doing it, and you are annoyed with them: *What do you think you're playing at?*

Grammar

Do not use **the** before the names of sports and games. Do not say 'We played the football/the tennis.' Say *We played football/tennis.*

Word Choice: play, go, or do?

You use **play** about sports in which you throw, kick, or hit a ball, for example tennis, soccer, golf, and basketball: *I used to play rugby when I was at school.| Do you play volleyball?*

You use **go** before sports activities that use the form v+ing, for example running, cycling, skiing, and swimming: *Mick goes jogging every morning.*

You use **do** about other sports activities, for example judo, karate, aerobics, and tai chi: *Tim does karate.*

PHRASAL VERBS

play around (*also* **play about** *BrE*)
1 *informal* to have a sexual relationship with someone who is not your husband or wife
2 to try doing something in different ways to see which is best: **[+with]** *Play around with the images until you are satisfied.*
3 to behave in a silly way: *I wish those kids would stop playing around outside our house.*

play around with sth (*also* **play about with** sth *BrE*) to keep touching or moving something SYN **fiddle with**: *Stop playing around with the remote control!*

play at sth to do something without being serious about it or doing it properly: *He's just playing at being an artist.*

play sth ↔ **back** to play something that has been recorded on a machine so that you can listen to it or watch it

play sth ↔ **down** to try to make something seem less important or bad than it really is: *The government was anxious to play down the latest unemployment figures.*

play sb **off against** sb to encourage two people or groups to argue or compete with each other, in order to get advantages for yourself

play on sth to use someone's fears or weaknesses in order to get what you want: *The film plays on people's fears and prejudices.*

play up
1 play sth ↔ **up** to make something seem better, more important etc than it really is: *He was obviously keen to play up his relationship with her.*
2 play (sb) up *BrE informal* if children play up, they behave badly

play with sth to keep touching or moving something: *Stop playing with the light switch!*

play² *n*
1 [C] a story that is written to be performed by actors, especially in a theatre: *We went to see a new play by Tom Stoppard. | He wrote the play in 1964. |* **put on/perform a play** *The play was put on by a local school.*
2 [U] things that people, especially children, do to enjoy themselves: *a **play area** with slides and swings |* **at play** *the sounds of children at play (=playing)*
3 [U] the activity of playing a game or sport: *Rain stopped play.* → FAIR PLAY, FOUL PLAY

PHRASES

come into play/be brought into play to affect or influence a situation: *Many different factors may come into play.*

a play on words a use of a word or phrase that is interesting or amusing because it can have two meanings → **pun**: *Children like jokes that are a play on words.*

COLLOCATIONS

verbs

to write a play *The play was written by Shakespeare.*
to go to a play *While we were in New York, we went to a play.*
to see a play *I've never seen the play.*
to watch a play *Some of the audience were talking instead of watching the play.*
to perform a play *The play was performed by Brighton Youth Theatre.*
to act/appear in a play *She has acted in plays and films.*
to put on a play (=to arrange for it to be performed) *The school puts on a play every year.*
⚠ Do not say 'give a play'. Say **put on a play**.

'play-,acting *n* [U] when someone pretends to be serious or sincere, but is not

playboy /ˈpleɪbɔɪ/ *n* [C] a rich man who spends his time enjoying himself

player /ˈpleɪə $ -ər/ *n* [C]
1 someone who plays a game or sport: *a football player*
2 someone who plays a musical instrument: *a piano player*
3 one of the people, countries etc that are involved in a situation: **a major/key etc player** *a major player*

in the UN peace talks → **CASSETTE PLAYER, CD PLAYER, MP3 PLAYER, RECORD PLAYER**

playful /ˈpleɪfəl/ *adj* **1** intended to be fun rather than serious: *playful teasing* **2** very active and happy: *a playful little kitten* —**playfully** *adv* —**playfulness** *n* [U]

playground /ˈpleɪɡraʊnd/ *n* [C] an outdoor area where children can play, especially while they are at school

playgroup /ˈpleɪɡruːp/ *n* [C] *BrE* an organized group where small children go to play, learn etc in the years before they go to school

playhouse /ˈpleɪhaʊs/ *n* [C] **1** a theatre - used especially in the names of theatres: *the Oxford Playhouse* **2** a small house or tent that children can play in

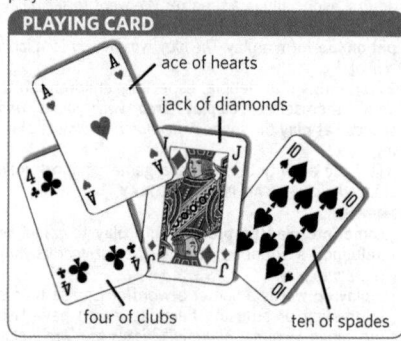

PLAYING CARD

ace of hearts

jack of diamonds

four of clubs   ten of spades

ˈ**playing card** *n* [C] one of a set of 52 cards that is used for playing games

ˈ**playing field** *n* [C] an area of ground used for playing football, baseball etc → **a level playing field** at **LEVEL²**

playmate /ˈpleɪmeɪt/ *n* [C] a friend that a child plays with

ˈ**play-off** *n* [C] a game between the best teams or players in a competition, played in order to choose the final winner

playpen /ˈpleɪpen/ *n* [C] a thing that you put young children in to play safely, surrounded by wooden bars or a net

playroom /ˈpleɪrʊm, -ruːm/ *n* [C] a room for children to play in

plaything /ˈpleɪθɪŋ/ *n* [C] **1** *formal* a toy **2** a person that you use for your own amusement or advantage, without caring about them

playtime /ˈpleɪtaɪm/ *n* [C] a period of time when children can play, especially at school

playwright /ˈpleɪraɪt/ *n* [C] someone who writes plays

plc /ˌpiː el ˈsiː/ *n* [C] *BrE* (**Public Limited Company**) used after the name of a big company in Britain which has SHARES that you can buy: *British Telecom plc*

plea /pliː/ *n* [C] **1** a request that is urgent or full of emotion: **[+for]** *Her mother ignored her pleas for help.* **2** *law* a statement by someone in a court of law

saying whether they are guilty or not guilty

ˈ**plea- bargaining** *n* [U] when someone agrees to admit in court that they are guilty of one crime if another crime that they are connected with is not mentioned

plead /pliːd/ (*also* **pled** /pled/ *AmE*) *v* (*past tense and past participle* **pleaded**) **1** [I] to ask for something in an urgent and anxious way: **plead with sb (to do sth)** *Amy pleaded with him to stay.* **2** **plead ignorance/illness/insanity etc** to give a particular excuse for your actions: *She stayed home from work, pleading illness.* **3** [I,T] *law* to state in a court of law whether or not you are guilty of a crime: **plead guilty/not guilty/innocent** *The defendant pleaded not guilty.* —**pleadingly** *adv*

pleasant /ˈplezənt/ *adj* enjoyable, nice, or friendly OPP **unpleasant** → **pleasure**: *They spent a pleasant evening together.* | *a pleasant young man* | *Kate! What a **pleasant surprise**!* | **[+to]** *He's always been very pleasant to me.* THESAURUS **NICE** —**pleasantly** *adv*: *She smiled pleasantly.*

pleasantries /ˈplezəntriz/ *n* [plural] *formal* polite things that you say when you meet someone

please¹ /pliːz/
1 used when you are politely asking for something: *Please could I have a glass of water?* | *Can you all sit down, please?* | *Please be quiet!*
2 **yes, please** *spoken* used to politely accept something that someone offers you: *'More coffee?' 'Yes, please!'*
3 *spoken* used when you think someone has said something silly or unreasonable

please² *v* **1** [I,T] to make someone feel happy or satisfied: **be hard/easy/impossible etc to please** *She's hard to please. Everything has to be perfect.* **2** used in some phrases to show that someone can do or have anything they want: **whatever/however etc you please** *He can buy whatever he pleases.* | *She does **what** she **pleases**.*
PHRASES
please yourself *spoken* used when telling someone to do whatever they like, even though you think they are making the wrong choice: *'I don't want any dinner.' 'OK, please yourself.'*

pleased /pliːzd/ *adj* happy about something or satisfied with something: **[+with/about]** *Are you pleased with the result?* | **[+for]** *That's wonderful. I'm really pleased for you.* | **[+(that)]** *I was pleased that he agreed to see me.* | **pleased to hear/see/know etc sth** *You'll be pleased to hear that you've got the job.* THESAURUS **HAPPY**
PHRASES
(I'm) pleased to meet you *spoken* a polite expression used when you meet someone for the first time: *'Pleased to meet you,' he said, shaking my hand.*
pleased with yourself *disapproving* feeling proud and satisfied because you think you have done something clever: *She's a bit too pleased with herself.*

pleasing /ˈpliːzɪŋ/ *adj* giving pleasure, enjoyment, or satisfaction: *a pleasing view* —**pleasingly** *adv*

pleasurable /'pleʒərəbəl/ *adj formal* enjoyable: *a pleasurable experience*

pleasure /'pleʒə $ -ər/ *n*
1 [U] a feeling of happiness, satisfaction, or enjoyment → **pleasant: with pleasure** *She sipped her drink with pleasure.* | **for pleasure** *I often read for pleasure.* | *She took great pleasure in telling him that he was wrong.* | *The garden has given pleasure to many people.*
2 [C] an experience or activity that you enjoy very much: *the simple pleasures of life* | **be a pleasure (to do)** *My new car is an absolute pleasure to drive.* | *It's a pleasure to do business with you.*
PHRASES
> **my pleasure/it's a pleasure** *spoken* used when someone has thanked you for doing something, and you want to say that you were glad to do it: *'Thanks for your help.' 'My pleasure.'*

pleat /pliːt/ *n* [C] a flat fold in a skirt, pair of trousers, dress etc

pleated /'pliːtɪd/ *adj* a pleated skirt, dress etc has a number of flat narrow folds

pleb /pleb/ *n* [C usually plural] *informal humorous* someone who belongs to a low social class

plebiscite /'plebəsət $ -saɪt/ *n* [C,U] *formal* a system by which everyone in a country votes on an important decision that affects the whole country → **referendum**

pled /pled/ *v AmE* a past tense and past participle of PLEAD

pledge¹ /pledʒ/ *n* [C] a serious or public promise: **[+of]** *a pledge of support* | **pledge to do sth** *the president's pledge to end the war* | *a Labour election pledge*

pledge² *v* [T] **1** to make a formal, usually public, promise to do or give something: **pledge (yourself) to do sth** *They have pledged to cut inflation.* **2** to make someone formally promise something: *We were all pledged to secrecy.*

plentiful /'plentɪfəl/ *adj* more than enough in quantity: *a plentiful supply of fruit and vegetables* —**plentifully** *adv*

plenty /'plenti/ *pron, adv*
1 a large quantity that is enough or more than enough: **[+of]** *We have plenty of time to get to the airport.* | **plenty to do** *There's plenty to see in New York.* | *If you need more wine, we've plenty more in here.* **THESAURUS** ENOUGH
2 *AmE* very: *By then Ronah was plenty scared.*

plethora /'pleθərə/ *n* **a plethora of sth** *formal* a very large number of things: *a plethora of complaints*

pliable /'plaɪəbəl/ *adj* **1** able to bend easily without breaking or cracking **2** easily influenced by other people

pliers /'plaɪəz $ -ərz/ *n* [plural] a tool for cutting wire or pulling nails out of wood: *a pair of pliers* → see picture at **TOOL**

plight /plaɪt/ *n* [singular] a very bad situation that someone is in: **[+of]** *the plight of the refugees*

plimsoll /'plɪmsəl, -saʊl $ -səl, -soʊl/ *n* [C] *BrE* a cotton shoe with a flat rubber SOLE **SYN** **sneaker** *AmE*

plod /plɒd $ plɑːd/ *v* [I] (**plodded, plodding**) **1** to walk along slowly, especially when this is difficult: **[+on/along/up etc]** *The old dog plodded along behind him.* **2** to work slowly or make slow progress: **[+on/along/through]** *He plodded along in the same boring job for years.*

plonk¹ /plɒŋk $ plɑːŋk, plɔːŋk/ (*also* **plonk down**) *v* [T] *especially BrE informal* to put something down somewhere, especially in a careless way: **plonk sth on/onto/beside etc sth** *He plonked a mug of coffee down beside me.*

plonk² *n* [U] *BrE informal* cheap wine

plop¹ /plɒp $ plɑːp/ *v* [I,T] (**plopped, plopping**) to fall, or drop something somewhere, making a sound like something dropping in water: **[+into/out of etc]** *The frog plopped back into the pond.*
PHRASES
> **plop (yourself) down** to sit down heavily: *She plopped down onto the sofa.*

plop² *n* [C] the sound made by something when it falls or is dropped in liquid

plot¹ /plɒt $ plɑːt/ *n* [C]
1 **SECRET PLAN** a secret plan to do something illegal or harmful: **plot to do sth** *a plot to kill the king* **THESAURUS** PLAN
2 **STORY** the events that form the main story of a book, film, or play: *I didn't really understand the plot.*
3 **LAND** a small piece of land for building or growing things on: *a vegetable plot*

plot² *v* (**plotted, plotting**) **1** [I,T] to make a secret plan to harm someone or do something illegal: **plot to do sth** *He denied plotting to kidnap the girl.* | **[+against]** *The army were secretly plotting against him.* **2** (*also* **plot out**) [T] to draw marks or a line to represent facts, numbers etc: *We plotted a graph to show the increase in profits.*

plough¹ *BrE,* **plow** *AmE* /plaʊ/ *n* [C] a large piece of farm equipment used to turn over the earth so that seeds can be planted

plough² *BrE,* **plow** *AmE v* **1** [I,T] to turn over the earth using a plough so that seeds can be planted: *newly ploughed fields* **2** [I] to hit or move through something with a lot of force: **[+into/through etc]** *A truck ploughed into the back of my car.*
PHRASAL VERBS
plough sth ↔ **back** to use money that you have earned from a business to make the business bigger and more successful: **[+into]** *We ploughed the profits back into the business.*
plough on to continue doing something, even though it is difficult or boring
plough through sth to read all of something even though it is difficult or boring **THESAURUS** READ

ploy /plɔɪ/ *n* [C] a clever way of getting what you want, especially by deceiving someone: *His usual ploy is to pretend he's ill.*

pluck¹ /plʌk/ *v* [T] **1** to quickly pull something or someone from the place where they are: **[+from/off**

pluck

Ac = words from the Academic Word List

etc] *She plucked an apple off the tree.* | *Three yachtsmen were plucked from the Atlantic yesterday.* **2** to pull the feathers off a dead bird before cooking it **3** to play a musical instrument by pulling the strings with your fingers

PHRASES

| **pluck up (the) courage (to do sth)** to make yourself be brave and do something difficult or unpleasant: *I finally plucked up the courage to ask for a raise.*

PHRASAL VERBS

pluck at sth to pull something quickly several times with your fingers, especially to attract attention: *The little boy plucked at her sleeve.*

pluck² n [U] courage and determination —**plucky** adj

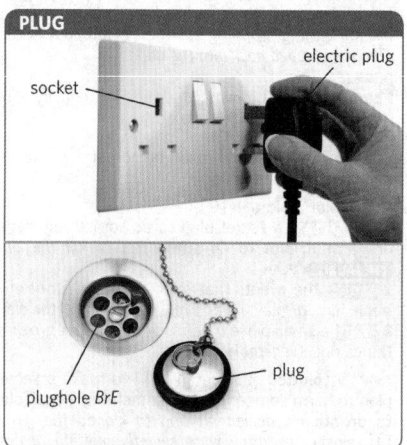

PLUG

electric plug

socket

plughole *BrE*

plug

plug¹ /plʌɡ/ n [C]

1 ELECTRICITY the thing that you push into a wall to connect a piece of electrical equipment to the electricity supply: *an electric plug*

2 BATH/SINK a round flat piece of rubber used for blocking the hole in a bath or SINK: *the bath plug*

3 ADVERTISEMENT informal a way of advertising a book, film etc by mentioning it publicly, especially on television or radio: **put/get in a plug (for sth)** *During the show she managed to put in a plug for her new book.* → SPARK PLUG

plug² v [T] (**plugged, plugging**) **1** (*also* **plug up**) to fill or block a hole **2** informal to advertise a book, film etc by mentioning it on television or radio

PHRASAL VERBS

plug away informal to continue working hard at something: *He's been plugging away at his essay all week.*

plug sth ↔ **in** to connect a piece of electrical equipment to the electricity supply, or to another piece of equipment OPP **unplug**: *Is the TV plugged in?*

plughole /ˈplʌɡhəʊl $ -hoʊl/ n [C] *BrE* a hole in a bath or SINK, where the water flows out → see picture at **PLUG¹**

plum /plʌm/ n [C] a soft round fruit which is purple, red, or yellow → see picture on page A4

plumage /ˈpluːmɪdʒ/ n [U] a bird's feathers

plumber /ˈplʌmə $ -ər/ n [C] someone whose job is to repair water pipes, baths, toilets etc

plumbing /ˈplʌmɪŋ/ n [U] **1** the pipes that water flows through in a building **2** the work of fitting and repairing water pipes, baths, toilets etc

plume /pluːm/ n [C] **1** a cloud of smoke, dust etc which rises up into the air: *a plume of smoke* **2** a large feather

plummet /ˈplʌmɪt/ v [I] **1** to suddenly and quickly decrease in value or amount: *House prices have plummeted over the past year.* **2** to fall quickly from a very high place

plump¹ /plʌmp/ adj slightly fat or round: *a cheerful plump woman* | *plump juicy strawberries* THESAURUS FAT

plump² (*also* **plump up**) v [T] to make PILLOWS, CUSHIONS etc rounder and softer by shaking or hitting them

PHRASAL VERBS

plump for sth informal to choose something after thinking carefully about it: *In the end I plumped for the tuna steak.*

plunder¹ /ˈplʌndə $ -ər/ v **1** [I,T] to steal large amounts of money or property from somewhere, especially during a war: *The city was plundered by invaders in 1793.* **2** [T] to use up all or most of a supply of something in a careless way: *We cannot continue to plunder the Earth's resources.*

plunder² n [U] literary the act of stealing things, or the things that someone steals, especially during a war

plunge¹ /plʌndʒ/ v **1** [I] to fall forwards and DOWNWARDS, especially into water: **[+into/off etc]** *The van plunged into the river.* **2** [T] to push something into another thing using a lot of force: **plunge sth into sth** *He plunged the knife into the man's chest.* **3** [I] to suddenly decrease by a large amount: *Oil prices have plunged to a new low.*

PHRASAL VERBS

plunge (sb/sth) **into** sth to suddenly experience a difficult or unpleasant situation, or to make someone suddenly do this: *A strike would plunge the country into chaos.*

plunge² n [singular] a sudden large decrease in the price, value etc of something: *a plunge in house prices*

PHRASES

| **take the plunge** to decide to do something important and risky, especially after thinking about it carefully: *She took the plunge and set up her own business.*

plunger /ˈplʌndʒə $ -ər/ n [C] a tool for clearing waste that is blocking a kitchen or bathroom pipe

pluperfect /pluːˈpɜːfɪkt $ -ɜːr-/ n **the pluperfect** the PAST PERFECT

plural /ˈplʊərəl $ ˈplʊr-/ n [C] the form of a word that shows you are talking about more than one person, thing etc. For example, 'dogs' is the plural of 'dog'. —**plural** adj

plus¹ **Ac** /plʌs/ prep, linking word
1 used to show that one number or amount is added to another **OPP** minus: *Three plus six equals nine (3+6=9).* | *The jacket costs $49.95 plus tax.*
2 and also: *There are numerous clubs plus a casino.*
PHRASES
| **plus or minus** used to say that a number may be more or less by a particular amount: *The final cost may be plus or minus 5%.*

plus² **Ac** adj **1** [only before noun] used to talk about something that is good about a thing or situation: *One of the hotel's **plus points** is that it's right in the middle of town.* **2** more than a particular amount: *She makes $50,000 a year plus.* | *a temperature of plus 12°* (=more than 12 degrees above zero)

plus³ **Ac** n [C] **1** something that is good about something: *The restaurant's location is a real plus.* **2** a plus sign **OPP** minus

plush /plʌʃ/ adj comfortable, expensive, and of good quality: *a large plush office*

'plus sign (also **plus**) n [C] the sign (+), used to show that two or more numbers or amounts are added together

Pluto /'pluːtəʊ $ -toʊ/ n the small PLANET that is furthest from the Sun

plutonium /pluː'təʊniəm $ -'toʊ-/ n [U] a metal used to produce NUCLEAR power

ply /plaɪ/ v (**plied, plying, plies**) **ply your trade** literary to do your usual work, especially by trying to sell things to people
PHRASAL VERBS
ply sb **with** sth to give someone large amounts of food or drink

plywood /'plaɪwʊd/ n [U] a material made from several thin layers of wood stuck together

p.m. (also **pm** BrE) /ˌpiː 'em/ used after numbers expressing time, to show that it is between NOON and MIDNIGHT → **a.m.**: *I leave work at 5.30 p.m.*

PM /ˌpiː 'em/ n [C] BrE informal the PRIME MINISTER

PMS /ˌpiː em 'es/ (also **PMT** BrE /ˌpiː em 'tiː/) n [U] (**premenstrual syndrome/tension**) the unpleasant physical and emotional feelings that many women have before their PERIOD

pneumatic /njuː'mætɪk $ nʊ-/ adj **1** technical filled with air: *a pneumatic tyre* **2** worked by air pressure: *a pneumatic drill*

pneumonia /njuː'məʊniə $ nʊ'moʊ-/ n [U] a serious disease of the lungs

poach /pəʊtʃ $ poʊtʃ/ v **1** [T] to cook food, especially eggs, in gently boiling liquid → see picture at **EGG¹** **THESAURUS** **COOK 2** [I,T] to illegally catch or hunt animals or fish on someone else's private land **3** [T] to take and use someone else's ideas unfairly or illegally

poacher /'pəʊtʃə $ 'poʊtʃər/ n [C] someone who illegally catches or hunts animals or fish on private land

PO Box /ˌpiː əʊ bɒks $ -oʊ baːks/ n [C] (**Post Office Box**) used before a number as an address at a post office where letters to you can be sent: *Write to PO Box 714, Accra, Ghana.*

pocket¹ /'pɒkɪt $ 'paː-/ n [C]
1 a small cloth bag sewn into or onto a piece of clothing, that you put your money, keys etc in: **shirt/trouser etc pocket** *There's some money in my jacket pocket.* | *Luke came in with his hands in his pockets.*
2 a small bag or piece of material fastened to something so that you can put things into it: *Please read the air safety card in the pocket of the seat in front.*
3 the amount of money that you have to spend: *There are eight hotels, with a price range to **suit every pocket**.* | **from/out of/into your own pocket** *He had to pay for the repairs out of his own pocket.*
4 a small area or amount of something that is different from what surrounds it: **[+of]** *pockets of resistance* | *pockets of air* → **pick sb's pocket** at **PICK¹**
PHRASES
| **out of pocket** if you are out of pocket, you have less money than usual because you have made a mistake or been unlucky: *I was actually out of pocket after the deal.*

pocket² v [T] **1** to put something in your pocket: *He locked the door and pocketed the keys.* **2** to get an amount of money, especially in a way that is illegal or seems very easy: *Baines pocketed $2,500 in prize money.*

pocket³ (also **'pocket-sized**) adj small enough to fit in a pocket: *a pocket calculator*

pocketbook /'pɒkətbʊk $ 'paː-/ n [C] AmE old-fashioned a HANDBAG or WALLET

pocketful /'pɒkətfʊl $ 'paː-/ n [C] the amount that can fit in a pocket: **[+of]** *a pocketful of coins*

'pocket knife n [C] a small knife with a blade that you can fold into its handle

'pocket ,money n [U] BrE a small amount of money that parents give regularly to their children, usually every week or month **SYN** allowance AmE: *How much pocket money do you get?*

pockmarked /'pɒkmaːkt $ 'paːkmaːrkt/ adj covered with hollow marks or holes

pod /pɒd $ paːd/ n [C] the long green part of plants such as beans and PEAS which the seeds grow in: *a pea pod*

podcast /'pɒdkaːst $ 'paːdkæst/ n [C] a radio programme that can be DOWNLOADed from the Internet —**podcast** v [T]: *The show is to be podcast.*

podiatrist /pə'daɪətrɪst/ n [C] AmE a doctor who takes care of people's feet and treats foot diseases **SYN** chiropodist BrE —**podiatry** n [U]

podium /'pəʊdiəm $ 'poʊ-/ n [C] a small raised area for a performer, speaker etc to stand on, sometimes with a high surface to put a book or notes on

poem /'pəʊɪm $ 'poʊ-/ n [C] a piece of writing that is written in short lines, especially using words that RHYME (=have similar sounds at the end) → **poetry**: *a famous poem by Wordsworth*

poet /'pəʊɪt $ 'poʊ-/ n [C] someone who writes poems → **poetry**

poetic

poetic /pəʊˈetɪk $ poʊ-/ *adj* relating to poetry or typical of poetry: *poetic language* —**poetically** /-kli/ *adv*

po,etic ˈjustice *n* [U] a situation in which someone suffers, and you think they deserve it because they did something bad

po,etic ˈlicence *BrE,* **poetic license** *AmE n* [U] the freedom that poets and other artists have to change facts because what they are making is poetry or art

poetry /ˈpəʊətri $ ˈpoʊ-/ *n* [U] poems in general, or the art of writing poems → **poet, prose**: *Shelley's poetry* | *a poetry class* | *a poetry reading* (=when someone reads poetry to an audience)

poignant /ˈpɔɪnjənt/ *adj* making you have strong feelings of sadness or sympathy: *a poignant scene near the end of the film* —**poignancy** *n* [U] —**poignantly** *adv*

point¹ /pɔɪnt/ *n*

1 STH YOU MENTION [C] an idea, fact, or opinion that someone mentions in a talk, discussion, or piece of writing: *Before I stop, I'd like to **make** one final **point*** (=mention one more thing). | *I agree with that point.* | *'Have you spoken to Alan?' '**That's a point*** (=a good thing to mention)*! I completely forgot to tell him.'*

2 MOST IMPORTANT THING **the point** the most important fact, idea, or part of a situation: ***The point is** we just don't have enough money.* | *I wish she'd hurry up and **get to the point*** (=talk about the most important thing). | **that's not/beside the point** (=that's not really important) *'But I gave you the money back.' 'That's not the point; you shouldn't have taken it.'*

3 PURPOSE [U] (*also* **the point**) the purpose or reason for doing something: **[+of]** *What's the point of this meeting anyway?* | *The **whole point** of travelling is to experience new things.* | *There's no point in going now – we're already too late.*

4 PLACE [C] a particular position or place: *the point where two lines cross each other* | *Dover is a major **point of entry** into Britain.* THESAURUS▶ PLACE

5 IN TIME/DEVELOPMENT [C usually singular] a time or part of a process when something happens: ***At that point** I began to get seriously worried.* | *I will probably sell the car **at some point** in the future.* | **high/low point** (=the best or worst part of something) *the high point of his career* | **reach/get to a point** *It got to the point where we both wanted a divorce.*

6 QUALITY/FEATURE [C] a particular quality, ability, or feature that someone or something has: **sb's/sth's good/bad points** *He has his good points.* | *The low price was one of its **selling points** (=features that will help to sell it).* | *Driving is not one of my **strong points.*** THESAURUS▶ DISADVANTAGE

7 IN A GAME [C] a unit used for showing the score in a game or competition: *He is now only three points behind the leader.* | **score/lose a point** *You lose a point if you do not finish on time.*

8 SHARP END [C] the sharp end of something: *the point of a needle*

9 TEMPERATURE **boiling/freezing/melting point** the temperature at which something boils, freezes, or melts: *Heat the water until it reaches boiling point.*

10 MEASURE ON A SCALE [C] a mark or measure on a scale: *Stocks were down 12 points today at 4,298.*

11 BETWEEN NUMBERS [C] the sign (.) used for separating a whole number from the DECIMALS that follow it

12 DIRECTIONS **the points of the compass** directions such as north, south, east, and west: *The ships made their way towards us from all points of the compass.*

13 LAND [C] a long thin piece of land that stretches out into the sea

14 SMALL SPOT [C] a very small spot: *a tiny point of light* → **BREAKING POINT, DECIMAL POINT, POINT OF VIEW, STARTING POINT, TURNING POINT**

PHRASES

in point of fact *formal* used when emphasizing, correcting, or adding something: *They said that the prisoner was being well treated. In point of fact, he looked sick and hungry.*

make a point of doing sth to do something deliberately, even when it involves making a special effort: *I always make a point of being early.*

be on the point of (doing) sth to be going to do something very soon, when something happens: *I was just on the point of leaving for work when the phone rang.*

the point of no return the time when it becomes impossible to stop something from happening: *I knew that we had **passed the point of no return.***

to the point mentioning only the most important things: *Her next letter was short and to the point.*

to the point of sth so much that something almost happens or is almost true: *The bird has been hunted to the point of extinction.*

up to a point partly, but not completely: *He's right, but only up to a point.*

COLLOCATIONS

adjectives

a good point *I think that's a very good point.*
an interesting point *He made some interesting points.*
an important point *There are two important points to remember.*

verbs

to make a point *I want to make the point that children's books can be enjoyed by adults too.*
to put/get your point across (=to make people understand it) *Do you think we got our point across?*
to see/take/get sb's point (=to understand it) *I take your point, but there's nothing I can do.*
to have a point (=to be right, or partly right) *Maybe she has a point.*

---

point² *v*

1 [I,T] to show something to someone by holding up one of your fingers or a thin object towards it: **[+to/at/towards etc]** *John pointed to a chair. 'Please sit down.'* | *'That's my car,' she said, pointing at a white Ford.* | *He **pointed his finger** at me.* → see picture on page A10

2 [T] to hold something so that it is aimed towards a person or thing: **point sth at sth** *He pointed a gun at the old man's head.*

3 [I] to face or be aimed in a particular direction: [+to/towards/at etc] *Hold the bat so that your fingers point towards the end.* | *The hands of the clock pointed to one o'clock.*
4 [T] to show someone which direction to go: *There should be signs **pointing the way** to her house.*
PHRASES
| **point the/a finger at sb** *informal* to blame someone [SYN] **accuse**: *I knew that they would point the finger at me.*

PHRASAL VERBS
point sb/sth ↔ **out**
1 to tell someone something that they did not already know or had not thought about: *He was always keen to point out my mistakes.* | [+that] *He pointed out that we did not have enough money to buy the house.* | [+to] *Thank you for pointing this out to me.*
2 to show a person or thing clearly to someone by pointing at them: [+to] *I'll point him out to you next time we see him.*
point to sb/sth to show that something is probably true: *The study points to stress as a cause of heart disease.*

point-'blank *adj, adv* if you say something point-blank, you say it in a direct way and without explaining your reasons: *She refused point-blank to help.*
PHRASES
| **at point-blank range** from an extremely close position: *The victim was **shot at point-blank range.***

pointed /ˈpɔɪntɪd/ *adj*
1 a pointed object has a point at the end: *pointed teeth*
2 criticizing in an indirect way: *a pointed remark*

pointedly /ˈpɔɪntɪdli/ *adv* in a way that shows clearly that you disapprove of something or that you are annoyed: *He pointedly ignored him.*

pointer /ˈpɔɪntə $ -ər/ *n* [C] **1** a useful piece of advice or information that helps you to do or understand something [SYN] **tip**: [+on] *Ruth can **give** you a few **pointers** on using the equipment.* **2** a small symbol such as an ARROW that you use to point to a place, for example on a computer screen

pointless /ˈpɔɪntləs/ *adj* without any useful purpose or effect: *a pointless argument* | *It is pointless trying to explain it to him.*

point of 'view *n* [C] (*plural* **points of view**) **1** one way of thinking about a situation: *From a financial point of view, this is a good idea.* **2** someone's personal opinion or attitude in a situation: *Try to see it from my point of view.* [THESAURUS] ▶ **OPINION**

pointy /ˈpɔɪnti/ *adj informal* a pointy object has a point at the end

poise /pɔɪz/ *n* [U] **1** calm confident behaviour: *She showed great poise in an awkward situation.* **2** a graceful way of moving or standing: *the poise of a ballet dancer*

poised /pɔɪzd/ *adj* **1** ready to do something or to move soon: *The army was poised to attack.* **2** behaving in a calm confident way

poison¹ /ˈpɔɪzən/ *n* [C,U] a substance that can kill or harm you if you eat it, drink it etc: *Arsenic is a deadly poison.*

poison² *v* [T] **1** to try to kill someone by giving them poison, especially by adding it to their food or drink: *He tried to poison his parents.* | *She killed him by poisoning his tea.* **2** to make water, air, land etc dangerous by adding harmful chemicals to it: *Pesticides are poisoning our rivers.* **3** to have a very harmful and unpleasant effect on something: *The quarrel had poisoned their relationship.* | *He tried to **poison** their **minds against** their mother.* —**poisoned** *adj* —**poisoner** *n* [C]

poisoning /ˈpɔɪzənɪŋ/ *n* [C,U] an illness that is caused by swallowing, touching, or breathing a poisonous substance: *lead poisoning*

poisonous /ˈpɔɪzənəs/ *adj* **1** containing poison or producing poison: *Many household chemicals are poisonous.* | *a poisonous snake* **2** full of very unpleasant and unfriendly feelings: *the poisonous atmosphere in the office*

poke /pəʊk $ poʊk/ *v* **1** [I,T] to push your finger or an object into something: *Stop poking me!* | [+at] *He poked at the ground with a stick.* → see picture on page A10 [THESAURUS] ▶ **PUSH 2** [T] to push something through a space or opening: **poke sth into/through/out of etc sth** *Dave poked his head around the door.* **3** [I] to appear through a hole or opening: [+up/through/out etc] *Weeds poked through cracks in the ground.* **4** [T] to show someone on a SOCIAL NETWORKING SITE such as Facebook that you want to communicate with them —**poke** *n* [C] → **poke your nose into sth** at **NOSE¹**
PHRASES
| **poke fun at sb/sth** to joke about someone in an unkind way: *Some kids were poking fun at Judy.*

poker /ˈpəʊkə $ ˈpoʊkər/ *n* **1** [U] a card game that people usually play for money **2** [C] a metal stick used for moving coal or wood in a fire

poker-'faced *adj* showing no expression or emotion on your face

poky, pokey /ˈpəʊki $ ˈpoʊ-/ *adj BrE informal disapproving* a poky place is too small: *a poky apartment*

polar /ˈpəʊlə $ ˈpoʊlər/ *adj* relating to the North or South Pole: *polar ice caps*

polar 'bear / $ ˈ.../ *n* [C] a large white bear that lives near the North Pole → see picture on **BEAR²**

polarize (*also* **-ise** *BrE*) /ˈpəʊləraɪz $ ˈpoʊ-/ *v* [I,T] *formal* to make people divide into two groups with completely opposite opinions: *The war polarized public opinion.* —**polarization** /ˌpəʊləraɪˈzeɪʃən $ ˌpoʊlərə-/ *n* [U]

Polaroid /ˈpəʊlərɔɪd $ ˈpoʊ-/ *n* [C,U] *trademark* a camera that uses a special film to produce a photograph very quickly, or a picture taken using this camera

pole /pəʊl $ poʊl/ *n* [C]
1 a long piece of wood or metal: *tent poles*
2 North/South Pole the most northern and southern point on Earth: *an expedition to the North Pole* → **TELEGRAPH POLE**

polemic

PHRASES

be poles apart to be completely different: *Their political views are poles apart.*

polemic /pəˈlemɪk/ n **1** [C] a statement that criticizes or defends an idea **2** [U] (*also* **polemics**) the practice or skill of making such statements —**polemical** adj

'pole vault n **the pole vault** a sport in which you jump over a high bar using a special long pole

police¹ /pəˈliːs/ n [plural]
1 the police the official organization whose job is to catch criminals and make sure that people obey the law: *The police are looking for him.*
2 members of the police: *Police surrounded the building.* | *Several police were hurt.*

COLLOCATIONS

verbs

to call the police *We can call the police if there's any trouble.*
to tell the police *Why didn't you tell the police?*
the police catch sb *The police are determined to catch the killer.*
the police arrest sb *The police arrested Mr Fox as he tried to leave the country.*
the police question/interview sb *Police are questioning two men about the deaths.*
the police charge sb (with sth) (=say officially that someone may be guilty of a crime) *The police have charged the parents with murder.*

police + noun

the police force *He joined the police force in 1990.*
a police officer *The police officer asked to see his driving licence.*
a police car *They were being followed by a police car.*

police² v [T] to make sure that laws or rules are obeyed in an area or activity: *an agency that polices the nuclear power industry*

po,lice 'constable n [C] BrE formal (abbreviation **PC**) a police officer of the lowest rank

po'lice de,partment n [C] AmE the official police organization in an area or city

po'lice force n [C] the official police organization in a country or area

policeman /pəˈliːsmən/ n [C] (plural **policemen** /-mən/) a male police officer

po'lice ,officer n [C] a member of the police

po'lice state n [C] disapproving a country where the government strictly controls people's freedom, for example to travel or to talk about politics

po'lice ,station n [C] a local office of the police

policewoman /pəˈliːsˌwʊmən/ n [C] (plural **policewomen** /-ˌwɪmɪn/) a female police officer

policy Ac /ˈpɒləsi $ ˈpɑː-/ n (plural **policies**)
1 [C,U] a way of dealing with something, especially one that has been officially decided by a political party or an organization: **foreign/economic/social etc policy** *a foreign policy adviser to the government* | **[+on]** *What is the school's policy on bullying?* | *The*

company operates a strict **no-smoking policy**. | **it is sb's policy to do sth** *It was her policy not to lend money to friends.*
2 [C] a written agreement with an insurance company: *a **life insurance policy***

polio /ˈpəʊliəʊ $ ˈpoʊlioʊ/ n [U] a serious disease that can make you unable to move your muscles

polish¹ /ˈpɒlɪʃ $ ˈpɑː-/ v [T] to make something clean and shiny by rubbing it: *Dad polished his glasses.* —**polishing** n [U]

PHRASAL VERBS
polish sth ↔ **off** informal to quickly eat or finish all of something: *Who polished off the pizza?*
polish sth ↔ **up** to improve a skill by practising it: *I need to polish up my French.*

polish² n **1** [C,U] a substance used for polishing things: *shoe polish* → **NAIL POLISH 2** [singular] if you give something a polish, you polish it

polished /ˈpɒlɪʃt $ ˈpɑː-/ adj **1** shiny because of being rubbed with polish: *polished shoes* **2** done with a lot of skill and with no mistakes: *a polished performance*

polite /pəˈlaɪt/ adj speaking or behaving in a way that shows respect for other people OPP **impolite, rude**: *He was always very polite.* | *a polite question* | **It is polite** *to cover your mouth when you yawn.* —**politely** adv: *'It's very nice,' she said politely.* —**politeness** n [U]

THESAURUS

polite speaking or behaving in a way that shows respect for other people, or is considered socially correct: *It's polite to say 'good morning' or 'hello' when you meet someone.* | *A polite young man showed me to my seat.*
tactful careful not to say something that might embarrass or upset someone: *She was very tactful and didn't say anything about the divorce.*
courteous formal polite and showing respect for other people, especially in formal situations: *Staff should be courteous towards customers at all times.* | *a courteous answer*
have good manners someone who has good manners behaves politely when they are with other people: *Try and teach your children to have good manners at meals.*

political /pəˈlɪtɪkəl/ adj
1 relating to the government, politics, and public affairs of a country: *a time of great political change* | *The US has two main **political parties**.* | *People want a new **political system**.*
2 interested in or involved in politics: *I'm not very political.* —**politically** /-kli/ adv

po,litical a'sylum n [U] the right to stay in another country because the political situation in your own country makes it dangerous for you to live there

po,litically cor'rect adj (abbreviation **PC**) politically correct language or behaviour is carefully chosen so that it does not offend or insult anyone —**political correctness** n [U]

po,litical 'prisoner n [C] someone who is put in

prison because of their political activities or opinions

politician /ˌpɒləˈtɪʃən $ ˌpɑː-/ n [C] someone who works in politics, especially someone who is elected

---

THESAURUS

politician someone who works in politics, especially someone who is elected: *a Labour politician*

statesman a political leader who people admire: *a great statesman like Roosevelt*

MP/Member of Parliament someone who has been elected to parliament to represent people from a particular area of the country: *William Hague, the MP for Richmond*

congressman/congresswoman a man or woman who is a member of a CONGRESS, especially the US House of Representatives: *a Republican congressman*

senator a member of a SENATE, especially in the US: *the Senator for New York*

---

politicize (also **-ise** *BrE*) /pəˈlɪtɪsaɪz/ v [T] to involve politics in a situation, or to make a person more involved in politics: *He does not believe in politicizing sport.* —**politicized** adj

politics /ˈpɒlətɪks $ ˈpɑː-/ n
1 [U also + plural verb *BrE*] ideas and activities relating to how a place is governed and who has power → **political**, **politician**: *Are you interested in politics? | modern American politics | Politics have always interested Anita.*
2 [U] the job of being a politician: *She retired from politics at the age of 70.*
3 [plural] the activities of people in a group who are trying to get advantages for themselves: *I try not to get involved with* **office politics**.
4 [plural] someone's political beliefs: *Anna's politics are pretty left-wing.*

polka /ˈpɒlkə, ˈpəʊlkə $ ˈpoʊlkə/ n [C] a kind of dance, or the music for this dance

poll¹ /pəʊl $ poʊl/ n [C] **1** the process of finding out what people think about a subject by asking a lot of people the same questions SYN **opinion poll**: *Polls show that most people support the President.*
2 the polls [plural] the place where you go to vote in an election: *The polls have now closed and the results are being counted. | Tomorrow UK voters will* **go to the polls** (=vote).

poll² v [T] **1** to try to find out what people think about a subject by asking a lot of people the same questions: *Most of the teachers we polled support the changes.* **2** to get a particular number of votes in an election: *The Conservatives polled 35% of the vote.*

pollen /ˈpɒlən $ ˈpɑː-/ n [U] a powder produced by flowers, which is carried by the wind or insects to make other flowers produce seeds

'pollen count n [C] a measurement of the amount of pollen in the air

pollinate /ˈpɒləneɪt $ ˈpɑː-/ v [T] to make a flower produce seeds by giving it pollen —**pollination** /ˌpɒləˈneɪʃən $ ˌpɑː-/ n [U]

'polling day n [U] *BrE* the day when people vote in an election

'polling ˌstation *BrE*, **'polling place** *AmE* n [C] the place where you vote in an election

pollster /ˈpəʊlstə $ ˈpoʊlstər/ n [C] a person or company that carries out POLLS to find out what people think about a subject

pollutant /pəˈluːtənt/ n [C] a substance that pollutes the air, water etc

pollute /pəˈluːt/ v [T] to make air, water, soil etc dirty or dangerous: *companies that pollute the environment | The beach was polluted by an oil spill.* —**polluter** n [C]

polluted /pəˈluːtɪd/ adj full of pollution: **heavily/seriously/severely polluted** *The rivers are heavily polluted.* THESAURUS ▸ DIRTY

pollution /pəˈluːʃən/ n [U] damage caused to air, water, soil etc by harmful chemicals and waste: *tough laws to* **reduce pollution** | *The public are in danger from* **industrial pollution**. | **air/water pollution** → NOISE POLLUTION

Grammar

Pollution is an uncountable noun and has no plural form. Do not say 'Car pollutions are a big problem.' Say *Car pollution is a big problem.*

---

polo /ˈpəʊləʊ $ ˈpoʊloʊ/ n [U] a game played between two teams riding horses, who hit a small ball with long wooden hammers

'polo neck n [C] *BrE* a SWEATER with a high collar that fits closely around your neck and folds over SYN **turtleneck** *AmE* → see picture at NECK¹

poltergeist /ˈpɒltəgaɪst $ ˈpoʊltər-/ n [C] a GHOST that moves objects around, often noisily

polyester /ˌpɒliˈestə, ˌpɒliˈestə◂ $ ˈpɑːliestər/ n [U] an artificial material used to make cloth

polyethylene /ˌpɒliˈeθəliːn $ ˌpɑː-/ n [U] *AmE* POLYTHENE

polygamy /pəˈlɪɡəmi/ n [U] the custom of having more than one wife or husband at the same time —**polygamous** adj

polystyrene /ˌpɒliˈstaɪriːn◂ $ ˌpɑː-/ n [U] *BrE* a soft light plastic material, used especially to make containers SYN **Styrofoam** trademark *AmE*

polytechnic /ˌpɒliˈteknɪk $ ˌpɑː-/ n [C] a college in Britain where students could study for a degree, which existed until 1993

polythene /ˈpɒləθiːn $ ˈpɑː-/ n [U] *BrE* a thin plastic material, used especially to make bags SYN **polyethylene** *AmE*

pomegranate /ˈpɒmɪɡrænɪt $ ˈpɑːmə-/ n [C] a round fruit that has a lot of small juicy red seeds and a thick reddish skin

pomp /pɒmp $ pɑːmp/ n [U] *formal* the impressive clothes, decorations, music etc at an important official ceremony

pompous /ˈpɒmpəs $ ˈpɑːm-/ adj *disapproving* someone who is pompous tries to make people think they are important, especially by using formal language: *He's a pompous idiot.* —**pompously** adv —**pomposity** /pɒmˈpɒsəti $ pɑːmˈpɑː-/ n [U]

pond /pɒnd $ pɑːnd/ n [C] a small area of water, especially one that is made in a field or garden **THESAURUS** LAKE

ponder /ˈpɒndə $ ˈpɑːndər/ v [I,T] *formal* to think carefully and seriously about something: *She pondered her answer for a long time.*

ponderous /ˈpɒndərəs $ ˈpɑːn-/ *adj formal* **1** boring and too serious: *a long, ponderous explanation* **2** slow and awkward because of being big and heavy: *an elephant's ponderous walk*

pong /pɒŋ $ pɑːŋ/ n [C] *BrE informal* an unpleasant smell —**pong** v [I]

pontificate /pɒnˈtɪfɪkeɪt $ pɑːn-/ v [I] *disapproving* to give your opinion about something in a way that shows you think you are always right: *She's always pontificating about moral values.*

pony /ˈpəʊni $ ˈpoʊ-/ n [C] (*plural* **ponies**) a small horse

ponytail /ˈpəʊniteɪl $ ˈpoʊ-/ n [C] hair tied at the back of your head so that it hangs down like a horse's tail: *She had her hair in a ponytail.* → see picture at **HAIR**

ˈpony-ˌtrekking n [U] *BrE* the activity of riding through the countryside on ponies

poo /puː/ n [U] *informal* solid waste from the BOWELS

poodle /ˈpuːdl/ n [C] a type of dog with thick curly hair

pooh-pooh /ˌpuː ˈpuː/ v [T] *informal* to say that you think an idea is silly or useless: *He pooh-poohs everything I say.*

POOL

pool¹ /puːl/ n
1 FOR SWIMMING [C] a place that has been made for people to swim in SYN **swimming pool**: *Does the hotel have a pool?* **THESAURUS** LAKE
2 GAME [U] a game in which you use a long stick to hit balls into holes at the edge of a table
3 AREA OF LIQUID [C] a small area of water or another liquid on a surface: *Pools had formed among the rocks.* | **pool of water/blood/oil etc** *She was lying in a pool of blood.*
4 STH SHARED BY A GROUP [C] things such as money or cars that are available for a group of people to use: *the company car pool*
5 GAMBLING **the pools** a competition in Britain in which people try to win money by guessing the results of football games

pool² v [T] if people pool their money, knowledge etc, they combine it so that they can all use it: *a meeting to pool ideas*

poor /pɔː $ pʊr/ *adj*
1 a) someone who is poor has very little money and not many possessions OPP **rich**: *Her family were very poor.* | *a poor country* **b) the poor** people who are poor: *a charity that helps the poor*
2 not as good as it should be or could be: *Her health is poor.* | **poor quality/standard** *The work was of a very poor standard.* | *the team's* **poor performance** **THESAURUS** BAD
3 [only before noun] *spoken* used to show that you feel sorry for someone: *Poor Kate was sick.* | *Oh, you* **poor thing!**
4 not good at doing something: *a poor swimmer* | **[+at]** *He's always been poor at languages.*

THESAURUS

poor having very little money and not many possessions – used about people and the places where they live: *They were too poor to have a television.* | *It's one of the poorest areas of the city.*
hard up/broke *informal* having very little money, especially for a short time: *I'm broke until I get paid next week.* | *A lot of people are feeling hard up at the moment.*
deprived very poor and without the things that are necessary for a comfortable life – used especially about people's lives and the areas they live in: *She had a very deprived childhood.* | *one of the most deprived areas of Glasgow*
developing a developing country is poor and has very little industry: *the problems faced by developing countries* | *the developing world*

poorly¹ /ˈpɔːli $ ˈpʊrli/ *adv* badly: *a poorly paid job*

poorly² *adj BrE informal* ill: *I felt poorly.* **THESAURUS** ILL

pop¹ /pɒp $ pɑːp/ v (**popped**, **popping**)
1 COME OFF/OUT [I] to suddenly come off or out of something: **[+off/out/up etc]** *The button popped off my skirt.* | **out/up popped sth** *The egg cracked and out popped a chick.*
2 GO [I] *informal* to go somewhere for a short time: **[+in/out/along etc]** *I'm just popping out to get a newspaper.* | *Pop round and see me later.*
3 PUT [T] *BrE informal* to put something somewhere: **pop sth in/on/into etc sth** *I'll just pop the chicken in the oven.*
4 SOUND [I,T] to make a sound like a small explosion, for example by bursting: *A balloon popped.*
5 EARS [I] if your ears pop, you feel the pressure in them suddenly change, for example when you go up or down in a plane
PHRASES
sb's eyes pop (out) *informal* used to say that someone looks very surprised and excited: *His eyes nearly popped out of his head when he saw her in that dress!*
sth pops into your mind/head used to say that you suddenly think of something: *The idea just popped into my head.*

PHRASAL VERBS

pop up to appear suddenly or unexpectedly: *Click here, and a list of options pops up.*

pop² n **1** (also **'pop ˌmusic**) [U] modern music that is popular with young people: *Their music is a mixture of jazz and pop.* | **pop group/singer/concert etc** *Which pop bands do you like?* **2** [C] a sudden short sound like a small explosion: *The balloon went pop* (=burst with a pop). **3** [U] *informal* a sweet drink with bubbles in it SYN **soda** *AmE*

popcorn /ˈpɒpkɔːn $ ˈpɑːpkɔːrn/ n [U] corn that is heated until it swells. You eat it with salt or sugar.

Pope /pəʊp $ poʊp/ n [C] the leader of the Roman Catholic Church: *the Pope's recent visit* | *Pope John Paul II*

poppy /ˈpɒpi $ ˈpɑː-/ n [C] (*plural* **poppies**) a bright red flower with small black seeds → see picture at **FLOWER¹**

Popsicle /ˈpɒpsɪkəl $ ˈpɑːp-/ n [C] *trademark AmE* frozen fruit juice on a stick

populace /ˈpɒpjələs $ ˈpɑː-/ n **the populace** *formal* the ordinary people of a country

popular /ˈpɒpjələ $ ˈpɑːpjələr/ adj
1 liked by a lot of people OPP **unpopular**: *Is Ben popular at school?* | *the most popular team in the country* | **[+with]** *a cafe popular with teenagers* | *a hugely popular novel*
2 popular belief/opinion/view etc a belief etc that a lot of people have: *The government cannot ignore popular opinion.* | **Contrary to popular belief**, *many cats dislike milk.*
3 for ordinary people: *the popular press* | *She knows nothing about **popular culture** (=TV, pop music etc).*

popularity /ˌpɒpjəˈlærəti $ ˌpɑː-/ n [U] when someone or something is liked by a lot of people: *The popularity of the Internet has grown dramatically.*

popularize (also **-ise** *BrE*) /ˈpɒpjələraɪz $ ˈpɑː-/ v [T] to make something known and liked or understood by a lot of people: *He popularized reggae music.*

popularly /ˈpɒpjələli $ ˈpɑːpjələr-/ adv **popularly believed/called/known etc** believed, called something etc by many people: *It's popularly believed that people need eight hours sleep a night.*

populate /ˈpɒpjəleɪt $ ˈpɑː-/ v **be populated** if an area is populated by a group of people, they live there: *a region populated mainly by farmers* | **densely/heavily populated** (=a lot of people live there) | **sparsely/thinly populated** (=very few people live there)

population /ˌpɒpjəˈleɪʃən $ ˌpɑː-/ n [C]
1 the number of people living in an area, a country etc: **[+of]** *What's the population of Tokyo?* | *India has a population of over 1 billion.* | **population growth/ density** *a declining rate of population growth* THESAURUS **PEOPLE**
2 all of the people who live in an area: *Most of the world's population live in poverty.* | **the male/adult/ Jewish etc population** (=people in an area who are male, adult etc) *Only 30% of the male population have jobs.*

populist /ˈpɒpjəlɪst $ ˈpɑː-/ adj relating to or representing ordinary people, rather than rich or very highly educated people: *a populist campaign* —**populist** n [C]

populous /ˈpɒpjələs $ ˈpɑː-/ adj *formal* a populous area has a large population: *the most populous part of Germany*

porcelain /ˈpɔːslɪn $ ˈpɔːrsəlɪn/ n [U] a hard white substance made by baking clay: *a priceless porcelain vase*

porch /pɔːtʃ $ pɔːrtʃ/ n [C] **1** *BrE* an entrance covered by a roof built onto a house or church **2** *AmE* a structure built onto the front or back of a house, with a floor and roof but no walls

porcupine /ˈpɔːkjəpaɪn $ ˈpɔːr-/ n [C] an animal with long pointed parts on its back and sides

pore¹ /pɔː $ pɔːr/ n [C] one of the small holes in your skin that SWEAT can pass through

pore² v
PHRASAL VERBS
pore over sth to read or look at something very carefully for a long time: *I spent days poring over my lecture notes.* THESAURUS **READ**

pork /pɔːk $ pɔːrk/ n [U] meat from pigs: *roast pork* | *pork chops*

pornography /pɔːˈnɒɡrəfi $ pɔːrˈnɑːɡ-/ (also **porn** /pɔːn $ pɔːrn/) n [U] magazines, films etc that are intended to make people feel sexually excited —**pornographic** /ˌpɔːnəˈɡræfɪk◂ $ ˌpɔːr-/ (also **porn**) adj: *porn videos*

porous /ˈpɔːrəs/ adj porous material allows liquid or gas to pass through it slowly: *porous rock*

porpoise /ˈpɔːpəs $ ˈpɔːr-/ n [C] a sea animal that looks similar to a DOLPHIN

porridge /ˈpɒrɪdʒ $ ˈpɑː-, ˈpɔː-/ n [U] OATS that are cooked in milk or water and eaten hot for breakfast

port /pɔːt $ pɔːrt/ n
1 [C,U] a place where ships arrive and leave from: *a fishing port* | **in port** *The ship was back in port.* → see Word Choice at **HARBOUR**
2 [U] a strong sweet Portuguese wine
3 [U] the left side of a ship or aircraft when you are looking towards the front OPP **starboard**
PHRASES
port of call *informal* one of the places that you visit: *My next port of call was the City Records Department.*

portable /ˈpɔːtəbəl $ ˈpɔːr-/ adj easy to carry: *a portable television* —**portable** n [C]

portal /ˈpɔːtl $ ˈpɔːrtl/ n [C] a website that helps you find other websites

porter /ˈpɔːtə $ ˈpɔːrtər/ n [C] someone whose job is to carry bags at airports, stations, hotels etc

portfolio /pɔːtˈfəʊliəʊ $ pɔːrtˈfoʊlioʊ/ n [C] (*plural* **portfolios**) a set of pictures that an artist, photographer etc uses as examples of his or her work

porthole /ˈpɔːthəʊl $ ˈpɔːrthoʊl/ n [C] a small round window in a ship

portion

portion Ac /ˈpɔːʃən $ ˈpɔːr-/ n [C] **1** a part of something: **[+of]** *The return portion of the plane ticket can be used at any time.* | **large/substantial/ significant portion** *A large portion of the money has been spent on advertising.* **2** an amount of food for one person: **[+of]** *a small portion of ice cream*

portly /ˈpɔːtli $ ˈpɔːr-/ adj fat

portrait /ˈpɔːtrɪt $ ˈpɔːr-/ n [C] **1** a painting, drawing, or photograph of a person: **[+of]** *a portrait of a young woman* → see picture at **PAINTING** **THESAURUS** PICTURE **2** a description of someone or something in a book, film etc: **[+of]** *The novel is a portrait of life in Harlem in the 1940s.*

portray /pɔːˈtreɪ $ pɔːr-/ v [T] **1** to describe or show something or someone in a story, film etc: *a film that portrays the life of Charlie Chaplin* | **portray sb/sth as sth** *The incident was portrayed as a defeat for the President.* **2** to act the part of a character in a play, film etc **SYN** play: *In 'Out of It' he portrayed a high-school football hero.* —**portrayal** n [C,U]

pose¹ Ac /pəʊz $ poʊz/ v **1 pose a threat/ problem/risk/danger etc** to cause a problem, danger etc: *Officials claim the chemical poses no threat to health.* **2** [I] to sit or stand in a particular position in order to be photographed or painted: **[+for]** *The winning team posed for photographs.* **3 pose a question** *formal* to ask or present a difficult question: *Her book poses several interesting questions about the relationship between mental and physical health.*

PHRASAL VERBS

pose as sb to pretend to be someone else in order to deceive people: *He obtained the drugs by posing as a doctor.*

pose² Ac n **1** [C] the position in which someone stands or sits, especially in a photograph or painting: *She stood in an aggressive pose with one hand on her hip.* **2** [singular] when someone pretends to have a quality or opinion that they do not really have: *He looked confident but she knew it was a pose.*

posh /pɒʃ $ pɑːʃ/ adj *informal* **1** expensive and used by rich people: *a posh hotel* **2** *BrE* relating to people from a high social class: *a posh voice*

position¹ /pəˈzɪʃən/ n

1 [C usually singular] the situation that someone is in: **in a position** *He's in a difficult position.* | *changes in the company's financial position* | **be in a position to do sth** (=be able to do something) *I'm afraid I'm not in a position to advise you.*

2 [C] the way someone is standing, sitting, or lying, or the direction that an object is pointing in: **in a position** *Lie in a comfortable position.* | *Make sure the switch is in the 'off' position.*

3 [C] the place where someone or something is, in relation to other things: *The position of the hotel makes it popular with young families.* **THESAURUS** PLACE

4 [C,U] the place where someone or something should be: **into/in position** *The lid was put into position and screwed down.* | **out of position** *Some of the tiles had slipped out of position.*

5 [C] someone's level or importance in a society or organization: *Women's position in society has changed.* | **position of power/authority** *Voters are in a position of power.*

6 [C] the opinion that someone has, especially the opinion of a government or organization: **[+on]** *the US government's position on global warming*

7 [C] *formal* a job in a particular organization: *He became president of the club in 1952 and* **held the position** *for over 30 years.* | **[+of]** *Hart will shortly* **take up** *the* **position** *of marketing director.* **THESAURUS** JOB

8 [C] the place where you play in relation to other players in a sports team: *'What* **position** *do you* **play***?' 'Goalkeeper.'*

9 [C] your place in a race or competition in relation to other people: **(in) 2nd/3rd/4th etc position** *Alesi finished in third position.*

position² v [T] to put something or someone in a particular position: **position sth on/against/above etc sth** *He positioned the hat carefully on his head.* | **position yourself** *Two guards positioned themselves at the door.*

positive Ac /ˈpɒzətɪv $ ˈpɑː-/ adj

1 hopeful and confident **OPP** negative: *You should try and be more positive.* | **positive attitude/approach** *a positive attitude to life* **THESAURUS** SURE

2 good or useful **OPP** negative: *Reducing stress has a* **positive effect** *on health.* | *The school has made a* **positive contribution** *to the community.* | *I wanted to do* **something positive** *to help him.*

3 expressing support, agreement, or approval **OPP** negative: *We've had a* **positive response** *to our suggestions.*

4 showing that you definitely want to achieve something: *The situation requires* **positive action** *by the government.* | *We're taking* **positive steps** *to ensure that it doesn't happen again.*

5 [not before noun] very sure that something is true **SYN** certain: *'Are you sure you don't want a drink?' 'Positive.'* | **[+(that)]** *I'm absolutely positive I locked the door.*

6 showing that there can be no doubt that something is true: *the first positive evidence that life exists on other planets*

7 a scientific test that is positive shows that a chemical or medical condition is present **OPP** negative: *He* **tested positive** *for drugs.*

8 *technical* a positive number is higher than zero

9 *technical* having the type of electrical charge that is carried by PROTONS

positively Ac /ˈpɒzətɪvli $ ˈpɑː-/ adv **1** *spoken* used to emphasize what you are saying, especially when it is surprising: *Some of these diets for losing weight are positively dangerous.* **2** in a way that shows you agree with or approve of something: *Local people have responded positively to the news.* **3** in a way that shows you are thinking about the good parts of a situation rather than the bad parts: *Try and think more positively.*

possess /pəˈzes/ v [T] *formal* to own or have something: *The fire destroyed everything he possessed.* | *She possesses considerable skill.* **THESAURUS** OWN —**possessor** n [C]

PHRASES

what possessed you/him etc? *spoken* used when someone has done something stupid and you cannot understand why: *What possessed you to ask a question like that?*

possessed /pə'zest/ *adj* controlled by an evil SPIRIT

possession /pə'zeʃən/ *n*
1 [C usually plural] something that you own SYN **belongings**: *Prisoners were allowed no **personal possessions**.* | **treasured/prized possession** (=one that is very important to you) *One of my most treasured possessions is a book my grandfather gave me.*
2 [U] *formal* when you have or own something: **in sb's possession** *The land remained in the duke's possession for many years.* | **be in possession of sth** *He was found in possession of a stolen car.* | *How did the books **come into** your **possession**?* | *The court has **taken possession of** the documents.*

possessive /pə'zesɪv/ *adj* **1** wanting someone to love and spend time with you and no one else: *a possessive husband* | **[+of/about]** *She's very possessive of her children.* **2** not wanting other people to use your things **3** *technical* used in grammar to describe words that show who something belongs to: *'Ours' and 'mine' are possessive pronouns.*

possibility /ˌpɒsə'bɪləti $ ˌpɑː-/ *n* (*plural* **possibilities**)
1 [C,U] something that may happen or may be true: **[+of]** *the possibility of an enemy attack* | **[+(that)]** *She refused to consider the possibility that he was lying to her.* | **a real/distinct/strong possibility** (=something that is likely to happen or be true) *There's a distinct possibility that the victim knew her killer.*
2 [C] one of the things that you could do: *I'm not sure what I want to study but French is one possibility.* | **[+of]** *We're **exploring the possibilities** of opening a club in the city.*

possible /'pɒsəbəl $ 'pɑː-/ *adj*
1 if something is possible, it can be done OPP **impossible**: **Is it possible** to get tickets for the game? | *Computer technology **makes it possible for** many people to work from home.* | *I want to get back by 5 o'clock **if possible**.* | **as soon/quickly/much etc as possible** (=as soon etc as you can) *Please reply to the invitation as soon as possible.* | **wherever/whenever possible** *Get fresh air and some exercise whenever possible.*
2 something that is possible may happen or may be true, but is not certain: **It's possible that** *we might be late.* | *There seem to be only two **possible explanations**.* | *the **possible causes** of rising crime*
3 the best/worst/greatest etc possible the best, worst etc that can exist or be achieved: *She was determined to get the best possible price for her paintings.*

possibly /'pɒsəbli $ 'pɑː-/ *adv*
1 used to say that something may be true or likely, but you are not sure SYN **perhaps**, **maybe**: *The journey will take three hours – possibly more.* | *'Are you going to have a picnic?' 'Possibly. It depends on the weather.'* THESAURUS ▶ MAYBE
2 used to emphasize that something is impossible or very surprising: *I couldn't possibly eat all that!* | *How could anyone possibly find out?*
PHRASES
could/can you possibly *spoken* used to make a polite request: *Could you possibly open the window for me?*

post¹ /pəʊst $ poʊst/ *n*
1 [U] *BrE* the official system for sending letters, packages etc SYN **mail**: **in the post** *The letter's in the post.* | **by post** *He sent it by post.*
2 [U] *BrE* letters or packages that are delivered to your house SYN **mail**: *Is there any post for me?*
3 [C] *formal* a job in a particular organization → **position**: *She has **held** the **post** (=had the job) since 1999.* | **[+of]** *She **applied for** the **post** of tutor.*
4 [C] an upright piece of wood or metal that is fixed into the ground
5 [C] the place where a soldier or guard stands to do their job

post² *v* [T]
1 *BrE* to send a letter or package by post SYN **mail**: *She posted the letter on her way to work.* | **post sth (off) to sb** *Can you post this card to my Dad?*
2 to send someone to a place to work: **post sb to London/Germany etc** *He joined the army and was posted to Corsica.*
3 (*also* **post up**) to put a notice about something on a wall or board: *The students' test results were posted on the board.*
4 to put a message or document on the Internet, so that other people can see it
PHRASES
keep sb posted to regularly tell someone the most recent news about something: *You will keep me posted, won't you?*

post- /pəʊst $ poʊst/ *prefix* after: *the post-election period*

postage /'pəʊstɪdʒ $ 'poʊs-/ *n* [U] the money charged for sending a letter or package by post

postal /'pəʊstl $ 'poʊs-/ *adj* [only before noun] relating to the official system for sending letters, packages etc: *the postal service*

'postal order *n* [C] *BrE* an official document that you buy at a post office and send to someone so they can exchange it for money

postbox /'pəʊstbɒks $ 'poʊstbɑːks/ *n* [C] *BrE* a box in a public place where you put letters that you want to send SYN **mailbox** *AmE*

postcard /'pəʊstkɑːd $ 'poʊstkɑːrd/ *n* [C] a card that you can send by post without an envelope, often one with a picture on it: **[+of]** *a postcard of Paris*

postcode /'pəʊstkəʊd $ 'poʊstkoʊd/ *n* [C] *BrE* a group of letters and numbers that you write at the end of an address SYN **zip code** *AmE*

poster /'pəʊstə $ 'poʊstər/ *n* [C] a large notice, picture etc used to advertise something or as a decoration: *She was **putting up posters** in her bedroom.* | **[+of]** *posters of movie stars* THESAURUS ▶ ADVERTISEMENT

posterity /pɒ'sterəti $ pɑː-/ *n* [U] the people who will live after you are dead: **for posterity** *I'm saving these pictures for posterity.*

postgraduate /ˌpəʊst'grædʒuət $ ˌpoʊst'grædʒuət/ *n* [C] *BrE* someone who is studying at a university to get a MASTER'S DEGREE or PHD SYN **graduate student** *AmE* —**postgraduate** *adj*

posthumous /'pɒstjəməs $ 'pɑ:stʃə-/ *adj* happening after someone's death: *a posthumous collection of his articles* —**posthumously** *adv*

posting /'pəʊstɪŋ $ 'poʊs-/ *n* [C] *especially BrE* **1** a job in a foreign country that your employer sends you to do: [+to] *His first posting was to Jedda.* **2** a message sent to an Internet discussion group

'Post-it (*also* **'Post-it ,note**) *n* [C] *trademark* a small piece of coloured paper that sticks to things, used for leaving notes for people

postman /'pəʊstmən $ 'poʊst-/ *n* [C] (*plural* **postmen** /-mən/) *BrE* someone whose job is to collect and deliver letters SYN **mailman** *AmE*

postmark /'pəʊstmɑ:k $ 'poʊstmɑ:rk/ *n* [C] a mark on an envelope, package etc that shows the place and time it was posted —**postmark** *v* [T]

post-mortem /,pəʊst'mɔ:təm $,poʊst'mɔ:r-/ *n* [C] an official examination of a dead body to discover why the person died

postnatal /,pəʊst'neɪtl◂ $,poʊst-/ *adj* relating to the time after a baby is born: *postnatal care*

'post ,office *n* [C] a place where you can buy stamps, and send letters and packages

postpone /pəʊs'pəʊn $ poʊs'poʊn/ *v* [T] to change the date or time of an event to a later one: *The meeting has been postponed until July.* THESAURUS DELAY —**postponement** *n* [C,U]

postscript /'pəʊs,skrɪpt $ 'poʊs-/ *n* [C] a PS

posture /'pɒstʃə $ 'pɑ:stʃər/ *n* [C,U] the way that you sit or stand: **good/bad posture** *Bad posture can cause back problems.*

postwar /,pəʊst'wɔ:◂ $,poʊst'wɔ:r◂/ *adj* after a war, especially World War II

posy /'pəʊzi $ 'poʊ-/ *n* [C] (*plural* **posies**) a small BUNCH of flowers

POTS

teapot

pot

coffee pot

paint pots

pot¹ /pɒt $ pɑːt/ *n* [C]
1 a round container, especially one used for cooking or storing food → **saucepan**, **flowerpot**, **jar**: *pots and pans* | *a plant growing in a pot* | [+of] *a pot of honey* → see picture at CONTAINER
2 a container used to make tea or coffee. It has a handle, and a tube for pouring: [+of] *I'll make a pot of tea.* → MELTING POT

pot² *v* [T] (**potted**, **potting**) to put a plant in a pot filled with soil

potassium /pə'tæsiəm/ *n* [U] a chemical ELEMENT, used, for example, in substances that make crops grow

potato /pə'teɪtəʊ $ -toʊ/ *n* [C,U] (*plural* **potatoes**) a round white vegetable with a brown or pale yellow skin that grows under the ground: **mashed/roast/ boiled potato** | **baked/jacket potato** (=cooked with its skin on) | *I'll peel the potatoes.* → see picture on page A5 → COUCH POTATO, SWEET POTATO

po'tato chips *n* [plural] *AmE* very thin pieces of potato cooked in oil and eaten cold SYN **crisps** *BrE*

potent /'pəʊtənt $ 'poʊ-/ *adj* powerful and effective: *potent drugs* | *a potent influence* —**potency** *n* [U]

potential¹ Ac /pə'tenʃəl/ *adj* [only before noun] likely to become a particular type of person or thing in the future: **potential customers/buyers/clients etc** *The salesmen were eager to impress potential customers.* | *Potential buyers have expressed interest in the building.* | **potential problem/danger/threat etc** *a potential threat to international peace* —**potentially** *adv*: *a potentially dangerous situation*

potential² Ac *n* **1** [singular, U] the possibility that something will develop in a particular way or do something: [+for] *There is still considerable potential for development.* | [+of] *the potential of the Internet to create jobs* **2** [U] abilities or qualities that may make someone or something very successful in the future: [+as] *She was told she had great potential as a singer.* | **achieve/realize your (full) potential** (=become as successful as you can) *She wanted to achieve her full potential in her new job.*

pothole /'pɒthəʊl $ 'pɑ:thoʊl/ *n* [C] a hole in the surface of a road → see picture at HOLE¹ THESAURUS HOLE

potholing /'pɒt,həʊlɪŋ $ 'pɑ:t,hoʊl-/ *n* [U] the sport of climbing down into CAVES under the ground

potion /'pəʊʃən $ 'poʊ-/ *n* [C] *literary* a magic drink

,pot 'luck *BrE*, **potluck** *AmE* /,pɒt'lʌk◂ $,pɑːt-/ *n* **take pot luck** to choose something without knowing very much about it, and hope that it will be what you want: *We hadn't booked a hotel so we had to take pot luck.*

potted /'pɒtɪd $ 'pɑː-/ *adj* [only before noun] **1** a potted plant is grown in a pot indoors **2 potted history/biography/version** *BrE* a short account of something: *Your employer will have a personnel file containing a potted history of your career with the company.*

potter¹ /'pɒtə $ 'pɑːtər/ *n* [C] someone who makes pottery

potter² (*also* **potter around/about**) *v* [I] *BrE* to spend time slowly doing pleasant things: *I was just pottering in the garden.*

pottery /'pɒtəri $ 'pɑː-/ *n* [U] **1** pots, dishes etc made out of baked clay **2** the activity of making objects out of baked clay

potty¹ /'pɒti $ 'pɑːti/ *n* [C] (*plural* **potties**) a container used by very young children as a toilet

potty² *adj BrE informal* crazy or silly

pouch /paʊtʃ/ n [C] **1** a small leather or cloth bag **2** a pocket of skin that animals such as KANGAROOS carry their babies in

poultry /ˈpəʊltri $ ˈpoʊl-/ n [plural] birds such as chickens and ducks that are kept for their meat and eggs

pounce /paʊns/ v [I] to suddenly move forward and attack or catch someone or something: **[+on]** Police are hunting an attacker who pounced on a young woman.

PHRASAL VERBS

pounce on sb/sth **1** to criticize someone's mistakes or ideas quickly and eagerly **2** to accept or take something quickly and eagerly: She pounced on the opportunity to work in the Paris office.

pound¹ /paʊnd/ n [C]
1 (written abbreviation **lb**) a unit for measuring weight, equal to 16 OUNCES or 453.6 grams: **[+of]** a pound of apples | Mary **weighs** 130 **pounds**.
2 (written symbol **£**) the standard unit of money in Britain and some other countries: The dress cost £50. | a pound coin | a ten pound note

pound² v **1** [I,T] to hit something hard many times, making a lot of noise: **[+on]** She pounded on the door with both hands. **2** [I] if your heart pounds, it beats very quickly **3** [I] to walk or run quickly with heavy steps: **[+up/along etc]** He pounded up the stairs.

pour /pɔː $ pɔːr/ v

POUR

1 [T] to make a liquid flow out of a container: **pour sth into/over etc sth** Pour the milk into a jug. | **pour sb sth** He poured himself a drink.
2 [I] to flow or come out quickly and in large amounts: **[+out of/from etc]** Tears poured down her cheeks. | Smoke was pouring from the engine.
3 (also **pour down**) [I] to rain heavily: **It poured with rain** all afternoon. → RAIN², WEATHER¹
4 [I] if people or things pour into or out of a place, a lot of them arrive or leave at the same time: **[+in/out of]** Letters of complaint poured in.

PHRASAL VERBS

pour sth ↔ **out** to tell someone all your unhappy thoughts or feelings: Sonia poured out her grief in a letter to her sister. | I ended up **pouring** my **heart out** to a stranger.

pout /paʊt/ v [I] to push out your lower lip because you are annoyed, or in order to look sexually attractive —**pout** n [C]

poverty /ˈpɒvəti $ ˈpɑːvərti/ n [U] when people are extremely poor: Poverty and unemployment are increasing. | **in poverty** families living in extreme poverty

PHRASES

the poverty line (also the poverty level AmE) the income below which someone is officially considered to be very poor and in need of help: Nearly a

quarter of the city's residents live below the poverty line.

ˈpoverty-ˌstricken adj extremely poor

POW /ˌpiː əʊ ˈdʌbəljuː $ -oʊ-/ n [C] a PRISONER OF WAR

powder¹ /ˈpaʊdə $ -ər/ n [C,U] a dry substance in the form of very small grains: soap powder | curry powder → **TALCUM POWDER, WASHING POWDER** —**powdery** adj: powdery snow

powder² v [T] to put powder on your skin, usually in order to make it look better

powdered /ˈpaʊdəd $ -ərd/ adj in the form of powder: powdered milk

power¹ /ˈpaʊə $ paʊr/ n
1 [U] the ability to control or influence people or events → **powerful, powerless**: the power of the media | **[+over]** People want to feel they have some power over their future. | **political/economic power** Workers had little political power.
2 [U] the position of having political control of a country: **in power** The Socialist Party were in power for five years. | De Gaulle **came to power** (=began to control his country) in 1958. | **power base** (=an area or group of people whose support makes a politician or leader powerful) His strongest power base was in the northern state of Hayana.
3 [C,U] the legal right or authority to do something: **power to do sth** The police have the power to stop and search people. | **be in/within sb's power** (=be legally possible for someone) It's within the power of the council to make this payment. | The ambassador promised to **do everything in** his **power** to get the hostages released.
4 [U] energy that is used to make a machine work or produce light, heat etc: nuclear power | wind power | **power failure/cut** (=a time when the supply of electricity stops) The storm caused a power cut.
5 [C] a country that has a lot of influence over other countries: a meeting of world powers
6 [U] force or physical strength: the power of the explosion
7 [C,U] a natural or special ability to do something: After the accident he lost the **power of speech** (=ability to speak). | **powers of observation/concentration/persuasion** Her powers of concentration were not helped by the noise. → **BALANCE OF POWER, WORLD POWER**

PHRASES

the powers that be the people who have positions of authority: The powers that be would not want this story to become known.

power² v [T] to supply power to a machine: The camera is powered by a small battery. | **battery-powered/solar-powered etc** (=made to work by a particular type of power)

ˈpower ˌbroker n [C] a person or country that has a lot of political influence and power

powerful /ˈpaʊəfəl $ ˈpaʊr-/ adj
1 able to control and influence people and events **OPP powerless**: the most powerful man in Hollywood | rich and powerful nations
2 having a lot of physical power, strength, or force:

The engine is extremely powerful. | *powerful weapons* | *a powerful voice* THESAURUS STRONG

3 having a strong effect: *a powerful argument* | *a powerful influence* | *powerful drugs* —**powerfully** adv

powerless /'paʊələs $ 'paʊr-/ adj unable to stop or control something: **powerless to do sth** *The police were powerless to stop last night's shootings.* | **[+against]** *Local people were powerless against the rising flood water.* —**powerlessness** n [U]

'power ,station (also **'power plant**) n [C] a building where electricity is made

'power tool n [C] a tool that works by electricity

pp. (also **pp** BrE) the written abbreviation of **pages**: *Read pp 20–35.*

PR /,pi: 'ɑ: $ -'ɑːr/ n [U] (**public relations**) the work of explaining to people what an organization does, so that they will approve of the organization: *a PR company*

practicable /'præktɪkəbəl/ adj formal possible in a particular situation: *It's not practicable to publish all the results.*

practical¹ /'præktɪkəl/ adj
1 relating to real situations and events rather than ideas → **theoretical**: *He's had no practical experience of teaching.* | *the practical problems of old age* | *The charity offers practical help to homeless people.*
2 likely to succeed or be effective OPP **impractical**: *A practical solution has to be found.*
3 useful and suitable for a particular purpose OPP **impractical**: *Remember to wear practical shoes and warm clothing.*
4 good at planning and making decisions OPP **impractical**
5 good at repairing or making things: *I'm not very practical – I can't even change a lightbulb.*

practical² n [C] BrE a lesson or test where you do or make something rather than writing THESAURUS TEST

practicality /,præktɪ'kæləti/ n **1 practicalities** [plural] the real facts of a situation, rather than ideas about how it might be: **[+of]** *the practicalities of the job* **2** [U] how suitable something is, or whether it will be effective: *I'm not sure about the practicality of the idea.*

,practical 'joke n [C] a trick that is intended to surprise someone and make other people laugh at them

practically /'præktɪkli/ adv
1 practically all/every/no etc *That's practically everyone we know!* | *The theatre was practically empty.* THESAURUS ALMOST
2 in a sensible way

practice /'præktɪs/ n
1 a) [U] the activity of doing something regularly to improve your skill: *It takes a lot of practice to be a good piano player.* **b)** [singular, U] a regular occasion when people meet to improve their skill at doing something: **football/rugby/choir etc practice**
2 [C,U] something that people do often, especially in a particular way: *dangerous working practices* | **common/standard/normal practice** (=the usual way of doing something) *The use of chemical sprays*

has become common practice. | **the practice of doing sth** *the widespread practice of dumping waste in the sea*
3 [C] the work of a doctor or lawyer, or the place where they work: **private practice** (=the business of a professional person that is independent of a bigger or government-controlled organization) | **legal/medical practice**

PHRASES
in practice used to say what really happens, instead of what people think may happen: *It looks difficult to make, but in practice it's quite easy.*
be out of practice to be unable to do something well because you have not done it for a long time: *I'd like to sing with you, but I'm so out of practice.*
put sth into practice to start using an idea, plan etc: *It gave him the chance to put his ideas into practice.*

practise BrE, **practice** AmE /'præktɪs/ v
1 [I,T] to do something a lot in order to improve your skill: **practise doing sth** *Today we're going to practise parking.* | **[+for]** *He's practicing for his driving test.* | **practise sth on sb** *Everyone wants to practise their English on me.*
2 [I,T] to work as a doctor or lawyer: *He has been practising law for 15 years.* | **[+as]** *Gemma is now practising as a dentist.*
3 [T] to use a particular method or custom: *a technique not widely practised in Europe*

PHRASES
practise what you preach to do what you always say other people should do: *She didn't always practise what she preached.*

THESAURUS

practise BrE, **practice** AmE to do something a lot or regularly in order to improve your skill: *I want to practise my French.* | *He was practising hitting the ball over the net.*
train to prepare for a race or game by exercising and practising physical movements: *The team are training for the big match on Saturday.*
rehearse to practise a play, speech, or concert so that you will be ready to perform it: *The producer made us rehearse the last scene again.* | *The band are rehearsing for their world tour.*
work on sth to practise a particular skill so that your general ability in something improves: *You need to work on your pronunciation.*

---

practised BrE, **practiced** AmE /'præktɪst/ adj good at doing something because you have done it many times before: *a practised performer* | **practised in (doing) sth** *He was well practised in giving speeches.*

practising BrE, **practicing** AmE /'præktɪsɪŋ/ adj **practising Catholic/Jew/Muslim etc** someone who follows the rules and customs of a particular religion

practitioner Ac /præk'tɪʃənə $ -ər/ n [C] formal someone who works as a doctor or lawyer: **medical/legal practitioner** → GENERAL PRACTITIONER

pragmatic /præg'mætɪk/ adj dealing with problems in a sensible and practical way rather than following a set of ideas: *a pragmatic approach to education* —**pragmatism** /'prægmətɪzəm/ *n* [U] —**pragmatist** *n* [C]

prairie /'preəri $ 'preri/ *n* [C] a large area of flat land in North America that is covered in grass

praise[1] /preɪz/ *v* [T] to say that you admire someone or something they have done, especially publicly OPP **criticize**: **praise sb for (doing) sth** *The Mayor praised the rescue team for their courage.* | *a* **highly praised** *novel*

THESAURUS

praise to say that you admire someone or something they have done, especially publicly: *The critics praised the film.* | *His boss praised him for the way he handled the situation.*

congratulate to tell someone that you think it is good that they have achieved something: *I want to congratulate you on your exam results.*

compliment to say to someone that you like how they look, or something they have done: *Everyone complimented her on her new dress.* | *Mark complimented Gerry on his speech.*

flatter to praise someone in order to please them or get something from them, although you do not mean it: *I'll try flattering him a bit – that will probably work.*

---

praise[2] *n* [U] things you say to praise someone or something: *Most parents are* **full of praise for** *the school* (=praise it a lot). | **in praise of sth** *a poem in praise of freedom*

praiseworthy /'preɪzwɜːði $ -ɜːr-/ *adj formal* something that is praiseworthy deserves praise

pram /præm/ *n* [C] *BrE* a thing on wheels that a baby can lie in and be pushed along SYN **baby carriage** *AmE*

prance /prɑːns $ præns/ *v* [I] **1** to walk or dance around in a way that makes people notice you: **[+around]** *He started prancing around in front of the cameras.* **2** if a horse prances, it moves with high steps

prank /præŋk/ *n* [C] a trick that is intended to make someone look silly: *a childish prank*

prat /præt/ *n* [C] *BrE informal* a stupid person: *Of course it's not, you prat!*

prattle /'prætl/ *v* [I] to talk continuously about silly or unimportant things —**prattle** *n* [U]

prawn /prɔːn $ prɒːn/ *n* [C] a small pink sea animal that you can eat → see picture at SHELLFISH

pray /preɪ/ *v* [I,T]
1 to speak to God in order to ask for something or give thanks: **[+for]** *Let us pray for peace.* | **[+to]** *He prayed to God for forgiveness.*
2 to hope for something very strongly: **[+for]** *We're praying for good weather for the wedding.* | **[+(that)]** *Paul was praying that no one had noticed.*

prayer /preə $ prer/ *n*
1 [C] words that you say to God: *The children knelt down to* **say their prayers.** | **[+for]** *a prayer for the dead* | *a prayer book*
2 [U] when someone prays: *the power of prayer* | **in prayer** *They bowed their heads in prayer.*

3 prayers [plural] when people pray together at an arranged time: *morning prayers*

pre- /priː/ *prefix* before: *the prewar period* | *pre-school children*

preach /priːtʃ/ *v* [I,T] **1** to give a speech about a religious subject, usually in a church: *The pastor preached a sermon on forgiveness.* **2** to try to persuade other people to do, support, or believe something, often in an annoying way: *politicians who preach fairness and equality*

preacher /'priːtʃə $ -ər/ *n* [C] someone who gives talks at religious meetings

preamble /pri'æmbəl $ 'priːæmbəl/ *n* [C] *formal* a statement at the beginning of a book or speech, explaining what it is about

prearranged /ˌpriːə'reɪndʒd◂/ *adj* planned or decided before: *At a prearranged signal, everyone stood up.*

precarious /prɪ'keəriəs $ -'ker-/ *adj* **1** a precarious situation may easily or quickly become worse: *The club is in a* **precarious** *financial position.* **2** not held in place firmly and likely to fall —**precariously** *adv*

precaution /prɪ'kɔːʃən $ -'kɒː-/ *n* [C] something that you do to prevent something bad or dangerous from happening: *fire precautions* | **[+against]** *precautions against theft* | **as a precaution** *She was taken to hospital as a precaution.* | *I* **took the precaution of** *insuring my camera.* —**precautionary** *adj*: *Residents were evacuated as a precautionary measure.*

precede Ac /prɪ'siːd/ *v* [T] *formal* to happen or exist before something else OPP **follow**: *The fire was preceded by a loud explosion.* —**preceding** *adj* [only before noun]: *an increase of 18% on the preceding year*

precedence Ac /'presɪdəns/ *n* **take/have precedence (over sth)** to be considered more important or urgent than something else: *This project takes precedence over everything else.*

precedent Ac /'presɪdənt/ *n* [C,U] an action or official decision that is used as an example for similar actions or decisions taken in the future: *The trial* **set a precedent** *for civil rights.*

precinct /'priːsɪŋkt/ *n* [C] **1 shopping/pedestrian precinct** *BrE* an area of a town where cars are not allowed and where people can walk and shop **2** *AmE* a part of a city that has its own police force, local government etc: *the 12th precinct* **3 precincts** [plural] the area around an important building: *the precincts of the cathedral*

precious[1] /'preʃəs/ *adj* **1** something that is precious is valuable or important and should not be wasted: **precious seconds/minutes/time etc** *We cannot afford to waste precious time.* | *the planet's precious resources* **2** precious memories or possessions are very important to you because they remind you of people or events in your life: **[+to]** *I know it's old, but it's very precious to me.* **3** valuable because of being rare: **precious metal** (=a metal such as gold or silver) | **precious stone** (=a jewel such as a diamond or ruby) THESAURUS VALUABLE

precious[2] *adv* **precious little/few** *informal* very little or very few: *We had precious little time left.*

precipice /'presɪpɪs/ n [C] a very steep side of a mountain or cliff

precipitate /prɪ'sɪpɪteɪt/ v [T] *formal* to make something happen suddenly: *The President's death precipitated a political crisis.*

precipitation /prɪˌsɪpɪ'teɪʃən/ n [U] *formal* rain or snow

precipitous /prɪ'sɪpɪtəs/ adj *formal* **1** dangerously steep or high: *precipitous cliffs* **2** very sudden: *a* **precipitous decline** *in profit*

précis /'preɪsi/ $ preɪ'si:/ n [C] (*plural* **précis**) *formal* a piece of writing giving only the main ideas of a longer piece of writing, speech etc

precise Ac /prɪ'saɪs/ adj **1** precise information, details etc are exact, clear, and correct: *We don't yet have* **precise details** *of the agreement.* **2** [only before noun] used to emphasize that you are talking about an exact thing: *No one seems to know the precise cause of the illness. | At that precise moment, her husband walked in.*

PHRASES

to be precise used to add exact details about something: *It's 9 o'clock, or 9.02 to be precise.*

precisely Ac /prɪ'saɪsli/ adv **1** exactly: [+what/how/why etc] *That's precisely what I mean.* | *at precisely 4 o'clock* **THESAURUS** EXACTLY **2** used to emphasize that something is completely correct or true: *The photos are fascinating* **precisely because** *they are of such ordinary situations.* **3** *spoken* used to say that you agree completely with someone: *'So you want them to give it all back.' 'Precisely.'*

precision Ac /prɪ'sɪʒən/ n [U] when something is done in a very exact way: **with precision** *Some animals can find their way in the dark with great precision.*

preclude /prɪ'klu:d/ v [T] *formal* to make it impossible for something to happen: **preclude sb from (doing) sth** *Bad eyesight may preclude you from driving.*

precocious /prɪ'kəʊʃəs $ -'koʊ-/ adj a precocious child shows skill or intelligence at a young age, or behaves in an adult way —**precociously** adv

preconceived /ˌpri:kən'si:vd◀/ adj [only before noun] preconceived ideas are formed before you know what something is really like: *He has a lot of preconceived ideas about life in America.*

preconception /ˌpri:kən'sepʃən/ n [C] an idea that is formed before you know what something is really like

precondition /ˌpri:kən'dɪʃən/ n [C] something that must happen before something else can happen: [+for/of] *An end to the fighting is a precondition for talks.*

precursor /prɪ'kɜ:sə $ -'kɜ:rsər/ n [C] *formal* something that existed or happened before something else and influenced its development: [+of] *a machine that was the precursor of the computer*

predate /pri:'deɪt/ v [T] to happen or exist before something else: *Many of the changes predate the 1981 reforms.*

predator /'predətə $ -ər/ n [C] an animal that kills and eats other animals

predatory /'predətəri $ -tɔ:ri/ adj **1** predatory animals kill and eat other animals **2** *disapproving* trying to use someone's weakness to get an advantage for yourself

predecessor /'pri:dəsesə $ 'predəsesər/ n [C] **1** the person who had a job before the person who has it now: *My predecessor worked here for ten years.* **2** a machine, system etc that existed before another one

predetermined /ˌpri:dɪ'tɜ:mɪnd $ -ɜ:r-/ adj *formal* already decided or arranged: *Schools cannot exceed a predetermined level of spending.*

predicament /prɪ'dɪkəmənt/ n [C] a difficult situation when you do not know what is the best thing to do: **in a predicament** *Many other young couples are in a similar predicament.*

predicate /'predɪkət/ n [C] the part of a sentence that gives information about the subject. In the sentence 'He ran out of the house', 'ran out of the house' is the predicate. → **subject**

predicative /prɪ'dɪkətɪv $ 'predəkeɪ-/ adj a predicative adjective comes after a verb and describes the subject, for example 'sad' in 'She is sad' → **attributive**

predict Ac /prɪ'dɪkt/ v [T] to say that something will happen, before it happens → **prediction**: *Organisers are predicting a close race.* | [+(that)] *We predict that student numbers will double in the next ten years.* | [+what/how/whether etc] *It's difficult to predict exactly what the effects will be.*

THESAURUS

predict to say that something will happen, before it happens: *It's impossible to predict how people will behave in a crisis.*

forecast to say what is likely to happen in the future with the weather, or the economic or political situation, when it is your job to do this: *They're forecasting snow next week. | Economists forecast that there would be a recession.*

know to realize that someone would do something, or something would happen: *I knew you'd say that! | No one could have known that there would be a fall in oil prices.*

foresee to know that something is going to happen before it happens, so that you are ready to deal with it: *The government was criticized for not foreseeing the problem earlier.*

predictable Ac /prɪ'dɪktəbəl/ adj behaving or happening in the way that you expect, and not different or interesting: *an entertaining but predictable film* —**predictably** adv: *Predictably, they rejected the plan.* —**predictability** /prɪˌdɪktə'brləti/ n [U]

prediction Ac /prɪ'dɪkʃən/ n [C,U] when you say what you think will happen in the future: *It's hard to* **make a prediction** *about who'll win the championship this year.* | [+of] *predictions of climate change*

predilection /ˌpri:dɪ'lekʃən $ ˌpredl'ek-/ n [C] *formal* a strong liking for something: [+for] *a predilection for chocolate*

predisposed /ˌpriːdɪsˈpəʊzd $ -ˈpoʊzd/ *adj* **be predisposed to/towards sth** to be likely to behave in a particular way, or to have particular problems: *Some people are predisposed to depression.*

predisposition /ˌpriːdɪspəˈzɪʃən/ *n* [C] a tendency to behave in a particular way, or to have particular problems: **[+to/towards]** *a predisposition to violence*

predominance Ac /prɪˈdɒmənəns $ -ˈdɑː-/ *n* **1** [singular] when there is more of one type of thing or person in a group than of any other type: **[+of]** *the predominance of boys in the class* **2** [U] the most power or importance in a place or situation: *rival supermarkets fighting to achieve predominance*

predominant Ac /prɪˈdɒmɪnənt $ -ˈdɑː-/ *adj* more powerful or common than other people or things: *In this painting, the predominant colour is black.*

predominantly Ac /prɪˈdɒmənəntli $ -ˈdɑː-/ *adv* mostly or mainly: *a college in a predominantly working class area*

predominate Ac /prɪˈdɒməneɪt $ -ˈdɑː-/ *v* [I] *formal* if something predominates in a group or area, it is more important or more common than other things: *areas where industries such as mining predominate*

pre-eminent /priˈemɪnənt/ *adj* much more important or powerful than other people or things of the same kind: *a pre-eminent expert in cancer treatment* —**pre-eminence** *n* [U]

pre-empt /priˈempt/ *v* [T] to make what someone has planned to do unnecessary or not effective by doing something first: *The deal pre-empted a strike by rail workers.* —**pre-emptive** *adj: a pre-emptive attack*

preen /priːn/ *v* **1 preen yourself** to spend a lot of time making yourself look attractive: *He's always preening himself in the mirror.* **2** [I,T] if a bird preens, or preens itself, it makes its feathers clean and smooth

pre-existing /ˌpriːɪɡˈzɪstɪŋ◂/ *adj* existing already, or before something else: *a pre-existing arrangement*

prefabricated /priːˈfæbrɪkeɪtɪd/ *adj* a prefabricated building is built by putting together large parts which have already been made

preface /ˈprefɪs/ *n* [C] an introduction at the beginning of a book

prefect /ˈpriːfekt/ *n* [C] *BrE* an older student in a school who has special powers and duties

prefer /prɪˈfɜː $ -ˈfɜːr/ *v* [T] (**preferred, preferring**) to like or want someone or something more than someone or something else → **preference**: *Would you prefer a hot or a cold drink?* | **prefer sb/sth to sb/sth** *She prefers walking to driving.* | **prefer to do sth** *I'd prefer not to talk about it at the moment.* | **prefer doing sth** *Most kids prefer wearing casual clothes.* | *Or,* **if you prefer,** *you can email us.* | **[+(that)]** *formal: The firm would prefer that the details were not made public.*
PHRASES
I would prefer it if *spoken* used to tell someone politely not to do something: *I'd prefer it if you didn't smoke in the house.*

preferable /ˈprefərəbəl/ *adj* better or more suitable: **[+to]** *Anything is preferable to war.*

preferably /ˈprefərəbli/ *adv* used to show which person, thing, place etc would be the best or most suitable: *You'll need some form of identification, preferably a passport.*

preference /ˈprefərəns/ *n* [C,U] when someone likes something more than something else: *Which style you choose is just a matter of **personal preference.*** | **[+for]** *Some parents **have** a strong **preference** for one school or another.* | **in preference to sth** *He drinks coffee in preference to tea.* | *You can list up to five choices,* **in order of preference.**
PHRASES
give/show preference (to sb) to treat someone better or give them an advantage over other people: *Preference will be given to candidates who speak foreign languages.*

preferential /ˌprefəˈrenʃəl◂/ *adj* if you are given preferential treatment, you are treated better than another person, and have an advantage over them: *Why should she get preferential treatment?*

prefix /ˈpriːfɪks/ *n* [C] a group of letters added to the beginning of a word to make a new word → **affix, suffix**

pregnancy /ˈpregnənsi/ *n* [C,U] (*plural* **pregnancies**) when a woman is pregnant: *You should try to avoid alcohol during pregnancy.* | *a pregnancy test*

pregnant /ˈpregnənt/ *adj* if a woman or female animal is pregnant, she has an unborn baby growing in her body → **pregnancy**: *a pregnant woman* | *She's three months pregnant.* | *I **got pregnant** when I was only 16.* | **[+with]** *Maria was pregnant with her second child.*
PHRASES
pregnant silence/pause a silence or pause which is full of meaning or emotion: *A pregnant silence filled the air before the winner was announced.*

preheat /ˌpriːˈhiːt/ *v* [T] to heat an OVEN to a particular temperature before it is used to cook something: ***Preheat** the **oven** to 375 degrees.*

prehistoric /ˌpriːhɪˈstɒrɪk◂ $ -ˈstɔː-, -ˈstɑː-/ *adj* relating to the time in history before anything was written down: *prehistoric cave drawings*

prejudge /ˌpriːˈdʒʌdʒ/ *v* [T] *disapproving* to form an opinion about someone or something before you know or have considered all the facts

prejudice¹ /ˈpredʒədɪs/ *n* [C,U] *disapproving* an unreasonable dislike and distrust of people who are different from you, especially because of their race, sex, religion etc: **[+against]** *There's still a lot of prejudice against gay people.* | *the problem of **racial prejudice** in the police force*

THESAURUS
prejudice an unreasonable dislike and distrust of people who are different from you, especially because of their race, sex, religion etc: *racial prejudice* | *prejudice against women* **discrimination** the practice of treating one group of people differently from another in an

unfair way: *It is important to end discrimination against older people.*
racism unfair treatment of people because they belong to a different race: *the struggle against racism*
sexism the belief that one sex, especially women, is weaker, less intelligent etc than the other: *She accused him of sexism.*

prejudice² *v* [T] **1** to influence someone so that they have an unfair opinion about someone or something: **prejudice sb against sth** *I didn't want to say anything that might prejudice him against her.* **2** to have a bad effect on someone's opportunities or chances of success: *Stories in the newspapers are prejudicing their chances of a fair trial.*

prejudiced /ˈpredʒədɪst/ *adj* having an unfair dislike of someone or something, especially because they belong to a particular group: **[+against]** *He's prejudiced against anyone who doesn't have a degree.*
THESAURUS UNFAIR

prejudicial /ˌpredʒəˈdɪʃəl◂/ *adj formal* having a bad effect on someone or something

preliminary¹ Ac /prɪˈlɪmənəri $ -neri/ *adj* [only before noun] happening before something that is more important, often in order to prepare for it: *European leaders meet tomorrow for preliminary talks.* | *the preliminary stages of the competition*

preliminary² Ac *n* [C usually plural] (*plural* **preliminaries**) something that is done or said to introduce or prepare for something else later: *the preliminaries of the competition*

prelude /ˈpreljuːd/ *n* **1 be a prelude to sth** to happen just before something else, often as an introduction to it: *The attack may be a prelude to full-scale war.* **2** [C] a short piece of music that comes before a longer musical piece

premature /ˈpremətʃə, -tʃʊə, ˌpreməˈtʃʊə $ ˌpriːməˈtʃʊr◂/ *adj* **1** happening too early or before the usual time: *Smoking is one of the major causes of premature death.* **2** a premature baby is born too early and is small or weak: *The baby was six weeks premature.* —**prematurely** *adv*: *The sun causes your skin to age prematurely.*

premeditated /priːˈmedɪteɪtɪd $ prɪ-/ *adj* a premeditated attack or crime is planned before it happens: *a premeditated murder* —**premeditation** /priːˌmedɪˈteɪʃən $ prɪ-/ *n* [U]

premenstrual /priːˈmenstruəl/ *adj* happening or relating to the time just before a woman's PERIOD (=the time each month when blood flows from her body)

premier¹ /ˈpremiə $ prɪˈmɪr/ *n* [C] the leader of a government: *the Chinese premier*

premier² *adj* [only before noun] best or most important: *one of Dublin's premier hotels* | *football's Premier League*

premiere /ˈpremieə $ prɪˈmɪr/ *n* [C] the first public performance of a film or play: *a movie premiere* —**premiere** *v* [I,T]

premiership /ˈpremiəʃɪp $ prɪˈmɪrʃɪp/ *n* [C,U] the period when someone is the leader of a government

premise /ˈpremɪs/ *n* **1 premises** [plural] the buildings and land that a shop, company etc uses: **on/off the premises** *No smoking is allowed on the premises.* **2** [C] *formal* a statement or idea that you consider to be true and use to develop other ideas: **[+that]** *The argument is based on the premise that men and women are equal.*

premium¹ /ˈpriːmiəm/ *n* [C] **1** an amount of money that you pay for insurance: *health insurance premiums* **2** an additional amount of money above the usual rate or amount: *The shares are being sold at a premium.*
PHRASES
be at a premium to be difficult to get because there is only a limited amount available: *Parking space is at a premium in most cities.*
put/place a premium on sth to think that one quality or type of thing is much more important than others: *schools that put a premium on exam results*

premium² *adj* **1** of very high quality: *consumer demand for premium products* **2** **premium price/rate** premium prices and rates are higher than the usual ones: *premium rate phone calls*

premonition /ˌpreməˈnɪʃən, ˌpriː-/ *n* [C] a feeling that something bad is going to happen: **[+of/that]** *She had a premonition that her daughter was in danger.*

prenatal /ˌpriːˈneɪtl◂/ *adj* prenatal care is the medical care given to a woman who is going to have a baby SYN antenatal *BrE* → **postnatal**

preoccupation /priːˌɒkjəˈpeɪʃən $ -ɑːk-/ *n* **1** [singular, U] when you think or worry about something all the time: **[+with]** *the artist's preoccupation with death* **2** [C] something that you give all your attention to: *Their main preoccupation was how to feed their families.*

preoccupied /priːˈɒkjəpaɪd $ -ɑːk-/ *adj* thinking or worrying about something a lot, so that you do not pay attention to other things: **[+with]** *I was too preoccupied with my own problems to notice.* —**preoccupy** *v* [T]

prep. (*also* **prep** *BrE*) the written abbreviation of **preposition**

prepaid /ˌpriːˈpeɪd◂/ *adj* if something is prepaid, it is paid for before it is needed or used: *a prepaid envelope*

preparation /ˌprepəˈreɪʃən/ *n*
1 [U] the work of preparing something or preparing for something: **[+for]** *The England team have begun their preparation for next week's game.* | **in preparation for sth** *We've had extra training sessions in preparation for the tests.* | **[+of]** *the preparation of the report* **2 preparations** [plural] arrangements for something that is going to happen: **[+for]** *preparations for the wedding* | *Preparations are being made for the President's visit.* **THESAURUS** PREPARE

preparatory /prɪˈpærətəri $ -tɔːri/ *adj* done in order to get ready for something: *a preparatory meeting*

prepare /prɪˈpeə $ -ˈper/ v
1 [I,T] to make plans or arrangements for something that will happen soon, or to get yourself ready for it: **[+for]** *I haven't even begun to prepare for tomorrow's test.* | **prepare yourself (for sth)** *Prepare yourself for a shock.* | **prepare to do sth** *Just as we were preparing to leave, the phone rang.*
2 [T] to make something ready to be used: **prepare sth for sth/sb** *Carol was upstairs preparing a room for the guests.*
3 [T] to give someone the training or skills that they need to do something: **prepare sb for sth** *The course prepares students for a career in business.*
4 [T] to make a meal: *This dish can be prepared the day before.* | *Anna was in the kitchen preparing vegetables.*
5 [T] to write a document: *The inspector will **prepare** a report for the minister.*

THESAURUS

for an event

prepare to make plans or arrangements for something that will happen: *It's always important to prepare for an interview.* | *I have to prepare some lessons for tomorrow.*
get ready to prepare for an event. **Get ready** is less formal than **prepare** and is very common in everyday English: *She's upstairs getting ready for the party.*
make preparations for sth to prepare for an event that needs a lot of planning: *They're busy making preparations for their wedding.*

make sth ready

prepare to make something ready to be used: *I've prepared a list of questions.* | *The room is all prepared.*
get sth ready to prepare something. **Get sth ready** is less formal than **prepare** and is very common in everyday English: *I need to get the place ready for the party tonight.*
set (sth) up to prepare equipment so that it is ready to be used: *The band began setting up their equipment.*

---

prepared /prɪˈpeəd $ -ˈperd/ adj **1** [not before noun] ready to deal with a situation: **[+for]** *He wasn't really prepared for all their questions.* **THESAURUS** READY **2** be prepared to do sth to be willing to do something, especially something difficult or unpleasant: *You have to be prepared to take risks in this kind of work.* **3** [only before noun] already planned, written etc and ready to be used: *His lawyer read out a **prepared statement**.* —**preparedness** /prɪˈpeədnəs, -ˈpeərəd- $ -ˈperəd-, -ˈperd-/ n [U]

preponderance /prɪˈpɒndərəns $ -ˈpɑːn-/ n [singular] *formal* when there is more of one type of person or thing in a group than any other: **[+of]** *There was a preponderance of students in the audience.*

preposition /ˌprepəˈzɪʃən/ n [C] a word or phrase used before a noun or PRONOUN to show place, time, direction etc. 'At', 'with', and 'into' are all prepositions.

preposterous /prɪˈpɒstərəs $ -ˈpɑːs-/ adj completely unreasonable or silly **SYN absurd**: *That's a preposterous suggestion!*

'prep school n [C,U] **1** a private school in Britain for children between 7 and 13 **2** a private school in the US that prepares students for college

prequel /ˈpriːkwəl/ n [C] a book or film that tells the story of what happened before the events covered in an existing book or film → **sequel**

prerequisite /priːˈrekwəzət/ n [C] *formal* something that is necessary before another thing can happen or be done: **[+for/of/to]** *A degree in French is a prerequisite for the job.*

prerogative /prɪˈrɒgətɪv $ -ˈrɑː-/ n [C usually singular] *formal* a special right that someone has: **[+of]** *Owning a motor car used to be the prerogative of the rich.*

presage /ˈpresɪdʒ, prəˈseɪdʒ/ v [T] *formal* to be a sign that something bad is going to happen: *Heavy clouds presaged the coming of snow.*

preschool /ˈpriːskuːl/ n [C] *AmE* a school for children between two and five

'pre-school adj relating to the time in a child's life before they are old enough to go to school: *a pre-school playgroup*

prescribe /prɪˈskraɪb/ v [T] **1** to say what medicine or treatment an ill person should have: **prescribe sb sth** *The doctor prescribed him tranquilizers.* **2** *formal* to state officially what must be done in a situation: *a punishment prescribed by the law*

prescription /prɪˈskrɪpʃən/ n **1** [C] a piece of paper on which a doctor writes what medicine a sick person should have, or the medicine itself: **[+for]** *a prescription for painkillers* **2 on prescription** *BrE*, **by prescription** *AmE* a drug that is only available on prescription can only be obtained with a written order from a doctor → **over-the-counter**

prescriptive /prɪˈskrɪptɪv/ adj *formal* saying how something should be done

presence /ˈprezəns/ n [singular] when someone or something is somewhere at a particular time, or a group of people who are somewhere at a particular time **OPP absence**: **in sb's presence** *The document should be signed in the presence of a witness.* | **[+of]** *Tests revealed the presence of drugs in his blood.* | *A heavy **police presence** (=a group of police sent to a place to control a situation) prevented further trouble.*
PHRASES
make your presence felt to have a strong effect on a situation or the people you are with: *Hanley has certainly made his presence felt since joining the company.*
presence of mind the ability to deal with a dangerous or difficult situation quickly and calmly: **have the presence of mind to do sth** *Luckily, she had the presence of mind to phone for an ambulance.*

present¹ /ˈprezənt/ adj
1 [not before noun] in a particular place **OPP absent**: **[+in/at]** *How many people were present at the meeting?*
2 [only before noun] happening or existing now:

This is the best we have **at the present time**. | Many people are unhappy with **the present situation**.

3 the present tense the form of a verb that you use to talk about what exists or is happening now: *Some writers choose to write in the present tense.*

PHRASES

the present day *the time now, or modern times: a collection of musical instruments from the sixteenth century to the present day*

present² /prɪˈzent/ v [T]

1 GIVE SB STH to give something to someone, especially at an official occasion: **present sb with sth** *She was presented with an award by the mayor.* | **present sth to sb** *We will present a cheque for £5,000 to the winner.* THESAURUS GIVE

2 PROBLEM/THREAT to cause a problem, threat etc: *Heavy rain has presented a new difficulty for tournament organisers.*

3 REPORT/EVIDENCE ETC to show people facts or information for them to consider: *The evidence was presented to the court by Conor's lawyer.* | *The committee will present its report.*

4 INTRODUCE SB to introduce someone formally to someone else to consider: *May I present my parents, Mr and Mrs Benning.*

5 TV/RADIO PROGRAMME especially BrE to introduce a television or radio programme, by announcing the performers on it and saying what is going to happen SYN **host** AmE: *Tonight's show will be presented by Jay Williams.*

6 PLAY/FILM/SHOW to organize or make a play, film, show, or programme: *The Lyric Theatre is presenting a brand new production of 'Hamlet'.*

7 BEHAVE **present yourself** the way you present yourself is the way you talk and behave when you meet new people: *She presents herself as willing and efficient.*

8 OPPORTUNITY **sth presents itself** if an opportunity or situation presents itself, it suddenly starts to exist: *If the opportunity ever presented itself, I'd love to go and work abroad.*

present³ /ˈprezənt/ n

1 [C] something that you give to someone on a special occasion SYN **gift**: *He got the computer as a birthday present.* | *He didn't even give me a present.*

2 the present the time that is happening now: *Live in the present – don't worry about the past!*

3 the present the form of a verb that you use to talk about what exists or is happening now SYN **the present tense**

PHRASES

at present at this time SYN **now**: *We have no plans at present for closing the factory.* THESAURUS NOW

for the present if something is true or happening for the present, it is true now, but may change in the future: *She tried to put it out of her mind, for the present anyway.*

COLLOCATIONS

verbs

to give sb a present *Everyone gave me presents and cards.*

to buy/get sb a present *She always buys him a birthday present.*

to get a present *She got a present from her boyfriend.*

to wrap a present *She spent the afternoon wrapping Christmas presents.*

to open a present (=to take it out of its wrapping or box) *It's time to open your presents.*
⚠ Do not say 'unpack a present'. Say **open a present**.

noun + present

a birthday/Christmas/wedding etc present
What would you like for your Christmas present?

presentable /prɪˈzentəbəl/ adj looking clean and tidy enough to be seen by other people: *Do I look presentable?* | *We need to make the house presentable.*

presentation /ˌprezənˈteɪʃən $ ˌpriːzen-, -zən-/ n **1** [C] when someone is given a prize or present at a formal ceremony: **[+of]** *the presentation of the awards* | *a presentation ceremony* **2** [C] an event at which someone describes and explains a new product or idea: *The managing director gave a short presentation.* **3** [U] the way something looks because of how it has been arranged: *You need to improve the presentation of your work.*

present-day adj [only before noun] existing now, not in the past: *present-day technology*

presenter /prɪˈzentə $ -ər/ n [C] someone who introduces a television or radio programme SYN **host** AmE

presently /ˈprezəntli/ adv formal **1** soon: *The doctor will be here presently.* **2** now: *He's presently living in London.*

present participle n [C] the form of a verb that ends in '-ing'

present perfect n **the present perfect** the verb tense that you use to talk about a time up to and including the present. It is formed with 'have' and the PAST PARTICIPLE, as in 'he has gone'.

preservation /ˌprezəˈveɪʃən $ -zər-/ n [U] when you prevent something from being harmed or damaged: **[+of]** *the preservation of the environment*

preservative /prɪˈzɜːvətɪv $ -ɜːr-/ n [C,U] a substance that is added to food to keep it in good condition: *foods that contain artificial preservatives*

preserve¹ /prɪˈzɜːv $ -ɜːrv/ v [T]

1 to stop something from being harmed, damaged, or destroyed → **preservation**: *It is important to preserve the rain forests.* | *The college wants to preserve its independence.* THESAURUS PROTECT

2 to add something to food so that it will stay in good condition: *fruit preserved in alcohol*

preserve² n **1** [C] a food that is made by cooking fruit or vegetables with sugar, salt, or other substances, so that they will remain in good condition: *jams and other fruit preserves* **2** [singular] if an activity is the preserve of one group of people, only that group does it: *Politics is no longer a male preserve.* | **[+of]** *a sport which used to be the preserve of the middle classes* **3** [C] an area of land or water that is kept for private hunting or fishing

preside /prɪˈzaɪd/ v [I] to be in charge of a formal meeting or ceremony: **[+at]** *He agreed to preside at the meeting.* | **[+over]** *the judge who will preside over this trial*

PHRASAL VERBS

preside over sth to be in control of a country at a time when something is happening in the country: *This government has presided over two major recessions.*

presidency /ˈprezədənsi/ n [C] (plural **presidencies**) the job of being a president, or the period of time when someone is a president: *his first attempt to win the presidency* | *the economic problems that developed during his presidency*

president, President /ˈprezɪdənt/ n [C]
1 the official leader of a country that does not have a king or queen: *President Lincoln* | *the US President* | **[+of]** *the President of France*
2 someone who is in charge of a large organization: **[+of]** *the President of the Royal Geographical Society*
THESAURUS BOSS → VICE PRESIDENT

presidential /ˌprezɪˈdenʃəl◂/ adj [only before noun] relating to the president of a country: *a* **presidential election** | *the party's* **presidential candidate**

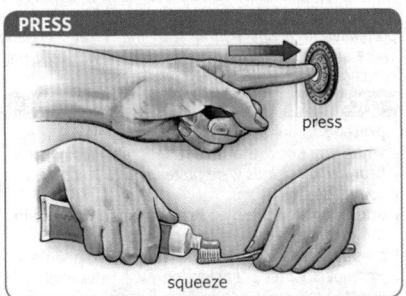

PRESS

press

squeeze

press¹ /pres/ v
1 [I,T] to push something firmly: *What happens if I* **press** *this* **button**? | **[+down]** *Press down with your left foot and pull back the lever.* | **press sth into/against/to sth** *He pressed some money into her hand.* | *Their faces were pressed against the window.*
2 [I,T] to try very hard to persuade someone to do something: **[+for]** *Nurses are pressing for a pay rise.* | **press sb to do sth** *He pressed me to accept the job.* | **press sb for sth** *I pressed her for an answer.* | *workers who are* **pressing** *their* **claim** *for more money* (=trying to persuade their employers to give them more money)
3 [I] to move forward by pushing against other people: **[+forward]** *The crowd continued to press forward.*
4 [T] to use something heavy to crush something or make it flat: *a machine for pressing grapes*
PHRASES
press charges to say officially that someone has done something illegal and must go to a court of law: *The police have decided not to press charges against him.*

PHRASAL VERBS
press on/ahead to continue doing something in a determined way: *Shall we press on?* | **[+with]** *Let's press ahead with the meeting.*

THESAURUS

press to push something firmly: *I pressed the switch and a light came on.*
squeeze to press something inwards from both sides: *If you squeeze the ball, it makes a funny noise.* | *He squeezed her arm.*
crush to press something hard so that it breaks into very small pieces, or is very badly damaged: *Crush two cloves of garlic.* | *The front of the car was crushed.*
squash to press something against a surface accidentally and damage it by making it flat: *He sat on my hat and squashed it.* | *Be careful not to squash the strawberries.*
compress formal to press something or make it smaller so that it takes up less space: *He tried to compress the clothes so that they would fit into his suitcase.*

press² n
1 the press [also + plural verb BrE] newspapers and magazines, and the people who write for them: *He agreed to give an interview to the press.* | *The press have been very nasty about him.* | *a press report* about the tragedy | **the national/local press** *I read about it in the local press.* | **the gutter press** BrE disapproving (=newspapers that like to print shocking and frightening stories) *fears stirred up by the gutter press*
THESAURUS NEWSPAPER
2 [C] a piece of equipment used to crush something or make it flat: *a trouser press*
3 [C] a machine used for printing books or newspapers → PRINTING PRESS
PHRASES
get a good/bad press to be praised or criticized in newspapers and on radio or television: *The government has been getting a bad press recently.*
go to press when a newspaper or book goes to press, it is printed: *The story came out just as the newspaper was going to press.*

'press ˌconference n [C] a meeting at which someone answers questions asked by people from newspapers, television etc: *The police will* **hold** *a* **press conference** *later today.*

pressed /prest/ adj **be pressed for time/money** informal to not have enough time or money

pressing /ˈpresɪŋ/ adj a pressing problem needs to be dealt with very soon: *one of the country's most pressing problems*

'press ˌoffice n [C] the office of an organization or government department which gives information to the newspapers, radio, or television —**press officer** n [C]

'press reˌlease n [C] an official statement giving information to newspapers, radio, television etc

'press-up n [C] BrE an exercise in which you lie facing the ground and push your body up using your arms SYN **push-up** AmE: *He does 50 press-ups every morning.*

pressure¹ /'preʃə $ -ər/ n

1 [U] attempts to make someone do something by threatening them or making them believe that they should do it: *Her family are **putting pressure on** her to stay at home.* | **be/come under pressure to do sth** *The director is now under pressure to resign.* | **[+from]** *The school agreed to the changes after pressure from parents.* | **[+on]** *There is pressure on the government to increase spending on health.* **THESAURUS ▶ FORCE**

2 [C,U] conditions in your life that make you feel worried because you have too much to do or think that you must do well: **[+of]** *the pressures of modern life* | **[+on]** *There is a lot of pressure on children these days.* | *I've been **under a lot of pressure** at work recently.*

3 [C,U] conditions that cause something to change or fail, especially in business or politics: *in response to **commercial pressures***

4 [C,U] the force that a gas or liquid has when it is pushed and held inside a container: *The air pressure in the tyres was too high.*

5 [U] the force or weight that is produced by pressing against something: *the pressure of the water against the sea walls* → **BLOOD PRESSURE**

pressure² v [T] *especially AmE* to try to make someone do something by threatening them or making them believe that they should do it **SYN** **pressurize** *BrE* —**pressured** *adj*

'pressure group n [C] a group of people who try to influence public opinion and persuade the government to do something: *an environmental pressure group*

pressurize (*also* **-ise** *BrE*) /'preʃəraɪz/ v [T] to try to make someone do something by threatening them or making them believe that they should do it: *I was pressurized into lending him the money.*

pressurized (*also* **-ised** *BrE*) /'preʃəraɪzd/ *adj* if a place is pressurized, the air inside it is kept at a controlled pressure: *a pressurized aircraft cabin*

prestige /pre'stiːʒ/ n [U] if you have prestige, you are respected and admired because of your job or something that you have achieved

prestigious /pre'stɪdʒəs $ -'stiː-, -'stɪ-/ *adj* a prestigious job or prize is one that people admire and respect a lot: *a prestigious literary award*

presumably Ac /prɪ'zjuːməbli $ -'zuː-/ *adv* used to say that you think something is probably true: *Presumably, the match will be cancelled.*

presume Ac /prɪ'zjuːm $ -'zuːm/ v **1** [T] to think that something is true, although you do not know for certain: **[+(that)]** *I presume you'll be there.* | *The three soldiers are missing and **presumed dead**.* **2** [I] *formal* to behave rudely by doing something that you have no right to do: **presume to do sth** *I would never presume to tell you what to do.*

presumption Ac /prɪ'zʌmpʃən/ n *formal* **1** [C] something that you suppose is true because it seems very likely, although you do not know for certain: *There is a general presumption that he is guilty.* **2** [U] rude behaviour in which you do something that you have no right to do

presumptuous /prɪ'zʌmptʃuəs/ *adj formal* doing something that you have no right to do, in a way that seems rude

presuppose /ˌpriːsə'pəʊz $ -'poʊz/ v [T] *formal* to accept as a fact that something is true or will happen, even though this might not really be true: **[+that]** *The sales projections presuppose that the economy will continue to grow.*

pre-tax /ˌpriː'tæks◂/ *adj* pre-tax profits or losses are the profits or losses of a company before tax has been taken away

preteen /ˌpriː'tiːn◂/ *adj* relating to or made for children who are 11 or 12 years old: *preteen clothing* —**preteen** /'priːtiːn/ n [C]

pretence *BrE*, **pretense** *AmE* /prɪ'tens $ 'priːtens/ n [C usually singular, U] when you pretend that something is true: *We had to **keep up the pretence** that we were married.* | *She **made no pretence of** being surprised* (=she did not pretend to be surprised).

PHRASES

under false pretences if you do something under false pretences, you do it by telling people things that are not true: *You brought me here under false pretences.*

pretend¹ /prɪ'tend/ v [I,T] to behave as though something is true when you know that it is not: *He's not really angry – he's just pretending.* | **[+(that)]** *She pretended that she hadn't seen me.* | *Let's pretend we're soldiers.* | **pretend to do sth** *He was only pretending to be asleep.*

THESAURUS

pretend to behave as though something is true when you know that it is not: *I pretended not to hear her.* | *The kids were pretending to be doctors and nurses.*

impersonate to copy a famous person's voice in order to make people laugh, or to behave and dress like someone in order to deceive people: *He impersonates politicians on TV.* | *Jones was arrested for impersonating a police officer.*

be putting it on *informal* to be pretending to be ill, upset, or hurt: *Don't take any notice of her – she's just putting it on.*

do a role-play to pretend that you are in a situation, when you are practising in class: *I want you to do a role-play in which you are trying to buy something in a shop.*

pretend² *adj* imaginary or not real – used especially by children: *We sang songs around a pretend campfire.*

pretense /prɪ'tens $ 'priːtens/ n the American spelling of PRETENCE

pretension /prɪ'tenʃən/ n [C usually plural, U] when someone tries to seem more important or more intelligent than they really are: *his honesty and lack of pretension*

pretentious /prɪ'tenʃəs/ *adj* trying to seem more important or more intelligent than you really are: *a pretentious young man* | *a pretentious film*

pretext /'priːtekst/ n [C] a false reason for doing something, which you give in order to hide the real reason: **[+for]** *The terrorist attack gave them a pretext for war.* | **on a pretext** *He left immediately on the pretext that he had to catch a train.*

pretty¹ /'prɪti/ *adv* spoken fairly or quite: *She looks pretty miserable.* | *I'm pretty sure he'll agree.*
THESAURUS RATHER
PHRASES
pretty much/pretty well almost completely: *They all look pretty much the same.* | *The streets were pretty well empty.* **THESAURUS** ALMOST

pretty² *adj*
1 a woman or girl who is pretty is attractive: *a very pretty girl* | *You look really pretty with your hair long.*
THESAURUS BEAUTIFUL
2 attractive to look at or pleasant to listen to: *a pretty vase* | *a pretty tune* —**prettily** *adv*
PHRASES
not a pretty sight very unpleasant to look at: *His face was covered in spots and he was not a pretty sight!*

prevail /prɪ'veɪl/ *v* [I] *formal* **1** if a belief or opinion prevails, it is common among a group of people: *the beliefs which still prevail in our society* **2** if something prevails, it is successful after a struggle: *Justice prevailed in the end.*
PHRASAL VERBS
prevail on/upon sb *formal* to persuade someone to do something: **prevail on/upon sb to do sth** *He prevailed upon the committee to reconsider its decision.*

prevailing /prɪ'veɪlɪŋ/ *adj* **1** [only before noun] most common or accepted at a particular time: *the prevailing views on education* **2** **the prevailing wind** the wind that usually blows over a particular area: *The direction of the prevailing wind had changed.*

prevalent /'prevələnt/ *adj* very common in a particular place or among a particular group of people: **[+in]** *a problem that is prevalent in Britain* | **[+among]** *a disease that is prevalent among young people* —**prevalence** *n* [U]

prevaricate /prɪ'værɪkeɪt/ *v* [I] *formal* to hide the truth by not answering questions directly: *Stop prevaricating and tell me what you know.*

prevent /prɪ'vent/ *v* [T] to stop something from happening, or stop someone from doing something: *an accident that could have been prevented* | **prevent sb from doing sth** *A knee injury prevented him from playing.* | *We were prevented from entering the building.* —**preventable** *adj*: *preventable diseases*

preventative /prɪ'ventətɪv/ *adj* PREVENTIVE

prevention /prɪ'venʃən/ *n* [U] when something is prevented: **[+of]** *the prevention of accidents* | *crime prevention*

preventive /prɪ'ventɪv/ (*also* **preventative**) *adj* intended to prevent something bad from happening: *preventive medicine* (=actions that prevent people from becoming ill)

preview /'priːvjuː/ *n* [C] **1** an occasion when you see a film, play, or painting before it is shown to the public **2** an advertisement for a film or television programme that shows short parts from it

previous Ac /'priːviəs/ *adj* [only before noun] happening or existing before now, or before the time you are talking about: *She has two children from a previous marriage.* | *I had seen him on the previous day* (=the day before that day).

THESAURUS

previous happening or existing before now, or before the time you are talking about: *The situation is better than in previous years.* | *the previous owner of the car* | *His previous jobs included selling computers and working in a restaurant.*
last used about the one before this one: *What happened to your last mobile phone?* | *Did you see the film last night?*
old used about things you had or people you knew in the past, or about things that existed in the past: *He's one of my old boyfriends.* | *The old theatre was pulled down years ago.*
former *formal* used about someone who used to have a particular job or position in the past. Also used about a place that used to have a different name in the past: *the former president of Chile* | *her former husband* | *the former Soviet Union*
ex-wife/ex-boyfriend/ex-soldier etc someone who used to be someone's wife, used to be a soldier etc, but is not any more: *She never talks about her ex-husband.*

previously Ac /'priːviəsli/ *adv* before now or before a time in the past: *She had previously lived in Cambridge.* **THESAURUS** BEFORE

prewar /ˌpriː'wɔː◄ $ -'wɔːr◄/ *adj* before a war, especially World War II: *life in prewar Britain*

prey¹ /preɪ/ *n* [U] an animal that is hunted and eaten by another animal: *a tiger stalking its prey* → BIRD OF PREY
PHRASES
fall prey to sth to be harmed by something: *More and more teenagers are falling prey to drugs.*

prey² *v*
PHRASAL VERBS
prey on sb/sth **1** if an animal preys on another type of animal, it hunts it and eats it **2** to deceive or harm someone who is not as clever or experienced as you are: *drug dealers who prey on young people* **3** **prey on sb's mind** if something preys on your mind, it worries you a lot

price¹ /praɪs/ *n*
1 [C,U] the amount of money you have to pay for something: **[+of]** *The price of fuel has come down.* | **in price** *Lots of things have gone up in price.* **THESAURUS** COST
2 [singular] something unpleasant that you must suffer in order to have something: *Being followed around by the press is **the price** you have to **pay** for success.* | *This was **a small price to pay** for his freedom.* | *She was determined to have a child **at any price*** (=even if there were a lot of difficulties).

COLLOCATIONS

adjectives

a high/low price *Their prices are too high.*
a reasonable price (=not too high) *The restaurant serves great food at reasonable prices.*
an astronomical price (=extremely high) *Many fans paid astronomical prices for their tickets.*
at half price *They're selling computers at half price.*

verbs

a price goes up/rises *In a time of inflation, prices go up.*
a price comes down/falls *House prices have fallen again.*
to put up/raise a price *Manufacturers have had to put their prices up.*
to cut/lower a price *The company recently cut the price of its best-selling car.*
to charge a high/low etc price *They charge higher prices than other shops.*

price + noun

a price rise/increase *There were protests about the price rises.*
a price cut *They hope that price cuts will increase sales.*

noun + price

house/food/oil etc prices *A poor harvest led to higher food prices.*

Word Choice: price or cost?
The **price** is how much it costs to buy something: *The price of this car is $20,000 including tax.*
The **cost** is how much you have to pay in order to do something: *The cost of manufacturing each car is about $10,000.*

---

price² *v* [T] to say how much something you are selling costs: *Tickets are priced at $25.*

priceless /'praisləs/ *adj* **1** worth a lot of money: *priceless antiques* **THESAURUS** **VALUABLE 2** very important or useful: *a priceless asset*

pricey, pricy /'praisi/ *adj informal* expensive: *The food's a bit pricey.* **THESAURUS** **EXPENSIVE**

prick¹ /prik/ *v* [T] **1** to make a small hole in the surface of something, using a sharp point: *Prick the sausages with a fork before cooking them.* | *I pricked my finger on a pin.* **2** if tears prick your eyes, your eyes sting slightly because you are going to cry
PHRASES
  prick (up) its ears if an animal pricks up its ears, it lifts them up so that it can listen: *The rabbit stopped suddenly, pricking up its ears.*
  prick up your ears to start listening to what someone is saying because it is interesting: *Jay pricked up his ears when I mentioned a vacation.*

prick² *n* [C] a slight pain you feel when something sharp goes into your skin: *I just felt a slight prick as the needle went into my arm.*

prickle¹ /'prikəl/ *n* [C] a sharp point on the skin of an animal or the surface of a plant

prickle² *v* [I,T] if your skin prickles, you feel slight stinging pains: *My skin prickled with tension.*

prickly /'prikli/ *adj*
1 covered with thin sharp points: *prickly bushes*
2 making your skin sting slightly: *a prickly woollen sweater* **3** *informal* someone who is prickly gets annoyed or offended easily

PRICKLY

a prickly plant

pricy /'praisi/ *adj* another spelling of PRICEY

pride¹ /praid/ *n* [U]
1 the feeling you have when you are proud of something that you or someone connected with you has achieved
→ **proud**: *His father smiled with pride.* | [+in] *They have a strong **sense of pride** in their country.* | *She **takes** great **pride in** her work* (=she is very proud of it).
2 the feeling that you like and respect yourself and want other people to respect you: *Losing his job really **hurt** his **pride**.*
3 the feeling that you are better or more important than other people and do not need their help: *I had too much pride to ask for money.* | *In the end I had to **swallow** my **pride** (=forget about my pride) and apologize.*
PHRASES
  have/take pride of place to be in the best place for people to see: *A family photograph took pride of place on the wall.*
  sb's pride and joy a person or thing that someone is very proud of: *His garden is his pride and joy.*
  the pride of sth something that people in a place are very proud of: *The football team is the pride of the town.*

Word Choice: pride or arrogance?
Pride is a good feeling about what you have achieved, or someone connected with you has achieved: *a mother's pride in her son* | *He looked at his work with pride.*
Arrogance is annoying behaviour that shows that someone thinks they are better, more important, or know more than other people: *the arrogance which some politicians have*

---

pride² *v* **pride yourself on (doing) sth** to be very proud of something that you can do well: *a restaurant that prides itself on serving top quality food*

priest /pri:st/ *n* [C] someone who performs religious duties and ceremonies in some religions

priestess /'pri:stes/ *n* [C] a woman who performs religious ceremonies in some religions

priesthood /'pri:sthʊd/ *n* **the priesthood** the job of being a Christian priest: *his decision to **enter the priesthood***

prim /prim/ *adj* always behaving in a polite and formal way, and easily shocked by anything rude: *a very **prim and proper** young lady* —**primly** *adv*

primacy Ac /ˈpraɪməsi/ n [U] formal when something is considered to be more important than anything else: We must give primacy to education.

prima donna /ˌpriːmə ˈdɒnə $ -ˈdɑːnə/ n [C] someone who thinks that they are very important, and so expects other people to admire and praise them even when they behave badly

primal /ˈpraɪməl/ adj formal primal feelings are basic and seem to come from ancient times when humans were more like animals: primal fears

primarily Ac /ˈpraɪmərəli $ praɪˈmerəli/ adv mainly: an advertisement that is aimed primarily at children

primary[1] Ac /ˈpraɪməri $ -meri/ adj [only before noun] **1** most important: Our primary concern is the safety of the children. **2** especially BrE primary education is for children between 5 and 11 years old SYN **elementary** AmE: a good primary school

primary[2] (also ˌprimary eˈlection) n [C] (plural **primaries**) an election in the US when people vote to decide who will be their political party's CANDIDATE in the main election

ˌprimary ˈcolour n [C] one of the three colours, red, yellow, and blue, that you can mix together to make any other colour

ˈprimary ˌschool n [C,U] a school in England and Wales for children between 5 and 11 years old → **junior school**

primate /ˈpraɪmeɪt/ n [C] a member of the group of animals that includes monkeys and humans

prime[1] Ac /praɪm/ adj [only before noun] **1** most important: Smoking is the prime cause of lung disease. | the prime suspect in the police investigation **2** very good: a house in a prime location | This is a prime example of this government's incompetence.

prime[2] n be in your prime/be in the prime of life to be at the time in your life when you are strongest and most active

prime[3] v [T] to prepare someone for a situation so that they know what to do: He was well primed for the interview.

ˌprime ˈminister, Prime Minister n [C] the leader of the government in some countries with a PARLIAMENT

ˌprime ˈnumber n [C] a number such as 5 or 13 that can be divided only by itself and 1

primer /ˈpraɪmə $ -ər/ n **1** [C,U] paint that you put on the surface of unpainted wood, metal etc before you put on the main layer of paint **2** [C] AmE a book that contains basic information about something

ˈprime ˌtime n [U] the time in the evening when the largest number of people watch television —prime-time adj: a prime-time TV show

primeval /praɪˈmiːvəl/ adj belonging to a very early time in the history of the world: primeval forests

primitive /ˈprɪmətɪv/ adj **1** having a simple way of life without modern machines: a primitive society | the tools used by primitive people **2** very simple, old-fashioned, and uncomfortable: The living conditions were a bit primitive.

primrose /ˈprɪmrəʊz $ -roʊz/ n [C] a small wild plant with pale yellow flowers

prince, Prince /prɪns/ n [C] **1** the son of a king or queen: Prince William **2** the male ruler of a small country: Prince Rainier of Monaco

princely /ˈprɪnsli/ adj **princely sum** a large amount of money – often used humorously to mean a very small amount of money: We now have the princely sum of £26.

princess, Princess /ˌprɪnˈses◂ $ ˈprɪnsəs/ n [C] **1** the daughter of a king or queen: Princess Anne **2** the wife of a prince

principal[1] Ac /ˈprɪnsəpəl/ adj [only before noun] most important SYN **main**: the principal character in the book | our principal reason for making this journey

THESAURUS IMPORTANT

principal[2] n [C] AmE the person in charge of a school or college SYN **head teacher** BrE

principality /ˌprɪnsəˈpæləti/ n [C] (plural **principalities**) a country that is ruled by a prince

principally Ac /ˈprɪnsəpli/ adv mainly: It's principally a language college, but they do teach some other subjects.

principle Ac /ˈprɪnsəpəl/ n
1 [C,U] a moral rule that you believe is right, and you use to guide the way you behave: the need to teach children **moral principles** | be against sb's **principles** It's against my principles to eat meat. | She refused to accept the money as **a matter of principle**. | **on principle** He wouldn't pay the fine on principle (=because he thought it was wrong).
2 [C] a basic rule or idea that controls or explains the way something works or is organized: the principles of economics | **general/basic principle** The general principle is that education should be available to all children equally. | **on the principle that** The machine works on the principle that air will expand when heated.

PHRASES

in principle 1 if something is possible in principle, there is no reason why it should not happen, but it has not actually happened yet: In principle, the new computer system should make our job easier. **2** if you agree in principle, you agree with the main parts of a plan before you know the details: They have accepted the idea in principle.

principled Ac /ˈprɪnsəpld/ adj someone who is principled has strong beliefs about what is morally right and wrong

print[1] /prɪnt/ v
1 [T] to produce words or pictures on paper, using a machine: I'm printing the document now. | a notice printed on bright blue paper
2 [T] to produce copies of a book, newspaper etc: The book was first printed in 1879.
3 [T] to include a piece of writing in a newspaper or magazine SYN **publish**: The magazine should never have printed this article.
4 [I,T] to write words by hand without joining the letters: Please print your name clearly at the top of the page.

print

PHRASAL VERBS

print sth ↔ **off/out** to produce a printed copy of a computer document: *I'll print out a copy of the letter for you.*

print² n **1** [U] writing that has been printed in books or newspapers: *I can't read small print without my glasses.* | **in print** *It was really exciting to see my name in print.* **2** [C] a picture or copy of a painting that has been printed onto paper **3** [C] a photograph: *I got an extra set of prints free.* **4** [C] a mark that is left on a surface when something is pressed onto it → **fingerprint**, **footprint**: *His feet left prints in the snow.* → **FINE PRINT, SMALL PRINT**

PHRASES

| **be in print/be out of print** if a book is in print, it is still being printed and you can buy new copies of it. If it is out of print, it is no longer being printed: *After 50 years, the book is still in print.*

printer /'prɪntə $ -ər/ n [C]
1 a machine that prints documents from a computer onto paper: *a laser printer*
2 a person or company whose work is printing books, magazines etc

printing /'prɪntɪŋ/ n [U] the process of making a book, magazine etc, using a machine

'printing press n [C] a machine used for printing newspapers, books etc

printout /'prɪnt,aʊt/ n [C,U] a piece of paper containing information printed from a computer

prior Ac /'praɪə $ praɪr/ adj [only before noun] formal a prior arrangement, agreement etc was planned or made earlier: *He is unable to attend due to a prior engagement.*

PHRASES

| **prior to sth** before: *the weeks prior to the election*

prioritize Ac (also **-ise** BrE) /praɪ'ɒrətaɪz $ -'ɔːr-/ v [I,T] to put several things in order of importance, so that you can do the most important first: *Try to prioritize your work.*

priority Ac /praɪ'ɒrəti $ -'ɔːr-/ n (plural **priorities**)
1 [C] the thing that you think is most important and that needs your attention first: **(sb's) top/first/main priority** *The government's top priority is education.* | **high/low priority** (=something that is considered very important or not very important) *Road repairs are a low priority.*
2 [U] when something is given or should be given more attention than other people or things: **have/take priority (over sth/sb)** *Your family should take priority over your job.* | *Security is given high priority in military establishments.*

prise /praɪz/ v [T] BrE to force something open or away from something else SYN **pry** AmE: **prise sth off/open etc** *I managed to prise the lid open.*

prism /'prɪzəm/ n [C] a block of glass with three sides that separates white light into different colours

prison /'prɪzən/ n [C,U] a building where criminals are kept as a punishment SYN **jail**: *a women's prison* | **in prison** *He spent two years in prison.* | *He*

attacked two **prison officers**. | *a five-year **prison sentence***

prisoner /'prɪzənə $ -ər/ n [C]
1 someone who is kept in a prison as a punishment
2 someone who is kept somewhere by force, for example during a war: **hold/keep sb prisoner** *The rebels kept him prisoner for three months.* | *Hundreds of soldiers were **taken prisoner**.* → **POLITICAL PRISONER**

,prisoner of 'war n [C] (abbreviation **POW**) a soldier etc who is caught by an enemy during a war and kept as a prisoner

pristine /'prɪstiːn/ adj extremely clean and looking as good as when new: *a 1973 Volkswagen in pristine condition*

privacy /'prɪvəsi, 'praɪ- $ 'praɪ-/ n [U] when you are alone and not seen or heard by other people: *Teenagers need some privacy.* | *I read the letter **in the privacy of** my own room.*

private¹ /'praɪvət/ adj
1 for only one person or group to use, not for everyone OPP **public**: *a room with a private bath* | *A sign said 'Private property. Keep out.'*
2 not owned or paid for by the government: *a private company* | *private health care*
3 a private meeting, conversation etc is for a few particular people, and nobody else: *Heads of state met for **private talks**.*
4 private feelings, information etc are secret or personal and not for other people to know about: *Don't read that – it's private.* | *'What are you laughing at?' 'It's **a private joke** (=a joke that only a few particular people will understand).'*
5 not related to your work: *The president made a private visit to Mexico.* | *He's had some problems in his **private life** (=his life with family and friends).*
6 used to describe someone who is not publicly known, or does something for themselves rather than for the government or another organization: *donations from **private individuals*** | *The painting was sold to a **private collector**.*
7 quiet and without other people there: *a private corner of the garden* —**privately** adv

private² (also **Private**) n [C] a soldier of the lowest rank in the army

PHRASES

| **in private** without other people listening or watching: *Can I speak to you in private?*

,private de'tective (also **,private in'vestigator**) n [C] someone who can be employed to look for information or missing people, or to follow people and report on what they do

,private 'enterprise n [U] when private businesses are allowed to compete freely with each other, and the government does not own or control them

'private school n [C] a school that is not supported by government money, where education must be paid for by the children's parents

privatize (also **-ise** BrE) /'praɪvətaɪz/ v [T] to sell an organization, industry etc that was previously owned by a government OPP **nationalize** —**privatization** /,praɪvətaɪ'zeɪʃən $ -tə-/ n [U]

privet /'prɪvɪt/ n [U] a bush with leaves that stay green all year, often grown to form a HEDGE

privilege /'prɪvəlɪdʒ/ n **1** [C,U] a special advantage that only one person or group has: *Leisure travel used to be a privilege of the rich.* | *positions of privilege and power* **2** [singular] something that you are lucky to have the chance to do: *It's **been a privilege** to meet you, sir.* —**privileged** adj: *students from **privileged backgrounds***

privy /'prɪvi/ adj **be privy to sth** formal to know about something that is secret: *Only Colby was privy to the deal.*

prize¹ /praɪz/ n [C] something that is given to someone who is successful in a competition, race etc: *He **won** a prize of £3,000.* | **first/second/third etc prize** *First prize was a weekend for two in Paris.* → BOOBY PRIZE

prize² adj [only before noun] good enough to win a prize: *prize cattle*

prize³ v [T] to think that something is very important or valuable: *These coins are prized by collectors.* —**prized** adj: *our most **prized possession***

pro /prəʊ $ proʊ/ n [C] (plural pros) informal someone who earns money by playing a sport: *a tennis pro*

PHRASES

the pros and cons (of sth) the advantages and disadvantages of something: *We have to weigh up the pros and cons of the proposal.*

pro- /prəʊ $ proʊ/ prefix supporting or approving of something or someone OPP **anti-**: *pro-government troops*

proactive /prəʊ'æktɪv $ proʊ-/ adj proactive actions are done to make something happen or change, not as a reaction to an event: *Banks need to take a more proactive approach to fraud.*

probability /ˌprɒbə'bɪləti $ ˌprɑː-/ n (plural probabilities) **1** [C,U] how likely it is that something will happen: *There's **a high probability** of success.* | **[+(that)]** *What's the probability that she will inherit the disease?* **2** [singular] something that is likely to happen or exist: *War is a real probability now.*

PHRASES

in all probability very probably: *In all probability, he's missed the bus.*

probable /'prɒbəbəl $ 'prɑː-/ adj likely to happen or be true: *The probable cause of the crash was engine failure.* | **It's probable that** *more people will be infected.*

probably /'prɒbəbli $ 'prɑː-/ adv used when saying that you think something will happen or be true, although you are not sure: *We'll probably go to France next year.* | *'Are you going to come?' 'Yes, probably.'*

THESAURUS

probably used when saying that you think something will happen or be true, although you are not sure: *I'm probably going to see Greg tonight.* | *The meeting is probably in room 2.*
likely if something is likely to happen, you think it will happen: *Prices are likely to rise again next*

year. | **It is likely that** they will win.
it looks as if/it looks like used when saying that the present situation makes you think something will happen or be true: *It looks as if the phone isn't working.* | *It looks like it will rain.*
may/might/could well used when saying that you think something will probably happen or is probably true: *You may well be right.* | *We might well lose.* | *It could well be too late.*

probation /prə'beɪʃən $ proʊ-/ n [U] **1** a system that allows some criminals not to go to prison if they behave well and see a probation officer regularly: **on probation** *He's on probation for theft.* **2** a period of time when someone starts a new job, when they must show that they are suitable for that job —**probationary** adj

pro'bation ˌofficer n [C] someone whose job is to help criminals who are on probation, and check that they are behaving well

probe¹ /prəʊb $ proʊb/ v [I,T] **1** to ask questions in order to get secret or personal information: **[+into]** *She didn't want him probing into her past.* **2** to look for or examine something, using a long thin object —**probing** adj

probe² n [C] **1** a long thin tool that doctors and scientists use to examine parts of someone's body **2** a spacecraft without people in it, sent into space to collect information **3** an official investigation that tries to find the truth about something: *The State Department ordered a probe into the allegations.*

problem /'prɒbləm $ 'prɑː-/ n [C]
1 something that causes difficulty or trouble: **[+of]** *the problem of unemployment* | *I've been having a few problems with the kids.* | **the (only) problem is (that)** spoken (=used before saying what the main difficulty is) *The problem is, there isn't enough time.*
2 a question for which you must find the right answer: *a **mathematical problem*** | *Can you **solve** this **problem**?*
PHRASES

that's your/his etc problem spoken used to say that someone else is responsible for dealing with a situation, not you: *If you're late, that's your problem.*

COLLOCATIONS

verbs

to have a problem *Call me if you have any problems.*
to cause/create a problem *Heavy rain has been causing problems for drivers.*
to deal with/solve a problem *Do you need advice on how to deal with the problem?*
a problem arises/occurs (=it happens) *A problem arose when the computer system crashed.* ⚠ Do not say 'a problem happens'. Say **a problem arises** or **occurs**.

adjectives

a big/major/serious problem *Our biggest problem is that we don't have enough space.*
a small/minor problem *We had a small problem with the delivery.*

personal problems (=relating to your private life and relationships) *I'm not interested in your personal problems.*

health/family/money etc problems *Smoking causes health problems.*

a drug/crime problem (=in an area) *The city has a huge crime problem.*

THESAURUS

problem something that causes difficulty or trouble: *If you have any problems, give me a call. | Crime is a big problem here.*

difficulty a problem that makes it difficult to do what you want: *If it doesn't rain soon, farmers will face serious difficulties. | We've had difficulty selling the house.*

issue a subject or problem that needs to be discussed. People often use **issue** instead of **problem** in more formal contexts: *Global warming is one of the most important issues facing all countries.*

snag *informal* a problem that seems small, but spoils your plans and prevents you from doing something: *There's just one snag – we don't have a car.*

setback something that happens that stops you from making progress: *The peace talks have had a series of setbacks.*

problematic /ˌprɒbləˈmætɪk◂ $ ˌprɑː-/ (also **problematical** /-tɪkəl/) *adj* full of problems, or causing problems: *a problematic relationship*

procedure Ac /prəˈsiːdʒə $ -ər/ *n* [C,U] the correct or normal way of doing something: **[+for]** *the procedure for getting a visa* —**procedural** *adj*

proceed Ac /prəˈsiːd/ *v* [I] *formal* **1** to continue to do something or happen: **[+with]** *The company decided to proceed with the project.* | *Talks are **proceeding smoothly**.* THESAURUS ▷ GO **2 proceed to do sth** to do something after you have done something else: *He stood up and proceeded to give an embarrassed speech.*

proceedings /prəˈsiːdɪŋz/ *n* [plural] **1** a series of events: *We watched the proceedings from the window.* **2** legal actions in a law court: ***divorce proceedings***

proceeds Ac /ˈprəʊsiːdz $ ˈproʊ-/ *n* [plural] the money that you get from selling something or from an organized event: *The proceeds from the concert will go to charity.*

process¹ Ac /ˈprəʊses $ ˈprɑː-/ *n* [C]
1 a series of things you do in order to achieve a particular result or to produce something: **[+of]** *the process of learning a language* | *the Israeli-Egyptian **peace process*** | *the car **production process***
2 a series of events or changes that happen naturally: **[+of]** *the **natural process** of evolution*

PHRASES

in the process while you are doing something else, or while something else is happening: *I ran, twisting my ankle in the process.*

be in the process of (doing) sth to have started doing something and not yet finished: *We're in the process of buying a house.*

process² Ac *v* [T] **1** to add chemicals to a substance or food in order to give it colour, keep it fresh etc: *processed cheese* **2** to deal with an official document, information etc by putting it through a system or into a computer: *Your application is still being processed.* **3** to print a photograph or film —**processing** *n* [U]

processed Ac /ˈprəʊsest $ ˈprɑː-/ *adj* [only before noun] processed food has substances added to it before it is sold in order to preserve it, improve its colour etc

procession /prəˈseʃən/ *n* [C] **1** a line of people or vehicles moving slowly as part of a ceremony → **parade**: *a funeral procession* **2** many people or things of the same kind, appearing or happening one after the other: **[+of]** *an **endless procession** of visitors*

processor /ˈprəʊsesə $ ˈprɑːsesər/ *n* [C] the part of a computer that deals with information → **FOOD PROCESSOR**

proclaim /prəˈkleɪm $ proʊ-/ *v* [T] *formal* to officially tell people something important: *The new government proclaimed independence immediately.* —**proclamation** /ˌprɒkləˈmeɪʃən $ ˌprɑː-/ *n* [C]

procrastinate /prəˈkræstəneɪt/ *v* [I] *formal* to delay doing something that you ought to do: *The government cannot procrastinate any longer on this issue.* THESAURUS ▷ DELAY —**procrastination** /prəˌkræstəˈneɪʃən/ *n* [U]

procreate /ˈprəʊkrieɪt $ ˈproʊ-/ *v* [I,T] *formal* to produce children or baby animals SYN **reproduce** —**procreation** /ˌprəʊkriˈeɪʃən $ ˌproʊ-/ *n* [U]

procure /prəˈkjʊə $ proʊˈkjʊr/ *v* [T] *formal* to get something, especially something that is difficult to get: *Clark had been procuring guns for the rebels.*

prod /prɒd $ prɑːd/ *v* [I,T] (**prodded, prodding**) **1** to push someone or something with your finger or a pointed object: *He prodded the snake with a stick.* → see picture on page A10 **2** to persuade or remind someone to do something that they are not eager to do: *We had to prod Ed into applying for the job.* —**prod** *n* [C]: *a cattle prod*

prodigious /prəˈdɪdʒəs/ *adj formal* very large or impressive: *a **prodigious amount** of money* —**prodigiously** *adv*

prodigy /ˈprɒdɪdʒi $ ˈprɑː-/ *n* [C] (plural **prodigies**) a young person who is extremely good at doing something → **genius**: *Mozart was a **child prodigy**.*

produce¹ /prəˈdjuːs $ -ˈduːs/ *v* [T]
1 to cause a particular thing to happen: *Research in the US produced similar results. | The drug can produce serious side effects.*
2 to make something using a particular process or skill → **product, production**: *The factory produces 100 cars an hour. | wine produced in California | The children produced some wonderful paintings.* THESAURUS ▷ MAKE
3 to make or grow something naturally: *Plants produce oxygen. | a snake that produces a deadly poison*
4 to bring out or show something so that someone can see it: *He suddenly produced a gun.*
5 to control how a film, play, record etc is made → **producer**: *James Cameron produced 'Terminator 2'.*

produce² /'prɒdjuːs $ 'proʊduːs/ n [U] food that is grown in large quantities to be sold: *dairy produce*

producer /prə'djuːsə $ -'duːsər/ n [C] **1** someone who controls the making of a film, play, record etc: *Hollywood producers* **2** a company or country that makes or grows something: **[+of]** *Spain is a large producer of olive oil.*

product /'prɒdʌkt $ 'prɑː-/ n [C]
1 something that is made in a factory or grown to be sold: **agricultural/dairy/software etc products** *a list of new food products*
2 be the product of sth to be the result of something: *The system is the product of two years' development.*

production /prə'dʌkʃən/ n
1 [U] the process of making things in a factory or growing food to be sold, or the amount produced → **produce**, **product**: **[+of]** *the production of consumer goods* | **food/oil/milk etc production** *Industrial production rose by 0.1%.* | **in production** (=being produced) *The old model was in production for about 30 years.* | *production costs*
2 [U] when something is produced through a natural process: **[+of]** *the body's production of red blood cells*
3 [C,U] a film, play etc, or the process of producing it: *a modern production of Romeo and Juliet* | *video production*

pro'duction ,line n [C] a line of machines and workers in a factory, each doing one job in the process of making a product before passing it to the next machine or worker

productive /prə'dʌktɪv/ adj producing or achieving a lot: *a productive meeting* —**productively** adv

productivity /,prɒdʌk'tɪvəti, -dək- $,prɑː-/ n [U] the speed at which goods are produced, and the amount that is produced: *ways to increase productivity*

Prof. the written abbreviation of **Professor**

profane /prə'feɪn/ adj formal showing a lack of respect for God or holy things: *profane language*

profess /prə'fes/ v [T] formal to say something about yourself, especially when it is not true: *He professes to love her.*

profession /prə'feʃən/ n
1 [C] a job that needs special education and training: **the legal/medical/teaching etc profession** | *I spent most of my life in the teaching profession.* | **enter/go into/join a profession** *My father wanted me to go into the legal profession.* | **by profession** *He's an architect by profession.* **THESAURUS** JOB
2 [singular also + plural verb BrE] all the people in a particular profession: *the nursing profession*

professional¹ Ac /prə'feʃənəl/ adj
1 [only before noun] relating to a job that needs special education and training: *You'll need professional legal advice.* | *professional qualifications* | *We rented the house to a professional couple.*
2 showing that someone has been well trained and is good at their work: *Your report looks very professional.* | *a professional approach to the job*
3 doing a sport or activity as your job: *a professional*

tennis player | *In 1990 he **turned professional*** (=started to do a sport etc as a job).
4 [only before noun] professional sports are played by people who are paid → **amateur**: *a professional golf championship* —**professionally** adv

professional² Ac n [C] **1** someone who works in a job that needs special education and training: *a health care professional* **2** someone who earns money by doing a sport or activity that other people do for enjoyment → **amateur**

professionalism Ac /prə'feʃənəlɪzəm/ n [U] the skill and high standards that a professional person is expected to have

professor /prə'fesə $ -ər/ n [C] **1** BrE a teacher at the highest level in a university department **THESAURUS** TEACHER **2** AmE a teacher at a university or college

proffer /'prɒfə $ 'prɑːfər/ v [T] formal to offer something to someone

proficient /prə'fɪʃənt/ adj able to do something very skilfully: *Gwen is proficient in three languages.* —**proficiency** n [U]: *Nick's proficiency with computers* —**proficiently** adv

profile¹ /'prəʊfaɪl $ 'proʊ-/ n [C] **1** a view of someone's head from the side, not the front: **in profile** *a drawing of her in profile* **2** a short description that gives the main details of what someone or something is like: **[+of]** *a profile of the singer* | *a job profile* → **HIGH-PROFILE**

PROFILE

PHRASES
a high profile if something or someone has a high profile, the public are very interested in them: *Drugs education **has a high profile** right now.*
keep a low profile to avoid doing things that will make people notice you: *Kendall keeps a low profile, refusing to do interviews with newspapers.*

profile² v [T] to write or give a short description of someone or something

profit¹ /'prɒfɪt $ 'prɑː-/ n [C,U] the money that you get when you sell something for more than you paid for it, especially in business → **loss**: **at a profit** *They sold the house at a big profit.*

COLLOCATIONS
verbs
to make a profit *We are in business to make a profit.*
profits rise/fall *The company's profits rose last year to $17 million.*
adjectives
a big/large/huge profit *Drug companies make huge profits.*
a small profit *The business managed to make a small profit last year.*

P

profit² v [I,T] *formal* to get something good or useful from a situation: **[+by/from]** *Wealthy people will profit from the new tax laws.*

profitability /ˌprɒfətəˈbɪləti $ ˌprɑː-/ n [U] the amount of profit that a business makes

profitable /ˈprɒfətəbəl $ ˈprɑː-/ adj producing a profit or a useful result: *profitable investments* —**profitably** adv

profiteering /ˌprɒfəˈtɪərɪŋ $ ˌprɑːfəˈtɪr-/ n [U] when a person or company makes a large profit by selling something that is difficult to obtain at an unfairly high price —**profiteer** n [C]

ˈprofit-ˌmaking adj a profit-making organization or business makes a profit

profound /prəˈfaʊnd/ adj **1** a profound effect, feeling etc is very great or serious: *The story had a profound effect on me.* | *Her death was a profound shock.* **2** showing a lot of knowledge and understanding: *a profound remark* —**profoundly** adv

profuse /prəˈfjuːs/ adj produced or present in large amounts: *Moira phoned with profuse apologies.* —**profusion** /prəˈfjuːʒən/ n [U]: *Wildlife is here in profusion.* —**profusely** adv

prognosis /prɒɡˈnəʊsɪs $ prɑːɡˈnoʊ-/ n [C] (*plural* **prognoses** /-siːz/) *formal* the way something, especially an illness, seems likely to develop in the future: *With some cancers the prognosis is good.*

program¹ /ˈprəʊɡræm $ ˈproʊ-/ n [C]
1 a set of instructions given to a computer to make it do something: *The students learnt how to write a computer program.* | *a graphics program* | *The program will run on Windows.*
2 the American spelling of PROGRAMME THESAURUS► PROGRAMME

program² v [T] (**programmed**, **programming**) to give a set of instructions to a computer to make it do something —**programming** n [U]

programme¹ BrE, **program** AmE /ˈprəʊɡræm $ ˈproʊ-/ n [C]
1 SCHEME a series of planned actions that are intended to develop or improve something: **training/investment/building etc programme** *the US space program* | *my new fitness programme* | **[+of]** *our programme of reforms* | **programme to do sth** *a programme to improve living conditions in the region* THESAURUS► PLAN
2 ON TV/RADIO a show, play, discussion etc that you watch on television, or listen to on the radio: *What's your favourite TV programme?* | **[+on/about]** *I watched a programme on killer whales.*
3 SET OF EVENTS a series of planned activities or events, or a list showing what order they will come in: *Tomorrow's programme includes drama, music, and dance.* | **[+of]** *a programme of exhibitions* THESAURUS► LIST
4 AT A CONCERT/PLAY a small book or piece of paper that you get at a concert, play etc which tells you about the performance: *a theatre programme*
5 COURSE AmE a course of study: *Stanford's MBA program*

programme BrE, **program** AmE a show, play, discussion etc that you watch on television, or listen to on the radio: *There's an interesting programme on TV tonight.*

show a programme that is intended to be entertaining or funny: *Welcome to tonight's show.* | *a comedy show* | *a game show* | *a talk show* (=in which famous people talk about themselves, their latest films etc)

documentary a programme that gives you facts and information about a serious subject: *a documentary about life in South Africa*

cartoon a film that shows a series of drawings of people and animals that seem to move, especially one that is made for children: *He was famous for making cartoons such as 'Tom and Jerry'.*

soap opera/soap a television or radio story about a group of imaginary people and their lives, which is broadcast regularly for many years: *the Australian soap opera 'Neighbours'*

sitcom an amusing programme with a different story each week about the same group of people: *'Friends' was one of the most popular sitcoms of all time.*

reality TV television programmes that film real people rather than actors in different situations, often for weeks or months: *the reality TV show 'Big Brother'*

programme² BrE, **program** AmE v [T] **1** to give a set of instructions to a machine to make it do something: *I've programmed the video to record tonight's movie.* **2 be programmed to do sth** to naturally behave or think in a particular way: *Cats are programmed to hunt.* **3** to arrange for something to happen at a particular time: *The festival is programmed for later this year.*

programmer /ˈprəʊɡræmə $ ˈproʊɡræmər/ n [C] someone whose job is to write programs for computers

progress¹ /ˈprəʊɡres $ ˈprɑː-/ n [U]
1 the process of getting better at doing something, or getting closer to finishing or achieving something: *Nick has made a lot of progress at school.* | **[+of]** *Millions of people watched the progress of the trial on TV.* | **[+towards]** *There's been steady progress towards a peace settlement.*
2 useful change or improvement in society: *Do we need all this technology? Is it really progress?* | **social/technological/economic etc progress**
PHRASES
| **in progress** *formal* happening now: *The class was already in progress.*

COLLOCATIONS
verbs

to make progress *I feel we're not making any progress.* ⚠ Do not say 'have progress'. Say **make progress**.
to check on sb's progress *He came home early to check on our progress.*

great/good progress *She has made good progress in reading and writing.* ⚠ Do not say 'big progress'. Say **great progress** or **good progress**.

slow/steady progress *The task is a difficult one and progress has been slow.*

rapid progress *From this small start, the company made rapid progress.*

progress² /prəˈgres/ v [I] **1** to develop and move to a further stage: *He soon progressed to more difficult exercises.* **2** to continue or move forward slowly: *As the meeting progressed, I became bored.*

progression /prəˈgreʃən/ n [C,U] change or development: *the rapid progression of the disease*

progressive¹ /prəˈgresɪv/ adj **1** supporting or using modern ideas and methods: *progressive teaching methods* **2** a progressive change happens gradually over a period of time: *the **progressive increase** in air travel* —**progressively** adv

progressive² n the progressive the form of a verb that shows that an action is continuing to happen. In English, it has the verb 'be' followed by the PRESENT PARTICIPLE, for example, 'I was waiting for a bus.'

prohibit Ac /prəˈhɪbɪt $ proʊ-/ v [T] *formal* to say that something is not allowed because of a rule or law SYN **forbid**: *Smoking is prohibited in the building.* | **prohibit sb from doing sth** *women were prohibited from remarrying.* **THESAURUS** FORBID —**prohibition** /ˌprəʊɪˈbɪʃən $ ˌproʊ-/ n [U]

prohibitive Ac /prəˈhɪbətɪv $ proʊ-/ adj prohibitive prices are very high and prevent people from buying or doing something —**prohibitively** adv

project¹ Ac /ˈprɒdʒekt $ ˈprɑː-/ n [C] **1** a piece of work that is carefully planned and done over a period of time: *a three-year **research project*** | **project to do sth** *a project to build new houses* | *a **project manager*** **2** a piece of school work for which students have to collect information about a subject over a period of time: *a geography project* | [+on] *a project on pollution*

project² Ac /prəˈdʒekt/ v **1** [T usually passive] to plan or calculate what will probably happen in the future: *The President's visit is projected for March.* | *Inflation was projected to rise to 8.9%.* **2** [I] *formal* to stick out beyond an edge or surface SYN **protrude**: *The roof projects over the driveway.* **3** [T] to make a picture, film etc appear on a large screen, using light

projectile /prəˈdʒektaɪl $ -tl/ n [C] *formal* an object that is thrown at someone, or fired from a weapon

projection Ac /prəˈdʒekʃən/ n **1** [C] a statement about what is likely to happen, using information you have now: *projections of an increase of 3%* **2** [C] something that sticks out beyond an edge or surface **3** [U] the use of light to make a picture, film etc appear on a large screen

projector /prəˈdʒektə $ -ər/ n [C] a piece of equipment that uses light to make a picture, film etc appear on a large screen

proliferate /prəˈlɪfəreɪt/ v [I] *formal* to increase very quickly in number —**proliferation** /prəˌlɪfəˈreɪʃən/ n [U]: *the proliferation of shopping centres*

prolific /prəˈlɪfɪk/ adj producing a lot of something: *a prolific writer* —**prolifically** /-kli/ adv

prologue /ˈprəʊlɒg $ ˈproʊlɔːg, -lɑːg/ n [C] the introduction to a book, film, or play → **EPILOGUE**

prolong /prəˈlɒŋ $ -ˈlɔːŋ/ v [T] to make something continue for longer: *There was no point in prolonging the conversation.*

prolonged /prəˈlɒŋd $ -ˈlɔːŋd/ adj continuing for a long time: *a prolonged illness*

prom /prɒm $ prɑːm/ n [C] a formal dance party for HIGH SCHOOL students in the US

promenade /ˌprɒməˈnɑːd◂, ˈprɒmənɑːd $ ˌprɑːməˈneɪd◂/ n [C] *BrE* a wide path next to the sea where people walk for pleasure

prominence /ˈprɒmənəns $ ˈprɑː-/ n [U] when someone or something is important and well-known: **come to/rise to prominence (as sth)** *She came to prominence as an artist in 1993.*

prominent /ˈprɒmɪnənt $ ˈprɑː-/ adj **1** well-known or important: *a prominent politician* **2** easy to see or notice: *a prominent nose* —**prominently** adv

promiscuous /prəˈmɪskjuəs/ adj having many sexual partners: *promiscuous sexual behaviour* —**promiscuity** /ˌprɒməˈskjuːəti $ ˌprɑː-/ n [U]

promise¹ /ˈprɒmɪs $ ˈprɑː-/ v [I,T] **1** to say that you will definitely do something or that something will definitely happen: **promise to do sth** *She promised to write to me.* | **promise (that)** *I promise that I won't be late.* | **promise sb (that)** *He promised me the car would be ready by then.* | **promise sb sth** *The company promised us a bonus.* | **promise sth to sb** *I've promised that book to Ian.* **2** to seem likely to be something in the future: **promise to be sth** *The meeting promises to be difficult.*

Grammar
Do not say 'My parents promised me to buy a new computer.' Say *My parents promised to buy me a new computer.* or *My parents promised (me) that they would buy me a new computer.*

THESAURUS

promise to say that you will definitely do something or that something will definitely happen: *She promised to call me today.* | *I promise that I'll be there by six.*

swear to make a very serious promise, especially publicly or in a law court: *Do you swear to tell the truth?*

give sb your word to promise very sincerely – used when you are trying to persuade someone that they can trust you: *I give you my word that I won't tell anyone.*

guarantee to say that something will definitely happen, especially when you feel very certain of this: *I guarantee that you will enjoy the film.* | *Can you guarantee the safety of the passengers?*

vow *especially written* to make a very serious promise, often to yourself: *He believed she was still alive and he vowed to find her.*

promise² n
1 [C] a statement that you will definitely do something or that something will definitely happen: [+of] *a promise of help* | [+to] *his promise to me* | **promise to do sth** *I have not forgotten my promise to help you.* | [+that] *his promise that the job would be mine*
2 [U] signs that something or someone will be good or successful: *He **shows** a lot of promise as a writer.*

COLLOCATIONS

verbs

to make a promise *I made a promise not to tell anyone.*

to give sb your promise *He gave me his promise that he would help me.*

to keep a promise (=to do what you promised) *Anna kept her promise to be back early.*

to break a promise (=to not do what you promised) *They accused the mayor of breaking his promise.*

adjectives

a solemn promise (=very serious) *He gave them his solemn promise to return.*

a vague promise (=not definite) *She made a vague promise to do her best.*

a false promise (=that will not be kept) *We have had enough of these false promises.*

---

promising /ˈprɒmɪsɪŋ $ ˈprɑː-/ adj likely to be good or successful: *a promising young actor* THESAURUS→ SUCCESSFUL —**promisingly** adv

promo /ˈprəʊməʊ $ ˈproʊmoʊ/ n [C] (plural **promos**) informal a short film that advertises an event or product

promontory /ˈprɒməntəri $ ˈprɑːməntɔːri/ n [C] (plural **promontories**) a long narrow piece of land which goes out into the sea

promote Ac /prəˈməʊt $ -ˈmoʊt/ v [T] **1** to help something happen or be successful SYN **encourage**: *a meeting to promote trade between Taiwan and the UK* **2** to give someone a higher job: **promote sb to sth** *Helen was promoted to manager.* **3** to help sell a new product, film etc, especially by advertising it: *She's in London to promote her new book.* **4** [usually passive] BrE if a sports team is promoted, they play in a better group of teams the next year

promoter Ac /prəˈməʊtə $ -ˈmoʊtər/ n [C] **1** someone who arranges and advertises concerts or sports events **2** someone who tries to persuade people to support or use something: *promoters of organic farming*

promotion Ac /prəˈməʊʃən $ -ˈmoʊ-/ n **1** [C,U] when you are given a higher job: *his promotion to manager* **2** [C,U] an advertisement or special attempt to sell something: *a **sales promotion*** **3** [U] when you help something happen or try to persuade people to support something: [+of] *the promotion of equal rights* **4** [U] BrE if a sports team gets promotion, they play in a better group of teams the next season

promotional /prəˈməʊʃənəl $ -ˈmoʊ-/ adj promotional films, events etc advertise something

prompt¹ /prɒmpt $ prɑːmpt/ v [T] **1** to make

someone decide to do something: **prompt sb to do sth** *What prompted you to buy that suit?* | *The accident prompted an investigation into rail safety.* **2** to remind someone, especially an actor, of what they should say next

prompt² adj **1** done quickly or immediately: *Prompt action must be taken.* **2** someone who is prompt is not late: *The meeting starts at 11, so please be prompt.* —**promptly** (also **prompt** BrE informal) adv

prompt³ n [C] **1** a word or words said to actors to help them remember what to say **2** a sign on a computer screen that shows the computer is ready for the next instruction

pron. (also **pron** BrE) the written abbreviation of **pronoun**

prone /prəʊn $ proʊn/ adj **1** likely to do something bad, or likely to suffer from something: *These plants are very prone to disease.* | **prone to do sth** *She's prone to eat too much.* | **accident-prone/injury-prone etc** *He's always been accident-prone.* **2** formal lying with the front of your body facing down

prong /prɒŋ $ prɔːŋ/ n [C] **1** one of the thin sharp parts of something such as a fork **2** one of two or three ways of achieving something which are used at the same time: **two-pronged/three-pronged** *a two-pronged attack*

pronoun /ˈprəʊnaʊn $ ˈproʊ-/ n [C] a word such as 'he' or 'themselves' that is used instead of a noun → PERSONAL PRONOUN, RELATIVE PRONOUN

pronounce /prəˈnaʊns/ v [T]
1 to make the sound of a word → **pronunciation**: *How do you pronounce your name?*
2 formal to state something officially: **pronounce sb/sth sth** *The doctor pronounced him dead.*
3 formal to give a judgment or opinion: *The scheme was pronounced a failure.*

pronounced /prəˈnaʊnst/ adj very noticeable: *He walks with a **pronounced** limp.*

pronouncement /prəˈnaʊnsmənt/ n [C] formal an official statement

pronunciation /prəˌnʌnsiˈeɪʃən/ n [C,U] the way in which a language or word is pronounced: [+of] *What's the **correct pronunciation** of this word?* | *His pronunciation is poor.*

proof /pruːf/ n
1 [C,U] something that proves something is true: [+of] *proof of the existence of life on other planets* | **proof of purchase/ownership/identity** *Do you have any proof of purchase* (=something to prove that you have paid for something)? | [+(that)] *This letter is proof that he knew about the robbery.*
2 [C usually plural] technical a first copy of a printed page that you correct mistakes on

-proof /pruːf/ suffix not able to be harmed or damaged by something, or not letting something through: *a waterproof jacket* | *a bulletproof car*

proofread /ˈpruːfriːd/ v [I,T] (past tense and past participle **proofread** /-red/) to read something in order to correct mistakes in it —**proofreader** n [C]

prop¹ /prɒp $ prɑːp/ v [T] (**propped, propping**) to support something and make it stay in a particular position: **prop sth against/on sth** *He propped his bike against the tree.*

PHRASAL VERBS

prop sth ↔ **up 1** to prevent something from falling by putting something against it or under it: *We propped the fence up with old bits of wood.* **2** to help an ECONOMY, industry, or government to continue to exist, especially by giving money: *government measures to prop up the stock market*

prop² *n* [C] **1** an object that you put under or against something to hold it in position **2** an object used in a play or film

propaganda /ˌprɒpəˈɡændə $ ˌprɑː-/ *n* [U] false information that a political organization gives to the public to influence them

> **Grammar**
> Do not say 'The government made propaganda about him.' Say *The government put out propaganda about him.*

> **Word Choice: propaganda or publicity?**
> **Propaganda** is untrue information that is intended to make you support a government or other organization: *The newspapers were full of propaganda about the government's achievements.*
> **Publicity** is advertisements, announcements, and other things that a company does in order to advertise something: *There has been a lot of publicity for the film in newspapers and magazines.*

propagate /ˈprɒpəɡeɪt $ ˈprɑː-/ *v* **1** [T] *formal* to spread your ideas or beliefs to many people: *The group uses its website to* **propagate** *its* **ideas**. **2** [I,T] *technical* if you propagate plants, or if they propagate, new plants are produced —**propagation** /ˌprɒpəˈɡeɪʃən $ ˌprɑː-/ *n* [U]

propel /prəˈpel/ *v* [T] (**propelled, propelling**) **1** to move or push something forwards → **propulsion**: *a boat propelled by a small motor* **2** to move someone into a new situation or make them do something: *The film propelled her to stardom.*

propeller /prəˈpelə $ -ər/ *n* [C] the part of a boat or plane that spins around and makes it move

propensity /prəˈpensəti/ *n* [C] (*plural* **propensities**) *formal* a natural tendency to behave in a particular way: *his propensity to argue*

proper /ˈprɒpə $ ˈprɑːpər/ *adj*
1 [only before noun] right, suitable, or correct: *Everything was in its* **proper place**. | *the* **proper way** *to clean your teeth* **THESAURUS** SUITABLE
2 [only before noun] *BrE spoken* real, or of a good and generally accepted standard: *a proper job* | *a proper meal*
3 socially correct and acceptable **OPP** improper: *It wouldn't* **be proper** *for me to ask her.*
4 [only after noun] used to describe the main part of something: *a friendly chat before the interview proper* | *the city centre proper*

properly /ˈprɒpəli $ ˈprɑːpərli/ *adv especially BrE* correctly or in a way that is considered right **SYN** right *AmE*: *I can't see properly without my* glasses. | *The brakes aren't working properly.* | *properly trained staff*

proper 'noun (*also* **proper 'name**) *n* [C] a noun such as 'Mike' or 'Paris' that is the name of a person, place, or thing and is spelt with a capital letter

property /ˈprɒpəti $ ˈprɑːpər-/ *n* (*plural* **properties**)
1 [U] the things that a person, organization etc owns: *Police recovered some of the* **stolen property**. | *his* **personal property** → LOST PROPERTY
2 [C,U] a building or piece of land: *property prices*
3 [C] a natural quality that something has → **characteristic, quality**: *herbs with* **healing properties** | **physical/chemical etc properties** *the chemical properties of a substance*

> **THESAURUS**
> **property** the things that a person, organization etc owns - used especially in formal situations: *The boys were arrested and charged with damaging school property.* | *The documents were marked 'Property of the US Government'.*
> **possessions** all the things that you own, which you keep in your home or carry with you: *Many people lost all their possessions in the floods.* | *The monks have very few personal possessions.*
> **belongings** things you own such as clothes, bags, books etc, especially things you take with you when travelling: *I packed a few belongings into a small suitcase and left.*
> **things/stuff** *informal* things you own such as clothes, books etc: *Don't leave your things all over the floor!* | *Whose stuff is this?*
> **valuables** *formal* small things that you own such as jewellery or cameras, which may get stolen: *I wouldn't leave any valuables in your hotel room.*

prophecy /ˈprɒfəsi $ ˈprɑː-/ *n* [C,U] (*plural* **prophecies**) a statement saying what you believe will happen in the future —**prophesy** /-fəsaɪ/ *v* [I,T]

prophet /ˈprɒfɪt $ ˈprɑː-/ *n* [C] someone who people believe God has chosen to be a religious leader or teacher

prophetic /prəˈfetɪk/ *adj* correctly saying what will happen in the future: *His warnings* **proved prophetic**.

propitious /prəˈpɪʃəs/ *adj formal* likely to bring good results: *a propitious time to attack*

proponent /prəˈpəʊnənt $ -ˈpoʊ-/ *n* [C] *formal* someone who supports something or persuades people to do something: *a proponent of women's rights*

proportion Ac /prəˈpɔːʃən $ -ˈpɔːr-/ *n* **1** [C usually singular] a part of an amount or group: **[+of]** *The proportion of adults who smoke is decreasing.* | *a* **large proportion** *of the population* **2** [C,U] the relationship between two amounts: **proportion of sth to sth** *What's the proportion of boys to girls in your class?* | **in proportion to sth** *Taxes rise in proportion to the amount you earn.* **3 proportions** [plural] the size or importance of something: *a disaster of* **enormous proportions**

keep sth in proportion to react to a situation sensibly, and not think that it is worse than it really is: *Try to stay calm and keep things in proportion.*

in proportion (with sth) when the size of one part of something looks right in relation to other parts: *Make sure the head is in proportion with the body.*

out of (all) proportion (to sth) too big or strong in relation to something: *Fear of violent crime is out of proportion to the actual risk.* | **get/blow sth out of proportion** (=treat something as more serious than it really is)

out of proportion (with sth) when the size of one part of something looks wrong in relation to other parts: *The porch is out of proportion with the rest of the house.*

sense of proportion the ability to judge what is most important in a situation: *I know you feel upset, but keep a sense of proportion.*

proportional Ac /prə'pɔːʃənəl $ -'pɔːr-/ (also **proportionate** /-ʃənət/) adj if something is proportional to something else, its size, amount, importance etc is related to another amount: **[+to]** *The punishment should be proportional to the crime.*

proposal /prə'pəʊzəl $ -'poʊ-/ n [C] **1** a suggested plan: **[+for]** *his proposal for a change in the law* | **proposal to do sth** *a proposal to build a new road* **2** when you ask someone to marry you: *Did you accept his proposal?*

propose /prə'pəʊz $ -'poʊz/ v **1** [T] to officially suggest a plan → **proposal**: *The President proposed a 5% cut in tax.* | **[+(that)]** *I propose that we discuss this at a later meeting.* | **propose doing sth** *The report proposed extending the motorway.* **2** [I] to ask someone to marry you: **[+to]** *Tom proposed to me.* **3** [T] *formal* to intend to do something: **propose to do sth** *What do you propose to do?* **4** [T] to formally suggest someone for an official position: **propose sb for sth** *He proposed Jill for the position of Treasurer.*

proposition¹ /ˌprɒpə'zɪʃən $ ˌprɑː-/ n [C] **1** an offer or suggestion, especially in business or politics: *They came to me with a **business proposition**.* **2 be a ... proposition** used to give your opinion about a possible activity: *Setting up your own business is a very **attractive proposition**.* **3** *formal* a statement in which you express an idea or opinion

proposition² v [T] *formal* to suggest to someone that they have sex with you

proprietor /prə'praɪətə $ -ər/ n [C] *formal* the owner of a business

propriety /prə'praɪəti/ n [U] *formal* correct social or moral behaviour

propulsion /prə'pʌlʃən/ n [U] *technical* the force that moves a vehicle forward: *jet propulsion*

pro rata /ˌprəʊ 'rɑːtə $ ˌproʊ 'reɪtə/ adj, adv *technical* a pro rata payment is calculated according to how much of something is used, how much work is done etc

prosaic /prəʊ'zeɪɪk, prə- $ proʊ-, prə-/ adj *formal* boring or ordinary —**prosaically** /-kli/ adv

proscribe /prəʊ'skraɪb $ proʊ-/ v [T] *formal* to officially say that something is not allowed: *Child labor is proscribed by law.* —**proscription** /-'skrɪpʃən/ n [C,U]

prose /prəʊz $ proʊz/ n [U] ordinary written language, not poetry

prosecute /'prɒsɪkjuːt $ 'prɑː-/ v [I,T] to say officially that you think someone is guilty of a crime and must be judged by a court of law: **prosecute sb for (doing) sth** *The police prosecuted him for theft.*

prosecution /ˌprɒsɪ'kjuːʃən $ ˌprɑː-/ n **1** [C,U] when someone is charged with a crime and judged in a court of law **2 the prosecution** the lawyers who are trying to prove that someone is guilty of a crime in a court of law OPP **defence**: *The prosecution has a good case.*

prosecutor /'prɒsɪkjuːtə $ 'prɑːsɪkjuːtər/ n [C] a lawyer who is trying to prove in a court of law that someone is guilty of a crime

prospect¹ Ac /'prɒspekt $ 'prɑː-/ n **1** [C,U] the possibility that something will happen: **[+of]** *I see **no prospect** of things improving.* | **[+for]** *good prospects for increasing profits* **2** [singular] an event which will probably or definitely happen in the future – used when you say how you feel about it: **[+of]** *The prospect of marriage terrified Alice.* | *It's an exciting prospect.* **3 prospects** [plural] chances of future success: *His job prospects are not good.*

prospect² /prə'spekt $ 'prɑːspekt/ v [I] to look for things such as gold or oil in the ground or under the sea —**prospector** n [C]

prospective Ac /prə'spektɪv/ adj **prospective buyer/husband/employer etc** someone who is likely to do or be something

prospectus /prə'spektəs/ n [C] a small book that advertises a school, college, business etc

prosper /'prɒspə $ 'prɑːspər/ v [I] to be successful, especially financially: *Businesses are prospering.*

prosperity /prɒ'sperəti $ prɑː-/ n [U] when people have a lot of money

prosperous /'prɒspərəs $ 'prɑː-/ adj *formal* rich and successful: *a prosperous farmer* THESAURUS ▶ RICH

prostitute /'prɒstɪtjuːt $ 'prɑːstɪtuːt/ n [C] someone who earns money by having sex with people

prostitution /ˌprɒstɪ'tjuːʃən $ ˌprɑːstə'tuːʃən/ n [U] the work of prostitutes

prostrate /'prɒstreɪt $ 'prɑː-/ adj lying on your front with your face towards the ground

protagonist /prəʊ'tægənɪst $ proʊ-/ n [C] *formal* the main character in a play, film, or story

protect /prə'tekt/ v [I,T] to keep someone or something safe from harm, damage, or illness → **protection**, **protective**: *laws to protect the environment* | **protect sb/sth from sth** *The cover protects the machine from dust.* | **protect (sb/sth) against sth** *Sunscreen will protect your skin against sunburn.* | *a drug that will protect against the virus* —**protected** adj: *Owls are a protected species.* —**protector** n [C]

THESAURUS

protect to keep someone or something safe from harm, damage, or illness: *Don't worry – I'll protect you.* | *The painting is protected by thick glass.*

give/offer/provide protection if something gives protection, it protects you, but often not completely: *The wall gave some protection from the wind.* | *The drug can offer protection against the disease.*

guard to stay near to a person, place etc and watch carefully, to make sure they do not escape, or get attacked or stolen: *The whole area is guarded by soldiers with guns.*

shield to protect something from danger or damage by putting something else in front of it: *He used a towel to shield his face from the heat of the flames.*

safeguard to protect something important such as people's rights, jobs, health etc: *Companies have a duty to safeguard the health and safety of their employees.*

save to stop someone or something from being harmed or destroyed: *They managed to save a few possessions from the fire.* | *We must save the polar bear from extinction (=from dying and disappearing completely).*

preserve to keep land, buildings, the environment etc from being harmed, destroyed, or changed too much: *The organization aims to preserve the forest for future generations.*

protection /prəˈtekʃən/ *n* [singular, U] when someone or something is protected, or something that protects you: **[+of]** *the protection of the environment* | **[+against/from]** *Vitamin C gives protection against cancer.* | **[+for]** *This law provides protection for threatened animals.* | **as (a) protection (against sth)** *He pulled up his collar as protection against the wind.* **THESAURUS** PROTECT

protective /prəˈtektɪv/ *adj* **1** [only before noun] used to protect someone or something from damage: *protective clothing* **2** wanting to protect someone from harm: *She is very protective towards her children.*

protégé /ˈprɒtəʒeɪ $ ˈprou-/ *n* [C] a young person who is taught and helped by an older and more experienced person

protein /ˈprəʊtiːn $ ˈproʊ-/ *n* [C,U] a substance in food such as meat and eggs which helps your body to grow and be healthy

protest¹ /ˈprəʊtest $ ˈproʊ-/ *n* [C,U]
1 when you do something to show publicly that you think something is wrong: **[+against/over]** *protests against the war* | **in protest (at/against sth)** *She resigned in protest at this behaviour.* | *Demonstrators staged a protest outside the UN headquarters.* → see Word Choice at **DEMONSTRATION**
2 words or actions which show that you do not want someone to do something, or that you dislike a situation very much: **[+from]** *I turned off the TV, despite loud protests from the kids.* | *He ignored her protests.* | **do sth under protest** *She paid the bill under*

protest (=while making it clear that she did not want to pay).

protest² /prəˈtest/ *v* [I,T]
1 if people protest against something, they show publicly that they think it is wrong: **[+against/at/about]** *a group protesting against the war* | **protest sth** *AmE: Students protested the decision.* **THESAURUS** **COMPLAIN**
2 to say that you strongly disagree with or are angry about something because it is wrong or unfair: *'Why should I take the blame for this!' she protested.* | *She protested her innocence (=she kept saying that she was innocent).*

Protestant /ˈprɒtəstənt $ ˈprɑː-/ *n* [C] a Christian who is not a Roman Catholic —**Protestant** *adj* —**Protestantism** *n* [U]

protestation /ˌprɒtəˈsteɪʃən ˌprəʊ- $ ˌprɑː-, ˌproʊ-/ *n* [C] *formal* a strong statement saying that something is true or not true, when other people believe the opposite

protester, protestor /prəˈtestə $ -ər/ *n* [C] one of a group of people who are showing publicly that they think something is wrong or unfair: *anti-war protesters*

protocol Ac /ˈprəʊtəkɒl $ ˈproʊtəkɔːl, -kɑːl/ *n* [U] rules about the correct way to behave on official occasions

proton /ˈprəʊtɒn $ ˈproʊtɑːn/ *n* [C] *technical* a part of the NUCLEUS of an atom which carries positive electricity → see picture at **ATOM**

prototype /ˈprəʊtətaɪp $ ˈproʊ-/ *n* [C] the first form of a new car, machine etc, which is used to test the design before it is made in large numbers

protracted /prəˈtræktɪd/ *adj* continuing for a long time, usually longer than necessary: *protracted negotiations*

protractor /prəˈtræktə $ proʊˈtræktər/ *n* [C] a flat object shaped like a half-circle, used for measuring and drawing angles

protrude /prəˈtruːd $ proʊ-/ *v* [I] *formal* to stick out from somewhere: *a rock protruding from the water* —**protrusion** /prəˈtruːʒən $ proʊ-/ *n* [C]

proud /praʊd/ *adj*
1 feeling pleased with something you, your family, or your country have achieved, or with something you own → **pride**: **[+of]** *Her parents are very proud of her.* | **proud to do/be sth** *I'm proud to receive this award.* | **[+(that)]** *She was proud that her book was going to be published.* | **proudest moment/achievement/possession** *His proudest moment (=the one he is most proud of) was winning the cup final.*
2 having respect for yourself, so that you are embarrassed to ask for help when you are in a difficult situation: *She was too proud to ask him for money.*
3 *disapproving* thinking that you are better, more important etc than other people —**proudly** *adv*
PHRASES
| **do sb proud** to make people feel proud of you by doing something well: *The team did their fans proud.*

THESAURUS

proud feeling pleased with something you, your family, or your country have achieved, or with something you own: *I'm very proud of my son.* | *The people are proud of their culture.*

arrogant behaving in an unpleasant and annoying way that shows you think you are better and know more than other people: *His arrogant manner was beginning to annoy me.* | *Don't be so arrogant!*

vain very pleased with yourself, especially your appearance, in a way that annoys people: *She's so vain – she's always looking in the mirror.*

conceited thinking that you are very intelligent, skilful, attractive etc, especially without good reason: *He was so conceited that he thought he couldn't fail.*

prove /pruːv/ v (past tense **proved**, past participle **proved** or **proven** especially AmE /ˈpruːvən/)
1 [T] to show that something is definitely true → **proof**: *You're wrong and I can prove it.* | **[+(that)]** *Tests have proved that the system works.* | **prove sth to sb** *I knew she had done it, but I couldn't prove it to Joe.* | **prove sb's guilt/innocence** *evidence that proves his guilt* | **prove sb right/wrong** *They said I was too old, but I proved them wrong.* | *To prove* his **point** (=show that he was right), *he showed me the results.*
2 [linking verb] if something proves useful, difficult etc, it is found to be useful, difficult etc: *Getting a job proved difficult.* | **prove to be sth** *The design proved to be a success.*

3 prove yourself/prove sth (to sb) to show that you can do something well: *When I first started this job, I felt I had to prove myself.*

proven /ˈpruːvən, ˈprəʊvən $ ˈpruːvən, ˈpruːvən/ *adj* shown to be good or true: *a player of proven ability*

proverb /ˈprɒvɜːb $ ˈprɑːvɜːrb/ *n* [C] a short well-known sentence that tells you something about life, such as 'Many hands make light work' **THESAURUS** PHRASE

proverbial /prəˈvɜːbiəl $ -ɜːr-/ *adj* **the proverbial sth** said when describing something using part of a well-known expression: *There is little sign of light at the end of the proverbial tunnel.* —**proverbially** *adv*

provide /prəˈvaɪd/ *v* [T] to give someone something they need → **provision**: *Tea and biscuits will be provided.* | **provide sth for sb** *The hotel provides a shoe-cleaning service for guests.* | **provide sb with sth** *I can provide you with a place to stay.* —**provider** *n* [C]: *an Internet service provider*
PHRASAL VERBS
provide for sb/sth
1 to give someone the things they need to live, such as money, food etc: *He has to provide for a family of five.*
2 *formal* if a law, rule, or plan provides for something, it makes it possible for it to be done or dealt with

provided /prəˈvaɪdɪd/ (also **provided that**) *linking word* used to say that something will happen only if another thing happens: *You will get good marks, provided you do the work.*

Providence, providence /ˈprɒvɪdəns $ ˈprɑː-/ *n* [U] *literary* a force which some people believe controls our lives and protects us

providing /prəˈvaɪdɪŋ/ (also **providing that**) *linking word* used to say that something will happen only if another thing happens **SYN provided**

province /ˈprɒvəns $ ˈprɑː-/ *n* [C] **1** one of the large areas into which some countries are divided: *a Chinese province* **2 the provinces** the parts of a country that are not near the capital

provincial /prəˈvɪnʃəl/ *adj* **1** relating to a province or the provinces: *the provincial capital* **2** someone who is provincial is not modern or fashionable, because they do not live in a large city

provision /prəˈvɪʒən/ *n* **1** [C usually singular, U] when you provide something that someone needs: *the provision of childcare facilities* **2 make provision for sb/sth** to make arrangements for someone or something: *He made provision for his wife in his will* (=arranged for her to have money etc when he dies). **3 provisions** [plural] food supplies: *We had enough provisions for a week.* **4** [C] a part of an agreement or law: *the provisions of the treaty*

provisional /prəˈvɪʒənəl/ *adj* likely or able to be changed in the future: *a provisional government* —**provisionally** *adv*

proviso /prəˈvaɪzəʊ $ -zoʊ/ *n* [C] (*plural* **provisos**) *formal* something that you say must happen before you allow another thing to happen

provocation /ˌprɒvəˈkeɪʃən $ ˌprɑː-/ *n* [C,U] an action that makes someone angry or upset, or is intended to do this: *He attacked me totally without provocation.*

provocative /prəˈvɒkətɪv $ -ˈvɑː-/ *adj* **1** intended to make someone angry or upset, or to cause a lot of discussion: *a provocative comment* **2** intended to make someone sexually excited: *provocative images of young women* —**provocatively** *adv*

provoke /prəˈvəʊk $ -ˈvoʊk/ *v* [T] **1** to cause a reaction or feeling: *The plan provoked widespread criticism.* **2** to deliberately make someone angry: *The dog wouldn't have attacked him if it hadn't been provoked.*

provost, Provost /ˈprɒvəst $ ˈproʊvoʊst/ *n* [C] an important official at a university

prow /praʊ/ *n* [C] the front part of a ship or boat

prowess /ˈpraʊɪs/ *n* [U] *formal* great skill at doing something: *athletic prowess*

prowl¹ /praʊl/ *v* [I,T] to move around an area quietly, especially when hunting: *a tiger prowling through the jungle*

prowl² *n* **be on the prowl** to be moving around quietly, hunting for another animal, or looking for someone to attack

prowler /ˈpraʊlə $ -ər/ *n* [C] someone who moves around quietly at night, especially in order to steal things or attack someone

proximity /prɒkˈsɪməti $ prɑːk-/ *n* [U] *formal* closeness to something: **[+to]** *We chose this house because of its proximity to the school.*

proxy /'prɒksi $ 'prɑːksi/ n **by proxy** if you do something by proxy, you arrange for someone else to do it for you

prude /pruːd/ n [C] *disapproving* someone who is easily shocked by anything relating to sex —**prudish** adj —**prudishness, prudery** n [U]

prudent /'pruːdənt/ adj sensible and careful: *prudent use of resources* —**prudence** n [U]

prune¹ /pruːn/ (*also* **prune back**) v [T] to cut branches off a tree or plant

prune² n [C] a dried PLUM

prurient /'prʊəriənt $ 'prʊr-/ adj *formal disapproving* showing too much interest in sex —**prurience** n [U]

pry /praɪ/ v (**pried, prying, pries**) **1** [I] to try to find out about someone's private life in an impolite way: *I don't want to pry, but are you still seeing Tom?* **2** [T] *AmE* to force something open or away from something else SYN **prise**: *pry sth open/off etc* I *used a screwdriver to pry off the lid.*

PS /ˌpiː 'es/ n [C] (**postscript**) a note added to the end of a letter: *PS I love you*

psalm /sɑːm $ sɑːm, sɑːlm/ n [C] a song in the Bible praising God

pseudo- /sjuːdəʊ $ suːdoʊ/ *prefix* not real: *pseudoscience*

pseudonym /'sjuːdənɪm $ 'suː-/ n [C] a name used by a writer, artist etc instead of his or her real name

psych /saɪk/ v

PHRASAL VERBS

psych yourself **up** *informal* to prepare for something difficult by telling yourself that you can do it —**psyched up** adj

psyche /'saɪki/ n [C] your mind and deepest feelings: *the human psyche*

psychedelic /ˌsaɪkə'delɪk◂/ adj producing or having bright colours and strange patterns

psychiatrist /saɪ'kaɪətrɪst $ sə-/ n [C] a doctor who treats people who have a mental illness → **psychologist** THESAURUS DOCTOR

psychiatry /saɪ'kaɪətri $ sə-/ n [U] the study and treatment of mental illness —**psychiatric** /ˌsaɪki'ætrɪk◂/ adj: *a psychiatric hospital*

psychic¹ /'saɪkɪk/ adj related to strange events or things that cannot be explained by science: *psychic phenomena* | *She claims to have psychic powers.*

psychic² n [C] someone with special powers, such as knowing what people are thinking

psycho /'saɪkəʊ $ -koʊ/ n [C] (*plural* **psychos**) *informal* a crazy person who is violent and dangerous

psychoanalysis /ˌsaɪkəʊ-ə'næləsɪs $ -koʊ-/ n [U] a treatment for mental illness that involves talking to the patient about their life, dreams, feelings etc

psychoanalyst /ˌsaɪkəʊ'ænəl-ɪst $ -koʊ-/ n [C] someone who treats mental illness using psychoanalysis

psychological Ac /ˌsaɪkə'lɒdʒɪkəl $ -'lɑː-/ adj relating to your mind, or the study of people's

minds: *psychological problems* —**psychologically** /-kli/ adv

psychologist Ac /saɪ'kɒlədʒɪst $ -'kɑː-/ n [C] someone who studies the way people's minds work → **psychiatrist**

┌───┐
Word Choice: psychologist or psychiatrist?
A **psychologist** studies the mind. A **psychiatrist** treats people who have a mental illness.
└───┘

psychology Ac /saɪ'kɒlədʒi $ -'kɑː-/ n (*plural* **psychologies**) **1** [U] the study of the way people's minds work **2** [C,U] the way that a particular kind of person thinks and behaves: *the psychology of child killers*

psychopath /'saɪkəpæθ/ n [C] someone who has a mental illness that makes them violent and dangerous —**psychopathic** /ˌsaɪkə'pæθɪk◂/ adj

psychosis /saɪ'kəʊsɪs $ -'koʊ-/ n [C,U] (*plural* **psychoses** /-siːz/) a serious mental illness

psychosomatic /ˌsaɪkəʊsə'mætɪk◂ $ -kəsə-/ adj *technical* a psychosomatic illness is caused by your mind, not by a real physical problem

psychotherapy /ˌsaɪkəʊ'θerəpi $ -koʊ-/ n [U] the treatment of mental illness by talking to someone about their problems, rather than using drugs —**psychotherapist** n [C]

psychotic /saɪ'kɒtɪk $ -'kɑː-/ adj relating to serious mental illness: *psychotic behaviour*

pt. 1 the written abbreviation of **part 2** the written abbreviation of **pint**

PTA /ˌpiː tiː 'eɪ/ n [C] *BrE* (**Parent Teacher Association**) an organization of the teachers and parents of children at a school SYN **PTO** *AmE*

PTO¹ /ˌpiː tiː 'əʊ $ -'oʊ/ (**please turn over**) used at the bottom of a page

PTO² n [C] *AmE* (**Parent-Teacher Organization**) an organization of the teachers and parents of children at a school SYN **PTA** *BrE*

pub /pʌb/ n [C] *BrE* a building where you can buy and drink beer, wine etc, and where meals are often served SYN **bar**: *Are you going to the pub?* | *He'd been in the pub* (=drinking in a pub) *all day.* | *a pub lunch*

puberty /'pjuːbəti $ -ər-/ n [U] the time when your body changes from being a child to being an adult

pubic /'pjuːbɪk/ adj relating to the sex organs: *pubic hair*

public¹ /'pʌblɪk/ adj
1 relating to the ordinary people in a country: ***Public opinion** is in favor of the war.* | *public health risks* | *Can you prove your actions were in the public interest* (=useful or helpful to ordinary people)?
2 available for anyone to use OPP **private**: *a public telephone* | *public toilets* | *a ban on smoking in public places* | *damage to public property*
3 relating to the government and the services it provides: *cuts in public spending* | *She was elected to public office* (=an important government job).
4 known, seen, or talked about by most people: *There is to be a public inquiry into the incident.* | *We need a wider public debate on gay issues.* | *His job puts*

him **in the public eye** (=people know about what he does). | **go public/make sth public** (=tell people something that was secret) *The name of the killer was made public.* —**publicly** adv: *The matter was never discussed publicly.*

public² n **the public** [also + plural verb *BrE*] people in general: *The museum is open to the public every day.* | *Police appealed to **members of the public** for help.* | *They are not yet on sale to **the general public** (*=ordinary people*).* | *The public are fed up with the Government's feeble excuses.* | **the travelling/ viewing/record-buying etc public** (=people who travel, watch television etc) *a campaign aimed at the record-buying public* **THESAURUS** PEOPLE

PHRASES

> **in public** if you do something in public, you do it where other people can see you: *I hate having rows in public.*

,public ad'dress ,system n [C] a PA

publican /'pʌblɪkən/ n [C] someone who owns or manages a PUB

publication Ac /ˌpʌblɪ'keɪʃən/ n **1** [U] the process of printing a book, magazine etc and offering it for sale → **publish**: [+of] *the publication of her latest novel* | *His article was accepted for publication.* **2** [U] when information is made available to people: [+of] *the publication of exam results on the Web* **3** [C] *formal* a book, magazine etc that is printed and sold: *a monthly publication* | *scientific publications*

,public 'figure n [C] someone who is often on television, in newspapers, and magazines etc

,public 'holiday n [C] *BrE* a day when people do not work and many shops are closed **SYN** **national holiday** *AmE*

,public 'house n [C] *BrE formal* a PUB

publicist /'pʌblɪsɪst/ n [C] someone whose job is to make sure that people know about a new film, book, event etc

publicity /pʌ'blɪsəti/ n [U]
1 attention that someone or something gets from newspapers, television etc: **good/bad etc publicity** *They had hoped to **avoid bad publicity**.* | **attract/receive publicity** *The trial received **widespread publicity**.*
2 the business of making sure that people know about a new film, book, event etc: *We launched a **publicity campaign** for the new range of sports shoe.* | **advance publicity** | *The fight was just a **publicity stunt** (*=something only done to get publicity*).*

publicize (also **-ise** *BrE*) /'pʌblɪsaɪz/ v [T] to tell people about a new film, book, event etc: **well/ highly publicized** *His visit has been highly publicized.*

,public re'lations n (abbreviation **PR**) **1** [U] the work of explaining to people what an organization does, so that they will understand and approve of it **2** [plural] the relationship between an organization and ordinary people

,public 'school n [C] **1** in Britain, an expensive private school for children aged between 13 and 18 **2** in the US, a school that the government pays for

> **Word Choice: public school or private school?**
> In Britain, you have to pay money to go to a **public school** or a **private school**, and they mean the same thing. **State schools** are free and are provided by the government.
> In the US, a **public school** is free and is provided by the government. You pay to go to a **private school**.

,public-'spirited adj willing to help people and society in general

,public 'television n [U] a television service in the US that the government, large companies, and ordinary people pay for

,public 'transport *BrE*, **public transpor'tation** *AmE* n [U] trains, buses etc that are available for everyone to use

publish Ac /'pʌblɪʃ/ v
1 [I,T] to print a book, magazine etc and offer it for sale → **publication**: *The book was published in 1968.*
2 [T] if a newspaper, magazine etc publishes a story, photograph etc, it prints it: *We publish as many of your letters as we can.*
3 [T] to make information available: *The results will be published this week.*
4 [I,T] if a writer, musician etc publishes his or her work, their work is printed in a book, magazine etc: *She's published a few short stories.*

publisher Ac /'pʌblɪʃə $ -ər/ n [C] a person or company that produces books, magazines etc and offers them for sale

publishing Ac /'pʌblɪʃɪŋ/ n [U] the business of producing books, magazines etc and offering them for sale

puck /pʌk/ n [C] the hard flat piece of rubber used in the game of ICE HOCKEY

pudding /'pʊdɪŋ/ n [C,U]
1 a sweet food made with milk, eggs, sugar, flour etc: *chocolate pudding*
2 *BrE* sweet food eaten at the end of a meal: *What's for pudding?*

puddle /'pʌdl/ n [C] a small pool of liquid, especially rain water: *children splashing through the puddles* **THESAURUS** LAKE

pudgy /'pʌdʒi/ adj disapproving fat

puff¹ /pʌf/ v **1** [I] to breathe quickly after running, carrying something heavy etc: *George **puffed and panted** as he ran.* **2** [I,T] to smoke a cigarette, pipe etc: [+at/on] *He puffed thoughtfully on his pipe.* **3** [I,T] if something puffs smoke, steam etc, small amounts of smoke, steam etc keep coming out of it: *a chimney puffing out black smoke*
PHRASAL VERBS
puff sth ↔ **out** to make your cheeks or chest bigger by filling them with air
puff up if part of your body puffs up, it becomes swollen: *His ankle had started to puff up.*

puff² n [C] **1** when you breathe smoke in and out: *He took a puff on his cigar.* **2** a small amount of air, smoke, wind etc: *puffs of smoke*

puffy /ˈpʌfi/ *adj* if part of your body is puffy, it is swollen: *Her eyes were red and puffy from crying.* —**puffiness** *n* [U]

pugnacious /pʌgˈneɪʃəs/ *adj formal* very eager to argue or fight with people

puke /pjuːk/ *v* [I,T] *informal* to VOMIT —**puke** *n* [U]

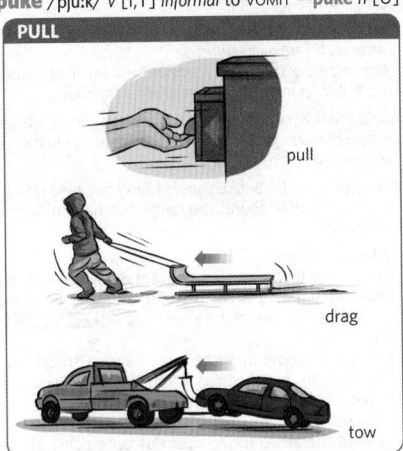

PULL

pull

drag

tow

pull¹ /pʊl/ *v*

1 [I,T] to hold someone or something firmly and move them in a particular direction, especially towards you OPP **push**: *He pulled her close and kissed her.* | **pull sb/sth out/from/away etc** *A motorist stopped and helped to pull him from the water.* | *Some kids had pulled up all the flowers.* | *Pulling on her coat, she ran outside.* | **pull sth open/shut** *Pull the door shut behind you.* | **pull the curtains/blinds etc** (=open or close them)

2 [T] to move while attached to something so that it moves along behind: *a car pulling a trailer*

3 [I,T] to move away from someone or something: **pull (sth) away/free** *He struggled to pull free.* | **pull sth out of/from sth** *She pulled her arm from his grasp.* | **[+back]** *As he moved, she pulled back.*

4 pull a knife/gun (on sb) to take out a weapon and threaten someone with it: *The defendant claimed that the boy had pulled a gun on him.*

5 [T] to attract a lot of people, interest, attention etc: *a singer who can always **pull** the **crowds** → make/ pull a face at FACE¹*

PHRASES

pull a fast one *spoken* to secretly try to trick someone in order to get what you want: *Don't try to pull a fast one on me.*

pull sb's leg to tell someone something that is untrue, as a joke: *Don't worry – I'm only pulling your leg.*

pull a muscle to injure a muscle by stretching it: *Paul pulled a muscle in training.*

pull out all the stops to do everything you can to make something succeed: *The doctors are pulling out all the stops.*

pull strings to secretly use your influence with important people to get what you want: *His Dad pulled strings to get him the job.*

pull your weight to do a fair share of the work: *The girls accused us of not pulling our weight.*

PHRASAL VERBS

pull sth ↔ **apart**
1 to separate something into pieces: *The dogs pull the fox apart.*
2 to criticize someone's work very strongly: *The tutor pulled my assignment apart in class.*

pull away
1 to start to drive away from a place: *She watched the car pull away.*
2 to start to win in a race or game, by going faster or getting more points: *Chicago pulled away in the third quarter to win 107–76.*

pull back to decide not to do something that you had intended to do: **[+from]** *He has decided to pull back from funding the project.*

pull sth ↔ **down** to destroy a building, wall etc: *My old school was pulled down.*

pull in
1 to drive to the side of the road and stop: *A police car pulled in behind me.*
2 if a train pulls in, it arrives at a station

pull off
1 pull sth ↔ **off** to succeed in doing something difficult: *The goalkeeper pulled off six terrific saves.*
2 pull off (sth) to drive a car off the road you are on so that you can stop, change direction etc: *Shall we pull off at the next junction?*

pull out
1 if a car pulls out, it moves away from the side of a road into a line of traffic: *Some idiot pulled out in front of me.*
2 if a train pulls out, it starts to leave a station
3 to not be involved in something that you had agreed to do: **[+of]** *The injury may force him to pull out of the championship.*
4 to leave a place or situation: **[+of]** *The country is just pulling out of a bad year.* | **pull sb/sth ↔ out** *US troops were pulled out on Sunday.*

pull (sb/sth) **over** if a car pulls over, it moves to the side of the road and stops: *The cops pulled him over for speeding.*

pull through *informal* to stay alive after you have been very ill or badly injured: *Do the doctors think he'll pull through?*

pull together
1 if a group of people pull together, they work hard together to succeed: *If we all pull together, we can win.*
2 pull yourself together *informal* to force yourself to be calm and stop behaving in an uncontrolled way: *Pull yourself together, man!*

pull up if a car pulls up, it stops: *Another car pulled up at the lights.* THESAURUS STOP

THESAURUS

pull to hold someone or something firmly and move them in a particular direction, especially towards you: *He pulled the blanket off the bed.*
drag to pull something along the ground, especially because it is too heavy to carry: *They managed to drag the sofa across the room.*
haul to pull something big and heavy using a lot of effort, especially using a rope: *The fishermen were hauling in their nets.*

tug to pull something with a short quick movement: *The little girl was tugging at her mother's coat.*

heave to pull or lift something very heavy, especially with one movement: *Somehow he heaved the bag onto his shoulders.*

tow to pull a vehicle along using a rope or chain: *Our car had to be towed to the nearest garage.*

pull² n 1 [C] the movement you make when you pull something towards you OPP **push**: *Give the rope a pull.* 2 [singular] a force such as GRAVITY that makes things move in a particular direction: *the gravitational pull of the Moon*

pulley /'pʊli/ n [C] a piece of equipment used for lifting things, which has a rope and a wheel

pullout, pull-out /'pʊlaʊt/ n [C] 1 when an army, organization etc leaves a place: *the pullout of troops* 2 part of a book or magazine that you take out and read separately

pullover /'pʊl,əʊvə $ -,oʊvər/ n [C] a SWEATER

pulp /pʌlp/ n [U] 1 a soft wet substance made by crushing something: *wood pulp* 2 the soft part inside fruit or vegetables SYN **flesh**

pulpit /'pʊlpɪt/ n [C] a high place where the priest in a church stands to speak to the people

pulsate /pʌl'seɪt $ 'pʌlseɪt/ v [I] to move, change, or make sounds in a strong regular way: *pulsating lights* —**pulsation** /pʌl'seɪʃən/ n [C,U]

pulse¹ /pʌls/ n 1 [C usually singular] the regular beat that your heart makes as it pumps blood around your body: *a fast pulse rate* | **take sb's pulse** (=touch someone's wrist or neck to check how fast their heart is beating) 2 [C usually plural] seeds such as beans and LENTILS that you can eat

pulse² v [I] to move quickly with a strong regular beat or sound: *the blood pulsing through his veins*

pulverize (also **-ise** BrE) /'pʌlvəraɪz/ v [T] 1 to crush something into powder: *a machine that pulverizes rocks* 2 *informal* to defeat someone completely

pummel /'pʌməl/ v [T] (**pummelled, pummelling** BrE, **pummeled, pummeling** AmE) to hit someone or something many times with your FISTS (=closed hands)

pump¹ /pʌmp/ n [C]
1 a machine that forces liquid or gas into or out of something: **water/fuel/air etc pump** → see picture at BICYCLE
2 a type of plain light shoe: *a pair of black pumps*

pump² v
1 [I,T] if liquid or gas pumps somewhere, or if you pump it, it is forced to move in a particular direction: **[+from/out of]** *Blood was pumping from the wound.* | **pump sth into/out of etc sth** *Fire crews will pump the water out of the flooded homes.* | *Your heart pumps blood around your body.* | **pump gas** AmE (=put gasoline in a car)
2 [T] *informal* if you pump someone for information, you ask them lots of questions: **pump sb for sth** *Laura began to pump Ben for more details.*
3 [I] to move quickly up and down or in and out: *His legs pumped harder as he cycled up the hill.*

PHRASAL VERBS
pump sth **into** sth if you pump money into a business or project, you spend a lot of money on it: *The government has pumped millions into the space project.*
pump sth ↔ **out** to keep producing a lot of something: *bands that pump out three new records a month*
pump sth ↔ **up**
1 to fill a tyre, ball etc with air SYN **inflate**: *Pump up the tyres before a long journey.*
2 to increase the value, amount, or level of something: *Nick pumped up the volume on the stereo.*

pumpkin /'pʌmpkɪn/ n [C,U] a large round orange vegetable that grows on the ground: *pumpkin pie* → see picture on page A5

pun /pʌn/ n [C] a joke that is funny because it uses two words that sound the same but have different meanings

punch¹ /pʌntʃ/ v [T]
1 to hit someone or something hard with your FIST (=closed hand): **punch sb on/in sth** *He punched me in the face.* → see picture on page A11 THESAURUS **HIT**
2 to make a hole in something, using a sharp tool: *The inspector punched our tickets.* | *These bullets can* **punch a hole** *through 20mm of steel.*

PHRASES
punch the air to move your FIST up quickly above your head, to show that you are pleased: *He punched the air in triumph.*

punch² n 1 [C] when you hit someone once with your FIST (=closed hand): *a punch in the stomach* 2 [U] a drink made from fruit juice, sugar, and alcohol 3 [C] a sharp tool used to make a hole in something → see picture at STATIONERY

punch bag BrE, **punching bag** AmE n [C] a heavy leather bag that BOXERS hit when they are training

punchline, punch line /'pʌntʃlaɪn/ n [C] the last few words of a joke or story, which make it funny or clever: *Jake had forgotten the punchline.*

punch-up n [C] BrE *informal* a fight THESAURUS **FIGHT**

punctual /'pʌŋktʃuəl/ adj arriving at exactly the time that has been arranged: *Ted's always very punctual.* —**punctually** adv —**punctuality** /,pʌŋktʃu'æləti/ n [U]

punctuate /'pʌŋktʃueɪt/ v [T] 1 to divide writing into sentences, phrases etc, using COMMAS (,), FULL STOPS (.) etc 2 **be punctuated by/with sth** to be interrupted by something several times: *silence punctuated by cries*

punctuation /,pʌŋktʃu'eɪʃən/ n [U] the use of COMMAS (,), FULL STOPS (.) etc in writing: *The punctuation in this essay is awful.*

punctu'ation mark n [C] a sign, such as a COMMA (,) or a FULL STOP (.), used to divide writing into sentences, phrases etc

puncture¹ /'pʌŋktʃə $ -ər/ n [C] 1 a small hole made by a sharp point THESAURUS **HOLE** 2 BrE a hole in a tyre SYN **flat** AmE

puncture² v [I,T] if you puncture something, or if it punctures, a small hole appears in it

pundit /'pʌndɪt/ n [C] a person who often gives their opinion about something on television or in newspapers: *political pundits*

pungent /'pʌndʒənt/ adj having a strong taste or smell: *the pungent smell of garlic* —**pungency** n [U]

punish /'pʌnɪʃ/ v [T]
1 to do something unpleasant to someone because they have done something wrong → **punishment**: **punish sb for (doing) sth** *He was severely punished for lying to his father.* | *She deserves to be punished for her crimes.* | **punish sb by doing sth** *The class was punished by being given extra work.*
2 if a crime is punished in a particular way, anyone who is guilty of it receives that punishment: *Drug smuggling is punished by death.*

punishable /'pʌnɪʃəbəl/ adj a crime that is punishable by death, prison etc is punished in that way

punishing /'pʌnɪʃɪŋ/ adj difficult to do and making you tired: *a punishing schedule*

punishment /'pʌnɪʃmənt/ n [C,U] something that is done to punish someone → **punitive**: **[+for]** *The punishment for murder is life in prison.* | **as a punishment** *They had to stay late after school as a punishment.*

COLLOCATIONS

adjectives
a harsh/severe punishment *Do you think the punishment was too harsh?*
a light punishment (=not severe) *The punishment was too light.*
the maximum punishment *The maximum punishment is three months in prison.*
a suitable punishment *Cleaning up the mess seems a suitable punishment.*

verbs
to give sb a punishment *I don't think she deserved the punishment she was given.*
to receive a punishment *He received the maximum punishment.*
to escape/avoid punishment *The thieves managed to escape punishment.*

THESAURUS

punishment something that is done to punish someone: *The court decided the original punishment was too severe.* | *Billy was sent to bed early as a punishment.*
fine an amount of money that you must pay as a punishment: *If you park here, you'll get a fine.*
penalty an official punishment for someone who breaks a law, rule, or agreement: *There should be tougher penalties for athletes who take drugs.*
sentence a punishment given by a judge in a court, especially a period of time in prison: *The thief was given a two-year sentence.*
the death penalty/sentence (also **capital punishment**) the system of killing people as a punishment for crimes: *I don't agree with capital punishment.* | *He could face the death penalty.*

---

corporal punishment the system of punishing children by hitting them: *In those days, schools still used corporal punishment.*

punitive /'pju:nətɪv/ adj done to punish someone, or like a punishment: *punitive action* | *punitive price rises* —**punitively** adv

punk /pʌŋk/ n **1** [U] a type of loud music and strange fashions that were popular in the 1970s and 1980s: *punk music* **2** [C] *AmE informal* a young man who fights and breaks the law

punnet /'pʌnɪt/ n [C] *BrE* a small box in which small fruit is sold

punt /pʌnt/ n [C] a long narrow boat that you move by pushing a long pole against the bottom of the river —**punt** v [I,T]

punter /'pʌntə $ -ər/ n [C] *BrE informal* **1** someone who buys something SYN **customer** **2** someone who makes a BET on the result of a race, game etc

puny /'pju:ni/ adj small, thin, and weak: *a puny kid*

pup /pʌp/ n [C] a PUPPY

pupil /'pju:pəl/ n [C]
1 *BrE* a child in a school: *the star pupil* (=the best)
2 someone who learns from an experienced musician, artist etc: *a pupil of Yehudi Menuhin*
3 the round black part in the middle of your eye → **iris** → see picture at EYE[1]

puppet /'pʌpɪt/ n [C] **1** a model of a person or animal that you move by putting your hand inside it or by pulling strings attached to it: *a puppet show* **2** *disapproving* a person or organization that allows other people to control them and make their decisions: *a puppet leader*

puppy /'pʌpi/ n [C] (*plural* **puppies**) a young dog

purchase[1] Ac /'pɜːtʃɪs $ 'pɜːr-/ v [T] *formal* to buy something: *Where did you purchase the car?* THESAURUS ► BUY —**purchaser** n [C]

purchase[2] Ac n [C,U] *formal* something you buy, or the act of buying something: **[+of]** *money for the purchase of new equipment* | *Every time you make a purchase, you pay tax.*

pure /pjʊə $ pjʊr/ adj
1 SUBSTANCE/MATERIAL not mixed with anything else OPP **impure**: *pure gold* | *pure cotton/wool/silk etc pure wool blankets*
2 AIR/WATER clean and not containing anything harmful or unhealthy: *pure drinking water* | *In the mountains, the air is pure.* THESAURUS ► CLEAN
3 COMPLETE complete and total SYN **sheer**: *We met by pure chance.* | *a smile of pure joy*
4 INNOCENT *literary* without any sexual experience or evil thoughts: *a pure young girl*
5 MATHS/SCIENCE [only before noun] pure maths or science is concerned with increasing our knowledge of the subject rather than using it for practical purposes → **applied**: *pure mathematics*

puree /'pjʊəreɪ $ pjʊˈreɪ/ n [C,U] food that has been boiled or crushed until it is almost a liquid: *tomato puree* —**puree** v [T]

purely /'pjʊəli $ 'pjʊrli/ adv completely and only: *He did it for purely selfish reasons.* | *It happened **purely by chance**.*

Purgatory /ˈpɜːɡətəri $ ˈpɜːrɡətɔːri/ n in Roman Catholic belief, a place where the souls of dead people suffer until they are pure enough to enter heaven

purge /pɜːdʒ $ pɜːrdʒ/ v [T] to remove unwanted people or things from something: **purge sth of sb/sth** Local languages were purged of Russian words. —**purge** n [C]: a purge of the army

purify /ˈpjʊərɪfaɪ $ ˈpjʊr-/ v [T] (**purified, purifying, purifies**) to remove dirty or unwanted parts from something: purified water —**purification** /ˌpjʊərɪfɪˈkeɪʃən $ ˌpjʊr-/ n [U]

purist /ˈpjʊərɪst $ ˈpjʊr-/ n [C] someone who has very strict ideas about the correct way to do something

puritanical /ˌpjʊərəˈtænɪkəl◀ $ ˌpjʊr-/ adj disapproving very strict about moral matters, especially sex: Her parents had very puritanical views. —**puritan** n [C]

purity /ˈpjʊərəti $ ˈpjʊr-/ n [U] the quality of being pure: the purity of our water | moral purity

purple /ˈpɜːpəl $ ˈpɜːr-/ n [U] a dark colour made from red mixed with blue —**purple** adj: a purple shirt

purport /pɜːˈpɔːt $ pɜːrˈpɔːrt/ v [I,T] formal to claim to be or do something, even if this is not true: a man purporting to be a police officer —**purportedly** adv

purpose /ˈpɜːpəs $ ˈpɜːr-/ n
1 [C] the purpose of something is what it is intended to achieve: **the purpose of (doing) sth** What is the purpose of your visit to England? | The purpose of running a business is to make money.
2 [C usually plural] what something is used for: The planes may be used for military purposes.
3 [U] determination to succeed in what you want to do: She went back to her work with a new **sense of purpose**. → **to/for all intents and purposes** at INTENT²
PHRASES
on purpose deliberately [OPP] **by accident**: I'm sorry. I didn't hurt you on purpose. [THESAURUS] **DELIBERATELY**

purpose-'built adj BrE designed and made for a particular purpose: purpose-built toilets for disabled people

purposeful /ˈpɜːpəsfəl $ ˈpɜːr-/ adj having a clear aim or purpose [SYN] **determined**: He picked up his toolbox in a purposeful manner. —**purposefully** adv

purposely /ˈpɜːpəsli $ ˈpɜːr-/ adv deliberately [SYN] **on purpose**: They purposely left him out of the discussion.

purr /pɜː $ pɜːr/ v [I] if a cat purrs, it makes a soft low sound in its throat to show that it is pleased —**purr** n [C]

purse¹ /pɜːs $ pɜːrs/ n
1 [C] BrE a small container used for carrying money, especially by women [SYN] **wallet** AmE: I opened my handbag and took out my purse.
2 [C] AmE a bag used by women to carry money and personal things [SYN] **handbag** BrE → see picture at **BAG¹**
3 [singular] formal the amount of money that a

person, organization, or country has available to spend: demands on the public purse
PHRASES
the purse strings used to refer to the control of spending in a family, company, country etc: She **holds the purse strings**.

purse² v **purse your lips** to bring your lips together tightly, especially to show that you do not like or do not agree with something

pursue [Ac] /pəˈsjuː $ pərˈsuː/ v [T] **1** to continue doing something, or to try to achieve something over a long period of time: He hoped to **pursue a career** in film-making. **2 pursue the matter/question** to continue trying to find out about a particular subject or trying to persuade someone: Janet did not dare pursue the matter further. **3** to chase someone or something in order to catch them: The stolen car was pursued by police for several miles. [THESAURUS] **FOLLOW** —**pursuer** n [C]

pursuit [Ac] /pəˈsjuːt $ pərˈsuːt/ n **1** [U] when someone chases or follows someone else: There were four police cars **in hot pursuit** (=following closely behind). **2** [U] when someone tries to achieve something or get something: He left his home town in pursuit of sth He left his home town in pursuit of work. **3 pursuits** [plural] formal things that you spend time doing, especially to enjoy yourself: outdoor pursuits

purveyor /pɜːˈveɪə $ pɜːrˈveɪər/ n [C] formal a shop or company that sells or provides something: purveyors of fine cheeses

pus /pʌs/ n [U] yellow liquid produced in an infected part of your body

push¹ /pʊʃ/ v
1 [MOVE SB/STH AWAY] [I,T] to make something or someone move away from you, by pressing against them with your hands, arms etc [OPP] **pull**: The door didn't move, so she pushed harder. | **push sth/sb down/into sth** Lisa pushed Amy into the pool. | **push sth/sb away/back/aside etc** She pushed him away. | **push sth open/shut** I slowly pushed the door open. | Push the green button to start the engine. → see picture on page A11
2 [MOVE THROUGH PEOPLE] [I,T] to move forward, using your hands to move people or things away from you: Don't push. Everyone will get a turn. | **push (your) way past/through/into etc sth** Heather pushed past us without speaking. | She pushed her way to the front of the crowd.
3 [MAKE SB DO STH] [T] to encourage or force someone to do something or to work hard: **push sb into (doing) sth** My parents pushed me into going to college. | **push yourself** Mike has been **pushing** himself too **hard** lately.
4 [PERSUADE] [I,T] to try to persuade people to accept your ideas, opinions etc in order to achieve something: **[+for]** He was **pushing hard** for changes in education.
5 [INCREASE/DECREASE] [T] to make a number, amount, price etc greater or less: **push sth up/down** The new tax will push up the price of consumer goods.
6 [TRY TO SELL STH] [T] informal to try to sell more of a

product by advertising it a lot: *They're really pushing the new movie.*

7 DRUGS [T] *informal* to sell illegal drugs SYN **deal**

PHRASES

be pushing 40/50 etc *informal* to be nearly 40, 50 etc years old: *He's pushing 50, but he doesn't look it.*

push your luck *informal* to do something or ask for something when this is likely to annoy someone or involve a risk: *Don't push your luck.*

PHRASAL VERBS

push ahead to continue trying to do something you have planned to do: [+with] *He has promised to push ahead with reform.*

push sb **around** (*also* **push** sb **about** *BrE*) *informal* to tell someone what to do in a rude or threatening way

push in *BrE informal* to go in front of other people who are waiting for something, instead of joining the end of the line: *Don't push in!*

push off *BrE spoken* used to rudely tell someone to go away

push on to continue travelling somewhere or trying to achieve something: *The others stopped for a rest, but I pushed on to the top.*

push sb/sth ↔ **over** to make someone or something fall to the ground by pushing them: *He went wild, pushing over tables and chairs.*

push sth ↔ **through** to get a plan, law etc officially accepted, especially quickly

---

THESAURUS

push to make something or someone move away from you, by pressing against them with your hands, arms etc: *He pushed me and I fell.* | *We pushed the car up the hill.*

shove to push someone or something in a rough or careless way: *The man tried to shove me out of the way.* | *He shoved the money across the counter.*

poke to push someone or something with your finger or something sharp: *I poked him to see if he was awake.*

nudge to push someone beside you gently with your elbow to get their attention: *Sally nudged me. 'Look, he's coming,' she said.*

---

push² n [C usually singular] **1** when someone pushes something OPP **pull**: *If the door's stuck, give it a push.* **2** when people try very hard to achieve something: [+for] *the party's final push for victory*

PHRASES

at a push *BrE informal* used to say that something can be done if necessary, but it will be difficult: *We have room for five people, six at a push.*

give sb **the push** *BrE informal* **1** to end a relationship with someone: *She gave her boyfriend the push.* **2** to make someone leave their job: *His boss has given him the push.*

when/if push comes to shove if a situation becomes very difficult or action needs to be taken: *If push comes to shove, I can always rent out the house.*

pushbike /'pʊʃbaɪk/ n [C] *BrE* a bicycle

'push-button adj [only before noun] operated by

pressing a button with your finger: *a push-button telephone*

pushchair /'pʊʃ-tʃeə $ -tʃer/ n [C] *BrE* a chair on wheels, used for pushing young children in SYN **stroller** *AmE*

pusher /'pʊʃə $ -ər/ n [C] *informal* someone who sells illegal drugs

pushover /'pʊʃəʊvə $ -,oʊvər/ n **be a pushover** *informal* **a)** to be easy to persuade, influence, or defeat: *The team is no pushover.* **b)** *BrE* to be easy to do or win: *The exam was a pushover.*

'push-up n [C] *AmE* an exercise in which you lie on the floor and push yourself up with your arms SYN **press-up** *BrE*

pushy /'pʊʃi/ adj *disapproving* someone who is pushy does everything they can to get what they want from other people: *pushy salespeople*

pussycat /'pʊsikæt/ (*also* **puss** /pʊs/, **pussy** /'pʊsi/) n [C] *BrE informal* a cat – used especially by children

pussyfoot /'pʊsifʊt/ (*also* **pussyfoot around/ about**) v [I] *informal* to be too careful and afraid to deal with a situation firmly

---

PUT

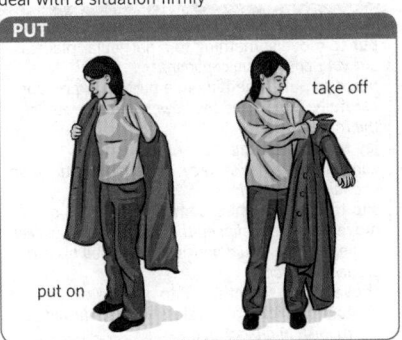

take off

put on

---

put /pʊt/ v [T] (*past tense and past participle* **put**, *present participle* **putting**)

1 PLACE/POSITION to move something to a particular place: **put sth in/on etc sth** *Just put the bags on the table.* | *Where did you put the newspaper?*

2 FEELING/SITUATION to make someone have a feeling, or make someone or something be in a particular situation: **put** sb **in a good/bad mood** *The long delay had put us all in a bad mood.* | *She's very good at* **putting** *people* **at ease** (=making them feel relaxed). | *They* **put** *him* **in charge of** *the company.*

3 WRITE STH to write or print something: **put sth in/on/under etc sth** *Put your name at the top of each answer sheet.* THESAURUS ▶ **WRITE**

4 SAY STH to say something in a particular way: *It is hard to* **put into words** *how I feel now.* | *It was an accident, an 'act of God' if you want to* **put it like that**. | *He's not very musical,* **to put it mildly** (=he's not musical at all).

5 SEND SB SOMEWHERE to arrange for someone to go to a place, or to make them go there: *I don't want to put my dad into hospital.* | *I'll* **put** *the kids* **to bed**. | *They* **put** *him* **in prison** *for life.*

6 QUESTION/SUGGESTION to ask a question or make a

suggestion, especially in order to get someone's opinion or agreement: *Can I put a question to you?*

PHRASES

I wouldn't put it past sb (to do sth) used to say that you think someone might do something wrong or illegal: *I wouldn't put it past him to black-mail them.*

put sth behind you to stop thinking about a bad experience or a mistake in the past: *She was strug-gling to put the affair behind her.*

put an end/a stop to sth to stop an activity that is harmful or unacceptable: *We must put an end to their threats.*

put sth into action/effect/practice to start using a plan, idea, knowledge etc: *James was keen to put the things he had learned into practice.*

put sth right to make a situation better, especially after someone has made a mistake or behaved badly: *Now we've discovered the problem, we intend to put it right.*

put sth to use to use something: *We can put this money to use immediately.*

put sb to work to make someone work: *He put the prisoners to work.*

THESAURUS

put to move something to a particular place: *I've put your coat in the cupboard.*

place to put something in a particular position carefully: *She placed the flowers in the centre of the table.*

lay to put something or someone down carefully on a flat surface: *Dad unfolded the map and laid it on the floor.*

slip to put something somewhere with a quick movement: *Lucy slipped the letter into her pocket, hoping no one would notice. | He slipped his arm around her waist.*

shove to put something into a space or container quickly or carelessly: *They shoved all the rubbish in a black bag.*

dump to put something down somewhere in a careless and untidy way: *Don't dump your dirty clothes on the floor.*

stick *informal* to put something somewhere quickly or carelessly: *Just stick the bags in the cupboard.*

PHRASAL VERBS

put sth ↔ **across** to explain your ideas, beliefs etc in a way that people can understand: *She's good at putting her ideas across.*

put sth ↔ **aside** to save money regularly in order to use it later: *We're trying to put some money aside for a new car.*

put sth ↔ **away** to put something in the place where it is usually kept: *Those kids never put anything away!*

put sth ↔ **back**

1 to return something to its place: *I put the letter back in the envelope.*

2 to delay something: *The publication date has been put back by three months.*

3 put a clock/watch back to make a clock or watch show an earlier time

put sb/sth ↔ **down**

1 to put something onto a surface such as a table or the floor: *She put down her knitting.* → see picture on page A11

2 to criticize someone and make them feel silly or stupid: *She's always putting him down.*

3 to write something on a piece of paper: *Put down your name and address.*

4 to kill an animal because it is old or ill

5 put down a revolution/revolt/rebellion etc to stop a REVOLUTION etc by using force

put sth **down to** sth to think that something is caused by something else: *She put her illness down to stress.*

put sb/sth ↔ **forward**

1 to suggest a plan or idea, or suggest someone for a job or position: *Milne has put his name forward as a candidate at the next election.*

2 put a clock/watch forward to make a clock or watch show a later time

put sth ↔ **in**

1 to add or replace equipment in your home SYN **install**: *They're having a new bathroom put in.*

2 to officially ask for something: *She put in an insur-ance claim.*

3 to spend time or effort doing something: *Doug's been putting in a lot of hours at work recently.*

4 put in an appearance to go to a social event, meeting etc for a short time

put sth **into** sth to spend time, effort, or money doing something: *We must put more money into education. | I put a lot of effort into writing that essay.*

put sb/sth ↔ **off**

1 to delay doing something SYN **postpone**: *You can't keep putting the decision off.* THESAURUS ▶ DELAY

2 to tell someone that you cannot do something that you had agreed to do: *I managed to put him off by promising to pay next week.*

3 *BrE* to make it difficult for someone to do some-thing by preventing them from thinking clearly about what they are doing: *Stop laughing - you're putting me off!*

4 *BrE* to make you dislike something or not want to do something: *Don't be put off by the title - it's a really good book.* THESAURUS ▶ DISLIKE

put sth ↔ **on**

1 to put clothes on your body OPP **take off**: *Put your coat on - it's cold.*

2 to put MAKE-UP, cream etc on your skin: *I need to put on some more lipstick.*

3 to make a machine or a piece of equipment start working SYN **turn on**: *Is it all right if I put the fire on?*

4 to put a record, video etc into a machine and start playing it: *Let's put some music on.*

5 put on weight/5 pounds/2 kg etc to become heavier → **gain**

6 to arrange or perform a concert, play etc: *They're putting on a concert to raise money for landmine vic-tims.*

7 to pretend to feel or believe something that you do not really feel or believe: *Don't take any notice of her - she's just **putting it on**. | I was trying to **put on a brave face** (=not show that I was sad or worried).* THESAURUS ▶ PRETEND

put sb/sth ↔ **out**

1 to make a fire or cigarette stop burning SYN **extinguish**

2 to make an electric light stop working by pressing a button: *Don't forget to put out the lights when you leave.*

3 to produce a book, record, film etc: *They're putting out a new album in the fall.*

4 to make extra work or problems for someone: *Will it put you out if I bring an extra guest?*

put sb **through**

1 put sb through sth to make someone experience something unpleasant: *She was put through a lot during her first marriage, so I'm glad she's happy now.*

2 to connect someone to someone else on the telephone

put sth ↔ **together**

1 to make a machine or model by joining the different parts SYN **assemble**: *It took us all day to put the table together.*

2 to prepare or produce something by collecting information, ideas etc: *The band are currently putting a new album together.*

3 more/louder etc than ... put together used to say that an amount is greater than a combined total: *Italy scored more points than the rest of the group put together.*

put sb/sth ↔ **up**

1 to build or make an upright structure SYN **erect**: *The kids were putting a tent up in the garden.* **THESAURUS ▶ BUILD**

2 to put a picture, sign etc on a wall so that people can see it: *Posters advertising the concert were put up on all the notice boards.*

3 to increase the cost of something SYN **raise**: *Our landlord keeps putting the rent up.* **THESAURUS ▶ INCREASE**

4 put up money/£500/$3 million etc to provide the money that is needed to do something: *Firth put up $42,000 in prize money for the contest.*

5 to let someone stay in your house for a short time: *Yeah, we can put you up for the night.*

6 put up resistance/a fight/a struggle to argue against something or fight against someone in a determined way: *The rebels have put up fierce resistance.*

put sb **up to** sth to encourage someone to do something stupid or dangerous: *It's not like Martha to steal – someone must have put her up to it.*

put up with sth to accept a bad situation without complaining: *I don't know how you put up with all this noise.*

'put-down n [C] *informal* something someone says that is intended to make you feel stupid or unimportant

,put 'out adj [not before noun] *BrE informal* upset and offended: *Of course she feels put out when you don't ask what she wants to do.*

putrid /'pju:trɪd/ adj dead animals, plants etc that are putrid are decaying and smell very bad: *a putrid odour*

putt /pʌt/ v [I,T] to hit a golf ball lightly a short distance along the ground towards the hole —**putt** n [C]

putty /'pʌti/ n [U] a soft substance used for fixing glass into window frames

a crossword puzzle

puzzle¹ /'pʌzəl/ n

1 [C] a game or toy that you have to think about carefully in order to solve it or put it together → **jigsaw**: *a crossword puzzle | a jigsaw puzzle*

2 [usually singular] something that is difficult to understand or explain: **[+of]** *the puzzle of how the Sun works | He thought he had solved the puzzle.*

puzzle² v [T] if something puzzles you, you feel confused because you do not understand it: *What puzzles me is why he never mentioned this before.*

PHRASAL VERBS

puzzle sth ↔ **out** to solve a confusing or difficult problem by thinking about it carefully: *I'm trying hard to puzzle things out.*

puzzle over sth to think about something for a long time in order to understand it: *Joe sat puzzling over the map.*

puzzled /'pʌzəld/ adj confused and unable to understand something: **puzzled look/expression/frown etc** *Dan had a puzzled expression on his face.*

puzzling /'pʌzlɪŋ/ adj difficult to understand or explain: *The results of the survey were a little puzzling.*

PVC /ˌpiː viː 'siː◂/ n [U] a type of plastic, used to make pipes, window frames, clothes etc

pyjamas *BrE*, **pajamas** *AmE* /pə'dʒɑːməz $ -'dʒæ-, -'dʒɑː-/ n [plural] light trousers and a shirt that you wear in bed

pylon /'paɪlən $ -lɑːn, -lən/ n [C] a tall metal structure that supports electric wires high above the ground

pyramid /'pɪrəmɪd/ n [C] a shape with a flat base and four sides in the shape of TRIANGLES that slope to a point at the top → see picture at **SHAPE¹**

PYLON

pyre /paɪə $ paɪr/ n [C] a high pile of wood on which a dead body is burned at a funeral ceremony: *a funeral pyre*

python /'paɪθən $ -θɑːn, -θən/ n [C] a large tropical snake that kills animals for food by crushing them

Qq

Q, q /kjuː/ *n* [C,U] (*plural* **Q's, q's**) the 17th letter of the English alphabet

qt. the written abbreviation of **quart**

quack[1] /kwæk/ *v* [I] if a duck quacks, it makes a loud noise from its throat

quack[2] *n* [C] **1** the sound a duck makes **2** *informal disapproving* someone who pretends to be a doctor **3** *humorous* a doctor

quad /kwɒd $ kwɑːd/ (*also* **quadrangle** /'kwɒdræŋgəl $ 'kwɑː-/) *n* [C] a square area with buildings all around it in a school or college

'quad bike *n* [C] *BrE* a small vehicle, similar to a MOTORCYCLE but with four wide wheels, usually ridden on rough paths or fields

quadruple /'kwɒdrʊpəl, kwɒ'druː- $ kwɑː'druː-/ *v* [I,T] if you quadruple an amount, or if an amount quadruples, it becomes four times as big: *The number of car owners has quadrupled in the last twenty years.*

quagmire /'kwægmaɪə, 'kwɒg- $ 'kwægmaɪr/ *n* [C] **1** an area of soft wet muddy ground **2** a very difficult or complicated situation: *a legal quagmire*

quail[1] /kweɪl/ *n* [C,U] a small bird that is hunted for food and sport, or this bird as food

quail[2] *v* [I] *literary* to feel afraid: *Our troops quailed at the size of his army.*

quaint /kweɪnt/ *adj* attractive in an old-fashioned way: *quaint narrow streets*

quake[1] /kweɪk/ *v* [I] *formal* to shake because you are afraid: **[+with]** *Kate stood in the doorway, **quaking with fear**.*

quake[2] *n* [C] *informal* an EARTHQUAKE

qualification /ˌkwɒlɪfɪ'keɪʃən $ ˌkwɑː-/ *n*
1 [C usually plural] *especially BrE* if you have a qualification, you have passed an examination or course to show you have a particular level of skill or knowledge in a subject: *He left school without any qualifications.* | *Do you have a teaching qualification?*
2 [C] a skill or quality that you need to do a job: **[+for]** *The mayor criticized his opponent's qualifications for the job.*
3 [U] when you achieve the necessary standard to work in a profession, enter a sports competition etc: **[+for]** *Portugal's qualification for the European Championships*
4 [C,U] something that you add to a statement to limit its meaning or effect **SYN** reservation: *He welcomed the proposal **without qualification**.*

qualified /'kwɒlɪfaɪd $ 'kwɑː-/ *adj* **1** having suitable knowledge, experience, or skills, especially for a particular job: **[+for]** *Gibbons is **highly qualified** for the job.* | **qualified to do sth** *He's not really well*

qualified to judge. **2** having passed an official examination that shows you are trained to do a particular job: *a qualified teacher*

qualifier /'kwɒləfaɪə $ 'kwɑːlɪfaɪər/ *n* [C] **1** a game that you have to win to take part in a sports competition: *a World Cup qualifier* **2** a person or team who achieves the standard that is needed to enter a sports competition: *Bronson was the fastest qualifier at the US Olympic Trials.*

qualify /'kwɒlɪfaɪ $ 'kwɑː-/ *v* (**qualified, qualifying, qualifies**) **1** [I] to pass an examination that shows you are trained to do a particular job: **[+as]** *Sue qualified as a solicitor last year.* **2** [I] to be successful at one stage of a sports competition so that you can continue to the next stage: **[+for]** *The US beat Nigeria to qualify for the finals.* **3** [I,T] to have the right to do something, or to give someone the right to do something: **[+for]** *Members qualify for a 20% discount.* **4** [T] to add information to something you have already said in order to limit its meaning or effect: *Let me qualify that statement.*

qualitative Ac /'kwɒlətətɪv $ 'kwɑːləteɪ-/ *adj formal* relating to the quality of something rather than to the amount or number → **quantitative**: *a qualitative study of the health care program*

quality[1] /'kwɒləti $ 'kwɑː-/ *n* (*plural* **qualities**)
1 [U] how good or bad something is: *the decline in air quality in our cities* | **of good/poor etc quality** *Much of the land was of poor quality.*
2 [U] a high standard: **[+of]** *I've been impressed by the quality of his work.*
3 [C usually plural] a good or bad part of someone's character → **characteristic**: **[+of]** *Stacy has all the qualities of a natural leader.*
4 [C] something that is typical of a person or thing: *Atkinson's novels all have a humorous quality.*

PHRASES

quality of life how good or bad someone's life is, shown, for example, by whether they are happy and healthy: *People don't just want more money – they want a better quality of life.*

COLLOCATIONS

adjectives

good/high/excellent quality *The quality of their work was very high.*
poor/low quality *They sell cheap food made with poor quality ingredients.*
top quality *We stock only top quality products.*

noun + quality

water/air quality *Scientists took samples to test the water quality.*
sound/picture quality *These TV sets have better picture quality.*

verbs

to improve quality *We want to improve the quality of our service.*
the quality improves *The quality of teaching has improved.*
the quality goes up/down (=becomes better or worse) *Most people think the quality of TV programmes has gone down.*

quality² adj [only before noun] very good: We sell quality clothing at a price you can afford.

qualm /kwɑːm $ kwɑːm, kwɑːlm/ n [C] a worry or doubt because you are not sure what you are doing is right: She **had no qualms** whatsoever **about** firing people.

quandary /ˈkwɒndəri $ ˈkwɑːn-/ n [C] (plural **quandaries**) a difficult situation in which you cannot decide what to do: **in a quandary** Ian's in a quandary about whether to accept their offer.

quantifier /ˈkwɒntɪfaɪə $ ˈkwɑːntɪfaɪər/ n [C] a word or phrase such as 'much', 'few', or 'a lot of' which is used with a noun to show an amount

quantify /ˈkwɒntɪfaɪ $ ˈkwɑːn-/ v [T] (**quantified, quantifying, quantifies**) to measure something and show it as a number: These kinds of improvement are hard to quantify. —**quantifiable** adj

quantitative /ˈkwɒntətətɪv $ ˈkwɑːntəteɪt-/ adj formal relating to amounts → **qualitative**: a quantitative analysis

quantity /ˈkwɒntəti $ ˈkwɑːn-/ n (plural **quantities**)
1 [C,U] an amount of something that you can measure or count: **[+of]** Police found a quantity of drugs hidden in their bags. | **large quantities** of money | **in quantity** It's cheaper **buying** goods **in quantity** (=in large amounts).
2 [U] the amount of something that is produced: It's quality that's important, not quantity.

quantum leap /ˌkwɒntəm ˈliːp $ ˌkwɑːn-/ n [C usually singular] a very big and important improvement: a quantum leap in medical science

quarantine /ˈkwɒrəntiːn $ ˈkwɔː-/ n [U] when a person or animal with a disease is kept apart from other people or animals so that they do not get the disease too: **in quarantine** Animals coming into Britain must be **kept in quarantine**. —**quarantine** v [T]

quarrel¹ /ˈkwɒrəl $ ˈkwɔː-, ˈkwɑː-/ n [C]
1 an angry argument: **[+with]** We've had a quarrel with our neighbours. | **[+about/over]** They had a quarrel about some girl. **THESAURUS** ARGUMENT
2 formal a reason to disagree with something or argue with someone: **[+with]** My only quarrel with the plan is that it will take too long. | We **have no quarrel with** the court's decision.

COLLOCATIONS

verbs

to have a quarrel We had a terrible quarrel last night.
a quarrel breaks out (=starts to happen) A quarrel broke out between the players.
to pick a quarrel with sb (=to deliberately start one) She's always picking quarrels with people.

adjectives

a bitter quarrel (=involving strong feelings of anger or hatred) After a bitter quarrel, they refused to speak to each other.

noun + quarrel

a family quarrel I didn't want to get involved in a family quarrel.
a lovers' quarrel Outside, two teenagers were having a lovers' quarrel.

---

quarrel² v [I] (**quarrelled, quarrelling** BrE, **quarreled, quarreling** AmE) to have an angry argument: **[+with]** She's always quarrelling with her sister.

quarrelsome /ˈkwɒrəlsəm $ ˈkwɔː-, ˈkwɑː-/ adj a quarrelsome person is always quarrelling with other people

quarry¹ /ˈkwɒri $ ˈkwɔː-, ˈkwɑː-/ n [C] (plural **quarries**) **1** a place where large amounts of stone or sand are dug out of the ground **2** a person or animal that is being hunted

quarry² v [I] (**quarried, quarrying, quarries**) to dig stone or sand from a quarry

quart /kwɔːt $ kwɔːrt/ n [C] (written abbreviation **qt**) a unit for measuring liquid, equal to two PINTS

quarter /ˈkwɔːtə $ ˈkwɔːrtər/ n [C]
1 one of four equal parts that you can divide something into: She cut the cake into quarters. | **[+of]** A quarter of Canada's population is French-speaking. | **three quarters (of sth)** (=75%) The house is about three quarters of a mile from the road.
2 15 minutes: Can you be ready in **a quarter of an hour**? | **(a) quarter to** (also **(a) quarter of** AmE) (=15 minutes before the hour) It's quarter to five. | **(a) quarter past** (also **(a) quarter after** AmE) (=15 minutes after the hour) It's a quarter past five. | The bus leaves at quarter after.
3 a period of three months: Profits increased in the first quarter.
4 a coin in the US and Canada worth 25 cents
5 AmE one of the four periods into which a year at school or college is divided → **semester**
6 AmE one of the four equal periods of time into which some sports games are divided
7 in/from ... quarters among or from different people: He received help from several quarters.
8 an area of a town where a particular group of people live: the Latin quarter
9 quarters [plural] rooms that are given to someone to live in as part of their job: the kitchen staff's **living quarters**

quarterback /ˈkwɔːtəbæk $ ˈkwɔːrtər-/ n [C] the player in American football who directs the team's attacking play, especially by throwing the ball

quarterfinal /ˌkwɔːtəˈfaɪnl $ ˌkwɔːrtər-/ n [C] one of four games near the end of a competition. The winners play in the two SEMI-FINALS.

quarterly /ˈkwɔːtəli $ ˈkwɔːrtər-/ adj produced or happening four times a year: a quarterly report —**quarterly** adv: The magazine is published quarterly.

quartet /kwɔːˈtet $ kwɔːr-/ n [C] four singers or musicians who perform together → **trio**, **quintet**: a **string quartet**

quartz /kwɔːts $ kwɔːrts/ n [U] a type of hard rock used for making electronic clocks

quash /kwɒʃ $ kwɑːʃ, kwɒːʃ/ v [T] formal **1** to officially say that a decision is not legal or correct any more: The Court of Appeal quashed Maloney's conviction. **2** to use force to stop fighting or protests: Troops loyal to the President quickly quashed the rebellion.

quaver /'kweɪvə $ -ər/ *v* [I] *literary* if your voice quavers, it shakes as you speak because you are nervous or upset

quay /kiː $ keɪ, kiː/ *n* [C] a place beside the sea or a big river for loading or unloading boats

queasy /'kwiːzi/ *adj* if you feel queasy, you feel as if you are going to be sick: *The sea got rougher, and I began to feel queasy.*

queen /kwiːn/ *n* [C]
1 Queen the female ruler of a country, or the wife of a king → **king**: *Queen Elizabeth II*
2 a playing card with a picture of a queen on it: *the queen of clubs*
3 a large female BEE that lays the eggs for a whole group

'queen-size *adj* a queen-size bed, sheet etc is a bed for two people that is larger than the standard size

queer /kwɪə $ kwɪr/ *adj* strange and not normal: *There's something a bit queer about him.*

quell /kwel/ *v* [T] *formal* to stop something: *Troops were called in to quell the riots.* | *Police tried to quell public fear about the murders.*

quench /kwentʃ/ *v* **quench your thirst** to drink something so that you no longer feel thirsty

query /'kwɪəri $ 'kwɪri/ *n* [C] (*plural* **queries**) *especially BrE* a question asking for more information: *Staff are always available to answer your queries.*
THESAURUS QUESTION —**query** *v* [T]: *Several players queried the referee's decision.*

quest /kwest/ *n* [C] *formal* a long and difficult search: **[+for]** *a quest for knowledge*

question¹ /'kwestʃən/ *n*
1 [C] something you say or write when you are asking for information OPP **answer**: *I must ask you one more question.* | **[+about/on]** *I have one or two questions about the timetable.*
2 [C] a subject that needs to be discussed or a problem that needs to be solved SYN **issue**: *Dunn's murder raises the question of whether more police should carry guns.*
3 [C,U] a feeling of doubt about something: *We've played poorly this season – there's no question about it* (=it is very certain). | *Her honesty is beyond question* (=certainly true). → **TRICK QUESTION**
PHRASES
call/bring/throw sth into question to make people feel uncertain about something: *Recent events have called into question the wisdom of the government's decision.*
(that's a) good question *spoken* used as a way of saying that you do not know the answer to a question: *'How can we afford this?' 'Good question!'*
in question the person or thing in question is the person or thing that is being discussed: *Where were you on the evening in question?*
be out of the question used to emphasize that something is not possible or not allowed: *A new washing machine is out of the question at the moment.* **THESAURUS** IMPOSSIBLE
there's no question of sth used to emphasize that something will definitely not happen: *There's no question of Gerrard leaving the team.*

without question 1 without complaining or asking why: *Soldiers must follow orders without question.*
2 used to say that something is definitely true: *It is without question the best show on television.*

verbs
to ask (sb) a question *Can I ask you a question?*
to answer a question *She tried to answer their questions honestly.*
to have a question (=to want to ask a question) *Does anyone have any questions?*
to put a question to sb (=to ask a question in a formal situation) *You will have the chance to put your questions to the director.*
to avoid/dodge a question (=to not give a direct answer) *Politicians are very good at avoiding questions.*

adjectives
a personal question (=a question relating to someone's private life) *Can I ask you a personal question?*
a difficult/hard/tough question *The questions were too hard for me.*
an easy/simple question *We'll start with some easy questions.*
a stupid/silly question (=one whose answer is obvious) *Did you win, or is that a stupid question?*

THESAURUS

question something that you ask someone, when you are either speaking or writing: *Do you have any questions about the homework?*
query *especially BrE* a question that you ask when you want more information about something, or you want to check that something is true or correct: *If you have any queries, contact the student accommodation office.*
inquiry (*also* **enquiry** *especially BrE*) a question that you ask officially, in order to find out more information about something: *There have been a lot of inquiries from members of the public.*
request a statement, letter etc in which you officially ask for something that you need: *The school has made a request for more money from the government.*

question² *v* [T]
1 to ask someone questions about something → **interrogate**: *Two men are being questioned by police.* | **question sb about sth** *Nelson was questioned about his activities on the night of the robbery.* **THESAURUS** ASK
2 to say that you have doubts about something: *Are you questioning my honesty?* —**questioning** *n* [U]: *The four men were held for questioning but later released.*

questionable /'kwestʃənəbəl/ *adj* something that is questionable does not seem to be completely true, correct, or honest: *Her motives are highly questionable.* | **It's questionable whether** *this research is actually useful.*

'question mark n [C] the sign (?) that you write at the end of a question

questionnaire /ˌkwestʃəˈneə, ˌkes- $ -ˈner/ n [C] a set of written questions that you answer in order to give information about something: *Students were asked to **fill out a questionnaire** (=answer it).*

'question tag n [C] a phrase such as 'isn't it?' or 'does she?' that you add to the end of a sentence to make it a question or check that someone agrees with you

queue¹ /kjuː/ n [C] *BrE* a line of people or vehicles that are waiting for something SYN **line**: *There was a long queue outside the cinema. | **be/stand/wait in a queue** We stood in a queue for half an hour. | We **joined the queue** at the ticket counter.*

queue² (*also* **queue up**) v [I] *BrE* to wait in a line of people SYN **line up**: **[+for]** *We had to queue for over an hour to get tickets.* THESAURUS **WAIT**

quibble /ˈkwɪbəl/ v [I] to argue about something that is not very important: **[+about/over/with]** *Let's stop quibbling over small details.*

quiche /kiːʃ/ n [C,U] a PIE without a top, filled with a mixture of eggs, cheese, vegetables etc

quick¹ /kwɪk/ adj

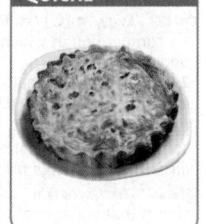
QUICHE

1 taking only a short time to do something → **fast**: *I'll just have a quick shower first. | The journey is much quicker by train. | What's the quickest way to the airport? | She felt she had to make a quick decision.*
THESAURUS **SHORT**

2 moving or happening fast: *She walked with short, quick steps.*

3 able to learn things fast: *Carolyn's a **quick learner**.*

4 be quick to do sth to react quickly to something someone says or does: *The President was quick to deny the rumours.*

> **THESAURUS**
>
> **quick** taking only a short time to do something: *Let's have a quick meal before the film.*
> **short** lasting only a short time: *It's quite a short journey.*
> **brief** lasting only a short time. **Brief** is more formal than **short**, and is used especially in written English: *There was a brief silence.*
> **rapid** happening in a short period of time – used about changes, increases, improvements etc: *It was a period of rapid change.*
> **hasty** deciding or doing something very quickly, especially when this has bad results: *I don't want to make a hasty decision.*

quick² adv *informal* quickly. Some people think that this use is not correct English: *Come quick! There's been an accident.*

quicken /ˈkwɪkən/ v [I,T] to become quicker, or to make something quicker: *Her heartbeat quickened when she saw him.*

quickie /ˈkwɪki/ n [C] *informal* something that you can do quickly and easily: *I've got a question for you – it's just a quickie.* —**quickie** adj: *a quickie divorce*

quickly /ˈkwɪkli/ adv moving fast, or doing something in a short amount of time: *He quickly put the money back in the box. | Get over here as quickly as you can.*

> **THESAURUS**
>
> **quickly** moving fast, or doing something in a short amount of time: *Richard ran quickly down the stairs. | I finished the book very quickly.*
> **fast** moving quickly or able to move very quickly: *You're walking too fast – I can't keep up! | a fast car*
> **rapidly** quickly – used especially about changes, increases, improvements etc. **Rapidly** is more formal than **quickly**: *Technology is changing rapidly.*
> **at high speed** very fast – used about cars, trains, machines etc: *The car was travelling at high speed on a narrow lane.*

quicksand /ˈkwɪksænd/ n [U] wet sand that is dangerous to walk on because you sink into it

quid /kwɪd/ n [C] (*plural* **quid**) *BrE informal* a pound in British money: *You owe me fifty quid.*

quiet¹ /ˈkwaɪət/ adj

1 not making a lot of noise OPP **loud, noisy**: *We'll have to be quiet – we don't want to wake your parents. | **(be) quiet!** spoken (=used to tell someone to stop talking or making a noise) Be quiet! I've got a headache.*

2 without much activity or without many people: *The shop has been really quiet this morning. | They live in a quiet part of town. | She wanted a **quiet life**.*

3 not speaking or not likely to say much: *Sam's a quiet hard-working boy. | You're awfully quiet today, Tania.* —**quietness** n [U]

PHRASES

> **keep sth quiet/keep quiet (about sth)** to not talk about something: *I have something to tell you, but you have to keep it quiet.*

> **THESAURUS**
>
> **quiet** not making a loud sound or a lot of noise: *a quiet voice | The engine is so quiet!*
> **silent** not speaking or making any sound at all: *Everyone in the room was silent. | He said a silent prayer.*
> **soft** quiet and pleasant to listen to: *a romantic evening with soft music | His voice was soft and gentle.*
> **low** a low voice is quiet because you do not want people to hear what you are saying. A low sound is deep or does not make much noise: *They were speaking in low voices. | There was a low rumbling sound. | The music was played at low volume.*
> **faint** quiet and difficult to hear, especially because the sound comes from a long way away: *the faint sound of church bells*

Q

peaceful quiet in a pleasant and relaxing way – used about a place where there is not much noise: *It's very peaceful here.*

quiet² n [U] when there is not very much noise and not many things are happening: *All I want is some peace and quiet.*

PHRASES

on the quiet *BrE* secretly: *He was doing some free-lance work on the quiet.*

quieten /'kwaɪətn/ *BrE*, **quiet** *AmE* (*also* **quieten down**, **quiet down**) v [I,T] to become quiet after making a lot of noise: *After a while, the children quietened down.*

quietly /'kwaɪətli/ *adv*
1 without making much noise: *Ron shut the door quietly.* | *'I'm sorry,' he said quietly.*
2 in a way that does not attract attention: *He quietly got on with his work.*

quilt /kwɪlt/ n [C] a cover for a bed that is filled with soft warm material

quilted /'kwɪltɪd/ *adj* quilted clothing has a thick layer of material sewn into it: *a quilted jacket*

quintessential /ˌkwɪntə'senʃəl◂/ *adj* being a perfect example of a particular type of person or thing: *New York is the quintessential big city.*

quintet /kwɪn'tet/ n [C] five singers or musicians who perform together → **trio**, **quartet**

quip /kwɪp/ v [I,T] (**quipped**, **quipping**) to say something clever and amusing —**quip** n [C]

quirk /kwɜːk $ kwɜːrk/ n [C] **1** a strange habit or feature that someone or something has: *one of her annoying little quirks* **2** something strange that happens by chance: **[+of]** *By a quirk of fate, I met him again the following day.*

quirky /'kwɜːki $ -ɜːr-/ *adj* slightly strange: *a quirky sense of humour*

quit /kwɪt/ v [I,T] (*past tense and past participle* **quit** *also* **quitted** *BrE, present participle* **quitting**) *informal*
1 to leave a job or school permanently: *I'm thinking about quitting school.* | *People are now calling on the chairman to quit.* THESAURUS▶ LEAVE
2 *especially AmE* to stop doing something bad or annoying → **give up**: *He quit smoking three years ago.* | *Quit complaining and get to work!* THESAURUS▶ STOP
3 to close a computer PROGRAM

quite /kwaɪt/ *adv*
1 *especially BrE* fairly or very, but not extremely SYN **pretty**: *She's quite tall for her age.* | *The food in the canteen is usually quite good.* | *Butch is out of the hospital and doing quite well.* | **quite a sth** *They live quite a long way from the nearest town.* | **quite like/enjoy** *BrE: I quite enjoyed that film.* THESAURUS▶ RATHER
2 *especially BrE* completely: *Although they're sisters, they're quite different.* | *I'm afraid that's quite*

impossible. | *I think you've had quite enough to drink already!*
3 not quite almost, but not completely or not exactly: *I'm not quite sure how much it costs.* | *Lewis isn't quite as fast as he used to be.* | *I'm not quite finished.* THESAURUS▶ ALMOST

PHRASES

quite a/an/some used to emphasize that something is especially good, bad etc: *He certainly made quite an impression on the kids.* | *Brad's quite some musician.*

quite a lot/bit/few a fairly large number or amount: *They've had quite a bit of snow this year.* | *This painting is worth quite a lot of money.*

quits /kwɪts/ *adj* [not before noun] *BrE informal* if two people are quits, neither one owes anything to the other: *I'll give you £10, and then we're quits.*

PHRASES

call it quits *informal* to stop doing something: *After 25 years as a teacher, he's decided to call it quits.*

quiver /'kwɪvə $ -ər/ v [I] to shake slightly, especially because you are angry, upset, or nervous: **[+with]** *His voice was quivering with rage.*

quiz¹ /kwɪz/ n [C] (*plural* **quizzes**)
1 a competition in which you have to answer questions: *a quiz show*
2 *AmE* a short test that a teacher gives to a class: *a math quiz* THESAURUS▶ TEST

quiz² v [T] (**quizzed**, **quizzing**, **quizzes**) to ask someone a lot of questions SYN **question**: *Reporters quizzed Harvey about his plans for the future.*

quizzical /'kwɪzɪkəl/ *adj* a quizzical look, smile etc shows that you do not understand something

quorum /'kwɔːrəm/ n [singular] the smallest number of people that must be at a meeting in order for official decisions to be made

quota /'kwəʊtə $ 'kwoʊ-/ n [C] an amount of something that someone is allowed to have: **[+on]** *a strict quota on imports*

quotation Ac /kwəʊ'teɪʃən $ kwoʊ-/ n [C]
1 words that come from a book, poem etc: **[+from]** *a quotation from the Bible* **2** a statement showing how much it will cost to do something: *Ask the builder to give you a written quotation for the job.*

quo'tation ˌmark n [C usually plural] a sign (" ") that you write before and after someone's speech

quote¹ Ac /kwəʊt $ kwoʊt/ v **1** [I,T] to repeat exactly what someone else has said or written: **[+from]** *She quoted from a newspaper article.* | *A company spokesman was quoted as saying that 2,000 people may lose their jobs.* **2** [T] to mention something as an example to support what you are saying: *Wilkins quoted several cases where errors had occurred.* **3** [T] to tell a customer the price you will charge them for something

quote² Ac n [C] a QUOTATION

Quran /kɔː'rɑːn, kə-$ kə'rɑːn, -'rɑːn/ n (*also* **Koran**, **Qur'an**) the holy book of the Muslims

Rr

R, r /ɑː/ $ ɑːr/ n [C,U] (*plural* **R's, r's**) the 18th letter of the English alphabet

R & B /ˌɑːr ən 'biː/ n [U] (**rhythm and blues**) a style of popular music that is a mixture of BLUES and JAZZ

rabbi /'ræbaɪ/ n [C] a Jewish religious leader

rabbit /'ræbɪt/ n [C] a small animal with long ears and soft fur that lives in holes in the ground → see picture at PET¹

rabble /'ræbəl/ n [singular] a noisy crowd of people who are behaving badly: **[+of]** *a rabble of angry youths*

rabid /'ræbɪd, 'reɪ-/ adj **1** *disapproving* having extreme opinions: *rabid right-wing fanatics* **2** a rabid animal has rabies

rabies /'reɪbiːz/ n [U] a disease that can kill animals and people that are bitten by an infected animal

raccoon /rə'kuːn, ræ- $ ræ-/ n [C] an animal with black fur around its eyes and black and white rings on its tail

race¹ /reɪs/ n
1 [C] a competition in which people, animals, cars etc try to go faster than each other: *He won the race easily.* | *She should do well in this race.*
2 [C,U] one of the main groups into which people are divided according to the colour of their skin and physical appearance: *The school welcomes children **of all races**.* | *people of **mixed race***
3 [C] a situation in which people compete with each other to obtain a position of power: *Davis had decided to enter the presidential race.* | **[+for]** *the race for city council*
4 [singular] a situation in which one group of people tries to obtain or achieve something before another group: **[+for]** *the race for the final playoff position* | **the race to do sth** *the race to find a cure for cancer*
5 the races an event at which horses race against each other: *Have you ever been to the races?* → ARMS RACE, HUMAN RACE, RAT RACE

PHRASES

a race against time when you must finish doing something in a short period of time: *He faces a race against time in order to be fit for the game.*

COLLOCATIONS

verbs
to win/lose a race *She won the race easily.*
to come first/last etc in a race *I used to come last in every race.*
to take part in a race *Runners from all over the world will take part in the race.*
to compete in a race *She's competing in the 10-kilometre race.*
to have a race *The children were having races in the playground.*
to finish a race *Tom finished the race in sixth place.*

types of race
a horse/boat/bike etc race *They were watching a horse race on TV.*
a 200-metres/10-kilometre etc race

race² v **1 a)** [I,T] to compete against someone or something in a race: **[+against]** *She will be racing against some of the world's top athletes.* **b)** [T] to use an animal or a vehicle to compete in a race: *My father has raced horses since he was 18.* **THESAURUS** RUN **2** [I,T] to go somewhere very quickly, or to move someone or something very quickly: **[+across/back/down]** *I raced down the stairs to answer the phone.* | **race sb to sth** *The crash victims were raced to Pacific Hospital.* **3** [I] if your heart or mind races, it works harder and faster than usual, for example because you are afraid or excited

racecourse /'reɪskɔːs $ -kɔːrs/ n [C] a place where horses compete in races

racehorse /'reɪshɔːs $ -hɔːrs/ n [C] a horse that competes in races

'race reˌlations n [plural] the relationship that exists between people from different countries, religions etc who are now living in the same place

racetrack /'reɪs-træk/ n [C] a track on which runners, cars etc race

racial /'reɪʃəl/ adj relating to someone's race or to the relationships between people of different races: *different **racial groups*** | *racial discrimination/prejudice* | *a rise in **racial tension*** —**racially** adv: *a racially motivated attack*

racing /'reɪsɪŋ/ n [U] the sport of racing horses, cars, dogs etc: **horse/motor/greyhound etc racing** | *a racing driver*

racism /'reɪsɪzəm/ n [U] when someone believes that people of their own race are better than people of other races, and they treat other races unfairly: **the struggle/fight against racism** **THESAURUS** PREJUDICE

racist /'reɪsɪst/ n [C] someone who believes that people of their own race are better than people of other races, and who treats other races unfairly —**racist** adj: *racist views*

RACKS

bicycle rack | spice rack

rack¹ /ræk/ n [C] a frame or shelf with bars, where you can put or keep things: *a **luggage rack*** | *a* *vegetable rack* | *a roof rack* (=for carrying luggage on top of a car)

rack² *v* **1 be racked with/by sth** if you are racked with pain or an emotion, it is causing you a lot of suffering: *Liza was racked with guilt.* **2 rack your brain(s)** to try very hard to remember something or think of something: *I racked my brains to remember her name.*

racket /'rækɪt/ *n* **1** (*also* **racquet**) [C] a piece of equipment that you use for hitting the ball in games such as tennis → see picture on page A9 **2** [C] *informal* an illegal way of making a lot of money: *a drugs racket* **3** [singular] *informal* a loud unpleasant noise: *Who's making that racket?* **THESAURUS ▶ NOISE**

racy /'reɪsi/ *adj* racy writing is exciting and entertaining and often about sex

radar /'reɪdɑː $ -ɑːr/ *n* [C,U] a method of finding the position of things such as planes and ships, using radio waves, or the equipment that does this
PHRASES
on sb's/the radar if something is on your radar, you have noticed it or are giving it some attention: *This problem was not on our radar.*

radiance /'reɪdiəns/ *n* [U] *literary* **1** happiness that shows in someone's face and makes them look attractive **2** a soft gentle light

radiant /'reɪdiənt/ *adj* **1** very happy and attractive: *The bride looked radiant.* | *a radiant smile* **2** [only before noun] *literary* very bright: *radiant light* —**radiantly** *adv*

radiate /'reɪdieɪt/ *v* **1** [I,T] if you radiate a feeling or quality, or if it radiates from you, people can see it very easily: *She radiated an air of calm.* **2** [I,T] to send out light or heat in all directions **3** [I] to spread out in different directions from a central point: **[+(out) from]** *Tiny lines radiated out from the corners of his eyes.*

radiation /,reɪdi'eɪʃən/ *n* [U] **1** a form of energy that comes especially from NUCLEAR reactions, which in large amounts can harm or kill people: *radiation sickness* **2** energy in the form of heat or light that is sent out as waves that you cannot see: *ultraviolet radiation from the Sun*

radiator /'reɪdieɪtə $ -ər/ *n* [C] **1** a piece of equipment, usually fastened to a wall, that heats a room. It consists of a metal container that fills up with hot water. **2** the part of a car that stops the engine from getting too hot

radical¹ Ac /'rædɪkəl/ *adj* **1** a radical change or difference is very big and important: *radical economic reforms* **2** if someone is radical, or if they have radical ideas, their ideas are very new and extreme: *radical feminists* —**radically** /-kli/ *adv*: *Life suddenly changed radically.*

radical² Ac *n* [C] someone who has new and extreme ideas, especially someone who wants complete social and political change —**radicalism** *n* [U]

radii /'reɪdi-aɪ/ *n* the plural of RADIUS

radio¹ /'reɪdiəʊ $ -dioʊ/ *n*
1 a) [C] a piece of equipment that you use to listen

to programmes that are broadcast, such as music and news: **put/switch/turn the radio on b)** [U] programmes that you can listen to using a radio: *Do you listen to the radio much?* | **on the radio** *I heard about it on the radio.* | *a radio station* | *local/national radio*

> **Grammar**
> Do not say 'I heard the news in the radio.' Say *I heard the news on the radio.*

2 a) [C] a piece of electrical equipment, for example on a plane or ship, that can send and receive spoken messages through the air **b)** [U] the method of sending and receiving messages in this way: **by radio** *We communicated by radio.* | *Suddenly, they **lost radio contact** (=could no longer send or receive messages).*

radio² *v* [I,T] to send a message using a radio: **[+for]** *The pilot radioed for help.*

radioactive /,reɪdiəʊ'æktɪv◄ $ -dioʊ-/ *adj* a radioactive substance sends out RADIATION (=a form of energy that can harm or kill people): *radioactive waste* —**radioactivity** /,reɪdiəʊæk'tɪvəti $ -dioʊ-/ *n* [U]: *high levels of radioactivity*

radiography /,reɪdi'ɒgrəfi $ -'ɑːg-/ *n* [U] the process of taking X-RAY photographs of people's bodies for medical purposes —**radiographer** *n* [C]

radiotherapy /,reɪdiəʊ'θerəpi $ -dioʊ-/ *n* [U] the treatment of illnesses using RADIATION

radish /'rædɪʃ/ *n* [C] a small round red vegetable that has a strong spicy taste and is eaten raw → see picture on page A5

radius /'reɪdiəs/ *n* [C] (*plural* **radii** /-diaɪ/) the distance from the centre to the edge of a circle
PHRASES
within a 10-mile/200-metre etc radius within a distance of 10 miles etc from a place in any direction: *They want to be within a 20-mile radius of the airport.*

RAF /,ɑːr eɪ 'ef, ræf/ *n* **the RAF** (**the Royal Air Force**) the British AIR FORCE

raffle /'ræfəl/ *n* [C] a competition in which you buy a ticket with a number on it and win a prize if your number is chosen: *a raffle ticket*

raft /rɑːft $ ræft/ *n* [C]
1 a flat structure that is used to travel on water. It is made from long pieces of wood tied together. **2 a raft of sth** a large number of people or things: *a raft of new taxes*

RAFT

rafter /'rɑːftə $ 'ræftər/ *n* [C usually plural] a sloping piece of wood that supports a roof

rafting /'rɑːftɪŋ $ 'ræf-/ *n* [U] the activity of travelling on a raft, especially as a sport: **white-water rafting** (=rafting where the water is flowing very fast)

rag /ræg/ n
1 [C,U] a piece of old cloth that you use to clean things
2 rags [plural] old torn clothes: **in rags** *children dressed in rags*
PHRASES
| **from rags to riches** becoming very rich after starting your life very poor: *his rise from rags to riches*

rage[1] /reɪdʒ/ n [C,U] a feeling of uncontrollable anger: *He was trembling with rage.* | *Sally flew into a rage* (=suddenly became very angry).
PHRASES
| **be all the rage** *informal* to be very popular and fashionable: *Short skirts were all the rage.*

rage[2] v [I] **1** to speak or behave in a way that shows you are extremely angry: **[+at/against]** *She raged at them in Arabic.* **2** to continue with great force: *The storm was still raging.* | *The battle raged on.*

ragged /ˈrægɪd/ adj **1 a)** old and torn: *ragged clothes* **b)** wearing clothes that are old and torn: *ragged children* **2** having a rough uneven edge: **ragged hole/edge/line**

raging /ˈreɪdʒɪŋ/ adj [only before noun] **1** very great or severe: *a raging appetite* | *The show was a raging success.* | *Nick had a raging headache.* **2** continuing with a lot of force or violence: *a raging blaze* | *a raging storm*

raid /reɪd/ n [C] **1** a short military attack on a place: **air/bombing raid** | **[+on]** *America's raid on Libya* **2** a sudden visit by the police to look for illegal goods or criminals: *a police raid* | *Uniformed police carried out the raid.* **3** an attack by criminals on a bank, shop etc to steal money or valuable things: *a bank raid* | *an armed raid* (=using guns) —**raid** v [T]

raider /ˈreɪdə $ -ər/ n [C] someone who attacks a place or steals things: **armed raiders**

RAILS

towel rail   handrail   railway line *BrE*

rail[1] /reɪl/ n **1** [U] the railway system: *the UK rail network* | **by rail** *people who travel by rail* **2** [C usually plural] one of the two long metal tracks that trains move along **3** [C] a bar along or around something, usually to stop you falling **4** [C] a bar that you use to hang things on: *a towel rail*

rail[2] v [I] *formal* to complain angrily

railcard /ˈreɪlkɑːd $ -kɑːrd/ n [C] *BrE* a small card that allows you to travel by train at a lower price than usual

railing /ˈreɪlɪŋ/ (*also* **railings** [plural]) n [C] a fence consisting of upright metal bars

railroad[1] /ˈreɪlrəʊd $ -roʊd/ n [C] *AmE* **1** the metal track that trains move along **SYN** **railway** *BrE* **2** a system of tracks and trains, or the company that operates this system **SYN** **railway** *BrE*

railroad[2] v [T] to force or persuade someone to do something without giving them enough time to think about it

railway /ˈreɪlweɪ/ n [C] *BrE*
1 (*also* **railway line**) the metal track that trains move along **SYN** **railroad** *AmE*
2 a system of tracks and trains, or the company that operates this system **SYN** **railroad** *AmE*: *the main East Coast railway* | *Mick met me at the railway station.* | *He worked on the railways.* → see picture at **RAIL**[1]

rain[1] /reɪn/ n
1 [U] water that falls in small drops from clouds in the sky → **rainy**: *There's been no rain for weeks.* | **in the rain** *You can't go out in the rain.* → **ACID RAIN**
2 the rains [plural] heavy rain that falls during a particular period in the year in tropical countries: *The rains came on time.*

COLLOCATIONS

adjectives

heavy rain (=a lot of water falling) *The rain became heavier.* ⚠ Do not say 'strong rain'. Say **heavy rain**.
light rain (=not much water falling) *A light rain began to fall.*
pouring/torrential rain (=very heavy rain) *He left us standing in the pouring rain.*

verbs

the rain falls *The rain was still falling steadily.*
the rain comes down/pours down (=a lot of rain falls) *The rain was coming down in torrents.*
it pours with rain *BrE*, **it pours rain** *AmE*: *We cancelled the picnic because it was pouring with rain.*
the rain stops *Let's wait for the rain to stop.*

noun + rain

a drop of rain *I felt a drop of rain.*

THESAURUS

rain water that falls in small drops from clouds in the sky: *There was heavy rain during the night.* | *I hope the rain stops soon.*
drizzle very light rain with very small drops of water: *A slight drizzle was falling.*
sleet a mixture of snow and rain: *The temperature fell and the rain turned to sleet.*
hail rain that falls as small balls of ice: *Hail and high winds have destroyed many crops.*
shower a short period of rain: *Tomorrow there will be heavy showers followed by sunny periods.*
downpour a short period of very heavy rain that starts suddenly: *A sudden downpour made us run for shelter.*

rain² v **it rains** if it rains, drops of water fall from clouds in the sky: *Is it still raining?* | *It started to rain.* | *It rained heavily* (=there was a lot of rain).

PHRASAL VERBS

rain down to fall in large quantities: **[+on]** *Bombs rained down on the city.*

be rained off *BrE*, **be rained out** *AmE* if an event or activity is rained off, it has to stop because there is too much rain

---

THESAURUS

it's raining drops of water are falling from clouds in the sky: *It's raining – you'd better take an umbrella.*

it's pouring (down) *BrE*, **it's pouring (rain)** *AmE* it is raining very heavily: *It's been pouring down all morning, so I haven't been out.*

it's drizzling it is raining a little, with very small drops of rain: *It's only drizzling – let's go for a walk anyway.*

---

rainbow /ˈreɪnbəʊ $ -boʊ/ n [C] a large curve of different colours in the sky that is caused by the sun shining through rain

'rain check n **I'll take a rain check** *spoken* used to say that you cannot accept an offer or an invitation now but you would like to at a later time

raincoat /ˈreɪnkəʊt $ -koʊt/ n [C] a coat that you wear when it rains

raindrop /ˈreɪndrɒp $ -drɑːp/ n [C] a single drop of rain

rainfall /ˈreɪnfɔːl $ -fɒːl/ n [C,U] the amount of rain that falls on an area in a particular period of time: *The annual rainfall is about 70 cm.*

'rain ˌforest n [C,U] a tropical forest with tall trees that are very close together, growing in an area where it rains a lot

rainstorm /ˈreɪnstɔːm $ -ɔːrm/ n [C] a storm with a lot of rain

rainwater /ˈreɪnwɔːtə $ -wɒːtər, -wɑː-/ n [U] water that has fallen as rain

rainy /ˈreɪni/ adj a rainy period of time is one when it rains a lot: *a rainy evening*

PHRASES

save sth for a rainy day to keep something, especially money, until a time when you will need it: *You could always save the money for a rainy day.*

raise¹ /reɪz/ v [T]

1 **LIFT** to move something to a higher position or into an upright position **OPP** **lower**: *Raise your hand if you know the answer.* | *I raised the lid.* | **raise your head/eyes/face** (=move your head, eyes etc so that you are looking up) | **raise yourself (up)** *I raised myself up on one elbow.* **THESAURUS** **LIFT**

2 **INCREASE** to increase an amount, number, or level **OPP** **lower**: *We had to raise our prices.* | *plans to raise taxes* | *an attempt to raise standards in primary schools* | **raise your voice** (=to speak loudly or shout because you are angry) **THESAURUS** **INCREASE**

3 **MONEY** to get people to give money that will be used to help other people or to do a particular job: *The event will **raise money** for charity.* | *We raised £900.*

4 **QUESTION/SUBJECT** **raise a question/issue/subject etc** to mention a question etc, or to bring something to someone's attention, so that it can be discussed or dealt with **SYN** **bring up**: *I plan to raise the issue with him face-to-face.* | *Thank you for raising that point.*

5 **HOPES/DOUBTS** **raise hopes/doubts/fears etc** to cause a particular emotion or reaction: *This attack raises fears of increased violence against foreigners.*

6 **CHILD** especially *AmE* to look after a child until they grow up **SYN** **bring up**: *His mother had raised five children by herself.*

7 **ANIMALS/CROPS** to keep animals or grow crops to sell or eat: *They used to **raise cattle**.*

PHRASES

raise the alarm to tell people there is a dangerous situation: *The alarm was raised by a passerby.*

raise your eyebrows/an eyebrow to show surprise, doubt, or disapproval by moving your EYEBROWS upwards

raise² n [C] *AmE* an increase in the money you earn **SYN** **rise** *BrE*: *It would be nice to **get a raise**.*

raisin /ˈreɪzən/ n [C] a dried GRAPE

rake¹ /reɪk/ n [C] a gardening tool with a row of metal teeth at the end of a long handle, used for gathering up dead leaves etc → see picture at **GARDEN**

rake² v [I,T] if you rake soil or dead leaves, you smooth the soil or gather the leaves with a rake

PHRASAL VERBS

rake sth ↔ in *informal* to earn a lot of money very easily: *He's absolutely **raking it in**.*

rally¹ /ˈræli/ n [C] (*plural* **rallies**) **1** a large public meeting that is held in support of something such as a political idea: *About 1,000 people attended the rally in Hyde Park.* **THESAURUS** **MEETING 2** a car race on public roads

rally² v (**rallied, rallying, rallies**) **1** [I,T] to come together, or to bring people together, to support an idea, a political party etc: **[+to]** *Fellow Republicans rallied to his defence.* | *attempts to **rally support** for his regime* **2** [I] to become stronger or higher again: *Share prices have rallied.*

PHRASAL VERBS

rally around (sb) (*also* **rally round** (sb) *BrE*) *informal* if a group of people rally around, they all try to help you when you are in a difficult situation: *My friends all rallied around when Mom died.*

ram¹ /ræm/ v (**rammed, ramming**) **1** [I,T] if a vehicle rams another, or rams into another, it crashes into it with a lot of force: *Thieves used his van to ram a police car.* **2** [T] to push something somewhere using great force: *I rammed my foot down on the brake.*

PHRASES

ram sth down sb's throat *informal* to try to force someone to accept an idea or opinion: *They're constantly trying to ram their beliefs down people's throats.*

ram² n [C] a male sheep

RAM /ræm/ n [U] technical (**Random Access Memory**) the part of a computer that keeps information temporarily so that it can be used immediately → ROM

Ramadan /'ræmədæn, -dɑːn, ˌræməˈdɑːn, -ˈdæn/ n [U] the ninth month of the Muslim year, when Muslims do not eat or drink during the day

ramble¹ /'ræmbəl/ v [I] **1** to talk for a long time in a confused and often boring way: *Sorry, I'm rambling.* | [+about] *Uncle Sid was always rambling on about the old days.* **2** to go for a walk in the countryside for pleasure

ramble² n [C] a walk in the countryside for pleasure

rambler /'ræmblə $ -ər/ n [C] someone who walks in the countryside for pleasure

rambling /'ræmblɪŋ/ adj **1** a rambling building has an irregular shape and covers a large area **2** rambling speech or writing is very long and does not seem to have any clear organization or purpose: *a long rambling letter*

ramifications /ˌræməfəˈkeɪʃənz/ n [plural] the additional results of something you do, which may not have been clear when you first decided to do it: [+of] *the ramifications of the new legislation*

ramp /ræmp/ n [C] **1** a slope that has been built to connect two places that are at different levels: *ramps for wheelchair users* **2** AmE a road for driving onto or off a large main road SYN **slip road** BrE

rampage¹ /ræmˈpeɪdʒ, 'ræmpeɪdʒ/ v [I] to rush about in groups, acting in a wild or violent way: [+through] *rioters rampaging through the streets*

rampage² n **on the rampage** rushing about in a wild and violent way: *gangs on the rampage*

rampant /'ræmpənt/ adj if something bad is rampant, there is a lot of it and it is very difficult to control: *rampant inflation*

rampart /'ræmpɑːt $ -ɑːrt/ n [C usually plural] a wide pile of earth or a stone wall built to protect a castle or city

ramshackle /'ræmʃækəl/ adj a ramshackle building is in very bad condition: *a ramshackle old farm house*

ran /ræn/ v the past tense of RUN

ranch /rɑːntʃ $ ræntʃ/ n [C] a large farm in the US or Canada where cattle, sheep, or horses are kept —**rancher** n [C]

rancid /'rænsɪd/ adj oily or fatty food that is rancid smells or tastes unpleasant because it is no longer fresh: *rancid butter*

rancour BrE, **rancor** AmE /'ræŋkə $ -ər/ n [U] formal an angry feeling towards someone when you hate them and cannot forgive them

random Ac /'rændəm/ adj happening or chosen without any definite plan, aim, or pattern: *a random sample of 120 families* —**randomly** adv
PHRASES
at random without any definite plan, aim, or pattern: **choose/select/pick sth at random** *Participants were chosen at random.*

randy /'rændi/ adj BrE informal full of sexual desire

rang /ræŋ/ v the past tense of RING

range¹ Ac /reɪndʒ/ n
1 OF DIFFERENT THINGS [C] a group of things that are different, but belong to the same general type: [+of] *The Centre provides a range of services for the elderly.* | **wide/whole/full etc range of sth** (=lots of very different things) *A wide range of subjects are on offer.*
2 OF PRODUCTS [C] a set of similar products made by a particular company or available in a particular shop: [+of] *a new range of tennis clothing*
3 LIMITS [C usually singular] the limits within which amounts, quantities, ages etc vary: **age/price/temperature etc range** *The age range of the patients was 39–97 years.* | **within/in your price range** (=that you can afford)
4 DISTANCE [singular, U] the distance over which a weapon can hit things, or the distance within which something can be seen or heard: [+of] *missiles with a range of 3,000 km* | **within range (of sth)** *We waited until the enemy was within range* (=near enough to be hit). | **out of range (of sth)** *Charles moved swiftly out of range.* | **at close range** (=very close to something) *We saw dozens of animals at close range.*
5 OF MOUNTAINS [C] a line of mountains or hills: *high mountain ranges* | **range of mountains/hills**
6 SHOOTING [C] an area where you can practise shooting: **rifle/firing/shooting range**

range² Ac v [I] **1** to include the two things mentioned and other things in between them: **range from sth to sth** *issues ranging from abortion to taxes* | *Toys range in price from $5 to $25.* **2** to deal with a large number of different subjects or ideas in a book, speech, conversation etc: [+over] *The conversation ranged over a variety of topics.*

ranger /'reɪndʒə $ -ər/ n [C] someone whose job is to look after a forest or area of public land

rank¹ /ræŋk/ n
1 [C,U] the position or level that someone has in an organization such as the police or army, or in society: [+of] *She held* (=had) *the rank of Inspector.* | **high/senior/low/junior rank** *an officer of junior rank* | *people of all ranks in society*
2 the ranks [plural] the ordinary members of an organization, for example soldiers who are not officers
3 ranks [plural] the ranks of a large organization or group are the people who belong to it: *The Democrats now face opposition from within their own ranks.* | [+of] *I joined the ranks of* (=became one of) *the unemployed.*
4 [C] a line of people or things: *a taxi rank* (=taxis waiting in a line to be hired)
PHRASES
break ranks to behave in a way that is different from other members of a group, especially when they expect your support: [+with] *In an angry speech, the senator broke ranks with the rest of his party.*
the rank and file the ordinary members of an organization rather than the leaders: *the Party's rank and file*

R

rank² v [I,T] to have a particular position on a list that shows how good or important people or things are, or to decide someone's or something's position in a list like this: **[+as/among]** *The lake must rank as one of the* most beautiful in Europe. | *The England team is ranked fourth in the world.*

ranking /ˈræŋkɪŋ/ n [C] a position on a list that shows how good someone or something is compared with others

rankle /ˈræŋkəl/ v [I,T] if something rankles, it continues to make you angry a long time after it happens: *an insult that still rankles*

ransack /ˈrænsæk/ v [T] **1** to go through a place stealing things and causing damage: *The whole house had been ransacked.* **2** to search a place very thoroughly

ransom /ˈrænsəm/ n [C,U] the money paid to free someone who is being kept as a prisoner: *The kidnappers demanded a ransom of $50,000.*
PHRASES
hold sb to ransom 1 to try to force someone to do what you want by threatening to do something if they do not do it: *He has accused the nurses of holding the government to ransom by threatening to strike.* **2** to keep someone as a prisoner until money is paid to you: *His daughter was kidnapped and held to ransom.*

rant /rænt/ v [I] *disapproving* to talk in a loud, excited, and angry way: **[+about]** *She was still ranting on about the unfairness of it all.* | **rant and rave** (=talk or complain very loudly and angrily)

rap¹ /ræp/ n **1** [C,U] a type of popular music in which the words are not sung but are spoken in time to music with a steady beat **2** [C] a series of quick sharp hits or knocks: *There was a rap on the door.*
PHRASES
take the rap (for sth) *informal* to be blamed or punished for a mistake or crime, especially unfairly: *She was left to take the rap for his murder.*

rap² v (**rapped, rapping**) **1** [I,T] to hit or knock something quickly several times: **[+on/at]** *Angrily, she rapped on the door.* **2** [T] *informal* to publicly criticize someone: *a film rapped by critics for its excessive violence*

rape¹ /reɪp/ v [T] to force someone to have sex, especially by using violence: *She had been raped and stabbed.*

rape² n [C,U] the crime of forcing someone to have sex, especially by using violence: *a rape victim* | **date rape** (=when the people involved have just spent time together socially)

rapid /ˈræpɪd/ adj done or happening very quickly **SYN** **fast**, **quick**: *rapid economic growth* **THESAURUS▶** FAST —**rapidly** adv —**rapidity** /rəˈpɪdəti/ n [U]

rapids /ˈræpɪdz/ n [plural] a part of a river where the water looks white because it is moving very fast over rocks

rapist /ˈreɪpɪst/ n [C] someone who forces someone else to have sex when they do not want to

rappel /ræˈpel/ v [I] (**rappelled, rappelling**) *AmE* to

go down a cliff etc by sliding down a rope and pushing against the cliff with your feet **SYN** **abseil** *BrE*

rapper /ˈræpə $ -ər/ n [C] someone who sings RAP songs

rapport /ræˈpɔː $ -ɔːr/ n [singular, U] friendly understanding and agreement between people: **[+with]** *She quickly established a rapport with her students.*

rapt /ræpt/ adj *written* so interested in something that you do not notice anything else

rapture /ˈræptʃə $ -ər/ n [U] *literary* great excitement, pleasure, and happiness: *a look of rapture on her face*

rare /reə $ rer/ adj
1 not happening often, or not common **OPP** **common**: *a disease that is very rare among children* | *rare plants such as orchids* | **it is rare (for sb/sth) to do sth** *It is very rare for her to miss a day at school.*
2 meat that is rare has been cooked for only a short time and is still red

rarely /ˈreəli $ ˈrerli/ adv not often: *She rarely goes out after dark.*

THESAURUS
rarely used when something happens on only a few occasions: *The people rarely ate meat.* | *This method is rarely used now.*
not (very) often another way of saying **rarely** that is very common in everyday English: *We don't get snow very often here.* | *I'm not often at home during the daytime.*
seldom rarely. **Seldom** sounds rather formal, and is used especially in written English: *Mr Brown seldom spoke about himself.* | *Karen had seldom seen him so angry.*
hardly ever/scarcely ever almost never: *We hardly ever speak to each other.* | *My grandmother scarcely ever goes out of the house.*

raring /ˈreərɪŋ $ ˈrer-/ adj **raring to do sth** *informal* very eager to do something: *We woke up early and were raring to go.*

rarity /ˈreərəti $ ˈrer-/ n **be a rarity** to not happen or exist very often: *Old cars in good condition are a rarity.*

rascal /ˈrɑːskəl $ ˈræs-/ n [C] a child who behaves badly but whom you still like

rash¹ /ræʃ/ n **1** [C] a lot of small red spots on someone's skin: **come/break out in a rash** *The baby broke out in a rash.* **2 a rash of sth** *informal* a lot of unpleasant things that suddenly start happening: *a rash of shootings*

rash² adj doing something too quickly, without thinking carefully first: *a rash decision* **THESAURUS▶** CARELESS —**rashly** adv

rasher /ˈræʃə $ -ər/ n [C] *BrE* a thin piece of BACON

rasp /rɑːsp $ ræsp/ v [I] to make a rough unpleasant sound: *Her breath rasped in her throat.* —**rasp** n [singular]

raspberry /ˈrɑːzbəri $ ˈræzberi/ n [C] (plural **raspberries**) a small soft sweet red fruit that grows on bushes → see picture on page A4

rat¹ /ræt/ n [C] an animal like a large mouse

rat² v [I] (**ratted, ratting**) informal if someone rats on you, they tell someone in authority about something wrong that you have done: **[+on]** They'll kill you if they find out you've ratted on them!

rate¹ /reɪt/ n [C]
1 the number of times something happens over a period of time: **birth/unemployment/crime etc rate** a country with a low birth rate
2 a charge or payment that is set according to a standard scale: Workers are demanding higher **rates of pay**. | What's **the going rate** (=the usual amount paid) for a piano teacher? | high **interest rates**
3 the speed at which something happens: Our money was running out **at an alarming rate** (=very quickly).
4 **first-rate/second-rate/third-rate** of good, bad, or very bad quality: a third-rate movie → **EXCHANGE RATE**
PHRASES
| **at any rate** spoken **1** used when you are stating one definite fact in a situation that you are not certain about SYN **anyway**: He's planning to come. At any rate, I think that's what he said. **2** used to introduce a statement that is more important than what was said before SYN **anyway**: Well, at any rate, the next meeting will be on Wednesday.
| **at this rate** spoken used to say what will happen if things continue in the same way: At this rate, we'll never finish on time.

rate² v **1** [T] to think that someone or something is good, bad etc: Johnson is rated one of the best basketball players in the world. **2** [I] to be considered good, bad etc: **[+as]** That rates as one of the best meals I've ever had.

rather /ˈrɑːðə $ ˈræðər/ adv especially BrE more than a little, but not very: I think she was rather upset last night. | It's a rather difficult problem. | I'm rather surprised to hear you say that.
PHRASES
| **or rather** spoken used to give more correct or exact information about what you have said: Mr Dewey, or rather his secretary, asked me to come to the meeting.
| **rather than** instead of something else: We decided to have the wedding in the summer rather than in the spring.
| **would rather** if you would rather do or have something, you would prefer to do or have it: I hate sitting doing nothing - I'd rather be working.

THESAURUS

rather/quite more than a little, but not very - used especially in British English: It's getting rather cold. | The test was quite difficult.
fairly rather - used in both British and American English: I'm fairly sure. | It's a fairly big house.
pretty informal rather. **Pretty** sounds a little stronger than **rather** and can sometimes also

mean 'very': I was pretty embarrassed. | It was pretty expensive.
reasonably rather - used especially when saying that someone or something is sure, good, healthy etc enough: I run every day, so I'm reasonably fit. | We feel reasonably confident that we'll win.
somewhat rather - used especially when comparing things: These figures are somewhat higher than average. | The situation is somewhat better now.

ratify /ˈrætɪfaɪ/ v [T] (**ratified, ratifying, ratifies**) to make a written agreement official: Both nations ratified the treaty. —**ratification** /ˌrætɪfɪˈkeɪʃən/ n [U]

rating /ˈreɪtɪŋ/ n **1** [C] a measurement of how popular, good, important etc someone or something is: The president's popularity rating has fallen. **2** **the ratings** a list that shows which films, television programmes etc are the most popular: The show is rapidly moving up the ratings.

ratio **Ac** /ˈreɪʃiəʊ $ ˈreɪʃoʊ/ n [C] (plural **ratios**) a relationship between two amounts, written as two numbers that show how much bigger one amount is than the other: **the ratio of sth to sth** a school where the ratio of students to teachers is about 5:1 (=five students for every teacher)

ration¹ /ˈræʃən $ ˈræ-, ˈreɪ-/ n [C] a limited amount of something such as food that you are allowed to have when there is not much available: the weekly meat ration

ration² v [T] to control the supply of something by allowing people to have only a limited amount of it: Coffee was rationed during the war. —**rationing** n [U]

rational **Ac** /ˈræʃənəl/ adj **1** based on real facts or scientific knowledge, and not influenced by feelings: There must be a **rational explanation** for their disappearance. **2** able to make decisions based on the facts of a situation, and not influenced too much by feelings OPP **irrational**: Let's try to discuss this like rational human beings. —**rationally** adv

rationale /ˌræʃəˈnɑːl $ -ˈnæl/ n [C,U] formal the reasons for a decision: **[+behind/for]** What's the rationale behind the President's decision?

rationalize **Ac** (also **-ise** BrE) /ˈræʃənəlaɪz/ v [I,T] to think of reasons to explain your behaviour, especially when you have done something wrong: He always finds a way to rationalize what he's done. —**rationalization** /ˌræʃənəlaɪˈzeɪʃən $ -lə-/ n [C,U]

'rat race n **the rat race** informal the unpleasant situation in business, politics etc in which people are always competing against each other

rattle¹ /ˈrætl/ v **1** [I,T] if something rattles, or if you rattle it, it makes a noise because it keeps shaking and hitting against something else: The wind was rattling the windows. THESAURUS ➤ **SHAKE 2** [T] informal to make someone lose their confidence and become nervous: Keep calm - don't let yourself get rattled.
PHRASAL VERBS
rattle sth ↔ **off** to say something very quickly and easily from your memory: She rattled off the names of all the American states.

rattle[2] *n* [C] **1** a baby's toy that makes a noise when it is shaken **2** a short repeated sound, made when something shakes: **[+of]** *the rattle of chains* → see picture on page A7

rattlesnake /'rætlsneɪk/ *n* [C] a poisonous American snake that makes a noise with its tail

raucous /'rɔːkəs $ 'rɒ:-/ *adj* a raucous voice or noise is very loud and unpleasant: *a raucous laugh*

raunchy /'rɔːntʃi $ 'rɒ:-/ *adj informal* sexually exciting, often in a way that is shocking: *a raunchy movie*

ravage /'rævɪdʒ/ *v* [T] to destroy or damage something very badly: *The forest was ravaged by fire.*

ravages /'rævɪdʒɪz/ *n* **the ravages of sth** *literary* damage or destruction caused by something such as war, disease, or time

rave[1] /reɪv/ *n* [C] a large party where young people dance to electronic music

rave[2] *v* [I] **1** to talk in an excited way about something because you think it is very good: **[+about]** *Everybody raved about the movie, but I hated it.* **2** to talk in an angry and uncontrolled way → **rant and rave** at RANT

rave[3] *adj* **rave reviews** strong praise for a new film, book, play etc

raven /'reɪvən/ *n* [C] a large black bird

ravenous /'rævənəs/ *adj* extremely hungry **THESAURUS** HUNGRY —**ravenously** *adv*

ravine /rə'viːn/ *n* [C] a deep narrow valley with steep sides

raving /'reɪvɪŋ/ (*also* ˌraving 'mad) *adj informal* completely crazy: *a raving lunatic*

ravings /'reɪvɪŋz/ *n* [plural] crazy things that someone says

ravishing /'rævɪʃɪŋ/ *adj* very beautiful

raw /rɔː $ rɒ:/ *adj*
1 FOOD not cooked: *raw onions* | *raw egg*
2 MATERIAL FOR MAKING STH raw cotton, sugar, and other materials are still in their natural state, and have not been prepared for people to use → **refined**: *raw materials* such as coal and iron
3 INFORMATION **raw data/material** information and facts that have been collected but have not been organized or examined: *This is just raw data.* | *He is still collecting the raw material for his novel.*
4 SKIN skin that is raw is red and sore
5 EMOTION/POWER raw emotion, power etc is very strong or powerful: *The film is full of raw emotion.* | *the raw power of their music*
6 NOT EXPERIENCED not experienced or trained: *raw recruits* in the army (=people who have just joined the army) | *She has plenty of raw talent.*
PHRASES
a raw deal unfair treatment: *She deserved a raise – I think she's getting a raw deal.*
hit/touch a raw nerve to accidentally upset or annoy someone by something you say: *I think I hit a raw nerve by asking him about his wife.*

ray /reɪ/ *n* [C] a narrow beam of light or energy from the sun, a lamp etc: *the rays of the sun*

PHRASES
ray of hope something that gives you a small amount of hope: *The treatment offers a ray of hope for cancer sufferers.*

rayon /'reɪɒn $ -ɑːn/ *n* [U] a smooth material like silk used for making clothes

raze /reɪz/ *v* [T] to destroy a city, building etc completely: *Their headquarters have been razed to the ground.*

razor /'reɪzə $ -ər/ *n* [C] a sharp instrument for removing hair from the body → **shaver**

'razor blade *n* [C] a small flat very sharp blade that is put inside a razor → see picture at BLADE

Rd., Rd the written abbreviation of **Road**: *5007 Rowan Rd.*

re /riː/ *prep written formal* used in business letters to introduce the subject: *Dear Sirs, re your enquiry of 19 October*

re- /riː/ *prefix* again: *plans to remake 'The Graduate'* | *We'll have to rethink our plans.*

're /ə $ ər/ the short form of 'are': *We're (=we are) ready now.*

reach[1] /riːtʃ/ *v*
1 PLACE [T] to arrive at a place: *It took four days for the letter to reach me.* **THESAURUS** ARRIVE

REACH

> **Grammar**
> Do not say 'We reached to New York at midnight.' Say *We reached New York at midnight.*

2 WITH YOUR HAND [I,T] to move your hand or arm in order to touch, hold, or pick up something: **[+for]** *He reached for his knife.* | **[+out]** *Mike reached out and took her hand.*
3 LEVEL/STANDARD [T] to increase, decrease, or develop to a particular level or standard over time: *Temperatures will reach 95° today.* | *I had reached the point where I was getting a good salary.*
4 HIGH PLACE [I,T] to be big enough, long enough etc to get to a particular level or point: *I can't reach the top shelf.* | *Will the ladder reach the roof?*
5 DECISION/AGREEMENT [T] to successfully agree with people about something: *We have finally reached a decision.* **THESAURUS** DECIDE
6 BY TELEPHONE [T] to speak to someone, especially by telephone **SYN** contact: *I wasn't able to reach him yesterday.*

reach[2] *n* [singular, U] **1** the distance that you can stretch out your arm to touch something: **out of/beyond (sb's) reach** *The box was just out of her reach.* | **within reach (of sb)** *Keep a glass of water within reach.* **2** the limit of someone's power or ability to do something: *He lives in Paraguay, well beyond the reach of the British authorities.*

PHRASES

within (easy) reach of sth close to a place: *The train is within easy reach of the hotel.*

react Ac /riˈækt/ v [I]

1 to behave in a particular way because of what someone has done or said to you, or because of the situation you are in → **respond**: **react by doing sth** *The audience reacted by shouting and booing.* | **react to sth** *How did she react to the news?*

2 to become ill when a chemical or drug goes into your body, or when you eat a particular kind of food: *Quite a lot of children react badly to antibiotics.*

3 *technical* if a chemical substance reacts, it changes when mixed with another substance

PHRASAL VERBS

react against sth to show that you do not like someone else's rules or ideas by deliberately doing the opposite: *Many teenagers react against their parents.*

reaction Ac /riˈækʃən/ n

1 [C,U] something that you feel or do because of what has happened to you or been said to you → **response**: **[+to]** *What was his reaction to the question?* | *The news brought an angry reaction from the unions.* | *My first reaction was to run away.*

2 [C] if you have a reaction to a drug or food that you have eaten, it makes you ill: *Some people have a very bad reaction to peanuts* (=peanuts make them ill). | **[+to]** *She had a severe **allergic reaction** to the drug.*

3 [singular] a change in people's attitudes, behaviour etc that happens because they disapprove of the way in which things were done in the past: **[+against]** *a reaction against his strict upbringing*

4 reactions [plural] *BrE* the ability to move quickly when something dangerous happens suddenly: *a driver with **quick reactions***

5 [C,U] *technical* a change that happens when two or more chemical substances are mixed together → **CHAIN REACTION**, **gut reaction** at **GUT¹**

reactionary Ac /riˈækʃənəri $ -ʃəneri/ adj disapproving strongly opposed to any social or political change —**reactionary** n [C]

reactor Ac /riˈæktə $ -ər/ n [C] a NUCLEAR REACTOR

read¹ /riːd/ v (past tense and past participle read /red/)

1 BOOK, NEWSPAPER ETC [I,T] to look at written words and understand what they mean: *Can Billy read yet?* | *She sat reading a magazine.* | **[+about]** *I read about the accident in the paper.* | **[+that]** *I read that the new drug is available now.* | *Her books are quite **widely read*** (=read by a lot of people).

2 MUSIC/MAP ETC [T] to look at signs or pictures and understand what they mean: *I can't actually read music, but I can play the guitar.* | *Can you read the map for me?*

3 SAY THE WORDS [I,T] to say the words written in a book, newspaper etc so that other people can hear you: *John read his report out loud.* | **read to sb/read sb a story** *Our mother used to read to us every evening.*

4 KNOW SB'S MIND **read sb's mind/thoughts** to guess what someone is thinking: *'Want some coffee?' 'You read my mind.'*

5 MEASUREMENT [T] if a measuring instrument reads a particular number, it shows that number: *The thermometer read 100°.*

6 SITUATION/COMMENT [T] to understand a situation or comment in a particular way: *The poem can be read as a protest against war.*

7 DISK [T] *technical* if a computer reads a DISK, it takes the information that is on the disk and puts it into its memory

8 SUBJECT AT UNIVERSITY [T] to study a subject at university: *He read chemistry at Oxford.*

PHRASES

read between the lines to guess what someone really feels or means, even when their words do not show it: *Reading between the lines, I don't think he is very happy.*

PHRASAL VERBS

read sth **into** sth to think that a situation, action etc means more than it really does: *You shouldn't read so much into what she says.*

read sth ↔ **out** to say the words you are reading to someone else: *He read out the names on the list.*

read sth ↔ **through/over** to read something carefully from beginning to end: *Read the contract over carefully before you sign it.*

read up on sth to read a lot about something because you will need to know about it: *We need to read up on the new tax laws.*

THESAURUS

read to look at and understand the words in a book, magazine etc, for interest and enjoyment: *I'm reading a book about China at the moment.*

look through sth to read something quickly, especially something containing information such as a report or document: *I'll look through your report tonight.* | *The police department spent days looking through old records.*

flick/flip through sth to turn the pages of a book, magazine etc quickly, looking for things that might interest you: *She sat in the waiting room and flicked through a magazine.*

plough through sth to read something long and boring: *I can't possibly plough through all these statistics.*

pore over sth to read something very carefully for a long time: *Chris was in his room, poring over a map.*

skim/scan to read something quickly to find a particular piece of information, or to get the main ideas: *I skimmed through the list, but my name wasn't there.* | *Rose scanned the TV programmes in the newspaper.*

read² n **a good read** something that you enjoy reading: *I thought his last book was a really good read.*

readable /ˈriːdəbəl/ adj **1** interesting and enjoyable to read: *a very readable history of Western philosophy* **2** clear and able to be read SYN **legible**

reader /ˈriːdə $ -ər/ n [C] **1** someone who reads books, or who reads in a particular way: *I've always been an **avid reader*** (=someone who likes to read a lot). | *a fast/slow reader* **2** someone who reads a particular newspaper or magazine regularly: *Many*

R

of our readers wrote in to complain about the article.
3 an easy book for children who are learning to read or for people who are learning a foreign language

readership /ˈriːdəʃɪp $ -ər-/ n [singular] the people who read a newspaper, magazine etc

readily /ˈredəli/ adv **1** quickly and easily: *The information is readily available on computer.* **2** quickly, willingly, and without complaining: *He readily agreed to help.*

readiness /ˈredinəs/ n [U] **1** willingness to do something: **readiness to do sth** *I admire his readiness to help people.* **2** when someone is prepared and ready for something that might happen: **in readiness (for sth)** *The army was standing by in readiness for an attack.*

reading /ˈriːdɪŋ/ n
1 [singular, U] the activity of looking at and understanding written words: *I enjoy reading in bed.* | *a careful reading of the contract*
2 [U] the books, articles etc that you read: *Her main reading seems to be romantic novels.* | *It's light reading* (=easy to read and not very serious).
3 [C] your way of understanding what a particular statement, situation, event etc means SYN **interpretation**: **[+of]** *What's your reading of the situation, Herb* (=what do you think has caused the situation, or what do you think might happen)?
4 [C] a number or amount shown on a measuring instrument: *The man came to take a reading from the electric meter.*
5 [C] an occasion when something is read to people: *a poetry reading*

readjust Ac /ˌriːəˈdʒʌst/ v **1** [I] to get used to a new job, situation, or way of life: **[+to]** *After the war, I needed time to readjust to life at home.* **2** [T] to make a small change to something, or move something to a new position: *She readjusted the microphone and began to sing.* —**readjustment** n [C,U]

readout /ˈriːdaʊt/ n [C] information produced by a computer that is shown on a screen or in print

ready /ˈredi/ adj [not before noun]
1 if you are ready, you have done everything necessary to prepare for something: *Go and get ready for bed.* | **ready to do sth** *We're just about ready to eat.* | **[+for]** *I don't think he's ready for marriage yet.*
2 something that is ready has been prepared and can be used, eaten etc immediately: *Is supper ready?* | *The computer is now set up and ready to use.* | **[+for]** *Is everything ready for the party?* | *I've got to get a room ready for our guests.* | *Have your passport ready for when we go through immigration.*
3 willing or likely to do something: **ready to do sth** *She's always ready to help in a crisis.*

THESAURUS

ready if you are ready, you have done everything necessary to prepare for something: *I'll be ready to go in a minute.* | *Let me know when you're ready for your lesson.*
prepared ready to deal with something, because you are expecting it or have made careful preparations: *I don't think he was prepared for*

that question. | *She was well-prepared for her interview.*
be all set informal to be completely ready for something that is just about to happen: *Right – are you all set for the match?*

ready-made adj already made or provided and ready for you to use: *a ready-made cake*

real¹ /rɪəl/ adj
1 actually existing and not just imagined: *The new system has real advantages.* | *Do your kids still think Santa Claus is a real person?* | *This kind of thing only happens in films, not in real life.*
2 true and not pretended: *What's the real reason you were late?* | *Jack isn't his real name.*
3 not false or artificial OPP **fake**: *real leather* | *I don't want a plastic Christmas tree – I want the real thing.* THESAURUS **GENUINE**
4 a real thing has all the qualities you expect something of that type to have: *I remember my first real job.* | *Simon was her first real boyfriend.*
5 used to emphasize what you are saying: *It's a real pleasure to meet you.*
PHRASES
for real seriously, not just pretending: *After two trial runs, we did it for real.*

real² adv AmE spoken very: *I'm real sorry!*

real estate n [U] especially AmE property such as houses or land

real estate agent n [C] AmE someone whose job is to sell houses or land SYN **estate agent** BrE

realisation /ˌrɪəlaɪˈzeɪʃən $ -lə-/ n a British spelling of REALIZATION

realise /ˈrɪəlaɪz/ v a British spelling of REALIZE

realism /ˈrɪəlɪzəm/ n [U] the ability to deal with situations in a practical or sensible way

realist /ˈrɪəlɪst/ n [C] someone who is realistic

realistic /rɪəˈlɪstɪk/ adj **1** someone who is realistic accepts the facts about a situation and realizes what is possible and what is not possible: **[+about]** *You need to be realistic about your chances of winning.* **2** showing things as they really are: *a very realistic TV drama* —**realistically** /-kli/ adv *We can't realistically hope for any improvement this year.*

reality /riˈæləti/ n (plural **realities**)
1 [C,U] what actually happens or is true, not what is imagined or thought: **[+of]** *Crime is one of the realities of living in the city.* | *She refuses to face reality.* | **the harsh/tough realities** (=unpleasant things that are real) *the harsh realities of unemployment*
2 **become a reality/make sth a reality** to begin to exist or happen, or to make something do this: *Her dream had become a reality.*
PHRASES
in reality used to say that something is different from what seems to be true: *He said he'd retired, but in reality he was fired.*

reality TV n [U] television programmes that film ordinary people doing their jobs or living their lives, or show what they do when put in a special situation THESAURUS **PROGRAMME**

realization (*also* **-isation** *BrE*) /ˌrɪəlaɪˈzeɪʃən $ -lə-/ *n* [singular, U] **1** when you understand something that you had not understood before: **[+that]** *She finally came to the realization that Jeff had been lying all the time.* **2** *formal* when you achieve something you had planned or hoped for: **[+of]** *the realization of a lifelong ambition.*

realize (*also* **-ise** *BrE*) /ˈrɪəlaɪz/ *v* [T]
1 to know and understand something, or suddenly begin to understand it: *He obviously didn't realize the dangers involved.* | **[+(that)]** *I'm sorry, I didn't realize that it was so late.* **THESAURUS** KNOW
2 realize a hope/goal/dream etc to achieve something you have been hoping to achieve: *She never realized her dream of becoming an actress.*
PHRASES
| **sb's (worst) fears were realized** used to say that the thing that you were most afraid of has actually happened: *His worst fears were realized when he received a phone call from the hospital.*

really¹ /ˈrɪəli/ *adv*
1 very or very much **SYN extremely**: *Yeah, he's a really nice guy.* | *I really like this place.*
2 used to make a negative statement less strong: *I don't really think it matters.*
3 if something is really true or really happens, it is true or it does happen: *Oliver's not really her cousin.* | *Now tell us what really happened.*

really² *spoken* **1 really?** used when you are surprised about or interested in what someone said: *'Jay's getting married.' 'Really? When?'* **2 not really** used to say no, especially when something is not completely true: *'Is it cold outside?' 'Not really.'*

realm /relm/ *n* [C] **1** *formal* an area of knowledge, interest, or thought: *new discoveries in the realm of science* **2** *literary* a country ruled over by a king or queen

'real-time *adj* [only before noun] *technical* a real-time computer system deals with information as fast as it receives it —**real time** *n* [U]

Realtor /ˈrɪəltə, -tɔː $ -ər, -ɔːr/ *n* [C] *trademark AmE* a REAL ESTATE AGENT

reams /riːmz/ *n* **reams of sth** a lot of something: *She took reams of notes in class.*

reap /riːp/ *v* **1** [T] to get something good because of the hard work you have done: *It will be some time before you reap the benefits of your hard work.* **2** [I,T] *old-fashioned* to cut and gather a crop of grain

reappear /ˌriːəˈpɪə $ -ˈpɪr/ *v* [I] to appear again after not being seen for some time: *Many of these ideas reappear in later books.* —**reappearance** *n* [C,U]

reappraisal /ˌriːəˈpreɪzəl/ *n* [C,U] *formal* when you think carefully about something again in order to decide whether you should change your opinion of it

rear¹ /rɪə $ rɪr/ *n* **1 the rear** the back part of an object, vehicle, building etc: **at the rear** *There are more seats at the rear of the hall.* **2** (*also* **rear end**) [C] the part of your body that you sit on —**rear** *adj*: *a rear window*

PHRASES
| **bring up the rear** to be at the back of a line of people or a group of people in a race: *Carole was left to bring up the rear.*

rear² *v* **1** [T] to look after a person or animal until they are fully grown **SYN raise**: *She reared seven children by herself.* **2** (*also* **rear up**) [I] if an animal rears, it rises up on its back legs: *The horse reared and threw me off.*
PHRASES
| **rear its ugly head** if a problem or something bad rears its ugly head, it appears or happens: *We must fight racism wherever it rears its ugly head.*

rearrange /ˌriːəˈreɪndʒ/ *v* [T] **1** to change the position or order of things: *Let's rearrange the furniture.* **2** to change the time of a meeting or event: *I can rearrange the appointment.* —**rearrangement** *n* [C,U]

reason¹ /ˈriːzən/ *n*
1 [C] a fact that explains why something happens or why someone does something: **[+for]** *He wouldn't give the reasons for his decision.* | **[+why]** *There are several reasons why the treatment didn't work.* | **[+(that)]** *The reason I'm calling is to see if you're free on Monday.* | **for a reason** *The bridge was closed for safety reasons.*

> **Grammar**
> Do not say 'the reason of the delay'. Say *the reason for the delay*.

2 [C,U] a fact that makes it right or fair to do something: **(no) reason to do sth** *There is no reason to panic.* | *I have no reason to believe that he's lying.* | *You had every reason* (=very good reasons) *to be suspicious.*
3 [U] sensible ideas or advice: *He won't listen to reason* (=be persuaded by sensible advice). | *He is the voice of reason.*
4 [U] the ability to think, understand, and make good judgments: *our powers of reason*
PHRASES
| **for obvious reasons** used to say that it is not necessary to explain why, because it is obvious: *This door must be kept locked, for obvious reasons.*
| **for some reason** used to say that you do not understand why: *For some reason, I felt like crying.*
| **within reason** within reasonable limits: *You can go anywhere you want, within reason.*

COLLOCATIONS
verbs
to have a reason *I had no reason to dislike her.*
to give a reason (=to say what the reason for something is) *Did she give any reason for being late?*
to explain the reasons for sth *Explain the reasons for your choice.*
to think of/see a reason *I can't see any reason why she would lie.*

adjectives
a good reason *There's a very good reason why you should listen to me.*

the main reason *Her main reason for leaving was that the pay was too low.*
the only reason *The only reason I came is that I wanted to help you.*
the real reason *Nobody knows the real reason why they split up.*
a simple reason (=one that is easy to understand) *We chose him for one simple reason: he was the best.*
legal/medical/personal etc reasons *The boy cannot be named for legal reasons.*

THESAURUS

reason something that explains why something happens, or why someone does something: *She told them the reason for her visit.* | *There are lots of good reasons for studying Chinese.*
explanation the reasons that help you understand why something happens, especially something that seems difficult to understand: *I can't think of any other explanation for his behaviour.*
excuse a reason you use to explain why you did something bad, or did not do something you should have done – especially a reason that is not completely true: *She always makes excuses for not doing her homework.*
motive a reason that makes someone decide to do something, especially a crime: *Police believe the motive for the murder was jealousy.*
justification a reason for doing something that seems wrong: *There is no justification for cruelty to animals.*
grounds a reason that makes it right or fair to do something, especially according to official or moral rules: *The court will decide if she has grounds for divorce.*

reason² v **1** [T] to decide that something is true by thinking carefully about the facts: **[+that]** *The jury reasoned that he could not have committed the crimes.* **2** [I] to think and make judgments: *the ability to reason*
PHRASAL VERBS
reason with sb to talk to someone in order to persuade them to be more sensible: *I tried to reason with her.*

reasonable /ˈriːzənəbəl/ *adj*
1 fair and sensible OPP **unreasonable**: *a reasonable excuse* | *a reasonable man* | *a perfectly reasonable* (=completely reasonable) *suggestion* | *It's reasonable to assume he must have known about this.*
2 reasonable prices are not too high SYN **fair**: *good furniture at very reasonable prices* THESAURUS ▶ **CHEAP**
3 quite big, good etc but not very big, good etc SYN **average**: *a reasonable amount of money* | *a reasonable standard of work* THESAURUS ▶ **SATISFACTORY**
—**reasonableness** n [U]

reasonably /ˈriːzənəbli/ *adv* **1** quite but not very: *I think I did reasonably well on the test.* THESAURUS ▶ **RATHER 2** in a way that is fair or sensible: *You can't reasonably expect people to work for such low wages.*

reasoned /ˈriːzənd/ *adj* [only before noun] based on careful thought SYN **logical**: *a reasoned argument*

reasoning /ˈriːzənɪŋ/ *n* [U] the process of thinking carefully about something in order to form an opinion or make a decision: *scientific reasoning*

reassurance /ˌriːəˈʃʊərəns $ -ˈʃʊr-/ *n* [C,U] something that you say or do to make someone feel less worried: **[+that]** *Many patients need reassurance that their condition will improve.*

reassure /ˌriːəˈʃʊə $ -ˈʃʊr/ *v* [T] to make someone feel less worried about something: **reassure sb (that)** *Police have reassured the public that the area is now perfectly safe.*

reassuring /ˌriːəˈʃʊərɪŋ◂ $ -ˈʃʊr-/ *adj* making you feel less worried: *a reassuring smile* —**reassuringly** *adv*

rebate /ˈriːbeɪt/ *n* [C] an amount of money that is paid back to you because you have paid too much rent, tax etc: *a tax rebate*

rebel¹ /ˈrebəl/ *n* [C] someone who opposes or fights against people in authority: *rebel soldiers*

rebel² /rɪˈbel/ *v* [I] (**rebelled, rebelling**) to oppose or fight against a person in authority, a law, an idea etc: **[+against]** *Teenagers often rebel against their parents.*

rebellion /rɪˈbeljən/ *n* [C,U] **1** when a group of people use violence to try to change the government: **[+against]** *an armed rebellion against the government* **2** when someone opposes ideas, rules, or people in authority: *teenage rebellion* | **[+against]** *a rebellion against middle-class values*

rebellious /rɪˈbeljəs/ *adj* opposing someone in authority or the rules of society: *young people with a **rebellious streak** (=a tendency to rebel)*

rebirth /ˌriːˈbɜːθ $ -ɜːrθ/ *n* [singular] when something becomes popular, important, or effective again: **[+of]** *the rebirth of British rock music*

reboot /ˌriːˈbuːt/ *v* [I,T] if you reboot a computer, you start it again after it has stopped working

rebound¹ /rɪˈbaʊnd/ *v* [I] to move quickly backwards after hitting a surface: **[+off]** *The ball rebounded off the wall.*
PHRASAL VERBS
rebound on sb if a situation or something you have done rebounds on you, it has a bad effect on you

rebound² /ˈriːbaʊnd/ *n* [C] a ball that has hit something and is moving back through the air
PHRASES
on the rebound feeling sad because your romantic relationship has ended, and looking for a new relationship in order to forget the old one: *My mother married my father on the rebound.*

rebuff /rɪˈbʌf/ *n* [C] formal an unfriendly answer to a suggestion or offer —**rebuff** *v* [T]

rebuild /ˌriːˈbɪld/ *v* [T] (past tense and past participle **rebuilt** /-ˈbɪlt/) **1** to build something again after it has been damaged or destroyed: *The church was completely rebuilt in the last century.* **2** to make something strong and successful again: *We try to help drug addicts **rebuild** their lives.*

rebuke /rɪˈbjuːk/ *v* [T] formal to speak angrily to someone because they have done something wrong —**rebuke** *n* [C,U]

rebut /rɪˈbʌt/ v [T] (**rebutted**, **rebutting**) *formal* to say or prove that a statement is not true —**rebuttal** n [C,U]

recalcitrant /rɪˈkælsətrənt/ *adj formal* refusing to obey rules or orders, even after being punished —**recalcitrance** n [U]

recall /rɪˈkɔːl $ ˈriːkɒːl/ v [T] **1** to remember something: [+(that)] *I seem to recall we had problems finding the place.* | *I don't recall meeting him.* **2** to officially order that something is returned or that someone should go back to a place: *The cars have been recalled because of a fault with the brakes.* —**recall** /rɪˈkɔːl, ˈriːkæp $ -ɒːl/ n [C,U]

recap /ˈriːkæp, riːˈkæp/ v [I,T] (**recapped**, **recapping**) to repeat the main points of something that has just been said —**recap** /ˈriːkæp/ n [C]

recapture /riːˈkæptʃə $ -ər/ v [T] **1** to make someone experience or feel something again: *a movie that recaptures the innocence of childhood* **2** to catch a prisoner or animal that has escaped

recede /rɪˈsiːd/ v [I] **1** to move further and further away and gradually stop being heard or seen: *The sound of the engines receded into the distance.* **2** to become less likely or less strong: *Hopes of finding the girls alive are receding.* **3** if your hair recedes, you gradually lose the hair from the front of your head: *his receding hairline* → see picture at **HAIR**

receipt /rɪˈsiːt/ n **1** [C] a piece of paper that shows you have paid for something: *Always keep the receipt.* | [+for] *the receipt for a pair of shoes* **2** [U] *formal* when someone receives something: [+of] *Please acknowledge receipt of the letter.* | **on/upon receipt of sth** (=when something is received) *The fee will be paid on receipt of an invoice.*

receive /rɪˈsiːv/ v [T]
1 to get or be given something SYN **get**: *She received an award for bravery.* | **receive sth from sb** *She received a letter from her mother.* | *The school receives strong support from parents.*
2 to react to something in a particular way → **reception**: *The speech was **well received** (=people said it was good).*
3 *formal* to accept or welcome someone officially as a guest: *Perez was formally received at the White House.*
PHRASES
be on/at the receiving end (of sth) to be the person who is affected by something, usually in an unpleasant way: *I would not want to be on the receiving end of his bad temper.*

receiver /rɪˈsiːvə $ -ər/ n [C] **1** the part of a telephone that you hold next to your mouth and ear → see picture on page A12 **2** someone who officially takes control of a business that is BANKRUPT (=does not have enough money to pay its debts) **3** a piece of equipment that receives television, radio, or other electronic signals

receivership /rɪˈsiːvəʃɪp $ -vər-/ n [U] if a business is in receivership, a receiver takes control of it because it has no money

recent /ˈriːsənt/ *adj* having happened or been done only a short time ago: *a recent photo* | **in recent**

years/months/weeks *Cases of skin cancer have increased in recent years.* THESAURUS NEW

recently /ˈriːsəntli/ *adv* not long ago: *They recently moved from South Africa.* | *Have you seen Anna recently?* | *He worked as a teacher **until recently**.*

THESAURUS

recently not long ago, especially a few days, weeks, or months ago: *I went there recently to do some shopping.* | *A new species of plant was recently discovered in Brazil.*
lately *especially spoken* during the last few weeks or months – often used in negative sentences and questions: *Gerry hasn't been feeling very well lately.* | *Have you seen her lately?*
just a very short time ago, especially only a few minutes, hours, or days ago: *It's just started raining.* | *They've just had a new baby.*
a short/little while ago not long ago – often used when you are not sure exactly when: *That hotel closed down a short while ago.* | *Apparently, they got married a little while ago.*
newly created, built, married etc not long ago: *a newly built stadium* | *the newly elected president*
freshly made, done etc not long ago – used especially about food, drink, and flowers: *freshly baked bread* | *freshly squeezed orange juice* | *The flowers were freshly picked.*
the other day *spoken* used in conversation when telling someone about something that happened to you recently: *I read an interesting article in the paper the other day.*

---

receptacle /rɪˈseptəkəl/ n [C] *formal* a container

reception /rɪˈsepʃən/ n
1 [C usually singular] a particular type of reaction or welcome that someone gets → **receive**: *The audience gave her an enthusiastic reception.* | *His paintings received a **mixed reception** (=some people liked them and some people did not).*
2 [U] the place where you go when you arrive at a hotel or large organization: *the **reception desk***
3 [C] a big formal party to celebrate something or to welcome someone: *a **wedding reception*** | *a **civic reception** for the US visitors* THESAURUS **PARTY**
4 [U] the quality of radio, television, or other electronic signals: *complaints of poor reception from mobile phone users*

receptionist /rɪˈsepʃənɪst/ n [C] someone whose job is to welcome and help people when they arrive at a hotel, office building etc

receptive /rɪˈseptɪv/ *adj* willing to consider new ideas and suggestions: *a receptive audience* | [+to] *Young people are usually very receptive to new ideas.*

recess /rɪˈses, ˈriːses $ ˈriːses, rɪˈses/ n **1** [C,U] a time when no work is done in a law court, parliament etc: *Parliament's summer recess* **2** [U] *AmE* a short period of free time between lessons at school SYN **break** *BrE* **3** [C] a space in a room, where part of the wall is further back than the rest

recession /rɪˈseʃən/ n [C,U] a time when there is much less trade and business activity than usual in a country: **out of/into recession** *ways to pull the country out of recession* | *the **economic recession** of the*

1970s | *a deep recession* (=one that lasts a long time)

> **Word Choice**: recession or depression?
> A **recession** is a situation in which there is less trade and more people are unemployed. It is much less severe than a **depression**, and does not have such a serious effect on people's lives: *The US economy went into recession earlier this year.*
> A **depression** is a very serious economic situation that lasts for many years. People use the phrase **the Great Depression** to talk about the economic situation in the 1930s, when millions of people had no jobs and there were great economic problems in Europe and the US.

recharge /ˌriːˈtʃɑːdʒ $ -ɑːr-/ *v* [T] to put a new supply of electricity into a BATTERY —**rechargeable** *adj*: *rechargeable batteries*
PHRASES
> **recharge your batteries** *informal* to get back your strength and energy again: *I'm going to spend a week in the mountains to recharge my batteries.*

recipe /ˈresəpi/ *n* [C] a set of instructions that tell you how to cook something: [+for] *a recipe for chocolate cake* | *a recipe book*
PHRASES
> **be a recipe for sth** to be very likely to cause a particular result: *Driving for too long without a break is a recipe for disaster.*

recipient /rɪˈsɪpiənt/ *n* [C] *formal* someone who receives something: [+of] *the recipient of the Nobel Peace Prize*

reciprocal /rɪˈsɪprəkəl/ *adj* a reciprocal arrangement, relationship etc is one in which two people or groups do or give the same things to each other —**reciprocally** /-kli/ *adv*

reciprocate /rɪˈsɪprəkeɪt/ *v* [I,T] *formal* to do or give something because something similar has been done or given to you

recital /rɪˈsaɪtl/ *n* [C] a performance of music or poetry, usually given by one person: *a piano recital*

recite /rɪˈsaɪt/ *v* [I,T] to say something that you have learned, for example a poem or list of facts —**recitation** /ˌresɪˈteɪʃən/ *n* [C,U]

reckless /ˈrekləs/ *adj* not caring about the possible bad effects of what you are doing: *reckless driving*
THESAURUS CARELESS —**recklessly** *adv* —**recklessness** *n* [U]

reckon /ˈrekən/ *v* [T]
1 *spoken* to think that something is true: *We've done all we can, I reckon.* | [+(that)] *I reckon he'll win.* | *Do you reckon you'll be able to come?* | *Moving house is reckoned to be one of the most stressful things you can do.*
2 to guess a number or amount without calculating it exactly: [+(that)] *Experts reckon profits will be around £280 million.* | *The car's speed was reckoned to be 180 kph when it left the road.*
PHRASAL VERBS
reckon on sth to expect something to happen and base your plans on it: *They had reckoned on profits of over a million dollars.* | **reckon on doing sth** *You can reckon on paying about £250,000 for a decent house in this area.*
reckon with sb/sth
1 sb/sth **to be reckoned with** someone or something that will not be easy to defeat or deal with: *He's a real force to be reckoned with.*
2 **not reckon with** sb/sth to not consider a possible problem when you are making plans: *I hadn't reckoned with the fact that the roads would be very busy.*

reckoning /ˈrekənɪŋ/ *n* [U] a calculation that is not exact: *By my reckoning, they should be here soon.*

reclaim /rɪˈkleɪm/ *v* [T] **1** to get back something you have lost or money you have paid: *Any lost property that is not reclaimed will be destroyed or sold.* **2** to make an area of land suitable for farming or building: *Large areas of derelict land have been reclaimed.* —**reclamation** /ˌrekləˈmeɪʃən/ *n* [U]

RECLINE

recline /rɪˈklaɪn/ *v* **1** [I] *formal* to lie back in a relaxed way **2** [I,T] if a seat reclines, you can move the back of the seat to a lower position so that you can lean back in it: *a reclining chair*

recluse /rɪˈkluːs $ ˈrekluːs/ *n* [C] someone who lives alone and avoids other people —**reclusive** /rɪˈkluːsɪv/ *adj*

recognition /ˌrekəgˈnɪʃən/ *n* **1** [singular, U] when you realize that something is important or true: [+of] *a growing recognition of the problems of homelessness* | [+that] *a general recognition that many prisons are failing* **2** [U] public respect or thanks for someone's work or achievements: *He gained international recognition after winning the competition.* | **in recognition of sth** *She was given the award in recognition of her work with animals.* **3** [U] when you know someone or something because you have seen them before: *He looked past me with no sign of recognition.*

recognize (*also* **-ise** *BrE*) /ˈrekəgnaɪz, ˈrekən-/ *v* [T]
1 to know who someone is or what something is because you have seen or heard them before: *He'd lost so much weight I hardly recognized him!* | *It can be difficult for doctors to recognize the symptoms of the disease.*
2 to accept officially that an organization, government, document etc is legal: *The UN refused to recognize the new government.*
3 to accept that something is true: [+that] *It's important to recognize that stress can affect your health.*

4 to realize that something that someone has done is good and to show approval: *His contribution to medical science should be recognized.* —**recognizable** /ˈrekəɡnaɪzəbəl/, -kən-, ˌrekəɡˈnaɪ-/ *adj* —**recognizably** *adv*

recoil /rɪˈkɔɪl/ *v* [I] to move back suddenly from something that you do not like or find frightening: **[+from/at]** *She recoiled in horror from his touch.*

recollect /ˌrekəˈlekt/ *v* [T] *formal* to remember something: *I don't recollect her name.*

recollection /ˌrekəˈlekʃən/ *n* [C,U] *formal* when you remember something from the past, or something you remember: **[+of]** *He had no recollection of the accident.*

recommend /ˌrekəˈmend/ *v* [T]
1 to advise someone to do something: **[+(that)]** *Dentists strongly recommend that you change your toothbrush every few months.* | **recommend doing sth** *The manufacturers recommend changing the filter every six months.* **THESAURUS** ADVISE

> **Grammar**
> Do not say 'They recommend to use gloves.'
> Say *They recommend using gloves.* or *They recommend that you use gloves.*

2 to say that someone or something is good: *Can you recommend a local restaurant?* | **recommend sth to sb** *I recommend this book to anyone who enjoys adventure stories.* **THESAURUS** SUGGEST

> **Word Choice**: recommend or suggest?
> If you **recommend** something, you tell someone that you think that it is a good choice, especially because you have used it, had it, or done it before: *A friend of mine recommended the hotel to us.* | *Which of his books do you recommend?*
> If you **suggest** something, you mention it as a possible idea for someone to consider: *She suggested that we should all go out for a meal.*

recommendation /ˌrekəmenˈdeɪʃən/ *n* **1** [C] an official statement advising people what to do about something: *The committee made detailed recommendations to the school.* | **[+that]** *the recommendation that babies should be laid to sleep on their backs* **2** [C,U] when you suggest that someone should choose a person or thing because they are very good: **on sb's recommendation** *We took the tour on a friend's recommendation.* **3** [C] *especially AmE* a letter or statement saying that someone is suitable for a job, course etc

recompense /ˈrekəmpens/ *n* [singular, U] *formal* something you give to someone for trouble or loss that you have caused them or as a reward for their help —**recompense** *v* [T]

reconcile /ˈrekənsaɪl/ *v* [T] **1** to find a way in which two different ideas, needs, situations etc can both happen or be true: **reconcile sth with sth** *difficulties in reconciling demands for leisure facilities with environment protection* **2** **be reconciled (with sb)** to have a good relationship with someone again after arguing with them: *The couple are now reconciled.* —**reconciliation** /ˌrekənsɪliˈeɪʃən/ *n* [singular, U]

PHRASAL VERBS
reconcile sb **to** sth to make someone accept an unpleasant situation: **reconcile yourself to sth** *He couldn't reconcile himself to the fact that his marriage was over.*

reconnaissance /rɪˈkɒnəsəns $ rɪˈkɑː-/ *n* [C,U] when aircraft and soldiers are sent somewhere in order to get information about the enemy

reconsider /ˌriːkənˈsɪdə $ -ər/ *v* [I,T] to think again about something in order to decide whether you should change your opinion: *Please reconsider your decision.* —**reconsideration** /ˌriːkənsɪdəˈreɪʃən/ *n* [U]

reconstitute /riːˈkɒnstɪtjuːt $ riːˈkɑːnstɪtuːt/ *v* [T] to change something so that it exists in a different form

reconstruct Ac /ˌriːkənˈstrʌkt/ *v* [T] **1** to produce a description or copy of an event, using the information you have: *Police were reconstructing the movements of the murdered couple.* **2** to build something again after it has been destroyed —**reconstruction** /-ˈstrʌkʃən/ *n* [U]: *the post-war reconstruction of Europe*

record¹ /ˈrekɔːd $ -ərd/ *n*
1 [C,U] information that is written down or stored in a computer so that it can be looked at in the future: *medical records* | **[+of]** *Keep a record of everything you spend.* | **on record** (=that has been recorded) *This month has been the wettest on record.*
2 [C] the fastest speed, longest distance, highest or lowest level etc that has ever been achieved: **[+for]** *He holds the world record for the 400 m.* | *We've had a record number of enquiries.*
3 [C,U] the facts about how good, bad etc someone or something has been in the past: *an airline with a good safety record* | **[+on]** *The government has a poor record on environmental issues.* | *He has a criminal record.*
4 [C] a round flat piece of plastic that music is stored on: *a large record collection* → TRACK RECORD
PHRASES
> **for the record** used to tell someone that what you are saying should be remembered: *For the record, the police never charged me.*
> **off the record** used to say that what you are saying is not official and you do not want someone to tell other people: *He told the reporter all about the incident, off the record.*
> **set/put the record straight** to tell someone the truth about something because you think they have false information: *I would like to set the record straight on a few points.*

> **COLLOCATIONS – sense 2**
> **verbs**
> **to break/beat a record** (=to do better or be greater than an existing record) *His jump broke the Olympic record.*
> **to hold a record** (=to have it) *George holds the record for the highest number of goals scored in a season.*
> **to set a record** (=to achieve it for the first time) *She set a new British record of 44.47 seconds.*

record

adjectives
an all-time record *Unemployment in Britain reached an all-time record.*
a world record *She holds two world records.*
an Olympic record *He broke the Olympic record by three seconds.*

record + noun
a record number/level/time etc *Temperatures this summer have reached record levels.*
a record high/low *Crime in the city fell to a record low.*

record² /rɪˈkɔːd $ -ɔːrd/ v
1 [T] to write down information or store it in a computer so that it can be looked at in the future: *All the events were recorded in a diary.*
2 [I,T] to store films, events, music etc on TAPE or DISCs so that you can watch or listen to them again: *The interview will be recorded.* | *The band has just finished recording their third album.*

ˈ**record-**ˌ**breaking** *adj* [only before noun] better, higher, faster etc than anything done before: *a record-breaking victory*

recorder /rɪˈkɔːdə $ -ˈkɔːrdər/ n [C]
1 tape/video/cassette etc recorder a piece of equipment that records sound or pictures **2** a musical instrument like a tube with holes that you play by blowing into it

recording /rɪˈkɔːdɪŋ $ -ɔːr-/ n [C,U] something that has been recorded on TAPE or DISC, or the process of recording something: [+of] *a recording of Mozart's 'Requiem'*

ˈ**record** ˌ**label** n [C] a company that records and produces music on DISCs or TAPES

ˈ**record** ˌ**player** n [C] a piece of equipment for playing records

recount¹ /rɪˈkaʊnt/ v [T] formal to tell a story or describe events

recount² /ˈriːkaʊnt/ n [C] the process of counting votes again

recoup /rɪˈkuːp/ v [T] to get back money that you have lost or spent

recourse /rɪˈkɔːs $ ˈriːkɔːrs/ n [U] formal something you can do or use to help you in a difficult situation: **have recourse to sth** *Did you have recourse to the data?* | **without recourse to sth** *a way of solving disputes without recourse to courts of law*

recover Ac /rɪˈkʌvə $ -ər/ v
1 [I] to get better after an illness, injury, shock etc: [+from] *My uncle is recovering from a heart attack.*
2 [I] to return to a normal condition after a period of trouble or difficulty: *The economy will take years to recover.*
3 [T] to get back something that was lost, taken etc: *The police managed to recover the stolen goods.*
4 [T] to get back control over your feelings, your movements etc SYN **regain**: *He never recovered the use of his arm.*

Word Choice: recover or get better/get well?
You **recover** from a serious illness or injury: *He is recovering from a knee injury.*

You **get better** or **get well** after any illness or injury. **Get better** and **get well** sound more informal than **recover** and are more common in everyday English: *'I've got a cold.' 'I hope you get better soon.'*

recovery Ac /rɪˈkʌvəri/ n **1** [singular, U] the process of getting better after an illness, injury etc: [+from] *He has made a remarkable recovery from the operation.* | **full/complete recovery** *Doctors expect her to make a full recovery.* **2** [singular, U] the process of returning to a normal condition after a period of trouble or difficulty: *economic recovery* **3** [U] when you get back something that has been lost or taken

recreate Ac /ˌriːkriˈeɪt/ v [T] to make something like it was in the past or like something in another place: *The zoo tries to recreate the animals' natural habitats.*

recreation /ˌrekriˈeɪʃən/ n [C,U] something you do for pleasure or fun: *outdoor recreation* —**recreational** adj

recrimination /rɪˌkrɪməˈneɪʃən/ n [C usually plural, U] when people blame and criticize each other: *bitter recriminations*

recruit¹ /rɪˈkruːt/ v [I,T] to find new people to work in a company, join an organization, do a job etc: *It's not easy to recruit well-qualified people.* —**recruitment** n [U]

recruit² n [C] someone who has recently joined a company or an organization

rectangle /ˈrektæŋgəl/ n [C] a shape with four straight sides and four angles of 90 degrees → **oblong** → see picture at SHAPE¹ —**rectangular** /rekˈtæŋgjələ $ -ər/ adj

rectify /ˈrektɪfaɪ/ v [T] (**rectified, rectifying, rectifies**) formal to correct something that is wrong: *efforts to rectify the problem*

rector /ˈrektə $ -ər/ n [C] a priest in some Christian churches

rectum /ˈrektəm/ n [C] technical the lowest part of your BOWEL —**rectal** adj

recuperate /rɪˈkjuːpəreɪt, -ˈkuː-/ v [I] to spend time getting better after an illness, injury etc: [+from] *people recuperating from major operations* —**recuperation** /rɪˌkjuːpəˈreɪʃən, -ˌkuː-/ n [U]

recur /rɪˈkɜː $ -ɜːr/ v [I] (**recurred, recurring**) to happen again: *a recurring dream* —**recurrence** /-ˈkʌrəns $ -ˈkɜːr-/ n [C,U] —**recurrent** adj

recycle /ˌriːˈsaɪkəl/ v [I,T] to put glass, paper etc through a special process so that it can be used again: *Glass bottles can be recycled.* —**recycled** adj: *recycled paper* —**recycling** n [U] —**recyclable** adj: *recyclable plastics* (=that can be recycled)

red¹ /red/ adj
1 having the colour of blood: *a red dress*
2 red hair is an orange-brown colour
3 if you go red, your face becomes pink because you are embarrassed, angry etc —**redness** n [U]

red² n [C,U] the colour of blood

PHRASES
be in the red to owe more money than you have OPP **be in the black**: *This is the airline's fourth straight year in the red.* THESAURUS▶ OWE
see red to become very angry: *She saw red when he admitted that he'd broken the window.*

red 'carpet *n* **the red carpet** special treatment that you give to someone important who is visiting you

redden /'redn/ *v* [I,T] to become red, or to make something do this

redeem /rɪ'diːm/ *v* [T] **1** to make something less bad: *Smith redeemed a poor game with a brilliant last-minute goal.* **2 redeem yourself** to do something that improves what other people think of you, after you have done something bad: *He redeemed himself by coming home that evening with flowers for her.* —**redeemable** *adj*

redemption /rɪ'dempʃən/ *n* [U] when someone is saved from the power of evil, especially according to the Christian religion
PHRASES
past/beyond redemption too bad to be saved or improved: *a criminal who is clearly beyond redemption*

redeploy /ˌriːdɪ'plɔɪ/ *v* [T] to move soldiers, workers, equipment etc to a different place or use them in a more effective way —**redeployment** *n* [U]

redevelop /ˌriːdɪ'veləp/ *v* [T] to make an area more modern by putting in new buildings and businesses or improving old ones —**redevelopment** *n* [C,U]

red-'handed *adj* **catch sb red-handed** *informal* to catch someone at the moment when they are doing something wrong

redhead /'redhed/ *n* [C] someone who has red hair

red 'herring *n* [C] a fact or idea that is not important but takes your attention away from something that is important

red-'hot *adj* extremely hot: *red-hot metal*

redid /riː'dɪd/ *v* the past tense of REDO

redirect, re-direct /ˌriːdaɪ'rekt, -də-/ *v* [T] **1** to send something in a different direction **2** to use something for a different purpose: *She needs to **redirect** her **energy** into something more useful.*

redistribute Ac /ˌriːdɪ'strɪbjuːt/ *v* [T] to share something between people in a different way from before —**redistribution** /ˌriːdɪstrə'bjuːʃən/ *n* [U]

red-'light ˌdistrict *n* [C] the area of a city where there is a lot of PROSTITUTION

red 'meat *n* [U] dark-coloured meat such as BEEF

redneck /'rednek/ *n* [C] *AmE informal* a man who lives in a country area who is not educated and who has strong unreasonable opinions

redo /riː'duː/ *v* [T] (*past tense* **redid** /-'dɪd/, *past participle* **redone** /-dʌn/, *third person singular* **redoes** /-'dʌz/) to do something again: *You'll have to redo this essay.*

redouble /riː'dʌbəl/ *v* **redouble your efforts** to greatly increase your efforts to do something

redress /rɪ'dres/ *v* [T] *formal* to correct something that is wrong, not equal, or unfair —**redress** /rɪ'dres $ 'riːdres/ *n* [U]

red 'tape *n* [U] official rules that seem unnecessary and prevent things from being done quickly

reduce /rɪ'djuːs $ rɪ'duːs/ *v* [T] to make the price, amount, or size of something less or smaller SYN **cut** → **reduction**: reduce the number/amount/level etc of sth *They're trying to reduce the number of students in the college.* | *attempts to reduce unemployment* | **reduce sth (from sth) to sth** *The jacket was reduced from £75 to £35.*
PHRASAL VERBS
reduce sb/sth to sth
1 reduce sb to tears to make someone cry: *Many staff were reduced to tears by the tragedy.*
2 reduce sb to doing sth to make someone do something that they would prefer not to, especially when it is worse than what they did before: *They were reduced to begging on the streets.*
3 reduce sth to rubble/ashes/ruins to destroy something, especially a building or city, completely

THESAURUS

reduce to make the price, amount, or size of something less or smaller: *I was hoping they would reduce the price a little.* | *Try to reduce the amount of energy you use in the home.*
cut to reduce the price, time, or number of something, especially by a large amount. **Cut** is often used in everyday English instead of **reduce**: *They've cut prices by 30%.* | *The company plans to cut hundreds of jobs.*
lower to reduce the amount or level of something – used especially in technical and formal English: *A healthy diet lowers the risk of heart disease.* | *The voting age was lowered to 18.*
bring sth down to reduce prices, costs, or the level of something, especially because they are too high: *Our aim is to bring down the level of unemployment.*
slash to reduce an amount or price by a very large amount – used especially in newspapers and advertisements: *In some areas, house prices have been slashed.*
relieve/ease to make pain or an unpleasant feeling less strong: *The doctor gave her some medicine to ease the pain.*

reduction /rɪ'dʌkʃən/ *n* [C,U] a decrease in the price, amount, or size of something, or when something is decreased: **[+in]** *a reduction in the number of students choosing science* | **[+of]** *targets for the reduction of pollution* | **[+on]** *There are 40% reductions on winter shoes.*

redundancy /rɪ'dʌndənsi/ *n* (*plural* **redundancies**) **1** [C,U] *BrE* when someone has to leave their job because there is not enough work: **compulsory/voluntary redundancy** *The company hopes that many staff will take voluntary redundancy.* | *Part-time workers may not be entitled to **redundancy payments**.* **2** [U] when something is not used or needed because something else does the same thing

redundant /rɪ'dʌndənt/ *adj* **1** *BrE* if you are made

R

redundant, you have to leave your job because there is not enough work: *Over 1,000 workers were made redundant.* **2** something that is redundant is no longer needed because something else does the same thing

reed /riːd/ n [C] **1** a tall plant like grass that grows near water **2** a thin piece of wood in some musical instruments that produces a sound when you blow air over it

reef /riːf/ n [C] a line of sharp rocks or a raised area near the surface of the sea, often made of CORAL

reek /riːk/ v [I] to smell of something unpleasant: *His breath reeked of garlic.* —**reek** n [singular]

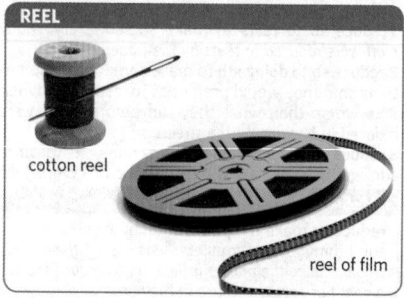

REEL

cotton reel

reel of film

reel¹ /riːl/ n [C] a round object that things such as thread or film can be wound onto

reel² v [I] **1** to walk in an unsteady way, almost falling over, as if you are drunk: *A guy came reeling down the hallway.* **2** to feel very shocked or confused: *The party is still reeling from its defeat in the election.*

PHRASAL VERBS

reel sth ↔ **off** *informal* to repeat a lot of information quickly and easily: *Andy can reel off the names of all the state capitals.*

re-elect /ˌriː ɪˈlekt/ v [T] to elect someone again —**re-election** /-ˈlekʃən/ n [C,U]

re-entry /riˈentri/ n [C,U] (*plural* **re-entries**) when someone or something enters a place again: *The shuttle made a successful re-entry into the Earth's atmosphere.*

ref /ref/ n [C] *spoken* a REFEREE

refer /rɪˈfɜː $ -ɜːr/ v (**referred, referring**)

PHRASAL VERBS

refer to sb/sth

1 to mention someone or something: *He referred to her several times.* | [**+as**] *Some people refer to them as 'gangsters'.*

2 to look at a book, map, piece of paper etc for information: *Refer to page 14 for instructions.*

3 refer sb **to** sb/sth to send someone to another person or place for information, advice etc: *Professor Harris referred me to an article she had written.* | *My doctor referred me to an eye specialist.*

referee¹ /ˌrefəˈriː/ n [C] **1** someone who makes sure that the rules are obeyed during some sports games → see picture at **FOOTBALL** **2** *BrE* someone who writes a letter saying that you are suitable for a job, course etc

referee² v [I,T] (**refereed, refereeing**) to be the referee for a game

reference /ˈrefərəns/ n

1 [C,U] something you say or write that mentions another person or thing: [**+to**] *Her writings contain references to members of her family.* | *In his letter, Sam made no reference to his illness.*

2 [C,U] when you look at something for information, or the place you get information from: *Keep this dictionary on your desk for easy reference.* | *The conversations are recorded for future reference* (=so that they can be looked at in the future).

3 [C] **a)** a letter saying that someone is suitable for a new job, course etc **b)** the person who writes a letter saying that someone is suitable for a new job, course etc **SYN** **referee**

'reference book n [C] a book, for example a dictionary, that you look at to find information **THESAURUS** **BOOK**

referendum /ˌrefəˈrendəm/ n [C,U] (*plural* **referenda** /-də/ or **referendums**) when people vote to make a decision on a particular subject, rather than for a person: [**+on**] *a referendum on independence* | *The assembly has agreed to hold a referendum on the issue.*

refill /ˌriːˈfɪl/ v [T] to fill something again: *A waiter refilled our glasses.* —**refill** /ˈriːfɪl/ n [C]: *He held out his glass for a refill.*

refine Ac /rɪˈfaɪn/ v [T] **1** to use an industrial process to make a natural substance more pure: *The sugar is refined and then shipped abroad.* **2** to improve a method, plan, system etc by making small changes to it —**refinement** n [U]

refined Ac /rɪˈfaɪnd/ adj **1** a refined substance has been made more pure using an industrial process: **refined sugar/oil/petroleum** **2** a method or process that is refined is improved and made more effective: *a more refined technique* **3** someone who is refined is polite and seems to be well educated: *a refined accent*

refinery /rɪˈfaɪnəri/ n [C] (*plural* **refineries**) a factory where something such as oil, sugar, or metal is refined

reflect /rɪˈflekt/ v **1** [I,T] if something such as a mirror or water reflects something, you can see the image of that thing in the mirror or water: **be reflected in sth** *The mountain was reflected in the waters of the lake.* **2** [T] if a surface reflects light, heat, sound etc, it sends back the light, heat, or sound that reaches it: *White clothes reflect more heat than dark ones.* **3** [T] to show or be a sign of something: *The new law reflects social changes in attitudes to marriage.* **4** [I] *formal* to think carefully: [**+on**] *Take some time to reflect on what I've said.*

PHRASAL VERBS

reflect on sb/sth to influence people's opinion about someone or something, especially in a bad way: *Behaviour like that always reflects very badly on the school.*

reflection /rɪˈflekʃən/ n **1** [C] an image that is reflected in a mirror or a similar surface: [**+in**] *We looked at our reflections in the pool.* **2** [U] when an image, light, sound etc is reflected **3** [C,U] careful and serious thought: *She paused for a moment's reflection.* **4** [singular] something that shows what something else is like, or is a sign of a particular situation: **[+of]** *The increase in ticket sales is a reflection of the popularity of the competition.* | **be a reflection on sb/sth** (=to show how good or bad someone or something is) *To some extent, students' grades are a reflection on the teacher.*

reflective /rɪˈflektɪv/ *adj* **1** reflective things reflect light: *reflective clothing* **2** thinking quietly: *a reflective mood*

reflector /rɪˈflektə $ -ər/ *n* [C] a piece of plastic that reflects light

reflex /ˈriːfleks/ *n* [C] a quick physical reaction that your body makes without you thinking about it: *Tennis players need to have quick reflexes.* | *Her reflex action was to pull her hand away.*

reflexive /rɪˈfleksɪv/ *adj* a reflexive verb or PRONOUN shows that an action affects the person or thing that does the action. In the sentence 'He cut himself', 'himself' is a reflexive pronoun. —**reflexive** *n* [C]

reform[1] /rɪˈfɔːm $ -ɔːrm/ *v* **1** [T] to change a law, system, or organization so that it is fairer or more effective: *plans to reform the voting system* **THESAURUS** CHANGE **2** [I,T] to change your behaviour and become a better person, or to make someone do this: *a reformed criminal* | *He doesn't drink any more – he's a reformed character.*

reform[2] *n* [C,U] a change that is made to a political or legal system in order to make it fairer or more effective: **[+of]** *the reform of local government* | **economic/political/educational reform**

reformer /rɪˈfɔːmə $ -ɔːrmər/ *n* [C] someone who works to improve laws or society

refrain /rɪˈfreɪn/ *v* [I] *formal* to not do something that you want to do: **[+from]** *Please refrain from smoking.*

refresh /rɪˈfreʃ/ *v* **1** [T] to make someone feel less tired or hot: *A shower will refresh you.* **2** [I,T] to make a computer screen show new information that has arrived since you began looking at it —**refreshed** *adj*
PHRASES
refresh sb's memory to make someone remember something: *He showed me some photographs to refresh my memory.*

refreshing /rɪˈfreʃɪŋ/ *adj* **1** making you feel less tired or less hot: *a refreshing drink* **2** pleasantly different and interesting: *The film made a refreshing change from the usual Hollywood blockbusters.* —**refreshingly** *adv*

refreshments /rɪˈfreʃmənts/ *n* [plural] food and drinks that are provided at a meeting, party, sports event etc: *Refreshments will be served at the interval.*

refrigerate /rɪˌfrɪdʒəreɪt/ *v* [T] to make food or drink cold so that it stays fresh for longer: *Cover the mixture and refrigerate it overnight.* —**refrigeration** /rɪˌfrɪdʒəˈreɪʃən/ *n* [U]

refrigerated /rɪˈfrɪdʒəreɪtɪd/ *adj* **1** a refrigerated

container, vehicle, ship etc keeps the food it contains cold **2** refrigerated food or drink has been kept cold in a refrigerator

refrigerator /rɪˈfrɪdʒəreɪtə $ -ər/ *n* [C] a piece of kitchen equipment like a cupboard that keeps food cold so that it stays fresh for longer **SYN** fridge → **freezer**

refuel /ˌriːˈfjuːəl/ *v* [I,T] (**refuelled, refuelling** *BrE*, **refueled, refueling** *AmE*) to fill a vehicle or plane with FUEL again before continuing a journey

refuge /ˈrefjuːdʒ/ *n* **1** [U] protection from danger, bad weather, trouble etc: **take/seek refuge** *A number of women and children took refuge in the French Embassy.* **2** [C] a place that provides protection from danger: **[+for]** *a refuge for abused women*

refugee /ˌrefjʊˈdʒiː/ *n* [C] someone who has had to leave their country to escape from danger or war: *a refugee camp near the border*

refund /ˈriːfʌnd/ *n* [C] money that is given back to you in a shop, restaurant etc, for example because you are not satisfied with what you bought: *If you're not completely satisfied, we'll give you a refund.* —**refund** /rɪˈfʌnd/ *v* [T]

refurbish /ˌriːˈfɜːbɪʃ $ -ɜːr-/ *v* [T] to repair and improve a building —**refurbishment** *n* [C,U]

refusal /rɪˈfjuːzəl/ *n* [C,U] when someone refuses to do, accept, or allow something: **refusal to do sth** *His refusal to pay the fine means he may go to prison.*

refuse[1] /rɪˈfjuːz/ *v*
1 [I,T] to say firmly that you will not do or accept something: *I asked her to marry me, but she refused.* | **refuse to do sth** *Cindy refuses to go to school.* | **flatly refuse/refuse point blank (to do sth)** (=refuse completely) *Mother flatly refused to go back into hospital.* | *The offer seemed too good to refuse.*
2 [T] to not give or allow someone something that they want: **refuse sb sth** *We were refused permission to enter the country.*

> **THESAURUS**
>
> **refuse** to say firmly that you will not do something, or that you do not want to accept an invitation, offer etc: *He refused to tell me how much he had paid.* | *Jenny decided to refuse the invitation.*
> **turn sth/sb down** to refuse an offer, invitation, or request – used especially when this is surprising or disappointing: *You'd be crazy to turn that job down!* | *For some reason, they turned down my application for a visa.*
> **say no** *spoken* to say that you will not do something when someone asks you: *You should ask him if he wants a date – I'm sure he won't say no.*
> **decline** *formal* to politely refuse to accept an offer or invitation, or refuse to do something: *They declined any offer of financial help.* | *He declined to comment on the rumours.*

refuse[2] /ˈrefjuːs/ *n* [U] *formal* waste material **SYN** rubbish: *refuse collection* | **domestic/household refuse**

refute

refute /rɪ'fju:t/ v [T] *formal* **1** to prove that a statement or idea is not correct: **refute an idea/hypothesis etc 2** to say that a statement is wrong or unfair: **refute an allegation/a charge etc**

regain /rɪ'geɪn/ v [T] to get something back: *The army has **regained control** of the area.* | *When he **regained consciousness**, he discovered he was in hospital.*

regal /'ri:ɡəl/ adj typical of a king or queen and therefore very impressive —**regally** adv

regard¹ /rɪ'ɡɑːd $ -ɑːrd/ n **1** [U] when you respect or consider someone or something: *Doctors are **held in high regard** (=respected a lot) by society.* | *She **has no regard for** (=does not consider) other people's feelings.* **2 regards** [plural] used to send good wishes to someone in a polite and slightly formal way: ***Give** my **regards to** your aunt.* | **(with) kind/best regards** (=used at the end of a letter or message)
PHRASES
| **with/in regard to sth** *formal* used to say what subject you are talking or writing about: *Several changes have been made **with regard to** security.*
THESAURUS ABOUT

regard² v [T] **1** to think about someone or something in a particular way: **regard sb as sth** *I've always regarded you as my friend.* **2** *formal* to look at someone or something: *She regarded him thoughtfully.*

regarding /rɪ'ɡɑːdɪŋ $ -ɑːr-/ prep *formal* a word used especially in business letters to introduce the subject you are writing about: *Regarding your recent inquiry, I've enclosed a copy of our new brochure.*
THESAURUS ABOUT

regardless /rɪ'ɡɑːdləs $ -ɑːr-/ adv **1 regardless of sth** in spite of something: *He'll sign that contract regardless of what anyone says!* **2** if you continue doing something regardless, you do it in spite of problems or difficulties: *You get a lot of criticism, but you just have to **carry on regardless**.*

regatta /rɪ'ɡætə/ n [C] a sports event in which there are boat races

regeneration /rɪˌdʒenə'reɪʃən/ n [U] when a thing or place is developed, improved, or grows strong again: *inner city regeneration* —**regenerate** /rɪ'dʒenəreɪt/ v [T]

reggae /'reɡeɪ/ n [U] a type of popular music from Jamaica with a strong regular beat

regime Ac /reɪ'ʒiːm/ n [C] a government, especially one that was not elected fairly or that you disapprove of: *a brutal **military regime*** **THESAURUS** GOVERNMENT

regiment /'redʒəmənt/ n [C] a large group of soldiers consisting of several BATTALIONS —**regimental** /ˌredʒə'mentl◂/ adj

regimented /'redʒɪmentɪd/ adj strictly controlled —**regiment** v [T]

region Ac /'riːdʒən/ n [C]
1 a large area of a country or of the world, usually without exact limits: **[+of]** *the north-eastern region of Russia* | **central/border etc region** *Snow is expected in mountain regions.*

2 an area of your body: *pain in the lower back region* —**regional** adj: *a regional accent* —**regionally** adv
PHRASES
(somewhere) in the region of sth used to describe an amount without being exact: *It will cost in the region of $750.*

register¹ Ac /'redʒɪstə $ -ər/ n **1** [C] an official list or record of something: **[+of]** *the register of births, marriages, and deaths* **THESAURUS** LIST **2** [C,U] a way of speaking or writing that is formal, informal, humorous etc that you use when you are in a particular situation → **CASH REGISTER**

register² Ac v **1** [I,T] to put the name of someone or something on an official list: **[+with]** *You need to register with a doctor.* | **[+for]** *How many students have registered for the course so far?* | *Is the car registered in your name?* **2** [T] *formal* to state an opinion or show a feeling: *The club has registered a formal protest about the decision.* **3** [I,T] if something registers, or you register it, you notice or realize it: *Then I remembered something that hadn't registered at the time.* **4** [I,T] if an instrument registers an amount, or an amount registers on it, it shows that amount: *The thermometer registered 74°F.*

'register ˌoffice n [C] a REGISTRY OFFICE

registrar /ˌredʒə'strɑː◂ $ 'redʒəstrɑːr/ n [C] **1** someone who is in charge of official records of births, marriages, and deaths **2** *BrE* a hospital doctor

registration Ac /ˌredʒə'streɪʃən/ n [U] when names and details are recorded on an official list, or when you add your name to an official list

regi'stration ˌnumber n [C] *BrE* the numbers and letters on a car's NUMBER PLATE

registry /'redʒəstri/ n [C] (plural **registries**) a place where official records are kept

'registry ˌoffice (also **'register ˌoffice**) n [C] a place in Britain where you can get married and where records of births, marriages, and deaths are kept

regress /rɪ'ɡres/ v [I] *formal* to go back to an earlier less developed state → **progress** —**regression** /-'ɡreʃən/ n [U]

regret¹ /rɪ'ɡret/ v (**regretted, regretting**)
1 to feel sorry about something you have done and wish you had not done it: **regret doing sth** *We've always regretted selling that car.* | **[+(that)]** *He regrets that he never went to college.* | **bitterly/deeply/greatly regret** *It was a stupid thing to do and I bitterly regret it.* | *If we don't deal with the problem now, we'll **live to regret it** (=will regret it in the future).*
2 *formal* to be sorry and sad about a situation: **[+(that)]** *Miss Otis regrets she's unable to attend today.*

regret² n [C,U] sadness that you feel about something because you wish it had not happened: *Carl said he **had no regrets about** his decision.* | *The company **expressed** deep **regret** at the accident.* —**regretfully** adv —**regretful** adj

regrettable /rɪ'ɡretəbəl/ adj something regrettable is something you wish had not happened: *a regrettable mistake* —**regrettably** adv

regular¹ /ˈreɡjələ $ -ər/ *adj*
1 happening every hour, every week, every month etc, usually with the same amount of time in between OPP **irregular**: *regular meetings* | *His heartbeat became slow and regular.* | *We hear from him* **on a regular basis.** | *War planes were taking off* **at regular intervals.** | *He already has a* **regular job** (=one he does every week).
2 happening or doing something very often OPP **irregular**: *He's one of our regular customers.* | *Regular exercise helps keep your weight down.*
3 normal or usual: *She's not our regular babysitter.*
4 with the same amount of space between one thing and the next OPP **irregular**: *The markers are spaced* **at regular intervals.**
5 of a normal or standard size: *fries and a regular Coke* THESAURUS **NORMAL**
6 especially AmE ordinary or normal and not special or different: *He's just* **a regular guy.** THESAURUS **NORMAL**
7 evenly shaped with parts or sides of equal size
8 a regular verb or noun changes its forms in the same way as most verbs or nouns. The verb 'walk' is regular, but 'be' is not. OPP **irregular** —**regularity** /ˌreɡjəˈlærəti/ *n* [U]

regular² *n* **1** [C] *informal* a customer who goes to the same shop, restaurant etc very often **2** [U] *AmE* petrol that contains LEAD → **unleaded**

regularly /ˈreɡjələli $ -ərli/ *adv*
1 often: *He visits the old man regularly.* THESAURUS **OFTEN**
2 at the same time every day, week, or month: *They are checked regularly, once a week.*
3 evenly arranged or shaped: *The plants are regularly spaced.*

regulate Ac /ˈreɡjəleɪt/ *v* [T] **1** to control an activity or process, especially by having rules: *rules regulating the use of chemicals in food* **2** to keep something at a particular speed, temperature etc

regulation Ac /ˌreɡjəˈleɪʃən/ *n* **1** [C] an official rule or order: *There seem to be so many* **rules and regulations.** THESAURUS **RULE 2** [U] when a system or process is controlled: [+of] *government regulation of arms sales*

regulator Ac /ˈreɡjəleɪtə $ -ər/ *n* [C] **1** an instrument that controls the temperature, speed etc of something works **2** someone who makes sure that a system works properly or fairly —**regulatory** /ˈreɡjəleɪtəri $ ˈreɡjələtɔːri/ *adj*

rehab /ˈriːhæb/ *n* [U] *informal* treatment to help someone who takes drugs or drinks too much alcohol: *Frank's* **been in rehab** *for six weeks.*

rehabilitate /ˌriːhəˈbɪlɪteɪt/ *v* [T] **1** to help someone to live a healthy or useful life again after they have been ill or in prison: *special help to rehabilitate stroke patients* **2** to improve a building, business, or area —**rehabilitation** /ˌriːhəbɪlɪˈteɪʃən/ *n* [U]: *a project for the rehabilitation of drug addicts*

rehash /riːˈhæʃ/ *v* [T] *informal* to use the same ideas again in a way that is not really different or better: *He keeps rehashing the same old speech.* —**rehash** /ˈriːhæʃ/ *n* [C]

rehearsal /rɪˈhɜːsəl $ -ɜːr-/ *n* [C,U] a time when all the people in a play, concert etc practise it before giving a public performance: *rehearsals for 'Romeo and Juliet'*

rehearse /rɪˈhɜːs $ -ɜːrs/ *v* [I,T] to practise, or make people practise, something such as a play or concert before giving a public performance THESAURUS **PRACTISE**

rehouse /ˌriːˈhaʊz/ *v* [T] to provide someone with a new or better home

reign¹ /reɪn/ *n* **1** [C] a period of time during which someone, especially a king or queen, rules a country: [+of] *the reign of Queen Anne* **2** [singular] a period of time during which someone is in control of an organization, business etc: *his 4-year reign as team coach*
PHRASES
reign of terror when a government, army etc uses violence to control people: *When he came to power, he started a reign of terror.*

reign² *v* [I] **1** to be the ruler of a country **2** *literary* to be the main feature or feeling of a situation: *For a few moments,* **confusion reigned.**
PHRASES
the reigning champion the most recent winner of a competition: *Next week, they take on the reigning champions, France.*

reimburse /ˌriːəmˈbɜːs $ -ɜːrs/ *v* [T] *formal* to pay money back to someone: **reimburse sb for sth** *The company will reimburse you for your travel expenses.* —**reimbursement** *n* [U]

rein /reɪn/ *n* [C usually plural] a long narrow band of leather that is fastened around a horse's head in order to control it
PHRASES
give sb (a) free rein to give someone complete freedom to say or do things the way they want to: *The company gave him a free rein to find the best design.*
keep a tight rein on sb/sth to strictly control someone or something: *They've promised to keep a tight rein on spending.*

reincarnate /ˌriːɪnˈkɑːneɪt $ -ɑːr-/ *v* **be reincarnated** to be born again in another body after you have died

reincarnation /ˌriːɪnkɑːˈneɪʃən $ -ɑːr-/ *n* **1** [U] the belief that people return to life in another body after they have died **2** [C] the person or animal that someone becomes when they return to life after they have died

reindeer /ˈreɪndɪə $ -dɪr/ *n* [C] (*plural* **reindeer**) a type of DEER with long horns that lives in very cold places

reinforce Ac /ˌriːənˈfɔːs $ -ˈfɔːrs/ *v* [T] **1** to support an opinion, feeling, system etc and make it stronger: *The minister's speech served to reinforce the government's policy on the environment.* **2** to make something such as a part of a building, a piece of clothing etc stronger —**reinforced** *adj*: *reinforced concrete*

reinforcements /ˌriːɪnˈfɔːsmənts $ -ˈfɔːrs-/ *n* [plural] more soldiers or police who are sent to help make a group stronger

R

reinstate /ˌriːɪnˈsteɪt/ v [T] to give someone their job back after they have lost it —**reinstatement** n [C,U]

reinvent /ˌriːɪnˈvent/ v **reinvent yourself** to completely change your appearance and image: *Pop stars constantly need to reinvent themselves.*

PHRASES

reinvent the wheel to waste time trying to find a way of doing something, when everyone already knows how to do it

reiterate /riːˈɪtəreɪt/ v [T] *formal* to say something important again

reject¹ Ac /rɪˈdʒekt/ v [T]
1 to not accept something or someone OPP **accept**: *Your application has been rejected.* | *He flatly rejected* (=completely rejected) *our offers of help.* | *I had expected my idea to be rejected outright* (=without even being considered). | **reject sth as sth** *The meat was rejected as unfit to eat.* | *Doctors say her body may reject the new kidney.*
2 to not give someone love or attention: *She felt rejected by her parents.*

reject² /ˈriːdʒekt/ n [C] a product that is damaged: *cheap rejects*

rejection Ac /rɪˈdʒekʃən/ n **1** [C,U] when someone does not accept something: **[+of]** *his rejection of his parents' values* | *She received many rejections before the novel was published.* **2** [U] when someone stops giving someone love or attention: *fear of rejection*

rejoice /rɪˈdʒɔɪs/ v [I] *literary* to be very happy because of something that has happened —**rejoicing** n [U]

rejoin /ˌriːˈdʒɔɪn/ v [T] to return to a group or person

rejuvenate /rɪˈdʒuːvəneɪt/ v [T] to make someone feel young and strong again: *I returned from holiday refreshed and rejuvenated.*

rekindle /riːˈkɪndl/ v [T] to make someone have feelings that they have had a long time ago

relapse /rɪˈlæps $ ˈriːlæps/ n [C,U] when someone becomes ill or worse after seeming to improve: **have/suffer a relapse** *He had a relapse and went back into hospital.* —**relapse** /rɪˈlæps/ v [I]

relate /rɪˈleɪt/ v **1** [T] if you relate two things, you show how they are connected: **relate sth to/with sth** *The report relates health with standards of living.* **2** [I] if one thing relates to another, it is connected with it in some way: **[+to]** *I collect anything that relates to baseball.* | *The doctor will ask some questions relating to your lifestyle.* **3** [T] *formal* to tell someone about something that has happened: **relate sth to sb** *He later related the whole story to us.*

PHRASAL VERBS

relate to sb/sth to understand how someone feels: *I find it hard to relate to kids.*

related /rɪˈleɪtɪd/ adj
1 things that are connected: *Police believe the murders are related.* | **[+to]** *I'm not sure if this is related to what we've just been talking about.* | **closely/directly related** *The ideas are closely related.* | **stress-related/drug-related etc** *stress-related illness*

2 belonging to the same family or group: **[+to]** *Are you related to Paula?* | *Dogs and wolves are closely related.*

> ### THESAURUS
>
> **related/connected** used about things that have a connection with each other. **Connected** is not used before a noun: *The two cases may be connected with each other.* | *banking and other related activities*
> **linked** having a direct connection - often used when one thing is the cause of the other: *Smoking is directly linked to cancer.*
> **relevant** related to what you are discussing, or to a particular subject: *Nick raised a very relevant point.* | *Their research is relevant to the education of children of all ages.*
> **have nothing to do with sth** especially spoken used when saying very firmly that two things are not connected in any way: *Your age has nothing to do with how good you are at your job.*

relation /rɪˈleɪʃən/ n
1 [C,U] a connection between things SYN **relationship** **[+between]** *the relation between drugs and mental illness* | *His statement bore no relation to the truth* (=it was not true at all).
2 [C,U] a member of your family SYN **relative**: **[+of]** *a distant relation of the Royal Family* | **[+to]** *What relation are you to John?* | *He's no relation to the film star Michael Douglas.* THESAURUS ▶ RELATIVE
3 relations [plural] the relationship between groups of people, countries, organizations etc - used when saying how friendly this relationship is: **[+between]** *Are the relations between the staff and students any better?* | **[+with]** *Relations with the local people are generally good.* | **diplomatic/international relations** *Britain broke off* (=ended) *diplomatic relations.* | *East–West relations* (=between countries in the East and the West) → **INDUSTRIAL RELATIONS, PUBLIC RELATIONS, RACE RELATIONS**

PHRASES

in relation to sb/sth 1 compared with someone or something else: *Women's earnings are still low in relation to men's.* **2** *formal* about a particular thing or person: *Is your enquiry in relation to an advertisement?*

relationship /rɪˈleɪʃənʃɪp/ n
1 [C] the attitude that two people or groups show towards each other: **[+with]** *I had a close relationship with my father.* | **[+between]** *the special relationship between the US and Britain*
2 [C] a situation in which two people have sexual or romantic feelings for each other: **[+with]** *Do you remember when I was having a relationship with Anna?* | *a sexual relationship*
3 [C,U] the way that things or people are connected: **[+between]** *the relationship between smoking and cancer* | **[+to]** *'What's your relationship to Sue?' 'She's my cousin.'*

relative¹ /ˈrelətɪv/ n [C] a member of your family SYN **relation**: *He's staying with relatives.* | *an elderly relative* | **close/distant relative** *She has no close relatives.*

THESAURUS

relative a member of your family, especially one who does not live with you: *We only invited close relatives to the wedding.*

relation a relative. You also use **relation** when talking about the family connection between you and another person: *Some of my relations live in Canada.* | *'What relation is she to you?' 'She's my cousin.'*

descendant someone who is related to a person who lived and died a long time ago: *He's a direct descendant of Shakespeare.*

ancestor a member of your family who lived a long time ago, especially hundreds of years ago: *Several of my family's ancestors are buried in this churchyard.*

next of kin the person who is most closely related to you, and who needs to be told if something serious happens to you: *The form asks you to give your next of kin.*

relative² *adj* having a particular quality when compared with similar things: *a period of relative peace*

PHRASES

relative to sth *formal* compared with something else: *Costs have gone up relative to wages.*

relative 'clause *n* [C] a part of a sentence that contains a verb and adds information about the person or thing you are talking about

relatively /'relətɪvli/ *adv* quite, when compared with other things: *Food is relatively cheap in the US.*

relative 'pronoun *n* [C] a PRONOUN such as 'who', 'which', or 'that' which connects a relative clause to the rest of a sentence

relativity /,relə'tɪvəti/ *n* [U] the relationship between time, space, and speed: *Einstein's theory of relativity*

relax Ac /rɪ'læks/ *v*
1 [I] to rest or do something you enjoy, especially after working: *What do you do to relax?*
2 [I,T] to feel calmer and less worried, or to make someone do this: *Sit down and relax!* | *The music will help relax you.*
3 [I,T] if you relax part of your body, or if it relaxes, it becomes less stiff: *Let your muscles relax.*
4 [T] to make rules, laws etc less strict: *plans to relax immigration controls*

relaxation Ac /,ri:læk'seɪʃən/ *n* [U] **1** a way of resting and enjoying yourself: **for relaxation** *I swim for relaxation.* **2** when rules, laws etc are made less strict: **[+of]** *the relaxation of drug laws*

relaxed /rɪ'lækst/ *adj*
1 feeling calm, comfortable, and not worried or annoyed: *Gail was lying in the sun, looking happy and relaxed.*
2 a situation or attitude that is relaxed is informal and not strict: *There's a **relaxed atmosphere** in school.*

THESAURUS

relaxed feeling calm, comfortable, and not worried or annoyed: *It was Friday night and I was feeling very relaxed.* | *I feel more relaxed about my job than I used to.*

comfortable/at ease feeling relaxed when you are doing something or when you are with someone: *Do you feel comfortable with speaking in front of a large group?* | *The doctor made her feel at ease.*

easy-going someone who is easy-going does not get easily annoyed and is not strict: *I liked Susie – she was lively, funny and easy-going.* | *an easy-going boss*

laid-back *informal* someone who is laid-back is always calm and does not seem to worry about anything: *He's a laid-back kind of guy.* | *a laid-back attitude to life*

relaxing /rɪ'læksɪŋ/ *adj* making you feel calm: *a relaxing bath*

relay¹ /'ri:'leɪ $ rɪ'leɪ, 'ri:leɪ/ *v* [T] to pass a message or signal from one person or place to another: *broadcasts relayed by satellite*

RELAY

a relay race

relay² /'ri:leɪ/ (*also* **'relay race**) *n* [C] a running or swimming race between two or more teams, each of which has several people in it. When one person finishes their part of the race, the next person starts and the race is over when everyone has finished.

release¹ Ac /rɪ'li:s/ *v* [T]
1 to allow someone to be free after you have kept them somewhere → **discharge, free**: *The hostages were released this morning.* | **release sb from sth** *He was released from hospital this morning.*
2 to give news or information to people after it has been secret: *The name of the victim has not been released.*
3 to make a film, record etc available for people to see or buy: *The film is released in May.*
4 to stop holding something: **release your grip/hold** *A sudden noise made him release his grip.*

release² Ac *n* **1** [singular] when someone is allowed to be free after they have been a prisoner: *the release of political prisoners* **2** [C] a new film or record that is available to see or buy: *her latest release* → **PRESS RELEASE**

PHRASES

be on general release if a film is on general release, it is being shown at most cinemas: *The movie is on general release throughout the UK.*

relegate /'relɪgeɪt/ *v* [T] **1** to put someone or something in a less important position: **relegate sb to sth** *He was relegated to the role of assistant.* **2** *BrE* if a sports team is relegated, it is moved to a lower

DIVISION: **relegate sb/sth to sth** *We were relegated to the Third Division last year.* —**relegation** /ˌreləˈgeɪʃən/ *n* [U]

relent /rɪˈlent/ *v* [I] to be less strict and allow something that you did not allow before

relentless /rɪˈlentləs/ *adj* not stopping or changing: *relentless pressure* —**relentlessly** *adv*

relevant Ac /ˈreləvənt/ *adj* **1** directly relating to the thing that is being discussed OPP **irrelevant**: [+to] *Are your qualifications relevant to the job?* THESAURUS RELATED **2** important and useful: *The teachings of Jesus are still relevant today.* —**relevance** (*also* **relevancy**) *n* [U]

reliable Ac /rɪˈlaɪəbəl/ *adj* if someone or something is reliable, you can trust and depend on them OPP **unreliable** → **rely**: *Rick is hard-working and very reliable.* | *a reliable computer* | *a reliable witness* THESAURUS HONEST —**reliably** *adv* —**reliability** /rɪˌlaɪəˈbɪləti/ *n* [U]

reliance Ac /rɪˈlaɪəns/ *n* [U] when someone or something depends on another thing → **rely**: [+on/upon] *our reliance on imported oil*

reliant Ac /rɪˈlaɪənt/ *adj* if you are reliant on someone, you depend on them → **rely**: *She's still reliant on her parents for money.*

relic /ˈrelɪk/ *n* [C] something from the past that still exists: [+of] *a relic of ancient times*

relief /rɪˈliːf/ *n*
1 [singular, U] the happy feeling you have when you are no longer worried or frightened → **relieved**: *a tremendous feeling of relief* | *It was a relief to be alone.* | *with/in relief I saw with relief that he wasn't hurt.* | *to sb's relief To my relief, she spoke English.* | *The news will come as a great relief to his family.* | *The car halted and I breathed a sigh of relief.*
2 [U] when pain or suffering is made less severe or stops for a time → **relieve**: *drugs for pain relief* | [+of] *the relief of suffering* | [+from] *relief from the intense heat*
3 [U] money, food, clothes etc given to people who need them: *famine/disaster/flood etc relief* | *Relief workers distributed rice.*

PHRASES
in relief a decoration that is in relief is higher than the surface around it: *A figure had been carved in relief on a stone pillar.*

relieve /rɪˈliːv/ *v* [T] to reduce pain, suffering, a bad feeling etc: *Exercise can help relieve stress.* THESAURUS REDUCE

PHRASAL VERBS
relieve sb of sth *formal* to take something from someone

relieved /rɪˈliːvd/ *adj* happy because you are no longer worried or frightened: **relieved to do sth** *I was relieved to be back home.* | [+(that)] *I felt relieved that Ben would be there to help.*

religion /rɪˈlɪdʒən/ *n* [C,U] a system of belief in one or more gods, or these beliefs in general: *the study of religion* | *people of different religions*

THESAURUS

religion a system of belief in one or more gods, or these beliefs in general: *'What religion are you?' 'I'm a Christian.'* | *We studied religion at school.*

faith a religion, especially one of the important world religions. Also used when talking about someone's belief in God: *There were people of all faiths.* | *He said his faith in God had kept him going.*

sect a group of people with their own religious beliefs, especially one that has separated from a large religion: *a Jewish sect*

the Catholic/Protestant etc Church one of the separate groups within the Christian religion: *the Baptist Church*

cult a religious group that is not part of an established religion – especially one that people disapprove of because of its extreme ideas: *He was a member of a strange religious cult somewhere in Texas.*

religious /rɪˈlɪdʒəs/ *adj*
1 relating to religion: *We don't share the same religious beliefs.*
2 having very strong religious beliefs: *a deeply religious woman*

religiously /rɪˈlɪdʒəsli/ *adv* if you do something religiously, you are always careful to make sure that you do it: *He phones her religiously every evening.*

relinquish /rɪˈlɪŋkwɪʃ/ *v* [T] *formal* to give your position, power, rights etc to someone else

relish¹ /ˈrelɪʃ/ *v* [T] to enjoy the thought that something good is going to happen: *Jamie didn't relish* (=did not like) *the idea of getting up so early.*

relish² *n* **1** [U] great enjoyment **2** [C,U] a thick cold spicy sauce, usually eaten with meat

relive /ˌriːˈlɪv/ *v* [T] to remember something so well that it seems to be happening again: *We spent the morning reliving our schooldays.*

reload /ˌriːˈləʊd $ -ˈloʊd/ *v* [I,T] **1** to put more bullets into a gun **2** to make a computer give you information again

relocate Ac /ˌriːləʊˈkeɪt $ riːˈloʊkeɪt/ *v* [I,T] *formal* to move to a new place: [+to] *Our company relocated to the West Coast.* —**relocation** /ˌriːləʊˈkeɪʃən $ -loʊ-/ *n* [U]

reluctant Ac /rɪˈlʌktənt/ *adj* unwilling to do something: *a reluctant smile* | **reluctant to do sth** *She was very reluctant to ask for help.* —**reluctance** *n* [U] —**reluctantly** *adv*

rely Ac /rɪˈlaɪ/ *v* (**relied, relying, relies**)
PHRASAL VERBS
rely on sb/sth to trust or depend on someone or something → **reliable**: *I knew I could rely on you.* | **rely on sb to do sth** *Can I rely on you to carry out my instructions?* | [+for] *He relies on the Web for the latest score.*

remain /rɪˈmeɪn/ *v*
1 [I, linking verb] to stay in the same place or condition: [+at/in/with] *The others left, while I remained at home.* | *The Communist Party remained in*

power for years. | **remain standing/seated etc** *Please remain seated until the train stops.* | *The boy remained silent.*
2 [I] to be left after other people, things, or parts have gone: *A pile of bricks was all that remained of our home.*
3 [I] if something remains to be done, said etc, it still needs to be done, said etc: *It remains to be seen whether the operation has been a success* (=we do not know yet whether it has succeeded).

remainder /rɪˈmeɪndə $ -ər/ *n* **the remainder** the part of something that is left after everything else has gone: **[+of]** *The remainder of the class stayed behind.*

remaining /rɪˈmeɪnɪŋ/ *adj* [only before noun] left when other things or people have gone

remains /rɪˈmeɪnz/ *n* [plural] the parts of something that are left after the rest has been destroyed: **[+of]** *the remains of a temple*

remake /ˈriːmeɪk/ *n* [C] a film that has the same story as one that was made before: **[+of]** *a remake of 'The Wizard of Oz'* —**remake** /riːˈmeɪk/ *v* [T]

remand¹ /rɪˈmɑːnd $ rɪˈmænd/ *v* [T] *BrE* to send someone away from a court of law to wait for their TRIAL: *Smith was remanded in custody* (=sent to prison) *until Tuesday.*

remand² *n* [U] *BrE* the period of time that someone spends in prison before their TRIAL: **on remand** *He committed suicide while on remand.*

remark¹ /rɪˈmɑːk $ -ɑːrk/ *n* [C] something that you say to express your opinion **SYN** comment: **[+about]** *Carl made a spiteful remark about her hair.*

remark² *v* [T] to say something that expresses your opinion: **[+that]** *One woman remarked that he was very handsome.* | *'It must be a very old house,' John remarked.* | **[+on/upon]** *Several people remarked on the poor service.*

remarkable /rɪˈmɑːkəbəl $ -ɑːr-/ *adj* excellent and unusual: *a remarkable achievement*

remarkably /rɪˈmɑːkəbli $ -ɑːr-/ *adv* in a way that is surprising: *Jane and her cousin look remarkably similar.*

remarry /ˌriːˈmæri/ *v* [I,T] (**remarried, remarrying, remarries**) to marry again —**remarriage** /riːˈmærɪdʒ/ *n* [C,U]

remaster /ˌriːˈmɑːstə $ -ˈmæstər/ *v* [T] to improve the quality of a film or musical recording, using a computer

remedial /rɪˈmiːdiəl/ *adj* intended to help, improve, or correct something: *a remedial class for students with learning difficulties*

remedy¹ /ˈremədi/ *n* [C] (*plural* **remedies**) **1** a successful way of improving a situation or solving a problem: **[+for]** *the remedy for rising crime rates* **2** a simple medicine to cure an illness that is not very bad: *cold and flu remedies*

remedy² *v* [T] (**remedied, remedying, remedies**) to improve a bad situation: *To remedy the situation, we need more teachers.*

remember /rɪˈmembə $ -ər/ *v*
1 [I,T] if you remember a fact, a name, or a person

or thing from the past, they come back into your mind → **forget**: **[+(that)]** *She suddenly remembered that she had an appointment.* | **[+what/why/how etc]** *Can you remember when you last saw him?* | **remember (sb) doing sth** *He couldn't even remember getting home.* | *Remember, you should never speak to strangers.* | **distinctly/clearly remember** *I distinctly remember reading about it in the paper.*
2 [I,T] to not forget something that you should do, get, or bring: **remember to do sth** *Did you remember to phone Nicky?*
3 [T] to think about and show respect for someone who has died: *a ceremony to remember those who died*

THESAURUS

remember if you remember a fact, a name, or a person or thing from the past, they come back into your mind: *I can't remember his name.* | *Do you remember Jo? She was in our class.*
memorize to learn something so that you can remember it later, for example facts, numbers, or a speech: *For some exams, you just need to be able to memorize things.* | *Don't write down your credit card number – memorize it.*
remind sb of sb/sth to make you think of another person, place etc by being similar to them: *He reminds me a bit of Daniel Craig.* | *The taste is delicious – it reminds me of strawberries.*

---

remembrance /rɪˈmembrəns/ *n* [U] when you think about and show respect for someone who has died: **in remembrance of sb/sth** *a tree planted in remembrance of her husband*

remind /rɪˈmaɪnd/ *v* [T] if you remind someone about something, you make them remember it or remember to do it: **remind sb to do sth** *Remind me to go to the bank.* | **remind sb about sth** *Thanks for reminding me about tonight's party.* | **remind sb that** *I had to remind her that we still had a lot of work to do.* | **remind sb of sth** *I reminded him of his promise.* | **that reminds me** *spoken* (=said when something makes you remember something) *Oh, that reminds me, we've run out of milk.*
PHRASAL VERBS
remind sb **of** sb/sth if someone or something reminds you of another person or place, they make you think of that person or place because they are similar: *She reminds me of my mother.* **THESAURUS►**
REMEMBER

reminder /rɪˈmaɪndə $ -ər/ *n* [C] something that makes you remember something else: **[+of]** *a painful reminder of the war* | *I received a reminder to return my library books* (=a message reminding me to return them).

reminisce /ˌreməˈnɪs/ *v* [I] to talk or think about pleasant events in your past: **[+about]** *We were reminiscing about our college days.* —**reminiscence** *n* [C,U]

reminiscent /ˌreməˈnɪsənt/ *adj* **be reminiscent of sth** making you think of something similar: *a scene reminiscent of a Hollywood movie*

remission /rɪˈmɪʃən/ *n* [C,U] a period of time when an illness improves: **in remission** *Her cancer is in remission.*

remit /'riːmɪt $ rɪ'mɪt, 'riːmɪt/ *n* [singular] *BrE* the work that you are responsible for in your job

remittance /rɪ'mɪtəns/ *n* [C] *formal* a payment for something

remnant /'remnənt/ *n* [C] a small part of something that is left after the rest has gone: **[+of]** *the remnants of our meal*

remodel /ˌriːˈmɒdl $ -'mɑːdl/ *v* [I,T] (**remodelled, remodelling** *BrE*, **remodeled, remodeling** *AmE*) to change the shape or appearance of something, especially a building: *The airport terminals have been remodelled.*

remonstrate /'remənstreɪt $ rɪ'mɑːn-/ *v* [I] *formal* if you remonstrate with someone, you tell them that you strongly disapprove of what they have done

remorse /rɪ'mɔːs $ -ɔːrs/ *n* [U] a feeling of being sorry because you have done something bad: **[+for]** *Keating* **showed** *no* **remorse** *for his crime.* | *Poor Dorothy was* **filled with remorse.** —**remorseful** *adj*

remorseless /rɪ'mɔːsləs $ -'mɔːr-/ *adj* **1** not stopping **2** very cruel or strict —**remorselessly** *adv*

remote /rɪ'məʊt $ -'moʊt/ *adj* **1** far away: *a remote village* | *in the remote past* **THESAURUS** ▶ **FAR 2** very slight or small: *The prospects for peace seem very remote.* **3** not friendly

re,mote con'trol *n* **1** (*also* **remote**) [C] a piece of equipment that you use to control a television, VIDEO etc from a distance **2** [U] a system for controlling something from a distance

remotely /rɪ'məʊtli $ -'moʊt-/ *adv* even to a very small degree: *He didn't sound remotely interested.*

removable Ac /rɪ'muːvəbəl/ *adj* able to be removed: *seats with removable covers*

removal Ac /rɪ'muːvəl/ *n* [C,U] **1** when something is taken away or someone gets rid of it: **[+of]** *the removal of rubbish* **2 removal firm/van/men** etc *BrE* a company, vehicle etc that is used to move all your furniture from your old house to a new house: *All our possessions were loaded into the removal van.*

remove Ac /rɪ'muːv/ *v* [T]
1 to take something away from the place where it is: *The police will remove any illegally parked cars.* | **remove sth from sth** *Dictionaries may not be removed from the library.*
2 to make something no longer exist: *This will remove the risk of infection.*
3 *formal* to force someone to leave their job: **remove sb from sth** *The college board has the power to remove a teacher from his post.*

PHRASES

far removed from sth very different from something: *The world of politics was far removed from the lives of ordinary people.*

THESAURUS - sense 2

remove to make something no longer exist, especially something that was causing problems: *How can I remove the stain?* | *A sea wall could remove the threat of flooding.*
get rid of sth to make something that you do not want go away. **Get rid of** is much more common than **remove** in everyday English:

I can't get rid of this sore throat I've got.
delete to remove something that has been written or stored on a computer: *I've deleted that email by mistake.*
erase to remove recorded sounds or pictures from a tape, or to remove writing: *Police say that the tape had been deliberately erased.*
cut to remove a part from a film, book, speech etc: *The film was too long and had to be cut.*

remover /rɪ'muːvə $ -ər/ *n* [C,U] **paint remover/ stain remover** etc a substance used to remove paint, dirt etc

remuneration /rɪˌmjuːnə'reɪʃən/ *n* [C,U] *formal* payment for a job, service etc

renaissance /rɪ'neɪsəns $ ˌrenə'sɑːns/ *n* [U] when something becomes popular or successful again

Renaissance *n* **the Renaissance** an important time in Europe between the 14th and 17th centuries when art, literature, music etc became very different from what they had been before

rename /ˌriːˈneɪm/ *v* [T] to give something a new name

render /'rendə $ -ər/ *v* [T] *formal* to cause someone or something to be in a particular condition: *The blow to his head rendered him unconscious.*

rendering /'rendərɪŋ/ *n* [C] someone's performance of a poem, play, piece of music etc

rendezvous /'rɒndəvuː, -deɪ- $ 'rɑːndeɪ-/ *n* [C] (*plural* **rendezvous** /-vuːz/) **1** an arrangement to meet someone at a particular time and place, especially secretly: **[+with]** *a midnight rendezvous with her lover* **2** a place where people arrange to meet: *a popular London rendezvous* —**rendezvous** *v* [I]

rendition /ren'dɪʃən/ *n* [C] someone's performance of a play, piece of music etc

renegade /'renəgeɪd/ *n* [C] *formal* someone who joins the opposing side in a war, argument etc: *a political renegade*

renege /rɪ'niːg, rɪ'neɪg $ rɪ'nɪg, rɪ'niːg/ *v* [I] *formal* to not do something that you promised to do: *He reneged on that promise.*

renew /rɪ'njuː $ rɪ'nuː/ *v* [T] **1** to arrange for an agreement or official document such as a licence to continue: *You can renew your library books on the Internet.* **2** to begin to do something again: *The search will be renewed in the morning.* **3** to replace something that is old or broken —**renewal** *n* [C,U]

renewable /rɪ'njuːəbəl $ rɪ'nuː-/ *adj* **1** renewable energy can be replaced as quickly as it is used **2** a renewable contract or official document can be continued after the date on which it ends: *My visa is renewable every six months.*

renewed /rɪ'njuːd $ -'nuːd/ *adj* starting again with greater energy or strength: *renewed efforts to tackle poverty*

renounce /rɪ'naʊns/ *v* [T] **1** to say publicly that you no longer believe in or support an idea: *They must renounce violence if the talks are to continue.* **2** to say publicly that you no longer have a right to something

renovate /ˈrenəveɪt/ v [T] to repair an old building or furniture so that it is in good condition again **THESAURUS** REPAIR —**renovation** /ˌrenəˈveɪʃən/ n [C,U]

renown /rɪˈnaʊn/ n [U] formal fame and respect that you get for something you have done

renowned /rɪˈnaʊnd/ adj famous and admired: **[+for]** an island renowned for its beauty **THESAURUS** FAMOUS

rent¹ /rent/ v
1 [I,T] if you rent a house, flat etc, you pay money regularly to the owner so that you can live there: **rent sth from sb** I rented a room from friends while I looked for work. | a rented apartment
2 [T] to pay money for the use of something for a short time **SYN hire** BrE: Will you rent a car while you're in Spain?
3 (also **rent out**) [T] to let someone live in a place that you own in return for money **SYN let** BrE: **rent sth (out) to sb** They've rented out their house to tourists this summer. —**rented** adj [only before noun]: rented accommodation —**renter** n [C] AmE

rent² n [C,U] money that you pay for the use of a house, room, car etc that belongs to someone else: How much do you pay in rent? | **for rent** (=available to rent) houses for rent

---

COLLOCATIONS

adjectives

a high/low rent Rents in the city centre are very high.
an affordable rent (=that people can easily pay) There is a need for more homes at affordable rents.
the annual/monthly/weekly rent The monthly rent is £550.

verbs

to pay the rent We can't afford to pay the rent.
to charge rent How much rent does he charge on the flat?
to increase/raise the rent (also **to put up the rent** BrE) The landlord has increased the rent again.
to fall behind with the rent (=to fail to pay your rent on time) You could lose your home if you fall behind with the rent.

---

rental /ˈrentl/ n **1** [C,U] money that you pay to use a car, television etc for a period of time: Ski rental is $14. **2** [C] AmE something that you rent, such as a house or car

renunciation /rɪˌnʌnsiˈeɪʃən/ n [U] formal when someone makes a decision to stop doing something, stop believing in something etc

reopen /riːˈəʊpən $ -ˈoʊ-/ v [I,T] if a place reopens, it opens again after a period when it was closed

reorganize (also **-ise** BrE) /riːˈɔːɡənaɪz $ -ˈɔːr-/ v [I,T] to organize something in a new and better way: The office needs reorganizing. —**reorganization** /riːˌɔːɡənaɪˈzeɪʃən $ -ˌɔːrɡənə-/ n [U]

rep /rep/ n [C] informal someone who sells things for a company

repaid /rɪˈpeɪd/ v the past tense and past participle of REPAY

---

repair¹ /rɪˈpeə $ -ˈper/ v [T]
1 to make something that is broken or damaged satisfactory again: How much will it cost to repair the car? | Your shoes **need repairing**. | I must **get** the roof **repaired** (=arrange for someone to fix it).
2 to do something to remove the harm that you have done: The government was left trying to **repair the damage**.

THESAURUS

repair to make something that is broken or damaged satisfactory again: They've repaired the fence. | He's good at repairing motorbikes.
fix to repair something, especially a piece of equipment. **Fix** is very common in everyday English: We'll have to get the car fixed on Monday.
mend especially BrE to repair something – often something that has a hole in it: Don't throw that shirt away – I'll mend it.
restore to repair something old and valuable, especially a building, piece of furniture, or painting, so that it looks like it did originally: The hotel was built in 1850 and has recently been restored. | She got a job restoring paintings.
renovate to repair an old building or furniture so that it is in good condition again: The house needed renovating when we bought it.

---

repair² n [C,U] something you do to fix something that is broken or damaged: **make/do repairs** They're doing repairs on the bridge. | **[+to]** repairs to the road | The roof is badly **in need of repair**. | **be under repair** (=being repaired)
PHRASES
in good/bad repair formal in good or bad condition: The power station was in poor repair.

reparation /ˌrepəˈreɪʃən/ n **1** **reparations** [plural] money paid by a country that loses in a war for the deaths, damage etc it has caused **2** [U] formal when you do something good for someone because you have done something bad to them in the past: Offenders must **make reparation for** their crimes.

repatriate /riːˈpætrieɪt $ riːˈpeɪ-/ v [T] to send someone back to the country that they came from —**repatriation** /riːˌpætriˈeɪʃən $ riːˌpeɪ-/ n [U]

repay /rɪˈpeɪ/ v [T] (past tense and past participle **repaid** /-ˈpeɪd/) **1** to pay back money that you have borrowed: How long will it take to repay the loan? **2** to reward someone for helping you: How can I ever repay you? —**repayment** n [C,U] —**repayable** adj

repeal /rɪˈpiːl/ v [T] to officially end a law: plans to repeal anti-immigration laws —**repeal** n [U]

repeat¹ /rɪˈpiːt/ v [T]
1 to say or do something again: Sally kept repeating, 'It wasn't me, it wasn't me.' | You'll have to repeat the course. | **repeat yourself** (=say something that you have said before, usually by mistake) Elderly people tend to repeat themselves.
2 to say something that you have heard someone else say: **repeat sth to sb** Please don't repeat this to anyone.

repeat² n **1** [singular] a situation or event that has happened before → **repetition**: **[+of]** Are you

R

expecting a repeat of last year's trouble? | It was a terrible journey – I hope we don't have a **repeat performance** *(=have the same thing happen again) on the way home.* **2** [C] *especially BrE* a television or radio programme that has been broadcast before SYN **rerun** *AmE*

repeated /rɪ'piːtɪd/ *adj* [only before noun] done or happening several times: *repeated attempts to kill him* —**repeatedly** *adv: Graham was repeatedly warned not to work so hard.*

repel /rɪ'pel/ *v* [T] (**repelled, repelling**) **1** to force someone to go away or to stop attacking you: *Tear gas was used to repel the rioters.* **2** if something repels you, you dislike it very much

repellent[1] /rɪ'pelənt/ *n* [C,U] a substance that keeps something, especially insects, away: *mosquito repellent*

repellent[2] *adj* extremely unpleasant: *The sight of blood is repellent to some people.*

repent /rɪ'pent/ *v* [I,T] *formal* to be sorry for something bad that you have done —**repentance** *n* [U] —**repentant** *adj*

repercussions /ˌriːpə'kʌʃənz $ -pər-/ *n* [plural] unpleasant effects or results of something that you do: *The collapse of the company will* **have repercussions** *for the whole industry.*

repertoire /'repətwɑː $ -pərtwɑːr/ *n* [C] the plays, songs, jokes etc that a performer knows and can perform: **[+of]** *a* **wide repertoire** *of songs*

repetition /ˌrepə'tɪʃən/ *n* [C,U] when something happens again or is done many times: **[+of]** *We don't want a repetition of this disaster.*

repetitive /rɪ'petətɪv/ (*also* **repetitious** /ˌrepə'tɪʃəs◄/) *adj* done many times in the same way and boring: *repetitive exercises*

rephrase /ˌriːˈfreɪz/ *v* [T] to say or write something in different words so that its meaning is clearer: *OK, let me* **rephrase** *the* **question**.

replace /rɪˈpleɪs/ *v* [T]
1 to start doing something instead of another person, or start being used instead of another thing: *I'm replacing Sue on the team.*
2 to remove someone from their job or something from its place, and put a new person or thing there: *Two of the tyres had to be replaced.* | **replace sb/sth with sb/sth** *They replaced thousands of permanent staff with part-timers.*
3 to put something back where it was before: *Please replace the books when you are finished.*
4 if you replace something that has been broken, stolen etc, you get a new one

replacement /rɪˈpleɪsmənt/ *n* **1** [C] someone or something that replaces another person or thing: *We're waiting for Mr Dunley's replacement.* **2** [U] when something is replaced: *the replacement of worn-out equipment*

replay[1] /ˈriːpleɪ/ *n* [C] **1** *BrE* a sports game that is played again because neither team won the first time: *The replay will be on Thursday.* **2** something that happens in a sports game on television that is immediately shown again → **action replay** —**replay** /ˌriːˈpleɪ/ *v* [T]

replenish /rɪˈplenɪʃ/ *v* [T] *formal* to make something full or complete again —**replenishment** *n* [U]

replica /ˈreplɪkə/ *n* [C] an exact copy of something: *replica guns*

replicate /ˈreplɪkeɪt/ *v* [T] *formal* if you replicate someone's work, a scientific study etc, you do it again, or try to get the same result again

reply[1] /rɪˈplaɪ/ *v* [I,T] (**replied, replying, replies**) to answer: *'Of course,' she replied.* | **[+to]** *I haven't replied to his letter yet.* | **[+that]** *When asked, he replied that he hadn't seen her.* THESAURUS ANSWER

reply[2] *n* [C,U] (*plural* **replies**) something that is said, written, or done as a way of answering SYN **answer**: *Stephen* **made no reply**. | **[+to]** *There have been no replies to our ad.* | **in reply (to sth)** *Marcy said nothing in reply.*

report[1] /rɪˈpɔːt $ -ɔːrt/ *n* [C]
1 a written or spoken description of a situation or event: **[+on/of/about]** *Martens gave a report on his sales trip to Korea.*
2 *BrE* a written statement by teachers about a child's progress at school SYN **report card** *AmE*

COLLOCATIONS

verbs

to write a report *He had written a report on the hurricane.*

to make a report *Teachers make regular reports to parents.*

to give a report (=to make a report, usually a spoken one) *I had to give a report to the board of directors.*

to publish a report *The committee will publish its report shortly.*

adjectives

a full/detailed report *I want a full report on how the accident happened.*

an official report *According to an official report, climate change is getting worse.*

a written report *The police officer had to make a written report.*

noun + report

a news report *I read all the news reports about the election.*

a progress report *My boss likes to have regular progress reports.*

report[2] *v*
1 [I,T] to tell people about an event or situation, especially in newspapers, on television, or on the radio → **reporter**: *We aim to report the news as fairly as possible.* | **[+on]** *She was sent to report on the floods in Bangladesh.* | **[+that]** *The newspaper wrongly reported that he had died.*
2 [T] **a)** to tell someone in authority that a crime or accident has happened: *Who reported the fire?* **b)** to officially complain about someone: *Somebody reported Kyle for smoking in school.*
3 **be reported to be/do sth** used to say that a statement has been made about someone or something, but you do not know if it is true: *The stolen necklace is reported to be worth $57,000.*
4 [I] to go somewhere and officially state that you

have arrived: **[+to]** *Visitors must report to the main reception desk.*

reportedly /rɪˈpɔːtɪdli $ -ɔːr-/ *adv* according to what people say: *She's reportedly one of the richest women in Europe.*

re,ported 'speech *n* [U] the style of speech or writing that is used for reporting what someone says, without repeating the actual words

reporter /rɪˈpɔːtə $ -ˈpɔːrtər/ *n* [C] someone whose job is to write about news events for a newspaper, or to tell people about them on television or on the radio → **journalist**

reporting /rɪˈpɔːtɪŋ $ -ɔːr-/ *n* [U] the activity of telling people about events in newspapers, on television, or on the radio: *news reporting*

repose /rɪˈpəʊz $ -ˈpoʊz/ *v* [I + adv/prep] *literary* to have been put somewhere, or to lie or rest somewhere —**repose** *n* [U]

repossess /ˌriːpəˈzes/ *v* [T] to take back something that someone has partly paid for, because they cannot pay the rest of the money they owe —**repossession** /-ˈzeʃən/ *n* [C,U]

reprehensible /ˌreprɪˈhensəbəl/ *adj formal* reprehensible behaviour is very bad

represent /ˌreprɪˈzent/ *v* [T]
1 to speak and do things for someone else because they have asked you to: *Craig hired a lawyer to represent him.*
2 if you represent a country, school etc in a competition, you compete in it for the country, school etc
3 to be a sign or mark that means something: *The green triangles on the map represent campgrounds.*
4 to form or be something: *This figure represents a 25% increase in wages.*
5 to describe someone or something in a particular way **SYN** **portray**: *The article represents the millionaire as a simple family man.*

representation /ˌreprɪzenˈteɪʃən/ *n* **1** [U] when you have someone to speak, vote, or make decisions for you: *Minority groups need more effective parliamentary representation.* **2** [C,U] the way that something is described or shown: **[+of]** *the representation of women in literature*

representative¹ /ˌreprɪˈzentətɪv◂/ *n* [C] someone who has been chosen to speak, vote, or make decisions for someone else

representative² *adj* typical of the people or things in a particular group: *a **representative sample** of New York residents* | **[+of]** *I don't claim to be representative of the majority of young people.*

repress /rɪˈpres/ *v* [T] **1** to stop yourself from expressing what you really feel: *It's not healthy to repress your emotions.* | *I repressed a smile.* **2** to control people by force —**repression** /-ˈpreʃən/ *n* [U]

repressed /rɪˈprest/ *adj* having feelings or needs that you do not express

repressive /rɪˈpresɪv/ *adj* cruel and very strict: *a repressive political system*

reprieve /rɪˈpriːv/ *n* [C] **1** an official order stopping a prisoner from being killed as a punishment **2** a delay before something bad happens or continues

to happen: *a temporary reprieve* —**reprieve** *v* [T]

reprimand /ˈreprəmɑːnd $ -mænd/ *v* [T] to tell someone officially that they have done something wrong —**reprimand** *n* [C]

reprint /ˈriːprɪnt/ *n* [C] **1** a book that has been printed again **2** an occasion when more copies of a book are printed because all the other copies have been sold —**reprint** /ˌriːˈprɪnt/ *v* [T]

reprisal /rɪˈpraɪzəl/ *n* [C,U] something that is done unofficially to punish someone: *They didn't tell the police **for fear of reprisal**.*

reproach¹ /rɪˈprəʊtʃ $ -ˈproʊtʃ/ *n* [C,U] blame or criticism: *His mother gave him a look of reproach.* —**reproachful** *adj* —**reproachfully** *adv*
PHRASES
| **above/beyond reproach** impossible to criticize: *The police should be above reproach.*

reproach² *v* [T] to blame someone and try to make them sorry for something they have done: **reproach sb for/with sth** *She reproached her son for his bad behaviour.*

reproduce /ˌriːprəˈdjuːs $ -ˈduːs/ *v* **1** [T] to make a copy of something or do it again in the same way: *an attempt by scientists to reproduce conditions on Mars* **2** [I] to produce babies, eggs etc: *Most birds and fish reproduce by laying eggs.*

reproduction /ˌriːprəˈdʌkʃən◂/ *n* **1** [U] the process of producing babies, eggs etc: *human reproduction* **2** [C] a copy of something, especially a work of art or piece of expensive furniture

reproductive /ˌriːprəˈdʌktɪv◂/ *adj* relating to reproduction: *the reproductive organs*

reprove /rɪˈpruːv/ *v* [T] *formal* to angrily criticize someone for doing something bad —**reproof** /rɪˈpruːf/ *n* [C,U]

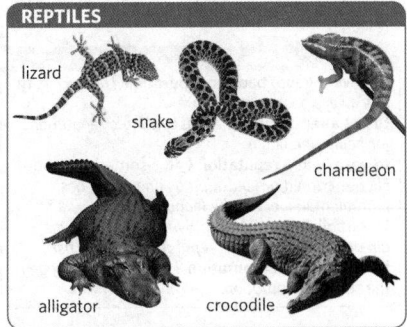

REPTILES

lizard

snake

chameleon

alligator   crocodile

reptile /ˈreptaɪl $ ˈreptl/ *n* [C] an animal such as a snake or LIZARD that lays eggs, and whose blood changes temperature with the temperature around it —**reptilian** /repˈtɪliən/ *adj*

republic /rɪˈpʌblɪk/ *n* [C] a country that has an elected government, and does not have a king or queen → **monarchy**

republican /rɪˈpʌblɪkən/ *n* [C] someone who believes in government by elected representatives only, with no king or queen —**republican** *adj*: *the spread of republican ideas*

Republican *n* [C] a member or supporter of the Republican Party in the US → **Democrat** —**Republican** *adj* [only before noun]: *a Republican candidate for the Senate*

Re'publican ,Party *n* **the Republican Party** one of the two main political parties of the US → **the Democratic Party**

repudiate /rɪˈpjuːdieɪt/ *v* [T] *formal* to refuse to accept something: *He repudiated all offers of friendship.*

repugnance /rɪˈpʌgnəns/ *n* [U] *formal* a strong feeling of dislike for something → **disgust**

repugnant /rɪˈpʌgnənt/ *adj formal* very unpleasant and offensive: *morally repugnant behaviour*

repulse /rɪˈpʌls/ *v* [T] **1** if something or someone repulses you, you think that they are extremely unpleasant **2** to defeat a military attack: *Enemy forces were repulsed with the help of French troops.* —**repulsion** /-ˈpʌlʃən/ *n* [singular, U]

repulsive /rɪˈpʌlsɪv/ *adj* extremely unpleasant: *What a repulsive man!* **THESAURUS** UGLY

reputable /ˈrepjətəbəl/ *adj* respected for being honest or for doing good work **OPP** disreputable: *a reputable company*

reputation /ˌrepjəˈteɪʃən/ *n* [C] the opinion that people have of a person, product, company etc: **[+for]** *a man with a reputation for honesty*

COLLOCATIONS

adjectives

a good/excellent reputation *The restaurant has an excellent reputation.*

a bad/poor reputation *He doesn't deserve his bad reputation.*

an international/a worldwide reputation *The department has a worldwide reputation for its research.*

verbs

to have a good/bad etc reputation *The university has a very good reputation.*

to get a reputation *She was getting a reputation for being unreliable.*

to earn/win a reputation (=for something good) *He has earned a reputation as one of the best football managers in the league.*

to establish a reputation *By then, Picasso was already establishing his reputation as an artist.*

to damage sb's reputation *The incident damaged the school's reputation.*

---

repute /rɪˈpjuːt/ *n* **of good/bad etc repute** *formal* having a good, bad etc reputation

reputed /rɪˈpjuːtɪd/ *adj* used to talk about a fact that most people think is true, although it is not definitely true: **be reputed to be/do sth** *He's reputed to be one of the wealthiest men in the world.* —**reputedly** *adv*

request¹ /rɪˈkwest/ *n* **1** [C,U] when someone politely or formally asks for something: **[+for]** *We've **made** a **request** for new equipment.* | **on**

request (=if you ask) *Drinks are available on request.* | **at sb's request** (=because someone asked for it to be done) *The study was done at the request of the Chairman.* **THESAURUS** QUESTION **2** [C] a piece of music that someone asks to be played

request² *v* [T] to ask for something officially or formally: *The pilot requested permission to land.* | **[+that]** *We request that everyone remain quiet.* | **request sb to do sth** *All club members are requested to attend the annual meeting.* **THESAURUS** ASK

requiem /ˈrekwiəm, -em/ *n* [C,U] a Christian ceremony of prayers for someone who has died, or music written for this ceremony

require Ac /rɪˈkwaɪə $ -ˈkwaɪr/ *v* [T]
1 to need something: *Pets require a lot of care.*
2 *formal* to officially demand that someone does something: **be required to do sth** *All passengers are required to show their tickets.*

requirement Ac /rɪˈkwaɪəmənt $ -ˈkwaɪr-/ *n* [C] something that is needed or asked for: *The refugees' main requirements are food and water.*

requisite /ˈrekwəzət/ *adj* [only before noun] *formal* needed for a particular purpose: *He lacks the requisite qualifications.*

requisition /ˌrekwəˈzɪʃən/ *v* [T] *formal* if someone in authority, especially a soldier, requisitions something owned by someone else, they demand to use it

re-release /ˌriːrɪˈliːs/ *v* [T] to produce a CD, record, or film for a second time and to sell or show it again —**re-release** /ˈriːrɪliːs/ *n* [C]

rerun /ˈriːrʌn/ *n* [C] *especially AmE* a television programme that is shown again **SYN** repeat *BrE*

resat /riːˈsæt/ *v* the past tense and past participle of RESIT

reschedule Ac /ˌriːˈʃedjuːl $ -ˈskedʒʊl, -dʒəl/ *v* [T] to arrange for something to happen at a different time from the one that was planned: **reschedule sth for sth** *The conference had to be rescheduled for March 19.*

RESCUE

---

rescue¹ /ˈreskjuː/ *v* [T] to save someone from harm or danger: **rescue sb from sth** *He rescued two people from the fire.* | *Survivors of the crash were rescued by helicopter.* —**rescuer** *n* [C]

rescue² *n* [C,U] when someone is saved from harm or danger: *his attempted rescue of a drowning* man | *A lifeboat* **came to** *our* **rescue** (=rescued us). | **rescue team/workers/boat etc**

research¹ Ac /rɪˈsɜːtʃ, ˈriːsɜːtʃ $ -ɜːr-/ n [U] serious and detailed study of a subject in order to find out new information: **[+on/into]** *scientific research into heart disease* **THESAURUS** STUDY → **MARKET RESEARCH**

COLLOCATIONS

verbs

to do/carry out research *He is doing research for a book on the Middle Ages.* ⚠ Do not say 'make research'. Say **do research** or **carry out research**.

adjectives

scientific/medical/historical research *Our conclusions are based on scientific research.*
basic research *Do some basic research before buying a new computer.*

research + noun

research findings (=what is discovered by a piece of research) *She presented her research findings at the conference.*
a research project/programme *The experiment was part of a research project into social attitudes.*

---

research² Ac /rɪˈsɜːtʃ $ -ɜːr-/ v [I,T] to study a subject in detail so that you can discover new facts about it: *Conner spent eight years researching the history of the group.* | *His book has been very well researched.* —**researcher** n [C]

resemblance /rɪˈzembləns/ n [C,U] a similarity between two people or things: **[+between]** *There's a slight resemblance between Mike and his cousin.*

resemble /rɪˈzembəl/ v [T] to be similar to someone or something: *She resembles her mother in many ways.*

resent /rɪˈzent/ v [T] to feel angry and upset about a situation or action: *I've always resented my father for leaving the family.* | **resent doing sth** *I resent having to work such long hours.* —**resentful** adj: *a resentful look* —**resentfully** adv —**resentment** n [U]: *a feeling of resentment*

reservation /ˌrezəˈveɪʃən $ -zər-/ n **1** [C] an arrangement you make so that a place in a hotel, on a plane etc is kept for you to use: *Have you* **made reservations** *at the restaurant yet?* **2** [C,U] a feeling of doubt because you do not completely agree with a plan, idea etc: *I still* **have reservations** *about promoting her.*

reserve¹ /rɪˈzɜːv $ -ɜːrv/ v [T]
1 to arrange for a place in a hotel, on a plane etc to be kept for you to use **SYN** **book**: *Do you have to reserve tickets in advance?* | *I'd like to reserve a table for two.*
2 to keep something separate so that it can be used for a particular purpose: **reserve sth for sb/sth** *a parking space reserved for the disabled*

reserve² n **1** [C usually plural] a supply of something that is kept to be used at a time when it is needed: *Water reserves are dangerously low.* **2** [U] when someone does not show or talk about their thoughts and feelings: *She found it difficult to overcome her* **natural reserve**. **3** [C] an area of land where wild animals, plants etc are protected: *a nature reserve* **4** [C] an extra player who plays in a team if one of the other players is injured or ill → **substitute**

PHRASES

in reserve ready to be used if needed: *We always* **keep** *some money* **in reserve**, *just in case.*

reserved /rɪˈzɜːvd $ -ɜːr-/ adj unwilling to show or talk about your thoughts and feelings

reservoir /ˈrezəvwɑː $ -ərvwɑːr, -vɔːr/ n [C] **1** an artificial lake where water is stored before it is supplied to people's houses **THESAURUS** LAKE **2 reservoir of sth** a supply of something that can be used if it is needed: *Students provide a reservoir of cheap labour.*

reset /ˌriːˈset/ v [T] (*past tense and past participle* **reset**, *present participle* **resetting**) to press the switches on a clock or other machine, so that it will work at a different time or in a different way, or so that it is ready to be used again: *I've reset the alarm for 7 o'clock.*

reshuffle /riːˈʃʌfəl, ˈriːʃʌfəl/ n [C] especially BrE when the jobs of people who work in an organization are changed around, especially in a government: *a Cabinet reshuffle*

reside Ac /rɪˈzaɪd/ v [I + adv/prep] formal to live or be somewhere

residence Ac /ˈrezɪdəns/ n formal **1** [C] a house, apartment etc where someone lives: *a private residence* **2** [U] when someone lives in a particular place: *He left home and* **took up residence** *in London.* | **in residence** *The emperor was in residence at his summer palace.*

residency /ˈrezɪdənsi/ n [U] **1** legal permission to live in a country for a certain period of time **2** formal when someone lives or works in a particular place

resident Ac /ˈrezɪdənt/ n [C] **1** someone who lives in a house, apartment, area etc: *a park for local residents* **2** AmE a doctor working at a hospital where they are being trained —**resident** adj

residential Ac /ˌrezɪˈdenʃəl◂/ adj a residential area consists of houses, not offices or factories

residual /rɪˈzɪdjuəl/ adj [only before noun] formal remaining after a process, event etc has finished: *the residual effects of exposure to radiation*

residue /ˈrezɪdjuː $ -duː/ n [C] a substance that remains after something else has disappeared or been removed: *an oily residue*

resign /rɪˈzaɪn/ v [I,T] to officially tell your employer that you are going to leave your job: **[+from]** *Burton resigned from the company yesterday.* | **[+as]** *He resigned as chairman in October.* **THESAURUS** LEAVE

PHRASES

resign yourself to (doing) sth to accept a situation that you do not like but cannot change: *I've resigned myself to living in the city for a while.*

resignation /ˌrezɪɡˈneɪʃən/ n **1** [C,U] when someone officially tells their employer that they are going to leave their job: *I'm planning to* **hand in** *my*

R

resignation. 2 [U] when you accept a situation that you cannot change although you do not like it

resigned /rɪˈzaɪnd/ adj willing to accept a situation you do not like —**resignedly** /rɪˈzaɪnɪdli/ adv

resilient /rɪˈzɪliənt/ adj **1** strong enough to get better quickly after problems, illness, damage etc: *Small babies can be remarkably resilient.* **2** a resilient substance will not break or get damaged easily —**resilience** n [U]

resin /ˈrezɪn/ n **1** [U] a thick sticky liquid produced by some trees **2** [C,U] a type of plastic

resist /rɪˈzɪst/ v [I,T] **1** to try to prevent yourself from doing something that you should not do, even though you want to: **cannot resist (doing) sth** *I just can't resist chocolate.* **2** to oppose or fight against someone or something: *British troops could not resist the attack any longer.* | *Residents were ordered to leave the area, but they resisted.*

resistance /rɪˈzɪstəns/ n [U] **1** when people oppose or fight against someone or something: **[+to]** *There is strong public resistance to the new taxes.* | *The rebels* **put up** fierce **resistance** *against the army.* **2** the natural ability of a person, animal, or plant to stop diseases or difficult conditions from harming them: **[+to]** *resistance to disease*

resistant /rɪˈzɪstənt/ adj **1** not easily harmed or damaged by something: *a water-resistant watch* **2** unwilling to accept new ideas or changes: **[+to]** *people who are resistant to change*

resit /ˌriːˈsɪt/ v [T] (*past tense and past participle* **resat** /-ˈsæt/, *present participle* **resitting**) *especially BrE* to take an examination again —**resit** /ˈriːsɪt/ n [C]

resolute /ˈrezəluːt/ adj formal determined not to change what you are doing because you are sure that you are right: *resolute leadership* —**resolutely** adv

resolution Ac /ˌrezəˈluːʃən/ n **1** [C] an official decision by a group or organization, especially after a vote: *a United Nations resolution* **2** [singular, U] a solution to a difficult situation: *a peaceful resolution to the crisis* **3** [C] a promise that you make to yourself to do something: *I made a New Year's resolution to stop smoking.* **4** [U] formal determination

resolve¹ Ac /rɪˈzɒlv $ rɪˈzɑːlv, rɪˈzɔːlv/ v **1** [T] to find a way of dealing with a problem or of ending a disagreement: *efforts to resolve the conflict in the Middle East* **2** [I,T] formal to make a definite decision to do something: **resolve to do sth** *He resolved to leave the country as soon as possible.*

resolve² Ac n [U] formal determination

resonant /ˈrezənənt/ adj having a loud pleasant strong sound: *a resonant voice* —**resonance** n [U]

resonate /ˈrezəneɪt/ v [I] to make a loud strong sound

resort¹ /rɪˈzɔːt $ -ɔːrt/ n [C] a place where a lot of people go for a holiday: *a beach resort*
PHRASES
| **as a last resort** if everything else fails: *I could borrow the money off my parents, but only as a last resort.*

resort² v
PHRASAL VERBS
resort to sth to do something that you do not want to do, in order to try to achieve something: *They may have to resort to court action.*

resound /rɪˈzaʊnd/ v [I] to make a loud sound, or be full of a loud sound: *His voice resounded throughout the house.*

resounding /rɪˈzaʊndɪŋ/ adj **1 a resounding success/victory/defeat etc** a great success, victory etc: *It was a resounding victory for the home team.* **2** very loud: *a resounding crash*

resource Ac /rɪˈzɔːs, -ˈsɔːs $ ˈriːsɔːrs/ n [C usually plural] something that a country, organization, person etc has that they can use: *South Africa's vast* **natural resources**

resourceful Ac /rɪˈzɔːsfəl, -ˈsɔːs- $ -ɔːr-/ adj good at finding ways to deal with problems effectively —**resourcefulness** n [U]

respect¹ /rɪˈspekt/ n [U]
1 when you admire someone, especially for their personal qualities → **admiration**: **[+for]** *I have great respect for her as a writer.*
2 when you treat someone in a polite way, especially because they are older or more important than you OPP **disrespect**: **[+for]** *He ought to show more respect for authority* (=for his parents, teachers, managers etc).
3 when you show by your behaviour that you think something is important: *countries where there is no respect for basic human rights*
PHRASES
| **in one respect/in many respects etc** used to say that something is true in one way, in many ways etc: *In some respects, José is right.*
| **pay your (last) respects** to go to someone's funeral: *We were there to pay our last respects to Uncle Frank.*
| **pay your respects** formal to visit someone: *I'd better pay my respects to Colonel Stewart while I'm here.*
| **with (all due) respect** spoken formal used before you say something to disagree with someone: *With all due respect, that's not the point.*
| **with respect to sth** (*also* **in respect of sth**) formal concerning a particular thing SYN **regarding**: *With respect to your question about jobs, all our positions are filled.*

respect² v [T]
1 to admire someone, especially for their personal qualities: *The students like and respect him.*
2 if you respect someone's wishes, rights, customs etc, you are careful not to do anything that they do not want, or that they think is wrong: *I would like you to respect my privacy.* | *the need to respect human rights*
3 if you respect the law or the rules, you obey them

respectable /rɪˈspektəbəl/ adj **1** someone who is respectable behaves in a way that is socially acceptable: *a respectable middle-aged lady* | *Try and make yourself look respectable.* **2** good or satisfactory: *We made quite a respectable profit.* —**respectability** /rɪˌspektəˈbɪləti/ n [U]

R

respected /rɪ'spektɪd/ adj admired by many people because of things you have achieved: *a **highly respected** journalist*

respectful /rɪ'spektfəl/ adj showing respect for someone or something OPP **disrespectful**: *The interviewer was very respectful.* —**respectfully** adv

respective /rɪ'spektɪv/ adj [only before noun] used to talk about things that belong to each of the people or things you have mentioned: *They all went back to their respective homes.*

respectively /rɪ'spektɪvli/ adv in the same order as the things you have just mentioned: *They've got two children, Sam and Ben, who are eight and ten respectively.*

respiration /ˌrespə'reɪʃən/ n [U] technical the process of breathing → ARTIFICIAL RESPIRATION

respirator /'respəreɪtə $ -ər/ n [C] a piece of equipment that helps you to breathe, for example if you are very ill or in a place where there is smoke or gas

respiratory /rɪ'spɪrətəri, 'respəreɪtəri, rɪ'spaɪərə- $ 'respərətɔːri, rɪ'spaɪrə-/ adj technical relating to breathing: *a respiratory illness*

respite /'respɪt, -paɪt $ -pɪt/ n [singular, U] a short period of time when something unpleasant stops happening: **[+from]** *The weekend away gave me a **brief respite** from the pressures of work.*

resplendent /rɪ'splendənt/ adj formal looking very attractive and impressive: **[+in]** *The guards looked resplendent in their uniforms.*

respond Ac /rɪ'spɒnd $ rɪ'spaːnd/ v [I] **1** to do something because of something that has happened: **[+to]** *How will the government respond to this latest development?* | **respond by doing sth** *The United Nations responded by sending troops to the area.* **2** to answer: *I called her name, but she didn't respond.* | **[+to]** *He didn't respond to my email.* THESAURUS ANSWER **3** to improve as a result of a medical treatment: **[+to]** *She is responding well to the drugs.*

respondent Ac /rɪ'spɒndənt $ rɪ'spaːn-/ n [C] formal someone who answers questions in a SURVEY

response Ac /rɪ'spɒns $ rɪ'spaːns/ n [C,U] a reply or reaction to something: *I knocked on the door but there was no response.* | **[+to]** *the government's response to the economic crisis* | **in response to sth** *I am writing in response to your advertisement.*

responsibility /rɪˌspɒnsə'bɪləti $ rɪˌspaːn-/ n (plural **responsibilities**)
1 [C,U] if something is your responsibility, it is your job or duty to do it: *It's your responsibility to pay the bills on time.* | *a job with a lot of responsibility* | **[+for]** *The committee will have responsibility for the budget.*
2 [U] the fact that you were the person who made something bad happen: **[+for]** *No one is willing to **accept responsibility** for the accident.* | *A terrorist group has **claimed responsibility** for the bombing.*

COLLOCATIONS
verbs
to have a responsibility *He already has a lot of responsibilities.*
to give sb responsibility *The students should be given more responsibility.*
to take responsibility for sth *Who is going to take responsibility for the project?*
to carry out your responsibilities (=do the things that it is your job to do) *They failed to carry out their responsibilities.*

adjectives
a big/great responsibility *The farm is a big responsibility.*
sb's main responsibility *One of his main responsibilities was organizing training.*
overall responsibility *The Department of Education has overall responsibility for schools and universities.*

noun + responsibility
a position of responsibility (=a job or role where you are responsible for something) *I can't imagine her coping with a position of responsibility.*
family responsibilities *Most women have jobs as well as family responsibilities.*

responsible /rɪ'spɒnsəbəl $ rɪ'spaːn-/ adj
1 [not before noun] if you are responsible for something bad that has happened, you caused it and you are the person who should be blamed: **[+for]** *a man who is responsible for the deaths of fifteen people* | *If anything goes wrong, I will **hold** you **responsible** (=blame you).* THESAURUS CAUSE
2 [not before noun] if you are responsible for something, you are in charge of it or it is your job to do it: **[+for]** *Local authorities are responsible for the schools in their area.* | *You will be responsible for training new staff.*
3 someone who is responsible is sensible and can be trusted OPP **irresponsible** → **reliable**: *a responsible young man*
4 **responsible job/position** a job in which you have to make important decisions: *He held a very responsible job.*
PHRASES
be responsible to sb if you are responsible to someone in your job, they tell you what to do and check your work: *Cabinet members are directly responsible to the Prime Minister.*

responsibly /rɪ'spɒnsəbli $ rɪ'spaːn-/ adv in a sensible way: *Can I trust you to **behave responsibly** while I'm away?*

responsive Ac /rɪ'spɒnsɪv $ rɪ'spaːn-/ adj someone who is responsive does what people want or need, or replies to them: **[+to]** *We must be responsive to the needs of our customers.* | *I tried talking to him, but he wasn't very responsive.*

rest¹ /rest/ n
1 the rest the part of something that still remains, or the people or things that still remain: **[+of]** *What shall I do with the rest of the pizza?* | *We spent the rest*

of the day at home. | There were a few people in the kitchen and the rest were in the garden.
2 [C,U] a period of time when you relax or sleep: *You can have a rest later.*

PHRASES

at rest *formal* resting or not moving: *Do you experience pain when the limb is at rest?*

come to rest to stop moving: *The truck came to rest at the bottom of the hill.*

put/set sb's mind at rest to stop someone from feeling worried: *She tried to put Alan's mind at rest about the money.*

COLLOCATIONS – sense 2

verbs

to have/take a rest *I'm going upstairs to have a rest.*

to get some rest *You'd better get some rest – you have a big day tomorrow.*

to need a rest *Just tell me if you need a rest.*

adjectives

a little/short rest *You'll feel better after a little rest.*

a good rest (=a complete rest that relaxes you) *What you need is a good rest.*

a well-earned rest (=a rest after working hard) *We sat down for a cup of tea and a well-earned rest.*

rest² *v*

1 [I,T] to stop working or moving and relax for a period of time: *We can stop for a minute if you need to rest.* | **rest your legs/feet/eyes** *I sat down to rest my feet.*

2 [I,T] to put something in a position where it is supported by something else, or to be in this position → **lean**: **rest (sth) on/against sth** *I rested my head on his shoulder.* | *Her head was resting against his chest.* | *She rested her bike against the wall.*

PHRASES

let sth rest to stop talking about something: *He wouldn't let the matter rest.*

rest assured (that) *formal* used to tell someone not to worry: *Rest assured that everything will be ready on time.*

rest on your laurels to be satisfied with your achievements and not try hard to succeed any more: *You can't rest on your laurels.*

PHRASAL VERBS

rest on/upon sth *formal* to depend on something or be based on something: *The whole case rests on his evidence.*

rest with sb *formal* if a decision rests with someone, they must make it: *The final decision rests with the chairman.*

restart /,ri:'stɑːt $ -'stɑːrt/ *v* [I,T] if something restarts, or if you restart it, it starts again: *new efforts to restart the peace process*

restate /,ri:'steɪt/ *v* [T] to say something again: *He restated his support for military action.*

restaurant /'restərɒnt $ -rənt, -rɑːnt/ *n* [C] a place where you can buy and eat a meal: **French/Italian/Indian etc restaurant** *a very good Chinese restaurant* |

in/at a restaurant *We had dinner in an Italian restaurant.*

THESAURUS

restaurant a place where you buy and eat a meal that is usually brought to your table, especially one that you go to as a social event: *Shall I book a table at the restaurant?*

cafe/coffee shop a place where you drink coffee, tea etc, and can also have cakes or small meals: *I'll meet you in the cafe at the station.* | *There's a great little coffee shop near here.*

cafeteria (also **canteen** *BrE*) a place at work or school where you can collect and eat meals: *The company has a staff cafeteria.* | *the school canteen*

fast food restaurant a restaurant where you get meals such as hamburgers, French fries etc: *fast food restaurants such as McDonald's*

self-service restaurant a restaurant where you collect the food yourself: *the self-service restaurant at the airport*

diner *AmE* a small restaurant where you can eat cheap meals: *They stopped for breakfast at a roadside diner.*

takeaway *BrE* a place where you buy meals to eat outside or at home: *There's a good Indian takeaway in town.*

rested /'restɪd/ *adj* [not before noun] feeling healthier, stronger etc because you have had time to relax

restful /'restfəl/ *adj* peaceful and quiet: *restful music* | *a restful weekend*

'rest home *n* [C] a place where people who are old or ill can be cared for

restive /'restɪv/ *adj formal* bored or unhappy with your situation and wanting it to change

restless /'restləs/ *adj* **1** unable to relax and keep still, especially because you are bored: *The children were getting restless.* **2** not satisfied with your situation and wanting new experiences: *After three years at college, I started to get restless.* —**restlessly** *adv* —**restlessness** *n* [U]

restore Ac /rɪ'stɔː $ -ɔːr/ *v* [T] **1** to make a situation, feeling etc exist again: **restore peace/order** *The police were called in to restore order.* | *the need to restore public confidence in the legal system* | **restore sth to sth** *an attempt to restore the company to profitability* **2** to repair something so that it looks new: *He spends hours restoring old cars.* | **restore sth to sth** *The clock has been restored to full working order.* **THESAURUS** REPAIR **3** *formal* to give something back to someone: **restore sth to sb** *The goods have now been restored to their rightful owner.* —**restoration** /,restə'reɪʃən/ *n* [C,U]: *an old building in need of restoration* | *the restoration of the death penalty*

restrain Ac /rɪ'streɪn/ *v* [T] **1** to prevent someone from doing something: *We had to restrain him physically.* | *I had to restrain myself from running after her.* **2** to control something: *efforts to restrain inflation*

restrained /rɪ'streɪnd/ *adj* calm and controlled: *She was quite restrained, although she was obviously angry.*

restraint Ac /rɪ'streɪnt/ n **1** [U] when you behave in a calm way, even though you are angry, excited, or frightened: *The police showed great restraint.* **2** [C,U] something that limits what you can do: *new restraints on public spending*

restrict Ac /rɪ'strɪkt/ v [T] to limit something: *laws that restrict people's freedom* | **restrict sth to sth** *The sale of alcohol is restricted to people over the age of 18.* | **restrict yourself to sth** *I usually restrict myself to one glass of wine.*

restricted Ac /rɪ'strɪktɪd/ adj limited or controlled: *He has a very restricted diet.*

restriction Ac /rɪ'strɪkʃən/ n [C,U] a rule or law that limits what you are allowed to do: **[+on]** *The government imposed new restrictions on imported goods.* | *a 50 mph speed restriction*

restrictive Ac /rɪ'strɪktɪv/ adj something that is restrictive limits people too much

restroom /'restrʊm, -ruːm/ n [C] *AmE* a room with a toilet, in a place such as a restaurant or theatre SYN **toilet** *BrE* THESAURUS TOILET

restructure Ac /ˌriː'strʌktʃə $ -ər/ v [T] to change the way in which a company, government, or system is organized —**restructuring** n [U]

'rest stop n [C] *AmE* a place near a road where you can stop and rest, use the toilet etc

result¹ /rɪ'zʌlt/ n
1 [C,U] something that happens or exists because of something else: **[+of]** *What was the result of their decision?* | *High unemployment is the **direct result** of the country's economic problems.* | **as a result (of sth)** *Did she die as a result of the doctor's mistake?* | **with the result that** *The crops failed, with the result that thousands of people starved.* THESAURUS THEREFORE
2 [C] the number of points or votes that each person or team has at the end of a game, competition, or election: **[+of]** *What was the result of the England–Italy game?* | *the election results* | *a good result for the Democrats*
3 [C] the information that you get from a scientific study or test: *The study has produced some very interesting results.* | **[+of]** *When will I get the results of my blood test?*
4 [C] *especially BrE* a number or letter that shows how well you have done in an examination SYN **score** *AmE: The exam results come out in August.*
5 [C] something good that you achieve: *We need a sales team that will **get results** (=achieve a lot).*
→ END RESULT

COLLOCATIONS

verbs

to get/achieve a result *We didn't get the result we were expecting.*
to have a result *The campaign did have some positive results.*
to produce a result *Using better ingredients produces better results.*

adjectives

a direct result *His death was a direct result of the accident.*
the end/final result *It costs less, but the end result is the same.*

the net result (=the final result, after everything has happened) *The net result was that we achieved nothing.*
with disastrous results *A computer disk was lost, with disastrous results.*

THESAURUS

result something that happens because of something else: *Fewer people are having children, with the result that the population is going down.* | *He died as a result of a heart attack.*
consequences the things that happen later as a result of a situation, decision etc, which are usually bad: *If we keep using oil at this rate, it could have serious consequences for the future of our planet.*
outcome the situation that exists at the end of a meeting, election, war etc: *What was the outcome of the meeting?*

result² v [I] to happen or exist because of something: **[+from]** *His illness resulted from excessive drinking.* | *He has coped well with his disability and the resulting loss of freedom.*
PHRASAL VERBS
result in sth to make something happen SYN **cause**: *a fire that resulted in the deaths of two children*

resultant /rɪ'zʌltənt/ adj [only before noun] *formal* happening or existing because of something else: *damage caused by the heavy rain and resultant flooding*

resume /rɪ'zjuːm $ rɪ'zuːm/ v [I,T] *formal* if something resumes, or if you resume it, it starts again: *The meeting will resume after lunch.* | *She'll resume work on Monday.* —**resumption** /rɪ'zʌmpʃən/ n [singular, U]: *the resumption of the war*

resumé, résumé /'rezjʊmeɪ, 'reɪ- $ ˌrezʊ'meɪ/ n [C] *AmE* a short list of your education and previous jobs, which you send to employers when you are looking for a new job SYN **CV** *BrE*

resurface /ˌriː'sɜːfɪs $ -ɜːr-/ v **1** [I] to appear again: *a problem which is likely to resurface* **2** [T] to put a new surface on a road **3** [I] to come back up to the surface of water

resurgence /rɪ'sɜːdʒəns $ -ɜːr-/ n [singular, U] when something starts to happen again: *a resurgence of racial violence*

resurrect /ˌrezə'rekt/ v [T] to bring back something that has not existed or been used for a long time: *an attempt to resurrect his singing career*

Resurrection /ˌrezə'rekʃən/ n **the Resurrection** when Jesus Christ started to live again after his death, according to the Christian religion

resuscitate /rɪ'sʌsɪteɪt/ v [T] to make someone start breathing again: *Doctors managed to resuscitate her.* —**resuscitation** /rɪˌsʌsɪ'teɪʃən/ n [U]

retail¹ /'riːteɪl/ (also **retailing** /'riːteɪlɪŋ/) n [U] the business of selling things to people in shops → **wholesale**: *a career in retail* | *retail profits*

retail² v [I] *technical* to be sold for a particular price in shops: **[+at/for]** *wine which retails at £4.50 a bottle*

retailer /'ri:teɪlə $ -ər/ *n* [C] a person or company that sells things to people in shops

retain Ac /rɪ'teɪn/ *v* [T] *formal* to keep something and not lose it or give it away → **retention**: *He wants to retain control of the business.*

retainer Ac /rɪ'teɪnə $ -ər/ *n* [C] **1** an amount of money that you pay to someone so that they will continue to work for you when you need them **2** *AmE* something that you wear inside your mouth to make your teeth stay straight SYN **brace** *BrE*

retake /ˌri:'teɪk/ *v* [T] *(past tense* **retook** /-'tʊk/, *past participle* **retaken** /-'teɪkən/) **1** to get control of a place again during a war: *Government forces have retaken the city.* **2** *BrE* to take an examination again because you failed it the first time

retaliate /rɪ'tælieɪt/ *v* [I] to do something bad to someone because they have done something bad to you: *The demonstrators threw stones and the police retaliated by firing tear gas into the crowd.* THESAURUS ATTACK —**retaliation** /rɪˌtæli'eɪʃən/ *n* [U]: *an attack in retaliation for last week's bombing*

retard /rɪ'tɑ:d $ -ɑ:rd/ *v* [T] *formal* to delay something or make it happen more slowly than usual: *Cold weather can retard the plant's growth.*

retarded /rɪ'tɑ:dɪd $ -ɑ:r-/ *adj* old-fashioned less mentally developed than other people. Many people think that this use is rude and offensive.

retch /retʃ/ *v* [I] to almost VOMIT: *The smell made me retch.*

retention Ac /rɪ'tenʃən/ *n* [U] *formal* when you keep something → **retain**: *the recruitment and retention of staff*

rethink /ˌri:'θɪŋk/ *v* [I,T] *(past tense and past participle* **rethought** /-'θɔ:t $ -'θɒ:t/) to think about a plan or idea again and decide what changes should be made: *The government needs to rethink its economic policy.* —**rethink** /'ri:θɪŋk/ *n* [singular]: *a complete rethink of our strategy*

reticent /'retəsənt/ *adj* not wanting to talk about something: **[+about]** *He was very reticent about his childhood.* —**reticence** *n* [U]

retina /'retənə/ *n* [C] the area at the back of your eye that receives light and sends messages to your brain

retinue /'retɪnju: $ -nu:/ *n* [C] a group of helpers who travel with a famous person: *the star's retinue of security guards*

retire /rɪ'taɪə $ -'taɪr/ *v* [I]
1 to stop working because you are old: **[+at]** *He retired at 65.* | **[+from]** *She retired from teaching last year.* | *She had to retire early because of poor health.* THESAURUS LEAVE
2 *formal* to go away to a quiet place: **[+to]** *He retired to his room.* —**retired** *adj*: *a retired police officer*

retirement /rɪ'taɪəmənt $ -'taɪr-/ *n* [C,U] when you stop working or have stopped working because you are old: *a party to celebrate her retirement* | *I hope you enjoy a long and happy retirement.* | **[+from]** *He*

has announced his retirement from politics.* | *She took **early retirement** because of her health.*

retiring /rɪ'taɪərɪŋ $ -'taɪrɪŋ/ *adj* shy

retook /ri:'tʊk/ *v* the past tense of RETAKE

retort /rɪ'tɔ:t $ -ɔ:rt/ *v* [T] to answer someone quickly in an angry or amusing way: *'It's easy for you to say that!' he retorted.* —**retort** *n* [C]: *a clever retort*

retrace /rɪ'treɪs, ri:-/ *v* [T] **1 retrace your steps/ path** to go back exactly the same way as you came: *We retraced our steps to the car.* **2** to repeat a journey made by someone else: *They will be retracing the route taken by Captain Cook.*

retract /rɪ'trækt/ *v* [T] *formal* to say that something you said before is not true: *He later retracted his confession.*

retractable /rɪ'træktəbəl/ *adj* a retractable part of something can be pulled back into the main part: *a knife with a retractable blade*

retraining /ri:'treɪnɪŋ/ *n* [U] when someone learns new skills so that they can do a different job —**retrain** *v* [I,T]

retreat¹ /rɪ'tri:t/ *v* [I] **1** if an army retreats, it moves back to avoid fighting OPP **advance**: *The British army was forced to retreat.* | *They retreated to the hills behind the city.* **2** to move away to a safe or quiet place: **[+to/into]** *She retreated into the kitchen.* | **[+from]** *He retreated from the busy office.*

retreat² *n* **1** [C,U] when an army moves back to avoid fighting: **[+from]** *the British retreat from Paris* **2** [C] a quiet place where you can go to rest or spend time alone: *a weekend retreat in the country*
PHRASES
beat a retreat *informal* to leave a place quickly: *We saw the teacher coming and **beat a hasty retreat**.*

retrial /ˌri:'traɪəl, 'ri:traɪəl $ ri:'traɪəl/ *n* [C] when a law case is judged for a second time in a court: *The judge ordered a retrial.*

retribution /ˌretrə'bju:ʃən/ *n* [singular, U] when someone is punished for something bad that they have done: *The victims are demanding retribution.*

retrieve /rɪ'tri:v/ *v* [T] to find something and bring it back: **retrieve sth from sth** *I retrieved my suitcase from the hall cupboard.* | *ways of retrieving information from the computer* —**retrieval** *n* [U]: *the storage and retrieval of data*

retriever /rɪ'tri:və $ -ər/ *n* [C] a type of dog

retro /'retrəʊ $ -troʊ/ *adj* based on a style from the past: *clothes with a retro look*

retrospect /'retrəspekt/ *n* **in retrospect** when you think about something that happened in the past, knowing more about it now than you knew then: *In retrospect, I shouldn't have given him the money.*

retrospective¹ /ˌretrə'spektɪv◂/ *adj* a law or decision that is retrospective is made now but will affect earlier things

retrospective² *n* [C] a show of the past work of an artist

retry /ˌri:'traɪ/ *v* [T] *(retried, retrying, retries)* **1** to judge a person or a law case again in court, for example because the original TRIAL was unfair in some way → **retrial 2** to try to do an action on a computer again

return¹ /rɪˈtɜːn $ -ɜːrn/ v

1 [I] to come back or go back to a place: *She didn't return until late.* | **[+to]** *I hope to return to Italy soon.* | **[+from]** *He had just returned from work.* | *We decided to return home.*

2 [T] to give, put, or send something back where it came from: **return sth to sb/sth** *I returned the books to the library.* | *The letter was returned unopened.* | *He returned the ball beautifully* (=hit it back to his opponent).

3 [I] to start to happen again: *Next morning, the pain had returned.*

4 [T] to do something to someone, after they have done the same thing to you: *He smiled warmly, and she returned his smile.* | *I phoned and left a message, but he hasn't returned my call.*

PHRASES

return a verdict when a JURY returns a verdict, they say whether someone is guilty or not: *The jury returned a verdict of guilty.*

PHRASAL VERBS

return to sth

1 to change back to a previous state: *After a couple of weeks, things had returned to normal.*

2 to start doing something again: *When will you return to work?*

return² n

1 COMING BACK [singular] when someone comes back or goes back to a place: **[+to]** *I was looking forward to my return to college.* | **on your return (to/from sth)** *He was arrested on his return to England.*

2 BRINGING STH BACK [singular] when something is given back, put back, or sent back: **[+of]** *a reward for the return of the stolen necklace*

3 IN TENNIS ETC [C] when someone hits the ball back to their opponent, especially in tennis: *She hit a brilliant return.*

4 STARTING AGAIN [singular] **a)** when someone starts doing something again: *her return to work* **b)** when something starts to happen again: *the return of high unemployment* | *a return to normal*

5 PROFIT [C,U] the amount of profit that you get from something: *a big return on our investment*

6 ON KEYBOARD [U] a key that you press on a computer at the end of an instruction or to move to a new line

7 TICKET [C] *BrE* a ticket for a journey to a place and back again SYN **round trip** *AmE* OPP **single** → DAY RETURN, TAX RETURN

PHRASES

in return (for sth) as a payment or reward for something: *What does he expect in return for his help?*

many happy returns *BrE* used to wish someone a happy BIRTHDAY

return³ adj [only before noun] **1** relating to a journey to a place and back again SYN **round trip** *AmE* → **single**: *a return ticket* | *The price includes a return flight.* **2** a return game, match etc is the second one played between two people or teams

reunification /ˌriːjuːnɪfɪˈkeɪʃən/ n [U] when different parts of a country are joined together again and become one nation: *the reunification of Germany*

reunion /riːˈjuːnjən/ n [C] a meeting of people who have not met for a long time: *a college reunion* | *a family reunion* | *He had an emotional reunion with his son.*

reunite /ˌriːjuːˈnaɪt/ v [T] to bring people together again: **reunite sb with sb** *He was at last reunited with his children.*

reuse /ˌriːˈjuːz/ v [T] to use something again: *The bottles may be reused up to 20 times.* —**reusable** adj: *reusable containers* —**reuse** /ˌriːˈjuːs/ n [U]

rev /rev/ (also **rev up**) v [I,T] (**revved, revving**) if an engine revs, or if you rev it, it works faster and makes a loud noise

Rev. the written abbreviation of **Reverend**

revamp /riːˈvæmp/ v [T] to change something in order to improve it and make it more modern

reveal Ac /rɪˈviːl/ v [T] **1** to tell people something that was secret: *The information was first revealed in a Sunday newspaper.* | **[+that]** *He revealed that he had spent five years in prison.* THESAURUS TELL **2** to show something that people could not see before: *The curtains opened to reveal a large stage.* THESAURUS SHOW

revealing Ac /rɪˈviːlɪŋ/ adj **1** telling people information that they did not know before, especially about a person's character or feelings: *Some of the answers he gave were very revealing.* **2** revealing clothes show parts of your body that are usually kept covered: *a very revealing nightdress*

revel /ˈrevəl/ v (**revelled, revelling** *BrE*, **reveled, reveling** *AmE*)

PHRASAL VERBS

revel in sth to enjoy something very much: *He was secretly revelling in his new fame.*

revelation Ac /ˌrevəˈleɪʃən/ n **1** [C] a surprising fact that was secret and has now been told to people: *revelations about the Prime Minister's private life* **2** **be a revelation** to be surprisingly good: *Her first book was a revelation to me.*

reveller *BrE*, **reveler** *AmE* /ˈrevələ $ -lər/ n [C] someone who is having fun singing, drinking etc in a noisy way

revelry /ˈrevəlri/ n [U] wild noisy dancing, eating, drinking etc

revenge¹ /rɪˈvendʒ/ n [U] when you hurt or punish someone because they have done something bad to you: *She was determined to get revenge.* | *He later took revenge on his employers.* | *an act of revenge* | **in revenge for sth** *The bombing was in revenge for the killing of two students by soldiers.*

revenge² v [T] *formal* to punish someone who has harmed you or someone else: **revenge yourself on sb** *He vowed to revenge himself on his attackers.*

revenue Ac /ˈrevənjuː $ -nuː/ (also **revenues** [plural]) n [U] money that a business or the government receives: *Most of the theatre's revenue comes from ticket sales.* | *an increase in tax revenues*

reverberate /rɪˈvɜːbəreɪt $ -ɜːr-/ v [I] if a sound

reverberates, you hear it many times in a place as it comes back off different surfaces: *Her voice reverberated around the empty warehouse.*

revere /rɪ'vɪə $ -'vɪr/ v [T] *formal* to respect and admire someone or something a lot —**revered** *adj*: *Ireland's most revered poet*

reverence /'revərəns/ n [U] *formal* a great respect and admiration for someone

Reverend /'revərənd/ used in the title of a Christian priest: *Reverend Larson*

reverent /'revərənt/ (*also* **reverential** /ˌrevə'renʃəl◂/) *adj formal* showing great respect for someone —**reverently** *adv*

reverie /'revəri/ n [C,U] *literary* when you are thinking about pleasant things and not noticing what is around you

reversal Ac /rɪ'vɜːsəl $ -ɜːr-/ n [C] a change so that something becomes the opposite of what it was before: *a sudden reversal of government policy*

reverse¹ Ac /rɪ'vɜːs $ -ɜːrs/ v **1** [T] to change something completely so that it is the opposite of what it was before: *The decision was later reversed by the Appeal Court.* | *Our roles have now been reversed.* **2** [I,T] if you reverse a car, or if it reverses, it moves backwards: *I reversed the car into a parking space.* | *She reversed into a side street.* | *The lorry was reversing.*

PHRASES

reverse the charges *BrE* to make a telephone call that is paid for by the person you are telephoning SYN **call collect** *AmE*: *Call me from London and reverse the charges.*

reverse² Ac n **1 the reverse** the complete opposite: *I wasn't disappointed by the film – **quite the reverse**.* **2** (*also* **reverse gear**) [U] if a car is in reverse, the controls are arranged so that it is ready to drive backwards: *Put the car in reverse.*

PHRASES

in reverse in the opposite way or the opposite order: *They're taking the same route, but in reverse.*

reverse³ Ac *adj* [only before noun] opposite to what is usual or expected: *The names were read out in reverse order.*

reversible Ac /rɪ'vɜːsəbəl $ -ɜːr-/ *adj* **1** something that is reversible can be changed back: *This decision is not reversible.* **2** a reversible piece of clothing can be worn with the inside part on the outside: *a reversible jacket*

revert /rɪ'vɜːt $ -ɜːrt/ v

PHRASAL VERBS

revert to sth to change back to a previous thing or situation: *The city reverted to its former name of St Petersburg.* —**reversion** /rɪ'vɜːʃən $ -'vɜːrʒən/ [singular, U]

review¹ /rɪ'vjuː/ n

1 [C,U] when someone examines something carefully in order to see if changes are necessary: **[+of]** *a review of training methods* | **carry out/conduct/undertake a review** *They're conducting a review of their safety procedures.* | **under review** *We're keeping this policy under review.*

2 [C] a report about a new book, film, or television show: *a film review* | **[+of]** *The paper published a review of her book.* | **good/bad review** *The band's new CD has had very good reviews.*

3 [C] a report on a series of events or a period of time that mentions the most important parts: **[+of]** *a review of the year*

review² v **1** [T] to examine something carefully in order to see if changes are necessary: *The school is reviewing its policy on homework.* **2** [T] to write a report about a new book, film, or television show **3** [I,T] *AmE* to prepare for a test by studying books and notes from your lessons SYN **revise** *BrE*

reviewer /rɪ'vjuːə $ -ər/ n [C] someone who writes about new books, films etc

revile /rɪ'vaɪl/ v [T] *formal* to express hatred of someone or something

revise Ac /rɪ'vaɪz/ v **1** [T] to change something in order to improve it: *We need to revise our plans.* | *the revised edition of the book* **2** [I] *BrE* to prepare for a test by studying books and notes from your lessons SYN **review** *AmE*: **[+for]** *She's revising for her history exam.* THESAURUS STUDY

revision Ac /rɪ'vɪʒən/ n **1** [C,U] when you change something in order to improve it **2** [U] *BrE* when you prepare for a test by studying books and notes from your lessons

revitalize (*also* **-ise** *BrE*) /riː'vaɪtəlaɪz/ v [T] to put new strength or power into something: *an attempt to revitalize the economy* —**revitalization** /riːˌvaɪtəlaɪ'zeɪʃən $ -tl-ə-/ n [U]

revival /rɪ'vaɪvəl/ n **1** [C,U] when something becomes popular or successful again: *economic revival* | **[+of/in]** *a revival of interest* in Picasso's work **2** [C] a new performance of a play that has not been performed for a long time: *a revival of 'Oklahoma!'*

revive /rɪ'vaɪv/ v **1** [T] to make something popular or used again: *This centuries-old tradition is being revived.* **2** [I,T] to become healthy and strong again, or to make someone or something healthy and strong again: *The economy is beginning to revive.* | *The doctors were unable to revive him* (=they couldn't make him conscious again).

revoke /rɪ'vəuk $ -'vouk/ v [T] *formal* to officially end a law or agreement, or change a decision

revolt¹ /rɪ'vəult $ -'voult/ v **1** [I] if people revolt, they take strong and often violent action against their government in order to change it: **[+against]** *The army revolted against the government.* **2** [T usually passive] if you are revolted by something, you feel sick and shocked because it is very unpleasant: *He was revolted by the smell.*

revolt² n [C,U] when people try to change the government, often by using violence, or refuse to obey someone in authority: *the Paris student revolt of May 1968*

revolting /rɪ'vəultɪŋ $ -'voul-/ *adj* very unpleasant: *The food was revolting.* THESAURUS TASTE

revolution Ac /ˌrevə'luːʃən/ n **1** [C] a complete change in the way people think or do something: **[+in]** *a revolution in scientific thinking* |

social/cultural/sexual etc revolution the sexual revolution of the 1960s

2 [C,U] when the people of a country change the government or the political system, using force: *the French Revolution*

3 [C,U] a circular movement around something → **revolve**: *a speed of 100 revolutions per minute*

revolutionary¹ Ac /ˌrevəˈluːʃənəri◂ $ -ʃəneri◂/ adj
1 completely new and different: *a revolutionary new product* **THESAURUS** NEW **2** [only before noun] relating to a political revolution: *a revolutionary leader*

revolutionary² Ac n [C] (plural **revolutionaries**) someone who takes part in a political revolution

revolutionize Ac (also **-ise** BrE) /ˌrevəˈluːʃənaɪz/ v [T] to completely change the way people think or do something: *The Internet has revolutionized the way people work.* **THESAURUS** CHANGE

revolve /rɪˈvɒlv $ rɪˈvɑːlv/ v [I] to move around in a circle: *The wheel began to revolve.* | *a revolving door* **THESAURUS** TURN

PHRASAL VERBS

revolve around sb/sth to have someone or something as the most important part: *Jane's life revolves around her children.*

revolver /rɪˈvɒlvə $ rɪˈvɑːlvər/ n [C] a small gun

revue /rɪˈvjuː/ n [C] a show in a theatre that includes singing, dancing, and jokes

revulsion /rɪˈvʌlʃən/ n [U] the feeling you have when you are very shocked by something unpleasant

reward¹ /rɪˈwɔːd $ -ˈwɔːrd/ n [C,U] something, especially money, that is given to someone to thank them for doing something: *She offered a £20 reward to anyone who could find her cat.* | **reward for (doing) sth** *Some parents give their children rewards for passing exams.*

> **Word Choice: reward or award?**
> A **reward** is something, especially money, that is given to someone because they have done something good or helpful: *A reward is being offered for information about the robbery.*
> An **award** is something such as a prize or a medal that is officially given to someone for their achievements: *They have just won an award for best website.*

reward² v [T] if you are rewarded for something you have done, something good happens to you or is given to you: **reward sb for** sth *He was rewarded for all his hard work.* | **reward sb with** sth *They rewarded him with a free ticket.*

rewarding /rɪˈwɔːdɪŋ $ -ɔːr-/ adj making you feel happy and satisfied: *a rewarding job*

rewind /riːˈwaɪnd/ v [I,T] (past tense and past participle **rewound** /-ˈwaʊnd/) to make a tape go back towards the beginning

rework /ˌriːˈwɜːk $ -ˈwɜːrk/ v [T] to make changes to something such as a piece of writing in order to improve it

rewrite /ˌriːˈraɪt/ v [T] (past tense **rewrote** /-ˈrəʊt $ -ˈroʊt/, past participle **rewritten** /-ˈrɪtn/) to write

something again in a different way —**rewrite** /ˈriːraɪt/ n [C]

rhapsody /ˈræpsədi/ n [C] (plural **rhapsodies**) a piece of music that is written to express emotion, and does not have a regular form

rhetoric /ˈretərɪk/ n [U] **1** words that sound impressive, but are not sincere: *political rhetoric* **2** the skill of using words effectively to influence people

rhetorical /rɪˈtɒrɪkəl $ -ˈtɔː-, -ˈtɑː-/ adj **1** a rhetorical question is one that you ask as a way of making a statement, without expecting an answer **2** used in rhetoric —**rhetorically** /-kli/ adv

rheumatism /ˈruːmətɪzəm/ n [U] a disease that makes your muscles and joints painful and difficult to move

rhinestone /ˈraɪnstəʊn $ -stoʊn/ n [C] a jewel made from glass or a rock that is intended to look like a DIAMOND

rhinoceros /raɪˈnɒsərəs $ -ˈnɑː-/ (also **rhino** /ˈraɪnəʊ $ -noʊ/) n [C] (plural **rhinoceros** or **rhinoceroses**) a large heavy African or Asian animal with thick skin and a horn on its nose → see picture on page A3

rhododendron /ˌrəʊdəˈdendrən $ ˌroʊ-/ n [C] a large bush with bright flowers

rhubarb /ˈruːbɑːb $ -ɑːrb/ n [U] a plant with red stems that are cooked and eaten as fruit → see picture on page A4

rhyme¹ /raɪm/ v [I] if two words or lines of poetry rhyme, they end with the same sound: **[+with]** *'Hat' rhymes with 'cat'.*

rhyme² n **1** [C] a short poem or song using words that rhyme **2** [U] when you use words that rhyme → **NURSERY RHYME**

rhythm /ˈrɪðəm/ n [C,U]
1 a regular repeated pattern of sounds or movements: *Drums are basic to African rhythm.* | **[+of]** *the rhythm of the music*
2 a regular pattern of changes: *the body's natural rhythms* —**rhythmic** /ˈrɪðmɪk/ adj —**rhythmically** /-kli/ adv

rib /rɪb/ n [C] one of the curved bones in your chest → see picture on page A2

ribald /ˈrɪbəld/ adj ribald humour is about sex in a rude way

ribbed /rɪbd/ adj something that is ribbed has raised lines on it: *a ribbed sweater*

ribbon /ˈrɪbən/ n [C,U] a narrow piece of attractive cloth that you use, for example, to tie your hair or hold things together

'rib cage n [C] the structure of RIBS in your chest

rice /raɪs/ n [U] food that consists of small white or brown grains that are cooked in water, or the plant that produces it: *We had chicken with boiled rice.* | *a few grains of rice*

rich /rɪtʃ/ adj
1 **HAVING A LOT OF MONEY a)** a rich person, country etc has a lot of money and valuable things **OPP poor**: *She found herself a rich husband.* | *Germany is one of Europe's richest countries.* | *an easy*

way to **get rich** (=become rich) **b) the rich** [plural] people who are rich

2 CONTAINING STH GOOD containing a lot of something good: **[+in]** *Citrus fruits are rich in vitamin C.* | *Red meat is a* **rich source** *of iron.*

3 FOOD rich food contains a lot of butter, cream, or eggs and makes you feel full very quickly: *a rich fruit cake* | *The sauce was very rich.*

4 SMELL/TASTE/COLOUR a rich smell, taste, or colour is strong and pleasant: *the rich smell of fresh coffee* | *a rich dark brown colour*

5 SOIL rich soil is good for growing plants in

THESAURUS

rich a rich person, country etc has a lot of money and valuable things: *By 33, he was a rich man.* | *The United States is one of the richest nations in the world.*

wealthy rich – used especially about a person, family, country etc that has been rich for a long time: *She came from a wealthy family.* | *a wealthy landowner* | *Britain is still a very wealthy country.*

well-off fairly rich compared to other people, so that you can live very comfortably: *He's a lawyer, so he's quite well-off.*

loaded informal very rich: *Her dad's loaded.*

affluent rich – used about a group of people, a society, or an area where people have nice houses and expensive possessions: *today's affluent society* | *People in affluent areas have two or three cars.*

prosperous rich – used about places and people, especially when their money is related to success in business: *Because of the oil industry, the city has become very prosperous in recent years.* | *prosperous farmers*

---

riches /ˈrɪtʃɪz/ *n* [plural] *literary* a lot of money or valuable things SYN **wealth**

richly /ˈrɪtʃli/ *adv* **1** in a beautiful and expensive way: *The room was richly decorated in marble.* **2 richly coloured/flavoured/scented** having a strong pleasant colour, taste, or smell: *richly scented flowers* **3 richly deserve sth** to completely deserve something: *They got the punishment they so richly deserved.*

richness /ˈrɪtʃnəs/ *n* [U] **1** when something contains a lot of interesting things: *the richness and diversity of the Amazonian rain forests* **2** the richness of a colour, taste, or smell is its quality of being strong and pleasant

rickety /ˈrɪkəti/ *adj* in a bad condition and likely to break: *a rickety old chair*

rickshaw /ˈrɪkʃɔː $ -ʃɔː/ *n* [C] a small vehicle used in South-East Asia for carrying one or two passengers. It is pulled by someone walking or riding a bicycle.

ricochet /ˈrɪkəʃeɪ/ *v* [I] if a bullet or stone ricochets off a surface, it hits it and moves away in a different direction —**ricochet** *n* [C]

rid¹ /rɪd/ *adj*

PHRASES

| **be rid of sb/sth** to have got rid of someone or something: *To be honest, I'm glad to be rid of him.*

get rid of sb to make someone leave a place or job: *Most people were glad to get rid of the old president.* | *Andy stayed for hours – we couldn't get rid of him!*

get rid of sth 1 to throw away, sell, or destroy something you do not want any more: *I got rid of all those old toys.* **2** to make something that you do not want go away: *We couldn't get rid of the smell in the house.* | *I can't get rid of this cough.* THESAURUS
REMOVE

rid² *v* (*past tense and past participle* **rid**, *present participle* **ridding**)
PHRASAL VERBS

rid sb/sth **of** sth to remove something bad: *a promise to rid the country of nuclear weapons* | **rid yourself of sth** (=stop having a feeling or problem) *He managed to rid himself of his fears.*

riddance /ˈrɪdns/ *n* **good riddance (to sb/sth)** *spoken* a rude way of saying you are glad that an annoying person or thing has gone away

ridden /ˈrɪdn/ *v* the past participle of RIDE

-ridden /rɪdn/ *suffix* having a lot of something unpleasant: *disease-ridden slums* | *a debt-ridden company*

riddle /ˈrɪdl/ *n* [C] **1** a joke or question that you try to guess the answer to for fun **2** something that you cannot understand or explain: *the riddle of Len's death*

riddled /ˈrɪdld/ *adj* **riddled with sth** containing a lot of something bad: *His essay was riddled with mistakes.*

ride a bicycle

rider

ride a horse

ride¹ /raɪd/ *v* [I,T] (*past tense* **rode** /rəʊd $ roʊd/, *past participle* **ridden** /ˈrɪdn/)

1 to move along on a horse, bicycle, motorcycle etc: *She learned to ride when she was five.* | *Can you ride a bicycle?* | **[+away/across/through etc]** *Paul jumped on his bike and rode off.*

2 to travel in a bus, car etc: *We got onto the bus and rode into San Francisco.* | *Ann rides the subway to work.*

PHRASAL VERBS

ride on sth if one thing is riding on another, it depends on it for success: *There's a lot riding on this match.*

ride sth ↔ **out** to come out of a difficult situation without being badly harmed by it: *He managed to ride out the scandal.*

> **Word Choice: ride or drive?**
> You **ride** a bicycle or motorcycle, or an animal such as a horse or a donkey.
> You **drive** a car, truck, bus, train etc.
> You **ride in** a car or bus when another person is driving. In American English, you also say **ride** a train, bus, subway etc.

ride² *n* [C] **1** a trip in a car, bus etc, or on a bicycle or horse: [+in] *We went for a ride in his new car.* | [+on] *Can I have a ride on your bike?* | **a car/bus/ train etc ride** *a fifteen-minute taxi ride* | **a smooth/ comfortable/bumpy etc ride** THESAURUS JOURNEY **2** a large moving machine that people go on for fun: *children's fairground rides*

PHRASES

rough/easy ride *informal* if people give someone, especially someone in authority, a rough or easy ride, they make them have a situation difficult or easy for them: *The president will not be given an easy ride when he meets with the unions.*

take sb for a ride *spoken* to trick someone, especially in order to get money from them: *After the deal was signed, I realized I'd been taken for a ride.*

rider /ˈraɪdə $ -ər/ *n* [C] someone who rides a horse, bicycle, or MOTORCYCLE → see picture at RIDE¹

ridge /rɪdʒ/ *n* [C] **1** a long narrow area of high land along the top of a mountain: *We could see climbers on the ridge.* **2** a raised line on a surface: *the ridges on the soles of his shoes*

ridicule¹ /ˈrɪdɪkjuːl/ *n* [U] *formal* when people laugh and say unkind things about someone or something: *She became an **object of ridicule** (=people laughed at her).*

ridicule² *v* [T] to laugh and say unkind things about someone or something: *His ideas were ridiculed.*

ridiculous /rɪˈdɪkjələs/ *adj* very silly: *That's a ridiculous idea!* THESAURUS STUPID —**ridiculously** *adv*

riding /ˈraɪdɪŋ/ *n* [U] the sport of riding horses

rife /raɪf/ *adj* [not before noun] if something bad is rife, it is very common: *Burglary is rife in large cities.*

riff-raff /ˈrɪf ræf/ *n* [U] an insulting word for people who are noisy or behave badly, or are of low social class

rifle¹ /ˈraɪfəl/ *n* [C] a long gun that you hold against your shoulder to shoot

rifle² (*also* **rifle through**) *v* [T] to search a place quickly, especially in order to steal something: *Somebody has been rifling through my desk.*

rift /rɪft/ *n* [C] **1** a serious disagreement: [+between] *a rift between the two men* **2** a crack in the ground, a mountain etc

rig¹ /rɪg/ *v* [T] (**rigged**, **rigging**) to make an election or competition have the result you want by doing something dishonest: *The election was rigged.*

PHRASAL VERBS

rig sth ↔ **up** *informal* to make something quickly from materials you can find easily: *We rigged up a shelter using a piece of plastic sheeting.*

rig² *n* [C] **1** a large structure used for getting oil or gas from under the bottom of the sea **2** *AmE informal* a large truck

rigamarole /ˈrɪgəmərəʊl $ -roʊl/ *n* an American spelling of RIGMAROLE

rigging /ˈrɪgɪŋ/ *n* [U] the ropes and chains that support a ship's sails

right¹ /raɪt/ *adj*

1 CORRECT correct or true OPP **wrong**: *Yes, that's the **right answer**.* | *Is that the **right time**?* | *I **got** most of the questions **right**.* | [+about] *You were right about Geoff getting married. Lisa told me the news yesterday.* | *'You live in London, don't you?' 'Yes, **that's right**.'* THESAURUS AGREE

2 SUITABLE suitable for doing something OPP **wrong**: *She is the **right person** for the job.* | *You need to use the right tools.* THESAURUS SUITABLE

3 NOT LEFT [only before noun] your right side is the side with the hand that most people write with OPP **left**: *He had a knife in his right hand.* | *a scar on the **right side** of her face* | *Take the next right turn.*

4 WITHOUT ANY PROBLEMS in normal condition, without any problems: *The engine's not quite right.* | *If anything goes wrong, the technicians are here to **put** it **right** (=correct it).* | *I don't feel right today.*

5 MORALLY CORRECT fair or morally good OPP **wrong**: **right to do sth** *I think you were absolutely right to report them to the police.*

6 VERY BAD/STUPID ETC [only before noun] *BrE spoken* used to emphasize how bad someone or something is SYN **total**, **complete**: *He made me feel a right idiot.* → ALL RIGHT¹

PHRASES

(as) right as rain *spoken* completely healthy, especially after an illness: *You'll soon be as right as rain.*

> ### THESAURUS
>
> **right** not wrong – used about an answer, decision etc, or about a person: *You made the right decision.* | *I'm sure you're right.*
> **correct** right. **Correct** sounds more formal than **right**: *The correct answer is 27.* | *Your father is absolutely correct.*
> **accurate** information, measurements, descriptions etc that are accurate are completely correct in every detail: *Are these measurements accurate?* | *Make sure you have accurate information about the weather conditions.*
> **exact** an exact number, amount, or time is completely correct and is no more and no less than it should be: *I can't remember the exact date we moved.* | *The exact number of deaths is not yet known.*

right² *adv*

1 EXACTLY exactly in a particular position: [+in/in front of/by etc] *She was standing right in the middle of*

the room. | **[+here/there]** *I left my bags right here.*
THESAURUS ▶ **EXACTLY**
2 **IMMEDIATELY** immediately: **[+after]** *The show is on right after the news.* | **right now/away** (=now or immediately) *I'll phone him right away.* | *I'm sorry, I can't talk to you right now.* | **I'll be right with you/ right there/right back** (=used to ask someone to wait for a short time) **THESAURUS** ▶ **IMMEDIATELY**
3 **NOT LEFT** towards the side nearest your right hand **OPP** **left**: *Turn right at the traffic lights.*
4 **WELL** informal in a good or satisfactory way **SYN** **well**: *Everything's **going right** for him.*
5 **CORRECTLY** correctly **OPP** **wrong**: *They didn't spell my name right.*
6 **COMPLETELY** **right along/through/round etc** all the way along, through etc: *Go right to the end of the road.* | *The bullet went right through the car door.*

right³ spoken **1** used to show that you have understood or agree with what someone has just said: *'You need to be there by ten o'clock.' 'Right.'* **2** used to ask if what you have said was correct: *You wanted to go to the show, right?* **3** *BrE* used when you want to make someone listen or get ready to do something: *Right, everyone! It's time to go!*

right⁴ n

1 **STH YOU ARE ALLOWED** [C] something that you are legally or morally allowed to do or have: **[+of]** *the rights and duties of citizens* | **right to do sth** *You have the right to consult a lawyer.* | **[+to]** *All children have the right to free education.* | **within your rights** (=legally or morally allowed) *You're within your rights to ask for your money back.*
2 **NOT LEFT** the side with the hand that most people write with **OPP** **left**: **on/to the right (of sth)** *Our car is just to the right of that white van.* | **on/to sb's right** *The school is on your right as you come into the village.*
3 **POLITICS** **the right/the Right** political groups that believe that the government should not own any business or try to control business by making too many rules: *This idea is popular with **the Right**.* | **the extreme/far right** *politicians on the extreme right*
4 **MORALLY GOOD BEHAVIOUR** [U] behaviour that is morally good and correct: *It's important to teach kids the difference between **right and wrong**.*
5 **BOOK/FILM ETC** **rights** [plural] if someone has the rights to a book, film etc, they are allowed to sell it or show it: **[+to]** *They paid £2 million for the **film rights** to the book.*
PHRASES

by rights spoken used to describe what should happen if things are done fairly or correctly: *By rights, the house should be mine now.*

have a right to be angry/upset etc to have a good reason to be angry, upset etc: *You had **every right** to be angry with them.*

have no right to do sth used to say that someone's behaviour is completely unreasonable or unfair: *You had no right to take money from my purse!*

be in the right to have the best reasons, arguments etc in a disagreement: *Both sides were convinced that they are in the right.*

in your own right without depending on anyone else: *She's a very wealthy woman in her own right.*

verbs
to have a right *We have a right to know what happened.*
to give sb a right *Being my boss doesn't give you the right to be rude to me.*
to deny sb a right (=to not allow someone to do something) *Women were denied the right to vote.*
to fight for your rights *The poor had to fight for their rights.*

types of right
a basic/fundamental right *We believe people have a basic right to choose where they live.*
a legal right *He has no legal right to be here.*
equal rights *Women demanded equal rights.*
human rights (=the rights that everyone should have) *He is a dictator with no respect for human rights.*
civil rights (=the rights that every person in a society should have) *African-Americans were campaigning for their civil rights.*
women's/workers'/animal rights *New laws have been passed to protect women's rights.*

right⁵ *v* [T] to put something, especially a boat, back into its correct upright position: *I managed to right the canoe.*
PHRASES

right a wrong to do something to stop an unfair situation from continuing: *He seems to think he can right all the wrongs of the world.*

'right ,angle *n* [C] an angle of 90°, like the angles at the corners of a square → see picture at **ANGLE¹**
—**right-angled** *adj*

righteous /ˈraɪtʃəs/ *adj* morally good
—**righteousness** *n* [U]
PHRASES

righteous indignation/anger etc strong feelings of anger when you think something is not morally right or fair

rightful /ˈraɪtfəl/ *adj* [only before noun] according to what is legally and morally correct: *He is the rightful owner of the house.* —**rightfully** *adv*

'right-hand *adj* [only before noun] on the right side of something: *the **right-hand side** of his body*

,right-'handed *adj* someone who is right-handed uses their right hand rather than their left hand to do most things

,right-hand 'man *n* [C] the person who supports and helps you the most, especially in your job

rightly /ˈraɪtli/ *adv* correctly or for a good reason: *Her father **quite rightly** said that she was too young to drive.*

,right of 'way *n* (plural **rights of way**) **1** [U] the right to drive into or across a road before other vehicles **2** [C] *BrE* **a)** the right to walk across someone else's land **b)** a path that people have the right to use

,right-'wing *adj* a right-wing person or group does not like changes in society, and supports **CAPITALISM**

rather than SOCIALISM: *right-wing parties* —**right-winger** *n* [C] —**right wing** *n* [singular]

rigid Ac /ˈrɪdʒɪd/ *adj* **1** rules or ideas that are rigid are strict and difficult to change: *a society with rigid traditions* **2** very unwilling to change your ideas **3** stiff and not moving or bending: *rigid plastic* —**rigidly** *adv*: *The laws were rigidly enforced.* —**rigidity** /rɪˈdʒɪdəti/ *n* [U]

rigmarole /ˈrɪgmərəʊl $ -roʊl/ (*also* **rigamarole** /ˈrɪgəmərəʊl $ -roʊl/ *AmE*) *n* [singular, U] a long confusing process or description: *I don't want to go through the rigmarole of taking him to court.*

rigorous /ˈrɪgərəs/ *adj* careful and thorough: *rigorous safety checks* —**rigorously** *adv*

rigour *BrE*, **rigor** *AmE* /ˈrɪgə $ -ər/ *n* **1 the rigours of sth** the problems and difficulties of a situation: *the rigors of a Canadian winter* **2** [U] great care and thoroughness in making sure that something is correct: *Their research is lacking in rigour.*

rile /raɪl/ *v* [T] *informal* to make someone very angry: *Don't let him rile you.*

rim /rɪm/ *n* [C] the outside edge of something round, such as a glass or wheel: **steel-rimmed/red-rimmed etc** *gold-rimmed glasses*

rind /raɪnd/ *n* [C,U] the thick skin on the outside of some foods, such as BACON or cheese → see Word Choice at PEEL

ring¹ /rɪŋ/ *n* [C]
1 JEWELLERY a circle of silver, gold etc that you wear on your finger: *a wedding ring* | *a diamond ring* → see picture at JEWELLERY
2 CIRCULAR OBJECT an object in the shape of a circle: *a key ring* | *a rubber ring for children to go swimming with*
3 OF PEOPLE/THINGS a group of people or things arranged in a circle: *A ring of armed troops surrounded the building.*
4 SOUND the sound made by a bell: *a ring at the doorbell* → see picture on page A7
5 CRIMINAL GROUP a group of people who illegally control a business or criminal activity: *a drugs ring*
6 ON A COOKER *BrE* one of the circular areas on top of a COOKER that is heated by gas or electricity SYN **burner** *AmE* → **hob**
7 CIRCUS/BOXING a square or circular area surrounded by seats where BOXING or a CIRCUS takes place: *a boxing ring*
PHRASES
give sb a ring *BrE informal* to telephone someone: *I'll give you a ring at the weekend.* THESAURUS PHONE
have the/a ring of sth if what someone says has a ring of truth, confidence etc, it seems to have this quality: *The story has the ring of truth.*
ring finger the finger next to the smallest finger on your hand that you usually wear your wedding ring on

ring² *v* (*past tense* **rang** /ræŋ/, *past participle* **rung** /rʌŋ/)
1 TELEPHONE SOUND [I] if a telephone rings, it makes a sound to show that someone is calling you: *The phone hasn't stopped ringing all day.* THESAURUS PHONE

2 BELL **a)** [I,T] if you ring a bell, you make it produce a sound: *I rang the doorbell, but no one came.* | **[+for]** *The sign said 'Ring for service'.* **b)** [I] if a bell rings, it makes a sound: *I heard the church bells ringing.*
3 CALL SB (*also* **ring up**) [I,T] *BrE* to telephone someone SYN **phone, call**: *I rang you yesterday, but you weren't in.* | *I rang up and made an appointment.* | **[+for]** *Sally rang for a taxi.*
4 EARS [I] if your ears ring, they are filled with a continuous sound after hearing something loud: *The explosion made our ears ring.*
PHRASES
not ring true if something does not ring true, you do not believe it: *His excuse didn't ring true.*
ring a bell *informal* if something rings a bell, it seems familiar but you cannot remember exact details about it: *Her name rings a bell, but I can't remember her face.*

PHRASAL VERBS
ring sb **back** *BrE* to telephone someone later SYN **call back**: *I'm busy at the moment. Can I ring you back?*
ring off *BrE* to end a telephone call: *He rang off without giving his name.*
ring out *written* to make a loud and clear sound: *The sound of a shot rang out.*

ring³ *v* [T] (*past tense and past participle* **ringed**)
1 to surround something: *The police ringed the building.* **2** *BrE* to draw a circular mark around something SYN **circle**: *Ring the mistakes in red.*

ringleader /ˈrɪŋliːdə $ -ər/ *n* [C] someone who leads a group that is doing something wrong: *Police caught three of the gang, but the ringleader escaped.* THESAURUS LEADER

ringlet /ˈrɪŋlɪt/ *n* [C] a long curl of hair

'ring road *n* [C] *BrE* a road that goes around a large town to keep traffic away from the centre THESAURUS ROAD

ringtone /ˈrɪŋtəʊn $ -toʊn/ *n* [C] the sound made by a MOBILE PHONE when someone is calling it

rink /rɪŋk/ *n* [C] an area where you can ICE SKATE or ROLLER SKATE

rinse /rɪns/ *v* [T] to wash something in clean water in order to remove soap or dirt from it: *Rinse the lettuce in cold water.* | **rinse sth out** *He rinsed out a glass and poured himself a whisky.* THESAURUS WASH —**rinse** *n* [C]: *I'll just give this shirt a quick rinse.*

riot¹ /ˈraɪət/ *n* [C] when a crowd of people behave violently in a public place: *His death triggered race riots.* THESAURUS FIGHT
PHRASES
run riot to become impossible to control: *Some parents just let their children run riot.*

riot² *v* [I] if a crowd of people riot, they behave violently in a public place —**rioter** *n* [C] —**rioting** *n* [U]: *Rioting broke out in the city last night.*

riotous /ˈraɪətəs/ *adj* **1** noisy, excited, and enjoyable in an uncontrolled way: *riotous celebrations* **2** noisy and violent in an uncontrolled way: *riotous crowds*

rip[1] /rɪp/ v (**ripped, ripping**) **1** [I,T] to tear something, or become torn: *Her clothes had all been ripped.* | *Don't pull the curtain too hard or it'll rip.* | *Sue ripped the letter open.* **2** [T] to remove something quickly and violently, using your hands: **rip sth out/off/away/down** *He ripped off his clothes and jumped into the pool.*

PHRASAL VERBS

rip sb/sth ↔ **off** *informal* **1** to charge someone too much money for something: *Banks have been ripping people off for years.* **2** to steal something: *Somebody had come in and ripped off the TV and stereo.*

rip sth ↔ **up** to tear something into a lot of pieces: *She ripped his photo up into tiny bits.*

rip[2] *n* [C] a hole in a piece of clothing or material where it has torn

ripe /raɪp/ *adj* fruit that is ripe is ready to eat: *Those peaches don't look ripe yet.* | *ripe tomatoes* —**ripen** *v* [I,T]: *The apples were ripened to perfection.*

PHRASES

be ripe for sth to be ready for a change to happen, especially when it should have happened sooner: *The area is ripe for development.* | **The time is ripe** (=it is the right time) *for trade talks.*

ripoff /'rɪpɒf $ -ɒːf/ *n* [C] *informal* something that is much too expensive: *The drinks in the hotel bar are a ripoff!*

RIPPLES

ripple /'rɪpəl/ *n* [C] **1** a small wave: *A gentle breeze made ripples on the lake.* **2** a feeling or sound that spreads from one person to another: **[+of]** *A ripple of laughter ran through the audience.* —**ripple** *v* [I,T]: *a flag rippling in the wind*

rise[1] /raɪz/ *v* [I] (*past tense* **rose** /rəʊz $ roʊz/, *past participle* **risen** /'rɪzən/)
1 INCREASE if an amount rises, it increases SYN **go up** OPP **fall**: *World oil prices are rising.* | *The population has risen steadily since the 1950s.* | **[+by]** *Salaries rose by 10% last year.* | **[+to/from]** *The research budget rose to £22.5 million.* | **rise from sth to sth** *The cost has risen from $100 to $200.* THESAURUS▶
INCREASE
2 MOVE UPWARDS (*also* **rise up**) to move upwards: *Flood waters are still rising in parts of Missouri.* | **[+from]** *Smoke rose from the chimney.*
3 STAND to stand up: *Everyone rose as the judge entered the courtroom.* | **[+from]** *Suddenly, Holmes rose from his chair and began shouting.* | *Thornton rose to his feet and turned to speak to them.*

4 BECOME IMPORTANT/POWERFUL to become important, powerful, successful, or rich OPP **fall**: **[+to]** *Mussolini rose to power in Italy in 1922.*
5 FEELING if a feeling or emotion rises, you begin to notice and feel it more and more strongly: *You could feel the excitement rising as we waited.*
6 SUN/MOON if the sun or moon rises, it appears in the sky OPP **set**: *The sun rises at around 6 am.*
7 BE TALL (*also* **rise up**) *written* if a mountain, building, tree etc rises, it is taller than anything else around it: *They could see Mount Shasta rising in the distance.*
8 REBEL (*also* **rise up**) *written* if a large group of people rise, they try to defeat the government, army etc that is controlling them: **[+against]** *In 1917 the Russian people rose against the Czar.*
PHRASES

rise to the occasion/challenge to deal successfully with a difficult situation, especially by working harder or performing better than usual: *She's a young athlete who can certainly rise to the occasion.*

PHRASAL VERBS

rise above sth to not let a bad situation affect you: *The President needs to rise above criticism of his administration.*

> **Word Choice**: rise or raise?
> If something **rises**, it increases: *Unemployment has risen by 800,000.* | *the rising cost of fuel*
> If you **raise** prices, taxes, profits etc, you make them increase: *The company raised the price of its coffee by 23%.*
> Do not say 'The government plans to rise the price of cigarettes.' Say *The government plans to raise the price of cigarettes.*

rise[2] *n* **1** [C] an increase OPP **fall**: *a tax rise* | **[+in]** *a sudden rise in temperature* | **[+of]** *a rent rise of more than 15%* **2** [C] *BrE* an increase in wages SYN **raise** *AmE*: *a pay rise* | *We got a 4% rise last year.* **3** [singular] when someone or something becomes more important, more successful, or more powerful OPP **fall**: **[+to]** *Stalin's rise to power* **4** [C] a slope that goes up: *a slight rise in the road*
PHRASES

give rise to sth *formal* to be the reason why something happens, especially something bad: *His speech gave rise to a bitter argument.*

riser /'raɪzə $ -ər/ *n* **early/late riser** someone who usually gets up early or late in the morning

risk[1] /rɪsk/ *n*
1 [C,U] a possibility that something bad or dangerous may happen → **danger**, **chance**: **[+of]** *the risk of serious injury* | **[+(that)]** *There is a real risk that the wheat crop may be lost.* | **[+to]** *Scientists believe there is no risk to public health.*
2 [C] something or someone that is likely to be dangerous: **[+to]** *Heart disease is the greatest **health risk** (=something likely to harm people's health) to women over 50.* | *The tire dump is a major **fire risk** (=something that could cause a fire).*
PHRASES

at your own risk if you do something at your own risk, you have been warned about the possible

dangers and you understand that no one else is responsible if something bad happens: *Cars are left at your own risk.*
at risk in a situation where you may suffer or be harmed: **[+from]** *people at risk from AIDS* | **[+of]** *Many high school boys are at risk of joining gangs.* | *The smallest mistake could put patients at risk.*
run the risk to be in a situation where there is a possibility that something bad could happen to you: **run the risk of doing sth** *Travellers without passports run the risk of being arrested.*
take a risk to do something even though you know it is dangerous or you may not succeed: *Are you willing to take the risk?* | **take the risk of doing sth** *I couldn't take the risk of leaving him alone.*

COLLOCATIONS
adjectives
a high/low risk *a high risk of failure*
a big/great/considerable risk *There's a big risk that something could go wrong.*
a small/slight risk *The risk of infection is small.*
a real risk *Thousands of people face a real risk of losing their homes.*
a serious risk (=real and big) *There is no serious risk to your health from this treatment.*

verbs
to carry/involve a risk *Most sports carry some risk.*
to pose a risk *formal: Smoking poses serious risks to health.*
to reduce/increase a risk *This diet could reduce your risk of certain cancers.*
to be worth the risk *It's not worth the risk to cycle without a helmet.*

noun + risk
an element/degree of risk (=some risk, but not much) *There is an element of risk in most investments.*

---

risk² *v* [T]
1 if you risk your life, money etc, you do something that may make you lose it: *He risked his life helping others to escape.* | **risk sth to do sth** *He had a dream and was willing to risk everything to follow it.* | **risk sth on sth** *You'd be crazy to risk your money on an investment like that!*
2 to do something that may be dangerous or may cause something bad to happen: **risk doing sth** *I wasn't prepared to risk losing my business.* | *You could slip out of school between classes, but I wouldn't risk it.*
3 risk death/punishment/defeat etc to do something that could result in your being killed, punished etc: *She was willing to risk arrest in order to protect her children.*

risky /ˈrɪski/ *adj* involving a risk that something bad or dangerous will happen: *a risky financial investment*
THESAURUS ▶ **DANGEROUS**

risqué /ˈrɪskeɪ $ rɪˈskeɪ/ *adj* a joke, remark etc that is risqué is slightly shocking because it is about sex

rite /raɪt/ *n* [C] a ceremony that is always performed in the same way, especially for religious purposes: *funeral rites*

---

ritual /ˈrɪtʃuəl/ *n* [C,U] a ceremony or set of actions that is always done in the same way: *church rituals* —**ritual** *adj: a ritual dance* —**ritually** *adv*

rival¹ /ˈraɪvəl/ *n* [C] a person or group that you compete with: *The two teams had always been rivals.* —**rival** *adj: rival gangs*

rival² *v* [T] (**rivalled, rivalling** *BrE*, **rivaled, rivaling** *AmE*) if one thing rivals another, it is as good as the other thing: *The college's facilities rival those of Yale or Harvard.*

rivalry /ˈraɪvəlri/ *n* [C,U] (*plural* **rivalries**) when people or groups try to show that they are better than each other: *There is a friendly rivalry between the two teams.*

RIVER

river

canal

stream

river /ˈrɪvə $ -ər/ *n* [C] a long area of water that flows into a sea → **stream**: *the River Thames* | *I went for a walk along the river.* | *We saw a group of boats sailing on the river.*

COLLOCATIONS
verbs
a river runs/flows *A river runs through the town.*
a river winds (=has many curves) *He could see the river winding across the plain.*
to cross a river *We looked for a safe place to cross the river.*
to go/sail down a river *They sailed down the River Nile.*

adjectives
a wide/broad river *The road continued across a wide river.*
a long river *The Sacramento is the longest river in California.*

---

riverside /ˈrɪvəsaɪd $ -ər-/ *n* [singular] the land along the sides of a river: *riverside apartments*

rivet¹ /ˈrɪvɪt/ *v* **be riveted** if you are riveted by something, you cannot stop looking at it or listening to it because it is very interesting: *People sat riveted to their TVs during the trial.* —**riveting** *adj: a riveting movie*

R

rivet² n [C] a metal pin used to fasten pieces of metal together

roach /rəʊtʃ $ roʊtʃ/ n [C] AmE a COCKROACH

road /rəʊd $ roʊd/ n [C,U] a hard surface that cars and other vehicles travel on: *Her address is 25 Park Road.* | *Is this **the road to** Stratford?* | **on/in the road** *There were loads of cars parked on the road.* | **up/down the road** *The boys go to the school down the road.* | *An old man cycled **along the road**.* | *We stopped and had something to eat **by the side of the road**.* | *There's a tyre **in the middle of the road**.* | *I saw some bushes **on the other side of the road**.* → A-ROAD, B-ROAD, RING ROAD, SLIP ROAD, TRUNK ROAD

PHRASES

by road in a car, bus etc: *If we go by road, it will take at least eight hours.*

be on the road to be travelling for a long distance, especially in a car: *We've been on the road since 7:00 a.m.*

COLLOCATIONS

adjectives

a busy/main road (=used by a lot of traffic) *The children have to cross a busy road to get to school.*

a quiet road (=with little traffic) *At that time of night, the roads were quiet.*

a side road/a back road (=a small road that is not used much) *Soon he turned down a side road that led to the house.*

a wide/narrow road *I couldn't turn the car round in the narrow road.*

noun + road

a country road *We drove along quiet country roads.*

a mountain road *The mountain roads are often blocked by snow.*

verbs

to go/drive along a road *I was going along the road at about 30 miles an hour.*

to cross a road (=to walk across it) *A group of children were waiting to cross the road.*

a road leads/goes somewhere *Which of these roads leads to the centre of town?*

road + noun

a road accident *I was badly hurt in a road accident.*

road safety *We aim to teach children about road safety.*

THESAURUS

types of road

road a hard surface that cars and other vehicles travel on: *Are we on the right road to Kingsgate?*

street a road in a town, usually with houses or shops on each side: *The streets were crowded with shoppers.*

avenue a road in a town, often with trees on each side: *the broad avenues of central Berlin*

high street BrE, **main street** AmE a road in the middle of a town where most of the shops, offices etc are: *We walked along the high street.*

lane a narrow road in the country: *a country lane*

track a narrow rough road in the country, which does not have a proper surface: *The farm is down a long dirt track.*

bypass a road that goes past a town, so that traffic can avoid the city centre

ring road a road that goes around the edge of a town

a big road

motorway BrE, **highway** AmE a wide road that connects towns and cities, for travelling fast over long distances: *It would be quicker to go on the motorway.*

freeway/expressway AmE a very wide fast road that takes traffic into and out of a big city: *They took the freeway to the airport.*

roadblock /'rəʊdblɒk $ 'roʊdblɑːk/ n [C] a place where the police or army have blocked the road: *The police have **set up roadblocks** to catch the two men.*

'road rage n [U] when drivers become angry and start shouting at or attacking other drivers

roadside /'rəʊdsaɪd $ 'roʊd-/ n [singular] the land at the edge of a road: *a roadside café*

roadway /'rəʊdweɪ $ 'roʊd-/ n [C] the part of the road used by vehicles

roadworks /'rəʊdwɜːks $ 'roʊdwɜːrks/ n [plural] BrE work that is being done to repair a road

roadworthy /'rəʊd,wɜːði $ 'roʊd,wɜːr-/ adj a vehicle that is roadworthy is in good condition and safe enough to drive

roam /rəʊm $ roʊm/ v [I,T] to walk or travel all over a place: *Teenage gangs **roamed the streets**.* | **[+around/over/through etc]** *bears roaming through the forest*

roar /rɔː $ rɔːr/ v **1** [I] to make a deep very loud noise: *We heard a lion roar.* | *The wind roared as she opened the front door.* THESAURUS NOISE **2** [I] if a vehicle roars somewhere, it moves very quickly and noisily: **[+past/off etc]** *A truck roared past.* **3** [I,T] to shout with a deep loud voice: *'Get out of here now!' he roared.* —**roar** n [C]: *a roar of laughter*

roaring /'rɔːrɪŋ/ adj **1** making a deep very loud continuous noise: *roaring floodwaters* **2** **roaring fire** a fire that burns with a lot of flames and heat **3** extremely successful: *The souvenir shops **do a roaring trade**.* | *The show was **a roaring success**.*

roast¹ /rəʊst $ roʊst/ v [I,T] to cook meat or vegetables in an OVEN or over a fire → see picture at COOK¹ THESAURUS COOK

roast² n [C] **1** a large piece of roasted meat **2** AmE an outdoor party where you cook food on an open fire: *a pig roast* —**roast** adj [only before noun]: *roast beef*

rob /rɒb $ rɑːb/ v [T] (**robbed, robbing**)

1 to steal money or other things from a bank, shop, or person → **burgle, steal**: *The two men were jailed for robbing a bank.* | **rob sb of sth** *Thieves robbed the woman of $70,000 in jewelry.* THESAURUS STEAL

2 rob sb/sth of sth to take away an important quality, ability etc from someone or something: *The disease has robbed him of his ability to speak.*

Word Choice: rob, steal, or take?
Someone **robs** a place or person: *The men robbed a bank and got away with over $2 million.* | *They robbed him of all his money.*
Someone **steals** something **from** a person or a place: *Thieves stole the car from outside his home.* Do not say 'They robbed all her money.' Say *They stole all her money.* or *They robbed her of all her money.*
In everyday English, people often use **take** in the same meaning as **steal**: *They took all her money.*

robber /'rɒbə $ 'rɑːbər/ n [C] someone who steals money or other things from a bank, shop etc: *a bank robber* THESAURUS **THIEF**

robbery /'rɒbəri $ 'rɑː-/ n [C,U] (*plural* **robberies**) the crime of stealing money or other things from a bank, shop etc: *They're in prison for **armed robbery*** (=robbery with a gun). THESAURUS **CRIME**

robe /rəʊb $ roʊb/ n [C] **1** a long loose piece of clothing that people wear especially for formal ceremonies: *a judge's robe* **2** *AmE* a DRESSING GOWN

robin /'rɒbɪn $ 'rɑː-/ n [C] a small brown bird with a red chest

robot /'rəʊbɒt $ 'roʊbɑːt, -bət/ n [C] a machine that can move and do jobs like a person: *cars built by robots* —**robotic** /rəʊ'bɒtɪk $ roʊ'bɑː-/ adj

robust /rə'bʌst, 'rəʊbʌst $ rə'bʌst, 'roʊ-/ adj strong and not likely to become ill or be damaged: *a surprisingly robust 70-year-old* | *a robust structure*

rock¹ /rɒk $ rɑːk/ n
1 [U] the hard substance in the Earth's surface that cliffs and mountains are made of → **stone**: *Pluto is made of ice and rock.* | *a tunnel cut through **solid rock*** **2** [C] a large piece of stone: *Jack stood on a rock for a better view.* | *The storm drove their ship onto **the rocks*** (=a line of rocks under or next to the sea).
3 (*also* **rock music**) [U] a type of popular modern music with a strong loud beat: *a rock band* | *a rock concert* | *Their music is a mixture of rock and disco.*
PHRASES
be on the rocks a relationship or business that is on the rocks is having a lot of problems and will probably fail soon: *I'm afraid Tim's **marriage is on the rocks.***

rock² v **1** [I,T] if something rocks, or if you rock it, it moves gently from side to side → **sway**: *Jane sat rocking the baby.* | *The boat rocked slowly.* THESAURUS **MOVE** **2** [T] *written* to shock and frighten a large number of people: *a city rocked by violence*
PHRASES
rock the boat *informal* to upset people in a group by criticizing or trying to change something that everyone else is satisfied with: *I didn't want to rock the boat, so I kept quiet.*

rock and roll /ˌrɒk ən 'rəʊl $ ˌrɑːk ən 'roʊl/ n [U] ROCK 'N' ROLL

rock 'bottom n **hit/reach rock bottom** *informal* to become as bad as it is possible to be: *By June, their marriage had hit rock bottom.*

rock-'bottom adj *informal* rock-bottom prices are as low as they can be

rocker /'rɒkə $ 'rɑːkər/ n [C] *AmE* a ROCKING CHAIR

rocket¹ /'rɒkɪt $ 'rɑː-/ n [C] **1** a long thin vehicle that carries people or scientific equipment into space: *a Soviet space rocket* **2** a long thin weapon that carries a bomb and is fired from a plane, ship etc: *anti-tank rockets* **3** a FIREWORK that goes high into the air and explodes

rocket² v [I] *informal* to increase very quickly: *The price of coffee has rocketed.*

'rocking chair n [C] a chair with curved pieces of wood on the bottom that allow it to move backwards and forwards when you sit on it → see picture at **CHAIR¹**

'rock ˌmusic n [U] a type of popular modern music with a strong loud beat

rock 'n' roll /ˌrɒk ən 'rəʊl $ ˌrɑːk ən 'roʊl/ n [U] a type of music with a strong loud beat for dancing

rocky /'rɒki $ 'rɑːki/ adj covered with rocks or made of rock: *the rocky coast of Maine*

rod /rɒd $ rɑːd/ n [C] a long thin pole or stick: *a fishing rod*

rode /rəʊd $ roʊd/ v the past tense of RIDE

rodent /'rəʊdənt $ 'roʊ-/ n [C] an animal such as a rat or a rabbit that has long sharp front teeth

rodeo /'rəʊdiəʊ, rəʊ'deɪ-əʊ $ 'roʊdioʊ, roʊ'deɪ-oʊ/ n [C] (*plural* **rodeos**) a show in which COWBOYS ride wild horses and catch cattle with ropes

roe /rəʊ $ roʊ/ n [C,U] fish eggs

rogue¹ /rəʊg $ roʊg/ n [C] *old-fashioned* a man or boy who behaves badly or is not honest

rogue² adj [only before noun] not behaving in the usual or accepted way and often causing trouble: *rogue regimes* that may have nuclear weapons

role Ac /rəʊl $ roʊl/ n [C]
1 the way in which someone or something is involved in an activity or situation: [+of] *What is the role of the sales manager?* | [+in] *the diet's role in the prevention of disease* | *The company **plays a** major **role in** the world's economy.*
2 a character in a play or film: [+of] *Brendan will **play the role** of Romeo.*

'role ˌmodel n [C] someone you admire and try to copy: *I try to be a **positive role model** for my kids.*

'role-play n [C,U] a training activity in which you pretend to be in a particular situation, especially to help you learn a language: *Language teachers often use role-play in the classroom.* THESAURUS **PRETEND** —**role-playing** n [U]

roll¹ /rəʊl $ roʊl/ v
1 TURN OVER [I,T] to move somewhere smoothly by turning over many times like a ball, or to make something do this: [+down/into/through etc] *The ball rolled across the lawn.* | *roll sth down/along/in etc sth They rolled the barrel down the hill.*
2 TURN YOUR BODY OVER (*also* **roll over**) [I,T] to turn your body over when you are lying down, or to turn someone else's body over: [+down/onto/off etc] *Beth's dog had been rolling in the mud.* | *roll sb onto/off sth We rolled him onto his back to see if he was still breathing.*
3 VEHICLE/STH WITH WHEELS **a)** [I] if a vehicle rolls, it

moves on its own, with no one driving it: **[+into/ forwards/past etc]** *The car was starting to roll down the hill.* **b)** [T] to make something that has wheels move: **roll sth to/around etc sth** *The waitress rolled the dessert trolley over to our table.*

4 TEARS ETC [I] if a drop of liquid rolls down, off etc something, it moves over a surface smoothly without stopping: **[+down/off/onto etc]** *Tears rolled down his cheeks.*

5 MAKE STH INTO TUBE/BALL [T] to make something into the shape of a tube or ball: *Bob rolled another cigarette.*

6 MAKE STH FLAT (*also* **roll out**) [T] to make something flat by moving a round and heavy object over it → **rolling pin**: *Roll the pastry out.*

PHRASES

(all) rolled into one if something or someone is several different things all rolled into one, they include qualities of all these things: *While making the film, he was the producer, director, and writer all rolled into one.*

be rolling in it/money *informal* to be very rich: *Her parents are rolling in it.*

PHRASAL VERBS

roll in *informal* to begin to arrive in large amounts: *The money soon came rolling in.*

roll up

1 roll sth ↔ up to bend something so that it is in the shape of a ball or a tube: *Painters arrived and rolled up the carpet.* | *a rolled-up newspaper*

2 roll your sleeves up to start doing a difficult or unpleasant job

3 *informal* to arrive late: *David rolled up after everyone else had left.*

roll² *n* [C] **1** a piece of paper, plastic etc that has been curled into the shape of a tube: **[+of]** *a roll of toilet paper* | *rolls of film* **2** a small round LOAF of bread for one person → **bun 3** an official list of names SYN **register**: *the union membership roll* **4 roll of fat** a layer of skin or fat around your waist → **ROCK AND ROLL, SAUSAGE ROLL, TOILET ROLL**

PHRASES

be on a roll *informal* to be having a lot of success with what you are doing: *We were on a roll, having won all six of our last games.*

'roll call *n* [C,U] when someone reads out all the names on a list to check who is there

roller /ˈrəʊlə $ ˈroʊlər/ *n* [C] **1** a tube-shaped piece of wood, metal etc that can be rolled over and over, used for painting, crushing etc: *a paint roller* **2** a small plastic or metal tube used for making hair curl

Rollerblade /ˈrəʊləbleɪd $ ˈroʊlər-/ *n* [C] *trademark* a boot with a single row of wheels fixed under it that you wear for SKATING → **roller skate** → see picture at **SKATE¹** —**rollerblade** *v* [I] —**rollerblading** *n* [U]

'roller ˌcoaster *n* [C] a small railway that carries people up and down a steep track very fast for fun → see picture at **FAIR³**

'roller skate *n* [C] a boot with four wheels fixed under it that you wear for SKATING → see picture at **SKATE¹** —**roller skate** *v* [I] —**roller skating** *n* [U]

rolling /ˈrəʊlɪŋ $ ˈroʊ-/ *adj* [only before noun] rolling hills have long gentle slopes

'rolling pin *n* [C] a long tube-shaped piece of wood used for making PASTRY flat and thin before you cook it → see picture at **KITCHEN**

ROM /rɒm $ rɑːm/ *n* [U] *technical* (**read-only memory**) the part of a computer where permanent instructions and information are stored → **RAM**

Roman /ˈrəʊmən $ ˈroʊ-/ *adj* relating to ancient Rome: *the Roman Empire* —**Roman** *n* [C]: *The Romans captured the city.*

ˌRoman ˈCatholic *adj* belonging or relating to the part of the Christian religion whose leader is the Pope —**Roman Catholic** *n* [C] —**Roman Ca'tholicism** *n* [U]

romance /rəʊˈmæns, ˈrəʊmæns $ roʊˈmæns, ˈroʊ-/ **1** [C,U] an exciting relationship between two people who love each other: *a summer romance* **2** [C] a story or film about two people who love each other **3** [U] the feeling of excitement and adventure that is related to a particular place, activity etc: **[+of]** *the romance of travelling to distant places*

ˌRoman ˈnumeral *n* [C] a number in a system that was used in ancient Rome, for example I, II, III, IV etc instead of 1, 2, 3, 4 etc

romantic¹ /rəʊˈmæntɪk, rə- $ roʊ-, rə-/ *adj* **1** related to love and with treating the person you love in a special way: *I wish my boyfriend was more romantic.* | *She enjoys romantic movies.*

2 based too much on the way you would like things to be, rather than on the way they really are OPP **realistic**: **romantic notion/view/idea etc** *her romantic dreams of becoming a famous writer* —**romantically** /-kli/ *adv*

romantic² *n* [C] someone who is not practical and thinks that things are better than they really are OPP **realist**: *an incurable romantic*

romanticize (*also* **-ise** *BrE*) /rəʊˈmæntəsaɪz, rə- $ roʊ-, rə-/ *v* [I,T] to talk or think about things in a way that makes them seem more attractive than they really are: *a romanticized idea of country life*

romp /rɒmp $ rɑːmp/ *v* [I] **1** to play in a noisy way, especially by running, jumping etc: **[+around/ about]** *They could hear the children romping around upstairs.* **2** to win a race, competition, election etc very easily: *Miano **romped to** an easy **victory**.* —**romp** *n* [C]: *the Yankees' 12–1 romp over the Red Sox*

roof /ruːf $ ruːf, rʊf/ *n* [C]

1 the part of a building or vehicle that covers the top of it: *He installed a satellite dish on the roof.* | **[+of]** *She had to jump from the roof of the building to escape.* | **flat/sloping/pitched roof**

2 the top of a PASSAGE under the ground: *The roof of the tunnel suddenly collapsed.*

PHRASES

a roof over your head somewhere to live: *I may not have a job, but at least I've got a roof over my head.*

hit the roof/go through the roof *spoken informal* to become very angry: *My wife is going to hit the roof when she finds out.*

the roof of your mouth the top part of the inside of your mouth
under one roof/under the same roof in the same building or house: *If we're going to **live under the same roof**, we need to get along.*

roofing /'ru:fɪŋ $ 'ru:f-, 'ruf-/ *n* [U] material used for roofs

'roof-rack *n* [C] *BrE* a metal frame fixed to the top of a car, used to carry bags etc SYN **luggage rack** *AmE* → see picture at **CAR**

rooftop /'ru:ftɒp $ 'ru:ftɑ:p, 'ruf-/ *n* [C] the top surface of a roof: *flying over the rooftops*

rook /ruk/ *n* [C] a large black bird

rookie /'ruki/ *n* [C] *AmE* someone who has just started doing a job or playing a sport: *rookie cops*

room¹ /ru:m, rum/ *n*
1 IN A BUILDING [C] a space in a building that is separated from the rest by walls and a door: *a hotel room* | *My brother is in the next room* (=the one beside the one you are in). | **sb's room** (=a room that someone uses regularly) *Which is Derek's room?* | **living/dining/meeting etc room** *the doctor's waiting room* | **single/double room** (=a hotel room for one person or for two) | **one-room(ed)/two-room(ed) etc** *a three-room apartment*
2 PEOPLE [singular] all the people in a room: *The whole room fell silent as he entered.*
3 SPACE [U] enough space for something or someone: **[+in]** *I hope there's room in the fridge.* | **[+for]** *Have you enough room for your legs?* | **room to do sth** *A bush needs plenty of room to grow.* | **make/leave room (for sb/sth)** (=move so that there is enough space) *Leave room for people to pass.* | *This desk takes up too much room* (=there is not enough space for it). | **leg/head room** (=space for your legs or head in a vehicle)
4 OPPORTUNITY [U] the possibility that something can happen or exist: **[+for]** *I always try to make room for meditation in my day.* | *The curriculum gives teachers little room for manoeuvre* (=the opportunity to change something). | *Good work is being done, but there's room for improvement* (=the possibility of doing better). → **CHATROOM, DRAWING ROOM, DRESSING ROOM, OPERATING ROOM, UTILITY ROOM**

room² *v* **room with sb** *AmE* to share a bedroom with someone who is not in your family, for example at college

roomful /'ru:mful, 'rum-/ *n* [C] a large number of people or things in a room: **[+of]** *a roomful of reporters*

roommate /'ru:m,meɪt, 'rum-/ *n* [C] someone who is not in your family who shares a bedroom with you, for example at college

'room ,service *n* [U] a service that a hotel provides to bring food, drinks etc to your room

roomy /'ru:mi/ *adj* with plenty of space inside: *a roomy car*

roost /ru:st/ *n* [C] a place where birds sleep —**roost** *v* [I]
PHRASES
rule the roost to be the most powerful and important person in a place: *She likes to think that she rules the roost.*

rooster /'ru:stə $ -ər/ *n* [C] a male chicken → see picture at **CHICKEN**

root¹ /ru:t/ *n* [C]
1 OF A PLANT the part of a plant that grows under the ground and gets water from the soil: *tree roots* | *Be careful not to break the roots.* → see picture at **PLANT¹**
2 OF TOOTH/HAIR the part of a tooth, hair etc that is under the skin
3 ORIGIN **roots** [plural] the place where someone or something began: **[+in]** *Jazz has roots in slave songs.* | **sb's roots** (=the connection someone feels with the place where their family came from) *She's very proud of her Jamaican roots.* | *He enjoys **returning to his roots**.* THESAURUS **ORIGIN**
4 CAUSE the basic cause of a problem: **at/to the root of sth** *Religion lies at the root of the conflict.* | *A good mechanic will get to the root of the problem.* | *the root causes of crime* → **GRASS ROOTS, SQUARE ROOT**
PHRASES
take root if something takes root, it starts to exist: *Economic recovery is beginning to take root.*

root² *v* [I] to search for something by moving things SYN **rummage:** **[+around/through/among etc]** *She rooted in her bag for a pen.*
PHRASES
be rooted in sth to have developed from something and to be strongly influenced by it: *feelings rooted in childhood*
rooted to the spot so shocked or frightened that you cannot move: *She stood rooted to the spot, staring in disbelief.*
PHRASAL VERBS
root for sb *informal* to support and encourage someone to succeed
root sth ↔ **out** to completely remove a problem: *We must root out bullying in schools.*

rope¹ /rəup $ roup/ *n*
1 [C,U] very strong thick string: *a skipping rope* | *pieces of rope tied to a tree* → see picture at **STRING¹**
2 the ropes [plural] the things someone needs to know in order to do a job: *I spent the first month learning the ropes.* | *Miss McGinley will show you the ropes.*
PHRASES
be at/near the end of your rope *AmE* to have no more strength or ability to deal with a difficult situation: *With three kids and no money, I'm at the end of my rope.*
on the ropes *informal* if you are on the ropes, you are likely to fail or be defeated: *The army says the rebels are on the ropes.*

rope² *v* [T] to tie things or people together, using rope: **rope sth to sth** | **rope sb/sth together** *The climbers were roped together for safety.*
PHRASAL VERBS
rope sb ↔ **in** *informal* to persuade someone to help you: **rope sb in to do sth** *I've been roped in to help.*

ropey, ropy /'rəupi $ 'rou-/ *adj BrE informal* not in good condition or not good quality

rosary /'rəuzəri $ 'rou-/ *n* [C] (*plural* **rosaries**) a string of BEADS (=small round balls), used by Roman Catholics when they pray

rose¹ /rəʊz $ roʊz/ n [C] a beautiful sweet-smelling flower that grows on a bush with sharp THORNS → see picture at **FLOWER¹**

rose² v the past tense of RISE

rosé /ˈrəʊzeɪ $ roʊˈzeɪ/ n [U] pink wine

rosemary /ˈrəʊzməri $ ˈroʊzmeri/ n [U] the narrow leaves of a bush, used as a herb

rosette /rəʊˈzet $ roʊ-/ n [C] a circular decoration made of coloured silk that you wear to show you have won a prize or to show that you support a particular political party

roster /ˈrɒstə $ ˈrɑːstər/ n [C] AmE a list of names showing the jobs that each person on the list must do and when they must do them **SYN** rota BrE

rostrum /ˈrɒstrəm $ ˈrɑː-/ n [C] a small raised area that someone stands on, for example to make a speech

rosy /ˈrəʊzi $ ˈroʊ-/ adj **1** showing hope of success or happiness: The company has a **rosy future**. **2** pink and healthy-looking: children with **rosy cheeks**

rot¹ /rɒt $ rɑːt/ v [I,T] (**rotted, rotting**) if something rots, or if something rots it, it goes bad and breaks into pieces because it is old, wet etc **SYN** decay: rotting vegetables | Sugary drinks **rot** your teeth. | The wooden stairs had **rotted away**.

rot² n [U] **1** the natural process that happens when something gets older and begins to go bad **SYN** decay: a tree full of rot **2** the rot informal a bad situation that is getting worse: how to **stop the rot** | **the rot set in** (=a situation started to get worse) After he left, the rot started to set in.

rota /ˈrəʊtə $ ˈroʊ-/ n [C] BrE a list of names showing the jobs that each person on the list must do and when they must do them **SYN** roster AmE

rotary /ˈrəʊtəri $ ˈroʊ-/ adj turning in a circle from a fixed point

rotate /rəʊˈteɪt $ ˈroʊteɪt/ v [I,T] **1** to turn around from a fixed point, or to make something do this: The Earth rotates on its axis. | **rotate sth to/towards/away from etc sth** Rotate the handle to the right. **THESAURUS** TURN **2** to change the use or position that things or people have, following a regular pattern: The presidency rotates yearly. | Rotating the type of crops you grow will improve the soil. —**rotation** /rəʊˈteɪʃən $ roʊ-/ n [C,U]: We work nights **in rotation**.

rote /rəʊt $ roʊt/ n **learn sth by rote** to learn something by repeating it but not really understanding it

rotor /ˈrəʊtə $ ˈroʊtər/ n [C] a part of a machine that turns around from a fixed point

rotten /ˈrɒtn $ ˈrɑːtn/ adj **1** rotten food or wood is in bad condition because it is old **SYN** decayed: rotten apples **2** informal old-fashioned unkind or unfair

rottweiler /ˈrɒtvaɪlə, -waɪlə $ ˈrɑːtwaɪlər/ n [C] a type of large strong dog

rotund /rəʊˈtʌnd $ roʊ-/ adj formal having a fat round body

rough¹ /rʌf/ adj

1 NOT SMOOTH not smooth or even **OPP** smooth: rough ground | rough skin | his rough voice → see picture at **SMOOTH¹**

2 NOT EXACT a rough description or idea is not exact and has few details → **approximate**: Can you give us a **rough idea** of the cost? | a **rough draft** of an essay

3 DIFFICULT if your life or a period of time is rough, it is difficult and unpleasant **SYN** tough: Sounds like you had a **rough day** at work. | We've seen some **rough times** together. | My boyfriend and I **hit a rough patch**. | Did you **have a rough night** (=did you sleep badly)?

4 VIOLENT violent, dangerous, or using too much force: Ice hockey is a rough sport. | a rough part of town | Don't be so rough with her. | A truck can withstand **rough treatment**. | The boat sank in rough seas. **THESAURUS** VIOLENT

5 NOT FAIR/NOT GENTLE unfair or unkind: **be rough on sb** I think you were a bit rough on her. | **rough justice** (=unfair or illegal punishment) rough justice handed out by street gangs

6 SIMPLY MADE simply made and often not completely finished: a rough wooden table | **rough and ready** (=not perfect, but good enough to use)

7 ILL BrE informal not feeling well: The next morning I felt pretty rough. —**roughness** n [U]

THESAURUS

rough having a surface that is not flat or smooth – used especially about the ground, a road, path etc. Rough is also used about skin: A rough path led down to the beach. | a cream for dry or rough skin

uneven an uneven surface has parts that are not all at the same level – used especially about the ground, the floor, or walls: It was an old house and the floor was uneven in places.

bumpy a bumpy road, path, or area of land is very rough, especially so that it makes you go up and down when you travel on it: The bus went along the bumpy road up the mountain.

coarse coarse cloth has a rough surface that feels slightly hard: He wore an old suit of coarse cloth.

---

rough² n **the rough** uneven ground with long grass on a golf course → **green**

PHRASES

take the rough with the smooth to accept the bad things in life as well as the good

rough³ v

PHRASES

rough it informal to live for a short time in uncomfortable conditions: She wasn't used to roughing it.

PHRASAL VERBS

rough sb ↔ **up** informal to attack and hurt someone by hitting them

rough⁴ adv **sleep/live rough** BrE to live outdoors because you have no home

roughage /ˈrʌfɪdʒ/ n [U] a substance in some foods that helps your BOWELS to work **SYN** fibre

rough-and-'tumble n [U] **1** noisy and violent play **2** a situation or activity that is busy and sometimes unpleasant for the people who are involved in it: [+of] the rough-and-tumble of political life

roughen /ˈrʌfən/ v [I,T] to make something uneven or not smooth

roughly /ˈrʌfli/ adv
1 not exactly **SYN about, approximately**: *roughly 100 people* | *I worked out the cost roughly.* **THESAURUS ▶ APPROXIMATELY**
2 violently or using force: *She pushed him away roughly.*

roughshod /ˈrʌfʃɒd $ -ʃɑːd/ adv **ride roughshod over sb/sth** *disapproving* to behave in a way that ignores other people's feelings or opinions

roulette /ruːˈlet/ n [U] a game in which you spin a ball on a moving wheel and people try to win money by guessing where the ball will stop

round¹ /raʊnd/ adj
1 shaped like a circle: *a round table* | *big round eyes* | *Cut a 2 cm round hole in the top.*
2 a round number is a whole number, often ending in 0: *Let's make it a round number, say $50?* | **in round figures** (=given as the nearest number to 10, 100, 1,000 etc) *In round figures, there are 30,000 students.* —**roundness** n [U]

round² *especially BrE* (also **around**) adv, prep
1 surrounding something: *We sat round the fire.* | *the path round the lake* | **Gather round** *for a story.* | *He put his arm round her waist.* → see picture on page A8
2 moving to face the opposite direction: **look/turn etc round** *I looked round to see who had come in.* | *Turn the picture* **the other way round.**
3 moving in a circle: *Bikes raced* **round and round.** | *fish swimming* **round in circles**
4 to different parts of a place: **go/travel etc round** *She spent her gap year travelling round Europe.* | **show sb round (sth)** (=show someone the different parts of a place) *A tour guide showed us round.*
5 on or to the other side of something: **[+to]** *She moved round to his side of the desk.* | *The two boys disappeared* **round the corner.**
6 to other people or positions: *Three men were* **passing** *a bottle* **round.**
7 if there is a way round a problem, there is a way to avoid it: *Somehow, the burglars had* **found a way round** *the alarm.*
8 *spoken* to someone's home: **come/go round** *What time are you coming round?* | *We've been invited round for dinner.*
9 *spoken* in a particular area: *Do you* **live round here?**
10 *spoken informal* **round about sth** nearly but not exactly: *I heard a scream round about midnight.*

round³ n [C]
1 **OF MEETINGS ETC** a set of related events that are part of a longer process: **[+of]** *the latest round of peace talks* | *endless rounds of meetings*
2 **OF A COMPETITION** a separate part of a competition, especially a sports competition → **heat, stage: first/ final/next etc round** *She made it to the second round.* | **[+of]** *the final round of the championship*
3 **OF GOLF** a complete game of golf: *We* **played** *a* **round** *of golf on Sunday.*
4 **OF DRINKS** if you buy a round of drinks in a bar, you buy a drink for each person in your group: **sb's round** (=when it is someone's turn to buy a round) *Whose round is it?*
5 **CLAPPING** **a round of applause** when people CLAP at the end of a speech, performance etc: *Let's give them* **a round of applause.**

6 **SHOT/BULLET** a shot from a gun, or a bullet you can fire from a gun: *He let off* **a round of ammunition.**

round⁴ v [T] to go around a bend, corner, piece of furniture etc: *The car* **rounded the bend** *at 75 mph.*

PHRASAL VERBS
round sth ↔ **down** to reduce a figure to the nearest whole number: **[+to]** *It cost £21.70, so we rounded it down to £20.*
round sth ↔ **off** to end something in a pleasant or suitable way: *Why not round off your visit at a night-club?*
round on sb to suddenly attack or criticize someone when they do not expect it: *After Miss Evans had left, Edward rounded on him angrily.*
round sb/sth ↔ **up 1** to find and bring together a group of people: *The police rounded 20 people up for questioning.* **2** to increase a figure to the nearest whole number

ROUNDABOUT *BrE/***TRAFFIC CIRCLE** *AmE*

roundabout¹ /ˈraʊndəbaʊt/ n [C] *BrE* **1** a circular area where roads meet and that cars must drive around **SYN traffic circle** *AmE: Turn left at the next roundabout.* **2** a round structure in a park that children sit on while it turns

roundabout² adj [only before noun] a roundabout way of saying or doing something is not clear, simple, or direct

rounded /ˈraʊndɪd/ adj curved

rounders /ˈraʊndəz $ -ərz/ n [U] a British ball game that is similar to baseball

roundly /ˈraʊndli/ adv if someone criticizes you roundly, they criticize you very strongly: *The administration has been* **roundly condemned** *for allowing it to happen.*

round-the-ˈclock adj happening all the time: *round-the-clock care*

round ˈtrip n [C] a journey to a place and back again —**round-trip** adj *AmE: a round-trip ticket*

roundup /ˈraʊndʌp/ n [C usually singular] **1** a short description of the main news on radio or television: **[+of]** *First, here's a roundup of the local news.* **2** when a lot of people or animals are brought together by force: **[+of]** *a roundup of criminal suspects*

rouse /raʊz/ v [T] **1** to make someone want to do something: *The speech roused King's supporters to action.* **2** *formal* to wake someone

rousing /ˈraʊzɪŋ/ adj making people excited and eager to do something: *a rousing speech*

rout /raʊt/ v [T] to defeat someone completely
—**rout** n [C]

route¹ Ac /ruːt $ ruːt, raʊt/ n [C]
1 the roads, paths etc that you follow to get from
one place to another: **[+to/from]** What's the quick-
est route to the station? | the most **direct route** home |
bus/shipping etc route a map of local bus routes |
take/follow a route Which is the best route to take? |
Cheering crowds **lined the route** (=stood in a line
along a road being used for a race, march etc).
2 a way of achieving something: **[+to]** Money is not
always the route to happiness. → **EN ROUTE**

route² Ac v [T] to send something or someone by
a particular route: Flights were routed through Paris
because of the snow.

routine¹ /ruːˈtiːn/ n **1** [C,U] the usual way that you
do things or the things you do regularly: **daily/
normal/usual routine** Making the beds was part of
her usual routine. | Try to **get into** a routine. **2** [C] a
series of movements or other actions that are performed regularly: my **exercise routine**

routine² /ruːˈtiːn◂/ adj happening as part of a
normal and regular process: a routine medical test |
routine jobs around the house **THESAURUS** **NORMAL**
—**routinely** adv

roving /ˈrəʊvɪŋ $ ˈroʊ-/ adj [only before noun]
travelling or moving from one place to another as
part of your job: **roving reporters**

row¹ /rəʊ $ roʊ/ n [C]
1 a line of things or people next to each other: **[+of]**
a row of houses | children standing **in a row**
2 a line of seats in a theatre, cinema etc → **DEATH
ROW**

PHRASES

twice/three times/four days etc in a row if something happens twice, three times etc in a row, it
happens twice, three times etc, and each occasion
is straight after the one before: She's lost three
times in a row.

row² v [I,T] to make a boat move across water,
using OARS (=long poles): They rowed across the lake.
→ see picture on page A9 —**rowing** n [U]

row³ /raʊ/ n BrE **1** [C] an argument **SYN** quarrel:
Anna and her boyfriend are **having** another row.
THESAURUS **ARGUMENT 2** [C] a situation in which
people disagree strongly about important public
affairs **SYN** controversy: **[+over]** a row over government cuts **3** [singular] an annoying loud noise
SYN racket, din

row⁴ /raʊ/ v [I] BrE to argue in an angry way
SYN quarrel: **[+about]** They rowed about money all
the time.

rowdy /ˈraʊdi/ adj behaving in a noisy and uncontrolled way: rowdy children **THESAURUS** **LOUD**

row house /ˈrəʊ haʊs $ ˈroʊ-/ n [C] AmE a house
that is joined to other houses on both sides
SYN terraced house BrE → see picture at **HOUSE¹**
THESAURUS **HOUSE**

rowing boat /ˈrəʊɪŋ bəʊt $ ˈroʊɪŋ boʊt/ BrE, row-
boat /ˈrəʊbəʊt $ ˈroʊboʊt/ AmE n [C] a small boat
that you move across water using OARS (=long
poles) → see picture at **TRANSPORT¹**

royal¹ /ˈrɔɪəl/ adj belonging to or connected with a
king or queen → **regal**: the royal family | the Royal
Navy

royal² n [C] a member of a royal family

,royal 'blue n [U] a strong bright blue colour
—**royal blue** adj

royalist /ˈrɔɪəlɪst/ n [C] someone who supports
the idea that a king or queen should rule their
country **OPP** republican

royalty /ˈrɔɪəlti/ n **1** [U] members of a royal family
2 royalties [plural] payment made to the writer of a
book or piece of music: How much did he get **in
royalties**?

rpm /ˌɑː piː ˈem $ ˌɑːr-/ (**revolutions per minute**)
used to describe how fast something such as an
engine or motor turns: 1200 rpm

RSI /ˌɑːr es ˈaɪ/ n [U] technical (**repetitive strain
injury**) pains in your hands, arms etc caused by
doing the same movements many times, especially
when using a computer

RSVP /ˌɑːr es viː ˈpiː/ used on invitations to ask
someone to reply

rub¹ /rʌb/ v [I,T] (**rubbed, rubbing**)
1 to move your hand, a cloth etc quickly backwards
and forwards over a surface: **rub sth with sth** She
rubbed her hair with a towel. | **rub sth into/onto etc
sth** Make sure you rub sunscreen into baby's delicate
skin. | **Rub** a bit **harder** (=with more force). | **rub
(sth) out/off** (=remove something by rubbing)
Don't worry, the marks will rub off. | **rub sth down**
(=rub something to make it dry, clean etc) Rub the
wood down with sandpaper.
2 to press against something and move backwards
and forwards: Are your shoes rubbing? | He smiled,
rubbing his hands at the prospect of a sale. | **rub (sth)
against/on sth** The cat rubbed against her legs, purr-
ing.

PHRASES

rub sb's nose in it/in the dirt informal to keep
reminding someone about something bad they
have done in order to punish or embarrass them:
There's no need to rub my nose in it!

rub salt into the wound to make a bad situation
even worse for someone: He didn't want to rub salt
into the wound. He just wanted to warn her.

rub shoulders with sb (also **rub elbows with sb**
AmE) informal to spend time with important or
famous people

rub sb up the wrong way informal to annoy someone by saying and doing things that make them
cross

PHRASAL VERBS

rub sth **in** to upset or annoy someone by reminding
them about something when you know that they
want to forget it: OK, there's no need to **rub it in**!

rub off if a person's behaviour rubs off on you, you
start to behave in the same way as them because
you are spending time together: **[+on]** Her positive
attitude rubs off on everyone.

rub² n **give sth a rub** to rub something for a short
time

rubber¹ /'rʌbə $ -ər/ n
1 [U] a strong substance used to make tyres, boots etc that is made from the juice of a tropical tree or chemicals: *The seal is **made of rubber**.*
2 [C] *BrE* a small piece of rubber used to remove pencil marks from paper SYN **eraser** *AmE* → see picture at **STATIONERY**
3 [C] a piece of wood or plastic with soft material on one side, used to remove marks from a BLACKBOARD SYN **eraser** *AmE*
4 [C] *informal* a CONDOM

rubber² *adj* made of rubber: *rubber gloves | a rubber ball* → see picture at **MATERIAL¹**

,rubber 'band n [C] a small thin circle of rubber, used to hold things together SYN **elastic band**

,rubber-'stamp v [T] *disapproving* to officially approve a plan or decision without considering it carefully

rubbery /'rʌbəri/ *adj disapproving* looking or feeling like rubber: *rubbery eggs*

rubbish /'rʌbɪʃ/ n [U] *BrE*
1 things that people throw away such as old food, dirty paper etc SYN **garbage** *AmE*: *household rubbish | a **rubbish bin** | a **pile of rubbish** | **rubbish dump/tip** (=a place to take rubbish)*
2 *informal* something you think is silly, wrong, or bad quality: *You do **talk rubbish** sometimes. | What **a load of rubbish**!*

rubble /'rʌbəl/ n [U] broken stones, bricks etc from a building that has been destroyed: *a **pile of rubble***

rubella /ruːˈbelə/ n [U] an infectious disease that makes red spots appear on your body SYN **German measles**

ruby /'ruːbi/ n [C] (*plural* **rubies**) a valuable dark red jewel —**ruby** *adj*: *a ruby ring*

rucksack /'rʌksæk/ n [C] *BrE* a bag that you carry on your back SYN **backpack** → see picture at **BAG¹**

rudder /'rʌdə $ -ər/ n [C] a flat part at the back of a boat or plane that you turn in order to change direction

ruddy /'rʌdi/ *adj* a ruddy face looks pink and healthy

rude /ruːd/ *adj*
1 speaking or behaving in a way that is not polite SYN **impolite**: *rude remark/comment The boys were making rude remarks about the teacher. | [+to] Don't be so rude to your mother! | It's rude to stare.*
2 rude words, jokes, songs etc are about sex SYN **dirty** —**rudely** *adv* —**rudeness** n [U]

THESAURUS

rude speaking or behaving in a way that is not polite: *It's rude to point at people. | a very rude woman*
impolite *formal* rude: *Elisa thought it would be impolite to refuse.*
cheeky *BrE*, **smart** *AmE* a little rude – used especially about children: *He's so cheeky sometimes. | Don't get smart with me!*
offensive making people feel upset or angry, especially because you do not show respect for their moral or religious beliefs: *Her remarks were deeply offensive to many Catholics.*

insulting speaking or behaving in a way that is very rude or offensive to someone: *His comments were insulting to women.*
bad-mannered behaving in a way that does not follow the rules of good social behaviour: *It's bad-mannered to leave the table while other people are still eating.*
tactless carelessly saying something that is likely to upset or embarrass someone, without intending to do this: *It was a bit tactless to bring up the subject of divorce.*

rudimentary /ˌruːdəˈmentəri◂/ *adj formal* very simple and basic: *a rudimentary knowledge of Chinese*

rudiments /'ruːdəmənts/ n [plural] *formal* the most basic parts of a subject: *[+of] the rudiments of grammar*

rueful /'ruːfəl/ *adj* showing that you wish something had not happened but that you accept it: *a rueful smile* —**ruefully** *adv*

ruffle¹ /'rʌfəl/ v [T] **1** to make a smooth surface uneven: *The wind **ruffled** his hair.* **2** to offend, annoy, or upset someone: *Don't let yourself get ruffled. | I don't want to **ruffle** his **feathers** (=upset him).*

ruffle² n [C] cloth sewn in folds as a decoration around the edges of a shirt, skirt etc

rug /rʌg/ n [C] **1** a piece of thick cloth or wool that is put on the floor as a decoration → carpet **2** *BrE* a type of BLANKET

rugby /'rʌgbi/ n [U] a game in which two teams carry, kick, or throw an OVAL ball → see picture on page A9

rugged /'rʌgɪd/ *adj* **1** land that is rugged is rough and uneven: *a rugged coastline* **2** a man who is rugged is attractive with strong features, which may not be perfect: *his rugged good looks* **3** a vehicle or piece of equipment that is rugged is strongly built

ruin¹ /'ruːɪn/ v [T]
1 to spoil or destroy something completely: *This new road will ruin the countryside. | One stupid comment had ruined everything.* THESAURUS **DESTROY**
2 to make someone lose all their money: *Jefferson was ruined by the court case against him.*

ruin² n **1** [U] a situation in which someone loses their social position or money, especially because of a business failure: *small businesses facing **financial ruin*** **2** [C] (*also* **ruins** [plural]) the part of a building that is left after the rest has been destroyed: *[+of] the ruins of the temple*

RUINS

PHRASES
fall/crumble into ruin if a building has fallen into ruin, it is in a bad condition because it has not been looked after: *The church had fallen into ruin.*
be in ruins to be badly damaged: *The country's economy is in ruins.*

ruinous /ˈruːɪnəs/ *adj* extremely damaging: *a ruinous decision*

rule¹ /ruːl/ *n*

1 [C] an official instruction about what is allowed, especially in a game, organization, or job → **law**, **regulation**: **[+of]** *Do you know the rules of the game?* | **[+about]** *There are strict rules about what you can wear.* | **against the rules** *It's against the rules* (=it's not allowed) *to pick up the ball.*

2 [C] what you should do in a particular situation: **The rule is:** *if you feel any pain, you should stop exercising.* | **The golden rule** (=the most important thing to remember) *in interviews is to listen carefully to the question.* | **[+of]** *the two basic rules of survival*

3 [singular] something that is normal or usually true: *I don't drink alcohol* **as a rule** (=usually). | **As a general rule,** *vegetable oils are much better for you than animal fats.* | *Not having a television is* **the exception rather than the rule** (=unusual).

4 [U] the government or control of a country: **under ... rule** (=controlled by that country or group) *At that time, Vietnam was under French rule.* | **colonial/military rule** *the end of British colonial rule*

5 [C] a statement of the correct way of doing something in a language, area of science etc: **[+of]** *the rules of grammar* → **GROUND RULES**

PHRASES

rule of thumb a general principle or method for calculating something: *As a rule of thumb, plant tall hedge plants two feet apart.*

COLLOCATIONS

verbs

to obey/follow a rule *If you don't obey the school rules, you get into trouble.*

to abide by/observe the rules *formal* (=to obey them) *All members agree to abide by the rules.*

to break/disobey a rule (=to not obey it) *He had broken one of the club rules.*

to make the rules *I'm only an assistant manager – I don't make the rules.*

to bend the rules (=to allow something that is not normally allowed) *She agreed to bend the rules and let me leave early.*

the rules say *The rules say that you must be 14 to use the gym.*

adjectives

strict rules *The rules about drinking on duty are very strict.*

petty rules (=unreasonable rules about unimportant things) *There are hundreds of petty rules.*

noun + rule

a school/prison/club etc rule

THESAURUS

rule an official instruction about what is allowed, especially in a game, organization, or job: *the rules of cricket* | *You are expected to obey the school rules.*

law an official rule that everyone in a country, city, or state must obey: *Congress has just passed a new law.*

regulation an official rule made by a government or organization, which is part of a set of rules: *the health and safety regulations*

guidelines rules or advice about the best way to do something: *guidelines for healthy eating*

rule² *v* **1** [I,T] to have the official power to control a country → **govern**: *The King ruled for 30 years.* **THESAURUS** **CONTROL 2** [T] if a feeling or desire rules someone, it has a powerful influence on their life: *Don't let your job* **rule your life.** **3** [I,T] to make an official decision about something such as a legal problem: **[+that]** *The judge ruled that the baby should live with his father.*

PHRASAL VERBS

rule sth/sb ↔ **out** to decide that something or someone is not possible or suitable: *We can't* **rule out the possibility** *that he may have left the country.*

ruled /ruːld/ *adj* ruled paper has lines printed across it

ruler /ˈruːlə $ -ər/ *n* [C]

1 someone such as a king who has official power over a country **THESAURUS** **LEADER**

2 a flat narrow piece of plastic, wood, or metal that you use for measuring things and drawing straight lines → see picture at **STATIONERY**

ruling¹ /ˈruːlɪŋ/ *n* [C] an official decision, especially by a law court: **[+on]** *the Supreme Court's ruling on the case*

ruling² *adj* [only before noun] the ruling group in a country or organization is the group that controls it: *the ruling classes*

rum /rʌm/ *n* [C,U] a strong alcoholic drink made from sugar

rumble /ˈrʌmbəl/ *v* [I] **1** to make a continuous low sound: *Thunder rumbled in the distance.* **2** if your stomach rumbles, it makes a noise because you are hungry —**rumble** *n* [singular]

rumbling /ˈrʌmblɪŋ/ *n* **1** **rumblings** [plural] remarks that show people are starting to become annoyed or that a difficult situation is developing: **[+of]** *rumblings of discontent* **2** [C usually singular] a long low sound

ruminate /ˈruːmɪneɪt/ *v* [I] *formal* to think about something carefully

rummage /ˈrʌmɪdʒ/ *v* [I] to search for something by moving things around: **[+in/through]** *Kerry was rummaging through a drawer looking for a pen.*

ˈrummage sale *n* [C] *AmE* an event at which old clothes, furniture, toys etc are sold **SYN** **jumble sale** *BrE*

rumour *BrE*, **rumor** *AmE* /ˈruːmə $ -ər/ *n* [C,U] information that is passed from one person to another and may not be true: **[+that]** *rumors that the President may have to resign* | **[+about]** *I heard a rumour about him and Sylvia.* | **Rumour has it** (=people are saying) *that Jean's getting married again.*

rumoured *BrE*, **rumored** *AmE* /ˈruːməd $ -ərd/ *adj* if something is rumoured to be true, people are saying that it may be true but no one is sure: *It was rumoured that a magazine offered £10,000 for her* *story.* | **rumoured to be/have done sth** *The actress is rumoured to be pregnant again.*

rump /rʌmp/ *n* [C,U] the part of an animal that is just above its back legs

rumpled /'rʌmpəld/ *adj* rumpled hair, clothes etc are untidy

run¹ /rʌn/ *v* (*past tense* **ran** /ræn/, *past participle* **run**, *present participle* **running**)

1 **MOVE FAST** [I] to move very quickly, moving your legs faster than when you walk: **[+down/up/to/ towards etc]** *Some kids were running down the street.* | *The boys ran off into the crowd.* | *Stephen came running down the stairs.* → see picture on page A11

2 **RACE** [I,T] to run in a race: *The horse ran a superb race.* | *He's training to run the marathon.*

3 **COMPANY/ORGANIZATION** [T] to control, organize, or operate a business, organization, activity etc: *My parents run their own business.* | **well-run/badly run** *The hotel is well-run and extremely popular.* **THESAURUS** CONTROL

4 **MACHINE/ENGINE** [I,T] if a machine, engine, or other piece of equipment runs, or if someone runs it, it is working: *Dad left the engine running.* | *She didn't realise the tape was still running* (=recording). | **run on coal/petrol/batteries etc** (=use coal, petrol etc to work)

5 **ROAD/RIVER/LINE ETC** [I,T] if something long, such as a road, river, or line runs somewhere, it continues in a particular direction: **[+along/through/past etc]** *The road runs along the coast.* | *a shelf that runs the length of one wall*

6 **FINGERS/COMB ETC** [T] to move your fingers or an object through or over something: *She ran her fingers through her hair.*

7 **FLOW** [I,T] to flow or to produce a stream of water etc: *Tears ran down her face.* | *Who left the tap running?* | *I'm just running a bath* (=filling it with water). | **sb's nose is running** (=liquid is coming out)

8 **HAPPEN/CONTINUE** [I] to happen in a particular way or for a particular time: *The tour guide helps to keep things running smoothly.* | **[+for]** *The play ran for two years* (=was performed for two years).

9 **BUSES/TRAINS** [I] to travel at a particular time, or on a particular route: *Trains run every ten minutes.*

10 **COMPUTER PROGRAM** [T] to start or use a computer program: *You can run this software on any PC.*

11 **TEST/CHECK** **run a check/test/experiment etc** to arrange for someone or something to be checked or tested: *My GP ran a test to check my blood sugar levels.*

12 **NEWS STORY** [I,T] to print or broadcast a story, piece of news etc: *They ran the item on the 6 o'clock news.*

13 **IN AN ELECTION** [I] to try to get elected: **[+for]** *He is running for President.*

14 **CAR** [T] to own and use a vehicle, especially a car: *I can't afford to run a car.*

15 **DRIVE SB** [T] to drive someone somewhere: *I'll run you home if you like.*

16 **BE AT A HIGH LEVEL** [I] to be at a particular level, amount, or price, especially one that is very high: **[+at]** *Inflation was running at 20% a year.* | **[+to/into]** *The bill could run to thousands of pounds.*

17 **COLOUR** [I] if a colour runs, it spreads to other parts of a piece of material when it is washed

PHRASES

run in the family if something such as a quality, disease, or skill runs in the family, many people in that family have it: *Diabetes appears to run in the family.*

be running late to be doing things late: *Sorry you had to wait – I've been running late all day.*

be running short (of sth) to have little of something left: *I'm running short of money.*

PHRASAL VERBS

run across sb/sth to meet or find someone or something by chance: *I ran across my old school photos the other day.*

run after sb/sth to chase someone or something: *She started to leave, but Smith ran after her.* **THESAURUS** FOLLOW

run away to leave a place in order to escape from someone or something: **[+from]** *Kathy ran away from home at the age of 16.*

run sth **by** sb *informal* to tell someone about something so that they can give you their opinion about it: *Can you run that by me again?*

run sb/sth ↔ **down**
1 to hit a person or animal with a car and kill or injure them: *As he was cycling into school, a car ran him down.*
2 to criticize someone or something: *Her boyfriend's always running her down.*

run into sb/sth
1 *informal* to meet someone by chance: *I ran into him the other day in town.*
2 **run into trouble/problems/debt etc** to begin to have trouble, problems etc: *She ran into trouble when she couldn't get a work permit.*
3 to hit someone or something with a car: *He lost control and ran into another car.*

run off
1 to leave a place or person when you should not: *Our dog keeps running off.*
2 **run off a copy** to quickly print a copy of something: *I'll need to run off a few more copies before the meeting.*

run off with sb/sth
1 *disapproving* to go away with someone to marry them or to live with them: *Her husband ran off with his secretary.*
2 to take or steal something: *A thief ran off with her mobile phone.*

run out
1 a) to use all of something, so that there is none left: *We've run out of sugar.* | *I'm running out of ideas.* **b)** if something is running out, there will soon be none left: *We'll have to make a decision soon – time is running out.*
2 if an official document, contract etc runs out, the period of time for which it is legal or you can use it ends: *My membership runs out in September.*

run sb/sth ↔ **over** to hit someone or something with your car, and drive over them: *The dog had been run over by a truck.*

run through sth
1 to read, check, or practise something quickly: *I'd like to run through the questions again before you start.*

2 if a quality or feature runs through something, it exists in all parts of it: *a theme which runs through the book*

run up sth if you run up a bill, debt etc, you then owe a lot of money: *We ran up a huge phone bill.*

run up against sth to suddenly have to deal with something difficult: *The team ran up against tough opposition.*

THESAURUS

run to move very quickly, moving your legs faster than when you walk: *I had to run to catch the bus this morning.*

jog/go jogging to run fairly slowly for exercise: *A few people were jogging in the park.* | *He goes jogging every morning.*

race/dash to run or move very quickly for a short distance, in order to do something urgent: *I dashed upstairs to give her the letter.*

charge to run quickly and with a lot of energy, with the result that you might knock someone over: *He was charging straight at me.*

sprint to run as fast as you can for a short distance: *I saw a policeman sprinting past.*

---

run² *n* [C]

1 when someone runs, or the distance that someone runs: *He usually goes for a run before breakfast.* | *a five-mile run*

2 [usually singular] a series of good or bad things that happen to you: **run of good/bad luck** *She has had a run of bad luck recently.* | **unbeaten/winning run** *an unbeaten run of 19 games*

3 the usual/normal/general run of sth the usual type of something: *It was just a bit different from the usual run of city centre bars.*

4 a point in a game such as BASEBALL or CRICKET: *He scored 218 runs.*

5 a period of time during which a play, film, or television programme is shown or performed regularly: *The play starts an 8-week run on Friday.*

6 a run on sth when a lot of people suddenly buy something at the same time: *There is a run on swimwear in hot weather.* → **HOME RUN, TEST RUN, TRIAL RUN**

PHRASES

have the run of sth to be allowed to use the whole of a place: *We had the run of the house for the weekend.*

in the short/long run in the near future, or later in the future: *Wood is more expensive, but in the long run it's better value.*

make a run for it to try to escape by suddenly running away: *The prisoners decided to make a run for it.*

be on the run to be trying to escape from someone, especially the police: **[+from]** *a criminal on the run from the police*

runaway¹ /'rʌnəweɪ/ *adj* [only before noun] **1** a runaway vehicle is out of control **2** happening quickly and suddenly: *The film was a **runaway success**.*

runaway² *n* [C] someone, especially a child, who has left their home, school etc secretly

rundown /'rʌndaʊn/ *n* [singular] a quick report or explanation of a situation or idea: **[+on]** *Can you give me a rundown on what happened while I was away?*

run-'down *adj* **1** if a building or area is run-down, it is in bad condition because it has not been looked after: *a run-down apartment block* **2** [not before noun] if a person is run-down, they feel tired and ill: *He's been feeling run-down lately.*

rung¹ /rʌŋ/ *v* the past participle of RING

rung² *n* [C] **1** one of the steps of a LADDER → see picture at **LADDER 2** *informal* a particular level or position in an organization: **first/lowest/bottom rung** *I started on the bottom rung in the company.*

'run-in *n* [C] an argument with someone in authority: **[+with]** *He had a run-in with his boss.*

runner /'rʌnə $ -ər/ *n* [C] **1** someone who runs as a sport, or a horse that runs in a race: *a long-distance runner* **2 gun/drug runner** someone who illegally takes guns or drugs from one country to another: *He was accused of being a drug runner.*

runner-'up *n* [C] (*plural* **runners-up**) the person or team that finishes second in a competition

running¹ /'rʌnɪŋ/ *n* [U] **1** the activity or sport of running: *a running track* | *Do you want to go running?* **2 the running of** sth the process of managing a business, organization etc: *the day-to-day running of the company*

PHRASES

be in/out of the running to have some chance or no chance of winning or being successful: **[+for]** *Is Sam still in the running for the swimming team?*

running² *adj* **1 running water** water that flows from a TAP: *hot and cold running water* **2 running battle** an argument that continues or is repeated over a long period of time **3 running commentary** a spoken description of an event while it is happening **4 running total** a total that gets bigger as new amounts are added to it

running³ *adv* **three years/five times etc running** for three years, five times etc without a change: *This is the fourth day running that it has rained.*

'running costs *n* [plural] the amount of money you have to pay to operate something

runny /'rʌni/ *adj informal* **1** if you have a runny nose, liquid is coming out of your nose because you are ill **2** food that is runny is not as thick as normal or as you want: *The sauce is far too runny.*

run-of-the-'mill *adj* not special or interesting: *a run-of-the-mill performance*

'run-up *n* **the run-up to** sth the period just before an important event: *political campaigning in the run-up to the election*

runway /'rʌnweɪ/ *n* [C] **1** a long wide road that planes land on and take off from **2** *AmE* the long narrow structure that models walk along in a fashion show **SYN** catwalk

rupture /'rʌptʃə $ -ər/ *v* [I,T] to break or burst open violently: *An oil pipeline ruptured.* —**rupture** *n* [C,U]

rural /'rʊərəl $ 'rʊr-/ *adj* relating to or happening in the country rather than in the city → **urban**: *a peaceful rural setting* | *a rural community*

ruse /ruːz $ ruːs, ruːz/ *n* [C] a clever trick

rush¹ /rʌʃ/ *v*

1 [I] to move or go somewhere quickly SYN **hurry**: *There's no need to rush – we have plenty of time.* | **[+into/along/from etc]** *David rushed into the bathroom.* THESAURUS **HURRY**

2 rush to do sth to do something eagerly and without delay: *People are rushing to buy shares in the company.*

3 [I,T] to do or decide something too quickly, especially without being careful or thinking about it: **rush into (doing) sth** *I don't want to just rush into buying the first house we see.* | *Take your time – don't rush it.*

4 [T] to take or send a person or thing somewhere very quickly: **rush sb/sth to sth** *We had to rush Helen to the hospital.*

5 [T] to try to make someone do something more quickly than they want to: *Don't rush me – let me think.* | **rush sb into (doing) sth** *I don't want to rush you into anything.*

PHRASAL VERBS

rush around to go to a lot of places or do a lot of things in a short period of time

rush² *n*

1 [singular] a sudden fast movement of things or people: **rush of air/water/wind** *She felt a cold rush of air as she wound down her window.* | **in a rush** *Her words came out in a rush.* | **[+for]** *There was a rush for the door.*

2 [singular, U] a situation in which you need to hurry: *We have plenty of time. There's no rush.* | **in a rush** *I can't stop – I'm in a rush.* | **rush to do sth** *There's a big rush to get tickets.*

3 the rush the time when a lot of people are doing something, for example travelling or shopping: *the Christmas rush*

4 [singular] a sudden strong feeling: **[+of]** *a sudden rush of emotion* | *Mark felt a rush of anger.*

5 rushes [plural] tall plants that grow near rivers and are used to make baskets etc

rushed /rʌʃt/ *adj* **1** if you are rushed, you are very busy because you have a lot to do quickly: *I've been*

rushed off my feet (=extremely busy) *all day.* THESAURUS **BUSY 2** done too quickly: *a rushed meeting*

'rush hour *n* [C,U] the time of day when there is a lot of traffic because people are going to and from work

rust¹ /rʌst/ *n* [U] the reddish-brown substance that forms on iron, steel etc when it gets wet

rust² *v* [I,T] to become covered with rust, or to make rust form on something

rustic /ˈrʌstɪk/ *adj* simple and old-fashioned in a way that is attractive and typical of the country: *The village has a certain* **rustic charm**.

rustle /ˈrʌsəl/ *v* [I,T] if papers, leaves etc rustle, or if you rustle them, they make a noise as they move against each other: *the sound of kids rustling ice-cream wrappers* → see picture on page A7 —**rustle** *n* [singular]

PHRASAL VERBS

rustle sth ↔ **up** *informal* to make something quickly, especially a meal

rusty /ˈrʌsti/ *adj* **1** covered with rust: *rusty nails* **2** if a skill is rusty, you are not as good at doing something as you were, because you have not practised: *My tennis is a little rusty.*

rut /rʌt/ *n* [C] a deep narrow track left in the ground by a wheel

PHRASES

> **in a rut** *informal* living or working in a boring situation that you cannot easily change: *Margaret felt she was* **stuck in a rut**.

rutabaga /ˌruːtəˈbeɪɡə/ *n* [C,U] *AmE* a round yellow vegetable that grows under the ground SYN **swede** *BrE* → see picture on page A5

ruthless /ˈruːθləs/ *adj* not caring if you have to harm other people to get what you want: *a ruthless dictator* THESAURUS **DETERMINED** —**ruthlessly** *adv* —**ruthlessness** *n* [U]

rye /raɪ/ *n* [U] a type of grain that is used for making bread and WHISKY

Ss

S, s /es/ *n* [C,U] (*plural* **S's, s's**) the 19th letter of the English alphabet

S 1 the written abbreviation of **south** or **southern 2** the written abbreviation of **small**, used on clothes to show the size

-'s /z, s/ **1** the short form of 'is' or 'has': *What's that?* | *He's gone out.* **2** used to make the POSSESSIVE form of nouns: *One of Jason's friends is going to UCLA.*

Sabbath /'sæbəθ/ *n* **the Sabbath** a day of the week for resting and praying, which is Sunday for Christians and Saturday for Jews

sabbatical /sə'bætɪkəl/ *n* [C,U] a period when someone, especially a university teacher, stops doing their usual work to travel or study: **on sabbatical** *Professor Burton is on sabbatical for two months.*

saber /'seɪbə $ -ər/ *n* the American spelling of SABRE

sabotage /'sæbətɑːʒ/ *v* [T] **1** to secretly damage or destroy something so that an enemy cannot use it: *The plane had been sabotaged and exploded in mid-air.* **THESAURUS** DAMAGE **2** to secretly spoil someone's plans because you do not want them to succeed: *He denied he was trying to sabotage the talks.* —**sabotage** *n* [U]: *deliberate acts of sabotage*

saboteur /ˌsæbə'tɜː $ -'tɜːr/ *n* [C] someone who deliberately damages, destroys, or spoils someone else's property or activities, in order to prevent them from doing something: *Saboteurs could have been on the train.*

sabre *BrE*, **saber** *AmE* /'seɪbə $ -ər/ *n* [C] **1** a thin pointed sword used in the sport of FENCING → see picture at **FENCING** **2** a heavy sword with a curved blade

saccharin /'sækərɪn/ *n* [U] a sweet chemical that is used in food instead of sugar

sachet /'sæʃeɪ $ sæ'ʃeɪ/ *n* [C] a small bag containing a liquid or powder: **[+of]** *a sachet of shampoo*

sack¹ /sæk/ *n* [C]
1 a large bag made of strong cloth, plastic, or paper in which you carry or store things: **[+of]** *a sack of potatoes*
2 get the sack/give sb the sack *BrE informal* to be told to leave your job or to tell someone to leave their job: *If someone complains to my manager about it, I could get the sack.*

sack² *v* [T] *BrE* to tell someone to leave their job **SYN** fire: *Campbell was sacked for coming in drunk.*

sacrament /'sækrəmənt/ *n* [C] an important Christian ceremony such as marriage or COMMUNION

sacred /'seɪkrɪd/ *adj* **1** relating to a god or religion, and believed to be holy: *sacred texts* | **[+to]** *The site*

is sacred to Muslims. → see Word Choice at **HOLY**
2 very important: *Human life is sacred.*
PHRASES
sacred cow something that is very important to some people, and which they will not change or allow anyone to criticize: *The painter attacked sacred cows such as ideas about good taste.*

sacrifice¹ /'sækrəfaɪs/ *n* [C,U] **1** when you give up something important or valuable in order to get something that is more important: *Her parents made a lot of sacrifices to give her a good education.* **2** something that is offered to a god in a ceremony, especially an animal that is killed —**sacrificial** /ˌsækrɪ'fɪʃəl◀/ *adj*

sacrifice² *v* **1** [T] to give up something important or valuable in order to get something else: **sacrifice sth for sth** *It's not worth sacrificing your health for your job.* **2** [I,T] to offer something, especially an animal, to a god in a ceremony, often by killing it

sacrilege /'sækrəlɪdʒ/ *n* [C,U] when something holy or important is treated in a way that does not show respect: *It would be sacrilege to demolish such a beautiful building.* —**sacrilegious** /ˌsækrɪ'lɪdʒəs◀/ *adj*

sacrosanct /'sækrəʊsæŋkt $ -roʊ-/ *adj* too important to be changed or criticized in any way: *Our time spent together as a family is sacrosanct.*

sad /sæd/ *adj*
1 not happy **OPP** happy: *Linda looks very sad today.* | **[+about]** *I was sad about the friends that I was leaving behind.* | **[+that]** *I am sad that you do not believe me.* | **sad to do sth** *I was sad to hear that he had died.*
2 a sad event, story etc makes you feel unhappy: *Have you heard the sad news about Mrs. Winters?* | *It's just so sad.* | **sad story/song/film etc** *a story with a sad ending*
3 very bad or unacceptable: *It's a sad state of affairs* (=bad situation) *when a person isn't safe in her own home.*
4 *informal* boring and unfashionable: *Stay in on a Saturday night? What a sad idea!*

THESAURUS
sad not happy: *She felt sad as she waved goodbye.*
unhappy sad, especially for a long time – used about people and periods of time: *I was unhappy at school.*	*He had an unhappy childhood.*
homesick sad because you are away from your home, family, and friends: *She had just moved to Paris and was feeling homesick.*
down *informal* feeling sad, often for no reason: *When you're feeling down, it sometimes helps to talk to other people.*
gloomy looking or sounding sad because you do not expect a situation to get better: *Why are you all looking so gloomy?*

very sad
miserable very sad – used about people and periods of time: *She had a miserable life.*	*Miranda sat alone in her room feeling miserable.*
depressed feeling very sad and without hope, either because things go wrong in your life or because of a medical condition: *Unemployed*

people often feel depressed and worthless.
heartbroken very sad, especially because a relationship has ended, someone you love has died, or what you wanted has not happened: *I was heartbroken when he left.*

sadden /'sædn/ v [T] *formal* to make someone feel sad or disappointed: *They were shocked and saddened by his death.*

saddle¹ /'sædl/ n [C] **1** a seat made of leather that is put on a horse's back so that you can ride it **2** a seat on a bicycle or a MOTORCYCLE → see picture at **BICYCLE**

saddle² (*also* **saddle up**) v [I,T] to put a saddle on a horse

PHRASAL VERBS
saddle sb with sth to make someone have a job or problem that is difficult or boring and that they do not want: *I've been saddled with organizing the whole party!*

sadism /'seɪdɪzəm/ n [U] when someone gets enjoyment or sexual pleasure from being cruel or violent → **masochism** —**sadist** n [C] —**sadistic** /sə'dɪstɪk/ adj: *a sadistic boss*

sadly /'sædli/ adv
1 in a sad way: *Jimmy nodded sadly.*
2 unfortunately: *Sadly, the concert was cancelled.*
3 in a way that seems wrong or bad: *Politeness is sadly lacking these days.* | *You're sadly mistaken if you think Anne will help.*

sadness /'sædnɪs/ n [U] a feeling of being unhappy, especially because something unpleasant has happened to you OPP **happiness**: *Most children feel great sadness if their parents separate.* | [+at] *He spoke of his sadness at the death of his friend.*

sae /ˌes eɪ 'iː/ n [C] *BrE* (**stamped addressed envelope**) an envelope that you put your name and address and a stamp on, so that someone can send you something in it

safari /sə'fɑːri/ n [C,U] a trip through the country areas of Africa in order to watch wild animals: **on safari** *We'll be going on safari in Kenya.*

safe¹ /seɪf/ adj
1 not likely to cause injury or harm: *Women are safer drivers than men.* | *Don't go near the edge – it isn't safe.* | **Is it safe** to swim here? | **a safe trip/drive/ journey** *Have a safe trip!* | **safe to use/drink etc** *Is the water safe to drink?*
2 [not before noun] not in danger of being lost, harmed, or stolen: *She doesn't feel safe in the house on her own.* | [+from] *The city is now safe from further attack.* | *Both children were found safe and sound* (=unharmed).
3 **safe place** a place where something is not likely to be stolen or lost: *Keep your passport in a safe place.*
4 not likely to be wrong or to fail: *Gold is a safe investment.* | *I think it's safe to say that everyone is happy with the arrangement.* —**safely** adv: *Drive safely!* | *Did the package arrive safely?*

PHRASES
be in safe hands to be with someone who will look after you very well: *Parents want to make sure they're leaving their children in safe hands.*

just to be safe/to be on the safe side in order to avoid a possible bad situation: *Take some extra money with you, just to be on the safe side.*

safe² n [C] a strong metal box or cupboard with a lock on it, where you keep money and valuable things

safeguard /'seɪfɡɑːd $ -ɡɑːrd/ n [C] a law, agreement etc that protects someone or something: [+against] *Copy the data as a safeguard against loss or damage.* —**safeguard** v [T]: *laws to safeguard endangered animals* THESAURUS ▸ PROTECT

safe haven n [C] a place where someone can go to escape from danger

safekeeping /ˌseɪf'kiːpɪŋ/ n **for safekeeping** if you put something somewhere for safekeeping, you put it in a place where it will not get damaged, lost, or stolen

safety /'seɪfti/ n [U]
1 the state of being safe from danger or harm: *Some students are concerned about safety on campus.* | **For your own safety**, please do not smoke inside the plane.* | *road safety* (=being safe on roads) | [+of] *There are fears for the safety of the hostages.*
2 how safe something is to use, do etc: [+of] *doubts about the safety of the drug* | **safety standards/ regulations/precautions etc** (=things that are done in order to make sure that something is safe) *The device meets safety standards.*

safety belt n [C] a SEAT BELT

safety net n [C] **1** a system that helps people when they are too ill, poor etc to help themselves: *the safety net of unemployment pay and pensions* **2** a large net that will catch an ACROBAT if they fall from a high place

safety pin n [C] a wire pin with a cover that its point fits into

safety valve n [C] **1** something that prevents a dangerous situation developing **2** a part of a machine that allows gas, steam etc to be let out when the pressure is too high

sag /sæɡ/ v [I] (**sagged**, **sagging**) to sink or bend down: *The branches sagged under the weight of the snow.*

saga /'sɑːɡə/ n [C] a long story or a description of a long series of events

sage¹ /seɪdʒ/ n **1** [U] a plant used to give a special taste to food **2** [C] *literary* someone who is very wise

sage² adj *literary* very wise —**sagely** adv

Sagittarius /ˌsædʒə'teəriəs $ -'ter-/ n **1** [U] the sign of the Zodiac of people born between November 23 and December 21 **2** [C] someone who has this sign

said /sed/ v the past tense and past participle of SAY

sail¹ /seɪl/ v
1 [I] to travel across water in a boat or ship: [+across/into/out of etc] *We sailed along the coast of Alaska.* THESAURUS ▸ TRAVEL
2 [I,T] to control the movement of a boat or ship: *The captain sailed the ship safely past the rocks.* | *I'd like to learn how to sail.*

S

3 [I] to start a trip by boat or ship: *What time do we sail?*

4 [I] to move quickly and gracefully, especially through the air: **[+into/out of/past etc]** *The ball sailed past the goalkeeper into the back of the net.*

PHRASAL VERBS

sail through sth to succeed very easily in a test, examination etc: *Adam sailed through his final exams.*

sail² *n* [C] a large piece of strong cloth fixed onto a boat, so that the wind will push the boat along: *a yacht with white sails* → see picture at **SAILBOAT**

PHRASES

set sail to begin a trip by boat or ship: *The ship set sail at dawn.*

sailing /'seɪlɪŋ/ *n* [U] the activity of sailing in boats: *They've invited us to **go sailing** this weekend.*

'sailing ˌboat *BrE*, **sail-boat** /'seɪlbəʊt $ -boʊt/ *AmE n* [C] a small boat with one or more sails

SAILING BOAT

sailing boat *BrE*/ sailboat *AmE*

sail

sailor /'seɪlə $ -ər/ *n* [C] someone who sails on boats or ships, especially as a job → **seaman**

saint /seɪnt/ *n* [C]
1 someone who is given the title 'saint' by the Christian Church after they have died, because they have been very good and holy: *Saint Patrick*
2 *spoken* someone who is very good, kind, and patient: *You're a real saint to help us like this.*

saintly /'seɪntli/ *adj* very good, kind, and patient

sake /seɪk/ *n*

PHRASES

for goodness'/Pete's/heaven's etc sake *spoken* used to emphasize what you are saying, when you are annoyed: *Why didn't you tell me, for heaven's sake?*

for sb's sake in order to help or please someone: *She only stays with her husband for the children's sake.*

for the sake of sth in order to help or improve a situation: *Both sides are willing to take risks for the sake of peace.*

salad /'sæləd/ *n* [C,U] a mixture of vegetables eaten cold and usually RAW: *a salad of lettuce, tomatoes, and cucumber* | *a large mixed salad*

salami /sə'lɑːmi/ *n* [C,U] a large SAUSAGE with a strong taste which is eaten cold in thin pieces

salary /'sæləri/ *n* [C,U] (*plural* **salaries**) money that you receive every month as payment from the organization you work for → **pay**, **wage**: *The average salary is $39,000 a year.* —**salaried** *adj*: *salaried workers*

COLLOCATIONS

verbs

to earn/get/receive a salary *She earns a good salary.*

to be on a salary *especially spoken* (=to earn a salary) *He's on a salary of £29,000 a year.*

adjectives

a high/good salary *They get paid higher salaries than we do.*

a large/big/huge salary *Does he deserve such a large salary?*

a low salary *Many office workers are on low salaries.*

a six-figure salary (=one over £100,000 or $100,000) *The top players earn six-figure salaries.*

sb's annual/monthly salary *He receives an annual salary of $500,000.*

THESAURUS

salary money that you receive every month as payment from the organization you work for. **Salary** is usually used for professional jobs such as teachers, managers etc: *Pilots earn a salary of around $120,000.*

wages (*also* **wage**) money that you receive every week as payment from the organization you work for. **Wages** is usually used for jobs such as factory or shop workers: *My wages were only £60 a week.*

pay money that you receive for doing a job: *The nurses want an increase in their basic pay.*

earnings used when talking about people's salaries in general, and all the money that you get from working: *Average earnings have gone up by 10%.* | *The star's earnings were estimated at around $20 million last year.*

income money that you get regularly from your job and from other things, which you use to live: *People on low incomes can get free dental care.* | *income tax*

sale /seɪl/ *n*
1 [C,U] an act of selling something, or when something is sold: **[+of]** *The sale of alcohol to under-18s is forbidden.* | *John showed the customer several jackets, trying to **make a sale** (=sell something).*
2 sales [plural] the total number of products that are sold during a particular period of time: **[+of]** *Sales of automobiles are up this year.*
3 sales [U] the part of a company that deals with selling products: *Sally got a job as sales manager.*
4 [C] a time when a shop sells its goods at lower prices than usual: *There's a great sale on at Macy's now.* | *I bought it in a sale.* → **CAR BOOT SALE, JUMBLE SALE, RUMMAGE SALE**

PHRASES

for sale available to be bought: *Is this table for sale?* | *They had to **put** their home **up for sale** (=make it available to be bought).*

on sale 1 available to be bought: *Tickets will **go on sale** tomorrow.* **2** *especially AmE* available to be bought at a lower price than usual: *Don's found a really good CD player on sale.*

saleable (*also* **salable** *AmE*) /'seɪləbəl/ *adj* something that is saleable can be sold, or is easy to sell: *salable products*

'sales as,sistant n [C] BrE someone who sells things in a shop SYN **shop assistant** BrE

salesclerk /'seɪlzklɑːk $ -klɜːrk/ n [C] AmE someone who serves customers in a shop SYN **shop assistant** BrE

salesman /'seɪlzmən/ n [C] (plural **salesmen** /-mən/) a man whose job is to sell things: a car salesman

salesperson /'seɪlzˌpɜːsən $ -ˌpɜːr-/ n [C] (plural **salespeople** /-ˌpiːpəl/) someone whose job is to sell things

'sales repre,sentative (also **'sales rep**) n [C] someone who travels around an area selling their company's products

saleswoman /'seɪlzˌwʊmən/ n [C] (plural **saleswomen** /-ˌwɪmɪn/) a woman whose job is to sell things

salient /'seɪliənt/ adj formal the salient points or features of something are the most noticeable or important ones —**salience** n [U]

saline /'seɪlaɪn/ adj containing salt: a saline solution (=liquid with salt in it)

saliva /sə'laɪvə/ n [U] the liquid that is produced naturally in your mouth

salivate /'sælɪveɪt/ v [I] to produce more saliva in your mouth than usual, especially because you see or smell food

sallow /'sæləʊ $ -loʊ/ adj sallow skin looks slightly yellow and unhealthy

salmon /'sæmən/ n [C,U] (plural **salmon**) a large fish with silver skin and pink flesh: smoked salmon

salmonella /ˌsælmə'nelə/ n [U] a kind of BACTERIA in food that makes you ill

salon /'sælɒn $ sə'lɑːn/ n [C] a place where you can get your hair cut, have BEAUTY TREATMENTS etc: a beauty salon

saloon /sə'luːn/ n [C] **1** a place where alcoholic drinks were sold and drunk in the US in the 19th century **2** BrE a car that has a separate enclosed space for bags, cases etc SYN **sedan** AmE: a four-door saloon

salsa /'sælsə $ 'sɑːl-/ n [U] **1** a hot-tasting SAUCE **2** a type of Latin American dance music

salt¹ /sɔːlt $ sɒːlt/ n [U] a natural white mineral that is added to food to make it taste better: Add a **pinch of salt** (=a small amount) to the mixture. | This might need some **salt and pepper**. | salt water (=water that contains salt)

PHRASES
take sth with a pinch/grain of salt to not completely believe what someone tells you because you have reason to think that it might not be true: His story must be taken with a pinch of salt.

salt² v [T] to add salt to food: salted peanuts

'salt ,cellar BrE, **'salt ,shaker** AmE n [C] a small container for salt

saltwater /'sɔːltˌwɔːtə $ -ˌwɒːtər, -ˌwɑː-/ adj living in salty water: saltwater fish

salty /'sɔːlti $ 'sɒːlti/ adj tasting of or containing salt THESAURUS TASTE —**saltiness** n [U]

salutary /'sæljətəri $ -teri/ adj formal a salutary experience is unpleasant but teaches you something

salute¹ /sə'luːt/ v [I,T] to move your right hand to your head to show respect to an officer in the army, navy etc

salute² n [C] **1** when someone salutes a person of higher rank: As they left, the Corporal **gave** them a respectful **salute**. **2** when guns are fired into the air as part of a military ceremony: a 21-gun salute

salvage /'sælvɪdʒ/ v [T] to save something from a situation in which other things have already been damaged, destroyed, or lost: **salvage sth from sth** They managed to salvage only a few of their belongings from the fire. —**salvage** n [U]: a salvage operation

salvation /sæl'veɪʃən/ n [U] **1** the state of being saved from evil by God, according to the Christian religion **2** something that prevents danger, loss, or failure: Donations of food and clothing have been the salvation of the refugees.

salve /sælv, sɑːv $ sæv/ v **salve your conscience** to make yourself feel less guilty about something you have done wrong

salvo /'sælvəʊ $ -voʊ/ n [C usually singular] (plural **salvos** or **salvoes**) formal **1** when several guns are fired during a battle or as part of a ceremony **2 opening/first salvo** the first in a series of things that you say or do to try to win an argument, competition etc: His speech was the opening salvo of the election campaign.

same¹ /seɪm/ adj **the same a)** the same person, place, thing etc is one particular person etc and not a different one: They go to the same place for their vacation every summer. | Kim's birthday and Roger's are on the same day. **b)** used to say that two or more people, things, events etc are exactly like each other: The same thing could happen again. | That's funny, Simon said **exactly the same** thing. | [+as] She does the same job as I do, but in a bigger company.

> Grammar
> You always say **the same**. Do not say 'We studied in a same class.' Say We studied in the same class.

PHRASES
at the same time 1 if two things happen at the same time, they happen together: How can you type and talk at the same time? **2** used when you want to say that something else is also true: She was a little suspicious of him, but at the same time she liked him.

the same old story/excuse etc informal something that you have heard many times before: It's the same old story – his wife didn't understand him.

THESAURUS

the same used to say that two or more people, things, events etc are exactly like each other: Jane and Rachel were wearing the same dress.
identical identical things are exactly the same in every way. **Identical** sounds stronger than **the same**: The two snakes have identical markings.

similar if things or people are similar, they are like each other: *Their voices are very similar on the phone.*

just like/exactly like *especially spoken* used to say that there is very little difference between two people or things: *She sounded just like my teacher.* | *He had a bag exactly like mine.*

matching [only before noun] having the same colour, style, pattern etc as something else: *She was wearing a diamond necklace with matching earrings.*

same² *pron* **1 the same a)** used to say that two or more people, actions, or things are exactly like each other: **look/sound/taste etc the same** *The houses may look the same, but one's slightly larger.* **b)** used to say that a particular person or thing does not change: *'How's Danny?' 'Oh, he's the same as ever.'* **2 (and the) same to you!** *spoken* used as a reply to a greeting or as an angry reply to a rude remark: *'Have a good weekend!' 'Thanks, same to you!'* **3 all/just the same** in spite of what has just been mentioned: *I realise she can be very annoying, but I think you should apologise all the same.* **4 same here** *spoken* used to say that you feel the same way as someone else: *'I hate shopping malls.' 'Same here.'*

same³ *adv* **the same (as sth)** in the same way: *'Rain' and 'reign' are pronounced the same even though they are spelt differently.*

sample¹ /ˈsɑːmpəl $ ˈsæm-/ *n* [C] a small part or amount of something that is examined or tried to find out what the rest is like: **[+of]** *free samples of a new shampoo* | *Doctors take a **blood sample** to test for HIV.* | *The questionnaire was given to a **random sample** of students.*

sample² *v* [T] **1** to taste food or drink to see what it is like: *We sampled several local cheeses.* **2** to do something for the first time to see what it is like: *Win a chance to sample the exotic nightlife of Paris!*

sanatorium /ˌsænəˈtɔːriəm/ (*also* **sanitarium** /ˌsænəˈteəriəm $ -ˈter-/ AmE) *n* [C] *old-fashioned* a hospital for people who are getting better but still need rest and care

sanctify /ˈsæŋktɪfaɪ/ *v* [T] (**sanctified, sanctifying, sanctifies**) to make something holy

sanctimonious /ˌsæŋktəˈməʊniəs◄ $ -ˈmoʊ-/ *adj* behaving as if you are morally better than other people: *a long and sanctimonious speech*

sanction¹ /ˈsæŋkʃən/ *n* **1 sanctions** [plural] official orders or laws stopping trade, communication etc with another country, as a way of forcing its leaders to make political changes: **[+against]** *US sanctions against Cuba* **2** [C] *formal* something such as a punishment that makes people obey a rule or law: *severe sanctions against those who avoid paying taxes* **3** [U] *formal* official permission or approval: *The protest march was held without government sanction.*

sanction² *v* [T] *formal* to officially approve of or allow something: *The UN refused to sanction the use of force.*

sanctity /ˈsæŋktəti/ *n* **the sanctity of sth** the fact that something is very important and must be respected and preserved: *the sanctity of marriage*

sanctuary /ˈsæŋktʃuəri, -tʃəri $ -tʃueri/ *n* (*plural* **sanctuaries**) **1** [C,U] a peaceful place that is safe and provides protection, especially for people who are in danger: **seek/find sanctuary** *The refugees were seeking sanctuary in Australia.* **2** [C] an area for birds or animals where they are protected and cannot be hunted: **[+for]** *a sanctuary for tigers*

sanctum /ˈsæŋktəm/ *n* **the inner sanctum** *humorous* a place that only a few important people are allowed to enter: *We were only allowed into the director's inner sanctum for a few minutes.*

sand¹ /sænd/ *n*
1 [U] the substance that forms deserts and beaches, which consists of many very small pieces of rock: *a **grain of sand***
2 sands [plural] a large area of sand

sand² *v* [T] to make a surface smooth by rubbing it with SANDPAPER

sandal /ˈsændl/ *n* [C] a light open shoe that you wear in warm weather: *a pair of leather sandals* → see picture at **SHOE¹**

sandbag /ˈsændbæg/ *n* [C] a bag filled with sand, used for protection against floods, explosions etc

sandbank /ˈsændbæŋk/ *n* [C] a raised area of sand in a river, sea etc

sandbox /ˈsændbɒks $ -bɑːks/ *n* [C] AmE a SANDPIT

sandcastle /ˈsænd,kɑːsəl $ -,kæ-/ *n* [C] a small model of a castle made out of sand, usually by children on a BEACH

'sand dune *n* [C] a DUNE

sandpaper /ˈsænd,peɪpə $ -ər/ *n* [U] strong paper covered with a rough substance, used for rubbing wood in order to make it smooth

sandpit /ˈsænd,pɪt/ *BrE,* **sandbox** *AmE n* [C] an enclosed area of sand for children to play in

sandstone /ˈsændstəʊn $ -stoʊn/ *n* [U] a type of rock formed from sand

sandtrap /ˈsændtræp/ *n* [C] AmE a wide hole on a GOLF COURSE filled with sand SYN **bunker** *BrE*

sandwich¹ /ˈsænwɪdʒ $ ˈsændwɪtʃ, ˈsænwɪtʃ/ *n* [C] two pieces of bread with cheese, meat, egg etc between them: *chicken sandwiches*

sandwich² *v* **be sandwiched between sth** to be in a very small space between two other things: *a motorcycle sandwiched between two vans*

sandy /ˈsændi/ *adj* covered with or containing sand: *a sandy beach* | *sandy soil*

sane /seɪn/ *adj* **1** not mentally ill OPP **insane**: *He seems perfectly sane* (=completely sane) *to me.* **2** reasonable and sensible: *a sane solution to a difficult problem*

sang /sæŋ/ *v* the past tense of SING

sanguine /ˈsæŋgwɪn/ *adj formal* happy and hopeful about the future

sanitarium /ˌsænəˈteəriəm $ -ˈter-/ *n* [C] AmE a SANATORIUM

sanitary /ˈsænətəri $ -teri/ *adj* **1** [only before noun] relating to health, especially to the removal of dirt, infection, or human waste: *Workers complained about sanitary arrangements at the factory.* **2** clean and not involving any danger to your health: *All food is stored under sanitary conditions.*

'**sanitary ,towel** *BrE*, '**sanitary ,napkin** *AmE n* [C] a piece of soft material that a woman wears when she has her PERIOD, to take up the blood

sanitation /ˌsænɪ'teɪʃən/ *n* [U] the protection of public health by removing and treating waste, dirty water etc

sanitize (*also* -**ise** *BrE*) /'sænətaɪz/ *v* [T] to make news, literature etc less offensive or shocking by taking out anything unpleasant

sanity /'sænəti/ *n* [U] **1** the quality of being reasonable and sensible **2** the condition of being mentally healthy [OPP] **insanity**: *He **lost** his **sanity** after his children were killed.*

sank /sæŋk/ *v* the past tense of SINK

Santa Claus /'sæntə klɔːz $ 'sænti klɔːz, 'sæntə-/, **Santa** *n* an imaginary old man with red clothes and a long white BEARD, who children believe brings them presents at Christmas [SYN] **Father Christmas** *BrE*

sap[1] /sæp/ *n* [U] the liquid that carries food through a plant

sap[2] *v* (**sapped, sapping**) **sap sb's/sth's strength/ energy/confidence etc** to gradually make someone or something weaker, less confident etc: *The illness sapped her strength.*

sapling /'sæplɪŋ/ *n* [C] a young tree → see picture at PLANT[1]

sapphire /'sæfaɪə $ -faɪr/ *n* [C,U] a bright blue jewel

sappy /'sæpi/ *adj AmE* expressing love and emotions too strongly [SYN] **soppy** *BrE*

Saran Wrap /sə'ræn ræp/ *n* [U] *trademark AmE* thin transparent plastic used to wrap food [SYN] **clingfilm** *BrE*

sarcasm /'sɑːkæzəm $ 'sɑːr-/ *n* [U] when you say the opposite of what you mean in order to make an unkind joke or to show that you are annoyed: *There was a touch of sarcasm in her voice as she thanked him.*

> **Word Choice: sarcasm or irony?**
> **Sarcasm** is deliberately saying the opposite of what you mean, as an unkind joke or to show that you are annoyed: *'You're early!' she said, her voice full of sarcasm.*
> **Irony** is saying the opposite of what you mean, in an amusing way. It is much gentler than **sarcasm**: *The writer often uses irony in his descriptions of the characters.* **Irony** is also used about a situation that seems strange or surprising, because it is the opposite of what you would expect: *The irony was that we never thought we would win the competition.*

sarcastic /sɑː'kæstɪk $ sɑːr-/ *adj* saying the opposite of what you mean in order to make an unkind joke or to show that you are annoyed: *a sarcastic comment* —**sarcastically** /-kli/ *adv*

sardine /sɑː'diːn◂ $ sɑːr-/ *n* [C,U] a small silver fish, often sold in cans

sardonic /sɑː'dɒnɪk $ sɑːr'dɑː-/ *adj* showing that you do not respect someone: *a sardonic smile*

sari /'sɑːri/ *n* [C] a long piece of cloth that you wrap around your body like a dress, worn especially by women from India

sash /sæʃ/ *n* [C] a long piece of cloth that you wear around your waist or over one shoulder

sass /sæs/ *v* [T] *AmE informal* to talk in a rude way to someone you should respect

sassy /'sæsi/ *adj especially AmE* **1** a sassy child is rude to someone they should respect [SYN] **cheeky** *BrE* **2** confident and full of energy: *a sassy young woman | sassy music*

sat /sæt/ *v* the past tense and past participle of SIT

Sat. (*also* **Sat** *BrE*) the written abbreviation of **Saturday**

Satan /'seɪtn/ *n* [singular] a name for the Devil

satanic /sə'tænɪk/ *adj* relating to practices that treat the Devil like a god: *satanic rituals* —**satanism** /'seɪtənɪzəm/ *n* [U]

satchel /'sætʃəl/ *n* [C] a leather bag that children in the past used for carrying their books to school

satellite /'sætəlaɪt/ *n* [C] **1** a machine that is sent into space and travels around the Earth, moon etc. Satellites are used to send radio or television signals, or for other forms of communication: **by/via satellite** *This broadcast comes live via satellite from New York.* **2** a natural object such as a moon that moves around a PLANET

'**satellite ,dish** *n* [C] a large circular piece of metal that is attached to a building and receives the SIGNALS for satellite television

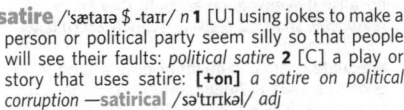
SATELLITE DISH

,**satellite 'television** (*also* ,**satellite T'V**) *n* [U] television programmes that are broadcast using satellites in space

satin /'sætɪn $ 'sætn/ *n* [U] a smooth shiny cloth

satire /'sætaɪə $ -taɪr/ *n* **1** [U] using jokes to make a person or political party seem silly so that people will see their faults: *political satire* **2** [C] a play or story that uses satire: **[+on]** *a satire on political corruption* —**satirical** /sə'tɪrɪkəl/ *adj*

satirist /'sætɪrɪst/ *n* [C] someone who writes satire

satirize (*also* -**ise** *BrE*) /'sætəraɪz/ *v* [T] to use jokes to make a person or political party seem silly so that people will see their faults

satisfaction /ˌsætəs'fækʃən/ *n* [C,U] a feeling of happiness or pleasure because you have achieved something or got what you wanted [OPP] **dissatisfaction**: **with satisfaction** *Jo looked around the room with satisfaction.* | *It gave me **a lot of satisfaction** to beat the world's No.1.*

S

satisfactory

PHRASES

to sb's satisfaction as well or as completely as someone wants: *I'm not sure I can answer that question to your satisfaction.*

COLLOCATIONS

verbs

to get/gain satisfaction from sth *I get a lot of satisfaction from teaching.*
to take satisfaction in/from sth *You can take some satisfaction in knowing that you were right.*
to have the satisfaction of doing sth *She finally had the satisfaction of seeing her book published.*
to give/bring sb satisfaction *It gives me great satisfaction when I find that I can play a difficult piece of music.*

adjectives

great satisfaction *Most nurses get great satisfaction from their work.*
deep/immense satisfaction (=great satisfaction) *His success was a source of immense satisfaction to me.*
real satisfaction (=used for emphasis) *I get real satisfaction from helping other people.*

noun + satisfaction

a sense/feeling of satisfaction *There was a great feeling of satisfaction when the film was finished.*

satisfactory /ˌsætəsˈfæktəri◂/ *adj* good enough OPP **unsatisfactory** SYN **acceptable**: *Your work this term has been satisfactory.* | [+to/for] *an agreement that is satisfactory to both sides* | **satisfactory explanation/solution/answer** *There seems to be no satisfactory explanation.* | **satisfactory result/ outcome** *We managed to achieve a satisfactory result.* —**satisfactorily** *adv*

THESAURUS

satisfactory good enough: *He has made satisfactory progress in class this year.* | *a satisfactory result*
all right/OK *spoken* not bad, but not very good: *'How was the film?' 'It was OK.'*
reasonable fairly good – used when saying that you do not want to complain about something because it seems good enough: *They had a reasonable standard of living.* | *I think £50 a day sounds reasonable.*
adequate enough in quantity, or of a good enough standard. **Adequate** sounds rather formal and is used especially in official contexts: *The accommodation was not adequate for such a big family.*
sth will do *informal* to be good enough for a particular purpose: *Any kind of paper will do.*

satisfied /ˈsætəsfaɪd/ *adj*
1 feeling that something is as good as it should be, or that something has happened in the way that you want OPP **dissatisfied**: [+with] *I'm not really satisfied with the way he cut my hair.* | *We have thousands of satisfied customers.* THESAURUS ▶ HAPPY

Grammar
Do not say 'He is satisfied about my work.' Say *He is satisfied with my work.*

2 feeling sure that something is right or true: [+(that)] *I'm satisfied that he's telling the truth.*

satisfy /ˈsætəsfaɪ/ *v* [T] (**satisfied, satisfying, satisfies**) **1** to make someone happy by doing what they want: *I felt that nothing I did would ever satisfy my father.* **2** if you satisfy someone's needs or demands, you provide what they need or want: **satisfy sb's needs/requirements/demands** *We aim to satisfy the needs of our customers.* | **satisfy sb's hunger/appetite/thirst** *A salad won't be enough to satisfy your hunger.* **3** *formal* to make someone believe that something is true or right: **satisfy sb/yourself (that)** *I want to satisfy myself that everything's OK.*

satisfying /ˈsætəsfaɪ-ɪŋ/ *adj* making you feel pleased and happy, especially because you have achieved something: *a satisfying job*

sat-nav /ˈsæt næv/ *n* [C,U] a piece of electronic equipment in a car which can tell you which way you need to go by using information received from a SATELLITE

satsuma /sætˈsuːmə/ *n* [C] a kind of small sweet orange with loose skin

saturate /ˈsætʃəreɪt/ *v* [T] **1** to make something completely wet SYN **soak**: *Rain had saturated the ground.* **2** to fill a place with a lot of things, so there is no space for any more: **saturate sth with sth** *The market is saturated with cheap imports.* —**saturation** /ˌsætʃəˈreɪʃən/ *n* [U]

saturated 'fat *n* [C,U] a kind of fat from meat and milk products

satu'ration ˌpoint *n* [singular] a situation in which no more people or things can be added because there are already too many: *The number of tourists has now reached saturation point.*

Saturday /ˈsætədi, -deɪ $ -ər-/ *n* [C,U] (*written abbreviation* **Sat.**) the day between Friday and Sunday → see examples at MONDAY

Saturn /ˈsætən $ -ərn/ *n* the second largest PLANET, sixth from the Sun

sauce /sɔːs $ sɒːs/ *n* [C,U] a thick liquid that is served with food to give it a nice taste: **tomato/ wine/cheese etc sauce** *spaghetti with tomato sauce* → SOY SAUCE

saucepan /ˈsɔːspən $ ˈsɒːspæn/ *n* [C] a round metal container with a handle that you use for cooking → see picture at PAN¹

saucer /ˈsɔːsə $ ˈsɒːsər/ *n* [C] a small round plate that you put under a cup: *a china cup and saucer* → see picture at CUP¹ → FLYING SAUCER

saucy /ˈsɔːsi $ ˈsɒːsi/ *adj* about sex in a way that is amusing but not shocking: *saucy pictures*

sauna /ˈsɔːnə $ ˈsɒːnə, ˈsaʊnə/ *n* [C] **1** a room that is heated to a very high temperature, where people sit and relax **2** **have/take a sauna** to spend time in a sauna

saunter /ˈsɔːntə $ ˈsɒːntər/ *v* [I] to walk in a slow relaxed way

sausage /'sɒsɪdʒ $ 'sɒ:-/ n [C,U] a mixture of meat and spices that is put into a small tube of skin and cooked: *beef sausages*

sausage 'roll n [C] a piece of sausage meat wrapped in PASTRY

sauté /'səʊteɪ $ soʊ'teɪ/ v [T] to cook something quickly in a little hot oil or fat

savage¹ /'sævɪdʒ/ adj **1** very cruel or violent: *a savage murder* **2** very severe: *a savage attack on the government* | *savage cuts in public spending* —**savagely** adv —**savagery** n [U]

savage² v [T] **1** if an animal savages someone, it attacks them and seriously injures them **2** to criticize someone or something very severely: *The movie was savaged by the critics.*

savage³ n [C] old-fashioned an offensive word for someone who does not live in a modern society

save¹ /seɪv/ v

1 FROM DANGER/HARM [T] to make someone or something safe from danger or harm → **rescue**: *The new speed limit could save many lives.* | **save sb/sth from sth** *Only three people were saved from the fire.* | *a campaign to save the old theatre* THESAURUS **PROTECT**

2 MONEY (also **save up**) [I,T] to keep money so that you can use it later: *I've saved $600 so far.* | **[+for]** *We're saving up for a new car.*

3 NOT WASTE (also **save on**) [T] to use less time, money, energy etc, so that you do not waste any OPP **waste**: *We'll save time if we take a taxi.* | *There are many ways to save on energy costs.*

4 TO USE LATER (also **save** sth ↔ **up**) [T] to keep something so that you can use or enjoy it in the future: *You can save up the vouchers and get free airline tickets.* | **save sth for sth** *We'd been saving the champagne for a special occasion.* THESAURUS **KEEP**

5 HELP SB AVOID STH [T] to help someone by making it unnecessary for them to do something unpleasant or inconvenient: **save sb (doing) sth** *If you get some bread, it will save me a trip to the shops.* | *I'll give you a lift to save you waiting at the bus stop.*

6 KEEP STH FOR SB [T] to stop people from using something, so that it is available for someone else SYN **keep**: **save sth for sb** *We'll save some dinner for you.* | **save sb sth** *Will you save me a seat?*

7 ON COMPUTER [I,T] to make a computer keep the work that you have done on it: *Don't forget to save the changes that you made.*

8 IN SPORT [I,T] to stop someone from scoring in games such as football: *The goalkeeper saved the shot.* → see picture at **FOOTBALL** → **save face** at **FACE¹**
PHRASES

 saving grace the one good thing that makes someone or something acceptable when everything else about them is bad: *His sense of humour was his only saving grace.*

save² n [C] when a player in a game such as football prevents the other team from scoring: *Martin made a brilliant save.*

saver /'seɪvə $ -ər/ n [C] someone who saves money in a bank

saving /'seɪvɪŋ/ n **1 savings** [plural] money that you have saved, usually in a bank: *He has savings of* over $150,000. | *a savings account* **2** [C] an amount of money that you have not spent or an amount of something that you have not used: **[+of]** *a saving of 25%* | **[+in]** *savings in fuel consumption*

savings and 'loan associ,ation n [C] AmE a business, similar to a bank, where you can save money or borrow money to buy a house SYN **building society** BrE

saviour BrE, **savior** AmE /'seɪvjə $ -ər/ n **1** [C] someone who saves you from a difficult or dangerous situation: **[+of]** *He was seen as the saviour of his people.* **2 the/our Saviour** in the Christian religion, Jesus Christ

savour BrE, **savor** AmE /'seɪvə $ -ər/ v [T] to make something last as long as possible, because you are enjoying it so much: *Drink it slowly and savour every drop.*

savoury BrE, **savory** AmE /'seɪvəri/ adj savoury food has a salty or spicy taste: *a savoury snack*

savvy /'sævi/ n [U] informal practical knowledge and ability: *political savvy*

saw¹ /sɔː $ sɒː/ v the past tense of SEE

saw² n [C] a tool that you use for cutting wood. It has a flat blade with a row of sharp points. → see picture at **TOOL**

saw³ v [I,T] (past participle **sawed** or **sawn** /sɔːn $ sɒːn/) to cut something using a saw: *Dad was outside sawing logs.* THESAURUS **CUT**

sawdust /'sɔːdʌst $ 'sɒː-/ n [U] very small pieces of wood that are left when you cut wood with a saw

sawmill /'sɔːmɪl $ 'sɒː-/ n [C] a factory where trees are cut into boards

saxophone /'sæksəfəʊn $ -foʊn/ (also **sax** /sæks/ informal) n [C] a curved musical instrument made of metal that you play by blowing into it and pressing buttons, used especially in JAZZ → see picture on page A6

say¹ /seɪ/ v (past tense and past participle **said** /sed/, third person singular **says** /sez/)

1 [I,T] to express an idea, feeling etc using words: *'I'm so tired,' she said.* | *I'm sorry, I didn't hear what you said.* | **[+(that)]** *Dave said he'd call back.* | *He didn't seem to understand a word I said (=anything I said).* | **say how/why/who etc** *Did she say what happened?* | **say sth to sb** *What did you say to them?* | **say hello/goodbye/thank you etc** *They left without saying goodbye.* | **say sorry/say you're sorry** (=apologize) *I've said I'm sorry, what more do you want?* | **a nice/nasty/silly etc thing to say** *That's a pretty mean thing to say.*

2 [T] to give information in writing, pictures, or numbers: *The clock said nine thirty.* | *What do the instructions say?* | **[+(that)]** *He received a letter saying the appointment had been cancelled.* | **It says here** *the concert starts at 8.* THESAURUS **ADVISE**

3 [T] used to talk about what someone means: *What do you think the writer is trying to say?* | **be saying (that)** *Are you saying I'm fat?*

4 [T] used when talking about something that people think is true: **they say/people say/it is said (that)** *They say she's the richest woman in the world.*

5 [I,T] to express something without using words: *Your clothes **say a lot about** the kind of person you are.*

> **Grammar**
> **Say** cannot have a person as its object. Do not say 'He said me that he was tired.' Say *He said that he was tired.* If you want to say who is being spoken to, use **tell**: *He told me that he was tired*

PHRASES

having said that *spoken* used when you are adding a different opinion to the one you have just expressed: *This isn't really a brilliant movie, but having said that, the kids should enjoy it.*

I must say/I have to say *spoken* used to emphasize what you are saying: *That cake does look good, I must say.*

it/that goes without saying used to say that the thing you have just mentioned is so clear that it really did not need to be said: *It goes without saying it will be a very difficult job.*

I would say/I'd say *spoken* used for giving your opinion: *I'd say he's jealous.*

(let's) say *spoken* used when suggesting or imagining something: *Say you were going to an interview. What would you wear?*

say to yourself to think something: *I was worried about it, but I said to myself, 'You can do this.'*

say 'when' *spoken* used when you are pouring a drink for someone and you want them to tell you when there is enough in their glass

you can say that again! *spoken* used to say that you agree with someone very strongly: *'I think we've been wasting our time.' 'You can say that again!'*

you don't say! *spoken* used to say that you are not at all surprised by what someone has told you: *'She used to work with the President.' 'You don't say!'*

THESAURUS

say to express an idea, feeling etc using words: *John said he's having a party.*

mention to talk about something or someone without giving many details: *He mentioned that he was hoping to visit Frankfurt.*

add to say something more after what has already been said: *Is there anything else you would like to add?*

point out to mention something important that other people have not noticed or thought of: *Someone pointed out that the picture was the wrong way up.*

announce to publicly tell people about something so that everyone knows: *They announced that the train would be late.*

state to say something publicly or officially – used about people, official documents, rules etc: *The report states that the problem could get worse.*

comment to give your opinion about something: *The company have refused to comment about these claims.*

---

say² *n* [singular, U] the right to help decide something: **have some/no/little say in sth** *Members felt that they had no say in the proposed changes.* | *Who has **the final say** (=the final decision)?*

have your say to give your opinion on something: *You'll all have the chance to have your say.*

saying /'seɪ-ɪŋ/ *n* [C] a well-known phrase that people use to give advice SYN **proverb** THESAURUS▶ PHRASE

scab /skæb/ *n* [C] a hard layer of dried blood that forms over a wound

scaffold /'skæfəld, -fəʊld $ -fəld, -foʊld/ *n* [C] **1** a structure of poles and boards that is built next to a building for workers to stand on while they build or repair the building **2** a wooden frame on which criminals were killed in the past by being hanged

scaffolding /'skæfəldɪŋ/ *n* [U] poles and boards that are made into a structure for workers to stand on when they are working on a building

scald /skɔːld $ skɒːld/ *v* [T] to burn someone with hot liquid or steam: *The coffee scalded his tongue.* —**scald** *n* [C]

scalding /'skɔːldɪŋ $ 'skɒːl-/ (*also* ,scalding 'hot) *adj* extremely hot: *scalding tea*

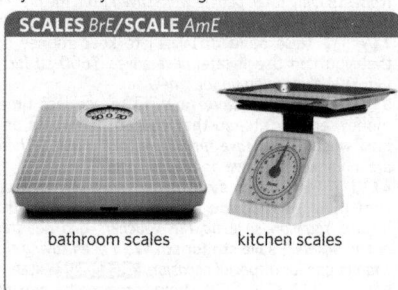

SCALES *BrE*/**SCALE** *AmE*

bathroom scales   kitchen scales

---

scale¹ /skeɪl/ *n*

1 HOW BIG/IMPORTANT [singular, U] how big or important something is: **large-/small-scale** *a large-scale development project* | *The house is built **on a grand scale**.* | *People underestimated the **sheer scale** (=very big size) of the problem.*

2 POSSIBLE RANGE [singular] the full range of different types of people or things: *One-third of the group had no qualifications at all while, **at the other end of the scale**, six were qualified teachers.* | *They came from opposite ends of the **social scale**.*

3 MEASURING SYSTEM [C usually singular] a system for measuring how strong, fast, or good something is: **on a scale** *The earthquake measured 5.8 on the Richter scale.* | *Your papers will be marked **on a scale of one to ten**.*

4 WEIGHING EQUIPMENT **scales** [plural] *BrE*, **scale** *AmE* a piece of equipment for weighing people or objects: *kitchen scales* | *a set of bathroom scales* (=for weighing things)

5 MARKS FOR MEASURING [C] a set of marks with regular spaces between them on a tool that is used for measuring things: *a ruler with a metric scale*

6 OF A MAP/MODEL [C,U] the relationship between the size of a map, drawing, or model and the actual size of the place or thing that it shows: *a scale of one inch to the mile*

7 IN MUSIC [C] a series of musical notes with a fixed distance between them that become gradually higher or lower

8 ON A FISH/SNAKE [C usually plural] the scales on a fish or snake are the small flat pieces of hard skin that cover its body

scale² v [T] to climb to the top of something that is high: *They scaled a 40-foot wall and escaped.*

PHRASAL VERBS

scale sth ↔ **back/down** to reduce the size or effectiveness of something → **decrease**: *Military operations in the area have been scaled down.*

scale sth ↔ **up** to increase the size or effectiveness of something: *Production at the factory is being scaled up.*

scallop /'skɒləp, 'skæ- $ 'skɑː-/ n [C] a small sea creature that has a shell and can be eaten

scalloped /'skɒləpt, 'skæ- $ 'skɑː-/ adj scalloped edges are cut in a series of small curves

scalp¹ /skælp/ n [C] the skin on the top of your head

scalp² v [T] **1** to cut the scalp off a dead enemy as a sign of victory **2** *AmE informal* to buy tickets for an event and sell them again at a much higher price SYN **tout** *BrE*

scalpel /'skælpəl/ n [C] a small, very sharp knife that is used by doctors during operations

scalper /'skælpə $ -ər/ n [C] *AmE* someone who buys tickets for a concert, sports match etc and sells them at a higher price SYN **tout** *BrE*

scaly /'skeɪli/ adj **1** an animal that is scaly is covered with small flat pieces of hard skin called SCALES **2** scaly skin is dry and rough

scam /skæm/ n [C] *informal* a clever but dishonest way to get money

scamper /'skæmpə $ -ər/ v [I] to run with short quick steps, like a small animal: **[+off/up/through etc]** *The boy scampered up the steps.*

scampi /'skæmpi/ n [plural] *BrE* PRAWNS covered in bread CRUMBS and cooked in oil

scan¹ /skæn/ v (**scanned**, **scanning**) **1** [T] to examine an area carefully, because you are looking for a particular person or thing: **scan sth for sth** *Lookouts were scanning the sky for enemy planes.* **2** [I,T] (*also* **scan through**) to read something quickly: *I scanned through the report on the plane.* THESAURUS **READ 3** [T] if a machine scans something, it produces a picture of what is inside it: *All luggage has to be scanned at the airport.* **4** [T] to copy a picture or piece of writing onto a computer by putting it into a machine attached to the computer: *You can scan the photos onto your PC.*

scan² n [C] a medical test in which a machine produces a picture of the inside of your body: *a brain scan*

scandal /'skændl/ n **1** [C] something dishonest or immoral that a famous or important person does which shocks a lot of people: **financial/political/ sexual etc scandal** *He was involved in a major financial scandal.* **2** [U] talk about dishonest or immoral things that famous or important people are believed

to have done: *The magazine is full of gossip and scandal.*

scandalize (*also* **-ise** *BrE*) /'skændəlaɪz/ v [T] to make people feel very shocked

scandalous /'skændələs/ adj very bad or wrong: *scandalous mismanagement*

scanner /'skænə $ -ər/ n [C] **1** a machine that passes electronic waves through something in order to produce a picture of what is inside it **2** a machine that copies a picture or piece of writing from paper onto a computer → see picture on page A12

scant /skænt/ adj very little: *The story has received scant attention in the press.*

scanty /'skænti/ adj **1** very little: *They had obtained only scanty information.* **2** scanty clothes are very small and do not cover much of your body: *a scanty bikini* —**scantily** adv: *scantily dressed*

scapegoat /'skeɪpgəʊt $ -goʊt/ n [C] someone who is blamed for something bad that happens, even if it is not their fault: *Our department has been **made a scapegoat** for the company's difficulties.* —**scapegoat** v [T]

scar¹ /skɑː $ skɑːr/ n [C] **1** a permanent mark on someone's skin from a cut or wound: *The cut will leave a permanent scar.* THESAURUS **MARK 2** a feeling of fear and sadness that stays with a person after a bad experience: *The community still **bears** the **scars** of the conflict.*

scar² v [T] (**scarred**, **scarring**) **1** if a wound or cut scars you, it leaves a permanent mark on your skin: *The fire had left him **scarred for life** (=for ever).* **2** if a bad experience scars you, it leaves you with a feeling of sadness and fear that continues for a long time: *She was deeply scarred by her father's suicide.*

scarce /skeəs $ skers/ adj if something is scarce, there is not enough of it available: *Food was often scarce in the winter.*

scarcely /'skeəsli $ 'sker-/ adv **1** almost not or almost none at all SYN **hardly**: *The city had scarcely changed since we were last there.* | *The country has **scarcely any** industry.* | *He **scarcely ever** (=almost never) leaves his house.* THESAURUS **RARELY 2** definitely not: *Owen is really angry, and you can scarcely blame him.*

scarcity /'skeəsəti $ 'sker-/ n [singular] when there is not enough of something: **[+of]** *a scarcity of clean water*

scare¹ /skeə $ sker/ v

1 [T] to make someone feel frightened SYN **frighten**: *The fireworks will scare the animals.* | **scare the life/living daylights/hell etc out of sb** (=scare someone very much) *The alarm scared the life out of me.*

2 scare easily to easily become frightened: *I don't scare easily, you know.*

PHRASAL VERBS

scare sb/sth ↔ **off/away**

1 to make someone or something go away by frightening them: *Move quietly or you'll scare the birds away.*

2 to make someone worried, so that they do not do

something they were going to do: *Customers are being scared off by high prices.*

scare² *n* **1** [singular] a sudden feeling of fear: *You really gave us **a scare**.* **2** [C] a situation in which a lot of people become frightened about something: *a **bomb scare***

scarecrow /'skeəkrəʊ $ 'skerkroʊ/ *n* [C] an object made to look like a person that is put in a field to frighten birds away

scared /skeəd $ skerd/ *adj* frightened or nervous about something SYN afraid: **[+(that)]** *We were scared that something terrible might happen.* | **scared of (doing) sth** *She's always been scared of flying.* | **scared stiff/scared to death** (=very frightened) *I'm scared stiff of spiders.* THESAURUS FRIGHTENED

SCARECROW

scarf /skɑːf $ skɑːrf/ *n* [C] (*plural* **scarves** /skɑːvz $ skɑːrvz/ *or* **scarfs**) a piece of material that you wear around your neck, head, or shoulders → see picture at CLOTHES

scarlet /'skɑːlɪt $ -ɑːr-/ *n* [U] a bright red colour —**scarlet** *adj*

scary /'skeəri $ 'skeri/ *adj informal* frightening: *a scary movie* THESAURUS FRIGHTENING

scathing /'skeɪðɪŋ/ *adj* criticizing someone or something very strongly: *a scathing attack on the government*

scatter /'skætə $ -ər/ *v* **1** [T] to throw or drop things over a wide area: **scatter (sth) over/around/across etc sth** *Scatter the seeds over the ground.* **2** [I,T] if people or animals scatter, or if something scatters them, they move quickly in different directions: *Guns started firing, and the crowd scattered in terror.*

scattered /'skætəd $ -ərd/ *adj* spread over a wide area or over a long period of time: *a scattered population* | *The weather forecast is for **scattered showers*** (=short periods of rain).

scattering /'skætərɪŋ/ *n* **a scattering of sth** *written* a small number of things or people spread out over a large area: *a scattering of isolated farms*

scavenge /'skævəndʒ/ *v* [I,T] to search for food or useful objects among things that have been thrown away: **[+for]** *Children were scavenging for food.* —**scavenger** *n* [C]

scenario Ac /sə'nɑːriəʊ $ -'nærioʊ, -'ner-/ *n* [C] (*plural* **scenarios**) a situation that could possibly happen: **worst-case/nightmare scenario** *The worst-case scenario would be if the college had to close.*

scene /siːn/ *n*
1 IN A PLAY/FILM [C] a short part of a play or film, when the events happen in one place: *the opening scene of the film* | *a love scene* THESAURUS PART
2 TYPE OF ACTIVITY [singular] a set of activities and the people who are involved in them: **the music/fashion/political etc scene** *the London music scene* | *I'm not into the **club scene*** (=going to nightclubs) at all.
3 OF AN ACCIDENT/CRIME [singular] the place where an accident or crime happened: **at the scene** *Firefighters arrived at the scene within minutes.* | **[+of]** *the scene of the crime*
4 VIEW/PICTURE [C] a view or picture of a place: *a peaceful country scene* THESAURUS SIGHT
5 ARGUMENT [C] a loud angry argument in a public place: *Sit down and stop **making a scene**!*
PHRASES
behind the scenes working secretly, while other things are happening publicly: *People are working hard behind the scenes.*
set the scene 1 to provide the conditions in which an event can happen: **[+for]** *This agreement sets the scene for democratic elections.* **2** to describe the situation before you tell a story: *The first shot, showing the family at home, sets the scene for the viewers.*

scenery /'siːnəri/ *n* [U]
1 the natural features of a place, such as the mountains, forests etc: **beautiful/spectacular/dramatic etc scenery** *Alaska's magnificent scenery* | *It's an area of wild **mountain scenery** and unspoilt villages.*
2 the large pictures of buildings, countryside etc used at the back of a theatre stage

scenic /'siːnɪk/ *adj* a scenic place or road has beautiful views of the countryside: *Let's take **the scenic coastal route**.*

scent¹ /sent/ *n* **1** [C] a pleasant smell: **[+of]** *the scent of roses* THESAURUS SMELL **2** [C] the smell that an animal or person leaves behind them: *The dogs soon **picked up** the fox's scent* (=were able to follow the smell). **3** [C,U] *especially BrE* a liquid with a pleasant smell that you put on your skin SYN perfume

scent² *v* [T] **1** if an animal scents another animal or a person, it knows that they are near because it can smell them **2** *written* to suddenly think that something is going to happen or exists: *We **scented danger** and decided to leave.*

scented /'sentɪd/ *adj* having a pleasant smell: *scented soap*

sceptic *BrE*, **skeptic** *AmE* /'skeptɪk/ *n* [C] someone who doubts whether something is true or right

sceptical *BrE*, **skeptical** *AmE* /'skeptɪkəl/ *adj* doubting whether something is true or right: **[+about/of]** *I'm **highly sceptical** about what I read in the press.* THESAURUS DOUBT

scepticism *BrE*, **skepticism** *AmE* /'skeptɪsɪzəm/ *n* [U] when someone doubts whether something is true or right

schedule¹ Ac /'ʃedjuːl, 'ske- $ 'skedʒʊl, -dʒəl/ *n*
1 [C,U] a plan of what someone is going to do, or when work is to be done: **on schedule** (=at the planned time) *The project looks like finishing on schedule.* | **ahead of/behind schedule** (=earlier or later than the planned time) *Meg's book was written well ahead of schedule.* | **busy/tight schedule** (=a

plan that includes a lot of things to be done in a short time) *I have a **busy schedule** this week.* | **[+of]** *a schedule of meetings*

2 [C] *AmE* a list that shows the times that buses, trains etc leave or arrive SYN **timetable** *BrE*

3 [C] a formal written list: **[+of]** *a schedule of postal charges*

schedule² Ac *v* [T usually passive] to arrange that something will happen at a particular time: **schedule sth for sth** *The meeting has been scheduled for Friday.* | **scheduled flight/service** (=a plane service that flies at the same time every day or every week) *daily scheduled flights to Paris*

scheme¹ Ac /skiːm/ *n* [C]

1 *BrE* an official plan that is intended to help people or to achieve something SYN **program** *AmE*: **[+for]** *a government **training scheme** for young people* | *a **pension scheme*** | **scheme to do sth** *schemes to encourage people to recycle waste* THESAURUS **PLAN**

2 an idea or plan that someone has, especially a slightly dishonest or stupid one: *a crazy scheme for making money*

scheme² Ac *v* [I] to make secret plans to get or achieve something, often dishonestly: **scheme to do sth** *politicians scheming to win votes* —**schemer** *n* [C]

schizophrenia /ˌskɪtsəʊˈfriːniə, -sə- $ -soʊ-, -sə-/ *n* [U] a serious mental illness in which someone thinks that imaginary events, conversations, ideas etc are really happening or true —**schizophrenic** /-ˈfrenɪk◂/ *adj, n* [C]

scholar /ˈskɒlə $ ˈskɑːlər/ *n* [C] someone who studies a subject and knows a lot about it: *a Latin scholar*

scholarly /ˈskɒləli $ ˈskɑːlərli/ *adj* relating to or involved with the serious study of a subject: *a scholarly journal*

scholarship /ˈskɒləʃɪp $ ˈskɑːlər-/ *n* **1** [C] an amount of money given to someone by an organization to help pay for their education **2** [U] the knowledge, work, or methods used in serious studying

school /skuːl/ *n*

1 [C,U] a place where children are taught: *I went to school in London.* | *Lizzie's starting a new school in September.* | **at school** *BrE*, **in school** *AmE* (=in the school building) *I work while the kids are in school.*

2 [U] **a)** the day's work at school: *School begins at 9 o'clock.* | *I'll meet you after school.* **b)** the time in your life that you spend at school: *She started school when she was four.* | **at school** *BrE* (=attending a school, not at university, doing a job etc) *John's only 14, so he's still at school.*

3 [singular] all the students and teachers at a school: *The whole school was sorry when she left.*

4 [C,U] *AmE* a university or college: *She was **going to school** in Boston.* | **in school** (=attending a university or school rather than having a job) *Are your boys still in school?*

5 [C,U] a college or a department at a university that teaches a particular subject: **law/business/medical school** *If I pass my exams, I'll **go to medical school**.* | *the London School of Economics*

6 [C] a group of painters or writers whose style of work is similar: *the Dutch school of painting*

7 riding/driving/language etc school an organization that teaches a particular skill or subject: *an English language school* | *the Amwell School of Motoring*

8 [C] a large group of fish etc swimming together: **[+of]** *a school of dolphins* THESAURUS **GROUP** → **COMPREHENSIVE SCHOOL, HIGH SCHOOL, NURSERY SCHOOL, PRIVATE SCHOOL, PUBLIC SCHOOL**

PHRASES

of the old school of the kind that used to exist or be typical: *a soldier of the old school*

school of thought an opinion that is shared by a group of people: *One school of thought is that red wine is good for you.*

Grammar

You say **the school** when talking about a particular school: *The local school is very good.* | *I pass by the school everyday on my way to work.* You do not use **the** with **school**, when you are talking about school in general: *School starts at 8.30.* | *What time do you go to school?* | *My dad left school when he was 15.*

COLLOCATIONS

verbs

to go to school (*also* **to attend school** *formal*) *I don't want to go to school today.* ⚠ Do not say 'go school'. Say **go to school**.

to start school *My little brother starts school next week.*

to leave school *What do you want to do when you leave school?*

school + noun

a school teacher *She became a school teacher.*

school children *He gives talks to local school children.*

a school friend *I got a letter from an old school friend.*

the school holidays *BrE What did you do in the school holidays?*

school uniform *Do you have to wear school uniform?*

school meals/lunches (*also* **school dinners** *BrE*) *I hated school meals.*

the school playground *We used to play games in the school playground.*

---

schoolboy /ˈskuːlbɔɪ/ *n* [C] *especially BrE* a boy who goes to school

schoolchild /ˈskuːlˈtʃaɪld/ *n* [C] (*plural* **schoolchildren** /-ˈtʃɪldrən/) a child who goes to school

schooldays /ˈskuːldeɪz/ *n* [plural] the time in your life when you go to school

schoolgirl /ˈskuːlɡɜːl $ -ɡɜːrl/ *n* [C] *especially BrE* a girl who goes to school

schooling /ˈskuːlɪŋ/ *n* [U] education at school

school-leaver *n* [C] *BrE* someone who has just finished their education at school

schoolteacher /ˈskuːlˌtiːtʃə $ -ər/ *n* [C] a teacher in a school

science /ˈsaɪəns/ n

1 [C,U] knowledge about the physical world based on testing and proving facts, or work that results in this knowledge: *the teaching of science in schools* | *the* **physical sciences** (=subjects such as physics and chemistry) | *developments in* **science and technology** | *the advances of* **medical science**

2 [U] the study of a particular type of human behaviour: *political science* → **EARTH SCIENCE, SOCIAL SCIENCE**

ˌscience ˈfiction n [U] books and stories about the future, for example about travelling in time and space **THESAURUS BOOK**

scientific /ˌsaɪənˈtɪfɪk◄/ adj

1 relating to science: *scientific discoveries* | *a* **scientific experiment** | *advances in* **scientific research**

2 using an organized system: *We keep records, but we're not very scientific about it.* —**scientifically** /-kli/ adv

scientist /ˈsaɪəntɪst/ n [C] someone who studies or works in science

sci-fi /ˌsaɪ ˈfaɪ◄/ n [U] informal SCIENCE FICTION

scintillating /ˈsɪntəleɪtɪŋ/ adj very exciting, impressive, or interesting: *a scintillating speech*

scissors /ˈsɪzəz $ -ərz/ n [plural] a tool for cutting paper or cloth, with two sharp blades that are joined together, and handles with holes for your finger and thumb: *a* **pair of scissors** → see picture at **STATIONERY**

scoff /skɒf $ skɔːf, skɑːf/ v **1** [I] to laugh at a person or idea and talk about them in a way that shows that you think they are stupid: **[+at]** *David scoffed at my fears.* **2** [T] *BrE informal* to eat a lot of something quickly

scold /skəʊld $ skoʊld/ v [I,T] to tell someone in an angry way that they have done something wrong: **scold sb for sth** *Her father scolded her for upsetting her mother.* —**scolding** n [C,U]

> **Word Choice**: scold or tell sb off?
> **Scold** sounds rather formal. In everyday English, people usually say **tell sb off**: *His mother told him off for being late.*

scone /skɒn, skəʊn $ skoʊn, skɑːn/ n [C] a small round cake that you eat with butter or cream and JAM

scoop¹ /skuːp/ n [C] **1** a deep spoon for serving food, or the amount that a scoop contains: *two scoops of ice-cream* **2** an exciting news story that is reported by one newspaper, television station etc before any of the others know about it

scoop² v [T] to remove or lift something with a spoon or with your curved hand: **scoop sth out/up** *Cut the melon and scoop out the seeds.*

scoot /skuːt/ v [I] *informal* to leave a place quickly: *You kids, get out of here – scoot!*

scooter /ˈskuːtə $ -ər/ n [C] **1** a small two-wheeled vehicle with an engine → see picture at **TRANSPORT¹** **2** a board on wheels with an upright handle. You stand on it with one foot and push against the ground with the other to make it move along.

scope Ac /skəʊp $ skoʊp/ n **1** [singular] the range of things that a subject, book, activity etc deals with: **within/beyond/outside the scope of sth** *Such questions are beyond the scope of this book.* **2** [U] the opportunity to do or develop something: **[+for]** *a house with scope for improvement*

scorch /skɔːtʃ $ skɔːrtʃ/ v [I,T] if you scorch something, or if it scorches, its surface burns slightly and becomes brown: *Even the walls were scorched by the fire.* —**scorch** n [C]: *scorch marks from the iron*

scorching /ˈskɔːtʃɪŋ $ ˈskɔːr-/ adj informal scorching weather is very hot: *the scorching heat of an Australian summer*

score¹ /skɔː $ skɔːr/ n [C]

1 IN SPORT the number of points that each team or player has won in a game or competition: **[+of]** *a score of 3–2* | *What's the score?* | *The final score was 35 to 17.*

2 IN A TEST the number of points that one person or group gets in a test SYN **mark**: **[+of]** *Sammy got a* **top score** *of 90%.* | *research based on children's* **test scores**

3 IN MUSIC a printed copy of a piece of music

4 A LOT **scores of sth** a large number of people or things: *Scores of buildings were damaged in the blast.*

PHRASES

know the score to know the facts about a person or situation, including any unpleasant ones: *You knew the score when you married him.*

on that score *spoken* concerning the thing you have just mentioned: *As for the cost – don't worry on that score.*

settle a score to do something to harm someone who has harmed you in the past: *Jack came back after five years to settle some old scores.*

score² v

1 [I,T] to get points in a game, competition, or test: *Dallas scored in the final minute of the game.* | **score a goal/point/run etc** *How many goals has he scored this year?* | *She scored 75% in the exam.* → see picture at **FOOTBALL**

2 [T] to give a particular number of points in a game, competition, or test SYN **mark**: *Teachers score the answers on a scale of 1 to 6.*

3 [I,T] *informal* to be successful or succeed in getting something you want: *Barnes has scored again with another popular book.* | *The JET project* **scored a** major **success.**

4 [T] to mark a line on a piece of paper, wood etc with something sharp

PHRASES

score points (off/over sb) (*also* **score off sb** *BrE*) to try to prove that you are better or cleverer than someone else: *The two guys were trying to score points off each other in front of her.*

scoreboard /ˈskɔːbɔːd $ ˈskɔːrbɔːrd/ n [C] a large board on which the score of a game is shown

scorer /ˈskɔːrə $ -ər/ n [C] **1** someone who scores a GOAL, point etc in a game **2** someone who officially records the number of points won in a game

scorn¹ /skɔːn $ skɔːrn/ n [U] complete lack of respect for someone or something because you think they are stupid or not good: **with scorn** *Scientists* **treated** *the findings* **with scorn.** | *Critics* **poured scorn on** *the idea* (=criticized it strongly). —**scornful** *adj* —**scornfully** *adv*

scorn² *v* [T] *formal* to show that you think that a person, idea, or suggestion is stupid or not worth considering: *young people who scorn the attitudes of their parents*

Scorpio /ˈskɔːpiəʊ $ ˈskɔːrpioʊ/ *n* (*plural* **Scorpios**) **1** [U] the sign of the Zodiac of people born between October 24 and November 22 **2** [C] someone who has this sign

scorpion /ˈskɔːpiən $ -ɔːr-/ *n* [C] a creature like a large insect with a curved tail which has a poisonous sting

Scotch /skɒtʃ $ skɑːtʃ/ *n* [C,U] a strong alcoholic drink made in Scotland, or a glass of this drink SYN **whisky**

,**Scotch ˈtape** *n* [U] *trademark AmE* thin clear TAPE used for sticking things together SYN **Sellotape** *BrE* → see picture at **CLASSROOM**

scoundrel /ˈskaʊndrəl/ *n* [C] *old-fashioned* a bad or dishonest man or boy

scour /skaʊə $ skaʊr/ *v* [T] **1** to search somewhere for something very carefully: **scour sth for sth** *I've scoured the whole area for a suitable house.* **2** to clean something by rubbing it with something rough

scourge /skɜːdʒ $ skɜːrdʒ/ *n* [C] *formal* something that causes a lot of harm or suffering: **[+of]** | *the scourge of war*

scout¹ /skaʊt/ *n* [C] **1 a) the Scouts** an organization that teaches young people practical skills and good behaviour **b)** (*also* **Boy Scout, Girl Scout**) a boy or girl who is a member of this organization → **guide 2** a soldier who is sent in front of an army to search an area and get information

scout² *v* [I] to look for something in an area: **[+for]** *I'll scout around for a place to eat.*

scowl /skaʊl/ *v* [I] to look at someone in an angry way: **[+at]** *Don't scowl at me!* —**scowl** *n* [C]

scrabble /ˈskræbəl/ *v* [I] to quickly feel around with your fingers in order to find something: **[+for]** *She scrabbled around for the light.*

scramble /ˈskræmbəl/ *v* [I] **1** to quickly climb up or over something difficult, using your hands to help you: **[+up/down/over etc]** *The kids were scrambling over the rocks.* **2** to move somewhere quickly, especially in order to compete with other people to get something: *Mick* **scrambled to** *his* **feet** (=stood up very quickly). | **[+for]** *Everyone was scrambling for shelter.* —**scramble** *n* [singular] *It was a tough scramble to the top.* | *the usual scramble for the bathroom*

,**scrambled ˈegg** *n* [C,U] one or more eggs which are mixed together and cooked → see picture at **EGG¹**

scrap¹ /skræp/ *n*
1 OF PAPER/CLOTH [C] a small piece of paper, cloth etc: **[+of]** *He wrote his address on a scrap of paper.*
THESAURUS ▶ PIECE

2 OF INFORMATION [C] a small amount of information, truth etc: **[+of]** *There isn't a scrap of evidence against him.*

3 OLD METAL [U] metal and parts from old or damaged cars and machines, which can be used again in another way: *Scrap metal fetched high prices after the War.* | *You'd better* **sell** *the car* **for scrap** – *it's not worth fixing.*

4 FIGHT [C] *informal* a short fight or argument: *He had a scrap with one of the boys at school.*

5 FOOD **scraps** [plural] pieces of food that are left after you have finished eating: *scraps for the dog*

scrap² *v* [T] (**scrapped, scrapping**) *informal* to decide not to do something or keep something: *We've* **scrapped the idea** *of renting a car.*

scrapbook /ˈskræpbʊk/ *n* [C] a book with empty pages where you can stick pictures, newspaper articles, or other things you want to keep

scrape¹ /skreɪp/ *v* **1** [T] to remove something from a surface using the edge of a knife, stick etc: **scrape sth away/off** *Scraping away the sand, they found a hidden entrance.* | **scrape sth off/into etc sth** *Scrape some of the mud off your boots.* **2** [T] to damage something slightly by rubbing it against a rough surface: *She fell and scraped her knee.* | **scrape sth against/on sth** *Careful! You nearly scraped the car on the wall!* **3** [I,T] to make an unpleasant noise by rubbing against a surface: *Chairs scraped loudly as they stood up.*

PHRASAL VERBS
scrape by to have enough money to live, but only with difficulty: *They have to scrape by on her tiny salary.*
scrape through (sth) to succeed in passing an examination, competition etc, but only with difficulty: *Nick just managed to scrape through his degree course.*
scrape sth ↔ **together/up** to get enough money for something with difficulty: *We're trying to scrape together enough money for a vacation.*

scrape² *n* **1** [C] slight damage or injury caused by rubbing against a rough surface SYN **graze**: *She wasn't badly hurt – only a few* **cuts and scrapes.** **2** [C] *informal* a situation in which you are in trouble or have difficulties: *He* **got into** *all sorts of* **scrapes** *as a boy.* **3** [singular] the unpleasant noise of one surface rubbing roughly against another: **[+of]** *the scrape of chalk on the blackboard*

scrapheap /ˈskræphiːp/ *n* **on the scrapheap** no longer wanted or considered useful: *When I lost my job, I felt I was on the scrapheap.*

scrappy /ˈskræpi/ *adj* **1** *BrE* untidy or badly organized: *a scrappy, badly written report* **2** *AmE informal* determined and always willing to compete, argue, or fight: *a scrappy team*

scratch¹ /skrætʃ/ *v* [I,T] **1** to rub your skin with your nails to stop it feeling uncomfortable: *Try not to scratch those mosquito bites.* → see picture on page A10 **2** to make a long thin cut on someone's skin with your nails, or a mark on something with a sharp object: *She bit him and scratched his face.* | *I'm afraid I've scratched your car.* **3** if an animal scratches, it rubs its foot against something, making a noise: **[+at]** *My dog scratches at the door when* it wants to come in. **4** to remove something from a surface using something sharp: **scratch sth off/away etc** *I managed to scratch off the paint.*

PHRASES

scratch the surface to deal with only a very small part of a problem: *Our aid can only scratch the surface of the problem.*

scratch² *n* **1** [C] a long thin cut or mark on something: *Her face was covered in scratches.* **2** [singular] *especially BrE* when you rub your skin with your nails: *Can you give my back a scratch?*

PHRASES

from scratch if you do something from scratch, you start it from the beginning, sometimes for the second time: *I deleted the file by mistake and had to start again from scratch.*

up to scratch *BrE informal* good enough: *Some of your work isn't up to scratch.*

scratchcard /ˈskrætʃkɑːd $ -kɑːrd/ *n* [C] *BrE* a card that you can buy which gives you a chance of winning money or a prize. You rub off the surface to see whether you have won.

scrawl /skrɔːl $ skrɒːl/ *v* [T] to write something in a careless or untidy way: *Charlie scrawled his name on the wall.* —**scrawl** *n* [C,U]: *The letter finished in a scrawl.*

scrawny /ˈskrɔːni $ ˈskrɒː-/ *adj* thin and weak: *a scrawny little kid*

scream¹ /skriːm/ *v*

1 [I] to make a loud high noise because you are hurt, frightened, angry, or excited: *There was a bang and people started screaming.* | **[+with/in]** *She jumped up screaming in terror.* | *kids in the playground* **screaming with laughter** **THESAURUS** ▶ SHOUT

2 (*also* **scream out**) [I,T] to shout something in a very loud high voice because you are afraid or angry **SYN** **yell**: **[+for]** *I screamed out for help.* | *'Get out!'* *she screamed.*

scream² *n* [C] a loud high noise that you make when you are hurt, frightened, angry, or excited: **[+of]** *a scream of rage* | *She saw the knife and* **let out a scream.**

PHRASES

be a scream *informal* to be very funny: *The play was a scream!*

screech /skriːtʃ/ *v* **1** [I,T] to shout loudly in an unpleasant high voice: *'Get out of my way!' she screeched.* **2** [I] if a vehicle screeches, its wheels make a high unpleasant noise as it moves along or stops: *A police car sped round the corner,* **tyres screeching.** | *The train* **screeched to a halt.** —**screech** *n* [C]

screen¹ /skriːn/ *n*

1 [C] the part of a television or computer where the picture or information appears → **monitor**: *a computer with an 18-inch screen* | **on (the) screen** *the flickering images on the screen* | *You can edit the text on screen.*

2 [C] a large white surface that a film is shown on in a cinema: *Her face fills the screen.*

3 [singular, U] films in general: **on screen** *his first*

appearance on screen | *The play is being adapted for* **the big screen** (=the cinema).

4 [C] an upright piece of furniture like a thin wall, used for dividing one part of a room from another

5 [C] something that hides a place or thing: **[+of]** *a house hidden behind a screen of trees*

screen² *v* [T] **1** to do medical tests on people to find out whether they have a particular illness: **screen sb for sth** *All women over 50 are screened for breast cancer.* **2** to find out information about people in order to decide whether they can be trusted in a particular job: *People wanting to work with children are thoroughly screened.* **3** (*also* **screen off**) to hide something, or separate it from another area, by putting something in front of it: *The garden is screened by tall hedges.* **4** to show a film or television programme

screenplay /ˈskriːnpleɪ/ *n* [C] a story written for film or television

'screen ,saver *n* [C] a moving picture that appears on a computer screen while you are not using the computer

screenwriter /ˈskriːnˌraɪtə $ -ər/ *n* [C] someone who writes plays for film or television

screw¹ /skruː/ *n* [C] a thin pointed piece of metal that you push and turn to fasten pieces of wood, metal etc together → **nail**

screw² *v* **1** [T] to fasten one thing to another, using a screw: **screw sth into/onto/to sth** *Screw the shelf to the wall.* **2** [I,T] to fasten or close something by twisting it around until it is tight **OPP** **unscrew**: **screw sth on/onto sth** *Don't forget to screw the lid on.* **3** (*also* **screw up**) [T] to twist paper or cloth into a small round shape: *She screwed the letter up and flung it in the bin.*

PHRASAL VERBS

screw up 1 *informal* to make a bad mistake **SYN** **mess up**: *You'd better not screw up again!* **2 screw sth ↔ up** *informal* to spoil something, especially something that you had planned or organized **SYN** **mess sth up**: *The bad weather screwed up our holiday plans.* **3 screw up your eyes/face** to make your eyes become narrow by changing the expression on your face

screwdriver /ˈskruːˌdraɪvə $ -ər/ *n* [C] a tool that you use for turning screws → see picture at **TOOL**

,screwed 'up *adj informal* very unhappy or anxious because you have had a lot of bad experiences

scribble /ˈskrɪbəl/ *v* **1** (*also* **scribble down**) [T] to write something quickly in an untidy way: *I scribbled his number on my hand.* **THESAURUS** ▶ WRITE **2** [I] to draw marks that do not mean anything —**scribble** *n* [C,U]

script /skrɪpt/ *n* **1** [C] the written form of a speech, play, film etc **2** [C,U] the letters used in writing a language: *Arabic script*

scripted /ˈskrɪptɪd/ *adj* a scripted speech or broadcast has been planned and written down before it is read

scripture /ˈskrɪptʃə $ -ər/ *n* [U] (*also* **the Scriptures**) the holy books of a religion, for example the Bible

scriptwriter /'skrɪptˌraɪtə $ -ər/ *n* [C] someone who writes the stories and words for films or television programmes

scroll¹ /skrəʊl $ skroʊl/ *n* [C] a long document that is rolled up

scroll² *v* [I] to move information up or down a computer screen so that you can read it: **[+up/down]** *If you scroll down the page, you'll find a link to the home page.*

scrooge /skruːdʒ/ *n* [C] *informal* someone who hates spending money

scrounge /skraʊndʒ/ *v* [T] to get money or something you want by asking other people for it: **scrounge sth off/from sb** *I'll try to scrounge some money off my dad.* —**scrounger** *n* [C]

scrub¹ /skrʌb/ *v* [I,T] (**scrubbed**, **scrubbing**) to clean something by rubbing it hard, especially with a brush: *Tom was on his knees, scrubbing the floor.* **THESAURUS** ▶ CLEAN

SCRUB

scrub² *n* **1** [U] low bushes and trees growing in a dry place **2** [singular] if you give something a scrub, you clean it by rubbing it hard

scruff /skrʌf/ *n* **by the scruff of the/your neck** by the back of a person's or animal's neck: *She grabbed him by the scruff of the neck.*

scruffy /'skrʌfi/ *adj* dirty and untidy: *a scruffy pair of jeans | a scruffy kid* **THESAURUS** ▶ UNTIDY

scrum /skrʌm/ *n* [C] when players in a game of RUGBY form a tight circle and push against each other, with their heads down, to try to get the ball

scrunch /skrʌntʃ/ *v*
PHRASAL VERBS
scrunch sth ↔ **up** to twist and press a piece of paper into a ball: *He scrunched up the letter and threw it in the bin.*

scruples /'skruːpəlz/ *n* [plural] a belief that something is wrong, which stops you from doing it: *He has no scruples about lying.*

scrupulous /'skruːpjələs/ *adj* **1** always careful to be honest and fair: *Not all car dealers are scrupulous.* **2** if you do something in a scrupulous way, you do it very carefully and well: *The names are all checked with scrupulous attention to detail.* —**scrupulously** *adv*: *The kitchen must be scrupulously clean.*

scrutinize (*also* -**ise** *BrE*) /'skruːtənaɪz/ *v* [T] to examine something very carefully: *He scrutinized the document closely.*

scrutiny /'skruːtɪni/ *n* [U] when people examine or watch something very carefully: *Her marriage has come under public scrutiny recently.*

scuba diving /'skuːbə ˌdaɪvɪŋ/ *n* [U] the sport of swimming under water using a container of air on your back to help you breathe → see picture at DIVE¹

scuff /skʌf/ *v* [T] if you scuff your shoes, you accidentally rub them against something rough and leave a mark on them

scuffle /'skʌfəl/ *n* [C] a short fight: *A scuffle broke out between demonstrators and the police.* **THESAURUS** ▶ FIGHT —**scuffle** *v* [I]: *Demonstrators scuffled with the police.*

sculptor /'skʌlptə $ -ər/ *n* [C] someone who makes sculptures

sculpture /'skʌlptʃə $ -ər/ *n* **1** [C,U] a work of art made from stone, wood, clay etc: *a bronze sculpture of a horse | an exhibition of modern sculpture* **2** [U] the art of making objects out of stone, wood, clay etc: *She teaches painting and sculpture.*

scum /skʌm/ *n* **1** [U] an unpleasant dirty layer that sometimes forms on the surface of a liquid: *a pond covered with green scum* **2** [plural] *informal* nasty, unpleasant people: *Scum like that should be locked away!*

scurrilous /'skʌrələs $ 'skɜːr-/ *adj* scurrilous remarks say unpleasant untrue things about a person

scurry /'skʌri $ 'skɜːri/ *v* [I] (**scurried, scurrying, scurries**) to move very quickly with small steps: **[+away/along/across etc]** *The mouse scurried away. | She scurried off to work.*

scuttle /'skʌtl/ *v* [I] to move quickly with small steps: **[+across/away/off etc]** *The spider scuttled away.*

scythe /saɪð/ *n* [C] a tool with a long curved blade that is used for cutting long grass or grain

SE the written abbreviation of **southeast** or **southeastern**

sea /siː/ *n* [C,U]
1 a large area of salty water: *the Mediterranean Sea | We swam **in the sea** every day. | I've always wanted to live **by the sea**. | **at sea** We spent the next six weeks at sea. | **by sea** It's cheaper to send goods by sea than by air. | **out to sea** The small boat drifted out to sea.* → see Word Choice at OCEAN
2 a sea of sth a very large number of people or things: *He stared at the sea of faces in front of him.*
PHRASES
| **go to sea** to go to work on a ship: *He went to sea when he was eighteen.*
| **be lost at sea** *formal* to be drowned in the sea: *His father had been lost at sea three months before.*
| **put to sea** to sail a boat away from land: *All the fishermen had put to sea.*

seabed /'siːbed/, **sea bed** *n* **the seabed** the land at the bottom of the sea

'sea change *n* [C] a very big change in something: *There's been a sea change in his attitude.*

seafood /'siːfuːd/ *n* [U] fish and animals from the sea that you can eat

seafront /'siːfrʌnt/ *n* [C usually singular] a part of a town next to the sea: *a hotel on the seafront*

seagull /'siːgʌl/ (*also* **gull**) *n* [C] a common grey and white bird that lives near the sea

S

seal¹ /siːl/ *n* [C] **1** a large sea animal that eats fish and lives by the sea in cold areas **2** a piece of paper or plastic that you break to open a container: *Do not use this product if the seal on the bottle is broken.* **3** a mark that has a special design and is put on documents to show that they are legal or official: *The letter had the seal of the Department of Justice at the top.* **4** a piece of rubber or plastic that keeps air or water out of something or inside something: *One of the seals was broken and oil was leaking out.*

SEAL

seal² *v* [T] **1** (*also* **seal up**) to close something very firmly so that people or things cannot get in or out: *The windows were sealed shut.* **2** to close an envelope and fasten the edges in place: *He sealed the envelope and handed it to me.* **3** **seal a deal/ agreement etc** to make an agreement definite and official: *Both companies were optimistic that an agreement would be sealed this month.* —**sealed** *adj*: *a sealed envelope*

PHRASAL VERBS

seal sth ↔ **in** to stop something that is inside something else from getting out: *Fry the meat quickly to seal in the flavour.*

seal sth ↔ **off** to stop people entering an area or building, because it is dangerous: *Police have sealed off the city centre.*

'sea ˌlevel *n* [U] the average level of the sea, used as a standard for measuring the height of an area of land: *a village 200 feet above sea level*

'sea ˌlion *n* [C] a type of large SEAL

seam /siːm/ *n* [C] **1** a line where two pieces of cloth have been sewn together: *an old jacket that was coming apart at the seams* **2** a layer of coal under the ground

seaman /ˈsiːmən/ *n* [C] (*plural* **seamen** /-mən/) a sailor

seamless /ˈsiːmləs/ *adj* happening so smoothly that you cannot tell where one thing stops and the next thing begins: *The show is a seamless blend of song, dance, and storytelling.*

seamy /ˈsiːmi/ *adj* involving bad things such as crime or violence: *the seamy side of life in the city*

seance /ˈseɪɑːns, -ɒns $ -ɑːns/ *n* [C] a meeting where people try to talk to the SPIRITS of dead people

sear /sɪə $ sɪr/ *v* [T] *literary* to burn something with a sudden powerful heat → **searing**

search¹ /sɜːtʃ $ sɜːrtʃ/ *n*
1 [C usually singular] an attempt to find someone or something: **[+for]** *The police are continuing their search for the missing girl.* | **[+of]** *We have carried out a search of the whole area.* | **in search of** (=attempting to find) *We set off in search of somewhere to eat.*
2 [C] an attempt to find information using a computer: *I did a search and found 16 websites.* | *online searches*

3 [singular] an attempt to find the explanation of a difficult problem: *the search for the meaning of life*

<table>
<tr><td colspan="2">COLLOCATIONS</td></tr>
<tr><td colspan="2">verbs</td></tr>
</table>

to do/make a search *I did a quick search for the keys around the office.*

to carry out/conduct a search (=to do a search, especially an official one involving a lot of people) *The police carried out a search of his home.*

to launch a search (=to start a big search) *A search was launched for the missing teenager.*

to call off/abandon a search (=to stop a search) *They called off the search when it got dark.*

adjectives

a thorough/careful search *They conducted a thorough search of the building.*

a desperate/frantic search (=for something that you want very much) *People began a desperate search for firewood.*

search² *v*
1 [I,T] to look carefully for someone or something: **[+for]** *Police are still searching for the missing children.* | *We searched the house from top to bottom.* | **search sth for sth** *Detectives are searching nearby woods for evidence.* | **[+through]** *I searched through the papers on my desk.*
2 [I,T] to use a computer to find information: **[+for]** *Try searching for information on the Internet.* | *searching the Web*
3 [T] if the police search someone, they look in their clothes or bags for weapons, drugs etc: *We were all searched before we were allowed to leave.*
4 [I] to try to find an answer or explanation for a difficult problem: **[+for]** *Scientists are still searching for a cure for this disease.*

'search ˌengine *n* [C] a computer program that helps you find information on the Internet

searching /ˈsɜːtʃɪŋ $ ˈsɜːr-/ *adj* a searching question or look is intended to discover the truth about something: *She asked some very searching questions.*

searchlight /ˈsɜːtʃlaɪt $ ˈsɜːrtʃ-/ *n* [C] a very large bright light that can be turned in different directions to find things or people at night

'search ˌparty *n* [C] a group of people who look for someone who is missing or lost

'search ˌwarrant *n* [C] a legal document that gives the police permission to search a building

searing /ˈsɪərɪŋ $ ˈsɪr-/ *adj* **1** searing heat is very hot: *the searing heat of the desert* **2** a searing pain is very painful **3** searing words criticize someone very strongly: *a searing attack on the government*

seashell /ˈsiːʃel/ *n* [C] the empty shell of a small sea animal

seashore /ˈsiːʃɔː $ -ʃɔːr/ *n* **the seashore** the sand and rocks along the edge of the sea

seasick /ˈsiːˌsɪk/ *adj* if you feel seasick, you feel ill because of the way a boat or ship is moving

seaside /ˈsiːsaɪd/ *n* **the seaside** *BrE* a place next to the sea where people go to enjoy themselves: *a day* at the seaside | *Shall we go* **to the seaside**? | *a seaside town*

season¹ /ˈsiːzən/ n [C]

1 one of the main periods into which a year is divided. In Europe, the four seasons are winter, spring, summer, and autumn: *Autumn is my favourite season.* | *the rainy season*

2 a period of time in a year when something usually happens: **the football/baseball etc season** *The cricket season starts in April.*

3 the time of year when a lot of people take their holiday: **the holiday/tourist season** *It gets very busy here during the holiday season.* | **the high/low season** (=the busiest or least busy time) *Prices go up in the high season.* | **the festive season** BrE (=Christmas and New year)

PHRASES

be in season 1 if vegetables or fruit are in season, they are ready to pick and eat and so are available to buy: *These tomatoes are in season from April to October.* **2** if a female animal is in season, she is ready to MATE

out of season 1 if vegetables or fruit are out of season, they are not ready to pick and eat and so are not available to buy: *You can now get fruit out of season, but it's so expensive.* **2** if you go somewhere out of season, you go when there are not many people there on holiday: *It's quite cheap if you go out of season.*

season² v [T] to add salt, pepper, or spices to food when you are cooking it: *Season the meat with salt and pepper.*

seasonal /ˈsiːzənəl/ adj happening or available only during one particular season: *You might be able to get seasonal work in the summer.*

seasoned /ˈsiːzənd/ adj [only before noun] with a lot of experience of doing something: *a seasoned traveller* | *seasoned musicians*

seasoning /ˈsiːzənɪŋ/ n [C,U] salt, pepper, and spices that you add to food when you are cooking it

ˈseason ˌticket n [C] a ticket that you can use for several journeys or events during a fixed period of time, without having to pay for each one

seat¹ /siːt/ n [C]

1 something that you can sit on, for example a chair: *Jo was driving and I was sitting in the back seat.* | **have/take a seat** (=used when telling someone to sit down) *Come in and have a seat.*

2 a place on a plane, train etc or a chair in a cinema etc that you pay to sit in: *I asked for a seat by the window.* | *I've booked two seats for Saturday's concert.*

3 the part of a chair, bicycle etc that you sit on: *a bike with a comfortable seat* → see picture at **BICYCLE**

4 a position as a member of a government or an official group: **[+in]** *a seat in the House of Commons* | **[+on]** *a seat on the company's board* | **win/lose a seat** (=gain or lose a position as member of a government) *She lost her seat at the last election.*

COLLOCATIONS

verbs

to have a seat *We had seats right at the front of the hall.*

to show sb to their seat *A flight attendant showed them to their seats.*

to book/reserve a seat *She had booked a seat on a flight from Edinburgh to London.*

to save sb a seat (=to keep a seat empty for someone) *I'll be a bit late – will you save me a seat?*

adjectives

a seat is taken (=not available for you to use) *Is this seat taken?*

a free/empty seat *There was an empty seat next to him.*

a good seat (=one from which you can see well) *I managed to get a fairly good seat.*

types of seat

the front seat (=in a car) *Can I sit in the front seat, Dad?*

the back/rear seat *Fred was asleep in the back seat.*

the driver's/passenger seat

a front-row seat (=in a theatre, sports ground etc)

seat² v [T] **1** if a place seats a particular number of people, it has enough seats for that number: *The new Olympic stadium seats over 70,000.* **2** formal if you seat yourself somewhere, you sit there: *He seated himself by the fire.*

ˈseat belt n [C] a strong belt that holds you safely in your seat in a car or plane

seated /ˈsiːtɪd/ adj formal if someone is seated, they are sitting down: *He was seated by the window.*

PHRASES

be seated used to ask people politely to sit down: *Please be seated.*

seating /ˈsiːtɪŋ/ n [U] the seats or chairs in a place, or the way that they are arranged: *a restaurant with seating for 40 customers* | *How shall we arrange the seating?*

seaweed /ˈsiːwiːd/ n [U] a plant that grows in the sea

sec /sek/ n [C] spoken informal a very short time: *Wait a sec – I'm coming too!* | *I'll be with you in a sec.*

secede /sɪˈsiːd/ v [I] formal if a country secedes from another country, it officially becomes independent from it

secluded /sɪˈkluːdɪd/ adj a secluded place is very quiet and private: *a secluded beach* | *a secluded corner of the garden*

seclusion /sɪˈkluːʒən/ n [U] when someone lives alone, away from other people: *I needed a few days of peace and seclusion.* | *He prefers to live in seclusion.*

second¹ /ˈsekənd/ adj the second person or thing is the one that is after the first one: *Joanna's in her second year at university.* | *We only saw the second half of the match.* | *He won second prize.* | *She* **came second** *in the 100 metres.* —**second** pron: *the second of August*

PHRASES

have second thoughts to have doubts about whether you have made the right decision about something: *I was having second thoughts about the whole idea.* **THESAURUS** ▶ DOUBT

not give sth a second thought/do sth without giving it a second thought to do something without worrying about it: *I used to stay out all night without giving it a second thought.*

on second thoughts *BrE*, **on second thought** *AmE spoken* used to say that you have just changed your mind about something: *On second thoughts, I will have a glass of wine.*

be second nature to sb if something is second nature to you, you have done it so often that you do it without thinking about it: *Lying was second nature to her.*

be second to none to be better than any others: *The food in this hotel is second to none.*

your second wind if you get your second wind, you suddenly feel less tired and have the energy to continue doing something: *He got his second wind and ran on.*

second² *n* [C]

1 a unit for measuring time. There are 60 seconds in a minute: *It takes about 30 seconds for the computer to start up.*

2 a very short period of time: *Can you just **wait a second**? | I'll be with you **in a second**. | Hang on **just a second** while I make a quick phone call.* **THESAURUS** TIME

3 something that is sold more cheaply than other goods because it is not quite perfect: *Most of the clothes they sell are seconds.* → SPLIT SECOND

second³ *v* [T] to formally support a suggestion that someone else has made at a meeting: **second a motion/proposal/amendment** *Sarah has proposed this motion – do we have someone who will second it?*

second⁴ /sɪ'kɒnd $ -'kɑːnd/ *v* [T] *BrE* to send someone to do someone else's job for a short time: *Jill's been seconded to the marketing department for six months.*

secondary /'sekəndəri $ -deri/ *adj* **1** [only before noun] secondary education is for children between 11 and 18 years old: *He's at **secondary school**. | a secondary teacher* **2** not as important as something else: *Work was always of secondary importance to him.* **3** a secondary problem or illness develops from another one: *She developed a secondary infection.*

,second 'best *adj* not quite best, but next best: *I'm the second best runner in the school.*

,second 'class *n* [U] **1** a way of travelling that is cheaper but not as comfortable as FIRST CLASS **2** a way of sending letters that is cheaper but slower than FIRST CLASS —**second class** *adv*: *to travel second class | I sent the letters second class.*

,second-'class *adj* [only before noun] **1** less important than other people or things, or not as good as them: *They treated us like second-class citizens. | We didn't want our children to have a second-class education.* **2** a second-class service costs less than a FIRST-CLASS one, but is not quite as good or as fast: *second-class post | a second-class train ticket*

,second-'guess *v* [T] **1** to try to say what will happen or what someone will do: *I'm not going to try*

and second-guess her decision. **2** *AmE* to criticize something after it has already happened: *The decision has been made – there's no point in second-guessing it now.*

secondhand /,sekənd'hænd◀/ *adj* **1** something that is secondhand is not new but has already been owned by someone else when you buy it: *We bought a cheap secondhand car. | shops selling second-hand clothes* **2** secondhand information is told to you by someone who did not do, say, or see something themselves but got the information from another person* OPP* **firsthand**: *We only have second-hand accounts of the attack.* —**secondhand** *adv*: *We bought it secondhand.*

,second 'language *n* [C] a language that you speak in addition to the language that you learned as a child

secondly /'sekəndli/ *adv* used to introduce the second fact or reason that you want to talk about: *Firstly, the cars are expensive to make and secondly, they are not very good.*

,second 'person *n* **the second person** the form of a verb that you use with 'you' → **first person**, **third person**

,second-'rate *adj* not very good: *a second-rate school*

secrecy /'siːkrəsi/ *n* [U] when something is kept secret: *The operation was carried out in total secrecy. | We were all **sworn to secrecy** (=made to promise that we would keep something secret).*

secret¹ /'siːkrɪt/ *adj*

1 if something is secret, only a few people know about it → **secrecy**: *a secret plan | a secret meeting | You must **keep** this **secret** (=not tell anyone). | He **kept** his marriage **secret from** his parents (=he did not tell his parents about it).*

2 [only before noun] doing something without telling anyone, because you do not want other people to know about it: *I think he's a secret gambler. | You've got a **secret admirer** (=someone who likes you romantically without telling you).* —**secretly** *adv*: *I secretly recorded our conversation.*

THESAURUS

secret if something is secret, only a few people know about it: *They kept the wedding secret.*

confidential used about information which is secret and not intended to be shown or told to other people: *confidential information about patients' medical history*

classified used about information that the government has ordered to be kept secret from most people: *The document contains classified information about US military bases.*

undercover working secretly in order to find out information for the government or the police: *Detectives arrested the man after a five-day undercover operation.*

underground an underground political organization operates secretly and illegally: *He was a member of the underground resistance movement in France during World War II.*

secret² n

1 [C] something that is only told to a few people → **secrecy**: *I can't tell you his name. It's a secret.*
2 the secret the best way to achieve something: **the secret to doing sth** *the secret to making good pastry* | **[+of]** *What's the secret of your success?*

PHRASES

in secret without other people knowing: *The meeting was held in secret.*

sth is an open secret used when saying that many people know about something, even though it is supposed to be a secret: *It was an open secret that the managers didn't like each other.*

COLLOCATIONS

verbs

to have a secret *Everyone has secrets.*
to know a secret (=about someone else) *Nobody knew her secret.*
to keep a secret (=to not tell it to anyone) *Tell me – I can keep a secret.*
to tell sb a secret *He told me all his secrets.*
⚠ Do not say 'say a secret'. Say **tell sb a secret**.
to discover/find out a secret *He was afraid that someone would discover his secret.*

adjectives

a big secret (=an important secret or one that very few people know) *Why won't you tell me? What's the big secret?*
sb's little secret (=a personal secret that very few people know) *Don't worry – it will be our little secret.*
a dark/terrible secret (=a secret about something bad) *I'm sure every family has a few dark secrets.*
sb's secret is safe (=it will not be told to anyone) *Your secret is safe with me.*

---

secret ˈagent n [C] a SPY

secretary /ˈsekrətəri $ -teri/ n [C] (*plural* **secretaries**)
1 someone whose job is to write letters, arrange meetings, answer telephone calls etc in an office: *Please make an appointment with my secretary.*
2 (*also* **Secretary**) an official who is in charge of a large government department: *the Secretary of Education* —**secretarial** /ˌsekrəˈteəriəl◂ $ -ter-/ adj: *secretarial work*

Secretary of ˈState n [C] (*plural* **Secretaries of State**) **1** the head of an important department in the British government: *the Secretary of State for Transport* **2** the head of the US government department that deals with the US's relations with other countries

secrete /sɪˈkriːt/ v [T] if a plant or animal secretes a liquid, it produces it: *The leaves secrete a mild poison.* —**secretion** /-ˈkriːʃən/ n [C,U]

secretive /ˈsiːkrətɪv, sɪˈkriːtɪv/ adj unwilling to tell people things: **[+about]** *Why are you being so secretive about your job?* —**secretively** adv

secret poˈlice n **the secret police** a police force controlled by a government, that secretly tries to defeat the political enemies of the government

secret ˈservice n [singular] **1** a country's secret service is the government department that tries to discover secret information from other countries **2** a US government department that does special police work and protects the President

sect /sekt/ n [C] a group of people with their own religious or political beliefs that have become separate from a larger group **THESAURUS** ▸ RELIGION

sectarian /sekˈteəriən $ -ter-/ adj sectarian problems or fighting take place between people from different religious groups: *sectarian violence* | *a sectarian murder*

section Ac /ˈsekʃən/ n [C] one of the parts that something is divided into: **[+of]** *Some sections of the motorway are very busy.* | *One section of the bridge has collapsed.* | *the sports section of the newspaper* | *The rocket is built in sections and fitted together later.* **THESAURUS** ▸ PART → CROSS SECTION

sector Ac /ˈsektə $ -ər/ n [C] **1** one part of a country's ECONOMY: *the public sector* (=businesses controlled by the government) | *the private sector* (=businesses controlled by private companies) **2** one of the parts that an area is divided into: *the northern sector of the city*

secular /ˈsekjələ $ -ər/ adj not religious or not controlled by a religious authority: *secular education* | *a secular society*

secure¹ Ac /sɪˈkjʊə $ -ˈkjʊr/ adj **1** not likely to change or fail: *a secure job* | *Does the company now have a secure future?* **2** a place that is secure is locked so that people cannot get in or out: *Make sure the house is secure before you leave.* **3** if you feel secure, you feel safe, confident, and free from worries: *Children need to feel secure.* **4** firmly fastened and not likely to fall: *That mirror doesn't look very secure.* —**securely** adv: *Are the doors securely locked?*

secure² Ac v [T] **1** to get something important, especially after a lot of effort: *an attempt to secure the release of the hostages* **2** to make something safe from being attacked or harmed: *to secure the building against attack* **3** to fasten or tie something firmly: *We secured the boat with a rope.*

security Ac /sɪˈkjʊərəti $ -ˈkjʊr-/ n [U] **1** the things you do to keep someone or something safe from danger or crime: *the man in charge of airport security* | **Security** *around the President has been* **tightened**. | *security cameras* **2** when you are not likely to lose something, or something is not likely to fail: *People want* **job security**. | *financial security* **3** a feeling of being safe, confident, and free from worries: *Children need a sense of security.* **4** something valuable that you promise to give to someone if you fail to pay back money you have borrowed: *You can use your house as security for the loan.*

seˈcurity ˌservice n [C] a government organization that protects a country's secrets or government against enemies

sedan /sɪˈdæn/ n [C] AmE a large car that has four doors and a separate part at the back for bags and cases **SYN** **saloon** BrE

sedate¹ /sɪˈdeɪt/ adj calm and formal

sedate² v [T] to give someone a drug to make

sedative

= words from the Academic Word List

them feel calm or ready to sleep: *He was still sedated after his operation.* —**sedation** /-'deɪʃən/ *n* [U]

sedative /'sedətɪv/ *n* [C] a drug that doctors give you to make you feel calm or ready to sleep

sedentary /'sedəntəri $ -teri/ *adj* a sedentary job or life involves sitting down a lot rather than moving around

sediment /'sedəmənt/ *n* [singular, U] a solid substance that forms a layer at the bottom of a liquid

sedition /sɪ'dɪʃən/ *n* [U] *formal* when you do or say things that encourage people to disobey a government —**seditious** *adj*

seduce /sɪ'djuːs $ -'duːs/ *v* [T] **1** to persuade someone to have sex with you, especially someone young **2** to persuade someone to do something by making it seem very attractive or interesting: *people who were seduced into investing in the company* —**seduction** /-'dʌkʃən/ *n* [C,U]

seductive /sɪ'dʌktɪv/ *adj* **1** sexually attractive **2** making something very attractive and interesting to you: *highly seductive advertising*

see /siː/ *v* (*past tense* **saw** /sɔː $ sɒː/, *past participle* **seen** /siːn/)

1 WITH YOUR EYES [I,T] to use your eyes to look at and notice people or things: *Can you see that car over there?* | *I can't see without my glasses.* | **[+(that)]** *I could see that she looked upset.* | **[+who/what/where etc]** *I didn't see who she was with.* | **see sb do sth** *I saw a man come out of the building.* | **see sb doing sth** *I saw her walking towards the library.*

2 FILM/PROGRAMME/GAME ETC [T] to watch a film, television programme etc: *Have you seen any good films lately?* | *I didn't see last week's episode.* THESAURUS > WATCH

3 UNDERSTAND [I,T] to understand or realize something: *I can see why he's angry.* | *Oh, I see, the water goes in here.* | *I can't see the point of doing extra homework.* | *It looks broken, do you see what I mean* (=understand what I am saying)? | *I see what you mean about George now.* THESAURUS > UNDERSTAND

4 VISIT/MEET [T] to visit or meet someone: *I saw Helen in town.* | *You should see a doctor.* THESAURUS > VISIT

5 FIND OUT [T] to find out something: **see what/whether/if etc** *Let's phone him and see what he says.* | *I'll see what time the train leaves.*

6 CONSIDER [T] to think about someone or something in a particular way: **see sb/sth as sth** *Fighting on TV can make children see violence as normal.* | *He sees himself as a failure.*

7 EVENTS HAPPEN [T] to be the time when or the place where something happens: *The 20th century saw huge social changes.*

8 IMAGINE [T] if you can see something happening, you can imagine it and think that it will happen: *I can't see people accepting a cut in pay.*

9 MAKE SURE [T] to make sure that something is done correctly: **[+(that)]** *Please see that everything is put back in the right place.*

10 GO WITH [T] to go with someone to a place, usually to make sure they get there safely: **see sb to/into etc** *He saw me to my room.* | *I'll see you home.*

11 ROMANTIC RELATIONSHIP **be seeing sb** to be having a romantic relationship with someone: *I'm not seeing anyone at the moment.*

PHRASES

I'll/we'll see *spoken* used when you do not want to make a decision immediately: *'Can I have an ice cream?' 'We'll see.'*

let's see/let me see *spoken* used when you are trying to remember something or are thinking about something: *Let's see. When did you send it?*

see eye to eye (with sb) to agree with someone: *Those two don't always see eye to eye.* THESAURUS > DISAGREE

see you *informal* used when saying goodbye to someone: *See you, Ben.* | *I'll see you later.*

PHRASAL VERBS

see about sth to make arrangements or deal with something: *Fran went to see about her passport.*

see sb ↔ **off** to go to an airport, train station etc to say goodbye to someone who is leaving: *We saw her off from the airport.*

see sb **out** to go with someone to the door when they leave: *It's OK, I can see myself out.*

see through

1 see through sb/sth to know that someone is not telling you the truth: *Can't you see through his lies?*

2 see sth through to continue doing something difficult until it is finished: *Miller is determined to see the project through.*

see to sth to deal with something: *I must go and see to the food.*

THESAURUS

see to use your eyes to look at and notice people or things: *I saw a picture of him in the newspaper.* | *She can't see very well.*

look at sb/sth to keep your eyes fixed on someone or something, especially someone or something that is not moving: *He looked at the clock and it was 10.40.*

notice to see something interesting or unusual: *I noticed a man running out of the bank.*

spot to suddenly see someone or something, especially someone or something you are looking for: *Nick spotted the advertisement in the newspaper.*

catch sight of/catch a glimpse of to suddenly see someone or something for a short time, usually not clearly: *Fans waited outside the hotel, hoping to catch a glimpse of the singer.*

witness to see something happen, especially a crime or an accident: *Police are appealing for information from anyone who witnessed the attack.*

---

seed¹ /siːd/ *n* [C]

1 a small hard thing produced by a plant, from which a new plant will grow: *sunflower seeds* | **plant/sow seeds** (=put them in the ground) *Sow the seeds one inch deep in the soil.* → see picture at **PLANT¹**

2 seeds of sth something that makes a new situation start to develop: *the **seeds of change** in Eastern Europe* | *Something Lucy said began to sow **seeds of doubt** in his mind.*

3 a player that has been given a particular rank in a competition because of how likely they are to win: *She beat the number three seed yesterday.*

seed² v [T usually passive] to remove seeds from a fruit or vegetable: *Slice and seed the pepper.*

seedless /'si:dləs/ adj seedless fruit has no seeds in it: *seedless grapes*

seedling /'si:dlɪŋ/ n [C] a young plant grown from a seed → see picture at **PLANT¹**

seedy /'si:di/ adj informal a seedy person or place looks dirty and poor, and is often connected with illegal or immoral activity: *a seedy nightclub*

seeing /'si:ɪŋ/ linking word spoken **seeing as/that** because a particular fact is true: *I won't stay long, seeing as you're busy.*

,Seeing 'Eye ,dog n [C] trademark AmE a specially trained dog that blind people use to help them go to places SYN **guide dog** BrE → see picture at **GUIDE DOG**

seek Ac /si:k/ v (past tense and past participle **sought** /sɔːt $ sɒːt/) **1** [T] to try to find or get something: *The UN is seeking a political solution.* | **seek refuge/asylum/shelter etc** *People were crossing the border, seeking refuge from the war.* **2 seek (sb's) advice/help/assistance etc** to ask someone for advice or help: *You should seek advice from a lawyer.* **3** [I,T] to try to do something: *Do you think the President will **seek re-election**?* | **seek to do sth** *We're always seeking to improve our results.*

seem /si:m/ v [linking verb] how something seems is how it appears to you: *The house seemed very quiet after he'd left.* | **seem to be** *She seemed to be upset.* | **seem to do sth** *He seemed to hesitate before answering.* | **seem important/right/strange etc to sb** *Doesn't that seem strange to you?* | **it seems to sb (that)** *It seems to me that we're lost.* | **it seems (that)** *It seems that he forgot to tell her.* | **seem as if/as though/like** *York seems like a nice place to live.*

THESAURUS

seem used when talking about the feeling you have about what something or someone is like, because of the way they look, sound etc: *He seems nice.* | *It seemed a good idea at the time.*
appear a more formal word for **seem**: *These reports appear to be untrue.*
look to seem to be something, especially because of what you can see: *Jim looked fine when I saw him.* | *It all looks very suspicious.*
sound to seem to be something because of what you can hear, what someone has told you, or what you have read: *He sounded a bit annoyed.* | *It sounds like a good place for a picnic.*

---

seemingly /'si:mɪŋli/ adv used to say that something seems true, but is actually not true: *a seemingly endless list of jobs*

seen /si:n/ v the past participle of SEE

seep /si:p/ v [I] if a liquid seeps somewhere, it flows there slowly through small holes: *Water was seeping into the boat.*

seesaw¹ /'si:sɔː $ -sɒː/ n [C] a piece of equipment which children play on outdoors. It is made of a board that is balanced in the middle so that when one end goes up, the other end goes down.

SEESAW

seesaw² v [I] written to move from one state or condition to another and back again many times

seethe /si:ð/ v [I] to be very angry, but not show it: *He was seething with anger.*

segment /'segmənt/ n [C] one of the parts that something is divided into: *a large segment of the population* | *Cut the orange into segments.* → see picture on page A4

segmented /seg'mentɪd/ adj divided into separate parts

segregate /'segrɪgeɪt/ v [T usually passive] to separate one group of people from others: *They were segregated from the other prisoners.* —**segregation** /ˌsegrɪ'geɪʃən/ n [U]: *racial segregation*

segregated /'segrɪgeɪtɪd/ adj a segregated school or other institution can only be used by members of one particular race, sex, religion etc

seismic /'saɪzmɪk/ adj technical relating to EARTHQUAKES

seize /si:z/ v [T] **1** to take something in your hand suddenly and roughly: *He suddenly seized the gun from her.* **2** if someone seizes power or control, they take it, using force: *The rebels have seized power.* **3** if the police or government officers seize illegal things such as drugs or guns, they take them away: *Police seized 10 kilos of cocaine.*

PHRASAL VERBS

seize on/upon sth to suddenly become interested in an idea, what someone says etc: *His remarks were seized on by the press.*

seize up 1 if a machine seizes up, it stops working, for example because of lack of oil **2** if part of your body seizes up, you cannot move it and it is very painful

seizure /'si:ʒə $ -ər/ n **1** [C,U] when someone suddenly takes control of something, especially by force: *the Fascist seizure of power* **2** [C,U] when the police or government officers take away illegal goods such as drugs or guns: *drugs seizures* **3** [C] a sudden attack of an illness: *a heart seizure*

seldom /'seldəm/ adv not very often: *He seldom goes out.* THESAURUS ▶ RARELY

select¹ Ac /sə'lekt/ v [T] to choose something or someone: *He wasn't selected for the team.* THESAURUS ▶ CHOOSE

select² Ac adj formal a select group is a small group of carefully chosen people: *a select group of students* | *Only a **select few** were invited.*

S

selection Ac /səˈlekʃən/ n **1** [U] when something or someone is chosen: **[+of]** *the selection of a new leader* **2** [C] a group of things that someone has chosen: *a selection of his favourite poems* **3** [C] a group of things that you can choose from: **[+of]** *The shop has a* **wide selection** *of books.*

selective Ac /səˈlektɪv/ adj **1** careful about the things you choose: *Be selective when you're shopping.* **2** relating to only a few specially chosen people or things: *children attending* **selective schools**

selector Ac /səˈlektə $ -ər/ n [C] *BrE* a member of a committee that chooses the best people for something such as a sports team

self /self/ n [C,U] (*plural* **selves** /selvz/) your nature and character: **sb's usual/normal self** *Sid was not his usual smiling self.* | **be/look/feel (like) your old self** (=be the way you usually are again) *You'll soon be back to your old self.*

self-apˈpointed adj disapproving giving yourself a responsibility or job without the agreement of other people, especially those you claim to represent

self-asˈsured adj confident about what you are doing —**self-assurance** n [U]

self-ˈcatering adj *BrE* a self-catering holiday is one in which you stay in a place where you can cook your own food: *a self-catering apartment*

self-ˈcentred *BrE*, **self-centered** *AmE* adj disapproving only interested in yourself **SYN** **selfish**

self-ˈconfident adj feeling sure that you can do things successfully **THESAURUS** CONFIDENT —**self-confidence** n [U]

self-ˈconscious adj uncomfortable and worried about what other people think about you or your appearance: *He felt self-conscious in his new suit.* —**self-consciously** adv —**self-consciousness** n [U]

self-conˈtained adj **1** something that is self-contained is complete and does not need other things to make it work **2** *BrE* a self-contained FLAT has its own kitchen and bathroom

self-conˈtrol n [U] the ability to behave calmly and sensibly even when you are angry, excited, or upset

self-deˈfence *BrE*, **self-defense** *AmE* n [U] the use of force to protect yourself when you are attacked: **in self-defence** *She shot the man in self-defence.*

self-destruct /ˌself dɪˈstrʌkt◂/ v [I] if something such as a bomb self-destructs, it destroys itself

self-deˈstructive adj deliberately doing things to yourself that are likely to seriously harm or kill you

self-determiˈnation n [U] the right of the people of a particular country to choose their own government or system of government

self-ˈdiscipline n [U] the ability to make yourself do the things you should do —**self-disciplined** adj

self-efˈfacing adj not wanting to attract attention to yourself or your achievements **SYN** **modest**: *her honesty and self-effacing modesty* —**self-effacement** n [U]

self-emˈployed adj someone who is self-employed has their own business rather than being employed by a company

self-esˈteem n [U] how you feel about yourself and whether, for example, you feel that you are a nice or successful person: **low/high self-esteem**

self-ˈevident adj clearly true and needing no more proof **SYN** **obvious**

self-exˈplanatory adj clear and easy to understand, and needing no more explanation

self-ˈhelp n [U] when you solve problems by yourself, instead of depending on other people: *self-help books*

self-ˈimage n [U] your opinions about yourself

self-imˈportant adj disapproving behaving in a way that shows you think you are more important than other people —**self-importance** n [U]

self-imˈposed adj a self-imposed rule, duty etc is one that you have made for yourself

self-inˈdulgent adj disapproving allowing yourself to have or do things that you enjoy but do not need —**self-indulgence** n [C,U]

self-inˈflicted adj a self-inflicted injury or problem is one that you have caused yourself

self-ˈinterest n [U] when you only care about what is best for you, and not for other people

selfish /ˈselfɪʃ/ adj disapproving caring only about yourself and not about other people **OPP** **unselfish**: *That was a very selfish thing to do.* | *selfish behaviour* —**selfishness** n [U] —**selfishly** adv

selfless /ˈselfləs/ adj approving caring about other people more than about yourself

self-ˈmade adj a self-made man or woman has become rich and successful by working hard: *a* **self-made millionaire**

self-ˈpity n [U] disapproving when you feel sorry for yourself, but without a good reason

self-ˈportrait n [C] a picture of yourself, done by you

self-posˈsessed adj approving calm, confident, and in control of your feelings

self-preserˈvation n [U] when you protect your own life in a threatening or dangerous situation

self-reˈliant adj able to do things by yourself without depending on other people

self-reˈspect n [U] a feeling of respect for yourself —**self-respecting** adj: *No self-respecting person would do that.*

self-ˈrighteous adj disapproving too sure that your moral behaviour or beliefs are right, in a way that annoys other people

self-ˈsacrifice n [U] when you decide not to have something in order to help someone else —**self-sacrificing** adj

self-ˈsatisfied adj disapproving too pleased with yourself

self-ˈservice adj a self-service restaurant, shop, garage etc is one where you get food, petrol etc for yourself before paying for it **THESAURUS** RESTAURANT

S

'self-styled adj [only before noun] disapproving having given yourself a title or position without having a right to it

self-suf'ficient adj able to provide for all your own needs without help from other people: Australia is 65% self-sufficient in oil. —**self-sufficiency** n [U]

sell¹ /sel/ v (past tense and past participle **sold** /səʊld $ soʊld/)
1 [I,T] to give something to someone and accept money from them for it → **buy**: **sell sth for £100/$50/30p etc** He sold his car for £5,000. | **sell sth to sb** I sold a ticket to Mary. | **sell sb sth** Sally's going to sell me her bike. | He had to sell the business at a loss.
2 [I,T] to offer something for people to buy: Do you sell stamps? | **sell at/for £100/$50/30p etc** The T-shirts sell at £10 each.
3 [T] to make someone want to buy something: Scandal sells newspapers.
4 [I,T] to be bought by people: Her book sold millions of copies. | **sell well/badly** These cakes are selling well.
5 [T] to try to persuade someone to accept a new plan or idea: **sell sth to sb** We have to sell the idea to the viewers.
6 sell yourself to make yourself seem impressive to other people: If you want promotion, you've got to sell yourself better.

PHRASAL VERBS
sell sth ↔ **off** to sell goods quickly and cheaply: The library is selling off some of its old books.
sell out
1 if a shop sells out of something, or if something sells out, the shop sells all of it and there is none left: **have/be sold out** Tickets for the show have sold out. | **[+of]** We've sold out of bread.
2 informal disapproving to do something against your beliefs in order to get money or some other advantage: ex-hippies who've sold out and become respectable businessmen
sell up to sell your house or your business: Liz decided to sell up and move abroad.

sell² n a **hard/tough sell** something that it is difficult to persuade people to buy or accept: This tax increase is going to be a hard sell to voters.

'sell-by date n [C] BrE the date printed on a food product, after which a shop should not sell it

seller /'selə $ -ər/ n [C] **1** someone who sells something → **buyer 2 good/bad/poor etc seller** a product that is popular or not popular etc with customers: The album remains one of the biggest sellers of all time.

'sell-off n [C] BrE the sale of a company or part of a company

Sellotape /'seləteɪp, -loʊ- $ -lə-, -loʊ-/ n [U] trademark BrE tape that you use for sticking pieces of paper or card together **SYN** Scotch tape AmE → see picture at CLASSROOM

sellout /'selaʊt/ n [singular] a performance, sports event etc for which all the tickets have been sold

selves /selvz/ n the plural of SELF

semantic /sɪˈmæntɪk/ adj formal relating to the meaning of words —**semantically** /-kli/ adv

semblance /'sembləns/ n **a/some semblance of** sth a situation that is slightly similar to another one: After the war, life returned to a semblance of normality.

semen /'siːmən/ n [U] the liquid containing SPERM (=substance produced by the male sex organs)

semester /sə'mestə $ -ər/ n [C] AmE one of two periods into which the school or college year is divided

semi /'semi/ n [C] (plural **semis**) BrE informal a SEMI-DETACHED house

semi- /'semi/ prefix **1** partly but not completely: semi-skilled labour | semi-automatic weapons | semi-darkness **2** exactly half: a semi-circle

'semi-,circle n [C] half a circle: The children sat **in a** semi-circle. —**semi-'circular** adj

semicolon /ˌsemɪˈkəʊlən $ 'semɪˌkoʊlən/ n [C] the mark (;) that you use in writing to separate different parts of a sentence or list

semi-de'tached adj BrE a semi-detached house is joined on one side to another house **THESAURUS** HOUSE → see picture at **HOUSE¹**

semi-'final BrE, **semifinal** /ˌsemiˈfaɪnl/ AmE n [C] the two games that are played in a competition before the last game. The winners of the two semi-finals play each other in the final game to find the winner.

seminar /'semɪnɑː $ -nɑːr/ n [C] a meeting in which a group of people discuss a subject

seminary /'semɪnəri $ -neri/ n [C] (plural **seminaries**) a college for training priests

senate, Senate /'senət/ n **the Senate** the smaller of the two parts of government in countries such as the US and Australia → **House of Representatives**

senator, Senator /'senətə $ -tər/ n [C] a member of a senate: Senator Dole **THESAURUS** POLITICIAN

send /send/ v [T] (past tense and past participle **sent** /sent/)
1 to arrange for something to go to a place or person: He sent the cheque last week. | **send sb sth** I'll send you an email confirming the date. | **send sth to sb/sth** I need to send some money to my family. | **send sth back/up/over etc** She signed the form and sent it back. | **send sth by post/sea/air etc** It's quicker to send parcels by air. | **send sth off** She sent the letter off this morning.
2 to make someone go somewhere: The UN is sending troops. | **send sb to sth** Al was **sent to prison** for stealing. | **send sb back/away/over/home etc** The refugees were sent back to Vietnam. | **send sb to do sth** I sent Joe to buy some food.
3 send your love/regards/best wishes etc spoken to ask someone to give your greetings, good wishes etc to someone else: Mother sends her love.
4 to cause someone or something to be in a particular state: His lectures **send** me to **sleep**. | **send sb/sth into sth** The tail broke off, sending the plane into a dive.

PHRASAL VERBS
send away/off for sth to send a letter to an organization asking them to post something to you: Send away for a free recipe booklet.
send for sb/sth to ask for someone or something to come to you: We sent for an ambulance.

send sb/sth ↔ **in**
1 to send something, usually by post, to a place where it can be dealt with: *Did you send in your application?*
2 to send soldiers, police etc somewhere to deal with a dangerous situation: *British troops were sent in as part of the peace-keeping force.*
send sb ↔ **off** *BrE* to order a sports player to leave a game because they have behaved badly
send sth ↔ **out**
1 to send things to several people so that they receive one each: *I sent out all the party invitations.* | *The school is sending a letter out to all the parents.*
2 if a machine sends out light, sound etc, it produces it: *The ship's radio sends out a powerful signal.*
send sb/sth ↔ **up** *BrE informal* to make someone or something look silly by copying them in a funny way: *The film sends up Hollywood disaster movies.*

sender /'sendə $ -ər/ n [C] the person who sent a particular letter, package, message etc

'send-off n [C] *informal* an occasion when a group of people say goodbye to someone who is leaving: *They gave her a good send-off when she retired.*

senile /'si:naɪl/ adj mentally confused because of old age —**senility** /sɪ'nɪləti/ n [U]

Senior (written abbreviation **Snr** *BrE*, **Sr.** *AmE*) used after the name of a man who has the same name as his son

senior¹ /'si:niə $ -ər/ adj a senior person has an important position or rank → **junior**: *senior management* | **[+to]** *She's senior to me (=she has a higher position than me).*

senior² n [C] **1** *AmE* a student in the last year of HIGH SCHOOL or college → **junior**, **freshman 2** *AmE* a senior citizen **3 be two/five/ten etc years sb's senior** to be two, five, ten etc years older than someone: *Her husband was nine years her senior.*

senior 'citizen n [C] someone who is over the age of 65

seniority /ˌsi:ni'ɒrəti $ -'ɔ:-, -'ɑ:-/ n [U] when you are older or higher in rank than someone else: *a position of seniority*

sensation /sen'seɪʃən/ n **1** [C,U] a feeling that you get from one of your five senses: *She had a tingling sensation in her hands.* **2** [C] a feeling caused by a particular experience, which you cannot describe: *Carol had the sensation that she was being watched.* **3** [singular] extreme excitement or interest, or something that causes this: *The film caused a sensation.*

sensational /sen'seɪʃənəl/ adj **1** very interesting, exciting, or good: *a sensational discovery* | *She looked sensational.* **2** *disapproving* intended to interest, excite, or shock people: *sensational newspaper stories* —**sensationally** adv

sensationalism /sen'seɪʃənəlɪzəm/ n [U] *disapproving* a way of reporting events that makes them seem as strange, exciting, or shocking as possible

sense¹ /sens/ n
1 [singular] a feeling about something: **[+of]** *I felt a great sense of relief.* | *She has a strong sense of loyalty.*
2 [singular] the ability to judge or understand

something: **sense of humour** *BrE*/**sense of humor** *AmE* (=the ability to understand and enjoy things that are funny) *She has a really good sense of humour.* | **sense of direction** (=the ability to judge which way you should be going) *It was dark and he had completely lost his sense of direction.* | *She has excellent business sense.* | **dress/clothes sense** (=the ability to judge what clothes look good)
3 [C] one of the five physical abilities of sight, hearing, touch, taste, and smell: **sense of smell/taste/touch etc** *Dogs have a good sense of smell.*
4 [U] when someone makes sensible or practical decisions, or behaves in a sensible practical way: **have the (good) sense to do sth** (=do the thing that is most sensible) *She had the sense to call the police.* | **Have some sense** (=be sensible). *We can't possibly have a picnic in this rain.* | **there is no sense in (doing) sth** *spoken* (=it is not sensible to do something) *There's no sense in getting upset.*
5 [C] the meaning of a word, phrase, sentence etc: *The word 'bank' has two main senses.*
6 [C] a way in which something can be true or real: *What he says is right in a sense (=in one way, but not every way).* → **COMMON SENSE, SIXTH SENSE**

PHRASES
come to your senses to start to think clearly and behave sensibly: *One day he'll come to his senses and realize what a fool he's been.*
make sense 1 to have a clear meaning and be easy to understand: *Read this and tell me if it makes sense.* **2** to be a sensible thing to do: **it makes sense (for sb) to do sth** *It would make sense to leave early, so that we miss the traffic.* **3** if something makes sense, there seems to be a good reason for it: *Why did she do a thing like that? It doesn't make sense.*
make (some) sense of sth to understand something difficult: *Can you make sense of the instructions?*

sense² v [T] to feel or know something without being told: *I could sense that something was wrong.* | *Cats can sense danger.*

senseless /'sensləs/ adj **1** a senseless action is bad and will not achieve anything: *senseless violence* | *The destruction of the rainforest is senseless.* **2** if someone is beaten senseless, they are hit until they are not conscious

sensibility /ˌsensə'bɪləti/ n [C,U] (*plural* **sensibilities**) *formal* the way that someone reacts to particular subjects or types of behaviour: *Avoid using words that might offend someone's religious sensibilities.*

sensible /'sensəbəl/ adj
1 someone who is sensible is able to make good decisions: *She's a very sensible girl.*
2 something that is sensible is a good idea: *He gave me some sensible advice.* | *It's sensible to keep a note of your passport number.* | *Moving house seemed like the sensible thing to do.* —**sensibly** adv: *If you won't behave sensibly, you must leave.*

Word Choice: sensible or sensitive?
If someone is **sensible**, they behave in a way that seems reasonable and practical: *He's normally very sensible with money.*

If someone is **sensitive**, they are able to understand other people's feelings and problems: *She's very sensitive to the needs of her students.*
You also use **sensitive** when saying that someone is easily upset or offended: *Teenagers are often very sensitive about their appearance.* Do not use **sensible** in this meaning.

sensitive /'sensətɪv/ adj
1 a sensitive person thinks of how other people will feel about something OPP **insensitive**: [+to] *He was very sensitive to other people's needs.*
2 easily offended or upset: *a sensitive child* | [+about] *She's sensitive about her weight.*
3 easily affected or damaged by something such as a substance or temperature: *sensitive skin* | [+to] *Older people tend to be very sensitive to cold.*
4 a situation or subject that is sensitive needs to be dealt with very carefully because it is secret or because it may offend people: *Abortion is a **politically sensitive** issue.* | *highly sensitive information*
5 reacting to very small changes in light, temperature, position etc: *a **highly sensitive** electronic camera* —**sensitively** adv: *an issue which needs to be handled sensitively* —**sensitivity** /ˌsensə'tɪvəti/ n [U]: *His comments show a lack of sensitivity.*

sensor /'sensə $ -ər/ n [C] a piece of equipment that is used to find light, heat, movement etc, even in very small amounts

sensory /'sensəri/ adj relating to your senses of sight, hearing, touch, taste, or smell

sensual /'senʃuəl/ adj relating to physical pleasure: ***sensual pleasures** such as massage* —**sensuality** /ˌsenʃu'æləti/ n [U]

sensuous /'senʃuəs/ adj making you feel physical pleasure: *the sensuous feel of silk*

sent /sent/ v the past tense and past participle of SEND

sentence¹ /'sentəns/ n [C]
1 a group of words that are written with a capital letter at the beginning and a FULL STOP at the end
2 a punishment that a judge gives to someone who is guilty of a crime: *She received an eight-year **prison sentence**.* | *He's **serving a life sentence** for murder.* | *The crime carries an automatic **death sentence**.*
THESAURUS PUNISHMENT

sentence² v [T] when a judge sentences someone, he or she gives them a punishment for a crime: *He was sentenced to six years in prison.*

sentiment /'sentəmənt/ n **1** [C,U] formal an opinion or feeling you have about something: *Similar sentiments were expressed by many politicians.* **2** [U] feelings of pity, love, or sadness that are often considered to be unsuitable for a particular situation: *There's no room for sentiment in business.*

sentimental /ˌsentə'mentl◂/ adj **1** showing emotions such as love, pity, and sadness too strongly or in a silly way: *sentimental love songs* | [+about] *People can be very sentimental about animals.*
2 relating to your feelings rather than practical reasons: *The ring has **sentimental value**.* —**sentimentality** /ˌsentəmen'tæləti/ n [U]

sentry /'sentri/ n [C] (plural **sentries**) a soldier who stands outside a building and guards it
THESAURUS GUARD

separable /'sepərəbəl/ adj two things that are separable can be separated OPP **inseparable**

separate¹ /'sepərət/ adj
1 separate things are different ones, not the same ones: *The sisters have separate bedrooms.* | *That's a separate issue.* | [+from] *I **keep** my work **separate from** my home life.*
2 not joined to or touching another thing: *The library is in a separate building.* | [+from] ***Keep** raw meat **separate from** cooked meat.* —**separately** adv: *His parents arrived separately.*

separate² /'sepəreɪt/ v
1 [I,T] to divide or split something into different parts: **separate sth into sth** *The class was separated into four groups.* | **separate sth from sth** *Separate the urgent letters from the rest.*
2 [T] to be between two things so that they cannot touch each other: **separate sth from sth** *A screen separates the dining area from the kitchen.* | *The two parts of the park are separated by a busy road.*
3 [I,T] to make people move apart, or to move apart: *A teacher separated the two boys.* | **separate sb from sb** *I got separated from my friends in the crowd.*
4 [I] to start to live apart from your husband, wife, or partner: *Her parents separated last year.* —**separated** adj

separation /ˌsepə'reɪʃən/ n **1** [U] when two things are different or are split into different parts: *There can be no separation of politics from morality.* **2** [C,U] when people spend time apart from each other: *a long separation from his mother* **3** [C] an agreement between a husband and wife to live apart

separatist /'sepərətɪst/ n [C] someone who wants part of a country to become separate and form a new country with its own government

Sept. a written abbreviation of **September**

September /sep'tembə $ -ər/ n [C,U] (written abbreviation **Sept.**) the ninth month of the year, between August and October: *next/last September He starts college next September.* | **in September** *He came here in September.* | **on September 6th** *My birthday is on September 6th.*

septic /'septɪk/ adj especially BrE infected with BACTERIA: *The wound **went septic**.*

sequel /'siːkwəl/ n [C] a film, book etc that continues the story of an earlier one: [+to] *the sequel to 'Silence of the Lambs'*

sequence Ac /'siːkwəns/ n **1** [C,U] the order that something happens or exists in: **in a ... sequence** *Ask the questions in a logical sequence.* | **in/out of sequence** (=in or not in the right order) *Read the chapters in sequence.* **2** [C] a series of events, numbers, letters etc that have a particular order: [+of] *a sequence of numbers* | *the **sequence of events** that led to war*

sequin /'siːkwɪn/ n [C] a small shiny piece of metal that is sewn on clothes for decoration

serenade /ˌserə'neɪd/ n [C] a song, especially a love song —**serenade** v [T]

serene /səˈriːn/ *adj* very calm and peaceful: *Her face was serene.* | *a serene mountain lake* —**serenity** /səˈrenəti/ *n* [U]

sergeant /ˈsɑːdʒənt $ ˈsɑːr-/ *n* [C] an officer of low rank in the army, air force, or police

serial¹ /ˈsɪəriəl $ ˈsɪr-/ *n* [C] a story that is broadcast or printed in several separate parts

serial² *adj* **serial killer/murderer/rapist etc** someone who commits the same crime several times

'serial ˌnumber *n* [C] a number put on things that are produced in large quantities, so that each one has its own number

series Ac /ˈsɪəriːz $ ˈsɪr-/ *n* [C] (*plural* **series**)
1 a series of sth several events or actions of the same kind that happen one after the other: *series of accidents* | *He was found guilty of a whole series of crimes.*
2 a set of television or radio programmes with the same characters or on the same subject: *a new comedy series*

serious /ˈsɪəriəs $ ˈsɪr-/ *adj*
1 a serious problem, situation etc is very bad and worrying: *Drugs are a serious problem here.* | *The damage was not serious.* | **serious illness/injury/accident etc**
2 be serious to really mean something that you say, and not be joking or pretending: *Are you serious about becoming a model?*
3 something that is serious is important and should not be laughed at: *Be quiet. This is serious.* | *Bullying is a serious matter.* | **serious thought/discussion etc** *We need to have a serious talk about your future.*
4 a serious person is always quiet and sensible and does not often laugh —**seriousness** *n* [U]

THESAURUS

serious very bad – used especially about problems, accidents, illnesses, or crimes: *She had a serious car accident.* | *Knife crime is a serious problem.*
severe very serious – used especially about problems, injuries, and illnesses: *Companies face severe financial problems.* | *The fire caused severe damage to the building.*
grave used about a situation that is very serious and worrying, especially because it is dangerous or seems likely to get worse: *The soldiers were in grave danger.* | *The economic situation is very grave.*
acute an acute problem or situation has become very serious and needs to be dealt with quickly. An acute medical condition is very serious: *There is an acute shortage of nurses in many parts of the country.* | *acute liver failure*

---

seriously /ˈsɪəriəsli $ ˈsɪr-/ *adv*
1 very much or very badly: **seriously ill/injured/damaged etc** *Nobody was seriously hurt in the accident.* | *I'm seriously worried about Ben.*
2 in a way that is not joking, because something is important: *I'm thinking seriously about leaving my job.* | **take sb/sth seriously** (=think they are very important) *You shouldn't take what he says seriously.*
3 *spoken* used to say that you are not joking, or to

ask whether someone is joking: *Seriously, he likes you.*

sermon /ˈsɜːmən $ ˈsɜːr-/ *n* [C] a talk given as part of a Christian church service **THESAURUS** SPEECH

serpent /ˈsɜːpənt $ ˈsɜːr-/ *n* [C] *literary* a snake

serrated /səˈreɪtəd, se-/ *adj* a serrated knife has a sharp edge made from a row of V-shaped points

serum /ˈsɪərəm $ ˈsɪr-/ *n* [C,U] *technical* a liquid containing substances that fight infection → **vaccine**

servant /ˈsɜːvənt $ ˈsɜːr-/ *n* [C] someone, especially in the past, who was paid to do jobs such as cleaning and cooking in another person's house → **CIVIL SERVANT**

serve¹ /sɜːv $ sɜːrv/ *v*
1 FOOD/DRINKS [I,T] to give someone food or drinks as part of a meal: *Dinner is served at eight.* | **serve sth with sth** *Serve the soup with crusty bread.* | **serve two/four etc** (=be enough for two people, four people etc) *The recipe serves six.*
2 IN A SHOP [I,T] to help the customers in a shop: *There was only one girl serving customers.* | *Are you being served?*

SERVE

3 HAVE A PURPOSE [I,T] to be useful or suitable for a particular purpose: **[+as]** *The sofa also serves as a bed.* | **serve to do sth** *The incident served to emphasize the importance of security.*
4 WORK IN ARMY/ORGANIZATION [I,T] to spend time in the army or in an organization doing useful work: **serve in the army/navy/air force etc** *They served in the same regiment.* | **[+on]** *She serves on the student committee.*
5 IN PRISON [T] to spend time in prison: *He served two years for theft.*
6 IN SPORT [I,T] to start playing in a game such as tennis, by throwing the ball in the air and hitting it over the net

PHRASES
  it serves sb right *spoken* used to say that someone deserves something bad, because they have done something wrong: *If you fail your exam, it will serve you right.*

serve² *n* [C] the action in a game such as tennis in which you throw the ball in the air and hit it over the net

server /ˈsɜːvə $ ˈsɜːrvər/ *n* [C] the main computer on a network that controls all the others

service¹ /ˈsɜːvɪs $ ˈsɜːr-/ *n*
1 OFFICIAL ORGANIZATION [C] the official system or organization that provides something, especially something that everyone needs: **the health/prison/postal etc service** *She works for the health service.* | **emergency/essential services** (=medical help, fire service, water supply etc)

2 `STH PROVIDED BY A COMPANY` [C] help or work that a business provides for customers, rather than goods produced by a business: **provide/offer a service** *We offer a free information service.* | *insurance and other* ***financial services***

3 `IN A SHOP/RESTAURANT` [U] the help that people who work in a restaurant, shop etc give you: **good/ poor/slow etc service** *The food is OK but the service is terrible.* | *Service is **included** in your bill.* | *We are proud of our **customer service**.*

4 `WORK` [U] (*also* **services** [plural]) work that you do for a person or organization: *He retired after 20 years of service.* | **[+as]** *You could **offer** your **services as** an English teacher.*

5 `HELP` [singular, U] *formal* help that you give someone: *Our trained assistants are **at your service** (=available to help).* | *Can I **be of service** (=help)?*

6 `ARMY` **the services** *BrE*, **the service** *AmE* a country's military forces

7 `RELIGIOUS CEREMONY` [C] a formal religious ceremony, especially in a church: *the evening service at St Marks*

8 `REGULAR CHECK` [C] a regular examination of a machine or car to make sure it works correctly: *My car needs a service.*

9 `IN TENNIS` [C] an act of hitting the ball over the net to start a game of tennis etc

10 `ON A MOTORWAY` **services** [plural] *BrE* a place where you can stop to buy petrol, food etc on a MOTORWAY `SYN` **service station** → CIVIL SERVICE, COMMUNITY SERVICE, FIRE SERVICE, LIP SERVICE, NATIONAL SERVICE

PHRASES

out of service not available for people to use: *Sorry, this bus is out of service.*

service² *v* [T] to examine a machine or vehicle and fix it if necessary: *I'm having the car serviced next week.*

'service ˌcharge *n* [C] *BrE* an amount that is added to a bill as a charge for the waiters that serve you

'service ˌindustry *n* [C,U] an industry that provides a service rather than a product, for example insurance or travel

serviceman /'sɜːvəsmən $ 'sɜːr-/ *n* [C] (*plural* **servicemen** /-mən/) a man who is a member of the military

'service ˌstation *n* [C] a place that sells petrol, food, and other goods `SYN` **gas station** *AmE*

servicewoman /'sɜːvəsˌwʊmən $ 'sɜːr-/ *n* [C] (*plural* **servicewomen** /-ˌwɪmɪn/) a woman who is a member of the military

serviette /ˌsɜːviˈet $ 'sɜːr-/ *n* [C] *BrE* a NAPKIN

servile /'sɜːvaɪl $ 'sɜːrvəl, -vaɪl/ *adj disapproving* very eager to obey and please someone

serving /'sɜːvɪŋ $ 'sɜːr-/ *n* [C] an amount of food that is enough for one person `SYN` **helping**

session /'seʃən/ *n* [C] **1** a period of time used for a particular activity, especially by a group of people: *We run **training sessions**.* | *There will be a **question-and-answer session** later.* **2** a formal meeting, or group of meetings, of a law court or parliament:

[+of] *a new session of Parliament* | **in session** (=meeting) *The court is now in session.*

set¹ /set/ *v* (*past tense and past participle* **set**, *present participle* **setting**)

1 `PUT` [T] *written* to carefully put something somewhere: **set sth down** *He brought in a jug and set it down.* | **set sth on sth** *She set the tray on the bed.*

2 `FILM/STORY/PLAY` [T] if a story, film etc is set in a particular place or at a particular time, the events in it happen in that place or at that time: **set sth in sth** *The film is set in Hong Kong.*

3 `FIX TIME/DATE/LIMIT ETC` [T] to decide or establish what something should be: **set a date/time** *Have they set a date for the wedding?* | **set a target/limit/ standard etc** *The target that was set was much too high.* | **set a pattern/trend etc** *Their computers set the trend for user-friendly graphics.* | *He **set** a new world record for the 100 metres.* | *I expect you to **set an example** (=show good behaviour for others to copy).*

4 `COMPARE` [T] to consider something in relation to other things: **set sth against/beside sth** *The number of accidents is small when set against the number of cars on the road.*

5 `BEGIN STH` [T] to start something happening: **set sth in motion/progress** *An inquiry into the incident was set in motion.* | **set sth on fire/alight/ablaze** (*also* **set fire to sth**) *Rioters set cars on fire.* | **set sb doing sth** *What she said has set me thinking.*

6 `CLOCK/MACHINE` [T] to move the switch on a machine, clock etc so that it will work in the way that you want: *Can you set the video recorder?* | *I forgot to **set the alarm**.* | **set sth to/on/at sth** *Set the oven to 180°.*

7 `BECOME HARD` [I] if a liquid mixture sets, it becomes hard and solid: *The concrete has set.*

8 `SUN` [I] when the sun sets, it moves lower in the sky until it disappears `OPP` **rise**

9 `SCHOOL WORK` [T] *BrE* to give a student a piece of work or a test to do: **set sb sth** *Did he set you any homework?*

PHRASES

set foot in sth to go into a place: *I had never set foot in a pub before.*

set a trap 1 to make a trap to catch an animal: *His father taught him how to fish and set traps.* **2** to invent a plan to catch someone: *She realized he had set a trap for her with the money.*

set sb free/loose to allow a person or animal to be free: *The hostages were finally set free.*

set (sb) to work to start doing something, or make someone start doing something: *I set to work clearing up.*

set the table to arrange plates, knives etc on a table so that it is ready for a meal

set your heart/sights/mind on sth (*also* **have your heart/sights/mind set on sth**) to want very much to achieve or get something: *I've set my heart on that pair of boots.* | *We now have our sights set on winning the championship.* → **set sb's mind at rest** at REST¹, **set sail** at SAIL², **set the ball rolling** at BALL

PHRASAL VERBS

set about sth **set about doing sth** to start doing something: *How do you set about getting a job?*

S

set sb against sb to make someone argue or fight with someone else: *The civil war set brother against brother.*

set sb/sth apart to make someone or something different from or better than other people or things: **[+from]** *His intelligence set him apart from the other students.*

set sth ↔ aside

1 to keep something for a special purpose: *I set aside a little money every week.* | **[+for]** *a room that had been set aside for visitors*

2 to decide not to consider a problem or feeling: *Let's set aside the question of payment for now.* | **set aside your differences** (=agree to stop arguing)

set back

1 set sb/sth ↔ back to delay something, or delay someone in doing something: *Her resignation set back the project.* | *I hurt my leg, which set me back a few days.*

2 set sb back $100/£100 etc to cost someone a lot of money: *Dinner set us back $300.*

set sth ↔ down to write something, especially in an official document: *We have set down clear guidelines.*

set forth

1 set sth ↔ forth to explain something clearly in writing or speech SYN **set out**: *The book sets forth her views on childcare.*

2 *literary* to start a journey

set in if something unpleasant sets in, it begins and is likely to continue: *Winter was setting in.*

set off

1 to leave and start going somewhere: *We'd better set off before it gets dark.* | **[+for]** *What time do you have to set off for the airport?* THESAURUS LEAVE

2 set sth ↔ off to make something start happening: *The news set off widespread panic.*

3 set sth ↔ off to make something explode or make a loud noise: *Some kids were setting off fireworks.* THESAURUS EXPLODE

set out

1 to start a long journey: **[+for]** *They set out for the border at dawn.*

2 to intend and try to achieve a particular result: **set out to do sth** *He set out to prove his innocence.* THESAURUS INTEND

3 set sth ↔ out to explain something clearly in writing or speech: *She set out her reasons for resigning in a letter.*

set up

1 to start a company or organization SYN **establish**: **set sth ↔ up** *She left the company to set up her own business.* | **set (yourself) up as sth** *John set himself up as a consultant.*

2 set sth ↔ up to make arrangements for something to happen: *Do you want me to set up a meeting?*

3 to get equipment ready to be used: *The DJ was still setting up when we arrived.* | **set sth ↔ up** *He had set up a computer in the classroom.* THESAURUS PREPARE

4 set sth ↔ up to place or build something somewhere, especially something that is not permanent: *The police set up roadblocks around the city.*

5 set sb ↔ up to deliberately make other people think that someone has done something wrong: *He believes his partner set him up.*

set² *n* [C]

1 GROUP a group of things that belong together or are related: **[+of]** *a set of tools* | *You need a different set of skills.* | *a chess set*

2 TV/RADIO a television or radio: *a TV/television set*

3 PLACE FOR FILMING a place where a film or programme is filmed: *He met her on the set of his latest movie* (=while filming it).

4 THINGS IN FILM/PLAY the furniture, scenery etc used in a film or television programme, or on stage in a play, OPERA etc: *She designed the set for the play.*

5 IN TENNIS one part of a game of tennis: *Murray won the set 6–4.*

6 BY BAND/SINGER a performance by a band, singer, or DJ: *They played a 90-minute set.*

set³ *adj* **1** in a particular place or position: **[+on/in/among etc]** *a village set high on a hill* | *The house is set back from the road.* **2** [only before noun] fixed and not changing: *You are given a set amount to spend.* | *We eat at a set time every day.* | *He has rather set ideas about religion.* **3** [not before noun] *informal* ready to do something: **[+for]** *Are you all set for your trip?* | **Get set** *for a fun evening!* THESAURUS READY **4 set to do sth** likely to do something: *The hot weather is set to continue.*

PHRASES

be set in your ways to be used to doing things in the same way and not want to change

be set on/upon/against sth to be determined about something: *Tina is set on becoming a teacher.* | *His parents were dead set against the marriage.*

setback /ˈsetbæk/ *n* [C] a problem that stops you from making progress: **[+for]** *Today's result was a major setback for the team.* THESAURUS PROBLEM

settee /seˈtiː/ *n* [C] *BrE* a comfortable seat for two or three people SYN **sofa**

setting /ˈsetɪŋ/ *n* [C usually singular] **1** the place where something is or happens, and the things that surround it: *a farmhouse in a beautiful setting* **2** the place or time in which the events in a book, film etc happen: **[+for]** *Ireland is the setting for his latest movie.* **3** a position in which you put the controls on a machine: *Turn the oven to its highest setting.*

settle /ˈsetl/ *v*

1 ARGUMENT [I,T] to end an argument or disagreement: **settle a dispute/lawsuit/conflict/argument etc** *a meeting to settle a pay dispute* | *I hope they can settle their differences* (=agree to stop arguing).

2 MAKE ARRANGEMENTS [T usually passive] to decide or arrange the details of something: *We need to agree a date so we can get things settled.* | **That settles it** (=helps to make a definite decision) – *I'm not going.*

3 LIVE SOMEWHERE [I] to start living in a place where you intend to live for a long time: **[+in]** *He finally settled in Madrid.* | *Many German families settled in the 19th century.*

4 SIT/LIE COMFORTABLY [I] to move into a comfortable position: **[+back/on/in etc]** *I settled back against my pillows.* | **settle yourself back/into etc** *Settle yourself down here and I'll bring you a drink.*

5 SNOW/DUST [I] to move or fall down and stay

there: **[+on]** *Snow had settled on the roofs.*
6 PAY DEBTS [I,T] to pay money that you owe: **settle a bill/account/claim** *Please settle your account within 30 days.* | **[+with]** *He managed to settle with his creditors.*

PHRASES

settle a score to do something bad to someone because they have done something bad to you: *I've got a score to settle with that guy.*

PHRASAL VERBS
settle down
1 settle (sb) down to become calm and quiet, or to make someone calm and quiet: *Settle down, class.* | *Laura is upstairs settling the baby down.*
2 to start living a quiet life in one place, especially when you get married: *I want to settle down and have children.*
settle for sth to accept something that is not as much or as good as you wanted: *We had to settle for a smaller car.*
settle in to start to feel happy in a new house, job, or school: *Adam seems to have settled in at his new school.*
settle on/upon sth to decide or agree on something: *Have you settled on a title for the book?*
settle up to pay money that you owe

settled /'setld/ *adj* **1 feel/be settled** to feel happy and comfortable in a situation because it is no longer completely new: *I still don't feel settled in my new job.* **2** not changing, and not likely to change: *a period of more settled weather*

settlement /'setlmənt/ *n* [C] **1** an official agreement that ends an argument or fighting: **a political/peace/peaceful settlement** *We still hope to reach a peaceful settlement.* **2** a group of buildings or houses where people live or lived: *a Stone Age settlement*

settler /'setlə $ -ər/ *n* [C] someone who goes to live permanently in an area where not many people have lived before: *the early settlers in the American West*

'set-top ˌbox *n* [C] *BrE* a piece of electronic equipment that is connected to your television, that allows it to receive DIGITAL signals

'set-up *n informal* **1** [C] the way that something is organized or arranged: *We have a new set-up at work.* **2** [C] a dishonest plan that is intended to trick someone: *I realized that the whole thing was a set-up.* **3** [U] the act of organizing a new business or computer system: *Our IT department will help with installation and set-up.*

seven /'sevən/ *number* the number 7: *We need seven chairs.* | *I got up at seven* (=seven o'clock). | *He's seven* (=7 years old). → **TWENTY-FOUR SEVEN**

seventeen /ˌsevən'tiːn◂/ *number* the number 17: *a group of seventeen soldiers* | *I'm nearly seventeen* (=17 years old). —**seventeenth** *adj, pron*: *her seventeenth birthday* | *I'm planning to leave on* **the seventeenth** (=the 17th day of the month).

seventh¹ /'sevənθ/ *adj* coming after six other things in a series: *his seventh birthday* —**seventh** *pron*: *I'm planning to leave on* **the seventh** (=the seventh day of the month).

seventh² *n* [C] one of seven equal parts of something

seventy /'sevənti/ *number*
1 the number 70
2 the seventies (*also* **the '70s, the 1970s**) [plural] the years from 1970 to 1979: **the early/mid/late seventies** *In the early seventies, Sag Harbor was still a peaceful village.* —**seventieth** *adj*: *her seventieth birthday*

PHRASES

be in your seventies to be aged between 70 and 79: **early/mid/late seventies** *Bill must be in his mid seventies now.*
in the seventies if the temperature is in the seventies, it is between 70 degrees and 79 degrees F: *The temperature is usually in the seventies in the summer.*

sever /'sevə $ -ər/ *v* [T] *formal* **1** to cut through something completely: *His finger was severed in the accident.* **2** to completely end a relationship or connection: *He severed all ties with his father.*

several /'sevərəl/ *determiner, pron* more than a few, but not a lot → **few**: *I called her several times.* | *Several people offered to help.* | **several hundred/thousand etc** *A computer costs several hundred pounds.* | **[+of]** *Several of his students complained.*

severe /sə'vɪə $ -'vɪr/ *adj*
1 a severe problem, injury etc is very bad: *severe head injuries* | *The damage to the building was severe.*
THESAURUS **SERIOUS**
2 severe weather is very extreme, for example very cold: *severe storms and gales*
3 severe punishment or criticism is very extreme or strict: *Drug smugglers face severe punishment.*
4 someone who is severe seems strict and not at all friendly SYN **stern**: *her severe expression* —**severity** /sə'verəti/ *n* [singular, U]

severely /sə'vɪəli $ -'vɪr-/ *adv*
1 very badly: *She was severely injured.*
2 in a very strict way: *Those who disobeyed were severely punished.*

sew /səu $ sou/ *v* [I,T] (*past tense* **sewed**, *past participle* **sewn** /səun $ soun/ *or* **sewed**) to use a needle and thread to make or repair clothes: *My mother taught me to sew.* | **sew sth on sth** *Will you sew a button on my shirt?* → see picture at **KNIT**

PHRASAL VERBS
sew sth ↔ **up**
1 [usually passive] to arrange or control something so that you get the result you want: *I've just sewn up a deal on a new account.* | *He* **has** *this election* **sewn up** (=is certain to win).
2 to close or repair something by sewing it

sewage /'sjuːɪdʒ, 'suː- $ 'suː-/ *n* [U] waste from the human body and used water that is carried away from buildings through pipes

sewer /'sjuːə,'suːə $ 'suːər/ *n* [C] a pipe under the ground that carries away sewage

sewing /'səuɪŋ $ 'sou-/ *n* [U] **1** the activity of making or repairing clothes with a needle and thread **2** something that you have been sewing

'sewing ma,chine *n* [C] a machine for sewing cloth together

sewn /səʊn $ soʊn/ *v* a past participle of SEW

sex Ac /seks/ *n*
1 [U] the physical activity that two people do together to produce babies or for pleasure: **[+with]** He **had sex** with his sister's friend. | *sex education* (=when young people are taught about sex) | *safe sex* (=when people use something that will protect them from sexual diseases)
2 [U] whether someone is male or female: *We don't want to know the sex of the baby before it's born.*
3 [C] all women considered as a group, or all men considered as a group: *people of **both sexes*** (=men and women) | He doesn't have much success with **the opposite sex** (=people that are not his own sex).

'sex ap,peal *n* [U] the quality of being sexually attractive

sexism Ac /'seksɪzəm/ *n* [U] when someone is treated unfairly because of the sex that they are: *sexism in education* **THESAURUS** PREJUDICE —**sexist** *adj*: *sexist attitudes*

'sex life *n* [C] someone's sexual activities

'sex of,fender *n* [C] someone who is guilty of a sexual crime such as RAPE

'sex ,symbol *n* [C] a famous person who a lot of people think is very sexually attractive

sexual Ac /'sekʃuəl/ *adj*
1 relating to the physical activity of sex: *sexual abuse* | *sexual partners*
2 relating to differences between men and women: *sexual stereotypes* —**sexually** *adv*: He was *sexually assaulted.*

,sexual 'harassment *n* [U] when someone makes sexual remarks to a person they work with, or touches them, when that person does not want them to

,sexual 'intercourse *n* [U] *formal* the activity of having sex

sexuality Ac /,sekʃu'æləti/ *n* [U] someone's sexual feelings and activities

sexy /'seksi/ *adj* (comparative **sexier**, superlative **sexiest**) sexually attractive or exciting: *sexy underwear* | *a sexy man*

Sgt. the written abbreviation of **Sergeant**

sh, shh /ʃ/ *spoken* used to tell someone to be quiet

shabby /'ʃæbi/ *adj* **1** old and in bad condition: *a shabby old coat* **THESAURUS** CONDITION **2** unfair or slightly dishonest: *shabby treatment* —**shabbily** *adv* —**shabbiness** *n* [U]

shack¹ /ʃæk/ *n* [C] a small simple building made of wood or metal

shack² *v*
PHRASAL VERBS
shack up with sb *informal* to start living with someone you have sex with, without marrying them

shackle /'ʃækəl/ *v* [T] **1** *literary* to prevent someone from being able to do what they want: *The government is opposed to shackling the media with privacy laws.* **2** to put shackles on someone

shackles /'ʃækəlz/ *n* [plural] **1** *literary* limits that something puts on your freedom: **[+of]** *the shackles of the past* **2** two metal rings joined by a chain, used to keep a prisoner's hands or feet together

shade¹ /ʃeɪd/ *n*
1 DARKER/COOLER AREA [U] an area that is cooler because the light of the sun cannot reach it: *a plant that needs shade* | **in the shade** *Let's find a table in the shade.* → see picture at SHADOW¹
2 FOR BLOCKING LIGHT [C] something used for reducing or keeping out light: *a lamp shade*
3 COLOUR [C] a particular type of a colour: **[+of]** *a room painted in shades of blue*
4 GLASSES **shades** [plural] *informal* SUNGLASSES
5 SLIGHTLY **a shade** very slightly: *The jacket was a shade too small.* | **a shade under/over/higher etc** *It weighed a shade over 5 kg.*
6 SLIGHT DIFFERENCE **shade of meaning/opinion etc** a meaning or opinion that is slightly different from others: *All shades of opinion are represented.*
PHRASES
| **put sb/sth in the shade** *informal* to be much better than someone or something else

> **Word Choice**: shade or shadow?
> A **shadow** is a dark shape made by something that blocks the sun or a light: *She saw his shadow on the wall.*
> **Shade** is a cool dark area where the sun does not reach: *We ate our lunch in the shade.*

shade² *v* [T] to protect something from light: *She lifted her hand to shade her eyes.* | *a courtyard shaded by trees*

SHADOW

shadow

shade

shadow¹ /'ʃædəʊ $ -doʊ/ *n*
1 [C] a dark shape on a surface, caused by a person or object being between the light and the surface: *the long shadow of a tree* | *The lamp **cast shadows*** (=made shadows) around the room.
2 [U] (also **shadows** [plural]) a part of an area that is dark, because light cannot reach it: **in shadow** *Most of the room was in shadow.* | **in the shadows** *He waited in the shadows.*

S

3 [singular] a bad effect or influence that something has: **under the shadow of sth** *families living under the shadow of unemployment* | *The financial problems will **cast a shadow over** the future of the project* (=make it less good).

PHRASES

without/beyond a shadow of (a) doubt used to say you are certain about something: *She knew without a shadow of doubt that he was lying to her.*

shadow² *v* [T] to follow someone in order to watch what they are doing

shadow³, Shadow *adj* [only before noun] having a particular job in the main party in the British parliament that is not in government: *the Shadow Chancellor*

shadowy /ˈʃædəʊi $ -doʊi/ *adj* **1** difficult to see because of shadows, or full of shadows: *a shadowy corner* | *a shadowy figure* **2** mysterious or unknown: *the shadowy forces of evil*

shady /ˈʃeɪdi/ *adj* **1** protected from the sun: *a shady corner* **THESAURUS** DARK **2** slightly dishonest or illegal: *a shady character*

shaft /ʃɑːft $ ʃæft/ *n* [C] **1** a passage that goes down through a building or down into the ground: *a mine shaft* **2** a long handle on a tool or weapon **3** a narrow beam of light

shaggy /ˈʃægi/ *adj* shaggy hair or fur is long and untidy

shake¹ /ʃeɪk/ *v* (past tense **shook** /ʃʊk/, past participle **shaken** /ˈʃeɪkən/)

SHAKE

shake hands

1 [I,T] to move up and down or from side to side with quick movements, or to make something do this: *His hands were shaking.* | *Shake the bottle before use.*
2 [T] to make someone feel shocked and upset: *Mark was clearly shaken by the news.* | *terrorist attacks that shook the whole world*
3 [I] if your voice is shaking, it is unsteady and you sound nervous or angry
4 shake sb's confidence/faith/belief to make someone feel less confident, or less sure about their beliefs: *Failing the test had shaken his confidence.* → **SHAKE-UP**

PHRASAL VERBS

shake sb ↔ **down** *AmE informal* to get money from someone by using threats

shake sb/sth ↔ **off**
1 to get rid of an illness or problem: *I can't shake off this cold.*
2 to escape from someone who is chasing you

shake sth ↔ **out** to shake something so that small pieces of dirt, dust etc come off it: *He shook out the blanket.*

shake sb/sth ↔ **up**
1 to make someone feel shocked and upset: *She was badly shaken up by the accident.*
2 to make changes to an organization so that it is

more effective: *plans to shake up the legal profession*

PHRASES

shake hands (with sb) to hold someone's hand and move it up and down, as a greeting or when you have made an agreement: *We shook hands and said goodbye.*

shake your head to move your head from side to side as a way of saying no → **nod**: *'Did she come back?' 'No,' he said, shaking his head sadly.*

THESAURUS

shake to move from side to side or up and down – used about people or things: *She was shaking with fear.* | *The ground shook with the force of the explosion.*

shiver to shake slightly, because you are cold or frightened: *He shivered in the cold night air.*

tremble to shake because you are frightened, worried, excited etc: *Her hands were trembling as she picked up the gun.*

wobble to move unsteadily from side to side – used about people or things: *The ladder wobbled and then started to fall.*

rattle to shake and make a noise: *The windows rattled in the wind.*

vibrate if something vibrates, it shakes continuously with small fast movements: *The music was so loud that the whole room vibrated.*

---

shake² *n* [C] **1** when someone shakes something: *He gave the bottle a shake.* **2** a MILKSHAKE

shakedown /ˈʃeɪkdaʊn/ *n* [C] *AmE informal* when someone gets money from another person by using threats

shake-up *n* [C] when big changes are made to the way something is organized

shaky /ˈʃeɪki/ *adj* **1** weak and unsteady because you are ill or old, or have had a shock: *My legs felt shaky.* **2** not very good and likely to fail: *a shaky economy* | *The team got off to a shaky start.* **3** not firm or steady: *a dangerously shaky elevator*

shall /ʃəl; strong ʃæl/ *modal verb especially BrE* (negative short form **shan't**)
1 I/we shall used to say what you are going to do: *We shall be away next week.*
2 shall I/we? used to make a suggestion or ask someone to decide about what to do: *Shall I make some coffee?* | *Where shall we meet?*

Usage

Shall is used especially in British English. You use it when talking about what you plan to do: *I shall be going to Tokyo next week.* It is often used when speaking in a determined way: *We shall get our land back one day.*
Shall is also very commonly used in the phrase **we shall see** (=we will find out soon).
You use **will** when talking about what you expect to happen, or what you plan to do: *Tomorrow will be sunny.* | *The next meeting will be on Thursday at 4 o'clock.* | *I'll be back soon.*

shallow /ˈʃæləʊ $ -loʊ/ *adj*
1 not deep **OPP** deep: *a shallow pool* | *a shallow bowl* → see picture at **DEEP¹**

2 not showing any serious or careful thought OPP **deep**: *a shallow argument*

shallows /ˈʃæləʊz $ -loʊz/ *n* **the shallows** a part of a river, lake etc which is not deep

sham /ʃæm/ *n* [singular] something that is not what it seems to be and is intended to deceive people: *Their marriage was a sham.* —**sham** *adj*

shamble /ˈʃæmbəl/ *v* [I + adv/prep] to walk slowly and awkwardly because you are weak or lazy

shambles /ˈʃæmbəlz/ *n* [singular] *informal* something that is very badly organized or very untidy: *The project was a complete shambles.*

shame¹ /ʃeɪm/ *n* [U] the feeling that you have when you know that you have behaved badly or have lost other people's respect → **ashamed**: *a deep sense of shame* | *He's **brought shame on** the whole family.* | *Have you **no shame**?* → see Word Choice at GUILT

PHRASES

it's a shame/what a shame *spoken* used to say that a situation is disappointing and you wish that it was different: **[+(that)]** *It's a shame you can't come.* | *It's a great shame to be indoors on such a nice day.*

put sb/sth to shame to be much better than someone or something else: *She has a knowledge of classical music that puts me to shame.*

THESAURUS

shame the feeling that you have when you know that you have behaved badly or have lost other people's respect: *He felt deep shame for what he had done.* | *She hung her head in shame* (=she looked down at the ground).

guilt the feeling that you are a bad person because you know that you have done something wrong: *Anna felt no guilt at leaving her husband.*

embarrassment the nervous and uncomfortable feeling that you have when you are worried about what other people will think of you, for example when you make a silly mistake, or you have difficulty doing something: *Imagine my embarrassment when I found out that I had left the bathroom door open.*

shame² *v* [T] to make someone feel ashamed

shamefaced /ʃeɪmˈfeɪst◄/ *adj* looking ashamed or embarrassed

shameful /ˈʃeɪmfəl/ *adj* so bad that someone should be ashamed: *a shameful waste of money* —**shamefully** *adv*

shameless /ˈʃeɪmləs/ *adj* behaving badly and not caring whether other people disapprove: *a shameless deception* —**shamelessly** *adv*

shampoo¹ /ʃæmˈpuː/ *n* [C,U] liquid soap for washing your hair

shampoo² *v* [T] to wash something with shampoo

shandy /ˈʃændi/ *n* [C,U] (*plural* **shandies**) a drink made of beer mixed with LEMONADE

shan't /ʃɑːnt $ ʃænt/ *BrE* the short form of 'shall not'

shanty town /ˈʃænti taʊn/ *n* [C] an area where very poor people live in small houses made from pieces of metal, wood etc

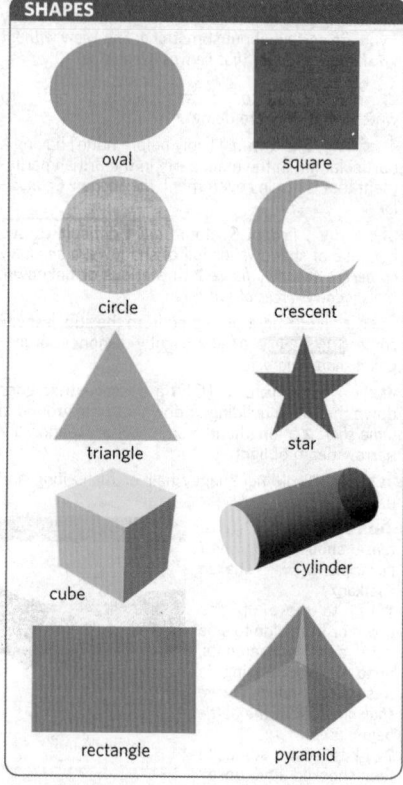

SHAPES

oval   square

circle   crescent

triangle   star

cube   cylinder

rectangle   pyramid

shape¹ /ʃeɪp/ *n*

1 [C,U] the form that something has, for example round, square etc: **in the shape of sth** *a card in the shape of a heart* | **in shape** *The room was square in shape.*

2 [U] the health or condition that someone or something is in: **in good/poor etc shape** *The business is in good shape.* | *How do you **keep in shape** (=stay healthy)?* | **out of shape** (=not healthy) *I'm out of shape these days.*

PHRASES

take shape to develop into a clear and definite form: *A plan was beginning to take shape in his mind.*

shape² *v* [T] **1** to influence something and make it develop in a particular way: *an event that will shape the country's future* **2** to make something have a particular shape: **shape sth into sth** *Shape the clay into small balls.*

PHRASAL VERBS

shape up *informal* to develop or improve: *The day was shaping up well.*

shaped /ʃeɪpt/ *adj* having a shape like a particular thing: **heart-shaped/oval-shaped etc** *heart-shaped leaves* | **[+like]** *a cake shaped like a butterfly*

shapeless /'ʃeɪpləs/ *adj* not having a clear or definite shape

shapely /'ʃeɪpli/ *adj* having an attractive shape: *shapely legs*

shard /ʃɑːd $ ʃɑːrd/ (*also* **sherd**) *n* [C] a sharp piece of broken glass, metal etc: **[+of]** *a shard of pottery*

share¹ /ʃeə $ ʃer/ *v*
1 [I,T] to have or use something with other people: **share sth with sb** *I shared a room with her when I was at college.* | *You'll have to share if there aren't enough books.*
2 (*also* **share out**) [T] to divide something between two or more people: **share sth between/among sb** *We shared the cake between us.*
3 [T] to have the same interests, opinion etc as someone else: *She didn't share my point of view.* | *a feeling shared by many people* **THESAURUS** AGREE
4 [I,T] to tell someone else about an idea, secret, problem etc: *The Internet allows people to share information.*

share² *n*
1 [singular] a part of something which has been divided between two or more people: **[+of]** *I paid my share of the bill and left.*
2 [C] one of the equal parts into which the value of a company is divided, which people can buy and sell → **stock**: **[+in]** *A lot of people are buying shares in the company.*
PHRASES

  have your (fair) share of sth to have quite a lot of something such as trouble or success: *I've had my share of bad luck this year.*

shareholder /'ʃeə,həʊldə $ 'ʃer,hoʊldər/ *n* [C] someone who owns shares in a company

shark /ʃɑːk $ ʃɑːrk/ *n* [C] a large sea fish with very sharp teeth → see picture on page A3

sharp¹ /ʃɑːp $ ʃɑːrp/ *adj*
1 KNIFE something that is sharp has a very thin edge or narrow point that can cut things easily OPP **blunt**: *a sharp knife* | **razor sharp** (=very sharp) → see picture at BLUNT¹
2 TURN/CORNER a sharp turn, bend, corner etc changes direction very suddenly
3 INCREASE/DECREASE a sharp increase, decrease etc is big and sudden SYN **steep**: *a sharp rise in profits*
4 DIFFERENCE sharp differences are very easy to notice: *There's a sharp contrast between his home and work life.*
5 CLEVER good at noticing things or thinking very quickly OPP **slow**: *a sharp mind*
6 VOICE/COMMENT a sharp voice, remark, expression etc shows that you are annoyed or being unkind: *His tone was sharp.* | *He gave her a sharp look.* | *She has a very sharp tongue* (=often says unkind things).
7 PAIN a sharp pain is sudden and bad OPP **dull**: *He felt a sharp pain in his chest.*
8 IMAGE a sharp image is clear and you can see all the details in it
9 TASTE a sharp taste is slightly bitter OPP **mild**

10 SOUND a sharp sound is sudden and loud: *a sharp cry*
11 IN MUSIC **a)** **F sharp/C sharp etc** the musical note that is slightly higher than F, C etc → **flat b)** a musical note that is sharp is played or sung slightly higher than it should be → **flat**
12 FASHIONABLE wearing clothes that are attractive and fashionable SYN **smart** *BrE: She was a sharp dresser.* —**sharply** *adv* —**sharpness** *n* [U]

sharp² *adv* **1** **at eight o'clock/two-thirty etc sharp** at exactly 8.00, 2.30 etc **2** **sharp left/right** *BrE* if you turn sharp left or right, you change direction suddenly to the left or right

sharp³ *n* [C] a musical note that is slightly higher than a particular note, shown by the sign (#) in written music → **flat**

sharpen /'ʃɑːpən $ 'ʃɑːr-/ *v* [T] to make something sharp: *She sharpened all her pencils.*

,sharp-'eyed *adj* good at noticing things

shatter /'ʃætə $ -ər/ *v* **1** [I,T] to break suddenly into very small pieces, or to make something do this: **[+into]** *The plate hit the floor and shattered into tiny pieces.* **THESAURUS** BREAK **2** [T] to destroy something completely, especially someone's hopes or beliefs: *An injury shattered his hopes of a baseball career.*

shattered /'ʃætəd $ -ərd/ *adj* **1** very shocked and upset **2** *BrE informal* very tired

shattering /'ʃætərɪŋ/ *adj* very shocking or upsetting: *a shattering experience*

shave¹ /ʃeɪv/ *v* [I,T] to cut off hair from the skin on your face, legs etc, using a RAZOR: *He washed and shaved.* | **shave sth off** *I've decided to shave off my beard.* —**shaven** *adj*: *his shaven head*

shave² *n* [C usually singular] if a man has a shave, he shaves the hair growing on his face
PHRASES

  a close shave a situation in which you only just avoid an accident or something bad: *That was a close shave. I nearly hit the car in front.*

shaver /'ʃeɪvə $ -ər/ *n* [C] a piece of electrical equipment used for shaving → **razor**

shavings /'ʃeɪvɪŋz/ *n* [plural] very thin pieces that have been cut from the surface of something, especially wood

shawl /ʃɔːl $ ʃɒːl/ *n* [C] a large piece of cloth that a woman wears around her shoulders or head

she /ʃi; *strong* ʃiː/ *pron* used to refer to a female person or animal that has already been mentioned: *'I saw Suzy today.' 'How is she?'* | *I was with Ann when she had the accident.*

sheaf /ʃiːf/ *n* [C] (*plural* **sheaves** /ʃiːvz/) **1** several pieces of paper held together **2** pieces of wheat, corn etc that have been cut and tied together

shear /ʃɪə $ ʃɪr/ *v* [T] (*past tense* **sheared**, *past participle* **sheared** *or* **shorn** /ʃɔːn $ ʃɔːrn/) to cut the wool off a sheep

shears /ʃɪəz $ ʃɪrz/ *n* [plural] a tool like a large pair of scissors → see picture at GARDEN

sheath /ʃiːθ/ n [C] (plural **sheaths** /ʃiːðz, ʃiːθs/) a cover for the blade of a knife or sword

she'd /ʃid; strong ʃiːd/ the short form of 'she had' or 'she would': She'd forgotten to close the door. | Paula said she'd love to come.

shed¹ /ʃed/ n [C] a small building used especially for storing things: a tool shed

shed² v [T] (past tense and past participle **shed**, present participle **shedding**) **1** to get rid of something that you do not want: He needs to shed some weight. | The company are planning to shed 200 jobs. **2** if a plant or animal sheds part of itself, that part falls off naturally: Many trees shed their leaves in winter.

PHRASES
shed blood literary to kill or injure people, especially during a war: Too much blood has been shed in this conflict.
shed light on sth to make something easier to understand by providing new information: This research sheds new light on possible causes of the illness.
shed tears literary to cry: I shed a few tears when I heard that he'd died.

sheen /ʃiːn/ n [singular, U] a smooth shiny appearance

sheep /ʃiːp/ n [C] (plural **sheep**) a farm animal that is kept for its wool and meat → see picture at LAMB → BLACK SHEEP

sheepish /ˈʃiːpɪʃ/ adj slightly embarrassed because you have done something silly or wrong: a sheepish smile —**sheepishly** adv

sheepskin /ˈʃiːpˌskɪn/ n [C,U] the skin of a sheep with the wool still on it: a sheepskin coat

sheer /ʃɪə $ ʃɪr/ adj **1** [only before noun] used to emphasize the amount, size, or degree of something: **the sheer size/weight/volume etc** The sheer size of some files caused problems. | **sheer delight/joy/luck etc** She giggled with sheer delight. **2** extremely steep: a sheer drop

sheet /ʃiːt/ n [C]
1 a large piece of thin cloth that you put on a bed → blanket, duvet: Have you **changed the sheets** (=put clean sheets on the bed)?
2 a piece of paper, glass, or metal: **[+of]** a sheet of paper with names on it → see picture at PIECE¹ → BALANCE SHEET

sheikh, **sheik** /ʃeɪk $ ʃiːk/ n [C] an Arab leader or prince

shelf /ʃelf/ n [C] (plural **shelves** /ʃelvz/) a long flat board fixed to a wall or in a cupboard, used for putting things on: **top/bottom shelf** Put the book back on the top shelf. | shelves of books | supermarket shelves

she'll /ʃil; strong ʃiːl/ the short form of 'she will': She'll be here soon.

shell¹ /ʃel/ n [C]
1 OF NUT/EGG the hard outside part of a nut, egg, or seed
2 OF SNAIL/CRAB the hard outside part that covers some animals, for example SNAILS and CRABS
3 IN GUN a metal container filled with an explosive

substance, which is fired from a large gun **SYN cartridge**
4 OF BUILDING/VEHICLE the outside structure of something such as a building or vehicle: the concrete shell of the building

PHRASES
come out of/go into your shell to become less shy or become shyer: Since she got her new job, she's started to come out of her shell a little.

shell² v [T] **1** to fire at something with shells from a gun: Rebel forces shelled the town. **THESAURUS** SHOOT **2** to remove the shell from something such as a nut

PHRASAL VERBS
shell out (sth) informal to pay a lot of money for something: We were forced to shell out $1,000 to get the car fixed.

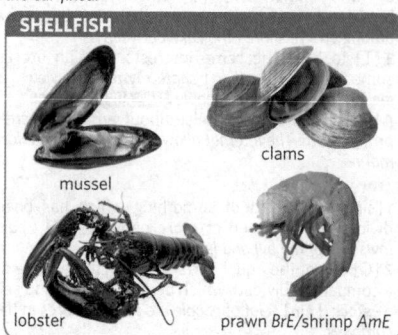

SHELLFISH

clams

mussel

lobster

prawn BrE/shrimp AmE

shellfish /ˈʃelfɪʃ/ n [C,U] (plural **shellfish**) an animal that lives in water, has a shell, and is eaten as food

shelter¹ /ˈʃeltə $ -ər/ n
1 [U] protection from danger or from the weather: **in/under the shelter of sth** He was standing in the shelter of a doorway. | They **took shelter** under a tree.
2 [C] a small building or covered place that protects you from bad weather or from attack: an **air-raid shelter** | a **bus shelter** (=where people wait for buses)
3 [C] a place where people or animals can stay if they do not have a home or are in danger: an animal shelter | a shelter for homeless people

shelter² v **1** [I] to stay somewhere in order to be protected from danger or the weather: **[+from]** People were in doorways, sheltering from the rain. **2** [T] to provide a place where someone or something is protected from danger or the weather: people who shelter criminals | **shelter sb/sth from sth** The trees shelter you from the sun.

sheltered /ˈʃeltəd $ -ərd/ adj **1** protected from extreme weather conditions: a sheltered bay **2** someone who has had a sheltered life has not experienced many things: Gina had a sheltered childhood.

shelve /ʃelv/ v [T] to decide not to continue with a plan, although you might continue with it later: Plans to build a new airport have been shelved.

shelves /ʃelvz/ n the plural of SHELF

shelving /ˈʃelvɪŋ/ n [U] a set of shelves

shepherd¹ /ˈʃepəd $ -ərd/ n [C] someone whose job is to take care of sheep

shepherd² v [T] to lead someone somewhere and make sure they go where you want them to: **shepherd sb out of/into etc sth** He took her arm and shepherded her to the taxi.

sherd /ʃɜːd $ ʃɜːrd/ n another spelling of SHARD

sheriff /ˈʃerɪf/ n [C] an elected law officer in a US COUNTY

sherry /ˈʃeri/ n [C,U] (plural **sherries**) a strong Spanish wine

she's /ʃiz; strong ʃiːz/ spoken the short form of 'she is' or 'she has': She's called Ruth. | She's arrived!

shh /ʃ/ another spelling of SH

shield¹ /ʃiːld/ n [C] a piece of metal or plastic that you hold in front of your body to protect yourself in a fight or battle: The police were carrying **riot shields**.

shield² v [T] to protect someone or something from being hurt or damaged: I tried to **shield** my **eyes** from the sun. **THESAURUS** PROTECT

shift¹ Ac /ʃɪft/ v 1 [I,T] to move from one place or position to another, or to make something do this: Paul **shifted uncomfortably** in his seat. | We'll have to shift the furniture. 2 [I] if your opinions or beliefs shift, they change 3 **shift the blame/responsibility** to say that someone else is responsible for something, especially something bad: My boss made a mistake, and now he's trying to shift the blame.

shift² Ac n [C] 1 a change in the way people think about something, or in the way something is done: [+in] a shift in public opinion 2 one of the periods during each day and night when workers in a factory, hospital etc do their work: the **night shift**

shifty /ˈʃɪfti/ adj someone who is shifty looks dishonest

shilling /ˈʃɪlɪŋ/ n [C] a British coin used in the past

shimmer /ˈʃɪmə $ -ər/ v [I] to shine with a soft light that seems to shake slightly: The sea shimmered in the sunlight.

shin /ʃɪn/ n [C] the front part of your leg between your knee and your foot → see picture on page A2

shine¹ /ʃaɪn/ v (past tense and past participle **shone** /ʃɒn $ ʃoʊn/)
1 [I] to produce bright light: The **sun** was **shining**.
2 [T] to point a light in a particular direction: **shine sth on/at/around etc sth** He shone his torch around the room.
3 [I] to look bright and smooth: her long **shining hair**
4 [I] if your eyes are shining, they are very bright because you are happy or excited
5 [I] if you shine at an activity, you do it very well: [+at] She shines at most sports.

THESAURUS

shine to produce bright light – used especially about the sun, the moon, or the stars: The sun shone in the sky.
flash to shine brightly for a very short time, or to shine on and off very quickly many times: Red warning lights were flashing.
flicker to shine with an unsteady light – used about a flame or light: The candle flickered and went out.
twinkle if stars or lights twinkle, they shine in the dark in a way that seems to change from bright to faint: I could see the harbour lights twinkling in the distance.
glow especially literary to shine with a warm soft light: A fire glowed in the hearth.
sparkle if something sparkles, it shines with many small bright points when light is on it: The diamond in her ring sparkled.
gleam to shine by reflecting the light – used especially about smooth clean surfaces, or about someone's eyes or teeth: Emily's eyes gleamed with pleasure.

shine² n [singular, U] the brightness that something has when light shines on it: hair with lots of shine
PHRASES
take a shine to sb informal to like someone and be attracted to them when you have only just met them: Ron took a shine to Amy the first time he met her.

shingle /ˈʃɪŋɡəl/ n [U] small round pieces of stone on a beach

shiny /ˈʃaɪni/ adj smooth and bright: shiny black shoes | shiny hair

ship¹ /ʃɪp/ n [C] a large boat used for carrying people or things across the sea: **cruise/cargo/supply etc ship** | **by ship** Supplies came by ship.

ship² v [T] (**shipped**, **shipping**) to send goods somewhere **THESAURUS** TAKE

shipment /ˈʃɪpmənt/ n [C,U] a load of goods sent by sea, road, or air, or the act of sending them: [+of] a shipment of grain | The goods are ready for shipment.

shipping /ˈʃɪpɪŋ/ n [U] 1 ships: The port is closed to all shipping. 2 the sending of goods from one place to another, especially by ship: a shipping company

shipwreck¹ /ˈʃɪp-rek/ n [C,U] an accident in which a ship is destroyed at sea

shipwreck² v **be shipwrecked** if you are shipwrecked, the ship you are travelling on is destroyed in an accident at sea

shipyard /ˈʃɪp-jɑːd $ -jɑːrd/ n [C] a place where ships are built or repaired

shirk /ʃɜːk $ ʃɜːrk/ v [I,T] to deliberately avoid working: He was accused of **shirking** his **duties**. —**shirker** n [C]

shirt /ʃɜːt $ ʃɜːrt/ n [C] a piece of clothing for the upper part of your body and your arms that usually has a collar and has buttons down the front → see picture at CLOTHES → TEE SHIRT, T-SHIRT

Word Choice: shirt or blouse?
A **shirt** is worn by men. A **blouse** is worn by women.

shiver /ˈʃɪvə $ -ər/ v [I] if you shiver, your body shakes slightly because you are cold or frightened **SYN** **tremble**: Come inside, you're shivering. | **shiver with cold/fear/delight** etc **THESAURUS** SHAKE

—**shiver** n [C]: *His words sent a **shiver down** her spine.* —**shivery** adj

> **Word Choice**: shiver or tremble?
> You usually **shiver** because you are cold: *He stood shivering in the cold night air.*
> You can also **shiver** because you are very frightened: *Anne hid behind the door, shivering with fear.*
> You **tremble** because you are very frightened, nervous, excited, angry, or upset: *He trembled as he opened the letter.* | *Her voice was trembling with anger.*

shoal /ʃəʊl $ ʃoʊl/ n [C] a large group of fish swimming together **THESAURUS** GROUP

shock¹ /ʃɒk $ ʃɑːk/ n
1 [C usually singular] if something is a shock, or if it gives you a shock, you did not expect it, and it makes you feel very surprised, and usually upset: *I got a terrible shock when I saw the bill.* | **[+of]** *I'm still recovering from the shock of his death.* | **it is a shock to discover/hear/realize etc (that)** *It was a shock to hear that she was leaving.*
2 [U] a state or feeling of being very surprised, and usually upset: **in (a state of) shock** *Everybody in the office is in shock.*
3 [U] a medical condition in which someone looks pale and their heart and lungs are not working correctly, usually after a sudden very unpleasant experience: *I was taken to hospital **suffering from shock**.* | **in (a state of) shock** *He was found in a state of shock.*
4 [C] an ELECTRIC SHOCK
5 [C,U] violent shaking caused by an explosion, a crash etc: *The rubber supports are designed to **absorb shock**.* → CULTURE SHOCK

> **COLLOCATIONS**
> **adjectives**
> **a big/great shock** *The news came as a great shock.*
> **a terrible/awful shock** *I know this must have been a terrible shock to you.*
> **a complete/total shock** *It was a complete shock when Jane said she wanted a divorce.*
> **a bit of a shock** *BrE especially spoken* (=a slight shock) *He expected to pass, so failure came as a bit of a shock.*
>
> **verbs**
> **to get/have a shock** *I opened the door and got a shock.*
> **to give sb a shock** *The accident gave us all a shock.*
> **to get over/recover from a shock** *She still hadn't got over the shock of seeing him again.*
> **to come as a shock** (=to be very unexpected) *His death came as a shock to his friends.*

shock² v
1 [T] to make someone feel very surprised and upset: *I was shocked by his arrogance.* | **be shocked to hear/learn/discover etc sth** *They were shocked to hear of his arrest.*
2 [I,T] to make someone feel very offended, by talking or behaving in an immoral or socially unacceptable way: *The play shocked audiences all over the country.* | *Ken loved to shock.*

shocked /ʃɒkt $ ʃɑːkt/ adj very surprised and upset: *John looked shocked when he heard the news.* | *He would be **deeply shocked** if he knew.* **THESAURUS** SURPRISED

> **THESAURUS**
> **shocked** very surprised and upset: *We were shocked when we saw the bill.*
> **horrified** very shocked because something unpleasant or frightening has happened: *His parents were horrified by his injuries.*
> **appalled** very shocked because you think something is very bad: *Most people were appalled by the shooting of an innocent man.*
> **outraged** extremely shocked and angry: *Viewers were outraged by the programme and called to complain.*
> **stunned** so shocked that you are unable to do or say anything immediately: *She was so stunned by the news that she didn't know what to say.*

shocking /ʃɒkɪŋ $ ʃɑːk-/ adj very upsetting, wrong, or immoral: *a shocking waste of money*

shock wave n [C] **1** a very strong wave of air pressure or heat from an explosion, EARTHQUAKE etc **2 shock waves** strong feelings of shock that people have when something bad happens unexpectedly – used especially in news reports: *His murder sent shock waves through the city.*

shod /ʃɒd $ ʃɑːd/ adj literary wearing shoes of the type mentioned

shoddy /ˈʃɒdi $ ˈʃɑːdi/ adj **1** badly or cheaply made: *shoddy goods* **2** unfair and dishonest: *He treated me in a pretty shoddy way.* —**shoddily** adv

SHOES
laces
sole heel
shoes
stilettos
clogs
trainers BrE/ sneakers AmE
slippers
boots sandals

shoe¹ /ʃuː/ n [C] something that you wear on your foot, made of leather or another strong material

be in sb's shoes to be in the situation that someone else is in: *I wouldn't like to be in your shoes when Kate gets home.*

shoe² v [T] (*past tense and past participle* **shod** /ʃɒd $ ʃɑːd/, *present participle* **shoeing**) to put HORSESHOES (=curved pieces of metal) on a horse's feet

shoelace /ˈʃuːleɪs/ n [C] a thin piece of string or leather used to fasten a shoe SYN **lace**

shoestring /ˈʃuːstrɪŋ/ n **on a shoestring** using very little money: *a movie made on a shoestring*

shone /ʃɒn $ ʃoʊn/ v the past tense and past participle of SHINE

shoo /ʃuː/ *spoken* used to tell a person or an animal to go away —**shoo** v [T]: *Gran shooed us back upstairs.*

shook /ʃʊk/ v the past tense of SHAKE

shoot¹ /ʃuːt/ v (*past tense and past participle* **shot** /ʃɒt $ ʃɑːt/)
1 GUN [I,T] to fire a gun at someone, or kill or injure someone with a gun: *She pulled out a gun and shot him.* | **Don't shoot!** | **[+at]** *Someone on the roof was shooting at her.* | *Three people were* **shot dead** *by police.* | **shoot yourself** *Finally, he shot himself.*
2 MOVE QUICKLY [I,T] to move quickly in a particular direction, or to make something move in this way: **[+out/through/into etc]** *I shot out of bed.* | **shoot sth out/into etc** *Most fountains shoot water into the air.*
3 FILM [I,T] to take photographs or make a film of something: *The movie was shot in Rome.*
4 BALL [I] to kick or throw a ball towards the place in a sports game where you can make points: *Giggs shot from outside the penalty box.* → see picture at **FOOTBALL**

shoot sb/sth ↔ down
1 to make an enemy plane crash to the ground, by firing weapons at it: *His plane was shot down over Russia.*
2 to tell someone that what they are saying or suggesting is wrong or stupid: *Whenever I suggest anything, I get* **shot down in flames.**
shoot up to increase very quickly: *Prices shot up by 60%.* THESAURUS **INCREASE**

THESAURUS

shoot to fire a gun at someone, or kill or injure someone with a gun: *He shot a police officer.* | *Someone shot at our car.*
fire to shoot bullets from a gun, or send an explosive object towards someone or something: *The police fired into the air.* | *The gunman fired three bullets – luckily all of them missed.* | *Dozens of rockets were fired.*
launch to send a large rocket or MISSILE into the air: *The country will soon be able to launch nuclear weapons.*
open fire to start shooting: *The soldiers opened fire, killing several protesters.*
shell to fire shells (=metal containers filled with explosives) in a war, using large guns: *They started shelling the hospital.*

---

shoot² n [C] **1** a new part of a plant **2** an occasion when someone takes photographs or makes a film: *a photo shoot*

shooting /ˈʃuːtɪŋ/ n **1** [C] a situation in which someone is injured or killed by a gun **2** [U] the sport of killing animals and birds with guns

shooting 'star n [C] a piece of rock or metal from space that burns brightly as it falls towards the Earth

'shoot-out n [C] a fight using guns: *a shoot-out with police*

shop¹ /ʃɒp $ ʃɑːp/ n
1 [C] *especially BrE* a building where you can buy things SYN **store** *AmE*: **toy/pet/shoe/gift etc shop** | *a* **shop window** | *I'm just* **going to the shops.** | **coffee/tea shop** (=where you can buy and drink coffee or tea)
2 [U] *AmE* a subject taught in schools that shows students how to use tools and machinery to make or repair things → **BETTING SHOP, CHARITY SHOP, CORNER SHOP, THRIFT SHOP**

shop² v [I] (**shopped**, **shopping**) to go to a shop to buy things: *Zoe wanted to* **go shopping.** | **[+for]** *I was out shopping for food.* | **[+at]** *I usually shop at Tesco's.* —**shopper** n [C]

shop around to compare the price and quality of different things before you decide which to buy

shopaholic /ˌʃɒpəˈhɒlɪk $ ˌʃɑːpəˈhɔː-/ n [C] *informal* someone who likes to go shopping a lot, and often buys things that they do not really need

'shop as,sistant n [C] *BrE* someone who serves customers in a shop SYN **salesclerk** *AmE*

,shop 'floor n [singular] the part of a factory where goods are made, or the people who work there

shopkeeper /ˈʃɒpˌkiːpə $ ˈʃɑːpˌkiːpər/ n [C] *especially BrE* someone who owns or is in charge of a small shop SYN **storekeeper** *AmE*

shoplifting /ˈʃɒpˌlɪftɪŋ $ ˈʃɑːp-/ n [U] the crime of taking things from shops without paying for them: *She was arrested for shoplifting.* THESAURUS **STEAL** —**shoplifter** n [C] —**shoplift** v [I]

shopping /ˈʃɒpɪŋ $ ˈʃɑː-/ n [U]
1 the activity of going to shops to buy things: **late-night shopping** | *I hate* **doing the shopping** (=buying the food and other things you regularly need). | **shopping trolley/cart/basket** | *a* **shopping list** (=a list of the things you need to buy)
2 *BrE* the things that you have just bought from a shop: *Shall I help you carry the shopping in?* → **WINDOW SHOPPING**

'shopping ,centre *BrE*, **shopping center** *AmE* n [C] a group of shops together in one area

'shopping mall n [C] a MALL

shore¹ /ʃɔː $ ʃɔːr/ n [C,U] the land along the edge of an ocean, sea, or lake: *We were still about a mile from shore.* | *Only a few survivors* **reached** *the* **shore.** | **on the shore(s) of sth** *a town on the shores of Lake Garda*

shore² v
PHRASAL VERBS
shore sth ↔ **up 1** to support a wall with pieces of wood or metal to stop it from falling down **2** to help or support something that is likely to fail or is not working well: *attempts to shore up the struggling economy*

shoreline /ˈʃɔːlaɪn $ ˈʃɔːr-/ *n* [C,U] the land along the edge of a large area of water such as an ocean or lake: *I stood silently on the shoreline.* | *the bay's 13,000 km of shoreline*

shorn /ʃɔːn $ ʃɔːrn/ *v* the past participle of SHEAR

short¹ /ʃɔːt $ ʃɔːrt/ *adj*
1 IN TIME happening for only a little time OPP **long**: *a short meeting* | *I've only lived here a short time.* | *Life is short.* | *People have short memories* (=they soon forget things that have happened). THESAURUS
QUICK
2 IN LENGTH/DISTANCE not very long in length or far in distance OPP **long**: *a short skirt* | *His hair was very short.* | *a short distance from the sea*
3 NOT TALL not very tall OPP **tall**: *a short fat man*
4 NOT ENOUGH **a)** if you are short of something, you do not have enough of it: [+of] *Are you short of money?* | *I'm a bit short of time.* | *be 5p/$10 etc short* | *Do you want to join our team? We're one short.* **b)** if something is short, there is not enough of it: *Money was short.* | *Water was in short supply* (=not enough was available).
5 SHORTER WAY TO SAY STH *be short for sth* to be a shorter way of saying a name: *Her name's Jo, short for Joanne.*
6 RUDE/UNFRIENDLY *be short with sb* to speak to someone using very few words, in a way that seems rude or unfriendly: *Sorry I was so short with you.*
—**shortness** *n* [U]
PHRASES
at short notice *BrE*, **on short notice** *AmE* with very little warning that something is going to happen: *The party was arranged at short notice.* THESAURUS
SUDDENLY
have a short temper someone who has a short temper gets angry very easily: *Mr. Stewart, who had a very short temper, told her to get out.*
in the short term/run having an effect for only a short time, not very far into the future → **short-term**: *The problem has been solved, at least in the short term.*

THESAURUS
lasting a short time
short happening for only a little time: *a short vacation* | *The film is very short.*
brief short, especially because there is not much time available. **Brief** is more formal than **short**: *The President will make a brief visit to Chicago today.* | *a brief pause*
quick taking a short time to do something: *He had a quick shower and then went out.* | *a quick look*
temporary expected to continue for only a short time, and not permanent: *a temporary job* | *The museum has an area for temporary exhibitions.*

with not many words
short a short piece of writing does not have many pages or many words: *a short novel* | *Keep your essay short.*
brief a brief note, description, comment etc is short and only gives the most important information, without a lot of details: *The book gives a brief description of the area.* | *I left a brief note saying what the problem was.*

person
short not as tall as most people: *He was short and fat.* | *I have rather short legs.*
not very tall quite short. This phrase sounds more polite than saying that someone is **short**: *He was about 40 and not very tall.*
small short and with a small body: *The girl was quite small for her age* (=smaller than other girls of the same age).

short² *adv* **short of doing sth** except for doing something: *They've done everything short of cancelling the project.* → **cut sth short** at CUT¹, **fall short** at FALL¹, **be running short (of sth)** at RUN¹, **stop short of (doing) sth** at STOP¹

short³ *n* **1 shorts** [plural] **a)** short trousers ending at the knees: *a pair of shorts* | *in shorts* *a boy in shorts* | *running/cycling/tennis etc shorts* → see picture at CLOTHES **b)** especially *AmE* men's underwear with short legs → **BOXER SHORTS 2** [C] *BrE* a glass of a strong alcoholic drink such as WHISKY SYN **shot** *AmE*
PHRASES
for short used as a shorter way of saying a name: *His name's Maximilian, or Max for short.*
in short used when you want to say the most important point in a few words: *In short, the answer is no.*

shortage /ˈʃɔːtɪdʒ $ ˈʃɔːr-/ *n* [C,U] a situation in which there is not enough of something: [+of] *a shortage of skilled labour* | *food shortages* | *There was no shortage of people applying for the job.*

shortbread /ˈʃɔːtbred $ ˈʃɔːrt-/ *n* [U] a hard sweet BISCUIT made with a lot of butter

short-'change *v* [T] **1** to treat someone unfairly by not giving them what they deserve: *Is society short-changing older people?* **2** to give back too little money to a customer who has paid for something

short 'circuit *n* [C] a failure of an electrical system, caused by a fault in the wires —**short circuit** *v* [I,T]

shortcoming /ˈʃɔːtˌkʌmɪŋ $ ˈʃɔːrt-/ *n* [C usually plural] a fault in someone or something that makes them less effective: [+of/in] *the shortcomings of the political system*

short 'cut / $ ˈ../ *n* [C] a quicker and more direct way of getting somewhere or achieving something: *He took a short cut across the fields.* | [+to] *There are no short cuts to becoming an actor.*

shorten /ˈʃɔːtn $ ˈʃɔːrtn/ *v* [I,T] to become shorter, or to make something shorter: *Smoking shortens your life.*

shortfall /ˈʃɔːtfɔːl $ ˈʃɔːrtfɒːl/ n [C] if there is a shortfall in something, there is not enough of it: **[+in]** *a $2.5 billion shortfall in funds*

shorthand /ˈʃɔːthænd $ ˈʃɔːrt-/ n [U] a fast method of writing using special signs and short forms of words

ˈshort list n [C] *BrE* a list of people or things that have been chosen from a larger group to be considered for a job or prize

ˈshort-list v **be short-listed** *BrE* to be put on a short list

short-lived /ʃɔːt ˈlɪvd◂ $ ˌʃɔːrt ˈlaɪvd◂/ adj existing or happening for only a short time: *His success was short-lived.*

shortly /ˈʃɔːtli $ ˈʃɔːrt-/ adv **1** soon: *The report will be published shortly.* | *We left shortly after two.* **THESAURUS** SOON **2** speaking impatiently: *'I know that,' he replied shortly.*

ˌshort-ˈrange adj [only before noun] short-range weapons are designed to travel or be used over a short distance

shortsighted /ʃɔːtˈsaɪtɪd◂ $ ˈʃɔːrt-, ˌshort-ˈsighted/ adj **1** *especially BrE* if you are shortsighted, you cannot see objects clearly unless they are close to you **SYN** **nearsighted** *AmE* **2** if a decision or action is shortsighted, it is not sensible because it does not consider the future effects of something: *short-sighted economic policies*

ˌshort-ˈstaffed adj having fewer than the usual or necessary number of workers

ˌshort ˈstory n [C] a short written story

ˌshort-ˈterm adj continuing for only a short time: *short-term benefits*

ˈshort wave n [U] a range of short radio waves used for broadcasting → **medium wave, long wave, FM**

shot¹ /ʃɒt $ ʃɑːt/ n [C]
1 **FROM GUN** when someone fires a gun, or the sound that this makes: *The gunman **fired** three **shots**.* | *We **heard** a **shot**.* | *He's a very **good shot** (=he can fire a gun well).*
2 **THROW/HIT/KICK** an attempt in sport to throw, kick, or hit the ball towards the place where you can get a point: *Good shot!* | **[+at]** *We only had one **shot** at goal in the whole match.*
3 **PHOTOGRAPH** a photograph, or a picture of something in a film: **[+of]** *I got a lovely **shot** of John.* | **opening/closing/final shot** *the opening shots of the movie*
4 **ATTEMPT** *informal* an attempt to do something: *I'm going to **have a shot at** decorating the house myself.* | *I'll **give it** my **best shot** (=try as hard as possible).*
5 **OF WHISKY/VODKA** a small amount of a strong alcoholic drink: **[+of]** *a shot of whisky*
6 **INJECTION** *especially AmE* when a doctor puts medicine into your body using a needle **SYN** **injection, jab** *BrE*: *Have you **had** your typhoid **shot**?* | **[+of]** *The doctor gave me a shot of antibiotics.*
→ **call the shots** at **CALL¹**, **long shot** at **LONG¹**
PHRASES
like a shot very quickly and eagerly: *I'd marry Pete like a shot.*

a shot in the arm something that makes you more confident or successful: *Being chosen was a real shot in the arm for Mike.*

shot² v the past tense and past participle of SHOOT

shotgun /ˈʃɒtɡʌn $ ˈʃɑːt-/ n [C] a long gun, used especially for shooting animals and birds

should /ʃəd; *strong* ʃʊd/ modal verb (*negative short form* **shouldn't**)
1 used to say what is the right or sensible thing to do: *You should see a doctor.* | *Children shouldn't be outside this late.* | *They **should have** called the police (=it would have been sensible, but they did not do it).*
2 used to give or ask for advice: *You should read his new book – it's fascinating.* | *Should I wear my black dress?*
3 used to say that you expect something to happen or be true: *Your Dad should be back soon.* | *It should be a nice day tomorrow.* | *It was an easy test and he **should have** passed (=he was expected to pass, but he did not).*
4 *formal* used to talk about something that may possibly happen or be true: *Should you (=if you) wish to complain, please use this leaflet.*
5 *especially BrE formal* used to ask politely for something, offer to do something, or say that you want to do something: *I should be grateful if you would send a receipt.*
PHRASES
I should think/imagine/hope used to say that you think or hope something is true, when you are not certain: *'Is that enough?' **'I should think so.'***

shoulder¹ /ˈʃəʊldə $ ˈʃoʊldər/ n [C]
1 one of the two parts of your body at each side of your neck where your arm is connected: *She rested her head on my shoulder.* | *When we asked what was wrong, she just **shrugged** her **shoulders** (=raised them to show that she did not know or care).* | **look/glance over your shoulder** (=to look behind you) *I looked over my shoulder to see if anyone was following me.* → see picture on page A2
2 the part of a piece of clothing that covers your shoulders: *a jacket with **padded shoulders*** → **HARD SHOULDER**
PHRASES
a shoulder to cry on someone who gives you sympathy: *Chris was always there when I **needed a shoulder to cry on**.*
on sb's shoulders if blame or a difficult job falls on someone's shoulders, they have to accept it or do it: *The responsibility for looking after my sisters fell on my shoulders.*

shoulder² v [T] **1** **shoulder the responsibility/blame/cost etc** to accept a difficult or unpleasant responsibility, duty etc: *Residents are being asked to shoulder the costs of the repairs.* **2** to lift something onto your shoulder to carry it

ˈshoulder bag n [C] a bag that hangs from your shoulder

ˈshoulder blade n [C] one of the two flat bones just below your shoulders on your back

shouldn't /ˈʃʊdnt/ the short form of 'should not'

should've /ˈʃʊdəv/ the short form of 'should have'

shout¹ /ʃaʊt/ v [I,T] to say something very loudly: *There's no need to shout.* | *'Over here!' he shouted.* | **[+at]** *I wish he'd stop shouting at the children.* | **[+for]** *They shouted for help.*

PHRASAL VERBS

shout sb ↔ **down** to shout so that someone who is speaking cannot be heard: *She tried to argue, but was quickly shouted down.*

shout sth ↔ **out** to say something suddenly in a loud voice: *Don't shout out the answer.*

THESAURUS

shout to say something very loudly: *I shouted at him to get down off the wall.*

yell to shout, especially because you are angry, excited, or in pain. **Yell** is more informal than **shout**: *The other driver started yelling at him.* | *The children were yelling with excitement.*

scream to shout in a very loud high voice, because you are frightened, unhappy, angry etc: *The baby has been screaming all day.* | *'Let me out!' she screamed.*

call (out) to shout in order to get someone's attention: *I heard someone call my name.*

cry (out) *written* to shout something, especially because you are in pain, frightened, or very excited: *'I don't want to leave,' Ari cried.*

raise your voice to say something more loudly than normal, especially because you are angry: *I never heard my father raise his voice.*

cheer if a group of people cheer, they shout as a way of showing their approval: *The crowd cheered when the band came on stage.*

---

shout² n [C] something that someone says very loudly: *She heard a shout.* | **[+of]** *He gave a shout of pain.*

PHRASES

give sb a shout *spoken* to go and find someone and tell them something: *Give me a shout if you need any help.*

shove /ʃʌv/ v **1** [I,T] to push someone or something in a rough or careless way: *He shoved her towards the car.* **THESAURUS** PUSH **2** [T] to put something somewhere carelessly or without thinking much: **shove sth into/in etc sth** *She shoved the books into her briefcase.* **THESAURUS** PUT —**shove** n [C]

shovel¹ /ˈʃʌvəl/ n [C] a tool with a rounded blade and a long handle used for moving earth, stones etc

shovel² v [I,T] (**shovelled, shovelling** *BrE*, **shoveled, shoveling** *AmE*) **1** to move earth, stones etc with a shovel **2 shovel sth into/onto sth** to put something, usually food, somewhere quickly: *He sat **shovelling** his dinner **into** his mouth.*

show¹ /ʃəʊ $ ʃoʊ/ v (past tense **showed**, past participle **shown** /ʃəʊn $ ʃoʊn/)
1 LET SB SEE [T] to let someone see something: **show sb sth** *She showed me her photos.* | **show sth to sb** *I showed the letter to Ruth.*
2 DEMONSTRATE [T] if you show someone how to do something, you do it and they watch, so that they learn how to do it: **show sb how/what etc** *Could*

you show me how to turn the oven on? | *I'll show you what to do.* **THESAURUS** EXPLAIN
3 GUIDE [T] to go with someone and guide them to a place: **show sb to/into sth** *Jill showed me to my room.* | *Did Rachel show you where to leave your coat?* | *I'll show you the way.* **THESAURUS** LEAD
4 PROVE [T] to make it clear that something is true or exists, by providing facts or information: **[+(that)]** *This study shows that poverty is increasing.* | **show how/what etc** *We wanted to show how united we were.*
5 FEELINGS [T] if you show your feelings, other people can see how you feel by the way that you look or behave: *Alan tried not to show his disappointment.*
6 PICTURE/MAP [T] if a picture, map etc shows something, you can see it on the picture, map etc
7 FILM/PROGRAMME [I,T] when a film or television programme is shown, people are able to see it in a cinema or on television: *The film will be shown on Channel 4.*
8 BE EASY TO SEE [I,T] if something shows, people can see or notice it easily: *His anger showed on his face.* | *Ellie was tired, and **it showed**.* | *Light-coloured clothes tend to **show the dirt**.*
9 STH CAN BE SEEN [T] if someone or something shows a particular quality, that quality can be seen: *The economy was **showing signs of** recovery.* | **show yourself (to be) sth** *Mr Peters has shown himself to be a fine teacher.*
PHRASES

have something/nothing to show for sth to have achieved something or nothing as a result of your efforts: *By the end of the day I was exhausted, but had nothing to show for all my work.*

show willing *BrE* to make it clear that you are willing to do something: *He hasn't done any cooking yet, but at least he's shown willing.*

PHRASAL VERBS

show sb **around** (sth) to go with someone around a place and show them what is important, interesting etc: *His wife showed us around the house.*

show off
1 *disapproving* to try to make people admire you and think you are attractive, clever, funny, or important, in a way that is annoying for other people: *Ignore him. He's just showing off.*
2 show sth ↔ off to show something to someone because you are very proud of it: *Jen proudly showed off her engagement ring.*

show up
1 *informal* to arrive somewhere, especially when someone is waiting for you SYN **turn up**: *It was 9.20 when he finally showed up.*
2 to be easy to see or notice: *The bacteria showed up under the microscope.*
3 show sb ↔ up to make someone feel embarrassed by behaving in a stupid or unacceptable way when you are with them: *She showed me up in front of my friends.*

THESAURUS

show to let someone see something, especially by holding it out in front of them: *Stephanie showed us her engagement ring.*

S

let sb see *especially spoken* to show something to someone: *Let me see the menu.*

reveal to let someone see something that has been hidden, or know about something that you usually keep secret: *He lifted the lid of the box to reveal a small snake.* | *Suzy looked away quickly in order not to reveal her true feelings.*

expose to let someone see something that is usually covered: *He opened his mouth, exposing two rows of yellow teeth.*

---

show² n

1 [C] a performance for the public, especially one that includes singing, dancing, or jokes: *The show starts at 7:30 pm.* | *a Broadway show*

2 [C] a programme on television or on the radio: *a TV show* **THESAURUS▶ PROGRAMME**

3 [C] an occasion when a group of things are brought together for people to look at: *the Chelsea Flower Show*

4 a show of sth an occasion when someone deliberately shows a particular feeling, attitude, or quality: *a show of force by the police*

5 [singular, U] something that you do to pretend to other people that something is true, or to make them think you are attractive or impressive: **[+of]** *Lucy put on a show of indignation.* | **for show** *Critics say such efforts are just for show.* → **CHAT SHOW, GAME SHOW, TALK SHOW**

PHRASES

on show being shown to the public: *The photographs will be on show until May 4.*

'show ,business (*also* **show biz** /ˈʃəʊ bɪz $ ˈʃoʊ-/ *informal*) n [U] the industry that makes money by entertaining people in films, the theatre etc: *a career in show business*

showcase /ˈʃəʊkeɪs $ ˈʃoʊ-/ n [C] an event that is designed to show the best qualities someone or something has: *a showcase for new musical talent*

showdown /ˈʃəʊdaʊn $ ˈʃoʊ-/ n [C] a final argument that will end a long disagreement: *a showdown between managers and staff*

shower¹ /ˈʃaʊə $ ˈʃaʊr/ n [C]

1 a piece of equipment that sends out water and that you stand under to wash yourself: *Are you in the shower?* | *a shower cubicle* → see picture at **BATHROOM**

2 when you wash your body under a shower: **have a shower** *BrE*/**take a shower** *AmE*: *Have I time to take a shower?*

3 a short period of rain: *a heavy shower* **THESAURUS▶ RAIN**

4 many small things that fall through the air together: **[+of]** *a shower of sparks*

5 *AmE* a party for a woman who is going to have a baby or get married

shower² v

1 [I] to wash yourself by standing under a shower: *Tom showered and changed.*

2 [I,T] to cover a person or place with a lot of small things: **shower sb/sth with sth** *Bystanders were showered with broken glass.*

3 [T] to give someone a lot of something: **shower sb with sth** *Mother showered us with gifts.*

showery /ˈʃaʊəri $ ˈʃaʊri/ *adj* with short periods of rain: *a showery afternoon*

showing /ˈʃəʊɪŋ $ ˈʃoʊ-/ n **1** [C] an occasion when a film is shown or a television programme is broadcast: *a second showing of this popular programme* **2** [singular] something that shows the level of your success: *He made a strong showing in his last race.*

showjumping /ˈʃəʊdʒʌmpɪŋ $ ˈʃoʊ-/ n [U] a sport in which horses with riders jump over fences

showman /ˈʃəʊmən $ ˈʃoʊ-/ n [C] (*plural* **showmen** /-mən/) someone who is good at entertaining people

shown /ʃəʊn $ ʃoʊn/ v the past participle of SHOW

'show-off n [C] *disapproving* someone who likes to show how clever, funny, or attractive they are

showpiece /ˈʃəʊpiːs $ ˈʃoʊ-/ n [C] something that an organization is proud of because it is a good example of its work

showroom /ˈʃəʊrʊm, -ruːm $ ˈʃoʊ-/ n [C] a room where you can look at things that are for sale: **car/furniture showroom**

showy /ˈʃəʊi $ ˈʃoʊi/ *adj* very big, bright, or expensive in a way that gets your attention

shrank /ʃræŋk/ v the past tense of SHRINK

shrapnel /ˈʃræpnəl/ n [U] small pieces of metal from a bomb or bullet that has exploded: *shrapnel wounds*

shred¹ /ʃred/ n **1** [C usually plural] a small thin piece that has been torn from something: **[+of]** *a shred of paper* | **rip/tear sth to shreds** *The puppy had ripped my shoes to shreds.* | **in shreds** *His shirt was in shreds.* **2 not a shred of sth** not even a small amount of something: *There is not a shred of evidence against him.*

shred² v [T] (**shredded, shredding**) to cut or tear something into small pieces → see picture at CUT¹ —**shredder** n [C]: *a paper shredder*

shrewd /ʃruːd/ *adj* good at understanding situations and making clever decisions: *a shrewd businesswoman*

shriek /ʃriːk/ v [I,T] to shout in a high voice **SYN scream**: *'Stop it!' she shrieked.* | **[+with]** *students shrieking with laughter* —**shriek** n [C]

shrill /ʃrɪl/ *adj* a shrill sound is high and unpleasant: *shrill voices*

shrimp /ʃrɪmp/ n [C,U] (*plural* **shrimp** or **shrimps**) a small pink sea creature that you eat → see picture at SHELLFISH

shrine /ʃraɪn/ n [C] a place that people visit for religious reasons or because it is connected with a special event or person: **[+of/to]** *the shrine of St John*

shrink¹ /ʃrɪŋk/ v (*past tense* **shrank** /ʃræŋk/, *past participle* **shrunk** /ʃrʌŋk/)

1 [I,T] if something shrinks, or if you shrink it, it becomes smaller: *Families have been shrinking since the 1970s.* | **shrink (sth) to sth** *Global warming has shrunk the ice cap to 13 km.*

2 [I] to move away because you are afraid: **[+back/ away from]** *She shrank back in fright.*

PHRASAL VERBS

shrink from sth to avoid doing something difficult or unpleasant: **shrink from doing sth** *She never shrank from doing her duty.*

shrink² n [C] *informal humorous* a PSYCHOANALYST or PSYCHIATRIST

shrink-'wrapped adj wrapped tightly in thin plastic

shrivel /ˈʃrɪvəl/ (*also* **shrivel up**) v [I,T] (**shrivelled, shrivelling** *BrE*, **shriveled, shriveling** *AmE*) if something shrivels, or if it is shrivelled, it becomes smaller and covered in lines because it is dry or old: *The flowers had shrivelled up.* | *her shriveled hands*

shroud¹ /ʃraʊd/ n [C] **1** a cloth that is wrapped around the body of a dead person before it is buried **2** *literary* something that hides or covers something: *a shroud of fog*

shroud² v *formal* **be shrouded in sth** to be hidden by something: *The hill was shrouded in mist.*

PHRASES

be shrouded in mystery/secrecy to be difficult to understand or explain: *His death was shrouded in mystery.*

shrub /ʃrʌb/ n [C] a small bush

shrubbery /ˈʃrʌbəri/ n [C] (*plural* **shrubberies**) part of a garden where many small bushes have been planted

shrug /ʃrʌɡ/ v [I,T] (**shrugged, shrugging**) to raise and lower your shoulders to show that you do not know or care about something: *Dan shrugged and returned to his book.* | *Melanie shrugged her shoulders.* —**shrug** n [C]

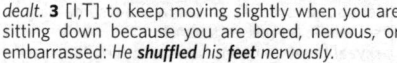

SHRUG

PHRASAL VERBS

shrug sth ↔ **off** to treat something as unimportant and not worry about it: *Mary tried to shrug off her failure.*

shrunk /ʃrʌŋk/ v the past participle of SHRINK

shrunken /ˈʃrʌŋkən/ adj something that is shrunken has become smaller: *a shrunken old woman*

shuck /ʃʌk/ v [T] *AmE* to remove the outer part of a vegetable such as corn or PEAS

shudder /ˈʃʌdə $ -ər/ v [I] **1** to shake because you are afraid or cold, or because you think something is unpleasant: **[+at]** *She shuddered at the thought.* | **[+with]** *Gwen shuddered with embarrassment.* **2** if a vehicle or machine shudders, it shakes —**shudder** n [C]

shuffle /ˈʃʌfəl/ v **1** [I] to walk slowly and without lifting your feet up properly: **[+across/away/into etc]** *The old man shuffled across the room.* **2** [T] to move papers, cards etc into a different position or order: *Joe shuffled the pack* (=of playing cards) *and*

dealt. **3** [I,T] to keep moving slightly when you are sitting down because you are bored, nervous, or embarrassed: *He shuffled his feet nervously.*

shun /ʃʌn/ v [T] (**shunned, shunning**) to deliberately avoid someone or something: *She shunned publicity.*

shunt /ʃʌnt/ v [T] **1** to move someone or something to another place or position in a way that seems unfair: *She was tired of being shunted to and fro.* **2** to push a vehicle from behind so that it is in a different position

shush /ʃʊʃ/ *spoken* used to tell someone to be quiet

shut¹ /ʃʌt/ v [I,T] (*past tense and past participle* **shut**, *present participle* **shutting**)
1 if you shut something, or if it shuts, it closes: *Would you mind shutting the window?* | *I heard the door shut with a bang.* | **Shut** your **eyes** and go to sleep. | **shut sth/sb in (sth)** (=close a door etc so that someone or something cannot get out) *Are the dogs shut in?* | *He shut his finger in the door.* | **shut sb/sth out** (=close a door etc so that someone or something cannot get in) *Close the curtains to shut out the noise.* **THESAURUS** ▶ CLOSE
2 *BrE* if a shop, bank etc shuts, it stops being open to people **SYN** **close**: *What time does the bank shut?*

PHRASAL VERBS

shut sb/sth **away** to put someone or something in a place where other people cannot see them: *He shut himself away in his office.*

shut down if a company, factory, machine etc shuts down, or if you shut it down, it stops operating: *Hundreds of local post offices have shut down.* | **shut sth ↔ down** *Did you shut the computer down?*

shut off
1 to stop a machine or supply of something from working, or to stop working **SYN** **turn off**: **shut sth ↔ off** *Don't forget to shut the gas off.*
2 **shut yourself off** to deliberately avoid other people: **[+from]** *After her death, he shut himself off from the world.*

shut (sb) **up** *informal* to stop talking, or to make someone stop talking: *Shut up a minute!* | *The chairman tried to shut us up.*

shut² adj [not before noun]
1 not open **SYN** **closed**: *Is the door shut?* | *Keep the windows shut.* | **slam/swing etc shut** *The gates swung shut behind him.*
2 *BrE* if a shop, bar etc is shut, it is not open for people to use

shutdown /ˈʃʌtdaʊn/ n [C] when a factory, business, or machine stops working

shutter /ˈʃʌtə $ -ər/ n [C] **1** a wooden or metal cover for a window: *a pair of wooden shutters* **2** a part of a camera that lets light in

shuttered /ˈʃʌtəd $ -ərd/ adj a shuttered window or building has closed shutters

shuttle¹ /ˈʃʌtl/ n [C] **1** a plane, bus, or train that makes regular trips between two places: *the Washington-New York* **shuttle service** | *a* **shuttle bus** **2** a spacecraft that goes into space and returns more than once

shuttle² v [I,T] to travel or move people regularly

between two places: **[+between/to and from]** *Graham shuttles between Rotterdam and Rome.* | *Guests are shuttled to and from the hotel by bus.*

shuttlecock /ˈʃʌtlkɒk $ -kɑːk/ *n* [C] a small light object with feathers attached that you hit across a net in BADMINTON **SYN** **birdie** *AmE*

shy¹ /ʃaɪ/ *adj*
1 nervous and embarrassed about meeting or talking to other people: **[+with]** *She's **painfully shy** with strangers.* | *He's **too shy** to speak up for himself.* **THESAURUS** CONFIDENT
2 unwilling to do or get involved in something: **not be shy about (doing) sth** *John has strong views, and he's not shy about voicing them.* | **publicity-shy/camera-shy** *He's publicity-shy and rarely gives interviews.* —**shyly** *adv* —**shyness** *n* [U]: *I gradually overcame my shyness.*

shy² *v* [I] (**shied**, **shying**, **shies**) if a horse shies, it suddenly moves away from something because it is frightened
PHRASAL VERBS
shy away from sth to avoid doing something because you are nervous or lack confidence: *He shies away from any sort of responsibility.*

shyster /ˈʃaɪstə $ -ər/ *n* [C] *AmE informal* a dishonest lawyer or politician

sibling /ˈsɪblɪŋ/ *n* [C] *formal* a brother or sister

sic /sɪk/ *adv written* (**sic**) used after a mistake to show that you know it is not correct

sick¹ /sɪk/ *adj*
1 a) ill: *a hospital for sick children* | **off sick** *BrE*, **out sick** *AmE* (=not at work because you are ill) *Steve's been off sick all week.* | **call in/ring in/phone in sick** (=telephone to say you are not coming to work because you are ill) *John called in sick this morning.* | *Mr Smith is **on sick leave** (=allowed to stay off work because of illness).* **b) the sick** people who are ill **THESAURUS** ILL
2 laughing about death and suffering in a cruel way: *a sick joke*
3 feel sick to feel ill in your stomach and as if you might VOMIT → **carsick**, **seasick**: *I felt really sick.* | *Coffee **makes** me **feel sick**.* | **[+with]** *Anna felt sick with fear.*
4 be sick if you are sick, food comes up from your stomach and out through your mouth **SYN** **vomit**: *The baby had been **violently sick** down her sweater.*
PHRASES
make sb sick *spoken* if something makes you sick, it makes you very angry: *Cruelty to animals makes me sick.*
be sick of sb/sth to be annoyed and bored with a person or situation: **be sick of doing sth** *I'm **sick and tired** of waiting.*
be worried sick to be very worried: *Why didn't you ring? I was worried sick!*

sick² *n* [U] *BrE* food that has come out of your mouth from your stomach **SYN** **vomit**

sick bay *n* [C] a room on a ship or in a building with beds for people who are ill

sicken /ˈsɪkən/ *v* [T] if something sickens you, it makes you feel shocked and angry: *men who were*

sickened by the war —**sickening** *adj*: *a sickening waste of life*

sickle /ˈsɪkəl/ *n* [C] a cutting tool with a curved blade for cutting long grass or grain crops

sickly /ˈsɪkli/ *adj* **1** weak and unhealthy **THESAURUS** ILL **2** a sickly smell, taste, or colour is very unpleasant

sickness /ˈsɪknəs/ *n* [U] **1** when you VOMIT (=bring food up from your stomach through your mouth) → **morning sickness**: *sickness and diarrhoea* | **travel/motion/sea sickness** (=caused by travel, movement etc) **2** the state of being ill **SYN** **illness**: *people suffering from radiation sickness*

side¹ /saɪd/ *n* [C]
1 one part or area of something: **[+of]** *Stop when you reach the **other side** of the field.* | **on this/that side** *the people on this side of the room* | **the left-hand/right-hand etc side** *Keep to the left-hand side of the stream.* | **the right/wrong side** *driving on the wrong side of the road* | **the east/north etc side** *the east side of the city* | **on/from all sides** (=on or from all directions) *We're **surrounded on all sides**.*
2 a position directly next to someone or something: **[+of]** *a house **by the side** of a lake* | **by/at sb's side** (=close to someone) *She stayed by his side throughout.*
3 the part of something that is furthest from the middle **SYN** **edge**: **[+of]** *She sat on the side of the bed.* | *Pull in at the **side of the road**.*
4 a part of something that is not the front, back, top, or bottom: **[+of]** *the side of the house* | *One of the carriages was lying on its side.*
5 one of the two surfaces of a thin object: **[+of]** *Use both sides of the paper.*
6 your sides are the parts of your body on your left and your right from your shoulders to the tops of your legs: *Turn over and **lie on your right side**.*
7 one of the flat surfaces something has: **six-sided/three-sided etc** *a six-sided shape*
8 the sloping part of a hill or valley
9 one separate part of a subject, problem, or situation: *the social side of the job* | *Can't you see **the funny side** (=the parts of a situation that are funny rather than serious)?* | *Always look on **the bright side** (=the good things about a situation).*
10 one person, group, or team in an argument, war, competition etc: **on sb's side** *Are you on our side?* | **the winning/losing side** *No one likes to be on the losing side.* | *Teachers should never **take sides** (=support just one person, group etc).*
11 one person's opinion **SYN** **point of view**: **sb's side of sth** *You never see my **side of the story** (=my opinion or account of an event).*
12 a part of someone's character: **[+of]** *a side of Karen I hadn't seen before* | **practical/emotional etc side** *All men have a feminine side.*
13 the part of your family that is related to either your mother or your father: **mother's/father's side** *There's a history of heart disease on my father's side.* → **FLIP SIDE**
PHRASES
from side to side moving left to right, then from right to left: *The lamp swung from side to side.*

get on the right/wrong side of sb *informal* to make someone pleased or angry with you

on the side secretly or dishonestly: *He was seeing another woman on the side.*

put/leave/set sth to one side to save something for later: *Put some money to one side each week.*

side by side 1 next to each other: *two cars parked side by side* **2** if people work or live side by side, they work or live close to each other peacefully

side² *adj* [only before noun]

1 in or on the side of something: **side door/exit** *The Prince left by a side door.* | *side pockets* | *a side view of the statue*

2 side street/road a small street or road that is attached to a main street: *a quiet side street*

PHRASES

side order/dish food that is served separately as part of a meal: *Would you like a side order of fries with that?*

side³ *v*

PHRASAL VERBS

side with sb to support someone in an argument: **[+against]** *Germany has sided with France against the other states.*

sideboard /ˈsaɪdbɔːd $ -bɔːrd/ *n* [C] a long low piece of furniture, used for storing plates, glasses etc

sideburns /ˈsaɪdbɜːnz $ -bɜːrnz/ *n* [plural] hair that has grown down in front of a man's ears

sidecar /ˈsaɪdkɑː $ -kɑːr/ *n* [C] a small vehicle for a passenger that is attached to a MOTORCYCLE

'side ef,fect *n* [C] **1** an additional effect that a drug has on your body as well as treating illness or pain: *a drug with **harmful side effects*** **THESAURUS** EFFECT **2** an unexpected result: **[+of]** *one side effect of the economic crisis*

sidekick /ˈsaɪdkɪk/ *n* [C] *informal* someone's sidekick is a friend or helper who is not as important as they are

sidelight /ˈsaɪdlaɪt/ *n* [C] one of the two small lights beside the main lights on a car

sideline¹ /ˈsaɪdlaɪn/ *n* **1** [C] something that you do to earn money in addition to your main job: *Mark does translations as a sideline.* **2 the sidelines** [plural] the area just outside the lines around the edge of a sports field

PHRASES

on the sidelines not taking part in an activity, even though you want to or should: *Alison had had enough of **standing on the sidelines.***

sideline² *v* [T] if you are sidelined, you are prevented from taking part in something: *Their quarterback was sidelined with an injury.*

sidelong /ˈsaɪdlɒŋ $ -lɒːŋ/ *adj* **sidelong look/glance** a way of looking at someone by only moving your eyes, not your head, to show that you do not trust or believe them: *He gave me a sidelong glance.* —**sidelong** *adv*

sideshow /ˈsaɪdʃəʊ $ -ʃoʊ/ *n* [C] part of an event or activity that is smaller, less important, or less serious than the thing it is connected with

sidestep /ˈsaɪdstep/ *v* [T] (**sidestepped, sidestepping**) to avoid a difficult question or decision: *The report sidesteps the environmental issues.*

sideswipe /ˈsaɪdswaɪp/ *v* [T] *AmE* to hit the side of another vehicle with your car

sidetrack /ˈsaɪdtræk/ *v* [T] if you sidetrack someone, you make them forget about doing what they should be doing by getting them interested in something else: *Don't **get sidetracked** by the audience's questions.*

sidewalk /ˈsaɪdwɔːk $ -wɒːk/ *n* [C] *AmE* the hard surface beside the road that people walk on **SYN** **pavement** *BrE*

sideways /ˈsaɪdweɪz/ *adv* **1** towards one side: *She moved her legs sideways to let him pass.* **2** with the side rather than the front or back facing forwards: *Mel's car slid sideways across the road.* —**sideways** *adj*

siding /ˈsaɪdɪŋ/ *n* **1** [C] *BrE* a short railway track next to a main track, where trains stay when they are not being used **2** [U] *AmE* long narrow pieces of metal or wood, used for covering the outside walls of a house

sidle /ˈsaɪdl/ *v* [I] to walk towards someone or something slowly because you do not want to be noticed: **[+up/over etc]** *Tom sidled up, looking embarrassed.*

siege /siːdʒ/ *n* [C,U] a situation in which the army, police, or a crowd of people surround a place to get control of it or to force people to come out: **[+of]** *the siege of Vienna* | **under siege (by/from sb)** *His apartment was under siege from journalists.* | **lay siege to sb/sth** *The army laid siege to the town.*

siesta /siˈestə/ *n* [C] a short sleep in the afternoon, often taken by people in warm countries: **take/have a siesta**

sieve /sɪv/ *n* [C] a tool made of a wire net and a handle that you use to separate solid things from liquids, or small things from larger things —**sieve** *v* [T]

sift /sɪft/ *v* [T] **1** (*also* **sift through**) to examine a lot of documents or information carefully: *Investigators are still **sifting through the evidence**.* **2** to put flour or sugar through a SIEVE

sigh /saɪ/ *v* [I] to take a deep breath and breathe out slowly and loudly because you are annoyed or unhappy: *Phil **sighed heavily** and shook his head.* | *'I'm so sorry,' she sighed.* **THESAURUS** BREATHE —**sigh** *n* [C]: *a **deep sigh** of relief*

sight¹ /saɪt/ *n*

1 [U] the ability to see **SYN** eyesight, vision: *She is **losing** her **sight** (=becoming blind).*

2 [singular, U] when you see something: **[+of]** *The sight of him made me tremble.* | *I **caught sight of** (=saw) a man in the garden.* | *They drove on ahead and we **lost sight of** (=could no longer see) them.* | *I **can't stand the sight of** blood.* | **on sight** (=as soon as you see something) *Rebel soldiers were **shot on sight**.* **THESAURUS** SEE

3 [U] if something is in sight, you can see it. If it is out of sight, you cannot see it: **in/within sight (of sth)** *There was no one in sight.* | **out of sight (of sth)**

We parked out of sight of the house. | *We waved until the train **disappeared from sight**.*

4 [C] something that you can see: **a common/rare/strange etc sight** *Street dentists are a common sight here.* → **at first sight** at FIRST¹

5 the sights the interesting places to visit in a town or city: *I hope we get a chance to **see the sights**.*

6 sights [plural] the parts of a gun that you look into to help you aim it

PHRASES

in/within sight likely to happen: *Peace is in sight.*

lose sight of sth to forget an important part of something because you are too concerned about the details: *We have **lost sight of the fact that** a computer is only a tool.*

not let sb out of your sight to make sure that someone stays near you: *Since the accident, she hasn't let the kids out of her sight.*

set your sights on (doing) sth to decide that you definitely want something: *She had set her sights on becoming a star.*

THESAURUS – sense 4

sight something that you can see: *The waterfall was certainly an impressive sight.*

view what you can see from a window or place, especially when it is beautiful: *The hotel has spectacular views of the ocean.*

scene what you see in a place, and what is happening there: *Imagine the scene – white sand, a beautiful sea, and palm trees bending gently in the breeze.*

---

sight² *v* [T] to see something that is far away or something you have been searching for: *The missing child was sighted in Manchester.*

sighted /'saɪtɪd/ *adj* able to see: *a school for blind and **partially sighted** children*

sighting /'saɪtɪŋ/ *n* [C] an occasion when someone sees something unusual or rare: **[+of]** *a sighting of a rare bird* | *UFO sightings*

sightseeing /'saɪtˌsiːɪŋ/ *n* [U] when you visit the famous or interesting places in a town or city: *In the afternoon, we **went sightseeing**.* —**sightseer** *n* [C]

SIGN

road sign

NO SMOKING sign

sign¹ /saɪn/ *n* [C]
1 a piece of wood, metal, plastic etc with words or pictures on it to give people information: *a 'No Smoking' sign* | *road signs* | *Follow the signs to*

Birmingham. | *What does that **sign say** (=what words are written on it)?*

2 an event or fact that shows that something exists or will happen: **[+of]** *Headaches are a sign of stress.* | *We searched, but **there was no sign of** them.* | **[+that]** *The marks are a sign that a tiger is close by.* | *She's smiling, which is a good sign.* | *a **sure sign** (=clear proof) of guilt* | **show signs of (doing) sth/show no sign of (doing) sth** *Auntie Meg showed no sign of leaving.*

3 a picture or shape that has a particular meaning SYN **symbol**: *a dollar sign*

4 a movement or sound made in order to tell someone something SYN **signal**: **give/make a sign** *He made a sign for me to follow him into the kitchen.* | **sign for sb to do sth** *The whistle was the sign for us to begin.* → **EQUALS SIGN, MINUS SIGN, PLUS SIGN, STAR SIGN**

sign² *v* [I,T]
1 to write your name on a letter, document etc to show that you wrote it or agree with it → **signature**: **Sign your name** *here please.* | *You forgot to **sign** the cheque.* | *a **signed photo*** | **sign a contract/treaty/agreement** (=make it legal by signing it) *France and Italy have signed a trade agreement.* **THESAURUS** WRITE

2 if a sports team or record company signs a player or musician, it gives the player or musician a job by signing a contract with them: *Virgin Records signed the band back in 1998.* | **[+to/with]** *The group eventually signed to Motown Records.*

PHRASAL VERBS

sign sth ↔ **away** to sign an official document that gives your property or rights to someone else

sign for sth to sign a document to prove you have received something

sign in to sign your name in a book when you enter a building, club etc: *Delegates must sign in at reception.* | **sign sb in** *I'll sign you in as my guest.*

sign on

1 to sign a document to say that you agree to work for someone, do a course etc: **[+for/with]** *I signed on with an IT agency.*

2 *BrE* to sign an official document to say that you have no job and can receive money from the government

sign out to sign your name in a book when you leave a building, club etc: **sign sb out** *I'll sign you out.*

sign sth ↔ **over** to sign an official document that gives your property or rights to someone else: **[+to]** *He signed the property over to his daughter.*

sign up

1 sign sb ↔ **up** to agree to give someone a job, for example in a sports team: *The Yankees signed him up when he finished college.*

2 to put your name on a list because you want to do something: **[+for]** *Ten people signed up for the trip to Paris.*

signal¹ /'sɪgnəl/ *n* [C]
1 a sound or something that you do to give information or to tell someone to do something: **signal (for sb) to do sth** *That was the signal for me to switch out the lights.* | *The headmaster **gave** the **signal** to start.*

2 something which shows what someone feels, what exists, or what is likely to happen: **[+that]** *The*

result is a **clear signal** that voters are not happy. | This will **send** the wrong **signal** to potential investors.
3 a series of light waves, sound waves etc that carry information to a radio, television etc: **send/ transmit/emit a signal** *Signals are sent via satellite.* | **receive/pick up/detect a signal** *a small antenna which receives radio signals*
4 a piece of equipment that tells a train driver whether to go or stop → **TURN SIGNAL**

signal² *v* (**signalled, signalling** *BrE*, **signaled, signaling** *AmE*) **1** [I,T] to move your hand, head etc as a way of telling someone something: **[+to/for]** *Tom signalled for the bill.* | **signal (to) sb to do sth** *She signalled to the children to come inside.* **2** [T] to be a sign or proof of something happening: *The elections* **signalled the end of** *a nine-year civil war.* **3** [T] to make something clear by what you say or do: *Carter has signalled his intention to resign.*

signatory /'sɪɡnətəri $ -tɔːri/ *n* [C] (*plural* **signatories**) *formal* a person or country that signs a formal agreement

signature /'sɪɡnətʃə $ -ər/ *n* [C] your name written the way you usually write it, for example at the end of a letter or on a cheque → **sign**

> **Word Choice**: signature or autograph?
> You write your **signature** at the end of a letter, or on a cheque or document, to show that you wrote it or that you agree to it: *Put your signature here, then print your name underneath.* An **autograph** is a signature by a famous person, which they write in a book, on a photograph etc, for someone to keep: *The singer was signing autographs for his fans.*

significance /sɪɡ'nɪfɪkəns/ *n* [U] the importance of something, especially something that might affect you in the future: **[+of]** *What is the significance of this new evidence?* | **of great/some/major etc significance** *a political agreement of some significance*

significant Ac /sɪɡ'nɪfɪkənt/ *adj* **1** noticeable or important OPP **insignificant**: **significant change/ difference/increase etc** *significant changes in the exam system* **2** a significant smile, look etc has a special meaning: *He gave me a significant look.* —**significantly** *adv*: *Her work has been significantly better this year.*

signify Ac /'sɪɡnɪfaɪ/ *v* [T] (**signified, signifying, signifies**) to mean or be a sign of something: *Does this signify a change in policy?*

signing /'saɪnɪŋ/ *n* **1** [U] when you write your name at the end of a document to show that you agree with it: **[+of]** *the signing of the ceasefire agreement* **2** [C,U] someone who has just signed a contract to join a sports team or work with a record company, or the act of doing this: **[+of]** *Birmingham City have completed the signing of Doug Bell from Shrewsbury Town.* **3** [U] the use of sign language

'**sign ,language** *n* [C,U] a language that uses hand movements instead of spoken words, used by people who cannot hear

signpost¹ /'saɪnpəʊst $ -poʊst/ *n* [C] a sign on a road that shows directions and distances

signpost² *v* **be signposted** *BrE* to have signposts showing you which way to go: *The village isn't very* **well signposted**.

Sikh /siːk/ *n* [C] a member of an Indian religious group that developed from Hinduism —**Sikh** *adj*

silence¹ /'saɪləns/ *n*
1 [C,U] when there is no sound or nobody is talking: **complete/total/dead silence** *There was a loud bang, then complete silence.* | **in silence** *The two men sat in silence.* | **[+of]** *the silence of the night*
2 [U] when someone refuses to talk about something: **[+on]** *So far, he has maintained his silence on the subject.*

silence² *v* [T] **1** to make someone stop criticizing or giving their opinions: *Critics of the system were quickly silenced.* **2** to stop someone from talking, or to stop something from making a noise

silencer /'saɪlənsə $ -sər/ *n* [C] **1** a thing that is put on the end of a gun so that it makes less noise **2** *BrE* a piece of equipment that makes an engine quieter SYN **muffler** *AmE*

silent /'saɪlənt/ *adj*
1 not saying anything: **keep/remain/stay silent** *They both remained silent, just looking at her.*
2 without any sound, or not making any sound: *The whole room* **fell silent** (=became silent). THESAURUS QUIET —**silently** *adv*

silhouette /ˌsɪluˈet/ *n* [C] a dark shape seen against a light background —**silhouetted** *adj*: *tall chimneys silhouetted against the sunset*

silicon /'sɪlɪkən/ *n* [U] an ELEMENT that is used for making glass, bricks, and computer parts: *a silicon chip*

silk /sɪlk/ *n* [C,U] soft cloth made from the threads produced by a type of CATERPILLAR: *a silk shirt*

silken /'sɪlkən/ *adj literary* soft and smooth like silk, or made of silk: *her silken hair*

silky /'sɪlki/ *adj* soft and smooth like silk: *silky fur*

sill /sɪl/ *n* [C] a WINDOWSILL

silly /'sɪli/ *adj* stupid or not sensible: *What a silly question!* | *That was a* **silly thing to do**, *wasn't it?* | **Don't be silly** – *it's only a spider.* | *She makes a fuss about such* **silly little** (=unimportant) *things.* THESAURUS STUPID —**silliness** *n* [U]

silo /'saɪləʊ $ -loʊ/ *n* [C] (*plural* **silos**) **1** a tall building on a farm, used for storing grain **2** a structure under the ground, from which a MISSILE can be fired

silt /sɪlt/ *n* [U] sand or mud in a river

silver¹ /'sɪlvə $ -ər/ *n* [U]
1 a valuable shiny white metal, used for making jewellery, spoons etc: *a tiny figure made of* **solid silver**
2 things that are made of silver SYN **silverware**

silver² *adj*
1 made of silver: *a silver spoon* → see picture at **MATERIAL¹**
2 having the colour of silver: *a shimmering silver dress*
3 **silver wedding/anniversary/jubilee** the date that is 25 years after something began: *They're having a party to celebrate their silver wedding anniversary.*

,silver 'medal n [C] a prize, especially a round piece of silver, that is given to someone who comes second in a race or competition

silverware /'sɪlvəweə $ -vərwer/ n [U] **1** things that are made of silver **2** AmE metal knives, forks, and spoons

silvery /'sɪlvəri/ adj shining like silver

SIM card /'sɪm kɑːd $ -kɑːrd/ n [C] a plastic card in a MOBILE PHONE that stores your personal information and allows you to use the phone

similar Ac /'sɪmələ, 'sɪmɪlə $ -ər/ adj almost the same OPP **different** → alike: They came from similar backgrounds. | The two brothers are very similar. | This one works **in a similar way**. | [+to] Your shoes are similar to mine. | [+in] All the apartments are similar in size. THESAURUS SAME

similarity Ac /,sɪmə'lærəti/ n [C,U] (plural similarities) when people or things are similar, or a way in which they are similar: [+between] There is some similarity between the styles of the two authors. | [+with/to] English has many similarities with German.

similarly Ac /'sɪmələli $ -ərli/ adv in a similar way

simile /'sɪməli/ n [C] an expression that describes something by comparing it with something else using the word 'like' or 'as', for example 'as red as blood'

simmer /'sɪmə $ -ər/ v [I,T] to cook food by boiling it very gently: Let the soup simmer for five minutes.

simper /'sɪmpə $ -ər/ v [I] literary to smile in a way that is silly and annoying —simper n [C]

simple /'sɪmpəl/ adj
1 EASY not difficult or complicated: a simple solution to the problem | **simple to use/make/operate etc** Modern cameras are very simple to use. | When planning what to cook, it's best to **keep it simple**. THESAURUS EASY
2 PLAIN made in a plain style, without unnecessary decorations or things added: a simple white dress
3 FOR EMPHASIS used to emphasize that something is the only reason, fact etc involved: She didn't answer **for the simple reason that** she couldn't think what to say. | It was a business decision, **pure and simple**.
4 ORDINARY ordinary and not special in any way: a simple country existence
5 VERB TENSE **simple past/present** a tense of a verb in English that is not formed with an AUXILIARY such as 'have' or 'be': The simple past of 'eat' is 'ate'.

simplicity /sɪm'plɪsəti/ n [U] when something is simple: [+of] the simplicity and effectiveness of the technique

simplify /'sɪmplɪfaɪ/ v [T] (simplified, simplifying, simplifies) to make something easier to do or understand: an attempt to simplify the tax system —simplification /,sɪmplɪfɪ'keɪʃən/ n [U]

simplistic /sɪm'plɪstɪk/ adj disapproving making something seem less complicated than it really is: a rather simplistic view of life

simply /'sɪmpli/ adv
1 used to emphasize what you are saying: But that simply isn't true! | His performance was **quite simply** dazzling.

2 only: Some students lose marks simply because they don't read the question properly.
3 in a way that is easy to understand: **To put it simply**, the bank won't lend us the money.
4 used to emphasize how easy it is to do something: Simply fill in the form and take it to the post office.
5 in a plain and ordinary way: a simply decorated room

simulate Ac /'sɪmjəleɪt/ v [T] to make or do something that seems like the real thing but is not: an experiment to simulate the effects of being weightless —simulator n [C]: a flight simulator

simulation Ac /,sɪmjə'leɪʃən/ n [C,U] something you do or produce in order to study or test what happens in a real situation: [+of] a **computer simulation** of an emergency landing

simultaneous /,sɪməl'teɪniəs◂ $,saɪ-/ adj happening or done at the same time as something else: a simultaneous broadcast on TV and radio —simultaneously adv

sin¹ /sɪn/ n **1** [C,U] something that is against religious laws: [+of] the sin of greed | He knew he'd **committed** a terrible **sin**. **2** a sin informal something that you think is very wrong: **It's a sin** to waste good food.

sin² v [I] (sinned, sinning) to do something that is against religious laws —sinner n [C]

since /sɪns/ linking word, prep, adv
1 from a particular time or event in the past until now, or in that period of time: I haven't seen him since we left school. | Jim's been working at Citibank since last April. | She phoned last week, but I haven't heard from her since. | He left the US in 1995 and **since then** he's lived in London. | We've had problems with the system **ever since** (=for all the time since) it was introduced.
2 used to give a reason or explanation for something: I'll do it myself since you're obviously not going to help.
PHRASES
since when spoken used in questions to show that you are annoyed or surprised about something: Since when have you been such a computer expert?

Word Choice: since or for?
You use **since** with a date or time: We've lived here since 2006. | I've been waiting since four o'clock.
You use **for** with a period of time: We've lived here for three years. | I've been waiting for two hours. Do not say 'We've lived here since three years.' or 'I've been waiting since two hours.'

sincere /sɪn'sɪə $ -'sɪr/ adj honest and really meaning what you say OPP **insincere**: **sincere thanks/apology/sympathy etc** Please accept my sincere apologies. | a sincere and loyal friend THESAURUS HONEST —sincerity /sɪn'serəti/ n [U]

sincerely /sɪn'sɪəli $ -'sɪr-/ adv in a sincere way: I sincerely hope we meet again.
PHRASES
Yours sincerely BrE, **Sincerely (yours)** AmE something you write at the end of a formal letter before you sign your name: Yours sincerely, Brian Cole

S

sinew /ˈsɪnjuː/ n [C,U] a part of the body that connects a muscle to a bone —**sinewy** adj

sinful /ˈsɪnfəl/ adj morally bad or wrong

sing /sɪŋ/ v [I,T] (*past tense* **sang** /sæŋ/, *past participle* **sung** /sʌŋ/) to produce musical sounds with your voice: *Sophie sings in a choir.* | *They sang a beautiful song.* | **[+to]** *a mother singing to her baby* —**singing** n [U]

singe /sɪndʒ/ v [T] (**singed**, **singeing**) to burn something slightly on its surface or edge: *I singed my hair on a candle.*

singer /ˈsɪŋə $ -ər/ n [C] someone who sings, especially as a job: *an opera singer*

single¹ /ˈsɪŋgəl/ adj

1 [only before noun] only one: *We lost the game by a single point.* | *a single-sex* (=for only girls or only boys) *school*

2 not married, or not involved in a romantic relationship: *Terry is 34 and still single.* **THESAURUS** MARRIED

3 single bed/room etc a bed, room etc to be used by only one person → **double**: *I've only got a single bed.* → see picture at **BED**

PHRASES

every single used to emphasize that you are talking about every person or thing: *My dad has every single Beatles album.*

not a single no people or things at all: *We didn't get a single reply to the advert.*

the single biggest/greatest etc used to emphasize that you are talking about the biggest, greatest etc thing of its kind: *The single biggest problem is lack of money.*

single figures *BrE*, **single 'digits** *AmE* the numbers from 1 to 9 → **double figures**: *The number of cases of the disease is now down to single figures.*

single² n **1** [C] a record or CD with only one song on it, or the song itself: *Madonna's new single* **2 singles** [U] a game, especially tennis, played by one person against another person → **doubles**: *the women's singles final* **3** [C] *BrE* a ticket to go from one place to another but not back again → **return**: *a single to Liverpool* **4 singles bar/club/night etc** a bar, club etc for people who are not married: *Chris spent the evenings hanging around in singles bars.*

single³ v

PHRASAL VERBS

single sb/sth ↔ **out** to choose someone or something from a group, especially in order to praise or criticize them: **[+for]** *The school was singled out for its excellent academic results.*

,single-'handedly, **,single-'handed** adv if one person does something single-handedly, they do it without help from anyone else: *She's brought up four kids single-handedly.* —**,single-'handed** adj [only before noun]

,single-'minded adj having one aim and working hard to achieve it: *a single-minded determination to succeed* **THESAURUS** DETERMINED —**single-mindedness** n [U]

,single 'parent n [C] a mother or father who looks after her or his children alone

singly /ˈsɪŋgli/ adv separately or one at a time: *The animals live singly or in small groups.*

'sing-song n [C] *BrE* when people sing songs together for fun, for example at a party

singular¹ /ˈsɪŋgjələ $ -ər/ adj

1 the singular form of a word is used when you are talking or writing about one person or thing → **plural**

2 *formal* very great or noticeable: *singular beauty*

singular² n **the singular** the form of a word that you use when you are talking or writing about one person or thing

singularly /ˈsɪŋgjələli $ -lərli/ adv *formal* very: *a singularly unattractive building*

sinister /ˈsɪnɪstə $ -ər/ adj making you feel that something bad or evil is happening: *There's something sinister about the whole thing.*

sink¹ /sɪŋk/ v (*past tense* **sank** /sæŋk/, *past participle* **sunk** /sʌŋk/)

1 [I,T] to go down, or make something go down, below the surface of water **OPP** float: *The boat sank after hitting a rock.* | *He watched his keys sink to the bottom of the river.* → see picture at **FLOAT¹**

2 [I] to fall or sit down heavily, because you are weak or tired: **[+into/down etc]** *Lee sank into a chair and went to sleep.*

3 [I] to move to a lower level **SYN** drop **OPP** rise: *The sun sank beneath the horizon.*

PHRASES

your heart sinks/your spirits sink used to say that you lose hope or confidence → **sinking**: *Her heart sank as she read the results.*

PHRASAL VERBS

sink in if information, news etc sinks in, you gradually understand it or realize the effect it will have: *He paused for a moment for his words to sink in.*

sink into sth

1 to gradually get into a worse state: *She could see him sinking into depression.*

2 sink sth into sth to spend a lot of money on a business, in order to make more money: *They had sunk thousands into the business.*

3 sink your teeth/a knife etc into sth to put your teeth or something sharp into someone's flesh, into food etc

sink² n [C] a piece of furniture in a kitchen or bathroom that you fill with water to wash dishes, your hands etc → **basin** → see picture at **BATHROOM**

sinking /ˈsɪŋkɪŋ/ adj **a sinking feeling** a feeling you get when you realize that something bad is going to happen

sinus /ˈsaɪnəs/ n [C] your sinuses are the hollow areas in the bones connected to your nose

sip /sɪp/ v [I,T] (**sipped**, **sipping**) to drink something slowly, taking only small amounts: *She sipped her tea.* **THESAURUS** DRINK —**sip** n [C]: *He took a sip of coffee.*

siphon¹ (*also* **syphon** *BrE*) /ˈsaɪfən/ n [C] a tube that you use to take liquid out of a container

siphon² (*also* **syphon** *BrE*) v [T] **1** to remove liquid from a container using a siphon **2** (*also* **siphon off**) to secretly take money from an organization over a period of time: *He had been siphoning money from his employer's account.*

sir /sə; strong sɜː $ sər; strong sɜːr/ n
1 *spoken* **a)** used when speaking politely to a man, for example a customer in a shop: *Can I help you, sir?* **b)** *especially AmE* used to get the attention of a man whose name you do not know: *Sir! You dropped your wallet!*
2 Dear Sir used at the beginning of a business letter to a man when you do not know his name: *Dear Sir, I am writing in reply to your advertisement.*
3 Sir used before the name of a KNIGHT: *Sir James*

siren /ˈsaɪərən $ ˈsaɪr-/ n [C] a piece of equipment that makes loud warning sounds: *the wail of* **police sirens**

sissy, cissy /ˈsɪsi/ n [C] (*plural* **sissies**) *informal disapproving* a boy who is thought to be weak or not brave, or like a girl —**sissy** *adj*

sister /ˈsɪstə $ -ər/ n [C]
1 a girl or woman who has the same parents as you → **brother**: *He's got two sisters.* | **older/big sister** *My older sister is a nurse.* | **younger/little sister** *I had to look after my little sister.*
2 Sister *BrE* a nurse who is in charge of a hospital WARD
3 Sister a title given to a NUN: *Sister Frances*
4 sister company/organization/paper etc a company, newspaper etc that belongs to the same group or organization: *We have a sister company in the United States.*
5 a woman who belongs to the same race, religion, or organization as you

'sister-in-law n [C] (*plural* **sisters-in-law**) **1** the sister of your husband or wife **2** the wife of your brother

sisterly /ˈsɪstəli $ -ər-/ *adj* typical of a loving sister: *a sisterly kiss*

sit /sɪt/ v (*past tense and past participle* **sat** /sæt/, *present participle* **sitting**)
1 a) [I] to be on a chair, on the ground etc with the top half of your body upright and your weight resting on your bottom: **[+on/in/by etc]** *The children were sitting on the floor.* | **sit at a desk/table etc** *I don't want to sit at a desk all day.* | **Sit still** (=sit without moving) *and let me fix your hair.* | *I spent half the morning sitting in a traffic jam.* → see picture on page A11 **b)** (*also* **sit down**) [I] to move to a sitting position after you have been standing: **[+by/beside etc]** *Come and sit by me.* **c)** [T] to make or help someone sit somewhere: **sit sb in/on sth** *She sat the boy in the corner.*
2 [I] to be in a particular position, especially not being used: **[+on/in etc]** *My walking boots were still sitting unused in the cupboard.*
3 [T] *BrE* to take an examination: *Anna's sitting her final exams this year.*
4 [I] if a committee, court, or parliament sits, it does its work in an official meeting: *The court sits once a month.*

PHRASES
sit on the fence to avoid saying which side of an argument you support or what you think is the

best thing to do: *You can't sit on the fence any longer – what's it going to be?*
sit tight to stay in the same place or situation and not do anything: *Investors should sit tight and see what happens in a few days.*

PHRASAL VERBS
sit around (*also* **sit about** *BrE*) to sit and not do very much: *Dan just sits around watching TV all day.*
sit back to let someone else do something or let something happen, without taking any action yourself: *You can't just* **sit back and** *wait for business to come to you.*
sit down to move into a sitting position after you have been standing: *Do sit down.*
sit in for sb to do a job instead of the person who usually does it
sit in on sth to watch a meeting or activity but not get involved in it: *Do you mind if I sit in on your class?*
sit sth ↔ **out** to stay where you are until something finishes and not get involved in it: *I'll sit this dance out.*
sit through sth to stay until a meeting, performance etc finishes, even if it is very long or boring: *We had to sit through a three-hour class this morning.*
sit up
1 to move to a sitting position after you have been lying down: *He sat up and rubbed his eyes.*
2 to stay awake and not go to bed: *We sat up all night talking.*

sitcom /ˈsɪtkɒm $ -kɑːm/ n [C,U] a funny television programme that has the same characters every week in a different story THESAURUS ➤ PROGRAMME

site¹ Ac /saɪt/ n [C] **1** a place where something important or interesting happened: **[+of]** *the site of the battle* **2** an area where something is being built, or was or will be built: *a construction site* | *an archaeological site* THESAURUS ➤ PLACE **3** a WEBSITE

site² v **be sited** *formal* to be put or built in a particular place

'sit-in n [C] a protest in which people refuse to leave a place until they get what they want

sitter /ˈsɪtə $ -ər/ n [C] *especially AmE spoken* a BABYSITTER

sitting /ˈsɪtɪŋ/ n [C] one of the times when a meal is served when it is not possible for everyone to eat at the same time

'sitting room n [C] *BrE* a LIVING ROOM

situated /ˈsɪtʃueɪtɪd/ *adj* **be situated** *formal* to be in a particular place: *The hotel is situated on the lakeside.*

situation /ˌsɪtʃuˈeɪʃən/ n [C]
1 the things that are happening at a particular time somewhere, or are happening to a particular person: **in a ... situation** *She's in a very difficult situation.* | *We will have to deal with very similar situations in the future.*
2 *formal* the position of a building or a town

COLLOCATIONS
adjectives
a difficult/tricky situation *We face a difficult situation.*

S

an **impossible situation** (=a very difficult one)
This is an impossible situation!
an **awkward/embarrassing situation** *How can we
get out of this embarrassing situation?*
a **dangerous situation** *If we don't act, the
situation could become dangerous.*
the **economic/political situation** *The economic
situation is getting worse.*

verbs

to **put sb in a situation** *This put me in a stressful
situation.*
to **deal with/handle a situation** *How would you
deal with this situation?*
a **situation arises/occurs** *formal: How has this
situation arisen?* ⚠ Do not say 'a situation
happens'. Say **a situation arises** or **occurs**.
a **situation changes** *The situation could change
very rapidly.*
a **situation improves/worsens** *Since then, the
situation has improved.*

'sit-up *n* [C usually plural] an exercise in which you
sit up from a lying position while keeping your feet
on the floor

six /sɪks/ *number* the number 6: *six months ago* | *She
arrived just after six* (=six o'clock). | *He learnt to play
the violin when he was six* (=6 years old).

sixteen /ˌsɪkˈstiːn◂/ *number* the number 16: *sixteen
years later* | *He moved to London when he was sixteen*
(=16 years old). —**sixteenth** *adj, pron: her sixteenth
birthday* | *Let's have dinner on **the sixteenth*** (=the
16th day of the month).

sixteenth /ˌsɪkˈstiːnθ◂/ *n* [C] one of sixteen equal
parts of something

sixth¹ /sɪksθ/ *adj* coming after five other things in a
series: *his sixth birthday* —**sixth** *pron: Let's have
dinner on **the sixth*** (=the sixth day of the month).

sixth² *n* [C] one of six equal parts of something

'sixth form *n* [C] the classes of school students
between the ages of 16 and 18 in Britain —**sixth
former** *n* [C]

ˌsixth 'sense *n* [singular] a special ability to know
something without using any of your five usual
senses such as hearing or sight

sixty /ˈsɪksti/ *number*
1 the number 60: *sixty years ago*
2 the sixties (*also* **the '60s, the 1960s**) [plural] the
years from 1960 to 1969: **the early/mid/late sixties**
the student riots in Paris in the late sixties —**sixtieth**
adj: her sixtieth birthday
PHRASES
be in your sixties to be aged between 60 and 69:
early/mid/late sixties *She's in her late sixties.*
in the sixties if the temperature is in the sixties, it
is between 60 degrees and 69 degrees F: *Today's
temperature will be in the sixties.*

sizable /ˈsaɪzəbəl/ *adj* another spelling of SIZEABLE

size¹ /saɪz/ *n*
1 [C,U] how big or small something is: *A diamond's
value depends on its size.* | *The Jensens' house is about
the same size as ours.* | [+of] *plans to reduce the size*

of the army | *I saw a spider **the size of*** (=as big as) *my
hand in the backyard.* | **medium-sized/normal-sized
etc** *a medium-sized car* | *Cut the chicken into **bite-
sized** pieces* (=pieces that will fit in your mouth).
2 [C] a measurement for clothes, shoes etc: *These
shoes are one size too big.* | *What size do you take?*

size² *v*
PHRASAL VERBS
size sb/sth ↔ **up** to look at a person or think about
a situation and make a judgment: *It only took a few
seconds for her to size up the situation.*

sizeable, sizable /ˈsaɪzəbəl/ *adj* fairly large: *a sizeable amount of money*

ˌsize 'zero *n* **1** [U] the smallest size of women's
clothing in the US **2** [C] a woman who is very thin
—**size zero** *adj: size zero models*

sizzle /ˈsɪzəl/ *v* [I] to make a sound like water
falling on hot metal: *bacon sizzling in the pan* → see
picture on page A7

SKATES

ice skates

Rollerblades™   roller skates

skate¹ /skeɪt/ *n* **1** [C] an ICE SKATE or ROLLER SKATE
2 [C,U] (*plural* **skate** or **skates**) a large flat sea fish

skate² *v* [I] to move around on skates: *I never
learned how to skate.* —**skating** *n* [U]: *Let's go skating.* —**skater** *n* [C] → see picture on page A9

skateboard /ˈskeɪtbɔːd $ -bɔːrd/ *n* [C] a board
with wheels on the bottom that you stand on and
ride on → see picture on BOARD¹ —**skateboarding** *n*
[U] —**skateboarder** *n* [C]

skatepark /ˈskeɪtpɑːk $ -pɑːrk/ *n* [C] an area for
skateboarders to use, which has special slopes or
other structures

skeleton /ˈskelətən/ *n* **1** [C] all the bones in a
human or animal body: *We found the skeleton of a
cat.* | *the human skeleton* → see picture on page A2
2 skeleton staff/crew/service only just enough
people to keep an organization working: *We will be
working with a skeleton staff during the Christmas
period.* —**skeletal** *adj technical: skeletal remains*
PHRASES
have a skeleton in the closet/cupboard to have a
secret about something embarrassing or unpleasant that you did in the past: *I think he may have a
few skeletons in the closet.*

skeptic /ˈskeptɪk/ the American spelling of SCEPTIC

skeptical /'skeptɪkəl/ the American spelling of SCEPTICAL

skepticism /'skeptɪsɪzəm/ the American spelling of SCEPTICISM

sketch¹ /sketʃ/ n [C] **1** a drawing that you do quickly and without a lot of details: **[+of]** *Cantor drew a **rough sketch** of his apartment.* **THESAURUS▶** PICTURE **2** a short humorous scene that is part of a longer performance: *a comic sketch* **3** a short description of something

sketch² v [I,T] to draw a sketch of something **THESAURUS▶** DRAW

PHRASAL VERBS

sketch sth ↔ **out** to describe something giving only the basic details: *Barry sketched out a plan for next year's campaign.*

sketch in sth to add more information or details: *I'll try to sketch in the historical background.*

sketchy /'sketʃi/ adj a sketchy account or description has very few details: ***Details** of the accident are still **sketchy**.*

skewed /skju:d/ adj if information is skewed, it contains only one opinion or point of view and so is not fair: *The media's coverage of the election has been skewed.*

skewer /'skju:ə $ -ər/ n [C] a metal or wooden stick that you put through pieces of food that you want to cook → see picture at STICK² —**skewer** v [T]

ski¹ /ski:/ n [C] (*plural* **skis**) skis are long narrow pieces of wood or plastic that you fasten to boots and use for moving across snow

ski² v [I] (**skied, skiing, skis**) to move over snow on skis: *Can you ski?* —**skier** n [C] —**skiing** n [U]: *We're going skiing in Colorado.* → see picture on page A9

skid /skɪd/ v [I] (**skidded, skidding**) if a vehicle skids, it suddenly slides sideways and you cannot control it: *The car skidded on ice.* → see picture at SLIDE¹ —**skid** n [C]

skilful *BrE*, **skillful** *AmE* /'skɪlfəl/ adj
1 good at doing something that you have learned and practised: *a skilful photographer*
2 done very well: *the skilful use of sound effects* —**skilfully** adv

skill /skɪl/ n [C,U] an ability to do something well, especially because you have learned and practised it → **talent**

COLLOCATIONS

verbs

to have a skill *It's easier to find work if you have computer skills.*
to learn a skill (*also* **to acquire a skill** *formal*) *Why not do a course to learn a new skill?*
to use a skill *He rarely gets the chance to use his language skills.*
to take skill *It takes a lot of skill to be a pilot.*

adjectives

great/considerable skill *They played with great skill.*

good/poor skills *We need someone with good communication skills.*
basic skills *She was trained in basic nursing skills.*
practical/technical skills *The students learn practical skills such as cooking and woodwork.*

noun + skill

reading/writing/language skills *Their reading skills are poor.*
computer/IT skills *We're looking for someone with good IT skills.*

THESAURUS

skill an ability to do something well, especially because you have learned and practised it: *He plays the game with great skill.* | *You need basic computer skills for this job.*
talent a natural ability to do something well, which can be developed with practice: *She was a young artist with a lot of talent.*
genius very great ability, which only a few people have: *The opera shows Mozart's genius as a composer.*

skilled /skɪld/ adj having the ability and experience needed to do something well **OPP** unskilled: *a skilled carpenter* | ***highly skilled** workers* | **[+at/in]** *She's very skilled in dealing with this kind of problem.*

skillet /'skɪlɪt/ n [C] a heavy cooking pan made of iron

skillful /'skɪlfəl/ adj the American spelling of SKILFUL

skim /skɪm/ v (**skimmed, skimming**) **1** [T] to remove something that is floating on the surface of a liquid: **skim sth off/from sth** *Skim the fat off the soup.* **2** (*also* **skim through**) [I,T] to read something quickly to find the main facts or ideas in it: *She skimmed through that morning's headlines.* **THESAURUS▶** READ **3** [I,T] to move along quickly, nearly touching the surface of something: *a plane skimming the tops of the trees*

skimmed 'milk *BrE*, **'skim milk** *AmE* n [U] milk that has had most of the fat removed from it

skimp /skɪmp/ v [I] to try to use or spend less than you really need to: **[+on]** *They try to save money by skimping on staff.*

skimpy /'skɪmpi/ adj skimpy clothes do not cover much of your body: *a skimpy little dress*

skin¹ /skɪn/ n [C,U]
1 the outside part of a human's or animal's body: *Strong sunlight can damage your skin.*
2 the skin of an animal used as leather, fur etc: *a tiger skin rug*
3 the outside part of a fruit or vegetable **SYN** peel: *banana skins* → see picture on page A4
4 a thin solid layer that forms on the top of a liquid, especially when it gets cold: *Cover the soup to stop a skin from forming.*

PHRASES

do sth by the skin of your teeth *informal* to only just succeed in doing something: *He escaped by the skin of his teeth.*

have (a) thin/thick skin to be easily upset or not easily upset by criticism: *You need to have thick skin to be a salesperson.*

COLLOCATIONS

adjectives

fair/pale/white skin *She had red hair and very fair skin.*

dark/brown/black skin *These bright colours look good against dark skin.*

bad/terrible skin (=with many spots or marks) *He had greasy hair and bad skin.*

good/clear skin (=smooth and without any red spots) *She's lucky because her skin is good.*

smooth/soft skin *She loved her baby's soft skin.*

rough skin *The skin on his hands was rough and dry.*

wrinkled skin (=covered in lines because of age) | **dry/oily skin** | **sensitive skin** (=becoming red or sore easily)

skin + noun

a skin condition/disease *He suffers from a skin condition that makes him itch.*

skin colour *Darker skin colour protects against the sun.*

skin² v [T] (**skinned, skinning**) to remove the skin from an animal, fruit, or vegetable

skinhead /'skɪnhed/ n [C] a young white person who has hair that is cut very short, especially one who behaves violently

-skinned /skɪnd/ suffix used to say that a person or animal has skin of a particular colour or kind: *a fair-skinned, red-haired woman*

skinny /'skɪni/ adj a skinny person is very thin
THESAURUS▶ THIN

skint /skɪnt/ adj [not before noun] BrE informal having no money: *I'm skint at the moment.*

skip¹ /skɪp/ v (**skipped, skipping**) **1** [I] to move forwards with little jumps between your steps: [+down/along etc] *children skipping down the street*
THESAURUS▶ JUMP **2** [I] (also **skip rope** AmE) to move a rope over your head and under your feet, jumping as it goes under your feet → see picture at JUMP¹ **3** [I,T] to avoid something or not do something: *You shouldn't skip breakfast.* | *Let's skip the next question.* | [+over] *I'll skip over the details.*

skip² n [C] **1** a quick light stepping and jumping movement **2** BrE a large container where you put waste such as bricks and broken furniture
SYN **Dumpster** AmE

skipper /'skɪpə $ -ər/ n [C] informal a CAPTAIN of a ship or of a sports team

'skipping ,rope n [C] BrE a long piece of rope with handles that children use for jumping over
SYN **jump rope** AmE

skirmish /'skɜːmɪʃ $ 'skɜːr-/ n [C] a fight between small groups of people or soldiers

skirt¹ /skɜːt $ skɜːrt/ n [C] a piece of clothing for girls and women that fits around the waist and hangs down like a dress → see picture at CLOTHES

skirt² (also **skirt around**) v [T] **1** to go around the outside edge of a place: *The train skirted around the lake.* **2** to avoid talking directly about a subject: *We cannot **skirt around** these **issues**.*

skit /skɪt/ n [C] a short performance or piece of writing that uses humour to criticize someone or something

skittle /'skɪtl/ n **1** [C] an object shaped like a bottle that you try to knock down with a ball **2** skittles [U] a British game in which you roll a ball to try to knock down skittles

skive /skaɪv/ (also **skive off**) v [I] BrE informal to not go to school or work when you should do: *He skived off work and went fishing.* —**skiver** n [C]

skulk /skʌlk/ v [I] to hide or move around quietly because you do not want people to see you: [+in/behind etc] *Two men were skulking in the shadows.*

skull /skʌl/ n [C] the bones of a person's or animal's head → see picture on page A2

'skull cap n [C] a small cap that some men wear for religious reasons

skunk /skʌŋk/ n [C] a small black and white animal that produces an unpleasant smell if it is attacked

sky /skaɪ/ n (plural **skies**)
1 [singular, U] the space above the earth where the sun, clouds, and stars are: **in the sky** *There wasn't a cloud in the sky.*
2 skies [plural] the sky – used especially to describe the weather: *Tomorrow there will be clear skies and some sunshine.*
PHRASES
the sky's the limit spoken used to say that there is no limit to what someone can achieve or spend: *If we can qualify for the Olympics, then the sky's the limit.*

skydiving /'skaɪˌdaɪvɪŋ/ n [U] the sport of jumping from a plane with a PARACHUTE

,sky-'high adj, adv extremely high: *sky-high prices*

skylight /'skaɪlaɪt/ n [C] a window in the roof of a building → see picture at WINDOW

skyline /'skaɪlaɪn/ n [C] the shape made by tall buildings or hills against the sky: *the famous New York skyline*

Skype /skaɪp/ n [U] trademark software that can be used to make telephone calls over the Internet —**Skype** v [T]: *I'll Skype you later.*

skyscraper /'skaɪˌskreɪpə $ -ər/ n [C] a very tall building

slab /slæb/ n [C] a thick flat piece of something: *a concrete slab*

slack¹ /slæk/ adj **1** loose and not pulled tight: *a slack rope* **2** with less business activity than usual: *Trade is slack at the moment.* **3** not taking enough care to do things correctly: *slack safety procedures* | *I've been slack about getting this work done.*

slack² n **1** take up/pick up the slack a) to do extra work because someone else is not doing it: *With McGill gone, I expect the rest of you to pick up the slack.* b) to pull a rope so that it is tight and not loose **2** slacks [plural] trousers

slack³ (*also* **slack off**) v [I] to not work as quickly as you should: *Don't let me see you slacking off!* —**slacker** n [C]

slacken /'slækən/ v [I,T] **1** (*also* **slacken off**) to gradually become slower, weaker, or less active, or to make something do this: *He **slackened** his **pace** so I could catch up.* **2** to make something looser, or to become looser: *Slacken the screw a little.*

slag¹ /slæg/ n [U] waste material that is left when metal has been taken from rock

slag² v (**slagged**, **slagging**)
PHRASAL VERBS
slag sb ↔ **off** *BrE informal* to criticize someone to another person

slain /sleɪn/ v the past participle of SLAY

slalom /'slɑːləm/ n [C,U] a race on SKIS or in CANOES in which people move down a curving course marked by flags

slam¹ /slæm/ v (**slammed**, **slamming**) **1** [I,T] if a door, gate etc slams, or if someone slams it, it shuts quickly and loudly: *He **slammed** the door shut.* **THESAURUS** CLOSE **2** [T] to put something somewhere roughly or violently: **slam sth down/against/onto** *Andy slammed the phone down angrily.*

slam² n [C usually singular] the action of hitting or closing something noisily or violently: *She shut the door with a slam.*

slander /'slɑːndə $ 'slændər/ n [C,U] a spoken statement about someone that is not true and is intended to damage the good opinion that people have of that person → see Word Choice at LIBEL —**slander** v [T] —**slanderous** adj

slang /slæŋ/ n [U] very informal language that uses new or rude words instead of the usual words for something **THESAURUS** LANGUAGE —**slangy** adj

slant¹ /slɑːnt $ slænt/ v [I] to slope, or move in a sloping line

slant² n [singular] **1** a way of writing about a subject that shows support for a particular set of ideas: **[+on]** *Each article has a slightly different slant on the situation.* **2** a sloping position or angle: **at/on a slant** *The pole was set at a slant.*

slanted /'slɑːntɪd $ 'slæn-/ adj **1** disapproving unfairly supporting only one person, opinion, or argument **SYN** biased: *a process heavily slanted towards the banks* **2** sloping: *slightly slanted eyes*

slap¹ /slæp/ v [T] (**slapped**, **slapping**) to hit someone with the flat part of your hand: *She **slapped** him across the face.* **THESAURUS** HIT
PHRASAL VERBS
slap sth ↔ **on** *informal* to put or spread something quickly onto a surface: *Just slap some paint on and it'll look a bit better.*

slap² n [C] a hit with the flat part of your hand
PHRASES
a slap in the face something someone does that makes you feel shocked and offended: *Gwyneth considered the salary they were offering a slap in the face.*

slapdash /'slæpdæʃ/ adj done quickly and carelessly: *slapdash work*

slapstick /'slæp,stɪk/ n [U] humorous acting in which the actors fall over and throw things at each other

slap-up adj **slap-up meal/dinner etc** *BrE informal* a big and good meal

slash¹ /slæʃ/ v [T] **1** to cut something violently, making a long deep cut: *He tried to kill himself by slashing his wrists.* **2** *informal* to reduce something by a lot: *Many companies are slashing prices.*
THESAURUS REDUCE

slash² n [C] **1** a long deep cut **2** (*also* **slash mark**) a line (/) used in writing to separate words or numbers

slat /slæt/ n [C] a thin flat piece of wood, plastic etc, used especially in furniture —**slatted** adj

slate¹ /sleɪt/ n **1** [U] a dark grey rock that can be split into thin flat pieces **2** [C] a piece of slate used as a roof covering → **clean slate** at CLEAN¹

slate² v [T] **1** *BrE* to criticize someone or something severely: *Leconte's latest film has been slated by the critics.* **2** *AmE* **be slated to do sth/be slated for sth** if something is slated to happen, it is planned to happen in the future: *He is slated to appear at the jazz festival next year.*

slaughter /'slɔːtə $ 'slɔːtər/ v [T] **1** to kill an animal for its meat **THESAURUS** KILL **2** to kill a lot of people in a violent way: *Hundreds of people were slaughtered.* —**slaughter** n [U]

slaughterhouse /'slɔːtəhaʊs $ 'slɔːtər-/ n [C] a building where animals are killed for their meat **SYN** abattoir

slave¹ /sleɪv/ n [C] someone who is owned by another person and must work for them without any pay
PHRASES
be a slave to/of sth to be influenced too much by something: *She's a slave to fashion.*

slave² (*also* **slave away**) v [I] to work very hard: *Michael's been slaving away in the kitchen all day.*

slave labour *BrE*, **slave labor** *AmE* n [U] **1** *informal* work for which you are very badly paid: *£2.00 an hour? That's slave labour!* **2** work done by slaves, or the slaves that do this work

slavery /'sleɪvəri/ n [U] the system of using slaves or the condition of being a slave: *Slavery was abolished* (=officially ended) *after the Civil War.*

slavish /'sleɪvɪʃ/ adj disapproving obeying or copying someone completely, without thinking: *slavish devotion to duty*

slay /sleɪ/ v [T] (past tense **slew** /sluː/, past participle **slain** /sleɪn/) *literary* to kill someone violently —**slaying** n [C]

sleaze /sliːz/ n [U] immoral behaviour in business or politics

sleazy /'sliːzi/ adj low in quality, immoral, and unpleasant: *a sleazy nightclub*

sledge /sledʒ/ *BrE*, **sled** /sled/ *AmE* n [C] a vehicle used for travelling on snow —**sledge** v [I]

sledge hammer n [C] a large heavy hammer

sleek

sleek /sliːk/ adj **1** sleek hair or fur is smooth and shiny **2** a sleek car is attractive and expensive

sleep¹ /sliːp/ v [I] (past tense and past participle **slept** /slept/)
1 to rest your mind and body, usually at night when you are lying in bed with your eyes closed: I normally sleep on my back. | Did you sleep well?
2 sleep two/four/six etc to have enough beds for a particular number of people: The cottage will sleep four easily.

PHRASES

not sleep a wink spoken to not sleep at all: I feel like I didn't sleep a wink last night.
sleep like a log/baby spoken to sleep very well: 'Did you hear anything last night?' 'No, I slept like a log.'
sleep on it spoken to not make a decision about something important until the next day: Sleep on it, and we'll discuss it tomorrow.
sleep rough BrE to sleep outdoors because you have no home: The city is full of people sleeping rough in shop doorways.
sleep tight! spoken used to say you hope someone sleeps well: Goodnight, sleep tight!

PHRASAL VERBS

sleep around informal disapproving to have sex with a lot of different people
sleep in to wake up later than usual in the morning: I slept in till 10:00 on Saturday.
sleep sth ↔ **off** to sleep until you do not feel ill or drunk any more
sleep through sth to continue to sleep while something is happening: Amazingly, Jim had slept through the storm.
sleep together informal if people sleep together, they have sex with each other
sleep with sb informal to have sex with someone: Everyone knows he's sleeping with her.

COLLOCATIONS
adverbs

to sleep well I didn't sleep very well last night.
to sleep badly She slept badly and felt tired the next day.
to sleep soundly/deeply (=in a way that means you are not likely to wake) The baby was still sleeping soundly.
to sleep peacefully A cat slept peacefully in his lap.
to sleep late (=to not wake up until late in the morning) We can sleep late tomorrow because it's Sunday.

THESAURUS

sleep to rest your mind and body with your eyes closed – used when talking about how long, how deeply, or where someone sleeps: Most people sleep for about eight hours. | I had to sleep on the sofa.
be asleep to be sleeping – used when saying that someone is not awake: The baby's asleep – don't wake her.
fall asleep/go to sleep to start sleeping: I fell asleep almost immediately.

oversleep to sleep for longer than you intended, especially when this makes you late: I overslept and was late for school.
take a nap (also **have a nap** especially BrE) to sleep for a short time during the day: Why don't you take a nap if you're tired?
doze to sleep lightly for a short time, for example in a chair: My grandmother spends a lot of time dozing in her chair.

sleep² n [singular, U] a time when you are sleeping: We didn't get much sleep last night. | I've only had four hours' sleep. | Her eyes were red from lack of sleep. | **in your sleep** Ed sometimes talks in his sleep.

PHRASES

go to sleep 1 to start sleeping: I went to sleep at nine o'clock and woke up at six. | It's nothing, just **go back to sleep** (=sleep again after waking up).
THESAURUS ▶ **SLEEP 2** informal if a part of your body goes to sleep, you cannot feel it for a short time, because it has not been getting enough blood: My leg has gone to sleep.
not lose (any) sleep over sth spoken to not worry about something: It's just a practice game – I wouldn't lose any sleep over it.
put sth to sleep to give an animal drugs so that it dies without pain: Our cat had to be put to sleep.

COLLOCATIONS
verbs

to go to sleep (=to start sleeping) Be quiet and go to sleep! ⚠ Do not say 'go sleep'. Say **go to sleep**.
to get to sleep (=to succeed in starting to sleep) I didn't get to sleep til two in the morning.
to send sb to sleep (=to make someone start sleeping) The film was so boring it sent me to sleep.
to get/have some sleep (=to sleep) I need to get some sleep.
to have a sleep BrE Grandad has a little sleep in the afternoon.

adjectives

a long/little sleep You've had a long sleep!
a good sleep (also **a good night's sleep**) Did you have a good sleep?
a deep sleep (=a sleep from which you cannot easily be woken) I was woken from a deep sleep by the phone ringing.

sleeper /ˈsliːpə $ -ər/ n [C] **1** BrE a train with beds for passengers to sleep on **2 a light/heavy sleeper** someone who wakes up easily or does not wake up easily from sleep: I've always been a light sleeper.

'sleeping bag n [C] a large warm bag for sleeping in

'sleeping pill n [C] a drug that helps you to sleep

sleepless /ˈsliːpləs/ adj unable to sleep: He spent a **sleepless night** (=a night when you do not sleep) worrying about what to do. —**sleeplessness** n [U]

sleepover /ˈsliːpəʊvə $ -oʊvər/ n [C] a party for children in which they stay the night at someone's house

sleepwalk /'sliːpˌwɔːk $ -ˌwɒːk/ *v* [I] to get out of bed and walk around while you are asleep —**sleepwalker** *n* [C]

sleepy /'sliːpi/ *adj* **1** tired and ready to sleep: *I felt really sleepy after lunch.* **THESAURUS** TIRED **2** a sleepy town or village is very quiet —**sleepily** *adv* —**sleepiness** *n* [U]

sleet /sliːt/ *n* [U] a mixture of rain and snow **THESAURUS** SNOW —**sleet** *v* [I]

sleeve /sliːv/ *n*
1 [C] the part of a piece of clothing that covers your arm: *a blouse with short sleeves*
2 long-sleeved/short-sleeved with long or short sleeves: *a long-sleeved sweater*
3 [C] *BrE* a cover for a record **SYN** jacket *AmE*
PHRASES
have sth up your sleeve *informal* to have a secret plan that you are going to use later: *Jansen usually has a few surprises up his sleeve.*

sleeveless /'sliːvləs/ *adj* without sleeves: *a sleeve-less dress*

sleigh /sleɪ/ *n* [C] a large vehicle that is pulled by animals, used for travelling on snow

sleight of hand /ˌslaɪt əv 'hænd/ *n* [U] **1** *disapproving* the use of skilful tricks and lies in order to deceive someone **2** quick and skilful movements with your hands when doing a magic trick

slender /'slendə $ -ər/ *adj* thin in an attractive way: *long slender fingers* **THESAURUS** THIN

slept /slept/ *v* the past tense and past participle of SLEEP

sleuth /sluːθ/ *n* [C] *literary* a DETECTIVE

slew¹ /sluː/ *n* *AmE informal* **a slew of sth** a large number of things: *A slew of companies reported increased profits in the last financial year.*

slew² *v* the past tense of SLAY

slice¹ /slaɪs/ *n* [C]
1 a thin piece of bread, meat etc that you cut from a larger piece: [+of] *a slice of bread* | **thin/thick slice Cut** *the tomato* **into** *thin* **slices.** → see picture at PIECE¹ **THESAURUS** PIECE
2 a slice of sth a share of something: *Everyone wants a slice of the profits.*

slice² *v*
1 (*also* **slice up**) [T] to cut meat, bread etc into thin pieces → **chop**: *Could you slice the bread?* | *Slice up the onions and add them to the meat.* → see picture at CUT¹ **THESAURUS** CUT
2 [I,T] to cut through something quickly and easily: [+through/into] *The knife is so sharp it can slice through bone.* | **slice sth in two/half** *Slice the lemon in half.* | **slice sth off** *She sliced off the top of her finger with a bread knife.*

slick¹ /slɪk/ *adj* **1** good at persuading people, often in a way that does not seem honest: *a slick salesman* **2** if something is slick, it is done in a skilful and attractive way, but is not important or interesting: *a slick Hollywood production*

slick² *n* [C] an OIL SLICK

SLIDE

slip

slide

skid

slide¹ /slaɪd/ *v* [I,T] (*past tense and past participle* **slid** /slɪd/)
1 to move smoothly over a surface, or to make something move in this way: [+along/around/down etc] *The children were sliding along the ice.* | **slide sth across/along etc sth** *She slid my drink along the bar.*
2 to move somewhere quietly and smoothly, or to move something in this way: [+into/out of etc] *Daniel slid out of the room when no one was looking.* | **slide sth into/out of etc sth** *He slid the gun into his pocket.*

slide² *n* **1** [C] a photograph in a frame. You shine light through it to show the photograph on a screen: *a slide show* **2** [C] a long metal slope with steps at one end, that children can climb up and slide down **3** [singular] a decrease in the price, level, standard etc of something: [+in] *a slide in profits* **4** [C] a piece of thin glass used for holding something under a MICROSCOPE

slight¹ /slaɪt/ *adj*
1 small in amount or degree: *a slight improvement* | *I have a slight headache.* | *There has been a slight change of plan.* **THESAURUS** SMALL
2 someone who is slight is thin and delicate **OPP** stocky
PHRASES
not in the slightest *spoken* not at all: *'You're not worried, are you?' 'Not in the slightest.'*
not the slightest chance/doubt/difference etc no chance, doubt etc at all: *I don't have the slightest idea where she is.*

slight² *n* [C] a remark or action that offends someone: [+on/to] *a slight to his authority*

slighted /'slaɪtɪd/ *adj* offended because you feel that someone has treated you rudely or without respect: *Meg felt slighted at not being invited to the party.*

slightly /'slaɪtli/ *adv* a little: *Each painting is slightly different.* | *Women make up slightly more than half the population.* | *slightly higher/lower/better/*

larger etc *She's slightly older than I am.* | *We know each other slightly.* | *He leaned forward ever so slightly.*

slim¹ /slɪm/ *adj*
1 someone who is slim is thin in an attractive way SYN **slender**: *You're looking a lot slimmer – have you lost weight?* | *a slim waist* THESAURUS▶ THIN
2 very small in amount or degree: *Doctors say she has only a slim chance of recovery.* | *a slim margin of profit*

> **Word Choice**: slim or skinny?
> **Slim** means thin in an attractive way: *He was tall, slim, and really good-looking.*
> **Skinny** means thin, especially in a way that is not very attractive: *I was really skinny when I was a teenager.*

slim² (*also* **slim down**) *v* [I] (**slimmed, slimming**) to make yourself thinner by eating less or by exercising → **diet**: *After he quit drinking, he slimmed to 210 pounds.* —**slimming** *n* [U]
PHRASAL VERBS
slim sth ↔ **down** to reduce the size or number of something: *Apex Co. is slimming down its workforce to cut costs.*

slime /slaɪm/ *n* [U] a thick sticky liquid that looks or smells unpleasant

slimy /'slaɪmi/ *adj* **1** covered with slime: *slimy rocks* **2** *informal* friendly in a way that is not sincere: *slimy politicians*

sling¹ /slɪŋ/ *v* [T] (*past tense and past participle* **slung** /slʌŋ/) **1** to throw or put something somewhere carelessly: *Duncan slung his suitcase onto the bed.* **2** to put something somewhere so that it hangs loosely: *Dave wore a tool belt slung around his waist.*

sling² *n* [C] **1** a piece of cloth that is put under your arm and then tied around your neck to support your arm or hand when it is injured **2** ropes or strong pieces of cloth used for lifting or carrying heavy objects: *a baby sling*

slingshot /'slɪŋʃɒt $ -ʃɑːt/ *n* [C] *AmE* a small Y-shaped stick with a thin band of rubber across the top, used to throw stones SYN **catapult** *BrE*

slink /slɪŋk/ *v* [I] (*past tense and past participle* **slunk** /slʌŋk/) to move somewhere quietly and secretly: *The cat slunk behind the chair.*

slip¹ /slɪp/ *v* (**slipped, slipping**)
1 FALL [I] if you slip, your feet move accidentally and you fall or almost fall: *Be careful not to slip – I just mopped the floor.* | [+on] *Joan slipped on the ice and broke her ankle.* → see picture at **SLIDE¹** THESAURUS▶ FALL
2 GO QUIETLY [I] to go somewhere quickly and quietly: [+out of/away/through etc] *Ben slipped quietly out of the room while his father was asleep.* | *No one saw Bill slip away when the police arrived.*
3 PUT [T] to put something somewhere quietly or secretly SYN **slide**: **slip sth into/around etc sth** *Ann slipped the book into her bag.* | *He slipped his arm around her waist and kissed her.* THESAURUS▶ PUT
4 MOVE ACCIDENTALLY [I] if something slips, it accidentally moves or falls: *The knife slipped as he cut into the wood.* | [+off/down/from etc] *The ring had slipped off Julia's finger.*

5 PUT ON/TAKE OFF [I,T] to put on a piece of clothing or take it off quickly and easily: **slip sth off/on** *Ken sat on the couch and slipped off his shoes.* | [+into/out of] *She slipped into her pyjamas.*
6 GET WORSE [I] to become worse or lower than before SYN **fall**: *Standards in our schools have been slipping.* | *The mayor's popularity is slipping.*
PHRASES
let sth slip *informal* to say something that is supposed to be a secret, without intending to: *Don't let it slip that I'm in town.*
slip your mind *spoken* if something slips your mind, you forget about it: *I was supposed to meet her for lunch, but it completely slipped my mind.* THESAURUS▶ FORGET

PHRASAL VERBS
slip away if an opportunity to do something slips away, the situation changes and the opportunity no longer exists: *This time, Radford did not let her chance slip away.*
slip out if something slips out, you say it without intending to: *Sorry, I shouldn't have said that – it just slipped out.*
slip up to make a mistake: *He can't afford to slip up again or he'll be fired.*

slip² *n* [C] **1** a small piece of paper: *He wrote his address on a slip of paper.* **2** a small mistake: *Molly knew she could not afford to make a single slip.* **3** a piece of clothing worn by women under a dress or skirt **4** an act of sliding accidentally so that you fall or almost fall
PHRASES
give sb the slip *informal* to escape from someone who is chasing you: *Palmer gave them the slip in the hotel lobby.*
a slip of the tongue/pen something that you say or write by accident, when you meant to say or write something else: *His comment was clearly a slip of the tongue.*

slipper /'slɪpə $ -ər/ *n* [C usually plural] a light soft shoe that you wear indoors → see picture at **SHOE¹**

slippery /'slɪpəri/ *adj* something that is slippery is difficult to walk on or hold because it is wet, oily, or covered in ice: *a slippery mountain path* | *Harry's palms were slippery with sweat.*
PHRASES
a/the slippery slope a process or habit that is difficult to stop and which will develop into something dangerous or harmful: [+to/towards] *He is on the slippery slope to a life in crime.*

'slip road *n* [C] *BrE* a road used when you drive onto or off a MOTORWAY

slit¹ /slɪt/ *n* [C] a long narrow cut or opening: *a slit in the curtains*

slit² *v* [T] (*past tense and past participle* **slit**, *present participle* **slitting**) to make a long narrow cut in something: *Guy slit open the envelope.*

slither /'slɪðə $ -ər/ *v* [I] **1** to slide somewhere: *He slithered down the muddy bank.* **2** if a snake slithers somewhere, it moves there

sliver /'slɪvə $ -ər/ n [C] a small thin pointed piece that has been cut or broken off something: [+of] a sliver of glass

slob /slɒb $ slɑːb/ n [C] informal someone who is lazy, dirty, or untidy

slobber /'slɒbə $ 'slɑːbər/ v [I] to let SALIVA (=the liquid produced in your mouth) come out of your mouth and run down: That dog slobbers everywhere.

slog /slɒg $ slɑːg/ v [I] (slogged, slogging) informal 1 to make a long hard journey somewhere, especially by walking: We had to slog through mud and dirt to get to the farm. 2 (also slog away) to work hard at something without stopping, especially when the work is difficult or boring: I don't want to slog away in a factory for the rest of my life. —slog n [singular, U]: The second day was a hard slog.

slogan /'sləʊgən $ 'sloʊ-/ n [C] a short phrase that is easy to remember and is used in advertising or politics

slop /slɒp $ slɑːp/ v [I,T] (slopped, slopping) if liquid slops, or if you slop it, it moves around or over the edge of a container: Water was slopping over the side of the bath.

slope¹ /sləʊp $ sloʊp/ n [C] a piece of ground or a surface that is higher at one end than at the other: The house was built on a slope. | a **steep slope** | a **gentle** (=not steep) slope | a **ski slope**

slope² v [I] if something slopes, it is higher at one end than at the other: [+up/down/away etc] The front yard slopes down to the street. | a sloping ceiling

sloppy /'slɒpi $ 'slɑːpi/ adj 1 not tidy or careful: sloppy work 2 sloppy clothes are large, loose, and not neat: a sloppy sweater —**sloppily** adv —**sloppiness** n [U]

slosh /slɒʃ $ slɑːʃ/ v [I] if liquid in a container sloshes, it moves against or over the sides of the container: [+around/about] Water was sloshing around in the bottom of the boat.

slot¹ /slɒt $ slɑːt/ n [C] 1 a long narrow hole in something, especially one for putting coins in: Put 20p in the slot and see how much you weigh. **THESAURUS** HOLE 2 a period of time allowed for one particular event: I was offered a slot on a local radio station.

slot² v [I,T] (slotted, slotting) to put something into a slot, or to go into a slot: The cassette slots in here. | The instructions tell you how to slot the shelf together.

'slot ma,chine n [C] a machine that you put coins into to play a game and try to win money

slouch /slaʊtʃ/ v [I] to stand, sit, or walk in a lazy way, with your shoulders bent forward: [+back/against/in etc] Jimmy slouched back in his chair. —**slouch** n [singular]

slovenly /'slʌvənli/ adj written dirty, untidy, and careless

slow¹ /sləʊ $ sloʊ/ adj, adv
1 NOT FAST not moving or happening quickly OPP fast: The slowest runners started at the back. | It's a very slow process. | My computer's very slow today. | Go slower.
2 NOT IMMEDIATELY **slow to do sth/slow in doing sth**

if you are slow to do something, you do not do it as soon as you can or should: We were slow to realize what was happening. | New ideas have been slow in coming.
3 CLOCK a clock that is slow shows a time earlier than the true time OPP fast: My watch is a few minutes slow.
4 BUSINESS if business is slow, there are not many customers: Business is usually slow this time of year.
5 NOT CLEVER someone who is slow does not understand things very quickly or easily: The school gives extra help for slower students.

slow² (also **slow down**) v [I,T] to become slower, or to make something slower: The traffic slowed to a crawl. | The ice on the road slowed us down.

slowdown /'sləʊdaʊn $ 'sloʊ-/ n [C] when an activity takes place more slowly than it did before: [+in] a slowdown in the tourist trade

slowly /'sləʊli $ 'sloʊ-/ adv at a slow speed OPP quickly: White clouds drifted slowly across the sky. | His voice became lower and he spoke more slowly.

THESAURUS

slowly at a slow speed: He walked slowly down the road.
gradually happening slowly over a long period of time: Many of our forests are gradually disappearing.
little by little/bit by bit slowly, in a series of small amounts or stages: The information came out bit by bit. | Little by little her health improved.

---

slow 'motion n [U] if part of a film or television programme is shown in slow motion, it is shown at a slower speed than the real speed: Let's look at that goal in slow motion.

sludge /slʌdʒ/ n [U] a soft thick unpleasant substance

slug¹ /slʌg/ n [C] a small soft creature with no legs that moves very slowly along the ground → snail → see picture at SNAIL

slug² v [T] (slugged, slugging) informal to hit someone hard with your closed hand
PHRASES
slug it out to argue or fight until someone wins: The two sides are slugging it out in court.

sluggish /'slʌgɪʃ/ adj moving or reacting more slowly than usual: Alex woke late feeling tired and sluggish.

slum /slʌm/ n [C] a house or an area of a city that is in very bad condition, where many poor people live: He had grown up in the slums of Chicago.

slumber /'slʌmbə $ -ər/ n [singular, U] (also **slumbers** [plural]) literary sleep: She awoke from her slumbers. —**slumber** v [I]

slump¹ /slʌmp/ v [I] 1 if a price or amount slumps, it suddenly becomes less: Car sales have slumped recently. 2 to fall or lean heavily against something because you are tired, ill, unhappy etc: [+against/over/back etc] Carol slumped back in her chair, defeated. | He was found slumped over the steering wheel of his car.

slump² n [C usually singular] **1** a sudden decrease in prices, sales, profits etc: [+in] *a slump in profits* **2** a period when there is a reduction in business and many people lose their jobs: *The war was followed by an economic slump.*

slung /slʌŋ/ v the past tense and past participle of SLING

slunk /slʌŋk/ v the past tense and past participle of SLINK

slur¹ /slɜː $ slɜːr/ v [I,T] (**slurred**, **slurring**) to speak in an unclear way without separating your words or sounds correctly: **slur your speech/words** *After a few drinks, he started to slur his words.*

slur² n [C] an unfair criticism that is intended to make people dislike someone or something: [+on/against] *a slur on his character* | *a racist slur*

slurp /slɜːp $ slɜːrp/ v [I,T] informal to drink in a noisy way ┃THESAURUS┃ DRINK —**slurp** n [C]

slush /slʌʃ/ n [U] snow on the ground that has partly melted ┃THESAURUS┃ SNOW

sly /slaɪ/ adj **1** someone who is sly tries to get what they want by not being completely honest ┃SYN┃ **cunning** ┃THESAURUS┃ DISHONEST **2** showing that you know something that others do not know: *a sly smile* —**slyly** adv

PHRASES
┃ **on the sly** informal secretly: *They'd been seeing each other on the sly for months.*

smack¹ /smæk/ v **1** [T] to hit someone, especially a child, with your open hand in order to punish them ┃THESAURUS┃ HIT **2** [I,T] to hit something: *The waves smacked against my knees.* —**smack** n [C]: *a smack on the head*

PHRASES
┃ **smack your lips** to make a short noise with your lips to show that you like a drink or some food: *He smacked his lips and picked up another piece of chicken.*

PHRASAL VERBS
smack of sth if a situation smacks of something unpleasant, it seems to involve that thing: *a policy that smacks of sex discrimination*

smack² adv informal **1** exactly in a place: *an old building **smack in the middle of** campus* **2** with a lot of force: *The van ran smack into a wall.*

small /smɔːl $ smɒːl/ adj
1 ┃LITTLE┃ not big: *She comes from a small town.* | *Smaller cars use less gas.* | *These shoes are too small.* | *Only a **small number** of people were affected.* | *Police found a **small amount** of drugs in the car.* ┃THESAURUS┃ SHORT
2 ┃NOT IMPORTANT┃ unimportant or easy to deal with ┃SYN┃ **minor**: *a small problem* | *We may have to make a few small changes.*
3 ┃YOUNG┃ a small child is young: *She has two small children.*
PHRASES
┃ **feel/look small** to feel or look stupid or unimportant: *She was always trying to **make** me **look small**.* ┃THESAURUS┃ YOUNG

the small hours the early morning hours, between about one and four o'clock: *The party went on until the small hours.*

┃**THESAURUS**┃

small not big: *a small boat* | *a small change of plan* | *a small mistake*
little [usually before noun] small – used especially with other adjectives to show how you feel about someone or something: *It's a very pretty little town.* | *a good little boy*
slight [usually before noun] very small and not very important or noticeable: *We've had a slight problem.* | *a slight movement of his hand*
minor small and not important or serious: *minor differences* | *minor changes* | *minor injuries* | *a minor traffic offence*
miniature [only before noun] made or grown to be much smaller than usual: *a miniature railway* | *miniature roses*

┃**extremely small**┃

tiny extremely small: *a tiny baby* | *They live in a tiny village in the mountains.*
minute extremely small and very difficult to see or notice: *The equipment is capable of detecting minute changes in air pressure.*

'small ad n [C] BrE an advertisement put in a newspaper by someone who wants to sell something, buy something etc

,small 'change n [U] coins of low value: *I didn't have any small change for the parking meter.*

'small fry n [U] informal people or things that are not important when compared to other people or things: *They're small fry compared to the real criminals.*

smallholding /'smɔːlˌhəʊldɪŋ $ 'smɒːlˌhoʊld-/ n [C] BrE a small farm

smallpox /'smɔːlpɒks $ 'smɒːlpɑːks/ n [U] a serious disease that killed a lot of people in the past

'small ,print (also **fine print**) n [U] all the rules and details relating to a contract or agreement: *Make sure you **read the small print** before you sign anything.*

,small-'scale adj not very big, or not involving a lot of people: *small-scale enterprises*

'small talk n [U] polite friendly conversation about unimportant subjects: *He's not very good at **making small talk**.*

'small-time adj a small-time criminal or BUSINESSMAN is not very important or successful

smart¹ /smɑːt $ smɑːrt/ adj
1 ┃CLEVER┃ intelligent ┃SYN┃ **clever** ┃OPP┃ **stupid**: *Jill's a smart kid.* | *Kelly didn't think she was smart enough to go to law school.* ┃THESAURUS┃ INTELLIGENT
2 ┃WELL-DRESSED┃ BrE someone who looks smart is wearing attractive clothes and looks very neat ┃SYN┃ **sharp** AmE ┃OPP┃ **scruffy**
3 ┃TIDY/ATTRACTIVE┃ BrE smart clothes, buildings etc are clean, tidy, and attractive ┃SYN┃ **sharp** AmE ┃OPP┃ **scruffy**: *a smart black suit* | *smart new offices*

4 FASHIONABLE *BrE* fashionable, or used by fashionable people: *one of London's smartest restaurants*

5 RUDE someone who is smart tries to be funny or clever in a way that is rude and does not show respect towards someone else: *Don't **get smart with** me, young lady! | He made some smart remark.* THESAURUS ▶ RUDE

6 CONTROLLED BY COMPUTER smart machines, weapons etc are controlled by computers —**smartly** *adv*

smart² *v* [I] **1** to be upset because someone has offended you: **[+from]** *He's still smarting from the insult.* **2** if a part of your body smarts, it hurts with a stinging pain

'smart card *n* [C] a small plastic card with an electronic part that can store information

smarten /'smɑːtn $ 'smɑːr-/ *v*

PHRASAL VERBS

smarten sb/sth ↔ **up** to make a person or place look neater and more attractive: *You'd better smarten yourself up.*

smash¹ /smæʃ/ *v* [I,T]

1 to break into a lot of small pieces, or to make something break in this way: *The plates smashed on the floor. | Rioters smashed store windows. | The boat was **smashed to pieces** on the rocks.* THESAURUS ▶ BREAK

2 to hit an object or surface violently, or to make something do this: *Murray smashed his fist against the wall. |* **[+against/down/into etc]** *A stolen car smashed into the bus.* THESAURUS ▶ DAMAGE

PHRASAL VERBS

smash sth ↔ **in** to hit something so violently that you break it and make a hole in it: *Pete's window was smashed in by another driver.*

smash sth ↔ **up** to deliberately destroy something by hitting it: *A group of young men started smashing the place up.*

smash² (*also* ,smash 'hit) *n* [C] a very successful new song, film, play etc: *The song became a smash hit.*

smashing /'smæʃɪŋ/ *adj BrE old-fashioned* very good: *We had a smashing holiday.*

smattering /'smætərɪŋ/ *n* [singular] a small number or amount of something: **[+of]** *a smattering of applause*

smear¹ /smɪə $ smɪr/ *v* [T] **1** to spread a liquid or soft substance on a surface: **smear sth on/over etc sb** *Jill smeared lotion on Rick's back. |* **smear sth with sth** *His face was smeared with mud.* **2** to tell an untrue story about someone important in order to harm them - used especially in newspapers: *an attempt to smear the party leadership*

smear² *n* [C] **1** a dirty mark made by a small amount of something spread on a surface: *It left a black smear on his forehead.* **2** an untrue story about someone important that is meant to harm them - used especially in newspapers

smell¹ /smel/ *v* (*past tense and past participle* **smelled** *or* **smelt** /smelt/)

1 [I] to have a particular smell: *The stew **smelled delicious**. |* **[+like]** *It smells like rotten eggs. |* **[+of]** *BrE: My clothes smelled of smoke.*

2 [I] to have an unpleasant smell: *Your feet smell!*

3 [T] to notice or recognize a smell: *I can smell something burning!*

4 [T] to put your nose near something in order to discover what kind of smell it has: *Come and smell these roses.*

smell² *n*

1 [C] a quality that you recognize using your nose: **[+of]** *the smell of fresh bread | The smell's getting worse.*

2 [U] the ability to notice or recognize smells: *Dogs have a good **sense of smell**.*

COLLOCATIONS

adjectives

a strong smell *There was a strong smell of paint.*
a faint smell (=not strong) *A faint smell of burning still hung in the air.*
a strange/funny smell *What's that funny smell?*
a nice/lovely smell *The soap had a lovely smell.*
a bad/awful/horrible smell *We opened the windows to get rid of the horrible smell.*
a delicious smell (=a pleasant smell of food) *There was a delicious smell of freshly baked bread.*
a sweet smell *She liked the sweet smell of hay in the barn.*

verbs

to have a smell *This shampoo has a nice fruity smell.*
to give off a smell (=to produce a smell) *The mixture gave off a strange smell.*
to notice/smell a smell *I noticed a smell of gas.*
a smell comes from somewhere *A nasty smell was coming from one of the apartments.*

THESAURUS

smell a quality that you recognize using your nose: *There's a funny smell in here.*
scent a smell - used especially about the pleasant smell from flowers, plants, or fruit. Also used about the smell left by an animal: *She smelt the sweet scent of the roses. | Cats use scent to mark their territory.*
fragrance/perfume a pleasant smell, especially from flowers, plants, or fruit. **Fragrance** and **perfume** are more formal than **scent**: *The air was filled with the sweet perfume of flowers.*
aroma a pleasant smell - used especially about the smell from food or coffee: *He could smell the aroma of fresh coffee.*
odour *BrE*, **odor** *AmE* a smell, especially an unpleasant one: *An unpleasant odour was coming from the dustbins.*
stink/stench a very strong and unpleasant smell: *I couldn't get rid of the stink of sweat.*

---

smelly /'smeli/ *adj* having a strong unpleasant smell

smidgen /'smɪdʒən/ (*also* **smidge** /smɪdʒ/) *n* [singular] *spoken informal* a very small amount of something

smile¹ /smaɪl/ *v*

1 [I] to have a happy expression on your face, with your mouth curving: *She came in, smiling. |* **[+at]** *Keith smiled sweetly at me.*

S

2 [T] to say or express something with a smile: *'Thanks,' she smiled.*

> **THESAURUS**
>
> **smile** to have a happy expression on your face, with your mouth curving: *Misha smiled at the boy.*
> **grin** to give a big happy smile: *He was grinning straight at the camera.*
> **beam** *especially written* to smile with a very wide smile for a long time, because you are very pleased or proud: *She beamed with pride as her son collected the award.*
> **smirk** *especially written* to smile in an unpleasant way, for example because you are pleased because of another person's bad luck: *He just smirked and said 'You should have listened to what I said.'*

smile² *n* [C] a happy expression on your face, with your mouth curving: *'Hello,' she said with a smile.*

smirk /smɜːk $ smɜːrk/ *v* [I] to smile in a satisfied and annoying way **THESAURUS** SMILE —**smirk** *n* [C]

smithereens /ˌsmɪðəˈriːnz/ *n* **smash/blow sth to smithereens** to destroy something or break it into very small pieces

smitten /'smɪtn/ *adj* [not before noun] loving someone very much: **[+with/by]** *He's absolutely smitten with her.*

smock /smɒk $ smɑːk/ *n* [C] a long loose shirt or a loose dress

smog /smɒg $ smɑːg, smɔːg/ *n* [U] unhealthy air in cities that contains a lot of smoke

smoke¹ /sməʊk $ smoʊk/ *n*
1 [U] the white, grey, or black gas that is produced by something burning: **Clouds** of black **smoke** billowed out. | **cigarette smoke**
2 [singular] when someone smokes a cigarette
PHRASES
> **go up in smoke** *informal* **1** if your plans go up in smoke, they fail: *Hopes of peace soon went up in smoke.* **2** to be destroyed by burning: *The whole factory went up in smoke.*

smoke² *v*
1 [I,T] to suck smoke from a cigarette or pipe: *I don't smoke any more. | He smokes a pipe.*
2 [I] to be producing smoke: *a smoking chimney*
3 [T] to prepare food by hanging it in smoke: *smoked salmon* —**smoking** *n* [U]

smoker /'sməʊkə $ 'smoʊkər/ *n* [C] someone who smokes OPP **non-smoker**: *He's a **heavy smoker** (=he smokes a lot).*

smokescreen /'sməʊkskriːn $ 'smoʊk-/ *n* [C] something that you do or say to hide your real plans or actions

smoky /'sməʊki $ 'smoʊ-/ *adj* **1** containing or producing smoke: *a smoky room | a smoky fire* **2** having the taste, smell, or appearance of smoke: *smoky cheese*

smolder /'sməʊldə $ 'smoʊldər/ *v* the American spelling of SMOULDER

smooch /smuːtʃ/ *v* [I] *informal* if two people smooch, they kiss and hold each other in a romantic way, especially while dancing —**smooch** *n* [singular]

> **SMOOTH**
>
> smooth
>
> rough

smooth¹ /smuːð/ *adj*
1 NOT ROUGH having an even surface OPP **rough**: *The road was wide and smooth. | She had lovely smooth skin. | The stone steps had been **worn smooth**.* **THESAURUS** FLAT
2 WITHOUT LUMPS a substance that is smooth has no big pieces in it OPP **lumpy**: *Beat all the ingredients together until smooth.*
3 GRACEFUL graceful or comfortable, with no sudden movements: *Swing the racket in one smooth motion. | It wasn't a very smooth ride.* **THESAURUS** COMFORTABLE
4 WITHOUT PROBLEMS happening or continuing without problems: *Sarah ensures the **smooth running** of the sales department. | a **smooth transition** from school to university*
5 CAN'T TRUST SB polite and confident in a way that people do not trust: *a smooth talker* —**smoothly** *adv* —**smoothness** *n* [U]

smooth² *v* [T] **1** to make something flat by moving your hands across it: *Tanya sat down, smoothing her skirt.* | **smooth sth back/down** *She smoothed back her hair.* **2** to take away the roughness from a surface: *a face cream that smooths your skin*
PHRASAL VERBS
smooth sth ↔ **out** to make something such as paper or cloth flat by moving your hands across it: *She smoothed out the newspaper.*
smooth sth ↔ **over** to end an unpleasant situation by talking to the people involved: *He depended on Nancy to smooth over any troubles.*

smoothie /'smuːði/ *n* [C] a thick drink made from fruit

smother /'smʌðə $ -ər/ *v* [T] **1** to cover someone's face so that they cannot breathe and they die **2** to put a large amount of a substance onto something: **smother sth in/with sth** *cakes smothered in chocolate* **3** to make someone unhappy by giving them more attention than they want **4** to stop yourself from having or expressing a feeling: *They tried to smother their giggles.* **5** to make a fire stop burning by preventing air from reaching it

smoulder *BrE*, **smolder** *AmE* /'sməʊldə $ 'smoʊldər/ *v* [I] **1** if a fire is smouldering, it is burning slowly without flames **THESAURUS** BURN

2 to have strong feelings which you are trying to hide: *Underneath he was smouldering with rage.*

SMS /ˌes em 'es/ *n* [U] (**short message service**) a feature on a MOBILE PHONE that allows a user to send and receive written messages

smudge¹ /smʌdʒ/ *n* [C] a dirty mark where something has been touched

smudge² *v* [I,T] if ink, paint etc on a surface smudges, or if you smudge it, its appearance is spoiled because it has been touched

smug /smʌg/ *adj* very satisfied with your situation, in a way that annoys other people: *a smug smile* —**smugly** *adv*

smuggle /ˈsmʌgəl/ *v* [T] to take something illegally from one place to another: *The guns were smuggled across the border.* —**smuggler** *n* [C] —**smuggling** *n* [U]

smutty /ˈsmʌti/ *adj* referring to sex in an unpleasant or silly way: *smutty jokes*

snack¹ /snæk/ *n* [C] food that you eat between meals or instead of a large meal: *The cafe serves drinks, snacks, and meals.* **THESAURUS** MEAL

snack² *v* [I] to eat small amounts of food between main meals or instead of a meal

'snack bar *n* [C] a place where you can buy snacks

snag¹ /snæg/ *n* [C] *informal* a difficulty or problem: *The only snag is lack of money.* **THESAURUS** PROBLEM

snag² *v* [I,T] (**snagged, snagging**) to damage something by getting it stuck on something sharp

SNAIL

snail

slug

snail /sneɪl/ *n* [C] a small creature with a long soft body and a round shell on its back
PHRASES
at a snail's pace extremely slowly: *The traffic was moving at a snail's pace.*

snake¹ /sneɪk/ *n* [C] a long thin animal that slides across the ground: *A snake slithered across the path.* | **poisonous/venomous snake** → see picture at REPTILE

snake² *v* [I,T] *written* to move in long curves or have long curves: [+through/across etc] *The convoy snaked through the city.* | *She saw the river **snaking** its **way** through the gorge.*

snap¹ /snæp/ *v* (**snapped, snapping**)
1 **BREAK LOUDLY** [I,T] if something snaps, or if you snap it, it breaks with a short loud noise: *Dry*

branches snapped under their feet. | **snap (sth) in half/two** *He snapped the chalk in two.* **THESAURUS** BREAK

2 **OPEN/CLOSE LOUDLY** [I,T] to move into a position with a short loud noise, or to make something do this: **snap (sth) together/open/shut** *She snapped her briefcase shut.*

3 **SPEAK ANGRILY** [I,T] to speak suddenly in an angry way: [+at] *I'm sorry I snapped at you.* | *'What?' she snapped.*

4 **LOSE TEMPER** [I] to be suddenly unable to control your anger: *He just snapped.*

5 **DOG** [I] if a dog snaps at you, it tries to bite you

6 **TAKE PHOTOGRAPH** [I,T] to take a photograph
PHRASES
snap your fingers to make a short loud noise with your finger and thumb: *He snapped his fingers in time to the music.*

PHRASAL VERBS
snap out of sth *informal* to stop being sad or upset: *Jane's still depressed – I wish she'd **snap out of it**.*
snap sth ↔ **up** to buy something immediately or take an opportunity to get something: *At that price, they'll be snapped up in no time.* **THESAURUS** BUY

snap² *n* **1** [singular] a sudden short loud noise, especially of something breaking or closing: *He shut the book with a snap.* **2** [C] a photograph that is taken quickly: *holiday snaps* **3** [U] a card game in which you say 'snap' when two cards are the same
PHRASES
be a snap *AmE informal* to be very easy: *The test was a snap.*

snap³ *adj* **snap judgment/decision** a judgment or decision made very quickly, without thought or discussion

snappy /ˈsnæpi/ *adj* a snappy phrase is short, clear, and often funny
PHRASES
make it snappy *spoken* used to tell someone to hurry: *Get me a drink, and make it snappy!*

snapshot /ˈsnæpʃɒt $ -ʃɑːt/ *n* [C] **1** a photograph that is taken quickly **SYN** snap **2** information that quickly gives an idea of a situation: [+of] *a snapshot of life during that time*

snare¹ /sneə $ sner/ *n* [C] a trap for catching birds or small animals

snare² *v* [T] **1** to catch an animal using a snare **2** to catch someone, especially by tricking them

snarl /snɑːl $ snɑːrl/ *v* **1** [I,T] to say something in a nasty angry way: *'Shut up!' he snarled.* **2** [I] if an animal snarls, it makes a low angry sound and shows its teeth: *The dog growled and snarled at me.* —**snarl** *n* [C]
PHRASAL VERBS
snarl sth ↔ **up** if traffic is snarled up, vehicles are not able to move

snatch¹ /snætʃ/ *v* [T] **1** to take something from someone with a sudden movement: **snatch sth from sb** *The boy snatched the note from her hand.* **2** to quickly do something or get something, when you have a short amount of time: *I managed to snatch an hour's sleep on the train.*

PHRASAL VERBS

snatch at sth to quickly put out your hand to try to take or hold something: *Jessie snatched at the bag.*

snatch² n **a snatch of conversation/song etc** a short part of a conversation, song etc that you hear

snazzy /'snæzi/ *adj informal* bright, fashionable, and attractive: *a snazzy jacket*

sneak¹ /sni:k/ v (*past tense and past participle* **sneaked** or **snuck** /snʌk/) **1** [I] to go somewhere quietly and secretly: **[+out/past/off etc]** *We managed to sneak past the guard.* **THESAURUS** WALK **2** [T] to take something somewhere secretly: *I'll sneak his present upstairs.* **3 sneak a look/glance at sth** to look at something quickly and secretly: *She sneaked a look at the diary.*

PHRASAL VERBS

sneak up to come close to someone very quietly, so that they do not notice you: **[+on/behind]** *Don't sneak up on me like that!*

sneak² n [C] *BrE informal disapproving* a child who tells adults when other children have done something wrong

sneaker /'sni:kə $ -ər/ n [C] *especially AmE* a soft sports shoe → see picture at SHOE¹

sneaking /'sni:kɪŋ/ *adj* **1 have a sneaking suspicion/feeling (that)** to think you know something without being sure: *I've a sneaking feeling this won't work.* **2 have a sneaking admiration for sb** to like someone, although you do not want to admit it

sneaky /'sni:ki/ *adj* done in a clever but unfair way: *a sneaky trick* **THESAURUS** DISHONEST

sneer /snɪə $ snɪr/ v [I,T] to smile or speak in a nasty unkind way: **[+at]** *She sneered at his taste in music.* | *'What happened to you?' he sneered.* —**sneer** n [C]

sneeze /sni:z/ v [I] when you sneeze, air suddenly comes out of your nose and mouth in a noisy and uncontrollable way: *The dust is making me sneeze.* —**sneeze** n [C]

snicker /'snɪkə $ -ər/ v [I] *AmE* to laugh quietly in an unkind way **SYN** **snigger** *BrE* **THESAURUS** LAUGH —**snicker** n [C]

snide /snaɪd/ *adj* a snide remark criticizes someone in a way which is unkind, although it may be clever: **snide comment/remark** *She started making snide remarks about him.*

sniff /snɪf/ v

1 [I] to breathe air into your nose noisily, for example when you are crying or have a cold: *Stop sniffing and blow your nose.*

2 [I,T] to breathe in through your nose in order to smell something: *'What's this?' he asked, sniffing it suspiciously.* | **[+at]** *The dog was sniffing at the carpet.* —**sniff** n [C]

PHRASES

not to be sniffed at *especially BrE spoken* worth considering or accepting: *An 8% salary increase is not to be sniffed at.*

'sniffer dog n [C] *BrE* a dog that has been trained to find drugs or explosives

sniffle /'snɪfəl/ v [I] to sniff a lot, especially when you are crying or ill —**sniffle** n [C]

snigger /'snɪgə $ -ər/ v [I] *BrE* to laugh quietly in an unkind way **SYN** **snicker** *AmE* **THESAURUS** LAUGH —**snigger** n [C]

snip¹ /snɪp/ v [I,T] (**snipped**, **snipping**) to cut something with quick small cuts, using scissors **THESAURUS** CUT

snip² n [C] **1** a quick small cut with scissors **2 be a snip** *BrE informal* to be surprisingly cheap: *This jacket is a snip at £15.*

snipe /snaɪp/ v [I] **1** to criticize someone in an unkind way: *I wish you two would stop sniping at each other.* **2** to shoot at people from a hidden position —**sniping** n [U]

sniper /'snaɪpə $ -ər/ n [C] someone who shoots at people from a hidden position

snippet /'snɪpɪt/ n [C] a small piece of news, information, or conversation: **[+of]** *The book contains some fascinating snippets of information.*

snivel /'snɪvəl/ v [I] (**snivelled**, **snivelling** *BrE*, **sniveled**, **sniveling** *AmE*) to cry and behave in a weak complaining way: *Stop snivelling!*

snob /snɒb $ snɑːb/ n [C] *disapproving* someone who thinks they are better than people from a lower social class

snobbery /'snɒbəri $ 'snɑː-/ n [U] the attitudes and behaviour of snobs

snobbish /'snɒbɪʃ $ 'snɑː-/ (*also* **snobby** /'snɒbi $ 'snɑːbi/) *adj* behaving like a snob

snog /snɒg $ snɑːg/ v [I,T] (**snogged**, **snogging**) *BrE informal* to kiss someone in a sexual way —**snog** n [singular]

snook /snuːk $ snʊk, snuːk/ n → **cock a snook at sb/sth** at COCK²

snooker /'snuːkə $ 'snʊkər/ n [U] a game played on a special table with long sticks, one white ball, and a set of coloured balls

snoop /snuːp/ v [I] to try to find out about someone's activities by secretly watching them or looking at their things: **[+on]** *He got a detective to snoop on her.* | **[+around]** *I caught him snooping around outside.* —**snooper** n [C]

snooty /'snuːti/ *adj* rude and unfriendly, because you think you are better than other people

snooze /snuːz/ v [I] *informal* to sleep lightly for a short time **SYN** **doze** —**snooze** n [singular]

snore /snɔː $ snɔːr/ v [I] to make a loud noise each time you breathe while you are asleep **THESAURUS** BREATHE —**snoring** n [U] —**snore** n [C]

snorkel¹ /'snɔːkəl $ 'snɔːr-/ n [C] a tube that you breathe through while swimming with your face under water

snorkel² v [I] (**snorkelled**, **snorkelling** *BrE*, **snorkeled**, **snorkeling** *AmE*) to swim using a snorkel —**snorkelling** n [U]

snort /snɔːt $ snɔːrt/ v [I,T] to make a noise by forcing air out through your nose, especially to express impatience or amusement: *She snorted with laughter.* —**snort** *n* [C]

snot /snɒt $ snɑːt/ *n* [U] *informal* the substance produced in your nose

snotty /'snɒti $ 'snɑːti/ *adj informal* **1** rude and believing you are better than other people **2** having snot on your nose

snout /snaʊt/ *n* [C] the long nose of a pig or other animal

snow¹ /snəʊ $ snoʊ/ *n* [U] soft white pieces of frozen water that fall like rain: *We had eight inches of snow last night.*

COLLOCATIONS

verbs

snow falls *The snow was still falling outside.*
snow covers sth *The ground was covered with snow.*
snow melts (=turns to water) *The snow was already melting.*

adjectives

deep snow *The snow was very deep on the lawn.*
heavy snow (=when a lot of snow falls) *Schools were closed because of the heavy snow.*
light snow (=when a little snow falls) *A light snow had begun to fall.*
fresh snow *They left footprints in the fresh snow.*

THESAURUS

snow soft white frozen water that falls from the sky: *The ground was covered with snow.*
snowflakes pieces of snow falling from the sky: *The snowflakes were larger now.*
sleet a mixture of snow and rain: *It was a freezing day with sleet and strong winds.*
slush snow on the ground that has partly melted: *Snow was turning to slush on the roads.*
blizzard a storm with a lot of snow and a strong wind: *We got caught in a blizzard on our way to school.*
frost a white powder of ice that covers things when the weather is very cold: *Overnight there had been a heavy frost.*

snow² *v* it snows when it snows, snow falls from the sky: *Look, it's snowing!* | *It snowed throughout the night.*

PHRASES

be snowed in to be unable to leave a place because so much snow has fallen: *We were snowed in for a week.*
be snowed under (with sth) to have too much work, so that you cannot deal with anything else **THESAURUS** BUSY

snowball¹ /'snəʊbɔːl $ 'snoʊbɔːl/ *n* [C] a ball made out of snow that children throw at each other

snowball² *v* [I] if a plan, problem, or activity snowballs, it develops or grows very quickly

snowboarding /'snəʊbɔːdɪŋ $ 'snoʊbɔːrd-/ *n* [U] the sport of coming down snowy mountains standing on a board —**snowboarder** *n* [C]

SNOWBOARDING

snowbound /'snəʊbaʊnd $ 'snoʊ-/ *adj* unable to leave a place because there is too much snow

snowdrift /'snəʊˌdrɪft $ 'snoʊ-/ *n* [C] a deep pile of snow formed by the wind

snowdrop /'snəʊdrɒp $ 'snoʊdrɑːp/ *n* [C] a plant with a small white flower that appears in early spring

snowfall /'snəʊfɔːl $ 'snoʊfɔːl/ *n* [C,U] when snow falls, or the amount that falls

snowflake /'snəʊfleɪk $ 'snoʊ-/ *n* [C] a piece of falling snow

snowman /'snəʊmæn $ 'snoʊ-/ *n* [C] (*plural* **snowmen** /-men/) a figure of a person made of snow

snowplough *BrE*, **snowplow** *AmE* /'snəʊplaʊ $ 'snoʊ-/ *n* [C] a vehicle for pushing snow off roads

snowstorm /'snəʊstɔːm $ 'snoʊstɔːrm/ *n* [C] a storm with a lot of snow **THESAURUS** STORM

snowy /'snəʊi $ 'snoʊi/ *adj* if it is snowy, the ground is covered with snow or snow is falling

Snr *BrE* the written abbreviation of **Senior**, used after someone's name: *James Taylor, Snr*

snub /snʌb/ *v* [T] (**snubbed**, **snubbing**) to be rude to someone, especially by ignoring them —**snub** *n* [C]

snuck /snʌk/ *v* a past tense and past participle of SNEAK

snuff¹ /snʌf/ *v*

PHRASES

snuff it *BrE informal* to die

PHRASAL VERBS

snuff sth ↔ out 1 to end something in a sudden way: *the violence which snuffed out his life* **2** to stop a CANDLE burning

snuff² *n* [U] tobacco powder, which some people breathe in through their noses

PHRASES

not be up to snuff *AmE informal* to not be good enough: *His performance was not up to snuff.*

snuffle /'snʌfəl/ *v* [I] to breathe noisily in and out through your nose

snug /snʌg/ *adj* **1** warm and comfortable: *It's nice and snug in here.* **2** snug clothes fit tightly —**snugly** *adv*

S

snuggle /'snʌgəl/ v [I] if you snuggle into a comfortable position, you get into that position: **[+up/down/into etc]** *We snuggled up together on the sofa.*

so¹ /səʊ $ soʊ/ adv

1 used before an adjective or adverb to emphasize what you are saying: *It was so embarrassing – everyone was looking at us!* | *She works so hard!* | **so much/many** *I've never seen so many people in one place before!* | **so ... (that)** (=used to mention a result) *He was so fat that he couldn't get through the door.*

2 used to refer back to something that has just been mentioned: *'Has she gone?' 'I believe so* (=I believe she has gone)'. | *'Will I need my coat?' 'I don't think so.'* | *Are you going into town? If so, can I come?*

3 so do I/so is he/so would Peter etc used to say that something is also true about someone else: *She's been ill, and so has her husband.* | *If you're going to have a drink then so will I.*

4 so it is/so he is etc especially BrE spoken used to agree with something that has just been mentioned: *'Look, she's wearing a hat like yours.' 'So she is.'*

5 spoken used to introduce the next part of what you are saying: *So anyway, he finally arrived.*

6 spoken informal definitely: *He is so not the right man for her.* | *I am so going to enjoy this.*

7 used with a movement of your hand to show how big, tall etc something or someone is, or how to do something: *It was about so big.* | *Then you fold the paper like so.*

8 be so to be true or correct: *People say that exams are easier now, but it isn't so!*

PHRASES

and so on/forth used after a list to show that there are other similar things that could be mentioned: *a room full of old furniture, paintings, and so forth*

not so big/good/bad etc not very big, good etc: *The news is not so good.*

only so much/many only a limited quantity: *Only so many people are allowed in at a time.*

or so used when you cannot be exact about a number, amount, or period of time: *He left a week or so ago.* **THESAURUS** APPROXIMATELY

so?/so what? used to say that you do not think that something is important, especially in a way that seems impolite: *Yes, I'm late. So what?*

so long! spoken used to say goodbye

so much for sb/sth spoken used to say that an action, idea, statement etc was not useful: *He's late again. So much for good intentions!*

so² linking word

1 used to say that someone does something because of the reason just stated: *I heard a noise so I got out of bed.* **THESAURUS** THEREFORE

2 so (that) a) in order to make something happen, or to make something possible: *I put your keys in the drawer so that they wouldn't get lost.* **b)** with the result that: *The groups are small, so everyone knows each other.*

PHRASES

so as to do sth formal in order to do something: *I drove at a steady 50 mph so as to save fuel.*

soak /səʊk $ soʊk/ v [I,T]

1 if you soak something, or if you let it soak, you cover it with liquid and leave it: *Soak the beans overnight.* | *Leave the dishes soaking.*

2 if water soaks somewhere, or if it soaks something, it makes something wet: **[+into/through]** *Sweat soaked into his collar.* | *The rain had soaked her shoes.*

PHRASAL VERBS

soak sth ↔ **up**

1 if something soaks up a liquid, it takes the liquid into itself **SYN** absorb: *The bread will soak up the milk.*

2 to let yourself experience or enjoy something: *Sit outside a cafe and soak up the atmosphere.* | *I just wanted to soak up the sun.*

soaked /səʊkt $ soʊkt/ adj very wet: *I'm soaked through* (=completely wet). **THESAURUS** WET

soaking /'səʊkɪŋ $ 'soʊ-/ (also ,soaking 'wet) adj completely wet

'so-and-so n **1** [U] used to refer to someone or something without saying who or what they are: *People ask, 'Where's Mrs So-and-So?'* **2** [C] spoken an unpleasant person

soap¹ /səʊp $ soʊp/ n

1 [U] a substance that you use to wash yourself with: *a bar of soap* | *Wash your hands with soap and water.* → see picture at BATHROOM

2 (also **soap opera**) [C] a television story about the ordinary lives of a group of people: *I don't watch any of the soaps.* **THESAURUS** PROGRAMME

soap² v [T] to rub soap on someone or something

soapbox /'səʊpbɒks $ 'soʊpbɑːks/ n **be/get on your soapbox** to talk about your opinion in a way that is boring and annoying for other people

'soap ,opera n [C] a television SOAP

'soap ,powder n [C,U] BrE a powder that is made from soap and other chemicals, used for washing clothes

soapy /'səʊpi $ 'soʊpi/ adj soapy water has soap in it

soar /sɔː $ sɔːr/ v [I] **1** to increase quickly to a high level: *The temperature soared to 32°.* **2** to fly fast and high: *Above her, an eagle soared.* **3** buildings or cliffs that soar are very high: *The cliffs soar 500 feet above the sea.*

sob /sɒb $ sɑːb/ v [I,T] (**sobbed**, **sobbing**) to cry noisily while taking short breaths: *She began to sob uncontrollably.* **THESAURUS** CRY —**sob** n [C]

sober¹ /'səʊbə $ 'soʊbər/ adj **1** not drunk **2** serious and calm: *a sober, hard-working man* **3** making you feel very serious: *a sober reminder of our duties* **4** plain and not brightly coloured: *a sober grey suit* —**soberly** adv

sober² v

PHRASAL VERBS

sober up to become less drunk, or to make someone become less drunk: **sober sb** ↔ **up** *A cup of coffee soon sobered him up.*

sobering /'səʊbərɪŋ $ 'soʊ-/ adj making you feel very serious: *It's a sobering thought that only 20% of new businesses survive their first year.*

'sob ,story n [C] *informal* a story that someone tells you to get sympathy

'so-called *adj* [only before noun] **1** used when you think the word used to describe something is wrong: *The so-called experts were no help.* **2** used to show that you are using a word that is new or that has a special meaning: *He was a victim of so-called 'Mad Cow Disease'.*

soccer /'sɒkə $ 'sɑːkər/ n [U] a game in which two teams try to kick a ball into a net at each end of a field SYN football *BrE*: *the soccer team* | *He's quite a good soccer player.* | *soccer fans*

sociable /'səʊʃəbəl $ 'soʊ-/ adj someone who is sociable is friendly and enjoys being with other people

social /'səʊʃəl $ 'soʊ-/ adj
1 relating to human society and the way it is organized: *social issues such as unemployment and homelessness* | *people from different social backgrounds*
2 social activities are ones in which you talk to other people and do things with them for enjoyment: *The social life at college is brilliant.* | *a range of social events for employees*
3 having the ability or opportunity to behave and speak properly with other people: *He has absolutely no social skills.* | *There were few opportunities for social interaction.*
4 social animals live together in groups OPP solitary —socially adv: *behaviour that is socially acceptable*

socialism /'səʊʃəl-ɪzəm $ 'soʊ-/ n [U] a political system that tries to give equal opportunities to all people, and in which many industries belong to the government → capitalism, communism —socialist adj, n [C]

socialite /'səʊʃəl-aɪt $ 'soʊ-/ n [C] a rich person who enjoys going to fashionable parties

socialize (also -ise *BrE*) /'səʊʃəl-aɪz $ 'soʊ-/ v [I] to spend time with other people for enjoyment: *I don't socialize with him.*

,social 'networking site (also ,social 'networking ,website) n [C] a website where people put information about themselves and can send messages to other people

,social 'science n [C,U] subjects such as history, politics, and ECONOMICS, or one of these subjects

,social se'curity n [U] a system run by the government to provide money for people when they are old, ill, or cannot work SYN welfare *AmE*

,social 'services n [plural] *BrE* the government department that helps people with problems, for example family or money problems: *Contact social services for help.*

'social ,studies n [plural] → SOCIAL SCIENCE

'social ,worker n [C] someone whose job is to help people who are having difficulties with money or their family —social work n [U]

society /sə'saɪəti/ n (plural societies)
1 [C,U] all the people who live in the same country and share the same laws and customs: *They are valued members of society.* | *important changes in the structure of society* | *a modern industrial society*

2 [C] an organization or club with members who have similar interests: *I joined the school film society.* THESAURUS ORGANIZATION
3 [U] the rich fashionable people within a country: *a society wedding* → BUILDING SOCIETY

socioeconomic /ˌsəʊsiəʊekəˈnɒmɪk, ˌsəʊʃiəʊ-, -iːkə- $ ˌsoʊsioʊekəˈnɑː-, ˌsoʊʃioʊ-, -iːkə-/ adj relating to social and economic conditions

sociology /ˌsəʊsiˈɒlədʒi, ˌsəʊʃi- $ ˌsoʊsiˈɑːl-/ n [U] the study of society and the way people behave towards each other —sociologist n [C]

sock¹ /sɒk $ sɑːk/ n [C] a piece of clothing that you wear on your foot: *Put your socks and shoes on.* | *a pair of socks* → see picture at CLOTHES
PHRASES
knock/blow sb's socks off *informal* to surprise and excite someone a lot: *Here is a new rock band that will knock your socks off.*
pull your socks up *especially BrE* to make an effort to improve your behaviour or your work: *He needs to pull his socks up if he wants to pass his exams.*

sock² v [T] *informal* to hit someone hard SYN thump: *Someone socked him in the mouth.*

socket /'sɒkɪt $ 'sɑː-/ n [C] **1** a place in a wall where you connect electrical equipment to the supply of electricity → see picture at PLUG¹ **2** the place on a piece of electrical equipment where you connect another piece of equipment **3** a place where one thing fits into another

soda /'səʊdə $ 'soʊ-/ n [C,U] **1** (also 'soda water) water that contains bubbles and is added to other drinks **2** (also 'soda pop) *AmE* a sweet drink containing bubbles SYN pop *BrE*

sodden /'sɒdn $ 'sɑːdn/ adj very wet: *His clothes were sodden.*

sodium /'səʊdiəm $ 'soʊ-/ n [U] a silver-white metal that produces salt when mixed with CHLORINE

sofa /'səʊfə $ 'soʊ-/ n [C] a comfortable seat with arms and a back, wide enough for two or three people SYN couch, settee *BrE*: *She sat down on the sofa.*

soft /sɒft $ sɒːft/ adj
1 NOT HARD not hard, firm, or stiff, but easy to press OPP hard: *a soft pillow* → see picture at HARD¹
2 GENTLE gentle: *She gave him a soft kiss.*
3 SKIN/FUR smooth and pleasant to touch OPP rough: *soft skin* | *a cat with lovely soft fur*
4 QUIET soft sounds are quiet OPP loud, harsh: *Her voice was softer now.* THESAURUS QUIET
5 COLOURS/LIGHTS soft colours or lights are not too bright OPP bright: *Soft lighting is much more romantic.*
6 NOT STRICT *informal* someone who is soft does not treat people severely enough when they have done something wrong OPP strict, tough: *[+on] The government does not want to seem soft on crime.*
7 TOO EASY *informal* a soft job or punishment does not involve hard work or difficulties: *Some people see this course as a soft option.*
8 SILLY *BrE informal* stupid or silly: *Don't be so soft!*
9 DRUGS soft drugs are illegal drugs that are considered to be less harmful than some other drugs

10 WATER soft water makes a lot of bubbles when you use soap —**softness** n [U]

PHRASES

have a soft spot for sb informal to like someone: *She's always had a soft spot for Chris.*

a soft touch informal someone whom you can easily control, especially someone from whom you can easily get money: *We always considered Uncle Jack to be rather a soft touch.*

THESAURUS

soft not hard, firm, or stiff, but easy to press: *She lay down in her soft, warm bed. | soft skin*

tender soft and easy to cut – used about cooked meat and vegetables: *Cook the carrots until tender. | a tender steak*

soggy soft and wet in an unpleasant way: *a soggy mass of fallen leaves*

---

softball /'sɒftbɔːl $ 'sɔːftbɒːl/ n **1** [U] a game like baseball, played with a larger and softer ball **2** [C] the ball used to play this game

'soft drink n [C] a cold drink that does not contain alcohol

soften /'sɒfən $ 'sɒː-/ v [I,T] **1** to become softer, or to make something softer OPP **harden**: *Cook the onion until it has softened.* **2** to become less severe and more gentle, or to make something do this OPP **harden**: *The government has softened its stance on this. | sb's face/voice softens His voice softened as he spoke to her.*

PHRASES

soften the blow to make something seem less unpleasant: *If you have bad news to tell someone, try to find a way to soften the blow.*

PHRASAL VERBS

soften sb ↔ up to be nice to someone so that they will do something for you

softhearted /ˌsɒftˈhɑːtɪd◂ $ ˌsɔːftˈhɑːr-/ adj kind and sympathetic

softie, softy /'sɒfti $ 'sɔːf-/ n [C] (plural **softies**) informal someone who is very kind, or who is easily persuaded: *He's just a big softie really.*

softly /'sɒftli $ 'sɔːftli/ adv quietly or gently: *She spoke softly, so that the baby did not wake.*

soft-'spoken adj especially AmE (also **softly 'spoken** BrE) having a quiet pleasant voice

software /'sɒftweə $ 'sɔːftwer/ n [U] computer programs → **hardware**: *a piece of software | software companies/development/packages etc*

softy /'sɒfti $ 'sɔːf-/ n (plural **softies**) another spelling of SOFTIE

soggy /'sɒgi $ 'sɑːgi/ adj wet, soft, and unpleasant: *The pie was all soggy.* THESAURUS ► **WET**

soil¹ /sɔɪl/ n [C,U] the earth in which plants grow SYN **earth**: *The soil here is very poor. | rich, fertile soil | plants that grow in sandy soil →* see picture at PLANT¹ THESAURUS ► **GROUND**

PHRASES

on American/French/foreign etc soil in America, France etc: *She stood on Irish soil for the first time.*

soil² v [T] formal to make something dirty —**soiled** adj: *soiled diapers*

solace /'sɒlɪs $ 'sɑː-/ n [U] formal comfort or happiness after you have been very sad or upset: *After the death of her son, Val found solace in the church. | Mary was a great solace to me after Arthur died.*

solar /'səʊlə $ 'soʊlər/ adj **1** relating to the sun → **lunar**: *a solar eclipse* **2** relating to energy obtained from sunlight: *solar energy/power | solar panels* (=equipment that gets energy from sunlight)

'solar ˌsystem n **the solar system** the Sun and all the PLANETs that move around it

sold /səʊld $ soʊld/ v the past tense and past participle of SELL

solder /'sɒldə, 'səʊl- $ 'sɑːdər/ v [T] to join metal surfaces together using melted metal

soldier¹ /'səʊldʒə $ 'soʊldʒər/ n [C] a member of the army, especially someone who is not an officer → **troop**

soldier² v

PHRASAL VERBS

soldier on to continue doing something in spite of difficulties: *He wasn't enjoying the course, but he soldiered on.*

ˌsold 'out adj if a concert, film etc is sold out, all the tickets have been sold

sole¹ Ac /səʊl $ soʊl/ adj **1** only: *He was the sole survivor of the crash. | The story was published for the sole purpose of selling newspapers.* **2** not shared with anyone else: *The women were forced to take sole responsibility for their children.*

sole² n **1** [C] the bottom surface of your foot or shoe → see picture at SHOE¹ **2** [C,U] a flat fish that you can eat

solely Ac /'səʊl-li $ 'soʊl-/ adv only: *Grants are awarded solely on the basis of need.*

solemn /'sɒləm $ 'sɑː-/ adj **1** serious and slightly sad: *His face grew solemn. | a solemn ceremony | solemn music* **2** [only before noun] a solemn promise is a promise that you will definitely keep —**solemnly** adv

solicit /sə'lɪsɪt/ v formal **1** [I,T] to ask someone for money, help, or information **2** [I] to offer to have sex with someone for money: *She was arrested for soliciting.*

solicitor /sə'lɪsɪtə $ -ər/ n [C] a lawyer in Britain who gives legal advice and works in the lower law courts → **barrister**, **lawyer**

solicitous /sə'lɪsɪtəs/ adj formal careful to make someone happy or comfortable

solid¹ /'sɒlɪd $ 'sɑː-/ adj

1 HARD/FIRM hard or firm, with a fixed shape, and not hollow: *solid rock | The milk was frozen solid.*

2 STRONG strong and well-made: *a good, solid chair*

3 METAL/WOOD **solid gold/silver/oak etc** completely made of gold etc → **pure**: *a solid gold necklace*

4 WITH NO SPACES/PAUSES continuous, without any spaces or pauses: *a solid white line | She didn't talk to me for three solid weeks.*

5 INFORMATION solid information is definitely correct: *We need solid evidence.*

6 HONEST someone who is solid is honest and can be trusted to do the right thing: *He seems very solid.* | *a firm with a solid reputation*

7 PERFORMANCE/ACHIEVEMENT a solid achievement or performance is very good: *It was a solid performance.* —**solidly** *adv*

PHRASES

on solid ground not likely to be criticized, damaged, or upset: *Legally the company is on solid ground.*

solid² *n* [C] **1** an object or substance that has a firm shape: *Water is a liquid and wood is a solid.* **2 solids** [plural] food that is not liquid: *He's still too ill to eat solids.* **3** *technical* a shape that has length, width, and height

solidarity /ˌsɒlɪˈdærəti $ ˌsɑː-/ *n* [U] support and agreement among people who share the same aim or opinions: *We are striking to show solidarity with the nurses.*

solidify /səˈlɪdɪfaɪ/ *v* [I,T] (**solidified, solidifying, solidifies**) to become solid, or to make a substance become solid

soliloquy /səˈlɪləkwi/ *n* [C] (*plural* **soliloquies**) a long speech made by an actor who is alone on the stage

solitaire /ˌsɒləˈteə $ ˈsɑːləter/ *n* [U] **1** a single jewel, or a piece of jewellery with a single jewel in it **2** *AmE* a card game for one player SYN **patience** *BrE* **3** a game for one player, in which you move small pieces around a board

solitary /ˈsɒlətəri $ ˈsɑːləteri/ *adj* **1** [only before noun] a solitary person or thing is the only one: *A solitary tree grew on the hilltop.* **2** a solitary activity is something that you do alone: *a long solitary walk* **3** solitary people and animals spend a lot of time alone

solitary con'finement *n* [U] a punishment in which a prisoner is kept alone

solitude /ˈsɒlɪtjuːd $ ˈsɑːlɪtuːd/ *n* [U] when you are alone, especially if you enjoy it: *She enjoyed the silence and solitude.*

solo¹ /ˈsəʊləʊ $ ˈsoʊloʊ/ *adj* **1** performed by one musician, rather than by a group: *I don't really like his solo album.* **2** done alone, without anyone else helping you: *his first solo flight* —**solo** *adv*

solo² *n* [C] (*plural* **solos**) a piece of music for one performer

soloist /ˈsəʊləʊɪst $ ˈsoʊloʊ-/ *n* [C] a musician who performs a solo

solstice /ˈsɒlstɪs $ ˈsɑːl-/ *n* [C] the longest or the shortest day of the year: *the summer/winter solstice*

soluble /ˈsɒljəbəl $ ˈsɑː-/ *adj* a soluble substance can DISSOLVE in liquid

solution /səˈluːʃən/ *n* [C]
1 a way of solving a problem or dealing with a difficult situation SYN **answer** → **solve**: [+to] *the perfect solution to all our problems* | *It was the ideal solution.* | *The only solution was to move into a quieter apartment.*

Grammar
Do not say 'They found the solution of the problem.' Say *They found the solution to the problem.*

2 the correct answer to a question → **solve**: *The solution to the puzzle is on page 14.*
3 a liquid in which a solid or a gas has been DISSOLVED: *a weak sugar solution*

solve /sɒlv $ sɑːlv/ *v* [T]
1 to find a way of dealing with a problem → **solution**: *Charlie thinks money will solve all his problems.* THESAURUS **DEAL**
2 to find the correct answer to a problem or the explanation for something that is difficult to understand → **solution**: **solve a mystery/crime/case** *Police are under great pressure to solve the case quickly.* | **solve an equation/puzzle/riddle**

solvent¹ /ˈsɒlvənt $ ˈsɑːl-/ *adj* someone who is solvent has enough money to pay their debts OPP **insolvent** —**solvency** *n* [U]

solvent² *n* [C,U] a chemical that is used to DISSOLVE another substance

'solvent a,buse *n* [U] when someone deliberately breathes in dangerous gases from glue or other substances for pleasure

sombre *BrE*, **somber** *AmE* /ˈsɒmbə $ ˈsɑːmbər/ *adj* **1** sad and serious: *a sombre mood* **2** dark or without any bright colours: *a somber room*

some¹ /səm; *strong* sʌm/ *determiner, pron*
1 an amount of something or a number of things, when you are not saying how much or how many: *Do you want some coffee?* | *I've made a cake; would you like some?* | *There were some children playing in the street.*
2 a number of people or things, but not most or all of them: *Most of the children enjoyed the film, but some didn't.* | *Some days, I just can't get out of bed.* | [+of] *Some of the roads were closed because of snow.*
3 some time/days/weeks etc quite a long time: *It was some time before the police finally arrived.*
4 used to talk about a person or thing without being specific: *I read about it in some magazine.* | **For some reason or other** (=it is not certain why) *he wasn't at work that day.*

Usage:
You use **some** in questions when you think the answer will be 'yes': *Would you like some coffee?* You use **any** when you do not know what the answer will be: *Were there any letters for me?*

some² *adv* **1 some 10 people/some 50%/some $600** about 10 people, about 50% etc: *Some 700 homes were damaged by the storm.* **2 some more** an additional number or amount of something: *Would you like some more cake?* **3** *AmE spoken* a little: *'Are you feeling better today?' 'Some, I guess.'*

somebody /ˈsʌmbɒdi, -bədi $ -bɑːdi, -bədi/ *pron* used to mention a person without saying who the person is SYN **someone** → **anybody**: *I want somebody who can help me.* | *She told me to ask somebody else.*

S

someday /'sʌmdeɪ/ *adv* at an unknown time in the future: *Maybe someday I'll be rich!*

somehow /'sʌmhaʊ/ *adv*

1 in some way, although you do not know how: *Somehow, he managed to escape.* | *We'll get there somehow.* | *Maybe we could mend it **somehow or other** (=in some way).*

2 for some reason, but you are not sure why: *Somehow it seemed the right thing to do.* | *I don't trust him somehow.*

someone /'sʌmwʌn/ *pron* used to mention a person without saying who the person is SYN **somebody → anyone**: *I want someone who can help me.* | *She told me to ask **someone else**.*

> **Usage**
> In negative sentences and questions, you usually use **anyone**: *I didn't see anyone I knew.* | *Have you told anyone about this?*

someplace /'sʌmpleɪs/ *adv AmE* SOMEWHERE: *Let's go someplace else.*

somersault /'sʌməsɔːlt $ -ərsɒːlt/ *n* [C] a movement in which you roll and your feet go over your head before you stand up again —**somersault** *v* [I]

something /'sʌmθɪŋ/ *pron* used to mention a thing without saying what it is → **anything**: *She said something that I found very interesting.* | *Would you like something to drink?* | *There's **something else** I wanted to talk to you about.* | *I was afraid **something like** this would happen.* | *He said **something about** a party.* | *There was **something wrong**.* | *I wish they would **do something about** that noise.*

PHRASES

be (really) something used to say that a thing, action, person etc is impressive or unusual: *It's really something to see all those jets taking off together.*

have/be something to do with to be connected with a person, thing, or activity in a way that you are not sure about: *High-fat diets may have something to do with the disease.*

... or something *informal* used when you cannot remember or cannot be sure: *Maybe I cooked it too long or something.*

something like used when giving a number or amount that is not exact: *It will take something like four hours.*

that's something *spoken* used to say that there is one thing that you should be glad about, even if everything else is wrong: *At least we've got some money left – that's something.*

there's something in ... used to admit that an idea is worth considering: *There's something in what you say.*

> **Usage**
> In questions and negative sentences, you usually use **anything**: *Is there anything else you wanted to talk about?* | *I don't know anything about computers.*
> However, when you are offering someone some food or drink, you often say: *Would you like something to eat/drink?*

sometime¹ /'sʌmtaɪm/ *adv* at an unknown time in the past or future: *I'll call you sometime next week.* | **[+in/during/after etc]** *Work will start sometime in July.*

sometime² *adj* [only before noun] **1** *formal* former: *a former governor and sometime presidential candidate* **2** *AmE* used to say that someone does something part of the time, but not always: *a gifted writer who has been my friend and sometime co-author for many years*

sometimes /'sʌmtaɪmz/ *adv* on some occasions, but not always: *Sometimes I don't get home until 9:00 at night.* | *'Do you miss your old school?' 'Sometimes.'*

> **THESAURUS**
> **sometimes** on some occasions but not always: *I sometimes walk to school.*
> **occasionally** used when something only happens a few times. You use **occasionally** when something happens more rarely than **sometimes**: *Tom's my cousin, but I only see him occasionally.*
> **every now and then/again** (*also* **every once in a while**) sometimes, but not often or regularly – used when there is a long period of time between each time something happens: *We still go out together every now and then.*
> **at times** sometimes, but not usually: *At times, the job can be difficult.*

somewhat Ac /'sʌmwɒt $ -wɑːt/ *adv* slightly, but not very much: *I was somewhat annoyed.* | *Things have changed somewhat.* THESAURUS ► RATHER

somewhere /'sʌmweə $ -wer/ (*also* **someplace** *AmE*) *adv* in or to a place, although you do not say exactly where → **anywhere**: *Go and play **somewhere else** – I'm trying to work.* | *The hotel's around here somewhere.* | *Let's find somewhere to eat.*

PHRASES

be getting somewhere to be making progress: *At last we're getting somewhere!*

somewhere along the line/way at some time: *Somewhere along the line they lost control.*

somewhere around/between etc sth used when stating an amount which is not exact SYN **approximately**: *It cost somewhere around $500.*

> **Usage**
> In questions and negative sentences, you usually use **anywhere**: *Have you seen my keys anywhere?* | *I haven't been anywhere very exciting.*

son /sʌn/ *n* [C]

1 someone's male child → **daughter**: *his/my etc son Her son was born in 1990.* | **the son of** *He was the son of a Welsh farmer.* | *She had two daughters and one son.*

2 used by an older person when they are speaking to a boy in a friendly way: *What's your name, son?*

sonata /sə'nɑːtə/ *n* [C] a piece of music written for a piano or for another instrument with a piano

song /sɒŋ $ sɒːŋ/ *n*

1 [C] a short piece of music with words: *Sing us a song.*

2 [U] songs in general: *a celebration of music, song and dance*
3 [C,U] the musical sounds made by birds: *the song of the blackbird*

PHRASES

burst/break into song to start singing: *The crowd burst into song.*

make a song and dance (about sth) if you make a song and dance about something, you say that it is very serious when it is not: *Surely he has better things to do than making a big song and dance about missing a dinner party?*

COLLOCATIONS

verbs

to sing a song *They sang songs to pass the time.*
to play a song *We're going to play a new song now.*
to write a song *The song was written by Bob Dylan.*

adjectives

a good/great/lovely song *That's a great song!*
an old/new song *The old songs are the best.*
a little song *He sang a happy little song.*
a sad/happy song *The song was so sad that I almost cried.*

noun + song

a pop song *I love all those 1960s pop songs.*
a folk song (=a traditional song) *They sang Russian folk songs.*
a love song *He is releasing an album of love songs for Valentine's Day.*
a Beatles/Madonna etc song *What's your favourite Beatles song?*

songwriter /ˈsɒŋˌraɪtə $ ˈsɒːŋˌraɪtər/ *n* [C] a person who writes songs

sonic /ˈsɒnɪk $ ˈsɑː-/ *adj technical* relating to sound

'son-in-law *n* [C] (*plural* **sons-in-law**) your daughter's husband

sonnet /ˈsɒnɪt $ ˈsɑː-/ *n* [C] a poem with 14 lines that RHYME with each other in a fixed pattern

sonorous /ˈsɒnərəs, səˈnɔːrəs $ səˈnɔːrəs, ˈsɑːnərəs/ *adj* a sonorous voice is deep and pleasantly loud

soon /suːn/ *adv* in a short time from now, or after a short time: *It will be dark soon.* | *Soon afterwards he realized his mistake.* | *I'll get it fixed as soon as possible.* | *How soon can you get here?*

PHRASES

as soon as immediately after something has happened: *I came as soon as I heard the news.*
I would sooner/I would just as soon ... used when you are saying what you would prefer to happen: *I'd just as soon stay in and watch TV.*
no sooner had ... than used to say that something happened immediately after something else: *No sooner had I stepped in the shower than the phone rang.*
sooner or later used to say that something will definitely happen but you are not sure when: *He's bound to find out sooner or later.*

the sooner (...) the better used to say that something should happen as quickly as possible: *The sooner we get this job finished the better.*
too soon too early: *It's too soon to say what will happen.*

THESAURUS

soon in a short time from now, or after a short time: *Speak to you soon!* | *I sat down and Katrina soon joined me.*
in the near future in the next few weeks or months. **In the near future** is more formal than **soon**: *The company plans to move its offices in the near future.*
shortly soon – used especially about something that you know will happen soon. **Shortly** is more formal than **soon**: *We will shortly be landing at Heathrow.*
in a minute *spoken* in a few minutes: *I'll be back in a minute.* | *The news will be on in a minute.*
any minute now *spoken* very soon – used especially when you are waiting for someone to arrive or something to happen: *They should be here any minute now.* | *The game will start any minute now.*
before long soon – used especially when something happens that you expected to happen: *I caught the waiter's eye and before long the drinks arrived.*

soot /sʊt/ *n* [U] black powder that is produced when something burns —**sooty** *adj*

soothe /suːð/ *v* [T] **1** to make someone feel calmer and less worried or upset: *He poured himself a drink to soothe his nerves.* **2** to make something less painful: *bath oil to soothe aching muscles* —**soothing** *adj*: *her soothing voice*

sophisticated /səˈfɪstɪkeɪtɪd/ *adj* **1** having a lot of experience of life, or knowledge about a subject: *a play for a sophisticated audience* | *today's more sophisticated investors* **2** a sophisticated machine or system is designed in a very clever way: *highly sophisticated weapons* —**sophistication** /səˌfɪstɪˈkeɪʃən/ *n* [U]

sophomore /ˈsɒfəmɔː $ ˈsɑːfəmɔːr/ *n* [C] *AmE* a student in the second year of HIGH SCHOOL or college

soporific /ˌsɒpəˈrɪfɪk $ ˌsɑː-/ *adj formal* making you feel ready to sleep

sopping /ˈsɒpɪŋ $ ˈsɑː-/ (*also* ˌsopping 'wet) *adj* very wet

soppy /ˈsɒpi $ ˈsɑːpi/ *adj BrE informal* expressing sadness or love in a way that seems silly SYN **sappy** *AmE*: *a soppy film*

soprano /səˈprɑːnəʊ $ -ˈprænoʊ/ *n* [C] (*plural* **sopranos**) a woman, girl, or young boy singer with a very high voice

sorbet /ˈsɔːbeɪ $ ˈsɔːrbɪt/ *n* [C,U] a sweet frozen food made from fruit juice, sugar, and water

sorcerer /ˈsɔːsərə $ ˈsɔːrsərər/ *n* [C] a person in stories who uses magic SYN **wizard**

sorcery /ˈsɔːsəri $ ˈsɔːr-/ *n* [U] magic, especially evil magic

sordid /ˈsɔːdɪd $ ˈsɔːr-/ adj **1** involving dishonest behaviour: all the **sordid details** of the scandal **2** a sordid place is dirty and unpleasant: a sordid hotel room

sore¹ /sɔː $ sɔːr/ adj a part of your body that is sore is painful: I've got a **sore throat** (=usually because of an illness). | [**+from**] Her fingers were sore from the cold. **THESAURUS** ▶ PAINFUL —**soreness** n [U]

PHRASES
sore point/spot (with sb) something that is likely to make someone upset or angry: Don't mention marriage – it's a sore point with him.

stand/stick out like a sore thumb to be very noticeable because of being very different from everyone or everything else: Being very tall, I always stuck out like a sore thumb in school photographs.

sore² n [C] a painful place on your body where your skin or a cut is infected

sorely /ˈsɔːli $ ˈsɔːrli/ adv very much: **sorely missed/ needed/tempted** I was sorely tempted to hit him.

sorority /səˈrɒrəti $ səˈrɔːr-/ n [C] (plural **sororities**) a club for women students at some American colleges and universities → **fraternity**

sorrow /ˈsɒrəʊ $ ˈsɑːroʊ, ˈsɔː-/ n [C,U] a feeling of great sadness, or an event that makes you feel very sad: a time of **great sorrow** | the joys and sorrows of family life —**sorrowful** adj

sorry /ˈsɒri $ ˈsɑːri, ˈsɔːri/ adj
1 sorry/I'm sorry spoken **a)** used to tell someone that you feel bad about doing something that has upset them, annoyed them etc: I'm sorry if I was rude. | [**+about**] Sorry about the mess! | [**+(that)**] I'm sorry I'm late. | **sorry for (doing) sth** Sorry for waking you up. | **Sorry to bother you**, but what's the address again? **b)** used when politely saying something disappointing, or disagreeing with someone: I'm sorry, but all the flights are booked. | 'Can I borrow the car?' 'Sorry, I'm using it myself.' | I'm sorry, I think you're wrong. **c)** used when correcting what you have just said: Turn right – sorry, left.
2 [not before noun] feeling sad about a situation and wishing it were different: [**+for**] She was sorry for what she had done. | [**+(that)**] Casey was sorry he'd been so angry with the kids. | **sorry to do sth** I was very **sorry to hear** about your accident. **THESAURUS** ▶ DISAPPOINTED
3 [only before noun] bad: The old house was **in a sorry state**.
4 sorry? especially BrE used to ask someone to repeat what they have just said because you did not hear it properly $\boxed{SYN}$ **pardon**

PHRASES
be/feel sorry for sb to feel sadness and sympathy for someone who has problems: He was lonely and I felt sorry for him. | Stop **feeling sorry for yourself** and do something!

sort¹ /sɔːt $ sɔːrt/ n
1 [C] a type or kind of something: [**+of**] What sort of work does he do? | There are many **different sorts** of mushrooms. | **all sorts (of sth)** (=a lot of different types) I like rock, jazz – all sorts of music. | On expeditions **of this sort** you must be well prepared.
2 [singular] if a computer does a sort, it arranges a list of things in order

PHRASES
of sorts/of a sort disapproving used to say that something is not very good: He's written an essay – of sorts.
sort of spoken used when what you are saying or describing is not very definite or exact: 'Do you like him then?' 'Sort of.' | The walls are sort of greeny-blue. | It was sort of a shock when I found out.

sort² v [T]
1 to put things in a particular order, or arrange them into groups: Eggs are **sorted according to** size. | **sort sth into sth** Our names were sorted into alphabetical order.
2 BrE spoken to deal with a situation so that there are no more problems and everything is organized: Don't worry, Jim'll **sort it**. | I want to **get** everything **sorted** before I go.

PHRASAL VERBS
sort sth ↔ **out**
1 to organize something that is untidy or in the wrong order: I must sort out my desk.
2 if you sort out a problem, you deal with it: It's a mistake – I'll sort it out and call you back.
sort through sth to look at a lot of things in order to find something or arrange things in order: We sorted through all his papers after he died.

sortie /ˈsɔːti $ ˈsɔːrti/ n [C] a short trip to find out what a place is like or to make an attack: The Tornado crashed on a sortie over Iraq.

SOS /ˌes əʊ ˈes $ -oʊ-/ n [singular] a signal used to call for help when a ship, plane, or person is in danger

so-so adj, adv spoken not very good

soufflé /ˈsuːfleɪ $ suːˈfleɪ/ n [C,U] a light food made from the white part of an egg and baked

sought /sɔːt $ sɔːt/ v the past tense and past participle of SEEK

sought-after adj wanted by a lot of people, but difficult to get: Her paintings are **highly sought-after**.

soul /səʊl $ soʊl/ n **1** [C] the part of a person which many people believe continues to exist after you die $\boxed{SYN}$ **spirit**: the inner areas of the **mind and soul 2** [C] a person: **not a soul** (=no one) Don't tell a soul! **3** (also **soul music**) [U] a type of popular music which often expresses strong emotions, usually performed by black singers and musicians

soulful /ˈsəʊlfəl $ ˈsoʊl-/ adj expressing strong sad emotions: a soulful song

soulless /ˈsəʊl-ləs $ ˈsoʊl-/ adj a soulless place has no interesting or attractive qualities

soul-searching n [U] careful thought about your feelings when you are not sure what is the right thing to do: After much soul-searching, I decided to resign.

sound¹ /saʊnd/ n
1 [C,U] something that you can hear: [**+of**] She could hear the sound of voices.
2 [U] the voices, music etc that come from a television, radio, film etc: **good/poor sound quality** (=clear or unclear sound) A hi-fi like this gives better sound quality. | **turn the sound down/up** (=make it quieter or louder)

PHRASES

by/from the sound of it/things *spoken* judging from what you have been told or have read about something: *It's a computer error, by the sound of it.*

not like the sound of sth to be worried about something that you have heard or read: *A teachers' strike? I don't like the sound of that.*

COLLOCATIONS

verbs

to hear a sound *She heard a sound behind her.*

to make a sound *Her shoes made a crunching sound on the gravel.*

a sound comes from somewhere *The sounds were coming from the bathroom.*

adjectives

a loud sound *There was a loud crashing sound.* ⚠ Do not say 'a strong sound'. Say **a loud sound.**

a faint/soft sound (=not loud) *From far away came the faint sound of music.*

a strange sound *The strange sounds of the jungle kept us awake.*

a banging/rustling/hissing etc sound *What's that clicking sound?*

sound² *v*

1 [linking verb] if someone or something sounds strange, interesting etc, they seem like that to you from what you have been told: *Your holiday sounds great.* | [+like] *Lou sounds like a nice guy.* | **it sounds as if/as though/like** *It sounds as if he's doing well at school.* **THESAURUS** SEEM

2 [linking verb] if someone sounds tired, upset etc, or if something sounds loud, strange etc, they seem like that to you when you hear them: *You sound tired. Are you OK?* | *Her breathing sounded steady.* | **sound as if/as though/like** *The noise sounded as if it was coming from next door.*

3 [I,T] if something such as a bell sounds, or if you sound it, it makes a noise as a signal: [+for] *A whistle sounded for half time.*

PHRASAL VERBS

sound off to complain angrily about something: [+about] *She was sounding off about the poor rail service.*

sound sb ↔ **out** to talk to someone in order to find out what they think about a plan or idea: *Why don't you sound her out about the job?*

sound³ *adj* **1** sensible and likely to produce good results: *Our helpline offers **sound advice** to new parents.* **2** complete and thorough: *a sound knowledge of English* **3** in good condition: *The roof leaks, but the floors are sound.*

sound⁴ *adv* **be sound asleep** to be completely asleep

'sound ,barrier *n* **the sound barrier** the point at which an aircraft reaches the speed of sound

'sound bite *n* [C] a short phrase that is easy to remember, especially one said by a politician

'sound ef,fects *n* [plural] the sounds produced artificially for a film, radio programme etc

soundings /'saʊndɪŋz/ *n* **take soundings** to ask

what people's opinion of something is, in a private and unofficial way

soundly /'saʊndli/ *adv* **1** completely or severely: *Our team was **soundly defeated.*** **2 sleep soundly** to sleep well without waking up: *Within seconds Maggie was sleeping soundly.* **3** in a strong way: *Their relationship is **soundly based.***

soundproof /'saʊndpruːf/ *adj* a soundproof wall, room etc does not allow sound to pass through it or into it —**soundproof** *v* [T]

'sound ,system *n* [C] a piece of equipment for playing music

soundtrack /'saʊndtræk/ *n* [C] the recorded music from a film

soup /suːp/ *n* [C,U] liquid food that usually has pieces of meat or vegetables in it: *tomato soup*

'soup ,kitchen *n* [C] a place where poor people are given free food

sour /saʊə $ saʊr/ *adj*

1 having an acid taste, like the taste of a LEMON **OPP** sweet → **bitter**: *sour green apples* **THESAURUS** TASTE

2 milk or other food that is sour is not fresh and has a bad taste and smell: *The milk has **gone sour.***

3 looking unfriendly and angry: **sour look/face/smile etc** *The waiter had a really sour expression.* —**sourly** *adv* —**sour** *v* [I,T]

PHRASES

go/turn sour *informal* if a relationship or situation goes sour, it becomes less enjoyable or is no longer what you want: *As time went on, their marriage turned sour.*

sour grapes *disapproving* used to say that someone is only pretending to dislike something because they cannot have it: *You may think this is sour grapes because I didn't get the job.*

source¹ Ac /sɔːs $ sɔːrs/ *n* [C] **1** the thing, place, or person that you get something from: [+of] *Tourism is our **main source** of income.* | **energy/information/food source** *a new energy source* **THESAURUS** ORIGIN **2** the cause of a problem, or the place where it starts: [+of] *Engineers have found the source of the trouble.* **3** a person, book, or document that you get information from: *Reliable sources say the company's in trouble.* **4** the place where a stream or river starts

source² Ac *v* [T] *technical* if something is sourced from a particular place, it is obtained from that place

south¹, **South** /saʊθ/ *n* [singular, U] (*written abbreviation* **S**)

1 the direction towards the bottom of a map: *Which way is south?* | **from/towards the south** *The army was approaching from the south.* | **to the south (of sth)** *Sandy beaches lie to the south.*

2 the south the southern part of a country or area: [+of] *the south of France*

south², **South** *adj* [only before noun] (*written abbreviation* **S**)

1 in the south or facing the south: *a village on the south coast* | *south Texas*

2 a south wind comes from the south

south³ adv (written abbreviation **S**) towards the south: *Most of the birds had already flown south.* | [+of] *a town 20 km south of London*

PHRASES

down south 1 BrE informal in or to the southern part of England: *They live down south near Brighton.* **2** (also **down South**) AmE in or to the southern US states: *His sister lives down south.*

southbound /'saʊθbaʊnd/ adj travelling or leading towards the south: *southbound traffic*

southeast¹, Southeast /ˌsaʊθˈiːst◂/ n [U] (written abbreviation **SE**) **1** the direction that is exactly between south and east **2 the southeast** the southeastern part of a country —**southeast** adv: *We continued southeast to Kells.*

southeast², Southeast adj [only before noun] (written abbreviation **SE**) **1** a southeast wind comes from the southeast **2** in the southeast of a place: *the southeast quarter of the city*

southeasterly /ˌsaʊθˈiːstəli $ -ər-/ adj **1** towards or in the southeast: *They set off in a southeasterly direction.* **2** a southeasterly wind comes from the southeast

southeastern /ˌsaʊθˈiːstən $ -ərn/ adj (written abbreviation **SE**) in or from the southeast part of a country or area: *southeastern Europe*

southerly /'sʌðəli $ -ər-/ adj **1** towards or in the south: *Keep going in a southerly direction.* **2** a southerly wind comes from the south

southern, Southern /'sʌðən $ -ərn/ adj (written abbreviation **S**) in or to the south of a country or area: *Southern Italy* | *a southern accent*

southerner, Southerner /'sʌðənə $ -ərnər/ n [C] someone from the southern part of a country

southernmost /'sʌðənməʊst $ -ərnmoʊst/ adj furthest south: *the southernmost tip of India*

South 'Pole n **the South Pole** the most southern point on the surface of the Earth → **North Pole** → see picture at **GLOBE**

southwards /'saʊθwədz $ -wərdz/ (also **southward** /'saʊθwəd $ -wərd/ adv towards the south: *We followed the coast southwards.* —**southward** adj: *the southward route to Charlestown*

southwest¹, Southwest /ˌsaʊθˈwest◂/ n [U] (written abbreviation **SW**) **1** the direction that is exactly between south and west **2 the southwest** the southwestern part of a country —**southwest** adv: *The plane flew southwest toward Egypt.*

southwest², Southwest adj [only before noun] (written abbreviation **SW**) **1** a southwest wind comes from the southwest **2** in the southwest of a place: *the southwest corner of France*

southwesterly /ˌsaʊθˈwestəli $ -ərli/ adj **1** towards or in the southwest: *They set off in a southwesterly direction.* **2** a southwesterly wind comes from the southwest

southwestern /ˌsaʊθˈwestən $ -ərn/ adj (written abbreviation **SW**) in or from the southwest part of a country or area: *southwestern Colorado*

souvenir /ˌsuːvəˈnɪə, 'suːvənɪə $ -nɪr/ n [C] an object that you keep to remind yourself of a special occasion or place that you have visited **SYN** memento: [+of] *a souvenir of Paris*

sovereign¹ /'sɒvrɪn $ 'sɑːv-/ adj a sovereign country or state is independent and governs itself —**sovereignty** n [U]

sovereign² n [C] formal a king or queen

Soviet /'səʊviət, 'sɒ- $ 'soʊ-, 'sɑː-/ adj relating to the former USSR (Soviet Union)

sow¹ /səʊ $ soʊ/ v [I,T] (past tense **sowed**, past participle **sown** /səʊn $ soʊn/ or **sowed**) to plant seeds in the ground: *Sow the seeds in early spring.*

sow² /saʊ/ n [C] a female pig

'soya bean /'sɔɪə biːn/ (also **soybean** /'sɔɪbiːn/) n [C] a bean that is often used in making other foods

,soy 'sauce /ˌsɔɪ 'sɔːs $ 'sɔɪ sɔːs/ n [U] a dark brown sauce used especially in Chinese cooking

spa /spɑː/ n [C] **1** a place where the water has special minerals in it. People go there to improve their health by drinking the water or swimming in it **2** (also **health spa**) a place where people go to exercise or have beauty treatments

space¹ /speɪs/ n
1 a) [C] an area that is empty or available to be used: [+for] *There's a space for the table here.* | *Write your name in this space.* | *a plan for 700 more parking spaces* | *the city's open spaces* **b)** [U] the amount of an area that is empty or available to be used **SYN** room: *Is there any more space in the car?* | *How much space is there on the disk?* | *The cupboard takes up too much space.* | *storage/cupboard/shelf etc space 6,900 square feet of office space*
2 [U] the area beyond the Earth where the stars and PLANETS are: *in/into space Who was the first American in space?* | *space travel/research/exploration etc the US space programme*
3 [C usually singular] a period of time: *in the space of an hour/two weeks etc All this happened in the space of a few weeks.* | *There's been a lot of rain in a short space of time.*
4 [U] time and freedom to do what you want: *She needed space to sort out her life.* → **BREATHING SPACE**, **OUTER SPACE**

space² (also **space out**) v [T] to arrange objects, events etc so that they have an equal amount of space or time between them: *Space the plants four feet apart.*

spacecraft /'speɪskrɑːft $ -kræft/ n [C] (also **spaceship** /'speɪsʃɪp/) a vehicle that can travel in space

'space ,shuttle n [C] a spacecraft that can go into space and return to Earth several times

spacious /'speɪʃəs/ adj a spacious room, house etc is large inside

spade /speɪd/ n [C]
1 a tool that you use for digging, with a long handle and a wide flat part at the end → **shovel** → see picture at **GARDEN**
2 spades [plural] in card games, the cards with black shapes like pointed leaves on them: *the queen of spades* → see picture at **PLAYING CARD**

spaghetti /spəˈgeti/ n [U] long thin pieces of PASTA that look like strings

spam /spæm/ n [U] unwanted email messages, especially emails that advertise something **THESAURUS** ADVERTISEMENT

span¹ /spæn/ n [C] **1** a length of time in which something happens or continues: **within/in/over a span (of sth)** Can the project be completed within that time span? | The mayfly has a two-day **life span** (=lives for two days). | **attention/concentration span** (=how long you can pay attention to something) **2** the distance from one side of something to the other: a bird with a large **wing span**

span² v [T] (**spanned, spanning**) **1** to include all of a period of time: a career which spanned 45 years **2** to go from one side of something to the other: a bridge spanning the river

spank /spæŋk/ v [T] to hit a child on the bottom with your open hand **THESAURUS** HIT

spanner /ˈspænə $ -ər/ n [C] BrE a tool used for turning NUTS (=small metal rings that fasten things together) SYN **wrench** AmE → see picture at TOOL

spare¹ /speə $ sper/ adj
1 spare key/tyre etc an extra key, tyre etc that you have so that it is available if it is needed: Leave a spare key with a neighbour. | Don't forget to take spare clothes. **THESAURUS** MORE
2 not being used and therefore available: We haven't much spare cash for holidays. | the spare bedroom
3 spare time/moment/hour etc time when you are not working: I play tennis in my spare time.

spare² v [T] **1** to let someone have or use something, because you do not need it: **spare sb sth** Can you spare me £5? | I'm sorry, I **can't spare the time** (=have not enough time to do something). **2** to prevent someone from having to do something difficult or unpleasant: **spare sb the trouble/difficulty/pain etc (of doing sth)** I wanted to spare you the trouble of picking me up. **3** to not damage or harm someone or something: The children's **lives** were **spared**.

PHRASES
  money/time etc to spare if you have money, time etc to spare, you have plenty or enough of it: We need volunteers with a few hours to spare each week.
  spare no expense/effort to spend a lot of money, time etc on something in order to make it a success: No effort was spared to find them.

spare³ n [C] an extra key, tyre etc that you have so that it is available if it is needed

sparingly /ˈspeərɪŋli $ ˈsper-/ adv if you use something sparingly, you use only a little of it —**sparing** adj

spark¹ /spɑːk $ spɑːrk/ n [C] **1** a very small piece of burning material, especially from a fire **2** a flash of light caused by electricity **3 spark of interest/intelligence/humour etc** a small amount of a good feeling or quality

spark² (also **spark off**) v [T] to make something start happening: The speech sparked off riots.

sparkle /ˈspɑːkəl $ ˈspɑːr-/ v [I] to shine with small bright flashes **THESAURUS** SHINE —**sparkle** n [C,U]

sparkling /ˈspɑːklɪŋ $ ˈspɑːr-/ adj a sparkling drink has bubbles of gas in it SYN **fizzy**: sparkling wine

'spark plug n [C] a part in a car engine that makes the petrol start burning

sparrow /ˈspærəʊ $ -roʊ/ n [C] a common small brown or grey bird

sparse /spɑːs $ spɑːrs/ adj existing only in small amounts, and often spread over a large area: sparse vegetation —**sparsely** adv

spartan /ˈspɑːtn $ -ɑːr-/ adj very simple and often uncomfortable: spartan living **conditions**

spasm /ˈspæzəm/ n [C,U] a movement that you cannot control in which your muscles suddenly become tight and painful: back spasms

spasmodic /spæzˈmɒdɪk $ -ˈmɑː-/ adj happening for short periods of time but not regularly or continuously: spasmodic efforts to stop smoking —**spasmodically** /-kli/ adv

spat /spæt/ v the past tense and past participle of SPIT

spate /speɪt/ n **a spate of sth** a large number of similar, usually bad things that happen in a short period of time: a spate of burglaries

spatial /ˈspeɪʃəl/ adj technical relating to the position, size, or shape of things

spatter /ˈspætə $ -ər/ v [I,T] if a liquid spatters or if it is spattered somewhere, drops of it fall all over a surface: **spatter sb/sth with sth** The walls were spattered with blood.

spawn¹ /spɔːn $ spɒːn/ v **1** [T] to make a series of things happen or start to exist: The book 'Dracula' has spawned several movies. **2** [I,T] if a fish or FROG spawns, it lays a lot of eggs

spawn² n [U] the eggs of a fish or FROG

speak /spiːk/ v (past tense **spoke** /spəʊk $ spoʊk/, past participle **spoken** /ˈspəʊkən $ ˈspoʊ-/)
1 [I] to say something or talk to someone about something: For a minute, nobody spoke. | **[+to]** I'll speak to Mr Hunt, please? | 'Can I speak to Mr Hunt, please?' 'Yes, speaking (=used on the telephone).' | **[+about]** Have you spoken to Mike about this? | **[+with]** especially AmE: Who did you speak with? | **[+of]** formal: He never spoke of his first wife. **THESAURUS** TALK
2 [T] to be able to talk in a particular language: **speak English/French/Spanish etc** Do you speak Italian? | **French-speaking/Spanish-speaking etc** (=using French, Spanish etc as a language) French-speaking countries
3 [I] to make a formal speech to a group of people: I get nervous if I have to **speak in public**. | **[+on/about]** The Prime Minister was speaking on education.
4 [I] to say something that expresses your ideas and opinions: **speaking as a parent/teacher/friend etc** He was speaking as a policeman with 20 years' experience. | **generally/technically etc speaking** Generally speaking, boys are noisier than girls.

PHRASES
  no ... to speak of very little of something: They've no money to speak of.
  so to speak spoken used to say that the expression you have used does not have its most basic

meaning: *My parents live on our doorstep* (=very close), *so to speak.*

be speaking (to sb) (*also* **be on speaking terms (with sb)**) to be willing to talk to someone again after an argument: *I'm surprised she's speaking to you after that.* | *Dan and Jo still aren't on speaking terms.*

speak your mind to say exactly what you think: *She's not afraid to speak her mind.*

speaking of ... *spoken* used when you want to say more about someone or something that has just been mentioned: *Speaking of birthdays, when's yours?*

PHRASAL VERBS
speak for sb/sth
1 to express the feelings, thoughts etc of a person or group of people: *You'll be missed, and I know I'm speaking for all of us.*
2 speak for yourself *spoken* used to tell someone that something that may be true for them is not true for you: *'I think we're too old now.' 'Speak for yourself!'*
3 speak for itself to show something very clearly: *A school's exam results speak for themselves.*
4 be spoken for to be promised to someone else: *The puppies are already spoken for.*
speak out to say publicly what you think about something, especially as a protest: **[+against]** *People are afraid to speak out against the government.*
speak up
1 *spoken* used to ask someone to speak more loudly: *Could you speak up, please?*
2 to say publicly what you think about something: *If we don't speak up, nothing will be done.*

speaker /'spi:kə $ -ər/ n [C] **1** someone who makes a speech **2** someone who speaks a language: **French/German etc speaker 3** the part of a radio or other machine where the sound comes out

spear[1] /spɪə $ spɪr/ n [C] a long pointed weapon that you can throw

spear[2] v [T] to push something pointed such as a spear or fork into something: *He speared a piece of meat with his fork.*

spearhead /'spɪəhed $ 'spɪr-/ v [T] to lead an attack or an organized action: *an anti-smoking campaign spearheaded by the government*

spearmint /'spɪəmɪnt $ 'spɪr-/ n [U] a strong fresh taste used in sweets and TOOTHPASTE

special[1] /'speʃəl/ adj different from other things or people in some way and often better or more important: *a special friend* | *special facilities for disabled students* | **anything/something/nothing special** *I want to do something special for my birthday.* | *Tonight is a very* **special occasion.** | *This plant needs* **special attention.** | *He's got his* **own special** *chair.* | *We try to make every child* **feel special.**

special[2] n [C] **1** a single special television programme: *a two-hour special on the election campaign* **2** a meal or cheaper price that a restaurant offers for one day only: *today's special*

special ef'fects n [plural] pictures and sounds that are made for a film or television programme to make it seem as if something exciting or impossible is really happening

specialist /'speʃəlɪst/ n [C] someone who knows a lot about a subject: *a cancer specialist* | **[+in]** *a specialist in international banking* **THESAURUS EXPERT**

speciality /ˌspeʃiˈæləti/ BrE, **specialty** /'speʃəlti/ AmE n [C] (*plural* **specialities**) **1** a type of food that is made in a particular restaurant or area and is always very good there: *Fish is our speciality.* | **[+of]** *a speciality of this region* **2** a subject that you know a lot about: *His speciality is American literature.*

specialize (*also* **-ise** BrE) /'speʃəlaɪz/ v [I] to study mainly one subject or do mainly one activity: **[+in]** *a lawyer who specializes in divorce* —**specialization** /ˌspeʃəlaɪˈzeɪʃən $ -lə-/ n [C,U]

specialized (*also* **-ised** BrE) /'speʃəlaɪzd/ adj used or made for doing one particular thing: *specialized equipment*

specially /'speʃəli/ adv
1 for one particular purpose or person: **specially made/designed/built** *a plane that is specially designed for speed* | **[+for]** *I bought this specially for you.*
2 *spoken* much more than usual, or much more than other people or things **SYN especially**: *I specially liked the ice cream.* | *I got up specially early.*

special 'needs n [plural] needs that someone has because they have mental or physical problems: *children with special needs*

special 'offer n [C] a special low price that is charged for something for a short period of time

specialty /'speʃəlti/ n [C] (*plural* **specialties**) AmE a SPECIALITY

species /'spi:ʃi:z/ n [C] (*plural* **species**) a group of animals or plants of the same kind: **[+of]** *Three different species of deer live in the forest.*

specific Ac /spəˈsɪfɪk/ adj **1** [only before noun] a specific thing or person is one particular thing or person: *toys and games for this specific age group* | *Do you have any specific problems?* **2** detailed and exact: *He gave us specific instructions.* | **[+about]** *Can you be more specific about what you're looking for?*

specifically Ac /spəˈsɪfɪkli/ adv **1** for one particular type of person or thing: *a campaign specifically aimed at young mothers* **2** if you specifically say something, you say it clearly because it is important: *I specifically told you to be here at two o'clock!*

specification Ac /ˌspesɪfɪˈkeɪʃən/ n [C usually plural] a detailed instruction about how something should be made or built: *furniture that is made to your own specifications*

specifics /spəˈsɪfɪks/ n [plural] exact details: **[+of]** *We can discuss the specifics of the deal later.*

specify Ac /'spesɪfaɪ/ v [T] (**specified, specifying, specifies**) to give information or instructions in an exact and detailed way: **[+that]** *The rules specify that competitors must be under 18 years of age.* | **[+what/how etc]** *He did not specify how this could be achieved.*

specimen /'spesɪmɪn/ n [C] **1** a small amount of something that you take so that you can test or examine it: *a blood specimen* | **[+of]** *a specimen of her clothing* **2** a single example of something: *The painting is a fine specimen of Pop Art.*

speck /spek/ n [C] a very small spot, or a very small piece of something: *The plane was just a tiny speck in the sky.* | **[+of]** *a speck of dirt* THESAURUS PIECE

speckled /'spekəld/ adj covered with a lot of small spots: *a speckled egg*

specs /speks/ n [plural] informal GLASSES

spectacle /'spektəkəl/ n [C] **1** something that is unusual or exciting to see: *the magnificent spectacle of a herd of elephants* **2 spectacles** [plural] old-fashioned GLASSES

spectacular¹ /spek'tækjələ $ -ər/ adj very impressive: *a spectacular view of the Grand Canyon* —**spectacularly** adv: *spectacularly beautiful scenery*

spectacular² n [C] a very big and impressive show or event

spectator /spek'teɪtə $ 'spekteɪtər/ n [C] someone who watches an event, especially a sports event

spectre BrE, **specter** AmE /'spektə $ -ər/ n [C] **1 the spectre of sth** something frightening that people think might happen: *the spectre of war* **2** literary a GHOST

spectrum /'spektrəm/ n [C] (plural **spectra** /-trə/) **1** all the different ideas, opinions, or situations that are possible: *They have support from right across the political spectrum.* **2** the set of different colours that light can be separated into: *all the colours of the spectrum*

speculate /'spekjəleɪt/ v **1** [I,T] to guess why something happened or what will happen next without knowing all the facts: **[+on/about]** *He refused to speculate on the cause of the accident.* | **[+that]** *Some economists have speculated that inflation will increase next year.* **2** [I] to buy things because you think you will make a profit when you sell them later —**speculator** n [C] —**speculation** /ˌspekjə'leɪʃən/ n [U]: *There has been a lot of speculation about his future.*

speculative /'spekjələtɪv $ -leɪ-/ adj involving guessing —**speculatively** adv

sped /sped/ v the past tense and past participle of SPEED

speech /spiːtʃ/ n **1** [C] a formal talk to a group of people, especially at an official meeting or ceremony: **[+to]** *The President will give a speech to Congress later today.* | **[+about/on]** *a speech on the environment* **2** [U] when someone speaks, or the way that they speak: *words that are used in speech as well as in writing* | *Her speech was slow and rather slurred.* → **DIRECT SPEECH, FIGURE OF SPEECH, INDIRECT SPEECH, PART OF SPEECH, REPORTED SPEECH**

PHRASES

freedom of speech/free speech the right to say or print whatever you want: *Minority groups have often had to fight for freedom of speech.*

COLLOCATIONS
verbs
to give/make a speech *She made a speech thanking her team.* ⚠ Do not say 'do a speech'. Say **give a speech** or **make a speech**.

to write a speech *He wrote most of his own campaign speeches.*
to listen to a speech *They listened to his speech in silence.*

adjectives
a long/short speech *Each member gave a long speech.*
a moving/powerful speech (=having a great effect on the audience) *She made a very moving farewell speech.*
a political speech *This was one of his most famous political speeches.*

THESAURUS
speech a formal talk to a group of people, especially at an official meeting or ceremony: *I had to give a speech at my brother's wedding.* | *a famous speech by Martin Luther King*
talk an occasion when someone speaks to a group of people about a particular subject: *I went to an interesting talk on the history of television.*
lecture a talk on a particular subject given to students in a university: *Students must not arrive late for lectures.*
sermon a talk given by a priest or a religious leader: *One Sunday, the priest preached a sermon about family.*

speechless /'spiːtʃləs/ adj unable to speak because you are so angry, shocked, or upset: *His answer left me speechless.* THESAURUS SURPRISED

'speech marks n [plural] the marks (" ") or (' ') that you use in writing to show when someone starts and stops speaking SYN quotation marks

speed¹ /spiːd/ n **1** [C,U] how fast something moves: **at a speed** *He was driving along at a speed of 60 mph.* THESAURUS QUICKLY **2** [U] the rate at which something happens: **[+of]** *the speed of change within the car industry* **3** [U] the quality of being fast: *She acted with speed and efficiency.* | *The train began to* **pick up speed** (=gradually move faster).

COLLOCATIONS
adjectives
high/great speed *The stolen car was being driven at high speed.*
low speed *Fortunately, the car was travelling at low speed when it hit her.*
full speed (=the highest speed possible) *He ran off at full speed.*
average speed *The average speed of cars in the city is less than 15 mph.*
a constant/steady speed *The motor should run at a constant speed.*
a top/maximum speed *He bought a sports car with a top speed of 120 mph.*

verbs
to reach a speed *These birds can reach speeds of more than 100 mph.*
to increase your speed *Gradually increase your speed.*

to reduce your speed *She reduced speed as she approached the village.*

speed² *v* (*past tense and past participle* **sped** /sped/) **1** [I] to move quickly: *The bus sped along the motorway.* **2 be speeding** to be driving faster than the legal limit: *I'm sure I wasn't speeding, officer.* —**speeding** *n* [U]

PHRASAL VERBS

speed up (*past tense and past participle* **speeded**) **1** to move faster [OPP] **slow down 2** to happen more quickly, or to make something happen more quickly [OPP] **slow down: speed sth ↔ up** *an attempt to speed up production at the factory*

speedboat /'spiːdbəʊt $ -boʊt/ *n* [C] a small fast boat with a powerful engine

'speed ,limit *n* [C] the fastest speed that you are legally allowed to drive at: *a 40 mph speed limit | motorists who break the speed limit* (=go faster than the speed limit)

speedometer /sprˈdɒmətə, spiː- $ -'dɑːmɪtər/ *n* [C] an instrument in a car that shows how fast it is going

speedy /'spiːdi/ *adj* happening quickly, without a delay: *He made a speedy recovery.* —**speedily** *adv*

spell¹ /spel/ *v* (*past tense and past participle* **spelt** /spelt/ *especially BrE*, **spelled** *especially AmE*) **1** [I,T] to form a word by writing or saying the letters in the correct order: *How do you spell 'necessary'? | I've never been able to spell. | They've **spelled** my name **wrong**.* **2** [T] if letters spell a word, they form it

PHRASES

spell trouble/defeat/danger etc if a situation spells trouble etc, it makes you expect trouble: *weather that could spell disaster for farmers*

PHRASAL VERBS

spell sth ↔ **out** to explain something in great detail: *Do I have to spell everything out for you?*

spell² *n* [C] **1** a piece of magic, or the special words that make magic happen: **cast/put a spell on sb** *They say that a witch cast a spell on her.* **2** a short period of time: **brief/short spell** *a short spell in jail |* **[+of]** *a spell of bad luck*

spellbound /'spelbaʊnd/ *adj* extremely interested in something you are listening to or watching: *The children listened spellbound to his story.* —**spellbinding** /-baɪndɪŋ/ *adj: a spellbinding story*

'spell-,checker *n* [C] a computer program that tells you when you have spelled a word wrongly

spelling /'spelɪŋ/ *n* **1** [U] the ability to spell words correctly: *Your spelling has improved. | a spelling mistake* **2** [C] the way that a word is spelled: *Who can give me the correct spelling?*

spelt /spelt/ *v especially BrE* a past tense and past participle of SPELL

spend /spend/ *v* [T] (*past tense and past participle* **spent** /spent/) **1** to use your money to pay for something: *I've **spent** all my money. |* **spend sth on sth** *I spent $40 on these shoes.*

> **Grammar**
> Do not say 'She spends all her money for clothes.' Say *She spends all her money on clothes.*

2 to use time doing something: *I want to **spend** more **time** with my family. | We spent two weeks in London. |* **spend sth doing sth** *I spent the morning working.*

spending /'spendɪŋ/ *n* [U] the amount of money that an organization or the government spends: **[+on]** *an increase in government spending on education*

'spending ,money *n* [U] money that you can spend on the things you want rather than things such as food or rent

spendthrift /'spendˌθrɪft/ *n* [C] someone who spends a lot of money in a careless way

spent /spent/ *adj* **1** already used and now empty or useless: *spent cartridges* **2** extremely tired

sperm /spɜːm $ spɜːrm/ *n* (*plural* **sperm** *or* **sperms**) **1** [C] a cell produced by the male sex organ that can join with an egg to produce new life **2** [U] the liquid from the male sex organ that contains sperm cells

spew /spjuː/ *v* [I,T] **1** (*also* **spew out**) if gas or liquid spews out of something, or if something spews gas or liquid, a large amount of gas or liquid flows out of it: *Smoke and gas were spewing out of the volcano.* **2** (*also* **spew up** *informal*) to VOMIT

sphere ⟨Ac⟩ /sfɪə $ sfɪr/ *n* [C] **1** the shape of a ball **2** an area of work, interest, knowledge etc: *in the sphere of international politics*

spherical ⟨Ac⟩ /'sferɪkəl/ *adj* shaped like a ball

spice¹ /spaɪs/ *n* **1** [C,U] a seed or powder from a plant which you add to food to give it a special taste: *herbs and spices* **2** [U] something that makes a situation or activity more interesting or exciting: *The argument added a bit of spice to the evening.* —**spiced** *adj: a dish of spiced plums*

spice² *v*

PHRASAL VERBS

spice sth ↔ **up** to make something more interesting or exciting: *I need a few jokes to spice up my speech.*

spick and span /ˌspɪk ən 'spæn/ *adj* very clean and neat

spicy /'spaɪsi/ *adj* spicy food has a strong taste because it contains a lot of spices [THESAURUS] TASTE

spider /'spaɪdə $ -ər/ *n* [C] a small creature with eight legs that makes nets of sticky threads to catch insects: *a spider's web*

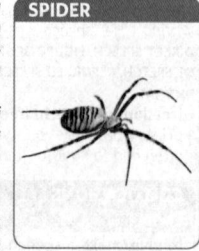
SPIDER

spidery /'spaɪdəri/ *adj* spidery writing is untidy and uses a lot of long thin lines

spiel /ʃpiːl, spiːl/ *n* [C] *informal* a speech that someone makes to try to persuade people to buy something

spike¹ /spaɪk/ n [C] a long thin piece of metal, wood etc with a sharp end

spike² v [T] to add alcohol or a drug to someone's drink without telling them

spiky /'spaɪki/ adj something that is spiky has a lot of thin points sticking out from it: *spiky hair* → see picture at HAIR

spill /spɪl/ v (past tense and past participle **spilt** /spɪlt/ especially BrE, **spilled** especially AmE)

SPILL

1 [I,T] if a liquid spills or if you spill it, it flows over the edge of a container by accident → **pour**: **spill (sth) on/over sth** *I spilled coffee on my shirt.* | **[+out]** *Some water had spilled out onto the floor.*
2 [I] if people spill out of a place, a lot of them leave at the same time [SYN] **pour**: **[+out/onto/into etc]** *The doors opened and people spilled out into the street.* —**spill** n [C]: *a huge oil spill in the Atlantic*

PHRASES
spill the beans informal to tell something that other people wanted you to keep secret: *The police were putting pressure on him to spill the beans.*

PHRASAL VERBS
spill over if a problem spills over, it begins to affect other places, people etc: **[+into]** *There's a danger that the fighting will spill over into other countries.*

spillage /'spɪlɪdʒ/ n [C,U] a spill

spin¹ /spɪn/ v (past tense and past participle **spun** /spʌn/, present participle **spinning**)
1 [I,T] to turn around very quickly, or to make something do this: **spin (sb/sth) round/around** *She spun round to face him.* | *He spun the rope around over his head.* [THESAURUS] TURN
2 [I,T] to make cotton, wool etc into thread by twisting it together
3 [T] to get water out of wet clothes by making them turn round and round very quickly in a washing machine
4 [T] if an insect spins a WEB or a COCOON, it produces the thread to make it

PHRASAL VERBS
spin sth ↔ **out** to make something last as long as possible

spin² n **1** [C,U] when something turns round and round very quickly: *The plane went into a spin.* **2** [C] informal a short trip in a car for pleasure [SYN] **drive**: *Shall we go for a spin?* **3** [singular, U] when someone talks about something in a way that makes it seem better than it really is, especially in politics: *He tried to put a positive spin on the situation.*

spinach /'spɪnɪdʒ, -ɪtʃ/ n [U] a vegetable with large dark green leaves

spinal /'spaɪnl/ adj relating to your SPINE: *a spinal injury*

'spinal cord n [C] the long string of nerves that goes from your brain down to the bottom of your back

spindly /'spɪndli/ adj long, thin, and not very strong: *spindly legs*

'spin doctor n [C] informal someone whose job is to make the public have a good opinion of an organization or politician, especially when there is a problem

spine /spaɪn/ n [C] **1** the row of bones down the centre of your back → see picture on page A2 **2** a stiff sharp point on an animal or plant: *the spines of a hedgehog*

spineless /'spaɪnləs/ adj not brave

'spin-off n [C] something that develops from something else, especially in an unexpected way

spinster /'spɪnstə $ -ər/ n [C] old-fashioned an old woman who has never been married

spiral¹ /'spaɪərəl $ 'spaɪr-/ n [C] **1** a curve that goes round and round as it goes up or down **2** a situation in which something gets worse and worse in a way that cannot be controlled: *a spiral of hatred and violence* —**spiral** adj: *a spiral staircase*

spiral² v [I] (**spiralled, spiralling** BrE, **spiraled, spiraling** AmE) **1** to move up or down in the shape of a spiral: **[+to]** *The plane spiralled to the ground.* **2** to become worse and worse in a way that cannot be controlled: *Crime is spiralling out of control.*

spire /spaɪə $ spaɪr/ n [C] a tall pointed tower on a church

spirit¹ /'spɪrɪt/ n
1 [C,U] a person's mind, including their thoughts and feelings: **in spirit** *I'm 85, but I still feel young in spirit.*
2 spirits [plural] the way you are feeling, for example whether you are happy or sad → **mood**: *The children were all in high spirits* (=very happy). | *We were all tired, and our spirits were low.* | *The warm sun lifted our spirits* (=made us feel happy).
3 [C] a dead person or a creature that is thought to exist in a form that is not physical → **ghost**, **soul**
4 [U] courage and determination: *You've got to admire her spirit.*
5 [singular] the attitude that you have towards something: **[+of]** *a spirit of cooperation* | *Everyone played the game in the right spirit.* | *Some people didn't enter into the spirit of the occasion* (=have the right attitude towards it).
6 team/community/public spirit the strong feeling that you belong to a particular group and want to help them
7 [C usually plural] a strong alcoholic drink such as BRANDY
8 the spirit of the law/an agreement etc the effect a law or agreement was intended to have, even though this may be different from its written details

spirit² v
PHRASAL VERBS
spirit sb/sth ↔ **away** to take someone or something away secretly

spirited /'spɪrɪtɪd/ adj full of courage and determination: *a spirited performance by the team*

spiritual /ˈspɪrɪtʃuəl/ adj **1** relating to your mind, thoughts, and feelings, rather than your body and the things that you own: *your spiritual needs* **2** relating to religion: *their spiritual leader* —**spiritually** adv —**spirituality** /ˌspɪrɪtʃuˈæləti/ n [U]

spiritualism /ˈspɪrɪtʃʊlɪzəm/ n [U] the belief that dead people can send messages to living people —**spiritualist** n [C]

spit¹ /spɪt/ v (past tense and past participle **spat** /spæt/ also **spit** AmE, present participle **spitting**) **1** [I,T] to push liquid or food out of your mouth: [+at/on] *That boy spat at me!* | **spit sth out** *He tasted the wine and then spat it out.* **2 it is spitting** used to say it is raining very lightly

PHRASES
spit it out *spoken* used to tell someone to say something they do not want to say: *Come on, spit it out.*

spit² n **1** [U] the liquid that is produced in your mouth **2** [C] a stick that you put through meat to cook it over a fire

spite¹ /spaɪt/ n [U] the feeling of wanting to annoy or upset someone: **out of spite** *She burned the letters out of spite.* | *an act of **pure spite***

PHRASES
in spite of sth although something exists or is true SYN **despite**: *We enjoyed ourselves in spite of the rain.* | *She stayed with him **in spite of the fact that** he had beaten her up.*

spite² v **do sth to spite sb** to annoy or upset someone deliberately

spiteful /ˈspaɪtfəl/ adj deliberately wanting to annoy or upset someone: *a spiteful remark* THESAURUS UNKIND —**spitefully** adv

splash¹ /splæʃ/ v [I,T] if a liquid splashes, or if you splash it, it falls on something or hits it: **splash sth on/over sth** *He splashed water on his face.* | [+against/on/over] *The waves splashed against the side of the boat.* | [+in/through/around] *children splashing through the puddles*

PHRASAL VERBS
splash out to spend a lot of money on something that you do not really need: [+on] *We've splashed out on a new kitchen.*

splash² n [C] **1** the sound that water makes when something hits it: *Jerry jumped into the water with a loud splash.* → see picture on page A7 **2** a small amount of a liquid that falls onto something: *splashes of paint on the floorboards* **3 splash of colour** a small area of bright colour

PHRASES
make a splash *informal* to do something that gets a lot of public attention: *His performance made quite a splash in New York.*

splatter /ˈsplætə $ -ər/ v [I,T] if a liquid splatters, or if you splatter it, drops of it fall onto something: *Blood splattered everywhere.*

splay /spleɪ/ v [T] to spread your fingers, arms, or legs wide apart

splendid /ˈsplendɪd/ adj old-fashioned very good: *a splendid idea*

splendour BrE, **splendor** AmE /ˈsplendə $ -ər/ n [U] very impressive beauty: *the splendour of the scenery*

splice /splaɪs/ v [T] to join the ends of two pieces of film, rope etc so that they form one continuous piece

splint /splɪnt/ n [C] a flat piece of wood or plastic that stops a broken bone from moving while it mends

splinter¹ /ˈsplɪntə $ -ər/ n [C] a small sharp piece of wood, glass, or metal: *I've got a splinter in my finger.* | *splinters of glass*

splinter² v [I] to break into a lot of thin sharp pieces

ˈsplinter group n [C] a group of people who have separated from a larger political or religious group because they have different ideas

split¹ /splɪt/ v (past tense and past participle **split**, present participle **splitting**) **1** [I,T] if a group of people split, or if something splits them, they disagree very strongly about something and divide into smaller groups: *an issue that could split the church* | **be split on/over sth** *The government is split over the question of immigration.* | [+from] *their decision to split from the Labour party* THESAURUS DISAGREE **2** (also **split up**) [I,T] to divide or separate something into different parts, or to be divided or separated in this way: **split (sth) into sth** *I'm going to split the class into three groups.* **3** [T] to share something between different people: **split sth between sb** *We decided to split the money between us.* | **split sth with sb** *He promised to split the profit with me.* | *We went for a pizza and **split the bill** (=shared paying for a meal).* **4** [I,T] if you split something, or if it splits, it tears or breaks into separate pieces: *He split the logs in half.* | *One of the bags had split.* THESAURUS BREAK

PHRASES
split hairs to argue about small unimportant details: *Let's stop splitting hairs and get back to the important issues.*

PHRASAL VERBS
split up if people split up, they end their marriage or relationship: *My parents split up when I was three.*

split² n [C] **1** a long cut or hole in something: [+in] *a split in the curtain* **2** a serious disagreement that divides an organization or group SYN **rift**: [+in] *a split in the Republican Party* **3** *informal* the end of a marriage or relationship – used especially in newspapers and magazines: [+with/from] *her recent split with her fiancé*

ˌsplit-ˈlevel adj a split-level house or room has floors at different heights in different parts

ˌsplit ˈsecond n [singular] an extremely short period of time: *He hesitated for a split second.* —**split-second** adj

splitting /ˈsplɪtɪŋ/ adj **splitting headache** a very bad HEADACHE

splutter /'splʌtə $ -ər/ v [I,T] to speak in a confused way because you are surprised, angry, or guilty

spoil /spɔɪl/ v (past tense and past participle **spoiled** or **spoilt** /spɔɪlt/)
1 [T] to make something less good or enjoyable **SYN** ruin: I'm not going to let him spoil my day. | She didn't want anything to spoil the look of the garden. **THESAURUS** DAMAGE
2 [T] to let a child have or do whatever they want, with the result that they behave badly
3 [T] to treat someone in a way that is kind or too kind: All these chocolates – you're spoiling me. | **spoil yourself** Go on, spoil yourself. Have another cake.
4 [I] if food spoils, it starts to decay

spoiled /spɔɪld/ (also **spoilt** /spɔɪlt/ BrE) adj someone who is spoiled behaves badly because they have always been allowed to have or do whatever they want

spoils /spɔɪlz/ n [plural] formal things that have been taken by thieves or by an army that has won a war

spoilsport /'spɔɪlspɔːt $ -spɔːrt/ n [C] informal someone who spoils other people's fun: Come and play, don't be such a spoilsport.

spoke[1] /spəʊk $ spoʊk/ v the past tense of SPEAK

spoke[2] n [C] one of the thin metal bars which connect the centre of a wheel to the outside edge → see picture at BICYCLE

spoken[1] /'spəʊkən $ 'spoʊ-/ v the past participle of SPEAK

spoken[2] adj **1** spoken English/language the form of language that you use rather than write **2** softly-spoken/well-spoken etc speaking quietly, in an educated way etc

spokesperson /'spəʊks,pɜːsən $ 'spoʊks,pɜːr-/, **spokesman** /'spəʊksmən $ 'spoʊks-/, **spokeswoman** /'spəʊks,wʊmən $ 'spoʊks-/ n [C] someone who has been chosen to speak officially for a group, organization, or government

sponge[1] /spʌndʒ/ n **1** [C] a soft object full of small holes that takes in and holds water, and is used for washing things **2** [C,U] BrE a sponge cake → **throw in the sponge** at THROW[1]

sponge[2] v **1** (also **sponge down**) [T] to wash something with a wet cloth or sponge **2** [I] informal disapproving to get money, food etc from someone without doing anything to help them: **[+off]** He's always sponging off his friends.

'sponge bag n [C] BrE a small bag for carrying soap, a TOOTHBRUSH etc when you are travelling

'sponge cake n [C,U] a light cake → see picture at DESSERT

spongy /'spʌndʒi/ adj soft and full of air or liquid like a SPONGE: the soft, spongy earth

sponsor[1] /'spɒnsə $ 'spɑːnsər/ v [T] **1** to give money to an event or institution, especially in exchange for the right to advertise: a competition sponsored by British Airways **2** to agree to give someone money for a CHARITY if they do something

difficult, for example walk a long way: a **sponsored walk** —**sponsorship** n [U]

sponsor[2] n [C] a person or company that pays for a show, sports event etc, especially in exchange for the right to advertise

spontaneous /spɒn'teɪniəs $ spɑːn-/ adj something that is spontaneous happens without being planned: a spontaneous reaction | spontaneous applause —**spontaneously** adv —**spontaneity** /,spɒntə'niːəti, -'neɪəti $,spɑːn-/ n [U]

spoof /spuːf/ n [C] a funny book, film etc that copies a serious one and makes it seem silly: **[+on/of]** a spoof on one of Shakespeare's plays

spooky /'spuːki/ adj informal strange and frightening: a spooky house **THESAURUS** FRIGHTENING

spool /spuːl/ n [C] an object shaped like a small wheel that you wind thread, wire, film etc around

spoon[1] /spuːn/ n [C] something that you use for eating and serving food. It has a small bowl-shaped part and a handle.

spoon[2] v [T] to move food with a spoon: **spoon sth into/onto/over sth** Spoon the sauce over the fish.

'spoon-feed v [T] (past tense and past participle **spoon-fed**) disapproving to give someone too much help and information: I don't believe in spoon-feeding students.

spoonful /'spuːnfʊl/ n [C] the amount that a spoon can hold: **[+of]** a spoonful of sugar

sporadic /spə'rædɪk/ adj not happening regularly, or happening only in a few places: sporadic fighting —**sporadically** /-kli/ adv

sport[1] /spɔːt $ spɔːrt/ n
1 [C] a game or physical activity that you do for enjoyment or in order to compete against other people: Swimming is a very popular sport.
2 [U] BrE sports in general: I always hated sport at school. → **BLOOD SPORT**

COLLOCATIONS

verbs

to play (a) sport Geoff plays a lot of sport. ⚠ Do not say 'make a sport'. Say **play a sport**.
to take part in (a) sport More people are taking part in sports.
to do sport BrE, **to do sports** AmE Do you do any sports?

types of sport

a team sport I prefer running or the gym to team sports.
a spectator sport (=one that people enjoy watching) Boxing is a popular spectator sport.
a winter sport (=skiing, ice skating etc) Switzerland is a great place for winter sports.
professional sport(s) There is a lot of money involved in professional sport.

sports + noun

a sports team She was in several university sports teams.
a sports club You could join a sports club.
sports facilities The resort has wonderful sports facilities.

S

sport

sports equipment *We sell all kinds of sports equipment.*

sport² *v* **be sporting sth** to be wearing something, especially something unusual or something that you seem proud of: *He walked in sporting an orange tie.*

sporting /ˈspɔːtɪŋ $ ˈspɔːr-/ *adj* [only before noun] relating to sports: *sporting events*

'sports car *n* [C] a low fast car, often with a roof that can be folded back

sportscast /ˈspɔːtskɑːst $ ˈspɔːrtskæst/ *n* [C] *AmE* a television broadcast of a sports game

'sports ,centre *BrE*, **sports center** *AmE n* [C] a building where you can do different sports

sportsman /ˈspɔːtsmən $ ˈspɔːrts-/ *n* [C] (*plural* **sportsmen** /-mən/) a man who plays sports: *Stuart is a keen sportsman.*

sportsmanlike /ˈspɔːtsmənlaɪk $ ˈspɔːrts-/ *adj* behaving fairly and honestly in a game or competition

sportsmanship /ˈspɔːtsmənʃɪp $ ˈspɔːrts-/ *n* [U] behaviour that is fair and honest in a game or competition

sportswear /ˈspɔːtsweə $ ˈspɔːrtswer/ *n* [U] clothes that you wear to play sports

sportswoman /ˈspɔːtsˌwʊmən $ ˈspɔːrts-/ *n* [C] (*plural* **sportswomen** /-ˌwɪmɪn/) a woman who plays sports: *a great all-round sportswoman*

sporty /ˈspɔːti $ ˈspɔːrti/ *adj* **1** a sporty car is designed to look attractive and go fast **2** *BrE* good at sport

spot¹ /spɒt $ spɑːt/ *n* [C]
1 PLACE a place: *This is the spot where the accident happened.* | [+for] *a great spot for a picnic* | **in a spot** *a plant that will flourish in a sunny spot* THESAURUS PLACE
2 COLOURED AREA a small round area on a surface, that is a different colour from the rest SYN **patch**: *a white dog with black spots*
3 MARK a small mark on something: *grease spots* | [+of] *a few spots of blood*
4 ON SKIN *BrE* a small raised red mark on someone's skin SYN **pimple**: *Many teenagers get spots.*
5 ON TELEVISION/RADIO a short time that is available for something on television or radio: *an advertising spot*
6 SMALL AMOUNT **a spot of sth** *BrE spoken informal* a small amount of something: **a spot of bother/ trouble** *I've been having a spot of trouble with the car.*
→ BEAUTY SPOT, BLIND SPOT, HOT SPOT, TROUBLE SPOT
PHRASES
on the spot 1 immediately: *He had to make a decision on the spot.* **2** at the place where something is happening: *Our reporter is on the spot.*
put sb on the spot to ask someone a difficult or embarrassing question: *I didn't want to put her on the spot in front of her Mom.*

spot² *v* [T] (**spotted**, **spotting**) to notice someone or something: *A pilot spotted the wreckage.* | *His talent was spotted at an early age.* THESAURUS SEE

,spot 'check *n* [C] a check that is done without warning, in order to make sure everything is being done correctly or legally: [+on] *Police are doing spot checks on cars.*

spotless /ˈspɒtləs $ ˈspɑːt-/ *adj* completely clean: *The kitchen was spotless.* THESAURUS CLEAN —**spotlessly** *adv*: *Her house is always spotlessly clean.*

spotlight¹ /ˈspɒtlaɪt $ ˈspɑːt-/ *n* **1** [C] a light with a very bright beam that can be directed at someone or something **2 the spotlight** a lot of attention from newspapers, television etc: **in/under the spotlight** *Education is once again under the spotlight.*

spotlight² *v* [T] (*past tense and past participle* **spotlighted** or **spotlit**) to put attention on someone or something: *The program spotlights the problems of the homeless.*

,spot-'on *adj BrE informal* exactly right: *Her prediction was spot-on.*

spotted /ˈspɒtɪd $ ˈspɑː-/ *adj* covered in small round marks, especially in a way that forms a pattern: *a red and white spotted dress* → see picture at PATTERN

spotty /ˈspɒti $ ˈspɑːti/ *adj* **1** *BrE* having a lot of raised red marks on your skin: *spotty schoolboys* **2** *AmE* good in some parts but not in others SYN **patchy** *BrE*

spouse /spaʊs, spaʊz/ *n* [C] *formal* your spouse is your husband or wife

spout¹ /spaʊt/ *n* [C] a part on the side of a container that you pour liquid out through: *The spout of the jug was broken.*

spout² *v* **1** [I,T] if a liquid spouts, or if something spouts a liquid, the liquid comes out of it very quickly with a lot of force: [+from] *Blood was spouting from her leg.* | *a whale spouting water* **2** [I] *informal* (*also* **spout off**) to talk a lot in a boring way: [+about] *He's always spouting off about politics.*

sprain /spreɪn/ *v* [T] to injure your wrist, knee etc by suddenly twisting it: *I fell and sprained my ankle.* THESAURUS HURT —**sprain** *n* [C]

sprang /spræŋ/ *v* the past tense of SPRING

sprawl /sprɔːl $ sprɒːl/ *v* [I,T] **1** if you sprawl or are sprawled somewhere, you lie or sit with your arms and legs stretched out: [+on/in etc] *Ian was sprawled on the sofa.* **2** if a building or town sprawls, it spreads out over a wide area —**sprawl** *n* [singular, U]: *miles and miles of urban sprawl*

spray¹ /spreɪ/ *v*
1 [T] to force liquid out of a container in a stream of very small drops: **spray sb/sth with sth** *She sprayed herself with perfume before going to the party.* | **spray sth on/onto/over sth** *Farmers were spraying chemicals onto crops.* → see picture at SQUIRT
2 [I] to scatter in small pieces or drops through the air: *The glass shattered and sprayed everywhere.*

spray² *n* [C,U] very small drops of liquid floating in the air: *spray blowing off the sea* | *hair spray*

SPREAD

spread¹ /spred/ v (*past tense and past participle* **spread**)

1 AFFECT LARGER AREA [I,T] to move and affect a larger area or more people, or to make something do this: **[+through]** *Fire spread quickly through the building.* | **[+to]** *The cancer had spread to her liver.* | *Rats often spread disease.*

2 NEWS/LIES ETC [I,T] to tell a lot of people about something, or to become known by a lot of people: **spread lies/rumours/gossip** *She's been spreading lies about me.* | *News of his arrest spread quickly.* | *The news spread like wildfire* (=became known very quickly).

3 MAP/CLOTH ETC (*also* **spread out**) [T] to open something or arrange a group of things so that they cover a flat surface: **spread sth over/across/on sth** *Spread the map out on the floor.* | *Books and papers were spread all over the table.*

4 BUTTER/CREAM ETC [T] to put a soft substance onto a surface: **spread sth on/over sth** *Spread the cream over the top of the cake.* | **spread sth with sth** *She spread the bread with butter.*

5 ARMS/LEGS ETC (*also* **spread out**) [T] if you spread your hands, arms, legs, or fingers, you move them wide apart: *He spread his hands in a gesture of confusion.*

6 DO STH OVER A LONG TIME (*also* **spread out**) [T] to do something over a period of time rather than at one time: **spread sth over sth** *You can spread the payments over a year.*

PHRASAL VERBS

spread out if a group of people spread out, they move apart from each other so that they cover a larger area: *They spread out to search the forest.*

spread² n **1** [singular] when something increases and affects a larger area or more people → **increase**: **[+of]** *the spread of disease* **2** [C,U] a soft food that you put on bread: *cheese spread* **3** [singular] a range of people or things: **wide/broad/good spread of sth** *books on a wide spread of subjects* **4** [C] a special article or advertisement that covers more than one page in a newspaper or magazine: *a two-page spread* | *a fashion spread*

spreadsheet /'spredʃiːt/ n [C] a computer program that can show and calculate financial information

spree /spriː/ n [C] a short period of time when you do a lot of something you enjoy: *He went on a shopping spree.* | **a shopping/spending/drinking spree**

sprig /sprɪg/ n [C] a small stem with leaves or flowers on it: **[+of]** *a sprig of parsley*

sprightly /'spraɪtli/ adj an old person who is sprightly is active and full of energy

spring¹ /sprɪŋ/ n

1 [C,U] the season between winter and summer: **in spring/in the spring** *The park is full of daffodils in spring.* | *spring flowers*

2 [C] a place where water comes up naturally from the ground: *hot springs*

3 [C] a twisted piece of metal that will return to its original shape after you have pressed or pulled it: *bed springs*

4 [C] a sudden quick movement or jump

spring² v [I] (*past tense* **sprang** /spræŋ/ *also* **sprung** /sprʌŋ/ *AmE, past participle* **sprung**) to move or jump suddenly and quickly SYN **leap**: **[+out/at/back etc]** *He sprang out of bed.* | *She sprang to her feet* (=stood up suddenly). | **spring open/shut** (=open or shut suddenly) THESAURUS JUMP

PHRASES

spring into life/action suddenly to become active or start doing something: *He sprang into action when he heard their screams.*

spring to (sb's) mind if something springs to mind, you immediately think of it: *Two questions spring to mind.*

tears spring to sb's eyes written if tears spring to someone's eyes, they are almost crying: *'Oh, Tom!' she cried, as tears sprang to her eyes.*

PHRASAL VERBS

spring from sth to be caused by something: *problems springing from childhood experiences*

spring sth **on** sb informal to tell someone something or ask them to do something that they are not expecting: *It's not fair to spring this on her now.*

spring up to suddenly appear or start to exist: *Hotels are springing up all over the city.*

springboard /'sprɪŋbɔːd $ -bɔːrd/ n [C] **1** something that helps you start doing something or helps something happen: **[+for/to]** *He hoped the course would be a springboard to success.* **2** a strong board, used to help you jump high, for example when you are jumping into water

spring-'clean v [T] to clean a place thoroughly —**spring-cleaning** n [U]

spring 'onion n [C] BrE a small white onion with a long green stem → see picture on page A5

springtime /'sprɪŋtaɪm/ n [U] the time of the year when it is spring

springy /'sprɪŋi/ adj something that is springy is soft and comes back to its usual shape after it has been pressed: *springy grass*

sprinkle /'sprɪŋkəl/ v **1** [T] to scatter small drops of liquid or small pieces of something onto something else: **sprinkle sth over/on sth** *Sprinkle the cheese over the salad.* | *a cake sprinkled with sugar* **2** it is sprinkling AmE if it is sprinkling, it is raining slightly —**sprinkle** n [C] → see picture on page 866

sprinkler /'sprɪŋklə $ -ər/ n [C] a piece of equipment that scatters water over an area

SPRINKLE

sprinkling /'sprɪŋklɪŋ/ n [singular] a small amount of something, especially something scattered over an area: **[+of]** a sprinkling of snow on the hills

sprint /sprɪnt/ v [I] to run very fast for a short distance: **[+up/across etc]** He sprinted up the stairs. **THESAURUS** RUN —**sprinter** n [C] —**sprint** n [C]

sprout¹ /spraʊt/ v **1** [I,T] to start to grow or produce new flowers, leaves etc **2** (also **sprout up**) [I] to appear suddenly and quickly: Office blocks seem to be sprouting up everywhere.

sprout² n [C] **1** a new stem or leaf that is starting to grow on a plant **2** (also **brussels sprout**) a green vegetable like a very small CABBAGE

spruce¹ /spruːs/ n [C,U] a tree with leaves shaped like needles, or the wood of this tree

spruce² v
PHRASAL VERBS
spruce up to make yourself or something look cleaner and neater: I want to spruce up before dinner. | **spruce sb/sth ↔ up** Sarah had spruced herself up.

sprung /sprʌŋ/ v a past tense and the past participle of SPRING

spry /spraɪ/ adj an old person who is spry is active and has a lot of energy

spud /spʌd/ n [C] informal a POTATO

spun /spʌn/ v the past tense and past participle of SPIN

spur¹ /spɜː $ spɜːr/ n [C] a fact or event that encourages you to do something: **[+to]** Ill health is often the spur to lifestyle changes.
PHRASES
on the spur of the moment suddenly and without any planning: We decided to go to Paris on the spur of the moment.

spur² v [T] (**spurred**, **spurring**) **1** (also **spur on**) to encourage someone and make them want to do something: The band were spurred on by the success of their last CD. **2** to make an improvement or change happen faster: The growth of the city was spurred by cheap housing.

spurious /'spjʊəriəs $ 'spjʊr-/ adj formal based on incorrect facts and reasons: spurious arguments

spurn /spɜːn $ spɜːrn/ v [T] literary to refuse an offer or someone's love: a spurned lover

spurt¹ /spɜːt $ spɜːrt/ v **1** [I,T] if liquid spurts from something, or if something spurts a liquid, the liquid flows out quickly and with a lot of force: **[+from/out of]** Blood spurted from his arm. **2** [I] to suddenly start moving more quickly: **[+to/along/past etc]** The Ferrari spurted to the top of the ramp.

spurt² n [C] **1** when a liquid comes out of something quickly and with a lot of force: **[+of]** a spurt of blood | **in spurts** (=a small amount at a time) Water was coming out in spurts. **2** a short sudden increase in activity, effort, or speed: **[+of]** a spurt of energy | a **growth spurt** (=when a child suddenly grows quickly)

sputter /'spʌtə $ -ər/ v **1** [I] to make sounds like a lot of small explosions: The engine sputtered and stopped. **2** [I,T] to talk with difficulty because you are so angry or shocked: 'What do you mean?' he sputtered.

spy¹ /spaɪ/ n [C] (plural **spies**) someone whose job is to find out secret information about a country or organization

spy² v (**spied**, **spying**, **spies**) **1** [I] to get information for a government or organization secretly **2** [T] literary suddenly to see someone or something: Ellen spied her friend in the crowd. —**spying** n [U]: He was arrested for spying.
PHRASAL VERBS
spy on sb to secretly watch someone **THESAURUS** WATCH

sq. the written abbreviation of **square**

squabble /'skwɒbəl $ 'skwɑː-/ v [I] to argue about something unimportant: **[+about/over]** What are you two squabbling about? **THESAURUS** ARGUMENT —**squabble** n [C]

squad /skwɒd $ skwɑːd/ n [C] **1** a team of police officers or soldiers who do a particular type of job: the police bomb squad **2** the group of people that a sports team is chosen from

'squad car n [C] a car used by police

squadron /'skwɒdrən $ 'skwɑː-/ n [C] a group of military aircraft or ships

squalid /'skwɒlɪd $ 'skwɑː-/ adj **1** dirty and unpleasant: squalid living conditions **2** dishonest or immoral: a squalid affair

squall /skwɔːl $ skwɒːl/ n [C] a sudden strong wind with rain or snow

squalor /'skwɒlə $ 'skwɑːlər, 'skwɒː-/ n [U] when a place is extremely dirty and unpleasant: **in squalor** people living in squalor

squander /'skwɒndə $ 'skwɑːndər/ v [T] to waste money, time, or opportunities: **squander sth on sth** They squandered their money on expensive cars.

square¹ /skweə $ skwer/ adj
1 something that is square has four straight sides of equal length and four angles of 90 degrees: a square room | **2 metres/5 feet etc square** The room is four metres square.
2 square metre/mile etc a measurement of an area equal to a square with sides a metre, mile etc long: two square acres of land
3 if part of someone's body is square, it is broad and strong: a square jaw

(all) square 1 if two people are square, they do not owe each other any money: *Here's your $20 so we're square.* **2** *BrE* having the same number of points as your opponent in a game: *The teams were all square at 2–2.*

a square deal honest and fair treatment, especially in business: *We want our customers to have a square deal.*

a square meal a big healthy meal: *Children should have three square meals a day.*

square² n [C]
1 a shape with four straight sides that are equal in length and four angles of 90 degrees → **rectangle** → see picture at **SHAPE¹**
2 an open area with buildings around it in the middle of a town: *Trafalgar Square* | *a market square*
3 the result of multiplying a number by itself → **square root: [+of]** *The square of 5 is 25.*
PHRASES
square one the situation from which you started to do something: **back to/back at square one** *He had spent all the money and was back to square one.* | **from square one** *The rehearsals went well from square one.*

square³ v [T] to multiply a number by itself
PHRASAL VERBS
square up to pay money that you owe: *I'll get the drinks, and you can square up later.*
square with sth **1 square (sth) with sth** if you square two ideas, facts etc with each other, or if they square with each other, they agree: *evidence that doesn't square with the facts* **2 square sth with sb** *BrE* to persuade someone to allow something: *I don't know if I can come. I'll have to square it with my Dad first.*

squarely /'skweəli $ 'skwer-/ adv **1** exactly or completely: *The report puts the blame squarely on senior managers.* **2** (also **square**) directly: *He looked her squarely in the eye.*

square 'root n [C] the number that produces another number when multiplied by itself: **[+of]** *The square root of nine is three.*

squash¹ /skwɒʃ $ skwɑːʃ, skwɒʃ/ v
1 [T] to damage something by pressing it until it is flat → **flatten**: *My hat got squashed on the bus.*
THESAURUS **PRESS**
2 [I,T] to push yourself or something into a space that is too small **SYN squeeze: [+into]** *Seven of us squashed into the car.*

squash² n **1** [U] a game played by two people who hit a small rubber ball against the four walls of an indoor court **2** [C,U] *AmE* a type of big hard fruit, such as a PUMPKIN, that you cook and eat as a vegetable → see picture on page A5 **3** [C,U] *BrE* a drink made from fruit juice, sugar, and water: *a glass of orange squash*
PHRASES
it's a squash *spoken* used to say that there is not enough space for everyone to fit in comfortably: *The boat's quite small, so it was a bit of a squash.*

squat¹ /skwɒt $ skwɑːt/ v [I] (**squatted, squatting**)
1 (also **squat down**) to balance on your feet with your knees bent and your bottom close to the ground: *He squatted down next to the child.* → see picture on page A11 **2** to live somewhere without permission and without paying rent —**squatter** n [C]

squat² adj short and wide: *small squat houses*

squat³ n [singular] *BrE* a home that people are living in without permission and without paying rent

squawk /skwɔːk $ skwɒːk/ v [I] if a bird squawks, it makes a loud angry sound —**squawk** n [C]

squeak /skwiːk/ v [I] to make a very high sound: *Is that your chair squeaking?* —**squeak** n [C] → see picture on page A7

squeaky /'skwiːki/ adj a squeaky sound or voice is very high
PHRASES
squeaky clean *informal* never having done anything morally wrong: *Most politicians are less than squeaky clean.*

squeal /skwiːl/ v [I] to make a long loud high sound: *children squealing with excitement* —**squeal** n [C]: *squeals of delight*

squeamish /'skwiːmɪʃ/ adj easily upset by seeing unpleasant things: *I couldn't be a nurse – I'm too squeamish.*

squeeze¹ /skwiːz/ v
1 [T] to press something from both sides, usually with your fingers: *She squeezed his hand reassuringly.* → see picture at **PRESS¹** THESAURUS **PRESS**
2 [T] to twist or press something in order to get liquid out of it: **squeeze sth out** *Can you squeeze a bit more juice out?*
3 [I,T] to try to make yourself or a thing fit into a small space **SYN squash: [+in/into/through etc]** *Can you squeeze in next to Rick?*

squeeze² n **1 a (tight) squeeze** when there is only just enough room for a group of people or things: *It'll be a tight squeeze with 14 of us at the table.* **2** [C] when you press something firmly with your hand: *Laurie gave his hand a little squeeze.*

squelch /skweltʃ/ v [I] to make a sucking sound by moving through something soft and wet, such as mud

squid /skwɪd/ n [C] (*plural* **squid** *or* **squids**) a sea creature with a soft body and ten long TENTACLES (=arms)

squiggle /'skwɪɡəl/ n [C] a short line that curls and twists —**squiggly** adj

squint¹ /skwɪnt/ v [I] **1** to look at something with your eyes partly closed in order to see better: *He squinted in the bright sunlight.* | **[+at]** *Stop squinting at the screen – put your glasses on.* **2** to have a condition in which each of your eyes looks in a different direction

squint² n [singular] a condition that makes each eye look in a different direction

squire /skwaɪə $ skwaɪr/ n [C] a wealthy man who, in the past, owned a lot of land in the countryside

squirm /skwɜːm $ skwɜːrm/ v [I] to twist your body

S

from side to side because you are uncomfortable or nervous: *I was squirming with embarrassment.*

squirrel /'skwɪrəl $ 'skwɜːrəl/ *n* [C] a small animal with a big tail that lives in trees and eats nuts

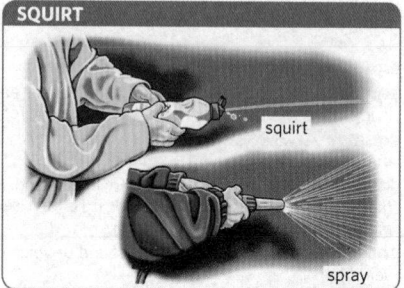

SQUIRT

squirt

spray

squirt /skwɜːt $ skwɜːrt/ *v* [I,T] if you squirt liquid or if it squirts, it is forced out of a narrow hole in a thin fast stream: **[+out/from/into]** *Water suddenly squirted out of a hole.* | **squirt sb/sth with sth** *He squirted me with water.* —**squirt** *n* [C]

squish /skwɪʃ/ *v* [I,T] *informal* to damage something by pressing it until it is flat [SYN] **squash**

squishy /'skwɪʃi/ *adj* something that is squishy feels soft when you press it

Sr. *AmE* the written abbreviation of **Senior**, used after someone's name: *Douglas Fairbanks, Sr.*

St., St 1 the written abbreviation of **Street**: *Oxford St.* **2** the written abbreviation of **Saint**: *St. John's church*

stab¹ /stæb/ *v* [T] (**stabbed, stabbing**) to push a knife into someone: *He was **stabbed to death** in a fight.* | **stab sb in the arm/chest etc** *The man had been stabbed several times in the stomach.*
[THESAURUS] ▶ **ATTACK**
PHRASES
| **stab sb in the back** *informal* to do something bad to someone who likes and trusts you: *I trusted him until he stabbed me in the back.*

stab² *n* **1** [C] when someone stabs someone else with a knife: *severe **stab wounds*** **2** **a stab at (doing) sth** *informal* an attempt to do something difficult: *Always **have a stab at** answering the questions.* **3** **a stab of pain/guilt/regret etc** *literary* a sudden feeling of pain etc: *Monique felt a stab of regret.*

stabbing¹ /'stæbɪŋ/ *n* [C] a crime in which someone is stabbed

stabbing² *adj* [only before noun] a stabbing pain is very sudden and strong

stability Ac /stə'bɪləti/ *n* [U] when a situation is steady and does not change [OPP] **instability**: *a long period of political stability*

stabilize Ac (*also* **-ise** *BrE*) /'steɪbəlaɪz/ *v* [I,T] to stop changing and to become steady, or to make something do this [OPP] **destabilize**: *The patient's condition has now stabilized.* —**stabilization** /ˌsteɪbəlaɪ'zeɪʃən $ -lə-/ *n* [U]

stable¹ Ac /'steɪbəl/ *adj* **1** not likely to change suddenly [OPP] **unstable**: *a stable marriage* | *He's **in a**

stable condition in hospital.* **2** in a firm position and not likely to move [OPP] **unstable**: *Make sure the ladder is stable.* **3** calm, reasonable, and not likely to be upset easily [OPP] **unstable**

stable² *n* [C] a building where horses are kept

stack¹ /stæk/ *n* [C] **1** a neat pile of things: **[+of]** *a stack of magazines* **2** **stacks of sth** *BrE informal* a lot of something: *I've got stacks of work to do.*

stack² *v* **1** (*also* **stack up**) [I,T] to make a neat pile: *Just stack the dishes in the sink.* | *chairs designed to stack easily* **2** [T] to put piles of things in a place: *Al has a job stacking shelves in the supermarket.*

stadium /'steɪdiəm/ *n* [C] (*plural* **stadiums** or **stadia** /-diə/) a large area for playing sports, surrounded by a building that has rows of seats: *a football stadium*

staff¹ /stɑːf $ stæf/ *n* [singular, U also + plural verb *BrE*] the group of people who work for an organization: *Lisa's the only female **member of staff.*** | *The staff were (=each member was) very helpful.* | **medical/academic/library etc staff** *a strike by hospital staff*

staff² *v* [T] to provide the workers for an organization: *a hospital staffed by experienced nurses*

staffer /'stɑːfə $ 'stæfər/ *n* [C] *AmE* one of the people who work for an organization: *a Mercury News staffer*

stag /stæg/ *n* [C] an adult male DEER

stage¹ /steɪdʒ/ *n*
1 [C] one part of a process or one time in the development of something → **phase**: **[+of]** *the first stage of the project* | *the early stages of the disease* | *They have now **reached** the halfway **stage** of the course.* | *the teams that **get to** the second **stage** of the competition* | *Children **go through** various **stages** of development.* | **at some/this/one stage** *At this stage, I'm not sure what the result will be.*
2 [C,U] the raised floor in a theatre where actors perform a play → **backstage**: **on stage** *I get very nervous before I go on stage.*
3 the stage the profession of acting: *I've always wanted to **go on the stage** (=become an actor).*

stage² *v* [T] to organize an event or performance: *They're staging a rock concert in the park.*

'stage fright *n* [U] the nervous feeling some people, especially actors, have before they perform in front of a lot of people

'stage ˌmanager *n* [C] a person in charge of what happens on the stage during a performance

stagger /'stægə $ -ər/ *v* **1** [I] to walk or move in an unsteady way, almost falling over: **[+along/back/down etc]** *Tom staggered drunkenly into the kitchen.*
[THESAURUS] ▶ **WALK** **2** [T] to make someone feel very surprised or shocked **3** [T] to arrange the time when things happen so that they do not all happen at the same time: *Student registration will be staggered to avoid delays.*

staggered /'stægəd $ -ərd/ *adj* [not before noun] very shocked or surprised: *I was staggered by the size of the bill.*

staggering /'stægərɪŋ/ *adj* very surprising or shocking: *She spent a staggering £2,000 on a new dress.* **THESAURUS** SURPRISING

stagnant /'stægnənt/ *adj* **1** stagnant water or air does not move and often smells bad **2** not changing or improving: *a stagnant economy*

stagnate /stæg'neɪt $ 'stægneɪt/ *v* [I] to stop developing or improving: *fears that the economy might stagnate* —**stagnation** /stæg'neɪʃən/ *n* [U]

'stag night (also **'stag party**) *n* [C] a social occasion when a man goes out with his male friends just before his wedding

staid /steɪd/ *adj* serious, old-fashioned, and boring: *a staid old bachelor*

stain¹ /steɪn/ *v* **1** [I,T] to accidentally make a mark on something, especially one that is difficult to remove, or to be marked in this way: *The carpet stains easily.* | **be stained with sth** *The tablecloth was stained with wine.* **2** [T] to paint wood with a stain

stain² *n* **1** [C] a mark that is difficult to remove: **[+on]** *coffee stains on the carpet* **THESAURUS** MARK **2** [C,U] a kind of paint used to colour wood and protect it

stained 'glass *n* [U] coloured glass that is used to make pictures and patterns in windows

stainless 'steel *n* [U] a type of steel that does not RUST

stair /steə $ ster/ *n* **1 stairs** [plural] a set of steps that you use to go from one level of a building to another: **up/down the stairs** *Kim ran up the stairs.* | *The office is up two flights of stairs.* **2** [C] one of the steps in a set of stairs: *Jane sat on the bottom stair.* → DOWNSTAIRS, UPSTAIRS, see picture at STAIRCASE

staircase /'steəkeɪs $ 'ster-/ (also **stairway** /'steəweɪ $ 'ster-/) *n* [C] a set of stairs inside a building

STAIRCASE

banister

stair/step

stake¹ /steɪk/ *n* **1 a stake in sth a)** a part or share in a business, plan etc: *She has a 5% stake in the company.* **b)** if you have a stake in something, you will get advantages if it is successful, and so you feel an important connection to it: *Many young people don't feel they have a stake in the country's future.* **2 stakes** [plural] the things you could lose in a game or uncertain situation: *I don't think you should get involved - the stakes are too high* (=you could lose a lot). **3** [C] a long sharp piece of wood or metal that you push into the ground to mark something or to support a plant **4** [C] money risked on the result of a game, race etc **SYN bet**: *a £10 stake*

be at stake if something is at stake, you will lose it if a plan or action is not successful: *We need this contract - hundreds of jobs are at stake.*

stake² *v* [T] to risk something on the result of a situation or competition: **stake sth on sth** *The President is staking his reputation on the peace plan.*
PHRASES
stake a claim to say that you think you have a right to have something: *Both countries have staked a claim to the islands.*

PHRASAL VERBS
stake sth ↔ **out** *informal* to watch a place secretly: *The police have been staking out the club for weeks.*

stale /steɪl/ *adj* **1** no longer fresh: *This bread's gone stale.* | *the smell of stale smoke* **2** no longer interesting: *stale news* **3** someone who is stale has no new ideas because they have been doing something for too long: *I was getting stale in my old job.*

stalemate /'steɪlmeɪt/ *n* [C,U] a situation when neither side in an argument, battle, or game can make progress or win: *The discussions ended in stalemate.*

stalk¹ /stɔːk $ stɒːk/ *n* [C] the main stem of a plant → see picture at PLANT¹

stalk² *v* **1** [T] to follow a person or animal in order to watch or attack them: *a tiger stalking its prey* **THESAURUS** FOLLOW **2** [I] to walk in a stiff, proud, or angry way: **[+off/out etc]** *She rose from her chair and stalked out of the room.*

stalker /'stɔːkə $ 'stɒːkər/ *n* [C] a person who follows and watches someone for a long time in a way that annoys or frightens them —**stalking** *n* [U]

stall¹ /stɔːl $ stɒːl/ *n* **1** [C] a large table on which you put things you want to sell: *a market stall* **2** [C] *AmE* a small enclosed area for washing or using the toilet: *a shower stall* **3 the stalls** [plural] the seats on the lowest floor nearest to the stage in a theatre

stall² *v* [I,T] **1** if an engine stalls, or if you stall it, it suddenly stops working: *The car stalled at the junction.* **2** *informal* to deliberately delay doing something, or to make someone else delay: *Quit stalling and answer my question!*

stallion /'stæljən/ *n* [C] an adult male horse

stalwart /'stɔːlwət $ 'stɒːlwərt/ *n* [C] someone who is very loyal in their support for an organization: *Labour Party stalwarts*

stamina /'stæmɪnə/ *n* [U] physical or mental strength that lets you continue doing something for a long time: *exercises to improve speed and stamina*

stammer /'stæmə $ -ər/ *v* [I,T] to repeat the first sound of a word when you speak: *'N-n-no,' he stammered.* —**stammer** *n* [singular]: *She has a bad stammer.*

stamp¹ /stæmp/ *n* [C]
1 (also **postage stamp**) a small piece of paper that you buy and stick on a letter before you post it: *a first-class stamp* | *Don't forget to put a stamp on the letter.*
2 a) an official mark that has been printed on a document using a tool covered with ink: *a stamp in*

my passport **b)** the tool that you press onto paper to make a mark

3 have/bear the stamp of sth to clearly have a particular quality: *a speech that definitely bore the stamp of authority* → **FOOD STAMP**

stamp² v

1 [I,T] to put your foot down very hard on the ground, or to walk in this way: **[+in/out/through etc]** *She stamped out of the room.* | *She was **stamping** her **feet** to keep warm.*

2 [T] to print an official mark on a document by pressing a tool covered with ink onto it: *Did they stamp your passport?*

PHRASAL VERBS

stamp sth ↔ **out** to end something bad completely: *efforts to stamp out drug abuse*

stampede /stæm'piːd/ *n* [C] **1** when a large number of animals suddenly start running together **2** when a lot of people suddenly want to do the same thing or go to the same place —**stampede** *v* [I]

stance /stɑːns $ stæns/ *n* [C] **1** an opinion that someone states publicly: **[+on]** *Senator, what is your stance on nuclear tests?* **2** *formal* a way of standing

stand¹ /stænd/ *v* (*past tense and past participle* **stood** /stʊd/)

1 BE ON YOUR FEET [I] to be on your feet with your body in an upright position: **[+in/by etc]** *Anna was standing in front of me.* | *Jo **stood still** (=stood without moving) and listened.* | **stand doing sth** *Hundreds of people stood watching.* | *Don't just **stand there** (=stand doing nothing) – help me!* | **stand back/ aside** (=move and stand further away) *A policeman told everyone to stand back.*

2 GET UP (*also* **stand up**) [I] to rise onto your feet after you have been sitting, bending, or lying down: *She finished her drink and stood to leave.* | *She stood up and put her coat on.*

3 PAIN/BAD SITUATION [T] to be able to accept or deal with something unpleasant or difficult SYN **tolerate**: *She **couldn't stand** the pain any longer.* | **stand (sb) doing sth** *How can she stand him treating her like that?*

4 BE IN A POSITION [I,T] to be in a place or position, or to put something in a place or position: **[+in/on/by etc]** *Their house stood on a corner near the park.* | **stand sth in/on sth** *We stood the lamp in the corner.* | *Few buildings were **left standing** after the explosion.*

5 BE IN A CONDITION [linking verb] to be in a particular state or condition: *The kitchen door **stood open**.* | *old houses **standing empty*** | *I'm not happy with **the way things stand** (=the situation) at the moment.* | *Your proposal, **as it stands**, is not acceptable.*

6 BE STRONG ENOUGH [T] to be strong enough or good enough not to be damaged or destroyed by something: *jeans that can stand the rough wear kids give them* | *Their marriage has certainly **stood the test of time** (=stayed strong).*

7 LIKELY TO DO STH [I] **stand to do sth** to be likely to get or do something: **stand to gain/lose/make/win** *They stand to make more than £12 million if the deal is successful.*

8 LEVEL [linking verb] to be at a particular level or amount: **[+at]** *The unemployment rate stands at 8%.*

9 HEIGHT [linking verb] *formal* to have a particular height: *The Eiffel Tower **stands** 300 metres **high**.* | *John **stood** 6 feet **tall**.*

10 IN AN ELECTION [I] *BrE* to try to be elected SYN **run** *AmE*: **[+for]** *He stood for parliament in 1959.* | **[+against]** *She stood against John Woodford for the party leadership.*

11 OFFER [I] if an offer still stands, it is still available for someone to accept

12 OPINION ABOUT STH **where/how you stand (on sth)** what your opinion about something is: *Where do you stand on the issue of immigration?* → **stand guard** at GUARD¹

PHRASES

can't stand *spoken* to hate someone or something: *Dave can't stand dogs.* | **can't stand (sb) doing sth** *I can't stand being late.* | *I know he **can't stand the sight of** me (=really hates me).* THESAURUS ▶ HATE

it stands to reason (that) used to say that something is clearly true: *It stands to reason that children will want to do what their friends do.*

know where you stand (with sb) to know what someone's feelings or intentions towards you are: *You never know where you stand with Debbie.*

stand a chance (of doing sth) to be likely to succeed in doing something: *You don't stand a chance of winning.* | **stand a better/a good/little/no chance (of doing sth)** *Short letters stand a better chance of publication.*

stand in line *AmE* to wait in a line of people until it is your turn to do something SYN **queue** *BrE*: *Fans stood in line waiting for the doors to open.* THESAURUS ▶ WAIT

stand in the way/stand in sb's way to prevent someone from doing something, or prevent something from happening: *There are a few problems that stand in the way of the agreement.*

stand on your own two feet to be independent and not need help from other people: *It's about time you learned to stand on your own two feet.*

stand trial if you stand trial for a crime, people try to prove that you are guilty of the crime in a court of law: *The judge ruled that the former president was too ill to stand trial.*

PHRASAL VERBS

stand around to stand somewhere and not do anything: *Everybody was just standing around waiting.*

stand by

1 stand by sth if you stand by something, you still believe in it and say that it is true: *I stand by what I said earlier.*

2 stand by sb to stay loyal to someone and support them in a difficult situation: *Matt's parents have stood by him throughout his drug treatments.*

3 to be ready to do something → **standby**: *Fire crews are now standing by.*

4 to allow something bad to happen by doing nothing: *People just stood by and watched him being attacked.*

stand down *BrE* to leave an important job or position SYN **step down** *AmE*: *The chairman stood down last month.*

stand for sth

1 to be a short form of a word or phrase: *What does ATM stand for?*

2 to support an idea, principle etc: *I don't like her, or what she stands for.*

3 not stand for sth *BrE* not to allow something to happen or continue: *I won't stand for this behaviour.*

stand in for sb to do someone else's job while they are away → **stand-in**: *Lyn stood in for me while I was ill.*

stand out

1 to be clearly better than other things or people: **[+as]** *Morrison stands out as the most experienced candidate.*

2 to be very easy to see or notice: *She really stood out in her bright green dress.*

stand up

1 to be on your feet, or to rise to your feet: *I've been standing up all day.* | *We stood up when the judge came in.* | *Stand up straight* *and put your shoulders back.* **THESAURUS** ► **STAND**

2 to be proved to be true, useful, or strong when tested: *The accusations will never stand up in court.*

3 stand sb up to not meet someone when you have promised to meet them: *Tom stood me up last night.*

stand up for sb/sth to defend a person or idea when they are being criticized or attacked: *Why didn't you stand up for me?*

stand up to sb to refuse to accept unfair treatment from someone: *He became a hero for standing up to the local gangs.*

THESAURUS

stand to be on your feet with your body in an upright position: *A policeman was standing by the door.*

be on your feet to be standing, especially for a long time: *I've been on my feet all day and I need to sit down.*

get up to stand after you have been sitting or lying down: *Get up and help me with the dishes.*

stand up to stand after you have been sitting, or to be in a standing position: *We all stood up when he came into the room.* | *There were no free seats on the train and I had to stand up all the way home.*

get to your feet to stand up, especially slowly or when it is difficult for you: *I helped her get to her feet.*

---

stand² *n* [C] **1** a piece of furniture or equipment for supporting something: *a music stand* **2** a table used for selling or showing things to people SYN **stall** *BrE*: *a hotdog stand* **3** an opinion that you state publicly: *The prime minister took a firm stand on the issue of import controls.* **4** a strong attempt to defend yourself or to oppose something: **make/take a stand (against sth)** *We have to take a stand against racism.* **5 the stands** [plural] a building where people sit or stand to watch a game in a sports ground → **grandstand 6 the stand** *AmE* the place in a court of law where someone sits when the lawyer asks them questions → **ONE-NIGHT STAND, WITNESS STAND**

standard¹ /'stændəd $ -ərd/ *n*

1 [C,U] a level that measures how good something is or how well someone does something: **[+of]** *We must improve standards of food hygiene.* | **up to/below**

standard (=good enough or not good enough) *Her work was not up to standard.*

2 standards [plural] moral principles about what is acceptable: *He has very high moral standards.* → **DOUBLE STANDARD**

PHRASES

by ... standards compared to the normal or expected level of something else: **by modern/ today's standards** *By today's standards, I earned very little.* | *Prices are low by Western standards.*

standard² *adj* normal or usual → **non-standard**: *The shoes are available in all standard sizes.* | **standard practice/procedure** *Security checks are now standard procedure.* **THESAURUS** ► **NORMAL**

standardize (*also* **-ise** *BrE*) /'stændədaiz $ -ər-/ *v* [T] to change things so that they are all the same as each other: *an attempt to standardize the tests* —**standardization** /ˌstændədaɪˈzeɪʃən $ -dərdə-/ *n* [U]

ˌstandard of 'living *n* [C] the amount of money that people have to spend, and how comfortable their life is: *Japan has a very high standard of living.*

standby /'stændbaɪ/ *n* [C] (*plural* **standbys**) something that is ready to be used if needed —**standby** *adj*: *a standby generator*

PHRASES

on standby 1 ready to be used if needed: *The police have been kept on standby in case of trouble.* **2** if you are on standby for a plane ticket, you will be allowed to travel if there are any seats that are not being used: *We can put you on standby.*

ˈstand-in *n* [C] someone who does another person's job or does something instead of them for a short time

standing¹ /'stændɪŋ/ *n* [U] the opinion that people have about someone, and how good and important they are: **[+in]** *This has improved the president's standing in the opinion polls.*

standing² *adj* **1 standing invitation** when someone has invited you to come whenever you want **2 standing ovation** when people stand up to CLAP after a performance because they think it is very good: *He was given a standing ovation.* **3 standing joke** something that happens often and that people make jokes about

ˌstanding 'order *n* [C] an arrangement in which your bank pays a fixed amount of money to someone regularly from your account → **direct debit**

ˈstand-off *n* [C] a situation in which a fight or battle stops because neither side can win

standpoint /'stændpɔɪnt/ *n* [C] one way of thinking about a situation SYN **point of view**: *Let's look at this from a practical standpoint.*

standstill /'stændstɪl/ *n* [singular] a situation in which nothing is moving or happening: *The funeral brought the city to a standstill.* | *The traffic came to a standstill.*

ˈstand-up *adj* [only before noun] a stand-up COMEDIAN stands alone in front of a group of people and tells jokes

stank /stæŋk/ *v* the past tense of STINK

stanza /ˈstænzə/ n [C] a group of lines that form part of a poem SYN **verse**

staple¹ /ˈsteɪpəl/ n [C] **1** a small piece of thin wire used to fasten pieces of paper together **2** a food that people use all the time: *staples like flour and rice* —**staple** v [T]: *Staple the pages together.*

staple² adj [only before noun] staple foods are very important and used all the time: *staple foods like potatoes* | *a staple diet of* (=consisting mainly of) *rice*

stapler /ˈsteɪplə $ -ər/ n [C] a machine that puts staples through paper → see picture at STATIONERY

star¹ /staː $ staːr/ n [C]

1 IN THE SKY a large ball of burning gas in space that you can see as a point of light in the night sky: *I looked up at the stars.*

2 a famous actor, singer, sports player etc: **movie/ film/Hollywood star** *photographs of movie stars* | **pop/rock star** THESAURUS ▶ ACTOR

3 IN A FILM/PLAY someone who has one of the main parts in a film, show, or play: **[+of]** *Tom Kay, star of the TV comedy 'Tom's World'*

4 THE BEST the best in a group of players, students etc: **star player/student/performer etc** *Jim is one of our star salesmen.* | *Louise was the star of the show* (=gave the best performance).

5 SHAPE a shape with five or six points: *paper decorated with silver stars* → see picture at SHAPE¹

6 HOTEL/RESTAURANT **two-star/four-star etc** a mark used in a system for showing how good a hotel or restaurant is: *a three-star hotel*

7 ASTROLOGY **the stars** [plural] *BrE* the way that some people believe that your life is affected by the position of the stars when you were born → SHOOTING STAR

THESAURUS

star a ball of burning gas in space, which can be seen at night as a point of light in the sky: *We looked up at the stars.*

planet one of the large objects that go around the Sun, for example the Earth, Saturn, or Mars: *the planet Jupiter*

sun the star that gives us light and heat, around which the planets move: *The sky was blue and the sun was shining.*

moon the round object that moves around the Earth every 28 days, or a similar object that goes around another planet: *The moon lit up the night sky.* | *the moons of Saturn*

constellation a group of stars that form a particular pattern and has a name: *the constellation of Aquarius*

---

star² v [I,T] (**starred, starring**) if a film, play etc stars someone, or if someone stars in a film, play etc, they have one of the main parts in it: *a movie starring Mel Gibson* | **[+in]** *She starred in her own TV series.* | **[+as]** *Nicole Kidman stars as Emma.* | **star sb as sb** *The film starred Hugh Grant as Will.*

starboard /ˈstɑːbəd $ ˈstɑːrbərd/ n [U] the right side of a ship or aircraft when you are facing the front OPP **port**

starch /stɑːtʃ $ stɑːrtʃ/ n **1** [C,U] a substance in foods such as bread, rice, and potatoes **2** [U] a substance used for making cloth stiff

starchy /ˈstɑːtʃi $ ˈstɑːr-/ adj starchy foods contain a lot of starch

stardom /ˈstɑːdəm $ ˈstɑːr-/ n [U] when someone is a very famous performer: *He rose to stardom.*

stare /steə $ ster/ v [I] to look at someone or something for a long time: **[+at]** *She stared at me in horror.* | *He sat there bored, staring into space* (=looking at nothing). THESAURUS ▶ LOOK —**stare** n [C]: *She gave him a hard stare.*

starfish /ˈstɑːfɪʃ $ ˈstɑːr-/ n [C] (*plural* **starfish**) a flat sea animal that has five arms forming the shape of a star

stark¹ /stɑːk $ stɑːrk/ adj **1** very plain in appearance, with no decoration: *the stark beauty of the desert* **2** unpleasantly clear and impossible to avoid: *a stark choice between life and death* —**starkly** adv

stark² adv **stark naked** not wearing any clothes

starlight /ˈstɑːlaɪt $ ˈstɑːr-/ n [U] the light that comes from stars at night —**starlit** /-lɪt/ adj: *a starlit sky*

starry /ˈstɑːri/ adj a starry sky has a lot of stars

starry-'eyed adj hopeful about things in a way that is silly or unreasonable, especially because you are young: *a starry-eyed teenager*

Stars and 'Stripes n **the Stars and Stripes** the national flag of the US

'star sign n [C] one of the 12 signs of the ZODIAC (=a system based on the belief that the time you were born affects what will happen to you)

'star-ˌstudded adj including many famous performers: *The film has a star-studded cast.*

start¹ /stɑːt $ stɑːrt/ v

1 [I,T] to begin doing something: *Now you're here, we can start.* | *When does she start college?* | **start doing sth** *He started laughing.* | **start to do sth** *It's started to rain.* | **start by doing sth** *I'll start by introducing myself.* | *I did it wrong, so I had to start again.* | *It's late, we should get started.* | **[+on]** *I'd better start on my homework.*

2 (*also* **start off**) [I,T] to begin happening or existing, or to make something begin happening: *The show starts soon.* | *The fire was started by a candle.* | **Starting from** tomorrow, this will be your room. | **start (sth) with sth** *The meal started with soup.* | *He always starts off the lesson with a test.* | **start (off) by doing sth** *Let's start off by saying why we're here.* | **[+as]** *The website started as a school project.*

3 (*also* **start up**) [T] to form a new business or organization: *We started our own record company.*

4 (*also* **start up**) [I,T] if you start an engine or machine, or if it starts, it begins to work: *The car wouldn't start this morning.*

5 **start at/from etc sth** if prices start at or from an amount, that is the lowest amount that you can pay to get something: *Tickets start from £12.*

PHRASES

to start with *spoken* **1** at the beginning of a situation: *You'll need some help to start with.* **2** used to emphasize the first of a list of things you want to mention: *I can't join the police – to start with, I'm too short.*

PHRASAL VERBS

start sb **off** to make someone begin doing something: **start sb off doing sth** *That started me off crying.*

start out to begin life, existence, work etc in a particular way or form: *When we started out, my bedroom was our office.* | **[+as]** *The book started out as a short article.*

start over *AmE* to start doing something again from the beginning

---

THESAURUS

to start doing something

start to begin doing something: *Start singing whenever you're ready.*

begin to start doing something. **Begin** is more formal than **start**, and is used especially in written English: *He picked up a pen and began to write.*

get down to sth to finally start doing something, especially your work: *It's time you got down to some schoolwork.*

set off to start a journey: *We set off after breakfast.*

to start happening

start to begin: *Has the play started yet?*

begin to start. **Begin** is more formal than **start** and is used especially in written English: *Building work has already begun.*

open to start being shown to the public – used about a play, show, or exhibition: *The show opens next week.*

commence *formal* to start happening: *The work is scheduled to commence in April.*

break out to start happening – used especially about a fire, a fight, war, or a disease: *War broke out in September.*

---

start² n

1 [C usually singular] the beginning of something: **[+of]** *Hurry, or we'll miss the start of the show.* | *She came here at the start of 2001.* | *The project has had problems **from the start**.* | **get off to a good/bad start** (=start well/or start badly) *The year got off to a good start.* **THESAURUS ▶ BEGINNING**

2 [singular] a sudden movement of your body, caused by fear or surprise: *Ed woke **with a start**.*

3 the start the place where a race or game begins

4 [C usually singular] an advantage you have when you start something before other people: **give sb/have a start** *He had a 100-metre **start on** his pursuers.*

5 be a start used to say that something may not be impressive, but it will help: *I go to the gym once a week, which is a start.* → **HEAD START**

PHRASES

for a start *BrE spoken* used to emphasize the first of several reasons or other things you want to mention: *I hated it. The food was awful, for a start.*

make a start to begin doing something: **[+on]** *I'll make a start on the cleaning.*

---

starter /ˈstɑːtə $ ˈstɑːrtər/ n [C] *BrE* a small amount of food that you eat as the first part of a meal **SYN** **appetizer**: *We had soup as a starter, followed by steak.*

PHRASES

for starters *spoken informal* used to emphasize the first thing in a series of things: *You've spelled the title wrong, for starters.*

'starting ˌpoint n [C] something from which a discussion or situation can develop: **[+for]** *The article is a good starting point for debate.*

startle /ˈstɑːtl $ ˈstɑːrtl/ v [T] to make someone suddenly feel surprised or shocked: *Sorry, I didn't mean to startle you.* —**startled** adj: *a startled expression*

'start-up¹ adj [only before noun] connected with starting a new business: *start-up costs*

'start-up² n [C] a new small company: *an Internet start-up*

starvation /stɑːˈveɪʃən $ stɑːr-/ n [U] suffering or death caused by lack of food: *people dying of starvation*

starve /stɑːv $ stɑːrv/ v [I,T] to suffer or die because you do not have enough to eat, or to make someone do this: *Thousands of people could **starve to death**.* | *starving refugees*

PHRASAL VERBS

starve sb/sth **of** sth not to give something that is needed: *Schools have been starved of funding.*

starving /ˈstɑːvɪŋ $ ˈstɑːr-/ adj

1 someone who is starving has not had enough food for a long time and could die: *starving children* **THESAURUS ▶ HUNGRY**

2 *BrE spoken*, **starved** /stɑːvd $ stɑːrvd/ *AmE* very hungry: *Let's have lunch – I'm starving.*

stash¹ /stæʃ/ v [T] *informal* to store something secretly somewhere: **stash sth away** *The money is stashed away in a bank account.*

stash² n [C] *informal* an amount of something, especially drugs or money, that is kept in a secret place

state¹ /steɪt/ n

1 **CONDITION** [C] the condition that someone or something is in: **[+of]** *We are concerned about the state of the economy.* | *The house was **in a terrible state**.* | *They found him **in a state of shock**.* | *You are in no fit state to drive.* **THESAURUS ▶ CONDITION**

2 **GOVERNMENT** **the state** (*also* **the State**) the government of a country: *the power of the state* | **state-owned/state-funded etc** *state-owned industries*

3 **PART OF A COUNTRY** (*also* **State**) [C] one of the parts that the US and some other countries are divided into, which each have their own government: *the state of Texas*

4 **THE UNITED STATES** **the States** *spoken* the US: *Have you been to the States?*

5 **COUNTRY** (*also* **State**) [C,U] a country considered as a political organization: *EU **member states*** | *a meeting between **heads of state** (=leaders of countries)* **THESAURUS ▶ LEADER**

6 OFFICIAL CEREMONY **state visit/ceremony/opening etc** an important official visit, ceremony etc involving governments or rulers → **NATION STATE, POLICE STATE, WELFARE STATE**

PHRASES

be in/get into a state *BrE informal* to be or become very nervous or upset: *Don't let yourself get into a state.*

state of affairs a situation: *The government got us into this sorry state of affairs* (=bad situation) *in the first place.*

state² *v* [T] *formal* to say something publicly or officially: *Please state your name.* | **[+(that)]** *The rules state that contestants must be over 18.* THESAURUS **SAY**

stately /'steɪtli/ *adj* formal and impressive: *a stately mansion*

stately 'home *n* [C] a large old house in the countryside in Britain, especially one that is open to the public

statement /'steɪtmənt/ *n* [C]
1 something that you say or write publicly or officially: **[+on/about]** *the President's statements on the economy* | *The minister will **make** a **statement** later today.* | *He **gave** a **statement** to the police.*
2 a list showing amounts of money that have been paid and received: *According to my **bank statement**, I haven't been paid.*

state of e'mergency *n* [C] (*plural* **states of emergency**) a situation in which a government uses special powers to limit people's freedom

state of 'mind *n* [C] someone's feelings, for example whether they are happy or upset

state-of-the-'art *adj* using the newest methods, materials, or knowledge: *state-of-the-art technology* THESAURUS **MODERN**

state ,school *n* [C] *BrE* a school which provides free education and is paid for by the government

statesman /'steɪtsmən/ *n* [C] (*plural* **statesmen** /-mən/) a political leader, especially one who is respected and admired THESAURUS **POLITICIAN** —**statesmanship** *n* [U]

static¹ /'stætɪk/ *adj* not changing or moving: *Prices have remained static.*

static² *n* [U] **1** noise caused by electricity in the air that spoils the sound on the radio or television **2** (*also* **static elec'tricity**) electricity that collects on an object and gives you a small electric shock when you touch it

station¹ /'steɪʃən/ *n* [C]
1 a building where trains or buses stop so that passengers can get on and off: **at a station** *We get off at the next station.* | **bus station/train station/ railway station** *BrE*/**railroad station** *AmE*
2 a building where a service or activity is based: **police/fire station** *He was interviewed at the police station.* | **petrol station** *BrE*/**gas station** *AmE* (=where petrol is sold)
3 a company that broadcasts on radio or television: **radio/TV station** → **FILLING STATION, POLLING STATION, POWER STATION, SERVICE STATION**

station² *v* [T usually passive] to send a soldier to a place as part of their duty: *He was stationed in Germany.*

stationary /'steɪʃənəri $ -neri/ *adj* not moving: *a stationary vehicle*

stationer's /'steɪʃənəz $ -ərz/ *n* [C] *BrE* a shop that sells stationery

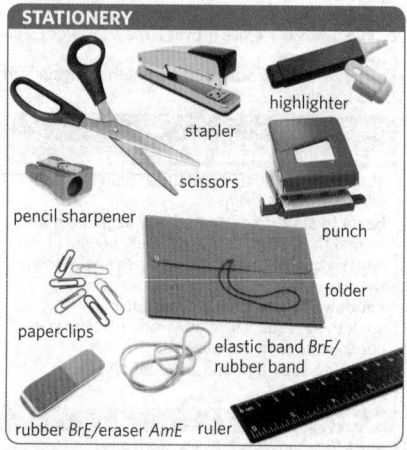

STATIONERY

highlighter
stapler
scissors
pencil sharpener
punch
folder
paperclips
elastic band *BrE*/
rubber band
rubber *BrE*/eraser *AmE*   ruler

stationery /'steɪʃənəri $ -neri/ *n* [U] things such as paper or pens that you use for writing

Word Choice: stationary or stationery?
Do not confuse the adjective **stationary** (=not moving) with the noun **stationery** (=paper, pens, and other things you need for writing).

station ,wagon *n* [C] *AmE* a large car with extra space at the back SYN **estate car** *BrE*

statistic Ac /stə'tɪstɪk/ *n* **1** [C] a number which represents a fact or measurement: *the government's official crime statistics* | *1 in 3 people get cancer – a frightening statistic.* **2 statistics** [U] the science of collecting and studying numbers which represent facts or measurements: *an expert in statistics* —**statistical** *adj*: *statistical analysis* —**statistically** /-kli/ *adv*

statistician Ac /,stætə'stɪʃən/ *n* [C] someone who works with statistics

statue /'stætʃuː/ *n* [C] a large image of a person or animal made of stone, wood, or metal → **sculpture**: **[+of]** *a statue of Queen Victoria*

stature /'stætʃə $ -ər/ *n* [U] *formal* **1** when someone is important and well respected: *a musician of great stature* **2** someone's height

status Ac /'steɪtəs $ 'steɪtəs, 'stæ-/ *n* [U]
1 the official or legal importance that someone or something has: *the status of women in society* | *This document has no **legal status** in the UK.* | *your name, age, and **marital status** (=whether you are married or not)*
2 respect or importance that is given to someone or something: *Caring for children should have more status.*

status quo /ˌsteɪtəs ˈkwəʊ $ ˌsteɪtəs ˈkwoʊ, ˌstæ-/ n **the status quo** the situation that exists at a particular time

'status ˌsymbol n [C] something that you own that suggests you are rich or important

statute /ˈstætʃuːt/ n [C] formal a law or rule

statutory /ˈstætʃətəri $ -tɔːri/ adj formal fixed or controlled by law: your statutory rights

staunch¹ /stɔːntʃ $ stɒːntʃ, stɑːntʃ/ adj very loyal: a staunch supporter of the Liberal Party —**staunchly** adv

staunch² (also **stanch** AmE) v [T] to stop a flow of blood from a wound

stave /steɪv/ v (past tense and past participle **staved** or **stove** /stəʊv $ stoʊv/)
PHRASAL VERBS
stave sth ↔ **off** to stop something unpleasant from happening for a short time: She ate an apple to stave off hunger.

stay¹ /steɪ/ v
1 [I] to remain in the same place, job, school etc, and not leave: He came to see me and stayed all day. | **[+at/in]** I stayed at school late. | He stayed in his job for ten years. | **stay at home** BrE/**stay home** AmE: She decided to stay home. | **stay here/there** Stay here in case anybody calls. | **stay and do sth** I want to stay and help. | **stay for dinner/lunch etc** Why don't you stay for tea?
2 [I, linking verb] to continue to be in a particular state, and not change: It was hard to **stay awake**. | Try to **stay calm**. | This town has **stayed the same** for centuries. | I hope we can **stay friends**.
3 [I] to live in a place for a short time as a visitor or guest: **[+at/in]** They're staying at her mother's. | How long are you staying in Paris? | **[+with]** We're going to stay with friends this weekend.
PHRASES
stay put informal to remain in one place and not move: Stay put until I get back.
PHRASAL VERBS
stay away to not go near someone or something: **[+from]** Stay away from my sister! THESAURUS ▶ AVOID
stay behind to stay in a place after the other people have left: I had to stay behind after school.
stay in to stay in your home and not go out: Let's stay in and watch TV.
stay on to continue to do a job or to study after the time when people can leave: Rachel is staying on for another year in college.
stay out
1 to remain away from home during the evening or night: She stayed out till midnight.
2 stay out of sth spoken to not get involved in an argument: He told me to stay out of it.
stay up not to go to bed: We **stayed up late** last night.

stay² n [C] a short period of time that you spend somewhere: We hope you enjoy your stay. | **[+in/at]** a short stay in hospital

STD /ˌes tiː ˈdiː/ n [C,U] (**sexually transmitted disease**) a disease that one person passes to another through having sex

stead /sted/ n **1 stand sb in good stead** to be very useful for someone in the future: Her training stood her in good stead. **2 do sth in sb's stead** formal to do something instead of someone else

steadfast /ˈstedfɑːst $ -fæst/ adj literary refusing to change your opinion or your support for someone

steady¹ /ˈstedi/ adj
1 continuing or developing at the same rate, without stopping or changing: He has made steady progress. | a steady speed of 50 mph | **hold/remain steady** Inflation held steady at 3%.
2 not moving or shaking → **stable**: Keep the ladder steady. | Her voice remained steady.
3 a steady job a job you get paid regularly for, and is likely to continue for a long time
4 steady boyfriend/girlfriend someone that you have had a romantic relationship with for a long time —**steadily** adv —**steadiness** n [U]

steady² v [I,T] (**steadied, steadying, steadies**) to control someone or something so that they do not shake or fall, or to become controlled like this: **steady yourself** He put out his hand to steady himself. | The ship steadied.

steak /steɪk/ n [C,U] a large thick piece of meat or fish

steal /stiːl/ v (past tense **stole** /stəʊl $ stoʊl/, past participle **stolen** /ˈstəʊlən $ ˈstoʊ-/)
1 [I,T] to take something that does not belong to you: Someone stole my passport. | **steal (sth) from sb/sth** He even stole from his friends. | Money was stolen from her purse. | a stolen car
2 [I,T] to use someone else's ideas and pretend that they are yours: She accused him of stealing her invention.
3 [I] to move secretly and quietly: **[+away/across/into etc]** Silently she stole away.

THESAURUS
steal to take something that belongs to someone else: Her bike has been stolen.
take to steal something – used when it is clear from the situation that you mean that someone takes something dishonestly: Someone's taken my purse!
nick BrE informal to steal something: Have you nicked my pen?
burgle BrE, **burglarize** AmE to go into someone's home and steal things: Our house was burgled while we were on holiday.
rob to steal money or other things from a person, bank, or shop: They robbed him of all his money. | The men were planning to rob a bank.
mug to attack someone in the street and steal something from them: He was mugged on his way home from school.
shoplifting stealing things from a shop: She was stopped at the pay desk and accused of shoplifting.

stealth /stelθ/ n [U] when you do something secretly or quietly —**stealthy** adj

steam¹ /stiːm/ n [U] the mist that hot water produces: The kitchen was full of steam. | **steam engine/boat/train etc** (=that uses power from steam)

PHRASES

let off steam to get rid of your anger or energy by doing something active: *She just needed to let off steam.*

under your own steam without help from anyone else: *I'll get to the restaurant under my own steam.*

steam² v **1** [I] to produce steam: *a cup of steaming coffee* THESAURUS ▷ COOK **2** [T] to cook something in steam → **boil**: *Steam the vegetables.*

steamed 'up adj **1** covered with steam: *My glasses were all steamed up.* **2** informal angry or worried

steamer /'sti:mə $ -ər/ n [C] **1** a ship that uses steam power **2** a pan in which you cook food by steaming it

steamroller¹ /'sti:m,rəʊlə $ -,rəʊlər/ v [T] informal to defeat someone or force someone to do something by using all your power

steamroller² n [C] a heavy vehicle used for making road surfaces flat

steamy /'sti:mi/ adj **1** full of steam or covered in steam: *steamy windows* **2** sexually exciting: *a steamy love scene*

steed /sti:d/ n [C] literary a horse

steel¹ /sti:l/ n [U] a strong metal that can be shaped easily and is used for making knives etc: *cutlery made of stainless steel* (=steel that remains shiny for a long time) | *a steel factory*

steel² v **steel yourself** to prepare yourself to do something unpleasant

steelworks /'sti:lwɜːks $ -wɜːrks/ n [C] (plural **steelworks**) a factory where steel is made

steely /'sti:li/ adj very determined and strong: *his steely determination*

steep¹ /sti:p/ adj

1 a steep road or hill goes down or up at a sharp angle: *a steep mountain track*

2 a steep increase or decrease is large: *a steep rise in profits*

3 informal very expensive —**steeply** adv —**steepness** n [U]

steep² v [T] to put food in a liquid and leave it for some time

PHRASES

be steeped in history/tradition etc to contain a lot of a particular quality: *The town is steeped in history.*

steeple /'sti:pəl/ n [C] a tall pointed tower on a church

steer¹ /stɪə $ stɪr/ v

1 [I,T] to control the direction a vehicle is going: **[+for/towards etc]** *I steered for the harbour.* | **steer sth towards/away from etc sth** *He steered the van through the traffic.*

2 [T] to influence someone's behaviour or the way a situation develops: **steer sb/sth towards/away from sth** *She steered me towards a medical career.* | *Helen tried to steer the conversation away from school.*

PHRASES

steer clear of sb/sth informal to try to avoid someone or something: *I steer clear of talking about politics.*

steer² n [C] a young male cow

steering /'stɪərɪŋ $ 'stɪr-/ n [U] the parts of a car, boat etc that control its direction: *power steering*

'steering wheel n [C] a wheel that you turn to control the direction of a car

stem¹ /stem/ n [C] the long thin part of a plant that grows up out of the ground → see picture at PLANT¹

stem² v [T] (**stemmed, stemming**) to stop something from spreading or growing: **stem the tide/flood/flow of sth** *an effort to stem the rising tide of crime*

PHRASAL VERBS

stem from sth to develop as a result of something

stench /stentʃ/ n [C] a very strong unpleasant smell SYN **stink** THESAURUS ▷ SMELL

stencil /'stensəl/ n [C] a piece of paper or plastic with patterns or letters cut out of it, which you use for painting patterns or letters onto a surface —**stencil** v [T]

step¹ /step/ n [C]

1 WHEN WALKING the movement you make when you put one foot in front of the other when walking: *He took a few steps, then stopped.* | **[+forwards/back/towards etc]** *Jamie took a step back and shook his head.*

2 STAGE one of a series of things that you do in order to deal with a problem or achieve something: **[+towards]** *an important step towards peace* | *We must take steps to make sure it never happens again.* | *Environmentalists called the change a step in the right direction* (=a good thing to do).

3 STAIR a flat narrow piece of wood or stone that you put your foot on when you are going up or down, especially outside a building: *Jenny sat on the step in front of the house, waiting.* | *We walked down a short flight of steps* (=set of steps) *to the car park.* → see picture at STAIRCASE

4 WHEN DANCING one of the movements you make with your feet when you are doing a dance → FOOTSTEP, STEP-BY-STEP

PHRASES

in step 1 thinking or behaving in the same way as other people: **[+with]** *The party needs to get in step with the voters.* **2** moving your feet at the same time as people you are walking with

out of step 1 thinking or behaving in a different way from other people: **[+with]** *Katy felt a little out of step with her schoolmates.* **2** moving your feet in a different way from people you are walking with: *The soldiers were completely out of step.*

watch your step BrE to be careful about what you say and how you behave: *You have to watch your step around the boss.*

step² v [I] (**stepped, stepping**)

1 to move somewhere by putting one foot down in front of the other: **[+back/forward etc]** *Everyone* stepped back to let the doctor through. | I opened the door and **stepped outside**.

2 BrE to put your foot on or in something SYN **tread** BrE: [+in/on etc] Sorry, I didn't mean to step on your foot.

PHRASES

step out of line to break the rules, or not do what you have been told to do: We were always punished if we dared to step out of line.

PHRASAL VERBS

step down/aside to leave an important job or official position

step forward to offer help SYN **come forward**: Several volunteers have kindly stepped forward.

step in to become involved in a situation, especially to stop trouble SYN **intervene**: The police stepped in and stopped the fight.

step up

1 step sth ↔ **up** to increase the amount of an activity or the speed of a process: Airlines are stepping up security checks.

2 (also **step up to the plate**) especially AmE to offer to help someone or be responsible for doing something: When we were in trouble, he stepped up.

stepbrother /'stepbrʌðə $ -ər/ n [C] the son of someone who has married one of your parents

step-by-'step adj a step-by-step plan, method etc deals with things carefully and in a fixed order: **step-by-step guide/instructions** a step-by-step guide to buying a house —**step by step** adv

stepchild /'steptʃaɪld/ n [C] (plural **stepchildren** /-,tʃɪldrən/) a STEPDAUGHTER or STEPSON

stepdaughter /'stepdɔːtə $ -dɔːtər/ n [C] a daughter that your husband or wife has from a previous marriage

stepfather /'stepfɑːðə $ -ər/ n [C] a man who is married to your mother, but who is not your father

stepladder /'step,lædə $ -ər/ n [C] a LADDER with two sloping parts that are joined at the top so that it can stand without support → see picture at **LADDER**

stepmother /'stepmʌðə $ -ər/ n [C] a woman who is married to your father, but who is not your mother

'stepping-,stone n [C] **1** something that will help you to achieve something else: a stepping-stone to a better job **2 stepping-stones** [plural] a row of stones that you walk on to get across a stream

stepsister /'stepsɪstə $ -ər/ n [C] the daughter of someone who has married one of your parents

stepson /'stepsʌn/ n [C] a son that your husband or wife has from a previous marriage

stereo /'steriəʊ, 'stɪər- $ 'steriou, 'stɪr-/ n (plural **stereos**) **1** [C] a machine for playing records, CDs etc that produces sound from two SPEAKERS **2** [U] a system for playing music or speech through two SPEAKERS

stereotype /'steriətaɪp, 'stɪər- $ 'ster-, 'stɪr-/ n [C] an idea of what a type of person is like, especially one which is wrong or unfair: **racial/sexual/cultural etc stereotype** —**stereotype** v [T] —**stereotypical**

/,steriə'tɪpɪkəl, ,stɪər- $,ster-, ,stɪr-/ adj: stereotypical images of women

sterile /'steraɪl $ -rəl/ adj **1** unable to have children SYN **infertile** OPP **fertile 2** completely clean and not containing any BACTERIA: a sterile bandage | **sterile equipment/needles/dressings etc 3** lacking new ideas or interest: **sterile debate/argument** —**sterility** /stə'rɪləti/ n [U]

sterilize (also **-ise** BrE) /'sterəlaɪz/ v [T] **1** to make something completely clean and kill any BACTERIA in it: a sterilized needle **2** if someone is sterilized, they have an operation that makes them unable to have children —**sterilization** /,sterəlaɪ'zeɪʃən $ -lə-/ n [C,U]

sterling¹ /'stɜːlɪŋ $ 'stɜːr-/ n [U] the standard unit of money in the United Kingdom, based on the pound

sterling² adj [only before noun] very good: **sterling work/service**

stern¹ /stɜːn $ stɜːrn/ adj very strict and severe: **stern voice/look/face etc** He was fined and given a stern warning. —**sternly** adv

PHRASES

be made of sterner stuff to have a strong character and be determined to succeed: Ann was made of sterner stuff than me.

stern² n [C] the back part of a ship → **bow**

steroid /'stɪərɔɪd, 'ste- $ 'stɪr-/ n [C] a chemical that is produced by the body or made as a drug. People sometimes use steroids illegally in sport to improve their performance.

stethoscope /'steθəskəʊp $ -skoup/ n [C] a piece of equipment that doctors use to listen to your heart or breathing

stew¹ /stjuː $ stuː/ n [C,U] a meal made by cooking meat or fish and vegetables together slowly for a long time SYN **casserole**: beef stew

stew² v [T] to cook something slowly in liquid: stewed apples

steward /'stjuːəd $ 'stuːərd/ n [C] **1** a man who serves food and drinks to people on a plane or a ship **2** BrE someone who helps to organize a race

stewardess /'stjuːədɪs $ 'stuːərd-/ n [C] old-fashioned a woman who serves food and drinks to people on a plane SYN **flight attendant**

stick¹ /stɪk/ v (past tense and past participle **stuck** /stʌk/)

1 JOIN WITH GLUE [I,T] to join something to something else, using a substance such as glue, or to become joined to something: **stick** sth **on/to/in etc** sth Did you remember to stick a stamp on the envelope? | The pages were all **stuck together**. | Put a drop of oil in the water to stop the pasta from sticking. THESAURUS ▶ PUT

2 PUSH [I,T] if a pointed object sticks into something, or if you stick it there, it is pushed into it: **stick** sth **in/into/through** sth The nurse stuck a needle in my arm.

3 PUT [T] informal to put something somewhere SYN **put**: Just stick your coat on that chair. | Clara stuck her head round the door to see who was there.

4 STH WON'T MOVE [I] if something sticks, it becomes fixed in one position and is difficult to move: *The door's stuck.*

5 TOLERATE [T] *BrE informal* to TOLERATE someone or something – used especially when you have done this for too long SYN **stand**: *I've stuck this job for as long as I can.* | **can't stick sb/sth** *I used to like him, but now I can't stick him.*

PHRASES

stick in sb's mind if something sticks in your mind, you remember it well because it was surprising, interesting etc: *It's the kind of name that sticks in your mind.*

stick your neck out *informal* to take the risk of saying or doing something that may be wrong, or that other people may disagree with: *Sometimes you have to stick your neck out and say what you think.*

PHRASAL VERBS

stick around *informal* to remain in a place, waiting for something to happen or someone to arrive

stick at sth to continue working hard in order to achieve something

stick by *informal*
1 stick by sb to help and support someone who is in a difficult situation: *Laura has always stuck by me.*
2 stick by sth not to change what you have decided to do, or not change what you have said: *The paper is sticking by its original story.*

stick out
1 if a part of something sticks out, it comes out much further than the rest of a surface: *Paul's legs were sticking out from under the car.*
2 stick sth ↔ out to deliberately make something come forward or out: *Don't stick your tongue out at me!*
3 stick it out *informal* to continue doing something that is difficult, boring etc
4 *informal* to be easily noticed because of being very different from everyone or everything else: *Here, any stranger sticks out like a sore thumb.*

stick to sth
1 to do what you said you would do, even when it is difficult SYN **keep to**: *We decided to stick to our original plan.*
2 stick to your guns to refuse to change your mind, even though other people say that you are wrong

stick together *informal* if people stick together, they continue to support each other when they have problems

stick up if a part of something sticks up, it is pointing up above a surface

stick up for sb *informal* to defend someone who is being criticized: **stick up for yourself** *You'll have to learn to stick up for yourself.*

stick with sb/sth *informal* to continue doing something or supporting someone: *He stuck with his job at the zoo.*

stick² *n* [C]
1 a long thin piece of wood, especially one that has fallen from a tree → **branch**, **twig**
2 a long thin piece of wood, plastic etc that you use for a particular purpose: *Grandad walks with a stick* (=uses a stick to help him walk).

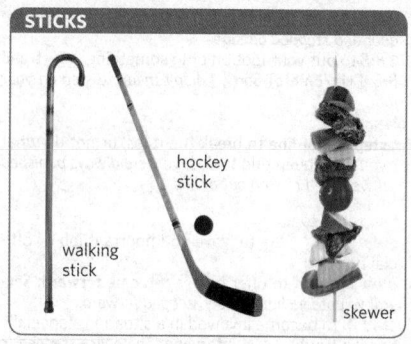

STICKS

hockey stick

walking stick

skewer

3 a long thin piece of something: **[+of]** *a stick of chewing gum*
4 a long thin piece of wood, plastic etc that you use in some sports to hit a ball: *a hockey stick* → **GEAR STICK**, **WALKING STICK**, **get (hold of) the wrong end of the stick** at **WRONG¹**

PHRASES

(out) in the sticks a long way from a town or city: *Living out in the sticks, a car is a necessity.*

sticker /'stɪkə $ -ər/ *n* [C] a small piece of paper or plastic with a picture or writing on it, that you can put onto something

stickler /'stɪklə $ -ər/ *n* [C] someone who is very strict about rules or small details: **[+for]** *She's a stickler for accuracy.*

'stick shift *n* [C] *AmE* a piece of equipment in a car that you move with your hand to control its GEARS → **automatic**

sticky /'stɪki/ *adj*
1 made of or covered with a substance that sticks to surfaces: *sticky cakes* | *Your hands are all sticky.* | **sticky tape/label etc** *BrE*
2 a sticky situation or problem is difficult to deal with
3 sticky weather is hot and damp, and makes you feel uncomfortable SYN **humid** —**stickiness** *n* [U]

stiff¹ /stɪf/ *adj*
1 NECK/ARM ETC if someone or a part of their body is stiff, their muscles hurt and it is difficult to move: *I've got a stiff neck.* | **[+with]** *Her fingers were stiff with cold.* THESAURUS **PAINFUL**
2 PAPER/MATERIAL/BRUSH hard and difficult to bend or move: *stiff cardboard* THESAURUS **HARD**
3 MIXTURE a stiff mixture is thick and almost solid: *Beat the egg whites until stiff.*
4 PUNISHMENT/COMPETITION very strict, severe, or difficult: **a stiff penalty/fine/sentence** | *Graduates face stiff competition in getting jobs.*
5 PERSON/BEHAVIOUR behaving in a formal and not very friendly way: *a stiff smile*
6 ALCOHOLIC DRINK **a stiff drink** a large amount of a strong alcoholic drink
7 WIND **a stiff wind/breeze** a fairly strong wind or BREEZE —**stiffly** *adv* —**stiffness** *n* [U]

stiff² *adv* **bored/worried/scared stiff** *informal* extremely bored, worried, or frightened

stiffen /'stɪfən/ v [I] to suddenly stop moving, especially because you are frightened or worried OPP **relax**

stifle /'staɪfəl/ v [T] to stop something from happening or developing: stifle a yawn/cry/grin etc | laws that stifle competition

stifling /'staɪflɪŋ/ adj a room or weather that is stifling is very hot and makes you feel uncomfortable

stigma /'stɪgmə/ n [singular, U] a strong feeling in society that being in a particular situation or having a particular illness is something to be ashamed of: the stigma of mental illness —**stigmatize** /-mətaɪz/ v [T]

stile /staɪl/ n [C] a set of steps that helps people climb over a fence in the countryside

stiletto /stə'letəʊ $ -toʊ/ n [C] (plural stilettos or stilettoes) a woman's shoe with a high thin heel, or the heel of this kind of shoe → see picture at SHOE¹

still¹ /stɪl/ adv
1 used when saying that a situation continues to be the same up to and including a particular point in time: Andy's still asleep. | I still haven't done my essay. → see Word Choice at YET
2 in spite of what has just been said or done: Clare didn't study much, but she still passed the exam. | The hotel was terrible. Still, the weather was OK.
3 used to say that something continues to be possible: We could still catch the bus if we hurry.
4 colder/harder/better etc still even colder, harder etc than something else: Dan found biology difficult, and physics harder still.

> **Grammar**
> You usually use **still** before a verb: We still love each other.
> You use **still** after the verb **to be**: It is still dark outside.
> If there are two or more verbs together, **still** comes after the first one: I can still remember that day.
> **Still** usually comes before any negative word: Still no sign of him!

still² adj
1 not moving: keep/stay/stand still The children wouldn't keep still.
2 quiet and calm: The forest was completely still.
3 BrE a still drink does not contain gas OPP **fizzy**: still lemonade —**stillness** n [U]

still³ n [C] a photograph of a scene from a film

stillborn /'stɪlbɔːn, ˌstɪl'bɔːn $ -ɔːrn/ adj born dead

still 'life n [C,U] (plural still lifes) a picture of objects, especially flowers or fruit → see picture at PAINTING

stilted /'stɪltɪd/ adj a stilted style of writing or speaking is formal and not natural

stilts /stɪlts/ n [plural] a pair of poles you can stand on, used for walking high above the ground

stimulant /'stɪmjələnt/ n [C] a drug or substance that makes you feel more active: Caffeine is a stimulant.

stimulate /'stɪmjəleɪt/ v [T] **1** to encourage an activity to grow and develop: These measures are designed to **stimulate** the economy. **2** to make someone interested and excited about something: We hope the project will **stimulate** students' **interest** in science. —**stimulation** /ˌstɪmjə'leɪʃən/ n [U]

stimulating /'stɪmjəleɪtɪŋ/ adj interesting and full of new ideas: a stimulating conversation

stimulus /'stɪmjələs/ n [C,U] (plural stimuli /-laɪ/) something that causes a development or reaction: [+to/for] a stimulus to industrial development | visual stimuli

sting¹ /stɪŋ/ v [I,T] (past tense and past participle stung /stʌŋ/)
1 if an insect, animal, or plant stings you, it hurts you by putting poison into your skin: Jamie got stung by a bee. THESAURUS BITE
2 to feel a sudden sharp pain, or to make someone feel this: The antiseptic might sting a little.
3 if you are stung by something someone says, it makes you feel upset: She was **stung** by his **criticism**.

sting² n [C] **1** a wound that is made when an insect, plant etc stings you: a bee sting **2** a pain that you feel in your eyes, throat, or on your skin **3** BrE the sharp part of an insect's or animal's body, with which it stings you SYN **stinger** AmE

> **Word Choice**: sting or bite?
> A bee, wasp, or scorpion can **sting** you. A mosquito, snake, or ant can **bite** you.

stinger /'stɪŋə $ -ər/ n [C] AmE the sharp part of an insect's or animal's body, with which it stings you SYN **sting** BrE

stinging /'stɪŋɪŋ/ adj criticizing someone very severely: a stinging attack

stingy /'stɪndʒi/ adj not generous, especially with money SYN **mean**

stink¹ /stɪŋk/ v [I] (past tense stank /stæŋk/, past participle stunk /stʌŋk/) **1** to have a very strong and unpleasant smell: [+of] The room stank of cigar smoke. **2** spoken used to say that something is very bad, unpleasant, or unfair: I think the whole thing stinks.

stink² n [C] a very bad smell THESAURUS SMELL
PHRASES
make/cause/kick up a stink to complain very strongly about something: I made a stink about it and got my money back.

stint /stɪnt/ n [C] a period of time that you spend doing something: [+in/at] a five-year stint in the army

stipulate /'stɪpjəleɪt/ v [T] formal if an agreement, law, or rule stipulates something, it must be done SYN **state**: [+that] The regulations stipulate that safety standards must be observed. —**stipulation** /ˌstɪpjʊ'leɪʃən/ n [C]

stir¹ /stɜː $ stɜːr/ v (stirred, stirring)
1 [T] to mix a liquid or food by moving a spoon around in it: Add milk, then stir for five minutes. | stir sth into sth Stir the flour into the mixture.
2 [I,T] to move slightly, or to make someone or

something do this: *A gentle breeze stirred the curtains.* | *He hadn't stirred from his chair all morning.*
3 [T] to make someone feel an emotion: *The music stirred childhood memories.*

PHRASAL VERBS

stir sth ↔ **up** to deliberately cause problems or arguments: *John was always* ***stirring up*** *trouble.*

stir² *n* [C usually singular] **1** a feeling of excitement or annoyance: **create/cause a stir** *The movie caused quite a stir.* **2** when you stir something: *Give the soup a stir.*

'stir-fry *v* [T] (**stir-fried, stir-frying, stir-fries**) to cook vegetables or meat quickly in a little hot oil **THESAURUS** COOK —**stir-fry** *n* [C]

stirring /ˈstɜːrɪŋ/ *adj* making people feel very excited or proud: *a stirring speech*

stirrup /ˈstɪrəp $ ˈstɜː-/ *n* [C] one of the two metal rings that you put your feet in when you are riding a horse

stitch¹ /stɪtʃ/ *n*
1 [C] a line of thread that has been sewn in a piece of cloth
2 [C] a piece of thread that a doctor uses to sew together a cut or wound: *Tony needed five stitches in his head.*
3 [C] one of the small circles of wool that you put round a needle when you are KNITTING
4 [singular] a pain that you get in the side of your body when you run too fast

PHRASES

in stitches laughing so much that you cannot stop: *Her jokes* ***had*** *us all* ***in stitches***.

stitch² *v* [T] to sew two things together, or to sew something onto a piece of cloth

stock¹ /stɒk $ stɑːk/ *n* **1** [C] a supply of something that you keep, which you can use when you need it: *How will the country's coal stocks last?* | **[+of]** *She kept a stock of candles in the cupboard.* **2** [C,U] a supply of a particular type of thing that a shop has available to sell: *Hurry – buy now while stocks last!* | **in stock/out of stock** (=available or unavailable to be sold) *Their new album is now in stock.* **3** [C,U] a SHARE or SHARES in a company **4** [C,U] a liquid made from boiling meat, bones, or vegetables, used to make soup: *chicken stock*

PHRASES

take stock (of sth) to think carefully about a situation so that you can decide what to do next: *We need to take stock of the situation.*

stock² *v* [T] **1** to have something available for people to buy: *Do you stock camping equipment?* **2** to fill something with a supply of something → **well-stocked**: **stock sth with sth** *The fridge was stocked with food.*

PHRASAL VERBS

stock up to buy a lot of something in order to keep it for when you need to use it later: **[+on]** *I need to stock up on groceries.*

stock³ *adj* **stock answer/remark etc** something that people usually say, but which is not interesting or original

stockade /stɒˈkeɪd $ stɑː-/ *n* [C] a fence built to defend a place, made from large pieces of wood

stockbroker /ˈstɒkˌbrəʊkə $ ˈstɑːkˌbroʊkər/ *n* [C] someone whose job is to buy and sell SHARES, STOCKS, and BONDS for other people —**stockbroking** *n* [U]

'stock exˌchange *n* [C usually singular] **1** the business of buying and selling STOCKS and SHARES **2** a place where STOCKS and SHARES are bought and sold **SYN** **stock market**

stocking /ˈstɒkɪŋ $ ˈstɑː-/ *n* [C] a very thin piece of clothing that fits closely around a woman's foot and leg: *a pair of silk stockings*

stockist /ˈstɒkɪst $ ˈstɑː-/ *n* [C] *BrE* a shop that sells the products of a particular company: *Telephone for details of your* ***nearest stockist***.

'stock ˌmarket *n* [C usually singular] **1** the business of buying and selling STOCKS and SHARES **2** a place where STOCKS and SHARES are bought and sold **SYN** **stock exchange**

stockpile /ˈstɒkpaɪl $ ˈstɑːk-/ *v* [T] to collect a large supply of something to use in the future: *Rebel troops have been stockpiling food and weapons.* —**stockpile** *n* [C]

stocktaking /ˈstɒkˌteɪkɪŋ $ ˈstɑːk-/ *n* [U] *BrE* when people in a shop or business check what goods they have **SYN** **inventory** *AmE*

stocky /ˈstɒki $ ˈstɑː-/ *adj* a stocky person is short and heavy and looks strong: *a stocky man with red hair*

stodgy /ˈstɒdʒi $ ˈstɑː-/ *adj* *BrE disapproving* stodgy food is heavy and makes you feel full very quickly **OPP** **light**: *a stodgy pudding*

stoic /ˈstəʊɪk $ ˈstoʊ-/ (*also* **stoical** /ˈstəʊɪkəl $ ˈstoʊ-/) *adj formal* not complaining when something bad happens to you: *a look of stoic resignation* —**stoicism** /-ɪsɪzəm/ *n* [U] —**stoically** /-kli/ *adv*

stoke /stəʊk $ stoʊk/ *v* [T] **1** to add more coal or wood to a fire **2** (*also* **stoke up**) to cause something to increase, especially something bad: *Rising oil prices stoked inflation.*

stole¹ /stəʊl $ stoʊl/ *v* the past tense of STEAL

stole² *n* [C] a long straight piece of cloth or fur that is worn over the shoulders

stolen /ˈstəʊlən $ ˈstoʊ-/ *v* the past participle of STEAL

stolid /ˈstɒlɪd $ ˈstɑː-/ *adj disapproving* not showing your emotions or becoming excited easily —**stolidly** *adv*

stomach¹ /ˈstʌmək/ *n* [C]
1 the part of your body where food goes when you have eaten it: *I hadn't eaten all day and my stomach felt empty* | *a* ***stomach upset*** *(=pain and illness after eating something bad)* | *a* ***stomach bug*** *(=illness that you get from someone else)* | *It was a long walk, especially* ***on an empty stomach*** *(=when you have not eaten).* | *The smell* ***turned my stomach*** *(=made me feel ill).* → see picture on page A2
2 the front part of your body, below your chest: *He punched Carlos in the stomach.*

have little/no stomach for sth used to emphasize that someone does not want to do something: *Their soldiers had no stomach for a fight.*

stomach² v [T] **can't stomach sth** to be unable to look at, accept etc something unpleasant → **bear**: *He couldn't stomach the sight of blood.*

'**stomach-ache** n [C] a pain in your stomach

stomp /stɒmp $ stɑːmp/ v [I] to walk with heavy steps, especially because you are angry: [**+off/out/through etc**] *She stomped out, slamming the door.*

stone¹ /stəʊn $ stoʊn/ n

1 SUBSTANCE [U] a hard solid mineral substance: *a stone wall | The house is **built of stone**.*

2 SMALL ROCK [C] a small piece of rock found on the ground: *Those boys **threw stones** at me.*

3 JEWEL [C] a jewel

4 UNIT OF WEIGHT [C] (*plural* **stone**) a British unit for measuring weight, equal to 14 pounds or 6.35 kilograms: *He weighs about 12 stone.*

5 IN FRUIT [C] *BrE* the large hard part at the centre of some fruits, containing the seed SYN **pit** *AmE* → **PAVING STONE** → see picture on page A4

PHRASES

a stone's throw from sth/away (from sth) very near to a place: *The beach is only a stone's throw away from the hotel.*

stone cold very cold: *This coffee's stone cold!*

stone² v [T] to throw stones at someone or something: *Christian martyrs who were **stoned to death***

'**Stone Age** n **the Stone Age** a very early time in human history, when only stone was used for making tools and weapons

stoned /stəʊnd $ stoʊnd/ adj informal **1** very relaxed or excited because you have used an illegal drug: *Everyone **got** completely **stoned**.* **2** very drunk

stonework /'stəʊnwɜːk $ 'stoʊnwɜːrk/ n [U] the parts of a building made of or decorated with stone

stony /'stəʊni $ 'stoʊ-/ adj **1** stony ground is covered with stones or contains stones: *stony soil* **2** not friendly or sympathetic: *They listened to him in **stony silence**. | The judge was **stony-faced**.*

stood /stʊd/ v the past tense and past participle of STAND

stool /stuːl/ n [C] a seat with three or four legs but no back or arms: *He was **perched on** a bar stool* (=sitting on it). *| a piano stool* → see picture at CHAIR¹

stoop /stuːp/ (*also* **stoop down**) v [I] to bend your body forward and down: *Dave stooped to pick up a pencil.* —**stoop** n [singular]

PHRASAL VERBS

stoop to sth to do something bad or wrong, which you would not normally do: **not stoop to doing sth** *I wouldn't stoop to taking money from a kid.*

stop¹ /stɒp $ stɑːp/ v (**stopped, stopping**)

1 NOT MOVE [I,T] not to walk or move any more, or to make someone or something do this: *Stop, come back! | We were stopped at the gate by security guards.* | [**+at/outside/in etc**] *Our driver stopped the*

car outside the hotel. | **watch/clock has stopped** (=is not working)

2 NOT CONTINUE [I,T] not to continue, or to make someone or something not continue: *Has the rain stopped yet? | What time do you **stop work** (=finish working at the end of the day)? | The referee stopped the fight.* | **stop doing sth** (=not do something any more) *Everyone stopped talking when she came in.* | **stop sb doing sth** *I couldn't stop her crying.* | **stop it/that** spoken (=used to tell someone to stop doing something annoying) *Stop it! You're hurting me.*

3 PAUSE [I] to pause in order to do something before you continue: [**+for**] *Do we need to stop for petrol? | I worked for three hours before stopping for a break.* | **stop to do sth** *She stopped to light a cigarette.* | **stop and do sth** *Let's stop and look at the view.* | **a bus/train etc stops** (=stops so that you can get off) *Does this train stop at Reading?*

4 PREVENT [T] to prevent someone from doing something, or something from happening: *efforts to stop the spread of AIDS | He's decided to go and you can't stop him.* | **stop sb/sth (from) doing sth** *With small kids you can't stop the place from being untidy.* | **stop yourself (from) doing sth** *I couldn't stop myself laughing.*

5 CHEQUE [T] if you stop a CHEQUE, you tell the bank not to pay it to someone: *I've asked the bank to stop the cheque.*

PHRASES

stop short of (doing) sth to decide not to do something, although you almost do it: *Tom stopped short of calling her a liar.*

will/would stop at nothing (to do sth) to be ready to do anything to achieve something that is important to you, even if it is dangerous or illegal: *We will stop at nothing in our fight against terrorism.*

PHRASAL VERBS

stop by to make a short visit to a friend: *It was nice of Judy to stop by.* | **stop by sth** *I stopped by her house yesterday.*

stop off to make a short visit to a place while you are going somewhere else: [**+at/in**] *We stopped off at the supermarket on the way home.*

stop over to stop somewhere and stay there for a short time before continuing a long journey: [**+at/in**] *The plane stopped over in Dubai.*

Grammar

You use **stop doing sth** when someone stops doing something, or something stops happening: *He's stopped calling me. | It's stopped raining.*

You use **stop to do sth** when saying that someone pauses in order to do something else: *We stopped to admire the view. | They stopped to have a rest.*

THESAURUS

stop doing something

stop to not do something any longer: *Stop annoying me!*

pause to stop speaking or doing something for a short time before starting again: *He paused briefly, then continued with his speech.*

S

have/take a break to stop working, studying, or driving for a short time in order to rest: *I'll finish this essay, then take a break.*

quit especially AmE informal to stop doing something: *Tell him to quit complaining.*

give sth up to stop doing something, especially something that you have been doing for a long time: *She's trying to give up smoking.*

stop happening

stop to not happen any longer: *Why has the music stopped?*

come to an end to stop – used about something that has continued for a long time: *His career was coming to an end.*

stop moving

stop to stop moving: *He stopped to look at a poster.*

come to a halt especially written to move more slowly and then stop – used about a vehicle: *The bus came to a halt outside the school.*

pull up to stop close to something – used about a vehicle or its driver: *We heard a car pulling up at the gate.*

stop² n

1 [singular] if a vehicle comes to a stop, or you bring it to a stop, it stops moving: *Our taxi came to a stop outside his house.* | *The driver brought the truck to a sudden stop.*

2 [singular] if an activity comes to a stop, or you bring it to a stop, it stops happening: *Work on the project has come to a stop.* | *efforts to bring the war to a stop*

3 [C] a place where you stop during a trip, or the short time you spend there: *Our first stop is Brussels.* | *The trip includes an **overnight stop** in London.*

4 [C] a place where a bus or train regularly stops for people to get on and off: *I get off at **the next stop**.* | *sb's stop* (=the place where someone usually gets off) *This is your stop, isn't it?* → **BUS STOP, FULL STOP, pull out all the stops** at **PULL¹**

PHRASES

put a stop to sth to prevent something from continuing or happening: *They tried to put a stop to the rumour.*

stopgap /'stɒpɡæp $ 'stɑːp-/ n [C] something you use or do for a short time until you can find something better: *a **stopgap measure** to deal with the parking problem*

stoplight /'stɒplaɪt $ 'stɑːp-/ n [C] AmE a set of red, yellow, and green lights, used for controlling traffic SYN **traffic lights**

stopover /'stɒp,əʊvə $ 'stɑːp,oʊvər/ n [C] a stop or short stay somewhere during a long plane journey: *a three-hour stopover in Atlanta*

stoppage /'stɒpɪdʒ $ 'stɑːp-/ n [C] when people stop working as a protest SYN **strike**

stopper /'stɒpə $ 'stɑːpər/ n [C] the thing that you put in the top of a bottle to close it SYN **cork**

stopwatch /'stɒpwɒtʃ $ 'stɑːpwɑːtʃ, -wɒːtʃ/ n [C] a watch used for measuring the exact time it takes to do something, especially to finish a race → see picture at **WATCH²**

storage /'stɔːrɪdʒ/ n [U] when things are kept in a special place until they are needed: **[+of]** *a shed for the storage of tools* | *There's plenty of **storage space** in the attic.* | **in storage** (=in a place where you pay to store things) *Our furniture's in storage until we find a new house.*

store¹ /stɔː $ stɔːr/ n [C]

1 a place where goods are sold to the public. In British English, a store is a large shop. In American English, a store is any kind of shop: **high street stores** BrE: *It costs £10.99 from leading high street stores.* | company-owned **retail stores** | **shoe/clothing/grocery etc store** especially AmE (=shop that sells one type of goods) *She worked in a book store during college.* | out-of-town furniture stores | **go to the store** AmE (=go to a shop that sells food) *I'm going to the store for some milk.*

2 a supply of something that you keep to use later: **[+of]** *a store of wood for the winter* → **CHAIN STORE, CONVENIENCE STORE, DEPARTMENT STORE**

PHRASES

in store (for sb) to be going to happen to someone in the future: *There's a surprise in store for you tomorrow!* | *We began to wonder what the future **had in store**.*

store² v [T]

1 to put things in a special place and keep them there: *All my old clothes are **stored away** in the loft.* | *The data is stored on a disk.* | **store sth up** (=keep a supply of something for the future) *animals that store up food for the winter* THESAURUS **KEEP**

2 **store up trouble/problems etc** to do something that will cause trouble for you later

storekeeper /'stɔː,kiːpə $ 'stɔːr,kiːpər/ n [C] AmE someone who owns or is in charge of a shop SYN **shopkeeper** BrE

storeroom /'stɔːrʊm, -ruːm/ n [C] a room for storing things

storey BrE, **story** AmE /'stɔːri/ n [C] (plural **storeys** BrE, **stories** AmE) a level of a building: *stairs leading to the **upper storey*** | **two-storey/three-storey etc** *a four-storey house*

stork /stɔːk $ stɔːrk/ n [C] a tall white water bird with long legs and a long beak

storm¹ /stɔːm $ stɔːrm/ n

1 [C] a period of very bad weather with a lot of wind or rain: *There was a terrible storm in the night.* THESAURUS **WIND**

2 [C,U] a situation in which people disagree strongly with something and express very strong feelings about it: **a storm of protest/criticism/disapproval etc** *There was a storm of protest over the government's decision.* | **cause/create/provoke etc a storm** *The scandal provoked a **political storm**.* → **RAINSTORM, SNOWSTORM, THUNDERSTORM**

PHRASES

take sth by storm to be very successful in a particular place: *The show took Broadway by storm.*

THESAURUS

storm a period of very bad weather with a lot of wind or rain: *The ship was damaged in a violent storm.*

thunderstorm a storm in which there is a lot of THUNDER and LIGHTNING: *Churches have been struck by lightning in thunderstorms.*

hurricane a storm that has very strong fast winds and that moves over water. **Hurricanes** start in the Atlantic Ocean: *Hurricane Andrew flattened thousands of homes when it hit Florida.*

typhoon a very violent tropical storm. **Typhoons** start in the Pacific Ocean: *A powerful typhoon hit southern China today.*

snowstorm a storm with strong winds and a lot of snow: *His car skidded on the road during a snowstorm.*

blizzard a severe snowstorm in which the snow is blown around by strong winds, making it difficult to see anything: *He had to drive home through the blizzard.*

---

storm² v **1** [T] to attack and enter a place: *Enemy troops stormed the city.* **2** [I] to walk somewhere in a very angry way: [+out of/off/past etc] *She stormed out of the meeting.*

stormy /ˈstɔːmi $ ˈstɔːr-/ adj **1** with strong winds, heavy rain, and dark clouds: *stormy weather* | *a stormy night* **2** a stormy relationship, meeting etc is one in which people argue a lot and have strong feelings

story /ˈstɔːri/ n [C] (plural **stories**)
1 a description of imaginary events and people, which is intended to entertain people: [+of] *the story of Romeo and Juliet* | [+about] *It's a story about a princess.*
2 an account of events that have really happened: *The film was based on a true story.* | *He's writing his life story.*
3 a report in a newspaper or news programme about something that has happened: *a front-page story in the 'Times'*
4 an explanation of how or why something has happened, which may be untrue: *Do you believe his story?* | *What's your side of the story* (=your personal explanation)? | *the full/whole story* (=all the facts) *I don't think you're telling us the whole story.*
5 the American spelling of STOREY → HORROR STORY, SOB STORY

PHRASES

it's a long story spoken used to say that something will take too long to explain: *It's a long story – I'll tell you later.*
to cut a long story short spoken used when you want to finish explaining something quickly: *To cut a long story short, she's leaving him.*

COLLOCATIONS

verbs

to tell a story *He told the children a story about a giant.* ⚠ Do not say 'say a story'. Say **tell a story**.
to read a story *Mummy, will you read me a bedtime story?*
to write a story *The story was written by Richard Yates.*

types of story

a short story *He has published two collections of short stories.*

---

a love story *'Jane Eyre' is one of the greatest love stories of all time.*
a children's story *She was like a wicked stepmother in a children's story.*
a fairy story (=a children's story in which magical things happen) | **an adventure story** | **a detective story** | **a ghost story** | **a horror story** (=a story about violent and frightening things) | **a bedtime story** (=a story that you read to a child before they go to sleep)

---

storyteller /ˈstɔːriˌtelə $ -ər/ n [C] someone who tells stories

stout¹ /staʊt/ adj **1** rather fat: *a stout middle-aged man* **2** strong and thick: *a stout pair of shoes*

stout² n [U] a strong dark beer

stove /stəʊv $ stoʊv/ n [C]
1 AmE a piece of kitchen equipment that you cook on [SYN] **cooker** BrE: *There's some soup on the stove.* → see picture at KITCHEN
2 a thing used for heating a room, which burns gas, wood, coal etc

stow /stəʊ $ stoʊ/ (also **stow away**) v [T] to put something in a particular space until you need it: *Please stow your bags under your seat.*

stowaway /ˈstəʊəweɪ $ ˈstoʊ-/ n [C] someone who hides on a ship or plane in order to travel without paying

straddle /ˈstrædl/ v [T] **1** to sit or stand with your legs on either side of something: *He sat straddling the fence.* **2** to be on either side of a place: *The town straddles the River Oder.*

straggle /ˈstrægəl/ v [I] to move more slowly than the other people in a group, so that you are behind them: *Ali straggled behind, carrying the shopping.*

straggly /ˈstrægəli/ adj growing or spreading out in an untidy way: *a straggly moustache*

straight¹ /streɪt/ adj
1 not bent or curved: *a straight road* | *The children stood in a straight line.* | *Keep your back straight.* | *My sister has straight hair* (=without curls). → see picture at HAIR
2 level or upright, and not leaning to one side: *Is my tie straight?* | *straight teeth*
3 honest and direct: *Just give me a straight answer, please.* | **be straight with sb** *I don't feel he's being straight with me.*
4 [only before noun] happening one after the other: *The Australian team had three straight wins.*
5 [not before noun] clean and tidy: *It took hours to get the house straight.*
6 informal someone who is straight is attracted to people of the opposite sex [SYN] **heterosexual** [OPP] **gay**
7 a straight alcoholic drink has no ice, water etc added to it: *a straight Scotch*
8 [only before noun] involving only two choices, people, or things: *It was a straight choice between my career and my family.* → set/put the record straight at RECORD¹

PHRASES

a straight face if you have a straight face, you are not laughing or smiling, although you would like to: *It was hard to keep a straight face.*

get sth straight *spoken* to understand completely the true facts about a situation: *Let's **get this straight**. You don't want to get married?*

get straight A's to get 'A' (=the highest possible mark) in all your examinations or school subjects: *Becky got straight A's all through high school.*

straight² *adv*

1 in a straight line, not curved or bent: **[+at/down/forwards etc]** *The truck was coming **straight** towards me.* | *She kept staring **straight ahead**.* | *Go **straight on** to the roundabout.* | **sit up/stand up straight** (=with your back straight, not curved)

2 immediately, without stopping to do something first: **[+to/back/past etc]** *Why didn't you **go straight** to the police?* | *Come **straight** back.* | **[+after]** *There's a meeting straight after lunch.*

PHRASES

go straight to stop being a criminal: *Tony's been trying to go straight for about six months.*

not see/think straight to be unable to see or think clearly: *It was so noisy I couldn't think straight.*

straight away (also **straightaway**) if you do something straight away, you do it immediately or without delay: *I phoned the hospital straight away.*

tell sb straight/straight out to tell someone something in an honest and direct way: *I told him straight that I wouldn't do it.*

straighten /'streɪtn/ *v* **1** (also **straighten out**) [I,T] to become straight, or to make something straight: *He straightened his tie.* | *The road straightened out.* **2** (also **straighten up**) [T] *especially AmE* to make something tidy: *Straighten your room!*

PHRASAL VERBS

straighten sth ↔ **out** to deal with a problem or difficult situation: *I'll see if I can straighten things out.*

straighten up to stand with your back straight

straightforward Ac /ˌstreɪt'fɔːwəd◀ $ -'fɔːrwərd◀/ *adj* **1** simple to do or easy to understand: *The questions seemed straightforward.* **THESAURUS** EASY **2** honest and not hiding what you think: *Is he being straightforward?*

straightjacket /'streɪtˌdʒækɪt/ *n* another spelling of STRAITJACKET

strain¹ /streɪn/ *n* **1** [C,U] the pressure or worry that is caused by a difficult situation, job, or problem: **the strain of sth** *He couldn't cope with the strain of being a teacher.* | **under (a) strain** *She's been under a lot of strain recently.* | **put a strain on sb/sth** (=cause them to be in a difficult situation) *The flu epidemic has put a huge strain on the health service.* | **break/crack/collapse etc under the strain** *Their relationship was cracking under the strain.* **2** [U] when something is pulled or stretched very tightly or has to carry a lot of weight: **under the strain** (=because of the strain) *The rope snapped under the strain.* **3** [C,U] an injury caused by using part of your body too much: *eye strain* **4** [C] a type of plant, animal, or disease: **[+of]** *a new strain of the virus*

strain² *v* **1** [T] to injure part of your body by stretching it too much: *Kevin **strained a muscle** in his neck.* **2** [I,T] to try very hard to do something: **strain to do sth** *She moved closer, **straining to hear** what they said.* **3** [T] to separate solid things from a liquid by

pouring the mixture through a strainer **4** [T] to make a situation or relationship more difficult: *It's an issue that's **straining relations** between the countries.*

strained /streɪnd/ *adj* **1** not relaxed or friendly: *a **strained conversation*** **2** worried and tired: *Alex looks strained.*

strainer /'streɪnə $ -ər/ *n* [C] a kitchen tool used for separating solid food from liquid

strait /streɪt/ *n* [C usually plural] a narrow area of sea that joins two larger areas of sea: *the Straits of Gibraltar*

PHRASES

be in dire straits to be in a very difficult situation: *The firm is now in dire financial straits.*

straitjacket, straightjacket /'streɪtˌdʒækɪt/ *n* [C] a special piece of clothing that is used to prevent someone who is violent from moving their arms

strand /strænd/ *n* [C] **1** a single thin piece of thread, hair, wire etc **2** one part of a story, problem, idea etc

stranded /'strændɪd/ *adj* unable to get away from a place: *Bad weather **left** travellers **stranded**.*

strange /streɪndʒ/ *adj*

1 unusual or surprising, in a way that is difficult to understand or explain: *I had a strange dream last night.* | *What's that strange noise?* | **It's strange that** *Brad isn't here.* | **[+about]** *There was something strange about him.* | **That's strange** – *I thought I left my keys on the table.*

2 not familiar or known to you: *I was alone in a strange country.* | *I never speak to strange men.*

—**strangely** *adv*: *She was looking at me very strangely.* —**strangeness** *n* [U]

THESAURUS

strange unusual or surprising, in a way that is difficult to understand or explain: *People do strange things when they're in love.* | *a strange woman*

funny *especially spoken especially BrE* a little strange: *What's that funny smell?* | *It seems a funny place for a holiday.*

curious strange, especially in an interesting way that makes you want to find out more: *The curious thing was that everyone believed him.*

mysterious used about something that people know little about: *the mysterious disappearance of a young girl*

eccentric strange in a way that seems slightly crazy and amusing – used about people and their behaviour: *an eccentric old man*

peculiar/odd slightly strange and different from what is normal: *Did you notice anything peculiar about him?*

weird/bizarre very strange: *She has some weird ideas.* | *The whole situation seems very bizarre.*

---

stranger /'streɪndʒə $ -ər/ *n* [C]

1 someone you do not know: *Don't get in a car with a stranger.* | **perfect/complete/total stranger** (=used to emphasize that you do not know them) *I didn't want to kiss a complete stranger.*

2 someone in a new and unfamiliar place: **[+to]** *He was a stranger to New York.*

Word Choice: stranger or foreigner?
A **stranger** is someone you do not know: *Children are taught not to speak to strangers.*
A **foreigner** is someone from another country: *Some British customs must seem very unusual to foreigners.*

strangle /ˈstræŋɡəl/ *v* [T] to kill someone by pressing their throat with your hands, a rope etc

stranglehold /ˈstræŋɡəlhəʊld $ -hoʊld/ *n* [C] complete control over a situation, organization etc: **[+on]** *The government had a stranglehold on the media.*

strap¹ /stræp/ *n* [C] a strong band of cloth or leather used to keep something in position or to carry something: *a watch strap* | *She slipped the strap of her bag over her shoulder.* → see picture at **WATCH²**

strap² *v* [T] (**strapped**, **strapping**) to fasten something in place using a strap: *Make sure your backpack is strapped on tightly.* | **be strapped in** (=have a belt fastened around you in a car) *Are the kids strapped in?*

strapped /stræpt/ *adj* **be strapped (for cash)** *informal* to have very little money to spend

strata /ˈstrɑːtə $ ˈstreɪtə/ *n* the plural of STRATUM

stratagem /ˈstrætədʒəm/ *n* [C] *formal* a plan or idea for defeating an enemy or gaining an advantage

strategic Ac /strəˈtiːdʒɪk/ *adj* **1** done as part of a plan, especially in business, politics, or war: *a strategic decision to sell off part of the company* **2** relating to fighting wars: *strategic weapons* (=powerful weapons for attacking other countries from your own) **3** a strategic position is good for a particular purpose: *He placed himself in a strategic position next to the door.* —**strategically** /-kli/ *adv*

strategy Ac /ˈstrætɪdʒi/ *n* (*plural* **strategies**) **1** [C] a plan used to achieve something: **business/political etc strategy** *the long-term economic strategy* **THESAURUS** PLAN **2** [U] the skill of making plans so that you are successful, especially in war: *an expert in military strategy* —**strategist** *n* [C]

stratum /ˈstrɑːtəm $ ˈstreɪt-/ *n* [C] (*plural* **strata** /-tə/) **1** *technical* a layer of rock or soil **2** *formal* a social class in society

straw /strɔː $ strɒː/ *n*
1 [C,U] the dried stems of plants such as wheat, used for animals to sleep on or to make things such as baskets → **hay**: *a straw hat*
2 [C] a thin tube of plastic or paper, used for sucking a drink from a bottle or cup
PHRASES
the last/final straw the last in a series of problems or bad events that finally makes you give

STRAW

straw

up or become angry: *Having to work late on a Friday was the last straw!*

strawberry /ˈstrɔːbəri $ ˈstrɒːberi, -bəri/ *n* [C] (*plural* **strawberries**) a small red juicy fruit that grows on plants near the ground: *strawberries and cream* → see picture on page A4

stray¹ /streɪ/ *v* [I] to move away from the safe place where you should be: *Some of the kids had strayed into the woods.*

stray² *adj* **1** a stray animal is lost or has no home: *a stray dog* **2** stray things have become separated from others of the same kind: *a few stray hairs*

stray³ *n* [C] an animal that is lost or has no home

streak¹ /striːk/ *n* [C] **1** a thin coloured line or mark: **grey/blond etc streak** *a few grey streaks in her hair* **2** a part of someone's character that is surprising, especially because it seems a little bad: **stubborn/mean/nasty etc streak** *Richard has a wild streak in him.* **3** a winning/losing streak a period when you are always successful or unsuccessful: *Our team was on a winning streak.*

streak² *v* **1** [I] to move or run very quickly: *A fighter jet streaked across the sky.* **2** be streaked with sth to be covered with thin lines of a colour, liquid etc: *Marcia's face was streaked with sweat.*

stream¹ /striːm/ *n* [C]
1 a very small river: *a mountain stream* → see picture at **RIVER**
2 a long series of people, vehicles, ideas etc coming continuously or one after another: **[+of]** *a stream of traffic* | *the stream of refugees crossing the border* | **endless/constant/steady etc stream** *an endless stream of questions*
3 a flow of liquid, gas, smoke etc: **[+of]** *A stream of cold air rushed in.*

stream² *v* [I] to move or flow continuously in one direction, especially in large amounts **SYN** pour: **[+out/past/through etc]** *Tears were streaming down his cheeks.* | *People streamed through the gates.*

streamer /ˈstriːmə $ -ər/ *n* [C] a long piece of coloured paper used to decorate a building for a special occasion

streamline /ˈstriːmlaɪn/ *v* [T] **1** to organize something so that it happens more quickly and effectively: *The college has streamlined entry procedures for new students.* **2** to improve the shape of something so that it moves more easily through the air or water —**streamlined** *adj*: *a streamlined sports car*

street /striːt/ *n* [C]
1 a road in a town or city with houses and shops on it: *24, West Street* | **on a street** *We live on Main Street.* | **up/down/along the street** *We walked down the street.* | **across the street** *They live just across the street.* **THESAURUS** ROAD
2 the streets [plural] the busy part of a city: *She shouldn't be out walking the streets after dark.* | *young people who live on the streets* (=have no home and sleep outside)
PHRASES
right up your street *BrE informal* exactly right for you: *The project should be right up your street.*

streets ahead BrE informal much better than other people or things: *He's streets ahead of the other children.*

COLLOCATIONS

adjectives

a busy street (=with a lot of traffic or people) *He looked out at the busy street.*

a crowded street (=with a lot of people) *It was market day and the streets were crowded.*

a quiet street (=with not many people or cars moving around) *We live on a quiet street.*

an empty/deserted street (=with no people) *It was 3 am, and the street was deserted.*

the main street *They drove slowly along the main street.*

a side/back street (=a small quiet street near the main street) *The restaurant is tucked away in a side street.*

the high street BrE (=the main street with shops)

street + noun

a street corner (=a place where streets meet) *Gangs of kids hang around on street corners.*

a street light/lamp *There were no street lights.*

a street map (=a map showing roads and streets) *I need a street map of Oxford.*

streetcar /'striːtkɑː $ -kɑːr/ n [C] AmE an electric bus that goes along metal tracks in the road **SYN** tram BrE → see picture at **TRANSPORT¹**

'street cred (also **street credi'bility**) n [U] popularity with young people because you have qualities, attitudes, and knowledge that they admire: *Around here, getting arrested gives you street cred.*

'street light, **streetlight** /'striːtlaɪt/ (also **'street lamp**) n [C] a light on a long pole in a street

streetwise /'striːtwaɪz/ adj able to deal with the situations and people that you meet in a big city: *streetwise kids*

strength /streŋθ, strenθ/ n

1 PHYSICAL POWER [U] physical power and energy **OPP** weakness: *a job which requires a lot of strength* | *They pushed with all their strength.* | **have the strength to do sth** *I didn't have the strength to lift it.*

2 DETERMINATION [U] determination to do something difficult: **have the strength to do sth** *She didn't have the strength to leave him.* | **strength of mind/character** *It took great strength of character to carry on.*

3 OF FEELING/BELIEF [U] how strong a feeling or belief is: *We hadn't realized the strength of feeling among parents about this issue.*

4 OF ECONOMY/ARMY ETC [U] how strong or powerful something is: *US military strength* | **[+of]** *the strength of the economy*

5 OF CURRENCY [U] the value of a country's CURRENCY (=the money used there) compared to other currencies: **[+of]** *the strength of the euro against the pound*

6 GOOD POINT [C] your strengths are the good things about you, or the things you are good at: *We have all got strengths and weaknesses.*

7 LIQUID/ALCOHOL [C,U] how strong a liquid is: *extra-strength beers*

PHRASES

at full strength/below strength with all the people that you need, or with fewer people than you need: *The French team is at full strength.*

go from strength to strength to become more and more successful: *The company has gone from strength to strength.*

on the strength of sth because of information or advice that you have: *She was hired immediately on the strength of his recommendation.*

strengthen /'streŋθən, 'strenθən/ v [I,T] to make something stronger, or to become stronger: *an exercise to strengthen your arms* | *We may need to strengthen the bridge.* | *government measures to strengthen the economy* | *The euro has strengthened against the dollar.*

strenuous /'strenjuəs/ adj using a lot of effort: *He is supposed to avoid strenuous exercise.* | *He's been making a strenuous effort to lose weight.*

stress¹ Ac /stres/ n

1 WORRY [C,U] a strong feeling of worry that prevents you from relaxing → **strain**: *a headache caused by stress* | *ways of coping with stress at work* | **under stress** *I've been under a lot of stress lately.* | *the stresses and strains of a doctor's life* | *a stress-related illness* (=one caused by stress)

2 SPECIAL IMPORTANCE [U] special importance that is given to something **SYN** emphasis: **lay/put stress on sth** *He lays particular stress on discipline in schools.*

3 FORCE [C,U] physical force or pressure on something: *Some sports put a lot of stress on joints.*

4 ON WORD [C,U] the stress on a word is the way you say one part more loudly than the rest: *The stress is on the last syllable.*

stress² Ac v [T] **1** to say that something is very important: *She stressed the need for more money for the project.* | **[+that]** *He stressed that the plan must be kept secret.* **2** to say one word or part of a word more loudly than others

stressed Ac /strest/ (also **stressed 'out**) adj [not before noun] so worried and tired that you cannot relax: *I was feeling really stressed out.* **THESAURUS** ▶ **WORRIED**

stressful Ac /'stresfəl/ adj a stressful job or situation makes you feel very worried and unable to relax

stretch¹ /stretʃ/ v

1 MAKE STH BIGGER/LOOSER [I,T] to make something bigger or looser by pulling it, or to become bigger or looser in this way: *Don't stretch my jumper!* | *Stretch the canvas so that it covers the whole frame.* | *Trainers tend to stretch when you wear them.*

2 ARMS/LEGS [I,T] to push your arms, legs, or another part of your body as far as they can go: *He sat up in bed and stretched.* | *an exercise to stretch the leg muscles* | **[+over/across/out/up]** *She stretched over and picked up the phone.* → see picture on page A11

3 COVER A LARGE AREA [I] to cover a large area of land: **[+away/to]** *The lake stretched away into the distance.*

4 CONTINUE A LONG TIME [I] to continue for a long

period of time: **[+into/to]** *The project will probably stretch into next year.*

5 MAKE SB WORK/THINK [T] to give someone difficult work so that they have to use all their intelligence and ability to do it: *It's important to stretch students.*

6 NOT HAVE ENOUGH **be stretched (to the limit)** not to have enough money, time etc: *We're really stretched for money at the moment.*

PHRASES

stretch your legs *informal* to go for a walk: *A few of the passengers got off the bus to stretch their legs.*

stretch² *n* [C] **1** an area of land or water: **[+of]** *a beautiful stretch of coastline* | *a dangerous stretch of road* **2** a continuous period of time: **[+of]** *a long stretch of dry weather* | *We worked for ten hours **at a stretch*** (=without stopping). **3** an action in which you stretch part of your body: *I stood up and **had a stretch.*** | *I usually do a few stretches before the game.*

PHRASES

(not) by any stretch (of the imagination) *spoken* used to say that something is definitely not true: *She isn't fat, not by any stretch of the imagination.*

stretcher /ˈstretʃə $ -ər/ *n* [C] a type of bed on which you carry someone who is injured

stretchy /ˈstretʃi/ *adj* material that is stretchy will stretch when you pull it

strew /struː/ *v* [T] (*past participle* **strewn** /struːn/ *or* **strewed**) to drop a lot of things over an area in an untidy way: **be strewn over/across sth** *Papers were strewn all over the floor.* | **be strewn with sth** *The streets were strewn with rubbish.*

stricken /ˈstrɪkən/ *adj formal* suffering from something very badly: **[+with/by]** *Half the class were stricken with flu.* | *a country stricken by economic problems* → **POVERTY-STRICKEN**

strict /strɪkt/ *adj*

1 a strict person makes sure that people always obey rules and behave well OPP **lenient**: *a strict teacher* | **[+with]** *She's very strict with her children.*

2 a strict rule or order must be obeyed completely: *I have **strict instructions** not to let anyone leave.* | *He's under **strict orders** to be home before dark.*

3 always behaving according to a set of rules or religious beliefs: *a strict Muslim* | *a strict vegetarian*

4 [only before noun] the strict meaning of a word is its exact meaning

strictly /ˈstrɪktli/ *adv* **1** **strictly prohibited/forbidden** definitely not allowed: *Smoking is strictly forbidden.* **2** in a strict way: *The children were brought up very strictly.* **3** exactly and correctly: *That's **not strictly true.*** | **strictly speaking** (=used when you are explaining something in a very exact way) *Strictly speaking, spiders are not insects.* **4** only for one purpose or one person: *Our meeting was strictly for business.*

stride¹ /straɪd/ *v* [I] (*past tense* **strode** /strəʊd $ stroʊd/, *past participle* **stridden** /ˈstrɪdn/) to walk with quick long steps: **[+into/across/out of etc]** *He strode across the room.* THESAURUS **WALK**

stride² *n* [C] a long step that you take when you are walking: *He was getting further away from me with every stride.*

PHRASES

get into your stride *BrE*, **hit your stride** *AmE* to start doing something confidently and well: *Once I've hit my stride I can finish an assignment in a few hours.*

make great strides to make a lot of progress: *We have made great strides in reducing poverty.*

take sth in your stride *BrE*, **take sth in stride** *AmE* to deal with a situation calmly without becoming annoyed or upset: *Neil took the criticism in stride.*

strident /ˈstraɪdənt/ *adj* **1** expressing opinions in a strong and determined way: *a strident critic of the reforms* **2** a strident voice is loud and unpleasant

strife /straɪf/ *n* [U] *formal* trouble or disagreement between people

strike¹ /straɪk/ *v* (*past tense and past participle* **struck** /strʌk/)

1 HIT [T] to hit someone or something: *The car struck a tree.* | *She struck him across the face.* | *He was struck on the head by a falling rock.* | *The church tower was **struck by lightning.*** THESAURUS **HIT**

2 THOUGHT [T] if a thought strikes you, you think of it: *The first thing that struck me was how few people were there.* | **it strikes sb that** *It suddenly struck me that we might lose the company.* | **be struck by sth** *I was struck by the friendliness of the local people.*

3 HOW STH SEEMS [T] the way that something strikes you is the way it seems to you: **strike sb as (being) sth** *His behaviour struck me as odd.* | *He strikes me as being very intelligent.*

4 STOP WORKING [I] if people strike, they stop working for a period of time because they want better pay or working conditions: *Teachers will vote today on whether to strike.* | **[+for]** *Nurses are striking for a shorter working week.*

5 ATTACK [I] to attack someone: *The police fear that the killer will strike again.*

6 BAD EVENT [I,T] if something bad strikes, it happens suddenly: *Later that evening **disaster struck.*** | *The hurricane struck the town just after dark.*

7 MATCH [T] to make a match start burning

8 OIL/GOLD [T] to discover oil, gold etc under the ground

9 CLOCK [I,T] if a clock strikes, its bell makes a number of sounds to show the time: **strike two/three/four etc** *The clock struck four.*

PHRASES

strike a balance to give the right amount of importance to two different things: *It's never easy to strike a balance between work and family.*

strike a bargain/deal if two people strike a deal, they each promise to do something for the other: *The company has struck a deal with the union.*

be within striking distance (of sth) to be close enough to a place to reach it easily: *By now the ships were within striking distance of the shore.*

PHRASAL VERBS

strike back to attack someone after they have attacked you

strike out

1 **strike sth ↔ out** to draw a line through part of a piece of writing

2 **strike out for sth** to try to reach a place: *They struck out for the coast.*

3 strike out on your own to start doing something new without other people's help
4 in the game of BASEBALL, to fail to hit the ball three times so that you are not allowed to continue, or to make someone do this: **strike sb ↔ out** *The first batter was struck out.*
strike up **strike up a conversation/friendship etc** to begin a conversation, friendship etc with someone

strike² *n* [C]
1 when a group of workers stop working for a period of time because they want better pay or better working conditions: **on strike** *The workers have been on strike for two months.* | **[+over]** *a strike over pay*
2 a military attack: **[+on/against]** *an air strike against military targets*
3 in the game of BASEBALL, an attempt to hit the ball that fails → **HUNGER STRIKE**

striker /'straɪkə $ -ər/ *n* [C] **1** someone who has stopped working because they want better pay or working conditions **2** a football player whose main job is to try to get GOALS

striking /'straɪkɪŋ/ *adj* **1** unusual and noticeable: *There's a striking similarity between the two girls.* **2** very attractive: *a very striking woman*

STRING

thread

string

rope

string¹ /strɪŋ/ *n*
1 [C,U] a strong thread that you use for tying or fastening things → **rope**: *The package was tied up with string.* | *a piece of string* | *a ball of string*
2 [C] a number of similar things that happen one after the other SYN **series**: **[+of]** *She's had a string of hit singles.*
3 [C] a set of things that are joined together on a thread: *a string of beads* | *a string of onions*
4 a) [C] the strings on a musical instrument are the pieces of wire that produce sound **b) the strings** [plural] the musicians in a group who play musical instruments with strings → **pull strings** at **PULL¹**
PHRASES
(with) no strings attached with no special conditions or limits: *The policy offers a high rate of interest with no strings attached.*

string² *v* [T] (*past tense and past participle* **strung** /strʌŋ/) to hang things up in a line, using string: *Dad was busy stringing up the Christmas lights.*
PHRASAL VERBS
string sb **along** *informal* to keep promising that you will do something for someone when you do not intend to do it: *I think he's just stringing you along.*
string sth ↔ **out** to do something very slowly so that it takes longer than it should

string sth ↔ **together** **string words/a sentence together** to form words into a sentence so that people can understand it: *He was so drunk he could hardly string a sentence together.*

stringed instrument *n* [C] a musical instrument that produces sound from strings, for example a VIOLIN

stringent /'strɪndʒənt/ *adj* stringent rules or laws are very strict and must be obeyed: *stringent new laws on gun ownership*

strip¹ /strɪp/ *v* (**stripped, stripping**) **1** (*also* **strip off**) [I,T] to take off your clothes, or take someone else's clothes off: *I stripped and got into the shower.* | *He was stripped and beaten.* | *She stripped off her sweater.* | *The men were all stripped to the waist.* **2** (*also* **strip off**) [T] to remove something that is covering the surface of something else: *I've stripped the old paint off the door.* | *We'll need to strip off the old wallpaper first.*
PHRASES
strip sb of sth to take property or rights away from someone: *If the drugs test proves positive, he could be stripped of his title.*

strip² *n* **1** [C] a long narrow piece of something: *Tear the paper into one-inch strips.* | **[+of]** *a narrow strip of land* **2** [singular] when someone takes their clothes off to entertain other people: *She did a strip.* | *a strip show*

stripe /straɪp/ *n* [C] a narrow line of colour: *a shirt with blue and white stripes* THESAURUS ▶ LINE

striped /straɪpt/ *adj* something that is striped has a pattern of stripes on it: *a red and white striped dress* → see picture at **PATTERN**

stripey /'straɪpi/ *adj* STRIPY

stripper /'strɪpə $ -ər/ *n* [C] someone who is paid to take off their clothes to entertain other people

striptease /'strɪptiːz, ˌstrɪp'tiːz/ *n* [C,U] a performance in which someone takes off their clothes

stripy, stripey /'straɪpi/ *adj* something that is stripy has a pattern of stripes on it: *stripy socks* → see picture at **PATTERN**

strive /straɪv/ *v* [I] (*past tense* **strove** /strəʊv $ stroʊv/, *past participle* **striven** /'strɪvən/) *formal* to try very hard to do something: **[+for]** *Don't always strive for perfection.* | *We are always striving to improve our efficiency.*

strode /strəʊd $ stroʊd/ *v* the past tense of STRIDE

stroke¹ /strəʊk $ stroʊk/ *n*
1 BRAIN INJURY [C] a medical condition in which your brain becomes damaged and you are unable to move part of your body: *He had a stroke last year.*
2 IN SWIMMING [C,U] a movement with your arms when you are swimming, often used after another noun to talk about a particular way of swimming: *backstroke* | *breaststroke*
3 IN TENNIS [C] a way of hitting the ball in a game such as tennis: *He played some beautiful strokes.*
4 IN DRAWING [C] a single movement of a pen or brush when you are writing or drawing

PHRASES

at a stroke/at one stroke with one single sudden action: *This would solve the problem at one stroke.*
not do a stroke (of work) *informal* to not do any work at all: *You haven't done a stroke of work all morning.*
a stroke of genius/inspiration an extremely clever thing to do
a stroke of luck/good fortune something lucky that happens to you: *Finding the key was a real stroke of luck.*

stroke² v [T] to move your hand gently over something: *He was stroking the cat.* | *She stroked his face gently.* **THESAURUS** TOUCH → see picture on page A10

stroll /strəʊl $ stroʊl/ v [I] to walk in a slow relaxed way: **[+along/down/across etc]** *We strolled along the beach.* **THESAURUS** WALK —**stroll** n [C]

stroller /ˈstrəʊlə $ ˈstroʊlər/ n [C] *AmE* a chair on wheels in which a small child can be pushed along **SYN** **buggy** *BrE*

strong /strɒŋ $ strɔːŋ/ adj
1 **PHYSICALLY** someone who is strong has big muscles and can lift heavy things, and is not weak or ill → **strength**: *a strong man* | **strong hands/arms/ muscles etc** **THESAURUS** BRIGHT
2 **MENTALLY** someone who is strong can deal with problems without becoming too upset or worried: *You have to be strong to cope with the death of a child.*
3 **NOT EASILY DAMAGED** something that is strong cannot be broken or damaged easily: *a strong rope* | *Is that branch strong enough to hold your weight?*
4 **GOOD AND NOT LIKELY TO FAIL** something that is strong is good, or has good qualities, and is not likely to fail: *a strong economy* | *They have a very strong relationship.*
5 **DETERMINED** powerful and determined: *a strong leader* | *We will take **strong action** against terrorists.*
6 **FEELING/BELIEF** strong feelings and beliefs are ones that you feel or believe a lot: *a strong belief in God* | *a strong desire for power*
7 **TASTE/SMELL** a strong taste or smell is one that you notice easily: *a strong smell of onions*
8 **DRINK** a strong drink contains a lot of alcohol, coffee, or tea
9 **WIND/CURRENT/SUN** a strong wind, current, or sun has a lot of force or power **THESAURUS** BRIGHT
10 **EVIDENCE/CASE** not likely to be proved wrong: *There's strong evidence to suggest he was innocent.* | *There is now a **strong case** for a change in the law.*
11 **CURRENCY** a strong CURRENCY (=the money used in a country) is worth a lot compared to others: *The dollar is quite strong at the moment.*
12 **MANY PEOPLE** **500/10,000 etc strong** having 500, 10,000 etc people: *The crowd was over 100,000 strong.*

PHRASES

be still going strong to still be working or living successfully: *a pop group that is still going strong*
strong point a good quality that someone has, or something that they can do well: *Science is not my strong point.*
strong language rude words that some people may find offensive: *Both sides criticized each other in very strong language.*

THESAURUS

person

strong having a lot of physical strength: *I'm not strong enough to lift you.* | *strong arms*
powerful very strong – used about someone's body, arms, muscles etc: *He has big powerful shoulders.*
muscular having big muscles and looking strong: *You could see his muscular chest through his shirt.* | *a tall muscular man*
well-built strong and tall, with a big body – often used in police descriptions: *Police say the man is well-built, with dark brown hair.*

thing

strong not easily broken or damaged: *Calcium keeps bones strong and healthy.* | *strong thread*
tough strong – used about something that can be used a lot without being damaged: *a pair of tough leather boots*
sturdy strong and often thick, and not likely to fall over or get broken: *a sturdy wooden bench*
indestructible impossible to break, damage, or destroy, and lasting forever: *The watch is virtually indestructible.*

stronghold /ˈstrɒŋhəʊld $ ˈstrɔːŋhoʊld/ n [C] **1** an area where there is a lot of support for a particular idea or political party: *a Conservative stronghold* **2** an area that is strongly defended: *a rebel stronghold*

strongly /ˈstrɒŋli $ ˈstrɔːŋ-/ adv **1** if you feel or believe something strongly, you think it is important or care a lot about it: *He is strongly in favour of capital punishment.* **2** tasting or smelling of something a lot: *The house smelled strongly of gas.* **3** if you say something strongly, you say it in a way that tries to persuade someone else: **strongly suggest/advise/ recommend** *I strongly advise you to see a doctor.*

strong-'minded adj not easily influenced by other people to change what you believe or want

strong-'willed adj determined to do what you want, even though other people tell you not to do it

stroppy /ˈstrɒpi $ ˈstrɑːpi/ adj *BrE informal* bad-tempered or easily annoyed

strove /strəʊv $ stroʊv/ v the past tense of STRIVE

struck /strʌk/ v the past tense and past participle of STRIKE

structural Ac /ˈstrʌktʃərəl/ adj relating to the structure of something: *structural damage*

structure¹ Ac /ˈstrʌktʃə $ -ər/ n
1 [C,U] the way in which the parts of something are put together or organized: **[+of]** *the structure of society* | *the structure of the company* | *the structure of an atom*
2 [C] something that has been built: *a large wooden structure*

structure² Ac v [T] to arrange something in a clear organized way **SYN** **organize**: *Students learn how to structure their essays.*

struggle¹ /ˈstrʌɡəl/ v [I] **1** to try very hard to achieve something difficult: **struggle to do sth** *parents who struggle to bring up children on a low income* |

[+with] *I really struggled with that homework.* **2** to fight someone who is attacking or holding you: **[+with]** *She struggled with her attacker.* **3** to move somewhere with a lot of difficulty: **[+up/down/along etc]** *He struggled up the stairs with the luggage.*

PHRASAL VERBS

struggle on to continue doing something, even though it is difficult

struggle² *n* [C] **1** when someone tries hard for a long time to achieve something: **[+for]** *their struggle for survival* **2** a fight between two people

strum /strʌm/ *v* [I,T] (**strummed, strumming**) to play an instrument such as a GUITAR by moving your fingers across the strings

strung /strʌŋ/ *v* the past tense and past participle of STRING

strut¹ /strʌt/ *v* [I] (**strutted, strutting**) to walk in a proud and annoying way

strut² *n* [C] a long piece of metal or wood that supports something

stub¹ /stʌb/ *n* [C] the part of a cigarette that is left after the rest has been used

stub² *v* (**stubbed, stubbing**) **stub your toe** to hurt your toe by hitting it against something

PHRASAL VERBS

stub sth ↔ **out** to stop a cigarette burning by pressing it against something

stubble /'stʌbəl/ *n* [U] **1** the very short hairs on a man's face when he has not SHAVEd → see picture at UNSHAVEN **2** short pieces of corn or wheat that are left in a field after it has been cut —**stubbly** *adj*: *his stubbly chin*

stubborn /'stʌbən $ -ərn/ *adj* refusing to change your mind even when other people criticize you or try to persuade you: *Steve can be very stubborn sometimes.* **THESAURUS** DETERMINED —**stubbornly** *adv*: *He stubbornly refused to join in.* —**stubbornness** *n* [U]

stubby /'stʌbi/ *adj* short and thick or fat: *stubby fingers*

stuck¹ /stʌk/ *v* the past tense and past participle of STICK

stuck² *adj* [not before noun] **1** if something is stuck, it cannot move: *I tried to open the window but it was stuck.* | *The car got stuck in the mud.* **2** if you are stuck, you cannot get away from a boring or unpleasant situation: **[+at/in]** *I was stuck at home with a cold.* **3** *informal* if you are stuck, you cannot continue with something because it is too difficult: *Can you help me with this? I'm stuck.* **4 be stuck with sth** *informal* to have to have something that you do not want: *It's an awful building but we're stuck with it.*

stud /stʌd/ *n* [C] **1** a small round piece of metal that is stuck into the surface of something as a decoration: *a leather jacket with silver studs* **2** a horse that is used for breeding, or a place where these horses are kept **3** a small round EARRING

studded /'stʌdɪd/ *adj* decorated with a lot of studs or jewels: *a diamond-studded watch* → STAR-STUDDED

student /'stjuːdənt $ 'stuː-/ *n* [C] someone who studies at a school or university → **pupil**

studio /'stjuːdiəʊ $ 'stuːdioʊ/ *n* [C] (*plural* **studios**) **1** a room where a painter or photographer works: *an art studio* **2** a room where television and radio programmes are made **3** a film company, or the place where films are made: *the big Hollywood studios*

studious /'stjuːdiəs $ 'stuː-/ *adj* someone who is studious spends a lot of time reading and studying: *a quiet, studious young man*

studiously /'stjuːdiəsli $ 'stuː-/ *adv* very carefully

study¹ /'stʌdi/ *n* (*plural* **studies**) **1** [C] a piece of work that someone does to find out more about something: *They are **carrying out** a study of the kinds of food that children eat.* | **[+of]** *a study of teenagers' language* **2** [U] when you spend time learning: *a period of study* **3 studies** [plural] **a)** the subjects that you study: *a degree in Business Studies* **b)** the work you do as a student: *He went on to continue his studies at Harvard.* **4** [C] a room in your house where you read, write, or study → **office** → CASE STUDY

study² *v* (**studied, studying, studies**) **1** [I,T] to spend time reading, going to classes etc in order to learn about a subject: *Her son's at university studying medicine.* | **study to be sth** *She's studying to be a lawyer.* **2** [T] to look at something carefully to find out more about it: *He studied the document carefully.* | **study how/when/why etc** *a way of studying how genes affect development*

stuff¹ /stʌf/ n [U] informal
1 a substance or material of any sort: *What's that blue stuff on the floor? | Where's all the camping stuff?*
THESAURUS MATERIAL
2 information, ideas, or activities of any sort: *He taught us all kinds of stuff. | I've got a lot of stuff to do this weekend. | He does skiing and **stuff like that**.*
3 sb's stuff the things that belong to someone **SYN** things BrE: *I need a place to store my stuff for a while.* **THESAURUS** PROPERTY
PHRASES
   know your stuff to know a lot about a subject: *He really knows his stuff.*

stuff² v [T] **1** to push things into a small space **SYN** shove: **stuff sth in/into sth** *She stuffed some clothes into a bag and left.* **2** to fill something until it is full: **be stuffed with sth** *a pillow stuffed with feathers | boxes **stuffed full** of papers* **3** to fill a chicken, vegetable etc with a mixture of food before cooking it: *stuffed tomatoes* **4** to fill the skin of a dead animal in order to make the animal look still alive: *a stuffed owl*
PHRASES
   stuff yourself/your face informal to eat a lot of food **THESAURUS** EAT: *The kids have been stuffing themselves all afternoon.*

stuffing /'stʌfɪŋ/ n [U] **1** a mixture of food that you put inside a chicken etc before you cook it: *lemon and herb stuffing* **2** soft material that is used to fill a piece of furniture, a toy, or a CUSHION

stuffy /'stʌfi/ adj **1** a room or building that is stuffy does not have enough fresh air in it **2** disapproving people who are stuffy are formal and old-fashioned: *Rob's family is really stuffy.*

stumble /'stʌmbəl/ v [I] **1** to almost fall while you are walking: **[+over/on]** *Vic stumbled over the step as he came in.* **THESAURUS** FALL **2** to stop or make a mistake when you are speaking: **[+over]** *I hope I don't stumble over any of the long words.*
PHRASAL VERBS
stumble on/across sb/sth to find someone or something by chance: *While clearing out a cupboard, she stumbled across one of her old diaries.*

'stumbling ,block n [C] a problem that stops you achieving something: **[+to]** *The question of disarmament is still the main stumbling block to peace.*

stump¹ /stʌmp/ n [C] the part of something that is left when the rest has been cut off: *an old tree stump*

STUMP

stump² v **1** [T] if you are stumped by a question or problem, you are unable to find an answer to it: *The police are stumped by this case.* **2** [I] to walk with very firm heavy steps: **[+off/out etc]** *He nodded and stumped off.*

PHRASAL VERBS
stump up (sth) BrE informal to pay money, especially when you do not want to: *We stumped up eight pounds each.*

stun /stʌn/ v [T] (**stunned, stunning**) **1** to surprise or shock someone very much: *Everyone was stunned by Betty's answer.* **2** to make someone unconscious for a short time

stung /stʌŋ/ v the past tense and past participle of STING

stunk /stʌŋk/ v the past participle of STINK

stunning /'stʌnɪŋ/ adj **1** extremely beautiful: *You look stunning in that dress.* **2** very surprising or shocking: *stunning news*

stunt¹ /stʌnt/ n [C] **1** something dangerous that a person does to entertain people, especially in a film: *an actor who does all his own stunts* **2** something that is done to get people's attention: *a **publicity stunt***

stunt² v [T] to stop something or someone from growing or developing properly: *Lack of sunlight will stunt the plant's growth.*

'stunt man n [C] a man who is employed to do the dangerous things in a film, instead of an actor

stupefied /'stjuːpɪfaɪd $ 'stuː-/ adj so surprised or tired that you cannot think clearly —**stupefy** v [T] —**stupefying** adj

stupendous /stjuːˈpendəs $ stuː-/ adj extremely large or impressive: *a stupendous achievement*

stupid /'stjuːpɪd $ 'stuː-/ adj
1 not very clever or intelligent → **silly**: *Don't be so stupid! | He understands – he's not stupid. | **It was stupid of me** to lose my temper. | a stupid mistake*
2 [only before noun] spoken used to talk about someone or something that annoys you: *I can't get this stupid door open! | What is that stupid idiot doing?* —**stupidly** adv —**stupidity** /stjuːˈpɪdəti $ stuː-/ n [C,U]

THESAURUS

stupid not very clever or intelligent – used when you are annoyed or when strongly criticizing someone's behaviour: *What a stupid question.*
silly a little stupid. **Silly** sounds much gentler than **stupid**: *a silly mistake | Don't be silly – it's only a game!*
crazy not at all sensible or reasonable – used when you are very surprised by someone's behaviour or what they have said: *You're going to jump out of a plane – are you crazy! | a crazy idea*
ridiculous extremely stupid: *It's ridiculous to spend so much money on a dress. | Don't be ridiculous!*
absurd/ludicrous extremely stupid – used especially when an idea or situation seems strange or illogical: *How can a return ticket cost less than a single? It's totally absurd! | a ludicrous suggestion*

stupor /'stjuːpə $ 'stuːpər/ n [C,U] when you are almost unconscious and cannot think clearly, especially because you have drunk too much alcohol: *a drunken stupor*

S

sturdy /ˈstɜːdi $ ˈstɜːr-/ adj strong and not likely to break or be hurt: sturdy shoes | sturdy legs **THESAURUS** STRONG —**sturdily** adv

stutter /ˈstʌtə $ -ər/ v [I,T] to repeat the first sound of a word when you speak: 'I'm D-d-david,' he stuttered. —**stutter** n [singular]

sty /staɪ/ n [C] (plural **sties**) **1** a place where pigs are kept **SYN** **pigsty** **2** (also **stye**) an infection at the side of your eye

style¹ Ac /staɪl/ n
1 [C] the way in which a person or group of people typically does something: He's trying to copy Picasso's style of painting. | architecture in the Gothic style | The dinner will be served buffet style.
2 [C] the particular way in which someone usually behaves or works: **[+of]** Children have different styles of learning. | his own personal style of management
3 a) [C] a particular design or fashion for something such as clothes, hair, or furniture: Shoes are available in several styles. | His hair was cut in a very strange style. **b)** [U] the quality of being fashionable: **in/out of style** Long skirts are back in style.
4 [U] a quality that people admire or think is attractive: You may not like him, but you have to admit he **has style**.

style² Ac v [T] to design clothing, furniture, or the shape of someone's hair in a particular way

stylish Ac /ˈstaɪlɪʃ/ adj attractive and fashionable: stylish clothes | a very stylish woman —**stylishly** adv

stylist /ˈstaɪlɪst/ n [C] **1** someone who cuts or arranges people's hair as their job **SYN** **hairdresser** **2** someone who chooses clothes, jewellery etc for fashion models or famous people when they are photographed

stylistic /staɪˈlɪstɪk/ adj relating to the style of a piece of writing, music, or art: I've made a few stylistic changes to your report.

stylized Ac (also **-ised** BrE) /ˈstaɪlaɪzd/ adj done in a style that does not look natural or like real life: a very stylized painting

Styrofoam /ˈstaɪərəfəʊm $ ˈstaɪrəfoʊm/ n [U] trademark AmE a soft light plastic material, used especially to make containers **SYN** **polystyrene** BrE

suave /swɑːv/ adj polite, attractive, and confident, especially in a way that is not sincere

sub /sʌb/ n [C] **1** a SUBMARINE **2** a SUBSTITUTE **3** AmE a long thin sandwich

sub- /sʌb/ prefix **1** under or below: subzero temperatures **2** smaller or less important: a subcommittee

subconscious¹ /sʌbˈkɒnʃəs $ -ˈkɑːn-/ adj subconscious feelings affect your behaviour although you do not realize that they exist: her subconscious fear of failure —**subconsciously** adv

subconscious² n [singular] the part of your mind that can affect the way you behave without you realizing it

subcontinent /sʌbˈkɒntɪnənt $ -ˈkɑːn-/ n [C] a large area of land that is part of a CONTINENT: the Indian subcontinent

subcontract /sʌbkənˈtrækt $ -ˈkɑːntrækt/ v [T] if a

company subcontracts work, they pay other people to do part of the work for them: Some of the work will be subcontracted to another company. —**subcontractor** n [C] —**subcontract** /sʌbˈkɒntrækt $ -ˈkɑːn-/ n [C]

subculture /ˈsʌbˌkʌltʃə $ -ər/ n [C] a particular group of people within a society who have their own beliefs and ways of behaving

subdivide /sʌbdəˈvaɪd/ v [I,T] to divide something into smaller parts —**subdivision** /-ˈvɪʒən/ n [C,U]

subdue /səbˈdjuː $ -ˈduː/ v [T] to stop someone from behaving violently, especially by using force: Police managed to subdue the angry crowd.

subdued /səbˈdjuːd $ -ˈduːd/ adj **1** someone who is subdued is quiet because they are sad or worried: her sad face and subdued manner **2** not as bright or loud as usual: subdued lighting | She spoke in a subdued voice.

subject¹ /ˈsʌbdʒɪkt/ n [C]
1 **TOPIC** something that you are talking or writing about: **[+of]** I don't want to talk about the subject of death. | **on/about a subject** She's written several books on this subject.
2 **STH YOU STUDY** something that you study at a school or university: 'What's your favourite subject?' 'Science.'
3 **IN GRAMMAR** the word that usually comes before the verb in a sentence and shows who is doing the action of the verb. In the sentence 'Jean loves cats', 'Jean' is the subject. → **object**
4 **IN AN EXPERIMENT** a person or animal that is used in a test or EXPERIMENT
5 **SB FROM A COUNTRY** someone who is from a country that has a king or queen: a British subject

---

COLLOCATIONS

verbs

to discuss/talk about a subject He refused to discuss the subject.
to change the subject (=to start talking about something different) Don't change the subject!
to bring up/raise a subject (=to deliberately start talking about it) Someone brought up the subject of payment.
to deal with/cover a subject (=to speak or write about it) We will deal with this subject in the following chapter.
a subject comes up (=people start talking about it) The subject of payment never came up.

adjectives

an interesting/fascinating subject He has spent years researching this fascinating subject.
a controversial subject Contraception is a controversial subject.
a sensitive/touchy subject (=one that people may get upset about) Try to avoid sensitive subjects.

THESAURUS

subject something that you are talking or writing about: We talked about all sorts of subjects.

topic a subject that people often discuss or write about, in books, in newspapers, at school etc: *a list of the topics we will be covering in history*
matter formal a subject: *This is a very serious matter.*
issue an important subject that people discuss and argue about: *the issue of racism*
theme the subject of a film, book etc: *The theme of the story is love.*

subject² adj **subject to sth a)** likely to be affected by something: *All prices are **subject to change**.* **b)** only happening if something else happens: *We're going to build a garage, subject to planning permission.*

subject³ /səbˈdʒekt/ v

PHRASAL VERBS

subject sb/sth **to** sth to make someone or something experience something unpleasant: *The victim was subjected to a terrifying ordeal.*

subjective /səbˈdʒektɪv/ adj influenced by your own opinions and feelings rather than facts OPP **objective**: *Try not to be too subjective when you write about the film.* —**subjectively** adv

ˈsubject ˌmatter n [U] the subject that is being discussed

subjugate /ˈsʌbdʒəɡeɪt/ v [T] formal to force a person or group to obey you —**subjugation** /ˌsʌbdʒəˈɡeɪʃən/ n [U]

subjunctive /səbˈdʒʌŋktɪv/ n [singular] a verb form used to express doubt, possibility, or a wish. In the sentence 'I suggested that Peter come with us', 'come' is in the subjunctive.

sublime /səˈblaɪm/ adj extremely beautiful: *a sublime view of the mountains* —**sublimely** adv

submarine /ˈsʌbməriːn, ˌsʌbməˈriːn/ n [C] a ship that can travel under water

submerge /səbˈmɜːdʒ $ -ˈmɜːrdʒ/ v [I,T] to go or put something below the surface of water: *Whole villages were submerged by the flood.* —**submerged** adj —**submersion** /-ˈmɜːʃən $ -ˈmɜːrʒən/ n [U]

submission Ac /səbˈmɪʃən/ n **1** [U] when someone obeys a person or group and is completely controlled by them: **into submission** *The prisoners were starved into submission.* **2** [C,U] when you give a document such as a legal contract to someone so that they can consider it, or the document itself

submissive /səbˈmɪsɪv/ adj ready to obey other people and do whatever they want

submit Ac /səbˈmɪt/ v (**submitted, submitting**) **1** [T] to give a plan or piece of writing to someone in authority so that they can consider it: *They submitted a report calling for changes in the law.* **2** [I] to agree to obey a person, group, set of rules, especially when you have no choice: **[+to]** *They were forced to submit to the kidnappers' demands.*

subordinate¹ Ac /səˈbɔːdənət $ -ˈbɔːr-/ n [C] formal someone who has a less important job than someone else in an organization

subordinate² Ac adj formal **1** in a less important position than someone else: **[+to]** *Women were subordinate to men.* **2** less important than something

else: **[+to]** *These aims were subordinate to the aims of the mission.*

subordinate³ Ac /səˈbɔːdəneɪt $ -ˈbɔːr-/ v [T] formal to put someone or something in a less important position —**subordination** /səˌbɔːdəˈneɪʃən $ -ˌbɔːr-/ n [U]

suˌbordinate ˈclause n [C] in grammar, a part of a sentence that begins with a word such as 'when' or 'because' and adds information to the main part

subpoena /səˈpiːnə, səb-/ n [C] law a legal document that orders someone to attend a TRIAL in a law court

subprime /ˌsʌbˈpraɪm/ adj [only before noun] a subprime LOAN is money that is lent to someone who may not be able to pay it back, usually at a higher than normal rate of interest

subscribe /səbˈskraɪb/ v [I] to pay money so that a newspaper or magazine is regularly sent to you: **[+to]** *What magazines do you subscribe to?* —**subscriber** n [C]

PHRASAL VERBS

subscribe to sth formal to agree with an idea or opinion

subscription /səbˈskrɪpʃən/ n [C] an amount of money that you pay to receive a newspaper or magazine regularly, or to belong to an organization

subsequent Ac /ˈsʌbsɪkwənt/ adj [only before noun] formal happening or coming after something else: *These skills were passed on to subsequent generations.* —**subsequently** adv

subservient /səbˈsɜːviənt $ -ˈsɜːr-/ adj too willing to obey other people in a way that makes you seem weak —**subservience** n [U]

subset /ˈsʌbset/ n [C] a small group of people or things that is part of a larger group

subside /səbˈsaɪd/ v [I] to become calmer or quieter: *The storm subsided around dawn.*

subsidence /səbˈsaɪdəns, ˈsʌbsɪdəns/ n [U] when the ground sinks to a lower level, especially when this causes damage to buildings

subsidiary¹ /səbˈsɪdiəri $ -dieri/ n [C] (plural **subsidiaries**) a company that is owned or controlled by a larger company: **[+of]** *a subsidiary of a large American firm* THESAURUS ▸ COMPANY

subsidiary² Ac adj relating to, but less important than, something else

subsidize Ac (also **-ise** BrE) /ˈsʌbsɪdaɪz/ v [T] to pay part of the cost of something: *Farming is **heavily subsidized** by the government.*

subsidy Ac /ˈsʌbsədi/ n [C] (plural **subsidies**) money that a government or organization pays to help with the cost of something

subsist /səbˈsɪst/ v [I] formal to stay alive using only small amounts of food or money: **[+on]** *The prisoners subsisted on rice and water.* —**subsistence** n [U]

substance /ˈsʌbstəns/ n
1 [C] any type of solid, liquid, or gas: *The bag was covered with a sticky substance.* | *a poisonous substance* THESAURUS ▸ MATERIAL
2 [singular, U] the most important ideas in a speech

or piece of writing: **[+of]** *The news report said little about the substance of the peace talks.* | **in substance** *What she said, in substance, was that the mayor should resign.*

3 [U] *formal* if something has substance, it is true: **There's no substance to** *the rumour.* | **without substance** *His remarks are completely without substance.*

substandard /ˌsʌbˈstændəd◂ $ -ərd◂/ *adj* not as good as the usual standard: *substandard health care*

substantial /səbˈstænʃəl/ *adj* **1** large in amount or number: *a substantial salary* | *a substantial breakfast* **THESAURUS** BIG **2** large and strongly made: *a substantial piece of furniture*

substantially /səbˈstænʃəli/ *adv* very much: *Prices have increased substantially.*

substantiate /səbˈstænʃieɪt/ *v* [T] *formal* to prove that something someone has said is true: *Can he* **substantiate** *his* **claims**?

substitute¹ Ac /ˈsʌbstɪtjuːt $ -tuːt/ *n* [C] a person or thing that takes the place of another: *a substitute teacher* | *a sugar substitute* | **[+for]** *You can use oil as a substitute for butter.*

substitute² Ac *v* **1** [T] to use something new or different instead of something else: **substitute sth for sth** *You can substitute olive oil for butter in the recipe.* **2** [I] to do someone's job for a short time until they are able to do it again: **[+for]** *I substituted for John when he was sick.* —**substitution** /ˌsʌbstɪˈtjuːʃən $ -ˈtuː-/ *n* [C,U]

subsume /səbˈsjuːm $ -ˈsuːm/ *v* [T] *formal* to include someone or something in a group or type

subterfuge /ˈsʌbtəfjuːdʒ $ -ər-/ *n* [C,U] *formal* a trick or dishonest way of doing something, or behaviour in which someone does this

subterranean /ˌsʌbtəˈreɪniən◂/ *adj formal* under the surface of the earth: *a subterranean lake*

subtitles /ˈsʌbˌtaɪtlz/ *n* [plural] the words printed over a film in a foreign language to translate what the actors are saying —**subtitled** *adj*

subtle /ˈsʌtl/ *adj* **1** not easy to notice or understand: *subtle changes in climate* | *subtle humour* | *a* **subtle form** *of racism* **2** a subtle taste, smell, sound, or colour is pleasant and delicate: *the subtle scent of mint in the air* **3** clever in a way that does not attract attention: *I think we need a more subtle approach.* —**subtlety** *n* [C,U] —**subtly** *adv*

subtract /səbˈtrækt/ *v* [T] to take one number away from another number OPP **add**: **subtract sth from sth** *If you subtract 15 from 25 you get 10.* —**subtraction** /-ˈtrækʃən/ *n* [C,U]

suburb /ˈsʌbɜːb $ -ɜːrb/ *n* [C] an area where people live which is on the edge of a city: **[+of]** *a suburb of Chicago* **THESAURUS** CITY

suburban /səˈbɜːbən $ -ˈbɜːr-/ *adj* **1** relating to a suburb: *a quiet suburban street* **2** boring and ordinary: *suburban attitudes*

suburbia /səˈbɜːbiə $ -ˈbɜːr-/ *n* [U] suburbs in general

subversive /səbˈvɜːsɪv $ -ˈvɜːr-/ *adj* subversive ideas or activities are secret and intended to damage or destroy a government or an established system —**subversive** *n* [C]

subvert /səbˈvɜːt $ -ˈvɜːrt/ *v* [T] *formal* to try to destroy the power and influence of a government or the established system

subway /ˈsʌbweɪ/ *n* [C] **1** *BrE* a path for people to walk under a road or railway SYN **underpass 2** *AmE* a railway that runs under the ground in a big city SYN **metro, underground** *BrE*

> **Word Choice**: subway, underground, or the Tube?
> A railway system that runs under the ground below a big city is called the **subway** in American English and the **underground** in British English.
> In British English, the informal name for the system of trains that run under the ground in London is **the Tube**.
> A path for people to walk under a road or railway is called a **subway** in British English.

succeed /səkˈsiːd/ *v*

1 [I] to do what you tried or wanted to do OPP **fail**: *I was determined to succeed.* | **succeed in doing sth** *Did you succeed in finding a place to stay?*

> **Grammar**
> Do not say 'I succeeded to catch him.' Say *I succeeded in catching him.*

2 [I] to reach a high position in something such as your job OPP **fail**: **[+as]** *She gave herself one year to succeed as a writer.*
3 [I] to have the result or effect that was intended OPP **fail**: *The negotiations are unlikely to succeed.*
4 [I,T] to take a position or do a job after someone else: **succeed sb as sth** *Mr Harvey will succeed Mrs Lincoln as chairman.*

> **THESAURUS**
> **succeed** to do something you tried or wanted to do: *They succeeded in reaching the top of the mountain.*
> **manage** to succeed in doing something, especially when this is difficult. **Manage** is often used instead of **succeed** in everyday English: *She managed to get a job on a fashion magazine.* | *I'm sure we can manage.*
> **achieve** to succeed in doing something good or important: *You should be proud of all you have achieved.*
> **make it** to succeed in your career, or to succeed in reaching a place or part of a competition: *She finally made it as a singer when she released her second album.* | *The team made it to the finals of the World Cup.*

succeeding /səkˈsiːdɪŋ/ *adj* coming after something else: *Sales improved in succeeding years.* | *succeeding generations*

success /səkˈses/ *n*

1 [U] when you achieve what you want to achieve OPP **failure**: *Her success is due to hard work.* | **without success** *I tried to contact him, but without success.* |

success in doing sth *Did you have any success in persuading Alan to come?*
2 [C] something that a lot of people like or buy OPP **failure**: *I'm sure the book will be a success.*
3 [C] something you do that has the result or effect that you wanted OPP **failure**: *The meeting was a success.*

COLLOCATIONS

adjectives

a great success *The party was a great success.*
a big/huge/major success *This product has been a huge success.*
great/considerable success *I have used this method myself, with great success.*
financial/commercial/economic success *Other artists envied his commercial success.*

verbs

to have/achieve success *He tried to bail the water out of the boat, but had little success.* ⚠ Do not say 'make success' or 'make a success'. Say **have success** or **achieve success**.
to meet with success (=to be successful) *This strategy has met with some success.*
to make a success of sth *They have both made a success of their lives.*

successful /sək'sesfəl/ adj
1 having the result or effect that you intended OPP **unsuccessful**: *If the operation is successful, you should make a full recovery.* | *a successful attempt to sail around the world*
2 a successful person earns a lot of money or is very well known and respected OPP **unsuccessful**: *a successful businesswoman*
3 a successful business, film, or product makes a lot of money OPP **unsuccessful**: *a **highly successful** product* | *The film was **hugely successful**.* —**successfully** adv

THESAURUS

successful achieving the result you wanted: *Their second attempt was successful.*
effective an effective method, treatment, drug etc is good because it does exactly what it is intended to do: *The tests showed that the drug was highly effective.* | *What is the most effective way of dealing with young criminals?*
victorious especially written successful because you win a game, election, war etc: *the captain of the victorious team*
promising a promising young player, student, artist etc is likely to be successful in the future: *The coach is always looking for promising young players.*
thriving a thriving business, industry, economy, city etc is very successful: *He has built up a thriving business.* | *The island's tourist industry is thriving.*
booming extremely successful - used about an economy, or when business or trade is increasing: *The economy is booming.* | *the booming market for modern art*

succession Ac /sək'seʃən/ n **1** [singular, U] a number of things that happen one after the other:

[+of] *She's had a succession of failed marriages.* | **in succession** *United have won four championships in succession.* **2** [U] when someone takes a position or job after someone else

successive Ac /sək'sesɪv/ adj happening one after the other: *The team had three successive victories.* —**successively** adv

successor Ac /sək'sesə $ -ər/ n [C] someone's successor is the person who has their job after they leave: *No one was certain who her successor would be.*

succinct /sək'sɪŋkt/ adj approving clearly expressed in a few words: *a succinct description* —**succinctly** adv

succulent /'sʌkjələnt/ adj juicy and good to eat: *a succulent steak* —**succulence** n [U]

succumb /sə'kʌm/ v [I] formal **1** to stop opposing someone or something that is stronger than you, and allow them to take control: **[+to]** *Eventually, she succumbed to his charms.* **2** to become ill or die from an illness

such /sʌtʃ/ determiner, pron
1 similar to the thing or person which has already been mentioned: *What would you do in such a situation?* | *Such behaviour is not acceptable here.* | *'You said you'd come.' 'I said **no such thing**!'*
2 used to emphasize your description of someone or something: *He's such an idiot.* | *It's such a long way from here.*
PHRASES

not ... as such spoken used to say that the word you are using to describe something is not exactly correct: *There isn't a garden as such, just a little vegetable patch.*
such as used to give an example of something: *big cities such as New York*
such ... that used to say what the result of something is: *The animal was such a nuisance that we had to get rid of it.*
there's no such thing/person (as sb/sth) used to say that something or someone does not exist: *There's no such thing as a perfect marriage.*

Word Choice: such a or so?
You use **such a** before a noun, or an adjective and a noun: *I feel such a fool!* | *We've had such a hard day!*
You use **so** before an adjective or an adverb: *Your dress is so pretty!* | *He talks so loudly.*

'such and ,such determiner, pron spoken used to talk about a certain thing, time, amount etc without saying exactly what it is: *They will ask you to come on such and such a day, at such and such a time.*

suck¹ /sʌk/ v [I,T]
1 to hold something in your mouth and pull on it with your tongue and lips: *Don't suck your thumb, Katie.* | **[+on]** *Barry was sucking on a candy bar.*
2 to take air or liquid into your mouth by making your lips form a small hole and then pulling the air or liquid in: **[+up]** *She sucked up the last of her lemonade with a straw.*
3 to pull someone or something with a lot of force: **suck sb under/down** *The river sucked him under.*

S

be sucked into (doing) sth to become involved in something unpleasant without wanting to: *He was quickly sucked into a life of crime.*

suck² *n* [C] an act of sucking

sucker /'sʌkə $ -ər/ *n* [C] *spoken* someone who is easily tricked: *Ellen always was a sucker.*

suction /'sʌkʃən/ *n* [U] the process of sucking air or liquid from a container or space

sudden /'sʌdn/ *adj* happening quickly, when you are not expecting it: *a sudden change in the weather | She felt a sudden rush of anger.* —**suddenness** *n* [U]

all of a sudden suddenly: *All of a sudden, the lights went out.* **THESAURUS** SUDDENLY

suddenly /'sʌdnli/ *adv* if something happens suddenly, it happens quickly, when you are not expecting it: *I suddenly realized that someone was following me. | George died very suddenly.*

THESAURUS

suddenly used when something happens very quickly and unexpectedly: *I suddenly felt tired.*

all of a sudden suddenly – used especially in stories or in descriptions of past events: *All of a sudden, the ground started to shake.*

without warning suddenly and with no signs that it was going to happen – used about bad things: *The attacks came completely without warning.*

out of the blue very suddenly and when you are not expecting it at all: *I can't just call her out of the blue!*

at short notice *BrE*, **on short notice** *AmE* suddenly, so that there is not much time to prepare or make arrangements: *I'm sorry to bring you here at short notice.*

sudoku /suː'dəʊkuː $ -'doʊ-/ *n* [C,U] a game in which you have to write numbers in a set of 81 squares. Each line of squares must contain the numbers 1 to 9 once only.

suds /sʌdz/ *n* [plural] the BUBBLES produced when soap and water are mixed together

sue /sjuː $ suː/ *v* [I,T] to start a legal process to get money from someone who has harmed you in some way: *She plans to sue the company for $1 million.*

suede /sweɪd/ *n* [U] soft leather with a slightly rough surface

suffer /'sʌfə $ -ər/ *v*
1 [I,T] to experience physical or emotional pain: *She's suffering a lot of pain. | He died in his sleep and didn't suffer.* | **[+from]** *David is suffering from a knee injury.*
2 [I,T] to experience and be badly affected by something OPP **benefit**: *Small businesses suffered financially because of the crisis.* | **[+from]** *He is suffering from financial problems.* | *We are suffering the consequences of other people's bad decisions.* | *In 1667 England suffered a defeat by the Dutch* (=they lost a battle to the Dutch).

3 [I] to become worse in quality because of something: *Safety will suffer if costs are cut.* —**sufferer** *n* [C] —**suffering** *n* [C,U]

suffice /sə'faɪs/ *v* [I] *formal* to be enough: *A light lunch will suffice.*

sufficient Ac /sə'fɪʃənt/ *adj* as much as you need for a particular purpose SYN **enough** OPP **insufficient**: *The police have sufficient evidence to charge him with murder.* **THESAURUS** ENOUGH —**sufficiently** *adv*

suffix /'sʌfɪks/ *n* [C] a letter or letters added to the end of a word to make a new word, for example 'ness' at the end of 'kindness' → **affix**, **prefix**

suffocate /'sʌfəkeɪt/ *v* [I,T] to die because there is not enough air, or to kill someone by preventing them from breathing —**suffocation** /ˌsʌfə'keɪʃən/ *n* [U]

suffocating /'sʌfəkeɪtɪŋ/ *adj* so hot that you have difficulty breathing: *the suffocating heat of the studio lights*

suffrage /'sʌfrɪdʒ/ *n* [U] *formal* the right to vote

sugar /'ʃʊɡə $ -ər/ *n*
1 [U] a sweet substance obtained from plants and used for making food and drinks sweet: *Do you take sugar in your tea? | a bag of sugar*
2 [C] *BrE* the amount of sugar that a small spoon can hold: *How many sugars do you want in your coffee?* —**sugar** *v* [T]

sugary /'ʃʊɡəri/ *adj* containing sugar or tasting like sugar: *sugary drinks*

suggest /sə'dʒest $ səɡ'dʒest/ *v* [T]
1 to tell someone your ideas about what should be done → **propose**: *My doctor suggested a week off work.* | **[+(that)]** *I suggest that you phone before you go over there.* | *He suggested that we should meet in London.* | **suggest doing sth** *Joan suggested asking her father for his opinion.* | **[+how/where/what etc]** *The teacher suggested how Andy could research the project.*

Grammar
Do not say 'They suggested me to take the bus.' Say *They suggested taking the bus.* or *They suggested that I should take the bus.*

2 to show that something might be true: **evidence/results/data etc suggest(s) that** *The evidence suggests that single fathers are more likely to work than single mothers.*
3 to say something in an indirect way: **[+(that)]** *Are you suggesting I'm too fat?*
4 to say that someone or something would be suitable for a particular job or activity: **suggest sb/sth for sth** *John Roberts has been suggested for the post of manager.*

THESAURUS

suggest to tell someone your ideas about what they should do, or what you could do together: *I suggested going to watch a movie.*

recommend to suggest that someone goes somewhere, tries something etc, because you know that it is good and you think they will like it: *Mary recommended this book to me.*

put forward to suggest an idea, plan, reason etc: *The company put forward plans for a new housing development.* | *No one has been able to put forward a satisfactory explanation.*

nominate to suggest someone or something should get an important job, prize etc, especially when people will vote to make the decision: *The film has been nominated for five Oscars.*

suggestion /sə'dʒestʃən $ səg-/ n
1 [C] an idea, plan, or possibility that someone suggests: **[+for/about/on]** *Do you have any suggestions about what we can do in New York?* | **[+that]** *the suggestion that we could go to war*
2 [singular, U] a sign or possibility of something: **[+of]** *There was never any suggestion of criminal activity.* | **[+that]** *There's some suggestion that he was the person that killed Angie.*
3 a suggestion of sth a slight amount of something: *There was just a suggestion of a smile on her face.*

COLLOCATIONS

verbs

to make a suggestion *Can I make a suggestion?*
to give sb a suggestion *Let me give you some suggestions.*
to have a suggestion *He had a suggestion for us.*
to come up with a suggestion (=to think of one) *They've come up with several suggestions.*
to follow a suggestion (=to do what is suggested) *I followed your suggestion and invited her.*

adjectives

a good/excellent suggestion *You've made some excellent suggestions.*
a helpful/useful suggestion *Thank you for your helpful suggestions.*

suggestive /sə'dʒestɪv $ səg-/ adj **1 suggestive of sth** similar to something: *Her symptoms are suggestive of an anxiety disorder.* **2** making you think of sex: *a suggestive remark*

suicidal /ˌsuːə'saɪdl◂, ˌsjuː- $ ˌsuː-/ adj **1** someone who is suicidal feels so unhappy that he or she wants to kill himself or herself: *She admits that she sometimes had suicidal thoughts.* **2** very dangerous or likely to have a very bad result: *It would be suicidal to attack in daylight.*

suicide /'suːəsaɪd, 'sjuː- $ 'suː-/ n [C,U]
1 when someone deliberately kills himself or herself: *There's been a rise in the number of suicides among young men.* | *Her brother **committed suicide** last year.* | *She left a **suicide note**.* **THESAURUS** ▶ **KILL**
2 political/economic suicide something that you do that ruins your good position in politics or the ECONOMY: *It would be political suicide to hold an election now.*
3 suicide bombing/attack/mission an attack in which someone deliberately kills himself or herself in the act of killing other people

suit¹ /suːt, sjuːt $ suːt/ n [C]
1 a jacket and trousers or a skirt that are made of the same material and are worn together: *a light-weight suit* | *I wear a suit to work.*
2 a LAWSUIT: *a civil suit*
3 bathing/jogging etc suit a piece of clothing or a set of clothes that you wear for swimming, running etc: *a ski suit*
4 one of the four types of playing cards in a set of playing cards → **BOILER SUIT, TROUSER SUIT, WET SUIT**

suit² v [T]
1 to be acceptable, right, or suitable for someone: *It's difficult to find a date that **suits everyone**. There's a range of restaurants to **suit all tastes** (=the different things that people like).* | *Either steak or chicken would **suit** me **fine**.*
2 clothes, colours etc that suit you make you look attractive: *I don't think that new hairstyle really suits her.*
3 be suited to/for sth to have the right qualities to do something: *Lucy's ideally suited for the job.*
PHRASES

suit yourself used to tell someone they can do whatever they want, even though it annoys you

suitable /'suːtəbəl, 'sjuː- $ 'suː-/ adj having the right qualities for a particular purpose, person, or situation **OPP** **unsuitable**: *We are hoping to find a suitable school.* | **[+for]** *The film isn't suitable for young children.* **THESAURUS** ▶ **UNSUITABLE** —**suitably** adv —**suitability** /ˌsuːtə'bɪləti, ˌsjuː- $ ˌsuː-/ n [U]

THESAURUS

suitable having the right qualities for a particular purpose, person, or situation: *a suitable person for the job* | *a suitable place to live*
right completely suitable in every way. **Right** is often used instead of **suitable** in everyday English: *This colour looks **just right**.* | *I still haven't met the right person.*
appropriate formal suitable for a particular purpose: *appropriate clothes for an interview* | *The doctor then decides on the most appropriate treatment.*
proper the proper equipment, clothes, or way of doing something is the one that most people think is the most suitable: *I didn't have the proper tools for the job.* | *Children need to be taught the proper way to behave in public.*

suitcase /'suːtkeɪs, 'sjuːt- $ 'suːt-/ n [C] a case with a handle, used for carrying clothes and possessions when you travel → see picture at **CASE**

suite /swiːt/ n [C] **1** especially BrE a set of matching furniture for a room: *a living-room suite* **2** a set of expensive rooms in a hotel: *the honeymoon suite*

suitor /'suːtə, 'sjuː- $ 'suːtər/ n [C] old-fashioned a woman's suitor is the man who wants to marry her

sulfur /'sʌlfə $ -ər/ n the American spelling of SULPHUR

sulk /sʌlk/ v [I] to show that you are annoyed by being silent and looking unhappy: *Stop sulking – you can go out and play later.* —**sulk** n [C] —**sulky** adj

sullen /'sʌlən/ adj being and looking angry but not saying anything: *a sullen expression* —**sullenly** adv

sulphur *especially BrE*, **sulfur** *AmE* /'sʌlfə $ -fər/ *n* [U] a yellow chemical powder that smells unpleasant —**sulphurous** *adj*

sultan /'sʌltən/ *n* [C] a ruler in some Muslim countries

sultana /sʌl'tɑːnə $ -'tænə/ *n* [C] *BrE* a dried white GRAPE, used in cooking

sultry /'sʌltri/ *adj* **1** sultry weather is hot with no wind **2** a woman who is sultry makes other people feel strong sexual attraction to her

sum¹ Ac /sʌm/ *n* [C] **1** an amount of money: *The city has spent a large sum of money on parks.* **2 the sum of sth** the total when you add two or more numbers together: *The sum of 4 and 5 is 9.* **3** *BrE* a simple calculation such as adding or dividing numbers

sum² Ac *v* (**summed**, **summing**)

PHRASAL VERBS

sum up 1 to end a discussion or speech by giving the main information about it in a short statement: *So, to sum up, we need to organize our time better.* | **sum sth ↔ up** *You should sum up your argument in the final paragraph.* **2 sum sb/sth ↔ up** to form an opinion about someone or something: *Pat summed up the situation at a glance.* —**summing-up** *n* [C]

summarize Ac (*also* **-ise** *BrE*) /'sʌməraɪz/ *v* [I,T] to give only the main information about something without the details

summary¹ Ac /'sʌməri/ *n* [C] (*plural* **summaries**) a short statement that gives the main information about something: *I've given a brief summary on a separate sheet.*

summary² Ac *adj* [only before noun] *formal* done immediately, without following the usual processes or rules: *summary executions*

summer /'sʌmə $ -ər/ *n* [C,U] the season between spring and autumn, when the weather is hottest: *Are you going away this summer?* | **in (the) summer** *Miriam likes to relax in the garden in summer.* → INDIAN SUMMER —**summery** *adj*

summertime /'sʌmətaɪm $ -ər-/ *n* [U] the time of year when it is summer: *It's really hot here in the summertime.*

summit /'sʌmɪt/ *n* [C] **1** a meeting between the leaders of several governments: *an economic summit* **2** the top of a mountain THESAURUS▶ MOUNTAIN

summon /'sʌmən/ *v* [T] *formal* **1** to officially order someone to come to a particular place: **summon sb to sth** *I was summoned to the principal's office.* **2** (*also* **summon up**) if you summon your courage, strength etc, you try to be brave, strong etc even though it is difficult: *Tom summoned up the courage to ask Kay to marry him.*

summons /'sʌmənz/ *n* [C] (*plural* **summonses**) an official letter that says you must go to a court of law —**summons** *v* [T]

sumptuous /'sʌmptʃuəs/ *adj* very impressive and expensive: *a sumptuous meal* —**sumptuously** *adv*

sun¹ /sʌn/ *n*
1 the Sun/sun the large bright object in the sky that gives us light and heat, and which the Earth moves

around: *The sun disappeared behind a cloud.* THESAURUS▶ STAR
2 [singular, U] the heat and light that come from the sun: **in the sun** *We sat in the sun, eating ice cream.*
3 [C] any star around which PLANETs move

COLLOCATIONS

verbs

the sun is shining *The sky was blue and the sun was shining.*
the sun comes out (=appears when cloud moves away) *In the afternoon the sun came out.*
the sun rises/comes up (=appears at the beginning of the day) *The sun had not yet risen.*
the sun sets/goes down (=disappears at the end of the day) *He watched the sun go down over the sea.*

adjectives

hot/warm sun *They felt the hot sun on their backs.*
bright sun *The sun was so bright it hurt my eyes.*
the sun is high/low *When she woke, the sun was high in the sky.*

noun + sun

the morning/afternoon/evening sun *The cat was sleeping in the afternoon sun.*
the midday sun *Avoid going out in the midday sun.*

sun² *v* (**sunned**, **sunning**) **sun yourself** to sit or lie outside when the sun is shining

Sun. (*also* **Sun** *BrE*) the written abbreviation of **Sunday**

sunbathe /'sʌnbeɪð/ *v* [I] to sit or lie outside in the sun in order to become brown —**sunbathing** *n* [U]

sunbeam /'sʌnbiːm/ *n* [C] a line of light shining down from the sun

sunbed /'sʌnbed/ *n* [C] a piece of equipment with special lights, that you lie on to make your body brown

'sun block *n* [C,U] SUNSCREEN

sunburn /'sʌnbɜːn $ -bɜːrn/ *n* [U] when your skin is red and sore from spending too much time in the sun —**sunburned**, **sunburnt** *adj*

'sun cream *n* [C,U] SUNSCREEN

sundae /'sʌndeɪ $ -di/ *n* [C] a dish made from ICE CREAM, fruit, nuts etc → see picture at DESSERT

Sunday /'sʌndi, -deɪ/ *n* [C,U] (*written abbreviation* **Sun.**) the day between Saturday and Monday → see examples at MONDAY

sundial /'sʌndaɪəl/ *n* [C] an object that shows the time by using the shadow made on it by the sun

sundown /'sʌndaʊn/ *n* [U] *old-fashioned* SUNSET

sundry /'sʌndri/ *adj* *formal* sundry people or things are all different, and cannot be considered as a group SYN **various**

PHRASES

all and sundry everyone, not just a few carefully chosen people: *I don't want all and sundry coming into our garden.*

sunflower /ˈsʌnˌflaʊə $ -ˌflaʊər/ n [C] a tall plant with a large yellow flower and seeds that you can eat → see picture at **FLOWER**[1]

sung /sʌŋ/ v the past participle of SING

sunglasses /ˈsʌnˌglɑːsɪz $ -ˌglæ-/ n [plural] dark glasses that you wear to protect your eyes from the sun → see picture at **GLASS**

sunk /sʌŋk/ v the past participle of SINK

sunken /ˈsʌŋkən/ adj [only before noun] **1** built or put at a lower level than the surrounding area: a sunken garden **2** having fallen to the bottom of the sea: sunken treasure **3** sunken cheeks or eyes have fallen inwards, making someone look ill

sunlight /ˈsʌnlaɪt/ n [U] natural light that comes from the sun: He stepped out into strong sunlight.

sunlit /ˈsʌnlɪt/ adj made brighter by light from the sun: a sunlit kitchen

sunny /ˈsʌni/ adj full of light from the sun → **bright**: a warm sunny day | I hope **it's sunny** tomorrow.

sunrise /ˈsʌnraɪz/ n **1** [U] the time when the sun first appears in the morning: **at sunrise** In the summer we start work at sunrise and finish at sunset. **2** [C] the coloured part of the sky where the sun first appears

sunroof /ˈsʌnruːf/ n [C] a part of the roof of a car that you can open to let in air and light

sunscreen /ˈsʌnskriːn/ n [C,U] a skin cream to stop the sun from burning you [SYN] **sun block, sun cream**

sunset /ˈsʌnset/ n **1** [U] the time when the sun disappears and night begins: **at sunset** In the summer we start work at sunrise and finish at sunset. **2** [C] the coloured part of the sky where the sun disappears

sunshine /ˈsʌnʃaɪn/ n [U] the light and heat that comes from the sun: Let's go out and enjoy the sunshine. | After a week of sunshine, it started to rain.

sunstroke /ˈsʌnstrəʊk $ -stroʊk/ n [U] an illness caused by being in the sun too long

suntan /ˈsʌntæn/ (also **tan**) n [C] when your skin goes brown from being in the sun —**suntanned** adj

sunup /ˈsʌnʌp/ n [U] old-fashioned SUNRISE

super[1] /ˈsuːpə $ -pər/ adj informal extremely good: a super idea

super[2] adv spoken extremely: a super expensive restaurant

super- /ˈsuːpə $ -pər/ prefix extremely or extreme: the super-rich | a super-efficient secretary | a superhero

superb /sjuːˈpɜːb, suː- $ sʊˈpɜːrb/ adj very good: a superb cook —**superbly** adv

supercilious /ˌsuːpəˈsɪliəs $ -pər-/ adj formal disapproving behaving as if you think that other people are less important than you

superficial /ˌsuːpəˈfɪʃəl◂ $ -pər-/ adj **1** not studying or looking at something carefully and only seeing the most noticeable things: a superficial knowledge of the culture **2** seeming to have a particular quality, although this is not true or real: The two animals have a **superficial resemblance** but they are actually different breeds. **3** superficial damage, injury etc only affects the skin or the outside of something and is not serious: superficial cuts —**superficially** adv

superfluous /suːˈpɜːfluəs $ -ˈpɜːr-/ adj formal not necessary, or more than is needed: superfluous details

superfood /ˈsuːpəfuːd $ -pər-/ n [C] a food that is believed to contain a lot of substances that make you healthy

superhuman /ˌsuːpəˈhjuːmən◂ $ -pərˈhjuː-, -ˈjuː-/ adj using powers that are much greater than those of ordinary people: It will take a superhuman effort to rebuild the country.

superimpose /ˌsuːpərɪmˈpəʊz $ -ˈpoʊz/ v [T] to put a picture, photograph etc on top of another one so that both of them can be seen

superintendent /ˌsuːpərɪnˈtendənt/ n [C] **1** a British police officer who has a fairly high rank **2** someone who is officially responsible for a building or place

superior[1] /suːˈpɪəriə $ sʊˈpɪriər/ adj **1** better than something or someone else [OPP] **inferior**: [+to] Today's computers are superior to those we had ten years ago. | a **vastly superior** (=very much better) army **2** disapproving showing that you think you are better than other people: his superior attitude

superior[2] n [C] someone who has a higher position than you at work: I'll have to discuss this with my superiors.

superiority /suːˌpɪəriˈɒrəti $ sʊˌpɪriˈɔː-, -ˈɑː-/ n [U] **1** the quality of being better than other things: [+of] the superiority of modern telecommunications **2** disapproving when you show that you think you are better than other people: She spoke with an air of superiority.

superlative[1] /suːˈpɜːlətɪv, sjuː- $ sʊˈpɜːr-/ adj extremely good: a superlative actor

superlative[2] n **the superlative** the form of an adjective or adverb that you use when saying that someone or something is the biggest, best, worst etc. For example 'fastest' is the superlative of 'fast', and 'most expensive' is the superlative of 'expensive'. → **comparative**

supermarket /ˈsuːpəˌmɑːkɪt $ -pərˌmɑːr-/ n [C] a large shop that sells food, drink, products for cleaning the house etc

supermodel /ˈsuːpəˌmɒdl $ -pərˌmɑːdl/ n [C] a very famous fashion MODEL

supernatural /ˌsuːpəˈnætʃərəl◂ $ -pər-/ n **the supernatural** events, powers, or creatures that are impossible to explain by science or natural causes —**supernatural** adj: supernatural powers

superpower /ˈsuːpəˌpaʊə $ -pərˌpaʊr/ n [C] a country that has a lot of military and political power **THESAURUS** COUNTRY

supersede /ˌsuːpəˈsiːd $ -pər-/ v [T] if a new product, idea, method etc supersedes another one, people start to use the new one because it is better: TV had superseded radio by the 1960s.

supersonic /ˌsuːpəˈsɒnɪk◂ $ -pərˈsɑː-/ adj faster than the speed of sound: supersonic jets

superstar /'suːpəstɑː $ -pərstɑːr/ n [C] an extremely famous actor, singer etc

superstition /ˌsuːpə'stɪʃən $ -pər-/ n [C,U] a belief that some objects or actions are lucky or unlucky: *the old superstition that the number 13 is unlucky*

superstitious /ˌsuːpə'stɪʃəs $ -pər-/ adj believing that some objects or actions are lucky or unlucky: *Are you superstitious?*

superstore /'suːpəstɔː $ -pərstɔːr/ n [C] *BrE* a very large shop, especially one that is built outside the centre of a city: *a DIY superstore*

supervise /'suːpəvaɪz $ -pər-/ v [I,T] to be in charge of an activity or person, making sure that work is done properly or that people behave correctly: *The engineer supervises all the construction work.* —**supervisor** n [C] —**supervisory** /'suːpəvaɪzəri $ ˌsuːpər'vaɪzəri/ adj: *The mayor has a supervisory role.*

supervision /ˌsuːpə'vɪʒən $ -pər-/ n [U] when you supervise someone or something

supper /'sʌpə $ -ər/ n [C] a meal that you eat in the evening SYN **dinner**: *We had supper in an Italian restaurant.* | *Have you eaten supper?*

supplant /sə'plɑːnt $ sə'plænt/ v [T] *formal* to take the place of another person or thing: *Smith was soon supplanted as party leader.*

supple /'sʌpəl/ adj able to bend and move easily: *supple leather*

supplement Ac /'sʌpləmənt/ n [C] something that you add to something else to improve it: *You may need vitamin supplements.* —**supplement** /'sʌpləment/ v [T]: *I supplement my income by teaching Italian at weekends.*

supplementary Ac /ˌsʌplə'mentəri◂/ adj added to something, or provided as well as something: *supplementary vitamins*

supplier /sə'plaɪə $ -ər/ n [C] a company that provides goods for shops and businesses: *medical suppliers*

supply¹ /sə'plaɪ/ n (*plural* **supplies**)
1 [C,U] an amount of something that can be used, or the process of providing this: **[+of]** *a week's supply of fresh meat* | *the supply of oxygen to the brain*
2 supplies [plural] food, clothes, and other things that are needed for an activity, journey etc: *emergency medical supplies*
3 water/electricity/power/gas supply a system of providing water, electricity etc

supply² v [T] (**supplied**, **supplying**, **supplies**) to provide people with something that they need, especially regularly over a period of time: **supply sb with sth** *Drivers are supplied with a uniform.* | **supply sth to sb** *He supplies information to the police.*

support¹ /sə'pɔːt $ -ɔːrt/ v [T]
1 to say that you agree with an idea, group, or person and want them to succeed: *I don't support any one political party.* | **support sb in (doing) sth** *We need to support teachers in their aims.*
2 to help and encourage someone or something: *My parents have always supported my decision to be an actor.*
3 to provide enough money for someone to have all

the things they need: *I have a wife and two children to support.* | **support himself/herself etc** *You've got to learn to support yourself.*
4 to give money to a group or organization or for an event: *Which charities do you support?*
5 to be under something, holding it up and preventing it from falling: *The bridge is supported by two columns.*
6 to help to show that something is true: *The results support our original theory.*
7 *BrE* to like a particular sports team and want them to win: *Which team do you support?*

support² n
1 [U] encouragement and help that you give to someone or something: *Many people have given us support in our campaign.* | **[+for]** *There was widespread support for the war.* | **the support of sb** *The board do not have the support of the shareholders.*
2 [U] sympathy and help that you give to someone: *I needed the support of my boyfriend.*
3 [U] money that provides help for people: *We will provide financial support for the trip.*
4 [C,U] something that holds something or something up, stopping them from falling: *supports for the roof* | *He leant against the wall for support.*
5 [U] facts showing that an idea or statement is correct: *My own research provides some support for this view.* → **CHILD SUPPORT, LIFE SUPPORT SYSTEM**

supporter /sə'pɔːtə $ -ɔːrtər/ n [C] **1** someone who supports a person, group, or plan **2** *especially BrE* someone who likes a particular team and wants them to win: *Manchester United supporters*

supporting /sə'pɔːtɪŋ $ -ɔːr-/ adj **1 supporting part/role/actor etc** a small part in a play or film, not one of the main characters **2 supporting wall** a wall that supports the weight of something

supportive /sə'pɔːtɪv $ -ɔːr-/ adj giving help or encouragement: *Mark and Sally are very supportive of each other.*

suppose /sə'pəʊz $ -'poʊz/ v [T]
1 to think that something is true, based on what you know: *No one answered, so she supposed that they must have gone home.*
2 be supposed to do sth a) used to say what someone should or should not do, according to rules or what someone has said: *You're not supposed to smoke in here.* **b)** used to say what is expected or intended to happen, especially when it did not happen: *The new laws are supposed to prevent crime.* **c)** if something is supposed to be true, many people believe it is true: *Mrs Carver is supposed to have a lot of money.*

PHRASES

do you suppose (that) ... ? used to ask someone their opinion or guess: *Do you suppose he was hurt?*
I don't suppose (that) used to ask a question in an indirect or polite way: *I don't suppose you know where my pen is?*
I suppose 1 used to say you think something is true, although you are not sure: **[+(that)]** *I suppose you're right.* | *'Aren't you pleased?' 'Yes, I suppose so.'*
2 used when agreeing to let someone do something, especially when you do not want to: *'Can we come with you?' 'Oh, I suppose so.'* **3** used when you

are angry with someone: **[+(that)]** *I suppose you thought that was funny!*

suppose/supposing (that) (*also* **let's suppose**) used when imagining a possible situation or condition: *Suppose you lost your job. What would you do?*

supposed /sə'pəʊzd, sə'pəʊzɪd $ -'poʊzd, -'poʊzɪd/ *adj* [only before noun] used to say that what you are talking about is believed to be true, but that you do not believe or agree with it yourself: *the supposed link between violent movies and crime*

supposedly /sə'pəʊzɪdli $ -'poʊ-/ *adv* used to say that you do not believe what you are saying about the thing or person you are describing, even though other people think it is true: *How can a supposedly intelligent person make so many mistakes?* | *He's quite well paid, supposedly.*

supposition /ˌsʌpə'zɪʃən/ *n* [C,U] *formal* something that someone believes is true even though they cannot prove it

suppress /sə'pres/ *v* [T] **1** to stop people from opposing the government, especially by using force: *The army was called in to suppress the revolt.* **2** to prevent important information or opinions from becoming known: *His lawyer illegally suppressed evidence.* **3** to control a feeling, so that you do not show it or it does not affect you: *Andy could barely suppress his anger.* —**suppression** /sə'preʃən/ *n* [U]

supremacy /sʊ'preməsi, sju- $ sʊ-, suː-/ *n* [U] when someone is more powerful or advanced than other people

supreme /sʊ'priːm, sju- $ sʊ-, suː-/ *adj* **1** having the highest position of authority or power: *the Supreme Commander of the UN forces* **2** the greatest possible: *He made a* **supreme effort**. | *a matter of* **supreme importance**

Su,preme 'Court *n* [singular] the most important court of law in some countries or some states of the US

supremely /sʊ'priːmli, sju- $ sʊ-, suː-/ *adv* extremely: *a supremely confident athlete*

surcharge /'sɜːtʃɑːdʒ $ 'sɜːrtʃɑːrdʒ/ *n* [C] money that you have to pay in addition to the basic price of something

sure /ʃɔː $ ʃʊr/ *adj, adv*
1 [not before noun] certain about something: **[+(that)]** *Are you sure you've had enough?* | **[+about]** *Are you* **quite** *sure (=completely sure) about this?* | **[+of]** *He wasn't sure of her name.* | *He* **felt** *sure he knew her.* | **not sure what/where/why etc** *I'm not sure what happened.* | **not sure if/whether ...** *I'm not sure if he's coming.*
2 certain to happen or be true: *This one's a sure winner.* | *Those clouds are a sure sign of rain.* | **sure to do sth** *He's sure to say something stupid.*
3 be sure of sth to be certain to get something or certain that something will happen: *You're sure of a warm welcome here.*
4 *spoken* used to say yes to someone: *'Can I read your paper?' 'Sure.'*
5 *informal* used to admit that something is true,

before you say something very different: *Sure, he's attractive, but I'm not interested.*

PHRASES
be sure to do sth *spoken* used to tell someone to remember to do something: *Be sure to write!*
for sure *informal* if you know something for sure, you are certain about it: *I think Jack's married, but I don't know for sure.*
make sure (that) 1 to check that something is true or that something has been done: *Can you make sure the door's locked?* **THESAURUS** CHECK **2** to do something so that you can be certain of the result: *Make sure you get there early.*
sure enough *informal* used to say that something happened that you expected to happen: *Sure enough, we got lost.*
sure of yourself confident about your own abilities and opinions **THESAURUS** CONFIDENT
sure thing *AmE spoken* used to agree to something: *'See you Friday.' 'Yeah, sure thing.'*
that's for sure used to emphasize that something is true: *It's a lot better than it was, that's for sure.*

THESAURUS

sure believing that something is definitely true or correct: *Are you sure Bill was there?*
certain completely sure. **Certain** is more formal than **sure**: *We are certain that you will find our website useful.*
convinced sure that something is true, even though you cannot prove it: *She became convinced that he was in love with her.*
positive *especially spoken* completely sure that something is true, especially when other people are not sure: *I'm positive you said we were meeting at seven.*
confident sure that something good will happen or that you will achieve something: *We are very confident of victory.* | *I'm confident that the show will be a great success.*
have no doubt (*also* **be in no doubt**) to have no doubts in your mind about something: *I have no doubt that you're right.*

'sure-fire *adj* [only before noun] *informal* certain to succeed: *a sure-fire way to make money*

surely /'ʃɔːli $ 'ʃʊrli/ *adv*
1 used to show that you are surprised at something: *Surely you're not leaving so soon?*
2 used to show that you think something must be true: *This will surely result in more problems.*

surf¹ /sɜːf $ sɜːrf/ *v* [I,T] **1** to ride on ocean waves standing on a board: *Matt* **goes surfing** *every day.* → see picture on page 902 **2 surf the Internet/ net/Web** to look for information on the INTERNET —**surfer** *n* [C] —**surfing** *n* [U]

surf² *n* [U] the white part that forms on the top of waves

surface¹ /'sɜːfɪs $ 'sɜːr-/ *n*
1 [C] the outside or top layer of something: **[+of]** *the surface of the vase* | *the Earth's surface*
2 the surface a) the top of an area of water: *The diver swam to the surface.* | **[+of]** *the surface of the lake* **b)** the way that someone or something seems

S

surface

SURF

surfing

windsurfing

to be, when their real qualities are hidden: **on the surface** *On the surface she seems happy enough.* | **below/beneath/under the surface** *I sensed a lot of tension beneath the surface.*
3 [C] a flat area, for example on top of a cupboard, on which you can work: *Keep kitchen surfaces clean and tidy.*

surface² v **1** [I] to rise to the surface of water: *Whales were surfacing near the boat.* **2** [I] to become known: *Rumours have **begun to surface** in the press.* | *No major problems have surfaced.* **3** [I] to appear again after being hidden or absent: *Three years later he surfaced again.* **4** [T] to put the surface on a road

surfboard /'sɜːfbɔːd $ 'sɜːrfbɔːrd/ n [C] a plastic board that you stand on to ride on ocean waves

surfeit /'sɜːfɪt $ 'sɜːr-/ n [singular] too much of something: **[+of]** *a surfeit of alcohol*

surge¹ /sɜːdʒ $ sɜːrdʒ/ v [I] **1** to suddenly move very quickly in a particular direction: **[+forward/through/ahead]** *The crowd surged forward.* **2** if a price or level surges, it suddenly becomes much higher **3** (*also* **surge up**) if a feeling surges in you, you suddenly feel it very strongly: *Rage surged up inside her.*

surge² n [C] **1** *a surge of anger/fear/excitement etc* a sudden and very strong emotion **2** a sudden increase: *a surge in oil prices* | *a new surge of interest* **3** a sudden movement of a lot of people

surgeon /'sɜːdʒən $ 'sɜːr-/ n [C] a doctor who does operations in a hospital **THESAURUS** DOCTOR

surgery /'sɜːdʒəri $ 'sɜːr-/ n (*plural* **surgeries**) **1** [U] medical treatment in which a doctor cuts open your body to repair or remove something: *heart surgery* | **in surgery** (=having/doing an operation) *He was in surgery for three hours.* **2** [C] BrE a place where you go to see a doctor or DENTIST

surgical /'sɜːdʒɪkəl $ 'sɜːr-/ adj relating to or used for medical operations: *surgical gloves* → see picture at MASK¹ —**surgically** /-kli/ adv

surly /'sɜːli $ 'sɜːrli/ adj unfriendly and rude

surmise /sə'maɪz $ sər-/ v [T] formal to guess

something, using the information that you have: *One can only surmise that she disagreed.*

surmount /sə'maʊnt $ sər-/ v [T] formal to deal successfully with a problem or difficulty **SYN** **overcome**

surname /'sɜːneɪm $ 'sɜːr-/ n [C] your family name **SYN** **last name**

surpass /sə'pɑːs $ sər'pæs/ v [T] formal to be better than someone or something else: *He had **surpassed** all our **expectations**.*

surplus¹ /'sɜːpləs $ 'sɜːr-/ n [C,U] more of something than is needed or used: **[+of]** *the country's huge surplus of grain*

surplus² adj more than what is needed or used: *surplus land* | *They said he was **surplus to requirements*** (=not needed).

surprise¹ /sə'praɪz $ sər-/ n
1 [U] the feeling you have when something unexpected or unusual happens: **in surprise** *Bill looked at him in surprise.* | **To my surprise**, *she agreed.*
2 [C,U] something that is unexpected or unusual → **shock**: *His decision to marry was a complete surprise.*
PHRASES
take/catch sb by surprise to happen in an unexpected way: *The snow caught everyone by surprise.*

COLLOCATIONS – sense 2

adjectives

a big/great surprise *The award was a big surprise.*
a complete/total surprise *Our defeat came as a complete surprise.*
a nice/pleasant/lovely surprise *What a lovely surprise!*
an unpleasant/nasty surprise *We don't want any unpleasant surprises.* ⚠ Do not say 'a bad surprise'. Say **an unpleasant surprise** or **a nasty surprise**.

verbs

to come as a surprise (*also* **to be a surprise**) (=to be surprising) *The news came as a surprise to many people.*
to get/have a surprise *I got a surprise when I opened the letter.*
to give sb a surprise *I wanted to give you a nice surprise.*
to have a surprise for sb (=to be planning a surprise for someone) *I think Jenny might have a surprise for you.*

surprise + noun

a surprise party *We planned a surprise party for Dad's 50th birthday.*
a surprise visit *We had a surprise visit from the boss.*
a surprise attack *They launched a surprise attack on the castle.*

---

surprise² v [T] **1** to make someone feel surprise → **shock**: *Her reaction surprised me.* | *It wouldn't surprise me if they got married.* **2** to catch or attack someone when they do not expect it: *A security guard surprised the robber.*

surprised /səˈpraɪzd $ sər-/ *adj* having a feeling of surprise: **[+(that)]** *We were surprised Tom wasn't there.* | **[+at/by]** *She was surprised at his attitude.* | **surprised to hear/see/find sth** *I'm surprised to hear you say that.* | *Jane **looked surprised**.*

PHRASES

I'm surprised at you/him etc *spoken* used to say that you are disappointed by someone's behaviour

THESAURUS

surprised having a feeling of surprise: *Are you surprised to see me?*
shocked surprised and upset by something unpleasant: *I was shocked when I heard he'd died.*
amazed/astonished extremely surprised: *I was amazed by her strength.* | *He was astonished at how difficult it was to open the door.* | *I'm amazed that you remembered.*
startled surprised and often a little frightened, because something has suddenly happened, or someone has just said something: *He had a startled expression on his face.* | *The birds are easily startled.*
taken aback surprised by what someone says or does, so that you are not sure how to react: *The man seemed a little taken aback by her question.*
speechless so surprised that you do not know what to say: *My mother was speechless when I told her that I was pregnant.*

surprising /səˈpraɪzɪŋ $ sər-/ *adj* unexpected or unusual: **It's hardly surprising that** *they lost the game.* | **It's surprising how** *well it works.* | *A surprising number of people came.* —**surprisingly** *adv*: *The test was surprisingly easy.*

THESAURUS

surprising making you feel surprised: *Then, a very surprising thing happened.*
extraordinary very unusual and surprising: *She looks exactly like her mother. It's quite extraordinary.*
amazing very surprising – used especially about good or impressive things: *He has made an amazing recovery.*
staggering very surprising, especially by being so large, so expensive etc: *My son eats a staggering amount of food.*
unbelievable so surprising that you can hardly believe it: *It's unbelievable how much these things cost.*

surreal /səˈrɪəl/ (*also* **surrealistic** /səˌrɪəˈlɪstɪk◂/) *adj* very strange, like something from a dream

surrender /səˈrendə $ -ər-/ *v* **1** [I] to say officially that you want to stop fighting, because you know you cannot win: *The rebel forces have surrendered.* | **[+to]** *The man finally surrendered to police.* **2** [T] *formal* to give something to someone in authority, for example weapons or official documents: *They had to **surrender** their **passports**.* —**surrender** *n* [U]: *their unconditional surrender to the Allied forces*

surreptitious /ˌsʌrəpˈtɪʃəs◂ $ ˌsɜː-/ *adj* done secretly so that other people do not notice: *She cast surreptitious glances backwards.* —**surreptitiously** *adv*

surrogate /ˈsʌrəgeɪt, -gət $ ˈsɜːr-/ *adj* [only before noun] taking the place of someone or something else: *a **surrogate mother** (=woman who has a baby for another woman)* —**surrogate** *n* [C]

surround /səˈraʊnd/ *v*
1 [T] to be or go all around someone or something: **be surrounded by sth** *The lake was surrounded by trees.* | *The police surrounded the house.*
2 be surrounded by sb/sth to have a lot of a particular kind of people or things near you: *She is surrounded by friends.* | **surround yourself with sb/sth** *He surrounds himself with exquisite objects.*
3 [T] to be closely related to a situation or event: *Some of the issues surrounding alcohol abuse are very complex.* —**surrounding** *adj*: *the **surrounding countryside***

surroundings /səˈraʊndɪŋz/ *n* [plural] the place where you are and all the things in it: *I soon got used to my new surroundings.*

surveillance /səˈveɪləns $ sər-/ *n* [U] when someone is being watched, for example by the police or by doctors: **under surveillance** *Police have the man under surveillance.*

survey¹ Ac /ˈsɜːveɪ $ ˈsɜːr-/ *n* [C]
1 a set of questions that you ask a lot of people in order to find out about their opinions or behaviour: **[+of]** *We **conducted** a **survey** of people's eating habits.* | *The **survey showed** that 61% backed the President.*
2 an examination of an area or building

survey² Ac /səˈveɪ $ sər-/ *v* [T] **1** to ask a lot of people questions in order to find out about their opinions or behaviour: *More than 50% of those surveyed agreed.* **2** to look at someone or something carefully: *I **surveyed** the **damage** to the car.* **3** to examine and measure land or a building

surveyor /səˈveɪə $ sərˈveɪər/ *n* [C] someone whose job is to examine and measure land or buildings

survival Ac /səˈvaɪvəl $ sər-/ *n* [U] when someone continues to live or exist, especially after a difficult or dangerous situation: *The operation will increase his **chances of survival**.* | *It's been a case of **survival of the fittest**.*

survive Ac /səˈvaɪv $ sər-/ *v* [I,T]
1 to continue to live after an accident, war, illness etc: *She **survived** the **war**.* | *They may not **survive** the **winter**.* | *Only one person survived.*
2 to continue to live normally or to exist in spite of problems: *A lot of firms did not survive the recession.* | *People are **struggling to survive**.* | **[+on]** *How do you survive on such a low salary?* | *I've had a tough few months, but **I'll survive**.*
3 to continue to exist after a very long time: **[+from]** *Several buildings have survived from medieval times.*

survivor Ac /səˈvaɪvə $ sərˈvaɪvər/ *n* [C]
1 someone who continues to live after an accident, illness etc: *There were no survivors.* **2** someone who will not fail or stop trying, even when life is difficult: *He's a survivor.*

susceptible /sə'septəbəl/ *adj* likely to be affected by an illness or problem: **[+to]** *I've always been very susceptible to colds.* —**susceptibility** /sə,septə'brɪləti/ *n* [U]

sushi /'su:ʃi/ *n* [U] Japanese food containing raw fish

suspect¹ /'sʌspekt/ *n* [C] someone who may be guilty of a crime: **main/prime/chief suspect**

suspect² /sə'spekt/ *v* [T] **1** to think that someone may be guilty of a crime: **suspect sb of sth** *She is suspected of murder.* **2** to think that something is true, may happen, or has happened: **[+(that)]** *I suspected that she would leave.* | *I strongly suspected he was lying.* **3** to think that something is not honest or true: *She suspected his motives.*

suspect³ /'sʌspekt/ *adj* difficult to believe or trust: *Her methods were highly suspect.*

suspend Ac /sə'spend/ *v* [T] **1** to stop or delay something: *The talks have been suspended.* | *I decided to* **suspend judgement. 2 suspend sb's sentence** to say that someone will go to prison for a crime, if they commit another crime within a specific period **3** to officially make someone leave their school or job for a short time, after something bad has happened **4** if something is suspended somewhere, it is hanging or floating there: *A light was suspended from the ceiling.*

suspenders /sə'spendəz $ -ərz/ *n* [plural] **1** *BrE* pieces of ELASTIC fixed to a woman's underwear and to her STOCKINGS to hold them up SYN **garters** *AmE* **2** *AmE* bands of cloth that hold up your trousers, worn over your shoulders SYN **braces** *BrE*

suspense /sə'spens/ *n* [U] the feeling you have when waiting for something exciting to happen: *Don't keep us in suspense. What happened?*

suspension Ac /sə'spenʃən/ *n* **1** [U] when someone stops or delays something for a period of time **2** [C,U] when someone is removed from a school or job for a short time as a punishment **3** [U] equipment fixed to the wheels of a vehicle to make it comfortable to ride in

sus'pension ,bridge *n* [C] a bridge that has no supports under it, but is hung from strong steel ropes fixed to towers → see picture at **BRIDGE¹**

suspicion /sə'spɪʃən/ *n* **1** [C,U] a feeling that someone has done something wrong: *He was arrested on suspicion of robbery.* | **under suspicion** (=thought to have done something wrong) *He felt he was still under suspicion.* **2** [C] a feeling that something may be true: *She had a suspicion that Steve might be right.*

suspicious /sə'spɪʃəs/ *adj* **1** something that is suspicious appears to involve a crime: *a* **suspicious package** | *the* **suspicious circumstances** *surrounding his death* THESAURUS> DISHONEST **2** if you are suspicious of someone, you do not trust them: *His behaviour made me suspicious.* —**suspiciously** *adv*: *They were* **acting suspiciously.**

suss /sʌs/ (*also* **suss out**) *v* [T] *BrE informal* to discover something about someone or something: *He finally sussed out the truth.*

sustain Ac /sə'steɪn/ *v* [T] **1** to make something

continue: *a strategy that would sustain economic growth* **2** to keep someone strong or healthy: *A good breakfast will sustain you through the morning.* **3** *formal* to suffer injury, damage, or loss: *Two people* **sustained minor injuries.**

sustainable Ac /sə'steɪnəbəl/ *adj* able to continue, especially without destroying the environment: **sustainable rural development**

sustained Ac /sə'steɪnd/ *adj* continuing without becoming weaker: *A* **sustained** *effort is needed.* | *sustained economic growth*

sustenance Ac /'sʌstənəns/ *n* [U] *formal* food that you need in order to live

svelte /svelt/ *adj* thin and graceful

SW the written abbreviation of **southwest** or **southwestern**

swab /swɒb $ swɑ:b/ *n* [C] a small piece of material, used to clean wounds or do medical tests

swagger /'swægə $ -ər/ *v* [I] to walk with a swinging movement, in a way that seems too proud and confident —**swagger** *n* [singular]

swallow¹ /'swɒləʊ $ 'swɑ:loʊ/ *v*
1 [I,T] to make food or drink go down your throat: *He swallowed a mouthful of coffee.*
2 [I] to make a movement in your throat, because you are nervous: *Lee* **swallowed hard** *and walked in.*
3 [T] *informal* to believe that something is true, especially when it is not true: *I found his story a bit* **hard to swallow.**
4 [T] to stop yourself from having or showing a feeling: *I* **swallowed** *my pride and phoned him.*
PHRASAL VERBS
swallow sth ↔ **up** to make something disappear or become part of something else: *As the city grew, nearby villages were swallowed up.*

swallow² *n* [C] **1** when you make food or drink go down your throat **2** a common small bird with pointed wings and a tail with two points

swam /swæm/ *v* the past tense of SWIM

swamp¹ /swɒmp $ swɑ:mp/ *n* [C,U] land that is always very wet or covered with water —**swampy** *adj*: *swampy ground*

swamp² *v* [T] **1** to suddenly give someone more work or problems than they can deal with: *We've been swamped with phone calls.* **2** to suddenly cover something with a lot of water: *Huge waves swamped the town.*

swan /swɒn $ swɑ:n/ *n* [C] a large white bird with a long neck that lives on lakes and rivers

swanky /'swæŋki/ *adj informal* very fashionable or expensive: *a swanky hotel*

swansong /'swɒnsɒŋ $ 'swɑ:nsɔ:ŋ/ *n* [C] the last piece of work that an artist or writer produces, or the last time someone gives a performance: *This concert will be her swansong.*

swap, swop /swɒp $ swɑ:p/ *v* [I,T] (**swapped, swapping**) to exchange something you have for something that someone else has: **swap (sth) with sb** *Can I swap seats with you?* | **swap sth for sth** *I'll swap my red T-shirt for your green one.* —**swap** *n* [C]: *Shall we do a swap?*

swarm¹ /swɔːm $ swɔːrm/ v [I + adv/prep] if people swarm somewhere, they quickly move there together

PHRASAL VERBS

swarm with sth if a place is swarming with people or things, many people or things are moving around there: *The beach was swarming with people.*

swarm² n [C] a large group of insects that move together: **[+of]** *a swarm of bees*

swarthy /ˈswɔːði $ -ɔːr-/ adj written someone who is swarthy has dark skin

swat /swɒt $ swɑːt/ v [T] (**swatted, swatting**) to hit an insect to try to kill it

swathe¹ /sweɪð $ swɑːð, swɒːð, sweɪð/ n [C] a long thin area of something, especially land

PHRASES

cut a swathe through sth to destroy a large amount or part of something: *The disease cut a swathe through the population.*

swathe² v [T usually passive] to wrap or cover something: *women swathed in expensive furs*

sway¹ /sweɪ/ v **1** [I] to move slowly from one side to another: *Trees swayed gently in the breeze.* THESAURUS ▶ MOVE **2** [T] to make someone change their opinion: *Nothing you say will sway her.*

sway² n [U] formal **hold sway** to have power or influence

swear /sweə $ swer/ v (past tense **swore** /swɔː $ swɔːr/, past participle **sworn** /swɔːn $ swɔːrn/)
1 [I] to use rude or offensive language: *She doesn't smoke, drink, or swear.* | **[+at]** *He swore at me.*
2 [T] to promise that you will do something: **swear to do sth** *Do you swear to tell the truth?* | **[+(that)]** *I swear I'll never leave you.* THESAURUS ▶ PROMISE
3 [I,T] to say very strongly that what you are saying is true: **[+(that)]** *She swore that she had never seen him before.* | *I never touched your purse, **I swear**.*

PHRASES

I could have sworn (that) spoken used to say that you were sure about something: *I could have sworn I left my keys here.*

PHRASAL VERBS

swear by sth informal to strongly believe that something is effective: *Heidi swears by aromatherapy.*

swear sb ↔ **in** if someone is sworn in, they make a public promise before beginning an important job or before speaking in court: *She was sworn in as president.*

swearing /ˈsweərɪŋ $ ˈswer-/ n [U] when people use rude or offensive language

'swear word n [C] a word that is considered rude or shocking

sweat¹ /swet/ v
1 [I] if you sweat, liquid comes out through your skin SYN **perspire**: *The heat was making us sweat.* | **sweat profusely/heavily**
2 [I,T] informal to work hard: *I **sweated blood** (=worked extremely hard) to get that report finished.*

PHRASAL VERBS

sweat sth ↔ **out** to continue in an unpleasant situation and wait anxiously for it to end: *We had to **sweat it out** until they arrived.*

sweat² n [singular, U] liquid that comes out through your skin, especially when you are hot or nervous SYN **perspiration**: *Beads of sweat appeared on his forehead.* | *He **broke out into a sweat** (=began to sweat).* | *She had **worked up** quite **a sweat** (=started sweating because of working hard).*

PHRASES

a cold sweat a state of fear or nervousness, in which you start to sweat even though you are not hot: *I woke up from the dream in a cold sweat.*

no sweat spoken informal used to say that you can do something easily: *'Can you give me a ride home?' 'Yeah, no sweat!'*

sweater /ˈswetə $ -ər/ n [C] a piece of clothing with long sleeves and no buttons for the top half of your body SYN **jumper** BrE → see picture at CLOTHES

sweatshirt /ˈswet-ʃɜːt $ -ʃɜːrt/ n [C] a thick soft cotton shirt with long sleeves, no collar, and no buttons → see picture at CLOTHES

sweatshop /ˈswet-ʃɒp $ -ʃɑːp/ n [C] a factory where people work in bad conditions for very little money

sweaty /ˈsweti/ adj covered with SWEAT, or smelling of sweat

swede /swiːd/ n [C,U] BrE a round vegetable that grows under the ground SYN **rutabaga** AmE → see picture on page A5

sweep¹ /swiːp/ v (past tense and past participle **swept** /swept/)
1 [I,T] to clean a floor or the ground, using a brush → **brush**: *I've just swept the kitchen floor.* → see picture at MOP²
2 [I] if a crowd of people sweeps somewhere, it moves there quickly: **[+through/across etc]** *The crowd swept through the gates.*
3 [I,T] if a feeling, idea, or type of weather sweeps an area, it spreads quickly across it: **sweep the country/nation** *the latest fitness craze to sweep the nation* | *Storms swept through the mountains.*
4 [I] to move quickly in a way that shows you are very confident or annoyed: *She swept into the room.*
5 [T] to move someone or something quickly in a particular direction: **sweep sb/sth into/out/along etc** *I swept the papers quickly into the drawer.* | *Jessie was swept along by the angry crowd.* | *He **swept his hair back** with his hand.*

PHRASES

sweep sb off their feet to make someone feel very attracted to you romantically, in a short time: *He absolutely swept me off my feet.*

sweep sth under the carpet especially BrE (also **sweep sth under the rug** especially AmE) to try to hide something bad that has happened: *All the evidence pointing to his guilt has been swept under the carpet.*

PHRASAL VERBS

sweep sth ↔ **away** to completely destroy something or make something disappear: *Many houses were swept away by the floods.*

sweep up to remove dirt from the floor or ground

using a brush: **sweep sth ↔ up** *Could you sweep up the leaves?*

sweep² *n* **1** [C usually singular] a long swinging movement: *She spoke with a sweep of her arm.* **2** [singular] a long curved line or area of land: *the sweep of the bay* **3** [C] someone whose job is to clean CHIMNEYS

sweeping /'swi:pɪŋ/ *adj* **1** affecting many things, or affecting one thing very much: *sweeping changes* **2 sweeping statement/generalization** *disapproving* a statement that is too general and does not consider all the facts: *sweeping generalizations about women drivers*

sweepstake /'swi:psteɪk/ *n* [C] a type of GAMBLING in which the winner gets all the money

sweet¹ /swi:t/ *adj*
1 having a taste like sugar → **sour, bitter**: *a cup of sweet tea* | *a sweet, sticky chocolate cake* **THESAURUS** TASTE
2 having a pleasant smell or sound: *a sweet-smelling rose* | *the sweet sounds of the cello*
3 kind, gentle, and friendly: **be sweet of sb** *It was sweet of you to help.* | *She's a sweet girl.* **THESAURUS** NICE
4 making you feel pleased or happy: *Goodnight, darling – sweet dreams.* | *Winning the match was sweet revenge.*
5 *especially BrE* pretty and pleasant – used when you are talking about children or small things **SYN cute**: *Her baby is so sweet!*
6 Sweet! *informal* used to show that you think something is very good: *'I got those tickets.' 'Sweet!'* —**sweetly** *adv*: *She smiled sweetly.* —**sweetness** *n* [U]
PHRASES
| **have a sweet tooth** to like to eat sweet foods: *I've always had a sweet tooth.*

sweet² *n BrE*
1 [C] a small piece of sweet food made of sugar or chocolate **SYN candy** *AmE*: *Don't eat too many sweets.*
2 [C,U] sweet food served after the meat and vegetables during a meal **SYN dessert**

sweetcorn /'swi:tkɔ:n $ -kɔ:rn/ *n* [U] *BrE* soft yellow seeds from MAIZE, cooked as a vegetable **SYN corn** *AmE* → see picture on page A5

sweeten /'swi:tn/ *v* [T] **1** to make something sweeter **2** (*also* **sweeten up**) to try to persuade someone to do something by giving them presents or being nice to them

sweetener /'swi:tnə $ -ər/ *n* **1** [C,U] a substance used instead of sugar to make food or drinks taste sweeter **2** [C] something that you give to someone to persuade them to do something: *The tax cut is just a sweetener.*

sweetheart /'swi:thɑ:t $ -hɑ:rt/ *n* [C] **1** a way of speaking to someone you love: *Good night, sweetheart.* **2** *old-fashioned* the person you love romantically: *He married his childhood sweetheart.*

sweetie /'swi:ti/ *n* [C] **1** *BrE* a SWEET, a word used by children **2** someone who is easy to love: *He's*

such a *sweetie.* **3** a way of speaking to someone that you love

,sweet po'tato *n* [C] a root that looks like a long red potato, cooked as a vegetable

swell¹ /swel/ *v* (*past tense* **swelled**, *past participle* **swollen** /'swəʊlən $ 'swoʊ-/) **1** (*also* **swell up**) [I] to increase in size: *My ankle swelled up like a balloon.* **2** [I,T] to increase to a much bigger amount or number: *The city's population has swollen to two million.*

swell² *n* [singular] the movement of the sea as waves go up and down

swelling /'swelɪŋ/ *n* [C,U] an area on your body that becomes bigger than usual because of injury or illness: *This should reduce the swelling.*

sweltering /'sweltərɪŋ/ *adj* unpleasantly hot: *sweltering heat*

swept /swept/ *v* the past tense and past participle of SWEEP

swerve /swɜ:v $ swɜ:rv/ *v* [I] to suddenly move to the left or right while you are driving: *She swerved but too late.* | [+across/off/into etc] *The car suddenly swerved off the road.*

swift /swɪft/ *adj* happening or moving quickly: *a swift recovery from illness* | *swift, agile movements* **THESAURUS** FAST —**swiftly** *adv*

swig /swɪg/ *v* [T] (**swigged, swigging**) *informal* to drink something by taking large amounts into your mouth —**swig** *n* [C]

swill /swɪl/ *v* **1** [T] to wash something by pouring a lot of water over or into it: *He swilled the yard down with water.* **2** [T] to make a liquid move around in a container: *He swilled the whisky round in his glass.* **3** (*also* **swill down**) [T] *informal* to drink a lot of something, especially beer

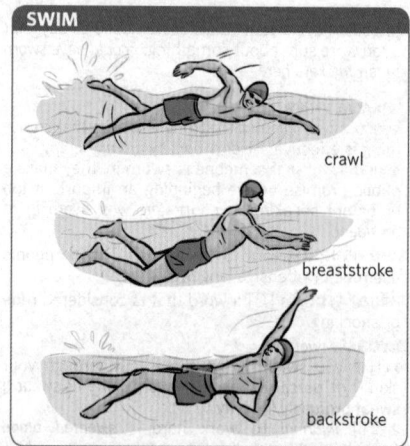

SWIM

crawl

breaststroke

backstroke

swim¹ /swɪm/ *v* (*past tense* **swam** /swæm/, *past participle* **swum** /swʌm/, *present participle* **swimming**)
1 [I,T] to move through water, using your arms and

legs: *Can Lucy swim?* | *Let's **go swimming**.* | *She swims 20 lengths every day.* | **[+in]** *We used to swim in the lake.* | **[+across/back/out etc]** *We swam across the bay.*

2 [I] if your head swims, you feel confused or as if everything is spinning around

3 [I] if something swims, it seems to be moving or turning, because you are ill, tired, drunk etc: *The room swam around her.* —**swimming** *n* [U]: *Let's all go swimming this afternoon.* —**swimmer** *n* [C]

PHRASES

be swimming in/with sth to be covered by a lot of liquid: *potatoes swimming in gravy*

swim² *n* [C] a time when you swim: *I **went for a swim** after school.*

'swimming ,costume *n* [C] *BrE* a swimsuit

'swimming pool *n* [C] a structure that has been built for people to swim in SYN **pool**

'swimming trunks *n* [plural] a piece of clothing that boys and men wear for swimming

swimsuit /'swɪmsuːt, -sjuːt $ -suːt/ *n* [C] a piece of clothing that girls and women wear for swimming

swindle /'swɪndl/ *v* [T] to get money from someone by tricking them —**swindle** *n* [C] —**swindler** *n* [C]

swine /swaɪn/ *n* [C] (*plural* **swine**) **1** *informal* someone who behaves very badly **2** *old-fashioned* a pig

'swine flu *n* [U] a type of INFLUENZA caused by a VIRUS that contains some parts from a virus that infects pigs

swing¹ /swɪŋ/ *v* (*past tense and past participle* **swung** /swʌŋ/)

1 [I,T] to move backwards and forwards while hanging from something, or to make something do this: *a sign swinging in the wind* | *They walked along, swinging their arms.*

2 [I,T] to move smoothly in a curved direction, or to make something move this way: **[+into/out of etc]** *A car swung into the drive.* | **swing sth into/out of sth** *Kate swung her legs out of bed.* | **swing open/shut** *The door swung shut.*

3 [I] if opinions or feelings swing, they change a lot: **swing from sth to sth** *Her mood swung from happiness to despair.*

PHRASAL VERBS

swing (sth) around/round to turn around quickly, or to make something do this: *Mike swung around to look at me.*

swing at sb/sth to try to hit someone or something: *He swung at me and missed.*

swing² *n* [C] **1** a seat that hangs from ropes or chains, for children to play on **2** an attempt to hit someone or something: *He **took a swing** at me.* **3** a fairly large change in feelings or opinions: *mood swings* | **[+in]** *a swing in public opinion* | **[+to/away from/towards etc]** *a swing towards left-wing ideas* → **be in full swing** at FULL¹

swipe /swaɪp/ *v* **1** [I,T] to hit or try to hit someone or something by swinging your arm at them: *She swiped me across the face.* **2** [T] *informal* to steal something **3** [T] to pull a plastic card through a machine that can read the electronic information on it —**swipe** *n* [C]

SWIPE

'swipe card *n* [C] a small plastic card that you pull through a machine in order to open a door

swirl /swɜːl $ swɜːrl/ *v* [I,T] to move around and around in a circular movement: **[+around/round]** *Smoke swirled around her.* —**swirl** *n* [C]

swish /swɪʃ/ *v* [I,T] to move or make something move through the air with a soft sound: *horses swishing their tails* —**swish** *n* [C]

switch¹ /swɪtʃ/ *v* [I,T]

1 to change from one thing to another thing SYN **change**: **[+to]** *If you switch to a low-fat diet, your health will improve.* | **switch from sth to sth** *He kept switching from one subject to another.* | **[+between]** *It is possible to switch between courses.* | *soldiers who **switch sides***

2 to exchange things, or replace one thing with another thing SYN **change**: **switch sth for sth** *I'm going to switch it for something newer.*

PHRASAL VERBS

switch off to turn off a machine, light etc, using a switch: **switch sth ↔ off** *My mobile phone was switched off.* | ***Switch off the lights** before you leave.*

switch on to turn on a machine, light etc using a switch: **switch sth ↔ on** *Switch the radio on.* | *The video will **switch on automatically**.*

switch over

1 to change to a different television CHANNEL

2 to start using a different product, system etc: **[+to]** *More and more people are switching over to internet banking.*

switch² *n* [C]

1 the thing you press to make a machine, light etc start or stop working: *a light switch*

2 a change from one thing to another: **[+to]** *Shoppers are **making the switch** to organic food.* | **[+in]** *a switch in emphasis*

switchboard /'swɪtʃbɔːd $ -bɔːrd/ *n* [C] a system used to connect telephone calls in an office building, hotel etc

swivel /'swɪvəl/ (*also* **swivel around**) *v* [I,T] (**swivelled, swivelling** *BrE*, **swiveled, swiveling** *AmE*) to turn around quickly, or to make something do this: *He swivelled his chair to face her.*

swollen¹ /'swəʊlən $ 'swoʊ-/ *v* the past participle of SWELL

swollen² *adj* **1** a part of your body that is swollen is bigger than usual, especially because you are ill or injured: *swollen glands* **2** a swollen river has more water in it than usual

swoop /swuːp/ v [I] **1** to move down suddenly through the air, especially to attack something: **[+down/over/across etc]** *The birds swooped down.* **2** if soldiers or the police swoop on a place, they go there quickly and without warning in order to find someone or something —**swoop** n [C]

swop /swɒp $ swɑːp/ v, n another spelling of SWAP

sword /sɔːd $ sɔːrd/ n [C] a weapon with a long sharp blade and a handle

swordfish /'sɔːdˌfɪʃ $ 'sɔːrd-/ n [C] (plural **sword-fish**) a large fish with a long pointed upper jaw → see picture on page A3

swore /swɔː $ swɔːr/ v the past tense of SWEAR

sworn¹ /swɔːn $ swɔːrn/ v the past participle of SWEAR

sworn² adj **1 sworn statement/evidence etc** a statement etc that you officially say is true **2 sworn enemies** two people or groups who hate each other

swot¹ /swɒt $ swɑːt/ n [C] BrE informal disapproving someone who studies too much

swot² v [I] (**swotted, swotting**) BrE informal to study hard, especially for an examination

PHRASAL VERBS
swot up to learn as much as you can about something: **[+on]** *Swot up on the company before your interview.*

swum /swʌm/ v the past participle of SWIM

swung /swʌŋ/ v the past tense and past participle of SWING

sycamore /'sɪkəmɔː $ -mɔːr/ n [C,U] a tree with seeds shaped like two wings, or the wood from this tree

sycophant /'sɪkəfænt/ n [C] formal disapproving someone who always praises an important person, but not in an honest way —**sycophantic** /ˌsɪkə'fæntɪk/ adj

syllable /'sɪləbəl/ n [C] a part of a word that contains a single vowel sound. 'Cat' has one syllable, and 'butter' has two.

syllabus /'sɪləbəs/ n [C] a plan of what students should learn in a particular subject

symbol Ac /'sɪmbəl/ n [C]
1 a picture, shape, letter etc that has a particular meaning or represents a particular chemical, amount etc → **sign**: *a symbol showing that the product is fire resistant* | **[+for]** *Fe is the chemical symbol for iron.*
2 someone or something that represents a particular quality or idea: **[+of]** *A suntan is not a symbol of fitness and health.* → **SEX SYMBOL, STATUS SYMBOL**

symbolic Ac /sɪm'bɒlɪk $ -'bɑː-/ adj **1** representing a particular idea or quality: **[+of]** *The fighting is symbolic of the chaos in the country.* **2** important but not having any real effect: *a symbolic victory* —**symbolically** /-kli/ adv

symbolism Ac /'sɪmbəlɪzəm/ n [U] the use of symbols to represent ideas or qualities: *religious symbolism*

symbolize Ac (also **-ise** BrE) /'sɪmbəlaɪz/ v [T] to represent a particular quality or feeling: *Crime often symbolizes a wider social problem.*

symmetrical /sɪ'metrɪkəl/ (also **symmetric** /sɪ'metrɪk/) adj having two halves that are exactly the same size and shape OPP **asymmetrical**

symmetry /'sɪmətri/ n [U] when both halves of something are exactly the same size and shape

sympathetic /ˌsɪmpə'θetɪk◂/ adj
1 showing that you understand and care about someone's problems OPP **unsympathetic**: *a sympathetic attitude* | **[+towards/to]** *Parents aren't always very sympathetic towards their children.* THESAURUS KIND
2 [not before noun] willing to support someone's ideas or actions: **[+to/towards]** *He wanted someone who was sympathetic to his views.* —**sympathetically** /-kli/ adv

sympathize (also **-ise** BrE) /'sɪmpəθaɪz/ v [I] **1** to show that you understand and care about someone's problems: **[+with]** *I can sympathize with the way you're feeling.* **2** to support someone's ideas or actions: **[+with]** *I don't sympathize with the party's views.*

sympathizer (also **-iser** BrE) /'sɪmpəθaɪzə $ -ər/ n [C] someone who supports the aims of an organization or political party

sympathy /'sɪmpəθi/ n [U] (also **sympathies** [plural])
1 the feeling you have when you understand why someone is unhappy and want to help them feel better: **[+for]** *I have a lot of sympathy for her.* | *My sympathies are with the victims' families.* → see Word Choice at PITY
2 belief in or support for an idea or action: **[+with]** *I do have some sympathy with their aims.* | **in sympathy with sth** *He is in sympathy with many Green Party policies.* | **liberal/left-wing/Republican etc sympathies**

symphony /'sɪmfəni/ n [C] (plural **symphonies**) a long piece of music written for an ORCHESTRA

symptom /'sɪmptəm/ n [C] **1** something that shows you have an illness: **[+of]** *Chest pain can be a symptom of heart disease.* **2** a sign that a serious problem exists: **[+of]** *Crime is often seen as a symptom of the breakdown in society.*

symptomatic /ˌsɪmptə'mætɪk◂/ adj formal showing that a serious problem exists: **[+of]** *The rise in unemployment is symptomatic of problems in the economy.*

synagogue /'sɪnəgɒg $ -gɑːg/ n [C] a building for Jewish religious meetings

sync /sɪŋk/ n informal
PHRASES
in sync working together at the same time or speed or in the same way
out of sync working at a different time or speed or in a different way

synchronize (also **-ise** BrE) /'sɪŋkrənaɪz/ v [T] to make two or more things happen at the same time —**synchronization** /ˌsɪŋkrənaɪ'zeɪʃən $ -nə-/ n [U]

syndicate /'sɪndəkət/ n [C] a group of people or companies that work together to achieve something: **[+of]** *a syndicate of banks*

syndrome /'sɪndrəʊm $ -droʊm/ n [C] **1** a medical condition that consists of a particular set of problems: *irritable bowel syndrome* **2** a set of feelings, qualities etc that are typical of a particular problem

synonym /'sɪnənɪm/ n [C] a word with the same meaning as another word in the same language OPP **antonym**

synonymous /sɪ'nɒnɪməs $ -'nɑː-/ adj **1** so closely related to something else that when you think of one thing you also think of the other thing: **[+with]** *His name has become synonymous with success.* **2** if two words are synonymous, they have the same meaning

synopsis /sɪ'nɒpsɪs $ -'nɑːp-/ n [C] (plural **synopses** /-siːz/) a short description of the main parts of a story

syntax /'sɪntæks/ n [U] technical the way words are arranged to form sentences or phrases

synthesis /'sɪnθɪsɪs/ n [C,U] (plural **syntheses** /-siːz/) formal when several things are combined to form something

synthesize (also **-ise** BrE) /'sɪnθɪsaɪz/ v [T] to combine different things in order to produce something: *Plants synthesize energy from sunlight.*

synthesizer (also **-iser** BrE) /'sɪnθəsaɪzə $ -ər/ n [C] an electronic instrument that can produce the sounds of various musical instruments

synthetic /sɪn'θetɪk/ adj made from artificial substances, not natural ones: *synthetic fabrics*
THESAURUS ARTIFICIAL

syphilis /'sɪfəlɪs/ n [U] a very serious disease that can be passed from one person to another during sex

syphon /'saɪfən/ n a British spelling of SIPHON

syringe /sə'rɪndʒ/ n [C] a tube and needle used for removing blood from your body, or for putting drugs into it → see picture at NEEDLE¹

syrup /'sɪrəp $ 'sɜː-, 'sɪ-/ n [U] thick sticky liquid made from sugar —**syrupy** adj

system /'sɪstɪm/ n [C]
1 a group of things or parts that work together: *an alarm system | your body's digestive system | our new computer system | the building's heating system*
2 a way of organizing or doing something: **[+of]** *a system of government* | **system for doing sth** *the system for electing a leader*
3 the system informal the rules and powerful organizations that restrict what you do → **IMMUNE SYSTEM, NERVOUS SYSTEM, OPERATING SYSTEM, SOLAR SYSTEM, SOUND SYSTEM**
PHRASES

get sth out of your system informal to do something that gets rid of an unpleasant emotion: *I was so angry that I went running to get it out of my system.*

COLLOCATIONS – sense 2
adjectives
a political/legal/economic system *Scotland has its own legal system.*
a complicated/complex system *The present system is far too complicated.*
the present/current system *The current system of taxation is unnecessarily complicated.*

noun + system
the education/health/tax etc system *The education system does not help these children.*

verbs
to use/run/operate a system *The system should be easy to use.*
to introduce a system (=to start to use it) *He introduced a new system of taxation.*
a system operates/works (=exists and is used) *Do you understand how the system works?*

systematic /ˌsɪstə'mætɪk◂/ adj organized carefully and done thoroughly: *a systematic approach to training* —**systematically** /-kli/ adv

Tt

T, t /tiː/ n [C,U] (plural **T's**, **t's**) the 20th letter of the English alphabet

ta /tɑː/ BrE spoken informal thank you

tab /tæb/ n [C] a small piece of metal, plastic, paper etc that is attached to something so that you can open it or find it easily

PHRASES

keep (close) tabs on sb/sth informal to watch someone or something carefully to check what they are doing: *The police are keeping close tabs on the suspect.*

pick up the tab to pay for something, especially a meal in a restaurant: *George generously offered to pick up the tab.*

tabby /'tæbi/ n [C] (plural **tabbies**) a cat with light and dark lines on its fur

---

TABLES

coffee table

dining table

bedside table   dressing table BrE

---

table¹ /'teɪbəl/ n [C]
1 a piece of furniture which has a flat top resting on legs: *We sat at a table in the corner.* | *There was a vase of flowers on the bedside table.*
2 a table in a restaurant that you arrange to use at a particular time: *I've booked a table for 8 o'clock.*
3 snooker/billiard/ping-pong etc table a special table, used for playing a particular game
4 a set of numbers or facts that are arranged in rows → **DRESSING TABLE**

PHRASES

the table of contents a list of the parts of a book and the pages they are on

turn the tables (on sb) to change a situation completely so that someone loses an advantage and you gain one: *The tables were turned when she married a younger man.*

---

table² v [T] **1 table a proposal/question etc** BrE to formally suggest something to be discussed at a meeting **2 table an offer/idea etc** AmE to decide to wait until a later time to discuss an offer, idea etc

tablecloth /'teɪbəlklɒθ $ -klɒːθ/ n [C] a cloth for covering a table

tablespoon /'teɪbəlspuːn/ (written abbreviation **tbsp**) n [C] a large spoon, or the amount it holds

tablet /'tæblɪt/ n [C] a small round piece of medicine that you swallow **SYN** **pill**: *She took a couple of sleeping tablets.*

'table ˌtennis n [U] a game in which people hit a ball to each other over a net that is stretched across a table **SYN** **ping-pong** → see picture on page A9

tableware /'teɪbəlweə $ -wer/ n [U] formal the plates, glasses, knives etc used when eating a meal

tabloid /'tæblɔɪd/ n [C] a newspaper that has small pages, a lot of photographs, and not very much serious news **THESAURUS** **NEWSPAPER**

taboo /tə'buː, tæ-/ n [C,U] (plural **taboos**) something that you must not do or talk about because it offends or embarrasses people —**taboo** adj: *Sex is a taboo subject in many homes.*

tacit /'tæsɪt/ adj tacit agreement, approval, or support is given without anything actually being said

taciturn /'tæsətɜːn $ -ɜːrn/ adj a taciturn person does not talk a lot, and seems unfriendly

tack¹ /tæk/ n **1** [C] a small nail with a sharp point and a flat top **2** [C] AmE a short pin with a large round flat top, for attaching notices to boards, walls etc **SYN** **thumbtack** AmE, **drawing pin** BrE **3** [C,U] a method that you use to achieve something: *If polite requests don't work, you'll have to try a different tack.*

tack² v [T] to attach something to a wall, board etc using a tack

PHRASAL VERBS

tack sth ↔ **on** to add something new to something that is already complete: *a small porch tacked on to the front of the house*

tackle¹ /'tækəl/ v [T] **1** to deal with a difficult problem: *a new attempt to tackle the problem of homelessness* | *Firemen tackled the blaze at the factory.* **THESAURUS** **DEAL 2 a)** to try to take the ball away from someone in a game such as football → see picture at **FOOTBALL b)** to force someone to the ground so that they stop running, in a game such as American football **3** to talk to someone about a difficult subject or something that they have done: **tackle sb about sth** *When I tackled her about it, she admitted that she had lied.*

tackle² *n* **1** [C] **a)** an attempt to take the ball away from another player in a game such as football **b)** an attempt to stop an opponent by forcing them to the ground, in a game such as American football **2** [U] the equipment used in some sports, especially FISHING

tacky /'tæki/ *adj* **1** cheap and badly made: *tacky furniture* **2** slightly sticky

tact /tækt/ *n* [U] the ability to be careful not to say or do things that will upset other people

tactful /'tæktfəl/ *adj* careful not to say or do something that will upset someone **OPP** **tactless** **THESAURUS** POLITE —**tactfully** *adv*

tactic /'tæktɪk/ *n* [C usually plural] a method that you use to achieve what you want: *aggressive business tactics*

tactical /'tæktɪkəl/ *adj* relating to what you do to achieve what you want: *For **tactical reasons** we won't ask for help.* | **tactical voting** (=voting in any way that will prevent a particular party from winning an election) —**tactically** /-kli/ *adv*

tactless /'tæktləs/ *adj* carelessly saying something that is likely to upset or embarrass someone **OPP** tactful **THESAURUS** RUDE

tad /tæd/ *n spoken* **a tad a)** a small amount: *'Would you like some milk?' 'Just a tad.'* **b)** slightly: *She looks a tad nervous.*

tadpole /'tædpəʊl $ -poʊl/ *n* [C] a small creature that will become a FROG or TOAD → see picture at FROG

taffeta /'tæfɪtə/ *n* [U] a shiny stiff cloth made from silk or NYLON: *a taffeta dress*

tag¹ /tæg/ *n* [C] a small piece of paper, plastic etc that is fastened to something and gives information about it: *I can't find the **price tag** on these jeans.* → QUESTION TAG

tag² *v* [T] (**tagged**, **tagging**) to attach a tag to something

PHRASAL VERBS

tag along *informal* to go somewhere with someone, especially when they have not asked you to go with them: *Is it all right if I tag along?*

tail¹ /teɪl/ *n*
1 [C] the long thin part on the back end of an animal's body: *The dog was **wagging** its **tail**.* → see picture on page A3
2 [C] the back part of a plane → see picture at AEROPLANE
3 tails [U] the side of a coin that does not have a picture of someone's head on it **OPP** heads
4 tails [plural] a man's suit coat with two long parts that hang down the back, worn to very formal events
PHRASES
the **tail end of sth** the last part of something: *the tail end of the century*

tail² *v* [T] *informal* to secretly follow someone and watch what they do, where they go etc **THESAURUS** FOLLOW

PHRASAL VERBS

tail off to become gradually quieter, smaller, less etc, and often stop or disappear completely: *His voice tailed off as he saw his father approaching.*

tailback /'teɪlbæk/ *n* [C] *BrE* a line of cars on a road that are moving very slowly or not moving at all

tail-light, tail light *n* [C] one of the two red lights at the back of a vehicle → see picture at CAR

tailor¹ /'teɪlə $ -ər/ *n* [C] someone whose job is to make men's clothes that are measured to fit each customer exactly

tailor² *v* [T] to make something so that it is exactly what someone wants or needs: *Courses are specially tailored to the needs of each student.*

tailored /'teɪləd $ -ərd/ *adj* a piece of clothing that is tailored is made to fit very well: *a tailored suit*

tailoring /'teɪlərɪŋ/ *n* [U] the way that clothes are made, or the job of making them

tailor-'made *adj* very suitable for someone or something: *The job's tailor-made for you.*

tailpipe /'teɪlpaɪp/ *n* [C] *AmE* an EXHAUST pipe → see picture at CAR

taint /teɪnt/ *v* [T usually passive] **1** if something bad taints a situation or person, it makes the person or situation seem bad: *Baker argues that his trial was tainted by negative publicity.* **2** to damage something by adding an unwanted substance to it: *hamburger meat tainted with harmful bacteria* —**taint** *n* [singular]

take¹ /teɪk/ *v* [T] (*past tense* **took** /tʊk/, *past participle* **taken** /'teɪkən/)
1 MOVE STH/SB to move something from one place to another, or to help someone go from one place to another: **take sb/sth to/into etc sth** *Can you take me to the airport?* | *The policeman took him into a tiny room.* | **take sth off/from etc sth** *Take your feet off the seats.* | **take sb/sth with you** *His wife went to Spain, taking the children with her.* | **take sb to do sth** *Howard took me to meet his parents.* **THESAURUS** BRING
2 REMOVE WITHOUT PERMISSION to steal something or borrow it without permission: *Did you take my soda?* **THESAURUS** STEAL
3 CARRY WITH YOU to carry something or have it with you when you go somewhere: *Make sure you take an umbrella when you leave.*
4 PERFORM AN ACTION used with some nouns instead of using a verb to say that someone does something, or that something happens: *Here, take a look.* | *I took a shower and got ready to go out.* | **take a holiday/break/rest etc** *Let's take a short break and meet again in ten minutes.* | **take a picture/photograph/photo** (=use a camera to make a picture)
5 TO A RESTAURANT/FILM ETC (*also* **take out**) to go with someone to a restaurant, film etc and pay for them or be responsible for them: *I'm taking her to a movie.* **THESAURUS** LEAD
6 HOLD to hold something: *Let me take your coat.* | *She took his arm.*

7 NEED TIME/MONEY ETC if something takes a particular amount of time, money, effort etc, you need that amount of time etc for it to happen or succeed: *Looking after children takes hard work.* | *It took a few minutes for his eyes to adjust to the dark.* | **take (sb) ages/forever** *informal*: *The drive to the airport took forever.* | **take courage/guts** *Starting your own business takes a lot of guts.* | *They can still win, but it'll* **take some doing** (=be difficult and take a lot of effort).

8 ACCEPT to accept something that is offered or given to you: *Are you going to take the job?* | *Jim took all the credit, even though he didn't do much of the work.* | **take credit cards/a cheque etc** (=accept them as a way of paying) *Do you take American Express?*

9 TEST/EXAM **take a test/exam** to do a test or examination SYN **sit** *BrE*: *I'm taking my driving test next week.*

10 STUDY A SUBJECT to study a particular subject in school or college: *Are you taking French next year?*

11 MEDICINE/DRUG to swallow or use a medicine or drug: *A lot of kids start* **taking drugs** (=using illegal drugs) *when they're 14 or 15.*

12 CAR/BUS/TRAIN ETC to use a car, bus, train etc to go somewhere, or to travel along a particular road: *Let's take the bus.* | *Take the M6 to Junction 19.* THESAURUS TRAVEL

13 ACCEPT STH BAD to accept an unpleasant situation SYN **stand**: *I can't take any more of her complaining.*

14 HAVE A FEELING to have a particular feeling about something: **take pleasure/pride/an interest etc in (doing) sth** *You should take pride in your work.* | **take pity on sb** (=help someone because you feel sorry for them) *Howard took pity on the man and gave him food.*

15 HOW SB REACTS to think about someone or something in a particular way, or react to them in this way: **take sth badly/personally/seriously etc** *Try not to take his criticism personally.* | **take sb seriously** *I was joking but he took me seriously.* | **take sth as sth** *I shall take that as a compliment.*

16 SIZE to be a suitable size, type etc for a particular person or thing: *Our car can take up to six people.* | *What size shoe do you take?*

17 BUY to choose to buy something: *We'll take a pound of ham and a half pound of cheese.* | *'It's $50.' 'OK, I'll* **take it**.'

18 GET CONTROL to get possession or control of something: *Rebel forces have taken the airport.* | **take control/charge/power** *Republicans hope to take control of Congress this fall.* | *Six soldiers were* **taken prisoner** (=captured by an enemy).

19 SUGAR/MILK ETC to use something such as sugar, milk, salt etc in your food or drinks: *Do you* **take milk and sugar** *in your coffee?*

20 REMOVE NUMBER to make a number smaller by a particular amount SYN **subtract**: **take sth away/take sth (away) from sth** *Take 2 from 9 and you get 7.*

21 NOTE/MESSAGE to write down information: *Sue offered to take notes.* | *He's not here right now – can I* **take a message** (=write down information from someone on the telephone and give the information to someone else)? THESAURUS WRITE

22 MEASURE AMOUNT/LEVEL to measure the amount,

level, rate etc of something: *The doctor took her blood pressure.*

PHRASES

I take it (that) *spoken* used to check with someone that something is true or has been done: *I take it you two have already met.*

take a lot out of you to make you very tired: *My job takes a lot out of me.*

take place to happen: *The robbery took place last night.* THESAURUS HAPPEN

take sb's word for it/take it from sb *spoken* used to tell someone to accept that what someone says is true: *He'll be there on time tomorrow, take my word for it.* THESAURUS BELIEVE

THESAURUS

take to move something from one place to another, or to help someone go from one place to another: *Don't forget to take your passport with you.* | *She's taken Ben to the doctor.*

bring to take someone or something to the place where you are now: *He's bringing his new girlfriend to meet us.* | *I'll bring a bottle of wine.*

deliver to take letters, newspapers, goods etc to someone's home or office: *The letter was delivered to the wrong address.*

transport to take a lot of goods, people etc from one place to another in a plane, train, ship etc: *It's cheaper to transport goods by ship.* | *The plane is used for transporting military personnel.*

ship to take goods from one place to another, especially over a long distance: *80% of the vegetables are shipped to grocery stores in the Northeast.*

drive to take someone from one place to another in a car: *My friend has offered to drive me to the airport.*

guide to take someone to a place and show them the way: *He guided us around the old city.*

escort to take someone to a place and protect or guard them: *The President was escorted by members of the armed forces.*

PHRASAL VERBS

take after sb to look or behave like an older member of your family: *Jenny takes after her dad.*

take sth ↔ **apart** to separate something into all its different parts: *Jim took apart the faucet and put in a new washer.*

take sb/sth ↔ **away** to remove someone or something from a place: *Hyde was taken away in handcuffs.*

take sth ↔ **back**

1 to return something to the place or person it came from: *If the shirt doesn't fit, take it back to the shop.*

2 to admit that you were wrong to say something: *All right, I'm sorry, I take it back.*

take sth ↔ **down**

1 to remove something that is attached to a wall: *Our teacher made us take down all the posters.*

2 to separate something into all its different parts and move it to a different place: *Would you help me take down the tent?*

3 to write information on a piece of paper: *The receptionist took down his name.*

T

take sb/sth ↔ **in**

1 to understand and remember new facts and information: *There was so much happening in the film, it was difficult to take it all in.*

2 be taken in (by sb/sth) to be deceived by someone or something: *The bank had been taken in by the forged receipts.* **THESAURUS** BELIEVE

3 to let someone stay in your house because they have nowhere else to stay: *The Humane Society took in almost 38,000 cats and dogs last year.*

4 to make a piece of clothing narrower, so that it fits you

take off

1 **REMOVE** **take** sth ↔ **off** to remove something **OPP** put on: *He took off his shoes.* → see picture at **PUT**

2 **AIRCRAFT** if an aircraft takes off, it leaves the ground and goes up into the air **OPP** land

3 **FROM WORK** **take some time/a day/a week etc off** to not go to work for a period of time

4 **LEAVE** *informal* to leave somewhere quickly and suddenly: *We packed everything in the car and took off.* **THESAURUS** LEAVE

5 **BE SUCCESSFUL** to suddenly start being successful: *The song became a surprise hit and his career suddenly took off.*

take sb/sth ↔ **on**

1 to compete or fight against someone, especially someone bigger or better than you: *The winner of this game will take on Miami.*

2 to start doing some work or start being responsible for something: *I've taken on far too much work lately.*

3 to start to employ someone: *We're taking on 50 new staff this year.*

take sb/sth ↔ **out**

1 take sth ↔ **out** to remove something from inside a building, your body etc: *The dentist says she may have to take out one of my back teeth.*

2 to go with someone to a restaurant, film etc, and pay for them: **[+for]** *Rich wants to take me out for Chinese food.*

3 take sth ↔ **out** to officially arrange to get something from a bank, insurance company etc: **take out a policy/loan etc** *The couple took out a £20,000 loan.*

4 take sth ↔ **out** to borrow books from a library: *You can take out six books at a time.*

take sth **out on** sb to treat someone badly when you are angry, tired etc, even though it is not their fault: *Don't take it out on me just because you've had a bad day.*

take over to take control of something → **takeover**: **take** sth ↔ **over** *His son will take over the business.*

take to sb/sth

1 to start to like someone or something: *We took to each other right away.*

2 take to doing sth to begin doing something regularly: *Sandra has taken to getting up early to go jogging.*

take up sth

1 take sth ↔ **up** to start doing a new job or activity: *I've just taken up golf.*

2 take up sb's offer/invitation to accept someone's offer or invitation: *I've decided to take up their offer.*

3 to use or fill an amount of time or space: *The program takes up a lot of memory on the hard drive.*

take up on sth to accept an invitation or suggestion: *Thanks for the offer. I might take you up on it.*

take sth **up with** sb to discuss something with someone, especially a complaint or problem: *If you're unhappy, you should take it up with your supervisor.*

take² n **1** [C] an occasion when a scene from a film or a song is recorded: *We had to do six takes for this particular scene.* **2** [singular] *AmE* an American word for TAKINGS → **DOUBLE TAKE, GIVE AND TAKE**

takeaway /ˈteɪkəweɪ/ n [C] *BrE* a meal that you buy from a restaurant to eat at home, or a restaurant that sells this food **SYN** takeout *AmE*: *a Chinese takeaway* **THESAURUS** MEAL —**take-away** adj

'take-home ,pay n [U] the amount of money that you receive from your job after taxes etc have been taken out

taken /ˈteɪkən/ v the past participle of TAKE → **be taken aback** at ABACK

PHRASES

be taken with sb/sth to like someone or something very much: *Chris was very taken with her.*

'take-off, takeoff /ˈteɪkɒf $ -ɒːf/ n [C,U] when a plane moves off the ground into the air

takeout /ˈteɪk-aʊt/ n [C] *AmE* a TAKEAWAY **THESAURUS** MEAL —**take-out** adj

takeover /ˈteɪkˌəʊvə $ -ˌoʊvər/ n [C] **1** when a company gets control of another company by buying over half of the SHARES: *The takeover bid was rejected by shareholders.* **2** the act of getting control of a country or political organization, using force

takings /ˈteɪkɪŋz/ n [plural] the amount of money that a shop, bar etc gets from selling things over a particular period of time: *the day's takings*

talcum powder /ˈtælkəm ˌpaʊdə $ -dər/ (also talc /tælk/) n [U] a powder with a nice smell that you put on your skin after washing

tale /teɪl/ n [C] a story about things that happened long ago, or things that may not have really happened: *a book of fairy tales* (=children's stories in which magical things happen) | *old Japanese folk tales* (=traditional stories from a country) | **[+of/about]** *Roger was always telling tales about life in the army.* → **OLD WIVES' TALE**

talent /ˈtælənt/ n [C,U] a natural ability to do something well: *Turner has more talent than any other player on the team.* | **[+for]** *Lee has always had a natural talent for public speaking.* **THESAURUS** SKILL

talented /ˈtæləntɪd/ adj having a natural ability to do something well: *a talented musician*

talisman /ˈtælɪzmən/ n [C] (plural talismans) an object that is believed to have magic powers to protect the person who owns it

talk¹ /tɔːk $ tɒːk/ v

1 [I] to say things to someone as part of a conversation: *I could hear Sarah and Andrew talking in the next room.* | **[+to/with]** *Tara's talking with a customer.* | *She's very easy to talk to.* | **[+about]** *Grandpa never talks much about the war.* | *Sue and Bob* still **aren't talking** (=are refusing to talk to each other).

> **Grammar**
> Do not say 'She talked me about her plans.' Say
> *She talked to me about her plans.* or *She told me about her plans.*

2 [I,T] to discuss something serious or important with someone: *Joe, we need to talk.* | **[+to/with]** *I'd like to talk with you in private.* | **[+about]** *My wife and I are talking about buying a new car.* | **talk sport/ politics/dinner etc** *Casey likes to drink beer and talk politics.*

3 [I] to use your voice to say words SYN **speak**: *How old are babies when they start to talk?* | *She was talking so fast I could hardly understand her.*

4 [I] to tell someone secret information because they force you to: *They threatened to shoot him, but he still refused to talk.*

PHRASES

talk about lazy/lucky etc *informal* used to emphasize that someone is very lazy, lucky etc: *Talk about annoying! I thought she was never going to shut up.*

know what you are talking about *spoken* to know a lot about a particular subject: *I know what I'm talking about, because I was there when it happened.*

talk sense/nonsense/rubbish etc used to say that you think someone is saying something sensible or stupid

talk (some) sense into sb to talk to someone and make them start behaving in a sensible way: *She hoped Father McCormack would be able to talk some sense into her son.*

talk to yourself to say your thoughts out loud: *'What did you say?' 'Nothing, I was just talking to myself.'*

talk your way out of sth *informal* to avoid an unpleasant situation by giving an explanation or excuse: *He usually manages to talk his way out of trouble.*

what are you talking about? *spoken* used when you think someone has said something stupid or wrong: *What are you talking about? I gave you the money weeks ago.*

PHRASAL VERBS

talk back if a child talks back to an adult, they answer the adult rudely: **[+to]** *Don't talk back to your father!*

talk down to sb to talk to someone in a way that shows you think they are not important or not intelligent: *The teachers talked down to us and treated us like children.*

talk sb **into** sth to persuade someone to do something that they do not really want to do: *I didn't want to go, but my friends talked me into it.* THESAURUS PERSUADE

talk sb **out of** sth to persuade someone not to do something that they wanted to do: *No one could talk Luis out of joining the army.*

talk sth ↔ **over** to discuss a problem with someone before deciding what to do: **[+with]** *I'm going to have to talk it over with your father first.*

> **THESAURUS**
>
> **talk** to say things to someone as part of a conversation: *Danny was talking to a girl in his*

class. | *They talked about the weather.*

speak to talk to someone, especially because there is something you need to say or ask. Also used when saying that someone **speaks** a language, or when describing the way someone **speaks**: *May I speak to Mr. Harrison?* | *She can speak French.* | *The man spoke with a foreign accent.*

have a conversation to talk to someone about everyday things: *I had a really interesting conversation with Paul the other day.*

chat/have a chat *informal* to have a friendly conversation, especially with someone you know well: *She's been chatting to him on the phone for hours.*

discuss to talk about a subject, especially so that you can make a decision or make plans: *They discussed the arrangements for the wedding.* | *Is there anything more we need to discuss?*

gossip to talk about other people's private lives when they are not there, especially about things that you have heard but are not really true: *People in the village are always gossiping.*

whisper to talk quietly, usually because you do not want other people to hear what you are saying: *The girls were whispering about something in the corner.*

go on *informal* to talk too much about something, in a way that makes you bored: *He's always going on about money.*

talk² n

1 [C] when people talk to each other about a subject: **[+about]** *We must have a talk about money.* | **[+with]** *After a long talk with her husband, Teri decided to get a divorce.*

2 [C] a speech on a particular subject: **[+on/about]** *Professor Mason will be **giving a talk** on the Civil War.* THESAURUS SPEECH

3 [U] when people say that something may be true or may happen: **[+of]** *Tickets sold so quickly there's talk of a second concert.*

4 talks [plural] formal discussions between different countries, organizations, leaders etc: **peace/ pay/trade talks** *Management and workers are holding pay talks.* → PEP TALK, SMALL TALK

> **COLLOCATIONS**
>
> **verbs**
>
> **to have a talk** *We need to have a talk about Paul.*
>
> **adjectives**
>
> **a long talk** *I met Jo for lunch and we had a long talk.*
>
> **a little talk** *Could we have a little talk later?*
>
> **a serious talk** (=about something important) *Then Mum said she wanted to have a serious talk with me.*
>
> **a quiet/private talk** *Sam's teacher had a quiet talk with him about his work.*

talkative /ˈtɔːkətɪv $ ˈtɒːk-/ *adj* a talkative person talks a lot

talker /ˈtɔːkə $ ˈtɒːkər/ *n* [C] *informal* someone who talks a lot or talks in a particular way: *Will's a fast talker.*

'talk show n [C] *AmE* a television or radio show in which people answer questions about themselves SYN **chat show** *BrE*

tall /tɔːl $ tɒːl/ *adj*
1 a tall person, building, tree etc is a greater height than normal OPP **small**: *the tallest boy in the class* | *a house surrounded by tall trees* THESAURUS → HIGH
2 used to talk about the height of someone or something: **5ft/2m/12 inches etc tall** *My brother's almost 6 feet tall.* | *How tall is that bookcase?*

tally¹ /'tæli/ n [C] (*plural* **tallies**) a record of how much you have won, spent, used etc by a particular point in time

tally² (*also* **tally up**) v (**tallied, tallying, tallies**) **1** [I] if numbers or statements tally, they match each other: *The witnesses' statements didn't tally.* **2** [T] to calculate the total number of something

talon /'tælən/ n [C] a bird's CLAW → see picture on page A3

tambourine /ˌtæmbə'riːn/ n [C] a small drum that you hold in your hand and play by hitting or shaking it → see picture on page A6

tame¹ /teɪm/ *adj* **1** a tame animal is not wild any more because it has been trained to obey people and not to fear them **2** disappointing and not exciting

tame² v [T] to train a wild animal to obey people

tamper /'tæmpə $ -ər/ v
PHRASAL VERBS
tamper with sth to change something without permission: *Someone had tampered with the switches.*

tampon /'tæmpɒn $ -pɑːn/ n [C] a tube-shaped piece of cotton that a woman uses to collect the blood during her PERIOD (=monthly flow of blood)

tan¹ /tæn/ n
1 [C] if you have a tan, your skin is darker than usual because you have spent time in the sun SYN **suntan**
2 [U] a pale yellow-brown colour

tan² v [I,T] (**tanned, tanning**) to get darker skin by spending time in the sun: *I don't tan easily.* —**tanned** *adj*

tan³ *adj* **1** pale yellow-brown in colour **2** *AmE* having darker skin after spending time in the sun SYN **tanned**

tandem /'tændəm/ n [C] a bicycle for two people
PHRASES
in tandem (with sb/sth) *formal* doing something at the same time as someone or something else: *Practical treatment of the disease must run in tandem with health education.*

tangent /'tændʒənt/ n **go off on a tangent** to suddenly start talking about something completely different

tangerine /ˌtændʒə'riːn/ n [C] a small sweet orange

tangible /'tændʒəbəl/ *adj* definite and able to be seen or touched OPP **intangible**: *tangible proof*

tangle¹ /'tæŋgəl/ n [C] a mass of hair, wires etc that are twisted together: **[+of]** *a tangle of cables*

tangle² (*also* **tangle up**) v [I,T] if hair, wires, string etc tangle, or if you tangle them, they become twisted together untidily: *Don't tangle all the electrical wires.* —**tangled** *adj*: *tangled hair*

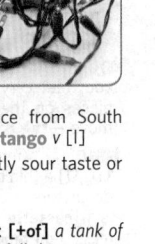
TANGLE
tangled Christmas lights

PHRASAL VERBS
tangle with sb *informal* to argue or fight with someone

tango /'tæŋgəʊ $ -goʊ/ n [C] (*plural* **tangos**) a fast dance from South America, or music for this dance —**tango** v [I]

tangy /'tæŋi/ *adj* having a pleasantly sour taste or smell

tank¹ /tæŋk/ n [C]
1 a large container for liquid or gas: **[+of]** *a tank of water* | *The plane's **fuel tanks** were full.* | *a **storage tank*** | *petrol tank* *BrE*, **gas tank** *AmE* (=a tank in a vehicle to hold petrol)
2 a large military vehicle that has a big gun and moves on metal belts that fit over the wheels → THINK TANK

tank² v
PHRASAL VERBS
tank sth ↔ **up** *AmE* to fill a car's tank with petrol SYN **fill up** *BrE*

tankard /'tæŋkəd $ -ərd/ n [C] a large metal cup

tanker /'tæŋkə $ -ər/ n [C] a ship or vehicle used for carrying liquid or gas: *an oil tanker*

tannoy /'tænɔɪ/ n [singular] *trademark BrE* a system of LOUDSPEAKERS: **over the tannoy** *We heard an announcement over the tannoy.*

tantalizing (*also* **-ising** *BrE*) /'tæntəl-aɪzɪŋ/ *adj* making you want something: *the tantalizing smell of fresh coffee* —**tantalizingly** *adv*

tantamount /'tæntəmaʊnt/ *adj* **be tantamount to** sth if something is tantamount to a bad or harmful action, it has the same effect or is equally bad

tantrum /'tæntrəm/ n [C] a short period when a child becomes very angry: **have/throw a tantrum** *Jenny threw one of her **temper tantrums**.*

tap¹ /tæp/ v (**tapped, tapping**)
1 [I,T] to gently hit something, often making a slight noise: **tap (sb/sth) on sth** *I tapped him on the shoulder.* | *Carol tapped her foot in time to the music.* THESAURUS → HIT → see picture on page A10
2 (*also* **tap into**) [T] to use or take what you need from a supply of something: *Youngsters tap the knowledge of more experienced players.*
3 [T] to use special equipment to listen secretly to a telephone conversation from a distance: *They've probably **tapped** our **phone**.*
PHRASAL VERBS
tap sth ↔ **in** (*also* **tap** sth **into** sth) *BrE* to put information into a computer or machine by pressing buttons

tap² n [C]
1 *especially BrE* a piece of equipment that you turn to control the flow of a liquid or gas SYN **faucet** *AmE*:

turn a tap on/off *You forgot to turn off the tap.* | **hot/cold (water) tap** | **kitchen/bath/garden tap** | *The tap's dripping* (=letting out drops of water continuously). | **tap water** (=water that comes out through a tap) → see picture at **BATHROOM**
2 when you hit something gently, especially to get someone's attention: **[+on/at]** *a tap on my shoulder*
PHRASES

| **on tap** available for use: *They have plenty of money on tap.*

'tap ,dancing n [U] dancing in which you move your feet very quickly and wear shoes with metal pieces on the bottom that make a noise as you move —**tap dancer** n [C] —**tap dance** v [I]

tape¹ $\boxed{\text{Ac}}$ /teɪp/ n
1 [C,U] a thin band of plastic used to record sounds or pictures, or the plastic box that contains it $\boxed{\text{SYN}}$ **cassette** → **videotape**: **[+of]** *a tape of African music* | **on tape** *I've got that film on tape.* | *Have you any* **blank tapes** (=tapes with nothing recorded on them)?
2 [U] a band of sticky material that you use to fasten things together
3 [C,U] a long thin piece of material, used to mark out an area or show where a race ends → **MASKING TAPE, RED TAPE**

tape² $\boxed{\text{Ac}}$ v [I,T] **1** to record sounds or pictures on a tape → **videotape**: *Are you taping this movie?* **2** to fasten or cover something using tape

'tape deck n [C] the part of a STEREO on which you can record and play music tapes

'tape ,measure n [C] a long thin piece of cloth or plastic marked with centimetres, metres etc that you use to measure things

taper¹ /'teɪpə $ -ər/ v [I,T] to become gradually narrower at one end —**tapered** adj
PHRASAL VERBS
taper off to decrease gradually: *The rain had tapered off.*

taper² n [C] a long thin CANDLE, used to light lamps, fires etc

'tape re,corder n [C] a piece of equipment on which you can record and play sounds on a TAPE —**tape recording** n [C,U]

tapestry /'tæpəstri/ n [C,U] (plural **tapestries**) a piece of heavy cloth that is woven with coloured threads to make a picture

tar /tɑː $ tɑːr/ n [U]
1 a black sticky substance that is used to cover roads and roofs
2 a harmful sticky substance that gets into the lungs of people who smoke —**tar** v [T]

tarantula /təˈræntʃələ $ -tʃələ/ n [C] a large poisonous SPIDER from Southern Europe and tropical America

target¹ $\boxed{\text{Ac}}$ /'tɑːɡɪt $ 'tɑːr-/ n [C]
1 an amount, level, or result that you try to achieve $\boxed{\text{SYN}}$ **goal**: *I didn't meet* (=achieve) *my sales target last month.* | **[+of]** *a target of £2 million profit* | **on target** *We're on target to finish by 2012.* **THESAURUS** ▶ **AIM**

2 a person or place that people attack or criticize: **[+for/of]** *Airports are* **prime targets** (=very likely targets) *for terrorist attacks.* | *His country has recently been the* **target of criticism.** | **easy/soft target** *Tourists are an easy target for thieves.*
3 the people that someone is trying to influence: *Who is the* **target audience** *for this show?*
4 something that you shoot, throw, or kick something at: *The arrow* **missed** *the* **target**.
PHRASES

| **target language** the language you are learning or translating into

COLLOCATIONS

verbs

to meet/reach/achieve a target (=achieve what you want to achieve) *How can the UK meet its target of cutting greenhouse gases by 50%?*
to set a target *She set herself a target of reading two chapters a day.*
to exceed a target (=achieve more than you wanted or expected) *I am confident that we will exceed our sales targets.*

adjectives

an ambitious target (=difficult to achieve) *Raising £1,000 is an ambitious target.*
a realistic target (=one that you can achieve) *Try to set yourself realistic targets.*
a financial target *Detailed financial targets were set.*

target² $\boxed{\text{Ac}}$ v [T] **1** to aim something at someone or something: **target sth at sth** *fears that they might target missiles at major cities* **2** to choose a particular person or place to attack: *The bombers are targeting tourist resorts.* **3** to offer something to a particular group because you want them to buy or accept it: **target sth at sb** *a magazine targeted at teenagers*

tariff /'tærɪf/ n [C] **1** a tax on goods coming into a country **2** *BrE* a list or system of prices for a particular service: *mobile phone tariffs*

Tarmac /'tɑːmæk $ 'tɑːr-/ n [U] trademark **1** *BrE* a mixture of TAR and small stones, used to cover the surface of roads $\boxed{\text{SYN}}$ **blacktop** *AmE* **2 the tarmac** the large area at an airport where planes land and take off

tarnish /'tɑːnɪʃ $ 'tɑːr-/ v **1** [T] to damage the opinion people have of someone or something: *The scandal* **tarnished** *his* **reputation** *forever.* **2** [I] if metal tarnishes, it becomes dull

tarot /'tærəʊ $ -roʊ/ n [singular, U] a set of 78 cards that some people use to find out what will happen in the future

tarpaulin /tɑːˈpɔːlɪn $ tɑːrˈpɒː-/ n [C,U] a large WATERPROOF cloth, used to protect things from the rain

tart¹ /tɑːt $ tɑːrt/ n [C] **1** a food with PASTRY on the bottom and a filling on the top: *jam tarts* **2** an offensive word for a woman who you think has sex with a lot of men

tart² v

PHRASAL VERBS

tart sth ↔ **up** BrE informal to try to make something old or ugly look more attractive

tart³ adj food that is tart has a sour taste **THESAURUS** TASTE

tartan /ˈtɑːtn $ ˈtɑːrtn/ n [C,U] a traditional Scottish pattern with coloured squares and lines → see picture at PATTERN

task Ac /tɑːsk $ tæsk/ n [C] a piece of work you must do: My first task was to paint the whole house. | Our tutor sets us some difficult tasks. | **the task of doing sth** I was given the task of handing out the cups.

PHRASES

be no easy task used for saying that something is difficult: Bringing up a child on your own is no easy task.

take sb to task (for/over sth) to criticize someone angrily: He was taken to task for not reporting the problem earlier.

task force n [C] a group of people who work together for a short time to solve a particular problem

tassel /ˈtæsəl/ n [C] a decoration made of a lot of threads tied together at one end

taste¹ /teɪst/ n

1 [C,U] the taste of food or drink is what it is like when you put it in your mouth, for example how sweet or salty it is: **the taste of sth** I don't like the taste of garlic. | **sweet/sour/sharp/bitter taste** The soup had a slightly sweet taste. | He's got a good **sense of taste** (=an ability to recognize different tastes). → see Word Choice at FLAVOUR

2 [C] a small amount of something that you put in your mouth to see what it is like: Can I **have a taste of** your ice cream?

3 [C,U] the kind of things that you like: **[+in]** We had **similar tastes** in music.

4 a taste for sth if you have a taste for something, you like it: a young man with a taste for adventure

5 [U] the ability to judge what is attractive, suitable, good quality etc: 'You've **got** good **taste**' said Eva, looking round the flat.

6 [singular] a short experience of something new: **[+of]** The weekend gave us a taste of university life.

7 be in good/bad/poor taste to be appropriate or inappropriate for a particular occasion: Her dress was in very bad taste for a funeral.

THESAURUS

describing the taste of something

delicious if something is delicious, it tastes very good: The fruit was delicious. | a delicious salad

tasty informal having a good taste: a tasty snack | That was really tasty!

disgusting/revolting/horrible having a very bad taste: I had some disgusting meat that I couldn't eat.

sweet containing a lot of sugar: a sweet sticky pudding

bitter bitter coffee, chocolate etc has a strong taste that is not sweet and is often not very nice: The coffee had a bitter, rather burnt taste.

sour/tart having a strong taste like a lemon does, especially when this does not taste very nice: This apple is a bit sour.

hot/spicy containing spices that make you feel as though your mouth is burning: I love hot curries. | spicy Mexican food

salty containing a lot of salt: The soup was too salty.

mild not having a strong or hot taste: mild cheeses | a mild curry

bland food that is bland is boring because it does not have enough taste: The fish was dry and bland.

taste² v

1 [linking verb] food that tastes sweet, sour etc has that quality when you put it in your mouth: The soup tasted lovely. | **taste good/sweet/sour etc** This milk tastes sour. | **[+of]** The stew tasted of garlic. | **taste like sth** What does the soup **taste like**? | **sweet-tasting/strong-tasting etc**

2 [T] to recognize what something is when you put it in your mouth: You **can taste** the spices in this curry.

3 [T] to eat or drink a small amount of something, to find out what it is like: Have you tasted the wine?

4 taste success/freedom/victory etc to experience success etc for a short time

taste bud n [C usually plural] the part of your tongue that can taste things

tasteful /ˈteɪstfəl/ adj attractive and of good quality: tasteful Christmas decorations —**tastefully** adv: tastefully furnished apartments

Word Choice: tasteful or tasty?
You use **tasteful** about things such as clothes or furniture which show that someone is good at choosing things that look attractive: The room was filled with tasteful modern furniture.
You use **tasty** about food that has a nice taste: This bread's really tasty.

tasteless /ˈteɪstləs/ adj **1** clothes, furniture etc that are tasteless are unattractive and show that the person who chose them has bad judgment: tasteless ornaments **2** slightly offensive: a tasteless joke **3** tasteless food is unpleasant because it does not have a strong taste

taster /ˈteɪstə $ -ər/ n [C] **1** someone whose job is to judge the quality of food or drink by tasting it: wine tasters **2** a small example of something that you try to see whether you like it: college taster courses

tasty /ˈteɪsti/ adj food that is tasty has a nice taste, but is not sweet **THESAURUS** TASTE

tattered /ˈtætəd $ -ərd/ adj old and torn **THESAURUS** CONDITION

tatters /ˈtætəz $ -ərz/ n **in tatters** very badly damaged or spoiled: Her self-confidence was in tatters.

tattoo /təˈtuː, tæˈtuː/ n [C] (plural **tattoos**) a picture or writing that is permanently marked on your skin, using a needle and ink —**tattooed** adj —**tattoo** v [T] —**tattooist** n [C]

tatty /ˈtæti/ adj BrE informal in bad condition

taught /tɔːt $ tɔːt/ v the past tense and past participle of TEACH

taunt /tɔːnt $ tɔːnt/ v [T] to try to upset someone by continuously saying unkind things about them: **taunt sb about sth** The other kids taunted him about his weight. —**taunt** n [C]

Taurus /'tɔːrəs/ n **1** [U] the sign of the Zodiac of people born between April 21 and May 21 **2** [C] someone who has this sign

taut /tɔːt $ tɔːt/ adj **1** stretched tight: a taut rope **2** showing signs of anxiety: a taut smile —**tautly** adv

tavern /'tævən $ -ərn/ n [C] old-fashioned a PUB

tawdry /'tɔːdri $ 'tɔː-/ adj cheap or badly made: tawdry jewels

tawny /'tɔːni $ 'tɔː-/ adj yellowish brown in colour: tawny fur

tax /tæks/ n [C,U] money that you pay to the government and that is used to provide public services: How much tax do you pay? | **[+on]** plans to increase the tax on alcohol | a tax-free salary (=with no tax to pay) | **before/after tax** She earns about $50,000 a year, after tax. —**tax** v [T]: Cigarettes are heavily taxed.

COLLOCATIONS

verbs

to pay tax Most people pay tax on their income.
to raise/increase taxes The government said it would have to raise taxes.
to cut/lower/reduce taxes He supports the idea of cutting taxes.

adjectives

high/low tax Many countries pay higher taxes than we do.

noun + tax

income tax (=tax you pay on money you earn) People who earn a lot pay more income tax.
sales tax (=tax you pay on things you buy)

tax + noun

a tax increase The changes will result in a big tax increase.
a tax cut The Republicans proposed a 15% tax cut.

taxable /'tæksəbəl/ adj if something is taxable, you must pay tax on it

taxation /tæk'seɪʃən/ n [U] the system of charging taxes, or the money that is collected

taxi¹ /'tæksi/ (also **taxicab** /'tæksikæb/) n [C] a car with a driver that you pay to take you somewhere **SYN** cab: **by taxi** We went by taxi. | **take/get a taxi** We'll get a taxi to the airport. | a **taxi driver** | How much was the **taxi fare**? → see picture at **TRANSPORT¹**

Grammar
Do not say 'She got on a taxi.' Say She got in a taxi.

taxi² v [I] (**taxied, taxiing, taxis** or **taxies**) if a plane taxies, it moves slowly along the ground

taxing /'tæksɪŋ/ adj needing a lot of effort: a taxing job

'taxi rank, **'taxi-stand** AmE n [C] a place where taxis wait

taxpayer /'tæks,peɪə $ -ər/ n [C] **1** someone who pays taxes: It will cost taxpayers 1.3 million. **2 the taxpayer** all the people who pay taxes

'tax re,turn n [C] an official form that you fill in to say how much you have earned so that the amount of tax you must pay can be calculated

TB /,tiː 'biː/ n [U] the abbreviation of **tuberculosis**

tba written **to be announced** used to say that the time or place of an event will be given at a later date

tbsp the written abbreviation of **tablespoon**: 1 tbsp sugar

tea /tiː/ n [C,U]
1 a drink made by pouring boiling water onto dried leaves, or the leaves used to make this drink: a **cup of tea** | Are you **making tea**? | I don't like **strong tea**. | herbal teas
2 BrE a meal eaten in the afternoon or early evening

teabag /'tiːbæɡ/ n [C] a small paper bag containing dried leaves, used to make tea

teach /tiːtʃ/ v (past tense and past participle **taught** /tɔːt $ tɔːt/)
1 [I,T] to give classes or instructions in a particular subject: **teach (sb) sth** He taught physics for 15 years. | the woman who taught us French | **teach sth to sb** I taught English to Italian students. | **teach sb (sth) about sth** They teach us about all the different religions. | **[+at]** She teaches at the Institute of Technology. | **teach school/college etc** AmE (=teach in a school etc)
2 [T] to tell or show someone how to do something: **teach sb (how) to do sth** We kids were taught to behave politely. | **teach sb what/where etc** Will you teach me what to do? | **teach sb sth** My grandfather tried to teach me chess.
3 [T] if an experience teaches you something, it helps you understand something about life: **teach sb that** It taught me that money can't buy happiness.

teacher /'tiːtʃə $ -ər/ n [C] someone who teaches as their job: **history/physics/English etc teacher** Mr Paulin is my history teacher. → **HEAD TEACHER**

THESAURUS

teacher someone who teaches as their job, especially in a school: She's training to be a teacher.
tutor someone who gives private lessons to one student or a small group of students. In Britain, a **tutor** also teaches small groups of students in a university: I had a few extra maths lessons with a private tutor.
lecturer a teacher in a university or college: a lecturer in economics
professor a university teacher – used in Britain about a university teacher of the highest rank, and in the US about any university teacher who has a higher degree such as a PhD: a professor at Stanford Law School | Professor Jones
instructor someone who teaches a sport or a practical skill: a ski instructor | a swimming instructor | a driving instructor

coach someone who trains a person or team in a sport, and helps them to improve their skills: *our football coach*
trainer someone who teaches people the special skills they need to do something: *a computer trainer*

,teacher's 'pet *n* [singular] *informal* a child who other students do not like because they think he or she is the teacher's favourite student

teaching /'tiːtʃɪŋ/ *n* **1** [U] the work or job of being a teacher: *I decided to go into teaching* (=become a teacher). | *the teaching profession* | *language/science/English etc teaching* **2 teachings** [plural] the important moral, political, or religious ideas of a famous person: **[+of]** *the teachings of Marx*

teacup /'tiːkʌp/ *n* [C] a small cup used for drinking tea

teak /tiːk/ *n* [C,U] a type of wood, used to make expensive furniture

team¹ Ac /tiːm/ *n* [C also + plural verb *BrE*]
1 a group of people who play a sport or game against another group: *The best team won.* | *Which football team do you support?* | *in/on a team Do you want to be on our team?* | *The team are* (=each member is) *confident.*
2 a group of people who work together: **[+of]** *a team of doctors* | *the team leader* | *sales/design/management etc team a member of the sales team*

COLLOCATIONS

types of team

a football/basketball etc team *She was captain of the hockey team.*
the school team *I was never on any of the school teams.*
the national team *He plays for Pakistan's national cricket team.*
the winning/losing team *The winning team will get a trophy.*

verbs

to play for/in a team *You're playing for the best team in the country.*
to support a team (=to want a particular team to win) *Which team are you supporting?*

team + noun

the team captain *The cup was presented to the team captain.*
a team member *He's the eldest team member.*
a team game/sport (=one that is played by teams) *I enjoy running and tennis, rather than team sports.*

---

team² Ac *v*
PHRASAL VERBS
team up to join another person, company etc in order to work together: **[+with]** *Can I team up with you?*

teammate /'tiːm-meɪt/ *n* [C] someone who is in your team in a game

'**team ,player** *n* [C] an office worker who works well as part of a team

teamwork /'tiːmwɜːk $ -wɜːrk/ *n* [U] the ability of a group to work well together

teapot /'tiːpɒt $ -paːt/ *n* [C] a container used for making and serving tea, which has a handle and a SPOUT → see picture at **POT¹**

tear¹ /teə $ ter/ *v* (*past tense* **tore** /tɔː $ tɔːr/, *past participle* **torn** /tɔːn $ tɔːrn/, *present participle* **tearing**)
1 [I,T] if you tear paper, cloth etc, or if it tears, you make a hole in it or it breaks into small pieces → **rip**: *Be careful the bag doesn't tear.* | *I've torn my trousers.* | *tear sth off Tear off the slip at the bottom of the page.* | *tear sth out (of sth) Someone had torn the last two pages out of the book.* | *tear sth to pieces/shreds She tore his letter to pieces.*
2 [I] to move quickly in a dangerous or careless way: **[+around/into/out of etc]** *The kids were tearing round the house.*
3 be torn if you are torn, you cannot decide which of two things you should do: **[+between]** *Anne was torn between her love for Alex and her duty.*

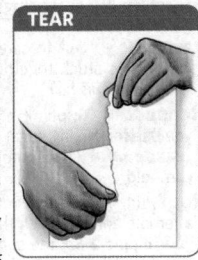
TEAR

PHRASES
be tearing your hair out *informal* to feel very anxious or upset: *He was tearing his hair out because the computer wasn't working properly.*

PHRASAL VERBS
tear sb/sth **apart** to make people argue or fight with each other: *a country torn apart by civil war*
tear sb **away** to force yourself or someone else to leave a place: *I was having so much fun I could hardly tear myself away.*
tear sth ↔ **down** to deliberately destroy a building: *The old school has been torn down.*
tear sth ↔ **off** to remove something roughly: *He tore off his wet clothes.*
tear into sb *informal* to criticize someone strongly
tear sth ↔ **up**
1 to tear paper into a lot of small pieces
2 if you tear up an agreement, contract etc, you refuse to accept it

tear² /tɪə $ tɪr/ *n* [C usually plural] a drop of liquid that falls from your eye when you cry: *She had tears in her eyes.* | *The children were in tears* (=crying). | *Brian burst into tears* (=started to cry). | *He was close to tears* (=almost crying). | *We all shed a few tears.*
THESAURUS ► **CRY**

tear³ /teə $ ter/ *n* [C] a hole in a piece of cloth or paper where it has torn: **[+in]** *There was a big tear in the sheet.*

tearaway /'teərəweɪ $ 'ter-/ *n* [C] a young person who is often in trouble because they behave badly

teardrop /'tɪədrɒp $ 'tɪrdraːp/ *n* [C] a single drop of liquid that falls from your eye when you cry

tearful /'tɪəfəl $ 'tɪr-/ *adj* crying or almost crying
—**tearfully** *adv*

teargas /'tɪəɡæs $ 'tɪr-/ *n* [U] a gas that hurts your

eyes, used by the police to control violent crowds

tease /tiːz/ v [I,T] if you tease someone, you say amusing or slightly unkind things to them about their appearance, behaviour etc: *Don't cry, I was **only** teasing.* | **tease sb about sth** *The other kids teased her about her hair.* —**teasingly** adv

PHRASAL VERBS

tease sth ↔ **out** to carefully separate thread, hair etc that is stuck together: *She carefully teased the knots out of his hair.*

teaspoon /'tiːspuːn/ n [C] **1** a small spoon that you use for mixing sugar into tea, coffee etc **2** (*also* **teaspoonful** /'tiːspuːnfʊl/) the amount this spoon can hold

teat /tiːt/ n [C] **1** the small red part on the breast of a female animal which their babies suck to get milk **SYN** **nipple 2** *BrE* the soft rubber part attached to a baby's bottle **SYN** **nipple** *AmE*

teatime /'tiːtaɪm/ n [U] *BrE* a time in the afternoon or early evening when people have a meal

'tea ,towel n [C] *BrE* a cloth that you use to dry cups, plates etc **SYN** **dish towel** *AmE*

techie /'teki/ n [C] *informal* someone who knows a lot about computers

technical Ac /'teknɪkəl/ adj
1 relating to machines and methods that are used in science or industry: *a **technical** problem* | *We provide **technical** training for our staff.* | ***technical** support for Internet subscribers*
2 relating to a particular subject or profession: *a document full of **technical** terms* | *The **language** is very **technical**.*

technicality /ˌteknə'kæləti/ n [C] (*plural* **technicalities**) **1 technicalities** [plural] the small details of how something works **2** one small detail in a law or agreement

technically Ac /'teknɪkli/ adv **1** according to the exact details of a rule or law: *What you have done is technically illegal.* **2** relating to the way machines are used in science and industry: *methods which are technically quite advanced*

technician /tek'nɪʃən/ n [C] someone whose job involves practical work relating to science or technology

technique Ac /tek'niːk/ n [C,U] a special skill or way of doing something: *guitar-playing techniques* | [+of] *techniques of problem solving* | **technique for doing sth** *a new technique for dealing with air pollution* **THESAURUS** WAY

techno /'teknəʊ $ -noʊ/ n [U] a type of popular electronic dance music with a fast strong beat

technology Ac /tek'nɒlədʒi $ -'nɑː-/ n [C,U] (*plural* **technologies**) modern machines and equipment: *the use of new computer technology* | *the achievements of modern technology* → **INFORMATION TECHNOLOGY** —**technological** /ˌteknə'lɒdʒɪkəl $ -'lɑː-/ adj: *technological advances*

COLLOCATIONS
adjectives
new/modern technology *New technology has changed the way we work.*

the latest technology *The hospital is equipped with all the latest technology.*
advanced technology (=very modern) *They work in a lab using the most advanced technology.*
digital technology *the growth of digital technology*

noun + technology
computer technology *The company has invested £700,000 in computer technology.*
advances/developments in technology *It was a period of great advances in technology.*

teddy bear /'tedi beə $ -ber/ (*also* **teddy** *BrE*) n [C] a soft toy shaped like a bear

tedious /'tiːdiəs/ adj very boring: *a tedious discussion* **THESAURUS** BORING —**tediously** adv

tee /tiː/ n [C] a small object used for holding a GOLF ball on the ground before you hit it

teem /tiːm/ v **be teeming with sth** to be full of people or animals that are all moving around: *The lake was teeming with fish.* —**teeming** adj: *the teeming streets of Cairo*

teen /tiːn/ n [C] *AmE informal* a teenager

teenage /'tiːneɪdʒ/ (*also* **teenaged** /'tiːneɪdʒd/) adj [only before noun] aged between 13 and 19, or suitable for people between 13 and 19: *She's got two teenage sons.* | *teenage fashion* **THESAURUS** YOUNG

teenager /'tiːneɪdʒə $ -ər/ n [C] someone who is between 13 and 19 years old → **adolescent**: *a TV series aimed at teenagers*

Word Choice: teenager or adolescent?
A **teenager** is someone between the ages of 13 and 19: *a magazine for teenagers*
An **adolescent** is a young person who is developing into an adult. You often use **adolescent** when talking about the problems that these young people have: *Adolescents are very conscious of their personal appearance.*

teens /tiːnz/ n [plural] the time in your life when you are aged between 13 and 19: **be in your teens** *She got married when she was still in her teens.*

teeny /'tiːni/ (*also* **teeny-weeny** /ˌtiːni 'wiːni/) adj *informal* very small: *I was just a teeny bit disappointed.*

'tee shirt n [C] a T-SHIRT

teeter /'tiːtə $ -ər/ v [I] to stand or walk moving from side to side, as if you are going to fall: *She teetered along in her high-heeled shoes.*
PHRASES
be teetering on the brink/edge of sth to be close to a very bad situation: *The country teetered on the brink of war.*

teeth /tiːθ/ n the plural of TOOTH

teethe /tiːð/ v [I] if a baby is teething, his or her teeth are starting to grow
PHRASES
teething troubles/problems *BrE* small problems that you have when you first start doing a new job or using a new system: *There were a lot of teething troubles in the first year.*

teetotaller *BrE*, **teetotaler** *AmE* /tiːˈtəʊtələ $ -ˈtoʊtələr/ n [C] someone who never drinks alcohol —**teetotal** *adj*

TEFL /ˈtefəl/ n [U] the teaching of English as a foreign language

tel. the written abbreviation of **telephone number**

telecommunications /ˌtelɪkəmjuːnəˈkeɪʃənz/ (*also* **telecoms** /ˈtelɪkɒmz $ -kɑːmz/) n [plural] the sending and receiving of messages by telephone, radio, television etc

teleconference /ˈtelɪˌkɒnfərəns $ -ˌkɑːn-/ n [C] a discussion in which people in different places talk to each other using telephones or video equipment —**teleconference** v [I]

telegram /ˈtelɪɡræm/ n [C] a message sent by telegraph

telegraph /ˈtelɪɡrɑːf $ -ɡræf/ n [U] an old-fashioned method of sending messages using radio or electrical signals

'**telegraph ,pole** n [C] *BrE* a tall wooden pole for supporting telephone wires

telepathy /təˈlepəθi/ n [U] the ability to communicate your thoughts directly to someone else's mind without speaking or writing —**telepathic** /ˌteləˈpæθɪk◂/ *adj*

telephone¹ /ˈteləfəʊn $ -foʊn/ (*also* **phone**) n
1 the telephone the system of communication that you use to have a conversation with someone in another place: **on the telephone** *I spoke to him on the telephone.* | a **telephone call** | **by telephone** *Reservations can be made by telephone.*
2 [C] the piece of equipment that you use when you are talking to someone by telephone: *The **telephone** rang just as I was leaving.* | *Could you **answer** the **telephone**?* | *Do you know her **telephone number**?* → see picture on page A12

telephone² v [I,T] *formal* to talk to someone by telephone **SYN** **call** **THESAURUS** PHONE

'**telephone ,box** *BrE*, '**telephone ,booth** *AmE* n [C] a structure containing a public telephone

'**telephone di,rectory** n [C] a book containing a list of the names, addresses, and telephone numbers of all the people in a particular area **SYN** **phone book**

'**telephone ex,change** n [C] an office where telephone calls are connected so that people can talk to each other

telesales /ˈteliseɪlz/ (*also* **telemarketing** /ˈteliˌmɑːkətɪŋ $ -ɑːr-/) n [U] selling things by telephone

telescope /ˈteləskəʊp $ -skoʊp/ n [C] a piece of scientific equipment shaped like a tube that you look through to make distant objects look larger and closer

Teletext /ˈtelitekst/ n [U] *trademark* a service that provides news and other information in written form on television

televise /ˈteləvaɪz/ v [T] to broadcast something on television: *Is the game going to be televised?*

television /ˈteləˌvɪʒən, ˌteləˈvɪʒən/ n
1 (*also* **tele'vision ,set**) [C] a thing shaped like a box with a screen, which you use to watch programmes **SYN** **TV**: *We need a new television.* | *Turn the television off!* → see picture on page A12
2 [U] the programmes that you can watch on a television: *He's been watching television all day.* | **on television** *What's on television tonight?*

> **Grammar**
> Do not say 'I watched a good programme in the television.' Say *I watched a good programme on television.*

3 [U] the business of making and broadcasting programmes for television: *a job in television* → **CABLE TELEVISION, CLOSED CIRCUIT TELEVISION, PUBLIC TELEVISION, SATELLITE TELEVISION**

COLLOCATIONS

verbs

to watch television *The kids usually watch television after school.*
to see/watch sth on television *Did you see the game on television last night?*
to put the television on *As soon as he gets home he puts the television on.*
to turn the television on/off (*also* **to switch the television on/off**) *Why don't you turn the television off and do something else?*

television + noun

a television show/programme *What's your favourite television programme?*
a television series (=a set of programmes with the same characters or subject) *A new television series is starting in the autumn.*
a television presenter *BrE* (=someone who introduces the different parts of a television show) *She's a television presenter on a breakfast show.*

types of television

national television (=shown all over the country) *The interview appeared on national television.*
satellite/cable television *The games will only be shown on satellite television.*
digital television *Soon everyone will have digital television.*

---

teleworker /ˈteliwɜːkə $ -wɜːrkər/ n [C] someone who works from home and communicates with their employer, customers etc using a computer or telephone —**teleworking** n [U]

tell /tel/ v (past tense and past participle **told** /təʊld $ toʊld/)
1 [T] to give someone information by speaking or writing to them: **tell sb about sth** *Have you told John about the party?* | **tell sb sth** *Tell me your phone number again.* | **tell sb (that)** *She told me she can't come on Friday.* | **tell sb how/where/when etc** *Could you tell me when he left?* | **tell (sb) a story/joke/secret/lie** *She's been telling lies again.* **THESAURUS** EXPLAIN

Grammar
Do not say 'She told to me about her new boyfriend.' Say *She told me about her new boyfriend.*
Do not say 'He told that he was sorry.' Say *He told me that he was sorry.* or *He said that he was sorry.*

2 [T] to say that someone should or must do something: **tell sb to do sth** *He told me to come in and sit down.* | **tell sb (that)** *His doctor told him he should take more exercise.* | **tell yourself sth** *I keep telling myself not to worry.* **THESAURUS ▶ ORDER**

3 [T] to give information in a way that does not use speech or writing: **tell sb (that)** *The machine's red light tells you it's recording.* | **tell sb how/where/who etc** *The survey tells us how young people spend their money.*

4 [I,T] *informal* to tell a teacher, parent etc about something wrong that someone else has done: **[+on]** *Please don't tell on me!* | *I'll tell Dad if you do that again!*

PHRASES

can/could tell to know that something is true because you can see it, hear it etc: **[+(that)]** *I could tell that Jo was in a bad mood.* | *Can you **tell the difference** between the twins?* **THESAURUS ▶ KNOW**

I tell you/I'm telling you *spoken* used to emphasize something: *I'm telling you, the food was unbelievable!*

I told you (so) *spoken* used when someone does something you have warned them not to do, and it has had a bad result: *I told you so – I told you it wouldn't work.*

tell the time *BrE*, **tell time** *AmE* to be able to know what time it is by looking at a clock: *The children are being taught how to tell the time.*

(I'll) tell you what used to suggest something: *Tell you what, call me on Friday.*

tell the truth to say what really happened: *It's always better to tell the truth.*

there's no telling what/how/whether etc *spoken* used to say that it is impossible to know what will happen: *There's just no telling what he'll say next.*

you never can tell/you can never tell *spoken* used to say that you can never be certain about what will happen in the future: *They're not likely to win, but you never can tell.*

PHRASAL VERBS

tell sb/sth **apart** to be able to see the difference between two people or things, even though they are similar: *It's difficult to tell them apart.*

tell sb ↔ **off** *informal* to talk angrily to someone because they have done something wrong: **be/get told off** *Sean's always getting told off at school.*

THESAURUS

tell to give someone information by speaking or writing to them: *Can you tell me how much this will cost?* | *She wrote to tell me that her husband had died.*

let sb know to tell someone something when you know more about it: *Let me know when you arrive and I'll pick you up.*

inform *formal* to officially tell someone about

something: *You must inform your bank if you change your address.*

announce to tell people publicly and officially about something: *The government has announced plans to build 300,000 new houses.*

pass a message on to sb to tell another person the information that has been told to you: *The meeting's been cancelled – could you pass the message on to everyone?*

reveal to tell people about something that was previously a secret: *Markov revealed that he had once worked for the CIA.*

teller /ˈtelə $ -ər/ *n* [C] *especially AmE* someone whose job is to take and pay out money in a bank

telling /ˈtelɪŋ/ *adj* showing what someone really thinks or what a situation is really like: *a telling remark*

telltale /ˈtelteɪl/ *adj* clearly showing something that is unpleasant or supposed to be secret: *the **telltale signs** of drug addiction*

telly /ˈteli/ *n* [C] (*plural* **tellies**) *BrE informal* a television

temp¹ /temp/ *n* [C] someone who works in an office for a short time, doing someone else's job while they are away

temp² *v* [I] to work as a temp: *Anne's temping until she can find another job.*

temper¹ /ˈtempə $ -ər/ *n*
1 [C,U] a tendency to become suddenly angry: *Mark needs to learn to **control** his **temper**.* | *Robin **has** quite **a temper**.* | *I **lost** my **temper** and shouted at them.* | *As a teacher, you have to be able to **keep** your **temper** (=not get angry).*
2 [singular, U] the angry or happy way that you feel: **be in a bad/foul/good temper** *You're certainly in a foul temper this morning.* → **BAD-TEMPERED**
PHRASES
in a temper very angry: *He was in a terrible temper.*

temper² *v* [T] *formal* to make something less severe or extreme

temperament /ˈtemprəmənt/ *n* [C,U] your character, or the type of person that you are: *He hasn't got the right temperament to work with children.*

temperamental /ˌtemprəˈmentl◂/ *adj* disapproving someone who is temperamental changes suddenly from being happy to being sad, angry etc

temperate /ˈtempərət/ *adj* temperate weather is never very hot or very cold: *a temperate climate*

temperature /ˈtemprətʃə $ -ər/ *n*
1 [C,U] how hot or cold something is: **[+of]** *Check the temperature of the water.* | *a temperature of 100°C*
2 sb's temperature the temperature of your body, used as a sign of whether you are ill: *The nurse **took** my **temperature**.*
PHRASES
have a temperature to be hot because you are ill: *Susie has a temperature and has gone to bed.*

adjectives

a high/low temperature *The temperature of the room was too high.*

a constant temperature (=one that stays the same rather than changing) *Snakes can keep their bodies at a constant temperature.*

nouns + temperature

the air/water temperature *The outside air temperature fell below freezing.*

body temperature *A high body temperature can be a sign of illness.*

a rise in temperature *Fish do not like a sudden rise in temperature.*

a drop/fall in temperature *The storm was followed by a drop in temperature.*

verbs

the temperature rises *The temperature rose to 25°C.*

the temperature falls/drops *At night, the temperature falls rapidly.*

tempest /'tempɪst/ n [C] *literary* a storm

tempestuous /tem'pestʃuəs/ *adj* full of anger and strong emotions: *a tempestuous relationship*

template /'templeɪt, -plət/ n [C] **1** a piece of paper, plastic etc that you use to help you cut other materials in the same shape **2** *technical* a computer document that you use as a model for producing many similar documents

temple /'tempəl/ n [C]
1 a building where people in some religions go to pray
2 the area on the side of your head, between your eye and your ear

tempo /'tempəʊ $ -poʊ/ n [C,U] (*plural* **tempos**)
1 the speed at which something happens: *the tempo of city life* **2** the speed at which music is played

temporary Ac /'tempərəri, -pəri $ -pəreri/ *adj* existing or happening only for a short time OPP **permanent**: *a temporary job* | *She was employed on a temporary basis.* **THESAURUS** ▶ SHORT —**temporarily** /'tempərərəli $ ˌtempə'rerəli/ *adv*: *The library is temporarily closed.*

tempt /tempt/ v **1** [T] to make someone want to do something: *He was tempted by the big profits of the drugs trade.* | **tempt sb to do sth** *They're offering free gifts to tempt people to join.* **2** **be tempted to do sth** to feel you would like to do something: *I was tempted to tell him the whole truth.* —**tempting** *adj*: *a tempting offer*

temptation /temp'teɪʃən/ n **1** [C,U] a strong feeling that you want to have or do something, although you know you should not: *I had to **resist the temptation** to slap him.* | *I finally **gave in to temptation** and had a cake.* **2** [C] something that you want to have or do, even though you know you should not: *Having chocolate in the house is a great temptation!*

ten /ten/ *number* the number 10: *Snow had been falling steadily for ten days.* | *I need to be home by ten* (=ten o'clock). | *She's about ten* (=ten years old).

tenacious /tə'neɪʃəs/ *adj* very determined to do something, even when it is difficult —**tenaciously** *adv* —**tenacity** /tə'næsəti/ n [U]

tenancy /'tenənsi/ n [C,U] (*plural* **tenancies**) the period of time that someone rents a house or piece of land

tenant /'tenənt/ n [C] someone who pays rent to live in a room or house

tend /tend/ v
1 tend to do sth to usually do something: *My car tends to overheat.* | *People tend to need less sleep as they get older.*
2 (*also* **tend to sth**) [T] *formal* to take care of someone or something: *farmers tending their cattle*

tendency /'tendənsi/ n [C] (*plural* **tendencies**) **1** if someone or something has a tendency to do something, they are likely to do it: **tendency to do sth** *He has a tendency to talk too much.* | **[+towards]** *Some people may inherit a tendency towards alcoholism.* **2** a general change or development in a particular direction: **There is an** *increasing* **tendency** *for women to have children later in life.*

tender¹ /'tendə $ -ər/ *adj* **1** tender food is soft and easy to cut and eat OPP **tough THESAURUS** ▶ SOFT **2** a tender part of your body is painful if someone touches it **THESAURUS** ▶ PAINFUL **3** gentle in a way that shows love: *a tender look* —**tenderly** *adv* —**tenderness** n [U]

PHRASES

at a tender age young and without much experience of life: *He lost his father at the tender age of seven.*

tender² v **1** [T] *formal* to formally offer something to someone: *Maria has **tendered** her **resignation*** (=said formally that she will leave her job). **2** [I] *BrE* to make a formal offer to do a job or provide goods and services

tender-hearted /ˌtendə 'hɑːtɪd◂ $ -dər 'hɑːr-/ *adj* very kind and gentle

tendon /'tendən/ n [C] a thick strong part inside your body that connects a muscle to a bone

tenement /'tenəmənt/ n [C] a large building divided into apartments, especially in a poor area of a city

tenet /'tenɪt/ n [C] a principle or belief: *the tenets of Buddhism*

tenner /'tenə $ -ər/ n [C] *BrE spoken* £10 or a ten pound note: *Can you lend me a tenner?*

tennis /'tenɪs/ n [U] a game for two people or two pairs of people who use RACKETS to hit a small ball to each other over a net: *Let's **have a game of tennis**.* → **TABLE TENNIS** → see picture on page A9

tenor /'tenə $ -ər/ n **1** [C] a male singer with a high voice **2** **the tenor of sth** *formal* the general meaning or attitude behind something: *the tenor of her argument*

tenpin bowling /ˌtenpɪn 'bəʊlɪŋ $ -'boʊ-/ n [U] *BrE* an indoor sport in which you roll a heavy ball along a floor to knock down bottle-shaped wooden objects SYN **bowling** *AmE*

tense¹ Ac /tens/ adj
1 nervous and anxious → **tension**: *You seem really tense – what's wrong?* | *This has been a tense two weeks.* THESAURUS **NERVOUS**
2 tense muscles feel tight and stiff → **tension**: *Massage helps to relax tense neck muscles.*

tense² n [C,U] a form of a verb that shows whether something happens in the past, the present, or the future

tense³ (*also* **tense up**) v [I,T] to become tight and stiff, or to make your muscles do this

tension Ac /'tenʃən/ n **1** [C,U] the feeling that exists when people do not trust each other and may suddenly attack each other: *an effort to calm racial tensions in the city* **2** [U] a nervous and anxious feeling: *The tension as we waited for the news was unbearable.* **3** [U] tightness or stiffness in a wire, rope, muscle etc: *Muscle tension can be a sign of stress.*

tent /tent/ n [C] a shelter consisting of a sheet of cloth supported by poles and ropes, used especially for camping: *We looked for a place to put up our tent.*

tentacle /'tentɪkəl/ n [C] one of the long parts like arms of a sea creature such as an OCTOPUS → see picture at **OCTOPUS**

tentative /'tentətɪv/ adj **1** a tentative idea or plan is not definite or certain **2** done without confidence: *a tentative smile* —**tentatively** adv

tenterhooks /'tentəhʊks $ -ər-/ n **be on tenterhooks** to feel nervous and excited because you are waiting for something to happen

tenth¹ /tenθ/ adj coming after nine other things in a series: *her tenth birthday* —**tenth** pron: *I'm planning to leave on the tenth* (=the tenth day of the month).

tenth² n [C] one of ten equal parts of something

tenuous /'tenjuəs/ adj a situation or relationship that is tenuous is uncertain or weak: *There is only a tenuous connection between the two events.* —**tenuously** adv

tenure /'tenjə, -juə $ -jər/ n [U] **1** the legal right to use land or buildings for a period of time **2** the period of time when someone has an important job: *during his tenure as chairman*

tepid /'tepɪd/ adj tepid liquid is slightly warm

tequila /tə'kiːlə/ n [U] a strong alcoholic drink made in Mexico

term¹ /tɜːm $ tɜːrm/ n [C]
1 POINT OF VIEW **in ... terms** if you explain or think about something in particular terms or in terms of a particular thing, you explain or think about it from that point of view: *A million years isn't a very long time in geological terms.* | *What do these statistics mean in simple terms?* | *In terms of profits, the project was a disaster.*
2 TECHNICAL WORD a word or phrase that has a particular technical or scientific meaning: **legal/medical/technical term** *I don't understand all the legal terms.* THESAURUS **WORD**
3 RULES **terms** [plural] the rules of an agreement: *Sign here to say you agree to the terms and conditions.*
4 TIME PERIOD a fixed period of time during which someone does something or something happens:

The President hopes to be elected for a second term. | **[+of]** *the maximum term of imprisonment*
5 AT SCHOOL/UNIVERSITY *BrE* one of the periods of time that a school or university year is divided into → **HALF TERM**
PHRASES
come to terms with sth to understand and deal with a difficult situation: *It was hard to come to terms with Marie's death.*
in no uncertain terms in a direct and often angry way: *I told him to leave in no uncertain terms.*
in the long/short/medium term during a long, short, or middle-sized period from now → **long-term, short-term**: *Things don't look good in the short term.*
be on good/bad/friendly etc terms (with sb) to have a good, bad etc relationship with someone: *We're on good terms with our neighbours.*
be on speaking terms to be able to talk to someone and have a friendly relationship with them: *We're barely on speaking terms now.*

term² v [T usually passive] *formal* to use a particular word or expression to describe something: *The meeting could hardly be termed a success.*

terminal¹ Ac /'tɜːmɪnəl $ 'tɜːr-/ n [C] **1** a building where you get onto planes, buses, or ships: *They're building a new terminal at the airport.* **2** a KEYBOARD and screen connected to a computer

terminal² Ac adj a terminal disease cannot be cured, and causes death: *terminal cancer* —**terminally** adv: *terminally ill*

terminate Ac /'tɜːməneɪt $ 'tɜːr-/ v [I,T] *formal* if something terminates, or if you terminate it, it ends —**termination** /ˌtɜːmə'neɪʃən $ ˌtɜːr-/ n [C,U]

terminology /ˌtɜːmə'nɒlədʒi $ ˌtɜːrmə'nɑː-/ n [C,U] (*plural* **terminologies**) the technical words that are used in a subject: *computer terminology* THESAURUS **LANGUAGE**

terminus /'tɜːmɪnəs $ 'tɜːr-/ n [C] (*plural* **termini** /-naɪ/) the station or stop at the end of a railway line or bus service

termite /'tɜːmaɪt $ 'tɜːr-/ n [C] an insect that eats and destroys wood from trees and buildings

terrace /'terɪs/ n [C] **1** a flat area next to a building or on a roof, where you can sit **2** *BrE* a row of houses that are joined to each other THESAURUS **HOUSE**

terraced 'house n [C] *BrE* a house that is one of a row of houses joined together THESAURUS **HOUSE** → see picture at **HOUSE¹**

terracotta /ˌterə'kɒtə◂ $ -'kɑː-/ n [U] hard red-brown baked clay: *a terracotta pot*

terrain /te'reɪn, tə-/ n [C,U] a particular type of land: *mountainous terrain*

terrestrial /tə'restriəl/ adj *technical* **1** relating to the earth rather than space: *terrestrial TV* (=TV broadcast from the earth, not through space using a SATELLITE) **2** living on or relating to land rather than water

terrible /'terəbəl/ adj very bad SYN **awful**: *The food at the hotel was terrible.* | *a terrible accident* | *You're* *making a terrible mistake.* | **[+at]** *I'm terrible at maths.* **THESAURUS** BAD

> **Usage**
> Do not say 'very terrible'. Just say **terrible**.

terribly /'terəbli/ *adv* **1** very badly: *He missed his mother terribly.* **2** *BrE* extremely: *I'm terribly sorry.*

terrier /'teriə $ -ər/ *n* [C] a type of small dog

terrific /tə'rɪfɪk/ *adj informal* **1** very good: *a terrific opportunity* | *She looked terrific.* **THESAURUS** GOOD **2** very big: *Losing his job was a terrific shock.* —**terrifically** /-kli/ *adv*

terrified /'terɪfaɪd/ *adj* very frightened: **[+of]** *I'm absolutely terrified of spiders.* | **terrified to do sth** *He was terrified to stay in the house alone.* **THESAURUS** FRIGHTENED

terrify /'terɪfaɪ/ *v* [T] (**terrified, terrifying, terrifies**) to make someone extremely frightened: *That dog terrifies me.* —**terrifying** *adj*

territorial /ˌterə'tɔːriəl◂/ *adj* [only before noun] relating to land that is owned or controlled by a particular country: *US territorial waters*

territory /'terətəri $ -tɔːri/ *n* (*plural* **territories**) **1** [C,U] land that a particular country owns and controls: *Canadian territory* | *The plane was flying over **enemy territory**.* **THESAURUS** LAND **2** [U] an area of business, experience, or knowledge: *We are moving into **unfamiliar territory** with the new software.* **3** [C,U] the area that an animal thinks is its own

terror /'terə $ -ər/ *n* [U] a feeling of extreme fear: *She screamed in terror.*

terrorism /'terərɪzəm/ *n* [U] the use of bombs and violence, especially against ordinary people, to try to force a government to do something

terrorist /'terərɪst/ *n* [C] someone who uses bombs and violence, usually against ordinary people, to try to force a government to do something → **freedom fighter**

terrorize (*also* **-ise** *BrE*) /'terəraɪz/ *v* [T] to deliberately frighten people by threatening them with violence: *Gangs have been terrorizing the community.*

terse /tɜːs $ tɜːrs/ *adj* said with few words, often in an unfriendly way: *a terse answer* —**tersely** *adv*

tertiary /'tɜːʃəri $ 'tɜːrʃieri, -ʃəri/ *adj technical* third in place, degree, or order

test¹ /test/ *n* [C] **1** a set of questions or exercises for measuring your knowledge of a subject, or your skill: *I've got a history test tomorrow.* | *I failed my driving test twice.* | *The children are doing a French test today.* **2** a medical check on part of your body: *an eye test* | *a blood test* **3** a process used to find out whether something works, whether it is safe etc: *safety tests on diving equipment* **4** a situation that shows how good, bad etc something is: **[+of]** *Today's race is a real test of skill.*

COLLOCATIONS

verbs
to take a test (*also* **to do a test** *BrE*) *All students have to take a test in English.* ⚠ Do not say 'make a test'. Say **take a test** or **do a test**.
to give sb a test *Shall I give you a test on your vocabulary?*
to pass/fail a test (=to succeed in it, or to not succeed) *All the children passed the maths test.*
to do well/badly in a test *BrE,* **to do well/badly on a test** *AmE I didn't do very well in the chemistry test.*

types of test
a biology/history etc test *I got 80% in the geography test.*
a spelling/reading/listening test *Part of the exam is a listening test.*
a written test *The written test involves doing two short essays.*
a driving test *When are you taking your driving test?*

THESAURUS

test a set of questions or exercises for measuring your knowledge of a subject, or your skill: *Our teacher gave us a maths test today.* | *He failed his driving test.*
exam (*also* **examination** *formal*) an important test that you do at the end of a course of study, or at the end of the school year: *Good luck in your exams!*
oral exam (*also* **oral** *BrE*) an exam in which you answer questions by speaking instead of writing: *It's my French oral exam tomorrow.*
practical *BrE* an exam that tests your ability to do or make things: *The chemistry practical will involve doing a simple experiment.*
finals *BrE* the last exams that you take at the end of a British university course: *I worked all through the Easter holidays before my finals.*
quiz *AmE* a quick test that a teacher gives to a class: *Mr. Morris might give us a quiz on that chapter we had to read.*

---

test² *v* [T] **1** to measure someone's skill or knowledge by giving them questions or activities to do: **test sb on sth** *We're being tested on grammar tomorrow.* **2** to use or check something to find out whether it works or is successful: *None of our products are tested on animals.* | *It's time to test our theory.* **3** to do a medical check on part of someone's body: *You need to get your eyes tested.* **4** to show how good or strong something is: *The next six months will test her powers of leadership.*

testament /'testəmənt/ *n formal* **a testament to sth** something that shows or proves something else very clearly: *His latest CD is a testament to his growing musical abilities.*

'test case *n* [C] a legal CASE that makes a principle of law clear and is used to judge future cases

testicle /'testɪkəl/ *n* [C] (*plural* **testicles** *or* **testes** /-tiːz/) a man's testicles are the two round organs below his PENIS

testify /'testɪfaɪ/ *v* [I,T] (**testified, testifying, testifies**) to make a statement in a law court: **[+that]** *He testified that he saw the two men fighting.* | **[+against]** *She refused to testify against her husband.*

testimonial /ˌtestə'məʊniəl $ -'moʊ-/ *n* [C] a written statement about someone's character and abilities

testimony /'testəməni $ -moʊni/ *n* [C,U] (*plural* **testimonies**) **1** a formal statement that someone makes in a law court **2** a testimony to sth something that shows or proves that something is true: *This achievement is a testimony to your hard work.*

testosterone /te'stɒstərəʊn $ -'stɑːstəroʊn/ *n* [U] the HORMONE in men that gives them their male qualities

'test run *n* [C] when you do a particular thing or use a machine before you really need to, in order to make sure that everything works properly

'test tube *n* [C] a small glass container shaped like a tube that is used in scientific tests

testy /'testi/ *adj* impatient and easily annoyed

tetanus /'tetənəs/ *n* [U] a serious disease that you can get when dirt gets into a cut on your body

tether /'teðə $ -ər/ *n* [C] a rope or chain used to tie an animal to something —**tether** *v* [T]: *a dog tethered to a post*

PHRASES

be at/reach the end of your tether to feel that you cannot deal with your problems any more: *I was at the end of my tether because the car wouldn't start and I was already late.*

text¹ Ac /tekst/ *n*
1 [U] words or writing: *a disk that can store huge quantities of text* | *a book with pictures but no text*
2 [C] a work of literature that you study at school or college: *There are three **set texts** this year.*
3 [C] a TEXT MESSAGE
4 the text of sth the exact words of a speech: *Some newspapers printed the full text of the speech.*

text² *v* [T] to send someone a TEXT MESSAGE: *I'll text you later.*

textbook¹ /'tekstbʊk/ *n* [C] a book about a subject which students use: *a history textbook* → see picture at **CLASSROOM THESAURUS ▸ BOOK**

textbook² *adj* **textbook example/case of sth** something that happens or is done in exactly the way that you would expect

textile /'tekstaɪl/ *n* [C] any cloth that is made by weaving threads together: *colourful textiles* | *the textile industry*

'text ,message *n* [C] a written message that you send to someone using a MOBILE PHONE —**text message** *v* [T] —**text messaging** *n* [U]

texture /'tekstʃə $ -ər/ *n* [C,U] the way that something feels when you touch it: *the smooth texture of silk*

textured /'tekstʃəd $ -ərd/ *adj* having a surface that is not smooth

than /ðən; *strong* ðæn/ *linking word, prep* used to compare two things or people: *She's taller than her sister.* | *a car that costs less than £5,000* | *He earns more than I do.*

thank /θæŋk/ *v* [T] to tell someone that you are grateful for something that they have given you or done for you: **thank sb for (doing) sth** *I thanked him for the flowers.* | *They thanked us for helping them.*

PHRASES

thank God/goodness/heavens *spoken* used to say that you are very glad about something: *Thank God no one was hurt!* | **[+for]** *'We're nearly there.' 'Thank goodness for that!'*

thankful /'θæŋkfəl/ *adj* [not before noun] glad that something good has happened: **[+for]** *I was thankful for a chance to rest.* | **[+that]** *I'm just thankful that no one was hurt.*

thankfully /'θæŋkfəli/ *adv* used to say that you are glad that something good has happened: *Thankfully, they all got home safely.*

thankless /'θæŋkləs/ *adj* a thankless job is difficult and you do not get much praise for doing it: *Cleaning is always a **thankless task**.*

thanks¹ /θæŋks/ *informal*
1 used to tell someone that you are grateful for something they have given you or done for you **SYN** **thank you**: *Can I borrow your pen? Thanks.* | *The flowers are lovely. **Thanks very much.*** | **[+for]** *Thanks for the drink.* | **thanks for doing sth** *Thanks for helping out.*
2 *spoken* used when answering someone's question politely: *'How are you?' 'Fine, thanks.'*

PHRASES

no, thanks *spoken* used to say politely that you do not want something: *'Would you like a drink?' 'No, thanks.'*

thanks² *n* [plural] something that you say or do to show that you are grateful to someone: *I did all that tidying up, but I didn't **get any thanks**.* | *He left without **a word of thanks**.*

PHRASES

thanks to sb/sth because of someone or something: *The church now has a new clock, thanks to the generosity of local people.*

Thanksgiving /ˌθæŋks'gɪvɪŋ/ *n* [U] a holiday in the US and Canada in November, when families have a large meal together

'thank you
1 used to tell someone that you are grateful for something they have given you or done for you: *I really liked the book. Thank you.* | ***Thank you very much.*** | **[+for]** *Thank you for the perfume.* | **thank you for doing sth** *Thank you for coming today.*

2 *spoken* used when answering someone's question politely: *'Did you have a nice holiday?' 'Yes, thank you.'*

PHRASES

no, thank you *spoken* used to say politely that you do not want something: *'Would you like another piece of cake?' 'No, thank you.'*

'thank-you n [C] something that you say or do to thank someone for something: **[+for]** *They bought me some flowers as a thank-you for looking after the children.* | *I want to* **say a big thank-you to** *everyone who helped organize this event.*

that¹ /ðæt/ *determiner, pron* (plural **those** /ðəuz $ ðouz/)

1 used to talk about someone or something that is a distance away from you → **this**: *My office is in that building.* | *What's that?* | *Who are those boys over there?*

2 used to talk about someone or something that has already been mentioned → **this**: *I've never seen that film.* | *We met for coffee later that day.* | *Who told you that?* | *Those were her exact words.*

3 used as a RELATIVE PRONOUN instead of 'which' or 'who': *the books that I bought yesterday* | *the man that I spoke to on the phone*

PHRASES

that is (to say) used to correct something you have just said: *Everyone was there – everyone, that is, except Paul.*

that's it *spoken* **1** used to say that something is completely finished: *That's it, then. We can go home.* **2** used to tell someone that they are doing something correctly: *Turn the wheel to the left, yes, that's it.*

that's that *spoken* used to tell someone that a situation will not change: *I'm not going and that's that!*

Grammar

The relative pronoun **that** is often left out when it is the object of a verb. You can say either *She's the woman that I love.* or *She's the woman I love.*

You can use **that** instead of **which** or **who** when you want to say which thing or person you mean *This is the man that/who told the police.* | *Here is the magazine that/which I was telling you about.* **Which** is used especially in more formal writing.

Do not use **that** instead of **which** or **who** if you are simply adding extra information. Do not say 'This is my father, that lives in Dublin.' Say *This is my father, who lives in Dublin.* Do not say 'She owns an old Rolls Royce, that she bought in 1954.' Say *She owns an old Rolls-Royce, which she bought in 1954.*

that² /ðət; strong ðæt/ *linking word*

1 used after some verbs, adjectives, and nouns to start a CLAUSE: *He promised that he would be here.* | *Is it true that you're leaving?* | *There is no proof that he stole the money.*

2 used after a phrase with 'so' or 'such' to say what the result of something is: *I was so tired that I could*

hardly walk. | *They were making such a noise that I didn't hear the phone.*

that³ /ðæt/ *adv*

1 that long/much/big etc used when you are talking about the size of something and showing it with your hands: *It's about that long.*

2 that good/bad/difficult etc as good, bad etc as someone has already mentioned: *I didn't realize things were that bad.*

3 not (all) that much/long/big etc not very much, long, big etc: *It won't cost all that much.*

thatch /θætʃ/ n [C,U] dried STRAW used for making roofs —**thatched** *adj*: *a thatched cottage*

thaw /θɔː/ $ θɔː/ v **1** (*also* **thaw out**) [I,T] if something frozen thaws, or if heat thaws it, it becomes warmer and softer: *The snow was beginning to thaw.* | *Is the meat properly thawed?* **2** [I] to become more friendly or less formal: *Relations between the two countries are beginning to thaw.* —**thaw** n [singular]: *a thaw in relations*

the /ðə; before vowels ðɪ; strong ðiː/ *determiner*

1 used before nouns when you are talking about a person or thing that has already been mentioned or is already known about, or that is the only one → **a**: *the shop next to our school* | *the woman I saw yesterday*

2 used as part of the names of some countries, rivers, oceans etc: *the United States* | *the Pacific Ocean*

3 used before an adjective to make it into a noun that refers to a particular group of people: *a hotel with facilities for the disabled* | *shelter for the homeless*

4 used before a singular noun to show that you are talking about that thing in general: *The computer has changed our lives.*

5 each or every: *He's paid by the hour.* | *How many euros are there to the pound?*

6 used before the names of musical instruments: *I enjoy playing the piano.*

7 used to talk about a part of the body: *The ball hit him right in the eye!*

8 used before a particular date or period of time: *the third of April* | *the 1960s*

PHRASES

the ... the ... used to show that two things happen together and depend on each other: *The more you practise, the better you'll play.*

Grammar

Do not use **the** when you are talking about something in general using an uncountable noun or a plural noun *I like ice cream.* | *Cats often hunt at night.*

You use **the** when you are talking about a particular thing *I like the ice cream you bought.* | *The cats on our street make a lot of noise.*

Do not use **the** before the names of airports, railway stations, or streets *We arrived at Gatwick Airport.* | *The train leaves from Euston Station.* | *She lives in Spencer Road.* Do not say 'the Gatwick airport', 'the Euston Station' etc. You use **the** when you are talking about a particular airport, station, or street without naming it *We arrived at the airport.* | *The train* *was just leaving the station. | She lives in the same street as me.*

theatre *BrE*, **theater** *AmE* /ˈθɪətə $ -ər/ *n*
1 [C] a building with a stage where plays are performed: *Shall we **go to the theatre** this evening?* | **at a theatre** *There's a good play on at the Apollo Theatre.*
2 [U] writing or performing plays as entertainment: *a study of modern Russian theatre*
3 [C] *AmE* a building where you go to see films **SYN** **cinema** *BrE*
4 [C,U] *BrE* the room in a hospital where doctors do operations **SYN** **operating room** *AmE*: **in theatre** *The patient is in theatre now.* → **OPERATING THEATRE**

theatrical /θiˈætrɪkəl/ *adj* **1** relating to the theatre and the performing of plays: *a theatrical production* **2** speaking or moving in a way that is intended to make people notice you: *He let out a theatrical sigh.*

theft /θeft/ *n* [C,U] the crime of stealing something: *Car theft is on the increase in this area.* | **[+of]** *the theft of two valuable paintings* **THESAURUS** **CRIME**

their /ðə; strong ðeə $ ðər; strong ðer/ *adj*
1 relating to or belonging to the people or things that have already been mentioned: *The children closed their eyes.* | *Their daughter is a teacher.*
2 used instead of 'his' or 'her' after words such as someone, anyone etc: *Everybody brought their own wine to the party.*

theirs /ðeəz $ ðerz/ *pron*
1 the POSSESSIVE form of 'they': *When our computer broke Tom and Sue let us use theirs.*
2 used instead of 'his' or 'hers' after words such as someone, anyone etc: *There's a coat left. Someone must have forgotten theirs.*

them /ðəm; strong ðem/ *pron*
1 the object form of 'they' - the people, animals, or things that have already been mentioned: *Has anybody seen my keys? I can't find them.* | *My friends want me to go out with them tonight.*
2 the object form of 'they' - used instead of 'him' or 'her': *If anyone phones, can you tell them to call back later?*

theme Ac /θiːm/ *n* [C]
1 the main subject or idea in a book, film, discussion etc: **[+of]** *Love is the **main theme** of the book.* | *Education has become a **central theme** of this election campaign.* **THESAURUS** **SUBJECT**
2 **theme music/song/tune** music that is always played with a particular television or radio programme

'theme park *n* [C] a place where you can have fun riding on big machines, which are all based on one subject such as water or space travel

themselves /ðəmˈselvz/ *pron*
1 the REFLEXIVE form of 'they': *People usually like to talk about themselves.*
2 used to emphasize a plural subject or object of a sentence: *Doctors themselves admit that the treatment does not always work.*

PHRASES
(all) by themselves 1 alone: *Many old people live by themselves.* **2** without help from other people: *The kids made the cake all by themselves.*

then[1] /ðen/ *adv*
1 at a particular time in the past or future: *I was still at university then.* | **by/until/since then** *He's coming at eight, but I'll have left by then.* | **Just then** (=at that exact moment) *I heard the door open.*
2 used to say what happens next: *We had lunch and then went shopping.*
3 used to say what the result of something will be: *Have something to eat now, then you won't be hungry later.* | *If the others want to go, then I'll go too.*
4 *spoken* used when you are adding something to what has been said before: *He's in bed? Is he not very well then? | If you can't come on Friday, then how about Saturday?* → **but then (again)** at **BUT**[1], **(every) now and then** at **NOW**[1]

PHRASES
now/OK/right then *spoken* used when you have finished talking about one subject and want to end the conversation or talk about something else: *Right then, shall we go? | OK then, I'll see you tomorrow.*

then and there/there and then immediately: *He demanded the money there and then.*

then[2] *adj* [only before noun] used when talking about someone who did a job at a particular time in the past: *George Bush, the then president of the US*

thence /ðens/ *adv formal* from that place: *They travelled to Paris, and thence by train to Rome.*

theology /θiˈɒlədʒi $ θiˈɑː-/ *n* [C,U] (*plural* **theologies**) the study of religion, or a particular set of religious beliefs —**theological** /ˌθiːəˈlɒdʒɪkəl◂ $ -ˈlɑː-/ *adj*: *theological arguments*

theorem /ˈθɪərəm $ ˈθiːə-/ *n* [C] *technical* a statement that you can prove is true, especially in mathematics

theoretical Ac /ˌθɪəˈretɪkəl $ ˌθiːə-/ *adj* **1** relating to scientific ideas rather than practical situations: *a good theoretical understanding of physics* **2** a theoretical situation could exist but does not exist yet: *There is a theoretical risk of an explosion.*

theoretically Ac /ˌθɪəˈretɪkli $ ˌθiːə-/ *adv* if something is theoretically possible, it could happen but has not happened yet

theorist Ac /ˈθɪərɪst $ ˈθiːə-/ *n* [C] someone who develops ideas that explain why particular things happen

theorize (*also* **-ise** *BrE*) /ˈθɪəraɪz $ ˈθiːə-/ *v* [I,T] to think of a possible explanation or reason for something: **[+about]** *We can only theorize about the cause of the fire.*

theory Ac /ˈθɪəri $ ˈθiːəri/ *n* (*plural* **theories**)
1 [C] an idea that tries to explain something → **theoretical**: **[+of]** *Darwin's theory of evolution* | **[+about]** *different theories about how the brain works | One theory is that he was killed by members of a rival gang.* **THESAURUS** **IDEA**
2 [U] the general principles of a subject: *studying economic theory*

PHRASES
in theory something that is true in theory should be true, but may not actually be true: *In theory, I don't work on Saturdays.*

therapeutic /ˌθerəˈpjuːtɪk◂/ *adj* **1** making you feel calm and relaxed: *I find walking very therapeutic.* **2** [only before noun] relating to the treatment of diseases: *therapeutic drugs*

therapy /ˈθerəpi/ *n* [C,U] (*plural* **therapies**) the treatment of a mental or physical illness over a long period of time, especially without using drugs or operations: *He's **having therapy** to help with alcohol addiction.* —**therapist** *n* [C]: *She's been seeing a therapist to help her get over the death of her child.*

there[1] /ðeə, ðə $ ðer, ðər/ *pron* **there is/are/was/ were etc** used to say that something exists or happens: *There's a bank just round the corner.* | *There are two biscuits left.* | *Is there a telephone here?* | *Suddenly, there was a loud crash.* **THESAURUS** HAPPEN

there[2] /ðeə $ ðer/ *adv*
1 in or to another place, not the place where you are → **here**: *I know Edinburgh well because I used to live there.* | **in/out/over/under there** *It's raining out there.* | *Look at that man over there.*

Grammar
Do not say 'We went to there by train.' Say *We went there by train.*

---

2 at a particular point in time or in a situation: *We'll stop there for today.* | *She left her husband, but her troubles didn't end there.*
3 if something is there, it exists: *The next morning the pain was still there.* | *The money's there if you need it.*
4 there is/are *spoken* used when you have just seen something or someone: *Oh look, there's Kate.* → **here and there** at HERE
PHRASES
  there and then/then and there immediately: *They offered me the job there and then.*
  be there for sb to be ready to help someone when they need you: *You know I'll always be there for you.*
  there it is/there he is etc *spoken* used when you have found someone or something that you were looking for: *I'm sure I put my keys here somewhere – oh, there they are.* | *There he is, over by the bar.*
  there you are *spoken* used when you are giving something to someone or when you have done something for them: *I'll just get you the key – there you are.*

there[3] /ðeə $ der/ *spoken* used when you have finished something: *There, that's done.*

thereabouts /ˌðeərəˈbaʊts $ ˈðer-/ *adv* near a particular number, amount, or time, but not exactly: *We'll arrive at 10 o'clock, or thereabouts.*

thereafter /ðeərˈɑːftə $ ðerˈæftər/ *adv formal* after a particular event or time: *He became ill in May and died shortly thereafter.*

thereby Ac /ˌðeəˈbaɪ, ˈðeəbaɪ $ ðerˈbaɪ, ˈðer-/ *adv formal* with the result that something happens: *Expenses were cut 12%, thereby increasing efficiency.*

therefore /ˈðeəfɔː $ ˈðerfɔːr/ *adv* for the reason that has just been mentioned: *The car is smaller and therefore cheaper to run.*

THESAURUS

therefore for the reason that has just been mentioned: *She had more experience and*
---

therefore seemed to be the best person for the job.
so therefore. **So** is less formal than **therefore**, and is more common in everyday English: *The teacher was ill, so the class was canceled.*
thus *formal* therefore: *The new scheme would be more efficient and thus reduce the cost.*
as a result (*also* **as a consequence** *formal*) used when saying that something happens because of a particular situation or action: *As a result of global warming, sea levels appear to be rising.* | *The company's profits were down by 20%. As a consequence, they have announced plans to close one of their factories.*

therein /ðeərˈɪn $ ðer-/ *adv formal* in that place, or in that piece of writing: *We have studied the report and the information contained therein.*
PHRASES
  therein lies sth used in order to say what the cause of something is: *The two sides will not talk to each other, and therein lies the problem.*

thereupon /ˌðeərəˈpɒn, ˈðeərəpɒn $ ˌðerəˈpɔːn, -ˈpɑːn, ˈðerə-/ *adv formal* immediately after something happens and as a result of it

thermal /ˈθɜːməl $ ˈθɜːr-/ *adj* **1** relating to heat or caused by heat: *thermal energy* **2** thermal clothes are made of a special cloth to keep you warm

thermometer /θəˈmɒmɪtə $ θərˈmɑːmɪtər/ *n* [C] a piece of equipment that measures the temperature of something, for example your body

Thermos /ˈθɜːməs $ ˈθɜːr-/ (*also* ˈThermos flask) *n* [C] *trademark* a container like a bottle that keeps drinks hot or cold → see picture at FLASK

thermostat /ˈθɜːməstæt $ ˈθɜːr-/ *n* [C] a piece of equipment that keeps a room or machine at a particular temperature

thesaurus /θɪˈsɔːrəs/ *n* [C] (*plural* **thesauruses** or **thesauri** /-raɪ/) a book that contains lists of words with similar meanings

these /ðiːz/ *determiner, pron* the plural form of THIS

thesis Ac /ˈθiːsɪs/ *n* [C] (*plural* **theses** /-siːz/) **1** a long piece of writing that you do for a university degree: **[+on]** *He wrote a thesis on children's literature.* **2** *formal* an idea that tries to explain why something happens

they /ðeɪ/ *pron*
1 the people or things that have already been mentioned or that are already known about: *Ken gave me some flowers, aren't they beautiful?* | *I called on my parents, but they weren't in.*
2 the group of people who organize something or are in charge of something: *They're going to build a new road round the town centre.*
3 used instead of 'he' or 'she' after words such as someone, everyone etc: *Someone at work said they saw you at the party.*
4 they say/think used to say what people in general say or think: *Nowadays, they say it's wrong to be too strict with children.*

they'd /ðeɪd/ **1** the short form of 'they had': *They'd been missing for three days.* **2** the short form of 'they would': *They'd like to visit us.*

they'll /ðeɪl/ the short form of 'they will': *They'll have to wait.*

they're /ðə; *strong* ðeə, ðeɪə $ ðər; *strong* ðer, ðeɪər/ the short form of 'they are': *They're very nice people.*

they've /ðeɪv/ the short form of 'they have': *They've been here before.*

THICK

thin
thick

thick¹ /θɪk/ *adj*

1 WIDE something that is thick is wide and not thin OPP **thin**: *a thick slice of bread | thick stone walls | thick woollen material | a thick layer of paint*

2 GIVING MEASUREMENT **5 cm/1 m etc thick** used to say exactly how thick something is: *The walls are 30 cm thick.*

3 LIQUID a thick liquid does not have much water in it: *a thick sauce*

4 FOG/SMOKE difficult to see through: *driving through **thick fog***

5 FOREST/HAIR growing close together with not much space in between: *a thick forest | his thick black hair*

6 STUPID *BrE informal* stupid: *Don't be so thick!* —**thickly** *adv*: *She sliced the bread thickly.*

thick² *n*

PHRASES

be in the thick of sth to be in the busiest or most dangerous part of a situation: *US troops are right in the thick of the action.*

through thick and thin in spite of any difficulties or problems: *The family has **stuck together through thick and thin**.*

thick³ *adv* **thick and fast** happening quickly, one after the other: *Letters have been coming in thick and fast.*

thicken /'θɪkən/ *v* [I,T] to become thick, or to make something thick: *The fog was beginning to thicken. | Thicken the soup with flour.*

thicket /'θɪkɪt/ *n* [C] a group of bushes or small trees growing close together

thickness /'θɪknəs/ *n* [C,U] how thick something is: *the different thicknesses of the old stone walls*

thick-'skinned *adj* not easily upset by criticism or insults

thief /θiːf/ *n* [C] (*plural* **thieves** /θiːvz/) someone who steals things: *Thieves broke in and stole some valuable jewellery. | a car thief | a petty thief* (=someone who steals things that are not valuable)

THESAURUS

thief someone who steals things from a person or place: *The thief grabbed her camera and ran off with it.*

burglar someone who goes into houses, offices etc to steal things: *Burglars often break into houses while people are away on holiday.*

robber someone who steals from banks, shops, houses etc, especially using threats or violence: *Two armed robbers hit the man over the head.*

shoplifter someone who steals things from shops, especially by quickly hiding them in their clothes or in a bag: *Store detectives have the job of stopping shoplifters.*

pickpocket someone who steals from people's pockets, especially in a crowded public place: *Tourists are being warned to watch out for pickpockets.*

mugger a thief who violently attacks someone in the street and robs them: *He was beaten up and robbed by a gang of muggers.*

thigh /θaɪ/ *n* [C] the top part of your leg above your knee → see picture on page A2

thimble /'θɪmbəl/ *n* [C] a small hard cap that you put over the end of your finger to protect it when you are sewing

thin¹ /θɪn/ *adj*

1 NOT THICK something that is thin is not very wide or thick OPP **thick**: *a thin slice of bread | a thin layer of paint | a thin summer jacket* (=one made of light material) → see picture at **THICK¹**

2 NOT FAT someone who is thin has very little fat on their body OPP **fat**: *He was tall and thin. | a long, thin face*

3 HAIR if someone has thin hair, they do not have very much hair OPP **thick**: *His hair's getting a bit **thin on top**.*

4 AIR thin air is difficult to breathe because there is little OXYGEN in it

5 LIQUID a thin liquid has a lot of water in it OPP **thick**: *thin soup* —**thinness** *n* [U]

PHRASES

the thin end of the wedge *BrE informal* the first stage of something that will get much worse later: *Are these job cuts the thin end of the wedge?*

be thin on the ground *informal* to be very few: *Good restaurants are very thin on the ground here.*

vanish/disappear into thin air to disappear suddenly and completely in a mysterious way: *He and his kidnappers had vanished into thin air.*

THESAURUS - sense 2

thin someone who is thin does not have much fat on their body: *He looked old and thin. | thin legs*

slim thin in an attractive way: *His girlfriend was tall and slim. | Women had slim waists in those days.*

skinny very thin in a way that is not attractive or healthy: *The little boy was small and skinny. | his skinny arms*

slender *literary* thin in an attractive and graceful way - used especially about women: *A slender* *young woman came in.* | *Her arms were long and slender.*

thin² *v* (**thinned**, **thinning**) **1** (*also* **thin down**) [T] to make a liquid weaker by adding water or another liquid: *You need to thin the paint down a little bit.* **2** (*also* **thin out**) [I] to become fewer in number: *The crowd was beginning to thin out.*

thing /θɪŋ/ *n* [C]
1 something that happens, or something that someone says or does: *A funny thing happened last week.* | *She did a very stupid thing.* | *That was a terrible thing to say.*
2 an object, especially when you do not know what it is, or what its name is: *What's that thing on the kitchen table?*
3 sb's things *especially BrE* someone's clothes or possessions SYN **stuff**: *Pack your things – we have to leave right now.*
4 things [plural] the situation that exists in your life: *How are things?* | *Things have improved a lot since I last saw you.*
5 not see/hear/feel etc a thing not see, hear etc anything at all: *It was so dark I couldn't see a thing.*
6 silly/poor etc thing used to talk about a person or animal: *You look tired, you poor thing.*
PHRASES
do your own thing *informal* to do what you want, and not what other people tell you to do: *During the day we each do our own thing, then we come together in the evenings.*
first thing *informal* at the beginning of the day: *I'll call you first thing tomorrow, OK?* THESAURUS **EARLY**
for one thing *spoken* used to give one of the reasons why you think something is true: *I don't think she'll get the job – for one thing she can't drive!*
not sb's thing *informal* not something that a person enjoys: *I'm afraid sport's not really my thing.*
the thing is *spoken* used to explain what a particular problem is: *I'd like to come, but the thing is, I promised to see Jim tonight.*

thingy /'θɪŋi/ *n* [C] (*plural* **thingies**) *informal* **1** used when you cannot remember or do not know the name of something you want to mention: *What are those plastic thingies for?* **2** *BrE* used when you cannot remember or do not know the name of someone you want to mention: *Is thingy coming?*

think¹ /θɪŋk/ *v* (*past tense and past participle* **thought** /θɔːt $ θɒːt/)
1 [T] to have an opinion about someone or something: [+(that)] *I think it's a brilliant film.* | *I don't think the food here is very good* (=I think it is not very good). | *What do you think of my new hairstyle?* | **think well/highly/a lot of sb** (=have a good opinion of someone) *His teachers seem to think highly of him.* | *The hotel was OK, but I **didn't think much of** the food* (=I didn't think it was very good).
2 [I] to use your mind to decide about something, imagine something etc: [+about/of] *What are you thinking about?* | *I couldn't think of anything to say.* | *I'll be thinking of you tomorrow.* | **Think hard** (=think a lot) *before you make a decision.*
3 [T] to believe that something is true, although you

are not sure: [+(that)] *I think they've gone home.* | *'Is David still here?' '**I think so.**'*
PHRASES
think better of it to decide not to do something that you had intended to do: *He reached for a cigar, but then thought better of it.*
think nothing of doing sth to do something often or easily, even though other people think it is very difficult: *He thinks nothing of driving two hours to work every day.*
think of/about sb to consider the feelings and wishes of another person, rather than just doing what you want to do: *You never think about other people!*
think of/about doing sth to consider the idea of doing something: *We are thinking of moving to the countryside.* THESAURUS **INTEND**
think twice to think carefully before deciding to do something that may cause problems for you: *You should think twice before signing the contract.*

PHRASAL VERBS
think back to remember something from the past: [+to] *I thought back to the years I spent in London.*
think sth ↔ **out** to plan all the details of something very carefully: *Everything has been really well thought out.*
think sth ↔ **over** to consider something carefully before making a decision: *I'll need to think it over for a couple of days.*
think sth ↔ **through** to think carefully about the possible results of doing something: *It sounds like a good idea, but I don't think they've really thought it through.*
think sth ↔ **up** to produce a new idea: *It's a great idea. I wonder who first thought it up.*

THESAURUS

to have a particular opinion
think: *I think the tickets are too expensive.* | *She thinks that you're right.*
believe to have an opinion that you are sure is right, especially about an important subject such as religion or politics: *They believe that it is wrong to do experiments on animals.*
feel to have an opinion that is based on your feelings rather than on facts: *I just felt it was the right thing to do.*

to think about something
think: *I need some time to think.* | *Have you thought about what you're going to do after university?*
consider to think about something carefully before deciding what to do. **Consider** sounds more formal than **think about**: *Before you invest your money, it's important to consider the risks.* | *The committee will meet to consider the proposals.*
give sth some thought to think carefully about something, especially over a period of time: *I've given it a lot of thought and I've decided to accept their offer.*

think² *n* **have a think** to think carefully about something: *I need to have a think about this.*

thinker /'θɪŋkə $ -ər/ *n* [C] **1** someone who is

famous for the work they have done in a subject such as science or PHILOSOPHY **2 an independent/ positive/free etc thinker** a person who thinks in a particular way

thinking /'θɪŋkɪŋ/ n [U] **1** someone's opinions and ideas about a subject: *His thinking on the issue has changed.* **2** when you think about something: *Lance's **quick thinking** had saved her life.* → WISHFUL THINKING

'think tank n [C] a group of people with special skills or experience in a particular subject that an organization or government employs to give advice and suggest new ideas

thinly /'θɪnli/ adv **1** if something is cut thinly, it is cut into thin pieces: **thinly sliced** ham **2** with only a small number of people or things spread over a large area: *a **thinly populated** area*

thinning /'θɪnɪŋ/ adj if your hair is thinning, some of it has fallen out

third¹ /θɜːd $ θɜːrd/ adj coming after two other things in a series: *her third birthday* —**third** pron: *I'm planning to leave on **the third** (=the third day of the month).* —**thirdly** adv

third² n [C] one of three equal parts of something: *Divide it into thirds.* | **[+of]** *A third of these jobs are held by women.* | **one-third/two-thirds** *Two-thirds of the profits are given to charity.*

third 'party n [singular] someone who is not one of the two main people involved in something, but who is involved in it or affected by it

third 'person n **the third person** a form of a verb that you use with 'he', 'she', 'it', or 'they' → **first person, second person**

third-'rate adj of very bad quality

Third 'World n **the Third World** the poorer countries of the world that are not industrially developed. Some people now consider this expression offensive. —**Third World** adj: *Third World debt*

thirst /θɜːst $ θɜːrst/ n
1 [singular] the feeling of wanting or needing a drink → **hunger**: *a drink to **quench** your **thirst** (=get rid of it)*
2 [U] the state of not having enough to drink: *Many of the animals had **died of thirst**.*
3 [singular, U] a strong need or desire for something: **[+for]** *a thirst for knowledge*

thirsty /'θɜːsti $ 'θɜːr-/ adj if you are thirsty, you want or need to drink something → **hungry**: *I'm thirsty – can I have a glass of water?* | *All this digging is **thirsty work**.* —**thirstily** adv

thirteen /ˌθɜːˈtiːn◂ $ ˌθɜːr-/ number the number 13: *They've only sold thirteen tickets so far.* | *When it happened, I was thirteen (=13 years old).* —**thirteenth** adj, pron: *his thirteenth birthday* | *I'm planning to leave on **the thirteenth** (=the 13th day of the month).*

thirty /'θɜːti $ 'θɜːrti/ number
1 the number 30
2 the thirties (also **the '30s, the 1930s**) [plural] the years from 1930 to 1939: **the early/mid/late thirties** *The house was built in the early thirties.* —**thirtieth** adj, pron: *her thirtieth birthday* | *I'm planning to leave on **the thirtieth** (=the 30th day of the month).*

PHRASES
be in your thirties to be aged between 30 and 39: **early/mid/late thirties** *a good-looking guy in his early thirties*
in the thirties if the temperature is in the thirties, it is between 30 degrees and 39 degrees F: *The temperature is in the thirties today.*

this¹ /ðɪs/ determiner, pron (plural **these** /ðiːz/)
1 used to talk about something or someone that is near to you: *My mother gave me this necklace.* | *Where did you get this from?*
2 used to talk about something that has just been mentioned or that is already known about: *I'm going to make sure this doesn't happen again.*
3 used to talk about the present time or a time that is close to the present: *What are you doing this week?* | *We'll be seeing Malcolm this Friday (=on Friday of the present week).*
4 this is ... spoken used to introduce someone to a person they do not know: *Nancy, this is my wife, Elaine.*

this² adv as much as this: *I've never stayed up this late before.*

thistle /'θɪsəl/ n [C] a wild plant with leaves that have sharp points and purple flowers → see picture at **FLOWER¹**

thong /θɒŋ $ θɔːŋ/ n [C] **1** a piece of underwear for the lower part of your body which has a very narrow back part **2** [usually plural] AmE a type of summer shoe held on your foot by a V-shaped band that goes between your toes SYN **flip-flop** BrE

thorn /θɔːn $ θɔːrn/ n [C] a sharp pointed part on the stem of a plant such as a rose

thorny /'θɔːni $ 'θɔːrni/ adj **1 thorny question/ problem/issue etc** a difficult question, problem etc: *the thorny issue of immigration policy* **2** having a lot of thorns

thorough /'θʌrə $ 'θʌrou, 'θʌrə/ adj careful to check every part of something, or doing something carefully so that you do not make mistakes → **thoroughly**: *The police carried out a thorough search of the house.* | *As a scientist, Madison is methodical and thorough.* THESAURUS **CAREFUL** —**thoroughness** n [U]

thoroughbred /'θʌrəbred $ 'θʌrou-, 'θʌrə-/ n [C] a horse that has parents of the same very good BREED

thoroughfare /'θʌrəfeə $ 'θʌroufer, 'θʌrə-/ n [C] a main road through a city

thoroughly /'θʌrəli $ 'θʌrouli,'θʌrə-/ adv **1** very or very much: *Thanks for the meal. I thoroughly enjoyed it.* **2** carefully and completely: *Rinse the vegetables thoroughly.*

those /ðəʊz $ ðoʊz/ determiner, pron the plural of THAT

thou /ðaʊ/ pron a word meaning 'you' which was used in the past

though /ðəʊ $ ðoʊ/ linking word, adv
1 used to introduce a statement that is surprising, unexpected, or different from your other statements → **although**: *Though Beattie is almost 40, she still plans to compete.* | *I seem to keep gaining weight*

even though I'm exercising regularly. | It looks like fun. Isn't it risky, though?
2 used before you add something that makes what you have just said seem less strong or important SYN **but**: I thought he'd been drinking though I wasn't completely sure.

PHRASES
as though used to say how something seems: She was staring at me as though she knew me.

thought¹ /θɔːt $ θɒːt/ v the past tense and past participle of THINK

thought² n
1 [C] something that you think of, remember, or realize SYN **idea**: I've just had a thought. I'll ask Terry to come. | She hated the thought of leaving her son. | **The thought that** it might be illegal didn't worry him. | He put those thoughts behind him. THESAURUS **IDEA**
2 thoughts [plural] a person's ideas or opinions about something: **[+on]** What are your thoughts on the subject?
3 [U] the ideas that people have about a subject: modern scientific thought
4 [U] when you think about something: **lost/deep in thought** (=thinking so much about something that you do not notice what is happening around you) She was staring out of the window, lost in thought. | I've been **giving** your proposal some **thought** (=thinking about it). THESAURUS **THINK**
5 [C,U] a feeling of worrying or caring about something: **[+for]** He acted without any thought for his own safety. | You are always **in my thoughts** (=used to tell someone that you think and care about them a lot).

COLLOCATIONS

verbs
to have a thought Wait a minute – I've just had a thought.
to express your thoughts (=to say what you think) It's sometimes easier to express your thoughts in writing.
the thought crosses sb's mind/occurs to sb (=someone suddenly thinks something) The thought crossed my mind that he had another girlfriend.
can't bear the thought of sth I can't bear the thought of her being angry with me.

adjectives
sb's first thought My first thought was that I must let Dan know.
a sudden thought I was just going out when I had a sudden thought.
a horrible/awful thought A horrible thought struck her: what if she was wrong?

thoughtful /ˈθɔːtfəl $ ˈθɒːt-/ adj **1** serious and quiet because you are thinking about something: a thoughtful expression on his face **2** kind and always thinking of things you can do to make other people happy: It's very thoughtful of you to visit me. THESAURUS **KIND** —**thoughtfully** adv —**thoughtfulness** n [U]

thoughtless /ˈθɔːtləs $ ˈθɒːt-/ adj not thinking about other people or how your actions or words will affect them: a thoughtless remark THESAURUS **UNKIND** —**thoughtlessly** adv —**thoughtlessness** n [U]

ˈthought-proˌvoking adj a thought-provoking film, book etc makes you think deeply about the subject of the film, book etc

thousand /ˈθaʊzənd/ number (plural **thousand** or **thousands**)
1 the number 1,000: a journey of almost a thousand miles | **two/three/four etc thousand** The company employs 30 thousand people. | **thousands of pounds/dollars etc**
2 an extremely large number of things or people: **a thousand** I've driven this route a thousand times before. | **thousands of sth** There are thousands of things I want to do. —**thousandth** n [C]: ten thousandths of a second —**thousandth** adj

thrash /θræʃ/ v **1** [T] to hit someone violently, usually as a punishment **2** [I] to move violently from side to side: a fish thrashing around in the net —**thrashing** n [C,U]

PHRASAL VERBS
thrash sth ↔ **out** to discuss something thoroughly until you reach an agreement: Officials are still trying to thrash out an agreement.

thread¹ /θred/ n
1 [C,U] a long thin string of cotton, silk etc used to sew cloth: a needle and thread → see picture at STRING¹
2 [singular] an idea, feeling, or feature that forms the connection between the different parts of an explanation, story etc: There's a **common thread** linking the different chapters of the book. | Halfway through the film I started to **lose the thread** (=not understand the story).

thread² v [T] to put thread, string etc through a hole: Will you **thread** the **needle** for me?

PHRASES
thread your way through/along etc to move through a place by carefully going around things and people: He threaded his way through the traffic.

threadbare /ˈθredbeə $ -ber/ adj threadbare clothes, CARPETS etc are thin and in bad condition because they have been used a lot

threat /θret/ n
1 [C,U] an occasion when someone says they will hurt you or cause problems, especially if you do not do what they tell you to do: **Threats** were **made against** his life. | **[+of]** threats of violence | Nichols never **carried out** his **threat** to sue. | **death threats** | a **bomb threat**
2 [C usually singular] someone or something that may cause damage or harm to another person or thing: **[+to]** Pollution in the river **poses** a **threat** to fish.
3 [C usually singular] the possibility that something bad will happen: **[+of]** the threat of famine | **under threat** The countryside is under threat from a massive increase in traffic.

threaten /ˈθretn/ v
1 [T] to tell someone that you will hurt them or cause serious problems for them if they do not do what you want: **threaten to do sth** The hijackers

three

threatened to shoot him. | **threaten sb with sth** *I was threatened with jail if I published the story.*
2 [T] to be likely to harm or destroy something: *Illegal hunting threatens the survival of the white rhino.* | **be threatened with sth** *The rainforest is threatened with extinction.*
3 [I] if something unpleasant threatens to happen, it seems likely to happen: **threaten to do sth** *The fighting threatens to turn into a major civil war.* —**threatening** *adj: a threatening letter* —**threateningly** *adv*

THESAURUS

threaten to tell someone that you will hurt them or cause serious problems for them if they do not do what you want: *They threatened to kill us if we didn't hand over the money.* | *She's always threatening to leave me.*
blackmail to force someone to give you money or do what you want, by saying that you will tell embarrassing secrets about them: *Police believe that the girl was blackmailing him and threatening to tell his wife.*
intimidate to make someone feel afraid about what might happen to them or their family, so that they will do what you want: *The gang threw bricks at his windows and tried to intimidate him into moving away from the area.*

three /θriː/ *number* the number 3: *They've won their last three games.* | *We'd better go. It's almost three* (=three o'clock). | *My little sister's only three* (=three years old).

three-di'mensional (*also* **3-D** /ˌθriː ˈdiː◂/) *adj* having or seeming to have length, depth, and height: *a 3-D movie*

threefold /ˈθriːfəʊld $ -foʊld/ *adj* three times as much or as many: *a threefold increase in price* —**threefold** *adv*

three-'quarters *n* [plural] an amount equal to three of the four equal parts that make up a whole: **[+of]** *three-quarters of an hour*

threshold /ˈθreʃhəʊld, -fəʊld $ -oʊld/ *n* [C] **1** the floor of the entrance to a room or building **2** the level at which something starts to happen or have an effect: *I have a* **high pain threshold** (=am able to suffer a lot of pain before reacting to it). **3 on the threshold of sth** at the beginning of a new and important event or period: *We're on the threshold of a new era in telecommunications.*

threw /θruː/ *v* the past tense of THROW

thrift /θrɪft/ *n* [U] wise and careful use of money —**thrifty** *adj: thrifty shoppers*

'thrift shop *n* [C] *AmE* a shop that sells used things, especially old clothes, in order to make money for a CHARITY **SYN** **charity shop** *BrE*

thrill¹ /θrɪl/ *n* [C] a strong feeling of excitement and pleasure, or something that makes you feel this: **the thrill of (doing) sth** *the thrill of driving a fast car*

thrill² *v* [T] to make someone very excited and pleased: *His music continues to thrill audiences.* —**thrilled** *adj: We're thrilled with the results.* —**thrilling** *adj: a thrilling game*

thriller /ˈθrɪlə $ -ər/ *n* [C] an exciting film or book about murder or a crime

thrive /θraɪv/ *v* [I] (*past tense* **thrived** *or* **throve** /θrəʊv $ θroʊv/, *past participle* **thrived**) to become very successful or very strong and healthy: *a plant that is able to thrive in dry conditions* —**thriving** *adj: a thriving business*

throat /θrəʊt $ θroʊt/ *n* [C]
1 the back part of your mouth and the tubes that go down the inside of your neck: *I have a* **sore throat**.
2 the front of your neck: *His attacker held him by the throat.* → **clear your throat** at CLEAR² → see picture on page A2

throaty /ˈθrəʊti $ ˈθroʊ-/ *adj* a throaty sound is low and rough: *a throaty whisper*

throb /θrɒb $ θrɑːb/ *v* [I] (**throbbed**, **throbbing**)
1 if a part of your body throbs, you get a regular feeling of pain in it: **[+with]** *My head was throbbing with pain.* **2** to beat strongly and regularly: *the throbbing sound of the engines* —**throb** *n* [C]: *the low throb of distant war drums*

throes /θrəʊz $ θroʊz/ *n formal* **in the throes of sth** in the middle of a very difficult situation: *Nigeria was in the throes of a bloody civil war.*

thrombosis /θrɒmˈbəʊsɪs $ θrɑːmˈboʊ-/ *n* [C,U] (*plural* **thromboses** /-siːz/) *technical* a serious medical problem caused by a CLOT forming in your blood that prevents it from flowing normally

throne /θrəʊn $ θroʊn/ *n* **1** [C] the chair that a king or queen sits on **2 the throne** the position and power of being king or queen

throng¹ /θrɒŋ $ θrɔːŋ/ *n* [C] *literary* a crowd of people

throng² *v* [I,T] *literary* if people throng a place, they go there in large numbers: *crowds thronging St. Peter's Square*

throttle¹ /ˈθrɒtl $ ˈθrɑːtl/ *v* [T] to hold someone's throat tightly, stopping them from breathing **SYN** **strangle**

throttle² *n* [C] a piece of equipment that controls the amount of FUEL going into a vehicle's engine, making it go faster or slower

through¹ /θruː/ *adv, prep*
1 from one side or end of something to the other: *The train went through the tunnel.* | *I pushed my way through the crowd.* | *We found a gap in the fence and climbed through.* → see picture on page A8
2 from the beginning to the end, including all parts of something: *She slept through the film.* | *I've searched through all the papers but I can't find your certificate.* | **read/think etc sth through** *Make sure to read the contract through before you sign it.*
THESAURUS DURING
3 if you see or hear something through a window, wall etc, the window, wall etc is between you and it: *I could see him through the window.*
4 because of something or with the help of something or someone: *She succeeded through sheer hard work.* | *I got the job through an employment agency.*
5 past one stage in a competition to the next stage: **[+to]** *This is the first time they've ever made it through to the final.*

6 Friday through Sunday/March through May etc AmE from Friday until the end of Sunday, from March until the end of May etc
7 BrE connected to someone by telephone: Please hold the line and I'll **put** you **through**.

PHRASES

through and through completely: a typical Englishman through and through

through² adj **1 be through with sth** informal to have finished using something, doing something etc: Can I borrow the book when you're through with it? **2 be through (with sb)** informal to no longer have a relationship: That's it. Steve and I are through! **3 through train/road** a train or road that goes all the way to another place

throughout /θruːˈaʊt/ adv, prep
1 in every part of a place: Thanksgiving is celebrated throughout the US.
2 during all of an event or a period of time: She was calm throughout the interview. **THESAURUS** ▷ DURING

throve /θrəʊv $ θroʊv/ v a past tense of THRIVE

throw¹ /θrəʊ $ θroʊ/ v
[T] (past tense **threw** /θruː/, past participle **thrown** /θrəʊn $ θroʊn/)
1 BALL/STONE ETC to make an object such as a ball move quickly through the air by pushing your hand forward quickly and letting the object go: **throw sth to sb** Throw the ball to Daddy. | **throw sth at sb/sth** Demonstrators began throwing rocks at the police. | **throw sb sth** Throw me a towel, would you. → see picture on page A11

THROW

throw away

2 PUT STH CARELESSLY to put something somewhere quickly and carelessly: Just throw your coat on the bed.
3 MOVE ARMS/BODY ETC to suddenly move your body somewhere, or part of your body into another position: She threw her arms around him. | **throw yourself down/onto/into etc sth** When he got home, he threw himself into an armchair.
4 SUDDEN VIOLENT MOVEMENT to push someone or something suddenly and violently, or make them fall down: The bus stopped suddenly and we were all thrown forward. | They were **thrown to the ground** by the force of the explosion.
5 PARTY **throw a party** to organize a party: They threw a party to celebrate.
6 CONFUSE SB informal to make someone feel very confused: Her question **threw** me **completely** for a moment. | Everyone was thrown into confusion by this news.

PHRASES

throw sb into jail/prison informal to put someone in prison: He was arrested and thrown into prison.
throw yourself into sth to start doing an activity eagerly: She threw herself into her work.

throw in the towel/sponge to admit that you have been defeated: After two hours of unsuccessfully trying to repair the machine, he threw in the towel.

PHRASAL VERBS

throw sth ↔ **away**
1 to get rid of something that you do not want or need: Can I throw those boxes away?
2 to waste a chance, advantage etc: He had everything – a good job, a beautiful wife – but he threw it all away.
throw sth ↔ **in** informal to include something extra in something you are selling, without increasing the price: The computer is going for only £900 with a free software package thrown in.
throw sth ↔ **on** to put on a piece of clothing quickly
throw sth/sb ↔ **out**
1 to get rid of something: The meat smells bad – you'd better throw it out.
2 to make someone leave: **[+of]** Jim got thrown out of the Navy for taking drugs.
throw up
1 informal to make food come out of your mouth from your stomach because you are ill **SYN** vomit
2 throw sth ↔ **up** to make something fly up into the air: Passing trucks threw up clouds of dust.

THESAURUS

throw to make something move quickly through the air using your hand: Throw the ball over here!
toss (also **chuck** informal) to throw something in a careless or relaxed way: She tossed her coat on the bed. | Just chuck them in the bin.
pass to throw the ball to another member of your team: Nathan passed the ball to Johnny, who tried to score.
hurl to throw something heavy with a lot of force, especially because you are angry: The crowd began hurling rocks at the police.
fling to throw something quickly, especially with a lot of force or in a careless way: She flung her arms around his neck. | Ronnie flung a few clothes into a bag.

throw² n [C] an action in which you throw something

throwback /ˈθrəʊbæk $ ˈθroʊ-/ n [C] something that is like another thing that existed in the past: His music is a throwback to the 1970s.

thrown /θrəʊn $ θroʊn/ v the past participle of THROW

thru /θruː/ adv, prep, adj AmE a way of saying or writing 'through'. Some people consider this use to be incorrect.

thrush /θrʌʃ/ n [C] a brown bird with spots on its front

thrust¹ /θrʌst/ v [T] (past tense and past participle **thrust**) to push something somewhere suddenly or with a lot of force: Dean thrust his hands in his pockets.

thrust² n **1** [C,U] when something is pushed forward with force, or the power used to push something forward **2 the thrust of sth** the main meaning of what someone says or does: *What was the main thrust of his argument?*

thud /θʌd/ n [C] the low sound made when something heavy falls or hits another thing: *He hit the floor with a thud.* —**thud** v [I]

thug /θʌg/ n [C] a violent person who may attack people

thumb¹ /θʌm/ n [C] the short thick finger on the side of your hand which helps you to hold things → see picture at **HAND¹**

PHRASES

give sth the thumbs up/down to say you approve or disapprove of something: *The new housing project was given the thumbs up.*

be under sb's thumb if you are under someone's thumb, they control everything you do: *He's always been under his wife's thumb.*

thumb² v

PHRASAL VERBS

thumb through sth to quickly look at each page of a book, magazine etc

thumbnail¹ /'θʌmneɪl/ adj **thumbnail sketch/ portrait** a short description that gives only the main facts about a person, thing, or event

thumbnail² n [C] **1** the nail on your thumb **2** a small picture of a document on a computer screen

thumbtack /'θʌmtæk/ n [C] *AmE* a short pin with a wide flat top, used for fastening notices to walls SYN **drawing pin** *BrE*

thump /θʌmp/ v **1** [T] *informal* to hit someone or something hard with your hand closed: *I'm going to thump you if you don't shut up!* **2** [I,T] to make a repeated low sound by beating or by hitting a surface: *I could hear my heart thumping.* —**thump** n [C]

thunder¹ /'θʌndə $ -ər/ n [U] the loud noise that you hear during a storm after a flash of LIGHTNING: *a huge storm with **thunder and lightning** | a **clap/crack of thunder** (=one sudden noise of thunder)* —**thundery** adj

thunder² v **1 it thunders** if it thunders, a loud noise comes from the sky after LIGHTNING **2** [I] to make a very deep loud sound: *The guns thundered in the distance.*

thunderbolt /'θʌndəbəʊlt $ -dərboʊlt/ n [C] **1** a flash of LIGHTNING that hits something **2** something that shocks you

thunderous /'θʌndərəs/ adj extremely loud: *thunderous applause*

thunderstorm /'θʌndəstɔːm $ -dərstɔːrm/ n [C] a storm with THUNDER and LIGHTNING **THESAURUS** **STORM**

Thursday /'θɜːzdi, -deɪ $ 'θɜːrz-/ n [C,U] (written abbreviation **Thurs.** or **Thur.**) the day between Wednesday and Friday → see examples at **MONDAY**

thus /ðʌs/ adv formal **1** as a result of something that you have just mentioned SYN **so**: *Traffic will become heavier, thus increasing pollution.* **THESAURUS** **THEREFORE 2** in this way or like this: *Thus began one of the darkest periods in the country's history.*

thwart /θwɔːt $ θwɔːrt/ v [T] to prevent someone

from doing what they are trying to do: *His plans had been thwarted.*

thy /ðaɪ/ determiner a word meaning 'your' which was used in the past

thyme /taɪm/ n [U] a plant used for giving a special taste to food

tiara /ti'ɑːrə/ n [C] a piece of jewellery like a small CROWN

tic /tɪk/ n [C] a sudden uncontrolled movement of a muscle in your face

tick¹ /tɪk/ n [C] **1** the sound that a clock or watch makes every second → see picture on page A7 **2** *BrE* a mark (✔) used to show that something is correct or has been done SYN **check** *AmE* **3** *BrE spoken* a moment: *I'll be back in a tick.* **4** a small creature that sticks to animals and sucks their blood

tick² v **1** [I] if a clock or watch ticks, it makes a short sound every second **2** [T] *BrE* to mark something with a tick

PHRASES

what makes sb tick *informal* the thoughts, feelings, opinions etc that make someone behave in a particular way: *I can't figure out what makes him tick.*

PHRASAL VERBS

tick away/by if time ticks away or by, it passes

tick sb/sth ↔ **off 1** *BrE informal* to tell someone angrily that you are annoyed with them **2** *AmE informal* to annoy someone: *Her attitude is really ticking me off.* **3** *BrE* to put a tick next to something on a list to show that it has been done

tick over *BrE* to continue working at a slow steady rate without producing much: *We kept the business just ticking over until new orders arrived.*

ticket /'tɪkɪt/ n [C]

1 a printed piece of paper that shows that you have paid to do something, for example travel on a train or watch a film: [+for] *How much are tickets for the concert?* | [+to] *He bought a plane ticket to New York.* | **ticket to do sth** *I've got two tickets to see Madonna.*

2 a printed note that orders you to pay money because you have done something illegal while driving or parking your car: **speeding/parking ticket** → **SEASON TICKET**

COLLOCATIONS

types of ticket

a train/bus/coach/plane ticket *My train ticket was only £12.*

a theatre/concert/cinema ticket *You can book your theatre tickets online.*

a one-way ticket (also **a single ticket** *BrE*) (=a ticket to a place but not back again) *I bought a one-way ticket to Chicago.*

a return ticket *BrE*, **a round-trip ticket** *AmE* (=a ticket to a place and back) *A return ticket to Edinburgh, please.*

verbs

to reserve a ticket (also **to book a ticket** *BrE*) *I've booked tickets for the film on Friday night.*

tickle /'tɪkəl/ v **1** [T] to move your fingers gently over someone's body in order to make them laugh: *Stop tickling me!* THESAURUS ▶ TOUCH → see picture on page A10 **2** [I,T] if something touching your body tickles, it is uncomfortable in a way that makes you want to rub your body: *Your hair is tickling me.* **3** [T] to amuse someone: *I was really tickled by what she said.* —**tickle** n [C]

ticklish /'tɪklɪʃ/ adj someone who is ticklish laughs a lot when you tickle them

tidal /'taɪdl/ adj relating to the regular rising and falling of the sea: *tidal forces*

'tidal wave n [C] a very large wave that flows over the land, destroying things

tidbit /'tɪd,bɪt/ n [C] AmE a TITBIT

tide¹ /taɪd/ n **1** [C] the regular rising and falling of the level of the sea: *High tide* (=when the sea is highest) *is at 9 o'clock tonight.* | *You can walk across at low tide* (=when the sea is low). | *The tide was out* (=the sea was low), *so we played in the rock pools.* **2** [C usually singular] the way that events or people's opinions are developing: [+of] *The tide of public opinion turned against him.* | *the rising tide of crime*

tide² v
PHRASAL VERBS
tide sb **over** to help someone through a difficult period, especially by lending them money: *I'll lend you $50 to tide you over.*

tidy¹ /'taɪdi/ adj especially BrE
1 a tidy place, room etc is carefully arranged with everything in the right place → **neat** OPP **untidy, messy**: *a tidy house* | *Try to keep your room tidy.*
2 a tidy person keeps their things neat and clean SYN **neat** AmE: *I'm not very tidy.* —**tidily** adv —**tidiness** n [U]

> **THESAURUS**
>
> **tidy** especially BrE a tidy place, room etc is carefully arranged with everything in the right place: *She keeps the house very clean and tidy.* | *a tidy desk*
> **neat** tidy – often used about a tidy pile or a straight row of things. **Neat** is used instead of **tidy** in American English: *He put his clothes in a neat pile on the bed.*
> **immaculate** extremely clean and tidy: *Melanie had an immaculate apartment on the tenth floor.*

tidy² (also **tidy up**) v [I,T] (**tidied, tidying, tidies**) to make a place look tidy: *Tidy up after you've finished.*
PHRASAL VERBS
tidy sth ↔ **away** BrE to put things back in the place where they should be: *Please tidy your toys away.*

tie¹ /taɪ/ v (**tied, tying, ties**)
1 [T] to fasten something by making a knot in a piece of string, rope etc OPP **untie**: **tie sth to/onto/around etc sth** *Tie this label to your suitcase.* | *She tied a scarf around her head.* | **tie sth with sth** *a parcel tied with string* | **tie sb to sth** *They tied him to a chair.* | **tie sb's hands/feet**
2 [T] to make a knot in a rope, string etc OPP **untie**: *Can he tie his shoelaces?* | **tie a knot/bow** *She put a ribbon round it and tied a bow.*

3 (also **be tied**) [I] to have the same number of points in a competition: [+with] *San Diego are tied with Denver Broncos.* | [+for] *Jones and Beale tied for second place.*
4 be tied to sth to be dependent on something or restricted by a particular situation: *Salary increases are tied to inflation.* | **be tied to doing sth** *I don't want to be tied to doing paperwork all day.*
PHRASES
tie the knot informal to get married: *When are you two going to tie the knot?*

PHRASAL VERBS
tie sb **down** to stop someone from being free to do what they want to do: *I'm not ready to be tied down at my age.*
tie in with sth to be similar to or related to another thing: *How does the new job tie in with your long-term plans?*
tie sb/sth ↔ **up**
1 to tie someone's arms, legs etc so that they cannot move
2 to fasten something together using string or rope
3 to use something continuously, stopping other people from using it: *Don't tie up the phone with personal calls.*
4 be tied up to be very busy: *I'll be tied up all day.*

tie² n [C]
1 a long narrow piece of cloth that a man wears around his neck with a shirt: *He wore a suit and tie.* → **BLACK TIE, BOW TIE,** see picture at **CLOTHES**
2 [usually plural] a relationship between two people, groups, or countries: **close/strong ties** *close family ties* | [+between/with] *economic ties between the two countries*
3 the result of a game, competition etc when two people or teams get the same number of points SYN **draw** BrE: *There was a tie for first place.*

tiebreaker /'taɪbreɪkə $ -ər/ n [C] **1** an extra question in a game or QUIZ, used to decide who will win when two people have the same number of points **2** (also **tiebreak** /'taɪbreɪk/) the final game of a SET in tennis, played when each player has won six games

'tie-in n [C] a product such as a record, book, or toy that is related to a new film, TV show etc

tier /tɪə $ tɪr/ n [C] **1** one of several levels or layers, each one higher than the one in front: *the lower tier of seats* **2** one of several levels in an organization or system: *the senior tier of management*

tiff /tɪf/ n [C] a small argument between two people who know each other well: *Dave's had a tiff with his girlfriend.*

tiger /'taɪgə $ -ər/ n [C] a large wild cat with yellow and black lines on its fur → see picture on page 938

tight¹ /taɪt/ adj
1 fitting part of your body very closely OPP **loose**: *tight jeans* | *These shoes feel too tight.* → see picture at **LOOSE¹**
2 attached or pulled very firmly, so that nothing can move OPP **loose**: *Make sure the screws are tight.* | *She put a belt on and pulled it tight.* | *He had a tight grip on her arm.*
3 strictly controlled: *We have to keep a tight grip on*

TIGER

tiger

cheetah

leopard

panther

spending. | **Security** is **tight** for the Pope's visit.
4 with hardly enough time, money, or space: **a tight schedule/deadline/budget etc** We are working to a tight schedule. | **a tight squeeze/fit** Six in the car will be a tight squeeze. | **money/time etc is tight** Money's a bit tight this month. —**tightly** adv

tight² adv firmly or closely: **Hold tight** to the rail. | I kept my eyes **tight shut**.

tighten /'taɪtn/ v [I,T] to become tighter, or to make something tighter: Richard's grip tightened on her arm. | How do I tighten my seat belt?
PHRASAL VERBS
tighten sth ↔ **up** (also **tighten up on** sth) to make something stricter or more strictly controlled: We need to tighten up the rules.

tight-'knit adj a tight-knit group of people have a strong close relationship with each other: a tight-knit island community

tight-lipped /ˌtaɪt 'lɪpt◂/ adj unwilling to talk about something

tightrope /'taɪt-rəʊp $ -roʊp/ n [C] **1** a rope high above the ground that someone walks along, especially in a circus **2 walk a tightrope** to be in a difficult situation in which you have to be careful about what you say or do

tights /taɪts/ n [plural] a piece of women's clothing that fits closely around the feet and legs and up to the waist SYN **pantyhose** AmE

tile /taɪl/ n [C] a flat square piece of clay or other material, used for covering roofs, floors etc → see picture at **BATHROOM** —**tile** v [T]

till¹ /tɪl, tl/ prep, linking word until: Let's wait till tomorrow. | Don't move till I tell you.

till² /tɪl/ n [C] a machine used in a shop to show how much you have to pay, and to keep money in SYN **cash register**

tilt /tɪlt/ v [I,T] to move or make something move into a position where one side is higher than the other: She tilted her head. | His chair tilted back. —**tilt** n [C]

timber /'tɪmbə $ -ər/ n **1** [U] BrE wood used for building or making things SYN **lumber** AmE **2** [C] a wooden beam that forms part of a structure

time¹ /taɪm/ n
1 [U] the thing that is measured in minutes, hours, years etc, using clocks: measurements of space and time | **period/amount of time** We only have a short amount of time. | **time passes/goes by** Time went by so quickly. | **with/over time** (=as time passes) The landscape changes over time. THESAURUS ▶ PERIOD
2 [C,U] a particular point in time, shown on a clock in hours and minutes: a list giving the times of the exams | **what time is it?/do you have the time?** 'What time is it?' 'It's five o'clock.' | **What time** does school start? | Josh is learning to **tell the time** (=see what time it is, using a clock).
3 [C] an occasion when something happens or when you do something: **How many times** have you been there? | **the first/second/last etc time** That was the last time I saw him. | Tim failed his exam **for the** second **time**. | **last/next time** Next time we go to the cinema, I'll pay.
4 [singular, U] an amount of time: **a long/short time** It happened a long time ago. | I want to **spend** more **time** at home. | Making friends **takes time**. | Don't **waste time** talking about it.
5 [C,U] the particular time when something happens: **at the time/at that time** (=a time in the past when something happened) I was living in Mexico at that time. | **a good/bad/suitable etc time** Is this a convenient time to talk? | **dinner time/bed time etc** Seven o'clock is the children's bath time. | **it's time for sth/to do sth** Come on, it's time for lunch. | **at one time** (=in the past) At one time they were friends.
6 [U] time that is available to do something: **time to do sth** I don't **have time** to talk now. | [+for] There was **no time** for questions. | **waste/save time** I'll go on my bike to save time.
7 **have a good/great time** to enjoy yourself: We had a great time at the party.
8 [C] the amount of time taken by someone in a race: The winner's time was 2 hours 6 minutes.
9 [U] the time in a particular part of the world: The plane arrived at 5.30 local time.
10 **five/ten/many times bigger/more etc** used to say how much bigger, more etc one thing is than another: He earns three times as much as I do. → **at the same time** at SAME¹, BIG TIME², GREENWICH MEAN TIME, LOCAL TIME, PRIME TIME
PHRASES
(it's) about time spoken used to say that something should already have happened: It's about time you got a job!
all the time continuously or very often: He's getting better all the time.
any time (now) spoken very soon: She should be here any time now.
one/two etc at a time one, two etc at the same time: I'll answer questions one at a time.
at times sometimes: At times I wish I didn't live here. THESAURUS ▶ SOMETIMES
by the time when: By the time I arrived, he had left.
for the time being for a short period of time, but not permanently: You can stay here for the time being. THESAURUS ▶ NOW

from time to time sometimes, but not often: *We see each other from time to time.*

in no time very soon or quickly: *We'll be there in no time.*

in time early enough, before something happens: **[+for]** *She arrived in time for dinner.* **THESAURUS** EARLY

in 2 days'/5 years' etc time two days, five years etc from now: *Call back in ten minutes' time.*

most of the time very often or almost always: *Most of the time I'm right.*

the best/biggest etc of all time *spoken* the best, biggest etc that has ever existed: *What do you think is the best film of all time?*

on time at the correct time or the time that was arranged: *You must get to work on time.* | *At least the trains run on time.* **THESAURUS** EARLY

take your time to do something without hurrying: *We took our time walking to school.*

time after time again and again: *Time after time he failed to get a job.*

THESAURUS

a long time

hours/weeks/months/years many hours, weeks, months, or years: *We had to wait for hours at the hospital.* | *It's years since I last saw her.*

ages *BrE informal* a very long time: '*How long have you lived here?' 'Oh, ages.'*

a while/some time a fairly long time: *It's a while since I went to the dentist.* | *It will take some time to mend this.*

a short time

a minute/moment a very short time: *She was here a minute ago.* | *It will only take a moment.*

a second a very short time – used especially when asking someone to wait a short time: *Just a second – I've forgotten my keys.*

a little while/a short while a short period of time, especially a few hours, days, or weeks: *He'll be back in a little while.* | *The painting sold a short while ago for £20 million.*

---

time² *v* [T] **1** to arrange that something will happen at a particular time: *She timed her arrival perfectly.* | **be timed to do sth** *The book was timed to coincide with a new movie.* | **well-timed** (=said or done at a very suitable time) *a well-timed remark* **2** to measure the time taken to do something: *We timed our journey.*

'time bomb *n* [C] **1** a bomb that is set to explode at a particular time **2** a situation that is likely to become a very serious problem: *the population time bomb*

'time-con,suming *adj* taking a long time to do

'time frame *n* [C] the period of time during which you expect or agree that something will happen or be done

'time-,honoured *BrE*, **time-honored** *AmE adj* a time-honoured method is one that has been used for a long time

'time lag (*also* **'time lapse**) *n* [C] the period of time between two connected events

timeless /ˈtaɪmləs/ *adj* always remaining beautiful, attractive etc

'time ,limit *n* [C] the longest time in which you are allowed to do something: *The time limit for the exam is three hours.*

timely /ˈtaɪmli/ *adj* done or happening at exactly the right time

,time 'off *n* [U] time when you are allowed not to be at work or studying: **take/have/get time off** *Can you get some time off for the funeral?*

,time 'out *n* **1** [C,U] a short period during a sports match when the team can rest and get instructions from the COACH **2 take time out** to rest or do something different from your usual job or activities: *The president took time out from his busy schedule to speak to the crowds.*

timer /ˈtaɪmə $ -ər/ *n* [C] an instrument on a machine, used to measure, for example, how long food should be cooked in an OVEN

times /taɪmz/ *prep* multiplied by: *Two times two equals four.*

timescale /ˈtaɪmskeɪl/ *n* [C] the period of time in which something will or should happen: *The timescale for the project is 6 months.*

timetable /ˈtaɪmˌteɪbəl/ *n* [C]
1 *BrE* a list of the times of buses, trains etc **SYN** **schedule** *AmE* **THESAURUS** PLAN
2 a list of times of classes in a school or college → see picture at CLASSROOM —**timetable** *v* [T]

'time zone *n* [C] one of the 24 areas that the world is divided into, each of which has its own time

timid /ˈtɪmɪd/ *adj* shy and not showing courage or confidence —**timidly** *adv* —**timidity** /təˈmɪdəti/ *n* [U]

timing /ˈtaɪmɪŋ/ *n* [U] **1** the time when someone does something or when something happens: *the timing of the election* **2** the skill of doing something at exactly the right time: *Comedy depends on timing.*

timpani /ˈtɪmpəni/ *n* [plural] a set of large drums that are played in an ORCHESTRA

tin /tɪn/ *n*
1 [U] a soft light metal that is often mixed with other metals: *a tin can*
2 [C] *BrE* a small metal container in which food is sold **SYN** **can** *AmE*: *a tin of tuna* → see pictures at BOX¹, CONTAINER
3 [C] a metal container in which food is stored or cooked: *a biscuit tin*

tinfoil /ˈtɪnfɔɪl/ *n* [U] thin shiny metal that bends like paper, used for covering food

tinge /tɪndʒ/ *n* [C] a very small amount of a feeling or colour: **[+of]** *There was **a tinge of sadness** in her voice.* —**tinged** *adj*: *white tinged with pink*

tingle /ˈtɪŋgəl/ *v* [I] if your skin tingles, you feel a slight stinging in it: *a **tingling sensation** in my arm* —**tingle** *n* [C]

tinker /ˈtɪŋkə $ -ər/ *v* [I] to try and improve something by making small changes to it: *Joe was tinkering with his bike.*

tinkle /'tɪŋkəl/ v [I] to make quick high ringing sounds —**tinkle** n [C]

tinned /tɪnd/ adj BrE tinned food is sold in small metal containers SYN **canned**: tinned tomatoes

tinny /'tɪni/ adj a tinny sound is weak, unpleasant, and sounds like it comes from inside a metal container

'tin ˌopener n [C] BrE a tool for opening TINS SYN **can opener** → see picture at OPENER

tinsel /'tɪnsəl/ n [U] thin strings of shiny paper, used as Christmas decorations

tint¹ /tɪnt/ n [C] a small amount of colour

tint² v [T] to change your hair to a slightly different colour

tinted /'tɪntɪd/ adj tinted glass is coloured, so that less light goes through it

tiny /'taɪni/ adj extremely small: tiny fish | The increase was tiny. | I felt **a tiny bit** sad. THESAURUS SMALL

tip¹ /tɪp/ n [C]
1 END the narrow or pointed end of something: [+of] the tip of her nose
2 MONEY an additional amount of money that you give to someone such as a WAITER or taxi driver: I gave him a big tip.
3 ADVICE a helpful piece of advice: [+on/for] He gave me some tips on travelling alone.
4 FOR WASTE BrE an area where unwanted waste is taken and left SYN **dump**: a rubbish tip
5 UNTIDY PLACE BrE informal a very dirty or untidy place: This place is an **absolute tip**! → FELT TIP PEN
PHRASES

on the tip of your tongue if a word or phrase is on the tip of your tongue, you nearly say it but do not, because you cannot remember it or because you decide not to say it: His name was on the tip of my tongue.

the tip of the iceberg a small sign of a much larger problem: The arrest of these gangsters is just the tip of the iceberg.

tip² v (tipped, tipping)
1 [I,T] to move something so that one side is higher than the other, or to move in this way SYN **tilt**: **tip sth forward/back etc** She tipped her hat forward over her eyes. | [+forward/back etc] The seat tips back.
2 [T] to pour something out of a container: **tip sth onto/into etc sth** Tip the mixture into a dish. | **tip sth out** He grabbed her bag and tipped everything out.
3 [I,T] to give a small additional amount of money to a WAITER, taxi driver etc
4 be tipped to do sth to be thought most likely to succeed in doing something: He is tipped to become the next president.
PHRASAL VERBS

tip sb ↔ **off** informal to give someone such as the police a secret warning or piece of information: [+about/that] The police had been tipped off about the robbery.

tip over to fall or turn over, or to make something do this: A bucket had tipped over. | **tip sth ↔ over** A large wave tipped the boat over.

'tip-off n [C] informal a secret warning or piece of information, especially one given to the police about illegal activities

tipsy /'tɪpsi/ adj slightly drunk

tiptoe /'tɪptəʊ $ -toʊ/ n **on tiptoe** standing on your toes, with the rest of your feet above the ground THESAURUS WALK —**tiptoe** v [I]: They tiptoed silently out. → see picture on page A11

tirade /taɪ'reɪd, tə- $ 'taɪreɪd, tə'reɪd/ n [C] a long angry speech criticizing someone or something

tire¹ /taɪə $ taɪr/ n [C] the American spelling of TYRE → see picture at CAR

tire² v [I,T] to make someone feel tired, or to become tired: Even short walks tire her.
PHRASAL VERBS

tire of sb/sth to become bored with someone or something: She soon tired of him.

tire sb ↔ **out** to make someone very tired: Those kids tire me out.

tired /taɪəd $ taɪrd/ adj feeling that you want to sleep or rest: You look tired. | The children were **tired out** (=very tired). | I'm **too tired to** go out tonight.
PHRASES

tired of (doing) sth bored or annoyed with something: I'm tired of her constant criticism.

THESAURUS

tired feeling that you want to sleep or rest: I'll drive if you are tired. | My legs are tired.
sleepy feeling that you want to sleep very soon, so that your eyes start to close: By 11 o'clock, I was feeling sleepy.
drowsy starting to sleep, especially because you are in a warm place, have taken some medicine, or drunk alcohol: The wine had made her drowsy.
exhausted extremely tired: It was an 18-hour journey and we were all exhausted.
worn out very tired, so that you cannot do any more, especially because you have been working hard: Have a break. You look worn out.

tireless /'taɪələs $ 'taɪr-/ adj working very hard and not stopping —**tirelessly** adv

tiresome /'taɪəsəm $ 'taɪr-/ adj annoying or boring

tiring /'taɪərɪŋ $ 'taɪr-/ adj making you feel tired: a long, tiring journey

THESAURUS

tiring making you feel tired: The work was very tiring. | a tiring day at the office
hard tiring and difficult. **Hard** is often used instead of **tiring** in everyday English: Have you had a hard day? | It's a long hard climb.
exhausting extremely tiring: In three days, we cycled 250 miles. It was exhausting.
backbreaking backbreaking physical work is extremely tiring and needs a lot of effort: The labourers were paid $2 a day for backbreaking farm work.

tissue /'tɪʃuː, -sjuː $ -ʃuː/ n **1** [C] a piece of soft thin paper, used for cleaning your nose: a box of tissues **2** (also **'tissue ˌpaper**) [U] soft thin paper used for wrapping and packing things **3** [U] the material forming animal or plant cells

titbit /ˈtɪtˌbɪt/ n [C] BrE a small piece of food or interesting information SYN **tidbit** AmE

tit for tat /ˌtɪt fə ˈtæt $ -fər-/ n [U] informal when you do something unpleasant to someone because they have done something unpleasant to you

titillate /ˈtɪtəleɪt/ v [T] to make someone feel sexually excited —**titillation** /ˌtɪtəˈleɪʃən/ n [U]

title /ˈtaɪtl/ n [C]
1 the name given to a book, painting, play etc: [+of] The title of her novel is 'Zoo'.
2 a book: They publish thousands of titles.
3 a word such as Mr, Mrs, Dr, or Sir, that is used before someone's name
4 the official name of someone's job: Her title is editorial manager.
5 the position of being the winner of an important sports competition: He won the world heavyweight title.

titled /ˈtaɪtld/ adj **1** a titled person is a member of the ARISTOCRACY and has a title such as 'lord'
2 used to say what the name of a book, play etc is: a book titled 'A History of America'

'title-,holder n [C] the person or team that has won an important sports competition

'title role n [C] the main acting part in a film or play, which has the same name as the film or play

'title track n [C] the song on a CD, CASSETTE etc that has the same title as the whole CD etc

titter /ˈtɪtə $ -ər/ v [I] to laugh quietly, especially in a nervous way —**titter** n [C]

T-junction /ˈtiː ˌdʒʌŋkʃən/ n [C] BrE a place where two roads meet and form the shape of the letter T → see picture at INTERSECTION

TNT /ˌtiː en ˈtiː/ n [U] a powerful explosive

to¹ /tə; before vowels tʊ; strong tuː/
1 used before the basic form of a verb to show that it is in the INFINITIVE: I want to go home. | They decided to wait. | **how/where/whether etc to do sth** Show me how to print things.
2 used to show a purpose or intention: I left early to catch the first train.

to² prep
1 used to say the place or direction where someone or something goes: She walked to the door. | He flew to Florida. | We're going to a party. | Which is **the way to** the station? | **to the left/right/north etc** Can you move a little to the left?
2 used to say who receives something or is told or shown something: **say/call/whisper etc sth to sb** Did Liz say hello to you? | **give/pass/show etc sth to sb** Show your ticket to the inspector.
3 used to say where something is touching, facing, or connected: She held her finger to her lips. | He stood with his back to me. | **tie/stick/fasten etc sth to sth** Stick the label to the package.
4 a) as far as a particular point or limit: **from ... to ...** It's 30 miles from here to Toronto. | books on everything from cooking to camping | The water came up to our knees. | Read to page 45. **b)** until and including a particular time or date: **from ... to ...** The banks are

open from 9.30 to 3.00. | I work from Monday to Thursday.
5 used to say what something is connected with: the key to the front door | I don't know the answer to that question. | a danger to health
6 used to say who has a particular attitude or opinion: To some people, £20 is a lot of money. | It looks a bit strange to me.
7 used to compare two things or numbers: I prefer New York to LA. | Brazil won by 2 goals to 1.
8 used to say what state something is in as a result of an action or change: **turn/change to sth** Wait until the light turns to green. | Mix the ingredients to a smooth paste.
9 used to say how much time is left before a particular time or event: It's only two weeks to Christmas. | **ten to four/quarter to six etc** School starts at five to nine.
10 to sb's surprise/horror/relief etc used to say what someone's reaction is to something: To her surprise, they offered her the job.

to³ /tuː/ adv if you push a door to, you close or almost close it

PHRASES
to and fro moving in one direction and then in the other: The rope swung to and fro.

toad /təʊd $ toʊd/ n [C] a brown animal like a large FROG → see picture at FROG

toadstool /ˈtəʊdstuːl $ ˈtoʊd-/ n [C] a wild plant like a MUSHROOM, which can be poisonous

toast¹ /təʊst $ toʊst/ n **1** [U] bread that has been heated until it is brown: **piece/slice of toast** → see picture at BREAD **2** [C] when people lift their glasses and drink because they want to thank someone, wish someone luck etc: I'd like to **propose a toast** to the happy couple.

toast² v [T] **1** to make bread turn brown by heating it **2** to lift your glass and drink with other people because you want to thank someone, wish someone luck etc

toaster /ˈtəʊstə $ ˈtoʊstər/ n [C] a machine you use for making toast → see picture at KITCHEN

tobacco /təˈbækəʊ $ -koʊ/ n [U] the dried brown leaves that are smoked in cigarettes, pipes etc

tobacconist /təˈbækənɪst/ n [C] **1** (also **tobacconist's**) a small shop that sells cigarettes, sweets etc **2** someone who owns or works in a small shop that sells cigarettes, sweets etc

toboggan /təˈbɒɡən $ -ˈbɑː-/ n [C] a curved wooden board, used for sliding down hills that are covered in snow SYN **sledge** —**tobogganing** n [U]

today /təˈdeɪ/ adv, n [U]
1 this day → **yesterday, tomorrow**: Today is Wednesday. | Can we go to the park today? | today's newspaper | We're leaving **a week today** (=on this day next week).
2 the present period of time: today's athletic superstars | Today more and more girls are taking up smoking.

toddle /ˈtɒdl $ ˈtɑːdl/ v [I + adv/prep] informal to walk somewhere

toddler /'tɒdlə $ 'tɑːdlər/ *n* [C] a young child who has just learned to walk

toe¹ /təʊ $ toʊ/ *n* [C] one of the five parts at the end of your foot → **finger**: **your big/little toe** (=your largest/smallest toe) | *I just **stubbed** my toe* (=hurt it by kicking against something). → see picture on page A2

PHRASES

keep sb on their toes to make sure that someone is ready for anything that might happen: *They do random checks to keep workers on their toes.*

toe² *v* **toe the line** to do what people in authority tell you to do, whether you agree or not

toenail /'təʊneɪl $ 'toʊ-/ *n* [C] the hard part that covers the top of each of your toes

toffee /'tɒfi $ 'tɑːfi/ *n* [C,U] a sticky brown sweet food made from sugar and butter

together¹ /tə'geðə $ -ər/ *adv*
1 if people do something together, they do it with each other → **alone**, **separately**: *Kevin and I went to school together.* | *Together they went back into the house.*
2 if you put things together, you join them into one thing: *Mix the flour and the sugar together.* | *Glue the broken pieces together.*
3 if people or things are together, they are next to each other: *The children were all sitting together in a group.*
4 if you keep things together, you keep them in one place: *Keep all your important documents together.*
5 at the same time: *Why do all the bills seem to come together?*

PHRASES

together with sth in addition to something else: *Bring it back to the store together with your receipt.*

together² *adj informal approving* someone who is together is good at organizing his or her life: *Carla seems really together.*

togetherness /tə'geðənəs $ -ðər-/ *n* [U] a feeling that you have when you have a close relationship with other people

toggle /'tɒgəl $ 'tɑː-/ *n* [C] a small piece of wood or plastic that is used like a button to fasten coats, bags etc

toil /tɔɪl/ *v* [I] *literary* to work very hard for a long period of time —**toil** *n* [U]

toilet /'tɔɪlɪt/ *n* [C]
1 a large bowl that you sit on to get rid of waste substances from your body: *I need to use the toilet before we leave.* → see picture at **BATHROOM**
2 *BrE* a room with a toilet: *the men's toilet*

PHRASES

go to the toilet *BrE* to use the toilet

THESAURUS - sense 2

toilet *BrE* a room with a toilet in a house or public place: *Where's the toilet?* | *The toilets are on the first floor.*
bathroom a room with a toilet in someone's house: *He got up to go to the bathroom.*
restroom *AmE* a room in a public place with one

or more toilets: *the ladies' restroom*
lavatory *formal* a room with a toilet in a house or in a public place: *Is there a downstairs lavatory?* | *a public lavatory*
loo *BrE informal* a room with a toilet. **Loo** is very common in everyday British English: *I'm just going to the loo.*

'toilet bag *n* [C] a small bag in which you carry soap, TOOTHPASTE etc when you are travelling

'toilet ,paper *n* [U] soft thin paper used for cleaning yourself after you have used the toilet

toiletries /'tɔɪlətriz/ *n* [plural] things such as soap that you use when you wash yourself

'toilet roll *n* [C] toilet paper that is wound around a small tube → see picture at **BATHROOM**

token¹ /'təʊkən $ 'toʊ-/ *n* [C] **1** *formal* something that is intended to show your intentions or feelings: **[+of]** *He gave her the ring as a token of his love.* **2** a piece of metal or plastic, used instead of money in some machines **3 book/record/gift token** *BrE* a piece of paper that you can exchange for a book, record etc in a shop, given to someone as a present **SYN** gift certificate *AmE*

token² *adj* [only before noun] **1 token woman/black etc** someone who is included in a group to make everyone think that the group has all types of people in it, when this is not really true **2** a token action, change etc is small and not very important, and is usually only done so that someone can pretend that they are dealing with a problem

told /təʊld $ toʊld/ *v* the past tense and past participle of TELL

tolerable /'tɒlərəbəl $ 'tɑː-/ *adj* something that is tolerable is acceptable but not very good **OPP** intolerable: *tolerable levels of pollution* —**tolerably** *adv*

tolerant /'tɒlərənt $ 'tɑː-/ *adj* allowing other people to do or say what they want, without criticizing them or punishing them **OPP** intolerant: *a tolerant society* —**tolerance** *n* [U]: *religious tolerance*

tolerate /'tɒləreɪt $ 'tɑː-/ *v* [T] **1** to accept or allow something, especially something that you do not like or approve of → **stand**: *I will not tolerate this sort of behaviour.* **2** to not be harmed by something: *plants that will tolerate all kinds of weather conditions* —**toleration** /,tɒlə'reɪʃən $,tɑː-/ *n* [U]

toll¹ /təʊl $ toʊl/ *n* **1** [singular] the number of people killed or injured by something: *The death toll has risen to 83.* **2** [C] money you pay to use a road, bridge etc: *toll roads*

PHRASES

take its toll (on sb/sth) to have a bad effect on someone or something over a long period of time: *Years of smoking have taken their toll on his health.*

toll² *v* [I,T] if a bell tolls, it rings slowly

,toll-'free *adv*, *adj* if you telephone a number toll-free, you do not have to pay for the call

tomato /tə'mɑːtəʊ $ -'meɪtoʊ/ *n* [C] (*plural* **tomatoes**) a round soft red fruit eaten raw or cooked as a vegetable → see picture on page A5

tomb /tu:m/ n [C] a place above or below the ground in which a dead person is buried

tomboy /'tɒmbɔɪ $ 'tɑ:m-/ n [C] a girl who likes to play the same games as boys

tombstone /'tu:mstəʊn $ -stoʊn/ n [C] a stone on a GRAVE, showing the name of the dead person

tomcat /'tɒmkæt $ 'tɑ:m-/ n [C] a male cat

tome /təʊm $ toʊm/ n [C] formal a large heavy book

tomorrow /tə'mɒrəʊ $ -'mɔ:roʊ, -'mɑ:-/ adv, n [U]
1 the day after this day → today, yesterday: Tomorrow is Thursday. | What are you doing tomorrow? | **tomorrow morning/night etc** We're meeting for dinner tomorrow evening.
2 the future: the computers of tomorrow

ton /tʌn/ n [C]
1 a unit for measuring weight, equal to 2,240 pounds or 1,016 kilos in Britain, and 2,000 pounds in the US → **tonne**
2 **tons of sth** informal a lot: tons of letters | I've got tons of work to do.
PHRASES
> **weigh a ton** informal to be very heavy: Your bag weighs a ton!

tone¹ /təʊn $ toʊn/ n
1 [C,U] the way your voice sounds, which shows how you are feeling or what you mean: **in a ... tone** 'Hello,' she said in a welcoming tone. | He spoke in an angry **tone of voice**.
2 [singular, U] the general feeling of something: **[+of]** The tone of her letter was rather unfriendly.
3 [C] a sound made by a piece of electronic equipment, especially a telephone: Please leave a message after the tone. | **dialling tone** BrE, **dial tone** AmE (=the sound you hear from a telephone before you dial)
4 [C] one of the many types of a particular colour, which are lighter or darker SYN **shade**

tone² (also **tone up**) v [T] to improve the strength and firmness of your muscles, skin etc: I'm trying to tone up my stomach.
PHRASAL VERBS
tone sth ↔ **down** to reduce the effect of something such as a speech or piece or writing, so that people will not be offended

tone-'deaf adj unable to hear the difference between different musical notes

toner /'təʊnə $ 'toʊnər/ n [C] **1** a type of ink that is used in machines that print or copy documents **2** a liquid that you put on your face to make your skin feel soft and smooth

tongs /tɒŋz $ tɑ:ŋz, tɔ:ŋz/ n [plural] a tool for picking up small things. It has two movable bars that are joined together at one end.

tongue /tʌŋ/ n
1 [C] the soft part inside your mouth that you move and use for tasting and speaking: the taste of chocolate on her tongue | The girl **stuck out** her **tongue** (=put her tongue outside her mouth as a rude sign) at me.
2 [C] a language: **mother/native tongue** (=the first language you learned as a child)
3 [C,U] the tongue of a cow or sheep, cooked and eaten cold → **a slip of the tongue** at SLIP², **on the tip of your tongue** at TIP¹

tongue-in-'cheek adj, adv said or done as a joke, although you pretend to be serious

'tongue-tied adj unable to speak because you are nervous

'tongue-,twister n [C] a phrase or sentence with many similar sounds, which is difficult to say quickly

tonic /'tɒnɪk $ 'tɑ:-/ n **1** (also **'tonic ,water**) [C,U] a clear bitter-tasting drink that you can mix with alcoholic drinks such as GIN **2** [singular] something that makes you healthier, happier, or have more energy

tonight /tə'naɪt/ adv, n [U] this evening or night: Tonight should be fun. | Do you want to go out tonight? | We're meeting at nine o'clock tonight.

tonnage /'tʌnɪdʒ/ n [U] the total weight or amount of something, measured in TONS

tonne /tʌn/ n [C] (plural **tonnes** or **tonne**) a unit for measuring weight, equal to 1,000 kilograms → **ton**

tonsil /'tɒnsəl $ 'tɑ:n-/ n [C] your tonsils are the two small round pieces of flesh at the sides of your throat

tonsillitis /ˌtɒnsɪ'laɪtɪs $ ˌtɑ:n-/ n [U] an infection of the tonsils

too /tu:/ adv
1 more than is acceptable or possible: He was driving too fast. | It's too hot! | **too ... for sb/sth** This dress is **much too** small for me. | **too ... to do sth** He was too ill to travel. | **too much/many** $200 for a room? That's **far too much**. | I drank too many cups of coffee.
2 also: Sheila wants to come too. | 'I'm really hungry.' 'Me too!'
PHRASES
> **all too/only too** used to emphasize that a particular situation exists when you wish it did not exist: This kind of attack happens **all too often** these days.
> **not too** spoken not very: He wasn't too pleased when I told him I was leaving.
> **be too much for sb** used to say that something is so difficult, tiring, upsetting etc that someone cannot do it or bear it: The shock was too much for him.

took /tʊk/ v the past tense of TAKE

tool /tu:l/ n [C]
1 something such as a hammer that you hold in your hand and use to do a particular job: gardening tools | a tool kit (=a set of tools) → **POWER TOOL**
2 something that can be used for a particular purpose: Computers can be used as a tool for learning.

toolbar /'tu:lbɑː $ -bɑːr/ n [C] a row of small pictures at the top of a computer screen that allow you to do particular things in a document

toot /tu:t/ v [I,T] if you toot the horn in your car, or if it toots, it makes a short sound —**toot** n [C]

tooth /tu:θ/ n [C] (plural **teeth** /ti:θ/)
1 one of the hard white things in your mouth, used for biting food: She had perfect white teeth. | Did you remember to brush your teeth? → see picture on page A2

toothache

TOOLS

pliers

hammer

screwdrivers

axe/ax *AmE*

spanner *BrE*/ wrench *AmE*   electric drill

saw

2 one of the long narrow pointed parts of a comb, SAW etc → **have a sweet tooth** at **SWEET¹**, **WISDOM TOOTH**

toothache /'tu:θ-eɪk/ *n* [C] a pain in a tooth
THESAURUS ▸ PAIN

toothbrush /'tu:θbrʌʃ/ *n* [C] a small brush for cleaning your teeth → see picture at **BATHROOM**

toothpaste /'tu:θpeɪst/ *n* [U] a substance used for cleaning your teeth → see picture at **BATHROOM**

toothpick /'tu:θpɪk/ *n* [C] a small pointed stick, used for removing pieces of food from between your teeth

top¹ /tɒp $ tɑːp/ *n* [C]
1 HIGHEST PART the highest part of something **OPP bottom: [+of]** *Write your name at the top of the page.* | **on top (of sth)** *ice cream with chocolate sauce on top* | **at the top (of sth)** *He waited at the top of the stairs.* | **to the top** *I filled the glass right to the top.*
2 UPPER SURFACE the flat upper surface of an object **OPP bottom:** *The table has a glass top.* | **[+of]** *the top of my desk*
3 HIGHEST RANK **the top** the most successful or important position in a company or competition **OPP bottom:** *Everyone wants to get to the top.* | **at the top (of sth)** *United are at the top of the league.*
4 LID the lid or cover for a pen, container etc
THESAURUS ▸ CLOSE
5 CLOTHES a piece of clothing that you wear on the upper part of your body: *She was wearing a yellow top.*
6 TOY a toy that spins and balances on its point
PHRASES
from top to bottom completely and thoroughly: *They searched the house from top to bottom.*
get on top of sb if your work or a problem gets on top of you, it begins to make you feel unhappy and upset: *Don't let financial worries get on top of you.*
off the top of your head *informal* when you give an answer or opinion immediately, without checking that you are right: *Off the top of my head I'd say there were about 50.*

on top winning: *Australia were on top throughout the game.*
on top of sb very near you: *The truck was almost on top of us.*
on top of sth 1 in addition to something: *On top of everything else, I need $700 to fix my car!* **2** completely able to deal with a job or situation: *Don't worry, I'm back on top of things now.*
on top of the world *informal* extremely happy: *When I saw my grades, I was on top of the world!*
over the top too extreme and therefore unacceptable: *The player's celebration of the goal was a bit over the top.*
shout/scream etc at the top of your voice to shout etc as loudly as you can: *She screamed at the top of her voice when she saw the rat.*

top² *adj*
1 [only before noun] best or most successful: *the world's top tennis players* | *She got top marks.*
2 [only before noun] nearest to the top of something **OPP bottom:** *the top floor of the building* | *the top button of my shirt* | *the top drawer of the desk*
3 winning in a game or competition: **[+of]** *Barcelona are top of the league.*
4 top speed the fastest speed a vehicle can move at: *a sports car with a top speed of 155 mph*

top³ *v* [T] (**topped, topping**) **1** to be more than a particular amount: *Their profits have topped $9 million this year.* **2** to be in the highest position in a list of the most successful people or things: *Their single topped the charts for two weeks.* **3** if something is topped with another thing, it is covered with it: *ice cream topped with maple syrup*
PHRASAL VERBS
top sth ↔ **off** *informal* to finish something successfully by doing one last thing: *We topped off the evening with a visit to a local bar.*
top sth ↔ **up** to fill something that is partly empty: *Let me top up your glass.*

,**top 'brass** *n* [plural] the people of highest rank in a company, the army etc

,**top 'dog** *n* [C] *informal* the most powerful or important person in a group: *He's the top dog now, and doesn't have to prove himself any more.*

,**top 'hat** *n* [C] a tall hat with a flat top, worn by men on very formal occasions → see picture at **HAT**

,**top-'heavy** *adj* too heavy at the top and therefore likely to fall over

topic Ac /'tɒpɪk $ 'tɑː-/ *n* [C] a subject that people talk or write about: **[+of]** *Jackie's engagement was the main topic of conversation.* | *a wide range of topics*
THESAURUS ▸ SUBJECT

topical Ac /'tɒpɪkəl $ 'tɑː-/ *adj* relating to something that is important at the present time: **topical issues**

topless /'tɒpləs $ 'tɑːp-/ *adj* a woman who is topless is not wearing any clothes on the upper part of her body

topmost /'tɒpməʊst $ 'tɑːpmoʊst/ *adj* highest: *the topmost branches*

,**top-'notch** *adj* *informal* something that is topnotch is of the highest quality or standard

topography /təˈpɒɡrəfi $ -ˈpɑː-/ n [U] the shape of an area of land, including its hills, valleys etc —**topographical** /ˌtɒpəˈɡræfɪkəl◂ $ ˌtɑː-, ˌtoʊ-/ adj

topping /ˈtɒpɪŋ $ ˈtɑː-/ n [C,U] food that you put on top of other food to make it taste better: *pizza with extra toppings*

topple /ˈtɒpəl $ ˈtɑː-/ v **1** [I] to fall over: **[+over]** *Several trees toppled over in the storm.* **2** [T] to take power away from a leader or government: *The scandal could topple the government.*

top-'secret adj top secret documents or information must be kept completely secret

topsy-turvy /ˌtɒpsi ˈtɜːvi◂ $ ˌtɑːpsi ˈtɜːrvi◂/ adj in a state of complete disorder or confusion

torch¹ /tɔːtʃ $ tɔːrtʃ/ n [C] **1** *BrE* a small electric lamp that you carry in your hand SYN **flashlight** *AmE* → see picture at **LIGHT¹** THESAURUS **LIGHT 2** a long stick with burning material at one end that produces light: *the Olympic torch*

torch² v [T] *informal* to start a fire deliberately in order to destroy something: *Rioters had torched several cars.*

tore /tɔː $ tɔːr/ v the past tense of TEAR

torment¹ /tɔːˈment $ tɔːr-/ v [T] **1** if you are tormented by something, it makes you feel very worried and unhappy: *He was tormented by feelings of guilt.* **2** to be deliberately cruel to someone, and try to hurt them —**tormentor** n [C]

torment² /ˈtɔːment $ ˈtɔːr-/ n [C,U] great pain and suffering, or something that causes this

torn /tɔːn $ tɔːrn/ v the past participle of TEAR

tornado /tɔːˈneɪdəʊ $ tɔːrˈneɪdoʊ/ n [C] (plural **tornadoes** or **tornados**) an extremely violent storm consisting of air that spins very quickly and causes a lot of damage

torpedo /tɔːˈpiːdəʊ $ tɔːrˈpiːdoʊ/ n [C] (plural **torpedoes**) a long narrow weapon that is fired under the surface of the sea and explodes when it hits something —**torpedo** v [T]

torrent /ˈtɒrənt $ ˈtɔː-, ˈtɑː-/ n **1** [singular] **a torrent of sth** a lot of something: **[+of]** *He answered with a torrent of abuse.* **2** [C] a large amount of water moving very quickly in a particular direction —**torrential** /təˈrenʃəl/ adj: *torrential rain*

torrid /ˈtɒrɪd $ ˈtɔː-, ˈtɑː-/ adj **1** involving strong emotions, especially of sexual love: *a torrid love affair* **2** *literary* torrid weather is very hot

torso /ˈtɔːsəʊ $ ˈtɔːrsoʊ/ n [C] (plural **torsos**) the main part of your body, not including your arms, legs, or head

tortoise /ˈtɔːtəs $ ˈtɔːr-/ n [C] a slow-moving land animal that can pull its head and legs into the shell that covers its body → see picture at **TURTLE**

> **Word Choice**: tortoise or turtle?
> **Tortoises** live on land. **Turtles** live mainly in water.

tortuous /ˈtɔːtʃuəs $ ˈtɔːr-/ adj **1** very long, complicated, and difficult: *a tortuous process* **2** a tortuous road or path has a lot of turns and is very difficult to travel along

torture¹ /ˈtɔːtʃə $ ˈtɔːrtʃər/ v [T] to hurt someone deliberately in order to force them to give you information, to punish them, or to be cruel: *Resistance leaders were **tortured to death** in prison.* —**torturer** n [C]

torture² n [C,U] **1** when someone is tortured: *the torture of innocent civilians* | **under torture** *He confessed under torture.* **2** severe physical or mental suffering

Tory /ˈtɔːri/ n [C] (plural **Tories**) someone who belongs to or votes for the Conservative Party in Britain

tosh /tɒʃ $ tɑːʃ/ n [U] *BrE spoken informal* nonsense, used when you believe that something is not true or correct: *What a load of tosh!*

toss¹ /tɒs $ tɔːs/ v **1** [T] to throw something, especially in a careless way: **toss sth into/on/ onto etc sth** *He tossed his jacket on the bed.* | **toss sb sth** *Frank tossed her the newspaper.* | **toss sth to sb** *'Catch,' said Tom, tossing his bag to her.* THESAURUS **THROW 2** (also **toss up**) [I,T] *especially BrE* to throw a coin in the air, and then make a decision according to the side that faces upwards when it comes down SYN **flip** *AmE*: *Let's toss up to see who goes first.*

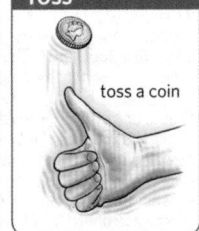

TOSS

toss a coin

PHRASES

| **toss and turn** to change your position a lot in bed because you cannot sleep: *I tossed and turned all night.*

| **toss your head (back)** to move your head back quickly: *She laughed and tossed her head.*

toss² n **1 a toss of a coin** when you throw a coin in the air and then make a decision according to the side that faces upwards when it comes down **2 a toss of his/her head** when someone moves their head backwards quickly and suddenly

tot¹ /tɒt $ tɑːt/ n [C] *informal* **1** a small child **2** *especially BrE* a small amount of an alcoholic drink

tot² v (**totted, totting**)

PHRASAL VERBS

tot sth ↔ **up** *informal* to add together numbers or amounts of money in order to find the total: *The waiter quickly totted up the bill.*

total¹ /ˈtəʊtl $ ˈtoʊ-/ adj

1 [only before noun] including everything: *His farm has a total area of 100 acres.* | *The total cost of the building will be $6 million.*

2 complete, or as great as is possible: *The sales campaign was a total disaster.* | *a total ban on cigarette advertising*

total² n [C] the final number or amount of things, people etc when everything has been counted: **a total of sth** *The city spent a total of two million dollars on the library.* | **in total** (=including everything) *In total, I spent £100.*

total³ v [T] (**totalled, totalling** *BrE*, **totaled, totaling**

AmE) **1** to add up to a particular amount: *Sales totalled nearly $700,000 last year.* **2** *AmE informal* to damage a car so badly that it cannot be repaired

totalitarian /təʊˌtæləˈteəriən $ toʊˌtæləˈter-/ *adj* based on a political system in which the government has complete control over everything —**totalitarianism** *n* [U]

totally /ˈtəʊtl-i $ ˈtoʊ-/ *adv* completely: *I totally agree.* | *The system was totally unfair.*

totter /ˈtɒtə $ ˈtɑːtər/ *v* [I] to walk or move in an unsteady way

touch¹ /tʌtʃ/ *v*

1 WITH YOUR HAND [T] to put your fingers or hand on something or someone: *Don't touch the paint – it's wet!* | **touch sb on the arm/leg etc** *Ricky touched her on the shoulder.*

2 VERY CLOSE [I,T] if two things touch, or one thing touches another, they come together physically: *Their lips touched* (=they kissed). | *He sat on the table, his feet not touching the ground.*

3 EMOTIONS [T] to make someone feel sad, sympathetic, or grateful → **touched, touching**: *The refugees' plight has touched the hearts of us all.* | *She knew that he cared and it touched her.*

4 NOT EAT/DRINK [T] to use, eat, or drink something – used when someone does not do this: *He never touches alcohol.* | *You haven't touched your breakfast.*

5 NOT BE INVOLVED [T] to deal with or become involved with something or someone – used when someone does not do this: *Several lawyers refused to touch the case.*

6 NOT HURT/DAMAGE [T] to hurt someone or damage something – used when saying that someone does not do this: *I didn't touch the kid!*

PHRASES

there's no one/nothing to touch sb/sth (also **no one/nothing can touch sb/sth**) *spoken* used to say that someone or something is the best

touch wood *BrE spoken* said when you do not want your good luck to end **SYN** **knock on wood** *AmE*

PHRASAL VERBS

touch down when a plane touches down, it lands on the ground

touch sth ↔ **off** to make a difficult situation or violent events begin: *The story touched off an international scandal.*

touch on/upon sth to mention something when you are talking or writing: *I'll be touching on that subject later.*

THESAURUS

touch to put your fingers or hand on something or someone: *You must not touch the glass.*
feel to touch something with your fingers in order to find out about it: *I felt his forehead to see if he had a fever.*
stroke to move your hand gently over a person's or animal's body in a loving way: *Most cats love it if you stroke them.*
pat to touch a person or animal lightly several times with your hand flat, to show them that you are pleased, or to comfort them: *'Good dog,' she said, patting him on the head.* | *She patted the little boy's shoulder.*

caress *written* to move your hands gently over part of someone's body in a loving way: *He gently caressed her hair.*
tickle to move your fingers lightly over someone's body in order to make them laugh: *Stop tickling my feet!*

touch² *n*

1 WITH HAND [C usually singular] the action of putting your hand, finger etc on someone or something: **[+of]** *Rita felt the touch of his hand on her arm.*

2 ABILITY TO FEEL [U] the sense that you use to feel something, by putting your finger, hand etc on it: *the sense of touch* | *firm/warm/soft etc to the touch* *The cake should be golden and firm to the touch.*

3 FEATURE [C] a small detail or change that improves something: *the final/finishing touches* *Becky put the finishing touches to the cake.* | *The flowers in the room were a nice touch.*

4 WAY OF DOING STH [singular] a particular way of doing something: *I like a hotel with a personal touch.*

5 A LITTLE **a touch** a small amount: **[+of]** *the touch of sadness in her voice* → **a soft touch** at **SOFT**

PHRASES

in touch (with sb) if you are in touch with someone, you speak or write to them regularly: *Are you still in touch with John?* | **keep/stay in touch** *Bye, Jane! Don't forget to stay in touch.* | *We'll get in touch* (=phone or write to you) *when we know the results of the test.*

in touch/out of touch (with sth) knowing or not knowing the most recent information about something, or what people think about something at the moment: *The government was accused of being out of touch.* | *I try to keep in touch with how the kids today feel.*

lose touch (with sb) to stop seeing, telephoning, or writing to someone you used to know: *I lost touch with Julie after we moved.*

lose your touch to lose your ability to do something well: *Her latest book proves she hasn't lost her touch.*

touch-and-go *adj informal* if a situation is touch-and-go, there is a risk that something bad could happen

touchdown /ˈtʌtʃdaʊn/ *n* [C] **1** the moment when a plane or spacecraft lands on the ground **2** when a player scores by moving the ball across the opposing team's GOAL line in American football or RUGBY

touched /tʌtʃt/ *adj* feeling happy and grateful because of what someone has done: **[+by]** *She was deeply touched by his kindness.*

touching /ˈtʌtʃɪŋ/ *adj* making you feel sad, sympathetic, or grateful: *a touching story*

touchline /ˈtʌtʃlaɪn/ *n* [C] one of the two lines that mark the longer sides of a sports playing area, especially in football

touchstone /ˈtʌtʃstəʊn $ -stoʊn/ *n* [C] something used as a test for whether something is good or not

touchy /ˈtʌtʃi/ *adj* **1** easily upset or annoyed: *Don't be so touchy!* **2** **touchy subject/question etc** a subject that might upset someone, so you should be careful when you talk about it

tough /tʌf/ adj

1 **DIFFICULT** difficult or involving problems: *It was a tough job.* | *They asked some **tough questions**.* | *Recently she's **had a tough time**.* | *It's tough being married to a cop.* | **be tough on sb** (=make things difficult for someone) *The divorce was tough on the kids.* **THESAURUS** DIFFICULT

2 **STRONG PERSON** a tough person is strong or determined, and not easily upset: *Bruce Willis plays the part of a tough cop.* | *a gang of teenage boys, trying to look tough* | *a tough businesswoman*

3 **STRICT** very strict: **[+on/with]** *The government said it was going to **get tough on** crime.* | *tough immigration laws*

4 **CLOTH/MATERIAL** tough material is not easily broken or damaged: *a tough waterproof jacket* **THESAURUS** STRONG

5 **MEAT** tough food, especially meat, is difficult to cut and eat **OPP** **tender**: *The steak was a bit tough.* **THESAURUS** HARD —**toughness** n [U]

PHRASES

tough!/tough luck! *spoken* used when a bad situation affecting someone cannot or will not be changed, and you do not care: *If you don't like it, tough!*

toughen /ˈtʌfən/ (also **toughen up**) v [I,T] to become stronger, or to make someone or something stronger: *The army toughened him up.*

toupee /ˈtuːpeɪ $ tuːˈpeɪ/ n [C] a small WIG

tour¹ /tʊə $ tʊr/ n [C]

1 a journey for pleasure in which you visit several different towns, areas etc: **[+of/around/round]** *We went on a 14-day tour of Egypt.* | *a walking/cycling/sightseeing etc tour a coach tour of Italy*

2 a short trip around a place to see it: **[+of/around/round]** *Shall I **give** you **a tour** of the house?* | *We **had a guided tour** of the cathedral* (=when someone shows you around a place and tells you about it).

3 a journey made by musicians, a sports team etc to perform or play in different places: **[+of]** *the cricket team's tour of India* | **on tour** *The group **went on tour** in America.* → **PACKAGE TOUR**

tour² v [I,T] to travel around an area to visit it or perform in different places there: *A few of us decided to tour the Greek islands.* **THESAURUS** TRAVEL

tourism /ˈtʊərɪzəm $ ˈtʊr-/ n [U] the business of providing people who are on holiday with places to stay, things to do etc: *The island depends on tourism for most of its income.* | *Morocco is still unspoilt by **mass tourism*** (=large numbers of tourists).

tourist /ˈtʊərɪst $ ˈtʊr-/ n [C] someone who is visiting a country or place for pleasure: *Oxford's full of tourists in the summer.* | *the **tourist industry*** | *Italy has so many **tourist attractions*** (=things that tourists want to see).

Usage

If you want to say that a place is popular with tourists, do not say that it is 'touristic'. This word does not exist in English.

Do not say 'Venice is a very touristic place.' Say *Venice is very popular with tourists.* or *Venice is a very popular tourist destination.*

tournament /ˈtʊənəmənt, ˈtɔː- $ ˈtɜːr-, ˈtʊr-/ n [C] a competition in which many players compete against each other until there is one winner: *a tennis tournament*

tourniquet /ˈtʊənɪkeɪ, ˈtɔː- $ ˈtɜːrnɪkət, ˈtʊr-/ n [C] a band of cloth that you twist tightly around an injured arm or leg to make it stop BLEEDing

tousled /ˈtaʊzəld/ adj tousled hair looks untidy

tout¹ /taʊt/ v [T] to praise something or someone in order to persuade people that they are good: **be touted as sth** *He is being touted as a possible future Wimbledon champion.*

tout² (also **ticket tout**) n [C] BrE someone who buys tickets for a concert, sports match etc and sells them at a higher price, usually near the street near a sports ground, theatre etc **SYN** **scalper** AmE

tow¹ /təʊ $ toʊ/ v [T] if one vehicle or ship tows another one, it pulls the other one along behind it: *Our car had to be towed away.* → see picture at **PULL¹** **THESAURUS** PULL

tow² n [singular, U] when a vehicle or ship is pulled somewhere by another vehicle or ship

PHRASES

in tow following closely behind someone: *Mattie arrived with her children in tow.*

towards /təˈwɔːdz $ tɔːrdz, twɔːrdz/ (also **toward** AmE /təˈwɔːd $ tɔːrd, twɔːrd/) prep

1 moving, facing, or pointing in a particular direction: *I saw Tim coming towards me.* | *She stood with her back towards me.* → see picture on page A8

2 used to say that someone is involved in a process that will lead to something: *Britain was moving towards war.* | *the first steps towards an agreement*

3 your attitude towards something or someone is how you feel about them or treat them: **Attitudes towards** *divorce have changed.* | *They were very sympathetic towards me at work.*

4 in order to help pay for something: *Mum gave me £500 towards a car.* | *The money from the sale **went towards** new computers.*

5 near a particular time or place: *I often feel tired toward 5 o'clock.* | *It's cooler towards the coast.*

towel /ˈtaʊəl/ n [C] a piece of cloth used for drying your skin: *She rubbed herself dry with a towel.* | **bath/beach/hand towel** → see picture at **BATHROOM** → **SANITARY TOWEL, TEA TOWEL, throw in the towel at THROW¹**

tower¹ /ˈtaʊə $ -ər/ n [C] a tall narrow building, or a tall narrow part of a castle, church etc: *the Eiffel Tower* | *a castle with four towers* | *a **church tower***

PHRASES

a tower of strength someone who gives you a lot of help, sympathy etc when you are in a difficult situation: *My mother has been a tower of strength these last few months.*

tower² v [I] to be much taller than someone or something else that is near: **[+over/above]** *The teacher towered above him.* | *the towering cliffs*

tower block n [C] BrE a tall building that contains apartments or offices **SYN** **high-rise** AmE

town /taʊn/ n
1 [C,U] a place that has many houses, shops, and offices but is smaller than a city: *a little town on the coast* | **[+of]** *the town of Bridgwater* | **in/into town** (=in or into the centre of a town, where the shops, restaurants etc are) *We had lunch in town.*
THESAURUS CITY
2 [singular] all the people who live in a town: *The whole town watched the procession.*
3 [U] *especially AmE* the town or city where you live: *Jodie's in town this week.* | *He left town yesterday.* →
GHOST TOWN, SHANTY TOWN
PHRASES
go to town (on sth) *informal* to spend a lot of money, time, or effort on something: *They really went to town on the decorations.*
on the town *informal* if you go out on the town, you go to a restaurant, bar, theatre etc and enjoy yourself: *They celebrated with a night on the town.*

COLLOCATIONS

types of town

a small town *The film is set in a small town in America.*
a quiet town (=without many people or much activity) *The town is much quieter at this time of year.*
a busy/bustling town *It's a very attractive and busy little town.*
a big/major town *Our bank has branches in most major towns and cities.*
a market town (=a town in Britain where there is a regular outdoor market) *Ashbourne is a pretty old market town.*
a seaside town *The pretty seaside town of Lyme Regis is on the south coast.*
a historic/ancient town *the historic town of Battle, near Hastings*
the old town (=the part of a town that was built a long time ago) *We had a look around the historic old town.*
sb's home town (=the town where someone comes from) *She went back to her home town of Leeds.*

town 'hall n [C] a public building used for a town's local government

townspeople /ˈtaʊnzpiːpəl/ (*also* **townsfolk** /ˈtaʊnzfəʊk $ -foʊk/) n [plural] all the people who live in a particular town

toxic /ˈtɒksɪk $ ˈtɑːk-/ adj poisonous: **toxic chemicals/substances/gases etc** | *toxic waste* (=from industry) **THESAURUS** DANGEROUS

toxin /ˈtɒksɪn $ ˈtɑːk-/ n [C] *technical* a poisonous substance

toy¹ /tɔɪ/ n [C] a thing for children to play with: *Anna was playing with her toys.* | *toy gun/soldier/truck etc* *a new toy car* | **soft/cuddly toy** *BrE* (=a toy that is like an animal, covered with fur)

toy² v
PHRASAL VERBS
toy with sth **1** to think about an idea, but not very seriously: *She had toyed with the idea of becoming an*

actress. **2** to move an object or food around rather than using it or eating it: *Roy toyed with his pen before he spoke.*

'toy boy n [C] *informal humorous* a woman's boyfriend who is much younger than she is

trace¹ Ac /treɪs/ v [T] **1** to find someone or something that has disappeared by searching for them carefully: *Police are trying to trace her husband.* **2** to find out where and when something began or how something has developed: **trace sth (back) to sth** *He traced his family history back to the 17th century.* | *The book traces the development of trade.* **3** to copy something by putting thin paper over it and drawing the lines that you can see through the paper **THESAURUS** DRAW

trace² Ac n **1** [C,U] a small sign that shows that someone or something has been in a place: **[+of]** *We found no trace of them on the island.* | **disappear/vanish without (a) trace** (=disappear completely) *The plane vanished without a trace.* **2** [C] a very small amount of something, which is difficult to notice: **[+of]** *Traces of the drug were found in his body.*

track¹ /træk/ n
1 **ROAD** [C] a narrow road or path with a rough surface: *a steep mountain track* **THESAURUS** ROAD
2 **MARKS ON GROUND** **tracks** [plural] marks on the ground made by a moving animal, person, or vehicle: *Ned followed the tracks of the fox in the snow.*
3 **FOR RACES** [C] a circular path or road used by people, cars etc for races
4 **RAILWAY** [C] the two metal lines that a train travels on **SYN** **railway line**: *Never try to cross the track.*
5 **ON CD/ALBUM** [C] one of the songs or pieces of music on a record, CD etc: *the best track on the album*
6 **SPORT OF RUNNING** [U] *especially AmE* the sport of running on a race track: *track events* → **FAST TRACK, TITLE TRACK**
PHRASES
keep/lose track of sth to know or not know the present state or position of something, when it keeps changing: *I can never keep track of how old their kids are.* | *I'm late. I lost track of the time.*
on track developing in the right way and likely to be successful: *I want to get my career back on track.*
be on the right/wrong track to be doing something in a way that is likely to be successful or unsuccessful: *Our profits are up, so we're on the right track.*

track² v [T] to follow someone or something by looking for signs of their movement, or by using special electronic equipment: *The whales were tracked across the Atlantic.*
PHRASAL VERBS
track sb/sth ↔ **down** to find someone or something by searching for a long time: *Detectives finally tracked her down.* **THESAURUS** FIND

track and 'field n [U] *especially AmE* all sports that involve running races, jumping, and throwing things **SYN** **athletics** *BrE*

'track ,record n [singular] the things that a person,

organization etc has done in the past which show how good they are at doing something

tracksuit /'træksu:t, -sju:t $ -su:t/ n [C] BrE loose trousers and a matching jacket or SWEATER, worn especially for sport → see picture at CLOTHES

tract /trækt/ n [C] a large area of land

traction /'trækʃən/ n [U] **1** the type of power needed to make a vehicle move, or to pull a heavy load **2** the force that prevents a wheel sliding on a surface **3** the process of treating a broken bone with special medical equipment that pulls it

tractor /'træktə $ -ər/ n [C] a strong vehicle with large wheels, used for pulling farm equipment

trade¹ /treɪd/ n
1 [U] the activity of buying and selling goods, especially from or to another country → **business, commerce**: [+with/between] They hope to increase trade with China. | trade between the two countries | [+in] the trade in cotton, sugar, and tobacco | **international trade** | The local shop doesn't seem to **do** much **trade** (=do much business).
2 the hotel/retail/motor etc trade a particular kind of business → **industry**: My first job was in the motor trade.
3 [C,U] a particular job, especially one needing skill with your hands: All my sons **learnt a trade**. | **by trade** Joe's a plumber by trade (=that is his job). → **FREE TRADE**

trade² v [I,T]
1 to buy or sell goods or services: [+with] Then India began trading with Europe. | [+in] The company traded in silk and tea. | Over a million shares were traded during the day.
2 AmE to exchange something you have for something another person has SYN **swap** BrE: We traded necklaces. | **trade sth for sth** He traded the cigarettes for food. —**trading** n [U]: the Christmas trading period

PHRASAL VERBS
trade sth ↔ **in** to give something that you own as part of the payment when you buy something new: [+for] I traded my Chevy in for a Honda.

'trade-in n [C] AmE a used car, piece of equipment etc that you give to the company from which you buy a new one, as part of the payment

trademark /'treɪdmɑːk $ -mɑːrk/ n [C] a special name, mark, or word on a product that shows it is made by a particular company

'trade name n [C] a name given to a particular product, that helps you recognize it from other similar products SYN **brand name**

'trade-off n [C] a balance between two very different things: [+between] There is a trade-off between the risks and the benefits involved.

trader /'treɪdə $ -ər/ n [C] someone who buys and sells goods, or STOCKS and SHARES

tradesman /'treɪdzmən/ n [C] (plural tradesmen /-mən/) BrE someone who brings goods to people's houses to sell, or who has a shop

trade 'union n [C] BrE an organization that represents the workers in a particular job, especially in meetings with employers SYN **union**

tradition /trə'dɪʃən/ n [C,U] a custom, belief, or way of doing something that has existed for a long time: The people are very proud of their traditions. | [+of] the Greek tradition of hospitality | **by tradition** By tradition, the oldest son inherited everything.

COLLOCATIONS

adjectives

a long tradition (=something that has been done for a long time) In Norway there is a long tradition of building with wood.

a strong tradition Spain has a strong tradition of small local shops.

an old/ancient tradition China's many ancient traditions

a family tradition It's a family tradition that we all get together once a year.

a local tradition There is a local tradition of decorating the well with flowers.

a cultural/religious tradition According to Mexican cultural tradition, refusing a gift is an insult.

verbs

to follow a tradition (=to do what has been done before) He didn't want to follow the family tradition of joining the navy.

to carry on/maintain a tradition (=to make a tradition continue) Both brothers carried on the tradition of cloth making.

traditional Ac /trə'dɪʃənəl/ adj relating to the traditions of a country or group of people: traditional Italian cooking | a **traditional way of life** | It's **traditional** to have a party after the wedding. —**traditionally** adv

traditionalist Ac /trə'dɪʃənəlɪst/ n [C] someone who likes traditional ways of doing things and does not like modern ones

traffic /'træfɪk/ n [U]
1 the vehicles moving along a road: On Sundays, there's usually less traffic on the roads. | Come on – we're holding up the traffic.
2 the movement of planes, ships etc from one place to another: air traffic control
3 the buying and selling of illegal drugs, weapons etc

COLLOCATIONS

verbs

to be stuck in traffic (also **to be held up in traffic**) I was stuck in traffic on the motorway for hours.

to avoid/miss the traffic We should leave early to avoid the traffic.

types of traffic

heavy/light traffic (=a lot of vehicles/not many vehicles) Heavy traffic made the journey very slow.

rush-hour traffic (=traffic at the time when a lot of people are going to or from work) We got stuck in rush-hour traffic.

bad/terrible traffic The traffic is really bad in town today.

traffic circle

> **traffic + noun**
> **a traffic jam** (=a line of cars that have stopped, or are moving very slowly) *I was sitting in a traffic jam for 45 minutes.*
> **a traffic accident** *We are getting reports of a bad traffic accident near exit 22.*
> **traffic congestion** (=when the roads are full of traffic) *Traffic congestion will only get worse.*

'traffic ,circle *n* [C] *AmE* a circular area where several roads meet, which all traffic must drive around **SYN** **roundabout** *BrE* → see picture at **ROUNDABOUT¹**

'traffic ,jam *n* [C] a long line of vehicles on the road that cannot move, or that move very slowly: *We were stuck in a traffic jam for hours.*

trafficking /'træfɪkɪŋ/ *n* [U] **1** the buying and selling of illegal goods, especially drugs **2** the crime of taking people to another country and forcing them to work, for example as PROSTITUTES —**traffic** *v* [T] —**trafficker** *n* [C]

'traffic ,lights *n* [plural] a set of red, yellow, and green lights that control the movement of traffic

'traffic ,warden *n* [C] *BrE* someone who checks that people's cars are parked legally

tragedy /'trædʒədi/ *n* (plural **tragedies**)
1 [C,U] a very sad event or situation, especially one involving death: *The evening ended in tragedy.* | *This tragedy could have been avoided.*
2 [singular] *informal* something that seems sad to you **SYN** **pity**: *It's a tragedy that this match wasn't shown on TV.*
3 [C,U] a serious play that ends sadly → **comedy**: *Shakespeare's tragedies*

tragic /'trædʒɪk/ *adj* a tragic event, situation, or story is very sad, especially because it involves death: *the tragic death of their only child* | *the tragic story of Romeo and Juliet* —**tragically** /-kli/ *adv*

trail¹ /treɪl/ *n* [C] **1** a rough path across countryside or through a forest: *a woodland trail* **2** a series of marks or signs that are left behind by someone or something as they move: **[+of]** *a trail of blood*
PHRASES
> **be on sb's/sth's trail** to be trying to find someone or something by getting information about them: *The police are on the trail of the robbers.*

trail² *v* **1** [I,T] to pull something behind you as you move along, or to be pulled in this way: *Her long dress trailed on the ground behind her.* **2** [I] to walk slowly, usually behind someone, because you are tired or bored: **[+behind/around]** *Sue trailed along behind her parents.* **3** [I,T] to be losing a game, competition, or election: *The Cowboys were trailing in the third quarter.* **4** [I] to hang down or lie across something: *a trailing plant* | **[+across/along/down]** *Wires trailed across the floor.* **5** [T] to follow someone to see where they go
PHRASAL VERBS
trail away/off if someone's voice trails away or off, it gradually becomes quieter and then stops

trailer /'treɪlə $ -ər/ *n* [C] **1** a container on wheels that can be pulled behind a vehicle, used for carrying things **2** *AmE* a vehicle that can be pulled behind a car, used for living and sleeping in during a holiday **SYN** **caravan** *BrE* **3** a short part of a film or television programme, shown to advertise it

'trailer ,park *n* [C] *AmE* an area where trailers are parked and used as people's homes

train¹ /treɪn/ *n* [C] a long vehicle which travels along a railway carrying people or goods. It consists of a line of carriages pulled by an engine: **[+to]** *What time's the next train to Birmingham?* | **by train** *We decided to go by train.* | *I always do my homework on the train.* → see picture at **TRANSPORT¹**
PHRASES
> **train of thought/events** a series of thoughts or events that are related to each other: *The phone rang and interrupted my train of thought.*

> ## COLLOCATIONS
>
> **verbs**
> **to go/travel by train** *It will be quicker to go by train.* ⚠ Do not say 'go by the train' or 'travel by the train'. Say **go by train** or **travel by train**.
> **to take/get a train** *We could drive, or we could take a train.*
> **to catch a train** (=to take a train, or to be in time to get on a train) *I'll try to catch the early train.*
> **to miss a train** (=to be too late to get on a train) *He overslept and missed his train.*
> **to get on/off a train** *A lot of people got on the train at Birmingham.*
> **a train arrives/leaves** (also **a train departs** *formal*) *The train arrived on time.*
>
> **types of train**
> **an express train/a fast train** (=one that does not stop at many places) *They took the 7.20 express train to Glasgow.*
> **a passenger train** *The passenger train was travelling at 125 mph.*
> **a freight/goods train** (=carrying goods not passengers) *a freight train carrying 1,000 tonnes of coal*
> **a commuter train** (=a train that people going to work use) *a crowded New York commuter train*
>
> **train + noun**
> **a train journey** *BrE*, **a train trip** *AmE* *He had a seven-hour train journey to get here.*
> **a train fare** (=the amount you pay to travel on a train) *Train fares have gone up a lot.*
> **a train crash** *Thirty-five people were killed in the train crash.*

train² *v*
1 [I] to learn the skills needed in a particular job: **[+as]** *She trained as a nurse for four years.* | **train to be sth** *You could train to be a policeman.*
2 [T usually passive] to teach someone how to do something, especially the skills they need to do a job: **train sb in sth** *Staff are trained in sales techniques.* | **train sb to do sth** *All teachers are trained to deal with minor accidents.* | *a highly trained pilot*
3 [I,T] to prepare for a sports event by practising

and exercising, or to help someone to do this: **[+for]** *He's training for the Olympics.* **THESAURUS▶ PRACTISE**
4 [T] to teach an animal to do something or to behave correctly

PHRASAL VERBS

train sth **on** sb/sth to aim something such as a gun or camera at someone or something

trainee /ˌtreɪˈniː◂/ n [C] someone who is being taught to do a job: *a trainee teacher*

trainer /ˈtreɪnə $ -ər/ n [C] **1** someone whose job is to train people or animals to do something **THESAURUS▶ TEACHER 2** *BrE* a type of shoe that you wear for sport or with informal clothes → see picture at **SHOE¹**

training /ˈtreɪnɪŋ/ n [U]
1 the process of teaching or learning the skills for a particular job or activity → **train: [+in]** *We all received training in first aid.* | *a staff training course* | *an international teacher training college*
2 physical exercises that you do to stay healthy or prepare for a sports event → **train: be in training for sth** *She's in training for the Olympics.* → **WEIGHT TRAINING**

trait /treɪ, treɪt $ treɪt/ n [C] a quality that is part of someone's character

traitor /ˈtreɪtə $ -ər/ n [C] someone who is not loyal to their country, friends etc

trajectory /trəˈdʒektəri/ n [C] (*plural* **trajectories**) *technical* the direction or line along which something moves when it goes through the air

tram /træm/ n [C] *especially BrE* a type of bus which carries passengers along the street on metal tracks **SYN streetcar** *AmE* → see picture at **TRANSPORT¹**

tramp¹ /træmp/ n [C] someone who has no home or job and moves from place to place

tramp² v [I,T] to walk slowly with heavy steps: **[+through/across etc]** *They tramped through the snow.*

trample /ˈtræmpəl/ v [I,T] to step heavily on something and damage it with your feet: **[+on/over/through etc]** *Don't trample on my flowers!*

trampoline /ˈtræmpəliːn/ n [C] a piece of equipment that you jump up and down on for sport or fun. It is made of a piece of material stretched across a metal frame.

trance /trɑːns $ træns/ n [C] a state in which you seem to be asleep, but can still hear and understand what is said

tranquil /ˈtræŋkwəl/ adj calm and peaceful: *a tranquil little town* —**tranquillity** /træŋˈkwɪləti/ n [U]

tranquillizer (also **-iser** BrE) /ˈtræŋkwəlaɪzə $ -ər/ n [C] a drug used to make someone calm or unconscious —**tranquillize** v [T]

trans- /træns, trænz/ prefix across or between: *trans-European transport networks* | *transcontinental travel*

transaction /trænˈzækʃən/ n [C] *formal* a business deal, such as buying or selling something: **financial transactions**

transatlantic /ˌtrænzətˈlæntɪk◂/ adj crossing the Atlantic Ocean, or involving countries on both sides of the Atlantic: *a transatlantic flight*

transcend /trænˈsend/ v [T] *formal* not to be limited by something: *the need to transcend barriers of race and religion*

transcribe /trænˈskraɪb/ v [T] to write down the words that someone has said, or the notes of a piece of music

transcript /ˈtrænskrɪpt/ n [C] a written copy of a speech, conversation etc

transfer¹ Ac /trænsˈfɜː $ -ˈfɜːr/ v [I,T] (**transferred, transferring**) to move from one place, part of an organization etc to another, or to make someone or something do this: **[+to]** *Stella's transferred to head office.* | **transfer sb to sth** *You will be transferred to your hotel by coach.* | **transfer sth to/into sth** *I'd like to transfer some money into my savings account.* —**transferable** adj

transfer² Ac /ˈtrænsfɜː $ -fɜːr/ n [C,U] when someone or something is moved from one place, part of an organization etc to another: **[+of]** *the transfer of electronic data* | **[+to]** *He's applied for a transfer to Hong Kong.*

transfixed /trænsˈfɪkst/ adj so shocked, interested, frightened etc by something that you cannot move: *She stood transfixed, unable to look away.*

transform Ac /trænsˈfɔːm $ -ˈfɔːrm/ v [T] to change something or someone completely, especially in a way that improves them: **transform sb/sth (from sth) into sth** *The movie transformed Amy from an unknown schoolgirl into a star.* **THESAURUS▶ CHANGE** —**transformation** /ˌtrænsfəˈmeɪʃən $ -fər-/ n [C,U]: *The city has undergone a total transformation* (=it has changed completely).

transformer /trænsˈfɔːmə $ -ˈfɔːrmər/ n [C] a piece of electrical equipment that changes electricity from one VOLTAGE to another

transfusion /trænsˈfjuːʒən/ n [C,U] if you have a blood transfusion, doctors put blood into your body

transgress /trænzˈgres $ træns-/ v [I,T] *formal* to break a rule —**transgression** /-ˈgreʃən/ n [C,U]

transient¹ /ˈtrænziənt $ ˈtrænʃənt/ adj *formal*
1 continuing or existing for only a short time: *transient fashions* **2** working or staying somewhere for only a short time

transient² n [C] *AmE* someone who has no home and moves from place to place

transistor /trænˈzɪstə, -ˈsɪstə $ -ər/ n [C] a small piece of electronic equipment in radios, televisions etc that controls the flow of electricity

transit Ac /ˈtrænsɪt, -zɪt/ n [U] when goods or people are moved from one place to another: *Goods often get lost in transit.*

transition Ac /trænˈzɪʃən, -ˈsɪ-/ n [C,U] *formal* when something changes from one form or state to another: **transition from sth to sth** *the smooth transition from work to retirement* —**transitional** adj: *a two-year transitional period*

transitive /ˈtrænsətɪv, -zə-/ adj in grammar, a transitive verb is followed by an object. In the sentence

'He hit the ball.', 'hit' is transitive and 'the ball' is the object. → **intransitive**

transitory Ac /'trænzətəri $ -tɔːri/ *adj formal* existing for only a short time

translate /træns'leɪt, trænz-/ *v* [I,T]
1 to change written or spoken words from one language to another → **interpret**: **translate sth (from sth) into sth** *I am translating the book into English.*
2 if one thing translates into another, the second thing happens as a result of the first: **translate (sth) into sth** *A rise in public spending could translate into a rise in taxation.*

translation /træns'leɪʃən, trænz-/ *n* [C,U] when you translate something, or something that has been translated: **[+of]** *a new translation of the Bible |* **[+from]** *a translation from Arabic*

translator /træns'leɪtə, trænz- $ -ər/ *n* [C] someone who changes written or spoken words into a different language

translucent /trænz'luːsənt $ træns-/ *adj* clear enough to allow light to pass through, but not transparent —**translucence** *n* [U]

transmission Ac /trænz'mɪʃən $ træns-/ *n*
1 [C,U] the process of broadcasting radio or television programmes, or a television or radio programme **2** [U] *formal* when something is sent or passed from one place, person etc to another: *the transmission of diseases* **3** [C,U] the system of GEARS in a car: *automatic transmission*

transmit Ac /trænz'mɪt $ træns-/ *v* [T] (**transmitted, transmitting**) **1** to send out electronic signals, messages etc using radio, television, or similar equipment **2** *formal* to send or pass something from one place, person etc to another: *The virus is transmitted through sexual contact.*

transmitter /trænz'mɪtə $ træns'mɪtər/ *n* [C] a piece of equipment that sends out radio or television signals

transparency /træn'spærənsi, -'speər- $ -'spær-, 'sper-/ *n* [C] (*plural* **transparencies**) a piece of plastic or film through which light can be shone to show a picture on a large screen

transparent /træn'spærənt, -'speər- $ -'spær-, -'sper-/ *adj*
1 clear and able to be seen through → **opaque**, **translucent**: *transparent plastic*
2 easy to recognize or understand —**transparently** *adv*

transpire /træn'spaɪə $ -'spaɪr/ *v* [I] *formal* **1** if it transpires that something is true, you discover that it is true **2** to happen

transplant¹ /'trænsplɑːnt $ -plænt/ *n* [C,U] a medical operation in which part of someone's body is put into the body of another person: **heart/liver/kidney transplant**

transplant² /træns'plɑːnt $ -'plænt/ *v* [T] **1** to remove part of someone's body and put it into the

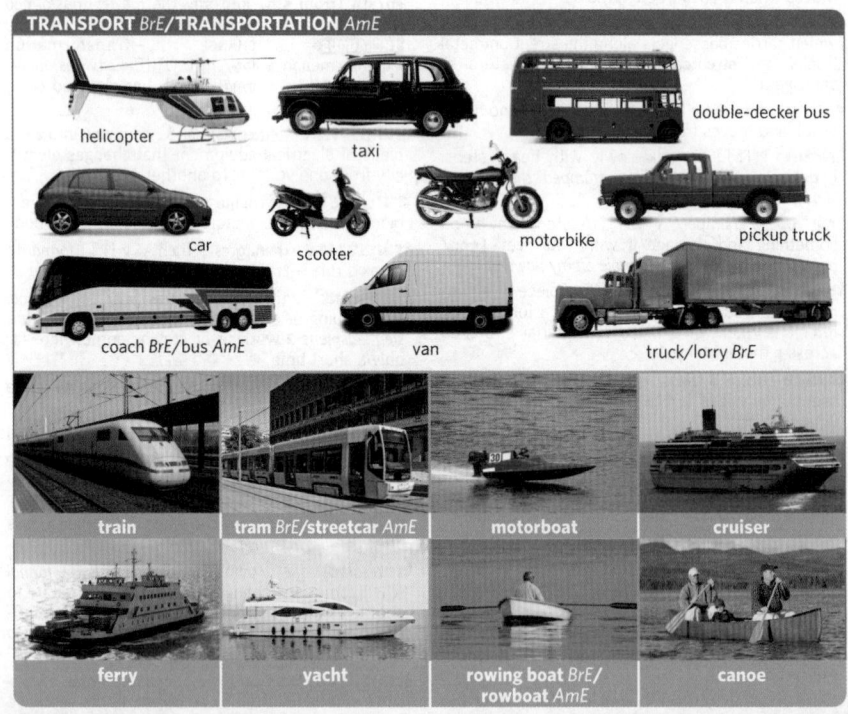

TRANSPORT *BrE*/**TRANSPORTATION** *AmE*

helicopter

taxi

double-decker bus

car

scooter

motorbike

pickup truck

coach *BrE*/bus *AmE*

van

truck/lorry *BrE*

train

tram *BrE*/streetcar *AmE*

motorboat

cruiser

ferry

yacht

rowing boat *BrE*/
rowboat *AmE*

canoe

body of another person **2** to move something to another place

transport¹ Ac /'trænspɔːt $ -ɔːrt/ (also **transportation** /ˌtrænspɔː'teɪʃən $ -spər-/ AmE) n [U]
1 BrE a system or method for carrying passengers or goods from one place to another: **air/rail/road transport** We need improved rail transport. | commuters who travel on **public transport** (=buses, trains etc) | **means/form/mode of transport** cars and other forms of transport | Do you have your own transport (=car, bicycle etc)?
2 especially BrE when people, goods etc are moved from one place to another: **[+of]** the transport of goods

> **Grammar**
> **Transport** is an uncountable noun. It is not used in the plural. Do not say 'I use public transports every day.' Say I use public transport every day.

transport² Ac /træn'spɔːt $ -ɔːrt/ v [T] to move goods, people etc from one place to another in a vehicle **THESAURUS** TAKE

transsexual /træn'sekʃuəl $ træns'sek-/ n [C] someone who has changed their sex or wants to be a different sex

transvestite /trænz'vestaɪt $ træns-/ n [C] someone who enjoys dressing like a person of the opposite sex

trap¹ /træp/ n
1 [C] a piece of equipment for catching animals: You should **set** a **trap** to catch mice.
2 [singular] a trick that is intended to make someone do something that they do not want to do: **fall/walk into a trap** Mr Smith had fallen into a **trap set** by the opposition.
3 [singular] an unpleasant situation from which it is difficult to escape: the **poverty trap** | the unemployment trap → **BOOBY TRAP, DEATH TRAP**

trap² v [T] (**trapped, trapping**)
1 [usually passive] if you are trapped in a dangerous place or a bad situation, there is something preventing you from escaping: Two people were trapped in the burning building. | Ann **felt trapped** in her marriage.
2 to catch an animal in a trap
3 to catch someone by forcing them into a place from which they cannot escape
4 to trick someone in order to make them do or say something that they do not want to: a series of questions intended to trap him | **trap sb into (doing) sth** He was trapped into signing a confession.
5 to prevent something such as gas or water from getting away: solar panels that trap the sun's heat

trapdoor /'træpdɔː $ -dɔːr/ n [C] a small door that covers an opening in a floor or roof

trapeze /trə'piːz $ træ-/ n [C] a short bar hanging from two ropes high above the ground, used by ACROBATS

trappings /'træpɪŋz/ n [plural] the things that someone gets because of their position, especially because they are rich, famous, successful etc: **[+of]** the trappings of stardom

trash¹ /træʃ/ n [U]
1 AmE waste material such as old food or paper that is thrown away **SYN** rubbish BrE
2 informal something that is of very poor quality: There's so much trash on TV these days.

trash² v [T] informal to destroy something completely

trashcan /'træʃkæn/ n [C] AmE a large container for keeping waste material in **SYN** dustbin BrE

trashy /'træʃi/ adj of extremely bad quality: trashy novels

trauma /'trɔːmə, 'traʊmə $ 'traʊmə, 'trɔː-/ n [C,U] the shock caused by an unpleasant and upsetting experience, or an experience that causes this feeling: the trauma of divorce

traumatic /trɔː'mætɪk $ trɔː-/ adj very shocking and upsetting: a traumatic experience

traumatized (also **-ised** BrE) /'trɔːmətaɪzd, 'traʊ- $ 'traʊ-, 'trɔː-/ adj so badly shocked by something that cannot forget it or have a normal life

travel¹ /'trævəl/ v (**travelled, travelling** BrE, **traveled, traveling** AmE) [I,T]
1 to go from one place to another, or to several places: Martha would like to **travel abroad**. | **[+to/across/through/around etc]** Jack spent the summer travelling around Europe. | **travel widely/extensively** He has travelled widely in China. | **travel by train/car/air etc** I usually travel to work by car. | The men travelled the country looking for work.
2 to move along, especially at a particular speed: **[+at]** The train was travelling at 100 mph. | shock waves travelling through the earth

> **THESAURUS**
>
> **travel** to go from one place to another, or to several places: Jack spent the summer travelling around Australia. | How do you travel to work?
> **go** to travel somewhere: We're going to Spain this summer. | He often goes there on business. | It's quicker to go by plane.
> **commute** to travel every day to work or school: I live in the country and commute to London every day.
> **cross** to travel across a wide area: They crossed the desert by camel. | The plane crossed the Atlantic Ocean.
> **tour** to travel to many different places in a country or area in a car, bus etc: Annie and I decided we'd like to tour Italy. | The band are currently touring Europe.
>
> **different ways of travelling**
> **go by car/bus/plane etc** to travel in a car, plane etc: Did you go by car?
> **take the train/bus/ferry etc** to travel by train or another form of public transport: Adam took the train to Scotland.
> **drive** to travel in a car: What about driving down to the sea for the day?
> **fly** to travel in a plane: My mother is afraid of flying.
> **sail** to travel in a ship or boat: We sailed from Malta to Alexandria.

travel² n

1 [U] the activity of travelling: **air/rail/road travel** *Heavy rain is making road travel difficult.*

2 travels [plural] journeys to places that are far away, usually for pleasure: **on your travels** *We met some interesting people on our travels.*

Word Choice: travel, journey or trip?

You use **travel** when talking about the activity of travelling in general: *Her interests are music, sport, and travel.*

You use **journey** or **trip** when talking about an occasion when you travel somewhere: *Hope you have a safe journey.* | *Did you have a good trip?*

Do not say 'Did you have a good travel?'

'travel ,agency (*also* **'travel ,agent's**) *n* [C] a shop or company that makes arrangements for people to travel or have holidays

'travel ,agent *n* [C] someone who works in a travel agency

traveller *BrE*, **traveler** *AmE* /'trævələ $ -ər/ *n* [C] someone who is on a journey or who travels a lot

'traveller's ,cheque *BrE*, **traveler's check** *AmE n* [C] a special cheque that can be exchanged for the money of a foreign country

traverse /'trævɜːs $ trə'vɜːrs/ *v* [T] *formal* to go across or over something

travesty /'trævəsti/ *n* [singular] if something is a travesty, it is very bad and not what it is claimed to be: **[+of]** *The trial was a travesty of justice.*

trawl /trɔːl $ trɒːl/ *v*

PHRASAL VERBS

trawl through sth to search through things in order to find something —**trawl** *n* [C]

trawler /'trɔːlə $ 'trɒːlər/ *n* [C] a large fishing boat that pulls a big net along the sea bottom

tray /treɪ/ *n* [C] a flat piece of plastic, wood etc with raised edges, used for carrying plates, food etc

treacherous /'tretʃərəs/ *adj* **1** someone who is treacherous cannot be trusted because they secretly intend to harm you **2** very dangerous because you cannot see the dangers easily: *treacherous mountain roads*

treachery /'tretʃəri/ *n* [U] when someone does something that harms someone they should have been loyal to

treacle /'triːkəl/ *n* [U] *BrE* a dark sweet sticky liquid made from sugar plants **SYN** *molasses* *AmE*

tread¹ /tred/ *v* (*past tense* **trod** /trɒd $ trɑːd/, *past participle* **trodden** /'trɒdn $ 'trɑːdn/)

1 [I,T] *especially BrE* to put your foot on something → **step**: **[+on/in]** *Sorry, did I tread on your foot?* | *He trod the narrow path between the trees.*

2 tread carefully/warily/cautiously etc to be very careful about what you say or do: *Politicians should tread carefully in this area.*

3 [T] to press something into the ground with your feet: *Look – you've trodden mud into the carpet.*

tread² *n* **1** [C,U] the pattern of deep lines on the surface of a tyre **2** [singular] the sound that someone makes when they walk: *She heard her father's heavy tread on the stair.*

treadmill /'tred,mɪl/ *n* **1** [C] a piece of exercise equipment that you walk or run on **2** [singular] a job or situation that seems very boring because you always have to do the same things

treason /'triːzən/ *n* [U] the crime of doing something that could cause great harm to your country or government, especially by helping its enemies

treasure¹ /'treʒə $ -ər/ n

1 [U] a group of valuable things such as gold, silver, jewels etc: **buried/hidden/sunken treasure**

2 [C] a very valuable and important object such as a painting: *the art treasures of the Uffizi Gallery*

treasure² *v* [T] to keep and care for something that is very special or important: *one of his most treasured memories*

treasurer /'treʒərə $ -ər/ *n* [C] someone who takes care of the money for an organization

Treasury /'treʒəri/ *n* **the Treasury** the government department that controls a country's money

treat¹ /triːt/ v [T]

1 **BEHAVE TOWARDS SB** to behave towards someone in a particular way → **treatment**: *She treats me like one of the family.* | **well/badly treated** *Tracy felt she had been badly treated.* | **treat sb with respect/contempt/courtesy etc** *Children must treat teachers with respect.*

2 **DEAL WITH STH** to deal with or consider something in a particular way → **treatment**: **treat sth as sth** *Please treat this information as confidential.*

3 **GIVE MEDICAL HELP** to give someone medical treatment for an illness or injury → **treatment**: **treat sb for sth** *Eleven people were treated for minor injuries.* | *Malaria can be treated with drugs.*

4 **DO STH SPECIAL** to buy or arrange something special for someone: **treat sb/yourself to sth** *We're treating Jill to dinner for her birthday.* | *I thought I'd treat myself to a new dress.*

5 **WITH A CHEMICAL/SUBSTANCE** to put a special substance on something or use a chemical process in order to protect it or clean it: *The metal has been treated against rust.*

treat² n

1 [C] something special that you give someone or do for them: **as a treat** *Stephen took his son to Disneyland as a treat.*

2 [singular] an event that gives you a lot of pleasure: *Getting your letter was a real treat.* → **TRICK OR TREAT**

PHRASES

my treat *spoken* used to tell someone that you will pay for something, especially a meal: *Let's all go to a movie – my treat.*

treatise /'triːtɪs, -tɪz/ *n* [C] a serious book or article about a subject: **[+on]** *a treatise on political philosophy*

treatment /'triːtmənt/ n

1 [C,U] something that is done to try to cure someone who is injured or ill: *Two of the boys needed*

treatment for head injuries. | *She was given emergency treatment.*
2 [U] a way of behaving towards someone or of dealing with them: *complaints about the treatment of prisoners*

COLLOCATIONS

verbs

to get/have treatment (*also* **to receive/undergo treatment** *formal*) *It's important that he gets treatment quickly.*
to give sb treatment *Patrick was given the best treatment available.*
to need/require treatment *Her injuries needed emergency treatment.*

adjectives

medical treatment *The cost of medical treatment is very high.*
effective treatment (=treatment that is successful) *The drug is an effective treatment for malaria.*

noun + treatment

hospital treatment *Some people have been waiting for over two years for hospital treatment.*
emergency treatment *The man was rushed to hospital for emergency treatment.*

---

treaty /'triːti/ n [C] (*plural* **treaties**) a formal written agreement between two or more countries: *They signed a **peace treaty**.* | *a treaty on nuclear weapons*

treble¹ /'trebəl/ *determiner BrE* three times as big, as much, or as many as something else **SYN triple**: *They sold the house for treble the amount they paid for it.*

treble² v [I,T] to become three times as much, or to make something do this **SYN triple**

treble³ n [U] the upper half of the whole range of musical notes

tree /triː/ n [C] a very tall plant that has branches and leaves: **cherry/peach/apple etc tree** *He has three apple trees in his garden.* | *the trunk (=main central part) of an old oak tree* → see picture at **PLANT**¹ → **CHRISTMAS TREE, FAMILY TREE, PALM TREE**

trek /trek/ v [I] (**trekked, trekking**) to make a long and difficult journey on foot —**trek** n [C]

trellis /'trelɪs/ n [C] a wooden frame for supporting climbing plants

tremble /'trembəl/ v [I] to shake slightly because you are afraid, worried, or excited: *Her voice trembled as she spoke.* | **tremble with anger/fear etc** *John was trembling with rage.* **THESAURUS SHAKE**

tremendous /trɪ'mendəs/ *adj* **1** very great: *I have tremendous respect for her.* **2** excellent —**tremendously** *adv*: *It was tremendously exciting.*

tremor /'tremə $ -ər/ n [C] **1** a small EARTHQUAKE **2** a slight shaking movement that you cannot control

trench /trentʃ/ n [C] a long narrow hole that is dug in the ground

trenchant /'trentʃənt/ *adj* very firm and clear: *a trenchant critic of big business*

trenchcoat /'trentʃkəʊt $ -koʊt/ n [C] a long RAIN-COAT with a belt

trend /trend/ n **1** [C] the way a situation is generally developing or changing: *There's a trend toward more part-time employment.* | *the latest fashion trends* **2 set the trend** to start doing something that other people copy: *To save the planet we must set the trend of caring for the environment.*

trendy /'trendi/ *adj* modern and fashionable: *a trendy bar* **THESAURUS FASHIONABLE**

trepidation /,trepə'deɪʃən/ n [U] *formal* anxiety or fear about something that is going to happen

trespass /'trespəs $ -pəs, -pæs/ v [I] to go onto someone's land without permission —**trespasser** n [C]

trestle /'tresəl/ n [C] a wooden support under a table

tri- /traɪ/ *prefix* three: *She's trilingual (=able to speak three languages).*

trial /'traɪəl/ n
1 [C,U] a legal process in which a court of law decides whether or not someone is guilty of a crime → **try**: *a murder trial* | **on trial (for sth)** (=being judged in a court) *He is on trial for armed robbery.*
2 [C,U] when something such as a drug is tested to find out how good, effective etc it is → **try**: *The drug is undergoing **clinical trials** (=tests involving sick people).*
3 [C usually plural] something that is difficult or unpleasant to deal with → **trying**: *the **trials and tribulations** of running a business*
4 trials [plural] *BrE* a sports competition that tests the ability of people who want to be included in a team **SYN tryout** *AmE*
PHRASES

on a trial basis/for a trial period if you use something or someone on a trial basis or for a trial period, you use them for a short period to find out whether they are satisfactory
trial and error when you test different methods or answers in order to find the most suitable one: *Students learn through a process of trial and error.*

COLLOCATIONS

verbs

to stand/face trial (=to be judged in a court of law) *Roche is standing trial for possession of heroin.*
to go on trial *A man has gone on trial for the murder of a security guard.*
a case goes/comes to trial *The legal costs could be as high as £250,000 if the case goes to trial.*
a trial is held *The trial will be held in a military court.*

types of trial

a murder/fraud etc trial *There were dramatic newspaper reports of the murder trial.*
a criminal trial (=for a case involving a crime) *She was called to be a witness in a criminal trial.*
a fair trial *He insists that he did not get a fair trial.*

trial 'run n [C] when something new is tested to see if it works

triangle /'traɪæŋɡəl/ n [C]
1 a flat shape with three straight sides and three angles → see picture at SHAPE¹
2 a small musical instrument shaped like a triangle. You hit it with a metal stick. —**triangular** /traɪˈæŋɡjələ $ -ər/ adj

triathlon /traɪˈæθlɒn/ n [C] a sports competition in which competitors run, swim, and cycle long distances

tribe /traɪb/ n [C] a group of people of the same race with the same language and customs, who usually live together in the same area —**tribal** adj: tribal art

tribulation /ˌtrɪbjəˈleɪʃən/ n [C,U] a problem in your life or work: the **trials and tribulations** of married life

tribunal /traɪˈbjuːnl/ n [C] a type of court that has official authority to deal with a particular situation or problem: a war crimes tribunal | He took his case to an **industrial tribunal** (=one that judges disagreements between workers and employers).

tributary /'trɪbjətəri $ -teri/ n [C] (plural **tributaries**) a river or stream that flows into a larger river

tribute /'trɪbjuːt/ n [C,U] something that you say or do to show how much you admire and respect someone: The concert was held as a tribute to Bob Dylan. | Today she **paid tribute to** the hospital staff who had treated her.
PHRASES
be a tribute to sb/sth to be a sign of how good, effective etc someone or something is: It's a tribute to her teaching that so many of the children love school.

'tribute band n [C] a group of musicians who play and sing the songs of a famous group, trying to sound and look like them

trick¹ /trɪk/ n [C]
1 something you do in order to deceive someone, or as a joke to make people laugh at someone: The phone call was just a trick to get him out of the office. | The girls were always **playing tricks** on their teacher.
2 something that seems like magic which is done in order to entertain people: a **card trick**
3 a clever and effective way of doing something: The trick is to keep your design simple. → HAT TRICK
PHRASES
do the trick spoken if something does the trick, it helps you to succeed in doing what you want: A little salt should do the trick.
it was a trick of the light used to say that something appeared to be different from the way it really is

trick² v [T] to make someone believe something that is not true, in order to get something from them or to make them do something: **trick sb into doing sth** He said he was tricked into carrying drugs.

THESAURUS

trick to make someone believe something that is not true, in order to get something from them

or to make them do something: She was tricked into signing the papers because she trusted her sons.
deceive to make someone who trusts you believe something that is not true, because it is useful to you if they believe it: This was a deliberate attempt to deceive the public.
fool to make someone believe something that is not true. **Fool** is more informal than **deceive**: He fooled me into thinking he loved me. | Some people are easily fooled.
mislead to make someone believe something that is not true, especially by deliberately not giving them all the facts: The company said that it had not intended to mislead customers about its products.

trickery /'trɪkəri/ n [U] the use of tricks to deceive or cheat people

trickle /'trɪkəl/ v [I] **1** if liquid trickles somewhere, it flows slowly in drops or in a thin stream: **[+down/ from etc]** Sweat trickled down his face. **2** if people or things trickle somewhere, they move there slowly in small groups or amounts —**trickle** n [C]: a trickle of blood

trick or 'treat v go trick or treating if children go trick or treating, they go to people's houses on HALLOWEEN (October 31) and say 'trick or treat' in order to get sweets and other small presents

trick 'question n [C] a question that seems easy, but which is intended to deceive you

tricky /'trɪki/ adj difficult to do or deal with: It was a tricky decision. **THESAURUS** DIFFICULT

tricycle /'traɪsɪkəl/ n [C] a bicycle with three wheels

tried¹ /traɪd/ v the past tense and past participle of TRY

tried² adj **tried and tested/trusted** used successfully many times

trifle /'traɪfəl/ n **1 a trifle** slightly: He looked a trifle unhappy. **2** [C,U] a cold DESSERT made of layers of cake, fruit, CUSTARD etc

trifling /'traɪflɪŋ/ adj small or unimportant

trigger¹ Ac /'trɪɡə $ -ər/ n [C] the part of a gun that you pull with your finger to fire it: He pointed the gun and pulled the trigger.

trigger² Ac (also **trigger off**) v [T] to make something start to happen: Heavy rain may trigger mudslides.

trillion /'trɪljən/ number (plural **trillion** or **trillions**)
1 the number 1,000,000,000,000: **two/three/four etc trillion** $5.3 trillion | **trillions of pounds/dollars etc** **2** an extremely large number of people or things: a trillion a shirt with a trillion holes in it. | **trillions of sth** We've made this mistake trillions of times before. —**trillionth** adj —**trillionth** n [C]

trilogy /'trɪlədʒi/ n [C] (plural **trilogies**) a series of three books, plays, films etc, which have the same subject or characters

trim¹ /trɪm/ v [T] (**trimmed, trimming**) **1** to cut a small amount off something to make it look neater: Get your hair trimmed regularly. **2** to reduce the size or amount of something: *We need to **trim costs**.* **3** to decorate something by adding something attractive: **be trimmed with sth** *The sleeves were trimmed with velvet.*

trim² *adj* **1** thin and healthy looking SYN **slim**: *a trim figure* **2** neat and attractive

trim³ *n* **1** [singular] when something is cut to make it look neater: *Your beard needs a trim.* **2** [singular, U] the decoration on something such as a piece of clothing

PHRASES

in trim in good physical condition: *If you want to get in trim, try aerobics.*

trimester /trɪˈmestə $ traɪˈmestər/ *n* [C] *AmE* one of three periods that a year at school or college is divided into

trimming /ˈtrɪmɪŋ/ *n* [C,U] decoration on the edge of a piece of clothing

PHRASES

with all the trimmings with all the other types of food that are traditionally served with the main dish of a meal: *a turkey dinner with all the trimmings*

Trinity /ˈtrɪnəti/ *n* **the Trinity** the three forms of God in the Christian religion, which are the Father, the Son, and the Holy Spirit

trinket /ˈtrɪŋkɪt/ *n* [C] a piece of jewellery or a small pretty object that is not worth much money

trio /ˈtriːəʊ $ ˈtriːoʊ/ *n* [C] (*plural* **trios**) a group of three people, especially a group of three musicians who play together

trip¹ /trɪp/ *n* [C] a visit to a place that involves a journey: **[+to]** *Did you enjoy your trip to Disneyland?* | *His wife was away on a **business trip**.* | **boat/coach/bus trip** | *a **day trip** to Brighton* THESAURUS **JOURNEY → FIELD TRIP, ROUND TRIP**

trip² *v* (**tripped, tripping**)
1 [I] to hit something with your foot while you are walking or running so that you fall or almost fall → **stumble**: *He tripped and fell.* | **[+on/over]** *I tripped over a chair.* THESAURUS **FALL**
2 (*also* **trip up**) [T] to make someone fall by putting your foot in front of them: *Baggio was tripped inside the penalty area.*

PHRASAL VERBS

trip up to make a mistake, or to make someone make a mistake: **trip sb ↔ up** *The interviewer tried to trip her up with a tricky question.*

triple¹ /ˈtrɪpəl/ *adj* [only before noun] consisting of three things or parts of the same kind, or doing something three times: *a triple gold medal winner*

triple² *v* [I,T] to become three times as big or as many, or to make something do this: *The population may triple in 20 years.*

triple³ *determiner* three times as big, as much, or as many as something else: *The rail system has triple the average number of accidents.*

triplet /ˈtrɪplɪt/ *n* [C] one of three children born at the same time to the same mother

tripod /ˈtraɪpɒd $ -pɑːd/ *n* [C] a piece of equipment with three legs, used for supporting something such as a camera

trite /traɪt/ *adj* a trite remark or idea has been used so much that it does not seem sincere or interesting

triumph¹ /ˈtraɪəmf/ *n*
1 [C] an important success or victory: **[+for]** *It was a diplomatic triumph for France.* | **[+over]** *the team's 5-2 triumph over England* | *Winning the championship was a great **personal triumph**.*
2 [U] the feeling of pleasure you get from victory or success: *a look of triumph* | **in triumph** *She smiled in triumph.* —**triumphal** /traɪˈʌmfəl/ *adj*

triumph² *v* [I] to win a victory or be successful: **[+over]** *people who've triumphed over pain and disability*

triumphant /traɪˈʌmfənt/ *adj* pleased because you have succeeded or won: *a triumphant smile* —**triumphantly** *adv*

trivia /ˈtrɪviə/ *n* [plural] unimportant details or facts: *We chatted about trivia.* | *a quiz of sporting trivia*

trivial /ˈtrɪviəl/ *adj* not serious or important: *a trivial matter* THESAURUS **UNIMPORTANT** —**triviality** /ˌtrɪviˈæləti/ *n* [C,U]

trivialize (*also* **-ise** *BrE*) /ˈtrɪviəlaɪz/ *v* [T] to make something seem less important or serious than it really is

trod /trɒd $ trɑːd/ *v* the past tense of TREAD

trodden /ˈtrɒdn $ ˈtrɑːdn/ *v* the past participle of TREAD

trolley /ˈtrɒli $ ˈtrɑːli/ *n* [C] **1** *BrE* a container on wheels, that you use for carrying things, for example in a SUPERMARKET SYN **cart** *AmE* **2** a small table on wheels, used for carrying food and drinks **3** *AmE* an electric vehicle that moves along the street on tracks SYN **tram** *BrE*

TROLLEY *BrE/* **CART** *AmE*

trombone /trɒmˈbəʊn $ trɑːmˈboʊn/ *n* [C] a large metal musical instrument that you play by blowing into it and sliding a long tube in and out → see picture on page A6 —**trombonist** *n* [C]

troop¹ /truːp/ *n* [C] **1 troops** [plural] soldiers: *Troops have been sent to the area to keep the peace.* **2** a large group of people or animals —**troop** *adj* [only before noun]: *troop movements*

troop² *v* [I] to walk somewhere in a group: **[+into/out of etc]** *We all trooped out of the classroom.*

trooper /ˈtruːpə $ -ər/ *n* [C] **1** a soldier **2** a member of a state police force in the US

trophy /ˈtrəʊfi $ ˈtroʊ-/ *n* [C] (*plural* **trophies**) an object such as a silver cup that you get for winning a race or competition

tropical /ˈtrɒpɪkəl $ ˈtrɑː-/ *adj* in or from the hottest parts of the world: *tropical rain forests* | *tropical fish*

tropics /ˈtrɒpɪks $ ˈtrɑː-/ *n* **the tropics** the hottest parts of the world, which are near the EQUATOR

trot¹ /trɒt $ trɑːt/ *v* [I] (**trotted, trotting**) to walk or run with quick short steps: **[+off/along/up etc]** *A group of horses trotted past.* | *He trotted along behind his parents.*

PHRASAL VERBS

trot sth ↔ **out** *informal disapproving* to give an opinion or idea that has been used too many times before: *They always trot out the same old excuses.*

trot² *n* [singular] a speed that is slightly faster than walking

PHRASES

on the trot happening one after the other: *The team have won five games on the trot.*

trouble¹ /'trʌbəl/ *n*

1 [C,U] problems or difficulties: **[+with]** *We've been having trouble with the new computer system.* | **have trouble doing sth** *We had no trouble getting here.* | *Mark was able to fix the tap without much trouble* (=easily). | *It's good to be able to talk to someone about your troubles.*

2 [singular] the thing that is causing a problem, or the thing that is bad about someone or something: *I'd love to come but **the trouble is** I can't afford it.* | **The trouble with** you **is that** you don't listen.

3 **in/into trouble** in a situation with a lot of problems: **get/run into trouble** *The project has already run into trouble.* | **in serious/deep trouble** *The company was in deep financial trouble.*

4 **in/into trouble** if someone is in trouble, they have done something wrong which they will be punished for: **[+with]** *He's been in trouble with the police.* | *I was always **getting into trouble** at school.*

5 [U] time and effort that is needed to do something: *It was a lovely meal. They'd obviously **gone to a lot of trouble**.* | *He'd **taken the trouble to** learn all our names.* | *Doing the course over the Internet **saves** you **the trouble of** attending classes.*

6 [C,U] a situation in which people fight or argue with each other: *crowd trouble* | **cause/make trouble** *English fans have a reputation for causing trouble.*

7 [U] problems with part of your body or part of a machine: *heart trouble* | *engine trouble*

COLLOCATIONS

verbs

to have trouble *She's been having a lot of trouble with her boyfriend.*

to have no trouble *We had no trouble selling our house.*

to cause trouble *A small electrical fault was causing the trouble.*

to give sb trouble *None of my kids ever gave me any trouble.*

to be asking for trouble (=to be likely to cause trouble) *Leaving your car unlocked is asking for trouble.*

adjectives

great/serious/terrible trouble *Hugh was having great trouble understanding her.*

endless trouble (=a lot of trouble) *This new computer has given me endless trouble.*

---

trouble² *v* [T] **1** if something troubles you, it makes you feel worried or upset: *She was troubled by feelings of guilt.* **2** *formal* to cause someone a slight

problem by asking them to do something, used especially when making a polite request **SYN** **bother**: *I'm sorry to trouble you, but could you open the door for me?*

troubled /'trʌbəld/ *adj* **1** worried: *a troubled expression* **2** having many problems: *a troubled marriage*

troublemaker /'trʌbəl,meɪkə $ -ər/ *n* [C] someone who deliberately causes problems

troubleshooter /'trʌbəl,ʃuːtə $ -ər/ *n* [C] someone whose job is to solve problems that an organization is having —**troubleshooting** *n* [U]

troublesome /'trʌbəlsəm/ *adj* causing problems: *troublesome symptoms*

'trouble ,spot *n* [C] a place where there is likely to be fighting or trouble: *Tourists have been warned to stay away from trouble spots.*

trough /trɒf $ trɔːf/ *n* [C] **1** a long container for animals to drink or eat from **2** a period when prices or economic activity are low

trounce /traʊns/ *v* [T] to defeat someone easily: *We trounced them 58-7.*

troupe /truːp/ *n* [C] a group of singers, actors, dancers etc who work together

trousers /'traʊzəz $ -ərz/ *n* [plural] a piece of clothing that covers the lower part of your body, with a separate part for each leg **SYN** **pants** *AmE*: *a pair of trousers* → see picture at CLOTHES —**trouser** *adj* [only before noun]: *The tickets are in my trouser pocket.*

Word Choice: trousers or pants?
British speakers usually say **trousers**. American speakers usually say **pants**. For British speakers, **pants** usually means UNDERPANTS.

'trouser suit *n* [C] *BrE* a woman's suit that consists of a jacket and trousers **SYN** **pant suit** *AmE*

trout /traʊt/ *n* [C,U] (*plural* **trout**) a fish that lives in rivers and can be eaten

trowel /'traʊəl/ *n* [C] **1** a small garden tool used for digging small holes → see picture at GARDEN **2** a small tool used for spreading CEMENT on bricks

truant /'truːənt/ *n* [C] a student who stays away from school without permission —**truancy** *n* [U]

PHRASES

play truant *BrE* to stay away from school without permission **SYN** **play hooky** *AmE*: *He was caught playing truant.*

truce /truːs/ *n* [C] an agreement to stop fighting or arguing for a short time: *They agreed to **call a truce**.*

truck /trʌk/ *n* [C] a large road vehicle used for carrying goods **SYN** **lorry** *BrE*: *a truck driver* → FIRE TRUCK → see picture at TRANSPORT¹

trucker /'trʌkə $ -ər/ *n* [C] *especially AmE* someone who drives a truck

trucking /'trʌkɪŋ/ *n* [U] *AmE* the business of taking goods from one place to another by truck

truckload /'trʌkləʊd $ -loʊd/ *n* [C] the amount that fills a truck: **[+of]** *a truckload of oranges*

truculent /ˈtrʌkjələnt/ *adj formal* bad-tempered and often arguing with people

trudge /trʌdʒ/ *v* [I] to walk with slow heavy steps, especially because you are tired: **[+through/up/off etc]** *He trudged up the stairs.* **THESAURUS** WALK

true /truː/ *adj*
1 based on real facts, and not imagined or invented **OPP false → truth: it is true (that)** *Is it true that you're moving to Denver? | a **true story** | The results appear to **hold true** (=still be correct) for other countries too.* **THESAURUS** GENUINE
2 [only before noun] real: *He's a **true friend**. | Is this **true love**? | The house was sold for a fraction of its **true value**. | the **true cost** of the holiday | the **true meaning** of the word*
3 *spoken* used to admit that something is correct, especially when saying that something else is also correct: *True, he has a college degree, but he doesn't have enough experience.*
4 true to sb/sth faithful and loyal, or doing what you have promised to do: *She remained true to him all her life. | He was **true to** his **word** and said nothing to anyone.*

PHRASES
come true if a dream, wish, or statement about the future comes true, the thing that someone thought or spoke about happens: *My dream of living in the country had finally come true.*
true to form/type used to say that someone is behaving exactly as they always do: *True to form, he disagreed with everything I said.*
true to life a book, film etc that is true to life seems similar to what really happens in people's lives **SYN** realistic

---

THESAURUS

true based on real facts, and not imagined or invented: *a true story | Is it true that they're getting married?*
accurate based on facts and not containing any mistakes: *Are these figures accurate? | Old guidebooks may no longer contain accurate information.*
be the truth to be true – used especially to tell someone that you are not lying: *I've never seen him before and that's the truth.*
it is a fact used when saying that some information is definitely correct: *It is a fact that women live longer than men.*

---

truffle /ˈtrʌfəl/ *n* [C] **1** a soft sweet made with chocolate **2** a FUNGUS you can eat that grows under the ground

truism /ˈtruːɪzəm/ *n* [C] a statement that is clearly true, so that there is no need to say it

truly /ˈtruːli/ *adv* **1** used to emphasize that the way you are describing something is really true: *a truly remarkable man | By now we were **well and truly** (=completely) lost.* **2** sincerely: *She truly believed he was innocent.* → **yours truly** at YOURS

trump /trʌmp/ *n* [C] a card that has a higher value than the other cards in some card games, for example BRIDGE

PHRASES
come/turn up trumps to provide what is needed, especially when you do not expect it: *The school came up trumps and said we could use the school hall.*

ˈtrump card *n* [C] something you can do or use in a situation which will give you an advantage

ˌtrumped-ˈup *adj* using false information to make someone seem guilty of doing something wrong: *He was sent to prison on trumped-up charges.*

trumpet /ˈtrʌmpɪt/ *n* [C] a metal musical instrument that you blow into, with three buttons that you press to change the notes → see picture on page A6 —**trumpeter** *n* [C]

truncate /trʌŋˈkeɪt $ ˈtrʌŋkeɪt/ *v* [T] *formal* to make something shorter: *a truncated version of the report*

truncheon /ˈtrʌnʃən/ *n* [C] *BrE* a short stick that police officers carry as a weapon **SYN** nightstick *AmE*

trundle /ˈtrʌndl/ *v* [I,T] to move slowly on wheels, or to make something do this by pushing or pulling it: **trundle (sth) along/out etc** *We trundled the luggage trolley onto the platform.*

trunk /trʌŋk/ *n* [C]
1 ON A TREE the thick main part of a tree, which the branches grow from: *a **tree trunk** →* see picture at PLANT[1]
2 ON A CAR *AmE* the space at the back of a car where you can put things **SYN** boot *BrE* → see picture at CAR
3 ON AN ELEPHANT the long nose of an ELEPHANT → see picture at ELEPHANT
4 BOX a large box used for storing or carrying things → see picture at BOX[1]
5 FOR SWIMMING trunks (*also* swimming trunks) [plural] a piece of clothing that men wear for swimming
6 BODY *technical* the main part of your body, not including your head, arms, or legs: *He had bruises all over his legs and trunk.*

ˈtrunk road *n* [C] *BrE* a main road between towns

trust[1] /trʌst/ *n*
1 [U] the belief that someone or something is honest or good: *There's a **lack of trust** between teachers and the government. | I had **put my trust in** the doctor.*
2 [C] an organization that controls how money will be used to help someone else: *a charitable trust*
3 [C,U] an arrangement in which someone legally controls your money or property, usually until you are old enough to have it: *The money is being **held in trust** until she's 21.*

PHRASES
take sth on trust to believe that something is true without having any proof: *I can't let you see the letter, so you'll have to take what I'm saying on trust.*

trust[2] *v* [T]
1 to believe that someone is honest and will not do anything bad or wrong **OPP** distrust, mistrust: *I don't trust her at all.*
2 trust sb to do sth to believe that someone will definitely do something: *I know I can trust you to keep this secret.*

3 to be sure that something is correct or right: *I'm not sure if I trust his judgment.*

PHRASES

I trust (that) *formal* used to say that you hope something is true: *I trust that these arrangements are satisfactory.*

trust you/him etc (to do sth)! *spoken* used to say that it is typical of someone to do something silly or bad: *Trust you to be late!*

PHRASAL VERBS

trust sb **with** sth to let someone have or control something because you believe they will be careful with it: *I wouldn't trust him with the keys.*

trustee /ˌtrʌˈstiː◂/ *n* [C] a person or company that legally controls someone else's property or money

'trust fund *n* [C] money belonging to someone, especially a child, that is controlled for them by a trustee

trusting /ˈtrʌstɪŋ/ *adj* believing that other people are good and honest: *a trusting young girl*

trustworthy /ˈtrʌstˌwɜːði $ -ɜːr-/ *adj* if someone is trustworthy, you can trust them completely

trusty /ˈtrʌsti/ *adj* [only before noun] *old-fashioned* a trusty person or object is one you can depend on

truth /truːθ/ *n*
1 the truth the true facts about something → **lie**: *I'm still trying to find out the truth.* | *The truth is I don't know what will happen.* | *He might be telling the truth.* **THESAURUS ► TRUE**
2 [U] if there is truth in something, it is true: **[+in]** *Do you think there's any truth in these accusations?*
3 [C] *formal* an important fact or idea that people accept as true: *scientific truths*

PHRASES

to tell (you) the truth *spoken* used when giving your opinion or admitting something: *To tell you the truth, I've never really liked him.*

truthful /ˈtruːθfəl/ *adj* honest and saying things that are true: *a truthful answer* | *a truthful witness* —**truthfully** *adv*

try¹ /traɪ/ *v* (**tried, trying, tries**)
1 [I,T] to attempt to do something: **try to do sth** *I'm trying to find out what happened.* | **try and do sth** *Try and take some exercise each day.* | *I tried hard not to smile.*
2 [T] to do, use, or taste something in order to find out if you like it or it is good: *You must try some of this cake!* | **try doing sth** *Try walking to work instead of driving.*
3 [T] to examine facts in a law court in order to decide if someone is guilty → **trial**: **try sb for sth** *Three men were tried for murder.*

PHRASES

try your hand at sth to try a new activity: *He was keen to try his hand at painting.*

PHRASAL VERBS

try sth ↔ **on** to put on a piece of clothing to find out if it fits or if you like it: *Can I try these jeans on, please?*

try sth ↔ **out** to test something to find out if it is effective or works properly: *I want to try out my new camera.*

THESAURUS

try to attempt to do something: *I've tried to call her several times today.*
attempt to try to do something, especially something difficult or dangerous. **Attempt** is more formal than **try**: *They are attempting to negotiate an agreement.*
make an effort to do sth to try to do something that you find difficult or do not really want to do: *I made an effort to sound interested in what he was saying.*
do your best to try as hard as you can to do something: *I'll do my best to finish it by Friday.*
have a go *BrE* (*also* **have a try**) *informal* to try to do something when you are not sure that you will succeed: *'I can't get this lid off.' 'Let me have a go.'* | *I'd love to have a try at skiing.*

try² *n* (*plural* **tries**) **1** [C] an attempt to do something: *He succeeded on his first try.* | *I don't know if I can do it but I'll have a try.* **THESAURUS ► TRY**
2 [singular] a test of something to see if it is suitable or successful: *I decided to give the job a try.*
3 [C] when a team gets points in RUGBY by putting the ball down behind the other team's goal line

trying /ˈtraɪ-ɪŋ/ *adj* annoying or difficult: *I've had a very trying day.*

tsar, tzar, czar /zɑː, tsɑː $ zɑːr, tsɑːr/ *n* [C] **1** a ruler of Russia before 1917 **2** someone who is chosen by the government to deal with a particular problem or activity: *the new anti-drugs tsar*

T-shirt /ˈtiː ʃɜːt $ -ʃɜːrt/ *n* [C] a soft shirt with short SLEEVES and no collar → see picture at **CLOTHES**

tsp. the written abbreviation of **teaspoon**

tsunami /tsʊˈnɑːmi/ *n* [C] a very large wave, caused for example by an EARTHQUAKE, which can cause a lot of damage when it reaches land

tub /tʌb/ *n* [C]
1 a container with a lid, in which food is sold: **[+of]** *a tub of margarine* → see picture at **CONTAINER**
2 a deep round container: *flowers growing in tubs*
3 *AmE* a container in which you sit to wash yourself **SYN** **bath** *BrE*

tuba /ˈtjuːbə $ ˈtuːbə/ *n* [C] a large metal musical instrument that consists of a curved tube and produces very low notes → see picture on page A6

tubby /ˈtʌbi/ *adj informal* slightly fat

tube /tjuːb $ tuːb/ *n* [C]
1 a pipe made of glass, rubber, metal etc that liquids or gases go through: *He had to be fed through a tube because he was so weak.*
2 a container for a soft substance that you press between your fingers to make the substance come out: **[+of]** *a tube of toothpaste* → see picture at **CONTAINER**
3 a long round hollow object: *a cardboard tube*
4 the Tube the railway system under the ground in London **SYN** **subway** *AmE*: *He took the Tube to Embankment.* | *Which is the nearest Tube station?*

tuberculosis /tjuːˌbɜːkjəˈləʊsɪs $ tuːˌbɜːrkjəˈloʊ-/ (also **TB**) n [U] a serious infectious disease that affects your lungs

tubing /ˈtjuːbɪŋ $ ˈtuː-/ n [U] tubes, usually connected together in a system: *copper tubing*

tubular /ˈtjuːbjələ $ ˈtuːbjələr/ adj made of tubes or shaped like a tube

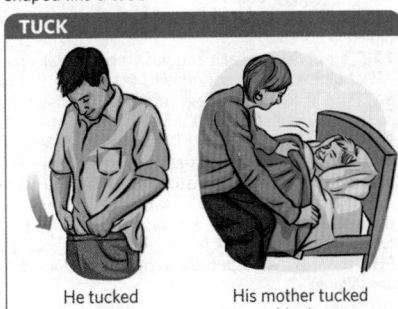

TUCK

He tucked his shirt in.   His mother tucked him in.

tuck /tʌk/ v [T] **1** to push the end of a shirt, sheet etc somewhere so that it looks tidy: **tuck sth in** *John tucked his shirt in.* | **tuck sth into/under/behind sth** *I tucked my T-shirt into my shorts.* | *She tucked a curl of hair behind her ear.* **2** to put something in a small space, especially so that it is safe or comfortable: **tuck sth into/under/behind sth** *She tucked the money into her pocket.*

PHRASAL VERBS

tuck sth **away 1** to put something in a safe place: *He tucked the letter away in a drawer.* **2 be tucked away** to be in a place that is far away or difficult to find: *a little village tucked away in the mountains*

tuck in 1 tuck sb in/up to make someone comfortable in bed by arranging the sheets around them **2** (also **tuck into** sth) BrE informal to eat something eagerly: *Come on, tuck in!*

tuck sb **up be tucked up (in bed)** to be sitting or lying in bed

Tuesday /ˈtjuːzdi, -deɪ $ ˈtuːz-/ n [C,U] (written abbreviation **Tues.** or **Tue.**) the day between Monday and Wednesday → see examples at **MONDAY**

tuft /tʌft/ n [C] a bunch of hairs, grass etc growing together: *a tuft of hair*

tug¹ /tʌg/ v [I,T] (**tugged**, **tugging**) to pull something suddenly and hard: **[+at/on]** *Alice tugged at my hand.* **THESAURUS ▶ PULL**

tug² n [C] **1** (also **'tug boat**) a boat used for pulling ships **2** a strong pull: *I gave the handle a tug.*

tug-of-'war n [singular] a competition in which two teams pull on the opposite ends of a rope

tuition /tjuˈɪʃən $ tu-/ n [U] **1** teaching, especially in small groups: **[+in]** *I had private tuition in English.* **2** AmE, **tu'ition fees** BrE the money you pay for being taught: *Tuition went up to $3,000 last semester.*

tulip /ˈtjuːlɪp $ ˈtuː-/ n [C] a flower that is shaped like a cup and grows from a BULB in spring. → see picture at **FLOWER¹**

tumble /ˈtʌmbəl/ v [I] **1** to fall somewhere suddenly: **[+down/into etc]** *She lost her balance and tumbled backwards.* **2** to move somewhere in an uncontrolled way: **[+into/out etc]** *The door opened and a group of students tumbled out.* **3** if prices tumble, they suddenly become much lower: *Share prices tumbled yesterday.* —**tumble** n [C]

,tumble 'dryer, tumble drier n [C] BrE a machine for drying clothes

tumbler /ˈtʌmblə $ -ər/ n [C] a glass with no handle or STEM

tummy /ˈtʌmi/ n [C] (plural **tummies**) informal your stomach

tumour BrE, **tumor** AmE /ˈtjuːmə $ ˈtuːmər/ n [C] a group of diseased cells in someone's body that grow too quickly: *He died of a brain tumor.*

tumult /ˈtjuːmʌlt $ ˈtuː-/ n [C,U] formal a situation in which there is a lot of noise, confusion, or excitement

tumultuous /tjuˈmʌltʃuəs $ tu-/ adj **1** very noisy because people are excited: *They received a tumultuous welcome from the crowd.* **2** full of activity, confusion, or violence: *the tumultuous years of the Civil War*

tuna /ˈtjuːnə $ ˈtuːnə/ n [C,U] (plural **tuna**) a large sea fish that can be eaten

tundra /ˈtʌndrə/ n [U] large flat areas of land in the north of Russia, Canada etc, where it is very cold and there are no trees

tune¹ /tjuːn $ tuːn/ n [C] a series of musical notes that are nice to listen to: *He started to play a tune on the piano.* → **change your tune** at **CHANGE¹**

PHRASES

in tune playing or singing the correct musical notes **OPP off-key**: *They sang perfectly in tune.*

be in tune with sb/sth to understand or realize what someone wants: *Teachers need to be in tune with their students' needs.*

out of tune playing or singing notes that are too high or low: *The guitar was badly out of tune.*

be out of tune with sb/sth to not understand or realize what someone wants: *a party that is out of tune with the people of this country*

tune² v [T]

1 MUSICAL INSTRUMENT to make changes to a musical instrument so that it plays the correct musical notes: *The piano needs tuning.*

2 RADIO/TV to make a television or radio receive broadcasts from a particular place: **be tuned to sth** *You're tuned to ABC Radio.* | **Stay tuned** (=keep listening or watching) *for more great music.*

3 ENGINE (also **tune up**) to make small changes to a car engine so that it works better

PHRASAL VERBS

tune in to watch a television programme or listen to a radio programme: **[+to]** *Over 3 million viewers tuned in to the show.*

tune up when musicians tune up, they prepare their instruments so that they will play the correct notes: *They're still tuning up.* | **tune** sth ↔ **up** *He was tuning up his violin.*

tuneful

tuneful /ˈtjuːnfəl $ ˈtuːn-/ *adj* music that is tuneful is pleasant to listen to

tungsten /ˈtʌŋstən/ *n* [U] a hard metal used in some lights

tunic /ˈtjuːnɪk $ ˈtuː-/ *n* [C] a long loose piece of clothing, usually without sleeves, that covers the top part of your body

tunnel¹ /ˈtʌnl/ *n* [C] a passage that has been dug under the ground, especially for cars or trains to go through

tunnel² *v* [I,T] (**tunnelled, tunnelling** *BrE*, **tunneled, tunneling** *AmE*) to dig a tunnel: [+under/through etc] *They managed to tunnel under the fence.*

tunnel ˈvision *n* [U] *disapproving* the tendency to think about only one part of something such as a problem or plan, instead of considering all the parts of it

turban /ˈtɜːbən $ ˈtɜːr-/ *n* [C] a long piece of cloth that you wind tightly around your head, often for religious reasons

turbine /ˈtɜːbaɪn $ ˈtɜːrbən, -baɪn/ *n* [C] an engine or motor which gets power from the pressure of a liquid or gas moving a wheel around

turbulent /ˈtɜːbjələnt $ ˈtɜːr-/ *adj* **1** a turbulent period or situation is one in which there are a lot of changes: *a turbulent time in European history* **2** turbulent air or water moves suddenly and violently —**turbulence** *n* [U]: *There was a lot of turbulence during the flight.*

tureen /tjʊˈriːn $ təˈriːn/ *n* [C] a large dish with a lid, used for serving soup or vegetables

turf¹ /tɜːf $ tɜːrf/ *n* [U] **1** thick short grass and the soil under it **2** *informal* someone's turf is the area that they control or that they know well: *She felt he was intruding on her turf.*

turf² *v*

PHRASAL VERBS
turf sb ↔ **out** *BrE informal* to force someone to leave a place or organization

turkey /ˈtɜːki $ ˈtɜːrki/ *n* [C,U] a bird that is like a chicken but larger, or the meat from this bird

turmoil /ˈtɜːmɔɪl $ ˈtɜːr-/ *n* [singular, U] a situation in which there is a lot of trouble or confusion: **in turmoil** *In 1968 the country was in turmoil.*

turn¹ /tɜːn $ tɜːrn/ *v*
1 MOVE YOUR BODY [I,T] to move your body so that you are looking in a different direction: *Ricky turned and walked away.* | *Ida turned her head slowly.* | [+around/round/away] *He turned around to look at Kim.* | [+to/towards] *Alison turned towards us.*
2 MOVE STH [T] to move something so that it is facing a new direction: *Turn the plant so it's facing the sun.* | **turn sth around/over/upside down etc** *You may turn over your exam papers.*
3 GO IN A DIFFERENT DIRECTION [I,T] to start going in a new direction, or to make the vehicle you are using do this: *The car turned a corner.* | **turn left/right** *Turn right at the next stop light.* | [+into/onto/down etc] *We turned onto a bumpy road.*
4 MOVE AROUND [I,T] to move around, or to make something move in this way: *The wheels turned slowly.* | **turn a handle/knob/key/tap etc** *She gently*

turned the handle of the door.
5 BECOME [linking verb, T] to become different, or to make something become different: *Helen turned bright red.* | *The weather will turn colder tonight.* | *Police are worried that the situation could turn violent.* | **turn (sth) into/to sth** *His disappointment turned to joy.* | *Hollywood discovered her and turned her into a star.* THESAURUS▶ BECOME
6 AGE [T] to become a particular age: *She's just turned 40.*
7 TIME [T] *BrE* to reach and pass a particular time: *'What time is it?' 'It's just turned 3.00.'*
8 PAGE [T] to move a page in a book or magazine so that you can see the next one
9 ATTENTION/THOUGHTS [I,T] if your thoughts, attention etc turn to something, you direct your attention to that thing instead of what you were thinking about or doing before: **turn your attention/thoughts/efforts etc to sth** *Brian looked up, then turned his attention back to the book he was reading.* | [+to/towards] *As usual, the conversation turned to her children.*

PHRASES
turn your back on sb/sth to refuse to help or be involved with someone or something: *She turned her back on all her old friends.*

THESAURUS – sense 4

turn to move around: *The wheels of the train began to turn.* | *The handle began to turn.*
go around (*also* **go round** *BrE*) to move in a continuous circular movement: *I watched the hands on the clock go slowly round until it was nearly 10 o'clock.*
revolve/rotate to move around continuously – used especially in technical contexts: *The Earth rotates around the Sun.*
spin to turn around many times very quickly: *She was spinning round and round on the ice.*
whirl to turn around extremely quickly, often in a powerful or uncontrolled way: *The blades of the helicopter whirled overhead.*

PHRASAL VERBS
turn (sb) **against** sb/sth to stop liking or agreeing with someone or something, or to make someone do this: *Many people had turned against the war.*
turn sth ↔ **around** (*also* **turn** sth ↔ **round** *BrE*) to make a company, business etc become successful again: *Gibson believes he can turn the struggling company around quickly.*
turn sb ↔ **away**
1 to not allow someone to enter a place: *Hundreds of fans were turned away at the door.*
2 to refuse to help someone: *Anyone who comes to us will not be turned away.*
turn back to go back in the direction you came from, or to make someone do this: *It's getting late – maybe we should turn back.* | **turn sb ↔ back** *Journalists are being turned back at the border.*
turn sb/sth ↔ **down**
1 to make a machine produce less sound, heat etc, using its controls OPP **turn up**: *Can you turn the radio down? I'm trying to work.*
2 to say no when someone offers you something:

She was offered a job there, but she turned it down.
THESAURUS ▶ REFUSE

turn in

1 turn sb ↔ in to tell the police where a person who is believed to be a criminal is: *Morris finally agreed to turn himself in.*

2 *informal* to go to bed

3 turn sth ↔ in *AmE* to give a piece of work you have done to a teacher, your employer etc: *Has everyone turned in last night's homework?*

turn off

1 turn sth ↔ off to make a light or piece of equipment stop working, or make a supply of water, gas etc stop flowing, by turning a switch, tap etc **OPP** turn on: *She turned off the computer and went to bed.*

2 turn off (sth) to leave the road you are travelling on and start travelling on a different road: *Turn off at the next light.*

turn on

1 turn sth ↔ on to make a light or piece of equipment start working, or make a supply of water, gas etc start flowing, by turning a switch, tap etc **OPP** turn off: *Could you turn on the TV? | He turned on the tap and washed the mugs.*

2 turn on sb to criticize or physically attack someone suddenly: *All of a sudden, the dog turned on him and bit him.*

turn out

1 to happen in a particular way or to be found to be something: *Joanna wished things had turned out differently. | turn out well/badly/fine etc I'm confident things will turn out all right in the end. | turn out to be sth The car turned out to be more expensive than we thought.*

2 turn sth ↔ out to make a light stop working by pressing a button, pulling a string etc **OPP** turn on: *Don't forget to turn out the lights when you leave.*

3 if people turn out for something, they go to watch it or be involved in it → **turnout: [+for]** *Only about 30 people turned out for the show.*

turn over

1 turn sb over to sb to take someone who is believed to be a criminal to the police or another official organization: *Benson was turned over to the FBI yesterday.*

2 turn sth over to sb to give someone the right to own or be responsible for something: *He'll turn the shop over to his son when he retires.*

3 *BrE* to change to a different CHANNEL on your television

turn to sb/sth

1 to ask someone for help or sympathy: **[+for]** *He still turns to us for advice.*

2 to look at a particular page in a book, magazine etc: *Turn to page 45 in your history book.*

3 to start to do or use something new, especially as a way of solving a problem: *Many consumers are turning to the Internet for their shopping needs. | turn to drugs/crime/drink etc Bored teenagers are more likely to turn to crime.*

turn up

1 turn sth ↔ up to make a machine produce more sound, heat etc, using its controls **OPP** turn down: *If you're cold, I can turn the heat up.*

2 if something turns up after you have been looking for it, you suddenly find it: *Eventually my watch turned up in a coat pocket.*

3 to arrive: **turn up late/early/on time etc** *Danny turned up late as usual.* **THESAURUS** ▶ ARRIVE

turn² *n* [C]

1 CHANCE TO DO STH if it is your turn to do something, it is the time when you can or should do it, not anyone else **SYN** go *BrE*: *It's your turn. Roll the dice. | Whose turn is it to walk the dog? | You'll just have to wait your turn* (=wait until it is your turn).

2 DIFFERENT DIRECTION a change in the direction you are moving in: **left/right turn** *The car made a left turn at the lights.*

3 JUNCTION a road that joins the road you are on **SYN** turning: *Take the first turn on your left.*

4 CURVE a curve in a road, river etc: *There's a sharp turn coming up ahead.*

5 CIRCULAR MOVEMENT when you turn something completely around a fixed point: *Give the wheel another turn.*

6 CHANGE a sudden or unexpected change that makes a situation develop in a different way: *this new turn of events | take a turn for the better/worse Two days after the operation, Dad took a turn for the worse.*

PHRASES

good turn something that someone does that is helpful to someone else: *He certainly did Patrick a good turn.*

in turn one after another: *He spoke to each of the students in turn.*

take turns (also **take it in turns** *BrE*) if a group of people take turns doing something, first one person does it, then another: **take turns doing sth** *They took turns caring for their mother. | take turns to do sth We took it in turns to do the driving.*

the turn of the century the beginning of a new century: *My ancestors moved to America at the turn of the century.*

turnaround /ˈtɜːnəraʊnd $ ˈtɜːrn-/ (also **turnround** *BrE*) *n* [C] a complete change from a bad situation to a good one: **[+in]** *a turnaround in the team's fortunes*

turning /ˈtɜːnɪŋ $ ˈtɜːr-/ *n* [C] *BrE* a road that joins the road you are on **SYN** turn: *Take the next turning on the left.*

'turning point *n* [C] the time when an important change starts to happen: **[+in]** *The film marked a turning point in Kubrick's career.*

turnip /ˈtɜːnɪp $ ˈtɜːr-/ *n* [C,U] a round white vegetable that grows under the ground → see picture on page A5

'turn-off *n* [C] a place where you can leave a main road to go onto a smaller one

turnout /ˈtɜːnaʊt $ ˈtɜːrn-/ *n* [singular] the number of people who go to an event such as a party, meeting, or election: **low/high turnout** *the low turnout in the elections*

turnover /ˈtɜːnˌəʊvə $ ˈtɜːrnˌoʊvər/ *n* **1** [singular, U] the amount of money a business earns during a particular period **2** [U] the rate at which people leave an organization and are replaced by others:

[+of] *The company has a high turnover of staff.* **3** [C] a small fruit PIE

turnpike /ˈtɜːnpaɪk $ ˈtɜːrn-/ *n* [C] *especially AmE* a large road that drivers have to pay to use

turnround /ˈtɜːnraʊnd $ ˈtɜːrn-/ *n* [C] *BrE* a TURNAROUND

ˈturn ˌsignal *n* [C] *AmE* one of the lights on a car that flash to show which way the car is going to turn SYN **indicator** *BrE* → see picture at **CAR**

turnstile /ˈtɜːnstaɪl $ ˈtɜːrn-/ *n* [C] a small gate that spins around and only lets one person at a time go through an entrance

turntable /ˈtɜːnˌteɪbəl $ ˈtɜːrn-/ *n* [C] a piece of equipment used for playing RECORDs

turpentine /ˈtɜːpəntaɪn $ ˈtɜːr-/ (*also* **turps** *BrE*) /tɜːps $ tɜːrps/ *n* [U] a strong-smelling type of oil used for removing paint

turquoise /ˈtɜːkwɔɪz, -kwɑːz $ ˈtɜːrkwɔɪz/ *n* [U] a greenish-blue colour —**turquoise** *adj*

turret /ˈtʌrɪt/ *n* [C] a small tower on a large building, especially a castle

TURTLE

tortoise

turtle

turtle /ˈtɜːtl $ ˈtɜːrtl/ *n* [C] an animal that lives mainly in water and has a hard flat shell

turtleneck /ˈtɜːtlnek $ ˈtɜːr-/ *n* [C] *AmE* a type of SWEATER or shirt with a collar that covers most of your neck SYN **polo neck** *BrE* → see picture at NECK[1]

tusk /tʌsk/ *n* [C] one of the two long pointed teeth that grow outside the mouth of some animals, such as ELEPHANTS → see picture at **ELEPHANT**

tussle /ˈtʌsəl/ *n* [C] a struggle or fight —**tussle** *v* [I]

tut /tʌt/ (*also* **tut-ˈtut**) a sound you make with your tongue to show disapproval —**tut** *v* [I]

tutor /ˈtjuːtə $ ˈtuːtər/ *n* [C] **1** someone who teaches one person or a small group of people: *a private tutor* THESAURUS **TEACHER 2** a teacher at a British university —**tutor** *v* [T]

tutorial /tjuːˈtɔːriəl $ tuː-/ *n* [C] a class, especially at a British university, in which a small group of students discuss a subject with their tutor

tuxedo /tʌkˈsiːdəʊ $ -doʊ/ (*also* **tux** /tʌks/ *informal*) *n* [C] (*plural* **tuxedos**) a type of man's suit or jacket, usually black, that is worn on very formal occasions

TV /ˌtiː ˈviː◂/ *n* [C,U] television: **on TV** *What's on TV tonight?*

TV ˈdinner *n* [C] a meal that is sold already prepared, so that you just need to heat it before eating it

twang /twæŋ/ *n* [C] **1** a way of speaking in which the sound seems to come from your nose as well as your mouth **2** a quick ringing sound like the one made by pulling a very tight wire and then suddenly letting it go —**twang** *v* [I,T]

tweak /twiːk/ *v* [T] **1** to pull or twist something suddenly: *Grandpa tweaked my nose and laughed.* **2** to make small changes to something in order to improve it —**tweak** *n* [C]

tweed /twiːd/ *n* [U] a thick wool cloth used especially for making jackets

tweet /twiːt/ *v* [I] **1** to make the short high sound of a small bird **2** to send a short message using the SOCIAL NETWORKING service Twitter SYN **twitter** —**tweet** *n* [C]

tweezers /ˈtwiːzəz $ -ərz/ *n* [plural] a small tool consisting of two thin pieces of metal joined at one end. You use tweezers to pull out hairs or pick up small things.

twelfth /twelfθ/ *n* [C] one of twelve equal parts of something

twelve /twelv/ *number* the number 12: *He received a twelve-month jail sentence.* | *Come at twelve* (=12 o'clock). | *Their son Dylan is twelve* (=12 years old). —**twelfth** *adj, pron:* *her twelfth birthday* | *I'm planning to leave on* **the twelfth** (=the 12th day of the month).

twenty /ˈtwenti/ *number*
1 the number 20: *a small village twenty miles from Nairobi* | *I'm nearly twenty* (=20 years old).
2 the twenties (*also* **the '20s, the 1920s**) [plural] the years from 1920 to 1929: **the early/mid/late twenties** *The photograph was taken in the late twenties.* —**twentieth** *adj, pron:* *her twentieth birthday* | *I'm leaving on* **the twentieth** (=the 20th day of the month).
PHRASES
be in your twenties to be aged between 20 and 29: **early/mid/late twenties** *She was in her late twenties.*
in the twenties if the temperature is in the twenties, it is between 20 degrees and 29 degrees F: *The temperature is expected to be in the twenties tomorrow.*

ˌtwenty-four ˈseven, 24-7 *adv informal* if something happens twenty-four seven, it happens all the time, every day

twice /twaɪs/ *adv* two times: *I've seen that movie twice already.*

twiddle /ˈtwɪdl/ *v* [I,T] to move or turn something around with your fingers many times, especially because you are nervous or bored
PHRASES
twiddle your thumbs to do nothing while you are waiting: *Let's go – there's no point in sitting here twiddling our thumbs.*

twig /twɪg/ n [C] a very thin branch that grows on a larger branch of a tree

twilight /'twaɪlaɪt/ n [U] the time when day is just starting to become night, or the small amount of light at this time

twin¹ /twɪn/ n [C] one of two children who are born at the same time and have the same mother: *My sister and I are **identical twins** (=twins that look exactly the same).*

twin² adj [only before noun] **1** used to describe a child who is a twin: **twin sister/brother 2** used to talk about two things of the same kind that are together or connected: *twin beds* **3** a twin room has two beds in it

twine /twaɪn/ n [U] thick strong string

twinge /twɪndʒ/ n [C] **1** a sudden slight pain **2 twinge of guilt/sadness/jealousy etc** a sudden slight feeling of guilt etc

twinkle /'twɪŋkəl/ v [I] **1** if a star or light twinkles, it shines very brightly, but not continuously **THESAURUS** SHINE **2** if someone's eyes twinkle, they look happy —**twinkle** n [C]

twinned /twɪnd/ adj **be twinned with sth** if a town in one country is twinned with a town in another country, an official relationship exists between them —**twinning** n [C,U]

twirl /twɜːl $ twɜːrl/ v [I,T] to turn around and around, or to make someone do this: *Elaine twirled across the dance floor.* —**twirl** n [C]

twist¹ /twɪst/ v
1 BEND INTO SHAPE [T] to bend or turn something around several times and change its shape: *He rolled up the paper and began twisting the ends.* | **twist sth into/in/around sth** *Her hair was twisted in a bun.*
2 MOVE BODY [I,T] to turn a part of your body around or change your position by turning: **[+around/round]** *He twisted around in order to get a better look.*
3 KNEE/ANKLE [T] to hurt your knee or ankle by suddenly turning it: *I slipped on the stairs and **twisted my ankle**.* **THESAURUS** HURT
4 KNOB/LID ETC [T] to turn something in a circle using your hand: **twist sth off (sth)** *Jack twisted the cap off the bottle.*
5 MEANING [T] to change the meaning of what someone says, especially in order to get some advantage for yourself: *Davis accused reporters of **twisting his words**.* **THESAURUS** CHANGE
6 ROAD/RIVER [I] if a road, river etc twists, it has a lot of curves in it
PHRASES
twist sb's arm to persuade someone to do something they do not want to do: *We had to twist her arm to get her to come.*

twist² n [C] **1** a sudden change in a story or situation that you did not expect: *Her disappearance added a **new twist** to the story.* **2** a small piece of something that is twisted into a particular shape: **[+of]** *a twist of lemon* **3** a bend in a river or road

twisted /'twɪstɪd/ adj **1** something twisted has been bent many times, so that it has lost its original shape: *twisted pieces of metal* → see picture at **BENT²**

2 seeming to enjoy things that are cruel or shocking, in a way that is not normal: *Whoever sent those letters has a twisted mind.*

twister /'twɪstə $ -ər/ n [C] AmE informal a TORNADO

twit /twɪt/ n [C] informal a stupid or silly person

twitch /twɪtʃ/ v [I] if a part of your body twitches, it suddenly moves slightly and you cannot control it **THESAURUS** MOVE —**twitch** n [C]

twitter /'twɪtə $ -ər/ v [I] **1** if a bird twitters, it makes a lot of short high sounds **2** to send a short message using the SOCIAL NETWORKING service Twitter **SYN** **tweet** —**twitter** n [singular]

Twitter trademark a SOCIAL NETWORKING service on the Internet, which allows people to send short text messages to other users

two /tuː/ number the number 2: *I'll be away for almost two weeks.* | *We have to be there by two (=two o'clock).* | *His family moved to Australia when he was two (=two years old).*

two-bit adj AmE informal not very good or important: *a two-bit actor*

two-di'mensional adj flat: *a two-dimensional shape*

two-'faced adj disapproving someone who is two-faced is not honest or sincere because they say different things about something to different people

twofold /'tuːfəʊld $ -foʊld/ adj two times as much or as many: *a twofold increase in price* —**twofold** adv

two-time v [T] informal if you two-time your boyfriend or girlfriend, you secretly have a sexual relationship with someone else

two-tone adj having two colours: *two-tone shoes*

two-'way adj **1** moving in two opposite directions: *two-way traffic* **2** a two-way radio sends and receives messages

tycoon /taɪˈkuːn/ n [C] someone who is very successful in business and has a lot of money

tying /'taɪ-ɪŋ/ v the present participle of TIE

type¹ /taɪp/ n
1 [C] a group of people or things that are similar to each other in some way → **kind**: **[+of]** *What type of food do you like?* | **a particular/certain/different etc type** *To run this program you need a special type of software.* | **of this/that/each etc type** *Accidents of this type are very common.*
2 [C usually singular] someone with particular qualities or interests: *He's not really the athletic type.*
3 [U] printed letters: *italic type* → **BLOOD TYPE**
PHRASES
be sb's type spoken to be the kind of person that someone is attracted to: *Alex is OK – but he's not really my type.*

type² v [I,T] to write something using a computer or typewriter: *Cindy can type 50 words a minute.*

typecast /'taɪpkɑːst $ -kæst/ v [T usually passive] (past tense and past participle **typecast**) if an actor is typecast, he or she is always given the same kind of characters to play: *In the early days of Hollywood, black actors were often typecast as servants.*

typeface /ˈtaɪpfeɪs/ n [C] letters, numbers etc of a particular style and size, used in printing

typewriter /ˈtaɪpˌraɪtə $ -ər/ n [C] a machine that prints letters, numbers etc on paper when you press its keys

typewritten /ˈtaɪpˌrɪtn/ adj written using a typewriter

typhoid /ˈtaɪfɔɪd/ (also ˌtyphoid ˈfever) n [U] a serious infectious disease that is caused by dirty food or drink

typhoon /ˌtaɪˈfuːn◂/ n [C] a tropical storm with very strong winds THESAURUS ▶ STORM

typical /ˈtɪpɪkəl/ adj
1 a typical person or thing has the usual qualities or features that people expect them to have: a typical American family | [+of] This painting is typical of his early work.
2 happening in the usual way: On a **typical day** I wake up at 6.

typically /ˈtɪpɪkli/ adv **1** used to say what usually happens: Prices typically start at around $600. **2** used to say that something is typical of a person, thing, or group: Typically, Lenny said nothing, keeping his feelings to himself. | a typically Japanese dish

typify /ˈtɪpɪfaɪ/ v [T] (**typified, typifying, typifies**) to be a typical example or feature of something

typing /ˈtaɪpɪŋ/ n [U] writing that you do using a TYPEWRITER or computer

typist /ˈtaɪpɪst/ n [C] someone whose job is to type letters and other documents in an office

typo /ˈtaɪpəʊ $ -poʊ/ n [C] (plural **typos**) a small mistake in the way something has been TYPEd or printed

tyranny /ˈtɪrəni/ n [U] when a government, leader etc uses their power in a cruel and unfair way —**tyrannical** /tɪˈrænɪkəl/ adj

tyrant /ˈtaɪərənt $ ˈtaɪr-/ n [C] someone who uses their power in a cruel and unfair way: Despite his friendly appearance, her father was a real tyrant.

tyre BrE, **tire** AmE /taɪə $ taɪr/ n [C] the round piece of rubber that fits around a wheel of a car, bicycle etc and is filled with air: I had a **flat tyre** (=all the air went out of it) on the way home. → see picture at **CAR**

tzar /zɑː, tsɑː $ zɑːr, tsɑːr/ n another spelling of TSAR

T

Uu

U, u /juː/ n [C,U] (plural **U's, u's**) the 21st letter of the English alphabet

ubiquitous /juːˈbɪkwɪtəs/ adj formal seeming to be everywhere

udder /ˈʌdə $ -ər/ n [C] the part of a cow, goat etc that hangs below its body and produces milk

UFO /ˈjuːfəʊ, juː ef ˈəʊ $ -foʊ, -ˈoʊ/ n [C] (**Unidentified Flying Object**) a moving object in the sky that some people believe could be carrying creatures from another world

ugh /ʊx, ʌg/ spoken the sound that people make when something is extremely unpleasant: *Ugh! This tastes foul!*

ugly /ˈʌgli/ adj
1 very unattractive or unpleasant to look at OPP **beautiful**: *ugly modern buildings* | *She's not pretty, but she's not ugly either.*
2 unpleasant and violent: *There were **ugly scenes** at the England-Italy game.* —**ugliness** n [U]

THESAURUS

ugly very unpleasant to look at – used about people, objects, and buildings: *He was short, fat, and ugly.* | *It was an ugly 1970s apartment building.*
unattractive not nice to look at. **Unattractive** sounds more formal and less strong than **ugly**: *Women found him unattractive.*
hideous extremely ugly: *a hideous concrete building* | *She looked hideous in that dress.*
repulsive extremely ugly, in a way that makes you feel uncomfortable or want to look away: *He loved her, but she found him repulsive and could not bear to be with him.*
grotesque extremely ugly in a strange and unnatural way: *The movie is full of grotesque images of violence.*
be an eyesore to be very ugly and spoil the appearance of an area – used especially about buildings, structures, or rubbish: *Local people think the factory is an eyesore.*

---

uh huh /ʌ ˈhʌ,ˈʌ hʌ/ spoken informal a sound that you make to say 'yes', or when you want someone to continue what they are saying: *'Can I sit here?' 'Uh huh.'*

uh-oh /ˈʌ əʊ $ -oʊ/ spoken informal a sound that you make when you have made a mistake, or when something bad is going to happen: *Uh-oh, I've deleted the wrong file.* | *Uh-oh! Here she comes.*

uh-uh /ˈʌ ʌ ʌ/ spoken informal a sound that you make to say 'no': *'Is Paul here yet?' 'Uh-uh.'*

ulcer /ˈʌlsə $ -ər/ n [C] a sore area on or inside your body, which may BLEED: *a stomach ulcer*

ulterior /ʌlˈtɪəriə $ -ˈtɪriər/ adj **ulterior motive** a secret reason for doing something

ultimate¹ [Ac] /ˈʌltəmət/ adj [only before noun]
1 better or greater than all other things or people of the same kind: *the ultimate rock and roll band* | *the ultimate disgrace* **2** final or coming at the end: *their ultimate objective* | *the ultimate failure of the project*

ultimate² n **the ultimate in sth** the best example or highest level of something: *Guy's home is **the ultimate in luxury**.*

ultimately [Ac] /ˈʌltəmətli/ adv finally, after everything else has been done or considered: *Their efforts ultimately resulted in his release from prison.* | *Ultimately it's your decision.*

ultimatum /ˌʌltəˈmeɪtəm/ n [C] a threat saying that if someone does not do what you want by a particular time, you will do something they do not want: **issue/give sb an ultimatum** *The government issued an ultimatum to the rebels to surrender.*

ultra- /ˈʌltrə/ prefix extremely: *an ultra-modern kitchen*

ultrasonic /ˌʌltrəˈsɒnɪk ◄ $ -ˈsɑː-/ adj technical ultrasonic sounds are too high for humans to hear

ultrasound /ˈʌltrəsaʊnd/ n [C,U] a medical process that produces an image of something inside your body

ultraviolet /ˌʌltrəˈvaɪəlɪt ◄/ adj ultraviolet light cannot be seen but makes your skin become darker when you are in the sun → **infra-red**

um /ʌm, əm/ spoken used when you cannot immediately decide what to say next: *Um, yeah, I guess so.*

umbilical cord /ʌmˈbɪlɪkəl ˌkɔːd $ -ˌkɔːrd/ n [C] the tube that connects a baby to its mother before it is born

umbrage /ˈʌmbrɪdʒ/ n **take umbrage (at sth)** old-fashioned to be offended by something, often without a good reason

umbrella /ʌmˈbrelə/ n [C]
1 a thing that you hold above your head to protect yourself from the rain → **parasol**: *It started to rain so I put up my umbrella.*
2 umbrella organization/group etc an organization that includes several smaller groups: *an umbrella organization of opposition groups*

umpire /ˈʌmpaɪə $ -paɪr/ n [C] the person who makes sure that the players of a sports game obey the rules —**umpire** v [I,T]

umpteen /ˌʌmpˈtiːn ◄/ determiner informal very many – used especially when you are annoyed there are so many: *umpteen reasons* —**umpteenth** /ˌʌmpˈtiːnθ ◄/ adj: **For the umpteenth time** *he checked his watch.*

UN, U.N. /ˌjuː ˈen/ n **the UN** the United Nations

un- /ʌn/ prefix **1** not: *unhappy* | *unexpected* **2** used to talk about the opposite of an action: *I undressed quickly* (=took my clothes off). | *You can unfasten your seat belt now.*

unabashed /ˌʌnəˈbæʃt ◄/ adj written not ashamed or embarrassed: *She stared at him with unabashed curiosity.*

U

unabated /ˌʌnəˈbeɪtɪd◄/ adj, adv if something continues unabated, it does not stop or become weaker: *The storm continued unabated.*

unable /ʌnˈeɪbəl/ adj **be unable to do sth** to not be able to do something → **inability**: *She was unable to sleep.* | *I'm sorry; I'm unable to help you.*

unacceptable /ˌʌnəkˈseptəbəl◄/ adj something that is unacceptable is wrong or bad and should not be allowed to continue: *Your behaviour is totally unacceptable.* —**unacceptably** adv

unaccompanied Ac /ˌʌnəˈkʌmpənid◄/ adj, adv **1** if you go somewhere unaccompanied, you go there alone **2** if you sing or play a musical instrument unaccompanied, no one plays with you

unaccountable /ˌʌnəˈkaʊntəbəl◄/ adj **1** very surprising and difficult to explain: *For some unaccountable reason he's moving to New York.* **2** not having to explain your actions or decisions to anyone else —**unaccountably** adv

unadulterated /ˌʌnəˈdʌltəreɪtɪd◄/ adj complete or pure: *sheer unadulterated pleasure*

unaffected Ac /ˌʌnəˈfektɪd◄/ adj not changed or harmed by something: *Parts of the city remained unaffected by the fire.*

unaided Ac /ʌnˈeɪdɪd/ adv without help: *She can no longer walk unaided.*

unanimous /juːˈnænɪməs/ adj a unanimous decision, vote etc is one in which everyone agrees THESAURUS **AGREE** —**unanimously** adv —**unanimity** /ˌjuːnəˈnɪməti/ n [U]

unannounced /ˌʌnəˈnaʊnst◄/ adj, adv if you arrive somewhere unannounced, your arrival was not expected

unanswered /ʌnˈɑːnsəd $ -ˈænsərd/ adj an unanswered letter, question etc has not been answered: *Many questions remain unanswered.*

unapproachable Ac /ˌʌnəˈprəʊtʃəbəl $ -ˈproʊ-/ adj not friendly and not easy to talk to

unarmed /ʌnˈɑːmd◄ $ -ˈɑːrmd◄/ adj, adv not carrying any weapons: *the killing of unarmed civilians*

unashamedly /ˌʌnəˈʃeɪmɪdli/ adv used to say that someone is not embarrassed or worried that other people will disapprove of what they are doing: *Their latest record is unashamedly commercial.* —**unashamed** /-ˈʃeɪmd◄/ adj

unassailable /ˌʌnəˈseɪləbəl◄/ adj formal impossible to be criticized or beaten: *The win gave the Yankees an unassailable lead.*

unassuming /ˌʌnəˈsjuːmɪŋ◄, -ˈsuː- $ -ˈsuː-/ adj not trying to be noticed or given special treatment SYN **modest**: *a quiet unassuming man*

unattached Ac /ˌʌnəˈtætʃt◄/ adj not married or involved in a romantic relationship → **single**

unattended /ˌʌnəˈtendɪd◄/ adj, adv formal left alone without being watched or looked after: *Please do not leave your bags unattended.* | *an unattended vehicle*

unattractive /ˌʌnəˈtræktɪv◄/ adj **1** not pleasant to look at **2** not good enough to be wanted

unauthorized (also **-ised** BrE) /ʌnˈɔːθəraɪzd $ -ˈɒː-/ adj done without official permission: *the unauthorized use of government funds*

unavailable Ac /ˌʌnəˈveɪləbəl/ adj **1** not able to be bought, obtained, or used: *an album previously unavailable on CD* **2** not able to be spoken to: *I'm afraid she's unavailable at the moment.* | **[+for]** *Officials were unavailable for comment* (=not able or willing to talk to reporters).

unavoidable /ˌʌnəˈvɔɪdəbəl/ adj impossible to prevent: *an unavoidable delay* —**unavoidably** adv

unaware Ac /ˌʌnəˈweə $ -ˈwer/ adj [not before noun] not noticing or realizing what is happening: **[+of]** *She seemed unaware of what was happening.*

unawares /ˌʌnəˈweəz $ -ˈwerz/ adv **catch/take sb unawares** if something catches you unawares, it happens when you are not expecting it: *The enemy had been caught unawares.*

unbalanced /ʌnˈbælənst/ adj **1** slightly crazy: *He's obviously mentally unbalanced.* **2** unfair or unequal: *unbalanced reporting*

unbearable /ʌnˈbeərəbəl $ -ˈber-/ adj too painful, unpleasant etc for you to accept or deal with SYN **intolerable**: *The pain was unbearable.* —**unbearably** adv: *an unbearably hot day*

unbeatable /ʌnˈbiːtəbəl/ adj something that is unbeatable is the best of its kind: *Their prices are unbeatable.*

unbeaten /ʌnˈbiːtn◄/ adj a team, player etc that is unbeaten has not been defeated

unbelievable /ˌʌnbəˈliːvəbəl◄/ adj **1** extremely bad, impressive, or surprising SYN **incredible**: *The noise was unbelievable.* | *an unbelievable amount of money* THESAURUS **SURPRISING 2** very difficult to believe and therefore probably untrue: *His story sounded completely unbelievable.* —**unbelievably** adv

unbending /ʌnˈbendɪŋ/ adj disapproving unwilling to change your opinions, decisions etc

unborn /ʌnˈbɔːn◄ $ -ˈbɔːrn◄/ adj not yet born: *an unborn child*

unbridled /ʌnˈbraɪdld/ adj literary disapproving extreme and not controlled: *unbridled passion*

unbroken /ʌnˈbrəʊkən $ -ˈbroʊ-/ adj continuing without being interrupted: *unbroken peace*

unbutton /ʌnˈbʌtn/ v [T] to unfasten the buttons on a piece of clothing

uncalled for /ʌnˈkɔːld fɔː $ -ˈkɔːld fɔːr/ adj behaviour or remarks that are uncalled for are not fair or suitable

uncanny /ʌnˈkæni/ adj very strange and difficult to explain: *an uncanny coincidence* —**uncannily** adv

uncaring /ʌnˈkeərɪŋ $ -ˈker-/ adj not caring about other people's feelings

unceremoniously /ˌʌnserəˈməʊniəsli $ -ˈmoʊ-/ adv in a way that shows no care or respect: *She dumped the flowers unceremoniously in the bin.*

uncertain /ʌnˈsɜːtn $ -ˈsɜːr-/ adj **1** [not before noun] feeling doubt about something SYN **unsure**: **[+whether/how/what etc]** *She was uncertain whether she would recognize him.* |

[+about/of] *I was uncertain about what to do next.*
2 not clear, definite, or decided SYN **unclear**: *His future with the company is uncertain.* —**uncertainty** *n* [C,U] —**uncertainly** *adv*

PHRASES
in no uncertain terms if you tell someone something in no uncertain terms, you tell them very clearly without trying to be polite: *I told Colin in no uncertain terms what I thought of him.*

unchanged /ʌnˈtʃeɪndʒd◀/ *adj* the same as before

unchanging /ʌnˈtʃeɪndʒɪŋ/ *adj* always staying the same

uncharacteristic /ˌʌnˌkærəktəˈrɪstɪk◀/ *adj* not typical of someone or something —**uncharacteristically** /-kli/ *adv*

uncharted Ac /ʌnˈtʃɑːtɪd $ -ɑːr-/ *adj* **uncharted territory/waters** a situation or activity that you have never experienced before

unchecked /ʌnˈtʃekt◀/ *adj, adv* if something bad continues unchecked, it is not stopped

uncle /ˈʌŋkəl/ *n* [C] the brother of your mother or father, or the husband of your AUNT

unclear /ʌnˈklɪə◀ $ -ˈklɪr◀/ *adj* **1** difficult to understand or be sure about: *The law is unclear on this issue.* **2 be unclear about sth** to not understand something clearly: *I'm a little unclear about what they mean.*

uncomfortable /ʌnˈkʌmftəbəl, -ˈkʌmfət- $ -ˈkʌmfərt-, -ˈkʌmft-/ *adj*
1 not feeling physically relaxed, or not making you feel physically relaxed: *The heat made her feel uncomfortable.* | *an uncomfortable chair*
2 embarrassed or worried, or making you feel embarrassed and worried SYN **awkward**: *There was an uncomfortable silence.* | [+about] *She felt uncomfortable about being photographed.* —**uncomfortably** *adv*

uncommon /ʌnˈkɒmən $ -ˈkɑː-/ *adj* rare or unusual: *It is not uncommon for patients to have to wait five hours to see a doctor.* —**uncommonly** *adv*

uncompromising /ʌnˈkɒmprəmaɪzɪŋ $ -ˈkɑːm-/ *adj* unwilling to change your opinions or intentions: *an uncompromising opponent of democratic reform*

unconcerned /ˌʌnkənˈsɜːnd◀ $ -ɜːrnd◀/ *adj* not worried about or interested in something: *Her parents seemed unconcerned by her absence.*

unconditional /ˌʌnkənˈdɪʃənəl◀/ *adj* not limited by or depending on any conditions: *unconditional surrender* —**unconditionally** *adv*

unconfirmed /ˌʌnkənˈfɜːmd◀ $ -ˈfɜːrmd◀/ *adj* if a report or story is unconfirmed, there is no definite proof that it is true

unconnected /ˌʌnkəˈnektɪd◀/ *adj* not related in any way: *The murders are probably unconnected.*

unconscious¹ /ʌnˈkɒnʃəs $ -ˈkɑːn-/ *adj*
1 unable to see, move, feel etc, especially because you have had an accident, been given drugs etc: *She was found alive but unconscious.* | *The driver was knocked unconscious.*
2 be unconscious of sth to not notice something or

realize what is happening: *She seemed quite unconscious of the attention her dress was attracting.*
3 an unconscious feeling is one that you do not realize you have → **subconscious**: *an unconscious desire* —**unconsciously** *adv* —**unconsciousness** *n* [U]

unconscious² *n* **the/sb's unconscious** the part of your mind in which there are ideas and feelings that you do not realize you have → **subconscious**

unconstitutional Ac /ˌʌnkɒnstəˈtjuːʃənəl $ -kɑːnstɪˈtuː-/ *adj* not allowed by the rules of a country or organization

uncontrollable /ˌʌnkənˈtrəʊləbəl◀ $ -ˈtroʊl-/ *adj* something that is uncontrollable cannot be controlled or stopped: *uncontrollable rage*

unconventional Ac /ˌʌnkənˈvenʃənəl◀/ *adj* very different from the kind that most people have, use etc: *unconventional teaching methods*

uncool /ʌnˈkuːl◀/ *adj* informal not fashionable or acceptable

uncountable /ʌnˈkaʊntəbəl/ *adj* an uncountable noun has no plural form, for example 'money', 'happiness', or 'furniture'

uncouth /ʌnˈkuːθ/ *adj* behaving or speaking in a rude unpleasant way

uncover /ʌnˈkʌvə $ -ər/ *v* [T] **1** to find out about something that has been kept secret: *They uncovered a plot to kill the president.* **2** to remove the cover from something

undaunted /ʌnˈdɔːntɪd $ -ˈdɒːn-/ *adj, adv* not afraid to continue doing something, in spite of difficulties or danger: [+by] *Fisher was undaunted by their opposition.*

undecided /ˌʌndɪˈsaɪdɪd◀/ *adj* [not before noun] not having made a decision: [+about] *Many people are still undecided about how they will vote.*

undeniable Ac /ˌʌndɪˈnaɪəbəl◀/ *adj* definitely true or certain —**undeniably** *adv*

under /ˈʌndə $ -ər/ *prep, adv*
1 below or at a lower level than something, or covered by something OPP **over**: *The cat was asleep under a chair.* | *She kept her head under the blankets.* | *We sailed under the Golden Gate Bridge.* | *He dived into the water and stayed under for over a minute.* → see picture on page A8
2 less than a particular number, amount, age, or price: *You can buy a good computer for under $1,000.* | *children aged 16 and under*
3 governed or controlled by a leader, political party etc: *Would things have been different under a Conservative government?*
4 used to say what is being done to something or how it is being dealt with: *The tunnel is still under construction.* | *We're under attack!* | *under discussion/consideration/review etc*
5 affected by a particular condition, influence, or situation: *She performs well under pressure.* | *under the influence of sth He was accused of driving while under the influence of alcohol.* | *I've got everything under control.*
6 if you are under someone, they are in charge of you: *She has a team of researchers under her.*

U

7 according to a law, agreement, system etc: *The trade is illegal under international law.*
8 used to say in which part of a book, list, or system something can be found: *You'll find her books under 'Modern Fiction'.*
9 using a particular name: *He writes under the name of Taki.*

PHRASES
under .... conditions/circumstances when particular conditions exist: *I wish I'd met him under different circumstances.*
under way if something is under way, it is being done or happening: *Important changes are now under way.*

THESAURUS

under below or at a lower level than something, or covered by something: *The shoes were under her bed.* | *He was wearing a jacket under his coat.*
below in a lower position than something else, though not always directly under it: *From the cliffs we could see the people on the beach below us.*
underneath directly under something, or covered by another thing: *The mechanic got down and looked underneath the car.* | *There are several pipes underneath the floor.*
beneath *formal* under or at a lower level: *They lay on the ground beneath the ash tree.* | *The people lived beneath the shadow of the mountain.*

---

under- /ˈʌndə $ -dər/ *prefix* **1** not enough: *undercooked cabbage* | *undernourished children* **2** beneath something else: *underwear* | *undersea exploration* **3** less important or lower in rank: *an under-secretary*

under-'age *adj* too young to legally buy alcohol, drive a car etc: *under-age drinking*

underarm /ˈʌndərɑːm $ -ɑːrm/ *n* [C] the area under your arm, where it joins your body SYN **armpit**

undercarriage /ˈʌndəˌkærɪdʒ $ -ər-/ *n* [C] the wheels of an aircraft or train and the structure that holds them

underclass /ˈʌndəklɑːs $ -dərklæs/ *n* [singular] a group of people in society who are very poor and cannot change the situation they are in

underclothes /ˈʌndəkləʊðz -kləʊz $ -dərkləʊðz, -kloʊz/ *n* [plural] *old-fashioned* clothes that you wear next to your body, under your other clothes SYN **underwear**

undercover /ˌʌndəˈkʌvə◂ $ -dərˈkʌvər◂/ *adj, adv* working secretly in order to find out information for the government or the police: *an undercover agent*
THESAURUS **SECRET**

undercurrent /ˈʌndəˌkʌrənt $ -dərˌkɜːr-/ *n* [C] a feeling, especially of anger or dissatisfaction, that people do not express openly: **[+of]** *an undercurrent of racism*

undercut /ˌʌndəˈkʌt $ -ər-/ *v* [T] (*past tense and past participle* **undercut**, *present participle* **undercutting**) to sell something more cheaply than someone else: *We've undercut our competitors by 15%.*

underdog /ˈʌndədɒg $ ˈʌndərdɔːg/ *n* [C] the person or team in a game or competition that is not expected to win

underestimate Ac /ˌʌndərˈestɪmeɪt/ *v* [T] **1** to think that something is smaller than it really is OPP **overestimate**: *They underestimated the size of the problem.* **2** to think that someone is less skilful, intelligent etc than they really are OPP **overestimate**: *Never underestimate your opponent.* —**underestimate** /-mət/ *n* [C]

underfoot /ˌʌndəˈfʊt $ -ər-/ *adv* under your feet when you are walking: *It's very wet underfoot.*

undergo Ac /ˌʌndəˈgəʊ $ ˌʌndərˈgoʊ/ *v* [T] (*past tense* **underwent** /-ˈwent/, *past participle* **undergone** /-ˈgɒn $ -ˈgɔːn/, *third person singular* **undergoes** /-ˈgəʊz $ -ˈgoʊz/) if you undergo a change, an unpleasant experience etc, it happens to you or is done to you: *He had to undergo major heart surgery.*

undergraduate /ˌʌndəˈgrædʒuət◂ $ -ər-/ *n* [C] a student who is doing their first degree at university → **postgraduate** —**undergraduate** *adj*

underground¹ /ˌʌndəˈgraʊnd◂ $ -ər-/ *adj, adv*
1 under the surface of the ground: *underground streams* | *an underground car park* | *animals that live underground*
2 an underground political organization is secret and illegal: *an underground resistance movement* | *The ANC was forced to **go underground** when its leaders were arrested.*

underground² /ˈʌndəgraʊnd $ -ər-/ *n* [singular] *BrE* a railway system under a city SYN **metro**, **subway** *AmE*: *the London Underground* → see Word Choice at **SUBWAY**

undergrowth /ˈʌndəgrəʊθ $ -dərgroʊθ/ *n* [U] bushes and plants that grow around bigger trees

underhand /ˌʌndəˈhænd◂ $ ˈʌndərhænd/ (*also* **underhanded** /ˌʌndəˈhændɪd◂ $ ˈʌndərhændɪd/) *adj disapproving* dishonest or done secretly: *underhand tactics*

underlie Ac /ˌʌndəˈlaɪ $ -ər-/ *v* [T] (*past tense* **underlay** /-ˈleɪ/, *past participle* **underlain** /-ˈleɪn/, *present participle* **underlying**) *formal* to be the basic cause of something, or the basic thing from which something develops: *the principle which underlies the party's policies* —**underlying** *adj*: *the underlying cause of the disease*

underline /ˌʌndəˈlaɪn $ -ər-/ *v* [T]
1 to draw a line under a word to show that it is important
2 to show or emphasize that something is important: *This tragic incident underlines the need for immediate action.*

undermine /ˌʌndəˈmaɪn $ -ər-/ *v* [T] to gradually make someone or something less strong or effective: *She totally undermined his self-confidence.*

underneath¹ /ˌʌndəˈniːθ $ -ər-/ *prep, adv*
1 directly under another object or covered by it: *I found the keys underneath a cushion.* | *She was wearing a jacket with a T-shirt underneath.*
2 on the lower surface of something: *The car was rusty underneath.*
3 used to say what someone is really like, when

their behaviour does not show this: *I think he's a nice person underneath.*

underneath² *n* **the underneath** the bottom surface of something THESAURUS> BOTTOM

underpaid /ˌʌndəˈpeɪd◂ $ -ər-/ *adj* earning less money than you should

underpants /ˈʌndəpænts $ -ər-/ *n* [plural] a piece of clothing that men wear under their trousers → see picture at CLOTHES

underpass /ˈʌndəpɑːs $ ˈʌndərpæs/ *n* [C] a road or path that goes under another road or a railway

underpin /ˌʌndəˈpɪn $ -ər-/ *v* [T] (**underpinned**, **underpinning**) to give strength or support to something

underprivileged /ˌʌndəˈprɪvəlɪdʒd◂ $ -dər-/ *adj* poor and having no advantages in society: *underprivileged children*

underrated /ˌʌndəˈreɪtɪd◂/ *adj* better than people think or say: *an underrated player* —**underrate** *v* [T]

underscore /ˌʌndəˈskɔː $ -dərˈskɔːr/ *v* [T] *especially AmE* to emphasize that something is important SYN **underline**

undershirt /ˈʌndəʃɜːt $ ˈʌndərʃɜːrt/ *n* [C] a piece of underwear worn under a shirt

underside /ˈʌndəsaɪd $ -ər-/ *n* **the underside (of sth)** the bottom surface of something: *white spots on the underside of the leaves* THESAURUS> BOTTOM

understaffed /ˌʌndəˈstɑːft◂ $ ˌʌndərˈstæft◂/ *adj* not having enough workers

understand /ˌʌndəˈstænd $ -ər-/ *v* [I,T] (*past tense and past participle* **understood** /-ˈstʊd/)

1 to know the meaning of what someone is telling you, or the language that they speak OPP **misunderstand**: *She spoke clearly, so that everyone could understand.* | *Most people there understand English.*

2 to know how something works, or why something happens: *Scientists still don't really understand this phenomenon.* | **[+how/why/where etc]** *You don't need to understand how computers work to be able to use them.*

3 to know how someone feels and why they behave in the way they do: *Believe me, John – I understand how you feel.* | *My parents don't understand me.*

4 to believe or think that something is true because you have heard it or read it: **[+(that)]** *I understand that you want to buy a painting.* | **It is understood that** *she is going to resign.*

PHRASES

make yourself understood to explain or say something in a way that people find easy to understand: *I'm not very good at German, but I can make myself understood.*

THESAURUS

understand to know the meaning of what someone is telling you, the language that they speak, or the reasons for something: *His books are difficult for ordinary people to understand.* | *Gila doesn't understand English very well.*

see *especially spoken* to understand something, especially the truth about a situation or the reasons for something: *Do you see what I mean?* | *I can see why you don't like him.*

follow to understand instructions, an explanation, a story, or what someone is talking about: *The instructions were easy to follow.* | *Do you follow me?*

comprehend *formal* to understand something, or understand why something is important: *The government failed to comprehend how serious the problem was.*

grasp to completely understand an idea or a fact, especially a complicated one: *I don't think Stuart really grasped the point I was making.*

understandable /ˌʌndəˈstændəbəl $ -dər-/ *adj* understandable behaviour etc seems reasonable because of the situation: *Of course he's upset. It's a perfectly understandable reaction.* —**understandably** *adv*

understanding¹ /ˌʌndəˈstændɪŋ $ -ər-/ *n* **1** [U] knowledge about something based on learning or experience: **[+of]** *major advances in our understanding of the brain* **2** [U] the ability to think or learn about something: *a concept that is beyond the understanding of a four-year-old* **3** [singular] an unofficial or informal agreement: *I thought we* **had an understanding** *about the price.* **4** [U] sympathy towards someone: *Harry thanked us for our understanding.*

understanding² *adj* showing sympathy towards someone who has problems: *an understanding boss*

understated /ˌʌndəˈsteɪtɪd◂ $ -dər-/ *adj* approving simple in style: *the understated elegance of her dress*

understatement /ˌʌndəˈsteɪtmənt $ -dər-/ *n* [C,U] a statement that is not strong enough to express how good, bad, impressive etc something really is: *To say the movie is bad is an understatement.*

understood /ˌʌndəˈstʊd $ -ər-/ *v* the past tense and past participle of UNDERSTAND

understudy /ˈʌndəˌstʌdi $ -ər-/ *n* [C] (*plural* **understudies**) an actor who learns the words of a character in a play so that they can perform if the usual actor is ill

undertake Ac /ˌʌndəˈteɪk $ -dər-/ *v* [T] (*past tense* **undertook** /-ˈtʊk/, *past participle* **undertaken** /-ˈteɪkən/) *formal* **1** to start to do a piece of work, especially one that is long and difficult: *Baker undertook the task of writing the report.* **2 undertake to do sth** to promise or agree to do something: *He undertook to pay the money back in six months.*

undertaker /ˈʌndəteɪkə $ -dərteɪkər/ *n* [C] someone whose job is to arrange funerals

undertaking Ac /ˌʌndəˈteɪkɪŋ $ ˈʌndərteɪ-/ *n* [C usually singular] **1** an important or difficult piece of work: *Starting a new business can be a risky undertaking.* **2** a legal or official promise to do something

undertone /ˈʌndətəʊn $ -dərtoʊn/ *n* [C] a feeling or quality that exists but is not very easy to recognize: *the political undertones of Sartre's work*

PHRASES

in an undertone in a low quiet voice: *The two women were speaking to each other in an undertone.*

undertook /ˌʌndəˈtʊk $ -ər-/ v the past tense of UNDERTAKE

undervalue /ˌʌndəˈvælju: $ -ər-/ v [T] to think that someone or something is less important or valuable than they really are

undervalued /ˌʌndəˈvælju:d◂ $ -ər-/ adj more important or valuable than people think

UNDERWATER

snorkel

goggles

swimming underwater

underwater /ˌʌndəˈwɔːtə◂ $ ˌʌndərˈwɒtər◂, -ˈwɑː-/ adj, adv below the surface of the water: underwater photography | He dived underwater and swam away.

underway /ˌʌndəˈweɪ $ -ər-/ adj if something is underway, it is being done or happening: The game was already **well underway**.

underwear /ˈʌndəweə $ -dərwer/ n [U] clothes that you wear next to your body under your other clothes

underweight /ˌʌndəˈweɪt◂ $ -ər-/ adj below the normal weight OPP **overweight**: an underweight baby

underwent Ac /ˌʌndəˈwent $ -ər-/ v the past tense of UNDERGO

underworld /ˈʌndəwɜːld $ ˈʌndərwɜːrld/ n [singular] **1** the criminals in a place and the activities they are involved in: the London underworld of the 1960s **2** the home of the dead, in ancient Greek stories

undesirable /ˌʌndɪˈzaɪərəbəl◂ $ -ˈzaɪr-/ adj formal something that is undesirable is not wanted because it may have a bad effect: The treatment has no undesirable side-effects.

undid /ʌnˈdɪd/ v the past tense of UNDO

undies /ˈʌndiːz/ n [plural] informal underwear

undisclosed /ˌʌndɪsˈkləʊzd◂ $ -ˈkloʊzd◂/ adj not known publicly: They bought the company for an undisclosed sum.

undisguised /ˌʌndɪsˈɡaɪzd◂/ adj an undisguised feeling is clearly shown and not hidden: She looked at me with undisguised hatred.

undisputed /ˌʌndɪˈspjuːtɪd◂/ adj **undisputed leader/champion/master etc** someone who everyone agrees is the leader etc

undisturbed /ˌʌndɪˈstɜːbd◂ $ -ɜːr-/ adj, adv not interrupted, moved, or changed: I was able to work undisturbed.

undivided /ˌʌndɪˈvaɪdɪd◂/ adj complete: I need your **undivided attention** (=full attention).

undo /ʌnˈduː/ v [T] (past tense **undid** /-ˈdɪd/, past participle **undone** /-ˈdʌn/, third person singular **undoes** /-ˈdʌz/)
1 to open something that is tied, fastened, or wrapped: He undid his shoelaces. | Have you undone all the screws? THESAURUS ▶ OPEN
2 to remove the bad effects of something: There's no way of undoing the damage done to his reputation.

undoing /ʌnˈduːɪŋ/ n **be sb's undoing** to cause someone's failure: His overconfidence proved to be his undoing.

undone /ʌnˈdʌn◂/ adj **1** not tied or fastened: Your shirt button has **come undone**. **2** not finished: Much of the repair work has been **left undone**.

undoubtedly /ʌnˈdaʊtɪdli/ adv used to emphasize that something is definitely true: Amis is undoubtedly one of the best writers of his generation. —**undoubted** adj: his undoubted talent

undress /ʌnˈdres/ v [I,T] to take your clothes off, or to take someone else's clothes off: He started to **get undressed**. —**undressed** adj

undue /ʌnˈdjuː◂ $ -ˈduː◂/ adj formal more than is reasonable or necessary: We don't want to cause undue distress to the animals.

undulating /ˈʌndjəleɪtɪŋ $ -dʒə-/ adj land that is undulating has gentle slopes and hills

unduly /ʌnˈdjuːli $ -ˈduː-/ adv formal more than is normal or reasonable: She wasn't unduly worried.

undying /ʌnˈdaɪ-ɪŋ/ adj literary continuing for ever: undying love

unearth /ʌnˈɜːθ $ -ˈɜːrθ/ v [T] **1** to find something that was buried in the ground: They unearthed a collection of Roman coins. **2** to find something that has been hidden or secret: New evidence has been unearthed that connects them to the crime.

unearthly /ʌnˈɜːθli $ -ˈɜːr-/ adj very strange and not seeming natural: an unearthly sound

unease /ʌnˈiːz/ n [U] a feeling of worry or slight fear

uneasy /ʌnˈiːzi/ adj worried because you think something bad may happen: **[+about]** We felt uneasy about his decision. —**uneasiness** n [U] —**uneasily** adv

uneconomical Ac /ˌʌniːkəˈnɒmɪkəl, ˌʌnekə- $ -ˈnɑː-/ adj costing too much money to use or operate: an old, uneconomical coal mine

unemployed /ˌʌnɪmˈplɔɪd◂/ adj
1 without a job: an unemployed teacher
2 **the unemployed** people who do not have jobs: We need to find jobs for the long-term unemployed.

unemployment /ˌʌnɪmˈplɔɪmənt/ n [U] when someone does not have a job, or the number of people who do not have a job: Many workers now face unemployment.

COLLOCATIONS
adjectives

high/low unemployment Wages are low and unemployment is high. ⚠ Do not say 'big unemployment' or 'great unemployment'. Say **high unemployment**.

U

long-term unemployment *It can be difficult to help people out of long-term unemployment.*

verbs

to reduce/cut unemployment *The government should do more to reduce unemployment.*
unemployment increases/rises *Unemployment has risen to its highest level in four years.*
unemployment falls *From 1986 to 1989 unemployment fell.*

unemployment + noun

the unemployment rate/level *The unemployment rate has gone up again.*
the unemployment figures *The latest unemployment figures show that 1 in 10 people are out of work.*

unending /ʌnˈendɪŋ/ *adj* something that is unending seems as if it will continue for ever: *an unending stream of people*

unequal /ʌnˈiːkwəl/ *adj* 1 unfair because people are treated differently and do not have the same rights or the same amount of power: *the unequal distribution of wealth* 2 not the same in size, amount, or level —**unequally** *adv*

unequivocal /ˌʌnɪˈkwɪvəkəl◄/ *adj formal* completely clear and definite: *unequivocal proof* —**unequivocally** /-kli/ *adv*

unerring /ʌnˈɜːrɪŋ/ *adj* completely right or always right: *He hit the target with unerring accuracy.*

unethical Ac /ʌnˈeθɪkəl/ *adj* morally wrong

uneven /ʌnˈiːvən/ *adj* 1 not flat, smooth, or level: *uneven ground* THESAURUS ROUGH 2 not equal, balanced, or regular: *Her breathing became slow and uneven.* —**unevenly** *adv*

unexpected /ˌʌnɪkˈspektɪd◄/ *adj* something that is unexpected is surprising because you did not expect it to happen —**unexpectedly** *adv*

unfailing /ʌnˈfeɪlɪŋ/ *adj* always there, even in times of difficulty or trouble: *Thank you for your unfailing support.*

unfair /ʌnˈfeə◄ $ -ˈfer◄/ *adj* not right or fair: *The other team had an unfair advantage.* | [+to] *Jenny was really being very unfair to him.* —**unfairly** *adv*: *They were treated unfairly.* —**unfairness** *n* [U]

THESAURUS

unfair/not fair not treating everyone equally, or in a way that most people think is right: *It's unfair that he gets paid more than me.* | *It's not fair to let an animal suffer.*
unjust unfair and against the moral principles of a society: *Many people believe that the law is unjust.* | *an unjust punishment*
biased supporting one person or group in an unfair way, when you should treat everyone fairly: *biased news reporting* | *The courts were accused of being biased against women.*
prejudiced having an unfair dislike of someone, for example because of their race, sex etc, or because they are old or disabled: *Maybe I'm prejudiced, but I think younger people are better at this sort of job.*

unfaithful /ʌnˈfeɪθfəl/ *adj* someone who is unfaithful has sex with someone who is not their wife, husband, or usual partner: [+to] *He had been unfaithful to his wife.*

unfamiliar /ˌʌnfəˈmɪliə◄ $ -ər◄/ *adj* 1 not known to you: [+to] *Some of the vocabulary was unfamiliar to me.* 2 be unfamiliar with sth to not have any experience of something: *I was totally unfamiliar with the equipment they were using.*

unfashionable /ʌnˈfæʃənəbəl/ *adj* not popular or fashionable

unfasten /ʌnˈfɑːsən $ -ˈfæsən/ *v* [T] to open something that is fastened or tied: *Don't unfasten your seat belt yet.* THESAURUS OPEN

unfathomable /ʌnˈfæðəməbəl/ *adj literary* too strange or mysterious to be understood

unfavourable *BrE*, **unfavorable** *AmE* /ʌnˈfeɪvərəbəl/ *adj* 1 not good and likely to cause problems for you: *unfavorable weather conditions* 2 showing that you do not like someone or something: *The play received unfavourable reviews.*

unfeeling /ʌnˈfiːlɪŋ/ *adj* showing that you do not care about other people

unfinished /ʌnˈfɪnɪʃt/ *adj* not finished

unfit /ʌnˈfɪt/ *adj* 1 not in a good physical condition: *He's still unfit after his injury.* 2 not suitable or good enough to do something or be used for something: *meat that is **unfit for human consumption** (=not suitable to eat)*

unfold /ʌnˈfəʊld $ -ˈfoʊld/ *v* 1 [I] if a story or event unfolds, it becomes clearer and you understand it: *The case began to slowly unfold in court.* 2 [T] to open something that is folded: *She unfolded the map.*

unforeseen /ˌʌnfɔːˈsiːn◄ $ -fɔːr-/ *adj* an unforeseen situation is one that you did not expect to happen: *unforeseen problems*

unforgettable /ˌʌnfəˈgetəbəl◄ $ -fər-/ *adj* something that is unforgettable is extremely good or exciting and you will remember it for a long time

unforgivable /ˌʌnfəˈgɪvəbəl◄ $ -fər-/ *adj* an unforgivable action is so bad that you cannot forgive the person who did it: *His behaviour was unforgivable.*

unfortunate /ʌnˈfɔːtʃənət $ -ˈfɔːr-/ *adj*
1 not lucky: *The teacher was yelling at some unfortunate student.* | *an **unfortunate accident*** THESAURUS UNLUCKY
2 used to say that you wish something had not happened or was not true: **it is unfortunate (that)** *It is unfortunate that so few people seem willing to help.* | *It's **most unfortunate** (=very unfortunate) that your father can't be here.*

unfortunately /ʌnˈfɔːtʃənətli $ -ˈfɔːr-/ *adv* used to say that you wish something had not happened or was not true: *Unfortunately, the show had to be cancelled.*

unfounded Ac /ʌnˈfaʊndɪd/ *adj* not true and not based on facts: *unfounded allegations*

unfriendly /ʌnˈfrendli/ *adj* not friendly: *I don't know why he was so unfriendly.* | [+to/towards] *The villagers were really quite unfriendly towards us.* —**unfriendliness** *n* [U]

THESAURUS

unfriendly not friendly – used about people, behaviour, places, or organizations: *The driver of the bus was very unfriendly.* | *The city seemed a large and unfriendly place.*

hostile very unfriendly in an angry way, and ready to argue or fight: *The other members of staff were openly hostile towards her.*

cold behaving towards other people as if you do not like them or care about them: *He gave me a cold hard stare.*

frosty unfriendly, especially because you are not pleased with someone: *When she spoke, her tone was frosty.*

---

unfurl /ʌnˈfɜːl $ -ɜːrl/ v [I,T] *literary* if a flag or sail unfurls, or if someone unfurls it, it unrolls and opens

unfurnished /ʌnˈfɜːnɪʃt $ -ɜːr-/ *adj* an unfurnished room, house etc has no furniture in it

ungainly /ʌnˈgeɪnli/ *adj* moving in a way that is not graceful: *an ungainly teenager*

ungracious /ʌnˈgreɪʃəs/ *adj* not polite or friendly —**ungraciously** *adv*

ungrammatical /ˌʌngrəˈmætɪkəl◂/ *adj* wrong according to the rules of grammar

ungrateful /ʌnˈgreɪtfəl/ *adj* not thanking someone for something they have given to you or done for you —**ungratefully** *adv*

unhappy /ʌnˈhæpi/ *adj*

1 not happy: *If you're so unhappy, why don't you change jobs?* | *an unhappy childhood* **THESAURUS** SAD

2 feeling worried or annoyed because you do not like what is happening in a situation: [+with/about] *O'Neill was unhappy with his team's performance.* | *I'm slightly unhappy about you using my car.* —**unhappiness** *n* [U] —**unhappily** *adv*

Word Choice: unhappy or sad?
Unhappy and **sad** have the same meaning. They are used in slightly different ways. You say that someone has an **unhappy childhood/marriage/time at school**. You do not use *sad* in this meaning.
You say a **sad song**, **story**, or **film**, not an unhappy one. You also usually say that a film or book has a **sad ending**.
When you wish that a situation was different, you say: *It's sad that she can't be here.*

---

unharmed /ʌnˈhɑːmd $ -ɑːr-/ *adj* [not before noun], *adv* not hurt or harmed

unhealthy /ʌnˈhelθi/ *adj* **1** likely to make you ill: *an unhealthy diet* | *an unhealthy lifestyle* **2** not healthy: *a rather unhealthy-looking child* **3** not normal or natural and likely to be harmful: *an unhealthy obsession with sex*

unheard-of /ʌnˈhɜːd ɒv $ -ˈhɜːrd ɑːv/ *adj* something that is unheard-of has never happened before and seems surprising: *Women pilots were practically unheard-of 20 years ago.*

unhelpful /ʌnˈhelpfəl/ *adj* not helping in a situation and sometimes making it worse: *The staff were unfriendly and unhelpful.*

---

unholy /ʌnˈhəʊli $ -ˈhoʊ-/ *adj* **1** [only before noun] very great and very bad: *an unholy row between the two families* | *an unholy mess* **2** not holy or not respecting what is holy

PHRASES

unholy alliance an agreement between people or groups who do not usually work together, for bad purposes: *They formed an unholy alliance with the Democrats.*

unhurt /ʌnˈhɜːt $ -ɜːrt/ *adj* [not before noun], *adv* not injured

unicorn /ˈjuːnəkɔːn $ -ɔːrn/ *n* [C] an imaginary animal like a white horse with one long straight horn on its head

unidentified /ˌʌnaɪˈdentɪfaɪd◂/ *adj* an unidentified person or thing is one that you do not know the name of

unification Ac /ˌjuːnɪfɪˈkeɪʃən/ *n* [U] when two or more countries or groups join together to form a single group or country: *the unification of Germany*

uniform¹ /ˈjuːnəfɔːm $ -ɔːrm/ *n* [C,U] a type of clothing worn by all the members of an organization, or all the children at a school: **school/army/ police etc uniform** *Do you like the new school uniform?* | *He wasn't wearing his uniform.* | **in uniform** *a police officer in uniform* —**uniformed** *adj*: *a uniformed police officer*

uniform² Ac *adj* things that are uniform are all the same size, shape etc —**uniformly** *adv* —**uniformity** /ˌjuːnəˈfɔːməti $ -ɔːr-/ *n* [U]

unify Ac /ˈjuːnɪfaɪ/ *v* [T] (**unified, unifying, unifies**) to join the parts of a country or organization together to make a single country or organization → **unification**: *Spain was unified in the 16th century.* —**unified** *adj*

unilateral /ˌjuːnəˈlætərəl◂/ *adj formal* a unilateral action or decision is taken by only one of the groups involved in a situation, without the agreement of the other groups: *The UN urged Washington not to take unilateral action.* —**unilaterally** *adv*

unimaginable /ˌʌnɪˈmædʒənəbəl◂/ *adj* very difficult to imagine: *unimaginable wealth*

unimportant /ˌʌnɪmˈpɔːtənt◂ $ -ɔːr-/ *adj* not important

THESAURUS

unimportant not important: *The details were unimportant.*

of no/little importance not important, or not very important. These phrases sound more formal than **unimportant**: *The issue was of no importance to her.* | *That fact is of little importance now.*

minor small and not very likely to have an important effect – used especially about changes, problems, injuries, damage, or differences: *The driver suffered minor injuries in the accident.* | *The storm caused minor damage.*

trivial very unimportant and not worth worrying about or spending time on: *They had a disagreement about a trivial matter.* | *a trivial sum of money*

unimpressed /ˌʌnɪmˈprest/ adj if you are unimpressed with something, you do not think it is very good

uninhabitable /ˌʌnɪnˈhæbətəbəl◂/ adj a place that is uninhabitable is impossible to live in

uninhabited /ˌʌnɪnˈhæbɪtɪd◂/ adj a place that is uninhabited has no one living there

uninhibited /ˌʌnɪnˈhɪbɪtɪd◂/ adj feeling free to behave how you want, without worrying about what other people think

unintelligible /ˌʌnɪnˈtelədʒəbəl◂/ adj impossible to understand

unintentional /ˌʌnɪnˈtenʃənəl◂/ adj not done deliberately —**unintentionally** adv

uninterested /ʌnˈɪntrɪstɪd/ adj not interested → **disinterested**

uninterrupted /ˌʌnɪntəˈrʌptɪd◂/ adj continuing without stopping or being interrupted: All I want is two hours of uninterrupted work.

union /ˈjuːnjən/ n [C]
1 (also **trade union** BrE, **labor union** AmE) an organization that is formed by workers in order to protect their rights: the car workers' union | [+of] the National Union of Teachers | Are you planning to **join** the **union**? **THESAURUS** → ORGANIZATION
2 [singular, U] formal when two countries or organizations join together: [+of] the union of East and West Germany
3 [singular] a group of countries or states with the same central government: the European Union

Union 'Jack n [C] the national flag of the United Kingdom

unique `Ac` /juːˈniːk/ adj
1 something that is unique is the only one of its kind: Every house is unique.
2 informal unusually good and special: a unique opportunity to study with an artist
3 unique to **sb/sth** existing only in a particular place, group etc: animals that are unique to Australia —**uniquely** adv —**uniqueness** n [U]

> **Usage**
> Do not say 'very unique'. Just say **unique**.

unisex /ˈjuːnɪseks/ adj intended for both men and women: a unisex jacket

unison /ˈjuːnəsən, -zən/ n **in unison** if a group of people do something in unison, they all do it at the same time

unit /ˈjuːnɪt/ n [C]
1 one part of something, that is whole or complete in itself but is also part of the bigger thing: the emergency unit at the hospital | The apartment building is split into eight units. | The book is divided into eight units. | The engine's cooling unit is broken.
2 an amount or quantity of something that is used as a standard of measurement: [+of] The dollar is the basic unit of money in the US.
3 a piece of furniture, especially one that can be fitted to others of the same type: a storage unit

unite /juːˈnaɪt/ v [I,T] to join together as a group, or to make people join together: Germany was united in

1990. | [+behind] Congress united behind the President.

united /juːˈnaɪtɪd/ adj **1** if people are united, they all want to stay together, or they all agree with each other: The Democrats are united on this issue. **2** a united country has been formed by two or more countries or states joining together: a united Europe

U,nited 'Nations n the United Nations (abbreviation the **UN**) the international organization that most countries belong to, which tries to find peaceful solutions to world problems

unity /ˈjuːnəti/ n [singular, U] when everyone in a group, country etc wants to stay together, or they all agree with each other: We must try to preserve party unity.

universal /ˌjuːnəˈvɜːsəl $ -ɜːr-/ adj **1** involving everyone in the world, or everyone in a group: a universal ban on nuclear weapons | There was almost universal agreement. **2** true or suitable in every situation: a universal truth —**universally** adv

universe /ˈjuːnəvɜːs $ -ɜːrs/ n **the universe** all the stars and PLANETs and all of space

university /ˌjuːnəˈvɜːsəti $ -ɜːr-/ n [C,U] (plural **universities**) a place where students study a subject at a high level to get a DEGREE: It is one of the best universities in the country. | **at university** I did physics at university.

> **Grammar**
> You say **the university** when talking about a particular university: The university has a good reputation. | He is studying at the University of Belfast.
> You do not use **the** before **university** when you are talking in general about the time when someone is studying there: His daughter is at university. | When do you start university?

> ## COLLOCATIONS
> **verbs**
> **to go to university** I want to go to university when I leave school.
> **to be at university** BrE My sister is at university in Brighton.
> **to do/study sth at university** What did you do at university?
> **to start/leave university** Some people take a year off before they start university.
>
> **university + noun**
> **a university student** We met a group of university students.
> **a university graduate** (=someone who has completed a university course) She is a university graduate who speaks three languages.
> **a university lecturer/professor** research done by an Australian university professor

unjust /ʌnˈdʒʌst◂/ adj not fair or reasonable: unjust laws **THESAURUS** → UNFAIR —**unjustly** adv

unjustified `Ac` /ʌnˈdʒʌstɪfaɪd/ adj happening without any good reason: Our fears were unjustified.

unkempt /ʌnˈkempt◂/ adj not neat or tidy: His hair looked dirty and unkempt.

unkind /ʌnˈkaɪnd◄/ *adj* treating people in an unpleasant and slightly cruel way: *an unkind remark* | **[+to]** *Her husband is very unkind to her.* —**unkindly** *adv* —**unkindness** *n* [U]

THESAURUS

unkind treating people in an unpleasant and slightly cruel way: *Children can be very unkind to each other.*
mean *especially spoken* unkind: *Don't be mean to your sister!*
nasty deliberately unkind, and seeming to enjoy making people unhappy: *He's a nasty little man!* | *a nasty letter from the bank*
hurtful unkind – used about remarks and actions: *Joe couldn't forget the hurtful things she had said.*
spiteful deliberately unkind to someone, especially because you are jealous of them or angry with them: *He made some spiteful comments about her work.*
hard-hearted not caring about other people's feelings: *She was a cold hard-hearted woman who was interested in only one thing – money.*
thoughtless/inconsiderate not thinking about how your actions or words will affect other people: *It was thoughtless of him to call so late at night.* | *An inconsiderate driver had parked too close to his car.*

---

unknowingly /ʌnˈnəʊɪŋli $ -ˈnoʊ-/ *adv* without realizing what you are doing or what is happening

unknown¹ /ʌnˈnəʊn◄ $ -ˈnoʊn◄/ *adj* **1** not known: *The number of people injured is still unknown.* | **[+to]** *His criminal history was unknown to us.* **2** not famous: *an unknown person*

unknown² *n* **1 the unknown** things that you know nothing about and have never experienced before: *a fear of the unknown* **2** [C] someone who is not famous

unlawful /ʌnˈlɔːfəl $ -ˈlɒː-/ *adj formal* not legal: *an unlawful act* —**unlawfully** *adv*

unleaded /ʌnˈledɪd/ *adj* unleaded petrol does not contain any LEAD

unleash /ʌnˈliːʃ/ *v* [T] to suddenly make something start happening which has a great effect: *The decision unleashed a storm of protest.*

unless /ʌnˈles, ən-/ *linking word* used to say that something will only happen if something else happens: *He won't go to sleep unless you tell him a story.* **THESAURUS** IF

unlike /ʌnˈlaɪk/ *prep*
1 completely different from another person or thing: *Unlike me, she's very intelligent.* **THESAURUS** DIFFERENT
2 not typical of the way someone usually behaves: *It's unlike Judy to leave without telling anyone.*

unlikely /ʌnˈlaɪkli/ *adj* not likely to happen or to be true: **it is unlikely (that)** *It's very unlikely that they'll win.* | *an unlikely explanation*

unlimited /ʌnˈlɪmɪtɪd/ *adj* without a fixed limit: *They seem to have unlimited funds.*

unlit /ʌnˈlɪt◄/ *adj* dark because there are no lights

unload /ʌnˈləʊd $ -ˈloʊd/ *v* **1** [I,T] to remove things from a vehicle or large container: *Can you unload the dishwasher for me?* | **unload sth from sth** *The driver unloaded some boxes from the back of the truck.* **2** [T] *informal* to get rid of something that you do not want by giving it to someone else: **unload sth on/onto sb** *Ben has a habit of unloading his work on others.*

unlock /ʌnˈlɒk $ -ˈlɑːk/ *v* [T] to open something by unfastening the lock on it **THESAURUS** OPEN

unlucky /ʌnˈlʌki/ *adj*
1 having bad luck: **[+with]** *We were unlucky with the weather this weekend.* | *The German team was unlucky not to win.*
2 happening because of bad luck: *an unlucky accident*
3 something that is unlucky is believed to make you have bad luck: *Thirteen is an unlucky number.* —**unluckily** *adv*

THESAURUS

unlucky if someone is unlucky, they have bad luck. If something is unlucky, people think it makes you have bad luck: *Matthews played well and was unlucky not to score.* | *Sailors believed that it was unlucky to have a woman on the ship.*
unfortunate unlucky because something bad happens to you that you do not deserve: **Unfortunate** sounds more formal than **unlucky**: *One unfortunate man lost all his money.*
be/bring bad luck if something is bad luck or brings bad luck, people think it makes you have bad luck: *It's supposed to be bad luck to walk under a ladder.* | *Crows were thought to bring bad luck.*
jinxed if something is jinxed, it seems to bring bad luck to everyone who is connected with it. If a person is jinxed, a lot of bad things happen to them and they seem very unlucky: *This place is jinxed!*

---

unmanned /ʌnˈmænd◄/ *adj* an unmanned vehicle or building does not have anyone in it

unmarked /ʌnˈmɑːkt◄ $ -ˈmɑːrkt◄/ *adj* something that is unmarked has no words or signs on it to show what it is: *an unmarked police car*

unmarried /ʌnˈmærid◄/ *adj* not married **SYN** single

unmistakable /ʌnməˈsteɪkəbəl◄/ *adj* if something is unmistakable, you know immediately what it is: *the unmistakable taste of garlic*

unmitigated /ʌnˈmɪtɪgeɪtɪd/ *adj* used to emphasize how bad something is: *an unmitigated disaster*

unmoved /ʌnˈmuːvd/ *adj* not feeling any sympathy, excitement, worry etc because of something

unnamed /ʌnˈneɪmd◄/ *adj* an unnamed person or thing is one whose name is not mentioned

unnatural /ʌnˈnætʃərəl/ *adj* different from normal, in a way that seems strange or wrong: *It's unnatural for a child to spend so much time alone.* —**unnaturally** *adv*

unnecessary /ʌnˈnesəsəri $ -seri/ *adj* not needed: *the unnecessary use of drugs* | *an unnecessary expense*

—**unnecessarily** /ʌn'nesəsərəli $ ˌʌn-nesə'serəli/ *adv*: *We don't want to take risks unnecessarily.*

unnerve /ʌn'nɜːv $ -ɜːrv/ *v* [T] to make someone frightened or nervous: *I was slightly unnerved by his behaviour.* —**unnerving** *adj*: *an unnerving experience*

unnoticed /ʌn'nəʊtɪst $ -'noʊ-/ *adj, adv* without being noticed: *She sat unnoticed at the back of the room.* | *His remark **went unnoticed** by everyone except me.*

unobserved /ˌʌnəb'zɜːvd $ -ɜːrvd/ *adj, adv* without being seen

unobtrusive /ˌʌnəb'truːsɪv◂/ *adj formal* not attracting attention and not likely to be noticed

unoccupied /ʌn'ɒkjəpaɪd $ -'ɑːk-/ *adj* a seat, house, room etc that is unoccupied has no one in it

unofficial /ˌʌnə'fɪʃəl◂/ *adj* **1** done or produced without formal approval or permission: *an unofficial biography* **2** not done as part of someone's official duties: *The Senator is in Berlin on an unofficial visit.* —**unofficially** *adv*

unorthodox /ʌn'ɔːθədɒks $ ʌn'ɔːrθədɑːks/ *adj* unusual and different from most people's ideas or ways of doing things: *her unorthodox lifestyle*

unpack /ʌn'pæk/ *v* [I,T] to take everything out of a box or bag: *I unpacked my suitcase.*

unpaid /ʌn'peɪd◂/ *adj* **1** an unpaid bill or debt has not been paid **2** working without receiving any money: *unpaid workers* | *unpaid work*

unparalleled Ac /ʌn'pærəleld/ *adj formal* much greater or better than anything else: *an unparalleled success*

unpleasant /ʌn'plezənt/ *adj*
1 not pleasant or enjoyable OPP **nice**: *an unpleasant surprise*
2 unkind or rude OPP **nice**: *What an unpleasant man!* | [+to] *She was rather unpleasant to me on the phone.* —**unpleasantly** *adv*

unplug /ʌn'plʌg/ *v* [T] (**unplugged, unplugging**) to disconnect a piece of electrical equipment by taking its PLUG out of a SOCKET

unpopular /ʌn'pɒpjələ $ -'pɑːpjələr/ *adj* not liked by most people: *an unpopular decision* | [+with] *He was unpopular with many of his colleagues.* —**unpopularity** /ˌʌnˌpɒpjə'lærəti $ -ˌpɑːp-/ *n* [U]

unprecedented Ac /ʌn'presɪdentɪd/ *adj* something that is unprecedented has never happened before: *an unprecedented achievement*

unpredictable Ac /ˌʌnprɪ'dɪktəbəl◂/ *adj* changing so much that you do not know what to expect: *unpredictable weather*

unprofessional /ˌʌnprə'feʃənəl◂/ *adj* not behaving in the way that people doing a particular job should behave: *His behaviour was extremely unprofessional.*

unprovoked /ˌʌnprə'vəʊkt◂ -'voʊkt◂/ *adj* unprovoked anger, attacks etc are directed at someone who has not done anything to deserve them

unqualified /ʌn'kwɒlɪfaɪd $ -'kwɑː-/ *adj* **1** not having the right knowledge, experience, or QUALIFICA-TIONS to do something: [+for] *She was totally unqualified for the job.* **2** completely and in every way: *The festival was an unqualified success.*

unquestionably /ʌn'kwestʃənəbli/ *adv* used to emphasize that something is certainly true: *He is unquestionably the world's greatest living composer.* —**unquestionable** *adj*

unravel /ʌn'rævəl/ *v* [I,T] (**unravelled, unravelling** *BrE*, **unraveled, unraveling** *AmE*) **1** if you unravel a complicated situation, or if it unravels, it becomes clear and you start to understand it: *Detectives are trying to unravel the mystery surrounding his death.* **2** if you unravel threads, or if they unravel, they stop being twisted together

unreal /ʌn'rɪəl◂/ *adj* **1** something that is unreal seems so strange that you think you must be imagining it: *The whole situation was completely unreal.* **2** not related to real things that happen: *Many people go into marriage with unreal expectations.* —**unreality** /ˌʌnri'æləti/ *n* [U]

unrealistic /ˌʌnrɪə'lɪstɪk◂/ *adj* unrealistic ideas are not sensible or based on what is really likely to happen: *She had rather unrealistic expectations of marriage.*

unreasonable /ʌn'riːzənəbəl/ *adj* **1** not fair or sensible about what you expect: *Do you think I'm being unreasonable?* **2** unreasonable prices, costs etc are too high —**unreasonably** *adv*

unrecognizable (also **-isable** *BrE*) /ʌn'rekəgnaɪzəbəl, -'rekə-/ *adj* looking completely different and difficult to recognize

unrelated /ˌʌnrɪ'leɪtɪd◂/ *adj* events, situations etc that are unrelated are not connected with each other: *The police think the attacks are unrelated.*

unrelenting /ˌʌnrɪ'lentɪŋ◂/ *adj formal* continuing without stopping and without becoming less unpleasant or difficult: *the unrelenting pressures of the job*

unreliable Ac /ˌʌnrɪ'laɪəbəl◂/ *adj* if someone or something is unreliable, you cannot trust them: *The buses here are often unreliable.*

unremarkable /ˌʌnrɪ'mɑːkəbəl◂ $ -ɑːr-/ *adj* ordinary and not very interesting

unremitting /ˌʌnrɪ'mɪtɪŋ◂/ *adj formal* never stopping, and never becoming less difficult or unpleasant: *Life here is an unremitting struggle.*

unrepentant /ˌʌnrɪ'pentənt◂/ *adj* not ashamed of your behaviour or beliefs, even though other people disapprove

unrequited /ˌʌnrɪ'kwaɪtɪd◂/ *adj* **unrequited love** *literary* when you love someone, but they do not love you

unreservedly /ˌʌnrɪ'zɜːvɪdli $ -ɜːr-/ *adv* completely: *He apologized unreservedly.* —**unreserved** /-'zɜːvd $ -'zɜːrvd◂/ *adj*

unresolved Ac /ˌʌnrɪ'zɒlvd $ -'zɑːlvd, -'zɒːlvd◂/ *adj* an unresolved problem or question has not yet been solved or dealt with: *an unresolved dispute*

unresponsive Ac /ˌʌnrɪ'spɒnsɪv◂ $ -'spɑːn-/ *adj* not reacting to something or not affected by it: *His manner was cold and unresponsive.* | [+to] *an illness that is unresponsive to drug treatment*

unrest /ʌn'rest/ *n* [U] when the people in a country feel angry about something and protest about it,

U

often violently: **political/social/civil unrest** *a period of social unrest* | *the **growing** student **unrest** before the election*

unrestrained Ac /ˌʌnrɪˈstreɪnd◂/ *adj* not controlled or limited: *unrestrained power*

unrivalled *BrE*, **unrivaled** *AmE* /ʌnˈraɪvəld/ *adj* better than any other: *an unrivaled collection*

unroll /ʌnˈrəʊl $ -ˈroʊl/ *v* [I,T] to open something that is in the shape of a tube or ball and make it flat, or to become open in this way: *He unrolled his sleeping bag.*

unruffled /ʌnˈrʌfəld/ *adj* calm and not upset by a difficult situation

unruly /ʌnˈruːli/ *adj* behaving badly and difficult to control: *unruly schoolchildren*

unsafe /ʌnˈseɪf◂/ *adj* **1** dangerous or likely to cause harm: *The river is unsafe to swim in.* **THESAURUS** DANGEROUS **2** likely to be harmed: *Many people **feel unsafe** in the streets at night.*

unsaid /ʌnˈsed/ *adj* **be left unsaid** if something is left unsaid, you do not say it although you think it

unsatisfactory /ˌʌnˌsætəsˈfæktəri/ *adj* not good enough or not acceptable

unsavoury *BrE*, **unsavory** *AmE* /ʌnˈseɪvəri/ *adj* unpleasant or dishonest: *The bar was full of **unsavoury characters** (=people).*

unscathed /ʌnˈskeɪðd/ *adj* [not before noun], *adv* not injured or harmed: *No one **escaped unscathed** from the accident.*

unscrew /ʌnˈskruː/ *v* [T] to remove or open something by twisting it round: *She unscrewed the light bulb.* **THESAURUS** OPEN

unscrupulous /ʌnˈskruːpjələs/ *adj* behaving in a dishonest way in order to get what you want

unseat /ʌnˈsiːt/ *v* [T] to remove someone from a powerful position

unseemly /ʌnˈsiːmli/ *adj formal* unseemly behaviour is not polite or not acceptable in a particular situation

unseen /ˌʌnˈsiːn◂/ *adj, adv formal* not noticed or seen: *She left the building unseen.*

unselfish /ʌnˈselfɪʃ/ *adj* caring about other people and thinking about them rather than yourself

unsettled /ʌnˈsetld/ *adj* **1** an unsettled political or social situation is one in which no one is sure what will happen next: *the unsettled financial markets* **2** worried, upset, or nervous: *Children often **feel unsettled** by moving home.* **3** still continuing without reaching any agreement: *The dispute **remains unsettled**.* **4** if the weather is unsettled, it keeps changing and there is a lot of rain: *Tomorrow will be cloudy and unsettled.* —**unsettle** *v* [T]

unsettling /ʌnˈsetlɪŋ/ *adj* making you feel nervous or worried: *It was slightly unsettling seeing so many people watching me.*

unshaven /ʌnˈʃeɪvən/ *adj* a man who is unshaven has short hairs growing on his face because he has not SHAVEd → see picture at **UNSHAVEN**

unsightly /ʌnˈsaɪtli/ *adj* something that is unsightly is ugly or unpleasant to look at

unskilled /ʌnˈskɪld◂/ *adj* **1** an unskilled worker does not have any special training for a job: *companies employing **unskilled labour** (=people with no training)* **2** unskilled work does not need people with special training

unsocial /ʌnˈsəʊʃəl $ -ˈsoʊ-/ (also **unsociable** /ʌnˈsəʊʃəbəl $ -ˈsoʊ-/) *adj* **unsocial hours** when someone has to work very late at night or early in the morning, when most people do not work

unsolicited /ˌʌnsəˈlɪsɪtɪd◂/ *adj formal* not asked for and not wanted: *unsolicited advice*

unsolved /ʌnˈsɒlvd◂ $ -ˈsɑːlvd◂, -ˈsɔːlvd◂/ *adj* an unsolved problem, mystery etc does not have an answer or explanation yet: *unsolved crimes*

unsophisticated /ˌʌnsəˈfɪstɪkeɪtɪd◂/ *adj* **1** having little knowledge or experience of life or of things like art, fashion etc: *She was 18 and quite unsophisticated.* **2** unsophisticated equipment, methods etc are very simple

unsound /ʌnˈsaʊnd◂/ *adj* **1** based on ideas or reasons that are wrong: *scientifically/politically etc **unsound** The method was educationally unsound.* **2** in bad condition and likely to fall down: *buildings that are **structurally unsound***

unspeakable /ʌnˈspiːkəbəl/ *adj* extremely bad: *unspeakable crimes*

unspecified Ac /ʌnˈspesɪfaɪd/ *adj* not known or not yet announced: *The painting was sold for an unspecified amount.*

unspoiled /ʌnˈspɔɪld◂/ (also **unspoilt** *BrE* /ʌnˈspɔɪlt◂/) *adj* an unspoiled place is beautiful because it has not changed and there are no buildings on it: *unspoiled countryside*

unspoken /ʌnˈspəʊkən $ -ˈspoʊ-/ *adj* not said or discussed with other people: *She nodded in answer to his unspoken question.* | *my unspoken fears*

unstable Ac /ʌnˈsteɪbəl/ *adj* **1** likely to change suddenly and become worse: *The political situation is still very unstable.* **2** someone who is unstable is not always in control of their feelings or behaviour, especially because there is something wrong with them mentally **3** likely to fall over: *an unstable wall*

unsteady /ʌnˈstedi/ *adj* **1** shaking when you walk or hold something, or when you speak, in a way that you cannot control: *I felt hot and **unsteady on my feet** (=as though I might fall over).* | *Her voice was unsteady.* **2** an unsteady object is not firmly in position and might fall

unstoppable /ʌnˈstɒpəbəl $ -ˈstɑːp-/ *adj* not possible to stop or beat: *The team seems unstoppable this year.*

unstuck /ʌnˈstʌk◂/ *adj* **come unstuck a)** *BrE* to fail or start to go wrong: *Our plans came unstuck.* **b)** if something comes unstuck, it becomes separated from the surface that it was stuck to

unsubstantiated /ˌʌnsəbˈstænʃieɪtɪd/ *adj* unsubstantiated reports, stories etc have not been proved to be true

unsuccessful /ˌʌnsəkˈsesfəl◂/ *adj* not achieving what you wanted to achieve: *an **unsuccessful attempt** to climb Everest* **THESAURUS** FAIL —**unsuccessfully** *adv*

unsuitable /ʌnˈsuːtəbəl, -ˈsjuː- $ -ˈsuː-/ adj not having the right qualities for a particular person, purpose, or situation: **[+for]** The movie is unsuitable for young children.

unsung /ʌnˈsʌŋ◄/ adj [only before noun] not praised or famous for something you have done, although you deserve to be: the **unsung heroes** of the revolution

unsure /ʌnˈʃɔː◄ $ -ˈʃʊr◄/ adj not certain about something: **[+of/about]** If you are unsure about anything, just ask. | **unsure what/whether etc** I was unsure what reaction I would get.

PHRASES

unsure of yourself not having very much confidence in yourself: Chris seemed nervous and unsure of himself.

unsurpassed /ʌnsəˈpɑːst◄ $ -sərˈpæst◄/ adj better than anyone or anything else

unsuspecting /ʌnsəˈspektɪŋ◄/ adj not knowing about something bad that is happening or going to happen: He would creep up from behind on his **unsuspecting victims**.

unsweetened /ʌnˈswiːtnd/ adj unsweetened food or drink has not had sugar added to it: unsweetened orange juice

unswerving /ʌnˈswɜːvɪŋ $ -ɜːr-/ adj an unswerving belief or attitude is very strong and never changes: his unswerving loyalty

unsympathetic /ʌnsɪmpəˈθetɪk/ adj **1** not kind or helpful to someone who is having problems: Dad was cold and unsympathetic. **2** not supporting or approving of an idea, aim etc: **[+to/towards]** The new committee was unsympathetic to these views. **3** an unsympathetic character in a book, film etc is unpleasant and difficult to like

untangle /ʌnˈtæŋɡəl/ v [T] **1** to separate pieces of string, wire etc that are twisted together **2** to understand something that is very complicated

untapped /ʌnˈtæpt◄/ adj an untapped supply of something has not yet been used: huge **untapped reserves** of oil and coal

untenable /ʌnˈtenəbəl/ adj formal an untenable position or idea no longer seems right and is impossible to continue with: His position as chairman proved to be untenable.

unthinkable /ʌnˈθɪŋkəbəl/ adj impossible to imagine or accept: **It is unthinkable that** a mistake like that could happen.

untidy /ʌnˈtaɪdi/ adj especially BrE
1 not neat **SYN** **messy**: an untidy room | untidy hair | Why's your desk always so untidy?
2 an untidy person does not keep their house, clothes, hair etc neat **SYN** **messy**: Most teenagers are pretty untidy.

THESAURUS

untidy BrE not neat – used about people, places, clothes, hair etc: His bedroom was always untidy. | My Dad is very untidy.
messy untidy or dirty: She was a messy child. | The kitchen was the messiest room in the house.
be a mess (also **be in a mess** BrE) to be very

untidy or dirty – used about places: The lounge was a mess, but she was too tired to clean up.
scruffy BrE wearing old and untidy clothes: My parents think I look scruffy in these jeans, but I like them.

untie /ʌnˈtaɪ/ v [T] (**untied**, **untying**, **unties**) to unfasten something that has been tied in a knot: Can you help me untie the rope?

until /ʌnˈtɪl, ən-/ (also **till**) prep, linking word if something happens until a time, it continues and then stops at that time: The banks are open until 3.30. | He waited until she had finished speaking.
PHRASES
not until used to say that something will not happen before a particular time: The movie doesn't start until 8. | We won't start until everyone's here.

untimely /ʌnˈtaɪmli/ adj happening too soon: her **untimely death**

untold /ʌnˈtəʊld◄ $ -ˈtoʊld◄/ adj [only before noun] very bad or very great: The floods caused **untold damage**.

untouched /ʌnˈtʌtʃt◄/ adj **1** not changed, affected, or damaged in any way: **[+by]** an area untouched by human activity **2** food or drink that is untouched has not been eaten or drunk

untoward /ʌntəˈwɔːd $ ʌnˈtɔːrd/ adj unpleasant or unacceptable: **nothing/anything untoward** Nothing untoward happened.

untrained /ʌnˈtreɪnd◄/ adj not trained to do a job: untrained staff
PHRASES
to the untrained eye/ear to someone who does not know a lot about something: To the untrained eye, the painting looks like a Van Gogh.

untreated /ʌnˈtriːtɪd/ adj **1** an untreated illness has not had medical treatment **2** an untreated substance has not been made safe: untreated water

untried /ʌnˈtraɪd◄/ adj new and not yet tested or proved to be good: a young untried actress

untrue /ʌnˈtruː/ adj not true: Most of what she said was untrue.

untruth /ʌnˈtruːθ, ˈʌntruːθ/ n [C] formal something that is not true **SYN** **lie**

untruthful /ʌnˈtruːθfəl/ adj saying things that are untrue

untying /ʌnˈtaɪ-ɪŋ/ v the present participle of UNTIE

unused¹ /ʌnˈjuːzd/ adj not being used at the moment, or never used: unused land

unused² /ʌnˈjuːst/ adj **unused to (doing) sth** not having any experience of something: She's unused to driving at night. | I was unused to the hot climate.

unusual /ʌnˈjuːʒuəl, -ʒəl/ adj different from what is usual or normal: a very unusual situation | **be unusual for sb/sth** He seemed sad, which was unusual for him. | **it is unusual for sb to do sth** It's unusual for Paul to be late. | **it is unusual to do sth** It's unusual to have snow in April.

unusually /ʌnˈjuːʒuəli, -ʒəli/ *adv* **1** in a way that is different from usual: **[+for]** *Unusually for Michael, he arrived on time.* **2 unusually hot/big/quiet etc** hotter, bigger etc than is usual: *That winter was unusually cold.*

unveil /ʌnˈveɪl/ *v* [T] to show the public something for the first time, or tell them about a new plan, product etc: *He unveiled a painting of the princess in a pink gown.* | *The chairman **unveiled plans** for a £100 million stadium.*

unwanted /ʌnˈwɒntɪd $ -ˈwɒːnt-, -ˈwɑːnt-/ *adj* not wanted: *an unwanted gift* | *an unwanted pregnancy*

unwarranted /ʌnˈwɒrəntɪd $ -ˈwɔː-, -ˈwɑː-/ *adj formal* done without any good reason: *unwarranted demands for further payment*

unwary /ʌnˈweəri $ -ˈweri/ *adj* not knowing about possible problems or dangers and easy to harm or deceive: *unwary tourists*

unwelcome /ʌnˈwelkəm/ *adj* not wanted: *unwelcome changes* | *an unwelcome visitor*

unwell /ʌnˈwel/ *adj* [not before noun] *formal* ill: *Anna's **feeling unwell** today.* **THESAURUS** ▶ ILL

unwieldy /ʌnˈwiːldi/ *adj* difficult to move or use: *a large, unwieldy shopping trolley*

unwilling /ʌnˈwɪlɪŋ/ *adj* not wanting to do something, or refusing to do it: **unwilling to do sth** *He's unwilling to admit he was wrong.* —**unwillingly** *adv* —**unwillingness** *n* [U]

unwind /ʌnˈwaɪnd/ *v* (*past tense and past participle* **unwound** /-ˈwaʊnd/) **1** [I] to relax and stop thinking about your work or problems: *Swimming helps me unwind.* **2** [I,T] to undo something that has been wrapped around something else, or to come undone: *He unwound the rope.* | *The snake slowly unwound.*

unwise /ʌnˈwaɪz◂/ *adj* not sensible and likely to cause problems: *an unwise decision* | ***It's unwise to** drink before driving.* —**unwisely** *adv*

unwittingly /ʌnˈwɪtɪŋli/ *adv* without knowing or realizing something: *Seb had unwittingly broken the law.* —**unwitting** *adj*

unworkable /ʌnˈwɜːkəbəl $ -ɜːr-/ *adj* a plan, idea etc that is unworkable cannot succeed

unwound /ʌnˈwaʊnd/ *v* the past tense and past participle of UNWIND

UNWRAP

unwrapping a present

unwrap /ʌnˈræp/ *v* [T] (**unwrapped**, **unwrapping**) to remove the paper that is covering something: *Sally was unwrapping her birthday presents.*

unwritten /ʌnˈrɪtn/ *adj* an unwritten rule or law is one that everyone knows about although it is not official

unyielding /ʌnˈjiːldɪŋ/ *adj* refusing to change what you believe or what you want: *The terrorists were unyielding in their demands.*

unzip /ʌnˈzɪp/ *v* [T] (**unzipped**, **unzipping**) to open something by undoing the ZIP on it

up¹ /ʌp/ *adv, prep*
1 towards or in a higher place **OPP** *down*: *They began walking up the hill.* | *Can you move the picture up a little higher?* | *Dave's up in his room.* → see picture on page A8
2 into an upright position: **get/sit/stand up** *The children stood up to sing.* | *He turned up his collar.*
3 further along something: **up the street/road/river etc** *She lives just up the street.* | *Can you **move up** (=move along) a little?*
4 if the amount or level of something is up, it has increased: **[+by]** *Inflation is up by 2%.* | *Violent crime **went up** last year.*
5 in or towards the north: *He lives up in Scotland.*
6 not in bed: *We were up all night.* | *They **stayed up** to watch the game.* | *He's **up and about** (=well and not in bed) again after his illness.*
7 beating your opponent by a particular number of points: **two goals/three points etc up** *United were two goals up at half time.*
8 *spoken* if a period of time is up, it has finished: *She left when two weeks were up.*
9 if a computer system is up, it is working: *Are the computers **up and running** yet?* → UPS AND DOWNS
PHRASES
it's up to sb used to say that someone has to decide about something: *'Should I go?' 'It's up to you.'*
be up against sth to have to compete against a very difficult opponent, or deal with a very difficult situation: *We're up against some of the biggest companies in the world.*
up and down 1 backwards and forwards: *He walked up and down, thinking carefully.* **2** to a higher position and then a lower one, several times: *The kids were jumping up and down on the bed.*
be up for sale/discussion etc to be available to be sold, discussed etc: *Their house is up for sale.*

up to sth 1 as much or as many as a particular number or amount: *I can get up to six people in the car.* **2** (*also* **up until**) until a particular date or time: *The offer is valid up to December 15.* **3** as good as a particular level or standard: *This essay isn't up to your usual standard.* **4** well enough to do something, or good enough to do a particular job: *Do you **feel up to** a walk?* | *He isn't really **up to the job**.* **5** doing something secret or something that you should not be doing: *I think Nick's **up to something**.*

walk/go/come etc up to move towards someone or something until you are very near them: *A man came up and asked me for a cigarette.* | **[+to]** *She drove **right up** to the door.*

up² v [T] (**upped, upping**) to increase the amount or level of something: **up sth to/by sth** *They've upped her salary to £35,000.*

up-and-'coming adj likely to become successful: *an up-and-coming actor*

upbeat /'ʌpbiːt/ adj cheerful and making you feel that good things will happen: *a movie with an upbeat ending*

upbringing /'ʌpˌbrɪŋɪŋ/ n [singular] the way that your parents care for you and teach you to behave when you are a child: *He had a **strict upbringing**.*

upcoming /'ʌpˌkʌmɪŋ/ adj [only before noun] happening soon: *the upcoming elections*

update¹ /ʌp'deɪt/ v [T] to add the most recent information to something, or to make something more modern: *We need to update some of the older files.*

update² /'ʌpdeɪt/ n [C] the most recent information about a news story: **[+on]** *an update on the earthquake*

upend /ʌp'end/ v [T] to turn something over so that it is upside down

upfront¹ /ʌp'frʌnt◀/ adv if you pay someone upfront, you pay them before they do any work

upfront² adj spoken behaving or talking in an honest and open way about something: **[+about]** *He was quite upfront about his feelings.*

upgrade /ʌp'greɪd/ v [T] to improve something, or change it for something better: *We need to upgrade our computer.* —**upgrade** /'ʌpgreɪd/ n [C]

upheaval /ʌp'hiːvəl/ n [C,U] a very big change, especially one that causes problems: *Moving house is a **major upheaval**.*

uphill /ʌp'hɪl◀/ adj, adv **1** towards the top of a hill `OPP` **downhill**: *an uphill climb* **2 an uphill struggle/ battle/task etc** something that is difficult to do and needs a lot of effort: *Encouraging children to eat vegetables can be an uphill struggle.*

uphold /ʌp'həʊld $ -'hoʊld/ v [T] (past tense and past participle **upheld** /ʌp'held/) formal to support a law or decision: *The job of the police is to uphold law and order.*

upholstery /ʌp'həʊlstəri $ -'hoʊl-/ n [U] material used to cover chairs: *leather upholstery*

upkeep /'ʌpkiːp/ n [U] the process and cost of keeping something in good condition, or looking after a child or animal: **[+of]** *The money went towards the upkeep of the church.*

uplands /'ʌpləndz/ n [plural] high areas of land —**upland** adj

uplifting /ʌp'lɪftɪŋ/ adj making you feel happier and more hopeful: *an **uplifting experience***

upload /ʌp'ləʊd $ -'loʊd/ v [I,T] to move information, a program etc from a computer to a computer network so that other people can see it or use it `OPP` **download**

upmarket /ʌp'mɑːkɪt◀ $ -ɑːr-/ adj especially BrE intended for or used by people who are rich and like expensive things: *an upmarket restaurant*

upon /ə'pɒn $ ə'pɑːn/ prep formal on: *The trip was dependent upon the weather.*

upper /'ʌpə $ -ər/ adj [only before noun] **1** in a higher position than another part of something `OPP` **lower**: *the upper jaw* | *the upper floors of the building* **2** more important than other parts in an organization, system etc: *the upper job levels in the company* | *areas **at the upper end of** the housing market* **3 upper limit** the most, highest etc that is possible or allowed: **[+of]** *an upper limit on spending*
`PHRASES`
| **have/get/gain the upper hand** to have more power than someone else, so that you are able to control a situation: *The Republicans seem to have the upper hand.*

upper 'case n [U] CAPITAL LETTERS (A, B, C etc not a, b, c etc) → **lower case**

upper 'class n **the upper class/classes** the group of people who belong to the highest social class

uppermost /'ʌpəməʊst $ -pərmoʊst/ adj **1 be uppermost in sb's mind** to be the thing that someone is thinking about most of all: *Exams were uppermost in my mind.* **2** [only before noun] highest: *the uppermost branches of the tree*

upright /'ʌpraɪt/ adj, adv **1** standing, sitting, or pointing straight up: **sit/ stand/walk upright** *When did man first walk upright?* | *Please put your seat in an **upright position**.* **2** always behaving in an honest way: *upright citizens*

uprising /'ʌpˌraɪzɪŋ/ n [C] an attempt by people in a country to change their government by force: *an **armed uprising** (=using weapons)*

upriver /ʌp'rɪvə $ -ər/ adv in the opposite direction to the way the river is flowing

uproar /'ʌprɔː $ -rɔːr/ n [singular, U] a lot of noise, shouting, or angry protest about something: *The announcement **caused an uproar**.* | **in (an) uproar** *The whole class was in uproar.*

uproot /ʌp'ruːt/ v [T] **1** to pull a plant and its roots out of the ground **2** to make someone leave their home and move to a new place: *If I take the job, I'll have to uproot the whole family.*

ups and 'downs n [plural] the good and bad things that happen in life, business etc: *Every marriage has its ups and downs.*

upscale /ˈʌpskeɪl/ adj AmE used by rich people from a high social class **SYN** **upmarket** BrE: *upscale housing*

upset¹ /ʌpˈset◄/ adj
1 [not before noun] unhappy because something unpleasant or disappointing has happened: **[+about/at]** *She's still very upset about her father's death.* | **[+that]** *He was upset that Helen had lied to him.* | *When I told him he'd failed, he* **got** very **upset**.
2 upset stomach/tummy when an illness affects your stomach

upset² /ʌpˈset/ v [T] (*past tense and past participle* **upset**, *present participle* **upsetting**) **1** to make someone feel unhappy or angry: *Kopp's comments upset many of his listeners.* **2** to change something in a way that causes problems: *I hope I haven't upset all your plans.* **3** to push something over, usually accidentally: *He upset the table and everything on it.*

upset³ /ˈʌpset/ n **1** [C,U] unhappiness, or something that causes it: *His decision caused great upset.* **2** [C] when a player or team unexpectedly wins: *There's been a big upset in the French Open tennis.* **3** [C] an unexpected problem **4 stomach/tummy upset** when your stomach is affected by an illness

upsetting /ʌpˈsetɪŋ/ adj something that is upsetting makes you feel shocked and unhappy: *an upsetting experience*

upshot /ˈʌpʃɒt $ -ʃɑːt/ n **the upshot (of sth)** the final result of a situation: *The upshot is that she's decided to take the job.*

upside /ˈʌpsaɪd/ n [singular] the good part of a situation: *The upside is that we got a free trip to Jamaica.*

upside 'down, upside-down adj, adv with the top at the bottom and the bottom at the top: *The picture is upside down.* | *an upside-down U shape*

UPSIDE DOWN

PHRASES
turn sth upside down 1 to move a lot of things and make a place untidy because you are looking for something: *The police turned the place upside down.* **2** to change something completely: *Her life had been turned upside down by the accident.*

upstage /ˌʌpˈsteɪdʒ/ v [T] to do something that takes people's attention away from a more important person or event

upstairs /ˌʌpˈsteəz◄ $ -ˈsterz◄/ adj, adv on or towards a higher floor of a building **OPP** **downstairs**: *The kids went upstairs to bed.* | *Her office is upstairs on your left.* | *an upstairs window*

upstart /ˈʌpstɑːt $ -ɑːrt/ n [C] disapproving someone who behaves as if they are more important than they really are and does not show enough respect to older more experienced people

upstate /ˈʌpsteɪt/ adj, adv AmE in or towards the northern part of a state: *She lives upstate.*

upstream /ˌʌpˈstriːm◄/ adv along a river in the opposite direction to the way the water is flowing

upsurge /ˈʌpsɜːdʒ $ -sɜːrdʒ/ n [C] a sudden increase: **[+in/of]** *the recent upsurge in crime*

uptake /ˈʌpteɪk/ n **be slow/quick on the uptake** informal to be slow or fast at understanding or learning things

uptight /ˈʌptaɪt, ʌpˈtaɪt/ adj informal behaving in an angry way because you are nervous and worried: *You shouldn't* **get** so **uptight about** it.

up-to-'date adj
1 up-to-date information includes the most recent facts available: *access to up-to-date medical information* | **keep (sb) up-to-date (with/on sth)** *Keep me up-to-date with the latest developments.*
2 modern: *the most up-to-date technology* | *The design has been* **brought** *bang* **up-to-date** (=made very modern).

up-to-the-'minute adj including the most recent information, details etc: *a service that provides up-to-the-minute information on share prices*

uptown /ˌʌpˈtaʊn◄/ adj, adv AmE to or in the northern area of a city or town, or the area where richer people live → **downtown**: *The Parkers live uptown.*

upturn /ˈʌptɜːn $ -tɜːrn/ n [C] when economic conditions improve and business activity increases: *an upturn in the economy*

upturned /ˌʌpˈtɜːnd◄ $ -ˈtɜːr-/ adj **1** pointing or facing upwards: *an upturned nose* **2** turned upside down: *I sat on an upturned box.*

UPVC, uPVC /ˌjuː piː viː ˈsiː/ n [U] (**unplasticized polyvinyl chloride**) a type of plastic, used especially to make window frames

upward /ˈʌpwəd $ -wərd/ adj [only before noun]
1 towards a higher position **OPP** **downward**: *an upward movement of his hand* **2** increasing to a higher level **OPP** **downward**: *the recent upward trend in house prices*

upwards /ˈʌpwədz $ -wərdz/ (*also* **upward** *especially AmE*) adv
1 towards a higher position **OPP** **downwards**: *Billy pointed upward at the clouds.*
2 increasing to a higher level **OPP** **downwards**: *Salaries have been moving steadily upwards.*
3 upwards of sth more than an amount: *paintings valued at upwards of $100 million*

uranium /juˈreɪniəm/ n [U] a RADIOACTIVE metal used to produce NUCLEAR power and weapons

Uranus /ˈjʊərənəs, jʊˈreɪnəs $ ˈjʊr-, jʊˈreɪ-/ n the seventh PLANET from the Sun

urban /ˈɜːbən $ ˈɜːr-/ adj in or relating to a town or city → **rural**: *urban areas* **THESAURUS** CITY

urbane /ɜːˈbeɪn $ ɜːr-/ adj behaving in a relaxed and confident way in social situations

urge¹ /ɜːdʒ $ ɜːrdʒ/ v [T] to strongly suggest that someone do something: **urge sb to do sth** *Her friends urged her to go to France.* | **[+that]** *The report urged that there should be no further cuts.* **THESAURUS** ADVISE

PHRASAL VERBS
urge sb ↔ **on** to encourage someone to try harder, go faster etc: *The crowd urged him on.*

urge² n [C] a strong wish or need: *sexual urges* | **urge to do sth** *I felt a sudden urge to hit him.*

urgent /ˈɜːdʒənt $ ˈɜːr-/ adj if something is urgent, it is very important and needs to be dealt with immediately: *an urgent message* | *She's **in urgent need of** medical attention.* | *calls for **urgent action** to tackle the situation* —**urgency** n [U]: *a **matter of** great **urgency*** —**urgently** adv

urinal /ˈjʊərənəl, jʊˈraɪ- $ ˈjʊrə-/ n [C] a toilet where men urinate

urinate /ˈjʊərəneɪt $ ˈjʊr-/ v [I] *technical* to make urine flow out of your body

urine /ˈjʊərɪn $ ˈjʊr-/ n [U] liquid waste that comes out of your body when you go to the toilet

urn /ɜːn $ ɜːrn/ n [C] **1** a large container in which tea or coffee is made **2** a decorated container used for holding the ashes of a dead person

us /əs, s; *strong* ʌs/ pron the object form of 'we': *I'm sure he didn't see us.* | *You four go in the car and the rest of us can get a taxi.* | *an issue affecting us all*

usable /ˈjuːzəbəl/ adj something that is usable is in a good enough condition to be used

usage /ˈjuːsɪdʒ, ˈjuːz-/ n **1** [C,U] the way that words are used in a language: *a book on modern English usage* **2** [U] the way in which something is used, or the amount that it is used: *Car usage has increased dramatically.*

USB drive /juː es ˈbiː draɪv/ n [C] a small piece of electronic equipment that stores information and can be fitted into a computer

use¹ /juːz/ v [T]
1 if you use something, you do something with it for a particular purpose: *Can I use your phone?* | **use sth to do sth** *Use a food processor to grate the vegetables.* | *The system is **easy to use**.*
2 to need or take an amount of electricity, petrol, food etc [SYN] **consume**: *These light bulbs use less electricity.* | *Our car's using too much oil.*
3 to treat someone in an unkind and unfair way in order to get something that you want: *Can't you see that Andy is just using you?*
4 to say or write a particular word or phrase: *Why did you use the word 'if'?* | *Don't **use** bad **language**.*

PHRASAL VERBS
use sth ↔ **up** to use all of something: *Who used up the toothpaste?*

THESAURUS

use if you use something, you do something with it for a particular purpose: *Many people use bicycles to get around the city.*
consume to use a particular amount of something, especially fuel, or resources: *The U.S. consumes more energy than any other country.*
employ *formal* to use a particular method or skill in order to achieve something: *The surgeons employed a new technique.*
utilize *formal* to use something that is available to you, for a practical purpose: *The company aims to utilize the skills and knowledge of its staff.*

exercise *formal* to use a power or right that you have: *Only 40% of people exercised their right to vote.*
apply to use an idea, method, law etc: *New technology is being applied to almost every industrial process.* | *It is satisfying to apply my knowledge to help people.*

use² /juːs/ n
1 [U] when people use something to do something: **[+of]** *Are you in favour of the use of animals for research?* | *an exit for emergency use*
2 [C] a purpose for which something can be used: *The drug **has many uses**.*
3 the use of sth the right or ability to use something: *Joe's given me the use of his office.* | *She lost the use of both legs.*
4 [C] one of the meanings of a word or phrase, or a way in which it is used → **usage**: *an interesting use of the word 'brave'*
PHRASES
in use being used: *The meeting room is in use all morning.*
it's no use (doing sth) (*also* **what's the use (of doing sth)**) *spoken* used to say that something will not have any effect: *It's no use arguing with her. She just won't listen.*
make use of sth to use something that is available: *Try to make good use of your time.* [THESAURUS] USE
be (of) no use (to sb) to not be useful to someone: *The ticket's of no use to me now.*
put sth to good use to use your knowledge, skills etc well: *a chance to put your medical training to good use*

used¹ /juːst/ adj **be used to (doing) sth** if you are used to something, you have experienced it many times before and it no longer seems surprising, difficult etc: *He's used to getting up early.* | *I soon **got used to** the Japanese way of life.*

used² /juːzd/ adj used cars, clothes etc have already been owned by someone and are then sold [SYN] **secondhand**

used to /ˈjuːst tuː/ modal verb if something used to happen, it happened often or regularly in the past but does not happen now: *We used to go to the movies every week.* | *Didn't you used to smoke?*

> **Word Choice: used to do sth or be used to doing sth?**
> You use **used to** to talk about something that you did regularly in the past: *I used to play tennis twice a week, but I don't have time now.*
> You use **be used to** and **get used to** to talk about feeling more comfortable with a situation or activity, so that it does not seem surprising or difficult: *I'm used to living in a cold climate.* | *Driving seems difficult at first, but you soon get used to it.*

useful /ˈjuːsfəl/ adj something that is useful helps you to do or get what you want [OPP] **useless**: *a useful book for travellers* | **[+for]** *Trade fairs are useful for meeting new clients.* | *It's useful to make a list before you start.* | *His knowledge of Italian was to **come in useful** (=be useful) later on.* —**usefully** adv —**usefulness** n [U]

THESAURUS

useful something that is useful helps you to do or get what you want: *The book is full of useful information.*

handy *informal* useful – used especially when something is easy to use, or in the phrase **come in handy**: *a handy little gadget for peeling potatoes* | *handy hints* | *The money could **come in handy** later on* (=be useful at that time).

helpful useful and helping you to do something: *Their website provides helpful advice for students.*

valuable very useful and important: *His information was very valuable to the police.* | *a valuable lesson*

useless /ˈjuːsləs/ *adj*
1 not useful or effective at all OPP **useful**: *useless information* | **virtually/completely/totally etc useless** *These scissors are completely useless.* | **[+for]** *The land is useless for growing crops.* | **it is useless doing sth/to do sth** *It's useless trying to talk to her.*
2 *informal* very bad at doing something: **[+at]** *I'm useless at golf.*

user /ˈjuːzə $ -ər/ *n* [C] someone who uses a product, service etc: *computer users*

user-'friendly *adj* something that is user-friendly is designed so that it is easy to use

'user name *n* [C] a name or word that you use to enter a computer system or use the Internet

usher[1] /ˈʌʃə $ -ər/ *v* [T] to take someone into or out of a room or building: *His secretary ushered us into his office.*

PHRASAL VERBS

usher in sth to make something new start happening: *Gorbachev ushered in a new era of reform.*

usher[2] *n* [C] someone who shows people to their seats in a theatre, at a wedding etc

usual /ˈjuːʒuəl, ˈjuːʒəl/ *adj* the same as what happens most of the time or in most situations → **unusual**: *Plant the bulbs in the **usual way**.* | *Let's meet at the usual place.* | **longer/bigger/worse etc than usual** *The food was even worse than usual.* | **It was usual** *for young mothers to stay at home.*

PHRASES
as usual in the way that happens on most occasions or most of the time: *They were late, as usual.*

usually /ˈjuːʒuəli, ˈjuːʒəli/ *adv* used to say what happens on most occasions or in most situations: *We usually go out for dinner on Saturday.* | *Usually I walk to work.*

usurp /juːˈzɜːp $ -ˈsɜːrp/ *v* [T] *formal* to take someone else's power, position, or job

utensil /juːˈtensəl/ *n* [C] *formal* a tool or object that you use for doing something, especially for cooking: *kitchen utensils*

uterus /ˈjuːtərəs/ *n* [C] (*plural* **uteruses**) *technical* the part of a woman or female MAMMAL where babies develop SYN **womb**

utilities /juːˈtɪlətiz/ *n* [plural] services such as gas or electricity provided for people to use: *Does the rent include utilities?*

u'tility ˌroom *n* [C] a room in a house where you can have your washing machine, FREEZER etc

utilize Ac (*also* **-ise** *BrE*) /ˈjuːtəlaɪz/ *v* [T] *formal* to use something THESAURUS USE

utmost[1] /ˈʌtməʊst $ -moʊst/ *adj* **the utmost importance/care etc** the greatest possible importance, care etc: *a matter of the utmost importance*

utmost[2] *n* [singular] the most that can be done: *The team **did** their **utmost** (=tried as hard as possible) to have it finished on time.* | *The course challenges drivers **to the utmost**.*

utopia /juːˈtəʊpiə $ -ˌtoʊ-/ *n* [C,U] an imaginary perfect world —**utopian** *adj*: *a utopian society*

utter[1] /ˈʌtə $ -ər/ *adj* complete or extreme: *That's **utter nonsense!** | *It was a **complete and utter** failure.* —**utterly** *adv*: *That's utterly ridiculous!*

utter[2] *v* [T] *literary* to say something: *No one uttered a word.* —**utterance** *n* [C]

U-turn /ˈjuː tɜːn $ ˌjuː ˈtɜːrn/ *n* [C] **1** if a driver does a U-turn, they turn their car around in the road and go back in the direction they came from **2** a complete change of ideas, plans etc: **[+on/over]** *a government U-turn on economic policy*

UV /juː ˈviː/ *adj* ULTRAVIOLET: *harmful UV rays*

Vv

V, v /viː/ *n* [C,U] (*plural* **V's, v's**) the 22nd letter of the English alphabet

v. (*also* **v** *BrE*) **1** the written abbreviation of **verb 2** a written abbreviation of **versus 3** the written abbreviation of **volt**

vacancy /'veɪkənsi/ *n* [C] (*plural* **vacancies**) **1** a job that is available for someone to start doing: *information about **job vacancies*** | [+for] *Are there any vacancies for cooks?* THESAURUS▶ JOB **2** a room that is available in a hotel

vacant /'veɪkənt/ *adj* **1** empty and available for someone to use: *vacant apartments* THESAURUS▶ EMPTY **2** if a position in an organization is vacant, the job is available because no one is doing it: *The post of Director became vacant.* **3** if someone has a vacant expression, they do not seem to be thinking about anything —**vacantly** *adv*

vacate /və'keɪt, veɪ- $ 'veɪkeɪt/ *v* [T] *formal* to leave a seat, room etc so that someone else can use it: *Guests must vacate their rooms by noon.*

vacation¹ /və'keɪʃən $ veɪ-/ *n* [C,U]
1 *AmE* a period of time that you spend in another place for enjoyment SYN **holiday** *BrE*: *We're thinking of **taking a vacation** in the Virgin Islands.* | **on vacation** *I went there once on vacation.*
2 *especially AmE* a period of time when you do not have to work or go to school SYN **holiday** *BrE*: *the summer vacation* | **on vacation** *They're on vacation for the next two weeks.* | *Contractors aren't entitled to paid **vacation time**.*

vacation² *v* [I] *AmE* to go somewhere for a holiday SYN **holiday** *BrE* —**vacationer** *n* [C]

vaccinate /'væksəneɪt/ *v* [T] to give someone a vaccine to protect them from a disease: *The children should all be vaccinated against measles.*

vaccination /,væksə'neɪʃən/ *n* [C,U] when someone is given a vaccine to protect them from a disease: *a vaccination against measles*

vaccine /'væksiːn $ væk'siːn/ *n* [C,U] a substance used to protect people from a disease. A vaccine contains a weak form of the VIRUS that causes the disease.

vacuum¹ /'vækjuəm, -kjʊm/ *n* **1** [C] a vacuum cleaner **2** [C] a space that is completely empty of all air or gas **3** [singular] a situation in which someone or something is missing or lacking: *His death left a vacuum in her life.*

vacuum² *v* [I,T] to clean a place using a vacuum cleaner THESAURUS▶ CLEAN

'vacuum ,cleaner *n* [C] a machine that cleans floors by sucking up the dirt from them

'vacuum ,flask *n* [C] *BrE* a container like a bottle that keeps drinks hot or cold

vagaries /'veɪgəriz/ *n* [plural] *formal* changes and events that cannot be controlled: *the vagaries of fashion*

vagina /və'dʒaɪnə/ *n* [C] the part that connects a woman's outer sexual organs to her UTERUS —**vaginal** /və'dʒaɪnl $ 'vædʒɪnl/ *adj*

vagrant /'veɪgrənt/ *n* [C] *formal* someone who has no home or work

vague /veɪg/ *adj* not clear or certain: [+about] *She's been a bit vague about her plans for the summer.* | **have a vague idea/feeling etc** *I had only a vague idea where the house was.* | *Looking closely, he could just see the vague outline of her face.*

vaguely /'veɪgli/ *adv* **1** slightly: *The woman's face looked vaguely familiar.* **2** in a way that is not clear or exact OPP **clearly**: *a vaguely worded statement* **3** in a way that shows you are not thinking about what you are doing: *He smiled vaguely.*

vain /veɪn/ *adj* **1** *disapproving* too proud of yourself, especially of your appearance → **vanity**: *Men can be so vain.* THESAURUS▶ PROUD **2** **vain attempt/hope etc** a vain hope or attempt is not successful —**vainly** *adv*
PHRASES
| **in vain** without success: *Doctors tried in vain to save his life.*

Valentine /'væləntaɪn/ (*also* **'Valentine's ,card**) *n* [C] a card that you send to someone you love on Valentine's Day (February 14)

valet /'vælət, 'væleɪ $ væ'leɪ/ *n* [C] **1** a male servant who takes care of a man's clothes, serves his meals etc **2** *AmE* someone who parks your car for you at a hotel or restaurant

valiant /'væliənt/ *adj* *formal* very brave: *a valiant rescue attempt* —**valiantly** *adv*

valid Ac /'vælɪd/ *adj* **1** a valid ticket, document, or agreement is legally or officially acceptable OPP **invalid**: *a valid passport* | *Your return ticket is valid for three months.* **2** a valid reason, argument etc is based on something reasonable or sensible: *a valid criticism* —**validity** /və'lɪdəti/ *n* [U]

validate Ac /'vælədeɪt/ *v* [T] *formal* to show that something is true or correct

valley /'væli/ *n* [C] an area of lower land between two lines of hills or mountains: *a village in the Loire Valley*

valour *BrE*, **valor** *AmE* /'vælə $ -ər/ *n* [U] *literary* great courage, especially in war

valuable /'væljuəbəl, -jəbəl $ 'væljəbəl/ *adj*
1 worth a lot of money OPP **worthless**: *a valuable ring*
2 help, advice etc that is valuable is very useful → **invaluable**: *volunteers who have made a valuable contribution to our work* THESAURUS▶ USEFUL

THESAURUS

valuable worth a lot of money: *Don't leave anything valuable in your hotel room.* | *a valuable gold coin*
priceless used when emphasizing that something is very valuable: *A priceless painting by Matisse was stolen from the gallery.*

valuables

precious a precious metal or stone is very rare and expensive. A precious person or thing is very special and important to you: *diamonds and other precious stones* | *His letters were very precious to me.*
irreplaceable very valuable or rare, and impossible to replace: *The books were irreplaceable.*

valuables /'væljuəbəlz, -jəbəlz $ -jəbəlz/ *n* [plural] things that you own that are worth a lot of money, such as jewellery or cameras: *Put your valuables in the hotel safe.* **THESAURUS** PROPERTY

valuation /ˌvælju'eɪʃən/ *n* [C,U] when people decide how much something is worth

value¹ /'vælju:/ *n*
1 [C,U] the amount of money that something is worth: **[+of]** *the value of the house* | **of value** (=worth a lot of money) *Did the thieves take anything of value?* **THESAURUS** COST
2 [U] the importance or usefulness of something: **[+of]** *the value of direct personal experience* | **of great/little value** *His research was of great value to doctors working with the disease.*
3 good/excellent etc value used to say that something is worth the amount you pay for it: *At only $45 a night, it's **great value for your money**.* **THESAURUS** CHEAP
4 values [plural] your beliefs about what is right and wrong, or about what is important in life: *traditional family values* → FACE VALUE

COLLOCATIONS

verbs
to increase/rise in value *His paintings have increased in value.*
to fall/go down in value *The dollar fell in value against the yen.*
the value of sth increases/rises *The value of the stock rose again.*
the value of sth falls *The value of your new car will fall as soon as you buy it.*
to put a value on sth (=to say how much it is worth) *How can you put a value on someone's life?*

adjectives
high/low value *They grow crops of high value.*

value² *v* [T] **1** to think that something is important and worth having: *I always value your advice.* **2** to say how much something is worth: *a painting valued at $5 million*

valve /vælv/ *n* [C] a part of a tube that opens and closes to control the flow of liquid, air etc passing through: *the valves of the heart* → see picture at BICYCLE

vampire /'væmpaɪə $ -paɪr/ *n* [C] in stories, a dead person who bites people's necks and sucks their blood

van /væn/ *n* [C] a vehicle used for carrying goods which is smaller than a truck, and which has a roof and metal sides: *a delivery van* → see picture at TRANSPORT¹

vandal /'vændl/ *n* [C] someone who deliberately damages things, especially public property

vandalize (*also* **-ise** *BrE*) /'vændəl-aɪz/ *v* [T] to deliberately damage things, especially public property **THESAURUS** DAMAGE —**vandalism** /-lɪzəm/ *n* [U]

vanguard /'vænɡɑːd $ -ɡɑːrd/ *n* **in the vanguard (of sth)** involved in the greatest way in something, especially in developing something new: *a group in the vanguard of political reform*

vanilla /və'nɪlə/ *n* [U] a substance with a slightly sweet taste, used in ICE CREAM and other foods

vanish /'vænɪʃ/ *v* [I] to disappear suddenly, especially in a way that cannot be easily explained: *When I looked again, he'd vanished.* | **[+from]** *The bird vanished from sight.* | *The smile vanished from her face.* | *The ship vanished without trace* (=disappeared, leaving no sign of what had happened to it). **THESAURUS** DISAPPEAR

vanity /'vænəti/ *n* [U] *disapproving* when someone is too proud of their appearance or their abilities → **vain**

vanquish /'væŋkwɪʃ/ *v* [T] *literary* to defeat someone or something completely

vantage point /'vɑːntɪdʒ pɔɪnt $ 'væn-/ *n* [C] a good position from which you can look at something

vaporize (*also* **-ise** *BrE*) /'veɪpəraɪz/ *v* [I,T] to be changed into a vapour, or to change a liquid into a vapour

vapour *BrE*, **vapor** *AmE* /'veɪpə $ -ər/ *n* [C,U] many small drops of liquid that float in the air: *water vapour*

variable¹ Ac /'veəriəbəl $ 'ver-/ *adj* likely to change often or to be different → **vary**: *a variable rate of interest* | *Hospital food is **highly variable** in quality.* —**variability** /ˌveəriə'bɪləti $ ˌver-/ *n* [U]

variable² Ac *n* [C] something that may be different in different situations: *economic variables*

variance Ac /'veəriəns $ 'ver-/ *n* **be at variance (with sth/sb)** *formal* if two things or people are at variance with each other, they are very different or do not agree

variant Ac /'veəriənt $ 'ver-/ *n* [C] something that is slightly different from the usual form of something: *a spelling variant* —**variant** *adj*

variation Ac /ˌveəri'eɪʃən $ ˌver-/ *n* **1** [C,U] a difference between similar things, or a change from the usual amount or form of something → **vary**: **[+in]** *variations in price from store to store* | **[+between/within/among]** *There is considerable variation between different areas.* **2** [C] something that is done in a slightly different way from normal: *This is the traditional recipe, but of course there are many variations.*

varicose veins /ˌværɪkəʊs 'veɪnz $ -koʊs-/ *n* [plural] a medical condition in which the VEINS in your leg become swollen and painful

varied Ac /'veərid $ 'ver-/ *adj* including many different types of things: *a varied diet*

variety /vəˈraɪəti/ n (plural **varieties**)
1 a variety of sth a lot of different types of things or people: *The college offers **a wide variety of** language courses.* | *Potatoes can be cooked in a variety of ways.*
2 [U] the different things or activities which something involves and which make it interesting: *I wanted a job with plenty of variety.*
3 [C] a type of something: **[+of]** *different varieties of lettuce*

various /ˈveəriəs $ ˈver-/ adj several different: *The coat is available in various colours.* | *He decided to leave school **for various reasons**.*

variously /ˈveəriəsli $ ˈver-/ adv in many different ways: *He's been variously called a genius and a madman.*

varnish¹ /ˈvɑːnɪʃ $ ˈvɑːr-/ n [C,U] a clear liquid that is painted onto wood to protect it and give it a shiny surface

varnish² v [T] to paint something with VARNISH

vary Ac /ˈveəri $ ˈveri/ v (**varied**, **varying**, **varies**)
1 [I] if things vary, they are all different from each other: **vary from sth to sth** *Prices vary from £15 to £25.* | **[+in]** *The flowers vary in colour and size.*
2 [I] to change: **[+according to]** *His moods seem to vary according to the weather.* | *'What do you wear when you go out?' 'Well **it varies**.'*
3 [T] to regularly change what you do or the way that you do it: *You need to vary your diet.* —**varying** adj: *varying degrees of success*

vase /vɑːz $ veɪs, veɪz/ n [C] a container used for putting flowers in

VASE

vasectomy /vəˈsektəmi/ n [C] (plural **vasectomies**) a medical operation to prevent a man from having children

vast /vɑːst $ væst/ adj extremely large **SYN** huge: *vast areas of rainforest* | *Refugees crossed the border **in vast numbers**.* **THESAURUS** ► BIG

PHRASES
the vast majority almost all of a group of people or things: *The vast majority of students work very hard.*

vastly /ˈvɑːstli $ ˈvæstli/ adv formal very much: *The two books are vastly different.*

vat /væt/ n [C] a very large container for keeping liquids in

VAT /ˌviː eɪ ˈtiː, væt/ n [U] (**value added tax**) a tax on goods and services in Britain and Europe

vault¹ /vɔːlt $ vɒːlt/ n [C] **1** a room in a bank with thick walls and a strong door, used for keeping money, jewels etc safely **2** a room where people from the same family are buried

vault² v [I,T] to jump over something in one movement, using your hands or a pole to help you: **[+over]** *He vaulted over the fence and ran off.*

VCR /ˌviː siː ˈɑː $ -ˈɑːr/ n [C] (**video cassette recorder**) a machine used for recording television programmes or playing videos

VD /ˌviː ˈdiː/ n [U] (**venereal disease**) a disease that is passed from one person to another during sex

VDU /ˌviː diː ˈjuː/ n [C] (**visual display unit**) a computer screen **SYN** monitor

-'ve /v, əv/ the short form of 'have': *We've finished.*

veal /viːl/ n [U] meat from a CALF (=very young cow)

veer /vɪə $ vɪr/ v [I] to change direction suddenly: *The car veered sharply to the left.*

veg¹ /vedʒ/ n [C,U] (plural **veg**) BrE informal vegetables

veg² v (**vegged**, **vegging**)
PHRASAL VERBS
veg out informal to relax and not do anything

vegan /ˈviːgən $ ˈviː-, ˈvedʒən/ n [C] someone who does not eat meat, fish, eggs, or milk products

vegetable /ˈvedʒtəbəl/ n [C] a plant such as a CARROT, CABBAGE, or potato, which you can eat

vegetarian /ˌvedʒəˈteəriən $ -ˈter-/ n [C] someone who does not eat meat or fish —**vegetarian** adj: *More and more people are becoming vegetarian.*

> **Word Choice**: vegetarian or vegan?
> **Vegetarians** do not eat meat or fish. They can eat cheese, butter, and eggs.
> **Vegans** do not eat anything that comes from an animal, including meat, fish, cheese, butter, and eggs.
> In informal English, you often say **veggie** instead of **vegetarian**: *Are you a veggie?*

vegetation /ˌvedʒɪˈteɪʃən/ n [U] the plants, flowers, trees etc that grow in a particular area: *dense vegetation*

veggie /ˈvedʒi/ n [C] informal **1** a VEGETARIAN **2** AmE a vegetable —**veggie** adj

vehement /ˈviːəmənt/ adj having very strong feelings or opinions about something: *his vehement opposition to the plan* —**vehemently** adv

vehicle Ac /ˈviːɪkəl/ n [C]
1 formal something such as a car or bus that is used for carrying people or things from one place to another: *a stolen vehicle*
2 a vehicle for (doing) sth something that you use as a way of spreading ideas, opinions etc: *The newspaper is a vehicle for government propaganda.* → MOTOR VEHICLE

veil /veɪl/ n [C] a thin piece of material that women wear to cover their faces: *a bridal veil*
PHRASES
draw a veil over sth formal to avoid talking about something because it is unpleasant or embarrassing: *She decided to draw a veil over the whole incident.*

veiled /veɪld/ adj veiled criticisms or threats are not said directly

vein /veɪn/ n [C]
1 one of the tubes through which blood flows to your heart from other parts of your body → artery

2 one of the thin lines on a leaf or on the wing of an insect

3 a thin layer of coal, gold etc in rock

4 in a ... vein in a particular style of speaking or writing: *She went on **in the same vein** for several minutes.*

> **Word Choice: vein or artery?**
> A **vein** is a tube that carries blood to your heart.
> An **artery** is a tube that carries blood away from your heart.

Velcro /'velkrəʊ $ -kroʊ/ n [U] trademark a material used for fastening shoes, clothes etc, made from two special pieces of material that stick to each other → see picture at **BUTTON¹**

velocity /və'lɒsəti $ -'lɑː-/ n [C,U] (plural **velocities**) technical the speed at which something moves in a particular direction: *the velocity of light*

velvet /'velvɪt/ n [U] cloth with a soft thick surface on one side: *velvet curtains | a velvet dress*

velvety /'velvəti/ adj pleasantly smooth and soft: *the cat's velvety fur*

vendetta /ven'detə/ n [C] when one person tries to harm another, or two people argue violently, over a long period of time

vending machine /'vendɪŋ məʃiːn/ n [C] a machine that sells cigarettes, drinks etc

vendor /'vendə $ -ər/ n [C] someone who sells something, especially on the street: *street vendors*

veneer /və'nɪə $ -'nɪr/ n **1** [C,U] a thin layer of wood that covers the outside of something that is made of a cheaper material: *oak veneer* **2 a veneer of sth** behaviour that hides someone's real feelings or character: *a veneer of politeness*

venerable /'venərəbəl/ adj formal a venerable person or organization is very old and respected: *venerable institutions*

venerate /'venəreɪt/ v [T] formal to honour or respect someone or something because they are old or holy

venereal disease /və,nɪəriəl dɪ'ziːz $ -'nɪr-/ n [C,U] VD

venetian blind /və,niːʃən 'blaɪnd/ n [C] a covering for a window made of bars of wood or plastic that can be raised or lowered to let in light

vengeance /'vendʒəns/ n [U] a violent or harmful action that someone does to punish someone for harming them or their family: *his desire for vengeance*

PHRASES
with a vengeance with great force or a lot of effort: *The hot weather is back with a vengeance.*

vengeful /'vendʒfəl/ adj literary very eager to punish someone who has done something bad

venison /'venəzən, -sən/ n [U] meat from a DEER

venom /'venəm/ n [U] **1** great anger or hatred: *a speech full of venom* **2** poison produced by some snakes, insects etc —**venomous** adj: *a venomous snake*

vent¹ /vent/ n [C] a special hole through which smoke or dirty air can go out, or fresh air can come in

PHRASES
give vent to sth formal to do something that shows how angry, annoyed etc you feel: *He gave vent to his anger and shouted at them.*

vent² v [T] to express strong feelings of anger, hatred etc: *She was **venting** her **frustration** by banging the pots.*

ventilate /'ventəleɪt $ -tleɪt/ v [T] to let fresh air into a room or building —**ventilated** adj —**ventilation** /,ventə'leɪʃən $ -tl'eɪ-/ n [U]: *the ventilation system*

ventilator /'ventəleɪtə $ -t-leɪtər/ n [C] a piece of equipment that pumps air into and out of someone's lungs so that they can breathe

ventriloquist /ven'trɪləkwɪst/ n [C] someone who speaks without moving their lips, in a way that makes the sound seem to come from somewhere else, especially from a PUPPET —**ventriloquism** n [U]

venture¹ /'ventʃə $ -ər/ n [C] a new activity that involves taking risks, especially in business: *The new venture was not a success.* → **JOINT VENTURE**

venture² v formal **1** [I] to go somewhere that could be dangerous: [+into/out (of) etc] *Kate rarely ventured beyond her nearest town.* **2** [T] to say or do something in an uncertain way because you are afraid it is wrong or will seem stupid: *No one else ventured an opinion.*

venue /'venjuː/ n [C] a place where a concert, sports game etc takes place: *a popular jazz venue*

Venus /'viːnəs/ n the second PLANET from the Sun

veracity /və'ræsəti/ n [U] formal the quality of being true

veranda, verandah /və'rændə/ n [C] an open area with a floor and a roof that is built on the side of a house

verb /vɜːb $ vɜːrb/ n [C] a word used to say what someone does or what happens, for example 'go', 'eat', or 'finish' → **AUXILIARY VERB, HELPING VERB, LINKING VERB, MODAL VERB, PHRASAL VERB**

verbal /'vɜːbəl $ 'vɜːr-/ adj **1** spoken, not written: *a verbal agreement* **2** relating to words or using words: *verbal skills* —**verbally** adv

verbatim /vɜː'beɪtɪm $ vɜːr-/ adj, adv repeating the actual words that were spoken or written

verbose /vɜː'bəʊs $ vɜːr'boʊs/ adj formal using too many words

verdict /'vɜːdɪkt $ 'vɜːr-/ n [C] **1** an official decision in a court of law about whether someone is guilty or how someone died: *Has the jury reached a verdict?* **2** an official decision about something or someone's opinion about something: [+on] *What's your verdict on the movie?*

verge¹ /vɜːdʒ $ vɜːrdʒ/ n [C] BrE a narrow area of grass at the side of a road

PHRASES
be on the verge of sth to be about to do something: *Helen was on the verge of tears.*

verge² v

PHRASAL VERBS

verge on/upon sth to be very close to a harmful or extreme state: *Their behaviour sometimes verged on insanity.*

verify /ˈverɪfaɪ/ v [T] (**verified, verifying, verifies**) to check or prove that something is true or correct: *There's no way of verifying his story.* THESAURUS CHECK —**verification** /ˌverɪfɪˈkeɪʃən/ n [U]

veritable /ˈverɪtəbəl/ adj formal used to emphasize your description of someone or something: *a veritable masterpiece*

vermin /ˈvɜːmɪn $ ˈvɜːr-/ n [plural] small animals, birds, and insects that are harmful because they destroy crops, spoil food, or spread disease

vernacular /vəˈnækjələ $ vərˈnækjələr/ n [singular] a form of a language that ordinary people use, especially one that is not the official language

versatile /ˈvɜːsətaɪl $ ˈvɜːrsətl/ adj 1 someone who is versatile has many different skills: *a versatile actor* 2 having many different uses: *a versatile computer system* —**versatility** /ˌvɜːsəˈtɪləti $ ˌvɜːr-/ n [U]

verse /vɜːs $ vɜːrs/ n 1 [C] a set of lines that forms one part of a song or poem: *the last verse of the poem* 2 [U] words arranged in the form of poetry: *a book of verse*

versed /vɜːst $ vɜːrst/ adj **be (well) versed in** formal to know a lot about a subject: *lawyers who are well-versed in these matters*

version Ac /ˈvɜːʃən $ ˈvɜːrʒən/ n [C]
1 one form of something that is slightly different from all other forms: **[+of]** *the original version of the film* | *a new version of an old Beatles song* | **English/German/electronic/film etc version** (=presented in a different language or form) *I think I preferred the television version.*
2 someone's version of an event is their description of it, when this is different from the description given by another person: **[+of]** *The newspapers all gave different versions of the story.* | *the official version of events* → COVER VERSION

versus /ˈvɜːsəs $ ˈvɜːr-/ prep (written abbreviation **v., vs.**) 1 used to say that two people or teams are playing against each other in a game or fighting a court case: *Connors versus McEnroe* 2 used when comparing the advantages of two different things or ideas: *It's a question of quantity versus quality.*

vertebra /ˈvɜːtəbrə $ ˈvɜːr-/ n [C] (plural **vertebrae** /-briː, -breɪ/) one of the small hollow bones down the centre of your back

vertical /ˈvɜːtɪkəl $ ˈvɜːr-/ adj pointing straight upwards → **horizontal**: *a vertical line* | **vertical cliff/climb/rock etc** (=one that is very deep) *a vertical rock face* —**vertically** /-kli/ adv

vertigo /ˈvɜːtɪɡəʊ $ ˈvɜːrtɪɡoʊ/ n [U] a feeling of sickness and DIZZINESS that you get when you look down from a high place

verve /vɜːv $ vɜːrv/ n [U] literary if someone does something with verve, they do it with energy, excitement, or great pleasure

very¹ /ˈveri/ adv used to emphasize an adjective, adverb, or phrase: *It's a very good book.* | *John gets embarrassed very easily.* | *I miss her very much.* | *I'm very, very pleased you could come.* | *My sister and I were married on the very same* (=exactly the same) *day.*

PHRASES
not very good/difficult/far etc not good, difficult, far etc at all: *I'm not very good at spelling.* | *'Was the talk interesting?' 'Not very* (=only slightly).'
your very own used to emphasize the fact that something belongs to one particular person and to no one else: **of your very own** *At last, a home of her very own.*

Usage
Do not use **very** with adjectives and adverbs that already have 'very' as part of their meaning, for example **huge** (=very big) or **terrible** (=very bad). Do not say 'a very huge cake'. Say *a huge cake*. For emphasis, you can use **really**: *a really huge cake*.

very² adj used to emphasize that you are talking exactly about one particular thing or person: *He died in this very room.*

vessel /ˈvesəl/ n [C] formal a ship or large boat → BLOOD VESSEL

vest /vest/ n [C] 1 BrE a piece of underwear that you wear under a shirt SYN undershirt AmE 2 a special piece of clothing without SLEEVEs that you wear to protect your body: *a bulletproof vest* 3 AmE a piece of clothing without SLEEVEs and with buttons down the front that you wear as part of a suit SYN waistcoat BrE

vested interest /ˌvestɪd ˈɪntrɪst/ n [C] if you have a vested interest in something happening, you have a strong reason for wanting it to happen because you will get money or advantages from it

vestibule /ˈvestɪbjuːl/ n [C] formal a wide PASSAGE or small room inside the front door of a public building

vestige /ˈvestɪdʒ/ n [C] a small part or amount of something that still remains when most of it no longer exists: **[+of]** *the last vestiges of the British Empire*

vet¹ /vet/ n [C]
1 especially BrE (also **veterinary surgeon** BrE formal) someone who is trained to give medical care and treatment to sick animals SYN **veterinarian** AmE: *We had to take our cat to the vet.* THESAURUS DOCTOR
2 AmE informal a veteran from a war: *Vietnam vets*

vet² v [T] (**vetted, vetting**) BrE to check details about a person in order to make sure they are suitable for a particular job: *All staff are vetted for security purposes.*

veteran /ˈvetərən/ n [C] 1 someone who has been a soldier, sailor etc in a war 2 someone who has had a lot of experience of doing something: *veteran Hollywood entertainer Bob Hope*

veterinarian /ˌvetərəˈneəriən $ -ˈner-/ n [C] AmE someone who is trained to give medical care and treatment to sick animals SYN **vet** BrE THESAURUS DOCTOR

veterinary /ˈvetərənəri $ -neri/ adj technical relating to the medical care and treatment of sick animals

ˈveterinary ˌsurgeon n [C] a VET¹

veto¹ /ˈviːtəʊ $ -toʊ/ v [T] (past tense and past participle **vetoed**, present participle **vetoing**, third person singular **vetoes**) to officially refuse to allow something to happen, especially something that other people or organizations have agreed: *The President vetoed the bill.* **THESAURUS** VOTE

veto² n [C,U] (plural **vetoes**) when someone officially refuses to allow something to happen: *The chairman can use his veto to stop the deal.*

vex /veks/ v [T] old-fashioned to make someone feel annoyed or worried

vexed /vekst/ adj **1 vexed question/issue/problem etc** a question or problem that is difficult to deal with and causes a lot of problems or discussion **2** old-fashioned worried or annoyed

via [Ac] /ˈvaɪə, ˈviːə/ prep **1** travelling through a place when you are going to another place: *We're flying to Denver via Chicago.* **2** using a particular machine, system, person etc to send, receive, or broadcast something: *The concert was broadcast around the world via satellite.*

viable /ˈvaɪəbəl/ adj something that is viable is able to exist or succeed: *a viable alternative to the petrol engine* | *At 28 weeks, the foetus is viable.* —**viability** /ˌvaɪəˈbɪləti/ n [U]

viaduct /ˈvaɪədʌkt/ n [C] a long high bridge across a valley

vibe /vaɪb/ n [C usually plural] informal a general feeling that you get from a person or a place: *I get bad vibes from that guy.*

vibrant /ˈvaɪbrənt/ adj **1** full of activity or energy in a way that is exciting and attractive: *a vibrant personality* **2** a vibrant colour is bright and strong

vibrate /vaɪˈbreɪt $ ˈvaɪbreɪt/ v [I,T] to shake with small fast movements, or to make something shake in this way: *The vocal cords vibrate as air passes over them.* **THESAURUS** SHAKE

vibration /vaɪˈbreɪʃən/ n [C,U] a continuous slight shaking movement: *vibration caused by passing traffic*

vicar /ˈvɪkə $ -ər/ n [C] a priest in the Church of England

vicarage /ˈvɪkərɪdʒ/ n [C] the house where a vicar lives

vicarious /vɪˈkeəriəs $ vaɪˈker-/ adj [only before noun] vicarious feelings are feelings that you get by watching or reading about someone else doing something rather than doing it yourself

vice /vaɪs/ n **1** [U] criminal activities that involve sex or drugs **2** [C] a bad habit or a bad part of someone's character: *Smoking is my only vice.* **3** [C] BrE, **vise** AmE a tool used to hold something firmly while you work on it, for example to hold a piece of wood while you cut it

vice- /vaɪs/ prefix **vice-president/chairman etc** the person next in rank below someone in authority, who can represent them or act instead of them

ˌvice ˈpresident, vice-president n [C] **1** the person who is next in rank to the president of a country **2** AmE someone who is responsible for one part of a company: *the vice president for marketing*

vice versa /ˌvaɪs ˈvɜːsə, ˌvaɪsɪ- $ -ɜːr-/ adv used to say that the opposite of a situation you have just described is also true: *The boys may refuse to play with the girls, and vice versa.*

vicinity /vəˈsɪnəti/ n **in the vicinity (of sth)** formal in the area near or around a place: *The stolen car was found in the vicinity of the station.*

vicious /ˈvɪʃəs/ adj **1** violent, cruel, and likely to harm someone: *a vicious attack* **THESAURUS** VIOLENT **2** cruel in a way that is intended to hurt someone's feelings or make their character seem bad: *a vicious rumour* —**viciously** adv —**viciousness** n [U]

ˌvicious ˈcircle n [singular] a situation in which one problem causes another problem which then causes the first problem again

victim /ˈvɪktɪm/ n [C] someone who has been hurt, attacked, or killed because of something bad: **[+of]** *victims of crime* | **rape/murder etc victims** *Most homicide victims are under 30.* | *an aid programme for the famine victims*

victimize (also **-ise** BrE) /ˈvɪktəmaɪz/ v [T] to deliberately treat someone unfairly: *People with AIDS have been victimized at work.* —**victimization** /ˌvɪktəmaɪˈzeɪʃən $ -mə-/ n [U]

victor /ˈvɪktə $ -ər/ n [C] formal the winner of a battle or competition

Victorian /vɪkˈtɔːriən/ adj connected with the period in British history between 1837 and 1901: *Victorian buildings* —**Victorian** n [C]

victorious /vɪkˈtɔːriəs/ adj successful in a battle or competition **THESAURUS** SUCCESSFUL

victory /ˈvɪktəri/ n [C,U] (plural **victories**) the success you achieve when you win a battle, game, election etc **OPP** defeat: **[+over/against]** *Poland's victory over France in the World Cup* | **[+for]** *This ruling represents a victory for all women.*

COLLOCATIONS

verbs

to win/score a victory *The young golfer won a great victory today.*
to lead sb to victory *He led his men to victory in battle.*
to celebrate a victory *The Democrats are celebrating their election victory.*

adjectives

a great/major victory *Local people regard the decision as a major victory.*
an easy victory *Nobody expected an easy victory.*
a narrow victory (=a win by a small amount) *Both sides claimed to have won a narrow victory.*
an election victory

---

video¹ /ˈvɪdiəʊ $ -dioʊ/ n (plural **videos**)
1 [C] a short film recording of something, which is shown on a television or computer screen: *It is currently the most watched video on the Internet.*
2 [C,U] a copy of a film or television programme, or

a film of an event, recorded on VIDEOTAPE: *Do you want to* **watch** *a* **video** *tonight?* | **on video** *I've got the whole ceremony on video.* | *The movie has just been* **released on video**.

3 [C] *BrE* a video cassette recorder: *Could you set the video to record the football match?*

video[2] *v* [T] (*past tense and past participle* **videoed**, *present participle* **videoing**, *third person singular* **videos**) *BrE* to record a television programme, film, or event on a video: *A friend videoed our wedding.* | *Are you going to video that film on TV tonight?*

video cas'sette re,corder *n* [C] *abbreviation* **VCR** (*also* '**video ,recorder**) a machine used for recording television programmes or showing videos

'**video ,conferencing** *n* [U] a system that makes it possible to have meetings with people in different parts of the world by sending pictures and sound electronically

'**video ,game** *n* [C] a game in which you move images on a screen using electronic controls

videophone /ˈvɪdiəʊfəʊn $ -dioʊfoʊn/ *n* [C] a type of telephone that allows you to see the person you are talking to on a screen

videotape[1] /ˈvɪdiəʊteɪp $ -dioʊ-/ *n* [C] a long narrow band of MAGNETIC material in a plastic container, on which films, television programmes etc can be recorded

videotape[2] *v* [T] to record a television programme, film, or event using a video

vie /vaɪ/ *v* [I] (**vied, vying, vies**) to compete with another person, company etc in order to get something: [+for] *The brothers vied for her attention.*

view[1] /vjuː/ *n*
1 [C] your opinion about something: [+about] *He has strong views about politics.* | [+on] *What's your view on this matter?* | **in sb's view** *In my view the government is wrong.*
2 [C,U] what you can see, or how well you can see something: [+of] *We had a really* **good view** *of the stage.* | **be in view/come into view** *Suddenly the pyramids were in view.* | **disappear/hide/vanish from view** *The gun had disappeared from view.* | *Fran hit him* **in full view of** *all the guests* (=where they could see him clearly). | *When we reached the top, we had a* **bird's eye view** (=a view of an area from high up) *of the city.*
3 [C] the area you can see from a place or window: [+of] *There was a beautiful view of the mountains from our hotel room.* **THESAURUS▸** SIGHT
4 [C] a photograph or picture that shows a beautiful or interesting place: [+of] *postcards showing views of New York* → **POINT OF VIEW**

PHRASES
in view of sth *formal* because of something: *In view of his behaviour the club has decided to suspend him.*
on view being shown to the public: *The painting is currently on view at the Museum of Modern Art.*
with a view to (doing) sth because you are planning to do something in the future: *We bought the house with a view to retiring there.*

view[2] *v* [T] *formal* **1** to think of someone or something in a particular way SYN see: **view sb/sth as**

sth *Women were viewed as sex objects.* **2** to look at or watch something: *The scenery was spectacular, especially when viewed from high ground.*

viewer /ˈvjuːə $ -ər/ *n* [C] someone who watches a television programme: *The series is watched by millions of viewers.*

viewfinder /ˈvjuːˌfaɪndə $ -ər/ *n* [C] the small square of glass on a camera that you look through when you are taking a photograph

viewing /ˈvjuːɪŋ/ *n* [C,U] **1** the activity of watching a television programme or a film: *young people's* **television viewing** *habits* **2** the activity of going to look at something, or an occasion when people can do this: *The palace is now open for* **public viewing**. | *a* **private viewing** *of the paintings*

viewpoint /ˈvjuːpɔɪnt/ *n* [C] a particular way of thinking about a problem or subject SYN **point of view**: *Try and think of it from the child's viewpoint.*

vigil /ˈvɪdʒəl/ *n* [C,U] a period of time when you stay quietly somewhere, especially in order to protest, pray, or be with someone who is ill: *Protesters* **held** *a* **vigil** *outside the embassy.*

vigilant /ˈvɪdʒələnt/ *adj* watching carefully what happens, so that you notice anything dangerous or illegal: *People should* **remain vigilant** *at all times and report suspicious packages to the police.* —**vigilance** *n* [U]

vigilante /ˌvɪdʒəˈlænti/ *n* [C] someone who tries to catch and punish criminals without having any legal authority to do so

vigor /ˈvɪgə $ -ər/ *n* the American spelling of VIGOUR

vigorous /ˈvɪgərəs/ *adj* using a lot of energy and strength or determination: **vigorous exercise** | *a vigorous campaign against dumping nuclear waste* —**vigorously** *adv*

vigour *BrE*, **vigor** *AmE* /ˈvɪgə $ -ər/ *n* [U] physical or mental energy and determination

vile /vaɪl/ *adj* very unpleasant: *The food* **tasted vile**.

vilify /ˈvɪlɪfaɪ/ *v* [T] (**vilified, vilifying, vilifies**) *formal* to say or write bad things about someone: *He was vilified by the press.*

villa /ˈvɪlə/ *n* [C] a house with a garden in the countryside or near the sea, used especially for holidays

village /ˈvɪlɪdʒ/ *n* [C] a group of houses usually with a church, shop etc in the countryside: *a fishing village* | **village school/shop/church etc** *The children go to the village school.*

villager /ˈvɪlɪdʒə $ -ər/ *n* [C] someone who lives in a village

villain /ˈvɪlən/ *n* [C] **1** the main bad character in a story, film etc **2** *BrE informal* a criminal

vindicate /ˈvɪndɪkeɪt/ *v* [T] *formal* to prove what someone said or did was right, even though many people believed that they were wrong —**vindication** /ˌvɪndɪˈkeɪʃən/ *n* [singular, U]

vindictive /vɪnˈdɪktɪv/ *adj* deliberately cruel and unfair —**vindictively** *adv* —**vindictiveness** *n* [U]

vine /vaɪn/ *n* [C] a climbing plant, especially one that produces GRAPES

vinegar /ˈvɪnɪɡə $ -ər/ *n* [U] a sour-tasting liquid made from MALT or wine that is used to improve the taste of food or preserve it

vineyard /ˈvɪnjəd $ -jərd/ *n* [C] an area of land where GRAPES are grown to make wine

vintage¹ /ˈvɪntɪdʒ/ *adj* [only before noun] **1** vintage wine is good quality wine that is made in a particular year **2** old but of high quality: *vintage cars* **3** showing all the best or most typical qualities of something: *a vintage performance by the champion*

vintage² *n* [C] the wine made in a particular year

vinyl /ˈvaɪnəl/ *n* [U] a type of strong plastic

viola /viˈəʊlə $ -ˈoʊ-/ *n* [C] a wooden musical instrument like a VIOLIN but larger and with a lower sound

violate Ac /ˈvaɪəleɪt/ *v* [T] *formal* **1** to do something against an official law, principle, agreement etc **2** to do something that makes someone feel that they have been attacked or have suffered a great loss of respect —**violation** /ˌvaɪəˈleɪʃən/ *n* [C,U]: *human rights violations*

violence /ˈvaɪələns/ *n* [U] **1** behaviour that is intended to hurt other people physically: *There's too much violence on TV these days.* | [+against] *violence against women* | *We condemn any act of violence.* **2** extreme force: *the violence of a tornado*

violent /ˈvaɪələnt/ *adj* **1** using force to hurt or kill people: *an increase in violent crime* | *violent clashes between police and demonstrators* | *Arthur was a violent and dangerous man.* **2** showing very strong angry emotions that are difficult to control: **violent quarrel/argument/row** *his violent temper* **3** a physical feeling or reaction that is painful or difficult to control: *a violent headache* **4 violent storm/earthquake/explosion etc** a storm etc that happens with a lot of force **5 violent film/play/drama** a film etc that contains a lot of violence —**violently** *adv*

THESAURUS

violent using force to hurt or kill people. Also used about films or books that contain a lot of violence: *When he was drunk he became violent.* | *The film is too violent for children.*
rough using a lot of force, but not causing serious injury: *Don't be too rough with him – he's only a little boy.*
vicious very violent and cruel – used especially when someone does something violent for no obvious reason: *It was a vicious attack on an unarmed man.* | *a vicious killer*
brutal very violent and cruel, and showing no pity: *He was a brutal dictator.* | *a brutal murder*
fierce a fierce animal looks frightening and likely to attack people: *The man had a fierce dog with him.*

---

gory involving a lot of violence and blood – used about films, stories, descriptions etc: *I couldn't watch the gory bits of the film.*

---

violet /ˈvaɪəlɪt/ *n* **1** [C] a small sweet-smelling dark purple flower → see picture at FLOWER¹ **2** [U] a purple colour —**violet** *adj*

violin /ˌvaɪəˈlɪn/ *n* [C] a wooden musical instrument that you hold under your chin and play by pulling a BOW (=special stick) across the strings → see picture on page A6 —**violinist** *n* [C]

VIP /ˌviː aɪ ˈpiː/ *n* [C] (**very important person**) someone who is famous or powerful and receives special treatment

viper /ˈvaɪpə $ -ər/ *n* [C] a small poisonous snake

viral /ˈvaɪərəl $ ˈvaɪrəl/ *adj* related to or caused by a VIRUS

virgin¹ /ˈvɜːdʒɪn $ ˈvɜːr-/ *n* [C] someone who has never had sex

virgin² *adj* virgin land, forest etc is still in its natural condition and has not been used or spoiled by people

virginity /vəˈdʒɪnəti $ vɜːr-/ *n* **lose your virginity** to have sex for the first time

Virgo /ˈvɜːɡəʊ $ ˈvɜːrɡoʊ/ *n* (*plural* **Virgos**) **1** [U] the sign of the Zodiac of people born between August 24 and September 23 **2** [C] someone who has this sign

virile /ˈvɪraɪl $ ˈvɪrəl/ *adj* approving a man who is virile is strong in a sexually attractive way —**virility** /vɪˈrɪləti/ *n* [U]

virtual Ac /ˈvɜːtʃuəl $ ˈvɜːr-/ *adj* **1** very nearly a particular thing: *He became a virtual prisoner in his own home.* **2** made, done, seen etc on the Internet or on a computer, rather than in the real world: *a virtual library*

virtually Ac /ˈvɜːtʃuəli $ ˈvɜːr-/ *adv* almost SYN **practically**: *The town was virtually destroyed.* | *He was virtually unknown before running for office.* **THESAURUS ▶ ALMOST**

virtual reality *n* [U] when a computer makes you feel as though you are in a real situation by showing images and sounds

virtue /ˈvɜːtʃuː $ ˈvɜːr-/ *n* [C,U] **1** behaviour that is morally good, or a good quality in someone's character: *a life of virtue* | *Stella has many virtues.* **2** an advantage that makes something better or more useful than other things: *the virtues of organic food* **PHRASES**
by virtue of sth *formal* by means of, or as a result of, something: *people who get promoted by virtue of their age*

virtuoso /ˌvɜːtʃuˈəʊsəʊ $ ˌvɜːrtʃuˈoʊsoʊ/ *n* [C] (*plural* **virtuosos**) someone who is a very skilful performer, especially in music: *a piano virtuoso* —**virtuoso** *adj*: *a virtuoso performance*

virtuous /ˈvɜːtʃuəs $ ˈvɜːr-/ *adj* behaving in a way that is morally good

virulent /ˈvɪrələnt/ *adj* **1** a virulent poison or disease is very dangerous and affects people very quickly **2** *formal disapproving* full of hatred for something, or expressing this in a strong way: *virulent anti-Semitism*

virus /ˈvaɪərəs $ ˈvaɪrəs/ *n* [C]
1 a very small living thing that causes diseases, or an illness caused by this: *the common cold virus*
2 a set of instructions secretly put into a computer that can destroy information stored in the computer

visa /ˈviːzə/ *n* [C] an official mark that is put on your PASSPORT that allows you to enter or leave another country: *She's here on a student visa.*

vis-à-vis /ˌviːz ɑː ˈviː, ˌviːz əˈ-/ *prep formal* concerning or compared with: *Where do we stand vis-à-vis last week's change in the law?*

viscous /ˈvɪskəs/ *adj technical* a viscous liquid is thick and does not flow easily —**viscosity** /vɪˈskɒsəti $ -ˈskɑː-/ *n* [U]

vise /vaɪs/ *n* [C] the American spelling of VICE

visibility Ac /ˌvɪzəˈbɪləti/ *n* [U] the distance that you can see, especially when this is affected by the weather conditions: *Dense fog led to **poor visibility** in many areas.*

visible Ac /ˈvɪzəbəl/ *adj* something that is visible can be seen or noticed OPP **invisible**: *The lights of the city were clearly visible below them.* | *a visible change in her attitude* —**visibly** *adv*: *She was visibly shocked by the news.*

vision Ac /ˈvɪʒən/ *n*
1 ABILITY TO SEE [U] the ability to see SYN **sight**: *Will the operation improve my vision?* | **good/normal/poor etc vision** *children who are born with poor vision*
2 AREA YOU SEE [U] the area that you can see, especially without turning your head: *a figure **at the edge of her vision***
3 IDEA [C] an idea about what something will be like: [+of] *He had a **clear vision** of how he wanted the company to develop.* | [+for] *The President outlined his vision for the future* (=what he wanted to happen in the future). | *I **had visions of** (=imagined) the children getting hurt.*
4 IN A DREAM/RELIGIOUS EXPERIENCE [C] a person or thing that appears to you in a dream, or as part of a powerful religious experience
5 ABILITY TO PLAN FOR THE FUTURE [U] the knowledge and imagination that are needed in planning for the future with a clear purpose: *We need a leader with vision.* → TUNNEL VISION

visionary /ˈvɪʒənəri $ -neri/ *adj approving* having clear ideas of what the world should be like in the future —**visionary** *n* [C]

visit¹ /ˈvɪzɪt/ *v*
1 PERSON/PLACE [I,T] to go and spend time in a place or with someone: *My aunt is **coming to visit** us next week.* | *Which cities did you visit in Spain?* | *She doesn't visit very often.*

> **Grammar**
> Do not say 'We visited to London.' Say *We visited London.*

2 GO AND CHECK [T] if someone visits a place, they go to examine something there as part of their job:

The building inspector will visit the site next week.
3 WEBSITE [T] to look at a WEBSITE on the Internet: *Over 1,000 people visit our site each week.*
4 TALK WITH SB [I] *AmE informal* to have a conversation with someone: [+with] *We watched TV while Mom visited with Mrs. Levison.*

> **THESAURUS**
> **visit** to go and spend time in a place or with someone: *I would love to visit Italy.* | *He was on his way to visit a friend in Edinburgh.*
> **go to** to visit a place. **Go to** is less formal than **visit**, and is very common in everyday English: *I'm going to Paris next week.*
> **see** to visit a doctor, lawyer etc in order to get their professional advice: *She should see a doctor.*
> **come around/by/over** (also **come round** *BrE*) to visit someone at their home for a short time, especially when you live near them: *You must come over for a meal some time.*
> **drop in/by** (also **call in/by** *BrE*) to visit someone at their home for a short time, especially on your way to another place: *Kate said she'd drop by later to give you the forms.*

visit² *n*
1 [C] when someone visits a place or person: [+to] *a visit to Chicago* | **on a visit** *We're only here on a **flying visit*** (=a very short visit). | *I decided to **pay Grandad a visit**.*
2 [singular] *AmE informal* a conversation with someone: *Barbara and I had a nice long visit.*

visitation /ˌvɪzɪˈteɪʃən/ *n* **1** [C,U] *formal* an official visit to a place or person **2** [C] an occasion when God or a SPIRIT is believed to appear to someone on earth

visitor /ˈvɪzɪtə $ -ər/ *n* [C] someone who visits a place or person: [+to] *visitors to Mexico City* | [+from] *visitors from overseas*

visor /ˈvaɪzə $ -ər/ *n* [C] **1** the part of a HELMET (=a hard hat) that can be lowered to protect your face **2** *AmE* the curved part of a cap that sticks out in front above your eyes **3** a flat object fixed above the front window of a car that you pull down to keep the sun out of your eyes

vista /ˈvɪstə/ *n* [C] *literary* a beautiful view of a large area of land

visual¹ Ac /ˈvɪʒuəl/ *adj* relating to seeing: *The movie has a strong **visual impact**.* | **the visual arts** (=art such as painting that you look at) —**visually** *adv*

visual² *n* [C usually plural] a picture or the part of a film, video etc that you can see, rather than the parts that you hear: *the film's stunning visuals*

visual 'aid *n* [C] something such as a picture, film etc that is used to help people learn

visualize Ac (also **-ise** *BrE*) /ˈvɪʒuəlaɪz/ *v* [T] to form a picture of someone or something in your mind SYN **imagine**: *I tried to visualize the house as she had described it.* —**visualization** /ˌvɪʒuəlaɪˈzeɪʃən $ -lə-/ *n* [U]

vital

vital /'vaɪtl/ *adj*
1 extremely important or necessary: **[+to]** *His evidence was vital to the defence case.* | *The work she does is* **absolutely vital.** **THESAURUS** ▶ IMPORTANT
2 full of energy, in a way that seems attractive —**vitally** *adv*: *The work is* **vitally important.**

vitality /vaɪ'tæləti/ *n* [U] energy and eagerness to do things

vitamin /'vɪtəmən, 'vaɪ- $ 'vaɪ-/ *n* [C] a chemical substance found in food that is necessary for good health

vitriolic /ˌvɪtri'ɒlɪk◀ $ -'ɑːlɪk◀/ *adj formal disapproving* vitriolic language or actions are full of anger and intended to hurt someone: *a vitriolic attack*

vivacious /və'veɪʃəs $ və-, vaɪ-/ *adj* someone, especially a woman, who is vivacious has a lot of energy and a happy attractive way of behaving

vivid /'vɪvɪd/ *adj* **1** vivid descriptions, memories, dreams etc are so clear that they seem real: *a vivid description of her childhood in Cornwall* | *She has a* **vivid imagination** (=she can imagine things clearly and easily).* **2** vivid colours are very bright —**vividly** *adv*

vivisection /ˌvɪvə'sekʃən/ *n* [U] when scientists operate on living animals in order to do scientific tests

vixen /'vɪksən/ *n* [C] a female FOX

V-neck /'viː nek/ *n* [C] **1** an opening for the neck in a piece of clothing, shaped like the letter V: *a V-neck sweater* → see picture at **NECK**¹ **2** a piece of clothing with a V-neck —**V-necked** /-nekt/ *adj*

vocab /'vəʊkæb $ 'vəʊ-/ *n* [U] *informal* VOCABULARY

vocabulary /və'kæbjələri, vəʊ- $ -leri, vəʊ-/ *n* (*plural* **vocabularies**)
1 [C,U] all the words that someone knows or uses: *I wanted to increase my English vocabulary.*
2 [singular] all the words in a language or all the words that are used in a type of language: *new words coming into the vocabulary of English* | *a specialized vocabulary*

> **Grammar**
> **Vocabulary** is usually used as an uncountable or a singular noun. Do not say 'I can learn new vocabularies from English songs.' Say *I can learn new vocabulary from English songs.*

COLLOCATIONS
adjectives
a large/wide vocabulary *She has a wide vocabulary.*
a limited/small vocabulary *It's hard to make conversation when your vocabulary is so limited.*
basic vocabulary *In the first lesson we learned some basic vocabulary.*
technical/specialized vocabulary *Engineers use a very specialized vocabulary.*

verbs
to have a vocabulary *The average two-year-old has a vocabulary of around 900 words.*
to use a vocabulary *Sports journalists use a different vocabulary.*

to learn vocabulary *We learned a lot of new vocabulary.*
to expand/increase/improve your vocabulary *You can expand your vocabulary by reading.*

vocabulary + noun
a vocabulary test/exercise *The teacher gave us a vocabulary test.*

vocal /'vəʊkəl $ 'voʊ-/ *adj* **1** expressing strong opinions publicly: *Mary was a* **vocal opponent** *of the plan.* **2** relating to the human voice, especially in singing: *vocal music* —**vocally** *adv*

'vocal cords *n* [plural] thin pieces of muscle in your throat that produce sound when you speak or sing

vocalist /'vəʊkəlɪst $ 'voʊ-/ *n* [C] someone who sings popular songs, especially with a band

vocals /'vəʊkəlz $ 'voʊ-/ *n* [plural] the part of a piece of music that is sung rather than played on an instrument: **on vocals** *The song features Elton John on vocals.*

vocation /vəʊ'keɪʃən $ voʊ-/ *n* [C,U] when you feel that the purpose of your life is to do a particular kind of work, or a job that gives you this feeling: *Teaching isn't just a job to her – it's her vocation.*

vocational /vəʊ'keɪʃənəl $ voʊ-/ *adj* relating to, or teaching, the skills needed to do a job: *vocational training*

vociferous /və'sɪfərəs, vəʊ- $ voʊ-/ *adj formal* expressing your opinions loudly and strongly: *a vociferous opponent of the plan* —**vociferously** *adv*

vodka /'vɒdkə $ 'vɑːdkə/ *n* [U] a strong alcoholic drink originally from Russia

vogue /vəʊg $ voʊg/ *n* [singular, U] when something is fashionable and popular: **be in vogue** *Japanese food is in vogue these days.*

voice¹ /vɔɪs/ *n*
1 [C,U] the sounds you make when you speak or sing, or the ability to make these sounds: **in a loud/soft etc voice** *'It's too late,' he said in a low voice.* | *the singer's beautiful voice*
2 [C,U] someone's opinion, or the right to express an opinion or influence decisions: *Parents should* **have a voice** *in deciding how their children are educated.*
3 [singular] a person, organization, newspaper etc that says publicly what a group of people think or want: **[+of]** *Dr King become the voice of the Civil Rights Movement.*
PHRASES
at the top of your voice as loudly as you can: *She shouted 'Help!' at the top of her voice.*
keep your voice down used for telling someone to speak more quietly: *Keep your voice down – the whole restaurant can hear you!*
speak with one voice if people speak with one voice, they all express the same opinion: *Europe must speak with one voice on European security.*
the voice of reason/experience etc when someone speaks in a way that seems sensible, that shows

they have had a lot of experience of doing something etc: *My mother was always the voice of reason in our house.*

COLLOCATIONS

adjectives

a loud voice *I heard loud voices in the next room.*

a quiet/low/soft voice (=not loud) *Her voice was so quiet I could hardly hear it.*

a deep/low voice (=near the bottom of the range of sounds) *He sang in his beautiful deep voice.*

a high/high-pitched voice (=near the top of the range of sounds) *His voice was surprisingly high-pitched.*

a good voice (=the ability to sing well) *My teacher thinks I've got a good voice.*

verbs

to raise/lower your voice (=to speak more loudly or more quietly) *She lowered her voice so Alex couldn't hear.*

to lose your voice (=to lose the ability to speak) *Jack's got a cold and he's lost his voice.*

sb's voice rises (=becomes louder or higher) *Her voice rose in panic.*

sb's voice trembles/shakes (=sounds unsteady) *His voice shook with anger.*

voice² *v* [T] *formal* to tell people your opinions or feelings about something

voice-'activated *adj* a voice-activated piece of equipment starts working at the sound of someone's voice

'voice box *n* [C] the part of your throat where your voice is produced

voicemail /'vɔɪsˌmeɪl/ *n* [U] a system that records telephone calls so that you can listen to them later

void¹ /vɔɪd/ *n* [singular] **1** a feeling of great sadness that you have when someone you love dies or when something is taken from you: *Work helped to* **fill the void** *after his wife died.* **2** a situation where something is needed or wanted but does not exist: *The team have not yet filled the leadership void left by the coach's resignation.*

void² *adj* **1** an agreement, result, or ticket that is void is not legally or officially acceptable **2 be void of sth** *literary* to be completely without something → **NULL AND VOID**

vol. the written abbreviation of **volume**

volatile /'vɒlətaɪl $ 'vɑːl̩tl/ *adj* **1** a volatile situation is likely to change suddenly and become worse **2** someone who is volatile can suddenly become angry or violent —**volatility** /ˌvɒlə'tɪləti $ ˌvɑː-/ *n* [U]

volcano /vɒl'keɪnəʊ $ vɑːl'keɪnoʊ/ *n* [C] (*plural* **volcanoes** *or* **volcanos**) a mountain with a large hole at the top, through which LAVA (=very hot liquid rock) is sometimes forced out: *The island has several active volcanoes.* **THESAURUS▶** **MOUNTAIN** —**volcanic** /-'kænɪk/ *adj*: *volcanic rocks*

volition /və'lɪʃən $ voʊ-, və-/ *n* *formal* **of your own volition** because you want to do something and not

because you are forced to do it: *She left the company of her own volition.*

volley /'vɒli $ 'vɑːli/ *n* [C] **1** a large number of bullets, rocks etc fired or thrown at the same time: *a volley of shots* **2 a volley of questions/abuse etc** a lot of questions, INSULTS etc that are all said at the same time **3** a hit in tennis, or a kick in football etc in which a player hits or kicks a ball before it touches the ground —**volley** *v* [I,T]

volleyball /'vɒlibɔːl $ 'vɑːlibɔːl/ *n* [U] a game in which two teams hit a ball to each other across a net with their hands and try not to let it touch the ground

volt /vəʊlt $ voʊlt/ (*written abbreviation* **v.**) *n* [C] a unit for measuring the force of an electric current

voltage /'vəʊltɪdʒ $ 'voʊl-/ *n* [C,U] the force of an electric current measured in volts

volume Ac /'vɒljuːm $ 'vɑːljəm/ *n*
1 SOUND [U] the amount of sound produced by a television, radio etc: **turn the volume up/down** *Can you turn down the volume on the TV?* | *He plays his music* **at full volume** (=as loudly as possible). **THESAURUS▶ LOUD**
2 TOTAL AMOUNT [C,U] the total amount of something: **[+of]** *an increase in the volume of traffic*
3 HOW MUCH SPACE [U] the amount of space that an object contains or that a substance fills: **[+of]** *an instrument for measuring the volume of a gas*
4 BOOK [C] a book, especially one that is part of a series of books: *a 12-volume set of poetry*

voluminous /və'luːmənəs, və'ljuː- $ və'luː-/ *adj* *formal* very large: *a voluminous cloak*

voluntary Ac /'vɒləntəri $ 'vɑːlənteri/ *adj*
1 working without being paid, especially to help people: **voluntary organization/association/agency** etc *a voluntary organization providing help for the elderly* | *She* **does voluntary work** *for the Red Cross.*
2 done willingly and without being forced → **compulsory**: *voluntary redundancy* —**voluntarily** /'vɒləntərəli, ˌvɒlən'terəli $ ˌvɑːlən'terəli/ *adv*

volunteer¹ Ac /ˌvɒlən'tɪə $ ˌvɑːlən'tɪr/ *n* [C] **1** someone who does work without being paid: *The helplines are manned by volunteers.* **2** someone who offers to do something without being told that they must do it: *I need someone to help me with the barbecue. Any volunteers?*

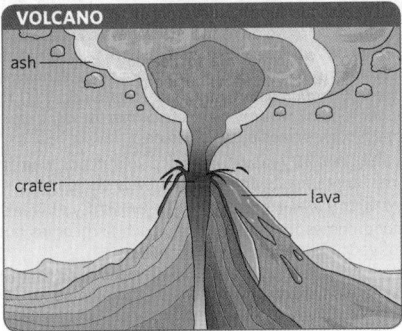

VOLCANO

ash

crater

lava

volunteer² Ac *v* **1** [I,T] to offer to do something without being told that you must do it: *Ernie volunteered to wash the dishes.* **2** [T] to tell someone something without being asked: *Michael volunteered the information before I had a chance to ask.* **3** [I] to offer to join the army, navy etc: *When the war began, my brother immediately volunteered.*

voluptuous /vəˈlʌptʃuəs/ *adj* a voluptuous woman has large breasts and an attractively curved body

vomit¹ /ˈvɒmɪt $ ˈvɑː-/ *v* [I,T] *formal* if you vomit, food comes up from your stomach and comes out of your mouth

vomit² *n* [U] the food or drink that comes out of your mouth when you vomit

voodoo /ˈvuːduː/ *n* [U] magical beliefs and practices used as a form of religion, especially in parts of Africa and the Caribbean

voracious /vəˈreɪʃəs, vɒ- $ vɔː-, və-/ *adj formal* wanting to do something a lot, especially eating: *He had a voracious appetite.* —**voracity** /-ˈræsəti/ *n* [U]

vote¹ /vəʊt $ voʊt/ *v*
1 [I,T] to show by marking a paper, raising your hand etc which person you want to elect, or whether you support a particular plan: **[+for/against/in favour of]** *He voted for the Labour candidate.* | **[+on]** *The people now had the chance to vote on the issue.* | **vote to do sth** *Congress voted to increase taxes.*
2 [T] to choose someone or something to win a particular prize by voting for them: *It was voted best film at Cannes.*

> ### THESAURUS
>
> **vote** to show that you want to choose a particular person or party, or that you support a particular plan: *Who are you going to vote for?* | *The people voted for independence.*
> **elect** to choose a government or leader by voting: *He was elected President of the United States.* | *The people will elect a new government.*
> **veto** to use your official power to refuse to allow a decision or plan, which other people have agreed: *The president has the right to veto any piece of legislation.*

vote² *n*
1 [C] an act of voting, or the choice that someone makes when they vote: *The bill was passed by 319 votes to 316.* | **[+for/against/in favour (of)]** *A vote for us is not a wasted vote.*

2 [singular] an occasion when people vote to choose or decide something: **[+on]** *There will be a vote on the matter.* | **take/have a vote (on sth)** *Let's take a vote then.* | **put sth to the/a vote** (=decide something by voting)
3 the vote a) the total number of votes in an election: *The Nationalists won 25% of the vote.* **b)** the right to vote: *In France, women didn't get the vote until 1945.* → CASTING VOTE

voter /ˈvəʊtə $ ˈvoʊtər/ *n* [C] someone who votes or has the right to vote

vouch /vaʊtʃ/ *v*
PHRASAL VERBS
vouch for sth/sb to say that something is true or good, or that someone can be trusted, which you know from your experience or knowledge of them

voucher /ˈvaʊtʃə $ -ər/ *n* [C] a kind of ticket that can be used instead of money to pay for things

vow¹ /vaʊ/ *n* [C] a serious promise: *The couple made their wedding vows.*

vow² *v* [T] to make a serious promise that you will definitely do something or not do something: *I vowed that I would never drink again.* THESAURUS
PROMISE

vowel /ˈvaʊəl/ *n* [C] one of the sounds shown in English by the letters a, e, i, o, or u, and sometimes y

voyage /ˈvɔɪ-ɪdʒ/ *n* [C] a long trip, especially in a ship or space vehicle: *The voyage from England to India used to take six months.* | *She made the voyage single-handed.* THESAURUS JOURNEY

voyeur /vwɑːˈjɜː $ -ˈjɜːr/ *n* [C] someone who gets sexual pleasure from secretly watching other people's sexual activities —**voyeurism** *n* [U] —**voyeuristic** /ˌvwɑːjəˈrɪstɪk◄/ *adj*

vs. (*also* **vs** *BrE*) a written abbreviation of **versus**

vulgar /ˈvʌlgə $ -ər/ *adj* **1** behaving in a way that is not polite, especially by talking in a rude way: *vulgar jokes* **2** *disapproving* not showing good judgment about what is attractive or suitable —**vulgarity** /vʌlˈgærəti/ *n* [U]

vulnerable /ˈvʌlnərəbəl/ *adj* easily harmed, hurt, or attacked: *The army was in a vulnerable position.* | *She looked so young and vulnerable.* —**vulnerability** /ˌvʌlnərəˈbɪləti/ *n* [U]

vulture /ˈvʌltʃə $ -ər/ *n* [C] a large wild bird that eats dead animals

vying /ˈvaɪ-ɪŋ/ *v* the present participle of VIE

W w

W, w /'dʌbəlju:/ n [C,U] (plural **W's, w's**) the 23rd letter of the English alphabet

W 1 the written abbreviation of **west** or **western** **2** the written abbreviation of **watt**

wacky /'wæki/ adj informal silly in an amusing way

wad /wɒd $ wɑːd/ n [C] **1** a thick pile of thin sheets of something, especially money: **[+of]** a wad of dollar bills **2** a thick soft mass of material that has been pressed together: **[+of]** a wad of cotton

waddle /'wɒdl $ 'wɑːdl/ v [I] to walk with short steps, with your body moving from one side to another, like a duck

wade /weɪd/ v [I] to walk through water: We waded across the stream. **THESAURUS** ▸ WALK

PHRASAL VERBS
wade through sth to read something that is very long and boring

wafer /'weɪfə $ -ər/ n [C] a very thin BISCUIT

waffle¹ /'wɒfəl $ 'wɑː-/ n
1 [C] a flat cake with a pattern of square holes in it, often eaten for breakfast in the US **2** [U] informal talk or writing that uses a lot of words but says nothing important

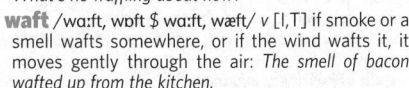
WAFFLES

waffle² (also **waffle on**) v [I] informal to talk or write using a lot of words but without saying anything important: **[+about]** What's he waffling about now?

waft /wɑːft, wɒft $ wɑːft, wæft/ v [I,T] if smoke or a smell wafts somewhere, or if the wind wafts it, it moves gently through the air: The smell of bacon wafted up from the kitchen.

wag /wæg/ v [I,T] (**wagged, wagging**) if a dog wags its tail, or if its tail wags, the tail moves quickly from one side to the other

wage¹ /weɪdʒ/ n [singular] (also **wages** [plural]) the money that someone receives every day or week as payment for working → **salary**: I'll get my wages on Friday. | the average **weekly wage** | He **earns** a good wage. | a **wage increase** | the national **minimum wage** (=the lowest wage that an employer is allowed to pay by law) **THESAURUS** ▸ SALARY

wage² v [T] to be involved in a war or battle against someone or something: The police are **waging war on** drug dealers.

wager /'weɪdʒə $ -ər/ n [C] an amount of money that you risk on the result of a game or race

waggle /'wægəl/ v [I,T] to move something quickly from side to side, or to move in this way

wagon /'wægən/ n [C] **1** a strong vehicle with four wheels, usually pulled by horses → **cart 2** BrE a vehicle used for carrying goods, which is pulled by a train **SYN** **freight car** AmE → STATION WAGON

PHRASES
be/go on the wagon informal to not drink alcohol any more: Do you want a beer, or are you still on the wagon?

waif /weɪf/ n [C] literary a child who is pale and thin and looks as if they do not have a home

wail /weɪl/ v [I] **1** to cry or complain loudly because you are sad or in pain: 'But what shall I do?' he wailed. **2** to make a long high sound: Police sirens were wailing. —**wail** n [C]

waist /weɪst/ n [C]
1 the narrow part in the middle of your body: a slim waist
2 the part of a piece of clothing that goes around your waist: trousers with an elasticated waist

waistband /'weɪstbænd/ n [C] the part of a skirt, trousers etc that fastens around your waist

waistcoat /'weɪskəʊt, 'weskət $ 'weskət/ n [C] BrE a piece of clothing with buttons down the front and no sleeves that a man wears over a shirt and under a jacket **SYN** **vest** AmE

waistline /'weɪstlaɪn/ n [C usually singular] **1** the measurement around your waist: his expanding waistline **2** the part of a piece of clothing that fits around the waist

wait¹ /weɪt/ v [I]
1 to stay somewhere or not do something until something else happens or someone arrives: Hurry up! Everyone's waiting. | **[+for]** Wait for me. | We had to wait 45 minutes for a bus. | **wait to do sth** Are you waiting to use the phone? | **[+till/until]** I'll wait till you come back. | I'm sorry to have **kept** you **waiting** (=made you wait).

> **Grammar**
> Do not say 'My father was waiting me at the station.' Say My father was waiting for me at the station.

2 if you are waiting for something, you expect or hope that it will happen but it has not happened yet: 'Have you heard about the job yet?' 'No, I'm still waiting.'
3 if something is waiting for you, it is ready for you to use or collect: I'll **have** dinner **waiting** for you.

PHRASES
sth can/can't wait if something can wait, it is not very urgent. If something can't wait, it is very urgent: The report can wait till tomorrow.
can't wait/can hardly wait (to do sth) used to emphasize that someone is very excited about something and is eager for it to happen: I can't wait to see him again. **THESAURUS** ▸ WANT
wait a minute/second/moment etc used to ask someone not to leave or start doing something immediately: Wait a moment, just let me think.
wait and see used to say that someone should be patient because they will find out about something later: The surgeons have done all they can – we just have to wait and see now.

wait tables *AmE* to serve food to people at their table in a restaurant: *I spent the summer waiting tables.*

(just) you wait *spoken* used to warn or threaten someone: *I'll get you back for what you've done. Just you wait.*

PHRASAL VERBS

wait around (also **wait about** *BrE*) to do nothing while you are waiting for something to happen: *The people at the embassy kept us waiting around for hours.*

wait on sb to serve food to someone at their table, especially in a restaurant

wait up
1 to wait for someone to come back home before you go to bed: **[+for]** *Please don't wait up for me.*
2 *AmE* to wait for someone: *Hey, wait up. I'm coming.*

THESAURUS
wait to stay somewhere or not do something until something else happens or someone arrives: *We've all been waiting for you! | I was waiting for a train.*
queue *BrE*, **stand in line** *AmE* to stand in a line of people who are all waiting for the same thing: *They queued for hours to get tickets.*
hang around *informal* to wait in a place, not doing anything, especially when this makes you waste time: *We were hanging around waiting for the taxi to arrive. | Men were hanging around on street corners.*
can you hang on/hold on? *spoken* used when asking someone to wait for a short time: *Can you hang on? I just need to shut the windows.*
hold the line *spoken* used when asking the person who is calling a company or organization to wait for a short time: *Hold the line, please, and I'll transfer you to our sales department.*

wait² *n* [singular] a period of time when you wait for something to happen, someone to arrive etc: **[+for]** *The average wait for an appointment was eight weeks. \| We had a three-hour wait before our flight.* → **lie in wait (for sb/sth)** at **LIE¹**

waiter /ˈweɪtə $ -ər/ *n* [C] a man who serves food and drink at the tables in a restaurant

'waiting list *n* [C] a list of people who have asked for something but who must wait before they can have it

'waiting room *n* [C] a room for people to wait in, for example to see a doctor

waitress /ˈweɪtrɪs/ *n* [C] a woman who serves food and drink at the tables in a restaurant

waive /weɪv/ *v* [T] to state officially that a right or rule can be ignored: *She waived her right to see a lawyer.*

wake¹ /weɪk/ (also **wake up**) *v* [I,T] (*past tense* **woke** /wəʊk $ woʊk/, *past participle* **woken** /ˈwəʊkən $ ˈwoʊ-/) to stop sleeping, or to make someone stop sleeping: *I woke up at 5.00 this morning. \| Try not to wake the baby.*

PHRASAL VERBS

wake up to sth to start to realize and understand something important: *It's time you woke up to the fact that it's a tough world out there.*

wake² *n* [C] the track made behind a boat as it moves through the water

PHRASES

in the wake of sth happening after something, usually as a result of it: *Famine followed in the wake of the drought.*

waken /ˈweɪkən/ *v* [I,T] *formal* to wake up, or to wake someone up

'wake-up ,call *n* [C] something that shocks you into realizing that you must do something to make a situation change: *Getting arrested for fighting was a real wake-up call.*

waking /ˈweɪkɪŋ/ *adj* **waking hours/moments etc** all the time when you are awake: *He spends every waking moment in front of his computer.*

walk¹ /wɔːk $ wɒːk/ *v*
1 [I,T] to move forward by putting one foot in front of the other: *We must have walked ten miles.* \| **[+into/down/up etc]** *She walked up to him and kissed him. \| We missed the bus and had to* **walk home**. *\| Is the school* **within walking distance** *(=near enough to walk to)?* → see picture on page A11
2 [T] to walk somewhere with someone: *It's late – I'll* **walk** *you home. \|* **walk sb to sth** *I'll walk you to the bus stop.*
3 [T] to take a dog out for exercise: *Jude's out walking the dog.* —**walker** *n* [C]: *an area popular with walkers and climbers* —**walking** *n* [U]: *We went walking in the hills.*

PHRASES

walk all over sb *informal* to treat someone very badly: *If you don't voice your opinion, people will walk all over you.*

PHRASAL VERBS

walk away to leave a situation without caring what happens: **[+from]** *You can't just walk away from 12 years of marriage!*

walk away with sth *informal* to win something easily: *Carrie walked away with the prize.*

walk into sth if you walk into a job, you get it very easily

walk off with sth *informal*
1 to steal something: *Someone's walked off with my new jacket!*
2 to win something easily: *He walked off with first prize.*

walk out to leave a place suddenly because you are angry

walk out on sb to leave your husband or wife: *Mary just walked out on him one day.*

THESAURUS
walk to move forward by putting one foot in front of the other: *He was walking along the street.*
go somewhere on foot to walk – used especially to compare this with going by car, bus etc: *It's quicker if you go on foot.*
go for a walk to walk somewhere for pleasure or for exercise: *It was a lovely day so we decided to go for a walk.*

stroll to walk in a relaxed way, especially for pleasure: *A few people were strolling along the beach.*

wander to walk with no particular aim or direction, often looking at things on the way: *We wandered around the old city.*

march to walk quickly with firm regular steps – used especially about soldiers: *Thousands of US soldiers marched through the streets.*

stride to walk with long steps in a determined or angry way: *He turned quickly and strode out of the room.*

creep/sneak to walk quietly because you do not want anyone to see or hear you: *He crept down the stairs.* | *We sneaked out of the back of the classroom.*

stagger to walk in a very unsteady way, especially because you are drunk or have been injured: *A man staggered out of the bar and fell on the ground.*

trudge to walk in a slow tired way, especially when it is difficult to continue walking: *She picked up her bags and continued trudging up the hill.*

tiptoe to walk quietly and carefully on your toes because you do not want to make a noise: *I tiptoed out trying not to wake the baby.*

limp to walk with difficulty because one leg hurts, putting most of your weight on the other leg: *He was limping slightly and leaning on his stick.*

wade to walk through water: *They got out of the boat and waded to the beach.*

walk² *n* [C]

1 when you walk somewhere: *Let's go for a walk on the beach.*

2 a path or road that you walk along, especially one that goes through an interesting or attractive area: *walks through the national park*

PHRASES

people from all walks of life people who have very different jobs or positions in society: *Our volunteers include people from all walks of life.*

COLLOCATIONS
verbs
to go for a walk *David and Sarah have gone for a walk.* ⚠ Do not say 'go a walk' or 'make a walk'. Say **go for a walk**.
to have/take a walk *We had a walk around town.*

adjectives
a long walk *She was tired after her long walk.*
a short walk *The school is only a short walk from his house.*
a five-mile/ten-kilometre etc walk *He began the five-mile walk home.*

walkie-talkie /ˌwɔːki ˈtɔːki $ ˌwɔːki ˈtɔːki/ *n* [C] a small radio that you can carry and use to speak to other people who have the same kind of radio

'walking stick *n* [C] a stick that you use to help support you when you walk → see picture at **STICK²**

walkout /ˈwɔːk-aʊt $ ˈwɔːk-/ *n* [C] an occasion when people stop working or leave a meeting as a protest

walkover /ˈwɔːkˌəʊvə $ ˈwɔːkˌoʊvər/ *n* [C] *informal* a very easy victory

walkway /ˈwɔːkweɪ $ ˈwɔːk-/ *n* [C] a path built for people to walk along, often above the ground

wall /wɔːl $ wɒːl/ *n* [C]

1 one of the sides of a room or building: *We've decided to paint the walls blue.* | **on a wall** *There were some lovely pictures on the wall.*

2 an upright structure made of stone or brick that divides one area of land from another → **fence**: *The garden is surrounded by a high wall.* —**walled** *adj*: *a walled city*

PHRASES

drive sb up the wall *informal* to make someone very angry: *That noise is driving me up the wall.*

wallet /ˈwɒlɪt $ ˈwɑː-/ *n* [C] a small flat case in which you carry paper money, bank cards etc
SYN billfold *AmE* → **purse**

wallop /ˈwɒləp $ ˈwɑː-/ *v* [T] *informal* to hit someone or something very hard —**wallop** *n* [singular]

wallow /ˈwɒləʊ $ ˈwɑːloʊ/ *v* [I] **1** if someone wallows in an unpleasant feeling or situation, they seem to enjoy it and want to be unhappy: *He was wallowing in self-pity.* **2** to lie or roll around in mud or water for pleasure

wallpaper /ˈwɔːlˌpeɪpə $ ˈwɒːlˌpeɪpər/ *n* [U] **1** paper that you stick onto the walls of a room in order to decorate it **2** the colour, pattern, or picture that you have as the background on the screen of a computer —**wallpaper** *v* [T]

'Wall Street *n* the New York City STOCK EXCHANGE: *Prices fell on Wall Street yesterday.*

ˌwall-to-'wall *adj* [only before noun] covering the whole floor: *wall-to-wall carpeting*

wally /ˈwɒli $ ˈwɑː-/ *n* [C] (*plural* **wallies**) *BrE informal* someone who behaves in a silly way

walnut /ˈwɔːlnʌt $ ˈwɒːl-/ *n* **1** [C] a nut that you can eat, shaped like a human brain → see picture at **NUT 2** [U] the dark brown wood of the tree on which this nut grows

walrus /ˈwɔːlrəs $ ˈwɒːl-, ˈwɑːl-/ *n* [C] a large sea animal with two long TUSKS (=long pointed teeth) coming down from the sides of its mouth

waltz¹ /wɔːls $ wɒːlts/ *n* [C] a fairly slow dance with a regular pattern of three beats

waltz² *v* [I] **1** to dance a waltz **2** *informal* to walk in a very confident way that annoys other people: **[+in/into/up to etc]** *Jeff waltzed up to the bar and poured himself a drink.*

wan /wɒn $ wɑːn/ *adj* looking pale, weak, or tired: *a wan smile*

wand /wɒnd $ wɑːnd/ *n* [C] a thin stick you hold in your hand to do magic tricks

wander /ˈwɒndə $ ˈwɑːndər/ *v*

1 **WALK SLOWLY** [I,T] to walk slowly across or around an area, usually without a clear direction or purpose: **[+around/in/through etc]** *We spent the*

morning wandering around the old part of the city. | He was found **wandering the streets** of New York. **THESAURUS** ▶ WALK

2 **WALK AWAY** (also **wander off**) [I] to walk away from where you are supposed to stay: *Don't let the children wander off.*

3 **THINK OF OTHER THINGS** [I] if your mind or your thoughts wander, you stop paying attention to something and start thinking about other things: *She's getting old, and sometimes her mind wanders.*

4 **LEAVE MAIN SUBJECT** [I] to start to talk or write about something not connected with the main subject: **[+from/off]** *I wish he'd stop wandering off the subject.* —**wander** n [singular]: *We had a little wander round the town.* —**wanderer** n [C]

wane¹ /weɪn/ v [I] to become gradually weaker or less important: *After a while his enthusiasm for the sport began to wane.*

wane² n **on the wane** becoming weaker or less important: *The president's popularity seems to be on the wane.*

wangle /ˈwæŋɡəl/ v [T] *informal* to succeed in getting something by using clever or slightly dishonest methods: *In the end she wangled an invitation to the wedding.*

wanna /ˈwɒnə $ ˈwɑː-/ *informal* a way of writing or saying 'want to' or 'want a', which many people think is incorrect

wannabe /ˈwɒnəbi $ ˈwɑː-/ n [C] *informal disapproving* someone who tries to look or behave like a famous or popular person: *Tom Cruise wannabes*

want¹ /wɒnt $ wɒːnt, wɑːnt/ v [T]

1 to have a desire for something: *Do you want a drink?* | *What do you want for your birthday?* | **want to do sth** *I want to go home.* | **want sb/sth to do sth** *Her parents want her to find a rich husband.* | *I don't want the holiday to end.* | **want sth done** *I want that report finished today.*

> **Grammar**
> Do not say 'She wants that her father buys her a car.' Say *She wants her father to buy her a car.*

2 *informal* used to say that something needs to be done: *The car wants a good clean.* | *Those plants want watering.*

3 to ask for someone to come and talk to you: *Sam, mum wants you!* | *You're wanted on the phone.*

4 *informal* used to tell someone what they should do **SYN** ought to: **want to do sth** *You want to be more careful with your money.*

THESAURUS

want to have a desire for something: *I really want to see that movie.* | *Do you want some more pizza?*

would like sth used as a polite way of saying that you want something, or asking someone if they want something: *I'd like to book a table for 8 o'clock, please.* | *Would you like some wine?*

feel like sth to have a feeling that it would be good to do something. **Feel like** sounds less definite than **want**: *Do you feel like going out tonight?* | *Sometimes she felt like giving up her job.*

be interested in sth to think that you may want

to do something, buy something etc: *If you're selling your car, I'd be interested in it.*

want something very much

wish to want something to happen or be true, especially when you know it is not possible or likely: *I wish I didn't have to do this essay.*

would love to want something very much – often used when politely accepting an invitation: *We'd love to come on Saturday.*

can't wait to feel excited and want something to happen as soon as possible because you know you will enjoy it: *I can't wait for the summer holidays.* | *She couldn't wait to see her family again.*

be dying for sth/to do sth *informal* to want something very much: *I'm dying for a drink.* | *I'm dying to meet her new boyfriend.*

want² n **wants** [plural] the things you want or need to have

PHRASES

for (the) want of sth because of a lack of something: *The gallery closed down for want of funding.*

'want ad n [C] *AmE* a CLASSIFIED AD

wanted /ˈwɒntɪd $ ˈwɔː-, ˈwɑː-/ adj someone who is wanted is being looked for by the police: **[+for]** *He is wanted for murder.*

wanting /ˈwɒntɪŋ $ ˈwɔː-, ˈwɑː-/ adj **be found wanting** *formal* if something is found wanting, it has been shown to be not good enough: *Traditional solutions had been tried and found wanting.*

wanton /ˈwɒntən $ ˈwɔː-, ˈwɑː-/ adj *formal* deliberately causing damage or harm for no reason: *wanton violence*

war /wɔː $ wɔːr/ n [C,U]

1 when there is fighting between two or more countries or between opposing groups within a country **OPP** peace: *He fought in the Vietnam War.* | **[+against/with]** *the war with Spain* | **[+between]** *the war between Iran and Iraq* | **be at war (with sb)** *In 1793 England was at war with France.*

2 a situation in which a person or group is fighting for power, influence, or control: *a trade war between Europe and the US*

3 a struggle over a long period of time to control something harmful: **[+against/on]** *the war against drugs* → PRISONER OF WAR

COLLOCATIONS

verbs

to fight a war *They fought a long war against the invaders.*

to fight in a war (=to take part as a soldier) *Her father was away fighting in the war.*

to win/lose a war *They won the war because they had a more disciplined army.*

to declare war *Italy declared war on Germany in 1943.*

war breaks out (=starts) *They married just before war broke out.*

types of war

a world war *He lived through two world wars.*

a **civil war** (=between opposing groups within a country) *He fought in the Spanish Civil War.*
a **nuclear war** (=involving nuclear weapons) *The effects of a nuclear war would be terrible.*

'war crime n [C] an illegal and cruel act done during a war —**war criminal** n [C]

ward¹ /wɔːd $ wɔːrd/ n [C] a large room in a hospital where people who need medical treatment stay

ward² v
PHRASAL VERBS
ward sth ↔ **off** to prevent something from affecting you or attacking you: *a spray to ward off insects*

warden /'wɔːdn $ 'wɔːrdn/ n [C] AmE the person in charge of a prison SYN **governor** BrE → TRAFFIC WARDEN

warder /'wɔːdə $ 'wɔːrdər/ n [C] BrE a prison guard

wardrobe /'wɔːdrəʊb $ 'wɔːrdroʊb/ n **1** [C] BrE a piece of furniture in which you hang clothes SYN **closet** AmE **2** [singular] the clothes that someone has: *the latest addition to her wardrobe*

warehouse /'weəhaʊs $ 'wer-/ n [C] a large building for storing goods before they are sold

wares /weəz $ werz/ n [plural] old-fashioned the things that someone is selling, usually not in a shop

warfare /'wɔːfeə $ 'wɔːrfer/ n [U] fighting in a war, especially fighting with a particular type of weapon: **nuclear/chemical/germ etc warfare**

warhead /'wɔːhed $ 'wɔːr-/ n [C] the explosive part at the front of a MISSILE

warlike /'wɔːlaɪk $ 'wɔːr-/ adj liking war and being skilful in it: *a warlike nation*

warlord /'wɔːlɔːd $ 'wɔːrlɔːrd/ n [C] the leader of an unofficial military group fighting against a government or other groups in a country

warm¹ /wɔːm $ wɔːrm/ adj
1 slightly hot, especially in a pleasant way OPP **cool** → **warmth**: *a nice warm bath* | *The weather was lovely and warm.* | *I've put your dinner in the oven to* **keep** *it* **warm**. | **keep/stay warm** *Make sure you keep warm!* THESAURUS HOT
2 clothes or buildings that are warm can keep in heat or keep out cold: *Here, put on your nice warm coat.*
3 friendly: *a* **warm** *welcome* | *The Hungarian people are* **warm and friendly.** THESAURUS FRIENDLY —**warmly** adv: *She smiled warmly.*

warm² v [T] to make someone or something warm: *I warmed my hands over the fire.*
PHRASAL VERBS
warm to sb/sth to start to like someone or something: *I must say I didn't warm to her.* | *They soon warmed to the idea.*
warm up 1 to become warm, or to make something warm: *The house will soon warm up.* | **warm sth ↔ up** *Shall I warm the soup up?* **2** to do gentle exercises to prepare your body for sport: *The athletes were warming up for the race.* **3** if a machine warms up, it becomes ready to work properly

warm-'blooded adj animals that are warm-blooded have a body temperature that remains fairly high whether the temperature around them is hot or cold OPP **cold-blooded**

warmed-'over adj AmE warmed-over food has been cooked before and then heated again for eating

warm-hearted /ˌwɔːm 'hɑːtɪd◄ $ ˌwɔːrm 'hɑːr-/ adj friendly and kind OPP **cold-hearted**: *a warm-hearted old lady*

warmonger /'wɔːˌmʌŋɡə $ 'wɔːrˌmɑːŋɡər, -ˌmʌŋ-/ n [C] disapproving someone who is eager to start a war —**warmongering** n [U]

warmth /wɔːmθ $ wɔːrmθ/ n [U] **1** the heat that something produces: **[+of]** *the warmth of the sun* **2** friendliness: **[+of]** *the warmth of her smile*

'warm-up n [C] a set of gentle exercises you do to prepare your body for sport

warn /wɔːn $ wɔːrn/ v [T]
1 to tell someone that something bad or dangerous may happen, so that they can avoid it or prevent it: *We tried to warn her, but she wouldn't listen.* | **warn sb (that)** *We warned them that there was a bull in the field.* | **warn sb about/of sth** *Travellers are being warned about the danger of HIV infection.* | **warn sb to do sth** *We warned them to be careful.*
2 to advise someone not to do something because it may have dangerous or unpleasant results: **warn sb against sth** *He warned her against such a risky investment.* | **warn sb not to do sth** *I warned her not to walk home alone.*
3 to tell someone about something before it happens so that they are not worried or surprised by it: **warn sb (that)** *Can you warn your mother that you'll be back late?*

warning /'wɔːnɪŋ $ 'wɔːrn-/ n [C,U] something that tells you that something bad, dangerous, or annoying is going to happen: **[+of/about]** *They have issued a warning about severe storms this evening.* | **[+that]** *a warning that the roads will be icy* | **without warning** (=suddenly, with no warning) *The planes attacked without warning.*

COLLOCATIONS

verbs
to give a warning *Did the police give a warning before they fired?*
to issue a warning (=to officially warn people) *The government issued a warning about terrorist activity.*
to ignore a warning *She ignored their warnings and set off into the fog.*

types of warning
a health warning (=a warning that something is bad for your health) *Packets of cigarettes carry a health warning.*
a flood/gale etc warning *A flood warning has been issued.*
advance/prior warning *I wish we had had some advance warning of the changes.*

warp /wɔːp $ wɔːrp/ v **1** [I,T] if wood or metal warps, or if something warps it, it becomes bent or twisted: *The wood had warped in the heat.* **2** [T] to have a bad effect on how someone thinks or behaves: *Don't let your emotions **warp** your **judgement**.*

warpath /ˈwɔːpɑːθ $ ˈwɔːrpæθ/ *n* **be on the warpath** to be angry and looking for someone to fight or punish

warped /wɔːpt $ wɔːrpt/ *adj* someone who is warped has ideas or thoughts that are unpleasant or cruel: *a warped mind*

warrant¹ /ˈwɒrənt $ ˈwɔː-, ˈwɑː-/ *n* [C] a legal document that is signed by a judge, allowing the police to do something: **[+for]** *The police have a warrant for his arrest.* | *a **search warrant***

warrant² *v* [T] *formal* to be a good enough reason for something to happen or be done → **unwarranted**: *The story doesn't warrant the attention it's been given in the press.*

warranty /ˈwɒrənti $ ˈwɔː-, ˈwɑː-/ *n* [C,U] (*plural* **warranties**) a written agreement in which a company selling something promises to repair it if it breaks within a particular period of time → **guarantee**: *The TV comes with a three-year warranty.*

warren /ˈwɒrən $ ˈwɔː-, ˈwɑː-/ *n* [C] **1** the underground holes that rabbits live in **2** a place with a lot of very narrow streets

warring /ˈwɔːrɪŋ/ *adj* [only before noun] fighting against each other: *the **warring countries***

warrior /ˈwɒriə $ ˈwɔːriər, ˈwɑː-/ *n* [C] someone who fought in battles in past times, especially someone who was very brave

warship /ˈwɔːʃɪp $ ˈwɔːr-/ *n* [C] a ship with guns, used in wars

wart /wɔːt $ wɔːrt/ *n* [C] a small hard raised part on your skin

wartime /ˈwɔːtaɪm $ ˈwɔːr-/ *n* [U] the period of time when a country is fighting a war [OPP] **peacetime**: *Things are different in wartime.*

ˈwar-torn *adj* a war-torn country, city etc is being destroyed by war

wary /ˈweəri $ ˈweri/ *adj* careful because you are worried that someone or something may be dangerous or harmful: **[+of]** *She was a bit wary of him at first.* —**warily** *adv*

was /wəz; *strong* wɒz $ wəz; *strong* wɑːz/ *v* the past tense of the verb BE in the first and third person singular

wash¹ /wɒʃ $ wɔːʃ, wɑːʃ/ *v*
1 [T] to clean something with soap and water: *He spent the morning washing the car.* | *These jeans need to be washed.* | **wash sth in sth** *I had to wash my hair in cold water.*
2 [I,T] to clean your body with soap and water: *You didn't wash this morning!* | *Go upstairs and wash your hands.* | *I **got washed** and went to bed.*
3 [I] if water washes somewhere, it flows there: **[+against]** *The waves washed softly against the shore.*
4 [T] if something is washed somewhere, the sea or a river carries it there: **wash sth out/into etc** *The body was washed out to sea.*

PHRASES

wash your hands of sth/sb to refuse to be responsible for something or someone: *His parents have washed their hands of him.*

PHRASAL VERBS

wash sth ↔ **away** if water washes something away, it carries it away

wash sth ↔ **down** to drink something with food or medicine: *a big plate of pasta washed down with red wine*

wash off
1 if something washes off, you can remove it from the surface of something by washing it: *Don't worry, the mud will wash off.*
2 wash sth ↔ off to clean dirt or dust from the surface of something by washing it

wash out
1 if a substance washes out, you can remove it from a material by washing it
2 wash sth ↔ out to wash the inside of something: *Wash the bowl out with warm water.*

wash up
1 *BrE* to wash the plates, dishes etc after a meal: *Will you help me wash up?* | **wash sth ↔ up** *It took ages to wash up all the pots.*
2 *AmE* to wash your hands: *Go wash up for supper.*
3 wash sth ↔ up if waves wash something up, they carry it to the shore: *His body was washed up on the beach.*

THESAURUS

wash to clean something with soap and water: *Can you wash the sheets?* | *I washed my face.*
do the washing *BrE*, **do the laundry** *AmE* to wash clothes that need to be washed: *I've cleaned the house and done the washing.*
do the dishes (*also* **wash up/do the washing-up** *BrE*) to wash all the cups, plates, knives etc that you have used during a meal: *It's your turn to do the dishes.* | *You cook and I'll do the washing-up.*
rinse to wash something in water in order to remove soap or dirt: *Shampoo your hair and rinse it well.*

---

wash² *n* [singular]
1 clothes that are to be washed, are being washed, or have just been washed: **in the wash** *All my jumpers are in the wash.*
2 a wash when you wash something, or wash yourself using soap and water: *I'm just going to **have a wash** (=wash myself).* | *I'll **give** the car a **wash** at the weekend.*

washable /ˈwɒʃəbəl $ ˈwɔːʃ-, ˈwɑːʃ-/ *adj* **1** washable clothes are not damaged by washing **2** washable paint can be removed from clothing by washing

washbasin /ˈwɒʃˌbeɪsən $ ˈwɔːʃ-, ˈwɑːʃ-/ *n* [C] *especially BrE* a small SINK for washing your hands and face

ˌwashed-ˈout *adj* **1** no longer having any colour: *washed-out jeans* **2** tired and pale: *You look washed-out.*

washer /ˈwɒʃə $ ˈwɔːʃər, ˈwɑː-/ *n* [C] a small flat ring of metal, plastic, or rubber, used between a NUT and BOLT or in a TAP

washing /'wɒʃɪŋ $ 'wɔː-, 'wɑː-/ n [singular, U] BrE clothes that need to be washed, are being washed, or have just been washed SYN **wash** AmE: I need to do the **washing**.

'washing line n [C,U] BrE a piece of string that you hang wet clothes on outside so that they can dry SYN **clothesline**

'washing ma,chine n [C] a machine that washes clothes

'washing ,powder n [C,U] BrE a powder used for washing clothes

,washing-'up n BrE 1 [U] plates, knives etc that need to be washed after a meal: a huge pile of washing-up 2 **do the washing-up** to wash the plates, dishes etc that have been used for a meal: It's your turn to do the washing-up.

,washing-'up ,liquid n [U] BrE a liquid used for washing plates, knives etc

washout /'wɒʃ-aʊt $ 'wɔːʃ-, 'wɑːʃ-/ n [singular] informal 1 a failure 2 when rain stops something from happening

washroom /'wɒʃrʊm, -ruːm $ 'wɔːʃ-, 'wɑːʃ-/ n [C] AmE a public toilet

wasn't /'wɒzənt $ 'wɑː-/ the short form of 'was not': He wasn't there.

wasp /wɒsp $ wɑːsp, wɒːsp/ n [C] a black and yellow insect that stings

wastage /'weɪstɪdʒ/ n [U] when something is wasted or lost: The aim is to reduce energy wastage.

waste¹ /weɪst/ n
1 [singular, U] when something such as money, time, or a skill is not used effectively or sensibly: **a waste of time/money/resources etc** My father thought college would be a complete waste of time. | **What a waste** of money!
2 [U] things that are left after people have used something: More household waste could be recycled.
3 **wastes** [plural] a large empty area of land: **icy/frozen/snowy etc wastes** the icy wastes of Antarctica

PHRASES
go to waste to be wasted: We can't let all this food go to waste.
a waste of space spoken someone or something with no good qualities: She thinks men are a waste of space.

waste² v [T]
1 to use something such as money, time, or a skill in a way that is not effective or sensible: They **wasted** a lot of **time** trying to fix it themselves. | **waste sth on sth** Don't waste your money on that junk!
2 **be wasted** if someone is wasted in a particular situation, their skills are not being fully used: He's wasted in that job.
3 **be wasted on sb** to have no importance for someone or no effect on someone: He thought education was wasted on women.

PHRASES
waste your breath spoken to say something that will have no effect: You're wasting your breath trying to tell her anything!
waste no time (in) doing sth to do something very quickly: He wasted no time in introducing himself.

PHRASAL VERBS
waste away to gradually become thinner and weaker, because you are ill

waste³ adj [only before noun] 1 having no use, or no further use: waste products | waste paper 2 waste ground is empty or not looked after by anyone

wastebasket /'weɪst,bɑːskɪt $ -,bæs-/ n [C] especially AmE a WASTEPAPER BASKET → see picture at **BIN**

wasted /'weɪstɪd/ adj 1 having no useful result: You've had a wasted trip – he's gone. 2 if someone's body is wasted, it is very thin and weak 3 informal very drunk or strongly affected by illegal drugs

wasteful /'weɪstfəl/ adj using more of something than you should: the wasteful use of resources

wasteland /'weɪstlænd, -lənd/ n [C,U] an area of land which is not looked after, for example with old factories on it: urban wasteland

wastepaper basket /,weɪst'peɪpə ,bɑːskɪt, 'weɪst,peɪpə- $ 'weɪst,peɪpər ,bæ-/ n [C] especially BrE a small container in which you put bits of paper and other things that you do not want SYN **wastebasket** AmE → see picture at **BIN**

watch¹ /wɒtʃ $ wɑːtʃ, wɒːtʃ/ v
1 [I,T] to look at someone or something and pay attention to what is happening: Watch me, I'll show you. | **Watch carefully** and you might learn something. | **watch sb do sth** She watched him drive away. | **watch sb doing sth** We watched the children playing. | **watch TV/a film etc** I was watching the news. | **[+what/how/where etc]** Watch what he does. → see picture at **LOOK¹**
2 [T] to be careful about something: **Watch yourself** (=be careful) when you cross the road. | **[+(that)]** Watch he doesn't run off on his own. | **[+where/what etc]** Watch what you're doing!
3 [T] to take care of someone or something for a short time: Can you watch my bags for me?
4 [T] to pay attention to a situation that interests or worries you: The government will watch the progress of these schemes with interest.

PHRASES
watch it spoken informal used to warn someone to be careful: Hey, watch it – you nearly hit that truck!
watch your step informal to be careful because you might make someone angry: You'd better watch your step if you want to keep your job.

PHRASAL VERBS
watch out to be careful and pay attention, because something unpleasant might happen: Watch out! You might cut yourself. | **[+for]** You can ride your bike here, but watch out for cars.
watch over sb/sth to take care of someone or something

THESAURUS

watch to look at someone or something and pay attention to what is happening: I watched the lion as it came closer.
see to watch a particular programme, film, game etc – used when saying whether you have watched it, or when you watched it: Did you see the news last night? | We saw the new Johnny Depp film on Saturday.

W

keep an eye on sb/sth to check that someone or something is safe, well etc by regularly looking at them: *Could you keep an eye on the house while we're away?*

spy on sb to watch someone secretly in order to find out what they are doing: *He hired a private detective to spy on her.*

WATCH

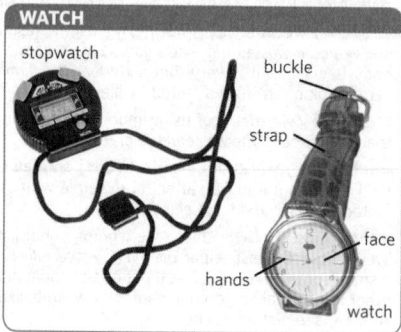

stopwatch

buckle

strap

face

hands

watch

---

watch² *n* [C] a small clock that you wear on your wrist: *My watch has stopped.* | *He looked at his watch.*

PHRASES

keep a (close) watch on/over sb/sth to watch someone or something carefully so that you are ready to deal with anything that happens: *The police are keeping a close watch on the area.*

keep watch to look around a place so that you can warn people if there is any danger: *Douglas kept watch while the others slept.*

watchdog /ˈwɒtʃdɒɡ $ ˈwɑːtʃdɔːɡ, ˈwɔːtʃ-/ *n* [C] a person or organization that checks that companies behave properly and protects the rights of ordinary people: *a consumer watchdog*

watchful /ˈwɒtʃfəl $ ˈwɑːtʃ-, ˈwɔːtʃ-/ *adj* careful to notice what is happening: *She cooked the meal under the watchful eye of her mother.*

watchword /ˈwɒtʃwɜːd $ ˈwɑːtʃwɜːrd, ˈwɔːtʃ-/ *n* [C] a word or phrase which expresses something that is very important: *Caution is still the watchword.*

water¹ /ˈwɔːtə $ ˈwɒtər, ˈwɑː-/ *n*

1 [U] the clear liquid that falls as rain and is used for drinking and washing: *Can I have a drink of water?* | *Wash your hands thoroughly with soap and water.*

2 [U] an area of water such as the sea or a lake: **shallow/deep water** *The ship ran aground in shallow water.*

3 waters [plural] a very large area of water, for example an ocean or large river: *the **coastal waters** of Alaska* | **international/Arctic/Korean etc waters** *We received permission to sail in Japanese waters.* | *The **flood waters** slowly receded.* → **keep your head above water** at HEAD¹, **not hold water** at HOLD¹

PHRASES

in hot/deep water in a lot of trouble: *He's in hot water after being caught cheating in the exam.*

uncharted/troubled waters a situation that is difficult, dangerous, or unfamiliar: *Troubled waters still lie ahead for the administration.*

be water under the bridge to belong to the past and no longer be important: *All that's water under the bridge now.*

water² *v*

1 [T] to pour water on a plant

2 [I] if your eyes water, liquid comes out of them: *The onions are making my eyes water.* **THESAURUS ▶ CRY**

PHRASAL VERBS

water sth ↔ **down**

1 to make a statement or plan less strong or less effective

2 to add water to a drink to make it less strong → **dilute**

watercolour *BrE*, **watercolor** *AmE* /ˈwɔːtəˌkʌlə $ ˈwɔːtərˌkʌlər, ˈwɑː-/ *n* [C,U] a kind of paint that you mix with water, or a painting done using this kind of paint

watercress /ˈwɔːtəkres $ ˈwɒtər-, ˈwɑː-/ *n* [U] a small green plant with strong-tasting leaves that grows in water → see picture on page A5

waterfall /ˈwɔːtəfɔːl $ ˈwɒtərfɒːl, ˈwɑː-/ *n* [C] a place where a river or stream drops down over a cliff or rock

WATERFALL

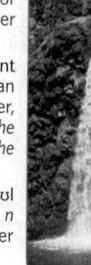

waterfront /ˈwɔːtəfrʌnt $ ˈwɒtər-, ˈwɑː-/ *n* [C] an area beside a lake, river, or the sea: *Most of the hotels are down on the waterfront.*

waterhole /ˈwɔːtəhəʊl $ ˈwɒtərhoʊl, ˈwɑː-/ *n* [C] a small area of water in a dry country

ˈwatering can *n* [C] a container used for pouring water on plants → see picture at GARDEN

waterlogged /ˈwɔːtəlɒɡd $ ˈwɒtərlɒːɡd, ˈwɑː-, -lɑːɡd/ *adj* land that is waterlogged is very wet or covered with water: *The pitch was waterlogged.*

watermark /ˈwɔːtəmɑːk $ ˈwɒtərmɑːrk, ˈwɑː-/ *n* [C] a design on a piece of paper, especially on money, that you can see when the paper is held up to the light

watermelon /ˈwɔːtəˌmelən $ ˈwɒtər-, ˈwɑː-/ *n* [C] a large round fruit with thick green skin, red flesh, and black seeds → see picture on page A4

ˈwater ˌpolo *n* [U] a ball game played in water between two teams

waterproof¹ /ˈwɔːtəpruːf $ ˈwɒtər-, ˈwɑː-/ *adj* not allowing water to enter: *waterproof boots* **—waterproof** *v* [T]: *Plastic sheeting was used to waterproof the shed.*

waterproof² *n* [C usually plural] waterproof clothing → see picture at CLOTHES

watershed /ˈwɔːtəʃed $ ˈwɒtər-, ˈwɑː-/ *n*

1 [singular] an event or time when very important changes happen: [+in] *The election marked a watershed in American politics.* **2 the watershed** the time in the evening after which programmes may be shown on British television which are not suitable for children

'water-,skiing *n* [U] a sport in which someone wearing SKIS is pulled over water by a boat —**water-ski** *v* [I] —**water skier** *n* [C]

watertight /'wɔːtətaɪt $ 'wɒːtər-, 'wɑː-/ *adj* **1** containing no mistakes or weaknesses, and therefore impossible to criticize: *a watertight explanation* **2** not allowing any water to get in or out: *a watertight container*

waterway /'wɔːtəweɪ $ 'wɒːtər-, 'wɑː-/ *n* [C] a river or CANAL that boats can travel on

watery /'wɔːtəri $ 'wɒː-, 'wɑː-/ *adj* **1** containing water, especially when this is unpleasant: *watery soup* **2** a watery light is very pale

watt /wɒt $ wɑːt/ (*written abbreviation* **W**) *n* [C] a unit for measuring electrical power: *a 100 watt light bulb*

wave¹ /weɪv/ *v*
1 [I,T] to raise your arm and move your hand from side to side as a signal or greeting: **[+to/at]** *Anne waved at us and we waved back.* | *She waved to me from the other side of the road.* | **wave sb through/away etc** (=show someone where to go by waving) *The policeman waved us through.* | *She* **waved goodbye** *to Tony.* | *They stood on the platform and* **waved us off** (=waved as we were leaving). → see picture on page A10
2 [I,T] if you wave something, or if it waves, it moves from side to side: **wave sth around/at/towards etc** *He started shouting and waving his gun around.* | *The crowd were waving flags and cheering.*

PHRASAL VERBS
wave sth ↔ **aside** to ignore what someone says

wave² *n* [C]
1 ON THE SEA a line of raised water that moves across the surface of the sea: *The children were playing in the waves.* | *She watched the* **waves breaking** *on the shore.* | *Huge* **waves** *were* **crashing** *into the boat.*
2 A LOT OF STH when something suddenly starts happening a lot: **wave of violence/attacks/bombings etc** *a wave of strikes* | *the latest crime wave to hit the city* | **Wave after wave** *of aircraft passed overhead.*
3 SUDDEN FEELING when someone suddenly feels a particular feeling very strongly: **wave of panic/fear/enthusiasm etc** *Harriet was overcome by a wave of homesickness.*
4 HAND MOVEMENT the movement you make when you wave your hand: *He* **gave** *us a quick* **wave.**
5 LIGHT/SOUND the form in which some types of energy move, for example light and sound: **sound/light/radio waves** → LONG WAVE, MEDIUM WAVE, NEW WAVE, SHOCK WAVE, SHORT WAVE, TIDAL WAVE

PHRASES
make waves to complain or cause problems: *I didn't want to make any waves.*

waveband /'weɪvbænd/ *n* [C] a set of sound waves of a particular length, used to broadcast radio programmes

wavelength /'weɪvleŋθ/ *n* [C] **1** the size of radio wave used by a radio company to broadcast its programmes **2** the distance between two waves of energy such as sound or light
PHRASES
be on the same wavelength to have the same opinions and feelings as someone else: *We all seemed to be on the same wavelength.*

waver /'weɪvə $ -ər/ *v* [I] **1** to be unable to make a decision: *The party wavered between free trade and protectionism.* **2** to become less definite or less strong: *He never wavered in his loyalty.* **3** to shake a little: *His voice wavered.*

wavy /'weɪvi/ *adj* with curves in, not straight: *wavy hair* | *a wavy line* → see picture at HAIR

wax¹ /wæks/ *n* [U]
1 a thick substance made of fats or oils, used for making CANDLES and for polishing surfaces
2 the sticky substance in your ears

wax² *v* [T] **1** to polish a surface using wax **2** to remove hair from your body using wax
PHRASES
wax and wane *literary* to increase and decrease: *Friendship can wax and wane like the moon.*
wax lyrical (about sth) *humorous* to talk about something in a way that shows you think it is excellent: *Journalists wax lyrical about the band.*

waxy /'wæksi/ *adj* having a shiny surface like wax: *waxy leaves*

way¹ /weɪ/ *n*
1 METHOD [C] a method of doing something: **way of doing sth** *There are different ways of doing this.* | **way to do sth** *What's the best way to get fit?* | *OK, do it* **your own way.** | **(in) the right/wrong way** *You're doing this the wrong way.* | **way (a)round sth** (=method of dealing with something) *There are several ways around this problem.* | **way out (of sth)** *There seemed to be no way out of the crisis.*
2 MANNER [C] the manner in which someone does something or in which something happens: **in a ... way** *He looked at me in a strange way.* | *The disease affects different people in different ways.* | *He had cooked the meat just the way I like it.* | **this/that way** *Try doing it this way.* | *I didn't know you felt that way.* | *Things are going to change* **in a big way** (=a lot).
3 HOW TO GO SOMEWHERE [C] the road, path etc that you follow in order to go to a place: **[+to]** *What's the quickest way to the beach?* | *Could you* **tell me the way** *to the station?* | *He offered to* **show us the way** *back.* | *I hope someone* **knows the way.** | *They* **lost their way** *coming down off the mountain.* | **way in/out** *We couldn't find the way out.*
4 POSITION/DIRECTION [C] a particular direction or position: *Which way is north?* | **the right/wrong way** *I think we might have gone the wrong way.* | *Face this* **way,** *please.* | *Is this picture* **the right way up**? | *You've got the letters* **the wrong way round.** | *Look both ways before crossing the road.*
5 DISTANCE/TIME [singular] a distance or a length of time, especially a long one: *We're still* **a long way** *from the airport.* | **a long way off/away/ahead etc** *A*

peace settlement seems a long way off. | *She slept **most of the way** home.* → NO WAY, RIGHT OF WAY

PHRASES

by the way *spoken* used when saying something that is not connected with what you were talking about before: *Oh, by the way, I saw Marie yesterday.*

sb can't have it both ways *spoken* used to say that someone cannot have the advantages of two opposite things and must choose one: *You can't have it both ways. Either you pay for the ticket yourself or you stay at home.*

get in the way of sth to prevent something from happening: *Don't let your social life get in the way of your studies.*

go out of your way to do sth to make a special effort to do something, especially to help someone or be kind to them: *Ben went out of his way to help us.*

sth has come a long way if something has come a long way, it has developed and improved a lot: *Psychiatry has come a long way since the 1920s.*

have a way with sb/sth to be especially good at dealing with people or things of a particular type: *He's always had a way with kids.*

have/get your (own) way to do what you want even if someone else wants something different: *They always let that kid get his own way.*

in a bad way ill: *He looked in a bad way.*

in a way/in some ways used to say that something is true about some parts of something: *Life is much easier now, in some ways.*

in the way/in sb's way if something is in the way, it is in front of you and prevents you from going somewhere or seeing something: *There was a big truck in the way.*

keep/stay out of sb's way to avoid someone: *It's best to stay out of her way when she's in this mood.*

know/find your way around to know or find out where things are: *It takes a few weeks to find your way around.*

make way 1 to move so that someone or something can pass: *People made way for the ambulance men.* **2** if one thing makes way for another thing, the other thing replaces it: *Several houses were torn down to make way for a new fire station.*

make your way to/towards/along etc sth to move towards something, especially when this takes a long time: *They made their way towards the exit.* **THESAURUS** GO

no way! *informal* used to say that you will definitely not do or allow something: *'Dad, can I borrow the car tonight?' 'No way!'*

be on its/his way to be arriving soon: *The taxi is on its way.*

on my/your way etc while you are going somewhere: *Could you get some milk on your way back home?*

out of the way if something is out of the way, it is finished or you have dealt with it: *I want to get my homework out of the way before we leave.*

push/force/fight etc your way somewhere to move somewhere in the way mentioned: *She elbowed her way to the front.*

split/divide sth two/three etc ways to divide something into two or three etc equal parts: *The robbers divided the money three ways.*

way to go! *AmE spoken, informal* used when CONGRATULATING someone: *Way to go, Sam! Nice hit!*

THESAURUS

way something that you do in order to do or achieve something: *Cycling is a good way to get fit.*

method a way of doing something, especially one that is well-known and often used: *modern farming methods* | *You can use various methods of payment, such as a credit card or by direct debit.*

means a method, system etc that someone uses in order to do something or achieve something: *They were prepared to use any means to get what they wanted.* | **a means of communication/transport** *The river was used as a means of transport.* | *It is better to find a solution **by peaceful means**.*

approach a general way of dealing with a particular problem or situation: *A different approach to youth crime is needed.*

technique a particular way of doing something, for which you need a skill that has to be learned: *You need to improve your exam technique.* | *We adopted some new techniques for improving staff performance.*

strategy a carefully planned way of achieving something difficult, that may take a long time: *the government's economic strategy*

---

way² *adv informal* **1** by a large amount: *The film was way too long.* | **way ahead/behind etc** *She was way ahead of us.* | *We met **way back** (=a long time ago) in the '70s.* | *Your guess was **way out** (=completely wrong).* **2** *informal* extremely: *This is way cool.*

waylay /ˈweɪleɪ/ v [T] (*past tense and past participle* **waylaid**) *literary* to stop or attack someone when they are going somewhere

way of 'life *n* [C] (*plural* **ways of life**) your way of life is the way that you live: *the American way of life*

way-'out *adj informal* very modern or unusual

wayside /ˈweɪsaɪd/ *n* **fall/go by the wayside** to stop being successful

wayward /ˈweɪwəd $ -wərd/ *adj* behaving badly: *his wayward son*

WC /ˌdʌbəljuː ˈsiː/ *n* [C] *BrE old-fashioned* (**water closet**) used on signs to show where there is a public toilet

we /wi; *strong* wiː/ *pron*
1 the person who is speaking and one or more other people: *We ordered our meal.* | *He didn't care, but we did.*
2 people in general: *Today we know much more about the disease.*

weak /wiːk/ *adj*
1 NOT PHYSICALLY STRONG not physically strong or not having much energy OPP **strong**: *She's too weak to feed herself.* | *Her knees **felt weak**.* | *He managed a **weak smile**.*

2 LIKELY TO BREAK unable to support a lot of weight, and likely to break: *The bridge was too weak to support the weight of the traffic.*
3 NOT SUCCESSFUL not very powerful or successful: *The president is now in quite a weak position.* | *a weak economy* | *The dollar is still quite weak* (=not worth very much) *compared to other currencies.*
4 EASILY INFLUENCED *disapproving* easily influenced by other people: *a weak and indecisive man*
5 NOT GOOD AT STH not very good at doing something: *His spelling was weak.* | *one of the weaker students in the class* | **[+at]** *I'm quite weak at maths.* | *Be honest about your* **weak points** (=things you are not good at).
6 EXCUSE/REASON a weak excuse or reason is not easy to believe
7 DRINK weak drinks have little taste because they contain a lot of water: *weak tea*
8 SOUND/LIGHT a weak sound or light is not very loud or bright SYN **faint** —**weakly** *adv*: *She smiled weakly.*

THESAURUS

person
weak not physically strong or not having much energy: *Women tend to be weaker than men.* | *He was feeling weak after his operation.*
frail weak and thin, especially because you are old: *My grandmother looked old and frail.*
feeble weak and not able to do much because you are very ill, very old, or very young: *He was still too feeble to get up.* | *She grew old and feeble.*
delicate weak and often becoming ill easily: *As a child, she had been rather delicate.*

thing
weak unable to support a lot of weight, and likely to break: *The branch was too weak to support his body.*
fragile made of a material that breaks easily – used about something you need to handle carefully: *a fragile glass bowl*
delicate easy to break or damage – used especially about things that are thin and attractive, or about someone's skin: *The flowers are incredibly delicate.* | *a soap for delicate skin*
flimsy not made from good strong materials and so easy to damage: *a flimsy plastic chair* | *a flimsy wooden building*

weaken /ˈwiːkən/ *v* [I,T] **1** to become less powerful or less strong, or to make someone or something do this: *The earthquake has weakened several buildings.* | *The president's position has weakened.* **2** to make someone less determined, or to become less determined: *Nothing could weaken her resolve.* | *He knew he would weaken.*

weakling /ˈwiːkˌlɪŋ/ *n* [C] someone who is very weak physically

weakness /ˈwiːknəs/ *n*
1 [U] when someone or something is not powerful, determined, or strong: *I dared not show any* **sign of weakness**. | *He caught me in a* **moment of weakness**. | *the weakness of the pound against the dollar*
2 [C] a problem or fault: **[+in]** *There are several weaknesses in their argument.* | *What are your main* **strengths and weaknesses**?
3 **have a weakness for sth** to like something very much, especially something that you should not have or do: *He had a weakness for chocolate.*

wealth /welθ/ *n*
1 [singular, U] a large amount of money or property that a rich person has: *She enjoyed sharing her wealth with her friends.* | *The purpose of industry is to* **create wealth**.
2 **a wealth of sth** a lot of something good: *The book contains* **a wealth of information**.

wealthy /ˈwelθi/ *adj*
1 rich: *an extremely wealthy family* | *the wealthy countries of the world* THESAURUS ▶ **RICH**
2 **the wealthy** people who have a lot of money or possessions

wean /wiːn/ *v* [T] to gradually stop feeding a baby on its mother's milk and start giving it ordinary food
PHRASAL VERBS
wean sb off sth to help someone to gradually stop doing or having something: *She wanted to wean him off junk food.*

weapon /ˈwepən/ *n* [C]
1 something that is used to attack people or to fight against people: *They were armed with knives and other weapons.*
2 something that you can use in order to achieve your aim: *The cameras are another weapon in the fight against car crime.*

weaponry /ˈwepənri/ *n* [U] weapons

wear¹ /weə $ wer/ *v* (*past tense* **wore** /wɔː $ wɔːr/, *past participle* **worn** /wɔːn $ wɔːrn/)
1 CLOTHES/SHOES ETC [T] to have something such as clothes, shoes, or jewellery on your body: *She was wearing jeans and a red jumper.* | *What are you wearing to the party?* | *He* **wears glasses** *for reading.* | *She never* **wears make-up**.
2 HAIR [T] to have your hair in a particular style: *Fay wore her hair in a bun.*
3 EXPRESSION [T] to have a particular expression on your face: *He came out wearing a big grin on his face.*
4 BECOME DAMAGED [I,T] to become thinner or weaker after continuous use, or to make something do this: *The carpet was starting to wear at the edges.* | *You've* **worn a hole in** *your sock.* → **WORN OUT**
PHRASES
wear thin if an excuse or joke is wearing thin, it has been used a lot and is no longer effective: *That excuse will soon wear thin.*
wear well to remain in good condition after being used: *This carpet has worn very well.*

PHRASAL VERBS
wear away to gradually become thinner or smoother because of being rubbed or touched, or to make this happen: **wear sth ↔ away** *Look how the rocks have been worn away by the sea.*
wear down
1 wear sb ↔ down to make someone weaker or less determined: *Lewis gradually wore down his opponent.*
2 to gradually become flatter or smaller because of being rubbed or used, or to make this happen: **wear sth ↔ down** *You've worn your shoes down at the heel.*

wear off if a feeling or effect wears off, it gradually stops: *The drug was starting to wear off.*

wear on **as the day/evening etc wore on** used to say that something happened gradually during a particular day, evening etc: *It became hotter as the day wore on.*

wear out

1 if something wears out, or if you wear it out, it becomes damaged and useless because it has been used so much: **wear sth out** *Terry had worn out the soles of his shoes.*

2 wear sb out to make someone feel very tired `SYN` **exhaust**: *The kids are wearing me out.*

wear² *n* [U] **1 children's/women's/casual etc wear** clothing worn by children, by women, on informal occasions etc **2** damage caused when something is used over a long period: *The carpets are showing signs of wear.* | *Check the equipment for wear and tear* (=damage). → **the worse for wear** at WORSE¹

wearing /'weərɪŋ $ 'wer-/ *adj* making you feel tired or annoyed: *He can be a bit wearing at times.*

wearisome /'wɪərɪsəm $ 'wɪr-/ *adj* formal making you feel tired or annoyed: *a wearisome task*

weary¹ /'wɪəri $ 'wɪr-/ *adj* **1** very tired: *She gave a weary sigh.* **2** wanting something to stop: **[+of]** *People were growing weary of the war.* —**wearily** *adv*: *We walked wearily home.* —**weariness** *n* [U]

weary² *v* [I,T] (**wearied, wearying, wearies**) formal to make someone tired, or to become tired: *The children wearied her.*

weasel /'wiːzəl/ *n* [C] a small wild animal with a long body

weather¹ /'weðə $ -ər/ *n* [singular, U] the temperature and other conditions such as sun, rain, and wind: *What's the weather like today?* → **RAIN¹, SNOW¹, SUN¹, WIND¹**

PHRASES

| **under the weather** slightly ill: *I was feeling a bit under the weather.* **THESAURUS** ▸ **ILL**

Grammar

Do not say 'We had a good weather.' Say *We had good weather.*

COLLOCATIONS

adjectives

hot/warm weather *I hope the weather stays hot.*
cold weather *He complained about the cold weather in London.*
good/nice weather (=not wet) *We had good weather, apart from one day of rain.*
fine/sunny/dry weather *If the weather is fine, we'll eat outside.*
bad/awful/terrible weather (=wet or stormy) *They had to cancel the match because of bad weather.*
wet/rainy weather *We've had a lot of wet weather recently.*
windy/stormy weather *The weather was cold and windy.*
severe weather formal (=very bad weather) *It would be too risky to fly in this severe weather.*

Word Choice: **weather or climate?**

The **weather** is the temperature and the conditions at a particular time, for example if it is sunny or snowing: *What's the weather like today?*

The **climate** is the usual weather conditions in a particular country or area: *Queensland has a warm tropical climate.* | *climate change*

---

weather² *v* **1** [T] if you weather a difficult period, you manage to continue until things improve: *We will have to weather the storm.* **2** [I,T] if a surface is weathered, or if it weathers, the wind, rain, and sun gradually change its appearance: *his weathered skin* | *The brick had weathered to a lovely pinky-brown.*

'weather-beaten *adj* damaged or changed by the wind and sun: *the sailor's weather-beaten face*

'weather ,forecast *n* [C] a report on the television or radio that says what the weather will be like: *It's going to rain, according to the weather forecast.*

'weather ,forecaster (*also* **weatherman** /'weðəmæn $ -ðər-/, **weathergirl** /'weðəgɜːl $ -ðərgɜːrl/) *n* [C] a person on the television or radio whose job is to say what the weather will be like

'weather vane *n* [C] a metal object that moves to show the direction of the wind

weave /wiːv/ *v*

1 [I,T] (*past tense* **wove** /wəʊv $ woʊv/, *past participle* **woven** /'wəʊvən $ 'woʊ-/) to make cloth, a CARPET, a basket etc by crossing threads or thin pieces under and over each other: *a beautifully woven carpet*

2 [T] (*past tense* **wove**, *past participle* **woven**) to join different ideas or subjects together in a clever way: *The plot weaves together fact and fiction.*

3 [I,T] (*past tense and past participle* **weaved**) to move somewhere by turning and changing direction a lot: **[+in and out/through]** *She watched him weaving in and out of the traffic on his bike.* | *The snake was weaving its way through the grass.* —**weaver** *n* [C]

web /web/ *n* **1** [C] a net of thin threads made by a SPIDER to catch insects **2 the Web** the system that connects computers around the world together so that people can find and use information on the Internet `SYN` **the World Wide Web** → **the Internet, the Net: on the Web** *a guide to the best education-related sites on the Web* **3** [singular] a set of things that are connected with each other in a complicated way: **[+of]** *a web of lies*

webbed /webd/ *adj* webbed feet have skin between the toes → see picture on page A3

'web ,browser *n* [C] a computer program that finds information on the Internet and shows it on your computer screen

webcam /'webkæm/ *n* [C] a video camera that broadcasts what it is filming on a website → see picture at **CAMERA**

'web page *n* [C] all the information that you can see in one part of a website

website /'websaɪt/ *n* [C] a place on the Internet

where you can find information about something, especially a particular organization: *For more information, visit our website.*

wed /wed/ v [I,T] (*past tense and past participle* **wedded** *or* **wed**) *literary* to marry

Wed. (*also* **Wed** *BrE*) a written abbreviation of **Wednesday**

we'd /wɪd; *strong* wiːd/ **1** the short form of 'we had': *We'd already eaten breakfast.* **2** the short form of 'we would': *We'd like to stay longer, but we have to get home.*

wedding /'wedɪŋ/ n [C] a ceremony in which two people get married → **marriage**, **honeymoon**

COLLOCATIONS

verbs
have a wedding *Where are you going to have the wedding?*
to go to a wedding (*also* **to attend a wedding** *formal*) *I went to a wedding last weekend.*
to invite sb to your wedding *Have you been invited to their wedding?*

types of wedding
a big wedding (=with a lot of guests) *They couldn't afford a big wedding.*
a quiet/small wedding (=with not many guests) *It's going to be a quiet wedding.*
a church wedding *She wanted a church wedding.*
a white wedding (=where the bride wears a white dress) *Many brides still want a traditional white wedding.*

wedding + noun
sb's wedding day *a picture of Edward and Nancy on their wedding day*
the wedding ceremony *There was a party after the wedding ceremony.*
a wedding dress (=the dress worn by the bride) *Have you chosen your wedding dress yet?*
a wedding cake *The bride and groom cut the wedding cake.*
a wedding present/gift *He gave them a painting as a wedding present.*
sb's wedding anniversary *It's our twentieth wedding anniversary next week.*
wedding reception (=a large formal meal or party after a wedding)

'wedding ring n [C] a ring that you wear to show that you are married

wedge¹ /wedʒ/ n [C] a piece of something which is thin and pointed at one end and thick at the other end: **[+of]** *a wedge of chocolate cake*

wedge² v [T] **1** to force something firmly into a narrow space: *She kept her hands wedged between her knees.* **2 wedge sth open/shut** to put something under a door, window etc to make it stay open or shut

Wednesday /'wenzdi, -deɪ/ n [C,U] (*written abbreviation* **Weds.** *or* **Wed.**) the day between Tuesday and Thursday → see examples at **MONDAY**

wee¹ /wiː/ adj very small – used especially in Scotland: *a wee child*

wee² v [I] *BrE spoken* to URINATE (=make liquid waste flow out of your body) – used by or to children —**wee** n [singular]

weed¹ /wiːd/ n [C] a wild plant that grows where you do not want it to grow: *She was pulling up weeds in the garden.*

weed² v [I,T] to remove weeds from a garden or other place
PHRASAL VERBS
weed sb/sth ↔ **out** to get rid of people or things that are not very good

weedy /'wiːdi/ adj *BrE informal* physically weak or having a weak character

week /wiːk/ n [C]
1 a period of seven days, especially one that begins on a Monday and ends on a Sunday: *The movie starts this week.* | **last/next week** (=the week before or after this one) *See you next week.* | *We had drawing lessons once a week.* | *I've been living here for six weeks.*
2 the part of the week between Monday and Friday, when people are working or studying: **during the week** *I don't see the kids much during the week.*
3 (on) Monday week/Tuesday week etc *BrE* a week after the day that is mentioned: *I'll be back Monday week.*

weekday /'wiːkdeɪ/ n [C] any day of the week except Saturday and Sunday

weekend /ˌwiːk'end◂ 'wiːkend $ 'wiːkend/ n [C] Saturday and Sunday: *What are you doing **this weekend** (=the weekend that is coming)?* | *We're going to Paris for a **long weekend** (=Saturday and Sunday and one or two more days).* | **last/next weekend** (=the weekend before or after this one) | **at the weekend** *BrE*, **on the weekend** *AmE: I like to play golf at the weekend.*

weekly¹ /'wiːkli/ adj happening or done every week: *a weekly newspaper* —**weekly** adv

weekly² n [C] (*plural* **weeklies**) a magazine or newspaper that appears once a week

weep /wiːp/ v [I,T] (*past tense and past participle* **wept** /wept/) *literary* to cry: *She wept with relief.*
THESAURUS CRY

weigh /weɪ/ v
1 [linking verb] to have a particular weight: *The baby weighs 12 pounds.* | *How much do you weigh?*
2 [T] to measure how heavy someone or something is: *Have you weighed yourself lately?*
3 (*also* **weigh up**) [T] to consider something carefully before making a decision: *It is my job to weigh the evidence.* | **weigh sth against sth** *You have to weigh the benefits against the extra costs.*
4 [I] *formal* to influence someone's opinion and the decision that they make: **[+against]** *Her age weighs against her.*
PHRASAL VERBS
weigh sb **down**
1 if something weighs you down, it is heavy and difficult to carry
2 if you are weighed down by your problems and responsibilities, you worry a lot about them
weigh on sb/sth to make someone feel worried and

upset: *I'm sure there's something weighing on his mind*.

weigh sth ↔ **out** to measure an amount of something by weighing it: *Could you weigh out half a pound of flour for me?*

weigh sb/sth ↔ **up** to consider someone or something carefully in order to make a judgment: *She weighed up the options before giving her decision.*

weight¹ /weɪt/ n

1 [C,U] how heavy someone or something is, or the quality of being heavy: *Your weight is about right. | The roof collapsed under the weight of the snow.*

2 [singular, U] something that makes you feel worried: **[+of]** *the weight of responsibility | The baby's healthy, so that's **a weight off** our **minds** (=it is no longer a cause of worry).*

3 weights [plural] heavy pieces of metal, usually fixed to a metal bar, that people lift to make their muscles bigger

4 [C] a piece of metal weighing a particular amount that is balanced against something to measure how much that thing weighs

5 [C] a heavy object: *Avoid lifting heavy weights.*
→ **pull your weight** at PULL¹

COLLOCATIONS

verbs

to put on/gain weight *He stopped going to the gym and put on weight.*

to lose weight *She's been trying to lose weight for months.* ⚠ Do not say 'lose your weight'. Say **lose weight**.

weight + noun

a weight problem (=a tendency to be too fat) *I've always had a weight problem.*

weight gain *Weight gain in pregnancy is completely normal.*

weight loss *Symptoms of the disease include weight loss and tiredness.*

weight²

PHRASAL VERBS

weight sth ↔ **down** to put something heavy on or in something so that it does not move: *The nets are weighted down with lead.*

weighted /ˈweɪtɪd/ adj **be weighted in favour of sb/against sb** if a system is weighted in favour of or against a group of people, it gives them advantages or disadvantages

weightless /ˈweɪtləs/ adj something that is weightless seems to have no weight, especially when it is floating in space or water —**weightlessness** n [U]

weightlifting /ˈweɪtˌlɪftɪŋ/ n [U] the sport of lifting weights attached to the ends of a bar —**weightlifter** n [C]

ˈweight ˌtraining n [U] a form of exercise in which you lift special pieces of metal

weighty /ˈweɪti/ adj important and serious: *a weighty problem*

weir /wɪə $ wɪr/ n [C] a wall or fence built across a river to control or stop the flow of water

weird /wɪəd $ wɪrd/ adj informal unusual and strange: *I had a really weird dream.* **THESAURUS** STRANGE —**weirdly** adv

weirdo /ˈwɪədəʊ $ ˈwɪrdoʊ/ n [C] (plural **weirdos**) informal someone who seems very strange

welcome¹ /ˈwelkəm/ spoken used to greet someone who has just arrived: **[+to]** *Welcome to Chicago! | Welcome back – it's good to see you again.*

welcome² adj

1 if you are welcome in a place, the other people want you to be there: *I had the feeling I wasn't welcome. | They all did their best to **make** me **feel welcome**.*

2 if something is welcome, people are pleased that it has happened, because it is useful, pleasant etc: *a welcome suggestion | a welcome breeze*

3 be welcome to do sth spoken used to invite someone to do something if they would like to: *You're welcome to stay for lunch.*

4 be welcome to sth spoken used to say that someone can have something if they want it, because you definitely do not want it: *If Rob wants that job, he's welcome to it!*

PHRASES

you're welcome! spoken used to reply politely to someone who has just thanked you for something: *'Thanks for the coffee.' 'You're welcome.'*

welcome³ v [T]

1 to say hello in a friendly way to someone who has just arrived → **greet**: *Jill was welcoming the guests at the door. | They **welcomed** us **warmly**.*

2 to be glad when something happens or is done, or to say that you are glad: *We would welcome a change in the law.*

welcome⁴ n [singular] the way in which you greet someone when they arrive at a place: *They **gave** him a very **warm welcome** when he returned to work.*

PHRASES

outstay/overstay your welcome to stay at someone's house longer than they want you to: *I had been there two hours, and had perhaps outstayed my welcome.*

welcoming /ˈwelkəmɪŋ/ adj pleasant and making you feel welcome: *a friendly hotel with a welcoming atmosphere* **THESAURUS** FRIENDLY

weld /weld/ v [T] to join metal objects to each other by heating them and pressing them together when they are hot —**welder** n [C]

welfare [Ac] /ˈwelfeə $ -fer/ n [U] **1** someone's welfare is their health and happiness: *We're only concerned with your welfare.* **2** help that is provided for people who have personal or social problems: *welfare services* **3** AmE money paid by the government in the US to people who are very poor or unemployed: **on welfare** *Most of the people in this neighborhood are on welfare.*

ˌwelfare ˈstate / $ ˈ.../ n **the welfare state** a system in which the government provides money, free medical care etc for people who are unemployed, ill, or too old to work

we'll /wɪl; strong wiːl/ the short form of 'we will' and 'we shall': *We'll have to leave soon.*

well¹ /wel/ adv (comparative **better** /ˈbetə $ -ər/, superlative **best** /best/)
1 in a good, successful, or satisfactory way: *Did you sleep well?* | *The business is doing well.* | *I hope the party goes well.*
2 thoroughly or completely: *Mix the flour and butter well.* | *I don't know her very well.* | *Summer is now well and truly* (=completely) *over.*
3 very much or a lot: [+before/after/above/below etc] *By the time they finished, it was well after midnight.* | *The village is well worth a visit.*
PHRASES
as well (as sb/sth) in addition to someone or something else: *My sister's going as well.* | *He's learning French as well as Italian.*
can't very well do sth *spoken* used to say that it does not seem sensible or fair to do something: *We can't very well just leave her on her own.*
may/might as well *spoken* used when you do not particularly want to do something but you decide you should do it: *We may as well get started.*
may/might/could well used to say that something is likely to happen or is likely to be true: *There may well be another earthquake very soon.* **THESAURUS** PROBABLY
might/could (just) as well used to say that a course of action that was easier, cheaper etc would have had an equally good result: *The taxi was so slow, we might just as well have gone on the bus.*
well done *spoken* used to praise someone when you think they have done something very well: *'I got an 'A' in Spanish.' 'Well done!'*

well² adj (comparative **better**, superlative **best**)
healthy: *You're looking well.* | *I should be better by this weekend.* | *I hope you get well soon.* | *'How are you?' 'Very well, thank you.'* **THESAURUS** HEALTHY
PHRASES
all is well used to say that a situation is satisfactory: *I hope all is well with you.*
it is as well to do sth used to give someone advice: *It would be as well to check.*
it's just as well (that) *spoken* used to say that it is lucky or good that things have happened in the way they have done: *It's just as well we didn't stay any longer, because it's just started raining.*
it's/that's all very well *spoken* used to say that you are not happy or satisfied with something: *It's all very well for you to say you're sorry, but I've been waiting here for two hours!*

well³ *spoken*
1 used to pause before saying something, or to emphasize what you are about to say: *Well, let's see now, I could meet you on Thursday.* | *'James doesn't want to come to the cinema with us.' 'Well then, let's go on our own.'*
2 (also **oh 'well**) used to say that you accept a situation, even though it is not a very good one: *Oh well, at least you did your best.*
3 (also **,well, 'well**) used when you are surprised about something: *'She's just got a job with CNN.' 'Well, well.'*
4 used when you want to start telling someone more about someone or something that you have

just mentioned: *You know that guy I was telling you about? Well, he's been arrested!*
5 **well?** used to ask someone to reply to you or tell you what has happened: *Well? What did he say?*

well⁴ n [C] a deep hole in the ground from which water or oil is taken → OIL WELL

well⁵ v
PHRASAL VERBS
well up *literary* if a liquid wells up, it rises and may start to flow: *I felt tears well up in my eyes.*

,well-'balanced adj **1** a well-balanced person is sensible and does not suddenly become angry, upset etc **2** a well-balanced meal or DIET contains all the things you need to stay healthy

,well-be'haved adj a well-behaved child behaves in the way he or she should

,well-'being n [U] a feeling of being comfortable, healthy, and happy

,well-brought-'up adj a well-brought-up child has been taught to be polite and behave well

,well-'built adj someone who is well-built is big and strong **THESAURUS** STRONG

,well-con'nected adj knowing a lot of powerful important people

,well-'done adj meat that is well-done has been cooked thoroughly → **rare**, **medium**: *He likes his steak well-done.*

,well-'dressed adj wearing good clothes

,well-'earned adj deserved, because you have worked hard: *He was enjoying a well-earned rest.*

,well-es'tablished adj something that is well-established has existed for a long time and is respected or trusted by people

,well-'fed adj a well-fed animal or person gets plenty of good food to eat

,well-'heeled adj *informal* rich

wellies /ˈweliz/ n [plural] *BrE informal* WELLINGTONS

,well-in'formed adj someone who is well-informed knows a lot about a subject or different subjects

wellingtons /ˈwelɪŋtənz/ (also **'wellington ,boots**) n [plural] *BrE* long rubber boots that stop your feet getting wet

,well-in'tentioned adj well-meaning

,well-'kept adj **1** something that is well-kept has been kept neat and tidy: *well-kept gardens* **2** a well-kept secret is one that few people know about

,well-'known adj known about by a lot of people: *a well-known artist and writer* **THESAURUS** FAMOUS

,well-'meaning adj trying to help, but often making the situation worse: *well-meaning advice*

,well-'off adj fairly rich: *Her family are quite well-off.* **THESAURUS** RICH

,well-'paid adj someone who is well-paid receives a lot of money for their work

well-read /,wel 'red◄/ adj someone who is well-read has read many books and knows a lot about different subjects

,well-'rounded adj someone who is well-rounded

has had a wide variety of experiences or is able to do many different things

,well-'spoken *adj* speaking in a correct and socially acceptable way

,well-'stocked *adj* having a large supply and variety of food or drink: *a well-stocked general store*

,well-to-'do *adj* rich and having a high position in society

'well-,wisher *n* [C] someone who does something to show that they want another person to succeed, become healthy again etc: *She received hundreds of cards from well-wishers.*

welter /'weltə $ -ər/ *n* **a welter of sth** *formal* a large and confusing number of different details or feelings: *a welter of information*

wend /wend/ *v* **wend your way** *literary* to go slowly from one place to another: *People began to wend their way home.*

went /went/ *v* the past tense of GO

wept /wept/ *v* the past tense and past participle of WEEP

we're /wɪə $ wɪr/ the short form of 'we are': *We're going home.*

were /wə; *strong* wɜː $ wər; *strong* wɜːr/ *v* the past tense of BE

weren't /wɜːnt $ wɜːrnt/ the short form of 'were not': *His parents weren't very pleased when they found out.*

werewolf /'weəwʊlf, 'wɪə- $ 'wer-, 'wɪr-/ *n* [C] (*plural* **werewolves** /-wʊlvz/) a person in stories who changes into a WOLF

west¹, West /west/ *n* [singular, U] (*written abbreviation* **W**)
1 the direction towards the place where the sun goes down: *Which way is west?* | **from/towards the west** *A damp wind blew from the west.* | **to the west (of sth)** *a village to the west of Brussels*
2 the west the western part of a country or area: *Rain will spread to the west later today.* | **[+of]** *the west of the island*
3 the West the western part of the world, especially western Europe and North America

west², West *adj* [only before noun] (*written abbreviation* **W**)
1 in the west or facing the west: *the west coast of the island* | *West Africa*
2 a west wind comes from the west

west³ *adv* (*written abbreviation* **W**) towards the west: *The window faces west.* | **[+of]** *The meeting took place in Rustenburg, 50 km west of Pretoria.*

westbound /'westbaʊnd/ *adj* travelling or leading towards the west: *westbound traffic*

westerly /'westəli $ -ərli/ *adj* **1** towards or in the west: *We set off in a westerly direction.* **2** a westerly wind comes from the west

western¹, Western /'westən $ -ərn/ *adj* (*written abbreviation* **W**) **1** in or from the west of a country or area: *the largest city in western Iowa* | *Western Australia* **2** in or from Europe or North America: *Western philosophies*

western², Western *n* [C] a film about life in the 19th century in the American West, especially about COWBOYS

westerner, Westerner /'westənə $ -tərnər/ *n* [C] someone from Europe or North America

westernize (*also* **-ise** *BrE*) /'westənaɪz $ -ər-/ *v* [T] if a country becomes westernized, it becomes like countries in North America and Western Europe —**westernization** /,westənaɪ'zeɪʃən $ -tərnə-/ *n* [U]

westernmost /'westənməʊst $ -tərnmoʊst/ *adj* furthest west: *the westernmost part of the island*

westwards /-wədz $ -wərdz/ (*also* **westward** /'westwəd $ -wərd/) *adv* towards the west: *The ship turned westwards.* —**westward** *adj*: *westward flights*

wet¹ /wet/ *adj*
1 covered in water or another liquid **OPP** dry: *wet clothes* | *I didn't want to get my hair wet.* | **soaking/dripping wet** (=extremely wet) *We arrived home soaking wet.* | *My jeans are wet through* (=completely wet).
2 a) rainy: *It's very wet outside.* **b) the wet** the rainy weather: *Come in out of the wet.*
3 not yet dry: *wet paint* —**wetness** *n* [U]

THESAURUS

wet covered in water or another liquid: *Don't sit on the grass – it's wet.* | *a wet towel*
damp slightly wet: *Clean the surfaces with a damp cloth.*
moist slightly wet, especially in a pleasant way – used about soil, food, or about someone's skin or eyes: *These plants like moist soil.* | *The cake was lovely and moist.*
soggy wet and soft in an unpleasant way – used especially about food or the ground: *a piece of soggy bread* | *The ground was soggy after all the rain.*
soaked/drenched very wet – used especially about people and their clothes: *We'll get soaked if we go out in this weather.* | *My clothes are drenched!*

---

wet² *v* [T] (*past tense and past participle* **wet** *or* **wetted**, *present participle* **wetting**) **1** to make something wet: *Wet this cloth and put it on her forehead.*
2 wet the bed/your pants etc to make your bed etc wet because you URINATE by accident

,wet 'blanket / $ '. ,.-/ *n* [singular] *informal* someone who spoils other people's enjoyment by not taking part in an activity

'wet suit *n* [C] rubber clothing that people wear to keep warm when swimming under water

we've /wɪv; *strong* wiːv/ the short form of 'we have': *We've got to leave soon.*

whack /wæk/ *v* [T] *informal* to hit someone or something hard —**whack** *n* [C]

whacked /wækt/ *adj spoken* very tired

whale /weɪl/ *n* [C] a very large animal that lives in the sea and looks like a fish → see picture on page A3

whaling /'weɪlɪŋ/ *n* [U] the activity of hunting whales —**whaler** *n* [C]

wharf /wɔːf $ wɔːrf/ n [C] (plural **wharves** /wɔːvz $ wɔːrvz/) a structure that is built out into the water so that boats can stop next to it SYN **pier**

what /wɒt $ wɑːt, wʌt/ determiner, pron
1 used to ask for information about something: *What are you doing?* | *What did Ellen say?* | *What kind of dog is that?*
2 used to talk about something that is not known or certain: *She asked them what they wanted for lunch.* | *Tell me what happened.* | **what to do/say/expect etc** *I'm not sure what to do.*
3 the thing which: *I like what you're saying.* | *What you need is a holiday.*
4 used at the beginning of a sentence to emphasize a description: *What an idiot!* | *What a nice day!*
5 what? *spoken* **a)** used to ask someone to repeat something they have just said because you did not hear it properly: *'Do you want a fried egg?' 'What?'*
b) used when you have heard someone calling to you and you are asking them what they want: *'Anita?' 'What?' 'Can you come here for a minute?'*
c) used when you are surprised or shocked → **guess what?** at GUESS[1], **so what?** at SO[1], **what about sb/sth?** at ABOUT[1]
PHRASES
... or what? *spoken* used to emphasize a question: *Are you afraid of him, or what?* | *Is she brilliant or what* (=she is brilliant)?
what if ...? *spoken* used to talk about something that might happen, especially something bad or frightening: *What if he got lost?*
what's more *spoken* used to add another thing to what you have just said, especially something interesting or surprising: *Gas is a very efficient fuel. What's more, it's clean.*
what's up (with sb/sth)? used to ask what is wrong with someone or something: *What's up with Denise?*
what with sth *spoken* used when you are giving the reasons for something, especially a bad situation: *I can't afford to run a car, what with petrol, insurance, and everything.*

whatever[1] /wɒtˈevə $ wɑːtˈevər, wʌt-/ determiner, pron
1 any or all of the things that are wanted, needed, or possible: *Just take whatever you need.* | *He needs whatever help he can get.*
2 used to say that it is not important what happens, what you do etc because it does not change the situation: *Whatever I say, she always disagrees.*
3 *spoken* used in a question when you are surprised or annoyed: *Whatever are you talking about?*
4 *spoken* used when you do not know exactly what something is: *He's doing Communication Studies, whatever that is.*
PHRASES
... or whatever *spoken* used to refer to other things of the same kind: *You can go swimming, scuba diving, or whatever.*

whatever[2] (also **whatsoever** /ˌwɒtsəʊˈevə $ -soʊˈevər, ˌwʌt-/) adv used to emphasize a negative statement: *She had no money whatsoever.*

wheat /wiːt/ n [U] a plant that produces grain

used for making flour, or this grain → **WHOLE WHEAT**

wheedle /ˈwiːdl/ v [I,T] to persuade someone to do something or give you something: *She managed to wheedle some money out of her parents.*

wheel[1] /wiːl/ n [C]
1 one of the round things under a car, bicycle etc that turn when it moves: **front/rear wheel** → see picture at **BICYCLE**
2 a STEERING WHEEL: *He had fallen asleep **at the wheel*** (=while driving).
3 a round object joined to a ROD in a machine, which turns when the machine operates: *a gear wheel*

wheel[2] v **1** [T] to move something that has wheels: *She wheeled her bike into the garage.* **2** [I] to turn around suddenly: **[+around]** *Anita wheeled around and started yelling at us.* → **WHEELING AND DEALING**

wheelbarrow /ˈwiːlˌbærəʊ $ -roʊ/ n [C] an open container with one wheel and two handles that you use outdoors to carry things, especially in the garden → see picture at **GARDEN**

wheelchair /ˈwiːltʃeə $ -tʃer/ n [C] a chair with large wheels, used by people who cannot walk → see picture at **CHAIR**[1]

'wheel clamp (also **clamp**) n [C] a metal object that is fastened to the wheel of an illegally parked car so that it cannot be driven away —**wheelclamp** v [T]

wheeler-'dealer n [C] someone in business or politics who uses complicated or slightly dishonest methods to achieve what they want

wheeling and 'dealing n [U] the making of complicated and sometimes dishonest deals, especially in business or politics

wheeze /wiːz/ v [I] to breathe with difficulty, making a noise in your throat and chest THESAURUS ► BREATHE —**wheezy** adj

when /wen/ adv, linking word
1 at what time: *When are we leaving?* | *When did you notice he was gone?* | **when to do sth** *I'll tell you when to stop.*
2 at or during the time that something happens: *He was nine when his father died.* | *He always wears glasses except when playing football.* | *The best moment was when Barnes scored the winning goal.*
3 after or as soon as something happens: *I'll phone you when I get home.*
4 even though something is true: *Why do you want a new camera when your old one's perfectly good?* → **since when** at SINCE

whenever /wenˈevə $ -ˈevər/ adv, linking word
1 every time: *Whenever we come here, we always see someone we know.*
2 at any time: *Come over whenever you want.* | *Use recycled paper **whenever possible**.*

where /weə $ wer/ adv, linking word
1 in or to which place: *Where do you live?* | *I think I know where he's gone.* | **where to do sth** *It's hard to know where to get help.*
2 used to talk about a particular place, or to give more information about it: *Stay right where you are.* |

W

In 1963 we moved to Boston, where my grandparents lived.
3 in or to any place SYN **wherever**: *You can sit where you like.*
4 used to talk about a part of a process or situation: *It had reached the point where both of us wanted a divorce.*

whereabouts¹ /ˌweərəˈbaʊts◂ $ ˈwerəbaʊts/ *adv* spoken used to ask about a place: *Whereabouts do you live?*

whereabouts² /ˈweərəbaʊts $ ˈwer-/ *n* [plural, U] the place where someone or something is: *His whereabouts are a mystery.*

whereas Ac /weərˈæz $ wer-/ *linking word, formal* used to say that one person, thing, or situation is different from another: *Nowadays the journey takes six hours, whereas then it took several weeks.*

whereby Ac /weəˈbaɪ $ wer-/ *adv formal* by or according to which: *a law whereby all children could receive free education*

wherein /weərˈɪn $ wer-/ *adv formal* in which place or part

whereupon /ˌweərəˈpɒn $ ˈwerəpɑːn, -pɔːn/ *linking word, formal* after which: *One of them called the other a liar, whereupon a fight broke out.*

wherever /weərˈevə $ werˈevər/ *adv, linking word*
1 in any place: *Sit wherever you like.*
2 in every place or situation: *I always have her picture with me wherever I go.* | *We try to use locally produced food wherever possible.*
3 spoken used in a question to show surprise: *Wherever did you find that old thing?*

wherewithal /ˈweəwɪðɔːl $ ˈwerwɪðɔːl/ *n* the wherewithal to do sth the money, skills etc you need in order to do something

whet /wet/ *v* (**whetted, whetting**) whet sb's appetite to make someone want more of something by letting them try it or see what it is like

whether /ˈweðə $ -ər/ *linking word*
1 used when talking about a choice you have to make or about something that is not certain: *He asked her whether she was coming.* | *I couldn't decide whether or not I wanted to go.* THESAURUS▸ IF
2 used to say that something definitely will or will not happen whatever the situation is: *Whether you like it or not, you have to take that test.*

whew /hjuː/ another spelling of PHEW

which /wɪtʃ/ *determiner, pron*
1 used to ask or talk about one or more members of a group of people or things, when you are uncertain about it or about them: *Which book is yours?* | [+of] *I don't know which of us was more scared.* | *I wondered which dress to buy.*
2 used to say what thing you are talking about, or to give more information about something: *I want a car which doesn't use too much petrol.* | *The house, which was built in the 16th century, is worth several million pounds.* | *One of the boys kept laughing, which annoyed Jane intensely.* | *She may have missed the train, in which case* (=if this has happened) *she won't arrive for another hour.*

Grammar
You can use both **which** and **what** when you are asking about one thing out of a number of possible things.
You use **which** when there is a small number of possibilities: *Which house does Tom live in?*
You use **what** when there is a very large number of possibilities: *What name have they given the baby?* | *What is the answer to question 12?*

---

whichever /wɪtʃˈevə $ -ˈevər/ *determiner, pron*
1 any of a group of things or people: *You can choose whichever one you like.*
2 used to say that it does not matter which thing or person is chosen because the result will be the same: *Whichever way you look at it, he's guilty.*

whiff /wɪf/ *n* [C] a slight smell: [+of] *As she walked past, I caught a whiff of her perfume* (=smelled it).

while¹ /waɪl/ *linking word*
1 during the time that something is happening: *They arrived while we were having dinner.* | *Thieves broke in while she was asleep.*
2 all the time that something is happening: *Would you look after the children while I go shopping?*
3 although: *While it was a good school, I was not happy there.*
4 used to say that one person, thing, or situation is different from another SYN **whereas**: *Schools in the north tend to be better equipped, while those in the south are relatively poor.*

while² *n* a while a period of time: **a short/little/long while** *He'll be back in a little while.* | *We talked on the phone for* **quite a while** (=a fairly long time). | *That hotel closed down* **a short while ago** (=not very long ago). → **(every) once in a while** at ONCE¹, **be worth sb's while** at WORTH¹

while³ *v* while away the hours/evenings/days etc to spend time in a pleasant and lazy way: *We whiled away the evenings playing cards.*

whilst /waɪlst/ *linking word especially BrE* while

whim /wɪm/ *n* [C] a sudden desire to do or have something, especially when there is no good reason for it: **on a whim** *I didn't just leave on a whim.*

whimper /ˈwɪmpə $ -ər/ *v* [I] to make low crying sounds, because you are sad or in pain: *The dog ran off whimpering.* —**whimper** *n* [C]

whimsical /ˈwɪmzɪkəl/ *adj* unusual or strange and often amusing: *his whimsical sense of humour*

whine /waɪn/ *v* [I] **1** to complain in a sad annoying voice about something: *Stop whining!* THESAURUS▸ COMPLAIN **2** to make a long high sound because you are sad or in pain: *He could hear the dog whining outside.* —**whine** *n* [C]

whinge /wɪndʒ/ *v* [I] (*present participle* **whinging** or **whingeing**) *BrE* to complain in an annoying way about something unimportant THESAURUS▸ COMPLAIN —**whinge** *n* [C]

whinny /ˈwɪni/ *v* [I] (**whinnied, whinnying, whinnies**) if a horse whinnies, it makes a high sound

whip¹ /wɪp/ *n* [C] a long thin piece of leather or

rope with a handle, used for making animals move faster or for hitting people as a punishment

whip² v (**whipped**, **whipping**) **1** [T] to hit a person or animal with a whip **2** (*also* **whip up**) [T] to mix cream or the clear part of an egg very hard until it becomes stiff **SYN** **beat**: *Whip the cream until thick.* **3** [I] to move quickly and violently: **[+round/across etc]** *A noise made him whip round.* **4** [T] to move or remove something with a quick sudden movement: **[+off/out/away]** *He whipped his gun out.*

PHRASAL VERBS

whip sb/sth ↔ **up 1** to try to make people feel strongly about something: *an attempt to whip up opposition to the plan* **2** *informal* to quickly make something n eat: *I could whip up a salad.*

'whip-round n **have a whip-round** *BrE informal* if a group of people have a whip-round, they all give some money so that they can buy something together

whir /wɜː $ wɜːr/ v the usual American spelling of WHIRR

whirl¹ /wɜːl $ wɜːrl/ v [I,T] to turn or spin around very quickly, or to make someone or something do this: *The leaves whirled around in the wind.* | *He whirled her around the dance floor.* **THESAURUS** TURN

whirl² n **1** [singular] a lot of activity of a particular kind: *the social whirl* | **[+of]** *The next two days passed in a whirl of activity.* **2** [C usually singular] a spinning movement or an amount of something that is spinning: **[+of]** *a whirl of dust*

PHRASES

give sth a whirl *informal* to try something that you are not sure you are going to like or be able to do: *It sounds like a great idea – let's give it a whirl.*

be in a whirl to feel very anxious or confused about something: *Debbie's head was all in a whirl.*

whirlpool /wɜːlpuːl $ 'wɜːrl-/ n [C] a powerful current of water that spins around and can pull things down into it

whirlwind /wɜːlˌwɪnd $ 'wɜːrl-/ n [C] **1** an extremely strong wind that moves quickly with a circular movement, causing a trail of damage **2 whirlwind romance/tour/campaign etc** something that happens or is done very quickly **3 a whirlwind of activity/work etc** a situation in which there is a lot of activity

whirr (*also* **whir** *AmE*) /wɜː $ wɜːr/ v [I] (**whirred**, **whirring**) if a machine whirrs, it makes a continuous low sound: *Helicopters whirred overhead.* —**whirr** n [singular]

whisk¹ /wɪsk/ v [T] **1** to mix liquid, eggs etc very quickly so that air is mixed in, using a fork or a whisk: *Whisk the yolks in a bowl.* **2** to take someone or something somewhere quickly: *They whisked her off to hospital.*

whisk² n [C] a small kitchen tool made of curved pieces of wire, used for whisking eggs, cream etc

whisker /wɪskə $ -ər/ n [C] **1** one of the long stiff hairs that grow near the mouth of a cat, mouse etc **2 whiskers** [plural] the hair that grows on a man's face

whisky, **whiskey** /wɪski/ n [C,U] (*plural* **whiskies** or **whiskeys**) a strong alcoholic drink made from grain, or a glass of this

whisper /wɪspə $ -ər/ v **1** [I,T] to say something very quietly, using your breath rather than your voice: **whisper sth to sb** *He leaned over to whisper something to her.* | *'I've missed you,' she whispered in my ear.* **THESAURUS** TALK **2** [I] *literary* to make a soft sound like a whisper: *The wind whispered in the trees.* —**whisper** n [C]: *He spoke in a whisper.*

whistle¹ /wɪsəl/ v **1** [I,T] to make a high or musical sound by blowing air out through your lips: **[+to]** *The man whistled to his dog.* | *He whistled a tune as he strolled home.* | *Janet whistled softly (=because she was shocked and impressed). 'That's pretty expensive!'* **2** [I] to move quickly, making a whistling sound: **[+through]** *Bullets were whistling through the air.* **3** [I] to make a high sound when air or steam is forced through a small hole: *a whistling kettle*

whistle² n [C] **1** a small object that produces a high sound when you blow into it: *The referee* **blew** *his* **whistle**. **2** a high sound made by blowing air through a whistle, your lips etc: *a piercing whistle*

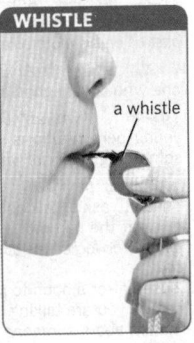

WHISTLE

a whistle

white¹ /waɪt/ adj **1** **COLOUR** having the colour of milk, snow, or salt: *white paint* **2** **PEOPLE** (*also* **White**) belonging to the race of people with pale skin → **black**: *Most of the students in this class are white.* **3** **PALE** looking pale, because of illness, strong emotion etc: *Her face* **went white**. | *Are you OK? You're* **as white as a sheet**. **4** **COFFEE** *BrE* white coffee has milk or cream in it → **black** **5** **WINE** white wine is a clear pale yellow colour → **red** —**whiteness** n [U]

white² n **1** [U] a white colour: *She was dressed in white.* **2** (*also* **White**) [C] someone who belongs to the race of people with pale skins → **black** **3** [C,U] the part of an egg which surrounds the YOLK (=yellow part), and becomes white when cooked

whiteboard /waɪtbɔːd $ -bɔːrd/ n [C] a large board with a white smooth surface that teachers write on → see picture at CLASSROOM

white-'collar adj [only before noun] white-collar workers do jobs in offices, banks etc → **blue-collar**

white 'elephant n [C] something that is not at all useful, although it may have cost a lot of money

'White House n **the White House** used to refer to the president of the US and the people who advise him: *The White House has refused to comment.* | *White House officials*

W

‚white 'lie n [C] a lie that you tell someone in order to protect them or avoid hurting their feelings

whiten /'waɪtn/ v [I,T] to make something white, or to become white

whitewash /'waɪtwɒʃ $ -wɒːʃ, -wɑːʃ/ n 1 [C usually singular] a report or examination of events that hides the true facts about something so that the person who is responsible will not be punished: *The newspapers are calling the report a whitewash.* 2 [U] a white liquid used for painting walls —**whitewash** v [T]

whittle /'wɪtl/ v 1 [I,T] to cut a piece of wood into a particular shape by cutting off small pieces 2 (also **whittle down**) [T] to gradually make something smaller by taking parts away: *I've whittled down the list of guests from 30 to 16.*

PHRASAL VERBS

whittle away to gradually make something smaller or less effective: **whittle sth ↔ away** *His power has been slowly whittled away.*

whizz¹ BrE, **whiz** AmE /wɪz/ v [I] *informal* to move very quickly: **[+past/by/through etc]** *Marty whizzed past us on his motorbike.*

whizz² BrE, **whiz** AmE n [singular] *informal* someone who is very good at doing something

whizzkid /'wɪzkɪd/ BrE, **'whiz kid** AmE n [C] a young person who is very skilled or successful at something: *financial whizzkids*

who /huː/ pron
1 used to ask or talk about which person is involved, or what the name of a person is: *Who do you work for? | Who locked the door? | I know who sent you that card.*
2 used after a noun to show which person or which people you are talking about, or to add more information about someone: *That's the woman who owns the house. | She asked her English teacher, who had studied at Oxford.*

whoa /wəʊ, həʊ $ woʊ, hoʊ/ *spoken* 1 said when you think something is impressive 2 used to tell someone to do something more slowly

who'd /huːd/ the short form of 'who had' or 'who would': *a young girl who'd been attacked*

whodunit, whodunnit /ˌhuːˈdʌnɪt/ n [C] a book, film etc about a murder, in which you do not find out who the killer is until the end

whoever /huːˈevə $ -ˈevər/ pron
1 used to talk about a specific person or people, although you do not know who they are: *Whoever did this is in big trouble.*
2 used to say that it does not matter who does something, is in a particular place etc: *Whoever gets there first can find a table.*
3 used in a question to show surprise: *Whoever would do a thing like that to an old woman?*

whole¹ /həʊl $ hoʊl/ adj
1 all of something → **entire**: *She drank a whole bottle of wine. | He had not told her **the whole truth**.*
2 not divided or broken into parts: *These birds swallow fish whole.*

PHRASES

a whole lot 1 very much: *I'm feeling a whole lot*

better. **2** a large quantity or number: **[+of]** *I've got a whole lot of problems.*

whole² n **the whole of sth** all of something: *The whole of my body ached.*

PHRASES

as a whole used to say that all the parts of something are being considered: *We must look at our educational system as a whole.*

on the whole generally or usually: *On the whole, life was much quieter after John left.*

wholefood /'həʊlfuːd $ 'hoʊl-/ n [U] food that does not contain harmful chemicals and artificial things, and is as natural as possible

wholehearted /ˌhəʊlˈhɑːtɪd◀ $ ˌhoʊlˈhɑːr-/ adj **wholehearted support/approval/co-operation etc** complete support, approval etc: *The plans met with our wholehearted approval.* —**wholeheartedly** adv

wholemeal /'həʊlmiːl $ 'hoʊl-/ adj BrE wholemeal flour or bread uses all of the grain, including the outside layer **SYN** whole wheat AmE

‚whole 'number n [C] a number such as 0, 1, 2 etc, not part of a number

wholesale /'həʊlseɪl $ 'hoʊl-/ adj 1 relating to the business of selling goods in large quantities at low prices to other businesses, rather than to the general public → **retail**: *wholesale prices* 2 affecting a lot of things or people, often in a bad way: *the wholesale destruction of the rainforest* —**wholesale** adv

wholesaler /'həʊlˌseɪlə $ 'hoʊlˌseɪlər/ n [C] a person or company that buys goods in large quantities and sells them to other businesses

wholesome /'həʊlsəm $ 'hoʊl-/ adj 1 good for your health: *a good wholesome breakfast* 2 morally good, or having a good moral effect: *good wholesome fun*

'whole wheat adj AmE whole wheat flour or bread uses all of the grain, including the outside layer **SYN** wholemeal BrE

who'll /huːl/ the short form of 'who will' and 'who shall': *Who'll be next?*

wholly /'həʊl-li $ 'hoʊl-/ adv formal completely: *The rumours are wholly untrue.*

whom /huːm/ pron
1 **many/all/some etc of whom** many, all etc of the people just mentioned: *They had four sons, one of whom died young.*
2 formal the object form of 'who': *To whom was the letter addressed?*

Grammar
You use **whom** only in written English and in very formal spoken English.

whoop /wuːp, huːp/ v [I] to shout loudly and happily —**whoop** n [C]

whooping cough /'huːpɪŋ kɒf $ -kɒːf/ n [U] a serious disease that mainly affects children, in which you make a loud noise after you cough

whoops /wʊps/ *spoken* used when you make a small mistake, drop something, or fall

whoosh /wʊʃ $ wuːʃ/ n [C] a sound like air or water moving very fast —**whoosh** v [I]

whopper /ˈwɒpə $ ˈwɑːpər/ n [C] *informal* something that is unusually large

whopping /ˈwɒpɪŋ $ ˈwɑː-/ adj [only before noun] *informal* very large: *a whopping fee*

who're /ˈhuːə $ ˈhuːər/ the short form of 'who are': *Who're those two guys?*

who's /huːz/ the short form of 'who is' or 'who has': *Who's sitting next to Reggie? | That's Karl, the guy who's come over from Germany.*

whose /huːz/ determiner, pron
1 used to ask which person or people a particular thing belongs to: *Whose jacket is this?*
2 used to say which person or thing you mean, or to add more information about a person or thing, by talking about something belonging to them: *families whose relatives have been killed | Jurors, whose identities will be kept secret, will be paid $40 a day.*

who've /huːv/ the short form of 'who have': *people who've been in prison*

why /waɪ/ adv, linking word used to ask or talk about the reason for something: *Why are these books so cheap? | I think I know why I didn't get the job. | Tell me the **reason why** you're leaving.*
PHRASES
why don't you/why not ... etc *spoken* used to make a suggestion: *Why don't you try this one? | Why not relax and enjoy yourself?*
why not? *spoken* used to agree with a suggestion or invitation: *'Do you want to come along?' 'Yeah, why not?'*

wick /wɪk/ n [C] the string that burns in a CANDLE or in an oil lamp

wicked /ˈwɪkɪd/ adj
1 very bad or evil: *the wicked stepmother in 'Cinderella'*
2 behaving badly in a way that is amusing → **mischievous**: *a wicked grin*
3 *spoken informal* very good: *That's a wicked bike!*
—**wickedness** n [U] —**wickedly** adv

wicker /ˈwɪkə $ -ər/ n [U] a material made from thin dry branches or stems woven together: *a wicker chair*

wicket /ˈwɪkɪt/ n [C] one of the sets of sticks that the BOWLER tries to hit with the ball in CRICKET

wide¹ /waɪd/ adj
1 measuring a large distance from one side to the other OPP **narrow** SYN **broad**: *a wide street | a wide grin | The earthquake was felt over a wide area.* → see Word Choice at **BROAD**
2 measuring a particular distance from one side to the other: **three feet/five metres etc wide** *The bathtub's three feet wide. | How wide is this room?*
3 including a large variety of different people, things etc: *We offer a **wide range** of vegetarian dishes.*
4 wide difference/gap etc a large and noticeable difference etc: *wide differences of opinion*
5 *literary* wide eyes are fully open, especially when someone is very surprised, excited, or frightened: *Her eyes grew wide in anticipation.*
6 wider wider problems, questions, or parts of a situation are more general and often more important: *The trial also raises a much wider issue.*

PHRASES
wide of the mark incorrect: *Their forecasts were hopelessly wide of the mark.*

wide² adv
1 if you open something wide, you open it as far as possible: *The windows had been opened wide. | Somebody left the door **wide open**. | He stood with his legs **wide apart**.*
2 be wide awake to be completely awake
3 away from the point that you were aiming at: *His shot went wide.*

wide-'eyed adj, adv **1** with your eyes wide open, especially because you are surprised or frightened: *a look of wide-eyed amazement* **2** too willing to believe, accept, or admire things because you do not have much experience of life: *wide-eyed innocence*

widely /ˈwaɪdli/ adv
1 in a lot of different places or by a lot of people: *products that are widely available | a widely read newspaper*
2 to a large degree: *Taxes **vary widely** from state to state.*

widen /ˈwaɪdn/ v [I,T] **1** to become wider, or to make something wider → **narrow**: *They're widening the road.* **2** to become greater or larger, or to make something do this → **narrow**: *The gap between rich and poor began to widen.*

wide-'ranging adj including a lot of different subjects, things, or people: *a wide-ranging discussion*

widescreen /ˈwaɪdskriːn/ adj a widescreen television is much wider than it is high

widespread Ac /ˈwaɪdspred/ adj happening in many places, among many people, or in many situations: *the **widespread use** of illegal drugs*

widow /ˈwɪdəʊ $ -doʊ/ n [C] a woman whose husband has died and who has not married again

widowed /ˈwɪdəʊd $ -doʊd/ adj **be widowed** if someone is widowed, their husband or wife dies
THESAURUS MARRIED

widower /ˈwɪdəʊə $ -doʊər/ n [C] a man whose wife has died and who has not married again

width /wɪdθ/ n [C,U] the distance from one side of something to the other → **length, breadth**: [+of] *the width of the window | a width of 10 inches | **two feet/three metres etc in width** It's about six metres in width.* → see picture at DIMENSION

wield /wiːld/ v [T] **1 wield power/influence/authority etc** to have a lot of power, influence etc and to use it: *the influence wielded by the church* **2** to use or hold a weapon or tool

wiener /ˈwiːnə $ -ər/ n [C] *AmE* a type of SAUSAGE

wife /waɪf/ n [C] (*plural* **wives** /waɪvz/) the woman that a man is married to → **husband**

wi-fi /ˈwaɪ faɪ/ n [U] a way of connecting computers or other electronic machines to a network using radio signals rather than wires

wig /wɪɡ/ n [C] artificial hair that you wear on your head

wiggle /ˈwɪɡəl/ v [I,T] to make small movements

from side to side or up and down, or to make something move this way: *Jo **wiggled** her **toes**.*
—**wiggle** *n* [C]

wigwam /'wɪgwæm $ -wɑːm/ *n* [C] a round tent used by some Native Americans

wild¹ /waɪld/ *adj*

1 ANIMALS/PLANTS wild animals and plants live or grow in natural conditions, without being changed or controlled by people → **tame**: *wild horses | wild flowers | wild mushrooms* THESAURUS NATURAL

2 LAND a wild area of land is in a completely natural state and does not have farms, towns etc on it: *the wild and beautiful landscape of Nepal*

3 STRONG FEELINGS feeling or expressing strong uncontrolled emotions, especially anger, happiness, or excitement: **[+with]** *He was wild with rage. | A **wild** look (=crazy look) came into her eyes. | The audience **went wild** (=they became very excited).*

4 BEHAVIOUR behaving in an uncontrolled way and not doing what other people tell you to do: *a wild teenager*

5 NOT CORRECT/TRUE [only before noun] done or said without thinking carefully or without knowing all the facts: *Take a **wild** guess. | wild accusations*

6 STORMY stormy and windy: *a wild night*

PHRASES

| **be wild about sb/sth** *spoken* to like someone or something very much: *I'm not wild about rap music.*

wild² *adv*

PHRASES

| **grow wild** if plants grow wild somewhere, they have not been planted by people
| **run wild** to behave in a very free way, without enough control: *Left on their own, the boys ran wild.*

wild³ *n* **1 in the wild** in natural conditions, without being changed or controlled by people: *animals in the wild* **2 the wilds** areas where there are no towns and not many people live: **[+of]** *the wilds of Canada*

wilderness /'wɪldənəs $ -dər-/ *n* [singular, U] a large natural area of land that has never been built on: *the Alaskan wilderness*

wildfire /'waɪldfaɪə $ -faɪr/ *n* [C,U] a fire that moves quickly and cannot be controlled → **spread like wildfire** at SPREAD¹

,wild 'goose ,chase *n* [singular] a situation in which you waste a lot of time looking for something that cannot be found

wildlife /'waɪldlaɪf/ *n* [U] animals and plants living in natural conditions

wildly /'waɪldli/ *adv* **1** in a very uncontrolled or excited way: *The audience cheered wildly.* **2** extremely: *wildly successful*

wiles /waɪlz/ *n* [plural] clever talk or tricks used to persuade someone to do what you want: *Men could not resist her **feminine** wiles.*

wilful *BrE*, **willful** *AmE* /'wɪlfəl/ *adj* **1 wilful damage/neglect etc** deliberate damage etc, when you know that what you are doing is wrong **2** doing what you want even though people tell you not to: *a wilful child* —**wilfully** *adv*

will¹ /wɪl/ *modal verb* (*negative short form* **won't**)

1 used to make future tenses: *I'm sure that will be OK. | What time will you arrive? | We'll call you later. | I hope she won't be angry.*

2 used to say that someone is willing or ready to do something, or that something is able to do something: *Dr Weir will see you now. | Sue won't agree. | The car won't start.*

3 used to ask someone to do something, or to offer something to someone: *Will you help me carry this? | Won't you have a cup of tea?*

4 used to say what always happens or what is generally true: *Some people will always complain.*

5 used to say that you think that something is true: *'Someone's at the door.' '**That'll** (=that will) be Nick.'*

6 used to describe someone's habits, especially when you think that they are annoying: *He **will keep on** whistling.*

will² *n*

1 [C,U] determination to do something that you have decided to do: **will to do sth** *I had lost the **will** to live. | She had a very **strong** will.*

2 [C] a legal document that says who you want your money and property to be given to after you die: *Have you **made** a will? | **in sb's will** Grandpa **left** me $7,000 **in** his **will**.*

3 [singular] what someone wants to happen in a particular situation: **[+of]** *the will of the people |* **against sb's will** (=when someone is forced to do something that they do not want to do) *Lucy was kept there against her will.* → **FREE WILL, ILL WILL**

PHRASES

| **at will** whenever you want and in whatever way you want: *He can't just fire people at will.*

will³ *v* [T] to try to make something happen by thinking about it very hard: **will sb/sth to do sth** *The crowd were all willing her to win.*

willful /'wɪlfəl/ *adj* the American spelling of WILFUL

willing /'wɪlɪŋ/ *adj*

1 be willing to do sth if you are willing to do something, you will agree to do it if someone asks you: *Are you willing to help? |* **quite/perfectly willing** *I'm perfectly willing to try.*

2 eager and wanting to do something very much: *willing helpers | a willing volunteer* —**willingly** *adv*: *I would willingly have accepted.* —**willingness** *n* [U]

willow /'wɪləʊ $ -loʊ/ *n* [C] a tree with very long thin branches that grows near water

willowy /'wɪləʊi $ -loʊi/ *adj* tall, thin, and graceful: *her young, willowy figure*

willpower /'wɪl,paʊə $ -,paʊr/ *n* [U] the ability to control your mind and body in order to do something: *It took all his willpower to remain calm.*

willy-nilly /,wɪli 'nɪli/ *adv* **1** if something happens willy-nilly, it happens whether you want it to or not **2** without planning

wilt /wɪlt/ v [I] if a plant wilts, it bends over because it is too dry or old

WILT

wily /'waɪli/ adj clever at getting what you want, especially by tricking people SYN **cunning**

wimp /wɪmp/ n [C] *informal disapproving* someone who is afraid to do anything that is slightly dangerous —**wimpish, wimpy** *adj*

win¹ /wɪn/ v (*past tense and past participle* **won** /wʌn/, *present participle* **winning**)
1 [I,T] to be the best or most successful in a competition, game, election etc OPP **lose**: *Who do you think will win the election?* | *Argentina won the World Cup that year.* | [+at] *I never win at cards.*
2 [T] to get something as a prize for winning in a competition or game: *He* **won** *a gold* **medal**. | *I won $200.*
3 [T] to get something good because of your efforts or abilities SYN **gain**: **win sb's approval/support/ trust etc** *Knight quickly won the respect of his colleagues.*
PHRASES
sb can't win *spoken* used to say that there is no satisfactory way of dealing with a particular situation: *We took the kids to California, and they complained it wasn't warm enough. You can't win, can you?*

PHRASAL VERBS
win sb ↔ **over** (*also* **win** sb ↔ **round/around** *BrE*) to persuade someone to agree with you, support you, or like you: *their attempt to win over voters*

THESAURUS

win to be the best or most successful in a competition, game, election etc: *Our team won 3–0.* | *Alex won the poetry competition.*
come first/be first to win a race or competition in which more than two people or teams are competing: *An Australian runner came first.*
be in the lead/be leading/be ahead to be winning a game, race, election etc at a particular moment: *Hamilton was in the lead.* | *Arsenal were ahead by two goals to one at the beginning of the second half.*
beat/defeat to win a game, battle, election etc against another person, army, party etc. **Beat** is more informal than **defeat**: *Brazil beat Italy 3–1.* | *Hitler's army was defeated by the Russians.*

win² n [C] a success or victory, especially in sport OPP **defeat**: [+over] *Ireland's 2–1 win over France*

wince /wɪns/ v [I] to suddenly change the expression on your face when you see or remember something painful or embarrassing

winch /wɪntʃ/ n [C] a machine with a rope or chain used for lifting heavy objects —**winch** v [T]

wind¹ /wɪnd/ n
1 (*also* **the wind**) [C,U] a natural current of air: *An icy wind was blowing.* | *The trees were swaying in the wind.* → RAIN¹, SNOW¹, SUN¹, WEATHER¹
2 [U] *BrE* when you have a lot of air in your stomach SYN **gas** *AmE*: *Baked beans always* **give** *me* **wind**.
3 [U] your ability to breathe properly: *I need to get my wind back.* → **your second wind** at SECOND¹
4 the wind section the people in an ORCHESTRA who play WIND INSTRUMENTS
PHRASES
get wind of sth to hear or find out about something secret or private: *Then the local press got wind of the affair.*

COLLOCATIONS

adjectives
a strong/high wind *A strong wind was bending the trees.*
a light wind (=not strong) *The wind was light and the sea was calm.*
a cold/icy/bitter wind *Protect the young plants from cold winds.*
a 20-/40- etc mile-an-hour wind *The walkers struggled in 35-mile-an-hour winds.*
the north/south etc wind (=coming from the north, south etc) *There was an east wind blowing.*

verbs
the wind blows *The wind was blowing from the north.*
the wind picks up (=becomes stronger) *The wind was starting to pick up.*
the wind drops/dies down (=becomes less strong) *The wind had dropped at last.*
the wind howls (=makes a lot of noise) *The wind howled all night.*

noun + wind
a gust of wind (=a strong movement of wind) *A gust of wind blew the door shut.*

THESAURUS

wind a natural current of air: *A strong wind was blowing from the north.*
breeze a gentle pleasant wind: *It was cooler in the evening, with a slight breeze.*
gale a very strong wind: *There are warnings of gales and icy conditions.*
storm a period of bad weather with a lot of wind and rain, snow etc: *Across the country, trees came down in the storm.*
hurricane a very bad storm with extremely fast winds, that starts in the Western Atlantic Ocean: *Many people were killed in the hurricane that struck Texas.*

wind² /waɪnd/ v (*past tense and past participle* **wound** /waʊnd/)
1 TURN STH AROUND [I,T] to turn or twist something long and thin several times, especially around something else: **wind sth around/round sth** *Wind the bandage around her arm.*
2 CLOCK/MACHINE/TOY (*also* **wind up**) [T] to make a

W

clock, machine, or toy etc work by turning a small handle several times

3 ROAD/RIVER [I] if a road, river etc winds somewhere, it has many smooth bends and is usually very long: *The road wound up into the hills.*

4 TAPE [T] to make a video CASSETTE tape go forwards or backwards

PHRASAL VERBS

wind down

1 wind sth ↔ **down** to gradually reduce the work of a business or organization so that it can be closed down completely

2 to rest and relax after a lot of hard work or excitement: *It's difficult to wind down after work.*

3 wind sth ↔ **down** BrE to make something, especially a car window, move down by turning a handle or pressing a button

wind up

1 to be in an unpleasant situation or place after a lot has happened: *He wound up in prison.*

2 wind sth ↔ **up** to end an activity, meeting etc: *Let's wind things up.*

3 wind sb ↔ **up** BrE to say something that will annoy or worry someone, as a joke

4 wind sth ↔ **up** BrE to make something, especially a car window, move up by turning a handle or pressing a button

wind³ /wɪnd/ v [T] if a fall, a blow, or exercise winds you, it causes you to have difficulty breathing —**winded** adj

windchill /ˈwɪndˌtʃɪl/ n [U] technical the cold effect of the wind

windfall /ˈwɪndfɔːl $ -fɒːl/ n [C] money that you get unexpectedly

winding /ˈwaɪndɪŋ/ adj curving or bending many times: *a winding path*

wind instrument /ˈwɪnd ˌɪnstrəmənt/ n [C] a musical instrument that you play by blowing into it

windmill /ˈwɪndˌmɪl/ n [C] a building or structure with parts that turn around in the wind, used for producing electrical power or crushing grain

window /ˈwɪndəʊ $ -doʊ/ n [C]

1 an area of glass in the wall of a building or vehicle that lets in light: *Let's open a window.* | *She looked out of the window.* | *a shop window* → BAY WINDOW, FRENCH WINDOWS

2 one of the areas on a computer screen where different programs operate

'window box n [C] a long narrow container attached to the bottom of a window, used for growing plants

windowpane /ˈwɪndəʊˌpeɪn $ -doʊ-/ n [C] a single whole piece of glass in a window

'window ˌshopping n [U] when you look at goods in shop windows without intending to buy them

windowsill /ˈwɪndəʊˌsɪl $ -doʊ-/ (also **'window ledge**) n [C] the shelf at the bottom of a window

windpipe /ˈwɪndpaɪp/ n [C] the tube through which air passes from your mouth to your lungs

windscreen BrE /ˈwɪndskriːn/, **windshield** AmE /-ʃiːld/ n [C] the large window at the front of a car, bus etc → see picture at CAR

WINDOWS

bay window

skylight

French windows

'windscreen ˌwiper BrE, **'windshield ˌwiper** AmE n [C] a long piece of metal with a rubber edge that moves across a windscreen to remove the rain → see picture at CAR

windsurfing /ˈwɪndsɜːfɪŋ $ -ɜːr-/ n [U] the sport of sailing across water by standing on a special board and holding onto a large sail → see picture at SURF¹ —**windsurfer** n [C]

windswept /ˈwɪndswept/ adj a windswept place is often very windy and has few trees or buildings

windy /ˈwɪndi/ adj if it is windy, there is a lot of wind: *a windy day*

wine¹ /waɪn/ n [C,U] an alcoholic drink made from GRAPES: *The waiter brought a bottle of red wine.*

wine² v **wine and dine sb** to entertain someone with good food, wine etc

winery /ˈwaɪnəri/ n [C] (plural **wineries**) a place where wine is made and kept

wing /wɪŋ/ n [C]

1 ON A BIRD/INSECT one of the parts of a bird's or insect's body that it moves in order to fly: *ducks flapping their wings*

2 ON A PLANE one of the two flat parts that stick out from the side of a plane and help it stay in the air → see picture at AEROPLANE

3 OF A BUILDING one of the parts of a large building, especially one that sticks out from the main part: *the east wing of the palace* | *the hospital's maternity wing*

4 IN POLITICS a group of people within a political party who have particular opinions or aims: *the liberal wing of the party* → LEFT-WING, RIGHT-WING

5 IN SPORT **a)** someone who plays on the far left or far right of the field in games such as football **b)** the far left or far right of a sports field

6 OF A CAR BrE the part of a car that is above a wheel SYN **fender** AmE → see picture at CAR

7 OF A STAGE **the wings** [plural] the parts at either side of a stage where the actors cannot be seen

W

PHRASES

(waiting) in the wings ready to do something or be used when the time is right: *Several junior managers are waiting in the wings for promotion.*

take sb under your wing to help or protect someone who is younger or less experienced than you: *Anna had taken the younger singer under her wing.*

winged /wɪŋd/ *adj* having wings: *winged insects*

wingspan /ˈwɪŋspæn/ *n* [C] the distance from the end of one wing to the end of the other

wink /wɪŋk/ *v* [I] if you wink at someone, you look towards them and quickly close and open one eye, in order to show them that you are joking or being friendly, or as a signal —**wink** *n* [C]: *She gave me a little wink.*

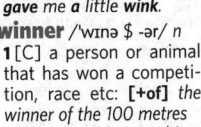

WINK

winner /ˈwɪnə $ -ər/ *n*
1 [C] a person or animal that has won a competition, race etc: **[+of]** *the winner of the 100 metres*
2 [C] *informal* something that is, or is likely to be, very popular and successful: *His latest book is another winner.*
3 [singular] a GOAL or point that makes someone win a game of tennis, football etc: *Moran scored the winner.*

winning /ˈwɪnɪŋ/ *adj* [only before noun] **1** the winning person or thing is the one that wins a competition or game: *the winning goal* **2** making someone attractive or making something successful: *a winning smile* | *As a business, they have found a winning formula.* → **a winning streak** at STREAK[1]

winnings /ˈwɪnɪŋz/ *n* [plural] money that you win in a game or competition

wino /ˈwaɪnəʊ $ -noʊ/ *n* [C] (*plural* **winos**) *informal* someone who drinks a lot of alcohol and lives on the streets

winter[1] /ˈwɪntə $ -ər/ *n* [C,U] the season after autumn and before spring, when the weather is coldest → **summer**: **in (the) winter** *It often snows in winter.* | *The lake froze last winter.*

COLLOCATIONS

adjectives

a cold winter *We had a very cold winter that year.*

a severe/harsh winter (=very cold) *Winters here are harsh and few plants can survive.*

a mild winter (=not very cold) *Some birds do not migrate in mild winters.*

winter + noun

the winter months *They lit fires to keep warm during the winter months.*

a winter night/evening *You need a good book to read on long winter evenings.*

winter sports (=skiing, sledging etc) *Many people come to these mountains to take part in winter sports.*

noun + winter

the depths of winter (=the middle of winter) *He never wore a coat, even in the depths of winter.*

winter[2] *v* [I] *formal* to spend the winter somewhere: *The birds usually winter in southern France and Spain.*

wintertime /ˈwɪntətaɪm $ -ər-/ *n* [U] the time of year when it is winter

wintry /ˈwɪntri/ *adj* typical of winter, especially because it is cold or snowing: *wintry weather*

win-'win *adj* [only before noun] a win-win situation is one that will be successful for everyone involved

wipe /waɪp/ *v* [T]
1 to remove liquid or dirt from a surface, especially using a cloth or your hand: **wipe sth with/on sth** *She wiped her eyes* (=removed the tears from her eyes) *with the back of her hand.* | **wipe sth from/off sth** *He wiped the sweat from his face.* | *Quickly, she wiped away her tears.* **THESAURUS** CLEAN
2 to remove all the information that is stored on a tape, video, or computer DISK —**wipe** *n* [C]

PHRASAL VERBS

wipe sth ↔ **down** to clean a surface completely, using a wet cloth

wipe sth ↔ **out** to destroy something completely: *Whole villages were wiped out by the floods.*

wipe sth ↔ **up** to remove liquid from a surface, using a cloth: *Could you wipe that mess up?*

wiper /ˈwaɪpə $ -ər/ *n* [C] a WINDSCREEN WIPER

wire[1] /waɪə $ waɪr/ *n*
1 [C,U] thin metal in the form of a thread, or a piece of this: *a wire fence* → **BARBED WIRE**
2 [C] a piece of metal like this, used for carrying electrical currents or signals: *electrical wires* | *telephone wires*

wire[2] *v* [T] **1** (*also* **wire up**) **a)** to connect wires inside a building or piece of equipment so that electricity can pass through: *instructions on how to wire a plug* **b)** to connect electrical equipment to the electricity supply, using wires: *I've wired up the speakers.* **2** to send money electronically: *Could you wire me $50?* **3** to fasten two or more things together using wire

wireless /ˈwaɪələs $ ˈwaɪr-/ *n* [C] *old-fashioned* a radio

wiring /ˈwaɪərɪŋ $ ˈwaɪr-/ *n* [U] the system of wires that carries electricity in a building, vehicle, or piece of equipment

wiry /ˈwaɪəri $ ˈwaɪri/ *adj* **1** someone who is wiry is thin but strong **2** wiry hair is stiff and curly

wisdom /ˈwɪzdəm/ *n*
1 [U] the ability to use your knowledge and experience of life to make good decisions and give good advice
2 the wisdom of sth whether something is sensible: *Some people doubted the wisdom of his decision.*

'wisdom tooth *n* [C] one of the four large teeth at the back of an adult's mouth

wise¹ /waɪz/ *adj*

1 a wise decision or action is sensible: **it is wise to do sth** *It would be wise to phone first.* **THESAURUS** INTELLIGENT

2 a wise person is able to use their knowledge and experience of life to make good decisions and give good advice: *He's **older and wiser** now.*

3 work-wise/price-wise/time-wise etc used to refer to a particular feature of a situation: *How are you managing money-wise?* —**wisely** *adv*

PHRASES

be none the wiser to not understand or know something even after it has been explained to you: *He tried to explain, but I was still none the wiser.*

wise² *v*

PHRASAL VERBS

wise up *informal* to realize the truth about a bad situation

wisecrack /ˈwaɪzkræk/ *n* [C] a quick, funny, and often slightly unkind remark

wish¹ /wɪʃ/ *v*

1 [T] to want something to be true, although you know it is impossible or unlikely: **[+(that)]** *I wish you hadn't invited him.* | *I wish I didn't have to go to work.* | *We wish we could have done more.* | *She wished Katie would stop crying.* **THESAURUS** WANT

2 [I,T] *formal* to want to do something: **wish to do sth** *I wish to make a complaint.* | *You may go, if you wish.*

3 [T] to say that you hope someone will be happy, successful, lucky etc: **wish sb sth** *They **wished** us a **happy Christmas**.* | *I **wish** you **luck**.*

4 [I] if you wish for something, you want it to happen or want to have it, although it seems unlikely or impossible: **[+for]** *It's no use **wishing for the impossible**.*

wish² *n* [C] a desire, or what someone wants to do or to happen: **wish to do sth** *her wish to emigrate* | **against sb's wishes** *He left school against his parents' wishes* (=his parents did not want him to leave school).

PHRASES

best/good/warmest etc wishes used, especially in cards and letters, to say that you hope someone will be happy, successful, or healthy: **[+for]** *Best wishes for your retirement!* | *Please **give** my best **wishes** to your parents.* | **(with) best wishes** (=used at the end of a letter before you sign your name) *With best wishes, Amy.*

COLLOCATIONS

verbs

to have no wish to do sth *formal I have no wish to upset them.*

to respect sb's wishes (=to do what someone wants) *A doctor should respect the wishes of his patient.*

to make a wish (=to silently ask for something to happen) *Close your eyes and make a wish.*

to get your wish (=to get what you want) *He wanted a baby sister, and he got his wish.*

to grant sb's wish (=to give someone what they want) *Now our wish has been granted.*

sb's wish comes true (=the thing that someone wants happens) *I hope all your wishes come true.*

adjectives

sb's greatest/deepest wish (*also* **sb's dearest wish** *BrE*) (=what someone wants most of all) *His greatest wish was to be a good father.*

sb's last/final/dying wish *Her last wish was to be buried in her husband's grave.*

wishful ˈthinking *n* [U] when you hope that something good will happen, when it is not possible

wishy-washy /ˈwɪʃi ˌwɒʃi $ -ˌwɔːʃi, -ˌwɑːʃi/ *adj informal disapproving* without any firm or clear ideas: *wishy-washy liberals*

wisp /wɪsp/ *n* [C] **1** a wisp of hair, grass, HAY etc is a thin piece of it that is separate from the rest **2** a wisp of smoke, cloud, steam etc is a small thin line of it that rises upwards —**wispy** *adj*

wistful /ˈwɪstfəl/ *adj* a little sad because you cannot have something you want: *a wistful smile* —**wistfully** *adv*

wit /wɪt/ *n*

1 [U] the ability to say things that are clever and amusing: *a woman of great wit*

2 wits [plural] your ability to think quickly and make good decisions: **keep/have your wits about you** (=be ready to think quickly to deal with any problems)

PHRASES

be at your wits' end to be very upset and not know what to do because you have tried everything possible to solve a problem: *I'm at my wits' end trying to fix this computer.*

frighten/scare/terrify sb out of their wits *informal* to frighten someone very much: *I was terrified out of my wits.*

witch /wɪtʃ/ *n* [C] a woman who is believed to have magic powers, especially to do bad things → **wizard**

witchcraft /ˈwɪtʃkrɑːft $ -kræft/ *n* [U] the use of magic to make strange things happen

ˈwitch ˌdoctor *n* [C] a man who is believed to be able to cure people, using magic

ˈwitch ˌhunt *n* [C] *disapproving* an attempt to find and punish people in a society or organization whose opinions are believed to be wrong or dangerous

with /wɪð, wɪθ/ *prep*

1 used to say that two or more people or things are together in the same place: *She lives with her Mom.* | *Will you come with me?* | *Put this bag with the others.* | *Mix the powder with boiling water.*

2 having or holding something: *a girl with dark hair* | *a house with a garden* | *She came back with an ice cream.*

3 using something: *Chop the onions with a sharp knife.* | *We decorated the church with flowers.*

4 used to say which other person, group, or country is involved in an action or activity: *Discuss the problem with your doctor.* | *She had been arguing with Kevin.* | *the war with France*

5 because of something, or as a result of something:

He was trembling with fear. | With Josh away (=because Josh is away), I have more time.
6 used to say what covers or fills something: His hands were **covered with** blood.
7 including: A double room with breakfast is £45.
8 used to say what an action or situation is related to: There's something wrong with the TV. | Be careful with that glass.
9 used to say who or what someone has a particular feeling towards: Are you angry with me? | She's delighted with her new car.
10 used to say how someone does something or how something happens: Prepare everything with great care. | The door closed with a bang. | 'Hello,' she said with a smile.
11 used to talk about the position of someone's body: He stood with his back to the class.
12 supporting someone or sharing their opinion: I'm with Harry on this one.

PHRASES

be with me/you spoken to understand what someone is saying: Sorry, I'm not with you.

withdraw /wɪðˈdrɔː, wɪθ- $ -ˈdrɔː/ v (past tense **withdrew** /-ˈdruː/, past participle **withdrawn** /-ˈdrɔːn $ -ˈdrɔːn/)
1 `STOP TAKING PART` [I,T] to stop taking part in a race, competition etc, or to leave an organization: **[+from]** Injury forced her to withdraw from the race.
2 `STOP SUPPORTING` [T] to stop giving support or money to someone or something: The government has **withdrawn** its **support** for the project.
3 `THREAT/OFFER ETC` [T] if you withdraw a threat, offer, request etc, you say that you no longer intend to do what you said or no longer want to do what you asked for
4 `CRITICISM/ACCUSATION` [T] formal if you withdraw something you have said, you admit that it was untrue
5 `MONEY FROM BANK` [T] to take money out of a bank account: I need to withdraw $200.
6 `ARMY` [I,T] if an army withdraws, or if it is withdrawn, it moves back away from a place

withdrawal /wɪðˈdrɔːəl, wɪθ- $ -ˈdrɔːəl/ n
1 `ARMY` [C,U] when military forces are moved back out of an area: **[+of]** the withdrawal of NATO forces from Bosnia
2 `STOP PROVIDING STH` [U] the removal or stopping of something such as support, an offer, or a service: **[+of]** the withdrawal of government aid
3 `FROM BANK` [C,U] the act of taking money from a bank account, or the amount you take out: I'd like to **make** a **withdrawal**.
4 `STOP TAKING PART` [U] the act of no longer taking part in an activity or being a member of an organization: **[+from]** Germany's withdrawal from the talks
5 `DRUGS` [U] when someone stops taking a drug that they were dependent on, and the unpleasant mental and physical effects that this causes: **withdrawal symptoms** (=the unpleasant effects of withdrawal)

withdrawn /wɪðˈdrɔːn, wɪθ- $ -ˈdrɔːn/ adj quiet and not wanting to talk to people

wither /ˈwɪðə $ -ər/ (also **wither away**) v [I] **1** if a plant withers, it becomes drier and smaller and

starts to die **2** to become weaker and then disappear: Without commercial sponsorship, sport would wither.

withering /ˈwɪðərɪŋ/ adj **withering look/remark etc** a look, remark etc that makes someone feel stupid or embarrassed

withhold /wɪðˈhəʊld, wɪθ- $ -ˈhoʊld/ v [T] (past tense and past participle **withheld** /-ˈheld/) to refuse to give someone something: **withhold sth from sb** He is accused of **withholding information** from Congress.

within /wɪˈðɪn $ wɪˈðɪn, wɪˈθɪn/ adv, prep
1 before a certain period of time has ended: Payment must be made within 28 days. | Within a year he was dead. `THESAURUS` ▶ **DURING**
2 less than a certain distance from a place: We live within four miles of each other.
3 inside a group, organization, building, or area: critics within the party | footpaths within the national park
4 if something stays within a particular limit or set of rules, it does not go beyond that limit: The company has acted **within the law**.
5 literary inside a person's body or mind: A feeling of happiness grew **within** her.

without /wɪˈðaʊt $ wɪˈðaʊt, wɪˈθaʊt/ adv, prep
1 not having, doing, or using something: a house without a garden | The soldiers fired **without warning**. | **without doing sth** He left without saying goodbye. | **do/go without (sth)** (=not have something important) We **had to do without** water for two days.
2 not with someone: If you're late, I'll go without you.

withstand /wɪðˈstænd, wɪθ-/ v [T] (past tense and past participle **withstood** /-ˈstʊd/) to be strong enough to remain unharmed by heat, pressure, a force etc

witness¹ /ˈwɪtnəs/ n [C]
1 someone who sees an accident, crime etc and can say what happened: **[+to]** Police have appealed for witnesses to the accident.
2 someone who tells a court of law what they know about the case that is being considered: Will she be **called as a witness** (=asked to speak in court)? | Few **witnesses** are willing to **testify** (=speak in court) against him. | **prosecution/defence witness**
3 someone who is present when an official document is signed, and who signs it to prove this

witness² v [T] **1** to see something happen, especially an accident or crime: Several people witnessed the attack. `THESAURUS` ▶ **SEE 2** to experience an important event or change: Our generation has witnessed a period of peace. **3** to be present when someone signs an official document, and to sign it to prove this

'witness stand (also **'witness box** BrE) n [C] the place where a witness stands when they speak in court

witticism /ˈwɪtɪsɪzəm/ n [C] a clever and amusing remark

witty /ˈwɪti/ adj funny and clever: **witty speech/ remark/story etc** `THESAURUS` ▶ **FUNNY**

wives /waɪvz/ n the plural of WIFE

wizard /ˈwɪzəd $ -ərd/ n [C] **1** a man who is thought to have magic powers **2** someone who is very good at something: *a financial wizard*

wizardry /ˈwɪzədri $ -ər-/ n [U] a very impressive skill or achievement in a particular subject: *technical wizardry*

wizened /ˈwɪzənd/ adj old and with dry and WRIN-KLEd skin: *wizened apples*

wobble /ˈwɒbəl $ ˈwɑː-/ v [I] to move unsteadily from side to side: *Celia wobbled past on her bike.* **THESAURUS** SHAKE —**wobbly** adj: *a wobbly chair* —**wobble** n [C]

woe /wəʊ $ woʊ/ n [U] *literary* great sadness
PHRASES
  woes [plural] very serious problems

woeful /ˈwəʊfəl $ ˈwoʊ-/ adj **1** very bad or disappointing: *The country has a woeful record on human rights.* **2** *literary* sad —**woefully** adv

wok /wɒk $ wɑːk/ n [C] a large round pan, used in Chinese cooking → see picture at PAN[1]

woke /wəʊk $ woʊk/ v the past tense of WAKE

woken /ˈwəʊkən $ ˈwoʊ-/ v the past participle of WAKE

wolf[1] /wʊlf/ n [C] (*plural* **wolves** /wʊlvz/) a wild animal similar to a large dog → see picture on page A3

wolf[2] (*also* **wolf down**) v [T] *informal* to eat something very quickly: *She wolfed down her breakfast.*

woman /ˈwʊmən/ n [C] (*plural* **women** /ˈwɪmɪn/) **1** a female adult person: *a beautiful woman | married women* | **woman priest/doctor etc** *the first woman president* | **women's clothes/magazines/groups etc** (=clothes etc for women) → MAN[1]
2 spokeswoman/businesswoman etc a woman who does a particular job or activity

THESAURUS

woman a female adult person: *An attractive woman of about 30 came in.*
lady a very polite word for a woman: *Never argue with a lady.*
girl a young female person – usually someone younger than about 20: *Who's that pretty girl over there?*

womanhood /ˈwʊmənhʊd/ n [U] the state of being a woman

womanizer (*also* **-iser** BrE) /ˈwʊmənaɪzə $ -ər/ n [C] a man who has sexual relationships with many women

womankind /ˈwʊmənkaɪnd/ n [U] all women, considered as a group

womanly /ˈwʊmənli/ adj *approving* behaving, dressing etc in a way that people think is right for a woman

womb /wuːm/ n [C] the part of a woman's body where a baby grows before it is born SYN **uterus**

women /ˈwɪmɪn/ n the plural of WOMAN

won /wʌn/ v the past tense and past participle of WIN

wonder[1] /ˈwʌndə $ -ər/ v [I,T] to think about something you do not know, and want to know it: **[+who/where/if etc]** *I wonder where she lives these days.* | *I wonder if he'll take the job.* | **[+about]** *She wondered about the bruise on his cheek.*
PHRASES
  I was wondering if/whether ... *spoken* used to ask for something politely, or to invite someone to do something: *I was wondering if you could help me – I'm looking for the City Hall.*

wonder[2] n **1** [U] surprise and admiration SYN **awe**: **in wonder** *They listened to her tale in wonder. We were* **filled with wonder**. **2** [C usually plural] something that makes you feel admiration: *the wonders of technology*
PHRASES
  do/work wonders to be very good at solving a problem: *This diet is supposed to work wonders.*
  it's a wonder (that) *spoken* used to say that something is surprising: *It's a wonder he didn't go mad.*
  (it's) no/small/little wonder (that) *spoken* used to say that something does not surprise you: *No wonder you feel sick after eating all that chocolate.*

wonder[3] adj [only before noun] very good or effective: *a new* **wonder drug**

wonderful /ˈwʌndəfəl $ -dər-/ adj very good SYN **great**: *wonderful news* | *We had a wonderful time.* **THESAURUS** GOOD —**wonderfully** adv

Usage
Do not say 'very wonderful'. Just say **wonderful**.

wondrous /ˈwʌndrəs/ adj *literary* wonderful

wonky /ˈwɒŋki $ ˈwɑːŋki/ adj BrE *informal* not straight or level

wont /wəʊnt $ wɔːnt/ adj **be wont to do sth** *formal* to have the habit of doing something

won't /wəʊnt $ woʊnt/ the short form of 'will not': *Dad won't like it.*

woo /wuː/ v [T] **1** to try to persuade someone to support you: *The politicians are busy wooing voters.* **2** *old-fashioned* to try to persuade a woman to love and marry you

wood /wʊd/ n
1 [U] the hard material that trees are made of → **wooden**: *a boat made of wood*
2 [C] (*also* **the woods**) an area of land that is covered in trees
PHRASES
  touch wood BrE, **knock on wood** AmE *spoken* used after you say you have been fortunate, because it is supposed to make your good luck continue: *Everything has gone well so far, touch wood.*

Word Choice: wood or forest?
A **forest** is much bigger than a **wood**.

wooded /ˈwʊdɪd/ adj covered with trees

wooden /ˈwʊdn/ adj made of wood: *a wooden box* → see picture at MATERIAL[1]

woodland /ˈwʊdlənd, -lænd/ n [C,U] an area of land that is covered with trees

woodpecker /'wʊd,pekə $ -ər/ n [C] a bird with a long beak that makes holes in trees

woodwind /'wʊd,wɪnd/ n [U] wooden or metal musical instruments that you play by blowing into them → **brass**

woodwork /'wʊdwɜːk $ -wɜːrk/ n [U] **1** BrE the skill or activity of making things out of wood SYN **woodworking** AmE **2** the parts of a building that are made of wood

PHRASES

crawl/come out of the woodwork disapproving to unexpectedly start to take part in a situation: As soon as he died, his relatives started crawling out of the woodwork.

woodworking /'wʊd,wɜːkɪŋ $ -ɜːr-/ n [U] AmE the skill or activity of making things out of wood SYN **woodwork** BrE

woodworm /'wʊdwɜːm $ -wɜːrm/ n [C,U] an insect that makes holes in wood, or the damage this insect causes

woody /'wʊdi/ adj **1** woody plants have thick hard stems **2** a woody area of land is covered with trees

woof /wʊf/ the sound a dog makes when it BARKS

wool /wʊl/ n [U] the soft thick hair of a sheep, used to make cloth or thread: a **ball of wool** | a pure wool skirt → **COTTON WOOL**

woollen BrE, **woolen** AmE /'wʊlən/ adj made of wool —**woollens** n [plural]

woolly BrE, **wooly** AmE /'wʊli/ adj **1** made of wool or a material similar to wool: a woolly hat → see picture at **MATERIAL**[1] **2** not showing clear thinking: a woolly argument

woozy /'wuːzi/ adj informal feeling weak and unsteady SYN **dizzy**

word[1] /wɜːd $ wɜːrd/ n

1 GROUP OF LETTERS [C] a separate group of letters or sounds that has a particular meaning: **[+for]** What's the English word for (=word that means)'casa'? | a 500-word essay | The weather was inclement. **In other words**, it was awful. | Say **in your own words** what happened.

2 STH YOU SAY [singular] something that you say to someone: **a word of warning/advice/thanks etc** He rode off without a word of thanks. | **a kind/angry etc word** His parents never exchanged an angry word. | **have a word (with sb)** (=have a short conversation with someone) Can I have a word with someone? | He **put in a good word for** me with the boss (=said good things about me to help me). | He found it hard to **put his feelings into words** (=say how he felt).

3 PROMISE sb's word someone's promise or statement that something is true: Can you trust her to **keep** her word? | I **give** you my **word** that you will not be harmed. | I'll have to **take** his **word for it** (=believe what he says because I do not know about something). THESAURUS ▶ PROMISE

4 NEWS [singular, U] news, information, or a message: Had any **word from** Andy? | **Spread the word** (=tell people) about the benefits of exercise. | **Word** soon **got round** about our engagement (=people soon heard about it). | I get most of my business **by word of mouth** (=by people talking to each other). | **the word**

is/word has it (that) (=people are saying that) The word is they're to marry.

5 TYPE OF LANGUAGE the spoken/written word spoken or written language → **FOUR-LETTER WORD, LINKING WORD, SWEAR WORD**

PHRASES

get a word in (edgeways) to manage to say something when other people are saying a lot: Once she starts talking, it's difficult to get a word in edgeways.

not say/understand/believe etc a word to not say, understand etc anything or any part of something: She didn't understand a word of Italian. | Don't **breathe a word** of what I've told you (=don't tell anyone).

not in so many words spoken used to say that although someone did not say something directly, you know what they meant: 'So Dad said he'd pay for it?' 'Not in so many words.'

the last word the last thing said in a discussion, argument etc: Why must you always **have the last word**?

word for word if you repeat something word for word, you say it using exactly the same words: He asked me to repeat word for word the instructions he'd just given me.

THESAURUS

word a separate group of letters or sounds that has a particular meaning: 'Sayonara' is the Japanese word for 'goodbye'.

name a word that people use for a particular thing, place, organization etc: Do you know the name of this flower? | The Big Apple is another name for New York.

term a word or group of words that is used in a technical or scientific subject: The medical term for losing your hair is 'alopecia'.

idiom a group of words that has a special meaning which you cannot guess from the meanings of each separate word: 'On top of the world' is an idiom that means 'very happy'.

cliché a group of words that people use a lot, so that it seems boring, annoying, or silly: 'You are what you eat' is a cliché but it's true.

slang very informal words used by a particular group of people, for example young people, criminals, or soldiers: 'Wicked' is slang for 'good'.

jargon disapproving words used by a particular profession or group of people, which are difficult for other people to understand: The document was written in complicated legal jargon.

---

word[2] v [T] to choose the words you use carefully SYN **phrase**: a carefully worded statement

wording /'wɜːdɪŋ $ 'wɜːr-/ n [U] the words and phrases used in a piece of writing or speech

wordless /'wɜːdləs $ 'wɜːrd-/ adj literary not using words: She embraced him in wordless grief. —**wordlessly** adv

'word-play n [U] using words in a clever amusing way

'word ,processor n [C] computer software or a small computer that you use for writing things —**word processing** n [U]

W

wordy /'wɜːdi $ 'wɜːrdi/ *adj disapproving* containing too many words

wore /wɔː $ wɔːr/ *v* the past tense of WEAR

work¹ /wɜːk $ wɜːrk/ *v*

1 DO A JOB [I,T] to do a job in order to earn money: **[+at/in]** *She works in a bank.* | **[+for]** *Do you enjoy working for the police?* | **[+as]** *Joe worked as a builder.* | **[+with/among]** *She wants to work with children.* | *Ted often works late* (=works after most people have finished). | **work days/nights/weekends** (=work during the day, night etc)

2 DO STH [I,T] to spend time and effort doing something: **[+on]** *She's working on a new book.* | **work to do sth** *The company is working hard to improve its image.* | *They work the land* (=grow crops) *to feed their families.*

3 OPERATE **a)** [I] if a machine works, it does what it is meant to do: *The CD player isn't working.* **b)** [T] to make a machine do what it is meant to do: SYN **operate**: *Do you know how to work the printer?*

4 BE EFFECTIVE [I] if a plan, method, medicine etc works, it gives you the results you want: *Most diets don't work.*

5 TO DIFFERENT POSITION [I,T] to gradually move to a new position: *The wheel must have worked loose.* | *He worked his way to the top.*

6 USE STH [I,T] to use a particular substance in order to make something: **[+in/with]** *a sculptor who works in steel*

PHRASES

| **work against sb/work in sb's favour** to stop someone succeeding, or to help someone to succeed: *Unfortunately, her low grades worked against her.*

PHRASAL VERBS

work sth ↔ **off** to do some physical exercise to make yourself feel less worried, angry etc: *Running is a good way of working off stress.*

work out

1 to calculate an amount, price, or value: **work sth ↔ out** *Let's work out how much beer we need.* | **[+at]** *It works out at $50 a night.*

2 **work sth ↔ out** to decide or plan something in order to solve a problem: *He still hasn't worked out where he'll live.*

3 if a situation works out in a particular way, it ends in that way: *Everything worked out OK in the end.*

4 to do exercises that make you stronger

work on sth to try very hard to improve or achieve something: *A trainer has been brought in to work on her fitness.* THESAURUS **PRACTISE**

work up sth to gradually make yourself have a particular feeling: **work up interest/energy/enthusiasm etc** *I'm trying to work up the courage to visit the dentist.* | **work up an appetite/thirst** (=make yourself hungry or thirsty)

work up to sth to prepare yourself for something difficult

work² *n*

1 JOB [U] your job or the activities that you do regularly to earn money: *I don't want to be late for work.* | **in/out of work** (=with or without a job) *He's been out of work for months.* | **after work** (=after you have finished working for the day) *Shall we go for a drink after work?* THESAURUS **JOB**

2 OFFICE ETC [U] the place where you do your job: **at work** *When do you have to be at work?*

3 EFFORT [U] physical or mental activity and effort: *Looking after children can be hard work.* | **[+on]** *Work on the bridge is continuing.* | **at work** (=working) *Dad was hard at work in the garden.* | **set/get to work** (=start working)

4 STH YOU HAVE DONE [U] something you produce for your job, as part of a course etc: *an excellent piece of work* | *The standard of work in colleges is improving.*

5 PAINTING/BOOK/MUSIC ETC [C] a painting, book, play, piece of music etc: *the works of Shakespeare* | *a great work of art* (=painting or sculpture)

6 ROADS ETC **works** [plural] activities that involve repairing roads, bridges etc

7 FACTORY **works** [plural] a large building where goods are produced or an industrial process takes place: **gasworks/ironworks etc** → DONKEY WORK

PHRASES

| **do sb's dirty work** to do an unpleasant or dishonest action for someone, so that they do not have to do it: *He didn't like having to do other people's dirty work.*

COLLOCATIONS

verbs

to go to work *He goes to work by train.*

to start/finish work (=to start or finish your day at work) *I usually finish work around six.*

to start work (=to start working in a new job or for the first time) *My dad started work when he was 16.*

to do work *Have you done this kind of work before?*

to look for work (*also* **to seek work** *formal*) *Young people come to town looking for work.*

to find work (=to get a job) *He found work in a local factory.*

types of work

part-time/full-time work *Many parents want part-time work.*

paid work *I would consider any kind of paid work.*

clerical/office work *I thought office work would be boring.*

manual work (=work done with your hands) *He was not used to manual work.*

temporary/casual work (=not a permanent job) *I managed to get some temporary work in a hotel.*

THESAURUS

work your job or the activities that you do regularly to earn money: *What time do you finish work today?* | *He's really enjoying his work.*

housework the work that you have to do in your home, for example cleaning and washing clothes: *Women still do most of the housework.*

homework the work that a student has to do at home: *I haven't finished my maths homework yet.*

duties *formal* all the things that you have to do as part of your job – used especially in official documents: *Your duties will include setting up the equipment in the laboratory.*

workable /ˈwɜːkəbəl $ ˈwɜːr-/ adj a workable plan, system, idea etc is practical and will work well OPP **unworkable**: a workable solution

workaholic /ˌwɜːkəˈhɒlɪk $ ˌwɜːrkəˈhɒː-/ n [C] someone who chooses to work so much that they do not have time for anything else

workbench /ˈwɜːkbentʃ $ ˈwɜːrk-/ n [C] a strong table used for working with tools

workbook /ˈwɜːkbʊk $ ˈwɜːrk-/ n [C] a school book with questions and exercises in it

ˌworked ˈup adj [not before noun] informal upset, nervous, or excited: [+about/over] Don't get so **worked up** over little things.

worker /ˈwɜːkə $ ˈwɜːrkər/ n [C]
1 someone who does a particular kind of job for an organization, but who is not a manager: a factory worker
2 a **good/hard/quick etc worker** someone who works well etc → DOCK WORKER, SOCIAL WORKER

workforce /ˈwɜːkfɔːs $ ˈwɜːrkfɔːrs/ n [singular] all the people who work in a country or company: a skilled workforce

working¹ /ˈwɜːkɪŋ $ ˈwɜːr-/ adj [only before noun]
1 relating to the situation or time when you work: **working conditions/environment etc** poor working conditions | **working day/week/hours etc** He spent most of his **working life** in the same firm. | a good **working relationship** between managers and staff
2 having a job: **working mothers** **3** **working party/group** a group of people formed to examine a particular situation or problem **4** a **working knowledge of sth** enough knowledge of a language, subject etc to be able to do something effectively: a working knowledge of Spanish
PHRASES
be in (good/perfect etc) working order to be working properly and not broken: The watch was still in good working order.

working² n **1** [singular] (also **workings** [plural]) the way that something works: the workings of government **2** [U] a particular way of working at your job: **part-time/flexible etc working**

ˌworking ˈclass n [singular] the group of people in society who usually do physical work and who do not have much money or power —**working-class** adj

workload /ˈwɜːkləʊd $ ˈwɜːrkloʊd/ n [C] the amount of work you must do: a **heavy workload** (=a lot of work)

workman /ˈwɜːkmən $ ˈwɜːrk-/ n [C] (plural **workmen** /-mən/) someone who does physical work, such as building or repairing things

workmanlike /ˈwɜːkmənlaɪk $ ˈwɜːrk-/ adj done in a practical and skilful way

workmanship /ˈwɜːkmənʃɪp $ ˈwɜːrk-/ n [U] the skill used to make something

workmate /ˈwɜːkmeɪt $ ˈwɜːrk-/ n [C] BrE someone you work with SYN **colleague**

workout /ˈwɜːkaʊt $ ˈwɜːrk-/ n [C] a period of physical exercise done to make your body stronger: a daily workout in the gym

ˈwork ˌpermit n [C] an official document that you must have to work in a foreign country

workplace /ˈwɜːkpleɪs $ ˈwɜːrk-/ n [C usually singular] the room or building where people work: the problem of bullying in the workplace

worksheet /ˈwɜːkʃiːt $ ˈwɜːrk-/ n [C] a piece of paper with questions and exercises on it

workshop /ˈwɜːkʃɒp $ ˈwɜːrkʃɑːp/ n [C] **1** a room or building where people use tools and machines to make or repair things **2** a meeting where people learn about a particular subject by discussing their experiences and doing practical exercises: **drama/writing/music etc workshop**

workstation /ˈwɜːkˌsteɪʃən $ ˈwɜːrk-/ n [C] a computer that is part of an office computer system

ˈwork-ˌsurface (also **ˈwork-top**) n [C] BrE a flat surface for working on SYN **counter** AmE: kitchen work-tops → see picture at KITCHEN

world¹ /wɜːld $ wɜːrld/ n
1 **the world** the PLANET we live on, and all the people, countries etc on it: Students from **all over the world** study here. | a common disease in some **parts of the world** | the world's tallest building | **in the world** (=used to emphasize) You're the best dad in the world! | I want **the whole world** (=everyone) to know how happy I am.

Grammar
Do not say 'It is the largest country on the world.' Say It is the largest country in the world.

2 [singular] our society, and the way that people live and behave: I want **a better world** for my kids. | **In an ideal world** everything would be recycled.
3 [C usually singular] all the things and people that are connected with a particular subject, activity, place, time, or person: **the world of fashion/politics/sport etc** | **the Arab/Western/English-speaking etc world** Opinion in the Western world is divided. | **the industrialized/developing world** | **the ancient/modern etc world** a history of the ancient world
4 **the animal/plant/insect world** animals etc considered as a group
5 [C] another PLANET that is not the Earth
PHRASES
the best of both worlds the advantages of two very different things: With instant access to your money and good interest rates, you **have the best of both worlds**.
do sb a world of good informal to make someone feel much better: A holiday would do you a world of good.
have the world at your feet to be very successful: In those days the band had the world at their feet.
in a world of your own thinking so much that you do not notice other people: She was a shy child who seemed to live in a world of her own.
mean the world to sb/think the world of sb if you mean the world to someone, or they think the world of you, they love or admire you very much: His children mean the world to him.

W

move/go up in the world to get a better job, more money etc: *Diamonds! You're going up in the world then?*

be/feel on top of the world to feel happy and healthy: *He felt on top of the world after winning the race.*

out of this world *informal* very good: *The graphics are out of this world!*

the outside world people and events in the rest of the world, where you cannot or do not go: *Prisoners are cut off from the outside world.*

a world of difference/worlds apart used to say that two things are very different from each other: *There's a world of difference between being alone and being lonely.*

Word Choice: world or earth?

The **world** is the planet we live on, and all the people, countries etc on it: *In some parts of the world, clean drinking water is very scarce.* | *You can buy Coca-Cola all over the world.*
You use **earth/Earth** especially when you are comparing our world with the Moon, stars, and other places in space: *Light from the stars can take millions of years to reach Earth.* | *The Earth revolves around the Sun.*

---

world[2] *adj* [only before noun] involving or affecting all or most of the world: *the world champion* | *World War Two* | *Bains set a new world record in the long jump.*

world-'class *adj* among the best in the world: *a world-class tennis player*

world-'famous *adj* known about by people all over the world

worldly /'wɜːldli $ 'wɜːrld-/ *adj* knowing a lot about life

PHRASES

worldly goods/possessions everything you own: *We care more about our worldly goods than we do about our relationships.*

'world ˌmusic *n* [U] traditional music from the different countries around the world, not the US or Britain

ˌworld 'power *n* [C] a country with power and influence over many other countries

worldwide /ˌwɜːld'waɪd◂ $ ˌwɜːrld-/ *adj, adv* everywhere in the world: *The company employs 2,000 people worldwide.* | *a worldwide campaign*

ˌWorld Wide 'Web *n* (*written abbreviation* **WWW**) **the World Wide Web** the system that connects computers around the World together so that people can find and use information on the Internet **SYN** the Web

worm[1] /wɜːm $ wɜːrm/ *n* [C]
1 a small long thin creature without bones or legs that lives in soil
2 worms [plural] long thin creatures that can live inside people or animals and make them ill → **can of worms** at **CAN**[2]

worm[2] *v* **1 worm your way into/through etc sth** to move through a narrow place slowly and with difficulty **2 worm your way into sb's heart/**

affections/confidence etc *disapproving* to gradually make someone love and trust you, especially in order to gain an advantage

PHRASAL VERBS

worm sth **out of** sb to persuade someone to tell you something

worn[1] /wɔːn $ wɔːrn/ *v* the past participle of WEAR

worn[2] *adj* old and rather damaged: *worn jeans*

ˌworn 'out, worn-out *adj* **1** very tired: *You look worn out.* **2** too old or damaged to use any more: *worn-out shoes*

worried /'wʌrid $ 'wɜːrid/ *adj* not happy or relaxed because you keep thinking about a particular problem or something bad that might happen: *You look worried.* | **[+about]** *I'm worried about my exam.* | **[+(that)]** *I was worried we'd be late.*

THESAURUS

worried not happy or relaxed because you keep thinking about a particular problem or something bad that might happen: *People are worried about losing their jobs.*
anxious worried, especially when you feel you have no control over the situation. **Anxious** is stronger and more formal than **worried**: *When people can't sleep, they become anxious about it.* | *Anxious relatives waited for news at the airport.*
nervous worried and slightly frightened about something you are going to do or something that is going to happen: *I felt a little nervous before the interview.*
concerned worried, especially about a problem affecting someone else, the country, or the world: *People are more concerned about the environment now.*
bothered worried because you think something is important – used especially in negative sentences: *I'm not bothered about what other people think.*
stressed/stressed out very worried and tired all the time, because you have too many problems or too much work: *If you're feeling stressed out, you should have a holiday.*

---

worry[1] /'wʌri $ 'wɜːri/ *v* (**worried, worrying, worries**)
1 [I] to keep thinking about a problem or about something bad that might happen so that you do not feel happy or relaxed: **[+about]** *Parents always worry about their children.* | **[+(that)]** *I worry that I won't have enough money.*
2 [T] if something worries you, it makes you feel worried: *Changes in the climate are worrying scientists.* | **it worries sb that** *It worries me that my dad lives alone now.*

PHRASES

don't worry *spoken* **1** used when you are trying to make someone feel less anxious: *Don't worry, Daddy's here.* **2** used to tell someone that they do not have to do something: **[+about]** *Don't worry about the washing-up. I'll do it later.*

worry[2] *n* [C,U] (*plural* **worries**) something that makes you feel worried, or the feeling of being worried: *My **main worry** is finding somewhere to live.* | *money worries* | *She was desperate with worry.*

worrying /ˈwʌri-ɪŋ $ ˈwɜː-/ *adj* making you feel worried: *worrying news*

worse¹ /wɜːs $ wɜːrs/ *adj* [the comparative of 'bad']
1 more bad or more unpleasant → **better**: [+than] *Your singing is even worse than mine!* | *The problem is **getting worse**.* | *The traffic is **much worse** after five o'clock.*
2 [not before noun] more ill: *If you **feel worse** tomorrow, go to the doctor.*
PHRASES
the worse for wear drunk or in a bad condition: *He arrived home at 5 am, looking the worse for wear.*

worse² *n* [U] something worse: *Worse was yet to come.*

worse³ *adv* [the comparative of 'badly']
1 in a more severe or serious way than before: [+than] *It's raining worse than ever.*
2 not as well → **better**: *He sings **even worse** than I do!*

worsen /ˈwɜːsən $ ˈwɜːr-/ *v* [I,T] to become worse or make something worse: *His condition is worsening.*

worse 'off *adj* poorer, or in a worse situation: *The tax increase will leave us worse off.*

worship /ˈwɜːʃɪp $ ˈwɜːr-/ *v* (**worshipped, worshipping** *BrE*, **worshiped, worshiping** *AmE*)
1 [I,T] to express respect and love for a god
2 [T] to love and admire someone very much: *He absolutely worships her.* **THESAURUS** ADMIRE
—**worship** *n* [U] —**worshipper** *n* [C]

worst¹ /wɜːst $ wɜːrst/ *adj* [the superlative of 'bad'] worse than any other person or thing → **best**: *the worst movie I've ever seen* | *It all happened at the **worst possible** time.*

worst² *n* the worst someone or something that is worse than every other person or thing → **the best**: *Of all the exams, that was the worst.* | **worst (that)** *This year's harvest is the worst I can remember.* | *Last month was **by far the worst** for road accidents.* | *When he didn't come home, I **feared the worst**.*
PHRASES
at (the) worst if things are as bad as they can be: *At worst, the repairs will cost you $700.*
if the worst comes to the worst *especially BrE*, **if worse comes to worst** *especially AmE* if the situation develops in the worst possible way: *If the worst comes to the worst, we'll have to sell the car.*

worst³ *adv* [the superlative of 'badly'] most badly: *the cities that were worst affected by the war* | *She was lost and, **worst of all**, she didn't have any money.*

worth¹ /wɜːθ $ wɜːrθ/ *adj*
1 be worth sth to have a particular value: *Our house is worth $350,000.* | *Each question is worth four points.* | **How much is** *it worth?*
2 a) used to say that something is interesting, useful, or enjoyable: **be worth (doing) sth** *The film is **well worth seeing**.* **b)** used to say that someone should do something because they will gain something from it: **it is worth doing sth** *It's worth checking the*

bill. | **be worth the time/effort/work** *It was a great show, and worth the hard work.*
PHRASES
it's (not) worth it *informal* used to say that you gain or do not gain something from an action: *Don't argue with her – it's just not worth it.*
be worth sb's while (to do sth) *spoken* used to say that someone should spend time or money on something because they will gain something from it: *It might be worth your while buying a new suit before the interview.*
make it worth sb's while *spoken* to offer someone money if they agree to do something for you: *He said he would help me if I made it worth his while.*

worth² *n* [U]
1 ten pounds' worth/$500 worth etc of sth an amount of something worth ten pounds, $500 etc: *£2,000 worth of computer equipment* | *The fire caused thousands of pounds' worth of damage.*
2 ten minutes' worth/a week's worth etc of sth something that takes ten minutes, a week etc to happen, do, or use: *We bought a week's worth of shopping.*
3 how good or useful something or someone is: *The new computer has **proved** its **worth**.*

worthless /ˈwɜːθləs $ ˈwɜːrθ-/ *adj* **1** something that is worthless has no value, importance, or use **OPP** valuable: *worthless rubbish* | *The information was worthless to me.* **2** a worthless person has no good qualities or useful skills: *She made him feel completely worthless.*

worthwhile /ˌwɜːθˈwaɪl◄ $ ˌwɜːrθ-/ *adj* if something is worthwhile, it is important or useful, even though you have to spend time, effort, or money doing it: *It's worthwhile comparing prices.*

worthy /ˈwɜːði $ ˈwɜːrði/ *adj* **1** [only before noun] deserving respect from people: *United are worthy winners.* | *a **worthy opponent*** **2 be worthy of sth** *formal* to deserve something: *A couple of other books are worthy of mention.*

would /wʊd/ *modal verb* (*negative short form* **wouldn't**)
1 used when describing what someone said or thought in the past: *He said he would call back later.* | *I never thought she would marry him.*
2 used when talking about a possible situation that you imagine or want to happen: *If I won the lottery, I'd buy a house.* | *I'd be amazed if I got the job.*
3 used when talking about something that might have happened, but it did not happen: *I would have phoned you, but there wasn't time.*
4 used when saying that something happened often in the past: *In summer he would sit out in the garden.*
5 *spoken* used when asking someone politely to do something: *Would you shut the door, please?*
6 *spoken* used when offering something to someone or inviting them politely: *Would you like a cake?*
7 *spoken* used when saying that someone wants something or wants to do something: **would like/love/prefer** *I'd love a coffee.* | *She'd like to meet you.*
8 would not a) used when saying that someone refused to do something: *He wouldn't give us any money.* **b)** used when saying that something did not

happen, even though someone was trying to make it happen: *The door wouldn't open, no matter how hard she pulled.*
9 *spoken* used when making a suggestion or giving advice politely: *I'd ask your teacher, if I were you.*
10 *spoken* used when you are annoyed about what someone has said or done, because it is typical of them: *You would say that, wouldn't you!* → **-'D**, **would rather** at RATHER

PHRASES

I **would think/imagine/guess/say** *spoken* used when saying what you think is probably true: *I would think she's gone back home.*

would-be *adj* a would-be writer, actor, student etc is someone who wants to be a writer, actor etc

wouldn't /'wʊdnt/ the short form of 'would not': *She wouldn't answer.*

would've /'wʊdəv/ the short form of 'would have': *You would've enjoyed the film.*

wound¹ /wuːnd/ *n* [C] a deep cut made in your skin by a knife or bullet: *gunshot wounds | It took a long time for his wounds to heal.* **THESAURUS** INJURY

wound² *v* [T] **1** to injure someone with a knife, gun etc: *Six people were wounded in the attack.* **THESAURUS** HURT **2** to make someone feel unhappy or upset —**wounded** *adj*

wound³ /waʊnd/ *v* the past tense and past participle of WIND

wound up /ˌwaʊnd 'ʌp/ *adj* [not before noun] very angry, nervous, or excited: *I was too wound up to sleep.*

wove /wəʊv $ woʊv/ *v* the past tense of WEAVE

woven /'wəʊvən $ 'woʊ-/ *v* the past participle of WEAVE

wow /waʊ/ *spoken* used when you think something is impressive or surprising: *Wow! Look at that!*

wrangle /'ræŋgəl/ *v* [I] to argue with someone angrily for a long time —**wrangle** *n* [C]

wrap¹ /ræp/ *v* [T] (**wrapped**, **wrapping**)
1 (*also* **wrap up**) to put paper or cloth over something to cover it completely: **wrap sth in sth** *The present was wrapped in gold paper.* | **wrap sth around sb/sth** *Wrap the blanket around you.*
2 if you wrap your arms, legs, or fingers around something, you use them to hold it: **wrap sth around sb/sth** *She sat with her arms wrapped around her legs.*

PHRASAL VERBS

wrap up

1 to put on warm clothes: *Make sure you **wrap up warm**.*

2 **wrap sth** ↔ **up** *informal* to finish a job, meeting etc: *The project was quickly wrapped up.*

3 **be wrapped up in sth** to give so much of your attention to something that you do not have time for anything else

wrap² *n*

PHRASES

under wraps being kept secret: *The details of the project are still under wraps.*

wrapper /'ræpə $ -ər/ *n* [C] the paper or plastic that covers something you buy

wrapping /'ræpɪŋ/ *n* [C,U] the cloth, paper, or plastic that is put around something to protect it

'wrapping ˌpaper *n* [U] coloured paper used to wrap presents

wrath /rɒθ $ ræθ/ *n* [U] *formal* extreme anger

wreak /riːk/ *v* (*past tense and past participle* **wreaked** *or* **wrought** /rɔːt $ rɔːt/) **wreak havoc (on sth)** to cause a lot of damage or problems

wreath /riːθ/ *n* [C] a circle of flowers and leaves used as a decoration or to show respect for someone who has died

wreathe /riːð/ *v literary* **be wreathed in sth** to be covered in something: *The mountains were wreathed in mist.*

wreck¹ /rek/ *v* [T] *informal* to destroy something completely: *The building was wrecked by an explosion.* | *Injury wrecked his career.* **THESAURUS** DESTROY

wreck² *n* [C] **1** a car, plane, or ship that has been very badly damaged **2** *informal* someone who is very tired, unhealthy, or worried: *The attack left her an emotional wreck.* **3** *AmE* a bad car accident or plane accident **SYN** crash *BrE: One person survived the wreck.*

wreckage /'rekɪdʒ/ *n* [singular, U] the broken parts of a vehicle or building that has been destroyed: *She pulled the driver from the wreckage.*

wren /ren/ *n* [C] a very small brown bird

wrench¹ /rentʃ/ *v* [T] **1** to twist and pull something from somewhere, using force: *I wrenched the box from his grasp.* **2** to injure part of your body by twisting it suddenly

wrench² *n* **1** [C] *especially AmE* a tool that you use for turning NUTS **SYN** spanner *BrE* → see picture at TOOL **2** [singular] if it is a wrench to leave someone or something, it makes you feel very sad: *It was a wrench to leave LA.* **3** (*usually singular*) a twisting movement that pulls something violently

wrest /rest/ *v* [T + adv/prep] *formal* to take something from someone with force

wrestle /'resəl/ *v* [I,T] to fight someone by holding them and trying to push them to the ground

PHRASES

wrestle with sth to try to understand or solve a difficult problem: *He wrestled with the problem for days.*

wrestling /'reslɪŋ/ *n* [U] a sport in which two people fight and try to push each other to the ground —**wrestler** *n* [C]

wretch /retʃ/ *n* [C] *old-fashioned* someone that you feel sorry for

wretched /'retʃɪd/ *adj* **1** someone who is wretched is very unhappy or ill, and you feel sorry for them **2** [only before noun] used when you feel angry with someone or something: *The wretched thing's broken!*

wriggle /'rɪgəl/ *v* [I,T] to twist quickly from side to side: *She wriggled into the tight dress.* —**wriggle** *n* [C]

W

PHRASAL VERBS

wriggle out of sth to avoid doing something by using clever excuses: *He wriggled out of paying.*

wring /rɪŋ/ v [T] (*past tense and past participle* **wrung** /rʌŋ/) **1** (*also* **wring out**) to twist wet cloth tightly to remove water **2 wring sth's neck** to kill an animal by twisting its neck

WRING

wrinkle /'rɪŋkəl/ n [C] a small line on your face that you get when you are old **THESAURUS** LINE —**wrinkled** *adj*: *his wrinkled face* —**wrinkle** v [I,T]

wrist /rɪst/ n [C] the joint between your hand and your arm → see picture at **HAND¹**

wristwatch /'rɪstwɒtʃ $ -wɑːtʃ, -wɒːtʃ/ n [C] a watch that you wear on your wrist

writ /rɪt/ n [C] a legal document that orders someone to do something

write /raɪt/ v (*past tense* **wrote** /rəʊt $ roʊt/, *past participle* **written** /'rɪtn/)
1 [I,T] to make letters or words on paper, using a pen or pencil: *We teach children to read and write.* | **write sth on/in sth** *Write your name on a piece of paper.* | **written report/agreement/reply etc** (=done on paper, not spoken)
2 [I,T] to produce a letter to send to someone: **[+to]** *Will you write to me?* | **write sth to sb** *I'm writing a letter to my mum.* | **write sb** *AmE: Ian hasn't written me for a long time.*
3 [I,T] to produce a book, song etc: *He wrote two books.* | *The article is well written.*
4 (*also* **write out**) [T] to write information on a cheque, form etc: *I wrote a cheque for £30.*
PHRASAL VERBS
write back to answer someone's letter by sending them a letter: *I sent them a long letter at Christmas, but they never wrote back.*
write sth ↔ **down** to write something on a piece of paper: *He wrote down her phone number.*
write in to send a letter to an organization
write off
1 to send a letter to an organization asking them to send you something: **[+for]** *I've written off for an application form.*
2 write sb/sth ↔ **off** to decide that someone or something is useless, unimportant, or a failure: *The critics wrote him off.*
3 write sth ↔ **off** to officially say that a debt no longer has to be paid, or officially accept that you cannot get back money that you have spent or lost: *The US wrote off debts worth billions of dollars.*
write sth ↔ **out** to write something on paper, especially in a neat and clear way, including all the details: *He wrote out the poem in his best handwriting.*
write sth ↔ **up** to write something using notes you made earlier: *I'm writing up my report.*

'write-off n [C] *BrE* a vehicle that is so badly damaged that it can never be used again

writer /'raɪtə $ -ər/ n [C] someone who writes books, stories etc, especially as a job → **playwright** → see Word Choice at **AUTHOR**

'write-up n [C] a piece of writing in a newspaper, magazine etc, in which someone gives their opinion about a new book, film etc: *The play got a good write-up.*

writhe /raɪð/ v [I] to twist your body, especially because you are in a lot of pain: *He lay writhing in agony.*

writing /'raɪtɪŋ/ n
1 [U] words that have been written or printed: *I can't read the writing on the envelope.* | *a T-shirt with Japanese writing on it*
2 [U] books, poems, articles etc by a particular writer or on a particular subject: *some of Greene's most powerful writing*
3 [U] the activity or skill of writing: *She took up writing as a career.*
4 writings [plural] the books, stories etc that an important writer has written
PHRASES
in writing if you get something in writing, it is official proof of an agreement, promise etc: *Ask them to put it in writing.*

written /'rɪtn/ v the past participle of WRITE

W

wrong¹ /rɒŋ $ rɔːŋ/ *adj*

1 NOT CORRECT not correct – used when someone has made a mistake OPP **right**: *Your calculations must be wrong.* | *The letter was delivered to the wrong address.* → **RIGHT¹**

2 OPINION **be wrong (about sb/sth)** to not be right in what you think about someone or something OPP **right**: *No, you're wrong. Sue wouldn't do a thing like that.*

3 PROBLEM used to describe a situation where there are problems, or when someone is ill or unhappy: **there is something wrong/something is wrong** *When he didn't come back, I knew that something was wrong.* | **[+with]** *He's got something wrong with his foot.* | *You look sad. What's wrong?*

4 NOT MORALLY RIGHT not morally right or acceptable OPP **right**: *it is wrong that It's wrong that people should have to sleep on the streets.* | *it is wrong to do sth It is wrong to treat children like that.*

5 NOT SUITABLE not suitable OPP **right**: *It's the wrong time of year to go skiing.*

6 NOT WORKING if something is wrong with a vehicle or machine, it stops working properly: **[+with]** *There's something wrong with the car.*

PHRASES

get on the wrong side of sb to make someone angry with you: *She knew not to get on the wrong side of her boss.*

get (hold of) the wrong end of the stick *BrE informal* to understand a situation in completely the wrong way: *I'm not angry. You've got the wrong end of the stick entirely.*

THESAURUS

wrong not correct – used when someone has made a mistake: *I think the shop has charged me the wrong amount.* | *He admitted he was wrong.*

incorrect something that is incorrect is wrong. *Incorrect* is more formal than **wrong**: *We apologize for the incorrect information in our report.*

inaccurate inaccurate information, figures etc need to be changed because they are not exact or no longer right: *Old guidebooks often contain inaccurate information.*

false not based on true facts: *Are the following statements true or false?*

misleading making people believe something that is wrong – used especially about information or a statement that does not give all the facts: *The advertisement was deliberately misleading.* | *misleading statistics*

mistaken mistaken ideas and beliefs are wrong. You also use **you are mistaken** when saying politely that someone is wrong: *There is a*

mistaken belief that animals do not have feelings. | *I think you must be mistaken.*

wrong² *adv* not in the correct way OPP **right**: *You spelt my name wrong.* | *Have I done it wrong?*

PHRASES

don't get me wrong *spoken* used when you think that someone may understand your remarks wrongly, or be offended by them: *Don't get me wrong – I like Tim.*

get sth wrong to make a mistake in the way you write, judge, or understand something: *He got the answer wrong.* | *We must have got the address wrong.*

go wrong if something goes wrong, it starts to have problems or it is unsuccessful: *Something's gone wrong with my watch.* | *His plan went wrong.*

wrong³ *n* **1** [U] behaviour that is not morally correct: *He's too young to know right from wrong.* **2** [C] an action or situation in which someone is treated badly or unfairly: *the wrongs done to these people during the war*

PHRASES

sb can do no wrong used to say that someone thinks that another person is perfect, especially when you know that they are not: *As far as Tammy was concerned, Nick could do no wrong.*

be in the wrong to make a mistake or deserve the blame for something: *He didn't want to admit that he was in the wrong.*

wrong⁴ *v* [T] *formal* to treat someone unfairly

wrongdoing /ˈrɒŋˌduːɪŋ $ ˌrɔːŋˈduːɪŋ/ *n* [C,U] *formal* when someone does something illegal or wrong —**wrongdoer** *n* [C]

wrongful /ˈrɒŋfəl $ ˈrɔːŋ-/ *adj* **wrongful arrest/imprisonment/dismissal etc** a wrongful arrest etc is unfair or illegal because the person affected by it has done nothing wrong —**wrongfully** *adv*

wrongly /ˈrɒŋli $ ˈrɔːŋ-/ *adv* **1** not correctly: *His name is wrongly spelt.* **2** in an unfair or immoral way: *He had been wrongly accused of murder.*

wrote /rəʊt $ roʊt/ *v* the past tense of WRITE

wrought /rɔːt $ rɒːt/ *v* the past tense and past participle of WREAK

wrought 'iron *n* [U] long thin pieces of iron formed into shapes: *a wrought iron gate*

wrung /rʌŋ/ *v* the past tense and past participle of WRING

wry /raɪ/ *adj* [only before noun] a wry expression or wry humour shows that you know a situation is bad, but you also think it is slightly amusing: *a wry smile* —**wryly** *adv*

WWW /ˌdʌbəljuː dʌbəljuː 'dʌbəljuː/ the written abbreviation of **World Wide Web**

W

X x

X, x /eks/ n (plural **X's, x's**) **1** [C,U] the 24th letter of the English alphabet **2** [C] a mark used on school work to show that an answer is wrong **3** [C] a mark used at the end of a letter to show a kiss **4** [U] a letter used instead of someone's name because you want to keep it secret, or you do not know it: *Ms X*

xenophobia /ˌzenəˈfəʊbiə $ -ˈfoʊ-/ n [U] strong fear or dislike of people from other countries —**xenophobic** adj

Xerox /ˈzɪərɒks $ ˈzɪrɑːks, ˈziː-/ n [C] trademark a PHOTOCOPY —**Xerox** v [T]

XL (**extra large**) used on clothes to show their size

Xmas /ˈkrɪsməs, ˈeksməs/ n [C,U] written informal Christmas: *Happy Xmas*

X-ray /ˈeks reɪ/ n [C] **1** a beam of RADIATION that can go through solid objects and is used for photographing the inside of the body **2** a photograph of the inside of someone's body, taken using X-rays to see if anything is wrong —**X-ray** v [T]

xylophone /ˈzaɪləfəʊn $ -foʊn/ n [C] a musical instrument with flat metal bars that you hit with a stick → see picture on page A6

Y y

Y, y /waɪ/ n [C,U] (plural **Y's, y's**) the 25th letter of the English alphabet

-y /i/ suffix having something or like something: *dusty shelves* (=covered in dust) | *a wintry day* (=typical of winter)

yacht /jɒt $ jɑːt/ n [C] **1** a boat with sails used for races or sailing for pleasure **2** a large expensive boat, used for travelling or pleasure → see picture at TRANSPORT¹

yachting /ˈjɒtɪŋ $ ˈjɑːtɪŋ/ n [U] especially BrE sailing or racing in a yacht

yachtsman /ˈjɒtsmən $ ˈjɑːts-/ n [C] (plural **yachtsmen** /-mən/) a man who sails a yacht

yachtswoman /ˈjɒtsˌwʊmən $ ˈjɑːts-/ n [C] (plural **yachtswomen** /-ˌwɪmɪn/) a woman who sails a yacht

yak¹ /jæk/ n [C] an animal of central Asia that looks like a cow with long hair

yak² v [I] (**yakked, yakking**) informal to talk a lot about unimportant things

yam /jæm/ n [C] **1** a tropical plant grown for its root which is eaten as a vegetable **2** AmE a SWEET POTATO

yank /jæŋk/ v [I,T] informal to suddenly pull something quickly and with force: *He yanked the door open.* —**yank** n [C]: *He gave the rope a yank.*

Yank n [C] informal someone from the US

yap /jæp/ v [I] (**yapped, yapping**) if a small dog yaps, it BARKS in an excited way —**yap** n [C]

yard /jɑːd $ jɑːrd/ n [C]
1 (written abbreviation **yd**) a unit for measuring length, equal to three feet or 0.9144 metres: *a hundred yards away* | *9,000 square yards*
2 AmE the area around a house, usually covered with grass [SYN] **garden** BrE: **front/back yard** *The kids were playing in the back yard.*
3 an area of land used for a particular purpose: *a builder's yard* | **prison/school yard** (=an area in a prison or school where people do activities outdoors)

yardstick /ˈjɑːdˌstɪk $ ˈjɑːrd-/ n [C] something that you compare another thing with, to show how good it is: *Profit is the main yardstick of success for a business.*

yarn /jɑːn $ jɑːrn/ n **1** [U] thread that you use to KNIT things **2** [C] informal a long story that is not completely true

yawn /jɔːn $ jɒːn/ v [I] to open your mouth wide and breathe deeply because you are tired or bored: *He looked at his watch and yawned.* —**yawn** n [C]

YAWN

yawning /ˈjɔːnɪŋ $ ˈjɒː-/ adj **yawning gap/gulf/chasm etc (between sth)** a very big space or difference between things: *the yawning gap between rich and poor*

yd the written abbreviation of **yard**

yeah /jeə/ adv spoken informal yes

year /jɪə, jɜː $ jɪr/ n [C]
1 [12 MONTHS] a period of 365 days or 12 months: *I've been teaching for six years.* | *They got married a year ago.* | **a/per year** (=each year) *How much does he earn a year?* | *Many birds return to the same spot year after year* (=every year for many years). | **all (the) year round** (=during the whole year) *It's sunny here all the year round.* | *The house is about 150 years old.* | **seven-year-old/twenty-year-old etc** (=someone who is seven years old etc)
2 [JANUARY TO DECEMBER] the period from January 1 to

December 31: *Where are you spending Christmas this year?* | *The movie's set in the year 2052.*

Grammar
Do not say 'I went there on last year.' Say *I went there last year.*
---

3 **FOR SCHOOLS/BUSINESSES ETC** school/financial/academic etc year a particular period of 12 months used by schools, businesses etc: *The tax year begins on April 6th.*

4 **A LONG TIME** years *informal* a very long time **SYN** ages: *It's years since I last saw him.* | **in/for years** *I haven't played tennis for years.*

5 **PERIOD IN LIFE/HISTORY** a particular time in someone's life or in history: **sb's early/later years** *In his later years he suffered from ill health.* | **sb's teenage/retirement etc years** *embarrassing memories of their teenage years* | **sb's years in/at/as sth** *She enjoyed her years as a student.* | **the war/depression/Clinton etc years** *Things were hard during the war years.*

6 **SCHOOL/UNIVERSITY** *BrE* **a)** a level at school or university which is related to how long you have been at school or university: *You have important exams in year 11.* | **the year above/below (sb)** *My brother's in the year above me.* | *John's in his third year at Oxford.* | **first-year students** **b)** **first-year/second-year etc** someone who is in their first, second etc year at school or university: *They must be first-years.* → GAP YEAR, LEAP YEAR, LIGHT YEAR, NEW YEAR

yearbook /ˈjɪəbʊk, ˈjɜː- $ ˈjɪr-/ *n* [C] a book that an organization or school produces every year, with information about its activities

yearly /ˈjɪəli, ˈjɜː- $ ˈjɪrli/ *adj* happening every year or once a year: *the yearly sum of £7,000* | **three-yearly/five-yearly etc** (=happening every three etc years) *a five-yearly review* —**yearly** *adv*: *A meeting is held* **twice yearly** (=two times every year).

yearn /jɜːn $ jɜːrn/ *v* [I] *formal* to want something very much, especially when it is difficult or impossible to get: **[+for]** *She yearned for a child.* | **yearn to do sth** *I yearned to go home.* —**yearning** *n* [C,U]

yeast /jiːst/ *n* [U] a substance used to make bread rise and to produce alcohol in beer and wine

yell /jel/ (*also* **yell out**) *v* [I,T] to shout very loudly: **[+at]** *Someone yelled at her to stop.* **THESAURUS** SHOUT —**yell** *n* [C]

yellow /ˈjeləʊ $ -loʊ/ *adj* having the colour of butter or the sun: **bright/pale yellow** *bright yellow curtains* —**yellow** *n* [C,U] —**yellow** *v* [I,T]: *yellowing newspaper cuttings*

yellow 'line *n* [C] *BrE* a yellow line at the side of a road which means you can only park there for a short time, or at a particular time: **double yellow lines** (=two lines that mean you cannot park there)

Yellow 'Pages *n trademark* a book containing the telephone numbers and addresses of businesses in an area

yelp /jelp/ *v* [I] to give a short high cry because of pain or excitement – used especially of dogs —**yelp** *n* [C]

yep /jep/ *adv spoken informal* yes

yes¹ /jes/ *spoken*
1 used as an answer to say that something is true, that you agree, that you want something etc **OPP** **no**: *'Is that real gold?' 'Yes.'* | *'The movie was great.' 'Yes, it was.'* | *'Would you like some wine?'* **'Yes, please.'** | **say yes** (=agree to something or allow something) *Ask Dad. I'm sure he'll say yes.*
2 used to show that you are ready to listen to someone when they call you or want your attention: *'Mum!' 'Yes?'*
3 used to say that a negative statement is not true: *'John doesn't love me any more.' 'Yes, he does!'*
4 used when you are very happy or excited: *Yes! I got the job!*

yes² *n* [C] (*plural* **yeses** *or* **yesses**) an answer, decision, or vote that agrees with or supports something: *Was that a yes?*

yesterday /ˈjestədi, -deɪ $ -ər-/ *adv, n* [U] the day before today → **tomorrow**: *Did you watch the game yesterday?* | *Yesterday was their anniversary.* | **yesterday morning/afternoon/evening** *I saw him yesterday afternoon.* | *They arrived* **the day before yesterday** (=two days ago).

yesteryear /ˈjestəjɪə, -jɜː $ ˈjestərjɪr/ *n* **the ... of yesteryear** *literary* things or people that existed in the past: *the beautiful cars of yesteryear*

yet¹ /jet/ *adv*
1 used in negative sentences and questions to talk about whether something has happened, especially something that you expect to happen: *Have you heard their new song yet?* | *I haven't finished yet.* | *'Is supper ready?' 'No,* **not yet.***'* | **As yet** (=until now) *there is no news.*
2 used in negative sentences to say that it is too early or soon for someone to do something: *You don't have to get up yet.*
3 **months/weeks/ages etc yet** used to say that a long time will pass before something happens: *My holiday's not for ages yet.* | *It'll be weeks yet before we know the result.*
4 used to emphasize that something could still happen in the future, or that there is still enough time to do something **SYN** **still**: **could/may/might yet do sth** *The plan may yet succeed.* | *There's plenty of* **time yet** *to enter the competition.*
5 **best/fastest/most etc yet** best etc until and including now: *This is their best record yet.*
6 **yet another/yet more/yet again** used to emphasize that something has increased or has happened again, especially when this is surprising or annoying: *I've spotted yet another mistake!* | *The meeting was cancelled yet again.*
PHRASES

---
have yet to do sth *formal* used to say that something you are expecting has not happened or been done: *He has yet to reply to my letter.*

Word Choice: yet or still?
You use **yet** when talking about whether something has happened. It is used especially at the end of questions and negative sentences: *Do you feel any better yet?* | *The post office isn't open yet.*
You use **still** when saying that a situation is the same as before. It is used especially before a
---

verb, or after the verb **to be**: *I've taken the medicine, but I still feel terrible.* | *He's still very good-looking.*

yet² *linking word* used to add something that is surprising after what you have just said: *It was past midnight, yet she still felt wide awake.* | *a simple yet effective solution*

yew /juː/ *n* [C] a tree with dark green leaves like needles

Y-fronts /'waɪ frʌnts/ *n* [plural] *trademark BrE* a type of men's underwear

yield¹ /jiːld/ *v* **1** [T] to produce something, especially a profit or a result: *Our research yielded important results.* **2** [I] to finally agree to do something because people have forced or persuaded you: **[+to]** *The minister yielded to pressure and resigned.* **3** [I] *AmE* to allow the traffic on another road to go first SYN **give way** *BrE*: **[+to]** *Yield to traffic on the left.* **4** [T] to allow someone else to have power or control over something: *The military promised to yield power.* **5** [I] *literary* to stop fighting and admit you have lost SYN **surrender** **6** [I] to bend or move when pressed

yield² *n* [C] the amount of profit, crops etc that something produces: **high/low yields** *investments with high yields*

yikes /jaɪks/ *spoken informal* said when you suddenly notice or realize something: *Yikes! I'm late!*

yippee /jɪ'piː $ 'jɪpi/ *spoken informal* said when you are very happy or excited

yo /jəʊ $ joʊ/ *spoken informal especially AmE* used to say hello to someone or get their attention

yob /jɒb $ jɑːb/ *n* [C] *BrE* a rude and often violent young man: *a gang of yobs*

yodel /'jəʊdl $ 'joʊdl/ *v* [I] (**yodelled, yodelling** *BrE*, **yodeled, yodeling** *AmE*) to sing while changing between your natural voice and a very high voice, as traditionally done in the mountains of Switzerland and Austria

yoga /'jəʊɡə $ 'joʊɡə/ *n* [U] a system of exercises which helps you to relax your body and mind

yoghurt, yogurt /'jɒɡət $ 'joʊɡərt/ *n* [C,U] a thick liquid food made from milk

yoke /jəʊk $ joʊk/ *n* [singular] something that limits your freedom: **[+of]** *the yoke of tradition*

yokel /'jəʊkəl $ 'joʊ-/ *n* [C] *humorous* someone who lives in the countryside and is not very intelligent or educated

yolk /jəʊk $ joʊk, jelk/ *n* [C,U] the yellow part of an egg → **white**

yonder /'jɒndə $ 'jɑːndər/ *adv, determiner literary* over there

you /jə, jʊ; *strong* juː/ *pron*
1 the person or people that someone is speaking or writing to: *Do you want a cigarette?* | *I can't hear you.* | *Can you all come a bit nearer?* | *You idiot!*
2 people in general: *As you get older, you often forget things.*

you'd /juːd/ **1** the short form of 'you had': *I wish*

you'd told me. **2** the short form of 'you would': *I didn't think you'd mind.*

you'll /juːl/ the short form of 'you will': *You'll feel better soon.*

young¹ /jʌŋ/ *adj*
1 someone who is young has not lived for very long OPP **old**: *a game for young children* | *I used to ski when I was young.* | *My brother's younger than me.* → **OLD**
2 seeming younger than you are → **youthful**: *I've always looked young for my age.* | *The show is ideal for children and people who are young at heart* (=who have the same attitudes, interests etc as young people).
3 a young country, organization etc has not existed for very long
4 intended for young people: *Is this dress too young for me?*

THESAURUS

young someone who is young has not lived for very long: *I was the youngest student in the class.* | *a quiet young man*
small/little a small child is very young: *Small children need plenty of sleep.* | *They have a little boy of about three.*
teenage between the ages of 13 and 19: *Clothes are very important to teenage girls.*
adolescent at the age when you change from being a child into an adult – used especially when talking about the problems people have at that age: *Adolescent boys find it hard to talk about their feelings.* | *adolescent behaviour*

---

young² *n* [plural] **1 the young** young people: *This kind of music is very popular among the young.* **2** the young animals produced by an animal: *The females care for their young alone.*

youngster /'jʌŋstə $ -ər/ *n* [C] a young person

your /jə; *strong* jɔː $ jər; *strong* jɔːr/ *determiner*
1 belonging or relating to you: *Is that your mother?* | *Don't worry, it's not your fault.*
2 belonging or relating to anyone – used when talking about people in general: *On entering the town, the church is on your right.*

you're /jə; *strong* jɔː $ jər; *strong* jʊr, jɔːr/ the short form of 'you are': *You're wrong.*

yours /jɔːz $ jʊrz, jɔːrz/ *pron* the POSSESSIVE form of 'you': *That bag's yours, isn't it?* | *Yours is the nicest car.* | **sth of yours** *Is he a friend of yours?*
PHRASES
Yours/Yours faithfully/Yours sincerely/Yours truly used at the end of a letter before you sign your name

yourself /jɔː'self $ jɔːr-/ *pron* (*plural* **yourselves** /-'selvz/)
1 the REFLEXIVE form of 'you': *Did you hurt yourself?*
2 used to emphasize 'you': *Why don't you do it yourself?* | *You yourself told me.*
PHRASES
(all) by yourself alone or without help from anyone else: *You're going to Ecuador by yourself?* | *Did you paint the house all by yourself?*

Y

you don't look/seem yourself *spoken* used to tell someone that they seem ill or worried: *Is something worrying you? You don't seem yourself.*
have sth (all) to yourself to be the only person in a place: *You'll have the house to yourself this weekend.*

youth /juːθ/ *n* (*plural* **youths** /juːðz $ juːðz, juːθs/)
1 [U] the time when someone is young, or the quality of being young → **old age: in your youth** *In his youth he lived in France.* | *He seemed confident, in spite of his youth.* **THESAURUS** MAN
2 [C] *disapproving* a boy or young man – used especially in news reports: *Three youths were arrested for stealing.*
3 [U] young people in general: **[+of]** *the youth of today* | *a youth training scheme*

'youth club *n* [C] a place where young people can meet, play games, dance etc

youthful /'juːθfəl/ *adj* **1** typical of young people: *youthful enthusiasm* **2** seeming younger than you are: *a youthful 50-year-old*

'youth ,hostel *n* [C] a place where people can stay cheaply when they are travelling

you've /juːv/ the short form of 'you have': *You've broken it.*

Yo-Yo /'jəʊ jəʊ $ 'joʊ joʊ/ *n* [C] (*plural* **Yo-Yos**) *trademark* a round toy that you can make go up and down on a string that you hold

yr. (*also* **yr** *BrE*) the written abbreviation of **year**

yuck /jʌk/ *spoken informal* said when you think something looks or tastes very unpleasant

yucky /'jʌki/ *adj informal* very unpleasant

Yuletide /'juːltaɪd/ *n* [C,U] *literary* Christmas

yum /jʌm/ *spoken informal* said when you think something tastes good

yummy /'jʌmi/ *adj informal* tasting very good **THESAURUS** DELICIOUS

yuppie /'jʌpi/ *n* [C] *disapproving* a young person who earns a lot of money and buys expensive things

Z, z /zed $ ziː/ *n* [C,U] (*plural* **Z's, z's**) the 26th letter of the English alphabet

zany /'zeɪni/ *adj* funny and unusual: *a zany new TV comedy*

zap /zæp/ *v* [T] (**zapped, zapping**) *informal* to attack or destroy something very quickly

zapper /'zæpə $ -ər/ *n* [C] *especially AmE informal* something you use for changing CHANNELS on a television from a distance **SYN** **remote control**

zeal /ziːl/ *n* [U] great eagerness to do something that you believe is important: *political zeal*

zealous /'zeləs/ *adj* having great energy and eagerness —**zealously** *adv*

zebra /'ziːbrə, 'ze-$ 'ziːbrə/ *n* [C] an animal like a horse but with black and white lines on its body

ZEBRA

,zebra 'crossing *n* [C] *BrE* a place on the road marked with black and white lines, where people can cross safely **SYN** **crosswalk** *AmE*

zenith /'zenəθ $ 'ziː-/ *n* [singular] the time when something is most successful: *The empire had reached its zenith.*

zero¹ /'zɪərəʊ $ 'ziːroʊ/ *number* (*plural* **zeros** *or* **zeroes**)
1 the number 0: *Make x greater than or equal to zero.*
2 the point between + and - on a scale for measuring something, or the lowest point on a scale that shows how much there is left of something: *The petrol gauge was already at zero.*
3 a temperature of 0°: **above/below zero** *It was five degrees below zero last night.*
4 none at all, or the lowest possible amount: *zero inflation* | *His* **chances** *of winning* **are zero** (=he has no chance of winning). | *The school has a* **zero tolerance** *policy on drugs* (=it does not accept any use of them).

zero² *v*
PHRASAL VERBS
zero in on sth to give your attention to something or move directly towards it: *She zeroed in on the weak point in his argument.*

zest /zest/ *n* [U] **1** a feeling of eagerness and enjoyment: **[+for]** *a zest for life* **2** the outer layer of the skin of an orange or LEMON

zigzag¹ /'zɪgzæg/ *n* [C] a line or pattern that looks like a row of w's joined together → see picture at PATTERN

zigzag² *v* [I] (**zigzagged, zigzagging**) to move forward by moving first to the left, then to the right etc at sharp angles: **[+up/down/through etc]** *The path zigzags up the mountain.*

zilch /zɪltʃ/ *n* [U] *informal* nothing

zillion /'zɪljən/ *number informal* an extremely large number or amount

zinc /zɪŋk/ *n* [U] a metal used to produce or cover other metals

zip¹ /zɪp/ *v* (**zipped, zipping**)
1 (*also* **zip up**) [T] to fasten something using a zip **OPP** **unzip**: *John zipped up his jacket.* | **zip sth shut/open** (=close or open something using a zip) *She zipped her case open.*

Zz

2 [I] to go somewhere or do something very quickly SYN **whizz, zoom: [+along/through/up etc]** *An ambulance zipped past us.*

zip² *n*
1 [C] *BrE* a thing for fastening clothes, bags etc, which consists of two lines of small pieces of metal or plastic that join together SYN **zipper** *AmE*: **do up/undo a zip** *Can you do up the zip on my dress?* → see picture at **BUTTON¹**
2 [U] *AmE informal* zero: *We beat them ten to zip.*

'zip code *n* [C] *AmE* a number you write below an address on an envelope, which helps the post office deliver the letter more quickly SYN **postcode** *BrE*

'zip drive *n* [C] *technical* a small piece of equipment that you connect to your computer and use with computer DISKs, that can store large amounts of information

zipper /'zɪpə $ -ər/ *n* [C] *AmE* a zip → see picture at **BUTTON¹**

zit /zɪt/ *n* [C] *informal* a small painful raised area on your skin SYN **spot**

zodiac /'zəʊdiæk $ 'zoʊ-/ *n* **sign of the zodiac** in ASTROLOGY, one of the 12 areas of the sky where the sun, the moon etc appear to be at different times of the year. They are named after groups of stars.

zombie /'zɒmbi $ 'zɑːm-/ *n* **like a zombie** in a very tired, slow, and confused way

zone /zəʊn $ zoʊn/ *n* [C] an area that is different from the areas around it, because of particular rules or something that is happening → **TIME ZONE**

zoo /zuː/ *n* [C] (*plural* **zoos**) a place where a lot of different animals are kept so that people can go to look at them

'zoo-,keeper *n* [C] someone who looks after animals in a zoo

zoology /zuːˈɒlədʒi, zəʊˈɒ- $ zoʊˈɑːl-/ *n* [U] the scientific study of animals and their behaviour —**zoologist** *n* [C]

zoom /zuːm/ *v* [I] *informal* to go somewhere or do something very quickly: **[+down/along/off etc]** *I saw a police car zooming along the highway.*
PHRASAL VERBS
zoom in if a camera zooms in, it makes the person or thing in the picture seem much closer and bigger

'zoom ,lens *n* [C] a camera LENS that can make the person or thing in the picture look bigger or smaller

zucchini /zʊˈkiːni/ *n* (*plural* **zucchini** or **zucchinis**) [C,U] *AmE* a long vegetable with dark green skin SYN **courgette** *BrE* → see picture on page A5

Z

Irregular verbs

Verb	Present participle	Past tense	Past participle
arise	arising	arose	arisen
be	being	was	been
bear	bearing	bore	borne
beat	beating	beat	beaten
become	becoming	became	become
begin	beginning	began	begun
bend	bending	bent	bent
bet	betting	betted or bet	betted or bet
bind	binding	bound	bound
bite	biting	bit	bitten
bleed	bleeding	bled	bled
blow	blowing	blew	blown
break	breaking	broke	broken
breed	breeding	bred	bred
bring	bringing	brought	brought
build	building	built	built
burn	burning	burned or burnt	burned or burnt
buy	buying	bought	bought
catch	catching	caught	caught
choose	choosing	chose	chosen
come	coming	came	come
cost	costing	cost	cost
creep	creeping	crept	crept
cut	cutting	cut	cut
deal	dealing	dealt	dealt
die	dying	died	died
dig	digging	dug	dug
dive	diving	dived, dove (AmE)	dived
do	doing	did	done
draw	drawing	drew	drawn
dream	dreaming	dreamed or dreamt	dreamed or dreamt
drink	drinking	drank	drunk
drive	driving	drove	driven
eat	eating	ate	eaten
fall	falling	fell	fallen
feed	feeding	fed	fed
feel	feeling	felt	felt
fight	fighting	fought	fought
find	finding	found	found
fly	flying	flew	flown
forbid	forbidding	forbade	forbidden
forget	forgetting	forgot	forgotten
freeze	freezing	froze	frozen
get	getting	got	got (BrE), gotten (AmE)
give	giving	gave	given
go	going	went	gone
grow	growing	grew	grown
hang	hanging	hung or hanged	hung or hanged

Verb	Present participle	Past tense	Past participle
have	having	had	had
hear	hearing	heard	heard
hide	hiding	hid	hidden
hit	hitting	hit	hit
hold	holding	held	held
hurt	hurting	hurt	hurt
keep	keeping	kept	kept
kneel	kneeling	knelt,	knelt,
		kneeled (esp AmE)	kneeled (esp AmE)
know	knowing	knew	known
lay	laying	laid	laid
lead	leading	led	led
lean	leaning	leaned or leant	leaned or lent
leap	leaping	leaped or leapt	leaped or leapt
learn	learning	learned or learnt	learned or learnt
leave	leaving	left	left
lend	lending	lent	lent
let	letting	let	let
lie¹	lying	lay	lain
lie²	lying	lied	lied
lose	losing	lost	lost
make	making	made	made
mean	meaning	meant	meant
meet	meeting	met	met
mistake	mistaking	mistook	mistaken
outgrow	outgrowing	outgrew	outgrown
overhear	overhearing	overheard	overheard
oversleep	oversleeping	overslept	overslept
overtake	overtaking	overtook	overtaken
panic	panicking	panicked	panicked
pay	paying	paid	paid
put	putting	put	put
quit	quitting	quit	quit
read	reading	read	read
repay	repaying	repaid	repaid
ride	riding	rode	ridden
ring	ringing	rang	rung
rise	rising	rose	risen
run	running	ran	run
saw	sawing	sawed	sawn
say	saying	said	said
see	seeing	saw	seen
seek	seeking	sought	sought
sell	selling	sold	sold
send	sending	sent	sent
set	setting	set	set
sew	sewing	sewed	sewn
shake	shaking	shook	shaken
shine	shining	shone	shone
shoot	shooting	shot	shot
show	showing	showed	shown

Verb	Present participle	Past tense	Past participle
shrink	shrinking	shrank	shrunk
shut	shutting	shut	shut
sing	singing	sang	sung
sink	sinking	sank	sunk
sit	sitting	sat	sat
sleep	sleeping	slept	slept
slide	sliding	slid	slid
sling	slinging	slung	slung
smell	smelling	smelt or smelled	smelt or smelled
sow	sowing	sowed	sown
speak	speaking	spoke	spoken
speed	speeding	speeded or sped	speeded or sped
spell	spelling	spelled or spelt	spelled or spelt
spend	spending	spent	spent
spill	spilling	spilled or spilt	spilled or spilt
spin	spinning	spun	spun
spit	spitting	spat	spat
split	splitting	split	split
spoil	spoiling	spoilt	spoilt
spread	spreading	spread	spread
spring	springing	sprang	sprung
stand	standing	stood	stood
steal	stealing	stole	stolen
sting	stinging	stung	stung
strike	striking	struck	struck
swear	swearing	swore	sworn
sweep	sweeping	swept	swept
swim	swimming	swam	swum
swing	swinging	swung	swung
take	taking	took	taken
teach	teaching	taught	taught
tear	tearing	tore	torn
tell	telling	told	told
think	thinking	thought	thought
throw	throwing	threw	thrown
thrust	thrusting	thrust	thrust
undergo	undergoing	underwent	undergone
understand	understanding	understood	understood
undertake	undertaking	undertook	undertaken
undo	undoing	undid	undone
unwind	unwinding	unwound	unwound
upset	upsetting	upset	upset
wake	waking	waked or woke	woken
wear	wearing	wore	worn
weep	weeping	wept	wept
wet	wetting	wet or wetted	wet or wetted
win	winning	won	won
wind	winding	wound	wound
withdraw	withdrawing	withdrew	withdrawn
write	writing	wrote	written